lonely planet

Japan

Rebecca Milner, Ray Bartlett, Andrew Bender, Stephanie d'Arc Taylor, Samantha Forge, Craig McLachlan, Kate Morgan, Thomas O'Malley, Simon Richmond, Phillip Tang, Benedict Walker

PLAN YOUR TRIP

ON THE ROAD

CHEN MIN CHUN/SHUTTERSTOCK ©

KATSURA RIKYŪ, KYOTO P337

SAHA ENTERTAINMENT/GETTY IMAGES ©

TOKYO SKYTREE P105

VINCENT ST. THOMAS/SHUTTERSTOCK ©

STREET FOOD, OSAKA P381

Contents

Contents

ON THE ROAD

JULIANNE.HIDE/SHUTTERSTOCK ©

KŌENJI AWA ODORI, TOKYO P122

Contents

COVID-19

We have re-checked every business in this book before publication to ensure that it is still open after the COVID-19 outbreak. However, the economic and social impacts of COVID-19 will continue to be felt long after the outbreak has been contained, and many businesses, services and events referenced in this guide may experience ongoing restrictions. Some businesses may be temporarily closed, have changed their opening hours and services, or require bookings; some unfortunately could have closed permanently. We suggest you check with venues before visiting for the latest information.

Right: Fushimi Inari-Taisha (p313), Kyoto

PATRYK KOSMIDER/SHUTTERSTOCK ©

WELCOME TO
Japan

I've lived in Tokyo for over 15 years now and am continuously surprised by something new. Such is the joy of living in a place that prides itself on constant renewal and reinvention; it seriously never gets old. Over the years I have had many opportunities to introduce visiting family and friends to Japan. The awe on their faces when first seeing Kyoto's golden temple, Kinkaku-ji, or experiencing the kindness of complete strangers never fails to take me back to the moment I first arrived and was instantly smitten.

By Rebecca Milner, Writer

For more about our writers, see p928

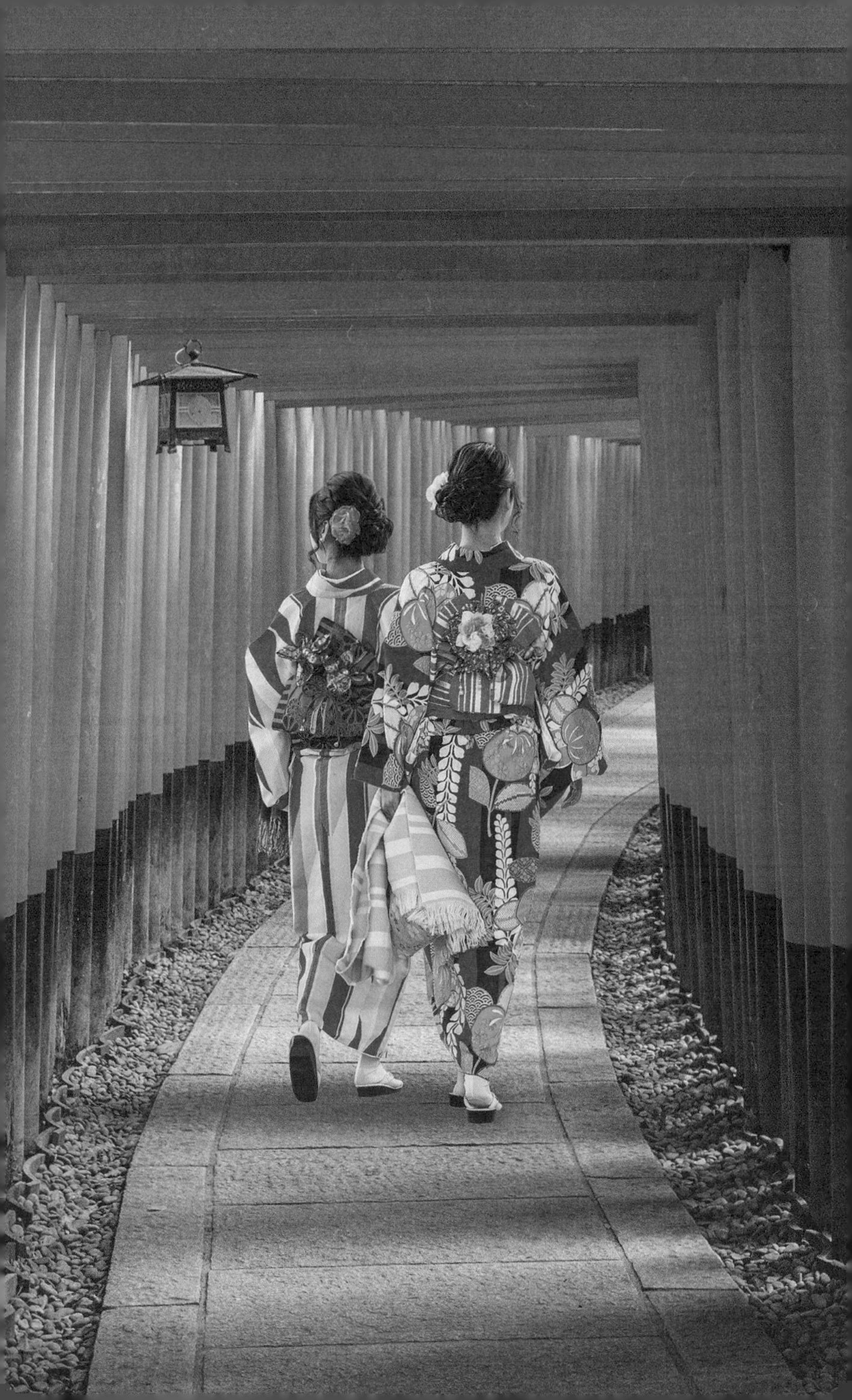

Japan

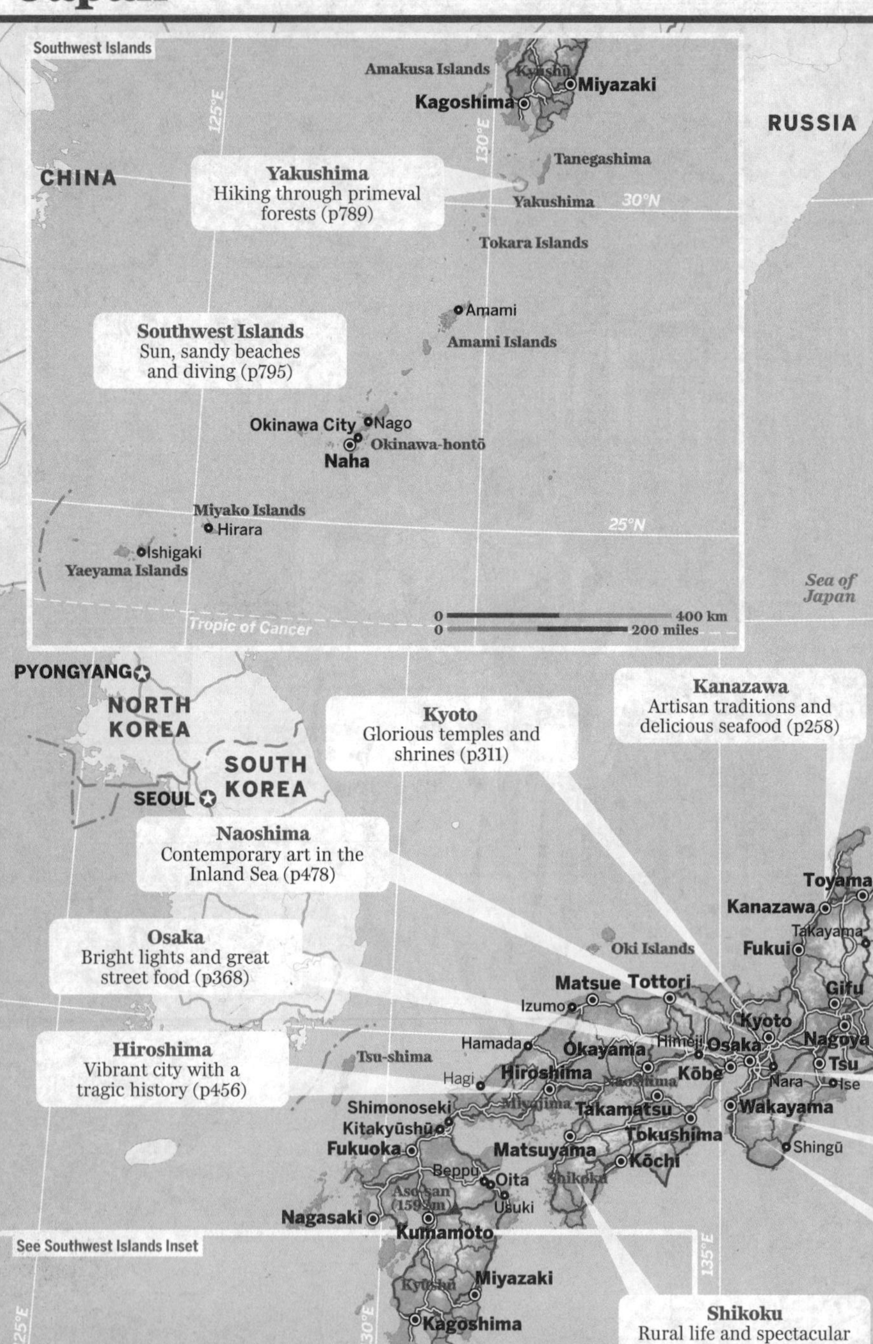

Southwest Islands
Amakusa Islands
Kyūshū
Miyazaki
Kagoshima
RUSSIA
CHINA
125°E
130°E
Yakushima
Hiking through primeval forests (p789)
Tanegashima
Yakushima
30°N
Tokara Islands
Amami
Southwest Islands
Sun, sandy beaches and diving (p795)
Amami Islands
Okinawa City
Nago
Okinawa-hontō
Naha
Miyako Islands
Hirara
25°N
Ishigaki
Yaeyama Islands
Sea of Japan
Tropic of Cancer
0 400 km
0 200 miles
PYONGYANG
NORTH KOREA
SOUTH KOREA
SEOUL
Kanazawa
Artisan traditions and delicious seafood (p258)
Kyoto
Glorious temples and shrines (p311)
Naoshima
Contemporary art in the Inland Sea (p478)
Osaka
Bright lights and great street food (p368)
Hiroshima
Vibrant city with a tragic history (p456)
Toyama
Kanazawa
Takayama
Fukui
Oki Islands
Matsue
Tottori
Izumo
Gifu
Kyoto
Nagoya
Hamada
Okayama
Himeji
Osaka
Kōbe
Tsu
Tsu-shima
Hagi
Hiroshima
Naoshima
Nara
Ise
Miyajima
Takamatsu
Wakayama
Shimonoseki
Kitakyūshū
Tokushima
Fukuoka
Matsuyama
Kōchi
Shingū
Beppu
Oita
Shikoku
Aso-san (1592m)
Usuki
Nagasaki
Kumamoto
See Southwest Islands Inset
135°E
Kyūshū
Miyazaki
Kagoshima
125°E
130°E
Shikoku
Rural life and spectacular scenery (p663)

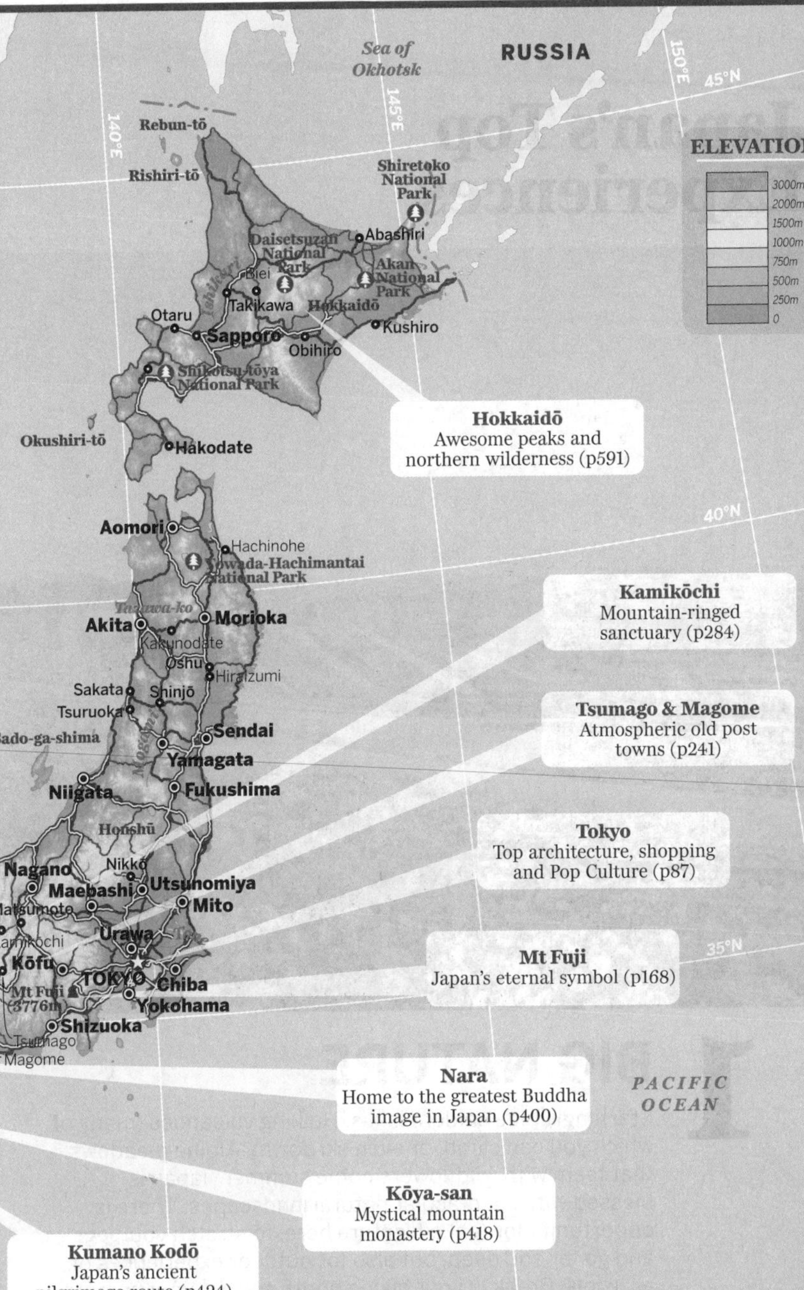

0
500 km
0
250 miles
Sea of Okhotsk
RUSSIA
ELEVATION
3000m
2000m
1500m
1000m
750m
500m
250m
0
Rebun-tō
Rishiri-tō
Shiretoko National Park
Abashiri
Daisetsuzan National Park
Akan National Park
Biei
Takikawa
Hokkaidō
Otaru
Sapporo
Kushiro
Obihiro
Shikotsu-tōya National Park
Okushiri-tō
Hakodate
Hokkaidō
Awesome peaks and northern wilderness (p591)
Aomori
Hachinohe
Towada-Hachimantai National Park
Tazawa-ko
Akita
Morioka
Kakunodate
Oshu
Hiraizumi
Sakata
Shinjō
Tsuruoka
Sado-ga-shima
Sendai
Yamagata
Niigata
Fukushima
Honshū
Kamikōchi
Mountain-ringed sanctuary (p284)
Tsumago & Magome
Atmospheric old post towns (p241)
Tokyo
Top architecture, shopping and Pop Culture (p87)
Nagano
Nikkō
Maebashi
Utsunomiya
Mito
Matsumoto
Urawa
Kamikōchi
Kōfu
TOKYO
Chiba
Mt Fuji (3776m)
Yokohama
Shizuoka
Tsumago
Magome
Mt Fuji
Japan's eternal symbol (p168)
Nara
Home to the greatest Buddha image in Japan (p400)
PACIFIC OCEAN
Kōya-san
Mystical mountain monastery (p418)
Kumano Kodō
Japan's ancient pilgrimage route (p424)
Ogasawara Archipelago (500km)
140°E
145°E
150°E
45°N
40°N
35°N

Japan's Top Experiences

1 BIG NATURE

Startlingly blue caldera lakes. Hulking volcanoes (many of which you can climb, or even ski down). Alpine meadows that teem with wildflowers come summer. Japan is blessed with spectacular natural landscapes. There is opportunity for real adventure here, to stretch your legs and go far and deep; but also for outdoor experiences of all levels. Break in your hiking boots and get your camera ready. Above: Biei (p627)

SEAN PAVONE/SHUTTERSTOCK ©

THANYA JONES/SHUTTERSTOCK ©

Hokkaidō

Hokkaidō is Japan's northernmost island: a largely untamed, highly volcanic landscape marked by soaring peaks, crystal-clear lakes and steaming hot springs. Hikers, cyclists and road trippers are all drawn to the island's big skies, wide open spaces and dramatic topography. p591

Right: Jōzankei (p614)

PIUS LEE/SHUTTERSTOCK ©

SKYEARTH/SHUTTERSTOCK ©

Kamikōchi

One of the most stunning natural vistas in Japan, Kamikōchi is a highland river valley enveloped by the soaring peaks of the Northern Japan Alps. It's the jumping off point for gentle, riverside day hikes and more challenging alpine ascents. p284

Above: Oku-hotaka-dake (p285), Northern Japan Alps

Mt Fuji

Even from a distance Mt Fuji (pictured above) will take your breath away. Close up, the perfectly symmetrical cone of Japan's highest peak is nothing short of awesome. Dawn from the summit? Pure magic. p168

2 BUDDHIST TEMPLES

Japan's Buddhist temples are not just active places of worship; they're also repositories of centuries of art, architecture and landscape design. Marvel at the monumental sculptures of the Buddha; the pagoda that have stood for a millennium; the stark, meditative Zen rock gardens; and the gilded pavilions of the medieval era. Let the incense wash over you. Or join the monks for morning rites. Below: Sensō-ji (p104), Tokyo

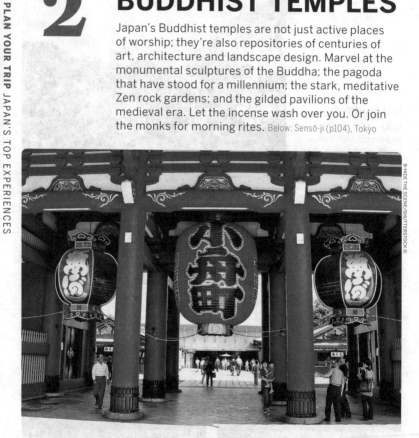

B-HIDE THE SCENE/SHUTTERSTOCK ©

LEONID ANDRONOV/SHUTTERSTOCK ©

THOMAS LA MELA/SHUTTERSTOCK ©

Kyoto

Kyoto, Japan imperial capital for a thousand years, has more than a thousand temples (including many of the country's most historically, culturally and artistically important). But part of the beauty of visiting Kyoto is finding your own quiet spot, overlooking a manicured garden, *matcha* (powdered green tea) in hand. p311

Left: Kinkaku-ji (p333), Kyoto

BEIBAOKE/SHUTTERSTOCK ©

Kōya-san

The most awe-inspiring site at mountain monastery Kōya-san is Oku-no-in (pictured left), a vast cemetery filled with moss-covered stone stupas set among towering cedars. Kōya-san is also the place to experience staying at a temple lodge, which includes meals of *shōjin-ryōri* (Buddhist vegetarian cuisine). p418

Nara

Nara's 15m-tall Daibutsu (Great Buddha; pictured left) was first cast in the 8th century, at the dawn of the Japanese empire. It's among the largest gilt-bronze effigies in the world and the temple that houses it, Tōdai-ji, is among the world's largest wooden structures. p400

3 SUSHI, SAKE & RAMEN

One of the joys of travelling in Japan is experiencing the true breadth of the country's cuisine. Sushi (raw fish on vinegar-seasoned rice) may be synonymous with Japan, but head to the mountains, for example, and you'll discover a hearty cuisine that draws from the land. It's hard not to eat well in Japan: such is the care and thought put into ingredients and presentation. A humble bowl of noodles can be sublime.

MATT MUNRO/LONELY PLANET ©

BANKOO/SHUTTERSTOCK ©

Tokyo

Tokyo is known as the best place in the world to get sushi: the highest quality ingredients arrive daily at the city's wholesale market; going for sushi breakfast at the fish market has long been a traveller tradition. p128 Top left: Sushi, Tokyo

Hiroshima

Hiroshima prefecture produces some of Japan's best sake, which pairs well with oysters from the Inland Sea. Saijō has been a sake-producing centre for centuries and has breweries you can visit. p467 Above right: Sake

Fukuoka

Fukuoka is arguably – Sapporo puts up a good fight – the Japan's most famous ramen city. Its signature style has a rich *tonkotsu* (pork bone) broth and thin noodles. Try it at a *yatai* (outdoor food stall). p720
Bottom left: Ramen, Fukuoka

4 CONTEMPORARY ART & ARCHITECTURE

Japanese architects are among the world's most celebrated. Their works – in concrete, wood and glass, riffing on traditional designs, motifs and materials or striving for something new – can be found in major cities and in far-flung destinations. There are also world-class contemporary art museums, galleries and public art works to see and explore. Japan has long been a source of inspiration for creators around the world; perhaps it will be for you, too.

Naoshima

This is one of Japan's great success stories: a rural island on the verge of becoming a ghost town, now a world-class centre for contemporary art. Top Japanese architects have contributed structures, including museums, a boutique hotel and even a bathhouse – all designed to enhance the island's natural beauty and complement its existing settlements. p478

Tokyo

Tokyo is a showcase city for Japan's leading and up-and-coming architects. See many examples of their works in one place, with a walk along the leafy boulevard Omote-sandō. Also: museums that blur the distinction between art, pop culture and technology. p119

Kanazawa

This attractive city on Honshū's Hokuriku Coast is best known for its 17th century garden and traditional crafts, but is also home to the excellent 21st Century Museum of Contemporary Art, Kanazawa. p258

The Swimming Pool (2004), Leandro Erlich

5 PILGRIM TRAILS

Centuries ago, religious ascetics carved trails through some of Japan's most remote territories; at the time, such places, deep in the mountains, must have felt like the ends of the earth. Some (or parts) of these trails still exist, drawing both modern-day pilgrims (recognisable by their white outfits) and also casual hikers. Join them for a fascinating blend of culture and outdoor activity.

Shikoku

Japan's fourth largest island is famous for its 88 temple pilgrimage. The 1400km-circuit is a months-long commitment if done on foot, but mini circuits can take in a few temples. p667

Below: Temple One (Ryōzen-ji; p675)

SEAN PAVONE/ALAMY STOCK PHOTO ©

Kumano Kodō

Deep in the interior of Kansai's Kii Peninsula, this network of trails links three Shintō shrines that were historic sites of nature worship. There are opportunities for short walks and week-long treks. p424

Above: Kumano Nachi Taisha (p431)

Dewa Sanzan

The 'three mountains of Dewa' are in Japan's northern Yamagata prefecture. Pilgrims completing the circuit (2–3 days) are said to undergo a symbolic cycle of death and rebirth. p572

Right: Haguro-san (p573)

6 HOT SPRINGS

SEAN PAVONE/SHUTTERSTOCK ©

AMEHIME/SHUTTERSTOCK ©

MANUEL ASCANIO/SHUTTERSTOCK ©

Some locals will tell you that the only distinctively Japanese aspect of their culture – that is, the only thing that didn't originate in mainland Asia – is the bath. Highly volcanic Japan has thousands of onsen (hot springs) scattered across the archipelago. The Japanese have turned the simple act of bathing into a folk religion and the country is dotted with temples to this most relaxing of faiths. Not convinced? Give it a try.

Kyūshū

The island of Kyūshū teems with onsen: there are whole resort towns devoted to bathing and also secluded *ryokan* (traditional inns) with their own springs, plus hot sand and mud baths. p713

Above: Kamado Jigoku (p755), Onsen Hells, Beppu

Kinosaki Onsen

At Kansai hot spring town Kinosaki Onsen you can hop between public bathhouses (with an all-you-can-bathe pass). Unlike some bathhouses, the ones in Kinosaki have no rules against tattoos. p448

Nyūtō Onsen

Nyūtō Onsen, in northern Honshū, has milky-white waters, rustic *rotemburo* (outdoor baths) and a gorgeous mountain setting. Visit the baths as a day-tripper or spend the night in one of the atmospheric inns here. p566

7 ISLAND ESCAPES

Japan's southwest islands, which include Okinawa, are a semi-tropical archipelago trailing from Kyūshū towards Taiwan. Life on the islands is slower, and different in other ways: in climate, dialect, culture and cuisine. Until the 19th century these islands made up the Ryūkyū Empire, distinct from Japan. This is also where you'll find Japan's best beaches, snorkeling and diving spots and surf breaks. Each island has its own distinct flavour; discover your favourite.

Yakushima

Yakushima, off the coast of southern Kyūshū is home to some of Japan's last primeval forest, where hiking trails pass under gnarly *yakusugi*, native cedars over a thousand years old. p789 Below: River, Yakushima

TORORO REACTION/SHUTTERSTOCK ©

Yaeyama Islands

The most remote of the southwestern islands, near the Tropic of Cancer, the Yaeyama Islands (pictured above) offer jungle trekking, kayaking among mangroves, Japan's best dive sites and plenty of sandy beaches. p819

Kerama Islands

An easy ferry ride from the Okinawan main island, the Kerama Islands have white sand beaches fringed with palm trees, turquoise waters with excellent snorkelling and little large-scale development. p810
Right: Zamami-jima (p811)

8 WINTER SPORTS

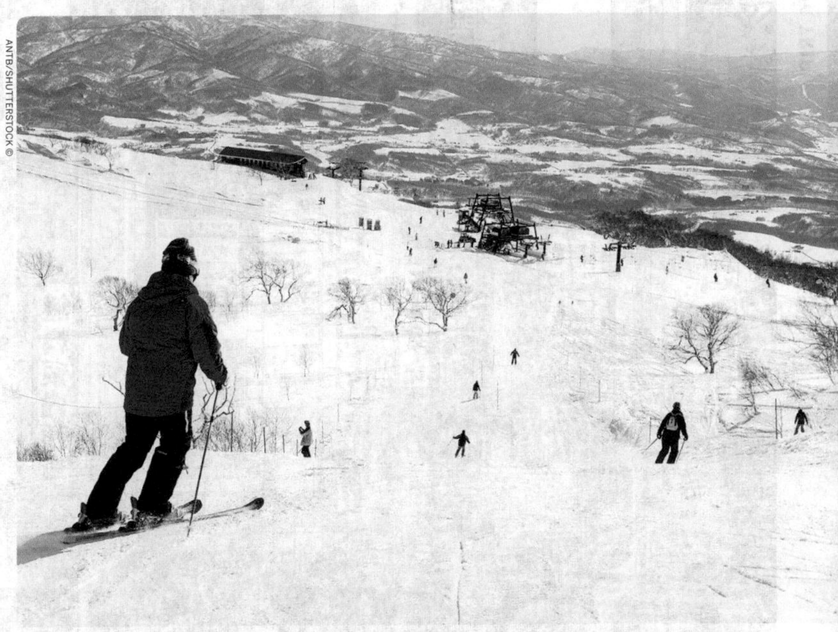

Come winter, copious dumps of dry, powdery snow turn the mountains of Japan into peaks of meringue. In recent decades, the country has emerged as a global destination for skiing and snowboarding. There are major resorts, which are easy to navigate in English, and also hundreds of smaller, local resorts where you'll have less competition for first tracks. For thrill-seekers, there are backcountry opportunities, too.

Niseko

Hokkaidō's famous ski destination checks all the boxes: tons of powdery snow; 60 runs across four interconnected resorts; a thriving après-ski scene; and English-speaking instructors and backcountry guides. p606

Above: Annupuri, Niseko

Hakuba

Hakuba is Nagano's signature ski resort, where the 1988 Winter Olympics were held. There is lots to choose from for all levels, plus onsen and a lively bar scene. p287

Zaō Onsen

In the mountains of northern Honshū, Zaō Onsen is known for its eerie-cool *juhyō* (ice monsters) – conifers that have been frozen solid by harsh Siberian winds, lit up at night – and its namesake hot springs. p569

9 CITY LIGHTS, CITY NIGHTS

Neon signs stacked several storeys high. Larger-than-life video screens. Alleyways flanked with small bars, *izakaya* (Japanese-style pubs) and *yakitori* (grilled chicken) stalls. The nightlife districts of Japan's larger cities have a visual signature that is distinct and highly photogenic. They're also a lot of fun, full of karaoke parlours, nightclubs and craft beer bars.

LUCIANO MORTULA/SHUTTERSTOCK ©

F1PHOTO/GETTY IMAGES ©

MICHAEL TANUJAYA/SHUTTERSTOCK ©

Tokyo

There's nothing quite like seeing one of the world's biggest cities from a couple of hundred metres in the air, cocktail in hand. By night, Tokyo appears truly beautiful, as if the sky were inverted and the glittering stars below. p87

Above left: Shinjuku (p144), Tokyo

Osaka

Osaka, Japan's third-largest city, has the most dramatic of nightscapes: a dazzling display of LED lights, animated signage and flashing video screens along the canal-side strip Dōtombori. It's also tops for street food. p368

Top right: Dōtombori (p372), Osaka

Sapporo

Japan's northernmost metropolis, Sapporo, the capital of Hokkaidō, gives you everything you want in a Japanese city, including a lively nightlife district in Susukino, and little of the hassles and crowds. p597

Bottom right: Ganso Ramen Yokochō (p603), Sapporo

10 SEASONAL SPECTACLES

Plum blossoms. Cherry blossoms. The first flush of spring green in the mountains. The sunset shades of fall foliage. Sparkling winter illuminations. Lively traditional festivals. Spectacular displays of fireworks. Whether this is your first visit to Japan or your tenth, there is always something new to experience – depending on the time of year. Whenever you visit, make sure to make the most of the season.

PATRICK HOCHNER/500PX ©

DAMADA/SHUTTERSTOCK ©

SEAN PAVONE/SHUTTERSTOCK ©

Cherry Blossoms

Come spring, cherry trees across the country burst into colour, a spectrum that runs from the palest of pink to a riotous magenta. Locals gather in parks and along river banks for cherry-blossom-viewing parties called hanami. p49

Left: Himeji-jō (p397)

Traditional Festivals

Japan's *matsuri* (festivals) are carried out much like they have for centuries, with participants (and many spectators) wearing colourful traditional clothing. Some see rollicking parades of portable shrines or floats go through the streets; others involve dancing, bonfires or drumming. Most take place during the summer months. For major events, book accommodation well in advance. p30

Above left and right: Gion Matsuri (p340)

Need to Know

For more information, see Survival Guide (p879)

Currency
Yen (¥)

Language
Japanese

Visas
Visas are issued on arrival for most nationalities for stays of up to 90 days.

Money
In cities, credit cards are widely accepted; rural areas are hit and miss. Post offices and most convenience stores have international ATMs.

Mobile Phones
Japan operates on the 3G and 4G (LTE) networks. Prepaid data-only SIM cards (for unlocked smartphones only) are widely available at the airport or electronics stores.

Time
Japan Standard Time (GMT/UTC plus nine hours)

When to Go

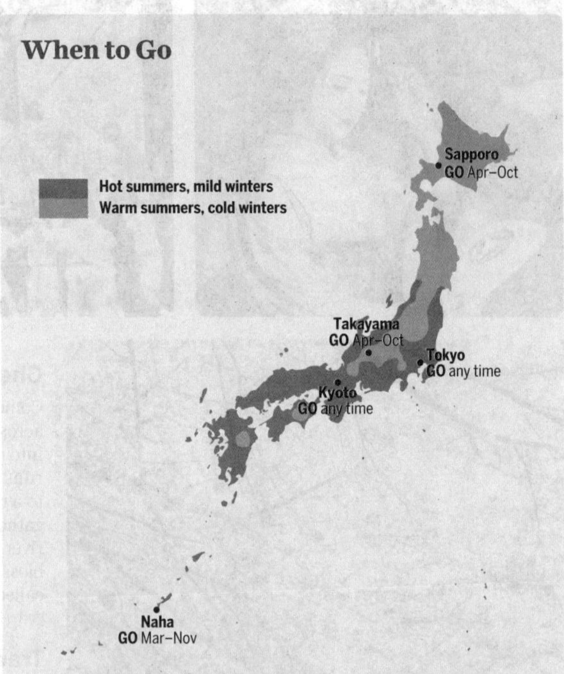

High Season (Apr & May, Aug)

- Cherry-blossom season (late March to early April), Golden Week (early May) and O-Bon (mid-August) are peak travel periods, when sights will be crowded and accommodation more expensive (and often fully booked).
- Mountain (read: cooler) destinations are most popular in August; this is also the month for many festivals.

Shoulder (Jun & Jul, Sep–Nov)

- Autumn foliage draws crowds during specific periods in October and November (depending on elevation).

Low Season (Dec–Mar)

- Sights are uncrowded and accommodation at its cheapest.
- The exception is the ski resorts, which are now hitting their stride.
- Many businesses close over the New Year period (end of December to early January).

Useful Websites

Lonely Planet (www.lonelyplanet.com/japan) Destination information, hotel reviews, traveller forum and more.

Japan National Tourism Organization (www.jnto.go.jp) Official tourist site with planning tools and events calendar; download its useful Japan Official Travel App.

Navitime Travel (https://travel.navitime.com) Tourist info; get its app, Japan Travel, for working out transit routes.

Japan Meteorological Agency (www.jma.go.jp) Get up-to-the-minute weather advisories – a must before heading out on hikes (especially during typhoon season).

Japan Cheapo (www.japancheapo.com) Full of tips for how to stretch your yen. has a comprehensive sister site www.tokyocheapo.com.

Important Numbers

Drop the 0 in the area code when dialling from abroad.

Ambulance and fire	☎119
Police	☎110
Country code	☎81
International access code	☎010

Exchange Rates

Australia	A$1	¥80
Canada	C$1	¥87
Europe	€1	¥130
New Zealand	NZ$1	¥76
UK	£1	¥152
US	US$1	¥109

For current exchange rates, see www.xe.com.

Daily Costs

Budget: Less than ¥8000 (Less than ¥10,000 in Tokyo & Kyoto)

- Dorm bed: ¥3000
- Bowl of noodles: ¥750
- Happy-hour beer: ¥500
- City one-day subway pass: ¥600
- One temple or museum entry: ¥500

Midrange: ¥8000–20,000 (¥10,000–25,000 in Tokyo & Kyoto)

- Double room at a business hotel: ¥10,000
- Dinner for two at an *izakaya* (Japanese pub-eatery): ¥6000
- Half-day cycling tour or cooking class: ¥5000
- Temple and museum entries: ¥1500

Top End: More than ¥20,000 (More than ¥25,000 in Tokyo & Kyoto)

- Double room in a nice hotel: from ¥25,000
- Dinner for two at a good sushi restaurant: from ¥15,000
- Taxi ride between city sights: ¥2500

Arriving in Japan

Narita Airport (Tokyo) Express trains and buses run frequently to central Tokyo (around ¥3000; one to two hours) between 6am and 10.30pm. Taxis cost ¥20,000 to ¥22,000.

Haneda Airport (Tokyo) Trains and buses (¥400 to ¥1200, 30 to 45 minutes) to central Tokyo run frequently from 5.30am to midnight; times and costs depend on your destination in the city. There are only a couple of night buses. For a taxi budget between ¥6000 and ¥8000.

Kansai International Airport (Osaka) Express trains run frequently to Kyoto (from ¥2850, 75 minutes) and Osaka (¥1430, 40 minutes). Buses cost ¥1050 to ¥1550 to central Osaka (50 minutes), ¥2550 to Kyoto (90 minutes). Trains and buses stop running close to midnight. A shared taxi service to Kyoto costs ¥4200; a standard taxi to Osaka starts at ¥14,000.

Getting Around

Train The most popular way to see Japan: trains are fast, efficient, reliable and can get you just about anywhere; discount rail passes make train travel very affordable.

Ferry Good for getting to far-flung islands or for fans of slow travel.

Bus The cheapest way to make long-haul journeys and the only way to get to some mountain and rural destinations.

Car Rental cars are widely available; roads are well-maintained and signposted in English. Especially recommended in Hokkaidō, Kyūshū and Okinawa. Drive on the left.

Air An extensive network of domestic flights and an increased presence of budget carriers makes air travel a good option for long distances or time-pressed itineraries.

For much more on **getting around**, see p891

First Time Japan

For more information, see Survival Guide (p879)

Checklist

➡ Work out which Japan Rail Pass works best for your itinerary and purchase a voucher online in advance for a discount.

➡ Get an international licence if you plan to rent a car.

➡ Check with your embassy or the Japanese customs agency if your prescription medicines are legal in Japan (and if any import procedures are required).

What to Pack

➡ Slip-on shoes, as you'll be taking off your shoes a lot.

➡ Any over-the-counter medications you might want, as finding local equivalents may be challenging.

➡ As little as possible! Hotel rooms are small and trains can get crowded. You can buy most things you'll need.

Top Tips for Your Trip

➡ The Japan Rail Pass offers unlimited use of the extensive, fast and efficient Japan Rail system; if your itinerary focuses on a limited area, look into regional rail passes, which are cheaper.

➡ Stay a night in a ryokan (traditional Japanese inn) and visit an onsen (hot spring), both ways to engage with local culture.

➡ Splurge at lunch. Many restaurants offer midday meals that cost half (or less!) of what you'd find at dinner, often for a meal that is not significantly smaller or lower in quality.

➡ Rent a pocket wi-fi device. Some places have free wi-fi networks but they can be frustratingly clunky. Constant internet access means you can rely on navigation apps to help you get around.

What to Wear

Dressing in layers is ideal. Japanese tend to dress smartly, but casual clothes are fine even in the cities. Some high-end restaurants and bars do have a dress code, but this usually just means no sleeveless shirts or sandals on men. Even during sandal season you may want to carry socks to slip into to avoid walking barefoot when you need to take your shoes off. You also may find yourself sitting on the floor, so dress comfortably for that. Many traditional inns can get chilly in the colder months; warm socks and a fleece are a good idea.

Sleeping

Japan offers a wide and excellent range of accommodation. Advance booking is highly recommended.

Hotels Midrange and luxury, domestic and international chains, and a few boutique properties can be found in all major cities.

Business hotels Compact, economic rooms clustered around train stations.

Ryokan Traditional Japanese inns, found usually in countryside and resort areas.

Hostels and guesthouses Affordable and plentiful in tourist destinations, often with English-speaking staff

Capsule hotels Sleeping berths the size of a single bed.

Bargaining

Bargaining is not common practice in Japan; flea markets are an exception, but a hard approach would still be considered rude.

Cash

Be warned that there are still places in rural Japan that don't accept credit cards. It's wise to assume you'll need to pay cash at ryokan and smaller restaurants and shops; stock up when you're in a town with an ATM.

Tipping

Tipping is not customary in Japan.

High-end restaurants & hotels usually add a 10% service fee to the bill.

Language

The level of English ability in Japan is generally low – or random at best. Cities and popular destinations are well signposted in English and will have Tourist Information Centres (TICs) with English-speaking staff; restaurants in these areas will also often have English menus. Rural areas are more hit or miss, though most TICs will have some English-language material, such as local maps. Most Japanese are more comfortable with written than spoken English, so whenever possible, email is often the best means of communicating, for example when booking accommodation.

See Language chapter (p903).

Phrases to Learn Before You Go

Is there a Western-/Japanese-style room?
洋室/和室はありますか?
yō·shi·tsu/wa·shi·tsu wa a·ri·mas ka

Some lodgings have only Japanese-style rooms, or a mix of Western and Japanese – ask if you have a preference.

Please bring a (spoon/knife/fork).
(スプーン/ナイフ/フォーク)をください。
(spūn/nai·fu/fō·ku) o ku·da·sai

If you haven't quite mastered the art of eating with chopsticks, don't be afraid to ask for cutlery at a restaurant.

How do I get to ...?
…へはどう行けばいいですか?
... e wa dō i·ke·ba ī des ka

Finding a place from its address can be difficult in Japan. Addresses usually give an area (not a street) and numbers aren't always consecutive. Practise asking for directions.

I'd like a nonsmoking seat, please.
禁煙席をお願いします。
kin·en·se·ki o o·ne·gai shi·mas

There are smoking seats in many restaurants and on bullet trains so be sure to specify if you want to be smoke-free.

What's the local speciality?
地元料理は何がありますか?
ji·mo·to·ryō·ri wa na·ni ga a·ri·mas ka

Throughout Japan most areas have a speciality dish and locals usually love to talk food.

Etiquette

Japan is famous for its etiquette, though it's not as strict (or as consistent) as you might think.

Greetings Japanese typically greet each other with a slight bow, but may greet foreigners with a handshake; hugging and cheek kissing is considered alarming.

Queuing Join the queue, usually a neat line.

Public transport It's bad form to eat or drink on public transport, except when riding the *shinkansen* (bullet train), or reserved-seat limited express trains; beverages in resealable containers are an exception.

Shoes off Many lodgings and restaurants (and some attractions) request you leave your shoes at the door. Just take a quick look around – for a sign or slippers in the foyer – to see if this rule applies. Never wear shoes or slippers on tatami (woven floor mats).

Religious sites There is no dress code for visiting a shrine or temple but it's polite to keep your voice down.

What's New

In the build-up to the 2020 (turned 2021) Summer Olympics in Tokyo, Japan set to work making the whole country more attractive and accessible to tourists. Unfortunately the COVID-19 pandemic prevented overseas visitors attending the games, but Japan will hope that the effort pays off in the years to come.

Best in Travel

Shikoku was awarded 6th place in Lonely Planet's list of Top Regions in 2022. Japan's fourth largest island sits below the main island of Honshū, separated by the Inland Sea. It's long been considered remote – an image that has stuck even though it's now easily accessible by train (and also by bus, plane, car or ferry).

Shikoku sees few tourists, and even fewer overseas travellers, which means visitors can enjoy all the island has to offer – culture, history, gorgeous natural landscapes and outdoor sports – without maddening crowds. Highlights include the vine bridges of the Iya Valley; the headline-making zero-waste village, Kamikatsu; and the temples that make up the 88 temple pilgrimage.

Update: Tōhoku

Japan's northeast coast was shattered by a devastating earthquake and tsunami in 2011. A decade on, the region is ready and eager to welcome visitors. There are new sights that memorialise the disaster, including the Takatamatsubara Memorial park for TSUNAMI Disaster, where the miracle pine (p544) – a lone tree that survived the tsunami – is located, and also new boutique hotels, like Hakoneyama Terrace (p544).

The final sections of the Michinoku Coastal Trail (p547) – a 1000km network of trails connecting Soma in Fukushima Prefecture and Hachinohe in Aomori Prefecture – were completed in 2019. Service on the Sanriku Railway, which runs along the coast has now been restored, making travel around the region easy.

LOCAL KNOWLEDGE

WHAT'S HAPPENING IN JAPAN

Rebecca Milner, Lonely Planet writer

The COVID-19 pandemic has created ripples throughout Japanese society. While the country did not see the devastating losses of life that other countries experienced, the hospitality industry took a serious hit. Locals were torn between following government guidelines to refrain from dining out and flouting them in order to support their beloved, struggling neighbourhood spots.

There were also mixed feelings about the absence of overseas visitors, which had skyrocketed in the years preceding the pandemic: on the one hand, many local businesses and economies depend on tourists; on the other hand, cities like Kyoto, that had been under strain from overtourism, could have a breather.

Many office workers were given the opportunity to work from home – revolutionary in a country that values face-to-face time – which has led to discussions about what the future of work-life in Japan could look like. Might it be possible live in a fixer-upper rural farmhouse, while earning a Tokyo salary?

New Openings in Tokyo

Popular Tokyo neighbourhood Shibuya is two-thirds through a massive redevelopment. The newest addition is Shibuya Scramble Square, a huge glass tower with a rooftop observatory and floors of shops and restaurants.

Other noteworthy new openings in Tokyo include: Toyosu Market (p114), which replaces Tsukiji Market as the city's central wholesale market (the 'outer' dry market (p91) at Tsukiji is still in place); the Yayoi Kusama Museum (p107), devoted to one of Japan's most prominent contemporary artists; and teamLab Borderless (p113), an immersive, interactive art experience created by Japan's leading digital-art collective, teamLab.

Guesthouses & Designer Hotels

Suddenly it seems every small city (and even some rural destinations) has at least one very cool guesthouse, usually run by a savvy, local English-speaker. This makes travelling outside the major cities cheaper, easier – and way more fun.

Meanwhile, in Tokyo and Kyoto the design wars are heating up, with several new properties, from both established international hoteliers, like Four Seasons (p343), and local upstarts, like BnA (p123), promising an all-encompassing aesthetic experience.

Sake, Tea & Mocktails

Japan went all in on the recent craft beer and third-wave coffee trends, but now we're seeing that same spirit of innovation and attention to detail being poured into two distinctly Japanese drinks: tea and sake. Keep an eye out for craft sake bars and third-wave-style teahouses, like Gem by Moto (p148) and Sakurai Japanese Tea Experience (p144) in Tokyo.

Non-alcoholic options are also getting more interesting, with more bars making original mocktails with the same enthusiasm they typically reserve for cocktails.

Restorations & Reopenings

Following more than two decades of work, the restoration process of Nikkō's spectacular shrines and temples is nearly complete. A few structures (none of the major ones) may still be under wraps but the rest gleam anew with brilliant colour (created using historical materials and techniques).

Restorations are also complete on Tokyo's signature shrine, Meiji-jingū (p108), and on the main hall of Kyoto's iconic temple, Kiyomizu-dera (p318). Work remains ongoing on the famous floating *torii* (shrine gate) of Miyajima; the main hall of Kyoto's Enryaku-ji; Dōgo Onsen Honkan (p693) in Matsuyama; and Kumamoto's castle, Kumamoto-jō (p744).

In 2019, Hiroshima's powerful Peace Memorial Museum reopened with new exhibits after two years of renovations.

LISTEN, WATCH & FOLLOW

For inspiration and up-to-date news, visit https://www.lonelyplanet.com/japan/articles

The Japan Times (www.japantimes.co.jp) Japan's long-running, English-language newspaper.

Outdoor Japan (www.outdoorjapan.com) Articles, videos and tips for exploring Japan's great outdoors.

National Parks of Japan (@nationalpark_japan) The park service's official Instagram.

Japan Eats (https://heritageradionetwork.org/series/japan-eats) Podcast on Japanese cuisine, from the essentials to the latest trends.

FAST FACTS

Food trend Vegan ramen

Number of convenience stores 55,828

Percentage of world's active volcanos 10%

Population 125.4 million

Month by Month

TOP EVENTS

Yuki Matsuri, February

Hanami (Cherry-Blossom Viewing), April

Sanja Matsuri, May

Gion Matsuri, July

Nebuta Matsuri, August

January

Japan comes to life again after the lull of the New Year holiday. Winter grips the country in the mountains and in the north, ushering in ski season (take care when driving in snow country).

Shōgatsu (New Year)

Families come together to eat and drink to health and happiness. The holiday is officially 1 to 3 January, but many businesses and attractions close the whole first week, and transport is busy. *Hatsu-mōde* is the ritual first shrine visit of the new year.

Coming-of-Age Day

The second Monday of January is Seijin-no-hi (Coming-of-Age Day), the collective birthday for all who have turned 20 (the age of majority) in the past year. Young women don gorgeous kimonos for ceremonies at Shintō shrines.

February

February is the coldest month and the peak of Japan's ski season.

Setsubun Matsuri

The first day of spring is 3 February in the traditional lunar calendar, a shift once believed to bode evil. As a precaution, people visit Buddhist temples, toss roasted beans and shout *'Oni wa soto! Fuku wa uchi!'* ('Devil out! Fortune in!').

Mantōrō

Nara's Kasuga Taisha celebrates Setsubun by lighting its 3000 stone and bronze lanterns during this festival, which also happens over O-Bon. (p406)

Yuki Matsuri

Two million visitors head to Sapporo's annual snow festival in early February. Highlights include the international snow sculpture contest, ice slides and mazes for kids, and plenty of drunken revelry. Book accommodation very early. (p601)

Plum-Blossom Viewing

Plum *(ume)* blossoms, which appear towards the end of the month, are the first sign that winter is ending.

March

Spring begins in fits and starts. The Japanese have a saying: *sankan-shion* – three days cold, four days warm.

Hina Matsuri

On and around 3 March (also known as Girls' Day), public spaces and homes are decorated with *o-hina-sama* (princess) dolls in traditional royal dress.

Anime Japan

Anime Japan (www.anime-japan.jp), the world's largest anime (Japanese animation) fair, takes place in Tokyo in late March. There are events and exhibitions for industry insiders and fans alike.

April

Warmer weather and blooming cherry trees make this a fantastic month to be in Japan, though places like Kyoto can get very crowded.

Hanami (Cherry-Blossom Viewing)

When the cherry blossoms burst into bloom, the Japanese hold rollicking *hanami* (blossom viewing) parties. The blossoms are fickle and hard to time: on average, they hit their peak in Tokyo or Kyoto between 25 March and 7 April.

Takayama Spring Matsuri

On 14 and 15 April the mountain town of Takayama hosts the spring installment of its famous festival. This is the more elaborate of the two (the other is in October), with parades of spectacular floats lit with lanterns and a lion dance. Book accommodation well in advance. (p248)

May

May is one of the best months to visit: it's warm and sunny in most places and the fresh green in the mountains is beautiful. Be wary of the travel crush during the Golden Week holiday.

Sanja Matsuri

The grandest Tokyo festival of all, this three-day event, held over the third weekend of May, attracts around 1.5 million spectators to Asakusa. The highlight is the rowdy parade of *mikoshi* (portable shrines) carried by men and women in traditional dress. (p121)

Roppongi Art Night

Held in late May, this weekend-long (literally, venues stay open all night) arts event (www.roppongiartnight.com) sees large-scale installations and performances taking over the museums, galleries and streets of Roppongi.

June

Early June is lovely, though by the end of the month *tsuyu* (the rainy season) sets in. As mountain snow melts, hiking season begins in the Japan Alps (though double-check for higher elevations).

Hyakumangoku Matsuri

In early June, Kanazawa's biggest festival celebrates the city's 16th-century glory days with period-costume parades, cultural performances and more. (p262)

July

When the rainy season passes, suddenly it's summer – the season for festivals and *hanabi taikai* (fireworks shows). It does get very hot and humid; head to Hokkaidō or the Japan Alps to escape the heat.

Mt Fuji Climbing Season

Mt Fuji officially opens to climbing on 1 July, and the months of July and August are ideal for climbing the peak. (p168)

Gion Matsuri

The most vaunted festival in Japan is held on 17 and 24 July in Kyoto, when huge, elaborate floats are pulled through the streets. Three evenings prior to the 17th, locals stroll through street markets dressed in beautiful *yukata* (light cotton kimonos). Accommodation is expensive and difficult to find. (p340)

Tenjin Matsuri

Held in Osaka on 24 and 25 July, this is one of the country's biggest festivals. On the second day, processions of *mikoshi* (portable shrines) and people in traditional attire parade through the streets, ending up in hundreds of boats on the river. (p377)

Fuji Rock Festival

Japan's biggest music festival takes place over one long (and often wildly muddy and fun) weekend at a mountain resort in Niigata in late July. Big-name acts on the large stages; indie bands on the smaller ones. (p585)

Peiron Dragon-Boat Races

In late July, dragon-boat races are held in the harbour of Nagasaki, a tradition introduced from China in the 17th century. (p737)

August

Hot, humid weather and festivals continuing apace. School holidays mean beaches and cooler mountain areas get crowded. Many Japanese return to their home towns (or take a holiday) around O-Bon, so transit is hectic and shops may close.

Summer Fireworks Festivals

Towns across Japan hold spectacular summer

BUSY TRAVEL TIMES

Most Japanese are on holiday from 29 April to 5 May, when a series of national holidays coincide (called 'Golden Week'). This is one of the busiest times for domestic travel, so be prepared for crowded transport and accommodation. Many businesses close for a week in mid-August, as Japanese return to their home towns for O-Bon festivities (or go on holiday instead). Restaurants and shops start shutting down from 29 December for the New Year holiday, which ends on 3 January (though many places close until 6 January). During this time, transport runs and accommodation remains open, but it's pricey.

fireworks festivals in late July and early August. Among the best: Sumida-gawa Fireworks festival (Tokyo, late July; p122), Lake Biwa Fireworks festival (near Kyoto, early August; p439) and Miyajima Water Fireworks Festival (near Hiroshima, mid-August; p4665).

World Cosplay Summit

Some 30 countries compete in early August (or late July) in Nagoya to see who has the best *cosplayers* (manga and anime fans who dress up as their fave characters). (p231)

Sendai Tanabata Matsuri

Sendai's biggest event celebrates a Chinese legend about the stars Vega and Altair, stand-ins for two star-crossed lovers who meet once a year on 7 July (on the old lunar calendar, early August on the modern one). Downtown is decorated with coloured streamers. (p526)

Nebuta Matsuri

Over several days in early August, enormous, illuminated floats are paraded through the streets of Aomori in Northern Honshū accompanied by thousands of rowdy, chanting dancers. A famous festival; book accommodation early. (p548)

Peace Memorial Ceremony

On 6 August a memorial service is held in Hiroshima for victims of the WWII atomic bombing of the city. Thousands of paper lanterns are floated down the river. (p460)

Matsumoto Bonbon

Matsumoto's biggest event takes place on the first Saturday in August, when hordes of people perform the city's signature 'bonbon' dance through the streets. (p279)

O-Bon (Festival of the Dead)

Three days in mid-August are set aside to honour the dead, when their spirits are said to return to the earth. Graves are swept, offerings are made and lanterns are floated down rivers, lakes or the sea to help guide spirits on their journey.

Awa-odori Matsuri

The city of Tokushima, on the southern island of Shikoku, comes alive in mid-August for the nation's largest and most famous *bon* dance. These dances, part of O-Bon celebrations, are performed to welcome the souls of the departed back to this world. (p670)

Rōsoku Matsuri

Kōya-san's already deeply atmospheric Oku-no-in is lit with some 100,000 candles on 13 August for Rōsoku Matsuri during O-Bon. (p422)

Daimon-ji Gozan Okuribi

Huge fires in the shape of Chinese characters and other symbols are set alight in the hills around Kyoto during this festival, which forms part of the O-Bon rites. It's one of Japan's most impressive spectacles. (p340)

Earth Celebration

The island of Sado-ga-shima, off the coast of northern Honshū, is the scene of this internationally famous festival of dance, art and music, held in late August. Highlights include *taiko* (drum) performances and workshops. (p579)

September

Days are still warm, hot even, though less humid. Though the odd typhoon rolls through this time of year, this is generally a great time to travel in Japan.

Jōzenji Street Jazz Festival

Over the second weekend in September, this festival draws buskers from all over the country to play in Sendai's streets and arcades. (p527)

Kishiwada Danjiri Matsuri

Osaka's wildest festival, held over the third weekend in September, is a kind of running of the bulls except with *danjiri* (festival floats), many weighing more than 3000kg – take care and stand back. Most of the action takes place on the second day. (p377)

Moon Viewing

Full moons in September and October call for *tsukimi,* moon-viewing gatherings. People eat *tsukimi dango* – *mochi* (pounded rice) dumplings, round like the moon.

October

Pleasantly warm days and cool evenings make this an excellent time to be in Japan. The autumn foliage peaks in the Japan Alps at this time.

Matsue Suitōro

Held on Saturdays, Sundays and holidays throughout October in the western Honshū city of Matsue, this festival of light and water takes place around the city's scenic castle. Lanterns are floated in the moat and rival drumming groups compete on the banks. (p500)

Asama Onsen Taimatsu Matsuri

In early October, Asama Onsen in Matsumoto holds this spectacular fire festival, which sees groups of men, women and children parade burning bales of hay through narrow streets en route to an enormous bonfire. (p279)

Yokohama Oktoberfest

For two weeks in early October much beer drinking goes down during this event held in Yokohama's historic harbour district. (p179)

Kurama-no-hi Matsuri

On 22 October, this festival sees loin-clothed men carrying huge flaming torches through the streets of the tiny hamlet of Kurama in the mountains north of Kyoto. (p340)

Performing Arts Festivals

Tokyo's annual performing arts festival, Festival/Tokyo (www.festival-tokyo.jp) is held over a month from mid-October to mid-November at venues around the city. Kyoto's edgier Kyoto Experiment (www.kyoto-ex.jp) is held around the same time.

Halloween

Japan has taken to Halloween in a big way. Tokyo's Shibuya Crossing (p109) draws thousands of costumed revellers on 31 October. Osaka's Amerika-Mura (p372) becomes one big street party.

November

Crisp and cool days with snow starting to fall in the mountains. Autumn foliage peaks in and around Tokyo and Kyoto, drawing crowds.

Shichi-go-san (7-5-3 Festival)

This adorable festival in mid-November sees parents dress girls aged seven *(shichi)* and three *(san)* and boys aged five *(go)* in wee kimonos and head to Shintō shrines for blessings.

December

December is cold across most of Japan. Year-end parties fill city bars and restaurants; commercial strips are decorated with seasonal illuminations. Many businesses shut down from 29 or 30 December to between 3 and 6 January.

Luminarie

Kōbe streets are lined with elaborate, illuminated arches every year for this event in early December, in memory of the victims of the 1995 Great Hanshin Earthquake. (p393)

Toshikoshi Soba

Eating buckwheat noodles on New Year's Eve, a tradition called *toshikoshi soba,* is said to bring luck and longevity – the latter symbolised by the length of the noodles.

Joya-no-kane

Temple bells around Japan ring 108 times at midnight on 31 December, a purifying ritual.

Plan Your Trip
Itineraries

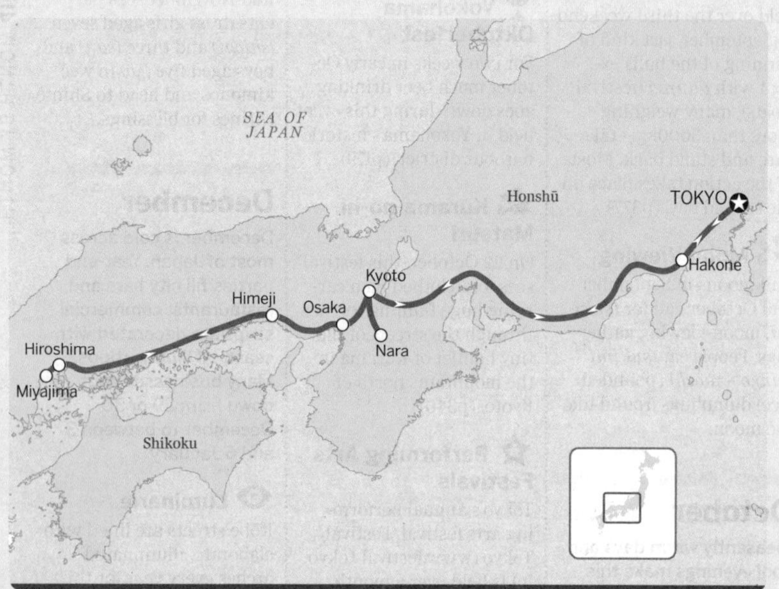

Tokyo, Kyoto & Hiroshima

This classic route for first-time visitors hits many of Japan's star attractions, can be done year-round and takes advantage of the excellent value and seamless travel offered by a Japan Rail Pass.

Start with a couple of days in **Tokyo**, getting your bearings and a taste of big-city Japan – the skyscrapers, the bustle and all those lights. Then hop on the bullet train for **Kyoto**. (If you wait until now to activate your rail pass, you can get by with a seven-day pass.)

You'll need two or three days to sample the best of Kyoto's temples and gardens. From here you can make side trips to **Nara**, home of the Daibutsu (Great Buddha), and **Osaka**, famous for its vivid nightscape and street food. Then head west on to **Himeji** to see Japan's best castle, Himeji-jō.

Next stop is **Hiroshima**, for the moving Peace Memorial Park. Further down the coast is **Miyajima**, with its photogenic floating shrine. You can spend the night in a ryokan (traditional Japanese inn) here before making the train journey back to Tokyo. On your way back there, drop into the mountain hot-spring resort of **Hakone** to get your onsen fix.

ARCHITECT NIKKEN SEKKEI: SEAN PAVONE/SHUTTERSTOCK ©

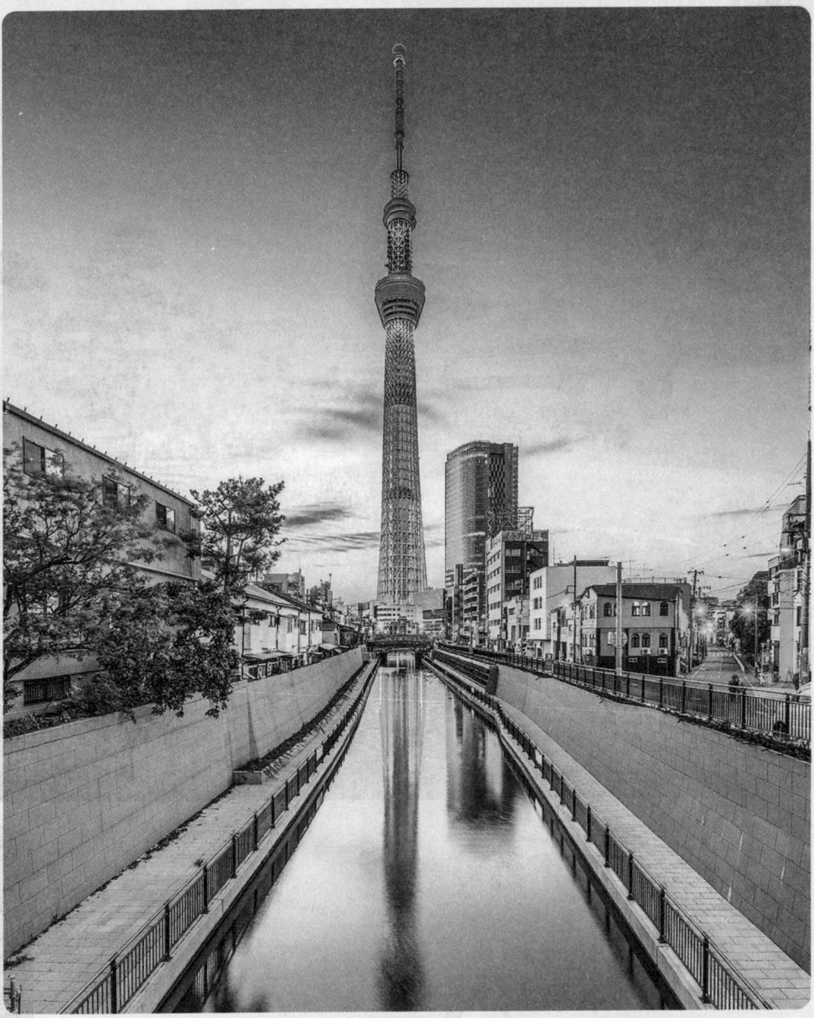

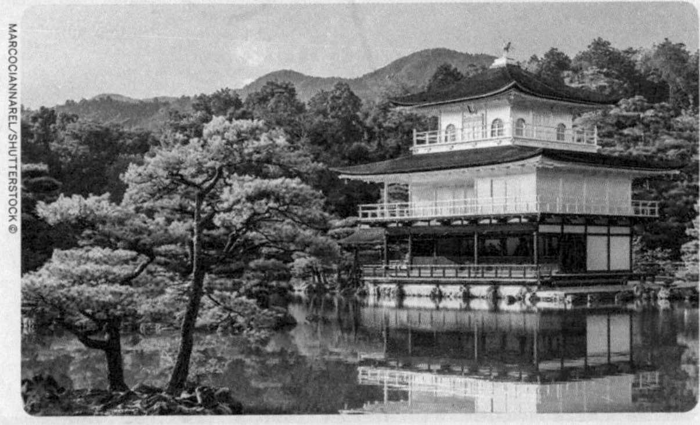

Top: Tokyo Skytree (p105)

Bottom: Kinkaku-ji, (p333), Kyoto

MARCOCIANNAREL/SHUTTERSTOCK ©

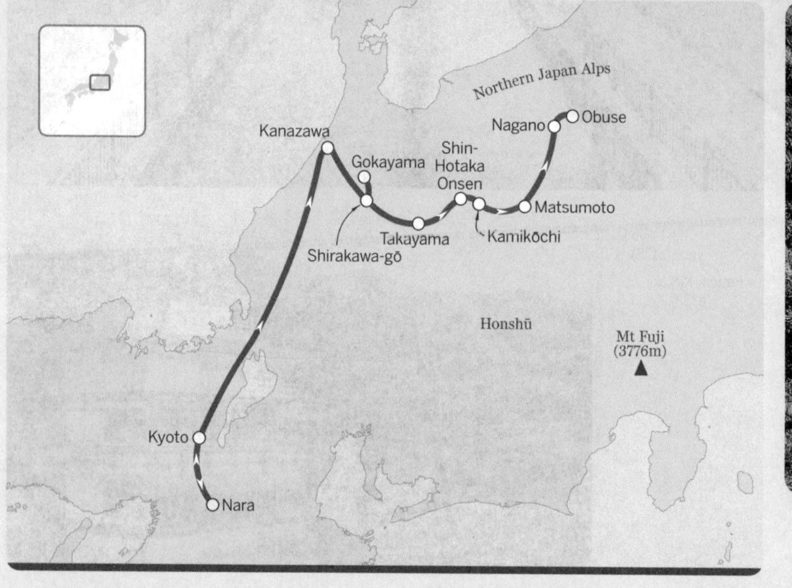

Northern Japan Alps
Nagano
Obuse
Kanazawa
Gokayama
Shin-Hotaka Onsen
Matsumoto
Takayama
Kamikōchi
Shirakawa-gō
Honshū
Mt Fuji (3776m)
Kyoto
Nara

PIUS LEE/SHUTTERSTOCK ©

Kyoto, Kanazawa & the Japan Alps

This route highlights Japan's traditional culture and its natural beauty. As snow can close mountain passes in winter, it is best undertaken in spring, summer or autumn.

Spend the first few days in **Kyoto** exploring the city's famous temples, shrines and gardens. Be sure to budget some time for the less-famous ones too, which are more peaceful, and for a day trip to **Nara**. Both Kyoto and Nara have excellent national museums with classical art and artefacts. In the evenings, stroll Kyoto's historic geisha district.

Next take the train to **Kanazawa**, a city that, in its heyday, rivalled Kyoto in its contributions to the arts. As befitting its location near the Sea of Japan, Kanazawa is known for excellent seafood, but also for its lasting artisan tradition and its strolling garden, Kenroku-en. Both Kyoto and Kanazawa are excellent places to shop for traditional crafts.

Now get a car and head for the mountains of Hida. The villages of **Shirakawa-gō and Gokayama** are famed for their farmhouses with dramatically angled thatched roofs. Continue to **Takayama**, a charming old post town with well-preserved wooden buildings (now housing galleries, sake breweries and craft shops) and narrow streets.

Then head to **Shin-Hotaka Onsen** for outstanding rustic onsen (hot springs) and ryokan (traditional Japanese inns), followed by a visit to **Kamikōchi** for alpine scenery and hiking (closed from 15 November to 22 April). You'll eat well travelling in the mountains: local specialities include soba (buckwheat noodles), beef, *hoba-miso* (sweet miso paste grilled on a magnolia leaf) and foraged mushrooms and shoots.

From here drive east to the castle town of **Matsumoto**, home to one of Japan's best original castles, Matsumoto-jō. Near Nagano, pretty **Obuse**, another well-preserved mountain town, is home to the Hokusai Museum. End your trip in **Nagano** with a visit to the city's impressive temple, Zenkō-ji.

Nagano has a *shinkansen* (bullet train) station, so you can catch a train onward or drive straight on to Narita Airport.

PHUONG D. NGUYEN/SHUTTERSTOCK ©

Top: Matsumoto-jō (p278)
Bottom: Zenkō-ji (p291)

Tokyo, Mt Fuji & Around

Japan often feels like a destination that requires a long trip and advance planning, but it needn't be. In and around Tokyo you can cover a lot of varied terrain, taking in both contemporary and traditional Japan.

Base yourself in **Tokyo** and do day trips or hop around. In three or four days you can take in the capital's highlights, eating well, and still have time to explore some of its less touristy neighbourhoods, like Shimo-Kitazawa and Kōenji.

Mt Fuji is open to hikers from June through mid-September; you can do it as one long overnight climb – to hit the summit for sunrise – or stay a night in a mountain hut. Year-round, visit the Fuji Five Lakes region for views of the iconic volcano.

For temples and shrines head north to **Nikkō**, with 17th-century structures set among cedars, or south to **Kamakura**, a one-time medieval capital with many Zen temples. On the Pacific coast, Kamakura is also a hip beach town with cafes and surf shops.

Round off your trip with a visit to the hot-spring resort **Hakone**. There are spa complexes here for day trippers, or you can splurge on a night in a ryokan.

BLANSCAPE/SHUTTERSTOCK ©

OMJAI CHALARD/SHUTTERSTOCK ©

Top: Mt Fuji (p168)
Bottom: Kamakura (p182)

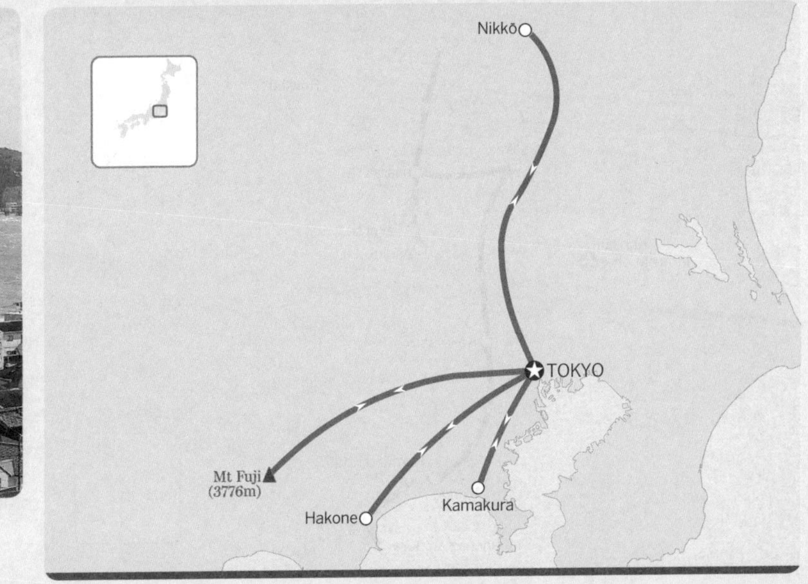
Nikkō
TOKYO
Mt Fuji
(3776m)
Hakone
Kamakura

大阪王将
名物元祖焼餃子
餃子
専門店
大阪王将
道頓堀本店
免税
平松ビル
おみやげ
よしもと芸人グッズ・大阪みやげ
大阪土产·오사카 선물
GAME
BAR OCEAN
ギョーザ

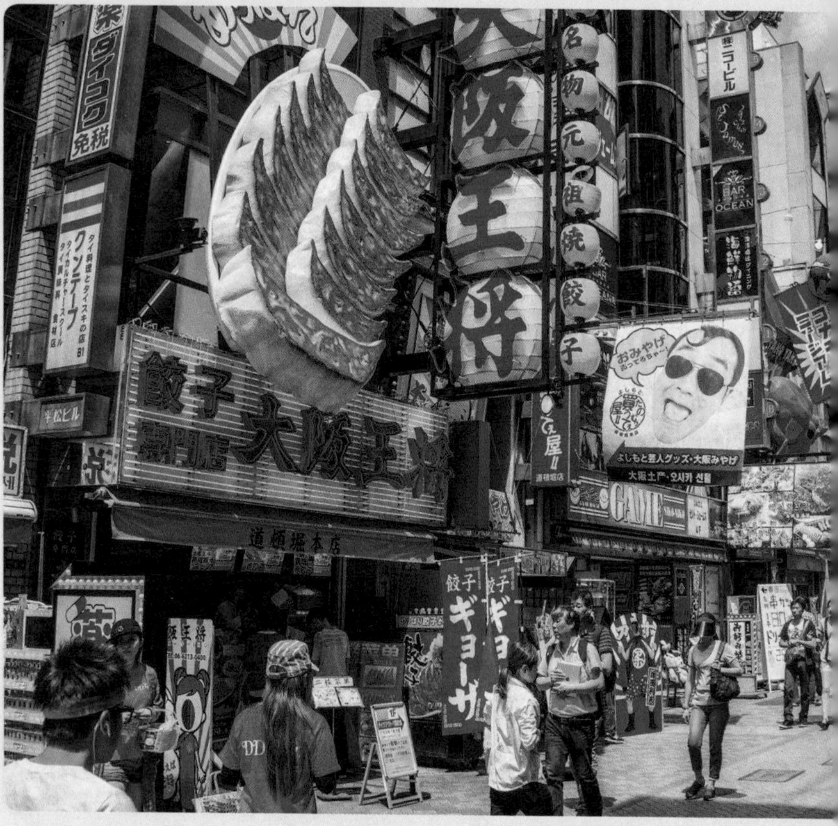

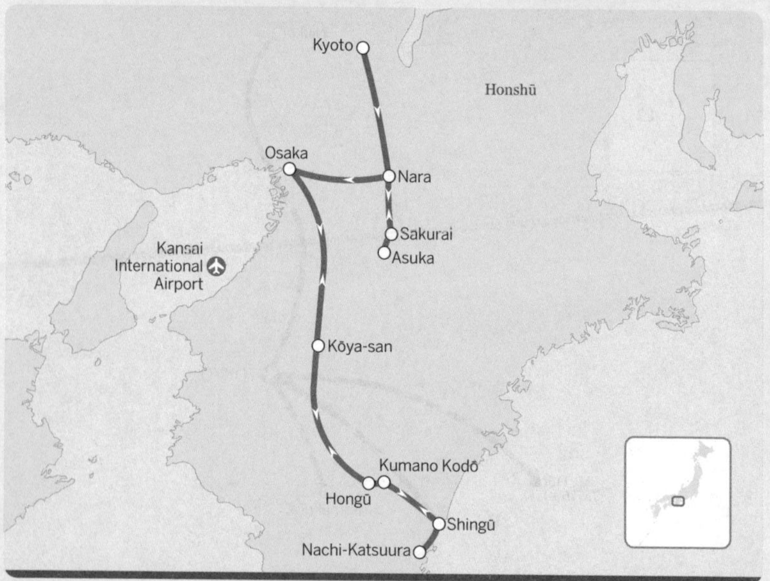

Kyoto
Honshū
Osaka
Nara
Sakurai
Asuka
Kansai International Airport
Kōya-san
Kumano Kodō
Hongū
Shingū
Nachi-Katsuura

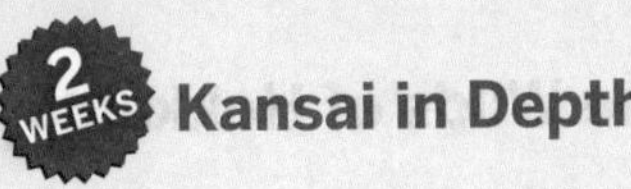

Kansai in Depth

Take a slow, deep dive into Japanese history and culture; you'll cover a lot without having to travel far. Arranged with public transport in mind, this itinerary is possible year-round, though Kōya-san will be cold and possibly snowy in winter. Fly in and out of Kansai International Airport.

Start with **Kyoto**, Japan's cultural storehouse, and spend several leisurely days exploring. Then head to **Nara** – not for the typical day trip – but for a few days' trip. Beyond the city there are fascinating historic temples, very old shrines and country rambles around **Sakurai** and pre-Buddhist burial mounds around **Asuka**.

Then pop over to **Osaka** for a jolt of city life, before taking the train to **Kōya-san**. This mountain monastery was founded in the 8th century and is still active today; spend the night in a temple for a taste of monk life.

Buses run April through November to your next destination, the ancient pilgrim trails of the **Kumano Kodō**. Outside of these months you'll need to do some backtracking via train. Spend a few days walking through woods and rural hamlets, to temples, shrines and some of Kansai's best onsen between **Hongū**, **Shingū** and **Nachi-Katsuura**.

Top: Dōtombori (p372), Osaka
Bottom: Konpon Daitō (p421), Garan, Kōya-san

The Wilds of Hokkaidō

Japan's northernmost island, Hokkaidō, has much of what you want out of Japan: steaming onsen and rugged, volcanic peaks, city lights and foodie cred, as well as something you wouldn't expect – the opportunity for an epic road trip. Snow falls early in Hokkaidō, so this is a summer trip.

Start in **Hakodate**, Hokkaidō's southernmost port, which has a charming 19th-century city centre. The journey here by *shinkansen* (bullet train) takes four hours from Tokyo (though it's probably cheaper to fly).

After a fresh seafood breakfast at Hakodate's fish market, pick up a rental car and drive to **Shikotsu-Tōya National Park**, home to caldera lakes and an active volcano. Budget time to soak in the springs of Noboribetsu Onsen inside the park.

Next stop: **Sapporo**, Hokkaidō's capital city (and Japan's fifth-largest). Get your city fix here, basking in the bright lights of the Susukino district. Then head to Hokkaidō's second city, **Asahikawa**, deep in the interior; also a famous ramen town. It's also the gateway for Daisetsuzan National Park, Japan's largest national park and a mostly untouched wilderness of dense forest high in the mountains.

There are three villages on the perimeter of the park: **Tokachidake Onsen**, **Asahidake Onsen** and **Sōunkyō Onsen**. All have hot springs, lodging and good day treks. Don't miss **Fukiage Roten-no-yu**, near Tokachidake Onsen, one of Japan's best in-the-wild onsen. It's also worth spending a night at **Daisetsu Kōgen Sansō**, a truly remote mountain lodge.

Continue east to the World Heritage–listed **Shiretoko National Park**, a spit of land that Hokkaidō's indigenous people, the Ainu, referred to as 'the end of the world'. There are hikes here through primeval woods and more hidden hot springs.

Akan National Park is most famous for its startlingly clear blue caldera lakes, Kussharo-ko and Mashū-ko. This is also the best place on Hokkaidō to connect with Ainu culture, starting with a visit to the village, Akan Kotan.

Finally head down to **Kushiro-shitsugen National Park**, home to the endangered Japanese red-crowned crane. From **Kushiro** it's easy work on the expressway back to New Chitose Airport, south of Sapporo.

Top: Hiking, Asahi-dake (p633)
Bottom: Ganso Ramen Yokochō (p603), Sapporo

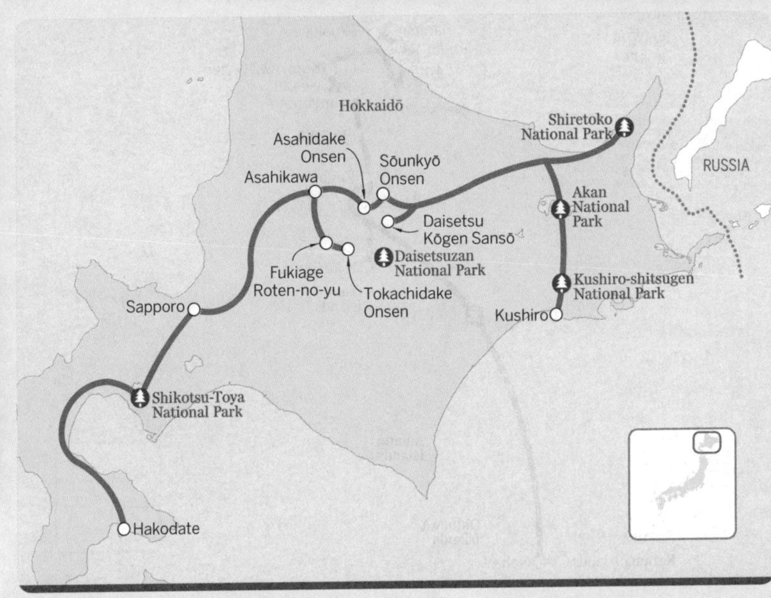
Hokkaidō
Shiretoko
National Park
Asahidake
Onsen
Sōunkyō
Onsen
Asahikawa
RUSSIA
Akan
National
Park
Daisetsu
Kōgen Sansō
Daisetsuzan
National Park
Fukiage
Roten-no-yu
Tokachidake
Onsen
Kushiro-shitsugen
National Park
Sapporo
Kushiro
Shikotsu-Toya
National Park
Hakodate

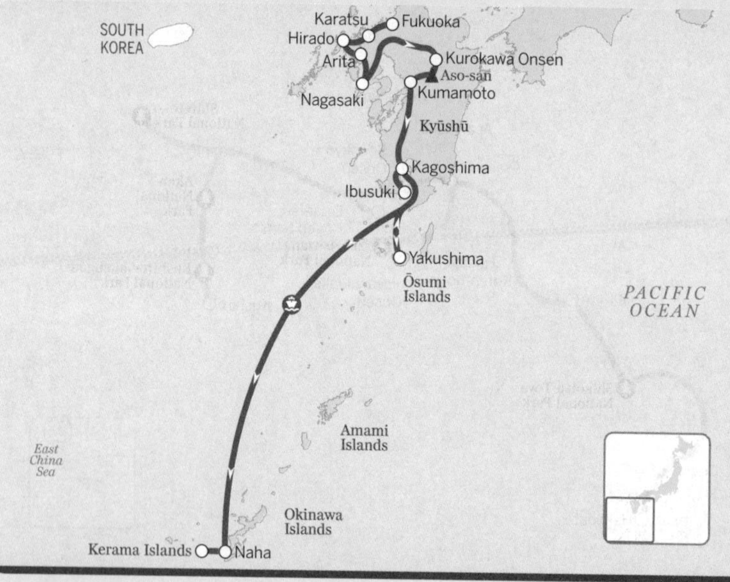
SOUTH
KOREA
Karatsu
Fukuoka
Hirado
Arita
Nagasaki
Kurokawa Onsen
Aso-san
Kumamoto
Kyūshū
Kagoshima
Ibusuki
Yakushima
Ōsumi
Islands
PACIFIC
OCEAN
Amami
Islands
East
China
Sea
Okinawa
Islands
Kerama Islands
Naha

Top: Waterfall, Yakushima (p789)
Bottom: Kurokawa Onsen (p751)

AIDO/SHUTTERSTOCK ©
DRYADPHOTOS/SHUTTERSTOCK ©

2 WEEKS Kyūshū & Okinawa

Considered off the beaten track, Kyūshū really delivers: it's got vibrant cities, layers of history, excellent onsen and smoking volcanoes. If you've been to Japan before, or want to see something totally different, this trip is for you.

Fly into **Fukuoka** from Tokyo and spend a day getting to know this hip young city, famous for its ramen. You can tour Kyūshū easily enough by train – there's a rail pass just for the island – but it helps to have a car. This will come in handy for working your way down the coast to Nagasaki through the pottery towns, **Karatsu** and **Arita**, with a detour to **Hirado**.

History, of course, weighs heavily on **Nagasaki**, the second Japanese city destroyed by an atomic bomb. But as Japan's only truly open port during the 200-year period of isolation in the 17th to 19th centuries, Nagasaki has cosmopolitan legacy that predates its historic tragedy and lives on today in its food and architecture.

From Nagasaki cut into the heartland to **Kurokawa Onsen**, one of Japan's best onsen towns, where you can stay in a ryokan. Continue south, past the active volcano **Aso-san** (if it's calm, you can get close) and the castle town **Kumamoto** (still recovering from a 2016 earthquake) to **Kagoshima**. This city at the tip of the Shimabara Peninsula is known for *tonkatsu* (breaded and fried pork cutlets), *shōchū* (strong distilled liquor) and Sakurajima – the smoking volcano that lords over the skyline. South of Kagoshima are the hot sand baths of **Ibusuki**.

Return the car and catch a speedboat from Kagoshima to magical **Yakushima**, an island with primeval, moss-strewn forests and seaside onsen. Make it an overnight trip (or longer – there are great hiking options here).

Back in Kagoshima, take the slow ferry for an epic overnight ride to Okinawa-hontō, the largest of the Okinawa Islands. Spend a day or two exploring the capital city **Naha**, the former seat of the Ryūkyū Empire, sipping fresh juice from the market and getting your fill of island delicacies. From Naha, it's a one-hour jet-foil ride to the idyllic, palm-fringed **Kerama Islands** – where you can get your beach fix. Then catch a flight back to Tokyo from Naha.

Off the Beaten Track: Japan

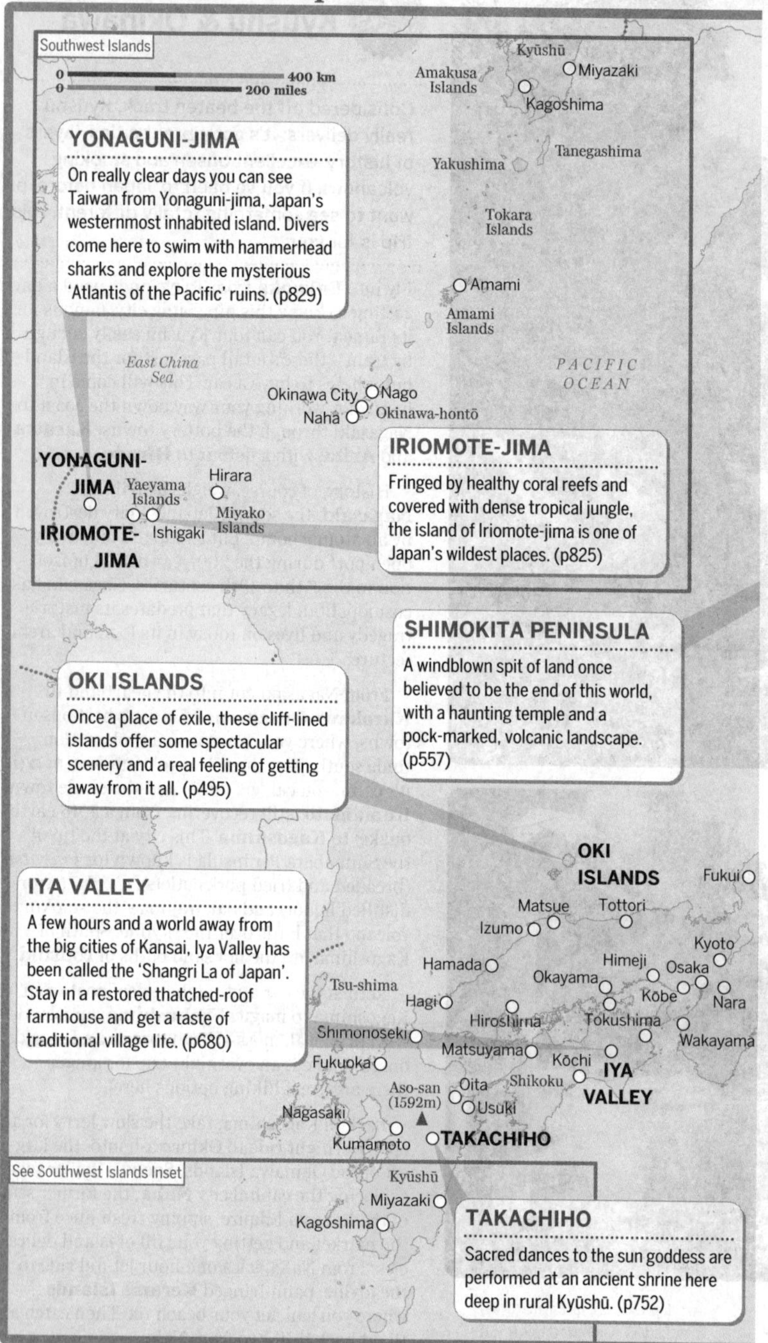
Southwest Islands
0 400 km
0 200 miles
YONAGUNI-JIMA
On really clear days you can see Taiwan from Yonaguni-jima, Japan's westernmost inhabited island. Divers come here to swim with hammerhead sharks and explore the mysterious 'Atlantis of the Pacific' ruins. (p829)
Kyūshū
Miyazaki
Amakusa Islands
Kagoshima
Yakushima
Tanegashima
Tokara Islands
Amami
Amami Islands
East China Sea
PACIFIC OCEAN
Okinawa City
Nago
Naha
Okinawa-hontō
IRIOMOTE-JIMA
Fringed by healthy coral reefs and covered with dense tropical jungle, the island of Iriomote-jima is one of Japan's wildest places. (p825)
YONAGUNI-JIMA
Yaeyama Islands
Hirara
Miyako Islands
Ishigaki
IRIOMOTE-JIMA
SHIMOKITA PENINSULA
A windblown spit of land once believed to be the end of this world, with a haunting temple and a pock-marked, volcanic landscape. (p557)
OKI ISLANDS
Once a place of exile, these cliff-lined islands offer some spectacular scenery and a real feeling of getting away from it all. (p495)
IYA VALLEY
A few hours and a world away from the big cities of Kansai, Iya Valley has been called the 'Shangri La of Japan'. Stay in a restored thatched-roof farmhouse and get a taste of traditional village life. (p680)
OKI ISLANDS
Fukui
Matsue
Tottori
Izumo
Kyoto
Hamada
Himeji
Osaka
Okayama
Tsu-shima
Kōbe
Nara
Hagi
Hiroshima
Tokushima
Shimonoseki
Wakayama
Matsuyama
Kōchi
IYA VALLEY
Fukuoka
Aso-san (1592m)
Oita
Shikoku
Usuki
Nagasaki
Kumamoto
TAKACHIHO
See Southwest Islands Inset
Kyūshū
Miyazaki
Kagoshima
TAKACHIHO
Sacred dances to the sun goddess are performed at an ancient shrine here deep in rural Kyūshū. (p752)

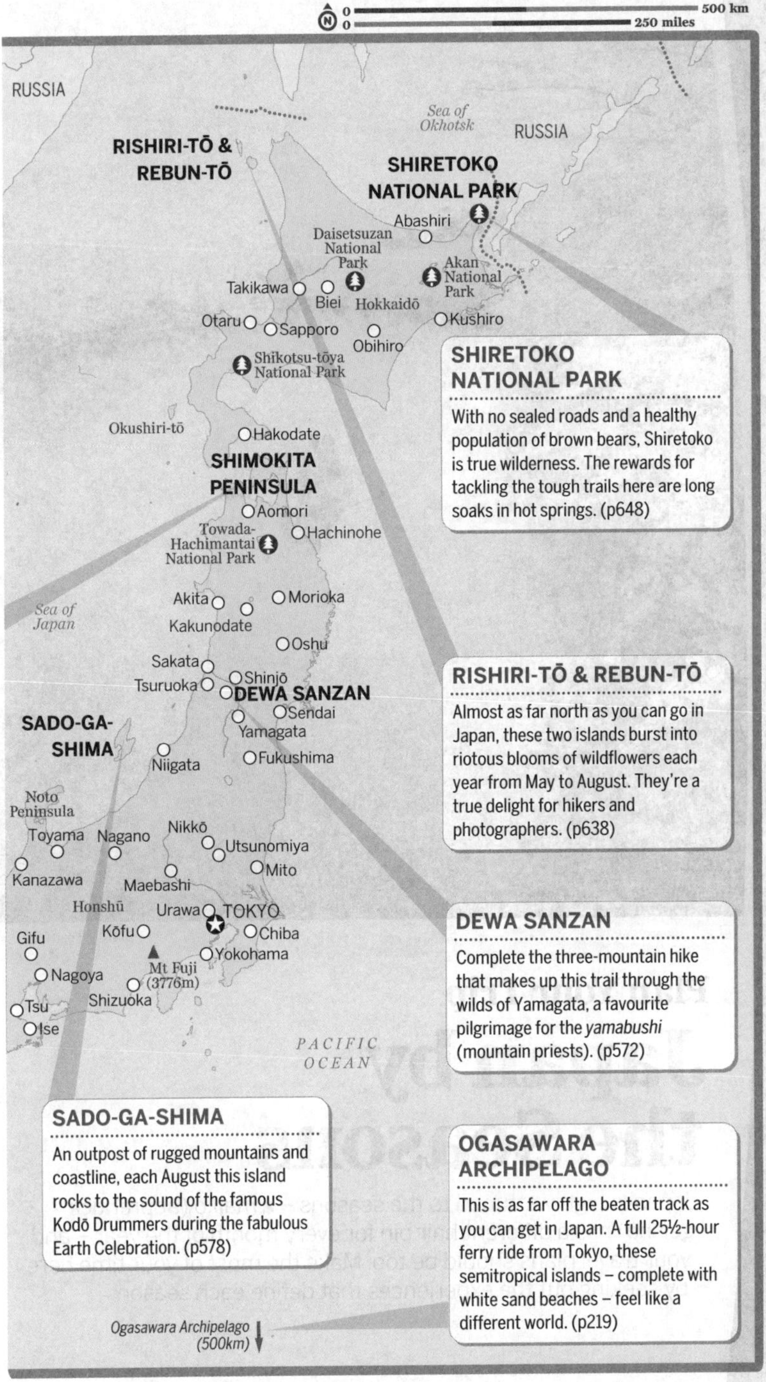

SHIRETOKO NATIONAL PARK

With no sealed roads and a healthy population of brown bears, Shiretoko is true wilderness. The rewards for tackling the tough trails here are long soaks in hot springs. (p648)

RISHIRI-TŌ & REBUN-TŌ

Almost as far north as you can go in Japan, these two islands burst into riotous blooms of wildflowers each year from May to August. They're a true delight for hikers and photographers. (p638)

DEWA SANZAN

Complete the three-mountain hike that makes up this trail through the wilds of Yamagata, a favourite pilgrimage for the *yamabushi* (mountain priests). (p572)

SADO-GA-SHIMA

An outpost of rugged mountains and coastline, each August this island rocks to the sound of the famous Kodō Drummers during the fabulous Earth Celebration. (p578)

OGASAWARA ARCHIPELAGO

This is as far off the beaten track as you can get in Japan. A full 25½-hour ferry ride from Tokyo, these semitropical islands – complete with white sand beaches – feel like a different world. (p219)

Hirosaki-kōen (p551), Hirosaki

Plan Your Trip

Japan by the Seasons

Japan is highly attuned to the seasons – a *maiko* (apprentice geisha) has a different hair pin for every month of the year – and your travel plans should be too. Make the most of your time here by seeking out the experiences that define each season.

Top Hanami Spots

Maruyama-kōen (p321)

Kyoto's classic *hanami* spot, known for its *yozakura* (night blossoms), when the trees are illuminated after dark.

Yoyogi-kōen (p108)

This big grassy Tokyo park becomes a week-long party scene.

Yoshino (p414)

Japan's most famous cherry-blossom viewing spot is this remote Kansai mountain village with its *hito-me-sen-bon* (1000 trees in a glance) viewpoint.

Hirosaki-kōen (p551)

There are over 5000 cherry trees in this park on the grounds of a castle in deep Tōhoku (northern Honshū).

Kakunodate (p562)

An old samurai district in Akita (Tōhoku) where the riverbank becomes a tunnel of pink.

Churei-tō Pagoda (p172)

The ultimate Japan photo-op is this hillside pagoda surrounded by cherry trees foregrounding Mt Fuji.

Spring (March–May)

Cherry Blossoms

Spring is, of course, the season for the *sakura* (cherry blossoms). The season starts in Kyūshū – Okinawa doesn't get the same blooms as the rest of Japan – in mid- to late-March, moving northward and hitting major cities in Honshū (like Kyoto and Tokyo) as early as late March; the season in Tōhoku starts in mid-April and in Hokkaidō in late April (these more remote areas that bloom later see fewer crowds).

The blossoms really peak ('full bloom' is called *mankai*) about a week after the buds start to open; the weekend nearest to *mankai* is when the biggest crowds gather for blossom-viewing parties called *hanami*. Over the next week or so the petals start to fall, covering parks and rivers in carpets of pink. Follow the forecast here: www.kyuhoshi.com/japan-cherry-blossom-forecast.

More Spring Blooms

Sakura are not the be all and end all of spring blooms: a few weeks later come the azaleas and the wisteria, followed by the irises in June – Kyoto's Kinkaku-ji (p333) is framed by them. Anytime in spring is a wonderful time to visit Japan's gardens; there's always something in bloom. Once rainy season sets in, around late June, the hydrangeas come out, big moon faces of colour against the misty grey skies; Kamakura (p182) and Hakone (p187) are both good places to see them.

Green Mountains

In the mountains fresh green appears in strata, moving higher up in elevation as May turns into June. It's still too early to go up too high, but destinations like Takayama (p245) are lovely in spring. So are Shikoku (p663) and Kumano Kodō (p424), both old pilgrimage destinations. Rural inns serve dishes with *sansai*, literally 'mountain vegetables' – fresh shoots and fern fronds collected in the mountains and served atop noodles or in tempura.

Summer (June–August)

Escaping the Heat

Summer in much of Japan is hot and sticky; this time of year the typical greeting is *'Atsui desu ne*?' (Hot, isn't it?). The cities in particular are scorching and many locals head to the hills to cool off. Popular destinations include Hokkaidō (p591) – which will be abloom with wildflowers – and mountain resort towns like Hakone (p187) and Karuizawa (p303). This is peak hiking season in the upper elevations, when you can summit Mt Fuji (p168) and head deep into the Alps and

HOW TO HANAMI

So you've planned your whole trip around the cherry blossoms, but how exactly is *hanami* (blossom viewing) done? There are essentially two different styles: a picnic in a park under the flowering trees or a stroll along a path lined with them; the latter are often lantern-lit in the evening. Picnics usually start early and the most gung-ho *hanami*-goers will turn up very early to secure a prime spot with a plastic ground sheet. However, you can usually find a good sliver of ground whenever you turn up, unless you've got a large group. You can get a ground sheet, along with food and booze, at a convenience store – or go upscale and stock up on picnic supplies at a *depachika* (department store food hall).

Hokkaidō's Daisetsuzan National Park (p632).

Japanese school holidays are short – from mid-July through August – and this is when beach destinations, like those on the Izu Peninsula (p195), the Izu Islands (p205) and the coasts of Kansai, will be full of students and families. Outside of this limited window many beaches are dead quiet; if that's what you prefer, visit just before or after.

Summer in the Cities

Of course not everyone gets away and city dwellers have come up with their own strategies – new and old – for beating the heat. One that you'll see in big cities around Japan is beer gardens held on department store rooftops, serving free-flowing lager and summer staples like fresh edamame.

Kyoto (p311) has a number of long-held summer traditions that make this a fantastic time of year to visit the old imperial capital. Restaurants along the city's central Kamo-gawa set up *kawayuka,* terraces suspended on stilts over the riverbank, for alfresco dining. Up in the foothills north of the city, in Kibune (p442), restaurants offer dining on *kawadoko* – temporary platforms set up just inches above the Kibune-gawa. It's best to book ahead for these experiences.

Tokyo (p87) also has its own tradition: *yakatabune*. These are traditional pleasure boats, strung with lanterns and open on the side – to let in a cool breeze – that cruise up and down the Sumida-gawa and around Tokyo Bay (p113).

Autumn (September–November)

Autumn Leaves

While they don't get parties, autumn leaves do draw phenomenal crowds to resort areas and temples and gardens that are known for their colourful displays for *momiji* (leaf-viewing). Most prized of all are the maples, which turn fiery red. The leaves start to change as early as late September in Hokkaidō (p591) and most mountain areas (depending on elevation) and last throughout October. The major coastal cities – Tokyo (p87), Nagoya (p226), Osaka (p368) and Kyoto (p311) – see their autumn colours in late November.

On the one hand, the scenery is spectacular; on the other, you might want to purposely steer clear of the crowds. Nikkō (p209) and Chūzen-ji Onsen (p216), for example, get clogged with traffic. Kyoto is very popular this time of year; Tokyo, not so much. Tokyo has its own autumn tree, the gingko, which turns gold the first week of December.

This is a good time of year to visit Northern Honshū (p521), where the leaves hit their stride in late October and early November; there are crowds, yes, but not like the more densely populated areas down south. It's also chilly enough to appreciate the region's fantastic onsen and belly-warming hotpot dishes, but not cold enough for snow to keep you off the roads. The temples and shrines of rural Nara (p400), fronting mountains, are also good off-the-beaten-track fall spots. Walk the Yama-no-be-no-michi (p411) past persimmon orchards and golden rice fields.

BLANSCAPE/SHUTTERSTOCK ©

Kyoto (p311)

Cultural Attractions

During the summer, most museums hold crowd-pleasing special exhibitions. It's in the fall that they tend to hold ones that appeal more to serious followers of the arts. There are performing arts festivals in Tokyo (p122) and Kyoto (p340), plus two film festivals in Tokyo at this time of year.

Of particular note in Kyoto in autumn is the Kyoto Heritage Preservation Association's Autumn Special Exhibit, when 20 or so historic structures generally closed to the public – like Tō-ji's five-storey pagoda (p314) – open their doors. Many temples around Japan hold special openings once or twice a year to display treasures that are too delicate to be shown year-round; while this varies from place to place, autumn is the most common time of year for this to occur. Temples in and around Nara (p400) have many special openings, too. Enquire at TICs.

Winter (December–February)

Quiet Time

Winter is considered the off-season for travel in Japan (skiing aside). It's cold, yes, but Japanese winters are relatively clear, and in the mornings at least, sunny. Sights are less crowded. Stripped of their vegetation, gardens, temples and shrines can take on a forlorn appearance; however, this time of year is conducive to the kind of private moments that can be hard to come by in Japan's more popular destinations like Kyoto (p311). Snow does come for Kyoto once or twice a year, in which case you should make a beeline for Kinkaku-ji (p333) – the golden temple really pops against a white backdrop.

CLUB4TRAVELER/SHUTTERSTOCK ©

Kinkaku-ji (p333), Kyoto

Winter Scenes

Blanketed in snow, the mountain monastery Kōya-san (p418) is a winter sleeper hit; it's bitterly cold, but some find the enchanting atmosphere worth it. Another classic winter snowscape: the villages of Shirakawa-gō and Gokayama (p254), with their steep thatched roofs coated in a thick layer of white. Unless you're a very experienced winter driver, you'll want to stay off the roads at higher elevations, sticking to places accessible by public transport.

Winter is also the best time to spot Mt Fuji: go to Fuji Five Lakes (p167) or Hakone (p187) – bonus: also a hot-spring resort – for views of the iconic volcano.

Seafood & Sake

This is the peak season for Kansai's signature hot-spring resort, Kinosaki Onsen (p448) – not only for its baths but also for the snow crabs that are pulled in this time of year from the Sea of Japan and served in the town's inns and restaurants. Fair warning: this experience doesn't come cheap. Actually anywhere on the Sea of Japan coast is a draw in winter for foodies: in addition to crab, the frigid waters produce fish rich in fat – considered the tastiest of all is *kan-buri* (winter yellow tail); try it in Kanazawa (p258).

Winter also means *shiboritate* – the fresh-pressed, first sake of the season, served chilled and usually unpasteurised. At the beginning of the season, breweries hang *sugidama* (balls of cedar fronds) from their eaves; as the fronds turn from green to brown they chart the maturation of the sake.

Plan Your Trip
Activities

Mountainous, volcanic Japan offers a wide range of outdoor activities: historic walking trails, epic hikes, powder skiing and cycling. Of course, Japan's signature activity is soaking in steaming onsen (hot springs) – a great follow-up to any of the above. In sub-tropical Okinawa, you can dive, snorkel and sunbathe.

Skiing

Japan is not the skiing and snowboarding world's best-kept secret any more. Those in the know come from around the globe to take advantage of the country's impressive snowfall, stunning mountain vistas, reasonable costs, friendly locals and great variety of après-ski options. Japan is a surprisingly reasonable place to ski or snowboard, with lift tickets and accommodation competitively priced.

The word for 'ski' in Japanese is the same as in English (though it's pronounced more like 'sukee'). At major resorts you won't encounter much of a language barrier: many employ a number of English-speaking foreigners and Japanese who have spent time overseas. All major signs and maps are translated into English, and provided you have some experience of large resorts back home, you'll find the layout and organisation of Japanese resorts to be pretty intuitive.

The season usually kicks off in December, though conditions are highly variable. January and February are peak months across the country. Things begin to warm up in March, heralding the close of the season in April. More snow falls on the Sea of Japan side of the mountains, with more snow the further north you go. Hokkaidō's Niseko ski area receives a whopping 15m of snow every year!

An excellent website for checking out the Japan ski scene is www.snowjapan.com.

Best Outdoor Destinations

Hokkaidō (p591)

World-class skiing in Niseko, Furano and beyond; hike for days in Daisetsuzan and Shiretoko National Parks.

Northern Japan Alps (p276)

High mountain trails and soaring views in Kamikōchi; excellent skiing in Hakuba.

Kumano Kodō (p424)

Walks and treks for all levels along ancient pilgrim trails on the Kii Peninsula.

Okinawa (p785)

Dive alongside sea turtles, manta rays and even hammerhead sharks; also some idyllic beaches.

Shimanami Kaidō (p696)

Japan's most famous cycling route crosses a chain of bridges over the Inland Sea from western Honshū to Shikoku.

Minakami Onsen-kyo (p306)

Central Honshū's hub for outdoor adventure sports, including canyoning, rafting and mountain biking.

Shikoku (p663)

Hiking, canyoning and zip-lining in the mountainous interior and a cool surf scene in Shishikui on the Anan Coast.

Where to Ski

Japan's best-known ski resorts are found in the Japan Alps, Nagano and on the northern island of Hokkaidō. The Japan Alps lay claim to the highest mountains, while Hokkaidō boasts the deepest and most regular snowfall in the country.

While the ski resorts of northern Honshū have seen tough times since the Great East Japan Earthquake, they offer up some wonderful options. And don't forget the Niigata mountains, easily accessed by *shinkansen* (bullet train) from Tokyo. In fact, many resorts can be reached by public transport, eliminating the need for a rental car.

There are some 500 ski areas in Japan. Here is our pick of the best:

Niseko (p606) As far as most foreign skiers are concerned, Niseko is how you say 'powder' in Japanese. This is understandable, as Niseko receives an average snowfall of 15m annually. Located on Hokkaidō, Niseko is actually four interconnected ski areas: Niseko Annupuri, Niseko Village (also known as Higashiyama), Grand Hirafu and Hanazono.

Furano (p629) More or less in the centre of Hokkaidō, Furano shot to world fame after hosting FIS World Ski and Snowboarding Cup events. Relatively undiscovered in comparison to Niseko, Furano rewards savvy powder fiends with polished runs through pristine birch forests.

TOP SKIING TIPS

- ➡ The majority of Japanese skiers start skiing at 9am, have lunch exactly at noon, and get off the hill by 3pm. If you work on a slightly different schedule, you may avoid a lot of the crowds.
- ➡ Midweek is good if you don't like lift lines.
- ➡ Off-piste and out-of-bounds skiing is often high quality but also illegal at many ski areas, resulting in the confiscation of your lift pass if you're caught by the ski patrol. Check out local policies.
- ➡ The information counter at the base of the mountain always has helpful and polite staff available to answer questions.

Sapporo Teine (p600) It's so close to Sapporo, Hokkaidō's capital, that buses run from downtown hotels to Sapporo Teine. You can swish down slopes used in the 1972 Sapporo Winter Olympics by day and enjoy the raucous restaurants, bars and clubs of Susukino by night.

Hakuba (p287) The quintessential Japan Alps ski resort, Hakuba offers eye-popping views in addition to excellent and varied skiing in six resorts. Hakuba hosted Winter Olympic events in 1998 and is led by the legendary Happō-One Ski Resort (pronounced 'hah-poh-oh-neh').

Shiga Kōgen (p301) Nagano Prefecture's Shiga Kōgen is one of the largest ski resorts in the world, with an incredible 18 different ski areas and 16 hotel areas, all interconnected by trails, lifts and shuttle buses – and accessible with one lift ticket. With such a variety of terrain on offer, there is something for everyone here.

Nozawa Onsen (p298) This quaint little village is tucked high up in the mountains northeast of Nagano city. It offers a good variety of runs, including some challenging mogul courses. Snowboarders will enjoy the terrain park and half-pipe, and there's even a cross-country skiing course that traverses the peaks.

Myōkō Kōgen (p300) Much less developed than the other resorts listed here, Myōkō Kōgen is directly north of Nagano city and close to the Sea of Japan. Head here for an off-the-beaten-path ski holiday in the powder-rich Myōkō mountain range.

Echigo-Yuzawa Onsen (p583) Talk about easy to get to! Echigo-Yuzawa Onsen has its own *shinkansen* station on the Jōetsu line to Niigata and you can literally go skiing as a day trip from Tokyo (77 minutes one way by the fastest service.) Gala Yuzawa is the resort to head to here.

Naeba (p584) Home to Dragondola, reportedly the longest gondola in the world (5.5km), Naeba has two massive ski areas, centred on the Prince Hotel Naeba, that cater to your every whim and fancy.

Zaō Onsen Ski Resort (p569) Arguably the top ski slopes in Northern Honshū, Zaō has a huge selection of beginner and intermediate runs, broad winding courses and excellent après-ski onsen options.

Tazawako Ski Park (p564) Akita Prefecture's largest winter sports destination, Tazawako Ski Park has slopes that wind down Akita Komagatake and overlook the shores of Tazawa-ko. Expect fewer foreigners but a friendly welcome.

Skiing in Japan

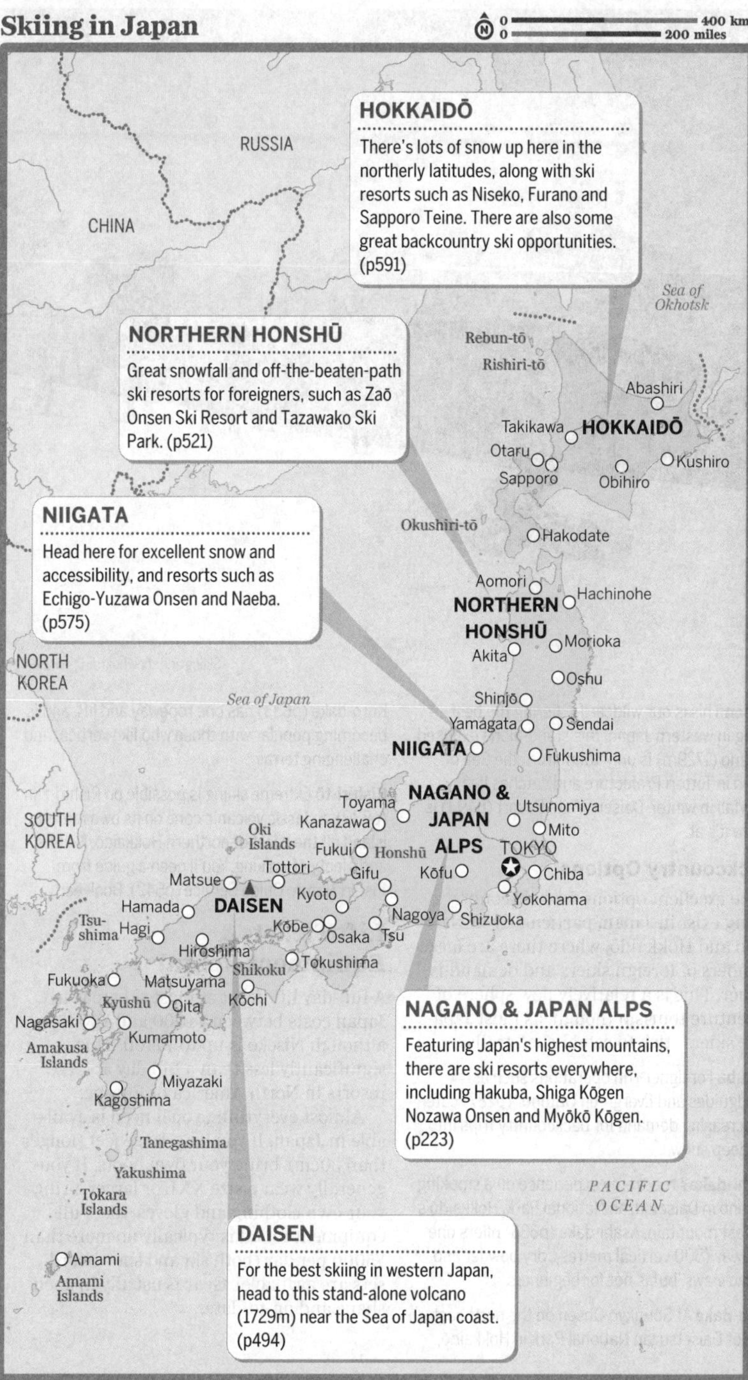
0 400 km
0 200 miles
HOKKAIDŌ
There's lots of snow up here in the northerly latitudes, along with ski resorts such as Niseko, Furano and Sapporo Teine. There are also some great backcountry ski opportunities. (p591)
NORTHERN HONSHŪ
Great snowfall and off-the-beaten-path ski resorts for foreigners, such as Zaō Onsen Ski Resort and Tazawako Ski Park. (p521)
NIIGATA
Head here for excellent snow and accessibility, and resorts such as Echigo-Yuzawa Onsen and Naeba. (p575)
NAGANO & JAPAN ALPS
Featuring Japan's highest mountains, there are ski resorts everywhere, including Hakuba, Shiga Kōgen Nozawa Onsen and Myōkō Kōgen. (p223)
DAISEN
For the best skiing in western Japan, head to this stand-alone volcano (1729m) near the Sea of Japan coast. (p494)
RUSSIA
CHINA
NORTH KOREA
SOUTH KOREA
Sea of Okhotsk
Sea of Japan
PACIFIC OCEAN
Rebun-tō
Rishiri-tō
Abashiri
Takikawa
HOKKAIDŌ
Otaru
Sapporo
Obihiro
Kushiro
Okushiri-tō
Hakodate
Aomori
Hachinohe
NORTHERN HONSHŪ
Morioka
Akita
Oshu
Shinjō
Yamagata
Sendai
NIIGATA
Fukushima
Toyama
NAGANO & JAPAN ALPS
Utsunomiya
Kanazawa
Mito
Oki Islands
Fukui
Honshū
TOKYO
Tottori
Gifu
Kōfu
Chiba
Matsue
Kyoto
Yokohama
Hamada
DAISEN
Nagoya
Shizuoka
Tsu-shima
Hagi
Kōbe
Tsu
Osaka
Hiroshima
Tokushima
Shikoku
Fukuoka
Matsuyama
Kyūshū
Oita
Kōchi
Nagasaki
Kumamoto
Amakusa Islands
Miyazaki
Kagoshima
Tanegashima
Yakushima
Tokara Islands
Amami
Amami Islands

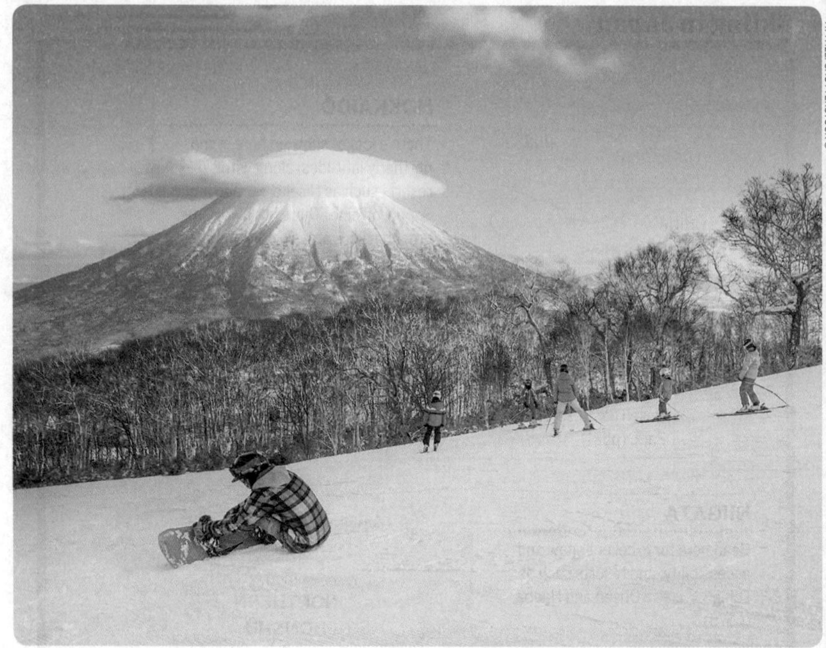

Skiing and snowboarding, Niseko (p606)

Daisen This is our wildcard. Offering the best skiing in western Japan, this stand-alone exposed volcano (1729m) is only 10km from the Sea of Japan in Tottori Prefecture and catches heavy snowfall in winter. Daisen White Resort (p494) is where it's at.

Backcountry Options

Some excellent options for backcountry skiing exist in Japan, particularly in Nagano and Hokkaidō, where there are large numbers of foreign skiers and demand is higher. This is a relatively new sphere of adventure tourism though, as most Japanese skiers stick to established trails.

Hakuba Foreigner-run operations such as Goodguides and Evergreen Outdoor (p287) cater to increasing demand for backcountry trips into the deep snow.

Asahi-dake An extreme experience on a smoking volcano in Daisetsuzan National Park. Hokkaidō's highest mountain, Asahi-dake (p633) offers one ropeway (500 vertical metres), dry powder and scenic views, but is not for beginners.

Kuro-dake At Sōunkyō Onsen on the northeastern side of Daisetsuzan National Park in Hokkaidō, Kuro-dake (p633) has one ropeway and lift, and is becoming popular with those who like vertical and challenging terrain.

Rishiri-tō Extreme skiing is possible on Rishiri-zan (p639), a classic volcanic cone on its own remote island off the coast of northern Hokkaidō. No lifts and plenty of walking. You'll need a guide from Rishiri Nature Guide Service (p642). Book early.

Lift Tickets & Equipment Rental

A full-day lift ticket at most ski areas in Japan costs between ¥4000 and ¥6000, although Niseko is up to ¥7400. This is significantly less than a full day at large resorts in North America or Europe.

Almost everything you'll need is available in Japan. If you have large feet (longer than 30cm), bring your own boots. If you generally wear a size XXL or larger, bring your own clothing and gloves, too. Full equipment rental is typically no more than ¥5000 per day (both ski and snowboard sets are available). Gear is usually in good shape and up-to-date.

Accommodation & Food

You can find plenty of decent accommodation in the ¥6500 to ¥10,000 range at major ski areas in Japan, and this price will often include one or two meals. This is well under what you'd expect to pay for similar accommodation in North America or Europe. In big resort areas you can find Western-style hotels (from midrange to as good as it gets) near the lifts.

For budget travellers, many resorts also have a variety of backpacker-type hostels, and families will be glad to know that young children (under six years of age) can usually stay for free or at a significant discount. Especially in Niseko and Hakuba, many accommodations are run by foreigners who've decided to stick around and well know the needs of overseas guests. Kamoshika Views (p288) in Hakuba is a great example.

On-slope meals mostly top out at around ¥1000. Restaurants serve local dishes like ramen, udon (wheat noodles), *karē-raisu* (curry rice) and *gyūdon* (sliced beef on rice), as well as sandwiches, pizza and burgers. In larger resorts with an après-ski scene there are plenty of restaurants around the accommodations; at smaller places, it's a safer bet to book meals at your accommodation.

Hiking

Blessed with a geography that is more than two-thirds mountain terrain, Japan offers outdoors enthusiasts the most diverse climate in all of Asia. From the rugged shores and wind-weathered peaks of Hokkaidō in the north to the tropical island jungles of Okinawa in the south, this country has it all. Mt Fuji is 3776m tall and 20 other peaks top 3000m. For more on hikes throughout Japan, check out www.hikinginjapan.com.

Where to Hike

Mt Fuji & Around Tokyo

Mt Fuji (p168) Japan's highest and best-known mountain, at 3776m. A gruelling climb that more than 300,000 people make each summer, many hiking overnight to be at the peak at sunrise.

Takao-san (p208) A popular day hike less than an hour west of Shinjuku. Can be walked year-round, has a high point of 599m and is good for families.

Oku-Tama Region (p208) One of Tokyo's top hiking getaway spots, with mountains, waterfalls, woodlands and walking trails. Head to Mitake-san for the day.

Kamakura (p182) The 3km Daibutsu hiking course winds its way past ancient temples and shrines in Japan's medieval capital to the giant Buddha statue at Hase.

The Japan Alps & Central Honshū

Home to the North, Central and South Alps, central Honshū is a hiking hot spot for Japan.

North Alps Excellent high-mountain trails. From Kamikōchi (p284), climb Yariga-take (3180m) and Oku-hotaka-dake (3190m). From Murodō on the Tateyama–Kurobe Alpine Route (p275), climb Tateyama (3015m) and Tsurugi-dake (2999m). From Hakuba (p287), take the gondola and chair-lifts to climb Karamatsu-dake (2695m).

Hakusan (p266) A sacred peak in Hakusan National Park, the 'white mountain' is criss-crossed with great hiking trails.

Nakasendō (p241) Walk the 8km hike from Magome to Tsumago in the historic and attractive Kiso Valley.

Kyoto

Daimonji-yama (p334) There is no finer walk in the city than the 30-minute climb to the viewpoint above Ginkaku-ji in Northern Higashiyama.

Fushimi Inari-Taisha (p313) A 4km pathway up Inari-yama in southeast Kyoto is lined with thousands of red *torii* (shrine gates) and hundreds of stone foxes.

Kurama & Kibune (p442) Only 30 minutes north of Kyoto, two tranquil valleys are linked by a trail over the ridge between them. A peaceful escape from the city.

Kansai

Kumano Kodō (p425) Walk on ancient pilgrimage routes in the wilds of the Kii Peninsula. Or go the whole way and walk the 500km 33 Sacred Temples of the Kannon Pilgrimage.

Yama-no-be-no-michi (p411) Ramble through the Nara countryside among farming villages, 1300-year-old emperors' tombs and a rich mix of rural sights.

Hiroshima & Western Honshū

Daisen (p494) A five-hour return climb of this 1729m stand-alone volcano affords excellent views of the San-in region.

Sandan Gorge (p462) An 11km ravine about 50km northwest of Hiroshima, Sandan-kyō gives access to waterfalls, forests and fresh air.

Miyajima (p464) There's good walking to be had on this well-known island not far from Hiroshima. Climb the high point of Misen (530m).

Kuniga Coast (p497) The coastal romp from Matengai cliff to Kuniga beach offers jaw-dropping scenery on the sleepy island of Nishino-shima, in the Oki Islands Geopark.

Northern Honshū (Tōhoku)

Dewa Sanzan (p572) The collective name for three sacred peaks – Haguro-san, Gas-san and Yudono-san – which represent birth, death and rebirth respectively. The climb up Gas-san (1984m) is a good challenge.

Bandai-san (p588) There are great tracks to climb this 1819m peak in Fukushima Prefecture.

Hakkōda-san (p556) Wildflower-filled marshes, a ridge trail and peaks in Aomori Prefecture.

Sapporo & Hokkaidō

There's so much hiking here that you could spend weeks in the northern wilds.

Daisetsuzan National Park (p632) Pick your walks in this massive park in the centre of Hokkaidō, with day trips to a weeklong challenge the length of the park.

Shiretoko National Park (p648) This World Heritage Site offers day walks of up to three days, plenty of hot springs and *higuma* (brown bears).

Akan National Park (p652) Brilliant day-trip options including Me-Akan-dake (p654; 1499m) and O-Akan-dake (p655; 1371m).

BEST...

- Iconic hike: Mt Fuji (p168)
- Remote volcano: Rishiri-zan (p639), Hokkaidō
- Island hike: Miyanoura-dake (p791), Yakushima
- Base for hiking: Kamikōchi (p284), North Alps
- Pilgrimage: 88 Temple walk (p667), Shikoku
- Scenery: Tateyama–Kurobe Alpine Route (p275), North Alps

Rishiri-zan (p639) A standalone volcano (1721m) on its own island off the northern coast of Hokkaidō.

Shikoku

Ishizuchi-san (p697) At 1982m, the highest peak in western Japan. Great day and overnight hikes in Ehime Prefecture.

Tsurugi-san (p685) At 1955m, Shikoku's second-highest peak provides both easy walks and multiday hiking opportunities.

88 Temple Pilgrimage (p667) 2015 was the 1200th birthday of Kōbō Daishi's legendary 1400km 88-temple pilgrimage around Shikoku.

Kyūshū

Kirishima-Kinkō-wan National Park (p777) Excellent options including climbing Karakuni-dake (1700m), Kirishima's highest peak.

Kaimon-dake (p775) This beautifully symmetrical 924m cone on the Satsuma Peninsula is a brilliant day walk.

Kujū-san (p759) Knock off Kyūshū's highest peak at 1791m, known for its spectacular pink azaleas in spring.

Aso-san (p747) Hiking at the world's largest volcanic caldera, 128km in circumference, is on hold following a devastating earthquake in 2016.

Okinawa & the Southwest Islands

Yakushima (p789) Lots of hiking options on this World Heritage–listed island. Climb Miyanoura-dake (1935m) or hike on myriad tracks that criss-cross the island.

Iriomote-jima (p825) A Japanese jungle hike on one of Okinawa Prefecture's westernmost islands.

Top Five Destinations for Experienced Hikers

If you're an experienced hiker and wandering around the mountains is one of your reasons for heading to Japan, look into the following hikes:

Kamikōchi (p284) This is the holy grail for Japanese hikers. This mountain-ringed village at the base of the North Alps offers plenty of options, none greater than a three-day circuit taking in Yariga-take (3180m) and Oku-Hotaka-dake (3190m) before returning to Kamikōchi.

Tateyama–Kurobe Alpine Route (p275) Take the opportunity to climb sacred Tateyama (3015m) and exhilarating Tsurugi-dake (2998m) in a two-

Hiking, Kamikōchi (p285)

day hike from Murodō (2450m) in the north of the North Alps. Or better yet, take six to seven days to hike south to Kamikōchi.

Yakushima (p789) There are wonderful options on this World Heritage–listed island off the tip of Kagoshima in Kyūshū. Climb Miyanoura-dake (1935m) in a day or consider a three-day traverse of the island.

Daisetsuzan National Park (p632) Lots of options here in spectacular Hokkaidō ranging from day trips using ropeways at Asahidake Onsen and Sōunkyō Onsen to the five- to seven-day 55km Daisetsuzan Grand Traverse.

Shikoku (p663) Put on your boots for a 40- to 60-day hike around the 88 Sacred Temples of Shikoku Pilgrimage (p667). Or with only a day free, climb western Japan's highest peak, Ishizuchi-san (p697; 1982m).

We emphasise that these hikes are for experienced and adventurous types only. Do your homework before you go, be well prepared, have the appropriate equipment, watch the weather forecasts, and never take the mountains lightly.

Mountain Huts & Camping

Japan's popular hiking routes typically have mountain huts that offer hot meals and a place to sleep, so weeklong hikes can be done with minimal gear. Rooms are shared and in most cases you'll be staking out a spot on the floor. Futons are provided, but you might want to bring your own sheet and pillow case.

The average price for a stay, including dinner and breakfast, is ¥8000 – in cash. Along popular trails during holiday times they fill up fast; try to reserve if you can (especially for Mt Fuji).

Mountain huts have their own culture: don't expect the same fawning service you get in a ryokan! Most people arrive around 3pm or 4pm and dinner is usually served at 5pm with lights out at 8pm. Your co-sleepers will begin to rise with the sun and start heading out around 5am.

Many hiking areas also have campgrounds, but you'll have to haul everything you need. It's okay to use a camp stove but no open fires. The cost is usually ¥500 to ¥1000 per person or tent.

Kinosaki Onsen (p448)

Hiking Seasons

Lower latitude and lower altitude hikes can be walked year-round. With heavy winter snowfalls, higher peaks such as the North, Central and South Alps and those in Hokkaidō have a July-to-October season; at the highest elevations in Hokkaidō snow can fall in early October. The official season for climbing Japan's tallest peak, Mt Fuji, is 1 July to mid-September.

Mountains in western Japan (Kansai, Western Honshū, Shikoku, Kyūshū), which have lower elevations than the Alps, have longer seasons, generally from April to November (if they get any snow at all).

A few other things to keep in mind: *tsuyu* (rainy season) strikes between early June and mid-July. The levels of rain aren't monsoonal and it won't necessarily rain everyday, but odds are high. *Tsuyu* has less effect the further north you go, and has little impact on Hokkaidō. The 10 days after the rainy season finishes, known as *tsuyu-aketōka* (the last 10 days or so of July) are considered the best for hiking – expect crowds!

More problematic are typhoons, which can roll through anytime between June and October. Check for typhoon warnings before heading out; do not hike during a typhoon.

Visiting an Onsen

Highly volcanic Japan has thousands of onsen (hot springs) scattered across the archipelago, which feed baths across the spectrum from humble to luxurious. The blissful relaxation that follows a good long soak can turn a sceptic into a convert and is likely to make you an onsen fanatic.

Onsen Styles

There are several different ways to experience an onsen. Many ryokan (traditional Japanese inns) are built on top of hot springs and have baths fed with onsen water. This is a great introductory experience: you can bath at your leisure, travelling between your room and the baths in a *yukata* (light cotton kimono, provided by inns to wear in-house). At some fancier ryokan you will have the option to upgrade to a room with its own private onsen bath.

Particularly abundant springs support whole resort towns, which will be made up of numerous ryokan, and sometimes Western-style hotels too, with baths. These may also have public bathhouses with onsen water, for which admission usually runs from ¥500 to ¥1000 – great for budget travellers.

Many inns, especially ones with famous baths, offer *higaeri-onsen* (日帰り温泉; bathing without accommodation), usually during the late morning and early afternoon; admission typically runs from ¥500 to ¥1500 and you'll need your own towel (or pay to rent one). It's a common sight at particular resort towns to see guests walking around town in *yukata* to the public baths or the baths of other inns – an act called *yu meguri* (making a round of the baths).

Some resort towns, and even some cities, will have day spas, with multiple baths and saunas. Admission to these runs from ¥1500 to ¥3000, with the option of additional treatments like massages or body scrubs. A few of these, like Tokyo's Ōedo Onsen Monogatari (p116), Hakone's Yunessun (p191) and Osaka's Spa World (p376), are more like onsen theme parks, with novelty baths and areas where mixed groups can hang out; they're popular with local families and couples.

There are also onsen in the wild. Hidden in the mountains or along undeveloped coasts, these humble baths may be no more than a pool in a riverbed blocked off with stones or a tidal basin beside crashing waves. Bathing is open-air, often co-ed and usually free. Hokkaidō, in particular, has some good ones, as do some of Japan's more far-flung islands. In many of these, it's okay to wear a swimsuit.

Ashi-yu (足湯; foot bath) Many onsen towns have free foot baths, often near the train station; roll up your trousers, take a seat on the bench and enjoy the body-warming effects. For such occasions, it's handy to have a small towel on hand.

Kashikiri-buro (貸切風呂; private bath) Some inns and day spas offer small, private baths that can be rented for a limited time (usually 40 to 60 minutes) for an additional fee; the fee varies depending on the luxe factor, but can be as low as ¥2000 and at some inns may be free. These baths, also sometimes called *kazoku-buro* (家族風呂; family bath), can be used alone or by up to two to four people.

Konyoku (混浴; co-ed bathing) A few rural inns and bathhouses, especially those in Tōhoku (Northern Honshū), are set up for co-ed bathing. In *konyoku*, women may be allowed to enter the baths wrapped in a larger towel – ask, or have a peek inside (or outside!) to see if this is the norm – but generally bathers of both sexes are respectful.

Rotemburo (露天風呂; outdoor bath) These offer the most delightful bathing experiences: the opportunity to soak while surrounded by mountain, river or ocean vistas. *Rotemburo* can be found at all styles of onsen.

Bathing Etiquette

First of all, relax...really. All you need to know to avoid causing alarm is to wash yourself before getting into the bath. But yes, you do need to get naked. With few exceptions, baths and changing rooms are gender-segregated. It's a good idea to memorise the characters for men (男) and women (女), which will be marked on the *noren* (curtains) hanging in front of the respective baths. (Some ryokan will swap the curtains in the mornings, so that guests can experience different baths, so do double-check the curtains).

If you're entering a day spa or public bathhouse, the first thing you'll encounter is a row of lockers for your shoes. Park your shoes, pay your admission and head to the correct changing room. At some larger day spas you'll be given a wristband, which can be used to open and close your locker in the changing room and also to charge any food, drinks or additional services to your tab, which you'll settle upon checking out. Some places may also keep your shoe locker key at the front desk as a deposit.

Next, head to the correct changing room. Take everything off here, storing your clothes, larger bath towel and belongings in the lockers or baskets provided. If there are no lockers, you can ask to leave valuables at the front desk.

Enter the bathing room with only a small towel; inns and days spas will provide these, otherwise you can purchase one at the front desk (around ¥100). While the towel – larger than a face cloth but smaller than a hand towel – seems too small to be useful, it is an important part of onsen etiquette. You can use it to wash (but make sure to give it a good rinse afterwards) or to cover yourself as you walk around. (It is not supposed to touch the

TATTOO WARNING

Some onsen and most day spas refuse entry to people with tattoos because of the association of tattoos with the *yakuza* (Japanese mafia). Those with strict policies will have signs posted that make their stance clear.

RACHIN MAPANYA/SHUTTERSTOCK ©

Cycling the Shimanami Kaidō (p470)

water though, so leave it on the side of the bath or – as the locals do – folded on top of your head). Most importantly, when you leave the bath, you'll use it to wipe yourself down before returning to the changing room, so as not to drip water on the floor.

Inside the bathing room, place a stool in front of one of the taps, sit down and give yourself a thorough wash. Make sure you rinse off all the suds. When you're done, it's polite to rinse off the stool for the next person. In the baths, keep splashing to a minimum and your head above the water (and your heart above water if you feel light-headed).

Top Onsen Destinations

Hakone (p187) Tokyo's favourite onsen escape, made up of seven small resorts nestled in the mountains about two hours from Tokyo. There are many gorgeous ryokan and day spas here.

The Japan Alps & Central Honshū There are several atmospheric onsen towns in the mountains here, with some lovely vistas from the outdoor baths. Some favourites include Shirahone Onsen (p284), Shin-Hotaka Onsen (p253) and Takaragawa Onsen (p306).

Kinosaki Onsen (p448) A quintessential onsen town, and Kansai's signature resort, with both public baths and onsen ryokan along a willow-lined river. Here guests ramble from bath to bath in *yukata*.

Northern Honshū The deep north is famous for its rustic wooden bathhouses and milky, mineral-rich waters. Remote Nyūtō Onsen (p566) is somewhere many Japanese would like to visit once in their lives.

Dōgo Onsen (p691) Storied Shikoku onsen – literally: it famously appears in Natsume Sōseki's classic novel *Botchan* – founded during 'the age of the gods' and currently housed in a castle-style building from 1894.

Kyūshū Several of Japan's most popular onsen resorts are here, including the rather commercial but fun Beppu (p755), more highbrow Yufuin (p762) and secluded Kurokawa Onsen (p751). In Ibusuki (p773), try immersing yourself in hot sand.

Public Bathhouses

As little as 50 years ago, many private homes in Japan did not have baths, so in the evenings people headed off to the local neighbourhood *sentō* (銭湯; public bath). More than just a place to wash oneself, the *sentō* served as a kind of community meeting hall, where news and gossip were traded and social ties strengthened. Most *sentō*-goers are neighbourhood regulars. This can be a little intimidating for first-timers, but don't let that put you off; just give your fellow bathers a brief nod and go about your business (correctly, of course!).

Bathhouses can be identified by their distinctive *noren* (half-length curtains over the doorway), which usually bear the hiragana (ゆ; *yu*) for hot water (occasionally, it may be written in kanji: 湯). If located where hot springs are present, the baths may use onsen water; most often it's ordinary tap water. You're expected to bring your own towel and toiletries; however, you can show up empty handed and rent a towel and purchase soap, shampoo etc for a small price.

Diving

Stunning both above and below the water's surface, the Southwest Islands set the scene for some excellent diving with an impressive variety of species, such as whale sharks, manta rays, sea snakes, turtles and corals. Keeping it even more interesting are underwater wrecks, cavern systems and even some mysterious ruins (...or very unusual rock formations).

Some operators run year-round, though winter water temperatures bottom out at 20°C (summer waters can get as warm 30°C). The water around the southernmost islands, the Yaeyama Islands, tends to be one or two degrees warmer than around the Okinawa main island. Advance bookings are recommended in July and August, as this is peak season. In general spring is best for marine life; go between April and October for the manta rays off Ishigaki-jima and in February for a chance to swim with hammerheads off Yonaguni-jima.

Costs for diving in the Southwest Islands are higher than you might pay in Southeast Asia, but equipment and guiding standards are fairly high. If you don't have a valid diving certification, many operators offer introductory diving courses. To rent equipment, you should know your weight in kilograms, your height in metres and your shoe size in centimetres.

Traveller-friendly operators with English-speaking staff include the following:

➡ Ishigaki-jima: Diving School Umicoza (p822)

➡ Okinawa-hontō: Piranha Divers (p810)

➡ Miyako-jima: Penguin Divers (p816)

➡ Yonaguni-jima: Yonaguni Diving Service (p830)

It's possible to dive in other spots around Japan, too. The *kuroshio* current brings warm waters (and colourful fish) up the Pacific coast of western Japan. Shikoku is an under-the-radar diving spot, where the marine landscape is different (more rocky than coral) from that of the Southwest Islands; it's a particularly good destination for fans of the nudibranch. The season here is May through October; water temps peak in September at 28°C but can be a chilly 20°C in May. Try English-speaking Kaanapali Diving Center (p677).

Cycling

Japan has a small but devoted cycling community. Bear in mind that roads can be narrow and lack shoulders, and that the terrain can be rather hilly with frequent tunnels. KANcycling (www.kancycling.com) is a good planning resource. The *Touring Mapple* (Shōbunsha) guide series, aimed at motorcyclists but also very useful for cyclists, has detailed maps (in Japanese) and is available at major bookstores. Cyclists can also stay at rider houses (p882), bare-bones guesthouses reserved for travellers on two wheels.

Outside of joining an organised tour, it is hard to rent touring bikes in Japan; Cycle Osaka (p377) is one operation that does. Another exception is the Shimanami Kaidō (p470), Japan's best developed cycling route. It travels from Onomichi (in Western Honshū) to Imabari (on Shikoku) crossing several bridges and islands in the Inland Sea. Bicycles (¥1000 per day, with a limited number of helmets available for free) can be rented at either end, and there are also ports along the way where you can return the bikes if you don't want to do the whole route. The 70km journey can be done in a day, or broken up into a longer trip, with more time to explore the small, rural islands.

There are also several tour operators (with rental bikes and helmets included) that can take you off the beaten track (literally) or on urban adventures:

➡ Takayama: Satoyama Experience (p251)

➡ Izu: Yamabushi Trail Tour (p203)

➡ Tokyo: Tokyo Great Cycling Tour (p120)

➡ Osaka: Cycle Osaka (p377)

➡ Minakami: MTB Japan (p307)

BEST ONSEN IN THE WILD

➡ Fukiage Roten-no-yu (p636), Hokkaidō

➡ Yudomari Onsen (p791), Yakushima (Okinawa & the Southwest Islands)

➡ Mizunashi Kaihin Onsen (p621), Hokkaidō

➡ Jinata Onsen (p207), Shikine-jima (Tokyo)

➡ Shin-Hotaka-no-yu (p253), Hida (Central Honshū)

Plan Your Trip

Eat & Drink Like a Local

As visitors to Japan quickly discover, the people here are absolutely obsessed with food. You'll find that every island and region of Japan has its own meibutsu (local speciality) that is a point of pride.

The Year in Food

At finer restaurants, not only does the menu change with the seasons but so does the crockery and the garnishes (which are often seasonal flowers, sprigs or leaves).

Spring (March–May)

The new growth of spring finds its way onto tables in the form of *takenoko* (bamboo shoots) and *sansei* (mountain vegetables). Especially good if you're in the mountains.

Summer (June–August)

The season for cooling dishes like *reimen* (cold ramen) and *zaru-soba* (cold buckwheat noodles served on a bamboo tray). And nothing says summer like *kakigōri* (shaved ice topped with sweet syrup).

Autumn (September–November)

The first sign of autumn is silvery *sanma* (Pacific saury) on menus. Other delicacies: matsutake mushrooms, ginkgo nuts, candied chestnuts and *shinmai*, the first rice of the harvest season.

Winter (December–February)

Friends come together for steaming *nabe* (hotpot) dishes; this is also the season for *fugu* (pufferfish) and oysters.

Dining Out in Japan

When you enter a restaurant in Japan the staff will likely all greet you with a hearty *'Irasshai!'* (Welcome!) In all but the most casual places, where you seat yourself, the waitstaff will next ask you *'Nan-mei sama?'* (How many people?). Indicate the answer with your fingers, which is what the Japanese do. You may also be asked if you would like to sit at a *zashiki* (low table on the tatami), at a *tēburu* (table) or the *kauntā* (counter). Once seated you will be given an *o-shibori* (hot towel), a cup of tea or water (this is free) and a menu.

There are two ways to order: *omakase* (chef's choice) and *okonomi* (your choice). It's common for high-end restaurants to offer nothing but *omakase* – the equivalent of a chef's tasting course – usually two or three options of different value. (Pricier doesn't necessarily mean more food; it often means more luxurious ingredients.) Most other restaurants will hand you a menu and expect you to choose what you like. If there's no English menu (and you're game) you can ask for the server's recommendation *'O-susume wa nan desu ka?'* and give the okay to whatever he or she suggests.

When your food arrives, it's the custom to say *'Itadakimasu'* (literally 'I will receive' but closer to 'bon appétit' in meaning) before digging in. All but the most extreme type-A chefs will say they'd rather have foreign visitors enjoy their meal than agonise over getting the etiquette right. Still, there's nothing that makes a Japanese chef grimace more than out-of-towners who over-season their food – a little soy sauce and wasabi go a long way.

Often a bill is placed discreetly on your table after your food has been delivered. If not, catch your server's eye with a *'sumimasen'* (excuse me) and ask for the check by saying, *'o-kaikei kudasai'*. Payment, even at high-end places, is often settled at a counter near the entrance, rather than at the table. On your way out, it's polite to say *'gochisō-sama deshita'* (literally 'it was a feast'; a respectful way of saying you enjoyed the meal) to the staff.

Eating Etiquette

➡ This is really the only big deal: do not stick your chopsticks upright in a bowl of rice or pass food from one pair of chopsticks to another – both are reminiscent of Japanese funeral rites.

➡ When serving yourself from a shared dish, it's polite to use the back end of your chopsticks (ie not the end that goes into your mouth) to place the food on your own small dish.

WORDS TO KNOW

If you're generally an adventurous (or curious) eater, don't let the absence of an English menu put you off. Instead, tell the staff (or ideally the chef), *'omakase de onegaishimasu'* (I'll leave it up to you).

This works especially well when you're sitting at the counter of a smaller restaurant or *izakaya* (Japanese pub eatery), where a rapport naturally develops between the diners and the cooks. It's best said with enthusiasm and a disarming smile, to reassure everyone that you really are game.

This isn't just a tourist hack: Japanese diners do this all the time. Menus might not reflect seasonal dishes and odds are the chef is working on something new that he or she is keen to test out on the willing.

It's probably a good idea to set a price cap, like: *hitori de san-zen-en* (one person for ¥3000).

➡ Lunch is one of Japan's great bargains; however, restaurants can only offer cheap lunch deals because they anticipate high turnover. Spending too long sipping coffee after finishing your meal might earn you dagger eyes from the kitchen.

➡ It's perfectly OK, even expected, to slurp your noodles. They should be eaten at whip speed, before they go soggy (letting them do so would be an affront to the chef); that's why you'll hear diners slurping, sucking in air to cool their mouths.

When to Eat

Breakfast The traditional Japanese breakfast consists of rice, miso soup and a few side dishes such as a small piece of cooked fish and *nattō* (partially fermented beans); this is what is served at a ryokan (traditional inn) or *minshuku* (traditional guesthouse). In cities you can source baked goods and coffee at cafes, but in rural areas eating in your inn may be your only option (or a convenience store run). Inns serve breakfast between 7am and 8.30am.

Lunch The midday meal is typically eaten between 11.30am and 1pm and in fact many restaurants stop serving by 2pm or 2.30pm. In cities with more options you can find food in the later afternoon, but in some rural areas you might get stuck waiting for dinner. The Japanese tend not to linger over lunch.

Dinner Unless they're urbanites doing overtime, most Japanese eat dinner fairly early, around 6pm; inns will serve meals at 6pm or 7pm. Given the option, most Japanese travellers choose to eat at their inns, which can mean that even resort areas have few to no dinner options. In cities, on the other hand, options are plentiful, with *izakaya* (Japanese pub-eateries) typically serving until at least 10pm.

Where to Eat

Shokudō

Shokudō (食堂) are casual, inexpensive eateries that serve homely meals – similar to what might be called a greasy-spoon cafe or diner in the United States. These offer quick and easy meals and usually enough variety to please everyone (including children). Like a lot of home-cooking in Japan, the food served at *shokudō* is often a mix of *washoku* (Japanese food), *yōshoku* (Western food) and *chuka-ryōri* (Chinese food) – the latter two usually with a liberal local interpretation.

MATT MUNRO/LONELY PLANET LP MAGAZINE ©

UV70/SHUTTERSTOCK ©

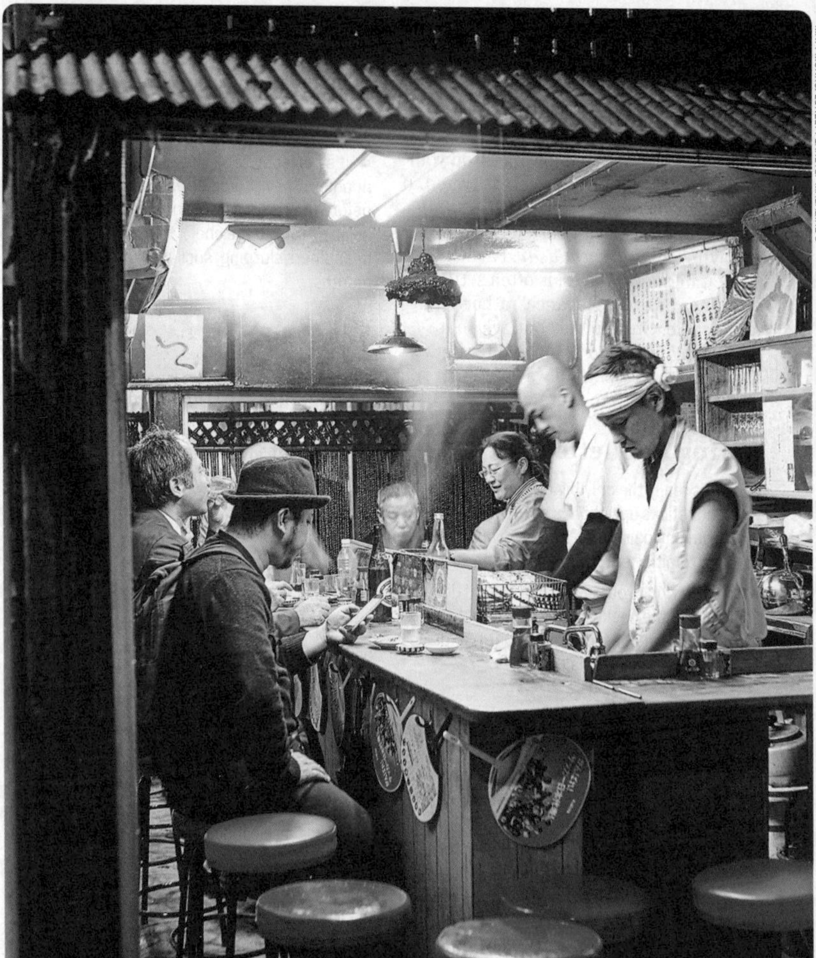

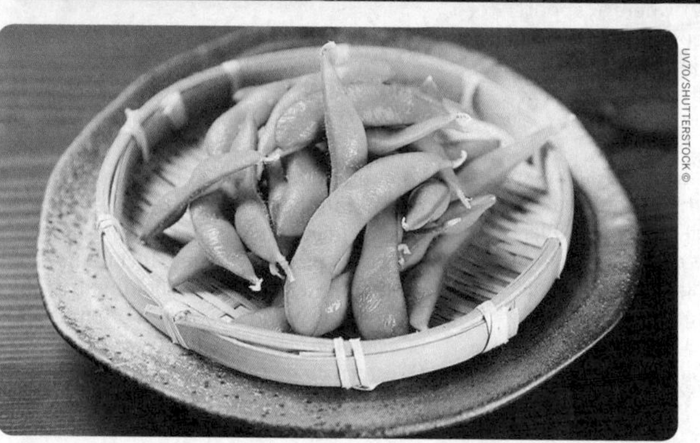

Top: Restaurant, Omoide-yokochō (p137), Tokyo

Bottom: *Edamame* (soybeans)

Meals are typically served as a set, called a *teishoku* (定食), which includes one main dish along with rice, miso soup and pickles, and sometimes a few other small sides. *Shokudō* are everywhere, and especially near train stations and tourist sights. They often have plastic food models displayed in their window; in a pinch, if there's no English menu, beckon the waitstaff outside and point to what you want. Meals typically cost ¥800 to ¥1500 per person.

Classic *shokudō* dishes:

ebi-katsu (海老カツ) breaded and fried prawns

katsu-don (かつ丼) rice topped with a fried pork cutlet

katsu-karē (カツカレー) rice topped with a fried pork cutlet and curry

omu-raisu (オムライス) omelette and fried rice, with ketchup

oyako-don (親子丼) rice topped with egg and chicken

shōga-yaki (生姜焼き) stir-fried pork and ginger

ten-don (天丼) rice topped with tempura prawns and vegetables

yaki-zakana (焼き魚) grilled fish

Some may also serve tempura or noodle dishes, and sometimes pasta, steak or hamburger patties.

Izakaya

Izakaya (居酒屋) translates as 'drinking house' – the Japanese equivalent of a pub – and you'll find them all over Japan. Visiting one is a great way to dig into Japanese culture. An evening at an *izakaya* is dinner and drinks all in one: food is ordered for the table a few dishes at a time along with rounds of beer, sake or *shōchū* (a strong distilled alcohol often made from potatoes). While the vibe is lively and social, it's perfectly acceptable to go by yourself and sit at the counter. If you don't want alcohol, it's fine to order a soft drink instead (but it would be strange to not order at least one drink).

There are orthodox, family-run *izakaya*, often with rustic interiors, that serve sashimi and grilled fish to go with sake; large, cheap chains, popular with students, that often have a healthy (er, unhealthy) dose of Western pub-style dishes (like chips); and there are also stylish chef-driven ones with creative menus. A night out at an average *izakaya* should run ¥2500 to ¥5000 per person, depending on how much you drink.

Chains often have deals where you can pay a set price for a certain amount of dishes and/or unlimited drinks. Look for the words *pātī puran* (パーティープラン; party plan) or *nomi-hōdai* (飲み放題; all-you-can-drink).

Note that *izakaya* often levy a small cover charge, called *otoshi* (お通し), of a few hundred yen per person. In exchange, you'll be served a small dish of food to snack on until the kitchen can prepare your order. But no, you can't pass it up even if you don't want to eat it.

Common *izakaya* dishes:

agedashi-tōfu (揚げだし豆腐) deep-fried tofu in a dashi (fish) broth

edamame (枝豆) salted and boiled fresh soy beans

hiyayakko (冷奴) a cold block of tofu with soy sauce and spring onions

karaage (唐揚げ) fried chicken

moro-kyū (もろきゅう) sliced cucumbers and chunky barley miso

poteto sarada (ポテトサラダ) potato salad

sashimi moriawase (刺身盛り合わせ) selection of sliced sashimi

tempura moriawase (天ぷら盛り合わせ) selection of tempura

yaki-zakana (焼魚) whole grilled fish

Kissaten

Kissaten (喫茶店) – or *'kissa'* for short – is the old word for coffee shop, the one used before chains like Starbucks arrived in Japan and changed the game. Today the word is used to describe independently run coffee shops that either date from the early or mid-20th century – when Japan's coffee first wave hit – or at least look like they do. In addition to pour-over or siphon-brewed coffee (you'll get no espresso drinks here), most *kissa* serve a 'morning set' (モーニング セット; *mōningu setto*), until around 11am, that includes thick, buttery toast and a hard-boiled egg for little more than the original price of a cup of coffee.

Street Food

Street-food stands, called *yatai* (屋台), don't have the same ubiquitous presence in Tokyo as they do in other Asian cities. However, you can find them in markets and at festivals. Popular street-food dishes include okonomiyaki, tako-yaki and *yaki-soba* (stir-fried buckwheat noodles).

Easy Options

Chain restaurants Found all over and good in a pinch; these stay open all afternoon and often until late and usually have English menus.

Department stores The upper levels have restaurants, often branches of famous ones; reliably good food and reasonably priced, usually with English menus. Takeaway and deli dishes can be purchased in the food halls in the basement.

Convenience stores Ubiquitous 24-hour suppliers of sandwiches, *bentō* (boxed meals, which you can ask to have microwaved) and *onigiri* (rice-ball snacks).

Food Experiences

Top Experiences

Breakfast at the fish market Go for sushi or *kaisen-don* (raw fish served on a bowl or rice) at one of Japan's famous fish markets, like Tokyo's Toyosu Market (p114) or Hokkaidō's Hakodate Morning Market (p621).

Kaiseki Japan's traditional haute cuisine is a full sensory culinary experience, a procession of seasonal dishes artfully arranged. Kyoto is tops for this and Kikunoi (p350) or Kitcho Arashiyama (p353) are among the top of the top.

Ramen Japan's top ramen pilgrimage sites are Fukuoka (p716), where the speciality is *tonkotsu* (pork bone) ramen, and Sapporo (p597), where the speciality is miso ramen.

Shōjin-ryōri This is Japanese Buddhist vegetarian cuisine, which specifies no meat, fish, onions or garlic be used; instead you'll be served tofu prepared in more ways than you may have imagined possible. Try it in Kōya-san (p418), at one of the mountain monastery's many *shukubō* (temple lodgings).

JAPANESE MENU DECODER

Kaiseki (haute cuisine) restaurants often serve different levels of courses with poetic names:

ume (梅) regular course

take (竹) special course

matsu (松) extra-special course

Sushi restaurants also sell sets of different grades:

nami (並) regular

jō (上) special

toku-jō (特上) extra-special

In most cases the difference is determined more by the value of the ingredients than by volume.

Many restaurants of all styles offer both prix fixe menu options (*kōsu menyu*; コースメニュー), which usually includes a starter, main, dessert and tea or coffee, and à la carte choices (*ippin ryōri*; 一品料理).

Kaiseki

Kaiseki (懐石) is Japanese cuisine at its finest, where ingredients, preparation, setting and presentation come together to create a highly ritualised, aesthetically sophisticated dining experience. Key to *kaiseki* is peak seasonal freshness; as the ingredients should be at the height of their flavour, only subtle seasoning is used to enhance them. The table settings and garnishes too are chosen to complement the ingredients and evoke seasonality.

The meal is served in several small courses, which usually include sashimi (raw fish), something steamed, something grilled, soup and finishes with rice and then a simple dessert (though there may be many, many more courses). Though fish is often served, meat never appears in traditional *kaiseki*.

For the most authentic *kaiseki* experience dine at a *ryōtei* (an especially elegant style of traditional restaurant). This is about as pricey as dining can get in Japan, ¥20,000 or more per person, with advance reservations required. There are less formal and less expensive places though, and lunch can be a good deal as some restaurants do boxed lunches (*bentō*; 弁当) containing a small sampling of their dinner fare for as little ¥2500. Many high-end ryokan serve a less orthodox version of *kaiseki* (meat is usually served), using local ingredients.

Sushi

Sushi (寿司 or 鮨) is raw fish and rice seasoned with vinegar. The most common style of sushi is called *nigiri-zushi,* which means hand-formed sushi, as it's made by deft-handed chefs who quickly press slivers of raw fish onto bite-sized mounds of rice. In truth, the fish isn't always raw; sometimes it's lightly seared or grilled.

Common *nigiri-zushi* toppings (called *neta*):

ama-ebi (甘海老) sweet shrimp

anago (穴子) conger eel

chū-toro (中とろ) medium-grade fatty tuna

ebi (海老) prawn or shrimp

hamachi (はまち) yellowtail

ika (いか) squid

ikura (イクラ) salmon roe

kai-bashira (貝柱) scallop

kani (かに) crab

katsuo (かつお) bonito

maguro (まぐろ) tuna

tai (鯛) sea bream

tamago-yaki (玉子焼き) slightly sweetened rolled omelette

toro (とろ) the choice cut of fatty tuna belly

uni (うに) sea-urchin roe

Unless otherwise instructed by the chef (who may have pre-seasoned some pieces), you can dip each piece lightly in *shōyu* (soy sauce), which you pour from a small decanter into a low dish specially provided for the purpose. *Nigiri-sushi* is usually made with wasabi, so if you'd prefer it without, order *wasabi-nuki* (わさび抜き). Sushi is one of the few foods in Japan that is perfectly acceptable to eat with your hands (even at high-end places.) Slices of *gari* (pickled ginger) are served to refresh the palate.

At an average *sushi-ya* (sushi restaurant) a meal should run between ¥2000 and ¥5000 per person. You can order à la carte – often by just pointing to the fish in the refrigerated glass case on the counter. But the most economical way to eat sushi is to order a set, usually of around 10 to 12 pieces, which may be served all at once or piece by piece. Another style of sushi you're likely to see is *chirashi-zushi* (ちらし寿司; bite-sized pieces of seafood scattered on a bowl of vinegar-seasoned rice), a whole meal unto itself.

Of course, you can spend much more at a high-end *sushi-ya,* where an *omakase* (chef's choice) course of seasonal delicacies could run over ¥20,000 per person. Sushi can also be had very cheaply, at *kaiten-zushi* (回転寿司), where ready-made plates of *nigiri-zushi* (about ¥200 each) are sent around the restaurant on a conveyor belt. Here there's no need to order: just grab whatever looks good.

Ramen

Ramen (ラーメン) originated in China, but its popularity in Japan is epic. If a town has only one restaurant, odds are it's a ramen shop.

Your basic ramen is a big bowl of crinkly egg noodles in broth, served with toppings such as *chāshū* (チャーシュー; sliced roast pork), *moyashi* (bean sprouts) and *menma* (fermented bamboo shoots). The broth can be made from pork or chicken bones or dried seafood; usually it's a top-secret combination of some or all of the above, falling somewhere on the spectrum between *kotteri* (thick and fatty – a signature of pork bone ramen) or *assari* (thin and light).

It's typically seasoned with *shio* (塩; salt), *shōyu* (醤油; soy sauce) or hearty miso (みそ) – though at less orthodox places, anything goes. Most shops will specialise in one or two broths and offer a variety of seasonings and toppings. Another popular style is *tsukemen,* noodles that come with a dipping sauce (like a really condensed broth) on the side.

Well-executed ramen is a complex, layered dish – though it rarely costs more than ¥1000 a bowl. Costs are minimised by fast-food-style service: often you order from a vending machine (you'll get a paper ticket, which you hand to the chef); water is self-serve. Many *ramen-ya* (ラーメン屋; ramen restaurants) also serve fried rice and *gyōza* (餃子; dumplings).

Yakitori

Putting away skewers of *yakitori* (charcoal-grilled chicken, but vegetables are served, too), along with beer, is a popular after-work ritual. Most *yakitori-ya* (焼き鳥屋; *yakitori* restaurants) are convivial counter joints where the food is grilled over hot coals in front of you. It's typical to order a few skewers at a time. They're usually priced around ¥100 or ¥200 a piece; one order may mean two skewers (and thus may mean double the price). The chef will ask if you want your skewers seasoned with *shio* (salt) or *tare* (sauce). *Yakitori-ya* are often located near train stations and are best identified by a red lantern outside (and the smell of grilled chicken).

Common *yakitori* dishes:

negima (ねぎま) pieces of white meat alternating with leek

kawa (皮) chicken skin

piiman (ピーマン) small green capsicums (peppers)

rebā (レバー) chicken livers

sasami (ささみ) skinless chicken-breast pieces

shiitake (しいたけ) Japanese mushrooms

tama-negi (玉ねぎ) round white onions

tebasaki (手羽先) chicken wings

tsukune (つくね) chicken meatballs

yaki-onigiri (焼きおにぎり) grilled rice ball

Soba & Udon

Soba (そば) are thin brown buckwheat noodles, which may or may not be cut with wheat (for 100% buckwheat look for the words 十割そば or *to-wari soba*). Udon (うどん) are thicker white wheat noodles. Some restaurants may specialise in one or the other; other places will serve both. In general, eastern Japan tends to favour soba while western Japan leans towards udon. There are also many regional variations.

Cheap noodle shops, where a meal costs less than ¥1000, are everywhere. At better shops, the noodles will be handmade (*te-uchi*; 手打ち) from premium flours and mountain spring water (and will cost twice as much). But even at their most refined, noodles are a reasonably affordable meal.

Both soba and udon may be served in a hot broth that is flavoured with bonito, kelp, soy sauce and *mirin* (sweet sake) – often with a choice of toppings, like *ebi-ten* (海老天; tempura prawns).

They may also be served cooled with dipping sauce (a more condensed broth) on the side, to which you can add aromatics like spring onions or wasabi. The weather may be a deciding factor but so is personal preference: if a place is famous for its noodles many customers would order them chilled, to better appreciate the flavour. (Also cooled noodles won't go mushy like those in hot broth so can be savoured rather than scoffed.)

When you order cooled noodles, the restaurant will often bring you a small kettle of hot water (the slightly starchy water used to boil the noodles). Pour it in the cup with the remaining dipping sauce and enjoy it like a hot broth.

Tempura

Tempura is seafood (fish, eel or prawns) and vegetables (like pumpkin, green pepper, sweet potato or onion) lightly battered and deep-fried in sesame oil. Season by dipping each piece lightly in salt or a bowl of *ten-tsuyu* (broth for tempura) mixed with grated *daikon* (Japanese radish).

At a speciality restaurant, tempura is served as a set (all at once, with rice and soup) or as a course, with pieces delivered one at a time freshly cooked; you can order extras on top of the set or course, but rarely just à la carte.

A tempura meal can cost between ¥1500 and ¥10,000, depending on the pedigree of the shop. *Shokudō* often serve cheaper *ten-don* (天丼; assorted tempura on rice) dishes. Tempura can also often be ordered as a side dish at *izakaya* and noodle restaurants.

Tonkatsu

Tonkatsu is a pork cutlet breaded in panko and deep-fried, almost always served as a set meal that includes rice, miso soup and a heaping mound of shredded cabbage. Season with *tonkatsu* sauce, a curious (and highly addictive) ketchupy condiment, or *karashi* (hot spicy yellow mustard). At around ¥1000 to ¥2000 a meal, it's perfect for when you want something hearty and filling. The best *tonkatsu* is said to be made from *kurobuta* (black Berkshire pork), from Kagoshima.

When ordering at a speciality shop, you can choose between *rōsu* (ロース; a fattier cut of pork) and *hire* (ヒレ; a leaner cut). *Tonkatsu* and other breaded and fried dishes are often served at *shokudō*. Look for *katsu-don* (かつ丼; rice topped with a fried pork cutlet), *katsu-karē* (カツカレー; rice topped with a fried pork cutlet and

JUNICHI MIYAZAKI/LONELY PLANET ©

TKYSZK/SHUTTERSTOCK ©

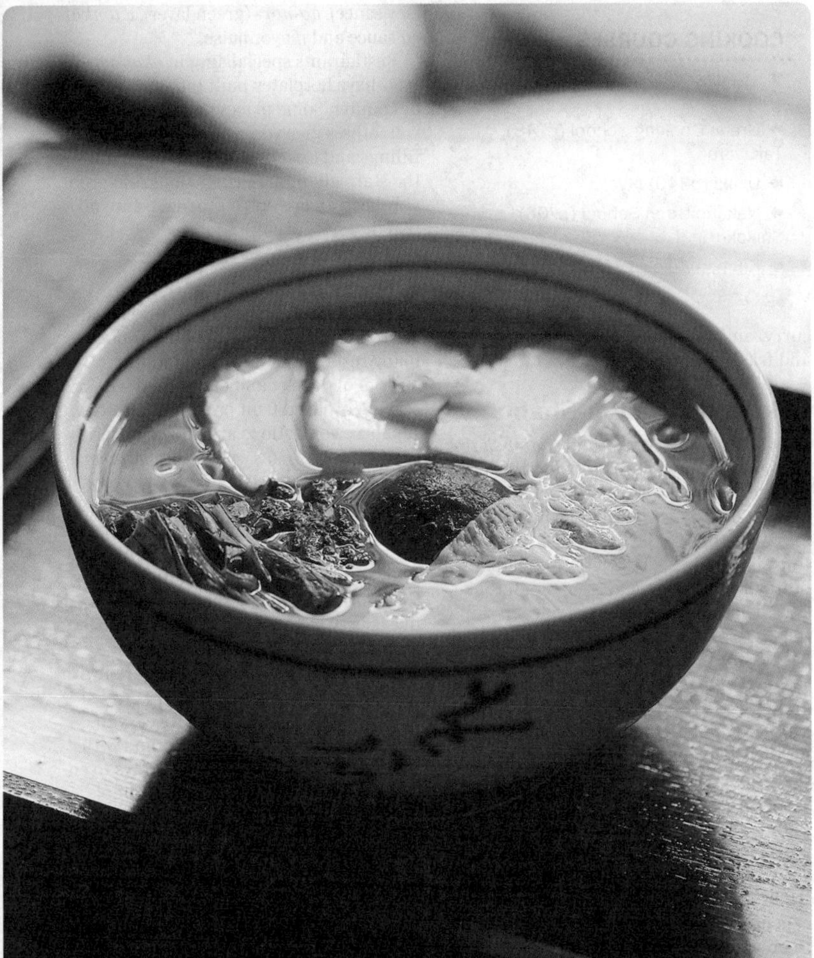

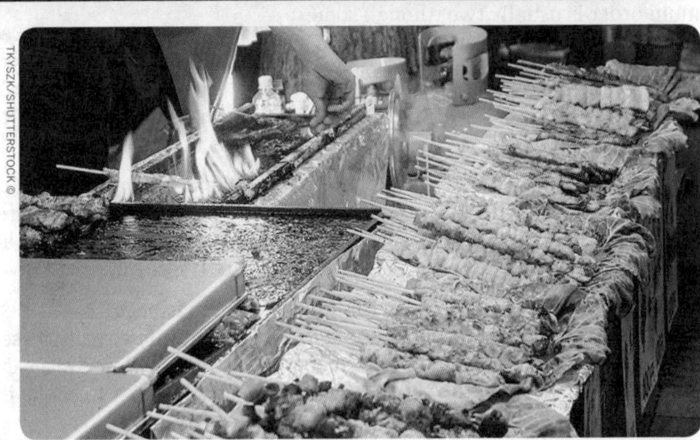

Top: Soba, Honke Owariya (p347), Kyoto

Bottom: *Yakitori* (charcoal-grilled chicken skewers)

COOKING COURSES

- Tsukiji Soba Academy (p117), Tokyo
- Green Cooking School (p248), Takayama
- Uzuki (p340), Kyoto
- Nakano Udon School (p708), Shikoku
- Kitchen Kujo (p118), Tokyo

curry) and *ebi-katsu* (海老カツ; breaded and fried prawns) on menus.

Sukiyaki & Shabu-Shabu

Both sukiyaki (すき焼き) and *shabu-shabu* (しゃぶしゃぶ) are hotpot dishes, cooked by diners at the table, and the same restaurant usually serves both (but may be known for one or the other). For sukiyaki, thin slices of beef are briefly simmered in a broth of *shōyu* (soy sauce), sugar and sake and then dipped in raw egg (you can skip the last part, though it makes the marbled beef taste even creamier).

For *shabu-shabu*, thin slices of pork and/or beef are swished around in boiling broth – *shabu-shabu* is the onomatopoeia for the sound of the meat being swished – then dipped in either a *goma-dare* (sesame sauce) or *ponzu* (citrus and soy sauce).

In either case, a healthy mix of veggies and tofu are added to the pot a little bit at a time followed by noodles at the end. So while sukiyaki and *shabu-shabu* can seem expensive (from around ¥3000 per person to upwards of ¥10,000 for premium beef), it is an all-inclusive meal.

One party shares the pot and the minimum order is usually two (though some places do lunch deals for solo diners). The waitstaff will set everything up for you and show you what to do.

Okonomiyaki

Okonomiyaki is a dish that flies in the face of the prevailing image of Japanese food being subtle. It's a thick, savoury pancake stuffed with pork, squid, cabbage, cheese, *mochi* (pounded rice cake) – anything really (*okonomi* means 'as you like'; *yaki* means 'fry'). Once cooked, it's seasoned with *katsuo-bushi* (bonito flakes), *shōyu* (soy sauce), *ao-nori* (green laver), a *tonkatsu* sauce and mayonnaise.

Restaurants specialising in *okonomiyaki* have hotplates built into the tables or counter. Some places do the cooking for you; others give you a bowl of batter and fillings and leave you to it. (Don't panic: the staff will mime instructions and probably keep an eye on you to make sure no real disasters occur.)

Sweets

Sweets in Japan are traditionally considered an accompaniment for tea, though many restaurants have adopted the custom of dessert and end a meal with a serving of sliced fruit or maybe ice cream. Japanese confections are known generically as *wagashi* (as opposed to *yōgashi*, Western-style sweets like cake and cookies). The basic ingredients are just rice and a sweetened paste of red *azuki* beans (called *anko*). Flavour (usually subtle) and design (often exquisite) are influenced by the seasons. In spring they may be shaped like cherry blossoms or wrapped in cherry leaves; in autumn they might be golden coloured, like the leaves, or flavoured with chestnut.

Okashi-ya (sweet shops) are easy to spot: they usually have open fronts with their wares laid out in wooden trays to entice passers-by. Buying sweets is simple – just point at what you want and indicate with your fingers how many you'd like.

Cheap Treats

Tako-yaki (たこ焼き) Bite-sized doughy dumplings stuffed with chunks of octopus. A popular street snack in Osaka; try them at Wanaka Honten (p383).

Curry pan (カレーパン) Deep-fried doughnuts filled with Japanese-style curry (thick, brown, often more sweet than spicy). Most bakeries sell them; Kōbe's Isuzu Bakery (p394) is especially famous for them.

Mitarashi dango (みたらし団子) Small silky rice dumplings stacked five on a skewer and lacquered in a sweet and savoury soy-based glaze. A Kyoto (p311) speciality.

Onsen tamago (温泉たまご) Literally eggs cooked in onsen water, these are commonly sold in onsen towns where the springs come in naturally very hot. Look for them in Beppu (p755)

Okonomiyaki (savoury pancake)

and Yunomine Onsen (p429), and at Hakone's Ōwakudani (p193).

Dare to Try

Nattō (納豆) These partially fermented soybeans with the scent of ammonia are the litmus test by which Japanese judge a foreigner's sense of culinary adventure. (Don't be surprised if someone asks you: 'Can you eat *nattō*?') It is often served at ryokan breakfasts.

Shirako (白子) Milt (the sperm sac) from cod or fugu is a winter delicacy. It can be found in sushi restaurants and *izakaya* around Japan, usually poached and served in a light, citrusy soy sauce.

Shiokara (塩辛) Chunks of seafood fermented in their own heavily salted viscera. *Shiokara* is a classic grandpa bar snack, washed down with sake at old-school *izakaya*.

Hoya (海鞘) Sea squirt (also called sea pineapple) is an alien-looking marine creature often served raw (but may also be grilled, dried, salted or smoked) and a specialty of Sanriku Kaigan (p542). Season: May through September.

Inago no tsukudani (いなごの佃煮) Rice grasshoppers braised in soy sauce and sugar were once a common source of protein; still eaten today around Nagano (p290).

Special Diets

Restaurants in Japan are not as used to catering to dietary restrictions as their counterparts in some other countries. Restaurants and inns that regularly get international guests are usually accommodating, as are the restaurants in international hotels.

State your restrictions at the earliest possible opportunity, like when you are booking a ryokan. Given time, most places will try to be accommodating. That said, in many cases your options will be defined by how strictly you adhere to restrictions; for example, unless explicitly noted otherwise, your vegetable tempura is going to be fried in the same oil as the prawns.

On the surface, Japan would appear to be an easy place for veggies and vegans, but the devil is in the details: many dishes (including miso soup) are seasoned with *dashi*, a broth made from fish.

Many cities in Japan do have restaurants that specifically offer vegetarian and vegan dishes. **Happy Cow** (www.happycow.net/asia/japan) is a good resource. In the countryside, you'll need to work a little bit harder and be prepared to explain what you can and cannot eat.

Of special note is *shōjin-ryōri*, the traditionally vegetarian cuisine of Buddhist monks; Kōya-san in Kansai is a good place for this.

Many chain restaurants and deli counters label their dishes with icons indicating potential allergens (such as dairy, eggs, peanuts, wheat and shellfish), but otherwise this can be tricky. You'll want to have a list of allergens written in Japanese on hand.

Gluten-free is particularly challenging, as there is a little awareness of coeliac disease in Japan and many kitchen staples, such as soy sauce, contain wheat (and even restaurant staff may not be aware of this). The Gluten-Free Expats Japan! Facebook group is a good resource.

Japan now has more halal options than it used to have. For certified halal restaurants, see Halal Gourmet Japan (www.halalgourmet.jp).

SAKE GLOSSARY

dai-ginjō (大吟醸) sake made from rice kernels with 50% or more of their original volume polished away

genshu (原酒) undiluted sake, often with an alcohol content close to 20%

ginjō (吟醸) sake made from rice kernels with 40% to 50% of their original volume polished away

junmai-shu (純米酒) 'pure rice sake', made from only rice, *kōji* and water

koshu (古酒) aged sake, often golden-hued and sweet

nama-zake (生酒) fresh, unpasteurised sake

nigori-zake (濁り酒) milky-white 'cloudy sake', often rather sweet

shiboritate (搾立て) young 'nouveau' sake that comes out in autumn

tokutei-meishōshu (特定 名称酒) premium sake; distinguished by being either *ginjō* or above or *junmai-shu*

What to Drink

Japan has a long history of, and love for, drinking. Sake, or *nihonshū*, as the Japanese call it, and *o-cha* (green tea) are the country's two signature drinks. There is also craft beer, award-winning whisky and meticulously brewed coffee to get excited about. Japan's cities have excellent bars and cafes; in rural areas, seek out local styles of sake.

Sake

What much of the world calls 'sake' the Japanese call *nihonshū* (日本酒; the drink of Japan). It's made from rice, water and *kōji*, a mould that helps to convert the starch in the rice into fermentable sugars.

Sake has existed for as long as history has been recorded in Japan (and odds are a lot longer). It plays an important part in a variety of Shintō rituals, including wedding ceremonies, and many Shintō shrines display huge barrels of sake in front of their halls (most of them are empty). Naturally, sake is the best pairing for traditional Japanese cuisine.

The rice used to make sake is different from the rice grown for eating: the grain is larger and starchier. It's polished before fermentation and – generally speaking – the greater the degree of polishing the better the sake will be. That which is made from only the innermost part of the kernel is the most prized. Sometimes the alcohol content is artificially regulated (either increased or reduced). On average the alcohol content of sake is around 15%; by law it can be no more than 22%.

The taste is often categorised as sweet (*ama-kuchi*; 甘口) or dry (*kara-kuchi*; 辛口), though these are just starting points. Sake can also be *tanrei* (crisp), *hanayaka* (fragrant), *odayaka* (mellow) and much more. Sake is always brewed during the winter, in the cold months that follow the rice harvest in September. Fresh, young sake is ready by late autumn.

Sake can be drunk *reishu* (冷酒; chilled), *jō-on* (常温; at room temperature), *nurukan* (ぬる燗; warmed) or *atsu-kan* (熱燗; piping hot), according to the season and personal preference. The top-drawer stuff is normally served chilled. Sake is traditionally presented in a ceramic jug known as a *tokkuri,* and poured into tiny cups known as *o-choko* or *sakazuki*. A traditional measure of sake is one *gō* (一合), which is a little over 180mL or 6oz. In speciality bars, you will have the option of ordering by the glass, which will often be filled to overflowing and brought to you in a wooden container to catch the overflow.

Beer

First brewed in Japan at the end of the 1800s, *biiru* (ビール; beer) is now the country's favourite tipple. Many a night out at an *izakaya* (Japanese pub-eatery) begins with the phrase, *'toriaezu biiru!'* ('first off, beer!'). Beer in Japan has long been ruled by what are known as the big five: Kirin, Asahi, Sapporo, Suntory and Orion (the latter is Okinawa's signature beer). Most bars and *izakaya* just serve one kind of lager (made by one of the above), either as mugs of draught beer (*nama biiru*; 生ビール) or in 633mL bottles (*bin-biiru*; 瓶ビール) meant to be shared among the table and drunk in glasses).

Japan does have a growing number of craft brewers; to sample their wares, seek out craft beer speciality bars – most cities have at least one. For the latest on the craft beer scene, check out blog Beer Tengoku (www.beertengoku.com) or follow @JapanBeerTimes.

Our favourites include the following:

- Baird Beer, Shizuoka
- Minoh Beer, Osaka
- Hitachino Nest, Ibaraki
- Yo-Ho Brewing, Nagano
- Shiga Kogen, Nagano

Tea

Japan is a treat for tea lovers. Here *o-cha* (お茶; tea) means green tea and broadly speaking there are two kinds: *ryokucha* (緑茶; steeped with leaves) and *matcha* (抹茶), which is made by whisking dried and milled leaves with water until a cappuccino level of frothiness is achieved. It's *matcha* that is served in the tea ceremony; it is quite bitter, so it is accompanied by a traditional sweet.

When you order *o-cha* in a Japanese restaurant (it's usually free, like water), you'll most likely be served *bancha* (番茶; ordinary tea). In summer, you might get cold *mugicha* (麦茶; roasted barley tea), instead. After a course meal, restaurants often serve *hōjicha* (ほうじ茶; roasted green tea), which is weaker and less caffeinated.

To really get to know Japanese tea, visit a teahouse or speciality shop, which will serve *matcha* and higher-grades of *ryokucha*, such as *sencha* (煎茶; medium-grade green tea) and *gyokuro* (玉露; the highest grade of green tea, shaded from the sun and picked early in the season). Cafes often serve black tea (*kōcha*; 紅茶), but rarely serve green tea. Department store food halls are also a good bet for quality tea to take home.

DRINKING CULTURE

In Japan it's considered bad form to fill your own glass. Instead, fill the drained glasses around you and someone will quickly reciprocate; when they do, raise your glass slightly with two hands – a graceful way to receive anything. 'Cheers!' in Japanese is *'Kampai!'*; glasses are raised though usually not clinked.

Nightlife

Any Japanese city of reasonable size will have a nightlife district. Famous ones include Tokyo's Kabukichō, Osaka's Minami (and especially Dōtombori) and Sapporo's Susukino. Such districts are stocked, often several storeys high, with a medley of drinking options that include *izakaya*, cocktail bars, Western-style pubs, jazz cafes, karaoke parlours, nightclubs and more – all awash in the colourful, LED-lit signage that forms Japan's urban signature.

The legal drinking age in Japan is 20. Bars generally don't require photo ID as proof of age, but nightclubs are required to check ID cards (of everyone, no matter how far past 20 you look). Though local governments have been cracking down on this practice, some establishments in well-known nightlife districts do employ street touts; though not all are employed by shady places (where bills may come inflated), it's best to steer clear of them.

Miso ramen

Karaoke

Karaoke (カラオケ; pronounced kah-rah-oh-kay) isn't just about singing: it's an excuse to let loose, a bonding ritual, a reason to keep the party going past the last train and a way to kill time until the first one starts in the morning. When words fail, it's a way to express yourself – are you the type to sing the latest J-pop hit (dance moves included) or do you go in for an Okinawan folk ballad? It doesn't matter if you're a good singer or not (though the tone-deaf might sign up for singing lessons – such is the important social function of karaoke), as long as you've got heart.

In Japan, karaoke is sung in a private room among friends. Admission is usually charged per person by the half-hour, though most places offer a variety of packaged deals that include a set number of singing hours with or without unlimited drinks. Food and drinks can be ordered from the phone in the room. To choose a song, use the touch-screen device to search by artist or title; most have an English function and plenty of English songs to choose from. Then let your inner diva shine!

All major cities will have karaoke parlours, usually in well-marked tower buildings around train stations or in nightlife districts.

Local Specialities

Tokyo

Sushi Tokyo's signature dish is *nigiri-zushi*, the style of sushi most popular around the world today: those bite-sized slivers of seafood hand-pressed onto pedestals of rice.

Nouveau ramen Creativity distilled in a bowl of noodles and the best budget gourmet experience around.

The Japan Alps & Central Honshū

Soba Nagano is famous for its soba (buckwheat noodles).

Mountain cuisine In and around the Alps local specialities include foraged mushrooms and shoots; game, like deer; and river fish, like *ayu* (sweetfish).

Seafood The Sea of Japan's cold waters produce excellent seafood, the most prized of which is *kanburi* (winter-fattened yellow tail).

Kyoto

Kaiseki Japan's haute cuisine developed in the old imperial capital. Kyoto has the most highly regarded *kaiseki* restaurants in the country (including some for diners on more modest budgets).

Tea and sweets The home of the tea ceremony is naturally the best place to sample green tea and the *wagashi* (Japanese sweets) served with it. Nearby Uji is Japan's most famous tea-producing region.

Kansai

Street food Don't miss Osaka speciality *tako-yaki* (grilled octopus dumplings), sold at street stalls; Osaka is also famous for *okonomiyaki* (a grill-it-yourself savoury pancake).

Kōbe beef Locally raised beef of the highest pedigree, in cosmopolitan Kōbe.

Vegetarian temple food The temple complex Kōya-san (p418) is an excellent place to sample *shōjin-ryōri*, the vegetarian cuisine of Buddhist monks.

Hiroshima & Western Honshū

Hiroshima-yaki You can't visit Hiroshima without sampling the city's distinctive style of *okonomiyaki*, topped with noodles and a fried egg.

Oysters In winter, oyster lovers from across Japan seek out the bivalves harvested from the Inland Sea near Hiroshima. Temporary *kaki-goya* (oyster houses) with makeshift grills appear in towns on the coast.

Northern Honshū (Tōhoku)

Hotpots Hotpot dishes are common in the remote and rugged deep north of Japan's mainland. Each area has its own style: in Yamagata it's made with taro; in Akita it's made with *kiritanpo* – kneaded rice grilled on bamboo spits.

Gyūtan Sendai's local speciality is thinly sliced, surprisingly tender beef tongue grilled over charcoal.

Sake Niigata is known for its distinctive style of crisp, dry sake (called *tanrei karakuchi*).

Sapporo & Hokkaidō

Shellfish Hokkaidō's cold waters are fertile breeding grounds for flavourful crab, scallops and surf clams in winter, and shrimp and sea urchin in summer.

Miso-ramen Sapporoites keep warm in winter with ramen spiked with pungent miso and topped with vegetables stir-fried with garlic.

Lamb BBQ Hokkaidō locals love lamb grilled over hot coals (a dish called *jingisukan*) paired with copious mugs of draught beer.

Shikoku

Largely rural Shikoku excels in simple pleasures, such as udon (in Kagawa) and *katsuo-tataki* (seared bonito; in Kōchi).

Kyūshū

Hakata ramen Fukuoka is Japan's top ramen pilgrimage spot. Here the signature style is thin noodles served in an intensely rich *tonkotsu* (pork bone broth). Eat it at one of the city's many *yatai* (open-air food stalls).

Shippoku-ryōri Nagasaki's formal cuisine is a blend of Japanese, Chinese and Portuguese – a legacy of the city's position as an open port. Also try *castella*, a sponge cake based on the recipe of a 16th-century Portuguese missionary.

Shōchū Kagoshima's signature tipple is this strong distilled spirit (p771).

Okinawa & the Southwest Islands

Okinawa, which was its own kingdom until the mid-19th century, has a food culture all its own. Local dishes to try include *umibudō* (sea grapes – a type of seaweed), *mimigā* (sliced pigs' ears marinated in vinegar) and *gōyā champurū* (stir-fry containing bitter melon, an Okinawan vegetable). *Awamori* (p811) is Okinawa's firewater, distilled from rice.

Plan Your Trip

Travel with Children

Japan is generally a great place to travel with kids: it's safe, clean, full of mod cons and easy to get around. Not many sights go out of their way to appeal to children, so you may have to get creative, but teens should be easily wowed by pop culture and dazzling cityscapes.

Best Regions for Kids

Tokyo (p87)

Pop culture galore: stay in a hotel with a giant Godzilla statue, explore the world of Japan's top animator, Miyazaki Hayao, at the Ghibli Museum or shop for character goods. Teens will love neighbourhoods like Harajuku and Shibuya.

Kansai (p365)

Meet the deer of Nara-kōen, see the castle in Himeji and bask in the colourful lights of Osaka.

Central Honshū (p223)

Hiking and skiing in the Alps, cycling past rice fields and exploring old farm villages outside Takayama and a fantastic castle in Matsumoto.

Sapporo & Hokkaidō (p591)

Great skiing, snowboarding, hiking and camping opportunities for outdoorsy families.

Okinawa & the Southwest Islands (p785)

Work in a little beach time in subtropical Okinawa – a popular destination for local families. Off-the-beaten-track island Taketomi is great for kids: there are no cars (bicycles only!) and great, low-key beaches.

Japan for Kids

Accommodation

Most hotels can provide a cot for an extra fee (providing there's enough room for one). Some hotels have triple rooms, but quads or rooms with two queen-sized beds are rare, as are conjoining rooms.

Local families often stay in traditional accommodation (ryokan and *minshuku*) with large tatami rooms that can hold up to four or five futons, laid out in a row. Unfortunately this can be pricey: if your child is old enough to require their own futon, the price is often the same or near to that of an adult (minus a discount for meals).

Hostels and guesthouses often have family rooms (or at worst, a four-person dorm room that you can book out); again there is usually no discounted child price. These also often have handy kitchen facilities.

Eating

Local families take a lot of meals at 'family restaurants' (ファミレス; *famiresu*). Chains like Gusto, Jonathan's, Saizeriya and Royal Host have kids' meals, high chairs, big booths and nonsmoking sections. High chairs are not as common as in the West. Supermarkets, bakeries, fast-food restaurants and convenience stores stock sandwiches and other foods that kids are likely to go for; supermarkets carry baby food. You might want to pack small forks and spoons, as not all restaurants have these on hand. If your child has allergies, get someone (perhaps at your accommodation) to write them down in Japanese. Chain restaurants often have common allergens marked on the menus with icons.

Getting Around

Trains have priority seating for pregnant passengers and those with small children. It's best to avoid trains during morning rush hour (7am to 9.30am). If you must, children under 12 can ride with mums in the less-crowded women-only carriages. Children between the ages of six and 11 ride for half-price on trains (including bullet trains); children under six ride for free.

Train stations and buildings in larger cities usually have lifts; many attractions, such as temples and shrines, do not have ramps (and prams do not get the same access to special elevators and back passages for visitors in wheelchairs). Beware that side streets often lack pavements.

Travelling by car (outside major cities) is often a good strategy for families, as it makes child and luggage-wrangling easier. Child seats in taxis are generally not available, but most car-rental agencies will provide one if you ask in advance.

Infants

Larger cities have more public facilities for nappy-changing and nursing; department stores, shopping malls and larger train stations are all good bets. Breastfeeding is generally not done in public, though some mums do (find a quiet corner and use a shawl). Pharmacies stock nappies (diapers) and wipes.

What to Pack

Do bring any medicines that your child takes regularly (or may need), as Japanese pharmacies don't sell foreign medications (though similar ones can be found). The *shinkansen* (bullet train) is very smooth and few travellers report feeling motion sickness, but if your child is very sensitive, you might consider preventative measures; winding mountain roads are as nausea-inducing as anywhere.

Children's Highlights

Amusement Parks

Tokyo Disney Resort, Tokyo (p114) Visit the only-in-Japan Disney Sea park (along with classic Disney attractions).

Universal Studios Japan, Osaka (p376) Japanese version of the American cinema theme park.

Sky Circus, Tokyo (p115) Experience being virtually shot out of a cannon over Tokyo.

Fuji-Q Highland, Fuji-Yoshida (p172) Best known for its thrill rides.

Trains

Japanese kids love trains; odds are yours will, too. Just getting to ride the *shinkansen* is a neat experience.

Kyoto Railway Museum, Kyoto (p314) The history of Japanese trains, from steam engines to *shinkansen*.

SCMAGLEV & Railway Park, Nagoya (p230) See an actual maglev (the world's fastest train) and test-ride a *shinkansen* simulator.

Skiing & Snowboarding

Niseko United, Niseko (p607) One of Japan's biggest resorts, with English-speaking instructors and children's ski camps.

Happō-One Ski Resort, Hakuba (p287) Another big resort, with lessons in English for kids and a snow park for little ones.

Cycling Tours

All of the following have child-sized bikes, though urban tours are better for older kids.

Satoyama Experience, Hida-Furukawa (p251) Cycle past rural scenes of rice fields and farmhouses.

Tokyo Great Cycling Tour, Tokyo (p120) Urban rides; the same company also does kayaking tours in Tokyo's canals.

Cycle Osaka, Osaka (p377) City tours around Osaka.

Baseball

Baseball is Japan's most popular sport and the crowds go wild for it, really putting on a show. This can be a really fun experience for kids, even if they're not already fans of the sport. All major cities have a local team. The season is March to October.

Plan Your Trip

Japan on a Budget

Japan has a reputation as an expensive place to travel to, but it's an image that doesn't hold up on the ground. With a little strategy, it can be very reasonable – budget-friendly, even. Many of the country's top sights, for example, cost nothing and free festivals take place year-round.

Top Free Sights

Fushimi Inari-Taisha

Kyoto's most photogenic shrine (p313), with hundreds of vermilion *torii* (gates).

Dōtombori

Osaka's famous neon strip (p373) with lots of snack vendors.

Nara-kōen

Sprawling park (p407) with historic temples and a herd of semi-wild deer.

Hiroshima Peace Memorial Park

Moving memorial (p456) to Hiroshima's tragic history.

Shibuya Crossing

Tokyo's famous intersection (p109), abuzz with youthful urban energy and lit by giant video screens.

Sapporo Beer Museum

The history of beer in Japan, in the original Sapporo factory (p597).

Zenkō-ji

Nagano's fascinating old temple (p291), full of legends.

Oku-no-in

Wooded paths pass moss-covered stupas in this ancient Buddhist cemetery (p420).

Budget Accommodation

Business hotels These economical (and to be honest, rather utilitarian) hotels offer the best prices for private rooms with en-suite facilities: it's possible to find double rooms for as low as ¥8000 (and single rooms for as low as ¥6000), though these will be a little more expensive in cities like Tokyo, Kyoto and Osaka. Look for places that include a free breakfast buffet – they can be substantial enough to keep you going for hours.

Guesthouses and hostels Japan has fantastic guesthouses and hostels all over; not only are they generally clean and well-maintained, friendly, English-speaking staff are usually on hand to offer near concierge-level service. A double or single room is comparative to a business hotel (but usually has shared facilities); dorm beds cost around ¥3000 (US$25). Some places do charge extra for towel rentals, so you can save a little yen by bringing your own. Note that rates are often slightly cheaper if you book directly rather than through a booking site.

Capsule hotels A capsule berth costs slightly more than a dorm bed in a hostel (maybe ¥4000 per night), but you get more privacy. You probably wouldn't want to stay every night in a capsule, but they're good for saving money in cities where hotels are pricier.

Camping If you really want to do Japan on the cheap, you can rely on its network of well-maintained campsites in rural or resort areas; prices start from ¥500 to ¥1000 per person or tent. Note that many sites are only open in the summer.

Getting Around on the Cheap

Japan Rail Pass (p899) Like the famous Eurail Pass, this is one of the world's great travel bargains and is the best way to see a lot of Japan on a budget. It allows unlimited travel on Japan's brilliant nationwide rail system, including the lightning-fast *shinkansen* (bullet train). There are also more regionally specific train passes that are cheaper, so examine your itinerary carefully before deciding.

Seishun Jūhachi Kippu (p898) Another great deal, but with very specific conditions: for ¥11,850 (US$100), you get five one-day tickets good for travel on any regular Japan Railways train (meaning not the *shinkansen* or any high-speed limited express trains) during a limited period of a few weeks; it's only available at certain times during the year. If the timing works, and you're a fan of slow travel, this is a unique, ultra-cheap way to get around.

Bus (p893) Long-distance buses are the cheapest way to get around and longer routes have night buses, which saves a night on accommodation. There are also bus passes, which can make this an even cheaper way to get around.

Car hire (p893) Highway tolls and petrol in Japan are expensive; however, renting a car can be economical if you're travelling as a family or are plotting an itinerary that takes you away from major rail hubs.

Discount flights (p891) Japan has several budget carriers that offer bus-like pricing on some routes – just be sure to factor in the time and cost of going to/from the airport.

Free Sights & Activities

Shrines and temples The vast majority of Shintō shrines in Japan cost nothing to enter. Likewise, the grounds of many temples can be toured for free (often, you only have to pay to enter the halls or a walled garden).

Traditional festivals Throughout the year festivals take place at shrines and temples and through city streets. They're free, an excellent way to see traditional culture come alive and are well attended by cheap food vendors. For a calendar, see JNTO's festivals page (www.jnto.go.jp/eng/location/festivals).

Walks and hikes These can be the most rewarding part of your trip: exploring an up-and-coming city neighbourhood, walking old pilgrimage trails or rural lanes, or getting up into the mountains.

Parks Urban parks are generally free to enter (and some gardens are, too) and are popular with locals on weekends; pack a picnic and settle in for an afternoon of people-watching.

Architecture Japan's cities, especially Tokyo, have some fantastic buildings designed by many of the big names in Japanese architecture.

Markets Many seaside towns have fish markets, some rural spots have morning markets and some cities still have their old-fashioned open-air markets – a great way to connect with local culture, and often a source of cheap, fresh food.

Eating on the Cheap

Shokudō You can get a good, filling meal in these all-round Japanese eateries for under ¥1000 (US$8.50). As is the case with all restaurants in Japan, tea and water are free and there's no tipping required.

Bentō These 'boxed meals', which include a variety of dishes, can be picked up for under ¥1000 at supermarkets. Department store food halls sell gourmet ones for a little bit more; visit just before closing to buy them on markdown.

Noodles You can get a steaming bowl of tasty ramen for as little as ¥600 (US$5). *Tachigui* (stand-and-eat counter joints) sell soba (buckwheat noodles) and udon (thick white wheat noodles) for even less – starting as low as ¥350 per bowl.

Lunch If you want to splurge, do it at lunch when many upscale restaurants offer a smaller course for significantly less than their dinner course.

Convenience stores The best friend to all budget travellers, convenience stores stock sandwiches, rice balls, hot dishes and beer, all of which you can assemble into a very affordable (if not exactly healthy) meal. Accommodations always have kettles so cup noodles are always an option.

Regions at a Glance

Tokyo

Food
Culture
Shopping

Sushi & More

Sushi is Tokyo's signature dish, but it's just the tip of the iceberg. There are restaurants here that excel at just about everything. Tokyoites love dining out; join them, and delight in the sheer variety of tastes and experiences the city has to offer.

Pop Culture

For fans of Japan's infectious pop culture – be it the enchanting anime films of Studio Ghibli (*Spirited Away*) or the old-school monster movies starring Godzilla – this is the place to be. Snap selfies with giant robots and cosplay while go-karting around the city.

Style City

Tokyo is one of the world's great shopping cities, with grand old department stores, avant-garde boutiques, vintage shops and style mavens who set global trends. There are some excellent shops for traditional crafts here, too.

p87

Mt Fuji & Around Tokyo

Onsen
Outdoors
Temples

Hot Spring Getaways

Some of Japan's favourite onsen retreats are all within easy striking distance of the capital: mountain hideaways to the north, lakeside resorts to the west and laid-back coastal villages to the south.

Mountains & Sea

In addition to climbing Mt Fuji, outdoor activities include hiking among cedar groves, strolling along bluffs, surfing and sea kayaking. Options range from easy Tokyo day trips to island excursions.

Temple Towns

There are two distinctly different destinations for temples here: Nikkō, in the mountains, has ornately decorated structures; and Kamakura, by the sea, is home to austere Zen temples.

p165

The Japan Alps & Central Honshū

Onsen
Villages
Outdoors

Mountain Hot Springs

The mountainous heart of Japan bubbles over with exquisite hot springs and fantastic inns in which to enjoy them. There's nothing like gazing up at snowy peaks while steam rises from your body.

Thatched Roofs

Travel to the remote village of Shirakawa-gō (or, even remoter, Ainokura) and fall asleep to the sound of chirping frogs in a centuries-old thatched-roof farmhouse.

Hiking & Skiing

In summer the Japan Alps is the country's top hiking destination. Come winter it offers some of Asia's best skiing. Après-ski soaking in hot springs is mandatory and there's nightlife in some ski towns, too.

p223

Kyoto

Temples
Culture
Food

Shintō & Buddhist Masterpieces

With over 1000 Buddhist temples and more than 400 Shintō shrines, Kyoto is the place to savour Japanese religious architecture and garden design. Find a quiet temple to call your own or join the throngs at a popular shrine.

Culture & Crafts

Japan's cultural capital for over a millennium has it all: historic geisha districts, classical theatre, excellent museums and venerable shops selling artisan crafts like lacquerware and *washi* (Japanese handmade paper).

Kaiseki, Tea & More

Kyoto is the place to try *kaiseki* (Japanese haute cuisine) and to get better acquainted with Japanese tea. Shop the city's central food market or try a cooking class.

p311

Kansai

Cities
Temples
History

Urban Pleasures

Get your city fix in one of Kansai's urban centres, like the bold commercial hub Osaka or the cosmopolitan port city Kōbe. Both have vibrant dining scenes, nightlife and shopping districts.

Buddhist Monuments

See the remains of Japan's earliest temples – and the famous Great Buddha – in Nara and Hōryū-ji or visit the mystical mountain monastery Kōya-san, established by Japan's most famous monk.

Castles & Tombs

There aren't many original castles left in Japan but two of the best are here: the 'White Egret Castle' of Himeji and Hikone-jō. The town of Asuka is home to burial mounds from the early days of Japanese history.

p365

Hiroshima & Western Honshū

Culture
History
Outdoors

Contemporary Art

Naoshima (and the islands in its orbit) in the Inland Sea has become synonymous in Japan with contemporary art and architecture. Come see works from international artists inside buildings that enhance the natural scenery.

Momentous Events

Hiroshima is a moving place to reflect on the history of the last century and the way forward. Other areas of western Honshū were key players in Japan's 19th-century modernisation.

Slow Travel

Cycle over bridges linking the tiny islands of the Inland Sea, rent a car and drive through the bucolic rural scenery of Yamaguchi, or head to Tottori's forlorn sand dunes.

p453

Northern Honshū (Tōhoku)

Onsen
Outdoors
Culture

Rustic Escapes

That image you have of bathing with stars overhead or the wooden bathhouse all by its lonesome in the mountains – that's Tōhoku. The onsen here are remote, isolated and among the best in the country.

Parks & Peaks

Northern Honshū is blessed with some spectacular mountains, including Dewa Sanzan – three peaks used for ascetic training (you can hike them). In winter there is skiing at established resorts and some less developed spots.

Festivals

Nobody in Japan does traditional festivals like they do up here; visit in the summer and book ahead. Ancient customs and beliefs live on in Tōhoku, preserved by centuries of isolation.

p521

Sapporo & Hokkaidō

Outdoors
Food
Culture

Pristine Wilderness

This is mountain country and big snow country, where skiers carve snow drifts reaching several metres in depth and hikes through old-growth forests can last for days. There's so much to explore here.

Seafood & Ramen

The cold northern waters produce excellent seafood, including prized delicacies like *uni* (sea urchin) and crab. Capital city Sapporo's specialities are *miso-rāmen* and its namesake beer.

Ainu Legacy

The culture of Hokkaidō's indigenous people, the Ainu, is represented in museums, in concerts of traditional folk songs and in shops, restaurants and inns run by Ainu descendants.

p591

Shikoku

Nature
Temples
Outdoors

Gorgeous Countryside

A short drive from the mainland madness, Iya Valley has dramatic gorges, ancient vine bridges and a hint of sustainable living. Raft along the pristine Yoshino-gawa.

Pilgrim Trails

The 88-temple pilgrimage is a rite of passage for many Japanese who, dressed in white and armed with a walking stick, lower the pulse, raise the gaze and seek to honour the great Buddhist saint, Kōbō Daishi.

Sand & Waves

There's good surfing, especially at Shishikui in Tokushima and Ikumi Beach in Kōchi; the crowd-free swells at Ōkinohama should be legendary. There's also a slow-life, beach-bum vibe to match.

p663

Kyūshū

History
Nature
Onsen

Nagasaki

Christian rebellions led to over two centuries of seclusion, during which Nagasaki's Dejima Island was Japan's window to the world. Visit the city to learn about its fascinating history.

Smoking Volcanoes

Kyūshū is home to two of Japan's most famous – and famously active – volcanoes: smoking Sakurajima, looming over the skyline of Kagoshima, and Aso-san, a hulking giant in the middle of the island.

In Hot Water & Hot Sand

Some of Japan's most popular onsen towns are here, including Beppu, Yufuin and Kurokawa Onsen (our favourite, for its secluded riverside location). In Ibusuki experience something different: getting buried in hot sand.

p713

Okinawa & the Southwest Islands

Beaches
Hiking
Food

Sun-Soaked

Japan's best beaches are naturally found on its semi-tropical islands. Laze about the gorgeous golden beaches of the Kerama or Ishigaki Islands, snorkel or go for a dive.

Ancient Cedars

Yakushima is a beacon for hikers who come to bask in the enormity of the island's towering cedars. Almost the whole island is forested, blanketed with one of Japan's most primitive natural environments.

Island Cuisine

Tuck into a plateful of *gōyā champurū,* Okinawa's signature stir-fry with bitter melon. Add some *awamori,* the local firewater, and you'll be ready to grab the *sanshin* (banjo) and party.

p785

On the Road

AT A GLANCE

POPULATION
13.96 million

TALLEST BUILDING
Tokyo Skytree (634m; p105)

BEST BOUTIQUE HOTEL
BnA STUDIO Akihabara (p123)

BEST SUSHI
Sushi Dai (p140)

BEST COCKTAILS
Bar BenFiddich (p144)

WHEN TO GO

Mar–Apr Cherry-blossom viewing is in full swing – bring a *bentō* and spread the picnic blanket.

May–Sep Hot and humid, but lively traditional festivals more than make up for it.

Oct–Dec Crisp, cool and sunny days; red maples in the gardens and golden gingkos along the streets.

Shinjuku (p105)
JONATHAN STOKES/LONELY PLANET

Tokyo

More than any one sight, it's Tokyo (東京) itself that enchants visitors. It's a sprawling, organic thing, always changing and stretching as far as the eye can see. No two experiences of the city are ever the same. Some areas feel like a vision from the future, with ever taller, sleeker structures popping up each year; others evoke the past with low-slung wooden buildings and glowing lanterns radiating warmth; elsewhere, drab concrete blocks hide art galleries and cocktail bars and every lane hints at possible discoveries. In Tokyo you can experience the whole breadth of Japanese culture, from centuries-old sumo wrestling and kabuki theatre to cutting-edge contemporary art and giant robots. And if eating and drinking are among your main travel inspirations, you've come to the right place.

INCLUDES

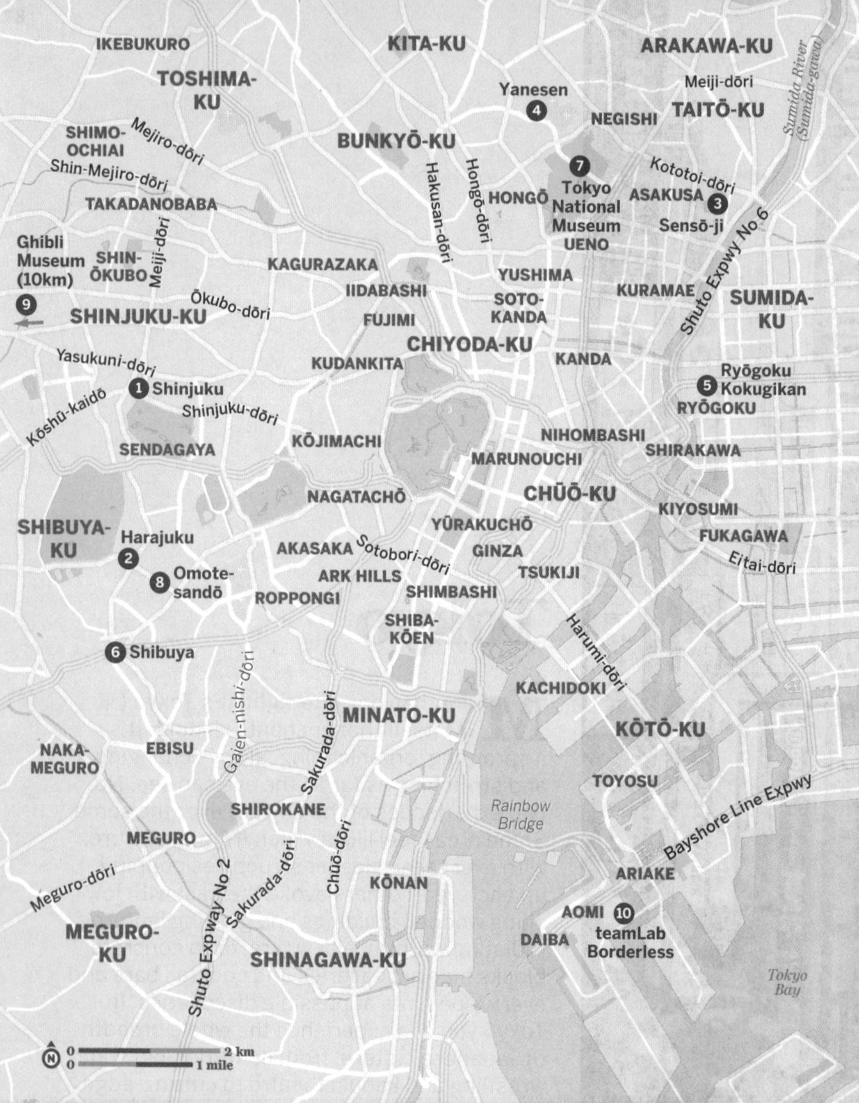

Tokyo Highlights

❶ **Shinjuku** (p144) Raising a glass in this colourful district.

❷ **Harajuku** (p156) Joining the city's eccentric fashion tribes as they shop.

❸ **Sensō-ji** (p104) Soaking up the atmosphere at Asakusa's centuries-old temple.

❹ **Yanesen** (p99) Losing yourself in the old city.

❺ **Ryōgoku Kokugikan** (p151) Catching the belly-slapping ritual of sumo.

❻ **Shibuya Crossing** (p109) Getting swept up in the crowds and neon lights.

❼ **Tokyo National Museum** (p98) Seeing the world's largest collection of Japanese artworks.

❽ **Omote-sandō** (p119) Checking out Tokyo's contemporary architecture.

❾ **Ghibli Museum** (p115) Visiting this enchanting museum.

❿ **teamLab Borderless** (p113) Experiencing the immersive, interactive art installations.

History

For most of its history, Tokyo was called Edo (literally 'Gate of the River') due to its location at the mouth of the Sumida-gawa. Until the warrior poet Ōta Dōkan put up a castle here in the 15th century, it was a remote fishing village. In 1603, warlord Tokugawa Ieyasu decided to make Edo Castle the centre of his new shogunate (military government). From that point, Edo quickly transformed into a bustling city and, by the late 18th century, had become the most populous city in the world.

In 1868, with the reversion of power to the emperor – an act known as the Meiji Restoration – the capital was officially moved from Kyoto to Edo, which was then renamed Tokyo, meaning Eastern Capital. At the same time, Japan ended its 250 years of self-prescribed isolation and began to welcome foreign influence with open arms. Western fashions and ideas were adopted as Tokyo eagerly sought to take its place among the pantheon of the world's great cities.

In 1923 the Great Kantō Earthquake and ensuing fires levelled much of the city; Tokyo was all but destroyed once more during the devastating Allied air raids in the final years of WWII. The city remade itself – and then some – in the decades after the US occupation. A soaring economic crescendo followed, culminating in the giddy heights of the 1980s 'bubble economy'. The humbling 'burst' in the '90s led to a recession that still continues today. Yet Tokyo remains the beating heart of its island nation, never ceasing to reinvent itself.

Sights

Tokyo can feel more like a collection of cities than one cohesive one. Pick just a couple of proximate neighbourhoods to explore in a day. The city is huge and while public transport is effortlessly smooth, you don't want to spend half the day on it.

Marunouchi & Nihombashi

Marunouchi is a high-powered business district with lots of gleaming skyscrapers. Nihombashi is a historic neighbourhood, home to many venerable old shops and restaurants.

★Intermediatheque MUSEUM
(インターメディアテク; Map p96; www.intermediatheque.jp; 2nd & 3rd fl, JP Tower, 2-7-2 Marunouchi, Chiyoda-ku; ⏲11am-6pm, to 8pm Fri & Sat, closed Mon & irregularly; 🚉JR Yamanote line to Tokyo, Marunouchi exit) FREE Dedicated to interdisciplinary experimentation, Intermediatheque cherry-picks from the vast collection of the University of Tokyo to craft a fascinating, contemporary museum experience. Go from viewing the best ornithological taxidermy collection in Japan to a giant pop art print or the beautifully encased skeleton of a dinosaur.

★Imperial Palace PALACE
(皇居, Kōkyo; Map p92; ☎03-5223-8071; http://sankan.kunaicho.go.jp; 1 Chiyoda, Chiyoda-ku; Ⓢ Chiyoda, Hanzōmon, Marunouchi or Tōzai line to Ōtemachi, exits C13b & C10) FREE The Imperial Palace occupies the site of the original Edo-jō, the Tokugawa shogunate's castle. In its heyday this was the largest fortress in the world, though little remains today apart from the moat and stone walls. Most of the 3.4-sq-km complex is off limits, as this is the emperor's home, but join one of the free tours organised by the Imperial Household Agency to see a small part of the inner compound.

Tours (lasting around 1¼ hours) run at 10am and 1.30pm usually on Tuesday to Saturday, but not on public holidays or mornings from late July through to the end of August. They're also not held at all from 28 December to 4 January or when Imperial Court functions are scheduled. Arrive no later than 10 minutes before the scheduled departure time at **Kikyō-mon** (桔梗門), the starting and ending point.

Reservations are taken – via the website, phone or by post – up to a month in advance (and no later than four days in advance via the website). Alternatively, go to the office at Kikyō-mon (open 8.45am until noon and 1pm to 5pm) where you can book for a tour up to seven days in advance; if there is space available on that day's tours, you'll be able to register. Bring photo ID.

The tour will take you past the present palace (Kyūden), a modest low-rise building completed in 1968 that replaced the one built in 1888, which was largely destroyed during WWII. Explanations are given only in Japanese; download the free app (www.kunaicho.go.jp/e-event/app.html) for

TOKYO IN...

Two Days

Pay a visit to **Meiji-jingū** (p108) in Harajuku, followed by a stroll along **Omote-sandō** (p119), to check out the contemporary architecture. Then walk down to Shibuya to see **Shibuya Crossing** (p109). Afterwards, head to Shinjuku to see the view from atop the **Tokyo Metropolitan Government Building** (p105), grab some *yakitori* in **Omoide-yokochō** (p137) and a drink (or a few) in **Golden Gai** (p000).

The following day, get an early start at either **Toyosu Market** (p114), where you can see the tuna auction and have sushi for breakfast, or **Tsukiji Market**, where you can cobble together a morning meal from the food vendors. Visit sights in central Tokyo or around Tokyo Bay, like **teamLab Borderless** (p113), the **Imperial Palace** (p89) and the landscape garden **Hama-rikyū Onshi-teien**, and catch an act of kabuki at **Kabukiza** (p150).

Four Days

On day three, visit the old side of town for some sightseeing in Asakusa, home to **Sensō-ji** (p104), and Ueno, home to the **Tokyo National Museum** (p98). Finish with an afternoon amble through atmospheric **Yanesen** (p000) and dinner at classic *izakaya* **Shinsuke** (p132).

The next day head west to the magical **Ghibli Museum** (p115). Get some onsen time in at **Spa LaQua** (p115) or explore pop culture centre **Akihabara** (p98), maybe via go-kart (p118). In the evening, head to Roppongi. The excellent **Mori Art Museum** (p95) stays open until 10pm, after which you can head out into the wilds of the neighbourhood's infamous nightlife.

explanations in English, Chinese, Korean, French or Spanish.

If you're not on the tour, head to the southwest corner of **Kōkyo-gaien Plaza** (皇居外苑広場, Kōkyo-gaien Hiroba; Map p96; www.env.go.jp/garden/kokyogaien; 1 Chiyoda, Chiyoda-ku; S Hibiya line to Hibiya, exit B6) to view two bridges – the iron **Nijū-bashi** (二重橋; Map p92) and the stone **Megane-bashi** (眼鏡橋; Map p92). Behind the bridges rises the Edo-era **Fushimi-yagura** (伏見櫓; Map p92) watchtower.

The main park of the verdant palace grounds is the **Imperial Palace East Garden** (東御苑; Kōkyo Higashi-gyoen; Map p96; 9am-4pm Nov-Feb, to 4.30pm Mar–mid-Apr, Sep & Oct, to 5pm mid-Apr–Aug, closed Mon & Fri year-round; S Chiyoda line to Ōtemachi, exits C13b & C10) FREE, which is open to the public without reservations. You must take a token upon arrival and return it at the end of your visit.

★National Museum of Modern Art (MOMAT) MUSEUM

(国立近代美術館, Kokuritsu Kindai Bijutsukan; Map p106; 03-5777-8600; www.momat.go.jp; 3-1 Kitanomaru-kōen, Chiyoda-ku; adult/child ¥500/free, after 5pm Fri & Sat adult/child ¥300/150; 10am-5pm, to 8pm Fri & Sat, closed Mon; S Tōzai line to Takebashi, exit 1b) Regularly changing displays from the museum's superb collection of more than 12,000 works are shown over floors 2 to 4; special exhibitions are mounted on the ground floor. All pieces date from the Meiji period onward and impart a sense of how modern Japan developed through portraits, photography, contemporary sculptures and video works. The museum closes in between exhibitions, so first check the schedule online.

Crafts Gallery MUSEUM

(東京国立近代美術館 工芸館; Map p106; www.momat.go.jp; 1 Kitanomaru-kōen, Chiyoda-ku; adult/child/student ¥250/free/¥130; 10am-5pm, closed Mon; S Tōzai line to Takebashi, exit 1b) This red-brick building, an annex of MOMAT, stages excellent changing exhibitions of *mingei* (folk crafts): ceramics, lacquerware, bamboo, textiles, dolls and much more. Some exhibits feature works by contemporary artisans, including some by Japan's officially designated 'living national treasures'. The museum closes between exhibitions.

Tokyo Station LANDMARK

(東京駅; Map p96; www.tokyostationcity.com; 1-9 Marunouchi, Chiyoda-ku; JR lines to Tokyo Station) Tokyo Station celebrated its centenary in 2014 with a major renovation and expansion. Kingo Tatsuno's original elegant brick building on the Marunouchi side has been expertly restored to include domes faithful to the original design, decorated inside with relief sculptures. It's best viewed straight on from the plaza on Miyuki-dōri.

Nihombashi BRIDGE

(日本橋, Nihonbashi; Map p96; 1 Nihombashi, Chūō-ku; S Ginza line to Mitsukoshimae, exits B5 & B6) Guarded by bronze lions and dragons, this handsome 1911-vintage granite bridge over the Nihombashi-gawa is partly obscured by the overhead expressway. During the Edo period, this was the beginning of the great trunk roads (the Tōkaidō, the Nikkō Kaidō etc) that took *daimyō* (domain lords) between the capital and their home provinces. It's still the point from which distances to Tokyo are measured.

Tokyo International Forum ARCHITECTURE

(東京国際フォーラム; Map p96; www.t-i-forum.co.jp; 3-5-1 Marunouchi, Chiyoda-ku; JR Yamanote line to Yūrakuchō, central exit) FREE This architectural marvel designed by Rafael Viñoly houses a convention and arts centre, with eight auditoriums and a spacious courtyard in which concerts and events are held. The eastern wing looks like a glass ship plying the urban waters; you can access the catwalks from the 7th floor (take the lift).

Ginza & Tsukiji

Ginza is Tokyo's most polished neighbourhood with luxury stores and art galleries.

★Hama-rikyū Onshi-teien GARDENS

(浜離宮恩賜庭園, Detached Palace Garden; Map p96; 03-3541-0200; www.tokyo-park.or.jp/teien; 1-1 Hama-rikyū-teien, Chūō-ku; adult/child ¥300/free; 9am-5pm; S Ōedo line to Shiodome, exit A1) This beautiful garden, one of Tokyo's finest, is all that remains of a shogunate summer villa next to Tokyo Bay. There's a large pond with an island, connected by a causeway, upon which sits the teahouse **Nakajima no Ochaya**, where you can sip matcha (¥740, traditional sweet included). Don't miss the spectacularly manicured 300-year-old black pine tree near the Otemon entrance.

★Tsukiji Market MARKET

(場外市場, Jōgai Shijō; Map p96; www.tsukiji.or.jp; 6-chōme Tsukiji, Chūō-ku; 5am-2pm, closed irregularly; S Hibiya line to Tsukiji, exit 1) Tokyo's main wholesale market may have moved to Toyosu (p114), but there are many reasons to visit its old home. The tightly packed rows of vendors (which once formed the Outer Market) hawk market and culinary-related goods, such as dried fish, seaweed, kitchen knives, rubber boots and crockery. It's also a fantastic place to eat, with great street food and a huge concentration of small restaurants and cafes, most specialising in seafood.

One must-visit is **Yamachō** (山長; Map p96; 03-3248-6002; 4-16-1 Tsukiji, Chūō-ku; omelette slices ¥100; 6am-3.30pm; S Hibiya line to Tsukiji, exit 1), a venerable purveyor of *tamagoyaki* (rolled omelettes). You can watch them being expertly made as you line up to buy. Sushikuni (p129) is here, too.

Note that some shops are closed on Sundays and Wednesdays.

Advertising Museum Tokyo MUSEUM

(アド・ミュージアム東京; Map p96; 03-6218-2500; www.admt.jp; basement, Caretta Bldg, 1-8-2 Higashi-Shimbashi, Minato-ku; 11am-6pm Tue-Sat; S Ōedo line to Shiodome, Shimbashi exit) FREE If you see advertising as art, this museum is a spectacle. Run by Dentsu, Japan's largest advertising agency, this fine collection runs from woodblock-printed handbills

ADVANCE PLANNING

- The best workshops and courses are designed for small groups, so sign up in advance (usually possible online).
- If you want to try go-karting (p118), get an international driving licence in your home country.
- Book tickets for sumo (p151), kabuki (p150) and Giants baseball games (p152) online to lock in good seats. Tickets usually go on sale one to two months prior.
- Tickets for the Ghibli Museum (p115) go on sale three months in advance; reserve yours ASAP.
- Other attractions that require advance reservations include the Imperial Palace (p89), if you want to tour the grounds.

Greater Tokyo

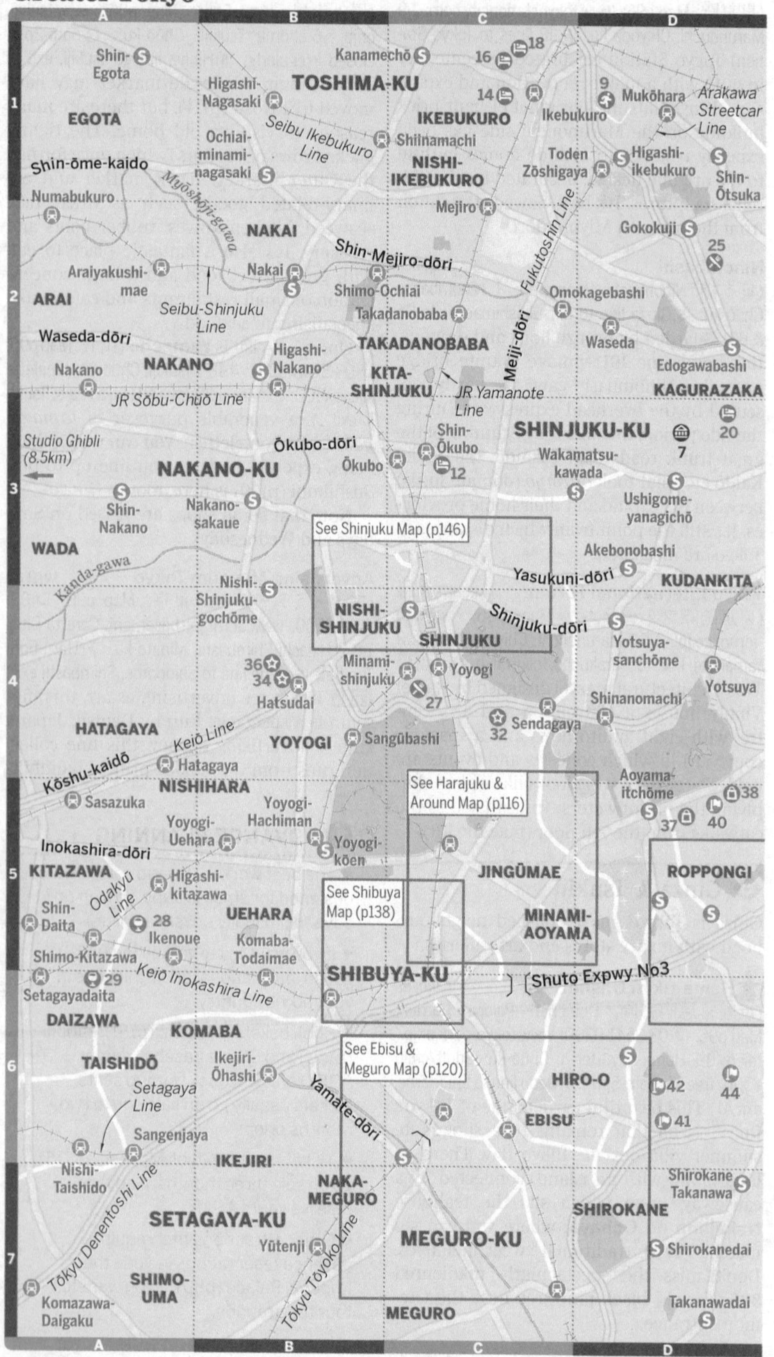

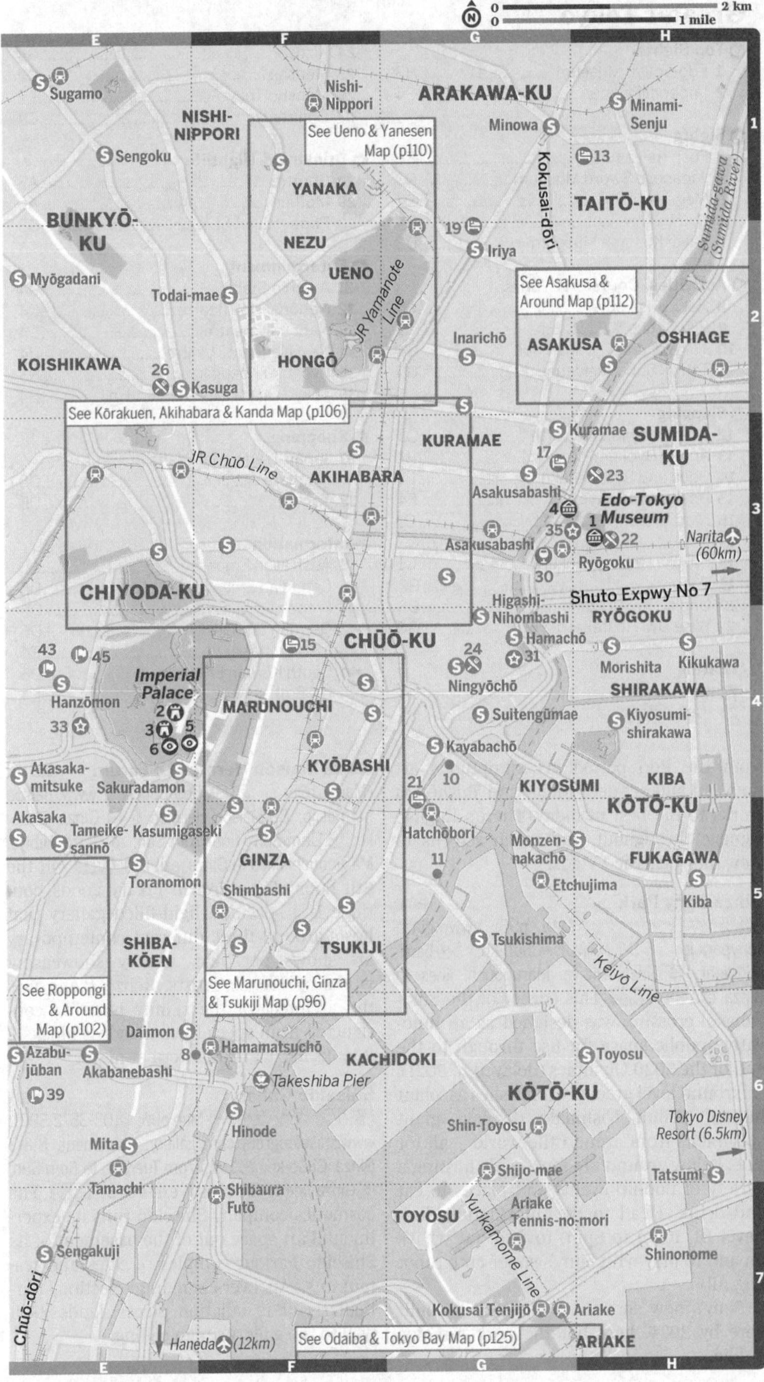
ARAKAWA-KU
NISHI-NIPPORI
BUNKYŌ-KU
TAITŌ-KU
KOISHIKAWA
YANAKA
NEZU
UENO
HONGŌ
ASAKUSA
OSHIAGE
KURAMAE
SUMIDA-KU
AKIHABARA
CHIYODA-KU
CHŪŌ-KU
RYŌGOKU
SHIRAKAWA
MARUNOUCHI
KYŌBASHI
KIYOSUMI
KIBA
KŌTŌ-KU
GINZA
FUKAGAWA
TSUKIJI
SHIBA-KŌEN
KACHIDOKI
TOYOSU
ARIAKE
Imperial Palace
Edo-Tokyo Museum
See Ueno & Yanesen Map (p110)
See Asakusa & Around Map (p112)
See Kōrakuen, Akihabara & Kanda Map (p106)
See Marunouchi, Ginza & Tsukiji Map (p96)
See Roppongi & Around Map (p102)
See Odaiba & Tokyo Bay Map (p125)
JR Yamanote Line
JR Chūō Line
Keiyō Line
Yurikamome Line
Kokusai-dōri
Chūō-dōri
Shuto Expwy No 7
Sumida-gawa (Sumida River)
Sugamo
Sengoku
Nishi-Nippori
Minowa
Minami-Senju
Myōgadani
Todai-mae
Iriya
Inarichō
Kasuga
Kuramae
Asakusabashi
Ryōgoku
Narita (60km)
Higashi-Nihombashi
Hamachō
Morishita
Kikukawa
Ningyōchō
Hanzōmon
Suitengūmae
Kiyosumi-shirakawa
Kayabachō
Akasaka-mitsuke
Sakuradamon
Akasaka
Tameike-sannō
Kasumigaseki
Hatchōbori
Monzen-nakachō
Toranomon
Etchujima
Shimbashi
Kiba
Tsukishima
Daimon
Hamamatsuchō
Azabu-jūban
Akabanebashi
Toyosu
Takeshiba Pier
Hinode
Shin-Toyosu
Tokyo Disney Resort (6.5km)
Mita
Shijo-mae
Tatsumi
Tamachi
Shibaura Futō
Ariake Tennis-no-mori
Shinonome
Sengakuji
Kokusai Tenjijō
Ariake
Haneda (12km)
0 2 km
0 1 mile

Greater Tokyo

Top Sights
1 Edo-Tokyo Museum H3
2 Imperial Palace E4

Sights
3 Fushimi-yagura E4
4 Japanese Sword Museum G3
5 Megane-bashi E4
6 Nijū-bashi E4
7 Yayoi Kusama Museum D3

Activities, Courses & Tours
8 Hato Bus Tours E6
9 Sky Circus D1
10 Tokyo Great Cycling Tour G4
11 Tsukiji Soba Academy G5

Sleeping
12 9 Hours Shinjuku-North C3
13 Andon Ryokan H1
14 Book and Bed Ikebukuro C1
15 Hoshinoya Tokyo F4
16 Kimi Ryokan C1
17 Nui G3
18 Sakura Hotel Ikebukuro C1
19 Toco G2
20 Unplan Kagurazaka D3
21 Wise Owl Hostels Tokyo G4

Eating
22 Hosokawa H3
23 Kappō Yoshiba H3
24 Kizushi G4
25 Mensho D2
26 Mensho Tokyo E2
27 Ohitotsuzen Tanbo C4

Drinking & Nightlife
28 Ghetto A5
29 Mother A6
30 Popeye G3

Entertainment
31 Arashio Stable G4
32 National Nō Theatre C4
33 National Theatre E4
34 New National Theatre B4
35 Ryōgoku Kokugikan H3
36 Tokyo Opera City Concert Hall B4

Shopping
37 Japan Traditional Crafts Aoyama Square D5
38 Toraya D5

Information
39 Australian Embassy E6
40 Canadian Embassy D5
41 French Embassy D6
42 German Embassy D6
43 Irish Embassy E4
44 South Korean Embassy D6
45 UK Embassy E4

from the Edo period via sumptuous art nouveau and art deco Meiji- and Taishō-era works to the best of today. There's English signage throughout, and touch screens to view many classic TV ads.

Ginza Sony Park PARK
(銀座ソニーパーク; Map p96; www.gingzasonypark.jp; 5-3-1 Ginza, Chūō-ku; 5am-midnight; S Ginza, Hibiya, Marunouchi lines to Ginza, exit B9) FREE This corner of the Sukiyabashi crossing was designed as an innovative public space for use through to the end of the 2020 Olympics (delayed to 2021). At ground level greenery flourishes as 'plant hunter' Seijun Nishihata displays giant specimens from around the world – all for sale. Below ground are four levels hosting a variety of pop-up events and places to eat and drink. Head to the information desk (level B1, 10am to 8pm) to find out what's on and to play with Sony's super-cute robot dog Aibo.

Sony's new showroom will also be built here by 2024, here but the park remains public.

Ginza Maison Hermès Le Forum GALLERY
(Map p96; 03-3569-3300; www.maisonhermes.jp; 8F Maison Hermès, 5-4-1 Ginza, Chūō-ku; 11am-8pm, until 7pm Sun; S Ginza, Hibiya, Marunouchi lines to Ginza, exit B9) FREE On the 8th floor of the French luxury goods boutique is a spacious, light-filled gallery that hosts around three different contemporary art shows per year, usually showcasing works by French artists. Renzo Piano was the architect of the skinny building constructed from specially made glass blocks – it looks like a giant lantern at night.

Shiseido Gallery GALLERY
(資生堂ギャラリー; Map p96; 03-3572-3901; www.shiseidogroup.com/gallery; basement, 8-8-3 Ginza, Chūō-ku; 11am-7pm Tue-Sat, to 6pm Sun; S Ginza line to Shimbashi, exit 1 or 3) FREE The cosmetics company Shiseido runs its experimental art space out of the basement of its Shiseido Parlour complex of cafes and restaurants. An ever-changing selection, particularly of installation pieces, lends itself well to the gallery's high ceiling.

Ginza Graphic Gallery GALLERY

(ギンザ・グラフィック・ギャラリー; Map p96; ☎03-3571-5206; www.dnp.co.jp/gallery; 7-7-2 Ginza, Chūō-ku; ⏰11am-7pm Tue-Fri, to 6pm Sat; Ⓢ Ginza line to Ginza, exit A2) FREE This gallery features monthly changing exhibits of graphic arts – focusing on advertising and poster art – from mostly Japanese artists but with the occasional Western artist. The annual Tokyo Art Directors Conference exhibition takes place here in July.

NI-Tele Really Big Clock PUBLIC ART

(日テレ大時計; Map p96; 1-6-1 Higashi-Shimbashi, Minato-ku; ⏰operates at noon, 3pm, 6pm & 8pm, also 10am Sat & Sun; 🚉 JR services to Shimbashi, Shiodome exit) FREE Studio Ghibli's animation director Miyazaki Hayao collaborated with sculptor Kunio Shachimaru on this fantastic, steampunk-style timepiece beside the entrance to Nippon Television Tower. Four times daily (with an extra morning show on weekends) various automaton elements spring to life as the clock strikes the hour and plays a jolly tune.

Roppongi & Around

Legendary for its nightlife, Roppongi also offers the chic Roppongi Hills and Tokyo Midtown complexes where you'll find several excellent art museums.

Keep your ticket stub for Mori Art Museum, Suntory Museum of Art or the National Art Center Tokyo, and when you visit one of the other two galleries you'll be entitled to a discount on admission. At any of these venues, pick up the *Art Triangle Roppongi* walking map, which lists dozens of smaller galleries in the area.

★ **Roppongi Hills** LANDMARK

(六本木ヒルズ; Map p102; ☎03-6406-6000; www.roppongihills.com; 6-chōme Roppongi, Minato-ku; ⏰11am-11pm; Ⓢ Hibiya line to Roppongi, exit 1) Roppongi Hills sets the standard for 21st-century real-estate developments in Tokyo. The centrepiece of the office, shopping, dining and entertainment complex is the 54-storey Mori Tower, home to the Mori Art Museum and the Tokyo City View observatory. Scattered around are several public artworks, such as Louise Bourgeois' giant, spiny **Maman spider sculpture** (Map p102). There's also an Edo-style strolling garden, **Mohri Garden** (毛利庭園, Mōri-teien).

Mori Art Museum MUSEUM

(森美術館; Map p102; www.mori.art.museum; 52nd fl, Mori Tower, Roppongi Hills, 6-10-1 Roppongi, Minato-ku; adult/child ¥1800/600; ⏰10am-10pm, to 5pm Tue; Ⓢ Hibiya or Toei Ōedo line to Roppongi, exit 1) Mori Art Museum is one of Tokyo's leading spaces for contemporary art, taking up a whole floor at the top of Mori Tower. It has no permanent exhibition; instead, large-scale, original shows introduce major local and global artists and movements. Past exhibitions have focused on the works of Chinese artist and dissident Ai Weiwei and native son Murakami Takashi, as well as themes like AI, protest and urbanism. Unlike most museums, Mori Art Museum is open late.

Tokyo City View VIEWPOINT

(東京シティビュー; Map p102; ☎03-6406-6652; www.roppongihills.com; 52nd fl, Mori Tower, Roppongi Hills, 6-10-1 Roppongi, Minato-ku; adult/child ¥1800/600; ⏰10am-11pm Mon-Thu & Sun, to 1am Fri & Sat; Ⓢ Hibiya line to Roppongi, exit 1) From this 250m-high vantage point, on the 52nd floor of Mori Tower, you can see 360-degree views of the seemingly never-ending city. Admission is included in the entry price for Mori Art Museum though you will pay the same fee to visit after the museum is closed. Weather permitting, you can also go out to the external rooftop **Sky Deck** (additional adult/child ¥500/300; 11am to 8pm) for alfresco views.

National Art Center Tokyo MUSEUM

(国立新美術館; Map p102; ☎03-5777-8600; www.nact.jp; 7-22-1 Roppongi, Minato-ku; admission varies; ⏰10am-6pm Wed, Thu & Sun-Mon, to 8pm Fri & Sat; Ⓢ Chiyoda line to Nogizaka, exit 6) Designed by Kurokawa Kishō, this architectural beauty has no permanent collection, but boasts the country's largest exhibition space for visiting shows, which have included Renoir and Modigliani. A visit here is recommended to admire the building's awesome undulating glass facade, its cafes atop giant inverted cones and the great gift shop, Souvenir from Tokyo (p154).

Suntory Museum of Art MUSEUM

(サントリー美術館; Map p102; ☎03-3479-8600; www.suntory.com/sma; 4th fl, Tokyo Midtown, 9-7-4 Akasaka, Minato-ku; admission varies, child free; ⏰10am-6pm Sun-Wed, to 8pm Fri & Sat; Ⓢ Ōedo line to Roppongi, exit 8) Since its original 1961 opening, the Suntory Museum of Art has subscribed to an underlying philosophy

Marunouchi, Ginza & Tsukiji

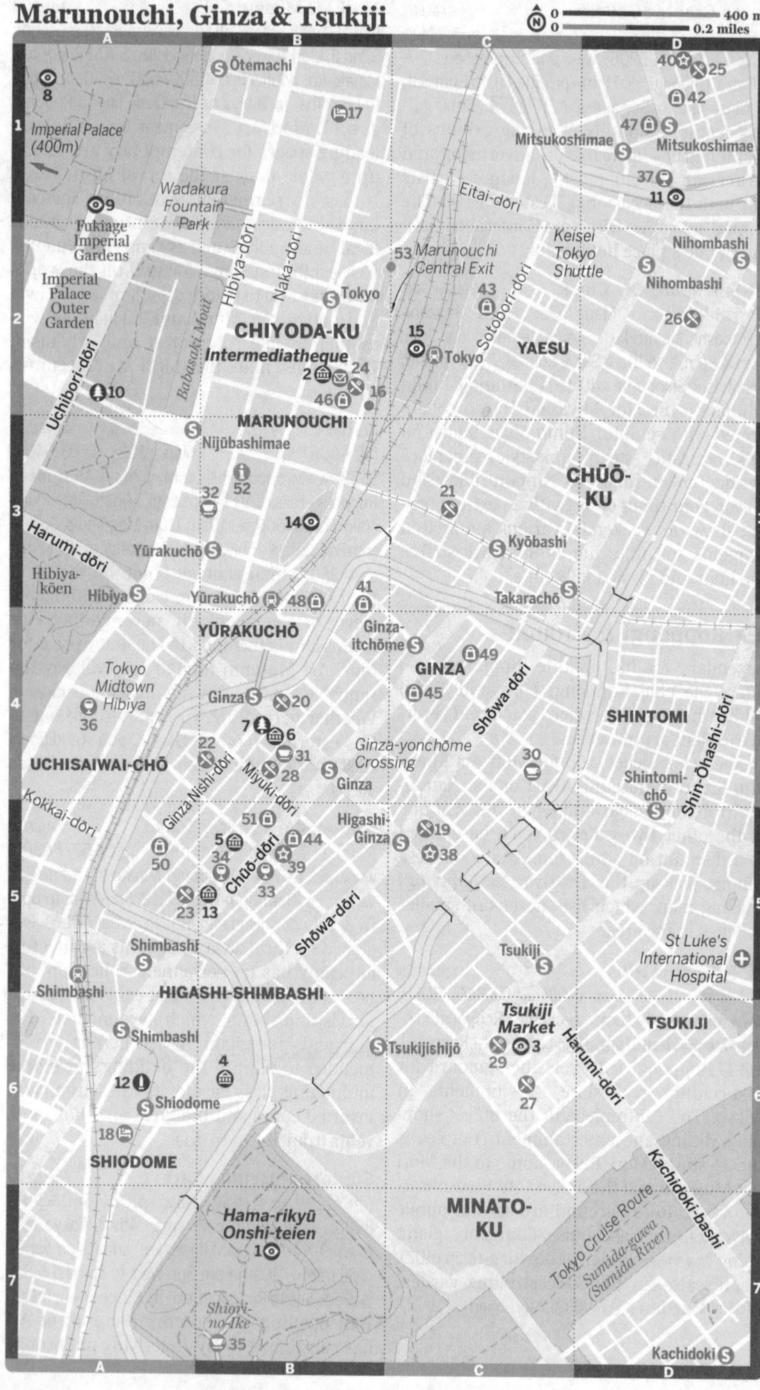

Marunouchi, Ginza & Tsukiji

Top Sights
1 Hama-rikyū Onshi-teien B7
2 Intermediatheque B2
3 Tsukiji Market C6

Sights
4 Advertising Museum Tokyo B6
5 Ginza Graphic Gallery B5
6 Ginza Maison Hermès Le Forum B4
7 Ginza Sony Park B4
8 Imperial Palace East Garden A1
9 Kikyō-mon A1
10 Kōkyo-gaien Plaza A2
11 Nihombashi D1
12 NI-Tele Really Big Clock A6
13 Shiseido Gallery B5
14 Tokyo International Forum B3
15 Tokyo Station C2

Activities, Courses & Tours
16 Hato Bus Tours B2
Imperial Palace East Garden Walking Tour .... (see 52)

Sleeping
17 Aman Tokyo B1
18 Park Hotel Tokyo A6

Eating
19 Ain Soph C5
20 Bird Land B4
21 Dhaba India C3
22 Ginza Sato Yosuke B4
23 Kyūbey A5
Meal MUJI Yūrakuchō .... (see 48)
24 Nemuro Hanamaru B2
25 Nihonbashi Dashi Bar Hanare D1
26 Nihonbashi Tamai D2
27 Sushikuni C6
28 Tempura Kondō B4
29 Yamachō C6

Drinking & Nightlife
30 Bongen Coffee C4
31 Cha Ginza B4
32 Chashitsu Kaboku B3
33 Ginza Lion B5
34 Ginza Music Bar B5
35 Nakajima no Ochaya B7
36 Old Imperial Bar A4
37 Toyama Bar D1

Entertainment
38 Kabukiza C5
39 Kanze Nōgakudō B5
40 Suigian D1

Shopping
41 Akomeya B3
42 Coredo Muromachi D1
43 Daimaru C2
Dover Street Market Ginza .... (see 51)
44 Ginza Six B5
45 Itōya C4
46 KITTE B2
47 Mitsukoshi D1
48 Muji B3
49 Okuno Building C4
50 Takumi A5
51 Uniqlo B5

Information
52 JNTO Tourist Information Center B3
53 JR East Travel Service Center C2

of lifestyle art. Rotating exhibitions focus on the beauty of useful things: Japanese ceramics, lacquerware, glass, dyeing, weaving and such. Its current Tokyo Midtown (p154) digs, designed by architect Kuma Kengō, are both understated and breathtaking.

21_21 Design Sight MUSEUM
(21_21デザインサイト; Map p102; 03-3475-2121; www.2121designsight.jp; Tokyo Midtown, 9-7-6 Akasaka, Minato-ku; adult/child ¥1100/free; 11am-7pm Wed-Mon; Ōedo line to Roppongi, exit 8) An exhibition and discussion space dedicated to all forms of design, the 21_21 Design Sight is a beacon for local art enthusiasts, whether they be designers or onlookers. The striking concrete and glass building, bursting out of the ground at sharp angles, was designed by Pritzker Prize–winning architect Andō Tadao.

Kōrakuen & Kanda

★Koishikawa Kōrakuen GARDENS
(小石川後楽園; Map p106; 03-3811-3015; www.tokyo-park.or.jp/teien; 1-6-6 Kōraku, Bunkyō-ku; adult/child ¥300/free; 9am-5pm; Ōedo line to Iidabashi, exit C3) Established in the mid-17th century as the property of the Tokugawa clan, this formal strolling garden incorporates elements of Chinese and Japanese landscaping. It's among Tokyo's most attractive gardens, although nowadays the *shakkei* (borrowed scenery) also includes the contemporary skyline of Tokyo Dome (p152).

Don't miss the **Engetsu-kyō** (Full-Moon Bridge), which dates from the early Edo period (the name will make sense when you see it), and the beautiful vermilion wooden bridge **Tsuten-kyō**. The garden is

LOCAL KNOWLEDGE

POP CITY AKIHABARA

Akihabara (Akiba to friends) is Tokyo's *otaku* (geek) subculture centre, full of shops selling manga (Japanese comics), anime (Japanese animation), cosplay ('costume play' – dressing up as your favourite character) outfits and accessories, models, figurines… and more. If this is up your alley, surely Akiba is already on your bucket list. Even if it's not, the neighbourhood is worth a visit: it's equal parts sensory overload and cultural mind-bender.

A must-visit is anime and manga megastore **Mandarake Complex** (まんだらけコンプレックス; Map p106; ☎03-3252-7007; www.mandarake.co.jp; 3-11-12 Soto-Kanda, Chiyoda-ku; ⊙noon-8pm; 🚇JR Yamanote & Sōbu lines to Akihabara, Electric Town exit), with eight storeys piled high with comic books, action figures, cosplay accessories and cel art just for starters. A fun pit stop is retro gaming centre **Super Potato Retro-kan** (スーパーポテトレトロ館; Map p106; ☎03-5289 9933; www.superpotato.com; 1-11-2 Soto-kanda, Chiyoda-ku; ⊙11am-8pm Mon-Fri, from 10am Sat & Sun; 🚇JR Yamanote line to Akihabara, Electric Town exit).

To get oriented, stop in at **Akiba Info** (Map p106; ☎080-3413-4800; www.akiba-information.jp; 2nd fl, Akihabara UDX Bldg, 4-14-1 Soto-Kanda, Chiyoda-ku; ⊙11am-5.30pm Tue-Sun; 📶; 🚇JR Yamanote line to Akihabara, Electric Town exit); staff usually speak English.

particularly well known for its plum blossoms in February, irises in June and autumn leaves.

TeNQ MUSEUM

(テンキュー; Map p106; ☎03-3814-0109; www.tokyo-dome.co.jp; 6F Tokyo Dome City, Yellow Bldg, 1-3-61 Kōraku, Bunkyō-ku; adult/child ¥1800/1200; ⊙11am-9pm Mon-Fri, from 10am Sat & Sun; 👪; 🚇JR Sobu line to Suidōbashi, west exit) This nifty, interactive museum is devoted to outer-space exploration and science. Timed entry tickets start you off with one of three impressive high-resolution videos projected across an 11m-diameter screen that you stand around. Good English captions throughout make it a fine educational experience. Set aside a couple of hours to do the museum justice.

Other fun things to do here include taking part in a Mars research project being run by Tokyo University (which has a lab on-site) and playing an astro-ball robot control game.

Kanda Myōjin SHINTŌ SHRINE

(神田明神, Kanda Shrine; Map p106; ☎03-3254-0753; www.kandamyoujin.or.jp; 2-16-2 Soto-kanda, Chiyoda-ku; 🚇JR Chūō or Sōbu lines to Ochanomizu, Hijiri-bashi exit) FREE Tracing its history back to 730 CE, this splendid Shintō shrine boasts vermilion-lacquered halls surrounding a stately courtyard. Its present location dates from 1616 and the *kami* (gods) enshrined here are said to bring luck in business and in finding a spouse. There are also plenty of anime characters, since this is Akiba's local shrine.

Ueno & Yanesen

Ueno is the cultural heart of Tokyo. Its central park, Ueno-kōen, has the city's highest concentration of museums, including the Tokyo National Museum. The neighbouring areas of Yanaka, Nezu and Sendagi are collectively known as Yanesen. It's a charming part of Tokyo that feels like time stopped several decades ago.

★**Tokyo National Museum** MUSEUM

(東京国立博物館; Map p110; ☎03-3822-1111; www.tnm.jp; 13-9 Ueno-kōen, Taitō-ku; adult/student ¥620/410, under 18yr and over 70yr free; ⊙9.30am-5pm, to 9pm Fri & Sat; Ⓢ Ginza or Hibiya line to Ueno, exit 7, 🚇JR Yamanote line to Ueno, Kōen exit) If you visit only one museum in Tokyo, make it the Tokyo National Museum. Here you'll find the world's largest collection of Japanese art, including ancient pottery, Buddhist sculptures, samurai swords, colourful *ukiyo-e* (woodblock prints), gorgeous kimonos and much, much more. Visitors with only a couple of hours to spare should focus on the **Honkan** (Japanese Gallery), which has a specially curated selection of artistic highlights on the 2nd floor.

With more time, you can explore the enchanting **Gallery of Hōryū-ji Treasures** (法隆寺宝物館; Map p110; ☎03-5777-8600; ⊙9.30am-5pm Tue-Thu, to 9pm Fri & Sat, to 6pm on Sun), which displays masks, scrolls and gilt Buddhas from Hōryū-ji (in Nara Prefecture, dating from 607); the **Tōyōkan** with

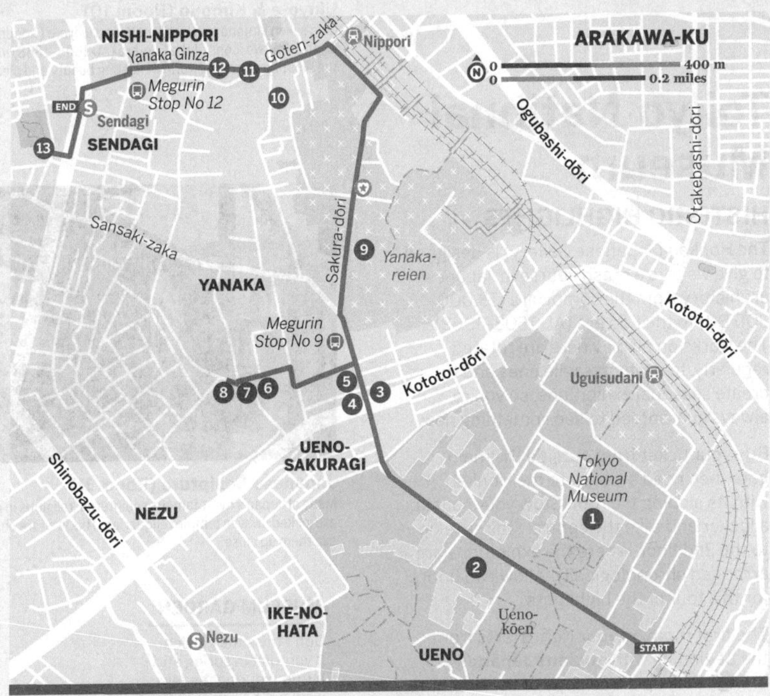

City Walk A Stroll Through Yanesen

START TOKYO NATIONAL MUSEUM
END SENDAGI STATION
LENGTH 3KM; TWO HOURS

If you have time, visit the ❶ **Tokyo National Museum** before you start exploring Yanaka If not, simply follow the road northwest out of ❷ **Ueno-kōen** (p103) until you hit Kototoi-dōri. At the corner is the ❸ **Shitamachi Museum Annex** (下町風俗資料館; Map p110; ☎03-3823-7451; www.taitocity.net/zaidan/shitamachi; 2-10-6 Ueno-sakuragi, Taitō-ku; ⏲9.30am-4.30pm Tue-Sun) FREE, actually a preserved, century-old liquor store. Across the street is ❹ **Kayaba Coffee** (p143), if you need a pick-me-up.

Nearby ❺ **SCAI the Bathhouse** (p103) is a classic old public bathhouse turned contemporary art gallery. Continue down to the studio of painter ❻ **Allan West** (p154). Beside it, on the corner, is an ancient, thick-trunked ❼ **Himalayan cedar tree**. Around here, you'll pass many temples, including ❽ **Enju-ji** (延寿寺; Map p110; http://nichika-do.jp; 1-7-36 Yanaka, Taitō-ku; ⏲10am-4pm), where Nichika-sama, the 'god of strong legs', is enshrined; it's popular with runners. Feel free to stop in any of the temples; just be respectful and keep your voice low.

Double back towards the entrance of ❾ **Yanaka-reien** (p103), one of Tokyo's most atmospheric and prestigious cemeteries. When you exit the cemetery, continue with the train tracks on your right, climbing until you reach the bridge, which overlooks the tracks.

Head left and look for the sign pointing towards the ❿ **Asakura Museum of Sculpture, Taitō** (p102), the home studio of an early-20th century sculptor and now an attractive museum. Back on the main drag, continue down the ⓫ **Yūyake Dandan** (夕やけだんん団; Map p110; JR lines to Nippori, Yanaka exit) – literally the 'Sunset Stairs' – to the classic mid-20th-century shopping street ⓬ **Yanaka Ginza** (p103). Pick up some snacks from the vendors here, then hunker down on a milk crate on the side of the road with the locals and wash it all down with a beer. Walk west and you can pick up the subway at Sendagi Station, after taking a peek at the gorgeous pocket park ⓭ **Sudo-kōen** (須藤公園; Map p110; 3-4 Sendagi, Bunkyō-ku) FREE.

Tokyo National Museum

HISTORIC HIGHLIGHTS

The Honkan (Japanese Gallery) is designed to give visitors a crash course in Japanese art history from the Jōmon era (13,000–300 BC) to the Edo era (AD 1603–1868). The works on display here are rotated regularly, to protect fragile ones and to create seasonal exhibitions, so you're always guaranteed to see something new.

Buy your ticket from outside the main gate then head straight to the Honkan with its sloping tile roof. Stow your coat in a locker and take the central staircase up to the 2nd floor, where the exhibitions are arranged chronologically. Allow two hours for this tour of the highlights.

The first room on your right starts from the beginning with **ancient Japanese art** ❶. Pick up a free copy of the brochure *Highlights of Japanese Art* at the entrance to the first room on your right. The exhibition starts here with the **Dawn of Japanese Art**.

Continue to the **National Treasure Gallery** ❷. 'National Treasure' is the highest distinction awarded to a work of art in Japan. Keep an eye out for more National Treasures, labelled in red, on display in other rooms throughout the museum.

Moving on into the Heian era (794–1185), considered the first flourishing of what we think of as Japanese culture, stop to admire the **courtly art** ❸. Next is the medieval art: ink brush scrolls, tea ceremony pottery and **samurai armour and swords** ❹; and then the ***ukiyo-e* and kimono** ❺ of the 17th and 18th centuries.

Head to the ground floor, where rooms are arranged by theme (such as lacquerware). Particularly noteworthy is the collection of **Buddhist sculptures** ❻ and the **Ainu and Ryūkyū cultural artefacts** ❼.

Finish your visit with a look inside the enchanting **Gallery of Hōryū-ji Treasures** ❽.

Ukiyo-e & Kimono (Room 10)
Chic silken kimono and lushly coloured *ukiyo-e* (woodblock prints) are two icons of the Edo-era (AD 1603–1868) *ukiyo* – the 'floating world', or world of fleeting beauty and pleasure.

TOKYO NATIONAL MUSEUM ©

Japanese Sculpture (Room 11)
Many of Japan's most famous sculptures, religious in nature, are locked away in temple reliquaries. This is a rare chance to see them up close.

MUSEUM GARDEN

Don't miss the garden if you visit in spring and autumn during the few weeks it's open to the public.

Gallery of Hōryū-ji Treasures
Surround yourself with miniature gilt Buddhas from Hōryū-ji, one of Japan's oldest Buddhist temples, founded in 607. Don't miss the graceful Pitcher with Dragon Head, a National Treasure.

TOKYO NATIONAL MUSEUM ©; PHOTO BY SATO AKIRA

TOKYO NATIONAL MUSEUM ©

Samurai Armour & Swords (Rooms 5 & 6)
Glistening swords, finely stitched armour and imposing helmets bring to life the samurai, those iconic warriors of Japan's medieval age.

Courtly Art (Room 3-2)
Literature works, calligraphy and narrative picture scrolls are displayed alongside decorative art objects, which allude to the life of elegance led by courtesans a thousand years ago.

5
4
1
3
2
7
6

Honkan (Japanese Gallery) 2nd Floor

Honkan (Japanese Gallery) 1st Floor

Museum Garden & Teahouses

Honkan (Japanese Gallery)

Tōyōkan (Gallery of Asian Art)

National Treasure Gallery (Room 2)
A single, superlative work from the museum's collection of 88 National Treasures (perhaps a painted screen, or a gilded, hand-drawn sutra) is displayed in a serene, contemplative setting.

GIFT SHOP

The museum gift shop, on the 1st floor of the Honkan, has an excellent collection of Japanese art books in English.

Dawn of Japanese Art (Room 1)
The rise of the imperial court and the introduction of Buddhism changed the Japanese aesthetic forever. These clay works from previous eras show what came before.

TOKYO NATIONAL MUSEUM ©

Ainu and Ryūkyū Collection (Room 16)
Japanese culture is often considered a monolith, but before Japan colonized Hokkaidō (home of the indigenous Ainu people) and the Ryūkyū Empire, each had its own rich culture.

Roppongi & Around

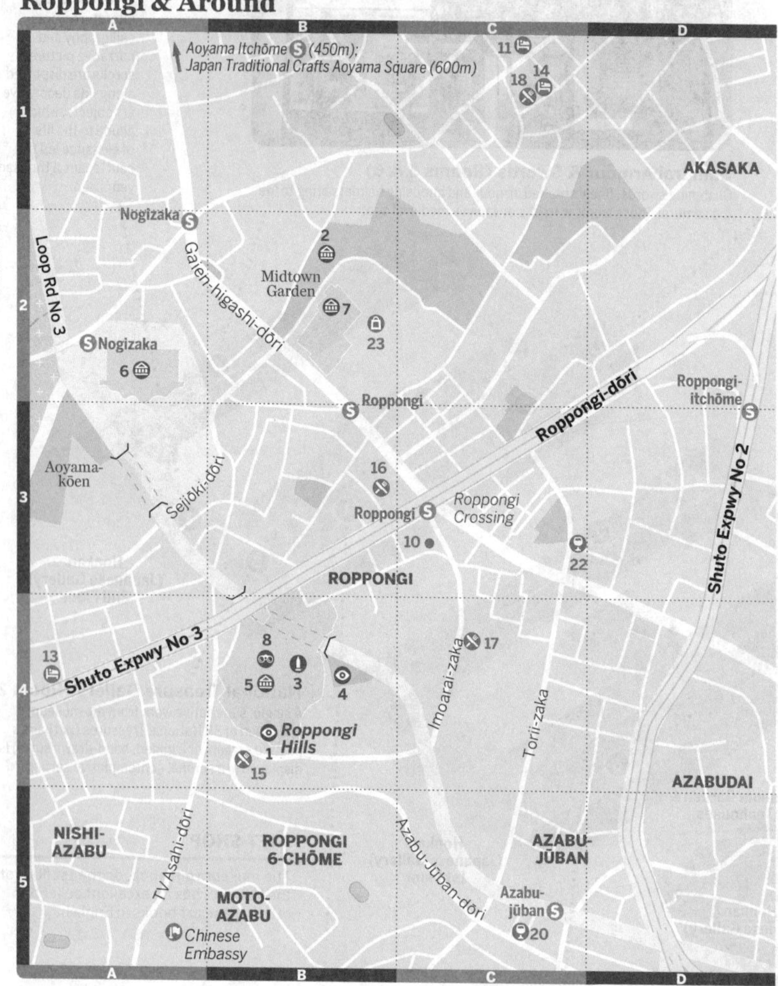

its collection of Asian art, including delicate Chinese ceramics; and the **Heiseikan** (平成館), which houses the **Japanese Archaeological Gallery**, full of pottery, talismans and articles of daily life from Japan's prehistoric periods.

Check whether it's possible to access the usually off-limits garden, which includes several vintage teahouses; it opens to the public from mid-March to mid-April and from late October to early December.

The museum regularly hosts temporary exhibitions (which cost extra); these can be fantastic, but sometimes lack the English signage found throughout the rest of the museum.

★Asakura Museum of Sculpture, Taitō

MUSEUM

(朝倉彫塑館; Map p110; ☎03-3821-4549; www.taitocity.net/taito/asakura; 7-16-10 Yanaka, Taitō-ku; adult/child ¥500/250; ⏲9.30am-4.30pm, closed Mon & Thu; 🚇JR Yamanote line to Nippori, north exit) Sculptor Asakura Fumio (artist name Chōso; 1883–1964) built his home studio in the early 20th century and it's very much representative of architecture of the time: part Japanese-style, with tatami rooms and open verandah facing an inner garden (his home) attached to a light-filled concrete space with vaulted ceilings (his studio). Now a museum, there are many of

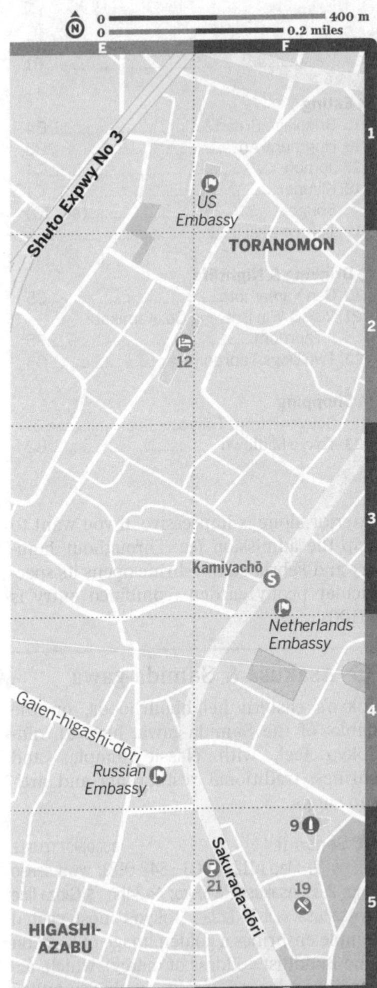

the artist's signature realist works, mostly of people and cats, on display throughout. Visit the roof terrace for views over the neighbourhood.

Nezu-jinja SHINTŌ SHRINE

(根津神社; Map p110; ☎03-3822-0753; www.nedujinja.or.jp; 1-28-9 Nezu, Bunkyō-ku; ⏰6am-5pm; Ⓢ Chiyoda line to Nezu, exit 1) Not only is this one of Japan's oldest shrines, it is also among the most beautiful – a tough call in a district packed with attractive, historic buildings. The vermilion-and-gold structure dates from the early 18th century and is offset by a long corridor of small red *torii* (shrine gates), which make for great photos.

Ueno-kōen PARK

(上野公園; Map p110; www.ueno-bunka.jp; Ueno-kōen, Taitō-ku; Ⓢ Ginza or Hibiya lines to Ueno, exists 6, 7 or 8, 🚆 JR Yamanote line to Ueno, Kōen or Shinobazu exits) Best known for its profusion of cherry trees that burst into blossom in spring (making this one of Tokyo's top *hanami* – blossom-viewing – spots), sprawling Ueno-kōen is also the location of the city's highest concentration of museums. At the southern tip is the large scenic pond, **Shinobazu-ike** (不忍池; Map p110; 🚆 JR Yamanote line to Ueno, Shinobazu exit), choked with lotus flowers in summer.

Ueno Zoo ZOO

(上野動物園, Ueno Dōbutsu-en; Map p110; ☎03-3828-5171; www.tokyo-zoo.net; 9-83 Ueno-kōen, Taitō-ku; adult/child ¥600/free; ⏰9.30am-5pm, closed Mon, enter by 4pm; 🚆 JR Yamanote line to Ueno, Ueno-kōen exit) Japan's oldest zoo, established in 1882, is home to animals from around the globe, but the biggest attractions are the giant pandas from China, Rī Rī and Shin Shin. Following several disappointments, the two finally had a cub, Xiang Xiang, in 2017. The zoo includes part of Shinobazu-iku and has a terrace right on the edge for good views. Across the causeway, there's a whole area devoted to lemurs, which makes sense given Tokyoites' general affection for all things cute.

Yanaka Ginza AREA

(谷中銀座; Map p110; www.yanakaginza.com; 🚆 JR Yamanote line to Nippori, north exit) Yanaka Ginza is pure, vintage mid-20th-century Tokyo, a pedestrian street lined with butcher shops, vegetable vendors and the like. Most Tokyo neighbourhoods once had stretches like these (until supermarkets took over). It's popular with Tokyoites from all over the city, who come to soak up the nostalgic atmosphere, plus the locals who shop here.

Yanaka-reien CEMETERY

(谷中霊園; Map p110; ☎03-3821-4456; www.tokyo-park.or.jp/reien; 7-5-24 Yanaka, Taitō-ku; 🚆 JR Yamanote line to Nippori, west exit) One of Tokyo's largest graveyards, Yanaka-reien is the final resting place of more than 7000 souls, many of whom were quite well known in their day. It's also where you'll find the tomb of Yoshinobu Tokugawa (徳川慶喜の墓), the last shogun. Come spring it is also a popular cherry-blossom-viewing spot.

Roppongi & Around

Top Sights
1 Roppongi Hills B4

Sights
2 21_21 Design Sight B2
3 Maman Spider Sculpture B4
4 Mohri Garden B4
5 Mori Art Museum B4
6 National Art Center Tokyo A2
7 Suntory Museum of Art B2
8 Tokyo City View B4
9 Tokyo Tower F5

Activities, Courses & Tours
10 Tokyo Cook C3

Sleeping
11 Apartment Hotel Mimaru Akasaka C1
12 Hotel Ōkura E2
13 Hotel S A4
14 Kaisu C1

Eating
15 Bricolage Bread & Co B4
16 Honmura-An B3
17 Jōmon C4
18 Kikunoi C1
Sougo .... (see 10)
19 Tofuya-Ukai F5

Drinking & Nightlife
20 Gen Yamamoto C5
21 Rise & Win Brewing Co. Kamikatz Taproom F5
22 Two Dogs Taproom C3

Shopping
Souvenir from Tokyo .... (see 6)
23 Tokyo Midtown B2

SCAI the Bathhouse GALLERY

(スカイザバスハウス; Map p110; ☎03-3821-1144; www.scaithebathhouse.com; 6-1-23 Yanaka, Taitō-ku; ⊙noon-6pm, closed Sun & Mon; Ⓢ Chiyoda line to Nezu, exit 1) FREE This 200-year-old bathhouse is now an avant-garde gallery, showcasing Japanese and international artists: the vaulted space just as suited for installations as it was for the rising steam of the baths that were once here. (You'll still see the old wooden shoe lockers at the entrance). Closed between exhibitions.

Shitamachi Museum MUSEUM

(下町風俗資料館; Map p110; ☎03-3823-7451; www.taitocity.net/zaidan/shitamachi; 2-1 Ueno-kōen, Taitō-ku; adult/child ¥300/100; ⊙9.30am-4.30pm Tue-Sun; 🚊JR lines to Ueno, Shinobazu exit) This small museum recreates life in the plebeian quarters of Tokyo during the Meiji and Taishō periods (1868–1926), before the city was twice destroyed by the Great Kantō Earthquake and WWII. There are old tenement houses and shops that you can enter.

Ueno Tōshō-gū SHINTŌ SHRINE

(上野東照宮; Map p110; ☎03-3822-3455; www.uenotoshogu.com; 9-88 Ueno-kōen, Taitō-ku; adult/child ¥500/200; ⊙9am-5.30pm, to 4.30pm Oct-Feb; 🚊JR Yamanote line to Ueno, Shinobazu exit) This shrine honours Tokugawa Ieyasu, the warlord who unified Japan; it's the (much smaller) Tokyo counterpart to Nikkō's grand Tōshō-gū (p212). Resplendent in gold leaf and ornate details, it dates to 1651 (though it has had recent touch-ups). The exterior alone is impressive, if you want to skip the admission fee. Throughout January and February, the shrine opens its spectacular peony garden (combined entry is ¥1100).

Asakusa & Sumida-gawa

Tokyo's eastern neighbourhoods, on the banks of the Sumida-gawa, have an old-Tokyo feel, with classic temples and shrines, traditional restaurants and artisan shops.

★ **Sensō-ji** BUDDHIST TEMPLE

(浅草寺; Map p112; ☎03-3842-0181; www.senso-ji.jp; 2-3-1 Asakusa, Taitō-ku; ⊙24hr; Ⓢ Ginza line to Asakusa, exit 1) FREE Tokyo's most visited temple enshrines a golden image of Kannon (the Buddhist goddess of mercy), which, according to legend, was miraculously pulled out of the nearby Sumida-gawa by two fishermen in 628 CE. The image has remained on the spot ever since but is never on public display. The present structure dates from 1958.

Sensō-ji is always busy, particularly on weekends; consider visiting in the evening to see it with fewer people and the buildings beautifully illuminated.

The main entrance to the temple complex is via the fantastic, red **Kaminari-mon** (雷門; Thunder Gate; Map p112) and busy shopping street **Nakamise-dōri**. Before passing through the gate, look to either side to see statues of Fūjin (the god of wind) and Raijin (the god of thunder), and under the giant red lantern to see a beautiful carved dragon.

Stalls along Nakamise-dōri sell everything from tourist trinkets to genuine Edo-style crafts. At the end of Nakamise-dōri is the temple itself, and to your left you'll spot the 55m-high **Five-Storey Pagoda** (五重塔; Map p112). The 1973 reconstruction of a pagoda built by Tokugawa Iemitsu was renovated in 2017.

It's a mystery as to whether or not the ancient image of Kannon actually exists, as it's not on public display. This doesn't stop a steady stream of worshippers from visiting. In front of the temple is a large **incense cauldron**: the smoke is said to bestow health and you'll see people wafting it onto their bodies.

At the eastern edge of the temple complex is **Asakusa-jinja** (浅草神社; Map p112; ☎03-3844-1575; www.asakusajinja.jp; ⏲9am-4.30pm), a shrine built in honour of the brothers who discovered the Kannon statue that inspired the construction of Sensō-ji. (Historically, Japan's two religions, Buddhism and Shintō, were intertwined and it was not uncommon for temples to include shrines and vice versa.) The current building, painted a deep shade of red, dates to 1649 and is a rare example of early Edo architecture. It's also the epicentre of one of Tokyo's most important festivals, May's Sanja Matsuri (p121).

★Edo-Tokyo Museum MUSEUM

(江戸東京博物館; Map p92; ☎03-3626-9974; www.edo-tokyo-museum.or.jp; 1-4-1 Yokoami, Sumida-ku; adult/child ¥600/free; ⏲9.30am-5.30pm, to 7.30pm Sat, closed Mon; 🚉JR Sōbu line to Ryōgoku, west exit) Tokyo's history museum documents the city's transformation from tidal flatlands to feudal capital to modern metropolis via detailed scale re-creations of townscapes, villas and tenement homes, plus artefacts such as *ukiyo-e* and old maps. Reopened in March 2018 after a renovation, the museum also has interactive displays, multilingual touch-screen panels and audio guides.

Japanese Sword Museum MUSEUM

(刀剣博物館; Map p92; ☎03-6284-1000; www.touken.or.jp; 1-12-9 Yokoami, Sumida-ku; adult/child ¥1000/free; ⏲9.30am-5pm Tue-Sun; 🚉JR Sōbu line to Ryōgoku, west exit) For visitors with a keen interest in Japanese sword-making – an art that continues to this day – this museum, which relocated to a new building in 2018, features exhibitions from contemporary craftspeople. There's good English information on the different styles and components (and more English-language references for sale in the small gift shop).

Tokyo Skytree TOWER

(東京スカイツリー; Map p112; ☎0570-55-0102; www.tokyo-skytree.jp; 1-1-2 Oshiage, Sumida-ku; 350m/450m observation decks ¥2060/3090; ⏲8am-10pm; Ⓢ Hanzōmon line to Oshiage, Tokyo Sky Tree exit) Tokyo Skytree opened in May 2012 as the world's tallest 'free-standing tower' at 634m. Its silvery exterior of steel mesh morphs from a triangle at the base to a circle at 300m. There are two observation decks, at 350m and 450m. You can see more of the city during daylight hours – at peak visibility you can see up to 100km away, all the way to Mt Fuji – but it is at night that Tokyo appears truly beautiful.

Shinjuku & Around

To the west of Shinjuku Station is Nishi-Shinjuku, a planned district of soaring skyscrapers; to the east, the city's largest entertainment district, aglitter with coloured LED lights.

★Tokyo Metropolitan Government Building OBSERVATORY

(東京都庁, Tokyo Tochō; Map p146; www.metro.tokyo.jp/english/offices; 2-8-1 Nishi-Shinjuku, Shinjuku-ku; ⏲observatories 9.30am-11pm; Ⓢ Ōedo line to Tochōmae, exit A4) FREE Tokyo's city hall – a landmark building designed by Tange

ASAKUSA TOURIST INFORMATION CENTER

The roof terrace of the **Asakusa Culture Tourist Information Center** (浅草文化観光センター; Map p112; ☎03-3842-5566; www.city.taito.lg.jp; 2-18-9 Kaminari-mon, Taitō-ku; ⏲9am-8pm; 📶; Ⓢ Ginza line to Asakusa, exit 2) has fantastic views of Tokyo Skytree and the Nakamise-dōri approach to Sensō-ji. Free guided **tours** (☎03-6280-6710; ⏲10.30am & 1.15pm Sat-Mon; Ⓢ Ginza line to Asakusa, exit 2) FREE of Asakusa depart from here. Free events are sometimes held here, including geisha dances and craft-making demonstrations – check with the centre for the schedule.

Kōrakuen, Akihabara & Kanda

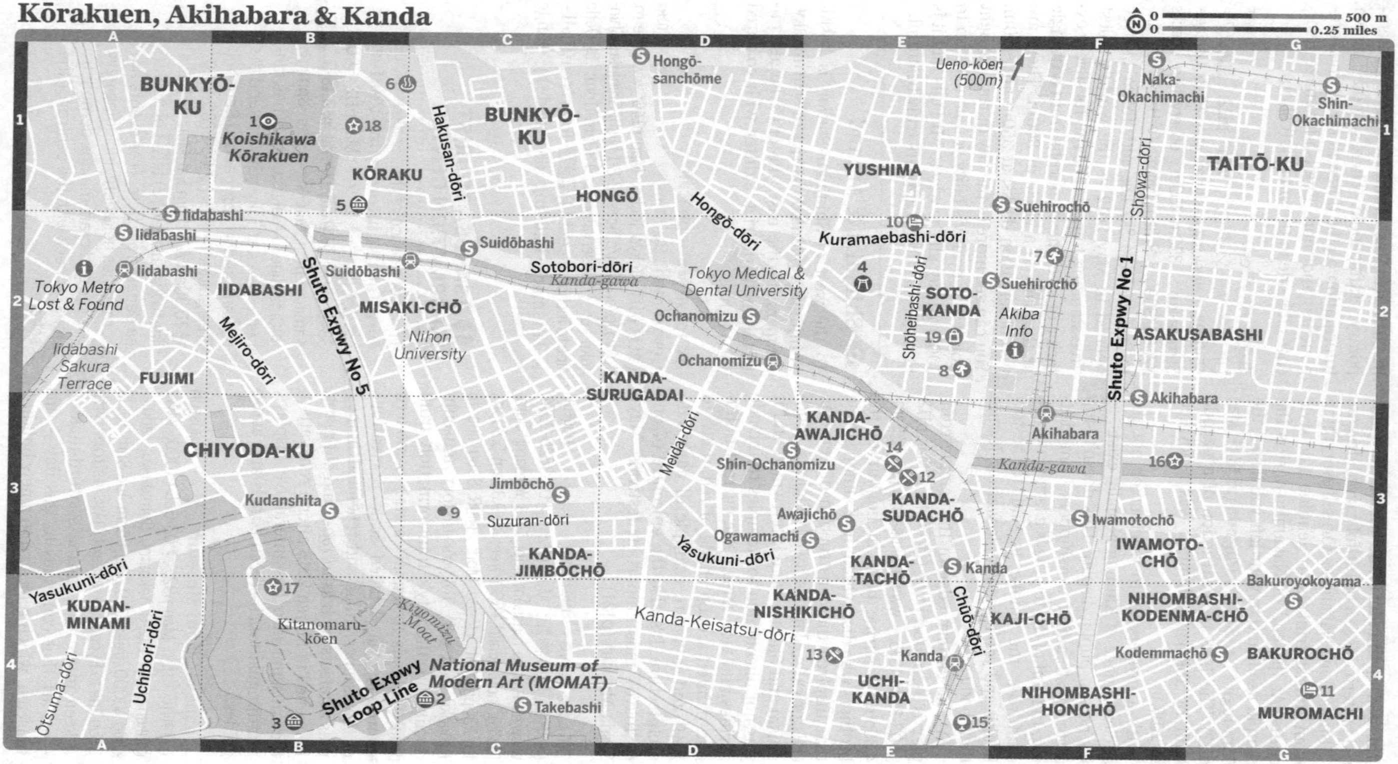

Kōrakuen, Akihabara & Kanda

Top Sights
1 Koishikawa Kōrakuen B1
2 National Museum of Modern Art (MOMAT) C4

Sights
3 Crafts Gallery B4
4 Kanda Myōjin E2
5 TeNQ B1

Activities, Courses & Tours
6 Spa LaQua B1
7 Street Kart F2
8 Super Potato Retro-kan E2
9 Toyokuni Atelier Gallery C3

Sleeping
10 BnA STUDIO Akihabara E2
11 Citan G4

Eating
12 Isegen E3
13 Kagawa Ippuku E4
14 Kanda Yabu Soba E3

Drinking & Nightlife
15 Beer-Ma Kanda E4

Entertainment
16 Club Goodman F3
17 Nippon Budōkan B4
18 Tokyo Dome B1

Shopping
19 Mandarake Complex E2

Kenzō – has observatories (202m) atop both the south and north towers of Building 1 (the views are virtually the same). On a clear day (morning is best), you may catch a glimpse of Mt Fuji beyond the urban sprawl to the west; after dark, it's illuminated buildings all the way to the horizon. Direct-access elevators are on the ground floor; last entry is at 10.30pm.

Shinjuku-gyoen PARK

(新宿御苑; Map p146; ☎03-3350-0151; www.env.go.jp/garden/shinjukugyoen; 11 Naito-chō, Shinjuku-ku; adult/child ¥200/50; ⏲9am-4.30pm Tue-Sun; Ⓢ Marunouchi line to Shinjuku-gyoen-mae, exit 1) Shinjuku-gyoen was designed as an imperial retreat (completed 1906); since opening to the public in 1951, it has become a favourite destination for Tokyoites seeking a quick escape from the hurly-burly of city life. The spacious manicured lawns are perfect for picnicking. Don't miss the greenhouse; the Taiwanese-style pavilion (Goryō-tei) that overlooks the garden's central pond; and the cherry blossoms in spring.

Yayoi Kusama Museum MUSEUM

(草間弥生美術館; Map p92; ☎03-5273-1778; www.yayoikusamamuseum.jp; 07 Benten-chō, Shinjuku-ku; adult/child ¥1000/600; ⏲11am-5.30pm Thu-Sun; Ⓢ Tōzai line to Waseda, exit 1 or Tōei Ōedo line to Ushigome-yanagichō, east exit) Kusama Yayoi (b 1929) is one of Japan's most internationally famous contemporary artists, particularly known for her obsession with dots and pumpkins. She cut her teeth in New York City's 1950s avant-garde scene and remains prolific today, working from a studio near this new museum dedicated to her work. Kusama is in possession of most of her works, and shows them in rotating gallery exhibitions. Tickets for one of the limited 90-minute viewing slots must be purchased in advance online. They become available on the first of the month at 10am and tend to go fast.

Godzilla Head STATUE

(ゴジラヘッド; Map p146; Shinjuku Toho Bldg, 1-19-1 Kabukichō, Shinjuku-ku; 🚉 JR Yamanote line to Shinjuku, east exit) Godzilla, a portmanteau of the Japanese words for gorilla *(gorira)* and whale *(kujira)*, is king of the *kaijū* (strange beasts) that ruled Japanese popular cinema for decades. This giant statue of him looking to take a bit out of a skyscraper is a (relatively new) Shinjuku landmark. Sometimes he roars to life, with glowing eyes and smoky breath.

There's an up-close view (and selfie opportunity) of the statue from the 8th-floor 'Godzilla Terrace' attached to the lobby of the Hotel Gracery Shinjuku (p126); access is limited to hotel guests and customers of the hotel's cafe (though we've never been stopped...).

Shinjuku I-Land PUBLIC ART

(新宿アイランド; Map p146; www.shinjuku-i-land.com; 6-5-1 Nishi-Shinjuku, Shinjuku-ku; Ⓢ Marunouchi line to Nishi-Shinjuku) This otherwise ordinary office complex is home to more than a dozen public artworks, including one of Robert Indiana's *LOVE* sculptures (on the southeast corner) and two *Tokyo Brushstroke* sculptures by Roy Lichtenstein (at the back, towards Ōme-kaidō). See the website for a complete photo directory of all the works.

RICKSHAW RIDES

Around the Kaminari-mon (p104) entrance to Sensō-ji (as well as elsewhere in Asakusa) you may well get approached by a scantily clad, strapping young man offering you…a ride in his *jinrikisha* (rickshaw). Rides start at ¥4000 per 10 minutes for two people (¥3000 for one person).

Harajuku & Aoyama

Harajuku is one of Tokyo's biggest draws thanks to its grand shrine, Meiji-jingū. It's also Tokyo's real-life catwalk, a world-renowned shopping destination where the ultra-chic (and chic in training) come to browse and be seen. Many boutiques here have been designed by influential architects – another draw. Neighbouring Aoyama is a shopping and dining district for the city's fashionable elite.

Harajuku, and especially the boulevard Omote-sandō, can be extremely crowded – with foot traffic moving at a slow, platform-shoe shuffle. If you want to seriously shop or zip around to see the museums and architecture, then head over on a weekday. If you want to get caught up in it all, check out the markets and people-watch, then come on a Saturday or Sunday afternoon.

★Meiji-jingū SHINTŌ SHRINE

(明治神宮; Map p116; www.meijijingu.or.jp; 1-1 Yoyogi Kamizono-chō, Shibuya-ku; dawn-dusk; S Chiyoda or Fukutoshin line to Meiji-jingūmae, exit 2, JR Yamanote line to Harajuku, Omote-sandō exit) FREE Tokyo's grandest Shintō shrine is dedicated to the Emperor Meiji and Empress Shōken, whose reign (1868–1912) coincided with Japan's transformation from isolationist, feudal state to modern nation. Constructed in 1920, the shrine was destroyed in WWII air raids and rebuilt in 1958; however, unlike so many of Japan's postwar reconstructions, Meiji-jingū has atmosphere in spades. Note that the shrine is currently undergoing renovations bit by bit in preparation for its 100th anniversary, but will remain open.

The main shrine, built of unpainted cypress wood with a copper-plated roof, is in a wooded grove accessed via a long winding gravel path. At the start of the path you'll pass through the first of several towering wooden *torii* (entrance gates). Just before the final *torii* is the *temizuya* (font), where visitors purify themselves by pouring water over their hands (purity is a tenet of Shintoism).

To make an offering at the main shrine, toss a ¥5 coin in the box, bow twice, clap your hands twice and then bow again. Nearby there are kiosks selling *ema* (wooden plaques on which prayers are written) and *omamori* (charms).

The shrine itself occupies only a small fraction of the sprawling forested grounds, which contain some 120,000 trees collected from all over Japan. Of this, only the strolling garden **Meiji-jingū Gyoen** (明治神宮御苑; admission ¥500; 9am-5pm, to 4.30pm Nov-Feb) is accessible to the public. The Meiji emperor himself designed the iris garden here to please the empress and the garden is most impressive when the irises bloom in June.

★Yoyogi-kōen PARK

(代々木公園; Map p116; www.yoyogipark.info; Yoyogi-kamizono-chō, Shibuya-ku; JR Yamanote line to Harajuku, Omote-sandō exit) If it's a sunny and warm weekend afternoon, you can count on there being a crowd lazing around the large grassy expanse that is Yoyogi-kōen. You'll usually find revellers and noisemakers of all stripes, from hula-hoopers to African drum circles to retro greasers dancing around a boom box. It's an excellent place for a picnic and probably the only place in the city where you can reasonably toss a Frisbee without fear of hitting someone.

★Ukiyo-e Ōta Memorial Museum of Art MUSEUM

(浮世絵太田記念美術館; Map p116; 03-3403-0880; www.ukiyoe-ota-muse.jp; 1-10-10 Jingūmae, Shibuya-ku; adult ¥700-1000, child free; 10.30am-5.30pm Tue-Sun; JR Yamanote line to Harajuku, Omote-sandō exit) This small museum (where you swap your shoes for slippers) is the best place in Tokyo to see *ukiyo-e*. Each month it presents a seasonal, thematic exhibition (with English curation notes), drawing from the truly impressive collection of Ōta Seizo, the former head of the Toho Life Insurance Company. Most exhibitions include a few works by masters such as Hokusai and Hiroshige. The museum closes the last few days of the month (between exhibitions).

★Nezu Museum — MUSEUM

(根津美術館; Map p116; ☎03-3400-2536; www.nezu-muse.or.jp; 6-5-1 Minami-Aoyama, Minato-ku; adult/child ¥1100/free, special exhibitions extra ¥200; ⏰10am-5pm Tue-Sun; Ⓢ Ginza line to Omote-sandō, exit A5) Nezu Museum offers a striking blend of old and new: a renowned collection of Japanese, Chinese and Korean antiquities in a gallery space designed by contemporary architect Kuma Kengo. Select items from the extensive collection are displayed in seasonal exhibitions. The English explanations are usually pretty good. Behind the galleries is a woodsy strolling garden laced with stone paths and studded with teahouses and sculptures.

Takeshita-dōri — STREET

(竹下通り; Map p116; Jingūmae, Shibuya-ku; 🚉JR Yamanote line to Harajuku, Takeshita exit) This is Tokyo's famous fashion bazaar. It's an odd mixed bag: newer shops selling trendy, youthful styles alongside stores still invested in the trappings of decades of subcultures past (plaid and safety pins for the punks; colourful tutus for the *decora;* Victorian dresses for the Gothic Lolitas). Be warned: this pedestrian alley is a pilgrimage site for teens from all over Japan, which means it can be packed.

Design Festa — GALLERY

(デザインフェスタ; Map p116; ☎03-3479-1442; www.designfestagallery.com; 3-20-2 Jingūmae, Shibuya-ku; ⏰11am-8pm; 🚉JR Yamanote line to Harajuku, Takeshita exit) FREE Design Festa has long been a champion of Tokyo's DIY art scene and its maze-like building is a Harajuku landmark. Inside there are dozens of small galleries rented by the day. More often than not, the artists themselves are hanging around, too.

Shibuya

Shibuya, the heart of Tokyo's youth culture, hits you over the head with its sheer presence: the continuous flow of people, the glowing video screens and the tangible buzz.

★Shibuya Crossing — STREET

(渋谷スクランブル交差点, Shibuya Scramble; Map p138; Ⓢ Ginza or Fukutoshin line to Shibuya, exit A8, 🚉JR Yamanote line to Shibuya, Hachikō exit) Rumoured to be the busiest intersection in the world (and definitely in Japan), Shibuya Crossing is like a giant beating heart, sending people in all directions with every pulsing light change. Nowhere else says 'Welcome to Tokyo' better than this. Hundreds of people – and at peak times upwards of 3000 people – cross at a time, coming from all directions at once, yet still to dodging each other with a practised, nonchalant agility.

Mag's Park (Map p138; 1-23-10 Jinnan, Shibuya-ku; admission ¥600; ⏰11am-11pm; 🚉JR Yamanote line to Shibuya, Hachikō exit), the rooftop of the Shibuya 109-2 department store, has the best views over the neighbourhood's famous scramble crossing. It's screened with plexiglass, so you can still get good photos, without having to worry about losing anything over the edge).

The intersection is most impressive after dark on a Friday or Saturday night, when the crowds pouring out of the station are at their thickest and neon-lit by the signs above. The rhythms here are, however, tied to the train station and after the last train pulls out for the night, the intersection becomes eerily quiet.

Shibuya Center-gai — STREET

(渋谷センター街, Shibuya Sentā-gai; Map p138; 🚉JR Yamanote line to Shibuya, Hachikō exit) Shibuya's main drag is closed to cars and chock-a-block with fast-food joints and high-street fashion shops. At night, lit bright as day, with a dozen competing soundtracks (coming from who knows where), wares spilling onto the streets and strutting teens, it feels like a block party – or Tokyo's version of a classic Asian night market.

d47 Museum — MUSEUM

(Map p138; www.hikarie8.com; 8th fl, Shibuya Hikarie, 2-21-1 Shibuya, Shibuya-ku; ⏰11am-8pm; 🚉JR Yamanote line to Shibuya, east exit) FREE Lifestyle brand D&Department combs the country for the platonic ideals of the utterly ordinary: the perfect broom, bottle opener or salt shaker (to name a few examples). See rotating exhibitions of its latest finds from all 47 prefectures at this one-room museum. The excellent d47 design travel store (p157) is next door.

Myth of Tomorrow — PUBLIC ART

(明日の神話, Asu no Shinwa; Map p138; 🚉JR Yamanote line to Shibuya, Hachikō exit) Okamoto Tarō's mural, *Myth of Tomorrow* (1967), was commissioned by a Mexican luxury hotel but went missing two years later. It finally turned up in 2003 and, in 2008, the haunting 30m-long work, which depicts the atomic bomb exploding over Hiroshima, was installed inside Shibuya Station. It's on the 2nd floor, in the corridor leading to the Inokashira line.

Ueno & Yanesen

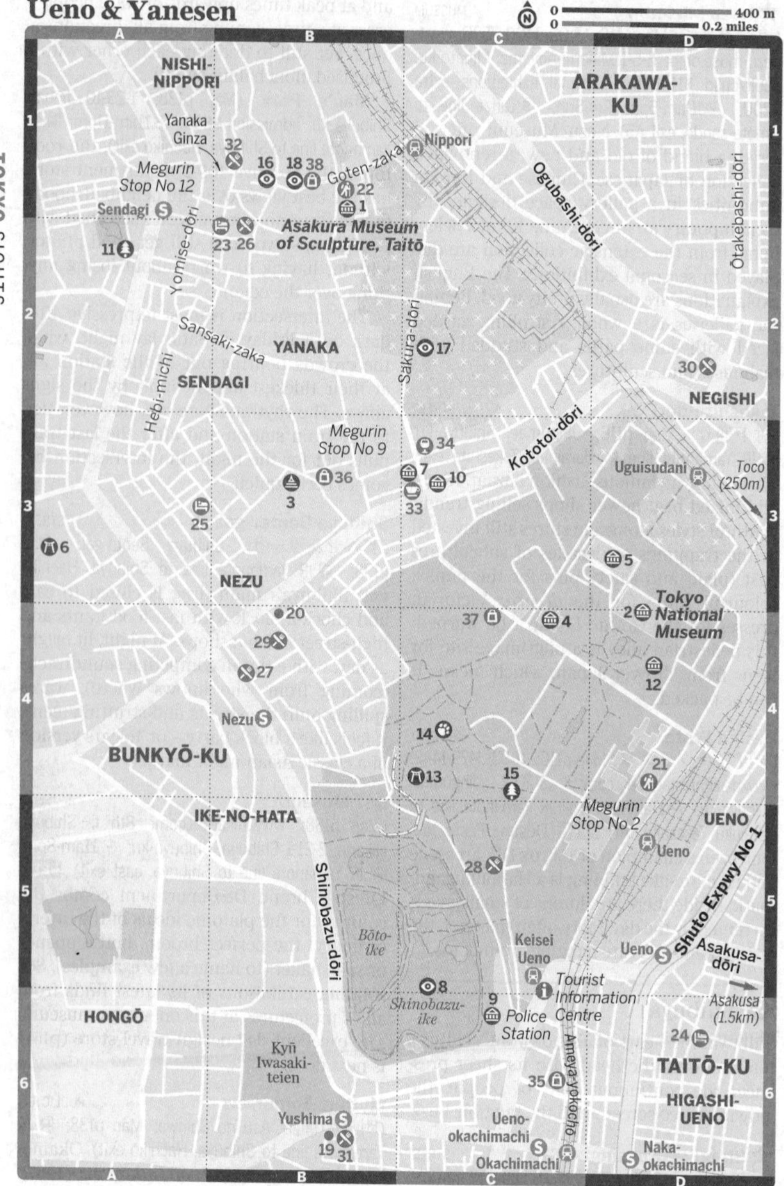

Shibuya Stream LANDMARK

(渋谷ストリーム; Map p138; https://shibuya stream.jp; 3-21-3 Shibuya, Shibuya; Ⓢ Ginza, Hanzōmon & Fukutoshin lines to Shibuya, exit 16b, Ⓡ JR Yamanote line to Shibuya, new south exit) It's hard to imagine, but Shibuya Crossing (p109) actually sits on the confluence of two rivers: the Shibuya-gawa and the Uda-gawa, which were diverted underground decades ago. Shibuya Stream, part of Shibuya's redevelopment, is a step towards bringing the city's waterways back. It's mostly a giant, glass multipurpose complex, but there's a lovely stretch of the

Ueno & Yanesen

Top Sights
1 Asakura Museum of Sculpture, Taitō B1
2 Tokyo National Museum D4

Sights
3 Enju-ji B3
4 Gallery of Hōryū-ji Treasures C4
5 Heiseikan D3
6 Nezu-jinja A3
7 SCAI the Bathhouse C3
8 Shinobazu-ike C5
9 Shitamachi Museum C6
10 Shitamachi Museum Annex C3
11 Sudo-kōen A2
12 Tōyōkan D4
13 Ueno Tōshō-gū C4
14 Ueno Zoo C4
15 Ueno-kōen C4
16 Yanaka Ginza B1
17 Yanaka-reien C2
18 Yūyake Dandan B1

Activities, Courses & Tours
19 Buddha Bellies B6
20 Kitchen Kujo Tokyo B4
21 Ueno Free Walking Tour D4
22 Yanaka Free Walking Tour B1

Sleeping
23 Hanare B2
24 Nohga Hotel D6
25 Sawanoya Ryokan A3

Eating
26 Hagi Cafe B2
27 Hantei B4
28 Innsyoutei C5
29 Kamachiku B4
30 Sasa-no-Yuki D2
31 Shinsuke B6
32 Tayori B1

Drinking & Nightlife
33 Kayaba Coffee C3
34 Yanaka Beer Hall C3

Shopping
35 Ameya-yokochō C6
36 Art Sanctuary Allan West B3
37 Geidai Art Plaza C4
38 Yanaka Matsunoya B1

newly liberated Shibuya-gawa flanked by terraces and some bars and restaurants.

Ebisu & Meguro

Ebisu and Meguro are gateways to largely residential (some artsy, some upscale, some both) districts, where Tokyo takes on a more human scale.

Beer Museum Yebisu MUSEUM
(エビスビール記念館; Map p120; ☎03-5423-7255; www.sapporoholdings.jp/english/guide/yebisu; 4-20-1 Ebisu, Shibuya-ku; ⊙11am-7pm Tue-Sun; 🚉JR Yamanote line to Ebisu, east exit) FREE Photos, vintage bottles and posters document the rise of Yebisu, and beer in general, in Japan at this small museum located where the actual Yebisu brewery stood from the late 19th century until 1988. At the 'tasting salon' you can sample four kinds of Yebisu beer (¥400 each or three smaller glasses for ¥800). It's behind the Mitsukoshi department store at Yebisu Garden Place.

TOP Museum MUSEUM
(東京都写真美術館, Tokyo Photographic Arts Museum; Map p120; ☎03-3280-0099; www.top-museum.jp; 1-13-3 Mita, Meguro-ku; ¥500-1000; ⊙10am-6pm Tue, Wed, Sat & Sun, to 8pm Thu & Fri; 🚉JR Yamanote line to Ebisu, east exit) Tokyo's principal photography museum usually holds three different exhibitions at once, drawing on both its extensive collection of Japanese artists and images on loan. Shows may include the history of photography, retrospectives of major artists or surveys of up-and-coming ones.

The museum is at the far end of Yebisu Garden Place, on the right side of the complex if you're coming from Ebisu Station. There's a branch of the excellent art bookshop **Nadiff** here, too.

Tokyo Metropolitan Teien Art Museum MUSEUM
(東京都庭園美術館; Map p120; www.teien-art-museum.ne.jp; 5-21-9 Shirokanedai, Minato-ku; adult/child ¥1200/960; ⊙10am-6pm, closed 2nd & 4th Wed each month; 🚉JR Yamanote line to Meguro, east exit) Although the Teien museum often hosts excellent exhibitions – usually of decorative arts – its chief appeal lies in the building itself: it's an art deco structure, a former princely estate built in 1933, designed by French architect Henri Rapin, with much of the original interior intact. Tip: budget time to lounge around on the manicured lawn. A recent renovation saw the addition of a modern annex designed by artist Sugimoto Hiroshi. Note that the museum is closed between exhibitions.

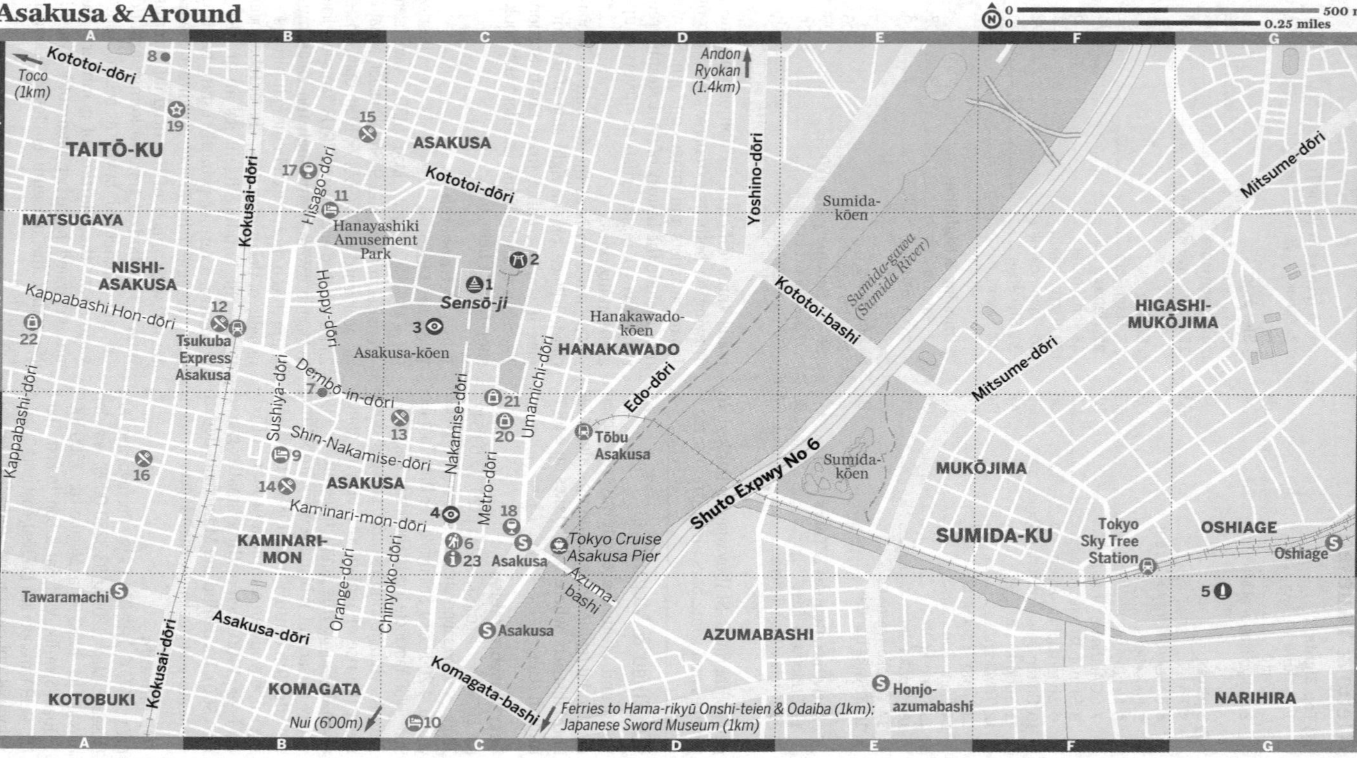
Asakusa & Around
0 500 m
0 0.25 miles
Kototoi-dōri
Toco (1km)
TAITŌ-KU
MATSUGAYA
NISHI-ASAKUSA
Kappabashi Hon-dōri
Kappabashi-dōri
Kokusai-dōri
Tsukuba Express Asakusa
Hisago-dōri
Hanayashiki Amusement Park
Hoppy-dōri
ASAKUSA
Kototoi-dōri
Sensō-ji
Asakusa-kōen
Dembō-in-dōri
Sushiya-dōri
Shin-Nakamise-dōri
ASAKUSA
Kaminari-mon-dōri
KAMINARI-MON
Orange-dōri
Chinyoko-dōri
Nakamise-dōri
Metro-dōri
Umamichi-dōri
Asakusa
Tawaramachi
Asakusa-dōri
Asakusa
KOTOBUKI
Kokusai-dōri
KOMAGATA
Nui (600m)
Komagata-bashi
Ferries to Hama-rikyū Onshi-teien & Odaiba (1km); Japanese Sword Museum (1km)
Andon Ryokan (1.4km)
Yoshino-dōri
Hanakawado-kōen
HANAKAWADO
Edo-dōri
Tōbu Asakusa
Tokyo Cruise Asakusa Pier
Azuma-bashi
Kototoi-bashi
Sumida-kōen
Sumida-gawa (Sumida River)
Shuto Expwy No 6
Sumida-kōen
AZUMABASHI
Honjo-azumabashi
MUKŌJIMA
SUMIDA-KU
Mitsume-dōri
Mitsume-dōri
HIGASHI-MUKŌJIMA
Tokyo Sky Tree Station
OSHIAGE
Oshiage
NARIHIRA

Asakusa & Around

Top Sights
1 Sensō-ji C2

Sights
2 Asakusa-jinja C2
3 Five-Storey Pagoda C2
4 Kaminari-mon C3
5 Tokyo Skytree G4

Activities, Courses & Tours
6 Asakusa Free Walking Tour C3
7 Mokuhankan B2
8 Wanariya A1

Sleeping
9 Bunka Hostel Tokyo B3
10 Hatago C4
11 Wired Hotel Asakusa B1

Eating
12 Asakusa Imahan B2
13 Daikokuya C3
14 Misojyu B3
15 Onigiri Yadoroku B1
16 Sometarō A3

Drinking & Nightlife
17 'Cuzn Homeground B1
18 Kamiya Bar C3

Entertainment
19 Oiwake A1

Shopping
20 Bengara C3
21 Fujiya C3
22 Kama-asa A2

Information
23 Asakusa Culture Tourist Information Center C3

Check the website for occasional performing arts events, sometimes held on the lawn.

Meguro-gawa RIVER
(目黒川; Map p120; Ⓢ Hibiya line to Naka-Meguro, main exit) Lined with cherry trees and a walking path, the Meguro-gawa (not so much a river as a canal) is what gives the neighbourhood Naka-Meguro its unlikely village vibe. On either side you'll find boutiques and a handful of eating and drinking spots.

Institute for Nature Study PARK
(自然教育園, Shizen Kyōiku-en; Map p120; ☎03-3441-7176; www.ins.kahaku.go.jp; 5-21-5 Shirokanedai, Meguro-ku; adult/child ¥310/free; ⊙9am-4.30pm Tue-Sun Sep-Apr, to 5pm Tue-Sun May-Aug, last entry 4pm; JR Yamanote line to Meguro, east exit) What would Tokyo look like were it left to its own natural devices? Since 1949 this park, affiliated with the Tokyo National Museum, has let the local flora go wild. There are wonderful walks through its groves, around ponds and on boardwalks over marshes. No more than 300 people are allowed in at a time, which makes for an even more peaceful setting.

Odaiba & Tokyo Bay

This collection of artificial islands on Tokyo Bay is a family-oriented entertainment district, with interactive museums, shopping malls and theme parks.

★ **teamLab Borderless** MUSEUM
(Map p125; ☎03-6406-3949; https://borderless.teamlab.art; 1-3-8 Aomi, Kōtō-ku; adult/child ¥3200/1000; ⊙10am-7pm, to 9pm Fri & Sat, closed irregularly; ; Yurikamome line to Aomi) Digital-art collective teamLab has created 60 artworks for this museum, open in 2018, that tests the border between art and the viewer: many are interactive. Not sure how? That's the point – go up to the artworks, move and touch them (or just stand still) and see how they react. There is no suggested route; teamLab Borderless is all about exploration. Admission is limited, so book online in advance.

Making your way from room to room feels like entering a sequence of discrete worlds – a bit like being in a fantasy role-playing game. Don't miss the maze-like **Crystal World**, where strands of shimmering light extend from floor to ceiling like disco stalagmites, and the **Forest of Lamps**, where Venetian glass lamps bloom into as you approach. The latter you'll likely have to queue for.

On the 2nd floor, the **Athletics Forest** is a collection of installations designed with kids in mind (but grown-ups can join in, too). Jump up and down on a bouncy plain and see your energy transformed into expanding stars. Add colour to a drawing of an animal or insect and watch as it is born into an animated creature – then follow it on its course along the crags and divots of this playful indoor landscape.

There are no minimum age or height requirements to enter teamLab Borderless; however, keep in mind the museum is dark and often crowded. Prams must be parked at the entrance.

Take a break at the **En Tea House**, where you can see digital flowers bloom inside your cup of tea (¥500).

Toyosu Market MARKET

(豊洲市場, Toyosu Shijō; Map p125; www.shijou.metro.tokyo.jp; 6-chōme Toyosu, Kōtō-ku; ⌚5am-5pm, closed Sun & irregularly (often Wed); 🚉Yurikamome line to Shijō-mae) In 2018, Tokyo's central wholesale market moved from its iconic Tsukiji location to this new facility in Toyosu, a structure clearly dreamed up by bureaucrats. The early-morning tuna auction and other parts of the market can be viewed by the public from glass-walled viewing platforms; entry to the market floor is limited to licensed buyers. The upper floors have some shops and restaurants, including sushi counters originally at Tsukiji. Get here early to make the most of your visit.

The market is divided into three blocks (5, 6 and 7), all connected via promenades that also run directly to the train station, and is well signposted in English.

At the tuna auction, *naka-oroshi* (intermediate wholesalers) gamble on bluefin tuna brought in from all over the world. The auction starts around 5am and finishes by 6.30am. A limited number of visitors can observe the auction up close from a mezzanine-level viewing platform that is only partially shielded by glass. Entry is by lottery, which opens one month in advance; for details see the market website. Otherwise anyone can watch it from the glassed-in corridors on the 2nd floor of block 7.

In block 6 is the produce market; auctions take place here at 6.30am and are also visible from the corridors above. The intermediate wholesaler market – where sushi chefs and fishmongers come to buy from the *naka-oroshi* – is in building 5. You can peer down into it from windows on the 3rd floor but the view isn't great. Also on the 3rd floor is another collection of restaurants; the 4th floor has shops selling tea, knives, *katsuo-bushi* (dried bonito flakes), miso and more. Above is a grassy rooftop garden.

Unicorn Gundam STATUE

(ユニコーンガンダム; Map p125; www.unicorn-gundam-statue.jp; 1-1-10 Aomi, Kōtō-ku; 🚉Yurikamome line to Daiba, south exit) This is truly an only-in-Tokyo sight: a 19.7m-tall model of an RX-0 Unicorn Gundam from the wildly popular Mobile Suit Gundam anime franchise. It undergoes a transformation four times a day (at 11am, 1pm, 3pm and 5pm) into 'destroy mode'; light shows take place on the half-hour between 7pm and 9.30pm. The statue is in front of the Diver City shopping mall.

National Museum of Emerging Science & Innovation (Miraikan) MUSEUM

(未来館; Map p125; www.miraikan.jst.go.jp; 2-3-6 Aomi, Kōtō-ku; adult/child ¥630/210; ⌚10am-5pm, closed Tue; 👪; 🚉Yurikamome line to Telecom Center, north exit) *Miraikan* means 'hall of the future', and the hands-on exhibits here present the science and technology that will possibly shape the years to come (including the chance to interact with androids!). Don't miss the demonstrations of robot ASIMO (at 11am, 1pm, 2pm and 4pm). The Gaia dome theatre-planetarium (adult/child ¥310/100) has an English audio option and is popular; book online one week in advance. A multilingual smartphone app turns your visit into a game.

Odaiba Kaihin-kōen PARK

(お台場海浜公園, Odaiba Marine Park; Map p125; www.tptc.co.jp; 1-4-1 Daiba, Minato-ku; ⌚24hr; 🚉Yurikamome line to Odaiba Kaihin-kōen) There are good views of the central Tokyo skyline from this park's promenades and elevated walkways – especially at night when old-fashioned *yakatabune* (low-slung wooden pleasure boats), decorated with lanterns, traverse the bay. Note that swimming here is not permitted.

Activities

Amusement Parks

Tokyo Disney Resort AMUSEMENT PARK

(東京ディズニーリゾート; ☎domestic calls 0570-00-8632, from overseas +81-45-330-5211; www.tokyodisneyresort.jp; 1-1 Maihama, Urayasu-shi, Chiba-ken; 1-day ticket for 1 park adult/child ¥7500/4800, after 6pm ¥4300; ⌚varies by season; 🚉JR Keiyō line to Maihama, south exit) Tokyo Disney Resort has two parks: Tokyo Disneyland, modelled after the one in California, and Tokyo DisneySea, an original theme park with seven 'ports' evoking locales real and imagined (the Mediterranean and 'Mermaid Lagoon', for example). DisneySea targets a more grown-up crowd, but still has many attractions for kids. Both resorts get extremely crowded, especially on weekends and during

DON'T MISS

THE MAGICAL GHIBLI MUSEUM

Master animator Miyazaki Hayao and his Studio Ghibli (pronounced 'jiburi') have been responsible for some of the best-loved films in Japan – and the world. Miyazaki himself designed **Ghibli Museum** (ジブリ美術館; www.ghibli-museum.jp; 1-1-83 Shimo-Renjaku, Mitaka-shi; adult ¥1000, child ¥100-700; ⏲10am-6pm, closed Tue & irregularly; 🚉JR Chūō-Sōbu line to Mitaka, south exit) and it's redolent of the dreamy, vaguely steampunk atmosphere that makes his animations so enchanting.

The building itself looks like an illustration from a European fairy tale. Inside there is an imagined workshop filled with the kinds of books and artworks that inspired the creator, as well as vintage machines from animation's history.

This museum rewards curiosity and exploration: peer through a small window, for example, and you'll see little soot sprites (as seen in *Spirited Away;* 2001); a spiral staircase leads to a purposefully overgrown rooftop terrace with a 5m tall statue of the Robot Soldier from *Laputa* (Castle in the Sky; 1986).

A highlight for children (sorry grown-ups!) is a giant, plush replica of the cat bus from the classic *My Neighbor Totoro* (1988) that kids can climb on. There's also a small theatre where original animated shorts – which can only be seen here – are screened (you'll get a ticket for this when you enter). The film changes monthly to keep fans coming back.

Tickets can be purchased up to four months in advance from overseas travel agents or up to one month in advance through the convenience store Lawson's online ticket portal. Both options are explained in detail on the website. For July and August visits especially, we recommend buying tickets as soon as you can from an agent as they will definitely sell out early. Tickets are non-transferable; you may be asked to show an ID.

The Ghibli Museum is located in the suburbs west of Shinjuku. Take the JR Chūō line from Shinjuku to Mitaka (20 minutes). From the south exit No 9 bus stop at Mitaka Station, get a shuttle bus (round trip/one way ¥320/210; every 20 minutes) for the museum.

summer holidays; you'll have to be strategic with your FastPasses. Book admission tickets online to save time.

Sky Circus AMUSEMENT PARK
(スカイサーカス; Map p92; ☎03-3989-3457; www.skycircus.jp; Sunshine 60, 3-1-1 Higashi-Ikebukuro, Toshima-ku; admission adult/child ¥1200/600, attractions ¥500 each; ⏲10am-10pm; 🚉JR Yamanote line to Ikebukuro, east exit) One of Tokyo's better virtual-reality parks, Sky Circus has an aerial roller-coaster that snakes between Ikebukuro's skyscrapers (Swing Coaster) and a cannon attraction that sends you bouncing around a futuristic version of Tokyo's more famous attractions (Tokyo Bullet Flight). Basic instructions are given in English. If you are prone to motion sickness, you will feel it, possibly acutely.

The admission ticket (purchase at the counter in the basement of Sunshine 60) gets you to the 60th-floor observatory, nice in its own right. To ride the attractions, children must be over seven years of age and taller than 130cm; grown-ups no bigger than 2m and 100kg.

Tokyo Joypolis AMUSEMENT PARK
(東京ジョイポリス; Map p125; http://tokyo-joypolis.com; 3rd-5th fl, DECKS Tokyo Beach, 1-6-1 Daiba, Minato-ku; adult/child ¥800/500, all-rides passport ¥4500/3500, passport after 5pm ¥3500/2500; ⏲10am-10pm; 🚉Yurikamome line to Odaiba Kaihin-kōen, north exit) This indoor amusement park is stacked with virtual-reality attractions and thrill rides, such as the video-enhanced Halfpipe Tokyo; there are rides for little ones, too. Separate admission and individual ride tickets (¥500 to ¥800) are available, but if you plan to ride more than a few, the unlimited 'passport' makes sense. Bring your passport for a slight discount on admission.

Onsen

★ **Spa LaQua** ONSEN
(スパ　ラクーア; Map p106; ☎03-5800-9999; www.laqua.jp; 5th-9th fl, Tokyo Dome City, 1-1-1 Kasuga, Bunkyō-ku; weekday/weekend ¥2900/3250; ⏲11am-9am; 🚉JR Sōbu line to Suidōbashi, west exit) One of Tokyo's few true onsen, this chic spa complex, renovated in 2017, relies on natural hot-spring

Harajuku & Around

water from 1700m below ground. There are indoor and outdoor baths, saunas and a bunch of add-on options, such as *akasuri* (Korean-style whole-body exfoliation). Towels included; visitors with tattoos will be denied admission. There's a surcharge of ¥1980 for guests using the facilities between 1am and 6am.

Ōedo Onsen Monogatari ONSEN
(大江戸温泉物語; Map p125; ☎03-5500-1126; https://daiba.ooedoonsen.jp/en/; 2-6-3 Aomi, Kōtō-ku; adult/child ¥2768/1078, surcharge Sat & Sun ¥220; ⏰11am-9am, last entry 7am; 👪; 🚉Yurikamome line to Telecom Center, south exit or Rinkai line to Tokyo Teleport, exit B with free shuttle bus) Come experience the truly Japanese phenomenon that is an amusement park centred on bathing. There are multiple tubs to choose from (indoor and outdoor), filled with real hot-spring water (pumped from 1400m below Tokyo Bay), and a lantern-lit re-creation of an old Tokyo downtown area. Come after 6pm for a ¥550 discount. Towels included; visitors with tattoos will be denied admission.

Thermae-yu ONSEN
(テルマー湯; Map p146; ☎03-5285-1726; www.thermae-yu.jp; 1-1-2 Kabukichō, Shinjuku-ku; weekdays/weekends & holidays ¥2365/2690; ⏰11am-9am; 🚉JR Yamanote line to Shinjuku, east exit) The best (and most literal) example to date that red-light district Kabukichō is cleaning up its act: this sparkling-clean onsen (hot springs) complex. The tubs, which include several indoor and outdoor ones (sex-segregated), are filled with honest-to-goodness natural hot-spring water. There are several saunas, including a hot-stone sauna (*ganbanyoku;* ¥810 extra). Towels included. No tattoos allowed.

You can stay the night here (sleeping on a reclining armchair) for an extra ¥1840.

Harajuku & Around

Top Sights
1 Meiji-jingū....A1
2 Nezu Museum....D4
3 Omote-sandō....C3
4 Ukiyo-e Ōta Memorial Museum of Art....B2
5 Yoyogi-kōen....A2

Sights
6 Design Festa....B2
7 Dior Omote-sandō....B3
8 Louis Vuitton Omote-sandō....C3
9 Meiji-jingū Gyoen....A1
10 Omotesandō Hills....B3
11 Prada Aoyama....D4
12 SunnyHills Minami-Aoyama....D3
13 Takeshita-dōri....B2
14 Tod's Omote-sandō....C3
15 Tokyu Plaza....B2

Activities, Courses & Tours
16 Ohara School of Ikebana....C4

Sleeping
17 Dormy Inn Premium Shibuya Jingūmae....A3

Eating
18 Agaru Sagaru Nishi-iru Higashi-iru....B2
19 Commune 2nd....C3
20 Eatrip....B2
21 Farmer's Market @UNU....B4
22 Gomaya Kuki....B2
23 Harajuku Gyōza-rō....B3
24 Maisen....C3
25 Mominoki House....C1
26 Narukiyo....B4
Sakura-tei....(see 6)

Drinking & Nightlife
27 Aoyama Flower Market Teahouse....C3
28 Koffee Mameya....C2
29 Sakurai Japanese Tea Experience....C4
30 Two Rooms....C4

Entertainment
31 Jingū Baseball Stadium....D1

Shopping
32 Arts & Science....D4
33 Comme des Garçons....C4
34 House @Mikiri Hassin....B3
35 KiddyLand....B3
36 Laforet....B2

Outdoors

ZAC KAYAKING

(☎03-6671-0201; www.zacsports.com; 1-7 Komatsugawa, Edogawa-ku; adult/child ¥5500/4500; 👪; Ⓢ Shinjuku line to Higashi-Ōjima, Komatsugawa exit) Tokyo was once a city of canals, and while few remain, a tour of them is a fascinating way to see the city from a different vantage point. Outdoor sports club Zac runs 1½-hour kayaking tours along Kyū-naka-gawa (actually a canal) on Tokyo's far east side. Choose from day or night tours and book online. Guides speak basic English.

Children aged six years and over are allowed to join (kayaks seat two). Solo travellers can book for an extra ¥1000. Life jackets provided; see the website for instructions about what to where.

Courses

★Toyokuni Atelier Gallery ARTS & CRAFTS

(豊國アトリエ; Map p106; ☎090-4069-8410; www.nekomachi.com; 3-1-13 Kanda-Jimbōchō, Chiyoda-ku; per person ¥2000; 👪; Ⓢ Toei Shinjuku line to Jimbōchō, exit A1) Try your hand at *sumi-e*, the delicate art of ink painting on *washi* (Japanese handmade paper), at this gallery displaying the artworks of master ink painter Honda Toyokuni. One-hour classes (at 1pm, 3pm or 5pm) are taught by his affable, English-speaking son Yuta, and is highly recommended for budding artists of all ages. Reservations are essential.

Classes with 74-year-old Toyokuni cost ¥15,000 and last two hours.

★Tsukiji Soba Academy COOKING

(築地そばアカデミー; Map p92; https://soba.specialist.co.jp; Hins Minato #004, 3-18-14 Minato, Chūō-ku; up to 3 people from ¥30,000, per additional person ¥10,000; 👪; Ⓢ Yūrakuchō line to Shintomichō, exit 7) Genial English-speaking chef Inoue Akila is a master of soba – noodles made from nutty buckwheat flour. He has taught chefs who have gone on to win Michelin stars for their versions of this classic Tokyo dish. Classes are held in a compact kitchen overlooking the Sumida-gawa.

Additional vegetarian and gluten-free menus and longer courses aimed at professionals are available for an extra fee upon request.

★Wanariya ARTS & CRAFTS

(和なり屋; Map p112; ☎03-5603-9169; www.wanariya.jp; 1-8-10 Senzoku, Taitō-ku; ⏲10am-7pm, closed irregularly; 👪; Ⓢ Hibiya line to Iriya, exit 1) Wanariya offers 45- to 60-minute indigo-dying workshops in English, meaning you get a traditional experience and unique souvenir all in one. Prices start at ¥2000

DON'T MISS

GO-KARTING

Experience Tokyo as if in a real-life video game on fun go-karting tours around the city with **Street Kart** (Map p106; https://kart.st; 1/2/3hr tours ¥7000/10,000/13,000; ⏲10am-8pm), where you can dress up in brightly coloured onesies. The two-hour course will get you out to Tokyo Skytree and down to Ginza.

Before you start there's only a short tutorial on how to drive the go-karts, then you're on the road with trucks and buses, so absolutely speak up if you're not comfortable; there's always an English-speaking guide and they are experienced at navigating the traffic and at pains to stress safety. You must have a valid international (or Japanese) driver's license.

Street Kart also has shops in Shibuya, Asakusa, Shinagawa and Shin-Kiba – each one offering different driving courses.

(per person) for a tea towel (materials included), and kids as young as three can participate. Reservations (minimum one day in advance) required. They also do weaving workshops.

★ Mokuhankan ARTS & CRAFTS
(木版館; Map p112; ☎070-5011-1418; https://mokuhankan.com; 1-41-8 Asakusa, Taitō-ku; ⏲10am-5.30pm, closed Tue; 👪; Ⓢ Ginza line to Asakusa, exit A4) Learn how *ukiyo-e* (woodblock prints) are made at this studio run by longtime Tokyo resident and printmaker David Bull. Hour-long 'print parties' (adult/child ¥2500/2000; tea included) are great fun – and you'll probably be more impressed with your artwork than you'd expect. Children should be 10 years or over to join.

There's a shop here too, where you can buy prints made from the professional workshop on the floor above, including high-quality replicas of famous works and Bull's and Jed Henry's humorous, original Ukiyo-e Heroes series – featuring video-game characters reimagined in classical styles.

Buddha Bellies COOKING
(Map p110; ☎080-5001-9395; www.buddhabelliestokyo.jimdo.com; ¥7500 per person; 👪; Ⓢ Chiyoda line to Yushima, exit 3) English-speaking professional sushi chef and sake sommelier Ayuko and her husband lead small hands-on classes in sushi, *bentō* (boxed lunch), udon and *wagashi* (Japanese sweets) making. Classes are held at Ayuko's home close to Yushima Station (she'll meet you at exit 3) and run usually from 11am, lasting 2½ hours. Book early.

Vegetarian, vegan and halal menus are also available.

Kitchen Kujo Tokyo COOKING
(Map p110; ☎03-5832-9452; www.kujo.tokyo; 1-2-10 Yanaka, Taitō-ku; classes ¥6000-12,000; ⏲classes 10.30am or 1.30pm, bar 6-10.30pm Mon-Sat; Ⓢ Chiyoda line to Nezu, exit 2) The Kobayashi family and their translator and ramen chef Jun offer an interesting variety of cooking and culture classes at this handy studio devoted to cooking with organic products. Learn how to make tofu, miso, vegan ramen and curry rice with guest instructor Curryman (who dresses in a wacky costume). Also available are calligraphy, tea-ceremony and yoga classes.

Ohara School of Ikebana ARTS & CRAFTS
(小原流いけばな; Map p116; ☎03-5774-5097; www.ohararyu.or.jp; 5th fl, 5-7-17 Minami-Aoyama, Minato-ku; classes ¥4000; Ⓢ Ginza line to Omote-sandō, exit B1) This established ikebana school pioneered the modern style of flower arrangement called *moribana* ('piled flowers', typically in a low, shallow dish) in the early 20th century. Two-hour, introductory classes are taught in English every Thursday at 10am and 1pm, and also two Sundays per month at 10am and 12.30pm. Sign up online by 3pm at least two days in advance.

Tokyo Cook COOKING
(Map p102; ☎03-5414-2727; www.tokyo-cook.com; 3rd fl, Roppongi Green Bldg, 6-1-8 Roppongi, Minato-ku; classes from ¥8640; Ⓢ Hibiya line to Roppongi, exit 3) Among the several types of cooking classes in English on offer here are ones focusing on making vegetarian dishes, the temple food *shōjin-ryōri* and soba noodles. Courses are led by professional chefs and are held inside the restaurant Sougo (p130).

☞ Tours

Free walking tours led by English-speaking volunteer guides take place weekly around Asakusa (p105), **Ueno** (Map p110; ☎03-6280-6710; www.tokyosgg.jp; 7-47 Ueno-kōen, Taitō-ku; ⏲10.30am & 1.30pm Wed, Fri & Sun; Ⓡ JR lines to

City Walk
Omote-sandō Architecture

START TOKYU PLAZA
END SUNNYHILLS
LENGTH 1.2KM; ONE HOUR

Omote-sandō is like a walk-through showroom featuring the who's who of contemporary architecture.

Start at the intersection of Omote-sandō and Meiji-dōri, at 1 **Tokyu Plaza** (東急プラザ表参道原宿), a castle-like structure built in 2012 and designed by up-and-coming architect Nakamura Hiroshi. The entrance is a dizzying hall of mirrors and there's a roof garden (with a Starbucks) on top.

Continue to Tadao Ando's deceptively deep 2003 2 **Omotesandō Hills** (表参道ヒルズ). This high-end shopping mall spirals around a sunken central atrium. Ando's architecture uses materials such as concrete to create strong geometric shapes, often drawn from Japan's traditional architecture.

Across the street, the five-storey glass 3 **Dior Building** designed by SANAA (Nishizawa Ryue and Sejima Kazuyo; 2003), has a filmy surface that seems to hang like a dress (an effect achieved with clever lighting and acrylic screens).

A couple of blocks down, Aoki Jun's 4 **Louis Vuitton Building** (2002) has offset panels of tinted glass behind sheets of metal mesh that are meant to evoke a stack of trunks. There's an art gallery on the 7th floor.

Climb onto the elevated crosswalk to better admire Itō Toyō's construction for 5 **Tod's** (2004). The criss-crossing strips of concrete take their inspiration from the zelkova trees below; they're also structural.

You can't miss the 6 **Prada Aoyama Building** (2003) with its curvaceous exterior of convex glass bubbles. Created by Herzog & de Meuron, this is the building that escalated the design race in the neighbourhood.

Turn the corner to see Kengo Kuma's design for Taiwanese pineapple cake shop 7 **SunnyHills** (2014). Kuma is an architect known for his use of wood and traditional Japanese joinery techniques, and this building represents his work at its most playful. The 3D-modelled latticework is supposed to evoke a bamboo basket, but also resembles a cross-hatched pineapple.

Ebisu & Meguro

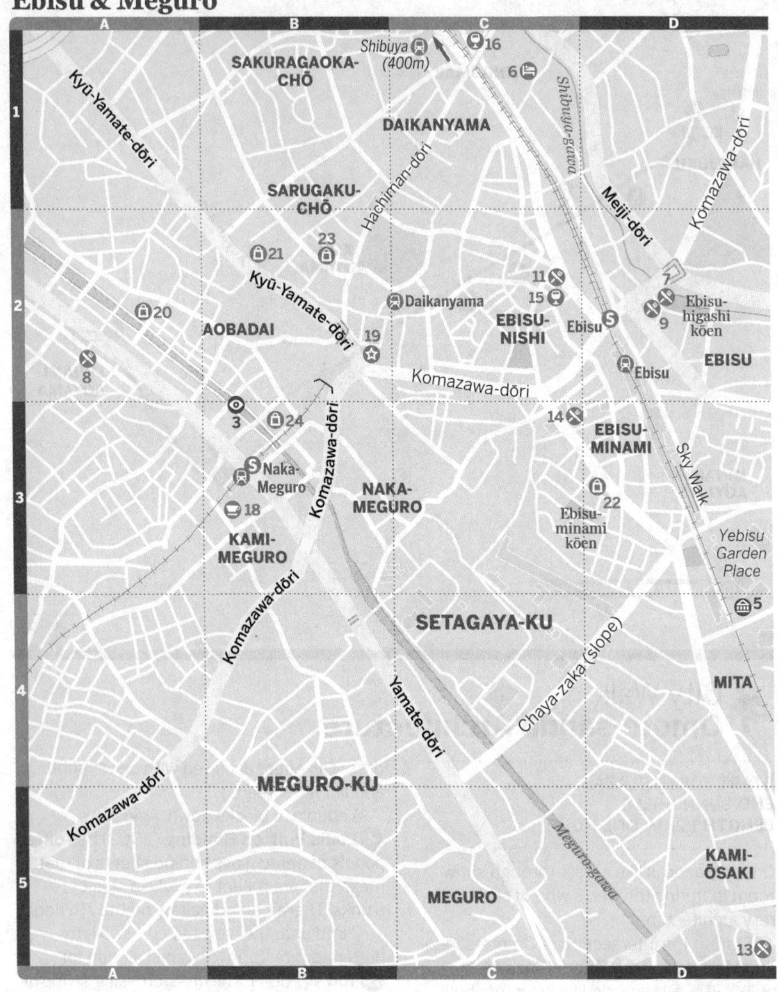

Ueno, Ueno-kōen exit) FREE, **Yanaka** (Map p110; ☎03-6280-6710; www.tokyosgg.jp; 7-8-10 Yanaka, Taitō-ku; ⏱10.30am & 1.30pm Sun; Yamanote line to Nippori, north exit) FREE and the **Imperial Palace East Garden** (Map p96; ☎03-6280-6710; JNTO Tourist Information Center, 3-3-1 Marunouchi, Chiyoda-ku; ⏱1pm Tue-Thu, Sat & Sun; S Chiyoda line to Nijūbashimae, exit 1) FREE. No advance reservations are required – just show up (though places are limited).

★**Tokyo Great Cycling Tour** CYCLING
(Map p92; ☎03-4590-2995; www.tokyocycling.jp; 1-3-2 Shinkawa, Chūō-ku; tours ¥5000-12,000; ; S Hibiya line to Kayabachō, exit 3) Cycling is a great way to see the city and this professional operation runs several different routes to suit different levels and interests, including alleyway tours or ones that take in architectural highlights. Guides speak English; lunch and bicycle rentals are included (child-sized bikes are available as are child's seats for very little ones). Reserve online in advance.

They also do running tours (www.tokyorunning.jp) and kayaking tours (www.tokyokayaking.jp).

Hato Bus Tours BUS

(Map p92; ☎03-3435-6081; www.hatobus.com; tours ¥1500-12,000; JR Yamanote line to Hamamatsuchō, south exit) This long-established bus-tour company offers hour-long, half-day and full-day bus tours of the city. Shorter tours cruise by the sights in an open-air double-decker bus; longer ones make stops. Tours leave from Hato Bus terminals in the annex of the World Trade Centre in Hamamatsuchō, as well as Shinjuku and from **Tokyo train station** (Map p96; ☎03-3435-6081; www.hatobus.com; per person ¥1800-12,000; JR lines to Tokyo, Marunouchi exit).

Ebisu & Meguro

Sights

1 Beer Museum Yebisu E3
2 Institute for Nature Study F5
3 Meguro-gawa B3
4 Tokyo Metropolitan Teien Art Museum E5
5 TOP Museum D4

Sleeping

6 Mustard Hotel C1

Eating

7 Afuri D2
8 Delifucious A2
9 Ebisu-yokochō D2
10 Ippo E2
11 Rangmang Shokudō C2
12 Ta-im E2
13 Tonki D5
14 Yakiniku Champion C3

Drinking & Nightlife

15 Bar Trench C2
16 Circus Tokyo C1
17 Gem by Moto E2
18 Onibus Coffee B3

Entertainment

19 Unit B2

Shopping

20 ...research General Store A2
21 Daikanyama T-Site B2
22 Kapital D3
23 Okura B2
24 Vase B3

Festivals & Events

Tokyo Marathon SPORTS

(www.marathon.tokyo; Mar) Tokyo's biggest running event happens on the first Sunday of March. Competition for slots is fierce; sign up the summer before.

Kanda Matsuri CULTURAL

(神田祭; May) Kanda Matsuri, put on by Kanda Myōjin (p98), was historically one of Tokyo's most important festivals – and it still puts on a good show, with a parade of *mikoshi* (portable shrines) around Kanda and Akihabara. It's held on the weekend closest to 15 May on odd-numbered years.

Sanja Matsuri PARADE

(三社祭; May) Tokyo's biggest festival is held over the third weekend of May and attracts about 1.5 million spectators to Asakusa-jinja (p105). The highlight is the rowdy parade of *mikoshi* (portable shrines) carried by men and women in traditional dress, with the grandest floats making the rounds on Sunday.

Roppongi Art Night ART

(www.roppongiartnight.com; ⏲May) Held in late May, this weekend-long (literally, as venues stay open all night) arts event sees large-scale installations and performances taking over the museums, galleries and streets of Roppongi. The vibe is more party than highbrow.

Sumida-gawa Fireworks FIREWORKS

(隅田川花火大会, Sumida-gawa Hanabi Taikai; www.sumidagawa-hanabi.com; ⏲Jul) Held the last Saturday of July, the largest of the summer fireworks shows sees 20,000 pyrotechnic wonders explode over Asakusa. The show starts around 7pm, but you'll have to get there way earlier to get a good spot.

Kōenji Awa Odori PARADE

(高円寺阿波おどり; www.koenji-awaodori.com; ⏲Aug) The most famous of Tokyo's *awa odori* (dance festivals for O-Bon) sees 10,000 participants in traditional costumes dancing their way through the streets of Kōenji over the last weekend of August.

TOKYO FOR CHILDREN

Odaiba is a popular destination for local families and is full of kid-friendly attractions, such as the hands-on National Museum of Emerging Science & Innovation (p114); the inspiring and immersive teamLab Borderless (p113); the virtual reality arcade Tokyo Joypolis (p115); and the awesome Unicorn Gundam model (p114). With the exception of the latter, these are all indoor attractions – perfect for rainy days. Odaiba's big malls all have food courts with family-friendly restaurants (including some international chains).

Tokyo Dome City, in Kōrakuen, with its baseball stadium (p152) and science museum (p98) is another good bet. And everyone loves the Ghibli Museum (p115).

Get older kids cycling (p120) around the city – or even kayaking (p117). Or trying their hand at traditional arts and crafts, like woodblock printmaking (p118).

Also fun (and good on a rainy day): karaoke.

Sleeping

Marunouchi & Nihombashi

★Citan HOSTEL ¥

(Map p106; ☎03-6661-7559; https://backpackersjapan.co.jp/citan; 15-2 Nihombashi-Odenmachō, Chūō-ku; dm/tw/d from ¥3000/8400/8500; ❄📶; Ⓢ Shinjuku line to Bakuro-Yokoyama, exit A1) The Bakurochō area has exploded with flashpacker hostels in the last few years – this is one of the biggest and the best. The trendy young staff are very helpful, and both dorms and private rooms (all share bathrooms) sport a pared-back contemporary look.

Also here is a spacious and buzzy basement cafe-bar (open 8am to 10.30pm), which serves craft beer and decent food and hosts occasional events and DJ nights.

Wise Owl Hostels Tokyo HOSTEL ¥

(Map p92; ☎03-5541-2960; www.wiseowlhostels.com; 3-22-9 Hatchōbori, Chūō-ku; dm/d from ¥2400/6000; 🚭❄📶) This industrial-looking hostel ticks all the boxes, with a super-convenient location above the subway and a relatively short walk or taxi ride from Marunouchi and Ginza. A clever configuration of wooden-cubicle bunks makes up the dorms; private rooms have one bunk bed. There's friendly service, a coffee stand in the lobby, a DJ bar in the basement and an attached *izakaya* (Japanese pub-eatery) for food.

★Hoshinoya Tokyo RYOKAN ¥¥¥

(星のや東京; Map p92; ☎050-3786-1144; www.hoshinoyatokyo.com; 1-9-1 Ōtemachi, Chiyoda-ku; r incl breakfast from ¥166,000; Ⓢ Marunouchi line to Ōtemachi, exit A1) In creating this contemporary ryokan in the heart of Tokyo, Hoshinoya has barely put a foot wrong, overcoming a location boxed in by office towers. Staying here is all about insulating yourself from the city in a building that incorporates timeless artisanship and the best of traditional Japanese design and service.

★Aman Tokyo DESIGN HOTEL ¥¥¥

(Map p96; ☎03-5224-3333; www.aman.com; 1-5-6 Ōtemachi, Chiyoda-ku; r from ¥120,000; 🚭❄@📶🏊; Ⓢ Marunouchi line to Ōtemachi, exit A5) Overlooking the Imperial Palace (p89) from atop Ōtemachi Tower, this outstanding hotel incorporates natural materials – including dark stone walls, blonde wood and white *washi* (Japanese handmade paper) – into its elegant, minimalist design. Enormous rooms all have baths with stunning city views – something you also get from the giant stone bath filled with onsen water in the spa.

Ginza & Tsukiji

★Park Hotel Tokyo DESIGN HOTEL ¥¥¥
(Map p96; ☎03-6252-1111; www.parkhotel tokyo.com; Shiodome Media Tower, 1-7-1 Higashi-Shimbashi, Minato-ku; s/d from ¥17,000/ 20,000, art rooms from ¥20,000/22,400; ; S Ōedo line to Shimbashi, exit 7) Kudos to the Park Hotel for commissioning 31 artists to decorate 31 of its 31st-floor rooms. The results are very impressive with all-Japanese themes ranging from sumo and Zen to *yokai* (monsters) and geisha. See the various themes online and book well in advance for popular rooms such as the cherry-blossom one.

Roppongi & Around

★Kaisu HOSTEL ¥
(Map p102; ☎03-5797-7711; www.kaisu.jp; 6-13-5 Akasaka, Minato-ku; dm/r without bathroom from ¥3900/10,500; ; S Chiyoda line to Akasaka, exit 7) Occupying a former *ryōtei* (geisha house), Kaisu is a flashpacker hostel with mid-century-modern and surfer-chic stylings. Dorms offer wooden bunks with the gorgeous old building's exposed beams on show. English-speaking staff are very friendly and there's a great cafe-bar (10am to 11pm) where you can mingle with locals.

★Apartment Hotel Mimaru Akasaka APARTMENT ¥¥
(Map p102; ☎03-6807-4344; www.mimaru hotels.com; 7-9-6 Akasaka, Minato-ku; apt from ¥18,000; ; S Chiyoda line to Akasaka, exit 7) Opened in 2018, Mimaru has beautifully designed rooms with fully equipped kitchens and proper bathrooms (no pokey unit baths!). Its apartment studios, some with Japanese tatami (tightly woven floor matting) areas, sleep up to four people. Online deals via its Facebook page can make it a great accommodation option, particularly for families or groups.

There are several other branches in the city, including three around Ueno.

★Hotel S BOUTIQUE HOTEL ¥¥
(ホテル S; Map p102; ☎03-5771-2469; www.hr-roppongi.jp; 1-11-6 Nishi-Azabu, Minato-ku; r from ¥16,000, apt per month from ¥216,000; ; S Hibiya line to Roppongi, exit 2) The various styles of room at this boutique property capture the arty design spirit of Roppongi. Some of the more expensive duplex-type rooms have Japanese design elements such as tatami (in charcoal) and circular *hinoki* (wooden baths). The entry-level rooms are also a cut above the usual.

★Hotel Ōkura HOTEL ¥¥¥
(ホテルオークラ東京; Map p102; ☎03-3582-0111; www.okura.com; 2-10-4 Toranomon, Minato-ku; s/d from ¥35,840/36,040; ; S Hibiya line to Kamiyachō, exit 4B) While the beloved original 1962 hotel has been demolished to make way for a new building, the Ōkura's elegant South Wing remains intact – and long may it do so! Rooms are bright, and large, with tasteful Japanese design touches. The public areas ooze retro glamour and service is courteous to a fault.

Kōrakuen & Kanda

★Unplan Kagurazaka HOSTEL ¥
(Map p92; ☎03-6457-5171; www.unplan.jp; 23-1 Tenjinchō, Shinjuku-ku; dm/r ¥3800/16,700; ; S Tōzai line to Kagurazaka, exit 2) A standout among Tokyo's new breed of flashpacker digs, Unplan offers comfy dorms in Scandinavian wood tones. The private rooms are very pleasant, and a superbly handy addition are the free smartphones for guests to use. There's a common room with cooking facilities as well as a pleasant cafe on the ground floor.

★BnA STUDIO Akihabara APARTMENT ¥¥¥
(Map p106; ☎03-5846-8876; www.bna-akiha bara.com; 6-3-3 Soto-Kanda, Chiyoda-ku; apt from ¥26,000; ; S Ginza line to Suehirochō, exit 4) Five different artists and artist groups have brought their creative visions to the studio apartments here. Designs are influenced by colourful street art and local culture – we love the minimalist Zen Garden from which you can gaze on a *kare-sansui* (dry landscape) on the balcony. All the rooms all spacious, with enormous bathrooms, fully equipped kitchens and washing machines.

Ueno & Yanesen

Toco HOSTEL ¥

(トコ; Map p92; 03-6458-1686; http://backpackersjapan.co.jp; 2-13-21 Shitaya, Taitō-ku; dm from ¥3000; ; Hibiya line to Iriya, exit 4) This is your chance to stay in a beautiful wooden building (which dates to 1920) that has been turned into one of Tokyo's most attractive hostels. Dorms with wooden bunks open onto a deck with a view of a traditional garden. The hostel is behind a trendy bar-lounge (open 7pm to 11.30pm) in a modern building at the front.

★ **Hanare** GUESTHOUSE ¥¥

(Map p110; 03-5834-7301; http://hanare.hagiso.jp; 3-10-25 Yanaka, Taitō-ku; s/d incl breakfast from ¥11,505/18,200; Chiyoda line to Sendagi, exit 2) A project of Tokyo University of the Arts, Hanare offers five immaculate tatami rooms in an old dormitory house, which has been tastefully upgraded to retain original features such as wooden beams. There is a shared bathroom, but you'll be given tickets to the local *sentō* (public bath), as the concept is to use Yanaka as an extension of the guesthouse.

Reception is in the nearby Hagiso building, the same location as Hagi Cafe (p132) where you'll be served a traditional breakfast.

★ **Sawanoya Ryokan** RYOKAN ¥¥

(旅館澤の屋; Map p110; 03-3822-2251; www.sawanoya.com; 2-3-11 Yanaka, Taitō-ku; s/d from ¥5615/10,585; ; Chiyoda line to Nezu, exit 1) Sawanoya is a gem in quiet Yanaka, run by a very friendly family and with all the traditional hospitality you would expect of a ryokan. The shared cypress and earthenware baths are the perfect balm after a long day (a couple of slightly more expensive rooms have their own bath, too). The lobby overflows with information about travel options in Japan.

Bicycles are available for rent, and lion-dance performances are occasionally held for guests.

★ **Nohga Hotel** DESIGN HOTEL ¥¥

(Map p110; 03-5816-0213; www.nohgahotel.com; 2-21-10 Higashi-Ueno, Taitō-ku; r from ¥20,000; JR lines to Ueno, Asakusa exit) Opened in November 2018, this super-stylish hotel ups the ante on midrange digs around Ueno. Fronted by attractive greenery and with a very pleasant restaurant-lounge area, Nohga's developers have incorporated products from local artisans and contemporary brands into the overall design. Rooms are comfortable and tastefully decorated in soft grey.

Asakusa & Ryōgoku

★ **Andon Ryokan** RYOKAN ¥

(行燈旅館; Map p92; 03-3873-8611; www.andon.co.jp; 2-34-10 Nihonzutsumi, Taitō-ku; s/d from ¥6500/7560; ; Hibiya line to Minowa, exit 3) About 2km north of Asakusa, the contemporary Andon Ryokan is fabulously designed in form and function. It has 20 tiny but immaculate tatami rooms, bathrooms decorated with specially commissioned manga art, and a spectacular upper-floor spa with a manga-style mural, which can be used privately. Toshiko, the friendly owner, collects antiques, which are displayed around the ryokan.

As of early 2019 Andon also has a new kitchen and cafe space on the ground floor in which a full program of cultural events are hosted. Bike rentals and laundry facilities are also available. It's a five-minute walk from the subway.

Nui HOSTEL ¥

(ヌイ; Map p92; 03-6240-9854; https://backpackersjapan.co.jp/nui; 2-14-13 Kuramae, Taitō-ku; dm/tw/d from ¥2800/8000/8500; ; Ōedo line to Kuramae, exit A7) In a former warehouse, this stylish hostel has rooms with high ceilings, translating to bunks you can comfortably sit up in. There's also an enormous shared kitchen and work space. Best of all is the ground-floor cafe-bar and lounge (open 8am to 1am), with furniture made from salvaged timber; it's a popular local hang-out.

Bunka Hostel Tokyo HOSTEL ¥

(Map p112; 03-5806-3444; www.bunkahostel.jp; 1-13-5 Asakusa, Taitō-ku; dm/f from ¥3000/16,800; Tsukuba Express to Asakusa, exit 4) This is one of the most stylish of the several Tokyo hostels that combine a cafe or a bar open to the public in the foyer with a hostel above. Bunka offers capsule-style bunks; roomier versions where you can stand up go for ¥5000 a bed.

The family room sleeping up to four offers great views across the area.

Wired Hotel Asakusa DESIGN HOTEL ¥¥

(Map p112; 03-5830-7931; www.wiredhotel.com; 2-16-2 Asakusa, Taitō-ku; tw/d from ¥13,000/14,000; ; Ginza line to Asakusa,

Odaiba & Tokyo Bay

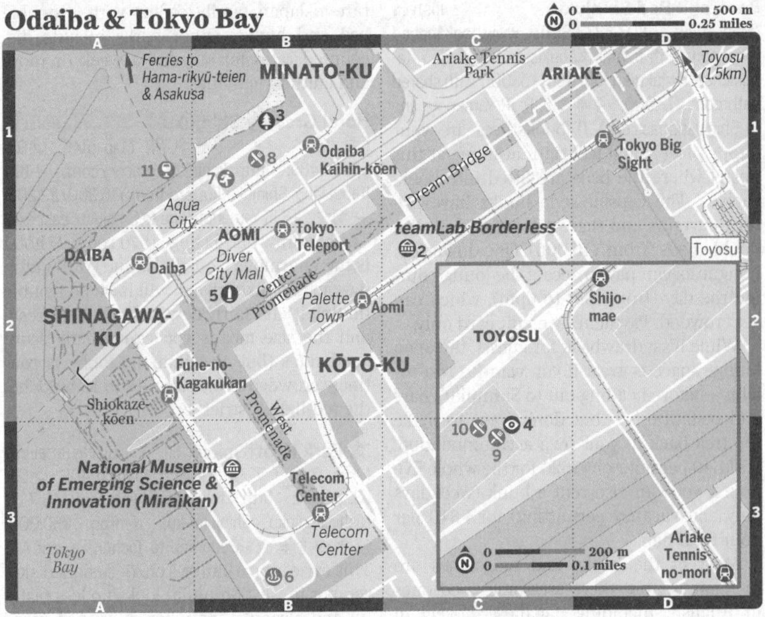

exit 1) This boutique-style hotel is an appealing mix of retro and contemporary design. Each room is decorated with subtly different decor, but all have decent-sized bathrooms and beds graced by a gorgeous indigo-dye throw. Events are sometimes held in the ground-floor cafe-bar.

Hatago BUSINESS HOTEL ¥¥
(旅籠; Map p112; ☎03-6802-7277; www.asakusahotel.org; 2-6-8 Komagata, Taitō-ku; s/tw incl breakfast from ¥7500/11,000; ; Ginza line to Asakusa, exit 4) The rooms at this well-run hotel with English-speaking staff are typically small but come with tatami floors (even though you sleep on beds) and other Japanese touches. Breakfast is served in the top-floor lounge, with spectacular views across the Sumida-gawa towards Tokyo Sky Tree – there's also a rooftop terrace.

Rates go up for Saturdays and the day before public holidays.

Shinjuku & Around

9 Hours Shinjuku-North CAPSULE HOTEL ¥
(Map p92; ☎03-5291-7337; https://ninehours.co.jp/en/shinjuku-north; 1-4-15 Hyakunin-chō, Shinjuku-ku; capsule from ¥4900; ; JR Yamanote line to Shin-Ōkubo) 9 Hours calls its capsules 'pods' which fits with the space-station sleek design, hushed vibe and views of the Shinjuku skyline (just one train stop away). As this is a capsule hotel, floors and facilities are gender segregated. You can stay for consecutive days but you must be out (with your stuff in one of the lockers) between 10am and 1pm.

Odaiba & Tokyo Bay

Top Sights
1 National Museum of Emerging Science & Innovation (Miraikan) B3
2 teamLab Borderless C2

Sights
3 Odaiba Kaihin-kōen B1
4 Toyosu Market C3
5 Unicorn Gundam B2

Activities, Courses & Tours
6 Ōedo Onsen Monogatari B3
7 Tokyo Joypolis B1

Eating
8 Bills B1
9 Daiwa Sushi C3
Mosuke Dango .... (see 9)
10 Sushi Dai C3

Drinking & Nightlife
11 Jicoo the Floating Bar A1

Book and Bed Shinjuku HOSTEL ¥
(Map p146; ☎03-6233-9511; www.bookandbedtokyo.com; 8th fl, AMP Kabukichō Bldg, 1-27-5 Kabukichō, Shinjuku-ku; dm from ¥5300, r with shared bathroom ¥12,000; ; JR Yamanote line to Shinjuku, east exit) If bookstores are your happy place you'll feel right at home at this hostel where the beds are fitted into bookshelves. The capsule-style bunks have privacy curtains and there are even ones with double beds (from ¥10,000). One downside: nonguests can pay to access the lounge during the day (from 1pm to 6pm), which can get crowded. Payment by credit card only.

While it's a drawback for guests, the open lounge space is great if you want to rest for a bit – before heading out to Shinjuku's bars and restaurants – but don't want to make the trek back to your own accommodation. It's ¥540 per hour or ¥1620 for the whole five hours; you can also rent a bunk (weekdays only and vacancy permitting) for ¥840 per hour for a nap.

Most of the books and magazines are in Japanese, but there are some good ones in English, including Japanese novels in translation.

Book and Bed also has a property in **Ikebukuro** (Map p92; ☎03-6914-2914; http://bookandbedtokyo.com; 7th fl, 1-17-7 Nishi-Ikebukuro, Toshima-ku; dm from ¥4100; ; JR Yamanote line to Ikebukuro, west exit).

Kimi Ryokan RYOKAN ¥
(貴美旅館; Map p92; ☎03-3971-3766; www.kimi-ryokan.jp; 2-36-8 Ikebukuro, Toshima-ku; s/d from ¥5400/8100; ; JR Yamanote line to Ikebukuro, west exit) Kimi Ryokan has been a traveller favourite for decades and it's easy to see why: the tatami rooms and shared bathrooms (including a Japanese cypress bath that can be used privately) are clean and well kept; the service (in multiple languages) is gracious and helpful; and there's a lounge and a rooftop terrace. Oh, and the eminently reasonable price. Book well in advance.

Sakura Hotel Ikebukuro HOSTEL ¥
(サクラホテル池袋; Map p92; ☎03-3971-2237; www.sakura-hotel.co.jp; 2-40-7 Ikebukuro, Toshima-ku; dm/s/d ¥3300/7000/9300; ; JR Yamanote line to Ikebukuro) This old standby lacks the designer charm of Tokyo's newer hostels but makes up for it with its multilingual, four-star-hotel-level front-desk service. There's a diverse spread of spartan room arrangements, including rare-in-Japan family rooms with a double bed and bunks. Other perks include discounted rates for stays of a week or more and cultural activities.

Hotel Gracery Shinjuku HOTEL ¥¥
(ホテルグレイスリー新宿; Map p146; ☎03-6833-2489; http://shinjuku.gracery.com; 1-19-1 Kabukichō, Shinjuku-ku; s/d from ¥16,200/22,200; ; JR Yamanote line to Shinjuku, east exit) The big draw of this huge (970 rooms!) hotel is the enormous Godzilla statue (p107) atop it (you, and taxi drivers, will have no trouble finding it). It's fairly new and still feels fresh, and the size means you can usually score good rates (but also that the lobby is routinely crowded). Note that it's in Kabukichō, the red-light district.

★ **Park Hyatt Tokyo** LUXURY HOTEL ¥¥¥
(パークハイアット東京; Map p146; ☎03-5322-1234; http://tokyo.park.hyatt.com; 3-7-1-2 Nishi-Shinjuku, Shinjuku-ku; d from ¥60,000; ; Ōedo line to Tochōmae, exit A4) This eyrie atop a Tange Kenzō–designed skyscraper in west Shinjuku looks no less tasteful and elegant than when it opened more than 20 years ago, and it remains a popular spot for visiting celebrities. The rooms are on the 42nd to 51st floors, meaning even the entry-level rooms have fantastic views; west-facing rooms look out towards Mt Fuji.

Hotel Century Southern Tower HOTEL ¥¥¥
(ホテルセンチュリーサザンタワー; Map p146; ☎03-5354-0111; www.southerntower.co.jp; 2-2-1 Yoyogi, Shibuya-ku; s/d from ¥16,400/20,520; ; JR Yamanote line to Shinjuku, south exit) This is the only upmarket accommodation in Shinjuku that seems to assume its guests will actually be getting around by public transport – it's just steps from Shinjuku Station's south exit. The hotel occupies the 20th to 35th floors, so the rooms (spacious with big beds) have views over Shinjuku. If you can lock in a good rate, this is a great deal.

Harajuku & Aoyama

Dormy Inn Premium Shibuya Jingūmae BUSINESS HOTEL ¥¥
(ドーミーインプレミアム渋谷神宮前; Map p116; ☎03-5774-5489; www.hotespa.net/hotels/shibuya; 6-24-4 Jingūmae, Shibuya-ku; s/d from ¥13,790/18,590; ; JR Yamanote line to Harajuku, Omote-sandō exit) Dormy is a popular chain of business hotels that offers some perks that others don't, like a

WHERE TO SLEEP: PICKING YOUR TOKYO BASE

Central neighbourhoods like Marunouchi – convenient for *shinkansen* (bullet train) hub Tokyo Station – and Ginza are typically pricey: this is where many of Tokyo's finest luxury hotels can be found. But increasingly, budget accommodation can be found everywhere (and often just a stop or two on the subway from a more famous address).

Roppongi and Shibuya, which both have solid midrange options, are good for night owls (otherwise give them a pass): both are nightlife centres. Roppongi is central and close to many sights; Shibuya has great transport links. Some cheaper Shibuya options are technically in nearby Shinsen, but still within walking distance (about 15 minutes) of Shibuya Station.

The busy western hub of Shinjuku is a traveller favourite, thanks to its many rail links and dining and drinking options. Note that many budget hotels in Shinjuku that target foreign travellers are in the red-light district, Kabukichō; while it's highly unlikely you'd encounter any real danger, some might find it unpleasant to walk past shady characters night after night. Ikebukuro, another big hub, north of Shinjuku, has good budget options.

Ueno and Yanesen abound with ryokan and good budget options, though these hoods can be sleepy at night. Asakusa, in the northeastern corner of Tokyo, is backpacker central with the best selection of hostels; on the downside, staying here can mean long train rides to other parts of the city.

Marunouchi (Tokyo Station), Shinjuku, Shibuya and Ikebukuro all have direct access to Narita Airport on the Narita Express; Ueno has its own direct line to Narita, the Skyliner.

traditional-style communal bath and sauna (in addition to in-room showers) and bicycle rentals (pending availability). Rooms are ordinary: typically small with double beds (140cm). There's a free morning shuttle service to Shibuya Station.

Shibuya

★Mustard Hotel DESIGN HOTEL, HOSTEL ¥¥
(マスタードホテル; Map p120; ☎03-6459-2842; www.mustardhotel.com; 1-29 Higashi, Shibuya-ku; dm/s/d with shared bathroom from ¥4000/10,000/15,000, s/d with bathroom from ¥20,000/25,000; ; JR Yamanote line to Shibuya, new south exit) Mustard is the most exciting of Shibuya's new crop of hotels. The glossy white interior is the work of design firm Tripstar, and there are a variety of sleeping spaces to accommodate different budgets. The hotel is within walking distance of Shibuya, Daikanyama and Ebisu (though 10 minutes from the nearest station, Shibuya). The English-speaking front desk staff have tips for local hang-outs.

Millennials CAPSULE HOTEL ¥¥
(Map p138; ☎03-6824-9410; www.themillennials.jp/shibuya; 1-20-13 Jinnan, Shibuya-ku; capsule incl breakfast from ¥8000; ; JR Yamanote line to Shibuya, Hachikō exit) This new Shibuya capsule hotel has cabin-style rooms: single-decker, divided on the sides by walls, but with curtains for doors; they're literally the size of a single bed (put your luggage underneath). It's located in the heart of Shibuya, and among the neighbourhood's cheapest options. Complimentary breakfast (continental style), happy-hour beer and all-day coffee sweeten the deal.

Unlike other capsule and cabin-style hotels, the Millennials doesn't require you to pack up daily for cleaning purposes. Actually if you want your bed redone with fresh sheets, you have to request it (¥1000).

Turntable HOSTEL ¥¥
(ターンテーブル; Map p138; ☎03-3461-7722; www.turntable.jp; 10-3 Shinsen-chō, Shibuya-ku; d/s/tw from ¥6750/12,000/20,000; ; Keio Inokashira line to Shinsen, south exit) This stylish, upscale hostel is pricier than average but has more amenities and services, like fresh towels every day and sheets changed every other day. The dorms are comfy and well designed, and the breakfast is a buffet of home-style Japanese cooking served in the ground-floor cafe. Shinsen is the closest station, but you can walk to Shibuya Station in 10 minutes.

Shibuya Stream Excel Hotel Tokyu HOTEL ¥¥¥
(渋谷ストリームエクセルホテル東急; Map p138; ☎03-3406-1090; www.tokyuhotelsjapan.com/global/stream-e; 3-21-3 Shibuya, Shibuya-ku;

s/d from ¥24,200/34,400; ; Ginza, Hanzōmon & Fukutoshin lines to Shibuya, exit 16b, JR Yamanote line to Shibuya, new south exit) Tokyu's new property in the Shibuya Stream complex (p110) is going for a boutique vibe with earthy textiles and mid-century furnishings, but honestly it could be dressed in potato sacks and we'd still take it: it's got direct access to Shibuya Station (via the subway) plus all the easy dining options at Shibuya Stream.

Hotel Mets Shibuya BUSINESS HOTEL ¥¥¥
(ホテルメッツ渋谷; Map p138; 03-3409-0011; www.hotelmets.jp/shibuya; 3-29-17 Shibuya, Shibuya-ku; s/d incl breakfast from ¥20,700/25,200; ; JR Yamanote line to Shibuya, new south exit) Hotel Mets is part of Shibuya Station's quiet south side, with direct access to the JR lines; the location can be confusing at first, but once you get the hang of it, it's convenient. Rooms are modern and comfortable, with the double beds clocking in at a roomy 160cm. JR Pass holders get a 10% discount. The free breakfast is good.

The hotel is especially convenient for the Narita Express airport train, as the platform is very near the south exit.

Eating

When it comes to Tokyo superlatives, the city's food scene tops the list. But we're not just talking about the famous restaurants and the celebrity chefs: what Tokyo excels at is consistency across the board. Wherever you are, you're usually within 100m of a good, if not great, restaurant. It's a scene that careens nonchalantly between the highs and lows: it's not unusual for a top-class sushi restaurant to share the same block as an oil-spattered noodle joint, and for both to be equally adored. Tokyoites love dining out; join them, and delight in the sheer variety of tastes and experiences the city has to offer.

Reservations are expected at high-end places and recommended at popular mid-range places and for groups of five or more.

AIRPORT ACCOMMODATION

For late-night arrivals and early-morning departures, sleeping at the airport is an economical option.

9 Hours (0476-33-5109; http://ninehours.co.jp/en/narita; Narita International Airport Terminal 2; capsule ¥4900;) Capsule hotel inside Narita Airport. It's also possible to stay for only a few hours (between 9am and 6pm; ¥1500 for the first hour, plus ¥500 per additional hour) or just use the shower room (24 hours; ¥1000).

Royal Park Hotel the Haneda (ロイヤルパークホテル ザ 羽田; 03-6830-1111; www.the-royalpark.jp/the/tokyohaneda; Haneda Airport International Terminal; s/d from ¥18,500/24,4100;) Attached to Haneda Airport's international terminal.

Marunouchi & Nihombashi

★ Dhaba India SOUTH INDIAN ¥
(ダバ インディア; Map p96; 03-3272-7160; www.dhabaindia.com; 2-7-9 Yaesu, Chūō-ku; lunch/mains from ¥850/1370; 11.15am-3pm & 5-11pm Mon-Fri, noon-3pm & 5-10pm Sat & Sun; Ginza line to Kyōbashi, exit 5) Indian meals in Tokyo don't come much better than those served at this long-established restaurant with deep-indigo plaster walls. The food is very authentic, particularly the curries served with basmati rice, naan or crispy *dosa* (giant lentil-flour pancakes). Set lunches are spectacularly good value.

Nihonbashi Dashi Bar Hanare JAPANESE ¥
(日本橋だし場はなれ; Map p96; 03-5205-8704; www.ninben.co.jp/hanare; 1st fl, Coredo Muromachi 2, 2-3-1 Nihombashi-Muromachi, Chūō-ku; set meals ¥1025-1950, dishes ¥650-1300; 11am-2pm & 5-11pm; Ginza line to Mitsukoshimae, exit A6) This casual restaurant from long-time producer (300-plus years!) of *katsuo-bushi* (dried bonito flakes), Ninben, naturally serves dishes that make use of the umami-rich ingredient. Set meals, with dishes such as hearty miso soups and *dashi takikokomi gohan* (rice steamed in stock), are good value, and healthy to boot.

Meal MUJI Yūrakuchō DELI ¥
(MealMUJI有楽町; Map p96; 03-5208-8245; http://cafemeal.muji.com/jp; 2nd fl, 3-8-3 Marunouchi, Chiyoda-ku; meals ¥850-1200; 10am-9pm; ; JR Yamanote line to Yūrakuchō, Kyōbashi exit) Those who subscribe to the Muji lifestyle will be delighted to know that the 'no name brand' experience goes beyond neutral-toned notebooks and linens. Meal MUJI follows the 'simpler is better' mantra with fresh deli fare uncluttered by chemicals and unpronounceable ingredients.

It's on the 2nd floor of Muji's flagship store (p152).

Nemuro Hanamaru SUSHI ¥

(根室花まる; Map p96; ☎03-6269-9026; www.sushi-hanamaru.com; 4th fl, KITTE, 2-7-2 Marunouchi, Chiyoda-ku; sushi per plate ¥140-630; ⊙11am-10pm, until 9pm Sun; Ⓡ JR lines to Tokyo, Marunouchi south exit) Nemuro is a fishing port in the far east of Hokkaidō (Japan's northern island), and visiting the original *kaiten-zushi* (conveyor-belt sushi restaurant) there earns you some serious bragging points. But really, you can also just go to this convenient, good-value branch inside the mall, KITTE. The trade-off is that there's usually a wait here.

Nihonbashi Tamai JAPANESE ¥¥

(玉ゐ 本店; Map p96; ☎03-3272-3227; www.anago-tamai.com; 2-9-9 Nihombashi, Chūō-ku; meals ¥1600-4000; ⊙11am-2.30pm & 5-9.30pm Mon-Fri, 11.30am-3pm & 4.30-8.30pm Sat & Sun; Ⓢ Ginza line to Nihombashi, exit C4) *Anago* (seafaring eel) has long been considered a super-food, rich in vitamins A and E (and fortunately, not endangered like its freshwater cousin *unagi*). Here it's served in lacquerware boxes (a style known as *hakomeshi*) and prepared either grilled or boiled – you can sample both cooking styles by asking for half and half.

★**Kizushi** SUSHI ¥¥¥

(喜寿司; Map p92; ☎03-3666-1682; 2-7-13 Nihombashi-Ningyōchō, Chūō-ku; lunch set ¥3850-5500, sushi course from ¥11,000; ⊙11.45am-2.30pm Mon-Sat, 5-9.30pm Mon-Fri, to 9pm Sat; Ⓢ Hibiya line to Ningyōchō, exit A3) While sushi has moved in the direction of faster and fresher, Kizushi, in business since 1923, is keeping it old school. Fourth-generation chef Yui Kazuhiro uses traditional techniques, such as marinating the fish in salt or vinegar, from back when sushi was more about preservation than instant gratification. The shop is in a lovely old timber-frame house.

Reserve through your accommodation; walk-ins are welcome though, if there's space.

Ginza & Tsukiji

Ginza is known to have some of the finest restaurants in the country.

Ginza Sato Yosuke NOODLES ¥¥

(銀座 佐藤養助; Map p96; ☎03-6215-6211; www.sato-yoske.co.jp/en/shop/ginza; 6-4-17 Ginza, Chūō-ku; noodles from ¥1300; ⊙11.30am-3pm & 5-10pm; Ⓢ Marunouchi line to Ginza, exit C2) A speciality of Akita Prefecture, *inaniwa* wheat noodles have been made by seven generations of the Sato family. As you'll be able to tell from the glossy, silky-textured results, they've pretty much got it down to perfection. Sample the noodles in a hot chicken broth or cold dipping sauces such as sesame and miso or green curry.

Ain Soph VEGAN ¥¥

(Map p96; ☎03-6228-4241; www.ain-soph.jp; 4-12-1 Ginza, Chūō-ku; mains from ¥1680, bentō boxes & set menus lunch/dinner from ¥2480/3250; ⊙11.30am-10pm Wed-Mon; Ⓢ Asakusa or Hibiya line to Higashi-Ginza, exit A7) Truly vegan restaurants are few and far between in Tokyo and ones that make so much effort over their food as Ain Soph are even rarer. Thank heavens then for this stylish place (bookings are essential for dinner) that serves delicious *bentō* box meals, vegan-cheese fondue, smoothies and fluffy American-style pancakes.

Ginza is the main branch but check its website for details of other ones in Shinjuku and Ikebukuro.

Sushikuni JAPANESE ¥¥

(鮨國; Map p96; ☎03-3545-8234; 4-14-15 Tsukiji, Chūō-ku; seafood rice bowls from ¥3000; ⊙10am-3pm & 5-9pm Thu-Tue; Ⓢ Hibiya line to Tsukiji, exit 1) *Kaisen-don* (bowls of rice topped with a variety of raw fish) is a common dish at Tsukiji's many seafood restaurants. The toppings of rich, creamy *uni* (sea urchin roe) and salty *ikura* (salmon roe) are generous here and straight from the market.

★**Kyūbey** SUSHI ¥¥¥

(久兵衛; Map p96; ☎03-3571-6523; www.kyubey.jp; 8-7-6 Ginza, Chūō-ku; lunch/dinner courses from ¥8250/11,000; ⊙11.30am-2pm & 5-10pm Mon-Sat; Ⓢ Ginza line to Shimbashi, exit 3) Kyūbey, running since 1935 is one of Tokyo's prestige sushi restaurants, where each piece of *nigiri-zushi* (hand-pressed sushi) is made and delivered one at a time. But there's no snobbery here: staff speak English (and deliver no side eyes) and the prices are very reasonable for Ginza. Reservations must be made through your accommodation. There's a 10% service charge.

★**Tempura Kondō** TEMPURA ¥¥¥

(てんぷら近藤; Map p96; ☎03-5568-0923; 9th fl, Sakaguchi Bldg, 5-5-13 Ginza, Chūō-ku; lunch/dinner course from ¥8800/14,300; ⊙noon-3pm

& 5-10pm Mon-Sat; S Ginza line to Ginza, exit B5) Nobody in Tokyo does tempura vegetables like chef Kondō Fumio. The carrots are julienned to a fine floss; the corn is pert and juicy; and the sweet potato is comfort food at its finest. Courses include seafood, too. Lunch servce is at noon or 1.30pm; last dinner booking is at 8pm. Reserve through your accommodation.

Bird Land YAKITORI ¥¥¥

(バードランド; Map p96; ☎03-5250-1081; www.ginza-birdland.sakura.ne.jp; 4-2-15 Ginza, Chūō-ku; course ¥6800-9240; ⏲5-9.30pm, closed Sun & Mon; S Ginza line to Ginza, exit C6) Most *yakitori* restaurants fall into the 'cheap and cheerful' category. Not Birdland: here chefs in whites grill heirloom free-range chicken (from Ibaraki prefecture) while diners sip wine. The course includes dainty serves of chicken liver pâté. Enter beneath Suit Company (yes, this is one of the upscale Tokyo restaurants in a nondescript basement). Reservations recommended.

Roppongi & Around

Honmura-An SOBA ¥

(本むら庵; Map p102; ☎03-5772-6657; www.honmuraantokyo.com; 7-14-18 Roppongi, Minato-ku; noodles from ¥950; ⏲noon-2.30pm & 5.30-10pm, closed Mon, 1st & 3rd Tue of month; 📶; S Hibiya line to Roppongi, exit 4) This fabled soba shop, once located in Manhattan, now serves its handmade buckwheat noodles at this small, elegant shop on a Roppongi side street. It's a restaurant for everyone: get simple *seiro-soba* (¥950; plain, cooled noodles) or go all out with the signature dish from the old NYC shop: soba topped with *uni* (sea urchin roe; ¥3900).

There is also a seasonal dinner course that include sashimi and tempura dishes (¥8900).

Sougo JAPANESE ¥

(宗胡; Map p102; ☎03-5414-1133; www.sougo.tokyo; 3rd fl, Roppongi Green Bldg, 6-1-8 Roppongi, Minato-ku; lunch from ¥1500, dinner course from ¥8000; ⏲11.30am-3pm & 6-11pm Mon-Sat; ✍; S Hibiya line to Roppongi, exit 3) Sougo is one of the few restaurants in Tokyo that prepares *shōjin-ryōri* (Japanese Buddhist vegetarian cuisine – what the monks eat). Not everything on the menu strictly adheres (it's all good though); if you want the real deal order the *shōji-kaiseki* (lunch/dinner ¥8000/10,000). Course reservations essential; give them at least two days' notice for dietary restrictions and allergies.

Bricolage Bread & Co CAFE ¥¥

(Map p102; ☎03-6804-3350; www.bricolagebread.com; 6-15-1 Roppongi, Minato-ku; mains ¥1200-1800; ⏲9am-7.30pm Tue-Sun; S Hibiya line to Roppongi, exit 1) A collaboration between coffee shop Fuglen (p140), Michelin-starred restaurant L'effervescence and Osaka-based bakery Le Sucré Coeur is naturally the perfect place for brunch. The thing to order here are the *tartines* (open-faced sandwiches), topped with, say, smoked salmon, *ikura* (salmon roe) and beetroot drizzled with salted plum sauce. Terrace seating is the cherry on top.

Jōmon IZAKAYA ¥¥

(ジョウモン; Map p102; ☎03-3405-2585; www.teyandei.com; 5-9-17 Roppongi, Minato-ku; skewers ¥250-500, dishes from ¥580; ⏲5.30-11.45pm Sun-Thu, until 5am Fri & Sat; ✍; S Hibiya line to Roppongi, exit 3) This cosy kitchen has bar seating, rows of ornate *shōchū* (liquor) jugs lining the wall and hundreds of freshly prepared skewers splayed in front of the patrons – don't miss the heavenly *zabuton* beef stick. Jōmon is almost directly across from the Family Mart – look for the name in Japanese on the door. Cover charge ¥300 per person.

★**Kikunoi** KAISEKI ¥¥¥

(菊乃井; Map p102; ☎03-3568-6055; www.kikunoi.jp; 6-13-8 Akasaka, Minato-ku; lunch course ¥11,000, dinner ¥16,500-33,000; ⏲lunch seating noon-12.30pm, dinner seating 5-7.30pm; S Chiyoda line to Akasaka, exit 7) Kikunoi is one of Japan's storied *ryōtei*, the high-class restaurants that serves *kaiseki* (Japanese haute cuisine). Its Akasaka branch is (relatively speaking) more casual and approachable. English-speaking staff are on hand to explain all the incredible seasonal delicacies served one at a time, each plated as works of art, over the two- to 2½-hour course.

Reservations are essential and must be made through your accommodation. 10% service charge.

★**Tofuya-Ukai** KAISEKI ¥¥¥

(とうふ屋うかい; Map p102; ☎03-3436-1028; www.ukai.co.jp/english/shiba; 4-4-13 Shiba-kōen, Minato-ku; set meals lunch/dinner from ¥5940/10,800; ⏲11.45am-3pm & 5-7.30pm Mon-Fri, 11am-7.30pm Sat & Sun; ✍; S Ōedo line to Akabanebashi, exit 8) One of Tokyo's most gracious restaurants is located in a former sake brewery (moved from northern Japan), with an exquisite traditional garden in the shadow of **Tokyo Tower** (東京タ

ワー; Map p102; www.tokyotower.co.jp/en.html; 4-2-8 Shiba-kōen, Minato-ku; adult/child/student main deck ¥900/400/500, incl special deck ¥2800/1200/1800; ⊙observation deck 9am-10.30pm; Ⓢ Ōedo line to Akabanebashi, Akabanebashi exit). Seasonal preparations of tofu and accompanying dishes are served in the refined *kaiseki* (Japanese haute cuisine) style. Make reservations well in advance. Vegetarians should advise staff when they book, and last orders for weekday lunch is 3pm, for dinner 7.30pm.

Kōrakuen & Kanda

★Kagawa Ippuku UDON ¥

(香川 一福 神田店; Map p106; ☎03-557-3644; www.udon-ippuku-kanda.com; 1st fl, Tokyo Royal Plaza,1-18-11 Uchikanda, Chiyoda-ku; udon ¥430-820; ⊙11am-8pm Mon-Sat, also closed 1st Mon of month; Ⓡ Yamanote line to Kanda, west exit) Proof you don't need to shell out a small fortune to eat well in Tokyo is this humble restaurant specialising in *Sanuki-udon*, wheat noodles from Kagawa in Shikoku. Pay at the vending machine; you'll be handed an English menu to help with the options, which include the amount of noodles you wish and the toppings. The curry noodles are excellent.

Mensho Tokyo RAMEN ¥

(Map p92; ☎03-3830-0842; http://menya-shono.com/tokyo; 1-15-9 Kasuga, Bunkyō-ku; noodles from ¥750; ⊙11am-3pm, 5-11pm, closed Tue; Ⓢ Namboku line to Kōrakuen, exits 5 & 6) Mensho is the new agitator in the Tokyo ramen scene, now with a couple of shops around town, each with a different speciality. At this one, it's a twist on *tonkotsu* ramen (with soup made from pork bones): lamb bones in the mix, for a similarly rich but slightly gamier broth (with a hint of spices).

If you like Mensho's style, be sure to check its branch near **Gokokuji** (Map p92; ☎03-6902-2878; http://menya-shono.com/mensho/; 1-17-16 Otowa, Bunkyō-ku; noodles from ¥1000; ⊙11am-3pm & 5-9pm Wed-Sun; Ⓢ Yūrakuchō line to Gokokuji, exit 6), which serves delicate seafood ramen.

Kanda Yabu Soba SOBA ¥

(神田やぶそば; Map p106; ☎03-3251-0287; www.yabusoba.net; 2-10 Kanda-Awajichō, Chiyoda-ku; noodles ¥825-2530; ⊙11.30am-8.30pm, closed Wed; Ⓢ Marunouchi line to Awajichō, exit A3) Kanda Yabu Soba has been in business since 1880. The restaurant was rebuilt after a fire in 2013, but the commitment to excellent soba remains the same: handmade, with a buckwheat-to-flour ratio of 10:1, for just the right bite. Get them simple, hot or cold, or with tempura shrimp or slices of duck breast.

DON'T MISS

BEST TOKYO RESTAURANTS FOR...

- ➡ Top-class sushi: Kyūbey (p129)
- ➡ Trend-setting ramen: Mensho Tokyo
- ➡ The classic *izakaya* experience: Shinsuke (p132)
- ➡ Vegetarians: Ain Soph (p129)

Isegen JAPANESE ¥¥

(いせ源; Map p106; ☎03-3251-1229; www.isegen.com; 1-11-1 Kanda-Sudachō, Chiyoda-ku; meals from ¥1600; ⊙11.30am-2pm & 5-9pm, closed Sat & Sun Apr-Oct; Ⓢ Marunouchi line to Awajichō, exit A3) This pocket of Kanda has several long-running restaurants in vintage wooden buildings. Isegen, in business since the 1830s, occupies a handsome one from 1930 with a communal tatami dining room. The speciality here is *ankō-nabe* (monkfish hotpot; ¥3500 per person, minimum order for two). Get a side of *kimo-zashi* (monkfish liver; ¥1400) – a prized delicacy, served pâté-style.

Cheaper lunchtime options include *yanagawa-nabe* (loach in rich egg and dashi stock; ¥1800).

Ueno & Yanesen

★Innsyoutei JAPANESE ¥

(韻松亭; Map p110; ☎03-3821-8126; www.innsyoutei.jp; 4-59 Ueno-kōen, Taitō-ku; lunch/dinner from ¥1680/5500; ⊙restaurant 11am-3pm & 5-9.30pm, tearoom 3-5pm; Ⓡ JR lines to Ueno, Ueno-kōen exit) In a gorgeous wooden building dating to 1875, Innsyoutei (pronounced 'inshotei' and meaning 'rhyme of the pine cottage') has long been a favourite spot for fancy *kaiseki*-style meals while visiting Ueno-kōen (p103). Without a booking (essential for dinner) you'll have a long wait, but it's worth it. Lunchtime *bentō* (boxed meals) offer beautifully presented morsels and are great value.

Between lunch and dinner the attached teahouse serves *matcha* (powdered green tea) and traditional desserts from ¥600.

Kamachiku UDON ¥

(釜竹; Map p110; ☎03-5815-4675; www.kamachiku.com; 2-14-18 Nezu, Bunkyō-ku; noodles from ¥935, small dishes ¥385-1155; ⊙11.30am-2pm Tue-Sun, 5.30-9pm Tue-Sat; Ⓢ Chiyoda line to Nezu, exit 1) *Kama-age* udon (wheat noodles served straight in the cook pot) is the speciality at this popular restaurant. It's part beautifully restored brick warehouse from 1910 and contemporary building by architect Kuma Kengo. In addition to noodles, the menu includes a good selection of sake and lots of small dishes (such as grilled fish, veggies and a delicious Japanese-style omelette).

Tayori JAPANESE ¥

(Map p110; ☎03-5834-7026; www.tayori-osozai.jp; 3-12-4 Yanaka, Taitō-ku; set meals ¥1000; ⊙11.30am-8pm Wed-Mon; ; Yamanote line to Nippori, Yanaka exit) Tucked down an alley off Yanaka Ginza (p103) is this design-savvy deli and cafe that subscribes to the farm-to-table ethos by telling customers all about its ingredients' provenance. The set meals are excellent value and the cool, artisan atmosphere makes it a prime spot to revive while you explore the area.

Call ahead or check its website for the weekly day off which changes occasionally.

Hagi Cafe CAFE ¥

(ハギカフェ; Map p110; ☎03-5832-9808; www.hagiso.jp; 3-10-25 Yanaka, Taitō-ku; mains ¥850-1445; ⊙8-10.30am & noon-9pm; Ⓢ Chiyoda line to Sendagi, exit 2) Part of the gallery and event space Hagiso, run by students from Tokyo University of the Arts (Geidai), this is a good all-rounder for meals, drinks and sweets in the heart of Yanaka. Its Japanese-style breakfast is a great deal at ¥325; later in the day there's curry, pasta, cakes and sundaes. Expect to wait on weekends as it's popular.

Hantei JAPANESE ¥¥

(はん亭; Map p110; ☎03-3287-9000; www.hantei.co.jp; 2-12-15 Nezu, Bunkyō-ku; lunch/dinner course ¥3200/4300; ⊙11.30am-3pm & 5-10pm, closed Mon; Ⓢ Chiyoda line to Nezu, exit 2) Housed in a beautifully wooden building from 1909, Hantei is a local landmark. It serves courses of *kushiage* (meat, fish and vegetables deep-fried in oil like tempura but coated in panko rather than batter) with palate-cleansing raw vegetables and miso dip on the side. The lunch set comes with eight skewers, dinner with 12, after which you can decide to order more.

Sasa-no-Yuki TOFU ¥¥

(笹乃雪; Map p110; ☎03-3873-1145; www.sasanoyuki.com; 2-15-10 Negishi, Taitō-ku; lunch/dinner course from ¥2400/5600; ⊙11.30am-8.30pm, closed Mon; JR Yamanote line to Uguisudani, north exit) Sasa-no-Yuki opened its doors in the Edo period and continues to serve its signature dishes with tofu made fresh every morning using water from the shop's own well. Some treats to expect: *ankake-dofu* (tofu in a thick, sweet sauce) and *goma-dofu* (sesame tofu). Vegetarians should not assume everything is purely veggie – ask before ordering. There is bamboo out front.

The best-value lunch set (¥2400) is served from 11.30am to 2pm Tuesday to Friday.

Shinsuke IZAKAYA ¥¥

(シンスケ; Map p110; ☎03-3832-0469; 3-31-5 Yushima, Bunkyō-ku; dishes ¥660-2750, cover charge ¥400; ⊙5-9pm Mon-Fri, to 8pm Sat; Ⓢ Chiyoda line to Yushima, exit 3) In business since 1925, Shinsuke has honed the concept of an ideal *izakaya* (Japanese pub-eatery) to perfection: long cedar counter, 'master' in *happi* (traditional short coat) and *hachimaki* (traditional headband), and smooth-as-silk *daiginjō* (premium-grade sake). The menu, updated monthly, includes house specialities (such as *kitsune raclette* – deep-fried tofu stuffed with raclette cheese) and seasonal dishes. Reservations recommended; cash only.

Also, unlike other storied *izakaya* that can be intimidating to foreigners, the staff here are friendly and go out of their way to explain the menu in English.

Asakusa & Ryōgoku

For more dining options east of the Sumida-gawa check www.oishii-sumida.tokyo.

Misojyu JAPANESE ¥

(Map p112; ☎03-5830-3101; www.misojyu.jp; 1-7-5 Asakusa, Taitō-ku; meal set ¥860-1400; ⊙8.30am-7pm; Ⓢ Ginza line to Asakusa, exit 1) When you just want something simple, filling and delicious: choose a soup (say, mushroom miso soup or a chunky pork soup with root vegetables) and an *onigiri* (rice ball; maybe stuffed with grilled salmon or pickled plum) and take a seat inside this stylish, cafe-style spot. Everything's organic. Come before 10am for the breakfast special (¥600).

★Onigiri Yadoroku JAPANESE ¥

(おにぎり 浅草 宿六; Map p112; ☎03-3874-1615; www.onigiriyadoroku.com; 3-9-10 Asakusa, Taitō-ku; set lunch 2/3 onigiri from ¥750/1010, onigiri ¥310-760; ⊙11.30am-5pm Mon-Sat, 6pm-2am Thu-Tue; Ⓢ Ginza line to Asakusa, exit 1) *Onigiri*, rice moulded into triangle and wrapped in sheets of *nori* (seaweed) is Japan's ultimate snack. You know, the ones at the convenience store; try them at Tokyo's oldest *onigiri* shop (opened in 1954), made-to-order with the high-grade rice still warm and the *nori* still deliciously crisp. Lunch sets include miso soup. Onigiri Yadoroku will close early when it runs out of rice.

Hosokawa SOBA ¥

(ほそ川; Map p92; ☎03-3626-1125; www.edosoba-hosokawa.jp; 1-6-5 Kamezawa, Sumida-ku; soba ¥1080-2650; ⊙11.45am-2.30pm & 5.30-8.30pm Tue-Sun, closed 3rd Tue of the month; Ⓡ JR Sōbu line to Ryōgoku, east exit) Chef Hosokawa Takashi grinds buckwheat fresh daily for the soba he kneads and cuts by hand. Get them in hot broth *(kake-soba)* or at room temperature on a bamboo tray *(seiro)* – and definitely with a side of crisp, seasonal tempura. With ochre walls and wildflowers on the table, Hosokawa brings a touch of country to the city.

No reservations and no small children.

Sometarō OKONOMIYAKI ¥

(染太郎; Map p112; ☎03-3844-9502; 2-2-2 Nishi-Asakusa, Taitō-ku; mains ¥700-1300; ⊙noon-10pm, closed irregularly; Ⓢ Ginza line to Tawaramachi, exit 3) Sometarō is a fun and funky place to try *okonomiyaki* (savoury Japanese-style pancakes filled with meat, seafood and vegetables that you cook yourself). This historic, vine-covered house is a friendly spot where the menu includes a how-to guide for novice cooks. Tatami seating; cash only. If it closes, it's often on a Tuesday or a Wednesday.

Daikokuya TEMPURA ¥

(大黒家; Map p112; ☎03-3844-1111; www.tempura.co.jp; 1-38-10 Asakusa, Taitō-ku; meals ¥1550-2100; ⊙11am-8.30pm; Ⓢ Ginza line to Asakusa, exit 1) This is the place to get old-fashioned tempura fried in pure sesame oil, an Asakusa speciality. It's in a white building with a tile roof. If there's a queue (and there often is), you can try your luck at the annex one block over.

★Kappō Yoshiba JAPANESE ¥¥

(割烹吉葉; Map p92; ☎03-3623-4480; www.kapou-yoshiba.jp; 2-14-5 Yokoami, Sumida-ku; dishes ¥650-7800; ⊙11.30am-2pm & 5-10pm Mon-Sat; Ⓢ Ōedo line to Ryōgoku, exit 1) The former Miyagino sumo stable is the location for this one-of-a-kind restaurant that has preserved the *dōyō* (practice ring) as its centrepiece. Playing up to its sumo roots, you can order the protein-packed stew *chanko-nabe* (for two people from ¥5200), but Yoshiba's real strength is its sushi, freshly prepared in jumbo portions.

The lunch *nigiri* set menu (¥1000) is a bargain, but you'll probably want to come in the evening when the *dōyō* becomes a stage for traditional live-music performances.

At 7.30pm on Monday, Wednesday, Friday and Saturday, former wrestlers sing *sumo jinku* (a type of folk song) for 15 minutes, while at 7pm on Tuesday and Thursday the female duo Kitamura Shimai plays a short concert on *shamisen* (three-stringed instruments resembling a lute or banjo). This is followed at 8pm by a pianist tinkling the ivories on the grand piano by the sushi counter (and stained-glass window of a sumo wrestler!).

★Asakusa Imahan JAPANESE ¥¥¥

(浅草今半; Map p112; ☎03-3841-1114; www.asakusaimahan.co.jp; 3-1-12 Nishi-Asakusa, Taitō-ku; lunch/dinner from ¥4200/8800; ⊙11.30am-9.30pm; Ⓢ Ginza line to Asakusa, exit 1) Among the oldest and most famous of Tokyo's *wagyū* (Japanese beef) restaurants, Imahan (in business since 1895), specialises in courses of sukiyaki and *shabu-shabu*, thin slices of marbled beef are cooked in hot broth at your table (followed up with vegetables and noodles). For sukiyaki, the broth has a deeper soy sauce flavour and the cooked meat is dipped in raw egg yolk.

Diners on a budget should arrive early for one of the 20 limited servings of a *gyūdon* (rice topped with beef; ¥1500) and other affordable options at lunch. Reservations recommended for courses.

Shinjuku & Around

Should you want to grab a quick bite to eat – without having to brave the crowded streets – head to one of the food courts on the top floors of the shopping centres in and around Shinjuku Station. **Takashimaya Restaurant Park** (レストランズパーク; Map p146; www.restaurants-park.jp; 12-14 fl, Takashimaya Times Sq; 11am-11pm; JR Yamanote line to Shinjuku, new south exit) has the nicest options.

Ohitotsuzen Tanbo JAPANESE ¥

(おひつ膳田んぼ; Map p92; 03-3320-0727; www.tanbo.co.jp; 1-41-9 Yoyogi, Shibuya-ku; meals ¥1580-2400; 11am-10pm; JR Yamanote line to Yoyogi, west exit) The speciality here is the least glamorous part of the meal – the rice, which comes from an organic farm the restaurant manages in Niigata Prefecture. It's served as *ochazuke,* a classic comfort food of rice topped with meat or fish, over which hot tea is poured. English instructions explain how to eat it. It's walkable from the south side of Shinjuku, with white door curtains out front.

Nagi RAMEN ¥

(凪; Map p146; 03-3205-1925; www.n-nagi.com; 2nd fl, Golden Gai G2, 1-1-10 Kabukichō, Shinjuku-ku; ramen ¥950-1350; 24hr; JR Yamanote line to Shinjuku, east exit) Nagi, once an edgy upstart in the ramen world, now has branches around the city. This tiny shop is one of the originals, located up a treacherous stairway in Golden Gai. It's still our favourite (we're clearly not alone as there's often a line). The house speciality is *niboshi* ramen (egg noodles in a broth flavoured with dried sardines). Look for the sign with a red circle.

Nakajima KAISEKI ¥

(中嶋; Map p146; 03-3356-4534; www.shinjyuku-nakajima.com; basement fl, 3-32-5 Shinjuku, Shinjuku-ku; lunch/dinner from ¥800/8640; 11.30am-2pm & 5.30-9.30pm Mon-Sat; S Marunouchi line to Shinjuku-sanchōme, exit A1) In the evening, Nakajima serves exquisite *kaiseki* (Japanese haute cuisine) dinners. On weekdays, it also serves a set lunch of humble *iwashi* (sardines) for one-tenth the price; in the hands of Nakajima's chefs, they're divine. The line for lunch starts to form shortly before the restaurant opens at 11.30am. Look for the white sign at the top of the stairs.

Berg CAFE ¥

(ベルグ; Map p146; www.berg.jp; basement fl, Lumine Est, 3-38-1 Shinjuku, Shinjuku-ku; morning set ¥410; 7am-11pm; JR Yamanote line to Shinjuku, east exit) Wedged inside the fashion-forward Lumine Est department store (itself inside the frenetic Shinjuku Station), Berg stands still. The cramped, cult-status coffee shop still charges just ¥216 for a cup (and ¥324 for a beer). The highly recommended 'morning set' *(mōningu setto),* served until noon, includes coffee, hard-boiled egg, potato salad and toast. The front is covered in picture menus.

Exiting the east exit ticket gates in JR Shinjuku Station, look for the 'Food Pocket' sign off to the left.

★Kanae IZAKAYA ¥¥

(鼎; Map p146; 050-3467-1376; basement fl, 3-12-12 Shinjuku, Shinjuku-ku; cover charge ¥550; dishes ¥660-1980; 5pm-midnight Mon-Sat, 4.30-11pm Sun; JR Yamanote line to Shinjuku, east exit) Kanae is a perfect example of one of Shinjuku-sanchōme's excellent and all but undiscoverable *izakaya:* delicious sashimi, seasonal dishes, simple staples (the potato salad is famous) and excellent sake in the basement of an unremarkable building (look for the white sign and then the cedar frond ball over the staircase). Seating is at the counter or at a handful of tables; reservations recommended.

Donjaca IZAKAYA ¥¥

(呑者家; Map p146; 03-3341-2497; 3-9-10 Shinjuku, Shinjuku-ku; cover charge ¥300, dishes ¥350-1000; 5pm-7am; S Marunouchi line to Shinjuku-sanchōme, exit C6) Donjaca, in business since 1979, has many telltale signs of a classic Shōwa-era (1926–89) *izakaya* (Japanese pub-eatery): red vinyl stools, lantern lighting and hand-written menus covering the wall. The food is equal parts classic (grilled fish and fried chicken) and inventive: a house speciality is *nattō gyōza* (dumplings stuffed with fermented soybeans). Excellent sake, too.

Warning: Donjaca can get smoky. If the main shop is full, staff will likely direct you around the corner to the larger annex.

★Kozue JAPANESE ¥¥¥

(梢; Map p146; 03-5323-3460; www.hyatt.com; 40th fl, Park Hyatt Tokyo, 3-7-1-2 Nishi-Shinjuku, Shinjuku-ku; lunch set menu ¥2530-11,000, dinner set menu ¥14,300-29,700; 11.30am-2.30pm & 5.30-9.30pm; S Ōedo line to Tochōmae, exit A4) It's hard to beat Kozue's combination of exquisite seasonal Japanese cuisine, artisan crockery and distractingly good views over Shinjuku. As the kimono-clad staff speak English and the restaurant caters well to dietary restrictions and personal preferences, this is a good splurge spot for diners who don't want to give up complete control. Reservations essential for dinner and recommended for lunch; 15% service charge.

The cheaper lunch options are only available on weekdays, when, for an extra ¥1000, you can follow your meal with coffee and dessert at the hotels's **Peak Lounge & Bar** (☎03-5323-3461; http://restaurants.tokyo.park.hyatt.co.jp/en/pbr.html; 41st fl, Park Hyatt; ⏰5-11.30pm).

Harajuku & Aoyama

Maisen TONKATSU ¥
(まい泉; Map p116; ☎0120-428-485; www.mai-sen.com; 4-8-5 Jingūmae, Shibuya-ku; lunch/dinner from ¥1000/1600; ⏰11am-10.45pm; 👪; Ⓢ Ginza line to Omote-sandō, exit A2) Maisen is famous both for its *tonkatsu* (breaded, deep-fried pork cutlets) and its setting (an old public bathhouse). There are different grades of pork on the menu, including prized *kurobuta* (black pig), but even the cheapest is melt-in-your-mouth divine; the very reasonable lunch set is served until 4pm. The *ebi-katsu* (breaded, deep-fried prawns), are excellent, too.

A takeaway window (10am to 7pm) serves delicious *tonkatsu sando* (tonkatsu sandwiches; from ¥430). There are branches (this is the main shop) all over town and many department store food halls sell Maisen sandwiches – always a great meal in a pinch.

Harajuku Gyōza-rō DUMPLINGS ¥
(原宿餃子楼; Map p116; 6-4-2 Jingūmae, Shibuya-ku; 6 gyōza ¥290; ⏰11.30am-4.30am Mon-Sat, to 10pm Sun; 🚉JR Yamanote line to Harajuku, Omote-sandō exit) *Gyōza* (dumplings) are the only thing on the menu here, but you won't hear any complaints from the regulars who queue up to get their fix. Have them *sui* (boiled) or *yaki* (pan-fried), with or without *niniku* (garlic) or *nira* (chives) – they're all delicious. Expect to wait on weekends or at lunchtime, but the line moves quickly.

Commune MARKET ¥
(Map p116; https://commune.tokyo; 3-13 Minami-Aoyama, Minato-ku; ⏰9.30am-8pm; Ⓢ Ginza line to Omote-sandō, exit A4) Commune is a food and event space, with a daily farmers market plus vendors selling fresh bread, curry, cold-pressed juice and herbal teas to eat and drink at one of the shared picnic tables. Lots of events are held here, including the pop-up hipster fleamarket **Raw Tokyo** (www.rawtokyo.jp); check their instagram for more (@commune_omotesando). Tents and tarps make it doable even on a rainy day.

FOOD ON THE GO

Heading off on the *shinkansen* (bullet train)? The basement of department store **Daimaru** (大丸; Map p96; ☎03-3212-8011; www.daimaru.co.jp/tokyo; 1-9-1 Marunouchi, Chiyoda-ku; ⏰10am-8pm, restaurants 11am-11pm; 🚉JR lines to Tokyo, Yaesu exit), on the eastern Yaesu side of Tokyo Station, is the best place to pick up *bentō* (boxed meals) for the journey.

For bus trips departing from Shinjuku Bus Terminal (p159) or before catching the Narita Express, there are a number of good takeaway vendors inside Shinjuku Station, just before the New South exit ticket gates.

Sakura-tei OKONOMIYAKI ¥
(さくら亭; Map p116; ☎03-3479-0039; www.sakuratei.co.jp; 3-20-1 Jingūmae, Shibuya-ku; okonomiyaki ¥1050-1500; ⏰11am-midnight; 📶🖉; 🚉JR Yamanote line to Harajuku, Takeshita exit) Grill your own *okonomiyaki* (savoury pancakes) at this funky place inside the gallery Design Festa (p109). In addition to classic options (with pork, squid and cabbage), there are some fun fusion-style ones. There's also a great-value, two-hour, all-you-can-eat plan (¥2500 plus one drink order).

Gomaya Kuki ICE CREAM ¥
(ごまや　くき; Map p116; http://gomayakuki.jp; 4-6-9 Jingūmae, Shibuya-ku; 2 scoops ¥550; ⏰11am-7pm; 🚉JR Yamanote line to Harajuku, Omote-sandō exit) *Goma* (sesame) ice cream is a must-try and this takeaway stand is the place to try it. There are two varieties, made from high-grade *kurogoma* (黒ごま; black sesame) or *shirogoma* (白ごま; white sesame), both from Mie Prefecture.

Mominoki House JAPANESE ¥¥
(もみの木ハウス; Map p116; www.mominoki-house.net; 2-18-5 Jingūmae, Shibuya-ku; lunch course ¥980-1480, dinner course ¥4500; ⏰11am-3pm & 5-10pm Mon-Sat, to 9pm Sun; 🖉; 🚉JR Yamanote line to Harajuku, Takeshita exit) 🌿 This pioneering macrobiotic restaurant has been running since 1976, long enough to see many a Harajuku trend come and go (and to see some famous visitors, like Sir Paul McCartney). Chef Yamada's menu is heavily vegan, but also includes free-range chicken and *Ezo shika* (Hokkaidō venison). Inside, the restaurant looks like a grown-up tree fort and features several cosy, semiprivate booths.

Agaru Sagaru Nishi-iru Higashi-iru JAPANESE ¥¥

(上下西東; Map p116; ☎03-3403-6968; basement fl, 3-25-8 Jingūmae, Shibuya-ku; small plates ¥500-900, dinner course ¥3500-5000; ⊙5.30-11.30pm Tue-Sun; 🚉JR Yamanote line to Harajuku, Takeshita exit) This chill little restaurant serves Kyoto-style food (deceptively simple, with the ingredients – always seasonal – taking centre stage) without pretense. The five-dish course (¥3500) – presented in succession and prettily plated – is perfect for when you want to indulge, but not too much. (The seven-dish course requires advance reservations.) Also, it looks like a cave.

★Eatrip BISTRO ¥¥¥

(Map p116; ☎03-3409-4002; www.restaurant-eatrip.com; 6-31-10 Jingūmae, Shibuya-ku; lunch/dinner course ¥2500/¥5500-8800; ⊙6pm-midnight Tue-Sat, 11.30am-3pm Sat, 11.30am-5pm Sun; 🚉JR Yamanote line to Harajuku, Omote-sandō exit) Eatrip is one of the big players in Tokyo's farm-to-table organic movement. Chef Shiraishi Takayuki works closely with domestic producers and his cooking is more about coaxing out the natural flavours than embellishment. The food is ostesibly Japanese but with some international inspiration. Sample dish: *mahata* (grouper; from Mie Prefecture) sautéed with harissa (made in-house), squid ink and *daikon* (radish).

When you find it (it's a little tricky; it's a house entered via a stone path past a flower shop), you'll be surprised that such a peaceful spot exists in Harajuku. Flowers from the adjacent shop adorn the interior. Bio wines by the glass (¥1000-2000). Course menu only; reserve ahead.

Shibuya

Sagatani SOBA ¥

(嵯峨谷; Map p138; 2-25-7 Dōgenzaka, Shibuya-ku; noodles from ¥320; ⊙24hr; 🚉JR Yamanote line to Shibuya, Hachikō exit) Proving that Tokyo is only expensive for those who don't know better, this all-night joint serves up bamboo steamers of delicious noodles for just ¥320. You won't regret 'splurging' on the *goma-dare soba* (ごまだれそば; buckwheat noodles with sesame dipping sauce) for ¥450. Look for the stone mill in the window and order from the vending machine.

Food Show SUPERMARKET ¥

(フードショー; Map p138; basement fl, Tokyu Department Store, 2-24-1 Shibuya, Shibuya-ku; ⊙10am-9pm; 🖉; 🚉JR Yamanote line to Shibuya, Hachikō exit) A best friend to harried and hungry commuters, Food Show has steamers of dumplings, crisp *karaage* (deep-fried chicken), sushi sets and heaps of salads from which to choose, all packaged to go. It's in the basement of Shibuya Station; look for the green signs near Hachikō and in the station pointing downstairs.

d47 Shokudō JAPANESE ¥

(d47食堂; Map p138; www.hikarie8.com; 8th fl, Shibuya Hikarie, 2-21-1 Shibuya, Shibuya-ku; meals ¥1680-1980; ⊙11.30am-2.30pm & 6-10.30pm; 🚉JR Yamanote line to Shibuya, east exit) There are 47 prefectures in Japan and d47 serves a changing line-up of *teishoku* (set meals) that evoke the specialities of each, from the fermented tofu of Okinawa to the stuffed squid of Hokkaidō. A larger menu of small plates is available in the evening; tea and coffee served in the afternoon hours.

Gyūkatsu Motomura TONKATSU ¥

(牛かつ もと村; Map p138; ☎03-3797-3735; www.gyukatsu-motomura.com; basement fl, 3-18-10 Shibuya, Shibuya-ku; set meal from ¥1300; ⊙10am-10pm; 🚉JR Yamanote line to Shibuya, east exit) You know *tonkatsu,* the deep-fried breaded pork cutlet that is a Japanese staple; meet *gyūkatsu,* the deep-fried breaded beef cutlet and currently much-hyped dish. At Motomura, diners get a small individual grill to cook the meat to their liking. Set meals include cabbage, rice and soup. It's just off Meiji-dōri, at the southern end of Shibuya Stream.

Motomura is exceedingly popular, with queues common. It has since opened other shops in Shibuya and around Tokyo to handle the overflow; check online for locations.

Katsu Midori SUSHI ¥¥

(活美登利; Map p138; ☎03-5728-4282; www.katumidori.co.jp; 8th fl, Seibu Bldg A, 21-1 Udagawa-chō, Shibuya-ku; ⊙11am-11pm; 👪; 🚉JR Yamanote line to Shibuya, Hachikō exit) This *kaiten-zushi* (conveyor-belt sushi restaurant) iis known to be far better than average, so there's nearly always a queue. Go at nontypical meal times (also convenient when you get hungry outside typical meal times). The menu is huge, including lots of non-seafood items; especially tasty is the sushi served *aburi* style – lightly seared with a blowtorch.

DON'T MISS

YOKOCHŌ: TOKYO'S EATING & DRINKING ALLEYS

Tokyo has (yet!) to completely erase all traces of an older city, the one of narrow alleyways and wooden buildings. Some of clusters of alleys – *yokochō* (literally 'side town') – harbour tiny restaurants and bars, and spending an evening in one is a must-do local experience. Two classic examples:

Omoide-yokochō (思い出横丁; Map p146; Nishi-Shinjuku 1-chōme, Shinjuku-ku; varies by shop; JR Yamanote line to Shinjuku, west exit) Literally 'Memory Lane' (and less politely known as Shonben-yokochō, or 'Piss Alley'), this Shinjuku landmark started as a post war black market and somehow managed to stick around. There are dozens of small restaurants, mostly serving *yakitori* (chicken, and other meats or vegetables, grilled on skewers), packed into the alley here; several have English menus.

Nonbei-yokochō (のんべえ横丁; Map p138; www.nonbei.tokyo; Shibuya 1-chōme, Shibuya-ku; JR Yamanote line to Shibuya, Hachikō exit) Shibuya's 'Drunkard's Alley' in the shadow of the elevated JR tracks. Note that some of the bars have cover charges (usually ¥500 to ¥1000). **Tight** (タイト; 2nd fl, 1-25-10 Shibuya, Shibuya-ku; 6pm-2am Mon-Sat; JR Yamanote line to Shibuya, Hachikō exit) is one that doesn't.

Maru Bengara JAPANESE ¥¥

(圓 弁柄; Map p138; 03-6427-7700; www.maru-mayfont.jp; 3rd fl, Shibuya Stream, 3-21-3 Shibuya, Shibuya-ku; lunch set ¥1265-3830, dinner course from ¥5500, small dishes ¥770-1700; 11am-3pm & 5-11pm; S Ginza line to Shibuya, exit 16b, JR Yamanote line to Shibuya, new south exit) Maru is a meal made easy: at lunch the restaurant does good grilled fish *teishoku* (set meals), among other things; in the evenings, courses with sashimi, seasonal sides, a main of meat or fish and a choice of Japanese-style desserts. If you want something lighter, you can also order small dishes (like grilled mushrooms or honeyed walnuts) designed to go with sake.

Matsukiya HOTPOT ¥¥¥

(松木家; Map p138; 03-3461-2651; 6-8 Maruyama-chō, Shibuya-ku; meals from ¥5400; 5-11pm Mon-Sat; JR Yamanote line to Shibuya, Hachikō exit) There are only two things on the menu at Matsukiya, established in 1890: *sukiyaki* (thinly sliced beef cooked in sake, soy and vinegar broth, and dipped in raw egg) and *shabu-shabu* (thin slices of beef or pork swished in hot broth and dipped in a citrusy soy or sesame sauce). The beef is top-grade *wagyū* from Ōmi. Meals include veggies and noodles cooked in the broths.

There's a white sign out front and the entrance is up some stairs. Reservations recommended.

★Narukiyo IZAKAYA ¥¥¥

(なるきよ; Map p116; 03-5485-2223; Basement fl, 2-7-14 Shibuya, Shibuya-ku; dishes ¥700-2700; 6pm-12.30am, closed irregularly; S Ginza line to Omotesando, exit B3) Narukiyo is many people's favourite 'secret' *izakaya*, serving all the classics (sashimi, charcoal grilled chicken, etc) with a low-key attitude that bellies the excellence of the food. It also comes with a side order of punk-rock cheek (the Pogues' Shane MacGowan is a regular). The menu, which changes daily, is handwritten on a scroll and undecipherable.

Sit at the counter (the best spot, anyway) and point, or leave the ordering up to chef Narukiyo Yoshida. Reservations recommended.

Ebisu & Meguro

There are lots of small, chef-run restaurants in this part of town. There's a lot of experimentation too, and many shops that started out here have gone on to open branches around the city, setting new dining trends along the way. What there isn't is pretence: many of the best restaurants in these districts are casual and moderately priced.

★Tonki TONKATSU ¥

(とんき; Map p120; 03-3491-9928; 1-1-2 Shimo-Meguro, Meguro-ku; meals ¥2100; 4-10.45pm Wed-Mon, closed 3rd Mon of the month; JR Yamanote line to Meguro, west exit) Tonki is a Tokyo *tonkatsu* (crumbed pork cutlet) legend, deep-frying with an unchanged recipe for over 80 years. The seats at the long counter – where you can watch the perfectly choreographed chefs – are the most coveted. There is usually a queue (no

Shibuya

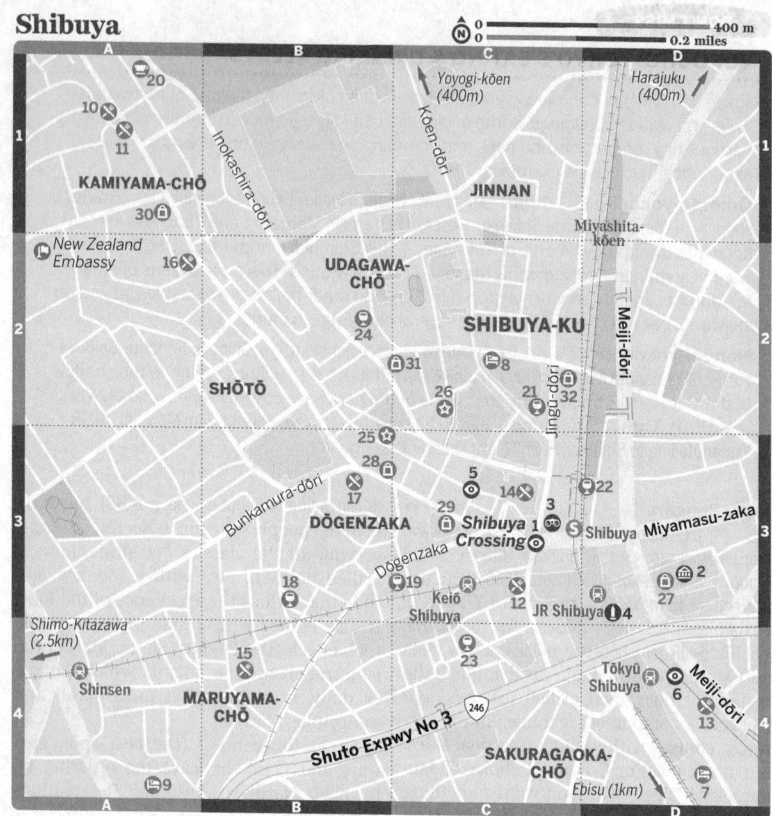

reservations accepted), but you can wait inside. There are tables upstairs for larger groups.

From the station, walk down Meguro-dōri, take a left at the first alley and look for a white sign and *noren* (doorway curtains) across the sliding doors.

Delifucious BURGERS ¥

(Map p120; ☎03-6809-0088; www.delifucious.com; 15-1 Udagawachō, Shibuya-ku; burgers from ¥1100; ⏲11am-11pm; 🚉JR Yamanote line to Shibuya, Hachikō exit) What happens when a former Ginza sushi chef turns his attention to – of all things – hamburgers? You get fish burgers and *anago* (seafaring eel) hot dogs prepared with the same attention to ingredients, preparation and presentation that you'd expect from a high-end sushi counter (but at a far more acceptable price). It's in the basement of **Shibuya Parco** (渋谷パルコ; https://shibuya.parco.jp; ⏲10am-9pm; 📶).

Afuri RAMEN ¥

(あふり; Map p120; www.afuri.com; 1-1-7 Ebisu, Shibuya-ku; ramen from ¥1080; ⏲11am-5am; 🖉; 🚉JR Yamanote line to Ebisu, east exit) Afuri has been a major player in the local ramen scene, making a strong case for a light touch with its signature *yuzu-shio* (a light, salty broth flavoured with *yuzu*, a type of citrus) ramen. They also do a vegan ramen (¥1380). It's since opened branches around the city, but this industrial-chic Ebisu shop is the original. Order from the touchscreen machine.

Rangmang Shokudō SHOKUDO ¥

(らんまん食堂; Map p120; ☎03-5489-4129; www.rangmang.com; 1-4-1 Ebisu-nishi, Shibuya-ku; dishes ¥460-660; ⏲11.30am-2.30pm & 6pm-midnight Mon-Fri, noon-2.30pm & 5-9.30pm Sat; 🚉JR Yamanote line to Ebisu) Fried chicken – which in Japan is lightly coated in a very fine starch – is having a moment and Rangmang

Shibuya

Top Sights
1 Shibuya Crossing C3

Sights
2 d47 Museum D3
3 Mag's Park C3
4 Myth of Tomorrow D3
5 Shibuya Center-gai C3
6 Shibuya Stream D4

Sleeping
7 Hotel Mets Shibuya D4
8 Millennials C2
Shibuya Stream Excel Hotel Tokyu .... (see 6)
9 Turntable A4

Eating
10 Ahiru Store A1
11 Camelback A1
d47 Shokudō .... (see 2)
12 Food Show C3
13 Gyūkatsu Motomura D4
14 Katsu Midori C3
Maru Bengara .... (see 6)
15 Matsukiya B4
16 Pignon A2
17 Sagatani B3

Drinking & Nightlife
18 Beat Cafe B3
19 Contact C3
20 Fuglen Tokyo A1
21 Karaoke Rainbow C2
22 Nonbei-yokochō D3
23 Oath C4
24 Rhythm Cafe B2

Entertainment
25 Club Quattro B3
26 WWW C2

Shopping
27 d47 design travel store D3
28 Mega Donki B3
29 Shibuya 109 .... C3
30 Shibuya Publishing & Booksellers A1
31 Tokyu Hands C2
32 Tower Records C2

Shokudō has a lot to do with that. Each order comes with four or five large bites, so you can eat light or go all out and sample several flavours. Staff recommend starting out with the classic *shio* (salt).

Ebisu-yokochō STREET FOOD ¥

(恵比寿横町; Map p120; www.ebisu-yokocho.com; 1-7-4 Ebisu, Shibuya-ku; 5pm-late; JR Yamanote line to Ebisu, east exit) Locals love this retro arcade chock-a-block with food stalls dishing up everything from humble *yaki-soba* (fried buckwheat noodles) to decadent *hotate-yaki* (grilled scallops). Seating is on stools; some of the tables are made from repurposed beer crates. It's loud and lively pretty much every night of the week; go early to get a table. Hours and prices vary by shop.

You won't find much English, but the adventurous can point at their fellow diners' dishes (you'll be sitting cheek-by-jowl with them). The entrance is marked with a rainbow-coloured sign.

Yakiniku Champion BARBECUE ¥¥

(焼肉チャンピオン; Map p120; 03-5768-6922; www.yakiniku-champion.com; 1-2-8 Ebisu, Shibuya-ku; dishes ¥780-3300, course from ¥5600; 5pm-midnight; JR Yamanote line to Ebisu, west exit) Champion is one of Tokyo's best spots for *yakiniku* – literally 'grilled meat' and the Japanese term for Korean barbecue. The menu runs the gamut from sweetbreads to the choicest cuts of grade A5 *wagyū;* there's a diagram of the cuts as well as descriptions (in English). It's very popular; reservations recommended.

This is the main shop bur there are other branches, too; see the website.

Ippo IZAKAYA ¥¥

(一歩; Map p120; 03-3445-8418; www.sakana-bar-ippo.com; 2nd fl, 1-22-10 Ebisu, Shibuya-ku; cover charge ¥500, dishes ¥500-1750; 6pm-3am; JR Yamanote line to Ebisu, east exit) This mellow little *izakaya* (Japanese pub-eatery) specialises in simple pleasures: fish and sake (there's an English sign out front that says just that). The friendly chefs speak English and can help you decide what to have grilled, steamed, simmered or fried; if you can't decide, the ¥2500 (plus tax) set menu is great value. The entrance is up the wooden stairs.

Ta-im ISRAELI ¥¥

(タイーム; Map p120; 03-5424-2990; www.ta-imebisu.com; 1-29-16 Ebisu, Shibuya-ku; lunch from ¥1180, dinner mains ¥1580-2580; 11.30am-2.30pm & 6-11pm Thu-Tue; ; JR Yamanote line to Ebisu, east exit) This tiny Israeli bistro, run by expat Dan Zuckerman, regularly draws a crowd for its authentic felafel (four

LOCAL KNOWLEDGE

HOTSPOT TOMIGAYA

For years Tomigaya, a largely residential part of what's known as Oku-Shibuya ('deep Shibuya'), was a well-kept secret, but with more and more creative cafes, bistros and boutiques opening, the buzz is too great to contain. Take a break from the brashness of central Shibuya – just 15 minutes away on foot – to see what locals are so excited about.

Walking northwest from central Shibuya, along the Kamiyama-chō *shōtengai* (market street), parallel to Inokashira-dōri, the first landmark you'll pass is indie bookshop **Shibuya Publishing & Booksellers** (SPBS; Map p138; 03-5465-0588; www.shibuyabooks.co.jp; 17-3 Kamiyama-chō, Shibuya-ku; 11am-11pm Mon-Sat, to 10pm Sun; JR Yamanote line to Shibuya, Hachikō exit). There's a small selection of books in English here, and also other stuff, like totes and accessories from Japanese designers.

Soon after (and off to the left) is **Camelback** (キャメルバック; Map p138; www.camelback.tokyo; 42-2 Kamiyama-chō, Shibuya-ku; sandwiches ¥450-900; 8am-5pm Tue-Sun; ; Chiyoda line to Yoyogi-kōen, exit 2), a creative sandwich shop run by a young and savvy English-speaking crew (among them a trained sushi chef). Get the omelette sandwich, made with the same kind of fluffy, rolled omelette served at sushi restaurants. Seating is on the bench outside.

A couple blocks later (and one block over, towards Yoyogi-kōen) is **Fuglen Tokyo** (Map p138; www.fuglen.no; 1-16-11 Tomigaya, Shibuya-ku; 8am-10pm Mon & Tue, 8am-1am Wed-Sun; ; Chiyoda line to Yoyogi-kōen, exit 2), Tomigaya's principal gathering spot. It does coffee by day and some of the city's most creative cocktails (from ¥1250) by night (Wednesday to Sunday).

In the evenings, Tomigaya is known for its fun neo bistros. Try **Pignon** (ピニョン; Map p138; 03-3468-2331; www.pignontokyo.jp; 16-3 Kamiyama-chō, Shibuya-ku; dishes ¥1700-4200; 6.30-10.30pm Mon-Sat; JR Yamanote line to Shibuya, Hachikō exit) or **Ahiru Store** (アヒルストア; Map p138; 03-5454-2146; 1-19-4 Tomigaya, Shibuya-ku; dishes ¥900-2800; 6pm-midnight Mon-Fri, 3-9pm Sat; Chiyoda line to Yoyogi-kōen, exit 2).

for ¥680), schnitzel, hummus and more – washed down with wine from the Golan Heights (¥980). Call ahead in the evening (in English is fine) as it's often full. Lunch is pita sandwiches.

Odaiba & Tokyo Bay

The best place to eat around Tokyo Bay is at the new Toyosu Market (p114), which has several floors of restaurants. Odaiba's malls are packed with easy, though largely uninspiring, options.

Mosuke Dango SWEETS ¥

(茂助だんご; Map p125; 03-6633-0873; 2nd fl, Bldg 7, Toyosu Market, 6-6-1 Toyosu, Kōtō-ku; per piece from ¥170; 5.30am-1pm, closed Sun & market holidays; ; Yurikamome line to Shijō-mae) The original Mosuke, a street vendor, began making *dango* (soft rice-flour balls) in 1898, back when the fish market was in Nihombashi. Now on its third market, Mosuke Dango still serves its famous *shōyu dango* (with soy-sauce glaze) and *tsubuan dango* (made from chunky *azuki*-bean paste), but with the addition of a cafe eat-in space (*matcha* ¥500).

★Sushi Dai SUSHI ¥¥

(寿司大; Map p125; 03-6633-0042; 3rd fl, Bldg 6, Toyosu Market, 6-5-1 Toyosu, Kōtō-ku; course meal ¥4800; 5.30am-1pm, closed Sun & market holidays; Yurikamome line to Shijō-mae) There is no better-value sushi in Tokyo than the *omakase* (chef's choice) course here. The menu changes daily (and sometimes hourly), but you're guaranteed to get 10 pieces of *nigiri* (hand-pressed) sushi made from seafood picked up from the fish market downstairs, prepared one at a time, pre-seasoned to perfection (and with zero boring fillers). Expect to queue.

You can order à la carte, but considering each piece costs ¥500 to ¥800 (based on market rates), the course is the way to go; you also get to choose your last piece. The shop also offers a course for customers who can't eat raw fish (¥4500) and a smaller children's course (¥3000). Staff speak some English and you'll be dining with plenty of fellow travellers, but don't write this off as a tourist spot – locals love it, too.

Cash-only Sushi Dai is one of the shops that made the move from Tsukiji to Toyosu; there's a big photo of the old shop on the wall. It's in the same building as the intermediate wholesalers market. Sushi Dai closes the same days as the market so check the market schedule online.

★Daiwa Sushi SUSHI ¥¥

(大和寿司; Map p125; ☎03-6633-0220; 1st fl, Bldg 5, Toyosu Market, 6-3-1 Toyosu, Kōtō-ku; course meal from ¥4400; ⏰5.30am-1pm, closed Sun & market holidays; Yurikamome line to Shijō-mae) One of Tsukiji's most famous sushi restaurants has made the move to the new Toyosu Market. The course meal includes seven pieces of *nigiri* (hand-pressed) sushi and one roll – all made with premium seafood. If you're still hungry you can order more sushi à la carte (¥300 to ¥800 per piece). Go early (before 9am), or there might be a queue.

Following the promenade from Shijō-mae to the fruit and vegetable market, look for a set of stairs (and an elevator) heading down. Daiwa Sushi is on the ground floor here, with blue door curtains.

Bills INTERNATIONAL ¥¥

(ビルズ; Map p125; www.bills-jp.net; 3rd fl, Seaside Mall, DECKS Tokyo Beach, 1-6-1 Daiba, Minato-ku; breakfast & lunch mains ¥1425-2375, dinner mains ¥1650-2700; ⏰9am-10pm Mon-Fri, 8am-10pm Sat & Sun; Yurikamome line to Odaiba Kaihin-kōen) Australian chef Bill Granger has had a big hit with his restaurant chain in Japan – unsurprising given how inviting and spacious a place this is. The menu includes his breakfast classics, like creamy scrambled eggs and ricotta hotcakes, and lunch and dinner mains like *wagyū* burgers and prawn and chilli linguine. The terrace has great bay views.

Drinking & Nightlife

Roppongi, Shibuya and Shinjuku are tops for a big night out. All have a high concentration of bars, music venues and karaoke parlours; Shibuya is best for clubs. Fridays and Saturdays are the big nights out, though you'll find people in bars most nights of the week. Most clubs don't get going until after midnight (and can keep going past dawn). You'll need to show photo ID to enter.

Marunouchi & Nihombashi

Chashitsu Kaboku TEAHOUSE

(茶室 嘉木; Map p96; ☎03-6212-0202; www.ippodo-tea.co.jp; 3-1-1 Marunouchi, Chiyoda-ku; tea ¥990-2090; ⏰11am-7pm; JR Yamanote line to Yurakuchō, Tokyo International Forum exit) Run by famed Kyoto tea producer Ippōdō, which celebrated 300 years of business in 2017, this teahouse is a fantastic place to sample top-quality *o-cha* (green tea). It's also one of the few places that serves *koicha* (thick tea), which is even thicker than ordinary *matcha* (powdered green tea). Add on a seasonal *wagashi* (Japanese sweet, ¥440) or two.

Toyama Bar BAR

(トヤマバー; Map p96; ☎03-6262-2723; www.toyamakan.jp; 1-2-6 Nihombashi-Muromachi, Chūō-ku; ⏰11am-9pm; S Ginza line to Mitsukoshimae, exit B5) This stylish, contemporary counter bar offers a selection of sakes from 17 different breweries located throughout Japan's Toyama prefecture, across the alps from Tokyo and bordering the Japan Sea. A set of three 30mL cups costs a bargain ¥700 (90mL cups from ¥700 each). English tasting notes are available.

It's part of the Nihonbashi Toyama-kan (日本橋とやま館), which promotes goods from the prefecture. Pick up a bottle of anything you like at the attached shop.

Ginza & Tsukiji

★Ginza Music Bar COCKTAIL BAR

(Map p96; ☎03-3572-3666; www.ginzamusicbar.com; 4F Brownplace, 7-8-13 Ginza, Chūō-ku; cover charge after midnight ¥1000; ⏰6pm-4am Mon-Sat; S Ginza line to Shimbashi, exits 1 & 3) A superb sound system showcases the 3000-plus vinyl collection that ranges from the likes of cool classic jazz to contemporary electronica. There are deep-blue walls and comfy seats in which to enjoy inventive cocktails (starting from ¥1400), such as the *matcha* and wasabi martini.

★Cha Ginza TEAHOUSE

(茶・銀座; Map p96; ☎03-3571-1211; www.uogashi-meicha.co.jp; 5-5-6 Ginza, Chūō-ku; ⏰teahouse noon-5pm Tue-Sat, shop 11am-6pm Tue-Sat; S Ginza line to Ginza, exit B3) Take a pause for afternoon tea (¥700 to ¥1400) at this slick contemporary tea salon. The menu is seasonal, but will likely include a cup of perfectly prepared *matcha* (powdered green tea) and a small sweet or two, or a choice of *sencha* (premium green tea). The ground-floor shop sells top-quality teas from various growing regions in Japan.

Old Imperial Bar BAR

(Map p96; Mezzanine, Main Bldg, Imperial Hotel, 1-1-1 Uchisaiwai-chō, Chiyoda-ku; ⏰11.30am-midnight; S Hibiya line to Hibiya, exit A13) This is one of the few parts of the Imperial Hotel

DON'T MISS

BEST TOKYO BARS FOR...

- Craft beer: Popeye
- Drinks with a view: New York Bar (p144)
- Creative cocktails: Gen Yamamoto
- Date night: Two Rooms (p145)
- Japanese Whisky: Zoetrope (p144)

to feature some of the designs and materials used in the original 1923 Frank Lloyd Wright building (note the architectural drawing behind the cash desk). The vintage early 20th-century interior suits the menu of classic cocktails (around ¥1500, plust 10% service charge).

There's no seating charge, but 10% service is added to the bill.

Ginza Lion BEER HALL

(銀座ライオン; Map p96; 050-5269-7095; https://ginzalion.net; 7-9-20 Ginza, Chūō-ku; 11.30am-11pm, until 10.30pm Sun; S Ginza line to Ginza, exit A2) So what if Sapporo's beers are not among the best you can quaff in Tokyo? Dating to 1934, the gorgeous art deco design at Japan's oldest beer hall – including glass mosaic murals – is to die for. The oompah-pah atmosphere, with waiters ferrying frothy mugs and plates of Bavarian-style sausages to the tables, is also priceless.

Bongen Coffee COFFEE

(Map p96; 03-6264-3988; www.ginza-bongen.jp; 2-16-3 Ginza, Chūō-ku; 10am-8pm; ; S Asakusa or Hibiya line to Higashi-Ginza, exit A7) Down a side street of Higashi-Ginza is this tiny third-wave coffee shop serving single-estate brews with side orders of *onigiri* (Japanese rice balls) or sandwiches of raisins and cream. An elegant traditional Japanese design pervades with warm woods and a spotlit bonsai tree behind the espresso machine.

Nakajima no Ochaya TEAHOUSE

(中島の御茶屋; Map p96; 1-1 Hama-rikyū Onshi-teien, Chūō-ku; tea ¥510 or ¥720; 9am-4.30pm; Ōedo line to Shiodome, exit A1) This beautiful teahouse from 1704 (and rebuilt in 1983) stands elegantly on an island in the central pond at Hama-rikyū Onshi-teien (p91), reached via a long cedar bridge. It's an ideal spot for a cup of *matcha* (powdered green tea) and a sweet while contemplating the very faraway 21st century beyond the garden walls.

Roppongi & Around

★Gen Yamamoto COCKTAIL BAR

(ゲンヤマモト; Map p102; 03-6434-0652; www.genyamamoto.jp; 1-6-4 Azabu-Jūban, Minato-ku; 3-11pm, closed Sun & Mon; S Namboku line to Azabu-jūban, exit 7) Gen Yamamoto takes the seaonal tasting menu concept and applies it to cocktails. Here they're made with fruits and herbs, with the same kind of devotion to presentation seen at restaurants serving *kaiseki* (Japanese haute cuisine). Choose from sets of four (¥4800), six (¥6900) or seven (¥7800). Fear not, they're designed to be savoured, not to get you sozzled (servings are small).

The bar is just eight seats at a counter made from a 500-year-old Japanese oak. Reservations (possible from one week in advance) recommended; cover charge ¥1000.

Two Dogs Taproom CRAFT BEER

(Map p102; 03-5413-0333; www.twodogs-tokyo.com; 2nd fl, 3-15-24 Roppongi, Minato-ku; 11.30am-2.30pm Mon-Fri, 5-11pm Sun-Thu, until 2am Fri & Sat; ; S Hibiya line to Roppongi, exit 3) This popular expat hang-out in Roppongi has 24 taps, roughly half of which are devoted to Japanese craft beers. Pints (US-size) start at a reasonable (for Tokyo) ¥850. We recommend starting with the tasting set of four half-pints (¥2000), or go all in on the two-hour all-you-can-drink special (¥3600). The kitchen turns out decent pizzas and pub dishes to line your stomach.

Rise & Win Brewing Co. Kamikatz Taproom CRAFT BEER

(Map p102; 03-6441-3800; www.kamikatz.jp; The Workers & Co, 1st fl, 1-4-2 Higashi-azabu, Minato-ku; noon-3pm Mon-Fri, 6-11pm Mon Sat; S Hibiya line to Kamiyachō, exit 2) This craft-beer brewery is based in a village in Tokushima Prefecture, Shikoku, that has adopted a zero-waste program. The bar features an appealing mishmash of country cabin design, plus a light fixture made from recycled bottles. There's usually six types of beer on tap, including an IPA, a porter and a leuven white; a flight of four costs ¥1400.

It also serves food, including specialities from Tokushima such as the breaded and deep-fried fish paste cakes.

Kōrakuen & Kanda

★**Beer-Ma Kanda** CRAFT BEER
(びあマ神田; Map p106; 03-3527-1900; www.facebook.com/kanda.wbm; 1-6-4 Kajichō, Chiyoda-ku; 4-11pm Mon-Sat, 3-9pm Sun; JR lines to Kanda, south exit) Down an alley of sketchy-looking drinking dens is this nirvana for craft-beer lovers. It's principally a bottle shop stocking hundreds of different beer brands, all of which you can buy and drink on the premises (corkage ¥200). There's also eight taps of barrel beer available with servings in a range of sizes.

Ueno & Yanesen

Kayaba Coffee CAFE
(カヤバ珈琲; Map p110; 03-3823-3545; http://kayaba-coffee.com; 6-1-29 Yanaka, Taitō-ku; coffee ¥500; 8am-6pm, to 9pm Fri & Sat; S Chiyoda line to Nezu, exit 1) This vintage 1930s coffee shop (the building is actually from the '20s) in Yanaka is a hang-out for local students and artists. Come early before 11am to get ¥100 off your coffee when you order toast (from ¥400) or a breakfast sandwich (from ¥550).

Yanaka Beer Hall CRAFT BEER
(谷中ビアホール; Map p110; 03-5834-2381; www.facebook.com/yanakabeerhall; 2-15-6 Ueno-sakuragi, Taitō-ku; noon-8.30pm Tue-Fri, from 11am Sat & Sun; S Chiyoda line to Nezu, exit 1) Exploring Yanesen can be thirsty work so thank heavens for this craft-beer bar, a cosy place with some outdoor seating. It's part of a charming complex of old wooden buildings that also houses a bakery-cafe, a bistro and an events space. It has several brews on tap, including a Yanaka lager (¥970) that's only available here.

Asakusa & Ryōgoku

Popeye PUB
(ポパイ; Map p92; 03-3633-2120; www.lares.dti.ne.jp/~ppy; 2-18-7 Ryōgoku, Sumida-ku; 5-11.30pm Mon-Fri, from 3pm Sat; JR Sōbu line to Ryōgoku, west exit) Popeye boasts an astounding 70 beers on tap, including a huge selection of Japanese beers – from Echigo Weizen

LGBTIQ+ TOKYO

Tokyo has a small but very lively gay quarter, Shinjuku-nichōme – or just Nichōme, for short. (Outside this and a handful of other scattered bars, the gay scene is all but invisible.) Some reliably welcoming and fun spots:

Aiiro Cafe (Map p146; www.aliving.net; 2-18-1 Shinjuku, Shinjuku-ku; 6pm-2am Mon-Thu, to 5am Fri & Sat, to midnight Sun; S Marunouchi line to Shinjuku-sanchōme, exit C8) Aiiro (formerly known as Advocates) has long been a hub in Shinjuku-nichōme, and is a good place to get an evening started – thanks to the all-you-can-drink beer for ¥1000 happy-hour special from 6pm to 9pm daily. The bar itself is teeny-tiny; the action happens on the street corner outside, which swells to block-party proportions when the weather is nice.

Arty Farty (アーティファーティ; Map p146; 03-5362-9720; www.arty-farty.net; 2nd fl, 2-11-7 Shinjuku, Shinjuku-ku; 8pm-4am Sun-Thu, to 5am Fri & Sat; S Marunouchi line to Shinjuku-sanchōme, exit C8) A fixture on Tokyo's gay scene for many a moon, Arty Farty welcomes all in the community to come shake a tail feather on its (admittedly small) dance floor. It gets going later in the evening. Weekend events sometimes have a cover charge (¥1000 to ¥2000), which includes entrance to sister club, **The Annex**, around the corner. Drinks from ¥700.

Bar Goldfinger (Map p146; www.goldfingerparty.com; 2-12-11 Shinjuku, Shinjuku-ku; 6pm-2am, to 5am Fri & Sat; S Marunouchi line to Shinjuku-sanchōme, exit C8) Goldfinger is a long-running ladies' spot in Shinjuku-nichōme (but open to all, save for Saturdays). The bar has a lowbrow-chic decor designed to look like a '70s motel, a friendly vibe and fun events, like Friday-night karaoke. Drinks from ¥700; no cover unless there's an event.

Eagle (Map p146; www.eagletokyo.com; 2-12-3 Shinjuku, Shinjuku-ku; 6pm-1am, to 4am Fri & Sat; JR Yamanote line to Shinjuku, east exit) Eagle has established itself as a popular hang-out in Shinjuku-nichōme, thanks to friendly staff, happy-hour prices (¥500 drinks from 5pm to 8pm; otherwise they're ¥700), an outdoor patio, but especially the instantly iconic mural from proudly out manga artist Inuyoshi and . Pick up a free copy of the artist's bilingual manga *Nippondanji* here.

to Hitachino Nest Espresso Stout. Pints start from ¥1020, but the real value is the excellent tasting sets, from ¥1750 for 10 small glasses. It's extremely popular and fills up fast; get here early to grab a seat.

From the station's west exit, take a left on the main road and pass under the tracks; take the second left and look for Popeye on the right.

Kamiya Bar BAR

(神谷バー; Map p112; 03-3841-5400; www.kamiya-bar.com; 1-1-1 Asakusa, Taitō-ku; 11.30am-10pm, closed Tue; S Ginza line to Asakusa, exit 3) Kamiya is one of Tokyo's oldest bars (open since 1880) and still hugely popular – thanks largely to the one-litre *dai-jokki* (大ジョッキ; 'big cups') of Asahi lager that cost only ¥1120. But the more interesting thing to order is the house 'Denki Bran' (¥380), a century-old secret mix of brandy, gin, wine, curaçao and medicinal herbs. Order from the counter reception counter.

'Cuzn Homeground BAR

(カズンホームグラウンド; Map p112; 03-5246-4380; www.homeground.jpn.com; 2-17-9 Asakusa, Taitō-ku; beer ¥900; noon-5am; ; S Ginza line to Tawaramachi, exit 3) Run by a wild gang of local hippies, 'Cuzn is the kind of bar where anything can happen: a barbecue, a jam session or all-night karaoke, for example.

Shinjuku & Around

★Bar BenFiddich COCKTAIL BAR

(バーベンフィディック; Map p146; 03-6279-4223; 9th fl, 1-13-7 Nishi-Shinjuku, Shinjuku-ku; 6pm-2am, closed Sun; JR Yamanote line to Shinjuku, west exit) Bar BenFiddich is dark and tiny, with vials of infusions on the shelves and herbs hung to dry from the ceiling. The English-speaking barman, Kayama Hiroyasu, in a white suit, moves like a magician. There's no menu, so just tell him what you like and he'll concoct something delicious for you (we like the gimlet with herbs). Expect to pay around ¥2000 per drink.

There's no sign on the street, but it's the building in between the karaoke parlour and the curry shop. You'll see the wooden door when you exit the elevator. Reservations are only accepted between 6pm and 8pm, on the day or the day before. Otherwise it's first come first served, so you may have to wait.

★Zoetrope BAR

(ゾートロープ; Map p146; 03-3363-0162; 3rd fl, 7-10-14 Nishi-Shinjuku, Shinjuku-ku; 5pm-midnight Mon-Sat; JR Yamanote line to Shinjuku, west exit) A must-visit for whisky fans, Zoetrope has over a hundred varieties of Japanese whisky behind its small counter, including many hard-to-find bottles and already sold-out limited editions. Cover charge ¥600; the average pour is ¥1500 to ¥2000 (reasonable, considering the going price for Japanese whisky these days) and there are some good-value tasting flights, too. Larger groups should come before 7.30pm.

New York Bar BAR

(ニューヨークバー; Map p146; 03-5323-3458; http://restaurants.tokyo.park.hyatt.co.jp/en/nyb.html; 52nd fl, Park Hyatt Tokyo, 3-7-1-2 Nishi-Shinjuku, Shinjuku-ku; 5pm-midnight Sun-Wed, to 1am Thu-Sat; Ōedo line to Tochōmae, exit A4) Head to the Park Hyatt's 52nd floor to swoon over the sweeping nightscape from the floor-to-ceiling windows at this bar of *Lost in Translation* fame. There's a cover charge of ¥2500 if you visit or stay past 8pm (7pm Sunday), when live music is performed. Better yet: go early and watch the sky fade to black.

Cocktails start at ¥2640. Unfortunately, New York Bar doesn't take bookings (so the earlier you arrive the better chance you have of scoring a coveted window seat). Note: dress code enforced and 15% service charge levied.

Harajuku & Aoyama

★Sakurai Japanese Tea Experience TEAHOUSE

(櫻井焙茶研究所; Map p116; 03-6451-1539; www.sakurai-tea.jp; 5th fl, Spiral Bldg, 5-6-23 Minami-Aoyama, Minato-ku; tea from ¥1650, course from ¥4900; 11am-11pm; S Ginza line to Omote-sandō, exit B1) Tea master (and former bartender) Sakurai Shinya's contemporary teahouse is a must-visit for anyone hoping to deeper their understanding of *o-cha* (Japanese tea). The course includes several varieties – you might be surprised how different tea can taste – paired with small bites, including some beautiful traditional sweets. Come in the evening (¥500 cover charge after 7pm) for tea cocktails. Reservations recommended.

DON'T MISS

GOLDEN GAI: TOKYO'S ICONIC BAR DISTRICT

Golden Gai – a Shinjuku institution for over half a century – is a collection of tiny bars, often literally no bigger than a closet and seating maybe a dozen. Each is as unique and eccentric as the 'master' or 'mama' who runs it. In a sense, Golden Gai, which has a strong visual appeal, with its low-slung wooden buildings, is their work of art. It's more than just a place to drink.

The district has long been a gathering spot for artists, writers and musicians. Originally many bars here functioned more like clubhouses for various creative industries. **La Jetée** (ラジェッティ; Map p146; ☎03-3208-9645; www.lajetee.org; 2nd fl, Hanazono 3-ban-gai; 1-1-8 Kabukichō, Shinjuku-ku; ⏰7pm-late Wed-Sat; 🚉JR Yamanote line to Shinjuku, east exit), named for the Chris Marker film, is a classic example: it's been the go-to spot for film industry veterans (the bar appears in Wim Wenders' 1983 documentary *Tokyo-Ga*) for four decades.

Some bars prefer to keep their doors closed to customers who aren't regulars (foreign tourists included) to preserve that old atmosphere; others, La Jetée included, will welcome you (if there is space, of course).

But recently there's been a changing of the guard, as new, younger owners take over, and the exclusive atmosphere of old is giving way to a lively scene of international bar-hoppers, instinctively drawn to Golden Gai's free spirit. **Albatross G** (アルバトロスG; Map p146; www.alba-s.com; 5-ban Gai, 1-1-7 Kabukichō, Shinjuku-ku; ⏰5pm-2am Sun-Thu, to 5am Fri & Sat; 🚉JR Yamanote line to Shinjuku, east exit), which drips with chandeliers, is a popular spot that welcomes foreign visitors; it's also comparatively spacious, with three floors (try to get the table on the 3rd floor). Ramen shop Nagi (p134) is here too, if you need fuel.

But these are just suggestions to get you started. The best way to experience Golden Gai is to stroll the lanes and pick a place that suits your mood. Bars that expressly welcome tourists have English signs posted on their doors. Note that most bars have a cover charge (usually ¥500 to ¥1500), which is often posted on the door.

Two Rooms BAR

(トゥールームス; Map p116; ☎03-3498-0002; www.tworooms.jp; 5th fl, AO Bldg, 3-11-7 Kita-Aoyama, Minato-ku; ⏰11.30am-2am, to 10pm Sun; Ⓢ Ginza line to Omote-sandō, exit B2) Expect a crowd dressed like they don't care that wine by the glass starts at ¥1540. The wine is good (and the bottle list deep), but more importantly, the terrace has sweeping views towards the Shinjuku skyline. Call ahead (staff speak English) on Friday or Saturday night to reserve a spot under the stars.

Two Rooms also has a full kitchen and champagne brunch on the terrace (from ¥5300), with eggs Benedict or crab cake sliders, is a Tokyo classic.

Aoyama Flower Market Teahouse TEAHOUSE

(Map p116; ☎03-3400-0887; www.afm-teahouse.com; 5-1-2 Minami-Aoyama, Minato-ku; ⏰11am-8pm Mon-Sat, to 7pm Sun; Ⓢ Ginza line to Omote-sandō, exit A5) Secreted in the back of a flower shop is this fairy-tale teahouse with flower beds running under the glass-top tables and more overhead, plus cut blooms in vases on every available surface. Tea comes by the pot and starts at ¥750; there are pretty sweets and salad spreads on the menu too. Reservations aren't accepted so you may have to queue.

Koffee Mameya COFFEE

(コーヒーマメヤ; Map p116; www.koffee-mameya.com; 4-15-3 Jingūmae, Shibuya-ku; ⏰10am-6pm; Ⓢ Ginza line to Omote-sandō, exit A2) At any given time, Koffee Mameya has 15 to 20 different beans on rotation from indie roasters around Japan (and some from overseas).

Get a cup brewed on the spot or purchase beans for home use; English-speaking baristas can help you narrow down the selection. There's no seating, but you can loiter at the counter.

It's a little tricky to find; look for a beige building with an alcove and a stone path.

Shinjuku

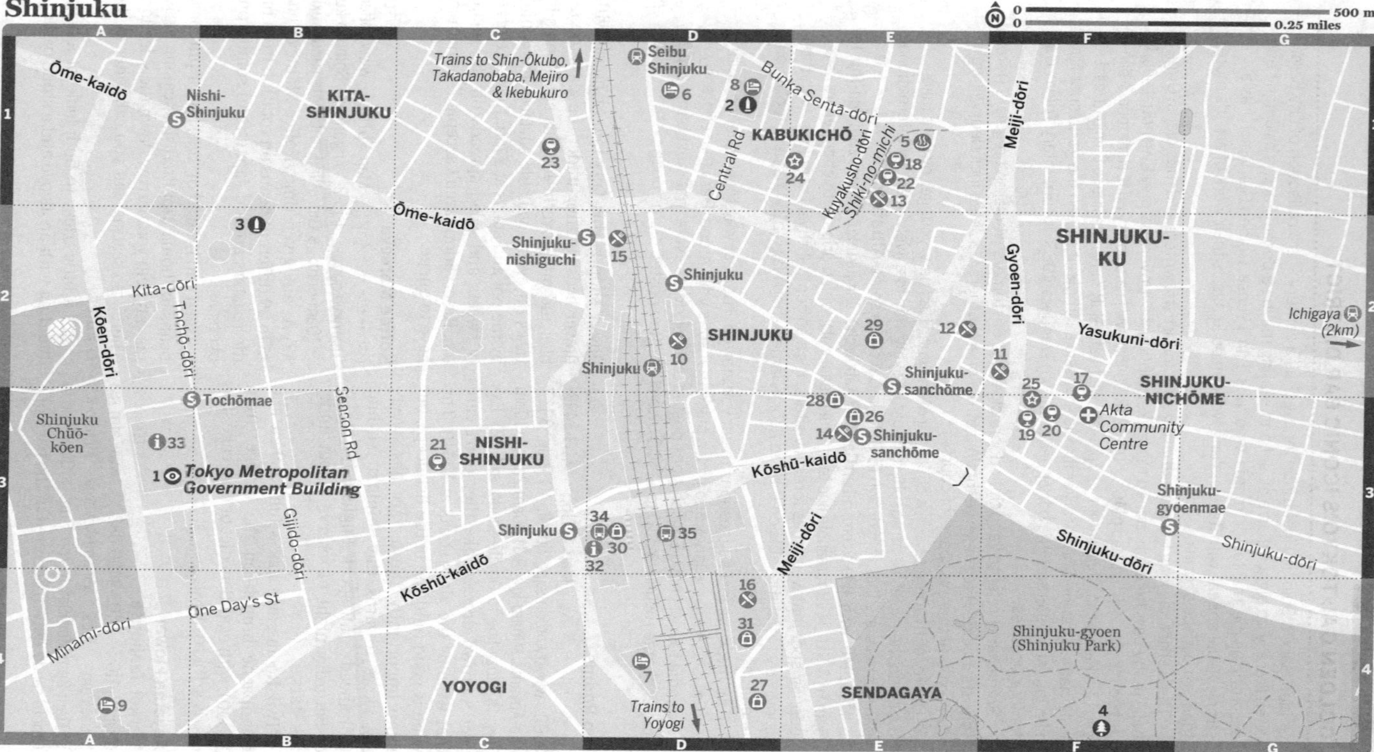
Ōme-kaidō
Nishi-Shinjuku
KITA-SHINJUKU
Trains to Shin-Ōkubo, Takadanobaba, Mejiro & Ikebukuro
Seibu Shinjuku
Bunka Sentā-dōri
KABUKICHŌ
Central Rd
Kuyakusho-dōri
Shiki-no-michi
Meiji-dōri
Ōme-kaidō
Shinjuku-nishiguchi
Shinjuku
SHINJUKU-KU
Gyoen-dōri
Kita-dōri
Kōen-dōri
Tochō-dōri
SHINJUKU
Yasukuni-dōri
Ichigaya (2km)
Shinjuku
Shinjuku-sanchōme
SHINJUKU-NICHŌME
Tochōmae
Season Rd
Akta Community Centre
Shinjuku Chūō-kōen
NISHI-SHINJUKU
Shinjuku-sanchōme
Kōshū-kaidō
Tokyo Metropolitan Government Building
Shinjuku-gyoenmae
Gijido-dōri
Shinjuku
Meiji-dōri
Shinjuku-dōri
Shinjuku-dōri
Kōshū-kaidō
One Day's St
Minami-dōri
Shinjuku-gyoen (Shinjuku Park)
YOYOGI
Trains to Yoyogi
SENDAGAYA
500 m
0.25 miles

Shinjuku

Top Sights
1 Tokyo Metropolitan Government Building ... A3

Sights
2 Godzilla Head ... D1
3 Shinjuku I-Land ... B2
4 Shinjuku-gyoen ... F4

Activities, Courses & Tours
5 Thermae-yu ... E1
Yamadōgu Rental ... (see 21)

Sleeping
6 Book and Bed Shinjuku ... D1
7 Hotel Century Southern Tower ... D4
8 Hotel Gracery Shinjuku ... D1
9 Park Hyatt Tokyo ... A4

Eating
10 Berg ... D2
11 Donjaca ... F2
12 Kanae ... E2
Kozue ... (see 9)
13 Nagi ... E1
14 Nakajima ... E3
15 Omoide-yokochō ... D2
16 Takashimaya Restaurant Park ... D4

Drinking & Nightlife
17 Aiiro Cafe ... F2
18 Albatross G ... E1
19 Arty Farty ... F3
20 Bar Goldfinger ... F3
21 BenFiddich ... C3
Eagle ... (see 20)
22 La Jetée ... E1
New York Bar ... (see 9)
23 Zoetrope ... C1

Entertainment
24 Robot Restaurant ... E1
25 Shinjuku Pit Inn ... F3

Shopping
26 Beams Japan ... E3
27 Books Kinokuniya Tokyo ... D4
28 Disk Union Shinjuku ... E3
29 Isetan ... E2
30 NEWoMan ... D3
31 Tokyu Hands Shinjuku ... D4

Information
32 Shinjuku Bus Terminal Tourist Information Center ... D3
33 Tokyo Metropolitan Government Building Tourist Information Center ... A3

Transport
34 Shinjuku Bus Terminal ... D3
35 Shinjuku Expressway Bus Terminal ... D3

Shibuya

Circus Tokyo CLUB

(Map p120; www.circus-tokyo.jp; 3-26-16 Shibuya, Shibuya-ku; JR Yamanote line to Shibuya, new south exit) Circus, the Tokyo offshoot of an Osaka club, is aggressively underground: small, out of the way, in a basement (of course), with no decor to speak of and all attention laser-focused on the often experimental music. It's open most Fridays and Saturdays from 11pm, and sometimes other nights; check the schedule online. Cover is ¥2000 to ¥3000 and drinks ¥600; ID required.

Wear your comfy shoes because there's nowhere to sit.

Oath BAR

(Map p138; www.djbar-oath.com; basement fl, 1-6-5 Dōgenzaka, Shibuya-ku; 8pm-5am, closed Sun; JR Yamanote line to Shibuya, Hachikō exit) Oath is a tiny space covered in gilt and mirrors, dripping with chandeliers and absolutely not taking itself seriously. It's a very popular spot for pre-partying and after-partying, thanks to cheap drinks (¥700), fun DJs and late hours. Cover charge is ¥1000 (one drink included; ¥1500 after 11pm on Friday and Saturday).

Karaoke Rainbow KARAOKE

(Map p138; 03-6455-3240; www.karaoke-rainbow.com; 8th fl, Shibuya Modi, 1-21-3 Shibuya, Shibuya-ku; per 30min before/after 7pm ¥155/420; 11am-5am; JR Yamanote line to Shibuya, Hachikō exit) This is Shibuya's most popular karaoke spot for two reasons: it doesn't have the same dated look as the generic chains and you get the first hour free (though, technically, you need to buy one drink; from ¥475). Staff speak some English and the English song list is extensive. It's on the 8th floor of the building with the Marui department store.

Contact CLUB

(コンタクト; Map p138; 03-6427-8107; www.contacttokyo.com; basement, 2-10-12 Dōgenzaka, Shibuya-ku; JR Yamanote line to Shibuya, Hachikō exit) Several storeys under a parking garage, Contact is as much a place to see and be seen as it is to dance. Come after 1am on a Friday or Saturday night to see it in top

LOCAL KNOWLEDGE

A NIGHT OUT IN SHIMO-KITAZAWA

For generations, Shimokita (as it's called here) has been a hang-out for musicians, artists and actors. It's among the city's last bastions of bohemia. If hippies – not bureaucrats – ran Tokyo, the city would look a lot more like Shimo-Kitazawa.

Unfortunately the massive (bureaucrat-led) redevelopment of the train station area is cramping its style a bit, but it's still a great place to wander – and bar-hop. Spend an evening here and raise your glass to (and with) the characters committed to keeping Shimokita weird.

Some favourite haunts include tiny dive bar **Ghetto** (月灯; Map p92; www.facebook.com/Ghetto.unko; 1-45-16 Daizawa, Setagaya-ku; ⏲8.30pm-late; 🚆Odakyū or Keiō Inokashira line to Shimo-Kitazawa, east exit), part of a collection of bars attached to a rundown fringe theatre, and cave-like rock-and-roll bar **Mother** (マザー; Map p92; www.rock-mother.com; 5-36-14 Daizawa, Setagaya-ku; ⏲5pm-2am, to 5am Fri & Sat; 🚆Odakyū or Keiō Inokashira line to Shimo-Kitazawa, southwest exit).

Shimo-Kitazawa (and the station of the same name) can be reached in less than 10 minutes from Shinjuku, via the Odakyū line, or from Shibuya, via the Keiō Inokashira line.

form. Music may be hip-hop, house or techno – it depends on the night. It has plenty of space for just lounging, too.

To enter, you must first sign up for a membership. ID required.

Beat Cafe BAR

(Map p138; www.facebook.com/beatcafe; basement fl, 2-13-5 Dōgenzaka, Shibuya-ku; ⏲8pm-5am; 🚆JR Yamanote line to Shibuya, Hachikō exit) Beat is a dive in the best sense of the word, comfortably shabby with cheap drinks (from ¥600), no cover, late hours, lipstick (blood?) red walls, random decor and an '80 and '90s cool-kid soundtrack. Look for Gateway Studio on the corner; the bar is in the basement, with scribbles on the door.

Rhythm Cafe BAR

(リズムカフェ; Map p138; 11-1 Udagawa-chō, Shibuya-ku; ⏲6pm-2am; 📶; 🚆JR Yamanote line to Shibuya, Hachikō exit) Rhythm Cafe is a fun little DJ bar secreted among the windy streets of Shibuya sub-district Udagawa-chō (known for its record shops). It's run by a record label and known for having offbeat event nights (like the one featuring retro Japanese pop). Drinks start at ¥600; some events have a cover, but not usually more than ¥1000.

Ebisu & Meguro

★Gem by Moto BAR

(ジェムバイモト; Map p120; ☎03-6455-6998; 1-30-9 Ebisu, Shibuya-ku; ⏲5pm-midnight Tue-Fri, 1-9pm Sat & Sun; 🚆JR Yamanote line to Ebisu, east exit) Gem specialises in boutique sakes collected from all over Japan. There's a menu, which is always changing, but if you're here to broaden your appreciation of the myriad styles of *nihonshū* (and that's why everyone is here), it's best to leave the choosing to the savvy people behind the counter. Tell them what you like and don't like; you're in good hands.

Most go for ¥750 to ¥1500 by the glass; small plates of food, designed to pair well, run about the same. Cover charge ¥800. Come early or make a reservation.

Bar Trench COCKTAIL BAR

(バートレンチ; Map p120; ☎03-3780-5291; www.small-axe.net; 1-5-8 Ebisu-nishi, Shibuya-ku; ⏲7pm-2am Mon-Sat, 6pm-1am Sun; 🚆JR Yamanote line to Ebisu, west exit) One of the pioneers of Tokyo's now flourishing cocktail scene, Trench (a suitable name for a bar hidden in a narrow alley) is a tiny place with an air of old-world bohemianism – but that might just be the absinthe talking. The always-changing original cocktails (from ¥1500) are made with botanical infusions and bitters. Cover charge ¥500; no reservations taken.

If it's full (and it often is), ask the staff to point you towards sister bar Tram, a block away.

Onibus Coffee COFFEE

(オニバスコーヒー; Map p120; ☎03-6412-8683; www.onibuscoffee.com; 2-14-1 Kami-Meguro, Meguro-ku; ⏲9am-6pm; Ⓢ Hibiya line to Naka-Meguro, south exit) Local hotspot Onibus Coffee perfectly nails two of Tokyo's current obsessions: third-wave coffee and vintage wooden buildings. The beans here are roasted in-house; the cafe is in a former tofu shop. There's outdoor seating, too.

Odaiba & Tokyo Bay

Jicoo the Floating Bar COCKTAIL BAR

(ジークザフローティングバー; Map p125; 11am-8pm 0120-049-490; www.jicoofloatingbar.com; cover from ¥2600; 8-10.30pm Thu-Sat; Yurikamome line to Hinode or Odaiba Kaihin-kōen, north exit) For a few nights a week, the futuristic cruise-boat *Himiko*, designed by manga and anime artist Leiji Matsumoto, morphs into this floating bar. Board on the hour at Hinode pier and the half-hour at Odaiba Kaihin-kōen (p114). The evening-long 'floating pass' usually includes some sort of live music; check the schedule online as sometimes events drive up the price.

Note that this won't run in the event of a typhoon or similarly inclement weather.

Entertainment

Live Music

★Shinjuku Pit Inn JAZZ

(新宿ピットイン; Map p146; 03-3354-2024; www.pit-inn.com; basement, 2-12-4 Shinjuku, Shinjuku-ku; matinee 2.30pm, evening show 7.30pm; S Marunouchi line to Shinjuku-sanchōme, exit C5) This is Tokyo's best jazz spot: intimate, unpretentious and with an always solid line-up of influential, avant-garde, crossover and up-and-coming musicians from Japan and abroad. If you're already a fan of jazz, you'll want to make a point to visit it; if you're not, Pit Inn is the kind of place that just might win you over.

★Unit LIVE MUSIC

(ユニット; Map p120; 03-5459-8630; www.unit-tokyo.com; 1-34-17 Ebisu-nishi, Shibuya-ku; Tōkyū Tōyoko line to Daikanyama) This subterranean club stages live music and DJ-hosted events (sometimes staggered on the same night). The solid line-up includes Japanese indie bands, veterans playing to a smaller crowd and overseas artists making their Japan debut. Unit has high ceilings and an intentionally industrial-cool interior (in addition to excellent sound), separating it from Tokyo's grungier live-music spots. Ticket prices vary.

WWW LIVE MUSIC

(Map p138; 03-5458-7685; https://www-shibuya.jp; 13-17 Udagawa-chō, Shibuya-ku; JR Yamanote line to Shibuya, Hachikō exit) In a former art-house cinema with the tell-tale tiered floor (but not the seats) still intact, this is one of those rare venues where you could turn up just about any night and hear something good. The line-up (of mostly local acts) varies from indie pop to hip-hop to electronica. Upstairs is WWW X, a bigger space. Tickets typically start at ¥3000 (more for international acts).

Tokyo Opera City Concert Hall CLASSICAL MUSIC

(東京オペラシティコンサートホール; Map p92; 03-5353-9999; www.operacity.jp; 3rd fl, Tokyo Opera City, 3-20-2 Nishi-Shinjuku, Shinjuku-ku; Keiō New line to Hatsudai, east exit) This beautiful, oak-panelled, A-frame concert hall, with legendary acoustics, hosts the Tokyo Philharmonic Orchestra among other well-regarded ensembles. Free lunchtime organ performances take place monthly, usually on Fridays. Get information and tickets from the box office next to the entrance to the Tokyo Opera City Art Gallery.

Kazunoya Oiwake TRADITIONAL MUSIC

(和ノ家追分; Map p112; 03-3874-0722; www.kazunoya-oiwake.com; 5-37-7 Asakusa, Taitō-ku; ¥2000 plus 1 food item & 1 drink; 5.30pm-midnight, closed Mon; S Hibiya line to Iriya, exit 3) Oiwake is one of Tokyo's few remaining *minyō izakaya,* pubs where traditional folk music is performed. It's a small, cosy place, where the waitstaff and the musicians – who play *shamisen* (a banjo-like instrument), hand drums and bamboo flute – are often one and the same. Sets start at 7pm and 9pm; children are welcome for the early show.

Check the website before heading out, as there is usually one special event per month with a higher entrance fee.

MISSED THE LAST TRAIN?

Missed the last train? You're not alone – or stuck for options. Nightlife districts such as Roppongi, Shinjuku and Shibuya have plenty of 24-hour options for night crawlers who were lured out late by the neighbourhood's charms but who'd rather not fork over the yen for a taxi ride home. In addition to love hotels and *manga kissa* (cafes where you pay by the hour to read manga, Japanese comic books), consider waiting for the first train at a karaoke parlour; most offer discounted all-night packages from midnight to 5am.

Club Quattro LIVE MUSIC

(クラブクアトロ; Map p138; 03-3477-8750; www.club-quattro.com; 4th & 5th fl, 32-13-4 Udagawa-chō, Shibuya-ku; JR Yamanote line to Shibuya, Hachikō exit) This small venue attracts a more grown-up, artsy crowd than the club's location – in the heart of Shibuya – might lead you to expect. There's no explicit musical focus, but the line-up leans towards indie rock and world music. It has the vibe of a stylish club (standing only). Ticket prices vary from ¥3000 to ¥6000, usually with one drink (¥600) minimum order.

Club Goodman LIVE MUSIC

(クラブグッドマン; Map p106; 03-3862-9010; www.clubgoodman.com; basement, AS Bldg, 55 Kanda-Sakumagashi, Chiyoda-ku; cover charge ¥100-5500; JR Yamanote & Sōbu lines to Akihabara, Shōwa-dōri exit) In the basement of a building with a guitar shop and recording studios, this small venue (capacity 230) is a long-running favourite with Tokyo's indie-scene bands and their fans. Entry charge (and crowd) depends on who is playing. Slightly (suitably?) grungy.

Performing Arts

★Kabukiza THEATRE

(歌舞伎座; Map p96; 03-3545-6800; www.kabukiweb.net; 4-12-15 Ginza, Chūō-ku; tickets ¥4000-20,000, single-act tickets ¥800-2000; Hibiya line to Higashi-Ginza, exit 3) The flamboyant facade of this venerable theatre is fitting for the extravagant dramatic flourishes that are integral to the traditional performing art of kabuki. Check the website for performance details and to book tickets; you'll also find an explanation about cheaper one-act day seats.

A full kabuki performance comprises three or four acts (usually from different plays) over an afternoon or an evening (typically 11am to 3.30pm or 4.30pm to 9pm), with long intervals between the acts. Be sure to rent a headset (single act/full program ¥500/1000) for blow-by-blow explanations in English, and pick up a *bentō* (boxed meal) to snack on during the intervals.

If four-plus hours sounds too long, 90 sitting and 60 standing tickets are sold on the day for each single act. You'll be at the back of the auditorium but the views are still good. Some acts tend to be more popular than others, so ask ahead as to which to catch, and arrive at least 1½ hours before the start of the performance.

★National Theatre THEATRE

(国立劇場, Kokuritsu Gekijō; Map p92; 03-3265-7411, box office 03-3230-3000; www.ntj.jac.go.jp; 4-1 Hayabusa-chō, Chiyoda-ku; S Hanzōmon line to Hanzōmon, exit 1) Japan's most important theatre for traditional performing arts stages kabuki, *gagaku* (music of the imperial court), *kyōmai* (Kyoto-style traditional dance), *bunraku* (classic puppet theatre) and more. Visit the website to see the schedule and purchase tickets. Premium tickets can cost over ¥10,000, while the cheap seats are indeed cheap (from ¥1800); student concessions available.

Earphones with English translation are available for hire (¥700, plus ¥1000 deposit) for kabuki performances. The theatre's 'Discover Bunraku' series runs with English subtitles and includes a brief introduction to the art form. For other performances an English synopsis is provided.

To the rear of the main building is the **Traditional Performing Arts Information Centre** (10am to 6pm) FREE where you can see exhibitions that include videos of performances.

National Nō Theatre THEATRE

(国立能楽堂, Kokuritsu Nō-gakudō; Map p92; 03-3423-1331; www.ntj.jac.go.jp; 4-18-1 Sendagaya, Shibuya-ku; tickets ¥2800-6400; JR Sōbu line to Sendagaya) This is Japan's only national theatre devoted to *nō*, a centuries' old mode of performing arts. It has a classically elegant, sparse cypress stage; meanwhile, each seat has a discrete screen displaying an English translation of the dialogue. Shows take place only a few times a month and can sell out quickly; purchase tickets online up to one month in advance.

Concessions available for students.

New National Theatre PERFORMING ARTS

(新国立劇場, Shin Kokuritsu Gekijō; Map p92; 03-5352-9999; www.nntt.jac.go.jp; 1-1-1 Honmachi, Shibuya-ku; Keiō New line to Hatsudai, central exit) This is Tokyo's premier public performing-arts centre, with state-of-the-art stages for drama, opera and dance. The plays are in Japanese and the operas and ballets are usually visiting international productions; however, Japanese contemporary dance performances are staged here a few times a year.

Purchase tickets online (in English) or at the box office. There are concession for seniors and students, including same-day, half-price tickets for students. The theatre is next to the Tokyo Opera City complex.

Suigian PERFORMING ARTS

(水戯庵; Map p96; ☎03-3527-9378; https://suigian.jp; basement fl, 2-5-10 Nihombashi-Muromachi, Chūō-ku; tickets ¥5000-12,000, plus 1 drink; Ⓢ Ginza line to Mitsukoshimae, exit A6) This chic lounge stages short acts (40 minutes) of traditional Japanese performing arts, including *nō, kagura* (sacred dance) and *Kyo-mai* (Kyoto-style traditional dance). While likely designed with international visitors in mind, the performers all belong to well-established schools. Shows are held nightly at 7pm (entrance from 5pm) and additionally at 11.15am and 1.45pm on Saturday, Sunday and Monday.

From 8.30pm (nightly except Sunday) the space becomes the **Momokawa Lounge** (cover charge ¥1000) and traditional dancers take the stage for three 10-to-15-minute performances. The easiest way to find Suigian, which is beneath the Coredo Muromachi 2 building, is to locate the steps down from ground level beside the Fukutoku shrine.

Kanze Nōgakudō PERFORMING ARTS

(観世能楽堂; Map p96; ☎03-6274-6579; www.kanze.net; Ginza Six B3, 6-10-1 Ginza, Chūō-ku; Ⓢ Ginza line to Ginza, exit A2) This venerable group specialising in *nō* dramas relocated to the bowels of the Ginza Six shopping complex in 2017. The theatre seats 48; if you haven't booked in advance and would like a taster, you can check on the day for ¥3000 'happy hour' tickets; one of these gets you an unreserved seat for the performance's last act.

Robot Restaurant CABARET

(ロボットレストラン; Map p146; ☎03-3200-5500; www.shinjuku-robot.com; 1-7-1 Kabukichō, Shinjuku-ku; tickets ¥8500; Ⓡ JR Yamanote line to Shinjuku, east exit) This Kabukichō spectacle has hit it big with its vision of 'wacky Japan': bikini-clad women ride around on giant robots against a backdrop of animated screens and enough LED lights to illuminate all of Shinjuku. The 90-minute shows are held at 3.30pm, 5.30pm, 7.30pm and 9.30pm. Book online for a ¥1000 discount; discount flyers can often be found at tourist spots.

If you've booked ahead, you must arrive 30 minutes prior to the start of the show or your ticket may be resold. Check the website for information about dress codes and small children.

> **ⓘ GETTING TICKETS**
>
> Ticket Pia is the source for concert and theatre tickets; there are kiosks located on the ground floor of Tower Records (p157) and on the 2nd floor of Shibuya 109 (p157). Staff may not speak English but if you write down the name and date of the event, they can usually manage. Note that some venues stop selling advance tickets one to three days before the show.

The show receives mixed reviews: some love it (you'll get great photos), while others recoil at the price and tourist-trappiness of it. You can have a small, free taste just by basking in the glow of the exterior, where two robo-glamazons are parked outside (also great for photos).

Spectator Sports

★ Ryōgoku Kokugikan SPECTATOR SPORT

(両国国技館; Map p92; ☎03-3623-5111; www.sumo.or.jp; 1-3-28 Yokoami, Sumida-ku; tickets ¥3800-14,800; Ⓢ Toei Ōedo line to Ryōgoku, exit A4, Ⓡ JR Sōbu line to Ryōgoku, west exit) If you're in town when a tournament is on, don't miss the chance to catch the big boys of Japanese wrestling in action at the country's largest sumo stadium. The main spectacle starts 3.40pm when the *makuuchi* (top division) wrestlers parade into the ring. Advanced tickets must be purchased through Ticket Oosumo (http://sumo.pia.jp/en), up to five weeks before the start of the tournament.

Tournaments run for 15 days each January, May and September. Doors open at 8.30am, but the action doesn't heat up until the senior wrestlers hit the ring around 2pm.

For the opening and closing days and the days in between that fall on the weekend you can expect advance purchase seats to sell out quickly. In addition to advanced tickets, 400 general-admission tickets (¥2200; cash only) are sold on the day of the match from 8am at the box office in front of the stadium. You'll have to line up very early (at the latest from 6am) to buy one and everyone in your party must be present (only one ticket purchase per person is allowed, children included); weekdays mid-tournament are your best bet.

If you arrive in the morning when the stadium is still fairly empty, you can usually

DON'T MISS

WATCHING SUMO PRACTICE

Not in town for a sumo tournament? You can still catch an early-morning practice session at a 'stable' – where the wrestlers live and practise. Overseas visitors are welcome at **Arashio Stable** (荒汐部屋, Arashio-beya; Map p92; ☎03-3666-7646; www.arashio.net; 2-47-2 Hama-chō, Nihombashi, Chūō-ku; Ⓢ Toei Shinjuku line to Hamachō, exit A2) FREE, so long as they mind the rules (check the website). Visit between 7.30am and 10am – you can watch through the window or on a bench outside the door.

There is no practice during tournament weeks.

sneak down to the box seats for a closer view. Rent a radio (¥200 fee, plus ¥3000 deposit) to listen to commentary in English. Stop by the basement banquet hall to sample *chanko-nabe* (the protein-rich stew eaten by the wrestlers) for just ¥300 a bowl.

★Tokyo Dome BASEBALL
(東京ドーム; Map p106; www.tokyo-dome.co.jp; 1-3 Kōraku, Bunkyō-ku; tickets ¥1700-6200; Ⓡ JR Sōbu line to Suidōbashi, west exit) Tokyo Dome (aka 'The Big Egg') is home to the Yomiuri Giants. Love 'em or hate 'em, they're the most consistently successful team in Japanese baseball. Tickets usually sell out in advance; get them early at www.giants.jp/en/ticket.

Jingū Baseball Stadium BASEBALL
(神宮球場, Jingū Kyūjo; Map p116; ☎0180-993-589; www.jingu-stadium.com; 3-1 Kasumigaoka-machi, Shinjuku-ku; tickets ¥2000-5900; Ⓢ Ginza line to Gaienmae, exit 3) Jingū Baseball Stadium, built in 1926, is home to the Yakult Swallows, Tokyo's number-two team (but number-one when it comes to fan loyalty; Swallows fans are famous for their 7th inning stretch routine). Get tickets from the booth next to Gate 9, open from 11am to 5pm (or until 20 minutes after a game ends), or online at www.yakult-swallows.co.jp/en.

Same-day outfield tickets can be had for as little as ¥1400 (¥500 for children); they're usually available, unless the Swallows are playing one of Japan's more famous teams (like the Giants).

Shopping

Marunouchi & Nihombashi

★Coredo Muromachi MALL
(コレド室町; Map p96; www.mitsui-shopping-park.com/urban/muromach; 2-2-1 Nihombashi-Muromachi, Chūō-ku; ⏲10am-9pm; Ⓢ Ginza line to Mitsukoshimae, exit A4) More like a purpose-built town than a mall, Coredo Muromachi is spread over three buildings and a terrace complex. It's stylish and upscale, focused more on homewares and food than clothes: there are branches of many famous artisan shops and gourmet purveyors here.

KITTE MALL
(Map p96; ☎03-3216-2811; www.jptower-kitte.jp; 2-7-2 Marunouchi, Chiyoda-ku; ⏲shops 11am-9pm Mon-Sat, to 8pm Sun; Ⓡ JR lines to Tokyo, Marunouchi south exit) This mall, within the restored facade of the 1930s Tokyo Central Post Office, has a partiuclarly good selection of boutiques specialising in homewares and lifestyle goods, including the **Good Design Store Tokyo by Nohara** (http://gdst.nohara-inc.co.jp).

★Mitsukoshi DEPARTMENT STORE
(三越; Map p96; ☎03-3241-3311; www.mitsukoshi.co.jp; 1-4-1 Nihombashi-Muromachi, Chūō-ku; ⏲10am-7pm; Ⓢ Ginza line to Mitsukoshimae, exit A2) Mitsukoshi's venerable Nihombashi branch was Japan's first department store. It's a grand affair with an entrance guarded by bronze lions and a magnificent statue of Magokoro, the goddess of sincerity, rising up from the centre of the ground floor. For the full effect, arrive at 10am for the bells and bows that accompany each day's opening.

Check out the floor dedicated to the art of the kimono or peruse the morsels in the incredible *depachika* (department-store food floor).

★Muji HOMEWARES
(無印良品; Map p96; https://shop.muji.com/jp/ginza; 3-3-5 Ginza, Chūō-ku; ⏲10am-9pm; Ⓢ Ginza line to Ginza, exit B4) You could hear the collective swoon of all devotees of functional design when this huge Muji flagship opened in 2019. Floors two through five carry the brand's signature clothing, accessories and homewares – simply elegant and utterly affordable. Muji is also particularly great for travel goods.

There are Muji all over Tokyo, including a branch in Coredo Muromachi.

Ginza & Tsukiji

★Akomeya FOOD

(アコメヤ; Map p96; ☎03-6758-0271; www.akomeya.jp; 2-2-6 Ginza, Chūō-ku; ⊙11am-8pm, to 9pm Fri & Sat; Ⓢ Yūrakuchō line to Ginza-itchōme, exit 4) Rice ('kome') is at the heart of Japanese cuisine. This stylish store sells not only many types of the grain but also products made from it (such as sake), plus all the classic Japanese pantry items (from artisan producers) and a choice collection of kitchen, home and bath items.

There's also an in-house **restaurant** (アコメヤ厨房; Akomeya Chūbō; ☎050-3184-0789; lunch 2500/4800; ⊙11am-10pm), and another branch in **Shinjuku** (Shinjuku Bus Terminal, Shinjuku-ku; ⊙11am-9.30pm, to 9am Sat & Sun; Ⓡ JR Yamanote line to Shinjuku, new south exit).

★Itōya ARTS & CRAFTS

(伊東屋; Map p96; ☎03-3561-8311; www.ito-ya.co.jp; 2-7-15 Ginza, Chūō-ku; ⊙10am-8pm, to 7pm Sun; Ⓢ Ginza line to Ginza, exit A13) Explore the nine floors (plus several more in the nearby annex) of stationery at this famed, century-old Ginza establishment. There are everyday items (notebooks and greeting cards) and luxuries (fountain pens and leather agendas). Also: *washi* (handmade paper), *tenugui* (hand towels, traditionally hand dyed or printed) and *furoshiki* (wrapping cloths) in gorgeous colours and patterns.

Okuno Building ARTS & CRAFTS

(奥野ビル; Map p96; 1-9-8 Ginza, Chūō-ku; Ⓢ Yūrakuchō line to Ginza-itchōme, exit 10) The Okuno Building (1932) is of a rare vintage in ever-redeveloping Tokyo; most such buildings have long come down. But a concerted effort by artists and preservationists has kept it standing, and the seven floors of rooms filled with boutiques and gallery spaces (most open noon to 7pm, closed irregularly). Climb up and down the Escher-like staircases or use the antique elevator to explore.

★Takumi ARTS & CRAFTS

(たくみ; Map p96; ☎03-3571-2017; www.ginza-takumi.co.jp; 8-4-2 Ginza, Chūō-ku; ⊙11am-7pm Mon-Sat; Ⓢ Ginza line to Shimbashi, exit 5) You're unlikely to find a more elegant selection of traditional folk crafts, including toys, textiles and ceramics from around Japan. Ever thoughtful, this shop also encloses information detailing the origin and background of the pieces if you make a purchase.

Ginza Six MALL

(Map p96; ☎03-6891-3390; http://ginza6.tokyo; 6-10-1 Ginza, Chūō-ku; ⊙10am-10pm; Ⓢ Ginza line to Ginza, exit A4) This high-end mall was designed by architect Taniguchi Yoshio, who also did the Gallery of Hōryū-ji Treasures. Large-scale art installations are held in the atrium and there's a garden on the roof with city views. Shopping-wise, it's mostly international brands, but Japanese craftwork and design is well represented on the 4th floor.

Dover Street Market Ginza FASHION & ACCESSORIES

(Map p96; ☎03-6228-5080; http://ginza.doverstreetmarket.com; 6-9-5 Ginza, Chūō-ku; ⊙11am-8pm; Ⓢ Ginza line to Ginza, exit A2) A department store as envisioned by Rei Kawakubo (of Comme des Garçons), DSM has seven floors of avant-garde brands, including several Japanese labels and everything in the Comme des Garçons line-up. The eccentric art installations alone make it worth the visit.

Uniqlo Ginza FASHION & ACCESSORIES

(ユニクロ銀座店; Map p96; ☎03-6252-5181; www.uniqlo.com; 5-7-7 Ginza, Chūō-ku; ⊙11am-9pm; Ⓢ Ginza line to Ginza, exit A2) Stop any Tokyoite on the street and odds are they're wearing at least one thing from Uniqlo, the ubiquitous retailer of indispensible basics. There are branches all over the city but this is the largest, stocking everything in the current line-up (which usually includes some collaborations with designers and artists).

If you're overwhelmed, start on the top floor, which has all the top-sellers in one place. The floor below carries limited-edition T-shirts.

Roppongi & Around

★Japan Traditional Crafts Aoyama Square ARTS & CRAFTS

(伝統工芸　青山スクエア; Map p92; ☎03-5785-1301; https://kougeihin.jp; 8-1-22 Akasaka, Minato-ku; ⊙11am-7pm; Ⓢ Ginza line to Aoyama-itchōme, exit 4) Supported by the Japanese Ministry of Economy, Trade and Industry, this is as much a showroom as a shop, exhibiting a broad range of traditional crafts from around Japan, including lacquerwork boxes, woodwork, cut glass, textiles and pottery. There are some exquisite heirloom pieces here, but also beautiful items at reasonable prices.

Summon videos of the artisans at work from the touch screens in the front of the shop.

Toraya FOOD & DRINKS

(とらや; Map p92; ☎03-3408-4121; https://global.toraya-group.co.jp; 4-9-22 Akasaka, Minato-ku; ⊙8.30am-7pm Mon-Fri, 9.30am-6pm Sat & Sun, tearoom 11am-6.30pm, to 5.30pm Sat & Sun; S) Founded in the 16th century in Kyoto, Toraya's traditional confectionery has long been patronised by the Imperial Court, giving it a cachet that other sweet-makers can only dream about. This is its impressive flagship store, reopened in 2018. It specialises in *yōkan*, a jelly made from red bean paste, but also sells other seasonal sweets, all beautifully packaged.

Souvenir from Tokyo GIFTS & SOUVENIRS

(スーベニアフロムトーキョー; Map p102; ☎03-6812 9933; www.souvenirfromtokyo.jp; basement, National Art Center Tokyo, 7-22-2 Roppongi, Minato-ku; ⊙10am-6pm Sat-Mon, Wed & Thu, to 8pm Fri; S Chiyoda line to Nogizaka, exit 6) There's always an expertly curated and ever-changing selection of home-grown design bits and bobs that make for unique souvenirs at this shop.

Tokyo Midtown MALL

(東京ミッドタウン; Map p102; www.tokyo-midtown.com; 9-7 Akasaka, Minato-ku; ⊙11am-9pm; ; S Ōedo line to Roppongi, exit 8) This upscale mall is good for homewares from Japanese designers. Check out **The Cover Nippon** (gorgeous and gallery-like) and **Wise-Wise** (clever designs and easier on the wallet), both on the on the 3rd floor of the Galleria section.

Ueno & Yanesen

Ameya-yokochō MARKET

(アメヤ横町; Map p110; www.ameyoko.net; 4-chōme Ueno, Taitō-ku; JR Yanamnote line to Ueno, main exit) One of Tokyo's few remaining open-air markets, Ameya-yokochō got its start as a black market, post-WWII, when American goods (which included *ameya* – candy and chocolates) were sold here. These days, vendors sell everything from fresh seafood to vintage jeans and bargain sneakers. There are also lots of cheap eateries in and around the market that stay open later than the shops.

Geidai Art Plaza ART

(Map p110; ☎050-5525-2102; www.artplaza.geidai.ac.jp; Tokyo University of the Arts, 12-8 Ueno-kōen, Taitō-ku; ⊙10am-6pm, closed Mon; JR lines to Ueno, Ueno-kōen exit) On the campus of Tokyo's top arts university this gallery-like space sells works in a range of media by the institute's staff, graduates and current students. Who knows: with a keen eye you might pick up something by a future living national treasure at a still reasonable price.

Yanaka Matsunoya HOMEWARES

(谷中松野屋; Map p110; ☎03-3823-7441; www.yanakamatsunoya.jp; 3-14-14 Nishi-Nippori, Arakawa-ku; ⊙11am-7pm, from 10am Sat & Sun, closed Tue; JR Yamanote line to Nippori, west exit) At the top of Yanaka Ginza (p103), Matsunoya sells beautifully simple, handmade household goods, such as baskets, brooms and bamboo strainers.

★**Art Sanctuary Allan West** ART

(繪処アラン・ウエスト; Map p110; ☎03-3827-1907; www.allanwest.jp; 1-6-17 Yanaka, Taitō-ku; ⊙1.30-4.30pm, from 3pm Sun, closed Thu; S Chiyoda line to Nezu, exit 1) FREE Long-time Yanaka resident Allan West, a graduate of Japan's prestigious Tokyo University of the Arts, paints gorgeous screens and scrolls in the classical Japanese styles, making his paints from scratch, just as local artists have done for centuries. Small votive-shaped paintings start at ¥5000; the screens are, uh, a lot more. Non-buyers are welcome to stop in to see the works.

Look for the dark wood, post and beam facade and sliding doors.

Asakusa & Ryōgoku

★**Kama-asa** HOMEWARES

(釜浅; Map p112; ☎03-3841-9355; www.kama-asa.co.jp; 2-24-1 Matsugaya, Taitō-ku; ⊙10am-5.30pm; S Ginza line to Tawaramachi, exit 3) A Japanese knife is not only a highly practical and prized piece of kitchenware, it can also be extremely beautiful in its design. Admire an excellent range at this upmarket store that has been in business since 1908. There are English- and French-speaking staff on hand, and there's a good range of other kitchen implements, including steel pans.

If you can wait for a week, they can engrave your name or choice of words onto a knife for free.

DON'T MISS

TOKYO'S WEEKEND MARKETS

Tokyo's best farmers market, **Farmer's Market @UNU** (Map p116; www.farmersmarkets.jp; 5-53-7 Jingūmae, Shibuya-ku; ⏲10am-4pm Sat & Sun; Ⓢ Ginza line to Omote-sandō, exit B2), sets up every weekend on the plaza in front of the United Nations University on Aoyama-dōri. There are always at least half a dozen food trucks here and the market is as much a social event as a shopping stop. Events pop up here too, including the monthly hipster flea market **Raw Tokyo** (www.rawtokyo.jp). Check the website for other events.

Another great market is the **Ōedo Antique Market** (www.antique-market.jp), which draws hundreds of dealers in retro and antique Japanese goods, from old ceramics and kimono to kitsch plastic figurines and vintage movie posters. It's held in the courtyard of Tokyo International Forum (p91), usually on the first and third Sunday of every month (check the website before you head out), from 9am to 4pm.

Bengara ARTS & CRAFTS

(べんがら; Map p112; ☎03-3841-6613; www.bengara.com; 1-35-6 Asakusa, Taitō-ku; ⏲10am-6pm, closed 3rd Thu of the month; Ⓢ Ginza line to Asakusa, exit 1) Spend any amount of time in Japan and you become quickly familiar with *noren*, the curtains that hang in front of shop doors. This shop sells beautiful ones, made of linen and coloured with natural dyes (such as indigo or persimmon) or decorated with ink-brush paintings. There are smaller items too, such as pouches and book covers, made of traditional textiles.

Fujiya ARTS & CRAFTS

(ふじ屋; Map p112; ☎03-3841-2283; 2-2-15 Asakusa, Taitō-ku; ⏲10am-6pm, closed Wed; Ⓢ Ginza line to Asakusa, exit 1) Fujiya specialises in *tenugui:* dyed cloths of thin cotton that can be used as tea towels, handkerchiefs, gift wrapping (the list goes on – they're surprisingly versatile). Here they come in both traditional and humorous modern designs.

Shinjuku & Around

Shinjuku is a major shopping hub, with department and electronic stores clustered around its train station.

★**Isetan** DEPARTMENT STORE

(伊勢丹; Map p146; ☎03-3352-1111; www.isetan.co.jp; 3-14-1 Shinjuku, Shinjuku-ku; ⏲10am-8pm; Ⓢ Marunouchi line to Shinjuku-sanchōme, exit B3, B4 or B5) Isetan is Tokyo's most fashion-forward department store. Head to the 2nd-floor Tokyo Closet and 3rd-floor Re-Style boutiques in the main building, and the 2nd floor of the men's building to discover new Japanese brands that haven't (yet) hit the big time. Other reasons to visit: the homewares from contemporary artisans (5th floor) and the excellent *depachika* (basement gourmet food hall).

★**Beams Japan** FASHION & ACCESSORIES

(ビームス·ジャパン; Map p146; www.beams.co.jp; 3-32-6 Shinjuku, Shinjuku-ku; ⏲11am-8pm; 🚉 JR Yamanote line to Shinjuku, east exit) Beams, a national chain of trendsetting boutiques, is a Japanese cultural institution and this multistorey Shinjuku branch has a particular audience in mind: you, the traveller. It's full of the latest Japanese streetwear labels, traditional fashions with cool modern twists, artisan crafts, pop art and more – all contenders for that perfect only-in-Tokyo souvenir.

Books Kinokuniya Tokyo BOOKS

(紀伊國屋書店; Map p146; ☎03-5361-3316; www.kinokuniya.co.jp/c/store/Books-Kinokuniya-Tokyo; 6th fl, Takashimaya Times Sq Minami-kan, 5-24-2 Sendagaya, Shibuya-ku; ⏲10am-8.30pm; 🚉 JR Yamanote line to Shinjuku, south exit) A long-time lifeline for Tokyo English-speakers, Kinokuniya stocks a broad selection of foreign-language books and magazines. Particularly of note is its fantastic collection of books on Japan in English and Japanese literature in translation; we love the notes handwritten by the staff with their recommendations.

Disk Union Shinjuku MUSIC

(ディスクユニオン新宿; Map p146; http://diskunion.net; 3-31-4 Shinjuku, Shinjuku-ku; ⏲11am-9pm Mon-Sat, to 8pm Sun; 🚉 JR Yamanote line to Shinjuku, east exit) Keeping the dream alive for fans of physical music, Disk Union has eight (cramped) storeys of used CDs and records, including whole floors for genres like '70s prog and '80s new wave. There are a few more branches nearby with even more specific (and obscure) foci, including one exclusively for vinyl; see the map out front.

NEWoMan MALL

(Map p146; www.newoman.jp; 4-1-6 Shinjuku, Shinjuku-ku; 11am-9.30pm, food hall 8am-10pm; JR Yamanote line to Shinjuku, new south exit) Awkward name and unlikely location (within the Shinjuku Bus Terminal complex) aside, this newish mall is one of Tokyo's swankiest places to shop. There's an outpost of excellent food and kitchenware shop Akomeya (p153) in the basement and a line-up of posh takeaway vendors on the 2nd-floor terrace (where you can sit a nd eat).

Harajuku & Aoyama

Harajuku is trend-central for young shoppers. Malls and department stores on the main drags carry international fast-fashion brands alongside home-grown ones. Edgier boutiques are located on the backstreets. Omote-sandō, the boulevard connecting Harajuku and Aoyama, has statement boutiques from pretty much all the famous European fashion houses. Many of the big names in Japanese fashion, such as Issey Miyake, Comme des Garçons and Yohji Yamamoto, have their flagship boutiques in Aoyama.

A&S Aoyama FASHION & ACCESSORIES

(Map p116; www.arts-science.com; 4-23-11 Minami-Aoyama, Minato-ku; noon-8pm; S Ginza line to Omote-sandō, exit A5) This is the flagship boutique from celebrity stylist Sonya Park, whose signature look is a vintage-inspired minimalism in luxurious, natural fabrics. It carries items both from her brand, Arts & Science, and also select international brands.

Park has more small stores in the nearby midcentury apartment building Palace Aoyama (across from the Nezu Museum). On the ground floor, look for: **Shoes and Things** (No 103; self-explanatory); **&SHOP** (No 105; more clothes and accessories) and **Over the Counter** (No 109; homewares).

★House @Mikiri Hassin FASHION & ACCESSORIES

(ハウス@ミキリハッシン; Map p116; 03-3486-7673; http://house.mikirihassin.co.jp; 5-42-1 Jingūmae, Shibuya-ku; noon-9pm, closed Wed; S Ginza line to Omote-sandō, exit A1) Hidden deep in the side alleys of Harajuku, House stocks an ever-changing selection of experimental Japanese fashion brands. Contrary to what the coolness of the clothes may suggest, the sales clerks are helpful and friendly – grateful, perhaps, that you made the effort to find the place. Look for 'ハウス' spelled vertically in neon.

Comme des Garçons FASHION & ACCESSORIES

(コム・デ・ギャルソン; Map p116; www.comme-des-garcons.com; 5-2-1 Minami-Aoyama, Minato-ku; 11am-8pm; S Ginza line to Omote-sandō, exit A5) Designer Kawakubo Rei threw a wrench in the fashion machine in the early '80s with her dark, asymmetrical designs. That her work doesn't appear as shocking today as it once did speaks volumes about her far-reaching success. This eccentric, vaguely disorienting architectural creation is her brand's flagship store.

KiddyLand TOYS

(キデイランド; Map p116; 03-3409-3431; www.kiddyland.co.jp; 6-1-9 Jingūmae, Shibuya-ku; 11am-9pm Mon-Fri, 10.30am-9pm Sat & Sun; JR Yamanote line to Harajuku, Omote-sandō exit) This multistorey toy emporium is packed to the rafters with character goods, including all your Studio Ghibli, Sanrio and Disney faves. It's not just for kids either; you'll spot plenty of adults on a nostalgia trip down the Hello Kitty aisle.

Laforet DEPARTMENT STORE

(ラフォーレ; Map p116; www.laforet.ne.jp; 1-11-6 Jingūmae, Shibuya-ku; 11am-9pm; JR Yamanote line to Harajuku, Omote-sandō exit) Laforet has been a beacon of Harajuku fashion for decades, where young brands cut their teeth and established ones hold court. Check out the avant-garde looks at ground-floor boutique **Wall**.

Shibuya

Shibuya is a popular shopping spot for teens and twenty-somethings. But the neighbourhood's position as a transport hub means there are branches of big-box electronics stores and department stores, too.

★Tokyu Hands DEPARTMENT STORE

(東急ハンズ; Map p138; http://shibuya.tokyu-hands.co.jp; 12-18 Udagawa-chō, Shibuya-ku; 10am-9pm; JR Yamanote line to Shibuya, Hachikō exit) This DIY and *zakka* (miscellaneous things) store is a Tokyo landmark, loved by locals and tourists alike. It has eight fascinating floors of everything you didn't know you needed – reflexology slippers, bee-venom face masks and cartoon-character-shaped rice-ball moulds, for example. Most stuff is inexpensive, making it perfect for souvenir and gift hunting. Warning: you could lose hours in here.

There's another branch in **Shinjuku** (東急ハンズ新宿店; Map p146; Takashimaya Times Sq, 5-24-2 Sendagaya, Shibuya-ku; ⏲10am-9pm; 🚉JR Yamanote line to Shinjuku, new south exit) that is usually less crowded and easier to navigate (but is less iconic than the Shibuya store).

d47 design travel store DESIGN
(Map p138; ☎03-6427-2301; 8th fl, Shibuya Hikarie, 2-21-1 Shibuya, Shibuya-ku; ⏲11am-8pm; 🚉JR Yamanote line to Shibuya, east exit) The folks behind the D&D Department lifestyle brand and magazine are expert scavengers, searching Japan's nooks and crannies for outstanding examples of artisanship – be it ceramics from Ishikawa or linens from Fukui. An ever-changing selection of finds is on sale here.

Adjacent the shop is the **d47 Museum**, which changing exhibitions showcasing products local to one particular prefecture out of Japan's 47.

Mega Donki VARIETY
(MEGAドンキ; Map p138; ☎03-5428-4086; 28-6 Udagawa-chō, Shibuya-ku; ⏲24hr; 🚉JR Yamanote line to Shibuya, Hachikō exit) You could show up in Tokyo completely empty-handed and this huge outpost of all-night, bargain retailer 'Don Quijote' would have you covered. There are groceries, toiletries, electronics and clothes – along with all sorts of random stuff, including the best selection of unusual flavoured Kit-Kat chocolates we've seen.

Tower Records MUSIC
(タワーレコード; Map p138; ☎03-3496-3661; http://tower.jp/store/Shibuya; 1-22-14 Jinnan, Shibuya-ku; ⏲10am-11pm; 🚉JR Yamanote line to Shibuya, Hachikō exit) Yes, Tower lives – in Japan at least! This eight-storey temple of music has a deep collection of Japanese and world music. Even if you're not into buying, it can be a great place to browse and discover local artists. There are lots of listening stations on the ground floor.

Shibuya 109 FASHION & ACCESSORIES
(渋谷109; Ichimarukyū; Map p138; www.shibuya109.jp; 2-29-1 Dōgenzaka, Shibuya-ku; ⏲10am-9pm; 🚉JR Yamanote line to Shibuya, Hachikō exit) Nicknamed *marukyū*, this cylindrical tower is a trend factory and teen institution. Inside are dozens of small boutiques, each with its own carefully styled look and competing soundtrack. Pose for photos with giant, pastel-coloured cupcakes and doughnuts in the top-floor studio **Moreru Mignon**.

Ebisu & Meguro

Ebisu and Naka-Meguro have fashionable boutiques and vintage stores. You'll have to do a bit of legwork, but finds are worth it.

★**Kapital** FASHION & ACCESSORIES
(キャピタル; Map p120; ☎03-5725-3923; www.kapital.jp; 2-20-2 Ebisu-Minami, Shibuya-ku; ⏲11am-8pm; 🚉JR Yamanote line to Ebisu, west exit) Cult brand Kapital is hard to pin down, but perhaps a deconstructed mash-up of the American West and the centuries-old Japanese aesthetic of *boro* (tatty-chic) comes close. Almost no two items are alike, and the textiles (particularly the shawls and socks) are gorgeous.

The shop itself is like an art installation, and the facade is always changing (just look for something that stands out). The staff, not snobby at all, can point you towards the other two shops nearby.

★**Okura** FASHION & ACCESSORIES
(オクラ; Map p120; ☎03-3461-8511; www.hrm.co.jp; 20-11 Sarugaku-chō, Shibuya-ku; ⏲11.30am-8pm Mon-Fri, 11am-8.30pm Sat & Sun; 🚉Tōkyū Tōyoko line to Daikanyama, central exit) Okura specialises in clothing and accessories dyed with indigo, which has a long tradition in Japan. There are contemporary T-shirts and hoodies and also items that riff on older silhouettes, like the trailing sleeves of a kimono. The natural fabrics are sturdy and/or sumptuous (unfortunately priced accordingly).

Note: there's no sign out the front, but the two-storey, plaster and tile building is distinct.

★**Daikanyama T-Site** BOOKS
(代官山T-SITE; Map p120; ☎03-3770-2525; http://real.tsite.jp/daikanyama/; 17-5 Sarugaku-chō, Shibuya-ku; ⏲7am-2am; 🚉Tōkyū Tōyoko line to Daikanyama, central exit) Tokyo's most famous bookstore, spread out over three buildings (with a cool basket-weave facade designed by KDa), has a dazzling collection of books on travel, art, design and food, including many books in English on Japan and Japanese fiction in translation. Reading at the

in-house Starbucks is a popular – and competitive; be quick on your feet for a seat! – local pastime.

...research General Store SPORTS & OUTDOORS

(Map p120; www.sett.co.jp; 1-14-11 Aobadai, Meguro-ku; ⌚noon-7pm; Ⓢ Hibiya line to Naka-Meguro, main exit) The revolution will have swag: ...research General Store sells original made-in-Japan outdoor wear and gear (and also cleverly branded t-shirts and totes) for what designer Kobayashi Setsumasa calls 'anarcho-mountaineers' and 'saunter punks'.

Vase FASHION & ACCESSORIES

(Map p120; ☎03-5458-0337; www.vasenakameguro.com; 1-7-7 Kami-Meguro, Meguro-ku; ⌚noon-8pm; Ⓢ Hibiya line to Naka-Meguro, main exit) Vase is a perfect example of one of Naka-Meguro's tiny, impeccably curated boutiques: a mix of vintage and one-off pieces from designers unknown to anyone but the most attentive hype-beast, plus the occasional trunk show. It's in a little white house set back from the Meguro-gawa (with the name on the post box).

ℹ Orientation

Generally speaking, Tokyo can be divided into central, east and west. The Imperial Palace is in the centre of the city; nearby sights include the kabuki theatre Kabuki-za, in Ginza, and Tsukiji Market, in Tsukiji. The eastern part of the city, around the Sumida-gawa, is often thought of as the old city. Major sightseeing centres here include Ueno, where the Tokyo National Museum is located, and Asakusa, home to the ancient temple, Sensō-ji. The west side, including neighbourhoods like Shinjuku, Harajuku and Shibuya, has more contemporary development. This is where you'll find the streetscapes that have become synonymous with modern Tokyo, aglow with colourful signs and giant video screens, skyscrapers, and attractions like Shibuya Crossing. On and around Tokyo Bay is the city that is still being built: islands of reclaimed land that host leisure and entertainment facilities, the new wholesale market on Toyosu, and many venues for the 2020 Summer Olympics.

ℹ Information

MEDICAL SERVICES

St Luke's International Hospital (聖路加国際病院; Seiroka Kokusai Byōin; Map p96; ☎appointments 03-5550-7120, general 03-3541-5151, international department 03-5550-7166; http://hospital.luke.ac.jp; 9-1 Akashi-chō, Chūō-ku; ⌚international department 8.30am-5pm Mon-Fri; Ⓢ Hibiya line to Tsukiji, exits 3 & 4) Tokyo's most foreigner-friendly hospital, with English-speaking doctors and translation services provided. Walk-ins accepted for primary care (8.30am to 11am weekdays) and paediatric care (8.30am to 11am and 6.45pm to 9.45pm weekdays); appointments are required for specialist care. Has 24-hour emergency care.

SAFE TRAVEL

➡ Drink-spiking continues to be a problem in Roppongi (resulting in robbery, extortion and, in extreme cases, physical assault). This is most often the case when touts are involved; never follow a tout into a bar, anywhere.

➡ Men are likely to be solicited in Roppongi and neighbourhoods that are considered red-light districts, including Kabukichō (in Shinjuku) and Dōgenzaka (in Shibuya). Women – particularly solo women – are likely to be harassed in these districts.

TOURIST INFORMATION

Tokyo Metropolitan Government Building Tourist Information Center (Map p146; ☎03-5321-3077; info@tokyo-tourism.jp; 1st fl, Tokyo Metropolitan Government Bldg 1, 2-8-1 Nishi-Shinjuku, Shinjuku-ku; ⌚9.30am-6.30pm; Ⓢ Ōedo line to Tochōmae, exit A4) Has English-language information and publications. There are additional branches in **Keisei Ueno Station** (Map p110; ☎03-3836-3471; 1-60 Ueno-kōen, Taitō-ku; ⌚9.30am-6.30pm; 📶; 🚊JR & Keisei lines to Ueno, Ikenohata exit), **Haneda Airport** (☎03-6428-0653; ⌚24hr; 📶) and **Shinjuku Bus Terminal** (Map p146; ☎03-6274-8192; 3rd fl, Shinjuku Bus Station, 5-24-55 Sendagaya, Shibuya-ku; ⌚6.30am-11pm; 🚊JR Yamanote line to Shinjuku, new south exit).

JNTO Tourist Information Center (Map p96; ☎03-3201-3331; www.jnto.go.jp; 1st fl, Shin-Tokyo Bldg, 3-3-1 Marunouchi, Chiyoda-ku; ⌚9am-5pm; 📶; Ⓢ Chiyoda line to Nijūbashi-mae, exit 1) Run by the Japan National Tourism Organisation (JNTO), this TIC has information on Tokyo and beyond. Staff speak English.

In addition to the nationally and municipally run Tourist Information Centers (TICs), there are many others around the city, run by individual wards, neighbourhood revitalisation NPOs (non-profits) and private enterprises.

Beyond general information in English, some offer luggage storage and shipping services, neighbourhood tours and cultural activities. Note that TICs cannot make accommodation bookings.

Asakusa Culture Tourist Information Center (p105), a ward-run TIC, has lots of info on Asakusa and Ueno, and a Pia ticket counter (for purchasing tickets to concerts and shows), near the entrance to Sensō-ji.

JR EAST Travel Service Centers

At all JR East Travel Service Centers, located at both airports and at JR Tokyo, Shinjuku, Shibuya, Ikebukuro, Ueno and Hamamatsuchō Stations, you can book *shinkansen* (bullet-train) tickets, purchase rail passes or exchange rail-pass vouchers and get tourist information in English. The main branch, at **Tokyo Station** (JR 東日本トラベルサービスセンター; Map p96; ☎03-5221-8123; www.jreast.co.jp; Tokyo Station, 1-9-1 Marunouchi, Chiyoda-ku; ⊙7.30am-8.30pm; 📶; 🚉JR Yamanote line to Tokyo, Marunouchi north exit), also offers currency exchange, same-day baggage storage (¥600), luggage forwarding, and booking services for ski and onsen getaways that are accessed via JR lines (and with lodgings at partner hotels); bookings can also be made at the Shinjuku branch.

USEFUL WEBSITES

Go Tokyo (www.gotokyo.org) The city's official website includes information on sights, events and suggested itineraries.

Tokyo Cheapo (www.tokyocheapo.com) Hints on how to do Tokyo on the cheap.

Time Out Tokyo (www.timeout.jp) Arts and entertainment listings.

ℹ Getting There & Away

AIR

Haneda Airport

Closer to central Tokyo, **Haneda Airport** (HND, 羽田空港; ☎Tokyo International Air Terminal Information 03-6428-0888; www.haneda-airport.jp; 📶) has two domestic terminals and one international terminal. Note that some international flights arrive at awkward night-time hours, between midnight and 5am, when the only public transport to central Tokyo will be infrequent night buses and taxis.

There's a tourist information centre in the international terminal, on the 2nd floor of the arrivals lobby.

Narita Airport

Though modern and well-run, **Narita Airport** (NRT, 成田空港; ☎0476-34-8000; www.narita-airport.jp; 📶) is inconveniently located 66km east of Tokyo. There are three terminals, with Terminal 3 handling low-cost carriers. All terminals have tourist information desks.

Only Terminals 1 and 2 have train stations; all terminals are accessible via coach lines.

A free shuttle bus runs between Terminal 2 and Terminal 3 approximately every five minutes (4.30am to 11.20pm); otherwise it is a 15-minute walk between the two terminals. Free shuttles also run between all terminals every 15 minutes (8am to 8pm) and every 30 minutes (7am to 8am and 8pm to 9.30pm).

When returning, note that there is a much better selection of shops and restaurants before security.

BUS

The easiest port of entry for travellers coming by bus from other parts of Japan is the new **Shinjuku Bus Terminal** (バスタ新宿, Busuta Shinjuku; Map p146; ☎03-6380-4794; www.shinjuku-busterminal.co.jp; 4th fl, 5-24-55 Sendagaya, Shibuya-ku; 📶; 🚉JR Yamanote line to Shinjuku, new south exit), part of the JR Shinjuku train station complex. There is a tourist information centre on the 3rd floor and direct access to JR rail lines on the 2nd floor. Another long-distance hub is the **JR Highway Bus Terminal** at Tokyo Station.

CAR & MOTORCYCLE

Driving in Tokyo, both on the *shutokō* (the city's convoluted expressway network) and the narrow lanes of residential neighbourhoods, can be challenging if you are not already used to driving such roads.

If your destination is a major hotel, arriving by rental car from other parts of Japan is a reasonable option; such hotels will have drop-off lanes and parking facilities (the latter at a cost).

Guesthouses and apartment rentals are often tucked deep in residential districts that are hard to navigate and will not have parking spaces – and may be located on roads so narrow that even brief (illegal) street parking would be tricky.

TRAIN

Tokyo Station (p91) is the terminus for all *shinkansen* that connect Tokyo to major cities all over Japan. From Tokyo Station you can transfer to the JR Chūō and JR Yamanote lines, as well as the Marunouchi subway line.

Shinkansen from points west (Kansai, Western Honshū and Kyūshū) will stop at Shinagawa (one stop before Tokyo Station for inbound trains), more useful for destinations on the city's west or south sides.

Meanwhile, *shinkansen* from points east (Tōhoku and Hokkaidō) will stop at Ueno (one stop before Tokyo Station for inbound trains), more useful for destinations on the city's east or north sides.

Both Shinagawa and Ueno are stops on the JR Yamanote line. From Shinagawa you can also get the Toei Asakusa subway line; From Ueno you can transfer to the Ginza and Hibiya subway lines.

Getting Around

TO/FROM HANEDA AIRPORT

Bus

Purchase tickets at the kiosks at the arrivals hall. In Tokyo, there's a ticket counter inside the Shinjuku Bus Terminal (p159).

Friendly Airport Limousine (www.limousine bus.co.jp) Coaches connect Haneda with major train stations and hotels in Shibuya (¥1030), Shinjuku (¥1230), Roppongi (¥1130), Ginza (¥930) and others, taking anywhere from 30 to 90 minutes depending on traffic. Buses for Shinjuku depart every 30 to 40 minutes (5am to 11.30pm) and at 12.20am, 1am, 1.40am and 2.20am; departures for other areas are less frequent. Fares double between midnight and 5am.

Monorail

Tokyo Monorail (www.tokyo-monorail.co.jp) Leaves approximately every 10 minutes (5am to midnight) for Hamamatsuchō Station (¥490, 15 minutes), which is a stop on the JR Yamanote line. Good for travellers staying near Ginza or Roppongi.

Train

Keikyū Airport Express (www.haneda -tokyo-access.com) Trains depart several times an hour (5.30am to midnight) for Shinagawa (¥410, 12 minutes), where you can connect to the JR Yamanote line. From Shinagawa, some trains continue along the Asakusa subway line, which serves Higashi-Ginza, Nihombashi and Asakusa Stations.

Note that the international and domestic terminals have their own stations; when travelling to the airport, the international terminal is the second-last stop.

Taxi

Fixed fares from designated airport taxi stands include: Ginza (¥5900), Shibuya (¥6600), Shinjuku (¥7100), Ikebukuro (¥8900) and Asakusa (¥7200), plus highway tolls (around ¥800). There's a 20% surcharge between 10pm and 5am. Credit cards accepted.

TO/FROM NARITA AIRPORT

Bus

Access Narita (www.accessnarita.jp; ¥1000) Discount buses depart roughly every 20 minutes (7.30am to 10.45pm) for Tokyo Station and Ginza (one to 1¼ hours). There's no ticket counter at the airport; just go directly to bus stop 31 at Terminal 1, or stops 2 or 19 at Terminal 2, and pay on board. Luggage is restricted to one suitcase of less than 20kg. For return trips to Narita, buses depart from platform 7 at the **JR Highway Bus Terminal** at Tokyo Station. You can reserve tickets online, but only in Japanese; departures are frequent, so if you leave yourself a little extra time, you should have no problem.

Friendly Airport Limousine (www.limousine bus.co.jp; adult/child ¥3100/1550) Coaches run to major hotels and train stations in central Tokyo. The journey takes 1½ to two hours depending on traffic. Travellers are allowed two bags up to 30kg each. No advance reservations are necessary but you must purchase a ticket before boarding. You can purchase tickets for the next available bus from one of the kiosks in any of the terminals' arrivals halls. At the time of research, discount round-trip tickets (¥4500), good for 14 days, were available for foreign tourists; ask at the airport ticket kiosk. From Tokyo, there's a ticket counter inside the Shinjuku Bus Terminal (p159); you can also reserve online up to the day before departure.

Train

Both Japan Railways (JR) and the independent Keisei line run between central Tokyo and Narita Airport Terminals 1 and 2. For Terminal 3, take a train to Terminal 2 and then walk or take the free shuttle bus to Terminal 3 (and budget an extra 15 minutes).

Tickets can be purchased upon arrival in the basement of either terminal, where the entrances to the train stations are located; you cannot buy tickets on the train. In general trains run slightly more frequently from the late morning to the late afternoon and less frequently earlier and later.

Seats on Narita Express and Skyliner trains are all reserved; purchase them at a ticket window or from the touch-screen machines. It's usually possible to get a seat on the next available train, though those with departure anxiety may want to book their outbound ticket in advance. Speed and comfort level are pretty much the same; both have space in the front of the cars to store luggage. Generally, the Skyliner is more convenient for destinations on the east side of Tokyo while the Narita Express gets you to the west side of the city faster.

Keisei Skyliner (www.keisei.co.jp) Nonstop direct trains to Nippori (36 minutes) followed by Ueno (41 minutes) run approximately twice an hour between 7.30am and 10pm (adult/child ¥2470/1240). Transfer is available at Nippori Station for the JR Yamanote line and at Ueno for the JR Yamanote line and Ginza and Hibiya subway lines. Foreign nationals can purchase advance tickets online for slightly less (one-way/return ¥2200/4300).

Narita Express (N'EX; www.jreast.co.jp) Trains run between 7.45am and 9.45pm, departing Narita Airport for Tokyo Station (¥3020, 60 minutes) before splitting and heading out to other parts of the city. The most useful route runs approximately every half-hour to Shibuya

(75 minutes) and Shinjuku (80 minutes); some trains stop first at Shinagawa (65 minutes) while others may continue to Ikebukuro (85 minutes). The price for all of the above destinations is the same: ¥3190. The ticket you purchase for your specific destination will ensure that you are in a seat in the right car – so it's pretty hard to mess this up! At the time of research, foreign tourists could purchase return N'EX tickets for ¥4000 (¥2000 for under 12s), which are valid for 14 days and can be used on any route. Check online or enquire at the JR East Travel Service Centers at Narita Airport for the latest deals. Long-haul JR passes are valid on N'EX trains, but you must obtain a seat reservation (no extra charge) from a JR ticket office.

Regular Keisei line trains run parallel to the Skyliner but make stops, and are a good budget option. There are no reserved seats on these trains; if you (and your bags) can squeeze in, you can ride. Purchase tickets from the touch-screen machines. These options can be a little bit more confusing, so pay attention to the signboards.

Keisei Main Line Rapid *tokkyū* (特急) trains run roughly every 20 minutes (from 6am to 10.30pm) to Nippori (¥1030; 66 minutes) and Ueno (¥1030; 71 minutes). There are also local trains that take significantly longer; make sure you get the *tokkyū*.

Keisei Access Express Approximately every 40 minutes (5.40am to 11pm) there are trains making limited stops on the same route until Aoto, after which they hook up with the Toei Asakusa line, running south to Asakusa (¥1290; 50 minutes), Nihombashi (¥1330; 59 minutes), Shimbashi (¥1330; 62 minutes) and Shinagawa (¥1520; 72 minutes).

Taxi

Fixed-fare taxis run ¥20,000 to ¥22,000 for most destinations in central Tokyo, plus tolls (about ¥2000 to ¥2500). There's a 20% surcharge between 10pm and 5am. Credit cards accepted.

BICYCLE

Tokyo is by no means a bicycle-friendly city. Bike lanes are almost nonexistent and you'll see no-parking signs for bicycles everywhere. (Ignore these at your peril: your bike could get impounded, requiring a half-day excursion to the pound and a ¥3000 fee.) Despite all this you'll see locals on bikes everywhere.

Cogi Cogi (www.cogicogi.jp; 24hr ¥2400) is a bike-sharing system with ports around the city, including some hostels. There are instructions in English, but it's a little complicated to use. You'll need to download an app, register a credit card and have wi-fi connection on the go to sync with the ports.

ℹ AIRPORT TRANSPORT & SUBWAY PASS PACKAGE DEALS

The following packages combine airport transport and an unlimited-ride Tokyo subway pass (good on Tokyo Metro and Toei lines, but not JR ones).

Limousine & Subway Pass (www.limousinebus.co.jp/en/guide/ticket/subwaypass.html) One-way travel on the Friendly Airport Limousine from Narita or Haneda Airports to most (but not all) stations and hotels serviced by coach routes and a 24-hour subway pass; or round-trip travel and a 48- or 72-hour subway pass. Coming from Narita this package is cheaper than buying a regular return ticket. Any ticket packages can be purchased on arrival at the airport; one-way packages can also be purchased at Shinjuku Bus Terminal.

Skyliner & Tokyo Subway Ticket One-way or round-trip travel on the Skyliner between Narita Airport and Ueno plus a 24-, 48- or 72-hour subway pass. Purchase online in advance or on arrival at the ticketing counter for a saving of ¥540 to ¥2240 off the total combined price of the individual tickets included in the deal.

Some accommodation has bikes to lend, sometimes for free or for a small fee. In Yurakuchō, Muji (p152) has bikes to rent.

PUBLIC TRANSPORT

Bus

Toei (www.kotsu.metro.tokyo.jp/eng/services/bus.html) runs an extensive bus network, though it's rarely more convenient than the subway.

➡ Fares are ¥210/110 per adult/child; there are no transfer tickets. Pay by IC pass (prepaid rechargeable Suica and Pasmo cards) or deposit your fare into the box as you enter the bus; there's a change machine at the front of the bus that accepts ¥1000 notes.

➡ Most buses have digital signage that switches between Japanese and English (otherwise listen for your stop). Signal the bus to stop in advance of the approaching stop by pushing one of the buttons near the seats.

Subway & Train

Tokyo's extensive rail network includes JR lines, a subway system and private commuter lines that depart in every direction for the suburbs,

TRAIN & SUBWAY TIPS

➡ Figure out the best route to your destination with the Japan Travel app (www.navitimejapan.com).

➡ Most train and subway stations have several different exits. Try to get your bearings and decide where to exit while still on the platform; look for the yellow signs that indicate which stairs lead to which exits.

➡ If you're not sure which exit to take, look for street maps of the area, usually posted near the ticket gates, which show the locations of the exits.

➡ Hub stations have lockers in several sizes and cost from ¥200 to ¥600. Storage is good for 24 hours, after which your bags will be removed and taken to the station office.

➡ Most train stations have toilets, almost all of which are free of charge and have toilet paper (though not always soap and towels).

like spokes on a wheel. Journeys that require transfers between lines run by different operators cost more than journeys that use only one operator's lines. Major transit hubs include Tokyo, Shinagawa, Shibuya, Shinjuku, Ikebukuro and Ueno stations.

Trains and subways run 5am to midnight. Trains arrive and depart precisely on time and are generally clean and pleasant, though they get uncomfortably crowded during rush hours. The morning rush (7am to 9.30am) for trains going towards central Tokyo (from all directions) is the worst. Until 9.30am women (and children) can ride in women-only cars, which tend to be less crowded. The evening rush (around 5pm to 8pm) hits trains going out of central Tokyo – though as many work late or stay out, it's not as bad as the morning commute. The last train of the night heading out of the city (around midnight) is also usually packed – with drunk people. Trains going the opposite directions during peak hours (towards central Tokyo in the evening, for example) are uncrowded, as are trains in the middle of the day.

Lines & Fares

The JR network covers the whole country and includes the *shinkansen* (bullet train). In Tokyo, the above-ground Yamanote (loop) and the Chūō–Sōbu (central) lines are the most useful. Tickets start at ¥133 and go up depending on how far you travel.

Tokyo has 13 subway lines, nine of which are operated by **Tokyo Metro** (www.tokyometro.jp) and four by **Toei** (www.kotsu.metro.tokyo.jp). The lines are colour-coded, making navigation fairly simple. Unfortunately a transfer ticket is required to change between the two; a Pasmo or Suica card makes this process seamless, but either way a journey involving more than one operator comes out costing slightly more. Rides on Tokyo Metro cost ¥170 to ¥240 (¥90 to ¥120 for children) and on Toei ¥180 to ¥320 (¥90 to ¥160 for children), depending on how far you travel.

Private commuter lines service some of the hipper residential neighbourhoods. Useful trains:

Keiō Inokashira line From Shibuya for Shimo-Kitazawa and Kichijōji.

Odakyū line From Shinjuku for Shimo-Kitazawa.

Tōkyū-Tōyoko line From Shibuya for Daikan-yama and Naka-Meguro.

Note that the commuter lines run *tokkyū* (特急; limited-express services), *kyūkō* (急行; express) and *futsū* (普通; local) trains, which can be a little confusing.

Lost & Found

Larger stations have dedicated lost-and-found windows (labelled in English); otherwise lost items are left with the station attendant. Items not claimed on the same day will be handed over to the operator's lost-and-found centre. Items not claimed after several days are turned over to the police.

JR East Infoline (☎ in English 050-2016-1603; ⏰10am-6pm)

Toei Transportation Lost & Found (☎03-3816-5700; www.kotsu.metro.tokyo.jp/eng/tips/found.html; ⏰9am-8pm)

Tokyo Metro Lost & Found (Map p106; ☎03-5227-5741; ⏰9am-8pm; 🚉JR Sōbu line to Iidabashi, west exit) Office located inside Iidabashi Station on the Namboku line.

Suica & Pasmo Cards

Prepaid re-chargeable Suica and Pasmo cards (they're interchangeable) work on all city trains, subways and buses. These make easy work of getting around all the different networks. Bonus: fares for pass users are slightly less (a few yen per journey) than for paper-ticket holders.

➡ Purchase from any touch-screen ticket-vending machine in Tokyo (including those at Haneda and Narita Airports); most have an English option. JR stations sell Suica; subway and independent lines sell Pasmo.

➡ Both require a ¥500 deposit, which is refunded (along with any remaining charge) when you return the pass to any ticket window.

➡ Passes can be topped-up at any touch-screen ticket-vending machine (not just, for example, at JR stations for Suica passes) in increments of ¥1000.

➡ To use the cards, just run them over the card readers at the ticket gates upon entering and exiting.

➡ If you somehow manage to invalidate your card, take it to the station window and staff will sort it out.

Single-Ride Tickets

➡ Single-ride paper tickets can be purchased at touch-screen ticket-vending machines outside station ticket gates.

➡ To purchase the correct ticket, you'll need to work out the fare from the chart above the machines. If you're unsure, just buy a ticket for the cheapest fare (you can sort it out when you exit).

➡ Insert your ticket in the slot at the gate (only some of the ticket gates will have slots for paper tickets). Make sure to pick it up when it pops out again.

➡ You'll do the same thing when you exit. If your ticket does not have sufficient charge to cover your journey, insert it into one of the 'fare adjustment' machines near the exit gates.

Unlimited-Ride Tickets

If you're planning a packed day, you might consider getting an unlimited-ride ticket.

Tokyo Subway Ticket Good for unlimited rides on both Tokyo Metro and Toei subway lines for 24 (¥800), 48 (¥1200) or 72 (¥1500) hours; half-price for children. This pass is only available to foreign travellers on a tourist visa; for more information and sales points see www.tokyometro.jp.

Tokyo Metro One-Day Open Ticket (adult/child ¥600/300) Unlimited rides over a 24-hour period on Tokyo Metro subway lines only. Purchase at any Tokyo Metro station; no restrictions apply.

TAXI

Taxis only make economic sense for short distances or groups of four.

➡ Fares start at ¥410 for the first 1km, then rise by ¥80 for every 237m you travel or for every 90 seconds spent in traffic.

➡ There's a surcharge of 20% between 10pm and 5am.

➡ Drivers rarely speak English, though most taxis have navigation systems. Have your destination written down in Japanese, or better yet, a business card with an address.

➡ Taxis take credit cards and IC passes.

Ride-Sharing Apps

Tokyo strictly regulates ride-sharing apps: only licensed chauffeurs can offer rides, meaning you're more likely to summon a town car that costs more than a regular taxi.

AT A GLANCE

POPULATION
Yokohama: 3.78 million

TALLEST WATERFALL
Kegon-no-taki (p216)

BEST VIEWPOINT
Panorama-dai (p176)

BEST ONSEN
Tenzan Tōji-kyō (p189)

BEST HOSTEL
K's House Itō Onsen (p198)

WHEN TO GO

Apr–May Experience the flush of spring in the mountains north and west of Tokyo.

Jul–Aug The official season for Mt Fuji climbing and beach-hopping around the Izu Peninsula.

Sep–Nov Pleasant temperatures and fewer crowds, save when the autumn leaves blaze red.

Kawaguchi-ko lake (p173) and Mt Fuji (p168)

Mt Fuji & Around Tokyo

Once you've succumbed to Tokyo's manifold pleasures, and the capital has chewed you up, Godzilla-style, worry not: there's a whole other world out there, where spiritual sanctuaries, invigorating hot springs and idyllic natural scenery awaits; and most of it is less than two hours away from the city. Rambling country ryokan (traditional Japanese inns), laid-back surf beaches, pristine lakes and cedar-lined trails are some of the delights in store, as well as the symbol of Japan itself, mighty Mt Fuji. There's history here too, including a medieval capital and ports that were among the first to open to the West.

INCLUDES

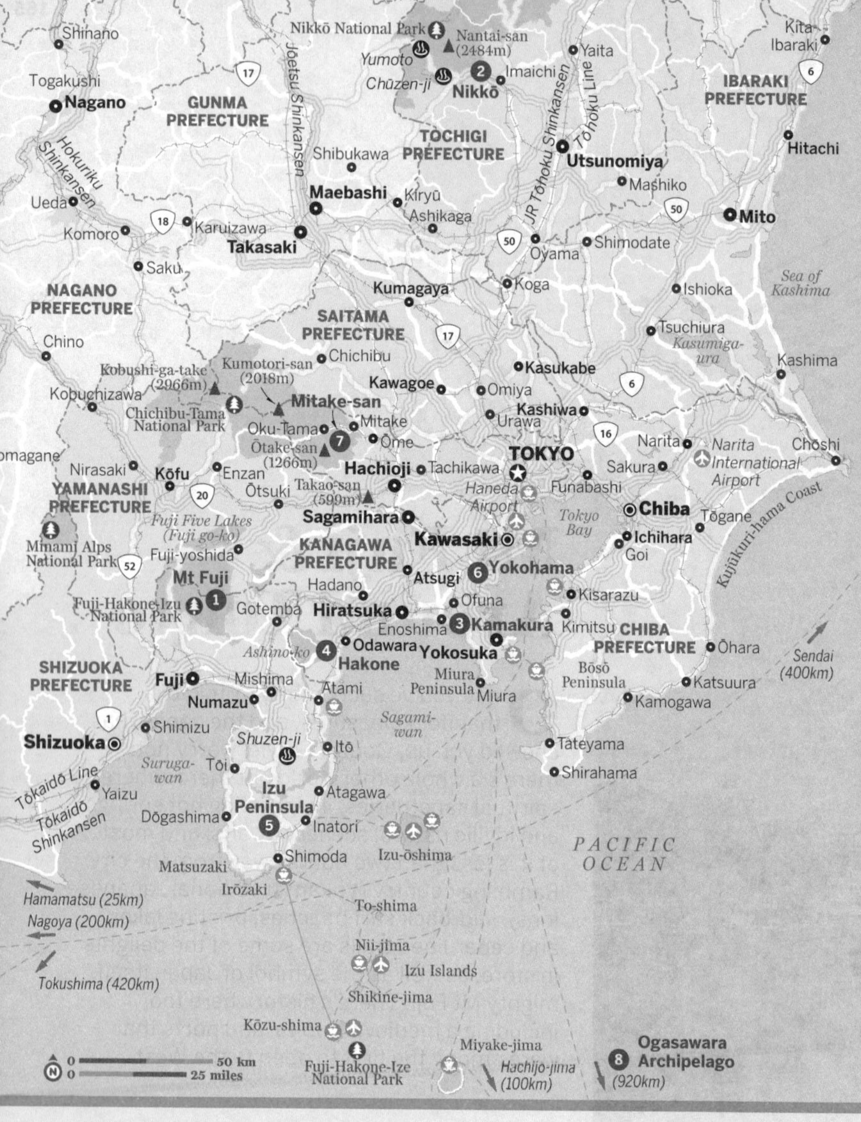

Mt Fuji & Around Tokyo Highlights

1. **Mt Fuji** (p168) Reaching the summit of Japan's highest mountain and national symbol.

2. **Nikkō** (p209) Taking in the grandeur of old Edo at this dazzling shrine complex.

3. **Kamakura** (p182) Resetting your senses in the Zen temples of Japan's medieval capital.

4. **Hakone** (p187) Hopping between onsen, art museums and hiking trails.

5. **Izu Peninsula** (p195) Flip-flopping between beaches and seaside hot springs.

6. **Yokohama** (p176) sampling craft beer, contemporary art and jazz in this cosmopolitan port city.

7. **Mitake** (p208) Hiking at Mitake-san, on the mountainous and forested western edge of Tokyo.

8. **Ogasawara Archipelago** (p219) Truly getting away from it all and back to nature on this pristine, subtropical island chain.

Getting There & Away

The greater Tokyo area is well served by trains going to and from the city; it's not as easy to get between places without having to double back to a transit hub. Useful train lines:

JR Chuō line Runs west from Tokyo; transfer at various stations for connecting trains to Takao-san, Oku-Tama and Fuji Five Lakes. The Chuō line continues on to destinations in Nagano Prefecture, but it's a long ride.

JR Tokaidō main line Runs south from Tokyo to Yokohama, then southwest to Odawara (transfer for trains to Hakone) and Atami, the gateway to the Izu Peninsula. Both Odawara and Atami are also stops on the Tokaidō *shinkansen* (bullet train), which continues west to Kyoto, Osaka and Hiroshima.

JR Yokosuka line Runs south from Tokyo to Kamakura via Yokohama.

Odakyu line Runs southwest from Shinjuku, on the west side of Tokyo, to Hakone.

Tobu Nikkō line Runs north from Asakusa, on the east side of Tokyo, to Nikkō.

For direct access to Mt Fuji, express buses, which depart from Shinjuku, are the most convenient.

The Izu Islands are a ferry, hydrofoil or plane ride away, either from Tokyo or towns along the Izu Peninsula. The only way to get to the Ogasawara Archipelago is via a 24-hour-long ferry trip from Tokyo.

MT FUJI & FUJI FIVE LAKES

☎0555

Japan's highest and most famous peak is the big draw of the Fuji Five Lakes (富士五湖) region, but even if you don't intend to climb Fuji-san, it's still worth coming here to enjoy the great outdoors around the volcano's northern foothills, and to admire the mountain photogenically reflected in the lakes. Culture buffs can also delve into the fascinating history of Mt Fuji worship at several sites.

Yamanaka-ko is the easternmost lake, followed by Kawaguchi-ko, Sai-ko, Shōji-ko and Motosu-ko. Particularly during the *kōyō* (autumn foliage season) season, the lakes make a good overnight trip out of Tokyo for leisurely strolling, lake activities and hiking in the nearby mountains.

Getting There & Away

The Fuji Five Lakes area is most easily reached from Tokyo by bus or train, with Fuji-Yoshida and Kawaguchi-ko being the principal gateways. It's also possible to bus in from Tokyo straight to the Fuji Subaru Line Fifth Station (alternatively known as Kawaguchi-ko Fifth Station or Yoshida-guchi Fifth Station) on the mountain during the official climbing season. If you want to combine travel to Mt Fuji and Hakone, consider the Fuji Hakone Pass (p191) from Tokyo.

Coming from western Japan (Kyoto, Osaka), you can take an overnight bus to Kawaguchi-ko.

BUS

Frequent **Keiō Dentetsu** (☎03-5376-2222; www.highwaybus.com) and **Fujikyū Express** (☎0555-72-6877; http://bus-en.fujikyu.co.jp) buses (¥1750, 1¾ hours) run directly to Kawaguchi-ko Station, and to Fujisan Station in Fuji-Yoshida, from the **Shinjuku Expressway Bus Terminal** (バスタ新宿; Map p146; ☎03-5376-2222; www.highway-buses.jp; Shinjuku Station; 🚉JR Yamanote line to Shinjuku, west exit).

Coming from Western Japan, the overnight bus departs from Osaka's Higashi-Umeda Subway Station (¥8700, 10.15pm) via Kyoto Station (¥8200, 11.18pm) to Kawaguchi-ko Station (arrives 8.37am).

TRAIN

JR Chūō line trains go from Shinjuku to Ōtsuki (*tokkyū* ¥2770, one hour; *futsū* ¥1320, 1½ hours), where you transfer to the Fuji Kyūkō line for Fujisan (the station for Fuji-Yoshida; ¥1020, one hour) and Kawaguchi-ko (¥1140, one hour and five minutes).

Getting Around

If you're relying on public transport, note that some inns may offer pick-up service from the nearest train station; enquire when booking.

BUS

The **Fuji Lakes Sightseeing Bus** (two-day passes adult/child ¥1500/750) has three looping routes that start and finish at Kawaguchi-ko Station, with numbered stops for all the sightseeing spots around the western lakes. It's a hop-on, hop-off service with buses every 15 to 30 minutes (seasonal). Pick up the excellent map and timetable from Kawaguchi-ko Station, where patient English-speaking staff can answer all sightseeing bus-related queries. The red line follows Kawaguchi-ko's northern shore and western area, the green line goes around Sai-ko and Aokigahara, and the blue line travels around Shōji-ko to the eastern end of Motosu-ko.

Buses run from both Kawaguchi-ko Station and Fujisan Station to the **Fuji Subaru Line Fifth Station** (Kawaguchi-ko Fifth Station) (one way/return ¥1540/2100, one hour) roughly mid-April to early December.

From Fujisan Station it's an eight-minute bus ride (¥240) to Kawaguchi-ko Station.

CAR

You'll find a branch of **Toyota Rent-a-Car** (☎0555-72-1100, in English 0800-7000-815; 4657 Funatsu; ⏰8am-8pm) a few minutes' walk from Kawaguchi-ko Station; head east from the station then bear right when you hit the main road.

TRAIN

The train is useful for making the short hop between Kawaguchi-ko and Fuji-Yoshida, and also for reaching Fuji-Q Highland amusement park.

Mt Fuji

Of all Japan's iconic images, **Mt Fuji** (富士山; www.fujisan-climb.jp; recommended donation per climber ¥1000) is the real deal. Admiration for the mountain (3776m) appears in Japan's earliest recorded literature, dating from the 8th century. Fuji-san was granted Unesco World Heritage status in 2013; these days, around 300,000 people make the ascent every year.

The Japanese proverb 'He who climbs Mt Fuji once is a wise man, he who climbs it twice is a fool' remains as valid as ever. While reaching the top brings a great sense of achievement (particularly at sunrise), be aware that it's a gruelling climb not known for its beautiful scenery or for being at one with nature. During the climbing season routes are packed, and its barren, apocalyptic-looking landscape is a world away from Fuji's beauty when viewed from afar. At the summit, the crater has a circumference of 4km, but be prepared for it to be clouded over.

Climbing Mt Fuji

The mountain is divided into 10 'stations' from base (First Station) to summit (Tenth). The original pilgrim trail runs from the base station, but these days most climbers start from the halfway point at one of the four active Fifth Stations, all of which can be accessed via bus or car. The intersection of trails is not well marked and it's easy to get lost, particularly on the way down, ending up at the wrong exit point; this is a good reason to climb with experienced guides.

To time your arrival for dawn you can either start up in the afternoon, stay overnight in a mountain hut and continue early in the morning, or climb the whole way at night. You do not want to arrive on the top too long before dawn, as it will be very cold and windy, even at the height of summer.

Fifth Station Routes

Around 90% of climbers opt for these more convenient, faster routes. The four routes are Yoshida Trail (2305m), Subashiri (1980m), Fujinomiya (2380m) and Gotemba (1440m). Allow five to six hours to reach the summit (though some climb it in half the time) and about three hours to descend, plus 1½ hours for circling the crater at the top.

The **Yoshida Trail** is by far and away the most popular route. It's accessed from Fuji Subaru Line Fifth Station (aka Kawaguchi-ko Fifth Station), and has the most modern facilities and is easiest to reach from Kawaguchi-ko town.

The less trodden, but more scenic, forested **Subashiri Trail** is a good alternative. As it merges with the Yoshida Trail at the

MT FUJI: KNOW BEFORE YOU CLIMB

Make no mistake: Mt Fuji is a serious mountain, high enough for altitude sickness, and on the summit it can go from sunny and warm to wet, windy and cold remarkably quickly. Even if conditions are fine, you can count on it being close to freezing in the morning, even in summer. Also be aware that visibility can rapidly disappear with a blanket of mist rolling in suddenly.

At a minimum, bring clothing appropriate for cold and wet weather, including a hat and gloves. Also bring at least 2L of water (you can buy more on the mountain during the climbing season), as well as a map and snacks. If you're climbing at night, bring a torch (flashlight) or headlamp, and spare batteries. Also bring plenty of cash for buying snacks, other necessities and souvenirs from the mountain huts and to use their toilets (¥200).

Descending the mountain is much harder on the knees than ascending; hiking poles will help. To avoid altitude sickness, be sure to take it slowly and take regular breaks. If you're suffering severe symptoms, you'll need to make an immediate descent.

For summit weather conditions, see www.snow-forecast.com/resorts/Mount-Fuji/6day/top.

Eighth Station, it's possible to combine the two by heading up via the Yoshida path and descending via Subashiri by schussing down its loose volcanic sand. Though be aware you'll end up at Subashiri Fifth Station, so it might not be an option if you've parked your car at Kawaguchi-ko Fifth Station.

Other Fifth Stations are **Fujinomiya**, which is best for climbers coming from the west (Nagoya, Kyoto and beyond) and the seldom-used and neglected **Gotemba Trail**, a tough 7½-hour climb to the summit.

Yoshidaguchi Trail

Historically, Fuji pilgrims began at Sengen-jinja near present-day Fuji-Yoshida, paying their homage to the shrine gods before beginning their 19km ascent up the sacred mountain. Today the Yoshidaguchi Trail offers climbers a chance to participate in this centuries-old tradition. Purists will tell you this is the only way to climb, saying that the lower reaches are the most beautiful, through lush forests along an isolated path.

It takes about five hours to reach the old Yoshidaguchi Fifth Station – you can cut this down by half by catching the climbing-season bus from Fujisan Station to Umagaeshi (¥500).

The trail meets up with the one leaving from the Fuji Subaru Line Fifth Station (also known as Kawaguchi-ko Fifth Station) at the Sixth Station. Count on around 12 hours to complete the climb from Fuji's base to summit.

Tours

Fuji Mountain Guides HIKING

(☎042-445-0798; www.fujimountainguides.com; 2-day tours per person from ¥49,500) Professional and experienced bilingual guides lead both group and private tours up the Subashiri Trail. Fees include round-trip travel from Shinjuku and a night in a mountain hut; gear rental is available for extra. They can also arrange trips outside the official season (in late June and late September to early October).

Fuji Mountain Guides can also assist independent travellers in making reservations at mountain huts for a fee of ¥1000 per booking.

Discover Japan Tours HIKING

(www.discover-japan-tours.com; tours per person from ¥10,000) Reputable company running self-guided overnight treks to/from Shinjuku, timed for sunrise arrival, on summer Saturdays, with a stop at a public hot spring on the way back. Groups of up to eight can arrange a private tour (¥60,000) any day of the week, including outside the climbing season.

Fujiyama Guides TOURS

(☎0555-23-7554; www.fujiyamaguides.com; 1/2 people 2-day tours from ¥84,000/92,000, 3-day tours ¥149,000/156,000) As well as standard two-day ascents of Fuji, this company also offers three-day pilgrim tours starting at Fuji Sengen-jinja. Prices do not include accommodation fees.

OUTDOOR GEAR RENTAL

Want to climb Mt Fuji (or any other mountain), but don't want to invest in (or schlep) all the requisite gear? **Yamadōgu Rental** (やまどうぐレンタル屋; Map p146; ☎call centre in English 050-5865-1615; www.yamarent.com; 6th fl, 1-13-7 Nishi-Shinjuku, Shinjuku-ku; ⊙noon-7pm, 6.30am-7pm during Jul & Aug; ⓡJR Yamanote line to Shinjuku, west exit) in Tokyo can set you up with individual items (shoes, poles, rain jacket etc) or a full kit including a backpack from ¥10,500 for two days. Most of the gear is from Japanese outdoor brand Montbell.

You can rent directly from the shop (same-day rental is possible, pending availability) or place an order online and have the gear shipped to your accommodation. During the Fuji climbing season, they have a shop at the Fifth Station of the popular Yoshida Trail where you can return your gear after coming down the mountain. All the details are online in English.

Sleeping & Eating

From the Fifth Stations up, dozens of mountain huts offer hikers simple hot meals in addition to a place to sleep. Most huts allow you to rest inside as long as you order something.

Conditions in mountain huts are spartan (a blanket on the floor sandwiched between other climbers), but reservations are recommended and are essential on weekends. It's also important to let huts know if you decide to cancel at the last minute; be prepared to pay to cover the cost of your no-show.

Camping on the mountain is not permitted, other than at the designated campsite near the Fuji Subaru Line Fifth Station (aka Kawaguchi-ko Fifth Station).

Mt Fuji Area

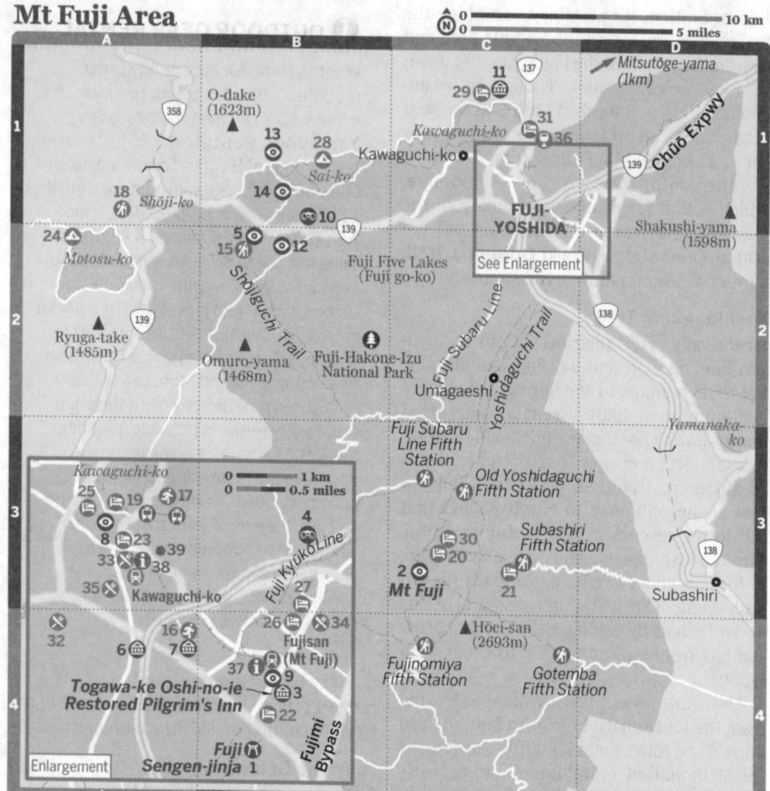

Higashi Fuji Lodge

LODGE ¥

(東富士山荘; ☎0555-75-2113; www4.tokai.or.jp/yamagoya; per person from ¥5000) This atmospheric rest hut at the Subashiri Fifth Station is convenient for off-season trekkers on Mt Fuji, and cooks up steaming soba (buckwheat noodles) with local mushrooms and Fuji herbs.

Taishikan

HUT ¥¥

(太子館; ☎0555-22-1947; www.mfi.or.jp/w3/home0/taisikan; per person incl 2 meals from ¥8500; ⏱1 Jul-early Sep; 🚭📶) Taishikan is located at just about the midway point, at the lower 8th Station (3100m), on Mt Fuji's Yoshida Trail. Sleeping is in warm sleeping bags rather than futons and vegetarian or halal meals are available if requested in advance. English-speaking staff are usually present; cash only. Reservations accepted from 1 April.

Fujisan Hotel

HUT ¥¥

(富士山ホテル; ☎hut 0555-24-6512, reservations 0555-22-0237; www.fujisanhotel.com; per person with/without 2 meals from ¥8350/5950; ⏱1 Jul-early Sep; 🚭📶) Fujisan Hotel is one of the most popular huts, thanks to its location at the Original 8th Station (at 3400m, where the Yoshida and Subashiri trails meet): from here it's only a short push (two hours) onwards to the summit. English-speaking staff are usually present; credit cards accepted.

Reservations required; bookings open from 1 April.

ℹ Information

Free wi-fi is available at Fifth Station access points and the summit, for 72 hours after you've acquired an access card at one of the Fifth Station information centres.

ℹ Getting There & Away

For those wanting to start trekking as soon as they arrive from Tokyo, Keiō Dentetsu (p167) runs direct buses (¥2700, 2½ hours; reservations necessary) from the Shinjuku Expressway Bus Terminal (p167) to Fuji Subaru Line Fifth Station (aka Kawaguchi-ko Fifth Station; it does not operate in winter).

Mt Fuji Area

Buses run from both Kawaguchi-ko and Fujisan Stations to the starting point at Fuji Subaru Line Fifth Station (one way/return ¥1540/2100, one hour), roughly mid-April to early December. In the trekking season, buses depart hourly from around 6.30am until 7pm (ideal for climbers intending to make an overnight ascent). Returning from Fifth Station, buses head back to town from 8am to 8.30pm.

In the low season, the first bus inconveniently leaves Kawaguchi-ko and Fujisan Stations at 8.50am, meaning most trekkers will need to get a taxi in the morning to have enough time (around ¥12,000, plus ¥2100 in tolls), before getting the bus back. The bus schedule is highly seasonal; call Fujikyū Express (p167) or your hotel for details.

In the low season you should be able to find other trekkers to share a taxi at hostels such as K's House (p174). Car hire is another option (particularly good if you're in a group), costing around ¥6800 per day plus fuel and tolls.

To get to the Subashiri Fifth Station trail, you can catch a bus from Kawaguchi-ko to Gotemba (¥1510), from where regular buses head to the Subashiri access point; Gotemba can also be accessed directly from Tokyo either by bus or train.

Fuji-Yoshida

☎0555 / POP 50,426

Fuji-Yoshida (富士吉田) was once teeming with *oshi-no-ie* (pilgrims' inns) where Fuji worshippers stayed before climbing the mountain, though these days only one or two still operate. There is more historic atmosphere here than at Kawaguchi-ko, but it's less convenient for sightseeing in the Fuji Five Lakes area. The central district, Gekkō-ji (月江寺), feels like the little town that time forgot, with original mid-20th-century facades. Fujisan Station is in the centre of Fuji-Yoshida, but if you're heading straight to one of the hostels, the closer stop is Gekkō-ji.

Sights & Activities

★**Fuji Sengen-jinja** SHINTŌ SHRINE

(富士浅間神社; ☎0555-22-0221; www.sengenjinja.jp; 5558 Kami-Yoshida; ⏲grounds 24hr, staffed 9am-5pm) FREE A necessary preliminary to the Mt Fuji ascent is a visit to this atmospheric shrine (8th century, rebuilt 1800s) dedicated to Sakuya-hime, the goddess of the mountain. An avenue of towering cedars leads to the main gate, which is rebuilt every

60 years (slightly larger each time); and its two one-tonne *mikoshi* (portable shrines), used in the annual Yoshida no Himatsuri festival. From Fujisan Station it's a 20-minute uphill walk, or take a bus to Sengen-jinja-mae (¥150, five minutes).

★Togawa-ke Oshi-no-ie
Restored Pilgrim's Inn HISTORIC BUILDING
(御師旧外川家住宅; 3-14-8 Kami-Yoshida; adult/child ¥100/50; ⊙9.30am-4.30pm Wed-Mon) Fuji-Yoshida's *oshi-no-ie* (pilgrims' inns) have served visitors to the mountain since the days when climbing Mt Fuji was a pilgrimage rather than a tourist event. Very few still function as inns but Togawa-ke Oshi-no-ie, dating to 1768 and wonderfully preserved, evokes the fascinating Edo-era practice of Mt Fuji worship, back when up to 100 pilgrims at a time would have shared the tatami floors here en route to the mountain. The audio guide is recommended.

Kanadorii GATE
(金鳥居) A symbol of Mt Fuji worship, this gate was first constructed in 1788 (though the present one dates to 1955), and in clear weather frames picture-postcard views of the mountain. Stroll uphill through the gate and you'll pass the old entranceways of *oshi-no-ie*, though only one or two still operate. It's a two-minute walk southeast of Fujisan Station.

Churei-tō Pagoda VIEWPOINT
(忠霊塔パゴダ) One of the classic Fuji postcard views has this five-tiered red pagoda in the foreground surrounded by cherry blossoms. It's actually a war memorial, accessed via a breathless set of 400 steps rising up through **Sengen Park** on the slopes of Arakura-yama. The park starts a few minutes up the hill from Shimoyoshida Station.

Fujiyama Art Museum MUSEUM
(富士山ミュージアム; ☎0555 22-8223; www.fujiyama-museum.com; 5-6-1 Shintanishi; adult/child ¥1000/500; ⊙10am-5.30pm Mon-Fri, to 8.30pm Sat & Sun) Should the weather thwart your chances of seeing the real thing, this contemporary gallery space contains a fine collection of Mt Fuji paintings by prominent Japanese artists, ranging from the romantic to the avant-garde. It's just outside the south entrance to the Fuji-Q Highland amusement park.

Fuji-Q Highland AMUSEMENT PARK
(www.fujiq.jp; 5-6-1 Shin-Nishihara; day passes adult/child ¥5700/4300; ⊙9am-5pm Mon-Fri, to 8pm Sat & Sun) The extreme roller coasters at this amusement park are not for the faint of heart – though they are a memorable way to bag Fuji views. Thomas Land, based on Thomas the Tank Engine, slows it down for the little ones, and there's also a resort hotel, onsen and shops. Fun for all the family, one stop west of Fujisan Station.

Admission to the park is free (you still have to obtain an entrance ticket at the booth), with individual rides costing between ¥800 and ¥2000. Get the day pass if you plan on going on more than a couple of rides.

Festivals & Events

Yoshida no Himatsuri CULTURAL
(Yoshida Fire Festival; ⊙26-27 Aug) This annual festival is held to mark the end of the climbing season and to offer thanks for the safety of the year's climbers. The first day involves a *mikoshi* (portable shrine) procession and the lighting of bonfires on Fuji-Yoshida's main street. On the second day, the focus is at Sengen-jinja (p171).

Sleeping & Eating

★Hitsuki Guesthouse HISTORIC HOTEL ¥
(☎080-1525-9125; hitsukiguesthouse@gmail.com; 7-12-16 Kami-Yoshida; r per person from ¥4000;) Just about the only remaining Fuji *oshi-no-ie* (pilgrims' inn) you can still stay in. The young owner is both a carpenter (hence the lovingly restored 440-year-old building) and an 18th-generation *oshi* (Shintō priest associated with Fuji worship). Stay as countless pilgrims before you: sleeping on tatami in rooms partitioned by *shōji* (sliding-screen doors).

★Maisan-chi GUESTHOUSE ¥
(まいさんち; ☎0555-24-5328; www.maisan-chi.com; 4-6-46 Shimo-Yoshida; dm/d with shared bathroom, incl breakfast ¥3000/8000;) On a quiet backstreet, this excellent choice combines an old Japanese-style house (where guests have breakfast) and a new build behind it housing fabulous capsule-style beds with paper-screen doors and windows, three private rooms, and a shared kitchen/lounge with Fuji views. The English-speaking owner also has bicycles to rent.

You need to pay in cash for your stay to qualify for the included breakfast (Japanese-style or fresh waffles).

Mt Fuji Hostel Michael's HOSTEL ¥
(☎0555-72-9139; www.mfi.or.jp/mtfujihostel; 2F 3-21-37 Shimo-Yoshida; dm/s/d ¥3000/3600/

TOP VIEWS OF MT FUJI

Mt Fuji has many different personalities depending on the season. Winter and spring months are your best bet for seeing it in all its clichéd glory; although even during these times the snowcapped peak may be visible only in the morning before it retreats behind its cloud curtain. Its elusiveness, however, is part of the appeal, making sightings all the more special. Here are some of our top spots for viewing, both in the immediate and greater area:

Kawaguchi-ko On the north side of the lake, where Fuji looms large over its shimmering reflection.

Motosu-ko The famous view depicted on the ¥1000 bill can be seen from the northwest side of the lake.

Hakone The mountain soars in the background of Ashino-ko and the red *torii* (shrine gate) rising from the water.

Izu Peninsula Journey along the west coast to catch glimpses of Fuji and the ocean, bathed in glorious sunsets.

Panorama-dai The end of this hiking trail (p176) rewards you with a magnificent front-on view of the mountain.

Kōyō-dai Mt Fuji can be seen from this lookout (p175), particularly stunning in the autumn colours.

7200;) Though this efficiently run, clean, Western-style hostel has no self-catering facilities or common space, it's upstairs from the expat and local favourite **Michael's American Pub** (マイケルズアメリカンパブ; 0555-24-3917; 3-21-37 Shimo-Yoshida; meals ¥600-1200; 11.30am-4pm Sun-Fri, 6pm-2am Fri-Wed), which serves reasonably priced Western and Japanese food. The English-speaking staff can also recommend some great local places to eat.

Sakurada Udon JAPANESE ¥
(桜井うどん; 0555-22-2797; 5-1-33 Shimo-Yoshida; noodles ¥350; 10am-2pm Mon-Sat) Just off the main drag, this tiny shop is a good spot to sample the local *te-uchi udon* (handmade wheat-flour noodles) while sitting cross-legged on tatami. Look for the blue *noren* (curtains) over the door.

Information

Fuji-Yoshida Tourist Information Center
(0555-22-7000; 9am-5pm) Next to Fujisan (Mt Fuji) train station; the clued-up staff can provide info on climbing, as well as brochures and maps of the area.

Kawaguchi-ko

0555 / POP 25,742

Even if you have no plans to climb Mt Fuji, the sprawling town of Kawaguchi-ko (河口湖), set around the lake of the same name, is a great base to hang out and enjoy all that the Fuji Five Lakes region has to offer, particularly as the three Fuji sightseeing bus lines all start from Kawaguchi-ko Station.

Sights & Activities

Kubota Itchiku Art Museum MUSEUM
(久保田一竹美術館; 0555-76-8811; www.itchiku-museum.com; 2255 Kawaguchi; adult/child ¥1300/400; 9.30am-5.30pm Wed-Mon Apr-Nov, 10am-4.30pm Wed-Mon Dec-Mar) In a Gaudí-influenced building above the lake, this charming museum displays the kimono art of Kubota Itchiku (1917–2003). You might see Mt Fuji in the wintertime, or the cherry blossoms of spring spread across oversized kimonos that have been painstakingly dyed, embroidered and hand-painted. The red-line bus stops here.

Fujisan World Heritage Center MUSEUM
(富士ビジターセンター; 0555-72-5502; www.fujisan-whc.jp; 6663-1 Funatsu; adult/child ¥420/free; 8.30am-5pm, to 6pm or 7pm in peak season, closed 4th Tue of month) The flashy South Hall of this visitor centre has imaginative, interactive displays detailing the spiritual and geological history of the mountain, as well as a dramatic video installation projected onto a fabric Mt Fuji suspended across the exhibition hall. The blue-line bus stops here. An observation deck at the North Hall (free) affords great views of Mt Fuji.

Ide Sake Brewery BREWERY
(井出醸造; ☎0555-72-0006; www.kainokaiun.jp; 8 Funatsu; tours ¥500) This small-scale brewery has been producing sake using Mt Fuji spring water for 21 generations. Tours (9.30am and 3pm; 40 minutes) provide a fascinating insight into the production process and include tastings and a souvenir glass. Reservations essential for English tours.

Kachi-Kachi Yama Ropeway CABLE CAR
(カチカチ山ロープウェイ; www.kachikachiyama-ropeway.com; 1163-1 Azagawa; one way/return adult ¥450/800, child ¥230/400; ⏲9am-5pm) On the lower eastern edge of the lake, this ropeway runs to the panoramic **Fuji Viewing Platform** (1104m). There's a hiking trail back down, or you can consider making the six-hour return hike from the top to **Mitsutōge-yama** (三つ峠山; 1785m); it's an old trail with excellent Fuji views. Ask at Kawaguchi-ko Tourist Information Center for a map. The red-line bus stops here.

Sleeping

Kawaguchi-ko Station Inn INN ¥
(河口湖ステーションイン; ☎0555-72-0015; www.st-inn.com; 3639-2 Funatsu; dm/s/d ¥2800/4200/8400; P⊖❄@≋) Directly across from Kawaguchi-ko Station is this cosy inn offering 16 great-value tatami rooms, a mixed dorm, English-speaking staff, a downstairs cafe and a fab top-floor bath (also open to nonguests, ¥600) looking out to Mt Fuji in the distance. Note the 11pm curfew.

K's House Mt Fuji HOSTEL ¥
(☎0555-83-5556; www.kshouse.jp; 6713-108 Funatsu; dm from ¥2500, d with/without bathroom from ¥8800/7200; P⊖❄≋) A popular place to hook up with other climbers, K's offers basic accommodation with plenty of common space and a large kitchen, though the 'deluxe' capsule dorms are rather cramped. Well-drilled staff can arrange a station pick-up, as it's a bit of a walk. If it's full, try its other location, **K's House Fuji View**, 1.5km due south.

Tominoko Hotel HOTEL ¥¥
(富ノ湖ホテル; ☎0555-72-5080; www.tominoko.net; 55 Asakawa; r per person incl 2 meals from ¥9180; P❄@≋) Given its views of Fuji across the lake, this retro hotel is a steal. Rooms are smart, Western-style twins with plenty of space, and all face the lake. Ask for one on an upper level to score a balcony. Also has a *rotemburo* (outdoor bath).

Buffet meal packages aren't a bad idea here, as there are few restaurants nearby and buses stop running in the early evening.

Sunnide Resort HOTEL ¥¥
(サニーデリゾート; ☎0555-76-6004; www.sunnide.com; 2549-1 Ōishi; r per person incl 2 meals from ¥10,000, cottages excl meals from ¥13,000; P⊖❄@≋) Offering views of Mt Fuji from the far side of Kawaguchi-ko, this homely complex has a wide range of accommodation, from basic twins to stylish suites, plus cottages that sleep up to four. A highlight is the bath complex looking out to Fuji across the lake (no tattoos permitted in baths). The red-line sightseeing bus stops here.

Note that in winter a heating surcharge of ¥3000 is tacked on to cottage rates.

★**Kozantei Ubuya** RYOKAN ¥¥¥
(湖山亭うぶや; ☎0555-72-1145; www.ubuya.co.jp; 10 Asakawa; r per person incl 2 meals from ¥29,310, with outdoor tub from ¥39,030; P⊖❄@≋) Elegant and ultrastylish, Ubuya offers panoramic views of Mt Fuji reflected in the lake that are simply unbeatable. Splash out on the more expensive suites to savour the scene while soaking in an outdoor tub on your balcony. One for honeymooners. The red-line sightseeing bus stops here.

Fuji Lake Hotel HOTEL ¥¥¥
(富士レークホテル; ☎0555-72-2209; www.fujilake.co.jp; 1 Funatsu; r per person incl 2 meals from ¥19,440; P❄@≋⛀) On Kawaguchi-ko's south shore, this sprawling vintage hotel (c 1932) offers either Mt Fuji or lake views from its Japanese-Western combo rooms. Some rooms have a private *rotemburo;* otherwise there's a common onsen and an outdoor swimming pool with lake views. Meals comprise a buffet-style breakfast and *kaiseki* (Japanese haute cuisine) dinner.

A free shuttle bus runs to and from Kawaguchi-ko Station.

Eating & Drinking

While in Kawaguchi-ko, be sure to try some *hōtō,* the local speciality of extra-thick wheat noodles in a hearty miso stock.

Idaten TEMPURA ¥
(いだ天; ☎0555-73-9218; 3486-4 Funatsu; meals from ¥800; ⏲11am-10pm) Load up on some delicious, deep-fried goodness pre- or post-hike at the Idaten counter, where you can watch the chefs prepare your tempura to order. Aside from Instagrammable Fujisan-themed sets (tempura arranged like a mountain) you

can also order à la carte (various vegetables are ¥90 to ¥180 apiece; a jumbo shrimp is ¥1000).

★ Sanrokuen JAPANESE ¥¥
(山麓園; ☎0555-73-1000; 3370-1 Funatsu; set meals ¥2160-4320; ⊙11am-7.30pm Fri-Wed) In this beautiful old thatched building, diners sit on the floor around traditional *irori* charcoal pits grilling their own meals – skewers of fish, meat, tofu and veggies. From Kawaguchi-ko Station, go west, then bear left (south) after the 7-Eleven; after 600m you'll spot the thatched roof on the west side of the road. Reservations strongly recommended.

Hōtō Fudō NOODLES ¥¥
(ほうとう不動; ☎0555-72-8511; www.houtou-fudou.jp; 707 Kawaguchi; hōtō ¥1080; ⊙11am-7pm) *Hōtō* are Kawaguchi-ko's local noodles, hand-cut and served in a thick miso stew with pumpkin, sweet potato and other vegetables. It's a hearty meal best sampled at this chain with five branches around town. This is the most architecturally interesting one, an igloo-like building in which you can also sample *basashi* – horsemeat sashimi (¥1080).

There's also a convenient branch directly opposite Kawaguchi-ko Station.

★ Sky Bar Moon Dance ROOFTOP BAR
(☎0555-72-1234; www.mzn.co.jp; 187 Azagawa; ⊙4-10.30pm Apr-Sep; 📶) When conditions are just right at this open-air rooftop bar, lights twinkling on the far shore of Kawaguchi-ko and mighty Fuji-san swathed in evening mist, you wouldn't want to be anywhere else in the world. Find it in the **Mizno**, a stylish boutique hotel on the hillside above the east shore of the lake.

ℹ Information

Kawaguchi-ko Tourist Information Center
(☎0555-72-6700; ⊙8.30am-5.30pm) To the right as you exit Kawaguchi-ko Station, the TIC has English speakers as well as maps, brochures, discount coupons and info about several public onsen in the area.

Sai-ko

Sai-ko (紅葉台) is a quiet lake area good for hiking, fishing and boating. Mt Fuji is mostly obstructed but there are great views from the Kōyō-dai lookout and from the western end of the lake. On the south side of the lake there are several interesting lava caves to explore, and hiking trails through Aokigahara Forest.

👁 Sights & Activities

Sai-ko Iyashi-no-Sato Nenba CULTURAL CENTRE
(西湖いやしの里根場; ☎0555-20-4677; 2710 Nenba; adult/child ¥350/150; ⊙9am-5pm, to 4.30pm Dec-Feb) On a serene wooded hillside facing Mt Fuji is this faithful re-creation of a peasant village that was washed away by a landslide in 1966. Visitors can wander in and out of the dozen or so thatched houses, some of which have museum displays, craft workshops and restaurants. The green-line bus has a stop here.

Sai-ko Kōmoriana CAVE
(西湖コウモリ穴, Bat Cave; 2068 Sai-ko; adult/child ¥300/100; ⊙9am-5pm) Despite being known as the Bat Cave, this 350m-long complex has neither bats nor caped crusaders. Nevertheless, it's still fun to scramble over the ancient lava flows, and in the car park you'll find a trailhead for marked hikes through Aokigahara Forest, including a 3km tramp to Fugaku Fuketsu. The green-line bus stops here.

Fugaku Fuketsu CAVE
(富岳風穴; ☎0555-85-2300; 2068-1 Aokigahara; adult/child ¥350/150; ⊙9am-4.30pm) The Wind Cave (also known as the Lava Cave) was used to store silk-worm cocoons in the past. Getting a combination ticket for this and Narusawa Hyōketsu makes sense, as they're a 15-minute walk from one another, or 30 minutes if you take the woodland trail.

Narusawa Hyōketsu CAVE
(鳴沢氷穴; ☎0555-85-2301; 8533 Narusawa-mura; adult/child ¥350/150; ⊙9am-5pm) Not for the claustrophobic, the Narusawa Hyōketsu (ice cave) was formed by lava flows from an eruption of Mt Fuji in 864. It takes about 10 minutes to walk through to the end to see the ice pillars, which are at their peak in April (no ice from September to December). Only the blue-line sightseeing bus stops here.

Kōyō-dai VIEWPOINT
(adult/child ¥200/150) There are good views of Mt Fuji from this lookout building, especially popular in autumn when the Aokigahara Forest is a sea of red. It's a 30-minute walk uphill from the Koyodai Ent bus stop on the blue line.

Aokigahara Forest HIKING
(青木ヶ原樹海) Aokigahara's expanse of forest stretches from just beyond the southern shore of Sai-ko up to the Mt Fuji

treeline, with lots of opportunities for hiking – though stick to the established trails, as you could easily get lost amid what is aptly called the 'Sea of Trees'. An easy jaunt is the marked 3km trail between Sai-ko Kōmoriana (p175) and Fugaku Fuketsu (p175).

Sleeping & Eating

Sai-ko is an excellent location for camping, with easy bus access to the nearby caves and hiking trails.

If you're self-catering, you'll want to bring supplies from Kawaguchi-ko, as there aren't many shops around the lake.

Saiko Camp Village Gnome CAMPGROUND ¥
(西湖キャンプビレッジノーム; ☎0555-82-2650; www.hamayouresort.com/gnome/index.html; 1030 Sai-ko; camping per person from ¥1000, 2-night tent rental ¥5000; P) Ex-model and outdoors author Tokichi Kimura is the convivial English-speaking owner of this campsite right in the centre of the lake's north shore, which also has barbecue facilities and canoe rental (¥3200/5400 per three hours/day). Note the ¥500 'garbage fee' levied per group.

Motosu-ko

☎0555, 0556 / POP 134

If you've ever examined the ¥1000 bill you'll recognise the iconic view of Fuji rising majestically from the northeast shore of Motosu-ko (本栖湖). Superlative vistas aside, the westernmost lake of Fuji Five Lakes can make for a peaceful escape, offering camping, kayaking, and hiking on panoramic trails in the surrounding hills.

Blue-line buses from Kawaguchi-ko Station only go as far as the east shore of Motosu-ko before looping back to the station. It's a further 5km to reach the north shore and the famous Fuji view. At the time of research, there was just one daily bus (10.18am, 50 minutes) from Kawaguchi-ko Station (bay 4), returning at 1.47pm.

Activities

Rent paddleboards (¥1500/4000 per hour/day) and kayaks (for two people ¥2000/5000 per hour/per day) from Kōan Motosu Inn.

Panorama-dai HIKING
(パノラマ台) This trail ends in a spectacular, head-on view of Mt Fuji and panoramic views of the surrounding lakes and mountains. Midway through, stop at the signed viewpoint to spot Fuji-san between the trees. It's a one-hour hike through the woods from the trailhead, which starts at the Panorama-dai-shita bus stop. Take a blue-line bus (38 minutes from Kawaguchi-ko).

Sleeping & Eating

Camping is the way to go on Motosu-ko, but you'll usually need your own tent and sleeping bags (most venues provide a tarp and can rent other gear like stoves, barbecues and even kayaks).

Local shops will have some basics, but you're best arriving with all the groceries you'll need.

Kōan Motosu Inn CAMPGROUND ¥
(浩庵キャンプ場; ☎0556-38-0117; www.kouan-motosuko.com; 2926 Nakanokura; camping per person ¥600, tent pitch ¥1000, 6-person cabins from ¥17,280; P) Kōan has two campgrounds on the lake, this one on the northeast corner has fine Fuji views, a jacuzzi, a helpful English-speaking owner and an attached **restaurant** and shop, as well as three cabins should you not wish to camp. Reservations are not required (nor accepted) for camping; just show up.

Having a car is the most convenient way to get to Kōan Motosu Inn. At time of research, only one daily bus (10.18am, 50 minutes) from Kawaguchi-ko Station comes here, returning at 1.47pm.

YOKOHAMA

☎045 / POP 3.78 MILLION

Even though it's just a 30-minute train ride south of central Tokyo, Yokohama (横浜) has an appealing flavour and history all its own. Locals are likely to cite the uncrowded, walkable streets or neighbourhood atmosphere as the main draw, but for visitors it's the breezy bay front, creative arts scene, multiple microbreweries, jazz clubs and great international dining.

History

Up until the mid-19th century, Yokohama was an unassuming fishing village. Things started to change rapidly, however, in 1853, when the American fleet under Commodore Matthew Perry arrived off the coast to persuade Japan to open to foreign trade.

From 1858, when it was designated an international port, through to the early 20th century, Yokohama served as a gateway for foreign influence and ideas. Among the city's firsts in Japan: a daily newspaper, gas lamps and a train terminus (connected to Shimbashi in Tokyo).

The Great Kantō Earthquake of 1923 destroyed much of the city, but the rubble was used to reclaim more land, including Yamashita-kōen. The city was devastated yet again in WWII air raids; occupation forces were initially based here but later moved down the coast to Yokosuka. Despite all this, central Yokohama retains some rather fine early 20th-century buildings.

Sights

Yokohama's frenetic Chinatown packs some 600 speciality shops and restaurants within a space of several blocks, marked by 10 elaborately painted gates. Adjacent is **Motomachi**, a pleasant, upscale shopping and dining area overlooked by the bluff of **Yamate**, the old foreign quarter where you can find several preserved Western-style residences from the early 20th century. The most convenient subway for all these areas is Motomachi-Chūkagai.

★Cup Noodles Museum MUSEUM
(☎045-345-0918; www.cupnoodles-museum.jp; 2-3-4 Shinkō, Naka-ku; adult/child ¥500/free; ⏲10am-6pm, closed Tue; 👪; Ⓢ Bashamichi) Dedicated to the 1956 invention of instant ramen by Momofuku Ando (the 'cup' came in 1971), this impressively slick attraction has a host of wacky exhibits that drive home the message to go against the grain, be creative and 'Never give up!'. The highlight is the chance to design your own Cup Noodle (additional ¥300) to take away.

★Yokohama Museum of Art GALLERY
(横浜美術館; ☎045-221-0300; www.yaf.or.jp/yma; 3-4-1 Minato Mirai, Nishi-ku; adult/child ¥500/free; ⏲10am-6pm, closed Thu; Ⓢ Minato Mirai) The focus of the Yokohama Triennale (to be held in 2023 and 2026), this museum hosts exhibitions that swing between safe-bet shows with European headliners to more daring contemporary Japanese and up-and-coming Southeast Asian artists. There are also permanent works, including by Picasso, Miró and Dalí, in the catalogue.

Hara Model Railway Museum MUSEUM
(原鉄道模型博物館; www.hara-mrm.com; 2nd fl, Yokohama Mitsui Bldg, 1-1-2 Takashima, Nishi-ku; adult/child ¥1000/500; ⏲10am-5pm Wed-Mon; 🚊Shin-takashima) Hara Nobutaro (1919–2014) was Japan's pre-eminent trainspotter, taking the pastime to a typically Japanese level of obsessiveness as this superb personal collection of model trains and other railway-associated memorabilia shows. Even if you don't care much for trains, the model railway – a mammoth gauge-one diorama of moving locomotives where you can act as train driver – is a delight.

> **TOKYO DAY-TRIP PLANNER**
>
> Many destinations can be done as day trips from Tokyo:
>
> **One-way travel up to an hour** Yokohama, Kamakura, Mt Takao, Oku-Tama
>
> **One-way travel up to two hours** Fuji Five Lakes, Hakone, Nikkō, Atami, Itō

Nippon Maru Sailing Ship MUSEUM
(日本丸; ship & museum adult/child ¥600/300; ⏲10am-5pm Tue-Sun; 🚊Sakuragichō) This magnificent, four-masted barque (built in 1930 as a training ship for naval cadets) sits in a wet dock adjacent to the **Yokohama Port Museum** (横浜みなと博物館; ☎045-221-0280; www.nippon-maru.or.jp; 2-1-1 Minato Mirai, Nishi-ku; museum only adult/child ¥400/200; ⏲10am-5pm Tue-Sun), and is fascinating to board and explore. Tickets also include entry to the museum building.

Shin-Yokohama Ramen Museum MUSEUM
(新横浜ラーメン博物館; ☎045-471-0503; www.raumen.co.jp; 2-14-21 Shin-Yokohama, Kohoku-ku; adult/child ¥310/100, dishes around ¥900; ⏲11am-10pm Mon-Sat, from 10.30am Sun; 🚊Shin-Yokohama) Nine ramen restaurants from around Japan were hand-picked to sell their wares in this theme-park-style replica of a 1958 *shitamachi* (downtown district) that's lit to feel like perpetual, festive nighttime. It's a short walk from Shin-Yokohama station – ask for directions at the station's information centre.

NYK Hikawa Maru MUSEUM
(氷川丸; www.nyk.com; Yamashita-kōen, Naka-ku; adult/child ¥300/100; ⏲10am-5pm Tue-Sun; Ⓢ Motomachi-Chūkagai) Moored at the eastern end of Yamashita-kōen, this 1930s luxury liner has stories to tell from its days conveying well-heeled Japanese passengers to

Yokohama

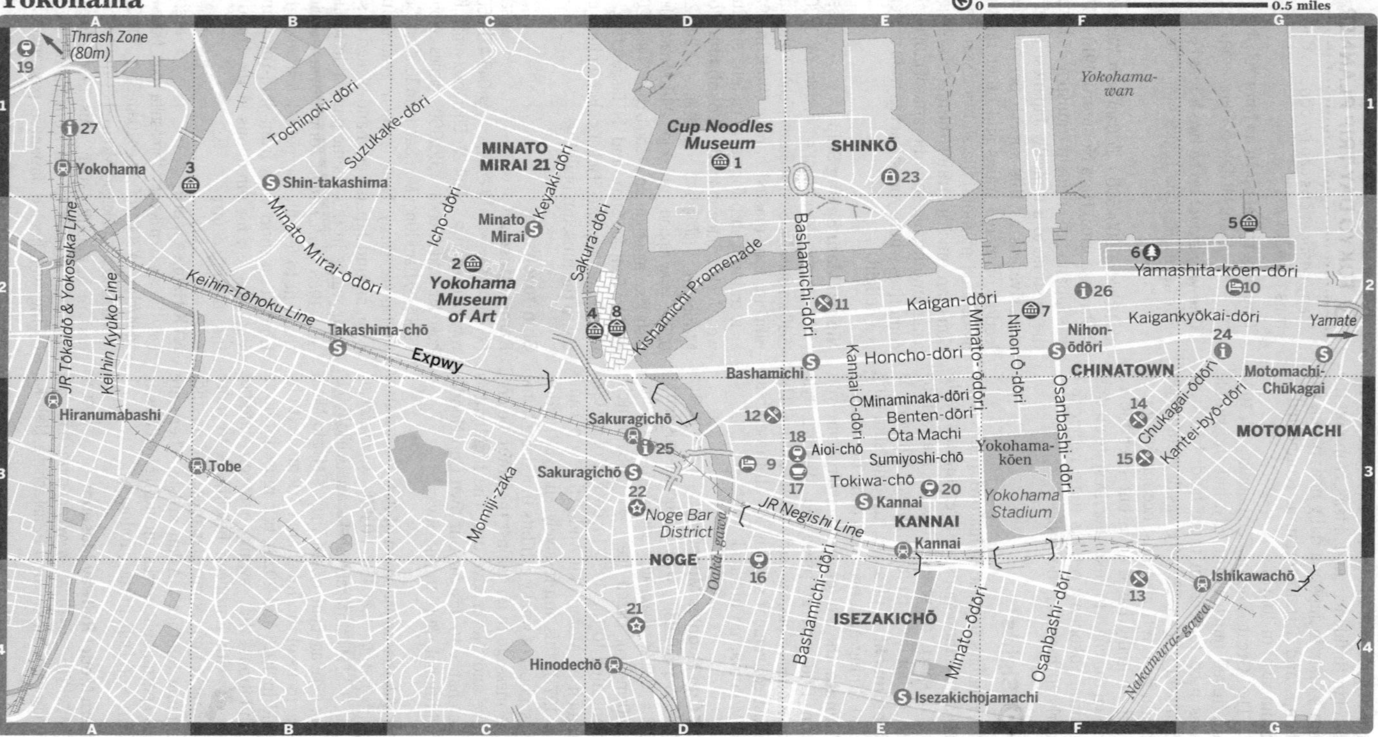

1 km
0.5 miles
Thrash Zone (80m)
Yokohama-wan
Cup Noodles Museum
SHINKŌ
MINATO MIRAI 21
Minato Mirai
Yokohama Museum of Art
Yokohama
Shin-takashima
Tochinoki-dōri
Suzukake-dōri
Keyaki-dōri
Icho-dōri
Sakura-dōri
Minato Mirai-ōdōri
Keihin-Tōhoku Line
Takashima-chō
Expwy
JR Tōkaidō & Yokosuka Line
Keihin Kyūko Line
Hiranumabashi
Tobe
Kishamichi Promenade
Bashamichi-dōri
Bashamichi
Kaigan-dōri
Yamashita-kōen-dōri
Kaigankyōkai-dōri
Yamate
Nihon-ōdōri
Honcho-dōri
Kannai Ō-dōri
Minato-ōdōri
Nihon Ō-dōri
Osanbashi-dōri
CHINATOWN
Motomachi-Chūkagai
MOTOMACHI
Chukagai-ōdōri
Kantei-byō-dōri
Minaminaka-dōri
Benten-dōri
Ōta Machi
Aioi-chō
Sumiyoshi-chō
Tokiwa-chō
Yokohama-kōen
Yokohama Stadium
Sakuragichō
Kannai
KANNAI
JR Negishi Line
Noge Bar District
NOGE
Ōoka-gawa
Momiji-zaka
ISEZAKICHŌ
Isezakichojamachi
Hinodechō
Ishikawachō
Nakamura-gawa

Yokohama

Seattle, and later as a hospital ship in WWII. Inside you can see cabins (one of the staterooms was used by Charlie Chaplin), lounges, the engine room and bridge.

Yokohama Archives of History MUSEUM
(横浜開港資料館; ☎045-201-2100; www.kaikou.city.yokohama.jp; 3 Nihon-ōdōri, Naka-ku; adult/child ¥200/100; ⊙9.30am-5pm Tue-Sun; Ⓢ Nihon-ōdōri) Inside the former British consulate, displays in English chronicle the saga of Japan's opening up at the Yokohama port following the arrival of Commodore Matthew Perry and his persuasively well-armed steamships.

A few steps away is the all-white **Yokohama Kaigan Church**, the first Protestant church in Japan, founded in 1872.

Yamashita-kōen PARK
(山下公園周辺; 279 Yamashitachō; Ⓡ Motomachi-Chūkagai) This elegant bayside park is ideal for strolling and ship-spotting. Moored at the eastern end is the 1930s passenger liner Hikawa Maru (p177).

Tours

Kirin Beer Yokohama Factory TOURS
(キリンビール 横浜工場; ☎045-503-8250; 1-17-1 Namamugi, Tsurumi-ku; ⊙10am-5pm Tue-Sun; Ⓡ Namamugi) FREE Even teetotallers will be charmed by this surprisingly hi-tech romp through one of the major breweries for Kirin beer. The free tour (in Japanese but with translation cards) takes an hour to explain the various stages of beer production with the help of touch screens and 3D goggles, finishing with a tasting of three beers. Reserve in advance (English spoken).

Don't miss the chance to have a meal (and more beer) in the rather fine **Spring Valley Brewery**, a red-brick building on-site with an open kitchen and tasty Western dishes paired with Kirin's new range of craft beers. Spring Valley Brewery was also the name of Japan's first brewery, the precursor to Kirin, established in Yokohama in 1869 by a Norwegian-American.

Festivals & Events

Great Japan Beer Festival Yokohama BEER
(www.beertaster.org; ¥5000; ⊙Apr & Sep) Held in mid-April and mid-September over two days, the Yokohama editions of this multi-city booze fest feature around 200 craft beers from across Japan at locations around the city.

Yokohama Oktoberfest BEER
(⊙Oct) Held over two weeks at **Akarenga Sōkō** (横浜赤レンガ倉庫; www.yokohama-akarenga.jp; 1-1 Shinkō, Naka-ku; ⊙11am-8pm; Ⓢ Bashamichi) in early October, this festival features dozens of beers and much carousing in the spirit of the German festival.

Sleeping

Hotel Edit HOTEL ¥¥

(☎045-680-0238; http://hotel-edit.com/en; 6-78-1 Sumiyoshi-chō; s/d incl breakfast from ¥7000/8500;) Priced like a business hotel but with an attractive, modern aesthetic and English-speaking staff, Hotel Edit is an excellent choice, especially since it's surrounded by great places to eat and to drink craft beer. If travelling solo, note that most of the singles lack proper windows; opt for the 'semi-double' category instead.

Hotel New Grand HOTEL ¥¥¥

(ホテルニューグランド; ☎045-681-1841; www.hotel-newgrand.co.jp; 10 Yamashita-chō, Naka-ku; r from ¥14,500; @; S Motomachi-Chūkagai) Dating from 1927, the New Grand has a prime waterfront location and elegant old-world charm, particularly in its original lobby and lavishly decorated ballrooms. It was once a favourite of visiting foreign dignitaries such as General McArthur and Charlie Chaplin. Note though that most rooms are housed in a modern tower annex, trading heritage atmosphere for bay views.

Eating

Colombus Okonomiyaki OKONOMIYAKI ¥

(お好み焼きころんぶす; ☎045-633-2748; 1-3-7 Matsukage-chō, Naka-ku; mains ¥890-1120; 11.30am-3pm & 5-10pm Mon-Thu, 11.30am-3pm & 5-11pm Fri, 11.30am-11pm Sat, 3-10pm Sun; Ishikawachō) Friendly staff grill up a wide range of *okonomiyaki* (savoury pancakes) at your table, with prawn, squid, pork or veg (the English menu has some cute manga to help). It's a two-minute walk from the Ishikawachō Station. Turn right from the north exit, left at the first traffic lights and Colombus is 40m on your right.

Masan-no-mise Ryūsen CHINESE ¥

(馬さんの店龍仙; ☎045-651-0758; www.ma-fam.com; 218-5 Yamashita-chō, Naka-ku; dishes from ¥700; 7am-2am; Ishikawachō) The walls at this cheerful little canteen are literally wallpapered with appetizing photos of the stir-fries, dumplings, noodle soups and salads on offer. It has two other branches in Chinatown.

Charcoal Grill Green GRILL ¥¥

(チャコールグリル グリーン 馬車道; ☎045-263-8976; www.greenyokohama.com; 6-79 Benten-dōri, Naka-ku; mains from ¥1380; 11.30am-2pm & 5pm-midnight; S Bashamichi) Char is the star at this hip grill restaurant and bar that serves pink-centred steaks and smoky chicken to go with craft beers on tap and a decent wine list. The lunch specials are a great deal.

Manchinrō Honten CHINESE ¥¥

(萬珍樓本店; ☎045-681-4004; www.manchinro.com; 153 Yamashita-chō, Naka-ku; lunch/dinner set menus from ¥2800/6000; 11am-10pm; Motomachi-Chūkagai) This palatial Cantonese restaurant is one of Chinatown's oldest (1892) and most respected. It serves a great selection of dim sum from 11am to 4pm, all in opulent surrounds, though it's a rather more formal affair for dinner. Book ahead on weekends.

★**Araiya** JAPANESE ¥¥¥

(荒井屋; ☎045-226-5003; www.araiya.co.jp; 4-23 Kaigan-dōri, Naka-ku; set lunch/dinner from ¥1540/2970; 11am-2.30pm & 5-10pm; S Bashamichi) Yokohama has its own version of the beef hotpot dish *sukiyaki*, called *gyūnabe*. This elegant restaurant, established in 1895, is the place to sample it.

Drinking & Nightlife

Bashamichi Taproom PUB

(馬車道 タップルーム; ☎045-264-4961; www.bairdbeer.com; 5-63-1 Sumiyoshi-chō, Naka-ku; 5pm-midnight Mon-Fri, from noon Sat & Sun; S Bashamichi) Set over three compact floors, this Baird Brewing Company pub offers at least a dozen of its own beers on tap, from session JPAs (Japan pale ale) to smoky stouts and hand-pumped cask ales. Try a sampler set of three for ¥1100. The kitchen barbecues delicious American-style beef brisket and pulled pork (meals from ¥1100).

Antenna America CRAFT BEER

(アンテナアメリカ; ☎45-315-5228; www.antenna-america.com; 5th fl, 5-4-6 Yoshida-machi, Naka-ku; 3-11pm Mon-Fri, from 11am Sat & Sun; Kannai) Sup imported cans of American craft beer for just ¥500 at this showroom-turned-bar attached to a beer distribution company. Nerdy staff know their hops and the selection is impressive; the decor less so. A tiny kitchen turns out respectable fish tacos. It also has a branch in Yokohama Station.

Bashamichi Jyuban-Kan CAFE

(馬車道十番館; ☎045-651-2621; www.yokohama-jyubankan.co.jp; 5-67 Tokiwa-chō, Naka-ku; 10am-10pm; S Bashamichi) Soak up the old Yokohama vibes at this former trading company building turned cafe-bar and French restaurant. You can join the well-to-do regulars for tea and pastries at dainty tables, or seek out the clubby little bar up the wooden staircase past old photographs of the port area.

Look for the five-storey building of red brick with stone portico and coloured-glass windows.

Thrashzone Meatballs CRAFT BEER
(www.beerdrinkinginternational.com; 2-15-1 Tokiwa-cho; 5-10pm Mon–Fri, from 1pm Sat & Sun) Pair your nano-brewed 'extreme beer' with a cheese-topped meatball sub or skillet at this heavy-metal-themed craft-beer bar, a (slightly) less divey spin-off from the original **Thrash Zone** (1F Tamura Bldg, 2-10-7 Tsuruyachō, Kanagawa-ku; 6-11.30pm, from noon Sat & Sun; Yokohama).

Grassroots BAR
(グラスルーツ; 045-312-0180; www.grassroots.yokohama; B1 fl, 2-13-3 Tsuruyachō, Kanagawa-ku; 5pm-2am; Yokohama) Gigs, live art shows, DJ events and pop-up vintage shops are held in this psychedelically decorated basement space a short walk north of Yokohama Station. The cool staff are tuned in to what's on around town.

It also serves tasty pub meals (¥750 to ¥2500) such as fish burgers and grilled tuna steaks with avocado mash.

Entertainment

Live music is prominent here, with Yokohama particularly noted for its love of jazz. The Kannai-Bashamichi area is considered the hub of jazz.

Club Sensation LIVE MUSIC
(045-241-3166; www.sensation-jp.com; 3-80 Miyagawachō; cover from ¥2500; 6-11.30pm; Hinodechō) Intimate British-themed rock cafe-bar, run by Japanese rockers, with live bands or DJs most evenings (check website for schedule) and English ales and cider to drink.

Airegin JAZZ
(エアジン; 045-641-9191; www.airegin.yokohama; 5-60 Sumiyoshi-chō, Naka-ku; cover incl 1 drink ¥2500; 7.30pm-midnight; Bashamichi) Up a flight of stairs, this atmospheric little live-music venue has been swinging since 1969. Run by a jazz-loving couple, the cluttered space draws a friendly, music-loving audience.

LOCAL KNOWLEDGE

NOGE BAR DISTRICT

Tiny, one-room bars with big personalities are stacked along a stretch of the Ōka River's west bank in the neighbourhood of Noge, a throwback to an earlier Japan. The rootsy vibe here couldn't be more different from high-rise Minato Mirai to the north – it's like Tokyo's Golden Gai, but without the tourists. Further west, narrow streets reward the intrepid with yet more micro bars, eclectic music venues and places to eat.

Downbeat Bar JAZZ
(ダウンビート; 045-241-6167; www.yokohama-downbeat.com; 2nd fl, Miyamoto Bldg, 1-43 Hanasaki-chō, Naka-ku; 4-11.30pm Tue-Sun; Sakuragichō) *Jazz kissa,* which fall somewhere between cafes and bars, boast extensive jazz-record collections. This is one of the oldest (1956) in Yokohama, with more than 3000 albums and some serious speakers. Occasional live music means an occasional cover charge. Look for the 2nd-floor red awning.

Information

See www.yokohamajapan.com and www.yokohamaseasider.com as well as the following tourist offices, all of which have an English speaker.

Chinatown 80 Information Center (横浜中華街インフォメーションセンター; 045-681-6022; 80 Yamashita-chō; 10am-8pm Sun-Thu, to 9pm Fri & Sat; Motomachi-Chūkagai) A few blocks from Motomachi-Chūkagai Station.

Sakuragichō Station Tourist Information (045-211-0111; Sakuragichō Station; 9am-6pm; Sakuragichō) Has maps and brochures and can help with hotel bookings. It's outside the south exit of Sakuragichō Station.

Yokohama Convention & Visitors Bureau (045-221-2111; www.yokohamajapan.com; 1st fl, Sangyō-Bōeki Center, 2 Yamashita-chō, Naka-ku; 9am-5pm Mon-Fri; Nihon-ōdōri) A 10-minute walk from Nihon-ōdōri Station, and is very helpful with recommendations, maps and brochures, all delivered in English. Check out its excellent website.

Yokohama Station Tourist Information Center (045-441-7300; Yokohama Station; 9am-7pm) Has helpful English-speaking staff who can book accommodation. It's in the east-west corridor at Yokohama Station.

Getting There & Away

JR Tōkaidō, Yokosuka and Keihin Tōhoku lines run from Tokyo Station (¥470, 25 to 40 minutes). Some Keihin Tōhoku line trains continue along the Negishi line to Sakuragichō, Kannai and Ishikawachō. From Shinjuku, take the Shōnan-Shinjuku line (¥550, 32 minutes).

The Tōkyū Tōyoko line runs from Shibuya to Yokohama (¥270, 30 minutes), after which it becomes the Minato Mirai subway line to Minato Mirai (¥450, 33 minutes) and Motomachi-Chūkagai (¥480, 39 minutes).

The Tōkaidō *shinkansen* stops at Shin-Yokohama Station, northwest of town, connected to the city centre by the Yokohama line.

Getting Around

The Yokohama City blue line *(shiei chikatetsu)* connects Yokohama with Shin-Yokohama (¥240, 11 minutes), Sakuragichō (¥210, four minutes) and Kannai (¥210, six minutes).

JR trains connect Yokohama with Shin-Yokohama (¥170, 14 minutes), Sakuragichō (¥140, four minutes) and Kannai (¥140, five minutes).

Although trains are more convenient, Yokohama has an extensive bus network. The cute, red-coloured Akai-kutsu ('red shoe') bus loops every 20 minutes from 10am to around 7pm through the major tourist spots (adult/child ¥220/110 per ride).

The **Minato Burari** day pass covers municipal subway and bus rides (including the Akai-kutsu bus, but not the Minato Mirai line) around Minato Mirai and Yamashita-kōen (adult/child ¥500/250); purchase at any subway (blue line) station.

KAMAKURA

0467 / POP 172,306

The glory days of Japan's first feudal capital (from 1185 to 1333) coincided with the spread of populist Buddhism in Japan. This legacy is reflected in the area's proliferation of stunning temples. Kamakura (鎌倉) also has a laid-back, earthy vibe complete with organic restaurants, summer beach shacks and surfers – which can be added to sunrise meditation and hillside hikes as reasons to visit. Only an hour from Tokyo, it tends to get packed on weekends and holidays, so plan accordingly.

History

In 1180 aspiring warlord Minamoto no Yoritomo set up his base at Kamakura, far away from the debilitating influences of Kyoto court life, close to other clans loyal to his family and, having the sea on one side and densely wooded hills on the other, easy to defend.

After victories over the old foes the Taira, Yoritomo was appointed shogun in 1192 and governed Japan from Kamakura. When he died without an heir, power passed to the Hōjō, the family of Yoritomo's wife. Ruling power remained in Kamakura until 1333, when, weakened by the cost of maintaining defences against threats of attack from Kublai Khan in China, the Hōjō clan was defeated by Emperor Go-Daigo. Kyoto once again became the capital.

By the Edo period, Kamakura was practically a village again. With the opening of a rail line at the turn of the last century, the seaside town was reborn as a summer resort. Summer homes of wealthy Tokyoites still line the Shōnan coast.

Sights

★Daibutsu — MONUMENT

(大仏; 0467-22-0703; www.kotoku-in.jp; Kōtoku-in, 4-2-28 Hase; adult/child ¥200/150; 8am-5.30pm Apr-Sep, to 5pm Oct-Nov) Kamakura's most iconic sight, an 11.4m bronze statue of Amida Buddha (*amitābha* in Sanskrit), is in Kōtoku-in, a Jōdo sect temple. Completed in 1252, it's said to have been inspired by Yoritomo's visit to Nara (where Japan's biggest Daibutsu holds court) after the Minamoto clan's victory over the Taira clan. Once housed in a huge hall, today the statue sits in the open, the hall having been washed away by a tsunami in 1498.

For an extra ¥20, you can duck inside to see how the sculptors pieced the 850-tonne statue together.

Buses from stops 1 and 6 at the east exit of Kamakura Station run to the Daibutsu-mae stop (¥200). Alternatively, take the Enoden Enoshima line to Hase Station and walk north for about eight minutes. Better yet, take the Daibutsu Hiking Course (p185).

★Kenchō-ji — BUDDHIST TEMPLE

(建長寺; www.kenchoji.com; 8 Yamanouchi; adult/child ¥300/100; 8.30am-4.30pm) Established in 1253, Japan's oldest Zen monastery is still active today. The central Butsuden (Buddha Hall) was brought piece by piece from Tokyo in 1647. Its Jizō Bosatsu statue, unusual for a Zen temple, reflects the valley's ancient function as an execution ground – Jizō consoles lost souls. Other highlights include a

Kamakura

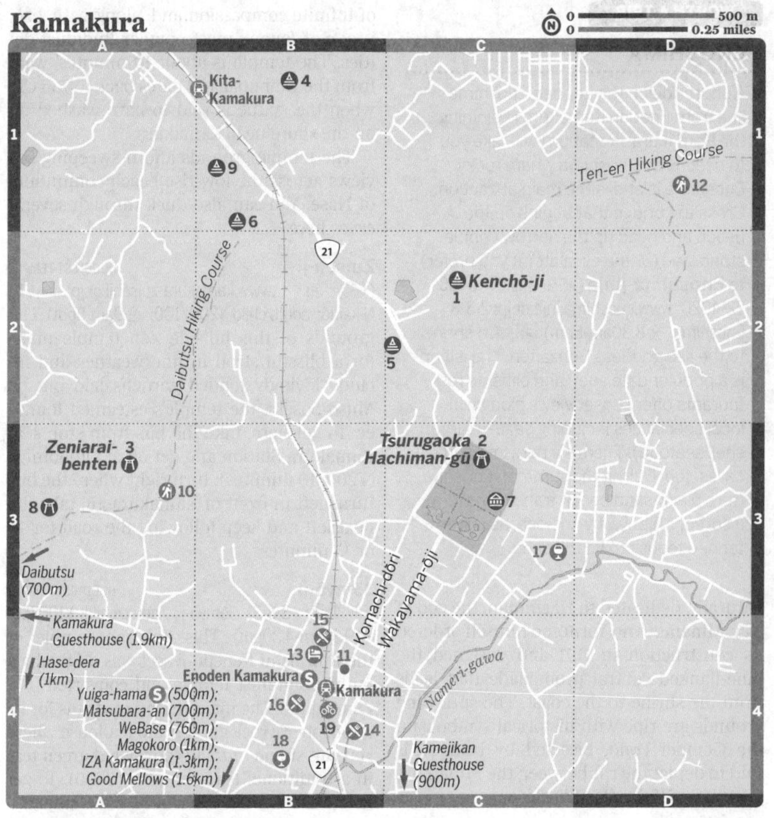

Kamakura

Top Sights
- 1 Kenchō-ji C2
- 2 Tsurugaoka Hachiman-gū C3
- 3 Zeniarai-benten A3

Sights
- 4 Engaku-ji B1
- 5 Ennō-ji C2
- 6 Jōchi-ji B1
- 7 Kamakura National Treasure Museum C3
- 8 Sasuke-inari-jinja A3
- 9 Tōkei-ji B1

Activities, Courses & Tours
- 10 Daibutsu Hiking Course A3
- 11 Kamakura Welcome Guides B4
- 12 Ten-en Hiking Course D1

Sleeping
- 13 Hotel New Kamakura B4

Eating
- 14 Cobakaba B4
- 15 Sông Bé Cafe B4
- 16 Wander Kitchen B4

Drinking & Nightlife
- 17 Magnetico C3
- 18 Univibe B4

Transport
- 19 Kamakura Rent-a-Cycle B4

bell cast in 1253 and a juniper grove, believed to have sprouted from seeds brought from China by Kenchō-ji's founder some seven centuries ago.

★ **Tsurugaoka Hachiman-gū** SHINTŌ SHRINE
(鶴岡八幡宮; 0467-22-0315; www.tsurugaoka-hachimangu.jp; 2-1-31 Yukinoshita; 5am-8.30pm Apr-Sep, from 6am Oct-Mar) FREE
Kamakura's most important shrine is,

WORTH A TRIP

ENOSHIMA

A short ride on the Enoden Enoshima line from Enoden Kamakura (adjoining the Kamakura JR station) will take you to beachside Enoshima where rocky Enoshima Island is the main attraction. Cross the bridge that begins on the beach and head up the narrow cobblestone lane (or the escalator if you prefer) to **Enoshima-jinja** (江島神社; ☎0466-22-4020; www.enoshimajinja.or.jp; 2-3-8 Enoshima; ⊙8.30am-5pm) FREE, a shrine to the sea goddess Benzaiten. The island is a popular date spot, and cliffside restaurants offer sunset views along with local specialities including *sazae* (turban shell seafood). There's a park and some caves, too. During the summer, Enoshima's black-sand beach transforms into a sort of Shibuya-by-the-sea, as super-tanned teens crowd the sand.

naturally, dedicated to Hachiman, the god of war. Minamoto no Yoritomo himself ordered its construction in 1191 and designed the pine-flanked central promenade that leads from the shrine to the coast. The sprawling grounds are ripe with historical symbolism: the Gempei Pond, bisected by bridges, is said to depict the rift between the Minamoto (Genji) and Taira (Heike) clans.

Engaku-ji BUDDHIST TEMPLE
(円覚寺; ☎0467-22-0478; www.engakuji.or.jp; 409 Yamanouchi; adult/child ¥300/100; ⊙8am-4.30pm Mar-Nov, to 4pm Dec-Feb) Engaku-ji is one of Kamakura's five major Rinzai Zen temples. It was founded in 1282 for Zen monks to pray for soldiers who lost their lives defending Japan against Kublai Khan. All of the temple structures have been rebuilt over the centuries; the Shariden, a Song-style reliquary, is the oldest, last rebuilt in the 16th century. At the top of the long flight of stairs is the Engaku-ji bell, the largest bell in Kamakura, cast in 1301.

Hase-dera BUDDHIST TEMPLE
(長谷寺; Hase Kannon; ☎0467-22-6300; www.hasedera.jp; 3-11-2 Hase; adult/child ¥300/100; ⊙8am-5pm Mar-Sep, to 4.30pm Oct-Feb) The focal point of this Jōdo sect temple, one of the most popular in the Kantō region, is a 9m-high carved wooden *jūichimen* (11-faced) Kannon statue. Kannon (*avalokiteshvara* in Sanskrit) is the Bodhisattva of infinite compassion and, along with Jizō, is one of Japan's most popular Buddhist deities. The temple is about 10 minutes' walk from the Daibutsu and dates back to 736 CE, when the statue is said to have washed up on the shore near Kamakura.

The temple grounds afford sweeping sea views across the low-rise beach community of Hase. You can also duck through several caves here.

Zuisen-ji BUDDHIST TEMPLE
(瑞泉寺; www.kamakura-zuisenji.or.jp; 710 Nikaidō; adult/child ¥200/100; ⊙9am-5pm) The grounds of this hillside Zen temple make for a blissful stroll in fine weather and include lovingly tended gardens laid out by Musō Soseki, the temple's esteemed founder. To get here, take the bus from stop 4 at Kamakura Station and get off at Ōtōnomiya (¥200, 10 minutes); turn right where the bus turns left in front of Kamakura-gū, take the next left and keep following the road for 10 or 15 minutes.

Jōmyō-ji BUDDHIST TEMPLE
(浄妙寺; 3-8-31 Jōmyō-ji; adult/child ¥100/50; ⊙9.30am-4.30pm) This Tokasan temple of the Rinzaishu Kenchō-ji sect was originally a tantric Buddhist temple and converted to a Zen temple. The main reason to visit is for its atmospheric rock garden and teahouse where you can sip on *matcha* (powdered green tea) in a traditional tea ceremony (¥600). To get here, take any bus from stop 5 at Kamakura Station's east exit and get off at the Jōmyō-ji stop, from where it's a two-minute walk.

Behind the main temple is the Tomb of Ashikaga Sadauji, the father of Takauji, the founder of the Muromachi era.

Ennō-ji BUDDHIST TEMPLE
(円応寺; 1543 Yamanouchi; ¥200; ⊙9am-4pm Mar-Nov, to 3pm Dec-Feb) Tiny Ennō-ji is distinguished by its statues depicting the judges of hell. According to the Juo concept of Taoism, which was introduced to Japan from China during the Heian period (794–1185), these 10 judges decide the fate of souls, who, being neither truly good nor truly evil, must be assigned to spend eternity in either heaven or hell. Presiding over them is Emma (Yama), a Hindu deity known as the gruesome king of the infernal regions.

Kamakura National Treasure Museum MUSEUM
(鎌倉国宝館; Kamakura Kokuhōkan; ☎0467-22-0753; www.city.kamakura.kanagawa.jp/kokuhoukan; 2-1-1 Yukinoshita; adult/child ¥400/200;

⌚9am-4.30pm Tue-Sun) This museum displays an excellent collection of Kamakura religious art and statuary. Some are the typically peaceful Jizō (Buddhist patron of travellers, children and the unborn), others more gruesome, like the demonic temple guardians.

Tōkei-ji BUDDHIST TEMPLE
(東慶寺; www.tokeiji.com; 1367 Yamanouchi; adult/child ¥200/100; ⌚8.30am-5pm Mar-Oct, to 4pm Nov-Feb) Across the railway tracks from Engaku-ji, Tōkei-ji is famed as having served as a women's refuge. A woman could be officially recognised as divorced after three years as a nun in the temple precincts. Today, there are no nuns; the grave of the last abbess can be found in the cemetery, shrouded by cypress trees.

Sugimoto-dera BUDDHIST TEMPLE
(杉本寺; www.sugimotodera.com; 903 Nikaidō; adult/child ¥200/100; ⌚8am-4.30pm) This small temple, founded in 734 CE, is reputed to be the oldest in Kamakura. Climb the steep steps up to the ferocious-looking guardian deities and statues of Kannon. Take a bus from stop 5 at Kamakura Station to the Sugimoto Kannon bus stop (¥200, 10 minutes).

Hōkoku-ji BUDDHIST TEMPLE
(報国寺; ☎0467-22-0762; www.houkokuji.or.jp; 2-7-4 Jōmyō-ji; bamboo garden ¥200; ⌚9am-4pm) This Rinzai Zen temple is popular for its small forest of towering *mōsō* bamboo, within which you can relax under a shelter with a cup of *matcha* and sweets (¥500). It's down the road from Sugimoto-dera, on the right-hand side.

Activities

Daibutsu Hiking Course HIKING
This 3km wooded trail connects Kita-Kamakura with the Daibutsu (p182) in Hase (allow about 1½ hours) and passes several small, quiet temples and shrines, including **Zeniarai-benten** (銭洗弁天; 2-25-16 Sasuke; ⌚8am-4.30pm) FREE via a slight detour, one of Kamakura's most alluring Shintō shrines.

The path begins at the steps just up the lane from pretty **Jōchi-ji** (浄智寺; 1402 Yamanouchi; adult/child ¥200/100; ⌚9am-4.30pm), a few minutes from Tōkei-ji. Near Zeniarai-benten a cavelike entrance leads to a clearing where visitors come to bathe their money in natural springs, with the hope of bringing financial success. From here, continue down the paved road, turning right at the first intersection, walking along a path lined with cryptomeria and ascending through a succession of *torii* (shrine gates) to **Sasuke-inari-jinja** (佐助稲荷神社; 2-22-10 Sasuke; ⌚24hr) FREE, a hilltop enclave strewn with *kitsune* (fox totems), before meeting up with the Daibutsu path once again. To hike in the opposite direction, follow the road beyond Daibutsu and the trail entrance is on the right, just before a tunnel.

Ten-en Hiking Course HIKING
(天園ハイキングコース) From Zuisen-ji you can access this trail, which winds through the hills for two hours before coming out at Kenchō-ji (p182). From Kenchō-ji, walk around the Hojo (Main Hall) and up the steps to the trail.

Tours

Kamakura Welcome Guides TOURS
(www.kamakurawelcome.guide) FREE Join free, hour-long tours on Fridays (10.30am and 1pm; English) which meet just outside the east entrance of Kamakura Station. The morning tour goes to Tsurugaoka Hachiman-gū (p183); the afternoon tour to Daibutsu (p182). You can also design your own half-day or day tour via the website at least two weeks in advance (multiple languages available). Guests pay their own admission and transport fees.

Sleeping

Kamakura Guesthouse GUESTHOUSE ¥
(鎌倉ゲストハウス; ☎0467-67-6078; www.kamakura-guesthouse.com; 273-3 Tokiwa; dm/q ¥3500/15,000; ⊖❄📶) While it's away from the action, this traditional cypress home with cheap Japanese dorms and a common area with an *irori* (fireplace) make it a nice

ZAZEN: SEATED MEDITATION

Too many temples and before you know it you're feeling anything but 'Zen'. *Zazen* (seated meditation) can help you discover what you're missing – after all, temples were originally designed for this purpose (and not sightseeing). Both Engaku-ji and Kenchō-ji (p182) hold beginner-friendly, public *zazen* sessions. Instruction is in Japanese, but you can easily manage by watching everyone else; arrive at least 15 minutes early. A book stand at Kenchō-ji sells English titles on *zazen* if you're keen to take your meditating skills to the next level.

place to hang out. Take the Enoden bus from stop 1 at the east gate of Kamakura Station to Kajiwaraguchi (¥240); it's a one-minute walk from here.

There are bicycles for rent (¥800 per day) and a communal kitchen; *zazen* meditation tours to Engaku-ji are offered during the week.

WeBase HOSTEL ¥
(☎0467-22-1221; www.we-base.jp; 4-10-7 Yuiga-hama; dm/d/f ¥3800/9600/28,000;) Steps from the beach is this campus-like former company retreat turned hostel, with capacious dorms, bags of socialising space and top spec facilities including bike and bodyboard rental and a yoga studio (classes from ¥1000). It's a five-minute walk south towards the beach from Yuiga-hama Station (Enoden Enoshima Line).

IZA Kamakura HOSTEL ¥
(IZA 鎌倉; ☎0467-33-5118; http://izaiza.jp; 11-7 Sakanoshita; dm/d/q ¥3800/8800/14,000;) This surfer hang-out is steps from the beach and handy for Hase's temples. Cramped but sociable, it also has a bar and bike rental (¥1000 per day).

★ Kamejikan Guesthouse GUESTHOUSE ¥¥
(亀時間; ☎0467-25-1166; www.kamejikan.com; 3-17-21 Zaimokuza; dm/d/q from ¥3500/9000/16000;) A three-minute walk to the beach, this lovely guesthouse occupies a restored wooden building that's almost a century old, with paper lampshades and a small cafe and bar (noon to 5pm Saturday and Sunday). Choose from a six-bed dorm or two private rooms, all with common tiled bathrooms. Catch bus 12, 40 or 41 to Kuhon-ji from Kamakura Station.

English-speaking owner Masa is a good source of information and rents bodyboards and bicycles (¥500 per day).

Hotel New Kamakura HOTEL ¥¥
(ホテルニューカマクラ; ☎0467-22-2230; www.newkamakura.com; 13-2 Onarimachi; s/d from ¥5000/8500;) Charming, slightly shabby and ultraconvenient, this hotel built in 1924 has both Western- and Japanese-style rooms, most of which share bathrooms. There's red carpet and a vintage vibe, though the economy rooms are rather plain – opt for Japanese-style. Exit west from Kamakura Station, then take a sharp right down the alley and up the left-hand stairs before the tunnel.

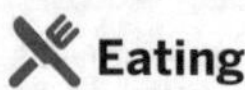

Eating

Kamakura has a wide range of touristy restaurants and cafes, including plenty of options for vegetarians.

Cobakaba JAPANESE ¥
(食堂コバカバ; ☎0467-22-6131; 1-13-15 Komachi; meals ¥500-1000; 7am-2pm) One of the few restaurants around town open for breakfast, Cobakaba serves Japanese-style breakfast sets – fried egg, rice, fish, miso soup, salad and simmered veggies – and lunch options that change seasonally.

Wander Kitchen INTERNATIONAL ¥
(ワンダーキッチン; ☎0467-61-4751; www.wanderkitchen.net; 10-15 Onarimachi; sweets/lunch from ¥400/1000; noon-8pm;) It's worth searching out this charmingly decorated, shabby-chic wooden house for its laid-back vibe, good coffee and tasty meals, cakes and crêpes. It's tucked away just off the main street, about five minutes' walk south of the west exit of Kamakura Station.

Sông Bé Cafe ASIAN ¥
(ソンベカフェ; www.song-be-cafe.com; 13-32 Onarimachi; dishes from ¥800; 11.30am-8pm Thu-Sun;) This mellow day-to-evening joint serves up dishes such as *pad thai* (stir-fried rice noodles) and green curry, with veggies sourced from the local farmers market, and Southeast Asian beers to match. The friendly owner also serves a good selection of teas and desserts like yuzu honey cheesecake and banana cake with coconut milk.

★ Matsubara-an SOBA ¥¥
(松原庵; ☎0467-61-3838; www.matsubara-an.com/shops/kamakura.php; 4-10-3 Yuiga-hama; mains ¥960-1850, set meals from ¥3200; 11am-10pm) Dinner reservations are recommended for this upscale soba restaurant in a lovely old house. Try the *goma seiro soba* (al dente noodles served cold with sesame dipping sauce). Dine alfresco or indoors where you can watch noodles being handmade. From Yuiga-hama Station (Enoden Enoshima line) head towards the beach and then take the first right. Look for the blue sign.

Magokoro FUSION ¥¥
(麻心; ☎0467-38-7355; www.magokoroworld.jp; 2nd fl, 2-8-11 Hase; meals ¥800-1400; 11.30am-8pm Tue-Sun;) Boho beachfront spot mixing ocean views with an organic hemp-based menu, including vegetarian hemp taco rice, several vegan options, macrobiotic cakes and hemp beer (no, it doesn't get you

high). From Hase Station, walk to the beach, then turn left on the coastal road.

Good Mellows CAFE ¥¥
(グッド　メローズ; ☎0467-24-9655; 27-39 Sakanoshita; burgers from ¥1000; ⊙10.30am-7pm Wed-Mon) Kick back in this California-style surf shack and enjoy charcoal-grilled burgers stacked with bacon, cheese and avocado, washed down with a Dr Pepper or a cold California microbrew.

Drinking & Nightlife

Magnetico BAR
(☎467-33-5952; 4-1-19 Yukinoshita; ⊙11.30am-3pm & 5.30-10pm Mon, Tue, Thu & Fri, 11.30am-11pm Sat & Sun; 📶) Run by a couple of relaxed reggae dudes, this louche hang-out has Japanese craft beers on tap, island rhythms on the stereo and a menu of tacos, fried chicken and other comfort food. It's a five-minute walk east from the main entrance of Tsurugaoka Hachiman-gū, Kamakura's main shrine.

Univibe BAR
(鎌倉; ☎0467-67-8458; www.univibe.jp; 2nd fl, 7-13 Onaricho; ⊙11am-3pm & 6pm-late; 📶) Surprisingly roomy upstairs bar kitted-out in retro vintage decor, with friendly owners, table football and a relaxed vibe. A five-minute walk from the Kamakura JR station.

Information

Just outside the east exit of Kamakura Station, the English-speaking staff at the **Tourist Information Center** (鎌倉市観光総合案内所; ☎0467-22-3350; www.kamakura-info.jp; 1-1-1 Komachi; ⊙9am-5pm) are helpful and can book accommodation. Pick up the detailed (and free) *Kamakura – A Historical and Cultural Mosaic* booklet for in-depth information on the region's temples and time periods, as well as umpteen brochures and maps for the area.

For information about Kamakura, see www.city.kamakura.kanagawa.jp (in Japanese).

Getting There & Away

JR Yokosuka–line trains run to Kamakura from Tokyo (¥920, 54 minutes) and Shinagawa (¥720, 46 minutes), via Yokohama (¥340, 25 minutes). Alternatively, the Shōnan Shinjuku line runs from the west side of Tokyo (Shibuya, Shinjuku and Ikebukuro, all ¥920) in about one hour, though some trains require a transfer at Ōfuna, one stop before Kita-Kamakura. The last train from Kamakura back to Tokyo Station is at 11.19pm and Shinjuku at 9.48pm.

JR Kamakura-Enoshima Free Pass (adult/child ¥700/350) Valid for one day from Ōfuna or Fujisawa Stations; unlimited use of JR trains around Kamakura, the Shōnan monorail between Ōfuna and Enoshima, and the Enoden Enoshima line.

Odakyū Enoshima/Kamakura Free Pass (from Shinjuku/Fujisawa ¥1470/610) Valid for one day; includes transport to Fujisawa Station (where it meets the Enoden Enoshima line), plus use of the Enoden.

Getting Around

You can walk to most temples and shrines from Kamakura or Kita-Kamakura Stations. Sites in the west, like the Daibutsu, can be reached via the Enoden Enoshima line from Kamakura Station to Hase (¥190) or by bus from Kamakura Station stops 1 and 6.

Kamakura Rent-a-Cycle (レンタサイクル; ☎0467-24-3944; www.jrbustech.co.jp/kamakura; 1-1 Komachi; per hr/day ¥800/1800; ⊙8.30am-5pm) is outside the east exit of Kamakura Station, and right up the incline.

HAKONE

☎0460 / POP 11,389

Offering serene onsen, world-class art museums, traditional inns and spectacular mountain scenery crowned by Mt Fuji, Hakone (箱根) can make for a blissful escape from Tokyo. Ashino-ko (芦ノ湖) is the lake at the centre of it all, the setting for the iconic image of Mt Fuji with the *torii* of Hakone-jinja rising from the water.

Naturally, this is all quite attractive, so it can feel crammed, particularly at weekends and holidays. If you follow the herd, it can also feel highly packaged. To beat the crowds, plan your trip during the week, go hiking and sample some of Hakone's offbeat gems.

Information

LUGGAGE FORWARDING

At Hakone-Yumoto Station, deposit your luggage with **Hakone Baggage Delivery Service** (箱根キャリーサービス; ☎0460-86-4140; 2nd fl, Hakone-Yumoto Station; S/M/L suitcase ¥800/1000/1500; ⊙8.30am-7pm) by 12.30pm, and it will be delivered to your inn within Hakone from 3pm. Alternatively, you can check your bag at your inn by 10am and pick it up after 1pm at Hakone-Yumoto Station. Hakone Freepass holders get a discount of ¥100 per bag.

TOURIST INFORMATION

Try www.hakone.or.jp for online information.

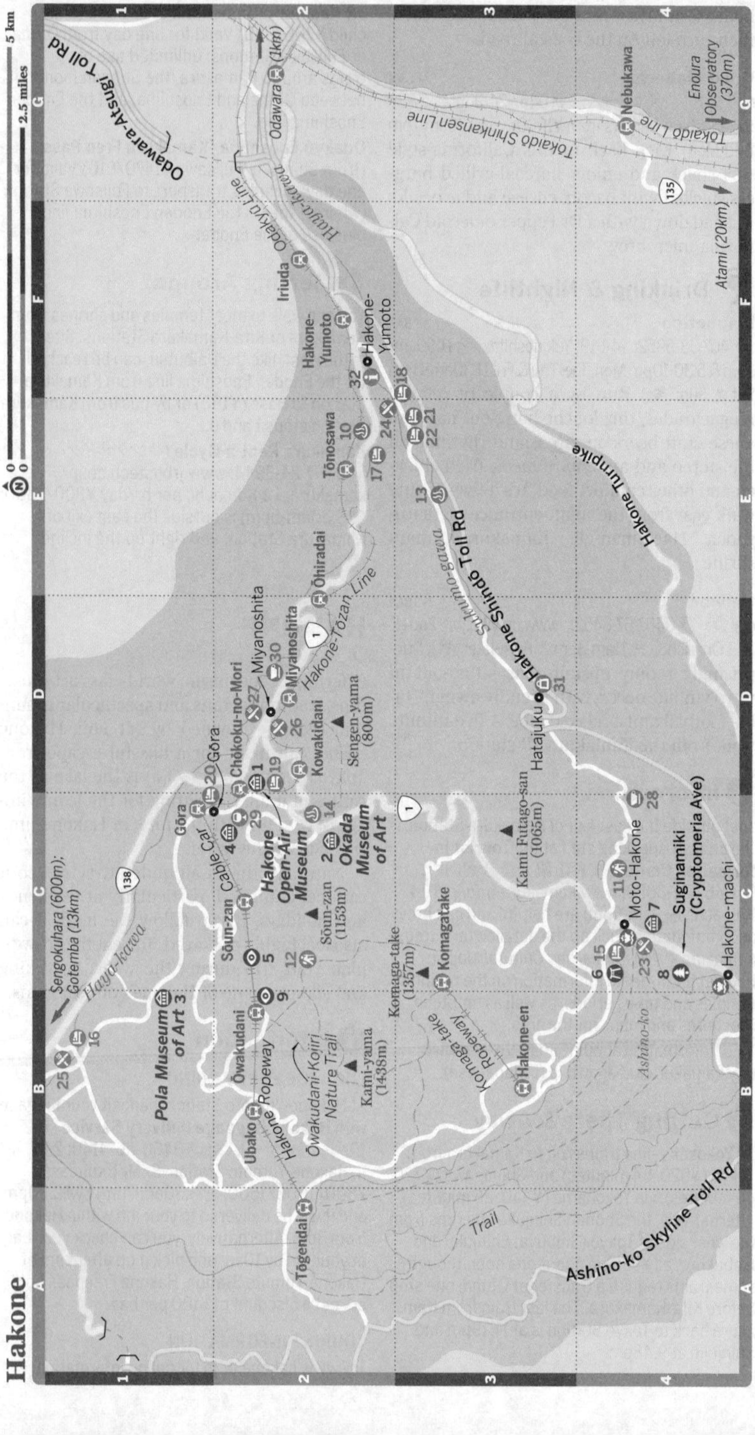

Hakone

0 — 5 km
0 — 2.5 miles

Sengokuhara (600m); Gotemba (13km)
25
16
Haya-kawa
138
Pola Museum of Art 3
Gōra
Cable Car
20 Gōra
Sōun-zan
4
Chōkoku-no-Mori
27
Miyanoshita
Ubako
Ōwakudani
5
29
1
Hakone Ropeway
9
Hakone Open-Air Museum
19
30
26
Miyanoshita
Tōgendai
12
Ōwakudani-Kojiri Nature Trail
Sōun-zan (1153m)
2
14
Kowakidani
Hakone-Tōzan Line
1
Ōhiradai
Okada Museum of Art
Sengen-yama (800m)
Kami-yama (1438m)
Komaga-take (1357m)
1
Komagatake
Komaga-take Ropeway
Trail
Hakone-en
Kami Futago-san (1065m)
Hatajuku
31
Hakone Shindō Toll Rd
Sukumo-gawa
13
Tōnosawa
10
17
24
22
21
18
32
Hakone-Yumoto
Hakone-Yumoto
Iriuda
Odakyū Line
Haya-kawa
Odawara (1km)
Odawara-Atsugi Toll Rd
Ashino-ko Skyline Toll Rd
6
15
11
Moto-Hakone
28
Ashino-ko
23
7
8
Suginamiki (Cryptomeria Ave)
Hakone-machi
Hakone Turnpike
Tōkaidō Shinkansen Line
Nebukawa
135
Tōkaidō Line
Atami (20km)
Enoura Observatory (370m)

Hakone

Top Sights
1 Hakone Open-Air Museum D2
2 Okada Museum of Art C2
3 Pola Museum of Art B1

Sights
4 Hakone Museum of Art C2
5 Hakone Ropeway C2
6 Hakone-jinja C4
7 Narukawa Art Museum C4
8 Onshi Hakone Kōen C4
9 Ōwakudani B2

Activities, Courses & Tours
10 Hakone Yuryō E2
11 Old Hakone Highway C4
12 Sōun-zan C2
13 Tenzan Tōji-kyō E3
14 Yunessun C2

Sleeping
15 Box Hotel C4
16 Fuji Hakone Guest House B1
17 Fukuzumirō E2
18 Guesthouse Azito F3
19 Guesthouse Tenmaku D2
20 Hakone Tent C1
21 K's House Hakone E3
22 Omiya Ryokan E3

Eating
23 Bakery & Table C4
24 Coco-Hakone E2
25 Hanasai B1
Itoh Dining by Nobu .... (see 4)
26 Miyafuji D2
Sukumo .... (see 13)
27 Yamagusuri D2

Drinking & Nightlife
28 Amazake-chaya C4
29 Gora Brewery & Grill C2
30 Naraya Cafe D2

Shopping
31 Hatajuku Yosegi Kaikan D3

Information
Hakone Baggage Delivery Service .... (see 32)
32 Hakone-Yumoto Tourist Information Center F2

Hakone-Yumoto Tourist Information Center (0460-85-8911; https://hakone-japan.com; 706-35 Yumoto; 9am-5.45pm) Make your first stop at the most clued-up of several tourist information centres scattered around Hakone. This is the best place for maps and information about hiking trails and all the attractions. Staffed by helpful English speakers, it's across the main road from the train station.

Getting There & Away

The Odakyū line (www.odakyu.jp) from Shinjuku Station goes directly into Hakone-Yumoto, the region's transit hub. Use either the convenient Romance Car (¥2280, 1½ hours) or *kyūkō* (regular-express) service (¥1190, two hours); the latter usually requires a transfer at Odawara.

JR Pass holders can take the Kodama *shinkansen* (¥3740, 35 minutes) from Tokyo Station to Odawara and change there for trains or buses for Hakone-Yumoto.

Getting Around

Part of Hakone's popularity comes from the chance to ride assorted *norimono* (modes of transport): switchback train (from Hakone-Yumoto to Gōra), cable car (funicular), ropeway (gondola), ship and bus.

The narrow-gauge, switchback Hakone-Tōzan line runs from Odawara via Hakone-Yumoto to Gōra (¥670, one hour).

From Gōra, a funicular (¥420, 10 minutes) heads up to near the 1153m-high summit of **Sōun-zan**, from where you can catch the Hakone Ropeway (p193) to **Ōwakudani** and **Tōgendai**.

From Tōgendai, sightseeing boats criss-cross Ashino-ko to **Hakone-machi** (0460-83-7550; Hakonemachi-ko) and **Moto-Hakone** (0460-83-6022; Motohakone-ko) between 9.30am and 5pm (one way/return ¥1000/1840, 30 minutes).

Of course you can do the whole circuit in reverse. For more details, see www.odakyu.jp/english/sightseeing/hakone.

Hakone-Yumoto

0460 / POP 3114

The onsen resort town of Hakone-Yumoto (箱根湯元温), spanning the Sukumo-gawa, is the starting point for most visits to Hakone. Though heavily touristed, it offers a high concentration of good onsen, the main attraction here.

Activities

★Tenzan Tōji-kyō ONSEN

(天山湯治郷; 0460-86-4126; www.tenzan.jp; 208 Yumoto-chaya; adult/child ¥1300/650; 9am-10pm) Tenzan Tōji-kyō is an upscale day spa in contemporary facilities with traditional design elements, set on the edge of the Sukamo-gawa. There's a variety of indoor and

WORTH A TRIP

ENOURA OBSERVATORY

Book well in advance to be sure of securing a ticket to **Enoura Observatory** (江之浦測候所; 0465-42-9170; www.odawara-af.com; 362-1 Enoura, Odawara; reserved/walk-up ticket ¥3300/3850; 10am-1pm & 1.30-4.30pm Thu-Mon; JR Tokaido line to Nebukawa), an extraordinary art, architecture and performing arts complex overlooking scenic Sagami Bay. A passion project of the artist Sugimoto Hiroshi, the Observatory showcase some of his beguiling seascape photography as well as his incredible collection of ancient stones, fossils and traditional architectural elements. Entry is limited to either the morning or afternoon session and there is a free transfer bus from Nebukawa Station.

You are free to wander the grounds, which include a bamboo forest, orange grove and traditional teahouse. Two of the buildings – a 100m-long gallery and a tunnel clad in weathered steel – are aligned with the rising sun for, respectively, the summer and winter solstice. There's also two outdoor stages – one stone, the other paved with optical glass and surrounded by a full-sized re-creation of a Roman ampitheatre – that are used for occasional events such as *nō*-plays (stylised dance-drama); check the website for further details.

There is no cafe here, but it is a lovely place to linger, so bring a packed lunch with you.

outdoor baths and saunas, as well as lounging areas with tatami floors and chaises. Private baths (for up to four people) can be booked for two hours (¥3900). Tattoos are allowed.

Take shuttle bus 'B' from Hakone-Yumoto Station to Tenzan-iriguchi (天山入り口).

Hakone Yuryō ONSEN

(箱根湯寮; 0460-85-8411; www.hakoneyuryo.jp; 4 Tōnosawa; adult/child ¥1500/750; 10am-9pm Mon-Fri, to 10pm Sat & Sun) Relax in spacious *rotemburo* (outdoor onsen) under the trees at this idyllic complex, or book yourself a private bath in advance (from ¥4300 for one hour for up to two people). Make use of the complementary shuttle bus (9am to 8pm, every 10 to 15 minutes) from Hakone-Yumoto Station. Visitors with tattoos will be denied admission.

You can also eat here before or after a soak (meal package ¥2500 including onsen).

Sleeping

K's House Hakone GUESTHOUSE ¥

(0460-85-9111; www.kshouse.jp; 12-1 Yumoto-chaya; dm/d from ¥3500/9000;) K's has the option of either Japanese-style futon dorms, capsules or bunks, along with neat tatami doubles. There's indoor and outdoor onsen, a shared kitchen, a lounge and a terrace with mountain views. It's a 15-minute slog uphill from Hakone-Yumoto Station on the south side of the Sukumo-gawa, or a ¥230 bus ride.

Friendly staff are clued up on all the Hakone travel questions you're wondering about.

Guesthouse Azito GUESTHOUSE ¥

(ゲストハウス　アジト; 0460-83-8557; www.guesthouseazito.com; 491 Yumoto; capsule ¥6800, s/d ¥4500/9000;) Azito means 'hideout', and there is indeed something playful and treehouse-like about the huge timber capsules here furnished with double beds. It also has Japanese-style private rooms and a sociable little bar (5.30pm-11.30pm) that opens onto the street. English spoken. It's a 10-minute walk uphill from Hakone-Yumoto Station on the south side of the Sukumo-gawa.

Omiya Ryokan RYOKAN ¥¥

(0460-85-7345; www.o-miya.com; 116 Yumoto-chaya; r incl 2 meals from ¥9300, Sat or Sun from ¥13,400;) Lower weekday prices make this cute ryokan with its tatami rooms an attractive proposition, especially as some have mountain views. There's also a small indoor onsen. To get here, take the 'B' course bus from Hakone-Yumoto Station. Limited English spoken.

★**Fukuzumirō** RYOKAN ¥¥¥

(福住楼; 0460-85-5301; www.fukuzumi-ro.com; 74 Tōnosawa; s/d incl 2 meals from ¥25,000/44,000;) Established in 1890 and lovingly maintained, Fukuzumirō embodies the aesthetics and spirit of a traditional inn. There's intricately carved, original woodwork throughout (look out for the lucky bats). Thoughtfully prepared seasonal meals, which include vegetarian and gluten-free options, are served in-room.

Facilities, including onsen baths of stone and pine, are shared.

Each of the 17 rooms has its own design; some have terraces over-looking the rushing Haya-kawa, though it was the quiet garden-facing room that was a a favourite of Nobel Prize–winning author Kawabata Yasunari.

Fukuzumirō is in Tōnosawa, which neighbours Hakone-Yumoto. Shuttle bus 'C' from Hakone-Yumoto Station stops in front of the inn.

Eating

Coco-Hakone CHICKEN ¥

(☎70-4006-5212; 475-8 Yumoto; meals around ¥1000; ⊙11am-4.30pm Wed-Sun) The 'Hakone lava' chicken over rice looks burnt to a crisp at this casual joint, but actually it's a juicy, tasty treat and simply a bit of gastronomic trickery. You can drink Hakone craft beer here, too, and nerds will appreciate the glass cabinet stuffed with vintage Star Wars toys (sorry, it's locked).

Sukumo SOBA ¥¥

(すくも; ☎0460-86-4126; 208 Yumoto-chaya; soba ¥800-1550; ⊙11.30am-4.30pm, closed Thu & every 2nd & 4th Fri; P) This serene riverside soba restaurant is perfect for a bite after visiting the neighbouring Tenzan Tōji-kyō onsen complex. Find it through an arched gate just beside the bridge. The chef speaks English.

Miyanoshita & Kowakidani

Miyanoshita (宮ノ下) is the first worthwhile stop on the Hakone-Tōzan railway heading towards Gōra, with antique shops, a small hiking trail and some good places to eat. The next stop along is Kowakidani (小涌谷), home to a giant onsen complex and the highly impressive collection of the Okada Museum of Art.

Sights & Activities

★Okada Museum of Art MUSEUM

(岡田美術館; ☎0460-87-3931; www.okada-museum.com; 483-1 Kowakidani; adult/student ¥2800/1800; ⊙9am-5pm) This mammoth museum showcases the dazzling Japanese, Chinese and Korean art treasures of industrialist Okada Kazuo. You could easily spend hours marvelling at the beauty of many pieces, including detailed screen paintings and exquisite pottery. Interactive, multilingual interpretive displays enhance the experience. The museum is opposite the Kowakien bus stop.

As well as admiring the treasures on display, you can explore the lush hillside garden and woodland, soak in the outdoor footbath or relax in the cafe-restaurant housed in a traditional wooden villa.

Yunessun ONSEN

(箱根小涌園ユネッサン; www.yunessun.com; 1297 Ninotaira; Yunessun adult/child ¥2900/1600, Mori-no-Yu ¥1900/1200, both ¥4100/2100; ⊙9am-7pm Mar-Oct, to 6pm Nov-Feb) This modern, family-oriented complex is more like an onsen amusement park, with outdoor water slides and a variety of baths (including some filled with coffee, green tea and even sake!) as well as indoor swimming pools with a retro leisure centre vibe. Mixed bathing so you'll need a swimsuit. The connected Mori-no-Yu complex (11am to 8pm) is traditional single-sex bathing.

Take a bus from Hakone-machi, Gōra or Hakone-Yumoto to the Kowakien bus stop. There's also a variety of accommodation here.

HAKONE TRAVEL PASSES

Odakyū's Hakone Freepass, available at Odakyū stations and Odakyū Travel branches, is an excellent deal, covering the return fare to Hakone and unlimited use of most modes of transport within the region, plus other discounts at museums and facilities in the area. It's available as a two-day pass (adult/child from Shinjuku ¥5140/1500; from Odawara, if you're not planning on returning to Shinjuku, ¥4000/1000) or a three-day pass (adult/child from Shinjuku ¥5640/1750, from Odawara ¥4500/1250). Freepass-holders need to pay an additional limited-express surcharge (¥890 each way) to ride the Romance Car.

If you plan to combine Hakone with Mt Fuji, also consider the Fuji Hakone Pass (adult/child ¥8000/4000), a three-day pass offering discount round-trip travel from Shinjuku as well as unlimited use of most transport in the two areas.

Eating & Drinking

Yamagusuri JAPANESE ¥¥

(山薬; ☎0460-82-1066; 224 Miyanoshita; meals ¥2300; ⏰7am-8pm) Yamagusuri is a popular spot for substantial, healthy meal sets featuring *tororo* (grated yam) that you pour over barley and rice. The dining room overlooks the forested gorge below.

Miyafuji SUSHI ¥¥

(鮨みやふじ; ☎0460-82-2139; www.miyanoshita.com/miyafuji; 310 Miyanoshita; meals from ¥1680; ⏰11.30am-3pm & 5.30-8pm Fri-Wed) This friendly sushi shop is known for its *aji-don* (horse mackerel over rice). If you know how to fold an origami crane, ask to try their special challenge – using their impossibly small origami, fold a crane in under 10 minutes (they provide tweezers) and they'll add it to the shop's teeny-crane-festooned decor. Look for the English sign.

Naraya Cafe CAFE

(ナラヤカフェ; 404-13 Miyanoshita; coffee from ¥350; ⏰10.30am-6pm, to 5pm Dec-Feb, closed Wed & 4th Thu of the month; 👪) Beside the station, this woodsy cafe and craft shop is a pleasant pit stop for drinks and light meals. You can also soak your toes in the footbath on the terrace looking out over the mountains, or unwind in the bookspace below.

Chōkoku-no-Mori & Gōra

Chōkoku-no-Mori (彫刻の森) is the station stop for the Hakone Open-Air Museum, one of the area's top attractions. The Hakone-Tōzan line terminates at the next station, Gōra (強羅), a characterful little mountain community and also the starting point for the funicular and cable-car trip to Tōgendai on Ashino-ko.

Sights

★**Hakone Open-Air Museum** MUSEUM

(彫刻の森美術館; ☎0460-82-1161; www.hakone-oam.or.jp; 1121 Ninotaira; adult/child ¥1600/800; ⏰9am-5pm) Occupying a verdant swath of Hakone hillside is this unmissable art safari, leading visitors past a rich array of 19th- and 20th-century sculptures and installations by leading Japanese artists as well as the likes of Henry Moore, Rodin and Miró, harmoniously plonked into the landscape. If it's raining, take shelter in the humongous Picasso Pavilion with more than 300 of his works inside, ranging from paintings and glass art to tapestry.

Kids will love the giant crochet artwork/playground with its Jenga-like exterior walls, as well as the spiral staircase of the stained-glass Symphonic Structure. End the day by soaking your feet in the outdoor footbath. Hakone Freepass holders get ¥200 off the admission price.

Hakone Museum of Art MUSEUM

(箱根美術館; ☎0460-82-2623; www.moaart.or.jp/hakone; 1300 Gōra; adult/child ¥900/free; ⏰9.30am-4.30pm Fri-Wed, to 4pm in winter) Sharing grounds with a lovely velvety moss garden and teahouse (¥700 *matcha* and sweet), this museum has a collection of Japanese pottery dating from as far back as the Jōmon period (some 5000 years ago). The gardens are spectacular in autumn. It's just across from Koenkami Station on the funicular.

Sleeping

★**Guesthouse Tenmaku** HOSTEL ¥

(囲炉裏ゲストハウス天幕; ☎0460-83-9348; 1121 Ninotaira; dm/tw/f from ¥3500/9000/18000, deluxe dorm 1/2 people ¥5500/8500; ⊖❄@📶) The centrepiece of this impeccably designed hostel is the *irori* (sunken hearth) in the bar-lounge, around which communal feasts of grilled fish, rice and miso soup are shared between guests (¥1000). The 'deluxe dorm' is worth considering – private timber cabins/capsules furnished with double beds. There's a good selection of rooms for families, too, and kids of all ages are welcome.

Tenmaku is from the same (exceedingly talented) folks behind Hakone Tent In an area low on nightlife, the bar here is a choice spot for a drink or three.

★**Hakone Tent** HOSTEL ¥

(温泉ゲストハウス; ☎0460-83-8021; http://hakonetent.com; 1320-257 Gōra; dm/s/d with shared bathroom from ¥3500/4000/9000; P⊖❄📶) A sociable hostel run by a team of friendly young staff, Tent offers Japanese-style futon dorms and private rooms in a stylishly renovated ryokan that has its own onsen baths. The smart lobby bar is a great place for an early-evening drink, or a tasty meal of pizza and pasta.

Eating & Drinking

Itoh Dining by Nobu JAPANESE ¥¥¥

(伊藤ダイニング バイノブ; ☎0460-83-8209; www.itoh-dining.co.jp; 1300-64 Gōra; lunch/dinner from ¥3000/7000; ⏰11.30am-3pm & 5-9.30pm; 📝) Savour premium Japanese beef, cooked *teppanyaki*-style in front of you by the chef, at this elegant restaurant, an outpost of the celeb chef Nobu's dining empire. It's just uphill from Koenshimo Station on the funicular, one stop from Gōra.

★Gora Brewery & Grill CRAFT BEER
(☎0460-83-8107; www.itoh-dining.co.jp; 1300-72 Gōra; ⊙1-4pm & 5-9.30pm; 📶) Sup on a Gora IPA or a Black Belt stout, among other ales from this stylish brewery venue, run by the folk behind Itoh Dining by Nobu. Grill treats include house-made sausages, Peruvian-style lamb and Nobu's signature black cod with miso. It's a three-minute walk from Koenshimo Station on the funicular, or a 10-minute uphill slog from Gora.

All beers are sold at the 'happy hour' price of ¥500 between 1pm and 4pm.

Sōun-zan & Sengokuhara

Sōun-zan (早雲) is where the top of Hakone's funicular railway meets the Hakone Ropeway for aerial journeys over the remarkable (and stinky) volcanic valley of Ōwakudani and onward to Ashino-ko. To the north, Sengokuhara (仙石原) is a sizeable town and a useful stopover between Hakone and the Mt Fuji area, with some good-value lodgings.

Sights & Activities

★Pola Museum of Art MUSEUM
(ポーラ美術館; www.polamuseum.or.jp; 1285 Kozukayama; adult/child ¥1800/700; ⊙9am-5pm) Showcasing the private collection of the late Suzuki Tsuneshi, son of the founder of the Pola Group (a cosmetics company), this impressive building displays works from Van Gogh, Cézanne, Renoir, Matisse, Picasso and Rodin, in addition to Japanese artists painting in the Western style, including Kuroda Seiki and Okada Saburosuke.

There's also a 700m nature trail winding through the museum's grounds.

Hakone Ropeway CABLE CAR
(箱根ロープウェイ; www.hakoneropeway.co.jp; one way/return ¥1450/2550; ⊙9am-5pm Mar-Nov, to 4.15pm Dec-Feb) The Hakone Ropeway is a 30-minute, 4km gondola ride, taking travellers to Tōgendai from Sōun-zan. It glides over the steaming crater of Ōwakudani, one of the stops along the way. At times, increased volcanic activity at Ōwakudani results in the ropeway not operating for the sake of public safety. In such cases, a bus runs from Tōgendai to Sōun-zan.

If you've bought a round-trip ticket and the ropeway is shut down before your return, there is a refund counter.

The ropeway is included on the Hakone Freepass.

Ōwakudani VOLCANO
(大桶谷; www.kanagawa-park.or.jp/owakudani) FREE The 'Great Boiling Valley' was created 3000 years ago when Kami-yama erupted and collapsed, also forming Ashino-ko. Hydrogen sulphide steams from the yellow ground here (the yellow is crystallised sulphur) and the hot water is used to boil onsen *tamago,* eggs blackened in the sulphurous waters, which you can buy to eat from the tourist shops beside the ropeway station. On rare occasions Ōwakudani might be closed due to volcanic activity.

Sōun-zan HIKING
(早雲山) There are various hiking trails on this mountain including one to Kami-yama, Hakone's highest peak (1¾ hours) and another up to Ōwakudani (1¼ hours). The latter is sometimes closed due to the mountain's toxic gases. Check at the tourist information office.

Sleeping & Eating

Fuji Hakone Guest House GUESTHOUSE ¥¥
(富士箱根ゲストハウス; ☎0460-84-6577; www.fujihakone.com; 912 Sengokuhara; s/tw/tr from ¥5550/10,950/16,350; P⊖❄@📶) Threadbare but exceedingly homely, this family-run guesthouse offers good-value tatami rooms, indoor and outdoor onsen with divine volcanic waters, and a wealth of information on local sights and hiking. Take the T-course bus to Senkyōrō-mae from the east exit of Odawara Station (lane 4; ¥1050, 50 minutes); it's a one-minute walk from there.

A smart choice, geographically-speaking, if you're planning onward travel by bus to the Fuji lakes region.

Hanasai JAPANESE ¥
(花菜; ☎0460-84-0666; 919 Sengokuhara; mains from ¥850; ⊙11.30am-2.30pm & 5.30-9pm Wed-Mon) Choose from a hodgepodge of Japanese favourites (*tonkatsu,* sashimi, curry rice) along with a few Western and even Chinese dishes in this retro family restaurant that's like dining in a late Showa-era (1970s) home.

Hakone-machi & Moto-Hakone

The kitsch sightseeing boats that ply the cobalt blue waters of Ashino-ko deposit you at either Hakone-machi (箱根町) or the adjacent Moto-Hakone (元箱根), two small lakeside communities both well touristed and with sights of historical interest.

Sights & Activities

Narukawa Art Museum MUSEUM
(成川美術館; ☎0460-83-6828; www.narukawamuseum.co.jp; 570 Moto-Hakone; adult/child ¥1300/600; ⊙9am-5pm) Art comes in two forms here – in the exquisite Japanese-style paintings, *nihonga,* on display, and in the stunning Mt Fuji views from the panorama lounge looking out across the lake, conditions permitting.

The website has ¥200 discount vouchers you can print out (one voucher good for four people).

Hakone-jinja SHINTŌ SHRINE
(箱根神社; ⊙9am-4pm) FREE Hakone-jinja, established in the 8th century, is set in the woods above Ashi-no-ko, but its red *torii* (shrine gate) is right on the water – and very photogenic. The shrine is a 10-minute walk from Moto-Hakone, around the perimeter of Ashi-no-ko.

Onshi Hakone Kōen PARK
(恩賜箱根公園; ☎0460-83-7484; 171 Moto-Hakone; ⊙9am-5pm) FREE Occupying a peninsula on Ashino-ko, this scenic park was formerly the grounds of an imperial summer retreat. The 'Lakeside Panorama Pavilion', said to offer Hakone's finest view of Mt Fuji, was built just behind the original palace building (destroyed in the Great Kanto Earthquake, but the foundations are still visible). Stop by for drinks and vistas.

Old Hakone Highway WALKING
(箱根旧街道; Hakone Kyū-kaidō) The Old Hakone Hwy is a rare, preserved section of the Tōkaidō, the feudal-era road that connected Tokyo (then called Edo) to Kyoto. It connects Moto-Hakone with the small settlement of Hatajuku (畑宿), a 4km (90-minute) walk over cobbles worn smooth from centuries of foot traffic (the shogun had banned the use of wheels). Unlike most of Hakone, this historic, wooded path is usually uncrowded.

The nearest bus stop is Hakone-jinja-iriguchi (箱根神社入り口), one stop before Moto-Hakone; from the bus stop, head up the small road (past the temple on the right) a few hundred metres to the wooden sign that marks the entrance to the trail. The route, which mostly runs gently downhill, is generally well-marked in English; however, there are some tricky parts where the trail meets up with the road, and you'll have to keep a keen eye out for signs. One note of caution: the cobbles, which are uneven in places, can get very slippery; it's good to have shoes with some traction and avoid walking during or the day after rain.

About 30 minutes' in, the path passes behind the teahouse, Amazake-chaya. Hatajuku is known for its marquetry craftsmanship and has a few shops, including **Hatajuku Yosegi Kaikan** (畑宿寄木会館; 103 Hatajuku; ⊙9am-4.30pm). Hakone Kyū-kaidō line buses return here to Hakone-Yumoto (¥400; 25 minutes; every 30 minutes).

Sleeping

Box Hotel BOUTIQUE HOTEL ¥¥
(☎0460-85-1113; www.boxhakone.com; 7-1 Moto-Hakone; r per person from ¥10,000;) All five of the lodge-style rooms have balconies at this thoughtfully-designed boutique hotel, but only the family rooms (which are more like small suites, complete with kitchenettes) overlook the lake. On ground level a folksy, American-style restaurant serves creative burgers, meatloaf, salads and great coffee.

Eating & Drinking

The shorefront streets of Moto-Hakone port are lined with places to eat.

Bakery & Table CAFE
(☎0460-85-1530; www.bthjapan.com; 9-1 Moto-Hakone; ⊙8.30am-5pm) This lakeside cafe, open early for those looking to beat the crowds, has great views inside and from the outside terrace. There's a bakery on the ground floor (open from 10am); order your pastries here first, then take them upstairs to the cafe.

There's also a restaurant on the 3rd floor (open from 11am Monday to Friday, from 9am Saturday and Sunday) serving sandwiches and crêpes.

★**Amazake-chaya** TEAHOUSE
(甘酒茶屋; ☎0460-83-6418; www.amasake-chaya.jp; 395-1 Futoko-yama; ⊙7am-5.30pm) Teahouses like Amazake-chaya were once common sights along the old Edo-era (1603–1868) foot highways that criss-crossed Japan. This one, with a thatched roof, is one of only a few that

remain, and run by the same family for 13 generations (and nearly four centuries). The speciality is the namesake *amazake* (¥400), a sweet, nonalcoholic, fermented rice milk.

Amazake-chaya can be reached on foot via the Old Hakone Highway in about 30 minutes from Moto-Hakone. It's also a stop on the Hakone Kyū-kaidō (K) bus line, which travels between Hakone-Yumoto and Moto-Hakone. If you visit in the chillier months, you can warm yourself around the *irori* (sunken fireplace).

IZU PENINSULA

The Izu Peninsula (伊豆半島, Izu-hantō), about 100km southwest of Tokyo in Shizuoka Prefecture, is where the famed Kurofune (Black Ships) of US Commodore Perry dropped anchor in 1854. Contemporary Izu has a cool surfer vibe, lush greenery, rugged coastlines and abundant onsen. Weekends and holidays see crowds descend on the east coast, particularly in summer. It's generally quieter on the west coast, which lacks a railway but has, weather permitting, Mt Fuji views over Suruga-wan (Suruga Bay).

Atami

☎0557 / POP 37,146

The onsen and seaside resort of Atami (熱海) is both the gateway to Izu and its largest town. Overbuilding in the 1980s unfortunately sullied Atami's picturesque bayside setting, but there's enough here to keep you occupied for a night or so while you plan onward travel or wait for a boat to the Izu Islands.

Sights & Activities

Coeda House ARCHITECTURE

(コエダハウス; ☎557-82-1221; 1027-8 Kamita-ga; garden ¥1000; ⏲9am-5pm) Resembling a parasol of cyprus and glass perched on a cliff above the ocean, this remarkable cafe space is the work of superstar architect Kengo Kuma (designer of the 2020 Tokyo Olympic stadium). You'll find it in the **Akao Herb and Rose Garden**, 5km south of Atami. The 'Yu-Yu' tourist bus stops here on its loop of Atami's sights.

A shuttle bus runs up to Coeda House from the garden's entrance, where you can while away an hour or two with coffee, orange custard tarts and ocean vistas before walking back down to the entrance via a series of terraced gardens.

MOA Museum of Art MUSEUM

(MOA美術館; ☎0557-84-2511; www.moaart.or.jp; 26-2 Momoyama-chō; adult/student ¥1600/1000; ⏲9.30am-4.30pm Fri-Wed) A small but refined collection of Japanese and Chinese pottery, paintings and Buddhist treasures spanning a millenia awaits at this museum, built dramatically into the hillside like a Bond villain lair. Artefacts are beautifully displayed in tatami-lined alcoves, the result of a design makeover by artist Sugimoto Hiroshi, while walls of glass at various junctures confer dizzying sea views.

Buses run here from platform 8 outside Atami Station (¥170, eight minutes).

Nikkotei Oyu ONSEN

(日航亭　大湯; ☎557-83-6021; 5-26 Kamijukuchō; ¥1000; ⏲9am-8pm Wed-Mon) Dip into the searing, mineral-rich waters of this old-school onsen with adjoining indoor and outdoor pools. It's a five-minute walk from Kinomiya station, one stop along from Atami. No tattoos.

Sleeping & Eating

Across from the station, the Heiwa-dōri shopping arcade has lots of little shops serving noodles or sushi.

★**Guesthouse Maruya** GUESTHOUSE ¥

(☎0557-82-0389; www.guesthouse-maruya.jp; 7-8 Ginza-chō; s/tw/tr from ¥3890/7775/10,800;) A terrific budget choice just three minutes from the beach, Maruya rocks a hip open-plan lounge-kitchen fronting a corridor of lockable sleeping capsules, each big enough to stand up in. The young staff are sweet and obliging, and they'll even barbecue you a fish on the front deck for breakfast.

Selfish Diner BURGERS ¥¥

(☎0557-52-6681; www.selfishdiner.jp; 15-11 Nagisa-chō; meals from ¥1500; ⏲10.30am-8pm) Grab a pavement table or counter seat at this smart little seafront joint for tuna cutlet burgers, stacked aesthetically with salad and sauce in a toasted bun, and served with fries or lotus root chips.

Information

Atami Tourist Office (☎0557-85-2222; http://travel.ataminews.gr.jp/en; 2018-8 Nagisa-chō; ⏲9am-5.30pm Apr-Sep, to 5pm Oct-Mar) Down on the waterfront; has town maps, 'Yu-Yu' bus timetables and discount vouchers for various sights.

Izu Peninsula

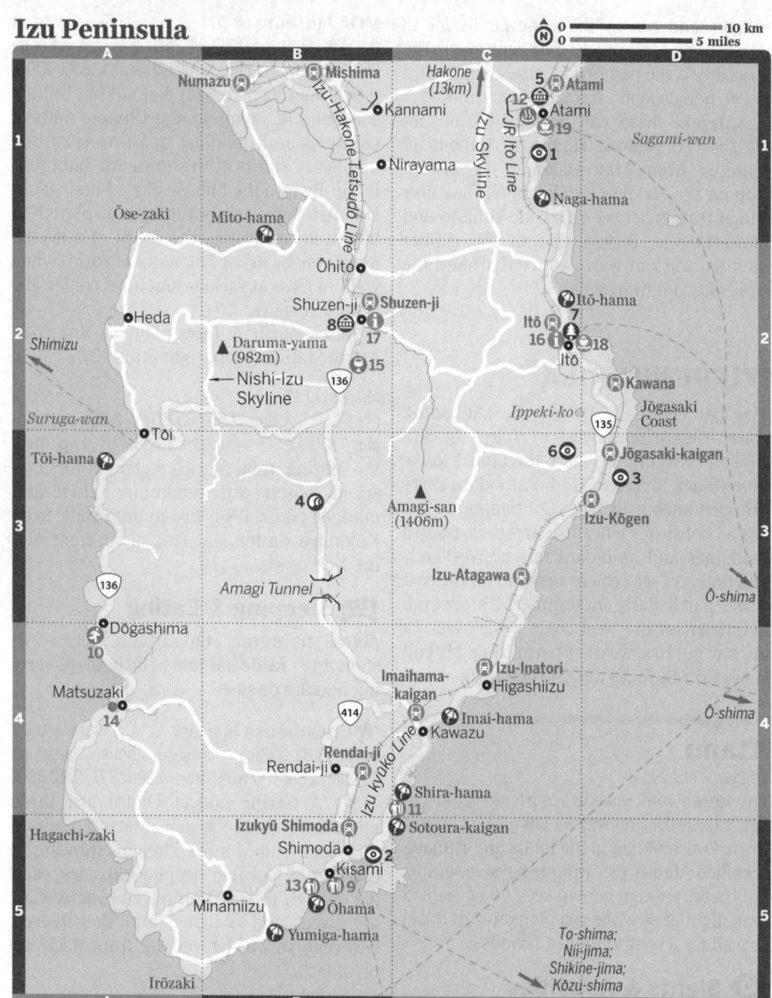

Getting There & Around

JR trains run from Tokyo Station to **Atami** (11 Taharahon-chō) on the Tōkaidō line (Kodama *shinkansen* ¥4190, 46 minutes; Odoriko sightseeing train ¥3800, 1¼ hours; *kaisoku* ¥1940, 1½ hours).

Tokai Kisen (東海汽船; ☎03-5472-9999; www.tokaikisen.co.jp; 6 Wadahamaminami-cho) hydrofoils travel daily from Atami port to the island of Ō-shima (¥4710, 45 minutes). Prices are seasonal. To reach Atami port, take the bus from lane 7 outside Atami Station (¥230, five minutes).

Atami's yellow 'Yu-Yu' sightseeing buses (day/single ¥700/250) depart from Atami Station and loop around town, climbing the headland for dramatic views, and also stopping at Akao Herb and Rose Garden for Coeda House (p195).

Itō

☎0557 / POP 68,541

A laid-back, low-rise seaside town with a few notable onsen, Itō (伊東) makes a good base for wider Izu Peninsula explorations, not least because of some excellent, affordable ryokan to overnight in. Flowing through town to the sea is the Matsu-kawa, along which runs a pretty riverside path.

Izu Peninsula

Sights

1 Coeda House ... C1
2 Gyokusen-ji ... B5
3 Jōgasaki-kaigan ... D3
4 Jōren-no-taki ... B3
5 MOA Museum of Art ... C1
6 Mt Ōmuro ... C3
7 Nagisa Park ... C2
8 Shoko Kanazawa Museum ... B2
Shuzen-ji ... (see 8)
Shuzen-ji Treasure Museum ... (see 8)
Tōkaikan ... (see 7)

Activities, Courses & Tours

9 Baguse Surf School ... B5
Dive & House Futo ... (see 3)
10 Dōgashima Marine ... A4
Hako-yu ... (see 8)
11 Irie Coffee & Sea ... C4
12 Nikkotei Oyu ... C1
13 Real ... B5
Ryokufuen ... (see 7)
Sawada-kōen Rotemburo ... (see 10)
Shirahama Mariner ... (see 11)
Tokko-no-yu ... (see 8)
14 Yamabushi Trail Tour ... A4
Yokikan ... (see 7)

Sleeping

A Million Roses ... (see 11)
Arai Ryokan ... (see 8)
Ernest House ... (see 13)
Goyōkan ... (see 8)
Guesthouse Maruya ... (see 12)
Hostel Knot ... (see 8)
K's House Itō Onsen ... (see 7)
Tabi Tabi ... (see 13)
Umibe-no-Kakureyu Seiryu ... (see 10)
Wabi Sabi ... (see 13)
Yamaki Ryokan ... (see 7)

Eating

Bora Noya ... (see 3)
Cafe Mellow ... (see 13)
Hamazushi ... (see 7)
Kunihachi ... (see 7)
Papa's Restaurant ... (see 11)
Selfish Diner ... (see 12)
South Cafe ... (see 13)
Wabi Sabi Cafe ... (see 13)
Zenfutei Nana ban ... (see 8)

Drinking & Nightlife

15 Baird Brewery Beer Garden ... B2
Freaks ... (see 7)

Information

Atami City Tourism Association ... (see 12)
Dōgashima Tourist Information Center ... (see 10)
16 Tourist Information Center ... C2
17 Tourist Information Office ... B2

Transport

Atami Station ... (see 12)
18 Ferry Terminal ... D2
Izu Velo ... (see 17)
19 Tōkai Kisen ... C1

Sights & Activities

If you plan on checking out Mt Ōmuro or hiking Jōgasaki-kaigan, pick up the one-day Itō Sightseeing Free Pass (adult/child ¥1300/650) at the bus terminal.

★ Jōgasaki-kaigan AREA

(城ヶ崎海岸) A cliffside hiking trail winds over volcanic rock and through pine forest along the gorgeous Jōgasaki coast south of Itō. Most visitors head to **Kadowaki Lighthouse** and the adjacent Kadowaki-no-Umi suspension bridge 23m above the waves; from there you can hike south 6km or so to Izu-Kōgen Station, or stop halfway at the **New York Lamp Museum** and bus back. From Itō Station, take the bus to Jōgasaki-guchi (¥700, 40 minutes) and walk the 1.2km to the lighthouse.

The first place of note you'll get to is Bora Noya (p198), where you can fortify yourself pre-hike with a delicious sashimi feast.

Tōkaikan HISTORIC BUILDING

(東海館; ☎0557-36-2004; www.itospa.com; 12-10 Higashi Matsubara-chō; adult/child ¥200/100; ⏲9am-9pm, tearoom 10am-5pm, onsen 11am-7pm Sat & Sun) This grand inn (c 1928) is now a national monument for its fine woodwork. Each of its three storeys was designed by a different master carpenter; architecture buffs will love comparing the styles. A highlight is the Grand Hall on the 3rd floor, an ocean of tatami (120 mats!) flanked by stages. An additional ¥500 will let you take a dip in its onsen baths (weekends only).

Several of the rooms house odd little museum exhibits, and there's a tearoom with river views on the ground floor.

Mt Ōmuro MOUNTAIN

(大室山; ☎0557-51-0258; return chairlift ¥500; ⏲chairlift 9am-5.15pm Apr-Sep, to 4.15pm Oct-Mar) Ten kilometres south of Itō is this dormant rice-bowl volcano, a perfectly smooth, steep-sided grassy mound. Ride the chairlift to the 580m summit where you can take in coastal views of Mt Fuji. There's a 1km walk around the crater, bizarrely enough with an archery centre in the middle. Take the bus bound for Shaboten Kōen and Ōmuroyama from Itō Station (¥710, 40 minutes).

Nagisa Park PARK
(なぎさ公園) At the southern end of **Orange Beach**, this little park is studded with photogenic bronze figurative sculptures by local artist Shigeoka Kenji.

Dive & House Futo DIVING
(☎0557-51-8113; dive@bj.wakwak.com; 855-3 Futo; half-day dive lesson ¥11,880, gear rental 2 people ¥14,040; ⏰8am-7pm) In the idyllic little harbour community of Futo is this shop that runs dive trips from neighbouring **Yokobama Beach**. Not much English is spoken, but licensed divers can rent all the necessary gear for an underwater adventure. It's a 20-minute walk from Jōgasaki-Kaigan Station.

Yokikan ONSEN
(陽気館; ☎0557-37-3101; www.yokikan.co.jp; 2-24 Suehiro-chō; ¥1000; ⏰11am-3pm) Part of a hotel, this rooftop *rotemburo* (outdoor onsen) has the novelty of only being accessible via a rickety in-house funicular. It's mixed bathing, with distant views over the town and the sea. Small tattoos aren't a problem.

Ryokufuen ONSEN
(緑風園; ☎0557-37-1885; www.ryokufuen.com; 3-1 Otonashi-chō; ¥1000; ⏰1.30-10pm) Soak away in this tranquil *rotemburo* (outdoor onsen) with its rocky waterfall under a canopy of trees. Follow the river inland from K's House (on the opposite bank) and you'll reach it in less than 10 minutes. K's House guests receive a 50% discount.

Sleeping

★K's House Itō Onsen HOSTEL ¥
(ケイズハウス伊東温泉; ☎0557-35-9444; www.kshouse.jp; 12-13 Higashi Matsubara-chō; dm ¥2950 s/d from ¥4800/7600;) Hugely popular with travellers, this 100-year-old riverside ryokan is an architectural treasure and an absolute steal. Japanese-style private rooms simply ooze history (book a river view), while the common areas are stylish and well-maintained. With a fully equipped kitchen, bicycle rental, helpful staff, and public and private onsen, K's is frankly the main reason to come to Itō. Book early.

The hostel shares the same architectural layout and fine carpentry as Tōkaikan (p197) next door (apparently the original owners were related); the difference being you can actually stay here.

Yamaki Ryokan RYOKAN ¥¥
(山喜旅館; ☎0557-37-4123; www.ito-yamaki.jp; 4-7 Higashi Matsubara-chō; s/d from ¥8790/16,200, without meals ¥5550/11,100;) A block east of Tōkaikan is this charming wooden inn from the 1940s with an onsen bath, old fashioned gym and pleasant rooms, some with ocean views. On weekends you can only book rooms with meals included. Almost no English; the Tourist Information Center can make a reservation for you.

Eating & Drinking

Hamazushi SUSHI ¥
(はま寿司; ☎557-35-5522; 546-40 Oyukawa; sushi from ¥100; ⏰11am-10.30pm;) This roadstop chain restaurant opposite the beach has zero character, but who cares when it's this cheap, tasty and fun? Choose from bargain-priced bites like *nigiri, maki,* fried chicken and ramen using a touch screen and watch them whiz to your table at high speed on a conveyor. Isn't technology wonderful?

Kunihachi IZAKAYA ¥
(国八; ☎0557-37-9186; 10-2 Higashimatsubara-chō; dishes ¥370-1000; ⏰5.30-11.30pm Wed-Sun;) A cute *izakaya* cluttered with eclectic decor. The menu caters to all with cheap and tasty dishes such as jumbo *okonomiyaki* (savoury pancakes), tempura and sashimi sets, alongside more outlandish options like fried crocodile and horse or deer sashimi. It has a great vegetarian selection, too.

Bora Noya JAPANESE ¥¥
(ぼら納屋; ☎0557-51-1247; www.boranaya.com; 833 Futo; meals ¥850-3200; ⏰9.30am-4pm Fri-Wed Apr-Sep, to 3.30pm Oct-Mar) Fish brought in to neighbouring Futo port supply the pearlescent sashimi platters at this former fishing lodge dating back to the 17th century. 'Bora' refers to the striped mullet that migrate along the coast and have sustained a fishing industry here since the Edo period. From Itō Station, take the bus to Jōgasaki-guchi (¥700, 40 minutes).

Freaks BAR
(☎0557-37-4560; 2-3 Matsukawa-chō; ⏰8pm-2am) Intimate bar spinning soul and funk vinyl, on the main road towards the station from the Matsukawa.

Information

For online info, check out www.itospa.com.

Tourist Information Center (☎0557-37-6105; 1-8-3 Yukawa; ⏱9am-5pm) Across from Itō Station, the TIC has loads of info on the Izu Peninsula and a detailed Itō map.

Getting There & Away

The JR limited-express Odoriko service runs from Tokyo Station to Itō (¥4510, one hour and 40 minutes). Itō is connected to Atami by the JR Itō line (¥320, 22 minutes).

From Itō, the Izukyūkō (aka Izukyū) line goes to Shimoda (¥1620, one hour and 10 minutes), stopping at Jōgasaki-kaigan (¥580, 20 minutes). There are six buses daily to Shuzen-ji (¥1130, one hour).

During summer and some major holidays, **Tōkai Kisen** (東海汽船; ☎03-5472-9999; www.tokaikisen.co.jp; ⏱9.30am-8pm) jetfoils depart from Itō's **tiny port** (http://itoport.info; 1-17-9 Wada) to Ō-shima (¥3560, 35 minutes) once a day. At other times, you'll have to go to Atami to reach Ō-shima.

Shimoda

☎0558 / POP 22,931

Shimoda (下田) holds a pivotal place in Japan's history as the spot where the nation officially opened to the outside world after centuries of near isolation. This legacy is preserved in shrines, culturally significant locations and folklore, as well as the ersatz 'black ships' that take tourists on harbour cruises. The small port's laid-back vibe is also perfectly suited to an exploration of its surrounding beaches, which are some of the best in Izu.

Sights

★Perry Road STREET

(ペリーロード) It takes less than 10 minutes to walk end-to-end of this quaint cobbled street shadowing a narrow stream leading to Ryōsen-ji temple. However, the appealing ambience of old houses under willow trees now occupied by cafes, jazz bars, boutique shops and restaurants will encourage you to linger.

At the east end, you can enter the old **Sawamura's House** (c 1915), overlooking the corner of the canal, which used to belong to a mayor of Shimoda.

Gyokusen-ji TEMPLE

(玉泉寺; 31-6 Kakisaki; museum adult/child ¥400/200; ⏱8am-5pm) Founded in 1590, this Zen temple is most famous as the first Western consulate in Japan, established in 1856. A small **museum** has artefacts of the life of American Townsend Harris, the first consul general. It's a 25-minute walk from Shimoda Station, or take bus 9 to Kakisaki-jinja-mae (¥240, five minutes).

Ryōsen-ji & Chōraku-ji BUDDHIST TEMPLE

(了仙寺・長楽寺; Perry Rd) **FREE** A 15-minute walk south of Shimoda Station is Ryōsen-ji, site of the treaty that opened Shimoda, signed by Commodore Perry and representatives of the Tokugawa shogunate. The temple's **Museum of the Black Ship** (了仙寺宝物館, Hōmotsukan; ☎0558-22-2805; www.mobskurofune.com; 3-12-12 Shimoda; adult/child ¥500/250; ⏱8.30am-5pm) stands streetside, with the temple beyond. Just beyond the temple's east gate at Perry Rd, a set of steps takes you up to Chōraku-ji, where a Russo-Japanese treaty was signed in 1854; look for the cemetery and *namako-kabe* (black-and-white lattice-patterned) walls.

Shimoda Kōen PARK

(下田公園・和歌の浦遊歩道; 3-1174 Sanchōme) If you keep walking east from Perry Rd, you can climb the steps into the hillside park of Shimoda Kōen, which overlooks the bay. It's loveliest in June, when the hydrangeas are in bloom.

Sleeping

Shimoda has a fair spread of accommodation, but if you don't mind being outside of the action (or have your own transport) there are nicer, more beachy places to stay in Shirahama or Kisami.

LOCAL KNOWLEDGE

SURFING SHIMODA

The beaches around Shimoda are some of Japan's best surf spots. While it's a year-round surfing destination, waves are best between June and September. Shirahama (p201) is the most popular and its small but constant break gets packed in summer. The beaches in Kisami (p202), just south of Shimoda, are among some of the best. Ōhama (大浜) has the largest stretch of sand and consistent waves, Irita (入田) is especially good when a southerly rolls in, and Tatado (多々戸) has arguably the most consistent waves on the peninsula. Board rentals are available in both Shirahama and Kisami.

Shimoda

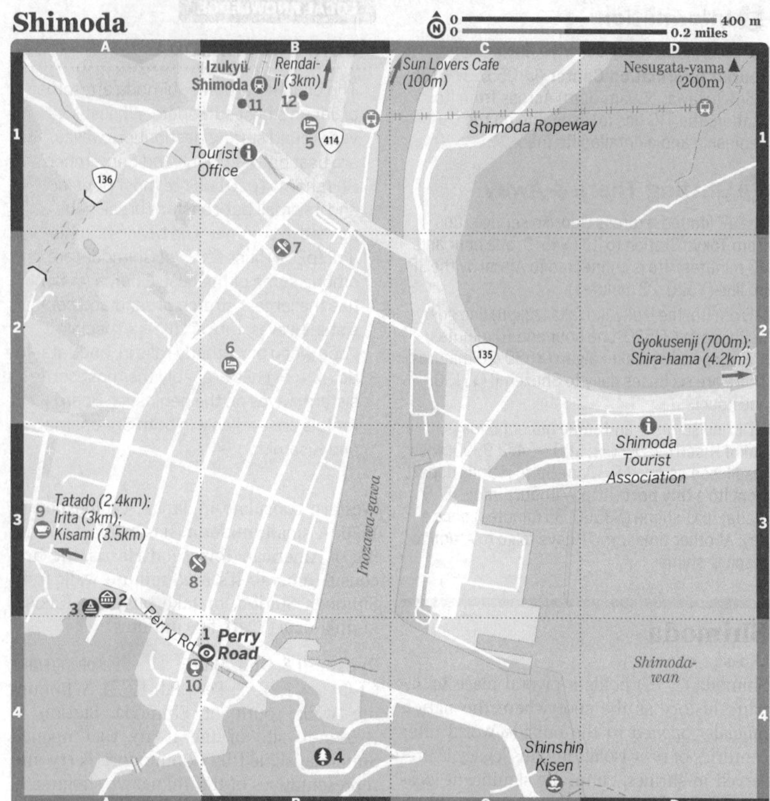

Shimoda

Top Sights
1 Perry Road B4

Sights
2 Museum of the Black Ship A3
3 Ryōsen-ji & Chōraku-ji A3
4 Shimoda Kōen B4

Sleeping
5 Hotel Marseille B1
6 Yamane Ryokan B2

Eating
7 Gorosaya B2
8 Nami Nami A3

Drinking & Nightlife
9 Cubstar A3
10 Soul Bar Tosaya A4

Transport
11 Nippon Rent-a-Car B1
12 Toyota Rent-a-Car B1

Yamane Ryokan RYOKAN ¥
(やまね旅館; ☎0558-22-0482; 1-19-15 Shimoda; r per person from ¥4750; P ❄) Neat Japanese-style rooms in a sprawling family home. The owners speak next to no English but are friendly and welcoming, and the central location is handy.

Hotel Marseille BUSINESS HOTEL ¥¥
(☎0558-23-8000; www.hotel-marseille.jp; 1-1-5 Higashi Hongo; s/d from ¥8000/15,500; ❄ 📶) Next to the station, the Marseille adds a little *je ne sais quoi* to the standard business-hotel offering with well-maintained, pleasant rooms and a tea lounge with free coffee in the morning.

Eating

★ **Gorosaya** JAPANESE ¥¥
(ごろさや; ☎0558-23-5638; 1-5-25 Shimoda; set menus ¥1700-3300; ⊙11.30am-2pm & 5-9pm) Elegant, understated ambience and fantastic seafood. The *isōjiru* soup is made from more than a dozen varieties of shellfish

and looks like a tide pool in a bowl. The *sashimi-don* (rice bowl), not on the English menu, is also excellent. Look for the wooden fish decorating the entrance. Book ahead on weekends and holidays, or arrive early.

Nami Nami IZAKAYA ¥¥
(開国厨房なみなみ; ☎0558-23-3302; 3-3-26 Shimoda; skewers/small plates from ¥150/550; ⏲5pm-midnight) This friendly counter bar has a retro vibe and an inventive menu including local fish *(honjitsu no sakana)* and assorted delicacies served *yakitori*-style or breaded and fried. Look for the yellow sign.

Drinking & Nightlife

Cubstar CAFE
(☎0558-27-3225; 4-7-22 Shimoda; coffee ¥500; ⏲11am-10pm, closed Tue & 2nd Mon of the month; 📶) Run by a cool couple who abandoned Tokyo for the slower life of Shimoda, this cafe-bar offers excellent coffee and alcoholic beverages, plus pasta and paninis (mains ¥1000). Look for it opposite the green church.

Soul Bar Tosaya BAR
(土佐屋; ☎0558-27-0587; 3-14-30 Shimoda; ⏲7pm-midnight) Halfway along Perry Rd, this atmospheric spot mashes up a traditional residence from the era of the Black Ships with a soul-music bar. Note the ¥500 'music charge' per person. It also serves meals.

Information

Shimoda's official online tourism portal can be found at www.shimoda-city.com.

The **Shimoda Tourist Association** (下田市観光協会; ☎0558-22-1531; www.shimoda-city.info; 2nd fl, 1-1 Sotogaoka; ⏲9am-5pm) in the port area has English-speaking staff and various maps and guides to the town.

At the **tourist office** (観光案内所; ☎0558-22-1531; www.shimoda-city.info; 1-1 Sotogaoka; ⏲10am-5pm) opposite the station, staff speak very little English, but they will arm you with maps and can call the English-speaking staff at the port branch for you to assist with accommodation booking.

The **Sun Lovers Cafe** (サンラバーズカフェ; ☎0558-27-2686; 1-21-9 Higashi-hongo; ⏲11.30am-5.30pm Tue-Sat; 📶👪) Offers free wi-fi, an English-language book swap, tourist info, a kids' playroom and light meals.

Getting There & Away

Bus Tōkai buses run to Dōgashima (¥1360, one hour) via Matsuzaki.

Car Rental is available at **Nippon Rent-a-Car** (ニッポンレンタカー; ☎0558-22-5711; www.nipponrentacar.co.jp; Shimoda eki-mae; per day from ¥6500; ⏲8am-7pm) and **Toyota Rent-a-Car** (トヨタレンタカー; ☎0558-27-0100, reservations in English 0800-7000-815; www.rent.toyota.co.jp; 1-5-30 Higashihongō; per day from ¥6500; ⏲8am-8pm Apr-Dec, to 6pm Jan-Mar) by the train station.

Ferry Serving the Izu Islands Kōzu-shima, Shikine-jima, Nii-jima and Tō-shima, **Shinshin Kisen** (神新汽船株式会社; ☎03-3436-1146, 0558-22-2626; www.shinshin-kisen.jp; 18 Sanchōme) ferries depart Shimoda at 9.30am daily (except Wednesdays) on a loop of the islands, returning at 4.30pm. You can purchase a ticket to the island of your choice (prices are seasonal) or, if you really like boat trips, do a return day cruise (adult/child ¥5760/2890, no disembarkation allowed).

Train Shimoda is as far as you can go by train on the Izu Peninsula. Limited-express Odoriko *tokkyū* run to Izukyu-Shimoda Station from Tokyo Station, on the hour between 9am and 1pm (¥6260 to ¥6640, 2¾ hours), and Atami (¥3480, 80 minutes); regular Izukyūko trains run from Atami (¥1940, 1½ hours) and Itō (¥1620, one hour). Try to catch Izukyū's *Resort 21* train or the *Super View Odoriko*, both with bigger windows and enhanced seating for those rugged coastal vistas.

Or if you want to travel in serious style, the **Royal Express**, a train launched in 2017, chugs between Yokohama and Shimoda, pulling designer carriages, a haute cuisine dining car, and even a bar carriage with piano and stained glass ceiling (from ¥25,000, www.the-royalexpress.jp).

Shirahama

☎0558 / POP 21,534

Five kilometres from Shimoda, Shirahama (白浜海岸; meaning 'white-sand beach') is a mellow resort town set back from the sea that fills up with Kantō-area surfers and students during holiday weekends. At the north end of the main beach you'll find the 2400-year-old **Shirahama-jinja** shrine with its photogenic *torii* (gate) overhanging the ocean.

Activities

Shirahama Mariner SURFING
(白浜マリーナ; ☎0558-22-6002; www.mariner.co.jp; 2752-16 Shirahama; board rental ¥1000-4000, surf lessons from ¥9000; ⏲9am-9pm) This surf school opposite the beach rents boards, conducts surf lessons, and has an attached shop selling surf accessories, magazines and clothing.

Irie Coffee & Sea SURFING

(☎0558-36-4333; 1737 Shirahama; board rental ¥1000-4000, 2hr surf lessons ¥8000; ⊙10m-7pm Wed-Mon, hours vary low season) Opposite the Shirahama-jinja is this surf school and cafe with board rental, surf lessons, speciality coffee and *karaage* (Japanese fried chicken) sandwiches. Also has hot showers and changing rooms.

Sleeping

★A Million Roses PENSION ¥

(百万本のバラ; ☎558-25-5522; 2733-9 Shirahama; s/tw ¥5400/7000, incl 2 meals ¥8000/13,600; P❄📶) A perfect hillside location means glorious sea views and easy beach access from this twee pension, which is all pink carpets, frilly lace and piped classical music inside. Most rooms have sea views, as does the terrace area. Book with meals to enjoy hearty Japanese and Western repasts in the communal dining room. Limited English spoken.

Papa's Restaurant CAFE ¥¥

(パパス; ☎0558-22-0225; 1262-3 Shirahama; pizzas from ¥1050; ⊙11am-3pm & 5-10pm, closed Tue) Cosy diner with vintage toy cars, gingham tablecloths and surfboards on the walls. Serves light fare such as pizza, salads and *omurice* (omelette and fried rice). It's about an eight-minute walk from Shirahama-jinja, away from the beach.

Getting There & Away

Bus 9 runs frequently from Izukyu-Shimoda Station to Shirahama (¥360, 10 minutes).

Kisami

☎0558 / POP 2276

Our pick of Izu's seaside getaways is laid-back Kisami (きさみ). Most famous for its long surf beach **Ōhama** (大浜), Kisami is also well placed for access to other nearby surf beaches **Irita** (入田) and **Tatado** (多々戸).

Activities

Real SURFING

(☎0558-27-0771; www.realsurf.jp; 1612-1 Kisami; board rental ¥4000, 90min lessons ¥9720; ⊙10am-7pm) Rents out shortboards and longboards, and conducts lessons at Ōhama. Also gives stand-up paddleboard lessons (¥9720). Its website has lots of English info on the surf scene. The shop sells boards, wetsuits and gear.

Baguse Surf School SURFING

(バグースタタド&サーフィンスクール; ☎0558-22-2558; www.baguse.jp; 58-8 Tatado; board rental from ¥3300, 90min lessons from ¥5500; ⊙10am-4pm Apr-Nov) This Tatado-based operation a few minutes up from the beach offers lessons and board rentals.

Sleeping

★Wabi Sabi GUESTHOUSE ¥

(☎0558-22-4188; www.wabisabishimoda.com; 2735 Kisami; dm/s/d with shared bathroom from ¥3500/5000/8000; ⊙Apr-Sep; ❄📶) An idyllic retreat enveloped by greenery but only five minutes' walk from Ōhama beach. The old Japanese house here perfectly embodies the *wabi-sabi* (beauty in imperfection) aesthetic and is expertly managed by Angela and Yasu, who also run nearby Tabi Tabi. Wabi Sabi has a large shared kitchen, a vegetarian cafe, tatami rooms and shared bathrooms in a peaceful setting.

Families and groups of four to five can also choose from two beautifully renovated rental cottages (from ¥25,000). Note that Wabi Sabi closes between October and April.

Tabi Tabi GUESTHOUSE ¥¥

(☎090-6513-5578; www.tabitabiizu.com; 1658 Kisami; s/d ¥6000/9000; 🚭❄📶) This relaxed four-room lodge, owned by the same folks who run Wabi Sabi, is on the road leading towards Ōhama and handy for the bus into Shimoda.

Ernest House B&B ¥¥

(アーネストハウス; ☎0558-22-5880; www.ernest-house.com; 1893-1 Kisami; r per person from ¥6480; P🚭❄@📶) Two minutes' walk from Ōhama surf beach, this clean clapboard pension, named after Hemingway, has a quaint beach-house vibe and bicycles for rent.

Eating

Kisami's restaurants are fun social hubs, especially during the summer when opening hours stretch later.

Wabi Sabi Cafe FUSION ¥

(☎0558-22-4188; www.wabisabishimoda.com; 2735 Kisami; dishes ¥850-1100; ⊙10am-8pm; 📶🍴) 🌿 Choose from chair or hammock to savour the serenity at this homespun cafe, part of Wabi Sabi guesthouse, serving veggie and vegan Japanese fusion food. Dishes like edamame hummus, vegan Massaman curry, and a sweet and spicy hot tofu sandwich are made with love and local ingredients. Hours are reduced outside of summer, so call ahead.

Cafe Mellow CAFE ¥

(☎0558-27-2327; 1893-1 Kisami; meals ¥1000-1500; ⏲11am-11pm, closed Tue, Fri & 2nd Wed of the month; 📶) Sun streams into this weatherboard cafe-bar where locals and tourists dine on beach fare such as burgers, pizza and seafood barbecues (order a day ahead). Attached to Ernest House. Open daily during July and August.

★**South Cafe** INTERNATIONAL ¥¥

(サウスカフェ; ☎0558-25-5015; www.southcafe.net; 918-2 Kisami; mains ¥1000-1130; ⏲11.30am-9pm, closed Thu; 📶) It's well worth dragging yourself away from the beach for the tasty sandwiches, burgers, salads and curries (not to mention the must-have brownies) at this stylish diner. The drip coffee (with free refills) is also excellent. It's a five-minute walk north along the main road from the Kisami bus stop.

Getting There & Away

From Izukyū Shimoda Station, take an Irōzaki-bound bus (lane 3 or 4; ¥270, 10 minutes) to Kisami, from where Ōhama beach is a 15-minute walk.

Dōgashima

☎0558

Dōgashima (堂ヶ島) has a dramatic coastline, best enjoyed from the steamy perspective of an onsen or on the tourist boats that squeeze thrillingly into sea caves. The cliff-edge park has excellent views too, and at low tide you can walk across the **tombolo**, a sandbar connecting the tiny island of Zo-jima.

Activities

Dōgashima Marine CRUISE

(堂ケ島マリン; ☎0558-52-0013; www.izudougasima-yuransen.com; 20/50min cruises ¥1200/2300) Dramatic rock formations and sea caves around the Dōgashima coast are best experienced from these cruises, which depart from the jetty just beyond the TIC, in front of the bus stop.

A highlight is sailing into the **Tensōdō** (天窓洞), a cave lit by a natural skylight in the rock (you can also peer down from the top by hiking the cliff path). In choppy seas only the 20-minute cave cruise operates.

Sawada-kōen Rotemburo ONSEN

(沢田公園露天風呂; 2817-1 Sawada Nishina; adult/child ¥600/200; ⏲9am-6pm Wed-Mon Oct-Feb, to 7pm Mar-May & Sep, to 8pm Jun-Aug) Set directly on a cliff overlooking an open view of the ocean is this small *rotemburo* (outdoor onsen; separate bathing). It's a 15-minute walk south from Dōgashima, or hop on a Matsuzaki-bound bus for one stop. Then skirt around the back of **Noribama Beach**, passing the fishing port on your left and head for the cliffs.

It can get very busy at sunset but at other times you may have the place to yourself.

OFF THE BEATEN TRACK

YAMABUSHI TRAIL TOUR

The mountains inland from Matsuzaki were once criss-crossed with pathways and trails, part of Izu's ancient charcoal industry. Overgrown and long forgotten, they were rediscovered by a band of bike-mad locals who have so far cleared 40km of trails for mountain biking. **Yamabushi Trail Tour** (☎0558-36-3737; www.yamabushi-trail-tour.com; 379-2 Matsuzaki; 1 day per person ¥8500, bike & safety gear hire ¥2000-3000; ⏲8am-5pm) has options from 'beginner' to 'epic' (the longest trail a 550m vertical descent from mountaintop to sea).

More experienced riders can opt for two-day tours that go further afield. Yamabushi also operates a guesthouse on the edge of town, Mondo Lodge, with dorms, private ensuites, and an onsen.

Sleeping & Eating

Dōgashima is a small onsen resort with limited accommodation, so book ahead or stay in neighbouring Matsuzaki. During the day, you'll find dining options near the jetty area.

Umibe-no-Kakureyu Seiryu RYOKAN ¥¥¥

(海辺のかくれ湯清流; ☎0558-52-1118; www.n-komatu.co.jp; 2941 Nishina; per person incl 2 meals from ¥17,800; P❄@📶) Enjoy sensational sea views from the tatami guestrooms at this cliffside ryokan. A variety of baths are on offer, including a men's *rotemburo* (outdoor onsen) down on the beach with crashing waves, and the women's overlooking the ocean slightly higher up. It's a five-minute walk north from the Dōgashima bus stop.

Information

Dōgashima Tourist Information Center
(☎0558-52-1268; www.nishiizu-kankou.com; 2910-2 Nishina; ⏲8.30am-5pm Mon-Fri Sep-Jun, daily Jul & Aug) Just up from the cruise pier, and can help with accommodation booking, though English is limited.

Getting There & Away

Buses run to Dōgashima from Shimoda (¥1400, one hour, every 30 minutes), via Matsuzaki (¥270, eight minutes).

Shuzen-ji Onsen

☎0558 / POP 16,328

Shuzen-ji Onsen (修善寺温泉) is a quaint hot-spring village in a central Izu valley bisected by the rushing Katsura-gawa. Narrow lanes, red-lacquered bridges and a bamboo forest path make it perfect for strolling, and it's a good base to explore the peninsula's lush heartlands. One of Japan's most esteemed onsen ryokan is here, and inns around town offer day-use bathing.

Sights

Shuzen-ji BUDDHIST TEMPLE

(修善寺; www.shuzenji-temple.com; 964 Shuzen-ji; ⊙8.30am-4pm) FREE In the middle of the village is its namesake temple, said to have been founded over 1200 years ago by Kōbō Daishi, the priest credited with spreading Buddhism throughout much of Japan. *Zazen* (zen meditation) sessions take place on Tuesdays at 9.30am (one hour) and are free to participate in.

You can wander the pleasant temple grounds for free but there's a fee if you wish to see inside the small **treasure museum** (修禅寺宝物殿; ☎0558-72-0053; adult/child ¥300/200; ⊙8.30am-4.30pm, closed Thu), which contains ancient carved buddhas and other religious works of art.

Shoko Kanazawa Museum MUSEUM

(金澤翔子美術館; ☎0558-73-2900; www.shokokanazawa.net; 970 Shuzen-ji; adult/child ¥600/300; ⊙11am-3pm, closed Thu) Kanazawa Shoko (www.k-shoko.org), who has Down syndrome, has been doing calligraphy since she was five years old. Her vividly expressive pieces, as well as a video of her creating calligraphic work, are displayed in an annex of the Arai Ryokan.

Jōren-no-taki WATERFALL

(浄蓮の滝; Yugashima; ⊙8.30am-5pm) FREE Half an hour by bus from Shuzen-ji Station is this 25m waterfall in a ravine. Wasabi plants thrive in the river here; the roadstop gift shop sells tasty (and mild) wasabi soft-serve ice cream. You can also pick up the 3km **Amagi Hiking Trail** from the falls to the village of Yugashima Onsen, and catch the return bus from there.

Activities

Tokko-no-yu ONSEN

(独鈷の湯, Iron-Club Waters; ⊙24hr) FREE Perched on the river is this picturesque thermal footbath. Legend says it was dug by hand by Kōbō Daishi himself.

Hako-yu ONSEN

(筥湯; ☎0558-72-5282; 925 Shuzen-ji; ¥350; ⊙noon-9pm) Soothe your aching limbs at this elegant, contemporary onsen facility that's identified by its 12m-high wooden tower.

Sleeping

Hostel Knot HOSTEL ¥

(☎055-878-0261; www.hostelknot.com; 985-1 Shuzen-ji; dm/tw ¥3200/6400; 🚭❄@📶) A beautifully restored old house with mixed and female-only capsule-style dorms, one tatami twin and friendly young staff.

Goyōkan RYOKAN ¥¥

(五葉館; ☎0558-72-2066; www.goyokan.co.jp; 765-2 Shuzen-ji; r per person incl/excl 2 meals from ¥16,000/9500; P🚭❄📶) Stylish tatami rooms, some with river views, are offered at this sleek, small contemporary ryokan. Shared (indoor) baths are made of stone and *hinoki* cypress. Some English is spoken.

★**Arai Ryokan** RYOKAN ¥¥¥

(新井旅館; ☎0558-72-2007; www.arairyokan.net; 970 Shuzen-ji; r per person incl 2 meals from ¥24,840; ❄📶) Long beloved by Japanese artists and writers, this gem of an inn was founded in 1872 and has kept its traditional, wood-crafted heritage. The main bath hall, designed by artist Yasuda Yukihiko, is grand, and the riverside rooms are particularly lovely in autumn when the maples are ablaze.

Eating & Drinking

Zenfutei Nana ban NOODLES ¥¥

(禅風亭な ゝ 番; ☎0558-72-0007; 761-1-3 Shuzen-ji; meals ¥630-1890; ⊙10am-4pm, closed Thu) This institution serves the local noodle speciality, *zendera soba* (¥1260), with a stalk of fresh wasabi root to grate yourself – they even give you a plastic bag in which to take home the precious wasabi root leftovers. Expect to queue in high season.

Baird Brewery Beer Garden BEER GARDEN

(ベアードブルワリーガーデン修善寺; ☎0558-73-1225; www.bairdbeer.com; 1052-1 Ōdaira; ⊙noon-7pm Mon-Fri, 11am-8pm Sat & Sun) Sample some lovely craft beers in a peaceful setting, or take a brewery tour (check the website for tour times). From Shuzen-ji Station, take a Laforet Shuzenji Iriguchi–bound bus from lane 3 or 4 (20 minutes).

Information

Tourist Information Office (631-7 Kashiwakubo; ☎0558-72-0271; www.shuzenji.info; ⏰9am-5pm) At Shuzen-ji Station, where you can pick up a sightseeing map in English.

Getting There & Away

Bus services connect Shuzen-ji Station to Shuzen-ji Onsen (¥220, 10 minutes), Itō (¥1130, one hour) and Dōgashima (¥2030, 1½ hours). For Shimoda, you can catch the bus to Kawazu Station (¥1700, 1½ hours) and change to the train for the last leg to Izukyu-Shimoda Station (¥490, 17 minutes).

By train From Tokyo, take the Tōkaidō line to Mishima (Kodama *shinkansen* ¥4520, 45 minutes) then transfer to the Izu-Hakone Tetsudō for Shuzen-ji (¥510, 35 minutes).

Getting Around

Battery-assisted bicycles can be hired from **Izu Velo** (いずベロ; ☎558-72-0111; www.izuvelo.com/en; 633-8 Kashiwakubo; half/full day ¥1000/2000; ⏰9am-5pm), just outside the train station.

IZU ISLANDS

The peaks of a submerged volcanic chain extending 300km into the Pacific make up the Izu Islands (伊豆諸島; Izu-shotō), a world away from Tokyo. Soaking in an onsen while gazing at the ocean is the classic Izu Islands activity, as is hiking up the mostly dormant volcanoes and along the pristine beaches. Snorkelling, surfing and fishing are also popular. Island-hopping is possible on daily ferries and hydrofoils that run up and down the archipelago, but check schedules carefully, as they change frequently.

Booking ahead for the limited accommodation on the islands is a must during the summer. All the islands have campsites with washing facilities.

For more information on the whole chain, which includes To-shima (利島), Kōzu-shima (神津島), Miyake-jima (三宅島) and Mikura-jima (御蔵島), where it's possible to swim with dolphins, see www.tokyo-islands.com.

Getting There & Away

Though you can fly to the Izu Islands, the most economical and convenient way to get there is by hydrofoil. If you plan to spend any time on the Izu Peninsula, it's faster and cheaper to travel from Atami, Itō or Shimoda than from Tokyo.

AIR

ANA (ww.ana.co.jp) has flights from Tokyo's Haneda Airport to Hachijō-jima (from ¥12,990, 55 minutes).

New Central Airservice (www.central-air.co.jp) flies between Chōfu Airport (on the Keiō line about 20 minutes from Shinjuku) and Ō-shima (¥11,800, 30 minutes) and Nii-jima (¥14,100, 40 minutes) as well as some of the other islands.

BOAT

Tōkai Kisen (p199) operates hydrofoils and ferries from Tokyo's **Takeshiba Pier** (竹芝桟橋; Takeshiba Sanbashi; Map p92; ☎03-3432-8081; www.tptc.co.jp; 1-16-3 Kaigan, Minato-ku; 🚉JR Yamanote line to Hamamatsuchō, north exit), a 10-minute walk from the north exit of Hamamatsu-chō Station. Takeshiba Station, on the driverless, elevated Yurikamome line, is directly next to the pier.

Hydrofoils service Ō-shima (¥7400, 1¾ hours), Nii-jima (¥9410, 2½ hours), Shikine-jima (¥9410, two hours 50 minutes) and the other inner islands; you can also use them to hop between islands. A slower, cheaper overnight passenger ferry departs mosts nights at 10pm for Ō-shima (¥4450, eight hours), Nii-jima (¥5980, 10½ hours) and Shikine-jima (¥5980, 11 hours); return service is during the day.

These islands are also serviced by ferries and hydrofoils from the Izu Peninsula – covering less distance, and thus cheaper than those from Tokyo – at Atami (p196) and Shimoda (p201) ports. From Atami, get a Tōkai Kisen hydrofoil to Ō-shima (¥4710, 45 minutes). From Shimoda, Shinshin Kisen (p201) ferries serve Nii-jima and Shikine-jima (three to four hours, ¥4110).

Tōkai Kisen's passenger ferry *Salvia-maru* departs from Tokyo for Hachijō-jima (¥8600, 10½ hours) once daily at 10.30pm, arriving at 8.50am, then returning to Tokyo at 9.40am.

Boat schedules change monthly and can be affected by adverse weather. The decision to cancel hydrofoils due to heavy seas or typhoons is made at 6am on morning of departure and posted online at www.tokaikisen.co.jp.

Note that prices change seasonally and to reflect fluctuating fuel prices.

Ō-shima

☎04992 / POP 7762

The largest of the Izu Islands, the closest to Tokyo and generally the most interesting to visit is Ō-shima (大島). It has a relaxed, rustic charm and is particularly known for its profusion of scarlet camellia flowers (best viewed in February and March) as well as its active volcano Mihara-san, which last erupted in 1990.

Sights & Activities

Hire a car or scooter in the main port of **Motomachi** (元町), or hop on one of the irregular buses to reach Ō-shima's rocky southernmost point, **Tōshiki-no-hana** (トウシキの鼻), with good swimming in sheltered pools below Tōshiki Camp-jō.

In unfavourable weather, ferries will dock at **Okata** (岡田), on the northern end of the island, rather than at the usual Motomachi port on the west coast.

★ Mihara-san VOLCANO

(三原山) A road runs to the slope of the volcano, from where you can see Mt Fuji on a clear day. From here, you can hike 45 minutes to the 754m summit to peer into the still-steaming crater. It's another 45-minute hike around the rim of the crater, with stellar views 360 degrees around – it's fascinating to observe the path of previous lava flows. The Ō-shima Tourist Association can help with taxis and bus schedules.

There's great interpretive signage in English at various points of interest (and concrete shelters, just in case).

Motomachi Hama-no-yu ONSEN

(元町浜の湯; 882 Motomachi; adult/child ¥300/150; ⊙1-7pm Sep-Jun, from 11am Jul & Aug) A short stroll from Motomachi port is this attractive outdoor onsen with great views of the ocean, and Mt Fuji, too, if the weather is clear. It's mixed, so bring your bathing suit, or you can rent one.

Sleeping & Eating

Tōshiki Camp-jō CAMPGROUND

(トウシキキャンプ場; ☎04992-2-1446) FREE At the very south of the island, this well-maintained stretch of grass has a nice location overlooking the sea, as well as showers and a communal cooking area. The Ō-shima Tourist Association can assist with advance booking (required) and transport arrangements.

A 10-minute walk from the campsite is a natural rock pool in the ocean, popular for snorkelling and swimming.

★ Book Tea Bed GUESTHOUSE ¥

(☎04992-7-5972; dm/s/d/q ¥4000/5000/12,000/22,000; ⊗❄📶) A few steps south of Motomachi port, this hip hang-out has sunny capsule dorms with partial sea views, and smart private rooms with a fridge, safe and TV – try to bag the one with a balcony facing the ocean and Mt Fuji. There's also a simple bar-cafe for cocktails, coffee and comfort food like curry udon (from ¥800).

Island Star House INN ¥¥

(アイランドスターハウス大島; ☎050-1227-7940; www.island-star-house.com; per person with shared bathroom from ¥5500; P❄📶) In the woods just north of Ō-shima's tiny airport is this bright-yellow 'secret house', a secluded lodge with just two Japanese-style rooms (each sleeping up to five), a shared kitchen, and free use of bikes, snorkels, fishing gear and a barbecue. Pick-up from either of Ō-shima's ports can be arranged in advance.

Minato Sushi SUSHI ¥¥

(港鮨; ☎04992-4-0002; 1 Habuminato; meals around ¥1500; ⊙11.30am-2pm & 5-9pm Wed-Mon) This sushi restaurant on the south coast is considered the island's best by locals, and so it pays to book ahead. A must-try is *bekko sushi,* made with fish marinated in soy sauce and island chilli peppers.

Information

For maps and detailed information on accommodation options and things to do, check out www.izu-oshima.or.jp.

Ō-shima Tourist Association (大島観光協会; ☎04992-2-2177; www.izu-oshima.or.jp; ⊙8.30am-5pm) Located near the pier in Motomachi. There are no English speakers but there is a free translation phone system, Gaikokugo 110, by which they can call English-speaking volunteers from 8am to 8pm. Otherwise, they can usually call English-speaking staff at the town office.

Nii-jima

☎04992

Nii-jima (新島) attracts surfers from all over Kantō who converge on **Habushi-ura** (羽伏浦), a blazing 6.5km stretch of white sand that runs over half Nii-jima's length. Aside from seductive beaches and surf spots, Nii-jima's other main attraction is **Yunohama Onsen** (湯の浜温泉; ⊙24hr) FREE, a whimsical *rotemburo* overlooked by faux Greek ruins which has several tubs built into the rocks. It's mixed bathing so you'll need a swimsuit. Popular after dark for steamy stargazing. It's a 1km walk south from the ferry pier.

The **Nii-jima Tourist Association** (新島観光協会; ☎04992-5-0001; Kuroishi; ⏰7.30am-5pm, 8.30am-5pm in winter) has a super-helpful tourist information counter inside the ferry terminal at Kurone port. Renting a bike from one of the shops near the port is a great way of getting around this small island.

If ocean conditions aren't ideal, ferries will dock at Wakago port at the northern end of the island; from there, free buses shuttle passengers to the regular port of Kurone.

Sleeping & Eating

Habushi-ura Camp-jo CAMPGROUND
(羽伏浦キャンプ場; ☎04992-5-1068) FREE With a stunning mountain backdrop and spacious, grassy sites, this campground is a winner, and it's only about 10 minutes' walk to the beach. There are showers and plenty of barbecue pits to go around. Check in at the campground clubhouse. It's 1km north of the airstrip.

B&B Seven INN ¥¥
(B&B セブン; ☎090-3304-5931, 04992-5-1106; per person ¥6000; ❄📶) While the second 'B' is no more (it doesn't offer any food), this simple inn is comfortable and friendly, with wood floors and a homely feel. The friendly owner here, Ōmura-san, is an English teacher. It's walkable from the port; call for directions.

Sakae Sushi SUSHI ¥¥
(栄寿司; ☎04992-5-0134; 5-2-9 Honson; meals ¥1850; ⏰11.30am-2pm & 6-10pm) This popular restaurant is a lovely spot to try *shimazushi*, the local speciality sushi using fish marinated in island soy sauce and green chilli peppers. Expect to queue at popular times.

Shikine-jima

☎04992

About 6km south of Nii-jima, tiny Shikine-jima (式根島) is not the island to visit if you're looking for some postcard-worthy, white-sand beaches, but its compact, rocky geography and several free, mixed-gender onsen makes it the perfect place to unplug, camp out and explore via bicycle.

The island's best baths are at **Jinata Onsen** (地鉈温泉; ⏰24hr) FREE, at the end of a narrow cleft in the rocky coastline. The waters, stained a rich orange from iron sulphide, are naturally 80°C; mixed with the cool ocean, they're just right. It's a 2km walk south from the ferry pier, or ask at the tourist office for transport options. The tide affects the temperature, so bathing times change daily; check before making the steep descent.

Camping is free at Shikine-jima's well-maintained campgrounds, but visitors are required to register with the town office; stop by the **Tourist Association** (式根島観光協会; ☎04992-7-0170; 923 Shikinejima; ⏰8am-5pm) counter at the pier to do so. A few steps from a quiet beach and two free onsen, **Kamanoshita Camp-jo** (釜の下キャンプ場; ☎04992-2-0004; ⏰Mar-Jun & Sep-Nov) FREE is a great little camping ground; in the low season you might have it to yourself. No showers. Ask at the tourist office for directions and transport options. Campers should bring most of their provisions from Tokyo.

Hachijō-jima

☎04996

About 290km south of Tokyo, Hachijō-jima (八丈島) has a culture all its own. With two dormant volcanos, 854m **Hachijō-Fuji** (八丈富士) and 700m **Mihara-yama** (三原山), and plenty of palms it attracts visitors for its hiking, diving and onsen. Hachijō-Fuji is the Izu Islands' highest mountain and affords fantastic views from the rim of the crater; in June, the island's forests light up at night with bioluminescent mushrooms.

At the southern end of the island, **Urami-ga-taki Onsen** (裏見ケ滝温泉; ⏰10am-9pm) FREE overlooks a waterfall and is not to be missed – it's pure magic in the early evening. Soap and shampoo are prohibited here, and it's a mixed-sex onsen, so bring your swimsuit. It's a 30-minute drive from Sokodo port, just below the road.

Sokodo Camp-jō (底土キャンプ場; ☎04996-2-1121; 4188 Mitsune) FREE is an excellent camping ground 500m north of Sokodo pier and near a beach, with toilets, cold showers and cooking facilities. If you're self-catering, it's wise to bring any special food items from Tokyo, as you won't find much variety on the island.

Hachijōjima Tourism Association (八丈島観光協会; ☎04996-2-1377; ⏰8.15am-5.15pm) is next to the town hall on the main road, in the centre of the island.

CHICHIBU & OKU-TAMA

Nature conquers concrete at the western edge of Tokyo, where there's great hiking in the mountains of Chichibu, which includes Takao-san, less than an hour from Tokyo, and Oku-Tama, once a popular destination for pilgrims (and today, Tokyoites).

Takao-san

Gentle Takao-san (高尾山; 599m) is a highly popular day trip from Tokyo with year-round hiking. It's rather built up compared with other regional hikes, but with several points of interest along the main hiking trail it can make for a perfect family outing if you avoid busy weekends and holidays.

The most popular route up Takao-san is **Trail No 1**, which is paved all the way and passes by all the major points of interest. If you're after more of a walk-in-the-woods experience, we recommend hiking up the lovely Trail No 6, and descending via Trail No 1. If following this route, wear sturdy shoes as there are some stream crossings and places where the trail is narrow or slippery. You can also take a funicular railway up the mountain from Takaosanguchi Station, and hike back down.

Sights

Yakuō-in BUDDHIST TEMPLE

(薬王院; ☎042-661-1115; www.takaosan.or.jp; 2177 Takao-machi; ⌚24hr) FREE One of the chief attractions on Takao-san is this temple near Takaosanguchi Station, best known for the **Hi-watari Matsuri** (Fire-crossing Ceremony), which takes place on the second Sunday in March. Priests walk across hot coals with bare feet in a ritual called *hiwatari*, amid the ceremonial blowing of conch shells. The public is also welcome to participate.

Takao 599 Museum MUSEUM

(☎042-665-6688; www.takao599museum.jp; 2435-3 Takao-machi, Hachioji-shi; ⌚8am-5pm Apr-Nov, to 4pm Dec-Mar; 👪) FREE With a wealth of natural history info on the Takao-san region, this beautifully designed museum is arranged with younger visitors in mind – display cases of insects and fungi have toddler step stools, and there's a kids play area and cafe.

Eating

The road leading to the base of the mountain is lined with soba and ice-cream shops.

Beer Mount BEER GARDEN

(ビアマウント; ☎042-665-9943; www.urban-inc.co.jp/tokyotakao/shop/beermt; admission men/women ¥3800/3600; ⌚1-9pm mid-Jun–mid-Oct) Fresh mountain air, serene temples and... all-you-can-drink beer. Day-trippers pack out the plastic chairs and tables at this scenic perch at the top of the funicular, gorging on buffet pasta, pizza, fried rice, ice cream and the aforementioned beer. The admission fee covers two hours, after which you can pay extra to extend. Discounts for children.

Information

Tourist Information Center (☎042-643-3115; Takaosanguchi Station; ⌚8am-5pm Apr-Nov, to 4pm Dec-Mar) There's usually an English speaker on hand at the helpful TIC just outside the station exit.

Getting There & Away

From Shinjuku Station, take the Keiō line (*jun-tokkyū*, ¥390, one hour) to Takaosanguchi. The tourist village, trail entrances, cable car and chairlift are a few minutes away to the right. JR Pass holders can travel to Takao Station on the JR Chūō line (48 minutes) and transfer to the Keiō line to Takaosanguchi (¥130, two minutes).

Oku-Tama

☎0428

Oku-Tama (奥多摩) is Tokyo's best spot for easy hiking getaways and for river activities along the Tama-gawa. From **Takimoto** (滝本) in the valley, you can either ride a cable car or hike up for an hour via a beautiful cedar-lined pilgrims' path to **Mitake-san** (御岳山; 939m), a charming old-world mountain hamlet that feels a world away from hyperkinetic Tokyo.

Sights & Activities

Near the Mitake Visitors Centre you'll find the pilgrims' lodge **Baba-ke Oshi-Jutaku**, an amazing thatched-roof building dating from 1866. From here, it's another 20-minute walk up the mountain and demon-riddled steps (look closely as you ascend) to Musashi Mitake-jinja.

Musashi Mitake-jinja SHINTŌ SHRINE

(武蔵御嶽神社; ☎0428-78-8500; www.musashimitakejinja.jp; 176 Mitake-san) FREE Musashi Mitake-jinja traces its history back over a thousand years and was a popular pilgrimage site during the feudal era. It's sits atop Mitake-san (御岳山; 929m), commanding stunning views of the surrounding mountains. The wolf imagery stems from folklore in which a lost pilgrim was led out of a blanket of fog on the mountain by a pair of wolves, who were then enshrined as gods of the mountain.

Ōtake-san HIKING

(大岳山) The five-hour round-trip hike from Musashi Mitake-jinja to the summit of Ōtake-san (1266m) is highly recommended. Although there's some climbing involved, it's a fairly easy hike and the views from the summit are excellent – Mt Fuji is visible on clear days.

Moegi-no-Yu ONSEN

(もえぎの湯; 0428-82-7770; www.okutamas.co.jp/moegi; 119-1 Hikawa, Okutama, Nishitama-gun; adult/child ¥780/410; 9.30am-8pm Tue-Sun Apr-Jun, Oct & Nov, to 9.30pm Jul-Sep, to 7pm Dec-Mar; JR Ome line to Okutama) This is a good onsen to relax in after a day hiking in the Oku-Tama region and includes *rotemburo* and footbaths. It's a 10-minute walk from the JR Oku-Tama station.

Sleeping & Eating

Most visitors come for a day trip, but spending a night or two on Mitake-san provides peace and luxurious quiet.

You'll find several small places to eat along the lane leading to Musashi Mitake-jinja.

Mitake Youth Hostel HOSTEL ¥

(御嶽ユースホステル; 0428-78-8774; www.jyh.or.jp; 57 Mitake-san, Ome-shi; dm member/non-member ¥2970/3570, incl 2 meals ¥4950/5550;) Bed down pilgrim-style on futon in tatami dorms (sleeping up to seven) at this hostel, a handsome old building that used to be a pilgrims' lodge. It's attached to and part of Reiun-sō ryokan. Find it midway between the top of the cable car and Musashi Mitake-jinja, about a minute beyond the visitors centre.

It's a good idea to choose the two-meal plan, or you can pay separately for meals (dinner is ¥1240).

Komadori Sansō MINSHUKU ¥¥

(駒鳥山荘; 0428-78-8472; www.komadori.com; 155 Mitake-san, Ome-shi; r per person with shared bathroom from ¥5940;) Below Musashi Mitake-jinja, towards the back end of the village, this former pilgrims' inn has been in the same family for 17 generations. Rooms and the verandah have mountain views, and the friendly English-speaking owners are a delight.

Meals (breakfast/dinner ¥1080/2700) are great, and you can also sometimes arrange to take a dawn hike to a stand under a waterfall, an ascetic practice known as *takigyō*.

Momiji-ya NOODLES ¥

(紅葉屋; 0428-78-8475; 151 Mitake-san, Ome-shi; mains ¥750-1200; 10am-3pm, closed irregularly) Near the gate of Musashi Mitake-jinja, this cosy shop has mountain views out the back windows. The house special is chilled soba (buckwheat noodles) with a dipping sauce of crushed walnuts.

Opening hours vary in the low season; call ahead.

Information

Mitake Visitors Centre (御岳ビジターセンター; 0428-78-9363; www.ces-net.jp/mitakevc/index.html; 38-5 Mitake-san; 9am-4.30pm, closed Mon) Pick up trail maps at this office 250m beyond the cable-car terminus, at the start of the village.

Getting There & Away

Take the JR Chūō line from Shinjuku Station, changing to the JR Ōme line at Tachikawa Station or Ōme Station depending on the service, and get off at Mitake (¥935, 90 minutes). Buses run from Mitake Station to Takimoto (¥290, 10 minutes) for the **cable car** (www.mitaketozan.co.jp; one way/return ¥600/1130; 7.30am-6.30pm) that runs up to the mountain area.

NIKKŌ & AROUND

North of Tokyo, the Kantō plain gives way to a mountainous, forested landscape providing a fine backdrop for the spectacular shrines of Nikkō and the beautiful nearby lake Chūzenji-ko. The whole area is within the 400-sq-km Nikkō National Park, sprawling over Fukushima, Tochigi, Gunma and Niigata Prefectures, offering some excellent hiking opportunities and remote onsen.

Nikkō

0288 / POP 84,197

A natural sanctuary that enshrines the glories of the Edo period (1603–1868), Nikkō (日光) is one of Japan's major attractions and a World Heritage Site. Pristine forests of towering cedars enclose a wealth of Shintō shrines and Buddhist temples that blend harmoniously with the topography of the setting, and reflect in their

Nikkō

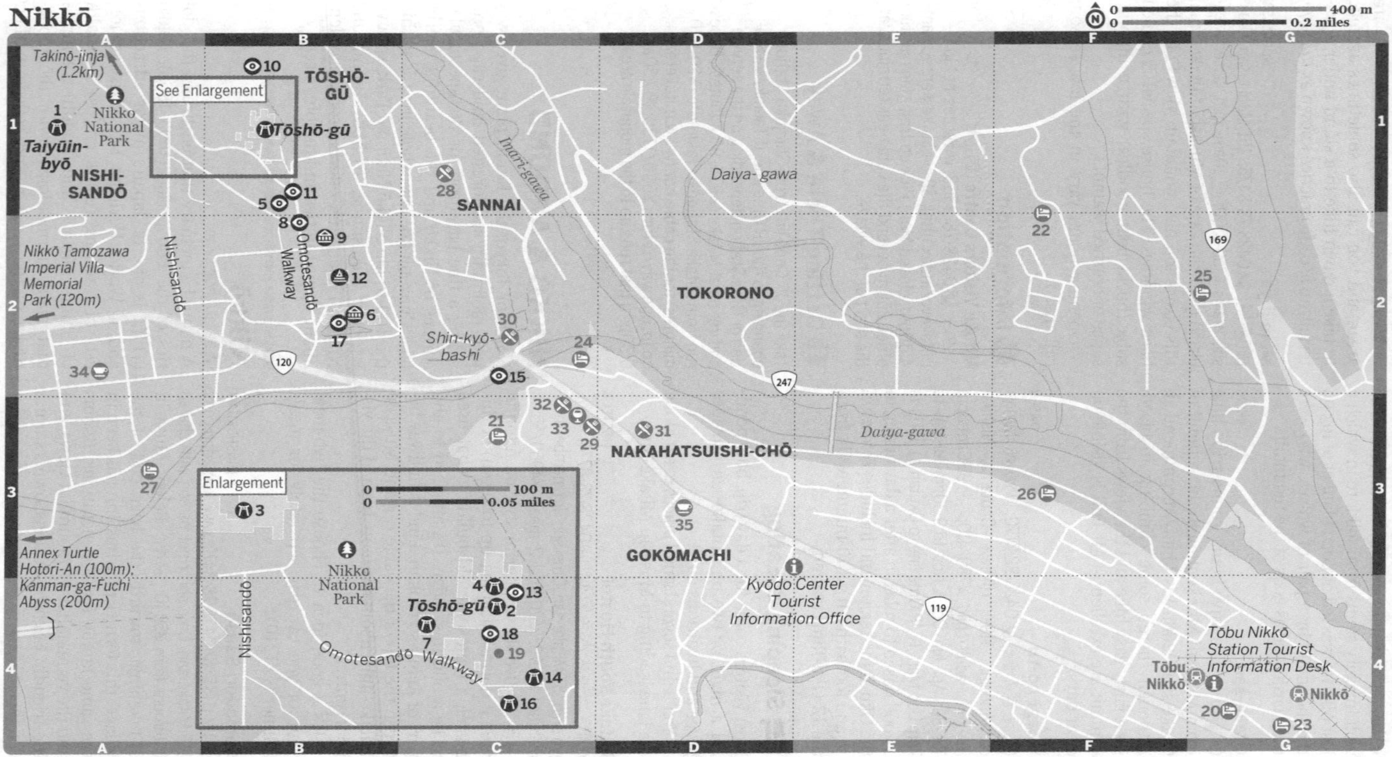

0 400 m
0 0.2 miles

A B C D E F G
1 2 3 4

Takinō-jinja (1.2km)
10
TŌSHŌ-GŪ
See Enlargement
Tōshō-gū
1
Taiyūin-byō
Nikko National Park
NISHI-SANDŌ
11
5
8
9
Omotesandō Walkway
Nishisandō
Nikkō Tamozawa Imperial Villa Memorial Park (120m)
12
6
17
28
SANNAI
Inari-gawa
Daiya- gawa
TOKORONO
22
169
25
30
Shin-kyō-bashi
24
15
120
34
247
32
33
29
21
31
NAKAHATSUISHI-CHŌ
Daiya-gawa
27
Enlargement
0 100 m
0 0.05 miles
3
Nikko National Park
4
13
Tōshō-gū
2
7
18
19
14
16
Nishisandō
Omotesandō Walkway
35
26
GOKŌMACHI
Kyōdo Center Tourist Information Office
119
Annex Turtle Hotori-An (100m); Kanman-ga-Fuchi Abyss (200m)
Tōbu Nikkō Station Tourist Information Desk
Tōbu Nikkō
Nikkō
20
23

Nikkō

Top Sights
1 Taiyūin-byō ... A1
2 Tōshō-gū ... C4

Sights
3 Futarasan-jinja ... B3
4 Gōhonsha ... C4
5 Gōjūnotō ... B1
6 Hōmotsu-den ... B2
7 Honji-dō ... C4
8 Ishi-dorii ... B2
9 Nikkō Tōshō-gū Museum ... B2
10 Okumiya ... B1
11 Omote-mon ... B1
12 Rinnō-ji ... B2
13 Sakashita-mon ... C4
14 Sanjinko ... C4
15 Shin-kyō ... C2
16 Shinkyūsha ... C4
17 Shōyō-en ... B2
18 Yōmei-mon ... C4

Activities, Courses & Tours
19 Tochigi Volunteer Interpreters & Guides Association ... C4

Sleeping
20 Nikkō Guesthouse Sumica ... G4
21 Nikkō Kanaya Hotel ... C3
22 Nikkō Park Lodge ... F2
23 Nikkō Station Classic Hotel ... G4
24 Nikkorisou Backpackers ... C2
25 Rindō-no-Ie ... G2
26 Stay Nikkō Guesthouse ... F3
27 Turtle Inn Nikkō ... A3

Eating
28 Gyōshintei ... C1
29 Hippari Dako ... C3
30 Hongū Cafe ... C2
31 Meguri ... D3
32 Nagomi-chaya ... C3

Drinking & Nightlife
33 Murmur Beer Stand ... C3
34 Nikkō Coffee ... A2
35 Yuzawaya ... D3

artistic splendour the awesome power of the Tokugawa shogunate.

All this, combined with the fact that Nikkō is only a couple of hours from Tokyo, means that in high season (summer and autumn) and at weekends, the magic of Nikkō can be somewhat lost amid the crowds. Spending the night here allows for an early start; a couple of nights and you can venture into the gorgeous mountain scenery, rivers, lakes and waterfalls of the surrounding area, much of it national park.

History

In the middle of the 8th century, the wandering Buddhist priest Shōdō Shōnin (735–817) established a hermitage at Nikkō. For centuries it attracted ascetics for whom the path to Buddha-hood lay in isolated meditations and deep mountain treks. Both the temple Rinnō-ji (p213) and the shrine Futarasan-jinja (p213) date to Shōdō Shōnin's time, as for much of history Shintō and Buddhism were considered complimentary practices. With time, however, Nikkō gradually faded into obscurity.

Until the early 17th-century: shortly before his death, Tokugawa Ieyasu (1543–1616), the shogun who unified Japan and kicked off the two-and-a-half centuries of relative peace known as the Edo period (1603–1868), left instructions for his final tomb to be erected in Nikkō. (His remains would first spend a year in his native Suruga, present-day Shizuoka). The spot had been chosen by Tenkai (1536–1645), a Buddhist priest of the highest rank, *fū-sui* (feng shui) master and trusted advisor to Ieyasu. The reason: Nikkō's location due north of Edo (Tokyo), a direction considered inauspicious. Ieyasu, deified upon death and renamed Tōshō Daigongen, would continue to protect the city he built, from his shrine, Tōshō-gū.

Sights

★Tōshō-gū SHINTŌ SHRINE

(東照宮; www.toshogu.jp/english/index.html; adult/child ¥1300/450; 8am-5pm Apr-Oct, to 4pm Nov-Mar) Tōshō-gū is Nikkō's biggest attraction, a shrine to the powerful shogun, Tokugawa Ieyasu (1543–1616). No expense was spared: when the original structure (completed in 1617) was deemed unsuitably grand, Ieyasu's grandson had it renovated two decades later, calling on the most celebrated artists of the day to work on the lavish structures, which are ornamented with gold leaf and black lacquer. It took 15,000 people to complete the project, at the modern equivalent of $100 million in manpower alone.

The compound was designed for maximum gravitas: visitors approach via a path lined with towering cedar trees, passing through a succession of ever more elaborate gates, decorated with carvings of mythical creatures like dragons, phoenixes and *baku* (a chimera who eats dreams). The shrine has been undergoing restoration work for over a decade, which was finally completed in 2019. As a result the structures are brilliant in colour, as they would have looked in the 17th century (when bold statement design was in vogue). The painstaking work was carried out using traditional materials (the white paint, for example, was made from powdered shells.

The first gate is **Ishi-dorii** (石鳥居), made of stone and dating to Tōshō-gū's original construction in 1619. To the left is 34.3m-tall **Gōjūnotō** (五重塔), an 1819 reconstruction of the the five-storey pagoda first built in the mid-17th-century. The next gate is **Omote-mon** (表門), guarded on either side by Deva kings.

In the outer courtyard are the **Sanjinko** (三神庫), the 'Three Sacred Storehouses', built in the *azekura-zukuri* style of architecture (horizontally-stacked logs, often triangle-shaped). On the upper storey of the **Kami-jinko** (upper storehouse) are relief carvings of elephants by the highly-esteemed artist, Kanō Tan'yū, as he imagined them to look (having never seen the real thing).

Look to your right to see the **Shinkyūsha** (神厩舎), the 'Sacred Stable' and the only building of unpainted wood in the whole complex. It is crowned with relief carvings of the allegorical 'hear no evil, see no evil, speak no evil' monkeys, which demonstrate principles of Buddhist morality. They're also Nikkō's unofficial symbol. Just past it is the *temizuya* (font), with a Chinese-style gabled roof.

In the far left corner of the courtyard is the **Honji-dō** (本地堂), which has a painting on its ceiling of the Nakiryū (Crying Dragon). Monks demonstrate the hall's acoustic properties by clapping two sticks together. The dragon 'roars' (a bit of a stretch) when the sticks are clapped beneath its mouth, but not elsewhere.

The next gate is Tōshō-gū's – and Japan's – most elaborately decorated one. **Yōmei-mon** (陽明門; Sunset Gate), a National Treasure, has over 500 carved images depicting folk tales, mythical beasts and Chinese sages, restored to its original brilliant white and gold. Worrying that its perfection might arouse envy in the gods, those responsible for the gate's construction had the final supporting pillar installed upside down as a deliberate error.

A second gate, **Kara-mon** (唐門), also a National Treasure, leads to the shrine's inner courtyard. It's less ornate than the Yōmei-mon but considered more elegant and refined, in white, black and gold with lacquer inlay. The walls on the sides of both gates also have fantastic carvings, including peony arabesques. There are also many stone lanterns around the complex, which were gifted by loyal *daimyō* (feudal lords).

Gōhonsha (御本社), the main shrine, is built in the H-shaped *gongen-zukuri* style, with its **Honden** (本殿; Main Hall) and **Haiden** (拝殿; Hall of Worship) connected by a stone corridor. Inside these halls are paintings of the 36 immortal poets of Kyoto, and a ceiling-painting pattern from the Momoyama period; note the 100 dragons, each different. *Fusuma* (sliding door) paintings depict a *kirin* (a mythical beast that's part giraffe and part dragon).

On the right, near the entrance to the inner courtyard, is another gate, **Sakashita-mon** (坂下門), from where 207 stone steps lead to **Okusha** (奥社), the inner shrine, where Ieyasu is entombed. It's decorated not with dragons or phoenixes but with a sleeping cat, **nemuri-neko** (眠猫). The diminutive carving is one of the most famous in Japan, attributed to the legendary (and possibly just a legend) artist Hidari Jingorō. Ieyasu is buried under a 5m-tall five-storey pagoda cast of gold, silver and bronze.

As Tōshō-gū is one of Japan's most famous attractions, it is routinely crowded, often with school groups and bus tours. Try to get here as early as possible.

★Taiyū-in BUDDHIST TEMPLE

(大猷院; adult/child ¥550/250; ⏲8am-5pm Apr-Oct, to 4pm Nov-Mar) Taiyū-in, completed in 1653, is the mausoleum of Tokugawa Iemitsu (1604–51), the third Tokugawa shogun and grandson of Ieyasu. (Ieyasu was deified, which earned him a shrine; Iemitsu was given an 'ordinary' temple burial). It has many of the same features as Tōshō-gū (p211): monumental gates, elaborate woodcarvings, lacquer and gold leaf, but is less grand (so as not to appear impudent). Many visitors find they prefer Taiyū-in for its comparatively restrained (though indeed still ornate) elegance, and also its fewer crowds.

Particularly impressive is its series of gates, **Niō-mon** (仁王門; 'Gate of the Virtuous Kings'), **Niten-mon** (二天門; 'Gate of the Heavenly Kings') and **Yasha-mon** (夜叉門; *yasha* are supernatural beings of

Hindu origin), all guarded by fearsome deities. As part of Nikkō extensive restoration work, the statues have been returned to their polychrome glory, and look straight from the pages of a comic book. The final gate, **Kara-mon** (唐門; 'Chinese-style gate'), is decorated with more demure carvings of dragons and cranes.

Taiyū-in's **Honden** (本殿; Main Hall) and **Haiden** (拝殿; Hall of Worship) are almost entirely encased in gold leaf (with a slightly red sheen) and glossy black lacquer. Inside the main hall, 140 dragons painted on the ceiling are said to carry prayers to the heavens; those holding pearls are on their way up, and those without are returning to gather more prayers.

Futarasan-jinja SHINTŌ SHRINE

(二荒山神社) Futarasan-jinja was founded over 1200 years ago as a place to worship the mountain Nantai-san (2484m), his mountain consort, Nyohō-san (2483m), and their mountainous progeny, Tarō-san (2368m). The current main hall dates to 1619, making it the oldest major structure in Nikkō. Though painted vermilion and with a sloping roof of lacquered copper, it is positively plain in comparison to its neighbours, and backed by cryptomeria trees. Admission (¥200) is required to enter a small garden of sacred trees and sub-shrines.

There is another Futarasan-jinja at the base of Nantai-san (on the shore of the lake, Chūzenji-ko) and also on the mountain's summit.

Nikkō Tamozawa Imperial Villa Memorial Park HISTORIC SITE

(日光田母沢御用邸記念公園; 0288-53-6767; www.park-tochigi.com/tamozawa; 8-27 Hon-chō; adult/child ¥510/250; 9am-4.30pm Wed-Mon) About 1km west of Shin-kyō bridge, this splendidly restored imperial palace (c 1899) of more than 100 rooms showcases superb artisanship, with parts of the complex dating from the Edo, Meiji and Taishō eras. Apart from the construction skills involved there are brilliantly detailed screen paintings and serene garden views framed from nearly every window.

Visit in autumn to see the gardens at their most spectacular.

Rinnō-ji BUDDHIST TEMPLE

(輪王寺; 0288-54-0531; www.rinnoji.or.jp; adult/child ¥400/200; 8am-5pm Apr-Oct, to 4pm Nov-Mar) Rinnō-ji's grand main hall, **Sanbutsu-dō** ('Hall of Three Buddhas'), was first built in 848; the current structure dates to 1645 and, with restoration work just completed in spring 2021, is now a brilliant shade of vermilion. Inside are a trio of gilded wooden statues, 8m-tall and seated on lotus pedestals. In the middle is Amida Nyorai (Buddha of Limitless Light); on the right is Senjū Kannon (thousand-armed bodhisattva of compassion); and on the left is Batō Kannon (horse-headed bodhisattva of compassion).

Each deity has its counterpart in Nikkō's one of the three sacred mountains: Nantai-san (Senjū Kannon), Nyohō-san (Amida Nyorai) and Tarō-san (Batō Kannon). Rinnō-ji is an important temple of Tendai sect (one of Japan's oldest sects, with a long history of patronage from the ruling class).

The sprawling grounds include Taiyūin-byō; purchase a combined ticket for ¥900. A separate admission ticket includes entrance to the temple's treasure hall, **Hōmotsuden** (宝物殿; ¥300; 8am-5pm, to 4pm Nov-Mar), and its strolling garden, **Shōyō-en** (逍遥園; ¥300; 8am-5pm Apr-Oct, to 4pm Nov-Mar).

Takinō-jinja SHINTŌ SHRINE

(滝尾神社) FREE Just to the left of the entrance to Futarasan-jinja is a 1km wooded path leading to Takinō-jinja, part of the greater shrine precinct. Just in front is the stone gate, **Undameshi-no-torii**. Before passing though, it's tradition to try your luck tossing three stones through the small hole near the top. More than the shrine itself, the attraction is the journey to get here; return following the path towards Tosho-gu, past small, humble pavilions, sacred natural features and stone effigies.

Detailed walking maps with explanations of the sights in English is available at the TIC (p216).

Kanman-ga-Fuchi Abyss NATURAL FEATURE

(憾満ガ淵) Along this particularly scenic stretch of the Daiya-gawa, where white rapids swirl around rocks, is a row of Jizō statues, the small stone effigies of the Buddhist protector of travellers and children. There were once 100, though many were damaged in a flood a century back, and remain in various states of crumble and mossiness. It's removed from the main sights, about 1km from the bridge, Shin-kyō (and is rarely crowded).

Nikkō Tōshō-gū Museum MUSEUM

(日光東照宮宝物館; 288-54-2558; www.toshogu.jp/shisetsu/houmotsu; adult/child ¥1000/400; 8am-5pm, to 4pm Nov-Mar) Opened in 2015 for the 400th anniversary of Tokugawa Ieyasu's death, this modern building behind Rinnō-ji contains artefacts relating to the shogun, including ceremonial armour, weapons and letters.

Shin-kyō HISTORIC SITE
(神橋; adult/child ¥300/100; ⏲8am-4.15pm) This much-photographed red footbridge over the Daiya-gawa is located at the sacred spot where Shōdō Shōnin is said to have been carried across the Daiya-gawa on the backs of two giant serpents. It's a 1907 reconstruction; the 17th-century original was washed away by floods.

The entrance fee allows you to walk upon it but not cross it.

Tours

Tochigi Volunteer Interpreters & Guides Association TOURS
(nikkotviga@hotmail.co.jp) FREE Offers free guided tours of Tōshō-gū between November and March (you pay the guide's entry fee and transport costs, as well as your own). Contact by email two weeks in advance.

Festivals & Events

Tōshō-gū Grand Festival CULTURAL
(⏲17 & 18 May) Nikkō's most important annual festival features horseback archery on the first day and a 1000-strong costumed re-enactment of the delivery of Ieyasu's remains to Nikkō on the second.

There's a slightly scaled-down version of this **festival** (⏲16 & 17 Oct) in October.

Sleeping

Nikkorisou Backpackers HOSTEL ¥
(にっこり荘バックパッカーズ; ☎080-9449-1545; www.nikkorisou.com; 1107 Kamihatsu-ishi-machi; dm/d with shared bathroom from ¥3000/7000; ❄📶) The closest hostel to Tōshō-gū offers a riverside location and a relaxed, friendly vibe. As it's run single-handedly by the English-speaking Hiro, guests need to be elsewhere between 10am and 4pm, but at any other hour the roomy kitchen, huge deck and cosy common area are havens for hanging out. Well-maintained hybrid mountain bikes are available for rent (¥500).

If checking in or moving on between 10am and 4pm, there are lockers by the front door to store your bags.

Nikkō Guesthouse Sumica GUESTHOUSE ¥
(日光ゲストハウス 巣み家; ☎090-1838-7873; www.nikko-guesthouse.com; 5-12 Aioi-chō; dm/r per person without bathroom from ¥3000/8000; 🚭📶) Run by a lovely, clued-up couple, this tiny guesthouse is set in an artfully renovated wooden house just steps from both train stations. The pair of dorms (male and female) are a bit cramped, but they're tidy, as are the two private tatami-mat doubles; all with fan only and shared bathrooms. There's an 11pm curfew.

Rindō-no-Ie MINSHUKU ¥
(りんどうの家; ☎53-0131; 1462 Tokorono; r per person without bathroom from ¥3500; 🚭❄@📶) Run by a lovely older couple, this small but well-maintained *minshuku* (guesthouse) offers spacious tatami rooms, generous meals and a pick-up service. Breakfast/dinner is ¥700. It's across the river, a 15-minute walk northwest of the train station.

Nikkō Park Lodge GUESTHOUSE ¥
(日光パークロッジ; ☎0288-53-1201; www.nikkoparklodge.com; 2828-5 Tokorono; dm/d from ¥2800/8980; 🚭❄@📶) In the wooded hills north of town, this guesthouse has sunny, Western-style rooms, a spacious dorm, a homely lounge with log fire and clued-up, English-speaking staff. There's an afternoon pick-up service, otherwise it's around ¥700 by taxi from the station.

Annex Turtle Hotori-An INN ¥¥
(アネックスーほとり庵; ☎0288-53-3663; www.turtle-nikko.com; 8-28 Takumi-chō; s/tw from ¥6700/13,100; P🚭❄📶) Only steps away from the trailhead to Kanman-ga-Fuchi Abyss, this tidy, comfortable inn offers Japanese- and Western-style rooms, plus river views from the house onsen. It's a lovely spot in a quiet neighbourhood that gives way to open space.

Stay Nikkō Guesthouse GUESTHOUSE ¥¥
(☎0288-25-5303; www.staynikko.com; 2-360-13 Inarimachi; r from ¥8200, house from ¥26,000; ❄📶) A Thai and Japanese couple run this comfortable guesthouse in a quiet spot close to the river, with just four rooms (tatami and Western-style) offering garden or river views and sharing bathroom facilities. Japanese-style breakfast costs ¥800, and there's a comfy communal lounge and garden seating. It's a 750m walk from the stations.

There's also a private house in the garden sleeping four to six people.

Turtle Inn Nikkō INN ¥¥
(タートル・イン・日光; ☎0288-53-3168; www.turtle-nikko.com; 2-16 Takumi-chō; s/tw without bathroom from ¥4950/9600, with bathroom from ¥6000/10,300; 🚭❄📶) A long-time

favourite with spacious rooms, both Japanese and Western style, the Turtle Inn is a cosy, well-run choice in a quiet neighbourhood close to the river. It's a 10-minute walk west from Shōyō-en, Nikkō's iconic red bridge, on the street closest to the river.

Nikkō Station Classic Hotel HOTEL ¥¥¥
(日光ステーションホテルクラシック; ☎0288-53-1000; www.nikko-stationhotel.jp; 31 Aioi-chō; s/tw incl breakfast from ¥11,500/20,000;) Opposite the JR station, this smart midrange hotel has comfortable Western-style rooms and beautiful onsen facilities that include outdoor baths. Day-use visitors can enjoy a soak for ¥700.

Nikkō Kanaya Hotel HOTEL ¥¥¥
(日光金谷ホテル; ☎0288-54-0001; www.kanayahotel.co.jp; 1300 Kamihatsu-ishimachi; tw from ¥17,820; P) This grand hotel from 1893 has hosted such notables as Albert Einstein, Helen Keller and King George V in its charming if slightly worn environs. The newer wing has Japanese-style rooms with excellent vistas, spacious quarters and private bathrooms; the cheaper rooms in the main building are Western style and have an appealing old-fashioned ambience.

The lobby bar is deliciously dark and particularly amenable to whisky drinkers. Rates rise steeply in high season.

Eating

A local speciality is *yuba* (the skin that forms when making tofu) cut into strips; it's a staple of *shōjin-ryōri* (Buddhist vegetarian cuisine). You'll see it all over town, in everything from noodles *(yuba soba)* to fried bean buns *(age yuba manjū)*.

Hongū Cafe CAFE
(本宮カフェ; ☎0288-54-1669; www.hongucafe.com; 2384 Sannai; drinks from ¥550; 10am-5pm, closed Thu) Stop by this cafe before or after visiting the shrines and temples for brewed-to-order coffee and matcha lattes. It's just inside the national park, in a historic house with indoor and outdoor seating. Desserts and light meals are available, too.

Hippari Dako YAKITORI ¥
(ひっぱり凧; ☎0288-53-2933; 1011 Kamihatsu-ishimachi; meals ¥550-900; 11am-8pm;) Refuel at this no-frills Nikkō staple that's been serving foreign travellers for almost three decades. Basic comfort food includes big bowls of curry udon, ramen, *yaki-udon* (fried noodles) and fried chicken.

OFF THE BEATEN TRACK

KANIYU ONSEN

In the midst of the mountainous Okukino region of 'secret onsen', you'll find **Kaniyu Onsen** (加仁湯; ☎0288-96-0311; www.naf.co.jp/kaniyu; 871 Kawamata; r per person with 2 meals from ¥12,360, onsen day visitor ¥800; day visitors 9am-3pm), a rustic ryokan with milky sulphuric waters in its multiple outdoor baths, a few of which are mixed bathing. To get here from Nikkō, take the Tōbu line to Shimo-imachi, change to a Kinugawa Onsen–bound train, then board the bus to Meoto-buchi (¥1540, 1½ hours, four daily). From here, it's a gentle 1½-hour hike up a beautiful river valley past several waterfalls.

You'll need to leave Nikkō before 9am to make it to Kaniyu and back in a day, and you'll still only get about one hour for the onsen. If you'd prefer to take it at a more leisurely pace, plan an overnight stay. Either way, check the latest transport details with one of Nikkō's tourist offices before setting off.

Meguri VEGAN ¥¥
(廻; ☎0288-25-3122; 909 Nakahatsu-ishimachi; meals ¥1420-1870; 11.30am-6pm, closed Thu;) Enjoy lovingly prepared vegan dishes in this former antique shop with a grand, faded ceiling fresco. Arrive as soon as it opens if you want to eat lunch – it's a popular place and once it's run out of food, it's sweets and drinks only. Look for the retro sign that says 'Oriental Fine Art & Curios'.

Nagomi-chaya JAPANESE ¥¥
(和み茶屋; ☎0288-54-3770; 1016 Kamihatsu-ishimachi; lunch set ¥1620-2700; 11.30am-4pm, closed Wed) This sophisticated arts-and-crafts-style cafe near the top of Nikkō's main boulevard serves beautifully plated meal sets with lots of small dishes to try. There are just two menu options: *kaiseki* lunch (懐石ランチ) and *yuba-kaiseki* (ゆば懐石), the latter featuring local specialty *yuba* prepared many different ways. Last order is 2.30pm.

★ **Gyōshintei** KAISEKI ¥¥¥
(尭心亭; ☎0288-53-3751; www.meiji-yakata.com/en/gyoshin; 2339-1 Sannai; meals ¥4180-6050; 11am-7pm, closed Thu;) Treat yourself to an elegant course of *shōjin-ryōri*, Japanese Buddhist vegetarian cuisine. Meals are

made from locally-sourced vegetables and bean curd and include Nikkō delicacy *yuba* (the thin skin that forms on the top of soy milk). The tatami-floored dining room overlooks a manicured garden.

While Gyōshintei looks like it requires reservations, walk-ins are welcome. It is part of the Meji-no-Yakata compound of chic restaurants, very close to Tōshō-gū and Rinnō-ji.

Drinking & Nightlife

Murmur Beer Stand CRAFT BEER
(1013 Kamihatsu-ishimachi; noon-10pm, closed Wed & Thu;) A one-person operation with five beers on tap, brewed right here on Nikkō's main street.

Nikkō Coffee Goyōteidōri CAFE
(日光珈琲・御用邸通; www.nikko-coffee.com; 3-13 Honchō; coffee from ¥550; 10am-6pm, closed Mon & 1st & 3rd Tue of every month;) This century-old rice shop was restyled into a retro-chic cafe serving house-roasted coffee, along with sweets and meals (like Japanese curry). It's famous for its shaved ice made from naturally harvested ice, served only in summer. There's often a queue.

Yuzawaya TEAHOUSE
(湯沢屋; www.yuzawaya.jp; 946 Kamihatsu-ishimachi; tea sets from ¥540; 11am-4pm, closed irregularly) In business since 1804, this teahouse specialises in *manjū* (bean-jam buns) and other traditional sweets; look for the green-and-white banners.

Information

Information desk (0288-54-0864; Tōbu Nikkō Station; 8.30am-5pm) Pick up a town map and get help in English to find buses, restaurants and hotels.

TŌBU NIKKŌ BUS FREE PASS

If you've already got your rail ticket, two-day bus-only passes allow unlimited rides between Nikkō and Chūzen-ji Onsen (adult/child ¥2000/1000) or Yumoto Onsen (adult/child ¥3000/1500), including the World Heritage Site area. The **Sekai-isan-meguri** (World Heritage Bus Pass; adult/child ¥500/250) covers the area between the stations and the shrine precincts. Buy these at Tōbu Nikkō Station.

Kyōdo Center Tourist Information Office (0288-54-2496; http://nikko-travel.jp; 591 Gokomachi; 9am-5pm;) Nikkō's main, flashy tourist information office, with English speakers (guaranteed between 10am and 2pm) and maps for sightseeing and hiking.

Getting There & Away

Nikkō is best reached from Tokyo via the Tōbu Nikkō line from Asakusa Station. You can usually get last-minute seats on the hourly reserved *tokkyū* (limited-express) trains (¥2800, 1¾ hours). *Kaisoku* (rapid) trains (¥1360, 2½ hours, hourly from 6.20am to 5.30pm) require no reservation, but you may have to change at Shimo-imaichi. Be sure to ride in the last two cars to reach Nikkō (some cars may separate at an intermediate stop).

JR Pass holders can take the Tohoku *shinkansen* (bullet train) from Tokyo to Utsunomiya (¥4930, 50 minutes) and change there for an ordinary train to Nikkō (¥760, 45 minutes).

Getting Around

Both JR Nikkō Station (designed by Frank Lloyd Wright) and the nearby Tōbu Nikkō Station lie southeast of the shrine area within a block of Nikkō's main road (Rte 119, the old Nikkō-kaidō). From the station, follow this road uphill for 20 minutes to reach the shrine area, past restaurants, souvenir shops and the main tourist information centre, or take a bus to the Shin-kyō bus stop (¥200). Bus stops are announced in English. Buses leave from both JR and Tōbu Nikkō Station; buses bound for both Chūzen-ji Onsen and Yumoto Onsen stop at Shin-kyō and other stops around the World Heritage Sites.

Chūzen-ji Onsen

0288

Accessed by a steep mountain road from Nikkō, Chūzen-ji Onsen offers natural seclusion, scenic waterfalls and striking views of Nantai-san from Chūzen-ji's lake, Chūzen-ji-ko. The lake itself is 161m deep and a fabulous shade of blue in good weather, topped by the usual flotilla of sightseeing boats. October and November, with autumn colours ablaze, are when Chūzen-ji is considered prettiest; it's also lovely under a blanket of snow.

Sights & Activities

Kegon-no-taki WATERFALL
(華厳ノ滝, Kegon Falls; 2479-2 Chūgūshi; adult/child ¥550/330; 7.30am-6pm May-Sep, 8am-5pm Oct-Apr) The big-ticket attraction of Chūzen-ji is this billowing, 97m-high

waterfall. Take the 1930s elevator down to a platform to observe the full force of the plunging water, or admire it from up high on the viewing platform.

Futarasan-jinja SHRINE
(二荒山神社; 2484 Chūgūshi; ⌚8am-4.30pm) FREE This shrine complements those at Tōshō-gū (p211) in Nikkō as part of the same Unesco World Heritage site, and is the starting point for pilgrimages up Nantai-san. The shrine is about 1km south along the lakeshore from the Chūzen-ji bus terminal.

Italian Embassy Villa Memorial Park PARK
(イタリアン大使館別荘記念公園; ☎0288-55-0388; 2482 Chūgūshi; ⌚9am-4pm Apr-Jun & Sep-Nov, to 5pm Jul-Aug) FREE The former summer residence of Italy's ambassadors (from 1928 to 1997) has a pleasant sun terrace with excellent views across Chūzen-ji lake. Walking here from the bus station takes around 25 minutes.

Nearby is the similar **British Embassy Memorial Park**, originally the lakeside residence of a British diplomat. Here you can have tea and scones.

Chūzen-ji Tachiki-kannon BUDDHIST TEMPLE
(中禅寺立木観音; 2578 Chūgūshi; adult/child ¥500/200; ⌚8am-3.30pm Dec-Feb, to 4pm Mar & Nov, to 5pm Apr-Oct) This eponymous temple, located on the lake's eastern shore, was founded in the 8th century and houses a 6m-tall Kannon statue from that time.

Lake Chuzenji Boat House CRUISE
(www.chuzenjiko-cruise.com; 1hr lake cruise ¥1250; ⌚9am-5pm Apr-Nov) Built in 1947, this rambling lakeside boat house contains a collection of antique dinghies and has a tearoom with a sun deck providing fine lake views. From here you can embark on various lake cruises. The Tobu Sightseeing Bus stops here en route to Yumoto Onsen.

Sleeping & Eating

There are a couple of restaurants scattered around Chūzen-ji lake, but most are clustered at the eastern corner.

KAI Nikko RYOKAN ¥¥¥
(界日光; ☎050-3786-0099; www.kai-nikko.jp; 1661 Chūgūshi; r per person incl 2 meals ¥30,000; P❄📶) Hoshino Resorts have given this 33-room mega-ryokan some contemporary sparkle, with spacious tatami rooms furnished with Western-style beds and lovely lake views, enormous onsen and delicious meals. Guests can also take part in *kumiko* woodcraft workshops and enjoy a nightly Nikko Geta folk-dance show. English spoken.

Getting There & Away

Buses run from Tōbu Nikkō Station to Chūzen-ji Onsen (¥1150, 45 minutes), before carrying on to Yumoto Onsen (¥860, 30 minutes). Consider purchasing the economical Tōbu Nikkō Bus Free Pass, available at Tōbu Nikkō Station.

Yumoto Onsen

☎0288 / POP 298

Yumoto Onsen (湯元温泉) is a sleepy hot-springs village on the shore of Lake Yuno-ko, high up in the mountains above Nikkō. It's quieter than nearby Chūzen-ji Onsen and offers easy access to several hiking trails.

Activities

★**Senjōgahara Shizen-kenkyu-rō** HIKING
(戦場ヶ原自然研究路, Senjōgahara Plain Nature Trail) Buses from Nikkō stop at **Ryūzu-no-taki** (竜頭ノ滝), a lovely waterfall overlooked by a teahouse that marks the trailhead. The hike follows the Yu-gawa across the picturesque marshland of **Senjōgahara** (mainly on wooden plank paths), passing the 75m-high falls of **Yu-daki** (湯滝) to the lake **Yuno-ko** (湯の湖), then around the lake to Yumoto Onsen.

It's less strenuous to do the hike in reverse (carrying on further to Chūzen-Ji Onsen if you wish), as you'll be walking downhill.

Yumoto Anyo-no-yu ONSEN
(⌚9am-8pm Apr–Dec) FREE Just behind the Yumoto Onsen bus stop is this large communal footbath under a shelter, which is free to use; blissful if you've just tackled the Senjōgahara Shizen-kenkyu-rō hike on a damp day.

Onsen-ji ONSEN
(温泉寺; adult/child ¥500/300; ⌚9am-4pm) Towards the back of Yumoto Onsen, this temple has a humble bathhouse (with extremely hot water) and a tatami lounge for resting weary muscles. Look for a row of stone lanterns near the final village bus stop that leads to the temple.

Sleeping & Eating

If you stay in Yumoto Onsen, you're likely to take your meals at your accommodation, as there isn't much else around.

Yu-no-Mori RYOKAN ¥¥¥

(ゆの森; 0288-62-2800; www.okunikko-yunomori.com; r per person incl 2 meals from ¥25,000; @) The 12 elegant rooms (Western-style on the 1st floor, Japanese-style on the 2nd) at this luxurious ryokan are decorated in natural tones, and each has a private wooden bath on a decked verandah. Free bicycle hire available.

Yumoto Rest House JAPANESE ¥

(dishes around ¥1000; 9am-4pm) Perched on the lakeside, this busy restaurant is of the picture-menu and vending-machine variety – choose your meal, pay at the machine, and then give your ticket to the servers and wait. Stake out a table in the sunny dining room and contemplate renting a rowing boat after lunch (¥1000 for 40 minutes).

Getting There & Away

There are regular buses between Yumoto Onsen and Nikkō (¥1700, one hour 20 minutes), which also stop at Chūzen-ji Onsen (¥860, 30 minutes).

You can also get to Yumoto Onsen from Chūzen-ji Onsen by a rewarding three-hour hike on the Senjōgahara Shizen-kenkyu-rō (p217).

LAYOVER IN NARITA?

Got a few hours to spare at Narita International Airport? Give duty-free the heave-ho and instead hop on a train to the charming town of Narita, 10 minutes away by rail. Omote-sandō, a historic commercial street, starts from just outside Narita and Keisei Narita Stations, winding past souvenir and craft shops on its way to Narita-san Shinshōji, a grand temple complex in expansive gardens. Here you can walk up an appetite for one last seafood feast at the affordable and highly regarded Edoko Sushi, back up Omote-sandō. Then it's time to grab any last-minute gifts on your way back to Narita Station, perhaps stopping off for a final farewell drink at the appropriately named Jet Lag Club, crammed full of aviation memorabilia donated by the regulars – almost entirely pilots and aircrew. *Sayonara*, Tokyo!

NARITA

0476 / POP 131,190

The home of Japan's main international airport, Narita (成田) is a surprisingly pleasant place to visit, with an esteemed temple, terrific places to eat and plenty of accommodation – perfect if you have an early-morning flight or would prefer to ease yourself into Japan after your arrival.

Sights

Narita-san Shinshōji BUDDHIST TEMPLE

(成田山新勝寺; www.naritasan.or.jp; 1 Narita; 24hr) FREE The landscaped grounds of this venerable temple, founded in 940, are among the largest in Japan, and are laced with walking paths. The temple buildings are splendid, particularly the Niomon entrance gate and three-storied pagoda.

Omote-sandō STREET

(表参道) Local ordinances have preserved the traditional architectural look of Narita's main shopping drag as it winds its way towards the Narita-san Shinshōji. Along the sinuous path you'll find souvenir, craft and medicinal shops, boutiques and restaurants.

Festivals & Events

Narita Gion Matsuri CULTURAL

(Jul) Going strong for over 300 years, the town's major festival features a parade of *mikoshi* (portable shrines) and large floats, embarking from Narita-san Shinshōji and drawing crowds of around 450,000. It's held on the Friday to Sunday closest to 8 July.

Sleeping

Ninehours Narita Airport CAPSULE HOTEL ¥

(0476-33-5109; http://ninehours.co.jp; Narita International Airport Terminal 2; capsules excl/incl breakfast from ¥5900/6440;) You can hardly get closer to the airport than this brilliant white, futuristic-styled capsule hotel, which is in the basement car park of Terminal 2. It books out early.

Wakamatsu Honten RYOKAN ¥¥

(若松本店; 0476-24-1136; www.wakamatsuhonten.jp; 355 Honchō; r per person incl 2 meals from ¥15,120;) Right smack across from the Narita-san complex, this ryokan is a great choice for a last night preflight. Though aspects of its public spaces could use updating, the spacious tatami rooms (try to book a temple-view room), communal baths and traditional meals are lovely. Staff don't speak much English, but there's a fair amount of explanatory material provided to guests.

Eating & Drinking

Kawatoyo Honten JAPANESE ¥¥
(川豊本店; ☎0476-22-2711; www.unagi-kawatoyo.com; 386 Naka-machi; meals from ¥2800; ⌚10am-5pm Tue-Sun) Sample *unagi* (freshwater eel) here, grilled on hot coals and served in lacquered boxes over rice. Eel numbers have plunged in recent years, and the species is endangered, but if you are keen to sample this Narita speciality, pay first, take a ticket and wait to be shown to your table. Chefs expertly carve up live eels in front, a testament to the restaurant's freshness; the squeamish can admire the period interiors instead.

Edoko Sushi JAPANESE ¥¥
(江戸ッ子寿司; ☎0476-22-0530; 536-10 Hanazakichō; set meals from ¥1200; ⌚11.30am-2.30pm & 5-10pm) Near the train station end of Omote-sandō is this locally-regarded and reasonably priced sushi joint with an English-speaking chef.

Jet Lag Club BAR
(☎0476-22-0280; 508 Kamichō; ⌚4pm-2am) Run by a former flight attendant and usually packed with a mix of flight crew and locals, this bar is a lively spot to get your bearings – or lose them. Plane spotters will love the array of aviation memorabilia – including dozens of pilot caps above the bar – donated by drinkers over the years.

Information

Narita Tourist Information Center (☎0476-24-3198; 839 Hanazaki-chō; ⌚8.30am-5.15pm) Pick up a map at the TIC just outside the eastern exit of JR Narita Station.

Getting There & Away

From Narita International Airport you can take the private Keisei line (¥260, 10 minutes) or JR (¥200/240 from Terminal 2/1, 10 minutes); Keisei-line trains are more frequent. From Tokyo, the easiest way to get to Narita is via the Keisei line from Keisei Ueno Station (¥840, 71 minutes). Note that most JR Narita Express trains do not stop at Narita.

OGASAWARA ARCHIPELAGO

About 1000km south of Ginza, but still within Tokyo Prefecture, the Unesco World Heritage-listed Ogasawara Archipelago (小笠原諸島; Ogasawara-shotō) is a nature-lover's paradise, with pristine beaches surrounded by tropical waters and coral reefs. Snorkelling, whale-watching, swimming with dolphins and hiking are all on the bill.

Just as fascinating as its natural attractions is the human history. Mapped by the Japanese in the 16th century, the islands' earliest inhabitants were a motley crew of Europeans and Pacific Islanders who set up provisioning stations for ships working the Japan whaling grounds in 1830. Around 100 descendants of these settlers, known as *obeikei,* still live on the islands, accounting for the occasional Western name and face. US Commodore Matthew Perry stopped here en route to Japan proper in 1853, when the archipelago was known as the Bonin Islands – it gained the name Ogasawara in 1875 when the Meiji government claimed the territory.

The only way to get here is by a 24-hour ferry ride (p221) from Tokyo. The ferry docks at Chichi-jima, the main island of the 30-strong group. A smaller ferry connects Chichi-jima to Haha-jima, the only other inhabited island.

Though it takes planning and a time commitment to get here, both Chichi-jima (Father Island) and Haha-jima (Mother Island) see a regular stream of visitors, so be sure to book accommodation in advance.

Note that camping is not permitted on either island.

Chichi-jima

☎04998 / POP 2061

Gorgeous, unspoilt Chichi-jima (父島) has plenty of accommodation, restaurants, and even a bit of tame nightlife. But the real attractions are the excellent beaches, outdoor activities and access to the Ogasawara's amazing natural heritage.

Activities

The two best beaches for snorkelling are on the north side of the island, a short walk over the hill from the village. **Miya-no-hama** (宮之浜) has decent coral and is sheltered, making it suitable for beginners. About 500m along the coast (more easily accessed from town) is **Tsuri-hama** (釣浜), a rocky beach that has better coral but is more exposed.

Good swimming beaches line the west side of the island, getting better the further south you go. The neighbouring coves of **Kopepe** (コペペ海岸) and **Kominato-kaigan** (小港海岸) are particularly attractive. From Kominato-kaigan, you can walk along a trail over the hill and along the coast to the beguiling white sand of **John Beach** (ジョンビーチ), but note that it's a two-hour walk in each direction and there is no drinking water – bring at least 3L per person.

Tours

Pelan Sea Kayak Club KAYAKING
(☎04998-2-3386; www.pelan.jp; full-day tours ¥9000, snorkelling gear rental ¥500) Run by Ryō-san from Pelan Village, this club offers tours to some of the island's more enchanting spots. Fees include rental of kayaking gear and meals cooked Pelan-style, on a wood-burning camp stove. Catching and grilling your own fish is optional.

Rao Adventure Tours TOUR
(☎04998-2-2081; jungle tours per half day ¥5000, surf school per day ¥15,000) Rao Adventure Tours at Ōgiura Beach is a surf shop that organises jungle tours and a surf school.

Sleeping

There are a few options for dining on the island, although it's wise to book meals at your accommodation where possible, or to self-cater.

★**Pelan Village** CABIN ¥
(☎04998-2-3386; www.pelan.jp; r per person with shared bathroom from ¥5000;) A Never-Never Land of rustic wooden cabins, walkways and ladders perched on a leafy mountainside, Pelan Village offers an eco-retreat designed for self-caterers. Free pick-up and drop-off to the ferry are provided. Also offers massage, yoga and sea kayak tours.

It's the closest you'll get to camping on the island, which is banned to protect the precious ecology. Pelon Village is committed to sustainable living, and conventional soaps and detergents are banned because water run-off goes directly to the crops.

Ogasawara Youth Hostel HOSTEL ¥
(小笠原ユースホステル; ☎04998-2-2692; www.oyh.jp; dm from ¥3800; @) Clean, well-run hostel with small bunk-bed dorms, about 400m southwest of the pier; book early during summer.

Tetsuya Healing Guest House GUESTHOUSE ¥¥
(てつ家; ☎04998-2-7725; www.tetuyabonin.com; r per person incl breakfast from ¥9,500; @) Offers thoughtfully designed rooms, open-air baths and multicourse meals that make innovative use of local ingredients. It's a five-minute walk from Kominato-kaigan Beach.

Rockwells GUESTHOUSE ¥¥
(ロックウェルズ; ☎04998-2-3838; www.rockwells.co.jp/ogasawara; s/d with shared bathroom incl half-board from ¥8200/14,400;) A young and friendly English-speaking family run this simple guesthouse and bar right on Ōgiura Beach. The meals are delicious.

Eating & Drinking

Cafe Hale JAPANESE ¥
(☎04998-2-2373; www.papasds.com; meals ¥1000; 9am-6pm Fri-Tue;) Hale's deck, facing Chichi-jima's port, is a top spot to enjoy a delicious lunch of sashimi on a bowl of rice, or a slice of lemon cheesecake. They also run a **diving school** from the same building, and an upmarket guesthouse (single/double with breakfast ¥14,580/28,080) with three smartly furnished en-suite rooms.

Bonina INTERNATIONAL ¥¥
(ニーナ; ☎04998-2-3027; mains from ¥1000; 11.30am-1.30pm & 6pm-midnight) Friendly restaurant and bar serving simple fare of rice dishes, pizza and tacos. Open for lunch on days when the Tokyo ferry is in town. It's in front of Futami Bay, steps from the port.

USK Coffee CAFE
(☎04998-2-2338; www.uskcoffee.com; Kita-fukurozawa; 1-5pm Thu & Fri, from 10am Sat & Sun) Out of an Airstream caravan on the road to Kominato-kaigan, English-speaking Ku and Yusuke serve thirst-quenching caffeinated drinks, made from beans grown on their adjacent plot, along with homemade cookies and cakes. A top spot to relax and refresh.

Yankee Town BAR
(ヤンキータウン; ☎080-2567-7168, 04998-2-3042; 8pm-midnight Thu-Tue) Follow the coastal road east of the main pier towards Okumura for around 10 minutes to find this convivial driftwood bar run by island-born, English-speaking Rance Ohira. It's a great place to chill with a beer or cocktail. There's occasional live music, too, making it the town's liveliest bar.

Information

Find the **Chichi-jima Tourism Association** (父島観光協会; ☎04998-2-2587; ⏰8am-noon & 1.30-5pm) in the B-Ship building about 250m west of the pier, near the post office (English spoken). Ask for the helpful *Guide Map of Chichi-jima*. Right on the beach past the village office, the **Ogasawara Visitor Center** (小笠原ビジターセンター; ☎04998-2-3001; www.ogasawaramura.com/visitorcenter; Ogasawara Village; ⏰8.30am-5pm) has displays in English about the local ecosystem and history.

Getting There & Around

Ogasawara Kaiun (小笠原海運; ☎03-3451-5171; www.ogasawarakaiun.co.jp/english) runs the *Ogasawara-maru*, which sails at least once a week between Tokyo's Takeshiba Pier (10 minutes' walk from Hamamatsu-chō Station) and Chichi-jima (2nd class from ¥26,990 one way, 24 hours); check the website for the exact departure schedule and current prices.

Rental scooters (from around ¥2000 per day) are the best way to get around as buses are infrequent, plus you'll be able to explore more of the island this way. You can rent them from **Ogasawara Kanko** (小笠原観光; ☎04998-2-3311; www.ogasawarakanko.com; Ogasawara Village; ⏰8am-6pm) if you have an international driving licence with the motorcycle permit included; they also have battery-assisted bicycles that don't require a license.

Haha-jima

☎04998 / POP 465

Around 50km south of Chichi-jima is the much less developed Haha-jima (母島). Outside the summer season, you may find yourself staring out over cerulean waters or spotting rare birds all by your lonesome.

Activities

Before leaving the only village on the island, scoot over to the **green turtle sanctuary** on the south side of the harbour – around 135 turtles are hatched here a year and released back into the sea.

From the village, a four-hour hike loops through rare indigenous flora to **Mt Chibusa** (乳房山; 463m), the highest peak on the island.

There are good snorkelling spots at the far north of the island at **Kita Minato** (北港湊).

Minami-zaki HIKING

(南崎) A road runs south from the village to the start of the **Minami-zaki Yūhodō** (南崎遊歩道), a hiking course that continues to Minami-zaki (literally 'southern point'). The route is jungly and at times slippery. Minami-zaki itself has a rocky, coral-strewn beach with ripping views of smaller islands to the south. Though tempting, the waters beyond the cove can whisk swimmers away.

Along the way you'll find **Hōraine-kaigan** (蓬莢根海岸), a narrow beach with a decent offshore coral garden, and **Wai Beach** (ワイビーチ), with a drop-off that sometimes attracts eagle rays. Above Minami-zaki you'll find **Kofuji** (小富士), an 86m-high peak with fantastic views in all directions.

Tours

Club Noah DIVING

(クラブノア母島; ☎04998-3-2442; www.hahajimamarine.wixsite.com/drhahajima; dive from ¥12,000, PADI course ¥100,000, eco-tours from ¥5200; ⏰cafe 9am-5pm) Dive shop Club Noah offers fun dives and open-water PADI courses, and runs jungle-hiking and marine-life eco-tours. It's in a white building next to the turtle sanctuary; inside there's a cafe serving light meals. Call ahead for reservations and current pricing.

Sleeping & Eating

It's best to book meals at your accommodation, as dining options on the island are limited.

Anna Beach Haha-jima Youth Hostel HOSTEL ¥

(アンナビーチ母島ユースホステル; ☎04998-3-2468; dm members/nonmembers incl 2 meals ¥5780/6380;) A friendly family runs this tidy, cheery youth hostel in a bright-yellow Western-style house overlooking the fishing port.

Information

Haha-jima Tourist Association (母島観光協会; ☎04998-3-2300; www.hahajima.com/en; Okikou Pier; ⏰8am-noon & 1-5pm) Located in the passenger waiting room at the pier and only open on ferry days.

Getting There & Around

The *Hahajima-maru* sails five times a week between Chichi-jima and Haha-jima (¥4520, two hours). Other operators run day cruises from Chichi-jima to Haha-jima.

Scooters (from ¥3000 per day) are the best way to get around the island. They can be rented from most lodgings.

AT A GLANCE

POPULATION
Nagoya: 2.32 million

TALLEST MOUNTAIN
Hotaka-dake (3190m)

BEST LOCAL MARKET
Asa-ichi (p269)

BEST RYOKAN
Yarimikan (p254)

BEST NOODLES
Uzuraya Soba (p296)

WHEN TO GO

Jan–Mar Nagano's slopes serve perfect snow days for a fraction of the price of European and American resorts.

Sep–Nov The many mountain onsen of Kamikōchi and Hida offer front-row seats for autumn's brilliant show.

Apr–May Come for cherry blossoms in Kanazawa's Kenroku-en and the great Takayama Matsuri.

Takaragawa Onsen (p306), Minakami Onsen-kyo
EAR IEW BOO/SHUTTERSTOCK ©

The Japan Alps & Central Honshū

Central Honshū (本州中部; Honshū Chūbu) is Japan's heartland, stretching out between the sprawling metropolises of Greater Tokyo and Kansai. The awesome Japan Alps rise sharply near the border of Gifu and Nagano Prefectures before rolling north to the dramatic Sea of Japan coast. World-class skiing, hiking and onsen can be found in the region's stunning alpine uplands. All but one of Japan's 30 highest peaks (Mt Fuji) are here. Kanazawa oozes culture: temples and tearooms that served lords and housed geisha are beautifully preserved. Takayama's quaint riverside streetscapes win admirers from Japan and abroad. Matsumoto's magnificent castle and alpine backdrop ensure its popularity.

INCLUDES

The Japan Alps & Central Honshū Highlights

❶ **Nakasendō** (p241) Walking this ancient post road between Tsumago and Magome.

❷ **Ainokura** (p256) Sleeping in a thatch-roofed house in this World Heritage village.

❸ **Asa-ichi** (p269) Haggling with vendors at the morning market in Wajima.

❹ **Matsumoto-jō** (p278) Climbing to the top of the castle for mountain vistas.

❺ **Zenkō-ji** (p291) Seeking enlightenment at this Buddhist temple in Nagano.

❻ **Kamikōchi** (p284) Hiking in some of Japan's most breathtaking scenery.

❼ **Tateyama-Kurobe Alpine Route** (p275) Getting around on high-altitude trolleys, cable cars and funiculars.

❽ **Takaragawa Onsen** (p306) Soaking your troubles away in the mineral-rich water at this Minakami onsen.

❾ **Haruna Jinja** (p305) Strolling through the forested river gorge to this ancient religious site in Gunma.

❿ **Zuiryū-ji** (p274) Admiring the fusion of Buddhist architectural styles at this Takaoka National Treasure.

⓫ **Kita-ke** (p267) Seeing the life of a feudal lord at this immaculately preserved house on the Noto Peninsula.

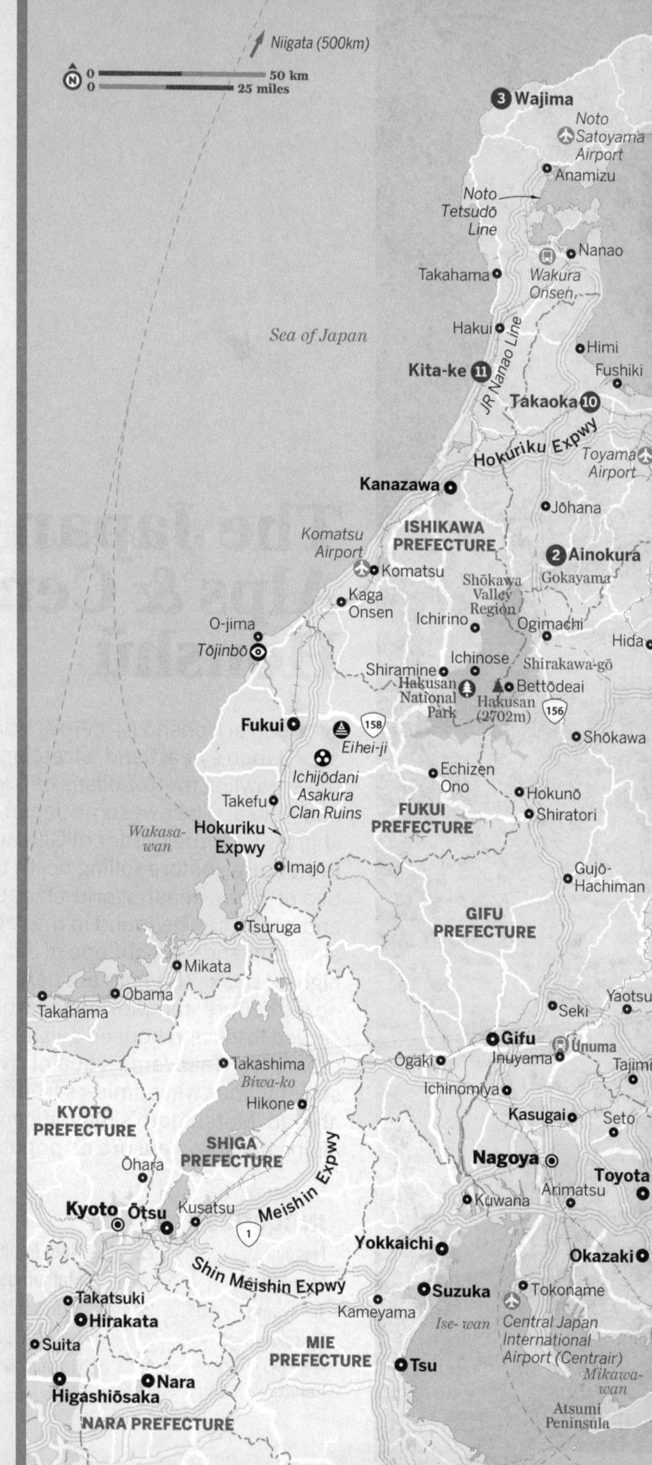

Noto Peninsula
Suzu
Sado-ga-shima (30km)
Nagaoka
Kashiwazaki
FUKUSHIMA PREFECTURE
NIIGATA PREFECTURE
Toyama-wan
Hokuriku Shinkansen Line
Jōetsu
Muikamachi
Toyama Chihō Tetsudō
Itoigawa
Nozawa Onsen
Iiyama
Uozu
Shinano
Naeba
8 Takaragawa Onsen
Shirouma-dake (2932m)
Toyama
Happō-One
Hakuba
Togakushi
Obuse
Shiga Kōgen
Tsukiyono
Numata
Tateyama
Nagano 5
Minakami
TOYAMA PREFECTURE
Kurobe Dam
Kusatsu Onsen
GUNMA PREFECTURE
Kan-Etsu Expwy
Tateyama–Kurobe Alpine Route 7
Shinano-ōmachi
Hokuriku Shinkansen
Shibukawa
Haruna Jinja 9
Joshin-etsu Expwy
Ueda
Maebashi
Kiryū
Chubu-Sangaku National Park
Bessho Onsen
Karuizawa
JR Ōito Line
Nakabusa Onsen
Usui Toge Railway Park
Takasaki
Isesaki
Ashikaga
Kamikōchi 6
Azumino
Shin-etsu Line
4 Matsumoto
Fukuji Onsen
Shinshū Matsumoto Airport
Shirahone Onsen
NAGANO PREFECTURE
Kumagaya
Takayama
Shiojiri
Koumi Line
Norikura-dake (3026m)
Suwa
Aidara
SAITAMA PREFECTURE
JR Takayama Line
JR Chūō-honsen Line
Chūō Expwy
Chichibu
Narai
Ontake-san (3067m)
Yabuhara
Azusayama
Chichibu-Tama National Park
Kawagoe
Kiso
Gero
Central Tokyo (22km)
Kōfu
YAMANASHI PREFECTURE
Hachioji
Nagiso
Tsumago
Matsukawa
Minami Alps National Park
Nakasendō 1
Magome
Nakatsugawa
Iida
Fuji-yoshida
KANAGAWA PREFECTURE
Yamato
Atsugi
Chigasaki
Mt Fuji (3776m)
Gotemba
Hiratsuka
Fujisawa
Odawara
Hakone
AICHI PREFECTURE
SHIZUOKA PREFECTURE
Fuji
Numazu
JR Iida Line
Tōmei Expwy
Shizuoka
Fujieda
Suruga-wan
Izu Peninsula
Dōgashima
Toyohashi
Hamamatsu
Sea of Enshū
148
19
41
299
151
153
52
1

Climate

Central Honshū's climate varies with its landscape. The best times to visit are generally April, May and late September to early November; temperatures are mild and clear skies prevail. Mid-April is the best time for *hanami* (cherry-blossom viewing) in the Alps. Expect heavy rains in the *tsuyu* (monsoon) season, typically a few weeks in June, then sticky summers capped with typhoons as late as October.

Road closures are commonplace in the Alps when the snow sets in from November to March, although higher peaks might remain snowcapped as late as June. Hiking season runs from July to September, until autumn ushers in a brilliant display of *kōyō* (turning leaves), peaking in mid-October.

Sleeping

Some of Japan's finest *onsen ryokan* (traditional hot-spring inns) are found in the hollows of this densely forested alpine region, or along the banks of its many rivers. In cities, modern, practical hotels offer midrange comforts. A newish development throughout the region is more guesthouses, which often offer the best value.

Getting There & Around

AIR

Central Japan International Airport (p234), outside Nagoya, is an excellent gateway to the region with a variety of global connections. Komatsu (p266) and Toyama (p274) airports to the north service domestic and a handful of intra-Asia routes, while Shinshū Matsumoto Airport (p282) has daily flights to Fukuoka, Osaka and Sapporo.

CAR & MOTORCYCLE

Renting a car is well suited for trips to the Noto Peninsula, the Japan Alps and for those wanting to get up high and off the beaten track. Be prepared for slow, steep and winding roads that can be treacherous at times and are not for the faint-hearted; plan your explorations carefully.

TRAIN

Rail access to this region is surprisingly good, given its often mountainous terrain.

Nagoya is a major rail hub on the Tōkaidō *shinkansen* (bullet train) line between Tokyo and Osaka.

Bullet trains also open up the nation's alpine interior with quick and easy access to the peaks from Tokyo. The Joetsu *shinkansen* connects runs to Niigata; the Hokuriku *shinkansen* to Kanazawa by way of Nagano and Toyama.

The JR Hokuriku line follows the Sea of Japan coast, linking Fukui, Kanazawa and Toyama, with connections to Kyoto and Osaka.

The north–south JR Takayama and Chūō lines have hubs in Takayama, Matsumoto and Nagano.

NAGOYA & AROUND

Understated and under-appreciated Nagoya is the jumping-off point for trips to the mountains and the sights of surrounding Aichi and Gifu Prefectures.

Inuyama and the nearby area has some excellent historical attractions, including a wonderful hilltop castle (p235), which is the oldest wooden castle in Japan, while Tokoname is a must for those interested in pottery and pre-industrial manufacturing. Almost a suburb of Nagoya, but a city in its own right, lovely Gifu is a good alternative base to Nagoya if you want to be close to the city, but not right in the heart of the action.

Nagoya

052 / POP 2.32 MILLION

Affable Nagoya (名古屋), birthplace of Toyota and *pachinko* (a pinball-style game), is a manufacturing powerhouse. Although Nagoya's GDP tops that of many small countries, this middle child has grown accustomed to life in the shadow of its older siblings, Tokyo and Osaka.

But its manufacturing roots don't mean that Nagoya is a city of factories: well-maintained parks and green spaces prevail in the inner wards. Nagoya has cosmopolitan aspects, including some fantastic museums, significant temples and excellent shopping, and Nagoyans are vivacious and unpretentious. It's an easy place to make friends.

Despite all this, the city still struggles to shake its reputation among Japanese (many of whom have never visited) as the nation's most boring metropolis.

In a prime spot between Tokyo and Kyoto/Osaka on the Tōkaidō *shinkansen* line, Nagoya is the gateway to Chūbu's big mountain heart and a great base for day trips.

History

As the ancestral home of Japan's 'three heroes' – Oda Nobunaga (unifier of Japan), Toyotomi Hideyoshi (second unifier of Japan) and Tokugawa Ieyasu (founder of Japan's last shogunate) – Nagoya's influence is long-standing, although it did not become a unified city until 1889.

In 1609 Tokugawa ordered the construction of Nagoya-jō, which became an important outpost for 16 generations of the Tokugawa family (also called the Owari clan), whose dictatorial yet prosperous reign in a time known as the Edo period held sway until 1868, when the restoration of Emperor Meiji saw the ultimate demise of feudal samurai culture in Japan.

Nagoya grew into a centre for commerce, industry and transport; during WWII some 10,000 Mitsubishi Zero fighter planes were produced here. Manufacturing prominence led to massive Allied bombing – almost 4000 citizens were killed, more than 450,000 were forced to leave their homes and roughly one quarter of the city was destroyed. From these ashes rose the Nagoya of today, with its subways, skyscrapers, parks and wide avenues.

Sights

Running east of Nagoya Station, Sakura-dōri, Nishiki-dōri and Hirokōji-dōri are the three main drags, intersected first by Fushimi-dōri, then by Otsu-dōri. The majority of the mainstream action is found within this grid. Just east of Otsu-dōri is the long, narrow Hisaya-ōdōri-kōen (aka Central Park), Nagoya's much-loved Eiffel-esque TV Tower (p229) and the wacky Oasis 21 (p230) complex. Following Otsu-dōri north will get you to Nagoya-jō (p229), while the vibrant Ōsu district, Atsuta-jingū shrine and the bustling Kanayama Station area are to the south.

Nagoya's subway system has English signs and services all the hot spots – Fushimi and Sakae stations are your mainstays for shopping, accommodation and nightlife. For the bohemian vibe around Ōsu Kannon (p229), alight at Kamimaezu.

★Tokugawa Art Museum GALLERY

(徳川美術館, Tokugawa Bijutsukan; ☎052-935-6262; www.tokugawa-art-museum.jp/english; 1017 Tokugawa-chō, Higashi-ku; adult/child ¥1400/500; ⏲10am-5pm Tue-Sun; 🚌Me-guru stop 11) A must for anyone interested in Japanese culture and history, this museum has a collection of over 10,000 pieces that includes National Treasures and Important Cultural Properties once belonging to the shogun family. A priceless 12th-century scroll depicting *The Tale of Genji* is usually locked away, except during a short stint in late November; the rest of the year, visitors must be content with a video.

★Atsuta-jingū SHINTŌ SHRINE

(熱田神宮; ☎052-671-4151; www.atsutajingu.or.jp; 1-1-1 Jingū, Atsuta-ku; Ⓢ Jingū-mae or Jingū-nishi, exit 2) Although the current buildings were completed in 1966, Atsuta-jingū has been a shrine for over 1900 years and is one of the most sacred Shintō shrines in Japan. Nestled among ancient cypresses, it houses the sacred *kusanagi-no-tsurugi* (grass-cutting sword), one of three regalia that, according to legend, were presented to the imperial family by the sun goddess Amaterasu. There's a changing collection of more than 4000 Tokugawa-era swords, masks and paintings on display in the **Treasure Hall** (宝物館; www.atsutajingu.or.jp/en/tre; adult/child ¥300/150; ⏲9am-4.30pm, closed last Wed & Thu of month).

Tokugawa-en GARDENS

(徳川園; ☎052-935-8988; www.tokugawaen.aichi.jp/english; 1001 Tokugawa-chō, Higashi-ku; ¥300; ⏲9.30am-5.30pm Tue-Sun; 🚌Me-guru, stop 10) This delightful Japanese garden adjacent to the Tokugawa Art Museum was donated by the Tokugawa family to Nagoya city in 1931 but destroyed by bombing in 1945. From that time until a three-year restoration project was completed in 2004, the site was used as a park. Water is its key element – there's a lake, a river, bridges and a waterfall. Each spring 2000 peonies and irises burst into bloom, and maples ignite in the autumn.

Nagoya City Science Museum MUSEUM

(名古屋市科学館, Nagoya-shi Kagaku-kan; ☎052-201-4486; www.ncsm.city.nagoya.jp; 2-17-1 Sakae, Naka-ku; adult/student ¥800/500; ⏲9.30am-4.30pm Tue-Sun; 👪; Ⓢ Fushimi, exit 5) This hands-on museum claims the world's largest dome-screen planetarium, with some seriously out-of-this-world projection technology. There's also a tornado lab and a deep-freeze lab complete with indoor aurora. Despite scheduled shows being kid-centric and in Japanese, the cutting-edge technology of this impressive, centrally located facility is worth experiencing.

Central Nagoya

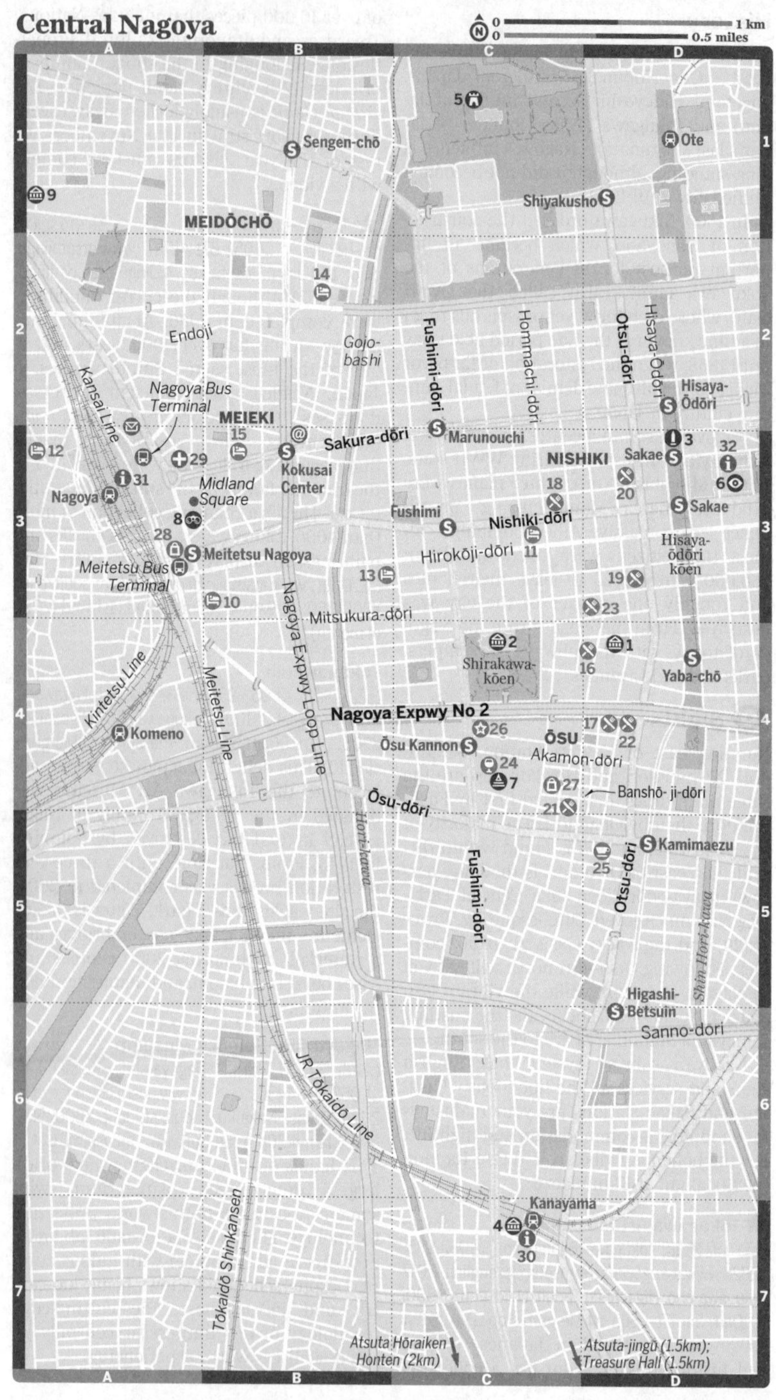

Central Nagoya

Nagoya-jō CASTLE

(名古屋城; ☎052-231-1700; www.nagoyajo.city.nagoya.jp; 1-1 Honmaru; adult/child ¥500/free; ⊙9am-4.30pm; Ⓢ Shiyakusho, exit 7) The original structure, built between 1610 and 1614 by Tokugawa Ieyasu for his ninth son, was levelled in WWII. Today's castle is a concrete replica (with elevator) completed in 1959. Renovations are ongoing. On the roof, look for the 3m-long gilded *shachi-hoko* (legendary creatures possessing a tiger's head and a carp's body). Inside, find treasures, an armour collection and the histories of the Oda, Toyotomi and Tokugawa families. Free English tours run every day at 1pm from the castle's east gate.

The beautiful year-round garden, **Ninomaru-en** (二の丸園) has a number of pretty teahouses.

International Design Centre Nagoya GALLERY

(国際デザインセンター, Kokusai Dezain Sentaa; ☎052-265-2105; www.idcn.jp; NADYA Park, 18-1, Sakae 3-Chome, Naka-ku; ⊙9am-5.30pm Mon-Fri; Ⓢ Yaba-chō, exit 5 or 6) FREE Housed in the swooping **Nadya Park** complex is this secular shrine to the deities of conceptualisation, form and function. Design touchstones from art deco to postmodernism, Electrolux to Isamu Noguchi, Arne Jacobsen to the Mini Cooper and everything in between is represented in these significant galleries.

Ōsu Kannon BUDDHIST TEMPLE

(大須観音; ☎052-231-6525; www.osu-kannon.jp; 2-21-47 Osu, Naka-ku; ⊙24hr; Ⓢ Ōsu Kannon, exit 2) The much-visited, workaday Ōsu Kannon temple traces its roots back to 1333. Devoted to the Buddha of Compassion, the temple was moved to its present location by Tokugawa Ieyasu in 1610, although the current buildings date from 1970. The library inside holds the oldest known handwritten copy of the *kojiki* – the ancient mythological history of Japan.

Coming from Kamimaezu Station, take exit 9 and walk north two blocks. Turn left onto Banshoji street (万松寺通), a covered shopping arcade that becomes Ōsu Kannon street and continues on to the temple. The streets either side are alive with activity.

Nagoya TV Tower TOWER

(名古屋テレビ塔; ☎052-971-8546; www.nagoya-tv-tower.co.jp; 3-6-15 Nishiki, Naka-ku; adult/child ¥700/300; ⊙10am-9pm; Ⓟ; Ⓢ Sakae, exit 4b or 5a) Nagoya's much-loved TV tower, completed in 1954, was the first of its kind in Japan. The tower's central location makes its 100m-high **Sky Balcony** a great place to get the lie of the land. Better still, the sprawling beer garden and Korean barbecue at its base is unrivalled in town. Check the website for special events and occasional night-time illuminations.

Nagoya/Boston Museum of Fine Arts MUSEUM

(名古屋ボストン美術館, Nagoya Boston Bijutsukan; ☎052-684-0101; www.nagoya-boston.or.jp; 1-1-1 Kanayama-chō, Naka-ku; adult/child ¥1300/free; ⊙10am-6.30pm Tue-Fri, to 4.30pm Sat & Sun; 🚇Kanayama, south exit) This collaborative effort between Japanese backers and the Museum of Fine Arts Boston showcases a small but impressive collection of Japanese and international masterpieces.

Sky Promenade VIEWPOINT

(スカイプロメナード; ☎052-527-8877; www.midland-square.com; 4-7-1 Meieki, Nakamura-ku; adult/child ¥750/500; ⊙11am-9.30pm; 🚇JR Nagoya) On levels 44 to 46 of **Midland Square** (ミッドランドスクエア⊙shops 11am-8pm, restaurants to 11pm), Sky Promenade features Japan's tallest open-air observation deck and a handful of high-altitude, high-priced eateries, from which you can overlook seemingly endless urban sprawl. Reach the promenade via strikingly lit passageways.

Oasis 21 LANDMARK

(オアシス21; ☎052-962-1011; www.sakaepark.co.jp; 1-11-1 Higashi-sakura, Higashi-ku; Ⓢ Sakae, exit 4a) Oasis 21 is a bus terminal and transit hub with a difference. Its iconic 'galaxy platform' – an elliptical glass-and-steel structure filled with water for visual effect and cooling purposes – caused quite a stir when it was built. Climb the stairs and walk around it while you're waiting for your next ride; it's most fun at night, when it's adventurously lit.

Around Nagoya

SCMAGLEV & Railway Park MUSEUM

(JR リニア・鉄道館, JR Rinia Tetsudō-kan; ☎050-3772-3910; http://museum.jr-central.co.jp; 3-2-2 Kinjo-futo, Minato-ku; adult/child ¥1000/200, *shinkansen*-driving simulator ¥500; ⊙10am-5.30pm Wed-Mon; Ⓟ; 🚇JR Aonami line to Kinjofuto) Trainspotters will be in heaven at this fantastic hands-on museum. Featuring actual maglev (the world's fastest train – 581km/h), *shinkansen* (bullet trains), historical rolling stock and rail simulators, the massive museum offers a fascinating insight into Japanese postwar history through the development of a railroad like no other. The 'hangar' is 20 minutes from Nagoya on the Aonami line, found on the Taiko-dōri side of JR Nagoya Station.

The *shinkansen*-driving-simulator tickets are assigned on a lottery basis. You must apply to the lottery on the day you wish to drive the simulator, and wait for the results.

Toyota Kaikan Museum MUSEUM

(トヨタ会館, Toyota Kaikan; ☎museum 0565-29-3345, tours 0565-29-3355; www.toyota.co.jp/en/about_toyota/facility/toyota_kaikan; 1 Toyota-chō; ⊙9.30am-5pm Mon-Sat, tours 11am; 🚇Aichi Kanjō line to Mikawa Toyota) FREE See up to 20 shiny examples of the latest automotive technology hot off the production line and witness firsthand how they're made here at Toyota's global HQ. Fascinating two-hour tours of Toyota Motor Corporation's main factory begin at the Exhibition Hall, with many exhibits fully revamped recently. You can visit the museum any time it's open, but free daily tours must be booked two weeks to three months ahead. Check the website for full details.

Allow two hours to get to Toyota city from central Nagoya; refer to the website for directions and reservations.

Toyota Commemorative Museum of Industry & Technology MUSEUM

(トヨタテクノミュージアム産業技術記念館, Toyota Techno-museum Zangyō Gijutsu Kinenkan; ☎052-551-6115; www.tcmit.org; 4-1-35 Noritake-shinmachi; adult/child ¥500/200; ⊙9.30am-4.30pm Tue-Sun; 🚇Meitetsu Nagoya line to Sako) The world's largest car manufacturer had humble beginnings in the weaving industry. This interesting museum occupies the site of Toyota's original weaving plant. Car enthusiasts will find things textile heavy before warming to the 7900-sq-metre automotive and robotics pavilion. Science-minded folk will enjoy the countless hands-on exhibits. Displays are bilingual and there's an English-language audio tour available.

Don't confuse this museum with the Toyota Exhibition Hall and factory tours.

Festivals & Events

There are plenty of lively festivals and events to enjoy in a city of this size. A good, up-to-date resource is www.nagoya-info.jp/en/event.

World Cosplay Summit CULTURAL

(www.worldcosplaysummit.jp; ⊙Jul/Aug) If you're in Nagoya in July or August, be sure to see if your stay coincides with some of the events of this truly unique visual feast, when *cosplayers* (costume players) and anime

(Japanese animation) fans from around the world come together to...well, play, in costume!

Nagoya Matsuri PARADE

(名古屋まつり; www.nagoya-festival.jp; ⊙mid-Oct) Nagoya's big bash takes place in Hisaya-ōdōri-kōen (Central Park). Celebrating Nagoya's 'three heroes', the lively procession includes costumes, *karakuri ningyō* (marionette) floats, folk dancing and decorated cars.

Grand Sumō Tournament Nagoya SPECTATOR SPORT

(日本相撲協会名古屋場所, Nihon Sumō Kyōkai Nagoya Basho; 052-971-2516; www.sumo.or.jp; Aichi-ken Taiiku-kan, 1-1 Ninomaru; tickets from ¥3000; ⊙Jul) One of six annual sumo championship tournaments, Nagoya Basho is held over two weeks in July at Aichi Prefectural Gymnasium. Arrive early in the afternoon to watch the lower-ranked wrestlers up close.

Sleeping

If you're passing through, stay near Nagoya or Kanayama Stations for convenience. The area between Fushimi and Sakae or around Kamimaezu subway station will suit you better if you want to hit the town.

Guesthouse Mado GUESTHOUSE ¥

(ゲストハウスMADO; 050-7516-6632; www.guesthousemado.com; 924 Arimatsu, Midori-ku; dm ¥3000; Meitetsu Arimatsu) This little guesthouse outside the hustle and bustle of downtown Nagoya in the pretty Arimatsu district really is an extension of the friendly owner's home, with two small shared rooms. If you're looking for a serene place to swap stories and experience day-to-day life in Japan, rather than city lights, you'll enjoy the vibe here.

Glocal Nagoya Hostel HOSTEL ¥

(グローカル名古屋ホステル; 052-446-6694; www.glocal-backpackers-hostel.aichihotels.com/en; 1-21-3 Noritake, Nakamura-ku; dm ¥3025; S Nagoya, JR Nagoya) This fabulously friendly hostel about seven minutes' walk from Nagoya Station has its own cafe and bar that's popular with locals and guests alike. Staff (some of whom live in) will make you feel welcome and are happy to dispense local advice and practise their already well-honed English skills.

Royal Park Canvas Nagoya HOTEL ¥¥

(052-300-1111; www.the-royalpark.jp/canvas/nagoya/en; 3-23-13 Meieki, Nakamura-ku; s/d from ¥6000/12,000; S Kokusai Center) This unpretentious, good-value hotel is steps away from Nagoya Station. It's been rebranded as part of Royal Park's less-stuffy Canvas line, and features cool drawings by Nagoya artist Yuka Takeda in guest rooms, the lobby and the exclusive onsen. It's popular with hip young Japanese families.

Dormy Inn Premium Nagoya Sakae HOTEL ¥¥

(ドーミーインPREMIUM名古屋栄; 052-231-5489; www.hotespa.net/dormyinn/english/list/nagoya.html; 2-20-1 Nishiki, Naka-ku; s/d from ¥8000/12,000; S Fushimi) Located in the heart of Nagoya's Sakae district, this busy tourist hotel is that little bit more luxe than the usual offering in the popular Dormy Inn chain, with stylish furnishings, a Japanese restaurant, a terrace and attractive communal baths. Relatively good value.

Kyoya Ryokan RYOKAN ¥¥

(京屋旅館; 052-571-2588; www.kyoya.to; 2-11-4 Habashita, Nishi-ku; s/d with 2 meals from ¥13,200/16,000; S Kokusai Center) This popular ryokan centred on an attractive Japanese garden can get a little noisy when busy, but it has a lovely common bath and an even lovelier self-contained private suite. It's a little far from the bustle of Nagoya (and the station), but the friendly owners are eager to help and they speak some English.

Daiwa Roynet Nagoya Ekimae HOTEL ¥¥

(ダイワロイネットホテル名古屋駅前; 052-541-3955; www.daiwaroynethotelnagoyaekimae.com/en-us; 1-23-20 Meieki-minami, Nakamura-ku; s/d from ¥7000/10,000; JR Nagoya, Sakura-dōri exit) If you're merely transiting in Nagoya and need cheap, clean (and yes, compact) digs near the station, look no further than this modern business hotel with refreshingly comfortable bedding. It's under 10 minutes' walk from JR Nagoya Station.

Hilton Nagoya HOTEL ¥¥¥

(ヒルトン名古屋; 052-212-1111; www.hilton.com; 1-3-3 Sakae, Naka-ku; s/d from ¥18,000/24,500; P @; S Fushimi, exit 7) This characteristic Hilton benefits from an excellent location and features spacious, stylish rooms with Japanese accents, a selection of suites and an executive floor. There's also complimentary bicycle rental, a courtesy station-shuttle service, two restaurants, three bars and a gym. Most rooms have good views.

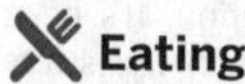

Eating

For cheap international eats, head to the storefronts of the Ōsu Shopping Arcade, where street vendors hawk everything from kebabs to *karaage* (deep-fried items), crêpes and pizza.

★ Misen TAIWANESE ¥
(味仙; ☎052-238-7357; www.misen.ne.jp; 3-6-3 Ōsu, Naka-ku; dishes ¥480-1500; ⏰11.30am-2pm & 5pm-1am Sun-Thu, to 2am Fri & Sat; ❄ ✍; Ⓢ Yaba-chō, exit 4) Folks line up for opening time at this jolly place, where the *Taiwan rāmen* (台湾ラーメン; a spicy concoction of ground meat, chilli, garlic and green onion, served over noodles in a hearty clear broth) induces rapture. Other faves include *gomoku yakisoba* (五目焼きそば; stir-fried noodles) and *kinoko-itame* (stir-fried mushrooms). It may be Taiwanese, but locals will tell you: 'this is real Nagoya food'.

Love Pacific Cafe VEGAN ¥
(ラブ・パシフィックカフェ; ☎052-252-8429; www.pacifit.jp/lovecafe.html; 3-23-38 Sakae; items from ¥600; ⏰11.30am-5pm Tue-Sun; ✍; Ⓢ Yaba-chō, exit 4) Lovers of wholesome, delicious, healthy foods are in for a treat at this trendy, friendly vegan cafe preparing lunch sets and cafe items that are free of dairy, egg and white sugars. The changing menu usually features a choice of two soups, access to the organic salad bar and a main: the tofu teriyaki burgers are delicious.

DON'T MISS

NAGOYA SPECIALITIES

The city is famous for bold specialities that translate well for non-Japanese palates: *kishimen* are soft, flat, handmade wheat noodles; *miso-nikomi udon* are noodles in a hearty miso broth; and *miso-katsu* is a fried breaded pork cutlet topped with miso sauce. *Kōchin* (a local heritage breed of chicken that's raised free range), *tebasaki* (chicken wings) and *hitsumabushi* (charcoal-grilled eel) are other local specialities.

Sōhonke Ebisuya Honten NOODLES ¥
(総本家えびすや本店; ☎052-961-3412; 3-20-7 Nishiki; dishes/sets from ¥760/900; ⏰11am-1am Mon-Sat; Ⓢ Sakae, exit 3) The massive noodle bowls at this, the head branch of one of Nagoya's best-known *kishimen* (flat, handmade wheat noodle) chains, are toasty, tasty and cheap. You can often see the noodles being made by the chef. There's a picture menu: try the *karē kishimen* (curry noodles).

★ Atsuta Hōraiken Honten SEAFOOD ¥¥
(あつた蓬莱軒本店; ☎052-671-8686; www.houraiken.com; 503 Gōdo-chō, Atsuta-ku; dishes ¥950, sets from ¥2500; ⏰11.30am-2pm & 4.30-8.30pm Thu-Tue; Ⓢ Temma-chō, exit 4) The head branch of this *hitsumabushi* chain, in business since 1873, is revered for good reason. Patrons queue during the summer peak season for *hitsumabushi* (eel basted in a secret *tare* (sauce) served atop rice in a covered lacquered bowl (¥3600); add green onion, wasabi and *dashi* (fish broth) to your taste. Other *teishoku* (set meals) include tempura and steak.

Yabaton Honten TONKATSU ¥¥
(矢場とん本店; ☎052-252-8810; http://english.yabaton.com; 3-6-18 Ōsu; dishes from ¥1200; ⏰11am-9pm; Ⓢ Yaba-chō, exit 4) This has been the place to try Nagoya's famed *miso-katsu* (a type of *tonkatsu* – deep-fried pork cutlet) since 1947. Signature dishes are *waraji-tonkatsu* (schnitzel-style flattened, breaded pork) and *teppan-tonkatsu* (breaded pork cutlet with miso on a sizzling plate of cabbage). Look for the massive pig over the door, just south of the overpass. It's next to McDonald's.

Check the website for other locations.

★ Suzunami Honten SEAFOOD ¥¥
(鈴波本店; ☎052-261-1300; www.suzunami.co.jp/shop/shop_honten.html; 3-7-23 Sakae, Naka-ku; lunch sets ¥1300; ⏰11am-2.30pm; ❄) Delightfully traditional but not overly formal, this Nagoyan *kappo* institution specialises in simple grilled fish lunches served with miso soup, rice and pickles, and finished off with *umeshu* (plum wine). You'll likely have a short wait for a table.

Trattoria Cesari ITALIAN ¥¥
(トラットリア　チェザリ; ☎052-238-0372; www.cesari.jp; 3-36-44 Ōsu, Naka-ku; pizza from ¥1000, mains from ¥1100; ⏰11am-3pm & 6-10pm Thu-Tue; Ⓢ Kamimaezu, exit 8) You may be

surprised to find an Italian trattoria of this calibre and value smack bang in the heart of Nagoya. Prepare to queue at weekends, as folks line up for chef Makishima's famous Napoletana pizzas. There's an extensive à la carte menu of Italian favourites, presented in an atmosphere reminiscent of the cuisine's homeland.

Yamamotoya Sōhonke Honke NOODLES ¥¥
(山本屋総本家本家; 052-241-5617; 3-12-19 Sakae, Naka-ku; dishes ¥980-1920; 11am-3pm & 5-10pm Thu-Tue; ; S Yaba-chō, exit 6) This is the place to go to for soupy *miso-nikomi udon* – the chain, which began here, has been doing it since 1925. From Yaba-chō station, take exit 6, turn left, cross Otsu-dōri and walk two blocks down Shirakawa-dōri. It's on your right and has a large white sign with black Japanese writing.

Torigin Honten JAPANESE ¥¥¥
(鳥銀本店; 052-973-3000; www.torigin.co.jp; 3-14-22 Nishiki; kaiseki courses from ¥5900; 5pm-midnight; S Sakae, exit 2) Come here for a unique *kōchin kaiseki* (haute cuisine featuring free-range chicken) experience with immaculately presented servers and a wonderfully traditional atmosphere. Courses consist of *kōchin* chicken served in many forms, including *kushiyaki* (skewered), *karaage* (deep-fried), *zōsui* (mild rice hotpot) and sashimi (raw).

Drinking & Nightlife

Trunk Coffee & Craft Beer COFFEE
(トランク コーヒーバー; 052-321-6626; www.trunkcoffee.com; 1-3-14 Kamimaezu, Naka-ku; 11am-11pm; ; S Kamimaezu, exit 6) Order your cold-brew coffee or regional Japanese craft beer downstairs, then head upstairs to soak in the David-Lynch-via-Stockholm design vibes at this year-old spot. Come evening, join the hipsters outside for a cigarette on the sidewalk. This is a welcome addition to the neighbourhood scene.

Smash Head PUB
(スマッシュヘッド; 052-201-2790; http://smashhead.main.jp; 2-21-90 Ōsu; 11.30am-9pm Wed-Sun, to 3.30pm Mon; S Ōsu Kannon, exit 2) Through the passageway to the left of the main Ōsu Kannon (p229) temple building you'll find this teeny motorcycle- and Vespa-repair shop-pub (that's right). Guinness and Corona are the beers of choice, the patrons are cool, and the bacon cheeseburgers cost ¥1100.

DON'T MISS

NAGOYA'S MARKETS

Ōsu Kannon (p229) temple hosts a colourful antique market on the 18th and 28th of each month, while **Higashi Betsuin** temple (just north of Higashi Betsuin subway station) has a flea market on the 12th of each month.

Entertainment

Electric Lady Land LIVE MUSIC
(エレクトリックレディランド; 052-201-5004; www.ell.co.jp; 2-10-43 Ōsu; S Ōsu Kannon, exit 2) An intimate live venue showcasing the underground music scene in a cool, post-industrial setting. Nationally known bands play the 1st-floor hall, while up-and-coming acts have a smaller one on the 3rd floor.

Shopping

Both Meieki and Sakae are home to huge malls and department stores, good for clothing, crafts and food. In Ōsu, along Akamon-dōri, Banshō-ji-dōri and Niomon-dōri, are hundreds of funky vintage boutiques and discount clothing shops. East of Ōsu, Otsu-dōri has a lot of manga (Japanese comic) shops.

Komehyō DEPARTMENT STORE
(コメ兵; 052-242-0088; www.en.komehyo.co.jp; 2-20-25 Ōsu; 10.30am-7.30pm Thu-Tue; S Ōsu Kannon, exit 2) Enjoy the genius of Komehyō, Japan's largest discounter of secondhand, well...everything. Housed over seven floors in the main building, clothes, jewellery and accessories are of excellent quality and are sold at reasonable prices. With patience, you can find some real bargains, especially at 'yen=g' on the 7th floor, where clothing is sold by weight.

Information

MEDICAL SERVICES

Aichi Prefectural Emergency Medical Guide (愛知県救急医療ガイド; 052-263-1133, automated service 050-5810-5884; www.qq.pref.aichi.jp) Phone or follow the English link on this prefectural homepage for a list of medical institutions with English-speaking staff, including specialities and hours of operation.

Tachino Clinic (たちのクリニック; 052-541-9130; www.tachino-clinic.com; 3F Dai-Nagoya Bldg, 3-26-8 Meieki; 9.30am-1pm & 2.30-6pm Mon-Wed & Fri, 9.30am-1pm Thu & Sat; JR Nagoya, Sakura-dōri exit) This clinic, a short walk from Nagoya Station, has English-speaking staff.

RESOURCES

Nagoya Convention and Visitors Bureau (www.nagoya-info.jp/en) English-language listings.

Nagoya International Center (www.nic-nagoya.or.jp) Brimming with information.

NAGMAG (www.nagmag.jp) English-language site with up-to-the-minute events and reviews.

TOURIST INFORMATION

English-language street and subway maps are widely available at Tourist Information Centers (TICs) and hotels. The *Nagoya Pocket Guide* (www.nagoyapocketguide.com) is particularly handy, as are the *Nagoya Navi Map* and *Nagoya Shopping & Dining Guide*, which you can also download at www.nagoya-info.jp/en/brochures.

Nagoya has three helpful TIC branches:

Tourist Information Center – Nagoya Station (名古屋駅観光案内所; ☎052-541-4301; 1-1-14 Meieki; ⏰9am-7pm; 🚉JR Nagoya)

Tourist Information Center – Kanayama (金山観光案内所; ☎052-323-0161; LOOP Kanayama 1F, 1-17-18 Kanayama; ⏰9am-7pm; 🚉JR Kanayama, north exit)

Tourist Information Center – Sakae (栄町観光案内所; ☎052-963-5252; Oasis 21 B1F, 1-11-1 Higashisakura; ⏰10am-8pm; Ⓢ Sakae)

ℹ Getting There & Away

AIR

On an artificial island in Ise-wan, 35km south of the city, **Central Japan International Airport** (NGO, Centrair; ☎056-938-1195; www.centrair.jp/en) is far friendlier and less frantic than its counterparts in Tokyo and Osaka. With excellent transport connections, it's a great arrival port into Japan from around 30 international destinations in Europe, North America and Asia. Domestic routes serve about 20 Japanese cities, though you'll find that some are reached more quickly by train.

It also has Japan's first in-airport onsen bath, **Fū-no-yu** (風の湯; ☎0569-38-7070; www.centrair.jp/interest/visit/relax/bath.html; SkyTown 4F, Central Japan International Airport; adult/child with towel ¥1030/620; ⏰8am-9pm; 🚉Central Japan International Airport), offering clear views of airline take-offs and landings.

BOAT

Taiheiyo Ferry (☎052-582-8611; www.taiheiyo-ferry.co.jp/english) sails snazzy ships between Nagoya and Tomakomai (Hokkaidō, from ¥9800, 40 hours) via Sendai (from ¥6700, 21¾ hours) every other evening at 7pm, with daily services to Sendai. Take the Meikō subway line to Nagoya-kō Station and go to Nagoya Port.

BUS

JR and Meitetsu highway buses operate services between Nagoya and Kyoto (¥2550, 2½ hours, hourly), Tokyo (from ¥2400, six hours, 14 daily) and Kanazawa (¥4180, four hours, 10 daily), and less frequently to Kōbe (¥3400, 3½ hours), Takayama (¥2980, 2¾ hours) and Nagano (from ¥3600, 4½ hours). Overnight buses run to Hiroshima (from ¥6400, nine hours).

Willer Express (www.willerexpress.com) offers airline-style seating and online reservations in English at heavily discounted rates. Key routes from Nagoya include Tokyo (from ¥3400, six hours, hourly) and Osaka (from ¥2200, three hours, hourly).

Departure points vary by carrier and destination, although almost all highway buses depart from somewhere in Meieki (JR Nagoya Station). Some routes also depart from Oasis 21 (p230). JR highway buses depart from the **Nagoya Bus Terminal** (名古屋バスターミナル) near the *shinkansen* (bullet-train) entrance (north side) of JR Nagoya Station.

Meitetsu highway buses depart from the **Meitetsu Bus Terminal** (名鉄バスターミナル). Willer Express buses depart from a variety of locations, depending on the route. Be sure to confirm your departure location with your carrier at the time of booking.

TRAIN

All lines lead to Meieki (JR Nagoya Station), a hybrid terminus of the JR and private Meitetsu and Kintetsu train lines, as well as subway and bus stations. Here you'll find a labyrinthine world of passageways, restaurants and retailers, and above, the soaring JR Central Towers and Midland Square (p230) complexes. Be sure to leave plenty of time if making a rail transfer!

Nagoya is a major *shinkansen* (bullet-train) hub, connecting with Tokyo (¥10,360, 1¾ hours), Shin-Osaka (¥5830, 50 minutes), Kyoto (¥5070, 35 minutes), Hiroshima (¥18,010, 2¼ hours) and Hakata/Fukuoka (¥22,530, 3¼ hours).

To get into the Japan Alps, take the JR Chūō-honsen line to Matsumoto on a *Shinano tokkyū* (limited express; ¥6030, two hours) or onwards to Nagano (¥7330, 2¾ hours). A separate line (JR Takayama) serves Takayama (*Hida tokkyū* ¥6030, 2¼ hours).

The private Meitetsu line has routes in and around Nagoya (Tokonome, Inuyama, Gifu) covered.

ℹ Getting Around

BUS

The gold **Me-guru** (名古屋観光ルートバスメーグル; www.nagoya-info.jp/en/routebus; day pass adult/child ¥500/250) bus follows a one-way loop near attractions in the Meieki, Sakae and castle areas. Ticket holders receive discounted admission to many attractions. It runs hourly from 9.30am to 5pm Tuesday to Friday and twice hourly at weekends. There's no bus on Monday.

SUBWAY

Nagoya has an excellent subway system with six lines, clearly signposted in English and Japanese. Fares are ¥200 to ¥330 depending on distance. One-day passes (¥740, including city buses ¥850), available at ticket machines, include subway transport and discounted admission to many attractions. On Saturday and Sunday the *donichi eco-kippu* (Saturday and Sunday eco-ticket) gives the same benefits for ¥600 per day.

Inuyama

☎0568 / POP 74,200

In Inuyama (犬山) the Kiso-gawa, aka the 'Japanese Rhine', paints a pretty picture beneath its castle, a National Treasure, and the oldest wooden castle still standing in Japan. By day, the castle, the quaint streets, manicured Uraku-en and the 17th-century Jo-an teahouse make for pleasant strolling, while at night fishermen perform the ancient art of *ukai* (cormorant fishing) by firelight.

Just beneath the castle are the picturesque Shintō shrines Haritsuna Jinja and Sankō-Inari Jinja, the latter with interesting statues of *komainu* (protective dogs) and a short pathway of red *torii* (gates).

Since 1635 townsfolk have celebrated the Inuyama Matsuri on the first weekend in April. The festival highlight is a parade of lantern-strewn floats.

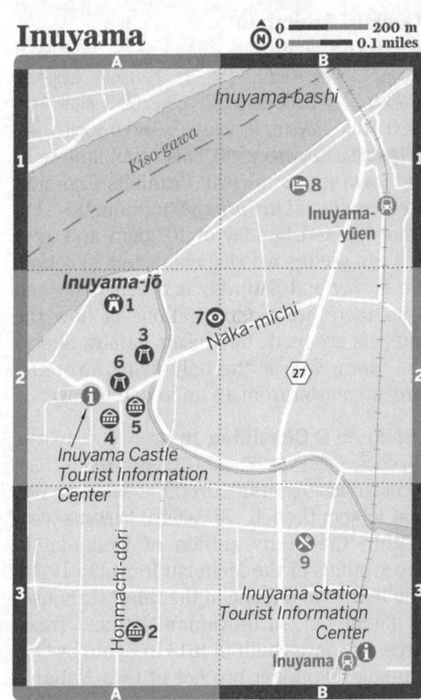

Inuyama

Sights

★Inuyama-jō CASTLE

(犬山城; ☎0568-61-1711; www.inuyama-castle.jp; 65-2 Kitakoken; adult/child ¥550/110; ⏲9am-4.30pm; Meitetsu Inuyama-yūen) A National Treasure, Japan's oldest standing castle is said to have originated as a fort in 1440. The current *donjon* (main keep), built atop a 40m rise beside the Kiso-gawa, dates from 1537 and has resisted war, earthquake and restoration, remaining an outstanding example of Momoyama-era architecture. Inside are steep, narrow staircases and military displays – the view from the top is worth the climb. The castle is 15 minutes' walk from Meitetsu Inuyama-yūen Station. Just south of Inuyama-jō, is picturesque **Haritsuna-jinja** (針綱神社; ☎0568-61-0180; 65-1 Kitakoken) FREE, with a particularly photogenic tunnel of 20-plus red *torii* (gates). Also nearby: **Sankō Inari-jinja** (三光稲荷神社; ☎0568-61-0702; 41-1 Kitakoken), with interesting statues of *komainu* (protective dogs) lovingly dressed in cloth collars.

Inuyama Artifacts Museum/Castle & Town Museum MUSEUM

(犬山市文化史料館・城とまちミュージアム, Inuyama-shi Bunka Shiryō-kan/Shiro to Machi Myūjiamu; ☎0568-62-4802; 8 Kitakoken; ¥100, with Inuyama-jō free; ⏲9am-4.30pm; Meitetsu Inuyama-yūen) This museum houses two float from the Inuyama Matsuri (p236) and various artefacts related to cormorant fishing (p237), Inuyama-jō and the town's history.

Karakuri Exhibition Room (Annexe) MUSEUM

(からくり展示館 (別館), Karakuri Tenji-kan (Bekkan); ☎0568-61-3932; 69-2/69-3 Kitakoken; ¥100, with Inuyama-jō free; ⏲9am-4.30pm; P; 🚉Meitetsu Inuyama-yūen) This small annexe of the town museum (p235) exhibits Edo- and Meiji-era *karakuri ningyō* (marionettes). On Saturday and Sunday at 10.30am and 2pm you can see the wooden characters in action. On Friday and Saturday between 10am and 4pm there are demonstrations of how the puppets are made by artisan Tamaya Shobei the ninth, who is the only living *karakuri ningyō* master from an unbroken lineage.

Uraku-en & Chashitsu Jo-an GARDENS

(有楽苑・茶室如安; ☎0568-61-4608; 1 Gomonsaki; adult/child ¥1000/600; ⏲9am-5pm Mar-Nov, to 4pm Dec-Feb; 🚉Meitetsu Inuyama-yūen) Within the pretty garden of Uraku-en in the grounds of the Meitetsu Inuyama Hotel, you'll find 'Jo-an', one of the finest teahouses in Japan. One of Inuyama's National Treasures, Jo-an was built in 1618 in Kyoto by Oda Urakusai, younger brother of Oda Nobunaga, and relocated here in 1972. You can enjoy tea in the grounds for an additional ¥500.

Dondenkan MUSEUM

(どんでん館; ☎0568-65-1728; 62 Higashi-koken; adult/child ¥100/free; ⏲9am-4.30pm; 🚉Meitetsu Inuyama) A rotating selection of three to four of the 13 impressive floats from Inuyama Matsuri are on year-round display in this custom-made building.

Around Inuyama

★Meiji-mura MUSEUM

(明治村; ☎0568-67-0314; www.meijimura.com; 1 Uchiyama; adult/child ¥1700/1000; ⏲9.30am-5pm Mar-Oct, to 4pm Nov-Feb, closed Mon Dec-Feb) Due to war, earthquakes and development, few Meiji-era buildings have survived here. In 1965 this open-air museum was created to preserve this unique style, known for unifying Western and Japanese architectural elements. Over 60 buildings from around Japan were painstakingly dismantled, transported and reassembled in this leafy lakeside location. Favourites include the entry facade of Frank Lloyd Wright's Tokyo Imperial Hotel, Kyoto's St Francis Xavier's Cathedral, and Sapporo's telephone exchange.

Buses to Meiji-mura (¥420, 20 minutes) depart every 20 to 30 minutes from Inuyama Station's east exit. If you're driving, parking is ¥800.

Ōagata-jinja SHINTŌ SHRINE

(大縣神社; ☎0568-67-1017; 3 Aza Miyayama; 🚉Meitetsu Komaki line to Gakuden) This ancient shrine on a lovely hillside is dedicated to female Shintō deity Izanami and attracts women seeking marriage or fertility. See if you can find the large *hime-ishi* (姫石; princess stone) and other items resembling giant female genitals. The popular **Hime-no-miya Matsuri** takes place here on the Sunday before 15 March (or on 15 March if it's a Sunday). Locals pray for good harvests and prosperity by parading through the streets bearing a *mikoshi* (portable shrine) with more replica vaginas.

Ōagata-jinja is a 25-minute walk from Gakuden Station (¥230 from Inuyama, seven minutes). To reach the shrine, turn right at the exit and follow Rte 177 east, all the way across the river and up the hill. Sadly, recent expansion of a nearby industrial landfill threatens the tranquillity of the shrine. Beware the many noisy, smelly dump trucks sharing the narrow road to your destination.

Tagata-jinja SHINTŌ SHRINE

(田県神社; 152 Tagata-chō; 🚉Meitetsu Komaki line to Tagata-jinja-mae) Izanagi, the male counterpart of female deity Izanami, is commemorated at this shrine, with countless wooden and stone phalluses to celebrate. You can buy souvenirs from ¥800. The **Tagata Hōnen-sai Matsuri** takes place on 15 March at Tagata-jinja, when the highly photogenic, 2m-long, 60kg 'sacred object' is paraded excitedly around the neighbourhood. Arrive well before the procession starts at 2pm. Tagata-jinja is five minutes' walk west of Tagata-jinja-mae Station on the Meitetsu Komaki line (¥300 from Inuyama, nine minutes).

Festivals & Events

Inuyama Matsuri CULTURAL

(犬山まつり) A government-designated Intangible Cultural Asset, this festival features a parade of 13 three-tiered floats strewn with 365 lanterns. Atop each float, elaborate *karakuri ningyō* (marionettes) perform to music. The festival has been held on the first weekend in April since 1635.

A scaled-down version is held on the fourth Saturday in October.

Sleeping & Eating

Inuyama has a few basic *minshuku* (guesthouses) and some tourist hotels that have frankly seen better days. If nothing suits, consider staying in nearby Gifu or Nagoya. Noodle and *bentō* (boxed meals) shops can be found at the train station.

Rinkō-kan RYOKAN ¥¥

(臨江館; ☎0568-61-0977; www.rinkokan.jp; 8-1 Nishidaimon; r per person incl 2 meals & without bathroom from ¥12,000; P ❄ @ 📶; 🚉 Meitetsu Inuyama-yūen, west exit) Overlooking the river, this cheery 18-room ryokan has stone common baths, including *rotemburo* (outdoor baths). Some rooms have in-room bathrooms, and a variety of packages are available, including good deals for single travellers. The retro avocado and coral upholstery is so unfashionable it's fashionable again.

Narita FRENCH ¥¥

(フレンチ創作料理なり多; ☎0568-65-2447; www.f-narita.com; 395 Higashikoken; 5-course meals from ¥4300; ⌚11am-9pm; 🚉 Meitetsu Inuyama, west exit) Fancy five-course French cuisine in an Edo-period building with an attractive garden – lovely! From the station, turn right at the lights, walk two blocks to the next set of lights, then turn right. It's on your right.

ℹ Information

Inuyama has two TICs that dispense English-language materials and assist with accommodation and activities reservations. Visit www.ml.inuyama.gr.jp.

Inuyama Station Tourist Information Center (犬山市観光案内所 (犬山駅); ☎0568-61-6000; ⌚9am-5pm)

Inuyama Castle Tourist Information Center (犬山市観光案内所 (犬山城); ☎0568-61-2825; 12 Kitakoken; ⌚9am-5pm)

ℹ Getting There & Away

Inuyama is connected with Nagoya (*tokkyū* ¥550, 37 minutes) and Gifu (¥450, 44 minutes) via the Meitetsu Inuyama line. The castle and *ukai* (cormorant-fishing) area are slightly closer to Inuyama-yūen Station than Inuyama Station.

Gifu

☎058 / POP 406,735

Historically, Gifu (岐阜) has a strong association with Oda Nobunaga, *daimyō* (domain lord) of the castle and bestower of the city's name in 1567. The city was later visited by famed haiku poet Matsuo Bashō, who witnessed *ukai* (cormorant fishing) here in 1688; Charlie Chaplin did the same in his day.

UKAI: THE ANCIENT ART OF CORMORANT FISHING

The cities of Inuyama and Gifu remain among the few places in the world where the ancient (and some say barbaric) practice of cormorant fishing continues as it has done for centuries. Estimates date the practice, which falls under the auspices of the Imperial Household Agency (the first and finest fish of the year are sent to the emperor), at over 1300 years old. The masters (called *ushō*) are so skilled that their craft is passed on from father to son.

During the *ukai* season (from May/June to 15 October), *ushō* set off after dusk in 13m traditional boats, with an iron basket containing a burning fire suspended by a pole at the front of the boat. Trained cormorants (large black, long-necked diving birds known for their voracious appetites) tethered by neck ropes to their masters, are released from the boats to dive for *ayu* (sweetfish). The ropes prevent the birds from swallowing the largest fish, which get lodged in their throats. Each bird will hold around six large fish until the master pulls it back into his boat and the fish are regurgitated. Although many object to this apparent cruelty, masters claim the birds are not harmed by their training.

While it's not for everyone, the spectacle of the fires reflected off the water and the opportunity to witness a relatively unchanged traditional livelihood, make watching *ukai* a memorable evening on the water. In Inuyama, cormorant fishing takes place close to Inuyama-yūen Station, by the Inuyama-bashi.

In Gifu, **Nagara-gawa Cormorant Fishing** (長良川鵜飼い, Nagara-gawa Ukai), attended by the glow of lanterns drifting along the river, can be glimpsed east of the Nagara-bashi. There are also exhibits on cormorant fishing at the **Nagara River Ukai Museum** (長良川うかいミュージアム, Nagara-gawa Ukai Myūjiamu; ☎058-210-1555; www.ukaimuseum.jp; 51-2 Choryo; adult/child ¥500/250; ⌚9am-6.30pm Wed-Mon May–mid-Oct, 9am-4.30pm Wed-Mon mid-Oct–Apr; 🚌city loop or N-line bus to Ukai-ya).

Contemporary Gifu shows little evidence of those historic times (due to a colossal earthquake in 1891 and the decimation of WWII); redevelopment has created a tidy and accessible downtown core. Skyscrapers give way to modest houses heading north toward the river; nearby, noteworthy attractions surround Gifu castle, including the beautiful Gifu park and one of the three Great Buddhas of Japan. Pretty mountains, a wide river and excellent transport links mean big-city convenience with small-town charisma.

Sights

Visitors generally arrive in Gifu at JR Gifu or Meitetsu Gifu Stations, but sightseeing is centred on **Gifu-kōen** (岐阜公園; P; N80, N32-N86 to Gifu-kōen), a 15-minute bus ride north of the train stations. At the foot of Kinka-zan, this is one of the loveliest city parks in Japan, with plenty of water and trees set into the hillside. People have been living and working here for centuries; you can see pottery excavations at the history museum on the park grounds.

Shōhō-ji (Gifu Great Buddha) BUDDHIST TEMPLE
(正法寺; 058-264-2760; 8 Daibutsu-chō; adult/child ¥200/100; 9am-5pm; N80, N32-N86 to Gifu-kōen) The main attraction of this orange-and-white temple is the papier-mâché *daibutsu* (Great Buddha; c 1832), one of the three Great Buddha statues of Japan. It's 13.7m tall and is said to have been fashioned over 38 years using a tonne of paper sutras.

Nawa Insect Museum MUSEUM
(名和昆虫博物館; 058-263-0038; 2-18 Omiyacho; adult/child ¥500/400; 10am-5pm Wed-Mon) On the grounds of Gifu-kōen is this quirky collection of more than 300,000 beetle, butterfly, moth and other insect specimens. It's the personal collection of Gifu-born entomologist Yasushi Nawa, who founded the museum in 1912. Between display cases are terrariums of well-camouflaged live insects. It's creepy fun even if your age is no longer in the single digits.

Gifu City History Museum MUSEUM
(岐阜市歴史博物館, Gifu-shi Rekishi Hakubutsu-kan; 058-265-0010; www.gifucvb.or.jp/en/01_sightseeing/01_05.html; 2-18-1 Ōmiya-chō; adult/child ¥300/150; 9am-4.30pm Tue-Sun; N80, N32-N86 to Gifu-kōen) Located within the grounds of Gifu-kōen, this museum focuses on the Sengoku period, when *daimyō* Oda Nobunaga was at the height of his power. Enthusiastic staff members are keen to show visitors wonderful DIY facsimiles of traditional crafts.

Gifu-jō CASTLE
(岐阜城; 058-263-4853; www.gifucvb.or.jp/en/01_sightseeing/01_02.html; 18 Tenshukaku; adult/child ¥200/100; 9.30am-4.30pm; N80, N32-N86 to Gifu-kōen) Perched atop Kinka-zan and with sweeping views over the cities of Gifu and Nagoya, this castle is a 1956 concrete replica of *daimyō* Oda Nobunaga's stronghold, destroyed in 1600, the ruins of which were finished off in WWII. There's an hour-long hiking trail from the park below.

Or you could take the **Kinka-zan Ropeway** (金華山ロープウエー; 058-262-6784; 257 Senjōjiki-shita; adult/child return ¥1080/540; 9am-5pm year-round, hours extended in holiday periods), also within the park, which whisks you 329m to the summit in less than five minutes.

Sleeping

There are plenty of modern, characterless-but-convenient business hotels around the JR and Meitetsu station areas.

Guesthouse Kiten GUESTHOUSE ¥
(ゲストハウス岐てん; 058-263-8218; http://gh-kiten.jugem.jp/?pid=1; 1-20 Chūsetsuchō; r per person without bathroom ¥4500; JR Gifu, north exit) Tiny Kiten, right on the Nagawa-kawa, is a welcoming place to rest your head. Cosy (read: small) Japanese-style tatami rooms set in a refurbished 50-year-old house are tidy and comfortable, as are shared bathrooms and common areas. Proprietor Osugi is a wealth of local knowledge and may whisk you off to dinner if you let him. It's a 30-minute walk north from JR Gifu Station.

Dormy Inn Gifu Ekimae HOTEL ¥¥
(ドーミーイン岐阜; 058-267-5489; www.hotespa.net/hotels/gifu; 6-31 Yoshino-machi; s/d from ¥7900/11,400; JR Gifu, north exit) This newish hotel is five minutes' stroll along the elevated walkway from JR Gifu Station. Bright rooms are functionally compact. There's an on-site onsen and the guest laundry has gas-powered dryers (so you can actually get a decent amount of clothing dried). Breakfast is available for ¥1500.

Eating

The narrow streets a few blocks north of JR Gifu Station and west of Meitetsu Gifu Station, between Kinkabashi-dōri and Nagarabashi-dōri, are dotted with open-air eateries and *izakaya* (pub-restaurants), and have a welcoming nocturnal vibe.

★Gyōza Gishū GYOZA ¥
(餃子専門店 岐州; ☎058-266-6227; 1-31 Sumidamachi; gyōza from ¥450; ⏲5.30pm until sold out Wed-Mon) This humming hole-in-the-wall place does soupy, fried *gyōza* (dumplings) and *ebi chahan* (shrimp fried rice) – and, of course, beer. Go straight from JR Gifu Station along the street between Kinkabashi-dōri and Nagarabashi-dōri. It's on the corner of the second block, to your right, behind Tokyo Mitsubishi UFJ Bank.

Sarashina SOBA ¥¥
(更科; ☎058-265-9594; http://tanuki-soba.com; 3-4 Kyomachi; mains from ¥1000; ⏲10.30am-7pm Fri-Wed) This 100-year-old shop is renowned among locals for delicious *tanuki soba* (buckwheat noodles topped with crunchy tempura bits left over from the deep fryer). *Tanuki* is the Japanese word for badger; the tenuous link is that badgers and the buckwheat used to make soba both come from the mountains. Meditate on ceramic badger figurines while slurping.

Senryū JAPANESE ¥¥¥
(潜龍; ☎058-231-1151; www.senryu.co.jp; 14 Nagara; set menus from ¥10,000; ⏲11.30am-9.30pm Wed-Mon) Since 1966 this delightful restaurant has been preparing succulent Hida beef in private tatami rooms in a traditional Japanese house. On the banks of the Nagara-gawa in view of Gifu-jō, and overlooking a manicured garden, the setting is delightful. If you're looking for an authentic *teppanyaki* experience (priced accordingly), you've found it. Some Japanese-language ability is advantageous.

Shopping

Gifu's craft tradition includes *wagasa* (oiled-paper parasols/umbrellas) and elegantly painted *chōchin* (paper lanterns), though the number of real artisans is dwindling – souvenir shops sell mass-produced versions. The Tourist Information Center has a map of high-quality makers and retailers. Expect to pay ¥10,000 and up for the good stuff.

Sakaida Eikichi Honten ARTS & CRAFTS
(坂井田永吉本店; ☎058-271-6958; 27 Kanōnakahiroe-chō; ⏲9.30am-5.30pm Mon-Sat) This high-end maker of *wagasa* (oiled-paper parasols/umbrellas) is a 10-minute walk from JR Gifu Station. Turn left from the south exit, then right at the second stoplight. It's on the next corner.

Ozeki Chōchin ARTS & CRAFTS
(オゼキ; ☎058-263-0111; www.ozeki-lantern.co.jp; 1-18 Oguma-chō; ⏲9am-5pm Mon-Fri; 🚌Ken-Sōgōchōsha-mae) Find beautiful paper lanterns here, by Higashi Betsuin temple.

Information

Tourist Information Center (観光案内所; ☎058-262-4415; JR Gifu Station; ⏲9am-7pm Mar-Dec, to 6pm Jan & Feb) Within JR Gifu Station; friendly staff can direct you to maps, accommodation and bicycle rentals (¥100 per day).

Getting There & Away

Gifu is a blink from Nagoya on the JR Tōkaidō line (*tokkyū* ¥470, 20 minutes). Meitetsu trains take longer and are more expensive (¥550, 28 minutes) but also serve Inuyama (¥450, 35 minutes) and Central Japan International Airport (*tokkyū* ¥1340, 64 minutes).

JR Gifu and Meitetsu Gifu Stations are a few minutes' walk apart, joined by a covered elevated walkway.

Getting Around

Buses to sights (¥200) depart from stops 11 and 12 of the bus terminal by JR Gifu Station's Nagara exit, stopping at Meitetsu Gifu Station en route. There's also a city-loop bus from stop 10. Check before boarding, as not all buses make all stops.

Gujō-Hachiman

☎0575 / POP 44,723

Nestled in the mountains at the confluence of several rivers, Gujō-Hachiman (郡上八幡) is a picturesque town that invites leisurely strolls along the river before *kaiseki* (haute cuisine) feasting and early to bed. Come summer, tourists flock to the town for the raucous Gujō Odori folk-dance festival. Rather incongruously, this is also where plastic food models were invented.

Following a tradition dating to the 1590s, townsfolk engage in frenzied dancing on 32 nights between mid-July and early September. Visitor participation is encouraged, especially during *tetsuya odori*, the four main days of the festival (13 to 16 August), when the dancing goes all night.

Otherwise, the town's good-value ryokan, sparkling rivers, well-preserved wooden storefronts and stone bridges beneath wooded peaks maintain appeal. Near the town centre, the famous spring Sōgi-sui is a pilgrimage site, named for a Momoyama-era poet. Spring connoisseurs place Sōgi-sui at the top of the list for clarity.

Sights & Activities

Resident Yuka Takada (Gujoinus) offers free English-language walking tours in the region. Contact her at pupi@zd.wakwak.com.

Gujō Hachiman-jō CASTLE

(郡上八幡城; 0575-65-5839; www.gujohachiman.com/kanko/history_e.html; 659 Hachiman-chō; adult/child ¥310/150; 9am-5pm) Twenty minutes' hike from Jōka-machi Plaza bus terminal you'll find the pride of Gujō, a 1933 reconstruction of the previous fortress, originally constructed in 1559 but destroyed in the Meiji period. The handsome hilltop castle contains various weaponry and has wonderful views across the valley. There's no access by public transport.

Shokuhin Sample Kōbō WORKSHOP

(食品サンプル工房創作館; 0575-67-1870; www.samplekobo.com; 956 Hachiman-chō; 9am-5pm Fri-Wed) FREE Realistic food models were one of life's great mysteries – until now. In an old merchant house, this hands-on workshop lets you see how it's done and try creating them yourself (reservations required). Tempura and lettuce (four pieces, ¥1200) and a spilled-ice-cream smartphone stand (¥900) make memorable souvenirs. It's about five minutes' walk from Jōka-machi Plaza, across the river.

Sleeping & Eating

The town's few inexpensive ryokan and *minshuku* (guesthouses) make spending a quiet night in this delightful hamlet a worthwhile consideration.

There are a few quaint riverside restaurants, but most close before dinnertime. Most overnight guests choose to dine at their lodgings.

Bizenya Ryokan RYOKAN ¥¥

(備前屋旅館; 0575-65-2068; www.gujyo-bizenya.jp; 264 Yanagi-machi; r per person without bathroom from ¥6400; P) This quietly upscale ryokan near Shin-bashi faces a lovely garden. Some rooms have private facilities; plans with or without meals are available.

Nakashimaya Ryokan RYOKAN ¥¥

(中嶋屋旅館; 0575-65-2191; www.nakashimaya.net; 940 Shinmachi; r per person without bathroom from ¥6500; P) Delightfully well kept, compact and comfortable, Nakashimaya Ryokan is between the train station and the Tourist Association. There's an organic cafe next door.

Drinking & Nightlife

Onabi-en TEAHOUSE

(郡上銘茶　小那比園; Hachimancho, btwn Shin-bashi & Miyagase-bashi; 10am-5pm Apr-Nov) Come for the Fukui Prefecture–grown green tea packaged for gifting, stay for the mind-blowing *matcha* (powdered green tea) soft ice cream. Onabi is 100m west of Bizenya Ryokan. You'll know it from the green-ice-cream cone out the front.

Information

Tourist Association (観光協会; 0575-67-0002; www.gujohachiman.com/kanko; 520-1 Shimadani; 8.30am-5pm) Pick up a walking map in English or rent a bicycle (¥300/1500 per hour/day) from this tourist office, located by Shin-bashi.

Getting There & Away

BUS

The most convenient access to Gujō-Hachiman is via bus from Gifu (¥1520, one hour). Be sure to get off at the Jōka-machi Plaza stop, which is not the end of the line. Nōhi Bus (p245) also operates services from Nagoya (¥1850, 1½ hours) and Takayama (¥1650, 1¼ hours), but these only stop at the Gujō-Hachiman Highway Interchange on the outskirts of town.

TRAIN

The private Nagaragawa Tetsudō line serves Gujō-Hachiman from Mino-Ōta (¥1350, 80 minutes, hourly), with connections via the JR Takayama line to Nagoya (*tokkyū* ¥2320, 45 minutes; *futsū* via Gifu ¥1140, one hour) and Takayama (*tokkyū/futsū* ¥3770/1940, 1¾/three hours), but the station is located a little inconveniently: about a 20-minute walk away from the sights.

In 2016 Nagaragawa Tetsudō (www.nagatetsu.co.jp) launched a new tourist train, Nagara, between Mino-Ōta and Gujō-Hachiman, with 1st-class seating, narration (in Japanese) and special French and Italian dining options (¥12,000 return). The train departs Mino-Ōta at 10.40am and arrives in Gujō-Hachiman at 12.16pm (Friday to Sunday). The ¥500 surcharge on top of the regular fare brings the total fare to ¥1850.

KISO VALLEY NAKASENDŌ

The Nakasendō (中仙道) was one of the five highways of the Edo period, and one of the two connecting Edo (now Tokyo) with Kyoto. This was the inland route, preferred by many to the Tōkaidō, which went around the coast and required many river crossings. Much of the route is now followed by national roads; however, in the thickly forested Kiso Valley there exist several sections of twisty, craggy post road that have been carefully restored. Most impressive is the 7.8km stretch of trail between Magome and Tsumago, two of the most attractive Nakasendō towns. Walking this route is one of Japan's most rewarding visitor experiences.

There were 11 post towns, each with the suffix *-juku* to its name, in the valley. Fukushima-juku (Kiso-Fukushima Station) and Narai-juku (Narai Station) boast areas evoking memories of the past and are easily reached by train.

Sleeping & Eating

Along this historic highway you'll find lovely, unpretentious *minshuku* (guesthouses) and ryokan that won't break the budget.

If you're only spending one night on the Nakasendō, Tsumago, which has a little more to choose from than the other towns in the valley, is the most popular choice.

Dining is limited to a handful of options in the evenings; most overnight visitors eat where they sleep.

Getting There & Around

The easiest way to reach the area is by *tokkyū* (limited express) Shinano trains on the JR Chūō line from Nagoya or Matsumoto. Key stations include Nakatsugawa (for Magome), Nagiso (for Tsumago), Kiso-Fukushima (for Kiso) and Narai (for Narai). Slower local trains will also do the trick.

This is also a great area to explore with your own wheels.

Magome

☎0264 / POP 460

Located in the administrative district of Nakatsugawa, in Gifu Prefecture, pretty Magome-juku (馬篭) is the furthest south of the Kiso Valley post villages. Its buildings line a steep, cobblestone pedestrian road (unfriendly to wheelie suitcases); the rustic shopfronts and mountain views will keep your finger on the shutter. This is the starting point for the popular 7.8km Magome-to-Tsumago hike (p242).

Sleeping

★**Magome-Chaya** MINSHUKU ¥¥
(馬籠茶屋; ☎0264-59-2038; www.magomechaya.com; 4296 Magome; r per person incl 2 meals from ¥8525; ❄☎) This popular *minshuku* (guesthouse) is almost halfway up the hill, just before the Tourist Information Office (p242). Room-only plans are available and English is spoken. Check out its excellent English website.

OFF THE BEATEN TRACK

HIKING IN THE CENTRAL ALPS

Officially called Kiso Sanmyaku (木曽山脈), the range of mountains east of the Kiso Valley is better known to the Japanese as the Chūō (Central; 中央) Alps. They may not be as high as the Northern and Southern Alps, but the Central Alps present a brilliant opportunity for just about anyone to climb 2956m Kiso-komagatake (木曽駒ヶ岳), one of Japan's 100 Famous Mountains, thanks to the **Komagatake Ropeway** (駒ヶ岳ロープウェイ; Map p292; ☎0265-83-3107; www.chuo-alps.com; 759-489 Akaho, Komagane; 1 way/return ¥1210/2260; ⏲every 30min 8am-5pm), which lifts visitors up to 2612m in the Senjōjiki cirque. This is the highest station in Japan, and even if you only make it this far you're in for a thrill: on a good day you can see virtually all the Southern Alps and even Fuji-san. Kiso-komagatake can be climbed from the top station in three hours return. Keen and well-prepared hikers can hike over the top and down into the Kiso Valley, not far from Kiso-Fukushima.

The Komagatake Ropeway is on the eastern side of the Central Alps. You'll need to make your way to Komagane (駒ヶ根), on the JR Iida line in the Tenryū river valley, then take a bus to Shirabidaira, where you'll find the bottom ropeway station. Check www.chuo-alps.com for bus, ropeway, accommodation and hiking details.

MAGOME–TSUMAGO HIKE

From Magome (elevation 600m), the 7.8km hike to Tsumago (elevation 420m) follows a steep, largely paved road until it reaches its peak at the top of Magome-tōge (pass) – elevation 801m. After the pass, the trail meanders by waterfalls, forest and farmland. The route is easiest in this direction and is clearly signposted in English; allow three to six hours to enjoy it.

Both towns offer a handy baggage-forwarding service from either Tourist Information Center to the other. Deposit your bags between 8.30am and 11.30am for delivery by 1pm.

Minshuku Tajimaya MINSHUKU ¥¥
(民宿但馬屋; 0264-69-2048; www.kiso-tajimaya.com; 4266 Magome; r incl 2 meals & without bathroom from ¥9800;) This pleasant historical inn has compact rooms and friendly staff. The array of local specialities served in the common dining area is impressive, as are the *hinoki* (cypress) baths.

Information

Tourist Information Office (観光案内館; 0264-59-2336; www.kiso-magome.com; 4300-1 Magome; 9am-5pm) Extremely helpful, with a good English map, but located somewhat inconveniently halfway up the hill, to the right. A baggage-forwarding service to Tsumago is available.

Getting There & Away

Nakatsugawa Station on the JR Chūō line serves Magome, though it's some distance from the town. Nakatsugawa is connected with Nagoya (*tokkyū* ¥2820, 55 minutes) and Matsumoto (*tokkyū* ¥4090, 1¼ hours).

Buses leave hourly from Nakatsugawa Station for Magome (¥560, 30 minutes). There's also an infrequent bus service between Magome and Tsumago (¥600, 25 minutes), via Magome-tōge.

Getting Around

If fitness or ability prevent you from appreciating the amazing walk between Magome and Tsumago, there's an easier way. The Magome–Tsumago bus (¥600, 25 minutes, two to three daily in each direction) also stops at Magome-tōge. If you alight and begin the walk there, it's a picturesque 5.2km downhill run to Tsumago.

Tsumago

0264 / POP 630

Tsumago (妻籠), about 15 minutes' walk from end to end, feels like an open-air museum village. Part of Nagiso town, it has been designated a protected area for the preservation of traditional buildings: modern developments such as telephone poles aren't allowed to mar the scene. The dark-wood glory of its lattice-front buildings is particularly beautiful at dawn and dusk. Film and TV crews are often spotted here.

On 23 November the **Fuzoku Emaki** parade, featuring townsfolk in Edo-period costume, is held along the Nakasendō in Tsumago.

Sights

Tsumagojuku-honjin HISTORIC BUILDING
(妻籠宿本陣; 2190 Azuma; adult/child ¥300/150; 9am-5pm) It was in this building that the *daimyō* (domain lords) themselves would spend the night, although the building's architecture is more noteworthy than its exhibits. A combined ticket (adult/child ¥700/350) includes admission to Waki-honjin (Okuya) and Local History Museum, opposite.

Waki-honjin (Okuya) & Local History Museum MUSEUM
(脇本陣（奥谷）・歴史資料館, Rekishi Shiryō-kan; 2159-2 Azuma; adult/child ¥600/300; 9am-5pm) This *waki-honjin* (rest stop) for the *daimyōs'* (domain lords') retainers was reconstructed in 1877 by a former castle builder under special dispensation from Emperor Meiji. It contains a lovely moss garden and a special toilet built in case Meiji happened to show up – he never did. The adjacent Local History Museum houses elegant exhibitions about Kiso and the Nakasendō, with some English signage.

Sleeping & Eating

★**Fujioto** RYOKAN ¥¥
(藤乙; 0264-57-3009; www.tsumago-fujioto.jp; 858-1 Tsumago; r per person incl 2 meals from ¥11,000;) The owner of this unpretentious, welcoming inn speaks some English, Italian and Spanish. It's a great place to have your first ryokan experience, as most staff are able to communicate well with travellers, especially over the wonderful *kaiseki* (Japanese haute cuisine) dinner. Corner

upstairs rooms have lovely views. You can also stop by for lunch – try the Kiso Valley trout (¥1350).

Oyado Daikichi MINSHUKU ¥¥
(御宿大吉; ☎0264-57-2595; www17.plala.or.jp/daikiti/english.html; 902-1 Azuma; r per person incl 2 meals from ¥8500;) Popular with foreign visitors, this traditional-looking inn benefits from modern construction and has a prime location on the top of the hill – all rooms have a lovely outlook. It's at the very edge of town. There's an English website and English is spoken.

Matsushiro-ya Ryokan RYOKAN ¥¥
(松代屋旅館; ☎0264-57-3022; http://matsushiroya.sakura.ne.jp; 807 Azuma; r per person with/without 2 meals ¥11,000/5500; Thu-Tue;) Showing signs of age, this is one of Tsumago's most historic lodgings (parts date from 1804). It has large tatami rooms and plenty of authentic charm.

Yoshimura-ya NOODLES ¥
(吉村屋; ☎0264-57-3265; 2176-1 Azuma; dishes from ¥720; 10am-5pm;) If you're hungry after a long walk, you can't go past a chilled bowl of handmade Kiso *zaru-soba* (cold buckwheat noodles with dipping sauce).

Information

Tourist Information Center (観光案内館; ☎0264-57-3123; www.tumago.jp/english; 2159-2 Azuma; 8.30am-5pm) In the centre of town. Some English is spoken and there's English-language literature. Ask here for any directions.

Getting There & Away

Nagiso Station, on the JR Chūō line, serves Tsumago, though it's 3.6km from Tsumago so you could walk it. Buses run between Tsumago and Nagiso Station (¥280, 10 minutes, eight daily).

You'll need to change to a local train at Nakatsugawa Station (¥320, 20 minutes) if you're coming from the Nagoya direction, or at Kiso-Fukushima (¥580, 40 minutes) if you're coming from the Matsumoto direction.

There's an infrequent bus service between Magome and Tsumago (¥600, 25 minutes), via Magome-tōge.

Kiso

☎0264 / POP 28,500

Kiso (木曽町; *kiso-machi*) is larger and considerably more developed than Magome, Tsumago or Narai. There's a full-on town here around Kiso-Fukushima Station and also an atmospheric historic district. Kiso was an important checkpoint on the Nakasendō, and in times requiring high security the road would be blocked off at Fukushima-juku.

These days, Kiso-Fukushima is the jumping-off point for hikers and sightseers heading to Ontake-san (p245), Japan's second-highest volcano (3067m).

Sights

From Kiso-Fukushima train station, turn right and head downhill towards the town centre and the Kiso-gawa. Sights are well signposted. Look for **Ue-no-dan** (上の段), the historic district of atmospheric houses and buildings.

Fukushima Checkpoint Site MUSEUM
(福島関所跡, Fukushima Sekisho-ato; ☎0264-23-2595; www.town-kiso.com/facility/100024; 4748-1 Sekimachi; adult/child ¥300/150; 8am-5pm Apr-Oct, 8.30am-4pm Nov-Mar) This is a reconstruction of one of the most significant checkpoints on the Edo-period trunk roads. From its perch above the river valley, it's easy to see the barrier's strategic importance. Displays inside show the implements used to maintain order, including weaponry and *tegata* (wooden travel passes), as well as the special treatment women travellers received.

Sleeping & Eating

There are a few good eateries in the village and by the train station.

Ryokan Sarashinaya RYOKAN ¥¥
(旅館 さらしなや; ☎0264-22-2307; http://sarashinaya.com; 6168 Nakajima; s/d without bathroom from ¥6000/10,000;) A short walk from Kiso-Fukushima Station, this ryokan offers simple Japanese-style rooms in a low-key, foreigner-friendly setting. The historic district of Ue-no-dan is only a short stroll away.

★**Kurumaya Honten** NOODLES ¥
(くるまや本店; ☎0264-22-2200; www.soba-kurumaya.com; 5367-2 Kiso-machi, Fukushima; mains from ¥670; 10am-5pm Thu-Tue;) One of Japan's most renowned soba shops, where the classic presentation is cold *mori* (plain) or *zaru* (with strips of *nori*) with a sweetish dipping sauce. It's near the first bridge at the bottom of the hill; look for the gears above the doorway.

Bistro Matsushima-tei ITALIAN ¥¥

(ビストロ 松島亭; ☎0264-23-3625; 5250-1 Ue-no-dan; mains from ¥1300, lunch sets from ¥1300; ⊙lunch & dinner daily Jul-Oct, Thu-Tue Nov-Jun) In the historic Ue-no-dan district, Bistro Matsushima-tei serves a changing selection of handmade pizzas and pastas in an atmospheric setting befitting the magnificent building's history.

Information

Kiso Tourist Information Center (木曽町観光協会; ☎0264-22-4000; https://en.visitkiso.com; 2012-10 Kiso-machi, Fukushima; ⊙9am-5pm) Across from the train station; the friendly staff here have English maps and brochures.

Getting There & Away

Kiso-Fukushima is on the JR Chūō line (*Shinano tokkyū*); it's easily reached from Matsumoto (¥2470, 40 minutes), Nakatsugawa (¥2470, 35 minutes) and Nagoya (¥4420, 1½ hours).

Narai

☎0264 / POP 580

A stunning example of a Nakasendō post town, little Narai (奈良井) is a gem tucked away in the folds of the northern end of the valley; it belongs to the city of Shiojiri, in Nagano Prefecture. Once called 'Narai of a thousand houses', it flourished during the Edo period, when its proximity to the highest pass on the Nakasendō made it a popular resting place for travellers.

Today it's a conservation area, with a preserved main street extending about 1.5km south from the station and showcasing some wonderful examples of Edo-period architecture. Look for **Nakamura House** (中村邸; ☎0264-34-2655; adult/child ¥300/free; ⊙9am-4pm), a wonderfully preserved former merchant's house and garden. Narai is famed for *shikki* (lacquerware). Plenty of quality souvenir shops line the main street, many with reasonable prices.

If you're not hiking from Magome to Tsumago, this is the easiest of the atmospheric old Nakasendō towns to visit on a day trip.

Sleeping & Eating

A handful of cafes cater to the village's slow but steady stream of tourists during the day.

★Echigo-ya RYOKAN ¥¥

(ゑちごや旅館; ☎0264-34-3011; www.naraijyuku-echigoya.jp; 493 Narai; r per person incl 2 meals from ¥15,000; ❄📶) In business for more than 220 years, this charming, family-run ryokan is one of a kind. With only two guest rooms, Echigo-ya provides an opportunity to experience the Japanese art of hospitality in its most undiluted form. You'll feel as though you've stepped back in time. Some Japanese-language ability will help make the most of your stay. Book well ahead. Cash only.

Oyado Iseya MINSHUKU ¥¥

(御宿伊勢屋; ☎0264-34-3051; www.oyado-iseya.jp; 388 Narai; r per person incl 2 meals from ¥9800; ❄📶) The street frontage of this former merchant house (built 1818) has been beautifully preserved. The site is now home to a pleasant 10-room inn, with guest rooms in the main house and a newer building out the back.

Matsunami SHOKUDO ¥

(松波; ☎0264-34-3750; 397-1 Narai; light meals from ¥650; ⊙11.30am-8pm Wed-Mon) This delightful little eatery on a corner serves simple favourites such as special-sauce *tonkatsu-don* (deep-fried pork cutlet on rice).

Information

Narai Tourist Information Center (奈良井宿観光協会; ☎0264-54-2001; www.naraijuku.com; ⊙9am-5pm May-Oct) Inside Narai Station. There's another office about halfway along Narai's preserved main street.

Getting There & Away

Only *futsū* (local) trains stop at Narai, which is on the JR Chūō line. It takes no more than an hour or three to see the sights, making it a neat day trip from Matsumoto (¥580, 50 minutes), but you could easily pass a peaceful evening here. From Nagoya, change trains at Kiso-Fukushima (¥410, 25 minutes).

HIDA REGION

Visitors flock to the dramatic mountains of the Hida region (飛騨地域) for their delightful *onsen ryokan* (traditional hot-spring inns); the World Heritage–listed villages of the Gokayama District, famed for their signature *gasshō-zukuri* (thatched-roof) architecture; and the region's centrepiece, Takayama, one of Japan's most likeable cities.

Getting There & Away

Located in the northernmost pocket of Gifu Prefecture, the Hida region is accessed by *tokkyū* services from Nagoya to the south and Toyama

WORTH A TRIP

CLIMBING ONTAKE-SAN

Sitting about 20km west of Kiso is Japan's second-highest volcano (after Fuji-san), the massive, active stratovolcano Ontake-san (御嶽山; 3067m). This stand-alone volcano can claim its own religion in the form of Ontake-kyō, a Shintō sect of mountain ascetics who wear white and practise harsh physical training. It's not as harsh as it used to be, though, as these days most practitioners and amateur hikers either whiz up to 2150m on the ropeway or start their climb at Ta-no-hara (田の原; 2180m), where there's a sizeable car park. Either way, they have only around 900 vertical metres to climb.

The road to Ta-no-hara and the hike to the peak, known as Ken-ga-mine (剣ヶ峰), make for an unforgettable experience, as both the road and the track are lined with small shrines, Shintō gates and religious statues. Throw in cobalt-blue lakes and magnificent views, and Ontake makes a great day-hike from Ta-no-hara – allow five to six hours return. Although there are a few buses from Kiso in summer, having your own wheels will be a blessing here. Early July to late September is the best hiking period.

Alternatively, take a bus from Kiso-Fukushima Station (one way/return ¥1500/2500) to the **Ontake Ropeway** (御嶽ロープウェイ; Map p292; ☎0264-46-2525; www.ontakerope.co.jp; one-way/return ¥1400/2600). Allow five to six hours for the return hike from the top of the ropeway, from where there are tracks to the peak. See the website for bus and ropeway details.

Keep in mind that Ontake-san is an active volcano. Unfortunately for the 63 hikers who lost their lives, Ontake erupted just before lunchtime on Saturday 27 September 2014, covering the mountain in ash. If it had erupted at 3am, very likely no lives would have been lost. Various hiking restrictions have been in place since; find out the latest by contacting the Kiso Tourist Information Center before heading out.

to the north, and also by buses. Both cities are linked to Tokyo by *shinkansen* lines.

Getting Around

Within Hida, there are two popular main routes, with frequent bus services operated by a number of carriers. The first connects Takayama to Okuhida Onsen-gō, Kamikōchi and sections of the northern Alps, and Matsumoto. The second links Takayama to Toyama/Kanazawa via the *gasshō-zukuri* villages of Shirakawa-gō and Gokayama. A wide range of bus tours is also available.

If you're planning to explore the area in some depth, the five-day Shōryūdō Highway Bus ticket (¥14,710), which must be purchased online or from a travel agent outside Japan, covers the Hida region extensively and includes travel to/from Nagoya, Matsumoto and Kanazawa.

You might benefit from purchasing the **Nohi Bus** (濃飛バス; ☎0577-32-1688; www.nouhibus.co.jp/english) four-day Hida Open ticket (adult/child ¥10,290/5150), offering unlimited travel around the region. It's one of a variety of discount passes available.

A car can be useful for explorations within and around the region, but note that in winter many roads become hazardous or impassable.

Takayama

☎0577 / POP 89,278

Takayama (officially known as Hida Takayama; 飛騨高山) has one of Japan's most atmospheric townscapes, with Meiji-era inns, hillside shrines and a pretty riverside setting. It's also home to one of the country's best-loved festivals. A trip here should be high on the list for anyone travelling in Central Honshū.

The town's present layout dates from the late 17th century and incorporates a wealth of museums, galleries andjapan temples for a place of its compact size. Excellent infrastructure and welcoming locals seal the deal. Although its recent rise in popularity can sometimes take the sparkle off what was a little-known hamlet just a decade ago, there's still plenty worth visiting for – a stay during the shoulder seasons will afford a little more tranquillity.

Takayama is easily explored on foot and is the perfect start or end point for sojourns into the Hida region and the northern Japan Alps.

Sights

Most sights are clearly signposted in English and are within walking distance of the train station, which sits between the main streets of Kokubunji-dōri and Hirokōji-dōri. Both run east and cross the Miya-gawa, where they become Yasugawa-dōri and Sanmachi-dōri, respectively.

Once across the river you're in the middle of the infinitely photogenic Sanmachi-suji district, which is made up of three main streets (Ichino-machi, Nino-machi and Sanno-machi). Among the immaculately preserved *furui machinami* (古い町並み; old private houses) are sake breweries, cafes and retailers. Sake breweries here are designated by spheres of cedar fronds hanging above their doors; some are open to the public in January and early February, but most sell their brews year-round.

Southeast of Sanmachi-suji, the Teramachi district has over a dozen temples and shrines you can wander around before taking in the greenery of Shiroyama-kōen. Various trails lead through the park and up the mountainside to the ruins of the castle, **Takayama-jō** (高山城跡; Shiroyama-kōen).

★ Kusakabe Folk Museum — HISTORIC BUILDING

(日下部民藝館, Kusakabe Mingeikan; ☎0577-32-0072; 1-52 Ōjin-machi; adult/child ¥500/300; ⏲9am-4.30pm Mar-Nov, to 4pm Wed-Mon Dec-Feb) This merchant and moneychanger's house, dating from the 1890s, showcases the striking craftsmanship of traditional Takayama carpenters. Inside is a collection of folk art. Rumour has it that a Rockefeller tried to buy the property after WWII; his offer was politely declined.

Karakuri Museum — MUSEUM

(飛騨高山獅子会館·からくりミュージアム; ☎0577-32-0881; www.takayamakarakuri.jp; 53-1 Sakura-machi; adult/child ¥600/400; ⏲9am-4.30pm) On display here are over 300 *shishi* (lion) masks, instruments and drums related to festival dances. The main draw is the twice-hourly puppet show where you can see the mechanical *karakuri ningyō* (marionettes) in action.

Hida Takayama Museum of Art — MUSEUM

(飛騨高山美術館, Hida Takayama Bijutsukan; ☎0577-35-3535; www.htm-museum.co.jp; 1-124-1 Kamiokamoto-chō; adult/child ¥1300/800; ⏲9am-5pm) Lovers of art-nouveau and art-deco glassware and furniture will appreciate this large private gallery set back from town with a ritzy cafe, its own London Bus shuttle (ask at the Tourist Information Center) and a spectacular glass fountain by René Lalique.

Takayama Shōwa-kan — MUSEUM

(高山昭和館; ☎0577-33-7836; www.takayama-showakan.com; 6 Shimoichino-machi; adult/child ¥800/500; ⏲9am-6pm) This nostalgia bonanza from the Shōwa period (1926–89) focuses on 1955 to 1965, a time of great optimism between Japan's postwar malaise and the 1980s economic boom. Lose yourself in the delightful mishmash, from movie posters to cars and everything in between, lovingly presented in a series of themed rooms.

Hida Folk Village — MUSEUM

(飛騨の里, Hida-no-sato; ☎0577-34-4711; www.hidanosato-tpo.jp; 1-590 Kamiokamoto-chō; adult/child ¥700/200; ⏲8.30am-5pm) The sprawling, open-air Hida-no-sato is a highly recommended half-day trip. It features dozens of traditional houses and buildings, which were dismantled at their original sites throughout the region and rebuilt here. Well-presented displays offer the opportunity to envision rural life in previous centuries. During clear weather, there are good views of the Japan Alps. To get here, hire a bicycle or catch a bus from Takayama bus station (¥210, 10 minutes); be sure to check return bus times.

Takayama Festival Floats Exhibition Hall — MUSEUM

(高山屋台会館, Takayama Yatai-kaikan; ☎0577-32-5100; 178 Sakura-machi; adult/child ¥900/450; ⏲9am-5pm Mar-Nov, to 4.30pm Dec-Feb) A rotating selection of four of the 23 multitiered *yatai* (floats) used in Takayama Matsuri (p248) can be appreciated here. These spectacular creations, some dating from the 17th century, are prized for their flamboyant carvings, metalwork and lacquerware. Some floats feature *karakuri ningyō* (marionettes) that perform amazing feats at the hands of of eight accomplished puppeteers manipulating 36 strings.

The museum is on the grounds of the stately **Sakurayama Hachiman-gū** (桜山八幡宮; ☎0577-32-0240; www.hidahachimangu.jp/english) FREE, which presides over the festival.

Takayama-jinya — HISTORIC BUILDING

(高山陣屋; ☎0577-32-0643; 1-5 Hachiken-machi; ¥430; ⏲8.45am-4.30pm Sep-Jul, to 6pm Aug) These sprawling grounds south

Takayama

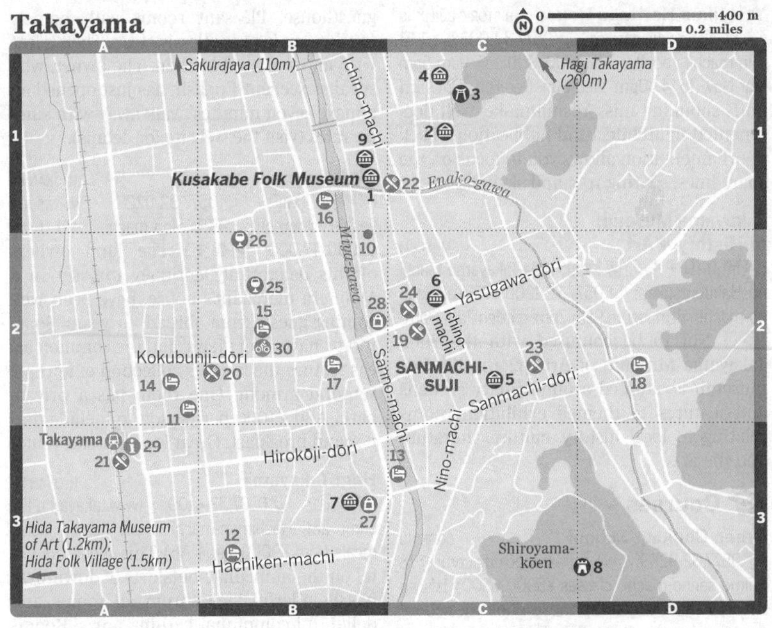

Takayama

Top Sights
1 Kusakabe Folk Museum........B1

Sights
2 Karakuri Museum........C1
3 Sakurayama Hachiman-gū........C1
4 Takayama Festival Floats Exhibition Hall........C1
5 Takayama Museum of History & Art........C2
6 Takayama Shōwa-kan........C2
7 Takayama-jinya........B3
8 Takayama-jō........D3
9 Yoshijima Heritage House........B1

Activities, Courses & Tours
10 Green Cooking School........B2

Sleeping
11 Guesthouse Tomaru........A2
12 Hida Takayama Temple Inn Zenkō-ji........B3
13 Honjin Hiranoya........C3
14 Oyado koto no Yume........A2
15 Rickshaw Inn........B2
16 Sumiyoshi Ryokan........B1
17 Tanabe Ryokan........B2
18 Yamakyū........D2

Eating
19 Ebisu-Honten........C2
20 Heianraku........B2
21 iCafe Takayama........A3
22 Kyōya........C1
23 Shōjin Ryōri Kakushō........C2
24 Takumi-ya........C2

Drinking & Nightlife
25 Bols........B2
26 Red Hill Pub........B2

Shopping
27 Jinya-mae Asa-ichi........B3
28 Miya-gawa Asa-ichi........B2

Information
29 Hida Takayama Tourist Information Center........A3

Transport
30 Hara Cycle........B2

of Sanmachi-suji house the only remaining prefectural office building of the Tokugawa shogunate, originally the administrative centre for the Kanamori clan. The present main building dates back to 1816 and was used as local-government offices until 1969. There's also a rice granary, a garden and a torture chamber with explanatory detail. Free guided tours in English are available (reservations advised).

Yoshijima Heritage House HISTORIC BUILDING
(吉島家, Yoshijima-ke; ☎0577-32-0038; 1-51 Ōjin-machi; adult/child ¥500/300; ⏰9am-5pm Mar-Nov, to 4.30pm Wed-Sun Dec-Feb) Design buffs shouldn't miss Yoshijima-ke, well documented in architectural publications. Lack of ornamentation allows you to focus on the spare lines, soaring roof and skylight.

Takayama Museum of History & Art MUSEUM
(飛騨高山まちの博物館, Hida-Takayama Machi no Hakubutsukan; ☎0577-32-1205; 75 Kamiichi-no-machi; ⏰museum 9am-7pm, garden 7am-9pm) FREE Not to be confused with the Hida Takayama Museum of Art (p246), this free museum is situated around pretty gardens and features 14 themed exhibition rooms relating to local history, culture, literature and the arts.

Courses

Green Cooking School COOKING
(☎0577-32-9263; www.green-cooking.com; 78 Shimo-sanno-machi; classes ¥6000-6500) It's so nice to discover a Japanese cooking school for foreign visitors in Takayama! Learn about the basics of Japanese cooking, then dine on your handiwork. Two days' notice and a minimum of two participants are required for classes to proceed.

Festivals & Events

Takayama Matsuri PARADE
One of Japan's great festivals, the Takayama Matsuri is in two parts. On 14 and 15 April there's the **Sannō Matsuri**, when a dozen decorated *yatai* (floats) are paraded through the town. **Hachiman Matsuri**, on 9 and 10 October, is a slightly smaller version.

In the evenings, the floats, with their carvings, dolls, colourful curtains and blinds, are decked out with lanterns and the procession is accompanied by sacred music.

Sleeping

If visiting during festival times, book accommodation months in advance and expect to pay a 20% premium. The Ryokan Hotel Association (www.takayamaryokan.jp) can assist with lodging enquiries.

Guesthouse Tomaru GUESTHOUSE ¥
(飛騨高山ゲストハウスとまる; ☎0577-62-9260; www.hidatakayama-guesthouse.com; 6-5 Hanasato-machi; dm ¥2500, s & d ¥7000, tr ¥9000; ❄@📶) Visitors love the friendly homestay vibe of this small, centrally located guesthouse. Pleasant rooms with homely touches are kept spotlessly clean. There's free wi-fi and a shared kitchen. The owner, who speaks excellent English, has just opened an annexe seven minutes' walk away with similar rates (visit the website for details).

★ **Sumiyoshi Ryokan** RYOKAN ¥¥
(寿美吉旅館; ☎0577-32-0228; www.sumiyoshi-ryokan.com; 4-21 Hon-machi; s/d from ¥9000/12,000; P@📶) The kind owners of this delightfully antiquey inn, set in a Meiji-era merchant's house, have been welcoming guests from abroad for years. Some rooms have river views, and the common areas feature the family's collection of antique samurai armour. One room has a private bath. Add ¥4000 per person to include dinner and breakfast. Great location and value.

Hagi Takayama RYOKAN ¥¥
(萩高山; ☎0577-32-4100; www.takayama-kh.com; 280 Hachiman-machi; r per person incl 2 meals from ¥9000; P❄📶) This elevated hotel on the immediate outskirts of downtown has wonderful views from all rooms and delightful communal bathing areas. Rooms in the main wing were refurbished most recently. Expect traditional service, fine local cuisine and a wonderful green location in the hills above Takayama, which makes it ideal for those with a car (parking in the town below can be tricky).

Honjin Hiranoya RYOKAN ¥¥
(本陣平野屋; ☎0577-34-1234; www.honjinhiranoya.co.jp; 1-5 Hon-machi; r per person incl 2 meals from ¥12,000; P❄📶) For a ryokan experience in a business-hotel setting, choose the contemporary elegance of the executive rooms in the Kachoan wing (from ¥25,000 per person including meals), which also features four newly refurbished suites. Otherwise opt for a river-view room in the Bekkan (Annexe) wing. There's a free shuttle bus from the train station, or it's a 10-minute walk. Service standards are high.

Rickshaw Inn HOTEL ¥¥
(力車イン; ☎0577-32-2890; www.rickshawinn.com; 54 Suehiro-chō; tw from ¥11,900, s without bathroom from ¥4200; ⊖❄@📶) Well positioned on the fringe of Takayama's entertainment district, this consistent travellers' favourite remains good value. There's a range of room types, a small kitchen, laundry facilities and a cosy lounge. The friendly English-speaking owners are fonts of information about Takayama. Breakfast is an extra ¥540.

Yamakyū RYOKAN ¥¥
(山久; ☎0577-32-3756; www.takayama-yamakyu.com; 58 Tenshōji-machi; r per person incl 2 meals from ¥9500; P@📶) Occupying a lovely hillside spot opposite Hokke-ji temple, Yamakyū is a 20-minute walk from the train station. Inside, antique-filled curio cabinets, clocks and lamps line the red-carpeted corridors. All 20 tatami rooms have a sink and a toilet, and the common baths are of a high standard. Some English is spoken.

This is an excellent choice for a ryokan experience without the expense.

★**Oyado koto no Yume** RYOKAN ¥¥¥
(おやど古都の夢; ☎0577-32-0427; www.kotoyume-peace.com; 6-11 Hanasato-machi; r per person incl breakfast ¥15,000; ❄📶) You'll be impressed by the friendly, professional staff at this wonderful hybrid of a boutique hotel and a traditional ryokan, whose all-tatami rooms are furnished with a stylish fusion of old and new. Be sure to book the indoor rooftop *kazoku-buro* (family bath). Conveniently located near the train station.

Hida Takayama Temple Inn Zenkō-ji HOTEL ¥¥¥
(飛騨高山善光寺宿坊; ☎0577-32-8470; www.takayamahostelzenkoji.com; 4-3 Tenman-machi; d from ¥28,000; P🚭📶) Good karma washes over this branch of Nagano's famous Zenkō-ji (p291), where donations are accepted in return for accommodation. Private rooms are generously proportioned and set around a courtyard garden. There's a shared kitchen and no curfew for respectful guests.

Tanabe Ryokan RYOKAN ¥¥¥
(旅館田邊; ☎0577-32-0529; www.tanabe-ryokan.jp; 58 Aioi-chō; r per person incl 2 meals from ¥20,000; 🚭❄@📶) This smart ryokan has a central location, and its tiny, elderly proprietress is worth a visit all on her own. All tatami rooms have an en-suite bath, although the lovely common baths with their beamed ceilings are worth enjoying. A sumptuous dinner of *kaiseki*-style Hida cuisine completes the experience.

Eating

Heianraku CHINESE ¥
(平安楽; ☎0577-32-3078; 6-7-2 Tenman-machi; dishes from ¥740; ⊙11.30am-1pm & 5-8pm Wed-Mon; 🖋) Atmospheric, inexpensive, welcoming and delicious are all words that spring to mind when describing this wonderful second-generation eatery serving up Chinese delights (including transcendent *gyōza*) in a traditional Japanese shopfront on Kokubunji-dōri. Special diets catered to and English spoken.

iCafe Takayama CAFE ¥
(www.icafe-takayama.com; 1-22-11 Showa-machi; light meals from ¥500; ⊙7.30am-7pm; 📶) Run by the inspiring crew from Satoyama Experience (p251) in neighbouring Hida-Furukawa, this new-in-2016 cafe in the slick Takayama Station is your one-stop shop for all things Hida. It's a great first port of call as you arrive in town, offering tasty snacks, good coffee and healthy servings of expert local knowledge. There's free wi-fi and oodles of baggage storage.

Ebisu-Honten NOODLES ¥
(恵比寿本店; ☎0577-32-0209; www.takayama-ebisu.jp; 46 Kamini-no-machi; noodle bowls from ¥880; ⊙10am-5pm Thu-Tue; 🖋) These folks have been making *teuchi* (handmade) soba since 1898. Try the *zaru soba,* which strips it bare so you can taste the flavour of the noodles. The *tororo nameko soba* is also very good: noodles in a hot soup with boiled mushroom and grated mountain potato. The building has an interesting red-glass sign with white characters and a little roof on it.

★**Sakurajaya** FUSION ¥¥
(さくら茶屋; ☎0577-57-7565; 3-8-14 Sowa-machi; dinner courses from ¥3000; ⊙11.30am-2pm & 6-10pm Thu-Tue; 🖋) Sakurajaya happens when you take a Japanese man to Germany, introduce him to European culinary arts, hone his craft, then return him to the quiet back lanes of Takayama. His artisanal creations draw from both German and Japanese lines. There's something for all palates and it's well worth the walk.

★**Kyōya** SHOKUDO ¥¥
(京や; ☎0577-34-7660; www.kyoya-hida.jp; 1-77 Ōjin-machi; mains ¥800-5200; ⊙11am-10pm Wed-Mon) This Takayama institution specialises in regional dishes such as *hoba-miso* (sweet miso paste grilled on a magnolia leaf) and *Hida-gyū* (beef) soba. Sit on tatami mats around long charcoal grills, under a dark-timber cathedral ceiling. It's on a corner, by a bridge over the canal. Look for sacks of rice over the door.

Takumi-ya BARBECUE ¥¥
(匠家; ☎0577-36-2989; 2 Shimo-ni-no-machi; mains downstairs ¥680-980, upstairs from ¥1500; ⊙11am-3pm & 5-9pm Thu-Tue) *Hida-gyū* (Hida

beef) on a burger budget. Adjacent to Takumi-ya's butcher shop is a casual restaurant specialising in ramen in beef broth and *Hida gyū-don* (beef and onion over rice). The upstairs restaurant serves *yakiniku* (Korean-style barbecue).

Shōjin Ryōri Kakushō VEGETARIAN ¥¥¥
(精進料理角正; ☎0577-32-0174; 2-98 Baba-machi; kaiseki dinner courses per person from ¥13,000; ⏲11.30am-1.30pm & 5-7pm; ✎) Experience the unique Japanese art of *shōjin-ryōri,* holistic vegetarian *kaiseki* dining in an atmospheric building and garden that's almost 200 years old, surrounded by ancient temples and mountains beyond. Sound dreamy? If you're a fan of the genre, it really, really is.

Drinking & Nightlife

Red Hill Pub PUB
(レッド・ヒル; ☎0577-33-8139; 2-4 Sowa-chō; ⏲7pm-midnight; 📶) You'll feel like you're walking into a friend's living room in this cosy, dimly lit basement bar. The hip and happy owner, Hisayo, deftly adjusts the vibe to suit the patrons present. It's sometimes soulful and smooth, sometimes rocking and raucous. If it's quiet and you're alone, you'll still have someone fascinating to talk to – Hisayo speaks excellent English.

Bols SPORTS BAR
(☎0577-35-1762; 72-1 Suehiro-machi; ⏲9pm-2am Tue-Sun) There's no cover charge at this friendly pub-sports bar with a great open patio out front. It's American-Euro styled but stocks a good selection of Japanese beer.

DON'T MISS

TAKAYAMA'S MORNING MARKETS

Daily *asa-ichi* (morning markets) are a wonderful way to wake up and get a sense of the place. The **Jinya-mae Asa-ichi** (陣屋前朝市; www.jinya-asaichi.jp; 1-5 Hachiken-machi; ⏲6am-noon) is in front of Takayama-jinya (p246); the larger **Miya-gawa Asa-ichi** (宮川朝市; www.asaichi.net; ⏲7am-noon) runs along the east bank of the Miya-gawa, between Kaji-bashi and Yayoi-bashi. Stalls range from farm-fresh produce to local arts and crafts. Autumnal apples are out of this world!

Shopping

Takayama is renowned for arts and crafts. Look for *ichii ittobori* (yew woodcarvings), *shunkei* lacquerware, and the rustic *yamada-yaki* and decorative *shibukusa-yaki* styles of pottery. Between Sanmachi-dōri and Yasugawa-dōri, near the Takayama Museum of History & Art (p248), are plenty of wonderful *kobutsu* (古物; antique) shops.

The city's most ubiquitous souvenirs, however, are *saru-bobo* (monkey babies). These little red dolls with pointy limbs and featureless faces recall the days when grandmothers fashioned dolls for children out of whatever materials were available.

Information

Tourist Information Center (飛騨高山観光案内所; ☎0577-32-5328; www.hida.jp/english; ⏲8.30am-5pm Nov-Mar, to 6.30pm Apr-Oct) Directly in front of JR Takayama Station, knowledgeable English-speaking staff dispense maps in English and other languages, and a wealth of pamphlets on sights, accommodation, special events and regional transport. Staff are unable to assist with accommodation reservations.

Free wi-fi is available for visitors throughout the downtown area. Check in with the TIC upon arrival for the wi-fi password, which gets you access for one week.

Getting There & Away

BUS

Nōhi Bus (p245) operates highway bus services between Takayama and Tokyo's Shinjuku Station (¥6690, 5½ hours, several daily; reservations required), Matsumoto (¥3190, 2½ hours) and Kanazawa (¥3390, 2¼ hours). Schedules vary seasonally and some routes don't run at all during winter, when many roads are closed.

TRAIN

From Tokyo or cities to the south (Kyoto, Osaka, Hiroshima, Fukuoka), Takayama can be reached by catching a frequent *shinkansen* (bullet-train) service to Nagoya, then connecting with the JR Takayama line (*tokkyū* ¥5510, 2½ hours).

Another option from Tokyo is to pick up the JR Takayama line from its northern terminus in Toyama (¥12,210, 1½ hours). Get to Toyama on the shiny, new-in-2015 Hokuriku *shinkansen:* the trains are fabulous.

Either way, the mountainous ride along the Hida-gawa is spectacular.

Getting Around

Most sights in Takayama can be covered easily on foot. You can amble from the train station to Teramachi in about 20 minutes. Takayama is bicycle friendly, but rentals can be expensive. Try **Hara Cycle** (ハラサイクル; ☎0577-32-1657; 61 Suehiro-chō; 1st hour ¥300, additional hour ¥200, per day ¥1300; ⊙9am-8pm Wed-Mon). Some lodgings lend bikes for free.

Hida-Furukawa

☎0577 / POP 24,726

Just 15 minutes by train from Takayama, Hida-Furukawa (飛騨古川) is a sleepy riverside town with a friendly, ageing population eager to preserve their local history and culture. Photogenic streetscapes, peaceful temples and interesting museums are framed by the dramatic Hida mountains. Each April the town comes to life for the Furukawa Matsuri.

Five minutes' walk from JR Hida-Furukawa Station, **Seto-kawa & Shirakabe-dōzō** (瀬戸川と白壁土蔵街) is a lovely, historic canal district with white-walled shops, storehouses, private homes and carp-filled waterways. Across the canal, **Ichino-machi** is sprinkled with woodworking shops, sake breweries (marked by spheres of cedar fronds above the entrance) and traditional storehouses.

Tours

★Satoyama Experience CULTURAL
(☎0577-73-5715; https://satoyama-experience.com; 8-11 Nino-machi; half-day tours from ¥4900; ⊙9am-6pm) The fantastic crew at Satoyama Experience are eager to introduce you to their beloved region, culture and people. Small-group cycling tours include a friendly, English-speaking guide, mountain-bike rental and insurance. A variety of tours (including walking) cater to different levels of fitness, but all capture the spirit and scenery of Hida. Highly recommended.

The team can also connect you with some unique, traditional accommodation (for longer stays) in town and around – just ask.

Festivals & Events

Furukawa Matsuri PARADE
(古川祭り; ⊙19 & 20 Apr) Furukawa Matsuri – informally known as Hadaka Matsuri (Naked Festival) – consists of parades of *yatai* (festival floats). The highlight is an event known as Okoshi Daiko: on the night of 19 April, squads of boisterous young men, dressed in *fundoshi* (loincloths) and fuelled by sake, parade through town. They compete to place small drums atop a stage bearing a giant drum.

OK, it's not *naked* naked, but you can see how the festival got its nickname.

Eating

Ichino-machi Cafe CAFE ¥
(壱之町珈琲店; ☎0577-73-7099; 1-12 Ichino-machi; cakes from ¥400; ⊙11am-5pm Wed-Mon; 📶) Chiffon cake, melon bread and local Hida-beef curry are all items you might find on the menu at this handsome cafe within a restored traditional *machiya* (merchant house). Free wi-fi is a bonus.

Information

There's a Tourist Information Center at the bus station with some English maps and leaflets, though little English is spoken.

Getting There & Around

Hida-Furukawa is serviced by the *tokkyū* (limited express) Hida trains between Nagoya (¥5510, 2¾ hours) and Toyama (¥1490, 1¾ hours).

Local trains run frequently between Hida-Furukawa and Takayama, three stops south (¥240, 15 minutes).

From the train station it's easy to stroll around central Furukawa, or you can hire bikes at nearby **Miyagawa Taxi** (宮川タクシー古川営業所; ☎0577-73-2321; 10-41 Furukawa-cho; bicycle rental per hour ¥200) or take a tour with Satoyama Experience.

Okuhida Onsen-gō

Meaning 'deep Hida hot springs', Okuhida Onsen-gō – comprising the villages of Hirayu Onsen, Fukuji Onsen, Shin-Hirayu Onsen, Tochio Onsen and Shin-Hotaka Onsen – has a tough battle with Shirakawa-gō for being the jewel in Hida's crown. Certainly it's where you'll find some of the loveliest *onsen ryokan* (traditional hot-spring inns) and alpine scenery in all of Japan.

DON'T MISS

HIDA CUISINE

Hida's culinary fame rests in *Hida-gyū* (Hida beef), *hoba-miso* (sweet miso paste grilled at the table on a magnolia leaf) and soba, but you'll find a wealth of seasonal local produce used in a variety of cooking in the area.

It's impossible to compare the two contenders, and you'd be well advised to visit as much of the Hida Region as you can, but if time is limited it's well worth taking the journey deep into the mountains to spend a tranquil evening here. Of the five villages, Hirayu, Fukuji and Shin-Hotaka Onsen have the most to offer visitors, by way of their wonderful ryokan. If the weather's clear, take a ride on the Shin-Hotaka Ropeway.

Sleeping & Eating

Some of Japan's most beautiful and peaceful *onsen ryokan* are found in the area's five villages: almost all are expensive, but they're worth every yen.

There are very few cafes and restaurants in these remote communities; most visitors dine on sumptuous *kaiseki* (Japanese haute cuisine) at their ryokan.

Getting There & Away

This remote alpine region can only be accessed by road; routes can become treacherous or impassable in winter. Bus services from Matsumoto are operated by Alpico (p282), those from Takayama by Nōhi Bus (p245).

If you don't get carsick and aren't scared of heights, consider renting a car in Takayama or Matsumoto for greater freedom to explore. However, self-driving is not recommended in winter.

Hirayu Onsen

0578

Hirayu Onsen (平湯温泉) is a hub for bus transport and the best base for day trips to Kamikōchi, neighbouring Shirahone and Fukuji Onsen, and the Shin-Hotaka Ropeway. There's a pleasant, low-to-the-ground cluster of onsen lodgings, about half of which open for day bathers. Even the bus station has a rooftop *rotemburo* (outdoor bath; ¥600).

Sleeping & Eating

Hirayu has a higher concentration of accommodation than elsewhere in the Alps, save for Kamikōchi. It's a good place to base yourself if you're a single traveller, you're on a budget or you can't get a room in the region's more famous ryokan.

There are a few basic eateries in the village and around the bus station, but not all tend to be open on the same days.

Hirayu Camping Ground CAMPGROUND ¥
(平湯キャンプ場; 0578-89-2610; www.hirayu-camp.com; 768-36 Hirayu; campsites per adult/child ¥600/400, bungalows from ¥5800, parking from ¥1000, hiking fee ¥300; late Apr-Oct; P) To reach the small Hirayu Camping Ground, turn right from the bus station – it's about 700m ahead, on the left.

Hirayu-no-mori RYOKAN ¥¥
(ひらゆの森; 0578-89-3338; www.hirayunomori.co.jp; 763-1 Hirayu; r per person incl 2 meals ¥7500; P) Practically in its own forest uphill from the bus station, this sprawling *onsen ryokan* (traditional hot-spring inn) boasts 16 *rotemburo* (outdoor baths), plus indoor and private baths. After 9pm baths are exclusively for overnight guests. Rooms are Japanese style, and meals are hearty and local.

Miyama Ouan RYOKAN ¥¥¥
(深山桜庵; 0578-89-2799; www.hotespa.net/hotels/miyamaouan; 229 Hirayu; r per person incl 2 meals from ¥17,000; P) This recently built chain ryokan has traditional service, modern technology and intimate personal touches. Seventy-two rooms in a variety of sizes and styles are beautifully finished with cypress woods and chic design – all have private facilities. The private *kazoku-buro* (family use) *rotemburo* (outdoor bath) is a little piece of heaven. Staff will even collect you from the bus station.

Information

Tourist Information Center (観光案内所; 0578-89-3030; 763-191 Hirayu; 9.30am-5.30pm) Opposite the bus station; has leaflets and maps, and can book accommodation. Little English is spoken.

Getting There & Away

Nōhi (p245) operates regular express buses that stop at Hirayu Onsen, which is almost midway between Takayama (¥1820, one hour) and Matsumoto (¥3190, 1½ hours).

Buses between Takayama and Shin-Hotaka Onsen also stop at Hirayu Onsen.

Fukuji Onsen

0578

Tiny Fukuji Onsen (福地温泉), a short ride north of Hirayu Onsen, follows a steep hill. The site has beautiful views and a handful of outstanding baths. Otherwise, there's not even a village here.

Activities

Mukashibanashi-no-sato (Isurugi-no-yu) ONSEN
(昔ばなしの里·石動の湯; ☎0578-89-2793; 110 Fukuji Onsen; bath ¥500; ⏲10am-4pm Thu-Tue) This restaurant-onsen is set back from the street in a traditional farmhouse with fine indoor and outdoor baths, free on the 26th of each month. Out front is an unmissable vintage knick-knack shop adorned with Shōwa-era movie posters and advertisements. If travelling by bus, get off at Fukuji-Onsen-Kami stop.

Sleeping

★**Yumoto Chōza** RYOKAN ¥¥¥
(湯元長座; ☎0578-89-0099; www.cyouza.com; 786 Fukuji; r per person with 2 meals from ¥19,000; P ❄) Opposite Fukuji-Onsen-shimo bus stop, the entrance to Yumoto Chōza is reached by a rustic covered walkway, as if to take you back in time. Bold, dark woods punctuate the handsome traditional architecture. Half of the 32 rooms have en suites and *irori* (fireplaces), and there are five indoor baths and two stunning *rotemburo* (outdoor baths). Reservations essential.

Day visitors can bathe between 2pm and 6pm for ¥750.

Yamazato-no-iori Soene RYOKAN ¥¥¥
(山里のいおり　草円; ☎0578-89-1116; www.soene.com; 831 Fukuji Onsen; r per person incl 2 meals from ¥19,000; P 📶) Atmosphere abounds here: this rustic ryokan is more than 100 years old. Its indoor and outdoor baths are absolutely delightful, as are the views. Rooms are spacious and have an air of romance. Delicious *kaiseki* (Japanese haute cuisine) is served in the dining room. A little English is spoken and there's wi-fi in the lobby.

Open year-round, this is one for all seasons.

Getting There & Away

By bus from Hirayu Onsen, you can get off at the Fukuji-Onsen-Kami stop and walk downhill to check out the ryokan, then pick up the bus to return to Hirayu or travel onward to Shirahone Onsen.

Shin-Hotaka Onsen

☎0578

The delightful sleepy hollow of Shin-Hotaka Onsen (新穂高温泉) is famed for the Shin-Hotaka Ropeway, Japan's longest, one of the largest *rotemburo* (outdoor baths) in the country, and its handful of magical lodgings, including an utterly lovable riverside *onsen ryokan* (traditional hot-spring inn).

DON'T MISS

BEST ONSEN

- Nakabusa Onsen (p283)
- Takaragawa Onsen (p306)
- Ōshirakawa Rotemburo (p255)
- Awanoyu (p284)
- Karukaya Sansō (p254)

Activities

★**Shin-Hotaka Ropeway** CABLE CAR
(新穂高ロープウェイ; ☎0578-89-2252; www.shinhotaka-ropeway.jp; one-way/return ¥1600/2900; ⏲8.30am-4.30pm) From a starting elevation of 1308m, two cable cars whisk you to 2156m, towards the peak of Nishi Hotaka-dake (2909m). Views from the top, from observation decks and walking trails, are spectacular. In winter, snows can be shoulder deep. In season, properly equipped hikers with ample time can choose from several hikes beginning from the top cable-car station (Nishi Hotaka-guchi).

The three-hour hike to Kamikōchi is much easier than going the other way.

Shin-Hotaka-no-yu ONSEN
(新穂高の湯; ☎0578-89-2458; Okuhida Onsen-go Kansaka; ⏲8am-9pm May-Oct) FREE Exhibitionists will love this bare-bones *konyoku* (mixed-bathing) *rotemburo* (outdoor bath) by the Kamata-gawa, visible from the bridge that passes over it. Entry is free (or by donation). Enter through segregated change rooms, and emerge into a single large pool. Women should bring their own modesty garment, and don't expect men to wear theirs. Be sure to mind your manners.

Nakazaki Sansou Okuhida-no-yu ONSEN
(中崎山荘奥飛騨の湯; ☎0578-89-2021; 710 Okuhida Onsengo Kansaka; adult/child ¥800/400; ⏲8am-8pm) More than 50 years old but completely rebuilt in 2010, this facility commands a spectacular vista of the mountains. The milky waters of its large indoor baths and *rotemburo* (outdoor baths) do wonders for dry skin.

Sleeping

Kazeya RYOKAN ¥¥

(風屋; ☎0578-89-0112; www.kazeyatakayamajapan.com; 440-1 Kansaka; r per person incl breakfast from ¥8000; P❄☜) Recently renovated, this gorgeous little 10-room traditional inn has atmospheric rooms with private baths and two blissful private *rotemburo* (outdoor baths). Deluxe rooms have their own onsen and offer some of the best value in this beautiful corner of rural Japan.

Karukaya Sansō HOTEL ¥¥

(佳留萱山荘; ☎0578-89-2801; www.karukaya.co.jp; 555 Kansaka; r per person incl 2 meals from ¥13,000; P❄☜) The tatami rooms at this friendly riverside inn with lots of open space to explore are clean, tidy and unexceptional, but for the better ones, which have lovely views. The enormous *konyoku rotemburo* (mixed-bathing outdoor baths), claimed to be the largest in Japan, are remarkable. However, add in the sweeping mountain views and they're quite extraordinary.

Campsites (adult/child ¥3000/1500) are available or you can come just to use the *rotemburo* (¥600; 10am to 3pm).

★**Yarimikan** RYOKAN ¥¥¥

(槍見舘; ☎0578-89-2808; www.yarimikan.com; Okuhida Onsen-gun Kansaka; r per person with meals from ¥17,000; P❄☜) Yarimikan is a wonderfully traditional *onsen ryokan* (hot-spring inn) on the Kamata-gawa, with two indoor baths, eight riverside *rotemburo* (outdoor baths; some available for private use) and 15 rooms. Guests can bathe 24 hours a day (it's stunning by moonlight) and day visitors (¥600 including towel rental) are accepted between 10am and 2pm. Cuisine features local Hida beef and grilled freshwater fish.

It's just off Rte 475, a few kilometres before the Shin-Hotaka Ropeway.

Information

Oku-Hida Spa Tourist Information Center (奥飛騨温泉郷観光案内所; ☎0578-89-2614; ⊙10am-5pm) On Hwy 471 before the bridge, as the road turns into Hwy 475 towards the ropeway.

Getting There & Away

Buses run from Takayama to Hirayu Onsen, then do a whistle-stop run to the Shin-Hotaka Ropeway (p253) terminus (¥2160, 1½ hours) at the far end of Shin-Hotaka Onsen.

From Matsumoto, an express bus to the Shin-Hotaka Ropeway terminus (¥2880, two hours) transits Hirayu Onsen.

Shirakawa-gō & Gokayama

The remote, mountainous districts of Shirakawa-gō (白川郷) and Gokayama, between Takayama and Kanazawa, are best known for farmhouses in the thatched *gasshō-zukuri* style. They're rustic and lovely whether set against the vibrant colours of spring, draped with the gentle mists of autumn, or peeking through a carpet of snow, and they hold a special place in the Japanese heart.

Most of Shirakawa-gō's sights are in Ogimachi, which has more tour buses than thatch-roofed houses. The less crowded, more isolated villages of Suganuma and Ainokura, in the Gokayama district of Toyama Prefecture, have the most ambience; other sights are spread over many kilometres along Rte 156. All three villages are Unesco World Heritage Sites.

Passionate debate continues around the impact tour buses have upon these unique communities, and how best to mitigate disruption to local life. To avoid the crowds, steer clear of weekends, holidays, and cherry-blossom and autumn-foliage seasons.

Sleeping & Eating

To best appreciate life here, stay overnight in a *gasshō-zukuri* inn. Accommodation is basic and advance reservations are recommended. Otherwise the area can be visited as a day trip from Takayama, Takaoka, Toyama or Kanazawa.

There's little in the way of dining options, save for a few touristy cafes in the 'day-tripper' villages. Meals are generally provided by your accommodation if you're staying overnight.

Information

Be sure to bring enough cash – ATMs are sparse and credit cards rarely accepted.

Getting There & Away

Access to the region is by road only. Self-driving is an increasingly popular way to explore. Ogimachi (Shirakawa-gō) is a quick and easy drive from Takayama if you have your own wheels. Beyond, the *gasshō* villages of Gokayama are a bit more of a trek and generally require an onward commitment towards the Sea of Japan, or that you approach from the north (Toyama).

Frequent bus services are operated by **Nōhi Bus** (濃飛バス; ☎0577-32-1688; www.nouhibus.

co.jp/english), from Takayama, and **Kaetsunou Bus** (加越能バス; ☎0766-22-4886; www.kaetsunou.co.jp), from Takaoka, and a plethora of day tours are available, departing from Takayama, Takaoka, Toyama and Kanazawa.

In colder months, check conditions in advance with regional tourist offices before setting out on any national roads.

Ogimachi

☎05769 / POP 1668

Ogimachi (荻町), the Shirakawa-gō region's central and most accessible settlement, has the largest concentration of *gasshō-zukuri* buildings – more than 110. Sadly, mass tourism has turned the village into a rather disheartening theme park; the valley is overrun with tour buses and many inhabitants seem hardened by the influx. Visit Ogimachi only if you're very motivated to take in *gasshō-zukuri* architecture but too pressed for time to travel to settlements further into the Gokayama mountains.

Wada-ke (和田家; ☎05769-6-1058; adult/child ¥300/100; ⌚9am-5pm) is Shirakawa-gō's largest *gasshō* house and a designated National Treasure. It once belonged to a wealthy silk-trading family and dates back to the mid-Edo period. Upstairs you'll find silk-harvesting equipment and a valuable lacquerware collection.

Generally, for tourism purposes the names Ogimachi and Shirakawa-gō are interchangeable.

Activities

Ōshirakawa Rotemburo ONSEN

(大白川露天風呂; ☎05769-6-1311; ¥300; ⌚8.30am-5pm mid-Jun–Oct, to 6pm Jul & Aug) This tiny, middle-of-nowhere onsen is 40km from Ogimachi, along a mountainous winding road with blind curves that's impassible much of the year. There's no public transport, which is part of the charm, as are the views of Lake Shiramizu. Getting here from Ogimachi takes at least 1½ hours and requires determination and a car, or a taxi and lots of cash.

Sleeping & Eating

For online reservations at one of Ogimachi's many *gasshō* inns, try www.japaneseguesthouses.com. Rates include two meals. Expect a nightly heating surcharge (¥400 and up) during cold weather.

Shirakawa-gō-no-yu HOTEL ¥¥

(白川郷の湯; ☎05769-6-0026; www.shirakawagou-onsen.jp; 337 Ogimachi; r per person incl 2 meals from ¥13,000; ❄📶) Day bathers (adult/child ¥700/300) at the town's only onsen can choose from a sauna, a small *rotemburo* (outdoor bath) and a large communal bath from 10am to 9.30pm. Overnight guests can enjoy the facilities without the crowds. Pleasant, modern tatami rooms have shared facilities; the more expensive rooms have private bathrooms. Western-style twin rooms are also available but lack appeal.

GASSHŌ-ZUKURI ARCHITECTURE

Hida winters can be unforgiving, and its people braved the elements long before the advent of propane heaters and 4WD vehicles. The most visible symbol of their adaptability is *gasshō-zukuri* architecture, as seen in the steeply slanted, straw-roofed homes that dot the regional landscape.

Sharply angled roofs prevent snow accumulation, a serious concern in an area where most mountain roads close from December to April. The name *gasshō* comes from the Japanese word for prayer, because the shape of the roofs was thought to resemble a pair of steepled hands. *Gasshō* buildings often feature pillars crafted from stout cedars to lend extra support. The attic areas are ideal for silk cultivation. Larger *gasshō-zukuri* buildings were inhabited by wealthy families, with up to 30 people under one roof. Peasant families lived in huts so small that today they'd only be considered fit for use as tool sheds.

The art of *gasshō-zukuri* construction is dying out. Most remaining buildings have been relocated to folk villages, including Hida-no-sato (p246) and those at **Ogimachi** (合掌造り民家園, Gasshō-zukuri Minka-en; ☎05769-6-1231; www.shirakawago-minkaen.jp; 2499 Ogimachi; adult/child ¥600/400; ⌚8.40am-5pm Apr-Nov, 9am-6pm Fri-Wed Dec-Mar), Suganuma (p256) and Ainokura (p256). Homes that are now neighbours may once have been separated by several days of travel on foot or by sled. These cultural-preservation efforts have made it possible to imagine a bygone life in the Hida hills.

Magoemon INN ¥¥

(孫右ェ門; ☎05769-6-1167; 360 Ogimachi; r per person incl 2 meals & without bathroom from ¥10,000; P❄📶) This building is 300 years old and oozes history and charm – great for an authentic and atmospheric retreat. The friendly family owners speak no English and appreciate your efforts to communicate in Japanese. Meals are served around the handsome *irori* (hearth). Three of the six large rooms face the river.

Kōemon INN ¥¥

(幸エ門; ☎05769-6-1446; 546 Ogimachi; r per person incl 2 meals from ¥10,000; P❄📶) In the centre of Ogimachi, Kōemon has five rooms with heated floors, dark-wood panelling and shared bathrooms. The fifth-generation owner speaks English well and his love of Shirakawa-gō is infectious.

Irori SHOKUDO ¥

(いろり; ☎05769-6-1737; 374-1 Ogimachi; dishes from ¥432, set menu from ¥1296; ⏲11am-3pm; 📝) At the entrance to Ogimachi, this bustling eatery serves regional specialities such as *hoba-miso* (sweet miso paste grilled at the table on a magnolia leaf), *yaki-dofu* (fried tofu) and soba or udon *teishoku* (set meals). You can eat at tables or around the *irori* (hearth).

Ochūdo CAFE ¥

(落人; ☎090-5458-0418; 792 Ogimachi; lunch ¥1000; ⏲10.30am-5pm) Set around a large *irori* (hearth) in a 350-year-old *gasshō* house, this delightful cafe serves curry rice, tea and coffee.

ℹ Information

Pick up free multilingual maps at the **Tourist Information Center** (白川郷観光協会; ☎05769-6-1013; 2495-3 Ogimachi; ⏲9am-5pm) by the main bus stop outside the Folk Village.

ℹ Getting There & Away

BUS

Nōhi Bus (p254) and its affiliates operate seven or more buses daily between Ogimachi (Shirakawa-gō) and Takayama (one way/return ¥2470/4420, 50 minutes), Kanazawa (¥1850/3290, 1½ hours) and Toyama (¥1700/3060, 1¾ hours). Some buses require a reservation. Weather delays and cancellations are possible between December and March.

Kaetsunou Bus (p255) operates at least four buses a day between Shin-Takaoka Station on the JR Hokuriku line and Ogimachi (¥1800, two hours), stopping at all major sights.

CAR & MOTORCYCLE

It's an easy drive on the Tokai-Hokuriku expressway from Takayama to Shirakawa-gō (Ogimachi). Parking in the official Ogimachi car park starts at an eye-watering ¥1000; best to find a spot just before you reach it and walk down the hill.

From June through mid-November, the Hakusan White Rd (formerly the Hakusan Super-Rindō) is a 34km stretch of scenic toll road (one way ¥1600) between Hakusan and Ogimachi.

Gokayama

☎0763

North along the Shōkawa-gawa, in Toyama Prefecture, Gokayama (五箇山) is isolated and sparsely populated. Although there are a number of *gasshō-zukuri* buildings scattered along Rte 156, the villages of Suganuma and Ainokura have the best examples. To get here, drive north on Rte 156 from Shirakawa-gō. You'll reach Suganuma first, then Ainokura.

👁 Sights

Down a steep hill off Rte 156, 15km north of Ogimachi, **Suganuma** (菅沼) is a pretty riverside collection of nine *gasshō-zukuri* houses and a World Heritage Site. It feels more like a residential museum than a working village, and there's no accommodation here.

Enchanting World Heritage–listed **Ainokura** (相倉) is the most impressive of Gokayama's villages. The valley is home to more than 20 *gasshō* buildings amid splendid mountain views. The village's remote location attracts fewer tour buses than Ogimachi, so it's much quieter. If you want to really step back in time and hear the sound of your thoughts, spend a night here – it's magical as afternoon turns into evening.

Murakami-ke HISTORIC BUILDING

(村上家; ☎0763-66-2711; www.murakamike.jp; 742 Kaminashi, Kaminashi; adult/child ¥300/150; ⏲8.30am-5pm Wed-Mon Apr-Nov, 9am-4pm Wed-Mon Dec-Mar) Between Suganuma and Ainokura, in the hamlet of Kaminashi, you'll find Murakami-ke, one of the oldest *gasshō* houses in the region (dating from 1578). It's now a small museum; the proud owner delights in showing visitors around and might sing you some local folk songs. Close by, the main hall of **Hakusan-gū shrine** dates from 1502. It's an Important Cultural Property.

Gokayama Washi-no-sato GALLERY
(五箇山和紙の里; ☎0763-66-2223; www.gokayama-washinosato.com; 215 Higashinakae; ⏲9am-5pm) North of Ainokura on Rte 156 you'll find this roadside attraction, which explains the art of making *washi* (handmade paper) and gives you the chance to try making some yourself (from ¥500; reservations required, limited English is spoken). There's also a gift shop.

Ainokura Minzoku-kan MUSEUM
(相倉民族館; ☎0763-66-2732; 352 Ainokura, Ainokura; ¥210; ⏲8.30am-5pm) Stroll through the village to this interesting folklore museum, with displays of local crafts and paper. The museum occupies two buildings, the former residences of the prominent Ozaki and Nakaya families.

Gokayama Minzoku-kan MUSEUM
(五箇山民俗館; ☎0763-67-3652; 436 Suganuma, Suganuma; adult/child ¥300/150; ⏲9am-4pm) You can see items from traditional life and displays illustrating gunpowder production, for which the area was once famed, at this folklore museum.

Activities

Kuroba Onsen ONSEN
(くろば温泉; ☎0763-67-3741; 1098 Kamitaira-hosojima, Nanto; adult/child ¥600/300; ⏲10am-9pm Wed-Mon) About 1km north of Suganuma along Rte 156, Kuroba Onsen is a complex of indoor-outdoor baths with a lovely view. Its low-alkaline waters are good for fatigue and sore muscles.

Sleeping & Eating

Remote Ainokura is a great place for a *gasshō-zukuri* stay. Some Japanese-language ability will help you with reservations and getting by. Rates may be higher in winter due to a heating charge.

Yamashita-ya GUESTHOUSE ¥
(山下や; ☎0763-77-3264; www.gokayama-yamashitaya.com/english.html; 839 Kaimukura, Nanto; dm/d/tr ¥3200/7500/9500; P ❄ 📶) The friendly proprietress of this cosy guesthouse knows just what the traveller wants after a long day: a cold beer while looking out over rice paddies and mountains, a heater to take the high-altitude chill off, and a discounted ticket to the nearest onsen. She also rents bicycles for ¥400 per day.

Ainokura Campground CAMPGROUND ¥
(五箇山国民休養地キャンプ場; ☎0763-66-2123; 611 Ainokura, Ainokura; per person ¥500; ⏲mid-Apr–late Oct; P) This lovely basic campground is about 1km from Ainokura.

Minshuku Chōyomon MINSHUKU ¥¥
(民宿長ヨ門; ☎0763-66-2755; 418 Ainokura, Ainokura; per person incl 2 meals ¥9200; 📶) You can't get much more rustic than this 350-year-old place in the centre of Ainokura village.

Minshuku Goyomon MINSHUKU ¥¥
(民宿五ヨ門; ☎0763-66-2154; www.goyomon.burari.biz; 438 Ainokura, Ainokura; per person incl 2 meals ¥9200; 📶) This is a small, family-oriented homestay.

Matsuya SOBA ¥¥
(まつや; 445 Ainokura, Ainokura; sets from ¥1400; P) Truly delicious soba and tempura set-lunch menus in a *gasshō-zukuri* house smack bang in the heart of Ainokura village. Try the house-made tofu, or the mountain vegetables steamed in soy and sake.

Information

You'll find the **Tourist Information Center** (五箇山観光総合案内所; ☎0763-66-2468; www.gokayama-info.jp; 754 Kaminashi; ⏲9am-5pm) for the Gokayama district in the village of Kaminashi. Yukie speaks good English and is extremely knowledgeable and passionate about the district.

Getting There & Away

BUS

Kaetsunou Bus (p255) operates at least four buses a day between Shin-Takaoka Station on the JR Hokuriku *shinkansen* (bullet-train) line and Ainokura (¥1000, 1½ hours), and then on to Suganuma (¥1200, 30 minutes) and Ogimachi (¥1800, 45 minutes). From the Ainokura-guchi bus stop it's about a 400m uphill walk to Ainokura before the descent into the village.

Some buses on the Kanazawa–Takayama route (via Ogimachi) operated by Nōhi Bus (p245) stop in Suganuma. Nōhi Bus also offers day-return **bus tours** of Shirakawa-gō and Ainokura (adult/child ¥6690/4420) from Takayama.

CAR & MOTORCYCLE

Ainokura (Gokayama) is directly accessible via the Tokai-Hokuriku expressway from Takayama.

For slower, more scenic explorations, get off the expressway at the Shirakawa-gō (Ogimachi) exit, then follow windy Rte 156 to the villages of Gokayama at your own pace.

KANAZAWA & THE HOKURIKU COAST

The Hokuriku (北陸) region stretches along the Sea of Japan coast, encompassing Fukui, Ishikawa and Toyama Prefectures. The opening of the Hokuriku *shinkansen* (bullet-train) line in 2015 greatly improved access to the region, and tourism is booming.

Kanazawa, in Ishikawa-ken (石川県), is the biggest draw. It was once the power base of the feudal Maeda clan, and this legacy can still be seen in the city's traditional architecture, artisan workshops and famous garden. To the north, the Noto Peninsula has sweeping seascapes and quiet fishing villages.

West is little Fukui-ken (福井県), with one of the world's most influential Zen centres, some pretty towns and fascinating architectural ruins.

Toyama-ken (富山県), at the eastern end, is a culinary and architectural draw. Its bayfront capital city, Toyama, features seafood specialities renowned throughout Japan. Neighbouring Takaoka is home to awesome National Treasure Zuiryū-ji, a fusion of Buddhist architectural traditions.

For more information on the region, see www.hot-ishikawa.jp/english.

Getting There & Away

Kanazawa is the main transport hub for the Hokuriku area.

Useful regional airports include Komatsu Airport (p266), west of Kanazawa, Toyama Airport (p274), and **Noto Satoyama (Wajima) Airport** (NTQ; ☎0768-26-2000; www.noto-airport.jp), on the Noto Peninsula.

Frequent trains on the Hokuriku *shinkansen* line travel between Tokyo and Kanazawa, via Toyama. The Hokuriku main line runs west from Kanazawa to Fukui and on to Kyoto and Osaka.

FERRIES FROM TSURUGA

From Tsuruga, a busy port and rail junction 60km south of Fukui city, Shin Nihonkai Ferry Company (www.snf.jp) has daily sailings to Tomakomai, Hokkaidō (19½ hours nonstop, 30½ hours with stops, from ¥9970). Several of these stop en route at Niigata (¥5550, 12½ hours) and Akita (¥7190, 20 hours). Buses timed to ferry departures serve Tsuruga-kō port from JR Tsuruga Station (¥350, 20 minutes).

Getting Around

A car is handy for exploring sights outside the larger cities. There are plenty of car-rental agencies around JR Kanazawa station.

Hokutetsu Kankō (☎076-237-5115; www.hokutetsu.co.jp/en) provides bus services within Kanazawa, around Ishikawa Prefecture and beyond. It has a variety of discount bus passes; see the website for details, fares and timetables.

Kanazawa

☎076 / POP 465,699

The array of cultural attractions in Kanazawa (金沢) make the city the drawcard of the Hokuriku region and a rival to Kyoto as the historical jewel of mainland Japan. Best known for Kenroku-en, a castle garden dating from the 17th century, it also boasts beautifully preserved samurai and geisha districts, attractive temples, a wealth of museums and a wonderful market (and far fewer tourists than Kyoto – for now). A two- or three-day stay is recommended to take it all in.

History

During the 15th century Kanazawa was under the control of an autonomous Buddhist government, ousted in 1583 by Maeda Toshiie, head of the powerful Maeda clan. Kanazawa means 'golden marsh' – in its heyday the region was Japan's richest, producing about five million bushels of rice annually. This wealth allowed the Maeda to patronise culture and the arts. Kanazawa remains a national cultural hot spot.

An absence of military targets spared the city from destruction during WWII. Its myriad historical and cultural sites are wonderfully preserved and integrate neatly with the city's contemporary architecture.

Sights

Kanazawa is a sprawling city with two almost parallel rivers traversing its core. Most areas of interest are located a good distance from the impressive JR Kanazawa Station area, where most visitors arrive. Since the arrival of the Hokuriku *shinkansen*, this area has been abuzz with activity. The terminus of the substantial regional bus network, which can at first seem a little confusing, is also here. Have patience: you'll orient yourself soon enough.

Heading south of the station along Hyakumangoku-dōri, you'll reach **Kōrinbō** (the shopping and business district) before arriving in **Katamachi**, by the banks of the Sai-gawa; this is the place to eat, drink and be merry. If you're staying near the station, note that buses stop early in the evening and taxis back from the action cost at least ¥1300. Tucked between Kōrinbō and the Sai-gawa is the stately former samurai district of **Nagamachi**.

Teramachi and **Nishi-chaya-gai** are just over the bridge from Katamachi, but the mainstay of sights, including Kanazawa Castle Park and Kenroku-en, are to the east. To their north, on opposite sides of the Asano-gawa, lie the pretty **Kazuemachi-chaya-gai** and **Higashi-chaya-gai** teahouse districts, in the shadow of hilly **Utatsuyama** and its many temples. Heading west will loop you back to the station, passing Ōmichō Market, a must-see.

★Kenroku-en — GARDENS

(兼六園; ☎076-234-3800; www.pref.ishikawa.jp/siro-niwa/kenrokuen/e; 1-1 Marunouchi; adult/child/senior ¥310/100/free; ⏲7am-6pm Mar–mid-Oct, 8am-4.30pm mid-Oct–Feb) This Edo-period garden draws its name (*kenroku* means 'combined six') from a renowned Sung-dynasty garden in China that dictated six attributes for perfection: seclusion, spaciousness, artificiality, antiquity, abundant water and broad views. Kenroku-en has them all. Arrive before the crowds.

It's believed that the garden, originally belonging to an outer villa of Kanazawa-jō, was developed from the 1620s to the 1840s and was so named in 1822. It was first opened to the public in 1871.

★DT Suzuki Museum — MUSEUM

(鈴木大拙館; ☎076-221-8011; www.kanazawa-museum.jp/daisetz; 3-4-20 Honda-machi; adult/child/senior ¥300/free/200; ⏲9.30am-4.30pm Tue-Sun) This spiritual museum is a tribute to Daisetsu Teitaro Suzuki, one of the foremost Buddhist philosophers of our time. Published in Japanese and English, Suzuki is largely credited with introducing Zen to the West. This stunning concrete complex embodies the heart of Zen.

★Gyokusen Inmaru Garden — GARDENS

(玉泉院丸庭園, Gyokusen Inmaru Teien; ☎076-234-3800; www.pref.ishikawa.jp/siro-niwa/kanazawajou/e/gyokusen-in; 1-1 Marunouchi; ⏲7am-6pm) FREE Adjacent to the Kanazawa Castle Park, this feudal pleasure garden was first constructed in 1634 but abandoned in the Meiji era. Its five-year reconstruction was completed in 2015. Features include a small waterfall, bridges and many traditional elements. While the garden's focal point is the **Gyokusen-an Rest House** (玉泉庵; tea ceremony ¥720; ⏲7am-6pm Mar-15 Oct, 8am-5pm 16 Oct-Feb), it's the overall picture of beauty and refinement that impresses most. The garden and teahouse are illuminated spectacularly on Friday and Saturday evenings between sunset and 9pm – have your camera at the ready.

Myōryū-ji — BUDDHIST TEMPLE

(妙立寺; Ninja-dera; ☎076-241-0888; www.myouryuji.or.jp/en.html; 1-2-12 Nomachi; adult/child ¥1000/700; ⏲by reservation only 9am-4pm Mon-Fri, to 4.30pm Sat & Sun) Completed in 1643 in Teramachi, the temple was designed to protect its lord from attack. It contains hidden stairways, escape routes, secret chambers, concealed tunnels and trick doors. Contrary to popular belief, it has nothing to do with ninja. Admission is by tour only (in Japanese with an English guidebook). Phone for reservations with English-speaking staff.

21st Century Museum of Contemporary Art — MUSEUM

(金沢21世紀美術館; ☎076-220-2800; www.kanazawa21.jp; 1-2-1 Hirosaka; ⏲10am-6pm Tue-Thu & Sun, to 8pm Fri & Sat) FREE A low-slung glass cylinder, 113m in diameter, forms the perimeter of this contemporary gallery, which celebrated its 10th birthday in 2014. Museum entry is free, but admission fees are charged for special exhibitions. Inside, galleries are arranged like boxes on a tray. Check the website for event info and fees.

Kaikarō — MUSEUM

(懐華樓; ☎076-253-0591; www.kaikaro.jp/eng/index.html; 1-14-8 Higashiyama; adult/child ¥750/500; ⏲9am-5pm) In Higashi-chaya-gai, Kaikarō is an early-19th-century geisha house refinished with contemporary fittings and art, including a red-lacquered staircase. Evening geisha performances include a short lecture in English by the proprietor, followed by a demonstration of traditional party games by geisha themselves. Performances last 1½ hours; tickets start at ¥6500.

Kanazawa

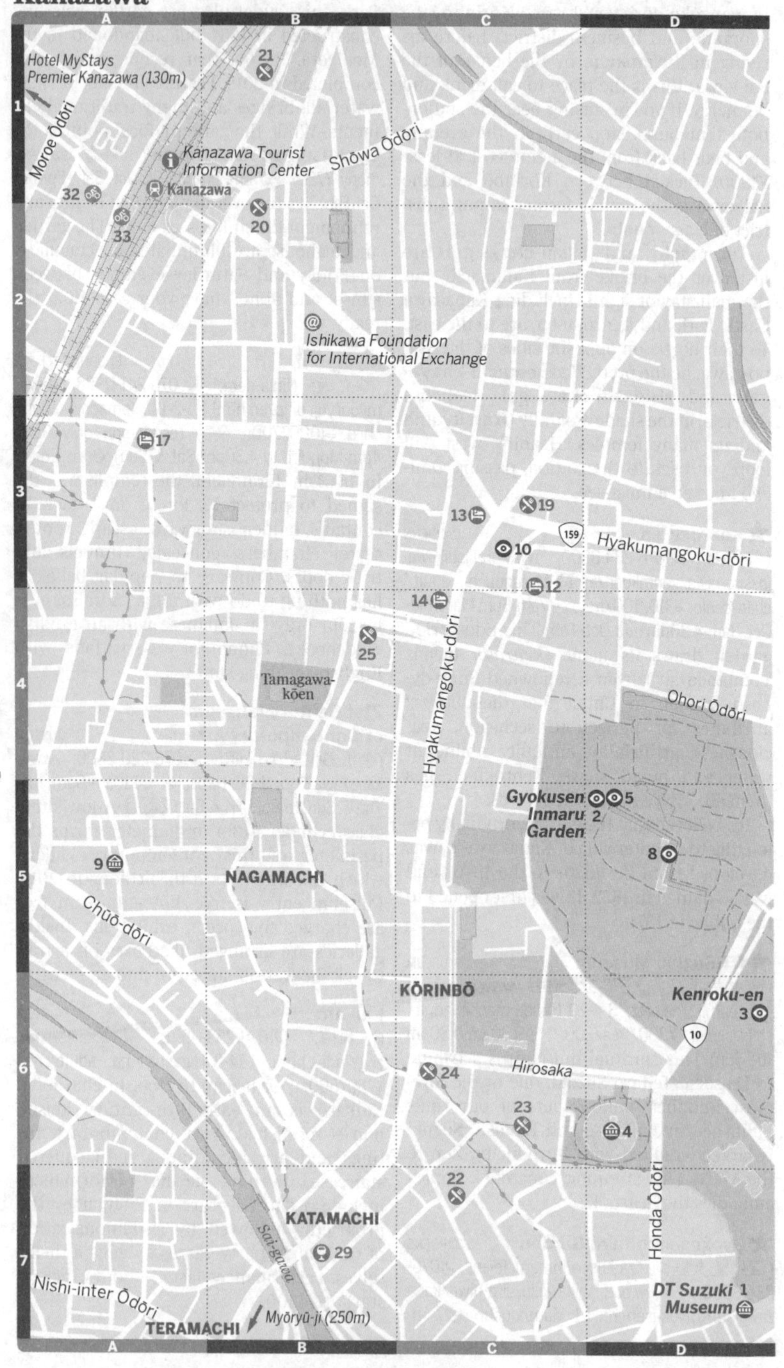
Hotel MyStays Premier Kanazawa (130m)
Moroe Ōdōri
Kanazawa Tourist Information Center
Kanazawa
Shōwa Ōdōri
21
20
32
33
Ishikawa Foundation for International Exchange
17
13
19
159
Hyakumangoku-dōri
10
12
14
25
Tamagawa-kōen
Hyakumangoku-dōri
Ohori Ōdōri
Gyokusen Inmaru Garden
2
5
8
9
NAGAMACHI
Chūō-dōri
KŌRINBŌ
Kenroku-en
3
10
24
Hirosaka
23
4
22
Honda Ōdōri
KATAMACHI
Sai-gawa
29
Nishi-inter Ōdōri
TERAMACHI
Myōryū-ji (250m)
DT Suzuki Museum
1

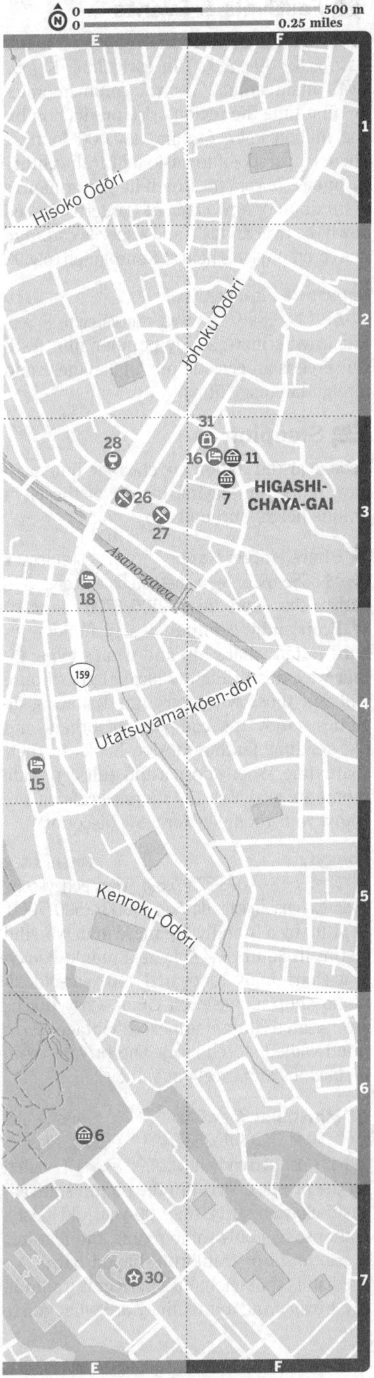

Kanazawa

Top Sights
1 DT Suzuki Museum D7
2 Gyokusen Inmaru Garden D5
3 Kenroku-en D6

Sights
4 21st Century Museum of Contemporary Art D6
5 Gyokusen-an Rest House D5
6 Ishikawa Prefectural Museum of Traditional Products & Crafts E6
7 Kaikarō F3
8 Kanazawa Castle Park D5
9 Nagamachi Yūzen-kan A5
10 Ōmi-chō Market C3
11 Shima F3

Sleeping
12 Asadaya Ryokan C3
13 Holiday Inn ANA Kanazawa Sky C3
14 Hotel Resol Trinity C4
15 Kanazawa Hakuchōrō Hotel E4
16 Minshuku Yōgetsu F3
17 Pongyi A3
18 Share Hotels Hachi E3

Eating
19 Curio Espresso & Vintage Design C3
20 Daiba Kanazawa Ekimae B2
21 Forus B1
22 Full of Beans C7
23 Itaru Honten C6
24 Janome-sushi Honten C6
25 Kaiseki Tsuruko B4
26 Kanazawa Todoroki-tei E3
27 Restaurant Jiyūken E3
Sentō .... (see 10)

Drinking & Nightlife
28 Oriental Brewing E3
29 Sturgis Rock Bar B7

Entertainment
30 Ishikawa Prefectural Nō Theatre E7

Shopping
31 Sakuda Gold Leaf Company F3

Transport
32 Hokutetsu Rent-a-Cycle A1
33 JR Kanazawa Station Rent-a-Cycle A2

Ōmi-chō Market MARKET
(近江町市場; 35 Ōmi-chō; ⏲9am-5pm) Between Kanazawa Station and Katamachi you'll find this market, reminiscent of Tokyo's old Tsukiji market. A bustling warren of fishmongers, buyers and restaurants, it's a great place to watch everyday people in action or indulge in the freshest sashimi and local produce. The nearest bus stop is Musashi-ga-tsuji.

Kanazawa Castle Park LANDMARK
(金沢城公園, Kanazawa-jō Kōen; ☎076-234-3800; www.kanazawa-tourism.com/eng/guide/guide1_1.php?no=2; 1-1 Marunouchi; buildings/grounds ¥310/free; ⏰grounds 7am-6pm Mar-15 Oct, 8am-5pm 16 Oct-Feb, castle 9am-4.30pm) Originally built in 1580, this massive structure was called the 'castle of 1000 tatami' and housed the Maeda clan for 14 generations until it was destroyed by fire in 1881. The elegant surviving gate, **Ishikawa-mon** (built in 1788), provides a dramatic entry from Kenroku-en; holes in its turret were designed for hurling rocks at invaders. Two additional buildings, the **Hishi-yagura** (diamond-shaped turret) and **Gojikken-nagaya** (armoury), were reconstructed using traditional means in 2001.

Shima MUSEUM
(志摩; ☎076-252-5675; www.ochaya-shima.com; 1-13-21 Higashiyama; adult/child ¥500/300; ⏰9am-6pm) An Important Cultural Asset, this well-known, traditional-style former geisha house dates from 1820 and has an impressive collection of elaborate combs, and picks for *shamisen* (three-stringed instruments resembling a lute or banjo).

Tours

Kanazawa Walking Tours WALKING
(☎803 044 3191; www.kanazawa-tours.com; half-day tours from ¥3700) KWT's English-speaking guides get rave reviews from happy customers. Public tours go ahead when a minimum of six people have booked; private tours start at ¥22,000 per half-day and are fully customisable.

DON'T MISS

KANAZAWA SPECIALITIES

Seafood is the staple of Kanazawa's *Kaga ryōri* (Kaga cuisine); even the most humble train-station *bentō* (boxed meal) usually features some type of fish. *Oshi-zushi*, a thin layer of fish pressed atop vinegar rice, is said to be the precursor to modern sushi. Another favourite is *jibuni*, flour-coated duck or chicken stewed with shiitake and green vegetables.

Festivals & Events

Hyakumangoku Matsuri PARADE
(百万石まつり; ⏰Jun) In early June Kanazawa's main annual festival commemorates the first time the region's rice production hit one million *koku* (around 150,000 tonnes). There's a parade of townsfolk in 16th-century costumes, *takigi nō* (torch-lit performances of *nō* drama), *tōrō nagashi* (lanterns floated down the river at dusk) and a special *chanoyu* (tea ceremony). It's held at Kenroku-en (p259).

Kanazawa Film Festival FILM
(かなざわ映画の会; www.eiganokai.com; ⏰Sep) Kanazawa's increasingly popular film festival screens an eclectic mix of Japanese and foreign-language films.

Sleeping

Beds near the station are cheaper, but you'll have more fun staying in one of the city's unique neighbourhoods.

★**Share Hotels Hachi** GUESTHOUSE ¥
(☎03-5656-6916; www.thesharehotels.com; 3-18 Hashiba-cho; dm/s from ¥2100/8700; ⊖❄📶) 🍃 Ecofriendly, communal, arty, funky – it's hard to tell what's hip and what's hype. Either way, this brilliantly located guesthouse will suit those who don't mind sharing facilities, enjoy the company of others and like reading Taschen design books in their spare time. Woody dorms and quirky private rooms are available and there's a cafe on-site (show your room key for a 5% discount).

Pongyi GUESTHOUSE ¥
(ポンギー; ☎076-225-7369; www.pongyi.com; 2-22 Rokumai-machi; dm/s/d ¥3000/3500/7000; @) Run by a friendly Japanese man who did a stint in Southeast Asia as a monk, Pongyi is a charmingly renovated 140-year-old kimono shop alongside a canal. Cosy dorms are located in an annexed vintage *kura* (mud-walled storehouse). The private room is spacious and excellent value.

★**Minshuku Yōgetsu** MINSHUKU ¥¥
(民宿陽月; ☎076-252-0497; 1-13-22 Higashiyama; r per person from ¥5000; ⊖❄) Located on the prettiest street in the picturesque Higashi-chaya district, this 200-year-old geisha teahouse has only three rooms and features a *goemonburo* (cauldron-shaped bath). No English is spoken, but it's perfect if tranquillity, history and authenticity are what you're after.

Hotel MyStays Premier Kanazawa HOTEL ¥¥
(☎076-290-5255; www.mystays.com/en/hotel/kanazawa/mystays-premier-kanazawa; 2-13-5 Hirooka; r from ¥8600) Spacious (guest rooms are 32 sq metres!), stylish, fresh and current: this tourist hotel a stone's throw from the station is a good-value choice. It has real king-size beds, a gym, a laundry and an on-site cafe.

Hotel Resol Trinity HOTEL ¥¥
(ホテルレソルトリニティ; ☎076-221-9629; www.resol-hotel.jp; 1-18 Musashi-machi; s/d from ¥6500/8200; ❄@📶) This lovely niche hotel is a breath of fresh air. Rooms have a splash of colour and have been designed to make you feel comfortable in a compact space. The hotel's location is central to everything; you can walk to JR Kanazawa Station, Katamachi and Kenroku-en (p259) in about 15 minutes.

Asadaya Ryokan RYOKAN ¥¥¥
(浅田屋旅館; ☎076-231-2228; www.asadaya.co.jp/ryokan; 23 Jikkenmachi; per person incl 2 meals ¥46,000; ❄📶) Although more expensive than some of Japan's most lauded *onsen ryokan* (traditional hot-spring inns), and without the views and outdoor baths, Asadaya's exceptional service, attention to detail and sublime *kaiseki* (Japanese haute cuisine) justify the rates. With only four rooms, the conveniently located inn (opened in 1867) has more staff than guests, to ensure your stay epitomises the Japanese art of hospitality.

Holiday Inn ANA Kanazawa Sky HOTEL ¥¥¥
(☎076-233-2233; www.holidayinn.com; 15-1 Musashi-machi; s/d from ¥10,000/18,000; ❄📶) Centrally located between JR Kanazawa Station and the sights, across the road from Ōmi-chō Market (p261), this recently renovated hotel is an excellent choice, with comfortable bedding and breathtaking views of Kanazawa and Hakusan National Park beyond. It's on top of the M'Za department store, whose basement-level food court is all too convenient.

Kanazawa Hakuchōrō Hotel HOTEL ¥¥¥
(金沢白鳥路ホテル; ☎076-222-1212; www.sanraku.premierhotel-group.com/kanazawa/en; 6-3 Marunouchi; s/tw from ¥14,000/20,000; P🚭@) This interesting hotel adjacent to Kanazawa Castle Park and near Higashi-chaya-gai is quiet and removed from the action. Formal, Western-style rooms are showing their age, but their generous dimensions compensate. There's a lovely lobby, a restaurant and common onsen. Free parking.

DON'T MISS

HIGASHI-CHAYA-GAI

Just north of the Asano-gawa, Higashi-chaya-gai (Higashi Geisha District) is an enclave of narrow streets established early in the 19th century for geisha to entertain wealthy patrons. The slatted wooden facades of the geisha houses are romantically preserved. It's very picturesque around sunset, but you won't be the only one snapping photos.

Eating

The shiny, architecturally stunning JR Kanazawa Station building is brimming with eateries. Its neighbour, **Forus department store** (☎076-265-8111; www.forus.co.jp/kanazawa; 3-1 Horikawa Shin-machi; ⏰11am-10pm), has excellent dining floors, as does the basement of Meitetsu M'Za department store, opposite Ōmi-chō Market (p261) with its fresh-from-the-boat restaurants. Otherwise, the locus of nocturnal dining is found in the lanes of Kōrinbō and Katamachi.

Full of Beans CAFE ¥
(フルオブビーンズ; ☎076-222-3315; www.fullofbeans.jp; 41-1 Satomi-chō; meals from ¥850; ⏰11.30am-3.30pm & 5-10pm Thu-Tue) A variety of Japanese dishes and *yōshoku* (Western-style meals) are served at this stylish cafe in the quieter backstreets of Katamachi – the website will give you a sense of the vibe. It's a good place to try inimitable Kanazawa speciality *hanton raisu:* a bowl of rice topped with an omelette, fried seafood, ketchup and tartare sauce (available at lunch).

Daiba Kanazawa Ekimae IZAKAYA ¥
(台場金沢駅前店; ☎076-263-9191; Kanazawa Miyako Hotel 1F, 6-10 Konohana-machi; items from ¥460; ⏰11am-3pm & 5pm-midnight) This trendy spot in the Kanazawa Miyako Hotel building has a comprehensive Japanese menu and a limited English one with all the Western favourites and some local specialities. It's a great place for your first *izakaya* (pub-restaurant) experience: lots of small plates and beer.

Curio Espresso & Vintage Design CAFE ¥
(☎076-231-5543; 1-13 Yasue-cho; sandwiches from ¥600; ⏲9am-6pm Sat-Mon, from 8am Wed-Fri) Brewing Seattle-style coffee that would satisfy even the most hardened coffee snob, this sweet little cafe is a quaint spot to grab a break near the station. The menu features Western favourites (including hummus and barbecue pulled pork) you'll be hard-pressed to find elsewhere in this part of Japan.

★ **Sentō** CHINESE ¥¥
(仙桃; ☎076-234-0669; 2F Ōmichō Ichiba, 88 Aokusa-machi; dishes from ¥650, set menus from ¥980; ⏲11am-3pm & 5-10.30pm Wed-Mon) Upstairs in Ōmi-chō Market (p261), chefs from Hong Kong prepare authentic Szechuan- and Hong Kong–style dishes (including dim sum) from scratch. Delicious lunch and dinner set menus are excellent value. The spicy, salted squid is exquisite, and the *tantanmen* (sesame-and-chilli ramen) will have you coming back for a second bowl.

Itaru Honten IZAKAYA ¥¥
(いたる 本店; ☎076-221-4194; www.itaru.ne.jp/honten; 3-8 Kakinokibatake; sashimi for 2 from ¥2400; ⏲5.30-11.30pm Mon-Sat) One of Kanazawa's favourite seafood *izakaya* (pub-restaurants) is as popular with locals as it is with international visitors, so you may have to queue for a spot. Expect superlative sushi and sashimi and daily specials based on the catch of the day. There's an English menu, and dinner sets start at ¥3000.

Janome-sushi Honten SUSHI ¥¥
(蛇之目寿司本店; ☎076-231-0093; 1-1-12 Kōrinbō; set menu ¥3000, Kaga ryōri sets from ¥4400; ⏲noon-2pm & 5.30-10.30pm Thu-Tue) Kanazawa institution Janome-sushi Honten has been known for sashimi and Kaga cuisine since 1931. Dinner *omakase* (chef's choice) menus start at ¥3000.

Restaurant Jiyūken SHOKUDO ¥¥
(レストラン自由軒; ☎076-252-1996; www.jiyuken.com; 1-6-6 Higashiyama; meals ¥700-1890; ⏲11.30am-3pm & 5-9pm) This *shokudō* (all-round, inexpensive restaurant) in the heart of Higashi-chaya-gai has been serving *yōshoku* (Western food) – or at least Japanese takes on Western food, like omelettes, hamburgers and curry rice – since 1909. Daily set lunches (¥995) are good value.

Kanazawa Todoroki-tei BISTRO ¥¥
(金沢とどろき亭; ☎076-252-5755; 1-2-1 Higashiyama; plates from ¥1500; ⏲11.30am-3.30pm & 6-11.30pm) The art-deco, woody, candelit atmosphere of this Western-style bistro near Higashi-chaya-gai is a big selling point. The Taisho-era (1912–26) building with vaulted ceilings is a little rough around the edges, but that's part of its charm: it's not too snooty. Eight-course dinners are good value, starting at ¥3500 per person.

★ **Kaiseki Tsuruko** JAPANESE ¥¥¥
(懐石 つる幸; ☎076-264-2375; www.turukou.com; 6-5 Takaoka-machi; lunch/dinner from ¥10,000/15,000; ⏲noon-3pm & 6-10pm) *Kaiseki* (Japanese haute cuisine) dining is a holistic experience of hospitality, art and originality. This outstanding restaurant is a true gourmand's delight, offering an experience beyond what you might enjoy in a ryokan. Dress to impress. A ¥5000 lunch course is available for groups of two or more.

Drinking & Nightlife

Sturgis Rock Bar BAR
(スタージス; ☎076-262-9577; 4F Kinrin Bldg, 1-7-15 Katamachi; ⏲8pm-3am) An original Kanazawan institution. With live rock bands and every manner of everything hanging from the ceiling, this place'll make you feel as though you're on a trip in San Francisco with a bunch of Japanese tourists, paying homage to the gods of rock and roll.

Oriental Brewing BREWERY
(☎076-255-6378; www.orientalbrewing.com; 3-2-22 Higashiyama; ⏲11am-10pm) You can't miss this trendy brewhouse at the entrance to Higashi-chaya-gai: it's always humming with Japanese and international guests, who love the mellow, friendly vibe and the original yeasty ales brewed on-site.

Entertainment

Ishikawa Prefectural Nō Theatre THEATRE
(石川県立能楽堂; ☎076-264-2598; www.nohgaku.or.jp; 3-1 Dewa-machi; performance prices vary; ⏲9am-4.30pm Tue-Sun) *Nō* theatre is alive and well in Kanazawa. Weekly performances take place here in summer.

Shopping

The Hirosaka shopping street, between Kōrinbō 109 department store and Kenroku-en, has some upmarket craft shops on its south side.

Sakuda Gold Leaf Company ARTS & CRAFTS
(金銀箔工芸さくだ; ☎076-251-6777; www.goldleaf-sakuda.jp; 1-3-27 Higashiyama; ⏲9am-6pm)

KANAZAWA'S TRADITIONAL CRAFTS

During the Edo period Kanazawa's ruling Maeda family fuelled the growth of important crafts. Many are still practised today.

For an introduction, visit the **Ishikawa Prefectural Museum of Traditional Products & Crafts** (石川県立伝統産業工芸館; ☎076-262-2020; www.ishikawa-densankan.jp; 2-1 Kenroku-machi; adult/child/senior ¥260/100/200; ⏲9am-5pm, closed 3rd Thu of month Apr-Nov, closed Thu Dec-Mar).

Gold Leaf

A lump of pure gold the size of a ¥10 coin is rolled to the size of a tatami mat, becoming as little as 0.0001mm thick. The gold leaf is then cut into squares of 10.9cm – the size used for mounting on walls, murals or paintings – or cut again for gilding on lacquerware or pottery. Kanazawa makes over 98% of Japan's gold leaf. See some of the many uses for gold leaf at Sakuda Gold Leaf Company.

Kaga Yūzen Silk Dyeing

The laborious, specialised method of *Kaga Yūzen* silk dyeing is characterised by strong colours and realistic depictions of nature, such as flower petals that have begun to brown around the edges. White lines between elements where ink has washed away are a characteristic of *Kaga Yūzen*.

The **Nagamachi Yūzen-kan** (長町友禅館; ☎076-264-2811; www.kagayuzen-club.co.jp; 2-6-16 Nagamachi; ¥350; ⏲9.30am-5pm Thu-Mon Mar-Nov) displays some splendid examples of Kaga Yūzen kimono dyeing and demonstrates the process. Enquire ahead about trying the silk-dyeing process yourself (¥4000).

Kutani Porcelain

Kutani porcelain is known for its elegant shapes, graceful designs and bright, bold colours. The style dates back to the early Edo period and shares design characteristics with Chinese porcelain and Japanese Imari ware. Typical motifs include birds, flowers, trees and landscapes. To learn more, visit the Kutaniyaki Porcelain Art Museum (p271) in Kaga Onsen.

Ōhi Pottery

The deliberately simple, almost primitive designs, rough surfaces, irregular shapes and monochromatic glazes of Ōhi pottery have been favoured by tea practitioners since the early Edo period. Since that time one family, with the professional name Chōzaemon, has been keeper of the Ōhi tradition.

Kanazawa & Wajima Lacquerware

To create Kanazawa and Wajima lacquerware, decoration is applied to luminous black lacquerware through *maki-e* (decorating with gold or silver power) or gilding. Artists must take great care that dust does not settle on the final product. In Wajima, see examples at the Ishikawa Wajima Urushi Art Museum (p269).

Here you can observe the *kinpaku* (gold-leaf) process and pick up all sorts of gilded souvenirs, including pottery, lacquerware and, er...golf balls. It also serves tea containing flecks of gold leaf, which is reputedly good for rheumatism. Even the toilet walls are lined with gold and platinum.

ℹ Information

Check out https://visitkanazawa.jp for general city information.

Kanazawa Tourist Information Center (石川県金沢観光情報センター; ☎076-232-6200, KGGN 076-232-3933; http://kggn.sakura.ne.jp; 1 Hirooka-machi; ⏲9am-7pm) This brilliant office inside Kanazawa Station, one of Japan's best, has helpful staff, a plethora of maps and pamphlets in a variety of languages, and the excellent, free English-language magazine *Eye on Kanazawa*. The friendly folk from the Goodwill Guide Network (KGGN) are also here to assist with hotel recommendations and free guiding in English – two weeks' notice is requested.

Ishikawa Foundation for International Exchange (☎076-262-5931; www.ifie.or.jp; 1-5-3 Honmachi; ⏲9am-8pm Mon-Fri, to 5pm Sat & Sun) Offers information, a library, satellite-TV

OFF THE BEATEN TRACK

HAKUSAN NATIONAL PARK

Geared to serious hikers and naturalists, stunning Hakusan National Park (白山国立公園) straddles four prefectures: Ishikawa, Fukui, Toyama and Gifu. Within are several peaks above 2500m, the tallest being Hakusan (2702m), a sacred mountain that has been worshipped since ancient times. In summer, folks hike and scramble uphill for mountain sunrises. In winter, skiing and onsen bathing take over. The alpine section of the park is criss-crossed with trails, offering treks of up to 25km. For well-equipped hikers, there's a 26km trek to Ogimachi in the Shōkawa Valley. For an overview of the hiking opportunities, check out www.kagahakusan.jp/en.

The closest access point is Bettōdeai. From here it's 6km to Hakusan Murodō (about 4½ hours' walk) and 5km to Nanryū Sansō (3½ hours).

Visiting Hakusan requires commitment. The main mode of transport is the Hokutetsu Kankō (p258) bus from the east exit of Kanazawa Station to Bettōdeai (¥2200, two hours). From late June to mid-October, up to three buses operate daily. If you're driving from the Shōkawa Valley, you can take the spectacular Hakusan White Rd toll route (one way/return ¥1600/2600).

There's limited accommodation on the peaks, primarily offered in giant dorms at **Hakusan Murodō** (白山室堂; ☎076-273-1001; www.kagahakusan.jp/en/murodo/index.html; dm ¥5300; ⊙May-Nov) and **Nanryū Sansō** (南竜山荘; ☎076-259-2022; http://city-hakusan.com/hakusan/naryusanso; dm incl 2 meals ¥8800, campsites ¥300, 5-person cabins ¥13,700; ⊙1 Jul–15 Oct). The latter has a campground and popular basic cabins – camping anywhere else is prohibited.

The villages of Ichirino, Chūgū Onsen, Shiramine and Ichinose have *minshuku* (guesthouses), ryokan and camping. Rates start at around ¥300 per person for campsites and around ¥8500 for lodge dorms or rooms in inns, each including two meals.

Dining options are limited to a handful of choices in each of the villages near the park's borders. Simple meals are available in the lodges atop the peaks.

news and free internet access. It's on the 3rd floor of the Rifare building, a few minutes' walk southeast of JR Kanazawa Station.

Getting There & Away

AIR

Nearby **Komatsu Airport** (KMQ; www.komatsuairport.jp) has air connections with major Japanese cities, as well as Seoul, Shanghai and Taipei.

BUS

JR Highway Bus operates express buses from in front of JR Kanazawa Station's east exit to Tokyo's Shinjuku Station (¥6600, 7½ hours) and Kyoto (¥3000, 4¼ hours).

Meitetsu (名鉄; ☎052-585-1111; 1-2-1 Meieki; ⊙10am-8pm; Ⓡ Meitetsu Nagoya), Hokutetsu Kankō (p258) and JR buses serve Nagoya (¥4180, four hours). Nōhi Bus (p245) takes you to Takayama (¥3390, 2¼ hours) via Shirakawa-go.

TRAIN

The arrival of the Hokuriku *shinkansen* in 2015 marked the beginning of a new period of prosperity for Kanazawa, slashing journey times from Tokyo by more than an hour. The direct trip between Kanazawa and Tokyo (¥14,120) now takes just 2½ hours.

The JR Hokuriku line links Kanazawa with Fukui (*tokkyū/futsū* ¥2500/1320, 45 minutes/1½ hours), Kyoto (*tokkyū* ¥6380, 2¼ hours), Osaka (*tokkyū* ¥7130, 2¾ hours) and Toyama (*futsū* ¥980, one hour).

Getting Around

BICYCLE

Full-size bikes can be rented from **JR Kanazawa Station Rent-a-Cycle** (駅レンタサイクル; ☎076-261-1721; per hour/day ¥200/1200; ⊙8am-8.30pm) and **Hokutetsu Rent-a-Cycle** (北鉄レンタサイクル; ☎076-263-0919; per 4hr/day ¥630/1050; ⊙8am-5.30pm), both by the train station's west exit.

There's also a pay-as-you-go bicycle-rental system called 'Machi-nori'. The bikes are a little small for larger bodies, and not the most comfortable to ride, but with a bit of planning the system functions well. For the low-down in English, a downloadable map is available at www.machi-nori.jp.

BUS

Buses depart from the circular terminus in front of the station's east exit. Any bus from station stop 7, 8 or 9 will take you to the city centre (¥200). The round-trip journey is free if you have a JR pass.

The Kanazawa Loop Bus (single ride/day pass ¥200/500, every 15 minutes from 8.30am to 6pm) circles the major tourist attractions in 45 minutes. On Saturday, Sunday and holidays, the Machi-bus goes to Kōrinbō for ¥100.

Airport buses (¥1130, 45 minutes) depart from Kanazawa station's west exit. Some services travel via Katamachi and Kōrinbō 109 but they take an hour to reach the airport.

Day passes (¥500) offer excellent value, but since the influx of non-Japanese-speaking visitors to town began to inadvertently cause lost-in-translation-style chaos across the network, they can no longer be purchased on board. Instead, purchase them from the Hokutetsu Kankō service centre inside JR Kanazawa Station; there's another centre opposite the Omi-chō Market bus stop.

For more information, see www.hokutetsu.co.jp/en/en_round.

Noto Peninsula

Rugged seascapes, rural life, seafood and a healthy range of cultural sights make Noto Peninsula (能登半島; Noto-hantō) a pleasant escape from Kanazawa's urban sprawl. The lacquer-making town of Wajima is the hub of the rugged north, known as Oku-Noto, and the best place to stay overnight. Famous products include *Wajima-nuri* (lacquerware), *Suzu*-style pottery (its black hue is due to iron in the indigenous clay), locally harvested sea salt and *iwanori* (seaweed harvested from rocks).

Sleeping & Eating

You'll find a handful of simple business hotels and *minshuku* (guesthouses) in the towns of Hakui and Himi, but it's worth going the extra few kilometres to stay in Wajima, with its wider variety of accommodation (and dining) options.

The furthermost tip of the peninsula is also the least populated, but you'll find some humble *minshuku* (guesthouses) here and a truly unique and impressive ryokan (p271).

Eating

Between them, Hakui and Himi have the peninsula's largest concentration of dining options, with seafood usually heavy on the menu. Both towns have branches of popular chain restaurants and some international flavours.

Wajima has dozens of *minshuku* known for seafood meals worth staying in for. There are nice restaurants by the harbour, though some are closed by early evening and finding an English speaker can be tricky.

Getting There & Around

In the centre of Oku-Noto, Noto Satoyama (Wajima) Airport (p258) connects the peninsula with Tokyo (Haneda).

From Kanazawa, the JR Nanao line goes up the west coast of the peninsula to Hakui and then across to Wakura Onsen on the east coast. From either station, you can connect to infrequent local buses to elsewhere.

Hokutetsu Kankō (p258) runs buses between Kanazawa and Wajima and, less frequently, Monzen (¥950, 35 minutes).

Self-driving from Kanazawa is easily the best way to see the peninsula. Most sights can be reached by road only: hiring a car in Kanazawa is recommended. The 83km Noto Yūryo (能登有料; Noto Toll Rd) speeds you as far as Anamizu (toll ¥1180).

Noto's mostly flat west coast appeals to cyclists, but cycling is not recommended on the Noto-kongō (mid-west) and east coasts because of steep, blind curves.

Lower Noto Peninsula

☎0767, 0766

The small town of **Hakui** (羽咋) is the Noto Peninsula's western transit hub, with frequent train connections to Kanazawa and less frequent bus connections along Noto's west coast. With about twice the population, the town of **Himi** (氷見) in neighbouring Toyama Prefecture, about 40 minutes' drive east, is also a viable starting point from which to tackle the peninsula.

Sights

★**Kita-ke** HISTORIC BUILDING

(喜多家; ☎0767-28-2546; Ra 4-1 Kitakawashiri, Hodatsushimizu; adult/child ¥500/200; ⏲8.30am-5pm Apr-Oct, to 4pm Nov-Mar) During the Edo period the Kita family administered over 200 villages from Kita-ke, the pivotal crossroads of the Kaga, Etchū and Noto fiefs. Inside this splendid, sprawling family home and museum are displays of weapons, ceramics, farming tools, fine and folk art, and documents. The garden has been called the Moss Temple of Noto.

Noto Peninsula

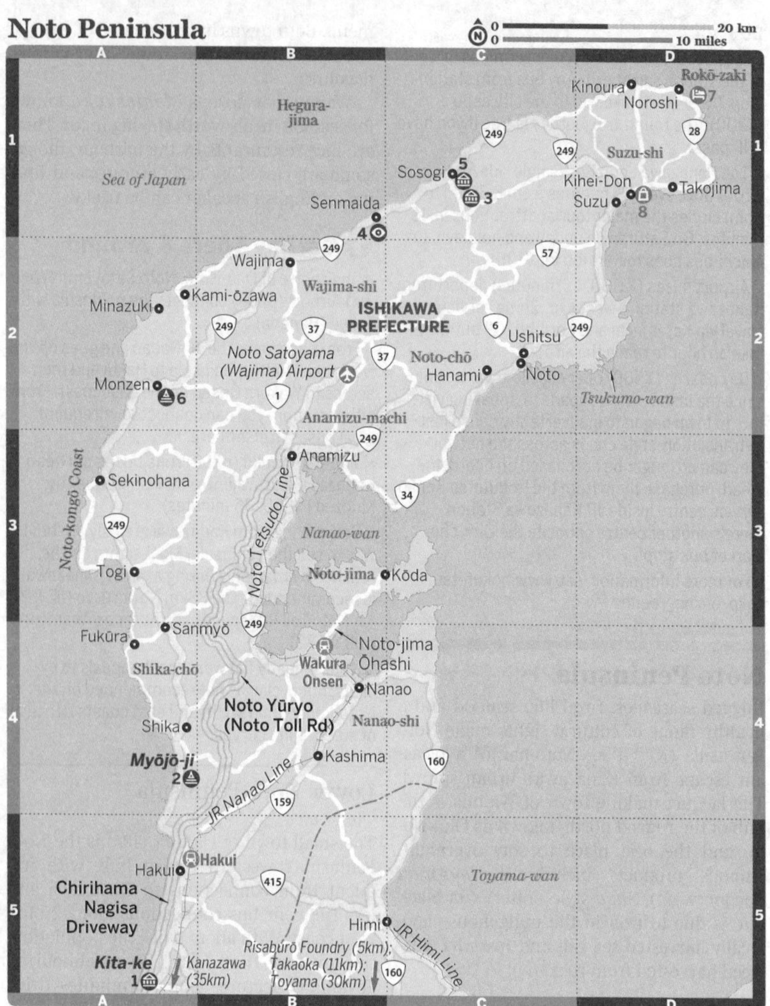

Noto Peninsula

Top Sights

1 Kita-ke A5
2 Myōjō-ji A4

Sights

3 Kami-tokikuni-ke C1
4 Senmaida Rice Terraces B1
5 Shimo-tokikuni-ke C1
6 Sōji-ji Soin A2

Sleeping

7 Lamp no Yado D1

Shopping

8 Road Station Suzunari D1

It's about 1km from the Komedashi exit on the Noto Yūryo (Noto Toll Rd). By train, take the JR Nanao line to Menden Station and walk for 20 minutes.

★ Myōjō-ji BUDDHIST TEMPLE

(妙成寺; ☎0767-27-1226; Yo-1 Takidani-machi; ¥510; ⊙8am-5pm Apr-Oct, to 4.30pm Nov-Mar) Founded in 1294 by Nichizō, a disciple of Nichiren's, the imposing Myōjō-ji remains an important temple for the sect. The peaceful grounds comprise 10 Important Cultural Properties, most notably the strikingly elegant five-storey pagoda. The Togi-bound bus from JR Hakui Station can drop you at Myōjō-ji-guchi bus stop (¥430, 18 minutes); from there it's less than 10 minutes' walk.

Getting There & Away

From Kanazawa, take the JR Nanao line to Hakui (¥820, one hour). The JR Himi line connects Takaoka (in Toyama Prefecture) with Himi (*futsū* ¥310, 33 minutes).

Car-rental companies can be found near Himi's and Hakui's train stations.

Noto-kongō Coast

☎0767, 0768

This rocky, cliff-lined shore extends for about 16km between Fukūra and Sekinohana, and is adorned with dramatic rock formations. The region's best explored by (narrow) road.

Sights

Sōji-ji Soin BUDDHIST TEMPLE

(総持寺祖院; ☎0768-42-0005; 1-18-1 Monzen, Monzen; adult/child ¥400/160; ⏰8am-5pm) This beautiful temple was established in 1321 as the head of the Sōtō school of Zen but now functions as a branch temple. The site's buildings were damaged by the 2007 Noto earthquake and remain under fastidious reconstruction. Sōji-ji Soin welcomes visitors to experience one hour of *zazen* (seated meditation; ¥300; 9am to 3pm), serves *shōjin-ryōri* (Buddhist vegetarian cuisine; ¥2500 to ¥3500) and can accommodate visitors (with two meals ¥6500; single women prohibited). Reserve at least two days ahead.

At time of research, the temple was undergoing renovations set to be completed in 2021.

Getting There & Away

To get to the coast from Kanazawa, take the JR Nanao line to Hakui (¥820, one hour), then connect to buses.

The manicured little town of Monzen is the area's transport hub, with buses servicing Kanazawa (¥2100, 2½ hours, four daily), Hakui (¥1560, 1½ hours, four daily) and Wajima (¥670, 45 minutes, nine daily).

Wajima

☎0768 / POP 27,698

The fishing port of Wajima (輪島), historically famed for delicate *Wajima-nuri* (lacquerware), is the largest town in the Noto Peninsula's north. The 2015 arrival of the Hokuriku *shinkansen* to Kanazawa has injected new energy into this fishing village; it's great fun seeing fashionable Japanese urbanites mingle with old salts. Wajima's fantastic Asa-ichi morning market is ground zero for people-watching and shopping for trinkets, snacks and antiques.

Sights

★**Asa-ichi** MARKET

(朝市, Morning Market; ⏰8am-noon, closed 10th & 25th of month) Among a few hundred elderly women selling fresh-off-the-trawler seafood, this entertaining morning market features cool boutiques offering tasteful lacquerware, pottery and souvenirs, and hip young Japanese families from Kanazawa and further afield. Haggle politely if you dare.

Kiriko Kaikan MUSEUM

(キリコ会館; ☎0768-22-7100; http://wajima-kiriko.com; 6-1 Marine Town; adult/child ¥620/360; ⏰8am-5pm) Here you can view a selection of the impressive illuminated, lacquered floats used in the **Wajima Taisai** (輪島大祭; ⏰late Aug) festival, some up to 15m tall. Take the bus to Tsukada stop (¥150, six minutes).

Ishikawa Wajima Urushi Art Museum MUSEUM

(石川輪島漆芸美術館; ☎0768-22-9788; www.city.wajima.ishikawa.jp/art/home_english.html; 11 Shijukari Mitomori-machi; adult/student ¥620/150; ⏰9am-4.30pm) This modern museum, about a 15-minute walk west of the former train station, has rotating exhibitions of its large lacquerware collection in galleries over two floors. Phone ahead, as it closes between exhibitions.

Festivals & Events

Gojinjō Daikō Nafune Matsuri MUSIC

(御陣乗太鼓名舟大祭; ⏰31 Jul) This festival features participants wearing demon masks and seaweed head gear and culminates in a frenzy of wild drumming.

Sleeping

Sodegahama Camping Ground CAMPGROUND ¥

(袖が浜キャンプ場; ☎0768-23-1146; 51 Sodegahama; campsites per person ¥1000; Ⓟ) Take the local *noranke* bus (¥100) or Nishiho bus (direction Zōza, 雑座) to Sodegahama, or hike for 20 minutes to reach this beachfront campground.

Route Inn Wajima HOTEL ¥¥
(ホテルルートイン輪島; 0768-22-7700; www.route-inn.co.jp; 1-2 Marine Town; s/d with breakfast from ¥7250/12,000; P ✱) With decent-size rooms and great views from the upper floors, this modern harbourside tourist hotel has all you need if you're passing through.

Oyado Tanaka RYOKAN ¥¥
(お宿たなか; 0768-22-5155; www.oyado-tanaka.jp; 22-38 Kawai-machi; r per person incl 2 meals from ¥13,000; P ✱) This immaculate 10-room inn has beds on tatami, hot-spring baths (including a private-use *rotemburo* – outdoor bath –for an extra charge), dark woodwork, paper lanterns and ambience aplenty. The *kaiseki* (Japanese haute cuisine) meals feature local seafood and lacquerware.

Eating & Drinking

Madara-yakata SEAFOOD ¥
(まだら館; 0768-22-3453; www.madara-yakata.com; 4-103 Kawai-machi; dishes from ¥870; 11am-7pm) This restaurant near the Asa-ichi market (p269) serves local specialities including *zōsui* (rice hotpot), *yaki-zakana* (grilled fish) and seasonal seafood, surrounded by folk crafts.

Umi-tei Notokichi SEAFOOD ¥¥
(海亭のと吉; 0768-22-6636; 4-153 Kawai-machi; dishes ¥620-2700; 11am-2pm & 5-8pm Thu-Tue) Umi-tei Notokichi has been a popular local haunt for generations – it's a quintessential Japanese seafood experience. Purists should keep it simple and go for the *sashimi moriawase* (sashimi of the day). It also does a mean version of *katsudon* (crumbed pork cutlet on rice).

Kalpa COFFEE
(0768-22-0036; 2-72-1 Kawaimachi; 8.30am-5pm Thu-Tue) What a delightful surprise to find excellent coffee in deepest Noto! The barista behind Kalpa's counter is also a third-generation lacquer craftsman; his and his father's handiwork is for sale in the shop.

Information

Tourist Information Center (輪島観光協会; 0768-22-1503; 8am-7pm) Limited English is spoken by the friendly staff at this office in the former Wajima train station, now the bus station. However, they do have English-language maps and can help with accommodation bookings.

Getting There & Away

Hokuriku Tetsudo runs buses between Kanazawa and Wajima (¥2200, two hours, 11 daily), although renting a car in Kanazawa or in the lower Noto Peninsula is by far the easiest way to explore the area.

Upper Noto Peninsula

0768

Travelling from Wajima towards the tip of the Noto Peninsula you'll pass the famous slivered *dandan-batake* (rice terraces) at **Senmaida** (千枚田) before arriving in the coastal village of **Sosogi** (曽々木), with its *mado-iwa* (窓岩; window rock) formation just offshore, and a number of hiking trails. In winter look for *nami-no-hana* (flowers of the waves): masses of foam that form when waves gnash Sosogi's rocky shore.

The road northeast from Sosogi passes sea-salt farms as it winds its way onward to **Rokō-zaki**, the peninsula's furthest point. Here, in the village of **Noroshi** (狼煙), you can amble up to the lighthouse for wonderful views before circling around the tip of the peninsula south to the outposts of **Suzu** and **Noto-chō**, from where the scenery becomes gradually less dramatic on the way back to more urban areas.

Sights

Senmaida Rice Terraces LANDMARK
(白米千枚田段々畑; http://senmaida.wajima-kankou.jp/en) Once a common sight in Japan, the ancient terraced method of rice farming is disappearing. These 'thousand' paddies snaking up the hillside are both fascinating and beautiful in all seasons.

Kami-tokikuni-ke HISTORIC BUILDING
(上時国家; 0768-32-0171; 13-4 Machino-machi, Minamitoki-kuni; adult/child ¥520/310; 8.30am-5pm) One of the few survivors of the Taira clan, Taira Tokitada was exiled to this region in 1185. His ancestors eventually divided and established separate family residences here, both now Important Cultural Properties – the other is Tokikuni-ke. Kami-tokikuni-ke has an impressive thatched roof and an elegant interior. It was completed in the early 19th century.

Shimo-tokikuni-ke (時国家; adult/child ¥600/300; 8.30am-5pm), the older residence, was built in 1590 in the style of the Kamakura period and has a *meishō tei-en* (famous garden).

Sleeping

★Lamp no Yado RYOKAN ¥¥¥

(ランプの宿; ☎0768-86-8000; www.lampnoyado.co.jp; 10-11 Jike, Misaki-machi; r per person with 2 meals from ¥21,000; P❄📶) Remote Lamp no Yado is a place all its own: a 13-room wooden village beneath a cliff (busy with tour buses, a snack hall and a vast asphalt parking lot). The cape's beach has been a destination for peace-seeking travellers for centuries; there's been an inn here since the 1970s. Rooms are decadent, and some have private *rotemburo* (outdoor bath).

This is a romantic destination ryokan.

Shopping

Road Station Suzunari ARTS & CRAFTS

(珠洲市観光協会; ☎0768-82-4688; https://notohantou.jp; 15 Nojemachi; ⏲8.30am-6pm) In the former Suzu train station (and attached to the current Suzu bus station), this shop sells well-priced crafts and products from around the Noto region. See if you can resist ordering another helping of the vanilla ice cream with Suzu salt.

Getting There & Away

From Wajima, Ushitsu-bound buses for the Senmaida Rice Terraces stop in Sosogi (¥760, 50 minutes), but renting a car will afford greater freedom to explore this sleepy, scenic coastline.

Kaga Onsen

☎0761 / POP 67,793

This broad area consisting of three hot-spring villages – Katayamazu Onsen, Yamashiro Onsen and Yamanaka Onsen – centres on Kaga Onsen (加賀温泉) and Daishōji Stations along the JR Hokuriku line and is famed for its *onsen ryokan* (traditional hot-spring inns), lacquerware and porcelain. The area is popular with local tourists, who spend most of their time relaxing in the onsen, enjoying *kaiseki* (Japanese haute cuisine) and getting to bed early. Kaga Onsen is not a party area.

Of the three villages, Yamanaka Onsen is the most scenic, straddling the Kakusenkei Gorge, through which the Daishoji-gawa flows.

Sights

Zenshō-ji BUDDHIST TEMPLE

(全昌寺; ☎0761-72-1164; 1 Daishōji Shinmei-chō; ¥500; ⏲9am-5pm) The Daishōji Station area is crammed with temples, including Zenshō-ji, which houses more than 500 amusingly carved Buddhist arhat sculptures.

Kutaniyaki Porcelain Art Museum MUSEUM

(石川県九谷焼美術館; ☎0761-72-7466; www.kutani-mus.jp/en; 1-10-13 Daishōji Jikata-machi; adult/child ¥500/free; ⏲9am-4.30pm Tue-Sun) Stunning examples of bright and colourful local porcelain are on display here, about an eight-minute walk from Daishōji Station.

Activities

Yamanaka Onsen ONSEN

The 17th-century haiku poet Bashō rhapsodised on the chrysanthemum fragrance of the mineral springs in Yamanaka Onsen. It's still an ideal spot for chilling at the **Kiku no Yu bathhouse** (菊の湯; 11 Yunodemachi, Yamanaka Onsen; ¥420; ⏲6.45am-10.30pm), and for river walks by the Kakusenkei Gorge, spanned by the elegant **Korogi-bashi** (Cricket Bridge) and the whimsical, modern-art **Ayatori-hashi** (Cat's Cradle Bridge).

Yamanaka Onsen is accessible by bus (¥420, 30 minutes) from Kaga Onsen Station.

Kosōyu ONSEN

(古総湯; Yamashiro Onsen; ¥500, Sōyu combined ticket ¥700; ⏲6am-10pm) Close to Kaga Onsen Station, Yamashiro Onsen is a sleepy town centred on a magnificent wooden bathhouse that was recently rebuilt. Kosōyu has beautiful stained-glass windows and a rest area on the top floor; neighbouring Sōyu is a larger, more modern bathhouse.

Sleeping & Eating

Ohanami Kyubei RYOKAN ¥¥

(お花見久兵衛; ☎0761-78-1301; www.ohanami-kyubei.jp; 138-1 Ni Shimotanimachi, Yamanaka Onsen; r per person ¥7000; P❄📶) Popular with Japanese tourists (the result of a ubiquitous television advert), the Kyubei *onsen ryokan* (traditional hot-spring inn) is a long, narrow property vertiginously perched on Kakusenkei Gorge. Rooms have good river views, and a bath-salt scrub in the public onsen will make your skin feel as soft as a baby's bottom.

★Kayōtei RYOKAN ¥¥¥

(かよう亭; ☎0761-78-1410; www.kayotei.jp; 1-20 Higashi-machi, Yamanaka Onsen; per person incl 2 meals from ¥30,000; P❄@📶) This opulent ryokan along the scenic Kakusenkei Gorge has only 10 rooms, centred on a delicate garden courtyard. Some rooms have views over the gorge and a beautiful hidden waterfall. Kitchen staff forage wild herbs from the mountains for meals, and wild boar are sometimes visible from private *rotemburo* (outdoor baths).

Beniya Mukayū RYOKAN ¥¥¥
(べにや無何有; ☎0761-77-1340; www.mukayu.com; 55-1-3 Yamashiro Onsen, Yamashiro Onsen; per person incl 2 meals from ¥34,000; P ❄ @ 📶) The friendly staff at this award-winning, gorgeously minimalist ryokan are committed to upholding the Japanese art of hospitality. A sense of Zen pervades every aspect of the guest experience here, from the welcoming private tea ceremony to the gentle morning yoga classes. Rooms are a beautiful fusion of old and new, and every room features a private *rotemburo* (outdoor bath).

Chōraku DUMPLINGS ¥
(手作り餃子　長樂; ☎0761-78-1087; http://choraku.net; 21 Yunohonmachi, Yamanaka Onsen; gyōza from ¥450; ⏲11.30am-1.30pm & 5-9.30pm) The family behind Chōraku has been making delicate *gyōza* (dumplings) by hand to order for more than 50 years, and their experience has deliciously paid off. The mapo tofu and ramen are also excellent. This is a refreshingly unpretentious place to eat in a town filled with gorgeous, precise *kaiseki* (Japanese haute cuisine).

Information

Yamanaka Onsen Ryokan Cooperative (山中温泉旅館協同組合; ☎0761-78-0330; www.yamanaka-spa.or.jp/global/eng; 5-1 Yamanaka Onsen)

Yamashiro Onsen Tourist Association (山代温泉観光協会; ☎0761-77-1144; www.yamashiro-spa.or.jp/foreign/en; 3-70 Hokubu; ⏲9am-5pm)

Getting There & Around

The JR Hokuriku line links Kaga Onsen with Kanazawa (*tokkyū/futsū* ¥1510/760, 25/44 minutes) and Fukui (*tokkyū/futsū* ¥1330/580, 21/33 minutes).

Willer Express (☎050-5805-0383; http://willerexpress.com) operates bus services from Tokyo to Kaga Onsen, from ¥5900.

Enquire at the tourism association or your accommodation about the irregular tour bus to Daihonzan Eihei-ji.

In Yamashiro Onsen, 'Can bus' (two-day pass ¥1200) operates a similar service around the area's various sights and onsen.

Fukui

☎0776 / POP 265,904

Unfortunate Fukui city (福井) was decimated in the 1940s, first by war, then by earthquake. Most of the sights of interest are scattered around the compact prefecture, a short drive from town, but the tidy city features a pretty park and castle grounds. Consider car rental and an overnight stay: country roads make for easy driving and the scenery is lovely.

Sights

★**Ichijōdani Asakura Clan Ruins** RUINS
(一乗谷朝倉氏遺跡, Ichijōdani Asakura-shi Iseki; ☎0776-41-2330; http://asakura-museum.pref.fukui.lg.jp; 4-10 Abaka; ¥230; ⏲9am-4.30pm) Designated a national historic site, this out-of-the-way place features one of the largest town ruins in Japan, dating from the early 15th century. It's easy to see why the Asakura clan would have built their small fortified city here: it's very beautiful, perched in a narrow valley between modest mountains. You're free to wander along the restored street of merchants' houses and stroll the lush grounds, following the building remnants up the hillside. It's a wonderful spot to sit, picnic and contemplate.

Daihonzan Eihei-ji BUDDHIST TEMPLE
(大本山永平寺; ☎0776-63-3640; https://daihonzan-eiheiji.com/en; 5-15 Shihi, Eiheiji; adult/child ¥500/200; ⏲8.30am-5pm) In 1244 the great Zen master Dōgen (1200–53), founder of the Sōtō sect of Zen Buddhism, established Eihei-ji, the 'Temple of Eternal Peace', in a forest outside Fukui. Today it's one of Sōtō's two head temples, a palpably spiritual place amid mountains, mosses and ancient cedars. That said, day trippers visiting the complex of more than 70 buildings might not find the constant buzz of visitors and activities as peaceful as they might desire.

Aspirants can participate in Eihei-ji's one-night stay or three-night sanzen-experience program, which follow the monks' training schedule.

The compound is often closed for periods varying from a week to 10 days for religious observance. Sanrō-temple stays cost from ¥9000 for a one-night stay to ¥20,000 for the full *sanzen* experience, and must be booked several months in advance.

To get to Eihei-ji from Fukui, take the Keifuku bus (¥720, 30 minutes, hourly); buses depart from the east exit of JR Fukui Station.

Fukui Dinosaur Museum MUSEUM
(福井県立恐竜博物館; ☎0779-88-0001; www.dinosaur.pref.fukui.jp; 51-11 Muroko-chō Terao, Katsuyama; adult/child ¥720/260; ⏲9am-5pm) Kids love the larger-than-life replicas and fossilised relics of the Jurassic Park–styled Fukui Dinosaur Museum, one of the three largest museums of its kind in the world. There are plenty of English explanations and more than 40 main exhibits (including interactive ones) concerned with natural history, prehistoric flora and fauna, and the dinosaurs that once roamed Japan and other parts of the world. The closest train station is Katsuyama on the privately owned Echizen line, but your best bet is self-driving.

Activities

Sanzen Experience Program MEDITATION
(☎0776-63-3640; https://daihonzan-eiheiji.com/en/guide-izw-beginners.html; 5-15 Shihi, Eiheiji; ¥20,000) Aspirants affiliated with a Sōtō Zen organisation can attend these four-day, three-night *sanzen* religious-experience programs at Daihonzan Eihei-ji, which follow the monks' training schedule, complete with 4.10am prayers, cleaning, *zazen* (seated meditation) and ritual meals in which not a grain of rice may be left behind. Knowledge of Japanese isn't necessary, but some self-discipline is helpful. Book well ahead.

Sleeping & Eating

Fukui city has a handful of moderately priced business and tourist hotels and some basic *minshuku* (guesthouses).

While Fukui lacks the range of dining options found in other, more popular tourist towns, there's still plenty to choose from around the train station's west and east exits and driving along Rte 158. The area is known for its *oroshi soba* (buckwheat noodles with a variety of dipping sauces).

Fukui Phoenix Hotel HOTEL ¥¥
(福井フェニックスホテル; ☎0776-21-1800; www.phoenix-hotel.jp; 2-4-18 Ote; s/d/tw from ¥9000/14,000/15,000; P❄📶) A hop, skip and jump from JR Fukui Station, this refurbished hotel has tastefully decorated rooms, free wi-fi, a coin laundry, and a variety of room types (including suites) for those wanting a little more room to spread out. Parking is available nearby for ¥1000.

Amida Soba Yūbuan NOODLES ¥¥
(あみだそば遊歩庵; ☎0776-76-3519; 1-9-1 Chūō; soba ¥600-1300; ⏲11.30am-7pm) On the Rekishi-no-michi street outside the west exit of Fukui Station, you'll find this delightful variation on a soba theme. The speciality is *oroshi soba sanmai* (¥1300), a double serve of thick, flattened soba noodles with three flavours to dip them into: *oroshi* (grated daikon), *tororo* (grated mountain potato) and wasabi.

Amida has another location on the ground floor of the food hall adjacent to the spanking-new station.

Information

Fukui Tourist Information Center (福井市観光案内所; ☎0776-20- 5348; 1-2-1 Chūō; ⏲8.30am-7pm) Enquire here, just outside the west exit of JR Fukui Station, for local maps and itineraries. The English-speaking staff members are super helpful and ready to show off their city.

Getting There & Away

JR trains connect Fukui with Kanazawa (*tokkyū/futsū* ¥2500/1320, 48 minutes/1½ hours), Tsuruga (*tokkyū/futsū* ¥2150/970, 35/52 minutes), Kyoto (¥4420, 1½ hours) and Osaka (¥5690, 2½ hours).

There are several car-rental options outside the east exit of JR Fukui Station, including Toyota Rent-a-Car.

Toyama

☎076 / POP 418,686

Toyama (富山) is the starting point for your journey on the Tateyama-Kurobe Alpine Route (p275). Its marine ecology also makes it a pilgrimage spot for seafood enthusiasts.

In October 2014 Toyama's picturesque mountain-ringed bay was inducted into the Unesco-endorsed Most Beautiful Bays in the World club, making it the second bay in Japan to be awarded this prestigious title, recognising the bay's natural beauty as well as its unique ecosystem. Toyama-wan's nutrient-dense waters are fed from nearby mountains and sustain a wide variety of marine life, including the uncommon *hotaruika* (firefly squid) and *shiroebi* (white shrimp). There aren't many opportunities to get out on the water, but sampling the unique seafood of Toyama, celebrated throughout Japan, is a special treat.

Sleeping & Eating

Thanks to the arrival of the Hokuriku *shinkansen*, Toyama's station area has been going through a facelift. The city has also seen the construction of some new hotels, most of which are around the station's south exit.

Sample Toyama's unique seafood at restaurants outside the station's south exit.

Toyama Excel Hotel Tōkyū HOTEL ¥¥¥
(富山エクセルホテル東急; ☎076-441-0109; www.toyama-e.tokyuhotels.co.jp; 1-2-3 Shintomichō; s/d from ¥15,000/20,000; P❄@) Toyama's fanciest place to stay has 210 rooms in a variety of configurations and two restaurants. Rooms on higher floors have fantastic views.

Shiroebi-tei SEAFOOD ¥¥
(白えび亭; ☎076-432-7575; www.shiroebiya.co.jp; 1-220 Meirin-cho; meal sets from ¥1200; ⊙10am-8pm) Locals swear by this high-volume institution on the ground floor of Toyama Station. The staple is *shiroebi ten-don* (white-shrimp tempura over rice; ¥1200). Order from the ticket-vending machine inside the restaurant; a server will be happy to help if you need it.

Information

Tourist Information Center (観光案内所; ☎076-432-9751; http://foreign.info-toyama.com/en; ⊙8.30am-8pm) Inside Toyama Station, this office stocks maps and pamphlets on Toyama and the Tateyama-Kurobe Alpine Route. Excellent English is spoken by blazer-wearing staff, and bicycles can be rented.

Getting There & Away

AIR

Daily flights operate between **Toyama Airport** (TOY; www.toyama-airport.co.jp/english) and major Japanese cities; there are less frequent flights to Seoul and Shanghai.

BUS

Buses are available between Toyama and Osaka, Toyko, and Gifu and Niigata Prefectures; see www.info-toyama.com for details.

TRAIN

The Hokuriku *shinkansen* connects Toyama with Kanazawa (¥3550, 20 minutes), Nagano (¥7100, one hour) and Tokyo (¥12,730, 2¾ hours).

The JR Takayama line runs south to Takayama (¥1660, 90 minutes) and Nagoya (¥8030, four hours). The JR Hokuriku line runs west to Kanazawa (¥1220, one hour) and Osaka (¥8350, 3¼ hours), and northeast to Niigata (¥6178, three hours).

Takaoka

☎0766 / POP 172,125

The pleasant city of Takaoka (高岡), famed for the production of copper temple bells, is home to one of Japan's three Great Buddhas, several well-preserved historic walking neighbourhoods, and the truly awesome Zuiryū-ji, a National Treasure. Unlike many cities of its size in Central Honshū, Takaoka has resisted modernisation and retains a mid-20th-century feel, from its covered sidewalk arcades right down to its adorable vintage tram cars that look as though they belong in a museum. It's a walkable, workaday town where you'll likely be one of only a few visitors.

Sights

★Zuiryū-ji BUDDHIST TEMPLE
(瑞龍寺; ☎0766-22-0179; www.zuiryuji.jp; 35 Sekihon-machi; adult/child ¥500/200; ⊙9am-4.30pm) One of Japan's National Treasures, the temple of the second generation of feudal lord Maeda Toshinaga's family is rightly famous for its manicured lawns, steep roofs, and all-round aesthetic that marries Indian and Japanese architectural styles. If you come just before 9am, there's every chance you'll have the place to yourself, with the exception of the temple *deshi* (apprentice), who'll be raking stones and opening *shōji* (sliding rice-paper-screen doors) before the day's visitors arrive.

Kojō Park PARK
(www.kojyo.sakura.ne.jp; 1-1-9 Kojō) This big park is the site of the old Takaoka castle (*kojō* means – you guessed it – 'old castle'), demolished in 1615 after being in use only six years. The moats and the large green lawns make for enjoyable strolling and picnicking. The park is also home to badminton, table-tennis and volleyball facilities (¥100 per hour).

Takaoka Great Buddha LANDMARK
(高岡大仏; ☎0766-23-9156; 11-29 Ōte-machi; ⊙6am-6pm) Construction of this great bronze Buddha statue began in 1907 and was completed in 1933. The statue was moved to its present location in 1981 after

TATEYAMA–KUROBE ALPINE ROUTE

From mid-April to November the popular seasonal 90km Tateyama–Kurobe Alpine Route (立山黒部アルペンルート) connects Tateyama (Toyama Prefecture) with Shinano-ōmachi (Nagano Prefecture) via a sacred mountain, a deep gorge, a boiling-hot spring and glory-hallelujah mountain scenery. It's divided into nine sections and uses different modes of transport, including your own two feet. Reservations are strongly advised.

Travel is possible in either direction; as the route is often only travelled one way, using it to travel between Toyama and Nagano is recommended. Full details can be found at www.alpen-route.com. There are hundreds of steps along the way and plenty of walking. Be sure to forward your baggage to your destination hotel before you set off (details are on the website).

The one way/return fare for the entire route is ¥10,850/18,260; tickets for individual sections are available. The trip takes at least six hours one way. If you're starting in Toyama and not heading to Nagoya, you may find a return trip to Murodō (¥6710), the route's highest point at 2450m, sufficient.

Start the journey before 9am at Toyama Station on the chug-a-lug regional Toyama Chiho line bound for Tateyama (¥1290, one hour). The first stage of the route is the cable car up to **Bijodaira** (美女平; seven minutes).

Next is a bus journey up to **Murodō** (室堂; 50 minutes) via the spectacular alpine plateau of **Midagahara Kōgen**, where you can break the trip and do the 15-minute walk to see **Tateyama caldera** (立山カルデラ), the largest nonactive crater in Japan. The upper part of the plateau is often covered with deep snow well into spring; snowploughs keep the road clear by pushing vast walls of snow to each side of the road, forming a virtual tunnel of ice.

Ten minutes' walk from Murodō is **Mikuri-ga-ike** (みくりが池) pond, where you'll find Japan's highest *onsen ryokan* (www.mikuri.com). Twenty minutes further on is **Jigokudani Onsen** (Hell Valley Hot Springs); there's no bathing here as the waters are boiling! To the east you can make the steep two-hour hike to the peak of **O-yama** (雄山; 3003m) for an astounding panorama. Experienced and equipped long-distance hikers can continue south to Kamikōchi.

When you're ready, board the trolley bus that tunnels through Tateyama-dake for 3.7km to **Daikanbō** (10 minutes). From here the Tateyama Ropeway whisks you 488m down to **Kurobe-daira** (seven minutes), offering breathtaking views of the valley below. You're free to stop between sections at your own pace, or go with the flow of the crowds. The next step is the underground Kurobe cable car to **Kurobeko** (five minutes). You'll emerge to see the massive **Kurobe Dam**: it's a 15-minute walk across the dam to the impressive observation deck.

When you're ready to proceed, trolley buses (16 minutes) whisk you through a 5.8km tunnel to the end of your journey at **Ogizawa**. From here there's a bus to **Ōmachi onsen-kyo** (40 minutes; elevation 712m) and then on to **Nagano Station** (90 minutes) – you made it!

the ground supporting it began to give way. It's now a symbol of the city and referred to as one of the three Great Buddhas of Japan.

Risaburō Foundry FACTORY
(鋳物工房利三郎, Imono Kōbō Risaburō; ☎0766-24-0852; www13.plala.or.jp/jinpachi; 8-11 Kanaya-machi; ⏰10am-5pm) FREE This factory has been producing traditional Takaoka bronzeware since the Meiji era and allows visitors a rare and fascinating glimpse of the casting process, as well as the opportunity to participate in the process themselves (¥3000).

Sleeping & Eating

Takaoka has some pleasant, well-priced business and tourist hotels by JR Takaoka Station.

Most of the city's dining options are clustered around the station area. Many restaurants showcase the variety of seafood sourced from nearby Toyama-wan.

Daibutsu Ryokan RYOKAN ¥¥
(☎0766-21-0075; www.ryokan.or.jp/english/yado/main/45780; 1276 Daibutsumachi; r per person from ¥4500; P ❄ 📶) Sweet Daibutsu Ryokan is run by a friendly, helpful family eager to

WORTH A TRIP

KUROBE GORGE RAILWAY

The **Kurobe Gorge Railway** (黒部峡谷トロッコ電車; Map p292; 0765-62-1011; www.kurotetu.co.jp; 11 Kurobe Kyokoku-guchi, Kurobe; one-way to Keyaki-daira ¥1980; 9am-5pm May-November) is a unique ride through the heart of the Kurobe Valley. It runs from Unazuki to Keyaki-daira in tiny carriages used for the construction of the Kurobe Dam. When you're not careening through tunnels, the mountain views are breathtaking, especially in autumn, and the opportunity to explore some truly remote and astounding mountain *rotemburo* and inns is definitely rewarding.

The new Kurobe Unazuki Onsen Station on the Hokuriku *shinkansen* line has dramatically improved access and increased visitor numbers. From Shin-Kurobe Station (adjacent to the *shinkansen* station), catch a local train to Unazuki Onsen Station (¥630, 30 minutes), from where it's a short walk to Unazuki Station, terminus of the Kurobe Gorge Railway.

You must purchase tickets for each leg of the journey separately at each station; due to high passenger demand, this is not a hop-on, hop-off service. The entire journey from Unazuki to Keyaki-daira takes about 80 minutes. It's suggested that you first take the full journey, and decide along the way which stops you'd like to get off at on the way back. For full details on how to get there, what to see and how it works, refer to the website.

The remote Kuronagi-onsen is a must-see: look out for bears along the path. Also recommended is the Iwa-buro cave bath, a short walk from Kanetsuri Station. The restaurant at Keyaki-daira can get very busy at times so bring snacks for the journey, as well as some warm clothing, even in summer it can get very chilly in the tunnels.

Try to get a seat on the right-hand side of the train for the outbound journey from Unazuki, and the left-hand side coming back, or you'll miss the best photo ops. Note that carriages are allocated, but seats aren't reserved: it's first come, first served.

share their knowledge of Takaoka. The rambling old house is built around two Japanese gardens, one featuring a personal, meditative koi (carp) pond. The ryokan's one-block proximity to the Great Buddha (p274) means you can have the large gentleman all to yourself in the evening or early morning.

Information

Takaoka Station Tourist Information Center (高岡駅観光案内所; 0766-20-1547; www.takaoka.or.jp/en; bike rental per day ¥200; 9am-5pm)

Getting There & Away

Takaoka is served by local trains from Himi, at the base of the Noto Peninsula (¥320, 29 minutes), and Toyama (¥360, 23 minutes). The Hokuriku *shinkansen* zooms into the new Shin-Takaoka Station, where you can change to the Johana line for a local train to Takaoka Station (¥140, three minutes).

Getting Around

It's easy to get around on bikes, which can be rented April to November from the Takaoka Station Tourist Information Center.

THE NORTHERN JAPAN ALPS

Boasting some of Japan's most magnificent peaks and dramatic scenery, the northern Japan Alps (北アルプス) are truly spectacular, with stunning 3000m peaks accessible even to amateur hikers. Also known as the Hida Range (飛騨山脈), the mountains are protected within Chūbu-Sangaku National Park (中部山岳国立公園). Put very simply, the northern Alps are in the shape of a big 'Y'. The northwestern arm is based around the Tateyama peaks and accessed from Murodō on the Tateyama–Kurobe Alpine Route. The lovely resort village of Kamikōchi, at the base of the 'Y', is the access point for hiking in the south, while the northeastern arm of the 'Y' is accessed from Hakuba, home to various events at the 1998 Winter Olympics.

For those coming from Tokyo, lovely Matsumoto, in the centre of north-south sprawling Nagano Prefecture, is the gateway city for the northern Alps and a fascinating destination in its own right.

Information

Make sure you have enough cash before setting out: to say that ATMs are scarce is an understatement – and bankcards rarely work at altitude.

Getting There & Away

Matsumoto is the key transport hub of the region, especially if you're coming from Tokyo. Those coming from points west, such as Nagoya or Osaka, may consider approaching the north Alps from Takayama, while the northwestern arm of the north Alps can be accessed from Toyama on the Sea of Japan coast.

Shinshū Matsumoto Airport (p282) services a handful of domestic destinations.

Alpico Group (www.alpico.co.jp) runs long-distance buses connecting Matsumoto, Nagano, Kamikōchi and Hakuba with Tokyo, Nagoya, Kyoto and Osaka.

JR's *tokkyū* Super Azusa trains link Matsumoto to Tokyo (Shinjuku) and its *tokkyū* Shinano trains twist their way through the mountains, onward to Nagoya.

Getting Around

BUS

Alpico Group runs buses connecting all the hot spots you're likely to want to get to. See its website for all the options.

If you're heading west into Kamikōchi, or through to Takayama, from Matsumoto, you can travel by bus, or take a ride on the private Alpico Line train to the end of the line at Shin-Shimashima and then a bus. Either way, the journey is breathtaking.

Within the Alps, schedules change seasonally. Alpico's Alps-wide Free Passport (www.alpico.co.jp/en/special; ¥12,000) gives you four days' unlimited travel on its network within Shinshu, Chūbu-Sangaku National Park and Hida (including Shirakawa-gō).

CAR & MOTORCYCLE

Hiring a car is a good option if winding roads don't bother you and you're not overnighting in Kamikōchi. Note that the road from the Naka-no-yu turnoff into Kamikōchi is only open to buses and taxis.

TRAIN

Matsumoto is the hub for trains in the region.

From Matsumoto, the JR Oito line runs north along the eastern side of the north Alps, stopping at Hotaka (30 minutes, ¥320), Shinano-Ōmachi (for the Tateyama–Kurobe Alpine Route; one hour, ¥670) and Hakuba (100 minutes, ¥1140).

Alpico Line trains run west as far as Shin-Shimashima (30 minutes, ¥700). Buses run from there into Kamikōchi and west through to Takayama.

JR Shinanoi line trains run northeast to Nagano city (*tokkyū* 50 minutes, ¥3040).

JR Shinano trains run southwest through the Kiso Valley to Kiso-Fukushima (40 minutes, ¥2870) and on to Nagoya. Local trains on the JR Chūō line also run through the valley, but at a much more leisurely pace.

NORTHERN JAPAN ALPS SAMPLE BUS FARES & DURATIONS

FROM	TO	FARE (¥, ONE-WAY)	DURATION (MINUTES, ONE-WAY)
Takayama	Hirayu Onsen	1570	55
	Kamikōchi	2600	80
	Shin-Hotaka	2150	90
Matsumoto	Shin-Shimashima	700 (train)	30
	Kamikōchi	2650	95
Shin-Shimashima	Naka-no-yu	1100	50
	Kamikōchi	1250	70
	Shirahone Onsen	1450	75
Kamikōchi	Naka-no-yu	770	15
	Hirayu Onsen	1160	25
	Shirahone Onsen	1350	35
Hirayu Onsen	Naka-no-yu	580	10
	Shin-Hotaka	920	30

Matsumoto

0263 / POP 245,000

The vibrant city of Matsumoto (松本) sits in a fertile valley, with the magnificent northern Japan Alps, in all their splendour, to the west. Formerly known as Fukashi, Nagano Prefecture's second-largest city has been here since the 8th century. In the 14th and 15th centuries it was the castle town of the Ogasawara clan and it continued to prosper through the Edo period to the present.

Matsumoto is an attractive, cosmopolitan place loved by both residents and admirers from around the globe, who come to enjoy its superb castle, pretty streets, galleries, cafes and endearing vistas. There seems to be some extra enthusiasm for life here, with a youngish population that includes those who have forsaken the massive cities for this regional beauty. The mountains are close, the air is fresh and the rivers are invigoratingly cold. Matsumoto makes a great stepping stone on your way to the Alps.

Sights

★Matsumoto-jō CASTLE

(松本城; 0263-32-9202; www.matsumoto-castle.jp; 4-1 Marunōchi; adult/child ¥610/300; 8.30am-5pm early Sep–mid-Jul, to 6pm mid-Jul–early Sep) Must-see Matsumoto-jō is Japan's oldest wooden castle and one of four castles designated National Treasures – the others are Hikone, Himeji and Inuyama. The striking black-and-white three-turreted *donjon* (main keep) was completed around 1595, earning the nickname Karasu-jō (Crow Castle). You can climb steep steps all the way to the top, with impressive views and historical displays on each level. Don't miss the recently restored *tsukimi yagura* (moon-viewing pavilion). The Goodwill Guide Group offers free one-hour tours by reservation.

Nawate-dōri STREET

(縄手道り) Nawate-dōri, a few blocks south from the castle, is a popular street for a stroll. Vendors along this riverside walk sell antiques, souvenirs, and delicious *tai-yaki* (filled waffles in the shape of a carp) of varying flavours. Look for the big frog statue by the bridge.

Matsumoto City Museum of Art MUSEUM

(松本市美術館, Matsumoto-shi Bijutsukan; Map p292; 0263-39-7400; www.matsumoto-artmuse.jp; 4-2-22 Chūō; adult/child ¥410/200; 9am-5pm Tue-Sun) This sleek museum has a good collection of the work of Japanese artists, many of whom hail from Matsumoto or whose art depicts scenes of the surrounding countryside. Highlights include the striking avant-garde works of local-born, internationally renowned Kusama Yayoi.

Japan Ukiyo-e Museum MUSEUM

(日本浮世絵美術館; Map p292; 0263-47-4440; www.japan-ukiyoe-museum.com; 2206-1 Koshiba; adult/child ¥1000/500; 10am-5pm Tue-Sun) Housing more than 100,000 woodblock prints, paintings, screens and old books, this renowned museum exhibits but a fraction of its collection. The museum is approximately 3km from JR Matsumoto Station (about ¥1600 by taxi) or 15 minutes' walk from Ōniwa Station on the Alpico line (¥180, six minutes).

Matsumoto Open-Air Architectural Museum MUSEUM

(松本市歴史の里, Matsumoto-shi Rekishi-no-sato; Map p292; 0263-47-4515; http://matsu-haku.com/rekishinosato/shisetsu; 2196-1 Shimadachi; adult/child ¥400/300; 9am-5pm Tue-Sun) Adjacent to the better-known Japan Ukiyo-e Museum, amid fields and rice paddies beneath the gaze of the Alps, stand these five examples of striking late-Edo- and early-Shōwa-era architecture for you to explore. The museum is approximately 3km from JR Matsumoto Station (about ¥1600 by taxi) or 15 minutes' walk from Ōniwa Station on the Alpico line (¥180, six minutes).

Kaichi School Museum MUSEUM

(旧開智学校, Kyū Kaichi Gakkō; Map p292; 0263-32-5725; http://matsu-haku.com/kaichi; 2-4-12 Kaichi; adult/child ¥300/150; 8.30am-4.30pm daily Mar-Nov, Tue-Sun Dec-Feb) A few blocks north of the castle, the former Kaichi School is both an Important Cultural Property and the oldest elementary school in Japan, founded in 1873. It opened its doors as an education museum in 1965. The building itself is an excellent example of Meiji-era architecture.

Around Matsumoto

Northeast of downtown, **Utsukushi-ga-hara Onsen** (美ヶ原温泉) – not to be confused with Utsukushi-ga-hara-kōgen – is a pretty spa village, with a quaint main street and views across the valley. **Asama Onsen** (浅間温泉) has a history that is said to date back to the 10th century and includes

Matsumoto

writers and poets, though it looks quite generic now. Both areas are easily reached by bus from Matsumoto's bus terminal.

East of Matsumoto, the alpine plateau of **Utsukushi-ga-hara-kōgen** (美ヶ原高原; 2000m) boasts more than 200 varieties of flora that come alive in summer. It's a great day trip from Matsumoto, reached via an ooh-and-aah drive along twisty mountain roads called Azalea Line and Venus Line (open late April to early November). A car will give you the freedom to explore the beauty, but there's also a bus in season (¥1500 one way, 1½ hours).

Utsukushi-ga-hara Open Air Museum MUSEUM
(美ヶ原美術館, Utsukushi-ga-hara Bijutsukan; Map p292; ☎0263-86-2331; www.utsukushi-oam.jp; adult/child/student ¥1000/700/800; ⏲9am-5pm late Apr-early Nov) Atop Utsukushi-ga-hara-kōgen plateau you'll find this seemingly random sculpture garden with some 350 pieces, mostly by Japanese sculptors. The surrounding countryside provides an inspiring backdrop. Nearby are pleasant walks and the opportunity to see cows in pasture (a constant source of fascination in Japan). Buses (¥1500, 1½ hours) run several times daily during the warmer months, although a rental car is a good option if winding roads don't faze you.

Matsumoto

Top Sights
1 Matsumoto-jō B1

Sights
2 Nawate-dōri B2

Sleeping
3 Alpico Plaza Hotel A3
4 Marunouchi Hotel B1
5 Nunoya Ryokan B2
6 Ryokan Marumo B2

Eating
7 Healthy Penguin Cafe B2
8 Katsu Gen Honten B1
9 Matsumoto Karaage Center A3
10 Menshō Sakura A2
11 Shin-Miyoshi A2
12 Shizuka B1

Drinking & Nightlife
Eonta Jazz Bar .... (see 8)
13 Matsumoto Brewery Taproom B2

Shopping
14 Belle Amie Doll Shop B2
15 Chikiri-ya Art & Craft Shop B2
16 Nakamachi Kura-chic-kan B2

Information
Matsumoto Tourist Information Center .... (see 9)

Transport
17 Matsumoto Bus Terminal A3

Tours

Goodwill Guide Group TOURS
(☎0263-32-7140; www.matsumoto-castle.jp/lang/eng/info/guide) Phone ahead to reserve free one-hour tours of Matsumoto-jō, in English. Reservations essential in busy holiday periods.

Festivals & Events

Matsumoto Bonbon PARADE
(松本ぼんぼん; https://visitmatsumoto.com/en/event; ⏲Aug) Matsumoto's biggest event takes place on the first Saturday in August, when over 25,000 people of all ages perform the 'bonbon' dance through the streets, well into the hot summer's night. Be prepared to be drawn into the action.

Asama Onsen Taimatsu Matsuri PARADE
(浅間温泉松明祭り; Torch Festival; https://asamaonsen.jp/en/eventsinformation/torchfestival; ⏲Oct) Around the start of October, Asama Onsen celebrates the spectacular and

DON'T MISS

MATSUMOTO'S NAKAMACHI DISTRICT

The charming former merchant district of Nakamachi (中町) by the Metoba-gawa, with its *namako-kabe kura* (lattice-walled storehouses) and Edo-period streetscapes, makes for a wonderful stroll. Many buildings have been preserved and transformed into cafes, galleries and craft shops specialising in wood, glass, fabric, ceramics and antiques. In particular, enjoy a stroll down Nakamachi-dōri.

slightly manic fire festival, wherein groups of men, women and children, shouting *'wa-sshoi!'* like a mantra, parade burning bales of hay through narrow streets to an enormous bonfire at Misha-jinja.

Seiji Ozawa Matsumoto Festival MUSIC
(小澤 征爾 フェスティバル松本; www.ozawa-festival.com; ⏲mid-Aug–mid-Sep) During this festival about a dozen classical-music concerts are held in memory of revered Japanese conductor and music educator Saitō Hideo (1902–72). Ozawa Seiji, conductor emeritus of the Boston Symphony Orchestra, is festival director.

Sleeping

With plenty of well-priced, quality accommodation and excellent access to, from and around the town, Matsumoto is an ideal base for exploring the Japan Alps and the Kiso and Azumino Valleys.

Matsumoto's downtown is compact enough that you can get around easily. Most business hotels are by the train station, but there are some great traditional options in picturesque Nakamachi.

★**Nunoya Ryokan** INN ¥
(ぬのや旅館; ☎0263-32-0545; www.mcci.or.jp/www/nunoya; 3-5-7 Chūō; r per person from ¥4500;) Few inns have more heart than this simple, traditional charmer, meticulously kept by its friendly owner. The spotless lodgings have shiny dark-wood floors, atmospheric tatami rooms, comfy futons and shared facilities right in the heart of Nakamachi. The rate is a bargain for this much character. You'll need to pay with cash here.

★**Ryokan Marumo** RYOKAN ¥
(まるも旅館; ☎0263-32-0115; www.avis.ne.jp/~marumo; 3-3-10 Chūō; r per person without bathroom ¥5000;) Between Nakamachi and the river, this creaky wooden ryokan dates from 1868 and has lots of traditional charm, including a bamboo garden and a coffee shop. Although the rooms aren't huge and don't have private facilities, it's popular, so book ahead.

Matsumoto BackPackers HOSTEL ¥
(松本バックパッカーズ; Map p292; ☎0263-31-5848; www.matsumotobp.com; 1-1-6 Shiraita; dm per person ¥3000;) By the river, just a few minutes' walk north from JR Matsumoto Station, you'll find this clean, friendly setup in a converted old house with tatami-mat rooms, futon bedding and shared facilities. There's a coin laundry, a kitchen and cooking utensils. These are the cheapest, most central dorm spots in town.

★**Marunouchi Hotel** HOTEL ¥¥
(丸の内ホテル; ☎0263-35-4500; www.matsumoto-marunouchi.com; 3-5-15 Ōte; s/d from ¥7000/11,000;) It's hard to fault this impressive hotel, occupying a prime spot near the castle. Reasonably priced rooms are refreshingly stylish and comfortable. Deluxe rooms approach Western standard sizes, while standard rooms are more compact but cheaper. Suites are a nice option for those who want something special. Some rooms even have castle views.

Alpico Plaza Hotel HOTEL ¥¥
(アルピコプラザホテル; ☎0263-36-5055; www.alpico-plaza-hotel.jp; 1-3-21 Fukashi; s/d from ¥7000/10,800; P) These folks have the bases covered: this is an extremely practical and convenient business hotel next to the Alpico Plaza building and bus terminal. No surprises here, with standard hotel rooms, laundry facilities (great if you've been hiking!), parking (¥1100 per night), and restaurants within a short stroll. Matsumoto Station is a two-minute walk away.

Eating

The area immediately opposite the train station is where you'll find *izakaya* (bar-restaurant) and restaurant mainstays. Cafes and eateries also line the banks of the Metoba-gawa and Nakamachi-dōri.

★**Shin-Miyoshi** IZAKAYA ¥
(新三よし; ☎0263-39-0141; http://sinmiyoshi.com; 1-7-17 Chūō; plates from ¥600; ⏲5-10.30pm Mon-Sat) Head to Shin-Miyoshi (New Miyoshi), established in 1999, to try everyone's favourite Nagano delicacy: horse meat. The first Miyoshi restaurant got going in 1899, and there are brilliant historical photos on the walls; the decor and furniture have been made to feel as if they're from older days. It's incredibly popular with locals. Try the *basashi* (horsemeat sashimi).

★**Healthy Penguin Cafe** CAFE ¥
(☎090-4153-8575; www.facebook.com/healthypenguincafe; 4-3-25 Ōte; plates from ¥700; ⏲11am-5pm Thu-Mon, to 7pm Sat & Sun; 🅥) This cute little cafe on a tiny side street off atmospheric old Nawate-dōri gets rave reviews for plates such as smashed avo toast (¥700) and cinnamon French toast (¥750). Desserts, plus organic coffees, teas, wine and craft beer round out an inspiring menu. A top spot for vegetarians and vegans. Look for the signboard out on Nawate-dōri.

★**Matsumoto Karaage Center** JAPANESE ¥
(松本からあげセンター; ☎0263-87-2229; www.karacen.com; 1-1-1 Fukashi; lunch & dinner sets from ¥780; ⏲10am-8.30pm) This wildly popular 4th-floor (above Midori in the station building) shrine to *karaage* (deep-fried chicken) is a must, with tender, juicy boneless chicken waiting to melt in your mouth. Try the local speciality, *Sanzoku-yaki* (山賊焼): crunchy chicken *katsu*. If you can't get a seat, there's a standing-only version of this place in the line-up out front of JR Matsumoto Station.

Katsu Gen Honten TONKATSU ¥
(かつ玄本店; ☎0263-32-2430; www15.plala.or.jp/katsugen; 4-9-7 Ōte; set lunch from ¥900; ⏲11.30am-2pm & 5-9pm) If you're into *tonkatsu* (deep-fried pork cutlet), try to find this place a block south of the southeastern corner of Matsumoto Castle park. There's a black pig on the sign hanging outside, plus an English menu. An old wooden interior with matching tables and chairs produces a soothing ambience, and the quality of the food is outstanding.

Menshō Sakura RAMEN ¥
(麺匠佐蔵; ☎0263-34-1050; 1-20-26 Chūō; ramen from ¥760; ⏲11.30am-3pm & 5.30-10pm) Miso and ramen fans shouldn't go past this purveyor of fine noodles in a cute little building opposite the Richmond Hotel. *Miso-rāmen* and black *Kuro-miso rāmen* are the specialities of the house: both are rated highly. The *gyōza* are crunchy and the beer is cold. Ask the friendly staff for help with the vending machine if you get stuck.

Shizuka IZAKAYA ¥
(しづか; ☎0263-32-0547; www.shiduka.co.jp; 4-10-8 Ōte; plates from ¥480; ⏲noon-10pm Mon-Sat) This wonderfully traditional *izakaya* (pub-restaurant) serves favourites such as *oden* (a stew comprising fishcakes, tofu, vegetables and eggs simmered in a kelp-flavoured broth) and *yakitori* (grilled skewers of meat or vegetables), as well as specialities that may be more challenging for Western palates, in a great location near the castle.

Drinking & Nightlife

★**Matsumoto Brewery Taproom** CRAFT BEER
(マツモトブルワリー タップルーム; ☎0263-31-0081; http://matsu-brew.com; 3-4-21 Chūō; ⏲1-7pm Wed-Mon) Tasty local brews, highlighted by the Awesome! Pale Ale, can be enjoyed in a delightful two-storey taproom in a lovely old building in Nakamachi. There's a second location on the 3rd floor of the new Media Building – you can relax on the terrace looking out over downtown Matsumoto.

★**Eonta Jazz Bar** BAR
(エオンタ; ☎0263-33-0505; 4-9-7 Ōte; ⏲4pm-midnight Thu-Tue) If you like jazz, it doesn't get any better than Eonta, a tiny 15-seater upstairs, directly above Katsu Gen restaurant. The friendly owner has been running his bar since 1974 and likes his jazz, chosen from over 4000 vinyl records and 1000 CDs, at a decent volume. He serves carefully brewed coffees as well as beer, wine and cocktails.

ALPINE–TAKAYAMA-MATSUMOTO AREA TOURIST PASS

The Alpine-Takayama-Matsumoto Area Tourist Pass (http://touristpass.jp/en/alpine; adult/child ¥17,500/8750) is very useful here. Valid for five consecutive days, it covers the Tateyama–Kurobe Alpine Route, Matsumoto, the Kiso Valley and parts west. It's ¥1000 more expensive when purchased in Japan.

WORTH A TRIP

A NIGHT ABOVE THE CLOUDS

If you're looking for something a little bit different, along the lines of isolation and indulgence, there are two very special places to rest your weary head in the mountains above Matsumoto. From April to November, consider a night at the singular **Ougatou Hotel** (王ヶ頭ホテル; Map p292; ☎0263-31-2751; www.ougatou.jp; d per person incl 2 meals from ¥16,500; P ❄ 📶) atop the beautiful Utsukushi-ga-hara-kōgen. Rooms are plush, comfy and reasonably priced for their standard. Oversized suites have decadent baths overlooking the plateau and the cloud line: you'll think you're on cloud nine as you wake.

For something a little pricier, fancier and more traditional, the exclusive **Tobira Onsen Myōjin-kan** (扉温泉明神館; Map p292; ☎0263-31-2301; http://myojinkan.tobira-group.com; 8967 Iriyamabe; s/d per person incl 2 meals from ¥32,500/26,000; P ❄ 📶) has been nestled quietly in the mountains above Matsumoto (en route to Utsukushi-ga-hara-kōgen) since 1931. There's a variety of room types: many have private onsen baths, and each enjoys wonderful vistas of the natural surrounds. The communal indoor and outdoor baths will leave you feeling as though you're floating on air. For your investment, expect nothing less than exquisite French food and *kaiseki* (Japanese haute cuisine) and the epitome of customer service.

Both rare gems are best enjoyed with the freedom of a rental car.

Shopping

Matsumoto is synonymous with *temari* (embroidered balls) and doll-making. Takasago street, one block south of Nakamachi, has several doll shops.

★Chikiri-ya Art & Craft Shop GLASS
(ちきりや工芸店; ☎0263-33-2522; 3-4-18 Chūō; ⏲10am-6pm Thu-Tue) Glass and pottery aficionados will find this wonderful boutique on Nakamachi-dōri a must.

Belle Amie Doll Shop ARTS & CRAFTS
(ベラミ人形店; ☎0263-33-1314; 3-7-23 Chūō; ⏲10am-6pm) *Temari* (embroidered balls) and dolls are found here, about 500m east of the station. Doll styles include Tanabata and *oshie-bina* (dressed in fine cloth).

Nakamachi Kura-chic-kan ARTS & CRAFTS
(中町・蔵シック館; ☎0263-36-3053; http://nakamachi-street.com/kurassickan; 2-9-15 Chūō; ⏲9am-5pm) A pun on 'classic' in English, '*kura* (storehouses)' in Japanese and 'chic' in French, Nakamachi Kura-chic-kan showcases locally produced arts and crafts on Nakamachi-dōri.

Information

Matsumoto Tourist Information Center (松本市観光案内所; ☎0263-32-2814; https://visitmatsumoto.com/en; 1-1-1 Fukashi; ⏲9am-5.45pm) This excellent TIC inside JR Matsumoto Station has friendly English-speaking staff and a wide range of well-produced English-language materials on the area.

Getting There & Away

AIR

Shinshū Matsumoto Airport (MMJ; Map p292; www.matsumoto-airport.co.jp) has daily flights to Fukuoka, Osaka and Sapporo.

An airport shuttle bus connects Shinshū Matsumoto Airport with downtown (¥600, 25 minutes); a taxi costs around ¥5000.

BUS

Alpico (www.alpico.co.jp) runs buses between Matsumoto and Shinjuku in Tokyo (¥3400, 3¼ hours, hourly), Osaka (¥5850, 5¾ hours, two daily; one longer overnight service) and Nagoya (from ¥3600, 3½ hours, 10 daily). Nōhi Bus (p245) services Takayama (¥3900, 2½ hours, at least six daily). Reservations are advised.

The **Matsumoto Bus Terminal** is in the Alpico Plaza building opposite and slightly to the right as you exit JR Matsumoto Station.

TRAIN

'Matsumotooo...Matsumotooo...' is connected with Tokyo's Shinjuku Station (*tokkyū* ¥6900, 2¾ hours, hourly), Nagoya (*tokkyū* ¥6030, two hours) and Nagano (Shinano *tokkyū* ¥2840, 50 minutes; Chūō *futsū* ¥1140, 1¼ hours).

Getting Around

Matsumoto-jō and the city centre are easily explored on foot and free bicycles are available for loan – enquire at the Tourist Information Center. Four 'Town Sneaker' loop bus routes operate between 8am and 5.30pm for ¥200 per ride (¥500 per day); the North and East routes cover the castle and Nakamachi.

Azumino

☎0263 / POP 95,000

An easy day trip north from Matsumoto, Azumino (安曇野) sits just east of the northern Japan Alps and has some interesting things going on. Hikers and onsen-seekers are close to heaven here, while foodies can visit Japan's largest wasabi farm to try wasabi wine and ice cream. Cute little JR Hotaka Station, 30 minutes north of Matsumoto, is the place to start your adventuring.

Sights

★Chihiro Art Museum Azumino MUSEUM

(安曇野ちひろ美術館; Map p292; ☎0261-62-0772; https://chihiro.jp/en/azumino; 3358-24 Nishi-hara, Matsukawa; ¥800; 9am-5pm Thu-Tue) This popular art museum showcases the work of Chihiro Iwasaki (1918–74), who became world-renowned while specialising in children's-book illustrations from the late 1950s until her death in 1974. Built in Azumino because Chihiro's parents came from Nagano, the museum is surrounded by a gorgeous park and is best accessed from Shinano-Matsukawa Station on the JR Ōito line. Its sister museum is the Chihiro Art Museum Tokyo, built on the site where the illustrator lived and worked in the capital.

Dai-ō Wasabi-Nōjo FARM

(大王わさび農場; Map p292; ☎0263-82-2118; www.daiowasabi.co.jp; 3640 Hotaka; 9am-5pm) FREE Fancy some wasabi wine or ice cream? This farm, a 15-minute bike ride from JR Hotaka Station, is a must for wasabi-lovers. An English map guides you among wasabi plants (130 tonnes of wasabi are grown in flooded fields here annually) amid rolling hills, restaurants, shops and workspaces. It's a fascinating and fun place for a stroll, but there's a huge bus park out the front, so be mentally prepared for lots of other visitors.

Rokuzan Bijutsukan GALLERY

(碌山美術館; ☎0263-82-2094; www.rokuzan.jp; 5095-1 Hotaka; adult/child ¥700/300; 9am-5pm) Ten minutes' walk north from JR Hotaka Station, Rokuzan Bijutsukan showcases the work of Meiji-era sculptor Rokuzan Ogiwara (1879–1910; aka the 'Rodin of the Orient') and his Japanese contemporaries in a delightful garden setting. Rokuzan is said to have learned the essence of sculpture from Rodin in Paris in the early 1900s and brought modern sculpture to Japan.

Activities

Jōnen-dake HIKING

(常念岳; https://japanhike.wordpress.com/2008/03/03/mt-jonen) From JR Hotaka Station it's a 30-minute (around ¥5000) taxi ride to reach the Ichinosawa trailhead, from where experienced hikers can climb Jōnen-dake (2857m), one of Japan's 100 Famous Mountains. This is a summer-only hike with a 1500m climb, so hikers must be properly prepared. Maps are available at the Tourist Information Center (p284), although the detailed ones are in Japanese.

There are many options for hikes extending over several days, but you must do your homework before you go.

Sleeping

There are some lovely ryokan dotted about the valley, plus rustic mountain lodgings as you edge your way towards the peaks and into the Hotaka Onsen area at the foot of the mountains.

★Nakabusa Onsen RYOKAN ¥¥

(中房温泉; ☎0263-77-1488; www.nakabusa.com; 7226 Nakabusa; r per person incl 2 meals from ¥10,000; Apr-Nov; P ❄) This rambling resort with indoor and outdoor onsen at the end of a twisting valley road to nowhere will delight anyone seeking a peaceful retreat. The older *honkan* (main building) has basic rooms, while the newer *bekkan* (annexe) is more comfortable. In late autumn gawk at stunningly colourful foliage from deep in the valley.

Day trippers can use one of the smaller *rotemburo* (¥700) between 9.30am and 4pm. Enquire at the Tourist Information Center (p284) for info on the limited buses (¥1700, one hour) from Azumino, or rent a car (and bring nerves of steel). This place is extremely remote. Nakabusa Onsen is also the trailhead for a stunningly steep climb up to Otensho-dake (大天井岳; 2922m) and Tsubakuro-dake (燕岳; 2762m).

Ariake-sō LODGE ¥¥

(有明荘; ☎0263-84-6511; www.enzanso.co.jp/ariakeso; Ariake-Nakabusa, Hotaka; r per person incl 2 meals from ¥10,000; Apr-late Nov; P ❄) Near the end of the road to Nakabusa Onsen, this seasonal forest lodge has basic, dorm-style rooms and a nourishing onsen (day use ¥600). The lodge is at 1380m and well out there in terms of remoteness. It's best to have your own wheels.

Oyado Nagomino RYOKAN ¥¥¥
(お宿なごみ野; Map p292; 0263-81-5566; www.oyado-nagomino.com; 3618-44 Hotaka-ariake; r per person incl 2 meals from ¥19,440; P ❄ 📶) In a lovely forested setting, this attractive modern ryokan is an oasis at the foot of the mountains in Hotaka Onsen. Although little English is spoken, staff members go to great lengths to ensure a pleasant stay. Guest rooms are typically styled, but the real draws are the delightful communal baths and the exceptional *kaiseki* (Japanese haute cuisine), with seasonal menus.

Information

Tourist Information Center (観光案内所; 0263-82-9363; www.azumino-e-tabi.net/en; 5952-3 Hotaka; 9am-5pm Apr-Nov, 10am-4pm Dec-Mar) This friendly, home-proud tourist office opposite JR Hotaka Station has helpful English-speaking staff and will sort out rental bicycles – a great way to explore the area. Its local-sightseeing map has a number of suggested bicycle routes. Be sure to check out the excellent English homepage.

Getting There & Away

Hotaka is the gateway city to the Azumino valley. JR Hotaka Station is 30 minutes (*futsū* ¥320) from Matsumoto on the JR Ōito line.

Shirahone Onsen

0263

Intimate, dramatic and straddling a deep gorge high in the mountains about halfway between Matsumoto and Takayama, Shirahone Onsen (白骨温泉) is one of Japan's most beautiful onsen hamlets – heavenly during autumn and a wonderland in winter. *Onsen ryokan* (traditional hot-spring inns) with open-air baths surround the gorge. It's said that bathing in the silky, milky-blue hydrogen-sulphide waters of Shirahone (meaning 'white bone') for three days ensures three years without a cold.

Activities

Kōkyō Notemburo ONSEN
(公共野天風呂; 0263-93-3251; ¥500; 8.30am-5pm Apr-Nov) Deep within the gorge, this exquisite, gender-segregated riverside *rotemburo* (outdoor bath) is a stunner. The entrance is by steep stairs near the bus stop. Brilliant for day trippers.

Sleeping

Lodging here is in a cluster of rustic ryokan, all with high rates and all extremely popular in the fall-foliage season around October. Book ahead.

Tsuruya Ryokan RYOKAN ¥¥
(つるや旅館; 0263-93-2331; www.shirahone-tsuruya.com; 4202-6 Shirahone Onsen; r per person incl 2 meals & without bathroom from ¥15,000; P ❄ 📶) Lovely Tsuruya Ryokan has both contemporary and traditional touches and great indoor and outdoor baths. Each of its 28 rooms has lovely views of the gorge; rooms with private toilet and sink are available for an extra charge. Book in advance.

★ **Awanoyu Ryokan** RYOKAN ¥¥¥
(泡の湯旅館; 0263-93-2101; www.awanoyu-ryokan.com; 4181 Shirahone Onsen; r per person incl 2 meals from ¥28,000; P ❄ 📶) Awanoyu Ryokan typifies mountain *onsen ryokan* (hot-spring inns). Uphill from Shirahone, it has been an inn since 1912 (the current building dates from 1940). Light-filled guest rooms have private facilities. There are also single-sex common baths and *konyoku* (mixed bathing); the waters are so milky that you can't see below the surface, so don't be shy. Reservations essential.

Information

Tourist Information Center (白骨温泉観光案内所; 0263-93-3251; www.shirahone.org; 4197-4 Azumino; 9am-5pm) The TIC, by the bus stop, maintains a list of inns that open their baths (from ¥600) to the public each day.

Getting There & Away

To get to Shirahone Onsen from Matsumoto, ask at Alpico Bus at the bus terminal. There are a few buses from Matsumoto per day, or take a train to Shin-Shimashima Station (¥700, 30 minutes), then catch a bus to Shirahone Onsen (¥1450, 70 minutes).

It takes just over an hour to drive from Matsumoto or Takayama to Shirahone Onsen.

Kamikōchi

0263

Mention Kamikōchi to Japanese outdoors enthusiasts and their eyes will light up. They'll tell you that this is where it's at and where you should be. In the late 19th century, foreigners 'discovered' this remote valley and mountainous region and coined the term 'Japan Alps'. British missionary Reverend Walter Weston toiled from peak to peak and sparked Japanese interest in mountaineering as a sport. He's now honoured with a festival on the first Sunday in June, the official opening of the hiking season.

It's feasible to visit as a day trip, but you'll miss out on the pleasures of staying in the mountains and taking uncrowded early-morning or late-afternoon walks. Stay overnight and savour the snowcapped peaks, bubbling brooks, wild monkeys, wildflowers and ancient forests.

Kamikōchi is closed from 15 November to 22 April. In midsummer and autumn-foliage season, the area around Kappa-bashi bridge may seem busier than Shinjuku Station.

Sleeping

Accommodation in hotels and lodges in Kamikōchi is expensive, and advance reservations are essential, especially during Japanese holiday periods. There are a number of camping areas in the valley at varying distances from Kappa-bashi, including at Konashidaira, Tokusawa and Yokō.

Dotted along the trails and around the mountains are dozens of *yamagoya* (huts), which provide two meals and a futon from around ¥8000 per person; some also serve simple lunches.

Konashishidaira Camping Retreat CAMPGROUND ¥

(森のリゾート小梨, Mori no rizōto Konashi; ☎0260-95-2321; www.nihonalpskankou.com; 4468 Kamikōchi; campsites/cabins per person from ¥800/6000; ⏰office 7am-7pm) About 200m past the Kamikōchi Visitor Centre (p286), this campground can get crowded. Rental tents are available from ¥7000, and there's a small shop, a restaurant and a public bath. There are lots of options: check them out on the good English website.

★Tokusawa-en INN ¥¥

(徳澤園; ☎0260-95-2508; www.tokusawaen.com; per person incl 2 meals dm ¥12,000, d from ¥16,500; ⏰May-Oct) This marvellously secluded place is in a wooded dell 7km northeast of Kappa-bashi. It's both a campground (¥700 per person) and a lodge, and has capsule-style dorm rooms, Japanese-style rooms (with shared facilities), and hearty meals served in a busy dining

HIKING & CLIMBING IN KAMIKŌCHI

If you're surprised by crowds of photo-taking visitors at Kamikōchi, especially at Kappa-bashi, keep in mind that 95% of visitors go no further than 500m from the bridge!

Kamikōchi and its Azusa river valley offer some extremely enjoyable, level, signposted walks. For a decent valley-walks map in English, check out www.kamikochi.org/plan/trekking. For a fun one-hour walk from the far side of Kappa-bashi, amble downriver to Weston Relief (a monument to Walter Weston; 15 minutes), cross the Azusa-gawa on the Hotaka-bashi and walk upriver back to Kappa-bashi.

A good four-hour hike begins at the bus-station side of Kappa-bashi and heads upriver past Myōjin-bashi (one hour). Over the far side of the Myōjin-bashi, the idyllic Myōjin-ike (pond) marks the innermost shrine of Hotaka-jinja (¥300). From Myōjin-bashi, continue on upriver to Tokusawa (another hour) before returning the same way.

Most serious hikers and climbers have the peaks of Oku-hotaka-dake and/or Yari-ga-take in their sights. These are Japan's third- and fifth-highest mountains, and the three-day hike from Kamikōchi, climbing 'Yari' (3180m), traversing the Daikiretto (a legendary hole in the ridge line), topping Oku-hotaka-dake (3190m) and then dropping back into Kamikōchi, is the holy grail for Japanese hikers. Be very well prepared, do your homework and watch the weather forecasts if you're going to take this on.

Long-distance hikes vary in duration and have access to mountain huts; enquire at the Tourist Information Center (p286) for details. Japanese-language maps of the area show routes and average hiking times between huts, major peaks and landmarks. Serious hikers could also consider a five- to seven-day length-of-the-north-Japan-Alps trek to Kamikōchi from Murodō on the Tateyama–Kurobe Alpine Route (p275).

In winter, deserted Kamikōchi makes a beautiful cross-country-skiing spot for the initiated: hike in from the entrance to the Kama Tunnel on Rte 158.

hall. There's a nice bath, a cafe and a small shop. Access is by walking only (about two hours).

★Kamikōchi Nishi-itoya Sansō INN ¥¥
(上高地西糸屋山荘; ☎0260-95-2206; www.nishiitoya.com; 4469-1 Kamikōchi; per person incl 2 meals dm from ¥9000, d from ¥22,000; ⊖❄📶) This friendly lodge, west of Kappa-bashi, dates from the early 20th century. The main-building rooms are a mix of Japanese and Western styles. The dorm rooms in the annexe building are the best deal in Kamikōchi if you're on a budget and don't want to go camping. The shared bath faces the Hotaka peaks. There's a cosy lounge.

Kamikochi Imperial Hotel HOTEL ¥¥¥
(上高地帝国ホテル; ☎0260-95-2001; www.imperialhotel.co.jp; Azumino Kamikochi; r from ¥30,700; ❄📶) Expect exceptional service and rustic, European Alps–styled rooms in this historic red-gabled lodge completed in 1933. Prices are elevated, but a wide range of stay plans are available, and the hotel occasionally offers excellent packages including French haute cuisine. You may have to book a year ahead.

Kamikōchi Gosenjaku Hotel & Lodge HOTEL ¥¥¥
(上高地五千尺ホテル・ロッヂ; ☎hotel 0260-95-2111, lodge 0260-95-2221; www.gosenjaku.co.jp; 4468 Kamikōchi; r per person incl 2 meals in lodge from ¥19,200, in hotel from ¥25,100; ❄📶) Part of the Alpico Group, this complex has things nicely covered with its hotel on the bus-station side of Kappa-bashi and its lodge on the far side. The lodge has Japanese-style rooms with sink and toilet; baths are shared. The hotel is more upscale, with a combination of comfortable Western and Japanese rooms, some with balconies.

NEED TO KNOW: KAMIKŌCHI

Be prepared before you arrive in Kamikōchi, especially if you're heading out hiking. Bring cash with you, as there's no ATM. There are souvenir shops, but no supermarket or convenience store. There's a baggage-storage counter at the bus terminal.

Eating

The bus station has a small selection of eateries, but there's little beyond that. Unless you're camping, you'll be dining at your lodge in the evenings.

Kamonji-goya SHOKUDO ¥
(嘉門次小屋; ☎0263-95-2418; www.kamonjigoya.wordpress.com; dishes from ¥600; ⏲8.30am-4pm) Kamikōchi's signature dish is *iwana* (river trout) grilled whole over an *irori*. This is the place to try it. The *iwana* set is ¥1500, or there's *oden*, soba and *kotsu-sake* (dried *iwana* in sake) served in a lovely ceramic bowl. There are also simple dorm rooms here. It's just outside the entrance to Myōjin-ike.

Information

INSURANCE

Serious hikers should consider insurance (保険, *hoken*; from ¥1000 per day), available at Kamikōchi bus station.

TOURIST INFORMATION

Kamikōchi Tourist Information Center (上高地インフォメーションセンター; ☎0260-95-2433; www.kamikochi.org; ⏲8am-5pm) This invaluable resource at the bus-station complex has English speakers on hand, provides information on hiking and weather conditions, and distributes the English-language *Kamikōchi Pocket Guide*, with a map of the main walking tracks.

Kamikōchi Visitor Centre (上高地ビジターセンター; ☎0260-95-2606; www.kamikochi-vc.or.jp/en; ⏲8am-5pm) Ten minutes' walk from Kamikōchi bus station along the main trail, this is the place for information on Kamikōchi's flora, fauna, geology and history. You can also book guided walks to destinations including Taishō-ike and Myōjin-ike (from ¥500 per person).

Getting There & Away

Visitors arrive at Kamikōchi's sprawling bus station. A 10-minute walk along the Azusa-gawa takes you to Kappa-bashi, a bridge named after a legendary water sprite.

Private vehicles are prohibited between Naka-no-yu and Kamikōchi; access is only by bus or taxi as far as the Kamikōchi bus station. Those with private cars can use car parks en route to Naka-no-yu in the hamlet of Sawando for ¥500 per day; shuttle buses (¥2500 return) run a few times per hour.

Buses run via Naka-no-yu and Taishō-ike to the bus station. Hiking trails commence at Kappa-bashi, which is a short walk from the bus station.

Hakuba

☎0261 / POP 9000

In a long north–south valley east of the northern Japan Alps, vibrant Hakuba (白馬), site of various skiing events at the 1998 Nagano Winter Olympics, is wholeheartedly embracing adventure tourism to become a year-round visitor hot spot. It's long been a winter destination, based on seven ski areas, but visitors now arrive in other seasons for hiking, mountain-biking, paragliding and all sorts of other activities. Hakuba's boom is the envy of other resort towns keen to make an all-season living. Foreigners are turning up in droves, especially in winter, spawning new development in restaurants, bars and low-cost accommodation. There are many onsen in and around Hakuba, and a long soak after a day of action is the perfect way to ease aching muscles.

Facilities are spread the length of the valley, close to the various ski areas, with popular Happō and the Hakuba Station area around mid-valley.

Activities

★Happō-One Ski Resort SKIING
(八方尾根スキー所; ☎0261-72-3066; www.happo-one.jp; 1-day lift ticket ¥5200; ⏲Dec-Apr) Host of the downhill races at the 1998 Winter Olympics, Happō-One is one of Japan's top ski areas, with superb mountain views and beginner, intermediate and advanced runs catering to skiers and snowboarders. For the low-down, check the excellent English-language homepage.

With a total of 23 lifts, half the terrain is rated intermediate. The resthouse at the top of the 'Adam' gondola, **Usagidaira 109**, is the ski area's centre point, with two chairlifts from there heading up to the highest elevation of 1830m.

From Hakuba Station, a five-minute bus ride (¥260) straight up the hill takes you into the middle of the lively little village of Happo-mura. In winter, shuttles make the rounds of the village, lodges and ski base.

Goodguides ADVENTURE SPORTS
(☎080-8629-3739; https://goodguides.co.nz; 14920-159 Ochikura) This outfit operates excellent backcountry skiing and snowshoeing adventures from a base near the Tsugaike slopes in Hakuba. With a ton of experience and qualified guides, it'll take you to where the snow is best and give you a top backcountry adventure to savour.

HIKING IN HAKUBA

In summer you can take the Happō Adam gondola and the two upper chairlifts, then hike up a trail for an hour or so to Happō-ike, on a ridge below Karamatsu-dake (唐松岳; 2695m). From here, follow a trail another hour up to Maru-yama, continue for 1½ hours to the Karamatsu-dake San-sō (mountain hut) and then climb to the peak of Karamatsu-dake in about 30 minutes. Come back down the same way.

Shirouma-dake (白馬岳; 2932m) is one of Japan's 100 Famous Mountains and looms high over Hakuba. For the well prepared it's a marvellous two-day hike with a 1700m climb and one of Japan's biggest mountain huts near the peak. Check www.japan-guide.com/blog/peaks/170904.html for details.

Mimizuku-no-yu ONSEN
(みみずくの湯; ☎0261-72-6542; www.hakuba-happo-onsen.jp/mimizukunoyu; 5480-1 Hokujō Happō-guchi; adult/child ¥600/300; ⏲10am-9.30pm, enter by 9pm) It's often said that this place – one of Hakuba's many onsen – has the best mountain views from the tub.

Hakuba47 Winter Sports Park & Hakuba Goryū Ski Resort SKIING
(Hakuba47ウインタースポーツパーク・白馬五竜スキー場; www.hakuba47.co.jp; 1-day lift ticket ¥5000; ⏲Dec-Apr) The interlinked areas of Hakuba47 Winter Sports Park and Hakuba Goryū Ski Resort form the second major ski resort in the Hakuba area, south of Happo. There's a good variety of terrain in both areas, with about an equal number of skiers and boarders. Like Happō-One, this area boasts fantastic mountain views.

A free shuttle bus from Hakuba-mura and JR Hakuba Station provides the easiest access.

Evergreen Outdoor OUTDOORS
(☎0261-72-5150; www.evergreen-hakuba.com; 4377 Hokujō; half-day tours from ¥4000) There are lots of things going on with these friendly, outdoorsy folk throughout the year. Winter offerings include ski school, backcountry tours and snowshoeing, while the green season brings canyoning, rafting, kayaking, stand-up paddle boarding, mountain biking, tree climbing, hiking and more.

HAKUBA VALLEY TICKET

The Hakuba Valley Ticket (www.hakubavalley.com; one day ¥6000) covers the following ski areas in Hakuba, Otari and Ōmachi towns: Hakuba Goryu Snow Resort, Hakuba47 Winter Sports Park, Hakuba Happō-One Snow Resort, Hakuba Iwatake Snow Field, Tsugaike Kogen Snow Resort, Hakuba Norikura Onsen Snow Resort, Hakuba Cortina Ski Resort, Kashimayari Snow Resort and Jiigatake Snow Resort. Check out the details online.

Headquarters is uphill from Hakuba Tokyu Hotel. Check out all the options on the English website.

Hakuba Cortina Ski Resort SKIING
(白馬コルチナスキー場; www.hakubacortina.jp/ski; 1-day lift ticket ¥4000; Dec-Apr) At the northern end of the valley, Hakuba Cortina is popular with Japanese families, who revel in the resort's facilities – a massive, ski-in European-style structure with hotel, restaurants, ski rental and deluxe onsen – and those who want quieter slopes. Its seven lifts and 16 courses cater to all levels of skier.

Sleeping

Hakuba has a huge selection of accommodation to suit all budgets. Book well ahead if you're arriving at busy times, such as January–March and July and August. Be aware that places to stay are spread the length of the valley: you may want to check exactly where you're staying before you book. Many places run free transfers to/from the station, the bus terminal and ski areas in winter.

★Kamoshika Views GUESTHOUSE ¥
(カモシカブユーズ; 070-4003-0723; www.skilodgehakuba.com; 9464-378 Oaza Hokujō; dm/r from ¥3000/8000; P) Russ the Kiwi has everything covered in Donguri, high above Hakuba. The dorm rooms are tight, but communal lounge, kitchen and party rooms make this a top spot. Russ runs complimentary train/bus-station and ski-area transfers, and also shuttles visitors on supermarket runs for food and drink supplies. If you're lucky, you might spot monkeys out the window.

Snowbeds B&B HOSTEL ¥
(0261-72-5242; www.snowbedsjapan.com; 2937-304 Hokujo; dm/d from ¥3900/9800; P) This foreign-run backpackers has decent budget bunk rooms, simple double rooms and a nice communal area with a wood stove. It's close to the nightlife in Echoland, with restaurants and bars just down the road.

★Backcountry Lodge Hakuba LODGE ¥¥
(バックカントリーロッジ白馬; 050-3497-9595; http://backcountry-hakuba.com; 14718-174 Hokujō; per person incl breakfast from ¥8000; P) Eric and Fumi's place is an extremely friendly spot to stay, away from the rush of resort-town Hakuba and north of most of the in-town action, near the Tsugaike slopes. They run free transfers from/to Hakuba Station and to the slopes and are lovingly refurbishing their backcountry lodge. Rooms are spacious, communal areas inviting, and the breakfast wonderful.

★Hotel Hifumi HOTEL, RYOKAN ¥¥
(ホテルひふみ; 0261-72-8411; www.hakubahifumi.jp; 4998 Happō; r per person incl breakfast from ¥12,000; P) This compact, family-run establishment extends the feeling of family to its guests and welcomes visitors from around the world. Beautifully designed and recently renovated rooms are a fusion of modern and traditional styles; some come with private outdoor baths, making this one of Hakuba's most rewarding places to stay. It's in Happō, near the bus terminal and Happo-One ski area (p287).

Shiroumaso RYOKAN ¥¥
(白馬荘; 0261-72-2121; www.shiroumaso.com; 5004 Happō; s/d incl breakfast from ¥10,030/17,900; P) This lovely little ryokan in Happō has smart, though compact, traditionally styled rooms with lots of *hinoki* (cypress) detailing and lovely views. Only a couple of minutes' walk from the bus terminal and close to Happō-One's (p287) Adam gondola.

Hakuba Panorama Hotel INN ¥¥
(白馬パノラマホテル; 0261-85-4031; www.hakuba-panorama.com; 3322-1 Hokujō; d per person incl breakfast from ¥7000; P) Not far from Happō-One Ski Resort (p287), this place has bilingual Japanese staff and a variety of room types. There's a guest laundry and a wonderful onsen. Best of all, though, is the ground-floor Hakuba Taproom, with craft beer, big screens for sports and frequent live music. You know it's good when locals come here, too.

★Ridge Hotel & Apartments HOTEL ¥¥¥
(☎0261-85-4301; www.theridgehakuba.com; 4608 Hakuba; d/apt from ¥25,000/42,000; P ❄ 📶) Sophisticated, sexy and stylish, this stunning property has it all, year-round: location, amenities, views. Room types range from the sublime (Western-style rooms with Japanese elements) to the ridiculous (a gorgeous loft balcony suite). Obliging, attentive staff speak English well. Built as accommodation in the upmarket Wadano area for the imperial family during the 1998 Winter Olympics.

Hakuba Tokyu Hotel HOTEL ¥¥¥
(白馬東急ホテル; ☎0261-72-3001; www.hakuba-h.tokyuhotels.co.jp; Happō-wadano; s/d with breakfast from ¥20,000/28,000; P ❄ 📶) This elegant, year-round, top-class hotel has large rooms with great views and a wonderful garden that's popular for weddings. The Grand Spa boasts the highest alkaline content in the area, and there are both French and Japanese restaurants. It's in a good location in the Wadano area, near the Happō-One (p287) lifts.

Eating

There's plenty to choose from around the area's resorts, with new options popping up all the time. Happō and Echoland offer plenty of eating, drinking and nightlife opportunities. Hours vary with the seasons.

★Hie Izakaya IZAKAYA ¥
(居酒屋 稗; ☎0261-72-8035; 3020-868 Hokujō; dishes from ¥400; ⏲6-11pm Fri-Wed) This lovely little *izakaya* (bar-restaurant) in Echoland is so popular that you'll need to make a booking; get your accommodation owner to set you up at least a day ahead. Expect all the usual *izakaya* fare here on a useful English menu, but you'll also find house specials such as seared tuna and avocado. Cosy atmosphere next to Mockingbird Bar.

★Zen SOBA ¥
(膳; ☎0261-72-3637; http://zen.artbi.net; 3020-49 Hokujō; dishes from ¥400; ⏲11am-2pm & 5.30-8.30pm Thu-Tue) A top spot both at lunchtime, when soba-noodle dishes are to the fore, and in the evening, when Zen morphs into an *izakaya* (bar-restaurant), this place oozes Japanese atmosphere, with both tatami-mat seating and tables. Extremely popular with locals and visitors, it's about halfway between Happō and Echoland. Try the seared Nagano beef (¥1170).

Sounds Like Cafe CAFE ¥
(☎0261-72-2040; 3020-504 Hokujō; coffee from ¥350, breakfast items from ¥450; ⏲8am-6pm Sat-Wed) Breakfast, lunch and lattes done Aussie-style keep hungry patrons coming back for more at this popular spot in Echoland. It's about as authentically Western as a cafe can be in Japan, and the food and coffee are top notch.

Ohyokkuri JAPANESE ¥
(おひょっくり; ☎0261-72-2661; 5081 Hokujō; meals from ¥650; ⏲11.30am-2pm & 5.30-9pm) Self-billed as 'Grandma's Hakuba home-style cooking', Ohyokkuri serves hearty soups and stews and traditional local dishes to an adoring crowd in the heart of Happō village.

Drinking & Nightlife

The rugged, sporty folk who hang around Hakuba have been known to down a beer or two at the end of a hard day's skiing or adventuring. Popular local brews from Hakuba Brewing Company (www.hakubabrewery.com) can be tried in bars all over town.

When the powder's deep, there's usually live evening entertainment somewhere on the slopes and nightclub-style shenanigans at weekends.

★Mocking Bird BAR
(モッキンバード; ☎0261-85-2450; www.mockingbird.jp; 3020-868 Hokujō; ⏲5pm-1am Thu-Tue) This Echoland favourite has a cosy, natural-wood, log-cabin vibe about it, offering a solid range of drinks and pub food on an English menu with great music. It's extremely popular: you might find it hard to get in during the winter months.

Hakuba Brew Pub PUB
(☎0261-85-2414; www.hakubabrewpub.com; 11420-1 Hokujō; ⏲noon-10.30pm winter) It's hard to go wrong when you're at the bottom of the Iwatake slopes and are home base for the local brew, Hakuba Beer. This winter-only place is a top spot, offering good pub food plus the full range of Hakuba Beer on tap, plus a pick-up and drop-off service (¥200).

Lucky Pete's Bar & Cafe SPORTS BAR
(☎0261-85-4458; Hakuba-eki; ⏲11am-9pm; 👪) This chilled-out, family-friendly, smoke-free bar to your right as you exit JR Habuka Station serves juicy original burgers and comfort-food favourites, along with plenty of snow-cold beer. Hours vary outside ski season.

Information

Northern Alps Information Center (北アルプス総合案内所; ☎0261-72-3000; www.kita-alps.com; ⏲8am-5pm) On the left as you exit JR Hakuba Station, this place has English pamphlets and maps – and if your timing is right, an English speaker.

Happō Information Center (☎0261-72-3066; ⏲6am-6pm summer, to 9pm winter) This place in the Happō Bus Station is a gold mine for visitors arriving by bus, with foreign-language brochures, maps and speakers. It also has rental bicycles that can be returned to Hakuba Sanroku Tours near the station.

Hakuba Sanroku Tours (白馬山麓ツアーズ; ☎0261-72-6900; www.hakuba1.com; ⏲9am-5pm) These folks run a tourist-information service for the town of Hakuba, over the main road and 100m up on the right straight ahead as you exit JR Hakuba Station. They run tours, can help with finding accommodation and have rental bicycles that can be returned to the Happō Information Center at the Happō Bus Station.

Getting There & Away

BUS

Alpico Group operates buses from Nagano Station (¥1800, approximately 70 minutes) and Shinjuku Nishi-guchi in Tokyo (¥4850, 4½ hours), as well as a direct service from Narita Airport (¥9500). See www.alpico.co.jp/traffic/express/narita_hakuba/en for details. Many visitors arrive by taking the *shinkansen* from Tokyo to Nagano, then the bus to Hakuba, arriving at **Happō Bus Terminal** (5734-1 Happō).

TRAIN

Hakuba is connected with Matsumoto by the JR Ōito line (¥1140, 1½ hours). Continuing north, change trains at Minami Otari to meet the JR Hokuriku line at Itoigawa; it's a pretty journey on a little two-carriage train, taking an hour from Minami Otari to Itoigawa, with connections to Niigata, Toyama and Kanazawa.

There's one direct service per day (Super Azusa 3) from Shinjuku to Hakuba, via Matsumoto (*tokkyū* ¥8300, four hours). It departs Shinjuku at 7.30am and returns from Hakuba at 2.37pm.

NAGANO PREFECTURE

Formerly known as Shinshū and often referred to as the 'Roof of Japan', Nagano Prefecture (長野県) is a wonderful place to visit for its regal mountains, rich cultural history, fine architecture and cuisine.

Nagano is a big prefecture, the fourth largest in Japan. Stretching in a north–south direction, yet with no coastline, Nagano is home to a hefty chunk of Chūbu-Sangaku National Park, as well as several quasi-national parks that attract skiers, mountaineers and onsen aficionados.

Nagano city, the prefectural capital and host of the 1998 Winter Olympic Games, is home to Zenkō-ji, a spectacular temple of national significance. Renowned resorts such as Kamikōchi, Hakuba, Nozawa Onsen, Shiga Kōgen and Karuizawa are all within Nagano's prefectural borders, as is Matsumoto, considered the gateway to the northern Japan Alps. The Kiso Valley, the Central Alps and northern parts of the Southern Alps are also in Nagano.

Getting There & Away

Willer Express (p272) operates services from Tokyo to a number of destinations in the prefecture.

Frequent *shinkansen* (bullet trains) depart Tokyo Station for Nagano city, with connections through to Toyama and Kanazawa.

The JR Shinonoi line connects Nagano to Matsumoto and through to Shiojiri, while the JR Chūō-honsen line links Shiojiri to Nagoya.

Super Azusa trains on the JR Chūō-honsen link Shinjuku (Tokyo) with Matsumoto and the JR Ōito line heads on from there to Hakuba.

Nagano & Around

☎026 / POP 375,000

The mountain-ringed prefectural capital of Nagano (長野) has been a place of pilgrimage since the Kamakura period, when it was a temple town centred on the magnificent Zenkō-ji, which draws a stunning number of visitors to the city each year. The highlights of town are Zenkō-ji and the 1.8km stretch of interesting Chūō-dōri that leads almost directly north to the temple from the station. *Monzen-machi* means 'a town that developed before the gates of a temple' and Nagano is a classic example.

Since the *shinkansen* and the upgraded station complex arrived in time for Nagano to host the Winter Olympics in 1998, the city has become a lot 'closer' to Tokyo: only 1½ hours away. It still has a friendly, small-town feel about it, though, while retaining plenty of accommodation and some appealing restaurants and bars. Many visitors use Nagano as a base for visiting Togakushi, Obuse and the Jigokudani Monkey Park.

Sights

★Zenkō-ji BUDDHIST TEMPLE

(善光寺; Map p294; ☎026-234-3591; www.zenkoji.jp; 491 Motoyoshi-chō; ⏰4.30am-4.30pm summer, 6am-4pm winter, hours vary rest of year) FREE Founded in the 7th century, National Treasure Zenkō-ji is home to the revered statue Ikkō-Sanzon, said to be the first Buddhist image to arrive in Japan (552 CE). Not even 37 generations of emperors have seen the image, though millions of visitors flock here to view a copy every seven years during the **Gokaichō Matsuri** (www.gokaicho.com; ⏰Apr/May). Zenkō-ji's immense popularity stems partly from its liberal welcoming of pilgrims, regardless of gender, creed or religious belief.

Its chief officiants are both a priest and a priestess. The current building dates from 1707.

Any bus from stop 1 in front of Nagano Station's Zenkō-ji exit will get you to the temple (¥150, about 10 minutes); alight at the Daimon stop. It takes about 30 minutes to walk up Chūō-dōri from the station to the temple.

Sleeping

Visitors have the unique opportunity to experience *shukubō* (temple lodging) at one of Zenkō-ji's 39 subtemples. Get a Japanese speaker to call the Zenkō-ji Shukubō Association on 026-237-7676 to book, at least one day ahead. Expect to pay ¥7000 to ¥10,000 per person with two traditional *shojin-ryori* (vegetarian) meals.

★Worldtrek Diner & Guesthouse Pise GUESTHOUSE ¥

(ワールドトレック ダイナー アンド ゲストハウス ピセ; Map p294; ☎026-214-5656; http://nagano-guesthouse.com; 2-1 Higashigo-chō; dm/r from ¥3000/7000; ❄📶) There's lots going on here on the main road up to Zenkō-ji, with mixed and female-only dorms, twin and family rooms, a super-cool cafe and a bar with a billiard table (open 3pm to 10pm), plus rental bikes (¥1000 per day). Rooms are simple, but there's everything you could need, including wi-fi, air-conditioning and laundry facilities.

★Matsuya Ryokan RYOKAN ¥¥

(松屋旅館; Map p294; ☎026-232-2811; http://matsuyaryokan.server-shared.com; Zenkō-ji Kannai; r per person from ¥6500, incl 2 meals from ¥11,000; ❄📶) Six generations of the Suzuki family

ZENKŌ-JI LEGENDS

Few Japanese temples inspire the fascination surrounding Zenkō-ji, thanks in part to the legends related to it. The following are just a few:

The Key to Salvation Visitors may descend Okaidan (¥500), a staircase to a twisting, pitch-black tunnel beneath the altar. The idea is that in the darkness, all are equal, seeking the same thing – a heavy metallic object said to be the key to salvation. Grope the right-hand wall while avoiding your fellow aspirants. Can you find it? (Claustrophobes, give this one a miss.)

Ikkō-Sanzon Three statues of the Amida Buddha were brought to Japan from Korea in the 6th century, and the one that resides at Zenkō-ji remains the temple's raison d'être. Wrapped like a mummy, it's kept in an ark behind the main altar. It's said that the image was not seen for 1000 years, but in 1702, to quell rumours that the ark was empty, the shogunate ordered a priest to confirm its existence and take measurements. That priest remains the last confirmed person to have viewed the image.

The Doves of San-mon Legend claims that there are five white doves hidden in the plaque of the San-mon gate; the five short strokes in the characters for Zenkō-ji do look remarkably dove-like. See if you can spot them, too. In the upper character (善, Zen), they're the two uppermost strokes; in the middle character (光, *kō*), they're the strokes on either side of the top; and in the 'ji' (寺), it's the short stroke on the bottom left.

Binzuru It is said that Binzuru, one of Buddha's disciples, a healer, had attained enlightenment but was instructed to remain on earth in service. You'll find his statue just inside, worn down where visitors have touched it to help heal ailments of the corresponding parts of their own bodies.

Nagano Prefecture

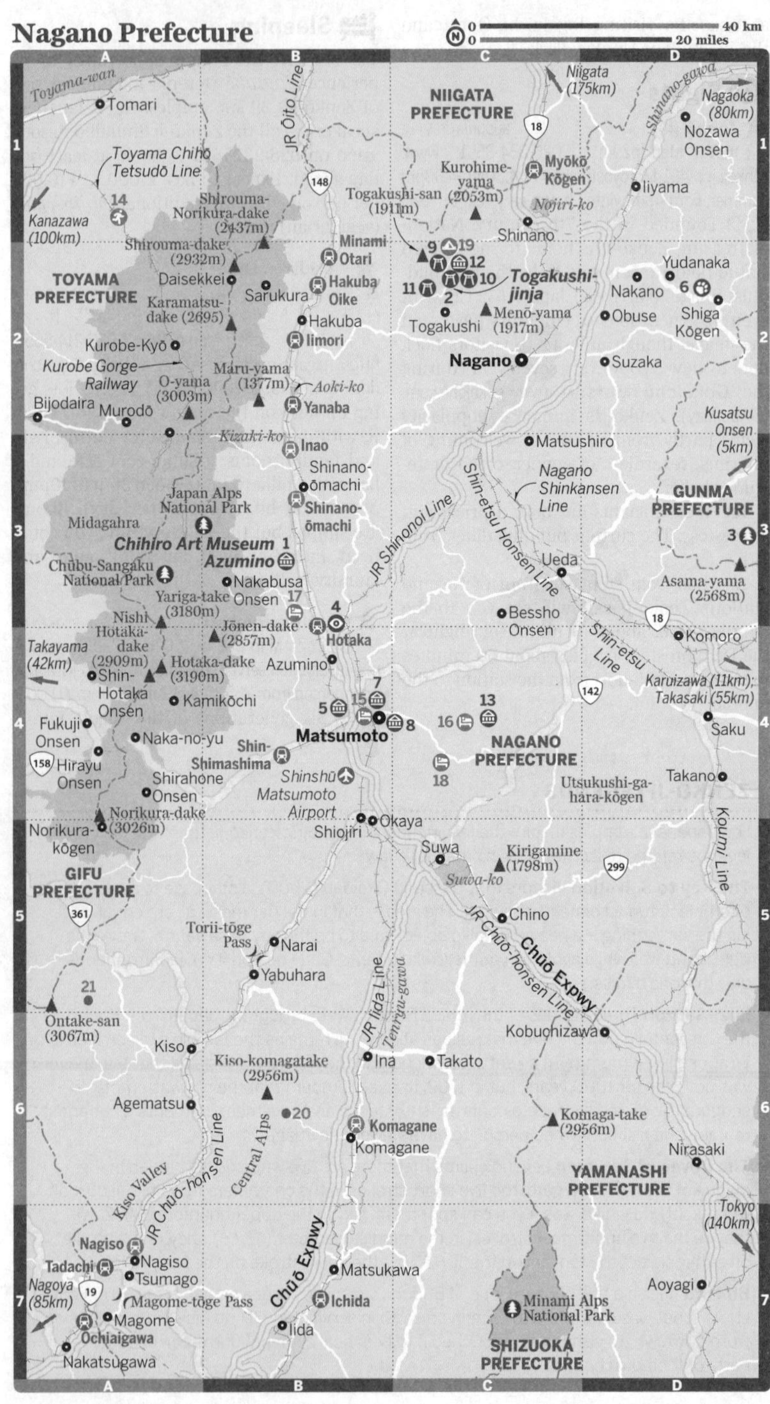

Nagano Prefecture

Top Sights
1 Chihiro Art Museum Azumino.............. B3
2 Togakushi-jinja.................................... C2

Sights
3 Asama-yama Magma Stone Park......... D3
4 Dai-ō Wasabi-Nōjo............................. B3
5 Japan Ukiyo-e Museum B4
6 Jigokudani Monkey Park..................... D2
7 Kaichi School Museum B4
8 Matsumoto City Museum of Art.......... C4
Matsumoto Open-Air Architectural Museum ....(see 5)
9 Togakushi Folk Museum & Ninja House C2
10 Togakushi-Chūsha C2
11 Togakushi-Hōkōsha C2
12 Togakushi-Okusha.............................. C2
13 Utsukushi-ga-hara Open Air Museum C4

Activities, Courses & Tours
14 Kurobe Gorge Railway A1

Sleeping
15 Matsumoto BackPackers.......................B4
16 Ougatou Hotel..C4
17 Oyado Nagomino....................................B3
18 Tobira Onsen Myōjin-kan C4
19 Togakushi Campground.........................C2
Yokokura Ryokan .... (see 10)

Eating
Uzuraya Soba................................ (see 11)

Information
Togakushi Tourist Information Center .... (see 2)

Transport
20 Central Alps Komagatake Ropeway.....B6
21 Ontake Ropeway A5

have maintained this traditional inn just inside Zenkō-ji's Niō-mon gate. Look for the statue of Enmei Jizō and the English signage indicating 'The original site of Zenkō-ji's Main Hall' out the front. It's the closest lodging to the temple and a great place to stay if you want to get into the Zenkō-ji (p291) atmosphere.

★ Chūō-kan Shimizuya Ryokan RYOKAN ¥¥
(中央館清水屋旅館; Map p294; ☎026-232-2580; www.chuoukan-shimizuya.com; 49 Daimon-chō; r per person incl breakfast & without bathroom from ¥6900; ❄ 📶) On Chūō-dōri a few blocks south of Zenkō-ji (p291), this ryokan has been in the family for 130 years and offers a friendly welcome to foreigners. The rustic, dark-wood interior has plenty of interesting ups, downs, nooks and crannies. There's a guest laundry. Meal plans are available.

Royal Hotel Nagano HOTEL ¥¥
(Royal Hotel 長野; ☎026-278-1811; www.daiwaresort.jp/en/nagano/index.html; 1372 Matsushiro-machi; r from ¥10,000; P ❄ 📶) This massive hotel is a good option if you're roving by rental car: it is right beside the highway's Nagano exit (9km from Nagano Station), has a huge, free car park, and runs a free shuttle from/to the station. Rooms are spacious, and there is a large bath and *rotemburo*, onsite restaurants and a big supermarket next door. Good rates are available online.

Hotel Metropolitan Nagano HOTEL ¥¥
(ホテルメトロポリタン長野; Map p294; ☎026-291-7000; www.metro-n.co.jp; 1346 Minami-Ishido-chō; s/d from ¥9500/13,300; P ❄ 📶) Adjacent to Nagano Station, the Metropolitan has elegant rooms that are spacious by Japanese standards. There's a cafe, a restaurant and a top-floor lounge with sweeping views.

Eating

Check out the area around the station's Zenkō-ji exit and along Chūō-dōri, especially towards the temple. Around the Zenkō-ji gates are vendors selling *oyaki* (steamed or baked wheat-flour dumplings filled with seasonal vegetables).

India the Spice CAFE ¥
(インディア・ザ・すぱいす; Map p294; ☎026-226-6136; 1418 Minami-ishido-chō; curries from ¥860; ⏱noon-2pm & 5pm-midnight Mon-Fri, noon-midnight Sat & Sun) This cafe is festooned with every kind of wall clock imaginable, and it specialises in variations on the theme of curry; lunch set menus include *omu-karē* (rice wrapped in an omelette in keema curry sauce). Look for the vines, Father Christmas, tubas and empty bottles outside – it's a tad eccentric but very popular!

★ Banikuman JAPANESE ¥¥
(バニクマン; Map p294; ☎026-228-0129; 1380 Kitaishido-chō; small plates from ¥500; ⏱5-11.30pm) This is the place to come to try a Nagano speciality: horse meat. Try it raw as

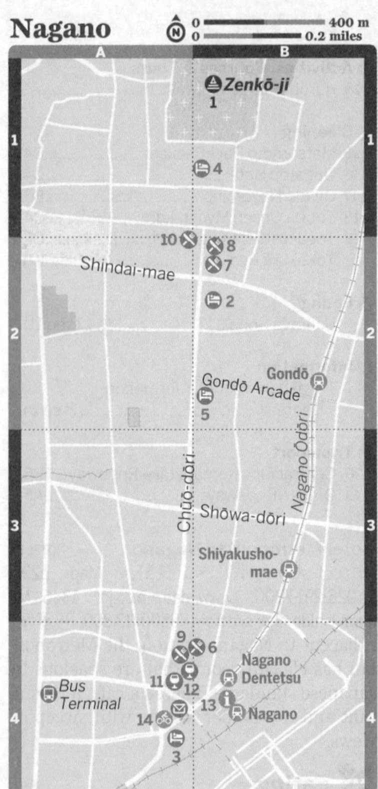

Nagano

Top Sights

1 Zenkō-ji B1

Sleeping

2 Chūō-kan Shimizuya Ryokan B2
3 Hotel Metropolitan Nagano A4
4 Matsuya Ryokan B1
5 Worldtrek Diner & Guesthouse Pise .. B2

Eating

6 Banikuman B4
7 Fujiki-an B2
8 Fujiya Gohonjin B2
9 India the Spice A4
10 Yayoiza A2

Drinking & Nightlife

11 James' Nagano Beer Market A4
12 Shinshū Nagaya Sakaba A4

Information

13 Nagano Tourist Information Center B4

Transport

14 Miyamoto Shōkai A4

basashi for ¥1480, in a *shabu-shabu* (hotpot) course for ¥3000 or grilled for ¥2200. Don't be confused if you hear the words *sakura-niku* – *sakura* means cherry and is used euphemistically for horse meat. There's lots of tasty Nagano sake here, too!

Fujiki-an SOBA ¥¥

(藤木庵; Map p294; ☎026-232-2531; www.fujikian.co.jp; 67 Daimon-chō; mains from ¥860; ⊙11am-3pm Wed-Mon; ✎) Fujiki-an has been making fresh soba in the north of Nagano Prefecture since 1827, but you wouldn't know it by the clean, contemporary lines of this outlet. *Seiro-mori soba* (cold soba on a bamboo mat) lets the flavour shine; other favourites are tempura, *kinoko* (mushroom) and *nishin* (herring). There's a picture menu.

Yayoiza JAPANESE ¥¥

(弥生座; Map p294; ☎026-232-2311; www.yayoiza.jp; 503 Daimon-chō; dishes from ¥600; ⊙11.30am-8.30pm Wed-Mon) This establishment just before the gates to Zenkō-ji (p291) has been serving *seiro-mushi* (ingredients steamed in a wood-and-bamboo box) for over 150 years. The standard is *monzen seiro-mushi* (local beef and vegetables). For dessert, try *kuri-an cream* (chestnut-paste mousse).

★ **Fujiya Gohonjin** FUSION ¥¥¥

(藤屋御本陣; Map p294; ☎026-232-1241; www.thefujiyagohonjin.com; 80 Daimon-chō; small plates from ¥750, courses from ¥4300; ⊙11.30am-3pm & 5.30-10pm Mon-Fri, 7-10pm Sat & Sun) *Gohonjin* means 'a residence for the lords', and in the Edo period Fujiya Gohonjin played host to the feudal lords of the Maeda family. The present 1925 building was Nagano's Hotel Fujiya but has since been transformed into the city's most elegant function centre. The spectacular dining room, Wisteria, is Nagano's top Western-style restaurant.

Drinking & Nightlife

★ **James' Nagano Beer Market** BAR

(ジェームス長野ビアマーケット; Map p294; ☎050-5861-8826; www.hotpepper.jp/strJ001026364; 1358 Suehiro-chō; ⊙5.30pm-midnight) This extremely popular beer-hall-type place is upstairs only a couple of minutes' walk from Nagano Station. Plenty of beer and wine from around the globe are on offer, but tops are the Shiga Kōgen Highland

Ales from Nagano. The food's good (try the Mexican fried chicken; ¥580) and the relaxed atmosphere will bring you back for more.

★ **Shinshū Nagaya Sakaba** PUB
(信州長屋酒場; Map p294; ☎026-269-8866; www.marutomisuisan.jpn.com/nagaya-shinsyu; 1418-12 Minami-ishidō-chō; dishes from ¥390; ⏲5pm-midnight) This lively *izakaya* (pub-restaurant) isn't far from the station and should be on your to-do list. You'll spot it by all the sake barrels plastered around the corner building – bring your sake-tasting gear because you can taste every sake made in Nagano in here! The ambience is straight out of another era.

Information

Nagano Tourist Information Center (長野市観光情報センター; Map p294; ☎026-226-5626; http://en.nagano-cvb.or.jp; ⏲9am-7pm Apr-Oct, to 6pm Nov-Mar) Inside JR Nagano Station, this friendly outfit has colour maps and guides to Nagano and the surrounding areas, and staff who speak good English.

Getting There & Away

BUS

Buses depart from the **bus terminal** (Map p294) outside the train station's Zenkō-ji exit.

Local destinations include Togakushi (one way/return from ¥1250/2250, one hour) and Hakuba (¥1800, approximately 70 minutes). Highway buses link Nagano with Shinjuku (Tokyo), Nagoya, Kyoto and Osaka. Check https://highway-buses.jp for up-to-date details.

TRAIN

Frequent *shinkansen* depart Tokyo Station for Nagano (¥8200, 1½ hours) and continue to Kanazawa (¥8960, 70 minutes).

The JR Shinonoi line connects Nagano with Matsumoto (Shinano *tokkyū* ¥2840, 50 minutes; Chūō *futsū* ¥1140, 1¼ hours) and Nagoya (Shinano *tokkyū* ¥7300, three hours).

Getting Around

Pick up a rental bicycle from **Miyamoto Shōkai** (宮本商会; Map p294; ☎026-226-3914; 1284 Minami-Ishidō-chō; per half-day/day ¥600/1000; ⏲9am-6pm), a two-minute walk from JR Nagano Station, or at Worldtrek Diner & Guesthouse Pise (p291), near Zenkō-ji. Don't attempt to cycle to Togakushi or the Jigokudani Monkey Park from Nagano.

Togakushi

☎026

High in the mountains northwest of Nagano city, Togakushi (戸隠) has long been visited by Shintō worshippers, who come to pray at Togakushi-jinja: first at its Lower Shrine (Togakushi-Hōkōsha); then, after a 2km uphill climb, at its Middle Shrine (Togakushi-Chūsha); then, a further 2km on, at the Upper Shrine (Togakushi-Okusha). These days, roads and trails link the three.

While most visitors today are still pilgrims, the Togakushi region is popular with hikers in spring, summer and autumn, and with skiers in winter. This pretty forested area of the mountains makes a lovely day trip or a peaceful overnight stay.

Sights

★ **Togakushi-jinja** SHINTŌ SHRINE
(戸隠神社; Map p292; ☎026-254-2001) Comprising three sub-shrines, **Togakushi-Hōkōsha** (戸隠宝光社), **Togakushi-Chūsha** (戸隠中社) and **Togakushi-Okusha** (戸隠奥社), each a few kilometres apart, Togakushi-jinja honours the 1911m-high Togakushi-san. According to legend, the mountain is where sun goddess Amaterasu hid in a cave behind a stone door, plunging the world into darkness, before another deity flung the door away, luring her out and restoring light. Chūsha, located in the middle of the village, is the easiest shrine to get to. Hōkōsha, the pretty lower sub-shrine of Togakushi-jinja, is reached via 274 ancient, steep stone steps.

From Okusha bus stop it's 2km (40 minutes' walk) to Okusha (meaning 'Upper Shrine') – the innermost of the three sub-shrines making up Togakushi-jinja – via a magnificent 500m-long cedar-lined path (杉並木; *suginamiki*) planted in 1612, with plenty of twists and turns and many stone stairs. It is not an easy walk for those with limited mobility, but it's certainly a rewarding one.

From Okusha, avid alpinists can make the strenuous climb to the top of the peak. In winter Okusha is inaccessible, except for hearty snowshoers.

Togakushi Folk Museum & Ninja House MUSEUM
(戸隠民俗館・忍者からくり屋敷, Togakushi Minzoku-kan & Ninja Karakuri Yashiki; Map p292; ☎026-254-2395; www.togakushi-ninja.com;

3688-12 Togakushi; adult/child ¥500/350; ⌚9am-5pm mid-Apr–mid-Nov; 🚌Okusha) Above the Okusha bus stop you'll find this museum housing artefacts from a time when local *yamabushi* (mountain monks) practised what became known as *ninpo* (the art of stealth). The Ninja House is the most fun, cleverly concocted with trick doors, hidden staircases and a room that slopes upwards.

Sleeping & Eating

Eating options are limited after dark; most overnight visitors dine at their accommodation. Togakushi has been famed for its soba for centuries, which are still said to be one of Japan's top three for tastiness. Try some at one of the 30 soba shops near Togakushi-Chūsha.

Togakushi Campground CAMPGROUND ¥
(戸隠キャンプ場; Map p292; ☎026-254-3581; www.togakusi.com/camp; 3694 Togakushi; sites/bungalows/cabins/cottages from ¥3000/5000/9000/18,000; ⌚late Apr-late Oct; P📶; 🚌Togakushi Kyanpu-jo) This beautiful, sprawling campground a few kilometres from Okusha (p295) has its own babbling brook, 350 campsites, 30 bungalows, 33 cabins and six self-contained cottages. It's best in October, when the leaves are turning and it's just about ready to close for the winter. Rental tents are available (¥4000). From Nagano, take the bus to Togakushi Kyanpu-jo stop.

Yokokura Ryokan RYOKAN ¥¥
(横倉旅館; Map p292; ☎026-254-2030; www.yokokura-inn.jp; 3347 Chūsha; dm with/without 2 meals from ¥5265/3245, r per person from ¥8000; P❄📶) Yokokura Ryokan is in a thatched-roof building from the early Meiji era, about 150m from the steps up to Chūsha shrine (p295). It's both a hostel and a ryokan, with gender-segregated tatami-room dorms, and private rooms. Room-only plans are available.

Uzuraya Soba NOODLES ¥
(うずら家そば; Map p292; ☎026-254-2219; 3229 Togakushi; soba from ¥780; ⌚10.30am-4pm Thu-Tue; 🚭) Revered in Japan by those who value soba (as many do), this wonderful noodle shop claims that Togakushi is the home of soba – and it may just be right. It's directly across from the steps to Chūsha shrine (p295). Tempura soba is king.

Information

Pick up English-language maps from the **Togakushi Tourist Information Center** (戸隠観光情報センター; Map p292; ☎026-254-2888; http://togakushi-21.jp; ⌚9am-5pm) near Togakushi-Chūsha (p295).

Getting There & Away

Buses depart Nagano hourly from 7am to 7pm and arrive at Chūsha-Miyamae bus stop by Togakushi-Chūsha in about an hour (one way/return ¥1250/2250). To Togakushi-Okusha shrine (p295) the one-way/return fare is ¥1350/2400.

Obuse

☎026 / POP 11,000

This lovely little town northeast of Nagano occupies a big place in Japanese art history and has a handful of interesting museums. The famed *ukiyo-e* (woodblock print) artist Hokusai (1760–1849) worked here during his final years. Obuse (小布施) is also famed for *kuri* (chestnuts), which you can sample steamed with rice or in ice cream and sweets.

The town is incredibly popular with Japanese day trippers, especially at weekends and on holidays. It's a 500m walk southeast from Obuse Station to the hot spots.

Sights

★**Hokusai Museum** GALLERY
(北斎館, Hokusai-kan; ☎026-247-5206; https://hokusai-kan.com; 485 Ōaza Obuse; adult/child ¥1000/free; ⌚9am-5pm) Japan's most famous *ukiyo-e* (woodblock print) artist, Hokusai, spent his final years in Obuse. There's an audiovisual presentation on his life in the theatre, and his '36 Views of Fuji' plus other works are exhibited in the gallery, which has recently undergone extensive renovation. You can buy everything Hokusai in the museum shop. It's a 10-minute, well-signposted walk from Obuse Station.

Takai Kōzan Kinenkan MUSEUM
(高井鴻山記念館; ☎026-247-4049; 805-1 Ōaza Obuse; ¥300; ⌚9am-6pm Apr-Sep, to 5pm Oct-Mar) Takai Kōzan, woodblock artist Hokusai's friend and patron, was a businessman and an accomplished classical artist specialising in elegant Chinese-style landscapes. His life and work are commemorated in this small museum.

JIGOKUDANI MONKEY PARK

Pleasant in winter when shrouded in snow, **Jigokudani Monkey Park** (地獄谷野猿公苑, Jigokudani Yaen-kōen; Map p292; ☎0269-33-4379; www.jigokudani-yaenkoen.co.jp; 6845 Ōaza-heian; adult/child ¥800/400; ⏲8.30am-5pm Apr-Oct, 9am-4pm Nov-Mar) is wildly popular. Made famous by the 1992 film *Baraka*, in which wild monkeys appear to bathe in natural onsen pools, the park sees thousands flock here each year to view the over-photographed troupe of wild Japanese macaques who are lured into the park with food. Many visitors are looking for that classic photo of a monkey in the steaming *rotemburo* with snow on its head.

While it's all good fun getting in there among the monkeys, a few points need to be noted beforehand. The monkeys are wild and not always there – confirm their presence before you start the 1.6km walk through the forest from the car park to the Monkey Park by asking the car-park attendant. The monkeys generally only go into the human-made onsen when the weather is cold. Keep in mind that these are wild monkeys and treat them as such: don't go in too close for that friendly photo. There's also a webcam link on the Monkey Park website where you can see what's going on. In winter, when snow hides the industrial debris, it's all quite appealing, but when there's no snow around, don't expect an overly attractive environment by the river.

A rental car will make life a lot easier here, but getting to the Monkey Park by public transport is also possible. Take the Nagano Dentetsu line from Nagano to the Yudanaka terminus (tokkyū ¥1260, 45 minutes), then take the bus for Kanbayashi Onsen Guchi and get off at Kanbayashi Onsen (¥230, 15 minutes, eight daily). Walk uphill along the road for about 400m until you see the sign reading 'Monkey Park', then begin your 1.6km walk through the forest.

Sleeping

Guest House Kokoro GUESTHOUSE ¥¥
(ゲストハウスココロ; ☎090-8843-9091; http://kokoro.obuse.jp; 1103 Obuse; s/d/tr without bathroom from ¥4200/7000/9000;) On the main road in the middle of Obuse, this little guesthouse boasts immaculate Japanese-style tatami rooms. It's only a couple of minutes' walk to the museums, and there are lots of eating options nearby.

★**Masuichi Kyakuden** RYOKAN ¥¥¥
(桝一客殿; ☎026-247-1111; www.kyakuden.jp; 815 Ōaza Obuse; d per person incl breakfast from ¥19,000; P) Delightful, original, stylish and enchanting: all describe this gem in the heart of Obuse. Twelve rooms – huge by Japanese standards – beautifully synergise old and new, and are constructed from antique *kura* (storehouses) around a chestnut garden. Disappear into the peace, tranquillity and refinement.

Eating

Obuse has a handful of imaginative eateries in line with the town's arty vibe. Expect to queue at weekends.

Cafe Gingadō CAFE ¥
(Cafe 銀河堂; ☎026-247-8130; 1444-1 Obuse; meals from ¥800; ⏲11.30am-5pm Tue-Sun) If you're struggling with the crowds on a busy day in Obuse, head back to the road in front of the station to find this lovely little cafe, offering set lunches such as daily pasta, pizza or omelette with salad for ¥800. It's a peaceful and attractive oasis, playing great jazz music.

Chikufūdō DESSERTS ¥
(竹風堂; ☎026-247-2569; http://chikufudo.com; 973 Ōaza Obuse; desserts from ¥300; ⏲8am-6pm) Sample chestnut confections at Chikufūdō, established in 1893. *Dorayakisan* (chestnut paste in pancake dumplings) are the standard here. It's on the main road near the Hokusai Museum.

Information

Obuse Tourist Information Center (☎026-214-6300; www.obusekanko.jp; ⏲9am-5pm) At Obuse station, this extremely helpful office has English brochures and maps, and rental bicycles (¥400 for first two hours, ¥100 per additional hour; available April to November) that can be returned at three other spots around town.

DON'T MISS

SHINSHŪ CUISINE

Nagano Prefecture is renowned for its food, and for Westerners the options range from familiar to downright challenging. Local foods are usually preceded by the region's ancient name, 'Shinshū' (信州).

ringo (りんご) Apples: the best in the world. Ubiquitous in autumn.

kuri (栗) Chestnuts, especially in Obuse.

teuchi soba (そば) Handmade buckwheat noodles, eaten either cold (*zaru-soba;* with wasabi and a soy-based dipping sauce) or hot (*kake-soba;* in broth).

oyaki (おやき) Wheat buns filled with vegetables, baked or steamed.

wasabi (わさび) Japanese horseradish, grown in bogs particularly in Hotaka. Look out for wasabi cakes and ice cream.

basashi (馬刺し) Raw horse meat.

hachinoko (鉢の子) Bee larvae.

inago(稲子) Crickets.

A la Obuse Guide Centre (ア·ラ·小布施ガイドセンター; ☎026-247-5050; 789-1 Ōaza Obuse; ⏲9am-5pm) You can get maps here, en route to the museums from Obuse Station. There's also a cafe, a gift store and a quaint guesthouse out the back (Petit Hotel a la Obuse; singles from ¥8000, twins from ¥12,000) if you decide to stick around.

Getting There & Away

Obuse is reached via the Nagano Dentetsu (Nagaden) line from Nagano (*tokkyū/futsū* ¥770/670, 25/40 minutes).

Nozawa Onsen

☎0269 / POP 3500

This wonderful working village tucked into a picturesque corner of the eastern Japan Alps is both a humming winter ski resort and a year-round onsen town – it's worth visiting at any time of year.

Settled as early as the 8th century, Nozawa Onsen (野沢温泉) is compact and quaint, with a maze of narrow streets. Dotted around the village are public onsen and a range of excellent accommodation. Outside the busy ski season, it's possible to briefly escape modernity and get a sense of life in an ancient mountain village. There's a strong sense of community here, epitomised by the 13 *soto-yu* onsen, each maintained by a different part of the village as bathing spots for locals. Onsen water is still used by many for laundry, cooking and heating. There's a refreshing desire to avoid unbridled development and maintain the uniqueness of the village.

Activities

★Nozawa Onsen Snow Resort SNOW SPORTS
(野沢温泉スキー場; www.nozawaski.com; 1-day lift ticket ¥4800; ⏲8.30am-4.30pm Dec-Apr) One of Honshū's best, this resort dominates the 'upper' village. It's easy to navigate and enjoy, with 21 lifts and a variety of terrain. The main base is around the Hikage gondola station, where there are beginner and kid-friendly runs. Snowboarders should try the Karasawa terrain park or the half-pipe at Uenotaira; advanced skiers will enjoy the steep Schneider Course.

The lively village is great for après-ski action.

Festivals & Events

Dōsojin Matsuri CULTURAL
(道祖神祭り; ⏲13-15 Jan) Each year crowds gather for the famous Dōsojin Matsuri, a kind of cleansing ritual for men aged 25 and 42 years, the so-called 'unlucky ages' in Japan. The 42-year-olds' task is to defend a purpose-built two-storey shrine, which they sit upon as it is besieged by fire at the hands of the 25-year-olds and onlookers.

The 13th and 14th are warm-up days for the big event on the 15th. Copious amounts of sake are imbibed by all, the defenders come down after a while, and then the shrine is set ablaze with great enthusiasm.

Sleeping

Nozawa Onsen has a variety of accommodation, including some wonderful rustic ryokan, open year-round. In winter it's buzzing; book ahead.

Lodge Nagano INN ¥
(ロッジながの; ☎050-5532-6026; www.lodgenagano.com; 6846-1 Toyosato; dm/r per person incl breakfast from ¥4500/6500; P❄📶) This popular foreign-run guesthouse attracts lots of Aussie skiers – everything is set up with exactly what you need. It's a friendly, fun place

with bunk dorms and tatami rooms, some with private bathroom.

★ **Address Nozawa** APARTMENT ¥¥
(アドレス野沢; ☎0269-67-0360; www.addressnozawa.com; 9535 Nozawa Onsen; studios from ¥12,000; P❄📶) This innovative, centrally located boutique property occupies what was a traditional inn. The new owners have created a space combining Japanese and European design elements, and the large, Western-style rooms feature fresh colours, downy beds, bright bathrooms and a full kitchen. There's an on-site onsen bath, a kids' room, ski storage and plenty of technology.

Nozawa Peaks LODGE ¥¥
(☎050-5539-8960; www.nozawapeaks.com; 6585 Toyosato; r without bathroom from ¥12,600; ❄📶) This foreigner-friendly place has Japanese-style tatami rooms with futon, some with bathroom, some with shared facilities. There's a large living room, along with drying and ski-storage rooms. The nearest resort lift is five minutes' walk away. Nozawa Peaks is a 10-minute walk south of the village centre.

Kiriya Ryokan RYOKAN ¥¥
(桐屋旅館; ☎0269-85-2020; www.kiriya.jp; 8714-2 Nozawa Onsen; r per person incl 2 meals & without bathroom from ¥14,500; P❄📶) This friendly ryokan has been in the family for generations. The owner's attentive service and excellent English ensure its abiding popularity with overseas guests. All rooms have private toilets; some have their own baths in addition to the large communal onsen baths. There's a guest laundry and a wonderful garden.

★ **Mura-no-hoteru Sumiyoshi-ya** RYOKAN ¥¥¥
(村のホテル住吉屋; ☎0269-85-2005; www.sumiyosiya.co.jp; 8713 Toyosato; r per person incl 2 meals & without bathroom from ¥18,820; ❄📶) This wonderful ryokan, the oldest in town, has a wide range of inviting traditional room types, many with private bathrooms and great views. The communal onsen baths with stained-glass windows are dreamy. Limited English is spoken, but the friendly staff is committed to excellence in service.

Eating & Drinking

Nozawa Onsen isn't so happening in the green season, when a nocturnal stroll around the village will leave you feeling decidedly calm and contemplative. It's a different scene entirely in the ski season, when you'll find no shortage of friendly little bars packed with playful punters.

★ **Sobadokoro Daimon** SOBA ¥
(そば処 大茂ん; ☎0269-85-2033; 9509 Toyosato; meals from ¥750; ⏲11.30am-2.30pm & 5.30-8.30pm) This superb soba shop, just of the main street in the middle of the village, offers a relaxed atmosphere, jazz music and a chance to try the superb soba that Nagano Prefecture is legendary for. Make sure you get a side dish of *nozawana* (¥350), the tasty local pickled vegetable.

Nappa 78 Cafe CAFE ¥
(なっぱ78カフェ; ☎080-1250-7878; http://nappa-cafe.com; 9301-2 Toyosato; plates from ¥400; ⏲10am-6pm Thu-Tue) This extremely cute little cafe is up at the top of town where the locals boil eggs in the onsen water. Set-menu lunches (¥780) and light meals are the go here, along with cakes, desserts and coffees. There's an *ashi-yu* (foot bath) right outside.

Kaze no Ie ITALIAN ¥
(風の家; ☎0269-85-3244; www.kazenoie.info; 9494 Toyosato; pasta ¥600-1000; ⏲6-10pm) You can't beat this little Italian trattoria in the heart of the village for hearty pastas, tasty pizzas and delicious bruschetta. Excellent

DON'T MISS

NOZAWA ONSEN'S BATHS

There are 13 onsen known as *soto-yu* (外湯; open 6am to 11pm) dotted about Nozawa Onsen. Historically, these are the locals' bathing houses: many older houses in the village still do not have a bath. While there's no-one to collect money, the correct etiquette for non-locals is to put some coins in the donation box on the wall outside.

Head through the correct door to get changed – to minimise mistakes, all the onsen have English signage on their Men and Women doors. Each place has two tiny baths; *nuru-yu* (ぬる湯) is the not-so-hot bath and *atsu-yu* (あつ湯) is the hot one – scaldingly hot at some of the 13. A favourite is Ō-yu, with its fine wooden building, followed by the steaming-hot Shin-yu and the atmospheric Kuma-no-te-arai-yu (Bear's Bath). Give as many as you can a try; you'll only need 10 minutes in each.

value, with a top wine list featuring Italian and French wines to boot!

★Libushi CRAFT BEER

(里武士; ☎080-6930-3992; http://libushi.com; 9347 Toyosato; ⊙4-11pm) Smack in the middle of the village, Libushi is Nozawa Onsen's very own artisan brewery. With a taproom up front, a brewery out the back and a very innovative attitude, this outfit is coming up with some intriguing one-off brews. Pints range from ¥1200 to ¥1600. You might find that hours vary outside the busy season.

Stay BAR

(ステイ; 9517 Toyosato; ⊙8pm-late) This cosy basement bar is open late and run by a music-loving Japanese man who has lived abroad. He's especially keen on Jackson Browne's 1977 classic 'Stay' – hence the name of the bar.

Information

Nozawa Onsen Visitor Centre (野沢温泉ビジターセンター; ☎0269-85-3155; www.nozawakanko.jp/english; 9780-4 Toyosato; ⊙8.30am-5.30pm) In the centre of the village. Has English-speaking staff who can assist with accommodation and tour bookings.

Getting There & Away

Since the arrival of the Hokuriku *shinkansen*, getting to Nozawa Onsen has become quicker and easier.

To get here from Tokyo, take a *shinkansen* direct to Iiyama station (¥8630, 110 minutes), then connect to the Nozawa Onsen Liner bus to Nozawa Onsen (¥600, 20 minutes).

Myōkō Kōgen

☎0255 / POP 33,200

The Myōkō mountain range (妙高高原) is a well-known destination among powder hounds – its proximity to the Sea of Japan means Myōkō gets snow before anywhere else – but there are plenty of other attractions in the many stylish, accessible resorts here for connoisseurs of alpine living. In the warmer months the lush, verdant forests of Myōkō Kōgen draw hikers and strollers alike to wander their many sunlit paths – the area is one of 48 certified 'forest therapy bases' in Japan, where walkers can practise the art of *shinrin-yoku* (forest bathing).

Activities

Akakura Onsen Ski Park SNOW SPORTS

(赤倉温泉スキー場, Akakura Onsen Sukī-Jō; ☎0255-87-2125; www.akakura-ski.com; 1-day lift ticket adult/child ¥4800/1000; ⊙Dec-Mar; 🚸) Akakura Onsen is one of the more popular resorts in Myōkō, especially among travellers with small children. All but two of the 20 runs were laid out with the needs of novice skiers in mind, and even the black diamonds are little more than short chutes. But the high-quality powder and picturesque setting ensure a good time for everyone.

Family restaurants, many drawing inspiration from European chalets, are scattered around the slopes. English signage is generally available.

Tours

Dancing Snow SNOW SPORTS

(ダンシングスノー; ☎090-1433-1247; www.dancingsnow.com) For off-piste excitement, check out these local experts for guided tours through the backwoods terrain and snowshoe treks, as well as personalised one-on-one instruction – all in English. Prices depend on the length and type of tour; summer hiking tours are also available. Check the website for details.

Sleeping & Eating

Akakura Onsen, a cosy mountain village nearby, is the perfect base for a long stay. Most places will pick you up from the station with advance notice.

There are plenty of restaurants in Akakura Onsen and around the train station, though many close down in the warmer months.

Hotel Alp INN ¥¥

(ホテルアルプ; ☎0255-87-3388; www.alp-myoko.com; 585-90 Akakura Onsen; r per person incl 2 meals from ¥12,750; P⊖@📶) The tranquil Hotel Alp lies at the base of the slopes and is extremely conducive to a ski-in, ski-out holiday. There are fewer than 20 rooms, allowing for a sense of intimacy not found at the resort hotels. Be sure to spend some quality time in the therapeutic sauna and hot-spring bath, perfect for thawing out your joints.

Red Warehouse LODGE ¥¥¥

(インターナショナルロッジ 赤の蔵; ☎0255-78-7828; www.red-warehouse.com; 25-549 Akakura

Onsen; s/d from ¥7900/14,900, closed Apr-Nov;) Knowledgeable, English-speaking hosts oversee this terrific homestyle retreat where guests stay in clean, simple rooms ideal for families. It's good value too, given the easy access to the ski fields, spotless communal areas and uncomplicated travel vibe.

Information

Tourist Information Center (妙高市観光協会; 0255-86-3911; www.myokotourism.com; 291-1 Taguchi; 9am-7pm) Enquire here about lift passes, accommodation, equipment rentals and ski schools with English-speaking instructors. In summer excellent walking maps are available, as is bike hire (¥3000 per day).

Getting There & Away

Myōkō Kōgen is actually in Niigata Prefecture but is best reached from Nagano. The Nagano *shinkansen* runs once or twice every hour between Tokyo and Nagano (¥7680, 1¾ hours). Nagano is connected to Myōkō Kōgen by the JR Shinano line; hourly *kaisoku* (rapid trains; ¥830, 45 minutes) ply this route. From Myōkō Kōgen Station, shuttle buses and taxis run to Akakura Onsen Ski Park and other ski resorts.

Shiga Kōgen

0269

The site of several events during the 1998 Nagano Winter Olympics, Shiga Kōgen (志賀高原) is Japan's biggest ski resort and one of the largest in the world: there are 18 linked areas covering an incredible amount of terrain. With a free shuttle connecting all the resorts and a 'key card' pass that can be used everywhere, skiers are swooning here.

Outside winter the mountain's lakes, ponds and overlooks make it an excellent destination for hikers. In 1980, some 130 sq km of land was designated a Unesco-protected Man and the Biosphere (MAB) Reserve.

If you don't ski or hike, the only compelling reason to visit are the glorious green-season vistas from Rte 292 as it winds its way up from Yudanaka, then around twisty peaks, past lakes and the craters of active volcanoes, and down to the village of Kusatsu Onsen: it's one of mainland Japan's most rewarding drives.

Activities

★ **Shiga Kōgen Ski Area** SKIING
(志賀高原スキー場; 0269-34-2404; www.shigakogen.gr.jp; 1-day lift ticket ¥5000; 8.30am-4.30pm Dec-Apr) This conglomeration of 18 ski areas is covered by one lift ticket, which gives access to all areas as well as the shuttle bus between various base lodges. Check out www.snowjapan.com for information on each of the areas.

There's a huge variety of terrain for all skill levels. In the Hasuike area, in front of the Shiga Kōgen ropeway station, the tourist office (p302) has English speakers who can help you navigate the slopes and book accommodation. Hasuike ski area is central and good for learners and families; Nishitate-yama has long courses and great views; Yakebitai-yama is one of the biggest areas, with a huge variety of terrain and panoramic views.

Sleeping & Eating

Ski resorts of all shapes and sizes dot the hills and valleys that make up Shiga Kōgen. There's no central village to speak of, but 16 hotel areas spread out around the mountains, so look at a map when you book your accommodation.

There's very little by way of dining options outside ski season. It's a good move to eat where you stay.

★ **Villa Ichinose** INN ¥¥
(ヴィラ・一の瀬; 0269-34-2704; www.villa101.biz; 7149 Hirao; per person incl breakfast & without bathroom from ¥6500;) In a great spot in front of the Ichinose bus stop, and with English-speaking staff and a friendly atmosphere, this inn is popular with overseas guests. Japanese-style rooms have toilet only; Western-style rooms have their own bathroom. There's wi-fi and a 24-hour public bath on the 2nd floor.

Hotel Shirakaba-sō HOTEL ¥¥
(ホテル白樺荘; 0269-34-3311; www.shirakaba.co.jp/english; 7148 Hirao; r per person incl 2 meals from ¥13,500;) Close to the cable-car base station and the Sun Valley ski area is this pleasant little hotel with a variety of rooms and its own indoor and outdoor onsen baths. It's in a great location virtually next to the Hasuike bus stop.

Chalet Shiga INN ¥¥
(シャレー志賀; 0269-34-2235; www.shigakogen.jp/chalet/en; r per person incl 2 meals from

¥10,200; P❄📶) Chalet Shiga is convenient to the slopes and has a popular sports bar on-site. Both Western- and Japanese-style rooms are available, plus onsen and sauna.

Information

Shiga Kōgen Tourist Office (志賀高原観光協会; ☎0269-34-2323; www.shigakogen.gr.jp; ⏲9am-5pm) In the Hasuike area, the Shiga Kōgen Tourist Office has English speakers who can help you navigate the slopes and book accommodation.

Getting There & Away

Nagaden runs direct buses between JR Nagano Station and Shiga Kōgen (¥1700, 70 minutes), with frequent departures in ski season. You can also take a train from Nagano to Yudanaka and continue to Shiga Kōgen by bus – take a Hasuike-bound bus and get off at the last stop (¥780, approximately 40 minutes).

Bessho Onsen

☎0268 / POP 2500

With some interesting temples and excellent hot-spring waters, mountain-ringed Bessho Onsen (別所温泉), part of Ueda city, is a charming little village well worth a visit. It lies at the end of its own train line, and it's a pleasure to hop off at the cute retro station and head uphill into the heart of the village.

Historically, Bessho Onsen has plenty of claims to fame. It has long been referred to as 'Little Kamakura' for the fact that it served as an administrative centre during the Kamakura period (1192–1333). It was also mentioned in *The Pillow Book* by the Heian-era poetess Sei Shōnagon, and the restorative properties of its onsen waters are said to have healed the arrow wounds of warriors through the ages.

Sights & Activities

There are three old onsen in the village (¥150), each open from 6am to 10pm: **Ō-yu** (大湯) has a small *rotemburo* (outdoor bath); **Ishi-yu** (石湯) is famed for its stone bath; and **Daishi-yu** (大師湯), most frequented by the locals, is relatively cool. A recent addition is **Aisome-no-yu** (あいそめの湯), a sizeable onsen complex just downhill from the station that charges ¥500. It's also open 6am to 10pm.

Kitamuki Kannon BUDDHIST TEMPLE
(北向観音; ☎0268-38-2023; ⏲24hr) FREE The grounds of this Tendai temple have some impressive ancient trees and sweeping valley views. The temple's name comes from the fact that this Kannon image faces north, a counterpart to the south-facing image at Zenkō-ji (p291) in Nagano.

Anraku-ji BUDDHIST TEMPLE
(安楽時; ☎0268-38-2062; adult/child ¥300/100; ⏲8am-5pm Mar-Oct, to 4pm Nov-Feb) Of the Sōtō Zen sect, Anraku-ji is the oldest Zen temple in Nagano. Dating from 824–34 CE, it's a National Treasure, renowned for its octagonal pagoda. The temple is a 10-minute walk from the Bessho Onsen train station.

Sleeping & Eating

There's a handful of reasonably priced eateries in the vicinity of the train station, but if you stay at a ryokan, it will be best to eat where you stay.

★ **Earthworks Guesthouse & Gallery** GUESTHOUSE ¥¥
(アースワークスギャラリー&ゲストハウス; ☎080-69370304; https://earthworksguesthouse.amebaownd.com; 1725 Bessho Onsen; s/d with shared bathroom from ¥5000/8000; P🚭❄📶) Run by Roberto and Rumi in a renovated old farmhouse behind their sensational Earthworks Gallery, this is a wonderful place to stay if you don't mind a shared bathroom. The tatami rooms are gorgeous, as are the communal rooms. It's all very tasteful, as you'd expect from top ceramic artists. It's in the middle of the village, 500m from the station.

Uematsu-ya INN ¥¥
(上松屋; ☎0268-38-2300; www.uematsuya.com; 1628 Bessho Onsen; r per person incl 2 meals from ¥10,000; P❄📶) Uematsu-ya is a well-kept, good-value inn occupying a nine-storey building atop a hill. It has both Japanese- and Western-style rooms; deluxe rooms are larger, on higher floors and have a private terrace. There are also indoor onsen and lovely *rotemburo* (outdoor baths). Good English is spoken.

Ryokan Hanaya RYOKAN ¥¥
(旅館花屋; ☎0268-38-3131; http://hanaya.naganoken.jp; 169 Bessho Onsen; r per person with 2 meals from ¥14,000; P) Ryokan Hanaya is a step back in time to the Taishō era (1912–26) – a traditional gem set among wonderful manicured Japanese gardens. Fourteen

beautiful, spacious tatami rooms open onto the scenery; each one has unique motifs and history. There's a blissful *rotemburo* (outdoor bath) in the garden.

Capitolino ITALIAN ¥
(カピトリーノ; ☎0268-38-3140; www.fresh-ikeda.com; 68-4 Bessho Onsen; meals from ¥800; ⏰11am-2.30pm & 5-8.30pm Thu-Tue) Bessho Onsen has a good Italian restaurant, whose proprietors are extremely proud of the quality of their pastas and pizzas. Just across from the station, the restaurant shares the building with a fresh-produce store and market.

ℹ Information

Bessho Onsen Ryokan Association (別所温泉旅館組合; ☎0268-38-2020; www.bessho-onsen.com; 1853-3 Bessho Onsen; ⏰9am-5pm) Located at the train station, this small office with enthusiastic staff provides tourist information and can assist with lodging reservations. It also has bicycles that visitors can use for free.

ℹ Getting There & Away

Access is by train, via Ueda. From Nagano, take the JR *shinkansen* (¥2940, 12 minutes) or the private Shinano Tetsudō line (¥770, 40 minutes). From Tokyo, take the JR *shinkansen* (¥6670, 1½ hours). Once at Ueda, change to the private Ueda Dentetsu line to Bessho Onsen (¥590, 28 minutes).

Karuizawa

☎0267 / POP 19,000

Karuizawa (軽井沢) is a picturesque resort town situated in a fertile valley beneath the shadow of Asama-yama, one of the most active volcanoes on Honshū. Its last minor eruption was in 2015, but the previous one in 2009 reportedly saw ash fall as far away as Tokyo (130km). Karuizawa has long been a popular retreat from Tokyo's summer heat for the rich and famous. In 1957 a young Emperor Akihito met his future bride, Empress Michiko, on a tennis court here. Since then, the town has been a popular spot for weddings and an even more popular weekend destination for Tokyoites.

With easy access from Tokyo and Nagano by *shinkansen*, a range of accommodation, restaurants, and a shopping outlet that even anti-shoppers will find hard to resist, Karuizawa makes a worthwhile day trip and a lovely, though expensive, place to spend a night or two.

◉ Sights

Old Karuizawa (旧軽井沢; Kyū Karuizawa), also known as 'Old Karuizawa Ginza', is an attractive main street lined with classy boutiques, galleries and cafes. Follow Karuizawa-hondōri north from JR Karuizawa Station for about 1km, then turn right onto Kyū Karuizawa Ginza-dōri – you can't miss it.

Asama-yama Magma Stone Park PARK
(鬼押出し園, Onioshidashi-en; Map p292; ☎0267-86-4141; www.princehotels.co.jp/amuse/onioshidashi; 1053 Kanbara, Tsumagoi-mura; adult/child ¥650/450; ⏰8am-4.30pm) Here's your chance to get up close and personal with Asama-yama – so close, you could almost touch it. Formed in 1783 by Asama's last violent eruption, this 'Hurled by Demons' park has a surreal landscape of jagged, hardened magma juxtaposed with verdant fields: volcanic soil is extremely fertile. Best accessed with your own wheels, the park is on the Onioshi Highway Toll Rd linking Naka-Karuizawa with Tsumagoi to the north. Ask at the Karuizawa Tourist Association office (p304) for bus details.

'Umi' Museum of Contemporary Art GALLERY
(軽井沢現代美術館, Karuizawa Gendai-bijutsukan; ☎0267-31-5141; www.moca-karuizawa.jp; 2052-2 Nagakura; adult/child/senior ¥1000/500/800; ⏰10am-5pm Jul-Sep, 10am-5pm Fri-Mon Apr-Jun, Oct & Nov) This light-filled gallery showcases an impressive collection of contemporary work by Japanese artists who have found fame abroad in genres such as oil painting, 3D art and sculpture. It's in a lovely forested spot between Karuizawa and Naka-Karuizawa Stations.

Usui Pass Lookout VIEWPOINT
(碓氷峠見晴台, Usui Tōge Miharadai) FREE On the border of Gunma and Nagano Prefectures, about 4km east of Karuizawa on Rte 18, you'll find the Usui Pass, historically an important point on the Nakasendō, one of the two routes of the Edo period that linked Tokyo and Kyoto. A train line ran through the pass from 1893 to 1997. The observation platform has stunning views of Asama-yama and surrounding mountains. There's no public transport; for directions, ask at the Karuizawa Tourist Association office (p304).

Sleeping

Occupancy is generally high and rates are among the dearest in Japan. As Karuizawa is very spread out, check that you're where you want to be when making a booking.

★Cottage Inn Log Cabin CABIN ¥¥
(☎0267-45-6007; www.log-cabin.co.jp; 3148-1 Naka-Karuizawa; cabins per person from ¥6000; P❄Wi-Fi) As the name suggests, these fully self-contained cabins, in a forested setting five minutes' walk from Naka-Karuizawa Station, have rustic appeal. This is a great option for travelling families, with a restaurant and *daiyokujō* (big bath) on-site.

Ikoisansō INN ¥¥
(いこい山荘; ☎0267-45-5254; www.ikoi-sanso.com; 3365-9 Nagakura; r with shared bathroom from ¥9000; P⊖❄Wi-Fi) A good midrange option 1km north of Naka-Karuizawa Station, Ikoisansō offers free pick-up and drop-off at the station. Choose from Japanese-style rooms with shared facilities in the older building or rooms with private bathroom in the new building. There's a decent *daiyokujō* (big bath) and rental bicycles (¥1000 per day). It's down a quiet side lane; there's free parking.

★Ancient Hotel HOTEL ¥¥¥
(☎0267-42-3611; www.ancient-hotel.com; 2126 Nagakura; d per person with 2 meals from ¥30,000; P❄Wi-Fi) About 10km north of Karuizawa Station, deep in the forest (there's a free shuttle bus!), this beautifully designed hotel blends gracefully into its surroundings. It's a place of understated luxury, relaxation and tranquillity. This attention to detail and aesthetic sensibility flow through to the cuisine, which is presented so elegantly you'll have to eat very slowly indeed.

Eating

★Kastanie Karuizawa Roast Chicken DINER ¥
(カスターニエ 軽井沢ローストチキン; ☎0267-42-3081; www.kastanie.co.jp; 23-2 Karuizawa-higashi; dishes from ¥600; ⌚11am-3pm & 5-9pm Wed-Mon) For something a little uncommon in Japan, pop into this original place for succulent and tender roast-chicken dinners, pizzas, pastas and sausage platters, all presented with Japanese attention to detail. This place is so popular that you'll need to book to get a table for dinner – do so online. It's about 400m north of Karuizawa Station.

Kawakami-an FUSION ¥¥
(川上案; ☎0267-42-0009; www.kawakamian.com/shopkaruizawa; 6-10 Karuizawa; plates from ¥480; ⌚11am-10pm) Just before the start of Ginza-dōri, this is a wonderful place to sample a wide variety of Japanese and Western dishes, including an excellent large serve of tempura soba (¥2090) or, for something different, avocado and Camembert salad (¥880). Otherwise, just stop in for coffee and dessert.

Shopping

Karuizawa Prince Shopping Plaza MALL
(軽井沢・プリンスショッピングプラザ; ☎0267-42-5211; www.karuizawa-psp.jp; ⌚10am-7pm) Just outside the south exit of JR Karuizawa Station, this gargantuan outlet shopping mall has most of the big names. Shopaholics should allocate plenty of time. It's set among an expanse of grassland, with its own lake, lots of dining options and great views to Asama-yama, so it's easy to lose time here, even if you're not a big shopper.

Information

Karuizawa Tourist Association (軽井沢観光協会, Karuizawa Kankō Kyōkai; ☎0267-42-2491; www.karuizawa-kankokyokai.jp; ⌚9am-5pm) Grab your English-language publications and maps at this office inside the JR Karuizawa Station building.

There are also tourist-information offices at Naka-Karuizawa Station and in Kyū Karuizawa Ginza-dōri.

Getting There & Away

Karuizawa is a stop on the Nagano *shinkansen* line from Nagano (¥3680, 30 minutes) or Tokyo (¥5910, 70 minutes). There are twice-hourly services in both directions at most times.

Alternatively, the private Shinano Tetsudō line from Nagano operates local trains (¥1640, 1¼ hours), and there are five buses per day from Tokyo's Ikebukuro Station (¥2600, three hours).

Getting Around

As the Karuizawa area is quite spread out, hiring a car will help you enjoy all the region has to offer.

There are four rental-bicycle outlets more or less right outside the north exit of Karuizawa Station and two more at Naka-Karuizawa Station. Many accommodation places also offer rental bikes.

GUNMA PREFECTURE

Mineral baths seem to bubble out of the ground at every turn in the dramatic forested mountain landscape of Gunma Prefecture (群馬県; Gunma-ken). Its most famous onsen town is Kusatsu, but there are many others that are less commercial. All that water and mountain adds up to great outdoor activities, ranging from skiing in winter to rafting and canyoning in spring and summer.

Getting There & Away

Gateway to Gunma Prefecture, Takasaki is an important transport hub where the Jōetsu and Hokuriku *shinkansen* lines branch out in the directions of Niigata and Kanazawa (via Nagano) respectively.

The most popular onsen villages are reached by a combination of local trains and buses, but, if you don't mind driving on winding mountain roads, renting a car here can make the journey vastly more pleasurable. Fair warning: it's hard to keep your eyes on the road with views this good.

Takasaki

0273 / POP 370,884

Takasaki (高崎) is a workaday city that feels increasingly like a Tokyo suburb due to the short 50-minute *shinkansen* (bullet-train) journey from the metropolis. Famous for *daruma* dolls, Italian-style pasta and as a gateway to Gunma's stunning mountain scenery, Takasaki is an excellent *norikaeru-machi* – the place to change trains or stop over if you're travelling between Tōhoku and the Japan Alps. You'll find cheap eats and beds near the train station, which is the branching-out point for the Jōetsu (to Niigata) and Hokuriku (to Nagano, Kanazawa and Toyama) *shinkansen* lines.

Sights

★Haruna Jinja SHINTŌ SHRINE

(上野國六之宮　榛名神社; 0273-74-9050; www.haruna.or.jp; 849 Harunasan-machi) Among gorgeously forested mountains and believed to be the home of the God of Water, Fire and Agriculture, this site has housed a shrine of some form for almost 1400 years. It's said that a visit brings good fortune in love and money. A 700m path to the shrine (situated under massive, carefully balanced boulders) takes you to a tree that some date as old as 1000 years. Take a bus from JR Takasaki Station (70 minutes) or drive.

Tomioka Silk Mill HISTORIC BUILDING

(富岡製糸場; 0274-64-0005; www.tomioka-silk.jp; 1-1 Tomioka, Tomioka; adult/child ¥1000/250; 9am-5pm) Listed as a World Heritage Site in 2014, Tomioka Silk Mill provides a look at the history of silk production, with some English-language narration. Completed in 1872, the mill was once one of the world's largest producers of silk. Today, its buildings are some of the only Meiji-era government factories preserved in excellent condition. It makes a fascinating day trip from Takasaki. To get here take the Joshin Dentetsu line to Joshu Tomioka Station, then walk 10 minutes.

Usui Tōge Railway Village MUSEUM

(碓氷峠鉄道文化村, Usui Tōge Tetsudō Bunka Mura; 0273-80-4163; 407-16 Yokokawa; adult/child ¥500/free; 9am-5pm) Fans of the iron horse will love this rail graveyard–locomotive museum, with rolling stock, stations, carriages, simulators and years of Japanese rail history in a lovely rural setting. Take the train from Takasaki to Yokokawa Station (¥500, 30 minutes), the end of the Shinetsu main line.

For self-drivers, the park is also within easy reach of Karuizawa (22km).

Sleeping

Takasaki has a wide variety of moderately priced business and tourist hotels clustered around the train-station area.

There's no shortage of places to eat near Takasaki Station.

Hotel Metropolitan Takasaki HOTEL ¥¥

(ホテルメトロポリタン高崎; 0273-25-3311; http://takasaki.metropolitan.jp; 222 Yashima-chō; s/d from ¥8700/14,000;) Adjoining JR Takasaki Station, this hotel is Takasaki's most stylish and convenient, with excellent views from higher floors, and well-appointed rooms.

Harappa Ekibiru-ten ITALIAN ¥

(はらっぱ駅ビル店; 0273-22-5445; www.harappa.co.jp; JR Takasaki Station Bldg 5F, 222 Yashima-chō; pasta from ¥960; 11am-3.30pm & 5-10pm) Dorothy, you're not in Emilia-Romagna any more. Upstairs inside the JR Takasaki Station building, this local favourite serves every pasta dish conceivable, from standard carbonara and marinara to Takasaki originals like *watari kani no tomato kuri-mu* (soft-shell-crab tomato cream). It's a welcome alternative slurp.

Information

Takasaki Tourist Information Center (高崎観光案内所; ☎0273-27-2192; www.gtia.jp/kokusai/english; ⊙9am-8pm) Inside JR Takasaki Station, these friendly folks have lots of English-language publications and can advise how to get to sights further afield.

Getting There & Away

Frequent *shinkansen* (bullet-train) services race into Takasaki from Tokyo (¥4410, one hour) and onward to Karuizawa (¥2600, 15 minutes), Nagano (¥4530, 45 minutes), Toyama (¥9850, two hours) and Kanazawa (¥11,460, 2¼ hours).

You can also travel from here on the Jōetsu *shinkansen* to Niigata (¥7470, 1¼ hours) to begin your explorations of the Tōhoku region.

Minakami Onsen-kyo

☎0278 / POP 19,573

In the northern region of Gunma Prefecture you'll find Minakami Onsen-kyo, a sprawling onsen collective formed by the amalgamation of three smaller villages: Minakami-machi, Tsukiyo-no-machi and Niharu-mura.

Surrounded by beautiful forests and mountains, and cut through by the gushing Tone-gawa, the broader area is home to two of Japan's most adored *onsen ryokan*, while the town of Minakami has become a year-round mecca for enthusiasts of outdoor-adventure sports, hiking and skiing.

As most people arrive at Jōmō Kōgen Station, about half an hour from Minakami, it's hard to get a handle on the place at first. Looking a little worse for wear (like most mountain villages once the snow has melted), Minakami-machi is Minakami Onsen-kyo's main town, itself spread out and hard to pin down.

Gunma Prefecture's top-billing retreats Takaragawa Onsen, formerly of Minakami-machi, and Hōshi Onsen, of Niharu-mura, are remote, isolated and located in opposing directions. Although both are part of the Minakami Onsen group, neither are within striking distance of Minakami town at all.

It would be difficult to visit all three in a day, but spending a night at Takaragawa Onsen's Ōsenkaku or Hōshi Onsen's Chōjūkan will solve your time problems – and, no doubt, countless others.

Activities

★Takaragawa Onsen ONSEN
(宝川温泉; ☎0278-75-2614; www.takaragawa.com; 1899 Fujiwara; ¥1500; ⊙9am-5pm) This stunning outdoor onsen offers four large rock pools cascading beside Tone-gawa and shaded by a lush forest with meandering paths, wooden huts, and folk and religious statues. All pools are mixed, except one that's for women only. Modesty towels are available (¥100) but seem to be used only by women. Buses run here hourly from Minakami Station (¥2900, 40 minutes).

Tanigawa-dake Ropeway CABLE CAR
(土合口駅; ☎0278-72-3575; www.tanigawadake-rw.com; return ¥2060; ⊙8am-5pm) Tanigawa-dake Ropeway takes you via gondola to the peak of Tenjin-daira, from where hiking trips, ranging from a couple of hours to all day, are available from May to November. There's skiing and snowboarding in winter. From Minakami Station, take a 20-minute bus ride to Ropeway-Ekimae bus stop (¥700). Discounted combined ropeway and return bus tickets are available.

Sleeping

Most local adventure-sports operators have their own lodges, but if you're not the adventuring kind, the town feels as though it has more ageing *minshuku* and ryokan than it does residents.

Tenjin Lodge LODGE ¥¥
(天神ロッジ; ☎0278-25-3540; www.tenjinlodge.com; 220-4 Yubiso; r per person from ¥8600; Wi-Fi) Ideally located at the foot of Tanigawa-dake, across from a lovely waterfall and nearby swimming holes, this lodge offers comfy, spacious Japanese- and Western-style rooms; ask for a riverside one. Welcoming hosts offer home-cooked meals (breakfast ¥800, dinner ¥1300) as well as plenty of local knowledge and adventure-sports options.

★Takaragawa Onsen Ōsenkaku RYOKAN ¥¥¥
(宝川温泉汪泉閣; ☎0278-75-2611; www.takaragawa.com; 1899 Fujiwara; r per person incl 2 meals & shared bathroom from ¥18,000; air-con, Wi-Fi, restaurant) They hardly come more traditional than this inn split over three buildings, the oldest of which is the riverside 1936 No 1 Annexe. Guests have 24-hour use of adjacent Takaragawa Onsen: early-morning bathing gives you the opportunity to experience that sense

ADVENTURE SPORTS IN MINAKAMI

Minakami is one of Japan's year-round adventure-sports destinations, with the exception of November, when many of the operators take a break before the start of the winter season.

In the spring melt (between April and June) the Tone-gawa (利根川) is the source of Japan's best white-water activities. Tour operators with English guides include **Canyons** (キャニオンズ ｜ラフティング,キャニオニング,ロッジ,カフェー&バー; ☎0278-72-2811; www.canyons.jp; rafting half-/full-day from ¥8500/15,500), **I Love Outdoors** (☎0278-72-1337; www.iloveoutdoors.jp/en; 169-1 Shikanosawa; half-day tours from ¥8000) and **H2O Guide Services** (エイチツーオーガイドサービス; ☎0278-72 6117; www.h2o-guides.jp; rafting/canyoning half-/full-day ¥8000/13,000). During summer, when water levels drop and it gets warmer, each outfitter offers canyoning trips. Both Canyons and I Love Outdoors can arrange packages in their own lodges.

A variety of mountain-biking tours are offered by **MTB Japan** (☎0278-72-1650; www.mtbjapan.com; tours from ¥6000), while the team at Tenjin Lodge offers hiking in the warmer months and off-piste skiing, snowboarding and snowshoeing in the winter. If none of that is heart-thumping enough for you, take a plunge with **Bungy Japan** (バンジージャパン 水上バンジー; ☎0278-72-8133; www.bungyjapan.com/minakami; 143 Obinata; 1st jump from ¥9000; ⏲10am-4pm Mon-Fri, 9am-5pm Sat & Sun Apr-Nov).

Serious climbers will want to tackle Tanigawa-dake (1977m), Tenjin-dake and Ichino-kura. Tanigawa-dake is suited to experienced climbers only: it is responsible for quadruple the number of deaths that have occurred on Mt Everest. When hiking, watch out for bears.

of real tranquillity that can be hard to grasp during crowded peak times.

Note that the dinner banquet may include bear-meat soup; if you'd prefer not to eat this, ask for no *kuma-jiru* (熊汁) when reserving. A shuttle service is available.

★ **Hōshi Onsen Chōjūkan** RYOKAN ¥¥¥
(法師温泉長寿館; ☎0278-66-0005; www.houshi-onsen.jp; 650 Nagai; r per person incl 2 meals from ¥18,000; P ❄ 📶) Remote, rustic and supremely photogenic, this lodging is one of Japan's finest *onsen ryokan*, with a stunning 1896 wooden bathhouse. From Gokan Station (two stops before Minakami), take a bus to Sarugakyō (¥1100, 40 minutes), then change to an infrequent bus for Hōshi Onsen (¥600, 15 minutes). Otherwise take a taxi (¥3000).

Bathing for nonguests is also available (¥1000; 10.30am to 1.30pm Thursday to Tuesday).

Eating & Drinking

Minakami is a sprawling town and its dining options are scattered, with many operating seasonally. Check at the nearest Tourist Information Center for recommendations, or dine where you sleep.

The area isn't known for its wild nightlife, but if you're overnighting with one of the outdoor-sports crews, you'll be sure to find fellow travellers to enjoy a drink with.

Kadoya SOBA ¥¥
(そば処角弥; ☎0278-72-2477; www.kadoya-soba.com; 189-1 Yubiso; soba ¥950-1500; ⏲11am-2.30pm) Expect to queue at this popular 'local' specialising in *hegi soba* (soba flavoured with seaweed and served on a special plate, a *hegi*). The noodles are hand-rolled fresh every day and the shop closes once they sell out.

Alpine Cafe BAR
(☎0278-72-2811; www.canyons.jp; 45 Yubiso; ⏲4pm-late Thu-Sun Dec-Oct; 📶) Run by the Canyons crew, this popular cafe-bar offers riverside barbecues in summer, a pool table, plenty of beer, hamburgers and occasional live music. It's also where you'll be put up if you're on one of Canyons' adventure-tour packages.

Information

Minakami Tourist Association (水上温泉旅館協同組合; ☎0278-62-0401; www.minakamionsen.com; ⏲8.30am-4.30pm Jun-Oct, 9am-4.30pm Nov-May) Adjacent to Jōmō Kōgen Station, this office has helpful English-speaking staff, brochures and bus schedules.

See also www.enjoy-minakami.jp.

Getting There & Away

From Ueno, take the Jōetsu *shinkansen* (¥4410, 50 minutes) or JR Takasaki line (¥1940, two hours) to Takasaki and transfer to the Jōetsu line (¥840, one hour).

Most JR Pass holders will elect to catch the Jōetsu *shinkansen* direct to Jōmō Kōgen from Tokyo/Ueno (¥5390/5180, 1¼ hours), from where buses run to Minakami (¥620, 25 minutes).

Getting Around

BUS

To get to Hōshi Onsen, take the bus from Jōmō Kōgen Station to Sarugakyō Onsen (¥880, 30 minutes) and change for the less frequent bus to Hōshi Onsen (¥600, 20 minutes).

If you're arriving by *tokkyū* train on the Jōetsu line, get off at Gokan Station (two stops before Minakami), then get the bus to Sarugakyō (¥1100, 40 minutes), where you should change to the bus for Hōshi Onsen (¥600, 15 minutes).

Buses depart regularly from both Jōmō Kōgen Station (¥3900) and Minakami Station (¥2900) for Takaragawa Onsen.

Timetables can be found at http://global.kan-etsu.net/en/minakami/yunokoya.html.

CAR & MOTORCYCLE

If you don't mind driving on winding mountain roads, renting a car from Jōmō Kōgen Station (or Takasaki) is by far the best way to experience the area, giving you freedom to explore the divine onsen, the town of Minakami and the ropeway.

See the friendly staff at **Toyota Rent-a-Lease** (トヨタレンタリース上毛高原駅前; ☎0278-62-0100; http://rent.toyota.co.jp; 766 Tsukiyono; ⏲8am-8pm), directly opposite Jōmō Kōgen Station.

Kusatsu Onsen

☎0279 / POP 6537

Consistently rated one of Japan's top onsen towns since the Edo period for its pungent, anti-bacterial, emerald-coloured waters, Kusatsu (草津温泉) is also a great base for winter skiing, suitable for all levels; see www.kusatsu-kokusai.com.

In the early 20th century, Emperor Meiji's German doctor Erwin von Bälz proclaimed the waters here 'very conducive to health'. The German connection endures with cheesy faux-Bavarian chalets sprinkled about the place, and a train station labeled 'Bahnhof'.

Sight & Activities

Yubatake HOT SPRINGS

(湯畑) Yubatake is the main attraction in the town centre and the source of hot-spring water in the area. Its milky-blue sulphuric water flows like a waterfall at 4000L per minute and is topped with wooden tanks from which Kusatsu's ryokan fill their baths. The area is atmospherically lit at night.

Sai-no-kawara Rotemburo ONSEN

(西の河露天風呂; ☎0279-88-6167; www.sainokawara.com; 521-2 Ōaza Kusatsu; adult/child ¥600/300; ⏲7am-8pm Apr-Nov, 9am-8pm Dec-Mar) In leafy Sai-no-kawara *kōen* (park) you'll find this atmospheric 500-sq-metre *rotemburo* separated into men's and women's baths by a bamboo wall. Each bath can hold at least 100 people and frequently does: early-morning visits afford greater privacy and tranquillity.

The baths are a 15-minute walk west from Yubatake or stop 15 on the Kusatsu Round Bus.

Ōtakinoyu ONSEN

(大滝乃湯; ☎0279-88-2600; www.ohtakinoyu.com; 596-13 Ōaza Kusatsu; adult/child ¥900/400; ⏲9am-9pm) Ōtakinoyu is known for its tubs at a variety of temperatures, some almost impossibly hot; try different ones for an experience known as *awase-yu* (mix-and-match waters). It's a five-minute walk downhill east of Yubatake.

Sleeping & Eating

Kusatsu gets extremely busy during holiday periods and at weekends, and there's little in the way of the contemporary style that you may find at other resorts. Several of the town's many towering onsen hotels are more suited to the Japanese tour-group market than DIY international visitors, and many have seen better days.

As you'd expect in such a popular tourist destination, there's no shortage of restaurants.

Kusatsu Onsen Boun RYOKAN ¥¥

(草津温泉望雲; ☎0279-88-3251; www.hotelboun.com; 433-1 Kusatsu-machi; r per person incl 2 meals from ¥14,040; ❄📶) Beautiful Boun offers traditional decor with elegant touches, featuring tatami rooms and common areas brightened with ikebana artwork, mossy gardens, waterfalls and a bamboo-decking atrium. There's a large onsen in a big wooden bathhouse and a *rotemburo* (outdoor bath) with a garden outlook. It's a three-minute walk from Yubatake.

Hotel Sakurai HOTEL ¥¥¥
(ホテル櫻井; ☎0279-88-3211; www.hotel-sakurai.co.jp; 465-4 Kusatsu-machi; r per person incl 2 meals from ¥28,000; P ❄ ☎) Unmissable in town, in a central location, this towering onsen hotel has a wide range of luxurious room types, dining options and baths. Rooms on higher floors in the newer wing feature lovely views over the town and countryside.

Mikuniya NOODLES ¥
(三国家; ☎0279-88-2134; 386 Ōaza Kusatsu; dishes from ¥680; ⊙11am-2pm) Fill up on tasty bowls of *sansai soba* (buckwheat noodles with mountain vegetables; ¥800) at this popular place on the shopping street that runs behind Yubatake towards Sai-no-kawara. Look for the renovated wooden building with the black door curtains, or the line out the front.

☆ Entertainment

Netsu-no-yu Yumomi LIVE PERFORMANCE
(☎0279-88-3613; www.kusatsu-onsen.ne.jp.e.uh.hp.transer.com/netsunoyu; 414 Kusatsu-machi; adult/child ¥600/300; ⊙performances 9.30am, 10am, 10.30am, 3.30pm, 4pm & 4.30pm) Although it's a touristy 30-minute show, this is a unique opportunity to see *yumomi,* in which local women stir the waters to cool them while singing folk songs. There's a chance to do it yourself at most shows (four or five daily) and the afternoon ones also include local dances. Visit the website for a ¥50 coupon off admission.

ℹ Information

For more town info, see www.kusatsu-onsen.ne.jp.

City Hall Tourist Section (☎0279-88-0001; ⊙8.30am-5.30pm) Next to the bus terminal, this tourist-information bureau has a touch-screen information terminal in English and the occasional English speaker on hand.

Kusatsu Onsen Ryokan Information Centre (草津温泉旅館案内センター; ☎0279-88-3722; ⊙9am-6pm Mon-Sat) Located in the white building opposite the bus station, this place can help with accommodation bookings and has a recommended walking map.

ℹ Getting There & Away

JR buses connect Kusatsu Onsen to Naganohara-Kusatsuguchi Station (¥700, free for JR Pass holders, 25 minutes). *Tokkyū* Kusatsu trains run from Ueno to Naganohara-Kusatsuguchi Station (¥4750, 2½ hours) two times a day. Alternatively, take the Jōetsu *shinkansen* to Takasaki (¥4410, one hour) and transfer to the JR Agatsuma line (¥1140, 1½ hours).

JR Bus Kantō (☎03-3844-1950; www.jrbuskanto.co.jp) offers direct service to Kusatsu Onsen (¥3450, four hours) from Shinjuku Station in Tokyo (departing from the New South exit); reservations required.

If you've rented a vehicle, you'll be stressed out trying to navigate the crowded, narrow streets of the village. However, the drive between Kusatsu Onsen and Karuizawa, 41km to the south, in the Nagano region, affords excellent views of the active volcano Mt Asama.

Heading northwest on Rte 292 towards Shiga Kōgen, and onward to Yudanaka in Nagano, offers some of Japan's most spectacular spring and autumn scenery, with no shortage of incredible vistas. The winding, high-altitude route is extremely popular (and slow) at weekends and is not recommended for those who get carsick easily.

AT A GLANCE

POPULATION
1.45 million

BIGGEST FESTIVAL
Gion Matsuri (p340)

BEST GARDEN
Saihō-ji (p336)

BEST RYOKAN
Tawaraya (p342)

BEST TEAHOUSE
Hiranoya (p357)

WHEN TO GO

Mar–May Cherry blossoms (late March to early April) are enchanting, as are spring geisha dances.

Jul–Sep Summer evenings are magical (though summer days are hot and humid).

Oct–early Dec Fall foliage makes the perfect backdrop for Kyoto's temples, shrines and gardens.

Arashiyama Bamboo Grove (p335)
PATRICK FOTO/SHUTTERSTOCK ©

Kyoto

Kyoto is old Japan writ large: quiet temples, sublime gardens, colourful shrines and geisha scurrying to exclusive engagements. With more than 1000 Buddhist temples and over 400 Shintō shrines it is one of the world's most culturally rich cities. But Kyoto is not just about sightseeing: while the rest of Japan has adopted modernity with abandon, the old ways are still clinging on here. Visit an old *shōtengai* (market street) and admire the ancient speciality shops: tofu sellers, *washi* (Japanese handmade paper) stores and tea merchants.

INCLUDES

Kyoto Highlights

❶ **Kinkaku-ji** (p333) Marvelling at the gold-plated hall of this temple.

❷ **Fushimi Inari-Taisha** (p313) Passing through the magical tunnel of vermilion gates at this shrine.

❸ **Gion** (p319) Exploring the atmospheric district at night for a glimpse of old Japan.

❹ **Ginkaku-ji** (p323) Taking the bamboo-lined path to see Kyoto's famed 'Silver Pavilion'.

❺ **Chion-in** (p320) Letting your soul be soothed by the chanting monks.

❻ **Kaiseki** (p350) Splurging on once-in-a-lifetime *kaiseki* (haute cuisine) at a restaurant like Kikunoi.

❼ **Nishiki Market** (p315) Grabbing local gourmet goods at Kyoto's central market.

❽ **Shopping** (p358) Finding that perfect souvenir, be it exquisite antique lacquerware or a bright umbrella.

❾ **Geisha dances** (p357) Seeing Kyoto's *geiko* (geishas) performing in all their finery.

History

Kyoto served as the capital of Japan for an almost unbroken stretch from the 8th century to the mid-19th century. (The city's nearly 1000-year reign was interrupted in the 12th and 13th centuries, when the first feudal government was established in Kamakura.) It was in Kyoto that the Heian-era (794–1185) court laid down the foundation for the Japanese aesthetic and here that the ascendant warrior class of the 15th and 16th centuries refined it, developing the tea ceremony, ikebana (art of flower arranging) and the elegant architectural style that can still be seen in the city's temples today.

When the emperor was reinstated as head of the country following the Meiji Restoration in 1868 and the imperial residence moved to Tokyo, the eastern city took on the mantle of nation's capital – though Kyoto remains in hearts and minds the cultural capital of the country.

Sights

Kyoto Station & South Kyoto

★Fushimi Inari-Taisha SHINTŌ SHRINE

(伏見稲荷大社; Map p316; 68 Yabunouchi-chō, Fukakusa, Fushimi-ku; dawn-dusk; JR Nara line to Inari or Keihan line to Fushimi-Inari) FREE With seemingly endless arcades of vermilion *torii* (shrine gates) spread across a thickly wooded mountain, this vast shrine complex is a world unto its own. It is, quite simply, one of the most impressive and memorable sights in Kyoto.

The entire complex, consisting of five shrines, sprawls across the wooded slopes of Inari-san. A pathway wanders 4km up the mountain and is lined with dozens of atmospheric sub-shrines.

Fushimi Inari was dedicated to the gods of rice and sake by the Hata family in the 8th century. As the role of agriculture diminished, deities were enrolled to ensure prosperity in business. Nowadays, the shrine is one of Japan's most popular, and is the head shrine for some 40,000 Inari shrines scattered the length and breadth of the country.

As you explore the shrine, you will come across hundreds of stone foxes. The fox is considered the messenger of Inari, the god of cereals, and the stone foxes, too, are often referred to as Inari. The key often seen in the fox's mouth is for the rice granary. On an incidental note, the Japanese traditionally see the fox as a sacred, somewhat mysterious figure capable of 'possessing' humans – the favoured point of entry is under the fingernails.

The walk around the upper precincts of the shrine is a pleasant day hike. It also makes for a very eerie stroll in the late afternoon and early evening, when the various graveyards and miniature shrines along the path take on a mysterious air. It's best to go with a friend at this time.

On 8 April there's a Sangyō-sai festival with offerings and dances to ensure prosperity for national industry. During the first few days in January, thousands of believers visit this shrine as their *hatsu-mōde* (first shrine visit of the new year) to pray for good fortune. For info on the shrine's many schedules, see www.inari.jp/en/rite.

★Tōfuku-ji BUDDHIST TEMPLE

(東福寺; Map p316; 075-561-0087; www.tofukuji.jp; 15-778 Honmahi, Higashiyama-ku; Hōjō garden ¥400, Tsūten-kyō bridge ¥400; 9am-4pm; Keihan line to Tōfukuji or JR Nara line to Tōfuku-ji) Home to a spectacular garden, several superb structures and beautiful precincts, Tōfuku-ji is one of the best temples in Kyoto. It is linked to Fushimi Inari-Taisha by the Keihan and JR train lines. The present temple complex includes 24 subtemples. The huge **San-mon** is the oldest Zen main gate in Japan, the **Hōjō** (Abbot's Hall) was reconstructed in 1890, and the gardens were laid out in 1938.

The northern garden has stones and moss neatly arranged in a chequerboard pattern. From a viewing platform at the back of the gardens you can observe the **Tsūten-kyō** (Bridge to Heaven), which spans a valley filled with maples.

Founded in 1236 by the priest Enni, Tōfuku-ji belongs to the Rinzai sect of Zen Buddhism. As this temple was intended to compare with Tōdai-ji (p400) and Kōfuku-ji (p401) in Nara, it was given a name combining characters from the names of each of these temples.

Tōfuku-ji offers regular Zen meditation sessions for beginners, but don't expect coddling or English-language explanations: this is the real deal. Get a Japanese speaker to enquire at the temple about the next session (it holds about four a month for beginners).

Note that Tōfuku-ji is one of Kyoto's most famous autumn-foliage spots, and it is invariably packed during the peak of colours in November. Otherwise, it's often very quiet.

KYOTO IN...

Two Days

Start your Kyoto experience by heading to the city's most important sightseeing district, Southern Higashiyama, to visit **Kiyomizu-dera** (p318), **Chion-in** (p320) and **Maruyama-kōen** (p321). If you've still got energy, walk off lunch with a stroll from **Nanzen-ji** (p325) up the **Path of Philosophy** (p327) to **Ginkaku-ji** (p323) in Northern Higashiyama. On the second day, head to the northwest corner of the city to see stunning **Kinkaku-ji** (p333) and the Zen garden at **Ryōan-ji** (p333). From here, hop in a taxi for Arashiyama, for the temple **Tenryū-ji** (p337) and its famous **bamboo grove** (p335). Finish up the evening with a stroll through the historic geisha districts, **Gion** (p319) and **Ponto-chō** (p318).

Four Days

With four days, we recommend doing the above in three days, rather than two, to give yourself more time to explore smaller sights en route and soak up the atmosphere. On the fourth day, take a break from temples to stroll around downtown, hitting the excellent **Nishiki Market** and nearby craft shops and department stores for souvenirs, maybe taking a walk along the Kamo-gawa or holding a picnic in **Kyoto Imperial Palace Park** (p331). Then head for a night out in the bars lining pretty **Kiyamachi-dōri** (p355).

Kyoto Station NOTABLE BUILDING
(京都駅; Map p321; www.kyoto-station-building.co.jp; Karasuma-dōri, Higashishiokōji-chō, Shiokōji-sagaru, Shimogyō-ku; Kyoto Station) The Kyoto Station building is a striking steel-and-glass structure – a kind of futuristic cathedral for the transport age – with a tremendous space that arches above you as you enter the main concourse. Be sure to take the escalator from the 7th floor on the east side of the building up to the 11th-floor glass corridor, Skyway (open 10am to 10pm), that runs high above the main concourse of the station, and catch some views from the 15th-floor Sky Garden terrace.

Tō-ji BUDDHIST TEMPLE
(東寺; Map p316; www.toji.or.jp; 1 Kujō-chō, Minami-ku; ¥800, grounds free; 8.30am-5pm mid-Apr–mid-Sep, to 4.30pm rest of year; Kyoto City bus 205 from Kyoto Station, Kintetsu Kyoto line to Tōji) One of the sights south of Kyoto Station, Tō-ji is an appealing complex of halls and a fantastic pagoda that makes a fine backdrop for the monthly flea market held on the grounds. The temple was established in 794 by imperial decree to protect the city. In 823 the emperor handed it over to Kūkai (known posthumously as Kōbō Daishi), the founder of the Shingon school of Buddhism.

Nishi Hongan-ji BUDDHIST TEMPLE
(西本願寺; Map p321; Horikawa-dōri, Hanayachō-sagaru, Shimogyō-ku; 5.30am-5pm; Kyoto Station) FREE A vast temple complex, Nishi Hongan-ji comprises several buildings that feature some of the finest examples of architecture and artistic achievement from the Azuchi-Momoyama period (1568–1603). The **Goei-dō** is a marvellous sight. Another must-see building is the **Daisho-in** hall, which has sumptuous paintings, carvings and metal ornamentation. A small garden and two *nō* (stylised Japanese dance-drama) stages are connected with the hall. The dazzling **Kara-mon** has intricate ornamental carvings.

Higashi Hongan-ji BUDDHIST TEMPLE
(東本願寺, Eastern Temple of the True Vow; Map p321; www.higashihonganji.or.jp; Karasuma-dōri, Shichijō-agaru, Shimogyō-ku; 5.50am-5.30pm Mar-Oct, 6.20am-4.30pm Nov-Feb; Kyoto Station) FREE Higashi Hongan-ji is the last word in all things grand and gaudy. Considering its proximity to the station, the free admission, the awesome structures and the dazzling interiors, this temple is the obvious spot to visit when near the station. The temple is dominated by the vast **Goei-dō** (Main Hall), said to be the second-largest wooden structure in Japan, standing 38m high, 76m long and 58m wide. An audio guide (¥500) is available at the information centre.

Kyoto Railway Museum MUSEUM
(梅小路蒸気機関車館; Map p316; www.kyotorailwaymuseum.jp; Kankiji-chō, Shimogyō-ku; adult ¥1200, child ¥200-500; 10am-5.30pm, closed Wed; Kyoto City bus 103, 104 or 110 from Kyoto Station to Umekōji-kōen/Kyoto Railway Museum-mae) This superb museum is spread

over three floors showcasing 53 trains, from vintage steam locomotives in the outside Roundhouse Shed to commuter trains and the first *shinkansen* from 1964. Kids will love the interactive displays and impressive railroad diorama with miniature trains zipping through the intricate landscape. You can also take a 10-minute ride on one of the smoke-spewing choo-choos (adult/child ¥300/100).

Kyoto Tower Observation Deck VIEWPOINT
(京都タワー; Map p321; Karasuma-dōri, Shichijō-sagaru, Shimogyō-ku; adult ¥770, child ¥150-520; 9am-9pm; Kyoto Station) Located opposite Kyoto Station, this retro tower (1964) looks like a rocket perched atop the Kyoto Tower Hotel. The observation deck provides excellent views in all directions and you can really get a sense for the Kyoto *bonchi* (flat basin). It's a great place to get oriented to the city upon arrival. There are free mounted binoculars to use and a cool touch screen information panel showing what the view looks like both day and night.

Downtown Kyoto

★Nijō-jō CASTLE
(二条城; Map p332; 541 Nijōjō-chō, Nijō-dōri, Horikawa nishi-iru, Nakagyō-ku; adult/child ¥600/200; 8.45am-5pm, last entry 4pm, closed Tue Dec, Jan, Jul & Aug; S Tōzai line to Nijō-jō-mae, JR line to Nijō) The military might of Japan's great warlord generals, the Tokugawa shoguns, is amply demonstrated by the imposing stone walls and ramparts of their great castle, Nijō-jō, which dominates a large part of northwest Kyoto. Hidden behind these you will find a superb palace surrounded by beautiful gardens. Avoid crowds by visiting just after opening or shortly before closing.

This castle was built in 1603 as the official Kyoto residence of the first Tokugawa shogun, Ieyasu. The ostentatious style of its construction was intended as a demonstration of Ieyasu's prestige and also to signal the demise of the emperor's power. As a safeguard against treachery, Ieyasu had the interior fitted with 'nightingale' floors (that sing and squeak at every move, making it difficult for intruders to move about quietly), as well as concealed chambers where bodyguards could keep watch.

After passing through the grand **Karamon gate**, you enter **Ninomaru Palace**, which is divided into five buildings with numerous chambers. The **Ōhiroma Yon-no-Ma** (Fourth Chamber) has spectacular screen paintings. Don't miss the excellent **Ninomaru Palace Garden**, which was designed by the tea master and landscape architect Kobori Enshū.

Audio guides are available (¥500) and English guided tours run daily at 10.30am and 12.30pm (¥2000, not including entry price).

★Nishiki Market MARKET
(錦市場; Map p322; Nishikikōji-dōri, btwn Teramachi & Takakura, Nakagyō-ku; 9am-5pm; S Karasuma line to Shijō, Hankyū line to Karasuma or Kawaramachi) Head to the covered Nishiki Market to check out the weird and wonderful foods that go into Kyoto cuisine. It's in the centre of town, one block north of (and parallel to) Shijō-dōri, running west off Teramachi covered arcade. Wander past stalls selling everything from barrels of *tsukemono* (pickled vegetables) and cute Japanese sweets to wasabi salt and fresh sashimi skewers. Drop into Aritsugu (p358) here for some of the best Japanese chef's knives money can buy.

MAIKO MANNERS

In Kyoto, *maiko* (apprentice geisha) are easily distinguished by their long trailing obi (sash) and okobo (towering wooden clogs that keep their kimono from trailing on the ground); they also wear their own hair sculpted in impressive poofs and swoops, accentuated with opulent (and extremely expensive) ornaments, called *kanzashi*.

No doubt spotting a *maiko* dressed to the hilt on the street in Kyoto is a wondrous experience, and a photo is a much-coveted souvenir of a visit to Japan. However, please keep in mind that these are young women – many of whom are minors – trying to get to work. Kyoto's *maiko* report feeling harassed by tourists blocking their path and cornering them, without permission, for photos. Let them through; *maiko* and geisha are professionals – if you want to get close to them, support their art and go to see them perform. You can also find plenty of tourists dressed as geisha on the streets of Higashiyama during the daytime; many are happy to be photographed if asked.

Greater Kyoto

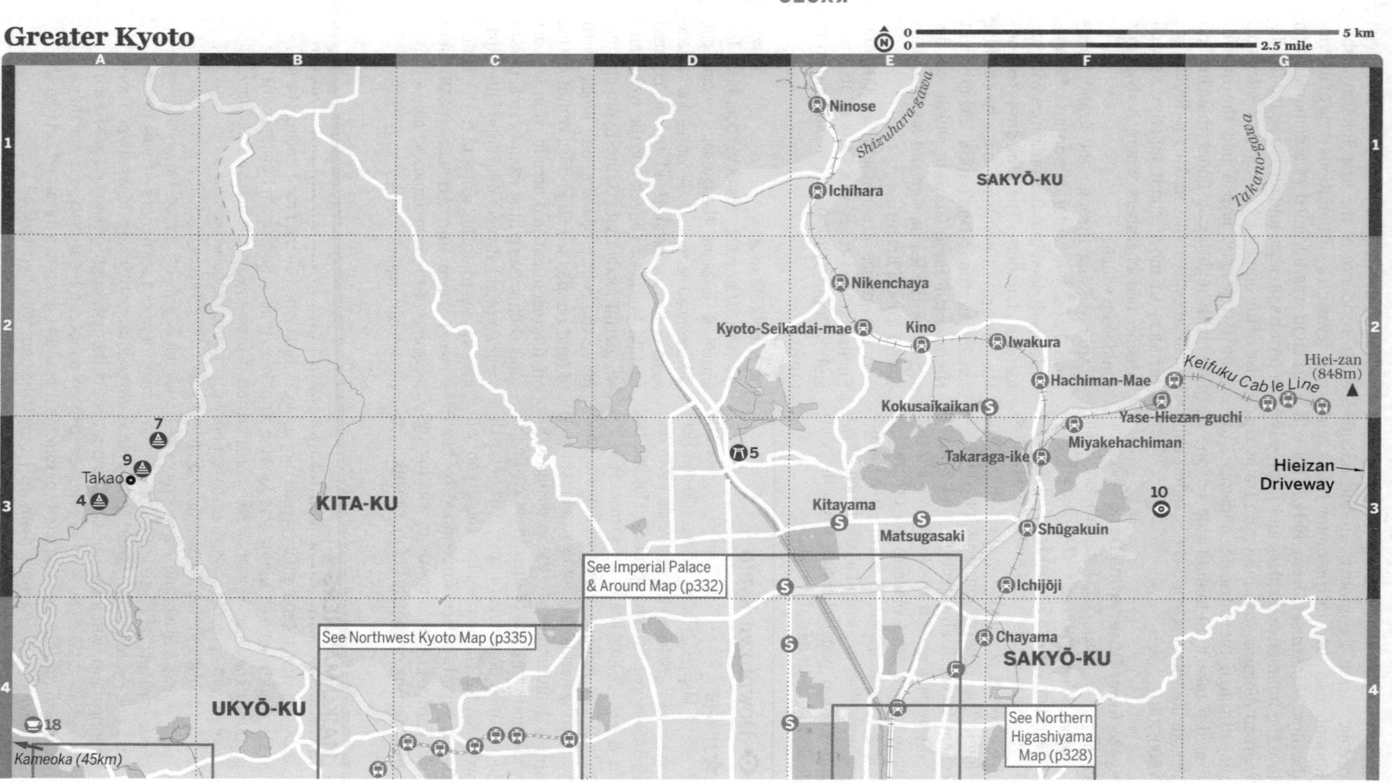

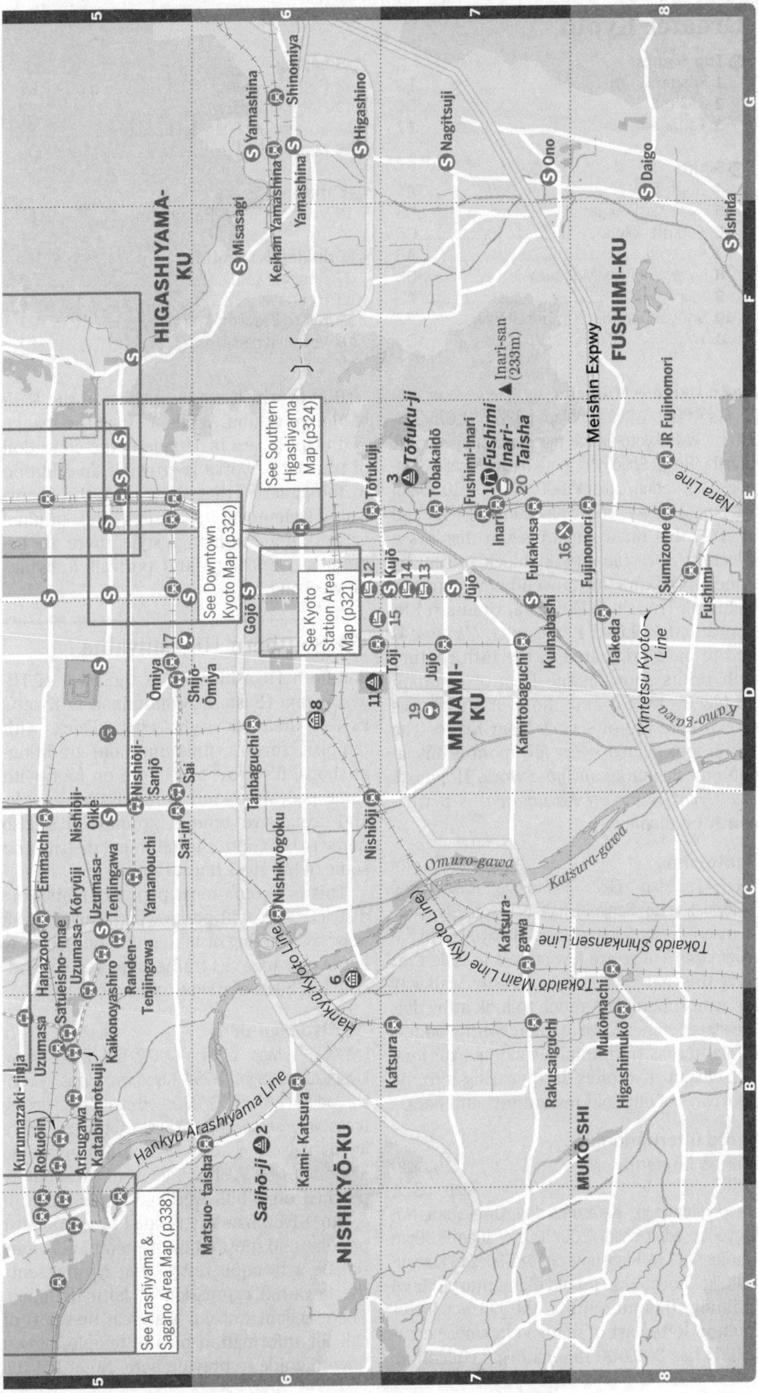

See Arashiyama & Sagano Area Map (p338)
See Downtown Kyoto Map (p322)
See Southern Higashiyama Map (p324)
See Kyoto Station Area Map (p321)

Kurumazaki-jinja
Rokuōin
Uzumasa
Hanazono
Emmachi
Satueisho-mae
Arisugawa
Katabiranotsuji
Uzumasa-Kōryūji
Nishiōji-Oike
Kaikonoyashiro
Uzumasa-Tenjingawa
Randen-Tenjingawa
Yamanouchi
Nishiōji-Sanjō
Ōmiya
17
Sai-in
Sai
Shijō-Ōmiya
HIGASHIYAMA-KU
Matsuo-taisha
Hankyū Arashiyama Line
Saihō-ji 2
Tanbaguchi
Gojō
Misasagi
Yamashina
Keihan Yamashina
Yamashina
Shinomiya
Nishikyōgoku
Kami-Katsura
Hankyū Kyoto Line
8
6
NISHIKYŌ-KU
Higashino
Nishiōji
11
12
Tōfukuji
Tōji
15
Kujō
3
Katsura
14
Tōfuku-ji
19
13
Jūjō
Tobakaidō
Nagitsuji
MINAMI-KU
Jūjō
Fushimi-Inari
Tōkaidō Main Line (Kyoto Line)
Omuro-gawa
1 Fushimi Inari-Taisha
Inari
Inari-san (233m)
Katsura-gawa
20
Kamitobaguchi
Fukakusa
Rakusaiguchi
Kuinabashi
Ono
Tōkaidō Shinkansen Line
Katsura-gawa
16
MUKŌ-SHI
Fujinomori
Meishin Expwy
Mukōmachi
Takeda
FUSHIMI-KU
Higashimukō
Kintetsu Kyoto Line
Daigo
Sumizome
JR Fujinomori
Kamo-gawa
Nara Line
Fushimi
Ishida

A B C D E F G
5 6 7 8

Greater Kyoto

Kyoto Ukiyo-e Museum MUSEUM
(京都浮世絵美術館; Map p322; ☎075-223-3003; www.kyoto-ukiyoe-museum.com; 2nd fl, Kirihata Bldg, Shijō-dōri, Teramachi Nishiiri, Shimogyō-ku; adult/child ¥1000/300; ⊙10.30am-6.30pm; Hankyū line to Kawaramachi) Opened in 2017, this one-room museum displays a selection of *ukiyo-e* (woodblock prints) by some of Japan's most well-known artists, including Hiroshige Utagawa, Utamaro Kitagawa and Hokusai Katsushika. *Ukiyo-e* is said to have originated in the 16th century with prints showing the lives of common people in Kyoto, and most of the works shown here are of scenes from Kyoto. The exhibitions change every few months but Japan's most famous *ukiyo-e* work, Hokusai's *The Great Wave off Kanagawa*, is permanently on display.

Ponto-chō AREA
(先斗町; Map p322; Ponto-chō, Nakagyō-ku; S Tōzai line to Sanjo-Keihan or Kyoto-Shiyakusho-mae, Keihan line to Sanjo, Hankyū line to Kawaramachi) There are few streets in Asia that rival this narrow pedestrian-only walkway for atmosphere. Not much to look at by day, the street comes alive at night, with wonderful lanterns, traditional wooden exteriors, and elegant Kyotoites disappearing into the doorways of elite old restaurants and bars.

Kyoto International Manga Museum MUSEUM
(京都国際マンガミュージアム; Map p322; www.kyotomm.jp; Karasuma-dōri, Oike-agaru, Nakagyō-ku; adult/child ¥800/100; ⊙10am-5.30pm Thu-Tue; ; S Karasuma or Tōzai lines to Karasuma-Oike) Located in an old elementary school building, this museum is the perfect introduction to the art of manga (Japanese comics). It has 300,000 manga in its collection, 50,000 of which are on display in the *Wall of Manga* exhibit. While most of the manga and displays are in Japanese, the collection of translated works is growing. In addition to the galleries that show both the historical development of manga and original artwork done in manga style, there are beginners' workshops and portrait drawings on weekends.

Southern Higashiyama

Southern Higashiyama, at the base of Higashiyama (Eastern Mountains), is Kyoto's richest area for sightseeing. Thick with temples, shrines, museums and traditional shops, it's great to explore on foot, with some pedestrian-only walkways plus parks and expansive temple grounds. It's also home to the Gion entertainment district and some of the city's finest ryokan.

This is Kyoto's most popular sightseeing district, so it will be crowded during peak seasons. Walking or taking the train/subway is the way to go as traffic comes to a standstill and buses are slow and overcrowded.

★**Kiyomizu-dera** BUDDHIST TEMPLE
(清水寺; Map p324; ☎075-551-1234; www.kiyomizudera.or.jp; 1-294 Kiyomizu, Higashiyama-ku; adult/child ¥400/200; ⊙6am-6pm, closing times vary seasonally; Kyoto City bus 206 to Kiyōmizu-michi or Gojō-zaka, Keihan line to Kiyomizu-Gojō) A buzzing hive of activity perched on a hill overlooking the basin of Kyoto, Kiyomizu-dera is one of Kyoto's most popular and most enjoyable temples. It may not be a tranquil refuge, but it represents the favoured expression of faith in Japan. The excellent website is a great first port of call for information on the temple, plus a how-to guide to praying here. Note that the

Main Hall is undergoing renovations and may be covered, but is still accessible.

This ancient temple was first built in 798, but the present buildings are reconstructions dating from 1633. As an affiliate of the Hossō school of Buddhism, which originated in Nara, it has successfully survived the many intrigues of local Kyoto schools of Buddhism through the centuries and is now one of the most famous landmarks of the city (for which reason it can get very crowded during spring and autumn).

The **Hondō** (Main Hall) has a huge verandah that is supported by pillars and juts out over the hillside. Just below this hall is the waterfall **Otowa-no-taki**, where visitors drink sacred waters believed to bestow health and longevity. Dotted around the precincts are other halls and shrines. At **Jishu-jinja**, the shrine up the steps above the main hall, visitors try to ensure success in love by closing their eyes and walking about 18m between a pair of stones – if you miss the stone, your desire for love won't be fulfilled! Note that you can ask someone to guide you, but if you do, you'll need someone's assistance to find your true love.

Before you enter the actual temple precincts, check out the **Tainai-meguri**, the entrance to which is just to the left (north) of the pagoda that is located in front of the main entrance to the temple (¥100 donation; open 9am to 4pm). We won't tell you too much about it as it will ruin the experience. Suffice to say that by entering the Tainai-meguri, you are symbolically entering the womb of a female bodhisattva. When you get to the rock in the darkness, spin it in either direction to make a wish.

The steep approach to the temple is known as **Chawan-zaka** (Teapot Lane) and is lined with shops selling Kyoto handicrafts, local snacks and souvenirs.

Check the website for the scheduling of special night-time illuminations of the temple held in spring and autumn.

★Gion AREA

(祇園周辺; Map p324; Higashiyama-ku; S Tōzai line to Sanjō, R Keihan line to Gion-Shijō) Gion is the famous entertainment and geisha quarter on the eastern bank of the Kamo-gawa. While Gion's true origins were in teahouses catering to weary visitors to the nearby shrine Yasaka-jinja, by the mid-18th century the area was Kyoto's largest pleasure district. The best way to experience Gion today is with an evening stroll around the atmospheric streets lined with 17th-century traditional restaurants and teahouses lit up

WORTH A TRIP

BYŌDŌ-IN: HEIAN ERA ART & ARCHITECTURE

Byōdō-in (平等院; 0774-21-2861; www.byodoin.or.jp; 116 Uji-renge, Uji-shi; adult/child ¥600/300; gardens 8.30am-5.30pm, Hōō-dō 9.30am-4.10pm; R JR Nara line or Keihan line to Uji) is home to one of the loveliest Buddhist structures in Japan: the Hōō-dō hall (Phoenix Hall), which is depicted on the back of the Japanese ¥10 coin. Perched overlooking a serene reflecting pond, this refurbished hall is a stunning sight. Paired with a stroll along the banks of the nearby Uji-gawa, this temple makes a good half-day trip out of Kyoto City.

This temple was converted from a Fujiwara villa into a Buddhist temple in 1052. The Hōō-dō, the main hall of the temple, was built in 1053 and is the only original building remaining. The phoenix used to be a popular mythical bird in China and was revered by the Japanese as a protector of Buddha. The architecture of the building resembles the shape of the bird and there are two bronze phoenixes perched opposite each other on the roof. Guided 15-minute tours (an extra ¥300) inside the hall are in Japanese but there is an English leaflet.

The Hōō-dō was originally intended to represent Amida's heavenly palace in the Pure Land. This building is one of the few extant examples of Heian-period architecture, and its graceful lines make you wish that far more had survived the wars and fires that have plagued Kyoto's past. Inside the hall is the famous statue of Amida Buddha and 52 *bosatsu* (Bodhisattvas) dating from the 11th century and attributed to the priest-sculptor Jōchō.

The modern Hoshokan Museum (9am to 5pm) contains the original temple bell and door paintings and the original phoenix roof adornments, along with a collection of Unchū Kuyō Bosatsu Buddhist statues. Allow about an hour all up for your visit.

with lanterns. Start off on the main street **Hanami-kōji**, which runs north–south and bisects Shijō-dōri.

★ **Chion-in** BUDDHIST TEMPLE

(知恩院; Map p324; www.chion-in.or.jp; 400 Rinka-chō, Higashiyama-ku; adult/child ¥500/250, grounds free; ⌚9am-4.30pm, last entry 3.50pm; Ⓢ Tōzai line to Higashiyama) A collection of soaring buildings, spacious courtyards and gardens, Chion-in serves as the headquarters of the Jōdo sect, the largest school of Buddhism in Japan. It's the most popular pilgrimage temple in Kyoto and it's always a hive of activity. For visitors with a taste for the grand, this temple is sure to satisfy.

Chion-in was established in 1234 on the site where Hōnen, one of the most famous figures in Japanese Buddhism, taught his brand of Buddhism (Jōdo – or Pure Land – Buddhism) and eventually fasted to death.

The oldest of the present buildings date to the 17th century. The two-storey **San-mon** temple gate is the largest in Japan. The immense **Miei-dō Hall** (Main Hall) contains an image of Hōnen. It's connected to another hall, the **Dai Hōjō**, by a 'nightingale' floor (that sings and squeaks at every move, making it difficult for intruders to move about quietly).

Up a flight of steps southeast of the main hall is the temple's **giant bell**, which was cast in 1633 and weighs 70 tonnes. It is the largest bell in Japan. The bell is rung by the temple's monks 108 times on New Year's Eve each year.

The temple has two gardens – the Hōjō garden designed around a pond in the *chisen kaiyūshiki* style, and the Yuzen-en featuring a *karesansui* (dry landscape garden).

★ **Shōren-in** BUDDHIST TEMPLE

(青蓮院; Map p324; 69-1 Sanjōbō-chō, Awataguchi, Higashiyama-ku; adult/child ¥500/free; ⌚9am-5pm; Ⓢ Tōzai line to Higashiyama) This temple is hard to miss, with its giant camphor trees growing just outside the walls. Fortunately, most tourists march right on past, heading to the area's more famous temples. That's their loss, because this intimate little sanctuary contains a superb landscape garden, which you can enjoy while drinking a cup of green tea (¥500; ask at the reception office, not available in summer).

Kōdai-ji BUDDHIST TEMPLE

(高台寺; Map p324; ☎075-561-9966; www.kodaiji.com; 526 Shimokawara-chō, Kōdai-ji, Higashiyama-ku; adult/child ¥600/250; ⌚9am-5.30pm; 🚌Kyoto City bus 206 to Yasui, Ⓢ Tōzai line to Higashiyama) This exquisite temple was founded in 1605 by Kita-no-Mandokoro in memory of her late husband, Toyotomi Hideyoshi. The extensive grounds include gardens designed by the famed landscape architect Enshū Kobori, and teahouses designed by the renowned master of the tea ceremony, Sen no Rikyū. The ticket also allows entry to the small Sho museum across the road from the entrance to Kōdai-ji.

Yasui Konpira-gū SHINTŌ SHRINE

(安井金比羅宮; Map p324; www.yasui-konpiragu.or.jp; 70 Simobenten-chō, Higashiyama-ku; ⌚24hr; 🚌Kyoto City bus 204 to Higashiyama-Yasui) This interesting little Shintō shrine on the edge of Gion contains one of the most peculiar objects we've encountered anywhere in Japan: the **enkiri/enmusubi ishi**. Resembling some kind of shaggy igloo, this is a stone that is thought to bind good relationships tighter and sever bad relationships.

If you'd like to take advantage of the stone's powers, here's the drill: purchase a special piece of paper from the counter next to the stone and write your name and wish on it. If you want to bind your love tighter (figuratively, of course), grasp the paper and crawl through the tunnel in the stone from front to back. If you want out of your present relationship, crawl through from back to front. Then, use the glue provided and stick your wishing paper to the ever-huge collection of wishes decorating the stone.

Sanjūsangen-dō Temple BUDDHIST TEMPLE

(三十三間堂; Map p324; ☎075-561-0467; 657 Sanjūsangendōma wari-chō, Higashiyama-ku; adult/child ¥600/300; ⌚8am-5pm Apr–mid-Nov, 9am-4pm mid-Nov–Mar; 🚌Kyoto City bus 206 or 208 to Sanjūsangen-dō-mae, 🚉Keihan line to Shichijō) This superb temple's name refers to the 33 *sanjūsan* (bays) between the pillars of this long, narrow edifice. The building houses 1001 wooden statues of Kannon (the Buddhist goddess of mercy); the chief image, the 1000-armed Senjū-Kannon, was carved by the celebrated sculptor Tankei in 1254. It is flanked by 500 smaller Kannon images, neatly lined in rows. The visual effect is stunning, making this a must-see in Southern Higashiyama and a good starting point for exploration of the area.

Kyoto Station Area

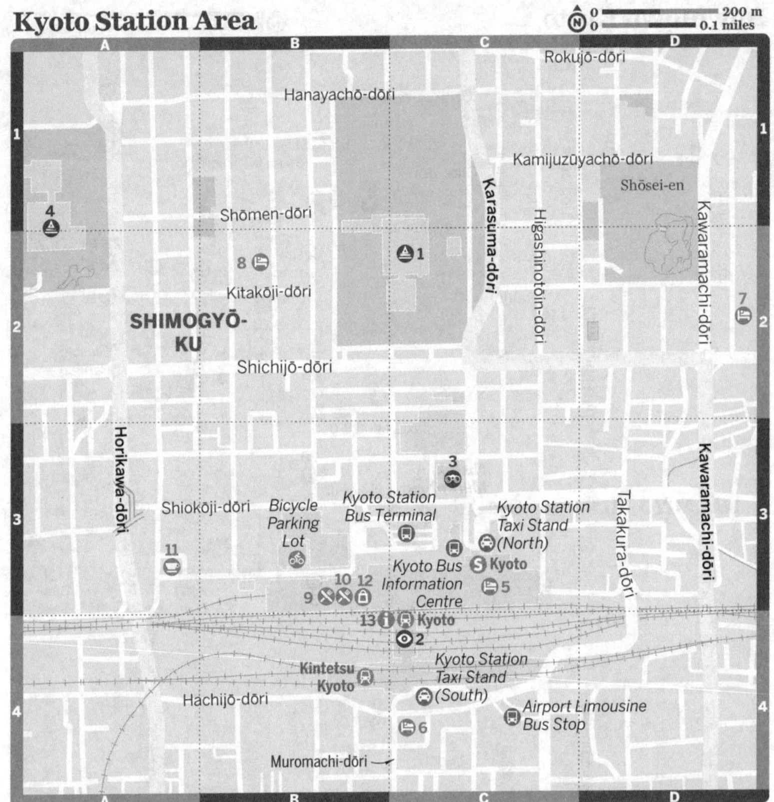

Kyoto Station Area

Sights
1 Higashi Hongan-ji.................C2
2 Kyoto Station.................C4
3 Kyoto Tower Observation Deck.................C3
4 Nishi Hongan-ji.................A1

Sleeping
5 Hotel Granvia Kyoto.................C3
6 Ibis Styles Kyoto Station.................C4
7 K's House Kyoto.................D2
8 Ryokan Shimizu.................B2

Eating
9 Eat Paradise.................B3
10 Kyoto Rāmen Kōji.................B3

Drinking & Nightlife
11 Kurasu.................A3
Roots of all Evil.................(see 3)

Shopping
12 JR Isetan Department Store.................B3

Information
13 Kyoto Tourist Information Center.................B4

Maruyama-kōen PARK

(円山公園; Map p324; Maruyama-chō, Higashiyama-ku; S Tōzai line to Higashiyama)

Maruyama-kōen is a favourite of locals and visitors alike. This park is the place to come to escape the bustle of the city centre and amble around gardens, ponds, souvenir shops and restaurants. Peaceful paths meander through the trees, and carp glide through the waters of a small pond in the park's centre.

For two weeks in early April, when the park's cherry trees come into bloom, the calm atmosphere is shattered by hordes of drunken revellers having *hanami* (cherry-blossom viewing) parties under the trees.

Downtown Kyoto

The centrepiece is a massive *shidare-zakura* cherry tree; this is one of the most beautiful sights in Kyoto, particularly the *yozakura* (night cherry blossoms) when lit up from below at night. For those who don't mind crowds, this is a good place to observe the Japanese at their most uninhibited. Arrive early and claim a good spot high on the east side of the park, from where you can peer down on the mayhem below.

Yasaka-jinja SHINTŌ SHRINE

(八坂神社; Map p324; 075-561-6155; www.yasaka-jinja.or.jp; 625 Gion-machi, Kita-gawa, Higashiyama-ku; 24hr; S Tōzai line to Higashiyama) FREE This colourful and spacious shrine is considered the guardian shrine of the Gion entertainment district. It's a bustling place that is well worth a visit while exploring Southern Higashiyama; it can easily be paired with Maruyama-kōen, the park just up the hill.

Kyoto National Museum MUSEUM

(京都国立博物館; Map p324; www.kyohaku.go.jp; 527 Chaya-machi, Higashiyama-ku; admission varies; 9.30am-5pm, to 8pm Fri & Sat, closed Mon; Kyoto City bus 206 or 208 to Sanjūsangen-dō-mae, Keihan line to Shichijō) The Kyoto National Museum is the city's premier art

Downtown Kyoto

Top Sights
1 Nishiki Market........B3

Sights
2 Kyoto International Manga Museum.....A1
3 Kyoto Ukiyo-e Museum........C3
4 Ponto-chō........D3

Sleeping
5 Citadines Karasuma-Gojō Kyoto........B5
6 Hiiragiya Ryokan........C1
7 Hotel Resol Kyoto Kawaramachi Sanjo........D2
8 Hotel Vista Premio Kyoto........C2
9 Len Hostel Kyoto Kawaramachi........C5
10 Millennials........D2
11 Royal Park Hotel The Kyoto........D2
12 Tawaraya........C1
Yoshikawa........(see 28)

Eating
13 Biotei........B2
14 Ganko........D2
15 Giro Giro Hitoshina........C5
16 Gyoza Chao Chao Sanjo-Kiyamachi....D2
17 Gyoza Chao Chao Shijo-Kawaramachi........D3
18 Honke Owariya........B1
19 Ippūdō........B3
20 Kiyamachi Sakuragawa........D1
21 Kyōgoku Kane-yo........C2
22 Menami........D2
23 Mishima-tei........C2
24 Roan Kikunoi........D3
25 Saryo Suisen........B4
26 Sushi no Musashi........C2
27 Tagoto Honten........C3
28 Yoshikawa........C1

Drinking & Nightlife
29 Atlantis........D3
30 Bee's Knees........D3
31 Kiln........D3
32 Nokishita 711........D4
33 Sake Bar Yoramu........B1
34 Taigu........D1
35 Weekenders Coffee........C2

Entertainment
36 Kamogawa Odori........D2
37 Taku-Taku........C4

Shopping
38 Aritsugu........C3
39 BAL........D2
40 Daimaru........B3
41 Kyūkyo-dō........C1
Maruzen........(see 39)
42 Mimuro........A5
43 Takashimaya........D3
44 Tokyu Hands........B3
45 Wagami no Mise........B4

museum and plays host to the highest-level exhibitions in the city. It was founded in 1895 as an imperial repository for art and treasures from local temples and shrines. The **Heisei Chishinkan**, designed by Taniguchi Yoshio and opened in 2014, is a brilliant modern counterpoint to the original red-brick **main hall** building, which was closed and undergoing structural work at the time of research. Check the *Kyoto Visitor's Guide* to see what's on while you're in town.

Kennin-ji BUDDHIST TEMPLE

(建仁寺; Map p324; www.kenninji.jp; 584 Komatsu-chō, Yamatoōji-dōri, Shijo-sagaru, Higashiyama-ku; ¥500; 10am-5pm Mar-Oct, to 4.30pm Nov-Feb; Keihan line to Gion-Shijō) Founded in 1202 by the monk Eisai, Kennin-ji is the oldest Zen temple in Kyoto. It is an island of peace and calm on the border of the boisterous Gion nightlife district and it makes a fine counterpoint to the worldly pleasures of that area. The highlight at Kennin-ji is the fine and expansive *kare-sansui* (dry landscape) garden. The painting of the twin dragons on the roof of the **Hōdō** hall is also fantastic.

Ninen-zaka & Sannen-zaka Area AREA

(二年坂・三年坂; Map p324; Higashiyama-ku; Kyoto City bus 206 to Kiyomizu-michi or Gojō-zaka, Keihan line to Kiyomizu-Gojō) Just downhill from and slightly to the north of Kiyomizu-dera (p318), you will find one of Kyoto's loveliest restored neighbourhoods, the Ninen-zaka–Sannen-zaka area. The name refers to the two main streets of the area: Ninen-zaka and Sannen-zaka, literally 'Two-Year Hill' and 'Three-Year Hill' (the years referring to the ancient imperial years when they were first laid out). These two charming streets are lined with old wooden houses, traditional shops and restaurants.

Northern Higashiyama

This area is packed with first-rate attractions and soothing greenery, making it one of the best parts of the city for relaxed sightseeing.

★**Ginkaku-ji** BUDDHIST TEMPLE

(銀閣寺; Map p328; 2 Ginkaku-ji-chō, Sakyō-ku; adult/child ¥500/300; 8.30am-5pm Mar-Nov, 9am-4.30pm Dec-Feb; Kyoto City bus 5 to Ginkakuji-michi stop) Home to a sumptuous

Southern Higashiyama

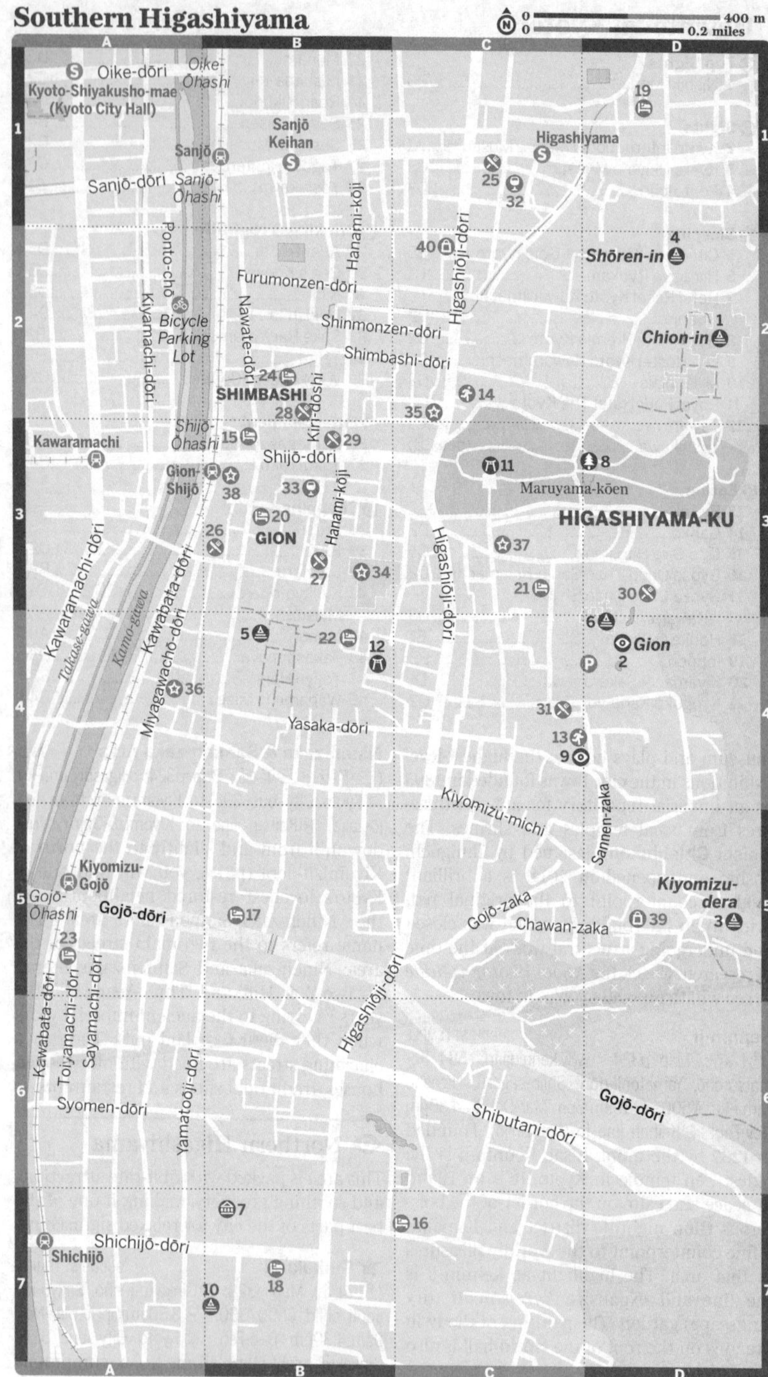

Southern Higashiyama

Top Sights

1 Chion-in....D2
2 Gion....D4
3 Kiyomizu-dera....D5
4 Shōren-in....D2

Sights

5 Kennin-ji....B4
6 Kōdai-ji....D4
7 Kyoto National Museum....B7
8 Maruyama-kōen....D3
9 Ninen-zaka & Sannen-zaka Area....C4
10 Sanjūsangen-dō Temple....B7
11 Yasaka-jinja....C3
12 Yasui Konpira-gū....B4

Activities, Courses & Tours

13 Camellia Tea Experience....C4
14 En....C2

Sleeping

15 Book + Bed Hostel....B3
16 Four Seasons....C7
Gion Hatanaka....(see 37)
17 Gojō Guest House....B5
18 Hyatt Regency Kyoto....B7
19 Koto Inn....D1
20 Kyoto Granbell Hotel....B3
21 Motonago....C3
22 Old Kyoto....B4
23 Seikōrō....A5
24 Shiraume Ryokan....B2

Eating

25 Bamboo....C1
26 Chidoritei....B3
27 Gion Karyō....B3
28 Gion Yuki....B2
29 Kagizen Yoshifusa....B3
Kasagi-ya....(see 9)
30 Kikunoi....D3
31 Omen Kodai-ji....C4

Drinking & Nightlife

32 Beer Komachi....C1
33 Gion Finlandia Bar....B3
Tōzan Bar....(see 18)

Entertainment

34 Gion Corner....B3
35 Gion Odori....C2
36 Kyō Odori....A4
37 Kyoto Cuisine & Maiko Evening....C3
38 Minamiza....B3
Miyako Odori....(see 34)

Shopping

39 Asahi-dō....D5
40 Ichizawa Shinzaburo Hanpu....C2

garden and elegant structures, Ginkaku-ji is one of Kyoto's premier sites. The temple started its life in 1482 as a retirement villa for shogun Ashikaga Yoshimasa, who desired a place to retreat from the turmoil of a civil war. While the name Ginkaku-ji literally translates as 'Silver Pavilion', the shogun's ambition to cover the building with silver was never realised. After Ashikaga's death, the villa was converted into a temple.

Walkways lead through the gardens, which include meticulously raked cones of white sand (said to be symbolic of a mountain and a lake), tall pines and a pond in front of the temple. A path also leads up the mountainside through the trees.

Note that Ginkaku-ji is one of the city's most popular sites, and it is almost always crowded, especially during spring and autumn. We strongly recommend visiting right after it opens or just before it closes.

★ Eikan-dō BUDDHIST TEMPLE

(永観堂; Map p328; ☎075-761-0007; www.eikando.or.jp; 48 Eikandō-chō, Sakyō-ku; adult/child ¥600/400; 9am-5pm; Kyoto City bus 5 to Eikandō-michi, S Tōzai line to Keage) Perhaps Kyoto's most famous (and most crowded) autumn-foliage destination, Eikan-dō is a superb temple just a short walk south of the famous Path of Philosophy. Eikan-dō is made interesting by its varied architecture, its gardens and its works of art. It was founded as Zenrin-ji in 855 by the priest Shinshō, but the name was changed to Eikan-dō in the 11th century to honour the philanthropic priest Eikan.

★ Nanzen-ji BUDDHIST TEMPLE

(南禅寺; Map p328; www.nanzenji.com; 86 Fukuchi-chō, Nanzen-ji, Sakyō-ku; adult/child from ¥300/150, grounds free; 8.40am-5pm Mar-Nov, to 4.30pm Dec-Feb; Kyoto City bus 5 to Eikandō-michi, S Tōzai line to Keage) This is one of the most rewarding temples in Kyoto, with its expansive grounds and numerous subtemples. At its entrance stands the massive **San-mon**. Steps lead up to the 2nd storey, which has a great view over the city. Beyond the gate is the main hall of the temple, above which you will find the **Hōjō**, where the Leaping Tiger Garden is a classic Zen garden well worth a look.

Nanzen-ji began as a retirement villa for Emperor Kameyama but was dedicated as a Zen temple on his death in 1291. Civil war in

City Walk
Highlights of Northern Higashiyama

START KEAGE STATION
END GINKAKU-JI-MICHI BUS STOP
LENGTH ABOUT 6KM; FOUR HOURS

Start at Keage Station on the Tōzai subway line, walk downhill, cross the pedestrian overpass, head back uphill and go through the tunnel under the old funicular tracks. This leads to a narrow street that winds towards **1 Konchi-in** (p330).

Just past Konchi-in, take a right on the main road and walk up through the gate into **2 Nanzen-ji** (p325). Continue east, up the slope and you'll soon see the brick Sōsui aqueduct on your right; cross under this, take a quick left and walk up the hill towards the mountains. You'll come first to the lovely **3 Kōtoku-an** subtemple. Beyond this, the trail enters the woods. Follow it up to the secluded **4 Nanzen-ji Oku-no-in**, a tiny shrine built around a waterfall.

Return the way you came and exit the north side of Nanzen-ji, following the road through a gate. You'll soon come to **5 Eikan-dō** (p325), a large temple famous for its artworks and pagoda. At the corner just beyond Eikan-dō, a sign in English and Japanese points up the hill to the Path of Philosophy. If you're hungry, take a short detour north to **6 Hinode Udon** (p352), a fine noodle restaurant. Otherwise, head up the hill to the **7 Path of Philosophy**, which is the pedestrian path that heads north along the canal.

It's then a straight shot up the lovely tree-lined canal for about 800m until you reach a small sign in English and Japanese pointing up the hill to **8 Hōnen-in** (p330). Follow the sign, take a left at the top of the hill, walk past a small park and you'll see the picturesque thatched gate of Hōnen-in. After checking out the temple (free), exit via the thatched gate and take a quick right downhill.

From here, follow the narrow side streets north to **9 Ginkaku-ji** (p323), the famed Silver Pavilion.

the 15th century destroyed most of the temple; the present buildings date from the 17th century. It operates now as headquarters for the Rinzai school of Zen.

While you're in the Hōjō, you can enjoy a cup of *matcha* (powdered green tea) and a sweet while gazing at a small waterfall (¥500; ask at the reception desk of the Hōjō).

Perhaps the best part of Nanzen-ji is overlooked by most visitors: **Nanzen-ji Oku-no-in** (南禅寺奥の院; Map p328) FREE, a small shrine hidden in a forested hollow behind the main precinct. It's here that pilgrims pray while standing under the falls, sometimes in the dead of winter.

To get here, walk up to the red-brick aqueduct in front of Nanzen-in. Follow the road that runs parallel to the aqueduct up into the hills, and walk past (or through) Kōtoku-an, a small subtemple on your left. Continue up the steps into the woods until you reach a waterfall in a beautiful mountain glen.

Path of Philosophy (Tetsugaku-no-Michi) AREA

(哲学の道; Map p328; Sakyō-ku; Kyoto City bus 5 to Eikandō-michi or Ginkakuji-michi, S Tōzai line to Keage) The Tetsugaku-no-Michi is one of the most pleasant walks in Kyoto. Lined with a great variety of flowering plants, bushes and trees, it is a corridor of colour throughout most of the year. Follow the traffic-free route along a canal lined with cherry trees that come into spectacular bloom in early April. It only takes 30 minutes to do the walk, which starts at Nyakuōji-bashi, above Eikan-dō, and leads to Ginkaku-ji.

Shūgaku-in Rikyū Imperial Villa NOTABLE BUILDING

(修学院離宮; Map p316; 075-211-1215; www.kunaicho.go.jp; Shūgaku-in, Yabusoe, Sakyō-ku; tours 9am, 10am, 11am, 1.30pm & 3pm Tue-Sun; Kyoto City bus 5 from Kyoto Station to Shūgakuinrikyū-michi) FREE One of the highlights of northeast Kyoto, this superb imperial villa was designed as a lavish summer retreat for the imperial family. Its gardens, with their views down over the city, are worth the trouble it takes to visit. The one-hour tours are held in Japanese, with English audio guides free of charge. You must be over 18 years to enter and bring your passport.

Construction of the villa was begun in the 1650s by Emperor Go-Mizunō, following his abdication. Work was continued by his daughter Akeno-miya after his death in 1680.

The villa grounds are divided into three enormous garden areas on a hillside – lower, middle and upper. Each has superb tea-ceremony houses: the upper, **Kami-no-chaya**, and lower, **Shimo-no-chaya**, were completed in 1659, and the middle teahouse, **Naka-no-chaya**, was completed in 1682. The gardens' reputation rests on their ponds, pathways and impressive use of *shakkei* (borrowed scenery) in the form of the surrounding hills. The view from Kami-no-chaya is particularly impressive.

You can book tickets in advance at the Imperial Household Agency office or online. Same-day tickets (for afternoon tours only) go on sale at the villa from 11am and are available on a first-come, first-served basis.

RESERVATION & ADMISSION TO KYOTO'S IMPERIAL PROPERTIES

Visitors no longer have to apply for permission to visit the Kyoto Imperial Palace (p333). The palace, situated inside the Imperial Palace Park, is open to the public from Tuesday to Sunday and you just need to go straight to the main gate for entry. Children are permitted with an accompanying adult.

Permission to visit the Sentō Imperial Palace (p333), Katsura Rikyū (p337) and Shūgaku-in Rikyū is granted by the Kunaichō, the **Imperial Household Agency** (宮内庁京都事務所; Map p332; 075-211-1215; www.kunaicho.go.jp; Imperial Palace Park, Kyoto Gyōen, Kamigyō-ku; 8.40am-5pm, closed Mon; S Karasuma line to Imadegawa), which is inside the Imperial Palace Park. You can book tours in advance at the Imperial Household Agency office or by filling out the application form on its website. You must be over 18 years to enter each property. For afternoon tours, it's also possible to buy tickets on the same day at the properties themselves from 11am. Only a certain number of tickets are issued each day, so it's first-come, first-served. Tours run for 60 minutes and you are required to arrive at least 20 minutes beforehand. All tours are free and are in Japanese with English audio guides available. The exception is Katsura Rikyū, which costs ¥1000 and also offers guided tours in English.

Northern Higashiyama

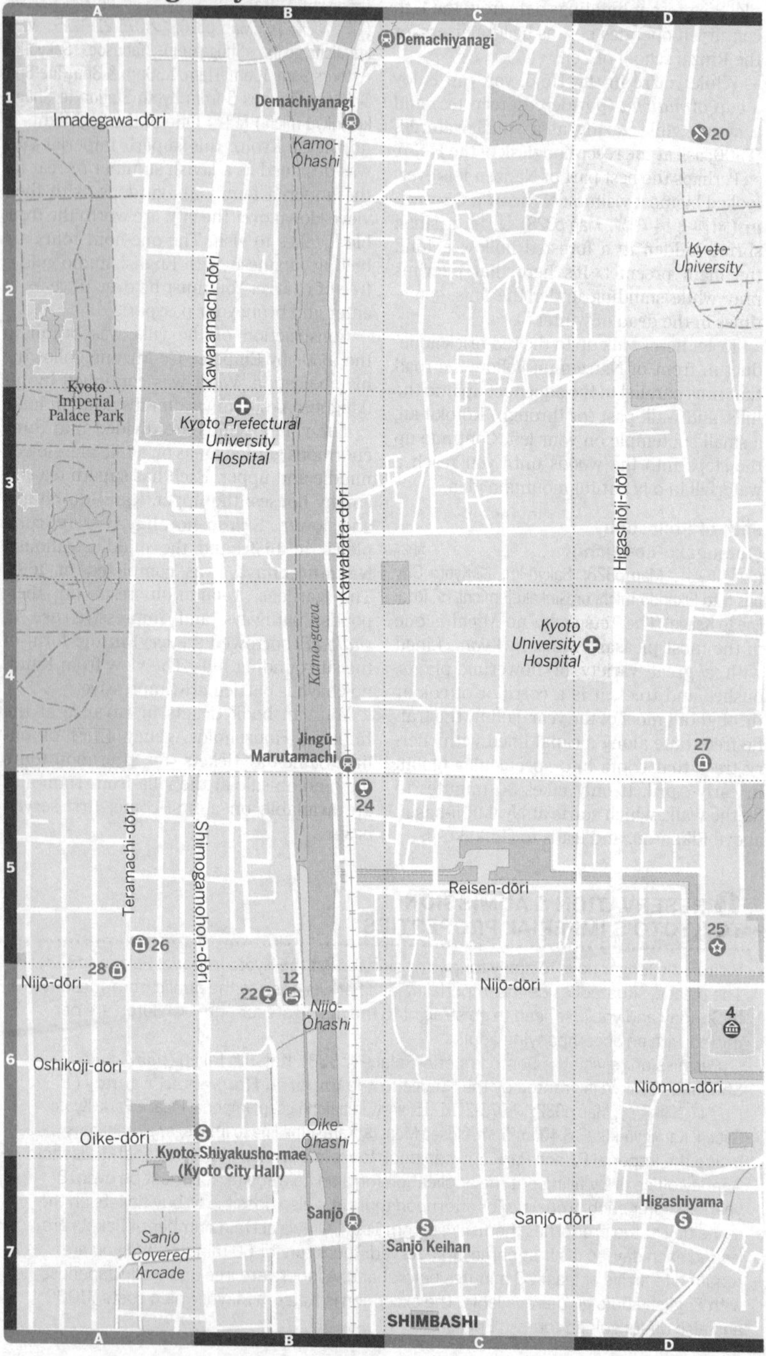

Demachiyanagi
Demachiyanagi
Imadegawa-dōri
Kamo-Ōhashi
Kyoto University
Kawaramachi-dōri
Kyoto Imperial Palace Park
Kyoto Prefectural University Hospital
Kawabata-dōri
Higashiōji-dōri
Kamo-gawa
Kyoto University Hospital
Jingū-Marutamachi
Teramachi-dōri
Shimogamohon-dōri
Reisen-dōri
Nijō-dōri
Nijō-dōri
Nijō-Ōhashi
Oshikōji-dōri
Niōmon-dōri
Oike-dōri
Oike-Ōhashi
Kyoto-Shiyakusho-mae (Kyoto City Hall)
Sanjō
Sanjō-dōri
Higashiyama
Sanjō Keihan
Sanjō Covered Arcade
SHIMBASHI

20, 27, 24, 25, 26, 28, 22, 12, 4

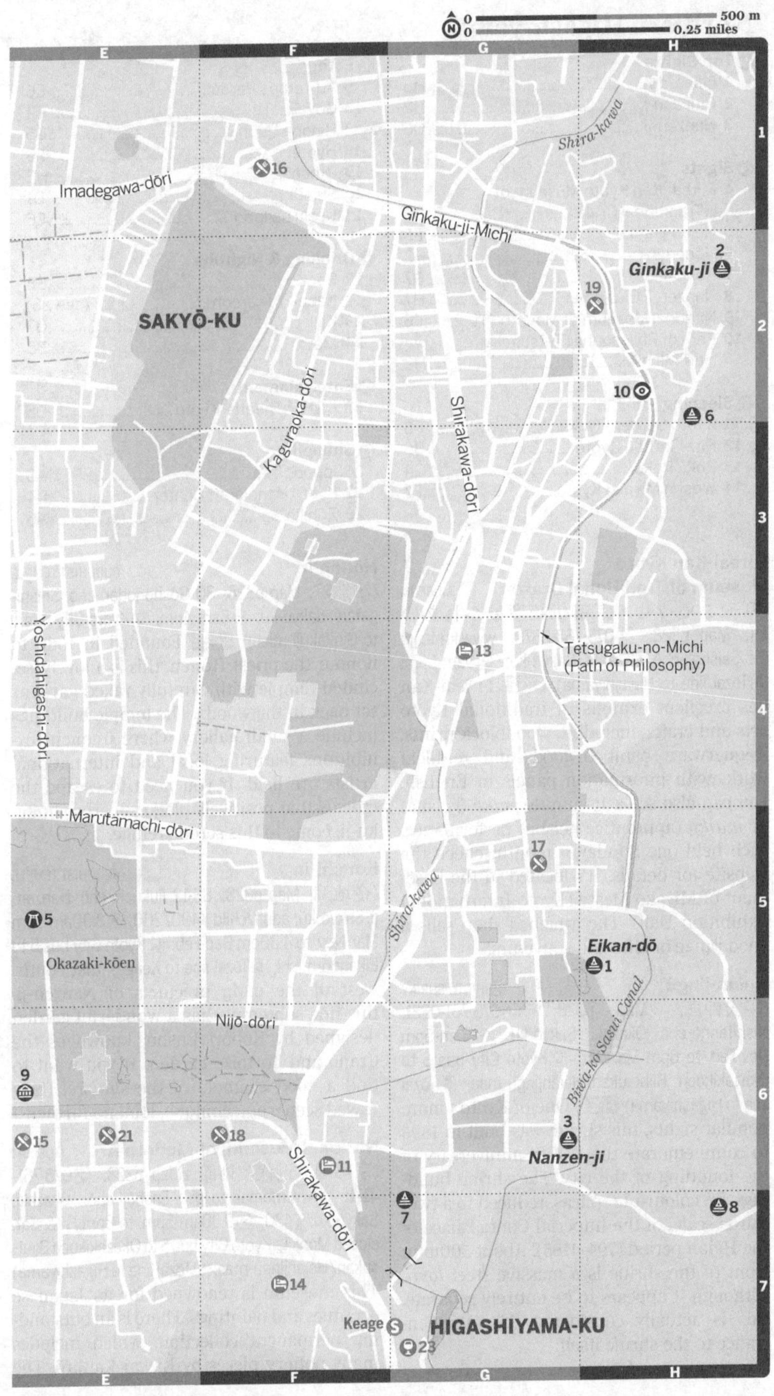

0 500 m
0 0.25 miles
E
F
G
H
1
2
3
4
5
6
7
Imadegawa-dōri
Ginkaku-ji-Michi
Shira-kawa
SAKYŌ-KU
Ginkaku-ji
Kaguraoka-dōri
Shirakawa-dōri
Yoshidahigashi-dōri
Tetsugaku-no-Michi (Path of Philosophy)
Marutamachi-dōri
Shira-kawa
Eikan-dō
Okazaki-kōen
Biwa-ko Sosui Canal
Nijō-dōri
Nanzen-ji
Shirakawa-dōri
Keage
HIGASHIYAMA-KU
1
2
3
5
6
7
8
9
10
11
13
14
15
16
17
18
19
21
23

Northern Higashiyama

Fureai-Kan Kyoto Museum of Traditional Crafts MUSEUM

(みやこめっせ・京都伝統産業ふれあい館; Map p328; 075-762-2670; www.kmtc.jp; 9-1 Seishōji-chō, Okazaki, Sakyō-ku; 9am-5pm; S Tōzai line to Higashiyama) FREE Fureai-Kan has excellent exhibits of traditional Kyoto arts and crafts, including woodblock prints, lacquerware, bamboo goods and gold-leaf work, with information panels in English. You can also see a 15-minute *geiko* (geisha) or *maiko* (apprentice geisha) performance, each held one Sunday a month; check the website for details. It's located in the basement of Miyako Messe (Kyoto International Exhibition Hall). The attached shop sells a good range of gifts and souvenirs.

Heian-jingū SHINTŌ SHRINE

(平安神宮; Map p328; 075-761-0221; Nishitennō-chō, Okazaki, Sakyō-ku; 6am-5pm Nov-Feb, to 6pm Mar-Oct; Kyoto City bus 5 to Okazakikoen Bijutsukan/Heianjingu-mae, S Tōzai line to Higashiyama) FREE One of Kyoto's more popular sights, this shrine was built in 1895 to commemorate the 1100th anniversary of the founding of the city. The shrine buildings are colourful replicas, reduced to a two-thirds scale, of the Imperial Court Palace of the Heian period (794–1185). About 500m in front of the shrine is a massive steel *torii*. Although it appears to be entirely separate, this is actually considered the main entrance to the shrine itself.

Hōnen-in BUDDHIST TEMPLE

(法然院; Map p328; 30 Goshonodan-chō, Shishigatani, Sakyō-ku; 6am-4pm; Kyoto City bus 5 to Ginkakuji-michi) FREE Founded in 1680 to honour the priest Hōnen, this is a lovely, secluded temple with carefully raked gardens set back in the woods. The temple buildings include a small gallery where frequent exhibitions featuring local and international artists are held. If you need to escape the crowds that positively plague nearby Ginkaku-ji, come to this serene refuge.

Konchi-in BUDDHIST TEMPLE

(金地院; Map p328; 86-12 Fukuchi-chō, Nanzen-ji, Sakyō-ku; adult/child ¥400/200; 8.30am-5pm Mar-Nov, to 4.30pm Dec-Feb; Kyoto City bus 5 to Eikandō-michi, S Tōzai line to Keage) Just southwest of the main precincts of Nanzen-ji, this fine subtemple has a wonderful garden designed by Kobori Enshū, known as the Crane and Tortoise garden. If you want to find a good example of the *shakkei* (borrowed scenery) technique, look no further.

National Museum of Modern Art MUSEUM

(京都国立近代美術館; Map p328; 075-761-4111; www.momak.go.jp; Enshōji-chō, Okazaki, Sakyō-ku; ¥430; 9.30am-5pm, to 8pm Fri & Sat, closed Mon; Kyoto City bus 5 to Okazakikoen Bijutsukan/Heianjingu-mae, S Tōzai line to Higashiyama) This museum is renowned for its Japanese ceramics and paintings. There is an outstanding permanent collection, which includes many pottery pieces by Kawai Kanjirō. The coffee shop here is a nice place for a break and overlooks a picturesque canal. The museum also hosts regular special exhibitions, so check the website for what's on.

Imperial Palace & Around

★Daitoku-ji BUDDHIST TEMPLE
(大徳寺; Map p332; 53 Daitokuji-chō, Murasakino, Kita-ku; Kyoto City bus 205 or 206 to Daitokuji-mae, S Karasuma line to Kitaōji) For anyone with the slightest fondness for Japanese gardens, don't miss this network of lanes dotted with atmospheric Zen temples. Daitoku-ji, the main temple here, serves as headquarters for the Rinzai Daitoku-ji school of Zen Buddhism. It's not usually open to the public but there are several subtemples with superb carefully raked *karen-sensui* (dry landscape) gardens well worth making the trip out for. Highlights include Daisen-in, Kōtō-in, Ryōgen-in and Zuihō-in.

Daitoku-ji is on the eastern side of the grounds. It was founded in 1319, burnt down in the next century and rebuilt in the 16th century. The **San-mon** gate (1589) has a self-carved statue of its erector, the famous tea master Sen no Rikyū, on its 2nd storey.

The Karasuma subway line to Kitaōji Station is the fastest way to get here. From Kitaōji Station, walk west along Kitaōji-dōri for about 15 minutes. You'll see the temple complex on your right. The main entrance is a bit north of Kitaōji. If you enter from the main gate, which is on the east side of the complex, you'll soon find Daitoku-ji on your right. Alternatively, take bus 205 or 206 from Kyoto Station to the Daitoku-ji-mae bus stop.

Daisen-in BUDDHIST TEMPLE
(大仙院; Map p332; 54-1 Daitokuji-chō, Murasakino, Kita-ku; adult/child ¥400/270; 9am-5pm Mar-Nov, to 4.30pm Dec-Feb; Kyoto City bus 205 or 206 to Daitokuji-mae, S Karasuma line to Kitaōji) The two small Zen gardens in this subtemple of Daitoku-ji are elegant examples of 17th-century *kare-sansui* style. Here the trees, rocks and sand are said to represent and express various spectacles of nature, from waterfalls and valleys to mountain lakes. It's one of the more popular subtemples here.

Ryōgen-in BUDDHIST TEMPLE
(龍源院; Map p332; 075-491-7635; 82-1 Daitokuji-chō, Murasakino, Kita-ku; adult/child ¥350/200; 9am-4.30pm; Kyoto City bus 205 or 206 to Daitokuji-mae, S Karasuma line to Kitaōji) Ryōgen-in is a fine subtemple in the Daitoku-ji complex. It has two pleasing gardens, one moss and one *kare-sansui*. The *kare-sansui* has an interesting island in its midst that invites lazy contemplation. When you enter the Daitoku-ji complex via the east (main) gate, it's on the left, just before Ōbai-in.

Zuihō-in BUDDHIST TEMPLE
(瑞峯院; Map p332; 075-491-1454; 81 Daitokuji-chō, Murasakino, Kita-ku; adult/child ¥400/300; 9am-5pm Mar-Nov, to 4.30pm Dec-Feb; Kyoto City bus 205 or 206 to Daitokuji-mae, S Karasuma line to Kitaōji) A subtemple of Daitoku-ji, Zuihō-in enshrines the 16th-century Christian *daimyō* (domain lord) Ōtomo Sōrin. In the early 1960s, a landscape architect named Shigemori Mirei rearranged the stones in the back rock garden into the shape of a crucifix. More interesting is the main rock garden, which is raked into appealing patterns reminiscent of water ripples. It's roughly in the middle of the complex; you may have to ask for directions.

★Kōtō-in BUDDHIST TEMPLE
(高桐院; Map p332; 73-1 Daitokuji-chō, Murasakino, Kita-ku; ¥400; 9am-4.30pm; Kyoto City bus 205 or 206 to Daitokuji-mae, S Karasuma line to Kitaōji) On the far western edge of the Daitoku-ji complex, the sublime garden of this subtemple is one of the best in Kyoto and worth a special trip. It's located within a fine bamboo grove that you traverse via a moss-lined path. Once inside there is a small stroll garden that leads to the centrepiece: a rectangle of moss and maple trees, backed by bamboo. Take some time on the verandah here to soak it all up.

Kyoto Imperial Palace Park PARK
(京都御苑; Map p332; Kyoto Gyōen, Kamigyō-ku; dawn-dusk; S Karasuma line to Marutamachi or Imadegawa) FREE The Kyoto Imperial Palace (Kyoto Gosho) and Sentō Imperial Palace (Sentō Gosho) are surrounded by the spacious Kyoto Imperial Palace Park, which is planted with a huge variety of flowering trees and open fields. It's perfect for picnics, strolls and just about any sport you can think of. Take some time to visit the pond at the park's southern end, which contains gorgeous carp. The park is most beautiful in the plum- and cherry-blossom seasons (late February and late March, respectively).

Imperial Palace & Around

Imperial Palace & Around

Top Sights
1 Daitoku-ji B1
2 Kōtō-in A1
3 Nijō-jō B4

Sights
4 Daisen-in B1
5 Kitano Tenman-gū A2
6 Kyoto Botanical Gardens C1
7 Kyoto Imperial Palace C3
8 Kyoto Imperial Palace Park C3
9 Ryōgen-in B1
10 Sentō Imperial Palace C3
11 Shimogamo-jinja D1
12 Zuihō-in A1

Activities, Courses & Tours
13 Funaoka Onsen B2
14 Haru Cooking Class C2

Sleeping
15 Bird Hostel C4
16 Mosaic Machiya Hostel A2
17 Noku Kyoto C4
18 Palace Side Hotel C3

Eating
19 Café Bibliotec Hello! C4
20 Falafel Garden D2
21 Kanei B2
22 Kazariya A1
23 Papa Jon's C2
24 Sarasa Nishijin B2
25 Toraya Karyō Kyoto Ichijō C3

Entertainment
26 Jittoku B3

Shopping
27 Aizen Kōbō B2

Kyoto Imperial Palace HISTORIC BUILDING
(京都御所, Kyoto Gosho; Map p332; ☎075-211-1215; www.kunaicho.go.jp; Kyoto Gyōen, Kamigyō-ku; ⊙9am-4.30pm Tue-Sun Mar-Sep, to 4pm Oct-Feb, last entry 40min before closing; S Karasuma line to Marutamachi or Imadegawa) FREE The Kyoto Imperial Palace, known as the Gosho in Japanese, is a walled complex that sits in the middle of the Kyoto Imperial Palace Park (p331). While no longer the official residence of the Japanese emperor, it's still a grand edifice, though it doesn't rate highly in comparison with other attractions in Kyoto. Visitors can wander around the marked route in the grounds where English signs explain the history of the buildings. Entrance is via the main Seishomon Gate where you'll be given a map.

Sentō Imperial Palace HISTORIC BUILDING
(仙洞御所, Sentō Gosho; Map p332; ☎075-211-1215; www.kunaicho.go.jp; Kyoto Gyōen, Kamigyō-ku; ⊙tours 9.30am, 11am, 1.30pm, 2.30pm & 3.30pm Tue-Sun; S Karasuma line to Marutamachi or Imadegawa) FREE The Sentō Gosho is the second imperial property located within the Kyoto Imperial Palace Park (the other one is the Imperial Palace itself). The structures are not particularly grand, but the gardens, laid out in 1630 by renowned landscape designer Enshū Kobori, are excellent. Admission is by one-hour tour only (in Japanese; English audio guides are free). You must be over 18 years old and bring your passport. Your ticket can be printed or shown on a smartphone.

Shimogamo-jinja SHINTŌ SHRINE
(下鴨神社; Map p332; www.shimogamo-jinja.or.jp; 59 Izumigawa-chō, Shimogamo, Sakyō-ku; ⊙6.30am-5pm; 🚌Kyoto City bus 205 to Shimogamo-jinja-mae, 🚆Keihan line to Demachiyanagi) FREE This shrine, dating from the 8th century, is a Unesco World Heritage Site. It is nestled in the fork of the Kamo-gawa and Takano-gawa, and is approached along a shady path through the lovely Tadasu-no-mori. This wooded area is said to be a place where lies cannot be concealed and is considered a prime location to sort out disputes. The trees here are mostly broadleaf (a rarity in Kyoto) and they are gorgeous in the springtime.

Kyoto Botanical Gardens GARDENS
(京都府立植物園; Map p332; Shimogamohangi-chō, Sakyō-ku; adult/child gardens ¥200/free, greenhouse ¥200/free; ⊙9am-5pm, greenhouse 10am-4pm; S Karasuma line to Kitayama) The Kyoto Botanical Gardens occupy 24 hectares and feature over 12,000 plants, flowers and trees. It is pleasant to stroll through the rose, cherry and herb gardens or see the rows of camphor trees and the large tropical **greenhouse**. This is a good spot for a picnic. It's also the perfect location for a *hanami* party, and the blossoms here tend to hold on a little longer than those elsewhere in the city.

Kamigamo-jinja SHINTŌ SHRINE
(上賀茂神社; Map p316; ☎075-781-0011; www.kamigamojinja.jp; 339 Motoyama, Kamigamo, Kita-ku; ⊙6am-5pm; 🚌Kyoto City bus 9 to Kamigamo-misonobashi) FREE Around 2km north of the Botanical Gardens is Kamigamo-jinja, one of Japan's oldest shrines, which predates the founding of Kyoto. Established in 679, it is dedicated to Raijin, the god of thunder, and is one of Kyoto's 17 Unesco World Heritage Sites. The present buildings (more than 40 in all), including the impressive Haiden hall, are exact reproductions of the originals, dating from the 17th to 19th centuries.

Northwest Kyoto

★Kinkaku-ji BUDDHIST TEMPLE
(金閣寺; Map p335; 1 Kinkakuji-chō, Kita-ku; adult/child ¥400/300; ⊙9am-5pm; 🚌Kyoto City bus 205 from Kyoto Station to Kinkakuji-michi, 🚌Kyoto City bus 12 from Sanjō-Keihan to Kinkakuji-michi) Kyoto's famed 'Golden Pavilion', Kinkaku-ji is one of Japan's best-known sights. The main hall, covered in brilliant gold leaf, shining above its reflecting pond is truly spectacular. Needless to say, due to its beauty, the temple can be packed any day of the year. It's best to go early in the day or just before closing, ideally on a weekday.

The original building dates from 1397 and was a retirement villa for shogun Ashikaga Yoshimitsu. His son converted it into a temple. In 1950 a young monk consummated his obsession with the temple by burning it to the ground. The monk's story was fictionalised in Mishima Yukio's *The Temple of the Golden Pavilion*. In 1955 a full reconstruction was completed that followed the original design, but the gold-foil covering was extended to the lower floors.

Ryōan-ji BUDDHIST TEMPLE
(龍安寺; Map p335; www.ryoanji.jp; 13 Goryōnoshitamachi, Ryōan-ji, Ukyō-ku; adult/child ¥500/300; ⊙8am-5pm Mar-Nov, 8.30am-4.30pm Dec-Feb; 🚌Kyoto City bus 59 from Sanjō-Keihan to Ryoanji-mae) You've probably seen a picture of the rock garden here – it's one of the symbols

of Kyoto and one of Japan's better-known sights. Ryōan-ji belongs to the Rinzai school and was founded in 1450. The garden, an oblong of sand with an austere collection of 15 carefully placed rocks, apparently adrift in a sea of sand, is enclosed by an earthen wall. The designer, who remains unknown to this day, provided no explanation.

Although many historians believe the garden was arranged by Sōami during the Muromachi period (1333–1568), some contend that it is a much later product of the Edo period. It is Japan's most famous hira-niwa (flat garden void of hills or ponds) and reveals the stunning simplicity and harmony of the principles of Zen meditation.

There is no doubt that it's a mesmerising and attractive sight, but it's hard to enjoy amid the mobs who come to check it off their 'must-see list'. An early-morning visit on a weekday is probably your best hope of seeing the garden under contemplative conditions. If you go when it's crowded, you'll find the less-famous garden around the corner of the stone garden a nice escape.

Myōshin-ji BUDDHIST TEMPLE

(妙心寺; Map p335; www.myoshinji.or.jp; 1 Myoshin-ji-chō, Hanazono, Ukyō-ku; main temple free, other areas of complex adult/child ¥500/100; ⏲9.10-11.40am & 1-4.40pm, to 3.40pm Nov-Feb; 🚌Kyoto City bus 10 from Sanjo-Keihan to Myōshin-ji Kita-mon-mae) Myōshin-ji is a separate world within Kyoto, a walled-off complex of temples and subtemples that invites lazy strolling. The subtemple of **Taizō-in** here contains one of the city's more interesting gardens. Myōshin-ji dates from 1342 and belongs to the Rinzai school. There are 47 subtemples, but only a few are open to the public.

From the north gate, follow the broad stone avenue flanked by rows of temples to the southern part of the complex. The eponymous Myōshin-ji temple is roughly in the middle of the complex. Your entry fee entitles you to a tour of several of the buildings of the temple. The ceiling of the **Hattō** (Lecture Hall) here features Tanyū Kanō's unnerving painting *Unryūzu* (meaning 'Dragon glaring in eight directions'). Your guide will invite you to stand directly beneath the dragon; doing so makes it appear that it's spiralling up or down.

Shunkō-in (p339), a subtemple of Myōshin-ji, offers 90-minute *zazen* (seated Zen meditation) sessions for foreigners with English explanations for ¥3500; highly recommended.

Kitano Tenman-gū SHINTŌ SHRINE

(北野天満宮; Map p332; www.kitanotenmangu.or.jp; Bakuro-chō, Kamigyō-ku; ⏲5am-6pm Apr-Sep, 5.30am-5.30pm Oct-Mar; 🚌Kyoto City bus 50 from Kyoto Station to Kitano-Tenmangū-mae) FREE The most atmospheric Shintō shrine in northwest Kyoto, Kitano Tenman-gū is also the site of Tenjin-San Market, one of Kyoto's most popular flea markets. It's a pleasant spot for a lazy stroll and the shrine buildings themselves are beautiful. The present buildings date from 1607 and were built by Toyotomi Hideyori; the grounds contain an extensive grove of plum trees, which burst into bloom in early March.

WORTH A TRIP

DAIMONJI-YAMA CLIMB

Length 5km; 1½ hours

Located directly behind Ginkaku-ji, Daimonji-yama is the main site of the Daimon-ji Gozan Okuribi. From almost anywhere in town the Chinese character for 'great' (大; *dai*) is visible in the middle of a bare patch on the face of this mountain. On 16 August this character is set ablaze to guide the spirits of the dead on their journey home. The view of Kyoto from the top is unparalleled.

Take Kyoto City bus 5 to the Ginkaku-ji Michi stop and walk up to Ginkaku-ji (p323). Here, you have the option of visiting the temple or starting the hike immediately. To find the trailhead, turn left in front of the temple and head north for about 50m towards a stone *torii* (shrine gate). Just before the *torii*, turn right up the hill.

The trail proper starts just after a small car park on the right. It's a broad avenue through the trees. You'll see a signboard and then a bridge after it. Cross the bridge to the right, then continue up a smaller, switchback trail. When the trail reaches a saddle not far from the top, go to the left. You'll climb a long flight of steps before coming out at the top of the bald patch. The sunset from here is great, but bring a torch.

Northwest Kyoto

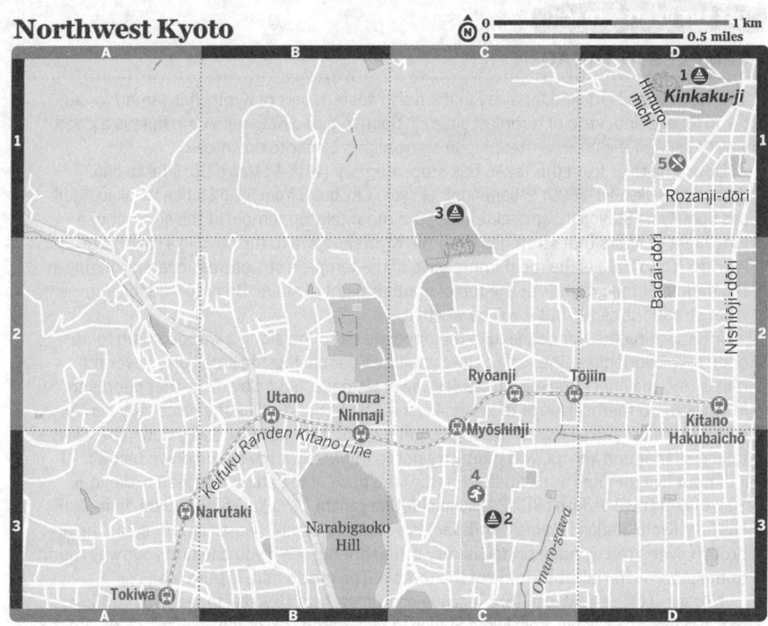

Arashiyama & Sagano

Most of Arashiyama and Sagano's sights lie on the north bank of the Hozu-gawa.

The main drag of Arashiyama and Sagano is overdeveloped and not particularly appealing, aside from its few eating and shopping options. As soon as you can, head west into the hills to escape into nature (via Tenryū-ji or straight through the Arashiyama Bamboo Grove).

★Arashiyama Bamboo Grove PARK

(嵐山竹林; Map p338; Ogurayama, Saga, Ukyō-ku; dawn-dusk; Kyoto City bus 28 from Kyoto Station to Arashiyama-Tenryuji-mae, JR Sagano/San-in line to Saga-Arashiyama or Hankyū line to Arashiyama, change at Katsura) FREE The thick green bamboo stalks seem to continue endlessly in every direction and there's a strange quality to the light at this famous bamboo grove. It's most atmospheric on the approach to Ōkōchi Sansō villa and you'll be unable to resist trying to take a few photos, but you might be disappointed with the results: photos just can't capture the magic of the place. The grove runs from outside the north gate of Tenryū-ji to just below Ōkōchi Sansō.

Northwest Kyoto

Top Sights

1 Kinkaku-ji D1

Sights

2 Myōshin-ji C3
3 Ryōan-ji C1

Activities, Courses & Tours

4 Shunkō-in C3

Sleeping

Shunkō-in .... (see 4)

Eating

5 Gontaro D1

★Ōkōchi Sansō HISTORIC BUILDING

(大河内山荘; Map p338; 8 Tabuchiyama-chō, Sagaogurayama, Ukyō-ku; adult/child ¥1000/500; 9am-5pm; Kyoto City bus 28 from Kyoto Station to Arashiyama-Tenryuji-mae, JR Sagano (San-in) line to Saga-Arashiyama or Hankyū line to Arashiyama, change at Katsura) This is the lavish estate of Ōkōchi Denjirō, an actor famous for his samurai films. The sprawling gardens may well be the most lovely in all of Kyoto, particularly when you consider the brilliant views eastwards across the city. The house and teahouse are also sublime. Be sure to

OFF THE BEATEN TRACK

TEMPLES IN TAKAO

The Takao area is tucked far away in the northwestern part of Kyoto. It is famed for autumn foliage and a trio of temples: Jingo-ji, Saimyō-ji and Kōzan-ji. A trip here is a good way to escape the crowds that plague some sights closer to downtown.

Down the river from the Takao bus stop, **Jingo-ji** (神護寺; Map p316; 5 Takao-chō, Umegahata, Ukyō-ku; ¥600; ⊙9am-4pm; 🚌Kyoto City bus 8 from Shijō Station to Takao, 🚌JR bus from Kyoto Station to Yamashiro-Takao) is a mountaintop temple at the summit of a long flight of stairs that stretches from the Kiyotaki-gawa to the temple's main gate. The **Kondō** (Gold Hall) is the most impressive of the temple's structures, located roughly in the middle of the grounds at the top of another flight of stairs. Be prepared for a somewhat strenuous climb, but it will be worth it.

After visiting the Kondō, head in the opposite direction along a wooded path to an open area overlooking the valley. Here you'll see people tossing small discs over the railing into the chasm below. These are *kawarakenage*, light clay discs that people throw in order to rid themselves of their bad karma. The trick is to flick the discs very gently, convex side up, like a Frisbee. When you get it right, they sail all the way down the valley – taking all that bad karma with them (try not to think about the hikers down below).

About five minutes' walk upstream from the base of the steps that lead to Jingo-ji, **Saimyō-ji** (西明寺; Map p316; 2 Makino-chō, Umegahata, Ukyō-ku; ¥500; ⊙9am-5pm; 🚌JR bus from Kyoto Station to Yamashiro-Takao) is a fine little temple worth stopping at. The approach over a red wooden bridge is very atmospheric; see if you can find your way round to the small waterfall at the side of the temple. The grotto here is pure magic.

Kōzan-ji (高山寺; Map p316; 8 Toganoo-chō, Umegahata, Ukyō-ku; to see scroll ¥800; ⊙8.30am-5pm; 🚌JR bus from Kyoto Station to Yamashiro-Takao or Toga-no-O), hidden amid a grove of towering cedar trees, is famous for the *chuju giga* scroll in its collection. It's an ink-brush depiction of frolicking animals that is considered by many to be the precursor of today's ubiquitous manga (Japanese comics). The temple is reached by following the main road north from the Yamashiro-Takao bus stop or, more conveniently, by getting off the JR bus at the Toga-no-O bus stop, right outside the temple. Note that there is an extra fee of ¥500 to visit the temple's gardens during the autumn-foliage season; other times of the year it's free to enter the grounds.

To reach Takao, take bus 8 from Nijō Station to the last stop, Takao (¥520, 40 minutes). From Kyoto Station, take the hourly JR bus to the Yamashiro-Takao stop (¥520, 50 minutes).

follow all the trails around the gardens. Hold onto the tea ticket you were given upon entry to claim the *matcha* and sweet that's included with admission.

★Saihō-ji BUDDHIST TEMPLE

(西芳寺; Map p316; http://saihoji-kokedera.com; 56 Matsuo Jingatani-chō, Nishikyō-ku; ¥3000; 🚌Kyoto bus 73 from Kyoto Station or 63 from Sanjō-Keihan to Koke-dera) Saihō-ji, one of Kyoto's best-known gardens, is famed for its superb moss garden, hence the temple's nickname: Koke-dera (Moss Temple). The heart-shaped garden, laid out in 1339 by Musō Kokushi, surrounds a tranquil pond and is simply stunning. In order to limit the number of visitors, you must apply to visit at least three weeks in advance, though the earlier the better to avoid disappointment.

To make a reservation to visit, you need to send a letter (or print and fill out the template on the website) and include your name, address, number of visitors and preferred dates, along with a self-addressed postcard for a reply to your address (in Japan or overseas). Note visitors must be at least 18 years old. The address to send it to is: Saihō-ji, 56 Matsuo Jingatanichō, Nishikyō-ku, Kyoto-shi 615-8286, JAPAN. Your return postcard will let you know the date and time of your visit. Payment is cash only on arrival.

When you arrive at Saihō-ji, visitors are required to copy a sutra with an ink brush. Foreigners are generally just required to write their name, address and a prayer, rather than attempt to copy the sutra. Once in the garden, you are free to explore on your own and at your own pace. The whole visit usually takes around one hour.

While the process might seem a little over the top, it's certainly worth the small effort to organise, particularly if you have a fondness for Japanese gardens.

★Tenryū-ji BUDDHIST TEMPLE

(天龍寺; Map p338; ☎075-881-1235; www.tenryuji.com; 68 Susukinobaba-chō, Saga-Tenryū-ji, Ukyō-ku; adult/child ¥800/600, garden only ¥500/300; ⏲8.30am-5pm; 🚌Kyoto City bus 28 from Kyoto Station to Arashiyama-Tenryuji-mae, 🚉JR Sagano (San-in) line to Saga-Arashiyama or Hankyū line to Arashiyama, change at Katsura) A major temple of the Rinzai school, Tenryū-ji has one of the most attractive gardens in all of Kyoto, particularly during the spring cherry-blossom and autumn-foliage seasons. The main 14th-century Zen garden, with its backdrop of the Arashiyama mountains, is a good example of *shakkei* (borrowed scenery). Unfortunately, it's no secret that the garden here is world class, so it pays to visit early in the morning or on a weekday.

Togetsu-kyō BRIDGE

(渡月橋; Map p338; Saga Tenryū-ji, Susukinobaba-chō, Ukyō-ku; 🚌Kyoto City bus 28 from Kyoto Station to Arashiyama-Tenryuji-mae, 🚉JR Sagano (San-in) line to Saga-Arashiyama or Hankyū line to Arashiyama, change at Katsura) The dominant landmark in Arashiyama, this bridge is just a few minutes on foot from either the Keifuku line or Hankyū line Arashiyama stations. The original crossing, constructed in 1606, was about 100m upriver from the present bridge. From July to mid-September, Togetsu-kyō is a good spot from which to watch *ukai* (fishing using trained cormorants) in the evening. To get close to the action you can join a passenger boat, the Kyoto Tourist Information Center (p361) can provide more details.

Kameyama-kōen PARK

(亀山公園; Map p338; Sagaogurayama, Ukyō-ku; ⏲24hr; 🚌Kyoto City bus 28 from Kyoto Station to Arashiyama-Tenryuji-mae, 🚉JR Sagano/San-in line to Saga-Arashiyama or Hankyū line to Arashiyama, change at Katsura) Just upstream from Tōgetsu-kyō and behind Tenryū-ji, this park is a nice place to escape the crowds of Arashiyama. It's laced with trails, one of which leads to a lookout over the Katsura-gawa and up into the Arashiyama mountains. It's especially attractive during cherry-blossom and autumn-foliage seasons. Keep an eye out for monkeys, which occasionally descend from the nearby hills to pick fruit.

Katsura Rikyū HISTORIC BUILDING

(桂離宮; Map p316; ☎075-211-1215; http://sankan.kunaicho.go.jp; Katsura Detached Palace, Katsura Misono, Nishikyō-ku; adult ¥1000, child 12-17yr free; ⏲tours 9.20am, 11.20am, 1.20pm, 3.20pm & 4.20pm Tue-Sun; 🚌Kyoto City bus 33 to Katsura Rikyū-mae, 🚉Hankyū line to Katsura) FREE Katsura Rikyū, one of Kyoto's imperial properties, is widely considered to be the pinnacle of Japanese traditional architecture and garden design. Set amid an otherwise drab neighbourhood, it is (literally) an island of incredible beauty. Book in advance for one-hour English guided tours. It also runs tours in Japanese with English audio guides free of charge; tours depart on the hour from 9am to 4pm and places are on a first-come, first-served basis until capacity is sold. Bring passport for ID. Note visitors must be at least 12 years old.

The villa was built in 1624 for the emperor's brother, Prince Toshihito. Every conceivable detail of the villa – the teahouses, the large pond with islets and the surrounding garden – has been given meticulous attention.

You can also book tickets for English guided tours in advance at the Imperial Household Agency office (p327).

It's a 15-minute walk from Katsura Station, on the Hankyū line. A taxi from the station to the villa will cost around ¥600. Alternatively, Kyoto bus 33 stops at Katsura Rikyū-mae stop, which is a five-minute walk from the villa.

Giō-ji BUDDHIST TEMPLE

(祇王寺; Map p338; www.giouji.or.jp; 32 Kozaka-chō, Sagatoriimoto, Ukyō-ku; adult/child ¥300/100; ⏲9am-5pm; 🚌Kyoto City bus 28 from Kyoto Station to Arashiyama-Tenryuji-mae, 🚉JR Sagano/San-in line to Saga-Arashiyama or Hankyū line to Arashiyama, change at Katsura) This tiny temple near the north end of the main Arashiyama sightseeing route is one of Kyoto's hidden gems. Its main attraction is the lush moss garden outside the thatch-roofed hall of the temple. Giō-ji was named for the Heian-era *shirabyōshi* (traditional dancer) Giō, who committed herself here as a nun at age 21 after her romance ended with Taira-no-Kiyomori, the commander of the Heike clan.

Arashiyama & Sagano Area

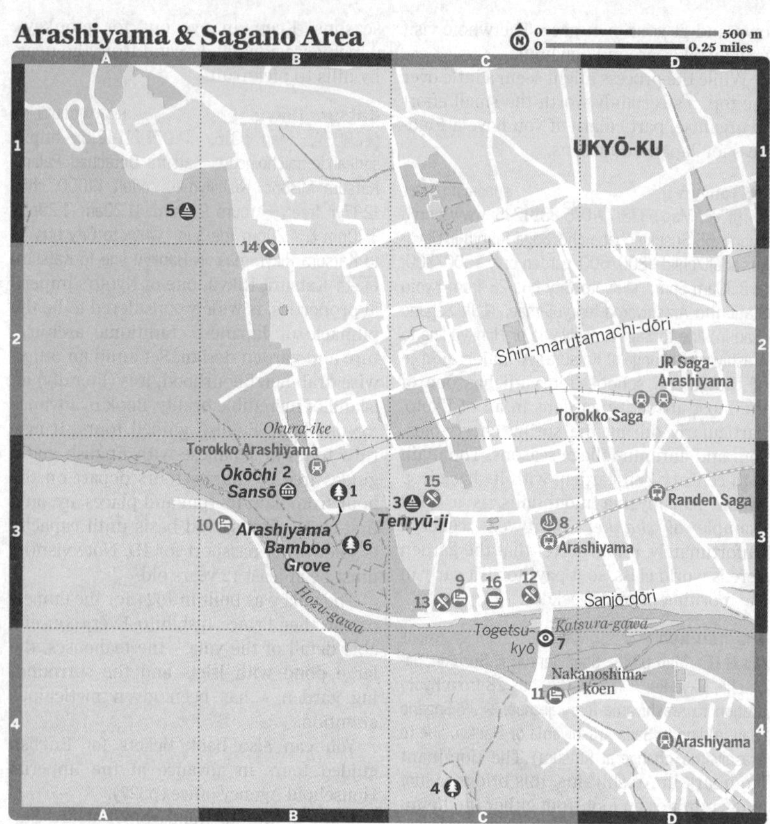

Arashiyama & Sagano Area

Top Sights
1 Arashiyama Bamboo Grove B3
2 Ōkōchi Sansō B3
3 Tenryū-ji C3

Sights
4 Arashiyama Monkey Park Iwatayama C4
5 Giō-ji A1
6 Kameyama-kōen B3
7 Togetsu-kyō C4

Activities, Courses & Tours
8 Keifuku Randen Arashiyama Station Foot Onsen C3

Sleeping
9 Arashiyama Benkei C3
10 Hoshinoya Kyoto B3
11 Japaning Hotel Liv Ranrokaku Kyoto C4

Eating
12 Arashiyama Yoshimura C3
13 Kitcho Arashiyama C3
14 Komichi B2
15 Shigetsu C3

Drinking & Nightlife
16 % Arabica C3

She was usurped in Kiyomori's affections by a fellow entertainer, Hotoke Gozen (who later deserted Kiyomori to join Giō at the temple). Enshrined in the main hall are five wooden statues: these are Giō, Hotoke Gozen, Kiyomori, and Giō's mother and sister (who were also nuns at the temple).

Giō-ji is also known for its autumn-foliage displays.

Arashiyama Monkey Park Iwatayama PARK

(嵐山モンキーパークいわたやま; Map p338; ☎075-872-0950; www.monkeypark.jp; 8 Genrokuzan-chō, Arashiyama, Ukyō-ku; adult/child ¥550/250; ⏲9am-5pm mid-Mar–Sep, to 4.30pm Oct–mid-Mar; 🚌Kyoto City bus 28 from Kyoto Station to Arashiyama-Tenryuji-mae, 🚆JR Sagano/San-in line to Saga-Arashiyama or Hankyū line to Arashiyama, change at Katsura) Though it is common to spot wild monkeys in the nearby mountains, here you can encounter them at a close distance and enjoy watching the playful creatures frolic about. It makes for an excellent photo opportunity, not only of the monkeys but also of the panoramic view over Kyoto. Refreshingly, it is the animals who are free to roam while the humans who feed them are caged in a box!

You enter the park near the south side of Tōgetsu-kyō, through the orange *torii* of Ichitani-jinja. Buy your tickets from the machine to the left of the shrine at the top of the steps. Just be warned: it's a steep climb up the hill to get to the monkeys. If it's a hot day, you're going to be drenched by the time you get to the spot where they gather.

Activities

★Camellia Tea Experience TEA CEREMONY

(茶道体験カメリア; Map p324; ☎075-525-3238; www.tea-kyoto.com; 349 Masuya-chō, Higashiyama-ku; per person ¥2000; 🚌Kyoto City bus 206 to Yasui) Camellia is a superb place to try a simple Japanese tea ceremony. It's located in a beautiful old Japanese house just off Ninen-zaka. The host speaks fluent English and explains the ceremony simply and clearly to the group, while managing to perform an elegant ceremony. The price includes a bowl of *matcha* and a sweet.

The 45-minute ceremonies are held on the hour from 10am to 5pm. Private tea ceremonies are held in a 100-year-old house with lovely gardens close to Ryōan-ji (p333) in northwest Kyoto (¥6000 per person).

Funaoka Onsen ONSEN

(船岡温泉; Map p332; 82-1 Minami-Funaoka-chō-Murasakino, Kita-ku; ¥430; ⏲3pm-1am Mon-Sat, from 8am Sun; 🚌Kyoto City bus 206 to Senbon Kuramaguchi) This old *sentō* (public bath) on Kuramaguchi-dōri is Kyoto's best. It boasts an outdoor bath, a sauna, a cypress-wood tub, an electric bath, a herbal bath and a few more for good measure. To get here, head west about 400m on Kuramaguchi-dōri from the Kuramaguchi and Horiikawa intersection. It's on the left, not far past Lawson convenience store. Look for the large rocks.

Be sure to check out the *ranma* (carved wooden panels) in the changing room. Carved during Japan's invasion of Manchuria, the panels offer insight into the prevailing mindset of that era. (Note the panels do contain some violent imagery, which may disturb some visitors.)

Shunkō-in MEDITATION

(春光院; Map p335; ☎075-462-5488; www.shunkoin.com; Myōshin-ji, 42 Myoshin-ji-chō, Hanazono, Ukyō-ku; class ¥3500; 🚆JR Sagano/San-in line to Hanazono) A subtemple of Myōshin-ji (p334), Shunkō-in is run by a monk who has studied abroad and made it his mission to introduce foreigners to his temple and Zen Buddhism. Regular introductory meditation classes are held in English; check the website for the schedule. You can also stay overnight in the accommodation (p346) here.

Tea ceremony (¥5500, 90 minutes) and Japanese calligraphy (¥3500, 90 minutes) courses are also on offer; check the website for schedules.

En TEA CEREMONY

(えん; Map p324; ☎080-3782-2706; www.teaceremonyen.com; 272 Matsubara-chō, Higashiyama-ku; per person ¥2500; 🚌Kyoto City bus 206 to Gion or Chionin-mae) A small teahouse near Gion where you can experience a Japanese tea ceremony with a minimum of fuss or expense. Check the website for times. English explanations are provided, and reservations recommended. It's a bit tricky to find: it's down a little alley off Higashiōji-dōri – look for the sign south of Tenkaippin Rāmen. Cash only.

Keifuku Randen Arashiyama Station Foot Onsen ONSEN

(Map p338; Keifuku Randen Arashiyama Station; ¥200; ⏲9am-8pm, to 6pm in winter; 🚌Keifuku Randen line to Arashiyama, 🚆JR Sagano/San-in line to Saga-Arashiyama or Hankyū line to Arashiyama, change at Katsura) Give your feet a soak after all the temple-hopping at this foot onsen located at the end of the Keifuku Arashiyama Randen Station platform. Price includes a souvenir towel.

KYOTO FOR CHILDREN

Great places for kids to run around include the Imperial Palace Park (p331), Kyoto Botanical Gardens (p333) and the Kamo-gawa riverbank. Museums that are likely to please all ages include the Kyoto Railway Museum (p314) and the Manga Museum (p318). And Kiyomizu-dera (p318), with its legends and hand-on experiences, is our pick for most fun temple.

Courses & Tours

Uzuki COOKING

(www.kyotouzuki.com; 2hr class per person from ¥5000) Learn how to cook some of the delightful foods you've tried in Kyoto with this highly recommended cooking class for groups of two to three people, conducted in a Japanese home. You will learn how to cook a variety of dishes (vegan courses are offered) and then sit down and enjoy the fruits of your labour.

The fee includes all ingredients. Reserve via website. The meeting point is the Kyoto University of Art and Design in the city's northeast.

Ninja Food Tours FOOD

(www.ninjafoodtours.com; 2hr tour from ¥7500) Runs enjoyable tours of Nishiki Market, a night food tour and a walking tour of Arashiyama.

Haru Cooking Class COOKING

(料理教室はる; Map p332; www.kyoto-cooking-class.com; 166-32 Shimogamo Miyazaki-chō, Sakyō-ku; per person from ¥6900;) Haru Cooking Class is a friendly one-man cooking school located in a private home a little bit north of Demachiyanagi. The school's teacher, Taro, speaks English and can teach both vegetarian (though fish stock may be used) and non-vegetarian cooking in classes that run for three to four hours. Reserve online.

Festivals & Events

Gion Matsuri PARADE

(Jul) Kyoto's most important festival, Gion Matsuri reaches a climax on 17 July with a parade of over 30 floats and a smaller parade on 24 July. On the three evenings preceding the 17th, people gather on Shijō-dōri dressed in beautiful *yukata* (light summer kimonos) to look at the floats and carouse from one street stall to the next.

Daimon-ji Gozan Okuribi CULTURAL

(16 Aug) This festival is celebrated as a means of bidding farewell to the souls of ancestors. Enormous fires, in the form of Chinese characters or other shapes, are lit on five mountains. The largest fire is burned on Daimon-ji-yama, just above Ginkaku-ji, in Northern Higashiyama. The fires start at 8pm and the best perspective is from the banks of the Kamo-gawa.

Kurama-no-hi Matsuri CULTURAL

(Kurama Fire Festival; 22 Oct) In perhaps Kyoto's most dramatic festival, the Kurama Fire Festival, huge flaming torches are carried through the streets of Kurama by men in loincloths on 22 October (the same day as the Jidai Matsuri). Note that trains to and from Kurama will be completely packed with passengers on the evening of the festival (we suggest going early and returning late).

Sleeping

A huge range of hotels and budget guesthouses are clustered around the Kyoto Station area, while the city's best ryokan (traditional Japanese inns) can be found downtown, spread out in Higashiyama, and in the hills of Arashiyama. Beware that Kyoto's accommodation can be booked out months in advance, especially during cherry-blossom season (late March to early April), Golden Week (29 April to 5 May), Gion Matsuri (mid-July), O-bon (mid-August) and the November autumn-foliage season. If you're truly stuck (or priced out), consider staying in Osaka (p368) or Ōtsu (p437) instead.

Kyoto Station & South Kyoto

★ Lower East 9 Hostel HOSTEL $

(ザ ロウワー イースト ナインホステル; Map p316; 075-644-9990; www.lowereastnine.com; 32 Minamikarasuma-chō, Higashi-kujō, Minami-ku; dm from ¥3800, tw ¥18,000; ; S Karasuma line to Kujō) LE9 is a design-savvy hostel in a quiet spot south of Kyoto Station. Dorms come with thoughtful details, while the private twin rooms are a little pricey for what you get. It's kitted out with mid-century furniture and has a cool downstairs cafe-bar and communal areas, so you mightn't want to leave. But if you do, you're right next to Kujō Station.

Mosaic Hostel HOSTEL $
(Map p316; ☎075-672-0511; www.mosaichostel.jp; 4-1 Kasuga-chō, Nishikuj, Minami-ku; dm/tw/q from ¥3000/7000/16,000; Karasuma line to Kujō, Kintetsu Kyoto line to Tōji) There's a lot to like about this well-run hostel close to Kyoto Station. Capsule-style dorms – a huge 30-bed, or eight-bed female only – come with thoughtful details like towel hooks, charging points and a privacy curtain, and there's a mix of private rooms. Staff are super friendly, the bar serves local craft beer and the rooftop terrace is perfect for a sundowner.

This is a great spot to meet other travellers.

Ryokan Shimizu RYOKAN $
(京の宿しみず; Map p321; ☎075-371-5538; www.kyoto-shimizu.net; 644 Kagiya-chō, Shichijō-dōri, Wakamiya-agaru, Shimogyō-ku; r per person from ¥5000; Kyoto Station) A short walk north of Kyoto Station, this friendly ryokan has a loyal following of foreign guests, and for good reason: it's clean and well run. Rooms are standard ryokan style and come with TV, private bathroom and toilet. Bicycle hire is available. Note there is a midnight curfew.

K's House Kyoto GUESTHOUSE $
(ケイズハウス京都; Map p321; ☎075-342-2444; www.kshouse.jp; 418 Naya-chō, Dotemachi-dōri, Shichijō-agaru, Shimogyō-ku; dm from ¥2400, s/d per person from ¥3800/3250; Kyoto Station) K's House is a large guesthouse with both private and dorm rooms, which are simple but adequate. The rooftop terrace, patio and attached bar-restaurant make this a very sociable spot and a good place to meet other travellers and share information. There's bicycle hire, internet terminals, free wi-fi and a guest-use kitchen. It's a short walk from Kyoto Station.

★Hotel Anteroom DESIGN HOTEL $$
(ホテルアンテルーム; Map p316; ☎075-681-5656; https://hotel-anteroom.com; 7 Aketa-chō, Higashi-kujō, Minami-ku; s/d from ¥5000/8000; Karasuma line to Kujō) If you're looking for traditional Japanese decor, Anteroom is not for you. This art-and-design hotel is as contemporary as it gets from its bright lobby gallery with changing exhibitions and whitewashed warehouse building to its artist concept rooms, including a dreamy Mika Ninagawa theme room. The terrace garden rooms (from ¥12,000) are the highlight with private Zen garden and a cypress wooden bathtub.

The breakfast spread is a real treat. It's a five-minute walk from Kujō Station and a 15-minute walk to Kyoto Station.

Ibis Styles Kyoto Station HOTEL $$
(イビススタイルズ　京都ステーション; Map p321; ☎075-693-8444; www.ibisstyles.com; 47 Higashikujō-Kamitonoda-chō, Minami-ku; s/d from ¥7800/10,000; Kyoto Station) While the bright, clean rooms may be a tight squeeze, they are packed with features at this great business hotel just outside the south entrance to Kyoto Station. The staff and management is extremely efficient, there's free wi-fi and laundry rooms, and breakfast is included, making this a fantastic option for the price.

Garnet Hotel HOTEL $$
(Map p316; ☎075-693-7600; 7-6 kitakarasuma-chō, Higashi-kujō, Minami-ku; d from ¥9000; Kyoto Station) Just a couple of blocks south of Kyoto Station, The Garnet Hotel offers a convenient location and good-value comfortable rooms that come with nifty gadgets, such as face steamers, leg massage boots and a smartphone. Friendly English-speaking staff go out of their way to help.

★Hotel Granvia Kyoto HOTEL $$$
(ホテルグランヴィア京都; Map p321; ☎075-344-8888; www.granviakyoto.com; Karasuma-dōri, Shiokōji-sagaru, Shimogyō-ku; d from ¥35,640; Kyoto Station) Imagine being able to step out of bed and straight into the *shinkansen* (bullet train). This is almost possible when you stay at the Hotel Granvia, which is located directly above Kyoto Station. The rooms are clean, spacious and elegant; some get a glimpse of the *shinkansen* on the tracks while others look out directly at Kyoto Tower.

Downtown Kyoto

Millennials CAPSULE HOTEL $
(Map p322; ☎075-212-6887; www.the-millennials-kyoto-jp.book.direct; Kawaramachi-dōri, Shijō-agaru, Nakagyō-ku; capsule from ¥3200; Keihan line to Gion-Shijō or Hankyū line to Kawaramachi) While you don't have to be a Millennial to stay here, it might help when it comes to the iPod-controlled 'rooms' at this modern take on a capsule hotel. Your iPod controls the lighting and bed tilt angle, while projector rooms turn your pull-down

door into a movie screen – just hook up your own device for streaming.

There's a cool industrial lobby/bar/lounge/co-working space, slick communal kitchen and free beer from 5.30pm to 6.30pm every evening.

★Royal Park Hotel The Kyoto HOTEL **$$**
(ロイヤルパークホテル ザ 京都; Map p322; ☎075-241-1111; www.rph-the.co.jp; Sanjō-dōri, Kawaramachi higashi-iru, Nakagyō-ku; s/tw/d from ¥12,000/15,000/15,000; ❄@📶; Ⓢ Tōzai line to Kyoto-Shiyakusho-mae, 🚇 Keihan line to Sanjō) Located on Sanjō-dōri, a stone's throw from the river, the Royal Park has a super-convenient location, with lots of shops and restaurants within easy walking distance. The hotel has a boutique-business feel, and rooms are larger than most in the city. The French bakery downstairs is a perfect stop for breakfast pastries.

Hotel Resol Kyoto Kawaramachi Sanjo HOTEL **$$**
(Map p322; ☎075-255-9269; www.resol-kyoto-k.com; 59-1 Daikoku-cho, Kawaramachi-dōri, Sanjō-sagaru, Nakagyō-ku; d from ¥10,000; 🚭❄@; 🚇 Keihan line to Gion-Shijō or Hankyū line to Kawaramachi) Perfectly placed for shopping, dining, nightlife and transport, Hotel Resol is a smart-looking boutique hotel offering great value. Rooms are compact (superiors offer more space) but well designed with Japanese touches, there's a small lounge with free coffee machine in the lobby, plus a laundry room. English-speaking staff are friendly and helpful.

Len Hostel Kyoto Kawaramachi HOSTEL **$$**
(Map p322; ☎075-361-1177; https://backpackersjapan.co.jp/kyotohostel; 709-3 Uematsu-chō, Kawaramachi-dōri, Shimogyō-ku; dm/tw/d from ¥2600/7000/8800; 🚭❄@📶; 🚇 Hankyū line to Kawaramachi or Keihan line to Kiyomizu-Gojō) Len has minimalist yet stylish mixed dorms, as well as a female-only dorm, and private rooms with shared bathroom. Rooms are on the small side, but who cares when you can hang out in the hip downstairs cafe-bar? The Kawaramachi-dōri location is convenient for Gion and downtown.

Hotel Vista Premio Kyoto HOTEL **$$**
(ホテルビスタプレミオ京都; Map p322; ☎075-256-5888; www.hotel-vista.jp; 457 Matsugae-chō, Kawaramachi-dōri, Rokkaku nishi-iru, Nakagyō-ku; s/d/tw from ¥16,000/20,000/22,000; ❄@📶; Ⓢ Tōzai line to Kyoto-Shiyakusho-mae) Tucked into a lane between two of Kyoto's main downtown shopping streets, this is a smart business hotel with excellent service. There are some nice Japanese design touches in the rooms, and the twin rooms are fairly roomy. You can find some good deals online and, overall, it's very good value for the money and a super-convenient location.

Citadines Karasuma-Gojō Kyoto HOTEL **$$**
(シタディーン京都 烏丸五条; Map p322; ☎075-352-8900; www.citadines.jp; 432 Matsuya-chō, Gojō-dōri, Karasuma higashi-iru, Shimogyō-ku; apt ¥15,000-45,000; ❄@📶; Ⓢ Karasuma line to Gojō) On Gojō-dōri, a bit south of the main downtown district but within easy walking distance of the Karasuma subway line (as well as the Keihan line), this serviced apartment-hotel is a great choice for those after self-catering rooms and a bit of space. Rooms are smart and bright with fully equipped kitchens, and there is a business centre and laundry room.

★Tawaraya RYOKAN **$$$**
(俵屋; Map p322; ☎075-211-5566; 278 Nakahakusan-chō, Fuyachō, Oike-sagaru, Nakagyō-ku; r per person ¥42,230-73,900; 🚭❄@📶; Ⓢ Tōzai line to Kyoto-Shiyakusho-mae or Karasuma-Oike) Operating for more than three centuries, Tawaraya is one of the finest places to stay in Japan. From the decor to the service to the food, everything is simply the best available, and this is reflected in the price. It's a very intimate, warm and personal place that has seen many loyal guests over the years, from Marlon Brando to Steve Jobs.

Rooms are kitted out in a mix of traditional Japanese-style and some mid-century decor, and the private wooden bathtubs have stunning garden views. It's centrally located within an easy walk of two subway stations and plenty of good restaurants. Book at least a few months in advance, much more if you plan to visit during peak periods.

★Hiiragiya Ryokan RYOKAN **$$$**
(柊家; Map p322; ☎075-221-1136; www.hiiragiya.co.jp; Nakahakusan-chō, Fuyachō, Aneyakōji-agaru, Nakagyō-ku; r per person incl 2 meals ¥34,000-90,000; 🚭❄@📶; Ⓢ Tōzai line to Kyoto-Shiyakusho-mae) This elegant ryokan has long been favoured by celebrities from around the world. Facilities and services are excellent and the location is hard to beat. Opt for the new wing if you prefer a polished sheen; alternatively, request an older room if you fancy some 'old Japan' *wabi-sabi* (imperfect beauty).

Room 14 played host to Japanese writer Yasunari Kawabata back in the day and is around 200 years old. You'll need to reserve months in advance and reservation is preferred by email.

Ritz-Carlton Kyoto HOTEL $$$
(ザ・リッツ・カールトン京都; Map p328; ☎075-746-5555; www.ritzcarlton.com; 543 Hokoden-chō, Nijō-Ōhashi-hotori, Nakagyō-ku; r ¥65,000-210,000; ; S Tōzai line to Kyoto-Shiyakusho-mae, Keihan line to Sanjō or Jingū-Marutamachi) The Ritz-Carlton is an oasis of luxury that commands some of the best views of any hotel in the city – it's located on the banks of the Kamo-gawa and huge windows in the east-facing rooms take in the whole expanse of the Higashiyama Mountains. The rooms are superbly designed and supremely comfortable, with plenty of Japanese touches.

Yoshikawa RYOKAN $$$
(吉川; Map p322; ☎075-221-5544; www.kyoto-yoshikawa.co.jp; 135 Matsushita-chō, Tominokōji, Oike-sagaru, Nakagyō-ku; s/d from ¥50,000/54,000; ; S Tōzai or Karasuma lines to Karasuma-Oike or Kyoto-Shiyakusho-mae) Located in the heart of downtown, within easy walking distance of two subway stations and the entire dining and nightlife district, this superb ryokan has beautiful rooms and a stunning garden. The ryokan is famous for its attached tempura restaurant (p349) and its meals are of a high standard. All rooms have private bathrooms with wooden tubs and toilets.

Southern Higashiyama

Book + Bed Hostel HOSTEL $
(Map p324; www.bookandbedtokyo.com/en/kyoto; 9th fl, Kamogawa Bldg, 200 Nakano-chō, Nishi-iru, Higashiyama-ku; bed from ¥4700; ; Keihan line to Gion-Shijō) With a cracking location and a 'novel' idea, this hostel is a unique option for those looking for budget accommodation in the heart of Gion. As expected, books dominate the decor; they hang from the ceiling and capsule-style beds nestle in among packed bookshelves. One bed comes with a river view, and views from the common area take in the Higashiyama.

Gojō Guest House GUESTHOUSE $
(五条ゲストハウス; Map p324; ☎075-525-2299; www.gojo-guest-house.com; 3-396-2 Gojōbashi higashi, Higashiyama-ku; dm/tw/tr from ¥2000/5500/9000; ; Keihan line to Kiyomizu-Gojō) This is a fine budget guesthouse in an old wooden Japanese house, which makes the place feel more like a ryokan than your average guesthouse. There are male and female dorms, as well as private rooms, and the dining area and cafe is a good place to meet other travellers. The staff speak English and can help with travel advice.

Kyoto Granbell Hotel HOTEL $$
(Map p324; ☎075-277-7330; www.granbellhotel.jp/kyoto; 27 Yamato-cho, Yamatooji-dori, Shigo-sagaru, Higashiyama-ku; d from ¥18,000; ; Keihan line to Gion-Shijō) Tucked in a quiet part of Gion, the Granbell comes with a knockout location, standout service and a lot of style. Snug rooms (the Japanese-style feel a bit more spacious) seamlessly blend traditional and modern design, and come with a smartphone. There's a free coffee machine in the hip lobby/lounge bar, and a lovely communal bath.

★**Four Seasons** HOTEL $$$
(Map p324; ☎075-541-8288; www.fourseasons.com/kyoto; 445-3 Maekawa-chō, Myohoin, Higashiyama-ku; r from ¥75,000; ; Keihan line to Shichijō) Extravagant and contemporary yet restrained and traditional, Four Seasons is an impressive new luxury hotel in the Higashiyama sightseeing district. The long bamboo-lined entrance brings you to a vast airy lobby with huge floor-to-ceiling windows looking out over the 800-year-old koi-filled pond and stunning gardens. The elegant rooms feature dark-wood floors, iPads, huge TVs, coffee-pod machines and marble bathrooms.

★**Shiraume Ryokan** RYOKAN $$$
(白梅; Map p324; ☎075-561-1459; www.shiraume-kyoto.jp; Gion Shimbashi, Shirakawa hotori, Shijōnawate-agaru higashi-iru, Higashiyama-ku; r per person incl 2 meals from ¥34,000; ; Keihan line to Gion-Shijō) Looking out over the Shirakawa Canal in Shimbashi, a lovely street in Gion, this ryokan offers excellent location, atmosphere and service. The decor is traditional with a small inner garden, and all five rooms have their own private bathroom with nice wooden bathtubs. This is a great spot to sample the Japanese ryokan experience. Note: there is no room-only option.

★**Hyatt Regency Kyoto** HOTEL $$$
(ハイアットリージェンシー京都; Map p324; ☎075-541-1234; www.kyoto.regency.hyatt.com; 644-2 Sanjūsangendō-mawari, Higashiyama-ku; r from ¥34,000; ; Keihan line to

WORTH A TRIP

HOZU-GAWA RIVER TRIP

The **Hozu-gawa river trip** (0771-22-5846; www.hozugawakudari.jp; Hozu-chō, Kameoka-shi; adult/child 4-12yr ¥4100/2700; JR Sagano/San-in line from Kyoto Station to Kameoka) is a great way to enjoy the beauty of Kyoto's western mountains without any strain on the legs. With long bamboo poles, boatmen steer flat-bottom boats down the Hozu-gawa from Kameoka, 30km west of Kyoto Station, through steep, forested mountain canyons, before arriving at Arashiyama.

Between 10 March and 30 November there are seven trips daily leaving on the hour from 9am to 2pm, with the last trip at 3.30pm. During winter the number of trips is reduced to four per day (10am, 11.30am, 1pm and 2.30pm) and the boats are heated.

The ride lasts two hours and covers 16km through occasional sections of choppy water – a scenic jaunt with minimal danger. The scenery is especially breathtaking during cherry-blossom season in April and maple-foliage season in autumn.

The boats depart from a dock that is eight minutes' walk from Kameoka Station. Kameoka is accessible by rail from Kyoto Station or Nijō Station on the JR Sagano (San-in) line. The Kyoto Tourist Information Center (p361) provides an English-language leaflet and timetable for rail connections. The fare from Kyoto to Kameoka is ¥410 one way by regular train (don't spend the extra for the express; it makes little difference in travel time).

Shichijō) Arguably one of Kyoto's best hotels, the Hyatt Regency sits at the southern end of the Southern Higashiyama sightseeing district. Elegant and contemporary rooms feature kimono tapestry walls and paper lanterns, and come packed with features such as a coffee-pod machine and tablet for ordering room service. Staff are extremely helpful, and the on-site restaurants and Tōzan Bar (p356) are excellent.

There is a 15-minute *maiko* (apprentice geisha) performance from 6.15pm each night in the lobby.

★ **Seikōrō** RYOKAN $$$
(晴鴨楼; Map p324; 075-561-1171; www.seikoro.com; 467 Nishi Tachibana-chō, 3 chō-me, Toiyamachi-dōri, Gojō-sagaru, Higashiyama-ku; r per person from ¥17,000; ; Keihan line to Kiyomizu-Gojō) The Seikōrō is a classic ryokan with a grandly decorated and homey lobby. It's spacious, with excellent, comfortable rooms, attentive service and a fairly convenient midtown location. Several rooms look over gardens and all have private bathrooms featuring wooden bathtubs.

Old Kyoto RENTAL HOUSE $$$
(Map p324; 075-533-7775; www.oldkyoto.com; 563-12 Komatsu-chō, Higashiyama-ku; per night from ¥32,000; ; Kyoto City bus 206 to Higashiyama-Yasui, Keihan line to Gion-Shijō) The Old Kyoto group manage three beautiful traditional Japanese houses that stand right on the edge of Gion and make for the perfect getaway for those seeking a more local experience. The Gion House, Amber House and Indigo House are all kitted out stylishly in Japanese meets mid-century decor and design, and can accommodate up to four people. Minimum stay five nights.

Step outside the door of each property and a few minutes' walk will bring you to Gion's most atmospheric lanes. The houses come with everything you need, including a phone with a local SIM.

Gion Hatanaka RYOKAN $$$
(祇園畑中; Map p324; 075-541-5315; www.thehatanaka.co.jp; 505 Gion-machi, Minami-gawa, Higashiyama-ku; r per person from ¥22,000; ; Kyoto City bus 206 to Higashiyama-Yasui) Gion Hatanaka is a fine ryokan right in the heart of the Southern Higashiyama sightseeing district, less than a minute's walk from Yasaka-jinja (p322). Despite being fairly large, this 21-room place manages to retain an intimate and private feeling. In addition to bathtubs in each room, there is a huge wooden communal bath. The rooms are clean, well designed and relaxing.

It also offers regularly scheduled geisha entertainment (p358) that nonguests are welcome to join. Note: there is a midnight curfew but guests can enter later if prearranged.

Motonago RYOKAN $$$
(旅館元奈古; Map p324; 075-561-2087; www.motonago.com; 511 Washio-chō, Kōdaiji-michi, Higashiyama-ku; r per person from ¥12,000; ;

Kyoto City bus 206 to Gion) This ryokan may have the best location of any in the city and it hits all the right notes for one in this class: classic Japanese decor, friendly English-speaking staff, nice wooden communal bathtubs and a few small Japanese gardens. There are 12 rooms; some have private bathroom, and one room has twin Western beds for those not comfortable on a futon.

Northern Higashiyama

Roku Roku HOSTEL $

(ろくろく; Map p328; 075-771-6969; www.rokuroku.kyoto.jp; 28-1 Nishiteranomae-chō, Shishigatani, Sakyō-ku; dm/tw per person ¥2500/4300; Kyoto City bus 5 to Shinnyodo-mae or 17 to Kinrinshako-mae) A great choice for budget digs, this modern hostel is within walking distance of the Path of Philosophy and many main temples. Dorms are a little cramped but have in-room bathrooms, while twin rooms come with a small tatami-mat sitting area. It has free laundry facilities and bicycle rental, plus a traditional house nearby with a lounge and garden views to relax in.

★ **Westin Miyako Kyoto** HOTEL $$$

(ウェスティン都ホテル京都; Map p328; 075-771-7111; www.miyakohotels.ne.jp/westinkyoto; Keage, Sanjō-dōri, Higashiyama-ku; d from ¥22,500; S Tōzai line to Keage, exit 2) Overlooking the Higashiyama sightseeing district (meaning it's one of the best locations for sightseeing in Kyoto), this *grande dame* of Kyoto hotels occupies a commanding position. Rooms on the north side have great views over the city to the Kitayama mountains. There is a fitness centre with a swimming pool (extra charge), as well as a private garden and walking trail.

The hotel even has its own ryokan section (rooms from ¥25,000) for those who want to try staying in a ryokan without giving up the convenience of a hotel. Rooms underwent a refurbishment finished in 2020.

Koto Inn RENTAL HOUSE $$$

(古都イン; Map p324; koto.inn@gmail.com; 373 Horiike-chō, Higashiyama-ku; per night for 2/3/4 people US$215/255/285; S Tōzai line to Higashiyama) Conveniently located near the Higashiyama sightseeing district in a lovely canal setting, this immaculate vacation rental is good for families, couples and groups who want a bit of privacy. It's got everything you need and is decorated with lovely Japanese antiques. While the building is traditionally Japanese, all the facilities are fully modernised. There's a two-night minimum stay.

Kyoto Garden Ryokan Yachiyo RYOKAN $$$

(旅館八千代; Map p328; 075-771-4148; www.ryokan-yachiyo.com; 34 Fukuchi-chō, Nanzen-ji, Sakyō-ku; r per person ¥10,000-50,000; S Tōzai line to Keage) Located just down the street from Nanzen-ji (p325), this beautiful ryokan has a choice of traditional or modern rooms, all with private bathroom and TV. Some rooms look out over private gardens and four rooms come with an open-air wooden bath. English-speaking staff are available.

Imperial Palace & Around

Bird Hostel HOSTEL $

(Map p332; 075-744-1875; www.birdhostel.com; 190 Joshinyo-chō, Marutamachi-dōri, Nagakyō-ku; dm/d/f incl breakfast from ¥2900/6800/16,000; S Karasuma line to Marutamachi) This cool, spotless and well-run hostel is just a short hop from the Imperial Palace Park and comes with a range of dorms, including a female-only option. Dorms are equipped with everything you need, there are a few compact double rooms and a family room with leafy views. It's rounded out with bicycle rental, a hip cafe-lounge area and laundry facilities.

Noku Kyoto BOUTIQUE HOTEL $$

(ノク京都; Map p332; 075-211-0222; www.nokuroxy.com; 205-1 Okura-cho, Karasuma-dōri, Maratumachi-sagaru, Nakagyō-ku; r ¥18,000-38,000; S Karasuma line to Marutamachi) Noku (also known as Noku Roxy) is a stylish boutique hotel set over six floors within sight of the Imperial Palace Park and located next to Marutamachi Station. The minimalist elegant rooms are all blonde wood with splashes of colour provided in the bedhead artwork. Some rooms have park views, and there is a basement bar and restaurant.

Palace Side Hotel HOTEL $$

(ザ・パレスサイドホテル; Map p332; 075-415-8887; www.palacesidehotel.co.jp; Okakuen-chō, Karasuma-dōri, Shimotachiuri-agaru, Kamigyō-ku; s/d from ¥6300/10,200; S Karasuma line to Marutamachi) Overlooking the Imperial Palace Park, this good-value hotel is looking a little dated but has a lot going for it, starting with friendly

English-speaking staff, great service, washing machines, an on-site restaurant and a communal guest-use kitchen. Free one-hour Japanese lessons are held in the evenings a couple of times a month.

Northwest Kyoto

Shunkō-in TEMPLE LODGE $

(春光院; Map p335; ☎075-462-5488; www.shunkoin.com; 42 Myōshinji-chō, Hanazono, Ukyō-ku; s ¥8800, d/tr per person ¥7500/6000; ; JR Sagano/San-in line to Hanazono) This is a *shukubō* (temple lodging) at a subtemple in Myōshin-ji (p334). It's very comfortable, with wi-fi and free bicycle hire, and the main priest here speaks fluent English. For an extra ¥1500 you can try Zen meditation and go on a guided tour of the temple. Being in the temple at night is a very special experience.

★**Mosaic Machiya Hostel** HOSTEL $$

(Map p332; ☎075-466-0510; www.mosaichostel.jp/mosaic-machiya-kamishichiken; 702 Shinsei-chō, Kamigyō-ku; tw/tr from ¥8000/15,000; ; Kyoto bus 50 to Kamishichiken) As the name suggests, this intimate hostel is set in a restored *machiya* (traditional Japanese townhouse) on an atmospheric street in the old geisha district of Kamishichiken near Kitano Tenman-gū. It offers five simple Japanese-style rooms and there's a lovely private bath and courtyard garden. Mingle with the friendly staff and other travellers in the small lobby bar.

It has another hostel (p341) close to Kyoto Station.

Arashiyama & Sagano

★**Japaning Hotel Liv Ranrokaku Kyoto** HOTEL $$

(ジャパニングホテル リヴ 嵐楼閣; Map p338; 54-2 Arashiyama Nakaoshita-chō, Nishikyō-ku; r ¥16,000-30,000; ; Kyoto City bus 28 from Kyoto Station to Arashiyama-Tenryuji-mae, JR Sagano/San-in line to Saga-Arashiyama or Hankyū line to Arashiyama, change at Katsura) It's not easy to find accommodation with a great location and spacious rooms for anything less than top-dollar in Arashiyama, so thankfully there is this hotel. Some rooms have separate tatami mat areas and the riverside rooms have sensational views. The on-site baths are perfect after a day on your feet.

Not much English is spoken but friendly staff go out of their way to help.

★**Hoshinoya Kyoto** RYOKAN $$$

(星のや京都; Map p338; ☎075-871-0001; www.hoshinoya.com/kyoto/en; 11-2 Arashiyama Genrokuzan-chō, Nishikyō-ku; r per person from ¥81,000; ; Kyoto City bus 28 from Kyoto Station to Arashiyama-Tenryuji-mae, JR Sagano/San-in line to Saga-Arashiyama or Hankyū line to Arashiyama, change at Katsura) Sitting in a secluded area on the south bank of the Hozu-gawa in Arashiyama (upstream from the main sightseeing district), this modern take on the classic Japanese inn is quickly becoming a favourite of well-heeled visitors to Kyoto in search of privacy and a unique experience. Rooms feature incredible views of the river and the surrounding mountains.

The best part is the approach: you'll be chauffeured by a private boat from a dock near Togetsu-kyō bridge to the inn (note that on days following heavy rains, you'll have to go by car instead). This is easily one of the most unique places to stay in Kyoto. If you tire of just relaxing with the views, it also offers meditation classes as well as incense ceremonies.

Arashiyama Benkei RYOKAN $$$

(嵐山辨慶旅館; Map p338; ☎075-872-3355; www.benkei.biz; 34 Susukinobaba-chō, Saga Tenryū-ji, Ukyō-ku; r per person incl meals from ¥28,000; ; Kyoto City Bus 28 from Kyoto Station to Arashiyama-Tenryuji-mae, JR Sagano/San-in line to Saga-Arashiyama or Hankyū line to Arashiyama, change at Katsura) This elegant ryokan, with kind and friendly service, has a pleasant riverside location and serves wonderful *kaiseki* (Japanese haute cuisine). It has three riverside rooms; one comes with a private bathroom, while other rooms have calming garden views. The open-air onsen is perfect for soaking in after walking around Arashiyama's temples.

Eating

Kyoto Station & South Kyoto

There are lots of choices on the 10th floor of Kyoto Station. Try **Kyoto Rāmen Kōji** (京都拉麺小路; Map p321; ☎075-361-4401; www.kyoto-ramen-koji.com; 10F Kyoto Station Bldg, Karasuma-dōri, Shiokōji-sagaru, Shimogyō-ku; ramen ¥840-1250; 11am-10pm; Kyoto Station), a collection of nine ramen restaurants. Buy tickets from the machines (in English, with pictures) before queuing.

Eat Paradise (イートパラダイス; Map p321; ☎075-352-1111; 10F Kyoto Station Bldg,

Karasuma-dōri, Shiokōji-sagaru, Shimogyō-ku; 11am-10pm; Kyoto Station) has more choices, including **Tonkatsu Wako** for *tonkatsu* (deep-fried breaded pork cutlet), **Tenichi** for sublime tempura, and **Wakuden** for approachable *kaiseki*.

Take the west escalators from the main concourse to get here – Eat Paradise is in front of you when you get to the 10th floor. Alternatively, take the north elevator in the JR Isetan department store to the 11th floor. Note that the restaurants here can be crowded, especially at lunchtimes on weekends.

There are plenty more eateries scattered all around Kyoto Station.

★ Vegans Cafe & Restaurant VEGAN $

(Map p316; 075-643-3922; www.veganscafe.com; 4-88 Nishiura-chō, Fukakusa, Fushimi-ku; meals ¥540-2500; 11.30am-5pm Thu-Tue, to 9pm Sat; ; Keihan line to Fujinomori) Who needs meat and dairy when food can taste this good without it? This light-filled cafe is a haven for vegans and vegetarians with a range of meals from healthy salad, rice and miso sets, to huge bowls of soy-milk miso ramen and deep-fried tofu pizza. There's organic beer, wine and coffee, too. It's a convenient detour when sightseeing around Fushimi-Inari.

Downtown Kyoto

Finding a good place to eat in Downtown Kyoto can be confusing (there are almost *too many* places to choose from). If you want a lot of choice in a small area, hit one of the *resutoran-gai* (restaurant floors) at Takashimaya or Daimaru.

★ Honke Owariya NOODLES $

(本家尾張屋; Map p322; 075-231-3446; www.honke-owariya.co.jp; 322 Kurumaya-chō, Nijō, Nakagyō-ku; dishes from ¥810; 11am-7pm; Karasuma or Tōzai lines to Karasuma-Oike) Set in an old sweets shop in a traditional Japanese building on a quiet downtown street, this is where locals come for excellent soba (buckwheat-noodle) dishes. The highly recommended house speciality, *hourai soba* (¥2160), comes with a stack of five small plates of soba with a selection of toppings, including shiitake mushrooms, shrimp tempura, thin slices of omelette and sesame seeds.

KYOTO CUISINE

Many of Kyoto's restaurants focus on local specialities, known as *kyō-ryōri* (Kyoto cuisine). In this style of cooking, the preparation of dishes makes ingenious use of fresh seasonal vegetables and emphasises subtle flavours, revealing the natural taste of the ingredients. *Kyō-ryōri* is selected according to the mood and hues of the ever-changing seasons, and the presentation and atmosphere in which it's enjoyed are as important as the flavour.

Different types of *kyō-ryōri* include *kaiseki* (Japanese haute cuisine), *obanzai-ryōri* (Kyoto home-style cooking) and *shōjin-ryōri* (Buddhist vegetarian cuisine). Kyoto is famed for its tofu, a result of the city's excellent water and large population of (theoretically) vegetarian Buddhist monks. Two dishes to look for: *yudōfu* (tofu cooked in a pot; especially good in winter) and *yuba* (the skin that forms when making tofu, and considered a delicacy).

Kyo-gashi is Kyoto's brand of *wagashi* (Japanese sweets).

★ Café Bibliotec Hello! CAFE $

(カフェビブリオティックハロー！; Map p332; 075-231-8625; 650 Seimei-chō, Nijō-dōri, Yanaginobanba higashi-iru, Nakagyō-ku; meals from ¥850; 11.30am-midnight; ; Tōzai line to Kyoto-Shiyakusho-mae) As the name suggests, books line the walls of this cool cafe located in a converted *machiya* attracting a mix of locals and tourists. It's a great place to relax with a book or to tap away at your laptop over a coffee (¥450) or light lunch. Look for the huge banana plants out the front.

There's a great little bakery attached where you can grab tasty takeaway pastries and breads (Tuesday to Sunday 11.30am to 11pm).

Saryo Suisen SWEETS, CAFE $

(茶寮翠泉; Map p322; 075-278-0111; 521 Takatsuji-chō, Shimogyō-ku; matcha parfait ¥1480; 10.30am-6pm; Karasuma line to Shijō) There are countless places in Kyoto to be restrained with your *matcha* and sweets...this teahouse isn't one of them. Roll up your sleeves, loosen your belt and get ready for a sugar high – it's all about the *matcha* parfaits here, piled as high as Kyoto Tower with sponge cake, *matcha* ice cream, sweet red-bean paste, *dango* (soft rice-flour balls) and more.

DON'T MISS

TEA & SWEETS

Kyo-gashi is Kyoto's brand of *wagashi* (Japanese sweets), which have a long association with the tea ceremony. The sweets are served alongside *matcha* to temper the bitterness of the tea. Two famous places to try tea and *kyo-gashi* are Kagizen Yoshifusa (p350) in Gion or and Toraya Karyō Kyoto Ichijō (p352) near the Imperial Palace Park.

Gyoza Chao Chao Sanjo-Kiyamachi DUMPLINGS $
(Map p322; ☎075-251-0056; Kiyamachi-dōri, Sanjō-sagaru, Nakagyō-ku; 3 pieces from ¥300; ⏲5pm-2am Mon-Fri, from 2pm Sat, 2pm-midnight Sun; Ⓢ Tōzai line to Kyoto-Shiyakusho-mae) In the heart of Kyoto's bar scene, it's no wonder Chao Chao draws long queues for its crispy *gyōza* (dumplings) – great as a pre-drink dinner, even better as a late-night drunken snack. Grab a counter seat or squish beside a table and try to stop chao chao chowing down plates of shrimp, boiled ginger, garlic kimchi or pork *gyōza*. Cash only.

Vegetarians will want to head to their other **branch** (Map p322; ☎075-353-2626; 312-1 Junpu-chō, Shijō-dōri, Kawaramachi higashi-iru, Shimogyo-ku; 3 pieces from ¥300; ⏲11.30am-3pm & 5-11pm Mon-Fri, 11.30am-11pm Sat & Sun; ✎; Ⓡ Hankyū line to Kawaramachi) at Shijo-Kawaramachi for meat-free options.

Biotei VEGETARIAN $
(びお亭; Map p322; ☎075-255-0086; 2nd fl, M&I Bldg, 28 Umetada-chō, Sanjō-dōri, Higashinotōin nishi-iru, Nakagyō-ku; lunch/dinner sets from ¥890/1385; ⏲11.30am-2pm Tue-Fri, 5-8.30pm Tue, Wed, Fri & Sat; ✎; Ⓢ Tōzai or Karasuma lines to Karasuma-Oike) Located diagonally across from Nakagyō post office, this is a favourite of Kyoto vegetarians, serving à la carte and daily sets with dishes such as deep-fried crumbed tofu and black seaweed salad with rice, miso and pickles. The seating is rather cramped but the food is excellent, beautifully presented and carefully made from quality ingredients.

It's on the corner. Go up the metal spiral staircase.

Ippūdō RAMEN $
(一風堂; Map p322; ☎075-213-8800; Higashinotō-in, Nishikikōji higashi-iru, Nakagyō-ku; ramen from ¥790; ⏲11am-3am, to 2am Sun; Ⓢ Karasuma line to Shijō) There's a reason that there's usually a line outside this place: the ramen is fantastic and the bite-sized *gyōza* are to die for. The *gyōza* set meal (from ¥1440) is great value. While it's not on the menu, you can request a vegetarian option.

Sushi no Musashi SUSHI $
(寿しのむさし; Map p322; ☎075-222-0634; www.sushinomusashi.com; Kawaramachi-dōri, Sanjō-agaru, Nakagyō-ku; plates from ¥146; ⏲11am-10pm; Ⓢ Tōzai line to Kyoto-Shiyakusho-mae, Ⓡ Keihan line to Sanjō) If you've never tried a *kaiten-sushi* (conveyor-belt sushi restaurant), don't miss this place – most dishes are a mere ¥146. Not the best sushi in the world, but it's cheap, reliable and fun. It's also easy to eat here: you just grab what you want off the conveyor belt. If you don't see what you want, there's an English menu to order from.

Musashi is just outside the entrance to the Sanjō covered arcade; look for the miniature sushi conveyor belt in the window.

★Giro Giro Hitoshina KAISEKI $$
(Map p322; ☎075-343-7070; 420-7 Nanba-chō, Nishi-kiyamachi-dōri, Matsubara-sagaru, Shimogyō-ku; kaiseki ¥4100; ⏲5.30pm-midnight; Ⓡ Hankyū line to Kawaramachi or Keihan line to Kiyomizu-Gojō) Giro Giro takes traditional *kaiseki* and strips any formality so you're left with great food but in a boisterous atmosphere and with thousands more yen in your pocket. In a quiet lane near Kiyamachi-dōri, things liven up inside with patrons sitting at the counter around the open kitchen chatting with chefs preparing inventive dishes.

The seasonal menu consists of eight courses. There are upstairs tables, too, but if you want a counter seat, book well in advance; for a Friday or Saturday night you'll need to allow a couple of months in advance. Cash only.

★Menami JAPANESE $$
(めなみ; Map p322; ☎075-231-1095; www.menami.jp; Kiyamachi-dōri, Sanjō-agaru, Nakagyō-ku; dishes ¥400-1600; ⏲5-11pm Mon-Sat; Ⓢ Tōzai line to Kyoto-Shiyakusho-mae, Ⓡ Keihan line to Sanjō) This welcoming neighbourhood favourite specialises in *obanzai-ryōri* – a type of home-style cooking using seasonal ingredients – done creatively and served as tapas-size plates. Don't miss the delicious spring rolls wrapped with *yuba* (tofu skin; 生ゆば春巻). Try to book a counter seat where you can eye off bowls filled with dishes to choose from while watching the chefs in action.

Otherwise, start with the *obanzai* taster plate (¥1200) and go from there. Book ahead.

Kyōgoku Kane-yo JAPANESE $$
(京極かねよ; Map p322; ☎075-221-0669; 456 Matsugaechō, Rokkaku, Shinkyōgoku higashi-iru, Nakagyō-ku; eel over rice from ¥2500; ⏰11.30am-9pm; Ⓢ Tōzai line to Kyoto-Shiyakusho-mae) This popular restaurant is a good place to try *unagi* (eel). You can choose to either sit downstairs with a nice view of the waterfall, or upstairs on the tatami. Look for the wooden facade.

Tagoto Honten KAISEKI $$
(田ごと本店; Map p322; ☎075-221-1811; www.kyoto-tagoto.co.jp; 34 Otabi-chō, Shijō-dōri, Kawaramachi nishi-iru, Nakagyō-ku; lunch/dinner from ¥1850/6000; ⏰11.30am-3pm & 4.30-9pm; 🚉 Keihan line to Shijō or Hankyū line to Kawaramachi) Across from Takashimaya department store, this long-standing Kyoto restaurant serves approachable *kaiseki* in a variety of rooms, both private and common. Its lunchtime *kiku* set (¥1850) includes some sashimi, tempura and a variety of other nibblies. You must reserve in advance for the evening *kaiseki*. Otherwise try the cheaper mini *kaiseki* lunch (¥3700).

Ganko SUSHI $$
(がんこ; Map p322; ☎075-255-1128; www.gankofood.co.jp; 101 Nakajima-chō, Sanjō-dōri, Kawaramachi higashi-iru, Nakagyō-ku; meals ¥645-4320; ⏰11am-11pm; 📶; Ⓢ Tōzai line to Kyoto-Shiyakusho-mae or Sanjō Keihan, 🚉 Keihan line to Sanjō) This giant four-storey dining hall is part of Kansai's biggest sushi chain. The ground floor is the sushi area, with a long sushi counter and plenty of tables. It's very popular with both tourists and locals. There's an extensive English/picture menu and good-value set meals. It may have the most plastic-looking food models of any restaurant window in Kyoto. Near Sanjō-Ōhashi bridge.

★ **Roan Kikunoi** KAISEKI $$$
(露庵菊乃井; Map p322; ☎075-361-5580; www.kikunoi.jp; 118 Saito-chō, Kiyamachi-dōri, Shijō-sagaru, Shimogyō-ku; lunch/dinner from ¥7000/13,000; ⏰11.30am-1.30pm & 5-8.30pm Thu-Tue; 🚉 Hankyū line to Kawaramachi or Keihan line to Gion-Shijō) Roan Kikunoi is a fantastic place to experience the wonders of *kaiseki*. It's a lovely intimate space located right downtown. The chef takes an experimental and creative approach and the results are a wonder for the eyes and palate. Highly recommended. Reserve through your hotel or ryokan or at least a few days in advance.

★ **Yoshikawa** TEMPURA $$$
(吉川; Map p322; ☎075-221-5544; www.kyoto-yoshikawa.co.jp; 135 Matsushita-chō, Tominokōji, Oike-sagaru, Nakagyō-ku; lunch ¥3000-25,000, dinner ¥8000-25,000; ⏰11am-1.45pm & 5-8pm; Ⓢ Tōzai line to Karasuma-Oike or Kyoto-Shiyakusho-mae) This is the place to go for delectable tempura with a daily changing menu. Attached to the Yoshikawa ryokan (p343), it offers table seating, but it's much more interesting to sit and eat around the small intimate counter and observe the chefs at work. Reservation is required for the private tatami room, and counter bar for dinner. Note: counter bar is closed Sunday.

Kiyamachi Sakuragawa KAISEKI $$$
(木屋町　櫻川; Map p322; ☎075-255-4477; Kiyamachi-dōri, Nijō-sagaru, Nakagyō-ku; lunch/dinner sets from ¥7000/16,000; ⏰noon-2pm & 6-10pm Mon-Sat; Ⓢ Tōzai line to Kyoto-Shiyakusho-mae) This elegant restaurant on a scenic stretch of Kiyamachi-dōri is an excellent place to try *kaiseki*. The modest but fully satisfying food is beautifully presented and it's a joy to watch the chef in action. The warmth of the reception adds to the quality of the food. Reservations are recommended and smart casual is the way to go here.

Mishima-tei JAPANESE $$$
(三嶋亭; Map p322; ☎075-221-0003; 405 Sakurano-chō, Teramachi-dōri, Sanjō-sagaru, Nakagyō-ku; sukiyaki lunch/dinner from ¥7720/14,850; ⏰11.30am-10.30pm Thu-Tue; Ⓢ Tōzai line to Kyoto-Shiyakusho-mae) Mishima-tei, around since 1873, is a good place to sample sukiyaki (thin slices of beef cooked in sake, soy and vinegar broth, and dipped in raw egg) as the quality of the meat is very high, which is hardly surprising when there is a butcher downstairs. It's at the intersection of the Sanjō and Teramachi covered arcades.

Southern Higashiyama

Offerings here fall into two categories: tourist eateries near the temples and refined places in Gion.

★ **Omen Kodai-ji** NOODLES $
(おめん　高台寺店; Map p324; ☎075-541-5007; 362 Masuya-chō, Kōdaiji-dōri, Shimokawara higashi-iru, Higashiyama-ku; noodles from ¥1150; ⏰11am-9pm; 🚌 Kyoto City bus 206 to

Higashiyama-Yasui) Housed in a remodelled Japanese building with a light, airy feeling, this branch of Kyoto's famed Omen noodle chain is the best place to stop while exploring the Southern Higashiyama district. Upstairs has fine views over the area. The signature udon (thick, white wheat noodles) served in broth with a selection of fresh vegetables is delicious.

★Kagizen Yoshifusa TEAHOUSE **$**
(鍵善良房; Map p324; ☎075-561-1818; www.kagizen.co.jp; 264 Gion machi, Kita-gawa, Higashiyama-ku; kuzukiri ¥1080, tea & sweet ¥880; ⏲9.30am-6pm, closed Mon; Hankyū line to Kawaramachi, Keihan line to Gion-Shijō) This Gion institution is one of Kyoto's oldest and best-known *okashi-ya* (sweet shops). It sells a variety of traditional sweets and has a lovely tearoom out the back where you can sample cold *kuzukiri* (transparent arrowroot noodles) served with a *kuro-mitsu* (sweet black sugar) dipping sauce, or just a nice cup of *matcha* and a sweet.

Chidoritei SUSHI **$**
(千登利亭; Map p324; ☎075-561-1907; 203 Rokken-cho, Donguri-dori, Yamato-oji Nishi-iru, Higashiyama-ku; sushi sets ¥600-2200; ⏲11am-8pm, closed Thu; Keihan line to Gion-Shijō) Family owned Chidoritei is a snug little sushi restaurant tucked away in the backstreets of Gion away from the bustle. It's a great place to try delicious traditional Kyoto *saba-zushi* – mackerel hand pressed into lightly vinegared rice and wrapped in *konbu* (a type of seaweed). In summer, the speciality here is conger-eel sushi.

Gion Yuki IZAKAYA **$**
(遊亀祇園店; Map p324; ☎075-525-2666; 111-1 Tominaga-chō, Higashiyama-ku; dishes ¥380-800; ⏲5-10pm Mon-Fri, to midnight Sat; Keihan line to Gion-Shijō) Squeeze in at the counter for front-row seats to watch the chefs do their thing at this lively *izakaya* (Japanese pub-eatery). Seafood is big on the menu, from sashimi plates and grilled fish to tasty tempura, and sake is the drink of choice – no surprise considering the owner is a sake brewer. Look for the short hanging red curtains.

Kasagi-ya TEAHOUSE **$**
(かさぎ屋; Map p324; ☎075-561-9562; 349 Masuya-chō, Kōdai-ji, Higashiyama-ku; tea & sweet from ¥650; ⏲11am-6pm, closed Tue; Kyoto City bus 206 to Higashiyama-Yasui) At Kasagi-ya, on Sannen-zaka near Kiyomizu-dera, you can enjoy a nice cup of *matcha* and a variety of sweets. This old wooden shop has atmosphere to boot and friendly staff – which makes it worth the wait if there's a queue. It's hard to spot; it's a few doors up from Starbucks up the stairs on the same side.

Bamboo IZAKAYA **$$**
(晩boo; Map p324; ☎075-771-5559; Minami gawa, 1st fl, Higashiyama-Sanjō higashi-iru, Higashiyama-ku; dishes from ¥500; ⏲5.30pm-midnight; S Tōzai line to Higashiyama) Bamboo is one of Kyoto's more approachable *izakaya*. It's on Sanjō-dōri, near the mouth of a traditional, old shopping arcade. You can sit at the counter here and order a variety of typical dishes, watching the chefs do their thing.

★Kikunoi KAISEKI **$$$**
(菊乃井; Map p324; ☎075-561-0015; www.kikunoi.jp; 459 Shimokawara-chō, Yasakatoriimae-sagaru, Shimokawara-dōri, Higashiyama-ku; lunch/dinner from ¥10,000/16,000; ⏲noon-1pm & 5-8pm; Keihan line to Gion-Shijō) Michelin-starred chef Mutara serves some of the finest *kaiseki* in the city. Located in a hidden nook near Maruyama-kōen, this restaurant has everything necessary for the full over-the-top *kaiseki* experience, from setting to service to exquisitely executed cuisine, often with a creative twist. Reserve through your hotel at least a month in advance.

Gion Karyō KAISEKI **$$$**
(祇園迦陵; Map p324; ☎075-532-0025; 570-235 Gion-machi, Minamigawa, Higashiyama-ku; lunch/dinner courses from ¥5800/11,600; ⏲11.30am-3.30pm & 6-10.30pm, closed Wed; Keihan line to Gion-Shijō) Take an old Kyoto house, make it comfortable for modern diners, serve excellent, reasonably priced *kaiseki* and you have Karyō's recipe for success. The chef and servers are welcoming and an English menu makes ordering a snap. There are counter seats where you can watch the chef working and rooms with *hori-kotatsu* (sunken floors) for groups.

Northern Higashiyama

★Goya OKINAWAN **$**
(ゴーヤ; Map p328; ☎075-752-1158; www.goya-asia.com; 114-6 Nishida-chō, Jōdo-ji, Sakyō-ku; dishes from ¥680; ⏲11.30am-4pm & 5pm-midnight, closed Wed; ; Kyoto City bus 5 to Ginkakuji-michi) This Okinawan-style restaurant has tasty food (with plenty of vegetarian options), a plant-filled stylish interior and comfortable upstairs seating. It's perfect for lunch while exploring Northern

KYOTO'S TRADITIONAL MACHIYA

Machiya are wooden row houses that functioned as both homes and workplaces for Japan's bourgeoisie, a class that grew in prominence during the Edo period. The shop area was located in the front of the house, while the rooms lined up behind it formed the family's private living quarters. This elongated shape, which came about because homes were once taxed according to the size of their street frontage, earned *machiya* the nickname *'unagi no nedoko'* (eel bedrooms). The affluent among Kyoto's merchants adopted design elements from *sukiya-zukuri* (a type of residential architectural style), such as delicate latticework. Even with space at a minimum, many *machiya* have small courtyard gardens, called *tsubo-niwa* – one *tsubo* being the standard size of two tatami mats.

Although well suited to Kyoto's humid, mildew-prone summers, a wooden *machiya* has a limited lifespan of about 50 years. In the decades after WWII, many families chose not to rebuild them and instead put up multistorey concrete buildings. In many ways this made sense: modern buildings were simpler to maintain and could easily be fitted out with the latest mod-cons, like air-conditioning; they were cheaper to build, as the cost of traditional materials and workmanship was rising; and the hardship of Japan's steep inheritance tax could be offset by income generated by rental units. The pendulum swung back around in the 1990s, when it became clear that the city was losing something dear. Since then there have been numerous efforts to restore old *machiya;* many of them now house restaurants, cafes and boutiques. Judith Clancy's *Kyoto Machiya Restaurant Guide* has over 100 suggestions, and Diane Durston's *Old Kyoto* features traditional cafes, shops and restaurants, many of which are housed in *machiya*.

Higashiyama and just a short walk from Ginkaku-ji. Choose from simple dishes, such as taco rice and *gōya champurū* (bitter melon stir-fry), or try the delicious *nasi champurū* – a plate of daily changing dishes.

★Omen NOODLES $

(おめん; Map p328; ☎075-771-8994; www.omen.co.jp; 74 Jōdo-ji Ishibashi-chō, Sakyō-ku; noodles from ¥1150; ⏰11am-9pm; 🚌Kyoto City bus 5 to Ginkaku-ji-michi) This elegant noodle shop, a five-minute walk from Ginkaku-ji, is named after the signature dish – thick white noodles that are served in broth with a selection of seven fresh vegetables. Choose from hot or cold noodles, and you'll be given a bowl of soup to dip them in and a plate of vegetables (put these into the soup along with the sesame seeds).

There's also an extensive à la carte menu. You can get a tasty salad here and brilliant *tori sansho yaki* (chicken cooked with Japanese mountain spice). Look for the traditional Japanese house with a lantern outside.

Usagi no Ippo JAPANESE $

(卯サギの一歩; Map p328; ☎075-201-6497; 91-23 Okazaki Enshōji-chō, Sakyō-ku; meals from ¥1400; ⏰11am-5pm, closed Wed; Ⓢ Tōzai line to Higashiyama) Perfectly located for a break when museum-hopping in the Okazaki-kōen area, this delightful restaurant is set in an old *machiya* with tatami-mat floors, a small pleasant garden and a cute rabbit theme. The delicious *obanzai* (home-style cooking) sets are great value and might include tasty dishes such as chicken tenderloin wrapped in *shiso* (Japanese basil). Group bookings only after 5pm.

Sujata VEGETARIAN $

(スジャータ; Map p328; ☎075-721-0789; www.sujata-cafe.com; 96-2 Tanaka Monzen-chō, Sakyō-ku; meals from ¥850; ⏰noon-4pm & 5-7.30pm Mon & Thu-Sat, closes 6pm Sun; 🖉; 🚌Kyoto City bus 206 to Hyakumanben) Opposite Kyoto University, this humble cafe is a godsend for vegetarians. The menu is limited but the food is fresh, tasty, mostly organic and nutritious, including Indian curries or a Japanese set. There's a few counter seats and tables downstairs and tatami-mat seating upstairs. Sip on authentic homemade chai and relax to the soothing background music. Ask about the free meditation classes.

Falafel Garden ISRAELI $

(ファラフェルガーデン; Map p332; ☎075-712-1856; www.falafelgarden.com; 15-2 Kamiyanagi-chō, Tanaka, Sakyō-ku; falafel from ¥450; ⏰11am-10pm; 🖉; 🚆Keihan line to Demachiyanagi) If you're in need of a break from Japanese food, head to this casual spot near Demachiyanagi Station for excellent and filling felafel pita sandwiches or plates with generous dollops of homemade hummus, or a side of green chilli sauce for more of a kick. There's a small garden courtyard for sunny days.

Au Temps Perdu FRENCH $

(オ・タン・ペルデュ; Map p328; ☎075-762-1299; 64 Enshōji-chō, Okazaki, Sakyō-ku; tea & cake set from ¥1100; ⏰11am-8.30pm Tue-Sun; Ⓢ Tōzai line to Higashiyama) Overlooking the Shirakawa Canal, just across the street from the National Museum of Modern Art, this tiny French-style cafe is a lovely spot to take a break when sightseeing in the area. Check out the delicious cakes on display and pair them with a pot of tea, or spring for a light lunch along the lines of quiche and salad.

Hinode Udon NOODLES $

(日の出うどん; Map p328; ☎075-751-9251; 36 Kitanobō-chō, Nanzenji, Sakyō-ku; noodles from ¥750; ⏰11am-3pm Tue-Sat; 🚌Kyoto City bus 5 to Eikandō-michi) Filling noodle and rice dishes are served at this pleasant shop with an English menu – the *nabeyaki udon* (pot-baked udon in broth) is a great choice. This is a good lunch spot when temple-hopping in the Northern Higashiyama area. It's popular so you'll probably have to queue. Cash only.

Hyōtei KAISEKI $$$

(瓢亭; Map p328; ☎075-771-4116; www.hyotei.co.jp/en; 35 Kusagawa-chō, Nanzen-ji, Sakyō-ku; kaiseki lunch/dinner from ¥23,000/27,000; ⏰11am-7.30pm; Ⓢ Tōzai line to Keage) The Hyōtei is considered one of Kyoto's oldest and most picturesque traditional restaurants. In the main building you can sample exquisite *kaiseki* courses in private tearooms; book months ahead for weekend evenings. If you wish to sample the cuisine on a tighter budget, the annexe building offers *shōkadō bentō* box lunches (¥5400; noon to 4pm Friday to Wednesday).

Closed second and fourth Tuesday of each month.

Imperial Palace & Around

★Kanei NOODLES $

(かね井; Map p332; ☎075-441-8283; 11-1 Murasakino Higashifujinomori-chō, Kita-ku; noodles from ¥950; ⏰11.30am-2.30pm, closed Mon; 🚌Kyoto City bus 206 to Daitoku-ji-mae) A small traditional place not far from Funaoka Onsen, Kanei is for soba connoisseurs – the noodles are made by hand and are delicious. The owners don't speak much English, so here's what to order: *zaru soba* (cold soba; ¥950) or *kake soba* (soba in a broth; ¥1000). Prepare to queue and note that noodles often sell out early.

★Kazariya SWEETS $

(かざりや; Map p332; ☎075-491-9402; Murasakino Imamiya-chō, Kita-ku; sweets ¥500; ⏰10am-5pm, closed Wed; 🚌Kyoto City bus 46 to Imamiya-jinja) There are two restaurants at the eastern entrance to Imamiya-jinja specialising in *aburi-mochi* (grilled rice cakes coated with soybean flour) served with *miso-dare* (sweet-bean paste). Kazariya is on the left side when facing the shrine gate. For over 300 years it has been serving plates of the skewered treats with a pot of tea to enjoy in its traditional teahouse.

★Papa Jon's CAFE $

(パパジョンズカフェ　本店; Map p332; ☎075-415-2655; 642-4 Shokokuji-chō, Karasuma-dōri, Kamidachiuri higashi-iru, Kamigyō-ku; lunch from ¥850; ⏰10am-9pm; 📶; Ⓢ Karasuma line to Imadegawa) A short walk from the north border of the Imperial Palace Park, this light-filled cafe serves brilliant New York cheesecake (¥550) and hot drinks. Other menu items include breakfast sets, homemade quiche, soup and tasty salads, as well as gluten-free cakes.

Sarasa Nishijin CAFE $

(さらさ西陣; Map p332; ☎075-432-5075; 11-1 Murasakino Higashifujinomori-chō, Kita-ku; lunch from ¥840; ⏰noon-11pm, closed irregularly; 📶; 🚌Kyoto City bus 206 to Daitoku-ji-mae) This is one of Kyoto's most interesting cafes – it's built inside an old *sentō* (public bathhouse) and the original tiles have been preserved. Light meals and coffee are the staples here. Service can be slow, but it's worth a stop for the ambience. Lines out the door are not uncommon. It's near Funaoka Onsen.

★Toraya Karyō Kyoto Ichijō CAFE $$

(虎屋菓寮　京都一条店; Map p332; ☎075-441-3113; 400 Hirohashidono-chō, Ichijō-dōri, Karasuma-nishi-iru, Kamigyō-ku; tea & sweet from ¥1296; ⏰10am-6pm; Ⓢ Karasuma line to Imadegawa) This gorgeous tearoom-cafe is a stone's throw from the west side of the Imperial Palace Park. It's fantastic for a break from sightseeing in this part of town. The menu has some pictures and simple English. You can enjoy a nice cup of *matcha* and its signature *yokan* (jelly sweet).

Northwest Kyoto

Gontaro NOODLES $

(権太呂; Map p335; ☎075-463-1039; www.gontaro.co.jp; 26 Hirano Miyaziki-chō, Kita-ku; meals from ¥850; ⏰11am-9.30pm, closed Wed; 🚌Kyoto

City bus 205 or 12 to Kinkakuji-michi) This is a great choice for a spot of lunch when visiting Kinkaku-ji and the temples in the area. The setting is traditional and relaxed and it serves filling noodle meals, such as the tempura prawn and soba noodle set or the popular *kitsune udon* (udon with fried tofu).

Arashiyama & Sagano

There are a bunch of great dining spots here. The majority of the area's restaurants are on the main street near the Keifuku Randen Arashiyama Station, as well as some stand-out spots along the Hozu-gawa between the main street and the start of Kameyama-kōen.

Arashiyama Yoshimura NOODLES **$**

(嵐山よしむら; Map p338; 075-863-5700; Togetsu-kyō kita, Saga-Tenryū-ji, Ukyō-ku; soba from ¥1000, sets from ¥1278; 11am-5pm; Kyoto City bus 28 from Kyoto Station to Arashiyama-Tenryuji-mae, JR Sagano/San-in line to Saga-Arashiyama or Hankyū line to Arashiyama, change at Katsura) For a tasty bowl of soba noodles and a million-dollar view over the Arashiyama mountains and the Togetsu-kyō bridge, head to this extremely popular eatery (prepare to queue at peak times) just north of the famous bridge, overlooking the Katsura-gawa. There's an English menu but no English sign; look for the big glass windows and the stone wall.

Komichi CAFE **$**

(こみち; Map p338; 075-872-5313; 23 Ōjōin-chō, Nison-in Monzen, Saga, Ukyō-ku; tea & sweet ¥650; 10am-5pm Thu-Tue; Kyoto City bus 28 from Kyoto Station to Arashiyama-Tenryuji-mae, JR Sagano/San-in line to Saga-Arashiyama or Hankyū line to Arashiyama, change at Katsura) This friendly little teahouse is perfectly located along the Arashiyama tourist trail. In addition to hot and cold tea and coffee, it serves *uji kintoki* (shaved ice with sweetened green tea) in summer and a variety of noodle dishes year-round. The picture menu helps with ordering.

★**Shigetsu** VEGETARIAN, JAPANESE **$$**

(篩月; Map p338; 075-882-9725; 68 Susukinobaba-chō, Saga-Tenryū-ji, Ukyō-ku; lunch sets ¥3500, ¥5500 & ¥7500; 11am-2pm; ; Kyoto City bus 28 from Kyoto Station to Arashiyama-Tenryuji-mae, JR Sagano/San-in line to Saga-Arashiyama or Hankyū line to Arashiyama, change at Katsura) To sample *shōjin-ryōri*, try Shigetsu in the precincts of Tenryū-ji (p337). This healthy fare has been sustaining monks for more than a thousand years in Japan, so it will probably get you through an afternoon of sightseeing, although carnivores may be left craving something more. Shigetsu has beautiful garden views. Prices include temple admission.

★**Kitcho Arashiyama** KAISEKI **$$$**

(吉兆嵐山本店; Map p338; 075-881-1101; www.kyoto-kitcho.com; 58 Susukinobaba-chō, Saga-Tenryūji, Ukyō-ku; lunch/dinner from ¥51,840/64,800; 11.30am-3pm & 5-9pm Thu-Tue; ; Kyoto City bus 28 from Kyoto Station to Arashiyama-Tenryuji-mae, JR Sagano/San-in line to Saga-Arashiyama or Hankyū line to Arashiyama, change at Katsura) Considered one of the best *kaiseki* restaurants in Kyoto (and Japan, for that matter), Kitcho Arashiyama is the place to sample the full *kaiseki* experience. Meals are served in private rooms overlooking gardens. The food, service, explanations and atmosphere are all first rate. Make bookings online via its website well in advance.

Drinking & Nightlife

For a night out, your best bet is to head to Kiyamachi-dōri and the surrounding streets where you'll find bars and clubs around the Shijō-dōri end, and a great selection of restaurants and nightlife around the Sanjo-dōri end. But it pays to do some exploring as there are great bars hidden away in streets elsewhere.

There are a number of places to stop in for a drink in the many backstreets around Gion and the main strip, Shijō-dōri. The luxury hotel bars in this area are also a good choice for something a bit next level.

Kyoto Station & South Kyoto

Kurasu COFFEE

(Map p321; 075-744-0804; www.kurasu.kyoto; 552 Higashiaburano-koji chō, Shimogyō-ku; 8am-6pm; ; Kyoto Station) Finally there's good coffee to be found near Kyoto Station! This minimalist cafe has a menu of monthly rotating coffee from speciality roasters in Japan, and offers filter coffee and espresso along with a *matcha* latte and Prana chai.

Roots of all Evil BAR

(Map p321; www.nokishita.net; Kyoto Tower, B1 Karasuma-dōri, Shichijō-sagaru, Shimogyō-ku; 11am-11pm; Kyoto Station) Stop by this standing bar in the Kyoto Tower Sando food

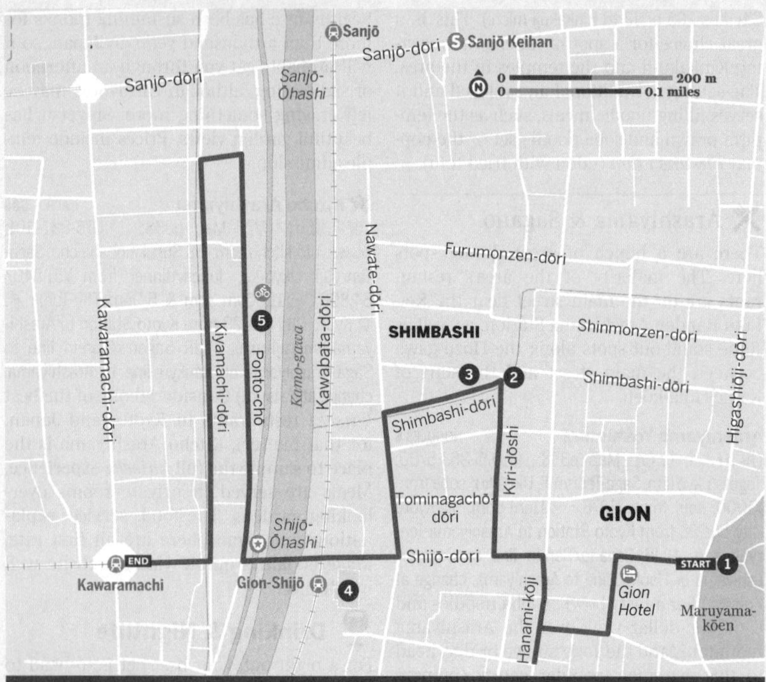

City Walk
A Night Stroll Through Gion and Ponto-chō

START YASAKA-JINJA
END KAWARAMACHI STATION
LENGTH 3KM; TWO HOURS

Start on the steps of ❶ **Yasaka-jinja** (p322), at the intersection of Shijō-dōri and Higashiōji-dōri, a 10-minute walk from Shijō (Keihan line) or Kawaramachi (Hankyū line) stations. Cross to the south side of Shijō-dōri and just after passing the APA Gion Hotel turn left. Walk 150m and take the second right. Another 100m brings you to Hanami-kōji, a picturesque street of *ryōtei* (traditional, high-class restaurants). Take a look then walk back north to Shijō-dōri.

Cross Shijō-dōri and go west for about 20m then turn right into Kiri-dōshi. As you continue along Kiri-dōshi, you'll cross Tominagachō-dōri, which is lined with buildings containing hundreds of hostess bars.

Kiri-dōshi crosses another street and then narrows to a tiny alley. You are now about to enter Gion's most lovely area, which lies just across ❷ **Tatsumi-bashi bridge**. This is the Shimbashi district, which features some of Kyoto's finest traditional architecture, most upmarket restaurants and exclusive hostess bars.

At the fork in the road you will find a small ❸ **Tatsumi shrine**. Take a left and walk west along the canal. Admire the views across the canal into some of the finest restaurants in Kyoto. You will occasionally spot geisha entertaining guests in some of these elite establishments.

At the end of Shimbashi, take a left onto gaudy Nawate-dōri. Head west on Shijō-dōri, passing ❹ **Minamiza** (p357), Kyoto's main kabuki theatre. Cross the Kamo-gawa on the north side of Shijō-Ōhashi and walk to the *kōban* (police box) on your right. You are now standing at the intersection of Shijō-dōri and ❺ **Ponto-chō**. Heading north brings you into an entirely different world of upmarket restaurants, bars, clubs and cafes.

At the north end of Ponto-chō at Sanjō-dōri, take a left and another left on Kiyamachi-dōri. This is a much more casual and inexpensive entertainment district.

basement for creative gin cocktails. It's run by the owner of Nokishita 711 and offers interesting herbal, spicy, floral gin infusions. Cocktails from ¥800.

Vermillion Espresso Bar CAFE

(バーミリオン; Map p316; www.vermillioncafe.com; 85 Onmae-chō, Fukakusa-inari, Fushimi-ku; ⏲9am-5pm; 📶; 🚉JR Nara line to Inari or Keihan line to Fushimi-Inari) A Melbourne-inspired cafe, tiny Vermillion takes its name from the colour of the *torii* of the nearby Fushimi Inari-Taisha shrine. It does standout coffee as well as a small selection of cakes, which can be taken away or enjoyed at the communal table. It's on the main street, just a short hop from Inari Station.

Kyoto Brewing Company BREWERY

(京都醸造株式会社; Map p316; ☎075-574-7820; www.kyotobrewing.com; 25-1 Takahata-chō, Nishikujō, Minami-ku; ⏲noon-6pm Sat & Sun; 🚉Kintetsu line to Jūjō) You'll find its beer in many of Kyoto's bars but it's worth a trip out to its tasting room to sample it in a friendly local setting in South Kyoto. Check out the brewery vats as you sip on a selection of 10 beers on tap, including a few seasonal releases. Open most weekends; check the website for the schedule.

Downtown Kyoto

★Bungalow CRAFT BEER

(バンガロー; Map p316; ☎075-256-8205; www.bungalow.jp; 15 Kashiwaya-chō, Shijō-dōri, Shimogyō-ku; ⏲3pm-2am Mon-Sat; 🚉Hankyū line to Ōmiya) Spread over two floors with an open-air downstairs bar, Bungalow serves a great range of Japanese craft beer along with natural wines in a cool industrial space. The regularly changing menu features 10 beers on tap from all over Japan and it also serves excellent food.

Weekenders Coffee COFFEE

(ウィークエンダーズ　コーヒー; Map p322; ☎075-746-2206; www.weekenderscoffee.com; 560 Honeyana-chō, Nakagyō-ku; coffee from ¥430; ⏲7.30am-6pm Thu-Tue; 🚉Hankyū line to Kawaramachi) Weekenders is a tiny coffee bar tucked away in a traditional-style building at the back of a parking lot in Downtown Kyoto. Sure, it's a strange location but it's where you'll find some of the city's best coffee being brewed by roaster-owner Masahiro Kaneko. It's mostly takeaway with a small bench out front.

Nokishita 711 COCKTAIL BAR

(Map p322; ☎075-741-6564; www.nokishita.net; 235 Atsumari-B, Sendo-chō, Shimogyō-ku; ⏲6pm-2am, to midnight Sun & Mon; 📶; 🚉Hankyū line to Kawaramachi) The sign inside says 'Kyoto Loves Gin' and if you do too, you won't want to miss this quirky little bar. Owner Tomo infuses gin with interesting ingredients, such as bamboo and smoked tea, and mixes up delicious cocktails with unique flavours – black sesame, yuzu pepper and truffle honey. There's a great range of gins from around the world.

Kaboku Tearoom TEAHOUSE

(喫茶室嘉木; Map p328; Teramachi-dōri, Nijō-agaru, Nakagyō-ku; ⏲10am-6pm; Ⓢ Tōzai line to Kyoto-Shiyakusho-mae) A casual tearoom attached to the Ippōdō Tea (p358) store, Kaboku serves a range of teas and provides a great break while exploring the shops in the area. Try the *matcha* and grab a counter seat to watch it being prepared.

Bee's Knees COCKTAIL BAR

(Map p322; ☎075-585-5595; www.bees-knees-kyoto.jp; 1st fl, Matsuya Bldg, 364 Kamiya-chō, Nishikiyamachi-dōri, Shijō-agaru, Nakagyō-ku; cocktails from ¥1300; ⏲6pm-1am Mon-Thu, to 2am Fri & Sat; 🚉Keihan line to Gion-Shijō or Hankyū line to Kawaramachi) Speakeasy-style cocktail bars have been popping up in Kyoto of late, and this one hits the mark with its 'secret entrance' (look for the subtle bee sign), pressed metal ceilings, dark wood and dim lighting. Chatty bartenders mix up Prohibition-era classics with a twist – try the *matcha* tiramisu or the smoked mojito with cherry-blossom wood smoke.

Kiln COFFEE

(Map p322; ☎075-353-3555; 194 Sendo-chō, Kiyamachi-dōri, Shimogyō-ku; ⏲11am-11pm Thu-Tue; 📶; 🚉Hankyū line to Kawaramachi) On a pretty stretch of canal on scenic Kiyamachi-dōri, Kiln's big windows frame the view and make it the perfect spot to stare lazily while waiting for your caffeine to kick in. The brew is made with single-origin beans and there's a selection of cakes and toasted sandwiches.

Atlantis BAR

(アトランティス; Map p322; ☎075-241-1621; 161 Matsumoto-chō, Ponto-chō-Shijō-agaru, Nakagyō-ku; cocktails from ¥900; ⏲6pm-2am, to 1am Sun; 🚉Hankyū line to Kawaramachi) This is a slick Ponto-chō bar that welcomes foreigners and draws a fair smattering of Kyoto's beautiful people, and wannabe beautiful people.

In summer you can sit outside on a platform looking over the Kamo-gawa (terrace closes at 11pm). It's often crowded so you may have to wait a bit to get in, especially if you want to sit outside.

Sake Bar Yoramu BAR

(酒バー よらむ; Map p322; ☎075-213-1512; www.sakebar-yoramu.com; 35-1 Matsuya-chō, Nijō-dōri, Higashinotoin higashi-iru, Nakagyō-ku; ⏲6pm-midnight Wed-Sat; Ⓢ Karasuma or Tōzai lines to Karasuma-Oike) Named for Yoramu, the Israeli sake expert who runs Sake Bar Yoramu, this bar is highly recommended for anyone after an education in sake. It's very small and can only accommodate a handful of people. If you're not sure what you like, go for a sake tasting set of three (¥1700). By day, it's a soba restaurant called Toru Soba.

Bar K6 BAR

(バーK６; Map p328; ☎075-255-5009; 2nd fl, Le Valls Bldg, Nijō-dōri, Kiyamachi higashi-iru, Nakagyō-ku; ⏲6pm-3am, to 5am Fri & Sat; Ⓢ Tōzai line to Kyoto-Shiyakusho-mae, Ⓡ Keihan line to Jingu-Marutamachi) Overlooking one of the prettiest stretches of Kiyamachi-dōri, this upscale modern Japanese bar has a great selection of single malts and some of the best cocktails in town. It's popular with well-heeled locals and travellers staying at some of the top-flight hotels nearby.

Taigu PUB

(ダイグ ガストロ パブ; Map p322; ☎075-213-0214; 1st fl, 498 Kamikoriki-chō, Nakagyō-ku; ⏲11.30am-11pm; 📶; Ⓢ Tōzai line to Kyoto-Shiyakusho-mae) Looking out on scenic Kiyamachi-dōri, Taigu (formerly Tadg's Gastro Pub) is a good spot for an evening drink. Choose from an extensive selection of craft beers (including several rotating Japanese beers on tap), a variety of wines, sake and spirits. It also does pub-style meals.

Southern Higashiyama

Beer Komachi CRAFT BEER

(ビア小町; Map p324; ☎075-746-6152; www.beerkomachi.com; 444 Hachiken-chō, Higashiyama-ku; ⏲5-11pm, from 3pm Sat & Sun, closed Tue; 📶; Ⓢ Tōzai line to Higashiyama) Located in the Furokawa-chō covered shopping arcade close to Higashiyama Station, this tiny casual bar is dedicated to promoting Japanese craft beer. There are usually seven Japanese beers on tap, which rotate on an almost daily basis. There's a great bar-food menu and a list of sake if you're not much of a beer drinker.

Tōzan Bar BAR

(Map p324; ☎075-541-3201; www.kyoto.regency.hyatt.com; Hyatt Regency Kyoto, 644-2 Sanjūsangendō-mawari, Higashiyama-ku; ⏲5pm-midnight; Ⓡ Keihan line to Shichijō) Even if you're not spending the night at the Hyatt Regency, drop by the cool and cosy underground bar for a tipple or two. Kitted out by renowned design firm Super Potato, the dimly lit atmospheric space features interesting touches, such as old locks, wooden beams, an antique-book library space and a wall feature made from traditional wooden sweet moulds.

Gion Finlandia Bar BAR

(ぎをん フィンランディアバー; Map p324; ☎075-541-3482; www.finlandiabar.com; 570-123 Gion-machi, Minamigawa, Higashiyama-ku; cover ¥500; ⏲6pm-3am; Ⓡ Keihan line to Gion-Shijō) This stylish, minimalist Gion bar in an old geisha house is a great place for a quiet civilised drink. There's no menu, so just prop up at the bar and let the bow-tied bartender know what you like, whether it's an expertly crafted cocktail or a high-end Japanese single malt. Friday and Saturday nights can get busy, so you may have to queue.

Northern Higashiyama

Metro CLUB

(メトロ; Map p328; ☎075-752-4765; www.metro.ne.jp; BF Ebisu Bldg, Kawabata-dōri, Marutamachi-sagaru, Sakyō-ku; ⏲8pm-3am; Ⓡ Keihan line to Jingū-Marutamachi) Metro is part disco, part live house and it even hosts the occasional art exhibition. It attracts an eclectic mix of creative types and has a different theme nightly. Metro is inside exit 2 of the Jingū-Marutamachi Station on the Keihan line.

Kick Up BAR

(キックアップ; Map p328; ☎075-761-5604; 331 Higashikomonoza-chō, Higashiyama-ku; ⏲7pm-midnight, closed Wed; Ⓢ Tōzai line to Keage) Located just across the street from the Westin Miyako Kyoto, this wonderful bar attracts a regular crowd of Kyoto expats, local Japanese and guests from the Westin. It's subdued, relaxing and friendly.

Arashiyama & Sagano

★Hiranoya TEAHOUSE

(平野屋; Map p316; ☎075-861-0359; 16 Sennō-chō, Saga-Toriimoto, Ukyō-ku; ⊙9am-9pm; 🚌Kyoto City bus 72 from Kyoto Station to Otaginenbutsu-ji-mae) Located next to the Atago Torii (a large Shintō shrine gate), this thatched-roof restaurant is about as atmospheric as they get. It serves *matcha* (powdered green tea) and a sweet for ¥840; the perfect way to cool off after a long slog around the temples of Arashiyama and Sagano. It also does a light lunch from 11.30am.

% Arabica COFFEE

(Map p338; ☎075-748-0057; www.arabica.coffee; 3-47 Susukinobaba-chō, Saga-Tenryūji, Ukyō-ku; ⊙8am-6pm; 🚌Kyoto City bus 28 from Kyoto Station to Arashiyama-Tenryuji-mae, 🚆JR Sagano (San-in) line to Saga-Arashiyama) Peer through the floor-to-ceiling windows that look across the Hozu-gawa and mountain backdrop as you order your coffee at this tiny cafe bringing excellent brew to Arashiyama. Grab a takeaway and stroll along the river or nab a bench out the front to take in the views.

☆ Entertainment

★Minamiza THEATRE

(南座; Map p324; www.kabukiweb.net; Shijō-Ōhashi, Higashiyama-ku; 🚆Keihan line to Gion-Shijō) This theatre in Gion is the oldest kabuki theatre in Japan. The major event of the year is the **Kaomise festival** in December, which features Japan's finest kabuki actors.

Taku-Taku LIVE MUSIC

(磔磔; Map p322; ☎075-351-1321; Tominokōji-dōri-Bukkōji, Shimogyō-ku; tickets ¥1500-4000; 🚆Hankyū line to Kawaramachi) One of Kyoto's most atmospheric live-music venues, with a long history of hosting some great local and international acts. Check the *Kyoto Visitor's Guide* and flyers in local coffee shops and record stores for details on upcoming events. It can be hard to spot: look for the wooden sign with black kanji on it and go through the gate.

DON'T MISS

GEISHA PERFORMANCES

The best way to experience geisha culture is to see one of Kyoto's annual public dance performances (known as *odori*), a city tradition for over a century.

Miyako Odori (都をどり; Map p324; ☎075-541-3391; www.miyako-odori.jp; Gion Kōbu Kaburen-jō Theatre, 570-2 Gion-machi, Minamigawa, Higashiyama-ku; tickets from ¥4000; ⊙shows 12.30pm, 2.20pm & 4.10pm; 🚌Kyoto City bus 206 to Gion, 🚆Keihan line to Gion-Shijō) Our top pick, held throughout April, usually at **Gion Kōbu Kaburen-jō Theatre**, but the building is under ongoing renovations until around 2021. Performances will be held at Minamiza in the meantime.

Kyō Odori (京おどり; Map p324; ☎075-561-1151; Miyagawachō Kaburenjo, 4-306 Miyagawasuji, Higashiyama-ku; with/without tea from ¥2800/2200; ⊙shows 1pm, 2.45pm & 4.30pm; 🚆Keihan line to Gion-Shijō) Performed by the geisha of the Miyagawa-chō district, from the first to the third Sunday in April at the **Miyagawa-chō Kaburen-jō Theatre** (宮川町歌舞練場), east of the Kamo-gawa between Shijō-dōri and Gojō-dōri.

Kamogawa Odori (鴨川をどり; Map p322; ☎075-221-2025; Ponto-chō, Sanjō-sagaru, Nakagyō-ku; seat ¥2300, special seat with/without tea ¥4800/4200; ⊙shows 12.30pm, 2.20pm & 4.10pm; Ⓢ Tōzai line to Kyoto-Shiyakusho-mae) Held 1 to 24 May at **Ponto-chō Kaburen-jō Theatre** in Ponto-chō (p318).

Gion Odori (祇園をどり; Map p324; ☎075-561-0224; Gion, Higashiyama-ku; with/without tea ¥4500/4000; ⊙shows 1.30pm & 4pm; 🚌Kyoto City bus 206 to Gion) Performed by the geisha of the Gion Higashi district 1 to 10 November at the **Gion Kaikan Theatre** (祇園会館), near Yasaka-jinja (p322).

In addition to these, there are a few more tourist-oriented performances in Kyoto that can be seen year-round, such as Kyoto Cuisine & Maiko Evening (p358).

ROHM Theatre Kyoto THEATRE

(京都観世会館; Map p328; ☎075-771-6051; www.rohmtheatrekyoto.jp; 44 Okazaki Enshōji-chō, Sakyō-ku; tickets from ¥3000; ⊙box office 10am-7pm; Ⓢ Tōzai line to Higashiyama) Housed in a striking modernist building, ROHM Theatre hosts everything from international ballet and opera performances to comedy shows, classical music concerts and *nō* (stylised dance-drama performed on a bare stage).

Jittoku LIVE MUSIC

(拾得; Map p332; ☎075-841-1691; 815 Hishiya-chō, Kamigyō-ku; ⊙5.30pm-midnight; Ⓢ Tōzai line to Nijōjō-mae) Jittoku is located in an atmospheric old *sakagura* (sake brewery). It plays host to a variety of shows – check *Kansai Scene* to see what's on. It also serves food.

Kyoto Cuisine & Maiko Evening DANCE

(ぎおん畑中; Map p324; ☎075-541-5315; www.kyoto-maiko.jp; 505 Gion-machi, Minami-gawa, Higashiyama-ku; per person ¥19,000; ⊙6-8pm Mon, Wed, Fri & Sat; 🚌Kyoto City bus 206 to Gion or Chionin-mae, 🚆Keihan line to Gion-Shijō) If you want to witness geisha perform and then actually speak with them, one of the best opportunities is at Gion Hatanaka (p344), a Gion ryokan that offers a regularly scheduled evening of elegant Kyoto *kaiseki* and personal entertainment by real Kyoto *geiko* (fully fledged geisha) as well as *maiko* (apprentice geisha). Children under seven years are not permitted.

Check the website for the schedule; Friday-night performances are guaranteed but other nights are subject to change.

Gion Corner THEATRE

(ギオンコーナー; Map p324; ☎075-561-1119; www.kyoto-gioncorner.com; Yasaka Kaikan, 570-2 Gion-machi, Minamigawa, Higashiyama-ku; adult/child ¥3150/1900; ⊙performances 6pm & 7pm, Fri-Sun only Dec–mid-Mar; 🚌Kyoto City bus 206 to Gion, 🚆Keihan line to Gion-Shijō) Gion Corner presents one-hour shows that include a bit of tea ceremony, koto (Japanese zither) music, ikebana (art of flower arranging), *gagaku* (court music), *kyōgen* (ancient comic plays), *kyōmai* (Kyoto-style dance) and *bunraku* (classical puppet theatre). It's a hugely touristy affair and fairly pricey for what you get. Tickets have been discounted from ¥3150 to ¥2500 for foreigners for quite some time.

Try to arrive early for front-row seats.

Shopping

Kyoto has a fantastic variety of both traditional and modern shops. Most are located in the Downtown Kyoto area, making the city a very convenient place to shop. Shijō-dōri, between Kawaramachi-dōri and Karasuma-dōri, is great for department stores, fashion boutiques and traditional arts and crafts.

Kyoto Station & South Kyoto

JR Isetan DEPARTMENT STORE

(ジェイアール京都伊勢丹; Map p321; ☎075-352-1111; Kyoto Station Bldg, Karasuma-dōri, Shiokōji-sagaru, Shimogyō-ku; ⊙10am-8pm; 🚆Kyoto Station) Isetan is an elegant department store located inside the Kyoto Station building, making it perfect for a last-minute spot of shopping before hopping on the train to the airport or your next destination. Don't miss the B1 and B2 food floors.

Downtown Kyoto

★**Aritsugu** HOMEWARES

(有次; Map p322; ☎075-221-1091; 219 Kajiya-chō, Nishikikōji-dōri, Gokomachi nishi-iru, Nakagyō-ku; ⊙9am-5.30pm; 🚆Hankyū line to Kawaramachi) While you're in Nishiki Market, have a look at this store – it has some of the best kitchen knives in the world. Choose your knife – all-rounder, sushi, vegetable – and the staff will show you how to care for it before sharpening and boxing it up. You can also have your name engraved in English or Japanese. Knives start at around ¥10,000.

Founded in 1560, Aritsugu was originally involved in the production of swords and the blacksmith skills have been passed down over the years through generation after generation. It also carries a selection of excellent and unique Japanese kitchenware and whetstones for knife sharpening.

★**Ippōdō Tea** TEA

(一保堂茶舗; Map p328; ☎075-211-3421; www.ippodo-tea.co.jp; Teramachi-dōri, Nijō-agaru, Nakagyō-ku; ⊙9am-6pm; Ⓢ Tōzai line to Kyoto-Shiyakusho-mae) This old-style tea shop sells some of the best Japanese tea in Kyoto, and you'll be given an English leaflet with prices and descriptions of each one. Its *matcha* makes an excellent and lightweight souvenir. Ippōdō is north of the city hall, on Teramachi-dōri. It has an adjoining teahouse, Kaboku Tearoom (p355); last order 5.30pm.

★Zōhiko ARTS & CRAFTS

(象彦; Map p328; ☎075-229-6625; www.zohiko.co.jp; 719-1 Yohojimae-chō, Teramachi-dōri, Nijō-agaru, Nakagyō-ku; ⊙10am-6pm; S Tōzai line to Kyoto-Shiyakusho-mae) Zōhiko is the best place in Kyoto to buy one of Japan's most beguiling art-and-craft forms: lacquerware. If you aren't familiar with just how beautiful these products can be, you owe it to yourself to make the pilgrimage to Zōhiko. You'll find a great selection of cups, bowls, trays and various kinds of boxes.

★Wagami no Mise ARTS & CRAFTS

(倭紙の店; Map p322; ☎075-341-1419; 1st fl, Kajinoha Bldg, 298 Ōgisakaya-chō, Higashinotōin-dōri, Bukkōji-agaru, Shimogyō-ku; ⊙9.30am-5.30pm Mon-Fri, to 4.30pm Sat; S Karasuma line to Shijō) This place sells a fabulous variety of *washi* for reasonable prices and is a great spot to pick up a gift or souvenir. Look for the Morita Japanese Paper Company sign on the wall out the front.

★Takashimaya DEPARTMENT STORE

(高島屋; Map p322; ☎075-221-8811; Shijō-Kawaramachi Kado, Shimogyō-ku; ⊙10am-8pm; 🚇Hankyū line to Kawaramachi) The *grande dame* of Kyoto department stores, Takashimaya is almost a tourist attraction in its own right, from the mind-boggling riches of the basement food floor to the wonderful selection of lacquerware and ceramics on the 6th. Check out the kimono display on the 5th floor.

Maruzen BOOKS

(丸善; Map p322; Basement, BAL, 251 Yamazaki-chō, Kawaramachi-sanjo sagaru, Nakagyō-ku; ⊙11am-9pm; 🚇Hankyū line to Kawaramachi) Occupying two basement floors of the BAL department store, this excellent bookshop has a massive range of English-language books across all subjects, plenty of titles on Kyoto and Japan, a great selection of Japanese literature, magazines from around the globe and travel guides.

Tokyu Hands DEPARTMENT STORE

(東急ハンズ京都店; Map p322; ☎075-254-3109; http://kyoto.tokyu-hands.co.jp; Shijō-dōri, Karasuma higashi-iru, Shimogyō-ku; ⊙10am-8.30pm; S Karasuma line to Shijō) While the Kyoto branch of Tokyu Hands doesn't have the selection of bigger branches in places like Tokyo, it's still well worth a browse for fans of gadgets and unique homewares. It's a good place for an interesting gift or souvenir, from Hario coffee equipment and lacquerware *bentō* boxes to stationery and cosmetics.

DON'T MISS

KYOTO'S MARKETS

Kōbō-san Market Held on the 21st of the month at Tō-ji (p314) to commemorate the death of Kōbō Daishi, who in 823 was appointed abbot of the temple. If you're after used kimonos, pottery, bric-a-brac, plants, tools and general Japanalia, this is the place.

Tenjin-san Market Takes place on the 25th of the month at Kitano Tenman-gū (p334). It's a sprawling flea market that marks the birthday (and the death) of the Heian-era statesman Sugawara Michizane (845–903). You'll find loads of ceramics, secondhand kimonos, antiques and food stalls.

Kyūkyo-dō ARTS & CRAFTS

(鳩居堂; Map p322; ☎075-231-0510; www.kyukyodo.co.jp; 520 Shimohonnōjimae-chō, Teramachi-dōri, Aneyakōji-agaru, Nakagyō-ku; ⊙10am-6pm Mon-Sat; S Tōzai line to Kyoto-Shiyakusho-mae) This old shop in the Teramachi covered arcade sells a selection of incense, *shodō* (calligraphy) goods, tea-ceremony supplies and *washi*. Prices are on the high side but the quality is good. Overall, this is your best one-stop shop for distinctively Japanese souvenirs.

Mimuro CLOTHING

(みむろ; Map p322; ☎075-344-1220; www.mimuro.net; Matsubara, Nishi-iru, Karasuma-dori, Shimogyo-ku; ⊙10am-6.30pm; S Karasuma line to Shijō) Mimuro is a great spot for anyone looking to take home a good-quality kimono or *yukata* (light cotton kimono). The English-speaking staff will go out of their way to help you find what you're looking for out of the huge range of colours and designs spread over five floors. *Yukata* prices start at ¥5000 and kimonos from ¥35,000.

BAL DEPARTMENT STORE

(バル; Map p322; www.bal-bldg.com; 251 Yamazaki-chō, Kawaramachi-dōri, Sanjō-sagaru, Nakagyō-ku; ⊙11am-8pm; 🚇Hankyū line to

Kawaramachi) For all your high-end fashion and homeware needs, the chic and elegant BAL department store is the place to go. You'll find designer fashion, botanical skincare from Neal's Yard, great souvenirs and gifts at Today's Special, and the ever popular lifestyle store Muji. The two basement floors house the huge Maruzen (p359) bookstore.

Daimaru DEPARTMENT STORE
(大丸; Map p322; 075-211-8111; Tachiuri Nishi-machi 79, Shijō-dōri, Takakura nishi-iru, Shimogyō-ku; 10am-8pm; Karasuma line to Shijō, Hankyū line to Karasuma) Daimaru has fantastic service, a brilliant selection of goods and a basement food floor that will make you want to move to Kyoto.

Southern Higashiyama

The stretch of Shijō-dōri from Gion-Shijō Station to Yasaka-jinja is packed with souvenir stalls and shops selling everything from tea and sweets to *kokeshi* (wooden Japanese dolls) and chopsticks. For ceramics, check out the stores lining the streets leading to Kiyomizu-dera.

★Ichizawa Shinzaburo Hanpu FASHION & ACCESSORIES
(一澤信三郎帆布; Map p324; 075-541-0436; www.ichizawa.co.jp; 602 Takabatake-chō, Higashiyama-ku; 9am-6pm, closed Tue; Tōzai line to Higashiyama) This company has been making its canvas bags for over 110 years and the store is often crammed with those in the know picking up a skillfully crafted Kyoto product. Originally designed as 'tool' bags for workers to carry sake bottles, milk and ice blocks, the current designs still reflect this idea. Choose from a range of styles and colours.

This is the one and only store that sells these bags making it the perfect souvenir.

Asahi-dō CERAMICS
(朝日堂; Map p324; 075-531-2181; www.asahido.co.jp/english; 1-280 Kiyomizu, Higashiyama-ku; 9am-6pm; Kyoto City bus 206 to Kiyōmizu-michi or Gojō-zaka, Keihan line to Kiyomizu-Gojō) Located in the heart of the Kiyomizu pottery area, Asahi-dō has been specialising in Kyōyaki-Kiyomizuyaki (Kyoto-style pottery) since 1870. The complex is called Asahi Touan and comprises the main store with the widest collection of Kyoto-style pottery in the city, as well as other stores selling a range of works, including some by the best up-and-coming ceramic artists in Japan.

Northern Higashiyama

Kyoto Handicraft Center ARTS & CRAFTS
(京都ハンディクラフトセンター; Map p328; 075-761-8001; www.kyotohandicraftcenter.com; 17 Entomi-chō, Shōgoin, Sakyō-ku; 10am-7pm; Kyoto City bus 206 to Kumano-jinja-mae) Split between two buildings, East and West, this place sells a good range of Japanese arts and crafts, including Hokusai woodblock prints (reproductions from ¥5000), Japanese dolls and a great selection of books on Japanese culture and travel guides. English-speaking staff are on hand and currency exchange is available. Within walking distance of the main Higashiyama sightseeing route.

Imperial Palace & Around

Aizen Kōbō CLOTHING
(愛染工房; Map p332; 075-441-0355; www.aizenkobo.jp; 215 Yoko Omiya-chō, Nakasuji-dōri, Omiya Nishi-iru, Kamigyō-ku; 10am-5.30pm, to 4pm Sat & Sun; Kyoto City bus 9 to Horikawa-Imadegawa) In the heart of the Nishijin textile district in a beautifully restored *machiya* (traditional Japanese townhouse), Aizen Kōbō has been producing its indigo-dyed handwoven textiles for three generations using the traditional dyeing method known as *aizome*. Products are hand-dyed using natural fermenting indigo and vegetable dye sourced from the Tade plant, native to Japan.

Information

MEDICAL SERVICES

Kyoto University Hospital (京都大学医学部附属病院; Map p328; 075-751-3111; www.kuhp.kyoto-u.ac.jp; 54 Shōgoinkawahara-chō, Sakyō-ku; walk-in appointments 8.15-11am Mon-Fri; Keihan line to Jingū-Marutamachi) The best hospital in Kyoto. There is an information counter near the entrance on the ground floor that can point you in the right direction.

Kyoto Prefectural University Hospital (Map p328; 075-251-5111; www.h.kpu-m.ac.jp/en; Kawaramachi-Hirokoji, Kamigyō-ku; walk-in appointments 8.15-11am Mon-Fri; Keihan line to Demachiyanagi) Can try to provide English-speaking staff to assist you and has English-speaking doctors.

TOURIST INFORMATION

Kyoto Tourist Information Center (京都総合観光案内所, TIC; Map p321; ☎075-343-0548; 2F Kyoto Station Bldg, Shimogyō-ku; ⌚8.30am-7pm; 🚉Kyoto Station) Stocks bus and city maps, has plenty of transport info and English speakers are available to answer your questions.

USEFUL RESOURCES

Kansai Scene (www.kansaiscene.com) Magazine with listings of foreigner-friendly bars and detailed upcoming events. Available at major bookshops and foreigner-friendly businesses. See website for places where you can grab a copy.

Deep Kyoto (www.deepkyoto.com) This website has listings on little-known Kyoto bars, cafes and restaurants, as well as some event information.

Getting There & Away

AIR

Coming directly to Kyoto, most foreign visitors arrive via Kansai International Airport (KIX), the nearest international airport. It's sometimes cheaper to fly into Tokyo than into KIX, and then take a connecting flight.

BUS

Overnight JR buses run between Tokyo Station (Nihombashi-guchi/arrival, Yaesu-guchi/departure long-distance bus stop) and **Kyoto Station Bus Terminal** (京都駅前バスターミナル; Map p321). The trip takes about seven hours and the one-way fare starts at around ¥5200. There is a similar service to/from Shinjuku Station's Shin-minami-guchi in Tokyo.

Other JR bus transport possibilities include Kanazawa (one way from ¥3100) and Hiroshima (one way from ¥4100).

You can purchase tickets from the bus information centre (p362) at Kyoto Station.

Willer Express (www.willerexpress.com) is a great budget option for long-distance and overnight buses. It operates between most major cities and Kyoto, and has comfortable reclining seats with a range of options from private seats to those with more legroom. From Tokyo's Shinjuku Station to Kyoto the fare starts at around ¥3200.

TRAIN

Train travel between Kyoto and other parts of Japan is a breeze. Kyoto Station is served by the Tōkaidō and San-yō *shinkansen* (bullet train) lines, which connect the city to Nagoya and Tokyo to the east and Kansai destinations Osaka (Shin-Osaka Station), Kōbe (Shin-Kōbe Station) and Himeji to the west (and beyond to Hiroshima, and other destinations in western Honshū and Kyūshū).

Private lines connect Kyoto Station with Nagoya, Nara, Osaka and Kōbe. Where they exist, private lines are always cheaper than JR. In particular, if you're travelling between Kyoto Station and Nara, you'll probably find a *tokkyū* (limited express) on the Kintetsu line to be faster and more comfortable than JR.

Getting Around

TO/FROM KANSAI INTERNATIONAL AIRPORT

Bus

Kansai International Airport Limousine Bus (☎075-682-4400; www.kate.co.jp/en; one-way adult/child ¥2550/1280) runs frequent buses between Kyoto and KIX (about 1½ hours). Buses from Kyoto Station to the airport depart from the **Hachijo-guchi exit** (Map p321) (in front of the Avanti department store and Keihan Hotel) every 20 to 40 minutes. There are also pick-up points at Shijō Karasuma and Sanjō Keihan departing roughly every 60 minutes. Purchase tickets from the ticket window near the boarding point.

Taxi

MK Taxi Sky Gate Shuttle limousine van service (☎075-778-5489; www.mktaxi-japan.com; one-way to Kansai airport ¥4200, to Itami airport ¥2900) is a door-to-door service that will drop you off at most places in Kyoto – simply go to the staff counter at the south end of the KIX arrivals hall and they will do the rest. From Kyoto to the airport it is necessary to make reservations two days in advance to arrange pickup from your hotel in Kyoto.

A similar service is offered by **Yasaka Taxi** (☎075-803-4800; www.yasaka.jp; adult/child one-way ¥4200/2100). Keep in mind that these are shared taxis (actually vans), so you may be delayed by the driver picking up or dropping off other passengers.

Train

The fastest and most convenient way to move between KIX and Kyoto is the special JR Haruka airport express (reserved/unreserved ¥3370/2850, 1¼ hours). It's actually cheaper to buy a JR West Kansai Area Pass as this is valid for unreserved seats on the JR Haruka express to KIX and costs ¥2300. Buy tickets at the JR ticket office inside the north entrance of Kyoto Station, to the left of the platform ticket gates (you'll need to show your passport).

First and last departures on the JR Haruka express from KIX to Kyoto are at 6.30am and 10.16pm Monday to Friday (6.40am on

KYOTO BUS & RAIL PASSES

One-day unlimited travel passes There's a one-day card valid for unlimited travel on Kyoto City buses and some of the Kyoto buses (these are different companies) that costs ¥600 and a one-day subway pass that also costs ¥600. A one-day unlimited bus and subway pass costs ¥900.

Kyoto Sightseeing Pass Allows unlimited use of the Kyoto City buses, subway and some of the Kyoto bus routes for one/two days for ¥900/1700.

One-day bus and Kyoto Sightseeing passes can be purchased at major bus terminals, at the Kyoto Bus Information Centre at Kyoto Station or at the Kyoto Tourist Information Center (p361). The one-day subway pass can be bought at subway ticket windows and the Kyoto Tourist Information Center.

For travelling around Kansai (including to and from Kansai International Airport), consider getting an ICOCA card or one of the many discount passes for the region.

The Kyoto City Subway Pass (adult/child ¥600/300) allows unlimited travel on the city's subway for one day, plus discounts on some sights. You can buy it from the Kyoto Tourist Information Center or any subway ticket office.

weekends); first and last departures from Kyoto to KIX are at 5.45am and 8.30pm.

If you have time to spare, you can save money by taking the *kankū kaisoku* (Kansai airport express) between the airport and Osaka Station, and then taking a regular *shinkaisoku* (special rapid train) to Kyoto. The total journey by this route takes about 95 minutes with good connections and costs around ¥1750.

BICYCLE

Kyoto is a great city to explore on a bicycle. With the exception of the outlying areas, it is mostly flat and there is a useful bike path running the length of the Kamo-gawa.

Many guesthouses hire or lend bicycles to their guests and there are also hire shops around Kyoto Station, in Arashiyama and in Downtown Kyoto. With a decent bicycle and a good map, you can easily make your way all around the city. Dedicated bicycle tours are also available.

Bicycle helmets are only required to be worn by law by children 12 years and under.

Note that cycling on the following streets is prohibited:

- Kawaramachi-dōri, between Oike-dōri and Bukkoji-dōri
- Shijo-dōri, between Higashioji-dōri and Karasuma-dōri
- Sanjo-dōri, between Kiyamachi-dōri and Kawaramachi-dōri

For more information, visit Cycle Kyoto (www.cyclekyoto.com).

BUS

Kyoto has an intricate network of bus routes providing an efficient way of getting around at moderate cost. Most of the routes used by visitors have announcements and bus-stop information displays in English. Most buses run between 7am and 10pm, though a few run earlier or later.

Kyoto's main bus terminals are also train stations: Kyoto Station, Sanjō Station, Karasuma-Shijō Station and Kitaōji Station. The bus terminal at Kyoto Station is on the north side and has three main departure bays (departure points are indicated by the letter of the bay and number of the stop within that bay).

Bus stops usually have a map of destinations from that stop and a timetable for the buses serving that stop.

The main **bus information centre** (京都バス案内所; Map p321; Kyoto Station; ⏲ city bus office 7.30am-7.30pm, JR office 9am-6pm; 🚇 Kyoto Station) is located in front of Kyoto Station. Here you can pick up bus maps, purchase bus tickets and passes (on all lines, including highway buses), and get additional information.

The Kyoto Tourist Information Center (p361) stocks the *Bus Navi: Kyoto City Bus Sightseeing Map,* which shows the city's main bus lines.

Bus entry is usually through the back door and exit is via the front door. Inner-city buses charge a flat fare (¥230 for adults, ¥120 for children ages six to 12, free for those younger), which you drop into the clear plastic receptacle on top of the machine next to the driver on your way out. A separate machine gives change for ¥100 and ¥500 coins or ¥1000 notes.

SUBWAY

Kyoto has two efficient subway lines, operating from 5.30am to 11.30pm. Minimum adult fare is ¥210 (children ¥110).

The quickest way to travel between the north and south of the city is the Karasuma subway line. The line has 15 stops and runs from Takeda in the far south, via Kyoto Station, to the Kyoto International Conference Hall (Kokusaikaikan Station) in the north.

The east–west Tōzai subway line traverses Kyoto from Uzumasa-Tenjingawa Station in the west, meeting the Karasuma subway line at Karasuma-Oike Station, and continuing east to Sanjō-Keihan, Yamashina and Rokujizō in the east and southeast.

TAXI

Taxis are a convenient, but expensive, way of getting from place to place about town. A taxi can usually be flagged down in most parts of the city at any time. There are also a large number of *takushī noriba* (taxi stands) in town, outside most train/subway stations, department stores etc.

During high seasons for tourism (cherry-blossom season in April and autumn-foliage season in November), the taxi ranks on the south and north side of Kyoto Station can be very long. If you're in a hurry, walk a few blocks north of the station and hail a cab off the street.

Foreigner-friendly taxis aim to make the taxi system more accessible to tourists, with drivers who can speak other languages, such as English and Chinese, and accepting payment by credit card. The taxis are clearly marked as 'foreigner friendly' and there are separate taxi stands in front of the JR Kyoto Station **north** (Map p321) and **south** (Map p321) exits.

TRAIN

The main train station in Kyoto is Kyoto Station, which is in the south of the city, just below Shichijō-dōri and is actually two stations under one roof: JR Kyoto Station and Kintetsu Kyoto Station.

In addition to the private Kintetsu line that operates from Kyoto Station, there are two other private train lines in Kyoto: the Hankyū line that operates from Downtown Kyoto along Shijō-dōri and the Keihan line that operates from stops along the Kamo-gawa.

AT A GLANCE

POPULATION
Osaka: 2.75 million

OLDEST BUILDING
Hōryū-ji (607 CE; p410)

BEST STREET FOOD
Wanaka Honten (p383)

BEST TEMPLE LODGE
Ekō-in (p422)

BEST WALK
Yama-no-be-no-michi (p411)

WHEN TO GO

Late Mar–mid-Apr The beauty of the cherry blossoms is over the top.

May–Sep July and August are hot and sticky, but summer's a great time for festivals and street life.

Oct–early Dec Kansai's sights are sublime against a backdrop of bright-red maple leaves.

Dōtombori (p372), Osaka
FOTOVOYAGER/GETTY IMAGES ©

Kansai

Kansai (関西) is the heart of Japan, where much of modern-day Japanese culture originated. Its highlights read like a greatest-hits list. Looking for a vibrant dining and drinking scene and the vivid colour that Japanese cities are famous for? Head to Osaka. Want to get out into remote mountains and hike for days? Follow the ancient trails of the Kumano Kodō. Famous works of art? See the Buddhist sculptures in Nara. Onsen? There's a whole town for that in Kinosaki. Castles? Check. There's enough to fill a whole itinerary here, and it's all easy to access by public transport. There's also much to discover beyond the highlights, including fascinating temples, shrines and archaeological sites that resonate through the ages.

INCLUDES

Kansai Highlights

❶ **Dōtombori** (p372) Getting the full sensory experience at Osaka's famous strip for street food, colourful neon and heaving crowds.

❷ **Tōdai-ji** (p400) Being awed by Japan's largest Buddha statue, housed in one of Nara's (many) fantastic temples.

❸ **Kumano Kodō** (p424) Walking the ancient pilgrimage trails in the remote interior of the Kii Peninsula.

❹ **Oku-no-in** (p420) Wandering through this deeply spiritual Buddhist cemetery with stone pagodas set among soaring cedars.

❺ **Himeji-jō** (p397) Seeing Japan's most magnificent castle, a rare original from the 16th century.

❻ **Kinosaki Onsen** (p448) Wrapping yourself in a *yukata* (light cotton kimono) and hopping from bath to bath at this historic hot-spring resort.

❼ **Ise-jingū** (p433) Feeling the gravitas emanating from Japan's most sacred Shintō shrine.

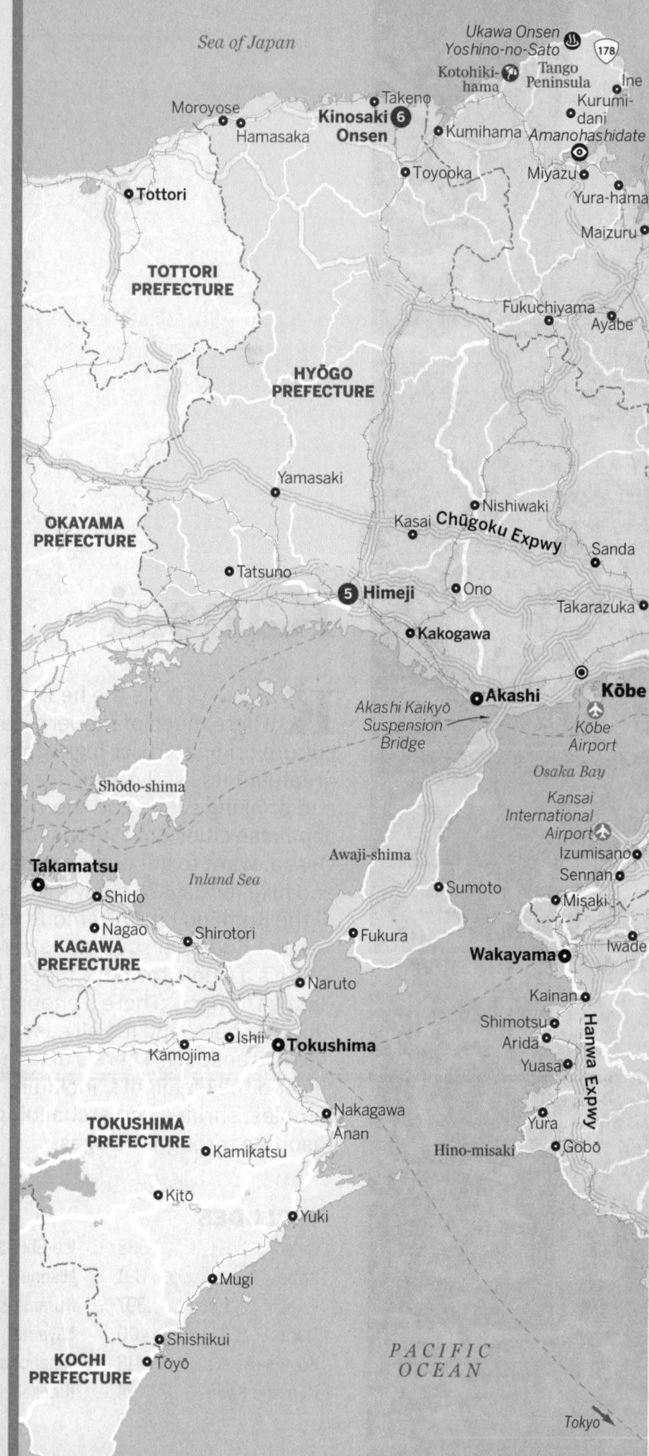

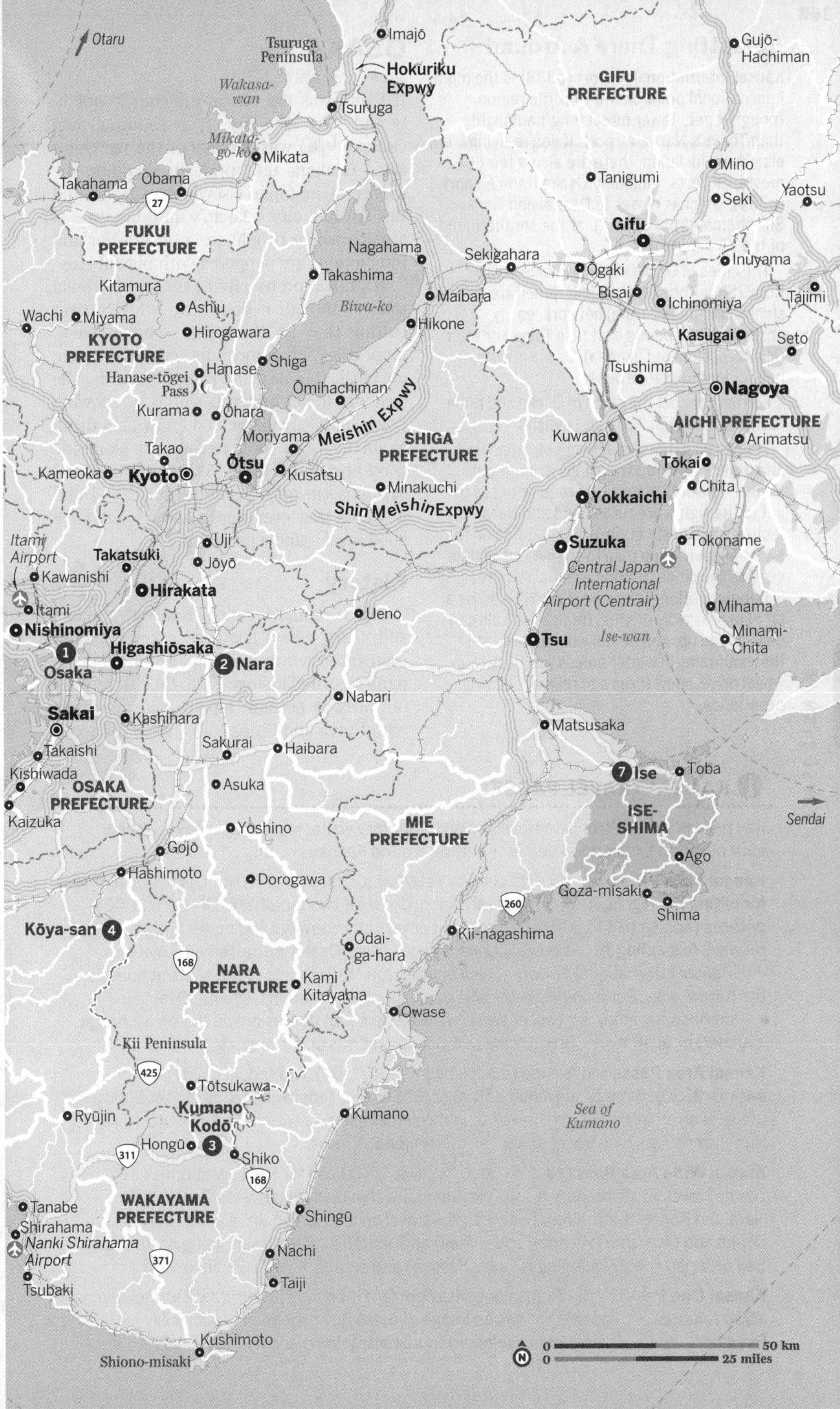

Otaru
Tsuruga Peninsula
Imajō
Hokuriku Expwy
Wakasa-wan
Tsuruga
GIFU PREFECTURE
Gujō-Hachiman
Mikata-go-ko
Mikata
Takahama
Obama
27
FUKUI PREFECTURE
Tanigumi
Mino
Seki
Yaotsu
Gifu
Nagahama
Sekigahara
Inuyama
Takashima
Ōgaki
Kitamura
Bisai
Tajimi
Maibara
Ashiu
Biwa-ko
Ichinomiya
Wachi
Miyama
Hikone
Hirogawara
Kasugai
Seto
KYOTO PREFECTURE
Shiga
Hanase
Hanase-tōgei Pass
Tsushima
Nagoya
Ōmihachiman
Meishin Expwy
Kurama
Ōhara
AICHI PREFECTURE
Moriyama
SHIGA PREFECTURE
Kuwana
Arimatsu
Takao
Ōtsu
Tōkai
Kameoka
Kyoto
Kusatsu
Minakuchi
Chita
Yokkaichi
Shin Meishin Expwy
Itami Airport
Uji
Suzuka
Tokoname
Takatsuki
Jōyō
Central Japan International Airport (Centrair)
Kawanishi
Hirakata
Itami
Ueno
Mihama
Nishinomiya
Tsu
Ise-wan
Minami-Chita
1
Higashiōsaka
2
Nara
Osaka
Nabari
Sakai
Kashihara
Matsusaka
Takaishi
Sakurai
Haibara
Kishiwada
7
Ise
Toba
OSAKA PREFECTURE
Asuka
Kaizuka
ISE-SHIMA
Sendai
Yoshino
MIE PREFECTURE
Gojō
Ago
Hashimoto
Dorogawa
Goza-misaki
260
Shima
Kōya-san
4
Kii-nagashima
Ōdai-ga-hara
168
NARA PREFECTURE
Kami Kitayama
Owase
Kii Peninsula
425
Tōtsukawa
Sea of Kumano
Ryūjin
Kumano Kodō
Kumano
Hongū
3
311
Shiko
168
Tanabe
WAKAYAMA PREFECTURE
Shingū
Shirahama
Nanki Shirahama Airport
Nachi
371
Tsubaki
Taiji
Kushimoto
Shiono-misaki
0
50 km
0
25 miles

Getting There & Around

Kansai International Airport (p388) is the main international point of entry for the region, though it gets fewer direct long-haul flights than Tokyo's Narita Airport. If you're flying from elsewhere in Japan, there are also a few domestic airports, including Osaka Itami Airport (p389), which is closer to Osaka, and Nanki Shirahama Airport (p417), at the southern end of the Kii Peninsula.

The cities of Osaka (Shin-Osaka Station), Kōbe (Shin-Kōbe Station) and Himeji are on the *shinkansen* (bullet-train) network, easily accessed from points east (like Tokyo) or west (like Hiroshima or Fukuoka). Osaka is a major hub for long-distance buses.

Ferries connect the cities of Osaka and Kōbe to the islands of Shikoku and Kyūshū.

There's an extensive network of Japan Rail and other ('private') train lines throughout Kansai. The only places that require buses to get to the sights are rural Kyoto and Nara Prefectures and parts of the Kumano Kodō on the Kii Peninsula. If you plan to spend a lot of time outside the cities, renting a car is an increasingly popular option. Take care if you'll be doing a lot of expressway driving, though, as tolls can quickly add up, and be wary of heading into the mountains in winter unless you have four-wheel drive, snow tyres and relevant driving experience.

OSAKA

06 / POP 2.75 MILLION

If Kyoto was the city of the courtly nobility and Tokyo the city of the samurai, then Osaka (大阪) was the city of the merchant class. Osakans take pride in shedding the conservatism found elsewhere in Japan, and this spirited city – Japan's third-largest – is a place where people are a bit brasher and interactions are peppered with playful jabs.

It's not a pretty city in the conventional sense – though it does have a lovely river cutting through the centre – but it packs more colour than most; its acres of concrete are cloaked in dazzling neon billboards. The best way to get under its skin is by chowing down on local cuisine and enjoying a drink at an *izakaya* (pub restaurant) alongside good-humoured locals. The city's unofficial slogan is *kuidaore* ('eat until you drop'), and it seems that everyone is always out for a good meal – and a good time.

History

Osaka (originally called 'Naniwa', a name still heard today) has been a key port and mercantile centre from the beginning of Japan's recorded history. From the 6th century onwards, it became Japan's base for trade with Korea and China – a gateway for goods

KANSAI TRAVEL PASSES

Rail passes, available only to travellers on temporary visitor visas (you'll have to show your passport), offer good deals for getting around Kansai.

Kansai Thru Pass (www.surutto.com/tickets/kansai_thru_english.html) is the best deal for hitting the highlights of the Kansai region. Good for two (adult/child ¥4000/2000) or three (adult/child ¥5200/2600) days, it covers city subways and buses and private railways (excluding JR lines) that connect Kyoto, Nara, Osaka, Kōbe, Himeji, Kōya-san and Kansai International Airport. It also entitles you to discounts at many attractions in the Kansai area. Purchase at the airport or a Tourist Information Center in Osaka.

Purchase the following two JR West (www.westjr.co.jp) passes online (for an exchange voucher) or at JR Kyoto, Shin-Osaka and Osaka Stations or the airport:

Kansai Area Pass Valid for one (adult/child ¥2300/1150), two (adult/child ¥4500/2250), three (adult/child ¥5500/2750) or four (adult/child ¥6500/3250) days of travel on JR intercity trains (excluding the *shinkansen*) between Osaka, Kyoto, Nara, Himeji and Ōtsu, plus travel to Kansai International Airport.

Kansai Wide Area Pass (adult/child ¥10,000/5000) Valid for five consecutive days; covers travel on JR intercity trains (excluding the *shinkansen*) between Osaka, Kyoto, Nara and Kansai International Airport, plus travel on the San-yō Shinkansen between Osaka and Okayama (via Kōbe and Himeji) and limited express trains going north to the Sea of Japan coast (including Kinosaki Onsen) and south to the Kii Peninsula.

Kansai One Pass (https://kansaionepass.com/en) is an ICOCA card (¥3000, including ¥500 refundable deposit) that has an image of Astro Boy on it and is specifically for foreigners. It offers discounts at selected tourist attractions and some temples.

but also ideas such as Buddhism and empire-building, and new technologies.

In the late 16th century, Osaka rose to prominence when the warlord Toyotomi Hideyoshi, having unified all of Japan after centuries of civil war, chose Osaka as the site for his castle. Merchants set up around the castle and the city grew into a busy economic centre. When Tokugawa Ieyasu moved the seat of power to Edo (now Tokyo) in the early 17th century, he adopted a hands-off approach to the city, allowing merchants to prosper unhindered by government interference. During the Edo period (1603–1868) Osaka served as Japan's largest distribution centre for rice (which was akin to currency at the time), earning it the nickname 'Japan's Kitchen'.

In the late 19th and 20th centuries, as economic influence became increasingly consolidated in Tokyo, Osaka reinvented itself as one of the most productive manufacturing centres in East Asia. Unfortunately this made it a bombing target during WWII. During the 1945 air raids, one-third of the city centre was levelled and upwards of 10,000 people were killed.

Today commerce remains vital to Osaka – it is the business hub of western Japan – while the greater Keihanshin Industrial Zone, of which Osaka is part, is one of Japan's great manufacturing centres.

Sights

Central Osaka is commonly divided into Kita (North) and Minami (South). The de facto dividing line is two rivers, Dōjima-gawa and Tosabori-gawa, and the island of Naka-no-shima. This area along the river is where the city's historic commercial district was established; Osaka-jō (Osaka Castle) sits about 1km east of here. Tennōji is even further south than Minami. The bayside Tempōzan neighbourhood and Universal Studios are west of the city centre. North of the city centre, is Banpaku-kinen-kōen, a sprawling park and home to a couple of worthwhile sights.

Kita

Kita (キタ; 'north') is the city's centre of gravity by day in office buildings, department stores and shopping complexes – plus the transit hubs of JR Osaka and Hankyū Umeda Stations (and the multiple train and subway lines converging here).

OSAKA IN ONE DAY

Start with a visit to **Osaka-jō** (p371); on the way, swing by **Gout** (p382) for pastries to eat on the castle lawns. Take the subway or enjoy a stroll along the river to Naka-no-shima for coffee with river views at **Brooklyn Roasting Company** (p384).

Then head down to Namba and have a wander through **Dōguya-suji Arcade** (p387), lined with kitchenware shops, and **Kuromon Ichiba** (p372), a food market. Sample Osaka speciality *tako-yaki* (octopus dumplings) at Wanaka Honten (p383) for lunch.

As the lights dim, head over to **Ebisu-bashi** (p372) before joining the nightly throngs in neon-lit **Dōtombori** (p372). There are plenty of places to eat here, like *okonomiyaki* (savoury pancakes) at **Chibo** (p383). See where the night takes you in bar- and club-packed **Amerika-Mura** (p372).

Umeda Sky Building NOTABLE BUILDING

(梅田スカイビル; Map p374; ☎06-6440-3855; www.kuchu-teien.com; 1-1-88 Ōyodonaka, Kita-ku; adult/child ¥1500/700; ⊙observation decks 9.30am-10.30pm, last entry 10pm; JR Osaka, north central exit) Osaka's landmark Sky Building (1993) resembles a 40-storey, space-age Arc de Triomphe. Twin towers are connected at the top by a 'floating garden' (really a garden-free observation deck), which was constructed on the ground and then hoisted up. The 360-degree city views from here are breathtaking day or night. Getting there is half the fun – an escalator in a see-through tube takes you up the last five storeys (not for vertigo sufferers). The architect, Hara Hiroshi, also designed Kyoto Station (p314).

O-hatsu Ten-jin SHINTŌ SHRINE

(お初天神, Tsuyu-no-Ten-jinsha; Map p374; ☎06-6311-0895; www.tuyutenjin.com; 2-5-4 Sonezaki, Kita-ku; ⊙6am-midnight; S Tanimachi line to Higashi-Umeda, exit 7, exit 15, JR Osaka, Sakura-bashi exit) FREE Hiding in plain sight amid the skyscrapers of Umeda, this 1300-year-old shrine owes its fame to one of Japan's best-known tragic plays (based on true events). Star-crossed lovers O-hatsu, a prostitute, and Tokubei, a merchant's apprentice, committed double suicide here in 1703, to remain together forever in the afterlife rather than live apart. The current shrine

Osaka

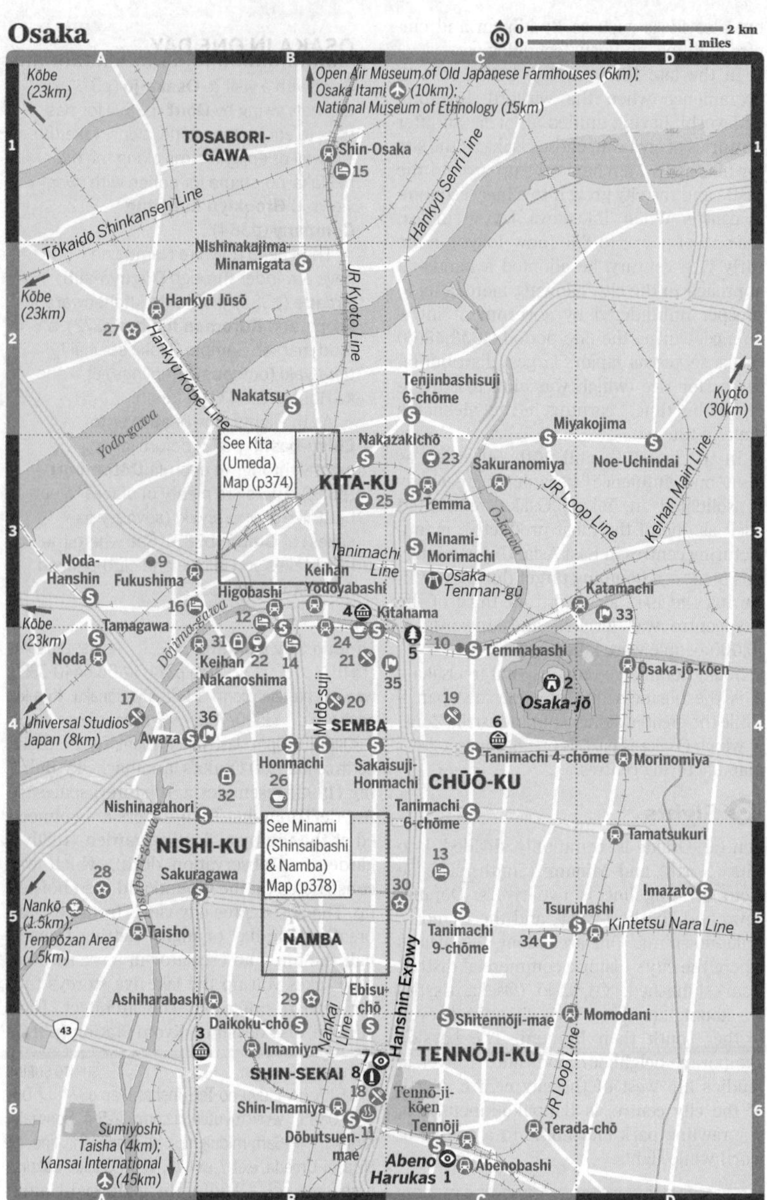

was constructed in 1957 (WWII destroyed the previous one); it's popular with couples, who come to pray for strength in love – and happier endings.

The shrine is just southeast of Ohatsutenjin-dōri arcade. There's a flea market here the first Friday of each month.

Naka-no-shima & Around

South of Kita, sandwiched between the rivers Dōjima-gawa and Tosabori-gawa, the island of Naka-no-shima (中之島) is a pleasant oasis, with riverside walkways, art museums, early 20th-century architecture and the

Osaka

park, **Naka-no-shima-kōen** (中之島公園; Map p370; Ⓢ Sakai-suji line to Kitahama, exit 26).

If you're coming from Kyoto, the Keihan line runs direct to Yodoyabashi Station; the island is a 15-minute walk south of JR Osaka Station.

★Osaka-jō CASTLE

(大阪城; Osaka Castle; Map p370; www.osakacastle.net; 1-1 Osaka-jō, Chūō-ku; grounds/castle keep free/¥600, combined with Osaka Museum of History ¥900; ⏲9am-5pm, open later at certain times in spring and summer; Ⓢ Chūō line to Tanimachi 4-chōme, exit 9, Ⓡ JR Loop line to Osaka-jō-kōen) After unifying Japan in the late 16th century, General Toyotomi Hideyoshi built this castle (1583) as a display of power, using, it's said, the labour of 100,000 workers. Although the present structure is a 1931 concrete reconstruction (refurbished in 1997), it's nonetheless quite a sight, looming dramatically over the surrounding park and moat. Inside is an excellent collection of art, armour, and day-to-day implements related to the castle, Hideyoshi and Osaka. An 8th-floor observation deck has 360-degree views.

Hideyoshi's original granite structure was said to be impregnable, yet it was destroyed in 1614 by the armies of Tokugawa Ieyasu (the founder of the Tokugawa shogunate). Ieyasu had the castle rebuilt, using the latest advancements to create terrifically imposing walls of enormous stones. The largest are estimated to weigh over a 100 tonnes; some are engraved with the crests of feudal lords.

Thirteen structures, including several turrets, remain from this 17th-century reconstruction. Osaka citizens raised money themselves to rebuild the main keep; in 1931 the new tower was revealed, with glittering gold-leaf tigers stalking the eaves.

At night the castle is lit with floodlights (and looks like a ghostly structure hovering above ground). Visit the lawns on a warm weekend and you might catch local musicians staging casual shows. The castle and park are at their colourful best (and most crowded) in the cherry-blossom and autumn-foliage seasons.

Museum of Oriental Ceramics MUSEUM

(大阪市立東洋陶磁美術館; Map p370; ☎06-6223-0055; www.moco.or.jp; 1-1-26 Naka-no-shima; adult/student/child ¥500/300/free, special exhibitions extra; ⏲9.30am-5pm, closed Mon; Ⓢ Midō-suji line to Yodoyabashi, exit 1) This museum has one of the world's finest collections of Chinese and Korean ceramics, with smaller galleries of Japanese ceramics and Chinese snuff bottles. At any one time, approximately 400 of the gorgeous pieces from the permanent collection are on display, and there are often special exhibits (with an extra charge). The permanent collection has good English descriptions.

Osaka Museum of History MUSEUM
(大阪歴史博物館, Osaka Rekishi Hakubutsukan; Map p370; www.mus-his.city.osaka.jp; 4-1-32 Ōtemae, Chūō-ku; adult/student/child ¥600/400/free, combined with Osaka-jō ¥900; ⌚9.30am-5pm, closed Tue; Ⓢ Tanimachi or Chūō line to Tanimachi 4-chōme, exit 9) Built above the ruins of Naniwa Palace (c 650), visible through the ground floor, this museum tells Osaka's story from the era of this early palace to the early 20th century. There are enough English explanations and many of the displays are highly visible, including a walk-through recreation of old city life. You can also rent an English-language audio guide (¥200). There are great views of Osaka-jō (p371) from the 10th floor.

Minami

Minami (ミナミ; 'south'), which includes the neighbourhoods Namba, Shinsaibashi, Dōtombori and Amerika-Mura, is the comic to Kita's 'straight man'. It's here that you'll see the flashy neon signs and vibrant street life that you expect of Osaka. By day, Minami is primarily a shopping district; after dark, restaurants, bars, clubs and theatres take over.

Namba and Shinsaibashi subway stations, both on the Midō-suji line, are convenient for this area.

★ **Dōtombori** AREA
(道頓堀; Map p378; www.dotonbori.or.jp; Ⓢ Midō-suji line to Namba, exit 14) Highly photogenic Dōtombori is the city's liveliest night spot and the centre of the southern part of town. Its name comes from the 400-year-old canal, Dōtombori-gawa, now lined with pedestrian walkways and with a riot of illuminated billboards glittering off its waters. Don't miss the famous **Glico running man** sign. South of the canal is a pedestrianised street that has dozens of restaurants vying for attention with the flashiest of signage.

For the best views, head to **Ebisu-bashi** (戎橋; Map p378), the bridge at the western end of the strip.

★ **Amerika-Mura** AREA
(アメリカ村, America Village, Ame-Mura; Map p378; www.americamura.jp; Nishi-Shinsaibashi, Chūō-ku; Ⓢ Midō-suji line to Shinsaibashi, exit 7) West of Midō-suji, Amerika-Mura is a compact enclave of hip, youth-focused and offbeat shops, plus cafes, bars, tattoo and piercing parlours, nightclubs, hair salons and a few discreet love hotels. In the middle is **Triangle Park** (三角公園, Sankaku-kōen; Map p378), an all-concrete 'park' with benches for sitting and watching the fashion parade. Come nighttime, it's a popular gathering spot.

Around the neighbourhood, look for street lamps resembling stick-figure people, some painted by artists; the **Peace on Earth** mural (1983), painted by Osaka artist Seitaro Kuroda, and, of course, a mini **Statue of Liberty**.

Ame-Mura owes its name to shops that sprang up after WWII, selling American goods such as Zippo lighters and T-shirts.

Kuromon Ichiba MARKET
(黒門市場, Kuromon Market; Map p378; www.kuromon.com; Nipponbashi, Chūō-ku; ⌚most shops 9am-6pm; Ⓢ Sakai-suji line to Nipponbashi, exit 10) An Osaka landmark for over a century, this 600m-long market is in equal parts a functioning market and a tourist attraction. Vendors selling fresh fish, meat, produce and pickles attract chefs and local home cooks; shops offering takeaway sushi or with grills set up (to cook the steaks, oysters, giant prawns etc that they sell) cater to visitors – making the market excellent for grazing and photo ops.

Hōzen-ji BUDDHIST TEMPLE
(法善寺; Map p378; www.houzenji.jp; 1-2-16 Namba, Chūō-ku; Ⓢ Midō-suji line to Namba, exit 14) This tiny temple hidden down a narrow alley houses a statue of Fudō Myō-ō (a deity of esoteric Buddhism), covered in thick moss. It's a favourite of people employed in *mizu shōbai* ('water trade' – a euphemism for the sexually charged night world), who pause before work to throw some water on the statue.

Hōzen-ji Yokochō (法善寺横丁, Hōzen-ji Alley; Map p378), the alley filled with traditional restaurants and bars, runs between the temple and the Sennichi-mae shopping arcade.

Tennōji

★ **Abeno Harukas** NOTABLE BUILDING
(あべのハルカス; Map p370; www.abenoharukas-300.jp; 1-1-43 Abeno-suji, Abeno-ku; observation deck: adult ¥1500; child from ¥500-700, under 4yr free; ⌚observation deck 9am-10pm;

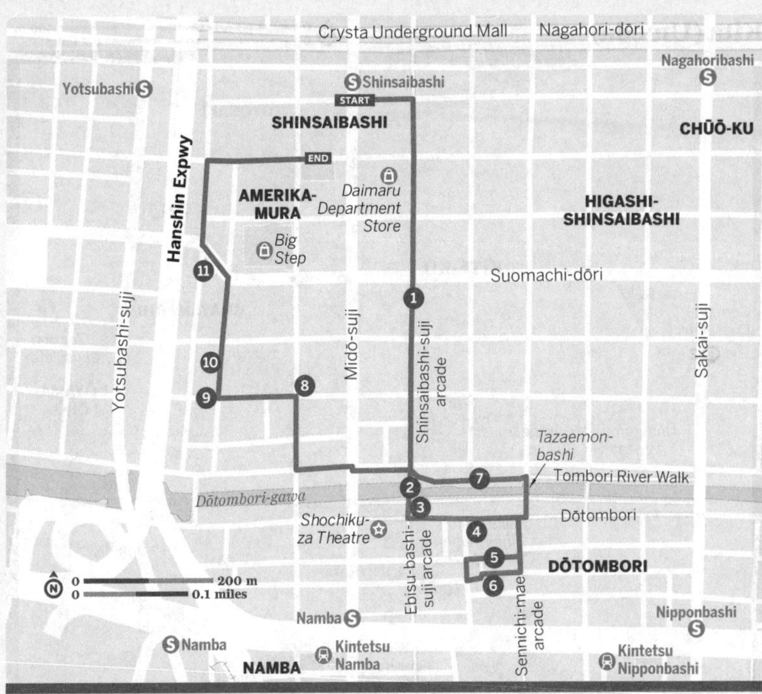

City Walk Sights of Minami

START SHINSAIBASHI STATION
END SHINSAIBASHI STATION
LENGTH 2.5KM; 2½ HOURS

Head out just before dusk to see the daylight fade and the neon lights of Dōtombori take over. Start with a stroll down ❶ **Shinsaibashi-suji** (p386), Shinsaibashi's famous covered *shōtengai* (market street). Emerging from the arcade, you'll hit the bridge, ❷ **Ebisu-bashi**, the most popular place for photos down the canal, Dōtombori-gawa.

Go left past ❸ **Kani Dōraku Honten** (かに道楽本店; Map p378; 1-6-18 Dōtombori; S Midō-suji line to Namba, exit 14), the crab restaurant with the giant animated crab suspended over the entrance – another local landmark. This will take you to the main Dōtombori strip, past restaurants and food stands marked with evermore outlandish signage that takes the plastic food model concept to a whole new level – a giant octopus indicates, for example, a *tako-yaki* (grilled octopus dumpling) stand. On your right look for the drumming mechanical clown Kuidaore Tarō at ❹ **Nakaza Cuidaore Building** (中座くいだおれビル; Map p378; 1-7-21 Dōtombori), the mascot for the city's eating culture.

Before the big cow, take a right down Sennichi-mae arcade. Turn again at the cobblestoned alley with the wooden signboard for ❺ **Hōzen-ji Yokochō**, and you're suddenly in an older, quieter Osaka, one charmingly lantern-lit in the evening. At the end, go left then through the temple gateway to tiny ❻ **Hōzen-ji**. Continue past the temple back around to the Dōtombori strip. Cross Tazaemon-bashi and head left on the ❼ **Tombori River Walk** – the promenade that runs alongside the canal.

Cross Shinsaibashi-suji and then turn right, into ❽ **Amerika-Mura**. Grab some *ika-yaki* (grilled squid) at ❾ **Za Ikaga** (p383) or *tako-yaki* at the branch of famed ❿ **Wanaka** (p383) next door. Eat them here on the street or get 'em to go and head to ⓫ **Triangle Park** – the district's popular local gathering spot. From here you can embark on an evening of bar-hopping in Amerika-Mura, or make your way back to Shinsaibashi Station.

Kita (Umeda)

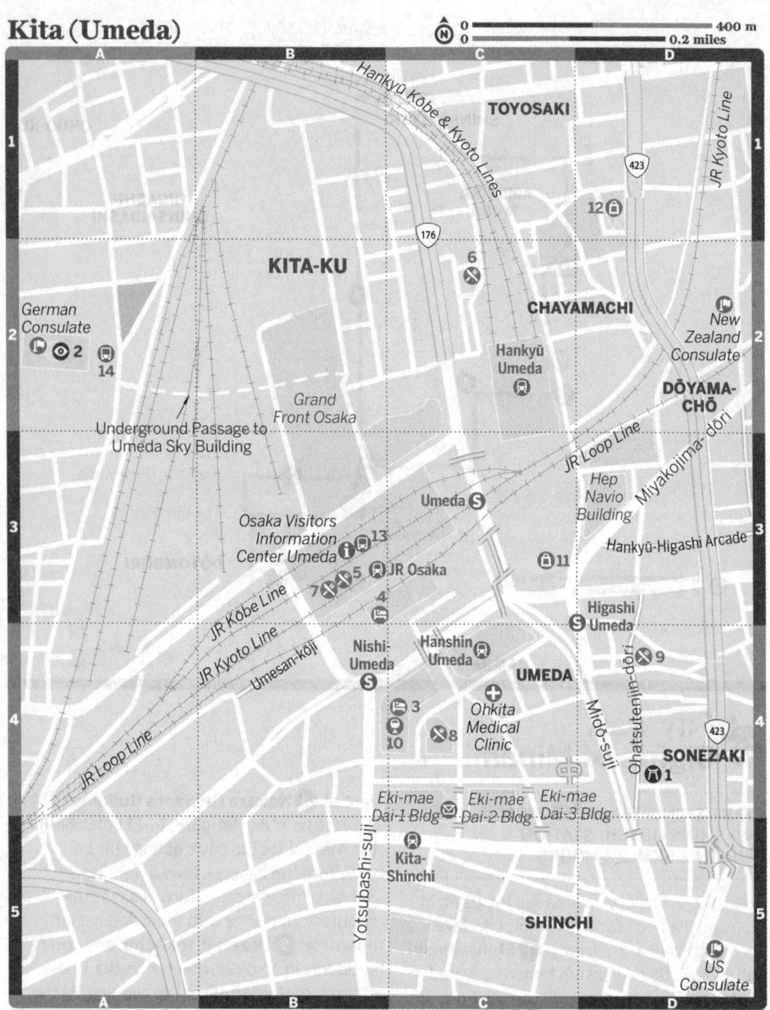

Kita (Umeda)

Sights
1 O-hatsu Ten-jin D4
2 Umeda Sky Building A2

Sleeping
3 Hilton Osaka C4
4 Hotel Granvia Osaka B3

Eating
5 Eki Marché B3
6 Ganko Umeda Honten C2
7 Kaiten Sushi Ganko B3
8 Osaka Maru Building C4
Robatayaki Isaribi .... (see 6)
9 Yukari D4

Drinking & Nightlife
10 Windows on the World C4

Shopping
11 Hankyū Umeda Department Store C3
King Kong Records .... (see 8)
12 Maruzen & Junkudō Umeda D1

Transport
13 JR Osaka Station Highway Bus Terminal B3
14 Willer Bus Terminal A2

(S Midō-suji to Tennōji, R JR Loop line to Tennōji) This César Pelli–designed tower, which opened in March 2014, is Japan's tallest building (300m, 60 storeys). The observatory on the 16th floor is free, but admission is required for the highly recommended top-level **Harukas 300 observation deck**, which has incredible 360-degree views of the whole Kansai region through windows that run several storeys high. There's also an open-air atrium. It houses Japan's largest department store (Kintetsu, floors B2–14), the **Abeno Harukas Art Museum** (あべのハルカス美術館; ☎06-4399-9050; www.aham.jp; admission varies by exhibition; ⏲10am-8pm Tue-Fri, to 6pm Sat & Sun), a hotel, offices and restaurants.

The brave can take part in **Edge of Harukas** (¥1000) where you walk the 20-metre-long ledge while tethered to the building; bring your passport. Although Abeno Harukas is Japan's tallest building, the tallest structure is Tokyo Sky Tree (p105), at 634m.

Shin-Sekai AREA

(新世界; Map p370; Naniwa-ku; S Midō-suji line to Dōbutsuen-mae, exit 5) A century ago, Shin-Sekai ('new world') was home to an amusement park that defined cutting edge. Now this entertainment district mixes down-at-heel with retro cool. It's centred on the crusty, trusty, 103m-high steel-frame tower **Tsūten-kaku** (通天閣; Map p370; ☎06-6641-9555; www.tsutenkaku.co.jp; 1-18-6 Ebisu-higashi, Naniwa-ku; adult/child ¥700/400; ⏲9am-9pm) – built 1912, rebuilt 1956 – and surrounded by ancient *pachinko* and mahjong parlours that draw some truly down-and-out characters. At the same time, Shin-Sekai draws plenty of visitors for nostalgia and cheap eateries behind over-the-top signage, especially for kushikatsu (deep-fried meat and vegetables on skewers; p382).

Sumiyoshi Taisha SHINTŌ SHRINE

(住吉大社; www.sumiyoshitaisha.net; 2-9-89 Sumiyoshi, Sumiyoshi-ku; ⏲6am-5pm Apr-Sep, from 6.30am Oct-Mar; Hankai line to Sumiyoshi-torii-mae, R Nankai line to Sumiyoshi-taisha) FREE Dedicated to Shintō deities of the sea and sea travel, this graceful shrine was founded in the early 3rd century and is considered the headquarters for all Sumiyoshi shrines in Japan. The buildings are faithful replicas of the ancient originals, with a couple that date back to 1810, and the grounds are criss-crossed by a tree- and lantern-lined waterway spanned by a bright orange drum bridge. It's a rare Shintō shrine that predates the influence of Chinese Buddhist architectural styles.

The Hankai line tram from Tennōji stops right in front of the *torii* (Shintō shrine gate).

Liberty Osaka MUSEUM

(大阪人権博物館, Osaka Human Rights Museum; Map p370; ☎06-6561-5891; www.liberty.or.jp; 3-6-36 Naniwa-nishi, Naniwa-ku; adult/student/child ¥500/300/200; ⏲10am-4pm Wed-Fri, 1-5pm Sat, closed Sun, Mon & every 4th Fri & Sat; S Midō-suji line to Daikoku-chō, exit 5, R JR Loop line to Imamiya) Japan's first human rights museum began in 1985 as an archive of documents relating to the *burakumin* – the lowest caste under the old feudal system (against whom discrimination continued into the modern age). The museum has since grown to cover a variety of topics, from sexual politics to the struggles of Japanese of Korean ancestry. Its portrait of contemporary Japan is unflinching. English is provided via an audio guide and a booklet with translations of some (though not all) exhibitions.

Tempōzan

Trudging through the urban morass of Kita or Minami, you could easily forget that Osaka is actually a port city. Remind yourself with a trip to Tempōzan (天保山), a bayside development with family-oriented attractions.

Osaka Aquarium Kaiyūkan AQUARIUM

(海遊館; ☎06-6576-5501; www.kaiyukan.com; 1-1-10 Kaigan-dōri, Minato-ku; adult ¥2300, child ¥600-1200; ⏲10am-8pm, last entry 7pm; S Chuō line to Osaka-kō, exit 1) Kaiyūkan is among Japan's best aquariums. An 800m-plus walkway winds past displays of sea life from around the Pacific 'ring of fire': Antarctic penguins, coral-reef butterflyfish, unreasonably cute Arctic otters, Monterey Bay seals and unearthly jellyfish. Most impressive is the ginormous central tank, housing a whale shark, manta rays and thousands of other fish. Note there are also captive dolphins here, which some visitors may not appreciate; there is growing evidence that keeping cetaceans in captivity is harmful for the animals.

There are good English descriptions, but the audio guide (¥500) gives more detail. Expect lots of families and school groups.

The Osaka Kaiyu Ticket (adult/child ¥2550/1300) combines entry to the aquarium with one-day unlimited transport on city subways and discounted admission to other sites. Purchase at any subway station. Check the schedule online, as the aquarium closes for a couple of days in January and February.

Banpaku-kinen-kōen

Banpaku-kinen-kōen, also called Senri Expo Park, was the site of the 1970 World Fair – the first such event to be held in Japan and a big moment for Osaka. Little remains of the futuristic (for the time) installations; today it's a sprawling park containing the city's best museum. Banpaku-kinen-kōen is a stop on the Osaka Monorail; the Midō-suji and Tanimachi subway lines intersect with the Osaka Monorail; so does the Hankyū Kyoto line. The sights are a 10-minute walk from the monorail station.

★National Museum of Ethnology MUSEUM

(国立民族学博物館; ☎06-6876-2151; www.minpaku.ac.jp; 10-1 Senri Expo Park, Suita; adult/child ¥420/free; ⏲10am-5pm, closed Wed; Osaka Monorail to Banpaku-kinen-kōen) This ambitious museum showcases the world's cultures, presenting them as the continuous (and tangled) strings that they are. There are plenty of traditional masks, textiles and pottery, but also Ghanaian barbershop signboards, Bollywood movie posters and even a Filipino jeepney. Don't miss the music room, where you can summon global street performances via a touch panel. There are also exhibits on Okinawan history and Japan's indigenous Ainu culture. There's English signage, but the audio guide gives more detail.

Tower of the Sun SCULPTURE

(太陽の塔, Taiyō-no-tō; Senri Expo Park, Suita; Osaka Monorail to Banpaku-kinen-kōen) The 70m-tall Tower of the Sun was created by Japanese artist Okamoto Tarō for Osaka's Expo '70. While the curious three-faced creature (there's one face in the back) has been open to interpretation (and critique) for decades, there's no doubt that it has become the symbol of the expo and of the energy and optimism that surrounded it.

Redhorse Osaka Ferris Wheel FERRIS WHEEL

(http://osaka-wheel.com; Expo City; ticket ¥1000; ⏲10am-11pm, last ride 10.40pm; Osaka Monorail to Banpaku-kinen-kōen) Japan's tallest Ferris wheel (123m), and the fifth tallest in the world, opened in 2016 and offers sweeping views over Expo Park and the Tower of the Sun statue. Not for acrophobes, the gondolas come with transparent floors to peer down through on the 18-minute rotation.

Greater Osaka

Momofuku Andō Instant Ramen Museum MUSEUM

(インスタントラーメン発明記念館; ☎072-752-3484; www.cupnoodles-museum.jp; 8-25 Masumi-cho, Ikeda; ⏲9.30am-4.30pm, last entry 3.30pm, closed Tue; Hankyū line to Hankyū Ikeda, east exit) FREE From its humble invention in 1958 by Andō Momofuku (1910–2007; later chair of Nissin Foods), instant rāmen has become a global business and one of Japan's most famous exports. Exhibits here illustrate the origin of Cup Noodles and how they're made; there's also a 'tunnel' of Nissin products that showcases a half-century of package design. The highlight, however, is getting to create your own custom-blend Cup Noodles to take away (¥300), including decorating the cup.

Get the free English-language audio guide (¥2000 deposit). Expect long queues at weekends. It's about a 10-minute walk from the station. Take the east exit and head down the stairs; go left and then right at the small tourist information centre, and the museum will be on your right shortly.

Activities

★Spa World ONSEN

(スパワールド; Map p370; ☎06-6631-0001; www.spaworld.co.jp; 3-4-24 Ebisu-higashi, Naniwa-ku; day pass ¥1300; ⏲10am-8.45am the next day; S Midō-suji line to Dōbutsu-en-mae, exit 5, JR Loop line to Shin-Imamiya) This huge, seven-storey onsen (hot-spring) complex contains dozens of options from saunas to salt baths, styled after a mini-UN's worth of nations. Gender-separated 'Asian' and 'European' bathing zones (bathe in the buff, towels provided) switch monthly. Swimsuits (rental ¥600, or BYO) are worn in swimming pools and *ganbanyoku* (stone baths; additional ¥800 Monday to Friday, ¥1000 Saturday and Sunday).

Many visitors stay and splash for hours; there are casual restaurants here and even 'relaxation rooms' with armchairs where you can choose to spend the night. Visitors with tattoos are not permitted.

Universal Studios Japan AMUSEMENT PARK

(ユニバーサルスタジオジャパン, Universal City; ☎0570-200-606; www.usj.co.jp; 2-1-33 Sakura-jima, Konohana-ku; 1-day pass adult/child ¥7400/5100, 2-day pass ¥13,400/9000; ⏲varies seasonally; JR Yumesaki line to Universal City) Modelled after sister parks in the US, 'USJ' bursts with Hollywood movie-related rides, shows, shops and restaurants. Top billing goes to the ¥45-billion (!) **Wizarding World of Harry Potter**, a painstakingly recreated Hogsmeade Village (shop for magic wands, Gryffindor capes and butterbeer) plus the 'Harry Potter and the Forbidden Journey' thrill ride through Hogwarts School.

Wizarding World admission is by timed ticket. Leaflet maps and signage are in English, though narrations and entertainment are in Japanese.

Long queues are common at the park's major venues (1½ hours, or more, is not unusual for the Harry Potter ride). To shorten waits, USJ offers a variety of express passes that allow you to bypass queues, at an (often significant) extra charge; check the website.

To get here, take the JR Loop line to Nishi-kujō Station, then switch to the JR Yumesaki line for Universal Studios (total trip ¥180, 15 minutes).

Tombori River Cruise CRUISE

(とんぼりリバークルーズ; Map p378; ☎06-6441-0532; www.ipponmatsu.co.jp/cruise/tombori.html; Don Quijote Bldg, 7-13 Sōemon-chō, Chūō-ku; adult/child ¥900/400; ⏲1-9pm Mon-Fri, from 11am Sat & Sun; Ⓢ Midō-suji line to Namba, exit 14) One way to beat the crowds in Dōtombori is to hop on a boat. Tombori's short, 20-minute trips past the neon signs run on the hour and the half-hour. Night time is best, though slots fill up quickly; tickets go on sale at the pier an hour before the first cruise of the day starts. Osaka Amazing Pass holders ride free.

Reception is on the 1st floor of the Don Quijote Bldg (identifiable by the oddly shaped Ferris wheel on top).

Tours

★Cycle Osaka CYCLING

(Map p370; ☎080-5325-8975; www.cycleosaka.com; 2-12-1 Sagisu, Fukushima-ku; half-/full-day tours ¥5000/10,000; Ⓡ JR Loop line to Fukushima) English-speaking guides lead well-organised tours to sights both well known and less well known, along the river banks and through the markets. The food route (¥8000) is particularly recommended. Fees include bicycle and helmet rental, water and food. It also rents out bikes (¥1500 per day).

Ninja Food Tours FOOD

(www.ninjafoodtours.com; tours ¥9500) Runs enjoyable evening food tours (in English) stopping in at local eateries to sample some of the city's specialities. The price includes dinner and two drinks.

Ofune Camome CRUISE

(御舟かもめ; Map p370; ☎050-3736-6333; www.ofune-camome.net; cruises ¥2100-4500, child half-price; Ⓢ Tanimachi line to Temmabashi, exit 18) This small wooden boat, with a few beanbags on the prow, cruises up and down the Yodo-gawa alongside Naka-no-shima; its small size means that, unless the tide is really high, it can go places that larger boats can't. The captain speaks some English and explains the significance of the buildings and bridges. Book at least three days in advance.

Opt for a breakfast cruise (¥3200) if you can; the lighting is best in the morning and the breakfast of organic farm-fresh fruits and homemade rice bread is delicious. Most cruises depart from the Hachikenya-hama Pier (八軒家浜船着場) near Tenma-bashi.

Festivals & Events

★Tenjin Matsuri CULTURAL

(天神祭; www.tenjinmatsuri.com; ⏲24 & 25 Jul) This is one of Japan's three biggest festivals and is dedicated to Sugawara Michizane, the Japanese deity of scholarship and learning. Try to make the second day, when processions of *mikoshi* (portable shrines) and people in traditional attire start at **Osaka Tenman-gū** (大阪天満宮; Map p370; ☎06-6353-0025; www.tenjinsan.com; 2-1-8 Tenjinbashi, Kita-ku; ⏲9am-5pm; Ⓢ Tanimachi line to Minami-Morimachi, exit 4b) and end up in hundreds of boats on the Ō-kawa. There's a huge fireworks display as night falls.

Summer Sonic MUSIC

(www.summersonic.com; Maishima Sonic Park; 1-day/2-day ticket ¥14,500/25,500; ⏲Aug) Held over two days in August, this annual music festival attracts an impressive line-up of international and Japanese bands. Past acts include Teenage Fanclub, Weezer, Radiohead, Beyonce, Beat Crusaders and the Pixies.

Kishiwada Danjiri Matsuri CULTURAL

(岸和田だんじり祭; ⏲Sep) Osaka's wildest festival, held over the 3rd weekend in September, is a kind of running of the bulls except with *danjiri* (festival floats), many weighing over 3000kg. The *danjiri* are hauled through the streets by hundreds of people using ropes – take care and stand back. Most of the action takes place on the second day. The best place to see it is west of Kishiwada Station on the Nankai main line (from Nankai Station).

Minami (Shinsaibashi & Namba)

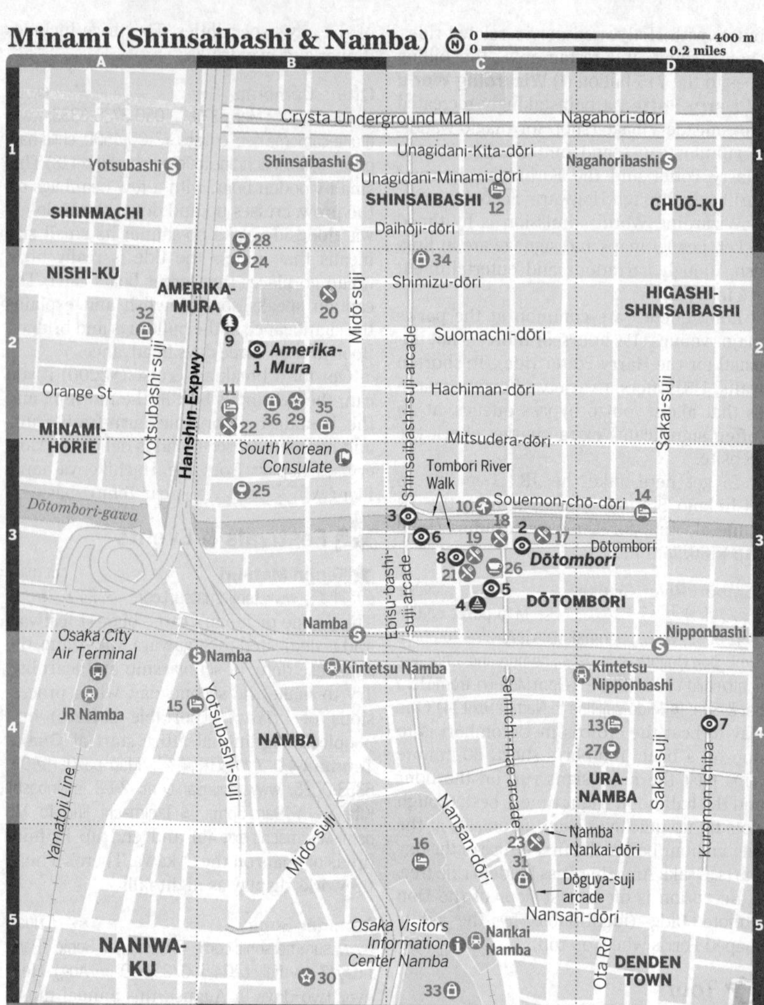

Sleeping

Check websites for discounted rates; expect prices to rise by 10% to 20% on weekends. Base yourself in Minami for access to a larger selection of bars, restaurants and shops, or in Kita for fast access to long-distance transport.

Kita

U-en GUESTHOUSE ¥
(由苑; Map p370; ☎06-7503-4394; www.hostelosaka.com; 2-9-23 Fukushima, Fukushima-ku; dm/d from ¥2800/6200; ; JR Loop line to Fukushima) Inside a restored, century-old townhouse down a quiet lane, U-en has seven upstairs rooms with a variety of bedding – futons and tatami mats in private rooms and bunks or capsules (with curtains, lockers and shelves) in dorms. It's beautifully done, though pretty touches like *shōji* (sliding rice-paper doors) mean that sound does travel. Staff speak English; bicycle rental available (¥500 per day).

All of this sits atop an attractive cafe, where you can get coffee (from ¥400) and croissants in the morning (or beer in the evening).

Minami (Shinsaibashi & Namba)

Top Sights
1 Amerika-Mura B2
2 Dōtombori C3

Sights
3 Ebisu-bashi C3
4 Hōzen-ji C3
5 Hōzen-ji Yokochō C3
6 Kani Dōraku Honten C3
7 Kuromon Ichiba D4
8 Nakaza Cuidaore Building C3
9 Triangle Park B2

Activities, Courses & Tours
10 Tombori River Cruise C3

Sleeping
11 Capsule Hotel Asahi Plaza Shinsaibashi B2
12 Hotel the Flag C1
13 Kamon Hotel Namba D4
14 Kaneyoshi Ryokan D3
15 Khaosan World Namba A4
16 Swissotel Nankai Osaka C5

Eating
17 Chibō C3
18 Daruma Dōtombori-ten C3
19 Imai Honten C3
20 Planet 3rd B2
21 Shoubentango-tei C3
22 Wanaka Amerika-mura-ten B2
23 Wanaka Honten C5
Za Ikaga ..... (see 22)

Drinking & Nightlife
24 Circus B2
25 Folk Rock Bar Phoebe B3
26 Jun-kissa American C3
27 Misono Building D4
28 Rock Rock B1

Entertainment
29 Hokage B2
30 Sumo Spring Tournament B5

Shopping
31 Dōguya-suji Arcade C5
32 Flake Records A2
33 Namba Parks C5
34 Shinsaibashi-suji Shōtengai C2
35 Standard Books B2
36 Time Bomb Records B2

Hilton Osaka HOTEL ¥¥¥
(ヒルトン大阪; Map p374; ☎06-6347-7111; http://osaka.hilton.com; 1-8-8 Umeda, Kita-ku; d/tw from ¥27,000; S Yotsubashi line to Nishi-Umeda, exit 6, JR Osaka, south central exit) The Hilton has spacious rooms with king-sized beds and lovely touches such as *shoji* (sliding rice-paper) window screens. Staff speak English and are at home with foreign guests. Facilities include a small fitness centre with a 15m pool and a **bar** (ウィンドーズオンザワールド; 5.30pm-12.30am Mon-Fri, to 1am Sat & Sun) with city views. The hotel is across from JR Osaka Station's southern side.

Hotel Granvia Osaka HOTEL ¥¥¥
(ホテルグランヴィア大阪; Map p374; ☎06-6344-1235; www.hotelgranviaosaka.jp; 3-1-1 Umeda, Kita-ku; s/d/tw from ¥13,600/20,600/20,600; JR Osaka, south central exit) Above JR Osaka Station, this hotel's 700-plus rooms (on floors 21 to 27) run the gamut from could-use-an-update to futuristic luxe (on the top-level 'Granvia' floor). A glass roof over the tracks cuts out virtually all train noise. Request an outward-facing room for skyline views.

Naka-no-shima & Around

Hotel Cordia BOUTIQUE HOTEL ¥¥
(Map p370; ☎06-6449-2030; www.cordia-osaka.com; 1-3-25 Edobori, Nishi-ku; s/d/tw/family ¥13,500/14,800/16,500/22,000; S Yotsubashi line to Higobashi, exit 3) Conveniently located a short hop from Higobashi Station, close to the river and Naka-no-shima's sights, and a 20-minute walk from the Umeda area, Cordia is a great-value hotel with a boutique feel. Rooms slot into the cool and contemporary category with blonde-wood and rainfall showers. Staff go out of their way to help.

★ **Conrad Osaka** LUXURY HOTEL ¥¥¥
(Map p370; ☎06-6222-0111; www.conradhotels3.hilton.com; 3-2-4 Nakanoshima, Kita-ku; r from ¥52,000-116,000; S Yotsubashi line to Higobashi, exit 2) Opened in 2017, the Conrad has injected some much-needed contemporary glamour into Osaka's hotel scene. Occupying floors 33 to 40 of the Festival Tower West skyscraper in Naka-no-shima, there are gobsmacking views throughout, from the eye-popping artwork-strewn lobby to the spacious, urban-chic rooms and striking pool. Plenty of dining options, a gym, a spa and exemplary service round it off.

OSAKA ACCOMMODATION TAX

The following accommodation tax is charged per person per night:

- ¥100 per person per night for lodgings that charge a rate of ¥10,000 to 14,999 per person per night
- ¥200 for lodgings that charge ¥15,000 to 19,999 per person per night
- ¥300 for lodgings that charge more than ¥20,000 per person per night

It is likely that accommodations will charge you these fees in addition to the stated nightly rates.

Minami

Kamon Hotel Namba HOTEL ¥
(カモンホテル; Map p378; 06-6632-3520; www.kamon-hotel.com; 3-3-3 Sennichi-mae, Chūō-ku; r from ¥5000; S Sakai-suji line to Nipponbashi, exit 5) Close to all the Dōtombori and Namba nightlife action, but tucked away in a quiet street, Kamon is a great choice for penny-pinchers. Some rooms are a little scruffy, but they are comfortable, and stylish decor brightens things up. There's a modern udon restaurant downstairs.

Osaka Hana Hostel HOSTEL ¥
(大阪花宿; Map p378; 06-6281-8786; http://osaka.hanahostel.com; 1-8-4 Nishi-Shinsaibashi, Chūō-ku; dm/tw/tr from ¥2200/6800/10,200; S Midō-suji line to Shinsaibashi, exit 7) This great budget option in the heart of Amerika-Mura has a variety of rooms. Besides four-bed and six-bed dorms, there are private Japanese- and Western-style rooms, some with ensuites and kitchenettes. Shared facilities include two kitchen-lounge areas and coin-operated laundry machines. It's expertly managed by a helpful team of well-travelled, English-speaking staff. The only downside is some street noise.

The downstairs sake bar is a great place to socialise.

Khaosan World Namba HOSTEL ¥
(カオサンワールドなんば; Map p378; 06-6632-7373; http://khaosan-tokyo.com/en/namba; 1-2-13 Motomachi, Naniwa-ku; dm/d/q from ¥2200/10,000/17,000; S Midō-suji line to Namba, exit 13) From the reliable Khaosan chain, this large hostel is run like an efficient hotel by a bevy of multilingual staff. The bunks are big and the more expensive six-bed rooms have showers. It also has private double and family rooms, and a spotless communal kitchen. Cultural events are held regularly and there's a ground-floor bar that encourages a social vibe.

Capsule Hotel Asahi Plaza Shinsaibashi CAPSULE HOTEL ¥
(カプセルホテル朝日プラザ心斎橋; Map p378; 06-6213-1991; www.asahiplaza.co.jp; 2-12-22 Nishi-Shinsaibashi, Chūō-ku; capsule from ¥3000; S Midō-suji line to Shinsaibashi, exit 7) This is a classic capsule hotel, with over 400 pods on separate floors for men and women as well as communal baths, conveniently located in Ame-Mura. They're quite used to foreign guests, so this is a good choice for capsule-hotel novices. Despite the capsules being nonsmoking there is a lingering smell of cigarette smoke through the building.

Luggage that doesn't fit in the lockers provided can be held at the front desk (¥200 per day).

Hotel the Flag BOUTIQUE HOTEL ¥¥
(Map p378; 06-6121-8111; www.hoteltheflag.jp; 1-18-30 Higashi-Shinsaibashi, Chūō-ku; standard/deluxe from ¥12,000/22,000; S Midō-suji line to Shinsaibashi) This hip design hotel ticks many boxes for those looking for a smart modern stay close to Shinsaibashi's shopping and nightlife. Rooms are stylish with a minimalist feel; 'deluxe' doubles are a tad bigger than standard options and come with a bath. Helpful staff are multilingual and there's an on-site library/lounge, a breakfast dining room and a sleek laundry.

Kaneyoshi Ryokan RYOKAN ¥¥
(かねよし旅館; Map p378; 06-6211-6337; www.kaneyosi.jp; 3-12 Sōemon-chō, Chūō-ku; s/d/tr/q from ¥6480/11,880/16,200/21,600; S Sennichimae line to Nipponbashi, exit 2) In business for nearly a century right by Dōtombori, Kaneyoshi's current (1980s) building feels a bit dated, but it's offset by eager-to-please staff, clean, comfy tatami (tightly woven floor matting) rooms with private bathrooms and a simple common bath on the top (6th) floor. Although it's in the nightlife district, doors close at 1am. Riverside rooms are excellent value.

Swissotel Nankai Osaka HOTEL ¥¥¥
(スイスホテル南海大阪; Map p378; ☎06-6646-1111; www.swissotel.com/hotels/nankai-osaka; 5-1-60 Namba, Chūō-ku; r from ¥31,000; ; S Midō-suji line to Namba, exit 4) Minami's most elegant hotel, with stunning views and direct connections to KIX airport via Nankai line trains that depart from Namba Station below the hotel. Rooms are spacious and well-appointed, the service is excellent and there's also a gym. In addition to the in-house restaurants, there are all the dining options in Namba Parks (p386), part of the same station complex.

Tennōji

Pax Hostel HOSTEL ¥
(Map p370; ☎06-6537-7090; www.thepax.jp; 1-20-5 Ebisu-Higashi, Naniwa-ku; dm from ¥2500; ; S Midō-suji line to Dōbutsuen-mae, exit 5) Housed in an atmospheric old wooden rice-store building, Pax Hostel is hidden away from the buzzing neon in Shin-Sekai. Dorms have coloured wooden bunk beds, a privacy curtain, a light, a charger and a security box. The downstairs cafe-record store is a chilled place to hang out, and serves great coffee and *bahn mi* (Vietnamese baguette).

There's bicycle hire (¥500 per day) too.

Greater Osaka

Shin-Osaka Youth Hostel HOSTEL ¥
(新大阪ユースホステル; Map p370; ☎06-6370-5427; www.osaka-yha.or.jp/shin-osaka-eng; Koko Plaza, 1-13-13 Higashi-Nakajima, Higashi-Yodogawa-ku; dm/tw ¥3500/9400; ; JR Shin-Osaka, east exit) Five minutes southeast of Shin-Osaka Station, this efficiently run hostel sits on the top floors of a contemporary, 10-storey tower with great views across the city. Rooms and common areas are big, well equipped and spotless; private rooms are good value. There's a daytime lockout (you can still use the lounge), a midnight curfew and breakfast for ¥500.

Hotel Nikkō Kansai Airport HOTEL ¥¥
(ホテル日航関西空港; ☎072-455-1111; www.nikkokix.com; Senshū Kūkō Kita 1, Izumisano-shi, Osaka-fu; s/d from ¥12,000/16,000; ; JR Haruka Airport Express to Kansai Airport) The excellent Hotel Nikkō Kansai Airport is connected to the main terminal building by a pedestrian bridge (you can even bring your luggage trolleys right to your room). The rooms here range from simple 'economy class' to 'first-class' suites; all are comfortable enough for a brief stay.

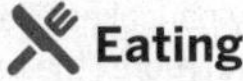

Eating

Kita

There are many options just within Osaka and Umeda stations, in the passages below ground and in the attached shopping centres. On the southwest side of JR Osaka Station, close to Daimaru and Hotel Granvia, look for food hall **Eki Marché** (エキマルシェ大阪; Map p374; ☎06-4799-3828; www.ekimaru.com; Osaka Station City, Kita-ku; 10am-10pm; JR Osaka, Sakurabashi exit); Kaiten Sushi Ganko is here.

South of the station (close to Higashi Umeda Station), **Ohatsutenjin-dōri** (お初天神通り) has lots of cheap local options, as does **Hankyū Higashi-dōri** (阪急東通り), which runs east of Hankyū Umeda Station. Both get lively in the evenings, with commuters grabbing food on their way home.

Kaiten Sushi Ganko SUSHI ¥
(回転寿司がんこ; Map p374; ☎06-4799-6811; Eki Marché, Osaka Station City, Kita-ku; plates ¥130-735; 11am-11pm; JR Osaka, Sakurabashi exit) This reliable *kaiten-sushi* (conveyor-belt sushi) shop is a popular choice for many a hungry commuter, meaning the two whirring tracks of plates are continuously restocked with fresh options. It can get crowded at meal times. It's inside JR Osaka's Eki Marché food court.

There are also branches in Shin-Osaka Station and Abeno Harukas (p372).

Ganko Umeda Honten JAPANESE ¥¥
(がんこ梅田本店; Map p374; ☎06-6376-2001; www.gankofood.co.jp; 1-5-11 Shibata, Kita-ku; meals ¥780-5000; 11.30am-2.30am Mon-Sat, to 11.30pm Sun; Hankyū Umeda) At the main branch of this Osaka institution, a large dining hall serves a wide variety of set-course meals and sushi (à la carte or in sets), reasonably priced and made with traditional, quality ingredients. It's on the street along the western side of Hankyū Umeda Station. Look for the logo of the guy wearing a headband.

Robatayaki Isaribi IZAKAYA ¥¥
(炉ばた焼き漁火; Map p374; ☎06-6373-2969; www.rikimaru-group.com/shop/isaribi.html; 1-5-12 Shibata, Kita-ku; dishes ¥300; 5-11pm; S Midō-suji line to Umeda, exit 2, Hankyū Umeda) Head downstairs to this spirited,

DON'T MISS

OSAKA SPECIALITIES

Okonomiyaki Thick, savoury pancakes filled with shredded cabbage and your choice of meat, seafood, vegetables and more (the name means 'cook as you like'), often prepared on a *teppan* (steel plate) set into your table. Slice off a wedge using tiny trowels called *kote*, and – warning – allow it to cool a bit before taking that first bite. Try it at Chibō in Dōtombori or Yukari in Umeda.

Tako-yaki Doughy dumplings stuffed with octopus (*tako* in Japanese) grilled in specially made moulds and often sold as street food. Nibble carefully first as the centre can be molten hot. Try it at Wanaka Honten in Namba.

Kushikatsu *Yakitori* refers to skewers of grilled meat, seafood and/or vegetables; *kushikatsu* is the same ingredients crumbed, deep-fried and served with a savoury dipping sauce (double-dipping is a serious no-no). Goes very well with beer. The Shin-Sekai neighbourhood is particularly famed for *kushikatsu* restaurants. Try Ganso Kushikatsu Daruma Honten (p384).

Kaiten-sushi This Osaka invention from the 1950s goes by many names in English: conveyor-belt sushi, sushi-go-round or sushi train. It's all the same – plates of sushi that run past you along a belt built into the counter (you can also order off the menu). Try it at at Kaiten Sushi Ganko (p381) in JR Osaka Station or at the branch in Abeno Harukas (p372).

Kappō-ryōri Osaka's take on high-end dining, with seasonal ingredients and meticulous presentation of *kaiseki* (traditional haute cuisine) but without the formality. Diners sit at the counter, chatting with the chef who hands over the dishes as they're finished. Despite the laid-back vibe these restaurants can be frightfully expensive; try Shoubentango-tei (p384), which is reasonable.

friendly *izakaya* (pub eatery) for standards such as skewered meats, seafood, veggies fresh off the grill and giant pieces of *tori no karaage* (fried chicken). The best seats are at semicircular counters, where your chef will serve you using a very, very long paddle.

It's on the street along the western side of Hankyū Umeda Station, to the left of the signage featuring a guy wearing a headband, and has white door curtains.

Yukari OKONOMIYAKI ¥¥

(ゆかり; Map p374; ☎06-6311-0214; www.yukarichan.co.jp; 2-14-13 Sōnezaki, Kita-ku; okonomiyaki ¥800-1450; ⊙11am-1am; ; Ⓢ Tanimachi line to Higashi-Umeda, exit 4, Ⓡ JR Osaka, south central exit) This popular restaurant in the Ohatsutenjin-dōri arcade serves up that great Osaka favourite, *okonomiyaki* (savoury pancakes), cooked on a griddle before you. There's lots to choose from on the picture menu, including veg options, but the *tokusen mikkusu yaki* (mixed *okonomiyaki* with fried pork, shrimp and squid) is a classic. Look for red-and-white signage out front.

Naka-no-shima & Around

Gout BAKERY ¥

(グウ; Map p370; ☎06-6585-0833; 1-1-10 Honmachi, Chūō-ku; bread from ¥200; ⊙7.30am-8pm, closed Thu; Ⓢ Tanimachi line to Tanimachi 4-chōme, exit 4) One of Osaka's best bakeries, Gout (pronounced 'goo', as in French) sells baguettes, pastries, croissants, sandwiches and coffee to take away or eat in. Perfect for picking up picnic supplies for nearby Osaka-jō.

★ **Endo Sushi** SUSHI ¥¥

(ゑんどう寿司; Map p370; www.endo-sushi.com/english.html; 1-1-86 Noda, Fukushima-ku; sushi set ¥1150; ⊙5am-2pm, closed Sun; Ⓢ Sennichimae line to Tamagawa, exit 3, Ⓡ JR Loop line to Noda) Trek out to Osaka's fish market to taste the exceptionally fresh sushi at cosy Endo, in business for over a century. You can choose from four different sushi sets of five pieces each; we recommend starting your day right with a sushi breakfast. It's in building three to the left of the market entrance where the large clock is. Staff speak some English and it's cash only.

★Yoshino Sushi SUSHI ¥¥

(吉野鯗; Map p370; ☎06-6231-7181; www.yoshino-sushi.co.jp; 3-4-14 Awaji-machi, Chūō-ku; lunch from ¥2700; ⊙11am-1.30pm Mon-Fri; Ⓢ Midō-suji line to Honmachi, exit 1) In business since 1841, Yoshino specialises in Osaka-style sushi, which is *hako-sushi* ('pressed sushi'). This older version of the dish (compared to the newer, hand-pressed Tokyo-style *nigiri-sushi)* is formed by a wooden mould, resulting in Mondrian-esque cubes of spongy omelette, soy-braised shiitake mushrooms, smokey eel and vinegar-marinated fish on rice. Reservations recommended.

On the ground floor, the shop sells reasonably priced takeaway boxes (less than ¥2000).

★Yotaro Honten TEMPURA ¥¥

(与太呂本店; Map p370; ☎06-6231-5561; 2-3-14 Kōraibashi, Chūō-ku; tempura set ¥2500, sea bream rice ¥4300; ⊙11am-1pm & 5-7pm, closed Thu; Ⓢ Sakaisuji line to Kitahama) This two-Michelin-starred restaurant specialises in exceptionally light and delectable tempura served at the counter, where you can watch the chefs, or in private rooms. The tasty sea bream dish serves two to three people and the filling tempura sets are fantastic value. Look for the black-and-white sign and black slatted bars across the windows. Reserve in advance through your hotel.

Minami

Lively Dōtombori has lots of street-food vendors and restaurants. As this area attracts a lot of tourists, English menus and English-speaking staff are common. Dōtombori can get extremely crowded in the evenings and you'll have to queue at the more popular spots.

Lots of Japanese chain restaurants can be found on Shinsaibashi-suji, while Ame-Mura has cheap *izakaya*, snack vendors and cafes popular with a young (though not exclusively so) crowd. In Namba, the Namba Parks (p386) mall has a good spread of restaurants as well.

★Wanaka Honten STREET FOOD ¥

(わなか本店; Map p378; ☎06-6631-0127; http://takoyaki-wanaka.com; 11-19 Sennichi-mae, Chūō-ku; tako-yaki per 8 from ¥450; ⊙10am-11pm Mon-Fri, from 8.30am Sat & Sun; Ⓢ Midō-suji line to Namba, exit 4) This famous *tako-yaki* (octopus dumplings) stand, just north of Dōguya-suji arcade, uses custom copper hotplates (instead of cast iron) to make dumplings that are crisper than usual (but still runny inside). There's a picture menu and tables and chairs in the back. One popular dish to try is *tako-sen* – two dumplings sandwiched between *sembei* (rice crackers).

There's also a convenient branch in **Ame-Mura** (わなかアメリカ村店; Map p378; ☎06-6211-3304; 2-12-8 Nishi-Shinsaibashi, Chūō-ku; ⊙10am-10pm Mon-Fri, 10.30am-10.30pm Sat & Sun; Ⓢ Midō-suji line to Shinsaibashi, exit 7).

Planet 3rd CAFE ¥

(プラネットサード心斎橋店; Map p378; ☎06-6282-5277; 1-5-24 Nishi-Shinsaibashi, Chūō-ku; breakfast buffet ¥1080, lunch & dinner mains from ¥880; ⊙7am-midnight; ❄📶; Ⓢ Midō-suji line to Shinsaibashi, exit 7) This large, comfortable cafe in Ame-Mura serves good coffee, drinks and eclectic light meals, including pastas, sandwiches, salads and rice bowls. It has trendy decor with big windows for people-watching and a few iPads for guest use.

Za Ikaga STREET FOOD ¥

(ザ・イカが; Map p378; ☎06-6212-0147; www.ikayaki.jp; 2-12-8 Nishi-Shinsaibashi, Chūō-ku; dishes from ¥350; ⊙6pm-late, closed Wed; Ⓢ Midō-suji line to Shinsaibashi, exit 7) The signature dish at this small food stand with a picture menu is *ika-yaki* – grilled squid, served here in a thin crêpe splattered with egg, mayonaise and savoury, *okonomiyaki*-style sauce. There are a few seats inside at the counter and a few folding chairs on the street (perfect for watching the comings and goings in Amerika-Mura).

★Chibō OKONOMIYAKI ¥¥

(千房; Map p378; ☎06-6212-2211; www.chibo.com; 1-5-5 Dōtombori, Chūō-ku; mains ¥885-1675; ⊙11am-1am Mon-Sat, to midnight Sun; Ⓢ Midō-suji line to Namba, exit 14) One of Osaka's most famous *okonomiyaki* restaurants, Chibō almost always has a queue, but it moves fast because there's seating on multiple floors (though you might want to hold out for the coveted tables overlooking Dōtombori canal). Try the house special *Dōtombori yaki*, with pork, beef, squid, shrimp and cheese (¥1650). Last orders are an hour before closing.

★Imai Honten UDON ¥¥

(今井本店; Map p378; ☎06-6211-0319; www.d-imai.com; 1-7-22 Dōtombori, Chūō-ku; dishes from ¥800; ⊙11am-10pm, closed Wed; Ⓢ Midō-suji line to Namba, exit 14) Step into an oasis of calm

LOCAL KNOWLEDGE

URA-NAMBA

Ura-Namba (literally 'behind Namba') is an unofficial district made up of clusters of small restaurants and bars in the shadow of Nankai Namba Station. It's becoming an increasingly cool place to hang out in. A good place to start is the **Misono Building** (味園ビル; Map p378; 2-3-9 Sennichi-mae, Chūō-ku; ⏲6pm-late; Ⓢ Sakai-suji line to Nipponbashi, exit 5), a once grand (and now wilting) structure with dozens of bars on the 2nd floor.

amid Dōtombori's chaos to be welcomed by staff at one of the area's oldest and most-revered udon specialists. Try *kitsune udon* – noodles topped with soup-soaked slices of fried tofu. Look for the traditional exterior and the willow tree outside.

★**Shoubentango-tei** KAISEKI ¥¥¥
(正弁丹吾亭; Map p378; ☎06-6211-3208; 1-7-12 Dōtombori, Chūō-ku; dinner course ¥3780-10,800; ⏲5-10pm; Ⓢ Midō-suji line to Namba, exit 14) That this *kappō-ryōri* (Osaka-style haute cuisine) restaurant isn't more expensive is surprising considering its pedigree: established over 100 years ago, it was a literati hangout in the early 20th century. Even the cheapest course, which includes five dishes decided that day by the chef, tastes – and looks! – like a luxurious treat; reservations are necessary for all but the cheapest course.

The restaurant is on Hōzen-ji Yokochō.

Tennōji

★**Ganso Kushikatsu Daruma Honten** JAPANESE ¥¥
(元祖串かつ だるま本店; Map p370; ☎06-6645-7056; www.kushikatu-daruma.com; 2-3-9 Ebisu-Higashi, Naniwa-ku; skewers ¥120-240; ⏲11am-10.30pm; Ⓢ Midōsuji line to Dōbutsuen-mae, exit 5) Daruma has branches around town, but for many Japanese a pilgrimage to the original shop in Shinsekai – opened in 1929 and said to be the birthplace of *kushikatsu* – is a necessary part of any visit to Osaka. There's room for maybe a dozen around the small counter. Start with the eight-piece assortment of perfectly crisp skewers.

There's a shop in **Dōtombori** (だるま 道頓堀店; Map p378; ☎06-6213-8101; 1-6-4 Dōtombori, Chūō-ku; ⏲11.30am-10.30pm; Ⓢ Midō-suji line to Namba, exit 14), but the queue can be long.

Yokozuna JAPANESE ¥¥
(横綱; Map p370; ☎06-6631-4527; 2-4-11 Ebisu-higashi, Naniwa-ku; kushikatsu ¥100-210, mains ¥780-1980; ⏲10am-11pm; Ⓢ Midōsuji line to Dōbutsuen-mae, exit 5) This lively local chain has a huge line-up of *kushikatsu* (skewers), from staples including *renkon* (lotus root) and *mochi* (rice cake) to unconventional options like chocolate banana. They're also known for their huge-portion versions of classic dishes (like *gyōza*) that could feed a family. Yokozuna couldn't be easier to find: look for the giant placards painted with sumo wrestlers.

If this location is full, two others with the same menu are just steps away, including a 24-hour branch. The staff, who usually speak some English, will direct you.

Drinking & Nightlife

Osakans love to let loose: the city is teeming with *izakaya*, bars and nightclubs.

Naka-no-shima & Honmachi

★**Brooklyn Roasting Company** COFFEE
(Map p370; ☎06-6125-5740; www.brooklynroasting.jp; 1-16 Kitahama, Chūō-ku; coffee from ¥350; ⏲8am-8pm Mon-Fri, 10am-7pm Sat & Sun; 📶; Ⓢ Sakaisuji line to Kitahama, exit 2) With its worn leather couches, big wooden communal table and industrial fittings, this is a little slice of Brooklyn in Osaka and the perfect pit stop while exploring Naka-no-shima. Sip well-crafted coffee (almond and soy milk available, too) on the wide riverside terrace and watch the boats go by. If hunger strikes, there's a small selcction of donuts and pastries.

★**Beer Belly** CRAFT BEER
(Map p370; ☎06-6441-0717; www.beerbelly.jp/tosabori; 1-1-31 Tosabori, Nishi-ku; ⏲5pm-2am Mon-Fri, 3-11pm Sat, 3-9pm Sun; Ⓢ Yotsubashi line to Higobashi, exit 3) Beer Belly is run by Osaka's best microbrewery, Minoh Beer, and features Minoh's award-winning classics and seasonal offerings (pints from ¥930). Pick up a copy of Osaka's *Craft Beer Map* here to further your local beer adventures. From the subway exit, double back and take the road that curves behind the APA Hotel.

There is another **branch** (Map p370; ☎06-6353-5005 7-4 Ikeda-chō, Kita-ku; half pint/full pint from ¥520/830; ⏲3pm-midnight; 🚉JR Osaka Loop Line to Temma) in Tenma.

40 Sky Bar & Lounge COCKTAIL BAR
(Map p370; ☎06-6222-0111; www.conradhotels3.hilton.com; 3-2-4 Nakanoshima, Kita-ku, Conrad Osaka; cover ¥1400 after 8.30pm; ⏲10am-midnight; Ⓢ Yotsubashi line to Higobashi, exit 2) If heights aren't your thing, you'll need a stiff drink once you've peered down over the city from the 40th floor at this ultrasuave hotel bar. Service is impeccable and there's a good range of food and bar snacks to go with well-made cocktails.

Minami

Visit Minami on a Friday night and you might think there's one bar for every resident – including *izakaya,* Irish pubs and cocktail lounges (as well as hostess and host bars, where the servers are flirtatious women and men, and the drinks are very pricey). Friday and Saturday nights are the big nights out (especially for clubs) but you'll usually have company on weeknights too. The English-speaking crowd tends to congregate in Amerika-Mura, which has lots of small, cheap bars that open onto the street; the nightclubs are mostly here too.

★**Circus** CLUB
(Map p378; ☎06-6241-3822; www.circus-osaka.com; 2nd fl, 1-8-16 Nishi-Shinsaibashi, Chūō-ku; entry ¥1000-2500; Ⓢ Midō-suji line to Shinsaibashi, exit 7) This small club is the heart of Osaka's underground electronic scene. The dance floor is nonsmoking. It's open on Friday and Saturday nights and sometimes during the week. Look up for the small sign in English and bring photo ID.

Jun-kissa American CAFE
(純喫茶アメリカン; Map p378; ☎06-6211-2100; 1-7-4 Dōtombori, Chūō-ku; ⏲9am-11pm; Ⓢ Midō-suji line to Namba, exit 15) With its 1940s interior intact and waitresses in long skirts, American is a classic *jun-kissa* – a shop from the first wave of cafes to open in Japan during the post-WWII American occupation. Come before 11am for a 'morning set' (¥620) of pillowy buttered toast, a hard-boiled egg and coffee. Look for the chrome sign out front.

Rock Rock BAR
(ロックロック; Map p378; www.rockrock.co.jp; 3rd fl, Shinsaibashi Atrium Bldg, 1-8-1 Nishi-Shinsaibashi, Chūō-ku; ⏲7pm-5am Mon-Sat, to 1am Sun; Ⓢ Midō-suji line to Shinsaibashi, exit 7) Serving the music-loving community since 1995, Rock Rock has a history of hosting after-parties for international acts and attracting celeb visitors. Regular events with a modest cover charge (usually ¥1500, including one drink ticket) showcase some of Osaka's finest rock DJs (and famous guests).

Mel Coffee Roasters CAFE
(メル・コーヒー・ロースターズ; Map p370; ☎06-4394-8177; https://melcoffee.stores.jp; 1-20-4 Shinmachi, Nishi-ku; coffee from ¥350; ⏲9am-7pm Tue-Fri, from 11am Sat & Sun; Ⓢ Yotsubashi line to Yotsubashi, exit 2) This tiny takeaway stand – the vintage Probat roaster takes up half of it – raised the bar for coffee in Osaka when it opened in 2016. The owner speaks good English and will happily discuss the taste profiles of the various single-origin hand-pours on offer.

Folk Rock Bar Phoebe BAR
(Map p378; 108 Dōtombori Heights, 2-7-22 Nishi-Shinsaibashi, Chūō-ku; ⏲7pm-2am; Ⓢ Midō-suji line to Namba, exit 14) Crammed with vinyl and knick-knacks, Phoebe looks like a drinks counter operated out of an old hippie's storage closet (we mean that in a good way). The friendly owner spins

LGBTIQ+ OSAKA

Dōyama-chō (堂山町), a district just east of JR Osaka Station, is where gay and lesbian bars are clustered. It's the second-largest scene in the country, after Tokyo's Shinjuku-nichōme. **Frenz Frenzy** (Map p370; ☎06-6311-1386; www.frenz-frenzy.website; 18-14 Kamiyama-chō, Kita-ku; ⏲8pm-1am; Ⓢ Tanimachi line to Higashi-Umeda, exit 3) calls itself a 'rainbow haven' and it means that literally: the whole place is awash in colour (including the front door, thankfully, because otherwise it would be impossible to find). Run by long-time expat Sari-chan, this is a welcoming first port of call for gay and lesbian travellers. There's no cover and drinks start at ¥500. It's on the ground floor of a building with other bars, set back from the road.

folk-rock tunes on the record player, mixes good cocktails and serves tasty food. There's an English sign out front.

☆ Entertainment

Osaka's lack of conservatism and boisterous sensibilities are evident in its underground music scene, which leans heavily towards raucous rock 'n' roll, punk, indie and experimental noise. The city has introduced the world to bands including Shonen Knife and the Boredoms, and it's home to a number of character-filled venues where you can catch up-and-coming and established bands.

★ Namba Bears LIVE MUSIC
(難波ベアーズ; Map p370; ☎06-6649-5564; http://namba-bears.main.jp; 3-14-5 Namba-naka, Naniwa-ku; ⊙hours vary; Ⓢ Midō-suji line to Namba, exit 4) For going on three decades this has been the place to hear underground music live in Osaka. It's a small, bare-concrete, smokey space – well suited to the punk, rock and indie bands that play here. In keeping with the alternative spirit, you can bring in your own beer. Most shows start at 7pm; tickets usually cost ¥2000 to ¥2500.

Fandango LIVE MUSIC
(Map p370; ☎06-6308-1621; www.fandango-go.com; 1-17-27 Juso-Honmachi, Yodogawa-ku; tickets ¥2000-3000; Ⓡ Hankyū line to Juso) This much-loved live house is an Osaka institution and favours Japanese punk rock and experimental noise bands; check the website for the gig schedule. Admission usually includes one free drink. It's two stops on the Hankyū local line from Umeda to Juso station.

Hokage LIVE MUSIC
(火影; Map p378; ☎06-6211-2855; www.musicbarhokage.net; Basement fl, 2-9-36 Nishi-Shinsaibashi, Chūō-ku; tickets around ¥1500; ⊙hours vary; Ⓢ Midō-suji line to Shinsaibashi, exit 7) Looking like an office with the inner walls ripped out (which is entirely likely), Hokage seems to be made for its rock, punk and noise bands. It's a small space, where the band might take up half the room, and a good place to discover local bands.

Sumo Spring Tournament SPECTATOR SPORT
(Haru Bashō; Map p378; www.sumo.or.jp; EDION Arena; ⊙Mar) The big fellas rumble into Osaka in March for this major tournament, held in the EDION Arena (Osaka Prefectural Gymnasium (府立体育会館) in Namba. Tickets (from ¥3800) go on sale in early February and can be purchased online.

Kyōcera Dome BASEBALL
(京セラドーム; Map p370; ☎06-6586-0106; www.kyoceradome-osaka.jp; 3-2-1 Chiyozaki, Nishi-ku; Ⓢ Nagahori Tsurumiryokuchi line to Domemae Chiyozaki) Also known as Osaka Dome, this futuristic stadium is home to the Orix Buffaloes baseball team. While the Buffaloes may not have the following of the mighty Hanshin Tigers, who play nearby in Kōbe (except for games in August, which they play here), they do have their own dedicated (and very vocal) fans.

Shopping

Osaka Station is ringed by malls and department stores – they're all interconnected by underground passages, making the Umeda district one big shopping conurbation. You'll find outlets of all of Japan's most popular national chains here, including Uniqlo, Muji and Tokyū Hands, along with literally hundreds of fashion boutiques.

In Minami, international high-end brands line Midō-suji, the main boulevard, between Shinsaibashi and Namba subway stations. A few blocks east, the jam-packed **Shinsaibashi-suji** (心斎橋筋商店街; Map p378; www.shinsaibashi.or.jp; Ⓢ Midō-suji line to Shinsaibashi, exit 4) arcade has popular local and international chain stores.

On the west side of Midō-suji, Ame-Mura has youthful streetware and secondhand shops while the Minami-Horie district has trendy boutiques.

Namba Station is anchored by the huge mall, **Namba Parks** (なんばパークス; Map p378; www.nambaparks.com; 2-10-70 Namba-naka, Naniwa-ku; ⊙shops 11am-9pm, dining to 11pm; Ⓢ Midō-suji line to Namba, exit 4).

★ Time Bomb Records MUSIC
(Map p378; ☎06-6213-5079; www.timebomb.co.jp; B1, 9-28 Nishi-Shinsaibashi, Chūō-ku; ⊙noon-9pm; Ⓢ Midō-suji line to Shinsaibashi, exit 7) One of the best record stores in the city, Time Bomb stocks an excellent collection of vinyl and CDs from '60s pop and '70s punk to alternative, soul and psychedelic. Find out about gigs around town here, too.

★ Tower Knives HOMEWARES
(タワーナイブズ; Map p370; ☎06-4301-7860; www.towerknives.com; 1-4-1 Ebisu-higashi, Naniwa-ku; ⊙10am-6pm; Ⓢ Midō-suji line to Dōbutsuen-mae, exit 5) Tower Knives has a fantastic selection of kitchen knives – both carbon steel and stainless steel; some are

DON'T MISS

BUNRAKU: TRADITIONAL PUPPET THEATRE

Bunraku, a not-at-all-childish form of puppet theatre, may not have originated in Osaka, but it became popular here and is still very much associated with the city. Bunraku's most famous playwright, Chikamatsu Monzaemon (1653–1724), wrote plays about Osaka's merchants and the denizens of the pleasure quarters, social classes otherwise generally ignored in the Japanese arts at the time. Not surprisingly, the art form found a wide audience among them, and a theatre was established to stage Chikamatsu's plays in Dōtombori.

Today the place to see it is Osaka's **National Bunraku Theatre** (国立文楽劇場; Map p370; ☎06-6212-2531, ticket centre 0570-07-9900; www.ntj.jac.go.jp; 1-12-10 Nipponbashi, Chūō-ku; full performance ¥2400-6000, single act ¥500-1500; ⏲opening months vary, check the website; Ⓢ Sakai-suji line to Nipponbashi, exit 7). Seeing a full performance is a half-day event: shows, which include scenes from different plays, top four hours. Too long? Unreserved, same-day single-act tickets are sold, when available, at the venue from 10am. Rent the English-language audio guide (full performance/single act ¥650/300). There's also an exhibition in the lobby about the history of bunraku and its puppeteers and main characters.

Purchase tickets from the box office or from the Japan Arts Council's website: www2.ntj.jac.go.jp/unesco/bunraku/en. Note that shows sell out quickly and single-act tickets are limited.

hand-forged by Osaka artisans. The English-speaking staff will walk you through the different styles, let you try them out on some veggies and show you how to care for them. Knives start from around ¥6000. Duty-free shopping available; bring your passport.

★Standard Books BOOKS
(スタンダードブックストア; Map p378; ☎06-6484-2239; www.standardbookstore.com; 2-2-12 Nishi-Shinsaibashi, Chūō-ku; ⏲11am-10.30pm; Ⓢ Midō-suji line to Shinsaibashi, exit 7) This cult-fave Osaka bookstore prides itself on not stocking any bestsellers. Instead, it's stocked with small-press finds, art books, indie comics and the like, plus CDs, quirky fashion items and accessories.

★Hankyū Umeda Department Store DEPARTMENT STORE
(阪急梅田本店; Map p374; www.hankyu-dept.co.jp/honten; 8-7 Kakuda-chō, Kita-ku; ⏲10am-8pm Sun-Thu, to 9pm Fri & Sat, restaurants to 10pm; Ⓢ Midō-suji line to Umeda, exit 6, Ⓡ Hankyū Umeda) Hankyū, which first opened in 1929, pioneered the now ubiquitous concept of the train-station department store. One of Japan's largest department stores, 'Ume-Han' is also among the most fashion-forward, with a few Japanese designers on the 3rd floor. Head to the 7th floor for artisan homewares and to the basement for a cornucopia of gourmet food items.

★Dōguya-suji Arcade MARKET
(道具屋筋; Map p378; www.doguyasuji.or.jp/map_eng.html; Sennichi-mae, Chūō-ku; ⏲10am-6pm; Ⓢ Midō-suji line to Namba, exit 4) This long arcade sells just about anything related to the preparation, consumption and selling of Osaka's principal passion: food. There's everything from bamboo steamers and lacquer miso soup bowls to shopfront lanterns, plastic food models and, of course, moulded hotplates for making *tako-yaki*. Hours vary by store.

Shimada-Shōten ALCOHOL
(島田商店; Map p370; ☎06-6531-8119; www.sake-shimada.co.jp; 3-5-1 Itachibori, Nishi-ku; ⏲9am-7pm Mon-Fri, to 6pm Sat; Ⓢ Chuō line to Awaza, exit 2) This third-generation-run sake store has narrow wooden stairs leading to a basement cellar where you can sample small glasses of sake (¥220 each), while sitting at tables made from sake barrel bottoms and snacking on cheese and pickles. Friendly, welcoming staff go out of their way to help you choose the right bottle to take home. Cash only.

Graf Studio HOMEWARES
(Map p370; www.graf-d3.com; 4-1-9 Naka-no-shima, Kita-ku; ⏲11am-7pm, closed Mon; Ⓢ Yotsubashi line to Higobashi, exit 3) Graf is a sleek furniture and design studio close to the National Museum of Art. Pick up some lovely homewares by Japanese and international designers; it stocks ceramics, jewellery and kitchenware. The attached cafe is a pleasant, quiet spot for a break.

NAVIGATING OSAKA

Osaka's larger stations can be disorienting, particularly Namba and the Umeda/JR Osaka Station area. Exits are often confusingly labelled, even for Japanese people, and English-language directional signage is lacking compared to similar stations in other big Japanese cities.

Adding to the confusion, *shinkansen* (bullet trains) don't stop at any of these hubs, but at Shin-Osaka Station, three subway stops (about five minutes) north of Umeda and JR Osaka Station on the Midō-suji line.

King Kong Records MUSIC
(キングコング本店; Map p374; ☎06-6348-2260; B1, Maru Bldg, 1-9-20 Umeda, Kita-ku; ⏲11am-8pm; Ⓢ Yotsubashi line to Nishi-Umeda, exit 6, 🚉 JR Osaka, south central exit) This small record store in the **Maru Building** (大阪丸ビル; Map p374; www.marubiru.com) packs in a great selection of vinyl and has a friendly and knowledgeable owner.

Flake Records MUSIC
(Map p378; ☎06-6534-7411; www.flakerecords.com; No 201, 2nd fl, Sono Yotsubashi Bldg, 1-11-9 Minami-Horie, Nishi-ku; ⏲noon-9pm; Ⓢ Yotsubashi line to Yotsubashi, exit 6) Flake is Osaka's most in-the-know music shop, selling new and used, Japanese and imported, CDs and vinyl. The owner speaks some English; ask him for his recommendations on local bands. This is also a good place to pick up flyers for live music events, and it has listening stations.

Maruzen & Junkudō Umeda BOOKS
(丸善&ジュンク堂書店梅田店; Map p374; www.junkudo.co.jp; Chaska Chayamachi Bldg, 7-20 Chayamachi, Kita-ku; ⏲10am-10pm; 🚉 Hankyū Umeda) This is the largest bookstore in Osaka, the result of two established chains joining forces. There's a big range of English-language books (on the 6th floor) and travel guides (3rd floor). It's in the Tadao Ando–designed Chaska Chayamachi building.

Information

MEDICAL SERVICES

Japan Red Cross Hospital (日本赤十字病院; Nihon Sekijyūji Byōin; Map p370; ☎06-6774-5111; www.osaka-med.jrc.or.jp; 5-30 Fudegasaki-chō, Tennōji-ku; ⏲24hr; 🚉 Kintestsu Ue-Honmachi) Emergency care; some doctors speak English.

Ohkita Medical Clinic (大北メディカルクリニック; Map p374; ☎06-6344-0380; www.ookita.com; 4th fl, Umeda Square Bldg, 1-12-17 Umeda, Kita-ku; ⏲10am-1.30pm & 3-7pm Mon-Fri, 10am-1.30pm Sat; 🚉 JR Osaka, south central exit) English-speaking doctor for non-emergency care, near JR Osaka Station.

POST

Osaka Central Post Office (大阪中央郵便局; Map p374; Basement fl, Eki-mae Dai-1 Bldg, 1-3-1 Umeda, Kita-ku; postal services 9am-9pm, ATM 7am-11.30pm Mon-Fri, 8am-11.30pm Sat, 8am-9pm Sun; Ⓢ Yotsubashi line to Nishi-Umeda, 🚉 JR Osaka, Sakurabashi exit)

SAFE TRAVEL

Osaka has a rough image in Japan, with the highest number of reported crimes per capita of any city in the country – though it remains significantly safer than most cities of comparable size. Still, it's wise to employ the same common sense here that you would back home.

➡ Purse snatchings are not uncommon, so be mindful.

➡ Nishinari-ku (also called Airin-chiku), south of Shinimamiya Station (just below Shin-Sekai), has a sizeable homeless population and an organised-crime presence. There are a number of budget accommodations here targeting foreign travellers; while it's unlikely you'd encounter any real danger, female travellers, particularly solo female travellers, do risk drawing unwanted attention, especially at night.

TOURIST INFORMATION

Osaka Visitors Information Center Umeda (大阪市ビジターズインフォメーションセンター・梅田; Map p374; ☎06-6345-2189; www.osaka-info.jp; JR Osaka Station; ⏲7am-11pm; 🚉 JR Osaka, north central exit) The main tourist office, with English information, pamphlets and maps, is on the 1st floor of the central north concourse of JR Osaka Station. There are also branches on the 1st floor of **Nankai Namba Station** (大阪市ビジターズインフォメーションセンター・なんば; Map p378; ☎06-6631-9100; ⏲9am-8pm; Ⓢ Midō-suji line to Namba, exit 4, 🚉 Nankai Namba) and at Kansai International Airport. Tourist offices can help book accommodation if you visit in person. The tourist information website (www.osaka-info.jp) is a good resource, too.

USEFUL RESOURCES

Kansai Scene (www.kansaiscene.com) For the lowdown on upcoming events, pick up a copy of this free English-language magazine at restaurants, nightspots, some hotels and major bookshops.

Getting There & Away

AIR

Two airports serve Osaka: **Kansai International Airport** (KIX; 関西空港; www.kansai-airport.or.jp) for all international and some domestic flights; and the domestic **Itami Airport** (ITM; 伊丹空港; ☎06-6856-6781; www.osaka-airport.co.jp; 3-555 Hotaru-ga-ike, Nishi-machi, Toyonaka), also confusingly called Osaka International Airport. KIX is about 50km southwest of the city, on an artificial island in the bay. Itami is located 12km northwest of Osaka.

BOAT

The following ferries depart from **Osaka Nankō Port** (大阪南港; ☎06-6613-1571; 2-1-10 Nan-kō-kita, Suminoe-ku; 🚇New Port Town line to Ferry Terminal) for destinations in Shikoku, Kyūshū and Okinawa:

Orange Ferry (www.orange-ferry.co.jp) Daily for Ehime (from ¥5660, eight hours), on Shikoku.

Ferry Sunflower (www.ferry-sunflower.co.jp) Daily for Beppu (from ¥11,510, 12 hours) and Kagoshima (from ¥13,420, 16 hours), on Kyūshū.

City Line (www.cityline.co.jp) Twice-daily for Kita-Kyūshū (from ¥4680, 12½ hours), north of Fukuoka

A Line Ferry (www.aline-ferry.com) Twice-weekly for Naha (¥19,330, 40 hours) on Okinawa via Amami-Oshima (¥15,120, 27 hours), off the coast of Kyūshū.

Tickets can be purchased online or from travel agencies.

BUS

Highway buses depart from the **Willer Bus Terminal** (Willerバスターミナル; Map p374; www.willerexpress.com; 1st fl, Umeda Sky Bldg Tower West, 1-1-88 Ōyodo-naka, Kita-ku; 🚇JR Osaka, north central exit), next to the Umeda Sky Building (p369) for:

Hakata (Fukuoka, Kyūshū; ¥3920 to ¥12,000, eight to 10 hours)

Hiroshima (¥3360 to ¥8000, six to eight hours)

Matsuyama (Ehime, Shikoku; ¥3760 to ¥9900, seven to eight hours)

Tokyo (¥4700 to ¥15,000, eight to 10 hours)

Longer routes have overnight buses; check the Willer website for more routes. Prices depend on the class of bus (nicer ones have roomy, reclining seats), season and day of departure (weekday travel is cheaper). Tickets can be purchased online in English.

Slightly pricier, but convenient, **JR West Highway Bus** (www.nishinihonjrbus.co.jp) runs to similar destinations from the **JR Osaka Station Highway Bus Terminal** (大阪駅ＪＲ高速バスターミナル; Map p374; www.nishinihonjrbus.co.jp; 🚇JR Osaka), outside the station's north-central concourse. Book online five days prior to travel for better rates.

TRAIN

Shin-Osaka Station is on the Tōkaidō-Sanyō *shinkansen* line (between Tokyo and Hakata in Fukuoka) and the eastern terminus of the Kyūshū *shinkansen* to Kagoshima. Departures are frequent.

Destinations include Tokyo (¥14,450, 2½ hours), Hiroshima (¥10,440, 1½ hours), Hakata (¥15,000, three hours) and Kagoshima (¥21,900, 4¾ hours).

To/From Kyoto

Tōkaidō-Sanyō shinkansen Runs from Shin-Osaka Station one stop east to Kyoto Station (¥1420, 14 minutes).

JR Kyoto line Cheaper and easier from central Osaka than getting the *shinkansen*. JR Osaka Station to Kyoto (¥560, 30 minutes).

Hankyū Kyoto line *Tokkyū* (limited express) trains run from Hankyū Umeda Station to Karasuma (¥400, 44 minutes) and Kawaramachi (¥400, 46 minutes) in Kyoto.

Keihan Main line *Tokkyū* trains run from Osaka's Yodoyabashi Station, a stop on the

OSAKA DISCOUNT PASSES

Enjoy Eco Card (エンジョイエコカード; weekday/weekend ¥800/600, child ¥300) One-day unlimited travel on subways, city buses and Nankō Port Town line, plus some admission discounts. At subway ticket machines, push the 'English' button, insert cash, select 'one-day pass' or 'one-day pass weekend'.

Osaka Amazing Pass (大阪周遊パス; www.osp.osaka-info.jp/en/) Foreign visitors to Japan can purchase one-day passes (¥2500), good for unlimited travel on city subways, buses and trains and admission to around 35 sights (including Osaka-jō and the Umeda Sky Building); or two-day passes (¥3300) that cover the same sights but only travel on city subways and buses. Passes are sold at tourist information centres and city subway stations.

Yokoso Osaka Ticket (www.howto-osaka.com/en/ticket/ticket/yokoso.html; ¥1500) Includes one-way fare on the Nankai Express Rapit from KIX to Nankai Namba Station and one-day travel on city subway and Nankō Port Town lines, plus some admission discounts. Must be purchased online in advance.

Midō-suji subway line, to Gion-Shijō and Sanjō stations (¥410, 45 to 55 minutes) in Kyoto.

To/From Kōbe

Tōkaidō-Sanyō shinkansen Runs from Shin-Osaka Station one stop west to Shin-Kōbe Station (from ¥1500, 13 minutes), but from central Osaka it's easier to get the JR Kōbe line from Osaka Station to Kōbe's central Sannomiya Station (¥410, 22 to 27 minutes).

Hankyū Kōbe line *Tokkyū* (limited express) trains run from Hankyū Umeda Station to Kōbe's Sannomiya Station (¥320, 30 minutes) and are usually less crowded than the JR trains.

To/From Nara

JR Yamatoji line *Kaisoku* (express) trains run from Tennōji Station to JR Nara Station (¥470, 35 minutes) via Hōryū-ji (¥460, 25 minutes).

Kintetsu Nara line *Kaisoku* trains run from Namba (Kintetsu Namba Station) to Kintetsu Nara Station (¥560, 40 minutes).

Getting Around

TO/FROM THE AIRPORT

Osaka Itami Airport

Osaka Monorail Connects the airport to Hotarugaike (¥200, three minutes) and Senri-Chūō (¥330, 12 minutes), from where you can transfer, respectively, to the Hankyū Takarazaka line or Hankyū Senri line for Osaka Station.

Osaka Airport Limousine (www.okkbus.co.jp) Frequent buses connect the airport with Osaka Station (¥640, 25 minutes), Osaka City Air Terminal (OCAT; ¥640, 35 minutes) in Namba and Shin-Osaka Station (¥500, 25 minutes). At Itami, buy your tickets from the machine outside the arrivals hall.

ICOCA CARD

This re-chargeable, prepaid transport pass with an IC-chip works on most trains, subways and buses in the Kansai area. Just wave it over the reader at the ticket gates. Purchase it at any ticket machine (¥2000, including ¥500 refundable deposit). If you're arriving at Kansai International Airport (KIX), you can buy a discounted ICOCA & Haruka combo ticket that includes travel from the airport to Shin-Osaka Station (¥3300) or Tennōji (¥3100) on the JR Haruka Kansai-Airport Express train and an ICOCA card with ¥1500 (and the ¥500 deposit). When you return the card to any station window, you are refunded the deposit and any remaining credit.

Kansai International Airport

KIX is well connected to the city with direct train lines and buses.

Nankai Express Rapit All-reserved twice-hourly service (¥1430, 40 minutes, 7am to 11pm) between Nankai Kansai-Airport Station (in Terminal 1) and Nankai Namba Station; Nankai Airport Express trains take about 10 minutes longer and cost ¥920. To reach Nankai Kansai-Airport Station from Terminal 2, you will need to take a shuttle bus to Terminal 1.

JR Haruka Kansai-Airport Express Twice-hourly service (6.30am to 10pm) between KIX and Tennōji Station (unreserved seat ¥1710, 30 minutes) and Shin-Osaka Station (¥2330, 50 minutes). More frequent JR Kansai Airport rapid trains also run between KIX, Tennōji (¥1060, 50 minutes) and Osaka Station (¥1190, 68 minutes); the last train departs at 11.30pm. All these stations connect to the Midō-suji subway line. It departs from Terminal 1; you need to take a free shuttle bus if you arrive at Terminal 2.

KATE (www.kate.co.jp) Airport limousine buses run to/from **Osaka City Air Terminal** (OCAT; Map p378; ☎06-6635-3000; www.ocat.co.jp) in Namba (¥1050, 50 minutes), JR Osaka Station (¥1550, one hour) and Tempōzan (¥1550, one hour). Note that the trip, especially to Umeda, can take longer depending on traffic. After midnight, there is only an hourly service to Osaka Station. Note that bus departures are more frequent from Terminal 1.

Taxi There are standard taxi fares to Umeda (¥14,500, 50 minutes) and Namba (¥14,000, 50 minutes). There is a late-night fare surcharge of ¥2500.

BICYCLE

Hub Chari (☎070-5436-2892; http://hubchari-english.jimdo.com; per hr/day ¥200/1000) rents city bikes at several stations around town. It's run by an NGO that supports Osaka's homeless community.

Cycle Osaka (p377) rents out city bikes; book online in advance and pick up from its Shin-Sekai branch.

TAXI

Taxis are your only option after midnight when public transport shuts down. Flagfall is ¥680, which covers the first 2km; then it's ¥80 for every additional 296m. Taxis can be hailed easily on the street; a red indicator means the taxi is available.

TRAIN & SUBWAY

Trains and subways should get you everywhere you need to go (unless you stay out past midnight, when they stop running).

The JR Kanjō-sen – the Osaka loop line – makes a circuit south of JR Osaka Station, though most sights fall in the middle of it.

OSAKA FERRIES TO/FROM SOUTH KOREA & CHINA

Ferries depart from the **Osaka Port International Ferry Terminal** (大阪港国際フェリーターミナル; Osaka-kō Kokusai Ferry Terminal; 06-6243-6345; 1-20-52 Nan-kō-kita, Suminoe-ku; S Chūō line to Cosmo Square, Nankō Port Town Line to Cosmo Square) for Shanghai, China, and Busan, South Korea. The ferry terminal is a 15-minute walk from the subway.

Japan China International Ferry (日中国際フェリー; 06-6536-6541; www.shinganjin.com) departs every other Tuesday (alternating with Kōbe) for Shanghai; **Shanghai Ferry Company** (上海フェリー; www.shanghai-ferry.co.jp) departs on Friday. One-way 2nd-class fares start from ¥20,000; the journey takes approximately 48 hours. Tickets can be booked online in English or through a travel agent.

Panstar Ferry (パンスターフェリー; 06-6614-2516; www.panstar.jp) leaves for Busan (one-way 2nd-class fares from ¥13,000, 19 hours) on Monday, Wednesday and Friday. As there's no English on the website, it's helpful to book through a travel agency.

There are eight subway lines, but the one that short-term visitors will find most useful is the Midō-suji (red) line, running north–south and stopping at Shin-Osaka, Umeda (next to Osaka Station), Shinsaibashi, Namba and Tennōji stations. Single rides cost ¥180 to ¥370 (half-price for children).

The Metro Osaka Subway app (available from the iTunes store) is very handy to have as some subway stations in Osaka don't have a route/fare map in English. You can search for fares using the app and plan your journey.

KŌBE

078 / POP 1,528,091

Perched on a hillside sloping down to the sea, Kōbe (神戸) is one of Japan's most attractive and cosmopolitan cities. It was a maritime gateway from the earliest days of trade with China and home to one of the first foreign settlements after Japan reopened to the world in the mid-19th century. Kōbe is compact, designed for walking, and easily visited as a day trip from Osaka or Kyoto, or as a stopover en route to points west. Stay overnight to immerse yourself in the city's distinct atmosphere and dining options.

Sights

Kōbe's sights can roughly be divided into three areas: Kitano-chō in the foothills to the north, near the Shin-Kōbe *shinkansen* station; central, around Sannomiya and Motomachi, including the former foreigners' settlement of Kyū-Kyoryuchi, and Nankin-machi (Chinatown); and the more recently developed waterfront, which includes shopping and dining complex Kōbe Harbor Land and bayside plaza Meriken Park.

Port of Kōbe Earthquake Memorial Park MONUMENT

(神戸港震災メモリアルパーク; Meriken Park; S Kaigan line to Minato Motomachi, Motomachi) FREE At 5.46am on 17 January 1995 the Great Hanshin Earthquake struck this region. It was Japan's strongest since the Great Kantō Quake of 1923 devastated Tokyo. Kōbe bore the brunt of the damage – 6000 killed, over 30,000 injured, toppled expressways and nearly 300,000 lost buildings. This simple, open-air, harbour-side museum tells the story through artefacts and a video presentation in English. Most striking is a section of the dock that was left as it was after that devastating day.

Nunobiki Falls WATERFALL

(布引の滝, Nunobikinotaki; S Shin-Kōbe, JR Shin-Kōbe) FREE You'd never guess that such a beautiful natural sanctuary could sit so close to the city. This revered waterfall in four sections (the longest is 43m tall) has been the subject of art, poetry and worship for centuries – some of the poems are reproduced on stone tablets at the site. It's accessible by a steep 400m path from Shin-Kōbe Station. Take the ground-floor exit, turn left and walk under the station building to the path.

You can also reach the falls from the midway station of the Nunobiki Ropeway (p393) in about 20 minutes; follow the road (it's signposted) and keep a lookout for the staircase on your right (not well signposted) that leads to the waterfall path.

Kitano-chō AREA

(北野町; S Shin-Kōbe, JR Shin-Kōbe) For generations of Japanese tourists, this pleasant, hilly neighbourhood is Kōbe, thanks to the dozen or so well-preserved homes of (mostly) Western trading families and diplomats who

Kōbe

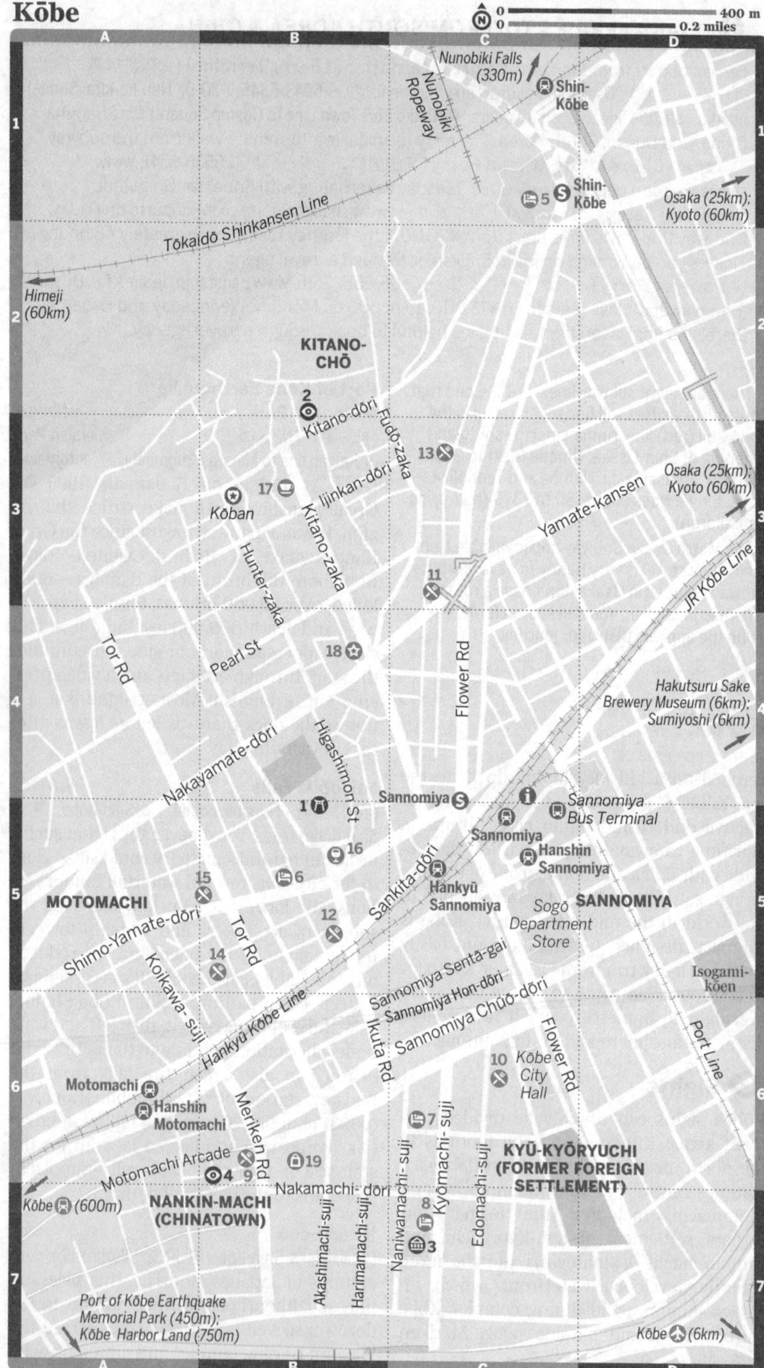

400 m
0.2 miles
Nunobiki Falls (330m)
Nunobiki Ropeway
Shin-Kōbe
Shin-Kōbe
Osaka (25km); Kyoto (60km)
Tōkaidō Shinkansen Line
Himeji (60km)
KITANO-CHŌ
Kitano-dōri
Fudō-zaka
Ijinkan-dōri
Kōban
Kitano-Zaka
Hunter-zaka
Yamate-kansen
Osaka (25km); Kyoto (60km)
JR Kōbe Line
Pearl St
Tor Rd
Flower Rd
Hakutsuru Sake Brewery Museum (6km); Sumiyoshi (6km)
Nakayamate-dōri
Higashimon St
Sannomiya
Sannomiya Bus Terminal
Sannomiya
Hanshin Sannomiya
Sankita-dōri
Hankyū Sannomiya
MOTOMACHI
SANNOMIYA
Sogō Department Store
Shimo-Yamate-dōri
Tor Rd
Isogami-kōen
Koikawa-suji
Sannomiya Sentā-gai
Sannomiya Hon-dōri
Sannomiya Chūō-dōri
Hankyū Kōbe Line
Flower Rd
Port Line
Ikuta Rd
Kōbe City Hall
Motomachi
Hanshin Motomachi
Meriken Rd
Motomachi Arcade
Nakamachi-dōri
Kyōmachi-suji
Naniwamachi-suji
Edomachi-suji
KYŪ-KYŌRYUCHI (FORMER FOREIGN SETTLEMENT)
Kōbe (600m)
NANKIN-MACHI (CHINATOWN)
Akashimachi-suji
Harimamachi-suji
Port of Kōbe Earthquake Memorial Park (450m); Kōbe Harbor Land (750m)
Kōbe (6km)

Kōbe

Sights

1 Ikuta-jinja B5
2 Kitano-chō B2
3 Kōbe City Museum C7
4 Nankin-machi B6

Sleeping

5 ANA Crowne Plaza Hotel Kōbe C1
6 B Kōbe B5
7 Hotel Trusty Kōbe Kyū-Kyoryuchi C6
8 Oriental Hotel C7

Eating

9 Daichi B6
10 Grill Jūjiya C6
11 Isuzu Bakery C3
12 Isuzu Bakery Ikuta Road Shop B5
Kōbe Plaisir .... (see 6)
13 Mikami C3
14 Modernark B5
15 Wanto Burger B5

Drinking & Nightlife

16 Sake Yashiro B5
17 Starbucks Ijinkan B3

Entertainment

18 Sone B4

Shopping

19 Daimaru Department Store B6

settled here during the Meiji period. These *ijinkan* (literally 'foreigners' houses') – strangely, though naturally, incongruent, as each is built in the architectural style of the owner's home country – are now mostly cafes, restaurants and souvenir shops.

Two of the best-preserved homes, the red-brick **Weathercock House**, built in 1909 for a German trader, and the wooden, jade-green **Moegi House**, built in 1903 for the former US consul, are open as museums (9am to 6pm; combined ticket ¥650). Much of the original furnishings are intact – you'll see the lengths that expats a century ago went to in order to maintain their native lifestyles.

Ikuta-jinja SHINTŌ SHRINE

(生田神社; ☎078-321-3851; 1-2-1 Shimo-Yamate-dōri, Chūō-ku; ⏰7am-sunset; 🚉JR Sannomiya) FREE Kōbe's signature shrine is said to date from 201, though it's been rebuilt many a time – a symbol of resilience for the city. It's right in the middle of Sannomiya, providing a peaceful retreat from the urban bustle.

Kōbe City Museum MUSEUM

(神戸市立博物館, Kōbe Shiritsu Hakubutsukan; ☎078-391-0035; www.kobecitymuseum.jp; 24 Kyō-machi, Chūō-ku; 🚉JR Sannomiya) Kōbe's local-history museum, in a Greek-revival-style building dating from 1935, is undergoing major renovations and scheduled to reopen in February 2022.

Nankin-machi AREA

(南京町, Chinatown; Sakaemachi-dōri, Chūō-ku; Ⓢ Kaigan line to Kyūkyoryūchi-Daimaru-mae, 🚉JR or Hanshin lines to Motomachi) Kōbe's Chinatown – Nankin comes from Nanjing; *machi* just means town – dates to the early days of the city opening its port to foreign traders. It was rebuilt after the 1995 earthquake and has all the visual signifiers of Chinatowns the world over: tiered gates at the cardinal entrances (except for the north side, guarded by lions) and lots of restaurants.

It's definitely touristy, but it's fun: most restaurants have stalls out the front selling street food, like *nikuman* (steamed buns, usually filled with pork; *baozi*) and *chimaki* (sticky rice wrapped in bamboo leaves, also often filled with pork; they're also called *zongzi*) for a few hundred yen each.

Nunobiki Herb Gardens & Ropeway VIEWPOINT

(布引ハーブ園&ロープウェイ; ropeway 1 way/return ¥950/1500, return after 5pm ¥900; ⏰10am-5pm Mon-Fri, to 8.30pm Sat & Sun 20 Mar-19 Jul & Sep-Nov, 10am-8.30pm daily 20 Jul-31 Aug, to 5pm Dec-19 Mar; Ⓢ Shin-Kōbe, 🚉JR Shin-Kōbe) Escape the city on a 400m-high mountain ridge, offering sweeping views across town to the bay. During the day (to 5pm) you can descend on foot through the landscaped herb gardens, which include some nicely placed benches and hammocks, to the mid-way station, from where you can return by ropeway or continue to the Nunobiki Falls (p391) and Shin-Kōbe Station.

Festivals & Events

Luminarie LIGHT SHOW

(神戸ルミナリエ; http://kobe-luminarie.jp; ⏰early Dec) Kōbe's biggest event takes place over 10 days in early December, when the streets southwest of Kōbe City Hall are decorated with illuminated archways that together look like an other-worldly cathedral. It's held in memory of the 6000 people who perished in the 1995 Great Hanshin Earthquake, and to celebrate the city's miraculous recovery. Check online for the exact dates.

Sleeping

There are lots of business hotels clustered around Sannomiya and some pricier options on the waterfront (with bay views).

ANA Crowne Plaza Hotel Kōbe HOTEL ¥¥
(ANAクラウンプラザ神戸; 078-291-1121; www.anacrowneplaza-kobe.jp; 1-chome, Kitano-chō, Chūō-ku; s from ¥12,800, d or tw from ¥14,800; S Shin-Kōbe, JR Shin-Kōbe) With direct access from Shin-Kōbe Station (via a passage on the station's 2nd floor) and spacious rooms, this 37-floor hotel is an easy choice, even if it feels a bit dated. There are English-speaking staff, restaurants, bars and a fitness centre (¥1080 surcharge for the pool).

There are also family rooms (¥22,800) with two double beds for up to four people.

B Kōbe BUSINESS HOTEL ¥¥
(ザ・ビー神戸; 078-333-4880; www.theb-hotels.com/the-b-kobe; 2-11-5 Shimo-Yamate, Chūō-ku; s/d from ¥11,000/12,700; S Sannomiya, JR Sannomiya) Centrally located steps from restaurants and nightlife and downhill from Kitano-chō, the B Kōbe is a good, modern, utilitarian choice. Staff speak some English, and there's free coffee in the lobby. Prices fluctuate wildly, rising at weekends, but great deals can be found during the week.

Oriental Hotel HOTEL ¥¥¥
(神戸旧居留地オリエンタルホテル; 078-326-1500; www.orientalhotel.jp; 25 Kyōmachi, Chūō-ku; s/d from ¥34,000/38,000; JR Sannomiya or Motomachi, Port Liner to Boeki Center) One of Japan's most historic hotels (1870), in Kyū-Kyoryuchi (the former foreigners' settlement), the Oriental was rebuilt after the 1995 earthquake and is now a sleek tower with elegant, designer rooms. Expect indulgent, English-speaking service and great views of the bay and mountains from the 17th-storey lobby and restaurant. Look for deals online. Note: this hotel is not affiliated with Oriental hotels in other countries.

Hotel Trusty Kōbe Kyū-Kyoryuchi BOUTIQUE HOTEL ¥¥¥
(ホテルトラスティ神戸旧居留地; 078-330-9111; http://ct.rion.mobi/trusty.kobe; 63 Naniwamachi, Chūō-ku; s/d/tw from ¥14,500/23,000/25,500; JR Sannomiya) The name screams 'standard-issue business hotel', but this is actually a boutique property with contemporary style in Kyū-Kyoryuchi (the former foreigners' settlement).

If you sign up for the breakfast buffet (¥1950), you can eat it on the terrace of the hotel's 2nd-floor cafe.

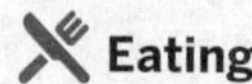

Eating

In addition to its premium beef, Kōbe is known for *yōshoku*, Western-style food as it was first interpreted in the late 19th and early 20th centuries, and Chinese food – both legacies of the city's cosmopolitan history. For *izakaya*, look no further than the nightlife district just north of Sannomiya Station.

The bayside mall **Kōbe Harbor Land** (神戸ハーバーランド; www.harborland.co.jp; Higashi Kawasaki-chō, Chūō-ku; 10am-9pm; S Kaigan line to Harbor Land, JR Kōbe line to Kōbe) has lots of family-friendly, if not terribly exciting, restaurants.

Isuzu Bakery BAKERY ¥
(イスズベーカリー; 078-222-4180; www.isuzu-bakery.jp; 2-1-4 Nunobiki-chō, Chūō-ku; bread & pastries ¥120-560; 8am-8pm; JR Sannomiya) The most famous of Kōbe's bakeries, Isuzu is particularly famous for its crisp, fluffy 'curry pan' (¥160; カレーパン), a deep-fried doughnut stuffed with beef curry. There's a huge variety of sweet and savoury options (and, with no English signs, you never quite know which you're going to get). Grab a tray and tongs and take your selections to the cashier.

This is the main shop, but there are other locations, such as the one on **Ikuta Road** (イスズベーカリー生田ロード店; 2-1-14 Kitanagasa-dōri, Chūō-ku; 9am-11pm; Sannomiya). Takeaway only.

Mikami SHOKUDO, INTERNATIONAL ¥
(味加味; 078-242-5200; 2-5-9 Kanō-chō, Chūō-ku; mains ¥480-1800, set meals from around ¥850; 11.30am-3pm & 5-11pm Wed-Mon; JR Sannomiya, JR Shin-Kōbe) Mikami is a beacon of good food in the otherwise forlorn zone between Shin-Kōbe Station and Sannomiya. For both lunch and dinner it does excellent *teishoku* (set meals); the '*katsu*' (crumbed and fried) dishes are especially good. At dinner it also does bistro-style fare like clams steamed in white wine and braised duck paired with wine, beer and cocktails.

It's on the street one block west of the main road connecting Shin-Kōbe Station and Sannomiya, about halfway between the two; look for an ivy-covered building.

Modernark CAFE ¥
(モダナーク; 078-391-3060; http://modernark-cafe.chronicle.co.jp; 3-11-15 Kitanagasa-dōri, Chūō-ku; mains ¥950-1150; 11.30am-10pm; Motomachi) This adorably funky cafe with a glassed-in verandah is Kōbe's go-to spot for organic vegetarian and vegan meals

and cakes, served with herbal tea or home-made sangria. Look for the thicket of potted trees out the front.

Grill Jūjiya INTERNATIONAL ¥¥
(グリル十字屋; 078-331-5455; www.grill-jujiya.com; 96 Edo-machi, Chūō-ku; mains ¥850-2300; 11am-8pm Mon-Sat; JR Sannomiya) In a city thick with east–west heritage, this old-fashioned charmer specialises in *yōshoku,* early Japanese takes on Western cooking, like *hayashi* rice (beef hash served with onions and demi-glace sauce over rice). It's been in business since the 1930s, though the exterior is newer (and so is the beer selection: you can get craft beer from Osaka brewery Minoh here).

Wanto Burger BURGERS ¥¥
(ワントバーガー; 078-392-5177; www.wantoburger.com; 3-10-6 Shimo-Yamate-dōri, Chūō-ku; burgers ¥1080-3800; noon-3pm & 5-10pm Tue-Fri, noon-10pm Sat, to 5pm Sun; JR Sannomiya) Wanto serves towering, teetering burgers made with Kōbe beef – and also somewhat less expensive varieties of *wagyū* (Japanese beef). It's run by a cool young crew and looks like a vintage US diner, with a long counter and a few tables.

Daichi STEAK ¥¥
(大地; 078-333-6688; www.koubegyuu.com/shop/daichi; 1-1-3 Motomachi-dōri, Chūō-ku; steak meals from ¥2500; 11am-9pm; S Kaigan line to Kyūkyorūchi-Daimaru-mae, JR Motomachi) A reliable place for Kōbe beef served *teppanyaki* (grilled on a steel plate) at entry-level prices: less-expensive cuts start at ¥2500 for 80g and a daily-special premium cut at ¥5800. Steak meals come with grilled vegetables and, for ¥800, salad, rice and miso soup (free before 3pm). Look for the giant bulls just inside Chinatown's east gate.

Kōbe Plaisir STEAK ¥¥¥
(神戸プレジール; 078-571-0141; https://kobe-plaisir.jp; 2-11-5 Shimo-Yamate-dōri, Chūō-ku; lunch/dinner Kōbe-beef set menus from ¥7500/11,000; 11.30am-3pm & 5-10.30pm; S Sannomiya, JR Sannomiya) This is a great place to try Kōbe beef prepared in a variety of styles, including teppanyaki or *shabu-shabu* (thinly sliced beef cooked with vegetables in boiling water and then dipped in sauce). It's managed directly by the local agriculture cooperative, and courses include plenty of veggies, too.

There are also less-expensive courses that use *Tajima-gyū* (high-quality beef that simply lacks the Kōbe brand name); there's a 10% service charge for dinner service.

The restaurant is rather nice inside, despite being on the ground floor of a business hotel, B Kōbe.

KŌBE BEEF

Kōbe is known worldwide for its top-class beef, considered by many to be the best in the world. Highly marbled, it's naturally tender and rich in flavour. It's also held to very strict regulations: to be accredited as *Kōbe gyū* (Kōbe beef), the meat must fulfill certain criteria for marbling, colour and texture; crucially, it must also come from a Tajima breed of Japanese black cow, born, raised and slaughtered in Kōbe's home prefecture, Hyōgo. There's a widespread belief that the cows are massaged, fed beer and played soothing music, though the Kōbe Beef Marketing & Distribution Promotion Association (www.kobe-beef.jp) disavows it. There are many places in the city to try it, though note that it is very expensive, especially for the best cuts (which really give you a taste for that famous marbling). Splurge on the cut rather than the size; the fat content makes Kōbe beef very filling.

Drinking & Nightlife

Kōbe has a lively nightlife scene, largely centred just north of Sannomiya Station.

Sake Yashiro BAR
(さけやしろ; 078-334-7339; 4-6-15 Ikuta-chō, Chūō-ku; 4-11.30pm; JR Sannomiya) This standing bar has a daunting selection of 90 kinds of sake, including about 50 from local brewers, on its (Japanese-only) menu. Anticipating your needs, staff have made a cheat sheet in English of their top five local picks, all priced ¥880 by the glass. Look for the denim door curtains.

If you need food to power you through your tasting session, try the 'sake yoshiro course' (さけやしろコース; ¥3800), a set of six small seasonal dishes.

Starbucks Ijinkan CAFE
(スターバックス異人館; 078-230-6302; 3-1-31 Kitano-chō, Chūō-ku; 8am-10pm; JR Sannomiya) A big chain wouldn't normally be worth listing, but this Starbucks is different: it's housed in a beautifully preserved former

ijinkan (foreigners' house), c 1907, in the Kitano-chō neighbourhood (p391). Buy a cuppa and ensconce yourself in period antiques and furniture (albeit amid some of the standard Starbucks decor). It can be crowded.

Entertainment

Sone JAZZ
(ソネ; ☎078-221-2055; www.kobe-sone.com; 1-24-10 Nakayamate-dōri, Chūō-ku; cover ¥1140; 5pm-midnight; JR Sannomiya) Sone is Kōbe's go-to spot for jazz (since 1969) and gathers four acts, of mostly Kansai-area artists, each night. The look is a bit old-timey Viennese cafe and the music is mostly standards, but there's a convivial atmosphere (and plenty of time for conversation between acts). One drink (from ¥700) or food (from ¥1000; mostly pub dishes) minimum order.

Information

Kōbe Information Centre (神戸市総合インフォメーションセンター; ☎078-322-0220; www.feel-kobe.jp; JR Sannomiya; 9am-7pm; Sannomiya) The city's main tourist information office is on the ground floor outside of JR Sannomiya Station's east gate. There's a smaller information counter on the 2nd floor of Shin-Kōbe Station, outside the main *shinkansen* gate. Both have good English city maps.

Getting There & Away

AIR

Kansai International Airport (p389) is the nearest international airport.

Kōbe Airport (www.kairport.co.jp) is served by ANA, Air Do, Skymark Airlines and Solaseed Air, with domestic flights to Tokyo (Haneda; one hour and 10 minutes), Sapporo (Chitose; two hours), Okinawa (Naha; 2¼ hours) and other cities. Osaka Itami Airport (p389) is also convenient for Kōbe.

BOAT

Overnight ferries depart from **Kōbe Rokko Port** for the following destinations:

Ehime (Niihama East Port, Shikoku; ¥6800, seven hours, Tuesday to Saturday) Departing around 1am, via **Orange Ferry** (☎06-6612-1811; www.orange-ferry.co.jp). Reservations can be made online in Japanese; otherwise use a travel agent.

Kita-Kyūshū (Shinmoji Port; ¥6680, 12½ hours, daily) Departing at 6.30pm (Sunday to Thursday) or 8pm (Friday and Saturday), via **Hankyū Ferry** (阪九フェリー; ☎0120-56-3268; www.han9f.co.jp); reservations can be made online.

Oita (Kyūshū; ¥11,820, 11½ hours, daily) Departing at 7pm (Sunday to Thursday) or 7.50pm (Friday and Saturday), via **Ferry Sunflower** (フェリーさんふらわあ; ☎toll free 0120-56-3268; www.ferry-sunflower.co.jp); reservations can be made online.

Buses (adult/child ¥230/120) make the 20-minute trip to Kōbe Rokko Port from JR Sumiyoshi Station; they're well timed for the Oita and Kita-Kyūshū ferries (see either ferry company for a schedule and more details).

BUS

Willer Express (http://willerexpress.com) overnight buses connect Kōbe's **Sannomiya Bus Terminal** and Tokyo (Shinjuku and Tokyo Stations). Prices start at ¥5000 and the journey takes eight or nine hours.

TRAIN

Centrally located Sannomiya Station is Kōbe's biggest rail hub, served by JR lines and the private Hankyū and Hanshin lines. The JR Kōbe line runs fast *shinkaisoku* (special rapid trains) for Osaka (¥410, 20 minutes) and Kyoto (¥1080, 50 minutes), and, in the other direction, for Himeji (¥970, 40 minutes). Hankyū-line trains connect Sannomiya and Osaka's Umeda Station (*tokkyū*; ¥320, 30 minutes).

Shin-Kōbe Station, north of Sannomiya, is on the Tōkaidō/San-yō and Kyūshū *shinkansen* lines. Destinations to the east include Shin-Osaka (¥1500, 15 minutes), Kyoto (¥2810, 30 minutes) and Tokyo (¥14,160, 2¾ hours); those to the west include Himeji (¥2700, 25 minutes), Hiroshima (¥9490, 70 minutes) and Fukuoka (Hakata Station; ¥14,160, 2¼ hours).

Getting Around

TO/FROM THE AIRPORT

Kansai International Airport

Boat A fun, if unusual, method: **Kōbe-Kansai Airport Bay Shuttle** (神戸関西空港ベイ・シャトル; www.kobe-access.jp; 5.30am-11.35pm) high-speed boats run between Kansai International Airport (KIX) and Kōbe Airport (adult/concession ¥1850/930, 30 minutes, approximately hourly). Purchase a ticket in the arrivals hall, then get the shuttle bus for the pier; at Kōbe Airport you can then take the Port Liner monorail the rest of the way to the city (fares for shuttle bus and monorail are included in the ticket, though when you purchase specify that you intend to take the Port Liner).

Bus Kate (www.kate.co.jp/en) runs direct limousine buses between KIX and Sannomiya Station (¥1950, 1¼ hours, every 20 minutes).

Train Take a JR Kansai Rapid Airport train to Osaka (¥1190, 70 minutes) and then change for a *shinkaisoku* train on the JR Kōbe line for Sannomiya (¥410, 20 minutes).

Kōbe Airport

The **Port Liner** (ポートライナー; www.knt-liner.co.jp) monorail connects Sannomiya (downtown Kōbe) and the airport (¥330, 18 minutes, frequent). A taxi costs between ¥2500 and ¥3000 (15 to 20 minutes).

Osaka Itami Airport

There are direct limousine buses (¥1050, 40 minutes, every 20 minutes) to/from Osaka's Itami Airport (p389). In Kōbe the buses stop on the southwestern side of Sannomiya Station.

BICYCLE

Kobelin (☎ toll free 0120-040-587; www.kobelin.jp; first hour ¥100, each additional 30min ¥100, per day ¥800) The city's bicycle-share scheme has ports all over town (look for the red bikes), though it's a little tricky to use: follow the instructions online and register in advance with a credit card.

BUS

The city-loop bus (per ride/day pass ¥260/660, children half-price) makes a circular tour of most of the city's sightseeing spots and its main stations several times an hour (10am to 6pm); look for the retro-style green buses. Purchase passes and tickets on board or at the tourist-information centre.

TRAIN

JR, Hankyū and Hanshin railway lines run east–west through town. The Seishin-Yamate subway line connects Shin-Kōbe and Sannomiya Stations (¥210, two minutes), or you can walk it in about 20 minutes. The Kaigan subway line runs from just south of Sannomiya Station to Minato Motomachi and Harbor Land stations for sights on the bay.

HIMEJI

☎ 079 / POP 531,300

Himeji (姫路), in Hyōgo Prefecture west of Kōbe, is on the map for one particular reason: it's home to Japan's biggest and best-preserved feudal-era castle, Himeji-jō. It's an easy day trip or stopover and well worth a visit.

Sights

★Himeji-jō CASTLE

(姫路城, Himeji Castle; www.himejicastle.jp/en; 68 Hon-machi; adult/child ¥1000/300, combination ticket with Kōkō-en ¥1040/360; ⏰ 9am-5pm Sep-Apr, to 6pm May-Aug) Himeji-jō is Japan's most magnificent castle, built in 1580 by general Toyotomi Hideyoshi and one of only a few original castles from that era (most are modern concrete reconstructions). Its white-plaster facade (and its elegant presence) earned it the nickname Shirasagi-jō (White Egret Castle). There's a five-storey main keep and three smaller keeps, all surrounded by moats and defensive walls. It takes about 1½ hours to follow the arrow-marked route around the castle. Last entry is an hour before closing.

The castle is often crowded – it's a popular destination for tour groups – in which case you might have to wait a little before entering some areas; if you're coming on a weekend especially, allow extra time.

While following the route through the keeps you'll get a good lesson in medieval defensive strategies, like the *ishiotoshi* – narrow openings that allowed defenders to pour boiling water or oil onto anyone trying to scale the walls after making it past the other defences. There are lovely city views from the top floor of the main keep. (You can also get close enough to the castle to appreciate the building, and get a good photo, before you reach the ticket gates.)

If Himeji-jō looks too good to be that old, it's because it underwent an extensive five-year renovation prior to reopening in 2014. And if it looks familiar, it's because it often appears in films, such as Kurosawa Akira's *Seven Samurai* (1954) and *Ran* (1985).

DON'T MISS

BEST TEMPLES & SHRINES

- Tōdai-ji (p400)
- Oku-no-in (p420)
- Ise-jingū (p433)
- Kumano Hongū Taisha (p427)
- Kasuga Taisha (p401)

Kōkō-en GARDENS

(好古園; 68 Hon-machi; adult/child ¥300/150, combination ticket with Himeji-jō ¥1040/360; ⏰ 9am-6pm May-Aug, to 5pm Sep-Apr) This is a modern recreation of an Edo-era samurai residence, with a lovely strolling garden complete with a central pond (filled with koi) and a teahouse (*matcha* ¥500). The layout and building design were based on archaeological excavation of the original residence.

Sleeping

Himeji is an easy day trip from any of Kansai's big cities, or on your way to/from points west – though if you stay over you can get an early start and avoid the crowds somewhat (and

see the castle lit up at night). There are many hotels (from budget to three star) around JR Himeji Station, mostly on the south side.

Daiwa Roynet Hotel Himeji BUSINESS HOTEL ¥¥
(ダイワロイネットホテル姫路; ☎079-287-0655; www.daiwaroynet.jp/himeji; 353 Ekimae-chō; s/d from ¥5600/9900;) In addition to being new (it opened in early 2018), this business hotel has a few other appealing things: walk-in showers (that are more accessible than the usual tub-shower combos); a fitness centre (albeit tiny); and a location on the north (castle) side of JR Himeji Station.

Himeji

Top Sights
1 Himeji-jō A1

Sights
2 Kōkō-en A2

Sleeping
3 Daiwa Roynet Hotel Himeji B4

Eating
4 Nadagiku Kappa-tei B4

Drinking & Nightlife
5 Hanamoto Coffee B3
6 Kokoromi B5

Transport
7 Bus Stop 6 .... A5
8 Harima Cycle Station A4
9 Highway Bus Terminal A5
10 Shinki Bus Information Desk A4

Eating & Drinking

Finding food in Himeji is easy: there are tons of options (with tourist-friendly English or picture menus) in the train station, along the main road to the castle and in the covered arcades between the two. Be sure to try some local sake here.

Nadagiku Kappa-tei SHOKUDO, IZAKAYA ¥
(灘菊かっぱ亭; ☎079-221-3573; www.nadagiku.co.jp/gourmet/nadagiku; 58 Higashi-ekimae-chō, Omizo-suji Shopping Arcade; set lunch ¥700-860, oden per piece ¥160-250, small plates ¥380-980; ⏰11.30am-2pm & 4.30-9.30pm Mon, Tue, Thu & Fri, 11.30am-9.30pm Sat, to 8.30pm Sun) A local sake brewery runs this casual spot specialising in *oden* (stew comprising fishcakes, tofu, vegetables and eggs simmered in kelp-flavoured broth), and other dishes that naturally pair well with sake. Choose a simple set at lunch (picture menu only) or visit in the evening to order à la carte. Look for the sake barrels out the front.

Hanamoto Coffee CAFE
(はまもとコーヒー; ☎079-282-2233; www.hamamoto-coffee.com; 49 Nikai-machi; ⏰7am-7pm Fri-Wed) Both locals and out-of-towners agree that this cafe (running since 1975) is the place for coffee (freshly ground and siphon brewed, from ¥430) in Himeji. Come before 11am and your drink order will arrive with a hard-boiled egg and toast at no extra charge. But most customers order extra 'almond-butter' toast (¥450) anyway.

Kokoromi BAR

(こころみ; ☎079-280-6172; Vierra Arcade, 125 Minami-ekimae; sake ¥110-1250; ⏰1-9pm Tue-Fri, noon-8pm Sat & Sun) It's all about local sake at this modern, sophisticated standing bar, which stocks 270 varieties from Hyōgo, Himeji's prefecture. Touch screens let you search and order in English by taste, price and grade (search West Harima for Himeji), and your 65mL pour comes with an English explanation card and a picture of the bottle for future reference.

It's in the Vierra arcade; from JR Himeji Station follow signs out the east exit until you can't go any further and hang a right to enter the arcade.

Information

Himeji Tourist Information Office (姫路市観光案内所; ☎079-287-0003; Ground fl, Himeji Station; ⏰9am-7pm) English maps and info. You may be able to book a volunteer English-speaking guide here, if the relevant desk is staffed.

Getting There & Away

Himeji is a stop on the San-yō *shinkansen* (bullet train), with connections to Shin-Kōbe (¥2700, 25 minutes), Shin-Osaka (¥3220, 35 minutes) and Kyoto (¥4750, 55 minutes) to the east, and Okayama (¥3220, 35 minutes) and Hiroshima (¥7770, one hour) to the west.

The fastest trains (*shinkaisoku*) on the ordinary JR Kōbe line travel to Kōbe's Sannomiya Station (¥970, 40 minutes), Osaka (¥1490, one hour) and Kyoto (¥2270, 1½ hours).

Long-distance buses to Tokyo (Shinjuku Bus Terminal; ¥8000, 10 hours) leave from the **Highway Bus Terminal**.

Getting Around

Himeji's attractions are a straight, flat 15-minute walk from the north side of JR Himeji Station. Arrive early to score one of the limited free rental bicycles offered at **Harima Cycle Station** (はりまサイクルステーション; ☎079-283-0006; ⏰9.30am-6pm, which also has a left-luggage service.

The retro-looking Himeji Castle Loop Bus runs from **bus stop 6** on the north side of JR Himeji Station to the castle, Kōkō-en and back (single ride/day pass ¥100/300; children half-price) every 30 minutes from 9am to 5pm daily March to November and at weekends December to February. Purchase passes from the **Shinki Bus Information Desk** (神姫バス案内所; ⏰7am-8pm Mon-Fri, 7.30am-7pm Sat, to 6pm Sun). The pass nets you a 20% discount on entry to sights (but does not apply to the already discounted combination ticket to the castle and gardens).

NARA PREFECTURE

History in Nara Prefecture (奈良県, Nara-ken) goes back further even than Kyoto's, as it was here in the Yamato basin that the forerunners of Japan's ruling Yamato dynasty consolidated power. In the early centuries of their reign they were building *kofun* (huge burial mounds for their emperors), some of which can still be seen today, especially in Asuka.

When the Yamato court finally chose a spot for a permanent capital, they chose Nara, and while Nara's time as capital was short, its cultural legacy was enormous. It was here that Buddhism first flourished in Japan, and the city's fantastic repository of temples and Buddhist art attests to that fact (Nara remains a thriving metropolis today).

In the southern reaches of the prefecture, Yoshino is a mountain hamlet with some sights of serious historic and cultural significance, but it's still better known as Japan's most famous cherry-blossom-viewing spot.

History

Until the 7th century the young Japanese empire had no permanent capital, as Shintō taboos concerning death stipulated that the capital be moved with the passing of each emperor. This changed under the influence of Buddhism and with the Taika reforms of 646. The court decreed that a permanent capital be built; two locations were tried before one was finally established at Nara (then known as Heijōkyō) in 710. 'Permanent' status, however, lasted a mere 75 years. When a priest named Dōkyō seduced an empress and nearly usurped the throne, it was decided to move the court out of reach of Nara's increasingly powerful clergy. The new capital was eventually established at Kyoto, about 35km north.

Although brief, the Nara period was extraordinarily vigorous in its absorption of influences from China, laying the foundations of Japanese culture. Except for an assault on the area by the Taira clan in the 12th century, Nara was spared the periodic bouts of destruction wreaked on Kyoto, and a number of magnificent buildings have survived.

Sleeping

Nara city has a great spread of accommodation across budgets, but the surrounding regions have fewer options (or none at all). It's best to base yourself in Nara and see the other sights as day trips. The exception is Yoshino, which has some nice inns – and if you're going to the trouble of visiting, it's worth staying there overnight.

Eating

Nara city has plenty of dining options. Outside the city, simple lunches are reasonably easy to find: towns with attractions have *shokudō* (all-round, inexpensive restaurants) and many of the major temples and shrines have snack stalls and teahouses lining their approaches. However, most places shut after dark; you'll have to work your way back to the nearest transit hub to find restaurants open for dinner.

The region has a long history of sake brewing, and Nara-style cuisine often uses sake lees (the leftover bits after brewing), which give a heady umami taste to pickles, marinated dishes, soups and hot pots. Another local speciality is *kakinoha-zushi* (individual pieces of sushi wrapped in persimmon leaves – don't eat the leaf!). This dish is especially associated with Yoshino (though you'll see it all over), as are gelatinous sweets made from the ground roots of kudzu (aka arrowroot).

Getting There & Around

Nara city is easily accessible by both JR and private Kintetsu-line trains from Kyoto and Osaka.

It's possible to access a lot of Nara Prefecture, even rural and mountain sights, via a combination of trains and buses, though having a car is convenient and more efficient, as local buses run infrequently.

The Kintetsu network is more thorough than JR, so not everywhere will be accessible by JR Pass. Useful JR stations include Sakurai (JR Man-yō Mahoroba line from Nara; transfer to the Kintetsu Osaka line) and Yoshino-guchi (JR Wakayama line; for travel to Yoshino).

Key Kintetsu hubs include Yamato-Saidaiji (Nara, Kyoto and Kashihara lines), Yamato-Yagi (Osaka and Kashihara lines) and Kashihara-jingū-mae (Kashihara and Yoshino lines).

Nara Kōtsū (www.narakotsu.co.jp) runs the bus network. The **Kintetsu Nara Bus Information Centre** (8.30am-8pm Mon-Fri, to 7pm Sat & Sun) is particularly helpful, with English-speaking staff who can help you with rural routes and schedules before you set out.

Nara

0742 / POP 357,412

Japan's first permanent capital, Nara (奈良) is one of the country's most rewarding destinations. The biggest draw is the awe-inspiring Daibutsu (Great Buddha), a towering effigy first cast in the 8th century. Historically important temples and shrines house treasures of Buddhist art, and more can be found in the excellent Nara National Museum. All of this occupies a compact area in and around Nara-kōen, a large, grassy park home to many (somewhat) tame deer.

Nara is popular as a day trip from Kyoto or Osaka – there's just enough time to see the highlights. If you stay longer, you can visit one or more of the temples on the city's outskirts (less crowded but no less rewarding), stroll through the old merchant district of Naramachi and really immerse yourself in early Japanese history, art and architecture, for which Nara is famous.

Sights

Nara retains its 8th-century Chinese-style grid pattern of streets. There are two main train stations: JR Nara and Kintetsu Nara. JR Nara Station is a little west of the city centre (but still within walking distance of the sights), while Kintetsu Nara is right in the centre of town. The main sights are clustered in and around Nara-kōen (奈良公園), east of Kintetsu Nara Station, and are easily walkable.

★Tōdai-ji — BUDDHIST TEMPLE

(東大寺; www.todaiji.or.jp; 406-1 Zōshi-chō; Daibutsu-den adult/child ¥600/300; Daibutsu-den 7.30am-5.30pm Apr-Oct, 8am-5pm Nov-Mar)

Nara's star attraction is its **Daibutsu** (Great Buddha; illustration p402), one of the largest bronze statues in the world. It was unveiled in 752, upon the completion of the **Daibutsu-den** (大仏殿, Great Buddha Hall), built to house it. Both have been damaged over the years; the present statue was recast in the Edo period. The Daibutsu-den is the largest wooden building in the world; incredibly, the present structure, rebuilt in 1709, is a mere two-thirds of the size of the original.

The Daibutsu stands just over 16m high and consists of 437 tonnes of bronze and 130kg of gold. It is an image of Dainichi Nyorai (also known as Vairocana Buddha), the cosmic Buddha believed to give rise to all worlds and their respective Buddhas. Historians believe that Emperor Shōmu ordered the building of the Buddha as a charm against smallpox, which ravaged Japan in preceding years. Over the centuries the statue took quite a beating from earthquakes and fires, losing its head a couple of times (note the slight difference in colour between the head and the body).

As you circle the statue towards the back, you'll see a wooden column with a hole through its base. Popular belief maintains that those who can squeeze through the hole, which is exactly the same size as one of the Great Buddha's nostrils, are assured of enlightenment. There's usually a line of children waiting to give it a try and parents standing ready to snap their picture. A hint for bigger 'kids': try going through with one or both arms above your head – someone on either end to push and pull helps, too.

Don't miss **Tōdai-ji Nandai-mon** (東大寺南大門, South Gate), which houses recently restored wooden images, carved in the 13th century by famed sculptor Unkei, are among the finest examples of guardian statues in the country – dynamic and full of character, with dramatic musculature.

Except for the Daibutsu-den, most of Tōdai-ji's grounds can be visited free. For a deep dive on the temple's history and to see some of its important artwork and relics, visit the **Tōdai-ji Museum** (東大寺ミュージアム; ☎0742-20-5511; 100 Suimon-chō; ¥600, joint ticket with Daibutsu-den ¥1000; ⏲9.30am-5.30pm Apr-Oct, to 5pm Nov-Mar).

★Nara National Museum — MUSEUM

(奈良国立博物館, Nara Kokuritsu Hakubutsukan; ☎050-5542-8600; www.narahaku.go.jp; 50 Noboriōji-chō; ¥520, special exhibitions ¥1100-1420; ⏲9.30am-5pm Tue-Sun) This world-class museum of Buddhist art is divided into two sections. Built in 1894 and strikingly renovated in 2016, the Nara Buddhist Sculpture Hall & Ritual Bronzes Gallery displays a rotating selection of about 100 *butsu-zō* (statues of Buddhas and bodhisattvas) at any one time, about half of which are National Treasures or Important Cultural Properties. Chinese bronzes in the ritual bronzes gallery date as far back as the 15th century BCE. Each image has detailed English explanations.

The newer east and west wings, a short walk away, contain the permanent collections (sculptures, paintings and calligraphy) and also host special exhibitions.

Particularly noteworthy is the fall special exhibition featuring the artefacts from Shōsō-in Hall, which holds the treasures of Tōdai-ji The exhibits include priceless items from the cultures along the Silk Road. This exhibit (admission ¥1100) is well worth it, but be prepared for crowds.

It's free to enter the underground passageway connecting the wings, where wall displays explain in detail the history, the making process and the symbolism of different styles of Buddhist sculpture – a good primer for appreciating Nara's sights.

★Kasuga Taisha — SHINTŌ SHRINE

(春日大社; www.kasugataisha.or.jp; 160 Kasugano-chō; ⏲6am-6pm Apr-Sep, 6.30am-5pm Oct-Mar) FREE Founded in the 8th century, this sprawling shrine at the foot of Mikasa-yama was created to protect the new capital, Nara. It was ritually rebuilt every 20 years, according to Shintō tradition, until the late 19th century and is still kept in pristine condition. Many of its buildings are painted vermilion, in bold contrast to the cedar roofs and surrounding greenery. The corridors are lined with hundreds of lanterns, which are illuminated during the twice-yearly Mantōrō lantern festival (p406).

Every morning at 9am (except for festival days), the public is welcome to observe the *chōhai* (morning prayer service), held in the Naoraiden (Ceremony Hall).

There are several subshrines around the main hall. It's worth walking a few minutes south to the nearby subshrine of **Wakamiya-jinja** (若宮神社).

Kōfuku-ji — BUDDHIST TEMPLE

(興福寺; www.kohfukuji.com; grounds free, Tōkondō ¥300, National Treasure Museum ¥600, combined ticket ¥800; ⏲grounds 24hr, Tōkondō 9am-5pm) Kōfuku-ji was founded in Kyoto in 669 and relocated here in 710. The original Nara temple complex had 175 buildings, though much has been lost over the years to fires and periods of medieval warfare. Of those that remain, the most impressive are the **Tōkondō** (東金堂; Eastern Golden Hall; adult/child ¥300/100; ⏲9am-5pm) and the temple's two pagodas: the **three-storey pagoda** (三重塔) dates to 1181 and is a rare example of Heian-era architecture, while the 50.1m **five-storey pagoda** (五重塔), last reconstructed in 1426, is Japan's second-tallest pagoda.

The Tōkondō is a National Treasure dating from 726; rebuilt in 1415 (but paying homage to older structures), it houses several important Buddhist statues. The temple's **Chūkondō** (Central Golden Hall) was rebuilt in 2018 – the first time it had been properly rebuilt since it burned down for the seventh time in 1717; that said, it does look a bit out of place among Kōfuku-ji's more historic structures.

The temple grounds are free to visit, though admission is required to enter some of the structures. If you have to pick just one, make it the **Kōfuku-ji National Treasure Museum** (国宝館; adult/child ¥700/300; ⏲9am-5pm), which houses the most outstanding pieces of the temple's vast collection of art.

Tōdai-ji

VISIT THE GREAT BUDDHA

The Daibutsu (Great Buddha) at Nara's Tōdai-ji is one of the most arresting sights in Japan. The awe-inspiring physical presence of the vast image is striking. It's one of the largest bronze Buddha images in the world and it's contained in an equally huge building, the Daibutsu-den hall, which is among the largest wooden buildings on earth.

Tōdai-ji was built by order of Emperor Shōmu during the Nara period (710–784) and the complex was finally completed in 798, after the capital had been moved from Nara to Kyoto. Most historians agree the temple was built to consolidate the country and serve as its spiritual focus. Legend has it that over two million labourers worked on the temple, but this is probably apocryphal. What's certain is that its construction brought the country to the brink of bankruptcy.

The original Daibutsu was cast in bronze in eight castings over a period of three years. It has been recast several times over the centuries. The original Daibutsu was covered in gold leaf and one can only imagine its impact on Japanese visitors during the eighth century AD.

The temple belongs to the Kegon school of Buddhism, one of the six schools of Buddhism popular in Japan during the Nara period. Kegon Buddhism, which comes from the Chinese Huayan Buddhist sect, is based on the Flower Garland Sutra. This sutra expresses the idea of worlds within worlds, all manifested by the Cosmic Buddha (Vairocana or Dainichi Nyorai). The Great Buddha and the figures that surround him in the Daibutsu-den Hall are the perfect physical symbol of this cosmological map.

FACT FILE

THE DAIBUTSU

Height 14.98m

Weight 500 tonnes

Nostril width 50cm

THE DAIBUTSU-DEN HALL

Height 48.74m

Length 57m

Number of roof tiles 112,589

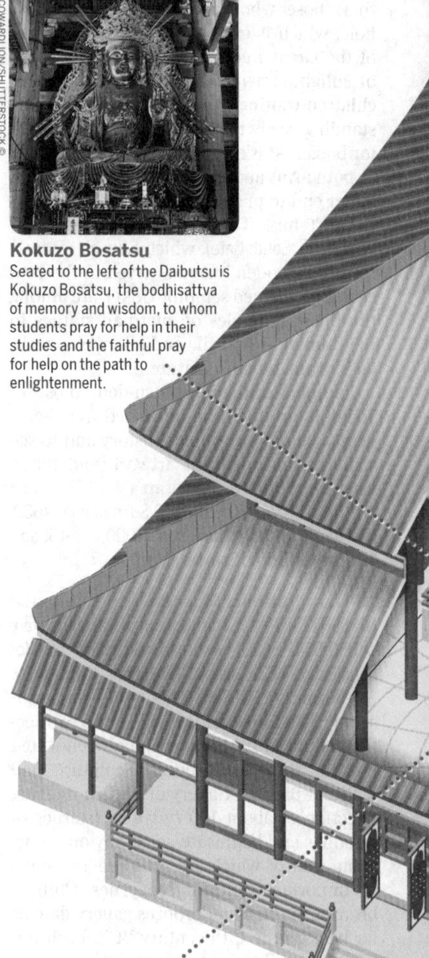

Kokuzo Bosatsu
Seated to the left of the Daibutsu is Kokuzo Bosatsu, the bodhisattva of memory and wisdom, to whom students pray for help in their studies and the faithful pray for help on the path to enlightenment.

The Daibutsu (Great Buddha)
Known in Sanskrit as 'Vairocana' and in Japanese as the 'Daibutsu', this is the Cosmic Buddha that gives rise to all other Buddhas, according to Kegon doctrine. The Buddha's hands send the messages 'fear not' (right) and 'welcome' (left).

Komokuten
Standing to the left of the Daibutsu is Komokuten (Lord of Limitless Vision), who serves as a guardian of the Buddha. He stands upon a *jaki* (demon), which symbolises ignorance, and wields a brush and scroll, which symbolises wisdom.

PATTILABELLE/GETTY IMAGES ©

Buddhas around Dainichi
Sixteen smaller Buddhas are arranged in a halo around the Daibutsu's head, each of which symbolises one of the Daibutsu's different manifestations. They are graduated in size to appear the same size when viewed from the ground.

Tamonten
To the right of the Daibutsu stands Tamonten (Lord Who Hears All), another of the Buddha's guardians. He holds a pagoda, which is said to represent a divine storehouse of wisdom.

COWARDLION/SHUTTERSTOCK ©

Hole in Pillar
Behind the Daibutsu you will find a pillar with a 50cm hole through its base (the size of one of the Daibutsu's nostrils). It's said that if you can crawl through this, you are assured of enlightenment.

PIUS99/GETTY IMAGES ©

Nyoirin Kannon
Seated to the right of the Daibutsu is Nyoirin Kannon, one of the esoteric forms of Kannon Bodhisattva. This is one of the bodhisattvas that preside over the six different realms of karmic rebirth.

Nara

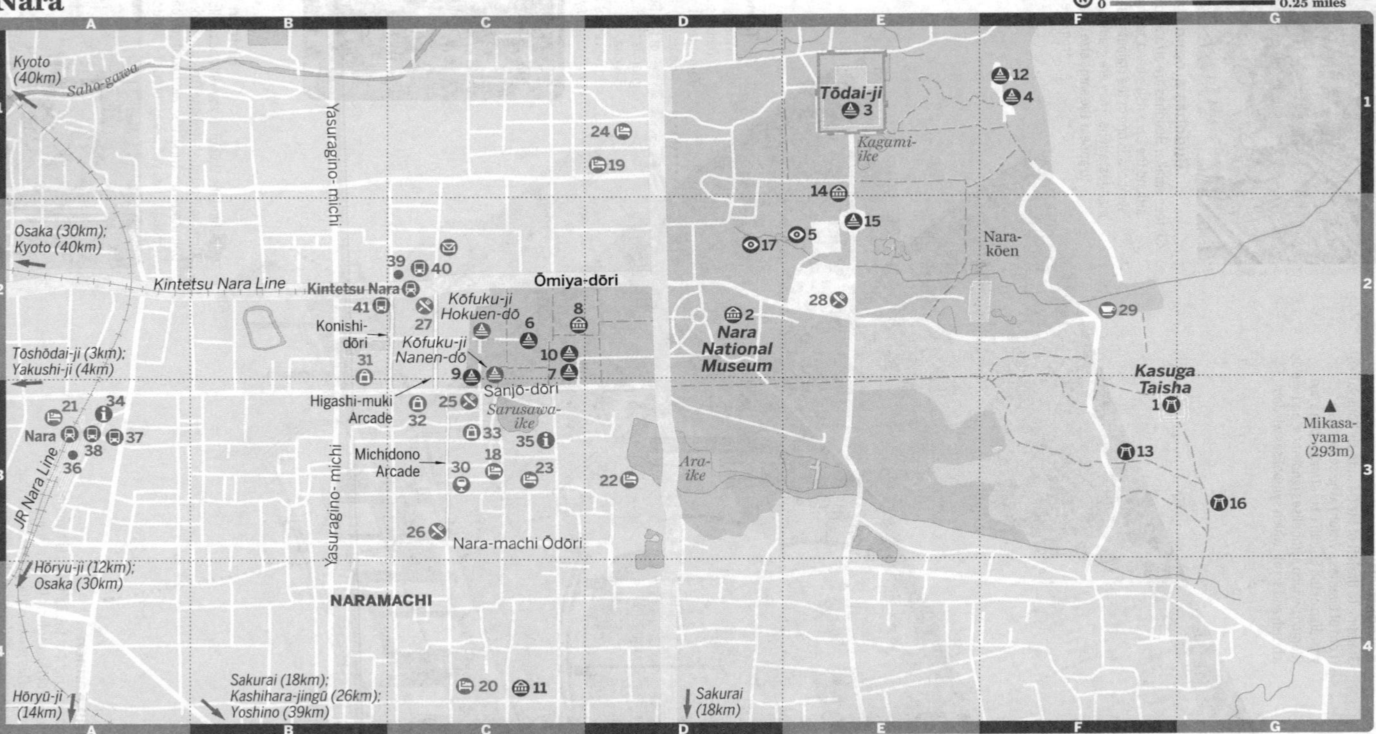
0 500 m
0 0.25 miles
Kyoto (40km)
Saho-gawa
Osaka (30km); Kyoto (40km)
Kintetsu Nara Line
Tōshōdai-ji (3km); Yakushi-ji (4km)
Nara
JR Nara Line
Hōryu-ji (12km); Osaka (30km)
Hōryū-ji (14km)
Sakurai (18km); Kashihara-jingū (26km); Yoshino (39km)
Yasuragino- michi
Kintetsu Nara
Konishi-dōri
Higashi-muki Arcade
Michidono Arcade
NARAMACHI
Kōfuku-ji Hokuen-dō
Kōfuku-ji Nanen-dō
Ōmiya-dōri
Sanjō-dōri
Sarusawa-ike
Nara-machi Ōdōri
Sakurai (18km)
Ara-ike
Nara National Museum
Tōdai-ji
Kagami-ike
Nara-kōen
Kasuga Taisha
Mikasa-yama (293m)
1 2 3 4 5 6 7 8 9 10 11 12 13 14 15 16 17 18 19 20 21 22 23 24 25 26 27 28 29 30 31 32 33 34 35 36 37 38 39 40 41
A B C D E F G

Nara

Isui-en & Neiraku Art Museum GARDENS
(依水園・寧楽美術館; 74 Suimon-chō; museum & garden adult/child ¥900/300; ⌚9.30am-4.30pm Wed-Mon Dec-Mar & Jun-Sep, daily Apr, May, Oct & Nov) Isui-en is an elegant garden in two parts: one created in the 17th century, in the style of an Edo-period (1603–1868) strolling garden, and another added in the early 20th century. Both make fantastic use of the technique of *shakkei* (borrowed scenery), incorporating the mountains behind Kasuga Taisha (p401) into the design. For ¥850 you can have *matcha* (powdered green tea) and a Japanese sweet in the teahouse. Admission covers the adjoining Neiraku Art Museum, displaying Chinese and Korean ceramics and bronzes.

Yoshiki-en GARDENS
(吉城園; ☎0742-22-5911; 60-1 Noboriōji-chō; ¥250, non-Japanese free; ⌚9am-5pm, closed last 2 weeks Feb) This garden was once part of Kofuku-ji (p401) and since 1919 has been a public garden, laid out in traditional fashion along paths around a pond. Most attractive is the moss garden with its teahouse. Admission is waived for foreign guests who show their passports.

Tours

Nara Walk TOURS
(奈良ウォーク; ☎090-9708-0036; www.narawalk.com; ⌚Mar-Nov or by appointment) Nara Walk does a popular three-hour morning tour with English-speaking guides around the highlights of Nara-kōen (Tōdai-ji (p400), Kasuga Taisha (p401) etc; adult/child ¥3000/1000); meet at 10am in front of JR Nara Station (no booking required). It also offers a two-hour afternoon stroll around Naramachi (adult/child ¥2000/free; booking required), and custom tours on request.

YMCA Goodwill Guides TOURS
(☎0742-45-5920; http://eggnara.tripod.com; ⌚9.30am-1pm Mon-Fri) Knowledgeable, English-speaking volunteer guides, keen to help you get the most out of your visit to Nara. Contact them to book.

Festivals & Events

Shuni-e Ceremony CULTURAL
(⌚early Mar) During this fire festival the monks of Tōdai-ji parade huge, flaming torches around the balcony of Nigatsu-dō

DON'T MISS

NARAMACHI

South of Sanjō-dōri and Sarusawa-ike pond, Naramachi (奈良町) is a traditional neighbourhood with many well-preserved *machiya* (shophouses) and *kura* (storehouses), including some business that have been around for generations. Usually uncrowded, it's a nice area to wander around.

Check out **Naramachi Kōshi-no-Ie** (ならまち格子の家; ☎0742-23-4820; 44 Gangōji-chō; ⏲9am-5pm Tue-Sun) FREE, a well-preserved *machiya* with lattice front, beamed ceilings, old kitchen, *tansu* (chest of drawers) stairs and inner garden. It's an excellent place to explore details of traditional Japanese architecture; an English-language leaflet is available.

for 10 nights straight, raining embers on spectators to purify them. On the following day they draw water from the temple well and at 2am (early on the final day) offer it to Kannon (the Buddhist goddess of mercy) and the public.

Yamayaki CULTURAL

(Grass-Burning Festival; ⏲6pm 4th Sat Jan) Though the origins of this festival are unclear (it's possibly a nod to a long-ago feud between the monks of Tōdai-ji and Kōfuku-ji), Nara's three big religious institutions, Tōdai-ji, Kōfuku-ji and Kasuga Taisha, come together to set alight Wakakusa-yama; a fireworks display follows. The whole city glows (and then the local fire brigade puts out the fire).

Mantōrō CULTURAL

(Lantern Festival; ¥500; ⏲5.30-8.30pm 3 Feb, 7-9.30pm 14 & 15 Aug) On 3 February, also known as Setsubun (the first day of spring on the old lunar calendar), Kasuga Taisha lights each and every one of its 3000 stone and bronze lanterns – it's unbelievably atmospheric. The festival is held again in August for O-Bon (a Buddhist observance honouring ancestral spirits).

Takigi Nō DANCE

(⏲May) Open-air performances of *nō* (stylised dance-drama) are held after dark by the light of blazing torches at Kōfuku-ji (on the third Friday of May) and Kasuga Taisha (on the third Friday and Saturday of May).

Sleeping

Many travellers pressed for time visit Nara as a day trip, but staying a night here is recommended: you'll have an early start on the day trippers at the main sights. There are lots of good accommodation options in all price ranges, and especially for budget travellers.

★Guesthouse

Nara Backpackers GUESTHOUSE ¥

(ゲストハウス 奈良バックパッカーズ; ☎0742-22-4557; www.nara-backpackers.com; 31 Yurugi-chō; dm ¥2400, s/d without bathroom ¥5800/7600;) An utterly charming stay in a traditional 1920s building, which was once a tea master's home. Choose from bunk-bed dorms or five different-size private tatami-mat rooms, some with garden views. Bathing facilities are shared (bring your own toiletries and towel, or buy or rent them here), and there's a shared kitchen for self-caterers.

Children under 10 years are not permitted, to preserve the home's *shōji* (sliding paper doors) and antique glass windows. It's about eight minutes on foot from Kintetsu Nara Station.

Guesthouse Makura GUESTHOUSE ¥

(ゲストハウス枕; ☎0742-24-2279; www.guesthouse-makura.com; 27-1 Imamikado-chō; dm/s/d ¥2500/3500/7000;) In Naramachi and close to the sights, Guesthouse Makura occupies a 90-year-old wooden *machiya* (shophouse). It's been lightly renovated but retains much of the flavour of an old Japanese house (which may charm or annoy you: the walls are thin). But it's very well maintained and the English-speaking owner goes out of his way to make guests feel at home.

Wakasa Bettei RYOKAN ¥¥

(和鹿彩別邸; ☎0742-23-5858; www.n-wakasa.com; 1 Kita-handahigashi-machi; r per person with/without 2 meals from ¥25,920/9720;) This friendly, contemporary ryokan (inn) aims to please. The 11 stylish, large Japanese- and Western-style rooms have private facilities, including a stone or wooden bathtub, and the top-floor common bath has views of Tōdai-ji (p400) and Wakakusa-yama. The newer Bettei is a better choice than the original (though still friendly) Hotel New Wakasa next door.

Guesthouse Sakuraya GUESTHOUSE ¥¥

(桜舎; ☎0742-24-1490; www.guesthouse-sakuraya.com; 1 Narukawa-chō; s/d incl breakfast & without bathroom ¥6200/10,400;) In a 160-year-old *machiya* (shophouse) with

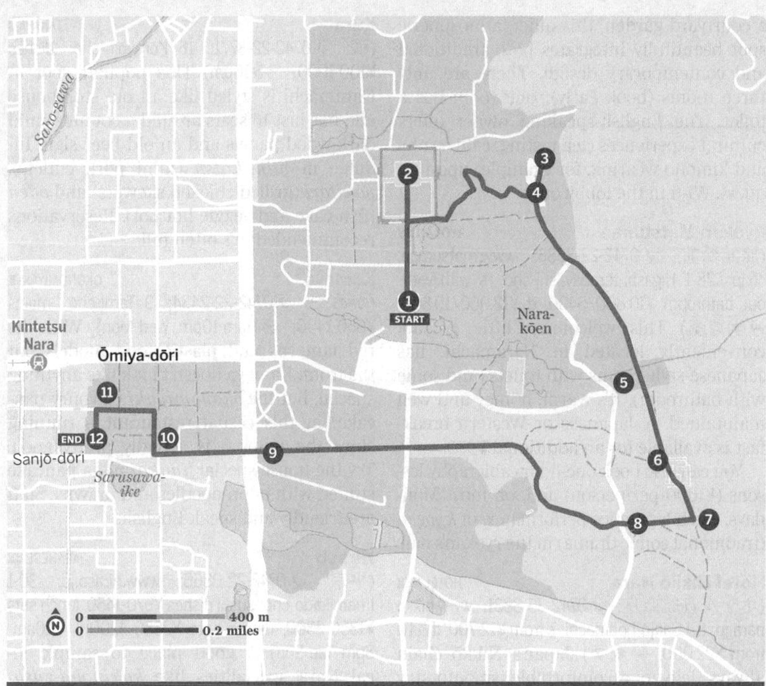

Town Walk Nara-kōen

START TŌDAI-JI'S NANDAI-MON
END KŌFUKU-JI
LENGTH 5KM; HALF A DAY

Get as early a start as possible to beat the crowds, and head straight for Tōdai-ji's ❶ **Nandai-mon** (p401), a 15-minute walk from Kintetsu Nara Station. Pause to admire the impressive Niō (guardian) statues – possibly the most impressive anywhere – then go on to Nara's star attraction, ❷ **Tōdai-ji** (p400), where the enormous Daibutsu (Great Buddha) has stood for more than 1250 years.

Exit to the east of the Daibutsu-den and follow the road until you see a path (and a sign) pointing up a hill to ❸ **Nigatsu-dō** (二月堂; ⏲24hr). Climb the steps to enjoy the view from the verandah, taking in the graceful curves of the Daibutsu-den and the Nara plain. Then continue to check out the adjacent ❹ **Hokke-dō** (法華堂; adult/child ¥600/300; ⏲8am-5pm Nov-Mar & Oct, 7.30am-5.30pm Apr-Sep), the oldest building on the grounds of Tōdai-ji.

From here, look for a path that runs south; there should be a shrine, Tamukeyama-hachimangū, on your left. Follow this past Wakakusa-yama until you see a set of descending stairs; take these. You will come to a clearing in the woods, where you can stop for tea and sweets at ❺ **Mizuya-chaya** (p409).

Continue south, following signs to ❻ **Kasuga Taisha** (p401), Nara's principal shrine, a bright-vermilion beacon of colour bedecked with lanterns. Leave the shrine via the main entrance and bear left up the path to ❼ **Wakamiya-jinja** (p401), passing several small shrines on the way.

Retrace your steps towards Kasuga Taisha and take a left down the steps that lead back towards the centre of town. You'll pass first through ❽ **Ni-no-Torii**, a large Shintō shrine gate, and then continue down the broad, wooded arcade to ❾ **Ichi-no-Torii**, another shrine gate. Cross the street and you'll soon see ❿ **Kōfuku-ji's five-storey pagoda** (p401). Finish with a wander around the temple's grounds, which have several historic structures, such as the ⓫ **Hokuen-dō** (北円堂) and the ⓬ **Three-Storey Pagoda** (p401) – the temple's two oldest structures. From here you can walk back to Kintetsu Nara Station in less than 10 minutes.

a courtyard garden, this quiet, atmospheric spot beautifully integrates both traditional and contemporary design. There are only three rooms (book early); one room has a toilet. The English-speaking owner offers cultural experiences (tea tasting, calligraphy and kimono wearing, for example) upon request. Wi-fi in the lobby only.

Ryokan Matsumae RYOKAN ¥¥
(旅館松前; ☎0742-22-3686; www.matsumae.co.jp; 28-1 Higashi-terabayashi-chō; s with/without bathroom ¥10,800/5400, d ¥12,960/10,800;) This welcoming little ryokan, conveniently located in Naramachi, has Japanese-style rooms with toilets (and some with bathroom). It's warm, homey and well maintained. A Japanese or Western breakfast is available for an additional ¥970.

You can also book one-hour calligraphy lessons (¥1000 per person) and, on most Mondays, catch a practice performance of *kyōgen* (traditional comic drama) in the ryokan's hall.

Hotel Nikkō Nara HOTEL ¥¥¥
(ホテル日航奈良; ☎0742-35-8831; www.nikkonara.jp; 8-1 Sanjō-honmachi; s from ¥12,700, d & tw from ¥22,000;) Japan's Nikkō chain always delivers a comfortable, smooth stay and this location is no different. It's conveniently connected to JR Nara Station by a pedestrian bridge and also has a big common bath (in addition to the en suites) and a small fitness centre.

Nara Hotel HOTEL ¥¥¥
(奈良ホテル; ☎0742-26-3300; www.narahotel.co.jp; 1096 Takabatake-chō; s/tw from ¥15,310/22,520; P) Founded in 1909, this grande dame has hosted everyone from Edward VIII and Albert Einstein to Audrey Hepburn and the Dalai Lama. It retains a Meiji-era style in its traditional exterior, high ceilings, gorgeous woodwork, refined Japanese and Western restaurants, a tea lounge and beautifully landscaped grounds. Rooms are spacious and comfortable, with big beds, though some have cramped bathrooms.

For historic atmosphere and all nonsmoking rooms, choose the Honkan (main building) over the Shinkan (new building). Rates can vary wildly by season.

Eating

The greatest selection of restaurants is around Nara Kintetsu Station.

Kura IZAKAYA ¥
(蔵; ☎0742-22-8771; 16 Kōmyōin-chō; dishes ¥100-1000; ⊙5-10pm) This popular spot in Naramachi is styled like an old storehouse and has just 16 seats around a counter amid dark-wood panels and an old beer sign. Indulge in *mini-katsu* (mini pork cutlets), *yakitori* (grilled chicken skewers) and *oden* (fish cake and veggie hot pot). Reservations recommended; it's often full.

Kameya OKONOMIYAKI ¥
(かめや; ☎0742-22-2434; 9 Tarui-chō; mains ¥650-1400; ⊙11am-10pm Wed-Mon) With its red lanterns and plastic food models out the front, Kameya doesn't look like anything special, but the *okonomiyaki* (savoury pancake) at this casual restaurant – running since the 1960s – is actually pretty good. Try the house special *'inakappe'*, a pancake stuffed with udon noodles and prawns. Staff are friendly and speak English.

Hirasō JAPANESE ¥¥
(平宗; ☎0742-22-0866; www.hiraso.jp; 30-1 Imamikado-chō; sushi dishes ¥970-1450, lunch sets ¥1350-2300, dinner sets ¥2650-4200; ⊙10am-8pm Tue-Sun) A good place to sample local Nara specialities like *kakinoha-zushi* (pressed sushi wrapped in persimmon leaf – don't eat the leaf!) and *chagayu* (rice porridge made with roasted green tea). Look for the lattice-wood front.

It also has a kiosk in front of JR Nara Station selling *kakinoha-zushi bentō* (boxed meals; from ¥1000); as this form of sushi was originally a preservation technique it lasts for up to three days – perfect to take along on trips into rural Nara Prefecture.

Washokuya Happoh JAPANESE ¥¥
(和食屋八寶; ☎0742-26-4834; www.happoh.com; 22 Higashimuki-nakamachi; lunch set meals ¥950-1380, dinner set meals from ¥3000, à la carte dishes ¥380-2800; ⊙11.30am-10.30pm Mon-Sat, to 10pm Sun) A reliable choice offering a variety of dishes, from sashimi to tempura to noodles to *wagyū* (Japanese beef). Try its speciality: dishes marinated in sake lees. The place is big enough for you to be able to get a table (and lunch is, generously, served until 4pm); ingredients are listed on the menu to help diners with allergies or dietary restrictions.

Look for the wooden beams on your right, inside the Higashimuki Arcade, a short walk south of Kintetsu Nara Station.

Yumekaze Plaza FOOD HALL ¥¥

(夢風ひろば; ☎0742-25-0870; www.yume-kaze.com; 16 Kasugano-chō; ⊙hours vary; 📶) Adjacent to Nara-kōen and across from the Nara National Museum (p401), this convenient collection of a dozen restaurants and cafes offers a variety of dishes (mostly Japanese, but also sandwiches and sweets). Most places serve lunch and dinner.

Drinking & Nightlife

Mizuya-chaya TEAHOUSE

(水谷茶屋; ☎0742-22-0627; www.mizuyachaya.com; 30 Kasugano-chō; ⊙10am-4pm Thu-Tue) In a small, wooded, brookside clearing between Nigatsu-dō (p407) and Kasuga Taisha (p401), this quaint thatched-roof teahouse is one of Nara's most atmospheric spots. Stop by for a cup of *matcha* (¥700 including a sweet), *onigiri* (rice balls; ¥350 to ¥400) or a bowl of udon (¥580 to ¥850).

In warm seasons, sit outside among the greenery and enjoy *kakigōri* (shaved ice with toppings of condensed milk, sweet red beans or fruit-flavoured syrups).

Nara Izumi Yūsai BAR

(なら泉勇斎; ☎0742-26-6078; www.naraizumi.jp; 22 Nishi-Terabayashi-chō; ⊙11am-8pm Wed-Tue) Drop in on this small standing bar in Naramachi for tastings (¥200 to ¥600) of sakes produced in Nara Prefecture (120 varieties from 29 makers, also available for purchase). There's a useful English explanation sheet.

Shopping

Yu Nakagawa Honten FASHION & ACCESSORIES

(遊中川本店; ☎0742-22-1322; 31-1 Ganrin-chō; ⊙10am-6pm) Nara's famed 300-year-old linen producer now creates beautiful bags, pouches and scarves out of natural materials, subtly adorned with traditional motifs. It's easy to miss, with no obvious sign; look for the building fronted by wooden lattice.

It also runs **Nipponichi** (日本市; ☎0742-23-5650; 1-1 Tsunofuri-shinyamachi; ⊙10am-7pm), which sells less expensive tea towels and totes with cute Nara-themed designs (lots of deer).

Ikeda Gankōdō ARTS & CRAFTS

(池田含香堂; 16 Tsunofuri-chō; ⊙9am-7pm, closed Mon Sep-Mar) This sixth-generation fan maker sells Nara-style *uchiwa*, paddle-style fans whose *washi* (Japanese handmade paper) covering has been intricately carved with local and nature scenes. Their silk backing makes them surprisingly durable. Prices run from ¥2000 to ¥25,000.

ℹ Information

Nara has several TICs with English-speaking staff, maps and more

Kintetsu Nara Station Information Office (☎0742-24-4858; ⊙9am-9pm; 📶) In front of Kintetsu Nara Station (near the top of the stairs above exit 3 from the station).

Nara City Tourist Information Center (奈良市観光センター; ☎0742-22-3900; ⊙9am-9pm) Located in the old Nara Station building just outside the east exit of JR Nara Station. This is the city's main tourist-information centre. You can store luggage here (¥600 per piece per day; counter open 9am to 7pm).

Nara Visitor Center & Inn (奈良県猿沢イン; Nara-ken Sarusawa Inn; ☎0742-81-7461; www.sarusawa.nara.jp; 3 Ikeno-chō; ⊙8am-9pm) On the southern side of Sarusawa-ike, with lots of useful info and free luggage storage. It also offers cultural experiences, including free origami lessons and, on Wednesday, a 45-minute tea ceremony (¥2000 per person).

ℹ Getting There & Away

BUS

Highway and limousine bus tickets can be purchased at Kintetsu Nara Bus Information Centre (p400) or **JR Nara Bus Information Centre** (⊙8am-8pm Mon-Fri, to 6.30pm Sat & Sun). These buses depart from **stop 4**, in front of JR Nara Station's east exit, and from **stop 20**, across the street from Kintetsu Nara Station.

To/From Tokyo

An overnight bus (from ¥6000, seven to eight hours) runs between Shinjuku Bus Terminal (p159) in Tokyo and both JR Nara and Kintetsu Nara Stations. See Nara Kōtsū (www.narakotsu.co.jp) for details.

To/From Kansai International Airport

Nara Kōtsū (www.narakotsu.co.jp) operates a limousine bus service between Nara and Kansai International Airport (¥2050, one to 1½ hours, hourly). Tickets can be purchased at the airport upon arrival.

TRAIN

To/From Kyoto

The Kintetsu Nara line is the fastest and most-convenient connection between Kyoto (Kintetsu Kyoto Station, in Kyoto Station) and central Nara (Kintetsu Nara Station). Comfortable, all-reserved *tokkyū* (limited-express) trains (¥1130, 35 minutes) run directly; *kyūkō* (express) trains (¥620, 50 minutes) usually require a change at Yamato-Saidaiji. For JR Pass holders, *kaisoku* (rapid) trains on the JR Nara line connect JR Kyoto Station with JR Nara Station (¥710, 45 minutes, several departures per hour).

To/From Osaka

The Kintetsu Nara line connects Osaka (Namba Station) with Nara (Kintetsu Nara Station; ¥560, 45 minutes). All-reserved *tokkyū* trains take five minutes less but cost almost double.

For JR Pass holders, the JR Yamatoji line links JR Nara Station with Osaka via *kaisoku* trains (Namba Station ¥560, 45 minutes; Tennō-ji Station ¥470, 30 minutes).

Getting Around

To skip the 15-minute walk between JR Nara Station and the temple and shrine districts (about five minutes from Kintetsu Nara Station), take the bus (¥210 per ride). Two circular bus routes cover the Nara-kōen area: bus 1 (anticlockwise) and bus 2 (clockwise). For more than two trips, a one-day Nara Park Nishinokyō pass costs ¥500; purchase it at either bus centre. On Saturday, Sunday and holidays, a tourist-friendly Gurutto Bus covers major sights (¥100 per ride) several times per hour from about 9am to 5pm.

Bus 98, for Tōshōdai-ji, Yakushi-ji and Hōryū-ji, departs from **stop 8** at Nara Kintetsu Station and **stop 6** at JR Nara Station for Hōryū-ji-mae (65 minutes, hourly).

Around Nara

Three temples southwest of Nara (in admittedly drab suburbs) take you to the roots of Buddhism in Japan: Hōryū-ji, Yakushi-ji and Tōshōdai-ji. Hōryū-ji is the most historically significant, though they are all great repositories of early Buddhist art. And because they're out of the way they're much less crowded than the main sights in Nara city.

Any of this trio of historic temples is worth a trip. If you plan ahead, you can see all three of them economically in one day. The Nara Park Nishinokyō Hōryū-ji one-day bus pass (¥1000) covers all the necessary routes. Start early and head first for the furthest of the three, Hōryū-ji. Bus 98 departs from stop 8 at Nara Kintetsu Station and stop 6 at JR Nara Station for Hōryū-ji-mae (65 minutes, hourly).

Then work your way back towards Nara to Yakushi-ji, taking bus 97 from platform 2 at the Hōryū-ji-mae bus stop to Yakushi-ji Higashi guchi (40 minutes, hourly 9am to 4pm), on the eastern side of the temple. Exit to the north of the temple's Kondō (Main Hall; past the Kōdō) and you can walk 10 minutes north to Tōshōdai-ji. Finally, pick up bus 77 or 97 from the Tōshōdai-ji Higashi-guchi bus stop for JR and Kintetsu Nara Stations (15 to 20 minutes, every 20 minutes); the last bus leaves at 4.42pm.

Purchase bus passes at the JR Nara Bus Information Centre (p409) or the Kintetsu Nara Bus Information Centre (p400).

★Hōryū-ji BUDDHIST TEMPLE

(法隆寺; www.horyuji.or.jp; adult/child ¥1500/750; 8am-5pm Mar-Oct, to 4.30pm Nov-Apr) Hōryū-ji was founded in 607 by Prince Shōtoku, considered by many to be the patron saint of Japanese Buddhism. It's renowned not only as one of the oldest temples in Japan but also as a repository for some of the country's rarest and most-outstanding examples of early Buddhist sculpture. There's an entire gallery of Hōryū-ji treasures at the Tokyo National Museum (p98). Some of the temple's buildings are considered to be the world's oldest existing wooden structures.

The temple is divided into two parts: **Sai-in** (West Temple) and **Tō-in** (East Temple); pick up a detailed map and guidebook in English. The main approach proceeds from the south along a tree-lined avenue and through the Nandai-mon and Chū-mon gates before entering the Sai-in precinct. As you enter, you'll see the **Kondō** (Main Hall) on your right (look up to see the fantastic carvings of mythical beasts on the eaves) and a pagoda on your left; both are considered the oldest of their kind, though they have been repaired over the years.

The Kondō houses several treasures, including the gilt-bronze triad of the Buddha Sakyamuni with two attendant bodhisattvas, created in 623 by one of the leading sculptors of the day; the Buddha's serene, enigmatic smile is captivating. There are many more works of art inside the **Daihōzō-in** (Great Treasure Hall).

Continue east through the Tōdai-mon to Tō-in. Here the **Yumedono** (Hall of Dreams), built in 739 as a place to pray for the repose of Prince Shōtoku's soul, houses another famous work of art: the Guze Kannon, a 7th-century sculpture of the bodhisattva Kannon (Buddhist goddess of mercy) carved from a single piece of camphor wood and sheathed in gold leaf.

The quickest way to get to Hōryū-ji is by train: take a JR Yamatoji-line train from JR Nara Station to Hōryū-ji Station (¥220, 11 minutes), then pick up bus 72 (¥180, eight minutes, every 20 minutes 9am to 4.45pm) to Hōryū-ji Sandō, right at the temple entrance.

Bus 98 departs from stop 8 at Nara Kintetsu Station and stop 6 at JR Nara Station

OFF THE BEATEN TRACK

YAMA-NO-BE-NO-MICHI

Yama-no-be-no-michi (山辺の道) is a fascinating ramble through rural Nara Prefecture that covers a lot of ground, both literally (13km, walkable in about four hours, plus stopping time) and figuratively: you'll pass by rice paddies and orchards, shrines and temples, the 1300-year-old tombs of ancient emperors and honesty stalls selling fruit and vegetables. The walk starts at JR/Kintetsu Tenri station and ends at JR Miwa Station.

Just outside Tenri Station, stop in at **CoFuFun** (コフフン; ☎0743-63-1001; 803 Kawaharajō-cho, Tenri-shi; ⌚9am-5pm; 📶), the visitor centre that was designed by hip Tokyo firm nendo and riffs on the appearance of the region's ancient *kofun* (burial mounds), to pick up an English map. (The path is fairly well signposted in English, but you might want to pick up a Japanese map, too.) Then head for the shopping arcade clearly labeled Tenri Main St; follow this and some more road until you hit **Isonokami-jingū** (石上神宮) and the start of the trail, which is a mixture of paved path and packed earth, with only gentle ups and downs.

Of all the shrines and temples on the route it's the final one, **Ōmiwa-jinja** (大神神社; ☎0744-42-6633; 1422 Miwa, Sakurai-shi), that is the most impressive. It's believed to be one of Japan's oldest Shintō shrines and is the official protector of sake breweries. After the shrine, sample *nyūmen* (にゅめん), a Miwa speciality of *sōmen* (very thin wheat noodles) in a hot broth, at **Sōmen-dokoro Morishō** (そうめん處 森正; ☎0744-43-7411; 535 Miwa, Sakurai-shi; noodles ¥850-1000; ⌚10am-4.30pm Mon & Wed-Fri, 9.30am-5pm Sat & Sun, closed irregularly), on a side street just off the main shrine approach. From here it's a five-minute walk to JR Miwa Station.

The JR Man-yō Mahoroba line connects Nara city to both Tenri (¥210, 15 minutes) and Miwa (¥320, 27 minutes) Stations; trains run once or twice an hour.

for Hōryū-ji-mae (¥760, 65 minutes, hourly 9am to 4pm). Returning to Nara, take bus 97 from platform 2 at the Hōryū-ji-mae bus stop. To save money, purchase a Nara Park Nishinokyō Hōryū-ji one-day bus pass (¥1000), which also includes bus travel to Yakushi-ji and Tōshōdai-ji and around Nara.

Yakushi-ji BUDDHIST TEMPLE

(薬師寺; ☎0742-33-6001; www.nara-yakushiji.com; 457 Nishinokyō; adult/child ¥1100/300; ⌚8.30am-5pm) Yakushi-ji was established by Emperor Temmu in 680 as a prayer for his ailing wife (who actually outlived him to accede to the throne). With the exception of the East Pagoda, which dates to 730, the present buildings either date from the 13th century or are very recent reconstructions. Inside, however, are some masterpieces of Buddhist art.

The temple's **Kondō** (Main Hall), rebuilt in 1976, houses several images, including the famous Yakushi Triad (the Yakushi Nyorai – healing Buddha – flanked by the bodhisattvas of the sun and moon), dating from the 8th century. The gilt-bronze statues were originally gold, but a fire in the 16th century turned the images a mellow black. In the **Tōin-dō** (East Hall), the famous 7th-century Shō-Kannon image shows the obvious influence of Indian sculptural styles. Exit to the north of the temple to walk to Tōshōdai-ji.

By train, take the Kintetsu Nara line to Yamato-Saidaiji Station and transfer to the Kintetsu Kashihara line to Nishinokyō Station (¥260, 20 minutes). The temple is about 200m southwest.

Bus 78 departs from stop 8 at Nara Kintetsu Station and stop 6 at JR Nara Station for Yakushi-ji (¥350, 20 to 25 minutes, 7am to 4.40pm). Bus 98 also departs from the same bus stops for Yakushi-ji Chūshajō (¥350, 20 to 25 minutes, hourly), the temple's parking lot. Returning to Nara, take bus 77 or 97 from the Yakushi-ji Higashi-guchi bus stop, on the eastern side of the temple. Bus travel to/from Yakushi-ji is covered by the Nara Park Nishinokyō one-day bus pass (¥500).

Tōshōdai-ji BUDDHIST TEMPLE

(唐招提寺; www.toshodaiji.jp; 13-46 Gojo-chō; adult/child ¥600/200; ⌚8.30am-5pm, last entry 4.30pm) Tōshōdai-ji was established in 759 by influential Chinese priest Ganjin (Jian Zhen), recruited by Emperor Shōmu to reform Buddhism in Japan. The main building, the **Kondō** (Golden Hall), dates from the 8th century and houses an impressive 5m-tall Thousand-armed (possibly literally) Kannon (Buddhist goddess of mercy),

Around Nara

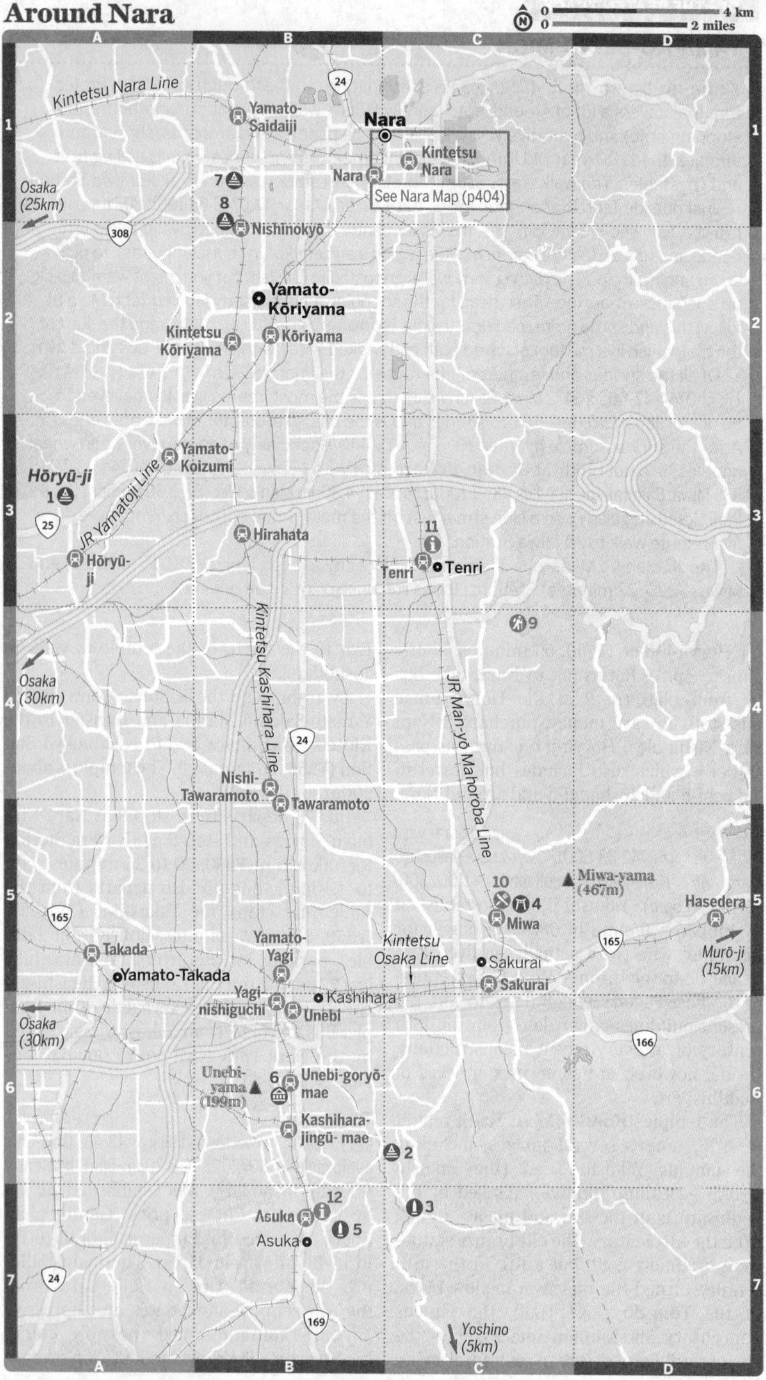

0 — 4 km
0 — 2 miles

A B C D
1 2 3 4 5 6 7

Kintetsu Nara Line
Yamato-Saidaiji
Nara
Kintetsu Nara
Nara
See Nara Map (p404)
Osaka (25km)
7
8
Nishinokyō
308
24
Yamato-Kōriyama
Kintetsu Kōriyama
Kōriyama
Yamato-Koizumi
Hōryū-ji
1
25
JR Yamatoji Line
Hōryū-ji
Hirahata
11
Tenri
Tenri
9
Osaka (30km)
Kintetsu Kashihara Line
JR Man-yō Mahoroba Line
24
Nishi-Tawaramoto
Tawaramoto
10
4
Miwa-yama (467m)
Miwa
Hasedera
165
Murō-ji (15km)
165
Takada
Yamato-Takada
Yamato-Yagi
Kintetsu Osaka Line
Sakurai
Sakurai
Yagi-nishiguchi
Kashihara
Unebi
Osaka (30km)
166
Unebi-yama (199m)
6
Unebi-goryō-mae
Kashihara-jingū-mae
2
12
Asuka
3
5
Asuka
24
169
Yoshino (5km)

Around Nara

Top Sights

1 Hōryū-ji A3

Sights

2 Asuka-dera C6
3 Ishibutai-kofun C7
4 Ōmiwa-jinja C5
5 Takamatsuzuka-kofun B7
6 The Museum, Archaeological Institute of Kashihara B6
7 Tōshōdai-ji B1
8 Yakushi-ji B1

Activities, Courses & Tours

9 Yama-no-be-no-michi C4

Eating

10 Sōmen-dokoro Morishō C5
Yumeichi-chaya .... (see 3)

Information

Asuka Rent-a-Cycle .... (see 12)
11 CoFuFun C3
12 Tourist Information Center B7

among other National Treasures. Behind it, the Kōdō (Lecture Hall), also built in the 8th century, was actually originally part of Nara's Imperial Palace – today it's all that remains of it.

By train, take the Kintetsu Nara line to Yamato-Saidaiji Station and transfer to the Kintetsu Kashihara line for Nishinokyō Station (¥260, 20 minutes). The temple is about 500m north.

Bus 78 departs from stop 8 at Nara Kintetsu Station and stop 6 at JR Nara Station for Tōshōdai-ji (¥260, 15 to 20 minutes, twice hourly 7am to 4.40pm). Bus 98 also departs from the same bus stops for Tōshōdai-ji Higashi-guchi (¥260, 15 to 20 minutes, hourly), at the temple's east entrance. Returning to Nara, take bus 77 or 97 from the Tōshōdai-ji Higashi-guchi bus stop. Bus travel to/from Tōshōdai-ji is covered by the Nara Park Nishinokyō one-day bus pass (¥500).

Asuka

0744 / POP 5339

Asuka (飛鳥; *Ahs*-ka), about an hour south of Nara, has some of Japan's best-preserved *kofun*, which were commonly built around the Nara basin as tombs for emperors and powerful nobles between the 3rd and 7th centuries. Asuka is also the site of what is considered to be Japan's first Buddhist temple, Asuka-dera. Now a village spread out over picturesque hills and rice paddies – it's strange to imagine that it was once a centre for culture and courtly intrigue – modern-day Asuka is particularly fun to tour by bicycle. For more context on the sights, visit The Museum, Archaeological Institute of Kashihara (p414) in nearby Kashihara.

Sights

Takamatsuzuka-kofun — MONUMENT

(高松塚古墳; 439 Hirata, Asuka-mura; museum ¥250; 9am-5pm; P) This *kofun* was discovered by accident in the 1960s, painstakingly excavated in the 1970s and then sealed for preservation. What you'll see is a grassy mound; however, in the hall next door you can see reproductions of the frescos found on the walls of the tomb. The images, especially of the guardian spirits of the four cardinal directions, are very similar to images found inside Korean and Chinese burial mounds. There are no clues as to who was buried here.

From the Takamatsuzuka bus stop it's a short walk up to the burial mound. You can also walk here from Asuka Station in about 15 minutes.

Ishibutai-kofun — MONUMENT

(石舞台古墳; 254 Shimasho, Asuka-mura; adult/child ¥250/100; 8.30am-5pm; P) Though other *kofun* remain covered in earth, Japan's largest stone burial chamber is laid bare and you can walk inside. The tomb was looted centuries ago, and it's unclear whose remains are interred here, though Soga no Umako, a powerful member of the influential Soga clan, is a likely candidate (which would date the tomb to the early 7th century).

Asuka-dera — BUDDHIST TEMPLE

(飛鳥寺; 0744-54-2126; 682 Asuka; adult/child ¥350/200; 9am-5.30pm Apr-Sep, to 5pm Oct-Mar; P) Considered the first Buddhist temple in Japan (founded 596), Asuka-dera houses Japan's oldest existing Buddhist statue, the Asuka Daibutsu (Great Buddha), a 15-tonne, seated bronze image of Shakyamuni (the historic Buddha). Though the temple has been rebuilt multiple times (most recently in the 19th century, based on archeological evidence), it's said that the statue has never been moved from this spot – meaning that many of the greats of Japanese history have likely stood before it.

The Museum, Archaeological Institute of Kashihara MUSEUM
(橿原考古学研究所附属博物館; ☎0744-24-1185; www.kashikoken.jp/museum/top.html; 50-2 Unebi-chō, Kashihara; Japanese/foreign visitors ¥400/free; ⏱9am-5pm, closed Mon & irregularly; P) FREE This museum and research centre is an important visit for students of ancient Japanese history. Artefacts come from various archaeological sites in the area, including several *kofun*, and date as far back as the Jōmon period (10,000 years ago). Foreign visitors can enter for free (bring your passport); you'll get a glossy pamphlet in English that explains the exhibits. It takes about an hour to see everything.

The museum is a five-minute walk west of Unebi Goryō-mae Station, one stop before Kashihara-jingū-mae on the Kintetsu Kashihara line.

Sleeping & Eating

Accommodation is extremely limited out this way; it's best to visit Asuka as a day trip from Nara, Osaka or Kyoto.

Scattered around Asuka's sights are plenty of cafes and restaurants open for lunch (from around 11am to 3pm). For food outside these hours, head to the nearest transit hub, Yamato-Yagi (a stop on the Kintetsu Kashihara line).

Yumeichi-chaya SHOKUDO ¥
(夢市茶屋; ☎0744-54-9450; 154-3 Shimasho, Asuka-mura; meals ¥860-1080; ⏱11am-4pm Mon-Fri, to 5pm Sat & Sun; P) A great spot for lunch in Asuka, above a local produce market and taking advantage of all those fresh ingredients in home-cooking-style dishes. Try the *kodai-mai gozen* lunch plate, which includes an heirloom variety of black rice and *godofu* (tofu mixed with kudzu, arrowroot starch).

It's just downhill from Ishibutai-kofun (p413).

Information

MONEY

The nearest ATMs are in Yamato-Yagi.

TOURIST INFORMATION

Tourist Information Center (☎0774-54-3240; https://asukamura.jp; Asuka Station; ⏱8.30am-5pm; 📶) Outside Asuka Station (to the left as you exit); pick up an English map of the area, purchase one-day bus passes or store your luggage (¥300 per item).

Getting There & Away

Asuka Station is on the Kintetsu Yoshino line. *Tokkyū* trains run to Asuka from Osaka-Abenobashi (¥1220, 40 minutes) and from Kintetsu Kyoto Station (¥1860, 65 minutes). Ordinary trains (from Osaka/Kyoto ¥710/960) take 10 to 15 minutes longer and require a transfer at Kashihara-jingū-mae (and maybe at Yamato Saidaiji as well).

From Nara, take the Kintetsu Nara line two stops to Yamato-Saidaiji and transfer to the Kintetsu Kashihara line to Kashihara-jingū-mae and then again to the Kintetsu Yoshino line (¥580, about an hour).

Getting Around

A sightseeing bus runs between Asuka Station and the east exit of Kashirahara-jingū-mae Station, stopping at Takamatsuzuka-kofun (¥190, two minutes), Ishibutai-kofun (¥270, 15 minutes) and Asuka-dera (Asuka Daibutsu-mae; ¥300, 25 minutes). If you plan to visit more than one sight, the one-day pass (adult/child ¥650/330) is a good deal.

The best (and most popular) way to tour Asuka (weather permitting) is by bicycle. The sights are each a few kilometres apart, linked largely by rural roads, which makes this both totally doable and very pleasant.

Asuka Rent-a-Cycle (明日香レンタサイクル; ☎0744-54-3919; http://k-asuka.com; 13-1 Koshi, Asuka-mura; weekday/weekend ¥900/1000; ⏱9am-5pm) has single-speed bicycles in adult and child sizes (helmet rental is included for children). There are several stations around Asuka, including one at Kashihara-jingū-mae Station, where you can return your bike if you don't want to do a full loop (extra charge ¥200). While Asuka is only lightly hilly, you can also rent an electric-assist bicycle here (¥1500 per day).

Yoshino

☎0746 / POP 7166

At the northern end of the Kii Mountain Range, Yoshino (吉野) is famous throughout Japan as the country's number-one spot for cherry-blossom viewing due to its *hito-me-sen-bon* (1000 trees at a glance) viewpoint. The mountain hamlet has also played an outsize role in Japanese history and culture: it was here that emperor Go-Daigo held his rival southern court during the schism of the 14th century; even earlier, Yoshino's temples incubated Japan's unique Shugendō religion, a belief system rooted in both Esoteric Buddhism and pre-Buddhist nature worship, influenced by Taoism and famous for its ascetic practices. Throughout April,

WORTH A TRIP

MURŌ-JI

Secluded in thick forest, **Murō-ji** (室生寺; ☎0745-93-2003; www.murouji.or.jp; 78 Murō, Uda-shi; adult/child ¥600/400; ⏲8.30am-5pm Apr-Nov, 9am-4pm Dec-Mar) is a Shingon temple founded in the 9th century. It's nicknamed 'Women's Kōya-san' because, unlike the more famous centre of Shingon Buddhism, it welcomed female students. The temple's Kondō (Golden Hall), restored in the 17th century (and far more humble than the name suggests), holds beautiful Heian-era Buddhist sculptures with some of their original colouring intact. Some 700 stairs lead further up to the Oku-no-in, the innermost sanctum.

To get here from Nara by public transport, take the JR Man-yō Mahoroba line to Sakurai (¥320, 30 minutes), change the Kintetsu Osaka line to Murōguchi-ōno Station (¥350, 20 minutes), then switch to a bus to Murō-ji-mae (¥430, 15 minutes, hourly).

when the cherry trees bloom (in strata along the slope of the mountain), Yoshino gets very, very crowded; otherwise it's pretty sleepy, drawing only visitors with a keen interest in the local history and culture.

Sights

★Kimpusen-ji — TEMPLE

(金峯山寺; 2498 Yoshino-yama; ¥500; ⏲8.30am-4.30pm, enter by 4pm) Kimpusen-ji, founded in the 7th century, is believed to be the incubator of Shugendō, a unique Buddhist sect that incorporates Shintō traditions and Taoism and is associated with the storied *yamabushi* (ascetic mountain priests). The main hall, called the Zaō-dō, was last rebuilt in 1592 and is Japan's second-largest wooden building, a National Treasure with a cedar-bark roof.

The principal deity is a bright-blue, three-bodied image of Zaō Gongen, protector of Yoshino-yama; it's only visible to visitors for a short period each year, in which case temple admission is ¥1000 (check at tourist offices for dates). The temple's Niō-mon, a gate with two fearsome Niō statues and the oldest structure at Kimpusen-ji, is undergoing restoration until 2026.

Early risers can observe morning *otsutome* (worship service), incorporating *taikō* drumming and the sounding of the *horagai* (giant conch).

Yoshimizu-jinja — SHINTŌ SHRINE

(吉水神社; 579 Yoshino-yama; ¥400; ⏲9am-4.30pm) It may not look like much, but this shrine, founded roughly 1300 years ago, has a serious historic pedigree: it has harboured general Minamoto Yoshitsune (taking refuge from his murderous brother Yoritomo, the first Kamakura shogun) and emperor Go-Daigo, and warlord Toyotomi Hideyoshi hosted a 5000-person *hanami* (blossom-viewing) party here in 1594. On display are a mishmash of artefacts from the shrine's long history.

From Kimpusen-ji, continue 300m to a side road to the left (the first turn past the post office), leading to the shrine. There are good views back to Kimpusen-ji and the *hito-me-sen-bon* (1000 trees at a glance) viewpoint.

Sleeping & Eating

There's a number of small inns around town. During cherry-blossom season, book well ahead.

Many restaurants are perched on a ridge for inspirational views. Eateries cluster near the steps to Kimpusen-ji and along the town's one main road, towards Yoshimizu-jinja. If you're staying overnight, book meals at your accommodation: restaurants generally close around 4pm.

Ryokan Katō — RYOKAN ¥¥

(旅館歌藤; ☎0746-32-3177; www.kato-yoshino.jp; 3056 Yoshino-yama; s/d ¥9000/15,100, incl 2 meals ¥18,000/32,000; P ⊖ ❄ 📶) In business for two centuries but marvellously up to date, Katō has English-speaking staff who cater well to international travellers. Especially appealing is the modern, log-house-style back building, with a glassed-in rotunda for cherry-tree viewing and communing around a wood stove. All 14 Japanese-style rooms have shared bathroom (there's a stone *rotemburo* – outdoor bath); half have private toilet.

Staff can pick you up from Yoshino Station if you ring them, except during cherry-blossom season, when the road's closed to traffic. Reservations for blossom time open at 9am on 10 January and go fast.

Chikurin-in Gumpō-en — RYOKAN ¥¥

(竹林院群芳園; ☎0746-32-8081; www.chikurin.co.jp; 2142 Yoshino-yama; r per person incl 2 meals from ¥12,960, single surcharge ¥5250; P ⊖ ❄ 📶) Chikurin-in is one of Yoshino's old Shugendō temples that now also operates as a ryokan. The simplest *shukubō* (temple-lodging) rooms have shared facilities, but there are also rather luxurious rooms with private *rotemburo*. Some staff speak English. Pick-up is available from Yoshino Station (except during cherry-blossom season, when the road's closed to traffic); request when you book.

Kakinohasushi Tatsumi SUSHI ¥¥
(柿の葉すしたつみ; ☎0746-32-1056; www.tatsumi-yoshino.jp; 559-3 Yoshinoyama; sushi set from ¥1150; ⏰9am-5pm, longer hours cherry-blossom season) This tiny, family-run takeaway shop serves *kakinoha-zushi*. Choose your fish – salmon *(sake)*, mackerel *(saba)* or both *(combi)* – and quantity (the smallest set includes seven pieces). Look for samples and a wooden sushi press in the window. It sometimes closes early if supplies run out.

Nakai Shunpūdō SWEETS ¥
(中井春風堂; ☎0746-32-3043; 545 Yoshino-yama; sweet set with tea ¥800; ⏰10am-5pm Thu-Tue Apr-Nov, Sat & Sun only Dec-Mar; ✎) You can watch the chef make *kuzu* (arrowroot gelatin) sweets in the shop window here – it's kind of like magic as the *kuzu* transforms from starch to edibles (a simple English translation explains the process). Then try it as *kuzumanju* (filled with bean paste) or *kuzukiri* (sliced into noodles and dipped in black honey) in the bright, airy contemporary cafe.

ℹ Getting There & Away

Yoshino is in the mountains, a 20-minute walk uphill from the nearest train station (Yoshino). There's also a shuttle bus that runs from the station to the Yoshino-yama stop at the top of the mountain and returns from the Senbon-guchi stop at the other end of the village (¥360, twice hourly 9am to 4pm).

Yoshino Station is on the Kintetsu Yoshino line. *Tokkyū* trains run here from Osaka-Abenobashi (¥1480, 1½ hours) and Kintetsu Kyoto Station (¥2550, 1¾ hours). Ordinary trains (from Osaka/Kyoto ¥970/1230) take 15 to 20 minutes longer and require a transfer at Kashihara-jingū-mae (and maybe at Yamato Saidaiji as well).

From Nara, take the Kintetsu Nara line two stops to Yamato-Saidaiji, then transfer to the Kintetsu Kashihara line to Kashihara-jingū-mae and then to the Kintetsu Yoshino line (¥580, about an hour).

The closest JR station is Yoshino-guchi on the JR Wakayama line; travel from Nara (¥760, 1¾ hours) and Osaka (¥9700, 1¾ hours) requires a transfer at Ōji. At Yoshino-guchi, transfer to the Kintetsu Yoshino line for Yoshino (*kyūkō/tokkyū* ¥380/890, 35/26 minutes).

KII PENINSULA

The remote and mountainous Kii Peninsula (紀伊半島, Kii-hantō) is a far cry from central Kansai's bustling urban sprawl. There are two top attractions here that make the area a worthy stop in your itinerary: the mountaintop temple complex of Kōya-san, one of Japan's most important Buddhist centres, and, further south, the ancient pilgrimage trails, sacred shrines and rustic onsen of the Kumano Kodō. With more time, you can explore the rocky southern coast, which makes up the Nanki Kumano Geopark and has some interesting geological formations.

Sleeping

Most of the accommodation here is in traditional-style inns – futons on the floor and shared bathrooms down the hall – and, in Kōya-san, *shukubō*. Some inns and temples offer Western-style beds and en-suite facilities, but you should expect to pay a fair bit extra. While they're remote, both Kōya-san and the Kumano Kodō are popular destinations for local and overseas travellers, and the best places can fill up early.

Eating

A speciality in Kōya-san is *shōjin-ryōri* (Buddhist vegetarian cuisine; no meat, fish, onions or garlic). The towns on the coast have restaurants around their train stations; in the interior there will be *shokudō* and teahouses, but many are only open for lunch – it's a good idea to book meals at your inn.

ℹ Information

MONEY

Many of the accommodation options, most of which are traditional inns, and restaurants here won't take credit cards. Post offices and convenience stores (with international ATMs) can be found in the larger towns on the coast and also in Kōya-san.

TOURIST INFORMATION

Kii Peninsula attractions fall within Wakayama Prefecture, which has a good tourism website: https://en.visitwakayama.jp.

ℹ Getting There & Away

AIR

Kansai International Airport

Kansai International Airport (p389), at the top of the peninsula, is convenient for Kii destinations. For Kōya-san, take the Rapi:t Airport

Kii Peninsula

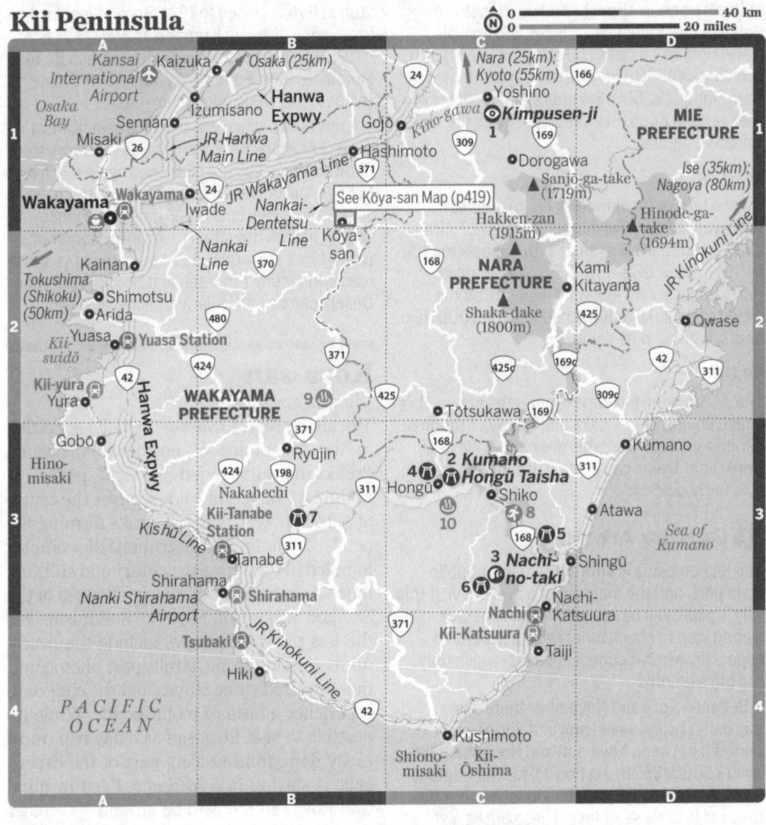

Kii Peninsula

Top Sights
1 Kimpusen-ji C1
2 Kumano Hongū Taisha C3
3 Nachi-no-taki C3

Sights
Hirō-jinja .... (see 3)
4 Hosshinmon-ōji C3
5 Kumano Hayatama Taisha C3
6 Kumano Nachi Taisha C3
Seiganto-ji .... (see 6)
7 Takijiri-ōji B3

Activities, Courses & Tours
8 Kumano River Boat Tour C3
9 Ryūjin Onsen Moto-yu B2
10 Sennin Buro C3

Sleeping
Fujiya .... (see 10)
Kamigoten .... (see 9)

Eating
Yuzuyume Cafe .... (see 9)

Express (¥1430, 40 minutes) or the Nankai Airport Express (¥920, 45 minutes) towards Namba (in Osaka) and get off at Tengachaya, where you can transfer to the Nankai Kōya line (*Tokkyū* Kōya Liner ¥1650, 80 minutes; *kyūkō* ¥870, 100 minutes) for Gokurakubashi and the cable car to the mountain.

For Tanabe, the nearest access point for the Kumano Kodō, take the JR Kansai Airport Rapid Service two stops to Hineno and transfer to the JR Kinokuni line for Kii-Tanabe; if you take one of the fast, hourly Kuroshio liner *tokkyū* trains, the journey takes 1¾ hours plus transit time (total cost ¥3890).

Nanki Shirahama Airport

On the southwestern coast of the peninsula, just south of Tanabe, **Nanki Shirahama Airport** (南紀白浜空港; ☎0739-43-0081; www.aikis.or.jp/~airport) has three flights daily to/from Haneda Airport in Tokyo. Buses are timed to meet most departures and arrivals; travel time to Tanabe is 50 minutes (¥770); a taxi costs ¥4290. One bus per day continues to/from Hongū (¥2500; 2½ hours), in the heart of the Kumano Kodō. See the airport website for schedule details.

BOAT

Nankai ferries (nankai-ferry.co.jp) connect **Wakayama Ferry Terminal** (☎073-422-2156; 2835-1 Minato, Wakayama) with **Tokushima** (南海フェリー; ☎088-636-0750; www.nankai-ferry.co.jp; 5-7-39 Minami-Okinosu), on the island of Shikoku (adult/child ¥2000/1000, two hours, eight to nine daily).

TRAIN

The JR Kinokuni line runs around the peninsula's coast, linking Shin-Osaka and Nagoya Stations. Limited-express Kuroshio liner and Wideview Nanki liner trains can get you around the peninsula fairly quickly.

Getting Around

The Kii Peninsula is entirely doable by public transport, and the majority of travellers visit this way. Unless you have a very loose schedule, it's a good idea to check timetables beforehand – especially when it comes to buses, which may run infrequently.

Between April and November there's one bus daily (two at weekends and during peak periods) between Kōya-san and Hongū (adult/child ¥5000/2500, 4½ hours), for the Kumano Kodō; there may be transfers involved, but the process is fairly seamless. These buses also stop at Ryūjin Onsen (p422). Book at least a day in advance, through **Kumano Travel** (熊野トラベル; ☎0739-22-2180; www.tb-kumano.jp; 14-6 Minato; 9am-6pm; wi-fi) or Japan Bus Online (https://japanbusonline.com/en).

A rental car, which you can pick up at Kansai Airport or in any Kansai city, gives you more freedom; however, you are cautioned against driving to Kōya-san between December and March, when snow is possible, unless you have experience driving narrow mountain roads in icy conditions (snow tyres are required). At this time of year the road connecting Kōya-san and Hongū, via Ryūjin Onsen, can be particularly treacherous.

ISE-KUMANO-WAKAYAMA AREA PASS

The Ise-Kumano-Wakayama Area Pass (http://touristpass.jp/en/ise_kumano; adult/child ¥12,000/6000) covers five days of travel on JR lines (including up to four rides on limited-express trains) around the Kii Peninsula and Ise-shima, including transit from Kansai International Airport and the gateway cities of Nagoya, Osaka and Nara, plus select Kumano Kotsu bus routes around the peninsula. It's only available to overseas visitors; purchase at the airport or at the main JR train station in any of the gateway cities, or in advance from a travel agent in your home country (for a discount of ¥1000). Unfortunately, this pass does not cover travel to Kōya-san, which is served by Nankai line trains.

Kōya-san

☎0736 / POP 3087

Thickly forested Kōya-san (高野山) is nestled in the mountains of northern Wakayama Prefecture, surrounded by eight peaks (in Buddhist iconography it resembles the centre of a lotus flower, with the peaks forming the petals). It's home to a large monastic complex founded in the early 9th century and still very much a centre of worship for followers of the Shingon school of Esoteric Buddhism. For the less pious, the draws include the peaceful mountain setting, strolls past photogenic, moss-covered stone stupas and the chance to experience a taste of monastic life. While it's possible to visit Kōya-san as a day trip (most easily done from Osaka), part of the experience is staying in a *shukubō*. Keep in mind that Kōya-san tends to be around 7°C colder than Kansai's cities. Much of the town shuts down between December and February, though most temples stay open.

History

The story of Kōya-san is the story of Kōbō Daishi, one of the most prominent figures in Japanese cultural history. In 804 a monk from Shikoku named Kukai – the man who would later be called Kōbō Daishi – joined an imperial mission to Chang-an, the capital of Tang-dynasty China. There he studied Esoteric Buddhism and upon his return to Japan in 806 began to promote its teachings. He was a success in the capital, establishing himself also as a scholar and a humanitarian – he's traditionally credited with creating the Japanese *kana* (phonetic writing system) – but longing for the mountains.

In 816, by imperial decree, he was granted permission to establish a monastery in Kōya-san and with it the Shingon sect of Buddhism (*shingon* means 'true word' and

Kōya-san

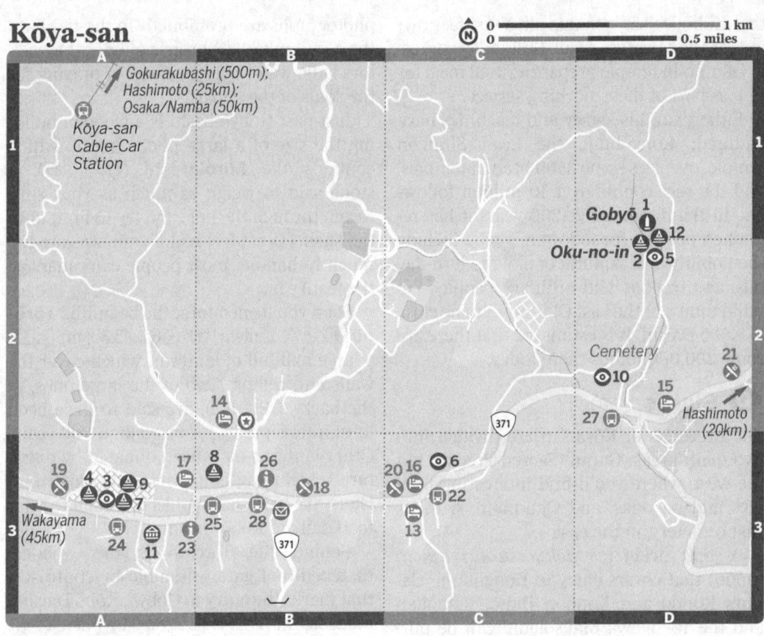

Kōya-san

Top Sights

1 Gobyō ... D1
2 Oku-no-in ... D2

Sights

3 Chūmon ... A3
4 Garan ... A3
5 Gobyō-bashi ... D2
6 Ichi-no-hashi ... C3
7 Kondō ... A3
8 Kongōbu-ji ... B3
9 Konpon Daitō ... A3
Miroku-ishi ... (see 2)
10 Naka-no-hashi ... D2
11 Reihōkan ... A3
12 Tōrō-dō ... D1

Sleeping

13 Ekō-in ... C3
14 Fukuchi-in ... B2
15 Koyasan Guest House Kokuu ... D2
16 Shōjōshin-in ... C3
17 Sōji-in ... A3

Eating

18 Bononsha ... B3
19 Kadohama ... A3
20 Kōmi Coffee ... C3
21 Tonkatsu-tei ... D2

Transport

22 Ichi-no-hashi-guchi ... C3
23 iKoya ... A3
24 Kondō-mae ... A3
25 Kongōbu-ji-mae ... B3
26 Kōya-san Shukubō Association ... B3
27 Oku-no-in-mae ... D2
28 Senjūin-bashi ... B3

is the Japanese translation of mantra). His choice of location enters the realm of legend: at the harbour in China, before his return passage to Japan, he tossed his *vajra* (a Buddhist ritual object) into the air and vowed to search for it upon his return. Wandering the forests, he met a hunter (said to be the mountain god Kariba Myōjin), whose dogs led him to the *vajra*, which had landed at the spot where the Garan temple now stands.

In 835, after fasting, he entered what is now the Gobyō gate and began a week-long concentrated meditation, after which, he told his followers, he would pass away and the crypt should be sealed. It was, and it has only been opened once since, when – again according to legend – sometime in the 10th century some curious monks are said to have discovered a still-living Kōbō Daishi, his hair and beard grown long. Among Shingon believers today, there are those who believe that Kōbō Daishi remains alive inside, praying for the salvation of all. Still today, monks at Oku-no-in temple prepare a ritual meal for him as part of their morning service.

Either way, his legacy and teachings have endured: Kongōbu-ji, the head Shingon temple, oversees some 3500 branch temples, and the sect counts over 10 million followers. In the intervening 1200 years it has remained popular for followers – who include the nobility and samurai of old, modern-day business tycoons and ordinary people – to build tombs in the vast Oku-no-in to be close to Kōbō Daishi. It is estimated that there are some 200,000 tombs there today.

Sights

The precincts of Kōya-san are divided into two main areas: Garan (Sacred Precinct) in the west, where you'll find interesting temples and pagodas, and Oku-no-in, with its vast cemetery, in the east.

A joint ticket (*shodōkyōtsu-naihaiken;* ¥1500) that covers entry to Kongōbu-ji, Garan's Kondō and Konpon Daitō, Reihōkan and the Tokugawa Mausoleum can be purchased at the Kōya-san Shukubō Association office and the venues themselves.

★Oku-no-in BUDDHIST TEMPLE

(奥の院; 24hr) FREE Oku-no-in, whose name means 'inner sanctuary', is perhaps the most intensely spiritual place in Japan. At its farthest reaches is the **Gobyō** (御廟), the crypt that Shingon Buddhism founder Kōbō Daishi entered to began his eternal meditation. Spread out before it are some 200,000 tombs, creating Japan's largest cemetery, built during various historical eras by people, prominent and otherwise, who wanted their remains (or at least a lock of hair) interred close to the legendary monk.

Enter the grounds at **Ichi-no-hashi** (一の橋), the bridge that marks the entrance to the cemetery, from where it's a 2km walk to the Gobyō. The grounds are thickly forested, sheltering countless five-tiered stupas, many of them worn with age and partly reclaimed by moss. It's a moody place: streaks of sunlight through the trees create enchanting contrast, though so does early-morning mist and, if you can brave the winter cold, blankets of snow.

Gobyō-bashi (御廟橋) is the final bridge before the Gobyō. It crosses the Tama-gawa, which runs down from Yōryū-san, the mountain behind the crypt. At this point it's customary to bow, and from here on photographs are prohibited. To the right are the Mizumuke Jizō, bronze effigies that visitors ladle water over as a way of praying for the souls of the departed.

Just past Gobyō-bashi is a wooden building the size of a large phone booth, which contains the **Miroku-ishi** (みろく石), a stone said to weigh as much as your sins. Reach through the hole and try to lift it onto the shelf. (Don't feel bad if your sins are too much to handle: most people can't manage the feat.)

Soon you'll encounter the beguiling **Tōrō-dō** (燈籠堂, Lantern Hall; 6am-5.30pm) FREE, a large hall full of lanterns, which cover the walls and ceiling. Two of the large ones, in the back of the hall, are said to have been lit uninterruptedly for more than 900 years. Other lanterns have been donated by dignitaries, including emperors and prime ministers. It's here that monks continue to offer food daily to Kōbō Daishi.

Behind the Tōrō-dō is the wooden, thatched-roof gate – humble by contrast – that marks the entry to Gobyō, Kōbō Daishi's mausoleum. This is as far as anyone can go. Pilgrims in a constant stream pause here to light incense and candles and chant sutras.

Oku-no-in is easily reached on foot from the town centre in 10 or 15 minutes, or you can take a bus east to the Ichi-no-hashi-guchi bus stop (p424). On return, you can take a shorter walk down, along the Naka-no-hashi route, which passes more modern tombs and leads you to the Oku-no-in-mae bus stop (p424), where you can catch a bus back to town (or walk it in about 30 minutes).

Garan BUDDHIST TEMPLE

(伽藍; per bldg ¥200; 8.30am-5pm) The name of this temple, which is sometimes called Danjo Garan or Dai Garan, derives from the Sanskrit *saṅghārāma,* which means monastery. With eight principal buildings (temples, pagodas), the complex was the original centre for teaching established by Kōbō Daishi in the 9th century. It's still a teaching centre today, and you might see groups of saffron-robed novices making the rounds. The buildings have burned several times in the intermediate centuries and what you see today are almost entirely modern-day reconstructions.

Chūmon (中門), the Garan's main gate, was renovated for Kōya-san's 1200th anniversary in 2015, after an 1843 fire. Two of the original statues of guardian kings enshrined in the gate were rescued from that fire, and two additional ones were carved to make the full set of four.

The most interesting structure in the grounds is the **Konpon Daitō** (根本大塔, Great Pagoda; ¥200), a 50m-tall, bright-vermilion pagoda seated at what is considered to be the centre of the lotus-flower mandala formed by Kōya-san's eight mountains. The main object of worship is Dainichi-nyōrai (Cosmic Buddha), surrounded by four attendant Buddhas and, painted on pillars, 16 bodhisattvas, which together compose a three-dimensional mandala of the Shingon Buddhist cosmos.

The **Kondō** (金堂, Golden Hall; ¥200; ⏲8.30am-5pm) is the Garan's main hall and enshrines Yakushi Nyorai, the Buddha of medicine and healing; the actual statue is hidden, but there are mandalas and paintings of bodhisattvas and Buddhist teachings on the walls.

Kongōbu-ji BUDDHIST TEMPLE

(金剛峯寺; ☎0736-56-2011; www.koyasan.or.jp; 132 Kōya-san; ⏲8.30am-5pm) This is the headquarters of the Shingon sect and the residence of Kōya-san's abbot. The main gate is the temple's oldest structure (1593); the present main hall dates from the 19th century. It's free to enter the grounds, but costs ¥500 to enter the main hall, which has several *fusuma* (opaque paper sliding doors) adorned with landscape paintings by famed 17th-century artists, including those of the Kanō school. Many of the temple's statues and ritual implements are displayed at the Reihōkan.

From inside the main hall you can see the *banryutei* (1984), Japan's largest rock garden. It contains 140 large granite stones brought from Shikoku (Kōbō Daishi's birthplace) and white gravel from Kyoto, which are collectively meant to represent two protector dragons rising from a sea of clouds.

The more recently built annexes (Betsuden and Shin-Betsuden) contain contemporary paintings of seasons and images inspired by Kōbō Daishi's sojourn in China.

Reihōkan MUSEUM

(霊宝館, Treasure Museum; ☎0736-56-2029; 306 Kōya-san; adult/child/student ¥600/250/350; ⏲8.30am-5.30pm May-Oct, to 5pm Nov-Apr) Several important artworks from Kōya-san's temples are collected here, most notably some Heian-era wooden sculptures of the Buddha and Fudō Myō-ō originally from Kongōbu-ji. Other works include scroll paintings depicting the life of Kōbō Daishi (p418).

The museum is in the centre of town, near the Garan. The original wing, built in 1921, is Japan's oldest wooden museum, and without heating gets quite chilly in winter.

Tours

★ **Awesome Tours** TOURS

(☎080-3108-4790; https://awesome-tours.jp/en; 1½hr night tour per person with/without return bus ¥2100/1800, 1½hr day tour per person ¥2500, children free) Let English-speaking monks guide you through Oku-no-in, telling you some of the stories and legends about the different graves. Eerie evening tours meet nightly at 7pm at Eko-in (p422); bookings are certainly

KŌYA-SAN'S SHOKUBŌ

The simplest *shukubō* (temple lodging) rooms (starting at ¥9720 per person including two meals, usually with a surcharge for solo guests) are very basic, with shared facilities; many do not have air conditioning (though they offer space heaters in winter and fans in summer). Most have a variety of room styles, and for a higher rate you can get a room with a private bath and more amenities. Some have gorgeous rooms with garden views.

Shukubō have a fairly set routine. Most expect you to check in by 5pm, and some have a curfew. Monks usually perform a morning prayer service, which guests can observe. The service is followed by breakfast; the timing of this depends on the time of year, but expect it to be early. Communal bathing facilities are often only available between check-in time and 10pm.

You can reserve online (at least a week in advance) through the **Kōya-san Shukubō Association** (高野山宿坊協会; ☎0736-56-2616; http://shukubo.net; 600 Kōya-san; ⏲8.30am-4.30pm Dec-Feb, to 5pm Mar-Jun & Sep-Nov, to 5.45pm Jul & Aug; Wi-Fi), though many *shukubō* are now using popular online-booking sites. Peak travel times include April and October, during which you should book well ahead.

OFF THE BEATEN TRACK

RYŪJIN

Deep in the mountains of Kii, Ryūjin (龍神) is a village of peaks and gorges along the Hidaka-gawa with onsen waters that are rich in sodium bicarbonate said to rank among Japan's most beautifying. It's roughly halfway between Kōya-san and the Kumano Kodō. If you'd like to spend the night in Ryūjin, stay at **Kamigoten** (上御殿; 0739-79-0005; www.kamigoten.jp; 42 Ryūjin; r per person incl 2 meals from ¥19,050; P ❄ wi-fi). Now in its 29th generation, the inn was built in 1657 for the local lord and member of the Tokugawa family. It's been updated over the years and now feels like a humbly elegant country home, with simple riverside baths, fresh tatami rooms, wooden corridors polished smooth and sprigs of fresh flowers everywhere. Meals, served in the rooms, are beautifully prepared feasts.

A once- or twice-daily bus running from April through November between Kōya-san (¥2900, 2½ hours) and Hongū (¥2500, two hours) stops at Ryūjin. It's easier to reach by car, but don't try it in winter. If you're just driving through, you can stop off for a soak at **Ryūjin Onsen Moto-yu** (龍神温泉元湯; 0739-79-0726; 37 Ryūjin; ¥700; 7am-9pm), the village's public bathhouse, fed by natural hot springs. Eat at **Yuzuyume Cafe** (ゆず夢カフェ; 0739-79-8025; 165-1 Ryūjin; mains ¥850-1200; 9am-6pm Sun, Mon & Wed, to 9pm Thu-Sat, closed irregularly; P), an unexpectedly eclectic indoor-outdoor place serving pizza, curry and coffee.

not required but recommended. Day tours (booking required), which include a ritual prayer at Gobyō (p420), are enriching and not at all stuffy. Tours are cancelled if it's raining.

Festivals & Events

Rōsoku Matsuri CULTURAL
(ろうそく祭り; 13 Aug) This captivating festival is held in remembrance of departed souls. Thousands of people come to light some 100,000 candles along the approaches to Oku-no-in (p420).

Sleeping

More than 50 temples in Kōya-san offer shukubō (p421), which serve *shōjin-ryōri* (Buddhist vegetarian cuisine).

Koyasan Guest House Kokuu GUESTHOUSE ¥
(高野山ゲストハウスKokuu; 0736-26-7216; http://koyasanguesthouse.com; 49-43 Kōya-san; capsules from ¥3500, s/d/tr from ¥6000/9000/12,000; closed Feb; P ⊖ wi-fi) A boon for budget travellers, this light and clean guesthouse has capsule-style bunks and a few private rooms, all with shared facilities. It's also a few minutes' walk from Oku-no-in-mae (p424) bus stop. Staff are super helpful and speak English.

You can order a breakfast of fresh bread, yoghurt, and coffee or chai (¥600) and an Indian-curry dinner (¥900).

★ **Shōjōshin-in** TEMPLE LODGE ¥¥
(清浄心院; 0736-56-2006; www.shojoshinin.jp; 566 Kōya-san; r per person incl meals from ¥9720; P ⊖ wi-fi) Among Kōya-san's most atmospheric temples, with a thatched roof and an old kitchen with exposed wooden beams, Shōjōshin-in is a wonderful choice for your *shukubō* experience. Rooms are simple, the cheapest divided only by *fusama*, but comfortable, and care goes into the meals. It's also the closest *shukubō* to Oku-no-in (p420).

★ **Ekō-in** TEMPLE LODGE ¥¥
(恵光院; 0736-56-2514; www.ekoin.jp; 497 Kōya-san; r per person incl meals & with/without bathroom from ¥18,000/12,000; P ⊖ @ wi-fi) This pretty hillside temple, set around a garden, offers both simple but nicely done-up rooms and pricier en-suite rooms with newly updated facilities. It's run by a bunch of friendly young monks keen to engage travellers in their culture. There are free evening meditation sessions in English and morning fire rituals. A single-traveller surcharge is ¥2000. The nearest bus stop is Ichi-no-hashi-guchi (p424).

Fukuchi-in TEMPLE LODGE ¥¥
(福智院; 0736-56-2021; www.fukuchiin.com; 657 Kōya-san; r per person with meals from ¥12,960, single travellers ¥16,200; P ⊖ ❄) Fukuchi-in has two standout features: a communal onsen bath, including a *rotemburo* (outdoor bath), and a garden designed by famous modernist landscape artist Shigemori Mirei. Upgrade for a room with garden view (and

for a little more for a room with a toilet). It's one of Kōya-san's larger *shokubō* (temple lodgings) and popular with bus tours. Some staff speak English.

Sōji-in TEMPLE LODGE ¥¥¥

(総持院; ☎0736-56-2111; www.soujiin.or.jp; 143 Kōya-san; r per person incl meals from ¥18,360, single travellers ¥29,380; P ❄ 📶) One of Kōya-san's smaller temples, with only 14 rooms, Sōji-in is also one of the most modernised: all rooms have air-conditioning, some have baths (and all have toilets) and there's a lift. All of this is set around a lovely garden, with English-speaking staff and a location across the street from the Garan (p420).

Eating

Kōya-san's local cuisine is, naturally, *shōjin-ryōri*, which means no meat, fish, onions or garlic. If you spend the night at a *shukubō*, this is what will be served for breakfast and dinner.

Many temples offer lunch, so if you're visiting as a day trip contact the Kōya-san Shukubō Association (p421) to make a reservation. Lunch prices at temples are fixed at ¥2700, ¥3800 and ¥5400, depending on the number of courses. Special dishes to look out for include *kōya-dōfu* (freeze-dried tofu – a natural preservation method in these cold mountain climes) – and *goma-dōfu* (sesame tofu).

There are also plenty of *shokudō* (all-round, inexpensive restaurants) in town; note that most of these close by late afternoon.

Tonkatsu-tei SHOKUDO ¥

(とんかつ亭; ☎0736-56-1039; 49-48 Kōya-san; set meals ¥900-1300; ⏲11am-2pm & 5-10pm Wed-Mon) Of course not everyone in Kōya-san follows a monk's diet: locals love this *tonkatsu* (deep-fried pork cutlet) shop, a five-minute walk beyond the Oku-no-in bus stop. Look for the yellow roof.

★ **Bononsha** CAFE ¥¥

(梵恩舎; ☎0736-56-5535; 730 Kōya-san; lunch set menu ¥1200; ⏲6.30am-5pm, closed irregularly & late Dec-Mar; 🌿) This chill spot – more Goa than rural Japan – with great wooden beams serves vegetarian dishes like tofu cheesecake that seem indulgent compared to temple food. Come after 11am for the daily lunch plate, only served until they run out. Good coffee and chai, too.

Kadohama TOFU ¥¥

(角濱; ☎0736-26-8700; 230 Kōya-san; lunch sets ¥1860, sweets ¥480; ⏲9am-5pm, closed irregularly) Kadohama specialises in *goma-dōfu* (sesame tofu) prepared several ways. The lunch sets come beautifully presented in bamboo baskets with eight small dishes around a larger one – evoking the eight-lotus-petal symbolism of Kōya-san. Vegetarians should note that, appearances aside, this is not *shōjin-ryōri*: some dishes are made with *dashi* (fish stock).

Sweet options include *matcha*-flavoured *goma-dōfu* served with *anko* (sweet red-bean paste). Look for the dark-wood building.

Kōmi Coffee CAFE ¥¥

(光海コーヒー; 571 Kōya-san; meals ¥1320-1650, sandwiches ¥600; 🌿) A cosy and convenient pit stop for curries, sandwiches and apple pie near the entrance to Oku-no-in (p420). Its namesake coffee comes from a small-batch roaster in Hokkaidō.

Information

MONEY

Kōya Post Office (770 Kōya-san; ⏲post 9am-5pm Mon-Fri, ATM 8.45am-6pm Mon-Fri, 9am-5pm Sat, to 3pm Sun) Has an international ATM. Note that few places here take credit cards.

TOURIST INFORMATION

iKoya (☎0736-56-2780; 357 Kōya-san; ⏲9am-5pm; 📶) English-speaking staff and lots of local info; rent electric-assist bicycles here for ¥1000 per day (return by 4.30pm).

Kōya-san Shukubō Association (p421) handles bookings for Kōya-san's *shukubō* and also temple meals; use its online system to book (you can just show up, but it's risky during peak periods like April and October). This office also has English info, including English-language audio guides (¥500) for major sights, and bicycle rental (¥1200 per day). It's in front of the Senjūin-bashi bus stop.

Getting There & Away

Access to Kōya-san is via the Nankai Railway from Osaka's Nankai-Namba Station; trains terminate at Gokurakubashi, at the base of the mountain. A cable car goes the rest of the way up the mountain. From the **cable-car station**, take a bus into town; walking is prohibited on the connecting road.

There are four daily (more frequent on weekends and holidays) reserved-seat limited-express Nankai Kōya line trains bound for

Gokurakubashi (¥1650, 1½ hours); otherwise, the journey takes 10 to 15 minutes longer on a regular express (¥870).

Nankai's Kōya-san World Heritage Ticket (¥3400; www.nankaikoya.jp/en/stations/ticket.html) covers return train fare (including one-way limited-express fare from Osaka), buses on Kōya-san for two days and discounted admission to some sites. Purchase at any major Nankai train station.

If you want to use a JR Pass, get to Hashimoto, on the JR Wakayama line, where you can connect to the Nankai line to Gokurakubashi (¥440, 45 minutes). This is most easily accomplished coming from Nara, via the JR Yamatōji line, with a transfer at Ōji for the JR Wakayama line (two hours plus transit time).

Getting Around

Buses run on three routes from Kōya-san Cable Car Station via the town centre (**Senjūin-bashi** bus stop; ¥290, 10 minutes), continuing either to Kongōbu-ji (**Kongōbu-ji-mae** bus stop; ¥290, 11 minutes) and Garan (**Kondō-mae** bus stop; ¥340, 15 minutes) or to Ichi-no-hashi (**Ichi-no-hashi-guchi** bus stop; ¥330, 14 minutes) and Oku-no-in (**Oku-no-in-mae** bus stop; ¥410, 16 minutes).

The bus office at the cable-car stations sells one-day bus passes (¥830), but once you're in town the sights are walkable: Kōya-san is only 3km west to east (and 2km north to south). Buses run a few times an hour; make a note of the schedule in advance if you're relying on them.

Both iKoya (p423) and the Kōya-san Shukubō Association (p421) rent bicycles, as do some lodgings.

Kumano Kodō

The Kumano Kodō (熊野古道) is an ancient network of roads – dating back more than 1000 years – running through the mountainous interior of the Kii Peninsula. These are pilgrim trails, connecting historic shrines and temples with deep spiritual significance. The most accessible and most popular route is the Nakahechi, also known as the Imperial Route (several emperors of old travelled along it), which crosses the width of the peninsula from Tanabe, a town on the western coast, to the towns of Shingū and Nachi-Katsuura on the eastern coast. There are hikes for all levels, quiet mountain hamlets and some excellent onsen in the villages around Hongū: Yunomine, Watarase and Kawa-yu.

Most travellers start in Tanabe and use a combination of buses – to skip the parts of the trails that have become major roads – and legwork to get around; there's also the option of finishing the pilgrimage by way of a traditional boat ride.

History

From the earliest times the Japanese believed the wilds of the Kii Peninsula to be inhabited by *kami*, the deities of its native Shintō belief system rooted in nature worship. When Buddhism arrived in Japan in the 6th century, it didn't wipe out the *kami;* instead, it enveloped them, transforming them into *gongen* – manifestations of the Buddha or a bodhisattva. A syncretic religion evolved and that is what was long practised in the mountains of Kii. Each of the Kumano Sanzan (three great shrines of Kumano) is rich in natural, Shintō and Buddhist significance.

It's believed that mountain ascetics called *yamabushi* established the first trails here as they engaged in tough acts of endurance, hiking and climbing for days on end. In the Heian period (794–1185) it became popular for retired emperors and members of noble families to make pilgrimages here (likely led by *yamabushi* guides). From Kyoto it would take 30 to 40 days. In the Edo period (1603–1868), when travel was heavily restricted by the shogunate, certain pilgrimages became popular among commoners because they were the only allowed form of travel.

Sights

The main sights are the Kumano Sanzan (three great shrines of Kumano) that anchor the Nakahechi route: Kumano Hongū Taisha (p427), Kumano Hayatama Taisha (p430) and Kumano Nachi Taisha (p431). Along the trails are numerous *oji,* subsidiary shrines that serve as mile markers and rest stops.

Sleeping

Lodgings are almost exclusively small, family-run *minshuku* (guesthouses). Booking through Kumano Travel (p418) is highly recommended: this is the only way to book most properties online and will allow you to pay up front by credit card; otherwise you'll need cash to pay at the inns. A room with no meals costs ¥4000 to ¥5000 per person; a room with two meals costs from ¥8000 to ¥10,000 per person.

HIKING THE KUMANO KODŌ

It's possible to hike the Nakahechi route of the Kumano Kodō year-round, though bear in mind that you'll have fewer daylight hours to work with in winter, so plan accordingly (it's a good idea to have a headlamp). Clearly signposted in English, the well-maintained trails are a mix of paved paths, packed earth and stone worn smooth after centuries of pilgrims treading them; the latter can get quite slippery when wet – poles can be a good hedge for balance. Otherwise, the gear you'll need depends on what level of hiking you plan to do. Bears are rare, though you do need to keep an eye out for pit vipers, *mukade* (big, poisonous centipedes) and aggressive hornets.

You can spend anywhere from a day to a week on the trails. For shorter visits, there are two good hikes around Hongū: the final stretch of the Nakahechi from Hosshin-mon-ōji (p427) to Kumano Hongū Taisha (p427), a gentle, 7.5km, mostly downhill hike that takes two to three hours and passes through a mix of farmland and forest, with stops at Fushiogami-chaya (p429) and a lookout point with views of Ōtorii (p427); buses run from town to the trailhead. There's also the **Dainichi-goe trail**, a short (2km) but steep up and down that connects the southern end of Hongū with Yunomine Onsen in an hour or two; you can follow the hike with a soak at Tsubo-yu (p427).

Longer itineraries often start at **Takijiri-ōji** (滝尻王子; 859 Kurisugawa) FREE, one of five major ōji (smaller shrines along the Kumano Kodō). Accessed by bus from Tanabe (p426), it marks the beginning of the passage into the mountains and today serves as the trailhead for the Nakahechi route of the Kumano Kodō. From Takijiri-ōji, it's a two-day trek to Hongū (p427), usually including an overnight stop in the village of **Chikatsu-yu**. There are a few villages along the way where you can pick up the Tanabe–Hongū bus, if you've hit bad weather or get in over your head.

From Hongū you can continue by bus to the embarkation port for the Kumano River Boat Tour (p428), which takes you to Kumano Hayatama Taisha (p430) in Shingū (p430) – the most fun way to end the journey (though weather can interfere). Alternatively, you can continue hiking for two more days along the **Kogumatori-goe** and the challenging **Ōgumatori-goe** to Kumano Nachi Taisha (p431), in the mountains at the edge of Nachi-Katsuura (p431).

For more detail about the trails, see www.kumano-travel.com. You can also visit the Kumano Travel office (p418) in Tanabe to ask questions and pick up detailed trail maps.

Eating

There are restaurants clustered around the train stations in Tanabe, Shingū and Nachi-Katsuura (around Kii-Katsuura Station), and Tourist Information Centers at each can offer suggestions. Hongū has some places to eat, though mostly just for lunch. If you're staying elsewhere, you'll need to book meals at your lodgings or pack your own food. Many inns can prepare *bentō* (around ¥600 to ¥1000) for lunch on the trails.

Information

MONEY

Very few accommodations along the Kumano Kodō accept credit cards. If you haven't booked online and paid in advance, be sure to get all the cash you'll need to cover food, lodging and incidentals at one of the gateway cities, which will have post offices with ATMs.

TOURIST INFORMATION

The best resources for travellers visiting the Kumano Kodō are Kumano Travel (p418) and the Tanabe Tourist Information Center (p426), both in Tanabe, and the Kumano Hongū Heritage Centre (p427) in Hongū.

Getting There & Away

Most travellers access the Kumano Kodō via Kii-Tanabe Station, on the western side of the peninsula, and end in Nachi-Katsuura (Kii-Katsuura Station) or Shingū, on the eastern side. All are connected to Osaka via the JR Kinokuni line, which runs along the rim of the peninsula.

Reserved-seat Kuroshio liner *tokkyū* trains run hourly from Shin-Osaka via Tennōji (in central Osaka) for Kii-Tanabe (¥4750, 2¼ hours). Some (six daily) travel all the way to Kii-Katsuura (¥6370, four hours) and Shingū (¥6690, 4¼ hours); there are more frequent local trains between Kii-Tanabe and Kii-Katsuura (¥970) and

Shingū (¥1400), but they take about an hour longer.

From Nagoya, JR Wideview Nanki liner *tokkyū* trains travel to Shingū (¥6870, 3½ hours, four daily) and Kii-Katsuura (¥7200, 3¾ hours, three daily). This route uses a small section of private-rail track, so JR Pass holders need to pay a surcharge of ¥820 to ride.

From Shingū you can also reach Ise with a change of trains (multiple options, from ¥4420, 2½ hours).

Getting Around

Buses depart from stop 2 in front of Kii-Tanabe Station for Shingū, stopping at Takijiri (for Takijiri-ōji; ¥960, 40 minutes) and Hongū Taisha-mae (¥2060, 2¼ hours) along the Kumano Kodō; the first bus in the morning (departing at 6.25am) and several in the afternoon also stop at Yunomine Onsen (¥1940, 1¾ hours), Watarase Onsen (¥1890, two hours) and Kawa-yu Onsen (¥1900, two hours).

Coming from Shingū, buses also depart from stop 2 (in front of Shingū Station) for Hongū Taisha-mae (¥1540, one hour 20 minutes, 14 daily). A few of these buses also stop at Kawayu Onsen (¥1540, one hour), Watarase Onsen (¥1540, one hour) and Yunomine Onsen (¥1540, one hour 10 minutes) en route.

A car can be useful for seeing the sights without being beholden to bus schedules, though travellers who want to hike as well will have to rely on some buses (or backtrack).

Tanabe

0739 / POP 74,405

Tanabe (田辺), a small city on the western coast of the Kii Peninsula, is the main gateway to the Kumano Kodō. You can bypass Tanabe if you have your trek all sorted, though many travellers stay a night here to get an early start the following morning. It's also worth visiting for the excellent resources provided by Kumano Travel (p418).

Sleeping

There are several small inns around town.

Miyoshiya Ryokan RYOKAN ¥
(美吉屋旅館; 0739-22-3448; www.miyoshiya-ryokan.com; 739-7 Minato; r per person from ¥3200; P ⊖ ❄) Miyoshiya is a simple travellers' ryokan from the 1940s, and the knowledgeable English-speaking owner makes a stay here worth it. Most of the Japanese-style rooms have shared facilities and there's a stone common bath. It's a three-minute walk from Kii-Tanabe Station (turn left at the first traffic signal, walk about 300m and it will be on your right).

There are coin laundry facilities; breakfast costs an extra ¥800.

Konyamachiya RENTAL HOUSE ¥¥
(紺屋町家; www.kumano-travel.com/en/accommodations/konyamachiya-townhouse; 74 Konyamachi; houses ¥9500-21,360; P ⊖ ❄) This beautifully renovated guesthouse, with exposed beams and traditional plaster walls, has two Japanese-style bedrooms and sleeps up to six; there's also a small kitchenette and washer and dryer. The downside: it's a bit far away, about a 15-minute walk or a five-minute taxi ride from Kii-Tanabe Station, and you must check in, at Kumano Travel (p418), between 3pm and 5pm.

The price varies according to the number of guests.

Eating

The epicentre of eating and drinking in Tanabe is Ajikōji ('Flavour Alley'), an atmospheric maze of narrow streets that connects dozens of *izakaya* a short walk from Kii-Tanabe Station. The vibe is very local but friendly; several spots have English menus.

Shinbe IZAKAYA ¥¥
(しんべ; 0739-24-8845; 12-45 Minato; dishes ¥300-2000; 5-10.30pm Mon-Sat) In the warren of tiny restaurants called Ajikoji ('Flavour Alley') near Kii-Tanabe Station and the tourist-information center, this boisterous, family-run *izakaya* is famous for its *ebi-dango* (shrimp-paste balls) and ridiculously fresh fish that the chef himself might have just pulled in from nearby waters. Sit at the counter for lots of local colour and tons of fun.

Information

Kumano Travel (p418) This community-run travel agency can help you organise your whole Kumano Kodō trek. You can book accommodation (and pay by credit card), store your luggage (¥500 per item per day) or have it shipped elsewhere on your route (price varies), pick up detailed maps, bus schedules and last-minute supplies, and have any questions addressed in fluent English. Walk straight out of Kii-Tanabe Station, cross the main intersection and it's on your right.

Tanabe Tourism Information Centre (田辺市観光センター; 0739-34-5599; www.tb-kumano.jp; 9am-6pm;) In front of Kii-Tanabe Station, with English-speaking staff and lots of local info, including a great map marked with restaurants that have English menus and bus schedules.

Getting There & Away

Reserved-seat Kuroshio liner *tokkyū* trains run hourly on the JR Kinokuni line to Kii-Tanabe from Tennōji (Osaka; ¥4320, two hours) and Shin-Osaka (¥4750, 2¼ hours). Some (six daily) continue along the peninsula from Kii-Tanabe to Kii-Katsuura (¥2630, 1¾ hours) and Shingū (¥3340, 2¼ hours); there are more frequent local trains that take about an hour longer (Kii-Katsuura/Shingū ¥970/1400).

Buses depart from stop 2 in front of Kii-Tanabe Station for Shingū, stopping at Takijiri (for Takijiri-ōji; ¥960, 40 minutes) and Hongū Taisha-mae (¥2060, 2¼ hours) along the Kumano Kodō; the first bus in the morning (departing at 6.25am) and several in the afternoon also stop at the onsen towns of Yunomine (¥1940, 1¾ hours), Watarase (¥1890, two hours) and Kawa-yu (¥1900, two hours).

Hongū

0735 / POP 2761

Hongū (本宮), in the interior of Kii, is the biggest hub along the Kumano Kodō. Still, it's more village than town, which suits its natural setting, on the sandy banks of the Kumano-gawa. One of the Kumano Sanzan (three great shrines of Kumano) is here, Kumano Hongū Taisha, which retains much of the character of an ancient shrine.

From Hongū you can easily reach the onsen villages of Yunomine (湯の峰), Watarase (わたらせ) and Kawa-yu (川湯) by bus, or even on foot. Yunomine is considered one of Japan's earliest onsen destinations, said to have been discovered some 1800 years ago; it's an attractive village, nestled around a rapidly flowing, narrow river in a wooded valley. Many travellers choose to stay a night or two in Hongū or Yunomine, to take advantage of the baths or to do one of the short day hikes around Hongū.

Sights

★Kumano Hongū Taisha SHINTŌ SHRINE

(熊野本宮大社; www.hongutaisha.jp; 6am-7pm; P) FREE Kumano Hongū Taisha is one of the Kumano Sanzan (three great shrines of Kumano) and if you're following the traditional pilgrim route, it's the first one you'll encounter. Though the shrine has been rebuilt many times over the years, it remains an excellent example of Japanese shrine architecture, made of unpainted wood using traditional carpentry techniques and with the signature *chigi* (cross-hatched beams) on the roof.

The shrine was originally located at Ōyunohara, a large sandbar in the Kumano-gawa and the original site of worship, but it was relocated here after flooding in 1889. It's now located on a tree-covered ridge, up a flight of stone steps.

In 2000 a giant *torii* (entrance gate to a Shintō shrine), **Ōtorii** (大鳥居), 33.9m tall and 42m wide, made out of steel, painted dramatic black and the largest in Japan, was erected at the entrance to Ōyunohara.

Kumano Hongū Heritage Centre MUSEUM

(世界遺産熊野本宮館; 0735-42-0751; 100-1 Hongū; 9am-5pm; P) FREE Part museum, part visitor centre, this contemporary multimedia complex has exhibits about Kumano's culture and natural environment, plus English-speaking staff and resources for travellers.

Hosshinmon-ōji SHINTŌ SHRINE

(発心門王子) The last of the five major *ōji* (smaller shrines along the Kumano Kodō) before Kumano Hongū Taisha, Hosshinmon-ōji marks the outer limits of the grand shrine's precincts and literally means 'spiritual awakening gate'. It's a small building, painted red, and has a stone *torii*.

Tōkō-ji BUDDHIST TEMPLE

(東光寺; Yunomine) This temple in the middle of Yunomine Onsen is just above Tsubo-yu Onsen, and like many hot springs adjacent to temples, is dedicated to Yakushi Nyorai, the medicine Buddha.

Activities

★Tsubo-yu ONSEN

(つぼ湯; Yunomine; ¥770; 6am-9.30pm) Right in the middle of Yunomine, this hot spring is inside a tiny wooden shack built on an island in the river. You can use it privately – it holds up to two people – on a first-come, first-served basis for up to 30 minutes. Rinse off at the tap before entering (no soap, shampoo or swimsuits allowed).

Admission includes entry to one of the baths at Yunomine Public Bathhouse (p428), which you can visit afterwards. For Tsubo-yu, first purchase a ticket at the public bathhouse; you'll be given a number card that indicates your place in the queue. When your number comes up, hang the card outside the bath; return it to the ticket counter when your time is up. Unfortunately, you can't pop into the public bathhouse while you're waiting.

DON'T MISS

KUMANO RIVER BOAT TOUR

The traditional way to end the Kumano Kodō pilgrimage is with a ride down the Kumano-gawa in a wooden vessel, re-created today in these 90-minute tours in old-fashioned sampans. Local guides narrate stories connected with the natural landmarks passed on the way; request an English-speaking guide (usually available; otherwise you'll get a pamphlet to help you follow along).

Boats require a minimum of three passengers (total) to depart. Reservations are a must, though if you're travelling solo you might be able to squeeze in; you can book directly (in Japanese) or through Kumano Travel (p418).

Boats depart from the **Kumano River Boat Centre** (熊野川川舟センター; ☎9am-5pm 0735-44-0987; http://kawabune.info; 47 Tanago, Kumano-gawa-chō; adult/child ¥3900/2000; ⊙10am & 2.30pm Mar-Nov, closed irregularly) at Dorokyō-kaidō Kumano-gawa Michi-no-eki, a road stop next to the river halfway between Hongū and Shingū, and arrive in Shingū, very near Kumano Hayatama Taisha (p430). Arrive at least 30 minutes before departure. Buses from Hongū (30 to 50 minutes) are timed perfectly; take a Shingū-bound bus at 8.30am or 1.20pm and get off at Michi-no-Eki Kumano-gawa stop, in front of the road stop.

There are a number of reasons the tour may be cancelled (such as too much or too little water in the river); have your lodging call ahead in the morning. In the event of a cancellation, and you have a booking and show up anyway, staff will be there to meet the bus to tell you to stay on and continue to Shingū.

Sennin Buro ONSEN

(仙人風呂; Kawa-yu; ⊙6.30am-10pm) FREE Kawa-yu Onsen is a natural wonder: geothermally heated water percolates up through the gravel banks of the river. In winter, from December to the end of February, bulldozers are used to turn the river into a giant *rotemburo*. It's known as the Sennin Buro (thousand-person bath), though whether it holds 1000 people is anyone's guess.

The rest of the year you can make your own bath by digging out some of the stones and letting the hole fill with hot water; then spend the day jumping back and forth between the bath and the cool river water. The best spots are in front of Fujiya ryokan. Bring a bathing suit year-round.

Yunomine Public Bathhouse ONSEN

(湯の峰温泉公衆浴場; Yunomine; regular bath ¥260, kusuri-yu ¥390; ⊙6am-10pm) There are two baths here: the *kusuri-yu* (literally 'medicine water') uses 100% pure hot-spring water; the regular one uses diluted water. Unlike most bathhouses, this one prohibits soap and shampoo (the sulphur content of the water does the trick instead); just rinse off at the taps before getting in.

Watarase Onsen Big Rotemburo ONSEN

(わたらせ温泉大露天風呂; 45-1 Watarase; ¥700; ⊙6am-9.30pm, private baths 8am-7pm) This sprawling onsen complex, in a wooded vale, contains multiple pools of clear sodium-chloride springs that get progressively cooler as you work your way out from the inside bath, which works well no matter the season. There are also private baths that can be rented (¥1500 per person per hour).

Sleeping

Hongū has the greatest selection of accommodations along the Kumano Kodō. There are a few convenient guesthouses in town and more clustered in the village of Yunomine. There are a few more isolated accommodations strung along the river in Kawa-yu. Watarase has some larger hotels that cater more to bus package travellers.

J-Hoppers Kumano Yunomine HOSTEL ¥

(ジェイホッパーズ熊野湯峰; 161 Yunomine; dm/r from ¥3500/10,000; P ⊖ ❄ 🛜) This old *minshuku* was recently converted into a hostel by the reliable J-Hoppers team. There are spacious, cabin-style bunks and private Japanese-style rooms, all with shared facilities, which include three small onsen baths that can be used privately. There's free rice porridge in the morning, cup noodles for sale, cooking facilities, coin-operated laundry machines and a social vibe.

It's located at the top of town, up the road from Tsubo-yu (p427).

★**Blue Sky Guesthouse** GUESTHOUSE ¥¥

(蒼空げすとはうす; ☎0735-42-0800; www.kumano-guesthouse.com; 1526 Hongū; r per person with breakfast from ¥6000, single travellers ¥7000; P ⊖ ❄ 🛜) An excellent modern B&B in a glen near central Hongū, with immaculate, comfortably minimalist design, lots of English-language sightseeing info and laundry machines. Its four Japanese rooms have private facilities.

The nearest bus stop is Dainichigoe Nobori-guchi; not all Hongū-bound buses stop here, so otherwise it's a 10-minute walk to the southern end of town from Hongū Taisha-mae bus stop. There's detailed information on the website.

Minshuku Yunotanisō MINSHUKU ¥¥

(民宿湯の谷荘; ☎0735-42-1620; www.kumano-travel.com; 168-1 Yunomine; r per person incl 2 meals from ¥9500; P ❄ 📶) At the upper end of the village of Yunomine, this seven-room *minshuku* is exactly what a *minshuku* should be: simple, clean and welcoming. Only one room has an en-suite toilet; the shared baths, both indoor and outdoor, are fed by hot springs. Meals include local ingredients cooked in onsen water. Reserve through Kumano Travel.

There's no surcharge for single travellers, but the inn does not usually accept single bookings on Saturday or national holidays.

Pension Ashita-no-Mori PENSION ¥¥

(ペンションあしたの森; ☎0735-42-1525; www.ashitanomori.jp; 1440-2 Kawa-yu; s/tw from ¥7000/14,000; P 🚭 📶) This Swiss chalet-style building sits across from the riverside hot springs in Kawa-yu. There's a big communal dining area on the ground floor and upstairs Western-style twin rooms; shared facilities include an onsen bath. Breakfast is ¥1000; for dinner, order from the à la carte menu (mains ¥780 to ¥4980), which includes simple curry dishes and Kumano-beef steaks.

Use the laundry machine for free (extra charge for the dryer).

Ryokan Yoshino-ya RYOKAN ¥¥

(旅館よしのや; ☎0735-42-0101; 359 Yunomine; r per person with/without 2 meals from ¥11,100/6950, single surcharge ¥1080/2600; P ❄ 📶) In Yunomine, just steps from Tsubo-yu (p427), is this modern ryokan perched above the river with lovely views. It's fairly new, the owners are very friendly, and the onsen *rotemburo* is especially nice. Rooms have no private facilities. Wi-fi in the lobby.

Fujiya RYOKAN ¥¥¥

(富士屋; ☎0735-42-0007; www.fuziya.co.jp; 1452 Kawa-yu; r per person with meals from ¥17,900, single surcharge ¥8400; P ❄ 📶) This upmarket ryokan features tasteful and spacious rooms, all with river views and private facilities in addition to onsen baths. There are some chic Western-style rooms, too (doubles with meals from ¥52,140), with en-suite *rotemburo*. Service is accommodating and there's a lift.

It's closest to the Sennin Buro.

Eating

Hongū has some restaurants, and even a small grocery store, though few options for dinner. In Yunomine, near Tsubo-yu (p427), look for the *yutzusu*, a public cooking facility where you can cook eggs and more in onsen water (Yunomine's spring comes out naturally at 93°C); some local shops sell eggs. There's a simple *shokudō* at Watarase.

Kumanoko Shokudō SHOKUDO ¥¥

(くまのこ食堂; ☎0735-30-0878; 452–1 Hongū; lunch set ¥1200-2750, dinner dishes ¥350-1200; ⏰11am-9pm Thu-Wed; P) This new restaurant – the only place in Hongū serving regularly after dark and naturally a gathering spot – dishes up small plates made with local ingredients, such as river fish, free-range eggs and venison, paired with craft beer and gin cocktails. At lunch it does set meals. Look for the white banner out the front.

Cafe Bonheur VEGAN ¥¥

(カフェボヌール; ☎0735-42-1833; www.bonheurcompany.com; 436-1 Hongū; lunch mains ¥750-1000, dinner set meal ¥1200-3000; ⏰noon-3pm, dinner by reservation from 5pm, closed Wed; P 📶 ✍) An unexpected treasure at Hongū's southern end is this vegan cafe in a former post office (with the wooden floors and clapboard walls to prove it). It does lunch plates with curry, tofu, salads, and bagel sandwiches. For dinner, ask your innkeeper to make a reservation.

Drinking & Nightlife

Fushiogami-chaya TEAHOUSE

(伏拝茶屋; 157 Fushiogami; coffee & juice ¥200; ⏰9am-5pm daily Apr, May & Nov, 9am-5pm Fri-Mon Jun-Aug, 9am-3.30pm Sat & Sun Dec-Mar) Along the Nakahechi trail halfway between Hosshinmon-ōji (p427) and Kumano Hongū Taisha (p427) – about an hour's walk from each – is this inviting pit stop run by a gang of local ladies. It serves homemade *shiso* (perilla-leaf) juice, which comes out a shocking-pink colour, and coffee brewed with water from the sulphur-rich springs of Yunomine. Seating is on benches out the front.

Cafe Alma CAFE
(カフェアルマ; www.kumano.shop; 195-3 Hongū; ⏲10am-4pm Mon-Fri, from 9am Sat & Sun; 📶) Get coffee (¥300), *castella* (Nagasaki-style sponge cake; ¥250) and a seat on the terrace, across the street from the Kumano Hongū Heritage Centre (p427).

Information

Kumano Hongū Heritage Centre (p427) Doubles as the town's tourist-information centre and post office.

Torii no mise (とりいの店; ☎0735-42-097; http://toriinomise.com; 195-3 Hongū; ⏲9am-5pm Fri-Wed) Store luggage here (¥500 per item per day) or have it shipped to Shingū (¥2300 per item) or Nachi-Katsuura (¥2600 per item). It's across the street from the heritage centre (p427).

Getting There & Away

The bus stop for Hongū is Hongū Taisha-mae, in front of the Kumano Hongū Heritage Centre and adjacent to the shrine (p427). Buses depart from stop 2 in front of Kii-Tanabe Station for Hongū Taisha-mae (¥2060, 2¼ hours, seven daily) and also from stop 2 in front of Shingū Station (¥1540, one hour 20 minutes, 14 daily). Many of these buses also stop at the nearby onsen towns of Yunomine, Watarase and Kawa-yu.

It's possible to travel directly to Hongū by local bus from JR Gojō Station (¥3200, four hours) and Kintetsu Yamato-Yagi Station (¥3950, five hours and 10 minutes), both in Nara Prefecture to the north (and accessible by train from Nara); these buses, operated by Nara Kotsu, run only a few times a day.

Getting Around

Ten buses daily running along various routes connect Hongū with the onsen villages Yunomine, Watarase and Kawa-yu (all ¥300). All buses depart from Hongū Taisha-mae, though the exact stop number and travel time (between 10 and 30 minutes) vary depending on the route. To double-check you're on the right bus, tell the driver where you'd like to get off. Buses also run to Hosshinmon-ōji (¥460, 15 minutes, seven daily April to November, five daily December to March).

It's possible to walk between the onsen villages. Yunomine is the closest to Hongū; from the southern end of town, pick up the Kumano Kodō Dainichi-goe trail, which goes to Yunomine in an hour or two (it's a steep up and down). From Yunomine to Watase it's another 40 minutes along a road. A tunnel (with a narrow sidewalk for pedestrians) connects Watarase and Kawa-yu; it's about a 10-minute walk between the two.

Shingū

☎0735 / POP 32,895

The small city of Shingū (新宮), on the eastern coast of the Kii Peninsula, is a useful transport hub for access to the Kumano Kodō and hosts one of its three main shrines, Kumano Hayatama Taisha. Many travellers arrive here via traditional sampan on the Kumano River Boat Tour (p428).

Sights

Kumano Hayatama Taisha SHINTŌ SHRINE
(熊野速玉大社; ☎0735-22-2533; 1 Shingū; ⏲6am-7pm; 🅿) FREE Located at the mouth of the Kumano-gawa, Kumano Hayatama Taisha is one of the Kumano Sanzan (three sacred shrines of Kumano), enshrining Hayatama-no-Okami, the god said to rule the workings of nature and, by extension, all life. Though ancient in origin, the current building is a 1951 reconstruction, painted a vibrant shade of vermilion. Look out for the impressively thick *shimenawa* (sacred rope) and what's said to be Japan's oldest conifer.

Gotobiki-iwa SHINTŌ SITE
(ゴトビキ岩) According to the Kumano faith, this large boulder, wedged on the side of Gongen-yama, was where the three principal gods descended to earth. It was the original site of worship, before Kumano Hayatama Taisha was built nearby. It's a somewhat tricky climb up the 538 uneven steps to the rock, where there's a small shrine, Kamikura-jinja.

It's about a 15-minute walk south to the start of the climb from Kumano Hayatama Taisha.

Sleeping & Eating

Shingū has a few business hotels and *minshuku* near the station.

There are several restaurants clustered around the station and on the way to the shrine; most are open for lunch and dinner.

Hotel New Palace BUSINESS HOTEL ¥¥
(ホテルニューパレス; ☎0735-28-1500; www.hotel-newpalace.com; 7683-18 Shingū; s/d/tw ¥7000/11,500/13,000; 🅿🚭❄@📶) For a break from *minshuku*, this contemporary business hotel with bigger-than-average rooms is the nicest place in town. There's a large common bath in addition to en-suite facilities, and coin-operated laundry machines. The breakfast buffet costs ¥800. It's a five-minute walk from Shingū Station.

Tensui JAPANESE ¥¥

(天酔; ☎0735-21-3175; 1-3-12 Isada-chō; dishes ¥630-840, set meals ¥1200-1500; ⏲11am-2pm & 5-10.30pm Tue-Sun) With its cluster of private rooms and regulars' personal whisky bottles kept on the shelves, Tensui has a local vibe, but it has happily embraced the trickle of overseas travellers passing though on the Kumano Kodō. The proprietress is quite proud of her reasonably priced *o-tsukuri teishoku* (sashimi set meal; ¥1500) and tempura *teishoku* (¥1200).

Information

Shingū Tourist Association (新宮市観光協会; ☎0735-22-2840; www.shinguu.jp; ⏲9am-5.30pm; 📶) Attached to JR Shingū Station, with English-speaking staff and useful maps of the town, including one with restaurants marked. Bike rental is available (¥500 per day; return by 5pm).

Getting There & Away

Shingū can be reached from Osaka to the west and Nagoya to the east. Reserved-seat Kuroshio liner *tokkyū* trains run six times daily on the JR Kinokuni line to Shingū from Tennōji (Osaka; ¥6690, four hours) and Shin-Osaka (¥6690, 4¼ hours).

From Nagoya there are four daily JR Wideview Nanki liner *tokkyū* trains bound for Shingū (¥6870, 3½ hours); this route uses a small section of private-rail track, so JR Pass holders need to pay a surcharge of ¥820 to ride.

Buses depart from stop 2 in front of Shingū Station for Hongū Taisha-mae (¥1540, one hour 20 minutes, 14 daily). A few of these buses also stop at the onsen villages of Kawa-yu (¥1540, one hour), Watarase (¥1540, one hour) and Yunomine (¥1540, one hour 10 minutes) en route.

Getting Around

Any of the local buses departing from platform 4 or the Kii-Katsuura Station–bound buses departing from platform 1 outside Shingū Station stop at Gongen-mae (¥200, five minutes), the stop for Kumano Hayatama Taisha; you can also walk there in 20 minutes.

Nachi-Katsuura

☎0735 / POP 15,273

The principal attractions in Nachi-Katsuura (那智勝浦) are Kumano Nachi Taisha, one of the Kumano Sanzan (the three sacred shrines of Kumano), and Japan's tallest waterfall, Nachi-no-taki. Beyond the shrine and the falls are the Nachi mountains, considered some of Japan's remotest. The town itself, centred on Kii-Katsuura train station, is on the coast and has a long fishing tradition; this is where you'll find food and lodging.

WHALE MEAT

The International Whaling Commission (IWC) bans commercial whaling, a stance the Japanese government opposes. Certain coastal communities on the Kii Peninsula, specifically Nachi-Katsuura, Kushimoto and especially Taiji, have a long tradition of whaling. In these areas, whale meat is likely to appear on some restaurant menus. It's unlikely that you'll be served it as part of the standard dinner course at a ryokan (inn) or *minshuku* (guesthouse), though either may offer it upon request. Travellers who feel strongly about not patronising businesses that serve whale meat should inquire when booking or before sitting down. Ask, *'Kujira no niku o dashimasu ka?'* ('Do you serve whale meat', クジラの肉を出しますか？).

Sights

★**Nachi-no-taki** WATERFALL

(那智の滝) At 133m, Nachi-no-taki is Japan's highest waterfall. It's the first of many still deeper in the Nachi mountains and has long been used in ascetic training.

For a close-up look at the falls, hike the 135 steps to a small shrine, **Hirō-jinja** (飛瀧神社; ¥300; ⏲7am-4.30pm), which has a viewing platform (it's also the spot from which to worship the falls). Drinking water from the dragon's mouth at the font (use your hands as a bowl) is believed to enhance longevity.

Kumano Nachi Taisha SHINTŌ SHRINE

(熊野那智大社; ⏲6am-4.30pm) FREE Built on the side of a mountain, facing the waterfall Nachi-no-taki, this shrine is one of Kii's most spiritual places, a site of ancient nature worship and one of the Kumano Sanzan (three great shrines of Kumano). The deity worshipped here is the waterfall itself, believed to be a *kami*. After visiting the shrine, walk down to the falls.

It's a 30-minute walk up 467 stairs from the nearest bus stop (Nachi-san) to the shrine. Get more atmosphere (and exercise) by starting at Daimon-zaka, the official approach (with another 267 steps), lined with cedar trees. At the entrance to Daimon-zaka are two particularly tall and sturdy trees nicknamed *meoto-sugi* ('married-couple cedars'); it's naturally a popular photo spot.

Seiganto-ji BUDDHIST TEMPLE

(青岸渡寺; ⊙5am-4.30pm) FREE This wooden temple, absent of colour and next to the Shintō shrine Kumano Nachi Taisha (p431), was last rebuilt in 1590, making it the oldest building in Kii (legend takes its founding back another 1000-plus years). The gong above the offering box in the main hall is the largest in Japan, a gift from warlord Toyotomi Hideyoshi.

The temple's three-storey pagoda, a vividly painted modern reconstruction, has views of Nachi-no-taki waterfall (p431) from the upper level (admission ¥300). The pagoda foregrounding the waterfall has become the classic image of Nachi.

Festivals & Events

Nachi-no-Ōgi Matsuri CULTURAL

(Nachi Fire Festival; ⊙14 Jul) *Mikoshi* (portable shrines) are brought down from Kumano Nachi Taisha (p431) on the mountain to the waterfall Nachi-no-taki (p431), where they're met by groups bearing dramatic, flaming torches (believed to have a purifying effect). This is one of Japan's three biggest fire festivals.

Sleeping & Eating

Accommodation here is limited to a handful of *minshuku* around Kii-Katsuura Station. Further south along the coast are some larger (though mostly dated) resort-style hotels, but you'll need your own transport to reach them.

A few small restaurants around Kii-Katsuura Station are open for lunch and dinner. Food near the sights is limited to the few *shokudō* and teahouses open during the day on the road between Kumano Nachi Taisha and Nachi-no-taki. The local speciality is *maguro* (bluefin tuna).

Minshuku Kosakaya MINSHUKU ¥¥

(民宿小坂屋; ☎0735-52-0335; http://kosakaya.jp; 1-18 Kita-hama; r per person with/without meals from ¥7950/5150; P ❄ 📶) The fourth-generation Kosaka family of innkeepers opened this modern and polished building in 2015. The current-generation Kosaka-san doesn't speak much English but makes up for it with enthusiasm. Hearty meals include local seafood. There are common onsen baths, and some rooms have a private bath (extra charge). Laundry machines are available.

From Kii-Katsuura Station, walk through the arch down the shopping street; it's about 300m ahead on the right.

Information

Nachi-Katsuura Tourist Information Centre (那智勝浦町観光協会; ☎0735-52-5311; www.nachikan.jp; 6-1-1 Tsukiji; ⊙8.30am-6pm) Inside Kii-Katsuura train station, with lots of English brochures. Get bus info at the adjacent bus stop.

Getting There & Away

Nachi-Katsuura has several train stations, the most useful of which are Kii-Katsuura (the largest, most central station) and Nachi, closest to the sights. Reserved-seat Kuroshio liner *tokkyū* trains run six times daily on the JR Kinokuni line to Kii-Katsuura from Tennōji (Osaka; ¥6370, 3¾ hours) and Shin-Osaka (¥6370, four hours). Local trains continue on the JR Kinokuni line north to Nachi (¥140, five minutes) and Shingū (¥240, 25 minutes); the limited express also continues to Shingū (¥890, 20 minutes). From Kii-Katsuura there are three daily JR Wideview Nanki liner limited-express trains bound for Nagoya (¥7200, 3¾ hours); this route uses a small section of private-rail track, so JR Pass holders need to pay a surcharge of ¥820 to ride.

Getting Around

Buses depart hourly from Kii-Katsuura (¥620, 25 minutes) and Nachi (¥480, 17 minutes) Stations for Nachi-san, the stop for Nachi Taisha shrine (for Nachi-no-taki waterfall, get off one minute earlier at Nachi-no-taki-mae; the price is the same). En route, buses also stop at Daimon-zaka (from Kii-Katsuura ¥420, 20 minutes; from Nachi ¥340, 10 minutes), the official approach to the shrine. If you're starting from Kii-Katsuura you can purchase a return bus ticket to Nachi-san for ¥1000 from the kiosk at the bus stop.

ISE-SHIMA

☎0596

Ise-Shima (伊勢志摩) is the bit of Mie Prefecture that juts out into the ocean. Far and away the top attraction here is Ise-jingū, Japan's most sacred Shintō shrine, believed to have been founded in the 3rd century. The buildings are rare examples of pre-Buddhist Japanese architecture: according to tradition, the shrines are rebuilt every 20 years, with exact imitations on adjacent sites according to ancient techniques – no nails; only wooden dowels and interlocking joints. The present

Ise-Shima

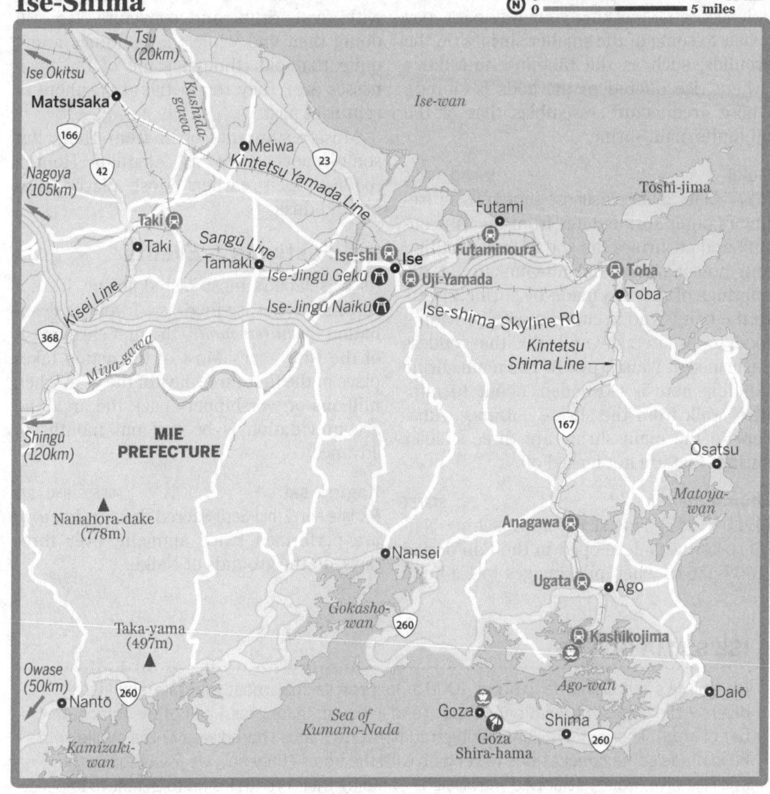

buildings were rebuilt in 2013. With a car you can travel further along the coast, for seaside views and seafood lunches with local *ama* (mostly female professional shellfish divers), who are famous in these parts.

Sights

Ise-jingū (伊勢神宮, Ise Grand Shrine) FREE is in two parts – Gekū (p434), the outer shrine, and Naikū, the more important inner shrine, several kilometres away – with both set in sprawling, deeply forested precincts. Unfortunately, the main sanctuaries at both Naikū and Gekū are almost completely hidden from view behind wooden fences – though you can just about make out their distinctive roofs, with their cross-hatched finials (called *chigi*) that are a hallmark of early Shintō architecture. Both shrine precincts have smaller subsidiary shrines that are visible to the public and are designed in the same style as the main sanctuaries.

Smoking is prohibited throughout the grounds of both shrines and photography is forbidden around their main halls. Information booths at the entrances to both shrines have English maps of the precincts.

★Naikū SHINTŌ SHRINE

(内宮, Inner Shrine) FREE Ise-jingū's inner shrine is dedicated to the sun goddess, Amaterasu-Ōmikami, considered the ancestral goddess of the imperial family and guardian deity of the Japanese nation. Naikū is particularly revered because it houses the sacred mirror of the emperor, one of three imperial regalia – the other two are the sacred beads – at the Imperial Palace (p89) in Tokyo, and the sacred sword, at Atsuta-jingū (p227) in Nagoya).

At the entrance to the precincts you'll cross the bridge **Uji-bashi** over the crystal-clear river Isuzu-gawa. The path continues along an avenue lined with towering cryptomeria trees, under several *torii*, to the

Goshōden, the main shrine building (which is fenced off). Working your way back, pay a visit to some of the smaller shrines on the grounds, such as the **Mishine-no-Mikura** (where rice offered to the gods is stored), whose architecture resembles that of the off-limits main shrine.

Gekū SHINTŌ SHRINE

(外宮, Outer Shrine; ⏲ sunrise-sunset) FREE Ise-jingū's outer shrine dates from the 5th century and enshrines the god of food, clothing and housing, Toyo'uke-no-Ōmikami. Daily offerings of rice are made by shrine priests to the deity, who is charged with providing food to Amaterasu-Ōmikami, the goddess enshrined at Naikū (p433). The main shrine building here is Goshōden, about 10 minutes' walk from the shrine entrance. Adjacent to the main shrine are three smaller shrines that are not fenced off.

Oharai-machi STREET

(おはらい町) This street approaching Naikū (p433) was developed in the Edo period (1603–1868), when pilgrimages to Ise-jingū were at an all-time high, to provide visitors with food, drink and souvenirs. It's still doing that, and while the buildings aren't quite that old (though some of the businesses are), they retain the atmosphere of centuries past.

Most restaurants open from 11am, but some spots, such as Akafuku Honten (p436), open earlier. Most places shut around dusk.

Festivals & Events

As it is Japan's most sacred shrine, it's not surprising that Ise-jingū is a favourite destination for *hatsu-mōde* (the first shrine visit of the New Year). Most of the action takes place in the first three days of the year, when millions of worshippers pack the area and accommodation is booked out months in advance.

Kagura-sai PERFORMING ARTS

(⏲ late Apr & mid-Sep) Sacred dances *(kagura)* are performed twice annually, over three days, on the grounds of Naikū.

ISE'S AMA DIVERS

Ise-Shima's Toba is home to about 1000 *ama:* professional, mostly female, shellfish divers – the largest population in Japan (and accounting for about half of the total number of *ama*). Theirs is a millennia-long tradition, one that is shared with Korea. While *ama* have made some concessions to keep up with the times (they now wear wetsuits), they still free dive, waists strapped with weights, holding their breath for up to a minute to pry *sazae* (turban shells) and other shellfish off rocks with a metal hook. In Ise's community, the oldest active divers are in their 80s.

The *ama* dive in the mornings and, because they're apparently indefatigable, cook lunches for visitors at their *ama-goya* (shellfish-divers' hut), **Osatsu Komado** (相差かまど; https://osatsu.org/en; Osatsu-chō, Toba; set meal adult/child ¥3500/1000; ⏲ 11.30am-2pm). Over a charcoal pit, the women grill seafood – including items from the morning haul – and entertain with stories about their (sometimes treacherous) lives at sea. Some Japanese ability is necessary to appreciate the latter, but they're warm and welcoming and eager to feed international visitors.

Book in advance online by 5pm the preceding day, and look out for a follow-up email (in English) from them to confirm. Unless your party is large, be sure to book Ozegosan, the smaller hut, perched on the cliff with spectacular views over the sea.

You can get to Osatsu Komado by public transport, but it's a bit of a trek. From Ise's Ujiyamada Station, take a Kintestu Toba line train to Toba (¥300, 15 minutes), arriving in time to get the 10.27am local 'Kamome' bus to Kuzaki (国崎; ¥600, 45 minutes), the nearest stop, from where it's a 10-minute walk to the *their* place. You'll have to wait until 3.26pm to get a return bus – better to have a car!

While you're in the neighbourhood, you can also visit **Shinmei-jinja** (神明神社; ☎ 0599-33-6873; 1237 Ōsatsu-chō, Toba-shi) FREE. Popularly known as Ishigami-san, this humble shrine is dedicated to the goddess Tamayori-hime and has long been a place for the area's *ama* to pray for safety. Between 9am and 5pm a kiosk sells handmade linen amulets marked with the divers' signature five-pointed star and lattice symbols for good luck. The same bus from Toba Station also stops here (¥600, 40 minutes).

Sleeping

Accommodation is clustered around Ise-shi Station, including guesthouses, ryokan and business hotels. Those on the south side of the station are more convenient for the sights. Considering its status as a major tourist attraction, Ise has fewer lodgings than you might expect; book in advance.

If you are travelling by car, you can consider staying further out on the peninsula, around Toba, where there are more resort-style hotels and ryokan, including some with ocean views.

★Ise Guest House Kazami GUESTHOUSE ¥¥

(風見荘, Kazami-sō; ☎0596-63-9170; www.ise-guesthouse.com; 1-6-36 Fukiage; dm/s/d/tr ¥3500/7000/8000/11,000;) Newly renovated, with natural timber paneling, contemporary amenities (including a kitchen and laundry facilities), a communal lounge and a very chill vibe, this guesthouse stands out among the business hotels near JR Ise-shi Station (a two-minute walk away). So long as you don't mind futons and shared baths. Check-in is 4pm–9pm; rental bikes (¥500 per day) are available.

Asakichi Ryokan RYOKAN ¥¥

(麻吉旅館; ☎0596-22-4101; iseasakichiryokan@gmail.com; 109 Nakano-chō, Ise-shi; r per person with/without 2 meals ¥12,960/7560;) This six-room ryokan, running for over 200 years, occupies a wonderfully rambling old building roughly halfway between Gekū and Naikū (p433). There's a nice common bath, and four rooms have en-suite bathrooms. Book through Japanese Guest Houses (www.japaneseguesthouses.com).

Take bus 1 or 2 from stop 7 outside Ise-shi Station (towards Urata-chō) and get off at Nakano-chō, in front of the inn (about 10 minutes); you can get buses to both shrines from the same stop. A taxi from the station should cost about ¥1000. If you're not eating at the inn, get dinner before you arrive as there are no restaurants nearby.

Hoshide-kan RYOKAN ¥¥

(星出館; ☎0596-28-2377; www.hoshidekan.jp; 2-15-2 Kawasaki; s/d/tr from ¥5350/10,500/15,575, with breakfast ¥6300/12,500/18,750;) A foreign-travellers' favourite, this 10-room ryokan in a nearly 100-year-old wooden building has heaps of traditional atmosphere and friendly, English-speaking staff. Facilities are shared, but the bath can be used privately. It's a 10-minute walk from Ise-shi Station, on the north side. Bicycle rental is ¥300 per day.

Look for Ise City Hotel and keeping going down the main road to the second light (400m); the ryokan will be on your right.

Denyō RYOKAN ¥¥

(伝洋; ☎0599-33-6166; www.denyou.gr.jp; 255-2 Ōsatsu-cho, Toba-shi; r per person incl 2 meals ¥8000-22,000;) Squat and concrete, family-run Denyō doesn't look like much but delivers on dinner, which features fresh local specialities such as *ise-ebi* (spiny lobster), oysters, sashimi and abalone (depending on season). Some of the simple tatami rooms have private toilets; all share the hot-spring-fed baths.

Very little English is spoken, but some written information in English is provided to guests. You'll want a car to get here.

Sanco Inn Iseshi Eki-mae BUSINESS HOTEL ¥¥

(三交イン伊勢市駅前; ☎0596-20-3539; www.sanco-inn.co.jp/ise; 1-1-1 Miyajiri; s/d from ¥7600/12,600) Only a few years old, this is the nicest of the business hotels clustered around Ise-shi Station, on the south side just a two-minute walk away. Book a deluxe double for a bigger (160cm wide) bed. There's a communal bath (in addition to in-room facilities) and coin-operated laundry machines.

Ise Shinsen RYOKAN ¥¥¥

(伊勢神泉; ☎0596-26-0100; www.iseshinsen.jp; 1-1 Hon-machi; r per person incl 2 meals from ¥25,000;) This contemporary ryokan has a mix of Japanese- and Western-style rooms, all with indoor showers and *rotemburo* on the balconies, discreetly hidden from outside view. It's right in front of Ise-shi Station (on the south side). Full-course dinners of traditional Japanese cuisine (included) are served in the ground-floor restaurant.

Todaya HOTEL ¥¥¥

(戸田家; ☎0599-25-2500; www.todaya.co.jp; 1-24-26 Toba, Toba-shi; d incl 2 meals from ¥25,000;) This sprawling, all-inclusive resort hotel on the waterfront in Toba has a huge variety of ocean view rooms (mostly Japanese-style, but some have beds), meal packages (buffet and in-room banquets) onsen baths and other entertainment facilities (like a karaoke room). Go for the more contemporary south wing, updated in 2018. It's a few minutes' walk from JR Toba Station.

Eating

Gekū-sandō, the approach to Gekū, is full of restaurants. Around Naikū, head to Oharai-machi (p434). There are lots of restaurants to choose from, but note that many close by early evening (or late afternoon). Local specialities are fish and seafood from Ise-wan and the dish *tekone-sushi* (bonito dipped in soy sauce and served atop a rice bowl).

Akafuku Honten SWEETS ¥
(赤福本店; ☎0596-22-7000; www.akafuku.co.jp; 26 Ujinakanokiri-chō; set with tea ¥210; ⊙5am-5pm) Akafuku has been making its signature style of *mochi* (pounded-rice cakes), coated in sweet adzuki-bean paste, for over three centuries. There are several branches around town, but it's worth visiting the main shop in Oharai-machi – the only one that opens at 5am for early-morning pilgrims – for its historic building and river-view terrace.

Sushi-kyū SUSHI ¥¥
(すし久; ☎0596-27-0229; 20 Ujinakanokiri-chō; set meal ¥1850-2380; ⊙10.30am-7pm, to 5pm Tue) Occupying a former ryokan from the early 19th century, Sushi-kyū is known as the go-to spot for Ise's speciality, *tekone-sushi* (bonito dipped in soy sauce and served atop a rice bowl). It's served as a set that goes up in grade (and number of side dishes) from *'ume'* to *'take'* to *'matsu'*.

The shop is in Oharai-machi (p434), just before the Okage-yokochō entrance.

Butasute JAPANESE ¥¥
(豚捨; ☎0596-23-8802; 52 Ujinakanokiri-chō; meals from ¥1000; ⊙restaurant 11am-6pm Apr-Sep, to 5pm Oct-Mar, takeaway counter from 9am) This local institution specialises in *gyū-don* (sliced beef on rice). Early-morning shrine visitors can pick up *menchi katsu* (croquettes stuffed with minced beef; ¥150) from the takeaway counter. The shop is in Okage-yokochō, a more contemporary cluster of restaurants connected to Oharai-machi (p434).

There's another **location** (豚捨外宮前店; ☎0596-25-1129; 1-1-33 Iwabuchi; meals from ¥1000; ⊙11am-3pm & 5-8pm Fri-Wed) which is open later by Gekū (p434).

Daiki SEAFOOD ¥¥
(大喜; ☎0596-28-0281; http://ise.ne.jp/daiki; 2-1-48 Iwabuchi; meals ¥800-4000; ⊙11am-9pm; Ⓟ) Signage reading 'Japan's most famous restaurant' may be an exaggeration, but this is a reliably polished place to sample a huge variety of local seafood dishes, including reasonably priced tempura and *tekone-sushi teishoku* (soy-dipped bonito set meals) – or splurge on an *ise-ebi* (Japanese lobster; market price). It's right in front of Uji-Yamada Station, in a wooden building.

Drinking & Nightlife

Isuzu-gawa Cafe CAFE
(五十鈴カフェ; ☎0596-23-9002; 52 Ujinakanokiri-chō; coffee ¥450; ⊙9am-5pm) This cafe is in one of Oharai-machi's (p434) beautifully maintained wooden buildings, but set back from the street, with window- and terrace-front views over the clear waters of the Isuzu-gawa. Come before 11am to get the 'morning set' (¥550), which includes coffee, toast, a hard-boiled egg and yoghurt.

Dandelion Chocolate CAFE
(ダンデライオン・チョコレート; ☎0596-63-6631; https://dandelionchocolate.jp; 20-24 Hon-machi; ⊙10am-5pm) Small-batch-chocolate speciality shop Dandelion serves decadent hot chocolates (¥580 to ¥630), along with cookies and brownies (¥330 to ¥450); the stylish cafe has several books on Ise-jingū to peruse, including a few in English.

It's across the street from the entrance to Gekū (p434).

Information

LEFT LUGGAGE

Ise-shi Station Baggage Storage Office (伊勢市駅手荷物預かり所; ☎0596-65-6861; ⊙9am-5.30pm) Offers luggage storage (¥500 per day per item) and forwarding to any Ise-Shima hotel (¥1000 per item); for the latter service, drop off your luggage by 1pm and it will be delivered by 5pm the same day. The office is outside the south side of Ise-shi Station, on the left as you exit.

MONEY

The post office adjacent to the main Tourist Information Center has an ATM that accepts international bankcards; there's also a post office in Oharai-machi.

TOURIST INFORMATION

The main **Tourist Information Center** (外宮前観光協会; ☎0596-23-3323; 16-2 Hon-machi, Ise-shi; ⊙8.30am-5pm) is across the street from Gekū (about 10 minutes' walk from Ise-shi Station). There's a smaller information office in Ise-shi Station; both offices have English-speaking staff and useful maps.

WORTH A TRIP

MIHO MUSEUM

Secluded amid hills and valleys near the village of Shigaraki, the knockout **Miho Museum** (ミホミュージアム; ☎0748-82-3411; www.miho.or.jp; 300 Tashiro Momodani, Shigaraki-chō; adult/child/student ¥1100/300/800; ⏲10am-5pm, closed Mon & btwn exhibitions; P) is most definitely worth a detour. It houses the Koyama family collection of Japanese, Middle Eastern, Chinese and South Asian art, and beautifully displayed special exhibitions. The facility is at least as impressive as the collection. The IM Pei–designed main building, reached from the ticket centre via a footpath and a long pedestrian tunnel opening onto a gorge, feels like a secret hideout in a futuristic farmhouse.

The museum's construction was quite an engineering feat: the top of the mountain was removed, the glass-and-marble building constructed, and the ground replaced as before around and above it, down to the massive red pine (a video explains it).

Teisan buses depart several times a day from JR Ishiyama Station for the museum (¥820, approximately 50 minutes). Check the museum calendar and bus times on the website before setting out. If you're driving here, note that the road is very curvy and narrow.

Getting There & Away

Ise-shi Station (JR and Kintetsu lines) is the most useful stop for sights and accommodation. Nagoya is the nearest transit hub.

The JR Rapid Mie train connects Nagoya and Ise-shi Station (¥2000, 1½ hours, hourly). This is the best way to go for Japan Rail Pass holders (even if you're coming from Kyoto/Osaka; take a *shinkansen* first to Nagoya), though you'll have to pay a ¥510 surcharge to ride the Rapid Mie (as it shares some non-JR tracks).

The Kintetsu line runs comfortable, reserved-seat *tokkyū* trains between Ise-shi and Nagoya (¥2770, one hour and 20 minutes, twice hourly), Osaka (Uehonmachi or Namba Stations; ¥3120, 1¾ hours, hourly) and Kyoto (¥3620, two hours, infrequent).

Getting Around

Gekū is a 10-minute walk south of Ise-shi Station; take the more attractive Gekū-sandō, one block east of the main street.

For Naikū, take bus 51 or 55 from bus stop 10 outside the south side of Ise-shi Station to Naikū-mae (¥430, 20 minutes); you can pick up the same bus from stop 2 in front of Gekū. The first bus departs for Naikū around 7am and by mid-morning they run every 10 minutes.

Return buses depart from Naikū-mae bus stop 2; the last one to Ise-shi Station goes at 6pm. A taxi between Ise-shi Station and Naikū should cost around ¥2000; there's a taxi stand at the train station and in front of the shrine.

A limited number of rental bicycles (¥800 for four hours) are available from the main Tourist Information Center and the Ise-shi Station Baggage Storage Office.

SHIGA PREFECTURE

Just across the Higashiyama mountains from Kyoto, Shiga Prefecture (滋賀県, Shiga-ken) is dominated by Biwa-ko (びわ湖), Japan's largest lake. Long an inspiration for poets, the lake was developed in the 20th century as a resort destination; concrete hotel blocks and tourist cruises now overshadow its lyrical charms. But Shiga has a few sights of note: temples that date to the early days of the Japanese empire, a well-preserved medieval castle and a fantastic (if remote) art museum. And while it's very close to Kyoto, you won't see Kyoto-level crowds out here.

Sleeping

Sights in Shiga can easily be visited as a day trips from Kyoto; however, given the premium on Kyoto accommodation, it makes economic sense to stay locally if you plan to take in several sights here. Ōtsu has the most accommodation options. It's also a good (cheaper!) alternative base for exploring Kyoto.

Getting There & Away

The JR Biwako line connects Kyoto to Ōtsu and Hikone. Some Kyoto Tōzai subway-line trains from Sanjō Keihan Station continue on the Keihan Keishin line to Hama-Ōtsu Station in Ōtsu.

Ōtsu

☎077 / POP 342,847

At the southern end of Biwa-ko, Ōtsu (大津) is the capital of Shiga Prefecture and a hub for transit and tourism around the lake. It has a long history – it was an imperial

Shiga Prefecture

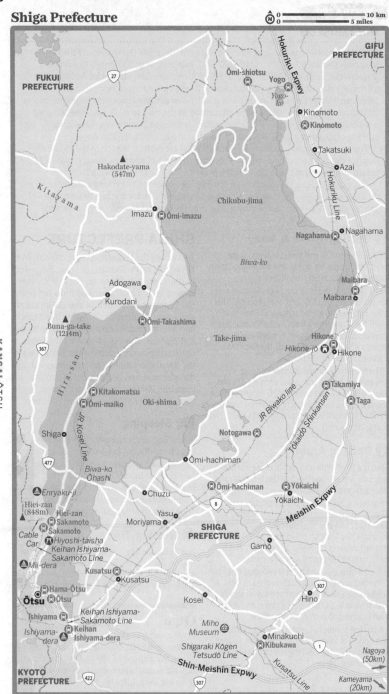

0 10 km
0 5 miles

GIFU PREFECTURE
FUKUI PREFECTURE
27
Hokuriku Expwy
Ōmi-shiotsu
Yogo
Yogo-ko
Kinomoto
Kinomoto
Takatsuki
Hakodate-yama (547m)
8
Azai
Hokuriku Line
Kitayama
Chikubu-jima
Imazu
Ōmi-imazu
Nagahama
Nagahama
Biwa-ko
Adogawa
Maibara
Maibara
Kurodani
Ōmi-Takashima
Buna-ga-take (1214m)
Take-jima
Hikone
Hikone-jō
Hikone
367
Hira-san
Takamiya
Kitakomatsu
JR Biwako line
Taga
Ōmi-maiko
Oki-shima
Tōkaidō Shinkansen
JR Kosei Line
Shiga
Notogawa
477
Ōmi-hachiman
Biwa-ko Ōhashi
Enryaku-ji
Chuzu
Ōmi-hachiman
Yōkaichi
Yōkaichi
Hiei-zan (848m)
8
Meishin Expwy
Hiei-zan Sakamoto
Yasu
Moriyama
Sakamoto
SHIGA PREFECTURE
Cable Car
Hiyoshi-taisha
Gamō
Keihan Ishiyama-Sakamoto Line
Mii-dera
Kusatsu
Kusatsu
Hama-Ōtsu
307
Ōtsu
Ōtsu
Kosei
Hino
Ishiyama
Keihan Ishiyama-Sakamoto Line
Keihan Ishiyama-dera
Miho Museum
Ishiyama-dera
Minakuchi
Kibukawa
Shigaraki Kōgen Tetsudō Line
1
Nagoya (50km)
Shin-Meishin Expwy
KYOTO PREFECTURE
422
307
Kusatsu Line
Kameyama (20km)

capital in the 7th century, before Kyoto – and a few noteworthy sights to show for it, including the impressive temples Mii-dera and Ishiyama-dera.

Sights

Mii-dera BUDDHIST TEMPLE
(三井寺; ☎077-522-2238; www.shiga-miidera.or.jp; 246 Onjōji-chō; adult/child ¥600/200; ⏲8am-5pm) Established in 672, over a century before the founding of Kyoto, Mii-dera gets its name for its three springs ('mi' means 'three' and 'i' means 'spring'). The highlight is the Hondō (main hall), last rebuilt in 1599, a National Treasure with a rare *hiwatabuki* (thatched cedar-bark) roof. Behind the main altar is a collection of Buddhist statues, the oldest of which date to the Heian era (794–1185). Adjacent to the main hall is a big temple bell you can ring (¥300).

There are many sub-temples, including one to Kannon (Buddhist goddess of mercy), around the forested grounds. Stop for some sweets and tea at **Chikara Mochi** (力餅; Mii-dera; mochi & tea ¥300; ⏲10am-5pm Thu-Tue).

The temple is a seven-minute walk from Mii-dera Station on the Keihan Ishiyama-Sakamoto line; you can also walk there in 15 minutes from Keihan Hama-Ōtsu Station and in 30 minutes from JR Ōtsu Station.

Ishiyama-dera BUDDHIST TEMPLE
(石山寺; www.ishiyamadera.or.jp; 1-1-1 Ishiyama-dera; adult/child ¥600/200; ⏲8am-4.30pm) This Shingon-sect temple, founded in the 8th century, has a lot going for it, including Japan's oldest pagoda (the Tahōtō, built in 1194) and an impressive location atop a stone outcrop, but it's most famous for hosting one of the world's earliest artists-in-residence: according to lore it was during a stay here that Murasaki Shikibu first dreamt up *The Tale of Genji*, in 1004.

There are also lovely walks through the grounds, partly forested and partly manicured, and views of Biwa-ko from the pavilion Tsukimi-tei. The temple is a 10-minute walk from Keihan Ishiyama-dera Station (continue along the road in the direction that the train was travelling).

Festivals & Events

Biwa-ko Dai-Hanabi Taikai FIREWORKS
(びわ湖大花火大会; www.biwako-visitors.jp/hanabi; ⏲early Aug) This display of 10,000 fireworks over Biwa-ko is a major summer event, drawing hundreds of thousands of visitors. You can get good views from the waterfront near Keihan Hama-Ōtsu Station, but you'll have to get there early in the day to secure a spot. Expect trains to/from Kyoto to be packed for hours before and afterward.

Sleeping & Eating

There are a few business hotels, restaurants and convenience stores near JR Ōtsu Station and Keihan Hama-Ōtsu Station.

Calendar Hotel CAPSULE HOTEL ¥
(☎077-526-9080; www.the-calendar.jp; Viera Ōtsu, 1-3 Kasuga-chō; capsules from ¥3300;) This recently opened, surprisingly stylish capsule hotel is attached to JR Ōtsu Station; it's a good base for exploring the sights in Shiga Prefecture and also a cheap alternative to staying in Kyoto. There's a cafe and bar below and a roof terrace (open in summer).

Information

Tourist Information Center (☎077-522-3830; www.otsu-guide.jp; ⏲9am-6pm;) Outside the north exit of JR Ōtsu Station, with brochures, rental bicycles (¥250/1800 per hour/day) and English-speaking staff.

Getting There & Away

From Kyoto, take the JR Biwako line from JR Kyoto Station to JR Ōtsu Station (¥200, 10 minutes), or travel on the Kyoto Tōzai subway line (which connects to the Keihan Keishin line) to Hama-Ōtsu Station (¥430, 25 minutes) from Sanjō Keihan Station. The JR Biwako line also goes to Ishiyama Station with *kaisoku* (rapid) or *futsū* (local) trains only (¥240, 13 minutes).

Getting Around

At Hama-Ōtsu Station connect to the Keihan Ishiyama-Sakamoto line, which runs along the western shore of Biwa-ko, stopping at Mii-dera Station (¥170, one minute) and Ishiyama-dera Station (¥240, 17 minutes).

Hikone

☎0749 / POP 113,073

On the eastern shore of Biwa-ko, Hikone (彦根) is best known for its castle, Hikone-jō – one of only a few castles in Japan with their original keep. It's surrounded by moats and more than 1200 cherry trees (which makes it a popular spot for springtime cherry-blossom viewing).

Sights

★Hikone-jō CASTLE

(彦根城; 1-1 Konki-chō; adult/child ¥800/200; 8.30am-5pm) Completed in 1622, this diminutive castle of the Ii family of *daimyō* (domain lords) is rightly considered a National Treasure; much of it remains in its original state. Two unusual features are the *teppōzama* and *yazama,* outlets for shooting guns and arrows, designed to be invisible from the outside until they're popped out for use. Upper storeys have great views across Biwa-ko.

The castle is a 10-minute walk up the street from the station (take a left before the shrine, then a quick right, or walk through the shrine grounds).

From the castle grounds you can continue directly to the garden **Genkyū-en** (玄宮園; ¥200, with Hikone-jō free; 8.30am-5pm). The path is tricky to find; look for signs in Japanese or ask for directions.

Eating

The best collection of restaurants near the castle can be found on Yumekyō-bashi Castle Rd (夢京橋キャッスルロード), across the moat from the castle's Ōte-mon (front gate).

Monzen-ya SOBA ¥

(もんぜんや; 0749-24-2297; 1-6-26 Honmachi; soba ¥840-1400; 11am-7pm Wed-Mon) This soba restaurant is the top pick along Yumekyō-bashi Castle Rd. Try the *nishin-soba* (soba with herring), a local speciality. From the castle end of the street it's about 100m along on the left – look for the white door curtains.

Information

Tourist Information Center (0749-22-2954; 9am-5pm) On the ground floor outside Hikone Station's west exit; ask for the English-language town map.

Getting There & Away

The JR Biwako line runs fast *shinkaisoku* trains five times a day to Hikone from Kyoto (¥1140, 50 minutes) via Ōtsu (¥970, 40 minutes); local trains run more frequently. If you have a JR Pass or are in a hurry, you can take the *shinkansen* to Maibara (¥2120, 20 minutes from Kyoto) and then backtrack on the JR Biwako line to Hikone (¥190, five minutes).

NORTHERN KANSAI

The northern reaches of Kansai are dramatically different from the densely populated urban areas to the south. Quiet hamlets like Miyama are found in the mountains north of Kyoto, and beyond lies a spectacular coastline with sandy beaches, rugged headlands and rocky islets (all part of the San-in Kaigan Geopark). Though the region is largely rural, there are some popular holiday destinations here, such as the hot-spring resort town of Kinosaki Onsen. Off-the-beaten-track spots include the Tango Peninsula.

Sleeping

Both Kinosaki Onsen and Kibune have excellent ryokan if you're looking to treat yourself. In the village of Miyama you can stay in a refurbished farmhouse. Beyond these highlights, accommodation is more limited in northern Kansai than elsewhere in the region. Major transport hubs have business hotels, and there are a few ryokan, guesthouses and hostels strung along the coast.

Eating

Kansai's northern coast, on the Sea of Japan, is famous for its seafood and especially for its *zuwaigani* (snow crab). Crab season runs from 6 November to 20 March, during which destinations like Kinosaki Onsen are very popular. In the mountains, specialities include foraged mushrooms, river fish and wild game. Restaurants can be hard to come by outside the resort towns; it's best to book meals at your accommodation.

Getting There & Around

Northern Kansai is largely accessible by public transport. Key train lines from urban Kansai include the JR Fukuchiyama line, which connects Osaka and Fukuchiyama, a major hub in northern Kyoto Prefecture, and the JR Sagano line, which runs from Kyoto via Hiyoshi (for buses to Miyama) to Fukuchiyama. In Fukuchiyama you can transfer to the JR San-in line for Kinosaki Onsen and Takeno or the private Kyoto Tango Railway for Amanohashidate.

Destinations closer to Kyoto, such as Ōhara, Kurama and Kibune, can be reached by Kyoto city public transport.

For the Tango Peninsula and other parts of Kansai's northern coast a rental car is recommended. Pick up one in Fukuchiyama or any other major city on the JR San-in line, such as Maizuru or Toyooka. A car is also ideal for exploring parts of rural Kyoto Prefecture, like Miyama.

OFF THE BEATEN TRACK

BUJŌ-JI

Bujō-ji (峰定寺; 075-746-0036; Hanase Harachi-chō, Sakyo-ku, Kyoto; ¥500, children under 12yr not permitted; 9am-3.30pm, closed rainy/snowy days & Dec-Mar; P) was founded in the 12th century by Emperor Toba, and while the main hall has been repaired over the years it stands pretty much the same as it always has: a simple wooden structure with a terrace overlooking Kyoto's northern mountains. The view is simply awesome; catch it on the right day – when the skies are clear and there's not another soul around – and you can have the kind of meditative experience that's so elusive at more famous temples.

It's a Shugendō (mountain asceticism) temple, reached via a 430-step climb. There's a formal entry procedure, where you surrender your personal items in exchange for a wooden staff and a special pilgrim's bag (you can keep bottled water and your wallet, to make an offering at the temple). Just before the hall, there's a bell you can ring.

Bujō-ji is most easily accessed by car, but you can take bus 32 from Demachiyanagi Station in Kyoto to the Daihizan-guchi bus stop (¥930, 95 minutes, three daily). At the bus stop a narrow road runs 2km to the temple (it's signposted in Japanese).

Ōhara

075 / POP 2526

Since ancient times Ōhara (大原), a quiet farming town about 15km north of Kyoto, has been regarded as a holy site by followers of the Jōdo (Pure Land) school of Buddhism. The region provides a charming glimpse of rural Japan, along with the picturesque Sanzen-in, Jakkō-in and several other fine temples, and is perfect for strolling. It's about a one-hour bus ride from Downtown Kyoto and makes for a pleasant day trip from the city. It's most popular in autumn, when the maple leaves change colour and the mountain views are spectacular.

Avoid Ōhara on busy autumn-foliage weekends in November. There's only one main road up there from Kyoto and you'll spend too much time sitting in traffic (and the temples will be crowded when you get there).

Sights

★Sanzen-in BUDDHIST TEMPLE

(三千院; 540 Raikōin-chō, Ōhara, Sakyō-ku; adult/child ¥700/150-400; 8.30am-5.30pm Mar-Nov, 9am-5pm Dec-Feb; Kyoto bus 17 or 18 from Kyoto Station to Ōhara) Famed for its autumn foliage, hydrangea garden and stunning Buddha statues, this temple is deservedly popular with foreign and domestic tourists alike. The temple's garden, **Yūsei-en**, is one of the most photographed sights in Japan, and rightly so.

Take some time to sit on the steps of the **Shin-den** hall and admire the beauty of the Yūsei-en. Then head off to see **Ōjō-gokuraku-in** (Temple of Rebirth in Paradise), the hall in which stands the impressive Amitabha trinity, a large Amida image flanked by attendants Kannon (goddess of mercy) and Seishi (god of wisdom). After this, walk up to the garden at the back of the temple where, in late spring and summer, you can wander among hectares of blooming hydrangeas.

Sanzen-in was founded in 784 by the priest Saichō and belongs to the Tendai school. Saichō, considered one of the great patriarchs of Buddhism in Japan, also founded Enryaku-ji.

If you're keen for a short hike after leaving the temple, continue up the hill to see the rather oddly named **Soundless Waterfall** (Oto-nashi-no-taki; 音無の滝). Though, in fact, it sounds like any other waterfall, its resonance is believed to have inspired Shōmyō Buddhist chanting.

The approach to Sanzen-in is opposite the bus stop; there is no English sign but you can usually just follow the Japanese tourists. The temple is located about 600m up this walk on your left as you crest the hill.

Jakkō-in BUDDHIST TEMPLE

(寂光院; 676 Kusao-chō, Ōhara, Sakyō-ku; adult/child ¥600/100-350; 9am-5pm Mar-Nov, to 4.30pm Dec-Feb; Kyoto bus 17 or 18 from Kyoto Station to Ōhara) Jakkō-in is a small temple on the opposite side of Ōhara from Sanzen-in. It's reached by a pleasant 15-minute walk from the bus station through an 'old Japan' village. Walk from the bus stop to the traffic lights on the main road, take the small road immediately to the left. Follow it over the bridge and across a road, then continue until you reach a T-intersection. Head left and continue around to the right a few minutes up the hill.

The history of the temple is exceedingly tragic. The actual founding date of the temple is subject to some debate (it's thought to be somewhere between the 6th and 11th centuries), but it acquired fame as the temple that harboured Kenrei Mon-in, a lady of the Taira clan. In 1185 the Taira were soundly defeated in a sea battle against the Minamoto clan at Dan-no-ura. With the entire Taira clan slaughtered or drowned, Kenrei Mon-in threw herself into the waves with her son Antoku, the infant emperor; she was fished out – the only member of the clan to survive.

Kenrei Mon-in was returned to Kyoto, where she became a nun and lived in a bare hut until it collapsed during an earthquake. She was then accepted into Jakkō-in and stayed there, immersed in prayer and sorrowful memories, until her death 27 years later. Her tomb is located high on the hill behind the temple.

The main building of this temple burned down in May 2000 and the newly reconstructed main hall lacks some of the charm of the original. Nonetheless, it is a nice spot.

Jakkō-in is also known for its autumn-foliage displays in November.

Shōrin-in BUDDHIST TEMPLE

(勝林院; 075-744-2537; 187 Shōrinin-chō, Ōhara, Sakyō-ku; adult/child ¥300/200; 9am-4.30pm; Kyoto bus 17 or 18 from Kyoto Station to Ōhara) This temple near Sanzen-in (p441) is worth a look, even if only through its admission gate, to admire the thatched roof of the main hall. It's a good option if you're trying to avoid crowds.

Hōsen-in BUDDHIST TEMPLE

(宝泉院; 075-744-2409; 187 Shōrinin-chō, Ōhara, Sakyō-ku; adult ¥800, child ¥600-700; 9am-5pm; Kyoto bus 17 or 18 from Kyoto Station to Ōhara) A quiet option, this temple is just down the path west of the entry gate to Shōrin-in. The main tatami room offers a view of a bamboo garden and the surrounding mountains, framed like a painting by the beams and posts of the building. There is also a fantastic 700-year-old pine tree in the garden. The blood-stained Chi Tenjō ceiling boards came from Fushimi-jō castle.

Eating

There are quite a few eating options on the walk up to Sanzen-in and close to the entrance. Many use local mountain vegetables and pickles in their dishes.

Seryō-Jaya SHOKUDO ¥

(芹生茶屋; 075-744-2301; 24 Shorinin-chō, Ōhara, Sakyō-ku; lunch sets from ¥1000; 11am-5pm; Kyoto bus 17 or 18 from Kyoto Station to Ōhara) Seryō-Jaya serves tasty soba noodles and other fare incorporating produce from the area, such as mountain-harvested mushrooms and pickled plums. There is outdoor seating in the warmer months. It's the first restaurant at the top of the stairs before the entrance to Sanzen-in (p441). Look for the English menu and food models in the window.

Getting There & Away

From Kyoto Station, Kyoto bus 17 or 18 runs to **Ōhara bus stop**. The ride takes about an hour and costs ¥550. From Keihan line's Sanjō Station, take Kyoto bus 16 or 17 (¥470, 45 minutes). Be careful to board a tan-coloured Kyoto bus, not a green Kyoto City bus of the same number. Note that the one-day bus pass can't be used for this trip as it's outside the zone.

Kurama & Kibune

Roughly 30 minutes north of Kyoto, Kurama (鞍馬) and Kibune (貴船) are a pair of tranquil valleys that have long been favoured as places to escape the city. Kurama's main attractions are its mountain temple and onsen. Kibune, a charming little hamlet just over the ridge, is a cluster of ryokan overlooking a mountain river. Kibune is best visited in summer, when the ryokan serve dinner on platforms built over the waters of Kibune-gawa.

The two valleys lend themselves to being explored together. In winter, start from Kibune, walk 30 minutes over the ridge, visit Kurama-dera, then soak in the onsen. In summer the reverse route is better: start from Kurama, walk up to the temple, then down the other side to Kibune to enjoy a meal above the cool river.

If you're in Kyoto on the night of 22 October, don't miss the Kurama-no-hi Matsuri fire festival.

Sights

★**Kurama-dera** BUDDHIST TEMPLE

(鞍馬寺; 1074 Kurama Honmachi, Sakyō-ku; ¥300; 9am 4.30pm; Eizan line from Demachiyanagi to Kurama) Located high on a thickly wooded mountain, Kurama-dera is one of the few temples in modern Japan that manages to retain an air of real spirituality. This magical place gains much of its power from its brilliant natural setting. The entrance to the temple is

Kurama & Kibune

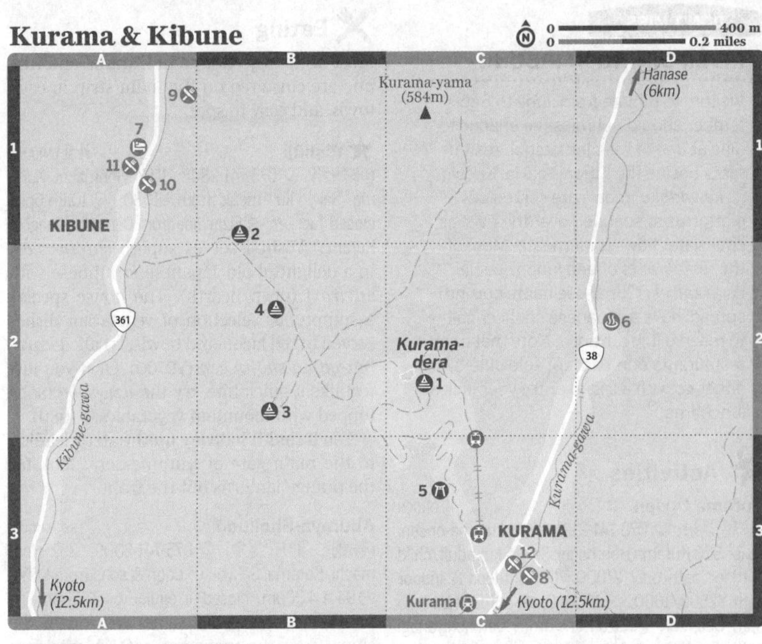

Kurama & Kibune

Top Sights
1 Kurama-dera C2

Sights
2 Okuno-in Maō-den B1
3 Ōsugi-gongen B2
4 Sōjō-ga-dani Fudō-dō B2
5 Yuki-jinja C3

Activities, Courses & Tours
6 Kurama Onsen D2

Sleeping
7 Ryokan Ugenta A1

Eating
8 Aburaya-Shokudō C3
9 Hirobun A1
10 Hiroya A1
11 Kibune Club A1
12 Yōshūji C3

just up the hill from Kurama Station. A cable car runs to/from the top (¥200 each way), or you can hike up in about 30 minutes (follow the path past the tram station).

The temple also has a fascinating history: in 770 the monk Gantei left Nara's Toshō-dai-ji in search of a wilderness sanctuary in which to meditate. Wandering in the hills north of Kyoto, he came across a white horse that led him to the valley known today as Kurama. After seeing a vision of the deity Bishamon-ten, guardian of the northern quarter of the Buddhist heaven, Gantei established Kurama-dera just below the peak of Kurama-yama. Originally belonging to the Tendai school of Buddhism, Kurama has been independent since 1949, describing its own brand of Buddhism as Kurama-kyō.

It's worth walking up the trail from the main entrance (if it's not too hot), since it winds through a forest of towering old-growth cryptomeria trees, passing by **Yuki-jinja**, a small Shintō shrine, on the way. Near the peak, there is a courtyard dominated by the **Honden** (Main Hall); behind this a trail leads off to the mountain's peak.

At the top, you can take a brief detour across the ridge to **Ōsugi-gongen**, a quiet shrine in a grove of trees. Those who want to continue to Kibune can take the trail down the other side. It's a 1.2km, 30-minute hike from the Honden to the valley floor of Kibune. On the way down are two mountain shrines, **Sōjō-ga-dani Fudō-dō** and **Okuno-in Maō-den**, which make pleasant rest stops.

DON'T MISS

RIVER DINING IN KIBUNE

Visitors to Kibune from June to September should not miss the chance to dine at one of the picturesque restaurants beside the Kibune-gawa. Known as *kawadoko*, meals are served on platforms suspended over the river as cool water flows underneath. Most of the restaurants offer a lunch special. For a *kaiseki* (Japanese haute cuisine) spread, have a Japanese speaker call to reserve it in advance. Note that most restaurants don't accept solo diners, so either go with a friend or try your luck at lunchtime.

Activities

Kurama Onsen ONSEN

(鞍馬温泉; 075-741-2131; www.kurama-onsen.co.jp; 520 Kurama Honmachi, Sakyō-ku; adult/child outdoor bath only ¥1000/700, outdoor & indoor bath ¥2500/1600; 10am-9pm, outdoor bath to 8pm Dec-Mar; Eizan line from Demachiyanagi to Kurama) One of the few onsen within easy reach of Kyoto, Kurama Onsen is a great place to relax after a hike. The outdoor bath has fine views of Kurama-yama, while the indoor bath area includes some relaxation areas in addition to the tubs.

To get to Kurama Onsen, walk straight out of Kurama Station and continue up the main street, passing the entrance to Kurama-dera on your left. The onsen is about 10 minutes' walk on the right. There's also a free shuttle bus between the station and the onsen, which meets incoming trains.

Sleeping & Eating

If you plan on spending the night in the area, Kibune is your best bet. It has a few lovely ryokan sitting opposite the river.

Ryokan Ugenta RYOKAN ¥¥¥

(旅館右源太; 075-741-2146; www.ugenta.co.jp; 76 Kibune-chō, Kurama, Sakyō-ku; r per person incl meals from ¥45,954; @; Eizan line to Kibune-guchi) The superb Ugenta is a stylish inn located in the village of Kibune, about 30 minutes north of Kyoto by taxi or train. There are only two rooms here, one Japanese-style and one Western-style. Both have private cypress-wood outdoor bathtubs. The perfect place for a secluded getaway or honeymoon, it offers a free shuttle bus to and from the station.

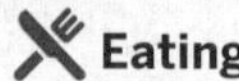

Eating

Most of the restaurants in Kurama and Kibune are clustered on the main strip in each town, and easy to spot.

★Yōshūji VEGETARIAN ¥

(雍州路; 075-741-2848; 1074 Honmachi, Kurama, Sakyō-ku; meals from ¥1080; 10am-6pm, closed Tue; ; Eizan line from Demachiyanagi to Kurama) Yōshūji serves superb *shōjin-ryōri* in a delightful old Japanese farmhouse with an *irori* (open hearth). The house special, a sumptuous selection of vegetarian dishes served in red lacquered bowls, is called *kurama-yama shōjin zen* (¥2700). Or if you just feel like a quick bite, try the *uzu-soba* (soba topped with mountain vegetables; ¥1080).

You'll find it halfway up the steps leading to the main gate of Kurama-dera; look for the orange lanterns out the front.

Aburaya-Shokudō SHOKUDO ¥

(鞍馬　油屋食堂; 075-741-2009; 252 Honmachi, Kurama, Sakyō-ku; udon & soba from ¥650; 9am-4.30pm, closed irregularly; Eizan line from Demachiyanagi to Kurama) Just down the steps from the main gate of Kurama-dera and on the street corner, this classic old-style *shokudō* is a reminder of Japan before it got rich. Limited English is spoken but there's an English menu and the service is very friendly. It offers soba, udon and *donburi* (dishes served over rice) bowls at good prices.

Kibune Club CAFE ¥

(貴船倶楽部; 075-741-3039; 76 Kibune-chō, Kurama, Sakyō-ku; coffee from ¥500; 11am-5pm, to 6pm Sat & Sun; Eizan line from Demachiyanagi to Kibune-guchi) The exposed wooden beams and open, airy feel of this rustic cafe make it a great spot to stop for a cuppa and cake while exploring Kibune. In winter it sometimes cranks up the wood stove, which makes the place rather cosy. Cash only.

Hirobun JAPANESE ¥¥

(ひろ文; 075-741-2147; 87 Kibune-chō, Kurama, Sakyō-ku; noodles from ¥1300, kaiseki courses from ¥8600; 11am-9pm; Eizan line from Demachiyanagi to Kibune-guchi) This is a good place to sample *kawadoko* 'above-river' dining on platforms. A friendly crew of ladies run the show and the food is quite good; they are known for their Nagashi *somen* noodles in summer (11am to 4pm), which are served via flowing cold water down sliced bamboo pipes – imagine a water slide for noodles.

Look for the black-and-white sign and the lantern. Book ahead for dinner. Note: it usually doesn't accept solo diners for the *kaiseki* courses.

Hiroya JAPANESE ¥¥¥

(ひろや; ☎075-741-2401; www.kibune-hiroya.com/multi/index.html; 56 Kibune-chō, Kurama, Sakyō-ku; kaiseki from ¥9500; ⊙11am-7.30pm May-Sep; 🚊Eizan line from Demachiyanagi to Kibune-guchi) One of the oldest restaurants offering *kawadoko* dining in Kibune, Hiroya is a fine choice for eating riverside in summer. It's well known for the speciality *ayu* (grilled sweet fish). Book ahead.

ℹ Getting There & Away

Take the Eizan line from Kyoto's Demachiyanagi Station. For Kibune, get off at the second-last stop, Kibune-guchi, take a right out of the station and walk about 20 minutes up the hill or jump on the shuttle bus. For Kurama, go to the last stop, Kurama, and walk straight out of the station. To reach both destinations by train from Kyoto costs ¥420/210 per adult/child and takes about 30 minutes.

ℹ Getting Around

Most people move between Kurama and Kibune by doing the hike over the Kurama-yama ridge between the two valleys. If you're not up for hiking, you can take the Eizan line between the two stations (two minutes, ¥210).

Miyama

☎0771 / POP 4000

Miyama (美山) is a collection of rural hamlets in the mountainous heartland of Kyoto Prefecture. The big sight here is Kayabuki-no-sato, a collection of farmhouses with traditional thatched roofs. Beyond that, Miyama's appeal lies in its slow pace, natural scenery and locally sourced food. You can see it in an afternoon, but to really experience it, stay for a night or two, rent a bicycle (or just walk) and explore the country lanes, dotted with small temples and shrines.

◉ Sights

Kayabuki-no-sato VILLAGE

(かやぶきの里; ☎0771-77-0660; www.kayabukinosato.com; Kita; ⊙shops & attractions 9am-5pm; P) FREE Miyama's star attraction is this hamlet, home to some 50 farmhouses with traditional *kayabuki-yane* (thatched roofs) in the local Kyoto Kitayama style (a hipped roof with a peaked gable on top). Many are still homes; others are now inns, cafes and shops. To see inside one that hasn't been modernised, and to get a sense of life in pre-modern Miyama, visit the Miyama Folk Museum (admission ¥300).

Kayabuki Art Museum & Folk Museum MUSEUM

(美山かやぶき美術館・郷土資料館; ☎0771-75-1777; http://miyama-kayabuki.org; 21 Shimahō-noki; ¥500; ⊙10am-4.30pm, closed Mon & Dec-Mar; P) There are two historic *kayabuki-yane* (thatched-roof) farmhouses here: one that displays artefacts from traditional life in Miyama and another that serves as a gallery for contemporary craftwork.

🛏 Sleeping

There are several ryokan and *minshuku*, an excellent youth hostel, and even whole houses you can rent out, scattered around Miyama. Accommodation can easily be booked online through Miyama's tourism homepage (https://kyotomiyama.jp/en).

Miyama Heimat Youth Hostel HOSTEL ¥

(美山ハイマートユースホステル; ☎0771-75-0997; http://miyama-heimat.com; 57 Obuchinakasai; dm members/nonmembers from ¥3800/4300, s/d from ¥5725/10,000; P⊖❄📶) This hostel is in a modernised *kayabukiya*, with both Japanese- and Western-style bedding. It's out by its lonesome in the far west of the village – ideal if you have a car or a bicycle (or just want to take local walks or relax on the porch swing). The friendly owners speak some English.

The food (breakfast ¥700, dinner ¥1240 to ¥4300), made with local ingredients, is excellent. If you're keen, the proprietor will run lunchtime cooking lessons for ¥1500 (lunch included!).

The nearest train station is Wachi (on the JR San'in line), from where you'll have to catch a local bus headed for Izumi and get off at Ikuseien-mae bus stop (¥600, 20 minutes). There are only a few buses daily; when you book, the hostel will help you work out the schedule.

Matabe MINSHUKU ¥¥

(またべ; ☎0771-77-0258; https://kyotomiyama.jp/stay/matabe; Kita; r per person incl 2 meals & without bathroom from ¥8700, solo travellers ¥9200; P⊖❄♨) In one of the thatched-roof homes within Kayabuki-no-sato, this three-room *minshuku* is traditional on the outside yet clean and modern on the inside, with Japanese-style rooms.

Dinners feature local free-range chicken. On Wednesday, Saturday and Sunday, Matabe also serves a set lunch with udon (¥1000) or grilled fish (¥1600).

Kigusuriya RYOKAN ¥¥¥

(きぐすりや; ☎0771-76-0015; www.kigusuriya.com; 8-1 Imayasu, Tsurugaoka; r per person incl 2 meals from ¥16,200; P ❄ 📶) In northern Miyama and surrounded by farmland, this four-room family-run inn started as a pharmacy on the old road connecting Kyoto with the sea; it also rents out a nearby renovated farmhouse. The kindly owners serve delicious meals using local ingredients, have free bicycles for guests to use, and have made an English-language map of nearby walking paths and sights.

If you don't have your own car, they will shuttle you to and from Hiyoshi Station.

Eating & Drinking

Local specialities include free-range chicken, wild venison, *ayu* (sweetfish), caught in the Yura-gawa, in spring, and *botan-nabe* (wild-boar hot pot) in winter. Note that many restaurants are open only for lunch or by appointment. If you're staying over, it's a good idea to book meals at your accommodation.

Morishige NOODLES ¥

(もりしげ; ☎0771-75-1086; 15 Tani-no-shimo, Uchikubo; noodle dishes ¥800-1000, set meals ¥1200-2100; ⏲11am-3pm Wed-Sun; P) In a 150-year-old thatched-roof farmhouse (and with tatami seating and a central hearth), Morishige serves soba, on its own or in a set with small dishes made from locally grown vegetables. Look for it behind the cluster of shrubs and pines.

★**Yururi** JAPANESE ¥¥¥

(ゆるり; ☎0771-76-0741; http://youluly.umesao.com; 15 Sano-mae, Morisato; lunch/dinner menus from ¥3240/5400; ⏲closed Jan & Feb; P) Miyama's natural bounty is a big draw, and this restaurant in an elegantly updated thatched-roof farmhouse serves menus of seasonal local ingredients (such as mountain vegetables in spring and mushrooms in fall). Reservations required (at least a day ahead), and only one party is served at dinner. You'll need a car to get here.

Saika CAFE

(采花; ☎0771-77-0660; https://kyotomiyama.jp/eat/saika; Kita; ⏲11am-5pm) Inside one of the farmhouses in Kayabuki-no-sato (p445), this cafe serves handmade local specialities like *dango* (soft rice-flour balls; ¥520 for a set with tea), made with millet and mugwort.

Information

MONEY

Miyama runs on cash. There are a few post offices with ATMs, but note that hours are limited (9am to 5.30pm Monday to Friday, to 12.30pm Saturday).

TOURIST INFORMATION

Kyoto Tamba Kōgen Quasi-National Park Visitors Centre (京都丹波高原国定公園ビジターセンター; ☎0771-75-9020; https://kyotomiyama.jp/en; 23 Shimo; ⏲9am-5pm; 📶) Miyama's excellent visitor centre can arrange tours and activities with English-speaking guides; book in advance through the website. You can also rent electric bicycles (¥1000/1500 per four hours/day); numbers are limited, so reserve ahead online. There's usually an English-speaking staff member here, and always maps and pamphlets in English.

Getting There & Around

It's possible to get to Miyama by public transport, but it requires some planning. From Kyoto Station, take the JR Sagano/San-in line to Hiyoshi Station (¥760, 50 minutes), then take a local bus for Agake (for the visitor centre; ¥600, 40 minutes) or Kita (for Kayabuki-no-sato; ¥600, 50 minutes). Buses run roughly hourly; the schedule is posted on www.miyamanavi.net.

Local buses do connect points around Miyama, but their infrequency can be frustrating. Having a car expands your options immensely. The fastest road to Miyama is Rte 162 (about 90 minutes), but there's a lovely but longer (two-hour) option (Rtes 38/477) via Kurama and over Hanase-tōge and Sasari-tōge passes.

Amanohashidate

☎0772 / POP 17,425 (MIYAZU-SHI)

Amanohashidate (天橋立, Bridge to Heaven) is a sandbar that runs across Miyazu-wan, on the northern coast of Kyoto Prefecture, at the base of the Tango Peninsula. Since the beginning of recorded history it's been considered to be among Japan's most beautiful sights. There's a tourist town at the southern end, and about 5km to the east is the transport hub and port city of Miyazu (宮津).

Sights

Amanohashidate WATERFRONT

(天橋立; Miyazu-shi) FREE Amanohashidate means 'bridge to heaven' and this narrow sandbar covered in some 5000 pine trees has long inspired poets and painters. It's also billed as one of Japan's 'top three views', along with Matsushima (p530) and Miyajima (p464), which means it's fated to underwhelm – especially with all the tourist trappings at the entrance. Still, the 3.5km-long stretch running across Miyazu-wan is lovely, with white-sand beaches for swimming on the eastern side. It takes about an hour to cross on foot, 15 minutes by bike.

To reach the bridge from the train station, take a right, walk along the main road for 200m until the first light and then take a sharp left.

Chion-in BUDDHIST TEMPLE
(知恩院; ☎0772-22-2553; www.monjudo-chionji.jp; 466 Monju, Miyazu-shi) FREE Steps from the southern end of the Amanohashidate footbridge, this busy temple is home to an Important Cultural Property pagoda from the Muromachi period (late 1500s). The temple's *o-mikuji* (fortunes; ¥300) are shaped like tiny folding fans, which is terribly photogenic when they're hung by the thousands from the branches of daintily pruned pines around the precincts.

Sleeping

There are several hotels and ryokan, many with onsen baths, clustered around the southern end of Amanohashidate. As this is considered a resort destination, they tend to be pricey (and especially so for bay views). Cheaper accommodation can be found in central Miyazu, about 5km from Amanohashidate.

Amanohashidate Youth Hostel HOSTEL ¥
(天橋立ユースホステル; ☎0772-27-0121; www.hashidate-yh.jp; 905 Nakano, Miyazu-shi; dm members/nonmembers ¥2750/3050; P ⊖ ❄ @ ☏) On a hill overlooking the bay, about a 10-minute walk from the northern end of Amanohashidate, this old but well-kept hostel has both Western- and Japanese-style dorms with shared bathroom, simple cooking facilities, rental bicycles (¥100 per hour), a cosy lounge, English-speaking owners and lots of helpful info. Breakfast/dinner costs ¥620/980.

To reach the hostel from Amanohashidate Station, take a local Tankai bus (¥400, 20 minutes, hourly) for Ine and get off at Jinja-mae; the last bus departs at 8.14pm. Follow signs toward Manai-jinja Shintō shrine. The hostel is just before the main *torii*.

Eating

There are many restaurants between Amanohashidate Station and the southern entrance to the sand bar; note that many close around dusk. The northern end has much fewer options. Local specialities include dishes with *asari* (clams), such as *asari-don* (clams on rice) and *asari udon* (clams in noodle soup); both cost around ¥1000 and most restaurants have at least picture menus.

310 Amanohashidate JAPANESE ¥¥
(☎0772-45-1870; 640-7 Benten; set meals ¥1800-2000; ⊙6-10pm, closed irregularly) This unexpectedly chic new spot does set meals of prettily plated grilled fish or sashimi, using seafood caught from the fish market in nearby Miyazu, paired with craft sake. It's on the road in front of Amanohashidate Station, with an English sign out the front. Cover charge ¥250.

Information

Tourist Information Centre (☎0772-22-8030; www.amanohashidate.jp; ⊙9am-6pm; ☏) Inside Amanohashidate Station, with English-speaking staff. There's also an ATM that works with international cards.

Getting There & Away

Amanohashidate Station is accessed via the Kyoto Tango Railway (also known as Tantetsu), which you can pick up at JR Fukuchiyama Station (*tokkyū/futsū* ¥1620/770, 40 minutes/one hour). From Kyoto, take the JR Kinosaki liner to Fukuchiyama (¥2460, 1½ hours), from Osaka the JR Kōnotori Liner (¥3340, 1¾ hours). There are two direct trains daily to/from Kyoto via Fukuchiyama (¥3880, two hours), but JR Pass holders will still have to pay ¥1420/1620 (unreserved/reserved seats) for the non-JR part of the route.

The Kyoto Tango Railway continues to Toyooka (*tokkyū/futsū*, ¥2040/1190, 30 minutes/1½ hours), where you can connect to a JR San-in line train for Kinosaki Onsen (¥200, 12 minutes).

Getting Around

You can cross Amanohashidate on foot, by bicycle or on a motorcycle of less than 125cc capacity. Bicycles (¥400/1600 per two hours/day) can be hired at a number of places.

Central Miyazu is about 5km from Amanohashidate Station. Kyoto Tango Railway connects Amanohashidate Station with Miyazu (¥210, five minutes).

OFF THE BEATEN TRACK

TANGO PENINSULA

Tango-hantō (丹後半島) juts into the Sea of Japan on the north coast of Kyoto Prefecture. Its serrated coast alternates between sandy beaches, gumdrop-shaped islands, bays, inlets and rocky points. If you're travelling between Amanohashidate and Kinosaki Onsen by car, it's a worthy detour

On the southeastern side of the peninsula (just north of Amanohashidate) is the quiet fishing village of **Ine** (伊根; Ine-chō). The village's signature houses, called *funaya*, are built right over the bay Ine-wan, so boats can moor underneath. The best way to see them up close is from the water.

Locally-run **Kameshima-maru** (亀島丸; 0772-32-0585; adult/child ¥1000/free) does 30-minute motorboat tours. Have your accommodation or the **Ine Tourist Information Centre** (伊根町観光案内所; 0772-32-0277; www.ine-kankou.jp/english; 491 Hirata; 9am-5pm;) make a reservation (two-person minimum). The boat will pick you up at the most convenient dock.

For food, head to **Aburaya** (油屋; 0772-32-0750; 459 Kameshima, meals from ¥1500; 11am-3pm Thu-Tue; P), a tiny counter restaurant inside the Funaya-no-sato *michi-no-eki* (road station). It looks utterly unremarkable, but locals swear that its *kaisen-don* (raw fish over rice) never disappoints. It often closes early when it runs out of ingredients. There's a picture menu. While you're here, steal views of the bay from the lookout point.

Buses from Amanohashidate Station will take you as far as Ine (¥400, about 55 minutes, hourly). After that, you're on your own. If you have your own wheels, you can follow the coastal Rte 178 around the peninsula and carry on to Kinosaki Onsen.

Kinosaki Onsen

0796 / POP 3519

Kinosaki Onsen (城崎温泉), on the Japan Sea coast, is the Kansai region's signature onsen resort. A willow-lined canal runs through the town centre, and many of the ryokan and restaurants here retain their traditional charm. Best of all about Kinosaki, however, is its public bathhouse culture; you can splash out on the full ryokan experience or just hop between baths – both, ideally. Though most inns have their own onsen baths, overnight guests clip-clop around the canal to the public ones, in *yukata* (light cotton kimonos) and *geta* (wooden sandals).

The most popular time of year to visit is winter (specifically November to March), when *matsuba-gani* (snow crab), a local speciality, is in season; this is Kinosaki's high season and many accommodations will be pricier.

Kinosaki Onsen is flat and easily walkable, about 20 leisurely minutes from end to end. Trains arrive at Kinosaki Onsen Station, in the southwestern corner of town. From here, Eki-dōri heads north and intersects with the willow-lined river Ōtani-gawa. Turn left on the streets paralleling the river, Kitayanagi-dōri and Minamiyanagi-dōri (north and south willow streets), to reach most onsen, inns and restaurants.

Sights

Genbudō CAVE

(玄武洞) Genbudō is the largest of the five caves at this site, part of San-in Kaigan National Park, with other-worldly surfaces of pillar-like ripples formed by basalt lava 1.6 million years ago.

It's about 5km south of Kinosaki Onsen, accessibly by car or bike, via a route the follows the Maruyama-gawa.

Kinosaki Strawcraft Museum MUSEUM

(城崎麦わら細工伝承館; 0796-32-0515; 376-1 Yushima, Kinosaki-chō; ¥300; 10am-4pm Thu-Tue) This tiny museum in a former *kura* (storehouse) displays *mugiwara-zaiku* (barley-straw crafts) practised locally since 1716. Straw is dyed and cut into tiny pieces, then applied to wood to form incredibly intricate, beautiful patterns. It's located off the river, a short walk from Ichi-no-yu onsen.

Activities

Kinosaki has seven *soto-yu* (public baths), large and small, simple and elaborate. If you visit more than one you'll want to get the *yu-meguri* pass (¥1200), which gives you entry to all of them. Most lodgings have their own *uchi-yu* (private baths) but offer complementary *yu-meguri* passes. All the baths are fed from the same springs, which are naturally alkaline and a little bit salty.

While some public bathhouses in Japan refuse entry to customers with tattoos, Kinosaki is totally cool with your ink.

★ Gosho-no-yu ONSEN
(御所の湯; 448 Yushima, Kinosaki-chō; ¥800; ⏲7am-11pm, closed 1st & 3rd Thu of month) This is Kinosaki's most famous bathhouse, with an entrance designed to look like the Kyoto Imperial Palace; inside it feels more like a countryside onsen, with exposed cypress beams and high ceilings, and a cascading set of rock-strewn outdoor baths. Note that it can get quite crowded.

It's on Yunosato-dōri; keep going past Ichi-no-yu, as the main street diverges from the canal.

Sato-no-yu ONSEN
(さとの湯; 290-36 Imazu, Kinosaki-chō; ¥800; ⏲1-9pm Tue-Sun) Kinosaki's largest bathhouse has a fantastic variety of baths and saunas, including a big rooftop *rotemburo* with waterfalls. The women's and men's baths shift floors daily, so you'll have to go two days in a row to sample all the offerings. It's right outside JR Kinosaki Onsen Station.

Kō-no-yu ONSEN
(鴻の湯; 610 Yushima, Kinosaki-chō; ¥600; ⏲7am-11pm Wed-Mon) At the far end of town (from the train station), this bathhouse has a *rotemburo* in a garden setting.

It's the waters here that form the setting for the legend of Kinosaki Onsen's founding: it's where an injured *kō* (oriental white stork) was discovered 1400 years ago healing its wounds – drawing attention to the restorative powers of this natural hot spring.

Ichi-no-yu ONSEN
(一の湯; 415-1 Yushima, Kinosaki-chō; ¥600; ⏲7am-11pm Thu-Tue) Ichi-no-yu's distinctive architecture – it's designed to look like a kabuki theatre – makes it a local landmark; it's also one of the bigger bathhouses, with an outdoor 'cave bath'.

Sleeping

Kinosaki is a great spot for your ryokan experience; there are many options, from fairly budget to splurge. The ryokan association operates a free shuttle bus, timed to train arrivals, to take you to member inns for check-in.

If you want to truly do Kinosaki on the cheap, consider staying at a business hotel in Toyooka, the nearest city, two stops before Kinosaki Onsen on the San-in line (¥200, 20 minutes).

Koyado Enn RYOKAN ¥¥
(小宿縁; ☎0796-32-4870; www.koyado.net; 219 Yushima, Kinosaki-chō; s/d from ¥8000/9000;) This fairly new inn, with both Japanese- and Western-style rooms, is well set up for solo travellers and those who don't want to be locked into a meal plan. Rooms have toilets and sinks; shared onsen baths can be used privately.

You can choose instead to take your meals at Irori Dining Mikuni (p450), on the 2nd floor, or at Cafe & Bar 3rd (p451), on the ground floor.

Ryokan Yamamotoya RYOKAN ¥¥
(旅館山本屋; ☎0796-32-2114; www.kinosaki.com; 643 Yushima, Kinosaki-chō; r per person incl meals from ¥17,800; P) Right on Yanagi-dōri, conveniently located for Kinosaki's *soto-yu* (public bathhouses), this long-running ryokan (350 years!) is well kept and welcoming. Rooms have river or mountain views but no private bath (sink and toilet only). Solo travellers are accepted in spring and autumn only and must pay a single supplement.

It runs brew-pub Gubigabu (p451) next door.

Mikuniya RYOKAN ¥¥
(三国屋; ☎0796-32-2414; www.kinosaki3928.com; 221 Yushima, Kinosaki-chō; r per person incl meals high/low season from ¥15,120/21,600; @) This long-time traveller favourite is a reliable choice and has friendly, English-speaking staff. Rooms have toilet and sink, and the communal onsen bath can be used privately. Dinner is served in the rooms; if you opt for the Western-style breakfast, it's served at Cafe & Bar 3rd (p451), next door.

Heading into town from the station, it's about 150m along on the right; look for the rickshaw.

Tsuruya RYOKAN ¥¥
(つるや; ☎0796-32-2924; 606 Yushima, Kinosaki-chō; r per person with/without meals from ¥12,550/6830; P) This is a great budget choice, with owners who love welcoming foreign guests. Rooms are simple (with shared facilities) but well cared for, and the onsen bath can be used privately. Book directly (English OK). There's a ¥1000 markup for solo travellers.

It's at the far end of town, a few metres before Kō-no-yu onsen as you approach from the station.

★Nishimuraya Honkan RYOKAN ¥¥¥

(西村屋本館; ☎reception 0796-32-2211, reservations 0796-32-4895; www.nishimuraya.ne.jp/honkan; 469 Yushima, Kinosaki-chō; r per person incl 2 meals high/low season from ¥42,000/32,000, single travellers from ¥48,000; P ❄ 📶) Running for seven generations, this is a fantastic ryokan for a splurge. It excels at everything: beautiful rooms arranged around a central garden; onsen baths made of cypress and stone; seasonal *kaiseki* meals using top local ingredients; and fluent-English-speaking concierges. All rooms have private facilities, and a few have their own *rotemburo* (outdoor baths).

While the building is not historic like the Honkan (main building), the ryokan's annexe, the Hiratakan, adheres to the same principles of traditional Japanese design and some guests may appreciate its quieter location, off the main road.

Nishimuraya Hotel Shōgetsu-tei RYOKAN ¥¥¥

(西村屋ホテル紹月庭; ☎0796-32-3535; www.nishimuraya.ne.jp/shogetsu; 1016-2 Yushima, Kinosaki-chō; r per person incl 2 meals from ¥28,000, single travellers from ¥38,000; P ❄ 📶) A bit far from town and in a rather ordinary building, this modern property is managed by the same family that runs Nishimuraya Honkan and offers a more entry-level luxury experience. The Japanese-style rooms are nicely done up (skip the Western-style ones), with en-suite facilities. Rather large, this is a good bet when other places are full.

There's an option to rent one of the private *rotemburo* (¥8640 for up to four guests, 70 minutes) that come with large tubs, rock saunas, gorgeous garden views and a complimentary bottle of sparkling wine.

Eating & Drinking

From November to March Kinosaki's ryokan and restaurants offer decadent crab feasts; prices are highest for fresh crab (some places use frozen). While many visitors choose to eat breakfast and dinner at their accommodation, there are enough restaurants staying open for dinner that you can skip the meal plan without getting stuck.

Thanks to the late hours of many of Kinosaki's *soto-yu* (public baths), there's a lot more life in this onsen resort than most after dark.

Okeshō SEAFOOD ¥¥

(おけしょう海中苑; ☎0796-29-4832; www.okesyo.com; 132 Yushima, Kinosaki-chō; meals from ¥1080; ⏰11am-6.45pm) Located above a fish market, this casual restaurant is a popular local spot for *kaisen-don* (raw seafood on rice; ¥1400 to ¥1950), but there are also tempura and grilled items on the menu. Between November and March you can splash out on crab feasts (from ¥10,000 per person). It's on a corner, with a ship's hull over the entrance.

You can also pick out your own seafood at the market and have the kitchen prepare it for you (at a roughly 40% mark-up from market rates).

Masuya NOODLES ¥¥

(ますや; ☎0796-32-2642; 654 Yushima, Kinosaki-chō; meals ¥900-1550; ⏰11am-9.30pm) Soba and udon are handmade here using local ingredients; try the house speciality, *kamo-zaru* (chilled soba served on a bamboo mat with hot broth and duck meat on the side). It's a small, cosy place that paints a picture of an older Kinosaki.

Orizuru SUSHI ¥¥

(をり鶴; ☎0796-32-2203; www.ori-zuru.com; 396 Yushima, Kinosaki-chō; lunch sets ¥1000-3200, sushi sets ¥1900-5300; ⏰11am-2pm & 5-9.30pm Wed-Mon) This is an elegant sushi counter, frequented by locals, offering reasonably priced set meals. In winter you can sample local crab sourced from Tsuiyama harbour, just 10 minutes away, in a variety of ways, from *kani-nigiri* (crab sushi; ¥2200) to a full-on crab feast (from ¥20,000 per person).

It's between Ichi-no-yu (p449) and Gosho-no-yu (p449) onsen, on the opposite side of the street, with a small, illuminated white sign with the kanji for sushi (鮨).

Irori Dining Mikuni STEAK ¥¥¥

(いろりダイニング三國; ☎0796-32-4870; 2nd fl, 219 Yushima, Kinosaki-chō; meal sets ¥1800-4600, steak sets ¥4800-31,200; ⏰11am-2.30pm & 6-10pm Thu-Tue) Mikuni serves local speciality *Tajima-gyū* (a high-end brand of Japanese beef). Different cuts are served different ways, and not just as steaks: sirloin, for example, is seared and sliced thin, served over rice (¥4600); you can also get a good curry made with the same premium beef for just ¥1800.

Reserve a day in advance for splurge-worthy *yakiniku* (grilled meat; ¥9180), *shabu-shabu* (¥11,340) and sukiyaki sets (thin slices of beef cooked in sake, soy and vinegar broth, and dipped in raw egg; ¥11,340).

Gubigabu PUB FOOD ¥¥

(グビガブ; ☎0796-32-4545; www.gubigabu.com; 646 Yushima, Kinosaki-chō; mains ¥800-2800; ⏰11.30am-10pm, closed Thu & 3rd Wed of month) This craft-beer pub near the town centre has four locally brewed house beers on tap and a diverse menu that includes dishes with Tajima beef, such as curry and *gyū-don* (simmered beef on rice).

There's also a counter at the ryokan next door where you can get takeaway paper cups of beer.

Cafe & Bar 3rd CAFE, BAR

(219 Yushima, Kinosaki-chō; coffee from ¥450, beer from ¥600; ⏰cafe 8am-7pm daily, bar 8pm-midnight Thu-Tue; 📶) With convenient early hours and open generously late, this simple spot serves pour-over coffee, with beans from cult-fave Tokyo roaster Onibus, and local Kinosaki beer. Breakfast (¥950), served until 10am, is toast and eggs or granola and yoghurt, plus a drink.

If you're staying at Koyado Enn (p449) or Mikuniya (p449) and sign up for the Western-style breakfast, it will be served here.

ℹ Information

There are two information centres opposite the station. Pick up a local map at either, or at the train station.

Ryokan Information Centre (お宿案内所; ☎0796-32-4141; 78 Yushima, Kinosaki-chō; ⏰9am-6pm) Accommodation booking, luggage storage (¥500 per item) or forwarding to your accommodation (¥100 per item), and bicycle rentals (¥400/800 per two hours/day; return by 5pm). Some English spoken.

Sozoro (そぞろ; ☎0796-32-0013; www.kinosaki-info.com; 96 Yushima, Kinosaki-chō; ⏰9am-6pm; 📶) Kinosaki's main tourist-information centre has English-speaking staff and bicycle rentals (¥500/1000 per two hours/day; return by 5pm). It also runs various sightseeing tours and activities; inquiries should be made in advance through the website.

ℹ Getting There & Away

Kinosaki is on the JR San-in line. There are three daily Kinosaki Liner limited-express trains from Kyoto (¥4320, 2½ hours); from Osaka or Shin-Osaka Station take the Kōnotori Liner (¥5080, three hours, seven daily). From Kyoto you can also take a limited express to Fukuchiyama and pick up one of the more frequent trains from Osaka.

From Kinosaki you can continue west along the San-in coast to Tottori (¥1320, two hours).

AT A GLANCE

POPULATION
Hiroshima: 1.19

NUMBER OF INLAND SEA ISLANDS
727

BEST PORT TOWN
Tomo-no-ura (p490)

BEST BOUTIQUE HOTEL
Benesse House (p480)

BEST OKONOMIYAKI
Okonomi-mura (p461)

WHEN TO GO

Mar–May & Sep–Nov Mild and photogenic, spring and autumn get most of the attention.

Jul–Sep Beach weather draws crowds to the Inland Sea islands and Sea of Japan coast.

Aug Hiroshima remembers 6 August with services and a river of lanterns.

Hiroshima-jō (p457)
COWARDLION/SHUTTERSTOCK ©

Hiroshima & Western Honshū

Travellers to Western Honshū (本州西部) will find a tale of two coastlines. San-yō (literally 'sunny side of the mountains'), looking southwards out over the Inland Sea, boasts the bigger cities, the narrow-laned portside and hillside towns, ceramic history and the fast train. This coast holds the region's big name – indelibly scarred but thriving and warm-hearted Hiroshima.

On the other side of the dividing Chūgoku mountain range, San-in (literally 'in the shade of the mountains') gazes northwards across the expanse of the Sea of Japan. Up here, it's all about an unhurried pace, onsen (hot spring) villages that see few foreigners, historic sites, wind-battered coastlines and great hospitality.

INCLUDES

Hiroshima & Western Honshū Highlights

1 Hiroshima (p456) Reflecting on a tragic past in this cosmopolitan city.

2 Naoshima (p478) Marvelling at the meeting of nature and contemporary art on this island.

3 Shimanami Kaidō (p470) Island-hopping by bicycle via this chain of bridges to Shikoku.

4 Taikodani-Inari-jinja (p509) Walking through the shrine gates in the mountain town of Tsuwano.

5 Onomichi (p469) Following in the footsteps of cats on a temple hunt.

6 Izumo Taisha (p503) Seeing where the gods go on holiday at this Shintō shrine.

7 Matsue (p498) Strolling around the moated castle and soaking up a gorgeous sunset.

8 Oki Islands (p495) Getting way off the beaten track in these nature- and culture-rich islands.

9 Iwami Ginzan (p504) Exploring the World Heritage–listed silver-mine district.

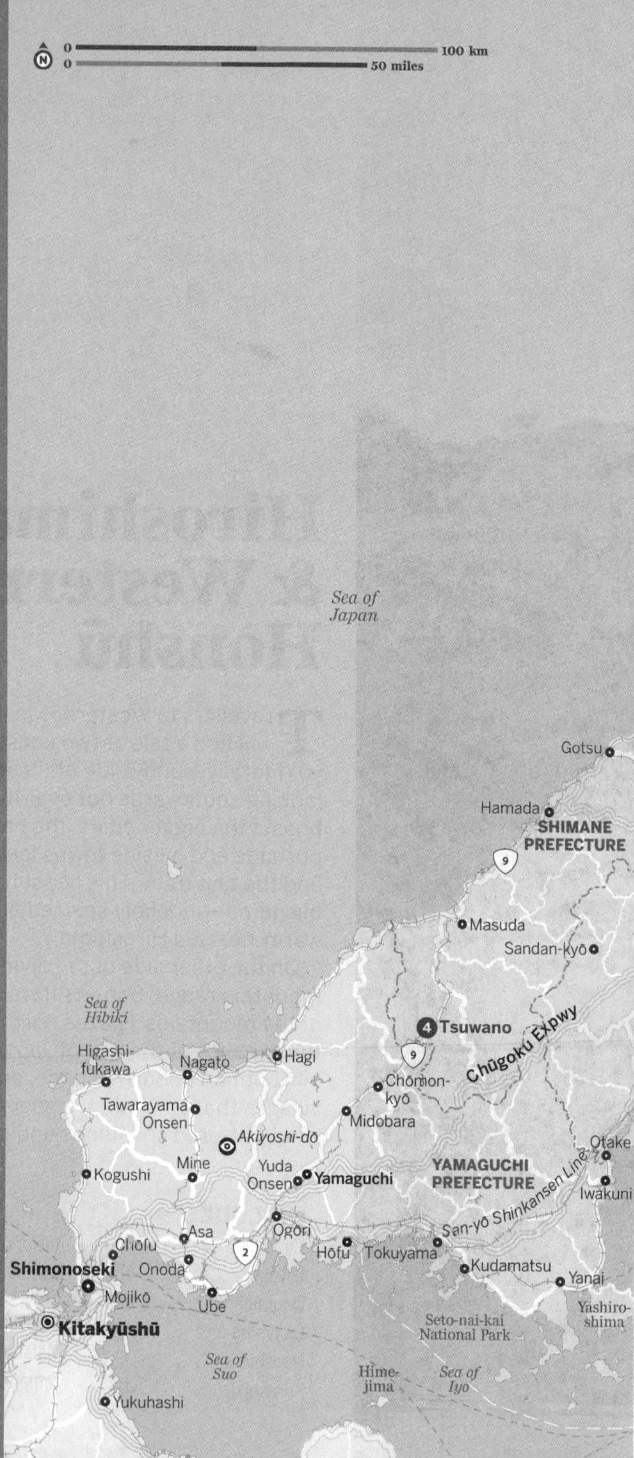

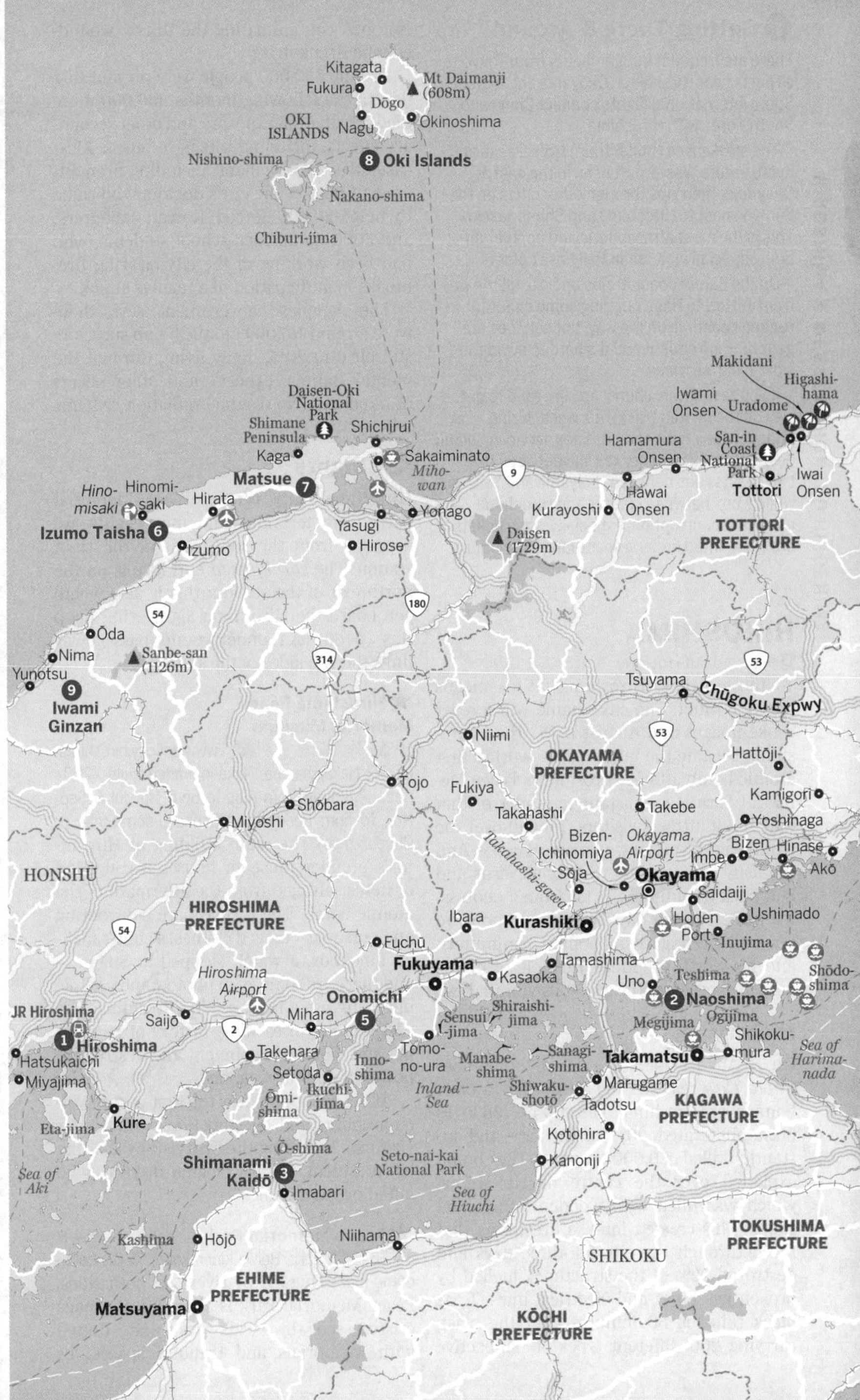

Kitagata
Fukura
Mt Daimanji (608m)
Dōgo
OKI ISLANDS
Nagu
Okinoshima
Nishino-shima
8 Oki Islands
Nakano-shima
Chiburi-jima
Makidani
Higashi-hama
Iwami Onsen
Uradome
Daisen-Oki National Park
Shimane Peninsula
Shichirui
Hamamura Onsen
San-in Coast National Park
Kaga
Sakaiminato
Iwai Onsen
Miho-wan
Matsue 7
Tottori
Hino-misaki
Hinomi-saki
Hirata
Hawai Onsen
Kurayoshi
Yonago
Yasugi
Izumo Taisha 6
Izumo
Hirose
Daisen (1729m)
TOTTORI PREFECTURE
Ōda
Nima
Sanbe-san (1126m)
Yunotsu
9 Iwami Ginzan
Tsuyama
Chūgoku Expwy
Niimi
OKAYAMA PREFECTURE
Hattōji
Tojo
Fukiya
Kamigori
Shōbara
Takebe
Miyoshi
Takahashi
Yoshinaga
Bizen-Ichinomiya
Okayama Airport
Bizen
Hinase
Takahashi-gawa
Imbe
Akō
HONSHŪ
Sōja
Okayama
Saidaiji
HIROSHIMA PREFECTURE
Ibara
Kurashiki
Hoden Port
Ushimado
Fuchū
Inujima
Fukuyama
Tamashima
Hiroshima Airport
Kasaoka
Teshima
Shōdo-shima
Onomichi
Uno
Shiraishi-jima
2 Naoshima
JR Hiroshima
Saijō
Mihara
Sensui-jima
Megijima
Ogijima
5
Shikoku-mura
1 Hiroshima
Takehara
Tomo-no-ura
Manabe-shima
Sanagi-shima
Takamatsu
Sea of Harima-nada
Hatsukaichi
Setoda
Inno-shima
Miyajima
Ikuchi-jima
Inland Sea
Shiwaku-shotō
Marugame
Ōmi-shima
Tadotsu
KAGAWA PREFECTURE
Eta-jima
Kure
Kotohira
Ō-shima
Seto-nai-kai National Park
Shimanami Kaidō 3
Kanonji
Sea of Aki
Imabari
Sea of Hiuchi
TOKUSHIMA PREFECTURE
Kashima
Hōjō
Niihama
SHIKOKU
EHIME PREFECTURE
Matsuyama
KŌCHI PREFECTURE
9
180
54
314
53
2

Getting There & Around

There are frequent budget flights from Tokyo to airports near Hiroshima, Okayama and Matsue. Some international flights connect China and South Korea with Hiroshima.

The *shinkansen* (bullet train) from Osaka and Kyoto enters Western Honshū in the east at Okayama, then zips through other cities on the San-yō coast to Hiroshima and Shimonoseki. This is the most atmospheric and popular option, especially for Japan Rail Pass holders.

On the San-in coast, trains operate all the way from Tottori to Hagi, hugging some beautiful rugged coastline on the way, but services are generally infrequent and it's hard to avoid the slow 'local' services.

If you're really in a hurry up here (and to get way off the beaten track), it's worth hiring a car. There are few train and bus lines servicing inland destinations: the major rail link between the two coasts runs between Okayama and Yonago, while a bus between Matsue and Hiroshima offers a second option, especially while tickets are discounted under a years-long promotion.

HIROSHIMA

082 / POP 1.19 MILION

To most people, Hiroshima (広島) means just one thing. The city's name will forever evoke images of 6 August 1945, when Hiroshima became the target of the world's first atomic-bomb attack. Hiroshima's Peace Memorial Park is a constant reminder of that day, and it attracts visitors from all over the world with its moving message of peace. And the leafy city, with its wide boulevards and laid-back friendliness, is far from a depressing place. Present-day Hiroshima is home to an ever-thriving cosmopolitan community, and it's worth spending a couple of nights here to experience the city at its vibrant best.

History

On 6 August 1945, the US B-29 bomber *Enola Gay* released the 'Little Boy' atomic bomb over Hiroshima. The 2000°C (3630°F) blast obliterated 90% of the city and instantly killed 80,000 people. The bomb exploded over the centre of Hiroshima, which was filled with wooden homes and shops. This created intense firestorms that raced through the city for three days and destroyed 92% of the structures, fuelled by broken gas pipes and electrical lines. Toxic black rain fell 30 minutes after the blast, carrying 200 different types of radioactive isotopes, contaminating the thirsty wounded who drank it.

Around 350,000 people were present that day. In the following months, 130,000 more died of radiation exposure and other secondary effects, including intensive burns. Most casualties were civilians, including firefighters and 90% of the city's doctors who came to help; 20,000 forced Korean labourers; and 6000 junior-high-school students, who had been working in the city clearing firebreaks in anticipation of a regular attack.

The Japanese government says there were around 187,000 atomic bomb survivors still alive in 2015, many living through the mental trauma, cancers, and other effects of radiation. (No residual radiation remains today.)

Sights

Hiroshima's city centre, Peace Memorial Park, tram terminus and most sights are accessed from the south exit of the train station. The *shinkansen* entrance is on the north exit of the station; this is also where you board the Hiroshima Sightseeing Loop Bus (p460). An underground passageway links the two sides of the station.

★Hiroshima Peace Memorial Museum MUSEUM

(広島平和記念資料館; www.pcf.city.hiroshima.jp; 1-2 Nakajima-chō, Naka-ku; adult/child ¥200/free; 8.30am-7pm Aug, to 6pm Mar-Jul & Sep-Nov, to 5pm Dec-Feb; Genbaku-dōmu-mae or Chūden-mae) The main building of Hiroshima's premier museum houses a collection of items salvaged from the aftermath of the atomic bomb. The displays are confronting and personal – ragged clothes, a child's melted lunchbox, a watch stopped at 8.15am – and there are some grim photographs. While upsetting, it's a must-see in Hiroshima. The east building presents a history of Hiroshima and of the development and destructive power of nuclear weapons.

At the exit, don't miss the first-person video accounts and guestbook of world-leader visitors – including the first visit by a sitting US president, Barack Obama in 2016, who gifted origami cranes.

★Peace Memorial Park PARK

(平和記念公園; Heiwa-kinen-kōen; Genbaku-dōmu-mae) Hugged by rivers on both sides, Peace Memorial Park is a large, leafy space crisscrossed by walkways and dotted with memorials and tranquil spaces for reflection. Its central feature is the long tree-lined Pond of Peace leading to the **cenotaph** (原爆死没者慰霊碑). This curved concrete monument holds the names of all the known victims of the bomb. Also at the pond is the **Flame of Peace** (平和の灯), set to burn on until all the world's nuclear weapons are destroyed.

Look through the cenotaph down the pond and you'll see it frames the Flame of Peace and the Atomic Bomb Dome across the river – the park was planned so that these features form a straight line, with the Peace Memorial Museum at its southern end.

Just north of the road through the park is the **Children's Peace Monument** (原爆の子の像), inspired by Sadako Sasaki, who was two years old at the time of the atomic bomb. When Sadako developed leukaemia at 11 years of age, she decided to fold 1000 paper cranes. In Japan, the crane is the symbol of longevity and happiness, and she believed if she achieved that target she would recover. She died before reaching her goal, but her classmates folded the rest. A monument was built in 1958. Sadako's story inspired a nationwide spate of paper-crane folding that continues to this day. Surrounding the monument are strings of thousands of colourful paper cranes, sent here by schoolchildren from around the country and all over the world.

Nearby is the **Korean Atomic Bomb Victims Memorial** (韓国人原爆犠牲者慰霊碑). Many Koreans were shipped over to work as slave labour during WWII, and Koreans accounted for more than one in 10 of those killed by the atomic bomb. Just north of this memorial is the **Atomic Bomb Memorial Mound** – the ashes of thousands of unclaimed or unidentified victims are interred in a vault below.

There are other monuments and statues throughout the park, and plenty of benches, including those along the riverside looking across to the Atomic Bomb Dome; they make this a pleasant area to take a break and take it all in.

★Atomic Bomb Dome — HISTORIC SITE

(原爆ドーム, Genbaku Dome; 1-10 Otemachi; ⏲24hr; 🚊Genbaku-dōmu-mae) FREE Perhaps the starkest reminder of the destruction visited upon Hiroshima in WWII is the Atomic Bomb Dome. Built by a Czech architect in 1915, it was the Industrial Promotion Hall until the bomb exploded almost directly above it. Everyone inside was killed, but the building was one of very few left standing near the epicentre. A decision was taken after the war to preserve the shell as a memorial.

The building has since become a haunting symbol of the city, and was declared a Unesco World Heritage Site in 1996. Try to wander past in the evening when it's quiet and the propped-up ruins are floodlit.

HIROSHIMA READING

- 'Hiroshima' (1946) by John Hersey – the article by the Pulitzer Prize–winning writer (available at www.newyorker.com).
- *Hiroshima: Three Witnesses* (1990); ed Richard H Minear – translation of first-hand accounts of three authors.
- *Black Rain* (1965) by Ibuse Masuji – a novel depicting the lives of those who survived.
- *Sadako and the Thousand Paper Cranes* (1977) by Eleanor Coerr – aimed at younger readers, based on the true story of Sasaki Sadako.

Hiroshima National Peace Memorial Hall for the Atomic Bomb Victims — MEMORIAL

(国立広島原爆死没者追悼平和祈念館; www.hiro-tsuitokinenkan.go.jp; 1-6 Nakajima-chō, Naka-ku; ⏲8.30am-7pm Aug, to 6pm Mar-Jul & Sep-Nov, to 5pm Dec-Feb; 🚊Genbaku-dōmu-mae or Hon-dōri) FREE A softly lit internal walkway leads down into this cool, contemplative space, where the walls show a circular panorama of Hiroshima and the names of its neighbourhoods at the time of the atomic bomb. The fountain at the centre represents the moment the bomb was dropped (8.15am), while the water offers relief to the victims. An adjoining room shows the names and photographs of those who perished. Before leaving, it's worth taking time to watch the evocative testimonies from survivors.

The memorial hall was built by architect Tange Kenzō, who also designed the nearby Peace Memorial Museum, Cenotaph and Flame of Peace.

Hiroshima-jō — CASTLE

(広島城, Hiroshima Castle; www.rijo-castle.jp; 21-1 Moto-machi; tower ¥370; ⏲9am-6pm Mar-Nov, to 5pm Dec-Feb; 🚊Kamiya-chō) Also known as Carp Castle (鯉城; Rijō), Hiroshima-jō was

Hiroshima

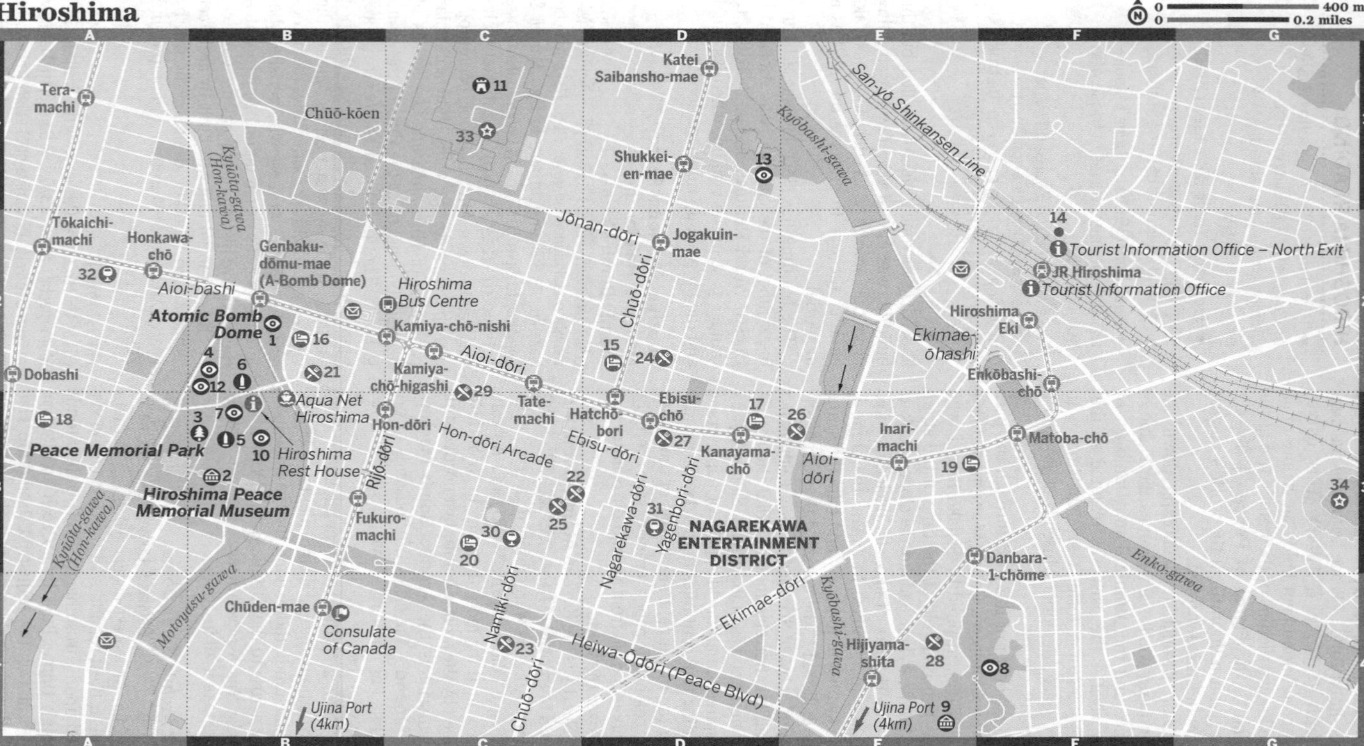
0 400 m
0 0.2 miles
Tera-machi
Chūō-kōen
11
33
Katei Saibansho-mae
Shukkei-en-mae
13
Kyōbashi-gawa
San-yō Shinkansen Line
Kyūōta-gawa (Hon-kawa)
Tōkaichi-machi
Honkawa-chō
32
Aioi-bashi
Genbaku-dōmu-mae (A-Bomb Dome)
Hiroshima Bus Centre
Kamiya-chō-nishi
Jōnan-dōri
Jogakuin-mae
Chūō-dōri
14
Tourist Information Office – North Exit
JR Hiroshima
Tourist Information Office
Hiroshima Eki
Ekimae-ōhashi
Enkōbashi-chō
Atomic Bomb Dome
1
16
4
6
12
21
Dobashi
Aioi-dōri
Kamiya-chō-higashi
29
15
24
Aqua Net Hiroshima
7
3
18
5
10
Peace Memorial Park
Hiroshima Rest House
Hon-dōri
Hon-dōri Arcade
Tate-machi
Hatchō-bori
Ebisu-chō
27
17
26
Kanayama-chō
Aioi-dōri
Inari-machi
Matoba-chō
19
2
Hiroshima Peace Memorial Museum
Rijō-dōri
Fukuro-machi
Ebisu-dōri
22
25
30
20
Nagarekawa-dōri
Yagenbori-dōri
31
NAGAREKAWA ENTERTAINMENT DISTRICT
34
Danbara-1-chōme
Enko-gawa
Kyūōta-gawa (Hon-kawa)
Motoyasu-gawa
Chūden-mae
Consulate of Canada
Namiki-dōri
23
Heiwa-Ōdōri (Peace Blvd)
Ekimae-dōri
Kyōbashi-gawa
Hijiyama-shita
28
8
Chūō-dōri
Ujina Port (4km)
Ujina Port (4km)
9

Hiroshima

originally constructed in 1589, but much of it was dismantled following the Meiji Restoration. What remained was totally destroyed by the bomb and rebuilt in 1958. In the north end there's a small five-level museum with historical items, but most visitors go for the tower with views over the impressive moat. The surrounding park is a pleasant (and free) place for a stroll. Enter from the east or south.

Shukkei-en GARDENS
(縮景園; www.shukkeien.jp; 2-11 Kami-nobori-chō, Naka-ku; ¥260; 9am-6pm Apr-Sep, to 5pm Oct-Mar; Shukkei-en-mae) Modelled after West Lake in Hangzhou, China, Shukkei-en was built in 1620 for *daimyō* (domain lord) Asano Nagaakira. The garden's name means 'contracted view', and it attempts to re-create grand vistas in miniature. Pathways lead through a series of 'landscapes' and views around an island-dotted pond.

Shukkei-en was destroyed by the bomb, though many of the trees and plants survived to blossom again the following year, and the park and its buildings have long since been restored to their original splendour.

Hiroshima City Manga Library LIBRARY
(広島市まんが図書館; 082-261-0330; www.library.city.hiroshima.jp/manga; 1-4 Hijiyama-kōen; 10am-5pm Tue-Sun; Hijiyama-shita) An obvious pit stop for manga (Japanese comics) enthusiasts, this library has a small section of foreign-language manga and a collection of vintage and rare manga. Grab the English-language pamphlet and head up to the 2nd floor.

It's closed on the last day of odd-numbered months.

Mazda Museum MUSEUM
(マツダミュージアム; 082-252-5050; www.mazda.com/about/museum; by reservation Mon-Fri; Mukainada) FREE Mazda is popular for the chance to see the impressive 7km assembly line. English-language tours (90 minutes) are available at 10am weekdays, but it's best to check the website or with the tourist office for the current times. Reservations are required and can be made online or by phone.

The museum is a short walk from JR Mukainada (向洋) Station, two stops from Hiroshima on the San-yō line.

Hiroshima City Museum of Contemporary Art GALLERY
(広島市現代美術館, MOCA; www.hiroshima-moca.jp; 1-1 Hijiyama-kōen; ¥300; 10am-5pm Tue-Sun; Hijiyama-shita) Fans of contemporary art should drop into this modern museum in Hijiyama-kōen, where the exhibits change regularly and may include anything from large-scale installations to video.

Outside is a sculpture garden. Check ahead before your visit, as there are sometimes special exhibitions (additional fees may apply).

Tours

Hiroshima Sightseeing Loop Bus BUS

(www.chugoku-jrbus.co.jp; single/day pass ¥200/400) The *meipurū-pu* (loop bus) has two overlapping routes – orange and green – taking in the main sights and museums of the city, including the Peace Memorial Park and Atomic Bomb Dome. Both routes begin and end on the *shinkansen* entrance (north) side of Hiroshima Station, running from about 9am to 6pm (the green route runs later during summer).

Passengers can get on and off the bus at any stop. There is a bus about every 15 minutes – both orange and green route buses run every half-hour. Tickets and day passes can be purchased from the driver. Those with a JR Pass (and JR West passes covering Hiroshima) can ride for free. On the bus there are announcements in English, though the background info on the sights is all in Japanese.

Festivals & Events

Peace Memorial Ceremony MEMORIAL SERVICE

(広島平和記念式典) On the anniversary of the atomic bombing, 6 Aug, a memorial service is held in Peace Memorial Park and thousands of paper lanterns for the souls of the dead are floated down the Kyūōta-gawa from in front of the Atomic Bomb Dome.

Sleeping

Hiroshima's accommodation is clustered around the station, near Peace Memorial Park, and along the main thoroughfares of Aioi-dōri and Heiwa-Ōdōri. The city is compact enough that, wherever you base yourself, you're never more than a short walk or tram ride away from the main sights.

★K's House Hiroshima HOSTEL ¥

(ケイズハウス広島; 082-568-7244; www.kshouse.jp/hiroshima-e; 1-8-9 Matoba-chō; dm/s/tw from ¥2600/5800/7900; Matoba-chō) K's House has a great location not far from the station. There are small dorms and comfortable tatami rooms with shared shower rooms, or you can pay a little more for a Western room with en suite. The kitchen-lounge is modern and a good size, there's a rooftop terrace, and staff are helpful.

The entrance is at the back of the block – turn left off Aioi-dōri to find it.

Santiago Guesthouse HOSTEL ¥

(サンチャゴゲストハウス広島; 082-545-8477; www.santiago-guesthouse-hiroshima-jp.book.direct; 4-18 Naka-machi; dm/tw without bathroom from ¥2500/7000, f from ¥25,000; Fukuro-machi) Its carpeted halls make Santiago feel hotel-like, but the sociable kitchen-lounge space promotes swapping travel tips, while being large enough to keep to yourself if you prefer. Dorms are in capsule-like bunks, and there are ample shower rooms, though you'll have to scurry to a different floor if staying in a private twin. The roof-terrace family room is immense.

J-Hoppers Hiroshima HOSTEL ¥

(ジェイホッパーズ広島ゲストハウス; 082-233-1360; https://hiroshima.j-hoppers.com; 5-16 Dobashi-chō; dm/tw without bathroom from ¥2500/5400; Dobashi) This clean old favourite near the Peace Memorial Park feels more like someone's house than a standard hostel. Private rooms and get tatami treatment, and the latter have private-feeling capsules. It's a small but cosy place with a friendly English-speaking crew and cheap laundry and bike use. Singles come at the price of a twin.

★Hotel Active Hiroshima HOTEL ¥¥

(ホテルアクティブ広島; 082-212-0001; www.hotel-active.com/hiroshima; 15-3 Nobori-chō; s/d incl breakfast from ¥8800/11,000; Kanayama-chō) With its satiny coverlets and backlit headboards, Hotel Active tries for a little more style than the average business hotel. It's right in the heart of things, and extras such as free-drink machines, a spa and an included buffet breakfast make this a good-value option.

Some English is spoken; it may be easier to book by phone than via the Japanese-only website.

Candeo HOTEL ¥¥

(082-511-1300; www.candeohotels.com; 14-1 Hatchō-bori; s/d incl breakfast from ¥11,185/14,325; Hatchō-bori or Ebisu-chō) Stylish Candeo has good-sized carpeted rooms with plush beds, impressive smart TVs, spacious desks, and small bathrooms with tech touches such as anti-fog mirrors. The extensive buffet breakfast is served in a ballroom-like space with floor-to-ceiling windows, and there's a spa upstairs. It's walkable to most attractions and one stop on the sightseeing bus from the station.

★**Hiroshima Inn Aioi** RYOKAN ¥¥¥
(広島の宿相生; ☎082-247-9331; www.galilei.ne.jp/aioi; 1-3-14 Ōtemachi; r per person with meals from ¥19,900; ; Genbaku-dōmu-mae) At this fine traditional inn, kick back in *a yukata* (light cotton kimono) and enjoy city and park views from your tatami room, or while lazing in the large bath on the 7th floor. The meals are an elaborate traditional spread of dishes, and you can opt for breakfast or dinner only.

Welcoming staff speak just a little English, but do their best to accommodate.

Eating

Hiroshima has an excellent range of Japanese and international eating options for all budgets, especially west of Peace Memorial Park and south of the Hon-dōri covered arcade. Many restaurants offer good-value set-lunch menus, and mall basements are budget-friendly. Hiroshima is famous for oysters and *Hiroshima-yaki* (noodle- and meat-layered *okonomiyaki*; savoury pancakes). Breakfast options are limited to bakeries.

★**Okonomi-mura** OKONOMIYAKI ¥
(お好み村; www.okonomimura.jp; 2nd-4th fl, 5-13 Shintenchi; dishes ¥800-1300; 11am-2am; Ebisu-chō) This Hiroshima institution is a touristy but fun place to get acquainted with *okonomiyaki* and chat with the cooks over a hot griddle. There are 25 stalls spread over three floors, each serving up hearty variations of the local speciality. Pick a floor and find an empty stool at whichever counter takes your fancy. Look for the entrance stairs off Chūō-dōri, on the opposite side of the square to the white Parco shopping centre.

★**Hassei** OKONOMIYAKI ¥
(八誠; ☎082-242-8123; 4-17 Fujimi-chō; dishes ¥600-1300; 11.30am-2pm & 5.30-11pm Tue-Sat, 5.30-11pm Sun; Chūden-mae) The walls of this popular *okonomiyaki* specialist are covered with the signatures and messages of famous and not-so-famous satisfied customers. The tasty, generous layers of cabbage, noodles and other ingredients are indeed satisfying – a half-order is probably more than enough at lunchtime.

Hassei is on a side street one block south of Heiwa-Ōdōri.

Maido Ōkini JAPANESE ¥
(まいどおおきに; ☎082-225-4477; 7-28 Teppōchō; dishes ¥108-410; 10.30am-9.30pm Mon-Fri, 11am-9pm Sat) If you want to get off the tourist circuit and eat with local workers, this *shokudō* (small budget restaurant) serves authentic and excellent-value dishes, conveniently on display. Take a tray and pick up the freshly cooked dishes you want, canteen style. Choices such as pork with bean sprouts, okra, grilled salmon, and spinach are simple and tasty.

Sushi-tei SUSHI ¥
(すし亭; ☎082-249-1808; 4-21 Ebisu-chō; dishes ¥100-700, set menus ¥865-2160; 5pm-midnight Mon-Sat, 11.30am-10pm Sun; Ebisu-chō) If choosing sushi and sashimi seems overwhelming, the good set menus at Sushi-tei can sort you out with eight to 12 pieces of artfully prepared fatty tuna, salmon, egg, shrimp, sea urchin, eel and squid. The bar and tables are equally popular with solo diners and groups, lingering over beers and sake. Ask for an English menu.

Antonio SEAFOOD ¥
(☎082-546-0777; http://antonio.owst.jp; 1-5-18 Ōtemachi; dishes ¥350-1280; Hon-dōri) A seafood restaurant that wants to give the impression of dining at a market somewhere in Portugal, complete with (Japanese) produce plucked from an ice display. The mood is folksy bistro though, with warm lighting and wooden tables. No meat dishes, just good fish carpaccio, squid pasta, salsa crab and shrimp-and-scallop skewers.

Bakudanya NOODLES ¥
(ばくだん屋; ☎082-546-0089; www.bakudanya.net; 2-12 Shintenchi; noodles ¥700-1060; 11.30am-midnight Mon-Thu, to 2am Fri & Sat; Ebisu-chō) Try the famous Hiroshima *tsukemen* at this simple street-corner eatery. *Tsukemen* is a ramen-like dish in which noodles and soup come separately. These restaurants invented the dish, and the chain has spread across the country. It's opposite a 'Don Quijote' store.

There are other branches around the city, including on the *shinkansen* side of Hiroshima Station.

★**Tōshō** TOFU ¥¥
(豆匠; ☎082-506-1028; www.toufu-tosho.jp; 6-24 Hijiyama-chō; set meals ¥2000-5000; 11am-3pm & 5-10pm Mon-Sat, to 9pm Sun; ; Danbara-1-chōme) In a traditional wooden building overlooking a large garden with a pond and waterfall, Tōshō specialises in homemade tofu, served in a variety of tasty and beautifully presented forms by kimono-clad staff. Even the sweets are tofu based. There is a

WORTH A TRIP

SANDAN GORGE

Sandan-kyō (三段峡, Sandan Gorge) is an 11km ravine about 50km northwest of Hiroshima, within the Nishi-Chūgoku-Sanchi Quasi-National Park (西中国山地国定公園). A trail follows the flow of the Shibaki-gawa through the gorge, offering visitors waterfalls, swimming holes, forests and fresh air. The hike is very popular in autumn, when the leaves change colour. Hiroshima tourist office has a hiking map in English.

A dozen buses a day run from the Hiroshima Bus Centre to Sandan-kyō – it's best to catch the one express service (¥1440, 80 minutes, 8am) which returns at 3pm. The bus terminates at the southern end of the gorge.

range of set courses, with some pictures and basic English on the menu.

From the tram stop, continue walking in the direction of the tram and turn left uphill after Hijiyama shrine.

Vegimo VEGAN ¥¥
(ベジモ野菜食堂; 082-236-1230; www.vegimo-yasai.com; 1-5-11 Kamiya-chō; lunch sets ¥860-1130, mains from ¥1200; 11.30am-3pm & 5.30-11pm;) This chic, bright restaurant is all blond wood and stone, serving mostly vegan deli plates of organic, local produce – salad, curry and veg with brown rice, or an excellent vegan burger. There's also grilled fish with olive tapenade, grass-fed beef stew, alcohol and juices.

Oyster Conclave Kaki-tei SEAFOOD ¥¥
(牡蠣亭; 082-221-8990; www.kakitei.jp; 11 Hashimoto-chō; mains ¥800-1800; 11.30am-2.30pm & 5-10pm Thu-Mon; Kanayama-chō) Come to this intimate riverside bistro for local oysters prepared in a range of mouth-watering ways. Lunch is a set menu (¥1800) of oysters in various guises, served with salad and soup; an à la carte menu is available in the evenings.

Drinking & Nightlife

Hiroshima is a great city for a weekend night out, with bars and pubs to suit whatever mood you're in. The city's main entertainment district is made up of hundreds of bars, restaurants and karaoke joints crowding the lanes between Aioi-dōri and Heiwa-Ōdōri in the city centre. Most places serve light meals or snacks, and some have live music.

★**Organza** BAR
(ヲルガン座; 082-295-1553; www.organ-za.com; 2nd fl, Morimoto Bldg, 1-4-32 Tōkaichi-machi; 5.30pm-2am Tue-Fri, 11.30am-2am Sat, 11.30am-midnight Sun; Honkawa-chō) Bookshelves, old-fashioned furniture, a piano and a stuffed deer head all add to the busy surrounds at this smoky lounge-bar. Organza hosts an eclectic schedule of live events (from acoustic guitar to cabaret), some with a cover charge, and food is also served. Lunch on weekends only.

★**Koba** BAR
(コバ; 082-249-6556; 3rd fl, Rego Bldg, 1-4 Naka-machi; 6pm-2am Thu-Tue; Ebisu-chō) It's bound to be a good night if you drop into this laid-back place, where the friendly metal-loving musician owner 'Bom-san' can be found serving drinks and cooking up small tasty meals. There is occasional live music.

It's up the stairs in a concrete building, just behind Stussy.

Ninjō Ganko Yatai PUB
(人情がんこ屋台; 082-247-7662; 6.30pm-7am; Kanayama-chō) Six small *izakaya* (Japanese pub-eateries) squeezed into one large room make up this convivial spot, where beer and sake come with the usual *izakaya* fare, as well as some local-style *okonomiyaki*. Look for the lanterns and rope curtain over the sliding-door entrance.

Entertainment

Mazda Zoom Zoom Stadium STADIUM
(Hiroshima Municipal Stadium; 2-3-1 Minami-Kaniya) This stadium is a good place to catch a baseball game and see the beloved local team, the Carp. It's a short walk southeast of Hiroshima Station – follow the signs and the red-marked pathways.

A love of baseball is not a prerequisite for having a great time – it's fun just watching the rowdy yet organised enthusiasm of the crowd, especially when the despised Yomiuri (Tokyo) Giants come to town. For schedule information in English, see www.japanball.com, or ask at the tourist office. Buy tickets (from ¥1700 unreserved) at the stadium a day in advance or at 7-Eleven stores.

Aki Hiroshima Busho-Tai PERFORMING ARTS
Performers in Mōri-clan samurai costumes give small shows of song and swordplay inside the south entrance of Hiroshima-jo (p457) every Sunday at 1.30pm and 3pm.

On Saturdays and holidays at 1pm and 3pm, the 'samurai' parade from the tower to the south entrance in photo-friendly regalia.

Information

In addition to the tourist offices, check out **Hiroshima Navigator** (www.hiroshimacvb.jp) for tourism and practical information, as well as downloadable audio guides to the sights. *Get Hiroshima* (http://gethiroshima.com), an expat-run website and magazine, has an events calendar, restaurant and bar reviews, and regular feature articles.

Hiroshima Rest House (広島市平和記念公園レストハウス; ☎082-247-6738; www.mk-kousan.co.jp/rest-house; 1-1 Nakajima-machi; ⏲8.30am-7pm Aug, to 6pm Mar-Jul & Sep-Nov, to 5pm Dec-Feb; 🚋Genbaku-dōmu-mae) In Peace Memorial Park next to Motoyasu-bashi bridge, this air-conditioned tourist office has comprehensive information, English-speaking staff, and a small shop selling souvenirs.

Tourist Information Office (観光案内所; ☎082-261-1877; ⏲9am-5.30pm; 📶) Inside Hiroshima Station near the south exit, with English-speaking staff. There is another branch at the **north (shinkansen) exit** (☎082-263-6822; ⏲9am-5.30pm).

Getting There & Away

AIR

Hiroshima Airport (☎082-231-5171; www.hij.airport.jp; 64-31 Hongō-chō, Mihara) is 40km east of the city, with bus connections to/from Hiroshima Station (¥1340, 45 minutes, every 15 to 30 minutes) via Hiroshima Bus Centre. Buses operate from the airport from 8.20am to 9.40pm; buses run from Hiroshima Station (*shinkansen* exit) from 6am to 7.20pm.

BOAT

There are connections from Hiroshima Port to Matsuyama in Shikoku with **Setonaikai Kisen Ferry** (瀬戸内海汽船フェリー; ☎082-253-1212; http://setonaikaikisen.co.jp), via standard car ferry (adult/child ¥3600/1800, 2¾ hours, 10 daily) or high-speed 'Super Jet' (adult/child ¥7100/3550, 1¼ hours, 12 daily). The port (広島港) is the last stop on trams 1, 3 and 5 bound for Ujina (宇品).

BUS

Long-distance buses connect Hiroshima with all the major cities. Buses depart from **Hiroshima Bus Centre** (広島バスセンター; www.h-buscenter.com; 3rd fl, 6-27 Motomachi; 🚋Kamiya-chō-nishi), located between the Sogo and AQ'A shopping centres in the city centre. There is a good food court while you wait.

Highway buses ply a popular route between Matsue Station and Hiroshima city (¥3900, three hours). At the time of writing, a years-long promotion to increase visitor numbers had been extended, offering tickets on the route to tourists for just ¥500! Enquire at the bus centre or tourist information offices to check if it is still available at this price.

TRAIN

Hiroshima Station is on the JR San-yō line, which passes westwards to Shimonoseki. It's also a major stop on the Tokyo–Osaka–Hakata *shinkansen* line. Note that if you're travelling from Tokyo or Kyoto, you may need to change trains at Osaka or Okayama en route. Example *shinkansen* journeys from Hiroshima:

Hakata ¥8420, 65 to 95 minutes

Shin-Osaka ¥9710, 1½ hours

Tokyo ¥18,040, four hours

Getting Around

Most sights in Hiroshima are accessible either on foot or with a short tram (streetcar) ride. There is also a convenient hop-on, hop-off sightseeing loop bus (p460) that links the main attractions.

Hiroshima's trams (www.hiroden.co.jp) will get you almost anywhere you want to go for a flat fare of ¥180. You pay by dropping the fare into the machine by the driver as you get off the tram. If you have to change trams to get to your destination, you should ask for a *norikae-ken* (transfer ticket).

DISCOUNT PASSES

If you'll be taking at least four tram trips in a day, get a one-day trip card, which gives you unlimited travel for ¥600. A one-day card that covers trams plus return ferry to Miyajima (not including Aqua Net Hiroshima from Ujina Port or Setonaikai Kisen Ferry from Peace Memorial Park) is ¥840. The three-day Visit Hiroshima Tourist Pass (Small Area) is a good deal at ¥1000 (for foreigners with ID), covering tram rides, the sightseeing bus, loop buses and Miyajima ferry. Buy passes from the tram terminal at the train station, from tram conductors on board (one-day cards only), in Hiroshima Bus Centre, or at various hotels and hostels.

AROUND HIROSHIMA

Miyajima

☎0829 / POP 2015

The small island of Miyajima (宮島) is a Unesco World Heritage Site and one of Japan's most visited tourist spots. Its star attraction is the oft-photographed vermilion *torii* (shrine gate) of Itsukushima-jinja, which seems to float on the waves at high tide – a scene that has traditionally been ranked as one of the three best views in Japan. It is also at its evocative best at sunset, or when lit up after dark.

Besides this fêted view, Miyajima has some good hikes on sacred Misen, as well as temples and cheeky deer that do what they want, when they want, and will eat your map (or JR Pass) right out of your pocket if you're not careful.

Sights

To head straight to the *torii* (shrine gate) of Itsukushima-jinja, turn right as you emerge from the ferry terminal and follow the waterfront for 10 minutes.

The main shopping street, Omotesando, is a block back from the waterfront and packed with souvenir outlets and restaurants. This is also where you'll find the world's largest *shakushi* (rice scoop).

★Floating Torii GATE

(大鳥居) This 16m-tall vermilion *torii* (shrine gate) is a symbol of Miyajima and the watery entrance to World Heritage shrine Itsukushima-jinja. At high tide, it appears to float on the water. There has been a *torii* at this site since 1168; the current gate dates from the late 1800s. Repair work on the *torii* began in June 2019 and was expected to last 2–3 years, during which the gate will not be visible to the public.

★Itsukushima-jinja SHINTŌ SHRINE

(厳島神社; 1-1 Miyajima-chō; ¥300; ⏱6.30am-5.30pm Jan-Nov, to 5pm Dec) With origins as far back as the late 6th century, Itsukushima-jinja gives Miyajima its real name. The shrine's unique and attractive pier-like construction is a result of the island's sacred status: commoners were not allowed to set foot on the island and had to approach by boat through the torii in the bay. Much of the time, though, the shrine and *torii* are surrounded by mud.

The shrine's present form dates from 1168, when it was rebuilt under the patronage of Taira no Kiyomori, head of the doomed Heike clan. On one side of the shrine is a **floating nō stage** (能舞台), built by local lord Asano Tsunanaga in 1680 and still used for *nō* (stylised dance-drama) performances every year from 16 to 18 April, as part of the Toka-sai Festival.

★Misen & Ropeway MOUNTAIN

(弥山; www.miyajima-ropeway.info; ropeway one way/return adult ¥1000/1800, child ¥500/900; ⏱ropeway 9am-5pm) Covered with primeval forest, the sacred, peaceful Misen is Miyajima's highest mountain (530m), and its ascent is the island's finest walk – especially in spring and autumn, when the valley is painted with cherry blossom or autumnal hues. You can avoid most of the uphill climb by taking the two-stage ropeway with its giddying sea views, which leaves you with a 30-minute walk to the top, where there is an excellent observatory.

At the summit observatory, you can kick off your shoes and laze on wooden platforms while enjoying 360-degree views – on clear days you can see across to the mountain ranges of Shikoku.

Close to the summit is a temple where Kōbō Daishi meditated for 100 days, following his return from China in the 9th century. Next to the main temple hall is a flame that's been burning continually since Kōbō Daishi lit it 1200 years ago. From the temple, a path leads down the hillside to Daishō-in and Itsukushima-jinja. The descent takes a little over an hour, or you can take the ropeway back down. While on the mountain you might see monkeys and deer around the ropeway station.

The ropeway station (Momiji-dani Station) to ascend Misen is about a 10-minute walk on from Momiji-dani-kōen, or a few minutes on the free shuttle bus, which runs every 20 minutes from a stop near Iwasō Ryokan.

★Daishō-in BUDDHIST TEMPLE

(大聖院; ☎0829-44-0111; 210 Miyajima-chō; ⏱8am-5pm) FREE Just south of town at the foot of Misen, Daishō-in is a worthwhile stopping point on the way up or down the mountain. This Shingon temple is crowded with interesting things to look at: from Buddhist images and prayer wheels to sharp-beaked *tengu* (bird-like demons) and a cave containing images from each of the 88

Miyajima

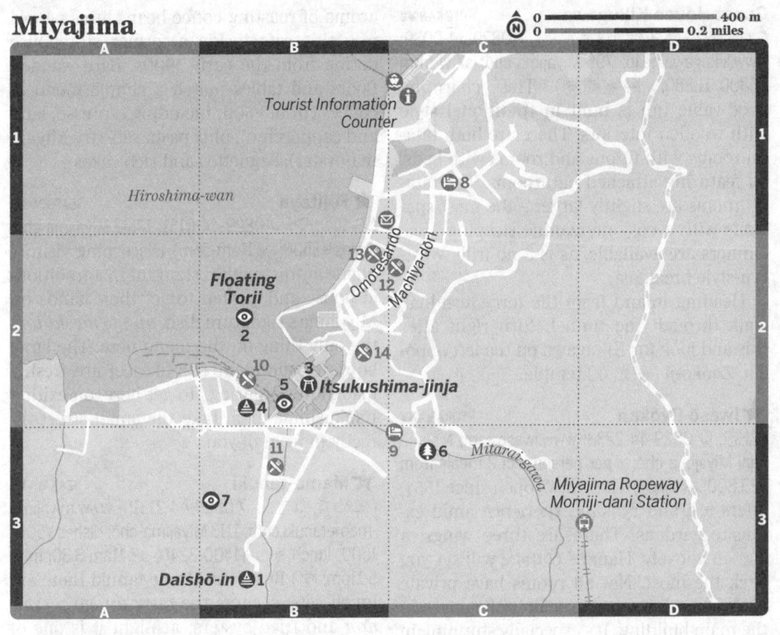

Miyajima

Top Sights

1 Daishō-in B3
2 Floating Torii B2
3 Itsukushima-jinja B2

Sights

4 Daigan-ji B2
5 Floating Nō Stage B2
6 Momiji-dani-kōen C3
7 Tahō-tō B3

Sleeping

8 Guest House Kikugawa C1
9 Iwasō Ryokan C3

Eating

10 Cafe Lente B2
11 Fujitaya B3
12 Kakiya C2
13 Mame-tanuki B2
14 Sarasvati B2

Shikoku pilgrimage temples. Daishō-in is a 15-minute walk from the ferry terminal; it's another 90 minutes if you intend to hike to Misen's summit.

Festivals & Events

Miyajima Water Fireworks Festival FIREWORKS

(☎0829-44-2011; ⊙mid-Aug) During Miyajima's most popular event, spectacular and imaginative fireworks are launched over the water, at a safe distance from the floating *torii* but still creating a one-of-a-kind visual. Come early and be prepared for crowds; around 40,000 people regularly attend, with an additional 200,000 watching from the mainland. Many spectators come dressed in *yukata*.

In the past, floods have forced the cancellation of the event, so check ahead.

Kangen-sai RELIGIOUS

(⊙late Jul/early Aug) This Shintō ritual sees decorated wooden boats float by to the sound of traditional drums and flutes. It's held in summer, starting early evening on the 17th of the sixth lunar-calendar month – check with the tourist office for exact dates for the year you're in town. Other ceremonies take place in the afternoon at Itsukushima-jinja.

Sleeping

It's worth staying overnight on the island to enjoy the evening quiet once the crowds have left and the floating *torii* is lit up.

Guest House Kikugawa RYOKAN ¥¥
(ゲストハウス菊がわ; 0829-44-0039; www.kikugawa.ne.jp; 796 Miyajima-chō; s/tw from ¥6800/11,880;) This charming good-value inn is built in traditional style with wooden interiors. There are both tatami rooms with futons and rooms with beds, all featuring attached bathrooms. The tatami rooms are slightly larger – the most spacious with a cosy mezzanine sleeping area. Dinners are available, as is a no-frills Western-style breakfast.

Heading inland from the ferry terminal, walk through the tunnel; turn right after this and look for Kikugawa on the left opposite Zonkō-ji (存光寺) temple.

★Iwasō Ryokan RYOKAN ¥¥¥
(岩惣; 0829-44-2233; www.iwaso.com; Momiji-dani Miyajima-chō; r per person incl 2 meals from ¥23,800;) The Iwasō, open since 1854, offers a grand ryokan experience amid exquisite gardens. There are three wings; a stay in a lovely 'Hanare' cottage will set you back the most. Not all rooms have private bathrooms, but you can soak in the onsen in the main building. It's especially stunning in autumn, when Momiji-dani (Maple Valley) explodes with colour.

It's about a 15-minute walk from the ferry port, or a pick-up can be arranged.

Eating

Plenty of restaurants line the main shopping strip of Omotesando and near the waterfront. One street back from Omotesando is the quieter Machiya-dōri, with a few cafes and eateries. Most restaurants shut down after the crowds go home – the tourist office has a list of those that stay open for dinner. Oysters are a speciality in Miyajima and Hiroshima; as is *anago* (saltwater eel) – try it on rice as *anago meshidon*.

★Cafe Lente CAFE ¥
(0829-44-1204; 1167-3 Miyajima-chō; mains ¥850; 11am-9pm Wed-Mon;) This comfortable cafe boasts excellent views of the *torii* and sea. Open and airy, it serves handsome-looking lunches, such as Japanese chicken curry and vegan risotto, to go with the quietly stylish decor. Organic coffee or wine are other excuses to drop by and chat to the English-speaking owner.

Sarasvati CAFE ¥
(0829-44-2266; www.sarasvati.jp; 407 Miyajima-chō; meals ¥990-1500; 8.30am-7pm) The aroma of roasting coffee beans lures people into this cafe inside a former storehouse dating from the early 1900s. Bare wooden floors and tables match a simple menu of coffees (from ¥500; including espresso, latte and cappuccino), plus pasta sets (try Miyajima-oyster), baguettes and rich cakes.

★Fujitaya SEAFOOD ¥¥
(ふじたや; 0829-44-0151; 125-2 Miyajima-chō; mains ¥2500; 11am-5pm) Discerning visitors queue at this small restaurant in a traditional house and garden to get their hands on Miyajima's signature dish, *anago meshidon*, the only thing on the menu here. The large bowls of succulent fish-like eel are freshly made after ordering. To get here, on exiting Itsukushima-jinja, take the small street directly in front of you.

★Mame-tanuki IZAKAYA ¥¥
(まめたぬき; 0829-44-2131; www.miyajima-mametanuki.com; 1113 Miyajima-chō; dishes ¥500-1500, lunch sets ¥1400-3240; 11am-3.30pm & 5-11pm;) By day at Mame-tanuki there are lunch sets, such as the tasty *anago meshidon* and fried oysters; at night it is one of the few places open late, serving drinks and *izakaya*-style small dishes. Look for the yellowish building; there's a menu signboard outside.

No smoking in the evening.

Kakiya SEAFOOD ¥¥
(牡蠣屋; 0829-44-2747; www.kaki-ya.jp; 539 Miyajima-chō; oyster sets ¥1200-2690; 10am-6pm) Kakiya is a sophisticated oyster bar on the main street, serving delicious local oysters freshly barbecued in their shells. For a taste of oysters done five ways, try the 'Kakiya set'. Wash them down with a glass of something from the well-stocked wine cellar.

Look for the white lantern.

Information

Tourist Information Counter (宮島観光案内所; 0829-44-2011; www.visit-miyajima-japan.com; 9am-6pm) Inside the ferry terminal on Miyajima. There is also a counter between the two ferry wharves on the mainland side.

Getting There & Away

Miyajima is accessed by ferry and is an easy day trip from Hiroshima.

The mainland ferry terminal is a short walk from Miyajima-guchi Station on the JR San-yō line, halfway between Hiroshima Station (¥410, 30 minutes) and Iwakuni. The ferry terminal can also be reached by tram 2 from Hiroshima (¥260, 1¼ hours; not JR), which runs from Hiroshima Station, passing the city's Atomic Bomb Dome on the way. Ferries operated by two companies shuttle regularly across to the island from Miyajima-guchi (¥180, 10 minutes). JR Pass holders can travel on the JR ferry for free. The bargain three-day Visit Hiroshima Tourist Pass Small Area covers trams and ferries to Miyajima (p463).

Setonaikai Kisen (p463) operates high-speed ferries (one way/return ¥1850/3300, 45 minutes, eight daily) direct to Miyajima from Hiroshima's Ujina Port, 5km south of central Hiroshima. To get to Ujina Port, take tram 1 or 3 from Hiroshima Bus Centre (¥180, 35 minutes, frequent) to the Hiroshimako stop. Another option is to take the **Aqua Net ferry** (☎082-240-5955; www.aqua-net-h.co.jp/en) directly from Peace Memorial Park in central Hiroshima (one-way/return ¥2000/3600, 45 minutes, 10 to 15 daily). These boats cruise under the bridges of the Kyūōta-gawa before coming out into the bay towards Miyajima. No reservation is required.

Getting Around

Everywhere on Miyajima is within easy walking distance. Hand-pulled rickshaws (from ¥4000 for two) are an atmospheric indulgence. There are also taxis on the island – ask at the tourist office for details.

Saijō

A short train ride east of Hiroshima is the town of Saijō (西条), where seven sake breweries are clustered within easy walking distance of the station. The brewers here know their stuff – Saijō has been producing sake for around 300 years – and most open up their doors to curious and thirsty visitors for free sake tastings. This is the place to try a tipple sipped by world leaders.

When you're done drink savouring, you can pay your respects to the god of sake at **Matsuo-jinja** (松尾神社; ☎0853-67-0007; 296 Saijō-chō), a short walk to the north of Saijō Station.

Sights

Kamotsuru BREWERY
(賀茂鶴; ☎082-422-2121; www.kamotsuru.jp; 4-31 Saijō-honmachi; ⏲8.30am-4.30pm) Founded in 1623 and among the best-known Saijō sake breweries, Kamotsuru is worth a look as it has a large tasting room, and screens a video about the district. Its other claim to fame is that, when Prime Minister Abe met US president Barack Obama in Japan in 2014, they toasted with a sake brewed here – namely Diginjo Tokusei Gold.

Hakubotan BREWERY
(白牡丹; ☎082-422-2142; www.hakubotan.co.jp; 15-5 Saijō-honmachi; ⏲9.30am-4pm Mon-Fri, from 10.30am Sat & Sun) One of Saijō's oldest sake breweries, Hakubotan has a lovely broad-beamed display and tasting room with Munakata woodblock prints on the wall.

Festivals & Events

Saijō Sake Matsuri FOOD & DRINK
(西条酒祭り; www.sakematsuri.com; ⏲Oct) If you're in the Hiroshima area on the second weekend of October, don't miss the Saijō Sake Festival, when crowds descend on Saijō for hours of sampling and events.

Sleeping & Eating

For a bite to eat and a freshly roasted coffee, stop in at **Kugurimon Cafe** (くぐり門; ☎082-426-3005; www.kugurimon.com; 17-1 Honmachi; meals ¥450-1180; ⏲10am-5pm, closed 2nd & 4th Tue of the month). Alternatively, try the handful of noodle and sushi joints at the station between trains, or the restaurants around the breweries.

Hiroshima Saijo Youth Hostel HOSTEL ¥
(広島西条駅前ユースホステル; ☎082-495-5306; www7b.biglobe.ne.jp/~hiroshimasaijoyha; 3-3 Saijō-oka-chō; dm ¥3500;) If you want to sip and stay in Saijō, this hostel next to the station is very handy. Dangerously, there is free sake in the communal kitchen's fridge, but the caring owner is usually on hand to take care of guests. Mattresses are thicker than most, and the coin laundry is handy for any spills.

Information

A beginner's guide to sake and what makes each local brewery special is available at www.saijosake.com.

Saijō Tourist Information Office (☎082-430-7701; 2nd fl, Saijō Station; ⏲9am-6pm;) Offers a good walking map in English, showing the location of each sake brewery.

Getting There & Away

Saijō is 40 minutes by train from Hiroshima (¥580) on the JR San-yō line.

Iwakuni

0827 / POP 137,120

Iwakuni (岩国), noteworthy for its five-arched bridge and old samurai quarters, is an easy day trip from Hiroshima (or stopoff en route between Yamaguchi and Hiroshima).

Sights

★**Kintai-kyō** BRIDGE

(錦帯橋; 0827-41-1477; 1 Iwakuni; return ¥300, combination incl cable car & castle ¥940; 8am-5pm) Iwakuni's chief claim to fame is this graceful bridge, built in 1673 during the rule of feudal lord Kikkawa Hiroyoshi. It has been restored several times since then, but its high arches remain an impressive sight over the wide river, with Iwakuni-jō atop the green hills behind.

Honke Matsugane HOUSE

(本家　松がね, Iwakuni City Visitors Center; 0827-28-6600; www.honke-matsugane.jp; 1-7-3 Iwakuni; 9am-6pm Apr-Aug, to 5pm Sep-Mar) FREE Both a tourist information office and a cultural experience, inside a traditional Japanese house dating from 1850 near the bridge entrance. The elegant building belonged to a family that produced hair oil used by samurai, and short free tours in English highlight decorative features such as nail covers in the walls. It's also possible to try reasonably priced Iwakuni *zushi* (local square sushi), *renkon* (lotus root) chips and Iwakuni sake. Excellent English spoken.

Kikkō-kōen PARK

(吉香公園; 2-6-51 Yokoyama) What remains of the old samurai quarter in Iwakuni now forms pleasant Kikkō-kōen, accessed via Kintai-kyō bridge. Within the park are old residences, a pavilion, a couple of museums, ice-cream vendors and spots for picnicking. Worth a look is the exterior of the **Mekata Family Residence** (旧目加田家住宅; 2-6 Yokoyama; 9.30am-4.30pm Tue-Sun) FREE, the former home of a middle-ranking samurai family from the mid-Edo period.

Information

MONEY

There is only one ATM near the bridge entrance, at the 7-Eleven reached by walking 10 minutes south along the water. Once you cross the bridge, there are no ATMs in Kikkō-kōen so come prepared with some cash, at least for small purchases.

TOURIST INFORMATION

There's a **tourist information office** (0827-24-9071; 10am-5pm Tue-Sun) inside JR Iwakuni Station, with another at **Shin-Iwakuni Station** (10.30am-3.30pm Thu-Tue).

Getting There & Away

JR Iwakuni Station is on the San-yō line, west of Hiroshima (¥760, 55 minutes). Shin-Iwakuni Station is on the San-yō *shinkansen* line, connecting to Hiroshima (¥1620, 15 minutes) and Shin-Yamaguchi (¥3390, 30 minutes).

The bridge and park are a 20-minute bus ride (¥300) from outside JR Iwakuni. There are also buses to the bridge (¥350, 15 minutes) from Shin-Iwakuni at stop 1. Buses leave regularly.

If coming from Hiroshima without a JR Pass, you may find it more convenient to get the Iwakuni bus from Hiroshima Bus Centre (stop 1), as it handily drops you at Kintai-kyō (one way/return ¥930/1700, 50 minutes, 12 daily).

ONOMICHI & THE SHIMANAMI KAIDŌ

For many travellers, Onomichi is the base from which to cycle the Shimanami Kaidō, the system of road bridges that allows people to island-hop their way across the Inland Sea to Shikoku.

Sleeping

Onomichi has some ryokan and hip guesthouses perched on the hillside behind the town, which is atmospheric, but only for those who can haul up their luggage. Most hostels along and off the tiled, covered shopping arcade are still a 15-minute walk from the station. Cyclists wanting a quick getaway are best staying near the port, where most of the accommodation is anyhow. Budget accommodation fills up quickly on weekends; book ahead.

Ikuchi-jima is a good place to overnight if you're cycling the Shimanami Kaidō (p470) chain of bridges. Tourist Information Setoda (p472) can help book accommodation, as can the office in Onomichi (p471).

Getting There & Around

BICYCLE

Onomichi Port Rent-a-Cycle (0848-22-5332; http://shimanami-cycle.or.jp/rental;

per day ¥1000, deposit ¥1000; ⏲7am-7pm Mar-Nov, 8am-6pm Dec-Feb) Located in the car park next to the ferry terminal, with multiple bikes. Bikes with gears and electric-assist bikes (¥1500 per day; must be returned here) are available. There are a dozen drop-off points on the Shimanami Kaidō route, useful if you get tired and decide to take a bus.

BOAT

Setouchi Cruising (☎0865-62-2856; www.s-cruise.jp) ferries travel from Onomichi Ekimae Port (in front of Onomichi Station) to Shigei-Higashi Port (¥600, 20 minutes, eight daily) on the east side of Inno-shima en route to Setoda Port (¥1200, 40 minutes, eight daily) on Ikuchi-jima. It is an additional ¥400 to take a bicycle. Ōmi-shima is not connected by ferry; the nearest port is Setoda on Ikuchi-jima.

If coming directly from Hiroshima Airport, take an airport bus (bicycles in a bag allowed; ¥820, 35 minutes, every 90 minutes) to Mihara Port, from where there are ferries to Setoda Port (¥820, 28 minutes, seven daily).

There are frequent ferries from Onomichi to Mukai-shima (¥100, five minutes), where the Shimanami Kaidō begins, which accept bicycles (¥10).

BUS

Regular buses run to Imabari (¥2330) in Shikoku from Onomichi Station (some originating in Shin-Onomichi Station), most with a 15- to 40-minute transfer at Inno-shima or Mukai-shima, but three daily run direct. It takes up to two hours, depending on the connection, or 90 minutes direct. Buses also run between Onomichi and Setoda Port on Ikuchi-jima (¥1030, 1¼ hours, four daily).

TRAIN

Onomichi is on the main JR San-yō line, east of Hiroshima (¥1490, 1½ hours). The Shin-Onomichi *shinkansen* station is 3km north. Regular buses (¥190, 20 minutes) connect the two.

Onomichi

☎0848 / POP 141,810

Onomichi (尾道) is an old-timey seaport town with hills full of temples, literary sites and cats. Local businesses increasingly embrace its retro-chic charm, and a visit is a glimpse of a quaint Japan of yesteryear. Film director Ōbayashi Nobuhiko was born in Onomichi, and the town has featured in a number of Japanese movies, notably Ozu's *Tokyo Story*.

Sights & Activities

★Temple Walk WALKING

(古寺めぐり) This picturesque trail takes in 25 old temples in the hills behind the town, following narrow lanes and steep stone stairways, where cats laze in the sunshine. Along the route is a **ropeway** (千光寺山ロープウェイ; one-way/return ¥320/500; ⏲every 15min, 9am-5.15pm) to an observation tower and a park area (Senkō-ji-kōen), home to Onomichi's best-known temple, **Senkō-ji** (千光寺). There are cute cafes, gift shops and galleries dotted between the temples.

The temple walk starts just east of the station: take the inland road from the station and cross the railway tracks by the statue of local author Hayashi Fumiko. To walk the whole trail takes a couple of hours. You can cut back down into town at various points along the way, or take the ropeway.

Sleeping

★Onomichi Guesthouse Anago no Nedoko HOSTEL ¥

(あなごのねどこ; ☎0848-38-1005; http://anago.onomichisaisei.com; 2-4-9 Tsuchidō; dm from ¥2800; ⊖❄@📶) Within a traditional old wooden house restored as part of an NPO project to give life to vacant dwellings, Anago is a budget option with character. As well as the dorms (accessed via narrow stairs) with firm beds and individual curtains, there are tatami family rooms (¥3300 per person), a kitchen and a schoolroom-themed cafe. Enter from the *shōtengai* (shopping arcade).

Pick up one of the excellent homemade maps.

★Hotel Cycle BOUTIQUE HOTEL ¥¥¥

(☎0848-21-0550; www.onomichi-u2.com; U2 complex, 5-11 Nishi-gosho-cho; tw from ¥17,000; ⊖❄@📶) Hotel Cycle, within the large U2 complex right on the waterfront boardwalk, is aimed at both the cycling crowd and those with an eye for design. The dark, minimalist tones suggest both boutique hotel and bicycle museum. The softly lit rooms (all twins) feature bike storage and spacious baths, perfect for a soak after a long day of pedalling.

U2 also houses a cafe (where you can 'ride through'), bar, restaurant and bakery, as well as a bicycle repair space and Giant bicycle shop.

CYCLING THE SHIMANAMI KAIDŌ

The **Setouchi Shimanami Kaidō** (瀬戸内しまなみ海道; Shimanami Sea Route) is a chain of bridges linking Onomichi in Hiroshima Prefecture with Imabari in Ehime Prefecture on Shikoku, via six Inland Sea islands. Besides being remarkable feats of engineering (the monster Kurushima-kaikyō trio at the Imabari end are among the longest suspension bridges in the world), the bridges make it possible to cycle the whole way across. Breezing along 50m or more above the island-dotted sea is an amazing experience, and a highlight of any trip to this part of Japan. Needless to say, it's best enjoyed when the weather is fine.

The Route

The route begins on Mukai-shima (a quick boat ride from Onomichi) and crosses Innoshima, Ikuchi-jima, Ōmi-shima (p472), Hakata-jima and Ōshima, before the final bridge to reach Imabari. The 'recommended' route is well marked with information boards and maps, but there's nothing stopping you from taking detours along the minor routes around the islands and plotting your own course from bridge to bridge. Much of the recommended route is fairly flat, with the odd minor hill, but there are long, thigh-burning inclines leading up to each bridge entrance. The ride takes you through towns, villages and rural areas, past citrus groves and along the coastline, but does also hit some less-pretty built-up industrial patches.

Distance & Time

The total recommended route from Onomichi to Imabari is roughly 70km and could be done in eight or so hours, depending on your fitness and propensity to stop and take pictures. You could take the ferry part of the way, such as to Ikuchi-jima, and bike the rest (where the ferry does not go). Alternatively, a good day trip from Onomichi is to cycle to Ikuchi-jima (about 30km) and return to Onomichi on the ferry in the afternoon. Some cyclists opt to spend a night on one of the islands on the way across – Ikuchi-jima is a popular stopover. Otherwise, take it easy and just spend a few hours cycling a section of the route on one of the islands.

Information

The tourist office in Onomichi, and those on each of the islands, can help with all the information you need, including an excellent map in English, showing the routes, distances, sights and locations of bike terminals along the way. There's information in English at www.go-shimanami.jp, from where you can download the English map. You'll also find basic maps, plus bus and ferry schedules, at www.city.onomichi.hiroshima.jp.

If you need to get heavy luggage across, try **Kuroneko Yamato** (www.kuronekoyamato.co.jp), whose *takkyūbin* (express shipping) service will deliver it for you by the next business day (from around ¥1000 depending on size). It picks up from many convenience stores.

Bikes & Costs

Bike hire is ¥1000 per day, plus ¥1000 deposit. You don't get the deposit back if you return the bike to a different rental place along the route. There are large bike-hire terminals in Onomichi (p468) and Imabari (p596), and on each island in between. Electric-assist bicycles are also available for ¥1500 per day; these have to be returned to the same rental terminal. It's not necessary to reserve a bike, though it's possible to do so and you may want to consider it if you're planning to cycle on a major holiday. Note that reservations can't be made less than a week in advance.

At the time of writing, cyclists did not need to pay bridge tolls and could cross for free, as fees had been waived. This years-long promotion is likely to be extended, but check tourist offices for the latest. Otherwise fees are between ¥50 and ¥200 per bridge. No one actually collects this money; you're trusted to drop the coins into the box at the bridge entrances. To take a bike on a ferry costs up to ¥300.

Uonobu Ryokan RYOKAN ¥¥¥
(魚信旅館; ☎0848-37-4175; www.uonobu.jp; 2-27-6 Kubo; r per person incl 2 meals from ¥18,900) Elegantly old-fashioned Uonobu is a good ryokan experience, but it's probably best if you can speak a little Japanese, although the hosts are welcoming anyhow. It's renowned for its seafood; nonguests can eat here if they reserve by 5pm the previous day. Find it about a 20-minute walk east from the station, just after the city hall (市役所).

Green Hill Hotel Onomichi HOTEL ¥¥¥
(グリーンヒルホテル尾道; ☎0848-24-0100; www.shimanami-gho.co.jp; 9-1 Higashi-gosho-machi; s/tw from ¥7910/17,700; P ⊖ ✻ @ ≋) Directly above the ferry port and a minute's walk from the station, this well-appointed hotel could hardly be better located. The neutral rooms have comfortable beds, and after a day's cycling there's a useful coin laundry and a free-to-use massage chair. Pay a little more for a room on the sea-view side.

Eating

Onomichi is known for its ramen, and you'll find plenty of places dishing up this speciality, which uses a soup base of chicken and *dashi* (dried fish stock), and sometimes also pork fat.

Go east from the station to find eateries along the waterfront and in the arcade one block inland.

Onomichi Rāmen Ichibankan RAMEN ¥
(尾道ラーメン壱番館; ☎0848-21-1119; www.f-ichibankan.com; 2-9-26 Tsuchidō; noodles ¥580-950; ⊙11am-7pm Sat-Thu) Opposite a shrine and facing the water, a 15-minute walk from the station, this popular noodle shop is a good place to try Onomichi ramen, characterised by thick slabs of juicy pork. Its best-seller is the *kaku-ni rāmen* (noodles with eggs and tender cuts of fatty pork).

Kome Doko JAPANESE ¥¥
(こめどこ食堂; ☎0848-36-5333; www.facebook.com/komedokoshokudou; 5-2 Higashi-gosho-chō; set lunch/dinner ¥1300/3500; ⊙11am-2pm & 6-11pm Tue-Sun) Slightly fancy, a rarity for Onomichi, this bistro-style restaurant uses locally sourced ingredients in excellent dishes that might make you wish portions were heftier, but allow you to sample more flavours such as tempura Okinawa bitter melon, miso-braised burger and seafood risotto. Dishes focus on rice and fermented ingredients. It's upstairs with sea views; look for 'Onomichi 2014' on the building.

Hana Akari SUSHI ¥¥
(花あかり; ☎0848-24-2287; 1-12-13 Tsuchidō; meals ¥1050-1630; ⊙11am-10pm) Every table has a sea view at this homely little seafood restaurant. The lively owner brightens up lunch, and it features excellent-value sashimi, sushi and tempura. Beware, the included seafood *chawanmushi* (savoury egg custard) is not a dessert. It's a five-minute walk east along the port road from Onomichi Station; look for the orange perspex sign.

Information

There is an ATM accepting international cards in the 7-Eleven on the port road east of the station.

Tourist Information Office (☎0848-20-0005; www.ononavi.com; ⊙9am-6pm) Supplies local maps, information on the Shimanami Kaidō, and can help with accommodation. English is spoken. It's inside JR Onomichi Station. There are also maps adjacent to the ticket counter for Senkō-ji-yama Ropeway.

Inno-shima

Famed for its flowers and fruit, Inno-shima (因島) is connected by bridge to Mukai-shima, facing Onomichi, and Ikuchi-jima to the west. The Inland Sea was once a haven for pirates, and Inno-shima was the base of one of the three Murakami pirate clans. Today you can get a taste for that time at the modern-replica **pirate castle** (因島水軍城, Suigun-jō; ☎0845-24-0936; 3228-2 Inno-shima Nakanosho-chō; ¥310; ⊙9.30am-5pm Fri-Wed), which has some displays of weaponry.

Worth cycling (then hiking) up to is **Shirataki-yama** (白滝山), a collection of sculptures of the 500 Rakan disciples of the Buddha. A picturesque bonus is the excellent panoramic view over the sea, islands and a bridge of the Shimanami Kaidō. Cycle (or drive) to the entrance (2km from Shigei-Higashi Port), where the steps begin; the ascent takes most people about 10 minutes.

For cyclists, Inno-shima is 22km from Onomichi.

Ikuchi-jima

Ikuchi-jima (生口島) is known for its citrus groves and beaches, including Sunset Beach on the west coast. The main port town is **Setoda**.

For cyclists, Ikuchi-jima is 31km from Onomichi. If you rented a bicycle from Onomichi Port and have had enough of riding, there are bicycle return points here.

Sights

★Ikuo Hirayama Museum of Art GALLERY
(平山郁夫美術館; www.hirayama-museum.or.jp; 200-2 Setoda-chō; ¥900; ⌚9am-5pm) The Ikuo Hirayama Museum of Art is dedicated to the life and work of the famous and well-travelled Setoda-born artist. The collection here includes several striking works inspired by Ikuo's journeys in India and along the Silk Road. A video overview of his life explains how his exposure to radiation in Hiroshima and illness led him to Buddhism, as seen in his paintings.

Kōsan-ji BUDDHIST TEMPLE
(耕三寺; www.kousanji.or.jp; 553-2 Setoda-chō; adult/child ¥1400/free; ⌚9am-5pm) Buddhist theme park, anyone? Shortly after the death of his beloved mother in 1934, local steel-tube magnate and arms manufacturer Kanemoto Kōzō became a Buddhist priest and sank his fortune into a series of vividly coloured temple buildings. The result is the remarkable Kōsan-ji, a sprawl of over-the-top Buddhist kitsch, consisting of some 2000 exhibits. Don't miss the 1000 Buddhas Cave and its series of graphically illustrated hells.

Kōsan-ji is a 15-minute walk from Setoda Port. The arty, white-marble cafe here has impressive sea views.

Sleeping & Eating

Casual eating options are clustered along the signposted 'Shiomachi' shopping street running east from Setoda Port, with local specialities of roast chicken, dried octopus and Setoda orange juice served in the fruit shell itself.

Setoda Private Hostel RYOKAN ¥
(瀬戸田垂水温泉, Setoda Tarumi Onsen; ☎0845-27-3137; http://setodashimanami.web.fc2.com; 58-1 Tarumi Setoda-chō; r per person with/without meals ¥4800/3000) This cheap and cheerful ryokan on Sunset Beach near the main sights has its own onsen and basic, individual tatami rooms; payment is by cash only. If you're not arriving on two wheels, pick-up can be arranged from Setoda ferry port. The tourist office in Onomichi can help with reservations. Breakfast (¥600) and dinner (¥1200) are also available separately.

Information

Tourist Information Setoda (尾道観光協会瀬戸田支部; ☎0845-27-0051; 200-5 Setoda-chō; ⌚9am-5pm; wi-fi) Tourist information office opposite Ikuo Hirayama Museum of Art, with maps and cycling information in English as well as bicycle rental (¥1000 per day), bike-repair tools, lockers and free wi-fi.

Ōmi-shima

The mountainous island of Ōmi-shima (大三島) is connected by bridge to Ikuchi-jima to the east and Ō-shima to the southeast. For such a modest, mandarin-growing island, some remarkable architectural gems have been grabbing the attention of visitors. Award-winning architect Itō Toyo has implemented ambitious building projects to revive the island's fortunes while honouring its natural environment. There are also rewarding sea views at every turn.

Ōmi-shima is 42km along the Shimanami Kaidō (p470) from Onomichi, or 36km from Imbari Station on the other end of the cycling road. Ōmi-shima is one of the hillier islands on the bicycle route so may take more time to explore.

Sights

★Tokoro Museum GALLERY
(ところミュージアム大三島; ☎0897-83-0380; http://museum.city.imabari.ehime.jp/tokoro; 2362-3 Urado, Ōmi-shima-chō; ¥300; ⌚9am-5pm Tue-Sun) This museum boasts a small but interesting collection of modern sculpture, often satirical, in a hilltop building with stunning sea views from the deck. The ride up is hilly but worth it.

Toyo Ito Museum of Architecture MUSEUM
(www.tima-imabari.jp; ¥800; ⌚9am-5pm Tue-Sun) This ode to architecture and Ōmi-shima showcases the natural beauty of the island through two buildings designed by internationally acclaimed architect Itō Toyo. Resembling a giant section of honeycomb, the black metallic Steel Hut exhibits photos covering Ōmi-shima culture and its inhabitants. It also displays the process of Itō's works, which include a Serpentine Gallery Pavilion structure in London, and the Mikimoto building in Ginza, Tokyo.

Ōyamazumi-jinja SHINTŌ SHRINE
(大山祇神社; ☎0897-82-0032; 3327 Miyaura, Ōmi-shima-chō; Treasure Hall & Kaiji Museum ¥1000; ⌚8.30am-5pm) Ōyamazumi-jinja is one of the oldest Shintō shrines in western Japan. The deity enshrined here is the brother of Amaterasu, the sun goddess. The

present structure dates from 1378, but in the courtyard is a 2600-year-old camphor tree, and the treasure hall contains the most important collection of ancient weapons found anywhere in Japan.

Sleeping & Eating

There are places to eat around Ōyamazumi-jinja, including good, cheap seafood joints. Look for the Ōmi-shima speciality cake, made with whole local mandarins, zest and all.

★Ōmi-shima Ikoi-no-Ie GUESTHOUSE ¥¥
(大三島 憩いの家; 0897-83-1111; www.ikoinoie.co.jp; 5208-1 Munakata, Ōmi-shima-chō; dm/d per person incl 2 meals from ¥5000/15,000; P) As young people abandoned the island, an Ōmi-shima family converted a deserted schoolhouse into this boutique guesthouse under the guidance of famous Japanese architect Itō Toyo. Original wooden beams, classroom signs, taps and lamps provoke nostalgia even in non-Japanese guests. Cedar-chic Western or tatami rooms are modern with black-tiled bathrooms. Staying here, complete with seafood meals, is a unique experience.

OKAYAMA & THE INLAND SEA

Okayama Prefecture (岡山県; Okayama-ken) is known for its rural character. The area is home to Kurashiki, with its well-preserved merchant quarter and picturesque canal, and the historic ceramic-making centre of Bizen – both within easy reach of prefectural capital Okayama. The coastline in this area also provides jumping-off points for some of the most popular islands in the Inland Sea, including arty Naoshima.

Getting There & Around

Okayama is the main transport hub for the region. The city is on the JR San-yō line and *shinkansen* line, connecting to Osaka in the east and Hiroshima to the west. Yonago in Tottori Prefecture is served by the limited express Yakumo and Sunrise Izumo.

Naoshima and the other 'art islands' can be accessed from Uno Port, south of Okayama, and Takamatsu in Kagawa, which can make a more convenient base for Naoshima than Okayama. There are rail links to Takamatsu, from where there are also ferries to Shōdo-shima.

MOMOTARŌ, THE PEACH BOY

Okayama Prefecture and Kagawa Prefecture, on the island of Shikoku, are linked by the legend of Momotarō, the Peach Boy, who emerged from the stone of a peach and, backed up by a monkey, a pheasant and a dog, defeated a three-eyed, three-toed people-eating demon. There are statues of Momotarō at JR Okayama Station, plus he and his sidekicks feature on manhole covers, and the city's biggest street is named after him. One of the most popular souvenir treats from Okayama is also Momotarō's favoured sweet, *kibi-dango*, a soft *mochi*-like dumpling made with millet flour.

Okayama

086 / POP 721,175

The jewel of Okayama (岡山) is Kōraku-en, one of Japan's three most attractive gardens. Its spring cherry blossoms and autumnal maple trees are overlooked by the city's crow-black castle. Together the striking pair make an enjoyable three-hour stroll and a good reason to step off the *shinkansen* on the way to Hiroshima. If you have a few days up your sleeve, make well-connected Okayama your base for day trips to other attractions in the region and side trips to the art islands in the Inland Sea.

The city is proud of its connection to Momotarō, the demon-quelling 'Peach Boy' hero of one of Japan's best-known folk tales. You'll spot his face beaming out at you all over town.

Sights

★Kōraku-en GARDENS
(後楽園; 086-272-1148; www.okayama-korakuen.jp; 1-5 Kōraku-en; ¥400, combination ticket with Okayama-jō ¥560; 7.30am-6pm Apr-late Jul & mid-Aug–Sep, to 9.30pm late Jul–mid-Aug, 8am-5pm Oct-Mar) Kōraku-en draws the crowds with its reputation as one of the three most beautiful gardens in Japan. It has expansive lawns broken up by ponds, teahouses and other Edo-period buildings, including a *nō* theatre stage; it even has a small tea plantation and rice field. In spring the groves of plum and cherry-blossom trees are stunning, in summer white lotuses unfurl, and in autumn the maple trees are a delight

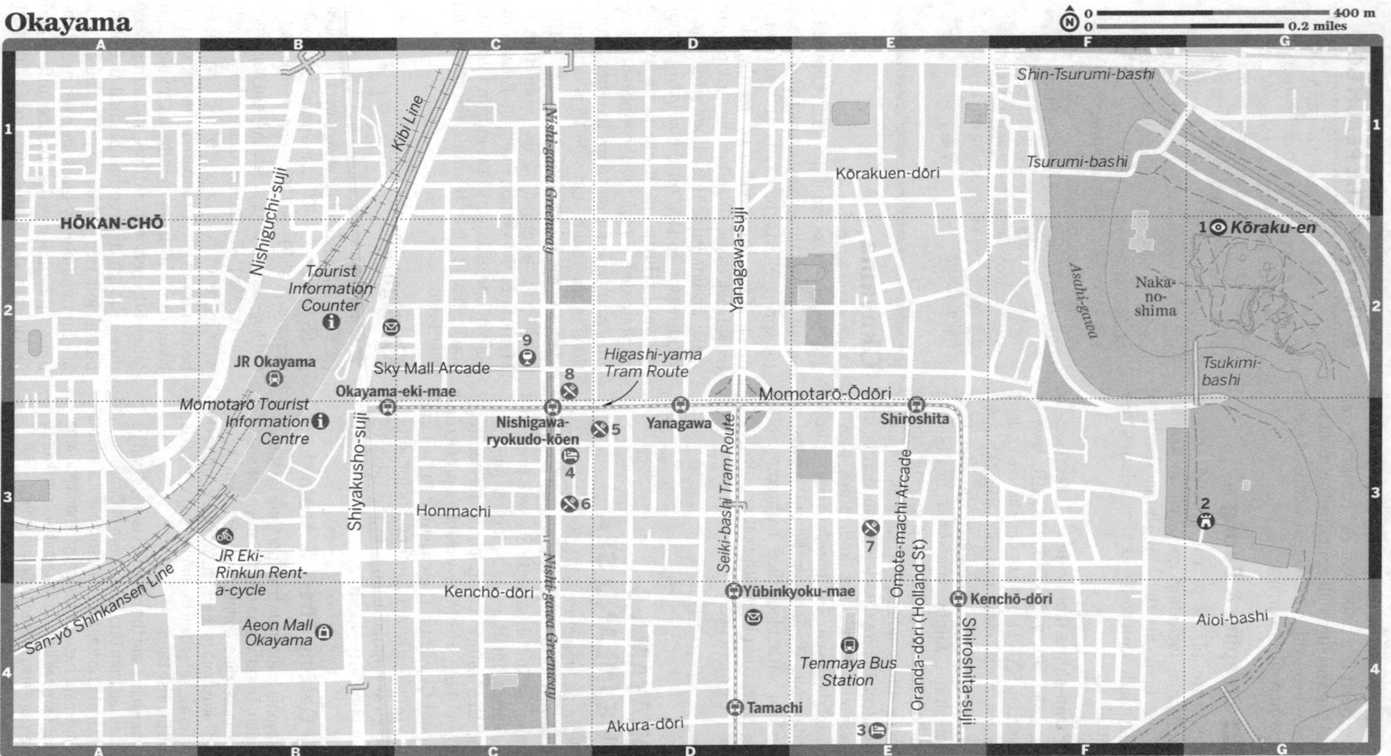
Okayama
0 400 m
0 0.2 miles
HŌKAN-CHŌ
Nishiguchi-suji
Kibi Line
Tourist Information Counter
JR Okayama
Momotarō Tourist Information Centre
Sky Mall Arcade
Okayama-eki-mae
Shiyakusho-suji
Nishi-gawa Greenway
Nishigawa-ryokudo-kōen
Honmachi
JR Eki-Rinkun Rent-a-cycle
San-yō Shinkansen Line
Aeon Mall Okayama
Kenchō-dōri
Higashi-yama Tram Route
Yanagawa
Yanagawa-suji
Seiki-bashi Tram Route
Yūbinkyoku-mae
Tamachi
Akura-dōri
Kōrakuen-dōri
Momotarō-Ōdōri
Shiroshita
Omote-machi Arcade
Oranda-dōri (Holland St)
Shiroshita-suji
Kenchō-dōri
Tenmaya Bus Station
Shin-Tsurumi-bashi
Tsurumi-bashi
Asahi-gawa
Naka-no-shima
Kōraku-en
Tsukimi-bashi
Aioi-bashi
1
2
3
4
5
6
7
8
9
A
B
C
D
E
F
G

Okayama

Top Sights
1 Kōraku-en G2

Sights
2 Okayama-jō G3

Sleeping
3 Hibari House E4
4 Kōraku Hotel C3

Eating
5 Ajitsukasa Nomura D3
6 Nodo Nobashi C3
7 Okabe E3
8 Teppan-Ku-Ya C2

Drinking & Nightlife
9 Izayoi no Tsuki C2

for photographers. There are also seasonal events (fancy some harvest-moon viewing?).

Built on the orders of *daimyō* Ikeda Tsunemasa, the garden was completed in 1700 and, despite suffering major damage during floods in the 1930s and air raids in the 1940s, it remains much as it was in feudal times. It was opened to the public in 1884.

In summer, from late July to mid-August, the garden and castle are dreamily lit up and stay open to 9.30pm.

From Okayama Station, take the Higashi-yama tram to the Shiroshita stop, from where it's about 10 minutes on foot. Bus 18 (¥100, 10 minutes) from the station will drop you right outside the garden (Kōraku-en-mae stop). Alternatively, walking the entire way will take about 25 minutes.

Okayama-jō CASTLE

(岡山城; http://okayama-kanko.net/ujo; 2-3-1 Marunouchi; ¥300, combination ticket with Kōraku-en ¥560, additional charge for special exhibitions; 9am-5pm, to 9.30pm late Jul–mid-Aug) Nicknamed U-jō (烏城; Crow Castle) because of its colour, the striking black Okayama Castle has an imposing exterior with gilded-fish gargoyles flipping their tails in the air. You can appreciate its impressive appearance for nix from either the grounds or across the river. In summer, the castle and nearby Kōraku-en are lit up and stay open late.

Inside the *donjon* (main keep), some modern finishes detract from the 16th-century feel, but there are a few interesting museum displays and views from the top floor. While it was first completed in 1597 under *daimyō* Ukita Hideie, much of the castle was dismantled after the Meiji Restoration and most of what remained burnt down during WWII air raids. It was rebuilt in 1966.

From Okayama Station, take the Higashi-yama tram to the Shiroshita stop, from where it's about 10 minutes on foot. Walking the entire way is also easy and takes about 25 minutes.

Sleeping

Modern midrange and budget hotels dominate the scene in Okayama. Book ahead for Fridays and Saturdays. Staying near the train station (and its buses) is the most convenient. Most options are southeast of the station, but be aware that staying further than the (lovely and walkable) Nishigawa Greenway means relying on the tram or long walks. For a more traditional ryokan experience, consider staying in nearby Kurashiki.

Hibari House HOSTEL ¥

(ヒバリハウス; 086-230-2833; www.hibari-t.com; 2-7-15 Omote-chō; dm ¥3500;) The Hibari building boasts a gallery, bookstore and coworking space, and the dorms are suitably attractive in dark wood with cream privacy blinds and USB ports. There are ample spotless bathrooms, a kitchen and a laundry. Hibari is in the slick shopping arcade next to Tenmaya bus station; otherwise from Okayama Station, walk 30 minutes or take the tram to Tamachi.

★**Kōraku Hotel** HOTEL ¥¥

(後楽ホテル; 086-221-7111; www.hotel.kooraku.co.jp; 5-1 Heiwa-chō; s/tw from ¥8275/10,200; @) Kōraku has classy touches such as local museum pieces displayed on each floor, and pampering extras such as complimentary aroma pots for your room. Beds are comfortable, and the corner rooms (twin from ¥14,000), with large curved windows, are especially spacious. Staff speak English, as does the enthusiastic manager, who you may find mingling with guests in the lobby.

There are good discounts for longer stays, and a buffet breakfast or lunch for ¥1080.

OFF THE BEATEN TRACK

FARMHOUSE GETAWAY IN HATTŌJI

Head up through the hills past the farms and thatched-roof houses to Hattōji (八塔寺) to stay at the restored farmhouse **Hattōji International Villa** (八塔寺国際交流ヴィラ; 086-256-2535; www.international-villa.or.jp; Kagami Yoshinaga-chō, Bizen-shi; s/d ¥4100/7200, whole house up to 8 people/9-13 people ¥25,700/41,000;).

Spending a night or two here is an excellent way to get a sense of Japan outside the well-trodden urban centres. In the farmhouse are four large tatami rooms separated by sliding doors, a shared bathroom and kitchen, and bicycles that are free to use. In the common area you can burn charcoal in the open hearth, and near the villa you'll find hiking tracks, shrines and temples (where it's possible to join morning meditation).

Check availability and make reservations online. Payment is cash only. There are a couple of eateries in the area, but hours are irregular – stock up on groceries in Okayama or Yoshinaga before you come to Hattōji.

Buses (¥200, 30 minutes, five to six daily Monday to Saturday) run to Hattōji from Yoshinaga (吉永), which is on the JR San-yō line, accessible by train (¥580, 35 minutes, roughly every hour) from Okayama. The bus drops you near the villa entrance. See the International Villa Group website (www.international-villa.or.jp) for the latest schedule.

Eating & Drinking

Okayama has the best range of eating options in the region. Even under the station, there are great modern, casual restaurants along the 'Kitchen Runway' – look for the signs. The streets southeast of the station, along and off Honmachi, have plenty of restaurants – including international, casual, budget, high-end sushi, and bars serving food into the wee hours.

★Okabe TOFU ¥

(おかべ; 086-222-1404; www.tofudokoro-okabe.com; 1-10-1 Omote-chō; set meals ¥820-870; 11.30am-2pm Mon-Wed, Fri & Sat) Squeeze in at the counter at this small, simple lunch joint and watch the team of women preparing delicious tofu meals as you wait. There are only three things on the (picture) menu; try the *okabe teishoku* for a set of several types of tofu. The menu is meat-free but contains fish stock.

The restaurant is on a corner – look for the big illustration of a heavily laden tofu seller in a straw hat.

Nodo Nobashi YAKITORI ¥

(串焼き のどのばし; 086-232-5959; www.facebook.com/nodonobashi; 5-23 Heiwa-chō; dishes ¥180-330; 5.30pm-midnight Thu-Tue) No, don't be intimidated. From the riverside street, it looks like it's bar-room only at this popular *kushiyaki* (grilled skewers) joint, but the tables out back, welcoming staff, English menu and whisky highballs will help you breathe easily. Chicken skin, shrimp, mushroom – all great on the hot coals.

Ajitsukasa Nomura TONKATSU ¥

(味司野村; 086-222-2234; 1-10 Heiwa-chō; mains ¥800-1100; 11am-9pm) Step into this quiet bamboo-themed restaurant to try Okayama speciality *demi-katsudon* – deep-fried pork cutlets with a thick, rich demi-glace sauce, served on rice. Place your order by purchasing a ticket from the machine inside the entrance. The machine doesn't have English, but the separate menu does and it's easy to match up the numbered items; button #1 is the classic.

★Teppan-Ku-Ya JAPANESE ¥¥

(テッパン クウヤ; 086-224-8880; http://teppan-ku-ya.com; 1-1-17 Nodaya-chō; mains ¥800-1950, set meals ¥2500-5000; 6pm-midnight;) An extremely popular fusion restaurant for Japanese classics such as *tako-yaki* (grilled octopus dumplings). The best bet is the set six-course meal, which includes French-leaning flavours in pumpkin soup, grilled prawn, *wagyū* beef or salmon steak, and sweet green-tea ice cream. The warm fuss-free atmosphere, English-speaking staff, wine options and Western-style service make this a foreigner-friendly, good-value choice.

Izayoi no Tsuki BAR

(いざ酔いの月; 086-222-2422; http://izayoinotuki.gorp.jp; 1-10-2 Ekimae-chō; 5pm-midnight) A convivial atmosphere (though it's fine to sit at the counter solo), walls decorated with sake labels, and an enormous drinks menu – just what you want from a local *izakaya*. There are numerous sakes from Okayama Prefecture and beers from local microbreweries. Try the Doppo pilsner or a Kibi Doteshita Bakushu ale.

From Sunday to Thursday, a set sushi menu with all-you-can-drink sake (in two hours) is available for ¥3000 – challenge accepted. Izayoi is just off the Sky Mall arcade. Look for the sign written across a yellow moon.

Information

Momotarō Tourist Information Centre (ももたろう観光センター; 086-222-2912; www.okayama-kanko.net; 9am-8pm;) Large office with maps and information on Okayama and the region, as well as coupons for small discounts on the major sights. The helpful staff speak some English and there's free wi-fi. It's in the basement complex below the station – follow the underground signs.

Tourist Information Counter (観光案内所; 9am-6pm) In the station, by the entrance to the *shinkansen* tracks.

Getting There & Away

BUS

Highway buses connect Okayama with major cities across the region. There are also buses between Okayama Station and Kansai International Airport (four hours, one way/return ¥4650/7700, seven daily); **Ryobi** (www.ryobi-holdings.jp/bus/kousoku/en) has timetables and maps for all three bus companies.

Buses to Shin-Okayama Port (¥490, 35 minutes, one or two per hour) leave from Okayama Station, stopping at **Tenmaya bus station** (天満屋バスステーション; 2-1-1 Omotesando) in the city centre on the way.

Buses leave from the stops outside the west exit of Okayama Station. Free wi-fi is available at stop 11.

TRAIN

Okayama is on the JR San-yō line and *shinkansen* line, connecting to Shin Osaka (¥6020, 45 minutes) in Osaka to the east and Hiroshima (¥6020, 40 minutes) to the west. There are also rail links to Uno (¥1100, 50 minutes) and Takamatsu in Kagawa (¥2030, 55 minutes), south of Naoshima, on the JR Marine Liner, and to Yonago in Tottori Prefecture on the limited express JR Yakumo (¥5270, 2¼ hours).

WORTH A TRIP

BIZEN POTTERY

The Bizen (備前) region has been renowned for its ceramics since the Kamakura period (1185–1333), and travellers with an interest in pottery will find the sleepy town of **Imbe** (伊部) and its kilns a worthwhile side trip from Okayama. The pottery produced here, which tends to be earthy and subdued, has been prized by dedicated tea-ceremony aficionados for centuries.

Most places of ceramic interest are within easy walking distance of Imbe Station. The **Imbe information counter** (0869-64-1001; www.touyuukai.jp; Imbe; 9am-6pm Wed-Mon), inside the souvenir shop on the left as you exit the platform, has a very good *Imbe Walk* map in English, showing the locations of kilns, shops and other sites.

Kibido (黄薇堂; 0869-64-4467; www.bizenyakikibido.com; 714 Imbe; 10am-5pm) FREE is a kiln and gallery-shop run by the Kimura family, one of the six original pottery-making families in the area. It's possible to take a free tour of the traditional step-style *nobori-gama* kiln and see the current generation of Kimura artists at work.

Free tours in English are available – they may be able to accommodate if you just drop in, but call or email in advance to avoid disappointment. Firings only happen once a year, so tours are unlikely to show a working kiln. The free information pamphlet has an excellent short explanation in English of the traditional process of producing Bizen ware – a good place to start a visit to Imbe.

Around Imbe Station, you can eat in a couple of *shokudō* (casual restaurants) on the busy road, where unexpectedly good sushi is available. Cute cafes serving snacks are dotted around the Bizen-ware stores, with one inside the station.

There is one direct train an hour to Imbe from Okayama (¥580, 40 minutes) on the Akō line (赤穂線), bound for Banshū-Akō (播州赤穂) and Aioi (相生).

Getting Around

Okayama can be seen on foot or with a couple of short tram rides. The Higashi-yama line takes you to the main attractions, going from the station's east exit all the way up Momotarō-Ōdōri (get out at the last stop on this street for nearly all of the sights), then turning right. The Seiki-bashi line turns right earlier at the large roundabout, passing Okayama Central Post Office. Travel within the central city area costs ¥100, or ¥140 further afield. Okayama is also a good city for cycling.

JR Eki-Rinkun Rent-a-cycle (レンタサイクル駅リンくん; 086-223-7081; www.ekiren.com; 1-2 Motomachi; rental per day ¥350; 7am-9.50pm) Bike rental on the east side of Okayama Station.

Naoshima

087 / POP 3120

As the location of the Benesse Art Site, the island of Naoshima (直島) has become one of the region's biggest tourist attractions, offering a unique opportunity to see some of Japan's best contemporary art in gorgeous natural settings. Museums and numerous outdoor sculptures are situated around the coast, including *Yellow Pumpkin* by Yayoi Kusama, which has become a symbol of Naoshima.

The Benesse project started in the early '90s, when the Benesse Corporation chose Naoshima as the setting for its growing collection of modern art. Once home to a dwindling population subsisting on the proceeds of a small fishing industry, Naoshima now has a number of world-class art galleries and installations, and has attracted creative types from all over Japan to set up businesses here. The art movement has not stopped at Naoshima's shores, either, with museums and art sites popping up on other islands in the Inland Sea.

Sights

★Art House Project — SCULPTURE

(家プロジェクト; www.benesse-artsite.jp/en; Honmura; single/combined ticket ¥410/1030; 10am-4.30pm Tue-Sun) In Honmura, half a dozen traditional buildings have been turned over to contemporary artists to use as the setting for creative installations, often incorporating local history. Highlights include Shinro Ohtake's shack-like **Haisha** (はいしゃ; 10am-4.30pm Tue-Sun), its Statue of Liberty sculpture rising up through the levels of the house; James Turrell's experiment with light in **Minamidera** (南寺; 10am-4.15pm Tue-Sun), where you enter in total darkness...and wait; and Hiroshi Sugimoto's play on the traditional **Go'o Shrine** (護王神社; 10am-4.30pm Tue-Sun), with a glass staircase and narrow underground 'Stone Chamber'.

The sites are within walking distance of each other. Take the Naoshima bus to the Nōkyō-mae stop to start exploring. Buy a ticket at the tourist counter in the Miyanoura ferry terminal, at Honmura Lounge, or at the tobacco shop near the bus stop.

★Yellow Pumpkin — SCULPTURE

(南瓜) This yellow pumpkin sculpture, by Japanese artist Yayoi Kusama, has become a symbol of Naoshima. It's perched on the end of a small jetty. Pumpkins are revered by Kusama for their quiet exuberance. Her style anticipated pop art and she claims to have influenced Andy Warhol.

The artist has also installed a larger **Red Pumpkin** (赤かぼちゃ), which you can walk inside, at Miyanoura Port.

Chichū Art Museum — GALLERY

(地中美術館; www.benesse-artsite.jp/en; adult/child ¥2060/free; 10am-6pm Tue-Sun Mar-Sep, to 5pm Oct-Feb) A work of art itself, this museum designed by Tadao Ando consists of a series of cool concrete-walled spaces sitting snugly underground. Lit by natural light, it provides a remarkable setting for several Monet water-lily paintings, some monumental sculptures by Walter De Maria and installations by James Turrell. Outside is the Chichū garden, created in the spirit of Monet's garden in Giverny.

During peak periods, a 'timed ticket' system may be in place, designating the time you are able to purchase a ticket and enter.

Benesse House Museum — GALLERY

(ベネッセハウスミュージアム; www.benesse-artsite.jp/en; adult/child ¥1030/free; 8am-9pm) Award-winning architect Tadao Ando designed this stunning museum and hotel on the south coast of the island. Among the works here are pieces by Andy Warhol, David Hockney, Jasper Johns and Japanese artists such as Shinro Ohtake. Art installations are dotted across the adjacent shoreline and forest, blending architecture into nature.

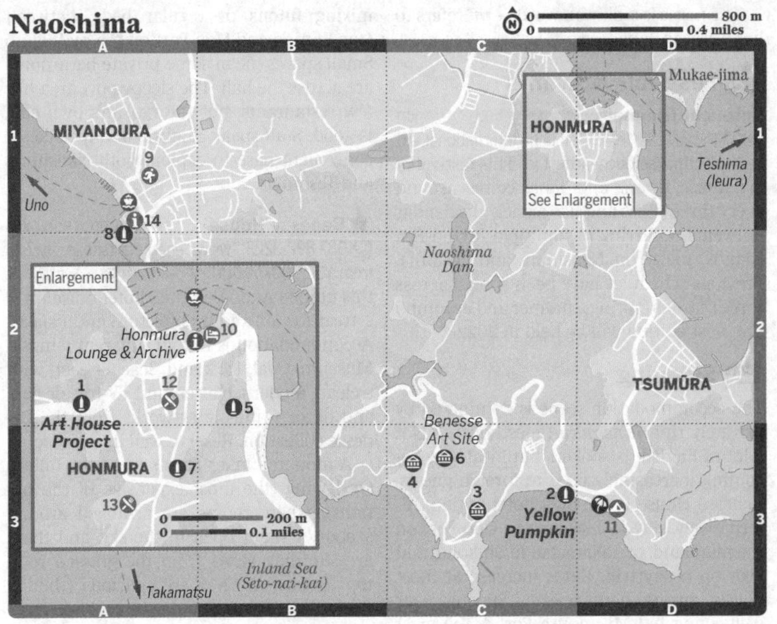

Naoshima

Top Sights
1 Art House Project A2
2 Yellow Pumpkin C3

Sights
3 Benesse House Museum C3
4 Chichū Art Museum C3
5 Go'o Shrine B2
Haisha .... (see 1)
6 Lee Ufan Museum C3
7 Minamidera A3
8 Red Pumpkin A2

Activities, Courses & Tours
9 Naoshima Bath "I Love YU" A1

Sleeping
Benesse House .... (see 3)
10 Naoshima Backpackers Guesthouse B2
11 Tsutsuji-sō D3

Eating
12 Apron Cafe A2
13 Cafe Salon Naka-Oku A3
Museum Restaurant Issen .... (see 3)

Information
14 Marine Station Tourist Information Centre A1

Transport
Cafe Ougiya Rent-a-Cycle .... (see 14)

Lee Ufan Museum GALLERY

(李禹煥美術館; www.benesse-artsite.jp/en; adult/child ¥1030/free; 10am-6pm Tue-Sun Mar-Sep, to 5pm Oct-Feb) Adding to the Benesse Art Site's suite of museums is yet another design from the irrepressible Tadao Ando. It houses works by the renowned Korean-born artist (and philosopher) Lee Ufan, who was a leading figure in the Mono-ha movement of the 1960s and '70s. Four rooms hold minimalist pieces that can be as simple as one brush-stroke or a gradient of colour.

Activities

★**Naoshima Bath "I Love YU"** BATHHOUSE

(直島銭湯 I♥湯; www.benesse-artsite.jp/en; 2252-2 Higashicho; adult/child ¥650/300; 1-9pm Tue-Sun) For a unique bathing experience, take a soak at this colourful fusion of Japanese bathing tradition and contemporary art, designed by Ōtake Shinrō, where there really is an elephant in the room. It's a couple of minutes' walk inland from Miyanoura Port. Look for the building with the palm trees out front.

The name is a play on words – *yū* refers to hot water in Japanese.

Festivals & Events

Setouchi Triennale ART
(瀬戸内国際芸術祭; Setouchi International Art Festival; http://setouchi-artfest.jp) This festival of art, music, drama and dance comes around every three years and has a packed calendar of events occurring on multiple Inland Sea islands, many on Naoshima and Teshima. Previous schedules have been spread across three seasons (spring, summer and autumn.) The next edition will be held in 2022.

Sleeping

The accommodation scene is dominated by privately run *minshuku* (guesthouses). Not a lot of English is spoken, but locals are becoming increasingly used to foreign guests. Benesse House is the only hotel option. Alternatively, stay in Okayama or Uno Port on the mainland, or Takamatsu in Shikoku, and visit on a day trip. Rates increase at most places during high season. Staying near well-connected Miyanoura Port is the most convenient.

★Tsutsuji-sō CAMPGROUND ¥
(つつじ荘; ☎087-892-2838; www.tsutsujiso.com; 352–1 Naoshima-chō; tents/cottages per person from ¥3780/4760;) Perfectly placed on the beachfront, not far from the Benesse Art Site area, is this encampment of Mongolian-style *pao* (yurt) tents. Cosy tents sleep up to four, have a small fridge and heater (but no air-con), and shared bathrooms. The tent-averse can opt instead for one of the caravans or cottages. Meals are available if reserved in advance. Cash only.

Naoshima Backpackers Guesthouse HOSTEL ¥
(☎080-9130-2976; www.naoshima-backpackers-guesthouse.com; 845-9 Naoshima-chō; dm ¥3000;) The dorms here may just be wooden capsules and there is only one shower, but it's cheap, with free bike use and an excellent location near Honmura Port and the sights. Prior reservations only, as they might not hear the doorbell! From the Honmura local bus stop, head straight towards the water and look for a white sign.

Uno Port Inn RYOKAN ¥¥
(☎0863-21-2729; www.unoportinn.com; 1-4-4 Chikko, Tamano; s/d from ¥6900/9900;) You'll find this cosy ryokan, with 12 rooms mixing futons or regular beds, between Uno Station and Uno Port on the mainland. Small spaces mean some private bathrooms are across the hall. The sleepy port area has few restaurants, but the ryokan's own cafe is good. Staff speak English, and it makes a convenient base to explore both Naoshima and Teshima.

★Benesse House BOUTIQUE HOTEL ¥¥¥
(☎087-892-3223; www.benesse-artsite.jp; tw/ste from ¥32,000/59,000; P@) A stay at this unique Ando-designed hotel-museum is a treat for art and architecture enthusiasts. Accommodation is in four different wings – Museum, Oval, Park and Beach – each with a clean, modern, clutter- and TV-free design, and decor featuring artworks from the Benesse collection. Reserve well in advance.

A monorail takes guests up to the hilltop Oval wing (the most expensive of the options), where rooms are arranged around a pool of water open to the sky, and there are stunning views from the grassed rooftop. Rooms in Oval are spacious (though the bathrooms are standard-issue) and large windows make the most of the views; you may not want to come back down once you're up here. The Beach wing is a newer building by the sea, from where you can see the *Yellow Pumpkin* sculpture. Alternatively, stick close to the art with a stay in the Museum lodgings.

Children under seven years old aren't permitted in the Oval and Museum wings. A guest-only shuttle bus runs between Miyanoura Port, the island's major art sites and the hotel.

Eating

In the Art House Project area in Honmura there are a few cafes, restaurants and bars serving food. Near Miyanoura Port, there are later-opening restaurants, plus a small supermarket and the only convenience store. Not many places open in the evenings, or at all on Mondays, and hours can be irregular.

★Cafe Salon Naka-Oku CAFE ¥
(カフェサロン中奥; ☎087-892-3887; www.naka-oku.com; Honmura; set lunch ¥650-800, dishes ¥480-980; 11.30am-3pm & 5.30-9pm Wed-Mon;) Up on a small hill at the rear of a farming plot, Naka-Oku is a good option in the Honmura area, and one of only a couple of places open in the evenings here. It's all wood-beamed warmth and cosiness, with homey specialities such as *omuraisu*

OFF THE BEATEN TRACK

CYCLING THE KIBI PLAIN

The largely rural Kibi plain west of Okayama is best explored on two wheels, following a mostly flat cycling route between Bizen-Ichinomiya (備前一宮) and Sōja (総社). Among the highlights are **Kibitsu-jinja** (吉備津神社; www.kibitujinja.com; 931 Kibitsu, Kita Ward; ⌚8.30am-4pm) FREE, a major shrine possibly connected to the Momotarō legend (p473); and the 5th-century **Tsukuriyama-kofun** (造山古墳; ☎086-270-5066; ⌚24hr) FREE, the fourth-biggest *kofun* (keyhole-shaped burial mound) in Japan, thought to mark the final resting place of a local king who ruled the Kibi region when this area was a rival power to the Yamato court.

Gearless bike rental is ¥1000 for the day (¥600 for three hours), available from **Uedo Rent-a-Cycle** (レンタサイクルウエド; ☎086-284-2311; Bizen-Ichinomiya Station; ⌚9am-6pm), on the right at the front of Bizen-Ichinomiya Station, and **Araki Rent-a-Cycle** (荒木レンタサイクル; ☎0866-92-0233; 2 Chome-1-5 Ekimae, Sōja; ⌚9am-6pm), at the side of the bus area in front of Sōja Station. It costs ¥200 extra if you hire from one office and drop it at the other. Uedo Rent-a-Cycle occasionally closes in bad weather; if no one is around, try asking the guard at the nearby bike parking lot, who may be able to call and get it opened up for you.

Follow the route map you receive with the bike, and the blue 'Kibiji District' road signs along the course. If you wander off track, locals will be able to set you straight – just ask them for the *Kibiji jitensha dōro* (Kibiji bike path). Allow at least three or four hours to cycle the roughly 15km route, past shrines, temples and rice fields, to give yourself time to wander the sights.

To reach Bizen-Ichinomiya take a local JR Kibi line train from Okayama (¥210, 12 minutes); for Sōja take either the JR Momotarō line (¥410, 40 minutes) or JR Hakubi line (¥500, 30 minutes) from Okayama.

(omelette filled with fried rice) at lunchtime and small dishes with drinks in the evening.

This is one of the few restaurants in the area open on Mondays.

Apron Cafe CAFE ¥¥

(☎087-892-3048; www.fb.me/aproncafe.naoshima; 777 Honmura; set meals ¥1380-1580; ⌚11am-4pm Tue-Sun; 📶🖉) You're here for art, so why not eat in a gallery-like space with polished timber, designer furniture, a faux-grass picnic area and even an in-house zine and giftware. The artfully arranged lunches function like tasting plates of quiche, tempura fish, samosas and Okayama black rice. Cranberry and coconut scones with local sea-salt butter are also attractive.

★Museum Restaurant Issen KAISEKI ¥¥¥

(ミュージアムレストラン日本料理一扇; ☎087-892-3223; www.benesse-artsite.jp/en/stay; breakfast ¥2613, lunch sets ¥2000-2900, dinner sets ¥7722-9504; ⌚7.30-9.30am, 11.30am-2.30pm & 6-9.45pm) The artfully displayed *kaiseki* dinners at this contrastingly austere restaurant in Benesse House Museum's basement (though with Andy Warhol works on the wall) are almost too pretty to eat. Courses feature Setouchi seafood, but there is a veg-dominated option (request a couple of days ahead) and the menu changes with the seasons. Breakfast and lunch are also served. Reservations are highly recommended.

ℹ Information

LEFT LUGGAGE

For day trippers, there are some luggage lockers at Miyanoura Port, and luggage can also be left at the Honmura Lounge & Archive.

MONEY

The ATMs at the post offices in Miyanoura and Honmura take international cards, as does the 7-Eleven near Miyanoura Port. Ask at the tourist office for directions.

TOURIST INFORMATION

Honmura Lounge & Archive (☎087-840-8273; ⌚10am-4.30pm Tue-Sun) Tourist information next to Honmura Port, with a rest area and left-luggage service. Tickets for the Art House Project can be purchased here.

Marine Station Tourist Information Centre (☎087-892-2299; www.naoshima.net; ⌚8.30am-6pm) At Miyanoura Port. Has a comprehensive bilingual map of the island (also downloadable from the website), a walking map

OFF THE BEATEN TRACK

BEYOND NAOSHIMA: MORE ARTY ISLANDS OF THE INLAND SEA

Naoshima and Teshima draw the largest art-loving crowds, leaving Inujima, Megijima and Ogijima for quieter exploration.

The drawcard on **Inujima** (犬島) is the excellent **Inujima Seirensho Art Museum** (犬島精錬所美術館; www.benesse-artsite.jp/en; incl Inujima Art House Project ¥2060; ⏲10am-4.30pm Wed-Mon, closed Wed & Thu Dec-Feb), a copper refinery converted into an eco-building displaying Yukinori Yanagi's surreal take on environmental issues. This is more an interactive experience than a traditional gallery – you enter through a dark maze of mirrors with the burning sun at its end and continue past floating furniture. Inujima also boasts smaller art sites (included in the museum ticket price) converted from Japanese houses, as well as cute little cafes.

Is **Megijima** (女木島) the mythical Onigi-shima, the 'Ogre's Island' where legendary Momotarō went to fight? Head up to the caves to see the comically colourful ogre statues and you might become a believer – or at least the kids will, while you appreciate the panoramic views. You can also explore the beach and Oni Cafe & Gallery, or *Mecon*, a work by Shinro Ohtake (of *Naoshima Bath "I Love YU"* fame) that places neon-coloured frameworks around actual school grounds to express the hope that locals remain on the island.

Tiny **Ogijima** (男木島) is only 2km long and has even less flat ground among the green mountaintops, but this makes it an interesting 'museum without walls'. The narrow roads, winding up in a maze through the sleepy village, suddenly open onto outdoor art installations. Look for a 'wallalley' – colourful paintings made from discarded lumber and scrapped vessels.

Ferries run between Inujima and Ieura Port (¥1230, 25 minutes, two daily) on Teshima (normally continuing to/from Miyanoura Port), or Hoden Port (¥300, 10 minutes, six to eight daily) on the mainland. A bus from Okayama Station (¥750, one hour, Saturday and Sunday only, three daily during Setouchi Triennale) terminates a two-minute walk from Hoden Port.

A ferry runs six times a day from Takamatsu, calling first at Megijima (¥370, 20 minutes) then Ogijima (¥510, 40 minutes). Warning: the last two ferries to Ogijima give you little or no time to catch the last return ferry.

and a full list of accommodation options. Note that staff don't make accommodation reservations. Tickets for the Art House Project can also be purchased here.

Getting There & Away

Naoshima can be visited on a day trip from Okayama or Takamatsu and it makes a good stopover if you're travelling between Honshū and Shikoku. Extra-large lockers or left-luggage services are available at the ports.

From Okayama, take the JR Uno line to Uno (¥580, one hour); this usually involves a quick change of trains at Chayamachi, crossing the same platform. Ferries go to Naoshima's main **Miyanoura Port** from the port near Uno Station (¥290, 15 to 20 minutes, hourly). There are also ferries from Uno to the island's **Honmura Port** (¥290, 20 minutes, five daily). Heading back to Okayama at night, you may find trains from Uno have finished or are two hours away, in which case it can be better to take a bus to Okayama Station (¥650, one hour, one to two hourly) from outside Uno Station at bus stop 1.

From March to November daily (except Tuesdays) high-speed boats connect Miyanoura Port to to the port on tiny Inujima island (¥1850, 40 to 55 minutes, three daily), with most services stopping off first at Ieura Port on Teshima (¥620, about 30 minutes, two daily). A daily (except Tuesdays) high-speed boat also connects Honmura Port to Ieura Port (¥620, 20 minutes) from April to November at 11.15am.

Takamatsu is connected to Miyanoura Port by standard ferry (¥520, 50 minutes, five daily) and high-speed boat (¥1220, 25 minutes, five daily). There is also one daily (except Tuesdays) high-speed boat to Honmura Port (¥1220, 30 minutes) at 10.45am from April to November.

Ferry route maps and the latest timetables can be found on the Benesse Art Site website (www.benesse-artsite.jp/en/access) or at the tourist offices in Okayama and Takamatsu.

Getting Around

Bicycle or the town bus are the best options for getting around Naoshima, though it's possible on foot if you have time; for example, it's just over 2km from Miyanoura Port to Honmura and the Art House Project area. There is one **taxi** (Japanese only 087-882-2424; 8.30am-10pm) on Naoshima, taking up to nine passengers – this has to be reserved in advance of coming to the island.

BICYCLE

Naoshima is great for cycling and there are a few rental places around Miyanoura Port. **Cafe Ougiya Rent-a-Cycle** (090-3189-0471; www.ougiya-naoshima.jp; bike per day ¥300-2000; 9am-6pm) is inside the Marine Station at the port. A few electric bikes (¥1000 per day) and scooters (¥1500 per day) are also available. Prices are similar at the other rental shops nearby.

BUS

Naoshima 'town bus' minibuses run between Miyanoura, Honmura, and the Benesse Art Site area (Tsutsuji-sō campground stop) in the south once or twice an hour – expect queues during the Setouchi Triennale festival. It costs ¥100 per ride (no change given). From Tsutsuji-sō, there's a free Benesse shuttle, stopping at all the Benesse Art Site museums. In busy seasons buses can fill up quickly, especially towards the end of the day, when people are returning to the port to catch ferries. Be sure to check the timetables and allow enough buffer time.

Teshima

Teshima (豊島), a small hilly island between Naoshima and Shōdo-shima, holds its own with a number of interesting art sites, especially its imposing spacecraft-like Teshima Art Museum squatting among the greenery. You can spot the larger sibling islands across the sea from lofty vantage points as you meander over the slopes, winding up past lemon trees and old Japanese houses.

Sights

★Teshima Art Museum MUSEUM

(豊島美術館; www.benesse-artsite.jp/en; ¥1540; 10am-5pm Wed-Mon Mar-Oct, to 4pm Nov-Feb, closed Wed & Thu Dec-Feb) Teshima's art 'museum' impresses for its architecture – a monumental concrete shell, forming a low teardrop-shaped dome on the hillside, designed by Tokyo-based architect Ryue Nishizawa. Visitors wander through the peaceful, contemplative space, where cutouts in the shell frame snapshots of blue sky, clouds, or the green of the surrounding hills. Look down to see small globules of water being rolled about the floor on the breeze, in an exhibit created by Hiroshima-born artist Rei Naito.

Teshima Yokoo House GALLERY

(豊島横尾館; www.benesse-artsite.jp/en; ¥510; 10am-5pm Wed-Mon Mar-Oct, to 4pm Nov-Feb, closed Wed & Thu Dec-Feb) Close to Ieura Port, an old house has been converted into exhibition spaces, with a colourful take on a traditional Japanese rock garden outside (which locals helped create). Don't miss stepping inside the tower 'waterfall' installation, which is lined with thousands of postcards of waterfalls and seems to go on forever below your feet. Even the giddying, all-chrome bathrooms are worth checking out.

Les Archives du Cœur MUSEUM

(心臓音のアーカイブ; www.benesse-artsite.jp/en; adult/child ¥510/free; 10am-5pm Wed-Mon Mar-Oct, to 4pm Nov-Feb, closed Wed & Thu Dec-Feb) For an oddly fascinating and unique museum experience, visit this 'heartbeat archive' on a small bay near the Karato Port area. There are tens of thousands of registered heartbeats from around the world, and you can listen to them played on a loop in surround sound in the very dark 'heart room'. While you're here, why not register and record your own heartbeat and get a keepsake CD (¥1540)?

Sleeping & Eating

Teshima can be visited as a day trip, but, if you want to soak up the island's natural charms, there are some *minshuku* and ryokan, although most are small homes with little English spoken. Staff at the tourist information office near the Ieura ferry terminal can help book accommodation.

Cafes dotted around the island offer *teishoku* (set-menu) lunches, and the Teshima Art Museum cafe serves simple olive rice. Sun-rich Teshima is known for its lemons, which you will find garnishing dishes or dried to take away as a souvenir.

Takamatsu-ya RYOKAN ¥

(古宿　たかまつ屋; 080-5275-8550; www.takamatsu-ya.jp; s/d/tr with shared bathroom ¥6000/10,000/12,000; P) This guesthouse has witnessed ample history as a sanatorium and ryokan for infants or the down and out. Not that you would know it now, looking at the seven immaculate tatami rooms. The English-speaking staff, breakfast (¥500) among the lemon trees, and location just a short walk from the Ieura ferry terminal make it as welcoming as ever.

Information

Pick up maps and information (some English spoken) at the tourist office near the Ieura ferry terminal.

Getting There & Away

Eight ferries a day travel from Uno Port on the mainland to Ieura Port (¥770, 25 to 40 minutes), with six continuing around to Karato Port (¥1030, 40 to 60 minutes); these ferries also continue to the island of Shōdo-shima. From Takamatsu, three to six ferries go to Ieura daily (¥1330, 35 to 50 minutes), some also stopping at Honmura on Naoshima. Two ferries a day go from Naoshima's Miyanoura Port to Ieura (¥620, 35 minutes; not every day in low season), continuing on to the island of Inujima.

Current timetables are available at www.benesse-artsite.jp/en/access.

Getting Around

Cycling on the island is highly recommended for getting around; travelling by bus and walking is easier, but more time-consuming. Bikes can be hired at the Ieura Port area for ¥500 per day; electric-assist bikes (¥1000 per four hours, ¥100 per additional hour) are also available (but go quickly during the Setouchi Triennale festival) and are a good idea if you're cycling across the hilly island to Karato. A shuttle bus connecting Ieura and Karato (¥200, 17 minutes) runs roughly hourly, with additional buses during the Triennale.

Shōdo-shima

☎0879 / POP 31,200

Famed for its olive groves and as the setting of the classic film *Nijūshi-no-hitomi* (Twenty-Four Eyes; telling the story of a village schoolteacher and her young charges), Shōdo-shima (小豆島) makes an enjoyable day trip or overnight escape from big-city Japan. It is mainly appealing for its mountainous landscape, scenic coastal roads and Inland Sea vistas, but also has a smattering of sights.

Tonoshō is the main town and port, and where you can see 'the world's narrowest navigable strait', Dobuchi Strait, which runs through the centre of town. The island is popular during summer and when the autumn leaves are at their prettiest in October and November. Come out of season and you'll find a sleepy isle with very few other travellers.

Sights & Activities

★Marukin Soy Sauce Historical Museum — MUSEUM

(マルキン醤油記念館; ☎0879-82-0047; http://moritakk.com/know_enjoy/shoyukan; ¥210; ⊙9am-4pm) Shōdo-shima was famous for its soybeans long before olives arrived, and several old soy-sauce companies are still in business here. Marukin has a small museum with displays of the sauce-making process, old implements, photos and interesting facts you never knew about the ubiquitous brown stuff. There are good English explanations, and you can try the surprisingly tasty soy-sauce-flavoured ice cream.

It's on the main road between Kusakabe and Sakate Ports.

Nakayama Rice Fields — LANDMARK

(中山千枚田, Nakayama Senmaida; 1486 Nakayama; ⊙24hr) FREE About 4km inland from the Ikeda ferry terminal are Nakayama's 'thousand rice fields'. The terraces are pretty in any season, but especially picturesque after rice planting in late April or early May, when the water-filled fields become a hillside of mirrors.

★Kanka Gorge & Ropeway — OUTDOORS

(寒霞渓; www.kankakei.co.jp; ropeway one way/return ¥980/1760; ⊙ropeway 8.30am-5pm) The cable car (寒霞渓ロープウエイ) is the main attraction at Kanka-kei in the central mountains, making a spectacular trip through the gorge – particularly impressive when the foliage is ablaze with autumn colours (drawing scores of leaf peepers). Hikers can also take in the breathtaking views of the Inland Sea from the area around the upper cable-car station without taking the ride.

Keen walkers can climb between the lower and upper cable-car stations via the Omote 12 Views (表12景; 2.3km) and Ura Eight Views (裏8景; 1.8km) tracks. There are other scenic walks from the upper station, including a hike to the eastern peak of Hoshigajō-yama (星ヶ城東峰; 817m).

On weekends, and on weekdays during peak periods, there are four buses a day from Kusakabe Port to the lower cable-car station (紅雲亭; Kōuntei), with additional services during the autumn leaf-viewing season. There are no buses during winter.

Shōdo-shima

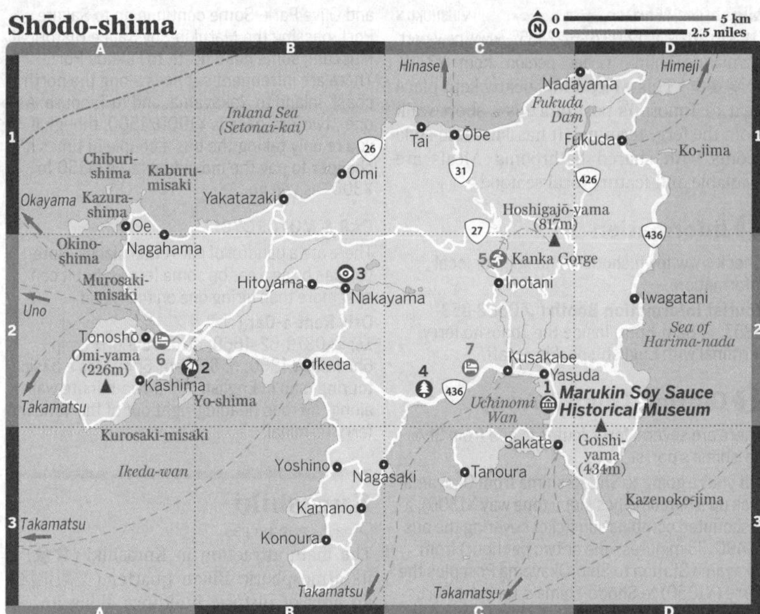

Shōdo-shima

Top Sights
1 Marukin Soy Sauce Historical Museum C2

Sights
2 Angel Road A2
3 Nakayama Rice Fields B2
4 Shōdo-shima Olive Park C2

Activities, Courses & Tours
5 Kanka Gorge & Ropeway C2
Sun Olive Onsen .... (see 4)

Sleeping
6 Minshuku Maruse A2
7 Shōdo-shima Olive Youth Hostel C2

Information
Tourist Information Booth .... (see 6)

Transport
Orix Rent-a-Car .... (see 6)

Sun Olive Onsen ONSEN
(サン・オリーブ温泉; 1941-1 Nishimura-misaki; ¥700; noon-9.45pm Thu-Tue) Enjoy fabulous views of the 'Japanese Aegean' from a variety of herbal baths. Located within Shōdo-shima Olive Park.

Sleeping & Eating

Shōdo-shima has a variety of hotels, particularly along the road running straight back from the waterfront in Tonoshō, which makes a good base. There are only a handful of hostels and guesthouses on the island. Accommodation further away from the port caters to visitors who want an escape and are not planning on moving about much.

Given its size, eating out on Shōdo-shima does not present the great number of options you might expect. Head to the road running straight back from the waterfront in Tonoshō for simple cafes and some *izakaya* and ramen joints. Resorts and large hotels usually include meals and have restaurants for nonguests.

Shōdo-shima Olive Youth Hostel HOSTEL ¥
(小豆島オリーブユースホステル; 0879-82-6161; www.jyh.gr.jp/shoudo; 1072 Nishimura, Uchinomi-chō; dm ¥3400, d tatami without bathroom ¥6800;) This pleasant hostel near the waterfront has bunk-bed dorms and tatami rooms. Meals, bike rental and laundry are available. Buses stop in front of the hostel (at the Shōdoshimi Orību-Yūsu-mae stop) or it's about a 20-minute walk from Kusakabe Port.

Minshuku Maruse MINSHUKU ¥
(民宿マルセ; ☎0879-62-2385; www.new-port.biz/maruse/1.htm; r per person from ¥3700;) This welcoming, neatly kept place next to Tonoshō's post office is a short walk from the ferry terminal. It has Japanese-style rooms with shared bathrooms. Meals are available and feature local seafood.

Information

Check www.town.shodoshima.lg.jp for local information.

Tourist Information Booth (☎0802-853-5857; ⏲8am-6pm) Inside the Tonoshō ferry terminal with English-speaking staff.

Getting There & Away

There are several ferry routes to and from Shōdo-shima's ports.

If you're going to Shōdo-shima from Okayama, pick up a *Kamome bus kippu* (one way ¥1300), a discounted combination ticket covering the bus (¥490, 35 minutes, one or two per hour) from Okayama Station to Shin-Okayama Port plus the ferry (¥1050) to Shōdo-shima's Tonoshō Port. They're sold at the booth of the bus terminal at Okayama Station, and at the Tonoshō Port ticket desk.

Getting Around

The most convenient way to see the island is by car and it's definitely worth hiring one for the day to take in all the scenic routes. Buses do not go everywhere and services are infrequent.

BUS

Shōdo-shima Olive Bus (小豆島オリーブバス; www.shodoshima-olive-bus.com) operates services around the island. The most frequent bus, at one or two per hour, runs between Tonoshō and Kusakabe Ports, passing Ikeda and Olive Park. Some continue on to Sakate Port, passing the Marukin Soy Sauce Historical Museum; some head north to Fukuda Port. There are infrequent services along the north coast, inland to Nakayama, and to Tanoura. A one-/two-day pass is ¥1000/1500, though if you're only taking the bus a couple of times it's cheaper to pay the individual fares (¥150 to ¥300) as you go.

CAR & MOTORCYCLE

There are a handful of car-rental places. Note you can bring a car on some ferries, but it can cost more than hiring one on the island.

Orix Rent-a-Car (オリックスレンタカー小豆島; ☎0879-62-4669; http://car.orix.co.jp; 6hr from ¥4860; ⏲8.30am-6pm) Has a basic touring map in English. It's a two-minute walk along the road heading right out of the Tonoshō ferry terminal.

Kurashiki

☎086 / POP 481,935

The main attraction in Kurashiki (倉敷) is its atmospheric Bikan quarter (美観地区), an area of historic buildings along an old willow-edged canal. A picturesque group of black-and-white warehouses has been converted into museums, and laneways are lined with old wooden houses and shops. By night, lamplight reflecting off the canal creates a cinematic mood in the small area.

In the feudal era, the warehouses here were used to store rice brought by boat from the surrounding countryside. Later, the town became an important textile centre, under the Kurabō Textile Company. Owner Ōhara Magosaburō built up a collection of European art and opened the Ōhara Museum of Art in 1930, which today draws many Japanese tourists.

FERRIES TO SHŌDO-SHIMA

ORIGIN	DESTINATION	FARE (¥)	DURATION	FREQUENCY (DAILY)
Himeji	Fukuda	1520	1hr 40min	7
Shin-Okayama	Tonoshō	1050	70min	13
Takamatsu	Tonoshō (regular)	690	1hr	15
Takamatsu	Tonoshō (high speed)	1170	30min	16
Takamatsu	Ikeda	690	1hr	8
Takamatsu	Kusakabe (regular)	690	1hr	5
Takamatsu	Kusakabe (high speed)	1170	45min	16
Uno	Tonoshō (via Teshima)	1230	1½hr	6

Kurashiki

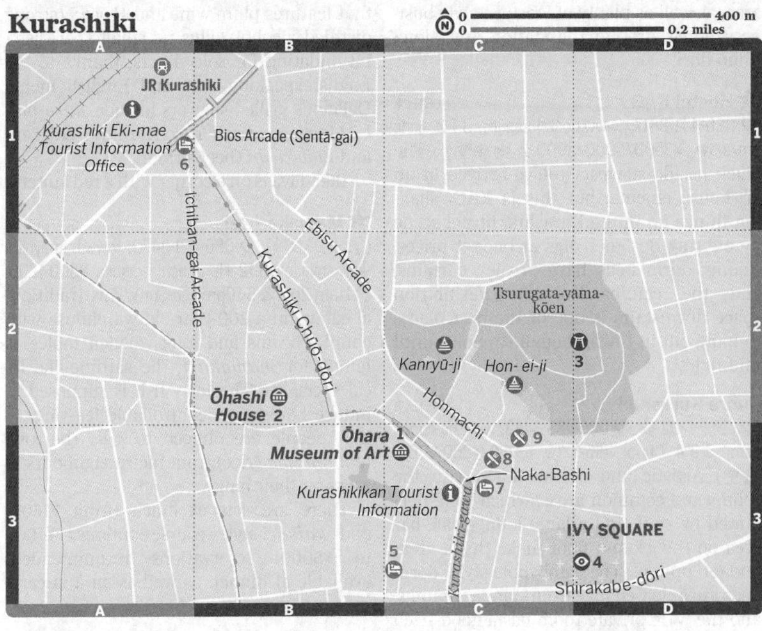

Kurashiki

Top Sights
1 Ōhara Museum of Art........C3
2 Ōhashi House........B2

Sights
3 Achi-jinja........D2
4 Ivy Square........D3

Sleeping
5 Cuore Kurashiki........C3
6 Hostel KAG........A1
7 Ryokan Kurashiki........C3

Eating
8 Mamakari-tei........C3
9 Takadaya........C3

Sights

★Ōhara Museum of Art GALLERY

(大原美術館; www.ohara.or.jp; 1-1-15 Chūō; adult/child ¥1300/500; ⊙9am-5pm Tue-Sun) This is Kurashiki's premier museum, housing the predominantly Western art collection amassed by local textile magnate Ōhara Magosaburō (1880–1943), with the help of artist Kojima Torajirō (1881–1929). The varied assemblage of paintings, prints and sculpture features works by Picasso, Cézanne, El Greco and Matisse, and one of Monet's water-lilies paintings (said to have been bought from the man himself, when Torajirō visited his home in 1920).

While no rival to the major galleries of Europe, it's an interesting collection and one of the town's biggest attractions for Japanese tourists. The valid-all-day ticket also gets you into the museum's **Craft & Asiatic Art Gallery**, the contemporary Japanese collection housed in an annexe behind the main building.

★Ōhashi House HISTORIC BUILDING

(大橋家住宅; www.ohashi-ke.com; 3-21-31 Achi; adult/child ¥550/350; ⊙9am-5pm) Built in 1793, this beautifully restored wooden house belonged to one of Kurashiki's richest families. It was built at a time when prosperous merchants were beginning to claim privileges that had previously been the preserve of the samurai.

Sleeping

Kurashiki is a good place to spend a night in a ryokan, soaking up the old-world atmosphere. There is an increasing number of stylish hostels in and around the historic area, as well as plenty of Western-style business hotels around the station and along Chūō-dōri.

★Hostel KAG HOSTEL ¥
(086-441-8817; www.hostel-kag.jp; 3-1-2 Achi; dm/s/tw ¥2500/5000/8000;) The black facade suggests you've arrived at an art-house cinema, but this is KAG, shaking things up in the Kurashiki hostel scene by offering designer digs at budget prices. Roomy dorm beds have privacy curtains, and the cafe/bar/live music/exhibition space downstairs is one of the best places to hang out in town, though it's noisy until midnight.

Cuore Kurashiki HOSTEL ¥
(クオーレ倉敷; 086-486-3443; www.bs-cuore.com; 1-9-4 Chūō; dm/s/tw ¥3780/4860/8100;) Artistic and quirky touches in the rooms and common areas, which were decorated by staff, and a large lounge-cafe-bar area on the ground floor make this a great budget option. The cubbyhole-style dorm beds are a cosy change from standard bunks, and the 'VIP' private room has a good-sized shower. The cafe opens to midnight, later than most in the area.

★Ryokan Kurashiki RYOKAN ¥¥¥
(旅館くらしき; 086-422-0730; www.ryokan-kurashiki.jp; 4-1 Honmachi; s/d incl 2 meals from ¥48,300/73,600;) By the canal in the heart of the historic district, this is the best ryokan in town, incorporating several beautifully restored Edo-period buildings. The spacious suites all have tatami lounge areas with attached twin-bed rooms and bathrooms. Dinner is a multicourse *kaiseki* affair, featuring Inland Sea delicacies – also available to nonguests (from ¥8000). Some English is spoken.

Eating

Within the historic area there are numerous eateries and you'll pay a little more for the atmosphere that goes with your food. You'll find cheaper, quick-eats options along Chūō-dōri and in the arcades running from the station.

Takadaya BARBECUE ¥
(高田屋; 0120-810-190; 11–36 Honmachi; skewers ¥120-420, set menu ¥1100-2110; 5-10pm Tue-Sun) This bar is in perfect balance: it manages to have loads of old-Japan charm, while maintaining a cocktail list that features plum wine and *shōchū* (strong distilled alcohol). Plus its small space isn't intimidating for solo diners, thanks to the English-speaking staff and English menu. Delicious grilled skewers include *shiso-maki* (Japanese basil rolled around chicken) and *gyū-kushi* (beef sirloin).

Takadaya is on a corner with a red lantern.

★Mamakari-tei SEAFOOD ¥¥
(ままかり亭; 086-421-3430; www.hamayoshi-kurashiki.jp; 3-12 Honmachi; dishes ¥800-1200; 11am-2pm & 5-10pm Tue-Sun) This traditional eatery, in a 200-year-old warehouse with chunky beams and long wooden tables, is famed for *mamakari,* the sardine-like local speciality. The tasty fish is supposed to induce bouts of uncontrollable feasting, so that people are obliged to *kari* (borrow) more *mama* (rice) from their neighbours to carry on their binge.

There are sets at lunch (from ¥1500) and *kaiseki*-style course options (¥4000 to ¥5000; reservations recommended) available at dinner, as well as an à la carte menu.

Information

MONEY

The Bikan historical area lacks 24-hour ATMs. The nearest machines accepting foreign cards are at the train station and nearby in the 7-Eleven on Chūō-dōri.

TOURIST INFORMATION

Kurashiki Eki-mae Tourist Information Office (倉敷駅前観光案内所; 086-424-1220; 2nd fl, Kurashiki City Plaza, 1-7-2 Achi; 9am-6pm;) Just out of the station on the second level and to the right.

Kurashikikan Tourist Information (倉敷館観光案内所; 086-422-0542; www.kurashiki-tabi.jp; 1-4-8 Chūō; 9am-6pm;) The main tourist centre, in the Bikan quarter, with multilingual staff.

Getting There & Around

Kurashiki is on the JR San-yō main line just west of Okayama (¥320, 17 minutes). Shin-Kurashiki, on the *shinkansen* line, is two stops from Kurashiki Station (¥200, nine minutes).

Kurashiki is easily explored on foot. It's possible to get around by bike, though this may end up being more of a nuisance than a convenience, as the lanes are narrow and often crowded.

Kasaoka Islands

Located between Kurashiki and Fukuyama, the port of Kasaoka (笠岡市) is the jumping-off point for six small islands connected to the mainland only by boat. In particular, the islands of Shiraishi-jima and Manabe-shima are worth visiting to enjoy the slower pace of life as it used to be lived all over the Inland Sea.

Sleeping & Eating

The two sleeping options on Manabe-shima are a ryokan and a guesthouse with futons, while Shiraishi-jima offers a villa and a family-run *minshuku*. It is worth organising your visit before you arrive, especially if you do not speak Japanese. Tourism offices can help book accommodation, and the owners of Shiraishi-jima's Moooo! Bar (p490) are very knowledgeable.

You will find the local speciality, Kasaoka ramen, sold in small restaurants on the islands. Rather than pork, pieces of chicken adorn the noodles and broth, which is also chicken based. Seafood is also big in these parts.

Getting There & Around

Kasaoka is 45 minutes west of Okayama (¥760) and 30 minutes west of Kurashiki (¥500) on the JR San-yō line. From the station, it's a seven-minute stroll down to the port for boats to Shiraishi-jima and on to Manabe-shima.

Eight **Sanyō Kisen** (三洋汽船; 0865-62-2866; www.en.sanyo-kisen.jp) ferries run a day to Shiraishi-jima, continuing on to Manabe-shima. There are four regular services (Shiraishi-jima ¥660, 35 minutes; Manabe-shima ¥1020, 72 minutes) and four high-speed services (Shiraishi-jima ¥1150, 22 minutes; Manabe-shima ¥1760, 45 minutes). Baggage charge: ¥210–230.

A water taxi is a convenient alternative option if heading to Santora ryokan on Manabe-shima, especially for groups, as these can take you from Kasaoka direct to the pier at the ryokan (saving you the 10-minute walk from Honura Port). Water taxis are ¥10,000 for up to 10 people – Santora can help with details.

Clear timetable and fare information in English is on the official Kasaoka Islands website, www.kasaoka-kankou.jp.

Manabe-shima

0865 / POP 325

Manabe-shima (真鍋島) is home to more cats than people, and its one small town is an atmospheric maze of old wooden houses, with a solitary village shop that has been in business since the Meiji period, and an old-fashioned school. As with everywhere in this part of Japan, Kōbō Daishi got here first – the great man spent time at the **Enpukuji** (円福寺) temple. More recently, the island and all its characters have been wonderfully captured in Florent Chavouet's illustrated book *Manabé Shima*. The locals are sure to show you a copy (and point themselves out in it).

There are few places to eat out on the island, most with irregular hours. The helpful staff at the Honura Port ferry terminal office can give you some tips, such as the seafood restaurants near there.

Inn the Camp GUESTHOUSE ¥

(www.manabeshima.info; 4073 Kabajima, Manabe-shima; dm ¥3500-4500; P ✻) Futons are sectioned off with tarps for privacy in this clean, modern addition to Manabe-shima, just 50m from Honura Port. The friendly couple who run the converted wooden house speak enough English to help guide you, which is useful on such a quiet island, and run a nearby cafe.

★ Santora RYOKAN ¥¥

(島宿三虎; 0865-68-3515; www.facebook.com/santora310ra; 2224 Manabe-shima; r per person incl 2 meals from ¥10,800;) At this waterfront ryokan, you can laze about in the outdoor saltwater bath while watching boats sail by. The rooms are spacious, the shared indoor bathroom has sea views, and the meals feature local seafood and veggies grown by the friendly owners (no English spoken). There is a range of rooms and plans. It's a 10-minute walk from Honura Port.

For something special, go for one of the *hanare* (separate) cabins (from ¥16,200 per person for two people with meals, with discounts for more people), which have private bathrooms and huge balconies.

Shiraishi-jima

0865 / POP 525

Sleepy Shiraishi-jima (白石島) is popular in the summer for its beaches and there are some good walking paths. Go-everywhere Buddhist saint Kōbō Daishi stopped off here on his way back from China in 806; the temple associated with him, **Kairyū-ji** (開龍寺; 0865-68-3014; 855 Shiraishi-jima; 24hr) FREE, incorporates a trail of small shrines leading to a huge boulder on top of the hill.

The Moooo! Bar rents out windsurfing boards and sea kayaks (¥1000 per hour).

There are a handful of eateries on the island, though hours are irregular outside of summer. If you're staying at the self-catering villa, make sure you bring groceries along with you.

Shiraishi Island International Villa RENTAL HOUSE ¥¥

(☎086-256-2535; www.international-villa.or.jp; 317 Shiraishi-jima; r per person ¥3500-4000; P ᯤ) This great-value villa is a large house atop a hill, with spacious living areas and kitchen, and an outdoor deck with views of the sea. There are four twin bedrooms, one Japanese room, and amenities are shared. It's particularly good for groups or families, though single occupancy is possible. Reservations can be made via the website or email (in English).

Moooo! Bar BAR

(www.mooooobar.com; 439 Shiraishi-jima; ⌚Mon-Sun Jul & Aug, Sun Jun & Sep; ᯤ) A popular bar on the beach, run by resident expat Amy Chavez, which only operates during summer.

Tomo-no-ura

☎084 / POP 5000

Tomo-no-ura (鞆の浦) is a sleepy port town with narrow cobbled streets that retain much of the flavour of its Edo-period heyday. Perfectly situated in the middle of the Inland Sea coast, the town flourished for centuries as a stopoff for boats travelling between western Japan and the capital, until the arrival of steam put an end to Tomo-no-ura's glory days.

Today, fishing boats quietly bob on the water at the old harbour, while a dozen or so temples, some tucked within residential streets, allow quiet meandering as you head up the hillside to views of the Inland Sea. It all makes for a good few hours of strolling.

For film buffs: Tomo-no-ura was the setting for some scenes in *The Wolverine* (2013). It also provided inspiration for renowned Studio Ghibli director Miyazaki Hayao, who spent two months here while developing *Ponyo* (*Gake no ue no Ponyo*; 2008).

Sights

★Sensui-jima ISLAND

(仙酔島) The island of Sensui-jima is just five minutes across the water from Tomo-no-ura town, though vastly different for its rugged natural beauty, as there are no residential homes. There's a walking path that hugs the coast, passing interesting volcanic rock formations, and offers lovely sunset views across the water. After a stroll or swim at the clear-water beach, drop into Kokuminshukusha Sensui-jima, where nonguests can soak in a range of baths for ¥540 (from 10am to 9pm).

The ferry that shuttles passengers across to the island is modelled on the Edo-era steamboat *Iroha Maru*. There are no English signs on the island, so check with the tourist office in Tomo-no-ura town if you have specific questions on where to go. The ferry (return ¥240) runs to the island every 20 minutes (7.10am to 9.35pm).

★Ōta Residence HISTORIC BUILDING

(太田家住宅; ☎084-982-3553; 842 Tomo-chō-tomo; ¥400; ⌚10am-5pm Wed-Mon) On the corner of a lane leading back from the harbour area, this former Ōta residence is a fine collection of restored buildings from the mid-18th century. Guided tours (included in the admission) take you through the impressive family home and workplace, where *hōmēshu* (sweet medicinal liquor) was once brewed. Some English information is available.

Iō-ji BUDDHIST TEMPLE

(医王寺) Up a steep hill on the western side of Tomo-no-ura, Iō-ji was reputedly founded by Kōbō Daishi in the 900s. A path leads from the temple to the top of a bluff, from where there are fabulous views.

Sleeping & Eating

If you're interested in spending the night, it's worth staying on the island of Sensui-jima, where there is a hotel and it is possible to camp on the beach. There are a few guesthouses in Tomo-no-ura town, and nearby Fukuyama has a bunch of decent hotels in the station area. The Fukuyama Station tourist office and the Tomo-no-ura tourist office can help with local accommodation bookings.

The greatest number of eating options are around or near the port. During the week, restaurants dotted around town may be closed.

Kokuminshukusha Sensui-jima RYOKAN ¥¥
(国民宿舎仙酔島; ☎084-970-5050; www.tomonoura.co.jp/sen; 3373-2 Ushiroji Tomo-chō; r per person incl 2 meals from ¥9505; P ⊖) This government-owned, reasonably priced ryokan option on Sensui-jima, right on the beach, has Japanese- and Western-style rooms and a range of baths (which nonguests can use from ¥540). Meals, unsurprisingly, feature local seafood.

★**Tabuchiya** CAFE ¥¥
(田渕屋; ☎084-983-5085; www.tomonoura-tabuchiya.com; 838 Tomo-chō-tomo; set lunch ¥1300; ⊙noon-5pm Thu-Tue) At this former merchant building, only one meal is served – *hayashi raisu* (beef in a rich tomato-based sauce on rice) – but it's served very well, and in a space filled with Japanese memorabilia. The set lunch comes with a tea or coffee. Walk past the Ōta Residence away from the harbour and look for the easel outside.

Information

Opposite the Tomo-no-ura bus stop, 500m from the central harbour area, **Tomo-no-ura Tourist Information Centre** (鞆の浦観光情報センター; ☎084-982-3200; 416-1 Tomo-chō-tomo; ⊙9am-7pm) doubles as a souvenir shop. It has English maps and information on the locations used in films, and rents out audio guides (¥500).

Getting There & Around

Bus 5 runs to Tomo-no-ura every 20 minutes from outside JR Fukuyama Station (¥520, 30 minutes). The tourist office is located at the Tomo-no-ura stop; the bus continues on another 450m or so to the Tomo-kō stop (Tomo Port), which is closest to the central harbour area. JR Fukuyama Station is a main hub and *shinkansen* stop on the San-yō line.

It's easy and most convenient to get around the town on foot. Bikes can be hired (¥300 for two hours) from a booth (open 10am to 4.30pm) next to the terminal where the ferries leave for Sensui-jima.

TOTTORI, SHIMANE & THE SAN'IN COAST

On the San-in coastline, alongside the Sea of Japan, the pace of life is decidedly slower than on the San-yō coast. Tottori Prefecture (鳥取県; Tottori-ken) is the least populous of Japan's 47 prefectures and probably gets less tourist love than most, although it has sand dunes, plenty of coastal scenery and a volcano to explore. Highlights of neighbouring Shimane Prefecture (島根県; Shimane-ken) include the capital city, Matsue, with its original castle; Izumo Taisha, possibly one of Japan's oldest Shintō shrines; and the far-flung Oki Islands. This is off-the-beaten-track Japan, but there is no shortage of reasons to visit.

Getting There & Around

The cities of Tottori and Matsue are the major hubs for the region. JR Super Hakuto trains connect Tottori and Kyoto (*tokkyū* ¥7550, three hours) via Osaka and Himeji. JR Yakumo trains connect Matsue and Okayama (*tokkyū* ¥5510, 2¾ hours), which is an interchange station on the main *shinkansen* trunk lines between Osaka and Tokyo to the north, and Fukuoka to the south.

The JR San-in line connects Tottori to points east, such as Kansai's Kinosaki Onsen, and continues west via Matsue into Yamaguchi Prefecture.

Hiring a car is recommended for exploring the region's diverse scenery.

Tottori

☎0857 / POP 193,770

If you're into camels, geological science, crumbling country railroads, fading post-WWII architecture and sand...little Tottori (鳥取) might be worth your while. Its big-in-Japan sand dunes and sand sculpture museum are the main draw here.

Most international visitors come en route to the prefecture's more rewarding natural attractions.

Sights

★**Sand Museum** MUSEUM
(砂の美術館; ☎0857-20-2231; www.sand-museum.jp; 2083-17 Yūyama, Fukube-chō; ¥600; ⊙9am-6pm Sun-Fri, to 8pm Sat May-Dec) You came to see sand? Well, there's truckloads at this impressive museum of sand sculptures, where sand aficionados from all over the world are invited to create huge, amazingly detailed works based on a particular theme. The exhibition changes each year: check at the tourist office for this year's theme and opening months. Unsurprisingly, the museum is near the sand dunes.

★**Tottori-sakyū (The Dunes)** DUNES
(鳥取砂丘; P) Used as the location for Teshigahara Hiroshi's classic 1964 film, *Woman in the Dunes,* the Tottori sand dunes are

on the coast about 5km from the city. There's a viewing point on a hillside overlooking the dunes, along with parking and the usual array of tourist schlock. You can even get a 'Lawrence of Arabia' photo of yourself accompanied by a camel. Pick up maps at the Sand Pal Tottori Information Centre.

The dunes stretch over 10km along the coast and, at some points, can be about 2km wide. Buses to the dunes also stop at the Sakyū-Sentā (砂丘センター; Dunes Centre) on the hillside, from where you can take a cable car (one way/return ¥200/300) across roads down to the entrance to the dunes. Otherwise it's an easy five-minute walk, or simply stay on the bus to the dunes.

Sleeping & Eating

Accommodation options in the city lack lustre, with most due for a thorough update. Staying near the station, not the dunes, is definitely the most convenient.

There's more choice here by way of dining than anywhere else in the prefecture, but that's not saying a lot. A neatly organised strip of good restaurants with international and Japanese options runs east along Suehiro-dōri, two blocks north of Tottori Station.

Drop Inn Tottori HOSTEL ¥
(ホステル ドロップイン鳥取; ☎0857-30-0311; www.dropinn-tottori.com; 2-276 Ima-machi; dm from ¥3900;) Tottori's only hostel has smart male- and female-only capsules with thick mattresses, flat-screen TVs, safes and, instead of bunks, cavernous personal lockers underneath each bed. The modern bathrooms are immaculately clean, and English-speaking staff in the stylish cafe serve great coffee and can guide you through their useful maps.

From Tottori Station's north exit, walk left along the main road and you'll find Drop Inn on a corner after a couple of minutes.

Matsuya-sō MINSHUKU ¥¥
(松屋荘; ☎0857-22-4891; 3-814 Yoshikata Onsen; s/tw from ¥3880/6580) This *minshuku*-style lodging has no wi-fi or mod cons, but offers large, clean tatami rooms with washbasins and shared bathrooms. From Tottori Station's north exit, go straight up the main street and turn right onto Eiraku-dōri (永楽通り). Look for Matsuya-sō on the left after six blocks; it's about a 15-minute walk from the station. The welcoming owners speak some English.

Green Hotel Morris HOTEL ¥¥
(グリーンホテルモーリス; ☎0857-22-2331; www.hotel-morris.co.jp; 2-107 Ima-machi; s/d/tw from ¥5835/8425/11,880;) Stylish, neutral-toned rooms, large spa baths and a sauna make Morris a good-value modern option. It's just two blocks north of the station, and there's a buffet breakfast for ¥565.

Gottsuo Ramen RAMEN ¥
(ごっつぉらーめん; ☎0857-35-0977; www.gottsuo.jp/about-tottori; 159-4 Suehiro-dōri, Onsen-chō; ramen ¥700-1050; 11am-2pm & 6pm-2am Mon-Sat) Get a taste of Tottori's take on ramen, which uses beef bones for the base rather than pork. This small joint is known for its flavoursome, thin, almost fresh broth and soft cuts of pork. Sit at the bar or tables with a beer and side of *gyōza*. Friendly English-speaking staff can help you navigate the menu.

It's on Suehiro-dōri, east of the intersection with Ekimae-dōri. Look for the door with the octagonal window.

Sumibi Jujuan GRILL ¥¥
(炭火焼ジュジュアン; ☎0857-21-1919; www.sumibi-jujuan.info; 751 Suehiro-dōri, Onsen-chō; mains ¥980-3000, set menus ¥4800-10,000; 5-11pm) Fresh seafood and local beef *sumibi-yaki* (charcoal grilled) are the specialities in this airy restaurant. It does *shabu-shabu* (thinly sliced beef or pork cooked with vegetables in boiling water and then dipped in sauce) and set courses, such as *wagyū* beef or *kaisen gozen* (grilled seafood and vegetables with sides), with a seasonal menu that may include crab and other locally sourced goodies.

It's on Suehiro-dōri, two blocks east of the intersection with Ekimae-dōri.

Information

Sand Pal Tottori Information Centre (サンドパルとっとり; ☎0857-20-2231; 083-17 Yūyama, Fukube-chō; 9am-6pm) Specialises in all things sand-sculpture and sand-dune related, but can also offer advice on excursions around the nearby coastline. Opposite the sand dunes entrance.

Tottori Tourist Support Center (鳥取市観光案内所; ☎0857-22-3318; www.torican.jp; 8.30am-5.30pm) To the right as you exit the station, with English-language pamphlets, maps, free wi-fi and English-speaking staff, who can book the 2000 Yen Taxi for tourists. Accommodation is only booked at the other tourism office, just inside the station entrance.

Getting There & Away

Tottori is on the coastal JR San-in train line. JR Pass holders going south and east (eg towards Himeji, Okayama, Osaka) must pay a cash fee on board or when booking of around ¥1820 for using non-JR tracks; JR-only alternatives add hours. JR West Pass holders do not need to pay this additional fee. Major destinations (completely covered by the JR Pass):

Matsue ¥2270, 2¼ hours; express service ¥4620, 1½ hours

Okayama express via Chizu and Kamigōri on the Super Inaba ¥5010, two hours

Toyooka (Hyōgo Prefecture) local service via Hamasaka and Kinosakionsen ¥1490, 2½ hours

There are also long-distance buses to major cities in the region.

Getting Around

BICYCLE

Rent-a-Cycle (per day ¥500; ⌚8am-6.30pm) is outside the station. You can also rent bikes at the Sand Pal Tottori Information Centre near the dunes.

BUS

The Kirinjishi loop bus (¥300/600 per ride/day pass; free for JR West Pass holders) operates on weekends, holidays and daily between 20 July and 31 August. It passes the main sights and goes to the dunes. Regular city buses depart from stop 0 (zero) outside the station and travel to the dunes area (¥360, 20 minutes). There are maps and timetables available at the information offices and inside the bus station.

CAR & MOTORCYCLE

Cal Rent-a-Car (キャルレンタカー; ☎0857-24-0452; www.cal-rent.net; 1-88 Tomiyasu; 24hr from ¥3800; ⌚8am-8pm) Take the main road leading straight out from the south side of the station, then take a left turn at the first major intersection; this rental outlet is in a petrol station on the right.

TAXI

2000 Yen Taxi (☎0857-22-7935; www.torican.jp; per car for foreigners with ID ¥2000; ⌚8.30am-5.30pm) A great deal for visiting a few sights in a short time. Up to four passengers can hire a taxi for up to three hours, including waiting time at any stops. Passengers are also given a coupon card that can be used at some sights for discounts and free souvenirs (mostly trinkets). Book at the Tottori Tourist Support Center.

San-in Coast National Park

The coastline east from the Tottori dunes, stretching all the way to the Tango Peninsula in Kyoto Prefecture, is known as the San-in Coast National Park (山陰海岸国立公園; San-in Kaigan Kokuritsu-kōen). The park boasts rugged headlands, sandy albeit polluted beaches, and pines jutting into the blue sky.

Near the edge of Hyōgo Prefecture, the **Uradome Kaigan** (浦富海岸; Uradome Coastline) features a scenic stretch of islets and craggy cliffs with pines clinging precariously to their sides. Three popular beaches lie a few kilometres further east: **Uradome** (浦富), **Makidani** (牧谷) and **Higashi-hama** (東浜). The last one is among the best swimming spots in the area.

The coast here forms part of the Chūgoku Shizen Hodō (中国自然歩道; Chūgoku Nature Walking Path), a network of 2295km of walking tracks that span the neighbouring prefectures of Shimane, Hiroshima, Okayama and Yamaguchi. There is scant information in English, but hikers can enquire at the tourism office for maps. Online maps showing the area are available from the Tottori Prefecture website (www.pref.tottori.lg.jp/81291.htm), and a detailed pamphlet in Japanese is available as a pdf from the Nature Lovers Club (http://bit.ly/2Jax44y).

Information

Uradome Tourism Association (浦富観光協会; ☎0857-72-3481; 783-8 Uradome, Iwami-chō; ⌚9am-6pm Tue-Sun) This info centre is located a stone's throw from JR Iwami Station. You can rent electric bicycles (¥500 a day with ¥500 deposit) and staff can help arrange accommodation in the area or show you how to you take a bus to the beach.

Getting There & Around

While it is possible to reach some of the area's sights by combinations of bus and train, services can be infrequent and stations aren't always conveniently located to what you want to see. If you're really keen to explore the area, your best bet is to rent a car: there's a number of car-rental companies around Tottori Station.

An exception is the swimming beach Higashi-hama (東浜), easily accessed by train from Tottori – it's just near Higashi-hama Station (¥410, 30 minutes).

Iwami, on the JR San-in line, is the closest station to the Uradome Kaigan from Tottori (¥320, 25 minutes), but still 4.5km away.

Daisen

☎0859

Although it's not one of Japan's highest mountains, at 1729m Daisen (大山) looks impressive because it rises straight from sea level – its summit is only about 10km from the coast. Daisen is part of the Daisen-Oki National Park (大山隠岐国立公園).

The popular climb up the volcano is a five- to six-hour return trip from Buddhist temple **Daisen-ji** (大山寺; ☎0859-52-2158; www.daisenji.jp; 9 Daisen; treasure hall ¥300; ⏲9am-4pm Apr-Nov). From the summit, there are fine views over the coast and, in perfect conditions, all the way to the Oki Islands.

The mountain catches the northwest monsoon winds in the winter, bringing lots of snow to what is western Japan's top skiing area. Among the slopes are **Daisen White Resort** (大山ホワイトリゾート; ☎0859-52-2315; www.daisen-resort.jp; day lift ticket adult/child from ¥4900/3900) and **Daisen Masumizu-kōgen Ski Resort** (大山ますみず高原スキー場; ☎0859-52-2420; www.masumizu.net/ski; 1067-2 Masumizu-kōgen; day lift ticket adult/child ¥4000/3000; ⏲lift 9am-5pm).

Bayside Square Kaike Hotel HOTEL ¥¥
(ベイサイドスクエア皆生ホテル; ☎0859-35-0001; www.kaikehotel.com; 4-21-1 Kaike-onsen, Yonago; s/d incl breakfast from ¥5950/14,050) In Yonago, about 17km from Daisen, you'll find this smart, modern beachfront hotel with simple, stylish rooms, a fabulous onsen, and lovely views over the Sea of Japan.

Information

Daisen-ji Information Centre (大山寺観光案内所; ☎0859-52-2502; 40-33 Daisen-cho; ⏲8am-6.30pm) Located at the temple; stocked with brochures, maps and hiking information. Staff can arrange bookings at the local ryokan.

For info online in English, check out http://en.go-to-japan.jp/daisenguide.

Getting There & Away

The closest station to Daisen is Yonago, about 30 minutes from Matsue (in Shimane) and one to 1½ hours from Tottori on the San-in line.

The Daisen Loop bus (one-/two-day pass ¥1000/1300) runs to Daisen-ji from Yonago Station on Saturdays, Sundays and holidays in early May, early August and late October. It stops at all the main sights around the mountain.

Nihon Kotsu (www.nihonkotsu.co.jp) buses run regularly to the temple from Yonago (¥830, 50 minutes, five daily).

Sakaiminato

☎0859 / POP 34,200

Sakaiminato (境港) is a beacon for fans of manga artist Mizuki Shigeru, who was born and raised here. There's a museum but also statues of many of his characters and other homages to the artist around town.

Sakaiminato station and port are adjacent, making the town a convenient boarding point for boats to the Oki Islands.

Sleeping & Eating

Onyado Nono SPA HOTEL ¥¥
(御宿野乃; ☎0859-44-5489; www.hotespa.net/hotels/sakaiminato; s/d from ¥9990/13,990; P❄☜) New in 2016, this towering 195-room, all-tatami (take off your shoes in the lobby) hotel looks like it has been plopped in the middle of nowhere. Popular with tour groups for its comfortable, compact rooms and convenient location by the station, the best bit is the rooftop *rotemburo* (outdoor bath) with sweeping views: you can even see Daisen on a clear day.

There are a handful of eateries a few minutes' walk from the station area, but don't expect too much in terms of variety. Turn left on exiting the station for a large supermarket a three-minute walk away for self-catering on your onward journey to the Oki Islands.

Genki-tei SEAFOOD ¥¥
(元気亭; ☎0859-42-3551; 38 Taisho-machi; dishes ¥600-2600; ⏲11am-3pm & 5.30-9pm Fri-Wed) This restaurant is proud that its *kaisen-don* (seafood over rice) has featured on Japanese TV. The friendly owner will help you navigate the menu and advise on the daily specials: fish fresh off the boat. There are a few *izakaya*-style items on the menu, or you can just stop in for some delicious *gyōza* and beer.

It's one block northeast of Sakaiminato Station. Look for the red writing on the black building.

THE GHOULISH WORLD OF MIZUKI SHIGERU

Eyeballs on taxis and ghostly murals on ferries and ports in the Oki Islands – this is the horror manga of artist Mizuki Shigeru (水木 しげる), Sakaiminato's most famous resident.

His adorably evil *yōkai* (spirit demons) from manga series *GeGeGe No Kitarō* are a take on Japanese folklore. They plaster four train exteriors and interiors from Yonago to Sakaiminato – even announcements are made by one of his characters.

Legions of fans make the trip especially to see Mizuki Shigeru Road – outside Sakaiminato Station – to pose with the 153 bronze *yōkai* statues and visit the **Mizuki Shigeru Museum** (水木しげる記念館; ☎0859-42-2171; http://mizuki.sakaiminato.net; 5 Hon-machi; ¥300; ⊙9.30am-5pm; Ⓟ), plus the inevitable souvenir stores. The multimedia museum explains all things ghoulish, with free English audio guides, and has rooms that re-create ancient Japan. Fans can pick up a *yōkai* stamp and guide booklet (¥100) from the **tourist information office** (☎0859-47-0121; www.sakaiminato.net; Sakaiminato Port; ⊙9am-6pm Mar-Oct, to 5pm Nov-Feb), adjacent to the ferry waiting room, to collect stamps from 37 stores corresponding to some of the statues.

Mizuki's undead cast includes Kitarō, the boy born in a cemetery; his father Medama-oyaji, a reborn eyeball; Neko Musume, the 'Cat Girl' with fangs and a Jekyll and Hyde personality; and Nezumi Otoko, the unwashed 'Rat Man' who uses flatulence as a weapon. Kids love it.

Getting There & Away

From Matsue, change at Yonago to the colourfully decked-out local trains of the JR Sakai line for Sakaiminato. The journey takes 90 minutes or so, depending on how long you have to transfer between trains, and costs ¥840.

You can also take a direct bus from Matsue Station stop 9 (¥1000, 40 minutes, nine daily; free with Perfect Ticket (p501)) to Sakaiminato, passing a scenic lake with onboard audio commentary in English.

Oki Islands

North of Matsue in the Sea of Japan are the remote and spectacular Oki Islands (隠岐諸島; Oki-shotō), once used to exile officials (including two emperors) who came out on the losing side of political squabbles. Being cut off from the mainland, there are cultural and religious practices preserved here that aren't observed elsewhere in Japan, the pace of life is decidedly slower, and there's a refreshing lack of development at the tourist spots. Four of the islands are inhabited: the three Dōzen Islands – Nishino-shima, Chiburi-jima and Nakano-shima – and the larger Dōgo island. Allow at least a couple of days to visit and keep in mind that ferry services are subject to change and halt in bad weather.

The islands are within the Oki Islands Geopark, with coastal areas that are part of the Daisen-Oki National Park (大山隠岐国立公園).

Sleeping & Eating

All the islands have ryokan, *minshuku* and campgrounds (you'll need to bring your own tent).

Before you set out, it's advisable to contact the tourism associations of the islands you wish to visit. Staff will be able to book your accommodation and tell you how to get there – essential, as lodgings can be spread out and resemble a regular house without any signs.

These are remote islands and much of the produce here is brought in by ferry: expect higher prices for regular commodities. You'll find an abundance of seafood on local menus. Each island's handful of eateries open irregular hours outside the busier summer season. Best to chill like the locals and play it by ear.

Information

MONEY

All of the four main islands have a post office with an ATM that accepts international cards.

TOURIST INFORMATION

Each island has a tourism association with a tourist information office offering free wi-fi and at least one native English speaker, who can book activities and accommodation.

For more on the natural and cultural features of the islands, the **Oki Islands Geopark Promotion Committee** (☎08512-2-9636; www.oki-geopark.jp) produces a very good English guide and map, with most of the information reproduced online.

Getting There & Away

AIR

The islands' **Oki Airport** (OKI; 08512-2-0703; www.oki-airport.jp; 1889-12 Misakimachi) on Dōgo is serviced by regular direct flights from Izumo and Osaka (Itami) airports.

BOAT

The most common way to reach the islands is by ferry or hydrofoil (the 'Rainbow Jet'). Services, operated by **Oki Kisen** (08512-2-1122; www.oki-kisen.co.jp) depart from Shichirui Port in Shimane Prefecture and Sakaiminato Port in Tottori Prefecture.

Depending on your port of embarkation and ultimate destination, boats do an island-hop en route. Sample routes and fares include Sakaiminato to Dōgo (ferry ¥3240, 2½ hours; hydrofoil ¥6170, 70 minutes) and Nishino-shima (ferry ¥3240, 1½ hours; hydrofoil ¥6170, one hour).

While there are some seated areas on the ferry, most locals sprawl out on the grubby carpet and sleep. Blanket rentals are available! Once on board, you can 'upgrade' to a private cabin from ¥4000 if you feel like a splurge. The Rainbow Jet is fully seated.

Buying tickets seems more complicated than it should be, even if you speak Japanese. You can reserve the Rainbow Jet in advance, but only pay for your ticket on the day. You'll need to fill in an embarkation card before proceeding to the ticket counter at all of the Oki Kisen offices. Make sure you allow yourself enough time before departure. When in doubt, phone a tourism office.

Buses go to Shichirui from Matsue Station stop 9 (¥1000, 40 minutes, twice daily) and Yonago Station stop 2 (¥870, 55 minutes, three daily). Sakaiminato is at the end of the JR Sakai train line, which connects with the JR San-in line at Yonago (¥320, 45 minutes). Direct buses from Matsue Station stop 9 (¥1000, 40 minutes, nine daily, free with Perfect Ticket) also run to Sakaiminato.

JR Passes cover trains but not buses or ferries.

Getting Around

It's possible to get to some of the main attractions by bike, but to see all of the islands it's best to hire a car or make use of a taxi or eco-tour guide service.

The **inter-island ferry** (089514-6-0016; 1 trip ¥300) service operates the Isokaze and Dōzen ferries between islands.

Dōgo

08512 / POP 14,850

While Dōgo (島後), the Oki group's largest island, has notably more signs of civilisation than the Dōzen trio, the pace here is as delightfully slow and there's still barely a franchised or recognisable brand to be found. The island is notable for its giant, wizened old cedar trees: the 800-year-old **Chichi-sugi** tree is believed to be the home of a deity; and the **Yao-sugi** tree at **Tamakawasu-no-mikoto-jinja** is thought to be 2000 years old, its gnarled and sprawling branches propped up with posts.

The island offers nature and coastal walks, and boat tours in the Saigō port area and along the northern Shirashima coast. 'Bull sumo' is an attraction throughout the year – not big guy versus bull, but bull versus bull in a tug-of-war, without harm to the animals.

Activities

Oki Onsen GOKA SENTO

(隠岐温泉GOKA; 08512-5-3200; 296-1 Nanpō; ¥500; 2-8pm Tue-Sun) Dōgo's only *sentō* (public bath) is delightfully dated and refreshingly quiet. It's on the northwest corner of the island, about 25 minutes' drive from Saigō Port. Unusually, in addition to sex-separated baths, there is a mixed bathing area (swimsuit required).

Sleeping & Eating

Dining options, though few, are mainly concentrated around the Saigō Port area in Okinoshima town and may have irregular hours. Pick up up a handy pamphlet from the Okinoshima Tourist Information Center.

Kichiura Campground CAMPGROUND ¥

(吉浦野営場, Kichiura yaeijō; 0852-22-6172; Hisami, Okinoshima-chō; campsites per person ¥300; Jun-Sep) Tucked away in the island's northwest, this attractive, isolated campground with modern facilities runs down a steep hill towards a little beach. Rental tents are available (¥1500).

Hotel Uneri CABIN ¥¥

(ホテル海音里; 08512-5-3211; www.gokanosato.jp; 1933-1 Minamigata; cabins from ¥12,420; P) Deliciously isolated on the island's northwestern flank, about 16km from Saigō Port, Hotel Uneri has log cabins in a peaceful location near the water and a waterfall. You can either self-cater with the open kitchen and outdoor barbecue or have a prearranged dinner and breakfast. The wooden beds are simple and firm but perfectly fine.

Yao-sugi SUSHI ¥¥
(八百杉; ☎08512-2-0028; 16 Menuki-no-ni; set menus ¥4000-6000; ⏲5-8pm Tue-Sun) The ample seafood dinner menus are a bounty of sushi, sashimi, crumbed shrimp skewers, plump oysters and sashimi. This is the way to dine on the Oki Islands. It's 500m north of the Saigō Port ferry terminal; look for the white building with an abstract picture of three cedar trees.

Information

Okinoshima Tourist Information Center (隠岐の島観光案内所; ☎8512-2-0787; www.oki-dougo.info; 54-3 Oki Port Plaza; ⏲8am-7pm; 📶) Opposite the Saigō Port ferry terminal – follow the signs.

Getting There & Away

Daily ferry services depart Sakaiminato in Tottori Prefecture (¥3240, 2½ hours) to Saigō Port in the southeast. For a faster trip, jump on the 'Rainbow Jet' hydrofoil at Shichirui Port in Shimane Prefecture (¥6170, 70 minutes).

Getting Around

Renting a car at Saigō Port is the best way to see the island. Contact the Okinoshima Tourist Information Center for advance reservations.

Dōzen Islands

West of Dōgo, **Nishino-shima** (西ノ島) boasts the stunningly rugged Kuniga coastline, with the sheer 257m Matengai cliff. The coastal hike here is a must-do. The island is also home to interesting shrines, including Yurahime-jinja, near a small inlet. Legend has it that squid come en masse to this inlet every autumn/winter to ask forgiveness from the deity (there are pictures at the shrine to prove it). Nishino-shima is also known for horses, which you'll see roaming the hillsides.

The small **Chiburi-jima** (知夫里島), or 'Chibu', where the local slogan is *nonbiri Chiburi* (carefree Chiburi), is home to more impressive coastline, featuring the striking Sekiheki, an expanse of rust-coloured cliffs. You can also see stone-wall remains on the island – what is left of a crop-rotation practice that began here in the Middle Ages.

The Akiya coast and Oki-jinja are draws on **Nakano-shima** (中ノ島), also known locally as Ama.

Activities

Club Noah Oki KAYAKING, DIVING
(クラブノア隠岐; ☎08514-6-0825; www.oki.club-noah.net; 3078-12 Mita, Nishino-shima; dives from ¥7600, sunset cave kayaking ¥5500; ⏲office 9am-6pm) Diving and kayaking, including sunset cave tours and night dives. Instructors know the essentials in English. If you are a beginner, try the 'Experience' dives (¥13,000 per person), which stick to the beach shallows and include all equipment rental.

Sleeping & Eating

Dining options outside the busier summer season are limited, spread out and open irregular hours. Pick up a pamphlet from the tourism office for the latest information, and dine at your accommodation.

★ **Kuniga-sō** RYOKAN ¥¥
(国賀荘; ☎08514-6-0301; www.kunigasou.com; 192 Urago, Nishino-shima; r per person with 2 meals from ¥12,000; P❄📶) Operated by a friendly family, Nishino-shima's best lodging features rooms with floor-to-ceiling windows overlooking the bay and a communal bath sharing the same vista. The decor in the shared spaces is delightfully outdated and islandy, while rooms are sleek (except for old TVs) and neutral-toned with comfortable twin beds. Meals include local rock oysters and scallops.

Oki Seaside Hotel Tsurumaru HOTEL ¥¥
(隠岐シーサイドホテル鶴丸; ☎08514-6-1111; www.oki-tsurumaru.jp; 771-1 Mita, Nishino-shima; r per person incl 2 meals from ¥10,800; P📶) On Nishino-shima, Oki Seaside Hotel Tsurumaru has a pleasant waterfront location and a large restaurant, and it runs regular cruises. The nautical theme continues to an on-site onsen with a boat-shaped bath.

Hotel Chibu-no-Sato HOTEL ¥¥¥
(ホテル知夫の里; ☎08514-8-2500; www.tibunosato.com; Chibu 1242-1, Chibun-jima; d incl 2 meals from ¥22,680; P❄📶) A great choice on Chiburi-jima, with balconied rooms featuring fabulous sea views. There's an open-air bath (open April to October) and free bicycle use for guests, though a beach is within walking distance. The included meals feature seafood.

Sawano CHINESE ¥
(さわの; ☎08514-6-0181; 367 Urago, Nishino-shima; dishes ¥680-1080, lunch ¥980; ⏲noon-1pm & 6-8pm) If you can speak some Japanese, you might indulge in a heartwarming conversation with the friendly owner of this cosy Chinese joint, who spent a year travelling the length and breadth of Japan in the '70s before starting a family on the island. He makes fat, juicy dumplings and delicious vegetable-laden *miso-rāmen,* among other dishes.

Information

Nishino-shima Tourist Information Office (☎08514-7-8888; www.nkk-oki.com; ⏲8.30am-7pm Jun-Oct, to 5pm Nov-May; 📶) English-speaking staff can help book accommodation.

Getting There & Away

Ferries and the faster 'Rainbow Jet' hydrofoil depart Shichirui Port in Shimane Prefecture and Sakaiminato Port in Tottori Prefecture for Chiburi-jima, Nakano-shima and Nishino-shima. The timetable is a little complicated; check www.oki-kisen.co.jp for the latest.

Ferries from the mainland to Dōgo via the Dōzen Islands take about 2½ hours and fares start at ¥3240.

Depending on the seasonal timetable, only a handful of hydrofoils stop at the Dōzen Islands. The most popular route in peak season is from the mainland to Nishino-shima (¥6170, one hour).

Getting Around

There's a local bus on Nishino-shima that goes to the Kuniga coast, though it's infrequent.

Bike hire on the smaller islands can suffice, but it's best to rent a car if you're planning to explore larger Nishino-shima. The tourism offices of each island can help with reservations.

It costs ¥300 to ride on the regular inter-island ferry service between the Dōzen Islands.

Matsue

☎0852 / POP 204,200

With its fine castle and crowd-pleasing sunsets over Shinji-ko (Lake Shinji), Matsue (松江) is an appealing city with some interesting historical attractions. The city straddles the Ōhashi-gawa, which connects Shinji-ko with Nakaumi, a saline lake. Most of the main attractions are in a compact area in the north, where you'll find the castle – a rare original. Matsue is also a good base for sojourns to other places of interest in Shimane Prefecture and you could easily spend a few lazy days here.

Sights

Bring your passport, as all of the main sights offer hefty discounts on admission for foreign visitors.

★Matsue-jō CASTLE
(松江城, Matsue Castle; ☎0852-21-4030; www.matsue-tourism.or.jp/m_castle; 1-5 Tono-machi; ¥670, foreigners with ID ¥330; ⏲8.30am-6.30pm Apr-Sep, to 5pm Oct-Mar) Dating from 1611, picturesque Matsue-jō has a wooden interior showcasing treasures belonging to the Matsudaira clan. Known as 'Plover Castle' for the graceful shape of its gable ornaments, Matsue-jō is one of only 12 original keeps left in Japan, making it well worth having a look inside. There are dioramas of the city and displays of armoury, including a collection of helmets – each helmet design is said to have reflected the personality of its wearer.

English explanations of how the castle proved it was an original are fascinating and detailed, highlighting the original structures. From the top of the castle there are great unobstructed views. It's also pleasant to walk around the castle grounds (free entry) and along the surrounding moat, with its charming bridges and pines reaching out across the water. A very enjoyable way to see the castle area is via a trip on a Horikawa Sightseeing Boat (p500).

Matsue History Museum MUSEUM
(松江歴史館; ☎0852-32-1607; www.matsu-reki.jp; 279 Tono-machi; ¥510, foreigners with ID ¥250; ⏲8.30am-6.30pm Apr-Sep, to 5pm Oct-Mar, closed 3rd Thu of the month) Matsue's excellent modern museum gives a broad-ranging introduction to the history of the regional clans and development of local industry and crafts. Among the displays are old town maps, ceramics, letters and the local speciality, Matsue *wagashi* (sweets) – you can taste modern versions in the attached shop, made famous in Japan by a TV show. The free English audio guide is very good.

Shimane Prefectural Art Museum GALLERY
(島根県立博物館; ☎0852-55-4700; www.shimane-art-museum.jp; 1-5 Sodeshi-chō; permanent/special collection ¥300/1000, foreigners with ID ¥150/500; ⏲10am-6.30pm Wed-Mon Oct-Feb,

Matsue

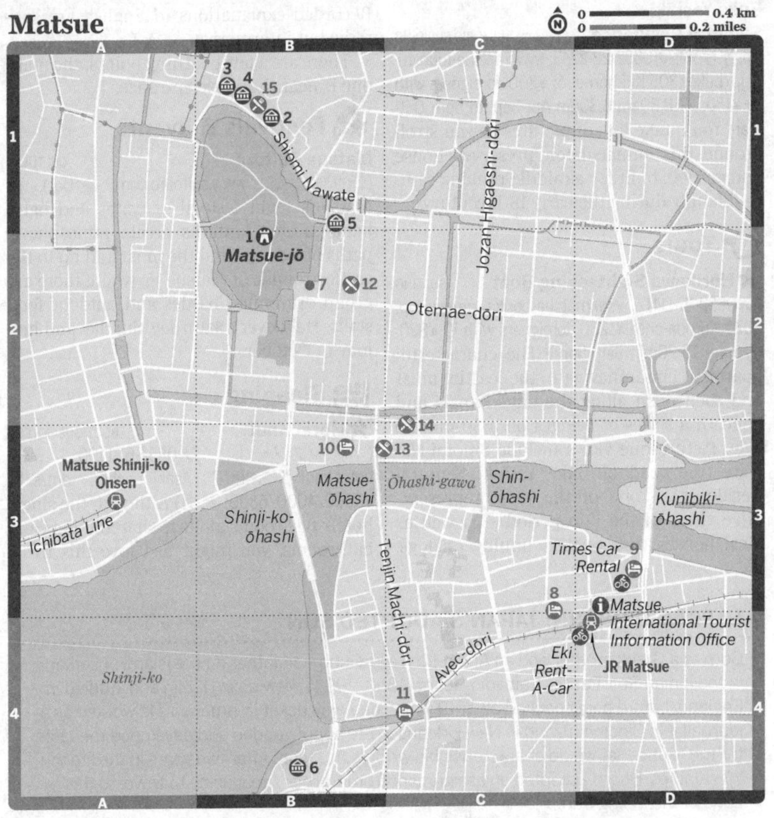

Matsue

Top Sights
1 Matsue-jō B2

Sights
2 Buke Yashiki Samurai Residence B1
3 Koizumi Yakumo (Lafcadio Hearn) Memorial Museum B1
4 Lafcadio Hearn Old Residence B1
5 Matsue History Museum B1
6 Shimane Prefectural Art Museum B4

Activities, Courses & Tours
7 Horikawa Sightseeing Boat B2

Sleeping
8 Hotel Knut C3
9 Matsue Urban Hotel D3
10 Minamikan B3
11 Ryokan Terazuya C4

Eating
12 Greens Baby B2
13 Kawa-kyō B3
14 Tsurumaru C3
15 Yakumo-an B1

to 30min after sunset Mar-Sep) With its white undulating roof and huge glass windows facing the lake, the museum building itself is an impressive sight. Inside, it displays rotating exhibits from its collection of woodblock prints (there are some Hokusai among them), as well as European paintings and contemporary art. The sunset views from the museum's 2nd-floor platform or outside by the water also draw crowds here. The museum is a 15-minute walk west of the station.

Buke Yashiki Samurai Residence HISTORIC BUILDING
(武家屋敷; ☎0852-22-2243; www.matsue-tourism.or.jp/buke; 305 Kitahori-chō; ¥300, foreigners with ID ¥150; ⊙8.30am-6.30pm Apr-Sep, to 5pm Oct-Mar) You'll take lots of pictures as you stroll around this immaculately preserved house and garden, built for a middle-ranking samurai family during the early 18th century.

Tours

★**Horikawa Sightseeing Boat** BOATING
(☎0852-27-0417; www.matsue-horikawameguri.jp; 507-1 Kuroda-chō; ¥1230, foreigners with ID ¥820; ⊙every 15-20min 9am-5pm) The characterful boatmen circumnavigate the castle moat and then push along the city's canals and beneath a series of bridges on a 50-minute ride. Picturesque views include Shiomi-Nawate (the road of Buke Yashiki Samurai Residence) – one of the most representative vistas of the Edo period – as well as local houses, and turtles sunning on logs. Recorded explanations in English are sporadic but informative.

There are a few boarding points; the main one is near the castle entrance.

Festivals & Events

Matsue Suitōro CULTURAL
(松江水燈路; www.suitouro.com; ⊙Oct) In Matsue's night festival of water and light, hand-painted lanterns create atmospheric paths of light around the moat and up to the castle grounds of Matsue-jō, where there are group drumming battles and outdoor food stalls. Held every Saturday, Sunday and holiday in October.

Sleeping

★**Hotel Knut** BOUTIQUE HOTEL ¥
(ホテルクヌート; ☎0852-61-1400; www.hotel-knut.jp; 481-7 Asahi-machi; dm/s/tw ¥3000/4000/6800; ❄📶) Although the single hotel-style rooms all have shared toilets and bathrooms, you might just love this fresh,

LAFCADIO HEARN: JAPAN'S ADOPTED SON

Born to a Greek mother and an Anglo-Irish army-surgeon father on the island of Lefkada in the Ionian Sea, Patrick Lafcadio Hearn (1850–1904) grew up in Dublin and studied in England, before being packed off at 19 with a one-way ticket to America. He worked as a journalist in Cincinnati, and in New Orleans wrote about voodoo and developed the taste for the exotic that would characterise his writing on Japan. After two years in the French West Indies, Hearn accepted an assignment from *Harper's* magazine to travel to the Land of the Rising Sun.

Hearn soon became famous for his articles and books about his new home. Eager to stay on after his contract with *Harper's* ran out, he took a job teaching English. For 15 idyllic months he lived in Matsue, where he married Koizumi Setsu, the daughter of a local samurai family. After stints elsewhere, he finally settled in Tokyo – 'the most horrible place in Japan' – where he was appointed Professor of English Literature at Tokyo Imperial University.

Although Japan has changed almost beyond recognition since Hearn lived here, his best pieces are still well worth reading today. His first Japan-themed collection, *Glimpses of Unfamiliar Japan* (1894), contains his famous essay on Matsue, 'Chief City of the Province of the Gods', as well as an account of his trip to Izumo, where he was the first European allowed inside the gates of the ancient shrine. Children still read Hearn's Japanese folk tales, ghost stories and legends, which may have been lost in time had Hearn not documented them.

In Matsue, visit the **Koizumi Yakumo (Lafcadio Hearn) Memorial Museum** (小泉八雲記念館; ☎0852-21-2147; www.hearn-museum-matsue.jp; 322 Okudani-chō; ¥400, foreigners with ID ¥200; ⊙8.30am-6.30pm Apr-Sep, to 5pm Oct-Mar). In addition to displays on the writer's life and work, there are some of his personal effects – including his dumbbells, spectacles and a stack of Japanese newspapers on which he wrote words and phrases to teach English to his son. Next door is the **Lafcadio Hearn Old Residence** (小泉八雲旧居; ☎0852-23-0714; 315 Kitahori-chō; ¥300, foreigners with ID ¥150; ⊙8.30am-6.30pm Apr-Sep, to 5pm Oct-Mar), the small late 19th-century samurai house with pretty gardens where the writer lived. Here you can see the desk where he penned *Glimpses of Unfamiliar Japan*.

young conversion of a business hotel, next to the station. Try for an airy corner double room. The foyer of the hotel hosts a popular cafe-bar with cheap eats and good drinks, creating a social meeting spot for those staying in the dorm.

Ryokan Terazuya RYOKAN ¥
(旅館寺津屋; ☎0852-21-3480; www.mable.ne.jp/~terazuya; 60-3 Tenjin-machi; r per person with/without breakfast ¥5300/4600; @ 📶) You'll find a warm welcome and simple tatami rooms at this family-run inn, opposite a shrine. The owners speak a little English and can collect you from the station. The bathroom is shared, there's a 10pm curfew, and coffee and toast are included if you haven't paid for the full breakfast. Cash only.

A canal runs behind the ryokan, as does the JR line – fortunately there's little traffic at night.

Matsue Urban Hotel BUSINESS HOTEL ¥¥
(☎0852-22-0002; www.station.matsue-urban.co.jp; 590-3 Asahi-machi; dm/s/d from ¥2970/4860/7300; ❄ 📶) Opposite Matsue Station, Urban Hotel is a total ugly duckling, resembling a tenement from the outside, but transforming into a sleek, modern hotel inside, with slick capsules, thick mattresses, and clean, modern furnishings that extend to the spacious, well-equipped shower rooms. English-speaking staff are professional, and the only slight letdown are the drab private rooms. Buffet breakfast is ¥1060.

★ **Minamikan** RYOKAN ¥¥¥
(皆美館; ☎0852-21-5131; www.minami-g.co.jp/minamikan; 14 Suetsugu Hon-machi; r per person incl 2 meals from ¥23,910; P ❄ 📶) A refined inn on the edge of the lake, Minamikan has a choice of 'modern', 'retro' and 'classic' rooms, all with broad views across the water. The top-end 'modern' has a tatami room with twin beds and private cypress-wood onsen. The cheaper 'classic' has seen the likes of literary great Kawabata Yasunari pass through.

There is also an excellent restaurant. The ryokan entrance is set back from the road.

KAI Izumo RYOKAN ¥¥¥
(会出雲; ☎0570-073-011; www.hoshinoresorts.com; 1237 Tamayu-chō, Tamatsukuri Onsen; r per person incl 2 meals from ¥34,125; P ❄ 📶) Whilst not in Izumo at all, this modern ryokan in Tamatsukuri Onsen, about 9km southwest of downtown Matsue, has a minimalist but traditional aesthetic along the (clean) lines of less is more. Each room has a private, onsen-fed indoor/outdoor bath, and the service and dining will leave you feeling elevated. One for those who like the finer things in life.

MATSUE PERFECT TICKET

The excellent-value **Perfect Ticket** (foreigners with ID ¥1500) is a three-day pass of unlimited travel within the Ensubu area (Izumo, Matsue and Sakaiminato in Tottori Prefecture) on transport (not JR) including Matsue City buses and Lake Line bus; Izumo and Yonago buses, including airport buses (¥1000 a ride alone); and the Ichibata bus between Matsue and Sakaiminato (¥1000 alone). Enquire at the Matsue International Tourist Information Office (p502).

Eating & Drinking

Turn left from the station's north exit and walk one block to the Asahi-chō intersection, then turn right to find a healthy selection of *izakaya* and the town's nightlife district radiating off from the main drag.

★ **Yakumo-an** NOODLES ¥
(八雲庵; ☎0852-22-2400; www.yakumoan.jp; 308 Kita-Horiuchi; dishes ¥700-1150; ⏲10am-3pm) This busy soba restaurant and its beautiful grounds are an excellent place to sample the local *warigo soba,* served in a stack of three round lacquerware trays. Pour some soup stock into the top tray, eat, then pour any leftover soup into the next tray. Also tasty is *soba kamo nanban* (noodles with slices of duck in broth).

Look for a sign on a piece of wood outside.

Greens Baby VEGETARIAN ¥
(☎0852-61-3208; http://restaurant-48211.business.site; 204 Tonomachi; lunch from ¥900; ⏲11am-4pm; 📶 🖉) If you have been craving vegetables in Japan, fill up at this cafe near the castle at a salad bar of pumpkin, peppers, okra and other veg. Vegetarian mains lean toward burritos, Thai green curry and 'taco' (spiced-bean) rice. There is sake cake or fig ice cream for dessert. Sit at the ethnic-chic upstairs tables or hammocks.

DON'T MISS

MATSUE'S SPECIALITIES

Matsue's *kyodo ryōri* (regional cuisine) includes the 'seven delicacies' from Shinji-ko:

- *suzuki* – bass, paper-wrapped and steam-baked
- *shirauo* – whitebait, as tempura or sashimi
- *amasagi* – smelt, as sweet tempura or teriyaki
- *shijimi* – freshwater clams, usually in miso soup
- *moroge ebi* – shrimp, steamed
- *koi* – carp, baked in sauce
- *unagi* – freshwater eel, grilled

★ **Kawa-kyō** IZAKAYA ¥¥
(川京; ☎0852-22-1312; 65 Suetsugu Hon-machi; dishes ¥800-1575; ⏰6-10.30pm Mon-Sat) You can count on a friendly welcome at this small *izakaya,* which specialises in the 'seven delicacies' from Shinji-ko and is a good place to try some local sake or homemade *umeshu* (plum wine). The owner's daughter speaks English. Look for the bamboo-roofed menu display outside. Weekends get busy so book ahead.

Tsurumaru SEAFOOD ¥¥
(鶴丸; ☎0852-22-4887; www.tsurumaru01.com; 1-79 Higashi Hon-machi; dishes ¥400-1200, set meals ¥2000-4000; ⏰5.30-10.30pm Mon-Sat) The smell of fish grilling over coals permeates this restaurant, which specialises in the cuisine of the Oki Islands. The menu features meals such as *eri-yaki konabe* (hot spicy soup cooked over a flame at your table) and sashimi. You'll know it by the *noren* (curtain) with the crane on it and the rustic folk singing that drifts into the street.

There's a limited English menu.

ℹ Information

Matsue International Tourist Information Office (松江国際観光案内所; ☎0852-21-4034; www.kankou-matsue.jp; 665 Asahi-machi; ⏰9am-7pm Jun-Oct, to 6pm Nov-May; 📶) Excellent, friendly assistance in English, French and other languages, directly in front of JR Matsue Station. Free wi-fi.

ℹ Getting There & Away

Matsue is on the JR San-in line, which runs along the San-in coast. You can get to Okayama on the limited express JR Yakumo (¥5510, 2¾ hours). A longer, but cheaper option (¥3350) is on a local train to Yonago and then transfer to the JR Hakubi line, taking 3½ to five hours depending on connections in Yonago.

Highway buses go to Japan's major cities from stop 9 at the terminal in front of Matsue Station. At the time of writing, the popular route to Hiroshima city (¥3900, three hours) was discounted for foreigners with ID to only ¥500! Enquire at the Matsue International Tourist Information Office to check if this years-long promotion is still available at this price.

ℹ Getting Around

It's possible to walk around the sights. Matsue is also a good place to explore by bicycle; these can be rented close to Matsue Station at **Times Car Rental** (タイムズカーレンタル; ☎0852-26-8787; 590-4 Asahi-machi; bicycle per day ¥300; ⏰8am-6.30pm), where you could also rent a car, and returned to your choice of six different locations. JR West Pass holders can rent bicycles for free from **Eki Rent-a-Car** (駅レンタカー西日本; ☎0852-23-8880; www.ekiren.com; 478-19 Asahi-machi; bicycle per day ¥500; ⏰8am-7pm), inside the station car park.

The easiest way to get to all the sights is via the handy city-loop bus. The red streetcar-like Lake Line buses follow a one-way set route around the attractions every 20 minutes, starting outside Matsue Station at stop 7. One ride costs ¥200; a day pass is available for ¥500, purchased on board. It's free to ride for holders of a JR West Pass or Perfect Ticket.

Izumo

☎0853 / POP 171,580

Breezy Izumo (出雲) is a lovely little city with one heavyweight attraction – the great Izumo Taisha shrine, which ranks as one of the most important shrines in Japan. The shrine and leafy surrounding area can be visited on a day trip from nearby Matsue.

👁 Sights

Izumo Taisha is 8km northwest of central Izumo. The shrine area is basically one street, lined with eateries and shops, that leads up to the shrine gates. The Ichibata-line Izumo Taisha-mae Station is at the foot of the street.

★Izumo Taisha SHINTŌ SHRINE
(出雲大社; ☎0853-53-3100; www.izumooyashiro.or.jp; 195 Kizuki-higashi, Taisha-chō; ⏲6.30am-8pm) FREE Izumo Taisha, also known as Izumo Ōyashiro, is perhaps the oldest Shintō shrine in Japan. This shrine, dedicated to Ōkuninushi, god of marriage and bringer of good fortune, is as old as Japanese recorded history – there are references to Izumo in the *Kojiki,* Japan's oldest book – and its origins stretch back into the age of the gods. It's second in importance only to Ise-jingū (in Kansai), the home of the sun goddess Amaterasu.

Visitors to the shrine summon Ōkuninushi by clapping four times rather than the usual two. According to tradition, the deity ceded control over Izumo to the sun goddess's line – on the condition that a huge temple would be built in his honour, one that would reach as high as the heavens.

Impressive as the structure is today, it was once even bigger. Records dating from 970 CE describe the shrine as the tallest building in the country; there is evidence that the shrine towered as high as 48m above the ground during the Heian period (794–1185). It may well have been too high for its own good – the structure collapsed five times between 1061 and 1225, and the roofs today are a more modest 24m high.

The current appearance of the main shrine dates from 1744. The main hall underwent one of its periodic rebuildings in 2013, to be repeated in another 60 years.

Huge *shimenawa* (twisted straw ropes) hang over the entry to the main buildings. Those who can toss and lodge a coin in them are said to be blessed with good fortune. Visitors are not allowed inside the main shrine precinct, most of which is hidden behind huge wooden fences. Ranged along the sides of the compound are the *jūku-sha,* which are long shelters where Japan's myriad deities stay when they come for their annual conference.

When former princess Noriko married the eldest son of the head priest of Izumo Taisha – a 'commoner' – in 2014 she relinquished her royal status. The couple now lives in a house near the shrine.

Shimane Museum of Ancient Izumo MUSEUM
(島根県立古代出雲歴史博物館; ☎0853-53-8600; www.izm.ed.jp; 99-4 Kizuki-higashi, Taisha-chō; ¥300; ⏲9am-6pm Mar-Oct, to 5pm Nov-Feb, closed 3rd Tue of the month) Just to the right of Izumo Taisha's front gate, this informative museum contains modern exhibits on local history. These include reconstructions of the shrine in its pomp, and recordings of the annual ceremonies held to welcome the gods to Izumo. There is also a superb collection of bronze from the ancient Yayoi period.

Festivals & Events

Kamiari-sai RELIGIOUS
The 10th month of the lunar calendar is known throughout Japan as Kan-na-zuki (Month without Gods). In Izumo, however, it is known as Kami-ari-zuki (Month with Gods), for this is the month when all the Shintō gods congregate at Izumo Taisha. This series of events, including lighting bonfires, mark the gods' arrival in Izumo.

Kamiari-sai runs from the 11th to the 17th of the 10th month according to the old calendar; exact dates vary from year to year.

WORTH A TRIP

ADACHI MUSEUM OF ART

The **Adachi Museum of Art** (足立美術館; ☎0854-28-7111; www.adachi-museum.or.jp; 320 Furukawa-chō, Yasugi-shi; tourists with passport ¥1150; ⏲9am-5.30pm Apr-Sep, to 5pm Oct-Mar; P 👪), located east of Matsue in Yasugi, was founded by local businessman and art collector Adachi Zenkō. The collection includes over 100 paintings by Yokoyama Taikan (1868–1958) and a good selection of works by other major 20th-century Japanese painters. There's also a delightful 'pictures for children' gallery. But for many the real attraction is the stunning gardens, regularly voted among the best in Japan.

Sit and contemplate the perfectly clipped mounds of the Dry Landscape Garden – in the distance, mountains rise up as though part of the garden itself.

From Matsue, take the JR line to Yasugi (安来; ¥410, 35 minutes), where there's a free shuttle bus (20 minutes, every 15 to 40 minutes from 8.50am) to the museum. The bus also leaves from Yonago Station (12.25pm and 1.15pm, 45 minutes).

Sleeping & Eating

For a city with such a well-known tourist attraction, accommodation options are limited. There are a couple of high-end ryokan with rooms for over ¥25,000 near the shrine, but the area is lifeless after 5pm. Your best bet is to grab a room at one of the low-cost but comfortable business hotels near Izumo-shi Station, or stay in Matsue.

There are plenty of well-priced restaurants on both sides of Izumo-shi Station, with seafood a common culinary theme. A higher concentration is found on the northern side. On the road leading from Izumo Taisha-mae Station to the shrine, the soba and other restaurants catering to tourists are overpriced but quite good.

Green Hotel Morris BUSINESS HOTEL ¥¥
(☎0853-24-7700; www.hotel-morris.co.jp/izumo; 2-3-4 Ekiminami-machi; s/d from ¥4900/7800; P@) With rooms bigger than typical business hotels in Japan, self-serve pillow bars, friendly and professional staff, a good communal bath with outdoor area, and an excellent breakfast buffet (¥570), all at a seriously reasonable price, it's hard to go past Green Morris. The hotel is just outside the station's south exit.

Gyōza-ya DUMPLINGS ¥
(餃子屋; ☎0853-22-5053; 1268-6 Imaichi-chō; gyōza ¥480-880; ⏲6.30pm-1am Mon-Thu, to 3am Fri & Sat) At that moment when you think you'll go crazy if you see another Izumo soba restaurant, proceed immediately to this cheap and late-opening station-area eatery specialising in humble *gyōza*: they're fat and juicy, and crispy fried on the outside, just the way they should be. Order a beer and...'*kampai!*' (cheers).

Uosensuisan Izumo-eki Minamiguchi-ten IZAKAYA ¥¥
(魚鮮水産出雲市駅南口店; ☎0853-24-7091; www.chimney.co.jp; 1-2-6 Ekiminami-machi; dishes ¥575-2380) This hulking seafood *izakaya* around the corner from the station is always loud and packed – you may have to wait. It'll be worth it if you're a fan of all-you-can-drink plans and seafood done every which way. The substantial picture menu has lots of other popular Japanese treats, from tofu to teriyaki, on offer.

Information

Izumoshieki Information Centre (☎0853-30-6015; ⏲8.30am-5pm) Inside Izumo-shi Station. Little English spoken but there are maps in English and guidance on taking the bus to the shrine.

Taisha Tourist Information Office (退社観光案内所; ☎0853-53-2298; 1346-9 Kizuki-minami, Taisha-chō; ⏲9am-5pm) On the main street halfway between Izumo Taisha-mae Station and the entrance to the shrine.

Getting There & Away

The private, old-fashioned Ichibata line starts from Matsue Shinjiko-onsen Station in Matsue and trundles along the northern side of Shinji-ko to Izumo Taisha-mae Station (¥810, one hour), with a transfer at Kawato (川跡).

The JR line runs from JR Matsue Station to JR Izumo-shi Station (¥580, 40 minutes), where you can transfer to an Ichibata train to Izumo Taisha-mae Station (¥490, 20 minutes), a five-minute walk to the shrine entrance, or to a bus from stop 1 to outside the shrine entrance (¥500, 25 minutes).

Long-distance buses run from a few major cities in the region, including Hiroshima, Okayama and Kyoto.

Iwami Ginzan

The former Iwami Ginzan (石見銀山) silver mine is a Unesco World Heritage Site dotted with shrines, mine shafts and an overgrown refinery that resembles a pyramid. In the early 17th century, the mine produced as much as 38 tonnes of silver annually, making it the most important mine in the country at a time when Japan was producing around a third of the world's silver every year. The Tokugawa shogunate had direct control over the 500 or so mines in the area. Iwami Ginzan is southwest of Izumo, about 6km inland from Nima Station on the San-in coast.

Sights

The site is spread along a valley, with the small town of **Ōmori** at its centre. The main streets and the walking path along the river roughly form a long narrow loop, with mine shafts, temples, historic residences and ruins dotted along it and in the wooded hillsides. It's about 2km from one end to the other; allow at least four hours to do the loop on foot and to see the various sites at leisure.

Gohyakurakan BUDDHIST SITE
(五百羅漢; Ōmori-chō; incl Rakan-ji ¥500) Crowded into two small caves at Gohyakurakan, there are 500 diminutive stone statues

of the Buddha's disciples, each showing a different expression – some smiling, some turning their head to chat to their neighbour. Built to memorialise fallen silver-mine workers, the collection was completed in 1766, after 25 years of work.

Kumagai Residence HISTORIC BUILDING
(熊谷家住宅; ☎0854-89-9003; http://kumagai.city.ohda.lg.jp; 63 Ōmori-chō; ¥500; ⏲9.30am-5pm, closed last Tue of the month) The lovingly restored Kumagai Residence was rebuilt in 1801 after an earthquake destroyed most of the town the previous year. The house belonged to a merchant family, who made their fortune as officials in the silver trade.

Iwami Ginzan World Heritage Centre MUSEUM
(石見銀山世界遺産センター; ☎0854-89-0183; http://ginzan.city.ohda.lg.jp; 1597-3 Ōmori-chō; ¥300; ⏲9am-5.30pm Mar-Nov, to 5pm Dec-Feb, closed last Tue of the month) This centre has exhibits with explanations in English on the history of the mines and the surrounding area.

Ryūgenji Mabu Shaft MINE
(龍源寺間歩; ☎0854-82-1600; ¥410; ⏲9am-5pm Apr-Nov, to 4pm Dec-Mar) This tunnel into the silver mine has been widened substantially from its original size, and a guide helps bring it to life. One glance at the old tunnel, which stretches beyond the fence at the end of the accessible area, should make most people glad they weren't born as 17th-century miners.

Shimizudani Refinery Ruins HISTORIC BUILDING
(清水谷製錬所跡; ☎0854-89-9090; Ōmori-machi) FREE These stepped, stone remains of a silver-mine refinery, now delightfully overgrown with apricot trees and grass, have a pyramid-like appearance.

Sleeping & Eating

Jōfuku-ji Youth House HOSTEL ¥
(城福寺ユースハウス; ☎0854-88-2233; www14.plala.or.jp/joufukuji; 1114 Nima-machi, Nima-chō; dm with/without meals ¥4500/3000; @) This is a great option for accommodation in comfortable tatami rooms in a Buddhist temple, a 20-minute walk east of Nima Station. Meals are available, and the owners can collect you from the station.

Chaya Yamabuki CAFE ¥
(茶屋やまぶき; ☎0854-89-0676; 28 Ōmori-chō; doughnuts ¥150; ⏲10am-5pm Thu-Mon Apr-Oct, to 4pm Nov-Mar) For a drink and a sweet treat, stop in at Yamabuki, where the speciality is sweet-potato doughnuts. It's a five-minute walk north of Shimizudani Refinery Ruins; look for the wooden sign.

Information

There is a booth near the Ōmori Daikansho Ato bus stop where you can pick up an audio guide (¥500) and map, also available at the **tourist information office** (☎0854-89-0333; 824 Ōmori-chō; ⏲8.30am-5pm May-Sep, to 4pm Oct-Apr) by the car park close to Rakan-ji.

Additional information can be found at www.ginzan-wm.jp.

Getting There & Around

Iwami Ginzan can be visited as a day trip from Matsue, but it would be a long day. Buses run to the Ōmori stop about every half-hour from Ōdashi Station (¥670, 25 minutes), and from Nima Station (¥480, 15 minutes, four or five per day). There is also a long-distance bus to Hiroshima.

Within the town area, shuttle buses (¥200, seven minutes, every 15 minutes) connect the Ōmori stop (next to the tourist information office) and the Iwami Ginzan World Heritage Centre.

While these buses connect the eastern length of the town, access to the mining area (along the western length) is only on foot or by bike. From the Ōmori bus stop, it's a picturesque 30- to 45-minute walk to the Ryūgenji Mabu Shaft.

Bike rental is available (¥500 for three hours, ¥700 for an electric-assist bike for two hours). Ask at the tourist information office.

YAMAGUCHI & AROUND

Honshū's southernmost prefecture doesn't get the attention it rightfully deserves. Temperate Yamaguchi Prefecture (山口県; Yamaguchi-ken) is full of surprises, with white sandy beaches that somehow avoid the float-up pollution that has spoiled Japan's coastline, as well as active volcanoes, a gargantuan limestone cave, rolling hills and farmland, historic villages and Unesco World Heritage Sites.

Dip your toes in with easy day trips: from Hiroshima to the curvaceous bridge and scenic samurai town of Iwakuni; or from Kyūshū to the morning seafood-market hustle in Shimonoseki, pufferfish capital of the world.

Yamaguchi

☎083 / POP 197,500

Yamaguchi (山口) is a surprisingly small prefectural capital with a handful of sights, most notably the many baths of Yuda Onsen and the five-storey pagoda of Kōzan-kōen. If you are whizzing by on the *shinkansen* between Hiroshima and Kyūshū during July or August, it's a worthy stopoff for the city's picturesque festivals.

During the 100 years of civil war that bedevilled Japan until the country was reunited under the Tokugawa in the early 17th century, Yamaguchi prospered as an alternative capital to chaotic Kyoto. In 1550, Jesuit missionary Francis Xavier paused here for two months on his way to the imperial capital, and quickly returned when he was unable to even find the emperor in Kyoto.

Sights

★Kōzan-kōen — PARK

(香山公園; ☎083-924-9139; 7-1 Kōzan-chō; ⏲24hr) FREE North of the town centre is Kōzan Park, where the five-storey pagoda of **Rurikō-ji** (瑠璃光寺), a National Treasure dating from 1442, is picturesquely situated beside a small lake. Its eaves are lit up dramatically at night (until 10pm). A small on-site museum displays miniatures of the 50-plus other five-storey pagodas in Japan. The park is also the site of the **Tōshun-ji** (洞春寺) and the graves of the Mōri lords.

★Saikotei — CULTURAL CENTRE

(菜香亭; ☎083-934-3312; www.c-able.ne.jp/~saikou; 1-2-7 Tenge; ¥100; ⏲9am-5pm Wed-Mon; P) This handsome building was originally a high-end restaurant named Gion Saikotei from 1878 to 1996. In 2004 it was converted into this cultural museum, where you can observe or learn calligraphy, wear a kimono (¥2800 for two hours), drink green tea (¥410, first and third weekends) or admire the garden. The homepage lists all that's on offer; reservations are required for activities.

St Francis Xavier Memorial Church — CHURCH

(ザビエル記念聖堂; ☎083-920-1549; www.xavier.jp; 4-1 Kameyama-chō; ⏲9am-5pm Thu-Tue) FREE Built in 1952 in honour of St Francis Xavier, this church burned down in 1991 and was rebuilt in 1998 with a clinically modern interior and geometric stained-glass windows. Sitting above the town in Kameyama-kōen, it resembles a large tent. The ground-floor **Christian museum** (¥300; ⏲9am-5pm) covers the life of Xavier, a Jesuit missionary, and the early history of Christianity in Japan, mostly in Japanese only. Yamaguchi was a major centre of Christian missionary activity before the religion was outlawed in 1589.

Steps opposite the church lead uphill to views of Yamaguchi.

Jōei-ji — BUDDHIST TEMPLE

(常栄寺; 2001 Miyano-shimo; garden ¥300; ⏲garden 8am-5pm) This temple is notable for its simple, stone-dotted Zen garden, **Sesshutei**, designed by the painter Sesshū. From the garden, a trail leads uphill through the woods to several more temples. About 4km northeast of JR Yamaguchi Station, you can reach the temple by bicycle or taxi (about ¥1300) from central Yamaguchi. Alternatively, take the train two stops to Miyano, from where it's a 1.5km walk.

Yamaguchi Furusato Heritage Centre — HISTORIC BUILDING

(山口ふるさと伝承総合センター; www.y-densho.sblo.jp; 12 Shimotatekōji; ⏲9am-5pm) FREE The ground floor of this 1886 sake-merchant building (Manabi-kan; まなび館) has a small display of local crafts, including some Ōuchi dolls (lacquerware speciality of Yamaguchi), and the building itself is interesting. Go upstairs to get a closer look at the large dark-wood beams, and look in the garden for the delightful tea-ceremony room made from old sake-brewing barrels. In the modern learning centre behind the old building, you can see lacquerware being made and try it yourself (¥860; by reservation).

Yamaguchi Prefectural Art Museum — GALLERY

(山口県立美術館; www.yma-web.jp; 3-1 Kameyama-chō; ¥300; ⏲9am-5pm Tue-Sun) This interesting gallery focuses on the art of the region, with three rooms showing work from its varied permanent collection; leafy grounds featuring modern sculpture; and regular special exhibitions (admission extra).

Activities

Just west of Yamaguchi city is the 800-year-old **Yuda Onsen** (湯田温泉). The area is full of hotels and bathing facilities, mostly along a busy main road, which isn't really a place for tottering between baths in your *yukata*. Still, a soak here is a pleasant way to spend a few hours.

Yamaguchi

Yamaguchi

Top Sights
1 Kōzan-kōen....B1
2 Saikotei....C1

Sights
Christian Museum....(see 3)
3 St Francis Xavier Memorial Church....B3
4 Yamaguchi Furusato Heritage Centre....C2
5 Yamaguchi Prefectural Art Museum....B3
6 Yasaka-jinja....C1

Eating
7 Sabō Kō....B4

You can take a dip in the six indoor and outdoor baths of **Tokiwa** (西の雅常盤; 083-922-0091; www.n-tokiwa.co.jp; 4-6-4 Yudaonsen; ¥800; 11am-10pm), use the baths at the large **Hotel Kamefuku** (ホテルかめ福; 083-922-7000; www.kamefuku.com; 4-5-2 Yudaonsen; ¥850; 11.30am-10pm) or, for a taste of luxury and a peaceful garden setting, head to **Sansui-en** (山水園; 083-922-0560; www.yuda-sansuien.com; 4-60 Midori-chō; ¥1600; 10am-10pm). All but Tokiwa include a towel.

For a full list and map of the baths and hotels, drop in first at the **tourist information office** (083-901-0150; 2-1-23 Yudaonsen; 9am-6pm, foot bath to 10pm;) on the main road, which also has a free foot bath and towels for sale.

JR and Bōchō Buses run regularly to Yuda Onsen bus stop from Yamaguchi Station (¥220, 15 minutes). They drop you on the main strip, Yuda Onsen-dōri, a short walk from the tourist office (just keep walking in the direction of the bus). Yuda Onsen also has a station, one stop on the local train line from Yamaguchi (¥140) or 20 minutes from Shin-Yamaguchi (¥240). From the station, follow the quiet red and then yellowish road for about 1km to get to the busy main intersection, and turn right for the tourist office.

Sleeping & Eating

There's not a great deal of choice in central Yamaguchi, but nearby Yuda Onsen is a good base, especially if you like the idea of an on-site onsen with your accommodation. There are also some good-value Western-style chain hotels clustered around unremarkable Shin-Yamaguchi Station.

Green Rich Hotel Yamaguchi Yuda Onsen BUSINESS HOTEL ¥¥
(083-923-6000; 4-7-11 Yudaonsen; s/d from ¥6805/8800; P) This smart business hotel, centrally located in Yuda Onsen, has above-average rooms, a coin laundry and plenty of parking. Guests receive discounted access (¥450) to a nearby onsen.

YAMAGUCHI BUS PASS

The **Yamaguchi Bus Pass** (1-/2-/3-day ¥2000/4000/5000) is available to tourists for unlimited travel by bus in Yamaguchi Prefecture, including Hagi's Circular Bus. It's excellent value if you plan on visiting other cities in the prefecture by bus. A one-way ticket between Hagi and Shimonoseki or Yamaguchi costs about the same as a one-day pass. Purchase passes from the bus counters at Yamaguchi, Shin-Yamaguchi and Shimonoseki Stations, Hiroshima Bus Center and Hagi Kanko Hotel. Passport required.

★ **Matsudaya Hotel** RYOKAN ¥¥¥
(ホテル松田屋; 083-922-0125; www.matsudayahotel.co.jp; 3-6-7 Yudaonsen; r per person incl 2 meals from ¥25,920; @) At this centuries-old, now-modernised ryokan, you can bathe in history – right in the tub where once dipped the plotters of the Meiji Restoration. The ryokan's gorgeous garden setting, complete with koi, and excellent service will likely ease any present-day rebellious thoughts.

Matsudaya is on the main drag in Yuda Onsen.

Sabō Kō CAFE ¥
(茶房幸; 083-928-5522; 1-2-39 Dōjōmonzen; dishes ¥680-980; 11.30am-6pm Wed-Mon) A cosy atmosphere prevails in this low-ceilinged little eatery, where customers perch on wooden stools sipping coffee. The speciality on the Japanese-only menu is the generous, rustic *omuraisu* (omelette filled with fried rice), but there are also curries and soba. Look for the small wood-covered hut with ceramic pots sticking out of the exterior plasterwork.

Mottimo Pasta Yuda Onsen ITALIAN ¥¥
(モッチモパスタ 山口湯田店; 083-941-6447; 2-5-41 Yoshikishimo-higashi; pastas ¥850-1200; 11am-3pm & 5-10pm Thu-Tue) In Yuda Onsen, Mottimo offers a variety of Japanese twists on Italian faves, including eight kinds of delicious hot, buttery, flavoured bread sticks (think honey, basil and custard cream!), a small selection of pizzas and a range of delicious pastas. Lunch specials are available and there's a picture menu.

Information

The **tourist office** (山口観光案内所; 083-933-0090; www.yamaguchi-city.jp; 9am-6pm) is inside Yamaguchi Station. There is also an office at **Shin-Yamaguchi** (083-972-6373; 9am-6pm), on the 2nd floor, *shinkansen* exit side.

Getting There & Away

AIR

It's a long way from Tokyo to Yamaguchi, even on *shinkansen*. You can often get good deals on flights from Haneda to **Yamaguchi Ube Airport** (UBJ; www.yamaguchiube-airport.jp) in Ube city, although access is a little inconvenient. There are also direct flights from Incheon in Seoul, South Korea.

BUS

Chūgoku JR Bus (083-922-2519; www.chugoku-jrbus.co.jp) runs nine to 11 buses daily to Hagi (Higashi-Hagi Station; ¥1760, free with JR Pass, 1½ hours) from Yamaguchi Station, some originating at Shin-Yamaguchi. **Bōchō Bus** (0834-32-7733; www.bochobus.co.jp) runs buses to Higashi-Hagi Station (¥2060, 95 minutes, at least hourly) from Shin-Yamaguchi.

TRAIN

Yamaguchi Station is on the JR Yamaguchi line. Shin-Yamaguchi Station is 10km southwest in Ogōri on the San-yō *shinkansen* line, which connects to Shimonoseki and Hiroshima, and to Osaka in the east. The Yamaguchi local service connects the Shin-Yamaguchi and Yamaguchi Stations (¥240, 25 minutes).

Getting Around

It's possible to walk to the central sights from Yamaguchi Station, but it's handy to hire a bicycle for the outlying temple areas. Jōei-ji, for example, is about 4km away (closer to Miyano Station). A taxi might be an easier option if you don't want to walk or cycle. For bikes, try **Fukutake** (福武; 083-922-0915; 1-4-6 Eki-dōri; per 2hr/day ¥300/700; 8am-7pm) just across from Yamaguchi Station.

Yuda Onsen is served by bus or train from Yamaguchi and Shin-Yamaguchi.

Tsuwano

0856 / POP 7660

A highlight of this region, utterly delightful Tsuwano (津和野) is a quiet, 700-year-old mountain town straddling a pretty river and boasting an important shrine, a ruined castle and an evocative samurai quarter. It also has a wonderful collection of carp swimming in the roadside water channels – in fact, there are far more carp here than people.

Sights

Only the walls and some fine old gates from the former samurai quarter of Tonomachi (殿町) remain, but it's an attractive area for strolling. The water channels that run alongside the picturesque Tonomachi Road are home to numerous carp, bred to provide food in case of emergency. As you're walking, look out for *sugidama* (cedar balls) hanging outside a few old sake breweries.

★Taikodani-Inari-jinja SHINTŌ SHRINE
(太鼓谷稲成神社; 24hr, store 8am-4.30pm; P) Within walking distance of town, this thriving shrine, built in 1773 by the seventh lord Kamei Norisada, is one of the five major Inari shrines in Japan. Walk up the hillside to it through a tunnel created by hundreds of *torii,* which are lit up at night, creating a beautiful sight from the town. At the top is a grand shrine complex, and fabulous views of the valley and mountains.

To get here, take Tonomachi Road and turn right before the river bridge, then follow the signs. The steps should take between 10 and 20 minutes to climb; or you can drive and park on-site.

Morijuku Museum MUSEUM
(杜塾美術館; 542 Morimura; ¥500; 9am-5pm Sat & Sun) This museum is housed in a 150-year-old building that once served as the home of a *shōya* (village headman). Downstairs is a collection of soft-edged scenes painted by local-born artist Nakao Shō, a roomful of bullfight sketches by Goya, and a framed set of beautifully embroidered Taishō-era kimono collars. The caretaker will gladly point out the features of the building, including the pinhole camera hidden away upstairs.

Tsuwano Catholic Church CHURCH
(津和野カトリック教会; Tonomachi; 8am-5.30pm Apr-Nov, to 5pm Dec-Mar) The church here is a reminder of the town's Christian history. 'Hidden Christians' from Nagasaki were exiled here in the early Meiji period. It's interesting to peep inside to see tatami mats instead of pews.

Chapel of St Maria CHAPEL
(乙女峠マリア聖堂, Otometoge Maria Kinenseido; 0856-72-0251; 9am-5pm) The tiny Maria-dō dates from 1951. More than 150 'hidden Christians' were imprisoned in a Buddhist temple on this site in the early years of the Meiji Restoration; 36 died before a law allowing freedom of religion was passed in 1873. A procession is held here on 3 May.

> **DRIVING IN YAMAGUCHI**
>
> Be sure to pick up a copy of the excellent *Enjoy Driving in Yamaguchi* brochure, produced by the **Yamaguchi Prefectural Tourism Federation** (www.oidemase.or.jp), from any of the region's tourist information centres. It's a must for anyone considering driving around the prefecture and contains a wealth of hidden gems.

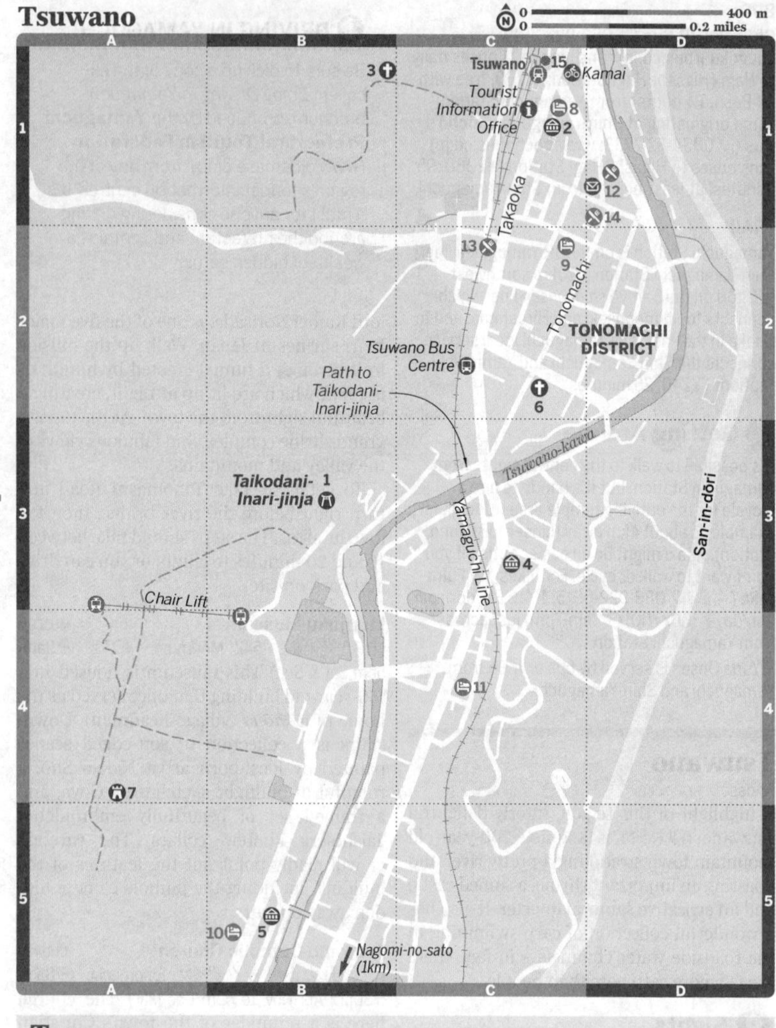

Tsuwano

Top Sights

1 Taikodani-Inari-jinja B3

Sights

2 Anno Art Museum C1
3 Chapel of St Maria B1
4 Morijuku Museum C3
5 Nishi Amane Former Residence B5
6 Tsuwano Catholic Church C2
7 Tsuwano-jō A4

Sleeping

8 Hoshi Ryokan C1
9 Noren Yado Meigetsu C2
10 Shokudō Minshuku Satoyama B5
11 Wakasagi-no-Yado C4

Eating

12 Pino Rosso D1
13 Tsurube C2
14 Yūki D1

Transport

15 SL Yamaguchi C1

Nishi Amane Former Residence HISTORIC BUILDING
(西周旧居; 13-2 Ushiroda Ro; ⌚9am-5pm) FREE It's a pleasant walk down the river from Tsuwano town centre to see the peaked-roof former residence of Nishi Amane (1829–97), a philosopher and political scientist prominent in the Meiji government.

Anno Art Museum GALLERY
(安野光雅美術館; ☎0856-72-4155; 60-1 Ushiroda; ¥800; ⌚9am-4.45pm, closed 2nd Thu in Mar, Jun, Sep & Dec) Tsuwano-born Anno Mitsumasa is famous for his wonderfully detailed illustrated books, including *Anno's Alphabet* and *Anno's Journey*. You can see his work at this traditional-looking white building near the station, where the large collection is rotated throughout the year.

Tsuwano-jō CASTLE
(津和野城; 477-20 Ushiroda; chairlift one way ¥450; ⌚chairlift 9am-4.30pm, irregular hours winter) The broken walls of Tsuwano-jō brood over the valley. A slightly rickety chairlift takes you slowly up the hillside, and there's a further 15-minute walk through the woods to the castle ruins. There's nothing here but the walls, but there are of course great views.

Activities

Nagomi-no-sato ONSEN
(なごみの里; www.nagomi-nosato.com; 256 Washibara; ¥600; ⌚10am-9pm Fri-Wed) After a day of sightseeing, take a soak at this onsen complex. It's about 2.5km from the centre of town, or a 15-minute walk from the Nishi Amane Former Residence. Buses do travel here from the station (¥200, eight minutes), but there are only three a day.

Festivals & Events

Sagi-mai Matsuri DANCE
(⌚Jul) The Heron Dance Festival sees processions of dancers dressed as herons on 20 and 27 July. The birds are a symbol of Tsuwano.

Sleeping

You could see Tsuwano on a day trip from Yamaguchi, but staying the night gives you the chance to enjoy one of the town's *minshuku* or ryokan and a walk through the quiet lamp-lit streets in the evening. For information in English, go to www.gambo-ad.com/english and click on 'Tsuwano' – a few of the local ryokan are listed.

> WORTH A TRIP
>
> **CHŌMON GŌRGE**
>
> If you're travelling between Yamaguchi and Tsuwano, consider a stop at Chōmon-kyō (長門峡), a gorge with a walking track, waterfalls, swimming pools and beautiful colours in autumn. The gorge entrance is just near Chōmon-kyō station on the JR Yamaguchi line.

Shokudō Minshuku Satoyama MINSHUKU ¥
(食堂民宿　さと山; ☎080-1913-9396; www.genki-ya.com/sato; 345 Washibara; s/tw from ¥2700/4700; P❄@🛜🐾) Satoyama has a spectacular countryside setting. The Japanese-style rooms have mountain views and strong wi-fi, though neglected shared bathrooms. The English-speaking owner cooks decent meals and there is a free-use clothes washer. The mountain-hugging road to Satoyama is flat and easy on a bike; it's walkable, but unlit at night. Look for the white house, blue *noren* and red banners.

★ **Hoshi Ryokan** MINSHUKU ¥¥
(星旅館; ☎0856-72-0136; 53-6 Ushiroda; r per person incl meals ¥7500; 🛜) You'll get a warm, family welcome at this big, creaky *minshuku* located a minute from the station. The tatami rooms are spacious and there's a shared family-style bathroom.

Noren Yado Meigetsu RYOKAN ¥¥
(のれん宿明月; ☎0856-72-0685; 665 Ushirodaguchi; r per person incl 2 meals from ¥10,800; ❄🛜) This is a traditional ryokan on a narrow lane in the Tonomachi area. *Fusuma* (sliding screen doors) glide open in the rooms to reveal a garden, and there are soothing, wood-panelled shared bathrooms. Some rooms have private bathrooms. Look for the old-fashioned gate with a red-tiled roof.

Wakasagi-no-Yado MINSHUKU ¥¥
(民宿わかさぎの宿; ☎0856-72-1146; 98-6 Morimura-guchi; r per person incl 2 meals ¥8000) This well-kept *minshuku* is on the main road south of the Tonomachi district. Bathrooms are shared. Walking from the station, look for the building with a diamond-pattern tile design on the facade and a curtain with a picture of a heron.

Eating

There are a few cafes and eateries on the main Tonomachi street, and more along the (less picturesque) street that runs directly south from the station. Not many places open at night as people tend to eat at their accommodation. Restaurants may also close if it's quiet, especially during winter.

★Tsurube NOODLES ¥
(つるべ; 384-1 Ushoroda-guchi; dishes ¥600-1050; ⌚11am-4pm Sat-Thu) The speciality here is fresh wheat noodles handmade on the premises, going into filling dishes such as *sansai udon* (noodles with wild vegetables) and *umeboshi udon* (noodles with dried plum). For a little extra, have a side of *omusubi* (rice ball).

Tsurube can be found next to a small graveyard.

Yūki SEAFOOD ¥¥
(遊亀; ☎0856-72-0162; 271-4 Ushiroda; meals ¥1400-2800; ⌚10.30am-3pm) The *Tsuwano teishoku* (a carp-themed sampler of local dishes) is recommended at this elegantly rustic restaurant, which has wooden tables and the sound of running water. There are koi (carp) in a pool in the floor, and more on the menu. Look for the old-fashioned building with a small pine tree outside. Dinner by reservation only.

Pino Rosso ITALIAN ¥¥
(ピノロッソ; ☎0856-72-2778; www.pinorosso.jp; 284 Ushiroda; lunch/dinner set menu from ¥1300/1700; ⌚10am-9pm Fri-Wed) The menu at this modern cafe-restaurant includes pastas and pizzas, plus there's a range of sweet bready items you can have with your coffee. Reservations are recommended in the evening.

YAMAGUCHI STEAM TRAIN

The **SL Yamaguchi** (☎0570-00-2486; www.c571.jp; adult/child ¥1660/830; ⌚Mar-Nov) steam train trundles through the scenic valleys from Shin-Yamaguchi to Tsuwano between mid-March and late November on weekends and holidays. It's a fun way to travel and is very popular; check the latest schedules and book well ahead at JR and tourist information offices.

Information

MONEY

The only convenience store with an ATM is outside Tsuwano Bus Centre.

Post Office (297 Ushiroda Ro; ⌚9am-4pm Mon-Fri; ATM 9am-6pm Mon-Fri, to 5pm Sat, to 1pm Sun) Has an ATM accepting international cards.

TOURIST INFORMATION

Tourist Information Office (津和野町観光協会; ☎0856-72-1771; www.tsuwano-kanko.net; ⌚9am-5pm; 📶) Immediately to the right as you exit the station. Basic English is spoken and there are maps in English, a rest area and free wi-fi, accessible even when closed.

Getting There & Away

Tsuwano is on the JR Yamaguchi line, which runs from Shin-Yamaguchi and Yamaguchi in the south, to Masuda on the Sea of Japan coast (which connects to the San-in line). The Super Oki service from Yamaguchi or Shin-Yamaguchi will shave about 25 to 35 minutes off the trip, but costs more than double the standard fare (or free for JR Pass holders).

Masuda ¥580, 45 minutes
Shin-Yamaguchi ¥1140, 1¾ hours
Yamaguchi ¥970, 80 minutes

Long-distance buses go from the **Tsuwano Bus Centre** (Takaoka) to Higashi-Hagi (¥2190, 1¾ hours, five daily 8.10am to 5.10pm; JR passes not valid). There are also overnight buses to Kōbe.

Getting Around

Most attractions are within walking or cycling distance of the station. There is a local bus service, but it's not of much use to travellers and runs only a few times a day. The easiest way to explore is to rent a bike from **Kamai** (貸自転車かまい; Takaoka; bike hire per 2/24hr ¥500/800; ⌚8am-sunset), across from the station.

Hagi

☎0838 / POP 49,580

The jewel in Yamaguchi's crown, Hagi (萩) is known for producing some of the finest ceramics in Japan and has a well-preserved old samurai quarter. During the feudal period, Hagi was the castle town of the Chōshū domain, which, together with Satsuma (corresponding to modern Kagoshima in southern Kyūshū), was instrumental in defeating the Tokugawa government and ushering in a new age after the Meiji

Hagi

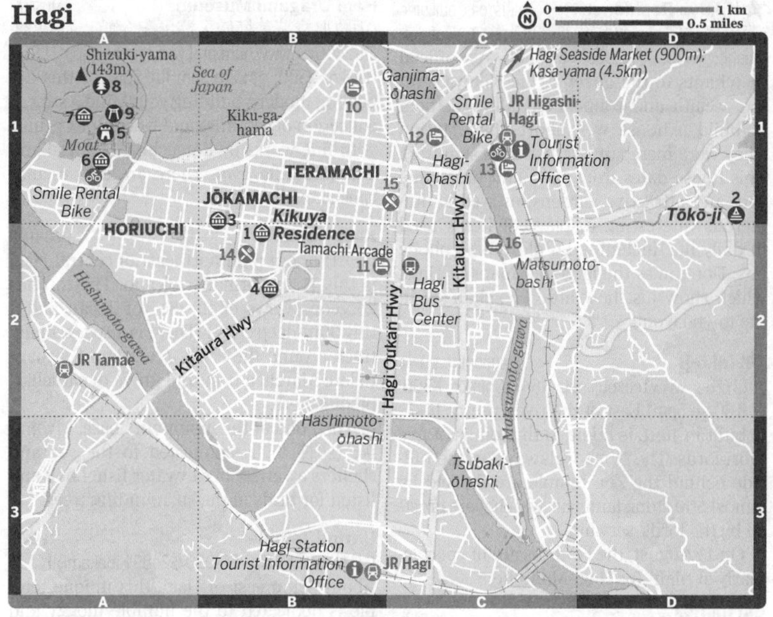

Hagi

Top Sights
1 Kikuya Residence B2
2 Tōkō-ji D1

Sights
3 Hagi Museum B1
4 Hagi Uragami Museum B2
5 Hagi-jō A1
6 Hagi-jō Kiln A1
7 Hanano-e Tea House A1
8 Shizuki-kōen A1
9 Shizuki-yama-jinja A1

Sleeping
10 Guesthouse Hagi Akatsukiya B1
11 Guesthouse Ruco B2
12 Hagi no Yado Tomoe C1
13 Hagi Royal Intelligent Hotel C1

Eating
Dining Mameta ..... (see 13)
14 Hotoritei B2
15 Maru C1

Drinking & Nightlife
16 Cafe Tikal C2

Restoration. The importance of Hagi's role in the modernisation of Japan was recognised in 2015 by Unesco, which decreed World Heritage status on five historical industrial sites.

Western and central Hagi are effectively an island, created by the two rivers Hashimoto-gawa and Matsumoto-gawa; eastern Hagi (with the major JR station Higashi-Hagi) lies on the eastern bank of the Matsumoto-gawa.

Hagi's proximity to the Sea of Japan, quiet pace and bucolic vistas make it the prefecture's most worthwhile destination.

Sights

Hagi is a sprawling city, which hugs every inch of land between the shoreline and its enfolding mountain range. The city's main areas of interest are its picturesque samurai district, **Jōkamachi** (also called 'Hagi Castle town' since its inclusion in the Unesco World Heritage camp) – the streets of which are lined with whitewashed walls enclosing beautiful villas – and its World Heritage Sites. Most attractions are spread apart and renting a car or bicycle can be a good idea.

★Kikuya Residence HISTORIC BUILDING
(菊屋家住宅; ☎0838-25-8282; 1-1 Gofuku-machi; ¥600; ⊙8.30am-5.30pm) As official merchants to the *daimyō,* the Kikuya family's wealth and connections allowed them to build a house well above their station (they were merchants rather than samurai). This house dates from 1604 and has a fine gate and attractive gardens, as well as numerous interesting displays of items used in daily life, including an old public phone box. Don't miss the large old maps of Hagi, which show just how little has changed in the town layout.

★Tōkō-ji BUDDHIST TEMPLE
(東光寺; www.toukouji.net; 1647 Chintō; ¥300; ⊙8.30am-5pm) East of the river, pretty Tōkō-ji, built in 1691, is home to the tombs of five Mōri lords. The stone walkways on the hillside behind the Zen temple are flanked by almost 500 stone lanterns, which were erected by the lords' servants.

On 15 August, the lanterns are lit spectacularly at night for Hagi Mantoue.

Shizuki-kōen PARK
(指月公園; incl Hagi-jō ¥210; ⊙8am-6.30pm Apr-Oct, to 4.30pm Nov-Feb, to 6pm Mar; P) Within this park, there's not much of the old **Hagi-jō** (萩城; ☎0838-25-1826; 1-1 Horiuchi; incl Shizuki-kōen ¥210; ⊙8am-6.30pm Apr-Oct, to 4.30pm Nov-Feb, to 6pm Mar) to see, apart from the castle's typically imposing outer walls and the surrounding carp-filled moat. The castle was built in 1604 and dismantled in 1874 following the Meiji Restoration. The inner grounds hold a pleasant park, with spring cherry blossoms; the **Shizuki-yama-jinja** (志都岐山神社); the mid-19th-century **Hanano-e Tea House** (花江茶亭; ☎0838-25-1750); and other buildings, including a *nagaya* (Japanese long house) known as Asa Mōri House.

From the castle ruins, you can climb the hillside to the 143m peak of **Shizuki-yama**.

Hagi-jō Kiln GALLERY
(萩城窯; ☎0838-22-5226; 2-5 Horiuchi; ⊙8am-5pm) FREE *Hagi-yaki* (Hagi ceramic ware) is noted for its fine glazes and delicate pastel colours, and connoisseurs of Japanese ceramics rank it as some of the best. At a number of shops and kilns, including this one within the walls of the old castle ruins, you can see *hagi-yaki* being made and browse the finished products.

The tourist office has a complete list of kilns in the area.

Hagi Uragami Museum MUSEUM
(山口県立萩美術館・浦上記念館; ☎0838-24-2400; www.hum.pref.yamaguchi.lg.jp; 586-1 Hiyako; ¥300; ⊙9am-5pm Tue-Sun) In this appealing modern building you'll find a superb collection of ceramics and woodblock prints, with fine works by Katsushika Hokusai and Utamaro Kitagawa. There are also regular special exhibitions.

Kasa-yama MOUNTAIN
(笠山) About 6km northeast of central Hagi is this 112m dormant volcano. The top has gorgeous views of the Sea of Japan and a tiny 30m-deep crater. There is also a walking track around the coast. From late February to late March, a beautiful grove of camellias blooms here.

The pond at the mountain's base, Myōjin-ike (明神池), is connected to the sea and shelters a variety of saltwater fish. Look and listen for birds in the surrounding trees.

Unrinji Temple TEMPLE
(雲林寺; ☎0838-86-0307; 2489 Kibekami) FREE About 22km east of Hagi, this unique temple is dedicated to the humble moggy and features cats, cats, everywhere! Well, carved ones, anyway. Serious cat people won't mind renting a car to get out here.

Hagi Museum MUSEUM
(萩博物館, Hagi Hakubutsukan; ☎0838-256-447; www.city.hagi.lg.jp/hagihaku; 355 Horiuchi; adult/child ¥510/100; ⊙9am-5pm; P) Hagi's impressive city museum features permanent displays on astrology, biology and local crafts, and hosts visiting exhibitions.

Festivals & Events

Hagi Mantoue CULTURAL
(万灯会, Hagi Lantern Festival; ⊙7.30-10pm 15 Aug) A promenade of 500 stone lanterns are lit up with candles at Tōkō-ji for the Hagi Lantern Festival, which honours the spirits of ancestors. The warm glow on a summer's night is atmospheric and worth seeking out if you are in Hagi around this time.

Sleeping

Guesthouse Hagi Akatsukiya HOSTEL ¥
(古民家ゲストハウス萩・暁屋; ☎050-3624-4625; www.facebook.com/hagi.akatsukiya.guest.house; 237-1 Hamasakimachi; dm ¥2600-2800;) This polished-up Japanese house, just two minutes from the beach, has a cute garden and soft bunk beds for a tranquil rest. The well-travelled owner provides

good local knowledge, speaks English and rents bikes (¥500 per 24 hours). Akatsukiya is beside a shrine – from the northernmost beach, go down the road opposite the blue-tiled toilets and cross the sawmill.

Guesthouse Ruco HOSTEL ¥
(ゲストハウスRuco; 0838-21-7435; www.guesthouse-ruco.com; 92 Karahi-chō; dm/s/d with shared bathroom ¥2900/4900/7900;) Ruco is a modern wonderland of handmade furniture and vintage decor, effortlessly stylish and minimalist from the cafe-bar to the bathrooms. Cramped but clean bunk beds have personal curtains, while the Japanese-style doubles are spacious. Helpful staff speak some English. Exit left from Hagi Bus Centre and then left again.

Hagi Royal Intelligent Hotel HOTEL ¥¥
(萩ロイヤルインテリジェントホテル; 0838-21-4589; www.hrih.jp; 3000-5 Chintō; s/d/tw incl breakfast from ¥6455/8100/10,500;) Walk out of Higashi-Hagi Station and straight into this modern hotel. The large rooms have some quirky features – the magnetic dartboard and puzzles will keep you entertained – plus spacious showers that spray you at all angles. There's an onsen on-site and some staff members speak English.

It also has a smart Japanese restaurant, Dining Mameta.

★Hagi no Yado Tomoe RYOKAN ¥¥¥
(萩の宿常茂恵; 0838-22-0150; http://tomoehagi.jp; 608-53 Kōbō-ji Hijiwara; r from ¥22,245;) The finest inn in Hagi, the historic Tomoe offers gorgeous Japanese rooms with garden views and luxurious baths, and beautifully prepared cuisine. Prices vary according to season, and there are discounted plans on the website (if you don't read Japanese, it may be easier to reserve via email). Cross the bridge from the station and take the road along the river.

★Hagi Kankō Hotel HOTEL ¥¥¥
(萩観光ホテル; 0838-25-0211; www.hagikan.com; 1189 Chintō; r from ¥15,120;) At the base of Kasa-yama, this solid tourist hotel has wonderfully friendly yet formal staff who'll do anything to assist, even if English is a challenge for them. Smart, ryokan-style rooms have beautiful views over the bay to the mountains in the distance, as does the gorgeous *rotemburo*.

Eating & Drinking

Hagi Seaside Market SEAFOOD ¥
(道の駅 萩しーまーと; 0838-24-4937; http://seamart.axis.or.jp; 4160-61 Chintō; 9.30am-6pm) There's all manner of fresh and wild delights to sample at this busy market, with plenty of eateries as well as straight-from-the-source sellers in case you're planning your own barbecue. Even if you just come for a gander, it's a good taste of local Hagi life.

★Hotoritei CAFE ¥¥
(畔亭; 0838-22-1755; www.facebook.com/hotoritei; 62 Minami-Katakawa; meals ¥1200-1850; 11am-4.30pm Fri-Wed Feb-Dec) A tranquil rest stop near the Jōkamachi area, Hotoritei is within a large house surrounded by gardens. It mainly serves coffees, teas and cakes – try the fluffy, cream-filled *matcha* roll. There are a few lunch sets, and the menu has some pictures. Look for the entrance set back from the road, next to Sam's Irish pub.

Maru IZAKAYA ¥¥
(まる; 0838-26-5060; 78 Yoshida-chō; dishes ¥750-1850; 5-11pm Mon-Sat) This lively *izakaya* specialises in dishes prepared using fresh local produce. There's a predictable seafood theme, with lots of sushi and sashimi to enjoy, but a range of other hot items are available. Reservations recommended on weekends.

Dining Mameta JAPANESE ¥¥
(ダイニング まめた; 0838-21-4689; http://diningmameta.com; 2nd fl, Hagi Royal Intelligent Hotel, 3000-5 Chintō; meals ¥600-1380; 11am-2pm & 5.30-10.30pm) This smart Japanese hotel restaurant, adjacent to Higashi-Hagi Station, happily welcomes international guests to sample its fresh local cuisine, including sushi, sashimi, salads and daily specials.

Cafe Tikal CAFE
(長屋門珈琲・カフェティカル; 0838-26-2933; www.facebook.com/nagayamoncoffee.cafetikal; 298-1 Hijiwara; 9.30am-8pm Tue-Sat, to 6pm Sun) Through the old gate of the Kogawa family residence is this small cafe with large windows overlooking a pleasingly unkempt garden. Sit among the games and books at one of the wooden tables and choose a coffee (from ¥400) from a range of 20 bean varieties. A toasted almond Bavarian cake is the speciality accompaniment.

Information

The **tourist information office** (萩市観光案内所; ☎0838-25-3145; www.hagishi.com; ⏲9am-5.45pm Mar-Nov, to 5pm Dec-Feb) is located inside Higashi-Hagi Station. Staff speak English and provide a good English cycling and walking map. They offer a free service with associated hotels (listed online) to store your luggage at the station and then later deliver it to your accommodation in time for check-in.

There's another tourist office near **Hagi Station** (萩駅観光案内所; ☎0838-25-1750; 3537-3 Tsubaki; ⏲9am-5.45pm Mar-Nov, to 5pm Dec-Feb).

Getting There & Away

BUS

Bus connections from Higashi-Hagi Station, via **Hagi Bus Center** (11-2 Karahimachi), include:

Shin-Yamaguchi Bōchō Bus ¥2060, 95 minutes, at least hourly; Super Hagi Bus ¥1550, 80 minutes, every one to two hours

Tsuwano ¥2190, 1¾ hours, five daily

Yamaguchi ¥1760 (free with JR Pass), 1½ hours, four daily

TRAIN

Hagi is on the JR San-in line, which runs along the coast from Tottori and Matsue. Get out at Higashi-Hagi Station for the main sights. Local services between Shimonoseki and Higashi-Hagi (¥1940) take up to 3½ hours, depending on transfers. If you're going to Tsuwano from Higashi-Hagi, go by train up the coast to Masuda (¥970, 1¼ hours), then change to the JR Yamaguchi line (¥580, 40 minutes) or *Super Oki* (¥580, 30 minutes) for Tsuwano. All these journeys are free with a JR Pass. If you have to wait long transferring at sleepy Masuda, try the hidden restaurant street one block north of the station.

Getting Around

It's easy to walk around central Hagi and the Jōkamachi area, but many sights, including the World Heritage locations, are on the edges of town. It helps to have wheels of some kind.

BICYCLE

Smile Rental Bike (スマイル貸自転車; ☎0838-22-2914; bike hire per 1/24hr ¥200/1000; ⏲8.30am-5.30pm) is the first of two rental sheds directly left as you exit Higashi-Hagi Station. A wide range of bikes is available, including child carriers. Smile allows taking bikes overnight.

Another Smile **branch** (スマイル貸自転車; ☎0838-22-2914; 83-27 Hidori Horiuchi; bike hire per 1/24hr ¥200/1000; ⏲8.30am-5.30pm) is just south of the castle ruins, if you are staying nearby and want to check in your luggage first.

BUS

The handy Māru Basu (まぁーるバス; Circular Bus; 7am to 6pm) takes in all of central Hagi's main attractions. There are east- (東回り) and west-bound (西回り) loops, with services every 30 minutes at each stop. One trip costs ¥100, and one-/two-day passes cost ¥500/700. Both routes stop at Higashi-Hagi Station.

Shimonoseki

☎083 / POP 268,620

At the southwestern tip of Honshū, Shimonoseki (下関) is on the visitor radar for an early-morning meal at its buzzing seafood market – the town is famous for its *fugu*, the potentially lethal pufferfish. Separated from Kyūshū by a narrow strait, the town is also known to Japanese for a decisive 12th-century clash between rival samurai clans. Nowadays it's friendly fireworks that sometimes take place across the waters, and you can even walk to Kyūshū through an underwater tunnel, with a foot on each side of the border. Shimonoseki is also an important connecting point to South Korea.

Sights

The area around Shin-Shimonoseki *shinkansen* station, where many visitors arrive, has little to offer by way of sights, services and restaurants. To explore the area, you need to change to a local train and head to Shimonoseki Station, two stops away.

Chōfu (長府), east of Shimonoseki Station along the coastal road, is home to the old castle town area. While little remains of the castle itself, there are earth walls and samurai gates, several temples and shrines, and inviting narrow streets, making it an atmospheric spot for a wander.

★**Karato Ichiba** MARKET

(唐戸市場; www.karatoichiba.com; 5-50 Karato; ⏲5am-1pm Mon-Sat, 9am-3pm Sun) A highlight of a trip to Shimonoseki is an early-morning visit to the Karato fish market. It's a great opportunity to try sashimi for breakfast or lunch, and fish doesn't get any fresher than this – a fair bit of it will still be moving. The best days to come are Friday to Sunday, when stallholders set up tables selling *bentō* of sashimi and cooked dishes made from the day's catch. Note that the market is closed on some Wednesdays.

You can take away meals or eat at the counters on the mezzanine level. Buses to Karato (¥220) leave from outside the station and take about seven minutes; the 'Karato' stop is announced in English.

Akama-jingū SHINTŌ SHRINE

(赤間神宮; 4-1 Amidaiji-chō; 24hr) FREE This shrine is dedicated to the seven-year-old emperor Antoku, who died in 1185 in the battle of Dan-no-ura. On the left is a statue of Mimi-nashi Hōichi (Earless Hōichi), the blind bard whose musical talents get him into trouble with ghosts in a story made famous by Lafcadio Hearn.

The bright vermilion shrine is between Karato and Hino-yama, about a five-minute walk from the Karato market area. Night lights emphasise its deep red colours. From the station, get off the bus at the Akama-jingū-mae bus stop (¥260, 10 minutes).

Hino-yama-kōen PARK

(火の山公園) About 5km northeast of Shimonoseki Station, this park has superb views over the Kanmon Straits from the top of 268m-high Hino-yama. To get to the lookout's **ropeway** (火の山ロープウエイ; 083-231-1351; one-way/return ¥300/500; 10am-5pm Thu-Mon Mar-Nov), get off the bus at Mimosusōgawa (¥260, 12 minutes). From here it's a steep 10-minute walk to the ropeway entrance. There are also buses from Shimonoseki Station (stop 3) that can drop you at the Hino-yama ropeway stop (¥260, 15 minutes, hourly).

Festivals & Events

Kanmon Straits Fireworks Festival FIREWORKS

(Hanabi Taikai; 13 Aug) A spectacular fireworks display occurring on both sides of the straits at the same time.

Sentei Festival CULTURAL

(4-1 Amidaiji-chō; 2-4 May) Held at Akama-jingū to remember the Heike women who worked as prostitutes to pay for rites for their fallen relatives. On 3 May, women dressed as Heian-era courtesans form a colourful procession at the shrine.

Sleeping

★ **Hinoyama Youth Hostel** HOSTEL ¥

(火の山ユースホステル; 083-222-3753; www.e-yh.net/shimonoseki; 3-47 Mimosusōgawa-chō; dm/tw ¥3500/8000;) Amazing views of the straits and welcoming service make this one of the best youth hostels in western Honshū. You can take a bus from the station to the Hino-yama ropeway stop (¥260, 15 minutes, hourly), from where it's a short walk. Note that the caretakers sometimes pop out – let them know if you're coming to drop off your bags.

Dormy Inn Shimonoseki HOTEL ¥¥

(ドーミーイン下関; 083-223-5489; www.hotespa.net/hotels/shimonoseki; 3-40 Shinmachi; s/d from ¥9445/14,395;) This modern hotel gets a vote for having a top-floor onsen, where you can look out over the straits and bathe under a *fugu*-shaped lantern. Rooms are stylish, though small, and it's in a good central location. There's a courtesy shuttle to the station in the morning and from the station in the evening (though it's not far to walk).

Kaikyō View Shimonoseki HOTEL ¥¥¥

(海峡ビューしものせき; 083-229-0117; www.kv-shimonoseki.com; 3-58 Mimosusōgawa-chō; r per person incl 2 meals from ¥10,800;) Perched up on Hino-yama, Kaikyō View has professional service and a choice of Japanese- or Western-style rooms, all with water views. Some of the Japanese-style rooms don't have private bathrooms. The hotel has a fabulous onsen with sea views – nonguests can also use it from 11am to 4pm Thursday to Tuesday (¥720, last entry 3pm).

FERRIES TO KOREA

The **Shimonoseki International Ferry Terminal** (下関港国際ターミナル; 083-235-6052; www.shimonoseki-port.com) is the boarding point for ferries to Busan, Korea. Check the ferry company websites for the latest schedules. Companies also have offices inside the terminal. The port website has some information, but it isn't regularly updated. Shimonoseki has no passenger ferry services to Shanghai (cargo services only), but Osaka does.

Kampu Ferry (関釜フェリー; 083-224-3000; www.kampuferry.co.jp) operates the Shimonoseki–Busan ferry. There are daily departures at 7.45pm (gate closes 7pm) from Shimonoseki, arriving in Busan at 8am the following morning. One-way fares start at ¥9000 (plus a ¥610 terminal fee, payable by cash only at check-in, and a ¥700 fuel surcharge) from Shimonoseki.

Shimonoseki

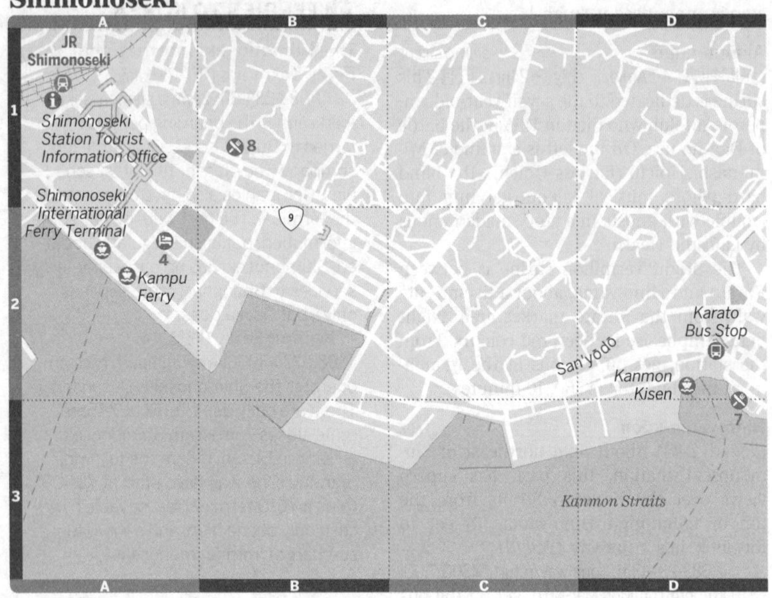

Shimonoseki

Top Sights
1 Karato Ichiba E3

Sights
2 Akama-jingū E2
3 Hino-yama-kōen H2

Sleeping
4 Dormy Inn Shimonoseki A2
5 Hinoyama Youth Hostel H2
6 Kaikyō View Shimonoseki H2

Eating
Kaiten Karato Ichiba Sushi .... (see 1)
7 Kamon Wharf D3
8 Yabure-Kabure B1

Eating

There are few noteworthy restaurants outside and around the station (apart from in the shopping centres), with plenty more options at Kamon Wharf and in the nearby Karato fish market. Note that whale meat *(kujira)* is on the menu at many seafood places in Shimonoseki. Check for くじら or クジラ if you'd rather avoid it.

Kaiten Karato Ichiba Sushi SUSHI ¥

(海転からと市場寿司; www.kaitenkaratoichibazusi.com; 2nd fl, 5-50 Karato; dishes ¥160-600; 11am-3pm & 5-9pm) This conveyor-belt sushi restaurant on the 2nd floor, right above the fish market, is a great place to get your hands on the freshest fish without needing to know what they're all called. It's closed when the market closes on some Wednesdays. Cash only.

Kamon Wharf SEAFOOD ¥

(083-228-0330; 6-1 Karato-chō; 9am-3pm & 5-10pm) Eateries and shops here specialise in local goodies. Seekers of only-in-Japan culinary experiences can look out for the *uni*-flavoured ice cream (うにソフトクリーム; sea urchin) and *fugu* burgers (ふぐバーガー).

★ Yabure-Kabure SEAFOOD ¥¥¥

(やぶれかぶれ; 083-234-3711; www.yaburekabure.jp; 2-2-5 Buzenda-chō; lunch sets ¥3240, dinner sets ¥5400-12,960; 11am-2pm & 5-9pm) There's only one thing on the menu in this boisterous spot: pick from a range of *fugu* sets, such as the dinner Ebisu course, which

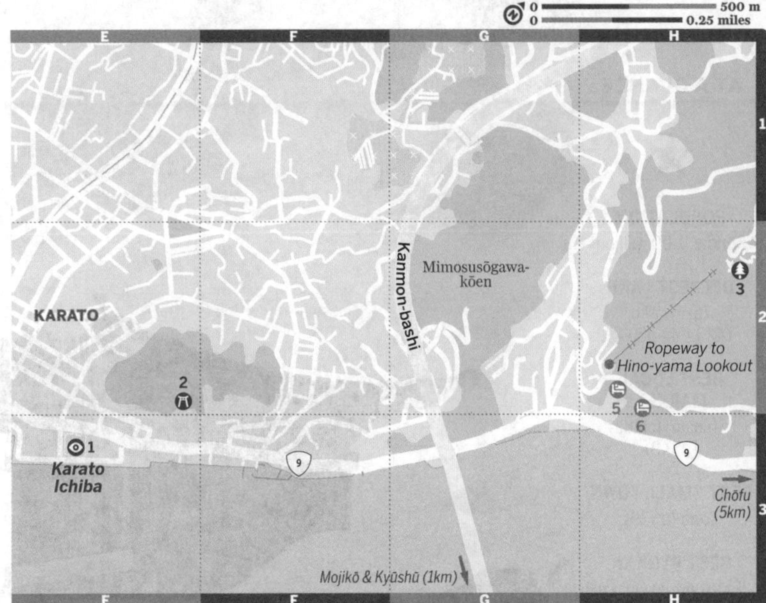

features the cute little puffer in raw, seared, fried and drowned-in-sake incarnations, or lunchtime *tetsuyaki setto* (set meal with grilled *fugu*). You can also order individual dishes. Look for the blue-and-white pufferfish outside.

Information

Shimonoseki Station Tourist Information Office (下関駅観光案内所; 083-232-8383; www.city.shimonoseki.lg.jp; 9am-6pm) Just downstairs upon exiting the ticket barriers, opposite a supermarket. English is spoken.

Shin-Shimonoseki Station Tourist Information Office (083-256-3422; 9am-6pm) A small booth as you exit the ticket gates.

Getting There & Away

BOAT

Kanmon Kisen (083-222-1488; www.kanmon-kisen.co.jp) ferries run about every 20 minutes (6am to 9.30pm) from the Karato wharf area of Shimonoseki to Mojikō in Kyūshū (adult/child ¥400/200, five minutes).

TRAIN

JR Shimonoseki is the end of the San-yō line and connects to the San-in line, which runs north to Nagato and beyond along the Sea of Japan coast.

JR Shin-Shimonoseki *shinkansen* station is two stops from JR Shimonoseki (¥200, 10 minutes).

There are a few restaurants around the spruced-up Shin-Shimonoseki Station area but little else, and it's a long walk through a tunnel connecting the local lines to the *shinkansen* lines. Trains don't always connect well so be prepared for a long and boring wait between trains.

Getting Around

Buses to **Karato** wharf and fish market area (¥220, seven minutes, frequent), and Chōfu (¥370, 22 minutes, frequent) leave from outside the station at stop 2.

If you're taking more than a couple of long bus rides in Shimonoseki, pick up a **one-day bus pass** (*ichi-nichi furī jōsha-ken;* ¥720).

It's good value – a trip to Chōfu and back alone normally costs more than ¥700 – and it saves you the hassle of paying coins each time you get off the bus.

A **one-day Strait Walking Ticket** (*kaikyō sansaku kippu;* ¥360) is also available and covers the Kanmon Tunnel and Karato wharf areas, with good savings if you take more than two rides.

Buy tickets from the booth at stop 5 of the bus terminal outside the train station, or at the Karato bus terminal.

AT A GLANCE

POPULATION
Sendai: 1.09 million

DEEPEST LAKE
Tazawa-ko (423.4m; p564)

BEST LOCAL MARKET
Shinsen Ichiba (p549)

BEST SMALL TOWN
Tōno (p539)

BEST RYOKAN
Tsuru-no-yu Onsen (p566)

WHEN TO GO

Dec–Feb Skiing galore, magnificent winter festivals and atmospheric snow-covered onsen villages.

Jun–Aug Dry summers, with a feast of food and cultural festivals, and lush green landscapes.

Sep–Oct Photographers and nature lovers alike flock here for spectacular displays of autumn foliage.

Risshaku-ji (p569), Yamadera
SEAN PAVONE/SHUTTERSTOCK ©

Northern Honshū (Tōhoku)

Stretching out above Tokyo is the fabled Tōhoku (東北; Northeast) – starring Miyagi, Yamagata, Iwate, Fukushima, Akita and Aomori Prefectures – where ice monsters and river imps inhabit the imagination (but hopefully not the onsen). Hugging the west coast is Niigata Prefecture, a skiing and hiking wonderland that also includes the rugged and remote island of Sado-ga-shima.

Three national parks, alternating between thick mountain forests, stark volcanoes and coastal marshes, offer year-round outdoor pursuits, while the spectacular caldera lakes of Tazawa-ko and Towada-ko welcome summertime pleasure-seekers. Stylish Sendai is the pick of the prefectural capitals for those seeking an uncomplicated urban fix.

INCLUDES

Northern Honshū (Tōhoku) Highlights

❶ **Dewa Sanzan** (p572) Following the footsteps of the *yamabushi* (mountain priests) through these lush, fabled peaks.

❷ **Kakunodate** (p562) Wandering the wide, feudal streets lined with cherry blossoms.

❸ **Towada-ko** (p553) Frolicking around this crater lake's verdant shores in summer.

❹ **Yamadera** (p569) Climbing the 1000 steps to this mountain temple in the footsteps of the poet Matsuo Bashō.

❺ **Nyūtō Onsen** (p566) Soaking your worries away at one of the numerous hot springs in the mountains above Tazawa-ko.

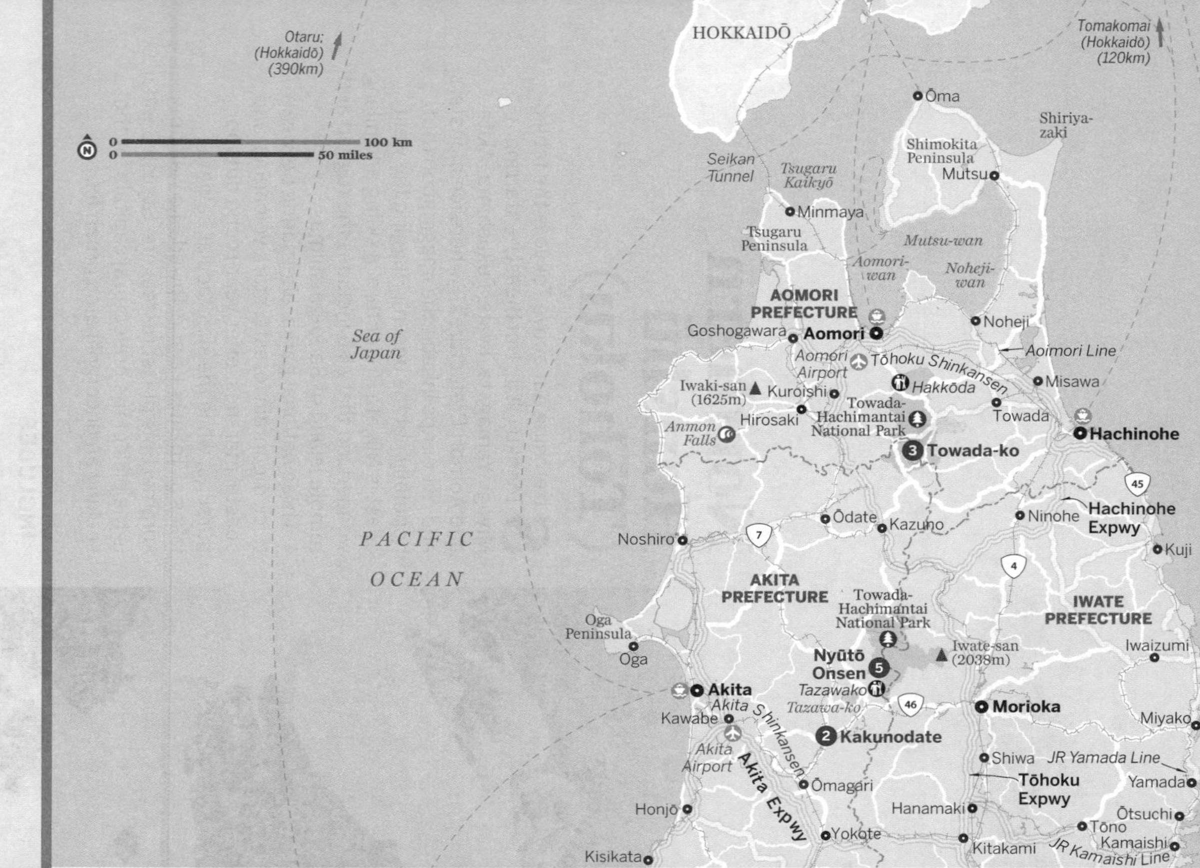

6 Zaō Onsen (p570) Dodging the 'ice monsters' at this pretty little onsen and ski town.

7 Matsushima (p530) Whiling away a weekend by this beautiful seaside town.

8 Naeba (p584) Shredding this famed mountain's slopes, or rocking out to world-class talent at Fuji Rock Festival.

9 Hiraizumi (p537) Marvelling at the golden glory of this untouched World Heritage Site.

10 Sanriku Kaigan (p542) Exploring one of Japan's coastal stretches in post-tsunami rebuild mode.

History

Tōhoku has been populated since at least the Jōmon period (13,000–400 BCE), but first entered historical records when, in the 8th century CE, the newly formed central government in Nara enlisted generals to subjugate the indigenous Emishi people. By the mid-9th century the land, then known as Michinoku (literally 'the land beyond roads'), was tenuously under imperial control.

In the 11th century the Ōshu Fujiwara clan established a short-lived settlement at Hiraizumi that was said to rival Kyoto in its opulence. However, it was the warrior and leader Date Masamune, in the 17th century, who would bring lasting notoriety to the region. Masamune transformed the fishing village of Sendai into the capital of a powerful domain. His descendants ruled until the Meiji Restoration brought an end to the feudal system, and an end to Tōhoku's influence, by restoring imperial control.

Blessed with rich alluvial plains, the coast along the Sea of Japan became an agricultural centre supplying rice to the imperial capital and, as a result, picked up more influence from Kyoto. Farming was less productive on the Pacific side, and the coastline was rocky, wind-battered and difficult to navigate, resulting in a strong culture of perseverance born of hardship and isolation.

JR EAST PASS

The JR East Pass (www.jreast.co.jp) has two options: 'Niigata & Nagano' (¥18,000) or 'Tōhoku' (¥20,000). Both offer unlimited rail travel around Tokyo and their respective regions. It's cheaper than the full JR Pass and good for five flexible days in a 14-day period. Passes can be purchased from JR East Travel Centres. Passes purchased before entering Japan are ¥1000 cheaper; exchange orders for passes should be surrendered for the actual pass at the JR ticket windows of Narita Airport station or JR Travel Service Centres at major train stations. Passes are only valid for foreign passport holders on a temporary visitor visa and do not cover travel on JR buses.

National Parks

Sprawling across Fukushima, Niigata and Yamagata Prefectures, **Bandai-Asahi National Park** (磐梯朝日国立公園), at 1870 sq km, is the third-largest protected area in Japan. The region is defined to the south by the Bandai-Azuma mountain range and to the north by the holy peaks of Dewa Sanzan.

Sanriku Fukkō National Park (三陸復興国立公園) runs along the Pacific coast, from Hachinohe in Aomori Prefecture and through Iwate Prefecture to Kesennuma in Miyagi Prefecture. It is characterised by sheer cliffs, crashing waves and, to the south, deep inlets and rocky beaches.

Further north, the 855-sq-km **Towada-Hachimantai National Park** (十和田八幡平国立公園) is a vast wilderness area of beech forests, volcanic peaks, crater lakes and alpine plateaus that straddles Akita and Aomori Prefectures.

The World Heritage–listed **Shirakami-sanchi** (白神山地) is a primeval beech forest, also on the Akita–Aomori border. One of the last of its kind in East Asia, it harbours a number of protected species, such as the Asiatic black bear and the golden eagle.

Getting There & Away

AIR

Decent domestic airports are found in Niigata, Sendai, Akita and Aomori.

BUS

Long distance bus connect many of the same hubs that the rail network does. Regional routes take you from hubs to some resort destinations that lack train access. The **Tōhoku Highway Bus Ticket** allows for unlimited bus travel in and between Aomori, Akita, Iwate, Yamagata, Miyagi and Fukushima Prefectures. Four-/seven-day tickets cost ¥10,000/13,000. See http://japanbusonline.com.

CAR & MOTORCYCLE

Exploring the more remote parts of Tōhoku is possible via public transport, but renting a car is a great way to discover the region. Be sure to confirm your rental has GPS with English capabilities (most now do). Have patience and *'go-yukkuri'* – take your time: speed limits are generally between 40km/h and 80km/h.

Tōhoku has a solid network of tolled expressways and well-maintained roads, signposted in *romaji* (romanised Japanese). Traffic is lighter than in central Honshū, although facilities can be more spread out. Between November and April roads can be closed by heavy snow and ice.

TRAIN

Though considered remote, Tōhoku has good rail access. The Tōhoku *shinkansen* (bullet train) line travels from Tokyo all the way to its northern terminus Shin-Aomori Station (on the outskirts of the city of Aomori); some trains continue to Hokkaidō. Key stops (and useful regional transit hubs) en route include, from south to north: Fukushima, Sendai, Ichinoseki (for destinations in Iwate prefecture), Morioka and Hachinohe.

At Morioka, the Akita *shinkansen* veers west for Akita, via Tazawa-ko and Kakunodate. The Yamagata shinkansen branches off at Fukushima for Yamagata. The Jōetsu *shinkansen* runs from Tokyo to Niigata, via Echigo-Yuzawa.

The JR Tōhoku main line follows roughly the same route as the Tōhoku *shinkansen*, with regular local and express trains as far as Morioka, after which private lines take over.

Along the Sea of Japan coast, JR limited express Inaho trains run between Niigata and Akita, via Tsuruoka (the jumping off point for trips to Dewa Sanzan) and Sakata.

On the Pacific coast, JR trains go as far as Kesennuma on the Sanriku Kaigan, after which a combination of buses and private train lines fill in the gaps until Hachinohe, where you can reconnect with the *shinkansen* network.

JR's Tōhoku network also includes a number of so-called 'Joyful Trains'; these cost more but come with perks like big picture windows and dining cars serving local cuisine. Some noteworthy ones include the SL Ginga (p539), Tōhoku Emotion (p543), Resort Shirakami (p562) and Genbi Shinkansen (p583).

MIYAGI PREFECTURE

When you reach Miyagi Prefecture (宮城県; Miyagi-ken) heading northbound, you have largely escaped the big-city life. Sendai, the smart capital, is the most happening city in Tōhoku, especially in summer, but it's nonetheless pretty laid-back and hassle-free. The archipelago around Matsushima has some superb ocean-facing ryokan (traditional Japanese inns), which make a great base for exploring the rejuvenated post-tsunami coastline at the southern end of Sanriku Kaigan, while Akiu Onsen and Naruko Onsen are justifiably popular for weekends in the mountains.

Sleeping

Sendai has the best range of hotel accommodation in northern Honshū. Elsewhere, Naruko Onsen has a wide range of options for rural getaways, while Matsushima has a long tradition of luxurious, sea-facing ryokan.

Sendai

☎022 / POP 1.09 MILLION

The capital of Miyagi Prefecture, Sendai (仙台) is a lively regional city and the pick of Tōhoku's urban centres. The city's wide, tree-lined streets fill up in summer for spectacular Tanabata Matsuri, one of Japan's most famous festivals. At other times the nightlife district is impressive for a relatively small city, and domestic visitors enjoy making this familiar entry into Tōhoku life en route to the wilder climes further north. Sendai is also a popular base for visits to the southern section of Sanriku Kaigan, as well as to Yamadera and Ginzan Onsen in nearby Yamagata Prefecture.

The samurai benefactor Date Masamune is synonymous with Sendai, and his lasting legacy is a ruined castle set in pleasant gardens.

History

Sendai, 'city of a thousand generations', was established by Date Masamune in 1600. A ruthless, ambitious *daimyō* (domain lord), Masamune turned Sendai into a feudal capital that controlled trade routes, salt supplies and grain milling throughout much of Tōhoku. The Date family ruled the Sendai-han until the Meiji Restoration brought an end to the feudal era in 1868.

Sights

Most sights can be reached by the Loople (p530) tourist bus.

★Zuihō-den Mausoleum HISTORIC BUILDING
(瑞鳳殿; ☎022-262-6250; www.zuihoden.com; 23-2 Otamaya-shita, Aoba-ku; adult/child ¥550/200; 9am-4.30pm Feb-Nov, to 4pm Dec-Jan; Loople stop 4) The mausoleum of Date Masamune sits majestically atop the summit of a tree-covered hill by the Hirose-gawa. Built in 1637 but destroyed by Allied bombing during WWII, the current building, completed in 1979, is an exact replica of the original, faithful to the ornate and sumptuous Momoyama style.

Sendai Castle Ruins CASTLE
(仙台城跡; ☎022-261-1111; 1 Kawauchi, Aoba-ku; Loople stop 6, regular bus stop Sendai Jō Ato Minami) Built on Aoba-yama in 1602 by Date Masamune and destroyed during Allied bombing, Sendai-jō still looms large over the city. Giant moss-covered walls, as imposing as they are impressive, remain intact and the grounds offer sweeping views over the city.

Miyagi Prefecture

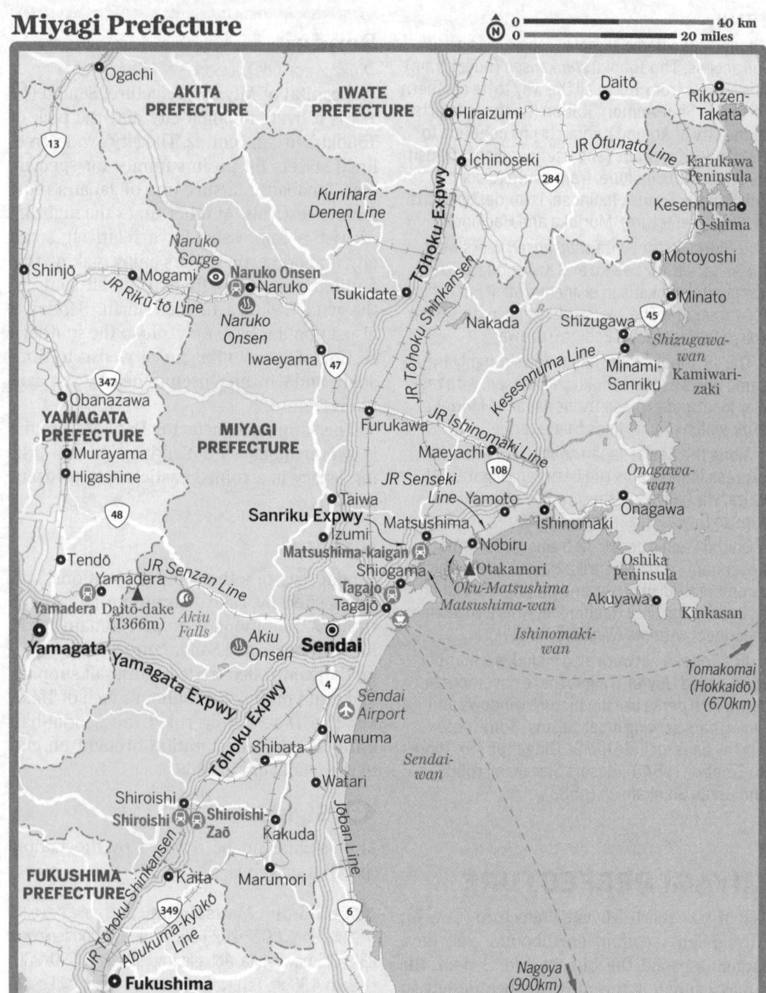

Sendai City Museum MUSEUM
(仙台市博物館; ☎022-225-3074; 26 Kawauchi, Aoba-ku; adult/child ¥460/230; ⏲9am-4.45pm Tue-Sun; 🚌Loople stop 5) The city museum offers a comprehensive account of samurai Masamune's epic life, as well as displaying more than 13,000 artefacts on loan from the Date family, with plenty of explanations in English.

Sendai Mediatheque LIBRARY
(仙台メディアテーク; ☎022-713-3171; www.smt.city.sendai.jp; 2-1 Kasuga-machi, Aoba-ku; ⏲9am-10pm, gallery hours vary) FREE Housed in an award-winning structure designed by Japanese architect Itō Toyō, this cultural hub includes a library, art galleries and event spaces. Check the website to see if anything is going on when you're in town.

Festivals & Events

Sendai Tanabata Matsuri CULTURAL
(仙台七夕まつり, Star Festival; www.sendaitanabata.com; ⏲6-8 Aug) The Tanabata Matsuri celebrates a Chinese legend about two stars: Vega, a king's daughter, who fell in love with Altair, a common herder. The king disapproved, so he formed the Milky Way between them. Once a year magpies are supposed to spread their wings across the universe so the

lovers can meet – traditionally on 7 July (on the old lunar calendar).

Sendai's Tanabata sees the city's streets draped with displays of brightly coloured streamers. Festivities include parades and live performances, culminating in a mammoth fireworks display on the last night of the festival.

Jōzenji Street Jazz Festival MUSIC
(定禅寺ストリートジャズフェスティバル; www.j-streetjazz.com; 2nd weekend Sep) Hundreds of buskers from across Japan perform in Sendai's streets and arcades. Book your accommodation way, way in advance.

Sleeping

★ Minshuku Keyaki MINSHUKU ¥
(民宿欅; 022-796-4946; www.keyaki2014.com; 13-4 Tachi-machi, Aoba-ku; dm/d ¥2800/5600;) Converted from an old restaurant into the best guesthouse in Sendai, Keyaki has sleek wooden floors, stylish, spotless dorms and a first-class bar. In the heart of Kokubunchō, this represents real value and is perfect for solo travellers or those on a budget.

Dōchū-an Youth Hostel HOSTEL ¥
(道中庵ユースホステル; 022-247-0511; www.jyh.or.jp; 31 Kita-yashiki, Ōnoda, Taihaku-ku; dm/s ¥3888/4644, breakfast ¥600;) You'll need some resolve to find this former farmhouse, but it's worth it. Go to Taishidō Station (¥180, eight minutes from Sendai Station) on the JR Tōhoku line, from where it's a six-minute walk (get a map at the station). Trees surround the humble property, which has been cleverly designed to accommodate independent travellers on a budget. There's a fantastic cedar bath.

Hotel Foliage HOTEL ¥¥
(ホテルフォーリッジ仙台; 022-221-3939; www.libraryhotel.jp; 4-7-1 Chūō; per person incl breakfast from ¥8000;) A step up from a generic business hotel, Foliage is handily located a few minutes' walk from the train station on a busy little street. The lobby and common areas show some design flair, while rooms are basic but comfortable. An excellent breakfast buffet is served in the sunny ground-floor dining area.

Bansuitei Ikoiso RYOKAN ¥¥
(晩翠亭いこい荘; 022-222-7885; www.ikoisouryokan.co.jp; 1-8-31 Kimachi-dori, Aoba; r per person incl breakfast from ¥8800) The best ryokan in Sendai is a humble, good-value establishment that will appeal to those seeking a more character-filled abode than the typical business hotel. The old creaky floorboards, fragrant oil burners and well-kept shared bathrooms make it a memorable Japanese experience.

★ Westin HOTEL ¥¥¥
(ウェスティンホテル仙台; 022-722-1234; www.westin.com; 1-9-1 Ichiban-chō, Aoba-ku; r from ¥17,700;) Set atop a chic shopping complex on the main thoroughfare running through Sendai, the Westin is the best five-star chain hotel in the whole far north. The cocktail bar affords magnificent views, while the rooms themselves are decadently comfortable and elegantly decorated.

WORTH A TRIP

AKIU ONSEN

Wonderful Akiu Onsen (秋保温泉) was the Date clan's favourite therapeutic retreat, with a natural saltwater spring that's said to be a curative for back pain and arthritis. There are dozens of inns here that offer their baths to day trippers.

Between dips stretch your legs along the rim of **Rairai Gorge** (磊々峡; Rairai-kyō), a 20m-deep gorge that runs through the village. Pick up maps and a list of bathhouses at the **Tourist Information Center** (秋保温泉観光案内所; 022-398-2323; www.akiuonsenkumiai.com; Akiu Sato Center; 9am-6pm;), where you can also borrow free bicycles (deposit ¥1000). In the hills west of town is **Akiu Falls** (秋保大滝; Akiu Ōtaki), a 6m-wide, 55m-high waterfall designated as one of Japan's three most famous waterfalls. View the falls from a scenic outlook, or hike down 20 minutes to the bottom.

Buses leave hourly for Akiu Onsen from stop 8 at Sendai Station's west bus pool (¥840, 50 minutes). On weekends there are two buses daily that continue to Akiu Falls (¥1100, 1½ hours). Otherwise catch one of the few buses for the falls from the Akiu Sato Center (¥670, 20 minutes), or borrow a bicycle (it's a 30km round trip).

Central Sendai

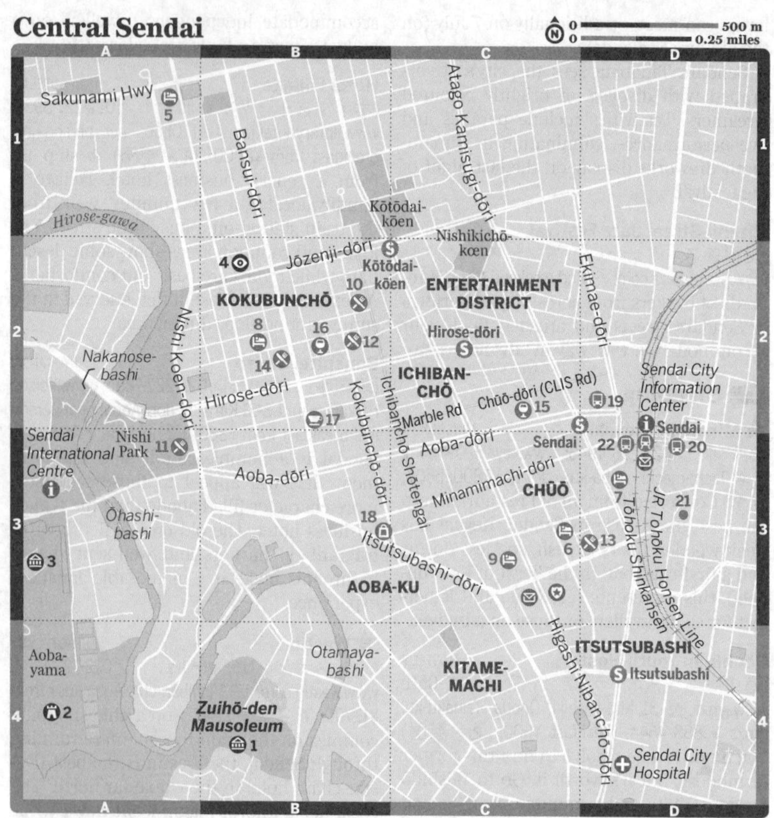

Central Sendai

Top Sights
1 Zuihō-den Mausoleum B4

Sights
2 Sendai Castle Ruins A4
3 Sendai City Museum A3
4 Sendai Mediatheque B2

Sleeping
5 Bansuitei Ikoiso A1
6 Hotel Foliage C3
7 Hotel Metropolitan Sendai D3
8 Minshuku Keyaki B2
9 Westin C3

Eating
10 Aji Tasuke B2
11 Gengo Chaya A3
12 Jiraiya B2
13 Ohisamaya D3
14 Santarō B2

Drinking & Nightlife
15 Craftsman Sendai C2
16 Peter Pan B2
17 Sendai Coffee Stand B2

Shopping
18 Kogensya B3

Transport
19 Bus Stop 34 .... D2
20 JR Tōhoku Bus Center D3
Loople .... (see 22)
21 Toyota Rent a Car D3
22 West Bus Terminal D3

Hotel Metropolitan Sendai HOTEL ¥¥¥
(ホテルメトロポリタン仙台; ☎022-268-2525; www.sendaimetropolitan.jp; 1-1-1 Chūō, Aoba-ku; s/d from ¥11,100/22,000;) Accessible from the pedestrian walkway attached to Sendai Station, the Metropolitan is the clear winner among the station business hotels. At the top end, Japanese-style

suites have serene garden views, but even basic rooms have plush furnishings and are recently renovated.

Eating

Gengo Chaya CAFE ¥

(源吾茶屋; ☎022-222-2830; 1-1 Sakuragaoka-kōen, Aoba-ku; snacks from ¥350; ⊙11am-6pm; ✎) In business for 130 years, this charming teahouse is known for its *zunda-mochi,* pounded rice cakes topped with a jam made from fresh soybeans – a Sendai speciality. The teahouse is on the eastern edge of Nishi Park, with white *noren* (sunshade) curtains out front.

★**Ohisamaya** VEGETARIAN ¥¥

(おひさまや; ☎022-224-8540; http://ohisama-nikoniko.sunnyday.jp; 4-8-17 Chūō, Aoba-ku; meals from ¥1200; ⊙11.30am-6.30pm Mon-Wed, to 8pm Thu & Fri, to 6pm Sat & Sun; ✎) Vegetable curries, macrobiotic tofu and fresh, colourful salads are the highlights of this delightful, minimalist cafe, which rotates its menu regularly from a library of cookbooks on display. The occasional fish product may sneak into view.

Aji Tasuke JAPANESE ¥¥

(味太助; ☎022-225-4641; www.aji-tasuke.co.jp; 4-4-13 Ichiban-chō, Aoba-ku; mains from ¥1200, lunch/dinner sets ¥1700/1800; ⊙11.30am-10pm Wed-Mon) In a city of fans of charcoal-grilled cow's tongue, this little *gyūtan* has been steadily among the top few purveyors for some time now. Perch at the counter to watch – and smell – the grilling in action. It's next to a small *torii* (shrine gate) and usually has a queue.

Jiraiya IZAKAYA ¥¥

(地雷也; ☎022-261-2164; www.jiraiya.com; basement fl, 2-1-15 Kokubunchō, Aoba-ku; dishes from ¥1100; ⊙5.30-11.30pm Mon-Sat, to 11pm Sun) Named after a Song-era fantasy epic, this classic *izakaya* specialises in charcoal-grilled *kinki* (rockfish; also called *kichiji*), which is nibbled by sake-sipping customers propped at the bar. Jiraiya's entrance is on a side street, marked by a giant red lantern.

Santarō JAPANESE ¥¥¥

(三太郎; ☎022-224-1671; www.santarou.jp; 1-20 Tachi-machi, Aoba-ku; dishes from ¥1200, sets from ¥1700, kaiseki courses per person ¥8000-16,000; ⊙11.30am-2pm & 5-10pm) Spectacular evening *kaiseki* (Japanese haute cuisine) courses and crunch-for-lunch tempura are served in this elegant traditional building in the heart of Kokubunchō. Best for dining with two or more.

Drinking & Nightlife

Sendai's Kokubunchō area is Tōhoku's largest entertainment district. It's noisy, slightly chaotic and bright, with everything from hole-in-the-wall bars and British-style pubs to raging dancing clubs and seedy strip shows. Note that there are a fair number of hostess and host clubs here, as well as seemingly ordinary bars, that levy steep cover charges.

★**Peter Pan** BAR

(ロックカフェ ピーターパン; ☎022-264-1742; 2-6-1 Chōme, Kokubunchō; ⊙5-10pm Sun-Thu, to midnight Fri & Sat) A music-loving father-and-son team runs this lounge-room-vibe 'rock' bar. Dad provides the soundtrack with his extensive, alternative-rock vinyl collection, while his son busies himself with the clientele. Coffee, booze, cake and conversation.

Sendai Coffee Stand COFFEE

(☎022-797-1015; www.coffee-stand.com; 1-3-12 Kokubunchō; ⊙10am-7pm) The best coffee in Sendai is brewed at this super-hip, one-room cafe at the edge of the entertainment district. A small rotating menu of baked goods and sandwiches keeps the caffeine shakes at bay.

Craftsman Sendai CRAFT BEER

(クラフトマン; ☎050-7576-4480; http://craftsman-sendai.com; 1F, 2-2-38 Chūō, Aoba-ku; ⊙5pm-1am Mon-Fri, from 11.30am Sat & Sun) When there's a global trend, like craft beer, the Japanese are never far behind. This small Craftsman outlet (a few are popping up around Japan) combines casual Italian dining (tapas plate ¥1450) with Japan's independent beer scene. Patrons prop at the bar or on leather seats around tiled tables and talk loudly over indie tunes and the regular chinking of glasses.

Shopping

Kogensya ARTS & CRAFTS

(光原社 仙台店; ☎022-223-6674; www.kogensya.sakura.ne.jp; 1-4-10 Ichiban-chō; ⊙10am-6.30pm Apr-Dec, to 6pm Jan-Mar) Buy handmade wares from all over Tōhoku at this elegant, perfectly curated shop. It's a lovely spot to pick up high-quality souvenirs for gifts (which will be beautifully wrapped while you wait). It's right on the corner; look for the sign with an image of a covered bowl.

SENDAI MARUGOTO PASS

The **Sendai Marugoto Pass** (仙台まるごとパス; adult/child ¥2670/1330) covers unlimited travel for two days on the Loople tourist bus, Sendai subway and area trains and buses going as far as Matsushima-kaigan, Akiu Onsen and Yamadera (in Yamagata Prefecture). Pick one up at JR Sendai Station, or from the ticket machines at Sendai airport.

Information

MEDICAL SERVICES

Sendai City Hospital (仙台市立病院; 022-266-7111, 24hr emergency hotline 022-216-9960; http://hospital.city.sendai.jp; 3-1 Shimizu-kōji, Wakabayashi-ku; outpatient service 8.30-11.30am Mon-Fri)

TOURIST INFORMATION

Sendai City Information Center (仙台市観光案内所; 022-222-4069; www.sentabi.jp; 2nd fl, JR Sendai Station; 8.30am-7pm) Helpful English-speaking staff dispense maps and brochures for all of Tōhoku.

Sendai International Centre (仙台国際センター; 022-265-2471; www.aobayama.jp; Aoba-yama, Aoba-ku; 9am-8pm) English-speaking staff, plus an international newspaper library and bulletin board.

Getting There & Away

AIR

From Sendai airport, 18km south of the city centre, flights head to Tokyo, Osaka, Nagoya, Hiroshima, Sapporo and many other destinations.

The Sendai Kūkō Access line leaves for the airport from Sendai Station roughly every 20 minutes (¥650, 25 minutes).

BOAT

From the port of Sendai-kō, **Taiheyo Ferry** (022-263-9877; www.taiheiyo-ferry.co.jp) has one daily ferry to Tomakomai on Hokkaidō (from ¥7200, 15 hours), and three to four ferries a week to Nagoya in Aichi Prefecture (from ¥6700, 22 hours).

Buses leave from **stop 34** (Sakurano Department Store) at Sendai Station for Sendai-kō (¥540, 40 minutes, four daily), but only until 6pm.

BUS

Highway buses depart from the **West Bus Terminal** outside the east exit of the train station, and connect Sendai to major cities throughout Honshū. Purchase tickets at the **JR Tōhoku Bus Center** (仙台駅東口バス案内所, Highway Bus Ticket Office; 022-256-6646; www.jrbustohoku.co.jp; Sendai JR Station, east exit; 7am-7pm), by the station's east exit.

CAR & MOTORCYCLE

Toyota Rent a Car (022-293-0100; https://rent.toyota.co.jp; 1-5-3 Tsutsujigaoka, Miyagino-ku; 8am-8pm) has several outlets within a few blocks of the train station, if you want to visit neighbouring destinations by car.

TRAIN

The JR Tōhoku *shinkansen* runs at least hourly between Tokyo and Sendai (from ¥10,890, 1½ to two hours), and between Sendai and Morioka (from ¥5940, 40 minutes to 1¼ hours).

There are several daily *kaisoku* (rapid trains) on the JR Senzan line between Sendai and Yamagata (¥1140, 1¼ hours), via Yamadera (¥840, one hour). Local trains on the JR Senseki line connect Sendai and Matsushima-kaigan (¥410, 40 minutes); make sure to get one going all the way to Takagi-machi, or you'll have to transfer at Higashi-Shiogama.

Getting Around

The **Loople** (www.loople-sendai.jp; single trip/day pass ¥260/620) tourist trolley leaves from the west bus pool's stop 15-3 every 20 minutes from 9am to 4pm, making a useful loop around the city in a clockwise direction.

Sendai's single subway line runs from Izumi-chūō in the north to Tomizawa in the south, but doesn't cover any tourist attractions; single tickets cost ¥200 to ¥350.

Matsushima

022 / POP 14,420

Matsushima (松島) is heavily romanticised by Japanese travellers due to its status as one of Japan's Three Great Sights (Nihon Sankei). It was also immortalised by the poet Matsuo Bashō, who revered its glorious bay's 260-odd pine-covered islands, battered by wind and sea to form a kind of Zen rock garden in the ocean. When the sun sets and a storm rolls in, the effect on the islands is mesmerising. The main village itself has some fine ancient temples, impressive ryokan, seafood shacks and a charming seaside feel. Try to avoid the high-summer weekend crowds.

Sights

Matsushima-kaigan, where the sights are, is essentially a small village, easily navigated on foot from the train station.

Zuigan-ji BUDDHIST TEMPLE
(瑞巌寺; www.zuiganji.or.jp; 91 Azachonai; adult/child ¥700/400; 8am-5pm Apr-Sep, closes earlier Oct-Mar) Tōhoku's finest Zen temple, Zuigan-ji was established in 828. The present buildings were constructed in 1606 by Date Masamune to serve as a family temple and the **Hondo** (main hall) has been beautifully restored to its former glory. Visitors pass by a series of dark-wood chambers illuminated by golden doors painted with exquisite images of flora and fauna. Nearby the excellent **Seiryūden** (temple museum) has a number of well-preserved relics from the Date family, including national treasures.

The temple is 500m north of Matsushima-kaigan Station.

Fuku-ura-jima ISLAND
(福浦島; ¥200; 8am-5pm Mar-Oct, to 4.30pm Nov-Feb) You can't miss the 252m-long red wooden bridge connecting Fuku-ura-jima to the mainland. The shady trails here, which wind around the island through native pines and a botanic garden, make for a pleasant hour-long stroll.

Activities

Matsushima-wan CRUISE
(松島湾; www.matsushima.or.jp; adult/child ¥1500/750; 9am-3pm) To get a sense of the bay's scale and appreciate its dense cluster of pine-topped islands, which sit like bonsai floating in a giant's backyard pond, cruise boats depart hourly from the central ferry pier, completing a 50-minute loop. Between April and October you can opt for a longer course (¥2700, 1¾ hours) that goes all the way to Oku-Matsushima.

Sleeping

Uchi Matsushima GUESTHOUSE ¥¥
(ゲストハウスUchi; 022-765-1397; www.uchi-matsushima.com; 121-3 Machiuchi; s/d ¥3800/7200;) A super-central location and a friendly communal atmosphere make this newly built guesthouse the pick of the bunch for budget travellers in Matsushima. Rooms are small but clean, and the communal bar area is great for socialising after dark.

Minshuku Kami-no-Ie MINSHUKU ¥¥
(奥松島 民宿 かみの家; 0225-88-4141; www.okumatsushima.wixsite.com/kaminoie; 16-1 Mura, Miyato, Higashi-Matsushima; per person incl 2 meals ¥8000; P@) This simple inn has become a symbol of post-tsunami sustainable tourism in the small community of Higashi-Matsushima, which bore the full force of the 2011 disaster. The tatami-mat rooms are bright and airy, while the seafood dinners are salty fresh. The owners also offer fishing tours in Matsushima Bay.

★**Komatsukan Kofu-tei** RYOKAN ¥¥¥
(松島小松館 好風亭; 0223-54-5065; www.new-komatsu.co.jp; 35-2 Matsushima; per person incl 2 meals from ¥16,000; P) This classy

DELICACIES OF THE DEEP NORTH

Eating in Tōhoku is all about simple seasonal pleasures – the bounty of the land and sea. Regional delicacies you might encounter include the following:

gyūtan (牛タン) Cow's tongue, grilled over charcoal (Sendai)

jaja-men (じゃじゃ麺) Flat wheat noodles topped with sliced cucumber, miso paste and ground meat (Morioka)

kamaboko (かまぼこ) Steamed fish paste (Sendai)

kiritanpo-nabe (きりたんぽ鍋) Kneaded rice wrapped around bamboo spits, barbecued over a charcoal fire then served in a chicken and soy-sauce hotpot with vegetables (Akita)

inaniwa udon (稲庭うどん) Thinner-than-usual wheat noodles (Akita)

wanko-soba (わんこそば) All-you-can-eat noodles (Morioka)

Aomori Prefecture's seafood is king:

hotate (ホタテ) Scallops

maguro (まぐろ) Tuna; the village of Ōma, at the tip of Honshū, is said to have the finest in the country

uni (うに) Sea urchin

Yonezawa-gyū (米沢牛) Yonezawa's premium-grade beef

seaside ryokan has inimitable, understated Japanese style. Elegant rooms are furnished sparingly with high-quality art and homewares. The outdoor onsen is pleasant, though small, but the bookable private outdoor bath with bay views is a treat. The *kaiseki* meals are as good as anything you'll find on your travels.

Eating

Matsushima has a few fine casual restaurants clustered near the train station and ferry terminal; most travellers dine at their acommodation.

Shōkadō SWEETS ¥
(松華堂菓子店; 022-355-5002; www.facebook.com/shokadomatsushima; 109-Chonai; set from ¥680; 10am-5pm) On the 2nd floor, with huge windows overlooking the bay, this light-filled, minimalist cafe specialises in *castella,* a moist, sponge-like cake originally brought to Japan by Portuguese merchants in the 16th century. Other options include *shōkadō* pudding (a caramel panna cotta–like creation) or milky soft-serve ice cream, all served alongside freshly brewed coffee or green tea.

Aizawa Bakery BAKERY ¥
(ぱんや　あいざわ; 022-354-0233; 156 Chōnai; pastries from ¥180; 8.30am-5pm Tue-Sun) Tucked away on a residential street a few blocks back from the main thoroughfare, this tiny, one-room bakery does a seriously good sourdough, as well as delectable croissants and pastries worthy of a Parisian boulangerie. Pick up a few choice items and head for the waterfront.

Santori Chaya JAPANESE ¥
(さんとり茶屋; 022-353-2622; www.santorichaya.com; 24-4-1 Senzui; oysters from ¥650; 11.30am-3pm & 5-9pm Thu-Tue) Perennial local favourites from land and sea such as *kaisen-don* (mixed sashimi on rice) and *gyūtan* (chargrilled cow's tongue) feature here, along with seasonal specialities such as Matsushima's famous oysters. Seating is on floor cushions on the 2nd level; try to get a window table. It's in a beige building with an indigo banner and has a picture menu.

Information

Tourist Information Center (松島観光協会; 022-354-2618; www.matsushima-kanko.com; 98-1 Azachonai; 9.30am-4.30pm Mon-Fri, 8.30am-5pm Sat & Sun;) Inside the sightseeing boat terminal, it has English brochures and accommodation bookings.

Getting There & Away

Frequent trains on the JR Senseki line connect Sendai and Matsushima-kaigan (¥410, 40 minutes).

Sights are at Matsushima-kaigan Station, not Matsushima Station – an easy mistake. To confuse further, Matsushima is on the Jōban line, while Matsushima-kaigan is on the Senseki line.

Ishinomaki

0225 / POP 147,200

Ishinomaki (石巻) is the largest city on Sanriku Kaigan, a beautiful stretch of coast that was decimated by the 2011 tsunami. Many travellers move on quickly, but this easily accessible place is a shining example of creative urban renewal in post-disaster Japan – loads of hip new businesses are opening up, inviting visitors to linger longer.

Sights

Ishinomori Mangattan Museum MUSEUM
(石ノ森萬画館; 0225-96-5055; www.mangattan.jp/manga; 2-7 Nakase; adult/child ¥800/200; 9am-6pm;) This popular manga museum's other-worldly spaceship structure survived the tsunami largely intact, while the collection has since been restored and rejuvenated. The work of influential *manga-ka* (cartoonist) and local hero Shōtarō Ishinomori, most famous for creating the *Cyborg 009* and *Kamen Rider* series, is the star attraction. It's a 20-minute walk from the train station.

Sleeping & Eating

There are only a handful of decent places to stay here, mostly business hotels near the station, but a few guesthouses are starting to emerge. Ask at the Tourist Information Center for the latest listings.

Long Beach House GUESTHOUSE ¥
(ロングビーチハウス; 0225-98-4714; www.longbeachhouse.wixsite.com/lbh314; 47-1 Watanoha Hamasone-no-ichi; dm/s/d from ¥2200/5000/7200;) Part of the new generation of socially conscious creatives setting up shop in Ishinomaki, the folk at Long Beach House have built a minimalist guesthouse with a terrific boho vibe. On-site is a Japanese and modern Spanish restaurant serving stiff cocktails, which may seduce you to spend the night.

THE GREAT EAST JAPAN EARTHQUAKE

At 2.46pm (JST) on 11 March 2011, a magnitude 9.0 earthquake struck off the eastern coast of Tōhoku.

During the Great East Japan Earthquake (東日本大震災; Higashi-nihon Dai-shinsai) – the most powerful to hit Japan since record keeping began in the early 20th century, and among the five strongest recorded worldwide – the ground shook for a mind-boggling six minutes. It is a testament to Japan's earthquake preparedness that many people received a warning on their mobile phones one minute prior to the event, with the same warning automatically stopping high-speed train services: both measures saved countless lives. Due to stringent building codes, few structures collapsed from the shaking.

It was, however, the series of tsunami that followed just 15 minutes later, with wave heights of a staggering 38m in some areas, that caused the devastation. Coastal communities along a 500km stretch of Sanriku Kaigan (p542) were levelled completely and more than 15,000 lives were lost.

Travelling in the Region

More than seven years on, the reconstruction efforts in this beautiful coastal region have been a testament to the resilience and community spirit of the Japanese people. Domestic tourists continue to support the rebuilding by spending time and money here – tourism is seen as one of the best ways to revitalise the local economies.

Ever-popular Matsushima, partly protected by one of Japan's most beautiful bays, escaped relatively unscathed, but other villages were far less fortunate. Oku-Matsushima, Ishinomaki, Minami-Sanriku, Kamaishi, Ofunato and Rikuzen-takata were near annihilated, but new guesthouses, onsen hotels, restaurants and community tourism initiatives have emerged and are helping survivors to move on with purpose.

It's a powerful experience to rent a car and drive along the coast here, visiting the towns that were most affected by the disaster – many travellers count it as a highlight of their visit to Japan.

Rail services are continuing to improve, with the entire Sanriku Railway from Ōfunato to Kuji reopened in 2019.

Common-ship Hashidori FOOD HALL ¥
(☎080-6006-9054; www.facebook.com/commonship.hashidori; 8-9 Chūō 2-chōme; burgers from ¥800; ⏲11am-10pm) Constructed haphazardly from caravans, pine beams, fake turf and fairy lights, this pop-up community dining and gathering space is emblematic of Ishinomaki's reconstruction. Burgers and other street-food-style bites are available all day long, while soulful tunes play to audiences of hip young things into the evening.

Information

Tourist Information Center (石巻観光案内所; ☎0225-93-6448; www.i-kanko.com; ⏲9am-5.30pm) Inside the JR train station.

Getting There & Away

A rapid service on the JR Senseki line connects Sendai and Ishinomaki (¥840, one hour). Direct highway buses for Ishinomaki depart roughly twice an hour from stop 33 in front of Sendai Station (¥800, 1½ hours).

Naruko Onsen

☎0229 / POP 8000

A lovely day trip or overnighter from Sendai, Naruko Onsen (鳴子温泉) is a spread-out rural town known for the magnificent Naruko Gorge. Most visitors take a leisurely hike through the 100m-deep gorge followed by a soak in one or more of the region's nine distinct springs – the waters of each have different compositions of minerals and thus different healing qualities.

Take advantage of the Yumeguri ticket (¥1300), which you can buy at the Tourist Information Center, to visit the baths at several different inns. The town is also known for its *kokeshi* (traditional wooden dolls).

Activities

★Taki-no-yu ONSEN
(滝の湯; 84 Yumoto Narukonsen; ¥150; ⏲7.30am-10pm) This fabulously atmospheric wooden bathhouse has hardly changed in 150 years and is a sheer delight. Water gushes in from

hinoki (cypress) channels, carrying with it various elements and minerals, including sulphur, sodium bicarbonate and sodium chloride. This onsen is particularly famous for its therapeutic relief of high blood pressure and hardened arteries.

Naruko Gorge HIKING

(鳴子峡, Naruko-kyō) Northwest of Naruko town, this 100m-deep gorge is particularly spectacular in autumn when the leaves change colour. Only some sections of the trail were open at the time of writing, due to landslides – check with the tourist office for maps and up-to-date trail information.

Another trail can be reached from Nakayama-daira Onsen Station, a short bus trip from Naruko Onsen Station (¥180, five minutes) or an easy, well-signed walk. This path also intersects with a 10km stretch of the old foot highway, walked by the haiku poet Matsuo Bashō, which is now a hiking trail.

Sleeping

You can eat a decent meal at one of the restaurants near the train station, or at the cafe at the Tourist Information Center. If you're staying overnight, fine meals will be included at your accommodation.

Ryokan Onuma RYOKAN ¥¥

(旅館大沼; ☎0229-83-3052; www.ohnuma.co.jp; 34 Narukonsen Akayu, Osaki; per person incl 2 meals from ¥16,000; P ❄ 📶) Alight the train at Naruko Goten-yu and walk 500m west until you reach this peaceful ryokan with an indefatigable staff who will soak, feed and replenish you in style. Each room has access to its own private onsen bath, plus there is an outdoor onsen on the forest floor. Rooms are large and spotless.

Yusaya Ryokan RYOKAN ¥¥

(ゆさや旅館; ☎0229-83-2565; www.yusaya.co.jp; 84 Yumoto; r per person incl 2 meals from ¥12,800; P @ 📶) Among the many charms of this country inn is its impressive *rotemburo* (outdoor bath) in an isolated building surrounded by a dense thicket of trees. The main building, dating to 1936, has tatami-lined sleeping quarters separated from Western-style sitting areas by *shoji* (sliding rice-paper screen doors). Meals are elegant banquets of river fish and mountain vegetables.

DON'T MISS

BEST ONSEN

- Nyūtō Onsen (p566)
- Aoni Onsen (p556)
- Ginzan Onsen (p571)
- Zaō Onsen (p569)
- Akiu Onsen (p527)

Information

Tourist Information Center (鳴子観光・旅館案内センター; ☎0229-83-3441; www.naruko.gr.jp; ⏲8.30am-6pm) Located just outside the train station. Offers walking maps of the town and of nearby Naruko Gorge.

Getting There & Away

There is an hourly service on the JR Tōhoku *shinkansen* between Sendai and Furukawa (¥1620, 15 minutes). The JR Tōhoku line also runs regular services from Sendai to Furukawa via Kogota (¥970, one hour). Hourly trains run on the JR Rikū-tō line between Furukawa and Naruko Onsen (¥670, 45 minutes).

IWATE PREFECTURE

The glorious temples of Hiraizumi are among only a few physical reminders of the turbulent feudal past of Iwate Prefecture (岩手県; Iwate-ken), but there are nonetheless plenty of opportunities for exploration in Japan's second-largest prefecture. Sleepy valleys, a rugged coastline and high, lush mountains attract discerning hikers and those looking for a tree-change, but it's perhaps the Tōno Valley, where countless folk tales are still born and told, where travellers will glimpse that all-too-rare Lost Japan.

The coastal communities here have regrouped admirably since the Great East Japan Earthquake and visitors with their own wheels, or the patience for the slow trains, will be rewarded with glorious sunrises and welcoming hosts.

Sleeping

Morioka and Ichinoseki (near Hiraizumi) have the usual cluster of business hotels, but most travellers opt for the traditional ryokan and guesthouses of the gorgeous Tōno Valley.

Iwate Prefecture

Morioka

☎019 / POP 297,631

Three rivers flow through Morioka (盛岡), an attractive park commands attention near the centre, and Iwate-san stands proudly in the background. The prefectural capital is a convenient transport hub and has a range of smart noodle restaurants. Morioka is also known for its cast-iron artisan work.

Sights

Iwate-kōen PARK

(岩手公園) If you head east on foot from the train station along Kaiun-bashi for about 2km, you'll eventually come to this landscaped park, where Morioka-jō once stood. All that remains of the castle, completed in 1633 and destroyed in 1874, are its moss-covered stone foundation walls. Still, you can get a sense of its scale.

Sleeping

Kumagai Ryokan RYOKAN ¥¥

(熊ヶ井旅館; ☎019-651-3020; www.kumagairyokan.com; 3-2-5 Ōsawakawara; s/d ¥5000/9000;) Travellers usually just pass through Morioka, but you'll find reason to linger in this spacious ryokan surrounded by a pleasant garden filled with various folk crafts. There's a lovely *iwa-buro* (rock bath) for evening soaks, and meals are a cut above the norm. The inn is located about 800m east of the train station (behind the large church).

Hotel Ace Morioka BUSINESS HOTEL ¥¥

(ホテルエース盛岡; ☎034-510-8651; www.hotel-ace.co.jp; 2-11-35 Chūō-dōri; s/d from ¥6000/8500;) This hotel was renovated in 2017 and is pretty stylish, despite having some of the pokiest rooms known to travel writers! The lobby and bathrooms are very spiffy, while management bows to your every need (even more than usual in Japan). The location is good, a 10-minute walk from the train station.

Morioka

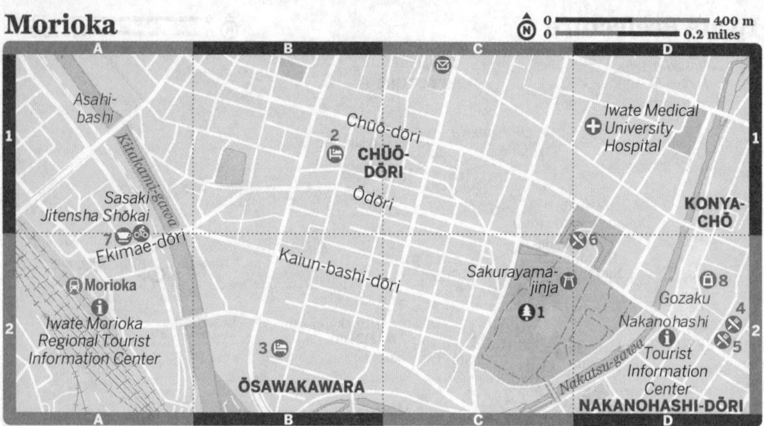

Morioka

Sights
1 Iwate-kōen C2

Sleeping
2 Hotel Ace Morioka B1
3 Kumagai Ryokan B2

Eating
4 Azumaya Honten D2
5 Karē Kōbō Chalten D2
6 Pairon Honten D2

Drinking & Nightlife
7 Cappuccino Shiki A2

Shopping
8 Kamasada Honten D2

✕ Eating

Karē Kōbō Chalten JAPANESE CURRY ¥

(カレー工房チャルテン; ☎019-651-1223; 1-8-1 Nakanohashi-dōri; curries from ¥850; ⌚11.30am-3pm & 6-8pm Mon-Sat) Serving the best curry we tried in the whole of northern Japan, this small, charming restaurant makes nothing except creamy plates of curry. The wonderful vegetarian option uses eight different vegetables diced to a near pulp. Choose your heat from one to five (three was pretty intense!). The *masala chai* (¥400) goes well.

Pairon Honten UDON ¥

(白龍本店; ☎019-624-2247; 5-15 Uchi-maru; noodles from ¥350; ⌚9am-9pm Mon-Sat, 11.30am-6pm Sun) *Jaja-men* (じゃじゃめん; noodle with miso and minced meat) joints are all over town, but this hole-in-the wall is still the leader. Ordering is a breeze: just ask for *shō* (small), *chū* (medium) or *dai* (large). When you're finished, crack a raw egg (¥50) into the bowl and the staff will add hot soup and more of that amazing miso paste.

It's down a side street opposite Sakurayama-jinja; you'll know you've found it when you find the queue.

Azumaya Honten SOBA ¥¥

(東屋本店; ☎019-622-2252; www.wankosoba-azumaya.co.jp; 1-8-3 Nakanohashi-dōri; wanko-soba from ¥2700; ⌚11am-8pm) Customers line up and tour buses roll in for this hugely popular *wanko-soba* restaurant. As per tradition, the waiter will refill your tiny bowl with soba as soon as you've put the last one down. Fifteen bowls are equivalent to one ordinary bowl, but the average customer will put away 50 (even 200 is not unheard of).

Cappuccino Shiki COFFEE

(☎019-625-3608; 10-6 Morioka Ekimae-dōri; coffee from ¥500; ⌚9am-10pm Mon-Sat, to 8pm Sun) Perfectly placed to catch caffeine addicts as they tumble off their train and out into the bustle of Morioka, this cosy, dark-wood coffee shop has great espresso and a hip vibe. Toasted sandwiches are also available.

Shopping

Kamasada Honten HOMEWARES

(釜定本店; ☎019-622-3911; 2-5 Konya-chō; ⌚9am-5.30pm Mon-Sat) Morioka is known for its *nanbu tekki* (cast ironware), notably tea kettles. There are some beautiful examples at this venerable shop, along with more affordable items such as wind chimes and incense holders.

Information

MEDICAL SERVICES

Iwate Medical University Hospital (岩手医科大学附属病院; 24hr emergency hotline 019-651-5111; www.iwate-med.ac.jp/hospital; 19-1 Uchi-maru; outpatient services 8.30-11am & 1-4pm Mon Fri)

TOURIST INFORMATION

Iwate Morioka Regional Tourist Information Center (いわて・盛岡広域観光センター; 019-625-2090; 2nd fl, JR Morioka Station, 1-48 Morioka Ekimae-dōri; 9am-5.30pm) On the 2nd floor of JR Morioka Station, this friendly office has English-speaking staff who can help you book accommodation.

Tourist Information Center (盛岡観光コンベンション協会; 019-604-3305; www.hellomorioka.jp; 2nd fl, Odette Plaza, 1-1-10 Nakanohashi-dōri; 9am-7pm, closed 2nd Tue of month;) The helpful staff near the Nakanohashi district speak some English and are happy to welcome you to Morioka.

Getting There & Away

There are hourly *shinkansen* on the JR Tōhoku line south to Tokyo (¥14,740, 2¼ hours) via Sendai (¥6670, 40 minutes), and north to Shin-Aomori (¥6130, one hour).

Frequent trains run on the JR Akita *shinkansen* line between Morioka and Akita (¥4620, 1½ hours) via Tazawa-ko (¥2030, 30 minutes) and Kakunodate (¥2840, 50 minutes). The local Tazawa-ko line covers the same route in about twice the time for around half the price; you may need to transfer at Ōmagari.

Regional buses depart from the JR Bus Station, which is outside the east exit of the train station, and connect Morioka with Sendai (¥2890, 2½ hours) and Hirosaki (¥2980, 2¼ hours). Night buses also go to Tokyo (¥7870, 7½ hours).

Getting Around

The charmingly named Denden Mushi ('electric transmission bug') tourist trolley makes a convenient loop around town (single ride/day pass ¥100/300), departing in a clockwise direction from stop 15 in front of JR Morioka Station (anticlockwise from stop 16) between 9am and 7pm. Buy a day pass from the Bus Information Office at the station before boarding.

Bicycles can be rented from **Sasaki Jitensha Shōkai** (佐々木自転車商会; 019-624-2692; 10-2 Morioka Ekimae-dōri; per hour/day ¥200/1000; 8.30am-6pm), near JR Morioka Station.

Hiraizumi

0191 / POP 7800

Home to Tōhoku's first Unesco World Heritage listing, Hiraizumi (平泉) is a handsome feudal town with architectural remnants courtesy of the gold-mining Ōshu Fujiwara clan who ruled here throughout the 12th century. Chief among the town's attractions is the Chūson-ji temple complex. Dedicated to the principles of Buddhism, the buildings have been thoughtfully integrated into the natural surrounds. While feudal strife eventually brought the old town's demise, visitors will appreciate modern Hiraizumi's understated charm.

Hiraizumi's fate is indelibly linked to that of Japan's favourite tragic hero, Minamoto no Yoshitsune. A great warrior, Yoshitsune earned the jealous contempt of his elder half-brother – Japan's first shogun, Minamoto-no-Yoritomo – and fled east, eventually taking refuge at Hiraizumi in 1187. This gave Yoritomo the perfect excuse to attack, resulting in both the defeat of the Ōshu Fujiwara clan and the death of Yoshitsune. Yoritomo was said to be so impressed with the temples of Hiraizumi that he allowed them to remain, and it was the Kamakura shogunate (military government) that later sponsored the construction of the first wooden hall to protect Konjiki-dō.

Sights

★**Chūson-ji** BUDDHIST TEMPLE
(中尊寺; 0191-46-2211; www.chusonji.or.jp; adult/child ¥800/300; 8.30am-5pm Mar-Oct, to 4.30pm Nov-Feb) Established in 850 by the priest Ennin, the Chūson-ji complex was expanded by the Ōshu Fujiwara family in the 12th century. A total of 300 buildings with 40 temples were constructed. Ironically, the family's grand scheme to build a Buddhist utopia was destroyed when a massive fire ravaged nearly everything in 1337. Only two of the original structures, the **Konjiki-dō** (金色堂, Golden Hall) and **Kyōzō** (経蔵; Sutra Repository), remain, alongside more recent reconstructions. The sprawling site is reached via a steep cedar-lined avenue.

Gilded and gleaming up to its eaves, with elaborate lacquerwork and mother-of-pearl inlay throughout, the **Konjiki-dō** was at the cutting edge of Heian-era artistry when it was created in 1124 – and still impresses

Hiraizumi

Hiraizumi

today. Beneath the three altars are the mummified remains of three generations of the Ōshu Fujiwara family. Given Hiraizumi's history, it seems a miracle that the Konjiki-dō has survived. To avoid tempting fate, the pavilion is now behind glass inside a fireproof enclosure.

The adjacent **treasury** (讃衡蔵; Sankōzō) contains the coffins and funeral finery of the Fujiwara clan – scrolls, swords and images transferred here from long-vanished halls and temples.

Kyōzō, the other original construction, is an understated building guarded by Kishi Monju Bosatsu and Four Attendants formerly stored sacred sutras and artefacts.

Mōtsū-ji GARDENS

(毛越寺; ☎0191-46-2331; adult/child ¥500/300; ⏲8.30am-5pm Apr-Oct, to 4.30pm Nov-Mar) Established by the priest Ennin in 850 at the same time as Chūson-ji (p537), Mōtsū-ji was once Tōhoku's largest and grandest temple complex. The buildings are all long gone, but the enigmatic 12th-century 'Pure Land' gardens, designed with the Buddhist notion of creating an earthly paradise, remain.

Hiraizumi Cultural Heritage Center MUSEUM
(平泉文化遺産センター; 44 Hanadate; ⏲9am-5pm) FREE This modest, friendly museum charts Hiraizumi's rise and fall through visual displays and artefacts, with English explanations throughout.

Activities

Geibi Gorge BOATING
(厳美渓, Geibi-kei; per person ¥1600; ⏲8.30am-4pm) Singing boatmen on flat-bottomed wooden boats steer passengers down the Satetsu-gawa, which cuts through a ravine flanked by towering limestone walls. Tours last 1½ hours and include some time on land halfway up the gorge.

Geibi Gorge is 15km east of Hiraizumi; between April and November, four daily buses travel from Hiraizumi (¥500, 35 minutes), otherwise take the *kaisoku* (rapid train) from Ichinoseki to Geibi-kei Station on the JR Ōfunato line (¥580, 30 minutes).

Sleeping & Eating

A couple of guesthouses in town cater to those wishing to stay overnight, but most travellers will likely visit on a day trip from Morioka or Sendai.

A cluster of Japanese tourist-type restaurants near the temples serve traditional fare, though fewer options are available at dinner.

Minpaku Hiraizumi MINSHUKU ¥
(民泊平泉町; ☎090-267-7889; 117-17 Hiraizumi Shirayama; per person incl breakfast ¥6000; P❄📶) The two rooms in this charming guesthouse are regularly booked out, for good reason. The friendly older couple in charge present their home in exquisite fashion, from the bright and stylish sleeping areas to the hearty breakfasts and peaceful sitting room.

Kanzan-tei JAPANESE ¥¥
(かんざん亭; ☎0191-46-2211; dishes from ¥980; ⏲10am-4.15pm) On top of the hill within the Chūson-ji (p537) complex, this glass-walled restaurant has lovely views of the surrounding countryside and is the perfect place to rest your temple-weary legs. Hot and cold soba dishes hit the spot.

Information

Tourist Information Center (平泉町観光協会; ☎0191-46-2110; ⏲8.30am-5pm) Located next to the train station, with English pamphlets available.

Getting There & Away

Hourly *shinkansen* run along the JR Tōhoku line between Sendai and Ichinoseki (¥3500, 35 minutes). Local trains (¥1660, two hours), running every hour or two, ply the same route on the JR Tōhoku main line and also connect Ichinoseki and Hiraizumi (¥200, 10 minutes).

Ichinoseki is connected to Morioka by the JR Tōhoku *shinkansen* (¥4120, 40 minutes) and the JR Tōhoku main line *futsū* (¥1660, 1½ hours).

Getting Around

The main sites are around a 30-minute walk from Hiraizumi JR Station. Alternatively you can hire a bicycle (four hours/one day ¥400/900) or catch the Loop Bus (single trip adult/child ¥150/80, twice hourly Monday to Friday, more frequent on weekends) from in front of the station.

Tōno

☎0198 / POP 28,062

Peaceful Tōno (遠野) has enjoyed a renaissance among domestic travellers in search of an antidote to a harried urban existence. It provides an accessible dip into agricultural life, watched over by a dramatic mountain range, and its folklore, the basis for so many spooky stories about *yōkai* (ghosts, demons, monsters and spirits), adds an intriguing spiritual dimension. The sights are spread out, so a car, or better yet a bicycle, is recommended to make the most of your stay.

Tōno is also a gateway for journeys south through the coastal region known as Sanriku Kaigan (p542).

Sights

More than any one sight, Tōno is a collective atmosphere. Get a feel for it by cycling (p541) through the area; you'll see many sights en route.

SL GINGA TRAIN

Train buffs should check out the rather special **SL Ginga** series steam locomotive, inspired by the novel *Night on the Galactic Railroad*, which runs on Saturdays from Hanamaki to Kamaishi (¥2480, 4½ hours) via Tōno, and back the other way on Sundays.

Tōno Valley

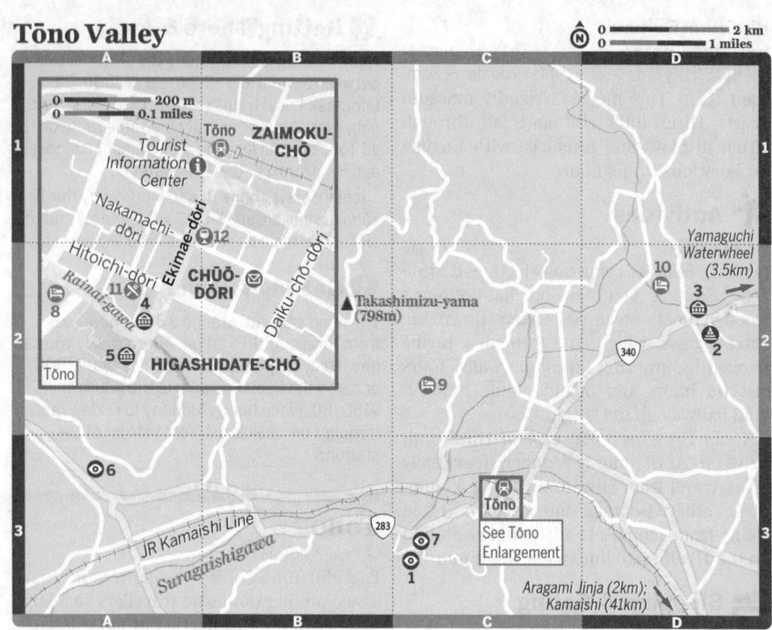

Tōno Valley

Sights
1 Gohyaku Rakan C3
2 Jōken-ji D2
3 Tōno Denshōen D2
4 Tōno Folktale and Storytelling Center A2
5 Tōno Municipal Museum A2
6 Tsuzuki-ishi A3
7 Unedori-sama C3

Sleeping
8 Aeria Tohno A2
9 Kuranoya C2
10 Tōno Youth Hostel D2

Eating
11 Itō-ke A2

Drinking & Nightlife
12 Tono Brewing B1

Tōno Folktale & Storytelling Center MUSEUM
(とおの昔話村, Tōno Mukashibanashi-mura; ☎0198-62-7887; 2-11 Chūō-dōri; adult/child ¥500/200; ⊙9am-5pm) Housed in the restored ryokan where Yanagita Kunio penned his famous work Legends of Tōno (p542), this evocative museum has audiovisuals of some of the tales and memorabilia pertaining to Yanagita. There is minimal English signage, but wandering the restored buildings is still worthwhile.

Sleeping

Tōno Youth Hostel HOSTEL ¥
(遠野ユースホステル; ☎0198-62-8736; 13-39-5 Tsuchibuchi-chō; dm from ¥4050; P ⊖ ❄ @ ☎) If you're after a gentle rural experience, then this hostel, set inside a converted farmhouse, is a worthy choice. The communal library and dining hall (breakfast/dinner ¥600/1200) invite lingering, and the open-air baths suggest a simpler time when mythical creatures stirred the locals' imaginations. The dorms are fairly plain, but the silence, soft pillows and Iwate wine will induce a restful sleep.

From Tōno Station, take a bus bound for Saka-no-shita to the Nitagai stop (¥290, 12 minutes). From there, it's a 10-minute walk, with the hostel clearly signposted along the way (look for the small wooden signs at knee level).

Aeria Tohno HOTEL ¥¥
(あえりあ遠野; ☎0198-60-1700; www.aeria-tohno.com; 1-10 Shin-machi; s/d incl breakfast from ¥8300/14,600; P ⊖ ❄ ☎) This is a very hospitable, upscale hotel near the town **museum**

(遠野市立博物館; ☎0198-62-2340; 3-9 Higashi-date-chō; adult/child ¥300/150; ⏲9am-5pm). Staff are highly knowledgeable about the local area and encourage guests to venture out from their spacious, elegant – if slightly dated – rooms. It's by far the pick of the town at the higher end. Dinner can be added for ¥4300.

Kuranoya MINSHUKU ¥¥
(くら乃屋; ☎0198-60-1360; www.kuranoya-tono.com; 45-136 Sanchiwari, Kōkōji, Matsuzaki-chō; s/d from ¥6800/12,600; P ❄ 📶) Guests rave about Kuranoya, a classic Japanese homestay with urbane owners who sought refuge from the city in Tōno's foothills. They speak magnificent English, are passionate about the history and future of their town, and are keen to share it with you. Accommodation is modern Japanese of the highest standard. A highly recommended dinner costs ¥1000. Call ahead for pick-ups.

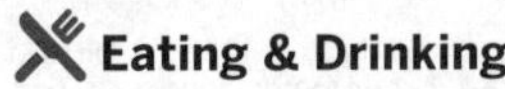

Eating & Drinking

There are a few local noodle places around town where you can grab a bowl at lunch. A handful of *izakaya* also serve dinner, but otherwise you'll need to depend on your hosts for an evening meal.

Itō-ke SOBA ¥
(伊藤家; ☎0198-60-1110; 2-11 Chūō-dōri; mains from ¥650; ⏲11am-5pm) Among the soba varieties served here, try *hitsuko soba* (ひっこそば), eaten with chicken, mushrooms, onion and raw egg. Otherwise go for *hittsumi* (ひっつみ), hand-cut noodles served with chicken-and-vegetable dumplings in a hot broth. The restaurant is in the traditional dark-wood building adjacent to the Tōno Folktale & Storytelling Center; look for the wooden sign over the sliding doors.

CYCLING AROUND TŌNO

A fantastic riverside trail draws leisure cyclists (no need for lycra), as the Tōno Valley opens up into some beautiful terrain, particularly to the east. Most of the sights following are dotted throughout the valley. Finding them is half the fun. Rent a bicycle, grab a walking map from the Tourist Information Center (p542) and don't be afraid to explore. The mythical world is well signposted in English, but don't let that stop you setting off down unmarked roads – you never know what you might find.

About 2.5km southwest of Tōno Station is **Unedori-sama** (卯子酉様; ☎0198-62-2111; Shimokumi-chō), the matchmaking shrine. According to legend, if you tie a strip of red cloth around one of the pines using only your left hand, you'll meet your soul mate. In the hills above, the **Gohyaku Rakan** (五百羅漢, 500 Buddhist Disciples) are eerie, moss-covered rock carvings of 500 disciples of Buddha that were fashioned by a priest to console the spirits of those who died in a 1754 famine. It's a unique site – approach respectfully.

If you continue west along Rte 283 towards Morioka for about 8km, you'll eventually come to **Tsuzuki-ishi** (続石), a curious rock that rests amid aromatic cedars; it's either a natural formation or a dolmen (primitive tomb). A short, steep hike rewards you with views across the valley, but take heed as bears – and hungry ogres (p542) – are reported to lurk in these parts.

About 5km east of the town centre is **Denshōen** (伝承園; ☎0198-62-8655; www.densyoen.jp; 6-5-1 Tsuchibuchi, Tsuchibuchi-chō; adult/child ¥320/220; ⏲9am-5pm; P), a traditional farmhouse containing a small cultural museum. The highlights here are the thousand Oshira-sama deities fashioned from mulberry wood. A few hundred metres southeast is **Jōken-ji** (常堅寺; 7-50 Tsuchibuchi, Tsuchibuchi-chō; ⏲8am-5pm Apr-Oct, 8.30am-4pm Nov-Mar), a peaceful temple dedicated to the deity image of Obinzuru-sama. Behind the temple is the **kappa-buchi pool**, where Tōno's famous water sprites (p542) lurk. It is said that if pregnant women worship at the shrine on the riverbank, they'll produce plenty of milk, but only if they first produce a breast-shaped offering. The tiny altar is filled with small red or white cloth bags, most complete with nipple.

Otherwise, see if you can find **Aragami Jinja** (荒神神社; 21 Nakazawa, Aozasa-chō), an insanely photogenic little shrine in the middle of a luminous yellow field of canola – you might need to ask for directions – or head on to the **Yamaguchi Waterwheel** (山口の水車), a delightful thatch-roofed waterwheel once used for milling crops, now preserved as a symbol of Tōno's past. From here it's a 12km ride back to town.

Tono Brewing BREWERY
(株式会社遠野醸造; ☎0198-66-3990; www.tonobrewing.com; 10-15 Chūō-dōri; 5-10pm Mon & Wed-Fri, from noon Sat, to 9pm Sun; 📶) Sleepy Tōno is a surprising home for this hip, friendly taproom, but it's a welcome addition to the city's drinking landscape nonetheless. Locally brewed beers include a 'coffee stout', as well as pale ales and lagers. There are also tasty bar snacks on offer, from fries and pickles to larger plates – the perfect end to a day's cycling.

ℹ Information

Tourist Information Center (遠野市観光協会; ☎0198-62-1333; www.tonojikan.jp; ⏲8.30am-5.30pm; 📶) Across from the train station, friendly, helpful staff await your arrival with bicycle rentals (¥1020 per day), English maps and free internet. They can also arrange accommodation in the area.

ℹ Getting There & Away

Trains run hourly on the JR Tōhoku line between Hiraizumi and Hanamaki (¥840, 45 minutes). The JR Kamaishi line connects Hanamaki to Tōno (¥840, one hour), and then onwards to Kamaishi (¥840, one hour), while the JR Tōhoku line connects Hanamaki to Morioka (¥670, 30 minutes).

If you're coming from Sendai, take the Tōhoku *shinkansen* to Shin-Hanamaki (¥5180, one hour) and transfer to the JR Kamaishi line for Tōno (¥760, 45 minutes). The *shinkansen* also connects Shin-Hanamaki to Morioka (¥3130, 11 minutes).

The Sennin-Tōge expressway links up with Rte 283 between Tōno and Kamaishi, for journeys around Sanriku Kaigan.

SANRIKU KAIGAN

Extending from Aomori Prefecture in the north, through Iwate and Miyagi Prefectures to the south, the vast Sanriku Kaigan (三陸海岸) is a rugged and beautiful stretch of coastline marked by steep rocky cliffs and a 'ria' topography. Rias are characterised by broad estuaries that funnel into long, narrow inlets. It is on the low-lying land around the rias of Sanriku Kaigan that communities developed. Ironically these peculiarities that sustain life here also amplify tsunami – sadly the Sanriku coast bore the brunt of the Great East Japan Earthquake (p533) and subsequent tsunami in March 2011.

Most of the low-lying areas of towns and villages here were levelled, and almost

LEGENDS OF TŌNO

At the beginning of the 20th century, writer and scholar Yanagita Kunio (1875–1962) published *Tōno Monogatari* (遠野物語; Legends of Tōno), a collection of local folk tales based on interviews with Sasaki Kyōseki, an educated man from a peasant family who had committed to memory more than 100 *densetsu* (local legends). The book captured the nation's imagination, bringing into focus the oral traditions of a region that had previously been ignored. Pick up the English translation before you visit, if you can.

A weird and wonderful cast of characters and situations draws heavily on the concept of animism, where an individual spirit is attributed to everything that exists, including animals and objects. Of particular importance to Tōno is the story of Oshira-sama. It begins with a farm girl who develops a deep affection for her horse; eventually the two marry, against her father's will. One night, the father finds her sleeping in the stables and, outraged, slaughters the animal. Distraught, the daughter clings to the horse's head and together they are spirited up to the heavens, becoming the deity Oshira-sama.

There are also shape-shifting foxes and *oni* (ogres) who live in the hills and eat lost humans; but best known are the *kappa* (yes, the inspiration for Kappa Mountain in Super Mario World): impish water sprites with thick shells, scaly skin and pointed beaks, responsible for all sorts of mischief and grief. Tōno's many *kappa* reputedly have a nasty habit of pulling people's intestines out through their bum to feed on their *shirikodama*, a mythical ball that humans would call a soul and *kappa* would call delicious.

Points to note: *kappa* love cucumbers, so keep some handy – they may earn your soul a temporary reprieve. (Astute connoisseurs of sushi will note that a *kappa-maki* is none other than a cucumber hand roll.) If you meet a *kappa* in the woods, remember to bow, as it will return the gesture, spilling out the water stored in its head and becoming temporarily powerless. *Kappa* will always repay a favour and are highly knowledgeable in medicine, agriculture and games of skill.

Throughout all of the *Tōno Monogatari* stories is a common theme: the struggle to overcome the everyday problems of rural life.

20,000 people lost their lives. It's a humbling experience to see what remains and to try to imagine what was here before. Mass reconstruction efforts have taken place, with much success: existing businesses have re-established themselves and new restaurants and hotels are popping up everywhere.

Those lucky enough to visit Sanriku Kaigan will not only enjoy the natural splendour of this ancient, ocean-facing landscape and its traditional seafaring communities, but will also be part of the rebirth of these towns and villages, with the people from them eager to protect and share their history and culture with the world. Many Japanese people travel here for this reason alone, especially young creatives and social activists, lending their energies, ideas and human capital to many communities. There's a real sense of resilience, and the appreciation of life here will touch the heart of anyone who visits.

Getting There & Around

Renting a car (from Morioka, Sendai or Ichinoseki) is highly recommended. Roads in, out and around the area are in excellent shape, with many new roads and highways now in action, including the newly completed Sanriku Expressway.

Rail services on the JR Kamaishi line are fully operational, but buses have replaced trains on a small section of the JR Ōfunato, Kesennuma and Yamada lines.

The private Sanriku Railway lines Kita-Riasu (between Miyako and Kuji) and Minami-Riasu (between Ōfunato/Sakari and Kamaishi), which were heavily damaged by the tsunami, are running full services again. A new section of railway opened in 2019, linking Miyako with Kamaishi and traversing the coast by rail all the way from Kuji to Ōfunato, linking north to Hachinohe and west to Ichinoseki.

Luxurious **Tōhoku Emotion** trains with gourmet cuisine served in dining cars run daily between Hachinohe and Kuji, mostly along the cost (round trip ¥11,900, including food).

Minami-Sanriku & Kesennuma

Kesennuma (気仙沼), in Miyagi Prefecture, is one of the Sanriku coast's larger cities. Life in the hilly suburbs above this port has returned to something like normal since 2000 people died here in 2011. Kesennuma was the site for the iconic photo of a ship – the *Kyotoku Maru 18* – beached atop an ocean of rubble. The eerie wreck was finally removed in 2013.

Around 40km south, 95% of the town of Minami-Sanriku (南三陸) was destroyed in the tsunami, yet thousands of people reached higher ground and survived. The area is still undergoing extensive land-reclamation works, with a memorial park due to open in 2020.

Sights

★RIAS Ark Museum of Art MUSEUM
(リアスアーク美術館; 0226-24-1611; www.riasark.com; 138-5 Akaiwamakisawa, Kesennuma; adult/child ¥500/150; 9.30am-5pm Wed-Sun) High in the hills above Kesennuma, this local art museum houses the largest collection of photographs and artefacts in existence relating to the 2011 Great East Japan Earthquake (p533) and tsunami. A comprehensive booklet containing an English translation of each exhibit is available. The sheer volume and nature of the collection is a little overwhelming.

Minami-Sanriku Crisis Management Centre MEMORIAL
(南三陸防災対策庁舎; Minami-Sanriku) The steel shell is all that remains of this three-storey building, standing alone in what once was central Minami-Sanriku. It has been preserved by the locals as a touching memorial to the lives that were lost here, and this whole area has now been turned into a memorial park.

Sleeping & Eating

There are a couple of business hotels and guesthouses in Kesennuma, which makes a handy base for exploring the surrounding area.

Accommo Inn Kesennuma BUSINESS HOTEL ¥¥
(アコモイン気仙沼; 0226-21-2565; www.accommo-inn.com; 2-1 Shinden, Kesennuma; s/d incl breakfast ¥6300/12,600;) Built in 2013 the low-rise Accommo Inn has modern rooms with soft colours, quality linen, small desks and lots of natural light. The complimentary breakfast is a Japanese take on a full English.

Sun Sun Shopping Village FOOD HALL ¥
(南三陸さんさん商店街; Shizugawa; dishes from ¥500; 9am-5pm) Atop reclaimed land near where the old centre of Minami-Sanriku stood, this new shopping village opened in 2017 to much fanfare. It represents the revitalisation of the tsunami zone, and is thronged with locals on weekends. A cluster

of restaurants serve local specialities, including excellent seafood rice bowls; the perfect lunch break.

Getting There & Away

Kesennuma is 50km east of Ichinoseki. Trains traverse the JR Ōfunato line between Kesennuma and Ichinoseki (¥1140, 1¼ hours, five daily).

JR also runs a bus rapid transit (BRT) service north to Ōfunato (¥840, one hour, five daily) and south to Minami-Sanriku (¥760, 1¼ hours, hourly).

Rikuzen-takata & Ōfunato

The small town of Rikuzen-takata (陸前高田) in southern Iwate was largely swept away in 2011. A vast network of conveyor belts subsequently ferried soil from neighbouring mountains into the town to raise the ground level. It's now an attractive seaside village with decent tourism infrastructure (namely hotels and restaurants) and makes a great base for trips around the region.

The port town of Ōfunato (大船渡), 15km north of Rikuzen-takata, saw 24m-high waves travel 3km inland during the 2011 tsunami. Residents heeded warnings and loss of life was comparatively small.

Sights

Goishi Kaigan BEACH

(碁石海岸; Ōfunato) This 6km scenic stretch of rocky coastline and picturesque beaches around Ōfunato is home to a number of geological attractions, including **Ranboya Gorge**, a watery canyon with 30m-high walls that is navigable by boats on calm days. Nearby **Kaminariiwa Rock** (雷岩; Thunder Rock) is one of the officially designated '100 Soundscapes of Japan' due to the deep rumbling sound produced when waves enter caverns in the rock. Around 4km of easily navigable walking trails hug the clifftops.

Campers can stay at the beachside **campground** (碁石海岸キャンプ場; ☎0192-29-2359; www.goishi.info; Ohama Suwaki-cho, Ōfunato; per person ¥500, campsite ¥1500, powered van site ¥4000; ⊙mid-Jul–Oct, reception 8.30am-5.15pm).

Ippon-matsu MEMORIAL

(陸前高田一本松, Miracle Pine; www.city.rikuzentakata.iwate.jp/kategorie/fukkou/ipponmatu/ipponmatu.html; Rikuzen-takata) More than 70,000 pine trees lined the coastline around Rikuzen-takata until 2011, when all but one were destroyed in the tsunami. That tree, known as the Miracle Pine, survived for over a year, until salination from the inundation caused its demise. A replica was constructed in its place and serves as a touching memorial, symbolising hope. A memorial park is under construction around the site, including the replanting of a pine grove from pine cones collected from the original trees.

Activities

Kurosaki Senkyo Onsen ONSEN

(黒崎仙境温泉; ☎0192-57-1126; www.kurosaki-onsen.com; 9-41 Hirotacho Kurosaki, Rikuzen-takata; 4hr/day ¥500/1000, towel ¥230; ⊙10am-8pm Thu-Tue) Right on the tip of the peninsula, this onsen has lovely views and an on-site noodle restaurant to fill tummies between plunges.

Sleeping

Rikuzen-takata and Ōfunato are home to some of the nicest accommodation options along Sanriku Kaigan; this area makes a great base for your travels.

Hakoneyama Terrace BOUTIQUE HOTEL ¥¥

(はこねやまテラス; ☎0192-22-7088; www.hakoneyama-terrace.jp; 1-Myoga, Otomocho; s/d incl breakfast Mon-Fri ¥8000/14,000, Sat & Sun ¥9000/16,000; P⊖❄📶) Set in the hills, among tall trees and with ocean views, this elegant guesthouse is the epitome of hip. Light-filled rooms are simple and supremely comfortable, but the main draw is the expansive sunset terrace. The main building also hosts a cafe, bar and workshop space. A healthy breakfast is included; other meals are available by reservation.

Capital Hotel 1000 HOTEL ¥¥¥

(キャピタルホテル1000; ☎0192-55-3111; www.capitalhotel1000.jp; 0-1 Nagasuna Takata-chō, Rikuzen-takata; s/d from ¥8250/15,500; P⊖❄📶) A symbol of the reconstruction effort, the Capital Hotel 1000 was reborn in 2013 and is now a grey rectangular building in an industrial style with excellent rooms, most with a small couch. The surrounding area is a hive of reconstruction. Breakfasts are delicious.

Tamanoyu Onsen HOTEL ¥¥¥

(霊泉玉乃湯; ☎0192-55-6866; www.tamanoyuonsen.com; 104-8 Takekoma-chō, Rikuzen-takata; per person incl 2 meals from ¥10,800; P❄📶) This is a lovely rural escape, with a number of piping-hot baths and a separate building for Japanese-style accommodation. Delicious meals are included. Day trippers can make use of the bathing facilities for ¥600.

Eating

There are some very hip, community-minded cafes springing up around this area, as well as excellent local seafood restaurants.

Riku Café JAPANESE ¥

(りくカフェ; ☎0192-22-7311; http://rikucafe.jp; 22-9 Naruishi Takata-chō, Rikuzen-takata; dishes from ¥900; ⊙9am-9pm;) The main community centre in Rikuzen-takata is also a lively cafe with home-cooked food, good coffee and the odd live performance. It's an unofficial information centre, too, so drop in if you're travelling independently.

Waiwai JAPANESE ¥

(わいわい; ☎0192-47-3102; 93-1 Osumi Takata-chō, Rikuzen-takata; dishes from ¥750; ⊙11am-2.30pm & 5.30-8.30pm) This friendly local eatery has novel food items, including *nattō*-filled fish cake and the refreshing alcoholic orange *nacchiku* drink. The owner is a mini celebrity around these parts.

Pechka CAFE

(☎0192-22-7162; www.life-with-pechka.com; 51-168 Naruishi, Takata-chō, Rikuzen-takata; ⊙11am-9pm;) Excellent coffee and delicious baked goods – such as Earl Grey scones with lemon butter – are the standouts at this hip cafe, which also hosts a lending library. The architect-designed space is constructed entirely of local materials.

Getting There & Away

Rikuzen-takata is 60km east of Ichinoseki. Hourly bus rapid transit (BRT) services run south to Kesennuma (¥500, 30 minutes) and north to Ōfunato (¥320, 35 minutes).

Ōfunato is also the southern end of the Sanriku Railway Minami-Rias line, which runs along the coast between Sakari Station in Ōfunato and Kamaishi (¥1080, one hour, five daily). The middle section of the Sanriku Railway, which links Kamaishi with Miyako, reopened in 2019 at making it possible to traverse the coast all the way north to Kuji.

Kamaishi & Ōtsuchi

Due east of Tōno, Kamaishi (釜石) is an industrial fishing town where low-lying areas were flattened in the tsunami and 1250 lives were lost. A famed Buddhist statue towers over the town. The town itself doesn't have much to hold travellers, but it makes a good base for journeys along the nearby coast, as its tourist infrastructure has received a hefty boost due to its role as one of the host venues for the 2019 Rugby World Cup. Just 10km down the road, flanked by Chojamori-san and Komagamori-san, the small fishing village of Ōtsuchi (大槌町) blooms with azaleas in spring. Roughly 10% of the town's 16,000 people were lost in 2011.

> **DON'T MISS**
>
> **GOURMET DINING**
>
> A few savvy chefs in Rikuzen-takata have created Hota-waka Go-zen, a 12-dish degustation menu of local produce, laid out on tiered wooden trays and served at a handful of venues along the coast. Check out www.rikuzentakata-hotatewakame.com.

Tours

★Oraga Otsuchi WALKING

(おらが大槌夢広場 大槌町語り部ガイド; ☎0193-55-5120; www.oraga-otsuchi.jp; 23-37-3 Ōtsuchi-cho; tours per person from ¥1000; ⊙by appointment) The resilient, forward-thinking and compassionate folk at this local organisation run individual and group tours around Ōtsuchi, sharing personal, firsthand accounts of the 2011 Tōhoku earthquake and tsunami, and educating visitors on disaster management and humanitarian concerns. Prepare to have your heart melt a little (OK, a lot). Very highly recommended.

Sleeping & Eating

Hamabeno Ryouriyado Houraikan RYOKAN ¥¥¥

(浜べの料理宿宝来館; ☎0193-28-2526; www.houraikan.jp; 2-1 Shinden, Kamaishi; r per person incl 2 meals from ¥15,000;) Expect superlative hospitality at this seaside gem. The dining experience at this ryokan is exceptional for such a remote place and the onsen facility includes a Zen garden surrounding a large wooden bath, and stunning views from the indoor hot and cold pools. Rooms are light and stylish, with a largely Western decor, save the tatami flooring.

The ryokan's owner, Akiko Iwasaki, was a leader of the local rehabilitation effort after the 2011 tsunami, and is a wealth of information on the region's history and highlights.

Sunfish Kamaishi MARKET ¥

(サン・フィッシュ釜石; www.sunfish-kamaishi.sakura.ne.jp; opposite Kamaishi Station; sushi set from ¥1100; ⊙7am-4pm Thu-Tue) A great spot to pick up fresh sushi on the way through Kamaishi, the Sunfish market also has a few small restaurants on the 1st floor.

Ririshiya JAPANESE ¥¥
(凜々家; 0193-44-2366; 1-3-53 Kiri Kiri, Ōtsuchi; dishes from ¥700; 11am-2.30pm & 5.30-10pm) When in Ōtsuchi, stop for a special seafood *donburi* (rice bowl) at this popular restaurant run by a former fisherman. Lots of local vegetables from the surrounding mountains also feature on the eclectic menu.

Information

Kamaishi Tourist Information Society (釜石観光物産協会; 0193-22-5835; 22-1 Suzuko-chō, Kamaishi; 9am-5pm) By Kamaishi Station, with friendly staff who speak little English but have excellent literature to disperse on Kamaishi and the surrounding area.

Getting There & Away

Kamaishi is 40km east of Tōno. Hourly trains traverse the JR Kamaishi line between Kamaishi and Tōno (¥840, one hour), continuing on to Hanamaki (¥1660, two hours).

Kamaishi is also the northern end of the Sanriku Railway Minami-Rias line, which runs along the coast between Kamaishi and Sakari in Ofunato (¥1080, one hour, five daily). The middle section of the Sanriku Railway, which links Kamaishi with Miyako, reopened in 2019 at making it possible to traverse the coast all the way north to Kuji.

Miyako

0193 / POP 56,700

The quiet port city of Miyako (宮古市) has a wealth of natural beauty on its doorstep, the jewel of which is the famed white-pebble beach of Jodogahama. This proximity to the coast also meant that Miyako suffered greatly during the 2011 tsunami, when much of the town, along with almost all of its fishing fleet, was destroyed, though loss of life was lower here than in towns further south. Most of the town's infrastructure is now back up and running, and the region once again draws large numbers of domestic tourists to its picturesque coastline.

Sights

Kitayamazaki Cliffs NATURAL FEATURE
(北山崎) Jagged, green-fringed cliffs plunge into the deep-blue Pacific Ocean along this 8km stretch of coastline known as the Kitayamazaki coast. Stunning in every season, whether shrouded in mist or bathed in sun, the cliffs have long drawn domestic tourists to this scenic region. Walking tracks meander through pine forests to various observation points; more serious walkers can use this as a starting point for a section of the Michinoku Coastal Trail.

The cliffs are a one-hour drive from Miyako. On public transport, take the Sanriku Railway to Tanohata (¥990, 45 minutes), from where buses depart for the cliffs (¥800, 20 minutes, hourly).

Jōdogahama BEACH
(浄土ヶ浜) Postcard-perfect Jodogahama ('pure land beach') sits on a sheltered inlet surrounded by jagged white-stone outcrops backed by deep-green pines. Walking tracks wend their way around the bay, while the beach itself has crystal-clear water perfect for peaceful bathing. Domestic tourists flock to the area in summer, when paddle boats are available for hire. To fully appreciate the seascape, take a short cruise to the nearby

DON'T MISS

TŌHOKU'S FAMOUS FESTIVALS

Tōhoku festivals are the stuff of Japanese legend, and many Japanese legends live on in Tōhoku's wild public celebrations. Particularly through the warmer months, you've a decent chance of passing a city, town or village in full flight. The following festivals, known as the Three Great Festivals of Tōhoku, are must-sees (just be sure to book accommodation months in advance):

Sendai Tanabata Matsuri (p526) Thousands of coloured streamers around Sendai's downtown area honour a tale of star-crossed lovers.

Aomori Nebuta Matsuri (p548) Local artists outdo each other in creating elaborate floats, and a multitude of merrymakers take to Aomori's streets.

Akita Kantō Matsuri (p560) Stunning acrobatics are performed in Akita, with towering bamboo poles hung with lanterns.

Blue Cave (¥1500, 20 minutes), departing from the pier below the visitor centre.

Buses run between Miyako Station and the visitor centre (¥180, 15 minutes, at least hourly), from where it's a 10-minute walk to the beach.

Sleeping & Eating

Seafood features heavily on Miyako menus, with a plethora of fresh catch available. The centre has plenty of local restaurants, though if you're visiting the coastal sights, you may wish to pack a picnic.

Park Hotel Jodogahama HOTEL ¥¥¥
(浄土ヶ浜パークホテル; 0193-62-2321; www.jodo-ph.jp; 32-4 Hitachihamacho; r per person from ¥14,500; P) The stunning location, only a short stroll from Jodogahama beach, is the biggest draw for this elegant oceanfront hotel. Most rooms are Japanese-style, and all feature small sitting areas – the ones with ocean views are obviously the pick, though those facing the pine forest offer a different kind of serenity. Friendly staff and excellent meals seal the deal.

Getting There & Away

Three daily trains run on the JR Yamada line between Miyako and Morioka (¥1940, 2¼ hours).

Miyako is also the southern end of the Sanriku Railway Kita-Rias line, which runs along the coast between Mikayo and Kuji (¥1850, 1¾ hours, five daily). The middle section of the Sanriku Railway, which links Miyako with Kamaishi, which links Kamaishi with Miyako, reopened in 2019 at making it possible to traverse the coast all the way to Ōfunato.

AOMORI PREFECTURE

Travellers to the northern tip of Honshū often speed through the peculiar-shaped prefecture of Aomori Prefecture (青森県; Aomori-ken) en route to the island of Hokkaidō. However, for geographic extremity – and remarkably few tourists – you needn't go so far. Disembark the bullet train before it reaches the sea, rent a car and explore the axe-shaped Shimokita Peninsula, the sacred volcanoes around Osore-zan, and the snowy Hakkōda highlands. It's seriously wild stuff. In summer the beaches around the deep blue caldera lake of Towada-ko make for a peaceful interlude. Hirosaki, the former capital, is a stylish little city with a hip downtown area and a rather fine park.

WORTH A TRIP

MICHINOKU COASTAL TRAIL

Stretching from Hachinohe in Aomori Prefecture to Soma in Fukushima Prefecture, the **Michinoku Coastal Trail** (みちのく潮風トレイル; http://tohoku.env.go.jp/mct) is a 700km hiking path through some of the most stunning coastal regions in Japan. Many sections of the trail are well established, but some linking pieces are much newer.

Sleeping

Aomori and Hirosaki have the most options for accommodation. Elsewhere in the prefecture, secluded onsen hotels abound, especially around Towada-ko and Hakkōda-san.

Aomori

017 / POP 287,648

In the upper reaches of Japan's main island is the quiet prefectural capital of Aomori (青森), with a very pleasant harbour-front and several excellent museums. The wilds of Hokkaidō draw many travellers here for a brief stopover, but the savvy wanderer will use it as a base for exploring this vastly under-visited prefecture. Aomori's most famous draw is its August Nebuta festival, but the rest of the time the city maintains a sleepy seaside feel. It's sunny and delightfully cooler than most of Japan in summer, but winter here is an icy, frigid state of affairs.

Sights

★ **Aomori Museum of Art** MUSEUM
(青森県立美術館; 017-783-3000; www.aomori-museum.jp; 185 Chikano, Yasuta; adult/child ¥510/100; 9am-6pm Jun-Sep, 9.30am-5pm Oct-May;) Looking like a modernist sculpture, the geometric white facade of the Aomori Museum of Art was designed to blend in with the landscape when blanketed with snow. The permanent collection features works by Aomori icons, including pop artist Yoshitomo Nara (and his 8.5m-tall dog) and master printmaker Munakata Shikō, alongside international artists. The showstopper is four huge ballet backdrops painted by Marc Chagall, which hang on the walls of the gallery's central atrium. Contemporary temporary exhibitions are elegantly staged.

Aomori Prefecture

The museum is about 5km west of JR Aomori Station, adjacent to Sannai Maruyama. City buses leaving from stop 6 at the JR station for Menkyō Center stop at Kenritsu-bijyutskan-mae (¥270, 20 minutes), across the road from the museum.

Sannai Maruyama ARCHAEOLOGICAL SITE
(三内丸山遺跡; ☎017-766-8282; www.sannaimaruyama.pref.aomori.jp; Sannai Maruyama 305; ⏲9am-6pm Jun-Sep, to 5pm Oct-May) FREE Excavation of this site turned up an astonishing number of intact artefacts from Japan's Jōmon era (10,000 to 2000 years ago), which are on display at the museum here. Clay figures, jade beads and large chestnut pillars head the collection, and there are also some reconstructed dwellings. Sannai Maruyama is approximately 5km west of JR Aomori Station. City buses leaving from stop 6 for Menkyō Center stop at Sannai Maruyama Iseki-mae (¥300, 20 minutes).

Nebuta no Ie Wa Rasse MUSEUM
(ねぶたの家ワ・ラッセ; ☎017-752-1311; www.nebuta.or.jp/warasse; 1-1-1 Yasukata; adult/child ¥600/250; ⏲9am-7pm May-Aug, to 6pm Sep-Apr) Even if you miss the Nebuta festival, you can still gawk at the awesome artisanship of the floats at this well-curated museum on the waterfront. On weekends there are dancing and drumming performances.

Festivals & Events

Aomori Nebuta Matsuri PARADE
(青森ねぶた祭り; www.nebuta.or.jp; ⏲2-7 Aug) Aomori's Nebuta Matsuri has parades of spectacular illuminated floats, accompanied by thousands of rowdy, chanting dancers. The parades start at sunset and last for hours; on the final day the action starts at about noon. This is one of Japan's most famous festivals; book accommodation way *way* in advance.

Sleeping

Aomori has the usual gamut of business hotels, mostly on the walk north from the train station along the Shinmachi covered arcade.

Hyper Hotels Passage HOTEL ¥¥
(ハイパーホテルズパサージュ; 017-721-5656; www.hyperhotel.co.jp; 1-8-6 Shin-machi; s/d from ¥5480/8000;) Sometimes the thought of exiting the train station can be too daunting. Luckily Japanese urban planners have perfected the covered arcade, which includes fabulous little hotels like this business number with a chandelier in the lobby, spotless rooms, bubbly management and an excellent breakfast.

Aomori Center Hotel HOTEL ¥¥
(青森センターホテル; 017-762-7500; http://aomori.atinnhotels.com; 1-10-9-1 Furukawa; s/d incl breakfast from ¥5600/9800;) The best reason to stay here is for the on-site onsen complex, complete with faux rocks and steaming hot baths. Rooms in the *bekkan* (annexe) are far nicer than those in the original building, which is starting to show its age. The hotel (not to be confused with the Aomori Central Hotel) is a 500m walk southeast from JR Aomori Station.

Eating & Drinking

Seafood is the star in this port city; there are loads of purveyors of the famed local scallop. If that's not your thing, there are plenty of other options on the streets near the station.

★**Shinsen Ichiba** MARKET ¥
(新鮮市場; 017-721-8000; basement fl, Auga Bldg, 1-3-7 Shin-chō; meals from ¥580; 5am-6.30pm) Cut out the middle man and head straight for the famed Aomori seafood market, where piles of fresh catch – as well as apples, pickled vegetables and a variety of other produce – are laid out for restaurateurs to hand-pick. A few counter restaurants also sell ramen and *sanshoku-don* (rice topped with scallops, fish roe and sea-urchin roe). Cheap and ridiculously cheerful.

Osanai SEAFOOD ¥
(おさない; 1-1-17 Shin-machi; items from ¥450; 7am-9.30pm Tue-Sun) In a town that knows how to handle a bivalve, Osanai has a stellar reputation for its simple and cheap *hotate* (scallops). The menu includes *marucchi tsumire soba* (dumplings made from apple and scallops on hot soba noodles). We preferred ours simply hot and buttery. Located at the beginning of busy Shinmachi-dōri.

A-Factory BREWERY
(エーファクトリー; 017-752-1890; 1-4-2 Yanagigawa; 11am-8pm) This rather hip complex features a cider brewery and food hall (meals from ¥600) alongside a lovely market space selling high-quality Aomori souvenirs. Sup sparkling cider made from Aomori-grown apples while downing excellent burgers and artisan gelati in front of high windows with water views. A delightful place to while away an afternoon.

Information

MEDICAL SERVICES

Aomori City Hospital (青森市民病院; 24hr emergency hotline 017-734-2171; 1-14-20 Katsuda; outpatient services 9am-5pm Mon-Fri)

TOURIST INFORMATION

Aomori Station Tourist Information Center (青森市観光交流情報センター; 017-723-4670; www.city.aomori.aomori.jp; 1-1-25 Shinmachi; 8.30am-7pm) Pick up useful English-language maps and brochures about Aomori – both the city and the prefecture. Staff speak English.

Shin-Aomori Station Tourist Information Center (あおもり観光情報センター; 017-752-6311; 140-2 Ishie Takama; 8.30am-7pm) On the 2nd floor of the *shinkansen* terminus; ask here for info on all things Aomori and journeys north to Hokkaidō.

Getting There & Away

AIR

From Aomori Airport, 11km south of the city centre, there are flights to and from Tokyo, Osaka, Sapporo and Seoul. Airport buses (¥700, 35 minutes) are timed for flights and depart from stop 11 in front of JR Aomori Station.

BOAT

Sii Line (シィライン; 017-722-4545; www.sii-line.co.jp) ferries depart at least twice daily for Wakinosawa on the Shimokita Peninsula (¥2610, one hour) from Aomori-kō Ryokyaku Fune Terminal (青森港旅客船ターミナル).

Tsugaru Kaikyō (津軽海峡; 017-766-4733; www.tsugarukaikyo.co.jp) operates eight ferries daily between Aomori and Hakodate (from ¥2020, 3½ hours) year-round. Ferries depart from Aomori Ferry Terminal (青森フェリーターミナル) on the western side of the city, a 10-minute taxi ride (around ¥2000) from JR Aomori Station. The Nebutan Gō (p550) shuttle also stops there.

BUS

JR highway buses connect Aomori to Sendai (¥6000, five hours) and Tokyo (from ¥9000, 9½ hours). Alight at the **JR highway bus stop** outside Aomori JR train station.

Aomori

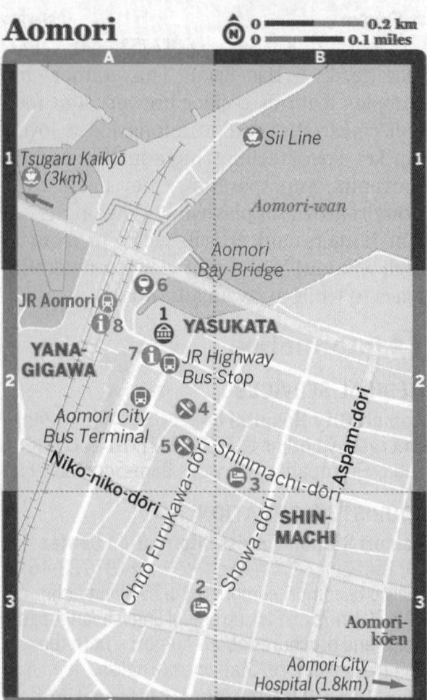

Aomori

Sights
1 Nebuta no Ie Wa Rasse ... A2

Sleeping
2 Aomori Center Hotel ... A3
3 Hyper Hotels Passage ... B2

Eating
4 Osanai ... A2
5 Shinsen Ichiba ... A2

Drinking & Nightlife
6 A-Factory ... A2

Information
7 Aomori Station Tourist Information Center ... A2
8 Shin-Aomori Station Tourist Information Center ... A2

Aomori city buses depart from stop 11 for Hakkōda (¥1100, one hour) and Towada-ko (¥3090, three hours); schedules vary seasonally and are infrequent in winter. See www.jrbustohoku.co.jp.

CAR & MOTORCYCLE

Toyota Rent a Car (トヨタレンタカー; ☎017-782-0100; http://rent.toyota.co.jp; 104-79 Ishie Takama; ⏲8am-8pm) can be found outside the west exit of the Shin-Aomori *shinkansen* station and also has branches a few blocks from JR Aomori Station.

TRAIN

The Tōhoku *shinkansen* runs roughly every hour from Tokyo Station, via Sendai and Morioka, to the terminus at Shin-Aomori Station (¥17,350, 3¼ hours).

Futsū (local) trains on the JR Ōu main line connect Aomori with Shin-Aomori (¥190, five minutes) and Hirosaki (¥670, 50 minutes). A few JR Tsugaru *tokkyū* (limited express) trains run daily between Aomori and Akita (¥5400, three hours) on the same line.

Hourly *tokkyū* (limited express) trains run on the JR Tsugaru-Kaikyō line between Aomori and Hakodate on Hokkaidō (¥3240, two hours), via the Seikan Tunnel.

One daily *kaisoku* (rapid train) on the JR Ōminato line connects Aomori and Shimokita (¥2700, 1½ hours). Otherwise take a *futsū* train on the private Aoimori Tetsudō line and transfer at Noheji for the JR Ōminato line (¥2180, 1¾ hours).

Getting Around

Nebutan Gō shuttle buses (single ride/day pass ¥200/500) circle the city, connecting Shin-Aomori Station, JR Aomori Station, Aomori Ferry Terminal and most city sights. They may be less direct than regular municipal buses, but are the most economical way to get around the city. Buy tickets on board, or from any of the tourist offices (p549). Buses depart from the **Aomori City Bus Terminal** (Aomori JR train station), plus numerous stops in between.

Hirosaki

☎0172 / POP 172,400

Surprisingly hip Hirosaki (弘前) is an enigmatic historic town with rightful claims as the cultural capital of the prefecture, a step up from the blander capital just a few stops down the train line. Set in the shadow of the impressive Iwaki-san (p555), the town has a youthful quality that belies its feudal past under the Tsugaru clan. Its semi-rural setting is complemented by beautiful parks, a wonderful temple district and some living history to be discovered in the spread-out backstreets, while its variety of boutique fashion stores, one-room bars and stylish cafes create a lasting impression.

Sights

Fujita Memorial Garden GARDENS
(藤田記念庭園; ☎0172-37-5525; 8-1 Kamishirogane; adult/child ¥310/100; ⏲9am-5pm Tue-Sun Apr-Nov) The former home and garden of the wealthy Fujita family, this beautiful example of a manicured Japanese garden is the second largest in Tōhoku. Meandering around

its many ponds, waterfalls and bridges is a delight. It also features a wonderful teahouse and a Western-styled Meiji-era mansion, which now serves as a cafe (dessert sets ¥770), replete with grand piano and lovely terrace with views of the gardens.

Hirosaki-kōen PARK

(弘前公園) Perfect for picnicking, this enormous public park has been shaped over the centuries by three castle moats, and landscaped with overhanging cherry trees (more than 5000 in total!) that bloom in late April or early May. The remains of Hirosaki-jō lie at the heart of the park. It's a lovely spot for cycling.

Apple Park PARK

(リンゴ公園; ☎0172-36-7439; www.city.hirosaki.aomori.jp/ringopark; Shimizu Tomita Aza Terasawa 125; ⏲apple season Aug-Nov; 👪) In season, an excursion to this working orchard in full view of regal Iwaki-san (p555) is an ideal family activity. Apple-picking tours leave every 30 minutes during the harvest season. It's possible to ride bikes here, but driving or catching the bus from the train station can be a better option. Check the website for details.

Neputa Mura MUSEUM

(ねぷた村; ☎0172-39-1511; 61 Kamenoko-machi; adult/child ¥500/300; ⏲9am-5pm) Come here to see some of Hirosaki's huge Neputa festival lanterns and try your hand at the giant *taiko* (drums). There are also exhibitions of local crafts. It's a short walk from the Bunka Center stop on the Dotemachi Loop Bus.

Hirosaki-jō CASTLE

(弘前城; adult/child ¥300/100; ⏲9am-5pm Apr-Nov) At the heart of Hirosaki-kōen lie the ancient remains of this castle, originally constructed in 1611. Rather tragically, only 16 years after it was built the castle was struck by lightning and burnt to the ground. Two centuries on, one of the corner towers was rebuilt and today it houses a small museum showcasing samurai weaponry.

Festivals & Events

Hirosaki Castle Snow Lantern Festival LIGHT SHOW

(ひろさきじょ　ゆきどうろう　まつり; Hirosaki-kōen; ⏲Feb) More than 200 snow lanterns and 300 miniature igloos light up the winter night in Hirosaki-kōen over five days in February.

DON'T MISS

BEST FOR SKIING

- Zaō Onsen (p569)
- Naeba (p584)
- Tazawa-ko (p564)
- Gala Yuzawa (p583)

Hirosaki Neputa Matsuri PARADE

(弘前ねぷたまつり; ⏲1-7 Aug) Giant illuminated floats parade through town, accompanied by flutes and drums for every night of Hirosaki's famed Neputa Matsuri. The festival is considered to signify ceremonial preparation for battle, expressing sentiments of bravery for what lies ahead and heartache for what lies behind.

Sleeping

★Ishiba Ryokan RYOKAN ¥

(石場旅館; ☎0172-32-9118; www.ishibaryokan.com; 55 Mototera-machi; r per person from ¥4860; P 📶) Ishiba is the only decent ryokan within Hirosaki itself, but luckily it's also excellent value. Set inside a late 19th-century property a block from the castle, the bright, large tatami rooms have attractive floor mats and drapes and face onto a tree-filled garden. Meals and rental bicycles are available.

Dormy Inn Hirosaki HOTEL ¥¥

(ドーミーイン弘前; ☎0172-37-5489; www.hotespa.net; 71-1 Hon-machi; s/d from ¥7500/10,000; P 🚭 ❄ 📶) The colourful Dormy Inn is perfectly placed on a hill near Hirosaki-kōen, affording glorious views from the rooftop onsen and *rotemburo*. Rooms are spotless and larger than average. Welcome touches include free coffee and apple juice in the lobby, complimentary ramen from 9pm to 11pm, and a shuttle bus to and from the station.

Super Hotel Hirosaki BUSINESS HOTEL ¥¥

(スーパー　ホテル弘前; ☎0172-35-9000; www.superhoteljapan.com; 148 Dote-machi; s ¥5000-7700, d ¥6200-12,800; P ❄ 📶) In the hip part of Dote-machi is this discreet business hotel, where the concrete facade belies the personal touches awaiting inside. Pillow menus, a small onsen, bicycle hire and an effortless check-in lift this hotel above its many competitors.

Eating

The best restaurants are found along Dote-machi.

Hirosaki

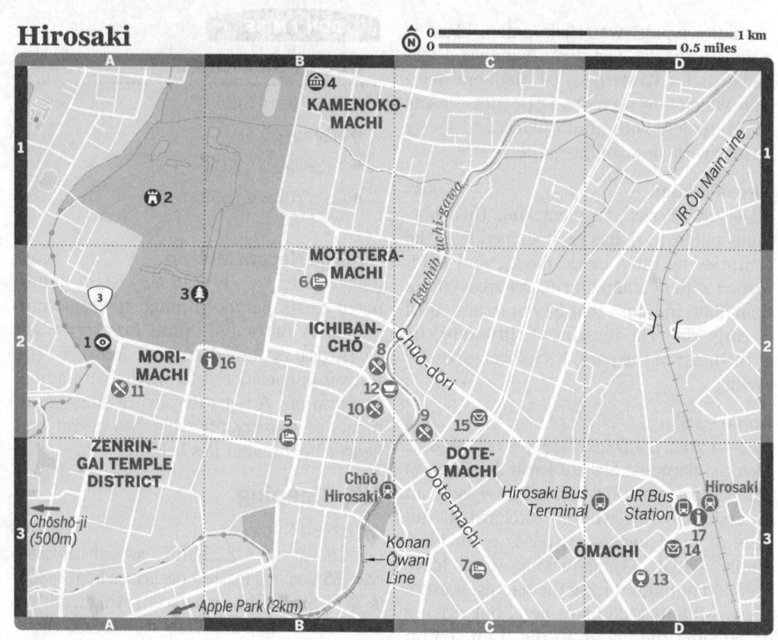

Hirosaki

Sights
1 Fujita Memorial Garden A2
2 Hirosaki-jō A1
3 Hirosaki-kōen A2
4 Neputa Mura B1

Sleeping
5 Dormy Inn Hirosaki B2
6 Ishiba Ryokan B2
7 Super Hotel Hirosaki C3

Eating
8 Kadare Yokochō B2
9 Kikufuji C2
10 Manchan B2
11 Rairai-ken A2

Drinking & Nightlife
12 Cembalo B2
13 Robbin's Nest D3

Shopping
Tanaka .... (see 8)

Information
14 Hirosaki Ekimae Post Office D3
15 Hirosaki Main Post Office C2
16 Hirosaki Sightseeing Information Center B2
17 Hirosaki Station Tourist Information Center D3

★ **Kadare Yokochō** FOOD HALL ¥

(かだれ横丁; ☎0172-38-2256; www.kadare.info; 2-1 Hyakkoku-machi; dishes from ¥400; ⏲3-11pm; 📶🌶) In the evening university students flock to this nondescript office building housing eight tiny restaurants, most doubling as bars. It's a lively local hang-out. **Hinata-bokko** (日向ぼっこ), with the orange *noren* curtains, is particularly recommended, turning out excellent *hotate misoyaki* (grilled scallops in miso; ¥600) and *ikamenchi* (fried minced squid; ¥400). English-language menus are available for most of the stalls.

Rairai-ken CHINESE ¥

(来々軒; ☎0172-32-4828; 16 Ōaza Shigemori-machi; dishes from ¥650; ⏲11am-2.30pm & 5-9pm Fri-Wed; 🌶) On the southern side of Hirosaki-kōen (p551), Rairai-ken is a lovely little Chinese restaurant in the temple district. There are lots of vegetarian options, including dark-green *yasai itame* (stir-fried vegetables) and a tofu-laden *yaki-soba* (soba noodle stir-fry), although most come for the pork-based ramen bowls, *gyōza* (dumplings) and beer.

Manchan CAFE ¥

(万茶ン; ☎0172-35-4663; 36-6 Dote-machi; apple pie ¥450; ⏰10am-6pm) In business since 1929, this old-fashioned cake and tea shop is said to be the oldest in Tōhoku. Expect to see arty types with pen in hand (or finger on screen), nibbling on a slice of famed apple pie coddled in cream. Coffee fiends shouldn't miss the siphon-brewed coffee (from ¥400). Look for the bifurcated cello out front.

Kikufuji JAPANESE ¥¥

(菊富士; ☎0172-36-3300; www.kikufuji.co.jp; 1 Sakamoto-chō; meals from ¥900; ⏰11am-3pm & 5-10pm) A true local restaurant offering a variety of set meals of hearty stews and delicate seafood concoctions. There's also an extensive list of Aomori sake, which you can try in an *otameshi* (sampler) set of three. Paper lanterns and folk music add atmosphere without being kitschy. Look for the vertical white sign out front.

Drinking & Nightlife

Cembalo COFFEE

(チェンバロ; ☎0172-33-6546; 42 Dote-machi; ⏰10.30am-5.30pm Thu-Tue) Hirosaki's students head to Cembalo to sip strong coffee and munch on cinnamon and honey toast while they type ostentatiously on their laptops. Light and bright, with friendly staff, it's a perfect break from wandering nearby Hirosaki-kōen.

Robbin's Nest PUB

(ロビンズネスト; ☎090-6450-1730; www.robbins-nest.jp; 1-3-16 Ōmachi; ⏰5pm-late) This is an excellent Japanese rendition of a British pub. It's intimate and there's no cover charge (except sometimes when bands are playing), frequent live music, Guinness on tap and a few tables on the outside terrace for alfresco drinking (in the warmer months).

Shopping

Tanaka ARTS & CRAFTS

(田中屋; ☎0172-36-0111; www.tanaka-meisan.jp; 24-10 Dote-machi; ⏰9am-6pm) Find beautiful examples of boldly coloured *tsugaru-nuri* (lacquerware from the Tsugaru region) at this elegant store. Even if you're not looking to buy (prices are high) it's worth stopping in to admire the handiwork of local artisans.

Information

Hirosaki Sightseeing Information Center (弘前市立観光館; ☎0172-37-5501; www.en-hirosaki.com; 2-1 Shimoshirogane-chō; ⏰9am-6pm) Situated inside the Kankōkan (tourism building), you can rent bikes and grab all manner of English-language materials here. There's also a cafe and a souvenir shop.

Hirosaki Station Tourist Information Center (弘前市観光案内所; ☎0172-26-3600; ⏰8.45am-6pm; 📶) On the ground floor of JR Hirosaki Station. The best way to see the city is by bicycle – rent one here (per day ¥500). Very helpful staff.

Getting There & Away

Tokkyū (limited express) trains on the JR Ōu main line run hourly between Aomori and Hirosaki (¥670, 50 minutes), and Hirosaki and Akita (¥4450, 2¼ hours).

For bus services to other cities, the **JR Bus Station** is directly in front of the JR Hirosaki Station.

Getting Around

The Dotemachi Loop Bus (single ride ¥100) traverses the downtown area every 30 minutes from 10am to 6pm; buy tickets on board (exact change only). It departs from in front of JR Hirosaki Station.

Catch buses around the town from the **Hirosaki Bus Terminal**, 200m west from the west exit of the JR station.

Bicycle rental (¥500 per day) is available at either tourist information centre from May to November.

The Tsugaru free pass (adult/child ¥2060/1030) covers area buses and trains, including those to Iwaki-san and Shirakami-sanchi, plus a few good nearby onsen, for two consecutive days. Enquire at the Hirosaki Station Tourist Information Center.

Towada-ko

☎0176

Hemmed in by rocky shores and dense forests, sparkling Towada-ko (十和田湖) is the largest crater lake in Honshū (52km in circumference) and a fabulous natural attraction for those seeking solitude. Towada-Hachimantai National Park once bore witness to a series of violent volcanic eruptions; today the only action is the quiet trickle of the Oirase Keiryū mountain stream, winding its way to the Pacific Ocean. The main tourist hub, Yasumiya, is a small village with a lovely waterfront promenade. The other lakeside village, Nenokuchi, is little more than a transport hub.

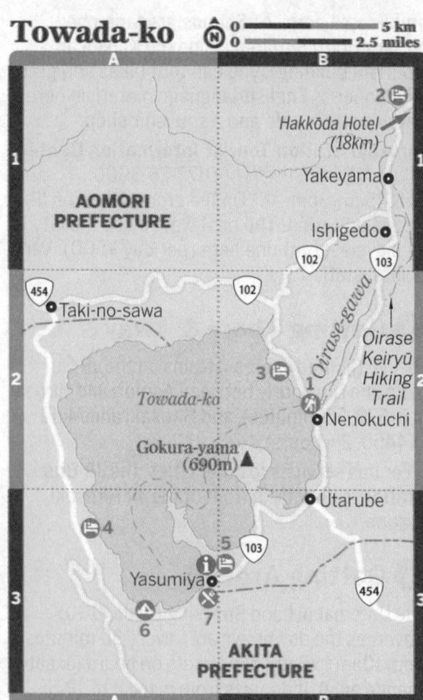

Towada-ko

Activities, Courses & Tours

1 Oirase Keiryū B2

Sleeping

2 Oirase Keiryū Hotel B1
3 That Sounds Good B2
4 Towada Hotel A3
5 Towadako Backpackers B3
6 Towadako Oide Camping Ground A3

Eating

7 Marine Blue A3

Activities

★ Oirase Keiryū HIKING

(奥入瀬渓流) This incredibly picturesque, meandering river is marked by cascading waterfalls, carved-out gorges and gurgling rapids. Walkers can follow its path for a 14km stretch connecting Nenokuchi, on the eastern shore of the lake, to Yakeyama, from where relatively frequent buses return to either Nenokuchi (¥610, 30 minutes) or the main lakeside tourist hub of Yasumiya (¥1130, one hour).

The entire hike should take about three hours. Set out in the early morning or late afternoon to avoid slow-moving coach parties.

Sleeping

Yasumiya is the lake's accommodation hub, with a smattering of hotels and guesthouses. Other options are scattered around the lakeshore. Rates peak during August (summer holidays) and October, when autumn leaves blaze red.

Towadako Backpackers HOSTEL ¥

(十和田湖バックパッカーズ; ☎0176-75-2606; www.laketowada.wordpress.com; 116-201 Yasumiya, Towada-ko; dm/s/d incl 2 meals ¥3100/6600/7200; P@Wi-Fi) This is a very unassuming hostel with a terrific communal atmosphere and hearty, simple meals. Shared facilities are clean and spacious, while the dormitories are Western-style and comfortable, if a little congested; the twin cottages are preferable. The location is great, just a steep 10-minute walk to the lake. Free bike rental available.

Towadako Oide Camping Ground CAMPGROUND ¥

(十和田湖生出キャンプ場; ☎0176-75-2368; www.bes.or.jp/towada; 486 Yasumiya, Towada-kohan; per person ¥300, campsite ¥200, powered sites ¥3000; ⏲25 Apr-5 Nov; P) This pretty riverside campground has well-maintained facilities, and rental gear (tents etc) available.

★ Oirase Keiryū Hotel HOTEL ¥¥¥

(奥入瀬渓流ホテル; ☎0176-74-2121; www.oirase-keiryuu.jp; 231 Tochikubo, Oirase; s/d incl 2 meals from ¥18,000/31,000; P Wi-Fi) One of our favourite hotels in Tōhoku sits by the trailhead for the lovely Oirase Keiryū hike. It's just the place to relax after tackling the trail in one of numerous wood-panelled riverside onsen baths. Rooms are a stylish mix of Japanese and Western decor, while dining occurs in a kind of forest-facing hardwood cathedral that fills with natural light.

Free transfers from Shin-Aomori Station are available.

Towada Hotel HOTEL ¥¥¥

(十和田ホテル; ☎0176-75-1122; www.towada-hotel.com; Namariyama, Kosaka-machi; r per person incl 2 meals from ¥14,000; P Wi-Fi) The pre-WWII Towada Hotel has a dramatic lobby of hulking timbers, rising to a chandelier-lit cathedral ceiling. The historic main building has elegant Japanese-style rooms (with and without baths); avoid the drab Western-style annexe. All have lake views, as do the communal baths. Dining is a treat.

A path leads from the hotel to the lake's secluded southwestern shore.

Eating

There are a few simple tourist restaurants and a grocery store in Yasumiya, but nothing stays open after sunset. Most travellers eat at their accommodation.

Marine Blue CAFE ¥
(マリンブルー; ☎0179-75-3025; www.marineblue.jp; Kosaka-machi, Yasumiya; apple pie ¥500; ⊙8am-6pm) All the coffee shops in Yasumiya have similar offerings – coffee, apple juice and locally made apple pie – but this one at the southern end of the village has the best location, right on the lakeshore, with a small terrace overlooking the water. It also rents out paddleboats (¥1000 per 20 minutes).

Information

Tourist Information Center (十和田ビジターセンター; ☎0176-75-1015; 486 Aza-Towadakohan, Yasumiya; ⊙9am-4.30pm Thu-Tue) In a large wooden building near the waterfront. Has English-language pamphlets and maps, and also some interesting displays on the region's flora and fauna.

Getting There & Away

Renting a car from Aomori or Hirosaki will give you the freedom to make the most of this picturesque and remote area. Rte 103 runs south from Aomori to Towada-ko.

JR buses run from Aomori, through Yakeyama (¥2300, two hours), to Towada-ko-eki in Yasumiya (¥3090, three hours); departures are highly seasonal and infrequent in winter. See www.jrbustohoku.co.jp for schedules.

Getting Around

A limited network of local buses run around the lakeside. Infrequent connections are reason enough to bring your own wheels.

Hakkōda-san

☎017

Honshū's northernmost volcanic range is a paradise for hikers between May and October, while in winter months, serious powder fiends descend, off-piste, for some of the best untapped skiing and snowboarding in Japan. For those needing to thaw, Hakkōda-san (八甲田山) is also home to one of Tōhoku's best onsen, Sukayu (p557).

The Hakkōda-san area is synonymous with a sad history: in 1902 a regiment of 210 Japanese soldiers on a winter training exercise were caught here in a severe snowstorm. All but 11 perished, carving out a place for Hakkōda-san in the collective Japanese psyche.

Sights & Activities

Hakkōda Ropeway CABLE CAR
(八甲田山ロープウェー; ☎017-738-0343; www.hakkoda-ropeway.jp; 1-12 Kansuizawa, Arakawa; one way/return ¥1180/1850; ⊙9am-4.20pm Mar-Oct, to 3.40pm Nov-Feb) For anyone wanting a taste of the alpine without having to brave the steep

OFF THE BEATEN TRACK

IWAKI-SAN & SHIRAKAMI-SANCHI

Looming over Hirosaki, sacred Iwaki-san (岩木山; Mt Iwaki; 1625m) looks remarkably like Fuji-san from certain angles and at times seems so close you could almost touch it. Should you wish to, daily buses depart the Hirosaki Station bus terminal for **Iwaki-san-jinja** (岩木山神社; ¥720, 40 minutes, April to October), where tradition dictates summit-bound travellers should first make an offering before attempting the ascent. The views from the top are remarkable. A different trail takes you down, past the smaller peak of **Tori-no-umi-san** (鳥ノ海山) to the village of **Dake-onsen** (岳温泉), from where infrequent buses chug back to Hirosaki (¥1050, one hour). The entire 9km hike should take you about seven hours. (If you were wondering, Iwaki-san's last recorded eruption was in 1863.)

Southwest of Iwaki-san is the isolated Shirakami-sanchi (白神山地), a World Heritage–listed virgin forest of Japanese beech trees. From the bus stop at Anmon Aqua Village, an hour-long trail leads into the woods to the three **Anmon Falls** (暗門の滝; Anmon-no-taki), the highest of which is 42m. This is part of the park's 'buffer zone', which is open to the public without permit. Two buses depart Hirosaki Station bus terminal each morning for Anmon Aqua Village (one way/return ¥1650/2470, one hour, May to October) and two return in the afternoon.

Enquire at the helpful Hirosaki Sightseeing Information Center (p553) for maps and timetables if you intend on making either of these trips.

OFF THE BEATEN TRACK

AONI ONSEN

You can't get much more romantic and isolated than **Rampu-no-yado** (ランプの宿; ☎0172-54-8588; www.yo.rim.or.jp/~aoni; 1-7 Aoni-sawa, Taki-no-ue, Okiura, Kuroishi; r per person incl 2 meals from ¥9870, day bathing ¥520; ⏲day bathing 10am-3pm; 🅿) in little Aoni Onsen (青荷温泉). Plopped in a deep valley surrounded by heavily forested mountains, this rustic ryokan is the ultimate escape from modernity: oil lamps *(rampu)* are used to light the corridors, though electricity has now reached the basic tatami rooms. As the sun goes down and the stars come out over the valley, the effect is magical. Have your camera and tripod at the ready.

Numerous indoor baths and *rotemburo* (outdoor baths) are spread over several small wooden buildings along both sides of a stream, crossed by a footbridge. With the lack of distractions, you'll have plenty of time to soak and think about what's important. Dining is a delicious and communal affair, featuring hearty, healthy, mostly vegetarian, locavore cuisine.

Aoni Onsen is located alongside Rte 102 between Hirosaki and Towada-ko. Getting here requires effort or a rental car. Without a car take the private Kōnan Tetsudō rail line from Hirosaki to Kuroishi (¥460, 30 minutes), then connect with a Kōnan bus for Niji-no-ko (¥830, 30 minutes), from where shuttle buses run to Aoni (free, 30 minutes, four daily). From December through March the narrow lane that winds down to Aoni Onsen is closed to private vehicles – if you're coming by car, park at the Niji-no-ko bus station and catch the free shuttle bus.

Advance reservations essential. Credit cards are not accepted; bring cash.

ascent, this scenic ropeway whisks you quickly up to the summit of Tamoyachi-dake (田茂萢岳; 1324m). From there you can follow an elaborate network of hiking trails, although purists prefer the magnificent one-day Hakkōda-san loop that starts and finishes just outside the Sukayu Onsen Ryokan.

★Hakkōda-san HIKING

(八甲田山) Hakkōda-san's gruelling but rewarding 12km day hike begins from the car park above Sukayu Onsen Ryokan, in the shadow of Ōdake (大岳; 1584m). The ridge trail continues to Ido-dake (井戸岳; 1550m) and Akakura-dake (赤倉岳; 1548m) before connecting with Tamoyachi-dake (田茂萢岳; 1324m) and looping via the ropeway (p555) back to Sukayu ryokan.

Things start out relatively flat as you wind through marshlands, but eventually the pitch starts to increase: a good level of fitness and some hiking experience is recommended. If you time your hike for mid- to late October, expect to whip your camera out for the early autumn foliage.

Hakkōda Ski Park SNOW SPORTS

(八甲田スキー場; ☎017-738-0343; www.hakkoda-ski.com; 5-ride pass ¥5050; ⏲9am-4.20pm) For all its fluffy white goodness, Tamoyachi-dake (田茂萢岳; 1324m) is a fairly modest set-up, with five official runs (three groomed, two ungroomed) beginning at the top of the Hakkōda Ropeway (p555). A two-seater chairlift serves two of the easier runs, while the 5km **Forest Course**, which cuts through the treeline, is for serious players only.

Note that weather conditions can suddenly become severe and getting lost is easy. Equipment rental (¥3500 per day) and a handful of dining options are available in the ropeway terminals.

Come spring it's possible to explore a network of unofficial hiking trails that extend to some of the nearby peaks. Even experienced alpinists should only go backcountry with a local guide.

Sleeping & Eating

Hikers and campers should bring their own supplies. Most accommodation options can provide proper meals.

Sukayu Camping Ground CAMPGROUND ¥

(酸ヶ湯キャンプ場; ☎017-738-6566; www.sukayu.jp/camp; per person ¥500, campsite from ¥500; ⏲Jun-Oct; 🅿) Campers will be pleased with this lush, open campsite, with clean facilities and rental equipment available. It's located at the end of a small access road immediately south of Sukayu Onsen Ryokan, a short stroll from the Hakkōda-san trailhead.

★Sukayu Onsen Ryokan RYOKAN ¥¥
(酸ヶ湯温泉旅館; ☎017-738-6400; www.sukayu.jp; 50 Arakawa; r per person incl 2 meals from ¥8100; P ⊖) Straight from an *ukiyo-e* (woodblock print), Sukayu's cavernous, dark-wooded bathhouse is a delight for the senses. The water is hot, acidic and sulphurous (don't get it in your eyes) – nothing beats the feel of its penetrating heat. Note that the main bath is *konyoku* (mixed bathing). Rooms in the sprawling old-fashioned inn are simple but comfortable, with shared facilities.

Recently updated, more expensive rooms (from ¥12,420 per person) have en suite toilets. Visitors can use the baths 7am–5.30pm (admission ¥1000).

Hakkōda-sansō LODGE ¥¥
(八甲田山荘; ☎017-728-1512; www.hakkoda-sanso.com; 1-61 Kansuizawa, Arakawa; r per person incl 2 meals from ¥6000; P ⊖ ⓦ) This basic ski lodge is conveniently located right at the base of the Hakkōda Ropeway (p555). Rooms have their own TV, but not all enjoy mountain views. The dining area, with picture windows facing the slopes, also serves lunch.

Hakkōda Hotel HOTEL ¥¥¥
(八甲田ホテル; ☎017-728-2000; www.hakkodahotel.co.jp; 1 Minami-arakawayama, Arakawa; s/d incl breakfast from ¥22,000/27,000; P ⊖ ❄ ⓦ) Great for powder hounds in winter and hikers in summer, this mountain lodge appeals to muscle-sore adrenaline junkies, who like to dump their gear and pass out, then wake up at dinnertime to eat like royalty. It's open and spacious, with beautiful views of the surrounding mountains. It's not cheap, but you can save by self-catering at dinner.

ℹ Getting There & Away

JR buses leave from stop 11 outside JR Aomori Station, stopping at Hakkōda Ropeway (p555) train station (¥1100, one hour) and the next stop, Sukayu Onsen (¥1340, 70 minutes). The bus continues to Towada-ko train station (from Sukayu ¥2080, 1½ hours). Bus schedules vary seasonally. See www.jrbustohoku.co.jp.

Shimokita Peninsula

☎0175

Wild, short-legged horses, craggy rock formations, lush, forested mountains and a frontier history give the remote, axe-shaped Shimokita Peninsula (下北半島; Shimokita-hantō) the air of travel legend. Jet-black ravens swarm about its sulphur-infused tributaries, where some locals believe Buddhist souls come if they cannot rest. The region is centred on Osore-zan (恐山; 874m), a barren volcano that is regarded as one of the most sacred places in Japan.

There are four main towns on the peninsula: Mutsu (first if arriving by car or train), Wakinosawa (first if arriving by ferry), Ōma (the furthest point north on the Japanese mainland) and Sai (the departure point for boats to Hotoke-ga-ura).

Sights

★Osorezan-bodaiji BUDDHIST TEMPLE
(恐山菩提寺; ☎0175-22-3825; adult/child ¥500/400; ⏲6am-6pm May-Oct) This holy shrine at Osore-zan's summit is a moving, mesmerisingly atmospheric and beautiful place honouring Jizō Bosatsu, protector of children and a much-loved deity in Japanese mythology. It's also said to be located at the entrance to hell: a small brook that flows into the beautiful crater lake, Usori, is said to represent the legendary Sanzu river, which souls must cross on their way to the afterlife. Fittingly people visit to mourn lost children or to commune with the dead.

Several stone statues of Jizō overlook hills of craggy, sulphur-strewn rocks and hissing vapour. Visitors are encouraged to help lost souls with their underworld penance by adding stones to the cairns. You can even bathe on hell's doorstep at the free onsen off to the side as you approach the main hall. Allow an hour or two to wander the landscape in deep contemplation.

Five daily buses run to and from JR Shimokita Station and Osore-zan (¥800, 45 minutes). If you'd like to spend more time on the mountain, it is possible to stay overnight at the temple (¥12,000 per person including two meals); reserve in advance.

Activities

Hotoke-ga-ura BOATING
(仏ヶ浦; www.saiteikikanko.jp) The western edge of the peninsula is a spectacular stretch of coastline dotted with 100m-high,

DON'T MISS

BEST HIKES

- Dewa Sanzan (p572)
- Hakkōda-san
- Iwaki-san (p555)
- Akita Komaga-take (p564)
- Oirase Keiryū (p554)

wind-carved cliffs, which are said to resemble images of Buddha. For non-drivers, five daily boats depart for 90-minute sightseeing round trips from Sai to Hotoke-ga-ura between May and October (¥2400). Services are often suspended in poor weather.

Sleeping

A few basic business hotels are found in Mutsu, close to the Shimokita JR train station. Most people, however, visit on a day trip from Aomori.

★**Wakinosawa Youth Hostel** HOSTEL ¥ (脇野沢ユースホステル; ☎0175-44-2341; www.wakinosawa.com; 41 Senokawame, Wakinosawa; dm ¥4200, breakfast/dinner ¥630/1050; P ⊖ 📶) Run by a wildlife photographer who takes pride in the region's natural attractions (including snow monkeys!), this remote hostel is perched on a hillside at Wakinosawa, about 15 minutes west of the ferry pier – call ahead for a pick-up. There's a homely feel about the wooden rooms, which are a touch above typical hostel standard.

While it helps to speak a bit of Japanese, the genial owners are extremely accommodating.

Getting There & Away

BOAT

Sii Line (p549) operates at least two daily ferries between Wakinosawa and Aomori (¥2610, one hour).

Tsugaru Kaikyō (p549) runs two to three ferries daily from Ōma to Hakodate on Hokkaidō (adult/car from ¥1810/9870, 1½ hours).

TRAIN

Trains traverse the JR Ōminato line between Aomori and Mutsu (¥2180, 1½ to two hours), with most requiring a change at Noheji. There are two stations in Mutsu: Shimokita and Ōminato. The first is of the most use to travellers, as most buses depart from there for other locations across the peninsula.

Getting Around

It's best to have a car to explore these parts.

From May to October there are up to five buses departing from JR Shimokita Station for Osorezan (¥800, 45 minutes). Year-round, buses connect Shimokita and Ōma (¥1990, two hours). There are a few buses each day to Wakinosawa from JR Ōminato Station (¥1800, 70 minutes).

AKITA PREFECTURE

Akita Prefecture (秋田県; Akita-ken) nestles between the Sea of Japan and the spectacular Ōu-sanmyaku and Dewa ranges, where hikers and pilgrims navigate their way to shrines and summits. In a prefecture overflowing with high-altitude hot springs, Nyūtō Onsen stands out for its variety of accommodation and its proximity to Tazawa-ko, an under-visited volcanic lake perfect for swimming in summer. The charming feudal city of Kakunodate is the cultural highlight of the region – its old samurai houses, pine-lined streets and cherry-tree-covered riverbanks make it one of the most photogenic historic towns in Japan.

ŌMA TUNA

Ōma, at the tip of the Shimokita Peninsula, may look like the end of the earth, but it's the centre of the universe when it comes to tuna. The frigid waters of the Tsugaru Strait directly off the coast are said to yield the tastiest *maguro* (bluefin tuna) in Japan. At the height of the season, prize catch can sell for up to ¥25,000 per kilogram.

Ōma's fishing co-ops catch fish the old-fashioned way, with hand lines and live bait (and a lot of muscle – these fish are enormous). It's a way of life that sets them squarely against large-scale commercial interests and in favour of greater regulation to protect the bluefin population.

Tuna is caught fresh between late August and January, although most shops close up by mid-November when the cold winds turn fierce.

You'll see it on the menu at restaurants all over the peninsula. If you make the trip up to Ōma, try **Kaikyōsō** (海峡荘; ☎0175-37-3691; 17-734 Ōma-taira, Ōma; meals from ¥1200; ⏲11am-3pm late Apr-early Nov). The bright-green building (which looks more like a hardware store than a purveyor of fine raw fish) does an excellent *maguro-don* (tuna sashimi over rice) with thick, melt-in-your-mouth cuts of *akami* (lean red meat), *chū-toro* (medium-grade fatty tuna) and *ō-toro* (top-grade fatty tuna).

Akita Prefecture

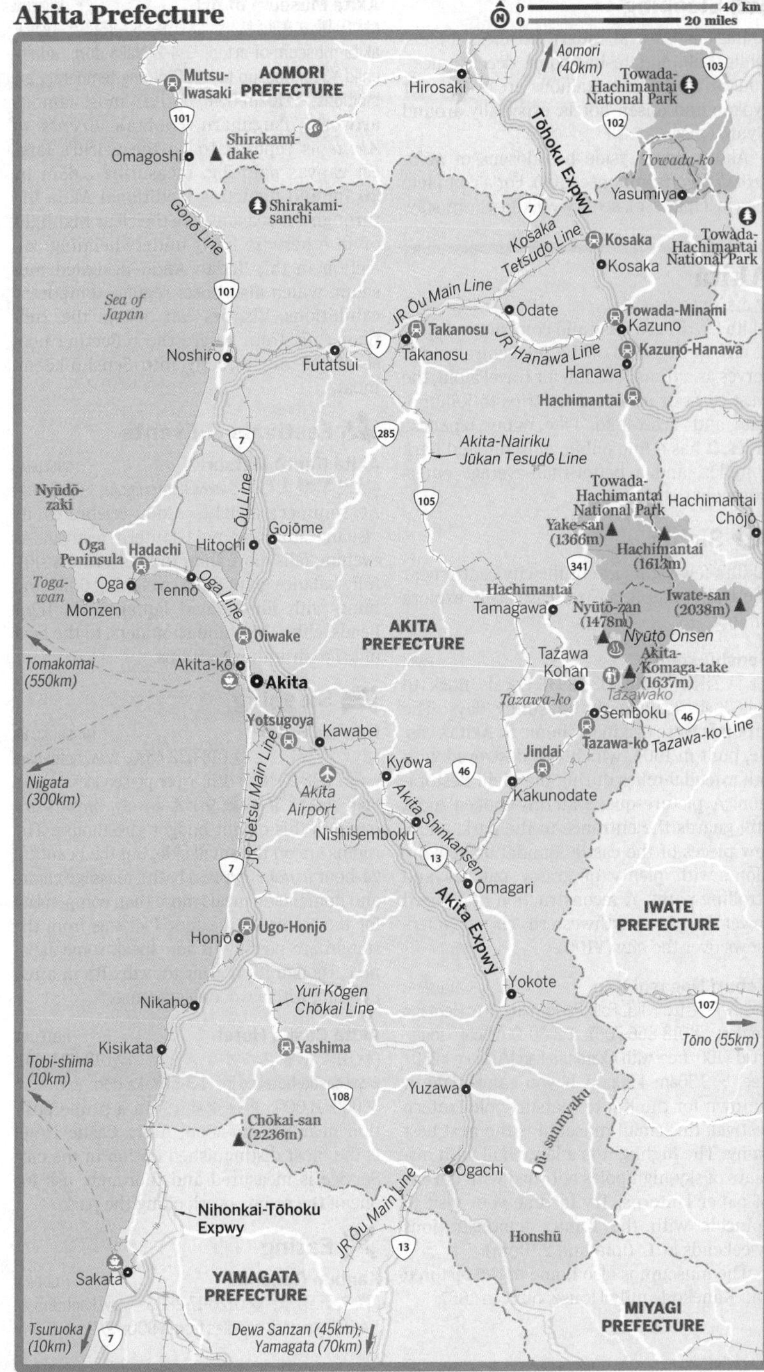

Sleeping

Akita has several smart business hotels, while Kakunodate has some decent guesthouses. In the mountainous areas, look for ryokan and onsen hotels, especially around Nyūtō Onsen.

Akita's countryside has dozens of *nōka minshuku* (farmhouse inns). For a complete list (in Japanese), see www.akita-gt.org/stay.

Akita

☎018 / POP 315,814

Akita (秋田) is a busy and compact industrial city in the west of the prefecture, which serves as a transport hub for travel along the west coast or as a base for trips to Kakunodate and Tazawa-ko. Like many Japanese cities, it has a fine public museum and park complex, and a better-than-average entertainment district.

Sights

Akita's few sights are in the city centre near the train station, so you can easily explore on foot.

Senshū-kōen PARK

(千秋公園; ☎018-832-5893) Locals flock to this lush, leafy oasis on sunny days. The grounds were originally home to Akita's castle, built in 1604, which was destroyed with other feudal relics during the Meiji Restoration. A picturesque, waterlily-choked moat still guards the entrance to the park, and a few pieces of the castle foundation remain, along with plenty of grassy patches and strolling paths. A reconstruction of a guard tower in the northwestern corner offers views over the city (¥100).

Neburi Nagashi Kan MUSEUM

(民俗芸能伝承館, Folk Performing Arts Heritage Center; ☎018-866-7091; 1-3-30 Ō-machi; adult/child ¥100/free, with Akarenga-kan Museum ¥250/free; ⏲9.30am-4.30pm) If you can't make it to town for the Kantō Matsuri pole lantern festival, this small museum is the next best thing. The highlight is a large hall with displays of sky-high poles adorned with dozens of paper lanterns. Try to time your visit to coincide with the Kantō demonstrations (weekends at 1.30pm and 2.10pm).

The museum is also home to the restored Old Kaneko Family House, built in 1887.

Akita Museum of Art MUSEUM

(秋田県立美術館; ☎018-853-8686; www.akita-museum-of-art.jp; 1-4-2 Naka-dōri; adult/child ¥310/free, up to ¥800 during temporary exhibitions; ⏲10am-6pm) Akita's most famous artwork, Tsuguharu Foujita's *Events of Akita*, is reputed to be the world's largest canvas painting, measuring 3.65m by 20.5m and depicting traditional Akita life through the seasons. It's the clear highlight of an otherwise fairly underwhelming collection in this Tadao Ando–designed museum, which also hosts regular temporary exhibitions. Visitors can rest in the 2nd-floor cafe, from where the reflecting pool seems to run directly into Senshū-kōen's moat.

Festivals & Events

Akita Kantō Matsuri CULTURAL

(秋田竿燈まつり; www.kantou.gr.jp; ⏲3-6 Aug) At summer's height, Akita celebrates its visually stunning pole lantern festival. As evening falls more than 160 performers skilfully balance giant poles, weighing 60kg and hung with illuminated lanterns, on their heads, chins, hips and shoulders, to the beat of *taiko* drumming groups.

Sleeping

Naniwa Hotel MINSHUKU ¥¥

(ホテルなにわ; ☎018-832-4570; www.hotel-naniwa.jp; 6-18-27 Naka-dōri; r per person incl 2 meals from ¥6000; P ⊖ ✻ ≋) A lovely *mama-san* oversees this quaint budget guesthouse. The rooms are on the small side, but the beautiful 24-hour *hinoki* (cypress bath), massage chairs and homemade meals more than compensate for the cramped quarters. Pick-ups from the station are possible if you speak some Japanese, though it's not far to walk. It's in a red building with a wooden entrance.

Akita Castle Hotel HOTEL ¥¥

(秋田キャッスルホテル; ☎018-834-1141; www.castle-hotel.co.jp; 1-3-5 Naka-dōri; s/d from ¥6000/11,000; P ⊖ ✻ @ ≋) In a prime position near Senshū-kōen, Akita Castle Hotel is the most distinguished option in the city. Service is measured and thorough; ask for one of the rooms overlooking the park.

Eating

Kanbun Gonendō UDON ¥

(寛文五年堂; ☎0120-17-2886; www.kanbun5.jp; 1-4-3 Naka-dōri; noodles from ¥800; ⏲11am-10pm;

Akita

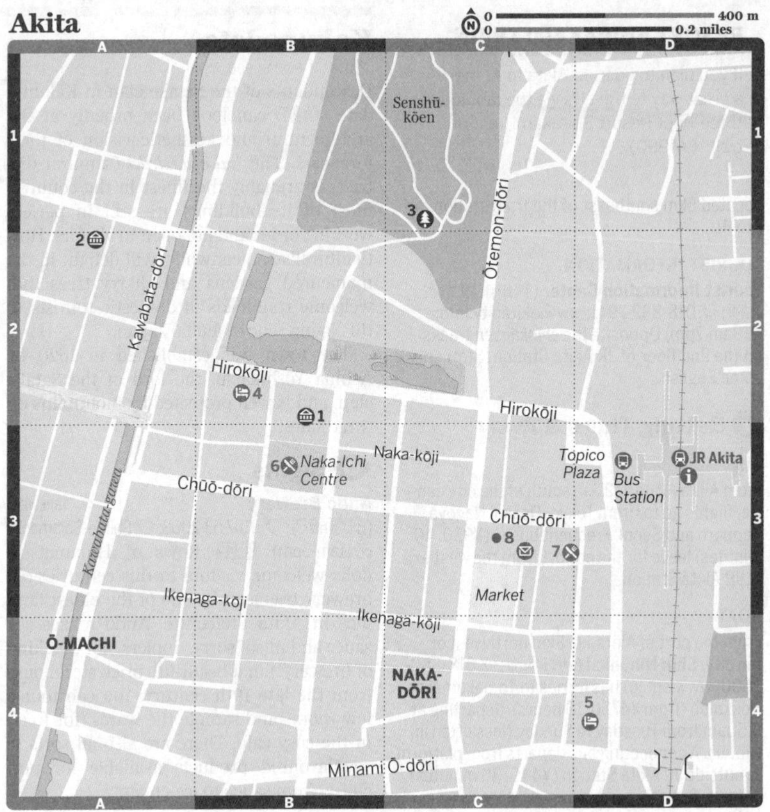

) This bright, well-regarded shop specialises in *inaniwa udon,* a thin chewy wheat noodle that originated in Akita Prefecture in the 1600s. Locals seek out the delicacy, often served cold with various sauces, while on shopping forays around the Naka-Ichi centre. Vegetarian dishes are available; ask before ordering.

Nagaya Sakaba IZAKAYA ¥¥
(秋田長屋酒場; 018-837-0505; www.marutomisuisan.jpn.com/nagaya-akita; 4-16-17 Naka-dōri; small dishes from ¥600; 5pm-late) Rebuilt after a 2017 fire, Nagaya Sakaba is easy to spot due to the massive Namahage demons above the entrance. Sake flows freely once you've negotiated the Japanese-only menu. If in doubt, just shout *'osusume'* (recommendation) and staff will happily bring various fish dishes accompanied by the signature pounded rice cake.

Akita

Sights

1 Akita Museum of Art B2
2 Neburi Nagashi Kan A2
3 Senshū-kōen C1

Sleeping

4 Akita Castle Hotel B2
5 Naniwa Hotel D4

Eating

6 Kanbun Gonendō B3
7 Nagaya Sakaba C3

Transport

8 Toyota Rent a Car C3

Information

MEDICAL SERVICES

Akita Red Cross Hospital (秋田赤十字病院; 24hr emergency hotline 018-829-5000; www.akita-med.jrc.or.jp; 222-1 Nawashiro-sawa; outpatient services 8-11.30am Mon-Fri)

RESORT SHIRAKAMI TRAIN

If you plan to go from Akita to Aomori, a great way to travel is via the fabulous three-hour Resort Shirakami 'resort train' (¥4950).

Located 5km southeast of the train station, off Rte 41.

TOURIST INFORMATION

Tourist Information Center (秋田市観光案内所; ☎018-832-7941; www.akitacity.info; ⏰9am-7pm) Opposite the *shinkansen* tracks on the 2nd floor of JR Akita Station. Staff speak some English.

 Getting There & Away

AIR

From Akita Airport, 21km south of the city centre, flights go to/from Tokyo, Osaka, Nagoya, Sapporo and Seoul. Frequent buses (¥930, 40 minutes) leave for the airport from the west exit at JR Akita Station.

BOAT

From the port of Akita-kō, 8km northwest of the city, **Shin Nihonkai** (新日本海; ☎018-880-2600; www.snf.jp) has ferries to Tomakomai on Hokkaidō (from ¥4730, 10 hours), departing at 6.50am from Tuesday to Sunday (less often in winter). A connecting bus departs from platform 11 outside JR Akita Station (¥440, 30 minutes).

BUS

Highway buses depart from the west exit of the train station, and connect Akita to major cities throughout Honshū.

CAR & MOTORCYCLE

Rental-car outlets are scattered around the train station, including the reliable **Toyota Rent a Car** (トヨタレンタカー; ☎018-833-0100; www.rent.toyota.co.jp; 4-6-5 Naka-dōri; ⏰8am-8pm), a few minutes' walk west.

TRAIN

The JR Akita *shinkansen* (bullet train) runs hourly between the northern terminus of Akita and the southern terminus of Tokyo (¥17,800, four hours) via Kakunodate (¥3020, 45 minutes) and Tazawa-ko (¥3360, one hour).

Infrequent local trains also run on the JR Ōu main line between Akita and Kakunodate (¥1320, 1½ hours), with a change at Ōmagari to the JR Tazawako line. There are a few *tokkyū* (limited express) trains each day on the JR Inaho line, connecting Akita with Niigata (¥7210, 3½ hours).

Kakunodate

☎0187 / POP 12,500

Descendants of the Satake clan in Kakunodate (角館) can look back proudly at the architectural and aesthetic vision of their forebears. The *buke yashiki* (samurai district) is arguably the finest in the country; most of its buildings are still in perfect working order and are open to visitors. Horticulturalists, meanwhile, will delight in the manicured gardens and cherry trees that welcome trainloads of domestic tourists to this living relic of feudal Japan.

The town was established in 1620 by Ashina Yoshikatsu, the lord of the Satake clan, and is well protected by mountains on three sides.

Sights

Andō Brewery BREWERY
(安藤醸造; ☎0187-53-2008; 27 Shimo-Shinmachi; ⏰11am-5pm) FREE Rows of Hinamatsuri dolls welcome visitors to this centuries-old brewery overseen by one of the oldest families in Akita Prefecture. Andō makes soy sauce and miso (sorry, tipplers, not that kind of brewery!) in a beautiful, brick storehouse from the late 19th century. You can tour a few rooms and sample the wares (for free!) in the cosy cafe. There are also all sorts of soy-flavoured products available for purchase, from sauce to ice cream.

Bukeyashiki Ishiguro-ke HISTORIC BUILDING
(武家屋敷石黒家; ☎0187-55-1496; 1 Omote-machi; adult/child ¥400/200; ⏰9am-5pm) Built in 1809 as the residence of the Ishiguro family, advisers to the Satake clan, this is one of the oldest buildings in the samurai district. Descendants of the family still live here, and offer tours around parts of the house. In addition to samurai gear, don't miss the weathered maps and the precision scales for doling out rice.

Aoyagi Samurai Manor Museum MUSEUM
(角館歴史村青柳家; Kakunodate Rekishi-mura Aoyagi-ke; ☎0187-54-3257; www.samuraiworld.com; 3 Omote-machi; adult/child ¥500/200; ⏰9am-5pm, to 4.30pm in winter) The restored Aoyagi family compound is impressive in its own right, but inside each well-maintained structure is a fascinating exhibition of family heirlooms. The collection spans generations and includes centuries-old samurai weaponry, folk art and valuable antiques, along with gramophones and classic jazz records.

Kakunodate Cherry-Bark Craft Center ARTS CENTRE
(角館樺細工伝承館, Kakunodate Kabazaiku Denshōkan; 0187-54-1700; 10-1 Omote-machi; adult/child ¥300/150; 9am-5pm Apr-Nov, to 4.30pm Dec-Mar) Inside this elegant building you'll find exhibits and demonstrations of *kabazaiku*, the craft of covering household or decorative items in fine strips of cherry bark. This pursuit was first taken up by lower-ranking and masterless samurai in times of hardship.

Festivals & Events

Kakunodate Sakura CULTURAL
(角館の桜; mid-Apr–early May) On the river embankment, a 2km stretch of cherry trees becomes a tunnel of pure pink during the *hanami* (blossom viewing) season. Some of the *shidare-zakura* (drooping cherry) trees in the *buke yashiki* (samurai district) are up to 300 years old.

Sleeping

Kakunodate has some lovely atmospheric places to stay, as well as a handful of business hotels. Room rates rise sharply during festivals and in cherry-blossom season (mid-April to early May).

Iori MINSHUKU ¥
(庵; 0187-55-2262; www.akita-gt.org/stay/minshuku/iori.html; 65 Maeda, Ogata; r per person incl 1/2 meals ¥5000/6000; P) Kakunodate is still a largely agricultural community, and this working farm nestled among rice paddies 3km north of the train station provides an authentic opportunity to experience its peaceful rural setting. Accommodation is in stylish, minimalist cabins with whitewashed walls, dark-wood beams, fresh tatami and indigo cushions; it's great value, especially with meals included.

Pick-up from Kakunodate Station is possible.

Tamachi Bukeyashiki Hotel BOUTIQUE HOTEL ¥¥
(田町武家屋敷ホテル; 0187-52-1700; www.bukeyashiki.jp; 23 Ta-machi; r per person from ¥13,500; P ❄ 📶) With an idyllic location in the historic Bukeyashiki area, Tamachi is a surprisingly modern hotel, blending Japanese and Western aesthetics. All rooms have the requisite dark wooden beams and paper lanterns, but the communal areas are largely typical of European boutique hotels.

★Wabizakura RYOKAN ¥¥¥
(わびざくら; 0187-47-3511; www.wabizakura.com; 2-8 Sasayama, Nishikichokadoya; r per person incl 2 meals ¥38,000; P ❄ 📶) Deep within the forest, surrounded by trees, this stunning ryokan is housed in a 200-year-old building that was carefully relocated from Iwate Prefecture. With distinct Western interior-design influences, Wabizakura (a type of cherry blossom) is popular with well-off Tokyoites seeking refined solitude in a historical setting. The 10 suites include outdoor onsen and stylish lounge areas. Very hard to leave.

It's 15km from Kakunodate; pick-up from the train station is available with advance reservation.

Eating

There are a number of pleasant places to eat near the train station, but the best options are in the old town.

Kosendō SOBA ¥¥
(古泉洞; 0187-53-2902; 9 Higashi-katsurakuchō; noodles from ¥1050; 10am-4pm) The best noodles in town are found in this 250-year-old Edo-era wooden schoolhouse. The house speciality is *buke-soba* served with *takenoko* (bamboo shoots) and tempura-fried *ōba* (large Japanese basil leaf). Little has changed here in years, including the regular clientele and the travellers who seek it out.

It's in the middle of the *buke yashiki* (samurai district); look for the wooden sign above the entrance. There's a pleasant gift shop out the back.

Nishi-no-miyake JAPANESE ¥¥
(西宮家レストラン北蔵; 0187-52-2438; www.nishinomiyake.jp; 11-1 Kami-chō, Tamachi; meals from ¥1100; 11am-5pm; P) Halfway between the train station and the sightseeing district, this samurai house has been partly converted into a stylish cafe. The menu spans the ages, but mostly serves elegant *yōshoku* (Japanese-style Western food). The tea and cake selection is equally tempting.

Information

Tourist Information Center (角館町観光協会; 0187-54-2700; 9am-6pm) Pick up very handy English walking maps and store luggage in this small building shaped like a *kura* (traditional Japanese storehouse) outside the train station.

Getting There & Around

Several of the *shinkansen* on the Akita line run hourly between Kakunodate and Tazawa-ko (¥1590, 15 minutes), and between Kakunodate and Akita (¥3020, 45 minutes).

Local trains also run infrequently on the JR Tazawako line between Kakunodate and Tazawa-ko (¥320, 20 minutes), and between Kakunodate and Akita (¥1320, 1½ hours), with a change at Ōmagari to the JR Ōu main line.

Bicycle hire (bikes per hour from ¥300) is available across from the train station.

Tazawa-ko

0187 / POP 3675

Cobalt-blue Tazawa-ko (田沢湖) feels isolated despite being accessible by *shinkansen*. There are some well-serviced beaches, plus a few where you'll have the natural world to yourself. Some strange creatures from the blue lagoon may have yet to surface – at 423m, Tazawa-ko is Japan's deepest lake.

The nearby mountains offer excellent views of the lake, and four seasons of activity, including skiing. It's highly recommended to pick up a rental car at Tazawa-ko Station for a night or two to make the most of the lake and nearby Nyūtō Onsen (p566).

Sights

Tazawa-ko LAKE

(田沢湖) The under-visited beach at **Shirahama** (白浜) is a real find for open-water swimmers and beach bums due to its clear-blue water, shallow entry and breathtaking mountain backdrop, but is only recommended during summer when the crispness has left the air. Rent paddle-boats at the nearby boathouse from spring to autumn. Romantic sunset strolls are highly recommended any time of year: on the lake's eastern shore, you'll find Tazawa-ko's famed bronze statue of the legendary beauty Tatsuko.

A 20km road wraps around the lake, perfect for a slow drive or vigorous cycle – bike rentals are available in the small village of Tazawa Kohan (¥400 per hour from). Sightseeing buses depart Tazawa-ko Station and loop around the lake, stopping for 15 minutes to admire the statue of Tatsuko. Scenic boat rides are available from Shirahama (¥1200, 40 minutes, every two hours May to October).

Tatsuko STATUE

Legend has it that long ago, a local woman, Tatsuko, believing that the spring water would make her beauty last forever, drank so much that she turned into a dragon, and remains in the lake to this day. She was joined by another dragon, formerly a prince, as her lover, and their passionate nocturnal antics are the reason Tazawa-ko doesn't freeze in winter! On the lake's western shore you'll find a large bronze statue of Tatsuko, sculpted by Funakoshi Yasutake.

Activities

★Akita Komaga-take HIKING

(秋田駒ヶ岳) These mountains, straddling the border with Iwate Prefecture, are admired for summer wildflowers, autumn foliage and a rare prevalence of both dry and wet plant species. Over two days you can pursue a 17km course that takes in three peaks, overnights in a picturesque mountain hut and ends with a rewarding soak in the healing waters of Nyūtō Onsen.

Access the trailhead at Komaga-take Hachigōme (eighth station) by taking one of seven daily buses (all departing before 1.30pm) from Tazawa-ko Station (¥1120, one hour). From the eighth station, it's a two-hour hike to the summit of Oname-dake (男女岳; 1637m) before pressing on to the eastern edge of the oval-shaped pond below and claiming your space at the Amida-ike Hinan Goya (阿弥陀池避難小屋) unstaffed mountain hut; it's recommended that you leave a small tip (¥1000). You can also double-back for 20 minutes or so and scale O-dake (男岳; 1623m).

On the second day, it's a seven-hour descent to Nyūtō Onsen, including first reaching the summit of Yoko-dake (横岳; 1583m). The trail down follows the ridge line most of the way before winding through expansive marshlands rich with bird life. Emerge at the Nyūtō Onsen bus stop, from where it's a short stroll to a heavenly bath.

Tazawako Ski Park SNOW SPORTS

(田沢湖スキー場; 0187-46-2011; www.tazawako-ski.com; 73-2 Shimo-takano; 1-day lift ticket adult/child ¥4000/1000, gear rental per day ¥3600; Dec-Apr) Skiers in northern Japan are spoiled for choice, so it's unsurprising that set-ups like Tazawako Ski Park, the venue for the 2016 World Cup Freestyle Moguls, are rarely visited by foreigners. Of the 13 or so trails, all but the 1.6km Kokutai and

Shirakaba runs are on the shorter side, but with an even mix of beginner, intermediate and advanced.

The views down the mountain to the nearby shores of Tazawa-ko are breathtaking.

There's English signage on the mountains and in the numerous eateries. In the winter months, buses leaving Tazawa-ko Station for Nyūtō Onsen stop at Tazawako Sukī-jō (¥550, 30 minutes).

Sleeping

There are a couple of hotels and ryokan scattered along the lakeshore, but many travellers elect to bed down in one of neighbouring Nyūtō Onsen's excellent ryokan (p566).

★That Sounds Good PENSION ¥¥
(ペンションサウンズグッド; ☎0187-43-0127; http://sounds-good.online; 160-58 Kata-mae; r per person incl breakfast from ¥6800; P ❄ 📶) Room options here range from quaint cottages with private bathrooms to split-level dwellings where you're just within snoring distance of your fellow nature lovers. Activity revolves around an open cafe-bar where meals are served and from where the sounds of weekend jazz billow out over the lake. One of the more cosmopolitan places to stay in this part of Japan.

Pick-ups from the train station are available. Drop in, tune out and relax…why not stay a few days?

Tamagawa Onsen Ryokan RYOKAN ¥¥
(玉川温泉旅館; ☎0187-58-3000; www.tamagawa-onsen.jp; Shibukurosawa, Tamagawa; r per person incl 2 meals from ¥8000, baths ¥600; ⏱day bathing 7am-5pm; P ❄ 📶) This very local onsen resort is affordable and fun, especially for those well versed in Japanese custom (or those happy enough to bumble along!). The long rows of baths are known for their high acidity, which is supposed to detox internal organs. The dining area is cafeteria-style, and the rooms are remarkably spacious, many with Western beds.

Hutte Birke RYOKAN ¥¥
(ヒュッテ ビルケ; ☎0187-46-2833; 72 Shimo-takano, Obonai; r per person incl 2 meals ¥8000; P ❄ 📶) This modest, very welcoming ryokan servicing the Tazawa-ko ski fields is well priced and perfect for families. Some of the spacious rooms (only eight available) interconnect, and the friendly owners are flexible with meal times.

Eating

A number of restaurants near the lake serve lunch and dinner, though ideally you'll need a car to reach them.

Soba Goro SOBA ¥
(そば五郎; ☎0187-43-3511; 59-40 Tazawako Obonai; dishes ¥600-1200; ⏱11am-5pm) The line of locals out the door at lunchtime is testament to the popularity of this small restaurant, tucked inside a grocery store opposite the Tazawa-ko JR station. The menu is simple – soba noodles, hot or cold, served a handful of ways – and the results simply delicious.

Orae CAFE ¥¥
(☎0187-58-0608; www.orae.net; 37-5 Haru-yama; meals from ¥1100; ⏱11.30am-8pm; P) Delicious, organic lakeside cafe known for its starring role in a Korean film. Salads, soups and locally made Kohan No Mori beer make for a very satisfying lunch – with the added bonus of expansive water views.

Information

Tourist Information Center (田沢湖観光情報センター; ☎0187-43-2111; ⏱8.30am-5.30pm; 📶) Inside the train station. Has English maps, bus timetables for both Tazawa-ko and Nyūtō Onsen, and free wi-fi.

Getting There & Away

BUS

Hourly buses run to Nyūtō Onsen (¥820, 45 minutes) between sunrise and sunset. Schedules are available from the Tourist Information Center.

CAR & MOTORCYCLE

Rte 46 connects the Akita Expressway (秋田自動車道) with Tazawa-ko.

TRAIN

JR Tazawa-ko Station is located a few kilometres southeast of the lake in Semboku and serves as the area's main access point.

The Akita *shinkansen* runs several times an hour between Tazawa-ko and Tokyo (¥16,170, three hours) and between Tazawa-ko and Akita (¥3360, one hour) via Kakunodate (¥1590, 15 minutes).

Getting Around

Frequent local buses run between JR Tazawa-ko Station and Tazawa Kohan (¥370, 10 minutes), the tourist hub on the eastern shore of the lake. Pick up a bus timetable from the Tourist Information Center.

Nyūtō Onsen

0187

Named for the bosom-shaped hills from where its famed milky-white waters spring, Nyūtō Onsen (乳頭温泉; *nyūtō* means 'nipple') is an isolated onsen village at the end of a mountain road. Offering the practice of *konyoku* (mixed-gender bathing), there's hardly a better place to enjoy nature in all its glory. Better yet, seven onsen can be visited on a single pass. When it all gets too hot, you can head downhill for a refreshing dip in, or a wander around, glittering Tazawa-ko (p564).

Activities

Kuroyu Onsen ONSEN

(黒湯温泉; 0187-46-2214; www.kuroyu.com; 2-1 Kuroyu-zawa; day bathing ¥600; day bathing 9am-4pm May–mid-Nov) Perhaps best visited as a 'day bather' (the accommodation is fairly underwhelming for the price), 300-year-old Kuroyu ryokan has a lovely old-fashioned feel. The sulphur smell may be a little strong for some, but the forest setting is the lushest in the area and little touches including waterfall jets, complimentary towels and rustic wooden changing rooms suggest a keen awareness of bathers' wants.

The nearest bus stop is Nyūtō Onsen, a 15-minute walk away.

Sleeping & Eating

There are seven ryokan (with attached onsen) tucked away in Nyūtō's hills. For the complete list, and some onsen eye-candy, see www.nyuto-onsenkyo.com. If you have the time, you'll appreciate spending a night in these divine surrounds; meals are uniformly special, and there's no better way to enjoy these fine outdoor baths than beneath moonlight without the crowds.

NYŪTŌ ONSEN PASS

It's possible to enjoy Nyūtō Onsen's waters as a day bather. The excellent-value *higaeri* (day visit) Yumeguri Pass (¥1800) is available from most inns, which open their baths to nonguests between check-out and check-in (usually between 10am and 3pm). The pass gets you entry to seven onsen. Otherwise, you'll need to pay admission (between ¥500 and ¥1000) at each onsen you visit. You'll also need to bring your own towel, or buy one. The caveat is that much of the ambience is lost when you're sharing your stunning mountain *rotemburo* (outdoor bath) with coach-loads of tourists with the same idea.

★Tsuru-no-yu Onsen RYOKAN ¥¥

(鶴の湯温泉; 0187-46-2139; www.tsurunoyu.com; 50 Kokuyurin, Sendatsui-zawa; r per person incl 2 meals ¥9830-19,950; P ❄) The jewel of Nyūtō, Tsuru-no-yu is the epitome of the Japanese ryokan: discreet, atmospheric and sumptuous. At every turn there's another picture-perfect moment, from the slick suites opening up to the forest floor to the Edo-era artworks lining the halls. Evenings are distinguished by memorable meals and guests in *yukata* (light cotton kimonos) socialising by lantern light. Reservations are essential.

The cheaper rooms have shared facilities. The newer Yamanoyado building is 1km back down the road towards the centre of Nyūtō, and very comfortable. Baths are open to visitors 10am to 3pm (admission ¥600) daily except Mondays.

According to lore, the onsen became the official bathhouse of Akita's ruling elite after a hunter once saw a crane *(tsuru)* healing its wounds in the spring. Its milky-white waters are rich in sulphur, sodium, calcium chloride and carbonic acid. The mixed *rotemburo* (outdoor bath) is positively jubilant, although shyer folk can take refuge in the indoor sex-segregated baths.

Ganiba Onsen RYOKAN ¥¥

(蟹場温泉; 0187-46-2021; 4-1 Komagatake; r per person incl 2 meals from ¥9870, day bathing ¥600; day bathing 9am-4pm; P ❄) 'Crab' Onsen is a delightfully unpretentious affair with a gorgeous mixed-gender onsen tucked back in the forest and superb Japanese cuisine. The rooms are large and comfortable, though a little worn. It's the last stop on the bus so the day trippers tend to stay away.

Tae-no-yu RYOKAN ¥¥

(妙乃湯; 0187-46-2740; www.taenoyu.com; 2-1 Komagatake; r per person incl 2 meals from ¥13,070, day bathing ¥800; day bathing 10am-3pm Wed-Mon; P ❄) This small ryokan is the most modern in Nyūtō Onsen. The stylish lodging combines urbane sensibility with a forest setting; think a Parisian apartment with tatami floors. Exquisite locavore meals incorporate wild plants foraged from the grounds. Bathing options are comprehensive, including private family onsen, reclining cypress tubs and a heavenly *rotemburo*. Single travellers are welcomed.

Getting There & Away

Buses run to Nyūtō Onsen (¥820, 45 minutes) from Tazawa-ko every hour from sunrise until sunset, stopping at several onsen en route. Pick up a bus schedule from the tourist office (p565) at Tazawa-ko train station.

Renting a car from Tazawa-ko, or Akita (p562), will give you the freedom to truly get the most out of a visit to this area.

YAMAGATA PREFECTURE

The three sacred peaks of Dewa Sanzan – and much of mountainous Yamagata Prefecture (山形県; Yamagata-ken) – have climbed into the consciousness of Japanese travellers thanks largely to the poct Matsuo Bashō (p570). His cherished accounts of the region's aesthetic beauty and his championing of the ascetic practices of the *yamabushi* (mountain priests) have elevated the prefecture to its current reputation as a place to seek tranquillity and reflection.

Further inland the remarkable clifftop temple of Risshaku-ji, above the village of Yamadera, makes a mesmerising day trip from the big cities, while Zaō Onsen, with its dramatic caldera lake, fine hiking trails and challenging ski slopes, attracts a more active wanderer. The coastal train from Tsuruoka to Sakata is utterly charming, as are many train lines weaving through the interior, but renting a car is the best way to explore the region's rural areas.

Sleeping

Yamagata and Tsuruoka have a decent smattering of business hotels, but most travellers will head for Zaō Onsen, Ginzan Onsen or Dewa Sanzan, where both luxurious and rustic mountain retreats await.

Yamagata

☎023 / POP 251,600

Yamagata (山形) is a pleasant, bustling *inaka* (rural) capital that makes a comfortable base for exploring the mountain trails around Yamadera and as a stopover en route to Zaō Onsen and Ginzan Onsen, tucked away in the surrounding countryside. The pottery district of Hirashimizu is definitely worth a peek, and when night falls there is plenty of action to be found in the entertainment district.

Sleeping & Eating

The usual range of business hotels lines the streets near the train station.

Plenty of *izakaya* can be found in and around the entertainment district.

Guesthouse Mintaro Hut GUESTHOUSE ¥¥
(ゲストハウスミンタロハット; ☎090-2797-1687; www.mintarohut.com; 5-13 Ōte-machi; s/d ¥4000/7000; P@☎) Guesthouses where hosts and guests interact freely with each other are a rarity in Japan, which makes the childhood home of English-speaking Sato-san all the more fabulous. The common area is built around a radiant stove, ensuring a warm and familial atmosphere conducive to chatting with fellow travellers, and the kitchen is stocked with supplies for self-caterers. Terrific value.

Sobadokoro Shōjiya SOBA ¥
(そば処庄司屋; ☎023-622-1380; 14-28 Saiwai-chō; noodles ¥700-1600; ⊙11-2.30pm & 5-8.30pm) Delicious chewy udon and signature soba bowls (hot or cold) are served with simple elegance at this friendly spot. The accompanying tempura and miso are respectively light and tangy. It's a worthwhile 10-minute walk from the entertainment district.

Kitanosuisan IZAKAYA ¥¥
(北野水産; ☎023-624-0880; www.marutomisuisan.jpn.com/kitano-yamagata; 2nd fl, 1-8-8 Kasumi-chō; dishes ¥500-2000; ⊙5pm-midnight) Come here to sample sake and local Yamagata specialities such as *imo nabe* (potato stew) and *dongara* (cod), as well as a variety of chargrilled seafood. The menu is on a wooden board and includes pictures. Take the first left outside the train station's east exit and look for the blue sign across the 2nd floor.

Information

Tourist Information Centre (山形市観光案内センター; ☎023-647-2333; www.yamagatakanko.com; 1st fl, Kajo Central, 1-1-1 Jonan-machi; ⊙8.30am-7pm) In the Kajo Central shopping complex, across the walkway from Yamagata Station.

Getting There & Away

The *shinkansen* between Tokyo and Yamagata (¥12,060, 2¼ hours) runs hourly, as do *kaisoku* (rapid trains) on the JR Senzan line between Yamagata and Yamadera (¥240, 20 minutes).

Alternatively, JR highway buses make an overnight trip between Yamagata and Tokyo (¥6500, 6½ hours).

Yamagata Prefecture

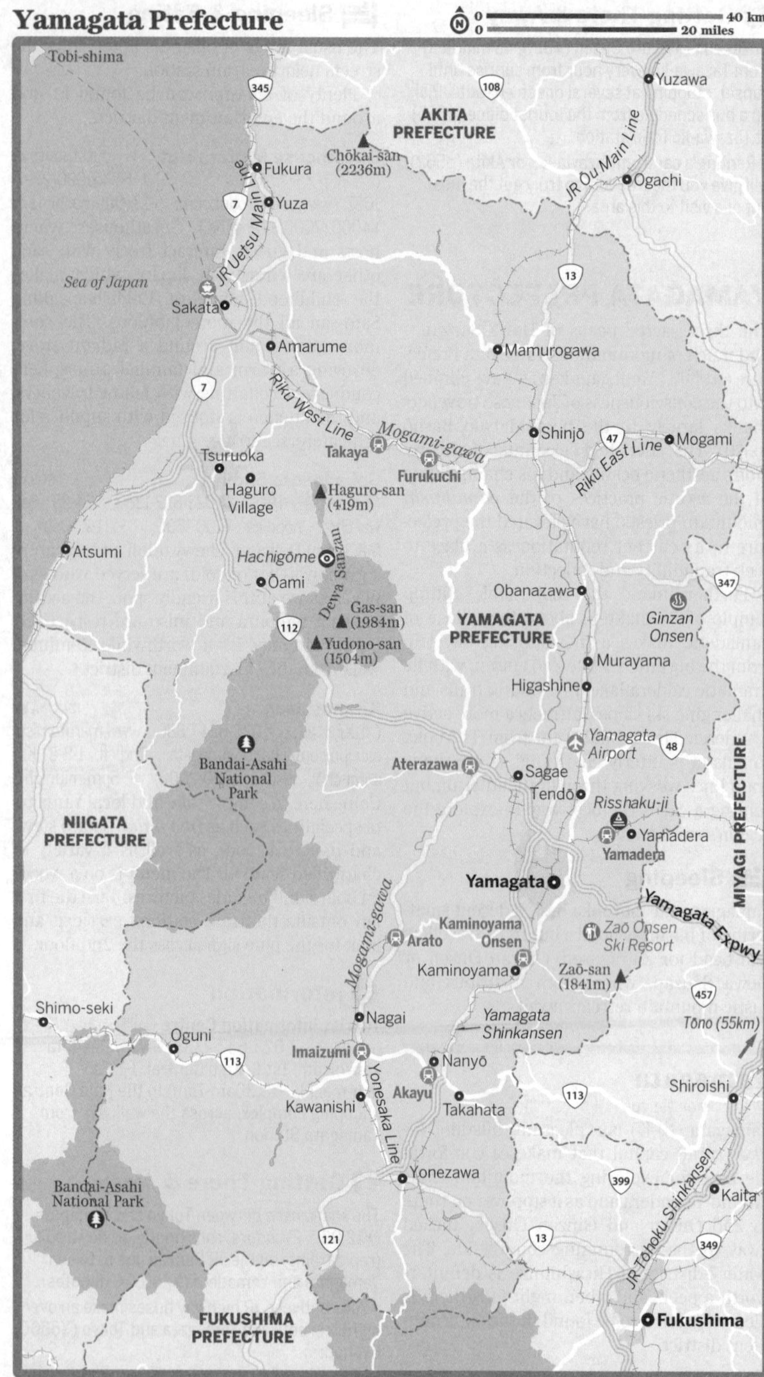

Yamadera

023

Immortalised by the itinerant haiku master, Matsuo Bashō, in *The Narrow Road to the Deep North* (1689), Yamadera (山寺), meaning 'mountain temple', is home to some very special temple buildings. The town was founded in 860 by priests who carried with them the sacred flame from Enryaku-ji near Kyoto, believing that Yamadera's rock faces were the boundaries between this world and the next. Supposedly that flame remains lit to this day.

The village's main attraction is the temple of **Risshaku-ji** (立石寺, Yamadera; 023-695-2843; www.rissyakuji.jp; adult/child ¥300/100; 8am-5pm). The 'Temple of Standing Stones', more commonly known as Yamadera, rests atop a rock-hewn staircase weathered over the centuries by unrelenting elements. At the foot of the mountain, guarded by a small lantern, is the sacred flame, Konpon-chūdō (根本中堂; ¥200), said to have been transported from Kyoto many centuries ago.

The San-mon (山門) gate marks the start of the climb – some 1000 steps that take you past carvings so mossy and worn they appear to be part of the landscape. It's a steep ascent – a sort of walking meditation – but one that makes the views from the top, of the surrounding mountains and bucolic countryside below, that much more spectacular. During the summer months, the electric whir of cicadas is almost overpowering.

Past the Nio-mon (仁王門), through which only those with pure souls may enter (be honest now!), the path splits, heading right to the Oku-no-in (奥の院; Inner Sanctuary) and left to the Godaidō (五大堂). The latter, an 18th-century pavilion perched on the cliffside, has the most arresting views.

For a better shot at a measure of the meditative bliss that so inspired Bashō, visit early in the morning or late in the afternoon. It's possible to visit Yamadera during winter, though if you arrive just after a snowfall, the paths (possibly precarious) may not yet be shovelled.

Sleeping & Eating

A few simple ryokan can be found near the train station, but most travellers visit on a day trip from Yamagata or Sendai.

Lots of street stalls sell yummy *tamakon* – gooey balls of pounded root vegetable on a stick. These, and a few pleasant noodle shops, are about the extent of Yamadera's culinary offerings.

Getting There & Away

Hourly *kaisoku* (rapid trains) travel the JR Senzan line between Yamagata and Yamadera (¥240, 20 minutes), continuing on to Sendai (¥840, one hour).

The temple is a 20-minute drive from Yamagata. Parking lots (from ¥500 per day) are plentiful.

Zaō Onsen

023 / POP 13,800

Hidden at the end of a winding, misty mountain road, Zaō Onsen (蔵王温泉) is a charming resort village equally suited to adventure and convalescence. In warmer months Zaō promises scenic hiking and the chance to soak in some special sulphur-infused *rotemburo* (outdoor baths). In ski season experts and beginners speed and stumble down huge slopes and dodge the creepy *juhyō* (ice monsters) – conifers that have been frozen solid by harsh Siberian winds – a phenomenon unique to the area.

Activities

★Zaō Onsen Ski Resort SNOW SPORTS

(蔵王温泉スキー場; 023-647-2266; www.zao-spa.or.jp; 1-day lift ticket adult/child from ¥5000/2500; Dec-Apr) Distinguished by its broad and winding runs (some up to 10km long!) and famous **Juhyō Kōgen** (樹氷高原; Ice Monster Plateau), which reaches peak ferocity in frigid February, Zaō has more than 40 ropeways and 14 spidery courses with multiple offshoots, including a huge breadth of beginner and intermediate runs. English signage is excellent and full equipment rental is available.

Nightly 'ice-monster' illuminations (January to February) are fun for all (adult/child ¥2800/1500). Newbies will love that it's possible to ski from the mountain's highest point to the base without accidentally turning down a black diamond or getting stuck in a field of moguls, while experienced skiers will appreciate the sheer scope and variety of terrain.

Zaō Ropeway CABLE CAR

(蔵王ロプウェー; 023-694-9518; www.zaoropeway.co.jp; one way/return adult ¥1500/3000, child ¥800/1500; 8.30am-5pm) This succession of cable cars whisks you over the conifers and up **Zaō-san** (蔵王山) to within spitting distance of **Okama** (御釜), a crater lake of piercing cobalt blue. The walk to the lake passes Buddhist statues and monuments hidden among the greenery, before the terrain breaks up into a sunset-coloured crumble of volcanic rock.

You can extend the hike (and save money) by taking one of the other two shorter ropeways, the **Zaō Chūō Ropeway** or the **Zaō Sky Cable**, up or down.

Zaō Onsen Dai-rotemburo ONSEN
(蔵王温泉大露天風呂; ☎023-694-9417; www.jupeer-zao.com/roten; adult/child ¥550/300; ⊙6am-7pm May-Oct) Above the village, at the base of the mountain, you'll find this huge open-air hot-spring pool. The sulphur-stained rocks set the stage for the spectacle of dozens of complete strangers bathing naked together in joyful unison. If you arrive for first light in the warmer months, you'll have the place to yourself.

Shinzaemon-no-Yu ONSEN
(新左衛門の湯; ☎023-693-1212; www.zaospa.co.jp; 905 Kawa-mae; adult/child ¥700/400; ⊙10am-6.30pm Mon-Fri, to 9.30pm Sat & Sun) An upmarket bathing option, this modern hot-spring complex has several spacious pools. The nicest are outside, set in stone with wooden canopies above.

Sleeping

Accommodation abounds, but reservations are essential if you're visiting during the ski season or on weekends in summer.

Yoshida-ya RYOKAN ¥
(吉田屋; ☎023-694-9223; www.zao-yoshidaya.com; 13 Zaō Onsen; r per person from ¥5800, incl 2 meals ¥8500; P 📶) Right in the heart of the modest action, Yoshida-ya has a more international feel than most due to the presence of young, foreign adventurers and helpful English-speaking staff. It's a modern building about a 500m uphill walk from the bus station.

Pension Boku-no-Uchi PENSION ¥
(ペンションぼくのうち; ☎023-694-9542; www.bokunouchi.com; 904 Zaō Onsen; r per person incl 2 meals from ¥7700; P 📶) This is a skiers' lodge through and through, from the posters on the wall of the sociable dining room to the prime location right in front of a convenience store and the Zaō Chūō Ropeway. Rooms are Japanese-style with communal facilities, including a 24-hour sulphur bath. Don't be put off by the weathered exterior.

Tsuruya Hotel HOTEL ¥¥
(つるやホテル; ☎023-694-9112; www.tsuruyahotel.co.jp; 710 Zaō Onsen; r per person incl 2 meals from ¥12,750; P ❄ 📶) Conveniently located opposite the bus terminal, this small hotel's friendly staff will do their best to ensure you have a wonderful stay. Handsome tatami rooms have beautiful views and a variety of indoor and outdoor baths are on hand to soak your troubles away. Great value for budget ski travellers; a shuttle to the ski lifts is available.

★**Miyamaso Takamiya** RYOKAN ¥¥¥
(高見屋; ☎023-694-9333; www.zao.co.jp/takamiya; 54 Zaō Onsen; r per person incl 2 meals from ¥39,000; P 📶) Takamiya is an atmospheric, upmarket ryokan that has been in business for nearly three centuries. There are several beautiful indoor and outdoor baths, while the spacious rooms have tatami sitting areas and fluffy *wa-beddo* (thick futons on platforms). Meals are traditional *kaiseki ryōri* (formal, multiple-course banquets) featuring top-grade local beef. Staff go above and beyond to offer exceptional hospitality.

MATSUO BASHŌ: CHRONICLER OF THE DEEP NORTH

Born into a samurai family, Matsuo Bashō (1644–94), regarded as Japan's master of haiku, is credited with elevating this poetic form's status from comic relief to Zen-infused enlightenment. Comparisons have been made between his haiku and Zen *kōan* (short riddles), intended to bring about a sudden flash of insight in the listener. Influenced by the natural philosophy of the Chinese Taoist sage Chuangzi, Bashō's work contemplated the rhythms and laws of nature. Later he developed his own poetic principle by drawing on the concept of *wabi-sabi*, a kind of spare, lonely beauty.

When he reached his 40s, Bashō abandoned his career in favour of travelling throughout Japan, seeking to build friendships and commune with nature as he went. He published evocative accounts of his travels, including *The Records of a Weather-Beaten Skeleton* and *The Records of a Travel-Worn Satchel*, but his collection *The Narrow Road to the Deep North*, detailing his journey throughout Tōhoku in 1689, is the most famous. Travellers in Tōhoku will encounter mentions of Bashō throughout the region.

It's not cheap, but it's a true destination and worth the splurge, especially with a loved one.

Zao Shiki no Hotel HOTEL ¥¥¥
(蔵王四季のホテル; ☎023-693-1211; www.zao-shikinohotel.jp; 1272 Zaō Onsen; per person incl 2 meals from ¥12,900; P) Massive Japanese- or Western-style rooms, many with mountain views, are the selling point of this fastidious ski hotel, with a wonderful outdoor onsen and lively communal dining area. It's very popular with Japanese weekenders, who come for the value, trail access and comfort.

Eating & Drinking

In winter the restaurants here often turn into unofficial drinking establishments, but there are are only a handful of bars and no real nightlife.

Robata BARBECUE ¥¥
(ろばた; ☎023-694-9565; 42-7 Kawara; courses from ¥1250; 11am-11pm Fri-Wed) The best Mongolian barbecue or *jingisukan* restaurant in Zaō (there are many) is a sharp operation where diners do the grunt work on plates of raw lamb and veggies. It's good smoky fun, well supported by a drinks menu that includes fruit sake and, everyone's favourite, yoghurt liqueur.

Oto-chaya CAFE ¥
(音茶屋; ☎023-694-9081; 935-24 Zaō Onsen; drinks from ¥400, meals from ¥880; 11am-8pm, closed Wed, open daily to midnight in winter;) Your one-stop shop for convivial pre- and post-ski rendezvous, Oto-chaya begins with coffee in the mornings and powers right through to sake and beer, with occasional live tunes, in the evenings. Hearty meals (from ¥850) are available, too. Look for the wooden sign with the teapot on the main road beyond the Zaō Chūō Ropeway.

Information

Tourist Information Center (蔵王温泉観光協会; ☎023-694-9328; www.zao-spa.or.jp; 708-1 Zaō Onsen; 9am-noon & 1-5pm, closed Tue & Wed) Tucked just inside the bus station; lots of English-language info is available here.

Getting There & Away

Buses run hourly between the **bus terminal** in Zaō Onsen and JR Yamagata Station (¥1000, 40 minutes).

During the ski season, private companies run overnight shuttles between Tokyo and Zaō. Prices can be as low as ¥7000 return – enquire at travel agencies in Tokyo.

Ginzan Onsen

☎0237 / POP 16,000

With century-old inns forming mirror images on either side of the peaceful Obana-zawa, Ginzan Onsen (銀山温泉), an out-of-the-way collection of ryokan in the classic Taishō-era style, was once the setting for *Oshin,* an enormously popular historical drama from the 1980s. Most romantic when draped in snow, Ginzan is a pleasant day trip from Yamagata, but overnight visitors can experience the real beauty of the village once the lamps are lit. Several ryokan open their baths for *higaeri* (day) bathing.

Sleeping

Ginzan Onsen's single heritage-listed street is filled with traditional Japanese ryokan. Reserve in advance, if you can.

Ginzan-so RYOKAN ¥¥¥
(銀山荘; ☎0237-28-2322; www.ginzanso.jp; r standard/deluxe incl 2 meals per person from ¥16,800/19,800; P) A picture of the artist Kenji Uchino greets guests to Ginzan-so, an enchanting mountain hotel with spacious, traditional accommodation where soft interiors are accentuated by beautiful paper lamps. Deluxe rooms have in-room spas overlooking the trees. It's a five-minute walk from the main riverside village.

Notoya Ryokan RYOKAN ¥¥¥
(能登屋旅館; ☎0237-28-2327; www.notoyaryokan.com; 446 Ginzan Shin-hata, Obanazawa; r per person incl 2 meals from ¥18,000; P) Right in the heart of the picturesque village, Notoya is a classical ryokan originally constructed in 1922, with three storeys complete with balconies, elaborate woodwork and a curious garret tower. Make sure you get a room in the main building overlooking the river.

Eating & Drinking

All ryokan offer at least half-board. There are a few restaurants serving local dishes for day trippers.

Coté de la Poste CAFE
(クリエ; ☎0237-28-2038; 410 Shinbata; 9am-6pm;) Tucked away on a corner near the bend in the river (next to the orange post box, hence the name), this petite coffee shop is the perfect spot for a post-soak tipple. Drinks are pricey, but the ambience is unbeatable. Head up the ladder-like stairs for river views and soft jazz.

Information

The small, friendly **tourist office** (9.30am-4pm Sat & Sun, hours vary Mon-Fri) has handy English-language maps, information on day-bathing options and bus timetables. It's on your left as you cross the bridge into the village.

Getting There & Away

From Yamagata take the *shinkansen* (¥1420, 30 minutes) or the JR Yamagata line towards Shinjo (¥670, 50 minutes), alighting in Ōishida, then transfer to one of up to nine daily buses leaving for Ginzan Onsen (¥710, 40 minutes) from the west-exit bus pool.

Tsuruoka

0235 / POP 129,600

Established by the Sakai clan, one of feudal Yamagata's most important families, Tsuruoka (鶴岡) is the second-largest city in the prefecture. This compact city on the Shōnai Plain is the base for visits to the mountains of Dewa Sanzan.

Sleeping

Hotel Route Inn Tsuruoka Ekimae HOTEL ¥¥
(ホテルルートイン鶴岡駅前; 0235-28-2055; www.route-inn.co.jp; 1-17 Suehiro-machi; s/d ¥7400/11,300;) The restaurant, lounge and lobby here befit a more expensive hotel, and the staff are invariably friendly and professional, though rooms are a little underwhelming in both size and style. Request a room on a high floor for views over Tsuruoka, the Shōnai Plain and enveloping mountains.

Tokyo Daiichi Hotel Tsuruoka HOTEL ¥¥
(東京第一ホテル鶴岡; 0235-24-7611; www.tdh-tsuruoka.co.jp; 2-10 Nishiki-machi; s/d from ¥6600/13,000;) This is a large, fairly impersonal hotel with comparatively spacious, stylish rooms and a rooftop sauna and *rotemburo* (outdoor bath), perfect for a post-hike soak. It's the huge yellow-brick building connected to the S-Mall shopping centre, a few minutes' walk from the train station (turn right as you exit the station).

Eating & Drinking

Downtown is pretty sleepy, though you'll find a handful of local restaurants scattered around. If you need a bite to eat or snacks for the road, try the S-Mall shopping centre, a few minutes on foot from the train station.

Ramen Kyuchan RAMEN ¥
(らーめんしょっぷ久ちゃん; 0235-23-6319; 6-48 Suehiro-machi; bowls from ¥650; 11.30am-2pm & 5pm-late) Ramen shops abound throughout Tsuruoka; this cheap and cheerful place is popular with locals for its flavoursome broth and late-night hours.

High Noon Diner BAR
(ハイヌーン ダイナー; 0235-25-0081; 15-18 Suehiro-machi; 7pm-late Wed-Mon) Two blocks left from the train station you'll spot the distinctive neon pink flamingo in the window of this cosy retro bar with Guinness on tap. Popular with foreign visitors and locals alike.

Information

Tourist Information Center (鶴岡市観光案内所; 0235-25-7678; www.tsuruokacity.com; 9.30am-5.30pm) Straight ahead as you exit the train station, with information, bus timetables and English maps for Dewa Sanzan and other attractions.

Getting There & Away

BUS

Buses leave from in front of Tsuruoka Station and from the bus depot at S-Mall for Haguro-san (¥820, 40 minutes). There are a few buses each day between Tsuruoka and Yamagata (¥2470, 1¾ hours), though services are often cut back during winter. See www.shonaikotsu.jp.

TRAIN

A few daily *tokkyū* (limited express trains) run on the JR Uetsu main line between Tsuruoka and Akita (¥3610, 1¾ hours) and between Tsuruoka and Niigata (¥3930, 1¾ hours).

Dewa Sanzan

0235 / POP 21,600

The mountains of Haguro-san (Birth), Gassan (Death) and Yudono-san (Rebirth) represent both the cycle of life and the stages you may go through when tackling the three famous peaks of Dewa Sanzan (出羽三山). The folk religion Shugendō's white-clad devotees worship a hybrid of Buddhism and Shintō and can be seen trekking the well-worn trail with wooden staffs, sandals and conical straw hats, alongside fleece-clad hikers equipped with poles, waterproof boots and bandanas.

Yamabushi (mountain priests) go that extra step in their unmistakable conch shells, chequered jackets and voluminous white pantaloons. Come winter you can join them beneath an icy waterfall to discipline both body and spirit, or just watch them pass from the comfort of your temple lodging at either end of the journey.

Sights & Activities

If you want to tackle all three mountains – possible from June through September – you need two full days, though three are advised and accommodation should be booked in advance. Tradition dictates that you start hiking at Haguro-san and finish at Yudono-san. You can do the pilgrimage in the opposite direction, though the ascent from Yudono-san to Gas-san is painfully steep. If you don't have that much time to spare, the hike up Haguro-san's 2446 stone steps (one hour) is a very rewarding alternative.

★Haguro-san MOUNTAIN

(羽黒山) The 2446 stone steps through ancient cedars to Haguro-san's summit (419m) have been smoothed by centuries of pilgrims. The climb, taking up to two hours, passes **Gojū-no-tō** (五重塔), a beautiful wooden five-storey pagoda dating from the 14th century. At the top marvel at the **Sanshin Gōsaiden** (三神合祭殿), a vivid red hall that enshrines the deities of Dewa Sanzan's three mountains.

If you're completing the circuit, you must catch the bus from the parking lot beyond the shrine bound for **Hachigōme** (八合目; eighth station), where the trail to the top of Gas-san picks up again. The last bus leaves just after 2pm. Most of the old 20km pilgrim trail along the ridge line to Gas-san became overgrown after a road was built in the 1960s.

★Gas-san MOUNTAIN

(月山) Accessible from July to September, Gas-san (1984m) is the highest of Dewa Sanzan's sacred mountains. From **Hachigōme** (八合目; eighth station) the route passes through an alpine plateau to **Kyūgōme** (九合目; ninth station) in 1¾ hours, then grinds uphill for another 1¼ hours to the top.

At the peak of Gas-san is the deeply spiritual Shintō shrine of **Gassan-jinja** (月山神社; ¥500; ⏲5am-5pm 1 Jul–15 Sep). Before entering you must be 'purifed': bow to receive the priest's benediction, then brush yourself head to toe with the slip of paper, placing it afterwards in the fountain. Beyond the gate, photography is prohibited.

From here the pilgrimage route presses on towards the steep descent to Yudono-san. This takes another three hours or so, and you'll have to carefully descend rusty ladders chained to the cliffs and pick your way down through a slippery stream bed at the end of the trail.

★Yudono-san MOUNTAIN

(湯殿山) Accessible from May to October, Yudono-san (1504m) is the spiritual culmination of the Dewa Sanzan trek. Coming from Gas-san it's a short walk from the stream bed at the end of the descent to Yudono-san-jinja.

To finish the pilgrimage, it's a mere 10-minute hike down the mountain to the trailhead at **Yudono-san Sanrōsho** (湯殿山参籠所), marked by a *torii* and adjacent to the Sennin-zawa (仙人沢) bus stop.

Yudono-san-jinja SHINTŌ SHRINE

(湯殿山神社; ☎0235-54-6133; 7 Haguro-yama; ¥500; ⏲8.30am-4pm, closed Nov-Apr; Ⓟ) Beyond the giant red *torii* of this shrine, ancient tradition (and stern-faced priests) forbids disclosure of what you witness. It's forbidden to photograph and taboo to discuss this sacred natural shrine, so you'll just have to find out for yourself. It's quite remarkable. Strict rituals prevail: remove your shoes, bow your head before the priest for purification rites then follow the other pilgrims.

A bus stop is a mere 200m from the shrine, though buses run only on weekends.

Yambushido MEDITATION

(大聖坊; www.yamabushido.jp; 99 Haguro-machi; 2-night training program ¥185,000) The new generation of *yamabushi* have opened up their *shukubō* (temple lodging) to everyday folk in need of reconnecting with nature. The masters dressed in white deliver three-day, two-night training programs twice monthly for those wanting to take their journey to the next level.

It's a tremendous opportunity to become versed in the austere spiritual practices of Shugendō devotees, revered across Japan for their mythical powers.

The sleeping quarters are more than pleasant, and the vegetarian meals come highly recommended. Guests can expect morning worship, educational nature walks, Shugendō incantations and even exorcism.

Festivals & Events

The peak of Haguro-san is the site of some lively festivals.

Shōrei-sai CULTURAL

(松例祭; ⏲31 Dec) On New Year's Eve, *yamabushi* novices perform similar rituals to those of the mountain priests at the Hassaku Matsuri, competing with each other after completing a 100-day-long period of cleansing and self-deprivation.

Hassaku Matsuri CULTURAL
(八朔祭; ⏲31 Aug) *Yamabushi* (mountain priests) perform ancient fire rites at the top of Haguro-san throughout the night to pray for a bountiful harvest.

Sleeping

Reservations are essential if you plan to stay on the mountains. You can choose to stay at either end of the pilgrimage path, in Haguro-san (p573) or Yudono-san (p573), and a few places in between. Otherwise you can base yourself in Tsuruoka.

★ **Saikan** LODGE ¥¥
(斎館; ☎0235-62-2357; 33 Haguro-yama; r per person incl 2 meals from ¥8640; P) Elegantly perched atop Haguro-san (p573), and accessed by an imposing gate, Saikan is a destination for reflective, quiet travel. The main building is sparingly furnished, but rooms are spotless and comfortable, and each is a few steps from valley views. Meals (lunch also available) are *shōjin ryōri* (Buddhist vegetarian cuisine) made with foraged mushrooms and mountain vegetables. A very special place.

It's the last left before the gate that signals the end of the stairs.

Midagahara Sanrōjo HUT ¥¥
(御田ヶ原参篭所; ☎090-2367-9037; per person incl 2 meals ¥8640; ⏲Jul-Sep) At the eighth station on Gas-san (p573), this mountain hut is a convenient place to break up the long three-mountain hike. Futons are laid out in one big communal room (sans shower), the meals are filling and the close quarters conducive for swapping stories. Catch the sunrise and you'll be on your way to the peak before the tour buses arrive.

Yudono-san Sanrōsho LODGE ¥¥
(湯殿山参籠所; ☎0235-54-6131; www.yudonosan-stay.com; 7 Rokujuri-yama, Tamugimata; r per person incl 2 meals from ¥8790; ⏲closed early Nov-late Apr; P) This airy mountain lodge at the bottom of Yudono-san (p573) has a hot bath and is full of jovial pilgrims celebrating the completion of their multiday circuit. Hearty meals, beer and sake are available and generally gratefully received. Tasty lunch sets (from ¥1640) are served here as well, even for non-lodgers.

Gas-san Shizu Onsen Ochimizu no Yu Tsutaya HOTEL ¥¥¥
(月山志津温泉変若水の湯つたや; ☎0237-74-4119; www.gassan-tsutaya.co.jp; r per person incl 2 meals from ¥14,000;) Perform some *toji* (restorative bathing) at this mellow onsen hotel in Shizu village, then walk the attractive streets in between feasting on mountain plants and river fish. The tatami rooms include a tea-drinking area. Day bathing is also available (¥800, 11.30am to 4pm).

Drinking & Nightlife

There are some delightful, welcoming noodle stands at the entrance to Haguro-san (p573), many serving fresh mountain-vegetable dishes. Each of the mountains has some dining options at the start and end of the trails, but trekkers should stock up on supplies in Tsuruoka.

Ni-no-saka-chaya TEAHOUSE
(二の坂茶屋; ⏲8.30am-5pm late Apr-early Nov) Halfway up the stone stairs of Haguro-san, as your calves are burning and your heart is pumping madly, this charming teahouse appears like a mirage. Here you'll be greeted by marvellous views and women selling refreshments to fuel the next stage of your hike.

Information

Stock up on maps at the tourist information center (p572) in Tsuruoka.

Getting There & Away

During the summer hiking months, there are up to 10 buses daily (the earliest leaving at 6am) from Tsuruoka to Haguro-san's Zuishin-mon stop (¥820, 40 minutes) at the base of the hike, most of which then continue to Haguro-sanchō (Haguro summit; ¥1180, 55 minutes). Outside the high season, the schedule is reduced.

From early July to late August, and then on weekends and holidays until late September, there are up to four daily buses from Haguro-sanchō to Gas-san (p573) as far as Hachigōme (¥1560, one hour).

On weekends three buses per day travel between the Yudono-san Sanrōsho trailhead and Haguro-san (¥1500, one hour). There is no public transport to Yudono-san on weekdays.

Sakata

☎0234 / POP 106,250

Sakata (酒田) flourished in the Edo period when it was a wealthy port cultivated by nobles and merchants. Today, while first glances might suggest a fading rural town, closer inspection reveals a wealth of cultural and historical attractions waiting to be uncovered. There's a surprising amount of English signage here and plenty to see and do if you have a few hours and sunny weather. It's also close enough to Dewa Sanzan to make a worthy alternative base to Tsuruoka.

Sights

Historical

Abumiya Residence HISTORIC BUILDING
(旧鐙屋; ☎0234-22-5001; www.abumiya.matizukuri.info; 14-20 1-chōme; adult/child ¥320/210; ⏰9am-4.30pm) Opposite the city hall, this private home once belonged to a wealthy shipping agent. With a beautiful garden and a variety of room divisions using *shōji* screens, it's a wonderful place to contemplate the Japanese aesthetic of bringing the outside in.

Hiyoriyama Park PARK
(日和山公園) This sprawling hilly park has views of the ocean and is a wonderful spot for a stroll or a picnic, especially at sunset. In April, 400 cherry trees burst into bloom and lanterns are lit all night in a spectacular display.

Sleeping

A few basic business hotels are found near the train station.

Wakaba Ryokan RYOKAN ¥¥
(若葉 旅館; ☎0967-44-0500; 2-3-9 Honcho; per person incl 2 meals from ¥7900) Friendly, English-speaking owners and a fine location within walking distance of shops and restaurants make Wakaba the pick of the town's ryokan. Rooms are bright and clean.

Eating & Drinking

Sakata Kaisen Ichiba SEAFOOD ¥
(酒田海鮮市場; ☎0234-23-5522; 5-10 2-chōme; sushi box from ¥1000; ⏰7am-7pm) A must-visit for seafood lovers. You can eat at a variety of places at this indoor seafood market or grab some mouth-watering sushi and picnic goodies.

Kachofugetsu JAPANESE ¥
(花鳥風月; ☎0234-24-8005; www.kachou.jp; 1-3-19 Higashi-cho; dishes from ¥630; ⏰11am-8.30pm) To the east of the centre, in a residential neighbourhood, this popular ramen joint does a roaring trade in steaming bowls of homemade noodles in a rich, umami broth. Place your order via the machine in the entryway and pass the resulting ticket to the waitstaff before finding a seat.

Of all the ramen restaurants in town (and there are many – pick up a map at the tourist office), this is one of the only ones that opens for dinner.

Kumura no Sakaba IZAKAYA ¥
(久村の酒場; ☎0234-24-1935; 1-41 Kotobukicho; dishes from ¥700; ⏰5-10pm Mon-Sat) While many believe Sakata is an underrated town, Kumura no Sakaba is definitely a much underrated *izakaya*. The atmosphere is propelled by buoyant, local Japanese sharing simple seafood, chicken and vegetable dishes, and the beer flows freely on most tables.

Kerun COCKTAIL BAR
(ケルン; ☎0234-23-0128; 2-4-20 Naka-machi; ⏰11.30am-2.30pm & 7-10pm) In business for decades, Kerun is run by an octogenarian Japanese man who whisks up frothy whisky sours from a well-stocked bar that's surrounded by mirrors and booth seating. You can also get lovely filter coffee and iced chocolates during the day.

Information

Tourist Information Office (酒田駅観光案内所; ☎0234-24-2454; www.sakata-kankou.com; ⏰9am-5pm) Within Sakata Station. Staff don't speak much English, but they rent bikes for free and have an excellent English-language walking map.

Getting There & Away

Sakata is an easy day trip from Tsuruoka on the local *fūtsū* train (¥500, 35 minutes), or a pleasant stop en route to Akita (limited express ¥1940, two hours) on the scenic, coast-hugging Uetsu main line.

Several daily buses go to Yamagata (¥2730, 2¾ hours) via Tsuruoka (¥820, 50 minutes).

NIIGATA PREFECTURE

Skirting the west coast of Tōhoku, Niigata Prefecture (新潟県; Niigata-ken) is known for its snow-covered mountains, rocky coastal stretches and established onsen villages. In summer thousands descend on the small mountain hamlet of Naeba for the famed Fuji Rock Festival (p585), while in winter city slickers carve up the slopes around Naeba and nearby Echigo-Yuzawa Onsen. The prefecture's sprawling capital city, Niigata, is an industrial and transport hub, with

Niigata Prefecture

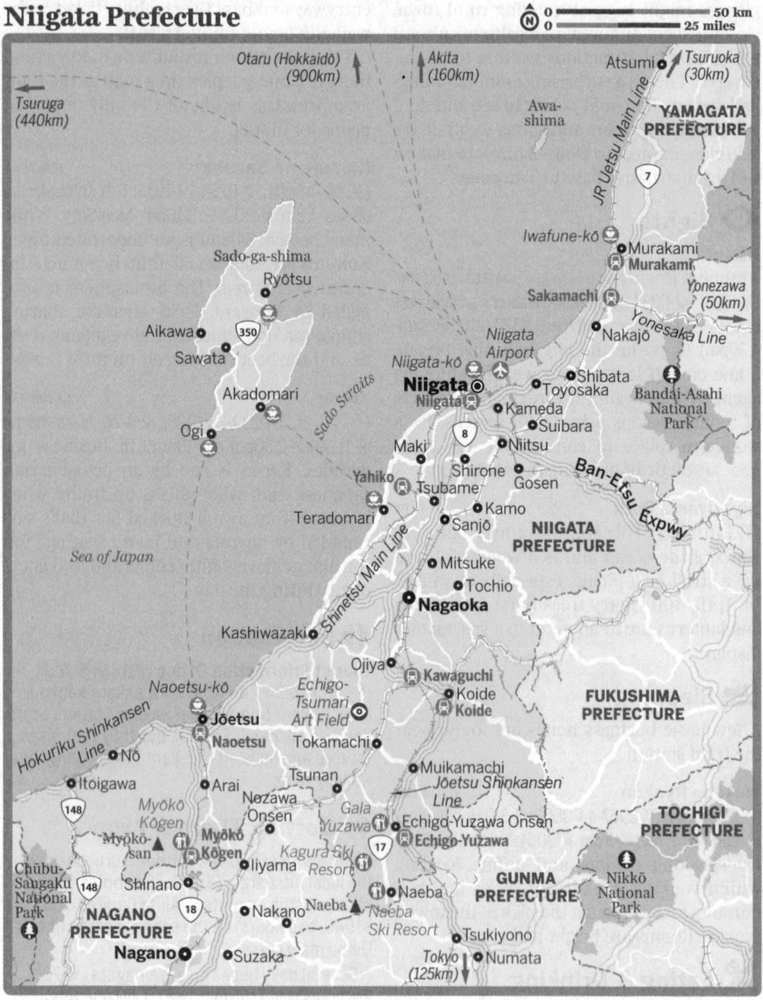

excellent transport connections, and is the gateway to quiet Sado-ga-shima, a working island with an interesting history and a rugged natural beauty.

Sleeping

As a major metropolitan centre, Niigata has the usual array of business hotels, as well as a handful of more atmospheric options. The mountain towns of Echigo-Yuzawa Onsen and Naeba are mainly populated by workhorse ski hotels, though Echigo-Yuzawa Onsen has some decent ryokan, which serve as good bases for ski trips.

Niigata

025 / POP 810,157

Niigata (新潟) is the prefectural capital, the largest city on Honshū's Sea of Japan coast and a welcoming place to spend a night or so en route to the ski fields or Sado-ga-shima. Highlights include a lively restaurant district serving the region's famed rice and sake, an attractive city park and the handsome Shinano-gawa running through the centre. Head up to the impressive Nippō observation deck to get a sense of where you are in the world.

Sights

Niigata City Art Museum MUSEUM
(新潟市美術館; ☎025-223-1622; www.ncam.jp; 5191-9 Nishiohata-cho; adult/child ¥200/100; ⏰9.30am-6pm Tue-Sun) This petite, elegant museum stages interesting temporary exhibitions by Japanese artists and also has a well-curated permanent collection of local and international works. The on-site organic cafe makes a great lunch stop.

Saito Family Summer Villa HISTORIC BUILDING
(旧齋藤家別邸, Kyū Saito-ke Bettei; ☎025-210-8350; www.saitouke.jp; 576 Nishi Ohata-chō; adult/child ¥300/100; ⏰9.30am-6pm Tue-Sun Apr-Sep, to 5pm Oct-Mar; 🚌3, 13 to Higashi-ōhata Niban-chō) Wander the polished wooden floors of this beautifully preserved Japanese summer house built in 1918, a luscious example of turn-of-the-century Japanese architecture and design. The grounds are home to a beautiful garden with huge Edo-period pines sheltering over 100 Japanese maples.

Nippō Media Ship Sora-no-hiroba VIEWPOINT
(新潟日報メディアシップそらの広場; ☎025-385-7500; 1-1-3 Chome, Bandai; ⏰8am-11pm) FREE Visit the observation deck on the 20th floor of this skyscraper for amazing 360-degree views over the Sea of Japan, Niigata city and the distant mountains. The elevator is to your right from the main entrance.

Sleeping

Niigata has the usual range of business hotels near the train station as well as by the Sado-ga-shima ferry terminal. North of the river you'll find a few more decent hotels (and love hotels) in the entertainment district.

Book Inn HOSTEL ¥
(ゲストハウス ブックイン; ☎025-290-7322; www.bookinn-niigata.com; 3-1-21 Benten, Chūō-ku; dm ¥2500-5000; ❄📶) Over 4000 books, including 1000 English-language titles, line the walls of this quirky hostel a five-minute walk from the train station. Guests sleep in capsule-like bunks in one large room. Spotless facilities, including a kitchenette with free tea and coffee, and friendly, English-speaking staff complete the story.

ANA Crowne Plaza Niigata HOTEL ¥¥
(ANAクラウンプラザホテル新潟; ☎025-245-3333; www.crowneplaza.com/niigata; 5-11-20 Bandai; s/d from ¥7695/10,165; P🚭❄📶) A 10-minute walk from the station and easy access to the river make the Crowne Plaza a convenient choice for affordable luxury. The Japanese suites are the best value if you have a friend or two, though guestrooms come in a variety of shapes and sizes.

Hotel Nikkō Niigata HOTEL ¥¥¥
(ホテル日光新潟; ☎025-240-1888; www.okura-nikko.com; 5-1 Bandai-jima; s/d from ¥7800/16,000; P🚭❄📶) Starting on the 23rd floor of the tallest building in the prefecture, the Nikkō looms over the mouth of Shinano-gawa and the Sado-ga-shima ferry terminal. Rooms are pushing five-star, with ample space, pleasing colour schemes and great views, while the breakfast buffet spans Japanese and Western tastes. It's perfectly located for an early-morning ferry departure to Sado.

Eating & Drinking

Pia Bandai MARKET ¥¥
(ピアBandai, Pier Bandai; ☎025-249-2560; 2-10 Bandai-shima, Chūō-ku; meals from ¥1000; ⏰9am-9pm) Conveniently located on the way to the Sado Kisen (p578) ferry terminal, this sprawling complex includes markets and eateries – so you can gawk at the bounty of Niigata's coast and sample it, too. If you're in Niigata with time to eat, a visit here is a must. You'll be spoiled for choice: from conveyer-belt sushi to Italian-style calzone to superb coffee.

Ponshukan DISTILLERY
(ぽんしゅ館; ☎025-240-7090; http://ponshukan-niigata.com; 3rd fl, 1-96-47 Hanazono; ⏰11am-10pm) This charming sake shop on the concourse just outside the train station sells hundreds of different types in the *kikizake* style, where you can purchase five small samples for ¥500. Gourmet nibbles are also served to line the stomach. Don't miss your train!

The tasting area is partitioned off inside the store, in the far corner – look out for the white *noren*.

Craft Beer Kan CRAFT BEER
(クラフトビールかん; ☎025-278-7622; ⏰noon-11pm) By the south exit of Niigata Station is this fun little stand-up beer bar at the forefront of the city's craft-beer renaissance. Forty-odd beers are on tap; buy tickets (500mL glass from ¥400) from a machine. The owners can point you towards their second branch in the entertainment district.

Information

MEDICAL SERVICES

Niigata University Medical & Dental Hospital (新潟大学医歯学総合病院; ☎025-227-2460, after hours 025-227-2479; www.nuh.niigata-u.ac.jp; 1-757 Asahimachi-dōri, Ichiban-chō; ⏲outpatient service 8.30-11am Mon-Fri)

TOURIST INFORMATION

Tourist Information Center (新潟駅万代口観光案内センター; ☎025-241-7914; www.nvcb.or.jp; ⏲9am-7pm) Lovely, helpful staff dispense English maps and information to the left of Niigata Station's Bandai exit. The website is good, too.

Getting There & Away

AIR

Niigata Airport (KIJ), 13km north of the city centre, has domestic flights to Sapporo, Nagoya, Osaka, Fukuoka and Okinawa and international flights to Khabarovsk, Vladivostok, Seoul, Shanghai, Harbin and Guam.

Buses to the airport run from stop 5 outside Niigata Station's south exit roughly every half-hour from 6.30am to 6.40pm (¥410, 25 minutes); a taxi should cost about ¥3000.

BOAT

From the port of Niigata-kō, **Shin-Nihonkai** (新日本海; ☎025-273-2171; www.snf.jp) ferries run daily (except Monday) to Otaru on Hokkaidō (from ¥6480, 18 hours). To get to Niigata-kō take bus line 10 at the Bandai exit bus pool in front of Niigata Station (¥210, 15 minutes).

Sado Kisen (佐渡汽船; ☎025-245-2311; www.sadokisen.co.jp) runs frequent car ferries (from ¥2170/10,910 per adult/car, three hours) and hydrofoils (¥6390, one hour) to Ryōtsu on Sado-ga-shima. Buses to the ferry terminal (¥210, 15 minutes) leave from stop 5 at the Bandai exit bus pool 45 minutes before sailing. A taxi should cost about ¥1000; alternatively, you can walk there in about 40 minutes.

Daily car ferries also run from the port of Naoetsu-kō, about 90km southwest of Niigata, to Ogi on Sado-ga-shima (from ¥3780/13,340 per adult/car, 2½ hours).

BUS

Highway buses depart from the **Bandai City Bus Terminal** (万代シテイバスセンター; 1-6-1 Bandai, Chuo-ku), a big yellow building 1km northwest of the train station, and connect Niigata to major cities throughout Honshū.

TRAIN

Shinkansen on the Jōetsu line run approximately twice an hour between Niigata and Tokyo (¥10,050, 2¼ hours), via Echigo-Yuzawa Onsen (¥4860, 45 minutes).

There are a few *tokkyū* (limited express trains) each day on the JR Uetsu line between Niigata and Tsuruoka (¥3930, 1¾ hours) and between Niigata and Akita (¥6690, 3½ hours).

To access the port of Naoetsu-kō, from where you can catch a ferry or hydrofoil to the town of Ogi on Sado-ga-shima, there are a few *tokkyū* each day on the JR Shinetsu line between Niigata and Naoetsu (¥4100, 1¾ hours). From Naoetsu Station, it's a 10-minute bus ride (¥210) or about ¥1000 for a taxi to the port.

NIIGATA SAKE

Niigata Prefecture is one of Japan's top sake-producing regions, known in particular for a crisp, dry style called *tanrei karakuchi*. The long, cold winters produce plenty of fresh mountain snowmelt for the valleys below, which translates into delicious rice and then delicious sake. Tipplers should be sure to treat themselves while passing through. In March a mammoth bacchanal in Niigata city, called **Sake-no-jin** (酒の陣; www.sakenojin.jp; ⏲Mar), highlights more than 90 varieties of sake from around the prefecture.

Sado-ga-shima

☎0259 / POP 57,255

Dramatic cliffs plunging into deep blue ocean, lush, dense forests marked by winding roads, and sleepy fishing villages backed by golden rice paddies are hallmarks of S-shaped Sado-ga-shima (佐渡島), a remote, sparsely populated island with a unique cultural heritage and dramatic natural landscape. Its history as a penal colony, gold mine, religious retreat and a bastion of cultural preservation gives Sado a special place in the Japanese psyche, but foreign travellers are mostly yet to discover its charms.

Crowds peak during the third week in August for the Earth Celebration, headlined by the world-famous Kodō Drummers. Outside of the summer holiday season, it's blissfully quiet.

History

Sado has always been something of a far-flung destination, just not always a voluntary one. During the feudal era, the island was a notorious penal colony where out-of-favour intellectuals were forever banished. The illustrious list of former prisoners includes Emperor Juntoku, *nō* (stylised dance-drama) master Ze-Ami and Nichiren, the founder of one of Japan's most influential Buddhist sects. When gold was discovered near the village of Aikawa in 1601, there was a sudden influx of miners, who were often vagrants press-ganged from the mainland and forced to work under slave-like conditions.

Sights

Ryōtsu (両津) serves as the main ferry access point to Sado-ga-shima. A short drive inland, the land gives way to rice fields, rustic farmhouses and ancient temples. The rustic wooden temple, **Konpon-ji** (根本寺; ☎0259-22-3751; www.sado-konponji.com; 1837 Niibo Ōno; adult/child ¥300/150; ⏰8am-4.30pm Apr-Oct, to 3.30pm Nov-Mar), with its thatched roof and pleasant gardens, is where the Buddhist monk Nichiren was first brought when exiled to Sado in 1271. Any bus on the Minami line from Ryōtsu can drop you off at the Konpon-ji-mae bus stop.

Villages on the west coast with sights include **Mano** (真野), which is a fantastic place for a ramble, and **Aikawa** (相川), an Edo-era gold-mining boom town and now a sleepy fishing village overlooking the Sea of Japan. A worthwhile sight here is **Sado Hanga-mura Museum** (佐渡版画村美術館; ☎0259-74-3931; 38-2 Aikawa Komeyamachi; adult/child ¥400/200; ⏰9am-5pm Mar-Nov), rambling gallery where local artists display vibrant *hanga* (woodblock prints) depicting country life in Sado.

North of Aikawa, Sado's **Sotokaifu** (外海府) coast is a dramatic landscape of sheer cliffs dropping into deep blue waters. Roads are narrow and windy; think harrowing/exhilarating coastal drives. Infrequent buses do pass by here, but you'll really want your own wheels.

Ogi (小木) is a small village on the southwestern tip of the island and one of the most popular places to visit. The drive along the beautiful rocky shoreline is cathartic if you crave remote destinations, and its splendid isolation is evident in the cultural practices that have changed little in 400 years.

Visit the **Ogi Folk Museum** (小木民俗博物館; Ogi Minzoku Hakubutsukan; ☎0259-86-2604; 270-2 Shukunegi; adult/child ¥500/200; ⏰8.30am-5pm), in a former 1920s schoolhouse, saved from demolition, to see cultural artefacts from Sado.

About 3km west the tiny hamlet of Shukunegi (宿根木), is a rarer jewel – the tiny, gated, traditional fishing village feels like a museum, with its weathered wooden merchant houses, narrow alleyways and stone staircases snaking up the hillside.

Activities

Sado Island Taiko Centre MUSIC
(佐渡太鼓体験交流館; Sado Taiko Taiken Tatakōkan; ☎0259-86-2320; www.sadotaiken.jp; 150-3 Ogi-kanetashinden; ⏰9am-5pm Tue-Sun) Come to this beautiful hall perched on a hill overlooking the ocean to have a drumming lesson with members of the elite Kodō Drummers. Pop in to have a look any time, but lessons must be booked in advance – generally ¥2000 per person, minimum five people.

Festivals

Earth Celebration CULTURAL
(アース・セレブレーション; www.earthcelebration.jp; ⏰mid-Aug) One of Sado's biggest drawcards is this three-day music, dance and arts festival, held during the third week in August. The event features *okesa* (folk dances), *onidaiko* (demon drum dances) and *tsuburosashi* (a phallic dance with two goddesses). The focal point, however, is the performance of the Kodō Drummers, considered one of the most elite drumming groups in the world.

The Kodō Drummers live in a small village north of Ogi but spend much of the year on tour around the globe. Members are required to adhere to strict physical, mental and spiritual training regimens.

Main concerts and workshops take place in and around the village of Ogi, but optional activities and tours are scheduled all over the island.

If you're interested in attending the festival, you will need to buy tickets and arrange accommodation well in advance.

Sleeping

Sado has a number of excellent ryokan, some smaller *minshuku* (guesthouses) and couple of hostels, but almost no typical business hotels. The best places to stay are in or around Ogi and Mano; for truly remote you can stay on the Sotokaifu coast or in central Sado.

So-bama Campground CAMPGROUND ¥
(素浜キャンプ場; ☎0259-86-3200; site per person/rental tent from ¥300/2500; ⏰May-Oct; Ⓟ) Right across the road from a tempting stretch of sand and only 6km from Ogi, this attractive campground reaches peak

Sado-ga-shima

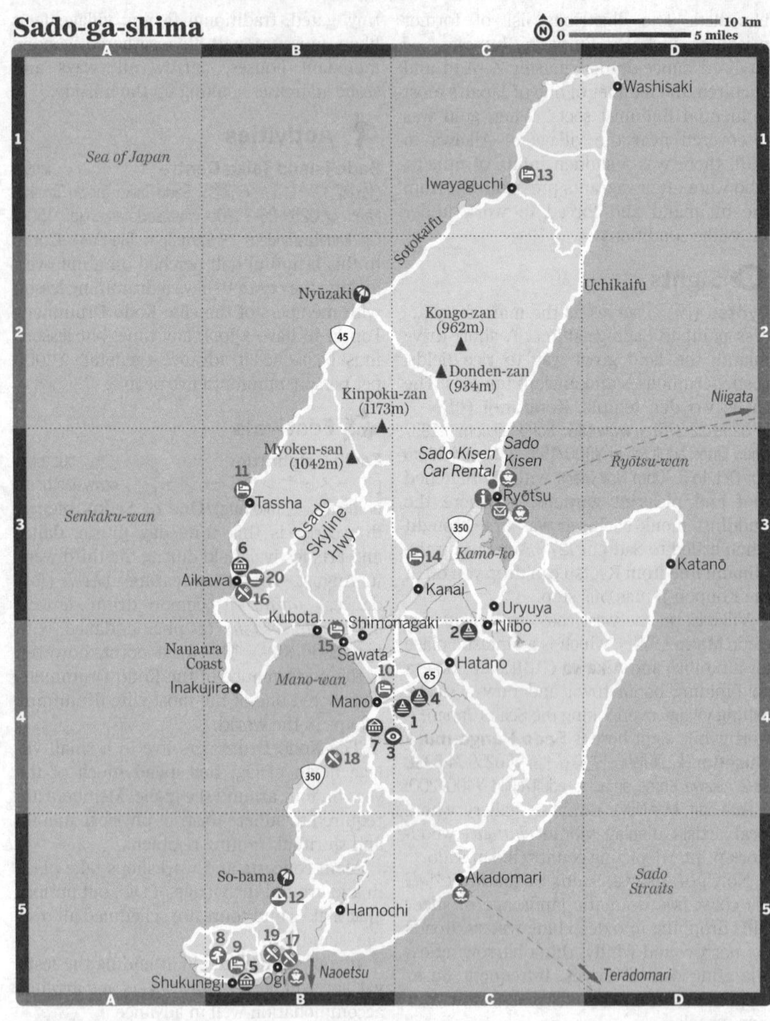

Sado-ga-shima

Sights
1 Kokubun-ji C4
2 Konpon-ji C4
3 Mano Go-ryō B4
4 Myōsen-ji C4
5 Ogi Folk Museum B5
6 Sado Hanga-mura Museum B3
7 Sado Museum of History & Tradition ... B4

Activities, Courses & Tours
8 Sado Island Taiko Centre B5

Sleeping
9 Hana-no-ki B5
10 Itōya Ryokan B4
11 Sado Belle Mer Youth Hostel B3
12 So-bama Campground B5
13 Sotokaifu Youth Hostel C1
14 Tōkaen C3
15 Urashima B4

Eating
16 Kimpuku B3
17 Shichiemon B5
18 Shimafumi B4
19 Uohara B5

Drinking & Nightlife
20 Kyōmachi Chaya B3

popularity during Earth Celebration (p579), when shuttle buses between it and festival events run several times a day. You'll need a car to access it easily.

Sado Belle Mer Youth Hostel HOSTEL ¥
(佐渡ベルメールユースホステル; ☎0259-75-2011; http://sado.bellemer.jp; 369-4 Himezu; dm incl 2 meals ¥6500; P ⊖ ᯤ) Fishing, hiking and hanging out by the windswept sea are the activities of choice at this established hostel, which immerses guests in Japanese village life. The owners know at least one fabulous secret beach. Rooms are basic dorms and almost all have sea views. Meals are available. It's near the Minami-Himezu bus stop.

Sotokaifu Youth Hostel HOSTEL ¥
(外海府ユースホステル; ☎0259-78-2911; www.sotokaifu.jp; 131 Iwayaguchi; dm incl 2 meals ¥6380; P ⊖) Tucked away in a tiny fishing hamlet, this cosy hostel will appeal to those looking for the quiet life. It's in a traditional Sado house, complete with central hearth, refitted with shared and private rooms. Filling meals include fresh seafood. The hostel is right in front of the Iwayaguchi (岩谷口) bus stop. Think remote.

★ **Hana-no-ki** RYOKAN ¥¥
(花の木; ☎0259-86-2331; www.sado-hananoki.com; 78-1 Shukunegi; s/d incl breakfast ¥6500/11,000; P ⊖ ᯤ) If you make it this far, you'll need to find somewhere worthwhile to rest your weary head. Luckily this 150-year-old former farmhouse has been relocated to the rice paddies of Shukunegi to serve exactly that purpose. Accommodation is in Japanese-style rooms in the main building, or detached cottages in the garden. Call ahead for pick-up from Ogi.

★ **Urashima** RYOKAN ¥¥
(浦島; ☎0259-57-3751; www.urasima.com; 978-3 Kubota; r per person from ¥8000, incl 2 meals from ¥13,000; P ❄ ᯤ) Sleek, modern architecture meets industrial chic at Urashima, housed in a former fishmongers redesigned by two prominent Japanese architects. The result is a total destination hotel, combining traditional Japanese elements with a distinct European sensibility. Superb meals and exceptional hospitality mean this is the best place on the island to stay for a few days.

It's about 400m west of Sawata, on the bus route to Mano.

Tōkaen MINSHUKU ¥¥
(桃華園; ☎0259-63-2221; www.on.rim.or.jp/~toukaen; 1636-1 Kanai-Shinbo; r per person ¥4500, incl 2 meals from ¥8800; P ᯤ) On the central plains outside Ryōtsu is this isolated *minshuku* where you can ride horses and receive salt therapy in a roasting sauna. The tatami-lined rooms are open and bright and you certainly won't go hungry at mealtime. Take a Hon-line bus from Ryōtsu to Undōkōen-mae and tell the driver you're going to Tōkaen; otherwise it's a 3km walk.

The owners are experts on Sado's many hidden hiking trails.

Itōya Ryokan RYOKAN ¥¥
(伊藤屋; ☎0259-55-2019; www.itouyaryokan.com; 278 Mano Shin-machi, Mano; r per person ¥5300, incl 2 meals ¥7300; P ᯤ) This welcoming ryokan in quiet Mano suits solo travellers. Rooms and common areas are full of handicrafts from across the island, and evening dishes feature seafood prominently. The inviting *hinoki* (wooden bath) is filled with ocean water to permeate your bones. It's just 50m southwest of the Shin-machi traffic signal.

Eating & Drinking

A few cafes line the exit from the ferry terminal in Ryōtsu, and there are a couple of simple restaurants within a 10-minute walk south. Mano has a handful of restaurants lining the attractive main thoroughfare. Aikawa has some spots too, like Kimpuku (p582) and Kyōmachi Chaya (p582). There are a few small noodle shops and seafood restaurants in Sotokaifu, but don't go looking for food after dark because you won't find any. Ogi has some delicious seafood, like Uohara, and noodle joints, like Shichiemon (p582); head for the main street, which winds up the hill opposite the port.

Shimafumi CAFE ¥
(しまふうみ; ☎0259-55-4545; www.shimafumi.com; 105-4 Dai-shō; cakes ¥200-600; ⏲9am-5pm Thu-Tue) On a bend in the road at the southern tip of Mano Bay, this unexpectedly excellent bakery-cafe serves a wide variety of baked goods as well as coffee, cold drinks and ice creams. The outside tables overlooking the water are a lovely spot on a sunny day.

Uohara SEAFOOD ¥¥
(魚晴; ☎0259-86-2085; 415-1 Ogi-machi; meals from ¥1100; ⏲11am-5pm, closed irregularly) The speciality here is *awabi* (abalone), grilled as a steak (at market rate) or, more affordably, barbecued with a sweet soy-sauce marinade and served over rice. Follow the shop-lined road snaking up the hill behind the tourist

DON'T MISS

STROLLING THROUGH THE COUNTRYSIDE IN MANO

Mano was the capital and cultural centre of the island from early times until the 14th century. It's now a quiet seaside village with a few attractive wooden buildings.

A peaceful 7km nature trail east of town winds through paddy fields and past Mano's attractions. The entrance is near the Danpū-jō bus stop, along the Minami bus route between Ryōtsu and Sawata. From the trailhead, it's a short walk to **Myōsen-ji** (妙宣寺; 0259-55-2061; dawn-dusk), which was founded by one of the Buddhist monk Nichiren's disciples and features a distinctive five-storey pagoda.

From Myōsen-ji, it's a 10-minute walk through farmland and up old wooden steps set into the hillside to **Kokubun-ji** (国分寺; 0259-55-2059; 113 Kokubun-ji; dawn-dusk), Sado-ga-shima's oldest temple, dating from 741. Another 3km takes you past marvellous lookout points to **Mano Go-ryō** (真野御陵; 10am-5pm), the tomb of Emperor Juntoku. From there it's a short walk down to the **Sado Museum of History & Tradition** (佐渡歴史伝説館; Sado Rekishi Densetsukan; 0259-55-2525; www.sado-rekishi.jp; 655 Mano; adult/child ¥800/400; 8.30am-5.30pm), where tireless animatrons act out scenes from Sado's dramatic past.

information centre for about 250m until you see a white building on the left with red and blue writing on the side. There's a picture menu.

Kimpuku YAKITORI ¥
(金福; 0259-74-3934; 2-9 Aikawa; dishes from ¥500; 5-11pm) Kimpuku operates on a simple premise: few seats, fast service, hot grill, quality meat, succulent sauces. Sado islanders often clock in here when passing through Aikawa.

Shichiemon SOBA ¥
(七右衛門; 0259-86-2046; 643-1 Ogi-machi; noodles from ¥550; 11am-2pm) This long-established eatery serves slightly flatter-than-usual *teuchi* (handmade) soba every which way.

Kyōmachi Chaya CAFE
(京町茶屋; 080-1093-6341; 5 Aikawa Yaoya-machi; 10am-4pm Wed-Mon) Grab a slice of fluffy chiffon cake and an iced coffee at this cafe and gallery in a restored merchant's house. The views and sea breezes from inside or the small plaza outside are delightful.

Information

MONEY

Ryōtsu Post Office (両津郵便局; 0259-27-3634; 2-1 Ryōtsu-ebisu; post office 9am-5pm Mon-Fri, ATM 8am-7pm Mon-Fri, from 9am Sat & Sun) Has an international ATM. Another branch opposite the ferry terminal has shorter hours.

TOURIST INFORMATION

Tourist Information Center (佐渡観光協会; 0259-27-5000; www.visitsado.com; 2nd fl, Sado Kisen Ferry Terminal; 8.30am-6pm) Be sure to stop in here on your way out of the ferry terminal. There's an excellent selection of English maps and pamphlets, including walking and cycling guides for all of the island's main areas. The helpful English-speaking staff can arrange car rental.

Getting There & Away

Sado Kisen (佐渡汽船; www.sadokisen.co.jp; Ryotsuminato 353) runs frequent car ferries (from ¥2170/10,910 per adult/car, three hours) and hydrofoils (¥6390, one hour) between Niigata and Sado's main port of **Ryōtsu** (Ryotsuminato 353). Service is greatly reduced outside the summer months. It's generally cheaper to rent a car on the island than take one on the ferry.

From Naoetsu-kō, about 90km southwest of Niigata, there are also up to three daily car-ferry services to **Ogi** (Ogi-machi 1950) (from ¥3780/13,340 per adult/car, 2½ hours); these are particularly useful during Earth Celebration (p579).

From March to November there are one to three daily high-speed ferries (¥2830, one hour) between **Akadomari** (Akadomari 2208) and Teradomari, 45km south of Niigata.

Getting Around

BICYCLE

Cycling is an enjoyable way to move around the towns, but steep elevations make long-distance cruising a challenge. Tourist information centres in Ryōtsu, Aikawa and Ogi rent electric bicycles (¥500/2000 per two/24 hours). One-way hire is also available (¥1100 per bike). Local shops in Ryōtsu and Ogi rent regular bikes for slightly less.

BUS

The island is well served by buses, though winding roads mean services are slow and can be confusing. Buses leave from Ryōtsu for destinations across the island from a well-marked bus terminal to the right as you exit the ferry.

The Minamisen line connects Ryōtsu with Mano (¥840, one hour) and Sawata (¥880, 1¼ hours), while the Honsen line runs from Ryōtsu to Aikawa (¥840, one hour), via Sawata.

There is one direct daily service between Ryōtsu and Ogi (¥1400, 1½ hours) departing at 6.50am from both Ogi and Ryōtsu. Otherwise buses from Ogi travel to Mano (¥840, 45 minutes) and Sawata (¥880, one hour), from where you can change for Ryōtsu and other destinations.

A multitude of other lines criss-cross the interior; be sure to pick up the English-language 'Sado Island Fixed Route Bus Map' before you leave the port.

Buy tickets on board the bus – take a numbered ticket as you enter, and pay the fare as you disembark at the end of your journey. The unlimited-ride bus pass (one/two/three days ¥1500/2500/3000) is good value; purchase one on board or at any of the island's information centres.

CAR & MOTORCYCLE

Renting a car on the island is probably the best way to explore: it's much cheaper than bringing a car over on the ferry. Expect to pay ¥6000 to ¥10,000 per day, depending on size and availability. **Sado Kisen Car Rental** (☎0259-27-5195) in the ferry terminal is a friendly, helpful operator. Petrol stations are few and far between outside the main towns, but you'll often pay a per-kilometre fee for petrol and not be required to return the car with a full tank. Unless you plan to circumnavigate the island or stay a long time, you're unlikely to use a full tank.

Echigo-Yuzawa Onsen

☎025 / POP 8046

If Kawabata Yasunari's famous novel *Yukiguni* (Snow Country), set here, is to be believed, Echigo-Yuzawa Onsen (越後湯沢温泉) was once a hot-spring retreat where geisha competed for guests' affections. Then came skiing and the *shinkansen*. Winter visitors generally head straight to the slopes of Gala Yuzawa and then back home, but there are plenty of great onsen here year-round.

Sights

Echigo-Tsumari Art Field PUBLIC ART

(越後妻有大地の芸術祭の里; www.echigo-tsumari.jp) FREE This open-air gallery was conceived in 2000 as a way to bring visitors to this enchantingly beautiful rural area of green fields and historical wooden farmhouses. Scattered over 770 sq km you'll find more than 160 art installations by Japanese and international artists, set as naturally as possible in the landscape. Catch a train from Echigo-Yuzawa Onsen to Tōkamachi (¥610, 30 minutes) and download maps online. You'll need a car to make the most of it all.

The area really comes to life during the summer-long Echigo-Tsumari Triennial (next up in 2024).

Yuzawa Town History Museum MUSEUM

(雪国館; Yukiguni-kan; ☎025-784-3965; 354-1 Yuzawa; ¥500; ⌚9am-5pm Thu-Tue) This lovely little museum displays memorabilia from the life of author Kawabata Yasunari, the first Japanese recipient of the Nobel Prize for Literature, in addition to interesting displays about life in snow country that bring his classic book to life. From the west exit of Echigo-Yuzawa Station, turn right and walk about 500m.

Activities

Gala Yuzawa SNOW SPORTS

(ガーラ湯沢; https://gala.co.jp/winter; 1-day lift ticket adult/child ¥4600/2300; ⌚8am-5pm Dec-Apr) With its own *shinkansen* stop at the base of the mountain, it's possible to wake up in Tokyo, hit the slopes here after breakfast and be back in the big smoke for dinner: the slopes can get predictably packed. Three quad lifts alongside six triple and double lifts help to thin the crowds. Expect queues at peak times.

Runs range the gamut from beginner to intermediate and advanced, with the longest stretching 2.5km. English is spoken everywhere, and you'll see plenty of other foreigners. Full equipment rental is available for ¥5000 per day. Tokyo travel agents can often arrange cheap packages that include lift and train fare, especially if you're planning to head up on a weekday.

GENBI SHINKANSEN

Art and/or train lovers should check out the *Genbi Shinkansen* 'art train', which operates between Niigata and Echigo-Yuzawa (¥4860, 50 minutes) six times daily. See www.jreast.co.jp/genbi.

Sleeping

Most visitors are day trippers from Tokyo, but there are plenty of options if you want to spend the night to take advantage of the hot springs and aim to be first on the slopes the following day.

Hotel Futaba HOTEL ¥¥
(ホテル双葉; ☎025-784-3357; www.hotel-futaba.com; 419 Yuzawa; per person from ¥8500, incl 2 meals from ¥14,600; P ❄ 📶) The full onsen hotel experience is accessible at Futaba, which also provides a free shuttle service to Gala Yuzawa (p583). The common areas are a little impersonal, but the Japanese-style rooms are large and cosy, and the food is excellent.

★ **Hatago Isen** RYOKAN ¥¥¥
(HATAGO井仙; ☎025-784-3361; www.hatago-isen.jp; 2455 Yuzawa; r per person incl 2 meals from ¥14,000; P ❄ 📶) This sumptuous ryokan perfects the aesthetic of an old-time travellers' inn with dim lighting and dark wood, while maintaining modern conveniences. Rooms vary from humble singles to deluxe suites with private *rotemburo*. Meals feature local ingredients and are unusually flexible: you can choose from three different dinner courses and even elect to swap breakfast for lunch and a later checkout.

NASPA New Ōtani RESORT ¥¥¥
(NASPAニューオータニ; ☎025-780-6111; www.naspanewotani.com; 2117-9 Yuzawa; r per person incl 2 meals & lift pass from ¥17,000; P @ 📶) This family- and foreigner-friendly resort has its own backyard ski park that is particularly suited to beginners and small children. Rooms are Western-style and reasonably spacious, and there's a whole range of resort facilities, including an onsen. Free shuttles take just five minutes to run between Echigo-Yuzawa Station and the resort.

Eating

The train-station area has some excellent restaurants that do a brisk trade during winter, but are often closed in the warmer months. Otherwise eat meals at your lodging up the mountain.

Kikushin SOBA ¥
(菊新; ☎025-784-2881; 1-1-2 Yuzawa; bowls from ¥950; ⏲11am-3pm & 5.30-9pm Thu-Tue) Just outside the train station's east exit, on the corner, Kikushin serves delicious soba (hot or cold) and crunchy tempura (including mountain mushrooms) – perfect on a cold day.

Moritaki UDON ¥¥
(森瀧; ☎025-784-3600; 357-5 Yuzawa; dishes from ¥620; ⏲11.30am-2pm & 5.30-9pm Thu-Tue) The family at this fabulous little *nabe* (hotpot) restaurant prepares handmade udon noodles and various small beer-drinking sides. It's intimate and always busy.

Information

Echigo-Yuzawa Tourist Information Center
(広域観光情報センター; ☎025-785-5678; www.e-yuzawa.gr.jp; Echigo-Yuzawa Station; ⏲8am-6pm) Friendly, English-speaking staff provide a plethora of English-language maps and brochures, including a *Gastronomic Guide* to nearby restaurants. Baggage storage is also available (¥500 per bag).

Getting There & Away

There are several hourly *shinkansen* on the Jōetsu line from Tokyo to Echigo-Yuzawa (¥6150, 1¼ hours). Trains continue from Echigo-Yuzawa to Niigata (¥4860, 45 minutes).

Echigo-Yuzawa Onsen is connected to Naeba by regular local buses (¥660, 40 minutes). A free shuttle runs between Echigo-Yuzawa Station and Gala Yuzawa (p583).

Naeba

☎025

Not much more than a bus stop and a ski resort, Naeba (苗場) nonetheless enjoys a gorgeous mountain location. Expect some serious talent on the slopes (and at the welcoming après-ski scene). Indie music lovers across the world know Naeba for the wondrous summertime Fuji Rock Festival, Japan's biggest outdoor music festival.

Activities

Naeba Ski Resort SNOW SPORTS
(苗場スキー場; ☎025-789-4117; www.princehotels.com; 202 Mikuni, Yuzawa; day lift ticket/combined with Kagura ¥5000/5700, equipment per day from ¥5000; ⏲Dec-Apr; 👪) The longest of Naeba's 20-plus runs (4km) winds through birch forests and mogul fields prior to dropping a full 1km. The snow tends to be dry and light, and there are plenty of ungroomed areas where you can carve up some serious powder. English is widespread.

There's also a snow park for kids and a freestyle snowboarding course complete with rails, halfpipes and kickers. At the bottom of the hill, you'll find the N-Plateau, a massive complex with food court, onsen, convenience store and ski shop.

The awesomely named **Dragondola** (ドラゴンドラ), covering a distance of 5.5km, is reportedly the longest gondola in the world and whisks you away to neighbouring Kagura resort in just 15 minutes.

Kagura Ski Resort SNOW SPORTS
(かぐらスキー場; ☎025-788-9221; www.princehotels.com; 742 Mitsumata, Yuzawa; day lift ticket/combined with Naeba ¥4700/5700, equipment per day from ¥4200; ⊙Nov-May) Contiguous with Naeba, Kagura is an impressive mountain in its own right, with an additional 20-plus runs from beginner to advanced and a lax policy on backcountry skiing: experienced alpinists can really have an extreme adventure up here. For those who feel more comfortable sticking to the trails, one of the courses here reaches an impressive 6km.

With the combined pass, you can travel freely between Naeba and Kagura on the Dragondola at any time. Free shuttle buses depart from the bottom of the Mitsumata area.

Festivals & Events

Fuji Rock Festival MUSIC
(www.fujirockfestival.com; ⊙late Jul) The Fuji Rock Festival now ranks among the most prominent music festivals in the world. Big-name acts across a variety of genres – with ample indie, pop and electronica – take the stage over three days. It's a peaceful scene and a gorgeous mountain setting. Certainly a must-do for contemporary music lovers.

Sleeping

A lot of folk choose to sleep down the mountain in Echigo-Yuzawa Onsen (p583), where there's more action, but if you like to beat the morning rush on the slopes there are some decent options in the village itself. Most places close in the warmer months (except during Fuji Rock).

Wadagoya Mountain Hut HUT ¥
(和田小屋; ☎025-789-2211; www.princehotels.com; Mt Kagura; dm per person incl 2 meals ¥7800; ⊙Dec-Apr) The Prince Hotel runs this mountain hut on Kagura. Sleeping elbow-to-elbow on futons in a communal room, you'll make friends and cut first tracks in the morning. Arrive in Naeba by 3pm in order to catch the sequence of lifts up to the hut.

Prince Hotel Naeba HOTEL ¥¥
(プリンスホテル苗場; ☎025-789-2211; www.princehotels.co.jp/naeba; 202 Mikuni, Yuzawa; r from ¥8078; P ⊖ ❄ @ ᯤ) All of the ski action in Naeba centres on this monolithic resort at the base of the mountain. On offer are a wide range of Western-style rooms and suites that vary considerably in size, amenities and price – check online for specials – in addition to a slew of bars, cafes, restaurants and health and fitness facilities.

Eating & Drinking

There is nowhere of note to eat here outside the resorts – head back down the mountain to Echigo-Yuzawa Onsen.

During the ski season the odd drinking venue pops up and the Prince Hotel in particular welcomes nonguests.

Getting There & Away

Naeba is connected to Echigo-Yuzawa Onsen by regular local buses (¥660, 40 minutes). There are free shuttle buses to the Prince Hotel from Echigo-Yuzawa Onsen for registered guests.

At the height of the ski season, **Seibu Travel** (☎03-5910-2525; http://bus.seibutravel.co.jp/en) runs the White Snow Shuttle Bus between the Shinagawa Prince Hotel in Tokyo and Naeba (¥3600, 4¼ hours).

FUKUSHIMA PREFECTURE

Fukushima Prefecture (福島県; Fukushima-ken), Japan's third-largest prefecture, runs from the Pacific Ocean in the east through to vast mountainous terrain in the west. In the centre nestles the lush, lake-spotted Bandai Plateau, a haven for hikers, campers and outdoor enthusiasts. The peaceful medieval capital, Aizu-Wakamatsu, makes an ideal base to explore the many traditional villages hidden along rickety train lines. In winter skiers seek out remote runs, and steaming onsen fill up on weekends.

The Fukushima Dai-ichi Exclusion Zone (p586) only applies to a small fraction of the prefecture, and is clearly signposted and safeguarded.

Aizu-Wakamatsu

☎0242 / POP 124,062

Aizu-Wakamatsu (会津若松) is a former feudal capital with a number of interesting historical attractions and a bucolic location on the Bandai Plateau. A leisurely cycle around its wide, quiet streets – Nanoka-machi-dōri has a number of old-fashioned shops selling local crafts – is a pleasant way to spend time between forays along rickety train lines to traditional villages in the surrounding foothills.

History

Aizu-Wakamatsu was once the capital of the Aizu clan, whose reign came to an end in the Bōshin civil war of 1868, when the clan sided with the Tokugawa shogunate against the imperial faction. The fall of Aizu is famous throughout Japan on account of the Byakkotai (White Tigers). This group of teenage samurai committed seppuku (ritual suicide by disembowelment) when they saw Tsuruga-jō castle shrouded in smoke. In reality it was the surrounding area that was ablaze and it took weeks before defeat was final, but the White Tigers emerged as a powerful symbol of loyalty and fraternity. Their story is commemorated at Iimori-yama, the mountain where they met their end.

Sights

The main sights in Aizu are arrayed around the fringes of downtown. English signage makes it easy to get around on foot; alternatively catch the Classic Town Bus (p588). Be sure to visit the area around Iimori-yama.

Aizu Bukeyashiki HISTORIC BUILDING
(会津武家屋敷; ☎0242-28-2525; Innai Higashiyama-machi; adult/child ¥850/450; ⏲8.30am-5pm Apr-Nov, 9am-4.30pm Dec-Mar; P) This is a superb reconstruction of the *yashiki* (villa) of Saigō Tanomo, the Aizu clan's chief retainer. Wander through the 38 rooms, which include a guestroom for the Aizu lord, a tea-ceremony house, quarters for the clan's judge and a rice-cleaning mill, presented here in full, noisy working order.

Iimori-yama HISTORIC SITE
(飯盛山) On the eastern edge of Aizu is Iimori-yama, the mountain where the White Tigers (Byakkotai) samurai killed themselves during the civil war of 1868. You can take an escalator (¥250) or walk to the top to visit their graves. There are also some creepy old monuments here, gifted by the former fascist regimes of Germany and Italy, in honour of the samurai's loyalty and bravery.

At the foot of Iimori-yama, **White Tigers Memorial Hall** (白虎隊記念館, Byakkotai Kinenkan; ☎0242-24-9170; 33 Bentenshita; adult/child ¥400/200; ⏲8am-5pm Apr-Nov, 9am-4pm Dec-Mar) tells the story of the dramatic suicides of the teenage samurai who died during the Bōshin civil war of 1868, and houses their personal possessions.

Halfway up the mountain, look for **Sazae-dō** (さざえ堂; ☎0242-22-3163; 1404

FUKUSHIMA POST-2011

Like Chernobyl, Fukushima (in English) has become a dirty word, far removed from its ancient origin. The characters *fuku* (福) and *shima* (島) mean 'luck, good fortune' and 'island'. It's a cruel irony for the people of this large region that their home has become synonymous with one of the great human-made misfortunes of our time.

Following the 2011 Great East Japan Earthquake (p533) and tsunami, the nuclear power plant Fukushima Dai-ichi experienced a meltdown in three of its reactors and an explosion in its fourth, severely damaging the building in which highly radioactive spent nuclear fuel is stored, causing an unprecedented and ongoing nuclear disaster. More than 55,000 people were permanently evacuated. Many still live in crowded, temporary housing and are not allowed to return to their homes. The government estimates the clean-up within the exclusion zone will not be completed for many decades to come.

For many travellers to this region, the big question is whether there are any risks. In general, risks faced by long-term residents far outweigh those encountered by short-term travellers and, according to the *Journal of Radiological Protection* (2015), there is essentially no health risk outside the 20km exclusion zone, which is on the coast 58km from the city of Fukushima and 80km from Sendai.

Read up on the event, the nuclear industry and how radiation affects humans, animals and plants at the Fairewinds Energy Education site at www.fairewinds.org; for up-to-the-minute scientific data and radiation readings, visit www.ieaa.org.

Fukushima is Japan's third-largest prefecture and the 20km exclusion zone is a fraction of the overall region. Your presence in this beautiful part of the country will help show locals they've not been forgotten.

WORTH A TRIP

RAMEN TOWN KITAKATA

An old Kitakata (喜多方) saying suggests that 'a man is not a man unless he has built at least one *kura* (mud-walled storehouse)', and scattered around town you'll find thousands of unique *kura*, constructed between the late 18th and early 20th centuries, as testament to this rule. Kitakata, however, is likely more famous for ramen than its *kura* obsession, and many tourists visit just to try the various varieties on offer at almost 120 different noodle shops in town. Kitakata-style ramen is made with wavy, wide noodles in a hearty pork-and-fish broth made with local spring water, soy sauce and sake. There's no 'best' in town: take your pick. The **tourist information centre** (喜多方観光案内所; ☎0241-24-2633; ⏲8.30am-5pm) has an excellent ramen map.

Kitakata can be reached from Aizu-Wakamatsu by frequent trains along the JR Ban-etsu West line (¥320, 20 minutes). For drivers, Rte 121 runs between Aizu and Kitakata.

The town is a little spread out, but is easily navigable with the TIC's English-language walking map. Bicycle rental (per day ¥500) is available across the street from the train station.

Bentenshita; ¥400; ⏲9am-5pm), a weird and wonderful hidden gem in a Buddhist temple complex. Built in 1796 the 16.5m-high hexagonal wooden structure houses 33 statues of Kannon, the Buddhist goddess of mercy. Once inside you follow a fabulous, spiral, Escher-esque staircase that allows you to journey up and back down again without retracing your steps.

Tsuruga-jō CASTLE
(鶴ヶ城; ☎0242-27-4005; www.tsurugajo.com; 1-1 Ōte-machi; castle & teahouse garden ¥510; ⏲8.30am-5pm) The towering 1965 reconstruction of Tsuruga-jō sits in sprawling grounds framed by the original moat and some ruins of the old castle walls. Inside is a museum with historical artefacts from battles and daily life, but the real drawcard is the view from the 5th-floor lookout. On the castle grounds is Rinkaku teahouse, with a small garden, where you can enjoy a cup of *matcha* (¥600).

Sleeping

Tagoto RYOKAN ¥¥
(料理旅館田事; ☎0242-24-7500; www.tagoto-aizu.com; 5-15 Johoku-machi; r per person from ¥7500; P⊖❄☜) Exceptional hospitality, delicious meals and elegant decor are the hallmarks of this traditional ryokan, located a few blocks' walk from the city centre. Reserve the private bath during check-in for a luxurious soak.

Minshuku Takaku MINSHUKU ¥¥
(民宿多賀来; ☎0242-26-6299; www.naf.co.jp/takaku; 104 Innai Higashiyama-machi; r per person ¥4500, incl 2 meals ¥6500; P⊖@☜) Minshuku Takaku is fairly modest, but the tatami rooms are adequate, and there's a pleasant *o-furo* (bath) and an elegant communal dining area. It's located just east of the Aizu Bukeyashiki bus stop; from there continue along the road, turn left at the post office and it's just behind, on the left.

Eating

Mitsutaya JAPANESE ¥
(満田屋; ☎0242-27-1345; www.mitsutaya.jp; 1-1-25 Ō-machi; skewers from ¥260; ⏲10am-5pm Thu-Tue; 🅥) The versatile soybean is pounded and skewered to perfection at this former bean-paste mill dating from 1834. The speciality here is *dengaku* – bamboo skewers of tofu, *mochi* (pounded rice cake) or vegetables basted in sweet miso paste and baked over charcoal. Just point at what you want, or go for the *dengaku cōsu* (tasting course; ¥1400).

Takino JAPANESE ¥¥
(田季野; ☎0242-25-0808; www.takino.jp; 5-31 Sakae-machi; wappa meshi from ¥1500; ⏲11am-9pm; 🅥) One of the most popular places to try the sublime *wappa meshi* (steamed fish or vegetables over rice, prepared in a container made from tree bark, which adds a woody fragrance). Takino offers several versions, including salmon, crab and wild mushroom. It's not particularly cheap for the size of the portions, but it's easy to order and quick to reach your table.

Information

MONEY

Aizu-Wakamatsu Post Office (会津若松郵便局; ☎0242-22-0840; 1-2-17 Chūō; ⏲9am-7pm Mon-Fri, to 3pm Sat, ATM 8am-9pm Mon-Sat, to 8pm Sun) Located on the main street, with an international ATM.

TOURIST INFORMATION

Tourist Information Center (会津若松観光案内所; ☎0242-33-0688; www.e.samurai-city.jp; ⌚9am-5.30pm) Inside the JR station. Staff speak limited English but have plenty of literature to dispense.

Getting There & Away

The JR Tōhoku *shinkansen* runs hourly between Tokyo and Kōriyama (¥7680, 1¼ hours). Kōriyama is connected to Aizu-Wakamatsu by the JR Ban-etsu-saisen line; hourly *kaisoku* (rapid trains; ¥1140, 1¼ hours) ply this scenic route. There are a couple of daily *kaisoku* on the JR Ban-etsu West line between Aizu-Wakamatsu and Niigata (¥2270, 2½ hours).

Highway buses depart from outside Aizu-Wakamatsu train station for Tokyo (¥4800, 4½ hours).

Getting Around

The retro **Classic Town Bus** (まちなか周遊バス; ☎0242-22-5555; www.aizubus.com; single/day pass ¥210/600) departs from outside the train station and does a slow loop of the main sights. There are two lines, the 'Akabe' and the 'Haikara-san'; pick up a route map from the tourist office.

Bicycle rental is available at several points around town for ¥500 per day; enquire at the tourist office.

Bandai Plateau

☎0241

The Bandai Plateau (磐梯高原) is part of the Bandai-Asahi National Park (磐梯朝日国立公園) and its spectacular scenery attracts all kinds of outdoor enthusiasts, including hikers, climbers, fishers, skiers and snowboarders. In the centre is Bandai-san (1819m), a once-dormant volcano that erupted suddenly in 1888, spewing forth a tremendous amount of debris that's said to have lowered the mountain's height by 600m. The eruption destroyed dozens of villages and completely rearranged the landscape, resulting in the vast, lake-dotted plateau now known as Bandai-kōgen.

Activities

Goshiki-numa HIKING

(五色沼) This popular 3.7km nature trail weaves around a dozen or so pools known as the Five Colours Lakes. Mineral deposits from the 1888 eruption imparted various hues to the waters – cobalt-blue, emerald-green, reddish-brown – which change with the weather. Trailheads begin at Goshiki-numa Iriguchi and Bandai-kōgen bus stops, the main transport hubs beside Hibara-ko, the largest of the Ura-Bandai lakes.

Buses depart from Inawashiro. In April the trail may still be covered in packed snow, and November marks the start of the long Tōhoku winter.

Bandai-san HIKING

(磐梯山) Six trails lead to Bandai-san summit and its panorama of mountain ranges and Inawashiro Lake; the summit is accessible from May to October. From JR Inawashiro Station, catch the bus to Bandai-kōgen to reach the **Ura-Bandai Tozan-guchi** (裏磐梯登山口) trail: this is the easiest to reach by public transport and the most challenging hike, at seven hours return.

After climbing through ski grounds, the path meets the **Happō-dai** (八方台) trail, the shortest, most popular route.

Snow Paradise Inawashiro SNOW SPORTS

(猪苗代スキー場; ☎0242-62-5100; www.inawashiro-ski.com; 7105 Hayama, Inawashiro-machi; 1-day lift ticket adult/child ¥4700/3900, equipment rental per day ¥3900; ⌚Dec-Mar; 👪) Bandai-san's original ski area, Inawashiro has 16 runs – most are beginner and intermediate, which, in conjunction with scant weekday crowds, makes this resort a great choice for novices and families. Veterans may grow bored with the limited options. The slopes are located in the hills above Inawashiro town. Frequent shuttles run between JR Inawashiro Station and the resort in season.

Sleeping

Inawashiro has the widest range of accommodation, while the winding roads around Bandai-kōgen are home to a plethora of resort-style complexes popular with bus tours and skiers.

Size Resort Hotel Urabandai HOTEL ¥¥

(サイズリゾートホテル裏磐梯; ☎0241-23-7776; www.sizeresorthotel-u.com; 1093 Kengamine, Hibara; r per person from ¥6300; P❄📶) Well located for hiking in the Urabandai region, this recently renovated hotel has a dozen small but pristine rooms, a light-filled dining room and a small attached onsen.

Bandai Plateau & Around

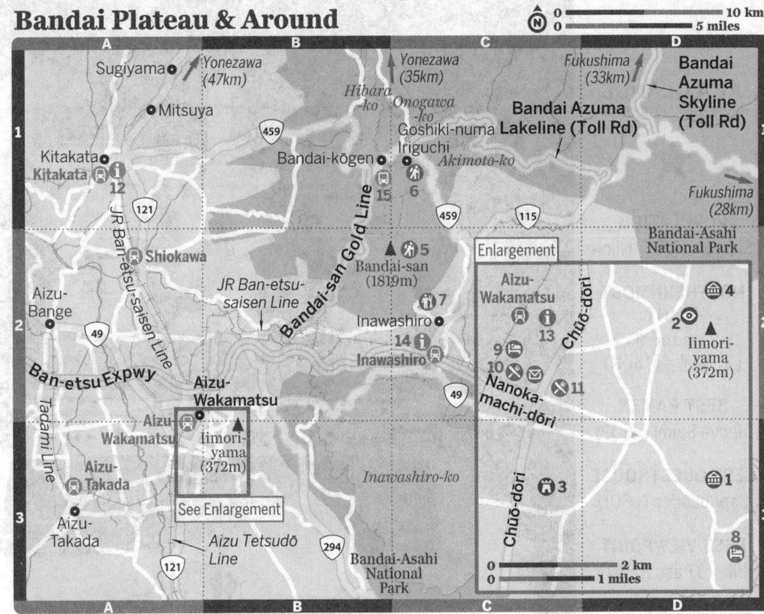

Bandai Plateau & Around

Sights

1 Aizu Bukeyashiki D3
2 Iimori-yama D2
Sazae-dō .... (see 4)
3 Tsuruga-jō C3
4 White Tigers Memorial Hall D2

Activities, Courses & Tours

5 Bandai-san C2
6 Goshiki-numa C1
7 Snow Paradise Inawashiro C2

Sleeping

8 Minshuku Takaku D3
Size Resort Hotel Urabandai .... (see 6)
9 Tagoto C2

Eating

10 Mitsutaya C2
11 Takino C2

Information

12 Tourist Information Center A1
13 Tourist Information Center C2
14 Tourist Information Center C2
Ura-Bandai Visitors Center .... (see 6)

Transport

15 Bandai-kōgen Bus Stop B1
Classic Town Bus .... (see 13)
Goshiki-numa Iriguchi Bus Stop .... (see 6)

Information

Tourist Information Center (裏磐梯観光協会; ☎0242-62-2048; www.bandaisan.or.jp; Ogida-1-4 Chiyoda, Inawashiro-machi; ⏲8.30am-5pm) Outside JR Inawashiro Station; get trail maps here for Bandai-san hikes and beyond.

Ura-Bandai Visitors Center (裏磐梯ビジターセンター; ☎0241-32-2850; 1093-697 Kengamine, Hibara; ⏲9am-4pm) Near the Goshiki-numa Iriguchi trailhead.

Getting There & Around

Several *kaisoku* (rapid trains) run daily along the JR Ban-etsu West line between Aizu-Wakamatsu and Inawashiro (¥500, 30 minutes).

From outside JR Inawashiro Station, frequent buses depart from stop 3 for the **Goshiki-numa Iriguchi** trailhead (¥770, 25 minutes), before heading on to the **Bandai-kōgen bus stop** (¥890, 35 minutes).

AT A GLANCE

POPULATION
Sapporo: 1.97 million

NORTHERNMOST POINT
Sōya-misaki (宗谷岬; 45°31'N)

BEST RAMEN
Menya Saimi (p602)

BEST GUESTHOUSE
SappoLodge (p601)

BEST VIEWPOINT
Bihoro Pass (p657)

WHEN TO GO

Jun–Aug Hiking season reaches its peak during the holidays of July and August.

Sep–Oct A brief but intense autumn is marked by changing leaves.

Dec–Mar Subzero chill and Siberian snowfalls herald the ski season.

View of Ōdōri-kōen (p597) from Sapporo TV Tower (p599)

Sapporo & Hokkaidō

Hokkaidō (北海道) is the Japan of wide-open spaces, with 20% of the country's land area but only 5% of its population. There are large swathes of wilderness here, with primeval forests, tropical-blue caldera lakes, fields of alpine wildflowers and bubbling, in-the-rough hot springs. In the summer, all this (plus the cooler, drier weather) draws hikers, cyclists and strollers.

Winter is a different beast entirely: cold fronts from Siberia bring huge dumps of light, powdery snow, which has earned Hokkaidō a reputation as a paradise for skiers and snowboarders; there are international-level resorts here, but also remote backcountry opportunities.

INCLUDES

Sapporo & Hokkaidō Highlights

❶ **Daisetsuzan National Park** (p632) Charting a path through the wilderness in Japan's largest national park, nicknamed the 'rooftop of Hokkaidō'.

❷ **Niseko** (p606) Carving fresh tracks in the famous powder of Asia's top ski destination.

❸ **Sapporo** (p597) Getting your urban fix in the restaurants and bars of Susukino and drinking Sapporo beer straight from the source.

❹ **Noboribetsu Onsen** (p618) Saying goodbye to stiff muscles in steaming baths of natural hot-spring water.

❺ **Rishiri-Rebun-Sarobetsu National Park** (p638) Taking the ferry to the remote islands of Rishiri-tō and Rebun-tō for hiking and *uni* (sea urchin).

❻ **Hakodate** (p621) Strolling through 19th-century streetscapes of a historic port city.

❼ **Shiretoko National Park** (p648) Getting close to *higuma* (brown bears) and spawning salmon at this Unesco World Heritage Site.

❽ **Akan National Park** (p652) Learning about Hokkaidō's indigenous people, the Ainu, in the park's lakeside *kotan* (village).

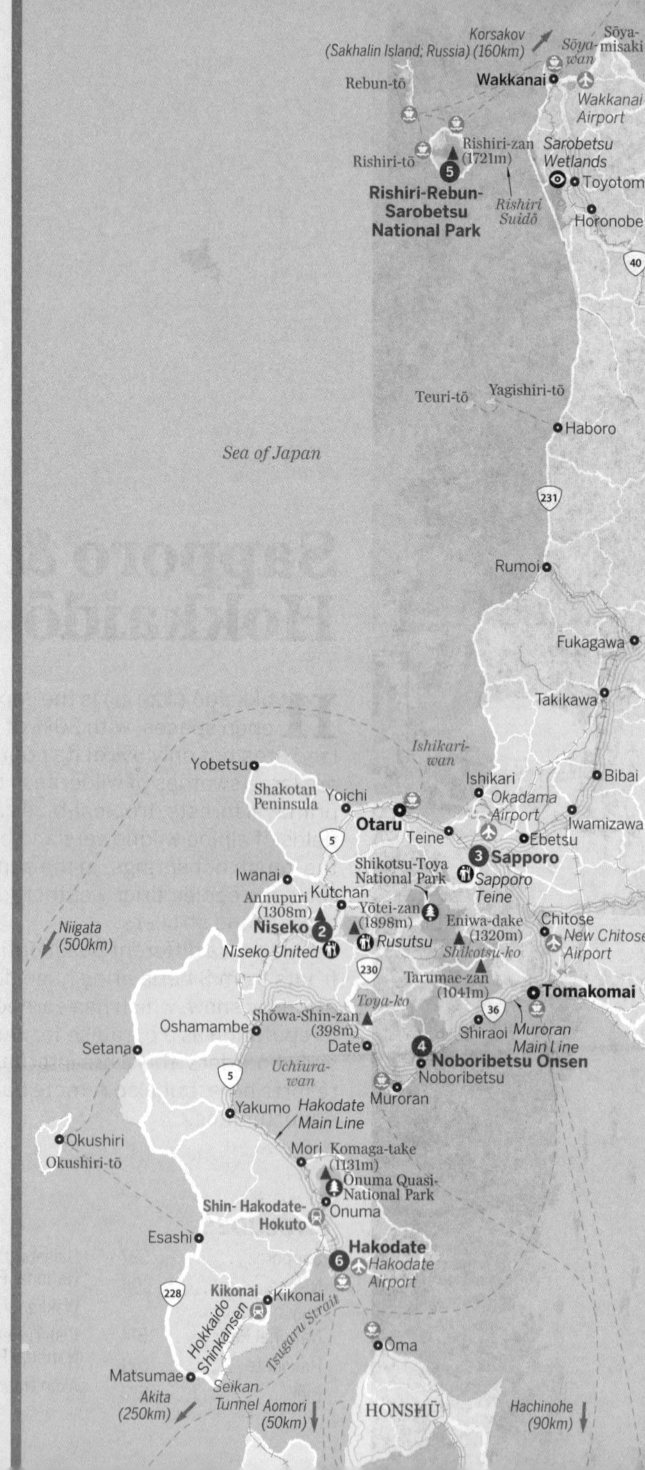

0
100 km
0
50 miles
Sea of Okhotsk
Esashi
Sōya Main Line
238
Nayoro
Monbetsu
Shibetsu
Saroma-ko
Engaru
Shiretoko-misaki
Shiretoko National Park 7
Iwaobetsu
Rausu-dake (1660m)
Utoro
Rausu
Nemuro Strait
RUSSIA
Abashiri
Memanbetsu Airport
Shari
334
335
Kamikawa
Sekihoku Main Line
Asahikawa
Asahikawa Airport
12
Sōunkyō
39
Kitami
Bihiro
Asahi-dake (2290m)
Kuro-dake (1984m)
Kussharo-ko
Kawayu Onsen
Shibetsu
Nokke Strait
Biei
Ashibetsu
Daisetsuzan National Park 1
HOKKAIDŌ
Akan National Park 8
Mashu-ko
Naka-Shibetsu
Akan-ko
Akanko Onsen
Teshikaga
Nosappu-misaki
Furano Line
38
Tokachi-dake (2077m)
Nukabira-ko
Akankohan
Me-Akan-dake (1499m)
O-Akan-dake (1371m)
Nemuro-wan
Nemuro
Furano
Shikaribetsu-ko
273
Senmō Main Line
Ashoro
274
Bear Mountain
Kushiro Wetlands National Park
Sekishō Main Line
39
44
Kushiro Airport
Shimizu
Kushiro
Obihiro
Ikeda
Shiranuka
Hidaka
38
Nemuro Main Line
Poroshiri-dake (2052m)
Obihiro Airport
Nibutani
Biratori
Shinhidaka
Hirō
Hidaka Main Line
Urakawa
Samani
Erimo-misaki
PACIFIC OCEAN
Sendai (430km);
Oarai (800km)

History

Hokkaidō was connected to northern Asia via Sakhalin, the large island to the north, and the Kuril Islands, a long archipelago reaching from the Kamchatka peninsula towards eastern Hokkaidō, during the glacial age. It is believed that humans moved into the region around 30,000 years ago, following the mammoths and bison that once roamed these parts. In the 12th or 13th century, influenced by both the burgeoning Japanese civilisation to the south and the hunting and fishing tribes to the north (in Sakhalin and beyond), a distinct culture formed. The people called themselves Ainu, which meant 'human' and their land Mosir, which meant 'world'.

Prior to 1869, the Japanese called the island Ezo (or Yezo) and its people *emishi* (basically, barbarians). Hokkaidō was a foreign land. As the Japanese empire solidified and expanded in the 14th and 15th centuries, many Japanese people moved north, lured by the promise of profit in trade. Conflicts erupted occasionally between the Ainu and the Japanese settlers, but they remained important trading partners: the Japanese coveted the dried fish, seaweed pelts and furs of the Ainu; the Ainu had come to depend on the iron goods imported from the south.

Then, in 1590, the Matsumae clan of northern Honshū was given permission by shogun Toyotomi Hideyoshi to extend their domain over the southern reach of Ezo – in order to better protect Japan from 'barbarian' attack. In 1604 the newly established Tokugawa shogunate granted the Matsumae clan exclusive trading rights in Ezo. With consolidated authority (and occasional force), the Matsumae were able to push forward with trade and production regulations that resulted in the Ainu working for the Japanese (in fisheries, for example) in order to receive the same goods they had previously acquired through trade.

Japanese authority crept ever northward throughout the 18th and 19th centuries, with colonialisation beginning in earnest following the Meiji Restoration. In 1869, the new government formally annexed Ezo, renamed it Hokkaidō ('northern sea territory'), and established the Kaitakushi (Development Commission) to promote settlement and introduce agriculture and manufacturing to the region. Among those who were encouraged to move north were the newly unemployed (and potentially troublesome) samurai class and luckless second sons (as first-born sons traditionally inherited everything).

The primary purpose of this push northward was to halt Russian expansion southward, but it was devastating for the Ainu. While the Ainu had previously been prohibited from dressing like Japanese – in order to distinguish them – new regulations demanded assimilation, banning the Ainu language and traditional ways of life.

Following the Japanese victory in the 1904–05 Russo-Japanese War, Japan took control of the whole of the island of Karafu-tō (now Sakhalin). By 1940, 400,000 Japanese were living there as part of a continuing colonial effort. In the final days of WWII, Russia recaptured Sakhalin, as well as the southern Kuril Islands, which were then part of Japan (and now referred to in Japan as the Northern Territories).

Still today Japan continues to dispute the ownership of the latter, which were captured after Japan's surrender to the Western European powers (Russia was not party to that treaty). The islands remain a point of contention between Japan and Russia, to the point that the two countries have yet to sign a peace treaty ending the war.

In September 2018, the island was hit by several major earthquakes, one of which caused a deadly landslide, ruptured highways, destroyed homes and buildings, and caused major power outages across the south and central parts of the island. Though the structural damage was quickly repaired, tourism dropped to a fraction of what it would have been as people avoided the area.

Climate

Surprisingly, Sapporo, at around 43°N, is about the same latitude as Marseille in the south of France and southern Oregon in the USA. The freezing winters for which Hokkaidō are known are a result of the island's proximity to Siberia and cold northwesterly winds, which bring significant snowfall, especially on the Sea of Japan side of the island.

Summers in Hokkaidō are relatively cool and dry compared to hot and humid Honshū to the south (making the island a popular escape). The typhoons that can wreck travel plans in the southern half of Japan don't usually reach this far – though one did, in 2016, causing enough damage to suspend some rail lines for months. Winter comes early: Daisetsuzan gets its first snowfall in October (and sometimes late September). This range of mountains in the dead centre of Hokkaidō is the coldest region in Japan, where temperatures can drop to -20°C.

National Parks

Hokkaidō has six national parks, including Japan's largest, Daisetsuzan National Park. As much of this protected landscape was formed by volcanic activity, all parks (except for Kushiro-shitsugen) have natural hot springs.

Akan (p652) Caldera lakes set in pristine forests of fir and spruce.

Daisetsuzan (p632) A true wilderness of primeval forests, covering more than 2300 sq km, with 15 peaks over 2000m.

Kushiro-shitsugen (p660) Japan's largest wetland and an important habitat for the endangered red-crowned crane.

Rishiri-Rebun-Sarobetsu (p638) Isolated islands and marshlands with endemic flora.

Shikotsu-Tōya (p614) Clear caldera lakes and active volcanoes.

Shiretoko (p648) A remote, wild peninsula with little human intervention (and lots of wildlife).

Sleeping

One of the joys of visiting Hokkaidō is getting to stay in some truly fantastic (and reasonably priced) lodgings run by eccentric characters. Outside of Sapporo and resort areas like Niseko, world-class hotels are basically non-existent; travelling here means roughing it a bit. In almost any city, you can find basic economy chains, of which Toyoko Inn (www.toyoko-inn.com) is the most reliable and prevalent. Hostels and campgrounds are plentiful, too.

Hokkaidō also has the greatest number of 'rider houses', bare-bones budget accommodation options reserved for travellers on two wheels.

Eating

Hokkaidō is a fantastic place to eat, serving up specialities different from what you might find elsewhere in Japan – thanks to its bountiful land, ample coast and a climate that favours belly-warming dishes. Sapporo has the liveliest dining scene, while Niseko, with its star rising ever higher, is becoming more than just a ski spot – it's got some decent restaurants year-round. In coastal areas, the fresh, seasonal seafood – particularly the shellfish – is tops.

In rural areas, restaurants may be hard to come by. Look for Michi-no-eki (道の駅; road stations), like highway service areas, but for country roads. In addition to toilets, tourist information and coffee, Michi-no-eki usually have cafeterias and shops selling local produce and homemade specialities. They're well signposted. Another lifesaver is the only-in-Hokkaidō convenience store chain Seico Mart.

Information

SAFE TRAVEL

Wildlife and weather pose the biggest threats in Hokkaidō. This is bear country and the bears up here are different to the small black bears that inhabit Honshū; they are *higuma* (Ussuri brown bear), thought to be the ancestor of the North American grizzly bear, and they're much bigger and more aggressive.

Take all precautions, especially in the early morning and at dusk, and avoid hoofing it alone. Make a lot of noise; like Japanese hikers, tie a *kuma-yoke* (bear bell) to your rucksack. The theory goes that bears want to meet you face to face about as much as you want to meet them face to face and if they hear you coming, they'll avoid you at all costs.

If you're camping, use the steel food bins or tie up your food and do not bury your rubbish. Bear activity picks up noticeably during early autumn when the creatures are actively foraging for food ahead of their winter hibernation. Be especially cautious at this time.

The Shiretoko Peninsula is home to the highest concentration of *higuma* on Hokkaidō, but they are also often sighted in Daisetsuzan National Park; really, they could be anywhere there are mountains. Only the remote islands of Rishiri-tō and Rebun-tō are bear-free.

Hikers need to also be wary of foxes. It's estimated that 40% of Hokkaidō's foxes carry the parasitic worm *echinococcus*, so keep away from them and boil your water if camping. If you're driving, keep an eye out for deer, especially at night, and enquire about road conditions if you're heading up into the mountains outside of the summer season.

Getting There & Away

AIR

Flying to Hokkaidō is often the cheapest way to get there. Sapporo's New Chitose Airport (p605) is the main port of entry, seeing an increasing number of direct international flights wing in from around Asia and the Pacific, including Taiwan, Hong Kong, China, Korea, Thailand, Guam and Hawaii.

Hokkaidō-based budget carrier **Air Do** (www.airdo.jp) flies direct from Tokyo's Haneda Airport

SEIKAN TUNNEL

A marvel of Japanese engineering, the Seikan railway tunnel travels beneath the Tsugaru Strait, connecting the islands of Honshū and Hokkaidō. With a total length of 53.85km, including a 240m-deep and 23.3km-long undersea portion, the Seikan Tunnel (青函トンネル), opened in 1988, is the deepest and longest undersea tunnel in the world.

to New Chitose and also to regional airports such as Asahikawa, Hakodate, Kushiro, Memanbetsu and Obihiro. It also flies to New Chitose from Hiroshima, Kōbe, Nagoya and Sendai.

ANA (www.ana.co.jp) has flights to New Chitose Airport from cities around Japan and also direct flights from Tokyo to some of Hokkaidō's regional airports, such as Asahikawa, Hakodate, Kushiro, Memanbetsu, Obihiro and Wakkanai.

The following budget airlines offer cheap flights, from as low as ¥4000 one way, to New Chitose Airport from Tokyo. If you buy a ticket from Narita, be sure to factor in the cost and time required for the trip to the airport.

Jetstar (www.jetstar.com) Also flies to/from Nagoya and Osaka.

Skymark (www.skymark.jp)

Vanilla Air (www.vanilla-air.com)

BOAT

Ferries make the journey from Honshū to Hokkaidō. This is pretty much never the cheapest way to get anywhere, and is always the least time-efficient, but the ferries themselves can be fun: long-haul ones have communal bathhouses, dining halls and even karaoke rooms.

Tomakomai is the main port of entry for long-haul ferries. Shorter runs from Aomori, the northernmost prefecture on Honshū, go to Hakodate. Ferries going up the Sea of Japan coast travel to Otaru.

The following companies operate ferries to/from Hokkaidō:

MOL Ferry (www.sunflower.co.jp) Between Tomakomai and Ōarai (Ibaraki-ken) – the closest port to Tokyo.

Seikan Ferry (www.seikan-ferry.co.jp) Runs between Hakodate and Aomori.

Shin-Nihonkai Ferry (www.snf.jp) Down the Japan Sea side of Honshū, between Tomakomai, Akita, Niigata and Tsuruga (Fukui-ken); and between Otaru, Niigata and Maizuru (Kyoto-fu).

Silver Ferry (www.silverferry.jp) Between Tomakomai and Hachinohe (Aomori-ken).

Taiheiyō Ferry (www.taiheiyo-ferry.co.jp) Down the Pacific coast of Honshū, between Tomakomai, Sendai and Nagoya.

Tsugaru Kaikyō Ferry (www.tsugarukaikyo.co.jp) Between Hakodate and Aomori, and Hakodate and Ōma (at the northernmost tip of Honshū).

TRAIN

With the opening of the Hokkaidō Shinkansen in 2016, it's now possible to take a *shinkansen* (bullet train) all the way from Tokyo to Hakodate, the terminus in southern Hokkaidō. Travel on the Hokkaidō Shinkansen is included in the country-wide Japan Rail Pass.

Getting Around

AIR

Flying is a good option if you are short on time and want to hit remote, and distant, points.

BICYCLE

Hokkaidō is a great place to tour by bike and cyclists are a common sight all over the island, especially during summer. The Cycle Tourism Hokkaido Promotion Network has a helpful booklet, called *Hokkaido Cycle Tourism*, that covers routes, climate, guidelines for taking bikes on public transport and more. Find it at www.hkd.mlit.go.jp.

BUS

Buses tend to be the cheapest way to get around Hokkaidō, based on individual fares, and there is an extensive network of routes. Most city-to-city coaches require reservations; purchasing a return ticket usually results in a slight discount. Bus terminals tend to be conveniently located: either next to the train station or, when the train station itself is outside of town, in a central location.**Chūō Bus** (中央バス; ☎Sapporo terminal 011-231-0600; www.chuo-bus.co.jp), based in Sapporo, is the biggest operator, connecting the capital with pretty much everywhere.

Regional operators include the following:

Dōhoku Bus (www.dohokubus.com) Between Asahikawa and Obihiro, Kushiro and Sapporo.

Dōnan Bus (www.donanbus.co.jp) Between Sapporo and points south, including Hakodate, New Chitose Airport, Tomakomai, Niseko, Rusutsu, Jōzankei, Tōya-ko Onsen and Noboribetsu Onsen.

Sōya Bus (www.soyabus.co.jp) Between Sapporo and Wakkanai.

CAR & MOTORCYCLE

With the advent of multilingual car navigation systems, more and more travellers are choosing to tour Hokkaidō by car. There is an expanding pay-your-way expressway system (高速道路; *kōsoku-dōro*), which is relatively expensive and you won't need to use unless you're in a hurry. A reduced-price **Hokkaidō Expressway Pass** (www.driveplaza.com/trip/drawari/hokkaido_

expass) is available for foreign visitors and can be purchased through rental-car companies.

The easiest place to pick up a car is at New Chitose Airport (p605). Shuttles take you directly to the airport car depots, where friendly English-speaking staff will get you on your way.

Prices are comparable among the major agencies, between ¥7000 and ¥10,000 per day (depending on the season), plus the cost of fuel. The following are reliable and can be booked online in English:

JR Hokkaido Rent a Car (www.jrh-rentacar.com) With outlets at major train stations, good for short-term rentals combined with rail travel.

Nippon Rent-a-Car Hokkaido (www.nrh.co.jp) Outlets in Sapporo, Hakodate and most regional airports.

Nissan Rent a Car (http://nissan-rentacar.com) Outlets in Sapporo, Hakodate and most regional airports.

Toyota Rent-a-Car (www.toyotarentacar.net) Outlets in Sapporo and Niseko.

Note that many Japanese companies have a clause that requires you to pay ¥50,000 or so if they are unable to rent the car immediately after you return it. This can be deceptive, as it may apply to a car that must be cleaned or (in the case of a minor accident) a ding or scrape that has to be repaired. Insurance against this is offered, but in otherwise-fair-and-reasonable Japan it seems usurious.

TRAIN

While the *shinkansen* only runs as far as Hakodate, a number of 'limited express' *(tokkyū)* trains make quick runs between major cities, as far north as Wakkanai and as far east as Kushiro. Sapporo is the main transit hub for these trains. Local trains ply the same routes and others, for less, but take much longer and often require multiple transfers.

In addition to the country-wide Japan Rail Pass, the following options are available for Hokkaidō-bound travellers. Passes can be purchased from travel agents abroad or from JR information centres in Hokkaidō and Tokyo, including those at Narita, Haneda and New Chitose Airports. For details, see: www2.jrhokkaido.co.jp/global.

Hokkaidō Rail Pass Unlimited fixed-day (three/five/seven ¥16,500/22,000/24,000, children half-price) and four-day flexible (¥22,000, children half-price) travel on Hokkaidō's network of limited express and local trains (*shinkansen* excluded).

JR East-South Hokkaidō Rail Pass (adult/child ¥27,000/13,500) Six-day unlimited, flexible travel (within 14 days) on *shinkansen* between Tokyo and Hakodate and limited express trains between Hakodate and Sapporo (via Niseko).

SAPPORO

☎011 / POP 1.97 MILLION

Japan's fifth-largest city, and the prefectural capital of Hokkaidō, Sapporo (札幌) is a dynamic urban centre that offers everything you'd want from a Japanese city: a thriving food scene, stylish cafes, neon-lit nightlife, shopping galore – and then some. While many travellers see the city as a transit hub from which to access Hokkaidō's mountains and hot springs, there are enough worthwhile attractions to keep you here for days. Summer is the season for beer and food festivals. In February, despite the bitter cold, Sapporo's population literally doubles during the famous Snow Festival.

Sights

High season runs from April to October; most attractions have reduced hours the rest of the year. Many spots close on Mondays.

★Sapporo Beer Museum MUSEUM
(サッポロビール博物館; ☎011-748-1876; www.sapporoholdings.jp/english/guide/sapporo; N7E9 Higashi-ku; ⊙10.30am-6.30pm; Ⓟ; 🚌88 to Sapporo Biiru-en, Ⓢ Tōhō line to Higashi-Kuyakusho-mae, exit 4) FREE This legendary Sapporo attraction is in the original Sapporo Beer brewery, a pretty, ivy-covered brick building. There's no need to sign up for the tour; there are plenty of English explanations throughout about Japan's oldest beer (the brewery was founded in 1876). At the end there's a tasting salon (beers ¥200 to ¥300) where you can compare Sapporo's signature Black Label with Sapporo Classic (found only in Hokkaidō) and Kaitakushi Pilsner, a re-creation of the original recipe (found only here).

Afterwards, head next door to the Sapporo Biergarten (p604) for more beer and *jingisukan* (all-you-can-eat lamb dish). Note that any drivers will not be allowed to drink.

From the subway it's a 10-minute walk; the bus stops right out front.

★Ōdōri-kōen PARK
(大通公園; www.sapporo-park.or.jp/odori; Ⓢ Tōzai, Tōhō & Namboku lines to Ōdōri) This haven in the heart of the city is fully 13 blocks (1.5km) long, with the TV Tower (p599) at its eastern end. Among the green lawns and flower gardens are benches, fountains and sculptures; don't miss Noguchi Isamu's elegant **Black Slide Mantra** (ブラックスライドマントラ; Ōdōri-kōen; Ⓢ Tōzai, Tōhō & Namboku lines to Ōdōri). This is also where many of the city's major events and festivals take place.

Sapporo

The park is a 10-minute walk south from JR Sapporo Station along Eki-mae-dōri.

Hokkaidō Ainu Center CULTURAL CENTRE
(北海道アイヌ協会, Hokkaidō Ainu Kyōkai; 011-221-0462; www.ainu-assn.or.jpx; 7th fl, Kaderu 2.7 Bldg, N2W7 Chūō-ku; 9am-5pm Mon-Sat; JR Sapporo, south exit; Ōdōri, exit 2) FREE In an office building across the street from Hokkaidō University Botanical Garden, this cultural centre is run by the Hokkaidō Ainu Association and has a small display of artefacts and historical information.

Sapporo

Top Sights
1 Ōdōri-kōen C3

Sights
2 Black Slide Mantra A4
3 Hokkaidō Ainu Center B3
4 Hokkaidō University Botanical Garden A2
5 Old Hokkaidō Government Office Building B2
6 Sapporo Clock Tower C3
7 Sapporo TV Tower D3

Sleeping
8 JR Tower Hotel Nikko Sapporo C1
9 Marks Inn Sapporo C6
10 Nakamuraya Ryokan B2
11 SappoLodge D5
12 Sapporo Grand Hotel C3

Eating
13 Daruma C5
14 Ganso Ramen Yokochō C5
15 Kani-honke C2
16 Kani-honke Susukino-ten C5
17 Milk Mura C5
18 Ramen Kyōwakoku C1
19 Saera C3

Drinking & Nightlife
20 Mugishutei C6
Riviera .... (see 16)

Information
21 Hokkaidō-Sapporo Food & Tourist Information Centre B2
22 JR Information Desk B1
23 Nomad C4
24 Sapporo International Communication Plaza C3

Transport
25 Chūō Bus Terminal D3
26 Ōdōri Bus Terminal D3
27 Porocle B2
28 Sapporo Eki-mae Bus Terminal C2

If you really want to learn more, the reading room here has pretty much every book published in English on the Ainu (past and present).

Hokkaidō Museum of Modern Art MUSEUM
(北海道立近代美術館, Hokkaidō Ritsukindai-bijutsukan; www.dokyoi.pref.hokkaido.lg.jp/hk/knb; N1W17, Chūō-ku; ¥510; 9.30am-5pm Tue-Sun; S Tōzai line to Nishi-juhatchōme, exit 4) Hokkaidō's top collection of modern art includes many works from artists who were born here, lived here or were inspired by the northern island. Exhibitions vary, so check the schedule ahead of time.

Moiwa-yama Ropeway CABLE CAR
(もいわ山ロープウェイ; 011-561-8177; http://moiwa.sapporo-dc.co.jp; 5-3-7 Fushimi; adult/child return ¥1700/850; 10.30am-10pm; Rōpuwei-iriguchi) At 531m, Moiwa-yama has fantastic, panoramic views over the city. Part of the fun is getting there. First you take a gondola for five minutes, then switch to a cute little cable car for two more minutes. Free shuttle buses run to the ropeway from the Rōpuwei-iriguchi tram stop; otherwise it's a 10-minute walk.

Old Hokkaidō Government Office Building NOTABLE BUILDING
(北海道庁旧本庁舎; 011-204-5019; N3W6 Chūō-ku; 8.45am-6pm; S Namboku & Tōhō lines to Sapporo-eki, exit 10) FREE Known by all as Akarenga (red bricks), this magnificent neo-baroque building was constructed of bricks in 1888 and is surrounded by lovely lawns and gardens. There are various historical exhibits and shows from local artists inside. While Akarenga closes at 6pm, the gardens are open until 9pm and are a popular place for a stroll.

Sapporo TV Tower TOWER
(さっぽろテレビ塔; Sapporo Terebi-tō; www.tv-tower.co.jp; Ōdōri-nishi 1-chōme; adult/child ¥720/300; 9am-10pm; S Tōzai, Tōhō & Namboku lines to Ōdōri, exits 2 & 7) Beating Tokyo Tower by two years, Sapporo TV Tower (147m) arrived in 1956, bringing with it the modern television age. It was designed by 'Dr Tower' Naitō Tachū, who also designed Nagoya TV Tower (1954), Osaka's Tsūtenkaku (1956) and Tokyo Tower (1958). The observation deck at 90m is rather cramped, but you do get a view straight down Ōdōri-kōen.

Hokkaidō University Botanical Garden GARDENS
(北大植物園, Hokudai Shokubutsuen; 011-221-0066; www.hokudai.ac.jp/fsc/bg; N3W8 Chūō-ku; adult/child ¥420/300; 9am-4pm Tue-Sun Apr-Sep, to 3.30pm Oct-Mar; JR Sapporo, south exit) Among the highlights of this meandering, 14-hectare outdoor garden maintained by Hokkaidō University, is a collection of 200 plants and herbs historically used by the Ainu as medicine, food and raw materials for clothing. There's also a landscaped section that evokes the alpine scenery of a mountain in Daisetsuzan, in northern Hokkaidō.

Sapporo Clock Tower HISTORIC BUILDING
(札幌市時計台; Sapporo Tokei-dai; www.sapporoshi-tokeidai.jp; N1W2 Chūō-ku; adult/child ¥200/free; ⏲8.45am-5pm; S Tōzai, Tōhō & Namboku lines to Ōdōri, exit 31) No Japanese tourist can leave Sapporo without snapping a photo of the city's signature landmark and oldest building, the clock tower. Built in 1878, the clock has not missed tolling the hour for more than 130 years. Inside is a **museum** on the tower.

Greater Sapporo

Ōkura-yama Ski Jump Stadium MUSEUM
(大倉山ジャンプ競技場; ☎011-641-8585; www.sapporowintersportsmuseum.com; 1274 Miyano-mori, Chūō-ku; combined lift & museum ticket ¥1000, museum only ¥600; ⏲9am-6pm late Apr-early Nov, 9.30am-5pm early Nov-late Apr; P) This ski-jump slope was built on the side of Ōkura-yama for the Sapporo 1972 Winter Games. At 133.6m it's just slightly shorter than Sapporo TV Tower, with a 33-degree incline. What would it feel like to whiz down that? You can hazard a guess after taking the rickety old lift up to the top and staring down the slope. Keep that image in mind when you try the highly amusing computerised simulator in the museum below.

There are a few other simulators in the museum, as well as photos and equipment from the 1972 Games – which show just how far winter sports technology (and fashion!) has come in the last 45 years.

The stadium is actually still in use and if you're lucky, you might catch a practice session.

To reach Ōkura-yama, take the Tōzai subway line to Maruyama Kōen (円山公園), and then take exit 2 for the Maruyama bus terminal. Next, take bus 14 to Ōkurayama-kyōgijō-iriguchi (大倉山競技場入り口; ¥210, 15 minutes); from here, it's a 10-minute walk uphill to the stadium.

Moerenuma-kōen PARK
(モエレ沼公園; ☎011-790-1231; www.sapporo-park.or.jp/moere; 1-1 Moerenuma-kōen; ⏲7am-10pm; P; 🚌69 or 79 to Moerunuma-kōen Higashi-guchi, S Tōhō line to Kanjo-dōri Higashi) FREE Completed in 2005, this former waste-treatment plant to the northeast of the central city is now an impressive reclaimed green belt. It was originally designed by the acclaimed Japanese-American artist Noguchi Isamu before his death in 1988. In addition to works by Noguchi in stone (on which children are free to climb), there are sculptures of land and water.

To reach the park, take bus 68, 69 or 79 (¥210, 25 minutes, every 10 to 30 minutes) from the Kanjo-dōri Higashi subway stop.

Hokkaidō Museum MUSEUM
(北海道博物館, Hokkaidō hakubutsukan; ☎011-898-0466; www.hm.pref.hokkaido.lg.jp; 53-2 Konopporo, Atsubetsu-chō, Atsubetsu-ku; adult/student/child ¥600/300/free; ⏲9.30am-5pm May-Sep, to 4.30pm Oct-Apr; P) This museum does an admirable job of explaining Hokkaidō's multilayered history, from the age of the woolly mammoths to the age of the steam locomotives, with English throughout. The museum is east of central Sapporo, in Nopporo Shinrin-kōen.

From Shin-Sapporo Station, take bus 新22 (¥210, 15 minutes, every 60 or so minutes) from bus stop 10 for Kaitaku-mura (開拓の村) and get off at the Hokkaidō hakubutsukan stop.

A short walk behind the museum is the modernist **Centennial Memorial Tower** (百年記念塔; Hyaku-nen Kinen-tō; 53-2 Konopporo, Atsubetsu-chō, Atsubetsu-ku; P) designed by architect Iguchi Ken, started in 1968 to mark Sapporo's centennial (it was completed in 1970). The footprint is a hexagon, to evoke a six-sided snowflake; a cross-section reveals the kanji for 'north' (北; kita).

Also in Nopporo Shinrin-kōen is **Kaitaku-mura** (開拓の村; ☎011-898-2692; www.kaitaku.or.jp; 50-1 Konopporo, Atsubetsu-chō, Atsubetsu-ku; adult/child/student ¥800/free/600; ⏲9am-5pm May-Sep, 9am-4.30pm Tue-Sun Oct-Apr; P), an expansive collection of historical buildings (and some re-creations), that show the diversity of experience in 19th-century Hokkaidō. There are ornate Victorian town halls; equally grand villas built by herring barons in the traditional Japanese style; and thatched-roof pioneer cabins. Most of the buildings you can enter. Entrance is free for international students living in Hokkaidō (with valid proof of residence). Kaitaku-mura is the last stop on bus 新22 from Shin-Sapporo Station (¥210, 15 minutes, every 60 minutes).

Activities

Sapporo Teine SNOW SPORTS
(サッポロテイネ; ☎011-223-5830, bus pack reservations 011-223-5901; www.sapporo-teine.com; day pass adult/child ¥5200/2600; ⏲9am-5pm Nov-May, to 9pm Dec-Mar; 👪) You can't beat Teine for convenience, as the slopes, which hosted skiing events for the 1972 Winter Olympics, lie quite literally on the edge of Sapporo.

Teine has two zones: the lower, more beginner- and family-oriented **Olympia Zone**; and the higher, more challenging **Highland Zone**. There are 15 runs and nine lifts. A variety of packages bring the price down.

If you're travelling as a family, take advantage of the 'family pack', which gives 10% off one adult-child combo, or 15% off three to five people, and drops adult equipment rental to ¥3900. The 'bus pack' (adult/child ¥6700/4300) gives you round-trip bus service from JR Sapporo Station plus a seven-hour lift ticket; this deal requires pre-booking by 3pm the day before. Full equipment rental for skiers/snowboarders is available for ¥5300 per day.

Just 10 minutes from Sapporo by local train, Teine can get very crowded, particularly on weekends and school holidays. Frequent trains on the JR Hakodate line run between Sapporo and Teine (¥260). From JR Teine Station, shuttle buses conveniently run to both zones.

Festivals & Events

For a list of festivals and events, see www.welcome.city.sapporo.jp.

★Sapporo Yuki Matsuri CULTURAL
(さっぽろ雪まつり, Sapporo Snow Festival; www.snowfes.com; Feb;) Held in early February, this is one of Japan's top festivals. From humble beginnings in 1950, when local high-school students built six snow statues in Ōdōri-kōen, the festival now hosts an international snow sculpture contest and draws more than two million visitors annually.

It's not just ice statues in Ōdōri-kōen and around town: there are frozen stages for musical acts and ice slides and mazes for kids. There are plenty of food and drink vendors and you can expect all kinds of drunken revelry, particularly once the sun sets (at these latitudes, it's quite early!). Finding reasonably priced accommodation can be extremely difficult, so book as far in advance as possible.

Sapporo Summer Matsuri BEER
(札幌夏まつり; www.sapporo-natsu.com; mid-Jul–mid-Aug) The big names plus microbrewers set up outdoor beer gardens in Ōdōri-kōen from mid-July to mid-August. A whole month of beer drinking in the sun! During the mid-August, weeklong **Obon Festival**, part of the summer *matsuri*, traditional dances are performed.

Sleeping

Budget options have gotten a whole lot better in Sapporo, with a slew of hip new hostels opening recently. There are a lot of midrange choices, too; prices often correlate with decor (if you're not picky, you can find very reasonable rooms). Book well in advance during festivals (especially the Snow Festival), holiday weekends and summer. Rates usually increase (by ¥1000 to ¥3000) on Friday and Saturday nights.

★SappoLodge GUESTHOUSE ¥
(サッポロッジ; 011-211-4314; www.sappolodge.com; S5E1-1-4 Chūō-ku; dm/tw from ¥3000/8000; ; S Namboku line to Susukino, exit 5; Tōhō line to Hōsui-susukino, exit 5) A little slice of mountain life a stone's throw from Susukino – you can use the climbing wall to get to the 2nd-floor dorms instead of the stairs – SappoLodge is a magnet for outdoorsy types who find themselves in the city. The only downside is the noise from the (fun, popular) ground-floor bar until 'quiet time' is enforced at 2am.

Owner (and Sapporo native) Nara-san is a real adventurer. He worked as a guide for 14 years and this is his form of 'retirement' – though he still takes guests on hiking and backcountry excursions to his favourite spots (shoot him an email if you're keen).

It's a great spot for a nightcap, even if you're not staying here.

Untapped Hostel HOSTEL ¥
(011-788-4579; www.untappedhostel.com; N18W4 Kita-ku; dm/d from ¥3500/9000, annexe dm ¥3700; ; S Namboku line to Kita-juhachi-jō, exit 2) This is one of Sapporo's new hipster hostels – think raw wood and concrete – inside an old *unagi* (eel) shop a minute's walk from the subway. The rooms, with Western-style beds and bunks, are spotless, though it's a hike up to the 3rd-floor dorms. Common space includes a lounge with cosy woodstove, kitchen and laundry room.

There are two buildings now, a newer annexe and the older *'honkan'*. It can also rent bikes, if you need one.

Ino's Place HOSTEL ¥
(イノーズプレイス; 011-832-1828; www.inos-place.com; 3-4-6-5 Higashi-Sapporo, Shiroishi-ku; dm/s/d from ¥3400/4800/8600; ; S Tōzai line to Shiroishi, exit 1) This is a popular backpackers' spot with all the fixings: friendly, bilingual staff, clean rooms with modern bunks, private lockers, free coffee and tea, no curfew, laundry facilities, a kitchen and a

communal lounge space. Bonus: the owner is a juggler and the hostel doubles as a shop for juggling goods.

From the subway exit (don't go to JR Shiroishi Station!), walk straight for a few minutes along the main street in the direction of the Eneos petrol station. Turn right at the fourth traffic light and you'll see a detached two-storey white building – you've arrived. The website tells you all you need to know.

Sapporo International Youth Hostel HOSTEL ¥
(札幌国際ユースホステル; ☎011-825-3120; www.youthhostel.or.jp/kokusai; 6-5-35 Toyohira 6-jō, Toyohira-ku; dm/r per person from ¥3200/3800; P ⊖ ❄ @ 📶; S Tōhō line to Gakuen-mae, exit 2) This oddly upmarket youth hostel – which looks like a modern apartment building – is great value, though it's a little out of the way. Both Western- and Japanese-style private rooms are available, as well as 'dorm rooms' featuring four full-sized beds that double as family rooms. It fills up quickly; be mindful of the midnight curfew.

The hostel is just two minutes from the subway station, behind the Sapporo International Student Centre.

Nakamuraya Ryokan RYOKAN ¥¥
(中村屋旅館; ☎011-241-2111; www.nakamura-ya.com; N3W7-1 Chūō-ku; s/d from ¥8640/14,800; ⊖ ❄ @ 📶; S JR Sapporo, south exit) Located on a side street near the entrance to the Hokkaidō University Botanical Garden, a 10-minute walk from JR Sapporo Station, this charming Japanese-style inn is a wonderful introduction to traditional hospitality. Sleeping is on futons on tatami floors and you can soak in the big communal *o-furo* (bath). The owner-managers are friendly and are used to foreign travellers.

Meals are available, too; enquire when booking. Be sure to read up on the inn's colourful beginnings on the website.

Marks Inn Sapporo HOTEL ¥¥
(マークスイン札幌; ☎011-512-5001; www.marks-inn.com; S8W3 Chūō-ku; s ¥4500-9000, d ¥5500-12,000; ⊖ ❄ @ 📶; S Namboku line to Nakajima-kōen, exit 1) For private accommodation, you really can't get cheaper or more convenient than this business hotel on the edge of the Susukino entertainment district, right across from the canal. It's a bit worn and rooms are a bit cramped, but the beds are comfy and the simple breakfast is free.

Sapporo Grand Hotel HOTEL ¥¥¥
(札幌グランドホテル; ☎011-261-3311; www.grand1934.com/english/index; N1W4 Chūō-ku; s/d from ¥23,166/35,046; ⊖ ❄ @ 📶; 🚉 JR Sapporo, south exit) Established in 1934 as the first European-style hotel in Sapporo, this grand old dame now occupies three adjacent buildings that lie at the southeast corner of the former Hokkaidō government building. Rooms vary considerably; those in the Honkan (main wing) offer the best balance of style and price. The newer wing is about ¥20,000 more expensive.

JR Tower Hotel Nikko Sapporo HOTEL ¥¥¥
(ＪＲタワーホテル日航札幌; ☎011-251-2222; www.jrhotels.co.jp/tower; N5W2-5 Chūō-ku; s/d/tw from ¥26,000/34,000/44,000; ⊖ ❄ @ 📶; 🚉 JR Sapporo, east exit) You can't beat the location of this lofty hotel, virtually on top of JR Sapporo Station. Rooms are plush, service is genteel and the views are fantastic. Downer: there's a spa with a natural hot spring but even staying guests pay an extra ¥1600 to use it.

Eating

You can eat well without leaving the JR Sapporo Station–Ōdōri–Susukino corridor, though there are some detour-worthy destination restaurants. Sapporo's signature dish is miso ramen (味噌ラーメン), *kotteri* (thick and rich), seasoned with pungent miso and topped with stir-fried vegetables. Another local dish is soup curry (スープカレー), a slurpy take on Japanese-style curry; usually mild but you can ask to up the spice factor.

★ **Menya Saimi** RAMEN ¥
(麺屋彩未; ☎011-820-6511; Misono 10-jō Toyohira-ku; ramen from ¥750; ⏱11am-3.15pm & 5-7.30pm Tue-Sun; P; S Tōhō line to Misono, exit 1) Sapporo takes its ramen very seriously and Saimi is oft-voted the best ramen shop in the city (and sometimes the country) – and it's not overrated. You will have to queue, which is annoying, but you will be rewarded with a mind-blowing meal for the same price as a convenience store *bentō*. Get the *miso ramen*.

Milk Mura ICE CREAM ¥
(ミルク村; ☎011-219-6455; S4W3-7-1; per serving ¥1300; ⏱noon-11pm Tue-Sun; S Namboku line to Susukino, exit 1) A grown-up twist on the classic ice-cream parlour, Milk Mura serves mugs of soft-serve ice cream accompanied by three tiny chalices of your choice of liquors – and there are dozens to choose from. Bottles, some ancient-looking, cover the counters, fairy lights twinkle and chansons

play in the background. Bonus: one free refill of ice cream.

Saera SANDWICHES ¥

(さえら; ☎011-221-4220; 3rd basement fl, W2 Ōdōri; sandwiches ¥660-940; ⏲10am-6pm Thu-Tue; Ⓢ Tōzai, Tōhō & Namboku lines to Ōdōri, exit 19) This Sapporo institution serves sandwiches of the genteel sort (crusts-off, lightly stuffed), with dozens of fillings. Two to try: the king-crab sandwich and the curious fruit sandwich, filled with mandarins and whipped cream. It's in Ōdōri subway station; at exit 19 go downstairs instead of up, then inside a department store, where the entry will be on your left. An extra ¥200 gets you coffee.

Kōhīhausu JAPANESE CURRY ¥

(こうひいはうす; ☎011-561-9115; S20W15-3; mains from ¥800; ⏲11.30am-7.30pm Mon, Tue & Thu-Sat, to 2.30pm Wed, to 8pm Sun; Ⓟ; 🚋Rōpuwei-iriguchi) This soup curry shop near the Moiwa-yama Ropeway comes highly recommended by Sapporo locals. Most popular: the chicken curry (チキンカレー; *chikin karē*) with a 'medium' (中; *chū*) spice level. Get it with coffee for ¥1000. Kōhīhausu is an unhurried, dimly lit place strewn with antiques.

Ganso Ramen Yokochō RAMEN ¥

(元祖さっぽろラーメン横丁; www.ganso-yokocho.com; S5W3 Chūō-ku; ramen from ¥800; ⏲11am-3am; Ⓢ Namboku line to Susukino, exit 3) This famous alleyway in the Susukino entertainment district is crammed with ramen shops, including branches of several venerable Hokkaidō shops. It's been around since 1952, and is keen to distinguish itself from all the 'imposter' ramen alleys.

It can be a little tricky to find (old as it is, it doesn't glow as bright as everything else in Susukino), but all locals know where it is. Look for 'Ganso' as there are other ramen alleys nearby. Hours for individual shops vary.

Ramen Kyōwakoku RAMEN ¥

(らーめん共和国, Ramen Republic; www.sapporo-esta.jp/ramen; 10th fl, ESTA Bldg; ramen from ¥780; ⏲11am-10pm; 🚉JR Sapporo, east exit) An easy option for a bite to eat in the train station, Ramen Kyōwakoku is a collection of ramen shops from all over Hokkaidō. It's all here: Sapporo *miso ramen*, Asahikawa *shōyu* ramen and Hakodate *shio* ramen. A mini option costs ¥600.

Daruma BARBECUE ¥¥

(だるま; ☎011-552-6013; www.best.miru-kuru.com/daruma; S5W4; plates from ¥750; ⏲5pm-3am; Ⓢ Namboku line to Susukino, exit 5) This is where

DON'T MISS

HOKKAIDŌ-STYLE RAMEN

Hokkaidō has no fewer than three ramen cities, each specialising in a different style. In Sapporo the signature style is hearty *miso ramen* (味噌ラーメン); in Asahikawa it's *shōyu* ramen (醤油ラーメン; soy-sauce-seasoned ramen); and in Hakodate, *shio ramen* (塩ラーメン), a light, salt-seasoned broth. In a nod to two of the prefecture's staple products, butter and corn, you'll often have the option to top off your ramen with either (or both!).

Sapporoites take friends visiting from out of town for the local speciality, *jingisukan* (all-you-can-eat lamb dish). There's nothing fancy here, just quality meat and a warm homely vibe. Daruma, in business for more than 60 years, is popular and has a few branches around town (see the website), which is good because the main shop draws long lines. Come early or late to beat the crowds.

Sushi-no-uo-masa SUSHI ¥¥

(鮨の魚政; ☎011-644-9914; www.asaichi-maruka.jp; Chūō Oroshi-uri-ichiba Maruka Centre 1F, N12W21, Chūō-ku; set ¥2800; ⏲6-11am Mon, Tue & Thu-Sat; Ⓟ; Ⓢ Tōzai line to Nijū-yonken, exit 5, 🚉JR Hakodate line to Sōen) This is something special: sushi for breakfast out at the fish market. It takes an effort to get here, but the sushi is excellent and you can wander around the market before and after eating. Sushi-no-uo-masa is smack in the middle of the stalls that lie between the two restrooms at either end on the ground floor of the Maruka Oroshiuri Centre.

Not to be confused with Ni-jō Ichiba, the Central Wholesale Market (Chūō Oroshi-uri-ichiba; 中央卸売市場) is a 10-minute walk from either the subway or the train station.

Kani-honke SEAFOOD ¥¥¥

(札幌かに本家; ☎011-222-0018; www.kani-honke.jp; N3W2 Chūō-ku; lunch/dinner mains from ¥2600/4400; ⏲11.30am-10pm; 🚉JR Sapporo, south exit) These are *the* crab guys! The frigid seas surrounding Hokkaidō are bountiful and yield some of the tastiest crustaceans around. Try the *kani-suki* (¥4600 per person), a crab version of sukiyaki; after the crab and vegetables are cooked in the pot, rice and egg are added to the remaining soup.

You can't miss it: there's a huge crab sign on the building. There's also a **branch** (か

に本家　すすきの店; ☎011-551-0018; S6W4 Chūō-ku; lunch/dinner mains from ¥2600/4400; ⏰11.30am-11pm; Ⓢ Namboku line to Susukino, exit 5) near Susukino crossing.

Drinking & Nightlife

Sapporo offers far and away the best nightlife in Hokkaidō. While bigger cities such as Tokyo have multiple nightlife districts catering to different demographics, in Sapporo it all comes together in Susukino, home to craft-beer bars, hostess bars, flashy nightclubs and jazz cafes.

★ Sapporo Biergarten BREWERY
(サッポロビール園; ☎reservation hotline 0120-150-550; www.sapporo-bier-garten.jp; N7E9 Higashi-ku; ⏰11.30am-10pm; 🚌88 to Sapporo Biiru-en, Ⓢ Tōhō line to Higashi-Kuyakusho-mae, exit 4) This complex next to the Sapporo Beer Museum has no fewer than five beer halls, the best of which is Kessel Hall, where you can tuck into *jingisukan* washed down with all-you-can-drink draught beer direct from the factory (¥3900 per person). Reservations highly recommended. From the subway it's a 10-minute walk; the bus stops right out front.

Riviera CLUB
(☎011-206-0226; www.riviera-sapporo.com; S6W4 Noguchi Bldg B1; cover varies; ⏰8pm-5am) Glitzy shows and elaborate, pricey cocktails make this a memorable night out. ID is mandatory, so travellers will need their passports on hand.

Mugishutei BAR
(麦酒停; ☎011-512-4774; www.mugishutei.com; S9W5 Chūō-ku; ⏰7pm-3am; Ⓢ Nakajima-kōen, exit 2) At Sapporo's original hub for craft-heads you can choose from a selection of 250 beers, including many from owner Phred Kauffman's line of Ezo beers, produced and bottled by Portland's Rogue Brewery. Beer aside, we love the off-beat vibe, from the bottle-cap mosaics to the '80s MTV clips played on the TV. Warning: cover charge ¥900.

Cafe Morihiko CAFE
(森彦; ☎011-622-8880; www.morihiko-coffee.com; S2W26-2-18 Chūō-ku; ⏰10am-9pm; Ⓢ Tōzai line to Maruyama-kōen, exit 4) Set in a teeny-tiny old wooden house, with red eaves and clinging ivy, this cafe delivers big on ambience. The hand-poured coffee (¥580 to ¥700) and homemade cakes are good, too.

☆ Entertainment

Sapporo Dome BASEBALL
(札幌ドーム; ☎011-850-1000, dome tour reservations 011-850-1020; www.sapporo-dome.co.jp; 1 Hitsujigaoka, Toyohira-ku; Ⓢ Tōhō line to Fukuzumi, exit 3) Built for the 2002 FIFA World Cup, Sapporo Dome is home to both baseball's Hokkaidō Nippon Ham Fighters (www.fighters.co.jp) and J-League soccer's Consadole Sapporo (www.consadole-sapporo.jp). The stadium switches surfaces depending on the sport being played: the Fighters play on an artificial surface; when Consadole has a match, a natural grass pitch is slid into the stadium.

The Fighters in particular have extremely boisterous crowds and a trip to the Dome is a great way to see parochial Japan in action. Check out the website for schedules. When nothing is on, tours of the dome are held on the hour from 10am to 4pm for ¥1050; reservations necessary. It's a 10-minute walk from the subway.

ℹ Orientation

Unlike most Japanese cities, Sapporo is laid out in a grid pattern. Centre city blocks are labelled East (東; *higashi*) or West (西; *nishi*) and North (北; *kita*) or South (南; *minami*). Addresses are generated accordingly; so, for example, the famous landmark Clock Tower is in the block of North 1, West 2 (Kita Ichi-jo, Nishi Ni-chōme) – or N1W2.

Ōdōri-kōen is the border between north and south; the canal-like Sōsei-gawa (創成川) divides east and west. Sapporo TV Tower is roughly the centre point, which makes it easy to get your bearings. South of Ōdōri is the downtown shopping district. Susukino, the entertainment district, is located mainly between the South 2 and South 6 blocks.

Sapporo is a very walkable city for much of the year – it gets bitterly cold in winter. This is the time to take advantage of the *chika-ho* (チカホ), the underground passageway that runs from JR Sapporo Station to the Susukino subway station.

ℹ Information

MEDICAL SERVICES

Sapporo City General Hospital (市立札幌病院; ☎011-726-2211; www.city.sapporo.jp/hospital; N11W13 1-1 Chūō-ku; ⏰outpatient reception 8.45-11am & 1-3pm, emergency room 24hr; 🚉Hakodate main line to Sōen)

TOURIST INFORMATION

There is a tourist help desk in the basement of the arrivals hall at New Chitose Airport.

Hokkaidō-Sapporo Food & Tourist Information Centre (北海道さっぽろ「食と観光」情

報館; 011-213-5088; www.sapporo.travel; JR Sapporo Station; 8.30am-8pm; JR Sapporo, west exit) This huge info centre has maps, timetables, brochures and pamphlets in English for Sapporo and all of Hokkaidō. Staff speak English and are helpful. It's located on the ground floor of Sapporo Stellar Pl, inside the north concourse of JR Sapporo Station.

JR Information Desk (JR Sapporo Station; 8.30am-7pm; JR Sapporo, west exit) English-language assistance regarding JR trains and rail passes, in the north concourse of JR Sapporo Station.

Sapporo International Communication Plaza (札幌国際プラザ; 011-211-3678; www.plaza-sapporo.or.jp; 3rd fl, MN Bldg, N1W3 Chūō-ku; 9am-5.30pm Mon-Sat; ; S Tōzai, Tōhō & Namboku lines to Ōdōri, exit 16) Directly opposite the Sapporo Clock Tower, this place is set up to cater for the needs of foreign residents and visitors, with an extensive list of English resources and helpful, friendly staff.

Getting There & Away

AIR

New Chitose Airport

New Chitose Airport (新千歳空港; CTS; 0123-23-0111; www.new-chitose-airport.jp) is located 45km southeast of Sapporo, in Chitose. With flights to more than 25 cities in Japan and many cities in Asia, this is where most travellers will arrive.

Rapid Airport trains (¥1070, 36 minutes) depart every 15 minutes for JR Sapporo Station.

Frequent buses (¥1030, 70 minutes) also make the trip, stopping not just at JR Sapporo Station but also at major hotels.

For a taxi to central Sapporo, budget about ¥14,000.

Okadama Airport

In Sapporo, **Okadama Airport** (丘珠空港; Okadama Kūkō; 011-785-7871; www.okadama-airport.co.jp; Okadama-chō, Higashi-ku) runs short-haul flights to Hakodate, Kushiri, Rishiri and Misawa (in Aomori).

Hokuto Airport Shuttle buses depart from the south side of JR Sapporo Station (¥400, 30 minutes) and are timed to match departures. A taxi from JR Sapporo Station should take 20 minutes (¥2500).

BUS

Highway buses tend to be cheaper than trains. Sapporo has three central bus stations:

Sapporo Eki-mae Bus Terminal (札幌駅前バスターミナル; JR Sapporo) Sapporo's main bus depot, beneath the Esta building on the south side of JR Sapporo Station.

> **TRANSIT PASSES**
>
> **Kitaca** (www2.jrhokkaido.co.jp/global) JR Hokkaidō's rechargeable pay-in-advance microchipped (IC) card that can be used on trains, subways, trams and buses in any zone that accepts IC cards (greater Sapporo and also cities like Tokyo). Enquire at JR info desks in New Chitose Airport or JR Sapporo Station. Even better, the little flying squirrel mascot is about as cute as can be.
>
> **Sapica** Rechargeable pay-in-advance IC card that covers Sapporo's subways, city buses and trams. Bonus: you accrue points for using the card. Get it in the subways or at other spots where tickets are sold.

Chūō Bus Terminal (中央バスターミナル; Ōdōri E1; S Namboku line to Bus Center-mae, exit 2) Most buses departing from Sapporo Eki-mae Bus Terminal also stop here, convenient for travellers staying around Ōdōri or Susukino.

Ōdōri Bus Terminal (大通バスターミナル; S1E1; S Namboku line to Bus Center-mae, exit 1) Mostly for destinations in greater Sapporo.

Buses run from Sapporo Eki-mae Bus Terminal, via Chūō Bus Terminal, to the following destinations:

Abashiri ¥6390, six hours, eight daily

Asahikawa ¥2060, two hours, every 20 to 30 minutes

Furano ¥2260, 2½ hours, every 60 to 80 mins

Hakodate ¥4810, 5½ hours, eight daily (including one night bus)

Niseko ¥2240, three hours, departures vary by season

Noboribetsu Onsen ¥1850, two hours, hourly

Shin-Hakodate-Hokuto (Hokkaidō Shinkansen station) ¥4810, five hours, eight daily (including one night bus)

Tōya-ko Onsen ¥2780, 2¾ hours, four daily

From Ōdōri Bus Terminal, buses run to Wakkanai (¥6240, six hours, six daily including one night bus).

TRAIN

From Sapporo Station, JR Limited Express trains run to the following destinations:

Abashiri (Okhotsk Liner) ¥9390, 5½ hours, four daily

Asahikawa (Limited Express Lilac) ¥4290, 90 minutes, every 30 minutes

Hakodate (Hokuto Liner) ¥8310, 3½ hours, hourly

Kushiro (Super Ōzora Liner) ¥8850, four hours, six daily

Noboribetsu Onsen (Hokuto Liner & Suzuran Liner) ¥3960, 70 minutes, hourly

Shin-Hakodate-Hakuto (Hokuto Liner) ¥8310, 3¼ hours, hourly

Wakkanai (Super Sōya Liner and Sarubetsu Liner) ¥9930, six hours, three daily

JR Hakodate line trains run to Kutchan (for Niseko; ¥1840, two hours) via Otaru (¥640, 45 minutes).

Getting Around

BICYCLE

Porocle (ポロクル; ☎011-242-4696; www.porocle.jp; 24hr ¥1200, after 3pm ¥700; ⏲7.30am-9pm) Sapporo's flat grid is made for cycling. With a smartphone and a passport you can access the city's easy-to-use bike-share program, which has 30-plus kiosks around downtown. Sign up at the Hokkaidō-Sapporo Food & Tourist Information Centre (p604), inside the train station, or at the Grand Hotel (p602).

BUS

Bus 88 loops around from JR Sapporo Station to the Sapporo Beer Museum, Ōdōri-kōen and the Clock Tower; a one-day pass costs ¥750, single trips are ¥210. Catch the bus from the south exit of the train station, in front of the Tokyū department store.

CAR & MOTORCYCLE

A car is a drag in central Sapporo as traffic and parking are constant hassles; however, some of the city's more far-flung (but worthwhile) sights are awkward to reach by public transport. It's worth renting a car for a day to hit those.

SUBWAY

Sapporo has three useful subway lines that run from 6am to midnight: the east–west Tōzai line; the north–south Namboku line; and the curving Tōhō line. Fares start at ¥200.

One-day passes cost ¥830 and only ¥520 on weekends (half-price for children).

TAXI

Taxis are easy to hail. Flagfall is ¥670, which gives you 1.6km; then ¥80 per 300m (or two minutes in traffic).

TRAM

Sapporo has a cute streetcar that loops from Ōdōri down to the base of Moiwa-yama and back (6.30am to 11.19pm). The fare is a flat ¥200.

CENTRAL HOKKAIDŌ

Given that the capital and transport hub Sapporo is here, central Hokkaidō (道央; Dō-ō) represents the island at its most accessible – perfect for a shorter trip. It's got everything you'd want and expect from Hokkaidō covered: for world-class ski slopes there is Niseko, with its legendary powder snow; for caldera lakes and steaming onsen towns there is Shikotsu-Tōya National Park; and for a bit of history, there's the 19th-century port town Otaru.

Getting There & Around

New Chitose Airport (p605) is the most obvious gateway to central Hokkaidō. Long-distance ferries from Honshū dock in Tomakomai, on the south-central coast of the island.

Of all the regions in Hokkaidō, this is the easiest one in which to get around by public transport. You can see and do more with a car, but trains and buses will get you pretty far.

The JR Hakodate line connects Sapporo with Otaru and Niseko. The Muroran line runs from Sapporo past New Chitose Airport to Tomakomai and to destinations in Shikotsu-Tōya National Park. Buses fill the gaps.

Niseko

☎0136 / POP 4940

Hokkaidō is dotted with world-class ski resorts, but the reigning prince of powder is unquestionably Niseko (ニセコ). There are four interconnected resorts with more than 800 skiable hectares along the eastern side of the mountain, Niseko Annupuri. Soft and light powdery snow and an annual average snowfall of more than 15m make Niseko extremely popular with international skiers. Many own second homes here – resulting in a diverse dining and nightlife scene that is atypical of far-flung rural Japan. English is spoken virtually everywhere. While it's possible to do Niseko on a budget, be warned that it is getting increasingly difficult, especially in winter (peak ski season).

Spread around the eastern base of the mountain are several towns and villages that compose Niseko 'resort'. Most of the restaurants and bars are clustered together in **Hirafu** (ひらふ), while **Annupuri** (アンヌプリ), **Niseko Village** (ニセコビレッジ; also called Higashi-yama Onsen) and **Hanazono** (花園) are much quieter and less developed. Further east are **Kutchan** (倶知安) and **Niseko** (ニセコ) proper, towns with more permanent population centres and less of a resort feel.

ROAD TRIPPING HOKKAIDŌ

Hokkaidō is punctuated by caldera lakes and soaring volcanoes, with vast fields and undeveloped land in between, and long stretches of forlorn sea. You can follow your nose to hot sulphur springs or be lured by the colourful siren banners of fishing town diners or wind your way through spectacular mountain passes. It's meant to be driven, and there's something to see at nearly every turn.

Best Drives

➡ Rte 334 between Utoro and Rausu, via the soaring Shiretoko Pass (p648) in Shiretoko National Park.

➡ Rte 237 from Furano to Biei with detours along the Patchwork Road and Panorama Road (p627), past flower-filled fields.

➡ Rte 243 from Abashiri to Kawayu Onsen, via the Bihoro Pass (p657), with fantastic views over Kussharo-ko in Akan National Park.

➡ The Ororon Line (オロロンライン; Rte 231), from Otaru to Wakkanai, with the Sea of Japan and the marshes of Sarobetsu (p638) on either side.

➡ Rte 273 on the eastern edge of Daisetsuzan National Park, through Mikuni Pass and Sōunkyō gorge.

➡ The Oiwake Soran Line (追分ソーランライン; Rte 228) along the winding coast of Dō-Nan, from Hakodate to Esashi.

➡ The long coastline from Wakkanai to Abashiri on the Okhotsk Line.

Tips for Drivers

➡ The best time for driving around Hokkaidō is mid-May through mid-October. Any later and snow can be a problem; coastal routes will be windy then, too. Note that Daisetsuzan is the first place in Japan to see snow, usually in September. Even if roads are open, use extreme caution driving in the mountains in winter. July and August will have the most crowds.

➡ Hokkaidō's roads are well paved and well signposted in English. What you won't see noted in English, however, is road closures or detours. Check before heading out.

➡ Keep an eye on the speedometer and look out for wildlife, such as deer.

➡ Most towns will have a petrol station and a convenience store, though many close around 7pm or 8pm.

➡ Outside of Sapporo, most places have free parking.

➡ It's often easiest to enter the phone number of your destination in the car's navigation system.

➡ For more information on driving in Hokkaidō, see the tourism bureau's downloadable handbook (www.hkd.mlit.go.jp), in English.

Activities

Niseko is making a big push to become a year-round destination. The buzz isn't quite there yet, but the infrastructure is building, with operators offering rafting, kayaking and mountain-biking tours. The combination of mountains and farmlands means Niseko is excellent for hiking and cycling, too. There are also 25 onsen in the area, from luxurious hotel baths to mountain hideaways.

★Niseko United SNOW SPORTS

(ニセコユナイテッド; www.niseko.ne.jp; adult/child ¥7400/4500; ⏲8.30am-8.30pm Nov-Apr) Niseko United covers the four resorts on Niseko Annupuri (1308m): Annupuri, Niseko Village, Grand Hirafu and Hanazono. While you can buy individual passes for each, part of what makes Niseko so great (in addition to that famous powder) is that you can buy a single all-mountain pass, an electronic tag that gives you access to 18 lifts and gondolas and 60 runs.

All the resorts have terrain for all levels, though quieter Hanazono is considered best for families. The all-mountain pass also gets you free rides on the hourly shuttle that runs between the resorts. Eight-hour and multi-day passes are available, too.

As so many skiers and snowboarders here are from abroad, there are plenty of English-speaking instructors and backcountry guides; rental shops (of which there are many) also typically have a few foreign staff on hand.

Niseko takes a pretty hard stance against rope ducking. Avalanches do happen; when conditions are deemed safe, gates to select off-piste areas are opened.

Moiwa SKIING

(モイワ; ☎0136-59-2511; www.niseko-moiwa.jp; 448 Niseko, Niseko-chō; lift ticket ¥4300; ⏰8am-4pm) Moiwa (not to be confused with Sapporo's Moiwa) is Niseko's 'fifth Beatle', right next to Annupuri but not part of Niseko United. It's a small resort that's quietly built up a loyal following for its deep powder and backcountry opportunities. Moiwa follows Niseko's policy of no rope-ducking – it just doesn't have any ropes.

Experienced skiers can ski from Moiwa over to Annupuri (if the gate is open). As always, check the daily avalanche report (http://niseko.nadare.info).

Goshiki Onsen ONSEN

(五色温泉; ☎0136-58-2707; 510 Niseko, Niseko-chō; ¥700; ⏰8am-8pm May-Oct, 10am-7pm Nov-Apr) At the base (750m) of active volcano Iwaonupuri, Goshiki Onsen has soaring views from the outdoor baths and sulphur-rich, highly acidic (pH 2.6!) waters. It's attached to a deeply rustic ryokan, but most visitors just come for the baths. You need a car to get here; some lodgings do excursions to the baths.

Niseko Circuit HIKING

Just above Goshiki Onsen, a trail heads off into the wilderness. At the first fork, you can opt for the 70-minute round-trip up Iwaonupuri (イワオヌプリ; 1116m) or go deeper towards the pond Ō-numa (大沼). From Ō-numa you can carry on, completing the epic nine-hour, 16km loop that goes up and over Nitonupuri (ニトヌプリ; 1080m) and Chisenupuri (チセヌプリ; 1134m) before returning to Goshiki Onsen.

Pick up a map and info on trail conditions at the Goshiki Onsen Information Centre (p611), at the start of the trail.

Niseko Adventure Centre (NAC) OUTDOORS

(ニセコアドベンチャーセンター; ☎0136-23-2093; www.nacadventures.jp; 179-53 Yamada, Kutchan-chō; ⏰8am-9pm) This outfit is an innovator in Japan, following examples set in other mountain resorts throughout the world. In winter it offers everything from ski and snowboard lessons to snowshoe and backcountry tours with experienced English-speaking guides. In summer it offers rafting, cycling, sea kayaking and canyoning tours...plus more!

It is based in a massive purpose-built building in Hirafu with an 11m indoor climbing wall and Jojo's Café & Restaurant (p610).

Sleeping

Hirafu, followed by Annupuri, has the most accommodation options, while Niseko Village is centred on the upmarket Hilton. Most places will provide pick-up and drop-off for the slopes in winter, or you can take buses and shuttles to move about. It's strongly recommended that you book well in advance in winter. Prices are increasing by the year, though low season remains a steal.

Eki-no-yado Hirafu MINSHUKU ¥

(駅の宿ひらふ; ☎080-5582-5241; www.hirafu-eki.com; 594-4 Hirafu, Kutchan-chō; d ¥3650-4000; P⊖📶) This is Japan's only train station *minshuku* (family-run guesthouse) and it is wonderfully eccentric. It's literally part of tiny JR Hirafu Station: to reach the bathhouse you need to walk out onto the platform. While it's convenient to arrive by train, the station is not convenient for Hirafu proper; however, the guesthouse offers ski field transfers for ¥200.

In summer, the station 'master' hosts barbecues on the train platform; there's a small kitchen, too, well set up for self-catering.

YHA Niseko Fujiyama Karimpani HOSTEL ¥

(ユースホステルカリンパニ・ニセコ藤山; ☎0136-44-1171; www.karimpani-niseko.com; 336 Niseko, Niseko-chō; dm ¥2800-4900, d ¥5600-9800, breakfast/dinner ¥600/1200; P@📶) In an 80-year-old converted schoolhouse, former classrooms now house dorms and concerts are held regularly in the gymnasium. Friendly owners Max and Yūko speak excellent English and do free pick-ups and transfers to the Annupuri slopes (a five-minute drive away). Six rooms are Western-style and two are Japanese; rates drop in the low season. Meals are first class.

WORTH A TRIP

CLIMBING YŌTEI-ZAN

The perfect conical volcano **Yōtei-zan** (羊蹄山; 1898m) is also known as Ezo-Fuji because of its striking resemblance to Fuji-san. One of Japan's 100 Famous Mountains, it sits in its own little pocket of Shikotsu-Tōya National Park, just 10km from Niseko. It's a stunning backdrop: the only way to miss it is if it's hidden in cloud.

Be prepared for a big climb if you want to tackle Yōtei-zan. The most popular of four trailheads is Yōtei-zan tozan-guchi (羊蹄山登山口), south of Kutchan near JR Hirafu Station at 350m. Do your maths and you'll calculate that you are in for more than 1500m of vertical climb. Most people climb and descend in a day – get an early start and allow six to nine hours return, depending on how fit you are. Be mentally and physically prepared – the weather can change quickly on this exposed volcano, especially above the 1600m tree line. Make sure you have enough food and drink. There is an emergency hut at 1800m.

The upper reaches of Yōtei-zan are covered in alpine flowers during the summer. From the peak, the Sea of Japan, the Pacific Ocean and Tōya-ko are all visible – unless, of course, you are inside a cloud!

If you want to attempt this by public transport, you have to catch the 6.40am bus (¥300, 11 minutes, Monday to Saturday) from JR Kutchan Station; the last return bus is at 8.07pm. Hiking season is roughly mid-June through mid-October.

Niseko Annupuri Guest House HOSTEL ¥
(ニセコアンヌプリゲストハウス; ☎0136-58-2084; www.annupuri-yh.com; 479-4 Niseko, Niseko-chō; dm from ¥4500; ⏲closed mid-Oct–early Dec; P ⊖ ᯤ) This friendly mountain lodge, which sees many repeat customers, is constructed entirely from hardwood and sits conveniently within a five-minute walk of the Annupuri ski grounds. In the evenings, guests congregate in front of the fire, swapping ski tips. Breakfast is available for ¥800.

Moiwa Lodge 834 CAPSULE HOTEL ¥¥
(☎050-3171-5688; www.nisekohotel-dh.com; 447-5 Niseko, Niseko-chō; capsule dm ¥7225-15,725; P ⊖ ❄ ᯤ) The world's only ski-in, ski-out capsule hotel, Moiwa Lodge 834, in front of the Moiwa lifts, is popular with powder hounds who have no patience for the morning queues in Hirafu. The lodge has done a pretty good job tweaking the capsule format: there's plenty of secure space for your gear. Capsule rooms are sex-segregated.

Buffet meals (of mostly Western food) are served in the cosy lounge, which looks out towards the mountain. The hotel does free pick-ups from the nearest highway bus stop at Kanronomori.

Outside the snow season, rates drop considerably, with no meals.

★ **AYA Niseko** HOTEL ¥¥¥
(☎0136-23-1280; Yamada 195-1; r/penthouse ¥55,000/720,000; P ⊖ ❄ ᯤ) Not for the budget minded, the AYA Niseko is there when you need to splurge and pamper yourself. Parents will love the kiddie playroom, and heck, they'll love the gym, the onsen, the art gallery, and the yoga room too. It's a sleek, modern, stylish spot well situated for anything Niseko offers. The restaurant on the 1st floor is tasty too.

Hotel Niseko Alpen HOTEL ¥¥¥
(ホテルニセコアルペン; ☎0136-22-1105; www.grand-hirafu.jp; 204 Aza-Yamada, Kutchan-chō; d incl breakfast from ¥40,000; P ⊖ ᯤ ≋) This utilitarian block is in need of an overhaul and we hope it never happens – because this is currently the most economical ski-in, ski-out option left in Niseko. It's right in front of the Grand Hirafu gondola, rooms are plain but comfortable and the breakfast buffet has a good spread. Look for package deals that include lift tickets.

Hilton Niseko RESORT ¥¥¥
(ヒルトンニセコビレッジ; ☎0136-44-1111; www.hiltonnisekovillage.jp; Higashi-yama Onsen; d from ¥30,000; P ⊖ ❄ @ ᯤ) The Hilton enjoys the best location of all – it is quite literally attached to the Niseko Gondola. Spacious Western-style rooms are complemented by a whole slew of amenities, including an onsen bath that faces Yōtei-zan, spread out across a self-contained village.

Check the website before arriving as special deals are usually available, which combine discounted room rates with breakfast and dinner buffets. Conversely, prices can balloon in peak ski season to more than twice the standard rate.

Eating & Drinking

The slopes have plenty of pizza, ramen and other snacks. After hours, Hirafu has an international spread of restaurants and buzzes during ski season (many places shut in the low season). Year-round, Kutchan town has lots of *izakaya*, especially on Miyako-dōri; there's a supermarket by JR Kutchan Station.

Sobadokoro Rakuichi SOBA ¥

(そば処 楽一; 0136-58-3170; www.rakuichisoba.com; 431 Niseko, Niseko-chō; lunch from ¥900; dinner course ¥8000; lunch from 11.30am, dinner from 5pm Fri-Wed; P) Niseko's most famous noodle shop is also famously hard to find, though its secluded location (accessed via a wooden boardwalk) is a big part of the appeal. The other part is watching chef Tatsuri Rai behind the counter hand-make the soba (buckwheat noodles) you just ordered. Simple is best: go for the *namako uchi seiro* (生粉打ちせいろ; fresh-made cold noodles) – just ¥900.

Rakuichi is known to draw huge lines for the first lunch seating at 11.30am (it stops serving lunch when it runs out). So unless you're willing to commit a lot of time, this is one for the low season. Dinner is reservations only, but lunch is better. It's off the access road to Annupuri; look for the banner. No children under 12.

Graubunden CAFE ¥

(グラウビュンデン; 0136-23-3371; www.graubunden.jp; 132-26 Yamada, Kutchan-chō; breakfast mains ¥600-1000, lunch mains ¥1000-1200; 8am-7pm Fri-Wed; P) This is Niseko's original hang-out spot in Hirafu East Village, a standby with season regulars and long-time expats for its sandwiches, omelettes and cakes. Service could be friendlier, especially at busy times, but the food is tasty enough to keep people coming back for more.

DON'T MISS

LOCAL DISH: JINGISUKAN

This dish of charcoal-grilled mutton is the unofficial symbol of Hokkaidō, a legacy of its short-lived 19th-century sheep-rearing program. Its name – a Japanese rendering of Genghis Khan – comes from the unique shape of the cast-iron hotplate used to grill the meat, thought to resemble the warlord's helmet. The meat is grilled on the peak of the hotplate, allowing the juices to run down the sides to the onions and leeks sizzling on the brim. *Jingisukan* (ジンギスカン) is served all over the island, though especially in the heartland, and is best accompanied by copious amounts of beer.

Jojo's Café & Restaurant CAFE ¥

(ジョジョズカフェ; 0136-23-2220; www.nacadventures.jp; 179-53 Yamada, Kutchan-chō; mains from ¥1080; 9.30am-10pm, to 5pm Jun-Sep; P) Atop the Niseko Adventure Centre (NAC), Jojo's offers typical casual fare, like burgers, filling salads, wraps and nachos. The terrace has a spot-on view of Yōtei-zan and there's a play area for kids in winter. Tasty pastries round out the offerings. Yum!

★Musu Bar + Bistro BISTRO ¥¥

(Mūsu バー+ビストロ; 0136-21-7002; www.musuniseko.com; 190-13 Yamada; mains ¥1000-1600; 7.30am-10pm) Musu offers great food, sweet service, and a lovely airy dining experience, plus easily the best cocktail menu in Niseko, with treats like the Yuzu Negroni (¥1400) or the Climber's Club (¥1400), the latter using a shiitake-mushroom-infused brandy. Breakfasts, whether a flaky croissant with homemade jelly or a yoghurt and fruit plate, hit the spot.

Niseko Loft Club BARBECUE ¥¥

(ニセコロフト倶楽部; 0136-44-2883; www.loftclub1989.com; 397-5 Sōga, Niseko-chō; per 300g ¥1900; 5-11pm; P) Down the road from the Annupuri slopes, Loft Club glitters with fairy lights and the warm, glowing promise of a filling meal washed down with beer and lively conversation. The speciality here is *yakiniku* (grill-it-yourself meat), but rather than just the usual beef and pork, there's lamb and venison on the menu, too. Dishes are to share.

Niseko Pizza ITALIAN ¥¥

(ニセコピザ; 0136-55-5553; www.nisekopizza.jp; 167-3 Yamada, Kutchan-chō; pizzas from ¥2100; 11am-11pm) This authentic family-run pizzeria headed by the affable Cezar does thin-crust, wood-fired pizzas with a mouth-watering variety of toppings (plus pastas and steaks). Bonus: it delivers. In central Hirafu, downhill from the gondola; reduced hours low season.

Ginger AMERICAN ¥¥

(0136-55-6293; www.ginger.restaurant; AYA Niseko 1F, Aza Yamada 195-1; mains ¥2200-3800; 7.30am-10pm; P) A newcomer to the Niseko scene, Ginger offers American-meets-*Izakaya* cuisine, with Japanese takes on burgers, steaks, salads, and so on. The orange-and-black decor and light wood panels make it feel more like a

WORTH A TRIP

SKIING IN RUSUTSU

Rusutsu gets snow that almost rivals Niseko's and **Rusutsu Resort** (ルスツリゾート; 0136-46-3331; www.hokkaido-rusutsu.com; 13 Izumi-kawa, Rusutsu; lift tickets adult/child ¥5900/3000, after 4pm ¥2600/1300; 9am-9pm Nov-Apr) has both well-groomed trails and fantastic tree runs. It caters equally to skiers and snowboarders of all levels, with18 lifts, more than three dozen runs, a half-pipe and numerous off-piste options. It's less developed and thus usually less crowded than Niseko, and makes for a good day trip.

You can also go all in and stay at **Rusutsu Resort Hotel** (ルスツリゾートホテル; 0136-46-3331; www.hokkaido-rusutsu.com; 13 Izumi-kawa, Rusutsu; d with breakfast from ¥32,500;), a self-contained facility, with restaurants and a very kitschy amusement park. It's great for families (and also a beacon for tour groups). Discounted packages including room, lift ticket and meal plan are often available. Note that there are few amenities outside the resort.

Rusutsu is only a 20- to 30-minute drive away from Niseko, off Rte 230, on the way to Tōya-ko. Various operators offer Rusutsu day trips if you don't have your own wheels.

sushi restaurant, despite the burgers and other Western mains.

Sprout CAFE
(スプラウト; 0136-55-5161; www.sprout-project.com; N1W3-10, Kutchan-chō; coffee from ¥400; 8am-8pm;) This popular hang-out run by a former outdoor guide serves Niseko's best coffee. It's 100m up the road from JR Kutchan Station, decked out like a very cool campsite. There's a huge library of outdoor books and magazines (in Japanese) here, too.

Information

Goshiki Onsen Information Centre (五色温泉インフォメーションセンター; 0136-59-2200; 510 Niseko, Niseko-chō; 8am-5pm Jun-Oct) English hiking maps and information on the latest weather and trail conditions. Just above Goshiki Onsen, at the start of the hiking trail.

Hirafu Welcome Centre (ひらふウエルカムセンター; 0136-22-0109; www.grand-hirafu.jp; 204 Yamada, Kutchan-chō; 8.30am-9pm) Near the Hirafu gondola (and where direct buses to/from New Chitose Airport originate and terminate), with English-language information. Open only during the snow season.

Information Centre Plat (くっちゃんまちの駅ぷらっと; 0136-55-5372; www.niseko.co.jp; Kita 1 Nishi 2, Kutchan-chō; 9am-6pm;) Lots of English brochures and maps (for Niseko and beyond), 200m down the street outside JR Kutchan Station. There's a smaller information centre (open 9am to 6pm) in the train station.

Niseko Tourist Information (ニセコ観光案内所; 0136-21-2551; www.niseko-ta.jp; 41-5 Aza Kabayama; 8am-5pm;) At JR Niseko Station, with pamphlets, maps, bus timetables; can help with bookings. It also has a centre at the View Plaza Michi-no-Eki on Rte 66 heading into town.

Getting There & Away

BUS

During the ski season, Chūō Bus (p596) coaches run from Sapporo Eki-mae Bus Terminal (¥2240/4000 one-way/return, three hours) and New Chitose Airport (one-way/return ¥2600/4500, 3¾ hours) to Niseko; travel times are dependent on weather conditions. Drop-off points include the Welcome Centre in Hirafu, the Hilton and Annupuri. Reservations are necessary, and it's recommended that you book well ahead of your departure date.

CAR & MOTORCYCLE

Scenic Rte 5 winds from Sapporo to Otaru around the coast, and then cuts inland through the mountains down to Niseko. Having a car will make it easier to move between the various ski slopes, though you'll need to drive with extreme caution. In summer (low season), public transport services drop off, which provides more incentive to pick up a car in Sapporo or at New Chitose Airport. There are also outlets of major car-rental companies in Hirafu.

TRAIN

The JR Hakodate line runs from Sapporo to Kutchan (¥1840, 2½ hours), Hirafu (¥1840, 3½ hours) and Niseko (¥2160, three hours) stations. You will need to transfer in Otaru, where you can also get trains directly to New Chitose Airport.

Note that JR Hirafu Station is actually inconvenient for central Hirafu, unless you've arranged for pickup.

Getting Around

BUS

Buses (¥300, 15 minutes) run irregularly (and infrequently in summer) between JR Kutchan Station and the ski villages; it's better to arrange pickup.

During snow season, **Niseko United Shuttle** (www.niseko.ne.jp) runs a service (roughly hourly 8am to 11pm) between Hirafu, Niseko Village and Annupuri (free for all-mountain pass holders). From 5pm to 11pm, the shuttle route extends to JR Kutchan Station, giving you more dining options. Pick up a schedule from any of the tourist information centres.

TAXI

Niseko suffers from a chronic taxi shortage during the ski season, as most are booked up in advance. Most likely your lodging will offer to shuttle you around (for a fee), which is usually cheaper than taxis and more reliable. If you do need to use a taxi, have your accommodation call ahead for you.

Otaru

0134 / POP 131,700

Otaru (小樽) was the financial centre of Hokkaidō – a bustling center of trade with Russia and China – in the early 20th century. The city's elite invested some of those riches in the construction of grand, Western-style buildings of stone and brick – the style of the time – many of which line the town's central canal. This atmosphere makes Otaru very popular with domestic visitors.

While the town is definitely touristy, with spots for selfie-taking and bus tours, its rich history, many preserved buildings, and overall uniqueness evoke a Hokkaidō of yesteryear that's well worth seeing, if only as a day trip out of Sapporo. Weekenders will find there's plenty to do, from museums to souvenir stores to restaurants and bars.

Sights

★Otaru Canal — CANAL

(小樽運河) Historic Otaru canal is lined with warehouses from the late 19th and early 20th centuries. This was a time when traditional Japanese architecture was infused with Western-style building techniques, so some of the buildings are quite interesting. Most have been restored and now house museums and cafes. Unfortunately the canal itself is half-buried by a major thoroughfare, despite the best lobbying efforts of local preservationists.

Nishin Goten — MUSEUM

(鰊御殿; 0134-22-1038; 3-228 Shukutsu; ¥300; 9am-5pm; Otaru Aquarium (Suizoukukan)) One of Otaru's must-see spots, this old herring house, once at the sea's edge, has been moved to a gorgeous bluff and has a number of artefacts and photos depicting the herring industry in its heyday. Most of it is in Japanese, but there's enough there to impress English-speaking visitors.

Otaru General Museum — MUSEUM

(小樽市総合博物館; 0134-22-1258; 2-1-20 Ironai; adult/child ¥300/free; 9.30am-5pm) This annexe of the Otaru Museum, known as the Ungakan (運河館), is housed in a restored warehouse dating from 1893 near the canal. It does a good job of illustrating (with an English-language supplement) Otaru's rise, thanks to the herring industry, its peak in the early 20th century and the city's subsequent decline.

Nichigin-dōri — AREA

(日銀通り) Once known as the 'Wall Street of the North', Nichigin-dōri is lined with elegant buildings that speak to Otaru's past life as a prominent financial centre.

Activities

Otaru Canal Cruise — CRUISE

(0134-31-1733; www.otaru.cc; 5-4 Minato-machi; adult/child day cruise ¥1500/500, night cruise ¥1800/500; 9am-9pm) The view of the canal is prettiest from this vantage point on the water. Cruises depart from Chūō-bashi and last 40 minutes; though recommended, no advance booking is necessary.

Sleeping

Otaru is an easy day trip from Sapporo, though it also works as a convenient stopover on the way to Niseko. There are plenty of places to stay here, the best (and priciest) of which have rooms overlooking the bay.

★Otarunai Backpackers' Hostel Morinoki — HOSTEL ¥

(おたるないバックパッカーズホステル杜の樹; 0134-23-2175; https://otaru-backpackers.com; 4-15 Aioi; dm ¥3000; P) While the sights of Otaru can be done in a day, if you're looking for somewhere to hole up for a few, this is a fantastic choice. Morinoki is an old, sprawling house perched on a stone embankment. Accommodation is in fairly simple mixed-gender dormitories, but there are kitchen and laundry facilities, bilingual staff and super-comfy lounging areas.

The hostel is about a 15-minute walk from JR Otaru Station, and can be a little tricky to find.

★Ginrinsō — RYOKAN ¥¥¥

(銀鱗荘; 0134-54-7010; www.ginrinsou.com; 1-1 Sakura; s/d incl 2 meals from ¥45,510/69,420;

Otaru

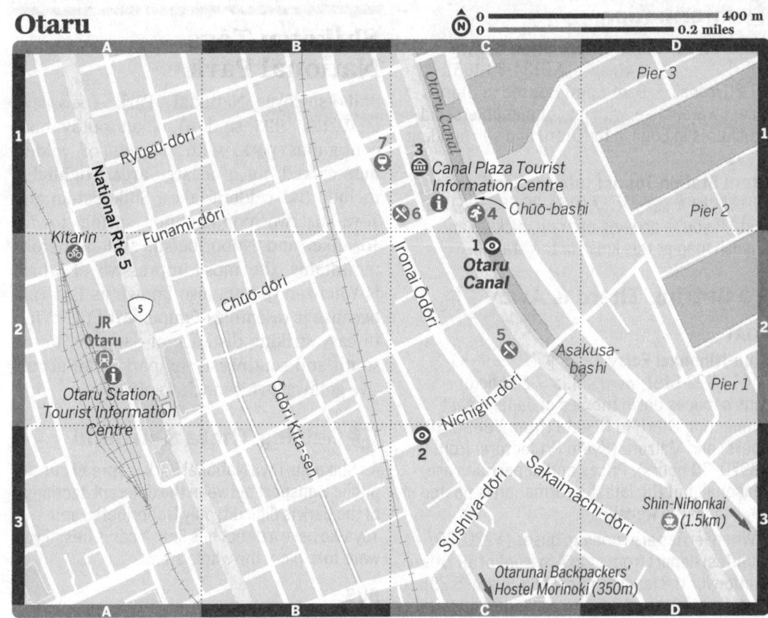

(P ❄ ☰) When Ginrinsō was constructed in 1873 it was among the most lavish of the herring estates. In 1938 it was relocated to a bluff overlooking Ishikari Bay and reborn as a (very) high-end ryokan. The sticker shock is real, but so is the beauty of this place, hewn of cedar and stone, with open-air natural hot springs facing the waters.

Eating & Drinking

★Kita-no Aisukurīmu-ya-san ICE CREAM ¥

(北のアイスクリーム屋さん; ☎0134-23-8983; 1-2-18 Ironai; ice cream from ¥300; ⏰9.30am-6pm) Housed in a converted warehouse that was built in 1892, just back from the canal, this legendary Otaru ice-cream parlour scoops up some seriously 'special' ice cream flavours, such as wasabi, beer, and *natto*. The *ika-sumi* (squid ink) is actually just mildly sweet. Melon, a more ice-cream friendly flavour, is divine.

Otaru Sushi-kō SUSHI ¥¥

(小樽 すし耕; ☎0134-21-5678; www.denshiparts.co.jp/sushikou; 2-2-6 Ironai; sushi sets ¥2000-3800; ⏰noon-9pm Thu-Tue) Come here for excellent sushi sets and *kaisen-don* (bowls of rice topped with sashimi) featuring Hokkaidō specialities such as *sake* (salmon), *ikura* (salmon roe), *uni* (sea urchin) and *kani* (crab). Note that it often closes for a few hours in the afternoon and fills up fast at dinner, so reservations are recommended.

ISO BAR

(☎0134-31-1888; www.otaruiso.jp; 2-2-14 Ironai; drinks from ¥800; ⏰11.30am-3pm & 5.30-10pm Thu-Tue) In a building with literary history sits ISO, one of the few bars Otaru offers. Dark leather seats, wood and brick walls, mellow bar staff, soft samba music in the background – it's a perfect spot to unwind with a whisky or cocktail after a hard day of sightseeing. The food is so-so, but the drinks are just fine.

Otaru

Information

Canal Plaza Tourist Information Centre (運河プラザ観光案内所; ☎0134-33-1661; 2-1-20 Ironai; ⊙9am-6pm) Housed in Otaru's oldest warehouse, with lots of pamphlets and brochures in English for Otaru and surrounding areas.

Otaru Station Tourist Information Centre (小樽駅観光案内所; ☎0134-29-1333; ⊙9am-6pm) If you're arriving by train, pick up an English map at this kiosk in the station.

Getting There & Away

BOAT

Shin-Nihonkai Ferry (新日本海フェリー; ☎0134-22-6191; www.snf.jp; 7-2 Chikkō) runs services down the Sea of Japan coast, connecting Otaru to Niigata (from ¥6680, 18 hours) and Maizuru (Kyoto Prefecture; from ¥9970, 20 hours). Prices and departures are seasonal, but the latest information is posted in English on the website.

When ferries are running, buses (¥220, 30 minutes) depart from stop 4 in front of JR Otaru Station for the ferry terminal at 8.59am, 5.29pm (Sundays only) and 9pm, to coincide with ferry departures. From the ferry terminal, buses depart at 9.30pm for Otaru.

TRAIN

Twice-hourly *kaisoku* (rapid) trains on the JR Hakodate line connect Otaru and Sapporo (¥1160, 30 minutes); hourly local trains take 45 minutes (¥640). Less frequent trains on the same line continue to Kutchan (¥1070, 1¼ hours).

Getting Around

Bikes are a great way to see more of the town; **Kitarin** (きたりん; ☎070-5605-2926; www.kitarin.info; 2-22 Inaho; 2 hours ¥900; ⊙9am-6.30pm Mon, Tue & Thu-Sat, from 6.30am Sun Apr-Nov, 9am-6.30pm daily, from 6.30am Sun Jul-Sep) is one of several bike rental shops near Otaru Station.

DON'T MISS

BEST ONSEN

- Hōheikyō
- Onsen Tengoku (p618)
- Goshiki Onsen (p608)
- Mizunashi Kaihin Onsen (p621)
- Fukiage Roten-no-yu (p636)

Shikotsu-Tōya National Park

Shikotsu-Tōya National Park (支笏洞爺国立公園; 993 sq km) is an oddly non-contiguous park, with pockets of wilderness carved out of a large area. Highlights include two caldera lakes, Shikotsu-ko and Tōya-ko, two popular hot spring towns, Jōzankei and Noboribetsu, and numerous mountains, the most impressive of which is Yōtei-zan (p609), also known as Ezo-Fuji, because it resembles famous Mt Fuji. Within easy striking distance of Sapporo, to the south and southwest, the park is an attractive getaway with much to offer.

Getting There & Around

As Shikotsu-Tōya National Park is spread out, public transport between the different sections of the park is difficult; only Noboribetsu and Tōya-ko have a direct bus link. A car is best if you want to explore the whole area.

BUS

Buses depart from Sapporo Eki-mae Bus Terminal (p605) for:

Jōzankei ¥770, one hour, five daily
Noboribetsu Onsen ¥1950, 100 minutes, once daily
Tōya-ko Onsen ¥2780, 2¾ hours, once daily

There are also direct buses from New Chitose Airport to Noboribetsu Onsen (¥1370, one hour). The bus terminals for Noboribetsu Onsen and Tōya-ko Onsen are in town.

There is no public transport to Shikotsu-ko, but if you pick up a car from New Chitose Airport the lake is only a 25km drive.

TRAIN

Noboribetsu and Tōya have train stations. Limited-express trains run 10 times daily on the JR Muroran line from Sapporo to Noboribetsu Station (¥2160, 1¼ hours) and Tōya Station (¥3240, two hours). The JR Muroran line also connects Tōya Station (¥5490, two hours) and Noboribetsu Station (¥3990, 2½ hours) with Hakodate. The fare for the 40-minute journey between Noboribetsu and Tōya is ¥2720. From the train stations, a local bus is required to get into town.

Jōzankei

☎011 / POP 1150

Jōzankei (定山渓) sits along the Toyohira-gawa, deep in a gorge. It's the closest major onsen town to Sapporo and an easy escape for those after some R&R. The resort is especially pretty (and popular) in autumn, when the leaves change colour – a sight that can be viewed from many an outdoor bath. Only an hour's bus or car ride from Sapporo, Jōzankei works well as a day trip. Most hotels and ryokan allow nonguests to use their onsen baths for a fee (¥500 to ¥1500). There's also Hōheikyō further up the road, often voted one of Hokkaidō's best onsen.

Sights & Activities

Ainu Culture Promotion Centre CULTURAL CENTRE
(札幌ピリカコタン, Sapporo Pirka Kotan; 011-596-5961; www.city.sapporo.jp/shimin/pirka-kotan/en; 27 Kogane-yu, Minami-ku; adult/child ¥200/free; 9am-5pm Tue-Sun; P) Unlike other museums, where artefacts are kept behind glass, exhibitions here consist of replicas, handmade by members of Sapporo's Ainu community using their own family heirlooms as models. As a result, you can touch everything on display, feeling, for example, the linen-like softness of textiles made from tree bark. The strangely shaped centre is in Kogane-yu, 3km east of Jōzankei.

The Sapporo–Jōzankei bus stops at Kogane-yu (¥650, 50 minutes); the museum is a short walk up from the bus stop.

Iwato Kannon-dō BUDDHIST TEMPLE
(岩戸観音堂; 011-598-2012; 3 Jōzankei Onsen-higashi; 7am-8pm) This small temple fronts a 120m-long cave that has 33 statues of Kannon, the Buddhist deity of compassion, and is dedicated to road workers who lost their lives constructing roads in the area. There are also lovely old photographs of Jōzankei on display and, next door, a free *ashi-yu* (foot bath).

★**Hōheikyō** ONSEN
(豊平峡; 011-598-2410; www.hoheikyo.co.jp; 608 Jōzankei; adult/child ¥1000/500; 10am-10.30pm) Home to Hokkaidō's largest outdoor bath, Hōheikyō is a stunner, set above town on the gorge's forested slope. The whole rambling structure is shack-like, which just adds to the appeal of having stumbled upon something great. The door curtains indicating which baths are for men and which are for women are swapped daily. These waters purportedly ideal for improving women's skin.

Oddly enough, there's an Indian restaurant on the ground floor. The Sapporo–Jōzankei bus continues on to Hōheikyō (¥840, 1¼ hours), its final stop.

DON'T MISS

BEST HIKES

- Rishiri-zan (p639)
- Shiretoko Traverse (p648)
- Rebun-tō Traverse (p643)
- Yōtei-zan (p609)
- Asahi-dake (p633)

Information

Tourist Information Centre (011-598-2012; www.jozankei.jp; 3-225 Jōzankei Onsen-higashi; 9am-5pm) Right on Rte 230, the main road through the valley, with English brochures and maps, an English-speaker, and a small museum with photos of Jōzankei in the booming years of days gone by.

Shikotsu-ko

Directly south of Sapporo and surrounded by soaring volcanoes, Shikotsu-ko (支笏湖) is the second-deepest lake in Japan and renowned for its clear water. While it is 250m above sea level, its deepest spot is 363m, 113m below sea level. You'll need your own wheels to get here, but it's a superb spot for independent exploration and excellent for campers.

Shikotsu-ko Onsen (支笏湖温泉), on the eastern side of the lake, is the only town. This compact little resort village has some nice short walks, including a nature trail for birdwatchers. Sightseeing boats head out onto the lake and there are rental bicycles, boats and canoes.

Activities

Marukoma Onsen ONSEN
(丸駒温泉; 0123-25-2341; www.marukoma.co.jp; 7 Poropinai, Chitose; ¥1000; 10am-3pm) On the surface, Marukoma Onsen is a typical ageing resort hotel, but the concrete facade hides a fantastic collection of baths – which are open to day trippers. The large *rotemburo* (outdoor bath) looks right over Shikotsu-ko.

The waters, high in sodium and calcium, are said to be good for fatigue. Shampoo etc is provided; bring your own towel.

Tarumae-zan HIKING
(樽前山) On the southern side of the lake is Tarumae-zan (1041m), an active volcano that is the area's most popular hike. The crater itself is usually closed – it has a still-smoking lava dome – but you can reach and go around the rim from the seventh station (650m; only

Niseko & Shikotsu-Tōya National Park

A B C D

1 2 3 4 5 6 7

Jōzankei
Jōzan-ko
Kutchan
See Enlargement
Hirafu
10
Yōtei-zan (1898m)
Kyōgoku
276
Nakayama Pass
230
Niseko
Kimobetsu
Makkari
19
8
Otaki
230
Tōya
Tōya-ko
Naka-jima
Shikotsu-Tōya National Park
Tōya-ko Onsen
Abuta
Tōya
Sōbetsu
Shōwa-Shin-zan (398m)
Usu-zan (729m)
2
Dō-ō Expwy
Noboribetsu Onsen
37
Date
Enlargement
6
3
27
7
28 23
15
22
24
21
12
18
5
11
17
26
Hirafu
14
25
20
0 4 km
0 2 miles
Mareppu
Horobetsu
Orofure Pass
Muroran Main Line
Sakimori
Higashi-Muroran
Muroran
Wanishi
Muroran
Chikyū-misaki

A B C D

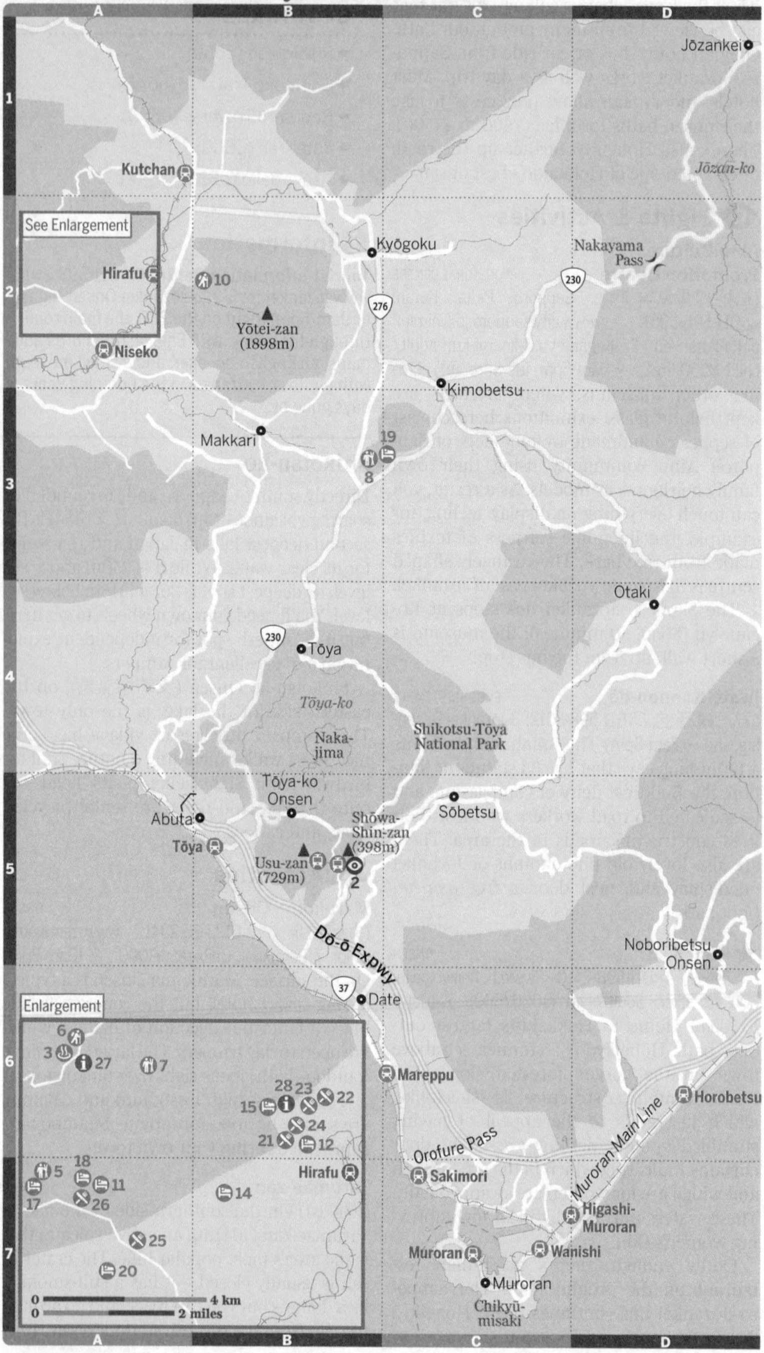

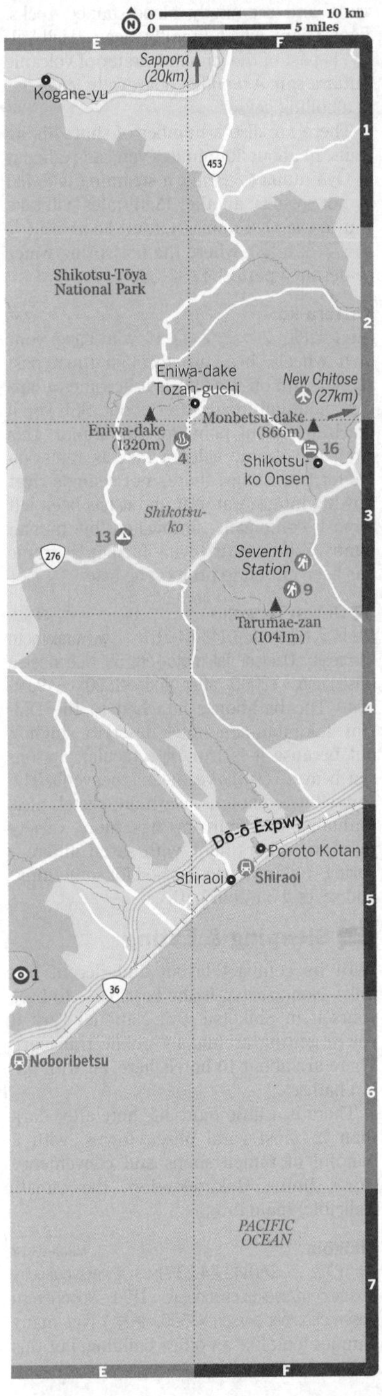

Niseko & Shikotsu-Tōya National Park

Sights

1 Kuttara-ko E5
2 Usu-zan B5

Activities, Courses & Tours

3 Goshiki Onsen A6
4 Marukoma Onsen E3
5 Moiwa A7
Niseko Adventure Centre (NAC) .... (see 23)
6 Niseko Circuit A6
7 Niseko United A6
8 Rusutsu Resort B3
9 Tarumae-zan F3
10 Yōtei-zan B2

Sleeping

11 Annupuri Village A7
12 AYA Niseko B6
13 Bifue Campsite E3
14 Hilton Niseko B7
15 Hotel Niseko Alpen B6
16 Log Bear F3
17 Moiwa Lodge 834 .... A7
18 Niseko Annupuri Guest House A7
19 Rusutsu Resort Hotel C3
20 YHA Niseko Fujiyama Karimpani A7

Eating

21 Ginger B6
22 Graubunden B6
23 Jojo's Café & Restaurant B6
24 Musu Bar + Bistro B6
25 Niseko Loft Club A7
Niseko Pizza .... (see 24)
26 Sobadokoro Rakuichi A7

Information

27 Goshiki Onsen Information Centre A6
28 Hirafu Welcome Centre B6
Shikotsu-ko Visitor Centre .... (see 16)

accessible by private car, off Rte 141). Allow 1½ hours for the return hike to the rim.

From the same trailhead you can also climb Fuppushi-dake (風不死岳; 1102m) in five to six hours return, which offers excellent views of the lake and park. Locals suggest a bear bell is essential for this hike.

Sleeping & Eating

There are very few places to eat here and they all close by 5pm or 6pm. Either secure meals at your lodging or pack food.

Bifue Campsite CAMPGROUND ¥

(美笛キャンプ場; 090-5987-1284; Bifue, Chitose; adult/child ¥1000/500; early May–mid-Oct) On a sandy bit on the lake's west shore among trees, this is the nicer of Shikotsu-ko's two campgrounds. There are showers and cooking facilities; four-person tent rentals are available for ¥1500. Accessible only by car.

Log Bear MINSHUKU ¥¥
(ログベアー; ☎0123-25-2738; http://logbear.moto-nari.com; Shikotsu-ko Onsen, Chitose; per person incl breakfast ¥5500; 📶) Log Bear is right in the middle of Shikotsu-ko Onsen, and is run by a real character called Robin. There are only two simple rooms: one twin and one quad. On the ground floor is a coffee shop (9am to 10pm), where breakfast is served along with the town's best coffee.

Information

Shikotsu-ko Visitor Centre (支笏湖ビジターセンター; ☎0123-25-2404; www.shikotsukovc.sakura.ne.jp; Shikotsu-ko Onsen; ⏲9am-5.30pm Apr-Nov, 9.30am-4.30pm Wed-Mon Dec-Mar) Before heading up any trails, check for closures and bear sightings on the map here. Staff are helpful and also rent out bicycles for ¥500 per day (9am to 5pm, mid-April to November).

Noboribetsu Onsen

☎0143 / POP 49,500

Noboribetsu Onsen (登別温泉) is a serious onsen: you can smell the sulphur from miles away. While the town is small, there are countless springs here, sending up mineral-rich waters. The baths received great fame when the town was designated as a health resort for injured soldiers following the 1904–05 Russo-Japanese War and remain Hokkaidō's most famous onsen today.

The source of the waters is Jigoku-dani, a hissing, steaming volcanic pit above town. According to legend, this hellish landscape is home to the *oni* (demon) Yukujin. Don't worry: he's kind and bestows luck. You'll find statues of him around town.

Sights & Activities

You can have a bath at just about all of the hotels without staying, with prices ranging from ¥400 all the way up to ¥2000. The Noboribetsu Gateway Center has a *higaeri-onsen* (day bathing) cheat sheet in English that includes opening hours and prices.

Jigoku-dani HOT SPRINGS
(地獄谷) FREE A short walk uphill from Noboribetsu town reveals what may await us in the afterlife: sulphurous gases, hissing vents and seemingly blood-stained rocks. Jigoku-dani, which literally means 'Hell Valley', is part of the smoking crater of volcanic Kuttara-san. A wooden boardwalk leads out to a boiling geyser.

There are also a number of short hiking trails. In about 30 minutes you can walk out to Ōyu-numa (大湯沼), a steaming lake fed by hot springs; another 15 minutes will take you to the Ōyu-numa Natural Footbath (大湯沼天然足湯), where the hot spring water comes up a perfect 42°C.

Kuttara-ko LAKE
(倶多楽湖; クッタラコ) If you have your own wheels, head up through town past Jigoku-dani on Rte 350 as it becomes a narrow mountain road. After about 4km you'll reach a lookout point for Kuttara-ko. This circular volcanic caldera lake is remarkable for two things: there's not a single river flowing into or out of it and it has been left almost completely untouched by human hands. You can't drive any further, as traffic has been cut off to protect the lake.

★**Onsen Tengoku** ONSEN
(温泉天国; ☎0143-84-2111; www.takimotokan.co.jp; Dai-ichi Takimoto-kan, 55 Noboribetsu Onsen-chō; ¥2000, after 4pm ¥1500; ⏲9am-6pm) The bathhouse attached to the Dai-ichi Takimoto-kan hotel deserves singling out because it is truly spectacular, an 'onsen heaven' (*tengoku* means 'heaven'). The sprawling complex, awash in pastel tiles, fountains and mirrors, has more variety than any others here, with seven different springs (all purportedly good for something) and several outdoor baths.

Sleeping & Eating

With its compact layout and decent bus links, Noboribetsu is the best place to base yourself in Shikotsu-Tōya National Park if you're getting around by public transport. There are about 10 hotels here, all with onsen baths.

There is a little more life here after dark than in most rural onsen towns, with a handful of ramen shops and convenience stores lining Gokuraku-dōri, the (small, walkable) main drag.

Shōkōin MINSHUKU ¥
(聖光院; ☎0143-84-2359; www.syoukouin.wixsite.com/syukubokannonji; 119-1 Noboribetsu Onsen-chō; per person ¥3500; P📶) Not many temples look like an office building, but this

one does! The entrance is on the ground floor, the temple rooms are on floor two, and the priest's wife runs a *minshuku* on floor three, with small but well-kept tatami rooms. The shared bath, which can be used privately and is open 24 hours, has onsen water.

The temple is also known locally as Kannon-ji (観音寺). Morning prayers (if you like) are at 8am.

Dai-ichi Takimoto-kan HOTEL ¥¥¥

(第一滝本館; ☎0143-84-2111; www.takimotokan.co.jp; 55 Noboribetsu Onsen-chō; s/d with 2 meals incl ¥18,910/24,940; P ❄ 📶) This sprawling onsen hotel, with its escalators and kiosks and constant buzz, feels a bit like a gaily decorated airport terminal. That's not meant to be critical: with 24-hour complimentary use of the excellent bathhouse, Onsen Tengoku, this is a fine place to stay. Go for the Japanese-style rooms (the Western rooms are rather dowdy). Meals are served buffet-style.

Note that wi-fi is only available in the Honkan (main wing) and Minami-kan (south wing).

Aji no Daiō RAMEN ¥

(味の大王; ☎0143-84-2415; 29-9 Noboribetsu Onsen-chō; ramen ¥800-1150; ⏲11.30am-3pm & 9pm-midnight, closed 1st, 3rd & 5th Tue of the month) Noboribetsu's landmark ramen shop serves up fiery red '*jigokudani*' noodles that would make the local *oni* (devils) proud. Entry level is a totally manageable kick; you can add ¥50 to step it up a notch, all the way to 10. (Warning: there are far more celebrity signings on the walls here than photos of customers who have successfully finished level 10 bowls.)

ℹ Information

Noboribetsu Gateway Center (登別ゲートウェイセンター; ☎0143-84-2200; 26 Noboribetsu Onsen-chō; ⏲8.30am-6pm) Part of the Noboribetsu Onsen bus terminal, with bus schedules, English maps and luggage storage (¥500 per day).

Noboribetsu Park Service Centre (登別パークサービスセンター; ☎0143-84-3141; www.noboribetsu-spa.jp; Noboribetsu Onsen-chō; ⏲8am-5pm) English brochures and hiking maps, at the entrance to Jigoku-dani.

ℹ Getting There & Away

Frequent buses (¥340, 18 minutes) connect JR Noboribetsu Station with Noboribetsu Onsen bus terminal, at the southern end of town; a taxi ride between the train station and town should cost ¥2200.

Tōya-ko

At the southwestern side of Shikotsu-Tōya National Park, Tōya-ko (洞爺湖) is an almost classically round caldera lake with a large island (Naka-jima) sitting in the middle. What sets it apart is its truly active volcano, Usu-zan (有珠山; 733m), which has erupted four times since 1910, most recently in 2000.

Usu-zan is a mixed blessing: residents know that it will erupt again, covering their town in ash, and possibly rock; however, it was the 1910 eruption that led to the discovery of hot springs here and the development of Tōya-ko Onsen (洞爺湖温泉), the small resort on the lake's southern shore.

👁 Sights & Activities

Tōya-ko Onsen has free hand baths and foot baths throughout town (think of it as an onsen treasure hunt!) and many hotels' baths can be used during the day (¥500 to ¥1500). There's a fireworks display on the lake every night from April to October at 8.45pm, and paddle steamers running lake cruises. The 50km circumference of the lake can be rounded by car or bicycle.

Volcano Science Museum MUSEUM

(火山科学館; ☎0142-75-2555; www.toyako-vc.jp; 142-5 Tōya-ko Onsen; adult/child ¥600/300; ⏲9am-5pm; P) The eruptions at Uzu-san were among the first to be recorded by modern means (and work here significantly advanced science in early detection). Here you can see video footage of eruptions in action, and before and after photos that clearly show new land masses forming. The museum is part of the Tōya-ko Visitor Centre (p620).

Usu-zan MOUNTAIN

(有珠山; ☎0142-74-2401; www.wakasaresort.com; 184-5 Shōwa Shin-zan, Sōbetsu-chō; ropeway adult/child return ¥1600/800; ⏲9am-4pm) Here's a rare chance to bear witness to modern mountain-making: Shōwa Shin-zan (昭和新山; 398m) – which means 'the new mountain of the Shōwa period' – arose from a wheat field following the 1943 eruption of Usu-zan. The **Usu-zan Ropeway** runs up to a viewing platform for Shōwa Shin-zan, with Tōya-ko behind it.

From the observation deck a trail heads out on a 90-minute circuit (open May to October) around the outer rim of Usu-zan, with views of Tōya-ko and Yōtei-zan. Buses (one way/round trip ¥340/620, 10.10am, 12.45pm, 1.40pm and 3.50pm) run four times a day from the Tōya-ko Onsen bus terminal to the ropeway. A taxi should cost ¥1800; all the way from JR Tōya-ko Station, ¥3000.

Sleeping & Eating

In addition to some pricier resorts, Tōya-ko Onsen has quite a few budget ryokan.

Though many restaurants only open for lunch in Tōya-ko Onsen, there are some *izakaya* and ramen shops that stay open well into the evening.

Daiwa Ryokan RYOKAN ¥¥
(大和旅館; 0142-75-2415; www.daiwa-ryokan.jp; 105 Tōya-ko Onsen; s/d from ¥5200/9200; P) Daiwa Ryokan is a simple, homely budget ryokan with character; adopting an early Shōwa (1926–89) theme, it's strewn with old knick-knacks and there's a hand onsen outside. The owners are friendly, the bath is 100% natural water and there's a small garden. Nonguests can use the onsen here for ¥500. Wifi's in the lobby only.

Boyotei JAPANESE ¥¥
(望羊蹄; 0142-75-2311; www.boyotei.com; 36-12 Tōyako Onsen; mains ¥1100-2000; 11am-3pm & 5-8.30pm) Festooned with a flower garden outside and romantic and cosy inside, Boyotei is a treat just five minutes' walk from the station. Hamburger-steaks, gratins, and other Japanese-Western food is on the menu, but it's the friendly service and ambience that really makes this place stand out.

Information

Tōya-ko Tourist Information Centre (洞爺湖観光情報センター; 0142-75-2446; www.laketoya.com; 142 Tōya-ko Onsen; 9am-5pm;) Inside the Tōya-ko Onsen bus terminal, with maps, pamphlets and bus schedules in English.

Tōya-ko Visitor Centre (洞爺湖ビジターセンター; 0142-75-2555; www.toyako-vc.jp; 142-5 Tōya-ko Onsen; 9am-5pm) Excellent (and free) information on the local topography as well as indigenous flora and fauna; a short walk west from the Tōya-ko Onsen bus terminal.

Getting There & Away

From the train station, it's a 15-minute bus (¥330, twice hourly) or taxi ride (¥2500) to the bus terminal in Tōya-ko Onsen.

Tomakomai

0144 / POP 174,200

Tomakomai (苫小牧) is actually a sizeable industrial city on Hokkaidō's south-central coast, though most travellers know it only as the main port for long-distance ferries.

Sleeping & Eating

There are restaurants near the hotels. If you're catching a ferry it's advisable to eat beforehand and stock up on snacks as the food on-board is terrible (if you just arrived by ferry, you already know that).

There really is no reason to stay in Tomakomai unless you are arriving or departing by ferry and won't be able to make your travel connections otherwise. There are plenty of business hotels here, including the major chains, for this very purpose.

Getting There & Away

JR Tomakomai Station is on the JR Muroran line, one hour from Sapporo (¥1450). **Dōnan Bus** (www.donanbus.co.jp) runs between the ferry terminal and JR Tomakomai Station (¥250, 15 minutes); a taxi should cost about ¥1500.

Chūō Bus (www.chuo-bus.co.jp) runs highway buses between Tomakomai Ferry Terminal and Sapporo Eki-mae Bus Terminal (¥1310, 1¾ hours).

FERRIES TO/FROM TOMAKOMAI

Four operators, Shin-Nihonkai Ferry (www.snf.jp), Silver Ferry (www.silverferry.jp), MOL Ferry (www.sunflower.co.jp) and Taiheiyō Ferry (www.taiheiyo-ferry.co.jp), run ferries between Tomakomai and the following destinations on Honshū. Note that schedules and prices are subject to seasonal fluctuations.

DESTINATION	COST (¥; 2ND CLASS)	DURATION (HR)	FREQUENCY	OPERATOR
Akita	4530	10	Mon-Sat	Shin-Nihonkai Ferry
Hachinohe (Aomori-ken)	5000	7½	4 daily	Silver Ferry
Nagoya	9800	40	alternate days	Taiheiyō Ferry
Niigata	6480	18	Mon-Sat	Shin-Nihonkai Ferry
Oarai (Ibaraki-ken)	8740	17	1-2 daily	MOL Ferry
Sendai	7200	15	daily	Taiheiyō Ferry
Tsuruga (Fukui-ken)	9570	19	daily	Shin-Nihonkai Ferry

HAKODATE

0138 / POP 275,500

Built on a narrow strip of land between Hakodate Harbour to the west and the Tsugaru Strait to the east, Hakodate (函館) is the southern gateway to the island of Hokkaidō. Under the Kanagawa Treaty of 1854, the city was one of the first ports to open up to international trade, and as such hosted a small foreign community. That influence can still be seen in the Motomachi district, a steep hillside that's sprinkled with European buildings and churches; the waterfront lined with red-brick warehouses; and in the nostalgic streetcar that still makes the rounds of the city.

Sights

Hakodate's highlights can easily be done in a day, as they're all time-specific: start early at the morning seafood market; spend the day strolling the attractive flagstone lanes of the Motomachi district; then head up Hakodate-yama for the famous night view over the bay.

Discounted combination tickets (two/three/four sights ¥500/720/840, half-price for children) are available for the Old British Consulate, the Old Public Hall of Hakodate Ward, the Hakodate Museum of Northern Peoples and the Hakodate Museum of Literature. Buy the tickets at participating sights.

★Hakodate-yama MOUNTAIN

(函館山) Mention you've been to Hakodate and every Japanese person you know will ask if you took in the night view from atop Hakodate-yama (334m) – it's that famous! You want to get up here for sunset or after dark: what's striking is seeing the lit-up peninsula (which locals say is shaped like Hokkaidō itself) against the pitch-black waters. In addition to the viewing platform and parking area, those who hunt will find the remains of an old fort behind the buildings, with interesting foundations intact.

There are a few ways to get here: by ropeway (p624), bus, car or foot. Buses for the ropeway (¥240, 10 minutes) and the summit (¥400, 30 minutes, mid-April to mid-November) depart from bus stop 4 at JR Hakodate Station. You can also walk to the ropeway in 10 minutes from the Jūjigai tram stop; alternatively you can hike up one of several trails (all take about an hour) between May and late October. Note that the road to the summit is often closed to private vehicles after sunset because it gets too crowded.

OFF THE BEATEN TRACK

MIZUNASHI KAIHIN ONSEN

Mizunashi Kaihin Onsen (水無海浜温泉) FREE is one of those hidden jewels – an onsen in the sea! You'll need to turn up at the right time as the two main rock pools are covered by the sea when the tide is in; check with the Hakodate Tourist Information Centre (p623) for bathing times. There are changing facilities. Bathing suits are not required, though you can wear them if you're feeling modest.

You'll need your own wheels to get here: head east from Hakodate on Rte 278 to the Kameda Peninsula. When the road heads inland, follow it up and over to the far coast, then turn right on Rte 231 and drive southeast to the end of the road.

★Hakodate Morning Market MARKET

(函館朝市, Hakodate Asa-ichi; www.hakodate-asaichi.com; 9-19 Wakamatsu-chō; 5am-noon; JR Hakodate) FREE With crabs grilling over hot coals, freshly caught squid packed tightly in ice-stuffed styrofoam and the sing-song call of vendors, Hakodate Morning Market does a fantastic impression of an old-time seafood market – though the visitors today are tourists not wholesale buyers. (The commercial market that was here originally has since moved to a bigger space.)

Orthodox Church CHURCH

(函館ハリストス正教会, Hakodate Harisutosu Seikyōkai; www.orthodox-hakodate.jp; 3-13 Motomachi; donation ¥200; 10am-5pm Mon-Fri, 10am-4pm Sat, 1-4pm Sun; Suehiro-chō) Dating from 1916, this Russian Orthodox church is adorned with distinctive copper domes and spires. It's still in use by the 300 or so (mostly elderly) members of the Japanese Orthodox community.

Goryō-kaku-kōen PARK

(五稜郭公園; Goryōkaku-kōen-mae) FREE Japan's first Western-style fort was built in 1864 in the shape of a five-pointed star (*goryō-kaku* means 'five-sided fort') designed to trap attackers in deadly crossfire. Nothing remains of the actual structure but the footprint – a park encircled by a star-shaped moat. To best appreciate this, visit the observatory atop the 98m **Goryō-kaku Tower** (五稜郭タワー; 0138-51-4785; www.goryokaku-tower.co.jp; 43-9 Goryōkaku-chō; adult/child ¥900/450; 8am-7pm mid-Apr–mid-Oct,

Central Hakodate

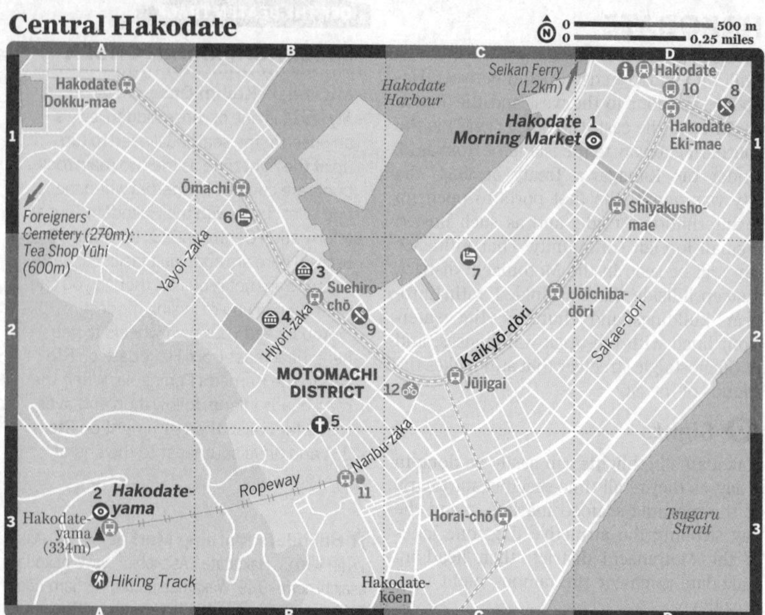

Central Hakodate

Top Sights

1 Hakodate Morning Market.................D1
2 Hakodate-yama.................A3

Sights

3 Hakodate Museum of Northern Peoples.................B2
4 Old British Consulate.................B2
5 Orthodox Church.................B2

Sleeping

6 Hakodate Perry House.................B1
7 La Vista Hakodate Bay Hotel.................C2

Eating

8 Daimon Yokochō.................D1
Kikuyo Shokudo.................(see 1)
9 Lucky Pierrot.................B2

Transport

10 Hakodate Eki-mae Bus Terminal.................D1
11 Hakodate-yama Ropeway.................B3
12 Hakorin.................C2

9am-6pm mid-Oct–mid-Apr; Goryōkaku-kōen-mae). Exhibitions in the observatory explain the history of the fort; you also get good views over Hakodate.

The park itself is a pretty green space, with 1600 cherry trees that bloom in April.

Hakodate Museum of Northern Peoples MUSEUM
(函館市北方民族資料館, Hakodate-shi Hoppōminzoku Shiryōkan; 0138-22-4128; www.zaidan-hakodate.com/hoppominzoku/#sisetu; 21-7 Suehiro-chō; adult/child ¥300/150; 9am-7pm Apr-Oct, to 5pm Nov-Mar; Suehiro-chō) Inside the old Japan Bank building (1926), this museum has interesting exhibitions (labelled in English) about Ainu culture and also other indigenous cultures from Sakhalin (the island north of Hokkaidō, now Russia) and further north.

Old British Consulate HISTORIC BUILDING
(旧イギリス領事館, Kyū-Igirisu Ryōjikan; 0138-27-8159; www.hakodate-kankou.com/british/en; 33-14 Motomachi; adult/child ¥300/150; 9am-7pm Apr-Oct, to 5pm Nov-Mar; Suehiro-chō) From 1913 to 1934, this whitewashed mansion served as the British consulate. You can see the restored interior and have tea (¥540) on the ground floor.

Festivals & Events

For more info on local festivals, see www.hakodate.travel/en/experience.

Hakodate Port Festival CULTURAL
(函館港祭り; Hakodate Minato Matsuri; Aug) In early August, thousands of locals gather to perform traditional dances in the streets, including Hakodate's signature squid dance.

Sleeping

Most of your standard budget chains are well represented here, located within a short walk of JR Hakodate Station. Fancier (if a bit overpriced) options overlook the bay. Winter is considered the low season in Hakodate and rates should drop.

B&B Pension Hakodate-mura PENSION ¥¥
(Ｂ＆Ｂペンションはこだて村; ☎0138-22-8105; www.bb-hakodatemura.com; 16-12 Suehiro-chō; s/d from ¥6300/10,800; P ⊜ @ ☜; 🚋Jū-jigai) This long-running traveller favourite has a great location near the harbour, and is within walking distance of Motomachi. The owners speak English and are very welcoming. There's a good spread of room options, including family rooms. Filling breakfasts (¥840) are served in the ground-floor lounge.

Hakodate Perry House GUESTHOUSE ¥¥
(函館ぺりーハウス; ☎0138-83-1457; www.hakodate-perryhouse.com; 3-2 Ōmachi; without bathroom s ¥3500-4500, d ¥7000; P ⊜ ☜; 🚋Ōmachi) Opened exactly 160 years after Perry's American navy ships visited Hakodate, this simple guesthouse is named after the great naval captain. Rooms are small and the bathroom and toilet facilities are shared, but the price is right and the location is conveniently near the Ōmachi tram stop.

La Vista Hakodate Bay Hotel HOTEL ¥¥¥
(ラビスタ函館ベイ; ☎0138-23-6111; www.hotespa.net/hotels/lahakodate; 12-6 Toyokawa-chō; s/d from ¥16,500/37,000; ⊜ ❄ ☜; 🚋Uōichiba-dōri) Rooms here are on the smallish side but they've been gussied up nicely to evoke an early 20th-century feel (while still being modern). The hotel is right on the waterfront, in the red-brick warehouse district, and has a rooftop onsen with outdoor tubs overlooking the bay.

Eating & Drinking

For many visitors, eating is the whole reason to come to Hakodate. Squid, caught in the Tsugaru Strait, is the city's speciality. Hakodate is also known for its *shio-ramen* (塩ラーメン; ramen in a light, salt-flavoured broth).

★Kikuyo Shokudo SEAFOOD ¥
(きくよ食堂; www.hakodate-kikuyo.com/asaichi; Hakodate Morning Market; mains from ¥1080; ⊙5am-2pm; 🚉JR Hakodate) Inside Hakodate Morning Market, Kikuyo Shokudo got its start in the 1950s as a counter joint to feed market workers and is now one of the top reasons to come to Hakodate. The speciality here is the *Hakodate tomoe-don* (函館巴丼; ¥1780), rice topped with raw *uni* (sea urchin), *ikura* (salmon roe) and *hotate* (scallops). There's a picture menu.

You can also custom-make *kaisen-don* (raw seafood over rice) from the list of toppings or sample another Hakodate speciality: *ika-sōmen* (raw squid sliced very thinly like noodles; ¥1150).

Lucky Pierrot BURGERS ¥
(ラッキーピエロ; ☎0138-26-2099; 23-18 Suehiro-chō; burgers ¥270-1100; ⊙10am-12.30am Sun-Fri, to 1am Sat; P; 🚋Suehiro-chō) Hakodate's iconic burger shop has been voted best in the nation several times – despite its cultivated dive image. The house special is the Chinese chicken burger, an oddly addictive combo of twice-cooked chicken, crisp lettuce and mayonnaise on a sesame bun. Much of the menu is similarly fusion; the decor is carnival diner c 1989.

It has several branches around the city, but this is one of the bigger ones, conveniently located near the bay front.

Daimon Yokochō STREET FOOD ¥
(大門横丁; www.hakodate-yatai.com; 7-5 Matsukaze-chō; ⊙5pm-midnight; 🚉JR Hakodate) This is a fun place to gather in the evening: a collection of 25 food vendors in an old-style marketplace, with outdoor seats (when it's not freezing). You can take your pick from ramen, *donburi* (rice bowl) dishes and typical *izakaya* fare. Most places have picture menus; figure about ¥2000 per person.

Walk straight out of JR Hakodate Station and turn left at the first traffic light.

★Tea Shop Yūhi TEAHOUSE
(ティーショップ夕日; ☎0138-85-8824; 25-18 Funami-chō; tea sets from ¥600; ⊙10am-dusk Fri-Tue mid-Mar–Nov; 🚌Funami-chō Kōryū-ji mae, 🚋Hakodate Dokku-mae) Filling the halls of a wooden building from 1885 (actually the old Hakodate Quarantine Office) is this magical teahouse overlooking the water. It's lit only by natural light so closes after the sun sets. In the meantime, you can while away the afternoon refilling your tiny pot of single-origin green tea, nibbling on the *wagashi* (Japanese sweets) and pickles that accompany it.

The teahouse is a short walk beyond the Foreigners' Cemetery.

Information

Hakodate Tourist Information Centre (函館市観光案内所; ☎0138-23-5440; ⊙9am-7pm Apr-Oct, 9am-5pm Nov-Mar) Inside JR Hakodate Station, with English brochures and maps.

DON'T MISS

HOKKAIDŌ'S SEASONAL SEAFOOD

For many Japanese travellers, Hokkaidō is synonymous with crab. Winter is the season for *tarabagani* (タラバガニ; king crab), *zuwaigani* (ズワイガニ; snow crab) and *kegani* (毛蟹; horse hair crab) from the frigid waters of the Sea of Okhotsk. Restaurants in Sapporo and resort areas like Niseko do lavish crab feasts. But you don't have to spend heaps: *kani-jiru* (かに汁) – miso soup made with crab – is a decadent treat that many *shokudō* will serve.

Summer, meanwhile, is *uni* (うに; sea urchin) season. The islands of Rebun-tō and Rishiri-tō are particularly famous for it. So is Shakotan, which means you can get good *uni* in season in southern and central Hokkaidō, too. Fish markets, sushi restaurants and *shokudō* serve *uni-don* (うに丼), a bowl of rice topped with a mountain of fresh roe; you can also get it with other toppings on a *kaisen-don* (海鮮丼; mixed seafood on rice). Summer is also the season for the blooming red *hanasakigani* (花咲ガニ; spiny king crab), found only around Nemuro. In autumn you can get fresh *ikura* (salmon roe).

Spring is the start of squid season, which moves slowly north through autumn. Hakodate, which peaks in June, is particularly known for squid (it even has a squid festival). Try *ika-sōmen* (イカそうめん), raw squid sliced thin like noodles.

Getting There & Away

AIR

From **Hakodate Airport** (函館空港; 0138-57-8881; www.airport.ne.jp/hakodate; 511 Takamatsu-chō), just a few kilometres east of the city centre, there are international flights to Seoul and Taipei, and domestic flights to various destinations including Sapporo, Tokyo and Kansai.

Frequent buses run direct between Hakodate Airport and JR Hakodate Station's bus stop 11 (¥450, 20 minutes), or you can simply take a taxi (¥2500).

BOAT

The **Tsugaru Kaikyō Ferry** (津軽海峡フェリー; www.tsugarukaikyo.co.jp) and the **Seikan Ferry** (青函フェリー; 0138-42-5561; www.seikan-ferry.co.jp; 5-11 Asanochō; adult/child Oct-May ¥1600/800, Jun-Sep ¥2000/1000) operate year-round. The former runs between Aomori and Hakodate (¥2220 to ¥3190, 3¾ hours, eight daily), and between Hakodate and Ōma (¥1810 to ¥2600, 1¾ hours, two daily) on the Shimokita Peninsula. The ferry terminal, where you also buy your tickets, is on the northeast corner of Hakodate Harbour. The Seikan Ferry (¥1600 to ¥2000, four hours, five to eight daily) also runs between Hakodate and Aomori, with a terminal close by.

Buses (¥320, 30 minutes) for the ferry terminal depart from bus stop 11 in front of JR Hakodate Station; a taxi should cost about ¥2000.

BUS

Chūō Bus (p596) coaches run eight times daily (including one night departure) between JR Hakodate Station and JR Sapporo Station (¥4810, 5½ hours); reservations required. The **bus terminal** (函館駅前バスターミナル) is in front of JR Hakodate Station; buses also stop at JR Shin-Hakodate-Hokuto Station.

CAR & MOTORCYCLE

If you've just arrived in Hokkaidō, Hakodate is a good place to pick up a rental car and start your road trip across the island. Major agencies have offices around JR Hakodate Station and in front of the JR Shin-Hakodate-Hokuto *shinkansen* station.

TRAIN

The JR Hokkaidō Shinkansen travels from Honshū to JR Shin-Hakodate-Hokuto Station, north of Hakodate, via the Seikan Tunnel. There are 10 trains daily to/from Tokyo (¥22,810, four hours). The JR Hakodate Liner connects JR Shin-Hakodate-Hokuto and JR Hakodate stations (¥360, 20 minutes, 16 times daily).

JR Limited Express Hokuto Liner trains run 12 times daily between Hakodate and Sapporo (¥8830, 3½ hours), via JR Shin-Hakodate-Hokuto Station.

A combination of *tokkyū* (limited express) and *kaisoku* (rapid) trains run on the JR Hakodate line between Hakodate and Niseko via Oshamambe (¥5560, about four hours with transfers).

Getting Around

Single-trip fares on trams and buses generally cost between ¥210 and ¥250, depending on how long you ride. One-day transport passes for bus (¥800), tram (¥600) or combined bus and tram (¥1000) can be purchased at the tourist information centre (p623) or on-board.

The **Hakodate-yama Ropeway** (函館山ロープウェイ; 0138-23-3105; www.334.co.jp; 19-7 Motomachi; adult/child return ¥1280/780; 10am-10pm 25 Apr-15 Oct, 10am-9pm 16 Oct-24 Apr) runs up to the top of Hakodate-yama.

You can rent bikes from **Hakorin** (はこりん; 0138-22-9700; 4-19 Suehiro-chō; per day ¥1600; 9am-6.30pm), which can be found at the community centre by JR Hakodate Station.

NORTHERN HOKKAIDŌ

Northern Hokkaidō (道北; Dō-hoku) is where the majestic grandeur of the natural world takes over. Southeast of Asahikawa, Hokkaidō's second-largest city, is Daisetsuzan National Park, Japan's largest national park. It's a raw virgin landscape of enormous proportions. Way up north, west of Wakkanai and in the shadow of Siberia, Rishiri-Rebun-Sarobetsu National Park is a dramatic island-scape famous for its wildflowers. For hikers and extreme skiers the possibilities here are tantalising. South of Asahikawa, Furano offers a somewhat mellower alternative: a family-friendly ski resort in winter and, in summer, picturesque fields through which you can drive, cycle or just stroll. Biei, nearby, is famous for its 'art fields' and a hot spot for photographers.

Sleeping

Asahikawa has the most diversity of sleeping options, and also the best deals. In winter (half the year) rooms can be had here for a song. Elsewhere, many lodgings are only open during the warmer months (and maybe ski season) and, because of this, can be pricier. Be wary though, of using Asahikawa as a base in winter, as roads can be icy.

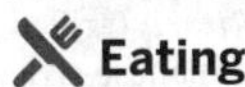

Eating

Furano is famous around Japan for its food production; you'll eat well here. Daisetsuzan National Park is trickier: with few restaurants near the park, you'll have to order meals at your lodging – though this can be a treat, as many serve river fish and mountain vegetables. Asahikawa, as to be expected of a major city, has plenty of options.

Getting There & Around

Asahikawa is the major transit hub for the region.

AIR

Northern Hokkaidō has two airports useful to travellers:

Asahikawa Airport (p627) In between Asahikawa and Biei and convenient for Daisetsuzan National Park and Furano; flights to/from Tokyo, Nagoya, Osaka and China.

Wakkanai Airport (p637) Convenient for Wakkanai and Rishiri-Rebun-Sarobetsu National Park; flights to/from Sapporo and Tokyo.

BOAT

Ferries depart from Wakkanai for Rishiri-tō and Rebun-tō, the islands of Rishiri-Rebun-Sarobetsu National Park.

BUS

Frequent highway buses run from Sapporo Eki-mae Bus Terminal to Asahikawa; there are less frequent buses to Wakkanai.

Buses run from Asahikawa to Asahidake Onsen and Sōunkyō Onsen in Daisetsuzan National Park.

CAR & MOTORCYCLE

The Hokkaidō Expressway runs from New Chitose Airport via Sapporo to Asahikawa.

It's very handy to have a car here, as buses have very limited schedules. However, snow comes early to northern Hokkaidō – as early as late September in the higher elevations – and you'll need to be mindful of road conditions and closures.

TRAIN

The following JR Limited Express trains run from Sapporo to northern Hokkaidō:

Super Kamui Liner For Asahikawa (¥4290, 90 minutes, every 30 minutes).

Super Sōya/Sarubetsu Liner For Wakkanai (¥9930, six hours, three daily), via Asahikawa.

JR Limited Express Super Sōya/Sarubetsu Liner trains run north from Asahikawa to Wakkanai. JR Furano line trains run south from Asahikawa to Biei and Furano.

Asahikawa

0166 / POP 352,100

Asahikawa (旭川), Hokkaidō's second-largest city, carries the dual honour of having the most days with snowfall in all of Japan, as well as the record for the coldest temperature (-40°C). It is mainly used by travellers as a transit point for Wakkanai to the north, Daisetsuzan National Park to the southeast, and Biei and Furano to the south. However, if you find your travel plans waylaid by bad weather, this a pleasant city in which to spend a day or two, with a handful of sights and plenty of eating and drinking options.

Heiwa-dōri, a large pedestrian strip, extends north of JR Asahikawa Station for eight blocks. Most hotels and many restaurants are around here, within easy walking distance of the station.

Sights

Kawamura Kaneto Ainu Memorial Hall MUSEUM

(川村カ子トアイヌ記念館; 0166-51-2461; www.ainu-museum.sakura.ne.jp; 11 Hokumon-chō; adult/child ¥500/300; 9am-5pm) Built in 1916 and thus just a few years past its 100th anniversary, this museum is less a collection of artefacts (though it has those too) and more the story of a local Ainu family desperate to keep the old ways alive; there are many fascinating, unstaged photographs from the early 20th century. Its founder was Kaneto Kawamura, an Ainu chief and master surveyor, who helped lay the tracks for many challenging rail projects in Japan; he used his savings to start the museum.

Take bus 24 from stop 14 in front of JR Asahikawa Station to the Ainu Kinenkan-mae stop (¥190, 15 minutes, hourly).

Festivals & Events

For local events, see www.asahikawa-daisetsu.jp/event.

Asahikawa Winter Matsuri CULTURAL
(旭川冬祭り; www.city.asahikawa.hokkaido.jp/awf; Feb) Into its sixth decade, Asahikawa's winter festival is second only to Sapporo's. The International Ice Sculpture Competition is a highlight, along with local food and fun events.

Kotan Matsuri CULTURAL
(こたんまつり; Sep) Held on the autumn equinox in September on the banks of the Chubestu-gawa, south of the city. There are traditional Ainu dances, music and prayer ceremonies offered to the deities of fire, the river, *kotan* (the village) and the mountains.

Sleeping

There's a good spread of national hotel chains around the train station.

Guesthouse Asahikawa Ride HOSTEL ¥
(ゲストハウス アサヒカワライド; 0166-73-7923; 7-31-10 6-jō-dōri; dm ¥3900; P @) On the 2nd floor of what used to be an office building, this hostel is about a 10-minute walk from JR Asahikawa Station, straight up the pedestrian strip. The world's smallest sign marks the entry; look for a grey building with a red sign on the corner. Those with pet allergies beware: there's a cat.

Art Hotel Asahikawa HOTEL ¥¥
(アートホテル旭川; 0166-25-8811; 6 7-jō-dōri; s/d from ¥8800/19,000; P) An easy-to-spot white tower block, the Art Hotel is Asahikawa's top hotel. It's not fancy, but it is clean and comfortable with very professional staff. Book early online for good deals. It's a 15-minute walk from JR Asahikawa Station, one block west of the pedestrian strip.

There's a spa in the basement, though admission is extra (¥1130; ask for a discount ticket at the front desk).

Eating & Drinking

Asahikawa is famous for its *shōyu* (soy sauce) ramen; there are countless shops, the best of which are highly debated. The shopping centre attached to JR Asahikawa Station has a food court and a supermarket. There are also options along Heiwa-dōri.

Ramen Aoba RAMEN ¥
(らーめん青葉; 0166-23-2820; 8 2-jō-dōri; ramen from ¥750; 9.30am-2pm & 3.30-7.45pm Thu-Tue) The city's oldest ramen shop (opened in 1947) serves delicious al dente noodles in a *shōyu* (soy sauce) seasoned *assari* (light) broth – classic Asahikawa-style. The proprietor truly loves foreign customers and may ask you to sign her notebook.

It's a five-minute walk from JR Asahikawa Station, one block east of the pedestrian strip, on Midori-bashi-dōri; look for the orange door curtains.

Furarīto Alley JAPANESE ¥¥
(ふらりーと小路; www.furari-to.com; 10am-11pm, individual shop times vary) This rambling collection of tiny restaurants runs the length of an alley between 4-jō-dōri and 5-jō-dōri, about a 10-minute walk north of the train station. Wander along (loosely translated, *furarīto* means wander) and see what looks good – options include *yakitori* (grilled chicken skewers), *izakaya* (Japanese-style pubs) and even a tapas restaurant. Prices vary, but none of these restaurants is expensive.

Mornings are quiet; head here after 5pm when things really start hopping.

★Coffee Shop Tirol CAFE
(珈琲亭ちろる; 0166-26-7788; www.cafe-tirol.com; 8-7 3-jō-dōri; 8.30am-7pm) Tirol may have only opened a few years ago, but the owner has kept the 70-year-old building lovingly intact, with a suitably vintage interior and jazzy soundtrack. The coffee (¥550), roasted in-house, is fantastic. Come before 11am to get the 'morning set' (モーニングセット; ¥750), which includes coffee, toast and a hard-boiled egg.

It's a five-minute walk from JR Asahikawa Station; walk up Midoribashi-dōri and turn left after the 7-Eleven. The shop will be on your left just after you turn.

Information

Asahikawa International Centre (旭川国際交流センター; 0166-25-7491; www.asahikawaic.jp; 7th fl, Feeeal Asahikawa Bldg, 8 1-jō-dōri;

10am-5pm;) This centre for foreign residents has a useful help desk and info-exchange bulletin board.

Tourist Information Counter (旭川観光物産情報センター; 0166-26-6665; JR Asahikawa Station; 8.30am-7pm Jun-Sep, 9am-7pm Oct-May) Inside JR Asahikawa Station on the ground floor, with English maps, brochures and bus timetables, and helpful English-speaking staff.

Getting There & Away

AIR

Asahikawa Airport (旭川空港; 0166-83-3939; www.aapb.co.jp/en; E2-16-98, Higashi-Kagura) is 10km southeast of the city, in between Asahikawa and Biei. There are domestic flights to Tokyo, Nagoya and Osaka, as well as international flights to Beijing, Shanghai and Taipei. Airport shuttle buses (¥650, 30 minutes) depart from bus stop 9 in front of JR Asahikawa Station and are timed to meet arrivals and departures. A taxi should run around ¥4100.

BUS

The following buses depart from the **Asahikawa Station Bus stops** (0166-25-3000; 5.45am-9.30pm):

- Buses leave every 30 minutes from bus stop 7 for Sapporo (¥2060, two hours; reservations necessary).
- There are four daily buses to/from Asahidake Onsen (¥1430, 1½ hours), departing from bus stop 9.
- **Furano Bus** (www.furanobus.jp) has eight daily runs to/from Furano (¥880, 1¾ hours) via Biei (¥620, 50 minutes), departing from bus stop 9.
- **Dōhoku Bus** (www.dohokubus.com) has seven daily runs to/from Sōunkyō Onsen (¥2100, two hours), departing from bus stop 8.

CAR & MOTORCYCLE

Rental cars are available at Asahikawa Airport or from agencies near JR Asahikawa Station.

TRAIN

JR Limited Express Super Kamui, Okhotsk, Super Sōya and Sarubetsu Liner trains run between Asahikawa and Sapporo (¥4290, 1½ hours, hourly).

Okhotsk Liner trains continue to Abashiri (¥7450, 3¾ hours, four daily). There are slightly more frequent trains on the JR Sekihoku line, but you'll need to transfer at Kamikawa.

Super Sōya and Sarubetsu Liner trains continue to Wakkanai (¥7780, four hours, three daily). Local trains require multiple transfers.

Hourly JR Furano trains run to Biei (¥540, 40 minutes); most continue to Furano (¥1070, 1¼ hours).

Biei

0166 / POP 10,000

More or less halfway between Asahikawa and Furano, with the dramatic mountains of Daisetsuzan National Park in the background, Biei (美瑛) boasts some of the prettiest countryside in Hokkaidō. There are plenty of meandering country lanes passing through fields of sunflowers, lavender and white birch. Biei is primarily a summer destination, with visitors coming to explore the countryside and maybe pick up local produce from farm stands and/or spend an afternoon in a cute, little cottage cafe.

There are two scenic routes, **Patchwork Road** (パッチワークの路) and **Panorama Road** (パノラマロード). The former stitches together a collection of small farms. The latter is a network of lanes with vistas over the countryside. Both are well signposted, and possible to traverse by car, bicycle or, if you get an early start, on foot.

The **Biei Tourist Information Centre** (美瑛観光案内所; 0166-92-4378; www.biei-hokkaido.jp; 8.30am-7pm Jun-Sep, 8.30am-5pm Nov-Apr, to 6pm Oct & May), to the left as you exit the train station, has an excellent map in English that even includes GPS map codes for key viewpoints.

Sleeping & Eating

Biei has a handful of pensions, the best of which are out in the countryside. The tourist information centre has a list, but it's better to book ahead in summer. Note that only a few places stay open year-round.

There are some places to eat around the train station, but the better options, which include restaurants, bakeries and cafes, are among the fields outside of town.

Biei Potato-no-Oka INN ¥¥
(美瑛ポテトの丘; 0166-92-3255; www.potatovillage.com; Ōmura Mura-yama; dm/d from ¥4850/22,800, breakfast/dinner ¥800/1500; closed mid-Nov–mid-Dec & mid-Mar–mid-Apr; P) Among the fields of Biei's pretty Patchwork Road, charming Potato-no-Oka, though small, has a big variety of accommodation, including dorm rooms, private Western- and Japanese-style rooms, and some cottages. Dinners are a treat, using fresh produce from Potato-no-Oka's neighbours. The owner is friendly and speaks English. Free shuttle service is possible from Biei station if you book 24 hours ahead.

Furano, Biei & Daisetsuzan National Park

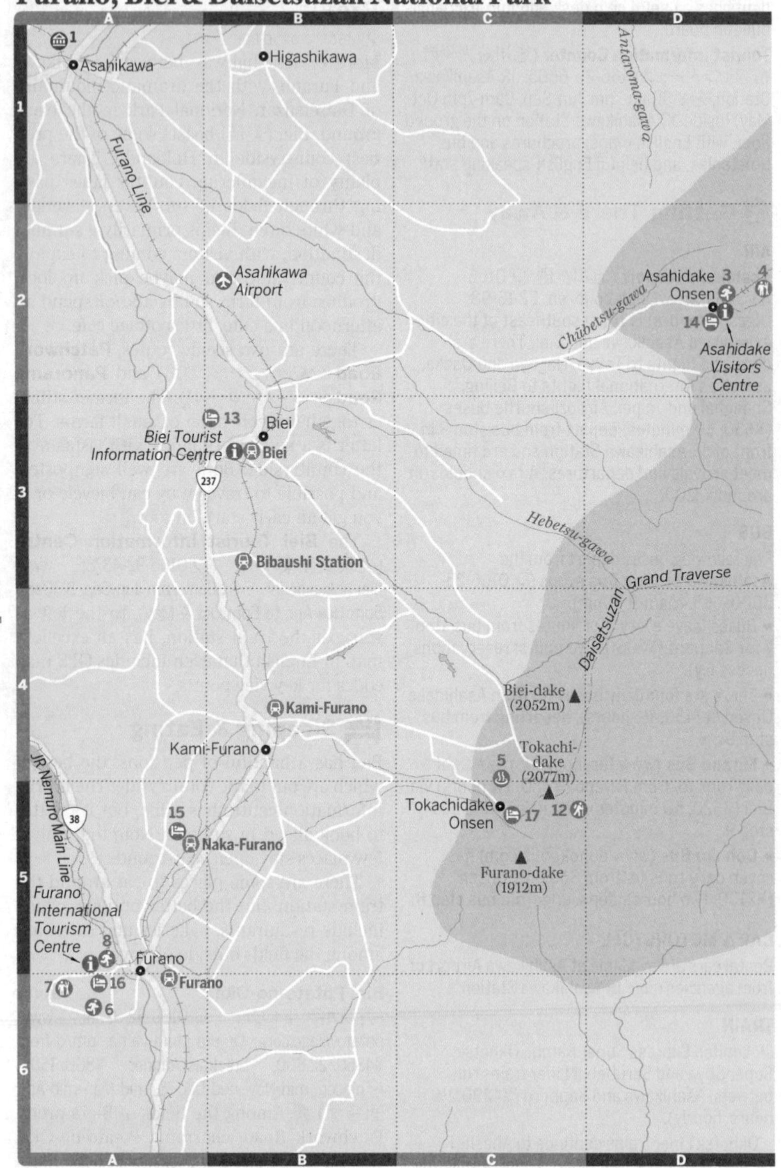

Getting There & Away

JR Furano line trains run hourly between Biei and Asahikawa (¥540, 32 minutes) and every two hours between Biei and Furano (¥640, 36 minutes).

Furano buses make eight runs daily between JR Asahikawa Station and JR Furano Station via Asahikawa Airport and Biei. The ride from Asahikawa Airport to Biei takes 15 minutes (¥370). To Furano it's 45 minutes and ¥640.

Rte 237 runs between Asahikawa, Biei and Furano.

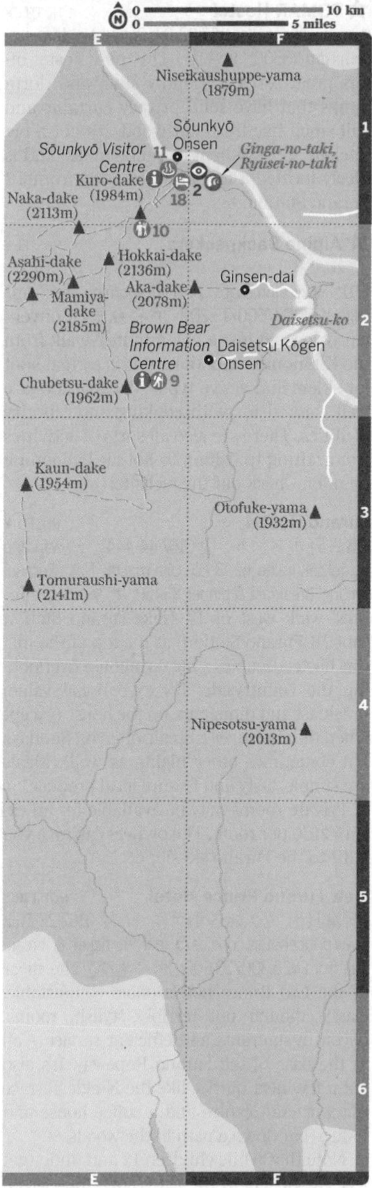

Getting Around

Pick up a car in Asahikawa if you plan on driving around Biei. Rental bicycles are available from a few shops around the station for ¥200/1000 per hour/day or battery-assisted bikes for ¥600/3000. Most bicycle rental shops will mind your bags for you.

Furano, Biei & Daisetsuzan National Park

Sights

1 Kawamura Kaneto Ainu Memorial Hall A1
2 Sōunkyō F1

Activities, Courses & Tours

Asahi-dake ..... (see 4)
3 Asahi-dake Ropeway D2
4 Asahi-dake Skiing D2
5 Fukiage Roten-no-yu C4
6 Furano Ropeway A6
7 Furano Ski Area A6
8 Kitanomine Gondola A5
9 Kōgen-numa Meguri Hike E2
Kuro-dake ..... (see 10)
10 Kuro-dake Skiing E2
11 Kurodake-no-yu E1
Sōunkyō Kuro-dake Ropeway ..... (see 11)
12 Tokachi-dake C5

Sleeping

Alpine Backpackers ..... (see 8)
13 Biei Potato-no-Oka B3
Daisetsu Kōgen Sansō ..... (see 9)
14 Daisetsuzan Shirakaba-sō D2
15 Furano Hostel A5
16 Furano Prince Hotel A6
17 Kamihoro-sō C5
New Furano Prince Hotel ..... (see 6)
Resort Pension Yama-no-ue ..... (see 11)
18 Sōunkyō Hostel E1

Shopping

Ningle Terrace ..... (see 6)

Furano

0167 / POP 22,700

Furano (富良野) is one of Japan's most inland towns and considered the centre of Hokkaidō – a distinction that has earned it the cute nickname Heso-no-machi (Belly-Button Town). Summers are almost hot (but not quite) and there are fields of flowers – especially lavender (which peaks in July and draws lots of domestic travellers) – farm-fresh produce and ice-cream stands to be enjoyed, plus plenty of opportunities for walking, hiking and cycling. Winters, on the other hand, are very cold – resulting in extreme amounts of powdery snow. Furano is one of the country's top skiing and snowboarding destinations, though it lacks the international recognition of rival Niseko.

Activities

Furano Ski Area SNOW SPORTS

(富良野スキー場; ☎0167-22-1111; www.princehotels.com; lift ticket full day/night ¥5500/1800; ⏲day 8.30am-7.30pm, night 4.30-7.30pm Dec-early May;) Furano gets excellent, light and dry snow, yet, compared to Niseko, remains relatively undiscovered by foreign visitors. The slopes are predominantly beginner and intermediate, though there are some steep advanced runs. If you're travelling as a family, a major bonus here is that children aged 12 and under get a free lift pass.

Eleven lifts, including the fastest gondola in Japan, help to keep the crowds in check. The resort is anchored by two large Prince hotels with ski-in, ski-out access, restaurants and bars. Full equipment rental is available for ¥9600 per day (¥6400 for children). English signage is adequate.

Kitanomine Gondola CABLE CAR

(北の峰ゴンドラ; ☎0167-22-1111; return ¥1900; ⏲6.30-9am Jul & Aug, 5.45-8.15am Sep) From July to September, this gondola makes early-morning runs up to 940m for day-break views over the sea of clouds below. It doesn't run every day or in bad weather, so call ahead. (During snow season, it's one of the two main Furano lifts.)

Furano Ropeway CABLE CAR

(富良野ロープウェー; ☎0167-22-1111; www.princehotels.com; one way/return ¥1300/1900; ⏲8am-4pm late Jun–mid-Oct, to 7pm mid-Jul–mid-Aug) The main lift in winter for skiers and boarders, the Furano Ropeway (a 100-person gondola) zips visitors up to 900m for magnificent views over the Furano valley. Outside ski season number of hiking options are available from the top, including walking back down.

Sleeping

Furano is full of pensions and *minshuku* and staying in one out in the countryside is one of the main reasons to visit (you'll need your own transport, though). If you're here to ski, zero in on lodging in the Kitanomine area, which is nearest the slopes. Note that many places close in the in-between season, from mid-November to mid-December and April. It's best to call ahead to confirm.

★TOMAR Hostel HOSTEL ¥

(トマール; ☎0167-22-0750; www.tom-eve.com; dm ¥3500;) This new hostel offers great service, friendly staff, and dorm bunks that have solid privacy curtains and still smell like fresh cut wood. It's got a big kitchen and excellent common areas, and is nicely located a few minutes away from JR Furano Station.

★Alpine Backpackers HOSTEL ¥

(アルパインバックパッカーズ; ☎0167-22-1311; www.alpn.co.jp; 14-6 Kitanomine-chō; dm/tw/q ¥3800/7600/15,200;) Conveniently located just a few minutes' walk from the Kitanomine Gondola, this is a great spot for skiers and active types. Backpackers are well catered for with cooking and laundry facilities. There are also all sorts of activities from rafting to fishing to hot-air ballooning on offer. Check out the website.

Furano Hostel HOSTEL ¥

(富良野ホステル; ☎0167-44-4441; www.furanohostel.sakura.ne.jp; 3-20 Oka-machi, Naka-Furano; dm incl breakfast & dinner ¥3450;) Six minutes' walk west of JR Naka-Furano Station (not JR Furano Station) at the top of the hill, this hostel occupies a big farmhouse overlooking the countryside. It's exceptional value: breakfast and dinner are on the house (except when the chef takes a break, often on Sundays but sometimes other nights as well). Meals are simple, tasty and feature local produce.

Private rooms may be available for an extra ¥2160 per room. The owners can give you a lift to the Furano ski slopes.

New Furano Prince Hotel HOTEL ¥¥¥

(新富良野プリンスホテル; ☎0167-22-1111; www.princehotels.com; s/d incl lift ticket & breakfast from ¥22,300/33,600;) The nicer of the two Prince hotels offers comfortable, classy, though not terribly stylish, rooms, decent restaurants and efficient service – all at the base of the Furano Ropeway. It's also got a few neat quirks, like the Ningle Terrace outdoor craft centre and a coffee house and lounge bar down a path in the woods.

Note that while children 12 and under get free lift tickets to the ski resort, those aged seven and above are charged the adult rate at this hotel. Book through the Japanese site for better rates.

The bus from Asahikawa Airport to Furano terminates here (¥930, 80 minutes), making this a good choice if you don't want to drive.

Furano Prince Hotel HOTEL ¥¥¥
(富良野プリンスホテル; ☎0167-23-4111; www.princehotels.como; 18-6 Kitanomine-machi; s/d with lift ticket & breakfast from ¥21,500/26,800; P❄@📶) This is the older of the two Prince hotels, old and relying mainly on its location: you're paying for the convenience here, as the hotel is right at the bottom of the Kitanomine Gondola. Hard to get closer than that.

Note that the same price caveats about the New Furano Prince Hotel apply here as well, and that wi-fi is currently in the lobby only.

Eating & Drinking

There are restaurants clustered around JR Furano Station and also in the Kitanomine district near the ski slopes. Furano actually produces some decent wines and cheeses, which you'll see on menus around town, along with more humble local specialities such as potatoes and onions.

Furano doesn't have anything close to the après-ski scene that Niseko has, though there are some bars in the Kitanomine district.

★**Soba Haru** SOBA ¥
(そば春; ☎0167-56-7096; 11-5 Hinodemachi; noodles ¥650-1300; ⏲11am-3pm & 5.30-8pm Wed-Mon) Not only does the owner Haru-san make the noodles here by hand, he made the wooden soba bar himself too. Stop by for a scrumptious handmade noodle meal at this spotless, lovely spot.

Chīzu Rāmen-no-mise Karin RAMEN ¥
(チーズラーメンの店かりん; ☎0167-22-1692; 9-12 Moto-machi; mains from ¥1000; ⏲11am-8pm, to 5pm Sep-May) Testing the adage that everything is better with cheese, Karin adds local Furano cheese to its ramen. Whether that sounds amazing or awful, you know you have to try it! It's in a nondescript brown-and-white building (look for the red curtain) a few minutes' walk southwest of JR Furano Station. The elderly owners will be ecstatic to greet you.

Shopping

Furano Marche FOOD & DRINKS
(フラノマルシェ; ☎0167-22-1001; www.furano.ne.jp/marche; 13-1 Saiwai-chō; ⏲10am-7pm, from 9am Jun-Sep) This one-stop shop for made-in-Furano food and drink is stocked with local wines, cheeses, cured meats, yoghurts and puddings. There's also a produce market and food court here.

Ningle Terrace ARTS & CRAFTS
(ニングルテラス; ☎0167-22-1111; www.princehotels.co.jp; ⏲10am-8.45pm Jul & Aug, noon-8.45pm Sep-Jun) The shopping centre at the New Furano Prince Hotel (p630) is a cute string of log cabins, each specialising in different crafts, connected by boardwalks in the forest. It stays open past dark, when it's lit with fairy lights. Ningles are a kind of forest fairy, at least according to the Furano folks.

Information

Furano International Tourism Centre (富良野国際観光センター; ☎0167-22-5777, off-season 0167-23-3388; 2nd fl, Kitanomine Terminal, 18-Kitanomine-chō; ⏲9am-6pm late Dec-late Mar) Tourist information counter inside the Kitanomine Gondola terminal.

Tourist Information Office (富良野観光案内所; ☎0167-23-3388; www.furanotourism.com; ⏲9am-6pm) Stock up on English maps and pamphlets here, next to JR Furano Station. Staff can also help with bookings.

Getting There & Away

BUS

Ten Chūō buses daily run between Sapporo and Furano (¥2260, 2½ hours), stopping at Kitanomine Iriguchi, for the Kitanomine district, before the terminus at JR Furano Station.

Furano Bus (www.furanobus.jp) makes eight runs daily between Furano and Asahikawa (¥880, 1½ hours), stopping at Biei and Asahikawa Airport. It takes one hour from Asahikawa Airport (¥770).

There are three buses daily between Furano and Obihiro (¥2160, 2½ hours). Reservations are necessary (0166-23-4161).

CAR & MOTORCYCLE

Rte 237 runs between Asahikawa, Biei and Furano. It is 59km to Asahikawa by road, 125km from New Chitose Airport and 142km to Sapporo. Be extremely careful in the winter months as roads in this area can be icy and treacherous.

TRAIN

JR Furano line trains run roughly hourly from Asahikawa to Furano (¥1070, 1½ hours), via Kami-Furano and Naka-Furano.

For Sapporo (¥4140, 2¼ hours), take a *futsū* (local train) on the JR Nemuro line to Takikawa, then change to the hourly JR Limited Express Super Kamui Liner.

Getting Around

Buses running from Asahikawa to JR Furano Station (¥880, two hours) continue to the Furano Prince Hotel and the New Furano Prince Hotel (¥1050), which are, respectively, at the bases for the Kitanomine Gondola and the Furano Ropeway. However, the earliest bus arrival in Furano is at 11.30am, so you'll miss the entire morning unless you arrange your own transportation. Additionally, if you're staying in town, you'll need to arrange with your hotel for a ride to the slopes, unless you have your own set of wheels.

Bicycle rentals (two hours regular/electric ¥500/1100) can be found around JR Furano and JR Naka-Furano Stations.

Daisetsuzan National Park

Daisetsuzan National Park (大雪山国立公園) is Japan's largest national park, designated in 1934 and covering more than 2300 sq km. It's a vast wilderness area of soaring mountains – Daisetsuzan literally means 'Big Snow Mountain' – active volcanoes, remote onsen, clear lakes and dense forests. Virtually untouched by human hands, the park has minimal tourism, with most visitors basing themselves in the hot-spring villages on the periphery. The three main access points into the park are Asahidake Onsen in the northwest, Sōunkyō Onsen in the northeast and Tokachidake Onsen in the southwest. Another special spot on the eastern side of the park is Daisetsu Kōgen Onsen.

Sleeping & Eating

Sōunkyō Onsen has the most sleeping options, though even this amounts to only a handful of lodges. Asahidake Onsen has a few; Tokachidake Onsen has two; Daisetsu Kōgen Onsen has exactly one. With limited space, book well in advance, especially during summer, around mid-September (when the autumn leaves peak) and in ski season. Note that most places don't accept credit cards and most towns don't have ATMs, so come with cash in hand.

Sōunkyō Onsen is the only gateway town to have restaurants and convenience stores (and still options are limited). It is highly recommended that you sign up for meals at your accommodation and pack plenty of snacks.

Getting There & Around

Buses run from Asahikawa to Asahidake Onsen and Sōunkyō Onsen. It's also possible to access Sōunkyō Onsen from Akan National Park in eastern Hokkaidō, as buses travelling from Akanko Onsen to Asahikawa stop there. To get to Daisetsu Kōgen Onsen, you'll need a car, though guests at the lodge there can take a shuttle bus from Sōunkyō Onsen. Furano, south of Asahikawa, is the access point for Tokachidake Onsen.

While public transport can get you to the various access points around the park, it's not good at getting you from one point to another. If you want to visit multiple places, you will have to do some serious back-tracking; it's better to have a car. If you're driving though, be aware that snow can fall on base roads as early as October.

Asahidake Onsen

☎0166

Asahidake Onsen (旭岳温泉) sits at 1100m, at the base of Asahi-dake, Hokkaidō's tallest peak. It's the easiest access point into the park, with regular buses from Asahikawa. There are plenty of hiking options in summer plus downhill and cross-country skiing in winter. All of this can be followed by a soak in the healing onsen found in the town's inns; most are open for day use to the general public for a fee (¥800 up to ¥2160).

HIKING & SKIING IN DAISETSUZAN NATIONAL PARK

Winter comes early to Daisetsuzan. While elevation may seem 'low' (at 2000m) compared to mountains in Honshū that top 3000m, conditions are similar. Snow is still common on trails through early July (and snowy gorges are visible year-round). High season is late July to early August, when the alpine flowers bloom. Coloured leaves appear in mid-September and the first snow falls later that month. By October, even the trailheads are snowed under and you'll need winter mountaineering experience and gear.

Staff at the visitor centres in both Asahidake Onsen and Sōunkyō Onsen can give you the latest information on trail and weather conditions, necessary gear, bear sightings etc. This is bear country, so you'll need to take precautions; a bear bell is advised.

Some ski and snowboard operators in Furano run backcountry tours to Asahi-dake and Kuro-dake (p634). If you come on your own, it's advisable to hire a local guide; your accommodation should be able to help with that (ask well in advance).

Be prepared: there are no ATMs, shops or restaurants at Asahidake Onsen. The nearest amenities are a 30-minute drive away in Higashikawa.

Activities

★Asahi-dake HIKING
(旭岳) Asahi-dake, Hokkaidō's tallest peak (2290m) and one of Japan's 100 Famous Mountains, offers amazing views and can be done in a day (June to September). Take the ropeway to Sugatami, from where it's a 2½-hour steep 6km hike to the top (allow four to five hours total for the return). Alternatively, you could do an easier, hour-long circuit around Sugatami-daira (姿見平), also from Sugatami.

From the summit of Asahi-dake it is possible to carry on over to Kuro-dake and take the ropeway down to Sōunkyō Onsen. Start early, check conditions at the visitors centre and allow seven to nine hours for this mission.

Asahi-dake Skiing SKIING
(www.asahidake.hokkaido.jp; day pass ¥4500; ⏲1 Dec-6 May) This is an extreme skiing experience on a smoking volcano – not for beginners. The only lift is the Asahi-dake Ropeway, but it is possible to hike up higher. There is plenty in the way of dry powder (best January to March) and scenic views, but it is recommended you ski with an experienced mountain guide, as visibility can be bad. There are no ski patrols to assist if you need help.

For up-to-date information, check out www.snowjapan.com.

Asahi-dake Ropeway CABLE CAR
(旭岳 ロープウェイ; ☎0166-68-9111; www.asahidake.hokkaido.jp; one way/return 1 Jun-20 Oct ¥1800/2900, 21 Oct-31 May ¥1200/1800; ⏲6am-5.30pm Jul–mid-Oct, 9am-4pm mid-Oct–Jun) This ropeway runs about every 15 mins from Asahidake Onsen up to Sugatami (姿見) at 1600m, the starting point for hikes up Asahi-dake. Even if you don't plan to hike (or ski), you can enjoy the alpine blooms (June and July), the brilliant gold and red foliage (September) or the snowy vistas (pretty much the rest of the year).

Note that it is closed yearly for maintenance between mid-November and mid-December. Parking costs ¥500. Simple meals such as curry, ramen or tempura are served in the Sugatami (姿見食堂) restaurant on the 2nd floor (11am to 4.30pm).

Sleeping & Eating

The ropeway has a simple cafe.

★Daisetsuzan Shirakaba-sō INN ¥¥
(大雪山白樺荘; ☎0166-97-2246; www.shirakabasou.com; with 2 meals dm from ¥7890, r per person ¥8940; Ⓟ📶) A cross between a youth hostel and a ryokan, this mountain lodge near the lower terminal of the ropeway offers comfortable Japanese- and Western-style rooms and hot-spring baths, plus a cool spiral staircase that goes up to a viewing deck. There is a large kitchen available if you're self-catering, but it's worth going for the meal plan.

Information

Asahidake Visitors Centre (旭岳ビジターセンター; ☎0166-97-2153; www.welcome-higashikawa.jp; ⏲9am-5pm) There are excellent maps here that the staff will mark with daily track conditions. If you're heading out on a long hike, inform them of your intentions.

Getting There & Away

There are four buses daily between bus stop 9 in front of JR Asahikawa Station and Asahidake Onsen (¥1430, 1½ hours). The first bus leaves Asahikawa at 7.40am, returning from Asahidake Onsen at 6pm. Buses run via the Asahikawa Airport (¥1000, either direction).

Sōunkyō Onsen

☎01658

Sōunkyō Onsen (層雲峡温泉; 658m), at the foot of Kuro-dake on the northeast side of the park, is a good base for forays into Daisetsuzan's interior. In addition to alpine treks, there is also the natural spectacle of the surrounding gorges.

There are more amenities here (including ATM facilities, restaurants and a couple of convenience stores) than in the other gateway villages. There's also a free foot bath in front of the Ginsenkaku Hotel. Still, if you are heading out into the backcountry, you'd be better off organising supplies before coming. There is no petrol station.

Sights & Activities

Sōunkyō GORGE
(層雲峡, Layer Cloud Gorge) Sōunkyō is a string of gorges 15km long formed by the Ishikari-gawa, the very same Ishikari River that empties out into the Sea of Japan just north of Sapporo. A few kilometres southeast of town on Rte 39, there's a popular viewing

station where you can see the waterfalls **Ryūsei-no-taki** (流星の滝; Shooting Stars Falls) and **Ginga-no-taki** (銀河の滝; Milky Way Falls). Well worth a detour if you're driving.

Kuro-dake HIKING
(黒岳) Take the **Sōunkyō Kuro-dake Ropeway** (大雪山層雲峡・黒岳ロープウェイ; ☎0165-85-3031; www.rinyu.co.jp/kurodake; one way/return ¥1100/1950; ⊙8am-7pm Jun-Aug, 7am-5pm Sep-May, closed intermittently winter) and chairlift to the mountain's seventh station (1520m), from where it's a 90-minute, 1km trek to the summit at 1984m. This hike, doable between June and early October (check at the visitor centre about early snow), is a favourite with alpine plant and flower enthusiasts.

From the summit of Kuro-dake it is possible to carry on over to Asahi-dake (p633) and take the ropeway down to Asahidake Onsen. Start early, check conditions at the visitor centre and allow seven to nine hours for this mission.

Kuro-dake Skiing SKIING
(☎0165-85-3031; www.rinyu.co.jp/kurodake; pass ¥3800) Kuro-dake gets heaps of fantastic snow and is becoming a word-of-mouth destination for hard-core enthusiasts who like vertical and challenging terrain. The season is December to early May, though the ropeway and chairlift close for maintenance for parts of January and February – time your visit well. This is not a place for beginners; avalanche gear is required for backcountry skiing.

A guide is recommended. For up-to-date info, check out www.snowjapan.com.

Kurodake-no-yu ONSEN
(黒岳の湯; ☎01658-5-3333; www.sounkyo.com/kurodakenoyu; ¥600; ⊙10am-9.30pm) After a hard day of play, Kurodake-no-yu offers handsome hot-spring baths, including a 3rd-floor *rotemburo* – it's on the town's main pedestrian street.

Sleeping

Sōunkyō Hostel HOSTEL ¥
(層雲峡ホステル; ☎080-2862-4080; Sōunkyō 39; dm/d ¥3200/8000; ⊙Jun-Oct; P) Expect a warm welcome at this humble wooden hostel, a 10-minute walk uphill from the bus station. There are bunk-bed dorms and a few private family rooms (book well ahead for the latter). This is a great place to meet other hikers before tackling the trails in the park. Summer season only.

Note that kitchen facilities are minimal, so it's best to sign up for the basic, but filling, meal plan.

Resort Pension Yama-no-ue PENSION ¥¥
(リゾートペンション「山の上」; ☎01658-5-3206; www.tabi-hokkaido.co.jp/p.yamanoue; tw with/without 2 meals ¥18,900/11,600; P) This friendly, family-run place is in the middle of the village, straight down from the ropeway terminal. There are nature photos everywhere and the meals are prepared with great care. Don't be fooled by 'resort' in the name: it's a humble place. Rooms are tatami-style with shared facilities; the bath gets the same hot-spring water as Kurodake-no-yu next door.

Information

Sōunkyō Visitor Centre (層雲峡ビジターセンター; ☎01658-9-4400; www.sounkyovc.net; ⊙8am-5.30pm Jun-Oct, 9am-5pm Nov-May) Near the bottom of the Sōunkyō ropeway, this is an excellent visitor centre with displays, photos and maps (some in English). Run your hiking plans by the helpful staff.

Getting There & Away

There are seven daily buses in both directions between Sōunkyō Onsen and Asahikawa (¥2100, two hours) via Kamikawa.

JR Rail Pass holders can take the JR Sekihoku line from Asahikawa to Kamikawa, and then catch the bus from Kamikawa to Sōunkyō Onsen (¥870, 30 minutes).

There are two buses daily to Kushiro (¥4930, five hours) via Akanko Onsen (¥3350, three hours) in Akan National Park and one bus daily to Obihiro (¥2260, 2¼ hours).

If you're driving, Rte 39 connects Sōunkyō Onsen to Asahikawa in the west and Abashiri in the east.

Daisetsu Kōgen Onsen

☎01658

On the eastern side of the park about 20km south of Sōunkyō Onsen, Daisetsu Kōgen Onsen (大雪高原温泉) is about as remote as it gets. Ten kilometres up an unsealed road in the middle of nowhere you'll find a couple of buildings in the heart of the national park. Make the effort – this is a highly recommended mountain adventure.

There are no shops, ATMs or petrol stations.

DAISETSUZAN GRAND TRAVERSE

The Ainu called the area now known as Daisetsuzan National Park *kamui mintara*, meaning 'the playground of the gods'. Those gods being the animals, most notably the brown bear – the god of the mountains – that had the run of the land. For experienced hikers, the park offers an amazing opportunity to really get out into the wilderness.

The 55km Daisetsuzan Grand Traverse covers the length of the park in anywhere from five to seven days, and as such, it's for expert hikers only. You could start at either Asahidake Onsen or Sōunkyō Onsen and you'll finish at Tokachidake Onsen. There are some extremely bare-bones huts along the way, but it's better to have a tent and camping gear. You'll need to carry in your own food and cooking supplies.

It is highly recommended to attempt this from mid-July through August, though it's feasible June to September. Any earlier and there will likely still be snow and ice; any later and you might have trouble finding water and be freezing your tush off. Check in with the staff at the visitor centre at either Asahidake Onsen or Sōunkyō Onsen, and carry a copy of Shōbunsha's *Yama-to-Kōgen Chizu Map 3: Daisetsuzan* (昭文社山と高原地図３大雪山).

It's also possible, with a very early start, to do a one-day traverse, from Asahi-dake, in Asahidake Onsen, to Kuro-dake, in Sōunkyō Onsen, going up one ropeway and down the other.

Activities

Kōgen-numa Meguri Hike HIKING
(高原沼めぐり登山コース; 22 Jun-10 Oct) This 6km four-hour hiking course around the Kōgen-numa (small lakes) is your best chance to see a brown bear in the wild. It's strictly regulated. Hikers must listen to a lecture at the **Brown Bear Information Centre** (ヒグマ情報センター; 7am-4pm late Jun–mid-Oct) and are only allowed to head out on the hike between 7am and 1pm. Hikers must be off the track by 3pm.

Staff are out on the track each day, radioing in bear whereabouts and keeping an eye on both the hikers and the bears. This is a wonderful day hike beneath the high peaks. Soak in the onsen at Daisetsu Kōgen Sansō after your walk.

Sleeping & Eating

★**Daisetsu Kōgen Sansō** LODGE ¥¥
(大雪高原山荘; 01658-5-3818; www.daisetsu-kogen.com; per person incl meals ¥17,280; 10 Jun-10 Oct; P) Make the most of your foray into the mountains: this inn, only open 123 days each year, is like staying at a mountain hut without having to walk five hours to get there. There are simple tatami rooms with shared facilities, but the food is good, the onsen is hot and the air is fresh. No English is spoken, so come prepared.

Note that early check-in is required (between 10.30am and 3pm) to ensure guests are not navigating the treacherous mountain road in the dark. Also, due to the remoteness, there is no telephone or mobile service, or wi-fi.

The lodge also operates a *shokudō* (casual eatery) between 11.30am and 1pm, with simple meals such as ramen and curry rice.

There are two shuttle buses per day from Sōunkyō Onsen for overnight guests (reservations necessary), but having your own wheels is the best option. If you're not staying, you can use the onsen for ¥700.

Getting There & Away

Daisetsu Kōgen Onsen is at the end of a 10km unsealed road off Rte 273 to the east of the park. The turn-off is signposted about 15km southeast from Sōunkyō Onsen.

Alternatively, make a booking for the night at Daisetsu Kōgen Sansō and use its twice-daily shuttle service for guests from Sōunkyō Onsen. There's a bus from Asahikawa Station (¥2100) seven times daily but only two match up with the shuttle.

Tokachidake Onsen

0167

At 1270m, remote Tokachidake Onsen (十勝岳温泉) is the highest of the gateway villages for Daisetsuzan. It is also the least developed, with no ropeway and just two inns, and is thus the least crowded – though it's relatively easy to access from Furano. In addition to being the end point for the epic Grand Traverse hike, Tokachidake Onsen is also a great spot for starting day hikes into the park. There are no shops, ATMs or petrol stations – not even a visitor centre – so you need to come prepared.

Activities

★Fukiage Roten-no-yu ONSEN

(吹上露天の湯) FREE If the idea of sitting naked in pools of hot steaming water surrounded by pristine forest appeals to you, then head to Fukiage Roten-no-yu. The turn-off, 2km before Tokachidake Onsen on Rte 291, is signposted. There's a parking lot, from where it's a 200m walk through the woods to the springs.

There's nothing there except two hot pools; the one higher up is hotter than the other. It's not for the shy: strip off and hop in! There's no charge…and this place is *konyoku*, meaning men and women bathe together. You can take a small 'modesty towel' if you prefer.

Tokachi-dake HIKING

(十勝岳) A return trip up Tokachi-dake (2077m), an active volcano and one of Japan's Hyakumeizan (100 Famous Mountains), will take six to eight hours return (16km) and reveal some marvellous volcanic landscapes – if you're lucky enough to get clear weather.

About 40 minutes in, the trail splits, with one branch heading up to the Tokachi-dake summit and another veering south to Furano-dake (富良野岳; 1912m); the 9.5km return trip up the latter will take four to six hours.

Sleeping

Kamihoro-sō LODGE ¥¥

(カミホロ荘; ☎0167-45-2970; www.tokachidake.com/kamihoro; d incl 2 meals from ¥15,000; P) A good place to unwind after hiking, with pleasant Japanese-style rooms, filling meals and hot-spring baths fronting the mountains. Nonguests can use the baths for ¥600.

When it's not crowded, it may be able to accommodate solo travellers – call ahead. Wi-fi in the lobby only.

Getting There & Away

Buses (¥500, 40 minutes) run three times daily to Tokachidake Onsen from JR Kami-Furano Station, 15 minutes north of Furano on the JR Furano line.

Wakkanai

☎0162 / POP 35,700

Wakkanai (稚内), Japan's northernmost city at 45°N, changes wildly with the seasons. From November to March, it's something akin to a remote Siberian outpost, home to hearty fishers, kelp farmers and a harp-seal colony. Outside the winter months, it's a pleasantly mild port city that serves as a departure point for ferries to the islands of Rishiri-tō and Rebun-tō. In addition to English, you'll see Cyrillic on the street signs – due to the frequent Russian travellers.

Sights & Activities

Fukukō-ichiba MARKET

(副港市場; ☎0162-29-0829; www.wakkanai-fukukou.com; 1-6-28 Minato; ⊙hours vary; P) About a 10-minute walk south of JR Wakkanai Station, this complex has restaurants, souvenir shops and the Minato-no-yu Onsen. It's designed to evoke the Wakkanai of bygone days. Poke around to see some historical photos and videos of the town – and also of Sakhalin (when it was Karafu-tō, and still part of Japan, prior to 1945).

Minato-no-yu Onsen ONSEN

(港の湯温泉; ☎0162-22-1100; 2nd fl, Fukukō-ichiba, 1-6-28 Minato; adult/child ¥750/420; ⊙10am-10pm; P) Wakkanai's best public onsen has outdoor baths that look over the harbour, and funky boat-shaped stairs for those who opt out of taking the elevator.

Sleeping

Considering it's the transit hub for Rishiri-tō and Rebun-tō, Wakkanai has relatively few sleeping options: a few good-value business hotels and one higher-end one.

Tenpoku no Yu Dormy Inn HOTEL ¥¥

(天北の湯ドーミーイン稚内; ☎0162-24-5489; www.hotespa.net/hotels/wakkanai/; 2-7-13 Chūō; s/d from ¥7590/11,790; P@) With an in-house onsen, free laundry machines (dryers extra) and a convenient location only four minutes' walk from JR Wakkanai Station, this is an easy choice. Rooms are standard issue but clean and not cramped.

ANA Crowne Plaza Wakkanai HOTEL ¥¥¥

(ANAクラウンプラザホテル稚内; ☎0162-23-8111; www.anacpwakkanai.com; 1-2-2 Kaiun; s/d incl breakfast from ¥18,500/32,000; @) Right on the waterfront and an easy walk to both the ferry and the train station, Wakkanai's only remotely upscale (though a bit weather-worn) option is a good bet – especially if you book an air-ticket package. Ask for an ocean-front room (plus ¥1000) when you book. Bonus: the airport bus stops here.

Eating

The JR Wakkanai Station building and Fukukō-ichiba are easy bets, as both have a selection of restaurants.

Pechika RUSSIAN ¥

(ペチカ; ☎0162-23-7070; Fukukō-ichiba, 1-6-28 Minato; mains from ¥400, set meals from ¥1500; ⏲5-10pm; P) If seeing all that Cyrillic on the street signs around Wakkanai has got you hankering for some *pelmeni* (dumplings; ¥700) or *pirozhki* (stuffed buns; ¥300), Pechika will help you out. There's plenty of Russian beer and vodka to wash it all down.

Take-chan SEAFOOD ¥¥

(竹ちゃん; ☎0162-22-7130; www.take-chan.co.jp; 2-8-7 Chūō; mains from ¥600, set meals ¥1400-3500; ⏲5-10pm) This popular seafood joint does good-value sushi sets as well as some seafood-themed variations on classic Japanese dishes, and some darned good fried chicken. Take-chan is a short walk from JR Wakkanai Station, with an illuminated, white vertical sign.

Information

There are info centres at the airport and ferry terminal, open from May to September.

Tourist Information Counter (☎0162-22-2384; www.welcome.wakkanai.hokkaido.jp; ⏲10am-6pm) Pick up maps and bus schedules from this counter located inside JR Wakkanai Station.

Wakkanai Post Office (稚内郵便局; 2-15-2 Chūō; ⏲8.45am-7pm Mon-Fri) If you're heading to Rishiri-tō or Rebun-tō, stock up on cash here, as few places on the islands accept credit cards. There is no 7-11, so the postal ATM is most travellers' best option for getting cash.

Getting There & Away

AIR

From **Wakkanai Airport** (稚内空港; ☎0162-27-2111; www.wkj-airport.jp; 6744 Koetoi-mura), about 10km east of the city centre, there are year-round daily flights to Sapporo and Tokyo, plus seasonal flights to Nagoya and Osaka. Buses (¥600, 30 minutes) run between the airport and the ferry terminal, stopping at JR Wakkanai Station, and are timed to meet departures and arrivals. A taxi costs ¥4000.

BOAT

Heartland Ferry (ハートランドフェリー; ☎0162-23-3780; www.heartlandferry.jp) Has sailings to Rishiri-tō and Rebun-tō.

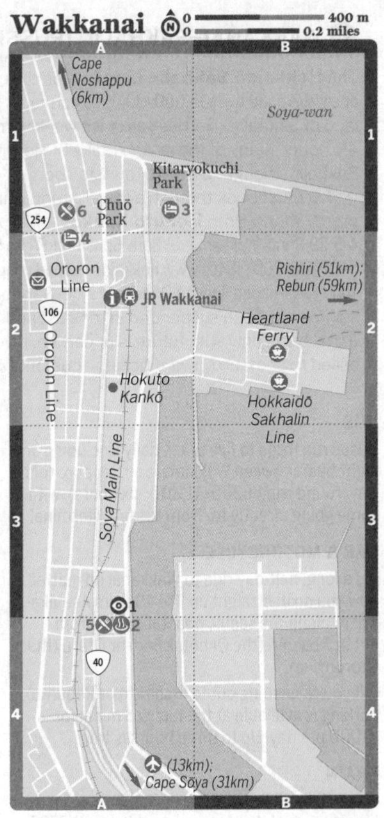

Wakkanai

Sights
1 Fukukō-ichiba ... A3

Activities, Courses & Tours
2 Minato-no-yu Onsen ... A4

Sleeping
3 ANA Crowne Plaza Wakkanai ... A1
4 Tenpoku no Yu Dormy Inn ... A2

Eating
5 Pechika ... A4
6 Take-chan ... A1

WAKKANAI–SAKHALIN (RUSSIA) FERRY

The **Hokkaidō Sakhalin Line** (北海道サハリン航路; 0162-22-2550; www.hs-line.com; one way/round trip ¥15,000/30,000) connects Wakkanai to Korsakov (on the Russian island of Sakhalin). Ferries sail twice weekly from August to mid-September; the trip takes 4½ hours. Many of those who make the journey are Japanese who have family ties to Sakhalin, though there are tourists, too.

You must book through a travel agent, which should also handle the necessary visa preparations. Both **Hokuto Kankō** (北都観光; 0162-23-3820; www.hoktokanko.co.jp; 4-5-29 Chūō, Wakkanai; 8am-6pm Mon-Fri, to 5pm Sat), in Wakkanai, and **Nomad** (ノマド; 011-200-8840; www.hokkaido-nomad.co.jp; S2W6 Chūō-ku; 9am-6pm Mon-Fri; Tōzai, Tōhō & Namboku lines to Ōdōri, exit 1), in Sapporo, are set up to do this. Note that this ferry service has been suspended in the past and at the time of research was operating on a trial basis only – its future is uncertain. If you are not returning to Japan, you may be asked to show an onward ticket at customs in Russia.

BUS

Buses run three to five times daily (including one night bus) between Wakkanai and Sapporo (one way/round trip ¥6200/11,300, six hours), with some going directly to/from the ferry terminal.

CAR & MOTORCYCLE

It's a long, half-day ride to Wakkanai no matter how you do it: straight up Rte 40 from Asahikawa, or along the scenic coastal routes from either Abashiri (the Okhotsk line) or Otaru (the Ororon line).

If you're heading out to Rishiri-tō or Rebun-tō, parking is available at the ferry terminal for ¥1000 per day. Up to three hours is free.

TRAIN

Three daily JR Super Sōya or Sarobetsu Liner trains connect Wakkanai to Asahikawa (¥7780, 3¾ hours) and Sapporo (¥9930, five hours).

Getting Around

Downtown Wakkanai is easy to get around on foot. JR Wakkanai Station is right next to the bus terminal and both are just a 10-minute walk from the ferry port.

Rishiri-Rebun-Sarobetsu National Park

The islands of Rishiri-tō and Rebun-tō are among the remotest in Japan, off the coast of the country's northernmost city, Wakkanai. Part of the Rishiri-Rebun-Sarobetsu National Park (利尻礼文サロベツ国立公園), they are largely undeveloped, save for a few scrappy fishing settlements and a small tourism industry. Geographically, they are totally different: Rishiri-tō is dominated by its volcano, Rishiri-zan; Rebun-tō is long and skinny, shaped by shifting plates. Most visitors come in summer, to climb Rishiri-zan, or to hike along the ridges in Rebun-tō, where wildflowers bloom in June and July.

Also part of the park are the **Sarobetsu Wetlands** (サロベツ原野; Sarobetsu Genya), on the mainland 40km southwest of Wakkanai. Fields of wildflowers bloom here in summer, which can be appreciated from boardwalks built over the marsh. There are also good views of Rishiri-zan from here – especially in winter, when eagles fly overhead and you can rent snowshoes (¥500) from the **Sarobetsu Wetlands Centre** (サロベツ湿原センター; 0162-82-3232; http://sarobetsu.or.jp/swc; 8662 Banchi Kami-sarobetsu, Toyotomi-chō; 9am-5pm May-Oct, 10am-4pm Nov-Apr, closed Mon Nov-Apr) to walk out over the snow pack.

Sleeping

On both Rishiri-tō and Rebun-tō there are campgrounds, hostels, pensions and hotels. The port of Oshidomari on Rishiri-tō is the largest settlement and has the most lodgings and amenities. Note that many accommodation options are seasonal, open roughly from May through early October.

Eating

Uni (sea urchin) is the islands' speciality. There are two kinds to sample: *kita-murasaki uni* (June to September) and *Ezo bafun uni* (July and August). The fresh seafood is delicious but don't expect bargain prices; the going rate for *uni-don* (urchin roe on rice) is ¥4000. There are some restaurants and a Seico Mart in both Oshidomari (Rishiri-tō) and Kafuka (Rebun-tō). Most visitors eat at their accommodation or bring food with them.

Getting There & Away

AIR

Rishiri-tō Airport, just a few kilometres west of Oshidomari, has flights to/from Sapporo on **ANA** (www.ana.co.jp) and **Japan Airlines** (JAL; www.jal.co.jp). Otherwise, Wakkanai is the transport hub for the park.

FERRY

Heartland Ferry (p637) operates two to four ferries daily (year-round) between Wakkanai and **Oshidomari** (0163-82-2201) on Rishiri-tō (from ¥2240, 1¾ hours) and between Wakkanai and **Kafuka Port** (0163-86-1662; 8am-5.30pm) on Rebun-tō (from ¥2470, two hours).

June to September, less frequent ferries (¥900, 45 minutes) run in both directions from Oshidomari and **Kutsugata** (0163-84-2349) ports on Rishiri-tō to Kafuka port on Rebun-tō. Tickets are available for purchase at any port.

For the Sarobetsu Wetlands, infrequent trains on the JR Sōya line run between Wakkanai and Toyotomi (*futsū* ¥930, 50 minutes; *tokkyū* ¥1550, 40 minutes). Buses (¥380, nine minutes) run from JR Toyotomi Station to the Sarobetsu Wetlands Centre at 8.30am, 1.25pm and 2.50pm June to September and at 9.15am and 1.50pm October to May.

Rishiri-tō

0163 / POP 2150

Seen from the distance, Rishiri-tō (利尻島) seems to be all mountain, a perfect volcanic cone, topped with snow most of the year, rising from the sea. This is Rishiri-zan, one of Japan's 100 Famous Mountains, and the island's main draw – it's on every Japanese hiker's bucket list. That said, its sheer remoteness means that Rishiri-tō never gets truly crowded. The weather on the island, however, is highly unpredictable: if you're keen on hiking, it's a good idea to stay for three or so nights, in the hope that on at least one of those days the weather will cooperate.

Activities

Cycling is a great way to see the island: circumnavigating the 60km perimeter on bicycle takes approximately seven to eight hours. There's also a 25km cycling path that runs through woods and coastal plains from Oshidomari to past Kutsugata.

★Rishiri-zan HIKING

(利尻山) Rishiri-zan (1721m) is also known as Rishiri-Fuji, as its solitary and perfect cone resembles famous Fuji-san. The hike to the top can be incredibly rewarding, with amazing views of Rebun-tō and even Sakhalin, but requires serious fitness. As the trailhead is at 220m, you've got to scale 1500 vertical metres. On average, the return trip takes 10 to 11 hours.

Unlike Fuji-san, Rishiri-zan is actually a beautiful mountain to climb, with fir, spruce and birch trees on the lower reaches and meadows of alpine flowers higher up. June through September is the best time to attempt an ascent, though even in the best of times the weather can be highly changeable, especially as the mountain is unshielded from winds. There are actually two peaks, Kita-mine (北峰) and Minami-mine (南峰), though the latter is closed for safety reasons.

There are no facilities on the mountain except for an unstaffed emergency shelter between the eighth and ninth stations. It is recommended to bring a minimum of 2L of water and you'll need to purchase a 'mobile restroom' kit (¥400) to use in designated booths on the mountain.

The main trailhead is 5km from the ferry port at Oshidomari (鴛泊) behind the Hokuroku Campground (p640). There is also a trailhead about 6km from Kutsugata, Rishiri-tō's other port. You can climb one and descend the other. The Kutsugata course is trickier, with a greater possibility of loose and falling rock, and should only be attempted by experienced mountaineers.

AINU LEGACY OF PLACE NAMES

While precious few people today can speak the Ainu language, the old tongue has left an indelible print on the map of Hokkaidō. You'll notice that many mountains are not 'san' or 'yama' (as they are in Japanese) but 'nupuri' – as in Niseko Resort's famous Annupuri – the Ainu word for 'mountain'. 'Nai' and 'pet' are the words for river; Wakkanai literally means 'cold water river' in Ainu. Rishiri-tō is actually redundant: both 'tō' (Japanese) and 'shir' (Ainu) mean the same thing – island.

Wakkanai & Rishiri-Rebun-Sarobetsu National Park

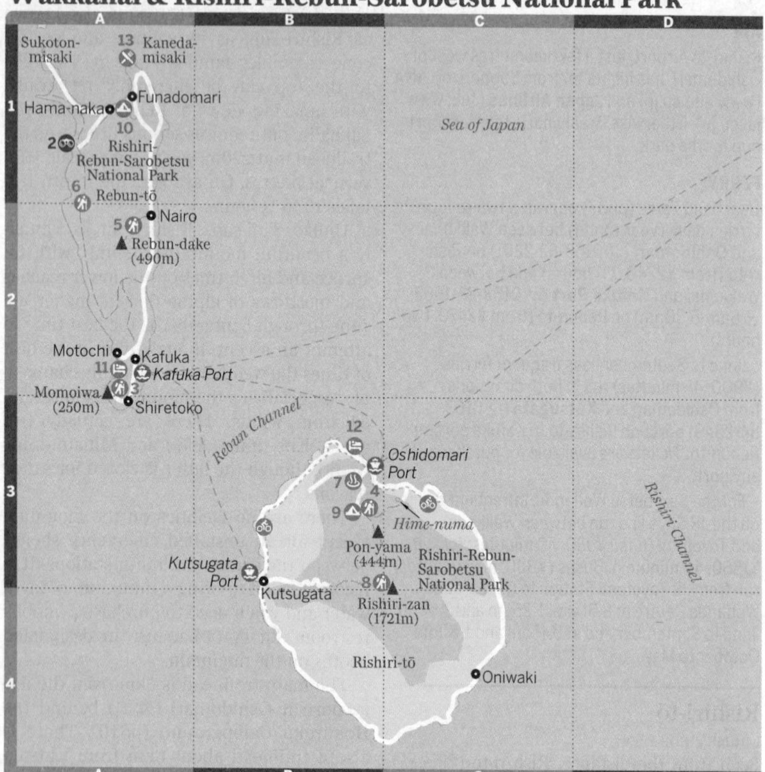

Buses, and even taxis, don't start up early enough to get you to the trailhead. As hiking is the most common reason to visit, most lodgings offer free shuttle service to the trailhead at around 5am.

The tourist information office (p642) at the Oshidomari ferry terminal has a pretty good English climbing guide, but the Shobunsha *Yama-to-kōgen Chizu 1 Rishiri; Rausu* (山と高原地図１利尻；羅臼) map (in Japanese) is far more detailed.

Pon-yama HIKING

(ポン山) For fantastic views of Rishiri-zan (and a far less challenging climb), you can scale neighbouring Pon-yama (444m) in about two hours, a 4km round trip. Start at the Rishiri-zan trailhead; the path to Pon-yama splits off 10 minutes into the hike, to the left.

Rishiri-Fuji Onsen ONSEN

(利尻富士温泉; 0163-82-2388; ¥500; 11am-9pm Jun-Aug, noon-9pm Sep-May) Could there be a better place to go to recover from climbing Rishiri-zan? We don't think so. This onsen is conveniently located on the road from Oshidomari to the trailhead. Pick it out on your way to the climb in the morning so you know where to go on the way back. There are a few local buses (¥150, seven minutes) to the onsen from Oshidomari Ferry Terminal, or it's about a 20-minute walk.

Sleeping & Eating

Hokuroku Campground CAMPGROUND ¥

(北麓野営場; 0163-82-2394; campsites per person ¥500, cabins ¥5000; mid-May–mid-Oct; P) Located at the Rishiri-zan trailhead, this camping ground is a good spot to stay if you want to get an early start to the hike. Cabins, which have blankets and pillows, sleep four. It's a 60-minute walk from the

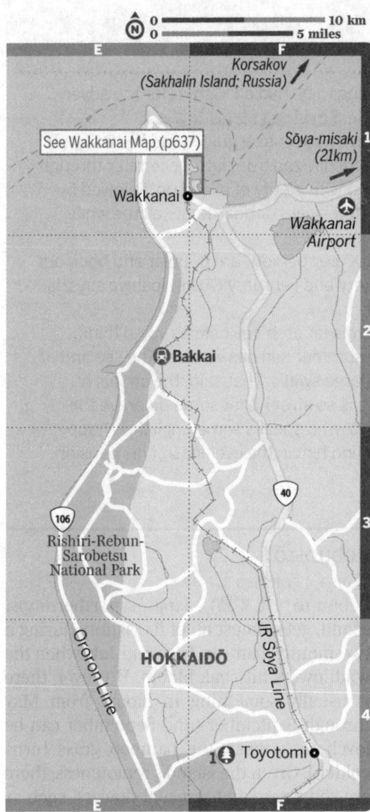

Wakkanai & Rishiri-Rebun-Sarobetsu National Park

Sights

1 Sarobetsu Wetlands F4
2 Sukai-misaki A1

Activities, Courses & Tours

3 Momoiwa Course A2
4 Pon-yama B3
5 Rebun-dake A2
6 Rebun-tō Traverse A1
7 Rishiri-Fuji Onsen B3
8 Rishiri-zan B3

Sleeping

9 Hokuroku Campground B3
10 Kushu-kohan Campground A1
11 Momoiwa-sō Youth Hostel A2
12 Rishiri Green Hill Inn B3

Eating

13 Kaisen-dokoro Atoi A1

Information

Sarobetsu Wetlands Centre .... (see 1)

ferry terminal, or you can take the local bus (¥150) as far as Rishiri-Fuji Onsen and walk the remaining 30 minutes.

Rishiri Green Hill Inn HOSTEL ¥
(利尻ぐりーんひるinn; ☎0163-82-2507; www.rishiri-greenhill.net; 35-3 Fujino, Oshidomari; dm/d ¥3800/9600; ⊙mid-Mar–mid-Oct; P⊖@☕) An excellent budget or backpacker option, this hostel has simple Japanese- and Western-style dorm rooms. There's free bread in the morning and a kitchen for cooking, but you'll have to walk 10 minutes to town to pick up supplies (or take advantage of the hostel's bicycle rentals; ¥1300 per day). The friendly owners will pick you up from the port and take you to the trailhead for Rishiri-zan.

★ **Maruzen Pension Rera Mosir** PENSION ¥¥
(マルゼンペンションレラモシリ; ☎0163-82-2295; www.maruzen.com/tic/oyado; 227-5 Sakae-chō, Oshidomari; per person with/without 2 meals ¥11,000/7460; P⊖❄@☕) Run by local adventure guide Watanabe Toshiya, Rera Mosir is the best place on the island for active types – whether you're here to climb Rishiri-zan in summer or ski the backcountry in winter. It's also one of the few places open year-round. Though small, it's modern and run like a hotel, and even has an onsen bath.

It does free shuttle runs to/from the port and the trailhead for Rishiri-zan; if you want to explore on your own, its rental cars are the cheapest on the island. The seafood dinners are good, too. Prices drop by ¥2000 to ¥2500 in the winter.

Tsuki Café CAFE ¥
(月カフェ; ☎0163-85-7474; www.tsukirishiri.wix.com/tsuki; 2nd fl, Oshidomari Ferry Terminal; ⊙11am-3pm Thu-Tue) A surprisingly tasty cafe for a ferry terminal, Tsuki serves up coffee, cakes and curries to waiting passengers. Service is so-so, and nonsmokers may have to cough their way through the meal, but the large picture windows look over the port and it's a great way to wait for the ferry to come.

It sometimes opens earlier and closes later during busy periods.

OFF THE BEATEN TRACK

SKIING & SURFING ON RISHIRI-TŌ

Yes, you read that right. There is skiing *and* surfing to be had on Rishiri (for the adventurous and experienced). **Rishiri Nature Guide Service** (利尻自然ガイドサービス; ☎0163-82-2295; www.maruzen.com/tic/guide), run by adventure guide (and Rishiri local) Watanabe Toshiya, offers backcountry tours on Rishiri-zan from late December through May. This is true backcountry stuff (think no lifts) with plenty of hiking up, followed by steep descents down the volcano – which sees few skiers or boarders – all the while taking in the breathtaking ocean views.

The tours (maximum six people; from ¥10,800 per person) are popular and book out fast, especially for peak powder season in January and February (April, Toshiya says, is best for sunny days). You'll need your own gear.

As for surfing, Toshiya swears the waters up this far aren't as cold as you'd think. September and October are the best, after the summer sun has warmed the sea and typhoons from the south drift north to deposit large swells. That said, the appeal of getting to ski or board and surf on the same trip is so strong that some do brave the waters off-season (you'll need a drysuit). Toshiya, who speaks some English, is happy to dispense tips on surf points. You can usually find him in the evenings at his pension, Maruzen Pension Rera Mosir (p641).

Information

Oshidomari Tourist Information Office
(☎0163-82-2201; www.rishiri-plus.jp; ⊙mid-Apr–Oct) On the ground floor of the ferry terminal. Pick up English-language climbing guides, maps and bus schedules. English-speaking staff can also help with bookings.

Getting Around

BICYCLE

Rental bicycles (both city and mountain bikes; ¥1500 per day) can be found in front of the ferry terminal in Oshidomari. Many accommodation places also rent bicycles.

BUS

Buses (¥370, 20 minutes) to the airport are timed to meet departures. Check at the tourist information office for exact times. A taxi into town costs around ¥2000.

Local buses run clockwise (six times daily) and counter-clockwise (five times daily) around the island. The trip from Oshidomari to Kutsugata (¥750) takes 30 to 45 minutes, depending on whether the bus stops at the airport. You can circumnavigate the island in about two hours (¥2260), but it's best to get a one-day pass (¥2260) from the driver if you plan to do so. The tourist information office has a current bus schedule in English.

CAR & MOTORCYCLE

There are car rental shops in front of the ferry terminal; however, rates are higher than elsewhere in Hokkaidō, starting at ¥5000 to ¥7000 for three hours. Motorcycles cost ¥3000 to ¥5000 per day.

Rebun-tō

☎0163 / POP 2650

Rebun-tō (礼文島), Japan's northernmost island, gets almost all of its visitors during a two-month span – in June and July when the wildflowers hit peak bloom. However, there is usually something in bloom from May through September (and September can be lovely, too, when the bamboo grass turns golden). Given the island's remoteness, there are some rare and unusual flowers, such as the Rebun Lady's Slipper Orchid. Rebun-tō is primarily a summer destination, as winter is cold and very windy.

Sights & Activities

Hiking is the main draw on Rebun-tō and there are several trails to suit different levels. You can also rent a scooter or car to visit the capes on the northern end of the island, which offer gorgeous sea views (when the weather cooperates). Year-round you can usually see spotted seals lazing on the rocks in **Funadomari Bay** (船泊湾) and at **Kaneda-misaki** (金田ノ岬).

Sukai-misaki VIEWPOINT
(澄海岬) This is the prettiest of the island's capes, where the waters are an almost tropical blue, framed by craggy rocks and grassy slopes. The Rebun-tō Traverse passes here; it's also accessible by road. As elsewhere on the island, it can be very windy. Hold onto that hat and keep trash tightly in hand.

★Rebun-tō Traverse HIKING

(8時間コース, Eight-Hour Course) This challenging but rewarding hike along the island's west coast starts at **Sukoton-misaki** (スコトン岬), the northernmost point on the island, passes beautiful Sukai-misaki and finishes down by the port in Kafuka, about 17km. Despite the name, it's best to budget 10 hours. You can also do an abridged version in four hours, returning northward from Sukai-misaki to the bus stop at Hama-naka (浜中).

To do the full hike, you'll need to catch the first bus of the day from the ferry terminal at 6.30am for Sukoton (¥1220), which means you'll need to sleep in Rebun two nights. Be sure to wear long pants and long sleeves as some of the local flora can cause skin irritation.

Momoiwa Course HIKING

(桃岩コース) The easiest and most popular of the island's hikes, and particularly beautiful when the wildflowers bloom, wends from the southernmost point in Shiretoko (知床) across a backbone of highlands to Momoiwa (桃岩; Peach Rock) and across to Kafuka. The 5.3km hike takes roughly three hours. From late April to mid-September, a bus (¥270) runs from the ferry to Momoiwa's lookout point.

Rebun-dake HIKING

(礼文岳) Rebun-dake (490m) is the highest point on the island. The not-too-challenging 4.5km hike to the top reaps big rewards, with 360-degree views over the island. The trail begins at the Nairo (内路) bus stop, a 20-minute bus ride (¥610) from the ferry terminal. The return hike takes three to four hours.

Usuyuki-no-yu Onsen ONSEN

(うすゆきの湯; ☎0163-86-2345; 961-1 Besshu, Kafuka-mura; ¥600; ⏲noon-10pm Apr-Sep, from 1pm Oct-Mar) The perfect place to rest after a hike, this onsen is right on the waterfront, just a couple of minutes' walk from the ferry terminal. From the *rotemburo* you can see Rishiri-zan. Families will enjoy the private bath, known as *kashikiriburo*.

Sleeping

Momoiwa-sō Youth Hostel HOSTEL ¥

(桃岩荘ユースホステル; ☎0163-86-1421; www.youthhostel.or.jp/n_momoiwaso; dm ¥3800, breakfast/dinner ¥600/1000; ⏲Jun-Sep; P) Part *Lost Boys* hideaway, part loopy summer camp, Momoiwa-sō is a very special place, which you will either love or hate. It has very strict rules, but also a lot of singing and dancing (for example, the 6am wake-up call includes bike horns and retro pop music blasting from loudspeakers). The location, on the remote western coast, is stunning.

The wooden building is a 150-year-old former fishery, and the accommodation, in bunks or on tatami mats, is basic. So are the meals, which you'll need unless you've packed food.

Momoiwa-sō organises group hikes along the Rebun-tō Traverse with shuttle service (¥700) at 5.40am to Sukoton. It also does free shuttle runs to and from the ferry terminal (otherwise it's an hour's walk). The atmosphere is very social; it's near impossible to leave without making friends.

Kushu-kohan Campground CAMPGROUND ¥

(久種湖畔キャンプ場; ☎0163-87-3110; Funadomari-mura; campsites per person ¥600; ⏲May-Sep; P) Beside Kushu-ko at the northern end of the island, this campground has grassy plots for tents and also some basic cabins that sleep four (¥2000, plus the standard per-person fee), and cottages that sleep up to five (¥15,000). The nearest bus stop is Byōin-mae, a 45-minute (¥960) ride from the ferry terminal. It does not have tents for rent.

If you ask, the bus driver can let you off a little closer to the campground, rather than at the bus stop. No pets.

★Pension Uni PENSION ¥¥

(ペンションうーにー; ☎0163-86-1541; www.p-uni.burari.biz; Tonnai, Kafuka-mura; per person with/without 2 meals ¥11,880/8860; P) Up the hill from the port, this immaculately clean pension with a big 'U-ni-!' sign has Western-style twin rooms. Meals include local seafood; rates with board drop when *uni* season finishes in September. The owners offer free shuttle service anywhere within a 5km radius (including the ferry terminal).

Eating

★Robata Chidori SEAFOOD ¥

(炉ばたちどり; ☎0163-86-2130; 1115-3 Tonnai; mains ¥800-1600; ⏲11am-9.30pm, closed irregularly Sep-May) Chidori does real *robata-yaki,* charcoal grilling in a pit built into the table. The speciality of the house is *hokke chanchan-yaki* (ホッケチャンチャン焼; ¥1000) – island-caught Okhotsk atka mackerel grilled with miso. The *ika-teppō-yaki* (いか鉄砲焼; stuffed and grilled squid; ¥1000) is good, too. The restaurant is along the waterfront in Kafuka, about five minutes' walk from the ferry terminal.

Kaisen-dokoro Atoi SEAFOOD ¥¥
(海鮮処あとい; ☎0163-87-2284; Funadomari-mura; mains ¥1500-4000; ⊙11am-2.30pm Apr-Sep; P) Run by the island's fishing collective (and closed the moment the sea urchin season ends), Atoi serves generously portioned *kaisen-don* (raw seafood over rice) using locally caught *uni* (sea urchin) and *ebi* (shrimp). There's a picture menu.

Information

Tourist Information Counter (☎0163-86-2655; www.rebun-island.jp; ⊙8am-5pm mid-Apr–Oct) Pick up trail maps and bus schedules in English. The staff, who usually speak some English, can assist with bookings, too. Open until the last ferry departs.

Getting Around

BICYCLE

Electric hybrid bicycles (¥700 per hour) – good for getting up the hills – are available for hire outside the ferry terminal.

BUS

Five to six buses daily run along the island's east coast from Kafuka in the south to Sukoton-misaki in the north (¥1220, one hour). There are also five buses daily (three on weekends) to the southern tip at Shiretoko (¥290, 10 minutes). Note that there is a gap in the middle of the afternoon; pick up a bus schedule (available in English) at the tourist information counter and plan accordingly – especially if you have a ferry to catch later.

CAR & MOTORCYCLE

Rental cars (from ¥7000 for three hours) and scooters (¥1000 per hour; ¥1500 per hour for 90cc two-seater) can be picked up just outside the ferry terminal. Note that rates are higher than elsewhere in Hokkaidō, but usually include gas and extra insurance. Some places only rent to Japanese-speakers, as they want understanding of the contract and rules.

EASTERN HOKKAIDŌ

Eastern Hokkaidō (道東; Dō-tō) is a harsh yet hauntingly beautiful landscape that has been shaped by volcanoes and vast temperature extremes. In the winter months, dramatic ice floes in the Sea of Okhotsk can be seen from the decks of ice-breakers off the coast of Abashiri. Both Akan National Park and Shiretoko National Park, the latter a World Heritage Site, are best explored during the mild summers when there are great hiking opportunities. Kushiro Wetlands National Park offers the chance to see the red-crowned white crane, the symbol of longevity in Japan.

Getting There & Around

AIR

Eastern Hokkaidō has three airports useful to travellers:

Kushiro Airport (p659) In Kushiro, convenient for Akan National Park and Kushiro Wetlands National Park; flights to/from Sapporo and Tokyo.

Memanbetsu Airport (p646) Near Abashiri and convenient for Shari and Shiretoko National Park; flights to/from Sapporo, Tokyo and Nagoya.

THE BLAKISTON LINE

It was an Englishman, Thomas Blakiston, who first noticed that the native animals of Hokkaidō are different species from those on the southern side of the Tsugaru Strait on Honshū. Blakiston lived in Japan from 1861 to 1884, spending most of his time in Hokkaidō in Hakodate, and his name is now used to describe the border in the distribution of animal species between Hokkaidō and the rest of Japan – 'the Blakiston Line'.

While Hokkaidō had land bridges to north Asia via Sakhalin and the Kuril Islands, southern Japan's land bridges primarily connected it to the Korean Peninsula. Bears found on Honshū are Asiatic black bears while Hokkaidō's bears are Ussuri brown bears, found in northern Asia. On the southern side of the straits, Japanese macaque monkeys are found on Honshū as far north as Aomori, but not in Hokkaidō. Among other species north of the Blakiston Line are Siberian chipmunks, Hokkaidō red squirrels, the *ezo-jika* (Hokkaidō deer), *kita-kitsune* (northern fox), northern pika and Blakiston's fish owl.

Tokachi Obihiro Airport (p661) In Tokachi; flights to/from Tokyo.

BUS

Highway buses run from Sapporo Eki-mae Bus Terminal (p605) to major hubs in eastern Hokkaidō, including Abashiri, Shari, Utoro (Shiretoko National Park), Kushiro and Obihiro.

CAR & MOTORCYCLE

If there is anywhere you need a car in Hokkaidō, it is Dō-tō. While there are buses running most places, they are infrequent (and almost nonexistent from November to March). There's little traffic out this way and almost everywhere offers free parking.

TRAIN

The following JR Limited Express trains run from Sapporo to eastern Hokkaidō:

Okhotsk Liner For Abashiri (¥9910, 5½ hours, four daily)

Super Ōzora Liner Six daily for Obihiro (¥6700, 2¾ hours) and Kushiro (¥9370, four hours)

The JR Senmō line runs north–south between Abashiri and Kushiro, via Kawayu Onsen (for Akan National Park) and Shiretoko-Shari (for Shiretoko National Park).

Abashiri

0152 / POP 39,000

To the Japanese, Abashiri (網走) is as synonymous with the word 'prison' as Alcatraz is to Americans – the mere mention can send a chill, implying gruelling punishment, harsh treatment, and hopelessness. Winters here are harsh, too: Abashiri is also known for its frozen seas, which can be explored on ice-breakers. Throughout the warmer months, the city serves as a jumping-off point for both Akan National Park and Shiretoko National Park.

Sights & Activities

Abashiri Prison Museum MUSEUM

(網走監獄博物館; 0152-45-2411; www.kangoku.jp; 1-1 Yobito; adult/child/student ¥1080/540/750; 8.30am-6pm Apr-Oct, 9am-5pm Nov-Mar) Some of the original Meiji-era prison buildings were restored and relocated to this oddly pleasant museum park. The Kangoku Hakubutsukan (penal museum) here details the reasons this historic prison was so feared: a sentence to Abashiri was a sentence to hard labour, as Abashiri prisoners laid much of the groundwork for Hokkaidō's infrastructure.

Hokkaidō Museum of Northern Peoples MUSEUM

(北海道立北方民族博物館; Hoppō-minzoku Hakubutsukan; 0152-45-3888; www.hoppohm.org; 309-1 Shiomi; adult/student/child ¥550/200/free; 9.30am-4.30pm Tue-Sun Oct-Jun, 9am-5pm Tue-Sun Jul-Sep) The examples here of traditional dress, tools and musical instruments from the indigenous cultures of the northern latitudes demonstrate the resourcefulness and joy that can be found in some of the world's harshest climates. Highlights include video footage of musical performances and celebrations shown on TV monitors around the museum.

★ **Aurora** CRUISE

(おーろら; 0152-43-6000; www.ms-aurora.com; adult/child ¥3300/1650; 9am-6pm) From 20 January to 31 March, the ice-breaker *Aurora* departs four to six times a day from Abashiri port for one-hour cruises into the frozen Sea of Okhotsk. Dress warmly.

Buses depart from stop 1 in front of JR Abashiri Station for the *Aurora* boarding dock.

Festivals & Events

Okhotsk Drift Ice Festival CULTURAL

(オホーツク流氷まつり; mid-Feb) An opportunity to celebrate the cold! Ice sculptures and statues, illuminated at night, plus lots of warm sake to keep your blood flowing.

Sleeping & Eating

Business hotels line the road in front of JR Abashiri Station, though most are pretty shabby. There are nicer options near scenic Notoro-ko, if you're not relying on public transport.

There's a handful of restaurants on the main drag running in front of JR Abashiri Station, although they are not worth going out of the way for.

Minshuku Lamp MINSHUKU ¥

(民宿ランプ; 0152-43-3928; 3-3-9 Shin-machi; per person ¥2800; P) Minshuku Lamp is well worn around the edges but the tatami rooms and shared facilities are clean, the owners are very friendly and the hallways are decorated with photos of old steam locomotives. There's a coin laundry and rental bicycles (¥1000 per day) too. Book ahead or ask the tourist information office (p646) to call for you.

NORTHERN TERRITORIES DISPUTE

A volcanic archipelago, the Kuril Islands stretch for 1300km from Kamchatka, Russia, towards Hokkaidō, separating the Sea of Okhotsk from the Pacific Ocean. The closest, the Habomai islets, uninhabited apart from a Russian border guard outpost, are barely 10km from Hokkaidō's easternmost point in Nemuro. The Habomai islets, along with three other islands in the southernmost Kurils, are known as the Northern Territories in Japan, and are the subject of a territorial dispute with Russia.

There have been tit-for-tat squabbles over who owned what between Japan and Russia since the early 1800s. Prior to WWII the islands belonged to Japan. At the close of the war, on 15 August 1945, Japan agreed to the terms of surrender in the Potsdam Declaration; however, Russia was not party to that agreement and had only just declared war on Japan on 9 August. Russian military forces started their invasion of the Kuril Islands on 18 August, and have occupied them since.

The ongoing dispute has blighted the Japan–Russia relationship ever since, to the point that the two countries have yet to sign a post-WWII peace treaty. Although sparsely populated, the Kurils have valuable mineral deposits, possibly oil and gas reserves, and are surrounded by rich fishing grounds.

It's a 10-minute walk from JR Abashiri Station, but can be tricky to find, as you'll have to walk over the train tracks. Ask the information office for directions.

Toyoko Inn Okhotsk Abashiri Eki-mae HOTEL ¥¥
(東横インオホーツク網走駅前; ☎0152-45-1043; www.toyoko-inn.com; 1-3-3 Shin-machi; s/d from ¥4160/7200; P ⊖ ❄ @ ᯤ) Directly opposite JR Abashiri Station, this is the nicest of Abashiri's business hotels. Simple, but clean and convenient, with free breakfast.

Abashiri Bīru-kan PUB FOOD ¥¥
(網走ビール館; ☎0152-41-0008; www.takahasi.co.jp/beer/yakiniku; S2W4-1-2; dishes ¥500-1800, beers from ¥400; ⏲5-11pm) Traditionalists should put aside all preconceptions when visiting this brewery-restaurant. The *yakiniku* (grilled meat) served here is pretty good. Abashiri Beer's signature brew is the Ryūhyō (drift ice) Draft, made with melted sea ice and coloured (with algae) acid blue.

ℹ Information

Tourist Information Office (☎0152-43-4261; www.abakanko.jp/en; ⏲noon-5pm Mon-Fri, 9am-5pm Sat & Sun) English-language maps and bus schedules. There's usually someone who can speak English and help with booking accommodation and tours. Inside JR Abashiri Station.

ℹ Getting There & Away

AIR

Memanbetsu Airport (女満別空港; ☎0152-74-3115; http://mmb-airport.co.jp.e.ug.hp.transer.com; 201–3 Memanbetsu, Abashiri), 15km south of the city centre, is the nearest airport, with flights to/from Sapporo, Tokyo, Nagoya and Osaka. Airport buses (¥910, 35 minutes) depart from bus stop 3 in front of JR Abashiri Station and are timed to arrive 40 minutes before plane departures.

BUS

Abashiri Bus (網走バス; ☎0152-43-4101; www.abashiribus.com) runs nine buses daily (including one night bus) between **Abashiri Bus Terminal** (網走バスターミナル; ☎0152-43-2606; S2W1-15; ⏲6.40am-6pm) and Sapporo (¥6390, six hours). Reservations required.

From Abashiri, buses run to Shari (¥1200 to ¥1400, one hour) and Utoro Onsen (¥2600, two hours).

CAR & MOTORCYCLE

There are several car rental shops around JR Abashiri Station, including **JR Hokkaido Rent-a-car** (JR北海道レンタカー; ☎0152-43-6197; www.jrh-rentacar.jp; 2-2 Shin-machi; ⏲8am-5pm). There are also counters at Memanbetsu Airport.

TRAIN

JR Limited Express Okhotsk Liner trains run four times daily between Abashiri and Asahikawa (¥7450, four hours), continuing on to Sapporo (¥9390, 5½ hours).

The JR Senmō main line runs between Abashiri and Kushiro (¥3670, 3½ hours, five to seven daily). On the way it passes through Shiretoko-Shari (¥840, 50 minutes), the closest station to Shiretoko National Park, and through Kawayu Onsen (¥1640, 1½ hours) in Akan National Park.

Getting Around

From June to October, a tourist-loop bus runs five to six times a day between the bus and train stations and the Abashiri Prison Museum, the Okhotsk Drift Ice Museum and the Hokkaidō Museum of Northern Peoples, which are a few kilometres southwest of town. Pick up a schedule at the tourist information office. A day pass costs ¥800/400 per adult/child.

Shari

0152 / POP 11,900

The small town of Shari (斜里) sits on the coast about 40km east of Abashiri and acts as a gateway to Shiretoko National Park. JR Shiretoko-Shari is the closest train station to the World Heritage Site, but you're still about an hour by bus or car from the entrance to the national park.

Sights & Activities

Shari-dake HIKING

(斜里岳) Shari-dake (1547m), south of town, is a spectacular volcanic cone and one of Japan's 100 Famous Mountains. Allow seven to eight hours for the return hike, which involves plenty of stream crossings plus spots with ropes and chains to help you. The views from the top are superb. Go between June and October, take supplies and use a bear bell.

Either use your own wheels to get to the trailhead (parking ¥500) at the Seigaku-sō (清岳荘) hut at 680m, or hop off the train at JR Kiyosato (清里町) station and take a taxi to the trailhead (¥4000, 30 minutes). If you get stuck, you can stay at the Kiyodake-sō for ¥1000 between June and September, but there are no meals.

Sleeping & Eating

There are some eating options clustered around the train station.

Clione Guesthouse & Campground CAMPGROUND ¥

(クリオネキャンプ場ゲストハウス; 0152-23-5108; www.campclione.jp; 4 Nishi; dm/r/cabin ¥1500/3000/4400; P ⊖ ᯤ) Named after the area's celebrity mollusc, this lovely campground and guesthouse offers an inexpensive overnight on the outskirts of Shari. It is quite strict about the rules; for example, no bathing happens after 10pm. Bungalows are simple and (unless you reserve a heater) unheated. But the onsen is toasty and the common areas inviting.

Minshuku Yumoto-kan MINSHUKU ¥

(民宿湯元館; 0152-23-3486; www.yumotokan.info; 13-11 Nishi-machi; s/d from ¥4480/7960; P ᯤ) This popular spot has a mountain-lodge vibe, Japanese-style rooms to accommodate different sized groups and an onsen bath (which nonguests can use for ¥400 between 7am and 8pm). Breakfast (¥500) is excellent. Yumoto-kan is a 20-minute walk from JR Shiretoko-Shari Station.

Route Inn Grantia Shiretoko-Shari Eki Mae HOTEL ¥¥

(ルートイングランティア知床　斜里駅前; 0152-22-1700; www.hotel-grantia.co.jp/shiretoko; 16-10 Minato-machi; s/tw from ¥8900/15,500; P ⊖ ❄ @ ᯤ) This is a convenient place to stay if you're relying on public transport – it's right in front of the train and bus stations in Shari. It's a modern tower hotel with comfortable rooms and an onsen; breakfast is ¥1000.

THE SEA OF OKHOTSK

The Sea of Okhotsk falls between Sakhalin (formerly known as Karafu-tō and part of Japan from 1905 to 1945), a long stretch of eastern Siberia, the Kamchatka Peninsula, the Kuril Islands and Hokkaidō. There are also many, many small, uninhabited islands here that are important breeding grounds for spotted seals and seabirds. The sea, which gets its name from the first Russian settlement in the Far East, is the coldest in East Asia and freezes as far south as Hokkaidō. In February, the coldest month, visitors come to Abashiri and Rausu to ride ice-breakers through the drift ice, hoping to spot seal pups on the ice.

This is just about as remote as it gets in Hokkaidō: the Okhotsk Line, the road that connects Wakkanai to Abashiri, is one long, lonely stretch of mostly nothingness. No towns, no traffic lights, few cars and only wind-battered coastline. For Tokyo drivers this is a dream come true and will shatter any thoughts you had that Japan is a densely populated, crowded country.

GVO BAR ¥¥

(☎0152-24-3040; www.infosnow.ne.jp/~bm/gvo; 91-5 Nishi Utoro; mains ¥1300-1700; ⏲11am-2.30pm & 6pm-11pm Sep-Mar; P) Guitars, motorcycles, CDs and 1960s folk all grace this cafe that's all about the sea urchin. If you've been craving sea urchin curry, sea urchin pasta, or sea urchin pretty-much-anything this is the place. Yet it's also a great spot for cakes and coffee, or a nice place to unwind in the evening, too.

GVO stands for 'Guitar' and 'VOcals'. Live music is here, and it does open mics as well.

Information

Tourist Information Centre (☎0152-23-2424; ⏲8.30am-5.30pm Apr-Oct & Feb) Maps, bus timetables and brochures; inside JR Shiretoko-Shari Station.

Getting There & Away

Infrequent trains run on the JR Senmō main line between Shiretoko-Shari and Abashiri (¥840, 50 minutes), and between Shiretoko-Shari and Kushiro (¥2810, 2½ hours). Between Shari and Kushiro is Kawayu Onsen (¥930, 45 minutes) in Akan National Park.

There are between five and eight buses daily between Shari and Utoro Onsen (¥1650, 50 minutes) in Shiretoko National Park. The bus terminal is right across from the train station.

Shiretoko National Park

Shiretoko-hantō, the peninsula that makes up Shiretoko National Park (知床国立公園), was known in Ainu as 'the end of the world'. This magnificent stretch of land, a Unesco World Heritage Site, is one of Japan's last remaining sections of true wilderness. It's mostly a draw for keen hikers; however, there are also some easier treks around lakes and to waterfalls, nature cruises up the coast and hidden hot springs in the woods. The park has two access points, at **Utoro** (ウトロ) on the northwestern side of the peninsula, and at **Rausu** (羅臼) on its southeastern side.

Sights & Activities

Shiretoko Pass VIEWPOINT

(知床峠) Rte 334, where it traverses the Shiretoko Pass, is considered one of Japan's most scenic stretches of road. It winds about 30km through the foothills of Rausu-dake between Utoro and Rausu, passing groves of Erman's birch and Japanese stone pines. There's a lookout point at 740m with parking. The road closes from November to April.

★ **Shiretoko Traverse** HIKING

(⏲Jul-Sep) The classic traverse is a two-day hike that stretches for 25km from **Iwaobetsu Onsen** (岩尾別温泉; 340m) FREE to Kamuiwakka-yu-no-taki (p650). You'll need to be properly equipped to tackle this route. Starting from the trailhead at Iwaobetsu Onsen, you'll climb Rausu-dake (羅臼岳; 1660m), traverse along the top to Iō-zan (硫黄山; 1563m; p657), then descend to Kamuiwakka-yu-no-taki, a 'waterfall onsen'.

There are four camping areas along the top that have steel food bins (think bears!). Don't underestimate the difficulty of the terrain. The last bit of this track has been reopened. Drop in at the Shiretoko Nature Centre (p651) for the latest on conditions and advise staff there of your intentions. The trail is officially open from mid-June through the September holiday period, though snow and extreme conditions make these shoulders inadvisable for all but the most extreme (and prepared) hikers.

Kuma-no-yu ONSEN

(熊の湯; ⏲7am-5am) FREE A few kilometres up and inland from Rausu, this pair of steaming pools on the far side of the river is superb. Park by the road and cross the bridge. Some locals come every day, and the facilities are maintained by a dedicated team of volunteers. The onsen is segregated by sex and has changing facilities.

Rausu-dake HIKING

(羅臼岳) One of Japan's 100 Famous Mountains, Rausu-dake (1660m) makes a great day hike, best tackled from the trailhead at Iwaobetsu Onsen. Allow seven to nine hours for the 7km return trip. From the top there are stunning views of one of the Northern Territories Southern Kuril Islands (Disputed Territories).

The trailhead is 4km from the closest bus stop at Iwaobetsu, so without your own wheels you'll have to walk (a taxi from Utoro Onsen costs ¥3000 to ¥4000). The trail officially opens 1 July (though there may still be snow then) and closes when snow begins to fall mid-November. There's a route from Rausu as well, but it's more challenging.

Shiretoko-go-ko Nature Trail WALKING

(知床五湖; www.goko.go.jp; ⏲7.30am-6pm late Apr-late Nov) This small area of five lakes *(go-ko)* is the most accessible part of Shiretoko,

Shiretoko National Park

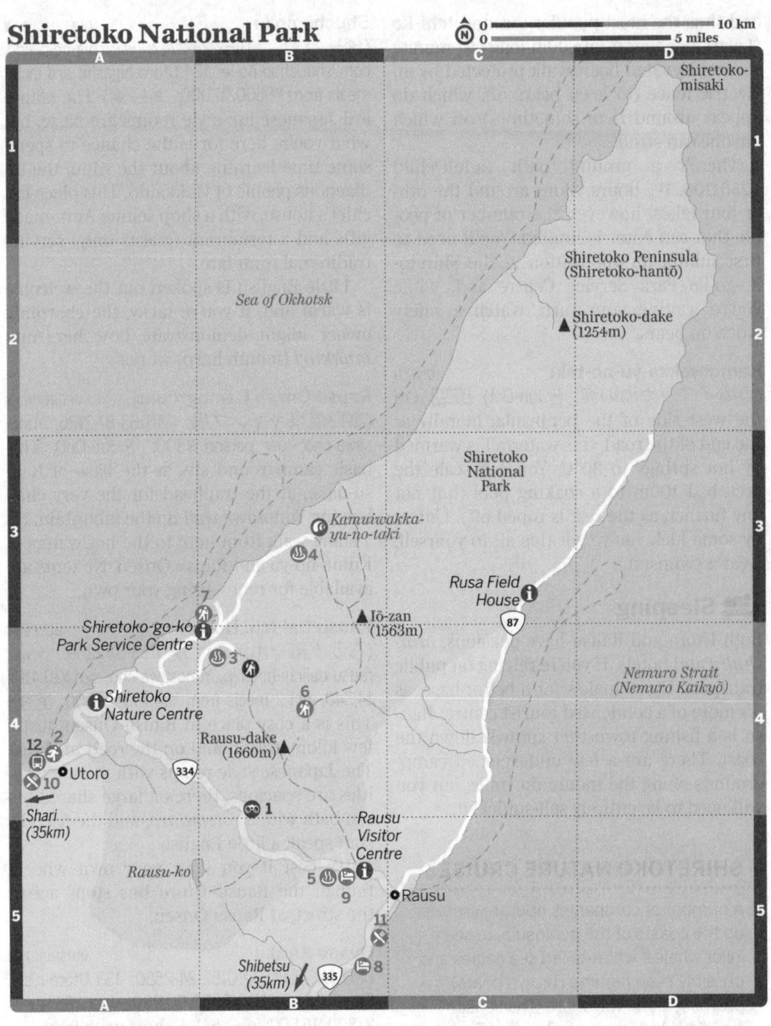

Shiretoko National Park

Sights

1 Shiretoko Pass B4

Activities, Courses & Tours

2 Aurora Cruises A4
Godzilla-Iwa Sightseeing .... (see 2)
3 Iwaobetsu Onsen B4
4 Kamuiwakka-yu-no-taki B3
5 Kuma-no-yu B5
Rausu-dake .... (see 3)
6 Shiretoko Traverse B4
7 Shiretoko-go-ko Nature Trail B3

Sleeping

8 Marumi B5
Oyado Kiraku .... (see 2)
9 Rausu Dai-Ichi Hotel B5
Rausu Onsen Campground .... (see 5)
Shūchō no Ie .... (see 2)

Eating

10 GVO A4
11 Rausu Maruo Hamada Shoten B5

Transport

Utoro Michi-no-eki .... (see 12)
12 Utoro Onsen Bus Terminal A4

and thus the most popular. Around **Ichi-ko** (Lake One), there's an 800m-long (40-minute return) elevated boardwalk protected by an electric fence (to keep bears off, which do appear around here sometimes) on which anyone can stroll.

There's a ground path (adult/child ¥250/100, 1½ hours, 3km) around the other four lakes; however, the number of people that can enter is limited. You'll need to first submit an application at the Shiretoko-go-ko Park Service Centre and, while you're waiting your turn, watch a safety video on bears.

Kamuiwakka-yu-no-taki ONSEN

(カムイワッカ湯の滝; Jun-Oct) FREE On the west side of the peninsula, literally at the end of the road, this waterfall is warmed by hot springs to 30°C. You can scale the rock bed 100m to a soaking pool (but not any further, as the rest is roped off). Unless by some luck you've got this all to yourself, wear a swimsuit.

Sleeping

Both Utoro and Rausu have pensions, *minshuku* and hotels. If you're relying on public transport, Utoro makes for a better base, as it's more of a condensed tourist centre; Rausu is a fishing town that sprawls down the coast. There are a few undeveloped campgrounds along the mountain trails, but you will need to be entirely self-sufficient.

SHIRETOKO NATURE CRUISES

A number of companies operate cruises up the coasts of the peninsula, to see killer whales, white-tailed sea eagles and possibly even *higuma* (brown bears) prowling along the shore. The season for this is May through October. Both **Aurora Cruises** (おーろら; 0152-24-2147; www.ms-aurora.com/shiretoko/en; 107 Utoro-higashi, Shari-chō) and **Godzilla-Iwa Sightseeing** (ゴジラ岩観光; 0152-24-3060; www.kamuiwakka.jp; 51 Utoro-higashi, Shari-chō) offer comparable trips, of either 90 minutes (as far as Kamuiwakka-yu-no-taki) or 3½ hours (all the way to the end of the cape). Godzilla-Iwa Sightseeing also runs hour-long cruises among the drift ice from Rausu between late January and mid-April. If you're lucky you'll see spotted seals chilling on the ice.

Shūchō no Ie GUESTHOUSE ¥

(酋長の家; 0152-24-2742; www.big-hokkaido.com/shuuchoo-no-ie; 124 Utoro-higashi; s/d incl 2 meals from ¥9500/17,000; P) The standard Japanese inn-style rooms are basic, but what you're here for is the chance to spend some time learning about the Ainu, the indigenous people of Hokkaidō. This place is a chief's house, with a shop selling Ainu-made gifts and a restaurant (guests only) serving traditional Ainu fare.

Little English is spoken but the welcome is warm and, if you're lucky, the charming owner might demonstrate how her Ainu *mukkuri* (mouth harp) works.

Rausu Onsen Campground CAMPGROUND ¥

(羅臼温泉キャンプ場; 0153-87-2126; Yunosawa-chō; per person ¥300; Jun-Oct) This basic campground sits at the base of Rausu-dake, at the trailhead for the very challenging Yunosawa trail up the mountain. It's a short walk from here to the hot waters of Kuma-no-yu and Rausu Onsen. No tents are available for rent – bring your own.

Rausu Dai-Ichi Hotel HOTEL ¥¥

(らうす第一ホテル; 0153-87-2259; www.rausu-daiichi-hotel.jp; Yunosawa-chō; s/d ¥10,410/14,340, incl 2 meals from ¥14,190/21,900; P) This is a cosy place in Rausu Onsen, just a few kilometres inland on the road to Utoro. The Japanese-style rooms with private facilities are spacious, there's a large shared onsen bath with a *rotemburo,* and the friendly staff speak a little English.

It's best if you have your own wheels, though the Rausu–Utoro bus stops across the street, at Rausu Onsen.

Oyado Kiraku MINSHUKU ¥¥

(お宿来羅玖; 0152-24-2550; 133 Utoro-nishi, Shari-chō; s/d ¥5000/10,000, incl 2 meals ¥7800/15,500; P) A short walk from the Utoro Michi-no-eki road stop (and one bus stop before the Utoro Onsen terminal), Kiraku is a good deal with tatami rooms, shared facilities and tasty meals. The staff at the information counter at the Utoro Michi-no-eki will call for you, but it pays to book ahead in summer.

Marumi RYOKAN ¥¥

(羅臼の宿まるみ; 0153-88-1313; www.shiretoko-rausu.com; 24 Yagihama-chō; s/d ¥7960/11,600, incl 2 meals from ¥9960/18,000; P@) Marumi prides itself on its gut-busting seafood banquets, making this a good choice if you've worked up a calorie deficit in the mountains. The Japanese-style rooms themselves are simple with shared facilities (you can upgrade for an ocean view and an en-suite bath), but there's an outdoor onsen facing the waters.

The modern, concrete ryokan is 8km southwest of Rausu on Rte 335. Marumi also does cruises to see whales and dolphins and, in winter, to see the drift ice; enquire about packages when you book.

Eating

There is a handful of small eateries in Utoro and Rausu, mostly serving local seafood (when in doubt, order *kaisen-don;* raw seafood on rice). Most have colourful banners out front so they're easy to spot. Rausu's *michi-no-eki* (road station) has a handy cheat sheet of restaurants in town and is also good for picking up packaged food.

Rausu Maruo Hamada Shoten SEAFOOD ¥¥
(☎0153-67-3111; www.rausu.co.jp; 361-5 Rebun-chō; mains ¥1700; ⏲10.30am-3pm Feb–mid-Oct; P) Choose your crab and have it served, or go for the menu, either way it's delicious seafood in a building that's four decades old. Note that the hours can be a bit wonky – your best bet is to call before heading over.

Information

Shiretoko National Park has several excellent information centres with knowledgeable staff. Whatever your plans are – from multiday treks to onsen soaks – stop into one of the centres to get the latest information on trail and road conditions, weather warnings and bear sightings. The information will be posted in English or in easy-to-understand images.

Rausu Visitor Centre (羅臼ビジターセンター; ☎0153-87-2828; www.rausu-vc.jp; 6-27 Yunosawa-chō; ⏲9am-5pm May-Oct, 10am-4pm Nov-Apr, closed Mon Oct-Jun) On the Rausu side of the peninsula, on Rte 334. Helpful staff.

Rusa Field House (ルサフィールドハウス; ☎0153-89-2722; http://shiretoko-whc.jp/rfh; 8 Kita-hama; ⏲9am-5pm May-Oct, closed Tue) This centre offers support for the truly intrepid and experienced, who plan to trek or kayak out to Shiretoko-misaki. If you have such aspirations, absolutely check in here first. Located on Rte 87, 13km northeast of Rausu, up the coast.

Shiretoko Nature Centre (知床自然センター; ☎0152-24-2114; http://center.shiretoko.or.jp/en; ⏲8am-5.30pm mid-Apr–mid-Oct, 9am-4pm mid-Oct–mid-Apr; 👪) Run by the Shiretoko Nature Foundation, this is the largest visitor centre; located 5km past Utoro.

Shiretoko-go-ko Park Service Centre (知床五湖パークサービスセンター; ☎0152-24-2306; www.utopia-shiretoko.co.jp; ⏲7.30am-6.30pm May-Jul, to 6pm Aug, to 5pm Sep, to 4pm Oct, to 3pm mid-Nov) Information and applications for the Shiretoko-go-ko Nature Trail.

Getting There & Away

AIR

Memanbetsu Airport (p646) is the most convenient for Shiretoko. Between mid-June and mid-October, three Shari Airport Liner buses depart a few times daily from Memanbetsu Airport, via Abashiri Station, for Shari (¥2100, 1½ hours) and Utoro (¥3300, two hours).

BUS

There is a night bus (one way/round trip ¥8230/15,430) from Sapporo's Chūō bus terminal departing at 11.15pm for **Utoro Onsen Bus Terminal** (ウトロ温泉バスターミナル; ☎0152-24-2054; 107 Utoro-nishi, Shari-chō; ⏲8.30am-4pm late Apr-Oct); reservations required. The return bus is at 9.20am. The bus also stops at the **Utoro Michi-no-eki** (ウトロ道の駅; ☎0152-22-5000; ⏲8.30am-6.30pm May-Oct, 9am-5pm Nov-Apr), one stop before arrival at Utoro bus terminal.

From May to October there are seven buses daily between Shari and Utoro Onsen (¥1650, 50 minutes), continuing to the Shiretoko Nature Centre (¥1800, 10 minutes), Iwaobetsu (¥1960, 15 minutes) and Shiretoko-go-ko (¥2000, 25 minutes); buses are timed to meet trains coming from Abashiri and Kushiro.

Daily buses also run between Rausu and Kushiro (¥4850, 3½ hours), departing from the bus stop behind the Rausu Michi-no-eki.

CAR & MOTORCYCLE

While it's possible to get around by public transport, buses are infrequent, so having your own wheels is better. Pick up a rental in Abashiri or Kushiro, before heading to the park.

Getting Around

BUS

A shuttle bus runs from Utoro Onsen via Shiretoko Nature Centre for Shiretoko-go-ko (¥1980, 25 minutes) and Kamuiwakka-yu-no-taki (¥1400, one hour) from 1 August to 25 August and again over the September holiday period (around the third week of the month).

From June through October, there are four buses daily between Utoro Onsen and Rausu Akan Bus Station (¥1380, 50 minutes) via the dramatic Shiretoko Pass.

CAR & MOTORCYCLE

When the summer shuttle bus is in operation, the road from Shiretoko-go-ko to Kamuiwakka-yu-no-taki is closed to private traffic. Daily road closures and conditions are posted at the Shiretoko Nature Centre (p651). Come November, beware of early snow-stopping traffic.

Akan National Park

Akan National Park (阿寒国立公園), designated in 1934 and covering 905 sq km, was one of Japan's first national parks. It's home to volcanic peaks, several large caldera lakes, thick forests of Sakhalin spruce, herds of sika deer, rejuvenating onsen and a small Ainu *kotan* (village). While the mountains are obviously a draw for hikers, those less inclined (and travelling by car) can drive out to a number of excellent lookout points around the park.

Sleeping

There are campgrounds, hostels, *minshuku* and resort-style onsen hotels here. Note that many of the hotels have seen better days – book only if the price is right. Many budget places, such as campgrounds and hostels, are only open in the summer.

Eating

Akan National Park is home to most of the few restaurants in Japan that serve dishes of Ainu origin. Look for *ruibe* (ルイベ), salmon that has been left out in the Hokkaidō midwinter freeze, sliced up sashimi style, and then served with soy sauce and water peppers; *pocche* (ポッチェ), traditional dumplings made from fermented potato mash; and *ohaw* (オハウ), a soup of salmon or venison and wild vegetables.

Getting There & Away

Kushiro and Abashiri are the main gateways to the park. There are two stations on the JR Senmō line, which runs between Kushiro and Shiretoko-Shari, that are convenient for Kawayu Onsen: Kawayu Station and Mashū Station. For Akanko Onsen, catch a bus from Kushiro, Abashiri or Asahikawa.

Getting Around

Akan Bus (阿寒バス; ☎0154-37-2221; www.akanbus.co.jp/foreign/en) does sightseeing runs (¥4600 to ¥5400 per person, nine hours) into the Akan area from Kushiro, stopping at Mashū-ko Viewpoint 1 as well as other viewpoints before returning to Kushiro. From April to October, a bus (one way ¥570) runs from Mashū-ko Station to the Viewpoint 1, waiting 30 minutes before returning. A Passport-only bus runs from Kawayu Onsen to the viewpoint between July and September.

While it is possible to get around the park with the limited public transport, you will have to be very mindful of timetables and plan on wasting lots of time, as buses and trains are infrequent, even during the peak summer season. It is highly recommended that you pick up a rental car in either Kushiro or Abashiri.

Akanko Onsen

☎0154 / POP 1350

The resort town of Akanko Onsen (阿寒湖温泉), in the western part of Akan National Park, is on the southern shores of Akan-ko. In addition to lakefront vistas and hot springs, Akanko is known for two things: *marimo*, a rare kind of algae that forms oddly perfect spheres; and its Ainu kotan (village), Japan's largest (though it's not big). If you have your own transport, you can use Akanko Onsen as a base for exploring the surrounding mountains.

Sights

★Ainu Kotan VILLAGE

(アイヌコタン) This collection of shops and households is actually the largest Ainu village in Hokkaidō. Residents make a living promoting their culture: dancing on the stage at Ikor (p656), cooking *pochie* (fermented potato dumplings) in restaurants, and selling wood and leather crafts, made with traditional techniques and motifs.

In the evenings (May to November) there's a procession around 8.30pm to light torches around the village.

Ainu Folklore Museum MUSEUM

(アイヌ文化伝承館, Ainu Bunka Denshō-kan; ☎0154-67-2727; www.akanainu.jp/; 4-7-19 Akanko Onsen; ⏲10am-9pm; P) FREE At the top of the hill in the Ainu *kotan*, this small museum has changing exhibitions of contemporary Ainu artisan work, and sometimes thought-provoking shows. There are some traditional dwellings here, too.

Akan Kohan Eco-Museum Centre MUSEUM

(阿寒湖畔エコミュージアムセンター; ☎0154-67-4100; http://business4.plala.or.jp/akan-eco; 1-1-1 Akanko Onsen, Akan-chō; ⏲9am-5pm Wed-Mon) FREE At the eastern edge of town, this centre has exhibitions on

AINU: HOKKAIDŌ'S INDIGENOUS PEOPLE

The Ainu draw their ancestry back to the earliest settlers of Hokkaidō, while a distinct Ainu culture is believed to have emerged around 700 years ago. They were hunters, fishers and gatherers, settling along salmon runs and coastal plains. Men wore long, bushy beards and women had distinctive blue tattoos on their hands and faces – especially around the lips, which gave them the appearance of always smiling.

Their gods, called *kamuy*, were found in the natural world, in the rocks and trees and especially in the animals around them. Of all their gods, the most important was *kim-un kamuy*, the god of the mountains – known in Japanese as *higuma* (Ussuri brown bear). Ritual ceremonies, called *iyomante*, were held to send spirits – of sacrificed bear cubs but also of plants and broken pots – back to the realm of the gods. Days began with prayer to the deity of fire, *apehuci kamuy*, who resided in the hearth.

While the Japanese and the Ainu had been trading partners for centuries, as the Japanese empire grew in military and economic might, the balance of power gradually shifted in favour of the southern nation. Following the formal annexation of Hokkaidō in 1869, the new Meiji government signed the Hokkaidō Former Aborigines Protection Act in 1899. Though well-meaning in name, it banned traditional practices, such as hunting and tattooing, along with the Ainu language. Ainu were given plots of land (typically small and ill-suited to cultivation) and instructed to take up the lives of sedentary farmers. Those who held out suffered discrimination; many who managed to assimilate feared being 'outed', leading many Ainu to bury their ancestry as deeply as possible.

Today there are roughly 25,000 people in Japan who claim Ainu descent. With the general cultural upheavals of the 1960s, more and more began to speak out against entrenched discrimination and poverty, finding pride and common cause with other indigenous peoples fighting for recognition and justice around the world. A number of community centres were founded; this coincided with a period of increased domestic tourism to Hokkaidō, and many Ainu found work performing their culture for tourists – singing folk songs for tour groups and selling traditional handicrafts. For some members of the community this was a breakthrough, an opportunity to draw positive recognition to their culture and, perhaps more importantly, to make a living. For others, these watered-down cultural displays were at best a distraction from the social justice movement and, at worst, a step backwards.

The way forward for Ainu descendants remains a thorny path. There are still battles being fought on the political front: after decades of lobbying, the Former Aborigines Protection Act was repealed in 1997, and as recently as 2009 activists finally succeeded in winning the passing of a Diet (Japan's national parliamentary body) resolution recognising the Ainu as an indigenous people of Japan.

There is also the question of what it means to be Ainu. There are only a handful of people who can still speak the language (though there are radio programs to learn), and traditional cultural practices can feel frozen in the past, especially to the younger generation who were raised like modern teens. There are, however, artists, musicians and chefs tinkering with the old ways, breathing new life into them. By all means, if you're able to catch acts like Oki Dub Ainu Band (www.tonkori.com) or Marewrew (www.facebook.com/marewrew) live, do!

Akan National Park, which has Ainu *kotan* (villages) in both Akanko Onsen and Kawayu Onsen (p657), is the best place in Hokkaidō to see Ainu culture in a contemporary context. The villages, with their folklore museums and restaurants serving Ainu dishes, are definitely touristy – though that is the modern reality. Akanko Onsen has a stage, Ikor (p656), for traditional folk music performances; Kawayu Onsen is the home base of modern Ainu musician Atuy, who runs the fantastic pension (and occasional performance space) Marukibune (p658).

If you're interested in digging deeper, visit the Hokkaidō Ainu Center (p598) in Sapporo. In addition to exhibitions on history and culture, there is a reading room with pretty much every book published in English on the Ainu.

Akan National Park

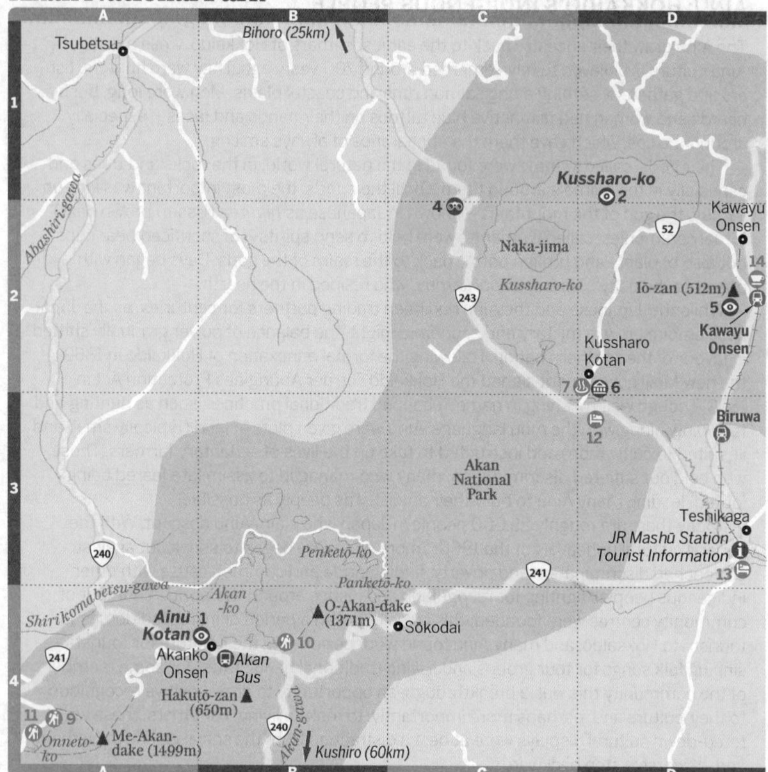

local flora and fauna, including *marimo* in aquarium tanks. It also has hiking maps in English and info on trail conditions and bear sightings.

Behind the centre, a trail makes a shaded, breezy loop out to Akan-ko and back through the forest to some volcanic bubbling clay pools (called *bokke*). The 3km walk takes about 40 minutes round-trip.

Activities

A number of hotels open their hot-spring baths to nonguests for a fee (¥500 to ¥1620); the tourist information office (p656) has a list. The town has been pushing other activities as well, such as fishing, kayaking, and adventure trekking. Info on all of these are available at the tourist information office or at Tsuruga Adventure. At the larger hotels, you can speak with the concierge.

★ Me-Akan-dake HIKING

(雌阿寒岳, Female Mountain) The highest mountain in the park, Me-Akan-dake (1499m) is an active volcano that is one of Japan's 100 Famous Mountains. There are three trails up it, though at the time of research the trail nearest Akanko Onsen was closed because of typhoon damage. We recommend driving around to **Me-Akan Onsen** (720m), from where it's a 10km, two-hour hike to the top.

There are some steep bits, over loose volcanic gravel, but the views from the top are spectacular. From the summit, you have the option to descend via the Onneto Nature Trail and loop back to your vehicle at Me-Akan Onsen (total journey four to five hours). Make sure you pick up a map.

Onneto Nature Trail WALKING

(オンネトーネイチャートレイル) The picturesque lake of **Onneto-ko**, emerald green and in the mountains to the west of

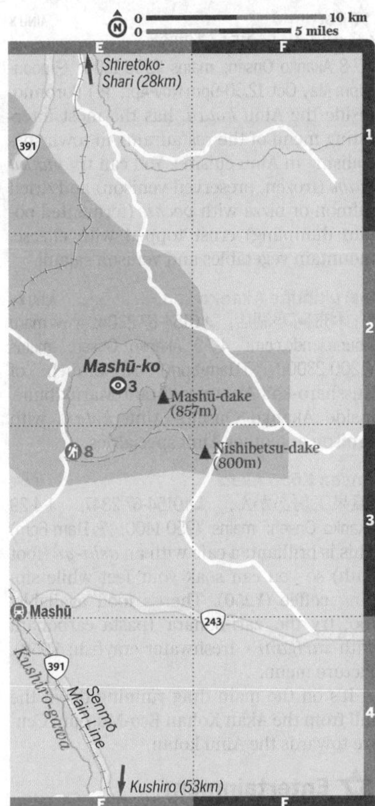

Akan National Park

Top Sights

1 Ainu Kotan B4
2 Kussharo-ko D1
3 Mashū-ko E2

Sights

4 Bihoro Pass C2
5 Iō-zan D2
6 Museum of Ainu Folklore D2

Activities, Courses & Tours

7 Kotan-yu D2
8 Mashū-dake Trail E3
9 Me-Akan-dake A4
10 O-Akan-dake B4
11 Onneto Nature Trail A4

Sleeping

12 Kussharo-Genya Youth Guesthouse D3
Marukibune .... (see 7)
13 Onsen Minshuku Mako D3

Eating

Marukibune Restaurant .... (see 7)

Drinking & Nightlife

14 Orchard Grass D2

Me-Akan-dake, can be circumnavigated on foot. There are viewing platforms, toilets, parking, a restaurant and a number of other short nature trails. Allow an hour to circle the lake (5km) and less than that for the return trip to **Yu-no-taki** (湯の滝) waterfall.

There is a campsite at the southern end of the lake, but no public transport here.

O-Akan-dake HIKING
(雄阿寒岳, Male Mountain) O-Akan-dake is the big volcano (1371m) to the east of Akanko Onsen. The 12.4km return hike to the top from the Takiguchi trail entrance at 450m takes five to six hours. From the peak there are great views of **Penketō-ko** and **Panketō-ko**, two small lakes formed when O-Akan's eruption separated them from Akan-ko.

If you're after a short walk, consider walking just the first kilometre of the trail, which passes alongside **Tarō-ko** (太郎湖) and **Jirō-ko** (次郎湖); the return walk takes 30 minutes. There are three buses (¥220, 10 minutes) daily between Akanko Onsen and the Takiguchi trailhead.

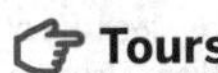

Tours

Tsuruga Adventure TREKKING
(☎0154-65-6276; www.en.tsuruga-adventure.com; 4-6-10 Akanko Onsen; treks ¥7000-70,000; ⏲9am-8pm) This tour outfitter offers a wide variety of fishing, trekking, birding, and other outdoor exploration options in the Akan park area.

Sleeping

Akan Lakeside Campsite CAMPGROUND ¥
(阿寒湖畔キャンプ場; ☎0154-67-3263; 5-1 Akan Onsen; campsites per adult/child ¥650/325; ⏲Jun-Sep; P) About a five-minute walk west of Akanko Onsen centre, across Rte 241 from the Ainu theatre, this campground has shady pitches, showers, laundry facilities and an *ashi-yu* (foot bath) for relaxing tired feet.

Minshuku Kiri MINSHUKU ¥
(民宿桐; ☎0154-67-2755; www10.plala.or.jp/kiriminsyuku; 4-3-26 Akanko Onsen; r per person with/without breakfast ¥4500/4000; P 📶) This *minshuku* has tiny, no-fuss rooms and a

MARIMO

Akan-ko is legendary throughout Japan for its *marimo* (まりも; *Cladophora aegagropila*), spheres of green algae that are both biologically intriguing – it takes as long as 200 years for them to grow to the size of a baseball – and very, very *kawaii* (cute). *Marimo* became endangered after being designated a national treasure: suddenly, everyone in Japan needed to have one. Members of the Ainu community came to the rescue by starting the **Marimo Matsuri** (まりも祭り), held in early October, which ceremonially returns *marimo* to Akan-ko.

There are *marimo* on display at the Akan Kohan Eco-Museum Centre (p652). You can also take a **lake cruise** (☎0154-67-2511; www.akankisen.com; per person ¥1900; ⏲6am-5pm May-Nov) out to the **Marimo Observation Centre**, where a monitor plays live footage of the velvety globes underwater.

great location – above a souvenir shop a couple of minutes' walk from the Ainu *kotan*. There is a wooden onsen and a friendly welcome here, too.

★Akan Yuku-no-sato Tsuruga RYOKAN ¥¥¥
(あかん遊久の里鶴雅, Lake Akan Tsuruga Resort Spa; ☎0154-67-4000; www.tsuruga.com; 4-6-10 Akan Onsen; s/tw incl 2 meals from ¥17,900/31,400; P ❄ @ 📶) This old-style resort is the fanciest spot in town and sprawls over three buildings. The *honkan* (main hall) rooms are the cheapest but don't have lake views; the rooms in the lavish *bekkan* (annexe) have en-suite outdoor onsen baths. Everyone gets to use the two big bathhouses, one of which has outdoor lake views. Look for sculptures from Ainu artists in the lobby.

This spot is ideal if you want a taste of the classic Japanese upscale *ryokan* experience. You'll be welcomed at check-in, the room has selected sweets and tea, and the service is impeccable.

Eating & Drinking

Your best bet is the Ainu kotan (p652); a handful of restaurants here serve Ainu cuisine (and more).

★Poronno AINU ¥
(ポロンノ; ☎0154-67-2159; www.poronno.com; 4-7-8 Akanko Onsen; mains ¥500-1500; ⏲noon-10pm May-Oct, 12.30-9pm Nov-Apr; P) Poronno, inside the Ainu *kotan*, has the most interesting menu of the restaurants in town specialising in Ainu cuisine. You can try *yukku ruibe* (frozen, preserved venison) and dried salmon or pizza with *pochie* (fermented potato dumpling) crust topped with cheese, mountain vegetables and venison salami.

Marukibune Akanko-ten AINU ¥¥
(丸木舟阿寒湖店; ☎0154-67-2304; www.marukibune.jimdo.com; 4-7-9 Akanko Onsen; mains ¥1200-2300; ⏲11am-8pm) A branch of Kussharo-ko's Ainu restaurant Marukibune, inside Akanko Onsen's Ainu *kotan*, with venison and other Ainu specialties.

Onsen Kōbō Akan CAFE
(温泉工房あかん; ☎0154-67-2847; 1-4-29 Akanko Onsen; mains ¥950-1400; ⏲11am-6pm) This is brilliant: a cafe with an *ashi-yu* (foot bath) so you can soak your feet while sipping coffee (¥250). There's food available, too; try the 'zari-bonara' (pasta carbonara with *zarigani* – freshwater crayfish; ¥950). Picture menu.

It's on the main drag running down the hill from the Akan Kohan Eco-Museum Centre towards the Ainu kotan.

☆ Entertainment

Ikor LIVE PERFORMANCE
(イコロ; ☎0154-67-2727; www.akanainu.jp; adult/child ¥1080/540) There are several shows daily of traditional singing and dancing at this theatre inside the *Ainu kotan*.

Information

Tourist Information Office (☎0154-67-3200; http://en.kushiro-lakeakan.com; 2-6-20 Akanko Onsen; ⏲9am-6pm; 📶) In the middle of the village, with bus and event schedules, hiking maps and info on accommodation and onsen – all in English. Helps with bookings, too.

Getting There & Away

Two buses daily run to/from Asahikawa (¥4710, five hours), via Sōunkyō Onsen (¥3350, four hours) in Daisetsuzan National Park. From April to November there are three to six buses daily to/from Kushiro (¥2700, two hours), via Kushiro Airport (¥2150, one hour).

From mid-July through mid-October, two buses daily run to/from Mashū Station (for Kawayu

Onsen; one hour, ¥1500), with a stop at Mashū-ko Viewpoint 1.

If you're driving, Akanko Onsen is on Rte 240, which (of course!) has been renamed Marimo Hwy (まりも国道).

Getting Around

A free shuttle bus runs around Akanko Onsen, from the bus terminal via the Ainu *kotan* and Akan Kohan Eco-Museum Centre. A few continue to Takiguchi, the trailhead for O-Akan-dake. The town is compact and very walkable.

Kawayu Onsen

0154 / POP 1050

Kawayu (川湯温泉) is a quiet onsen town with a dozen or so hot-spring hotels, but it's in the surrounding area that Akan National Park really comes to life. In the vicinity are two stunning caldera lakes, Kussharo-ko and Mashū-ko, hiking opportunities and plenty of hot springs – including some in-the-rough, free ones.

Sights

★Mashū-ko LAKE

(摩周湖) Considered by many to be Japan's most beautiful lake, Mashū-ko once held the world record for water clarity. The island in the middle was known by the Ainu as the Isle of the Gods. A road runs along the western rim. You can't get down to lake level, but there are two official viewing points called Viewpoint 1 and Viewpoint 3; there's no parking fee at the latter.

★Kussharo-ko LAKE

(屈斜路湖) Japan's largest caldera lake is a rich blue on sunny days. A small volcano peeks out from the centre, creating the island **Naka-jima** – best viewed from the Bihoro Pass.

The lake is also purportedly the home of a Loch Ness monster--like creature nicknamed Kusshi.

Bihoro Pass VIEWPOINT

(美幌峠) This lookout point on Rte 243, which runs between Abashiri and Mashū, has a fantastic panoramic view over Kussharo-ko, with Naka-jima in the middle.

Iō-zan VOLCANO

(硫黄山) This hissing mountain (512m), a couple of kilometres south of Kawayu Onsen, is stained sunshine-yellow in patches from sulphur. Locals steam eggs in the hot volcanic vapours for a speciality known as *onsen-tamago*. Chances are you'll hear the sellers calling *'Tamago! Tamago! Tamago!'* (Eggs!) even before you reach the car park.

Museum of Ainu Folklore MUSEUM

(コタンアイヌ民俗資料館; 0154-84-2128; www.town.teshikaga.hokkaido.jp; adult/child ¥420/280; 9am-5pm May-Oct) In the Kussharo *kotan* (village) on the southern shores of Kussharo-ko, this museum displays traditional Ainu tools and crafts. Ask the staff to play the 25-minute English video, which talks about Ainu history and contemporary Ainu culture.

Activities

★Mashū-dake Trail HIKING

(摩周岳) The 14.4km walk to the top of Mashū-dake (857m) takes you around the lake to its eastern side and back in four to six hours. The pay-off is big: you will be rewarded with amazing volcanic views for much of the hike. The trailhead is at Mashū-ko Viewpoint 1 (400m) at the southern end of the lake; the public bus stops here, though infrequently.

Kotan-yu ONSEN

(コタン湯; closed 2-3pm) FREE On the southern shores of Kussharo-ko, in the Ainu *kotan*, this *rotemburo* is right on the lake, with unobstructed views over the water. There's also unobstructed views from the road, so bring a swimsuit if that makes you squeamish! The bath is 'divided' into male and female sides by a rock. It's well maintained thanks to devoted volunteers.

Sleeping

Onsen Minshuku Mako MINSHUKU ¥

(温泉民宿摩湖; 0154-82-5124; www.onsenmako.com; 1-2-17 Sakuraoka, Teshikaga-chō; r per person with/without 2 meals ¥5300/3800; P) The owner of this simple, family-run place is a keen traveller and extends a warm welcome to foreign guests. Rooms are tatami or Western, with shared facilities (including an onsen bath). All-round good value. Best if you have your own wheels – it's a 20-minute walk from JR Mashū Station.

From November to April add ¥300 per night for heat.

Kussharo-Genya Youth Guesthouse HOSTEL ¥

(屈斜路原野ユースゲストハウス; 0154-84-2609; www.gogogenya.com; dm/r per person from ¥3500/5200, breakfast/dinner ¥750/1300;

(P ⊖ @ ≋) On a back road off Rte 243 near the southern shores of Kussharo-ko, this attractive youth hostel has vaulted ceilings, lofty skylights and polished wooden floors, plus an onsen bath. There's a restaurant here (but no private cooking facilities).

As it's a little out of the way, set back from the road among fields, it's better if you've got your own transport, although the English-speaking staff will pick you up from JR Mashū Station, if you request in advance. Meals are tasty, and for a bit extra they can add venison to the menu.

★Marukibune RYOKAN ¥¥
(丸木舟; ☎0154-84-2644; www.marukibune.jimdo.com; Kotan, Kussharo-Shigai, Teshikaga-chō; s/tw from ¥7710/17,580; P ⊖ ❄ ≋) This unique spot in the Ainu *kotan* at the southern end of Kussharo-ko is run by Ainu musician Atuy. It has just a handful of rooms decorated with traditional touches, some with lake views, and an onsen bath. The 'Ainu Room' (single/double ¥19,590/32,700), with wooden walls, carvings and colourful textiles, is a work of art. Meals can be taken in the ground-floor restaurant.

Kinkiyu Hotel HOTEL ¥¥
(欣喜湯; ☎0154-83-2211; www.kinkiyu.com; 1-5-10 Kawayu Onsen; s/d ¥7000/14,000, incl 2 meals from ¥15,000/30,000; P ⊖ ≋) This decades-old hotel in Kawayu Onsen may have seen better days, but the baths, known for their highly acidic waters, are fantastic. Day trippers can use them between 1pm and 9pm (¥700). Though the hotel is ageing, the Western-style or tatami rooms are well kept.

Eating & Drinking

There are a few eating options in front of Mashū and Kawayu Stations, and more scattered around Kussharo-ko. You will greatly increase your options by having a car. Note that outside summer (July and August) many places close.

Marukibune Restaurant AINU ¥¥
(丸木舟レストラン; ☎0154-84-2644; www.marukibune.jimdo.com; Kotan, Kussharo-Shigai, Teshikaga-chō; mains ¥1200-1800; ⏲11am-7pm; P) OK, the food here isn't dramatically different from what a Japanese diner would serve, but you can get a *donburi* (rice bowl) topped with Hokkaidō venison and *gyōja niniku* (alpine leek), the local aromatic that has a long history in Ainu cooking. Also available is *pochie* (ポッチェ; ¥700), fermented potato dumplings. The decor is an eclectic mix of Ainu items, drum sets, microphones, and so on.

Ask one of the staff to put on a video of owner Atuy and his group performing traditional music and dance.

There's another branch (p656) in the Ainu *kotan* in Akanko Onsen.

Orchard Grass CAFE
(オーチャードグラス; ☎0154-83-3787; Kawaya Onsen Station; coffee from ¥400; ⏲10am-5pm, closed Tue; ≋) This cafe is inside historic Kawayu Station (built in 1936), which retains much of its original character – in the form of high, wood-panelled ceilings, antique pendant lamps, stained-glass windows and an iron-and-tile stove. Food, such as hamburgers, soup and ice cream, is available too.

There's a free foot bath on the other side of the station.

Information

JR Mashū Station Tourist Information
(☎0154-82-2642; www.masyuko.or.jp; ⏲9am-5pm May-Oct, 10am-4pm Nov-Apr) In JR Mashū Station, with English maps and brochures. Staff can help with accommodation bookings. There's a smaller counter inside JR Kawayu Onsen Station.

Getting There & Away

BUS

From mid-July to early October, Akan Bus (p652) runs a tourist shuttle between Abashiri Station and Kushiro Station, stopping at Bihoro Pass, Kawayu Onsen, Mashū Station and Akanko Onsen. A four-day pass costs ¥4000/2000 per adult/child. A week pass costs ¥11,000/5500.

CAR & MOTORCYCLE

Your own wheels will allow you to fully explore the park. On Rte 241, between Mashū Station and Akanko Onsen, there's a particularly scenic stretch with a lookout point at Sokodai where you can see Penketō-ko and Panketō-ko.

TRAIN

Infrequent trains run north on the JR Senmō main line between Kawayu Onsen and Shiretoko-Shari (¥1270, one hour), and south between Kawayu Onsen and Kushiro (¥1640, 1¾ hours) via Mashū (¥360, 15 minutes). Abashiri (¥2050) is two hours away.

Getting Around

From mid-July to mid-October, Akan Bus (p652) has daily connections between JR Mashū Station and Mashū-ko (25 minutes, Passport holders only). There is also a circular route that runs three times daily to/from Kawayu Station via Mashū-ko, JR Kawayu Onsen Station, Iō-zan, Suna-yu, the Ainu Kotan and Bihoro Pass. This bus usually stops for 15 to 30 minutes so you have time to check stuff out.

Buses, timed to meet trains, make the 10-minute run between Kawayu Onsen Station and Kawayu Onsen town.

All of the above are covered by the **Teshikaga Eco Passport** (弟子屈えこパスポート; two/three/five/seven days ¥1500/2000/2500/3000) – a must if you are planning to use public transport to get around. The pass also includes free luggage storage and bicycle rental; drop off your bags and pick up wheels at either Mashū or Kawayu Onsen stations.

Kushiro

☎0154 / POP 174,900

The most populous city in eastern Hokkaidō, Kushiro (釧路) is an industrial port that came to prominence thanks to its harbour, which remains relatively free of ice in winter. For travellers, it is a key transit hub for nearby Kushiro Wetlands National Park and, further north, Akan National Park.

Sleeping & Eating

As a transport hub for the region, Kushiro has a good spread of hotels near the train station, mostly national chains.

There are cafes and bakeries in the train station, but few options in the streets nearby.

Getting There & Away

AIR

Kushiro Airport (釧路空港; ☎0154-57-8304; www.kushiro-airport.co.jp; 2 Tsuruoka), located about 10km west of the city, has flights to/from Sapporo and Tokyo. Buses between the airport and JR Kushiro Station (¥940, 45 minutes) are timed for arrivals and departures.

BUS

Two buses daily run between Kushiro and Asahikawa (¥5450, 6½ hours). Other buses go to Akanko Onsen (¥2700, 1½ hours) and Sōunkyō Onsen (¥4930, five hours). There are also five buses daily (two on weekends) between Rausu and Kushiro (¥4850, 3½ hours). The bus terminal is next to the train station.

TRAIN

There are six daily JR Limited Express Super Ōzora Liner trains between Sapporo and Kushiro (¥8850, 4½ hours), via Obihiro (¥4290, 1½ hours, from Kushiro). The JR Nemuro line runs east to Nemuro (¥2490, 2¼ hours).

Heading north from Kushiro, the JR Senmō line runs between Kushiro and Abashiri (¥3670, 3½ hours) via Kushiro-shitsugen (¥360, 20 minutes), Kawayu Onsen (¥1840, 1½ hours) and Shiretoko-Shari (¥2810, 2½ hours).

WORTH A TRIP

ALONG THE JR SENMŌ LINE

Travellers for whom train travel is part of the journey – rather than just a means to get around – will want to experience the JR Senmō line. It travels from Abashiri to Kushiro, passing some stunning scenery along the way: in summer, fields of flowers and the marshes of Kushiro Wetlands National Park (p660); in winter, plains of glistening white snow and the icy sea.

Alight at Gensei-kaen Station for **Koshimizu Gensei-kaen** (小清水原生花園; ☎0152-63-4187; ⏲8.30am-5.30pm May-Sep, 9am-5pm Oct & Apr) FREE, a spectacular 20km stretch of wildflowers along the coast between Abashiri and Shari. Visit in early summer and catch it at its peak, when more than 40 species of flowers bloom.

The line and its stations were constructed in the 1920s and '30s and many original stations remain. Few people actually take the Senmō line because they need to – it's usually only two cars long. Many stations are now unstaffed and have turned their former offices and waiting rooms into charming cafes.

Worth a visit are Orchard Grass, at Kawayu Onsen, and **Teishaba** (停車場; ☎0152-46-2410; Kita-Hama Station; drinks from ¥430, lunch mains ¥750-1200; ⏲11am-7pm Wed-Mon), inside the 90-year-old Kita-Hama Station, one stop west of Gensei-kaen. The latter is decked out to look like a vintage rail car, with wood and burgundy-velour booths and rotating fans overhead. With views of both the Sea of Okhotsk and the trains coming and going, it is an attractive place for a coffee break.

Kushiro-shitsugen National Park

☎0154

Kushiro-shitsugen National Park (釧路湿原国立公園; Kushiro Wetlands National Park), at 269 sq km, is Japan's largest undeveloped wetland. It was designated a national park in 1987 to combat urban sprawl and protect the habitat of numerous species, chiefly the *tanchō-zuru* (red-crowned white crane), the traditional symbol of both longevity and Japan.

In the early 20th century, the cranes were thought to be extinct due to overhunting and habitat destruction. In 1926, however, some 20 birds were discovered in the marshes here; with concentrated conservation efforts, they now number over 1000. Cranes can be seen year-round, but the best time to spot them is during winter when they gather at feeding spots.

Sights & Activities

Rte 53 runs up the park's western fringes. If you have your own wheels, you can explore the park at length, including various viewpoints.

Train-users can ride to JR Kushiro-shitsugen Station, then walk uphill for 15 minutes to the **Hosooka Marsh Viewpoint** (細岡展望台).

Kushiro Japanese Crane Reserve WILDLIFE RESERVE

(釧路市丹頂鶴自然公園, Tanchō-zuru Shizen-kōen; ☎0154-56-2219; www.kushiro-tancho.jp; 112 Tsuruoka; adult/child ¥470/110; ⏲9am-6pm Apr-early Oct, 9am-4pm early Oct-Mar) Run by Kushiro Zoo, this reserve has been instrumental in increasing the crane population. There are currently 14 *tanchō-zuru* living here, though they are free to leave anytime they like (the fences are for people, not the birds).

Akan International Crane Centre 'GRUS' WILDLIFE RESERVE

(阿寒国際ツルセンター【グルス】; ☎0154-66-4011; www.aiccgrus.wixsite.com/aiccgrus; 23-40 Kami-Akan, Akan-chō; adult/child ¥470/240; ⏲9am-5pm Apr-Oct, to 4.30pm Nov-Mar) You can see a few cranes in breeding pens here but the real attraction is the **Crane Observation Centre** (8.30am to 4.30pm November to March), a winter feeding ground that is your best chance to see cranes outside of a bird park. Inside there are lots of interesting photos and some fun exhibits.

Kushiro-shitsugen Norokko Train RAIL

(釧路湿原ノロッコ号; ⏲Jun-Oct) This is the best way to see the wetlands without a car: once or twice daily, a vintage train with large picture windows makes a slow journey from Kushiro via Kushiro-shitsugen (¥360) as far as Tōro Station (¥540). It's very popular so be sure to reserve a seat (plus ¥520). The tourist info booth at Kushiro Station can help.

In February, an old steam locomotive, the Fuyu-shitsugen Norokko Train, plies the same route; it doesn't run every day though and you'll need to book ahead.

Sleeping & Eating

Very few options here; head to Kushiro for more.

★**Kushiro-shitsugen Tōro Youth Hostel** HOSTEL ¥

(釧路湿原とうろユースホステル; ☎0154-87-2510; www.tohro.net; 7 Tōro, Shibecha-chō; dm/s/d from ¥4500/6500/9000, breakfast/dinner ¥600/1000; P) This hostel, run partly on solar power, was designed with birdwatchers in mind. A porch (partly glassed in) looks directly over the marshes and there are binoculars you can borrow. It's also a peaceful place to spend a few days, with good meals (book ahead, there's not much else around) and comfortable dorm rooms.

From May to November, the hostel runs canoe tours and offers a guiding service, while from December to March it offers tours to see the cranes. It's a few minutes' walk from JR Tōro (塘路) Station, two stops north of Kushiro-shitsugen on the JR Senmō line.

Getting There & Around

The JR Senmō main line runs from Kushiro to Kushiro-shitsugen (¥360, 20 minutes), on the east side of the park. From Kushiro-shitsugen, trains continue to Kawayu Onsen, Shiretoko-Shari and Abashiri.

The bus from Kushiro Station to Akanko Onsen stops at the Japanese Crane Reserve (¥910, one hour) and Akan International Crane Centre 'GRUS' (¥1450, 1¼ hours). Both are also along Rte 240, which runs between Kushiro and Akanko Onsen. Buses to Sapporo take 5½ hours and cost ¥5770.

Tokachi

Largely rural Tokachi (十勝) is known throughout Japan for its dairy farms, cattle ranches and vineyards. For travellers, this is mostly a place to pass through, en route to Daisetsuzan National Park or eastern Hokkaidō, though there is some lovely countryside here.

Obihiro (帯広) is the biggest city here and a useful transit hub.

Sleeping

Obihiro has the most options and the most convenient transport links; however, if you're driving, there are some lovely hostels in the countryside, not too far from the main towns.

Toipirka Kitaobihiro Youth Hostel HOSTEL ¥

(トイピルカ北帯広ユースホステル; ☎0155-30-4165; http://toipirka.eco.coocan.jp; N4E52-8 Shimo-Shihoro, Otofuke-chō; dm from ¥3500, breakfast/dinner ¥750/1300; P @) A great place to break for the night is this attractive log house with a hammock on the front porch and cosy sofas around a wood stove in the lounge. The meals, cooked from scratch with no additives, are fantastic. It's near Tokachi-gawa Onsen, a cluster of resort-style onsen and hotels along the Tokachi-gawa, a 15-minute drive east of Obihiro.

If you're coming by public transport, it's a little trickier: take bus 45 for Tokachi-gawa Onsen from stop 6 in front of JR Obihiro Station, alighting at Shimoshihoro Shōgakō (下士幌小学校前; 20 minutes). If you ring ahead, the hostel owners will pick you up at the bus stop. Note that buses only run eight times a day.

Ikeda Kita-no-Kotan Youth Hostel HOSTEL ¥

(池田北のコタンユースホステル; ☎0155-72-3666; www11.plala.or.jp/kitanokotan; 99-4 Toshibetsu Nishimachi; dm with/without 2 meals from ¥5600/3870; P) Friendly management and delicious dinners, including a complimentary glass of local wine (for dinner guests only), make Ikeda Kita-no-Kotan Youth Hostel a real treat. The hostel is a five-minute walk from JR Toshibetsu Station, one stop west of Ikeda (¥210, five minutes) on the JR Nemuro line.

Note that the hostel is closed sporadically between November and June. Reservations are thus required so you'll be sure to catch them when they're open.

Getting There & Away

Obihiro, which has **Tokachi Obihiro Airport** (十勝帯広空港; ☎0155-64-5320; www.tokachiobihiro-airport.jp; W9 Chūō 8-41, Izumi-chō) nearby, is the main transit hub for the region.

JR Limited Express Super Tokachi Liner and Super Ōzora Liner trains connect Sapporo and Obihiro (¥6700, 2¾ hours, 11 daily); Super Ōzora Liner trains continue from Obihiro to Kushiro (¥4810, 1½ hours, six daily). Obihiro and Ikeda are also stops on the JR Nemuro main line, running between northern Hokkaidō and the far eastern tip in Nemuro.

Car rentals from most major companies are available in Obihiro or at Tokachi Obihiro Airport.

AT A GLANCE

POPULATION
Matsuyama: 507,000

LONGEST RIVER
Shimanto-gawa (196km; p691)

BEST SURF TOWN
Ikumi (p678)

BEST RURAL STAY
Chiiori (p684)

BEST LOCAL MARKET
Hirome Ichiba (p689)

WHEN TO GO

Apr Enlightenment may know no weather, but any pilgrimage is best taken in spring.

Jul–Sep Rivers are running, surf is rolling, and the sun is, well, shining.

Aug Join every man, woman and child for Awa-odori Matsuri, Japan's wildest dance party.

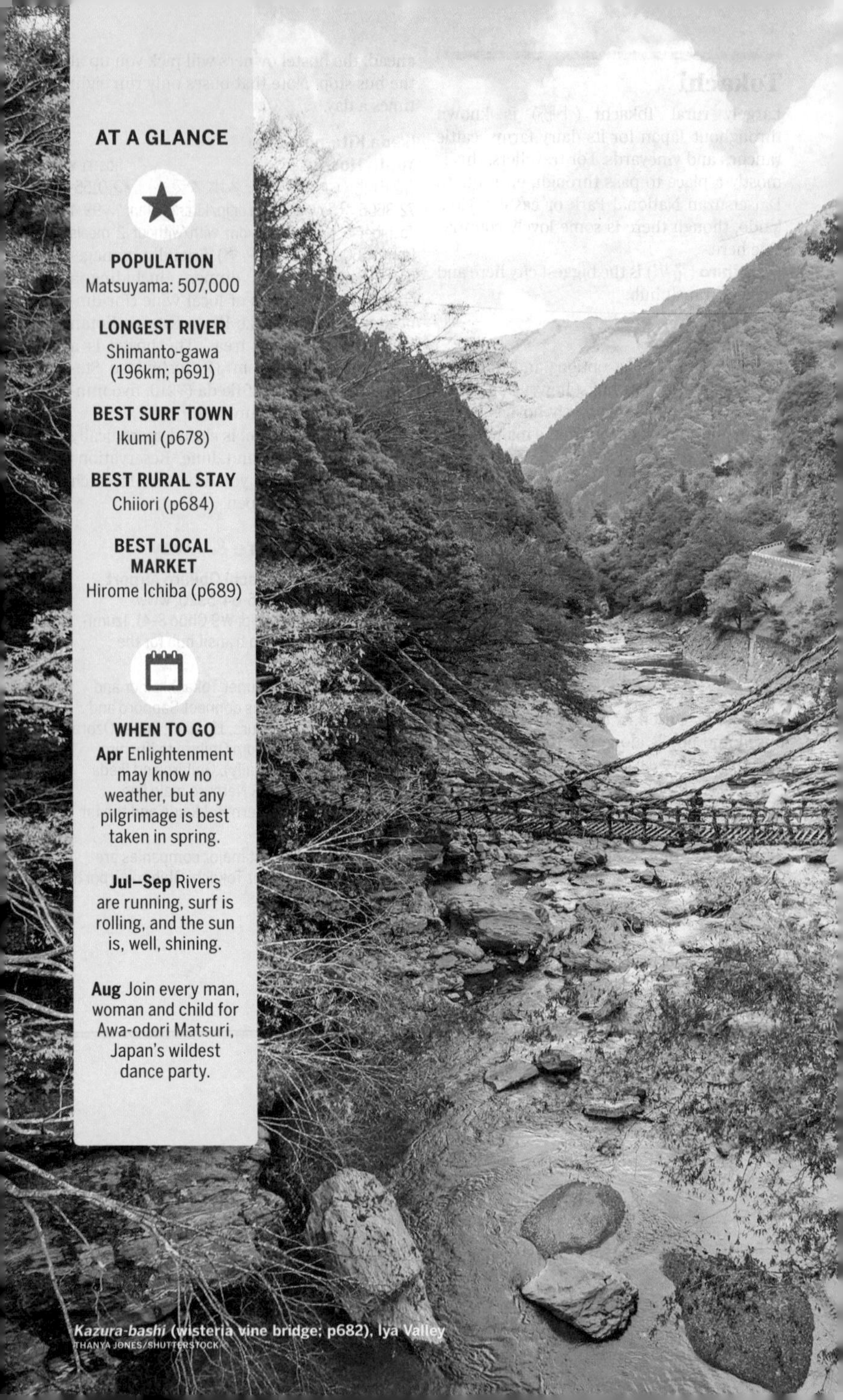

Kazura-bashi (wisteria vine bridge; p682), Iya Valley
THANYA JONES/SHUTTERSTOCK ©

Shikoku

The birthplace of revered ascetic and founder of the Shingon Buddhist sect Kōbō Daishi (774–835), Shikoku (四国) is synonymous with natural beauty and the pursuit of spiritual perfection. It's home to the 88 Sacred Temples of Shikoku, Japan's most famous pilgrimage. In Japan's feudal past, the island was divided into four regions; hence the name *shi* (four) and *koku* (region). Considered remote and isolated for centuries, Shikoku is now easy to access from Honshū via three impressive bridge systems built in the last three decades.

The island's stunning Iya Valley, rugged Pacific coastline, mountain ranges and gorgeous free-flowing rivers all beckon to be explored with hiking boots, kayaks, surfboards and your own earthly vessel.

INCLUDES

Shikoku Highlights

❶ 88 Temple Pilgrimage (p667) Walking the time-worn route.

❷ Muroto-misaki (p679) Finding seclusion, if not enlightenment, like Kōbō Daishi did.

❸ Ishizuchi-san (p697) Hiking up the sacred mountain, one of Japan's most gripping ascents.

❹ Iya Valley (p680) Picking your way across swaying vine bridges in gorgeous isolation.

❺ Dōgo Onsen (p693) Soaking in the venerable waters of the historic onsen in the castle-town metropolis of Matsuyama.

❻ Konpira-san (p708) Trekking up 1368 stone steps to pay homage to the god of seafarers.

❼ Ritsurin-kōen (p702) Walking off Japan's most famous udon with a stroll through Takamatsu's exquisite Edo-period garden.

❽ Tairyū-ji Ropeway (p680) Riding the spectacular ropeway up to mountaintop Temple 21 of the 88 Sacred Temples.

❾ Naruto (p675) Marvelling at the vitality of the whirlpools from close up while aboard a sightseeing boat.

❿ Ōkinohama (p688) Surfing beautiful swells or relaxing on the beach.

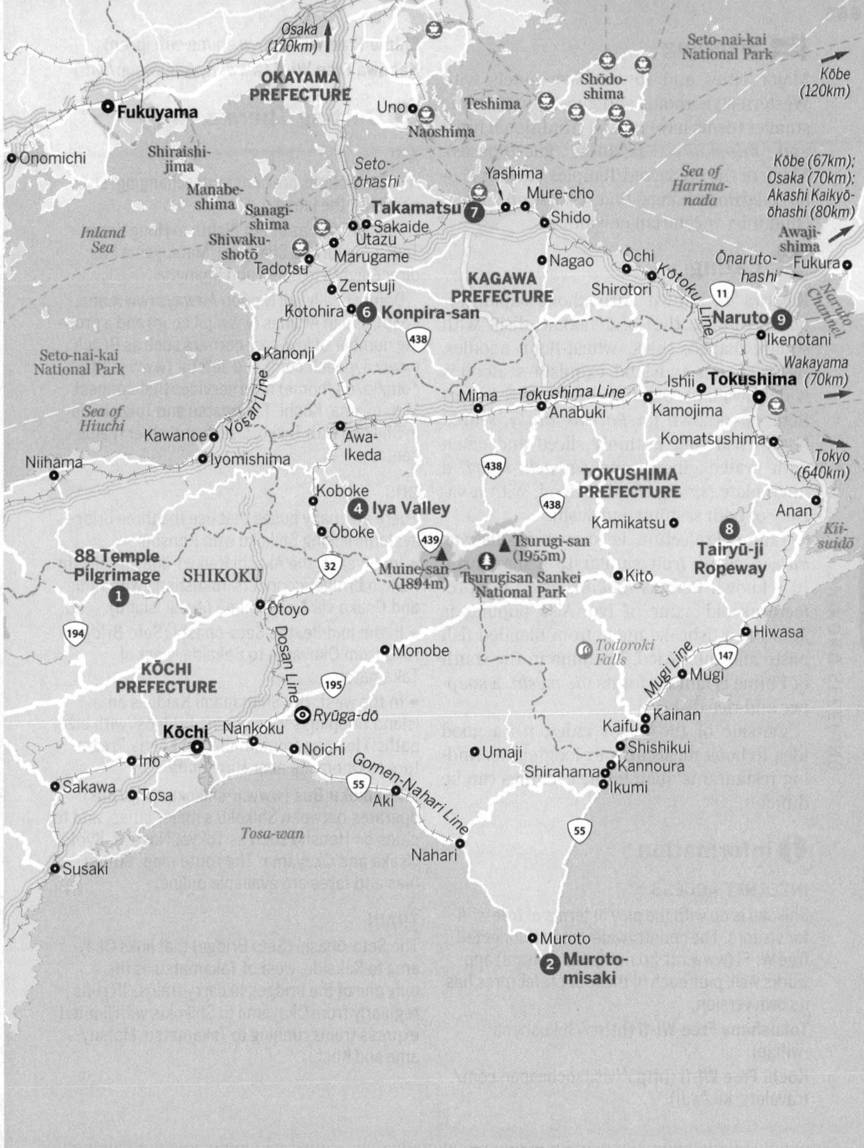
Osaka (170km)
OKAYAMA PREFECTURE
Fukuyama
Onomichi
Shiraishi-jima
Manabe-shima
Sanagi-shima
Shiwaku-shotō
Inland Sea
Tadotsu
Seto-ōhashi
Uno
Naoshima
Teshima
Shōdo-shima
Seto-nai-kai National Park
Kōbe (120km)
Kōbe (67km); Osaka (70km); Akashi Kaikyō-ōhashi (80km)
Sea of Harima-nada
Yashima
Mure-cho
Takamatsu
7
Shido
Sakaide
Utazu
Marugame
Zentsuji
Kotohira
6
Konpira-san
Nagao
KAGAWA PREFECTURE
Ōchi
Kōtoku Line
Shirotori
Awaji-shima
Ōnaruto-hashi
Fukura
Naruto Channel
11
Naruto
9
Ikenotani
438
Kanonji
Seto-nai-kai National Park
Yosan Line
Sea of Hiuchi
Kawanoe
Iyomishima
Niihama
Awa-Ikeda
Mima
Tokushima Line
Anabuki
Ishii
Tokushima
Wakayama (70km)
Kamojima
Komatsushima
Tokyo (640km)
Koboke
4
Iya Valley
Ōboke
TOKUSHIMA PREFECTURE
Kamikatsu
Anan
8
Tairyū-ji Ropeway
Kii-suidō
439
Tsurugi-san (1955m)
Muine-san (1894m)
Tsurugisan Sankei National Park
Kitō
32
88 Temple Pilgrimage
1
SHIKOKU
Ōtoyo
194
Dosan Line
Monobe
Todoroki Falls
Hiwasa
147
Mugi Line
Mugi
KŌCHI PREFECTURE
195
Ryūga-dō
Kainan
Kaifu
Kōchi
Nankoku
Noichi
Umaji
Shishikui
Kannoura
Shirahama
Ikumi
Ino
Sakawa
Tosa
55
Aki
Gomen-Nahari Line
Tosa-wan
Nahari
Susaki
Muroto
2
Muroto-misaki
PACIFIC OCEAN
N
0
50 km
0
25 miles

Sleeping

Major cities and towns have hotels with Western-style rooms and guesthouses, while smaller towns have ryokan (traditional inns) and *minshuku* (Japanese guesthouses). Many of the 88 Sacred Temples have *shukubō* (pilgrim lodgings) that serve *shōjin-ryōri* (Buddhist vegetarian cuisine).

Eating

Kagawa is known throughout Japan for *Sanuki-udon,* the local noodle dish, with square-shaped, thick, wheat-flour noodles. As Shikoku is an island, exquisite seafood is widely available too. Kōchi Prefecture in particular is known for *katsuo-tataki*, seared bonito fish that is thinly sliced and eaten with grated ginger; and *sawachi-ryōri,* a huge plate *(sawachi)* of seafood, with a variety of both sashimi and sushi.

Ehime Prefecture is known for its *mikan,* a citrus fruit similar to a mandarin. It is known here as *Iyokan,* using the prefecture's old name of Iyo. Also popular is *jakoten,* a fishcake made from blended fish paste and then fried. Uwajima in the south of Ehime is famous for its *tai-meshi,* a snapper and rice dish.

Outside of the major cities, it's a good idea to book meals at your lodgings as finding restaurants open in the evenings can be difficult.

Information

INTERNET ACCESS

Shikoku is up with the play in terms of free wi-fi for visitors. The countrywide Japan Connected-free Wi-Fi (www.ntt-bp.net/jcfw/en.html) app works well, plus each of the four prefectures has its own version.

Tokushima Free Wi-fi (http://tokushima-wifi.jp)

Kōchi Free Wi-fi (http://visitkochijapan.com/travelers_kit/wifi)

Ehime Free Wi-fi (www.ehime-wifi.jp/en)

Kagawa Free Wi-fi (www.my-kagawa.jp/wifi)

Getting There & Away

AIR

Air connections are constantly changing, so check for the latest.

Takamatsu has direct flights to Hong Kong, Taipei, Seoul and Shanghai; Matsuyama has direct flights to Seoul and Shanghai.

Domestically, All Nippon Airways (www.ana.co.jp), Japan Airlines (www.jal.co.jp) and a growing number of low-cost carriers such as Peach (www.flypeach.com) and Jetstar (www.jetstar.com/jp/en/home) have services that connect Matsuyama, Kōchi, Takamatsu and Tokushima in Shikoku with Tokyo, Osaka and other major centres.

BUS

There are many buses that use the three bridge systems linking Shikoku with Honshū.

- In the east, the Akashi Kaikyō-ōhashi (Akashi Kaikyō bridge) connects Tokushima with Kōbe and Osaka via Awaji-shima (Awaji Island).
- In the middle, the Seto-ōhashi (Seto Bridge) runs from Okayama to Sakaide, west of Takamatsu.
- In the west, the Shimanami Kaidō is an island-hopping series of nine bridges (with bike paths!) leading from Imabari in Ehime Prefecture to Onomichi near Hiroshima.

JR Shikoku Bus (www.jr-shikoku.co.jp/bus) operates between Shikoku's major cities, and to cities on Honshū such as Tokyo, Nagoya, Kyoto, Osaka and Okayama. The route map, timetables and fares are available online.

TRAIN

The Seto-ōhashi (Seto Bridge) that links Okayama to Sakaide, west of Takamatsu, is the only one of the bridges to carry trains. JR runs regularly from Okayama to Shikoku, with limited express trains running to Takamatsu, Matsuyama and Kōchi.

FERRIES TO SHIKOKU

Numerous ferry routes link Shikoku to destinations in Kansai, Western Honshū, Kyūshū and even Tokyo.

DEPARTING FROM	DESTINATIONS
Tokushima (p674)	Wakayama, Kita-Kyūshū and Tokyo
Matsuyama (p697)	Hiroshima, Kita-Kyūshū
Yawatahama (p699; south of Matsuyama)	Beppu and Usuki on Kyūshū
Takamatsu (p704)	Kōbe, Naoshima and Uno (in Okayama Prefecture)

WALKING THE 88 TEMPLE PILGRIMAGE

The *henro* (pilgrim on the 88 Temple walk) is one of the most distinctive sights of any trip to Shikoku. They're everywhere you go, striding along busy city highways, cresting hills in remote mountain valleys – solitary figures in white, trudging purposefully through heat haze and downpour alike on their way from temple to temple. Who are these people and what drives them to make a journey of more than 1400km on foot?

Although the backgrounds and motives of the *henro* may differ widely, they all follow in the legendary footsteps of Kōbō Daishi, the monk who attained enlightenment on Shikoku, established Shingon Buddhism in Japan and made significant contributions to Japanese culture. Whether or not it is true that Kōbō Daishi actually founded or visited all 88 sacred sites, the idea behind making the 88 Temple Circuit (map p872) is to do so accompanied by the spirit of Kōbō Daishi himself – hence the inscription on pilgrims' backpacks and other paraphernalia: 同行二人 *(dōgyō ninin)*, meaning 'two people on the same journey'.

Regardless of motivation of each *henro*, the pattern and routine of life on the road is very similar for everyone who undertakes the trail. The dress is uniform, too: *hakue* (white garments) to signify sincerity of purpose and purity of mind; the *sugegasa* (straw hat) that has protected pilgrims against sun and rain since time immemorial; and the *kongōzue* (colourful staff). The routine at each temple is mostly the same, too: a bang on the bell and a chant of the Heart Sutra at the Daishi-dō (one of the two main buildings in each temple compound), before filing off to the *nōkyō-jo* (desk), where the pilgrims' book is inscribed with beautiful characters detailing the name of the temple and the date of the pilgrimage.

If you're eager to become an *aruki henro* (walking pilgrim), you'll need to budget 40 to 60 days (allowing for an average distance of 25km a day) to complete the circuit. To plan your pilgrimage, the website www.shikokuhenrotrail.com and the guidebook *Shikoku Japan 88 Route Guide* (Buyodo Publishing) are both excellent English-language resources. The book, plus all the *henro* gear you'll need for your walk, can be purchased at Temple One: Ryōzen-ji (p675). For brilliant background reading on the pilgrimage, get a copy of *Japanese Pilgrimage*, by Oliver Statler, and for ideas on innovative sleeping spots, download Craig McLachlan's *Tales of a Summer Henro*.

Travellers who don't have the time or inclination to attempt the whole thing can get a taste of what it's all about by following one of the *henro*-for-a-day minicircuits. Aside from walking the first few temples at Naruto (p676), cities with concentrations of temples within easy reach of each other include Matsuyama (p692), Temples 46 through 53, and Zentsūji (p707), in Kagawa Prefecture.

If you're keen to do the pilgrimage, but walking doesn't appeal, take into account that most pilgrims these days travel around the 88 Temples on tour buses, in taxis or cars, on motorbikes or bicycles. It's making an effort that counts!

Getting Around

BUS

Buses link major Shikoku cities and reach points that trains don't get to, but times and connections can be difficult, especially in remote areas.

CAR & MOTORCYCLE

Shikoku is perfect for a road trip. Highlights such as the Iya Valley, the southern capes of Muroto-misaki and Ashizuri-misaki, and many of the 88 Temples have no train lines and tricky bus connections, so a car can make it a lot easier to see what Shikoku has to offer, especially with limited time.

Rent a car and head out on a voyage of exploration. You may also consider driving to Shikoku over one of the three bridge systems or putting your rental car on a ferry to get there.

A 'Car Pilgrimage' around the 88 Temples is perfectly feasible in 15 to 20 days. Navigation is easy – just enter the next temple's phone number in your English-speaking satnav and you'll be led right there.

Toyota Rent a Car (https://rent.toyota.co.jp/eng) Has offices in all four Shikoku prefectures.

Nissan Rent a Car (https://nissan-rentacar.com/english) In Shikoku's four major cities and airports.

TRAIN

Trains link all Shikoku's major cities, but do not reach as far as the southern capes of Muroto-misaki and Ashizuri-misaki or into the island's mountainous interior.

JR Shikoku offers an All Shikoku Pass. The options are all ¥500 cheaper when purchased outside of Japan. Passes can be bought after arrival on Shikoku, and besides unlimited use of JR trains, also offer discounts on a number of ferry and bus lines.

TOKUSHIMA PREFECTURE

The starting point for pilgrims over the past 1200 years, Tokushima Prefecture (徳島県), formerly known as Awa, is home to the first 23 of Shikoku's 88 Sacred Temples. Ryōzen-ji is Temple One as it is the first temple pilgrims came to after visiting Kōya-san in Wakayama Prefecture and asking for Kōbō Daishi's support on their journey. To *henro* (pilgrims), Tokushima is known as *Hosshin-no-dōjō*, the 'place to determine to achieve enlightenment'. If you haven't got time to walk the 88, the first five temples sit in an east–west line spanning about 15km to the north of the Yoshino River and make a worthy mini-pilgrimage.

These days, notable attractions of the prefecture include the lively Awa-odori Matsuri, which takes place in Tokushima in August; the mighty whirlpools of the Naruto Channel between Shikoku and Awaji-shima; the surf beaches of the Anan Coast (阿南海岸; Anan-kaigan) to the south; and the onsen and gorges of the remote Iya Valley.

Check out www.discovertokushima.net for information on the area.

Tokushima

088 / POP 270,000

With Mt Bizan looming in the southwest, and the Shinmachi-gawa cutting a gentle swath through the middle, bustling Tokushima city (徳島) is its prefecture's pleasant capital. With a number of nearby temples, the city makes a solid starting point for 88 Temple pilgrims. It's a modern, regional city with plenty going on between JR Tokushima Station in the city centre and the Bizan ropeway station.

In the southern part of the city, Bunka-no-mori-kōen is a great option for rainy days, as the complex houses several museums, including the Tokushima Modern Art Museum, the Tokushima Prefectural Museum and the prefectural library.

Every August, the Awa-odori Matsuri, a traditional dance festival, attracts thousands of Japanese visitors from across the country. Book accommodation well ahead and expect to pay a premium if you're visiting during this time.

Sights

★Bizan MOUNTAIN

(眉山) At the foot of Bizan, the 280m-high summit at the southwestern end of Shinmachibashi-dōri, the **Bizan Ropeway** (088-652-3617; one way/return ¥610/1020; 9am-5.30pm Nov-Mar, to 9pm Apr-Oct & during special events) whizzes you to the top for fine city views. A combined ticket for the cable car, museum and dance show at the Awa Odori Kaikan costs ¥1620.

Awa Odori Kaikan MUSEUM

(阿波おどり会館; 088-611-1611; www.awaodori-kaikan.jp; 2-20 Shinmachibashi; 9am-5pm, closed 2nd & 4th Wed of month) FREE Awa Odori Kaikan features extensive exhibits relating to the Awa-odori Matsuri (p670) and dance. The dance is performed for visitors at 2pm, 3pm and 4pm daily (and also at 11am on weekends), with a nightly performance at 8pm (afternoon/evening ¥600/800). From the 5th floor, a cable car whizzes you to the top of Bizan for fine city views. There's also a small Tourist Information Office with rental bicycles on the ground floor.

Chūō-kōen PARK

(中央公園) Northeast of the train station is Tokushima's central park, Chūō-kōen, a lovely place for a stroll. You'll find the scant ruins of **Tokushima-jō** (Tokushima Castle) and the beautiful **Senshūkaku-teien** (千秋閣庭園; ¥50, incl in museum ticket), an intimate 16th-century garden featuring rock bridges and secluded ponds. Get a glimpse into the castle's former grandeur at **Tokushima Castle Museum** (徳島城博物館; 088-656-2525; www.city.tokushima.tokushima.jp/johaku; 1-8 Jōnai; ¥300; 9.30am-5pm Tue-Sun), whose structure is based on the original castle's architecture and location. The museum contains a model of the castle town at its peak as well as artefacts.

Awa Jūrobe Yashiki Puppet Theatre THEATRE

(阿波十郎兵衛屋敷; 088-665-2202; www.joruri.info/jurobe; 184 Miyajima Motoura, Kawauchi-chō; ¥410; 9.30am-5pm, to 6pm Jul & Aug) For hundreds of years, puppet theatre thrived in the farming communities around Tokushima. Performances can still be seen here, in the former residence of Bandō Jūrobe, a samurai who allowed himself to be executed for a crime he didn't commit in order to preserve the good name of his

Tokushima

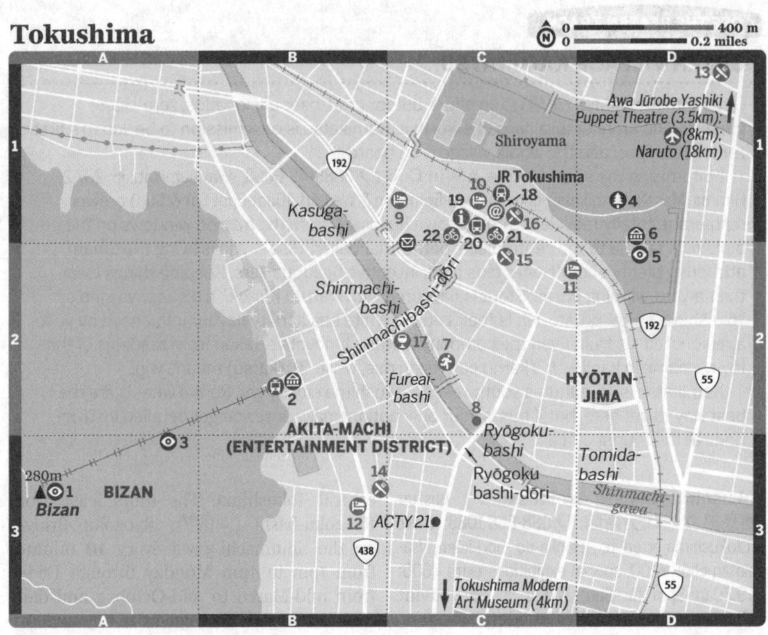

Tokushima

Top Sights
1 Bizan A3

Sights
2 Awa Odori Kaikan B2
3 Bizan Ropeway A3
4 Chūō-kōen D1
5 Senshūkaku-teien D2
6 Tokushima Castle Museum D1

Activities, Courses & Tours
7 Funride Tokushima C2
8 Hyōtan-jima Boats C2

Sleeping
9 Agnes Hotel Tokushima C1
10 Hotel Clement Tokushima C1
11 Sakura-sō C2
12 Tokushima Washington Hotel Plaza B3

Eating
13 Izakaya Ikiiki D1
14 Otona-no-Izakaya Kagoya-Tarō Kamuan B3
15 Tokushima Ramen Men Ō C2
16 Tokushima Station Bar Alley C1

Drinking & Nightlife
17 Awa Shinmachigawa Brewery C2

Information
18 Tokushima Prefecture International Exchange Association C1
19 Tourist Information Office C1

Transport
20 Bus Terminal C1
21 Rental Bicycles C1
22 Rental Electric-Assist Bicycle C1

master. The tale inspired the drama *Keisei Awa no Naruto*, first performed in 1768. Sections from the play are performed at 11am and 2pm daily.

To get to the museum, take a bus for Tomiyoshi Danchi (富吉団地) from bus stop 7 at Tokushima bus terminal and get off at the Jūrobe Yashiki-mae stop (¥270, 25 minutes). More puppets can be seen at the nearby **Awa Deko Ningyō Kaikan** (阿波木偶人形会館; Awa Puppet Hall; ☎088-665-5600; www3.tcn.ne.jp/~awadekoningyokk/top.html; 1-226 Miyajima Motoura, Kawauchi-chō; ¥400; ⏲9am-5pm, closed 1st & 3rd Mon of month). This small museum displays puppets made by the in-house master, who also gives talks (in Japanese) on the puppet-making process.

OFF THE BEATEN TRACK

GREEN VILLAGE KAMIKATSU

Getting to Kamikatsu (上勝) is an effort, but for craft-beer aficionados, zero-waste greenies and architectural fans, it's worth it. Kamikatsu is on a mission to be Japan's first zero-waste town and the whole village is on board.

Epitomising the effort is **Rise & Win Co's** (☎0885-45-0688; www.kamikatz.jp; 237-2 Hirama, Masaki, Kamikatsu-chō; ⊙11am-5pm Mon & Wed-Fri, 10am-6pm Sat & Sun) brewery restaurant, totally recycled from old town buildings, from the framed windows on the building's facade to the centrepiece 'bottle chandelier'. Rise & Win is living the dream, attracting plenty of craft-beer fans to its inventive headquarters. Keeping things local, their award-winning Porter Stout is flavoured with *Naruto Kintoki*, a distinctive kind of Tokushima sweet potato, while their Leuven White has a fruity flavour influenced by *yuko*, a regional citrus fruit. Even the company name is innovative, taken from readings of the town's name in kanji – 上 (kami) can mean rise, while 勝 (katsu) means win.

Kamikatsu is 45 minutes southwest of Tokushima city by car. Rental wheels are the best way to get here, but if bus is your only option, make sure you get detailed instructions at the tourist office.

Tokushima Modern Art Museum MUSEUM
(徳島県立近代美術館; ☎088-668-1088; www.art.tokushima-ec.ed.jp; Bunka-no-mori-kōen, Hachiman-chō; ¥200, special exhibitions extra ¥600; ⊙9.30am-5pm Tue-Sun) With a permanent collection that includes modern masters, both Japanese and Western, this surprisingly sophisticated prefectural museum houses two- and three-dimensional art by Picasso and Klee as well as by Kaburagi and Seishi. It is particularly interesting to compare the more familiar European works to their Japanese counterparts, especially the pieces reflecting Japan's postwar identity; the fusion of traditional and Western-influenced styles embodies the zeitgeist of the period.

Activities

★Funride Tokushima WATER SPORTS
(ファンライド徳島; ☎090-9772-7588; www.funride-tokushima.com; 3-18 Minami-uchi-machi; introductory paddle ¥4000) A very cool way to spend time in Tokushima is stand-up paddleboarding on the Shinmachi-gawa with Nanri-san at Funride Tokushima. This is flat-water SUP right in the middle of the city – a one-hour introduction costs ¥4000, including equipment, while if you're keen, there's a 2½-hour trip around Hyotanjima, the island that central Tokushima is built on.

Tours

Hyōtan-jima Boats BOATING
(ひょうたん島周遊船; ☎090-3783-2084; tours ¥200) Take the boat cruise around 'gourd-shaped' Hyōtan-jima (Hyōtan Island) in central Tokushima. The tours leave from Ryōgoku-bashi (両国橋; Ryōgoku Bridge) on the Shinmachi-gawa every 40 minutes from 1pm to 4pm Monday through Friday from mid-March to mid-October, and daily from 20 July to 31 August. In July and August there are additional departures every 40 minutes from 5pm to 8pm.

Festivals & Events

★Awa-odori Matsuri DANCE
(阿波踊り; ⊙12-15 Aug) The Awa-odori is the largest *bon* dance in Japan. Each evening men, women and children take to the streets to dance to the samba-like rhythm of the theme song 'Awa Yoshikono', accompanied by the sounds of *shamisen* (three-stringed guitars), *taiko* (drums) and *fue* (flutes). More than a million people turn up every year.

Sleeping

★Sakura-sō MINSHUKU ¥
(さくら荘; ☎088-652-9575; 1-25 Terashima-honchō-higashi; s/d without bathroom ¥3300/6000; ❄📶) The delightful owner readily welcomes foreigners to her charming place, which has a dozen large, good-value tatami rooms. There's free wi-fi, laundry facilities, parking and baggage storage at this budget bonanza right opposite the tracks, a few blocks east of the train station, just before the NHK TV tower. Get someone to call and book for you.

No English signage; look for the signage さくら荘.

★Agnes Hotel Tokushima
BOUTIQUE HOTEL ¥¥

(アグネスホテル徳島; ☎088-626-2222; www.agneshotel.jp; 1-28 Terashima-honchō-nishi; s/d from ¥7500/12,000; P⊖❄📶) Hip little Agnes lies 200m west of the station and offers a more sophisticated aesthetic than the usual business hotel. Rooms are sleek, with stylish interiors; the casual-yet-smart cafe is open all day; and the 'pastry boutique' is a destination in its own right.

Tokushima Washington Hotel Plaza
HOTEL ¥¥

(徳島ワシントンホテルプラザ; ☎088-653-7111; www.washingtonhotel.co.jp; 1-61-1 Ōmichi; s/tw from ¥5000/7000; P⊖❄📶) The Tokushima branch of this big nationwide chain is surprisingly friendly. The rooms are a decent size, the complimentary breakfast features freshly baked bread, soup and salt-flavoured boiled eggs, and there's take-out coffee at breakfast. It's convenient for the entertainment district with bars and restaurants only a short stroll away.

★Hotel Clement Tokushima
HOTEL ¥¥¥

(ホテルクレメント徳島; ☎088-656-3111; www.jrclement.co.jp/tokushima; 1-61 Terashima-honchō-nishi; s/d from ¥11,000/15,000; P⊖❄📶) Part of Tokushima Station building, the luxurious Hotel Clement boasts 18 floors and 250 comfortable, spacious, Western-style rooms. Although it's more expensive than other business hotels, it's the top hotel in town and the extra yen buys you a slew of amenities including a spa and a range of restaurants and bars.

Eating & Drinking

Options abound in the streets around JR Tokushima Station and in the station building itself. Head across the Shinmachi-gawa to Akita-machi for more choice.

★Tokushima Station Bar Alley
FOOD HALL ¥

(徳島駅バル横丁; www.clementplaza.com/floorguide/b1; ⏲11am-11pm) Definitely the hottest eating and drinking spot in Tokushima is downstairs in the Clement Plaza building, under the station. New in 2018 is Bar Alley, with nine impressive places offering set meals for lunch, then transforming into bar-type restaurants in the evening. There's everything from Ikinari Steak, Otokomae Kara-age chicken to an outlet of Awa Beer. Extremely popular with locals.

★Otona-no-Izakaya Kagoya-Tarō Kamuan
IZAKAYA ¥

(おとなの居酒屋　籠や太郎可夢庵; ☎088-602-1755; 2-15-1 Kagoya-machi; dishes from ¥400; ⏲6-11pm Mon-Sat) There aren't many nonsmoking *izakaya* out there! This place, up the white stairs almost at the end of the arcade, offers a smoke-free environment, healthy menu options and *nomi-kurabe* (compare the taste) sets of local sake. The name '*otona-no-izakaya*' means a 'pub for mature thinkers' – it's not a place for a raucous night out, but a relaxed spot for good food and drink.

Tokushima Ramen Men Ō
RAMEN ¥

(徳島ラーメン麺王; ☎088-623-4116; www.7-men.com; 3-6 Terashima-Honchō-higashi; dishes from ¥500; ⏲11am-midnight) There are about 20 seats in this Tokushima classic only a couple of minutes' walk from the station. Right outside the front door is a machine with the menu and photos of each dish – pick what looks good, put the appropriate amount of money in and pass over your ticket inside. Look for the red awning and lantern.

Izakaya Ikiiki
IZAKAYA

(活意気; ☎088-635-7130; www.hansyudokoro-ikiiki.com; 1-2-5 Minami-jōsanjima-chō; plates from ¥400; ⏲11.30am-2.30pm & 6pm-2am Mon-Sat, 5pm to midnight Sun) This slick little *izakaya* is well worth the adventure of having to battle Japanese-only menus. Just past the northeast corner of the park, Ikiiki has friendly, helpful staff, fresh seafood, and best of all, tasting trays of Tokushima-made sake – *nomi-kurabe*trays with three varieties for ¥900 each.

★Awa Shinmachigawa Brewery
MICROBREWERY

(麦酒工房Awa新町川ブリュワリー; ☎088-653-2271; www.awa-mugishu.com; 1-6 Higashi-senbachō; ⏲5pm-midnight Tue-Fri, from midday Sat & Sun) Head to this relaxed spot down by the river to try a few local brews such as the pale ale, stout and bitter. There's indoor and outdoor seating, plenty of eating options and a convivial atmosphere. A *nomi-kurabe* tasting set of three beers will set you back ¥800, while if you're in the mood, you can sample a beer cocktail.

88 Temples of Shikoku

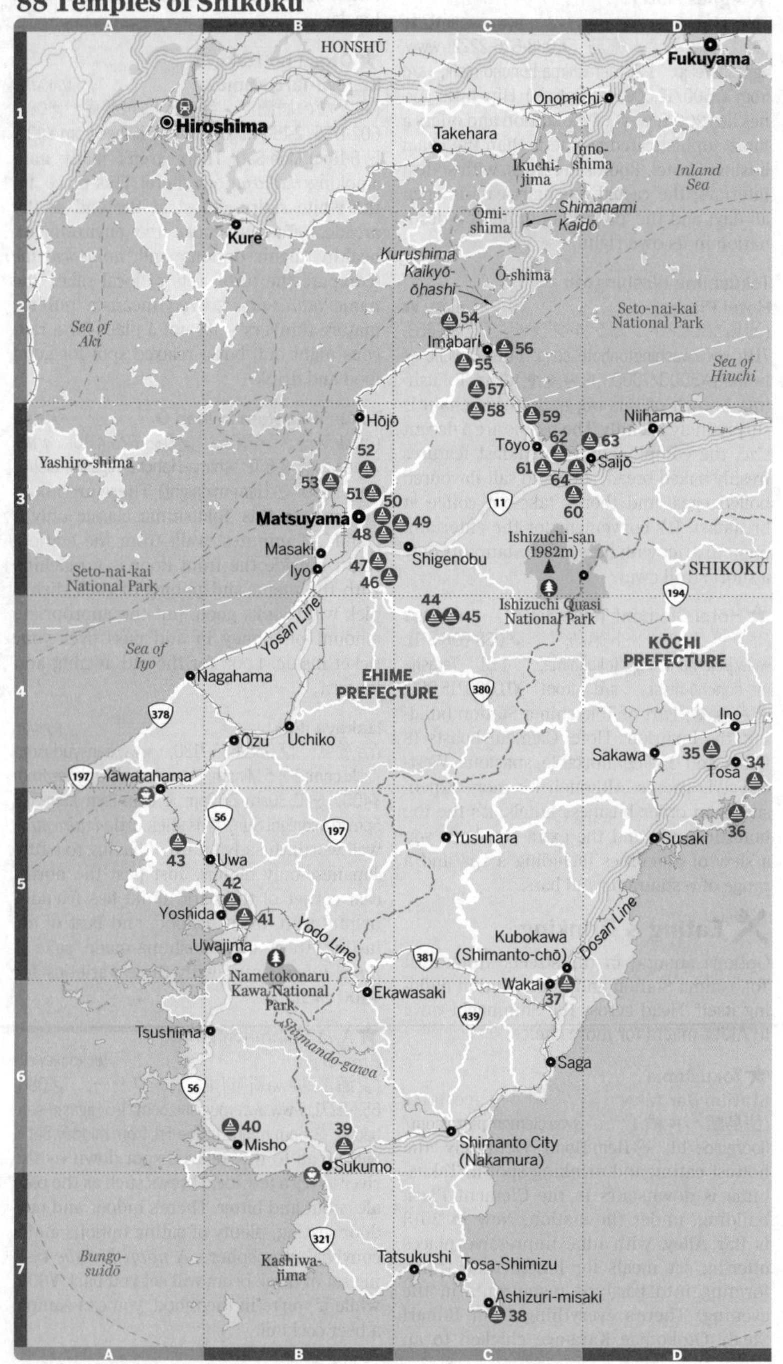

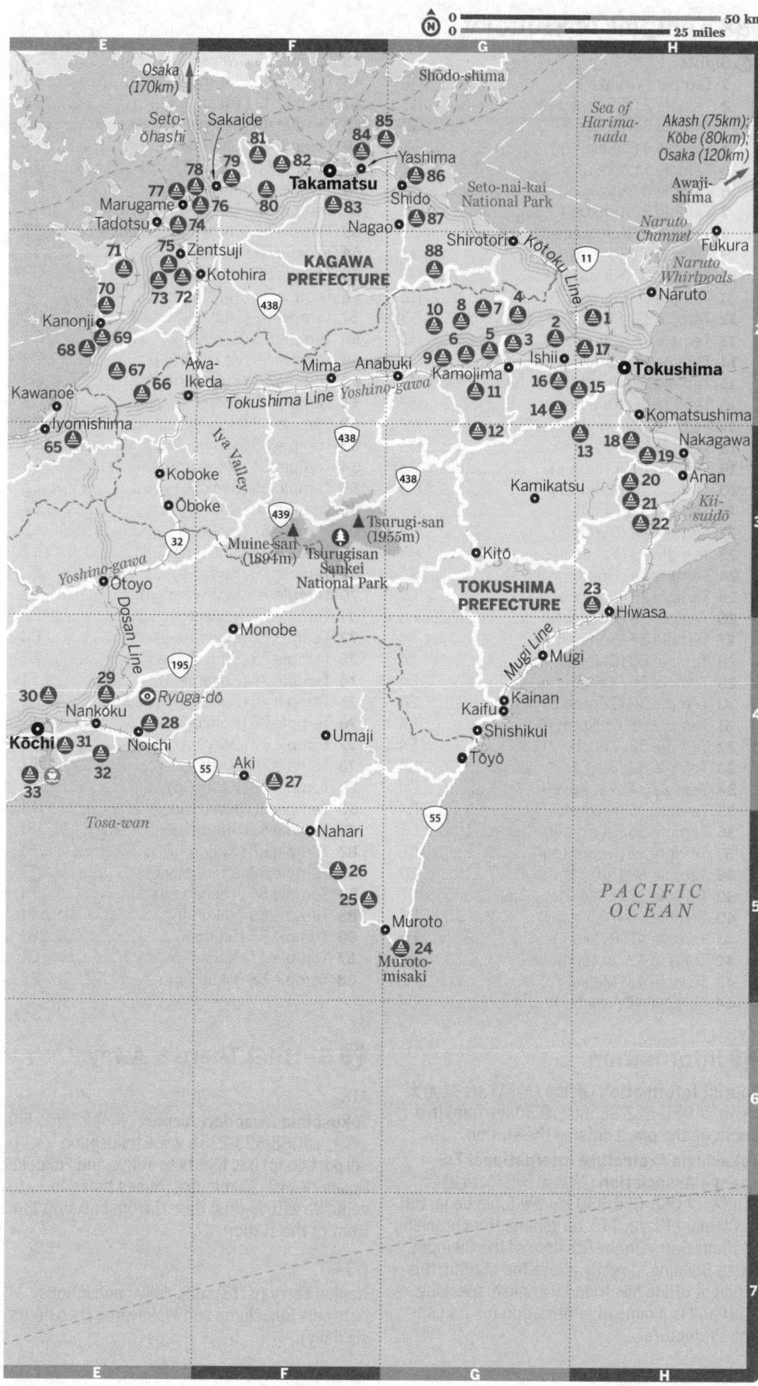
0 50 km
0 25 miles
Osaka (170km)
Shōdo-shima
Sea of Harima-nada
Akash (75km); Kōbe (80km); Osaka (120km)
Seto-ōhashi
Sakaide
Yashima
Takamatsu
Marugame
Tadotsu
Shido
Nagao
Seto-nai-kai National Park
Awaji-shima
Naruto Channel
Fukura
Naruto Whirlpools
Naruto
Zentsuji
Kotohira
KAGAWA PREFECTURE
Shirotori
Kōtoku Line
Kanonji
Awa-Ikeda
Mima
Anabuki
Kamojima
Ishii
Tokushima
Kawanoe
Iyomishima
Tokushima Line
Yoshino-gawa
Iya Valley
Komatsushima
Nakagawa
Anan
Koboke
Ōboke
Kamikatsu
Kii-suidō
Tsurugi-san (1955m)
Muine-san (1894m)
Tsurugisan Sankei National Park
Kitō
Yoshino-gawa
Ōtoyo
Dosan Line
TOKUSHIMA PREFECTURE
Hiwasa
Monobe
Mugi Line
Mugi
Ryūga-dō
Nankoku
Kainan
Kaifu
Kōchi
Noichi
Umaji
Shishikui
Tōyō
Aki
Tosa-wan
Nahari
PACIFIC OCEAN
Muroto
Muroto-misaki
SHIKOKU

88 Temples of Shikoku

Sights

1 Temple 1 (Ryōzen-ji) H2
2 Temple 2 (Gokuraku-ji) G2
3 Temple 3 (Konsen-ji) G2
4 Temple 4 (Dainichi-ji) G2
5 Temple 5 (Jizō-ji) G2
6 Temple 6 (Anraku-ji) G2
7 Temple 7 (Jūraku-ji) G2
8 Temple 8 (Kumadani-ji) G2
9 Temple 9 (Hōrin-ji) G2
10 Temple 10 (Kirihata-ji) G2
11 Temple 11 (Fujii-dera) G2
12 Temple 12 (Shōzan-ji) G3
13 Temple 13 (Dainichi-ji) H3
14 Temple 14 (Jōraku-ji) G2
15 Temple 15 (Kokubun-ji) H2
16 Temple 16 (Kannon-ji) G2
17 Temple 17 (Ido-ji) H2
18 Temple 18 (Onzan-ji) H3
19 Temple 19 (Tatsue-ji) H3
20 Temple 20 (Kakurin-ji) H3
21 Temple 21 (Tairyū-ji) H3
22 Temple 22 (Byōdō-ji) H3
23 Temple 23 (Yakuō-ji) H3
24 Temple 24 (Hotsumisaki-ji) G5
25 Temple 25 (Shinshō-ji) F5
26 Temple 26 (Kongōchō-ji) F5
27 Temple 27 (Kōnomine-ji) F4
28 Temple 28 (Dainichi-ji) E4
29 Temple 29 (Kokubun-ji) E4
30 Temple 30 (Zenraku-ji) E4
31 Temple 31 (Chikurin-ji) E4
32 Temple 32 (Zenjibu-ji) E4
33 Temple 33 (Sekkei-ji) E4
34 Temple 34 (Tanema-ji) D4
35 Temple 35 (Kiyotaki-ji) D4
36 Temple 36 (Shōryū-ji) D5
37 Temple 37 (Iwamoto-ji) C6
38 Temple 38 (Kongōfuku-ji) C7
39 Temple 39 (Enkō-ji) B6
40 Temple 40 (Kanjizai-ji) B6
41 Temple 41 (Ryūkō-ji) B5
42 Temple 42 (Butsumoku-ji) B5
43 Temple 43 (Meiseki-ji) A5
44 Temple 44 (Taihō-ji) C4
45 Temple 45 (Iwaya-ji) C4
46 Temple 46 (Jōruri-ji) B3
47 Temple 47 (Yasaka-ji) B3
48 Temple 48 (Sairin-ji) B3
49 Temple 49 (Jōdo-ji) C3
50 Temple 50 (Hanta-ji) B3
51 Temple 51 (Ishite-ji) B3
52 Temple 52 (Taisan-ji) B3
53 Temple 53 (Enmyō-ji) B3
54 Temple 54 (Enmei-ji) C2
55 Temple 55 (Nankō-bō) C2
56 Temple 56 (Taisan-ji) C2
57 Temple 57 (Eifuku-ji) C2
58 Temple 58 (Senyū-ji) C3
59 Temple 59 (Kokubun-ji) C3
60 Temple 60 (Yokomine-ji) C3
61 Temple 61 (Kōon-ji) C3
62 Temple 62 (Hōju-ji) C3
63 Temple 63 (Kichijō-ji) D3
64 Temple 64 (Maegami-ji) C3
65 Temple 65 (Sankaku-ji) E3
66 Temple 66 (Unpen-ji) E2
67 Temple 67 (Daikō-ji) E2
68 Temple 68 (Jinne-in) E2
69 Temple 69 (Kanon-ji) E2
70 Temple 70 (Motoyama-ji) E2
71 Temple 71 (Iyadani-ji) E2
72 Temple 72 (Mandara-ji) E2
73 Temple 73 (Shusshaka-ji) E2
74 Temple 74 (Kōyama-ji) E1
75 Temple 75 (Zentsū-ji) E2
76 Temple 76 (Konzō-ji) F1
77 Temple 77 (Dōryū-ji) E1
78 Temple 78 (Gōshō-ji) E1
79 Temple 79 (Kōshō-in) F1
80 Temple 80 (Kokubun-ji) F1
81 Temple 81 (Shiromine-ji) F1
82 Temple 82 (Negoro-ji) F1
83 Temple 83 (Ichinomiya-ji) F1
84 Temple 84 (Yashima-ji) F1
85 Temple 85 (Yakuri-ji) F1
86 Temple 86 (Shido-ji) G1
87 Temple 87 (Nagao-ji) G1
88 Temple 88 (Ōkubo-ji) G2

Information

Tourist Information Office (徳島総合観光案内所; ☎088-622-8556; ⊙9.30am-7pm) In a booth on the plaza outside the station.

Tokushima Prefecture International Exchange Association (徳島県国際交流協会; TOPIA; ☎088-656-3303; www.topia.ne.jp; 6th fl, Clement Plaza, 1-61 Terashima Honchō-nishi; ⊙10am-6pm) On the 6th floor of the Clement Plaza Building, directly above the station, this efficient office has friendly English-speaking staff and is a mine of information for Tokushima Prefecture.

Getting There & Away

AIR

Tokushima Awaodori Airport (徳島阿波おどり空港; ☎088-699-2831; www.tokushima-airport.co.jp) has flights to Tokyo and Fukuoka. Buses (¥440; 30 minutes; buses timed to coincide with flights) depart from bus stop 1 in front of the station.

BOAT

Nankai Ferry (p418) runs daily connections between Tokushima and Wakayama (two hours, six daily).

Ocean Tōkyū Ferry (オーシャン東九フェリー; ☎088-636-0109; www.otf.jp; 2-62-2 Higashi-Okinosu) departs once daily to/from Tokyo/Tokushima/Kita-Kyūshū (18 hours to Tokyo, 15 hours to Kita-Kyūshū).

BUS

Daily highway buses connect Tokushima with Tokyo (nine hours), Nagoya (five hours) and Kyoto (three hours); there are also 10 buses per day to Osaka (2½ hours) and Kansai airport (2¾ hours). They leave from the **bus terminal** outside the train station.

TRAIN

Tokushima is just over an hour by train (¥3360) from Takamatsu by *tokkyū* (limited express). For the Iya Valley and Kōchi, change trains at Awa-Ikeda (阿波池田, ¥3540, 1¼ hours).

Getting Around

Rental bicycles (貸し自転車; ☎088-652-6661; per half/full day ¥270/450, deposit ¥3000; ⏲9am-8pm) are available from the underground bike park to the left as you leave the station.

Electric-assist bicycles (ぐるとくサイクル; ☎088-655-6133; per 3hr/day/week ¥500/1000/3000; ⏲9am-7.30pm) are available just opposite the station, down the escalator at SOGO.

Naruto

POP 60,000

Naruto is a spread-out city in the northeast corner of Shikoku. While there's not much of interest in the township itself, Naruto is known throughout Japan for whirlpools in the sea underneath Ōnaruto Bridge, the impressive structure that connects Shikoku with Awaji-shima. The phenomena is best viewed as the tides change, either from a boat or from the observation platform under the bridge. Check www.uzusio.com for the best times to view them on a particular day.

Also within the city limits are the first two temples of the 88 Sacred Temples of Shikoku Pilgrimage.

Sights

★Temple One: Ryōzen-ji — BUDDHIST TEMPLE

(霊山寺; ☎088-689-1111; www.88shikokuhenro.jp/tokushima/01ryozenji; 126 Bandō, Ōasa-chō) FREE Ryōzen-ji is Temple One of the 88 Sacred Temples of Shikoku pilgrimage. It is called Temple One because it was the first that temple pilgrims came to after arriving on Shikoku following a visit to Kōya-san in Wakayama Prefecture to ask Kōbō Daishi for his support on their journey. Everything you need is here, from guidebooks (in English too) to pilgrim wear and temple stamp books. Savour the serenity and the history – the pilgrimage has been walked for 1200 years.

Take a local train from Tokushima to Bandō (板東; ¥260, 20 minutes). The temple is a 10- to 15-minute walk (about 700m) northwest of the station; the map at Bandō Station will point you in the right direction.

★Uzu-no-michi Viewing Walkway — VIEWPOINT

(渦の道; ☎088-683-6262; www.uzunomichi.jp; 772-0053 Naruto Park; ¥510; ⏲9am-6pm, to 5pm Oct-Feb) For an intriguing bird's-eye view of the whirlpools, you can walk out along this breezy 450m-long walkway hanging underneath the Naruto Bridge, which puts you 42m directly above the action. There is an observation gallery with glass floors through which you can gaze down at the whirlpools. Check the website for the best time to view the whirlpools on the day you go.

Otsuka Museum of Art — MUSEUM

(大塚国際美術館; ☎088-687-3737; www.o-museum.or.jp; Naruto Park; adult/child ¥3240/540; ⏲9.30am-5pm Tue-Sun) One from the 'only in Japan file', this incredible 'ceramic board masterpiece museum' features more than 1000 replicas of priceless Western art on ceramic boards in a five-storey museum built inside a mountain at **Naruto Park** (鳴門公園). Absolutely mind-boggling; there is even a life-size Sistine Chapel, built as part of Otsuka Pharmaceutical Group's 75th anniversary. See the *Mona Lisa*, the *Last Supper*, *Guernica* and more on ceramic boards that will keep them in perfect condition for an estimated 2000 years.

Ōnaruto-hashi — BRIDGE

(大鳴門橋) Linking Shikoku to Awaji-shima, impressive Ōnaruto-hashi was completed in 1985. Later, when the world's longest suspension bridge, the Akashi Kaikyō-ōhashi, linking northern Awaji-shima to Kōbe, was completed in 1998, Tokushima Prefecture finally had a road link to Honshū. It's 1629m long, its two towers are 145m in height, and the bridge itself is 42m above the water. On the Shikoku side and attached under the bridge, the Uzu-no-michi walkway takes viewers out above the Naruto Whirlpools.

THE FIRST FIVE TEMPLES: RYŌZEN-JI TO JIZŌ-JI

Naruto is the starting point for Shikoku's 88 Temple Pilgrimage. The first five temples are all within easy walking distance of each other, making it possible to get a taste of the *henro* (pilgrim) trail on a day trip from Tokushima.

To get to Temple One, Ryōzen-ji (p675), take a local train from Tokushima to Bandō (板東; ¥260, 25 minutes). The temple is a 10- to 15-minute walk (about 700m) along the main road; the map at Bandō Station should point you in the right direction. From Ryōzen-ji it's a short walk along the main road from the first temple to the second, **Gokuraku-ji** (極楽寺), and another 2km from here to Temple Three, **Konsen-ji** (金泉寺). There are more-or-less regular signposts (in Japanese) pointing the way. Look for the signs by the roadside marked *henro-michi* (へんろ道 or 遍路道), often decorated with a red picture of a *henro* in silhouette. From here, it's about 5km along an increasingly rural path to Temple Four, **Dainichi-ji** (大日寺), and another 2km to Temple Five, **Jizō-ji** (地蔵寺), where there's an impressive collection of statues (¥200) of the 500 Rakan disciples of the Buddha. From the Rakan (羅漢) bus stop on the main road in front of the temple you can catch a bus to Itano Station (板野), where a train will take you back to Tokushima (¥360, 30 minutes).

Tours

★Naruto Whirlpool Sightseeing Boats BOATING
(鳴門観光汽船; Naruto Kankō Kisen; ☎088-687-0101; www.uzusio.com/en; 264-1 Oge, Tosadomariura; per person from ¥1800; ⏲every 20min 9am-4.20pm) This company makes regular trips out to see the Naruto whirlpools from the small port next to the Naruto Kankō-kō (鳴門観光港) bus stop. If you're making the effort to do this, check their website to find the best time to head out that particular day. The whirlpools are at their most impressive roughly every six hours.

Sleeping & Eating

If you are overnighting in the Naruto area, it's best to take meals at your accommodation, unless you have a car and are willing to explore. During the day there are plenty of small, simple eating places primarily catering to Japanese tourists, such as in Naruto-kōen.

★Seaside Hotel Taimaru Kaigetsu RYOKAN ¥¥
(シーサイドホテル鯛丸海月; ☎050-3066-1001; www.taimaru-kaigetsu.com; 15-33 Azafukuike, Tosadomariura; s/tw from ¥9000/12,000; P ❄ 📶) Just south of Naruto Park, this ryokan has spotless Japanese- and Western-style rooms, most with a view of the sea and Naruto Bridge. There's an excellent onsen-with-a-view on the top floor, a good restaurant on the ground floor, and free parking. This is a great spot to stay if you have a rental car and are exploring.

Getting There & Around

JR Naruto Station is on the JR Naruto line, 40 minutes north from Tokushima (¥360). Naruto-kōen can be reached by bus from there in 20 minutes.

The Anan Coast

The highway running south from Tokushima city along the Anan Coast (阿南海岸) passes through prosperous little agricultural towns fronted by lazy surf beaches. It is flanked by hidden temples and spectacular rocky bluffs. Enjoy the laid-back atmosphere and relaxed attitudes as you get to Surf City, Japan, occupying both sides of the Tokushima–Kōchi prefectural border.

Getting There & Around

The JR Mugi line runs from Tokushima city down the coast as far as Kaifu, stopping at Hiwasa (¥1090, 1¼ hours). From Kaifu, the private Asa Kaigan railway runs to Shikisui (¥1880, 2½ hours total travel time from Tokushima) and Kannoura (for Shirahama).

Seven buses a day run from Kannoura to Muroto-misaki (¥1520, 40 minutes) via Ikumi. Buses then continue on as far as Nahari and Aki (安芸; ¥2880, 2½ hours), where you can transfer to a train to Kōchi.

Coming the other way, trains run from Kōchi as far as Nahari – but you'll have to rely on buses to get you around the cape and up to Kannoura.

Your own wheels are useful here. Rte 55 travels down the coast south of Tokushima connecting Hiwasa, Shishikui and Ikumi and all the way to Muroto-misaki.

Hiwasa

☎0884 / POP 5500

The small fishing town of Hiwasa (日和佐; also known as Minami) provides respite for road-weary pilgrims with a *michi-no-eki* (rest stop) on the main road in the middle of town, not far from the entrance gates to the town's main attraction, Yakuō-ji, Temple 23 of the 88. In addition to the usual food stalls, immaculate restrooms and small market, this place also has a free foot bath. Stop by and soak your feet. If you are interested in sea turtles, head out to attractive Ōhama Beach where's there's a very good museum and a secluded hotel.

If you're struggling with road signs, Hiwasa is the main town in what is now called Minami town, which covers a large area of southern Tokushima Prefecture. Road signs now label Hiwasa as Minami, though the train station is still called Hiwasa and that's what locals call their town.

Sights

★Sea Turtle Museum Caretta MUSEUM
(うみがめ博物館カレッタ; ☎0884-77-1110; www.caretta-hiwasa.com; 370-4 Hiwasa-ura; ¥600; ⏲9am-5pm) Dedicated to sea turtles, the museum's name – Caretta – comes from the scientific name for the Loggerhead Sea Turtle. Inside, there's a lot of turtle info, small tanks and a hatchery with baby turtles aged up to three years. The outside pools house turtles from age four upwards. The facility is on **Ōhama Beach** (大浜), known as a turtle egg-laying spot from May to August.

★Temple 23: Yakuō-ji BUDDHIST TEMPLE
(薬王寺; ☎0884-77-0023; www.yakuouji.net; 285-1 Teramae Okugawachi, Minami-chō) FREE The major attraction of Hiwasa, Yakuō-ji, Temple 23, is the last temple in Tokushima Prefecture. Yakuō-ji dates back to the year 726, and is famous as a *yakuyoke-no-tera* (a temple with special powers to ward off ill fortune during unlucky years). The unluckiest age for men is 42; for women, 33 is the one to watch out for. Kōbō Daishi is said to have visited in 815, the year of his own 42nd birthday.

The long set of stone steps leading up to the main temple building comes in two stages: 33 steps for the women, followed by another 42 for the men. The tradition is for pilgrims to put a coin on each step – when it's busy, you may find the steps practically overflowing with one-yen coins.

Shishikui

☎0884 / POP 3550

Just north of the Tokushima–Kōchi prefectural border, Shishikui (宍喰), formerly a rural village focused on fishing and farming, is becoming a hit with young visitors, particularly those interested in surfing, diving, sea kayaking and other ocean-based activities. Throw in an onsen, some seriously good little eateries and you've got a great place to stay for a couple of days.

Activities

★Kaanapali Diving Center DIVING
(カアナパリダイビングセンター; ☎0884-76-3243; http://kaanapali-diving.jp; 97-10 Matsubara) With friendly English-speaking staff, decades of experience diving in this region and a roadside shop in the middle of Shishikui, these are the people to go diving with. An introductory dive including equipment costs ¥13,500; a two-dive trip for experienced divers costs ¥15,000 with equipment. They also have rental gear and run snorkelling trips.

★Pavilion Surf School SURFING
(☎0884-76-3277; www.kaorimayaguchi.com; 215-1 Matsubara, Shishikui-ura; surfing/SUP lesson from ¥5400/6480) Based in Pavilion Surf's shop just east of Shishikui, Kaori Mayaguchi runs surfing and SUP lessons and tours with gear and wetsuits included. Her parents help run the place; the family lived in Honolulu for a number of years and speak English. Surfboard rentals cost ¥3240 per day. It's easy to spot, two doors east of 7-Eleven.

Shishikui Onsen ONSEN
(宍喰温泉; ☎0884-76-3300; www.hotel-riviera.co.jp; 226-1 Aza Matsubara; adult/child ¥600/300; ⏲6.30-9am & 11am-11pm) On the upper floor of the **Hotel Riviera** (ホテルリビエラ; ☎0884-76-3300; www.hotel-riviera.co.jp; 226-1 Aza Matsubara; r per person incl/excl breakfast from ¥8000/8500; P❄📶) complex on the main road in Shishikui, this onsen boasts that its natural water comes from 1km below the ground. The main baths look out to the sea. There is also a restaurant and a shop on-site.

Tours

Blue Marine Sea Kayaking KAYAKING
(ブルーマリンシーカヤック; ☎0884-76-3100; http://marine.kaiyo-kankou.jp; 28-45 Takegashima; guided kayaking trips ¥3000; ⏲10am & 2pm) Popular guided sea-kayaking tours

DON'T MISS

BEST TEMPLES

- Temple 45: Iwaya-ji (p692)
- Temple 51: Ishite-ji (p692)
- Temple 38: Kongōfuku-ji (p691)
- Temple 21: Tairyū-ji (p680)
- Temple 88: Ōkubo-ji (p708)
- Temple 66: Unpen-ji (p710)

around Takegashima island, a rocky island connected to the mainland by a bridge, 2km south of Shishikui. It also offers SUP (¥6000; 90 minutes) and Blue Marine underwater-viewing boat tours (¥1800; 45 minutes). Check out the various options online in Japanese.

Sleeping & Eating

★ **Pavilion Surf & Lodge** GUESTHOUSE ¥
(☎0884-76-3277; www.pavilion-surf.com; 215-1 Matsubara, Shishikuiura; r per person from ¥3000; P ⊖ ❄ ᯤ) This place only has basic surfer accommodation, but all are welcome. Rooms are simple, with beds, air-con and nothing else. Shared male and female bathroom facilities and a kitchen occupy other buildings. That said, this is a great place for budget travellers. The friendly and enthusiastic owners speak English, having lived in Hawaii.

It's next to the sea slightly north of Shishikui, two doors east of 7-Eleven.

Pension Shishikui PENSION ¥¥
(ペンションししくい; ☎0884-76-2130; www.p-shishikui.com; 84-18 Akazome; r per person incl meals from ¥9720; P ❄ ᯤ) Perfect for families or romantic getaways, charming Pension Shishikui, with an English-speaking owner, occupies a snug cove with a private beach (protected by a sea wall). All rooms, whether in the main house or in freestanding log cabins, have ocean views and private bathrooms. Check the location on the website; it's on the first road just south of Shishikui Bridge.

★ **Bahati** INTERNATIONAL ¥
(☎0884-76-2696; 222-1 Shishikui; mains from ¥800; ⊙11.30am-3pm & 6-9pm) A superb little spot a tad east of Shishikui, Bahati is run by keen surfer Tsuji-san. Serving everything from pasta to *katsu-kareē* (pork cutlet, curry and rice), Bahati has surfboards on the rafters, surf photos on the walls, indoor and outdoor seating, plus a cool and relaxed vibe. If Bahati is late opening, it's because Tsuji is out surfing.

Cafe Hikōsen CAFE ¥
(ひこうせん; ☎0884-76-3488; 82-2 Shishikuiura; breakfast ¥540; ⊙8.30am-5pm Fri-Tue) This small roadside cafe is a locals' favourite, particularly for the impressive Japanese/Western breakfast that will keep everyone satisfied. Expect a warm, friendly welcome, an English menu (and possibly an English speaker), and some gorgeous pottery pieces.

Ikumi

☎0887 / POP 800

On the Kōchi side of the prefectural border with Tokushima, Ikumi (生見) is beach-bum paradise. Surfers from all over Japan head to the lovely beach here, which is lined with some good budget accommodation, a few eateries that won't break the bank, and a surf shop or two. If you'd like a relaxed day or two looking at a different side of Japan, Ikumi is a great place to hang out. Lie back on the beach and enjoy the sun, catch a few waves, soak in the sea, thumb through surf magazines and enjoy a cool beverage – or two!

Shirahama (白浜), 2km north of Ikumi and just in Kōchi Prefecture, offers a wide, protected beach and is a good spot for families.

Activities

Surf Shop More SURFING
(☎0887-29-3615; www.surfshopmore.com; 575-1 Ikumi; 2hr surfing/body-boarding lessons ¥5000) Head to Surf Shop More for all your surfing needs, be they surf lessons, rentals or shopping. Rental costs are board-and-wetsuit/board-only ¥5000/3000, body-board and fins ¥3000. The shop is located in the heart of the action at Ikumi Beach.

Sleeping & Eating

★ **Ikumi White Beach Hotel** HOTEL ¥
(生見ホワイトビーチホテル; ☎0887-29-3018; www.wbhotel.net; 575-11 Ikumi; r per person from ¥4200; P ❄ ᯤ) This clean, laid-back Ikumi beachfront hotel has Japanese- and Western-style rooms more or less right on the beach. Fall out the door and into the waves. You'll need to bring your own towels. Olu-Olu is part of the complex and open for breakfast, lunch and dinner. There's plenty of parking.

South Shore INN ¥
(サウスショア; ☎0887-29-3211; www.southshore-ikumi.com; 12-10 Ikumi; r per person incl/excl meals ¥7250/3800; P ❄ 📶 ≋) A sunny, simple inn with shared bathrooms, South Shore sits about a block from the beach in Ikumi and has a relaxed Hawaiian-esque vibe. The cute attached cafe and tiny pool area are convivial spots to hang out après-surf.

Minshuku Ikumi MINSHUKU ¥
(民宿いくみ; ☎0887-24-3838; www.ikumiten.com; 7-1 Ikumi; r per person incl breakfast ¥4100; P ❄ 📶) This cosy, family-run *minshuku* (guesthouse) sits right alongside the highway in Ikumi. It's a popular surfer's choice, thanks to the well-presented rooms and the helpful, knowledgeable owner, Ten. Check out the website; there are often online specials.

Tōyō Shirahama Resort Hotel HOTEL ¥¥
(東洋白浜リゾートホテル; ☎0887-29-3344; www.shirahama-resort-hotel.amebaownd.com; 88-8 Shirahama, Tōyō-chō; s/d from ¥5400/10,800; P ❄ 📶) It's hard to miss this large hotel in Shirahama as you're driving along the coast. Set back from an attractive beach, it's a five-storey white building. Although it's dated, rooms are simple and clean. Protected by headlands on both sides, the nearby beach isn't a top surfing spot, but more of a splash-about-in-the-water place that's fun for families.

★ **Aunt Dinah** JAPANESE CURRY ¥
(アント・ダイナ; ☎0887-29-2080; 24-107 Kawauchi, Tōyō-chō; meals from ¥800; ⏲10am-3pm & 5.30-9pm Wed-Mon) Get ready for a friendly welcome, country music and a great range of curries, pastas and pizzas at this rustic spot on the main road near the impossible-to-miss white Tōyō Shirahama Resort Hotel at Shirahama. Aunt Dinah's has a useful English menu.

Olu-Olu CAFE ¥
(オルオル; ☎0887-29-3018; www.wbhotel.net; meals ¥800-1000; ⏲7am-2pm & 5-8pm) Ikumi White Beach Hotel runs an inexpensive restaurant called Olu-Olu, featuring a picture menu and plenty of dog-eared Japanese surf mags. Eat inside, or there's a hole-in-the-wall ordering spot and terrace for eating outside while gazing at the waves. It serves everything from hotdogs (¥420) to *katsu-kare* (¥1030).

Muroto-misaki

☎0887

Muroto-misaki (室戸岬) is one of Shikoku's two great capes that jut out into the Pacific. In Japanese literature, Muroto is famed as one of the wildest spots in the nation and as the 'doorway to the land of the dead'. To pilgrims, it is the place where Kōbō Daishi achieved enlightenment and many come to try to do the same. On a calm day, the Pacific is like a millpond; in bad weather Muroto is pounded by huge waves and buffeted by the wind. Visitors can explore Kōbō Daishi's bathing hole among the rock pools, and the cave where he meditated. A *henro* trail leads up through bush to Temple 24, Hotsumisaki-ji, founded by Kōbō Daishi in the early 9th century.

Muroto is a designated Unesco Global Geopark, where sites and landscapes of international geological significance are managed with a holistic concept of protection, education and sustainable development.

Sights

★ **Temple 24: Hotsumisaki-ji** BUDDHIST TEMPLE
(最御崎寺; Higashi-dera; ☎0887-23-0024; www.88shikokuhenro.jp/kochi/24hotsumisakiji; 4058-1 Muroto-misaki-chō) FREE This gorgeous hilltop temple is considered one of the most important on the 88 Temple Pilgrimage because it is here at Muroto that Kōbō Daishi achieved enlightenment. Either walk up on the

SURFING SHIKOKU

It's not the North Shore of O'ahu, but Southern Tokushima is a Japanese surfer's paradise, with great waves and relatively few surfers in the water. Despite the prevalence of concrete on the shoreline, this region has attractive beaches and relaxed, friendly locals – some of whom have been world travellers and can speak English. The area is growing as a destination, with alternative lifestylers moving in, setting up tourism-related lifestyle businesses and catering for a growing number of visiting foreigners. Shishikui (p677) in Tokushima and the two-street beach-bum town of Ikumi, just over the border in Kōchi are prime spots.

WORTH A TRIP

TEMPLE 21: TAIRYŪ-JI

For 1200 years, *henro* have struggled up steep mountain paths to get to the magnificent mountaintop temple, **Tairyū-ji** (太龍寺; ☎0884-62-2021; www.88shikokuhenro.jp/tokushima/21tairyuji; 2 Ryūzan Kamo-chō, Anan-shi) FREE. A 2.7km-long **ropeway** (太龍寺ロープウェイ; ☎0884-62-3100; www.shikoku-cable.co.jp; 76 Tano, Naka-chō; one way/return ¥1300/2470; ⏲every 20min 7.20am-5pm), the longest in western Japan, makes easy work of the ascent, giving one and all the opportunity to visit this atmospheric haven. Magnificent views justify the effort to get here. Getting to the rural ropeway base will be a lot easier with your own wheels, but you can also get here by bus from Tokushima Station in 1½ hours. There's a museum, a restaurant and a place to stay at the bottom of the ropeway. Make sure you take your passport as there is often a half-price discount to foreign visitors.

age-old *henro* trail that starts just northeast of the cape, or drive up the winding road a kilometre to the northwest of the cape. Ancient buildings and statues contribute to a sacred atmosphere.

Muroto Unesco Global Geopark Center MUSEUM
(室戸ユネスコ世界ジオパーク; ☎0887-22-5161; www.muroto-geo.jp/en; 1810-2 Muroto-misaki-cho; ⏲9am-5pm) FREE The Muroto Geopark was designed to help create a better understanding about how local people have been dealing with ever-changing landforms. The area's geography is fascinating and it possesses a rich heritage of diverse geological formations. The park has walking, cycling and driving routes – head to the Geopark Center to learn more and obtain maps.

Sleeping

Temple 24: Hotsumisaki-ji Shukubō GUESTHOUSE ¥¥
(☎0887-23-0024; Hotsumisaki-ji; per person incl/excl meals ¥6500/4200; P⊖❄📶) Run by Temple 24: Hotsumisaki-ji, this is a great opportunity to stay at a peaceful *shukubō* with spotless tatami rooms or bedrooms and a communal bath, and to try traditional vegetarian pilgrim food. Temples on the pilgrimage have been catering to pilgrims for 1200 years and as well as providing a service, they make extra income this way.

Iya Valley

The spectacular Iya Valley (祖谷渓) is a special place: its staggeringly steep gorges and thick mountain forests lure travellers to seek respite from the hectic 'mainland' lifestyle. Winding your way around narrow cliff-hanging roads as the icy water of the Iya-gawa shoots along the ancient valley floor is a blissful travel experience. Top-notch onsen are well within reach, while evening entertainment is nothing more strenuous than sampling the local Iya soba (buckwheat noodles) and reliving your day's visual feast.

The earliest records of the valley describe a group of shamans fleeing from persecution in Nara in the 9th century. At the end of the 12th century, Iya famously became the last refuge for members of the vanquished Heike clan following their defeat at the hands of the Minamoto in the Gempei Wars. Their descendants are believed to live in the mountain villages to this day.

Getting There & Around

This is one of those places where, if you're going to make the effort to get here, it's best to have your own wheels (p667).

Public transport can only get you so far out here. A few buses head out daily into the valley from Awa-Ikeda Bus Terminal near JR Awa-Ikeda Station, on the Dosan line (¥3340, 1¼ hours from either Takamatsu or Kōchi), which runs between Takamatsu and Kōchi. Get details at the **Miyoshi City Tourism Association** (三好市観光協会; ☎0883-76-0877; www.miyoshi-tourism.jp/en; 1810-18 Sarada, Ikeda-chō; ⏲9am-6pm).

Nishi Iya

Nishi Iya (西祖谷, West Iya) is the more accessible end of the Iya Valley, and tour buses stream over Rte 45 from Ōboke to fill the monstrous car-and-bus parking area that casts a huge shadow over the poor little vine bridge that people come to see. The good news is that most of those buses then fill up and head back over the hill.

Iya Valley

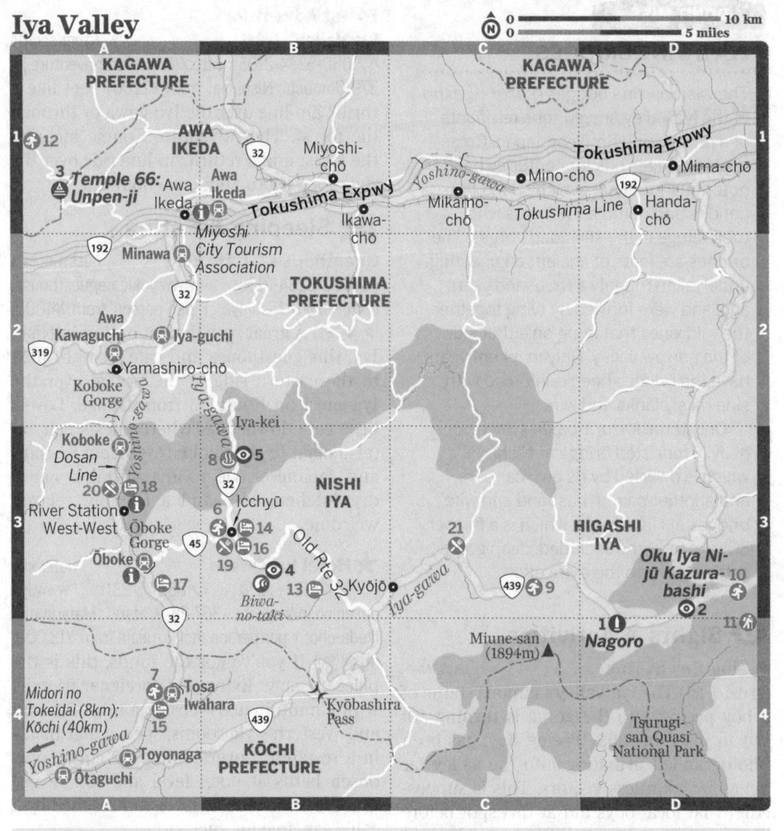

Iya Valley

Top Sights

1 Nagoro D4
2 Oku Iya Ni-jū Kazura-bashi D3
3 Temple 66: Unpen-ji A1

Sights

4 Kazura-bashi B3
5 Peeing Boy Statue B3

Activities, Courses & Tours

6 Forest Adventure Iya Valley B3
7 Happy Raft A4
8 Iya Onsen B3
9 Oku-Iya Monorail C3
10 Tsurugi-san Chairlift D3
11 Tsurugi-san Hiking D4
12 Unpenji Ropeway A1

Sleeping

13 Chiiori B3
14 Guesthouse & Cafe Yoki B3
15 Happy Guest House A4
Hotel Iya Onsen (see 5)
16 Hotel Kazura-bashi B3
Iyashi no Onsen-kyō (see 9)
17 Ku-Nel-Asob A3
18 Sunriver Ōboke A3
Tabi-no-yado Kiri-no-mine (see 10)
Tsurugi-san Chōjō Hutte (see 11)

Eating

19 Iya Bijin B3
20 Iya-soba Momiji-tei A3
21 Soba Dōjō C3

For a most pleasurable visit, use old Rte 32 from Iya-guchi, enjoy the cliff-hugging, winding road that requires plenty of concentration, and plan to overnight in the valley after the day trippers are gone. Nishi-Iya is nice, but head east, further up the valley for a more remote and 'away from it all' Iya experience.

DON'T MISS

IYA'S VINE BRIDGES

The wisteria vine bridges *(kazura-bashi)* of the Iya Valley are glorious remnants of a remote and timeless Japan. Crossing the bridges has for centuries been notoriously difficult, which suited the bandits and humbled warriors who took refuge in the secluded gorges. The bridges are feats of ancient engineering, undertaken roughly a thousand years ago, and were formed by tying together the wild vines that hung on either side of the narrow valley. Only in recent years have the bridges been reinforced with side rails, planks and wire.

Only three *kazura-bashi* survive, one heavily touristed bridge at Nishi Iya, which is dwarfed by its own car park, and another pair of 'husband and wife' bridges at Higashi Iya, which is a further 30km east – the secluded, deep gorge setting is worth the extra effort.

Sights & Activities

Peeing Boy Statue LANDMARK
(小便小僧) The Iya Valley's famous statue of a boy peeing into the gorge is turning 50! Put in place in 1968, 'Peeing Boy' has been photographed urinating into the valley far below by countless visitors. This is supposedly what local boys did at this spot before 'Peeing Boy' was erected. Guaranteed to put a smile on every visitor's face!

Kazura-bashi BRIDGE
(かずら橋; ¥550; 8am-5pm) This remarkable vine bridge is one of only three left in the valley – the other two are further east in Higashi Iya. If you do visit this bridge, also check out the nearby **Biwa-no-taki**, an impressive 50m-high waterfall.

★**Iya Onsen** ONSEN
(祖谷温泉; 0883-75-2311; www.iyaonsen.co.jp; 367-2 Matsuo Matsumoto; ¥1700; non-hotel guests 7.30am-6pm) On Rte 32, this onsen is a great experience. At Hotel Iya Onsen, a cable car descends a steep cliff-face to some sulphurous, open-air baths on the riverside. A fantastic place to slow down, enjoy spectacular views of the forested gorge and, of course, soak in the onsen, even if you're not staying there.

Forest Adventure Iya Valley ADVENTURE SPORTS
(080-6284-2105; http://fa-iya.foret-aventure.jp; 379 Oinouchi, Nishi-iya; from ¥2200) Feel like a thrill? Zip-line over the Iya-gawa or through the forest. The Adventure Course includes the forest and a return zip-line ride over the river for ¥4000. Allow two hours.

Sleeping & Eating

Guesthouse & Cafe Yoki GUESTHOUSE ¥
(080-6284-2105; www.yokicafeguesthouse.com; 375-3 Nishi-iya; r per person from ¥4000; P ❄) A great new budget option in Nishi Iya, this guesthouse and cafe sit right next to the eastern side of the bridge over the Iya-gawa on Route 45 from Ōboke. Lovely little cafe downstairs where guests can eat (also open to the public from 11am to 4pm) and Japanese-style rooms upstairs. Laundry, kitchen, wi-fi and a friendly, relaxed welcome.

★**Hotel Iya Onsen** HOTEL ¥¥¥
(ホテル祖谷温泉; 883-75-2311; www.iyaonsen.co.jp/english; 367-28 Matsuo Matsumoto, Ikeda-cho; r per person incl 2 meals from ¥18,000; P ❄) If you've got the funds, this is the place to stay. Extremely foreigner-friendly with a multilingual website, a mix of tatami and Western-style rooms, spectacular meals in a restaurant overlooking the gorge, plus onsen baths at hotel level and *rotemburo* that are close to river level and reached by a cable car (free for guests).

Hotel Kazura-bashi RYOKAN ¥¥¥
(ホテルかずら橋; 0883-87-2171; www.kazurabashi.co.jp; 33-1 Zentoku; r per person incl 2 meals from ¥16,000; P ❄) This lovely hotel not far from Kazura-bashi offers spacious, comfortable, Japanese-style rooms with mountain views. Beautifully prepared traditional meals are served by attentive staff. A funky cable car ferries guests up to the hotel's highlight: a gorgeous, open-air onsen on the hill. Nonguests are welcome to use the onsen (¥1200) between 10am to 4pm.

★**Iya Bijin** SOBA ¥
(祖谷美人; 0883-87-2009; www.iyabijin.jp; 9-3 Zentoku; meals from ¥700; 8am-5pm) For a taste of local Iya soba, head to Iya Bijin, in an attractive black-and-white building with lanterns hanging out the front, overlooking the gorge. Try a simple plate of *zaru soba* (cold noodles with dipping sauce), or a lunch set including regional dishes such as

dekomawashi (grilled skewers of taro, tofu and *konnyaku* – devil's tongue), boar and wild vegetables.

Getting There & Away

Come by bus from either JR Awa-Ikeda station or JR Ōboke station. With your own wheels either drive up the Iya-gawa valley on exciting old Rte 32 from Iya-guchi, or come over the hill from Ōboke on Rte 45.

Higashi Iya

Also known as Oku-Iya, meaning 'deep Iya', Higashi Iya (東祖谷, East Iya) is the area to go to for an extremely remote Shikoku experience. The valley narrows, the road climbs and craggy mountains encroach from both sides. The spectacular Kazura-bashi here are an absolute pleasure to visit, with minimal visitors getting this far, and the 'scarecrow village' of Nagoro is an enthralling eye-opener. Few reach here as Rte 439 is narrow, windy and requires great care – don't become a road statistic! If you carry on up to the head of the valley, you'll be at the foot of Tsurugi-san, Shikoku's second-highest peak.

Sights & Activities

★Oku Iya Ni-jū Kazura-bashi BRIDGE
(奥祖谷二重かずら橋; ¥550; ⏲7am-5pm) Away from the crowds and tour buses, the spectacular Oku Iya Ni-jū Kazura-bashi are two secluded vine bridges hanging side by side high over the river. Cross one and come back over the other. A self-propelled, two-seated wooden cable-cart is another fun way to cross the river; there's a small public camping area on the other side. There are also a couple of spots where you can get down to the river and enjoy the serenity.

★Nagoro PUBLIC ART
(名頃かかしの里; Nagoro Scarecrow Village) If you're travelling along Rte 439, it's not a matter of 'blink and you'll miss it', but blink, and blink again, because you may have a hard time believing your eyes when you hit Nagoro. Those 'people' – waiting at the bus stop, gossiping on a porch, toiling in the fields – are life-sized scarecrow-type dolls made by resident Ayano Tsukimi as a way of memorialising former inhabitants of her hometown. Nagoro is 12km west of Oku Iya Ni-jū Kazura-bashi.

The figures are surprisingly lifelike from afar and strikingly expressive up close, each with a unique posture and face. Equal parts eerie and sweet, the dolls of Nagoro create a surreal tableau amid the quiet river valley. For a look into the village, check out the beautiful short film *Valley of Dolls* (www.vimeo.com/92453765), created by the German filmmaker Fritz Schumann, who visited with Ayano-san.

Oku-Iya Monorail RAIL
(奥祖谷モノレール; ☎0883-88-2975; adult/child ¥2000/1000; ⏲8.30am-4pm) At Iyashi no Onsen-kyō, this is a cutesy little monorail with two-seater cars that slowly move passengers along a 4.6km course through the mostly untouched forest. Surprisingly, it also climbs nearly 600m in height and takes passengers up to 1400m on a loop track to see different vegetation. The gentle ride takes 70 minutes.

Sleeping & Eating

Iyashi no Onsen-kyō HOTEL ¥¥
(いやしの温泉郷; ☎0883-88-2975; http://iyashino-onsenkyo.com; 28 Sugeoi, Higashi Iya; r per person incl meals from ¥14,000; ⏲onsen 10am-9pm; P⊖❄📶) Off the main road between Kyōjō and the Higashi Iya vine bridges is this lovely and unpretentious hotel and hot-springs complex, with Japanese- and Western-style rooms, an onsen and a restaurant. A smattering of Japanese-language skills would be helpful here. Nonguests can eat at the attractive restaurant. They also run an intriguing 4.6km monorail up into the mountains.

Soba Dōjō SOBA ¥
(そば道場; ☎0883-88-2577; zaru soba ¥800; ⏲11am-5pm Fri-Wed) At Soba Dōjō on Route 439, you can sample a bowl of *zaru soba* and even make your own (¥2500; reservations required). The restaurant has a rusty reddish roof, and a brown curtain hanging over the door. If you're driving, you'll pass within a metre or two of the front door.

Getting There & Away

Get to Higashi Iya either by following Route 439 up the valley from Nishi Iya, or by heading down the valley from Mi-no-koshi, at the foot of Tsurugi-san.

The roads here are narrow, windy and too precarious for tour buses.

OFF THE BEATEN TRACK

CHIIORI: A RURAL RETREAT

Chiiori (The Cottage of the Flute; 篪庵; www.chiiori.org; 209 Higashi-iya-tsurui, Miyoshi-shi; high season s/d from ¥34,000/36,000, lower rates for groups; P) is a once-abandoned, 18th-century, thatched-roof farmhouse in the remote Iya Valley, looking out over forested hillsides and plunging gorges. The house was bought as a ruin by the author and aesthete Alex Kerr in the early 1970s (who went on to romanticise the Iya Valley in his award-winning book *Lost Japan*) and has been painstakingly restored to its original brilliance. The glistening red-pine floorboards surround *irori* (traditional hearths) under soaring rafters. There are *shōji* (sliding rice-paper screen doors) and antique furnishings, but also a gleaming, fully-equipped modern kitchen and a gorgeous bathroom, complete with *hinoki* (Japanese cypress) tub.

Part of the project's mission has been to work with residents to promote sustainable, community-based tourism and realise the financial potential of traditional life, which until recently many locals saw as backward and valueless. Since the establishment of the non-profit Chiiori Trust in 2005, the local government has approached the trust to help restore several smaller traditional houses in the area. These houses have been renovated to a similarly high standard and aesthetic as Chiiori and are also available as accommodation. All are outfitted with modern kitchens and bathrooms, and even washing machines. Follow the Higashi-Iya Ochiai link on the Chiiori Trust website for information and rates on these smaller houses.

To stay in these extraordinary environs, you must reserve in advance; payments must be made in cash. Because of the remote locations of Chiiori and the other houses, the Chiiori Trust strongly recommends that guests bring private vehicles. Hire a rental car and stock up on food at the supermarket before going, because it's very remote.

Ōboke & Koboke

Ōboke (大歩危) and Koboke (小歩危) are scenic gorges on the Yoshino-gawa, which fluctuates from languid green waters to Class IV rapids. These are the upper reaches of the same Yoshino River that flows out into the Pacific Ocean near Tokushima city.

The area has become a popular destination for adventure sports. Around 20 companies run white-water rafting and kayaking trips from mid-March to mid-October. **Happy Raft** (ハッピーラフト; 0887-75-0500; www.happyraft.com; 221-1 Ikadagi; mid-Mar–mid-Oct), steps from JR Tosa Iwahara Station, operates sensational rafting trips and canyoning adventures (¥9000) with English-speaking guides (half-day ¥5500 to ¥7500, full day ¥10,000 to ¥15,500).

With plenty of outdoor action, there's a revitalised vibe going on in this remote part of mountainous Shikoku. You'll find activity operators, new guesthouses and, especially on weekends and in holiday periods, plenty of young people, making the upper reaches of the Yoshino River the envy of other off-the-beaten-track villages.

Sleeping & Eating

Happy Guest House GUESTHOUSE ¥
(0887-75-0500; www.happyraft.com; guesthouses per person ¥4000; P) Run by the local outfit Happy Raft, these five small guesthouses can each accommodate up to 10 and all come with a kitchen, a stocked bathroom and fans. The original guesthouse is a self-contained and fully-restored farmhouse with a tatami room overlooking the Yoshino Valley. The guesthouses are scattered around the valley – check the website for details.

Ku-Nel-Asob GUESTHOUSE ¥¥
(空音遊; 090-9778-7133; www.k-n-a.com; 442 Enoki; r per person incl dinner/breakfast & dinner ¥9720/10,800; P) Four simple, attractive tatami rooms are available in this near-century-old house, perched on a beautiful bluff overlooking the river. Meals here are vegan and served family-style. Since the house doesn't have a bath, the friendly English-speaking owners provide transfers and entry to a local onsen. Reservations must be made at least three days in advance; reserve earlier if you can.

The owners also offer free pick-ups/drop-offs at JR Ōboke Station, 3km away.

Sunriver Ōboke HOTEL ¥¥
(サンリバー大歩危; ☎0883-84-2111; www.oobokeonsen.jp; 1259-1 Yamashiro-chō, Nishiu; s/tw from ¥6000/12,000; P ❄ ☎) This large riverside hotel between Ōboke and Koboke stations has had a new lease of life due to Japan's influx of international visitors. It's dated, but features free wi-fi in the lobby, free parking and a natural onsen on the high floors. There are both Western-style and tatami rooms. Good for those with a rental car.

★ **Iya-soba Momiji-tei** SOBA ¥¥
(祖谷そば　もみじ亭; ☎0883-84-1117; 1468-1 Yamashiro-chō Nishiu; meals ¥900-2000; ⊙10am-5pm Thu-Tue) At the West-West centre, Momiji-tei offers a good opportunity to try Iya soba. It's the lovely old building in the garden at the northern end of the complex. Try the tempura soba set (¥1450), either hot or cold.

Information

Ōboke Station Tourist Information Office
(大歩危駅観光内所; ☎0883-76-0877; www.miyoshi-tourism.jp/en; ⊙8.30am-3.30pm Mon, Tue, Thu & Fri, to 5.30pm Sat & Sun) This extremely efficient office with English-speaking staff on hand and tons of brochures and maps can be found in tiny Ōboke station. Staff can help with organising your trip over the hill and into the Iya Valley.

River Station West-West Information
(☎0887-84-1117; www.west-west.com) Stop by for tourist information, river gear at the Mont Bell shop and ramen or soba.

Getting There & Away

Both JR Ōboke and JR Koboke are stations on the JR Dosan line that connects Takamatsu with Kōchi. JR Ōboke is closer to Kōchi (¥3180, 50 minutes) than to Takamatsu (¥3710, 1½ hours).

Tsurugi-san

At 1955m, Tsurugi-san (剣山) is the second-highest mountain in Shikoku and one of Japan's 100 Famous Mountains. Unlike the sharp-edged peak of Shikoku's highest mountain, Ishizuchi-san to the west, which is said to represent a strict father, the summit of Tsurugi-san is gently rounded and frequently likened to a gentle mother.

The summit plain is known as Heike-no-baba and is said to have served as the 12th-century training field for military horses of local Heike warriors. When the Heike clan succumbed to the rival Genji warriors at the Battle of Dan-noura in 1185, legend tells us they buried their emperor's sword at the peak of Tsurugi-san; hence the mountain's nickname of *Ken-zan* (sword peak).

From Mi-no-koshi, either hike or take the **chairlift** (剣山観光登山リフト; ☎0883-62-2772; www.turugirift.com; Mi-no-koshi; one way/return ¥1030/1860; ⊙9am-5pm, last return 4.45pm; mid-Apr–late-Nov) up to the top station. If you're relatively fit, climbing to the peak is a breeze from there. Enjoy the views, and if the weather is good and you're up for more walking, head southwest and climb Jirōgyū (1929m) on an easily identifiable trail. Allow 1½ hours for the return hike.

There are trails all over these mountains and with careful planning, a three-day hike from Tsurugi-san west to Miune-san (1894m) and a descent into Kubo in Higashi Iya (p683) is possible.

Sleeping

Tabi-no-yado Kiri-no-mine MINSHUKU ¥
(旅の宿霧の峰; ☎0883-67-5211; www.kirinomine.jp; Mi-no-koshi; r per person incl/excl 2 meals ¥7000/4000; P ❄ ☎) This one-stop shop in the car park at Mi-no-koshi has all the bases covered, with a restaurant, a gift shop and a *minshuku,* all within a minute's walk of the chairlift station. Rooms are small and facilities shared, but there is a bath for tired hikers and laundry facilities that guests can use.

Tsurugi-san Chōjō Hutte HUT ¥¥
(剣山頂上ヒュッテ; ☎088-622-0633; www.tsurugisan-hutte.com; Tsurugi-san; per person incl/excl meals ¥8500/5300) Just below the peak, Tsurugi-san Chōjō Hutte offers basic lodgings. It's simple, as you'd expect at a mountain hut, but the food tastes great at 1955m, the bath is claimed to be the highest *ofuro* in western Japan and you'll sleep well as 'lights out' is at 9pm. Best of all, it's not far to go for a mountaintop sunrise.

Getting There & Away

Tsurugi-san is at the head of the Iya Valley, so if you've been exploring Iya, carry on up Rte 439 to Mi-no-koshi. Alternatively, head up the fascinating Rte 438 from the main Yoshino Valley to the north at Sadamitsu. For a long, mountainous approach, take Rte 438 from Tokushima city to the east.

It is possible to get to Mi-no-koshi by bus, but it's not easy. Check for the latest at a tourist information office.

KŌCHI PREFECTURE

The largest of Shikoku's four prefectures, Kōchi Prefecture (高知県) spans the Pacific coastline between the two capes of Muroto-misaki and Ashizuri-misaki. Cut off from the rest of Japan by the mountains and sea, the province once known as Tosa was traditionally regarded as one of the wildest and most remote places in the country. To pilgrims, Kōchi is known as *Shūgyō-no-dōjō*, the place of practice, and has a reputation as 'the testing ground'. Although the trip through Tosa makes up more than a third of the pilgrimage, only 16 of the 88 Temples are located in the province.

Kōchi Prefecture is a good place for outdoor types; it brims with scenic spots both in and along its rugged mountains and coastlines. Check out www.visitkochijapan.com.

Kōchi

088 / POP 350,000

Kōchi (高知) is a smart, compact city with a deserved reputation for enjoying a good time. The castle here is largely undamaged and remains a fine example of Japanese architecture. Excellent access to Muroto-misaki, Ashizuri-misaki and the Iya Valley, and easy day trips to caves, beaches and mountains make Kōchi a perfect base for travels around the island. Also claimed by Kōchi is a samurai of great national significance – during the Meiji Restoration, Sakamoto Ryōma was instrumental in bringing down the feudal government.

The central part of the city is 12km north and inland from the sea and the liveliest part of town is where the tramlines cross near Harimaya-bashi, a tiny red replica of a bridge made famous by song and film in Japan. The main Obiyamachi shopping arcade runs perpendicular to Harimayabashi-dōri. This action is about 1km south of JR Kōchi station.

Sights

★Kōchi-jō CASTLE

(高知城; 1-2-1 Marunouchi; ¥420; 9am-5pm) Kōchi-jō is one of just a dozen castles in Japan to have survived with its original *tenshu-kaku* (keep) intact. The castle was originally built during the first decade of the 17th century by Yamanouchi Katsutoyo, who was appointed *daimyō* by Tokugawa Ieyasu after he fought on the victorious Tokugawa side in the Battle of Sekigahara in 1600. A major fire destroyed much of the original structure in 1727; the castle was largely rebuilt between 1748 and 1753.

The castle was the product of an age of peace – it never came under attack and for the remainder of the Tokugawa period it was more like a stately home than a military fortress. The fee is for entry to the castle itself; it's free to walk in the surrounding grounds.

★Kōchi Castle Museum of History MUSEUM

(高知城歴史博物館; 088-871-1600; www.kochi-johaku.jp; 2-7-5 Ōtesuji; ¥500; 9am-6pm Mon-Sat, from 8am Sun) This new museum (opened in 2017), celebrating the history of Kōchi castle, is an architectural achievement in its own right. Entry is free to the museum shop (1st floor) and to the 2nd floor cafe and terrace – both with marvellous views of the castle and its grounds. The entry fee gives you access to the 3rd floor where you'll find interesting exhibitions on the history of the castle and the city of Kōchi.

★Sunday Market MARKET

(日曜市; Ōte-suji; 5am-6pm Sun Apr-Sep, 5.30am-5pm Sun Oct-Mar) Our favourite street market in Shikoku is 300 years old and takes place every Sunday along 1.3km of Ōte-suji, the main road leading to the castle. Around 430 colourful stalls sell fresh produce, tonics and tinctures, knives, flowers, garden stones, wooden antiques and everything else imaginable.

Temple 31: Chikurin-ji BUDDHIST TEMPLE

(竹林寺; 088-882-3085; www.chikurinji.com; 3577 Godaisan) FREE At Godaisan in the east of the city, you'll find Chikurin-ji, Temple 31 of the 88. The extensive grounds feature a five-storey pagoda and thousands of statues of the Bodhisattva Jizō, guardian deity of children and travellers. The temple's **Treasure House** (¥400; 8am–5pm) hosts an impressive collection of Buddhist sculpture from the Heian and Kamakura periods; the same ticket gets you in to see the temple's lovely Kamakura-period garden opposite.

The **My-Yū bus** (MY遊バス; www.visitkochijapan.com/about/Kochi_MYyou_EN.pdf; 1-/2-day pass ¥1000/1600) runs from Kōchi bus station (p689) to Godaisan. Purchase the pass at the tourist information office (p689) in front of Kōchi Station; show your foreign passport and you'll get the pass for half price.

Kōchi

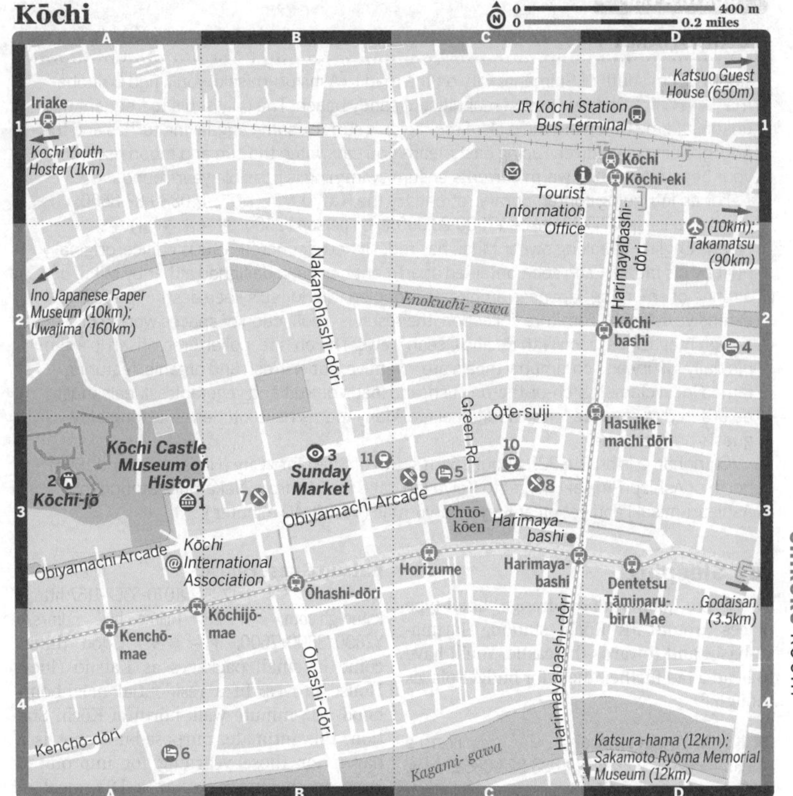

Kōchi

Top Sights

1 Kōchi Castle Museum of History A3
2 Kōchi-jō A3
3 Sunday Market B3

Sleeping

4 EN Hostel & Local Community D2
5 Richmond Hotel C3
6 Sansuien A4

Eating

7 Hirome Ichiba B3
8 Kinako Cafe C3
9 Tosa Binchōtanyaki Onomi C3

Drinking & Nightlife

10 Amontillado C3
11 Tosa-shu Baru B3

Ino Japanese Paper Museum MUSEUM
(いの町紙の博物館; ☎088-893-0886; www.kamihaku.com/en; 110-1 Saiwai-chō, Ino-chō; ¥500; ⊙9am-5pm Tue-Sun) Discover the history and development of *washi* (Japanese paper) at Ino, about 10km west of downtown Kōchi. There are demonstrations of *nagashizuki* papermaking techniques and on the first Sunday of every month, there's a papermaking class (¥400; in Japanese only). Check out the excellent English website for details. The museum is a 10-minute walk from both the Ino JR and tram stations.

Festivals & Events

Yosakoi Matsuri CULTURAL
(よさこい祭り; Yosakoi Festival; ⊙10 & 11 Aug) Kōchi's lively Yosakoi Matsuri on 10 and 11 August perfectly complements Tokushima's Awa-odori Matsuri (12 to 15 August). There's a night-before event on 9 August and a night-after effort on 12 August, but 10 and 11 August are the big days.

WORTH A TRIP

ŌKINOHAMA

About 25km south of Shimanto City on the road to Ashizuri-misaki, you'll find Ōkinohama (大岐の浜), Shikoku's most magnificent sandy beach. The only souls to frequent this unspoilt 2km stretch are the pick of the region's surfers, some egg-laying turtles and the odd, grinning clam diver. Facing east means you can watch the sun and moon rise from your beach towel, and warm currents ensure swimming is possible year-round.

For an intriguing contemporary retreat, try the **Kaiyu Inn** (海癒; ☎0880-82-8500; www.kaiyu-inn.jp; 2777-12 Ohki; s ¥7000-23,000, extra person ¥2500; P ⊖ ❄ ☎ 🐾) . Fluent-English-speaking owner Mitsu has redesigned a concrete 1960s edifice, originally built by his father. Each self-contained apartment has been designed either by Mitsu or a range of emerging Japanese architects. Coupled with Mitsu's keen aesthetic eye and extensive designer-furniture collection, the result is a collection of spaces worthy of design magazines, each with Pacific Ocean views. The on-site, boiler-fired onsen is a simple daily luxury and communal meals are inventive, super-fresh and organic, featuring famed local clams, catch-of-the-day fish, and loads of fruit and vegetables. Meals must be ordered in advance for an additional fee. Many rooms have kitchens and long-stay guests are welcome.

Ōkinohama is on Rte 321, about 25km south of Shimanto City (Nakamura) and 15km north of Ashizuri-misaki. To get to Kaiyu Inn, take the bus from Nakamura Station to Ashizuri-misaki and get off at Kaiyu-no-yu-mae (¥1100, 40 minutes).

Sleeping

There are plenty of midrange hotel-type places around JR Kōchi station, Harimaya-bashi and towards the castle. You'll have to head a tad further afield for budget places though.

★**Kochi Youth Hostel** HOSTEL ¥
(高知ユースホステル; ☎088-823-0858; www.kyh-sakenokuni.com; 4-5 Fukuihigashi-machi; dm/s ¥2500/3000; P ⊖ ❄ ☎) Sitting along a canal near Engyōjiguchi (円行寺口) Station, this immaculate wood-panelled hostel has simple, comfortable rooms and a welcoming, homely vibe. Spring for the excellent-value ¥400 breakfast. The friendly, English-speaking host Kondo Tomio is a former sake company rep and offers sake-sampling courses for ¥500. Find detailed directions in English on the website.

EN Hostel & Local Community HOSTEL ¥
(☎088-855-9888; www.enhostel.com; 1-12-2 Sakurai-chō; dm/tw from ¥3500/7400; ❄ ☎) Opened in 2018, EN provides stylish mixed and female-only dorms, plus a number of private rooms, in a totally refurbished building. It has been elegantly decorated in a lovely timber finish, and has a welcoming community lounge and bar, as well as a coin laundry. It's a 10-minute walk from JR Kōchi Station.

Katsuo Guest House GUESTHOUSE ¥
(かつおゲストハウス; ☎070-5352-1167; http://katuo-gh.com; 4-7-28 Hijima-chō; dm/s/d ¥2800/3800/7600; P ⊖ ❄ ☎) Good things come in small packages as Katsuo Guest House proves. In a residential neighbourhood a 15-minute walk north of Kōchi Station, this intimate, purpose-built spot is a haven for those yearning for impromptu jams on the house guitar, a DIY meal in the communal kitchen and a friendly Kōchi welcome.

★**Richmond Hotel** HOTEL ¥¥
(リッチモンドホテル高知; ☎088-820-1122; http://kochi.richmondhotel.jp; 9-4 Obiyamachi; s/d from ¥6500/8500; P ⊖ ❄ ☎) Kōchi's top business hotel has the spotless, modern rooms and professional service expected for accommodation of this class, plus it's located just off the main shopping arcade in the heart of the city. Parking (¥700 per day) is a short distance off-site, but the hotel's convenient location puts you in walking distance of restaurants, bars and city attractions.

Sansuien HOTEL ¥¥
(三翠園; ☎088-822-0131; www.sansuien.co.jp; 1-3-35 Takajō-machi; r per person incl breakfast from ¥7500; P ⊖ ❄ ☎) Three blocks south of the castle along Kenchō-mae Dōri is this classy multistorey hotel with luxurious onsen baths and a garden incorporating a series of buildings that once formed part of the residence

of the *daimyō*. The Japanese tatami rooms far outweigh their Western counterparts for both size and comfort. Nonguests can use the baths from 10am to 4pm (¥900).

Eating & Drinking

Kōchi's main eating and entertainment district is in the area around the Obiyamachi Arcade and the Harimaya-bashi junction where the tramlines meet, about 1km south of JR Kōchi station. Local specialities include *katsuo-tataki*.

★**Tosa Binchōtanyaki Onomi** GRILL ¥
(土佐備長炭焼き おの実; 088-875-9710; www.hitosara.com/0006069213; 1-15-17 Obiya-machi; dishes from ¥400; 5pm-midnight) You'll need to be a tad adventurous to eat here as there's no English menu, but it's a top spot for regional meat cuisine, especially wild venison shot by the owner. Other charcoal-grilled meats include Kōchi beef, pork, chicken and – in season – *inoshishi* (wild boar). Quench your thirst with Kōchi sake, *shōchu* or tasty cold beer.

★**Hirome Ichiba** JAPANESE ¥
(ひろめ市場; 088-822-5287; www.hirome.co.jp; 2-3-1 Obiyamachi; dishes from ¥300; 8am-11pm, from 7am Sun) Dozens of mini-restaurants and bars specialising in everything from *gomoku rāmen* (seafood noodles) to *tako-yaki* (octopus balls) surround communal tables; this is the hub of Kōchi's cheap-eats scene. On weekends, it positively heaves with young people drinking hard and happy. It's a full block of mayhem at the end of the main arcade, just before the castle.

Kinako Cafe CAFE ¥
(きなこCafe; 088-875-2255; www.hitosara.com/0006109127; 1-1-7 Obiyamachi; meals from ¥800; 11am-3pm & 5-11pm Tue-Sat, lunch only Sun) This tiny, lovingly run place serves tasty set meals at lunchtime, then morphs into a jazz and wine bar serving top-quality *otsumami* (snacks) in the evenings. A great little place to relax after time on your feet in the Obiyamachi shopping arcade.

★**Tosa-shu Baru** BAR
(土佐酒バル; 088-823-2216; 1-9-5 Ōte-suji; 6pm-midnight Tue-Sun) Without doubt, this nonsmoking bar with an extremely convivial atmosphere is the place to go to try Kōchi-made sake. Owner Kōji is passionate about sake and has offerings from all 18 breweries in Kōchi, three daily-changing *nomi-kurabe* (tasting sets) and serves superb small dishes featuring local produce. He is a fountain of sake knowledge and plays great jazz.

Amontillado PUB
(アモンティラード; 088-875-0599; www.irishpub-amontillado.owst.jp; 1-5-2 Obiyamachi; 5pm-1am) When you're *izakaya*'d out and crave fish and chips with a pint of Guinness (¥880), pop into this Irish pub in its new location right on Obiyamachi Arcade. There's always plenty going on as it's popular with locals.

Information

Tourist Information Office (高知観光案内所; 088-826-3337; www.visitkochijapan.com; 8.30am-5pm, accommodation info to 7.30pm) The helpful tourist information pavilion at the front of JR Kōchi Station provides English-language maps, Kōchi mini-guidebooks, accommodation help and more. There's always an enthusiastic English speaker on hand. Free bicycles are also available here from 8.30am-5pm (bring ID).

Kōchi International Association (高知県国際交流協会; 088-875-0022; www.kochi-kia.or.jp; 2nd fl, 4-1-37 Honmachi; 8.30am-5.15pm Mon-Sat) Free internet access, a library and English newspapers.

Getting There & Away

AIR

Kōchi Ryōma Airport (高知龍馬空港; www.kochiap.co.jp; 58 Hisaedaotsu, Nankoku-shi), about 10km east of the city, is accessible by bus (¥720, 35 minutes) from the station. There are daily flights to/from Tokyo, Nagoya, Osaka and Fukuoka.

BUS

The **JR Kōchi Station Bus Terminal** (高知駅バスターミナル) is on the north side of Kōchi Station.

TRAIN

Kōchi is on the JR Dosan line, and is connected to Takamatsu (*tokkyū* ¥4900, 2¼ hours) via Awa-Ikeda (*tokkyū* ¥3140, 70 minutes). Trains also run west to Kubokawa (*tokkyū* ¥2960, 70 minutes), where you can change for Shimanto City (formerly known as Nakamura; *tokkyū* ¥4670, 1¾ hours from Kōchi).

Getting Around

Kōchi's colourful tram service (¥200 per trip) has been running since 1904. There are two lines: the north–south line from the station intersects with the east–west tram route at the Harimaya-bashi (はりまや橋) junction. Pay when you get off and ask for a *norikae-ken* (transfer ticket) if you have to change lines.

Free rental bicycles can be picked up from the Tourist Information Office (p689) at the front of JR Kōchi Station. They're available 8.30am to 5pm (bring ID).

Shimanto City

☎0880 / POP 37,000

Shimanto City (四万十市), formerly called Nakamura, is easily confused with Shimanto town, further up the coast – don't worry, even locals get confused! Both Shimanto City and the town further north chose their name because the Shimanto-gawa (四万十川) is known throughout Japan for its beauty and as being the country's last remaining undammed river. Shimanto City claimed the name because this is where the river heads out to the sea. Shimanto town claimed the name because the river's headwaters are within its boundaries.

Shimanto City is a good place to organise trips on and around the beautiful Shimanto-gawa and the surrounding valley. The further up the river you go, the more remote and beautiful it all becomes.

Activities

Head to Shimanto City Tourist Information Office for info on the region's blossoming number of outdoor activities including kayaking, canoe trips and camping.

Several companies offer **river cruises** on boats called *yakata-bune* (¥2000 per 50 minutes) and kayak rental (half-/full-day from ¥3500/5000).

Bike rental is available here too (five hours/full-day ¥1000/1500), along with maps for five suggested cycling routes.

DON'T MISS

BEST OUTDOOR ADVENTURES

- Hiking Ishizuchi-san (p697)
- Surfing the Tokushima coastline (p679)
- Hiking Tsurugi-san (p710)
- Rafting Yoshino-gawa (p684)
- Canyoning in Nametoko Valley (p701)
- Swimming at Ōkinohama (p688)

Sleeping & Eating

Kawarakko CAMPGROUND ¥

(かわらっこ; ☎0880-31-8400; www.kawarakko.com; campsites from ¥3300) About 12km inland and upriver on Route 441, this is a neatly maintained riverside campground run by an adventure company. Canoes, mountain bikes and even tents are available to hire should you fancy a night under the stars. There are no shops around here, so take all the supplies you are likely to need.

★**Shimanto-no-yado Iyashi-no-sato** SPA HOTEL ¥¥

(四万十の宿　いやしの里; ☎0880-33-1600; www.shimantonoyado.co.jp; 3370 Shimoda; r per person from ¥8000; P⊖❄📶) Describing itself as a 'resort-type ecology hotel', this lovely spot out on a hill near Shimoda Port at the mouth of Shimanto-gawa features beautiful, individually designed rooms, superb meals and an onsen that is also open to nonguests (¥680). Iyashi-no-sato is well worth the price; it's best if you have your own wheels to get here.

Hotel Sunriver Shimanto HOTEL ¥¥

(ホテルサンリバー四万十; ☎0880-34-8875; www.hss-40010.com; 383-15 Uyama; s/d from ¥6000/6500; P⊖❄📶) This brand spanking new hotel (as of 2018) is an excellent place to stay in Nakamura and to use as a base to explore the Shimanto area. Rooms may be a tad small, but the facilities are excellent with free parking out front and a ¥500 buffet breakfast. It's a short walk from JR Nakamura Station on Rte 56.

Ichimonya JAPANESE ¥

(いちもん家; ☎0880-34-5552; www.sunriver-shimanto.com; 383-15 Uyama; meals from ¥750; ⏲11am-9pm) Part of the new Hotel Sunriver Shimanto complex, this place has good-quality Japanese regional cuisine with sizeable portions at very reasonable prices. Take your pick of booth, table or tatami-mat seating. Seafood options on the picture menu include *katsuo-tataki*, while the chicken and pork meals more than hit the spot.

★**Sanzenkai** JAPANESE ¥¥

(山川海; ☎0880-31-5811; www.shimantonoyado.co.jp; 3370 Shimoda; mains from ¥1500; ⏲11.30am-2pm & 5-9pm) The three kanji characters that make up this classy restaurant's name say it all – mountain, river, sea. Out at the spectacular Iyashi-no-sato eco-hotel, Sanzenkai uses locally sourced seasonal ingredients to tempt the palates of both hotel guests and visitors. If you're not staying here, get the tourist office to call ahead and make a booking. There's also an onsen.

Information

The **Shimanto City Tourist Information Office** (四万十市観光協会; ☎0880-35-4171; www.shimanto-kankou.com; ⌚8.30am-5.30pm) is on the left as you exit JR Nakamura station and has an English-speaker on hand, an excellent English-language guide to the area, and can help book local accommodation and trips.

Getting There & Away

Shimanto City's station is called Nakamura, and it is 1¾ hours from Kōchi by the fastest train (¥5070). This is it in terms of heading south by train. To get to Ashizuri-misaki, you'll need to use a bus or your own wheels. From Nakamura, the Tosa-Kuroshio Sukumo Line does continue west, however, as far as Sukumo (¥620; 30 minutes).

It is possible to get to Uwajima in Ehime Prefecture by train and then continue on around Shikoku. This will involve backtracking north from Nakamura to either Wakai station (若井駅) or Kubokawa station (窪川駅), then taking the JR Yodo line (予土線) west through the mountains to Uwajima.

Ashizuri-misaki

☎0880

Ashizuri-misaki (足摺岬) is a rugged, picturesque promontory that's famous for **Kongōfuku-ji** (金剛福寺; ☎0880-88-0038; www.88shikokuhenro.jp/kochi/38kongofukuji; 214-1 Ashizuri-misaki) FREE, Temple 38 of the 88, its lighthouse and violent weather. Walking pilgrims breathe a sigh of relief on arrival, as they have just survived the longest distance between temples – 94km from Iwamoto-ji in Kubokawa.

Ashizuri means 'foot stamping' and the cape got its name from the story of an old monk who stamped his foot in anguish when his young disciple set off looking for the promised land of Fudaraku in a boat. Fudaraku was believed to be the blessed realm of Kannon, goddess of mercy, and many set forth from the cape in their search for paradise in this lifetime, never to be heard from again. Centuries later, Ashizuri is famous for suicides, with stories such as that of a young geisha who danced off the edge onto the beckoning rocks below.

There are enjoyable short walks around the cape, including to an observation platform and the lighthouse.

DRIVING SHIMANTO-GAWA

Little traffic and stunning scenery make Shikoku one of the best driving destinations in Japan. There's also a lack of regular public transport services in some areas, namely around the two southern capes and the Iya Valley, so your international licence can at last come in handy. Our favourite drive is along the banks of the Shimanto-gawa. Here you vie with the odd truck for single-lane access to some of the narrowest, bendiest, prettiest roads in the country, boxed in by rocky cliffs on one side and the shimmering Shimanto-gawa on the other.

Sleeping

Ashizuri Youth Hostel HOSTEL ¥
(足摺ユースホステル; ☎0880-88-0324; www.jyh.or.jp; 1351-3 Ashizuri-misaki; dm from ¥3780; 📶) This hostel is run by a friendly older couple who have been providing large, well-cared-for tatami rooms to visitors for years. With advance notice meals are available – breakfast is ¥650, dinner is ¥1080. It's west of the temple.

Ashizuri Kokusai Hotel HOTEL ¥¥
(足摺国際ホテル; ☎0880-88-0201; www.ashizuri.co.jp; 662 Ashizuri-misaki; r per person incl meals from ¥11,500; P❄📶) With spacious Japanese-style rooms and onsen baths overlooking the sea, this hotel is one of many that are located along the main road in town and mainly cater to groups.

Getting There & Away

This is a place to have your own wheels (p667). Alternatively, there are buses to Ashizuri-misaki from Nakamura Station (¥1900, 1½ hours, eight daily).

EHIME PREFECTURE

Occupying the west of Shikoku and formerly known as Iyo, Ehime Prefecture (愛媛県) is home to Shikoku's largest city, Matsuyama, and has the greatest number of the 88 pilgrimage temples – 27, to be precise. Like Tosa (Kōchi Prefecture), the southern part of the prefecture has always been considered wild and remote; by the time pilgrims arrive in Matsuyama, they know that the hard work has been done and they are well on their way to completing their goal. To pilgrims, Ehime is known as *Bodai-no-dōjō*, the 'place for attainment of wisdom'.

Highlights include the immaculately preserved feudal castle and historic Dōgo Onsen in Matsuyama, and the sacred peak of Ishizuchi-san (1982m), the highest mountain in western Japan.

For prefectural information, check www.visitehimejapan.com.

Matsuyama

089 / POP 507,000

Located in a lush river basin, Shikoku's largest city is handsome and refined, with a hint of mainland hustle. Matsuyama (松山) is famed across Japan for Dōgo Onsen Honkan, a luxurious 19th-century public bathhouse built over ancient hot springs. The finest castle on the island towers above the stylish trams criss-crossing the city streets and the harbour glistening in the distance.

WORTH A TRIP

TEMPLE 45: IWAYA-JI

Pilgrims will be hoofing it through Shikoku's mountainous interior to get here, but if you're not a henro you'll need your own wheels to get to the isolated, but extremely atmospheric Temple 45, **Iwaya-ji** (岩屋時; 0892-57-0417; www.88shikokuhenro.jp/ehime/45iwayaji; 1468 Nanatori, Kuma-kōgen) FREE. Its cliffside buildings tower precariously above the valley and visitors might almost feel the presence of the holy men of long ago. A trail lined with age-old statues winds up to the temple, then up and over the mountain above. Beside the main hall, climb the wooden ladder up to the platform in the indentation in the cliff where pilgrims ascend to pray.

Matsuyama is also home to eight of the 88 Temples, including Ishite-ji, one of the most famous stops on the pilgrimage.

The castle sits on a hill in the middle of the city with JR Matsuyama Station to its west, the city centre to its south and Dōgo Onsen to its east. Trams connect all the areas, including circumnavigating the castle's hill. The ferry port and airport are both west of the city.

Sights

★Matsuyama-jō CASTLE

(松山城; 089-921-4873; www.matsuyamajo.jp; ¥510; 9am-5pm, to 5.30pm Aug, to 4.30pm Dec & Jan) Perched on top of Mt Katsuyama in the centre of town, the castle dominates the city, as it has for centuries. Matsuyama-jō is one of Japan's finest surviving castles, and one of the very few with anything interesting to peruse inside: the castle has a treasure trove of artefacts with excellent English-language displays. A **ropeway** (one way/return ¥270/510) is on hand to whisk you up the hill, though there is a pleasant pathway if you prefer to walk.

It's worth walking down via the back slopes of the castle and stopping off at **Ninomaru Shiseki Tei-en** (二之丸史跡庭園; ¥100; 9am-5pm, to 5.30pm Aug, to 4.30pm Dec & Jan) in the outer citadel of the fort, consisting of old gardens and modern water features.

★Temple 51: Ishite-ji BUDDHIST TEMPLE

(石手寺; 089-977-0870; www.88shikokuhenro.jp/ehime/51ishiteji; 2-9-21 Ishite) FREE East of Dōgo Onsen is Ishite-ji, the 51st of the 88 Temples and one of the most impressive in the circuit. *Ishite* means 'stone hand' and comes from a legend associated with Kōbō Daishi in which a baby was born with a stone in its hand. Don't miss exploring the tunnels and caves at the rear of the complex. A statue of Kōbō Daishi overlooks the temple from high on the hillside.

Botchan Karakuri Clock LANDMARK

(坊ちゃんからくり時計) At the start of the arcade at Dōgo Onsen you can check out Botchan Karakuri Clock, which was erected as part of Dōgo Onsen Honkan's centennial in 1994. It features figures based on the main characters from *Botchan*, who emerge to take a turn on the hour from 8am to 10pm. The spectacle is viewed hourly by crowds of excited Japanese visitors.

Activities

According to legend, Dōgo Onsen (道後温泉) was discovered during the age of the gods when a white heron was found healing itself in the spring. The mono-alkaline spring contains sulphur, and is believed to be particularly effective at treating rheumatism, neuralgia and hysteria. It is best known for being included in the famous 1906 novel *Botchan* by Natsume Sōseki, the greatest literary figure of Japan's modern age, who based his novel on his time as a schoolteacher in Matsuyama in the early 20th century.

While the venerable old Dōgo Onsen Honkan building is *the* place to go, it is undergoing a seven-year extensive refurbishment until 2026 which may mean that it doesn't meet your expectations when you visit. What is actually operating will depend on when you turn up.

If you don't want a full bath, there are also nine free **ashi-yu** (足湯; foot baths) scattered around Dōgo Onsen, where you can take off your shoes and socks and warm your feet.

★Dōgo Onsen Honkan ONSEN
(道後温泉本館; www.dogo.jp/en; 5-6 Dōgo-yunomachi; ⏲6am-10pm, kami-no-yu to 11pm) The main building at Dōgo Onsen, Dōgo Onsen Honkan, was constructed in 1894, and designated as an important cultural site in 1994. The three-storey, castle-style building incorporates traditional design elements, and is crowned with a statue of a white heron in commemoration of its legendary origins. The larger and more popular of the two baths here is *kami-no-yu*.

Dōgo Onsen Honkan can be a bit confusing as there are two separate baths (and four pricing options) from which to choose. There are English-language pamphlets to clarify the various options and correct sequence of steps. Regardless of which option you choose, you are allowed to explore the building after taking your bath.

Asuka-no-yu Dōgo Onsen Annex ONSEN
(道後温泉別館 飛鳥乃湯泉; www.dogo.jp/en; 19-22 Dōgo-yunomachi; adult/child from ¥600/300; ⏲7am-10pm) Dōgo Onsen is expanding and its new Asuka-no-yu annex, while having some gorgeous new regular-type baths, will really appeal to those who want to enjoy a private bathing experience, whether it be with family or friends. Reservations for 90-minute slots can be made online, costing ¥2000 plus ¥1650 per adult and ¥820 per child. Check out the new complex online.

Tsubaki-no-yu ONSEN
(椿の湯; www.dogo.jp/en; 19-22 Dōgo-yunomachi; ¥400; ⏲6.30am-11pm) If you want to escape the crowds at Dōgo Onsen Honkan, one minute away on foot (through the shopping arcade) is Tsubaki-no-yu, Dōgo Onsen's hot-spring annex, frequented primarily by locals.

Sleeping

You'll want to decide whether to stay at Dōgo Onsen in the east or in Matsuyama city when in the prefecture's capital. There are plenty of options in both parts of the city.

★Cinnamon Guest House Dōgo GUESTHOUSE ¥
(シナモンゲストハウス道後; ☎089-916-9252; www.cinnamon-guesthouse-dogo.com; 4-50 Dōgo-yunomachi; dm/r ¥3000/10,000; 🚭❄📶) Run by English-speaking Shimpei, this place is a joy for backpackers happy to stay in a cheap capsule-style mixed or women-only dorm. There is also a four-person room up on the 3rd floor. Expect a welcome reception and an extremely convivial atmosphere. It's only a few minutes' walk up from Dōgo Onsen.

Fujiya HOSTEL ¥
(ふじや; ☎080-1750-5454; www.yado-fujiya.com; 7-23 Dōgo-yunomachi; dm/r from ¥3000/6000; ❄📶) Fujiya offers simple stuff with men's and women's dormitories plus a couple of rooms, but it is incredibly convenient – only a couple of minutes' walk from Dōgo Onsen tram station and the various Dōgo baths. There's a community room plus a kitchen and shower facilities, all attractively put together.

★Dōgo Yaya HOTEL ¥¥
(道後やや; ☎089-907-1181; www.yayahotel.jp; 6-1 Dōgo-takōchō; s/d from ¥8000/11,000; P❄📶) Easy on the eyes and the budget, Dōgo Yaya is aesthetically pleasing as well as a smashing deal. The 68 rooms of various layouts are models of clean, contemporary style infused with traditional Japanese elements: raised tatami platforms for the cushy Western beds, sliding *shōji*-type doors and wood-slat embellishments. No onsen, but guests receive discounted entry to nearby Dōgo Onsen.

Matsuyama

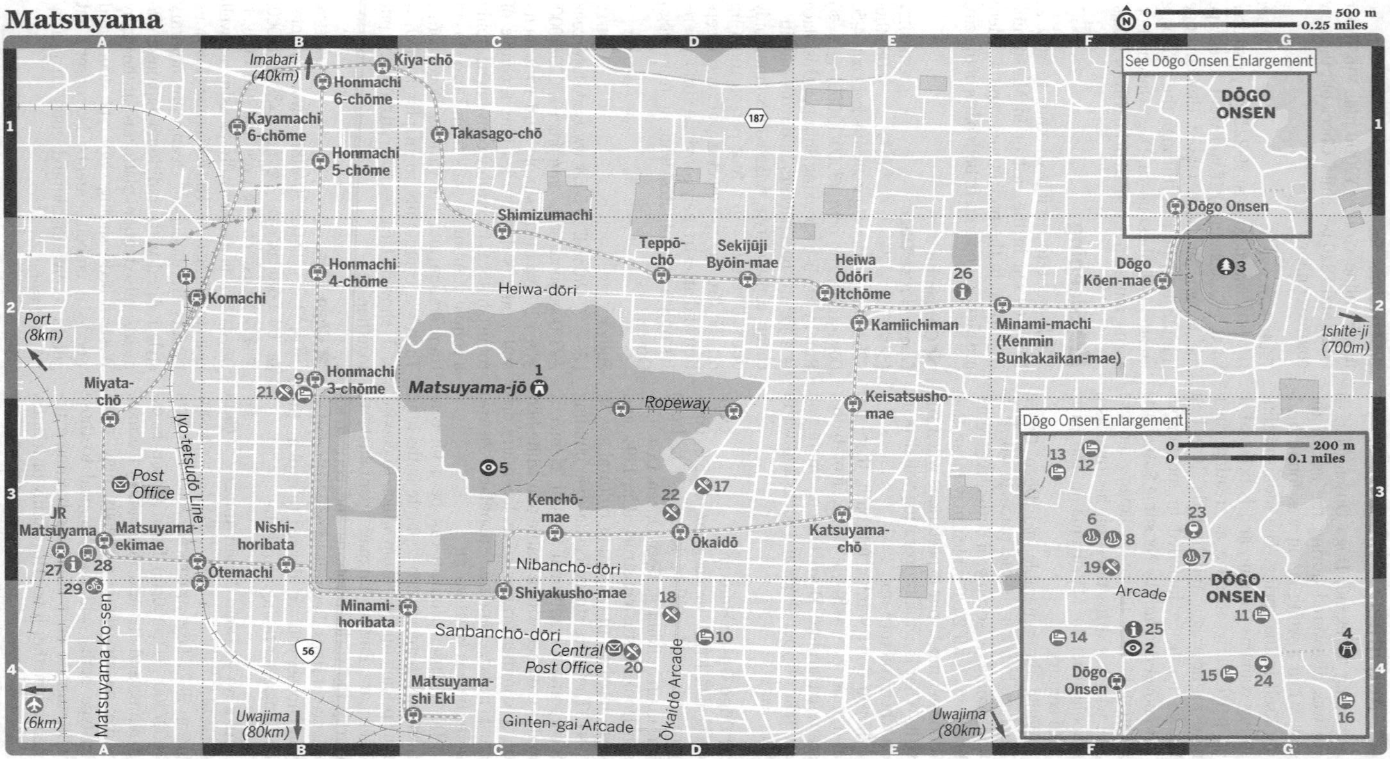

0 500 m
0 0.25 miles
A B C D E F G
1 2 3 4
Imabari (40km)
Kiya-chō
Honmachi 6-chōme
Kayamachi 6-chōme
Takasago-chō
Honmachi 5-chōme
187
See Dōgo Onsen Enlargement
DŌGO ONSEN
Dōgo Onsen
Shimizumachi
Teppō-chō
Sekijūji Byōin-mae
Heiwa Ōdōri Itchōme
26
Dōgo Kōen-mae
3
Honmachi 4-chōme
Heiwa-dōri
Komachi
Kamiichiman
Minami-machi (Kenmin Bunkakaikan-mae)
Port (8km)
Ishite-ji (700m)
Honmachi 3-chōme
9
21
1
Matsuyama-jō
Miyata-chō
Ropeway
Keisatsusho-mae
Iyo-tetsudō Line
5
Post Office
22
17
Kenchō-mae
Ōkaidō
Katsuyama-chō
JR Matsuyama
Matsuyama-ekimae
Nishi-horibata
27
28
Ōtemachi
Nibanchō-dōri
29
Shiyakusho-mae
Minami-horibata
18
Sanbanchō-dōri
10
Matsuyama Ko-sen
56
Central Post Office
20
Ōkaidō Arcade
Matsuyama-shi Eki
Uwajima (80km)
Ginten-gai Arcade
(6km)
Dōgo Onsen Enlargement
0 200 m
0 0.1 miles
13
12
6
8
23
7
19
Arcade
DŌGO ONSEN
11
25
2
14
4
15
24
Dōgo Onsen
16

Matsuyama

Hotel Mielparque Matsuyama HOTEL ¥¥

(ホテル　メルパルク松山; ☎089-945-6411; www.mielparque.jp/matsuyama; 123-2 Dogohimezuka; s/d from ¥7000/11,000; P ❄) A convenient place with a mix of large Western- and Japanese-style rooms a five-minute walk up from Dōgo Onsen (p693). This is a good option if you're driving as there is free parking, plus there's a nice onsen and you're only a short stroll from the heart of the Dōgo action.

Check Inn Matsuyama HOTEL ¥¥

(チェックイン松山; ☎089-998-7000; www.checkin.co.jp/matsuyama; 2-7-3 Sanban-chō; s/tw from ¥5500/8000; P ❄) This business hotel is excellent value for money. Well-equipped modern rooms have free wi-fi, there's a *konbini* (convenience store) in the lobby and an onsen on the roof (the women's onsen is on the 2nd floor). A short walk from the Ōkaidō arcade (大街道), the hotel is super convenient for the city's nightlife and restaurants.

Funaya RYOKAN ¥¥¥

(ふなや; ☎089-947-0278, toll-free 0120-190-278; www.dogo-funaya.co.jp; 1-33 Dōgo-yunomachi; r per person incl meals from ¥22,000; P ❄) Natsume Sōseki took refuge from his writer's block and aching limbs here, and so should you if you can afford it. The beauty lies inside, from the central garden and private onsen to the exquisite surrounding tatami rooms fit for Japanese royalty. It's a short walk from the Dōgo Onsen tram station along the road that leads up to Isaniwa-jinja.

Dōgo Kan HOTEL ¥¥¥

(道後舘; ☎089-941-7777; www.dogokan.co.jp; 7-26 Dōgo-takōchō; r per person incl meals Mon-Fri from ¥24,000, Sat & Sun from ¥28,000; P ❄) The Kurokawa Kishō–designed Dōgo Kan lies on a slope behind the Tsubaki-no-yu public baths. Indoor ponds and supremely gracious staff complement the grand tatami rooms and elaborate series of communal baths. The Western rooms are appreciably cheaper but lack any real 'Dōgo-ness', which is one of the attractions of this atmospheric spot. You may find better rates online.

Eating

★**Café Bleu** CAFE ¥

(カフェブルー; ☎089-907-0402; 4th fl, 2-2-8 Ōkaidō; meals ¥600-900; ⏲11.30am-midnight Mon-Sat) This lovely little music cafe serves tasty, simple sustenance with a picture menu and daily specials. The decor includes photos of Andy Warhol and Mick Jagger spying on you in the bathroom, vintage typewriters and shelves of art books. Beer (including Guinness on draught) and generous cocktails are also available. Spot the signboard out front; it's on the 4th floor.

Agetai FISH & CHIPS ¥

(揚げ鯛; ☎089-904-4515; www.agetai.net; 3-4-1 Ōkaidō; meals from ¥500; ⏲11am-8pm Thu-Tue) This is a new concept taking into

CYCLING OVER THE SEA

A fantastic way to travel between Shikoku and Hiroshima Prefecture is via the Shimanami Kaidō (p470), a bicycle route that crosses a series of bridges across six Inland Sea islands.

Sunrise Itoyama (サンライズ糸山; 0898-41-3196; www.sunrise-itoyama.jp; 2-8-1 Sunaba-chō, Imabari; bicycle rental per day from ¥1000, plus ¥1000 deposit; 7am-9pm) in Imabari, right at the base of the first bridge, is the most convenient starting point on the Shikoku side. Everything is very well set up here. Rental bicycles (normal, tandem and electric-assist), which you can drop off on the Honshū side, are available; you can stay here (singles/twins ¥4320/6500); and there is a restaurant and an information office. Check it all out online. JR Imabari Station is a 15-minute, ¥2000 taxi ride away.

consideration that Ehime Prefecture is well known for its *tai* (snapper). Agetai offers up tasty dishes such as deep-fried snapper fish and chips (from ¥500), and deep-fried snapper burgers (from ¥650), plus local drinks like Dōgo Beer in a casual spot on the road leading up to the castle ropeway. Relaxed and fun.

Dōgo-no-machiya CAFE ¥

(道後の町屋; 089-986-8886; www.dogonomachiya.com; 14-26 Dōgo-yunomachi; meals ¥650-1000; 10am-10pm Wed-Mon, closed every 3rd Wed) With a traditional shopfront along the Dōgo arcade, this former teahouse now serves as a bakery-cafe offering burgers, sandwiches and soul-satisfying coffee and tea drinks. Its shotgun-style layout leads through beautifully preserved dark-wood rooms to a Japanese garden and a tatami room out back.

★**Kappō Yano** SEAFOOD ¥¥

(割烹矢野; 089-931-6346; 2-5-8 Masaki-machi; meals from ¥1500; 11am-2.30pm & 5-10pm Mon-Sat) Yano-san and his family have been serving traditional meals at their popular seafood place a block back from **APA Hotel** (アパホテル松山城西; 089-943-1011; www.apahotel.com; 2-5-5 Honmachi; s/d from ¥6000/8000; P ⊖ ❄ ☜) for more than 30 years. Choose from his chef's *omakase* courses from ¥3000, or go for a *teishoku* set meal such as sashimi *teishoku* or *yakizakana teishoku* (grilled fish) for ¥1500. Top seafood at reasonable prices.

SOHSOH VEGETARIAN ¥¥

(お野菜食堂ＳＯＨＳＯＨ; 089-998-7373; www.greenlabel-group.com; 3-2-10 Ōkaido; set meal from ¥1050; 11am-10pm;) This is the first store of what has become a Japan-wide chain for Ehime-based SOHSOH. While meals are not completely vegetarian, they are vegetable and salad heavy with small fish and meat portions (which can be removed when you order). It's extremely popular, so there are often lines to get in. Another SOHSOH restaurant is underground by Takashimaya at Shi-eki station.

Goshiki Sōmen NOODLES ¥¥

(五志喜; 089-933-3838; https://s422500.gorp.jp; 3-5-4 Sanban-chō; meals ¥780-2000; 11am-3pm & 5-11pm) Next to the central post office is this elegant Matsuyama institution, which specialises in *goshiki sōmen* (thin noodles in five different colours). You'll recognise it by the piles of colourful noodles in the window waiting to be taken home as souvenirs. Set meals are around ¥1500; there is a picture menu with English descriptions of the most popular dishes.

Drinking & Nightlife

★**Dōgo Bakushukan** MICROBREWERY

(道後麦酒館; 089-945-6866; www.dogobeer.co.jp/bakusyukan.html; 20-13 Dōgo-yunomachi; 11am-10pm) Right by Dōgo Onsen Honkan, it's hard to walk past this brewery restaurant, a good spot for a locally made beer and a bite to eat after a relaxing soak. The names of the brews are allusions to novelist Natsume Sōseki and his famous novel, *Botchan*. There's also a decent range of food available from a picture menu.

Wani to Sai BAR

(ワニとサイ; 080-3319-2765; www.facebook.com/wanitosai; 1-39 Dōgo-yunomachi; drinks from ¥600; 6pm-late) Easily the funkiest little spot in Matsuyama, Wani to Sai is definitely easy to spot with a colourful facade featuring an alligator and a rhinoceros *(wani to sai)*. Wanting to hang with an arty crowd? You've come to the right place.

Information

Ehime Prefectural International Centre (愛媛県国際交流協会; EPIC; 089-917-5678; www.epic.or.jp; 1-1 Dōgo Ichiman; 8.30am-5pm Mon-Sat) Provides advice, internet access and bike rental. EPIC is near the Minami-machi (南町; aka Kenmin Bunkakaikan-mae) tram stop. Get off the tram, look towards the castle and you'll see a sign about 200m away above the road pointing to EPIC.

Tourist Information Office (☎089-931-3914; ⏰8.30am-8.30pm) The main office is located inside JR Matsuyama Station, while a **branch office** (☎089-943-8342; ⏰8am-8pm) is opposite the tram terminus for Dōgo Onsen.

ℹ Getting There & Away

AIR

Matsuyama airport (松山空港; www.matsuyama-airport.co.jp), 6km west of the city, is easily reached by bus (¥460, 15 minutes, every 30 minutes) from the front of the JR Matsuyama Station.

BOAT

The superjet hydrofoil, run by the **Setonaikai Kisen** (瀬戸内海汽船; ☎Matsuyama booking office 089-953-1003; www.setonaikaikisen.co.jp; ⏰7am-9pm) ferry, has regular hydrofoil connections between Matsuyama and Hiroshima (¥7100, 1¼ hours, 12 daily). Their Hiroshima–Matsuyama ferry (¥3600, 2½ hours, 10 daily) is also a popular way of getting to/from Shikoku.

The **Matsuyama Kokura Ferry** (松山・小倉フェリー; ☎089-967-7180; www.matsuyama-kokuraferry.co.jp; 5-2292-1 Takahama-chō) runs between Matsuyama and Kita-Kyūshū (seven hours, daily).

BUS

There are daily JR Highway buses from the **bus stop** at the train station that run to/from Osaka (5½ hours) and Tokyo (12 hours). Fares vary considerably depending on the date. There are frequent buses to major cities in Shikoku.

TRAIN

The JR Yosan line connects Matsuyama with Takamatsu (*tokkyū* ¥6390, 2½ hours) and there are also services across the Seto-ōhashi to Okayama (*tokkyū* ¥7030, 2¾ hours) on Honshū.

ℹ Getting Around

BICYCLE

Available at the **JR Matsuyama Rental Cycle Port** (per day ¥300; ⏰8.30am-5pm), to the right, out on the main road, as you exit JR Matsuyama Station. You can also pick up and drop off at the Ōkaidō Rental Cycle Port in the Ōkaidō Arcade, the Matsuyama-jō (Castle) Rental Cycle Port at the foot of the ropeway, and the Dōgo Onsen Station Rental Cycle Port.

TRAM

Tickets cost a flat ¥160 for each trip (pay when you get off). A day pass costs ¥600. Lines 1 and 2 are loop lines, running clockwise and anti-clockwise around Katsuyama (the castle mountain). Line 3 runs from Matsuyama-shi station to Dōgo Onsen; line 5 goes from JR Matsuyama station to Dōgo Onsen; and line 6 from Kiya-chō (木屋町) to Dōgo Onsen.

You can also ride the vintage Botchan Ressha (坊ちゃん列車), small trains that were imported from Germany in 1887. Named for Natsume Sōseki's famous novel, they ran up and down Matsuyama's streets for 67 years, and they're now back in use. Combo tickets for the Botchan Ressha plus a one-day tram pass cost ¥800.

Ishizuchi-san

At 1982m, Ishizuchi-san (石鎚山) is known as 'the roof of Shikoku' and is the highest peak in western Japan. With its name meaning 'stone hammer mountain', Ishizuchi is one of the Hyakumeizan, Japan's 100 Famous Mountains. Long a centre for mountain worship, Ishizuchi attracts pilgrims and climbers alike, particularly during the July and August climbing season. The first 10 days of July are marked with a 'mountain opening festival' attended by white-dressed pilgrims from all over Japan. Views from the peak are spectacular.

With a rental car, Ishizuchi-san can be climbed easily on a day trip from Matsuyama when approached from Tsuchi-goya. A day trip from Matsuyama without your own wheels will require a fair bit of planning and use of train, bus and cable car via Iyo-Saijo.

Skiing and snowboarding is possible using the Ishizuchi Tōzan Ropeway between January and April.

Activities

★**Ishizuchi-san** HIKING

(石鎚山) There are two good starting points for climbing Ishizuchi-san. For the easier hike, head to **Tsuchi-goya** at 1500m, to the east of the mountain and allow four hours for the return hike. For a more strenuous day, start at the Ishizuchi cable-car station at **Nishi-no-kawa**, to the north of Ishizuchi-san. The **cable car** (石鎚登山ロープウェイ; ☎0897-59-0331; www.ishizuchi.com; one way/return ¥1030/1950; ⏰8am-6pm Jul & Aug, hours vary Sep-Jun) carries hikers from 455m up to 1300m, followed by a six-hour round-trip hike to the summit.

The two tracks meet before a final climb to the peak of **Misen** (1974m), where you'll find **Ishizuchi-jinja** and a mountain hut where you can eat and stay the night.

The last sections before the peak can be climbed using *kusari,* steel chains that are embedded in the rock and head straight up. These are provided to help you test your mettle. If pulling yourself up chains doesn't appeal, there are alternate routes that bypass the chains. From the peak of Misen, there is a final test along a sharp ridge to **Tengu-dake** (1982m, the highest point).

Sleeping & Eating

If you are out hiking, there are places to eat at the top of the cable car, at the mountain hut at the peak and at Tsuchi-goya. Take hiking snacks with you.

Ishizuchi-san Summit Hut HUT ¥¥
(Chōjō-sansō; 石鎚山 頂上山荘; ☎0897-55-4168, bookings 080-1998-4591; www.ishizuchisan.jp/sansou/sub02-0.htm; per person incl 2 meals ¥8700) Open from the start of May to the start of November, this is an isolated mountain hut perched on the exposed peak of Ishizuchi-san. It sleeps 50. There's nothing luxurious here, but hot meals, a spot with bedding on a tatami mat in a warm shared room, and a solid roof and walls await. A real Japanese mountain experience.

Getting There & Away

Having your own wheels is the best way to get to Tsuchi-goya. There are buses from Matsuyama, requiring a change of buses at Kuma, but these only operate on weekends and public holidays.

To get to the Ishizuchi cable-car station, **Setouchi Bus** (せとうちバス; ☎0898-23-3450; www.setouchibus.co.jp; one way ¥1000) runs buses between JR Iyo-Saijo station (earliest departure is at 7.47am) and the Shimodani cable-car station (one hour). The latest departure back is at 5.23pm. There are plenty of places to park (¥400) at the bottom cable-car station if you come by car.

Uchiko

☎0893 / POP 20,500

Uchiko (内子) is undergoing a mini-renaissance, with a growing number of domestic travellers taking interest in this attractive town with a prosperous past. During the late Edo and early Meiji periods, Uchiko boomed as a major producer of vegetable wax – the Hon-Haga family established the production of fine wax in Uchiko, winning awards at World Expositions in Chicago (1893) and Paris (1900).

Sights

★Yōkaichi Historic District HISTORIC SITE
(八日市) Uchiko's picturesque and protected main street has a number of interesting buildings, many of which now serve as museums, souvenir stalls, craft shops, accommodation and charming teahouses. The old buildings typically have cream-coloured plaster walls and 'wings' under the eaves that serve to prevent fire spreading from house to house. As the street is in the Historic District Preservation Zone, there are strict regulations on how buildings are renovated.

Museum of Commerce & Domestic Life MUSEUM
(商いと暮らし博物館; ☎0893-44-5220; 1938 Uchiko; ¥200; ⏲9am-4.30pm) A few minutes' walk north along the main road from the visitors' centre is the Museum of Commerce & Domestic Life, which exhibits historical materials and wax figures portraying a typical merchant's home of the early 20th century. If you understand Japanese, the recorded voicing of various characters in the house is entertaining; otherwise, get the lowdown from the English flyer.

Uchiko-za THEATRE
(内子座; ☎0893-44-2840; www.town.uchiko.ehime.jp/site/uchikoza; 1515 Uchiko; ¥400; ⏲9am-4.30pm) About halfway between the station and Yōkaichi is Uchiko-za, a magnificent traditional kabuki theatre. Originally constructed in 1916, the theatre was completely restored in 1985, complete with a revolving stage. Performances are still held at the theatre; call ahead for a schedule.

Ōmori Wa-rōsoku FACTORY
(大森和ろうそく; ☎0893-43-0385; http://o-warousoku.com; 2214 Uchiko; ⏲9am-5pm, closed Tue & Fri) Here at Uchiko's last remaining candle manufacturer the candles are still made by hand, according to traditional methods; you can watch the candle makers at work.

Sleeping

★Uchikobare Guesthouse & Bar HOSTEL ¥¥
(内子晴れ; ☎0893-57-6330; https://uchikobare.jp; 3025 Uchiko; dm/d from ¥3000/10,000; P⊖❄☜) This lovely spot in a totally refurbished building right on Uchiko's Yōkaichi main street provides the town's cheapest accommodation with both mixed

and women-only dorm rooms and a private room with a shared bathroom. It's impressively done, with welcoming English-speaking hosts and a gorgeous tatami-mat cafe and bar in operation from 1pm-10pm.

★ Nakahaga Residence Guesthouse GUESTHOUSE ¥¥
(中芳我邸ゲストハウス; ☎0893-50-6270; www.we-love-uchiko.jp/stay/581; 2655 Uchiko; s/tw ¥8000/12,000;) Uchiko has some gorgeous traditional places to stay and the Nakahaga Residence on Yōkaichi tops the list. This stylish, remodelled storehouse is a classic and feels like a step back in time to the Edo period. It only has the one lodging room with twin beds. No meals on offer, but there are plenty of places to eat nearby.

Takahashi Residence MINSHUKU ¥¥
(文化交流ヴィラ高橋邸; ☎0893-44-2354; www.we-love-uchiko.jp/stay/562; 2403 Uchiko; per person with breakfast ¥6260; P) This lovely refurbished two-storey traditional place, just off Yōkaichi, is a registered 'cultural exchange house' and takes only one booking per night. It can sleep up to 10. There are huge stone walls at the entrance, an Edo period–style gate, and a well-kept garden. Enjoy a real Japanese experience.

Oyado Tsuki-no-ya GUESTHOUSE ¥¥
(御宿月乃家; ☎0893-43-1160; www.uchiko-tsukinoya.com; 2646 Uchiko; s/tw ¥6400/10,500;) A brilliant place to stay right on Yōkaichi in the protected area, Tsuki-no-ya is a beautifully restored traditional building with classic tatami rooms and Japanese-style shared bathroom and toilet facilities. Meals are available and lovingly prepared using local produce by the couple who run the place – dinner ¥2310, breakfast ¥1050. Order the meals for the full experience.

Eating

Nanze CAFE ¥
(☎0893-44-6440; 2023 Uchiko; meals from ¥700; ⏲10am-5pm Fri-Wed) Nice spot out the back of the visitors' centre with tons of parking. Offers interesting options including a seasonal set lunch, French toast, spaghetti and Locomoco (everyone's Hawaiian favourite!). Local products are also for sale.

Uchiko Fresh Park Karari MARKET ¥
(内子フレッシュパークからり; ☎0893-43-1122; www.karari.jp; 2452 Uchiko; ⏲9am-5pm) Above the Oda River, this farmers market offers fresh, locally grown produce, prepared *bentō* (boxed meals) and regional specialities. There's a restaurant serving good *teishoku* meals.

Restaurant Karari JAPANESE ¥¥
(レストランからり; www.karari.jp; 2452 Uchiko; Karari set ¥1200; ⏲11am-7.30pm) This lovely spot by the walking bridge serves good *teishoku* meals. Try the Karari set (¥1200) and choose a main, served with bread or rice, from the picture menu. Then head up to the salad bar for your fill of hearty greens.

Getting There & Away

Uchiko is 25 minutes south of Matsuyama by the fastest train (¥2230) and 55 minutes (¥2990) north of Uwajima.

Uwajima

☎0895 / POP 87,000

A pleasant, unhurried castle town, Uwajima (宇和島) draws a steady trickle of titillated travellers to its Shintō fertility shrine and attached sex museum. Though most travellers bypass Uwajima en route to Matsuyama, the town makes an enjoyable stop and retains some noteworthy traditions, such as pearl farming, terraced agriculture and bloodless bullfighting.

SHIKOKU–KYŪSHŪ FERRY

Throughout the centuries, pilgrims from Kyūshū traditionally arrived in Yawatahama (八幡浜) by ferry and then started and ended their pilgrimage at nearby Temple 43 – Meiseki-ji (明石寺).

The **Uwajima Unyu Ferry** (宇和島運輸フェリー; ☎0894-22-2100; www.uwajimaunyu.co.jp) connects Yawatahama to Beppu (¥3100, three hours, six daily) and Usuki (¥2310, 2½ hours, six or seven daily) on Kyūshū. You can also take your car.

By the fastest train, Yawatahama is 45 minutes from Matsuyama (¥3180) and 30 minutes from Uwajima (¥2130).

From the station, Yawatahama port is a five-minute bus ride (¥150) or taxi ride (around ¥630); because buses are so infrequent, the 25-minute (1.5km) walk from Yawatahama Station is often faster than waiting for a bus.

Uwajima

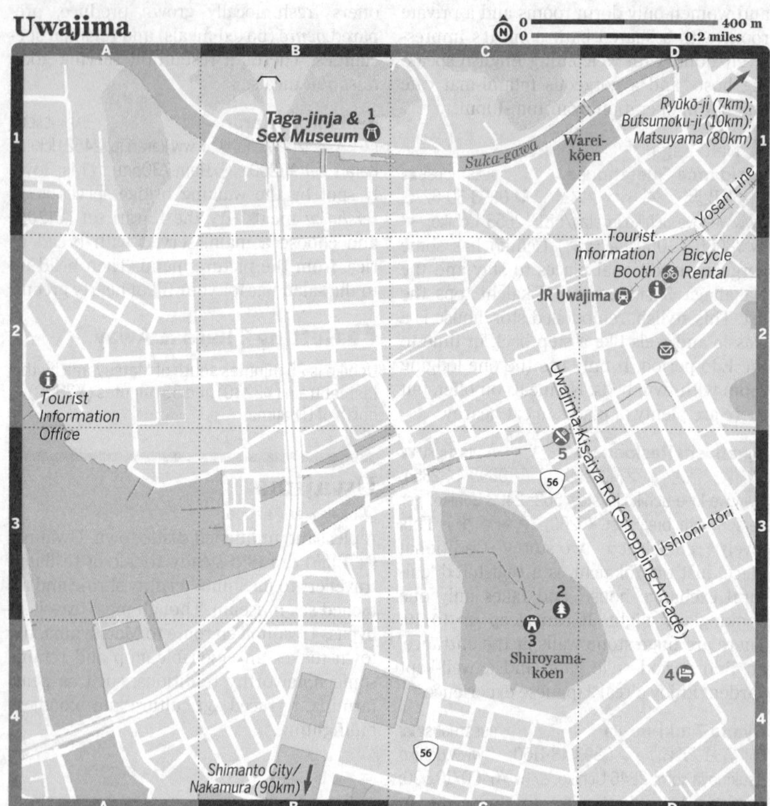

Sights

★Taga-jinja & Sex Museum
SHINTŌ SHRINE

(多賀神社・凸凹神堂; 0895-22-3444; www.geocities.jp/taga_shrine; 1340 Fujie; ¥800; 8am-5pm) Once upon a time, many Shintō shrines had a connection to fertility rites. Of those that remain, Taga-jinja is one of the best known. The grounds of the shrine have a few tree-trunk phalluses and numerous statues and stone carvings, but it's the notorious three-storey Sex Museum, packed with anthropological erotica from all corners of the procreating world, that brings 'em in.

Uwajima-jō
CASTLE

(宇和島城; 0895-22-2832; 1 Marunouchi; ¥200; 9am-4pm Tue-Sun) Dating from 1601, Uwajima-jō is a small three-storey castle on an 80m-high hill in the centre of town. The present structure was rebuilt in 1666 by the *daimyō* (regional lord) Date Munetoshi. The *donjon* (main keep) is one of only 12 originals left in Japan; there is nothing much to see inside. The surrounding park, **Shiroyama-kōen** (城山公園; sunrise-sunset), is a pleasant place for a stroll.

Activities

★Forest Canyon ADVENTURE SPORTS
(フォレストキャニオン; ☎0895-49-6663; www.nametoko.net; Meguro, Matsuno-chō; canyoning full-/half-day ¥11,000/7000) For an adrenaline rush, try canyoning in the beautiful Nametoko Valley (an easy day trip from Uwajima). Forest Canyon is dedicated to safety, with experienced guides, so guests can freely leap into deep pools, climb up some waterfalls, abseil down others and swoosh down natural slides (including one that's 40m long!) created by the river.

All equipment – including wetsuits, helmets and life jackets – is included in the rate. They also have a river-rafting option.

Sleeping & Eating

There are a few business hotels with standard rooms near the station in the centre of town.

There's eating and drinking action in the main street outside JR Uwajima Station and in and around the Uwajima Kisaiya Shopping Arcade between the station and the castle.

★Kiya Ryokan RYOKAN ¥¥¥
(木屋旅館; ☎0895-22-0101; www.kiyaryokan.com; 2-8-2 Honmachiōte; ryokan rental per night ¥21,600, plus per person ¥5400;) A rare opportunity to rent an entire house where literary greats have stayed, Kiya Ryokan offers a compelling reason for an Uwajima stop. Though not a traditional ryokan experience – no in-house staff or elaborate *kaiseki* (Japanese haute cuisine) dinners – it is uniquely modern and appealing. Best enjoyed by, and most economical for, groups (the house sleeps up to eight).

★Wabisuke SEAFOOD ¥¥
(和日輔; ☎0895-24-0028; www.sk-wabisuke.com; 1-2-6 Ebisu-machi; dishes ¥1000-1500; ⏲11am-10pm) This restaurant, just off the arcade, is an elegant spot to try the local *tai* (sea bream) specialities, available here as a *tai-meshi gozen* (sea bream set course; ¥1880). There is a picture menu, and plenty of small plates to choose from, and you'll find Wabisuke easy to spot with its red *ushi-oni* (red devil-bull) out front.

Information

Tourist Information Office (宇和島市観光協会; ☎0895-22-3934; www.uwajima-tourism.org; ⏲9am-6pm) At Kisaiya Hiroba at the port; find a more conveniently located **information booth** (☎0895-23-5530; ⏲9am-6pm) at the JR station.

There are international ATMs at the **post office** across from the station.

Getting There & Around

If you've come from points south, then from Uwajima you're back in the land of the trains. Uwajima is on the JR Yosan line, and you can head to Matsuyama (*tokkyū* ¥3710, 1½ hours) via Uchiko (*tokkyū* ¥2990, one hour). The JR Yodo line runs east to Kubokawa and Kōchi Prefecture.

You can hire **bicycles** (per hour ¥100; ⏲9.30am-5pm) at the station, in the corner office on the left after you exit the building.

KAGAWA PREFECTURE

Formerly known as Sanuki, Kagawa Prefecture (香川県) is the smallest of Shikoku's four regions and the smallest of the country's 47 prefectures. The region's hospitable weather and welcoming people have always been a comfort to pilgrims as they come to the end of their journey. To *henro*, Kagawa is known as *Nehan-no-dōjō*, the 'place of completion', because it has the last 22 of the 88 pilgrimage temples.

WORTH A TRIP

HIKING TEMPLES 41 & 42

A great way to get a taste of the 88 Temple Pilgrimage without having to slog it out along busy main roads is to follow this mini-circuit that starts and ends in Uwajima. This walk between **Temple 42 Butsumoku-ji** (佛木寺) and **Temple 41 Ryūkō-ji** (龍光寺) covers a little more than 5km.

Take a bus from Uwajima Station direct to Temple 42, Butsumoku-ji. After admiring the thatched bell-house and the statues of the seven gods of good fortune, follow the clearly marked *henro* trail back through picturesque farming villages and rice paddies to Temple 41, Ryūkō-ji. Here, a steep stone staircase leads up to a pleasant temple and shrine overlooking the fields. From outside Ryūkō-ji there are signs to Muden Station (務田駅), a 15-minute walk away. From here, you can catch a train or bus back to Uwajima.

Kagawa's attractions include the celebrated shrine of Konpira-san in Kotohira, the lively port city of Takamatsu with its world-renowned Japanese garden, Ritsurin-kōen, and the folk village of Shikoku-mura at Yashima. Today, the prefecture is a major point of arrival for visitors to Shikoku, since the only rail link with Honshū is via the Seto-ōhashi bridge to Okayama.

Takamatsu

☎087 / POP 420,500

The buoyant port city of Takamatsu (高松) hums a vibrant, many-part harmony – venerable castle grounds that host contemporary crafts fairs, the small-town-big-city energy of a prefectural capital, regional culinary specialities including *Sanuki-udon* and the heritage of traditional gems such as Ritsurin-kōen. It's urban Japan at its most pleasant.

While there has been a lot of modernisation around the station and port, the heart of Takamatsu still beats further south in the colourful entertainment district and arcades of the central city.

On a practical and pleasurable level, Takamatsu is also a transportation hub. It serves as a jumping-off point for day-trippers to catch ferries to the snowballing art scene on the islands of the Inland Sea, and good train links mean visitors can consider staying in Takamatsu to visit prefecture hot spots such as Kotohira, Zentsūji, Marugame and Yashima.

Sights

★Ritsurin-kōen PARK

(栗林公園; ☎087-833-7411; www.my-kagawa.jp/brochure; 1-20-16 Ritsurin-chō; ¥410; ⏲sunrise-sunset) One of the most beautiful gardens in the country, Ritsurin-kōen dates from the mid-1600s and took more than a century to complete. Designed as a walking garden for the enjoyment of the *daimyō* (regional lord), the park winds around a series of ponds, tearooms, bridges and islands. To the west, **Shiun-zan** (Mt Shiun) forms an impressive backdrop to the garden. The classic view of **Engetsu-kyō bridge** with the mountain in the background is one of the finest in Japan.

Enclosed by the garden are a number of interesting sights, including **Sanuki Folkcraft Museum** (讃岐民芸館; 1-20-16 Ritsurin-chō; ⏲8.30am-5pm) FREE, which displays local crafts dating back to the Tokugawa dynasty. There are a number of teahouses in the park, including 17th-century **Kikugetsu-tei** (掬月亭; ☎087-833-7411; 1-20-16 Ritsurin-chō; matcha ¥710; ⏲9am-4pm), where you can sip *matcha* with a traditional sweet and enjoy various garden tableaux from the tatami rooms. You can also try the lovely thatched-roof **Higurashi-tei**, which dates from 1898.

Takamatsu-jō CASTLE

(高松城; 2-1 Tamamo-chō; ¥200; ⏲sunrise-sunset) The site of Takamatsu's castle now forms delightful **Tamamo-kōen**, a park where the walls and seawater moat survive, along with several of the original turrets. Each spring a swimming race is held in the moat to honour an age-old chivalrous tradition. The original castle was built in 1588 for Itoma Chikamasa, and was the home of the region's military rulers until the Meiji Restoration, nearly 300 years later. The restored castle keep is open to the public.

Takamatsu City Museum of Art MUSEUM

(高松市美術館; ☎087-823-1711; www.city.takamatsu.kagawa.jp/museum/takamatsu; 10-4 Konya-machi; ¥200; ⏲9.30am-5pm Tue-Sun) This impressive inner-city gallery is testament to Takamatsu's quality art scene. The light and spacious refitting of a former Bank of Japan building is a stroke of curatorial genius, well served by interesting exhibitions on rotation from across Japan and the world. It's often open until 7pm during special exhibitions.

Sleeping

★Guest House Wakabaya GUESTHOUSE ¥

(ゲストハウス若葉屋; ☎070-5683-5335; www.wakabaya.main.jp/en; 603-1 Kankō-chō; dm/s/tw ¥3000/4000/8000; P❄📶) Wakabaya's many pluses include an English-speaking owner, reasonable rates, clean rooms and bathroom facilities, a living room and a kitchen, a washing machine (¥100), free parking, wi-fi and bicycle rental (per day ¥500); they'll even keep baggage for you. Best of all, it's a super-friendly place to stay. It's a five-minute walk from Hanazono Station on the Kotoden Nagao line.

Konyamachi Guesthouse Kuku HOSTEL ¥

(紺屋町ゲストハウス 久々; ☎087-887-5665; www.kuku81.com/; 3-13 Konya-machi; dm/apt ¥3500/20,000; ❄📶) This well-appointed three-storey hostel meets all requirements. It's spotlessly clean; convenient to the station, port and arcades; and has mixed and women-only dorm rooms, a communal kitchen,

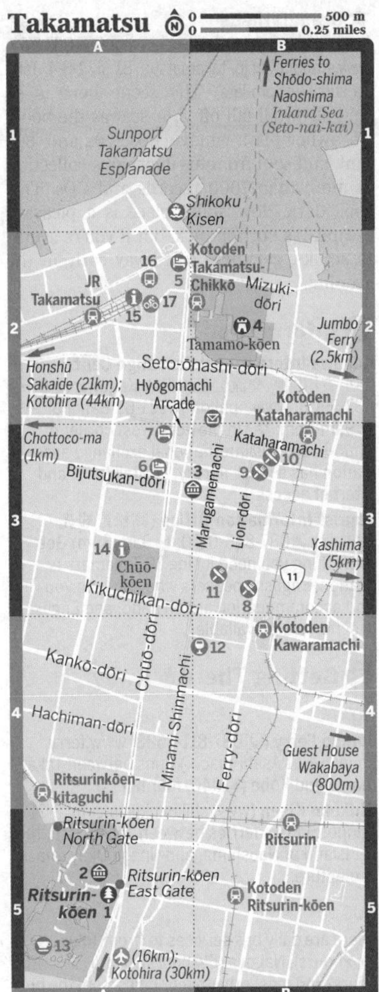

laundry facilities and wi-fi. Apartment-style rooms on the 3rd-floor sleep up to four and have a private bathroom and a kitchen.

Takamatsu Tokyu REI Hotel HOTEL ¥¥

(☎087-821-0109; www.tokyuhotels.co.jp/takamatsu-r; 9-9 Hyogomachi; r from ¥9500; P ⊜ ❄ 📶) This recently refurbished place in the Tokyu hotels stable is extremely convenient with quality, practical rooms and full amenities. No surprises here, but you know what you're getting will be decent. It's right on the corner of Chūō-dōri and the Hyogomachi arcade, a short stroll south from the station.

Takamatsu

Top Sights

1 Ritsurin-kōen A5

Sights

2 Sanuki Folkcraft Museum A5
3 Takamatsu City Museum of Art B3
4 Takamatsu-jō B2

Sleeping

5 JR Hotel Clement Takamatsu A2
6 Konyamachi Guesthouse Kuku A3
7 Takamatsu Tokyu REI Hotel A3

Eating

8 Bijin-tei B3
9 Kawafuku B3
10 Kawanishi Broiler B3
11 Ofukuro B3

Drinking & Nightlife

12 Grandfather's B4
13 Kikugetsu-tei A5

Information

14 Kagawa International Exchange Centre A3
15 Tourist Information Office A2

Transport

16 Bus Terminal A2
17 Takamatsu City Rent-a-Bicycle A2

JR Hotel Clement Takamatsu HOTEL ¥¥¥

(JRホテルクレメント高松; ☎087-811-1111; www.jrclement.co.jp; 1-1 Hamano-chō; s/d from ¥14,000/23,000; P ⊜ ❄ 📶) This eye-catching place is the top hotel in town and one of the first buildings you see as you exit JR Takamatsu Station. The rooms are spacious, and there's a good selection of bars and restaurants with sweeping views of the Inland Sea. Big convenience factor here, but you'll pay appropriately.

Eating & Drinking

Restaurants and bars cluster in the covered arcades to the west side of the tracks between Kotoden Kataharamachi and Kawaramachi stations. In particular, north-south running Lion-dōri and its side streets throw up an abundance of eating and drinking options. People here are serious about their udon and no trip would be complete without at least one bowl of *Sanuki-udon*. Look for the words *te-uchi udon* (手打ちうどん), meaning 'handmade noodles'.

★**Kawanishi Broiler** IZAKAYA ¥
(カワニシブロイラー; ☎087-811-6845; https://kawanishiburoiya.gorp.jp; 9-8 Kawara-machi; plates from ¥200; ⊙4pm-midnight) A top spot for beer, *yakitori* and just about anything featuring chicken. Relax inside at the counter or tables and enjoy the mayhem as locals come and go, or sit out at one of the three tables in the arcade and watch the world pass by. All drinks are ¥280, the beer is cold and the food is extremely tasty.

★**Ofukuro** IZAKAYA ¥
(おふくろ; ☎087-862-0822; 1-11-12 Kawara-machi; dishes ¥500-1500; ⊙5-11pm Mon-Sat) This fabulous *washofu* (local eating house) in the heart of the entertainment district offers a well-priced and hearty dining experience. A number of delicious, pre-prepared vegetarian and fish dishes sit on the counter, served with salad and miso soup. It might be a tad hard to find, but it's right on Tokiwa Shinmachi shopping street and worth the effort.

Kawafuku UDON ¥
(川福; ☎087-822-1956; www.kawafuku.co.jp; 2-1 Daiku-machi; udon lunch set ¥600; ⊙11am-11.30pm) One of Takamatsu's best-known udon shops, Kawafuku serves its silky *Sanuki-udon* in a variety of ways. Choose from the plastic food models outside. Look for the red-and-white striped lanterns in front, along Lion-dōri.

Bijin-tei IZAKAYA ¥¥
(美人亭; ☎087-861-0275; 2-2-10 Kawara-machi; dishes ¥700-1500; ⊙5-10pm Mon-Sat) Smiling *mama-san* sees all at this discreet seafood *izakaya*. Point to the menu items already plated – the pickled *tako* (octopus) is a mouthful – or ask for an *osusume* (recommendation). It's on the ground floor of a unobtrusive building containing several snack bars and karaoke joints. Look for the white sign with the shop's name written in black kanji.

BOAT EXCURSIONS

Takamatsu is a great base for exploring the olive groves of Shōdo-shima (p484), the art scene of Naoshima (p478) and the islands of the Inland Sea, all less than an hour by boat.

★**Grandfather's** BAR
(グランドファーザーズ; ☎087-837-5177; www.grandfather.jp/takamatsu; B1 fl, 1-6-4 Tokiwa-chō; ⊙6pm-late) The scene here is so smooth you'll fall off your seat as the bookish owner plays vintage '60s, '70s and '80s funk and soul from his enormous collection of more than 7000 records and CDs. This cool, dark, downstairs place is a pleasant escape. It's our top pick, but if you're averse to smoke, get there and away early in the evening.

Information

Kagawa International Exchange Centre (アイパル香川国際交流会館; I-PAL Kagawa; ☎087-837-5908; www.i-pal.or.jp; 1-11-63 Banchō; ⊙9am-5pm; 📶) In the northwest corner of Chūō-kōen, this international exchange association has a small library, a satellite TV and internet access.

Tourist Information Office (高松市観光案内所; ☎087-826-0170; ⊙9am-8pm) Get everything you need inside JR Takamatsu Station. English speakers who can help you find accommodation are on hand, and English brochures are available.

Getting There & Away

BOAT

Jumbo Ferry (☎087-811-6688; www.ferry.co.jp; 5-12-1 Asahi-machi) Runs between Takamatsu and Kōbe (¥1940, four hours).

Shikoku Kisen (www.shikokukisen.com; 8-21 Sanpōto) Runs ferries between Takamatsu, the art island of Naoshima, and Uno in Okayama Prefecture.

BUS

There are daily bus services to/from Tokyo (9½ hours), Nagoya (5½ hours), Kyoto (3½ hours) and most other major cities from the **bus terminal**.

TRAIN

Takamatsu has regular rail links to Honshū. There are frequent trains to Okayama (¥2030, 55 minutes), where you can connect to *shinkansen* services that will whiz you to any of Japan's major cities in just a few hours.

From Takamatsu, *tokkyū* trains on the JR Kōtoku line run southeast to Tokushima (¥3360, one hour); the JR Yosan line runs west to Matsuyama (¥6390, 2½ hours); and the JR Dosan line runs to Kōchi (¥5360, two hours). The private Kotoden line also runs direct to Kotohira (¥620, one hour).

Getting Around

BICYCLE

Takamatsu is flat and excellent for biking. The city offers a great deal on its rental bicycles (per 24 hours ¥100; photo ID is required), which can be picked up at **Takamatsu City Rent-a-Bicycle** (高松駅前広場地下レンタサイクルポート; 087-821-0400; 7am-10pm) in the underground bicycle park outside JR Takamatsu Station. Grab a pamphlet with a map showing six other spots around town where you can return the bike.

TRAIN

Kotoden (ことでん; 087-831-6008; www.kotoden.co.jp), a friendly and efficient local train company, runs trains on three lines:

- The yellow line runs from Takamatsu-Chikkō station, by the castle park in central Takamatsu to Kotohira (stops at Ritsurin-kōen)
- The green line runs from Takamatsu-Chikkō out to Nagao, where you'll find Temple 87, Nagao-ji
- The red line runs from Kawaramachi out east to Shido, stopping at Kotoden-Yashima and Yakuri on the way.

Yashima

About 5km east of Takamatsu and highly visible from the city is the 292m-high tabletop plateau of Yashima (屋島), where you'll find Yashima-ji, Temple 84 of the 88. Yashima, meaning 'roof island', is a peninsula of lava and is part of Seto-nai-kai National Park. There are great views over the Inland Sea and Takamatsu from various viewing spots.

Just to the east of Yashima and still in Seto-nai-kai National Park is Goken-zan, the mountainous stony peninsula that attracted Isamu Noguchi to live here with a source of stone for his sculptures. Here you'll also find Temple 85, Yakuri-ji and a fun retro cable car.

Sights

★Shikoku-mura — MUSEUM

(四国村; 087-843-3111; www.shikokumura.or.jp; 91 Yashima-nakamachi; ¥1000; 8.30am-6pm Apr-Oct, to 5.30pm Nov-Mar) About 500m north of Yashima station, Shikoku-mura is an excellent village museum that houses old buildings transported here from all over Shikoku and neighbouring islands. The village's fine kabuki stage came from Shōdo-shima, which is famous for its traditional farmers' kabuki performances. There is also an excellent restaurant serving, you guessed it, *Sanuki-udon* (from ¥450) in an old farmhouse building as you leave the village.

Temple 85: Yakuri-ji — BUDDHIST TEMPLE

(八栗寺; 087-845-9603; www.88shikokuhenro.jp/kagawa/85yakuriji; 3416 Mure, Mure-chō) FREE Half the fun of visiting Yakuri-ji may be riding the retro **cable car** (八栗ケーブル; 087-845-2218; www.shikoku-cable.co.jp; 3378-3 Mure, Mure-chō; one way/return ¥460/930; every 15min 7.30am-5.15pm) up and down to the temple, but this is a spectacular place in its own right, sitting in the forest under the high cliffs of Goken-san. As this is Temple 85 of the 88, most pilgrims at Yakuri-ji are excited as they get closer to their goal. This is a temple at which to pray for success in business, study and matchmaking! Take your passport as there's usually a 50% discount for foreigners on the cable car.

Temple 84: Yashima-ji — BUDDHIST TEMPLE

(屋島寺; 087-841-9418; www.88shikokuhenro.jp/kagawa/84yashimaji; 1808 Yashima-higashimachi) FREE Yashima-ji, Temple 84 of the 88, sits atop the tabletop mountain of Yashima, to the east of Takamatsu. This was the site of a decisive battle between the Genji and Heike clans in the late 12th century, and the temple's **Treasure House** (¥500) exhibits artefacts relating to the battle. Check out the Pond of Blood, where victorious Genji warriors washed the blood from their swords. You can either walk up from Yashima Station or drive up the scenic road.

Isamu Noguchi Garden Museum — MUSEUM

(イサムノグチ庭園美術館; 087-870-1500; www.isamunoguchi.or.jp; 3-5-19 Mure-chō; tours ¥2160; tours by appointment 10am, 1pm & 3pm Tue, Thu & Sat) Born in Los Angeles to a Japanese poet and an American writer, Noguchi (1904–1988) set up a studio and residence here in 1970. Today the complex is filled with hundreds of Noguchi's works, mostly unfinished. Inspiring sculptures are displayed in the beautifully restored buildings and in the surrounding landscape. You can also check out the house in which Noguchi lived. Email ahead for reservations, preferably two weeks or more in advance (see the website for reservations and access details). Tours in English are possible.

Eating

There are simple eating options (mainly specialising in udon) scattered about, particularly near the train stations of Yashima and Yakuri.

OFF THE BEATEN TRACK

UTAZU

For a taste of immersion in a small-town historic district where nothing caters to tourists, book a night or two in the town of Utazu. Along the old *henro* trail, the local government has teamed up with the Chiiori Trust (p684) to preserve and utilise two historic houses, known as **Co-machi-no-ie** (古街の家; ☎0877-85-6941; www.co-machi-no-ie.jp/english; s/d/tr from ¥14,000/16,000/21,000;).

The Co-machi houses are best for self-caterers looking to connect with the community – those who welcome the micro-adventures of interacting with the local shop owners, poking around **Gōshō-ji** (郷照寺; Temple 78) and checking out the landscape paintings housed in the waterfront Higashiyama Kaii Setouchi Art Museum. Utazu is a good base for self-driving visitors, with easy access to Marugame, Zentsū-ji and Konpira-san.

Udon Honjin Yamada-ya UDON ¥
(うどん本陣山田家; ☎087-845-6522; www.yamada-ya.com; 3186 Mure, Mure-chō; dishes from ¥800; ⊙10am-8pm) Something special not too far from the base of the Yakuri Cable Car east of Takamatsu. This is udon in a lovely setting in the old Yamada residence, a 'Cultural Property of Japan', eating in elegant tatami rooms and gazing out on a perfectly manicured Japanese garden. Tie in lunch here with a visit to Yakuri-ji, Temple 85 (p705).

Getting There & Away

Yashima is six stops from Takamatsu's Kawaramachi Station on the private Kotoden line (¥320). It's a very pleasant hour-long hike up the forested back side of the plateau to the temple. If you have your own wheels, the road up Yashima offers great views over Takamatsu and the Inland Sea and runs right up to the temple. At the time of research, the road was free, but it may become a toll road again.

Yakuri is eight stops from Kawaramachi on the Kotoden line (¥340). The Yakuri Cable Car station is easily reached by car from Takamatsu in 30 minutes.

Marugame

☎0877 / POP 110,500

Marugame (丸亀) is a bustling city that is only 25 minutes from Takamatsu by train. Home to Marugame-jō, a castle dating from 1597, the fascinating Uchiwa-no-Minato paper-fan museum and some top art museums, it makes an interesting day trip. Those wanting a true Shikoku experience for a few days might consider staying at one of the Co-machi-no-ie houses in Utazu, the next town north.

Sights

★Marugame-jō CASTLE
(丸亀城; ☎877-24-8816; www.marugame-castle.jp; ¥200; ⊙9am-4.30pm) This small castle dates from 1597. It took five years to build and is one of only 12 castles in Japan to have its original wooden *donjon* intact. It's known for its exquisite stone walls, moat and 1000 cherry trees that virtually explode with blossoms in spring. The entrance fee is for the castle keep; it's free to stroll inside the castle. Marugame Castle is a 10-minute walk southeast from JR Marugame Station.

Higashiyama Kaii Setouchi Art Museum MUSEUM
(東山魁夷せとうち美術館; ☎0877-44-1333; www.pref.kagawa.jp/higashiyama/english/museum; 224-13 Aza Minami-dōri, Shamijima, Sakaide; ¥300; ⊙9am-5pm Tue-Sun) Set on the waterfront of the Inland Sea with a sweeping view of Seto-ōhashi, this museum showcases the works of landscape painter Higashiyama Kaii (1908–99). It was Higashiyama who proposed the colour for the Seto Bridge.

Uchiwa-no-Minato Museum MUSEUM
(うちわの港ミュージアム; ☎0877-24-7055; www.city.marugame.kagawa.jp/sightseeing/spot/uchiwa_museum; 307-15 Minato-machi; ⊙9.30am-5pm Tue-Sun) FREE This museum has displays and demonstrations on how *uchiwa* (round paper fans) are made. Around 90% of Japan's *uchiwa* are still made in Marugame. You can learn how to make a paper fan in 50 minutes for ¥700. The museum is a 15-minute walk from the station, near the harbour.

Sleeping & Eating

Marugame Guesthouse HOSTEL ¥
(丸亀ゲストハウス; ☎0877-21-2942; www.marugame-guesthouse.com; 30-1 Fukushima-chō; dm from ¥3000;) This new place has

mixed, men's and women's dorms spread over three floors in a former office building within 50m of the North Exit of Marugame Station. SPACE Fukufuku is a very pleasant communal area for guests, plus there's a decent kitchen and laundry facilities

★ Ikkaku CHICKEN ¥
(一鶴; ☎0877-22-9111; www.ikkaku.co.jp; 317 Hamachō; plate from ¥750; ⌚11am-2pm & 4-10pm Mon-Fri, 11am-10pm Sat & Sun) *Honetsuki-dori* (spicy grilled chicken on the bone) is a Marugame speciality – try it at Ikkaku, a very popular local restaurant that has expanded its operations, taking Marugame's delicious dish as far as Osaka and Yokohama. Head out of the North Exit at the station, turn right and walk for 200m.

Information

Marugame Tourist Information Office (丸亀市観光案内所; ☎0877-22-0331; www.love-marugame.jp; ⌚9am-5.30pm) This office at JR Marugame Station has local maps and brochures, including in English. There is also an office at Marugame Castle.

Marugame Castle Tourist Information Office (丸亀城観光案内所; ☎0877-25-3881; www.love-marugame.jp; ⌚9am-4.30pm) Everything you could need in terms of maps and brochures is available at Marugame's second tourist office at the base of the castle.

Getting There & Around

Marugame is easily visited as a day trip by train (*tokkyū* ¥1070, 25 minutes) from Takamatsu (p702).

Across from the station, **bike hire** (☎0877-25-1127; www.love-marugame.jp; 42-6 Hamamachi; per day normal/electric ¥300/700; ⌚7am-7pm) is available from the bicycle park. By bike, it's five minutes to the castle and less than an hour to cycle from Marugame to Zentsuji.

Zentsuji

☎0877 / POP 35,000

The small town of Zentsuji is built up around Zentsū-ji, Temple 75 of the 88, and the place where Kōbō Daishi was born. The temple came first, then the town. If you're on a bike, there are several other pilgrimage temples within easy reach of this one, including Temple 72, Mandara-ji, and Temple 73, Shusshaka-ji. While these temples were originally sub-temples of Zentsū-ji, they soon became independent and part of the 88 Temple Pilgrimage in their own right.

Sights

★ Temple 75: Zentsū-ji BUDDHIST TEMPLE
(善通寺; ☎0877-62-0111; www.zentsuji.com; 3-3-1 Zentsūji-chō) FREE Zentsū-ji, Temple 75 of the sacred 88, is the largest of the temples – most of the other 87 could fit in its car park. This is where Kōbō Daishi was born, and the temple boasts a magnificent five-storey pagoda and giant camphor trees that are said to date back as far as Daishi's childhood. The temple is about 1.5km from the JR Zentsuji Station.

Visitors can venture into the basement of the **Mie-dō** and traverse a 100m-long passageway (戒壇めぐり; ¥500; 8am to 5pm) in pitch darkness. By moving carefully along with your hand pressed to the passageway's wall (painted with mandalas, angels and lotus flowers), you are said to be safely following Buddha's way.

Temple 73: Shusshaka-ji BUDDHIST TEMPLE
(出釈迦寺; ☎0877-63-0073; www.88shikokuhenro.jp/kagawa/73shusyakaji; 1091 Yoshiwara-chō) FREE Temple 73 on the 88 Temple Circuit, Shusshaka-ji was moved to the valley 200 years ago to make it more accessible to pilgrims. Before that, it was up a steep, precipitous mountain rising 500m above the plain. It is said that at the age of seven, Kōbō Daishi threw himself off this peak crying 'If I am called to save the people, save me Buddha!' Legend says he was saved by angels who carried him back to the top.

This is one of the places where magical powers are attributed to the mountains.

Sleeping & Eating.

A number of well-priced, casual restaurants are clustered around JR Zentsuji Station.

Kaze-no-Kuguru HOSTEL ¥
(風のくぐる; ☎0877-63-6110; www.kuguru.net; 306-1 Kami-yoshida-machi; dm ¥3000, s/d from ¥3800/6600; P❄📶) Located on a main road on the *henro* trail, this hostel is an excellent choice: friendly, immaculate and flooded with natural light. There are free laundry facilities and wi-fi. It's a brown building with lots of windows a 15-minute walk from the station; find a map on the website.

Getting There & Away

Kagawa is a very small prefecture. JR Zentsuji Station is only 45 minutes from Takamatsu (¥760) and only five minutes from Kotohira (¥210).

WORTH A TRIP

TEMPLE 88: ŌKUBO-JI

Ōkubo-ji (大窪寺; 0879-56-2278; www.88shikokuhenro.jp/kagawa/88ookuboji; 96 Tawa-kanewari, Sanuki-chō) FREE, the last of the Shikoku pilgrimage's 88 Temples, sits in the mountains in the southeast of Kagawa Prefecture and is well worth a visit. It's fitting that walking *henro* should face a stiff climb to get to the final temple, though if they are doing it properly, they still have to walk back to Temple one to complete the circle – for the search for enlightenment is, like a circle, never-ending.

Kotohira

0877 / POP 9800

The small village of Kotohira (琴平) is home to one of Shikoku's most famous tourist attractions, Konpira-san, a Shintō shrine dedicated to the god of seafarers. Ascending its 1368 steep stone steps is a rite of passage for many Japanese people, with plenty of interesting en-route distractions. Mention to any older Japanese person that you've been to Shikoku and one of the first things they'll ask you is whether you climbed Konpira-san.

Sights

★**Konpira-san** SHINTŌ SHRINE

(金刀比羅宮; 892-1 Kotohira-chō; Hōmotsu-kan ¥800, Shoin ¥800; Hōmotsu-kan & Shoin 8.30am-4.30pm) Konpira-san or, more formally, Kotohira-gū, was originally a Buddhist and Shintō temple dedicated to the guardian of mariners. It became exclusively a Shintō shrine after the Meiji Restoration.

A lot of fuss is made about how strenuous the climb (1368 steps) to the top is, but if you've made it this far in Japan, you've probably completed a few lengthy ascents to shrines already.

The first notable landmark on the long climb is **Ō-mon** (大門), a stone gateway that leads to **Hōmotsu-kan** (宝物館; Treasure House; ¥800; 8.30am-4.30pm), where the collection of treasures is pretty underwhelming for such a major shrine. Nearby you will find five traditional-sweets vendors at tables shaded by large white parasols. A symbol of ancient times, the vendors (the Gonin Byakushō – Five Farmers) are descendants of the original families who were permitted to trade within the grounds of the shrine. Further uphill is **Shoin** (書院; Reception Hall; ¥800; 8.30am-4.30pm), a designated National Treasure that dates from 1659 and has some interesting screen paintings and a small garden.

Continuing the ascent, you eventually reach large **Asahi-no-Yashiro** (旭社; Shrine of the Rising Sun) FREE. Built in 1837, this large hall is dedicated to the sun goddess Amaterasu and is noted for its ornate wood-carving. From here, the short final ascent, which is the most beautiful leg of the walk, brings you to **Gohonsha** (御本社; Gohon Hall) FREE and **Ema-dō** (絵馬堂; Ema Pavilion) FREE. The latter is filled with maritime offerings ranging from pictures of ships and models to modern ship engines. From this level, there are spectacular views that extend right down to the coast and over the Inland Sea.

Keen climbers can continue for another 500 or so steps up to **Oku-sha** (Inner Shrine), which features stone carvings of *tengu* (bird-like demons) on the cliff.

★**Kanamaru-za** THEATRE

(金丸座; 0877-73-3846; www.konpirakabuki.jp/index.html; ¥500; 9am-5pm) This is Japan's oldest kabuki playhouse, though it had a lengthy stint as a cinema before falling out of use. Nowadays it has sporadic shows, but can be visited daily. The restorations are superb; wander backstage and see the revolving-stage mechanism, basement trapdoors and a tunnel out to the front of the theatre. The playhouse is 200m east of the main approach to Konpira-san. There's a good English leaflet available, and English-speaking volunteer guides are sometimes on hand.

Courses

Nakano Udon School COOKING

(中野うどん学校; 0877-75-0001; www.nakanoya.net; 796 Kotohira-chō; ¥1500) This is pretty good fun, learning how to make the legendary *Sanuki-udon* in an hour in a shop on the main street leading up to the bottom of the steps to Konpira-san. You get to knead the dough, jump on it, cut it, cook it and finally eat it – and you receive a certificate to boot. Make a reservation online.

Sleeping

★**Kotobuki Ryokan** RYOKAN ¥¥

(ことぶき旅館; 0877-73-3872; 245-5 Kotohira-chō; r per person incl breakfast from ¥7200; P ❄) This welcoming ryokan, which has

Kotohira

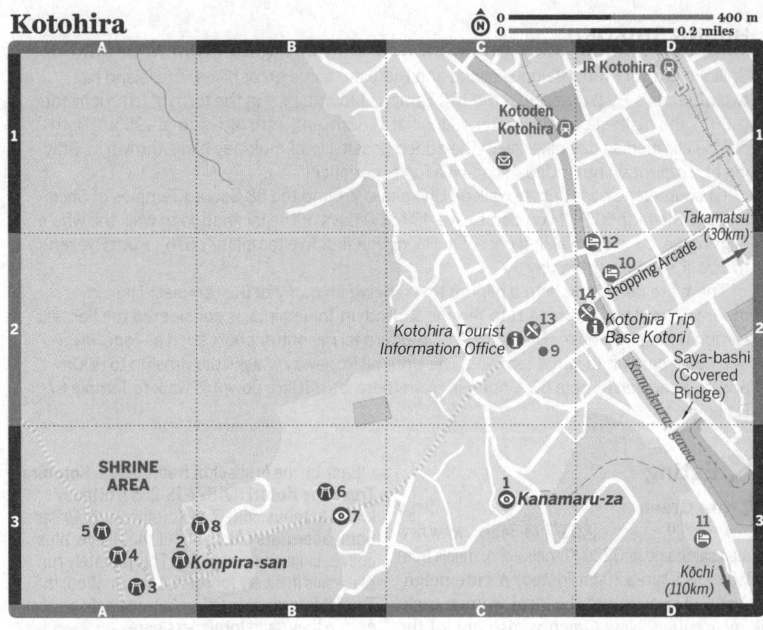

Kotohira

Top Sights

1 Kanamaru-za C3
2 Konpira-san A3

Sights

3 Asahi-no-Yashiro A3
4 Ema-dō A3
5 Gohonsha A3
6 Hōmotsu-kan B3
7 Ō-mon B3
8 Shoin B3

Activities, Courses & Tours

9 Nakano Udon School C2

Sleeping

10 Kotobuki Ryokan D2
11 Kotohira Kadan D3
12 Kotohira Riverside Hotel D2

Eating

13 Konpira Udon C2
14 New Green D2

comfortable tatami rooms and warm hospitality, is conveniently situated by the riverside, only a few minutes' walk from the start of the steps up to the shrine. Umbrellas, internet access and spotless shared bathrooms are all available. The wooden bathtub is gorgeous.

Kotohira Kadan RYOKAN ¥¥
(琴平花壇; ☎0877-75-3232; www.kotohira-kadan.jp; 1241-5 Kotohira-chō; r/villas per person from ¥12,000/24,000; P ⊖ ❄ 📶) A luxurious refuge after a climb up Konpira-san, this elegant ryokan is about three minutes' walk from the centre of Kotohira. Most of the rooms are Japanese style; there are three standalone villas too, all within a garden setting. Soak weary muscles in the house onsen or in your own tub (some of the tubs are open-air).

Beautifully presented meals feature local seafood and specialities of the region, and though the staff don't speak much English, they are extremely warm and accommodating.

Kotohira Riverside Hotel HOTEL ¥¥
(琴平リバーサイドホテル; ☎0877-75-1880; www.hananoyu.co.jp; 246-1 Kotohira-chō; s/d incl breakfast from ¥7500/13,000; P ❄ 📶) This well-run business hotel has comfortable Western-style rooms. There's an in-house bath, but guests also receive discounted rates at its sister property's onsen nearby. The hotel has a comfortable restaurant, a coin laundry and wi-fi throughout.

HIKING SHIKOKU

Shikoku is a very mountainous island and there are some great hikes. The island has two of Japan's Hyakumeizan – the 100 Famous Mountains – in the form of Ishizuchi-san (p697), the highest peak in western Japan at 1982m, and **Tsurugi-san** at 1955m. Both can be climbed as day hikes, with the added possibility of multiday hikes thrown in. Staying at a mountain hut in Japan can be a fun experience!

Of course, the best-known walk on Shikoku is around the 88 Sacred Temples of Shikoku Pilgrimage (p667). If you don't have 40 to 60 days or the inclination to walk the whole pilgrimage, consider walking part of it. Hiking the first five temples (p676), from Ryōzen-ji to Jizō-ji, will take half a day.

There are *henro-michi* (old pilgrim trails) between many of the temples. The old mountain trail from Temple 11 to Temple 12, both in Tokushima, is considered the hardest climb on the pilgrimage. There are even modern forms of transport such as ropeways and cable cars up to some temples. The Unpenji Ropeway whisks pilgrims up to 900m and spectacular Temple 66, Unpen-ji. From there it's a 10km downhill walk to Temple 67, Daikō-ji.

Eating

★New Green CAFE ¥

(ニューグリーン; ☎0877-73-3451; www.new-green.sakura.ne.jp; 722-1 Kotohira-chō; meals from ¥850; ⊙8.30am-8.30pm Fri-Wed) A cute neighbourhood spot where the local women cackle over coffee, New Green is also one of the few restaurants in town open for dinner. If the salads, *kaki-furai* (breaded, fried oysters) and *omu-raisu* (omelette filled with fried rice) leave you wanting, there's cake as well.

Konpira Udon UDON ¥

(こんぴらうどん; ☎0877-73-5785; www.konpira.co.jp; 810-3 Kotohira-chō; meals from ¥500; ⊙8am-5pm) Just short of the first set of steps leading up Konpira-san, this is one of dozens of *Sanuki-udon* joints in Kotohira. You can't miss it: the front window shows off the busy udon-makers rolling out dough and slicing noodles by hand. Try the *kake udon* (¥500), a simple dish of hot or cold noodles in broth.

Information

MONEY

The ATMs at the **post office** (665 Kotohira-chō; ⊙8am-8pm Mon-Fri, to 6pm Sat, 9am-3pm Sun) accept international cards.

TOURIST INFORMATION

Just before the start of the steps up Konpira-san, the small **Kotohira Tourist Information Office** (琴平観光協会; ☎0877-75-3500; www.kotohirakankou.jp; 811 Kotohira-chō; ⊙10am-6pm) offers up maps and English brochures for the town. A limited number of rental bicycles (¥100/500 per hour/day) are available too.

Back by the first set of traffic lights, **Kotohira Trip Base Kotori** (☎877-75-2657; https://kotori.kotobus.com; 725 Kotohira-cho; ⊙9am-6pm) offers lots of info about the village, plus coffee, cake and craft beer. This privately run place fills in nicely for tourist information; the Tourist Information Office has no English speakers, so they send foreigners here.

Getting There & Away

You can travel to Kotohira on the JR Dosan line from Kōchi (*tokkyū* ¥4650, 1½ hours) and Ōboke (¥2990, 45 minutes). For Takamatsu and other places on the north coast, change trains at Tadotsu. The private Kotoden line also has regular direct trains from Takamatsu (¥620, one hour).

Kanonji

☎0875 / POP 64,000

Named after Kannon, Goddess of Mercy, the town of Kanonji (観音寺) makes an interesting stop. In the town itself is Kotohiki-kōen, with an attractive beach and the Zenigata coin-shaped sand sculpture. Nearby are two of the 88 Temples, Jinne-in and Kanon-ji, Temples 68 and 69, in one compound – the only place on the pilgrimage where two temples share the same grounds. Inland, the Unpenji Ropeway whisks visitors up into the mountains to 900m and amazing Unpen-ji, Temple 66 of the 88.

Sights

★Temple 66: Unpen-ji BUDDHIST TEMPLE

(雲辺寺; ☎0883-74-0066; www.88shikokuhenro.jp/kagawa/66unpenji; 763-2 Hakuchi, Ikeda-chō) FREE Unpen-ji, aptly meaning 'Temple of the Surrounding Clouds', is the highest of the 88 Temples at 900m. Surprisingly, it actually sits in Tokushima Prefecture, although it's more or less right on the Kagawa Prefecture border. While walking pilgrims dreaded the climb for centuries, modern *henro* ride the **cable car** (雲辺寺ロープウェイ; ☎0875-54-4968; www.shikoku-cable.co.jp; 1974-57 Onohara-chō Marui; return ¥2060; ⏲every 20min 7.20am-5pm) up from the Kagawa side. There are 500 marvellous Rakan statues here. It is said that everyone has a lookalike among the 500 – see if you can find yours.

Zenigata LANDMARK

(銭形; Kotohiki-kōen) Zenigata is a 350m-circumference coin-shaped sculpture in the sand dating from 1633. The coin and its inscription are formed by huge trenches dug in the sand, and are said to have been dug overnight by the local population as a welcome present to their feudal lord. For the best views of the impressive sculpture, drive or climb the hill to the observation point in Kotohiki-kōen, directly behind Temple 68. There is a track up from the back of the temple.

Temples 68 & 69: Jinne-in & Kanon-ji BUDDHIST TEMPLE

(神恵院・観音寺; ☎0875-25-3871; www.shikoku88-6869.com; 3875 Yahata-chō) FREE These two temples, said to have been founded in 703 CE, are notable in that this is the only point on the pilgrimage trail where two of the 88 Temples share the same compound. Apparently this is a top spot to pray for victory in battle, as Emperor Kameyama held ceremonies here in the 13th century that helped repel an attempted Mongol invasion. There's a good little noodle shop on the grounds too.

Sleeping & Eating

Kanonji is only 45 minutes from Takamatsu by train. There isn't much in the way of sleeping options here, so it's best visited on a day trip.

You'll find small eating establishments serving standard Japanese fare scattered about town, especially near the station.

Information

The **tourist information office** (☎0875-25-3839; http://kanonji-kankou.jp; ⏲9am-5pm), over the bridge from the station in the Taishō-bashi Plaza building, has maps and information, plus regular/electric-assist rental bicycles (¥100/1000 per day) for use between 9am and 4.30pm.

Getting There & Away

JR Kanonji station is only 45 minutes from Takamatsu by the fastest train (¥2990) and 1¾ hours from Matsuyama (¥4980).

AT A GLANCE

POPULATION
Fukuoka: 1.60 million

MOST ACTIVE VOLCANO
Sakurajima (p772)

BEST VIEWPOINT
Inasa-yama (p735)

BEST RAMEN
Ippudō (p720)

BEST SHŌCHŪ
Honkaku Shōchū Bar Ishizue (p771)

WHEN TO GO

Apr–May Temperate weather and blooming azaleas on the volcanic slopes.

Jul–Aug Beat the night-time heat at tempting *yatai* (food stalls) in Fukuoka.

Oct–Nov Pleasant temperatures bring energetic festivals, such as Nagasaki's Kunchi Matsuri.

Kumamoto-jō (p744)
COLOURSINMYLIFE/SHUTTERSTOCK ©

Kyūshū

Kyūshū (九州), Japan's southern- and westernmost main island, is arguably its warmest and most beautiful, with active volcanic peaks, rocky, lush and near-tropical coastlines, and great onsen (hot springs) virtually everywhere. History and legend were made here: Jōmon ruins, Shintō's sun goddess, wealthy trading ports, cloistered foreigners, samurai rebels and one of the earth's greatest wartime tragedies all loom large. Today, burgeoning Fukuoka is a multicultural metropolis. In sweet, picturesque Nagasaki, tragedy contrasts with a colourful trading history. Kumamoto's castle is one of Japan's finest fortresses, and volcanic Aso is the world's largest caldera (both were heavily damaged in earthquakes in 2016).

INCLUDES

Kyūshū Highlights

1 Fukuoka (p720) Joining night owls for beer and ramen at a *yatai* (food stall).

2 Nagasaki (p730) being moved by stories of early European traders and WWII tragedy.

3 Hirado (p728) Exploring this remote island's unique history and charm.

4 Ibusuki (p774) Getting buried in warm volcanic sand at this hot-spring resort.

5 Kurokawa Onsen (p751) Recharging in a riverside *rotemburo* (outdoor bath).

6 Gunkanjima (p734) Touring the deserted 'ghost island' (aka Hashima).

7 Pottery towns (p728) Marvelling at Japan's ceramics traditions in Arita, Imari and Karatsu.

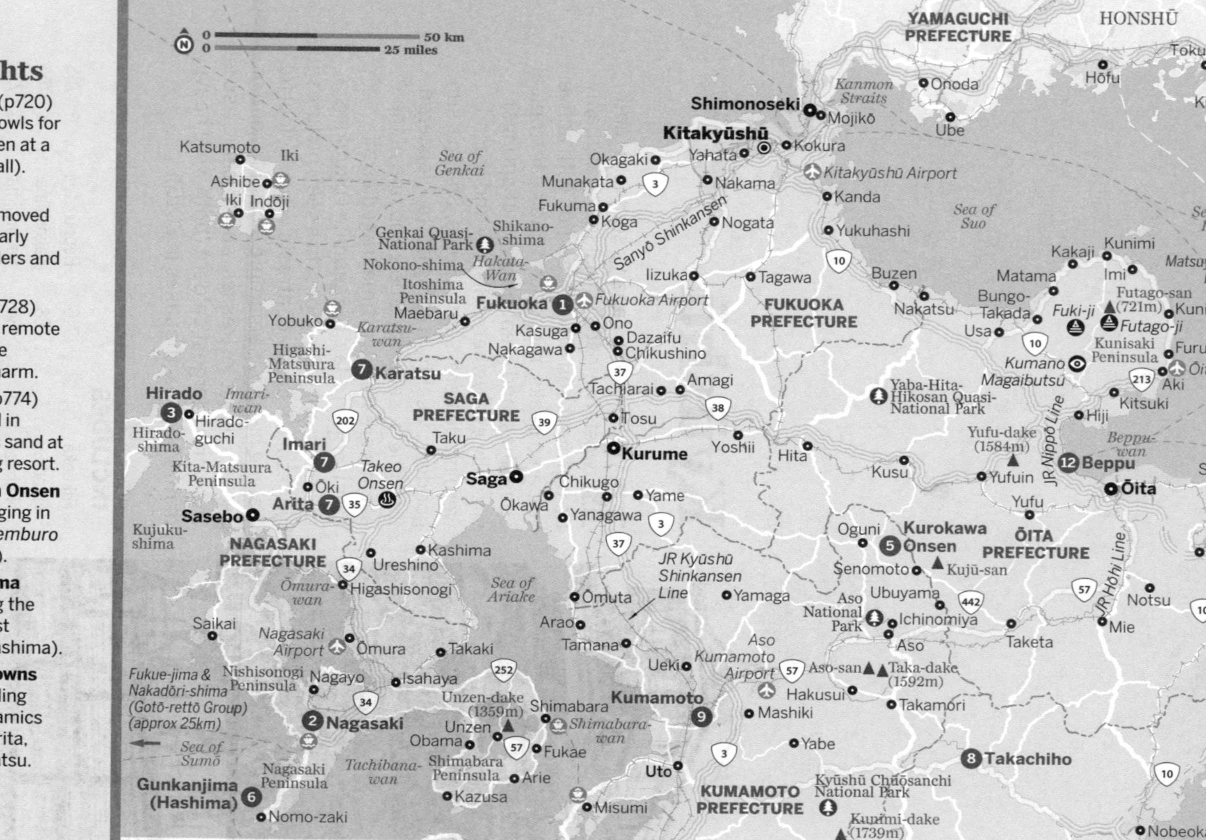

8 Takachiho Gorge (p753) Rowing amid waterfalls (and hungry ducks).

9 Kumamoto-jō (p744) Seeing where the last samurai made their final stand, at this earthquake-damaged, yet still impressive, castle.

10 Nichinan Coast (p783) Surfing local breaks along the coast.

11 Kagoshima (p768) Sipping sweet-potato *shōchū* as the Sakurajima volcano billows ash across the bay.

12 Beppu (p755) Soaking in onsen from the brash to the secluded.

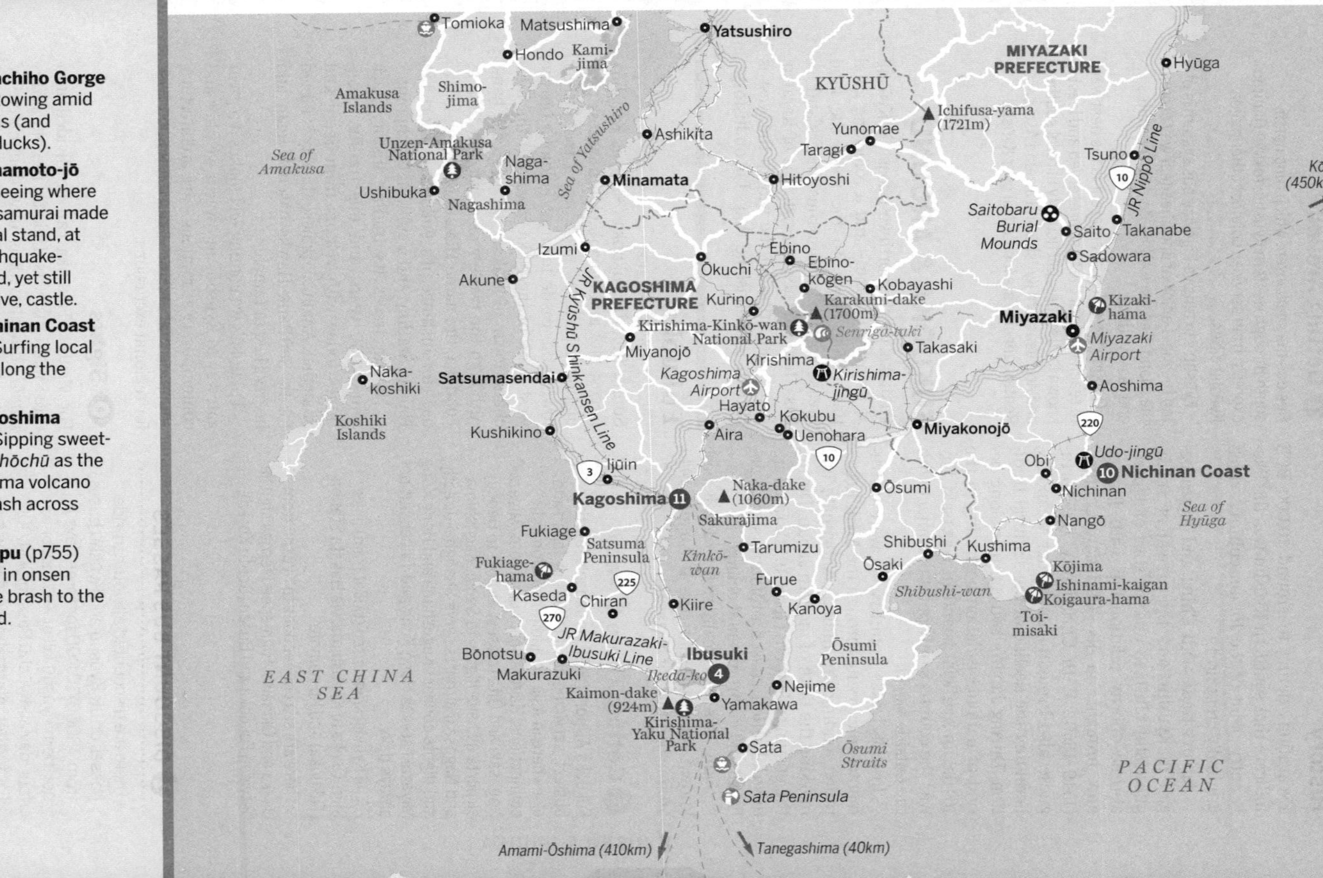

History

Excavations dating to around 10,000 BCE indicate that southern Kyūshū was the likely entry point of the Jōmon culture, which gradually crept north.

Japan's trade with China and Korea began in Kyūshū, and the arrival of Portuguese ships in 1543 was the start of Japan's at-times-thorny relationship with Europe and brought on its 'Christian Century' (1549–1650). With Christianity, the Portuguese also brought gunpowder weaponry, heralding the decline of the samurai tradition. During Japan's two-centuries-long period of national isolation beginning in the 1640s, an artificial island in Nagasaki Bay was the country's only point of contact with the outside world.

In 1868 rebels from Kyūshū were instrumental in carrying through the Meiji Restoration, ending the military shogunate and marking the birth of modern Japan. During the ensuing Meiji era (1868–1912), rapid industrialisation caused profound social, political and environmental change.

Sadly, this historically rich region is best known for one event: the 9 August 1945 atomic bombing of Nagasaki.

Getting There & Away

Fukuoka Airport (p722) is Japan's fourth-busiest, servicing destinations in Japan and elsewhere in Asia. In addition to domestic connections, Kagoshima, Kumamoto, Miyazaki, Nagasaki and Ōita (closest airport to Beppu) airports all have flights to Seoul. Kagoshima and Nagasaki airports serve Shanghai directly, and flights connect Kagoshima and Hong Kong. Miyazaki serves Hong Kong and Taipei, but not always daily.

The Kyūshū *shinkansen* (bullet train) links Shin-Osaka to Kagoshima, via Hakata Station (Fukuoka) and Kumamoto.

There are sea connections to Kyūshū from Osaka and Okinawa. High-speed ferries shuttle between Fukuoka and Busan (South Korea).

DISCOUNT BUS PASSES

There are discounted all-you-can-ride passes on JR Kyūshū and Kyūshū buses, from ¥8000/10,000 for three days in northern Kyūshū/all of Kyūshū, or a four-day all-Kyūshū Pass for ¥14,000. For further information visit www.sunqpass.jp.

Getting Around

Besides the *shinkansen*, which runs north–south through western Kyūshū, *tokkyū* (limited express) train services connect other major Kyūshū cities.

Kyūshū's extensive highway bus system is often the most efficient and cheapest way around the island. See www.atbus-de.com for routes and reservations.

Outside the cities, a rental car is the best way to reach many of the best-preserved and least-known landscapes, particularly in rural southern and northeastern Kyūshū and around Aso-san. Rental agencies are located all over Kyūshū.

FUKUOKA & AROUND

Fukuoka, on the northwest coast, is Kyūshū at its most urbane – and a rollicking good time. From there, to the west, the land breaks apart into numerous fingers and inlets. Here are the pottery towns of Karatsu, Imari and Arita. All the way to the west is Hirado, a small island that's big on history.

Fukuoka

092 / POP 1.60 MILLION

Sunny, friendly Fukuoka (福岡) is Kyūshū's largest city and Japan's eighth-largest population centre. It's made up of two former towns: the castle town of Fukuoka on the west bank of the Naka-gawa and the merchant town of Hakata on the east bank. Although the two towns merged in 1889 as Fukuoka, the name Hakata is still widely in use (for instance, it's Fukuoka Airport but Hakata Station) and a cultural touchpoint.

Hakata traces its trading history back some 2000 years, and this tradition continues today with visitors from Seoul and Shanghai. Among Japanese the city is famed for its SoftBank Hawks baseball team and hearty Hakata ramen.

Fukuoka's welcoming feel makes it a great gateway to Kyūshū, and warm weather and contemporary attractions – art, architecture, shopping and cuisine – make it a good base for regional excursions.

Sights

For visitors, Fukuoka can be divided into three main districts. Hakata, the old *shitamachi* (downtown), is now dominated by Fukuoka's *shinkansen* (bullet train) stop, the busy JR Hakata Station, within striking distance of several traditional shrines, temples, gardens and museums. Three subway stops away and across the Naka-gawa is Fukuoka's beating heart, the Tenjin district, bursting with department stores, boutiques, eateries and nightlife. Above ground, Tenjin centres on Watanabe-dōri, paralleled underground by Tenjin Chikagai, a long shopping arcade with mood lighting and cast-ironwork ceilings that make it a cool refuge from the summer heat. West of Tenjin is trendy Daimyō, Fukuoka's homage to Tokyo's Harajuku, minus the crowds, heading toward Fukuoka's former castle grounds.

★Fukuoka Asian Art Museum MUSEUM
(福岡アジア美術館; ☎092-263-1100; http://faam.city.fukuoka.lg.jp; 7th & 8th fl, Hakata Riverain, 3-1 Shimo-Kawabata-machi; adult/student ¥200/150; ⏰10am-8pm Thu-Tue; Ⓢ Nakasu-Kawabata) On the upper floors of the Hakata Riverain mall (p722), this large museum houses the world-renowned Asia Gallery, and additional galleries for special exhibitions (admission fee varies) and artists in residence. Changing exhibits show contemporary works from 23 countries, from East Asia to Pakistan.

★Hakata Machiya Furusato-kan MUSEUM
(博多町家ふるさと館, Hakata Machiya Folk Museum; ☎092-281-7761; www.hakatamachiya.com; 6-10 Reisen-machi; ¥200; ⏰10am-6pm; Ⓢ Gion) Spread over three *machiya* (traditional Japanese townhouses), this folk museum recreates a Hakata *nagare* (neighbourhood unit) from the late Meiji era. Inside the replica buildings, artisans are frequently on hand offering demonstrations of local crafts, and galleries show historical photographs and displays of traditional Hakata culture (festivals, crafts and performing arts), as well as recordings (more like lessons) of the impenetrable Hakata-ben dialect. The gift shop has an interesting selection of traditional toys and reasonably priced crafts.

Kushida-jinja SHINTŌ SHRINE
(櫛田神社; ☎092-291-2951; 1-41 Kami-kawabata; ⏰8am-6pm; Ⓢ Gion or Nakasu-Kawabata) FREE The intimate Kushida-jinja, municipal Shintō shrine of Hakata, traces its history to 757 CE and sponsors the Hakata Gion Yamakasa Matsuri, in which storeys-high floats make their way through the streets. There's a float visible outside that's well worth a gawk. A one-room **local-history museum** (博多歴史館; 1-41 Kami-kawabata; ¥300; ⏰10am-5pm Tue-Sun; Ⓢ Gion or Nakasu-Kawabata) has many displays about the festival, as well as swords, ancient pottery and more.

Ōhori-kōen Japanese Garden GARDENS
(大濠公園日本庭園, Ōhori-kōen Nihon-teien; ☎092-741-8377; 1-7 Ōhori-kōen; adult/child ¥240/120; ⏰9am-6pm Tue-Sun Jun-Aug, to 5pm Sep-May; Ⓢ Ōhori-kōen) Set within the expansive grounds of Ōhori-kōen, adjacent to the remains of Fukuoka's once grand castle, this traditional (though constructed in 1984) 12,000-sq-metre Japanese garden boasts a beautiful main pond, streams and a waterfall, a dry garden and a traditional teahouse, all within a border of whitewashed traditional walls. The design is by one of Japan's most famous 20th-century garden masters, Nakane Kinsaku, whose other works include the gardens at Kyoto's Nijo-jō (p315) and the Adachi Museum of Art (p503) in Shimane Prefecture.

Shōfuku-ji BUDDHIST TEMPLE
(聖福寺; 6-1 Gokushō-machi; ⏰24hr; Ⓢ Gion) FREE Shōfuku-ji is considered the oldest Zen temple in Japan, founded in 1195 by Eisai, who introduced Zen and tea to Japan; the nation's first tea plants are also said to have been planted here. Although its buildings are closed to the public, tree-lined stone paths make a nice ramble.

Fukuoka City Museum MUSEUM
(福岡市博物館; http://museum.city.fukuoka.jp; 3-1-1 Momochi-hama; ¥200; ⏰9.30am-5.30pm Tue-Sun; Ⓢ Nishijin) This smart museum displays artefacts from local history and culture. The pride of the collection is an ancient 2.3-sq-cm, 108g golden seal with an inscription proving Japan's historic ties to China.

Festivals & Events

Hakata Gion Yamakasa Matsuri CULTURAL
(博多祇園山笠祭; ⏰1-15 Jul) The city's main festival is held in July, climaxing at 4.59am on the 15th, when seven groups of men converge at Kushida-jinja to race along a 5km-long course carrying huge portable shrines called *yamakasa*. According to legend, the festival originated after a 13th-century Buddhist priest was carried aloft, sprinkling holy water over victims of a plague.

Sleeping

Stay near JR Hakata Station for convenience if railing around, although Tenjin is a better bet if you plan to spend a few days shopping and bar-hopping.

Central Fukuoka

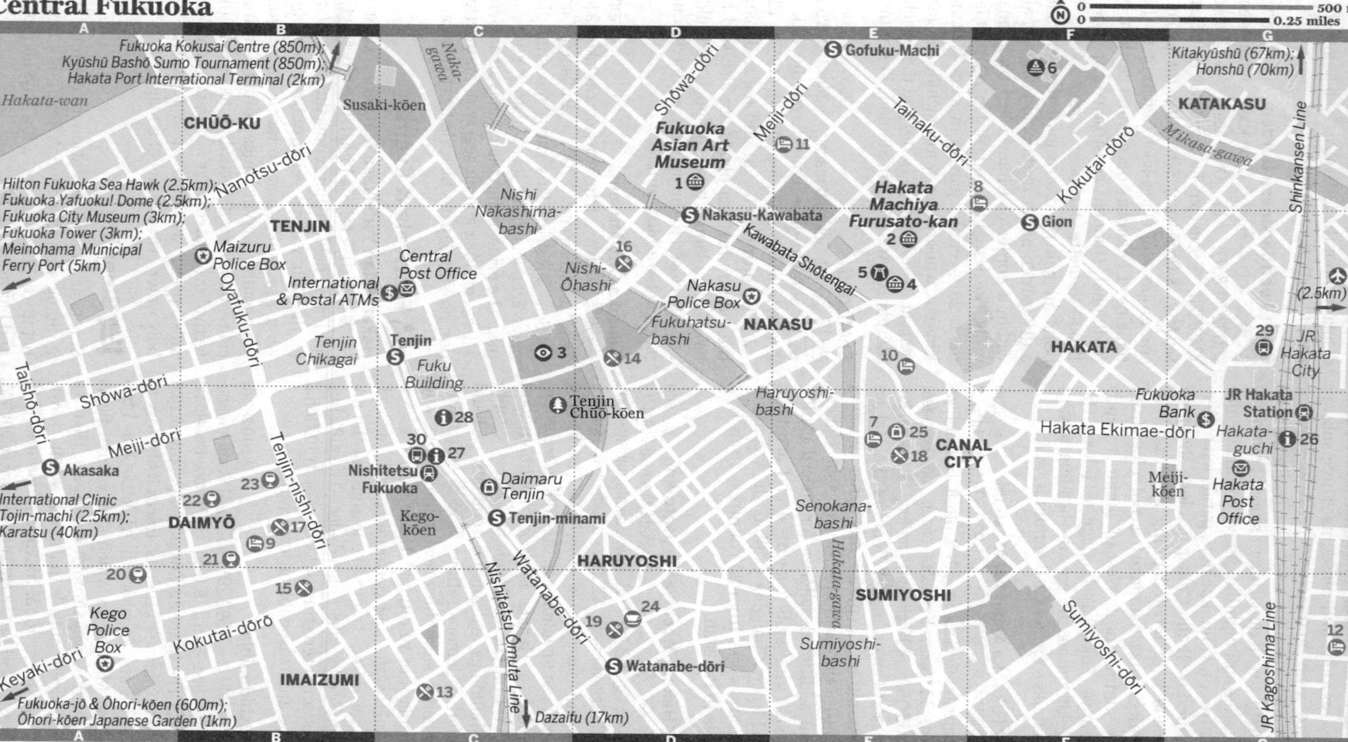
500 m
0.25 miles
Fukuoka Kokusai Centre (850m);
Kyūshū Bashō Sumo Tournament (850m);
Hakata Port International Terminal (2km)
Hakata-wan
Susaki-kōen
Naka-gawa
CHŪŌ-KU
Nanotsu-dōri
Hilton Fukuoka Sea Hawk (2.5km);
Fukuoka Yafuoku! Dome (2.5km);
Fukuoka City Museum (3km);
Fukuoka Tower (3km);
Meinohama Municipal Ferry Port (5km)
TENJIN
Maizuru Police Box
Oyafuku-dōri
Central Post Office
International & Postal ATMs
Nishi Nakashima-bashi
Nishi-Ōhashi
16
Tenjin Chikagai
Tenjin
Fuku Building
3
14
Taishō-dōri
Shōwa-dōri
Meiji-dōri
28
Tenjin Chūō-kōen
30
27
Nishitetsu Fukuoka
Akasaka
International Clinic
Tojin-machi (2.5km);
Karatsu (40km)
23
22
DAIMYŌ
Tenjin-nishi-dōri
17
9
21
20
15
Kego-kōen
Daimaru Tenjin
Tenjin-minami
Kego Police Box
Kokutai-dōrō
Keyaki-dōri
Fukuoka-jō & Ōhori-kōen (600m);
Ōhori-kōen Japanese Garden (1km)
IMAIZUMI
13
Nishitetsu Ōmuta Line
Dazaifu (17km)
Watanabe-dōri
HARUYOSHI
19
24
Shōwa-dōri
Fukuoka Asian Art Museum
1
Meiji-dōri
11
Nakasu-Kawabata
Kawabata Shōtengai
Nakasu Police Box
Fukuhatsu-bashi
NAKASU
Haruyoshi-bashi
Senokana-bashi
Hakata-gawa
Sumiyoshi-bashi
SUMIYOSHI
Gofuku-Machi
Taihaku-dōri
Hakata Machiya Furusato-kan
2
5
4
10
7
25
18
CANAL CITY
6
8
Gion
Kokutai-dōrō
HAKATA
Sumiyoshi-dōri
Kitakyūshū (67km);
Honshū (70km)
KATAKASU
Mikasa-gawa
Shinkansen Line
(2.5km)
29
JR Hakata City
Fukuoka Bank
JR Hakata Station
Hakata Ekimae-dōri
Hakata-guchi
26
Meiji-kōen
Hakata Post Office
JR Kagoshima Line
12

Central Fukuoka

Top Sights
1 Fukuoka Asian Art Museum ... D1
2 Hakata Machiya Furusato-kan ... E2

Sights
3 ACROS Fukuoka ... C2
4 Hakata Local History Museum ... E2
5 Kushida-jinja ... E2
6 Shōfuku-ji ... F1

Sleeping
7 Grand Hyatt Fukuoka ... E3
8 Kashima Honkan ... F1
9 Plaza Hotel Premier ... B3
10 The Life ... E2
11 WeBase Hakata ... E1
12 With the Style ... G4

Eating
13 Fish Man ... C4
14 Ganso Hakata Mentaijū ... D2
15 Hakatarou ... B4
16 Ichiran ... D2
17 Ippudō ... B3
18 Rāmen Stadium ... E3
19 Umeyama Teppei Shokudō ... D4

Drinking & Nightlife
20 Citadel ... A4
21 Fukuoka Craft ... B3
22 Morris' Black Sheep ... B3
23 Morris' Red Fox ... B3
24 Stereo Coffee ... D4

Shopping
25 Canal City ... E3
Hakata Japan ... (see 1)
Hakata Riverain ... (see 1)
Okano Hakata Riverain ... (see 1)

Information
26 Hakata Station General Information Center ... G3
27 Nishitetsu Tenjin Bus Center Tourist Information ... C3
28 Rainbow Plaza ... C3

Transport
29 Fukuoka Kōtsū Centre ... G2
30 Nishitetsu Tenjin Bus Terminal ... C3

★WeBase Hakata HOSTEL ¥
(092-292-2322; www.we-base.jp; 5-9 Tenyamachi; dm/s/d/q ¥3240/9720/8640/17,280; Nakasu-Kawabata) The 3m-tall sculpture of a cat in a diving suit standing guard outside is your first clue that this place is not like the others. Spanking-new, 164-bed, nine-storey WeBase pays tribute to Hakata's shipping history with clever nautical motifs throughout, and it calls the minimalist private rooms 'cabins'. The up-to-date bunk beds have built-in reading lamps and electrical outlets.

No meals are served, but the top-floor lounge has a kitchen, in addition to an extensive library and rooftop access.

The Life HOSTEL ¥
(ザライフホステル; 092-292-1070; www.thelife-hostel.com; 8-13 Gionmachi; dm/d from ¥2800/9000; Nakasu-Kawabata) The Life has a super-central location between Hakata Station and Canal City (and a soon-to-open subway stop), making this 130-bed hostel an easy base for exploring the city. Add post-industrial decor (exposed brick, concrete and ductwork) and a cool bar-restaurant with cheap happy hours, and it's a winning combination at a reasonable price. Check-in is 4pm to 10pm.

★Kashima Honkan RYOKAN ¥¥
(鹿島本館; 092-291-0746; 3-11 Reisen-machi; without bathroom s/d Sun-Thu ¥5500/7400, Fri & Sat ¥7000/12,000; Gion) This charmingly creaky, unpretentious Taishō-era ryokan is a historic landmark, pleasantly faded and focused on a small garden with a stone lantern. All that, tatami rooms and a sampling of knick-knacks make it a great place to sample traditional Japan. The friendly owners communicate well in English. Japanese breakfasts are available for ¥864.

Plaza Hotel Premier HOTEL ¥¥
(プラザホテルプルミエ; 092-734-7600; www.plaza-hotel.net; 1-14-13 Daimyō; s/d/tw from ¥8100/13,500/15,500; Tenjin or Akasaka) Location, location and location are reasons enough to stay here in trendy Daimyō, and this hotel gives you easy access from business-hotel-size rooms that rival those at far pricier properties. The busy, fashionable street vibe is reflected in the hotel's bistro, which serves *moules frites* (mussels and fries) and pizzas and would be at home on a Paris sidewalk.

★With the Style HOTEL ¥¥¥
(ウィズザスタイル福岡; 092-433-3900; www.withthestyle.com; 1-9-18 Hakataeki-minami; r incl breakfast from ¥45,000; Hakata) It's anyone's guess what the name means, but 'style' is indeed the byword at this sleek designer hotel. You could easily imagine yourself poolside in Hollywood around the fountain courtyard. Each of the 16 rooms

exude rock-star cool, all include breakfast, minibar and welcome drinks, and guests can reserve complimentary private use of the rooftop spa or penthouse bar.

Hilton Fukuoka Sea Hawk HOTEL ¥¥¥
(ヒルトン福岡シーホーク; ☎092-844-8111; www.hilton.com; 2-2-3 Jigyohama; s/d/tw from ¥15,000/15,000/16,000; P⊖❄@☎≋) If you want to make an impression, you can hardly do better anywhere else in Japan. The lobby restaurant of this César Pelli–designed hotel soars like its namesake bird, and at 1052 rooms, it's Asia's largest Hilton. From the right room, you can watch the baseball game at the Yafuoku Dome (p722) next door.

Eating

Fukuokans and non-Fukuokans alike salivate at the mention of Hakata ramen. The distinctive local version of these ubiquitous noodles is called *tonkotsu rāmen,* served in a hearty broth made from pork bones stewed for a day or more. Ichiran and Ippudō are two local shops that have spawned national chains.

For a quick bite, try the restaurants on the 9th and 10th floors of JR Hakata City (the Hakata Station building) or the *depachika* (food hall) in the basements of Hankyu or Amu, nearby.

★Ippudō RAMEN ¥
(☎092-771-0880; www.multilingual.ippudo.com; 1-13-14 Daimyō; ramen ¥790-1080; ⊙11am-10pm Mon-Fri, 10.30am-10pm Sat & Sun; S Tenjin, 🚉 Tenjin) Fukuoka's most famous ramen chain has efficient and always bustling branches in Tenjin, serving the best-selling Akamaru Modern (with black-sesame oil and a fragrant *umami-dama,* or flavour ball), Shiromaru Classic (with thin noodles) and Karaka (spicy ramen). This branch, Daimyō Honten, is the original, off Tenjin-nishi-dōri; there's another branch on the 10th floor of JR Hakata City (p723) shopping centre.

★Ichiran RAMEN ¥
(一蘭; ☎092-262-0433; www.ichiran.co.jp; 5-3-2 Nakasu; ramen ¥790-1200; ⊙24hr; S Nakasu-Kawabata, 🚉 Tenjin) This Fukuoka-born chain (since 1993) has a nationwide following. That's as much for its serving style as for its fresh noodles and 15-second kitchen-to-table rule. Customers fill out forms (available in English) requesting precisely how they want their noodles prepared: flavour strength, fat content, noodle tenderness, amount of special sauce and garlic, and eat at individual cubicles for zero distractions.

The corporate office/main location in Nakasu has two storeys: the upper floor has the signature individual booths, while the ground floor is more traditional, with sit-down tables and a bar. Look for the bright green-and-red awning.

Umeyama Teppei Shokudō SHOKUDO ¥
(梅山鉄平食堂; ☎092-726-6119; 3-1-16 Watanabe-dōri; teishoku ¥730-1880; ⊙11.30am-3.30pm & 5-10.30pm Mon, Thu, Fri & Sat, 11.30am-3.30pm & 5-9.30pm Tue, 11am-10.30pm Sun; S Watanabe-dōri) A humble-chic *shokudō* (everyday restaurant) run by some clever gourmets. The emphasis on fresh local ingredients means that the menu changes frequently; pictures and English-speaking staff can help you with ordering. Pretty much everyone orders *teishoku* (set meals) featuring fish like *saba* (mackerel) cooked in mirin (sweet rice wine) or the typically Fukuoka *goma-saba* (sashimi-style tossed with sesame).

There's no English sign, but look for the decorative *saba* hanging outside the door, just east of Watanabe-dōri.

Rāmen Stadium RAMEN ¥
(ラーメンスタジアム; ☎092-282-2525; 5th fl, Canal City; ramen ¥550-1290; ⊙11am-11pm) An entire floor of ramen outlets, with eight vendors imported from the length and breadth of Japan, including five from Fukuoka, such as **Jinanbō** (二男坊), serving the classic *tonkotsu rāmen.* In the mood for something unusual? Try the tomato ramen at **Sanmi** (三味); it's like ramen in tomato soup.

Take the escalator from the 4th floor.

★Hakatarou JAPANESE, IZAKAYA ¥¥
(博多廊; ☎092-687-5656; 5th fl, SouthSide Terrace Bldg, 1-1-38 Daimyō; most dishes ¥370-1800, 9-dish menus from ¥5000; ⊙11am-3pm & 5-11pm Sun-Thu, to midnight Fri & Sat; S Tenjin or Tenjin-minami) If you can't visit the rest of Kyūshū, try regional foods at this elegant *izakaya.* Look for dishes like *karashi renkon* (spicy, deep-fried lotus root) and *basashi* (horsemeat sashimi) from Kumamoto, grilled Shimabara chicken, Kagoshima *kurobuta* (black pork), and Hakata ramen salad and *mizutaki* and *gameni* chicken stews, plus a huge selection of Kyūshū sake and *shōchū* (strong distilled liquor).

Fish Man IZAKAYA ¥¥
(魚男フィッシュマン, Sakana Otoko; ☎092-717-3571; 1-4-23 Imaizumi; set meals ¥680-1500; ⊙11.30am-1am; S Yakuin) Fish Man's

post-industrial vibe features lacquered plywood and big windows, which show off the unconventional presentations of seafood fresh from the Nagahama market across town: *kaidan-zushi* (sushi served on a wooden spiral staircase), *tsubotai no misoyaki* (miso-grilled snapper) or a shrimp hamburg steak. The varied menu also covers *donburi* (rice bowls), tempura, and even meat and veg dishes.

Ganso Hakata Mentaijū SEAFOOD ¥¥
(元祖博多めんたい重; ☎092-725-7220; www.mentaiju.com; 6-15 Nishi-Nakasu; mentaiju from ¥1680, set menus from ¥3380; ⏰7am-10.30pm; Ⓢ Nakasu-Kawabata or Tenjin) Behind a geometric lattice facade, this shop specialises in *mentaijū* – *mentaiko* (spicy cod roe, a Fukuoka delicacy), wrapped with savoury kelp and served over rice and flaked seaweed in a wooden box. Pick up a tag at the entrance to choose your spice level. Set menus with seafood *tsukemen* (ramen noodles served with dipping sauce) are intense and satisfying.

Drinking & Nightlife

The weekend starts on Thursday in multicultural, party-friendly Fukuoka. The streets of Tenjin and Daimyō are safe, easy to explore and great for people-watching. The main drag, Oyafuko-dōri, roughly translates to 'street of unruly children' because of the cram schools that once lined it. In a way, the cap still fits.

Nakasu Island, while one of Japan's busiest entertainment districts, is often sleazy.

★ **Citadel** COCKTAIL BAR
(シタデル; ☎092-688-4190; www.facebook.com/citadeldaimyo; 2nd fl, 1-8-40 Daimyō; ⏰5pm-3am; Ⓢ Akasaka) At this classy upstairs bar, mellow out over coffee cocktails such as mojitos (with homemade coffee rum and coffee ice cubes) and espresso martinis. Liqueurs macerating on shelves above the bar lend a mad-scientist's-lab vibe (ginger gin, anyone?), yet it's not above serving more conventional drinks, plus tasty snacks.

Fukuoka Craft BREWERY
(フクオカクラフトブルワリー; ☎092-791-1494; 1-11-4 Daimyō; ⏰5pm-2am Mon-Fri, 3pm-2am Sat & Sun; Ⓢ Akasaka) This beer bar, opened in 2017, brews its own creations and offers dozens of other beers from around the world, along with eats like mixed grill and Mexican dishes. The intimate wood-and-brick space opens onto a Daimyō side street for great people-watching.

DON'T MISS

FUKUOKA'S FOOD CARTS

The Fukuoka way to eat is at *yatai* (屋台), mobile hawker-style food carts with simple kitchens surrounded by counters and seats; Fukuoka claims about 150 *yatai*, more than in the rest of Japan combined! Let the aromas and chatty conversation lead you to the best cooking and the best companions. The Tenjin and Nagahama neighbourhoods have the highest concentration, along pavements and canals. Get there early, as most seats are soon taken. (Note that if you talk too much without ordering enough you'll be asked to move on.)

Stereo Coffee CAFE
(ステレオコーヒー; ☎092-231-8854; 3-8-3 Watanabe-dōri; ⏰8am-10pm; Ⓢ Watanabe-dōri) This artful, art-filled cafe draws a hip, creative crowd for tasty espresso drinks, hot sandwiches and seasonal special drinks such as floats for summer. There are no seats – all the better to peruse the art on the walls of the loft-like gallery spaces upstairs and down, while cool beats play in the background.

Morris' Black Sheep BAR
(モーリスブラックシープ; ☎092-725-8773; 2-1-20 Daimyō; ⏰5pm-1am; Ⓢ Akasaka) This Morris bar is just down the street from its **Red Fox** (モーリスレッドフォックス; ☎092-771-4774; 7th fl, Stage 1 Nishidōri Bldg, 2-1-4 Daimyō; ⏰5pm-1am; Ⓢ Tenjin) 🍃 cousin. It's often packed, loud and fun, and may open even later on Friday and Saturday nights, depending on numbers. A generous patio opens onto the street, and pub grub includes pizza and fish and chips.

Entertainment

Kyūshū Bashō Sumo Tournament SPECTATOR SPORT
(www.sumo.or.jp; ⏰mid-late Nov) Held for two weeks at the **Fukuoka Kokusai Centre** (福岡国際センター; ☎092-272-1111; www.marinemesse.or.jp; 2-2 Chikkohon-chō; 🚌88 or 99 to Fukuoka Convention Centre, Ⓢ Gofukumachi). The main ticket sale is in October, and spectators start lining up at dawn for limited same-day tickets (*tōjitsu-ken;* ¥3400 to ¥15,000).

Fukuoka Yafuoku! Dome STADIUM
(福岡ヤフオク！ドーム; ☎092-847-1006; www.softbankhawks.co.jp; 2-2-2 Jigyohama; tours ¥1500; ⊙tours hourly 10am-4pm; Ⓢ Tojin-machi) This monolithic, retractable-roof stadium is the home field of Fukuoka's much-loved SoftBank Hawks baseball team. Tours (in Japanese) are offered and there's a museum of the life of Oh Sadaharu, the world's all-time home-run king (best for die-hard fans).

Shopping

Hakata Japan CLOTHING
(ハカタジャパン; ☎092-263-1112; 1st fl, Hakata Riverain, 301 Shimo-Kawabata-machi; ⊙10.30am-7.30pm; Ⓢ Nakasu-Kawabata) Hakata is renowned for it weaving tradition, called Hakata-ori, and this chic shop, to the right as you enter Hakata Riverain mall, has been producing intricately woven Hakata-ori for generations. Originally supplying obi (kimono sashes), it now puts the fabrics to more modern uses including accessories. It also sells used kimono (not Hakata-ori) – still expensive but a fraction of the cost of a new one.

Canal City SHOPPING CENTRE
(キャナルシティ; www.canalcity.co.jp; 1-2 Sumiyoshi; ⊙shops 10am-9pm, restaurants 11am-11pm) Canal City is Fukuoka's biggest mall, boasting an eponymous artificial canal with illuminated fountain symphony, a multiplex cinema, a playhouse and about 250 boutiques (large tenants include Muji, H&M, Uniqlo and Sanrio), the **Grand Hyatt** (グランドハイアット福岡; ☎092-282-1234; www.fukuoka.grand.hyatt.com; 1-2-82 Sumiyoshi; s/d/tw from ¥39,000/45,000/51,000; P⊖❄@🛜≋) and other hotels, bars and bistros, game arcades and Ramen Stadium (p720). It was designed by Jon Jerde, who later created Tokyo's Roppongi Hills (p95).

Hakata Riverain MALL
(博多リバレイン; ☎092-282-1300; www.riverain.co.jp; 3-1 Shimo-kawabata-machi, Hakata-ku; Ⓢ Nakasu-Kawabata) Modern, multistorey mall with some 70 shops for fashion, homewares and design, plus restaurants and cafes. The Fukuoka Asian Art Museum (p717) is on the top floors.

Okano Hakata Riverain CLOTHING
(OKANO 博多リバレイン店; ☎092-283-8111; www.okano1897.jp; B1 fl, Hakata Riverain, 3-1 Shimo-Kawabata-machi; ⊙10.30am-7.30pm; Ⓢ Nakasu-Kawabata) This elegant shop offers obi, kimonos and accessories from business-card holders to handbags in the distinctive Hakata-ori style. None of it is cheap (silk obi start at around ¥10,000), but it's meant to last generations.

Information

INTERNET ACCESS

Fukuoka has free public wi-fi at city hall, major train and subway stations, the airport, tourist information centres and in the Tenjin Chikagai (underground arcade).

MEDICAL SERVICES

International Clinic Tojin-machi (☎092-717-1000; www.internationalclinic.org; 1-4-6 Jigyo; ⊙9am-1pm & 2.30-5.30pm Mon, Tue, Thu & Fri, 9am-1pm Sat; Ⓢ Tōjin-machi, exit 1) Multilingual clinic for general medical services and emergencies. It's two blocks from Tojin-machi subway station.

TOURIST INFORMATION

Fukuoka City Tourist Information Counters (福岡市観光案内所) at Fukuoka Airport, **Hakata Station** (福岡市観光案内所JR博多駅支店; ☎092-431-3003; ⊙8am-9pm) and **Nishitetsu Tenjin Bus Center** (福岡市観光案内所天神支店; ☎092-751-6904; ⊙10am-6.30pm) dispense maps, coupons and the helpful *City Visitor's Guide*, and can help with lodging, transport and car-rental information. Information centres at **ACROS Fukuoka** (アクロス福岡; ☎092-725-9100; www.acros.or.jp; ACROS Bldg, 1-1-1 Tenjin; ⊙10am-6pm; Ⓢ Nakasu-Kawabata or Tenjin) and **Rainbow Plaza** (レインボープラザ; ☎092-733-2220; www.rainbowfia.or.jp; 8F, IMS Bldg, 1-7-11 Tenjin; ⊙10am-8pm, closed 3rd Tue of month; 🛜) are targeted mostly at foreign residents.

Fukuoka Now (www.fukuoka-now.com) is an indispensable monthly English-language street mag with detailed city maps.

Yokanavi.com (www.yokanavi.com) is a comprehensive Fukuoka/Hakata tourist-information site.

Getting There & Away

AIR

Fukuoka Airport (福岡空港, FUK; ☎domestic terminal 092-621-6059, international terminal 092-621-0303; www.fuk-ab.co.jp; ⊙domestic 6.20am-10.20pm, international 7am-9.30pm; Ⓢ Fukuoka Airport) is well connected, offering dozens of domestic routes including Tokyo (from Haneda/Narita airports), Osaka and Okinawa (Naha), and international routes serving East and Southeast Asia.

In addition to ANA and Japan Airlines with their numerous domestic and international connections, domestic airline **StarFlyer** (www.starflyer.jp) connects Fukuoka with Tokyo Haneda and

Nagoya, and **Skymark** (☎ Tokyo 0570-051-330; www.skymark.co.jp) flies to Haneda.

From the airport, the subway takes just five minutes to reach JR Hakata Station (¥260) and 11 minutes to Tenjin (¥260). Shuttle buses connect domestic and international terminals.

Taxis cost around ¥1600 to Tenjin/Hakata.

BOAT

Ferries from Hakata connect to Okinawa and other islands off Kyūshū. **Beetle** (☎ Japan 092-281-2315, Korea 051-469-0778; www.jrbeetle.co.jp) high-speed hydrofoils connect Fukuoka with Busan in Korea (one way/return ¥13,000/26,000, three hours, twice daily). The **Camellia line** (☎ in Japan 092-262-2323, in Korea 051-466-7799; www.camellia-line.co.jp) has a regular ferry service from Fukuoka to Busan (one way/return from ¥6200/12,500, 5½ hours, daily at 12.30pm). Both ships dock at **Hakata Port International Terminal** (博多港国際ターミナル; ☎ 092-282-4871; www.hakataport.com) – reach it via bus 88 from JR Hakata Station (¥230) or bus 80 from Tenjin (Solaria Stage-mae; ¥190).

BUS

Long-distance buses (☎ ask operator for English interpreter 0570-00-1010) depart from the **Fukuoka Kōtsū Centre** (福岡交通センター) next to JR Hakata Station (Hakata-gate) and also from the **Nishitetsu Tenjin Bus Terminal** (西鉄天神バスセンター). Destinations include Tokyo (economy/business ¥8300/12,000, 14½ hours), Osaka (from ¥8800, 10½ hours), Nagoya (¥7500, 11 hours) and many towns in Kyūshū; ask about discounted round-trip fares.

TRAIN

JR Hakata Station (JR博多駅; ☎ 092-471-8111, English info line 03-3423-0111) is a hub in northern Kyūshū and the terminus of *shinkansen* (bullet trains) to/from Tokyo (¥21,810, five hours). Other *shinkansen* connect with Shin-Osaka (¥14,480, 2½ hours), Hiroshima (¥8420, 62 minutes), Kumamoto (¥4610, 37 minutes) and Kagoshima-Chūō (¥9930, 84 minutes).

Within Kyūshū, non-*shinkansen* trains run on the JR Nippō line through Beppu to Miyazaki; the Sasebo line runs from Saga to Sasebo; and the Nagasaki line runs to Nagasaki. You can also travel by subway and JR train to Karatsu and continue to Nagasaki by train.

Getting Around

Fukuoka has three subway lines (http://subway.city.fukuoka.lg.jp; open from 5.30am to 12.25am), of which visitors will find the Kūkō (Airport) line most useful, running from Fukuoka Airport to Meinohama Station via Hakata, Nakasu-Kawabata and Tenjin stations. Fares start at ¥200; a one-day pass costs ¥620/310 per adult/child.

TOURIST CITY PASS

In addition to regular bus and subway passes, overseas visitors can purchase the Fukuoka Tourist City Pass. It costs ¥820/410 per adult/child and covers buses and subways within the city, though not Nishitetsu trains. Present it for discounted admission at attractions throughout town. For ¥1340/670 the pass also covers Dazaifu. Purchase at major stations, bus terminals and information counters. Passport required.

City bus services operate from the Fukuoka Kōtsū Centre, adjacent to JR Hakata Station, and from the Nishitetsu Tenjin Bus Terminal. Many stop in front of the station (Hakata-guchi). Specially marked buses have a flat ¥100 rate for city-centre rides; one-day passes cost ¥900.

Dazaifu

☎ 092 / POP 71,787

Dazaifu (太宰府), former governmental centre of Kyūshū, has a beautiful cluster of temples, a famous shrine and a striking national museum, making for a popular day trip from Fukuoka.

Sights

★Kyūshū National Museum MUSEUM
(九州国立博物館; ☎ 092-918-2807; www.kyuhaku.com; 4-7-2 Ishizaka; adult/student ¥430/130, additional charge for special exhibits; 9.30am-5pm Tue-Sun, to 8pm Fri & Sat) Built into the tranquil eastern hills of Dazaifu and reached through more escalators than can be found at the average airport, this striking structure (built 2005) resembles a massive space station and chronicles the cultural flow between Asia and Kyūshū (and, by extension, the rest of Japan). The permanent, 1500-sq-metre 'Cultural Exchange Exhibition' on the 4th floor includes priceless pieces from across the continent; English signage and an audio-guide help illuminate it all. A must-visit for architecture and history buffs.

★Dazaifu Tenman-gū SHINTŌ SHRINE
(太宰府天満宮; www.dazaifutenmangu.or.jp; 4-7-1 Saifu; 6.30am-7pm) FREE Among the countless visitors to the grand, sprawling Tenman-gū – shrine and burial place of poet-scholar Tenman Tenjin (p724) – are

students making offerings and buying amulets in hopes of passing college entrance exams.

The *hondō* (main hall) was rebuilt in 1591. Behind the shrine is the **Kankō Historical Museum** (菅公歴史資料館; ☎092-922-8225; ¥200; ⊙9am-4.30pm Thu-Mon), with dioramas showing Tenjin's life (an English leaflet provides explanations). Across the grounds, the **Dazaifu Tenman-gū Museum** (太宰府天満宮宝物殿; ¥400; ⊙9am-4.30pm Tue-Sun) has artefacts from his life, including some excellent swords.

Eating

Ume (Japanese pickled plum) is a local speciality due to its association with distinguished poet-scholar Tenman Tenjin. Dozens of shops up and down Tenjinsama-dōri, the main street to the shrine, serve *umegaemochi* (sweet-bean-paste-filled cakes with plum-branch insignia), symbolising the branch of blossoms given to Tenjin to 'cheer him up' during his Dazaifu exile.

Saifu Udon NOODLES ¥

(さいふうどん; ☎092-922-0573; http://kimura-saifuudon.wixsite.com/saifuudon; 3-4-31 Saifu; ⊙11am-4pm Wed-Mon; Nishitetsu Dazaifu) In business since 1948, the Kimura family makes such sought-after udon noodles that this tiny eight-seat shop closes whenever it runs out. Arrive early or prepare to wait. The reward is a bowl of broth and noodles that are as fresh and tasty as handmade food can be. If it's warm, additional outdoor seating is opened up.

TENMAN TENJIN

Poet-scholar Sugawara-no-Michizane (845–903 CE) was a distinguished Kyoto intellectual until he fell out of favour with the imperial court and was exiled to distant Dazaifu, where he died two years later. Shortly after his death, many disasters befell the imperial court, including plague, drought, heavy storms, lightning strikes and untimely deaths in the imperial family. Sugawara became deified as Tenman Tenjin (sometimes abbreviated 'Tenjin'), god of culture and scholars, and to calm his spirit, shrines around the country were built in his memory, including the grand Dazaifu Tenman-gū (p724). To this day, he remains Dazaifu's most prominent historical figure.

Information

Tourist Information Office (太宰府市観光案内所; ☎092-925-1880; ⊙9am-5pm) Adjacent to Nishitetsu Dazaifu Station; has helpful staff and an English-language map.

Getting There & Around

The private Nishitetsu train line connects Nishitetsu Fukuoka (in Tenjin) with Dazaifu (¥400, 30 minutes). Direct trains are rare; mostly you'll change trains at Nishitetsu Futsukaichi Station. A bus to Dazaifu leaves from JR Hakata station (¥600, 40 minutes) and Fukuoka Airport (¥500, 25 minutes).

Bicycles can be rented for ¥500 per day at Nishitetsu Dazaifu Station (9am to 6pm). Electric bikes cost ¥800 per day.

Karatsu

☎0955 / POP 122,785

Karatsu (唐津) is at the base of the scenic Higashi-Matsuura Peninsula, an ideal location for its historic pottery trade. Korean influences elevated the town's craft from useful ceramics to art.

Pottery fanatics will be in their element here as they view earth-toned vases and tea bowls. Some pieces sell for more than a luxury car, but work by junior artists can be more affordable. Other attractions include a hilltop castle, historic buildings, a simple Shōwa-era town centre and a pretty seaside cycling trail. Outside town, the coastline, pounded into shape by the roiling Sea of Genkai, makes for dramatic vistas and pleasant day hikes.

The Nakamachi shopping area, near Karatsu Station, offers good restaurants and souvenir shops, all within an easy stroll.

Sights

It's about a 25-minute walk from JR Karatsu Station to the sea or the castle. Ceramic shops are dotted around town, along with **kilns** and **studios** where you can see local potters at work.

★**Karatsu-jō** CASTLE

(唐津城; 8-1 Higashi-jōnai; adult/child ¥500/250, elevator one way ¥100/50; ⊙9am-6pm Jul & Aug, to 5pm Sep-Jun; P) Nicknamed Maizuru-jō (Dancing Crane Castle), this elegantly proportioned white castle (built 1608, rebuilt 1966 and refurbished 2017) is picturesquely perched on a hill overlooking the sea. Inside are antique ceramics, samurai armour and

WORTH A TRIP

TACHIARAI

From 1919 to 1945, the isolated farm village of Tachiarai (大刀洗) hosted a training school for Japanese fighter pilots, including some on kamikaze suicide missions. Expanded in 2009, **Tachiarai Heiwa Kinenkan** (大刀洗平和記念館, Tachiarai Peace Memorial Museum; ☎0946-23-1227; www.tachiarai-heiwa.jp; 2561-1 Takata, Chikuzen-machi; ¥500; ⊙9am-5pm; P; Amagi Railway to Tachiarai) shows the rigorous training these men endured. English signage is basic, but the museum's artefacts (uniforms, medals, gold-plated sake cups etc) are evocative. The centrepiece is a jet fighter shot down during the war and recovered from Hakata Bay in 1996. The museum also memorialises kamikaze pilots and townspeople who died during a USAF B-29 bombing on 27 March 1945.

The museum is across from Tachiarai Station. From Fukuoka, take the Nishitetsu line to Nishitetsu Ogōri (¥510, 30 minutes); from Dazaifu (¥340) it takes 25 minutes plus transfer time at Nishitetsu Futsukaichi. Then walk to Ogōri Station on the Amagi Railway for the trip to Tachiarai (¥290, 15 minutes). JR passengers can transfer to the Amagi Railway at Kiyama (¥340, 20 minutes).

archaeological displays, amid walls lined with Karatsu-yaki (Karatsu pottery) tiles. Download the Karatsu Castle app to scan QR codes for detailed English descriptions of select pieces. The climb up the hill can be a slog, especially in muggy summer heat, but there's a diagonal elevator.

Nakazato Tarōemon MUSEUM

(中里太郎右衛門; ☎0955-72-8171; www.nakazato-tarouemon.com; 3-6-29 Chōda; ⊙9am-5.30pm Thu-Tue) FREE Karatsu-yaki is defined by the work of 14 generations of the Nakazato family. Walk through the shop, which feels like a museum unto itself, and cross the wooden breezeway above a stream to see an exhibition of pieces by some of the family's recent generations. The shop is named for Nakazato Tarōemon (1923–2009), who is said to be responsible for the revival of Karatsu-yaki. Later, walk across the street to see the family's historic kiln.

Kyū-Takatori-tei HISTORIC BUILDING

(旧高取邸; 5-40 Kita-jōnai; adult/child ¥510/250; ⊙9.30am-5pm Tue-Sun) This fabulously restored late-Meiji period villa of a local trader is built in a mix of Japanese and Western styles, with lantern-filled gardens, a Buddhist altar room, a wealth of paintings on cedar boards and an indoor *nō* (stylised dance-drama) stage. English audioguide available (¥300).

Sleeping

Quiet Karatsu's sleeping options are limited mainly to business hotels and high-end ryokan.

★Yōyōkaku RYOKAN ¥¥¥

(洋々閣; ☎0955-72-7181; www.yoyokaku.com; 2-4-40 Higashi-Karatsu; r per person incl 2 meals from ¥21,600; P) In a word: gorgeous. Also: rambling and minimalist, with 100-year-old woodwork, a pine garden and Karatsu-yaki pottery for your in-room seafood meals. Koi swim lazily in the immaculate 200-year-old garden. This property is a real getaway, yet it's less-than-10-minutes' walk from the castle. Even if you can't stay here, visit the on-site gallery of Nakazato family pottery.

Rates are based on two people per room. Discounts available for accommodation-only plans.

Eating

Karatsu Bāgā BURGERS ¥

(からつバーガー; ☎090-6299-0141; burgers ¥310-490; ⊙9am-8pm) In the middle of nowhere (in a parking lot) in Niji no Matsubara is a brown-and-white Toyota serving burgers so famous people line up to buy them, and have for decades. The 'Special' is the most popular: a steaming cheeseburger topped with a fried egg and a ham slice. There's also a branch in **Nakamachi** (からつバーガー; ☎080-9101-6912; 1513-18 Nakamachi; ⊙9am-8pm; Karatsu), near Karatsu Station.

★Kawashima Tōfu TOFU ¥¥¥

(川島豆腐店; ☎0955-72-2423; www.zarudoufu.co.jp; Kyōmachi 1775; set meals lunch ¥1500-2500, dinner ¥5000-13,000; ⊙8am-10pm, meal seatings 8am, 10am, noon, 2pm & 5.30pm) On Kyōmachi covered arcade near the station, this renowned tofu shop has been in business since the Edo period and serves refined *kaiseki*,

WORTH A TRIP

YOBUKO MORNING MARKET

A colourful, daily **morning market** (朝市; ☎095-582-3426; Sasaichi-dōri, Yobuko; ⌚7.30-11am) for squid, fish and produce animates the quaint, dwindling fishing port of Yobuko (呼子), drawing visitors from all over the region. Buses (¥750, 30 minutes) connect from Karatsu's Ōteguchi Bus Centre.

starring tofu plus other seasonal specialities, around a 10-seat counter in its jewel box of a back room. Soft, warm, fresh – this is tofu as good as it gets.

Reservations are essential for *kaiseki*, or stop by to taste a scoop of the fresh, creamy tofu (called *zarudōfu;* top it with the lightest sprinkle of salt or a drop of soy sauce) or a cup of *tōnyū* (soy milk) for ¥100, or try frozen tofu 'soft cream' for ¥300.

Shopping

Karatsu Ware Federation Exhibition Hall GALLERY
(唐津焼総合展示場; ☎0955-73-4888; Arpino Bldg; ⌚9am-6pm) FREE Just outside Karatsu Station, this exhibition hall displays and sells local potters' work, with prices ranging from ¥500 to eye-watering. Potters have a display area and many have (Japanese only) info.

Information

Tourist Information Office (☎0955-72-4963; 2935-1 Shinkomachi; ⌚9am-6pm) Inside JR Karatsu Station; has a selection of English-language tourist maps and brochures, and some enthusiastic English-speaking staff who can book accommodation or show points of interest on the map. It's well worth stopping here before heading into the town.

Getting There & Away

From Fukuoka, take the Kūkō (Airport) subway line to the western end of the line at Meinohama. Many trains continue directly (or you may need to switch) to the JR Chikuhi line to reach Karatsu (¥1140, 70 minutes). From Karatsu to Nagasaki (¥3710, three hours), take the JR Karatsu line to Saga, and the Kamome *tokkyū* on the JR Nagasaki line from there. Note that severe winds and other weather may result in train cancellations.

From Karatsu's **Ōteguchi Bus Centre** (大手口バスセンター; ☎0955-73-7511), highway buses depart for Fukuoka (¥1030, 70 minutes) and Yobuko (¥750, 30 minutes).

At the **Arpino** (アルピノ; ☎0955-75-5155; www.karatsu-arpino.com; 2881-1 Shinkomachi) building, next to the station, you can rent bicycles (free) with your passport on the 1st floor; the station no longer rents bicycles.

Imari

☎0955 / POP 54,900

You can tell you're getting close to Imari (伊万里) by the blue-and-white tiles that start appearing everywhere: street signs, bridge totems, even crushed gravel has shards of Imari's signature item. This famous pottery town (p728) is best visited as a day trip from Karatsu. There are a few local eateries near the station.

Sights

★Ōkawachiyama VILLAGE
(大川内山) The area's renowned pottery kilns are concentrated in photogenic Ōkawachiyama, a 15-minute bus ride from the station. Around 30 workshops and public galleries make for a lovely ramble uphill alongside streams, cafes and a stunning bridge covered with local Imari-ware shards. Arrive by noon to allow for exploring and shopping.

Imari City Ceramic Merchant's Museum MUSEUM
(伊万里市陶器商家資料館; ☎0955-22-7934; 1-1-59 Jōnai; ⌚10am-5pm Tue-Sun) FREE In Imari town near the river, this museum houses some priceless pieces of Koimari (as old Imari ware is known) from the 18th and 19th centuries. It's in the handsomely preserved home of a merchant family.

Information

Imari City Information (伊万里市観光協会; ☎0955-23-3479; ⌚9am-6pm) Tourist brochures are available from this outlet on the regional Matsuura-tetsudō railway (MR), across the street from JR Imari Station.

Getting There & Around

Imari is connected to Karatsu (¥650, 50 minutes) by the JR Chikuhi line or bus (¥1030, 60 minutes), and also to Arita by the private Matsuura-tetsudō line (¥460, 25 minutes).

Five to six buses per day (¥170) make the trip to Ōkawachiyama. Alternatively, the taxi fare is approximately ¥1800 each way.

Arita

☎0955 / POP 20,153

Kaolin clay was discovered in Arita (有田) in 1615 by Ri Sampei, a naturalised Korean potter, enabling the manufacture of fine porcelain in Japan for the first time. By the mid-17th century, the porcelain was being exported to Europe.

Between the station and Kyūshū Ceramic Museum is the **Yakimono Sanpo-michi** (Pottery Promenade) of around 16 galleries. The tourist office has a map that's in Japanese but easy enough to follow. Arita's streets fill with vendors for the **pottery market**, held from 29 April to 5 May.

Out of the town centre, two of Arita-yaki's prime practitioners have been at it for more than 14 generations. The Imaemon Gallery and Kakiemon Kiln both have museums in addition to sales shops. **Genemon Kiln** (源右衛門窯; ☎0955-42-4164; www.gen-emon.co.jp; 2726 Maruohe; ⏲workshop 8am-5pm Mon-Fri, shop 8am-5pm daily) makes and sells more contemporary styles.

About a 15-minute train ride east of Arita, the hot-spring town of Takeo Onsen is a worthy side trip.

Sights

★Kyūshū Ceramic Museum MUSEUM
(九州陶磁文化館; ☎095-543-3681; http://saga-museum.jp/ceramic; 3100-1 Toshaku-ōtsu; ⏲9am-5pm Tue-Sun) FREE About 15 minutes on foot from Arita Station, this large, hilltop operation is the most comprehensive ceramics museum in the region. The Shibata Collection showcases the development and styles of Kyūshū's many ceramic arts, with excellent English signage. An entrance fee may be charged for some special exhibits.

★Kouraku Kiln FACTORY
(幸楽窯; ☎0955-42-4121; www.kouraku.jp.net; Marunohei 2512; ⏲9am-8pm) This fascinating pottery factory has something for everyone: you can try making simple pottery on the throwing wheel (your pieces can be fired and mailed to you within Japan); you can stay here longer in a residency to learn the craft (¥49,000/200,000 per week/month); or shoppers can go 'treasure hunting' in the vast seconds warehouse and spend as much time filling a box (¥5000) with whatever fits.

Imaemon Gallery GALLERY
(今右衛門ギャラリー; ☎0955-42-5550; 2-1-11 Akaemachi; ¥300; ⏲9.30am-4.30pm Tue-Sun) It looks humble from the outside, but stunning works of art are on display in the gallery of one of Japan's Living National Treasures, the 14th generation of his family to produce ceramics. The adjoining shop is open daily, even when the gallery is closed.

The shop and gallery are about halfway between two stations: Arita (1.8km) and Kami-Arita (1.1km).

Kakiemon Kiln FACTORY
(柿右衛門窯; ☎0955-43-2267; 352 Nanzan; ⏲9am-5pm) FREE This workshop of the Sakaida family (artist name: Kakiemon) is one of Arita's top sights. Now in its 15th generation and featured in its own exhibit at the British Museum in 2016, the family includes a Living National Treasure. Creamy-white porcelain tableware, vases and urns from wood-fired kilns are colourfully glazed with delicate images from nature. Facilities include an exhibit space and a shop.

Activities

Takeo Onsen ONSEN
(武雄温泉; ☎0954-23-2001; Moto-yu ¥400, Saginoyu ¥600, private baths per hour ¥3000-3800; ⏲Moto-yu & Sagino-yu 6.30am-midnight) East of Arita, this hot-spring town has a 1300-year history and is said to have refreshed the armies of Toyotomi Hideyoshi. Its oldest existing bathing building (Moto-yu; 1870) is a simple wooden hall with hot and very hot pools separated by gender. Sagino-yu has more modern facilities: sauna, *rotemburo* (outdoor baths) and *kashikiri* (private reservable baths), useful for families and couples.

The town's impressive lacquered Chinese-style entrance gate, Sakura-mon, was built without nails.

The bathing areas are a 15-minute walk west of Takeo Onsen Station's north exit. It's a 16-minute ride from Arita Station (¥260), or you can pay ¥1100 for a *tokkyū* (Midori Huis Ten Bosch) and get there two minutes faster.

Sleeping & Eating

There are a few nondescript hotels in central Arita. Takeo Onsen is a better spot to overnight.

Takeo Onsen Youth Hostel HOSTEL ¥
(武雄温泉ユースホステル; ☎0954-22-2490; www.e-yh.net/takeo; 16060-1 Nagashima; dm HI member/nonmember ¥3400/4000; P ⊖ ❄ @ ☎) This hostel has onsen, 14 rooms with sleeping space for 80, and a green-and-orange

KYŪSHŪ'S POTTERY TOWNS

In mountainous Kyūshū, many villages had difficulty growing rice and looked to other industries to survive. Access to good clay, forests and streams made pottery-making a natural choice, and a number of superb styles can be found here.

Karatsu, Arita and Imari are the major pottery towns of Saga Prefecture, on Kyūshū's northwestern coast. From the early 17th century, pottery was produced in this area by captive Korean potters, experts who were zealously guarded so that neither the artists nor the secrets of their craft could escape. When trade routes opened up to the West, potters in Japan began imitating the highly decorative Chinese-style ware popular in Europe. Pottery styles are often known by the town name with the suffix *-yaki* (pottery) added.

Arita (p727) Highly decorated porcelain, often with squares of blue, red, green or gold.

Imari (p726) Fine porcelain, originally blue and white, bursting into vibrant colours in the mid-Edo period.

Karatsu (p724) Marked by subtle earthy tones, and prized for its use in the tea ceremony.

In southern Kyūshū, Kagoshima Prefecture is known for Satsuma-yaki (Satsuma is the feudal name for that region). Styles vary from crackled glazes to porcelains painted with gleaming gold, and rougher, more ponderous 'black Satsuma' ware.

exterior so bright it's likely visible from space. The friendly owners can pick you up from the station if you ring ahead to say you'll be later than the 4pm check-in. A couple of rental bikes are available (¥500 each).

Gallery Arita CAFE ¥¥

(ギャラリー有田; ☎095-542-2952; Honmachi Ōtsu 3057; lunch set menu ¥950-1300, godōfu set menu ¥1350, coffee from ¥450; ⏲9am-7pm) The walls of this gallery-cafe are lined with more than 2000 cup-and-saucer sets from hundreds of Arita-yaki potters; choose your favourite set, and staff can serve your drinks in them and sell them to you afterwards. Coffee is brewed filter style, and lunch specials are a good deal; the house speciality is *godōfu* (kudzu-starch tofu).

Information

Kiln Arita Tourist Information Desk (キルンアリタ観光案内所; ☎0955-42-4052; www.arita.jp; 972-31 Honmachi-he; ⏲9am-5pm) Staff at the city's tourist information office, near Arita Station, can assist with maps in English, timetables, bicycle rentals and introductions to accommodation – predominantly small private *minshuku* (guesthouses).

Getting There & Around

The private Matsuura-tetsudō line connects Arita with Imari (¥460, 25 minutes). JR *tokkyū* trains between Hakata (¥2750, 85 minutes) and Sasebo (¥760, 30 minutes) stop at Arita and Takeo Onsen. JR trains connect Arita and Takeo Onsen (*futsū/tokkyū* ¥280/580, 20/15 minutes).

Infrequent community buses (¥200) cover most places, but you'll save time by taking taxis (about ¥1000 to most sights). Arita Station rents out bicycles (¥500 to ¥1000 per day).

Hirado

☎0950 / POP 32,000

Sweet, off-the-beaten-path Hirado (平戸) was once *the* spot where foreigners visited Japan before *sakoku* (Japan's national isolation period), after which they were confined to Nagasaki's Dejima Island (p733). Secluded yet lovely, with hills rising steeply from the sea, this island has many reminders of early Western engagement, particularly of the *Kakure Kirishitan* (hidden Christians) who lived in the region. It's also a popular beach getaway and has picturesque old streets, great seafood and beef, a castle and wonderful museums.

As trains, then planes, surpassed ships as the main means of entry to Japan, Hirado was all but forgotten, and now it takes some effort to get here; the main village lies several kilometres from the nearest private, non-JR rail line. It's worth it.

Sights

★Oranda Shōkan HISTORIC BUILDING

(オランダ商館, Dutch Trading Post; ☎0950-26-0636; 2477 Ōkubo; ¥300; ⏲8.30am-5.30pm, closed 3rd Tue, Wed & Thu Jun) Across from the waterfront, this building was the trading house of the Dutch East India Company.

Shogunal authorities took the Gregorian date on the front of the building (1639) as proof of forbidden Christianity, ordered it destroyed and used it to justify confining Dutch traders to Dejima (p733). It was recently rebuilt according to the original plans and now houses displays about the history and goods traded – textiles, ceramics, pewter ware, gin etc – with good English descriptions.

★Ji-in to Kyōkai no Mieru Michi STREET
(寺院と教会の見える道, Street for Viewing Temples & a Church) This street, rising up a steep hill from town, is one of the most photogenic vantage points in all of Kyūshū. The Buddhist temples and large Christian church are testament to the island's history and shared East-West heritage.

Matsuura Historical Museum MUSEUM
(松浦史料博物館; 0950-22-2236; www.matsura.or.jp; 12 Kagamigawa-chō; ¥510; 8.30am-5.30pm) This museum is housed in the stunning residence of the Matsuura clan, who ruled the island from the 11th to the 19th centuries. You'll find armour that you can don to pose for photos; *byōbu* (folding screen) paintings; and the thatched-roof **Kanun-tei** *chashitsu* (tearoom) where the unusual Chinshin-ryū warrior-style tea ceremony is still practised (10am to noon and 2pm to 4pm Friday). Other days, try *matcha* and local sweets for ¥500; ask for *taiken* (experience) to whisk the tea yourself. A shop on the premises rents kimonos to wear while you promenade around town.

A combination ticket with the Oranda Shōkan costs ¥650.

Sleeping & Eating

Kotonoha GUESTHOUSE ¥
(コトノハ; 0950-29-9442; 846-2 Sakagata-chō; dm/s/tw ¥3000/3900/6500;) Opened in 2017 by a friendly former Tokyoite, this humble guesthouse across the street from Hirado's ferry port shows its Taishō-era roots in quirky touches like steep stairs and tree-trunk ceiling beams. The six dorm beds look like wooden boxes fitted with futons – some have windows (with no curtains), others don't – and there's one single-bed room and a bunk-bed twin.

Hirado Seto Ichiba SEAFOOD, MARKET ¥¥
(平戸瀬戸市場, Seaside Market; restaurant 0950-57-1057; www.setoichiba.com; 345-15 Yamauchi-men, Tabira-chō; meals ¥800-2980; 11am-5pm; P; Hirado-guchi bus stop) Downstairs is a fish market selling colourful and bargain-priced local fish (gutted and filleted on request), while upstairs is a popular *shokudō* with indoor-outdoor seating and views across the strait to Hirado. There's no English menu, but the regular menu has pictures of local specialities, including *kaisen-don* (raw seafood over rice bowl) and *Hirado-gyū* (beef). For dessert, a stand outside sells ice cream and sorbet made from local fruit.

The market is across the street from Hirado-guchi bus stop.

Suzu STEAK ¥¥
(鈴; 0950-23-3808; 446-1 Kihikida-chō; dishes ¥480-2300, lunch specials ¥1150-2500; 11am-2pm & 5-9pm, closed most Wed) Local *Hirado-gyū*, marvellously marbled and tender, is highly prized. This place on Hirado's main shopping street does it *yakiniku* style: in a private room, you cook the beef over a grill set into your table. Weekday lunch specials are a great deal, or share the 'pair set' with your favourite co-chef.

Tsutaya SWEETS ¥
(蔦屋; 0950-23-8000; 431 Kihikida-chō; sweets ¥100-220; 9am-7pm; P) Tsutaya has been making gorgeous tea-ceremony sweets since 1502, as a supplier to Hirado's ruling Matsuura clan. Nowadays it reproduces those historic tastes and innovates others, including through the 'Sweet Hirado' collaboration with Dutch candy makers. Buy snacks by the piece or the package to take with you, or eat them in the shop's lovely tatami room.

Information

Tourist Information Center (平戸観光案内所; 0950-22-2015; 776-6 Sakigata; 8am-6pm;) Near the ferry terminal; has lots of English-language materials, free computers and wi-fi, and helpful staff who can assist with booking accommodation.

Getting There & Away

Hirado is joined to Kyūshū by a mini Golden Gate–lookalike bridge from Hirado-guchi. The closest train station, Tabira-Hirado-guchi on the private Matsuura-tetsudō line (to Imari ¥1230, 65 minutes; to Sasebo ¥1340, 80 minutes), is Japan's westernmost, and local buses cross the bridge to the island (¥260, 10 minutes). From Nagasaki, journey to Sasebo by JR/express bus (¥1600/1450, both 1½ hours) and continue to Hirado by bus (¥1500, 1½ hours).

Getting Around

Hirado township is small enough to navigate on foot, but you'll need your own transport for points elsewhere on the island.

Rental bikes are available at the Tourist Information Center (p729) for ¥500 per four hours. Rental cars, starting at ¥5300 per day, are well worth it if you plan to see the furthest sights or beaches.

NAGASAKI & AROUND

Nagasaki sits high on the list of Kyūshū's must-sees, and not just for the tragedy most often associated with it – the atomic bombing by the United States at the end of WWII. The city has a colourful cosmopolitan history, and a dynamic cuisine to match. Travelling east, there's more history (and volcanic landscapes) to explore on the Shimabara Peninsula.

Nagasaki

095 / POP 430,000

It's both unfortunate and important that the name Nagasaki (長崎) is synonymous with the dropping of the second atomic bomb. This history undeniably overshadows everything else, yet if that's all you experience during your visit you'll be missing the point. As paradoxical as it may seem, Nagasaki is vibrant and charming, and it begs to be explored far beyond the bomb museums, monuments and memorials.

Spend some time here and you'll find that this welcoming, peaceful city also boasts a colourful history of trade with Europe and China, interesting churches, shrines and temples, and a global fusion culinary scene, all set prettily around a gracious harbour. A few days will only let you scratch the surface.

Not that the WWII history can be overlooked: it's as much a part of the city's fabric as the hilly landscape and cobblestones, and a visit to the scenes of atomic devastation is a must.

History

Nagasaki Prefecture's multilayered role in Japanese history started when an off-course Chinese ship landed in Kagoshima Prefecture in 1543, carrying guns and Portuguese explorers. Catholic missionaries arrived soon thereafter, ushering in Japan's 'Christian Century' (1549–1650), centred on Nagasaki, Hirado and other local communities in Nagasaki Prefecture.

By 1570 Nagasaki had become a wealthy, fashionable port. While Portuguese traders shuttled between Japan, China and Korea, missionaries converted Japanese. In 1580 the *daimyō* (domain lord) briefly ceded Nagasaki to the Society of Jesuits.

THE ATOMIC BOMB OVER NAGASAKI

When USAF B-29 bomber *Bock's Car* set off from the Marianas on 9 August 1945 to drop a second atomic bomb on Japan, the target was Kokura on Kyūshū's northeastern coast. Due to poor visibility, the crew diverted to the secondary target, Nagasaki.

The B-29 arrived over Nagasaki at 10.58am amid heavy cloud. When a momentary gap appeared and the Mitsubishi Arms Factory was sighted, the 4.57-ton 'Fat Man' bomb, with an explosive power equivalent to 21.3 kilotonnes of TNT (almost twice that of Hiroshima's 'Little Boy'), was released over Nagasaki.

The bomb missed the arms factory, its intended target, and exploded at 11.02am, at an altitude of 500m, almost directly above the largest Catholic church in Asia (Urakami Cathedral). In an instant, it annihilated the suburb of Urakami and 74,000 of Nagasaki's 240,000 people. Ground temperatures at the hypocentre were estimated at between 3000°C and 4000°C, and as high as 600°C 1.5km away. Everything within a 1km radius of the explosion was destroyed, and searing winds up to 170km/h (typhoons generally top out at 150km/h) swept down the valley of the Urakami-gawa towards the city centre. With able-bodied men at work or at war, most victims were women, children and senior citizens, as well as 13,000 conscripted Korean labourers and 200 Allied POWs. Another 75,000 people were horribly injured (and it is estimated that as many people died due to the after-effects). After the resulting fires burned out, a third of the city was gone.

Yet the damage might have been even worse had the targeted arms factory been hit. Unlike in the flatlands of Hiroshima or the Nagasaki port itself, the hills around the river valley protected outlying suburbs from greater damage.

The shogun then reclaimed Nagasaki, expelled the Jesuits and, in 1597, crucified 26 European and Japanese Christians. Christianity was officially banned in 1613, yet some 'hidden Christians' (*kakure Kirishitan* in Japanese) continued to practise. In 2018 Unesco added sites related to the hidden Christians to its World Heritage list.

After a peasant uprising at Shimabara in 1637–38, the shogunate excluded all foreigners from Japan and forbade Japanese to travel overseas, beginning a period called *sakoku* (national seclusion) that lasted over two centuries. The single exception was Dejima, an artificial island in Nagasaki harbour where Dutch traders lived under close scrutiny; the Dutch were deemed to be more about trade than conversion or conquest.

When Japan reopened its doors to the world in the 1850s, Nagasaki was uniquely positioned to become a major economic force, particularly in shipbuilding, the industry that ultimately led to its tragic bombing on 9 August 1945.

Sights

Nagasaki's sights are scattered over a broad area, but once you're in a district it's easy to walk from one location to the next. The atomic-bomb hypocentre is in the suburb of Urakami, about 2.5km north of JR Nagasaki Station. Central and southern Nagasaki are where you'll find sights related to its history of trade and foreign influence. Main enclaves are around JR Nagasaki Station and about 2km south: Shinchi Chinatown, the Dutch Slopes and Glover Garden. Near Shinchi Chinatown, Shianbashi is the main nightlife and shopping district.

Parts of Nagasaki are quite hilly, so bring good walking shoes. Because of the hills, people rarely cycle, and even driving can be challenging.

Urakami (Northern Nagasaki)

Urakami, the hypocentre of the atomic explosion, is today a prosperous, peaceful suburb. While nuclear ruin seems comfortably far away seven decades later, many sights here keep the memory alive.

★Nagasaki National Peace Memorial Hall for the Atomic Bomb Victims MEMORIAL
(国立長崎原爆死没者追悼平和祈念館; Map p732; www.peace-nagasaki.go.jp; 7-8 Hirano-machi; 8.30am-6.30pm May-Aug, to 5.30pm Sep-Apr; Heiwa Kōen/Peace Park) FREE Adjacent to the Atomic Bomb Museum and completed in 2003, this minimalist memorial by Kuryū Akira is a profoundly moving place. It's best approached by quietly walking around the sculpted water basin, commemorating those who cried for water in their dying days. In the hall below, 12 'pillars of light', containing shelves of books of the names of the deceased, reach skyward. Listen to survivors' messages and leave your own digital message for peace at 'peace information counters'.

★Nagasaki Atomic Bomb Museum MUSEUM
(長崎原爆資料館; Map p732; 095-844-1231; www.nagasakipeace.jp; 7-8 Hirano-machi; ¥200, audioguide ¥154; 8.30am-6.30pm May-Aug, to 5.30pm Sep-Apr; Genshi Shiryokan/Atomic Bomb Museum) On 9 August 1945, the world's second nuclear weapon detonated over Nagasaki, and this sombre place recounts the city's destruction and loss of life through photos and artefacts, including mangled rocks, trees, furniture, pottery and clothing, a clock stopped at 11.02 (the time of the bombing), firsthand accounts from survivors, and stories of heroic relief efforts. Exhibits also include the post-bombing struggle for nuclear disarmament, and conclude with a chilling illustration of which nations bear nuclear arms.

★Peace Park PARK
(平和公園, Heiwa-kōen; Map p732; Ōhashi) North of the hypocentre, Peace Park is presided over by the 10-tonne bronze **Nagasaki Peace Statue** (平和祈念像; Map p732; Peace Park), designed in 1955 by Kitamura Seibō. It also includes the dove-shaped Fountain of Peace (1969) and the Peace Symbol Zone, a sculpture garden with contributions on the theme of peace from around the world. On 9 August a rowdy antinuclear protest is held within earshot of the more formal official memorial ceremony for those lost to the bomb.

Atomic Bomb Hypocentre Park PARK
(長崎爆心地公園; Map p732; Heiwa Kōen/Peace Park) A must-see for anyone coming to Nagasaki for its historic significance, this park houses a smooth, black-stone column that marks the point above which the atomic bomb exploded. Nearby are bomb-blasted relics, including a section of the wall of the Urakami Cathedral (p733).

Nagasaki

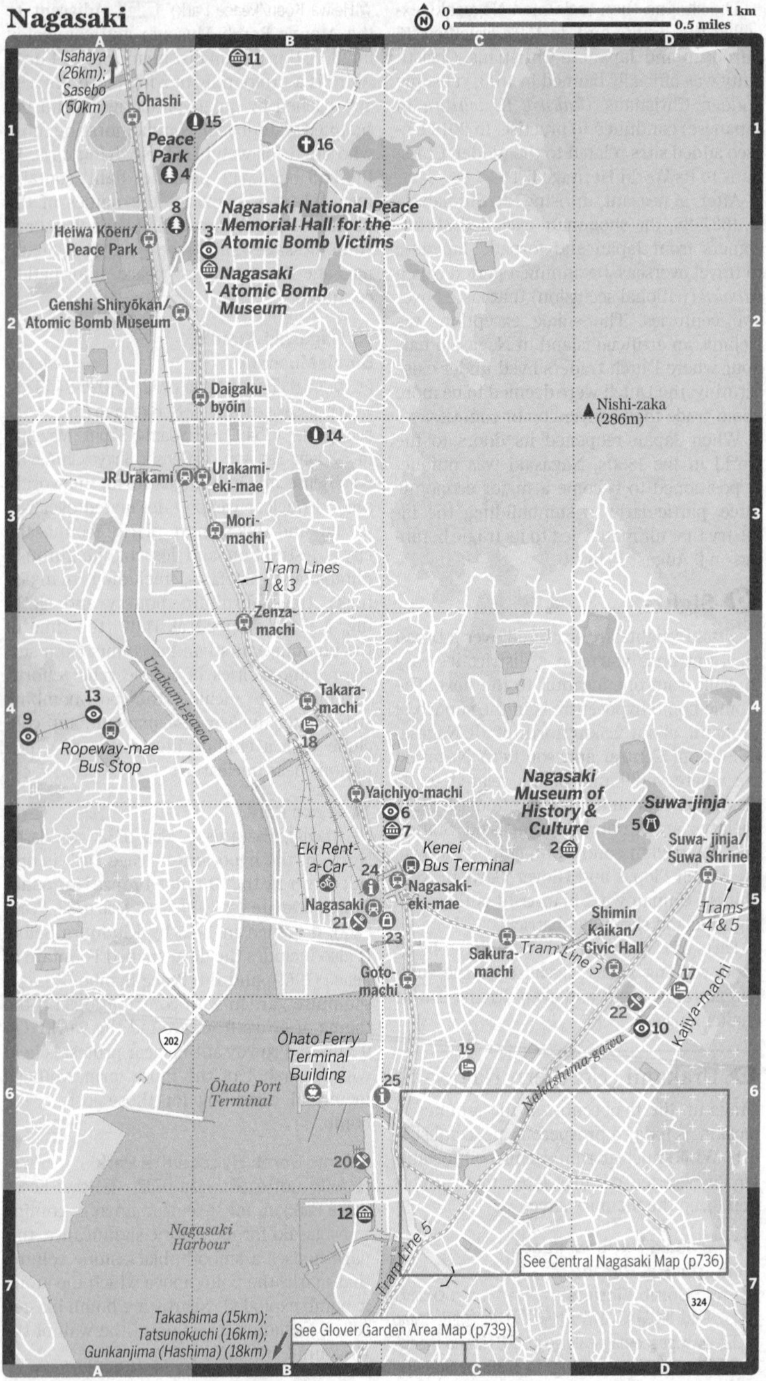

0 — 1 km
0 — 0.5 miles

Isahaya (26km); Sasebo (50km)
Ōhashi
11
15
Peace Park
4
16
8
Nagasaki National Peace Memorial Hall for the Atomic Bomb Victims
3
Heiwa Kōen/ Peace Park
1 Nagasaki Atomic Bomb Museum
Genshi Shiryōkan/ Atomic Bomb Museum
Daigaku-byōin
Nishi-zaka (286m)
14
JR Urakami
Urakami-eki-mae
Mori-machi
Tram Lines 1 & 3
Zenza-machi
Urakami-gawa
Takara-machi
13
9
Ropeway-mae Bus Stop
18
Yaichiyo-machi
6
7
Nagasaki Museum of History & Culture
2
Suwa-jinja
5
Suwa-jinja/ Suwa Shrine
Eki Rent-a-Car
24
Kenei Bus Terminal
Nagasaki-eki-mae
Nagasaki
21
23
Trams 4 & 5
Shimin Kaikan/ Civic Hall
Sakura-machi
Tram Line 3
Goto-machi
17
22
10
Kajiya-machi
202
Ōhato Ferry Terminal Building
19
Nakashima-gawa
Ōhato Port Terminal
25
20
12
Nagasaki Harbour
Tram Line 5
See Central Nagasaki Map (p736)
324
Takashima (15km); Tatsunokuchi (16km); Gunkanjima (Hashima) (18km)
See Glover Garden Area Map (p739)

Nagasaki

Top Sights
1 Nagasaki Atomic Bomb Museum B2
2 Nagasaki Museum of History & Culture C5
3 Nagasaki National Peace Memorial Hall for the Atomic Bomb Victims B2
4 Peace Park A1
5 Suwa-jinja D5

Sights
6 26 Martyrs Memorial C5
7 26 Martyrs Museum C5
8 Atomic Bomb Hypocentre Park A1
9 Inasa-yama A4
10 Megane-bashi D6
11 Nagai Takashi Memorial Museum B1
12 Nagasaki Prefectural Art Museum B7
13 Nagasaki Ropeway A4
Nakashima-gawa Bridges .... (see 10)
14 One-Pillar Torii B3
15 Peace Statue B1
16 Urakami Cathedral B1

Sleeping
17 Hostel Akari D5
18 Hotel Nagasaki B4
19 Sakamoto-ya C6

Eating
20 Dejima Wharf B6
21 No no Budo B5
22 Shōkandō D6

Shopping
23 Amu Plaza C5

Information
24 Nagasaki City Tourist Information Center B5
25 Nagasaki Prefectural Tourism Association & Visitors Bureau C6

Urakami Cathedral CHURCH
(浦上天主堂; Map p732; 1-79 Motō-machi; 9am-5pm; Atomic Bombing Museum) Once the largest church in Asia (1914), the cathedral took three decades to complete and three seconds to flatten. This smaller replacement cathedral was completed in 1959 on the ruins of the original. Walk around the side of the hill to see a belfry lying in state where the original building fell after the atomic blast.

Catholic visitors are welcome to worship, in a side chapel where the original *hibaku Maria* is kept, a charred figure of the Virgin Mary.

Nagai Takashi Memorial Museum MUSEUM
(永井隆記念館; Map p732; 095-844-3496; 22-6 Ueno-machi; ¥100; 9am-5pm; Ōhashi) This small but quietly moving museum celebrates the courage and faith of one man in the face of overwhelming adversity. Already suffering from leukaemia, Dr Nagai survived the atomic explosion but lost his wife to it. He immediately devoted himself to the treatment of bomb victims until his death in 1951. In his final days he continued to write prolifically and to secure donations for survivors and orphans, earning the nickname 'Saint of Nagasaki'. Ask to watch the video in English.

Next door is **Nyokodō** (如己堂), the simple hut from which Dr Nagai worked – its name comes from the biblical commandment 'love thy neighbour as thyself'.

One-Pillar Torii MONUMENT
(一本柱鳥居; Map p732; Daigaku-byōin or Urakami) The atomic blast knocked down half of the stone entrance arch to Sanno-jinja shrine, 800m southeast of the hypocentre, but the other pillar remains, a quiet testament to the power of human strength and resilience.

Central Nagasaki

★Dejima HISTORIC SITE
(出島; Map p736; 095-829-1194; www.nagasakidejima.jp; 6-1 Dejima-machi; ¥510; 8am-7pm mid-Jul–mid-Oct, to 6pm mid-Oct–mid-Jul; Dejima) In 1641 the Tokugawa shogunate banished all foreigners from Japan, with one exception: Dejima, a fan-shaped, artificial island in Nagasaki harbour. From then until the 1850s, this tiny, 15,000-sq-metre Dutch trading post was the sole sanctioned foreign presence in Japan. Today the city has filled in around the island and you might be tempted to skip it. Don't. Seventeen buildings, walls and structures (plus a miniature Dejima) have been painstakingly reconstructed.

Restored and reopened in 2006 and constantly being upgraded, the buildings are as instructive inside as they are appealing outside, filled with exhibits covering the spread of trade, Western learning and culture, archaeological digs, and rooms combining Japanese tatami (tightly woven floor matting) with Western wallpaper. There's excellent English signage. Allow at least two hours.

OFF THE BEATEN TRACK

GHOST ISLAND HASHIMA

From afar, the Unesco World Heritage island of **Hashima** (軍艦島) resembles a battleship, hence its nickname Gunkanjima ('battleship island'). Up close, this long-abandoned coal mine looks as though it's straight out of an apocalyptic manga (even appearing as the villain's lair in the 2012 James Bond film *Skyfall*). Once earth's most densely populated place, it became a ghost island when the mines were closed in 1974, and it's been left to nature since, now accessible only by guided tour.

Access is restricted because so many structures have collapsed or been damaged that much of the island is unsafe. Guided tours allow visitors to ramble on walkways among the long-disused skyscrapers. Some of the architecture (such as the iconic 'X' stairways – alas, not visible on the tour) was considered remarkable for its time, as engineers tackled the challenges of designing for such cramped living.

While most of the spoken guiding is in Japanese, English info is available. Three-hour cruises from Nagasaki run twice daily from April to October; there are fewer departures November to March. Contact **Gunkanjima Concierge** (軍艦島コンシェルジュ; Map p739; ☎095-895-9300; www.gunkanjima-concierge.com; Tokiwa Town, 1-60 Tokiwa Terminal Bldg 102; tour ¥4300) for reservations.

Bring sunscreen and make sure you've gone to the bathroom prior to exiting the boat: there are no facilities on the island.

For days when the island is inaccessible, the nearby **Gunkanjima Digital Museum** (軍艦島デジタルミュージアム; Map p739; ☎095-895-5000; www.gunkanjima-museum.jp; 5-6 Matsugae-machi; adult ¥1800; ⏲9am-6pm; 🚋Oura-Tenshudō) shows off the island from afar, through video presentations and virtual-reality experiences.

Free walking-tour maps of the entire site are available, and there's even a kimono-rental shop (¥2000/6000 per hour/day) for those who want to feel even more historically connected.

★Nagasaki Museum of History & Culture — MUSEUM

(長崎歴史文化博物館; Map p732; ☎095-818-8366; www.nmhc.jp; 1-1-1 Tateyama; ¥600; ⏲8.30am-7pm, closed 3rd Tue of month; 🚋Sakura-machi) This large museum with attractive displays focuses on Nagasaki's proud history of international exchange. Additionally, there's a fabulous, detailed reconstruction of a section of the Edo-period Nagasaki Magistrate's Office, which controlled trade and diplomacy. Be sure to get the free English-language audio guide.

★Suwa-jinja — SHINTŌ SHRINE

(諏訪神社; Map p732; ☎095-824-0445; 18-15 Kaminishiyama-machi; ⏲24hr; 🚋Suwa-jinja) FREE Situated on a forested hilltop and reached via multiple staircases with nearly 200 steps, this enormous shrine was established in 1625. Around the grounds are statues of *komainu* (protective dogs), including the *kappa-komainu* (water-sprite dogs), which you pray to by dribbling water onto the plates on their heads. The *gankake komainu* (turntable dog) was often called on by prostitutes, who prayed that storms would arrive, forcing the sailors to stay at the port another day.

The shrine comes to life each year with the dragon dance of Kunchi Matsuri (p737), Nagasaki's most important annual festival.

★Sōfuku-ji — BUDDHIST TEMPLE

(崇福寺; Map p736; 7-5 Kajiya-machi; ¥300; ⏲8am-5pm; 🚋Sōfuku-ji) In Teramachi, this Ōbaku temple (Ōbaku is the third-largest Zen sect after Rinzai and Sōtō) was built in 1629 by Chinese monk Chaonian. Its red entrance gate *(Daiippo-mon)* exemplifies Ming-dynasty architecture. Inside the temple you can admire a huge cauldron that was used to prepare food for famine victims in 1681, and a statue of Mazu (aka Maso), goddess of the sea, worshipped by early Chinese seafarers. There are excellent descriptions in English throughout the grounds.

Nakashima-gawa Bridges — BRIDGE

(中島川; Map p732; 🚋Shimin Kaikan/Civic Hall or Megane-bashi) Parallel to Teramachi, the Nakashima-gawa is crossed by a picturesque collection of 17th-century stone bridges. At one time each bridge was the distinct entrance to a separate temple. Best known is the double-arched **Megane-bashi** (め

がね橋, Spectacles Bridge; Map p732; Megane-bashi). Six of the 10 bridges, including Megane-bashi, were washed away by flooding in 1982 but later restored using the recovered stones.

Nagasaki Prefectural Art Museum MUSEUM

(長崎県美術館; Map p732; 095-833-2110; www.nagasaki-museum.jp; 2-1 Dejima-machi; ¥400; 10am-8pm, closed 2nd & 4th Mon of month; Shimin-Byōin-mae) Designed by Kuma Kengo (the architect behind Tokyo's Nezu Museum and 2020 Olympic Stadium), this museum straddles a canal in an environmentally friendly building (note the roof garden). The permanent collection covers both Nagasaki-related art and Spanish art, and special exhibits are eclectic, from Chinese art to Chagall. There's a lovely cafe in the bridge over the canal.

26 Martyrs Memorial MEMORIAL

(日本二十六聖人殉教地; Map p732) This memorial wall has reliefs of the 26 Christians – six Spanish friars and 20 Japanese – crucified in 1597 during a harsh crackdown. The youngest killed were boys aged 12 and 13. Behind the memorial is a simple **museum** (二十六聖人記念館; Map p732; 095-822-6000; www.26martyrs.com; 7-8 Nishisaka-machi; ¥500; 9am-5pm) with Christianity-related displays. The memorial is a 10-minute walk from JR Nagasaki Station.

Shinchi Chinatown AREA

(新地中華街; Map p736; Shinchi Chinatown) During Japan's long period of seclusion, Chinese traders were theoretically just as restricted as the Dutch, but in practice they were relatively free. Only a couple of buildings remain from the old area, but Nagasaki still has an energetic Chinese community, a fact evident in the city's culture, architecture, festivals and cuisine. Visitors come from far and wide to eat here and shop for Chinese crafts and ornaments.

Southern Nagasaki

Glover Garden GARDENS

(グラバー園; Map p739; 095-822-8223; www.glover-garden.jp; 8-1 Minamiyamate-machi; adult/student ¥610/300; 8am-9.30pm May–mid-Jul, to 6pm mid-Jul–Apr; Ōura Tenshudō) Some two dozen former homes of the city's Meiji-period European residents and other important buildings have been reassembled in this beautifully landscaped hillside garden, with breathtaking views across the harbour. Glover Garden is named after Scottish merchant and industrialist Thomas Glover (1838–1911), who built Japan's first railway and helped establish the shipbuilding industry, and whose arms-importing operations influenced the course of the Meiji Restoration.

Start by taking the moving walkways to the top of the hill, then work your way back down.

The **Mitsubishi No 2 Dock building** (旧三菱第２ドックハウス) is at the top, with panoramic views of the city and harbour from the 2nd floor. Next highest is **Walker House** (旧ウォーカー住宅), filled with artefacts donated by the Glover and Walker families, followed by **Ringer House** (旧リンガー住宅), **Alt House** (旧オルト住宅) and finally **Glover House** (旧グラバー住宅). Halfway down is the **Madame Butterfly Statue** of Japanese opera singer Tamaki Miura. Exit the garden through the **Nagasaki Traditional Performing Arts Museum** (長崎伝統芸能館), which has a display of dragons and floats used in Nagasaki's colourful Kunchi Matsuri (p737).

The 'audio pen' guide, available near the ticket office, gives lots of detailed commentary and costs ¥700, although the map that comes with it can be confusing.

★Ōura Cathedral CHURCH

(大浦天主堂; Map p739; 095-823-2628; 5-3 Minamiyamate-machi; ¥1000; 8am-6pm; Ōura Tenshudō) This hilltop church, Japan's oldest (1864), is dedicated to the 26 Christians who were crucified in Nagasaki in 1597. The former seminary and bishop's residence have recently been renovated to house a

DON'T MISS

INASA-YAMA

West of the harbour, the **Nagasaki Ropeway** (長崎ロープウェイ; Map p732; 095-861-3640; www.nagasaki-ropeway.jp; 8-1 Fuchi-machi; return ¥1230; 9am-10pm; Mori-machi) ascends every 15 to 20 minutes to the top of 333m-high **Inasa-yama** (稲佐山, Mt Inasa; Map p732), offering superb views over Nagasaki; it's been ranked as one of the world's top three night time views, alongside Hong Kong and Monaco. A tower at the top offers even more panoramic views.

Central Nagasaki

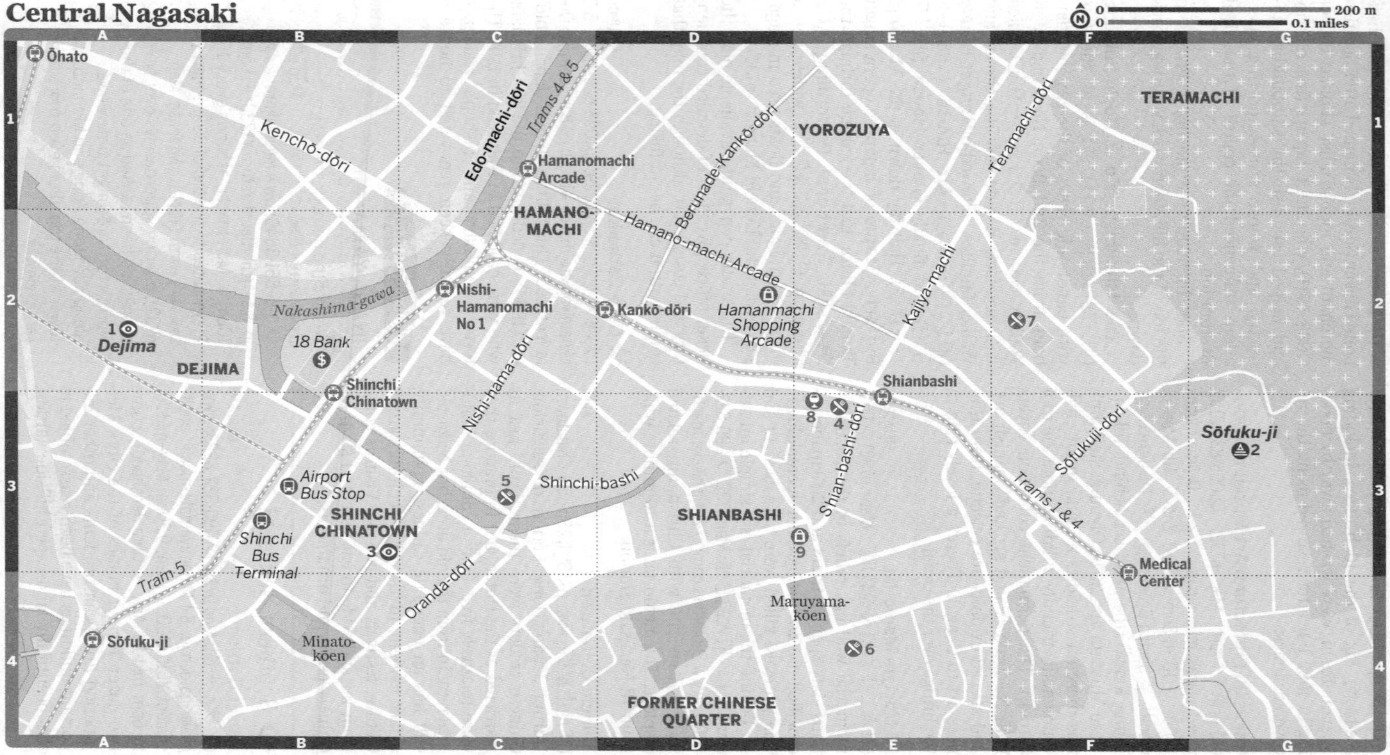

0 200 m
0 0.1 miles

Ōhato
Kenchō-dōri
Edo-machi-dōri
Trams 4 & 5
Hamanomachi Arcade
Berunade-Kankō-dōri
YOROZUYA
Teramachi-dōri
TERAMACHI
HAMANO-MACHI
Hamano-machi Arcade
Nakashima-gawa
Nishi-Hamanomachi No 1
Kankō-dōri
Hamanmachi Shopping Arcade
Kajiya-machi
7
1 Dejima
DEJIMA
18 Bank
Shinchi Chinatown
Nishi-hama-dōri
Shianbashi
8
4
Shian-bashi-dōri
Sōfukuji-dōri
Sōfuku-ji 2
Airport Bus Stop
5
Shinchi-bashi
SHINCHI CHINATOWN
Shinchi Bus Terminal
3
SHIANBASHI
9
Trams 1 & 4
Medical Center
Tram 5
Oranda-dōri
Maruyama-kōen
Sōfuku-ji
Minato-kōen
6
FORMER CHINESE QUARTER

Central Nagasaki

museum exhibiting items relating to the history of Christianity in Japan, with a special focus on hidden Christians (p842) and the suffering they endured under shogunal rule. The church and other Nagasaki Christian sites were named to Unesco's World Heritage list in 2018.

Dutch Slopes AREA
(オランダ坂, Oranda-zaka; Map p739; Oura Cathedral) The gently inclined flagstone streets known as the Dutch Slopes were once lined with wooden Dutch houses. Several buildings here have been beautifully restored and offer glimpses of Japan's early interest in the West. The Japanese name 'Oranda-zaka' comes from the Japanese word for Holland. It's a lovely stroll, and the quiet **Ko-shashin-shiryōkan** (古写真資料館, Museum of Old Photographs; combined admission ¥100; 9am-5pm Tue-Sun) and **Maizō-shiryōkan** (埋蔵資料館, Museum of Unearthed Artefacts; 9am-5pm Tue-Sun) museums showcase the area's history (note that most signage is in Japanese).

Festivals & Events

Peiron Dragon-Boat Races CULTURAL
(late Jul) Colourful boat races were introduced by the Chinese in the mid-1600s, and held to appease the god of the sea. They still take place in Nagasaki harbour.

Kunchi Matsuri CULTURAL
(くんち祭; 7-9 Oct) This energetic festival features Chinese dragons dancing all around the city, but especially at Suwa-jinja (p734). The festival is marked by elaborate costumes, fireworks, cymbals and giant dragon puppets. In addition, neighbourhood associations sponsor colourful floats, many shaped like boats and reflecting Nagasaki's Dutch and Chinese influences.

Sleeping

For ease of transport and access to restaurants and nightlife, it's most convenient to stay near JR Nagasaki Station or Shianbashi.

★ Hostel Akari HOSTEL ¥
(ホステルあかり; Map p732; 095-801-7900; www.nagasaki-hostel.com; 2-2 Kōjiya-machi; dm/s/d/tr from ¥2700/3900/¥6800/¥9900; reception 9am-1pm & 3-8pm; Shimin-kaikan) This commendably friendly 28-bed hostel sets the standard, with bright, clean Japanese-style rooms with Western-style bedding and bathrooms, uber-helpful staff, an open kitchen and a dedicated crew of local volunteers who lead free walking tours around the city. It's located by the lovely Nakashima-gawa. Towel rental is ¥100. Check-in can be tough between 1pm and 3pm.

★ Sakamoto-ya RYOKAN ¥¥¥
(料亭御宿坂本屋; Map p732; 095-826-8211; www.sakamotoya.co.jp; 2-13 Kanaya-machi; r per person incl 2 meals from ¥16,200; Goto-machi) This magnificent old-school ryokan has been in business since 1894. Offering *shippoku-ryōri* (Nagasaki-style *kaiseki*) and personalised service, Sakamoto-ya has just 11 rooms, each with a *hinoki-buro* (cypress bath). Hallways are lined with Arita-yaki pottery and there are postage-stamp-size gardens off 1st-floor rooms. From Goto-machi tram stop, walk past S-Peria Hotel and turn left; it's diagonally across from the TV tower.

Hotel Nagasaki HOTEL ¥¥¥
(ザ・ホテル長崎 BWプレミアコレクション; Map p732; 095-821-1111; www.landowner.jp/hotel-nagasaki; 2-26 Takaramachi; s/d/tw from ¥15,200/16,200/17,400; Takaramachi) This polished hotel, with spacious rooms and decent-size bathrooms, is about seven minutes' walk from Nagasaki Station and right across from a tram stop. Breakfast (¥1000 extra) is served in the 15th-floor dining room, with sweeping views south towards the harbour or north to the hills and Urakami. The best part, though, is the caring, practically doting, service.

Eating

Nagasaki cuisine reflects its rich international history, with influences from China and Europe popping up in what looks typically Japanese at first glance. There are restaurants throughout town, especially in shopping districts and around the station and harbour areas.

Hōuntei IZAKAYA ¥

(宝雲亭; Map p736; 095-821-9333; 1-8 Moto-shikkui-machi; dishes ¥380-540; 5.30-11pm; Shianbashi) Patrons have been ordering the *hito-kuchi gyōza* (¥380 for 10) at this rustic hole-in-the-wall place since the 1970s. Also try *butaniratoji* (pork and shallots cooked omelette style; ¥540) or beer or sake highball cocktails. There's a picture menu. Look for the red-letter signage and brown *noren* (door curtain) across from Hamanmachi Shopping Arcade.

★Organic Restaurant Tia JAPANESE ¥¥

(ティア; Map p736; 095-828-2984; www.tia-nagasaki.com; 7-18 Ginza-chō; set meals lunch/dinner from ¥900/1500; 11.30am-2.30pm & 6-10pm Thu-Sat, 11.30am-2.30pm Tue, Wed & Sun; Shinchi Chinatown) Tia serves a buffet of mouth-watering home-style Japanese cooking using local, organic products. It's on the 2nd floor, with an entry that's easy to miss on the corner of the Links Douza Building.

★Shippoku Hamakatsu KAISEKI ¥¥

(卓袱浜勝; Map p736; 095-826-8321; www.sippoku.jp; 6-50 Kajiya-machi; lunch/dinner from ¥1500/3500, shippoku courses ¥3900-7900; 11am-10pm; Shianbashi) Come here if you'd like to experience *shippoku-ryōri* (Nagasaki-style *kaiseki*) and still afford your airfare home. Menus are filling and varied, and there's a choice of Japanese- or Western-style seating.

No no Budo BUFFET ¥¥

(野の葡萄; Map p732; 095-895-8515; 5th fl, Amu Plaza, 1-1 Onouemachi; buffet lunch/dinner ¥1600/2100; 11am-11pm; Nagasaki-eki-mae, JR Nagasaki) Come for the buffet, stay for the view at the new Nagasaki branch of this much-loved casual buffet chain. Dozens of savoury and dessert offerings concentrate on organic and local, including an entire counter of Nagasaki specialities. The views from the far windows overlooking the harbour offer a great perspective on the city.

Higashi-yamate Chikyū-kan INTERNATIONAL ¥¥

(東山手「地球館」; Map p739; 095-822-7966; www.higashiyamate-chikyukan.com; 6-25 Higashiyamate-machi; cafe mains ¥800-850, restaurant prices vary; cafe 10am-5pm Thu-Mon, restaurant noon-3pm Sat & Sun; Ishibashi) In the Dutch Slopes a quirky 'World Foods Restaurant' operates most weekends; each week a different chef comes to prepare inexpensive meals from their home country – some 70 nations have been represented so far. This little gem is what cultural exchange is all about. Chess and language exchange are also reasons to stop by.

Dejima Wharf INTERNATIONAL ¥¥

(出島ワーフ; Map p732; 095-828-3939; www.dejimawharf.com; 1-1-109 Dejimamachi; Dejima) First things first: the wharf's not part of Dejima (p733); the land didn't even exist during those times. Still, Dejima Wharf is a picturesque harbour-side collection of indoor-outdoor restaurants (serving everything from seafood to Italian at a variety of price points), plus bars and galleries. Add sunset views over the bay – maybe with your sweetie – and it's well worth a visit.

Ryōtei Kagetsu KAISEKI ¥¥¥

(史跡料亭花月; Map p736; 095-822-0191; www.ryoutei-kagetsu.co.jp; 2-1 Maruyama-machi; lunch/dinner set meals from ¥10,370/14,260; noon-3pm & 6-10pm Wed-Mon; Shianbashi) Dating to 1642, this sky-high *shippoku-ryōri* restaurant started life as a high-class brothel. Japanese skills or a chaperone, and a love of food, will enhance the dining experience. There are beautiful gardens and an English sign with the building's history as you walk in, complementing the movie-set ambience. Reservations essential.

Drinking & Nightlife

Nagasaki nightlife can be hit or miss. You might find everyone partying on Friday or it could be dead. Little nightspots punctuate the narrow lanes around Hamano-machi and Shianbashi.

In the warmer months, Glover Garden (p735) hosts a beer garden with pretty views across the harbour. Check the website for opening times.

Barakamon BAR

(ばらかもん; Map p736; 2-19 Moto-Shikkuimachi; Shianbashi) This standing bar sits on the

Glover Garden Area

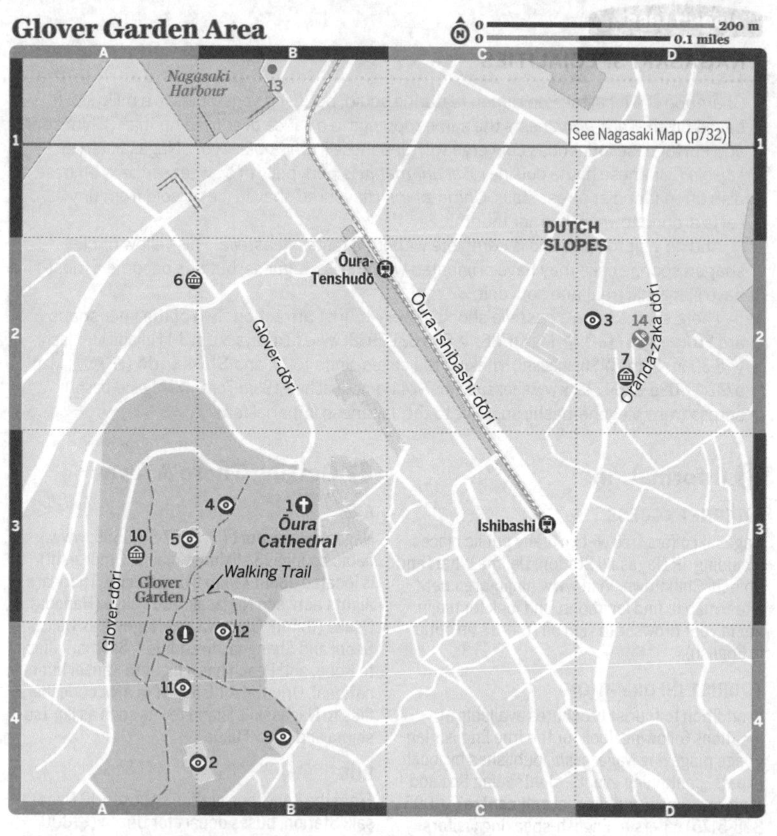

Glover Garden Area

Top Sights
1 Ōura Cathedral B3

Sights
2 Alt House B4
3 Dutch Slopes D2
4 Glover Garden B3
5 Glover House A3
6 Gunkanjima Digital Museum A2
7 Ko-shashin-shiryōkan D2
8 Madame Butterfly Statue A4
Maizō-shiryōkan .... (see 7)
9 Mitsubishi No 2 Dock Building B4
10 Nagasaki Traditional Performing Arts Museum A3
11 Ringer House A4
12 Walker House B4

Activities, Courses & Tours
13 Gunkanjima Concierge B1

Eating
14 Higashi-yamate Chikyū-kan D2

back alley of Shianbashi-yokochō and serves beers, highballs and 'strawberry milk' (with *shōchū* liquor). Look for the tiny storefront beneath the red sign.

Bar IWI BAR
(イーウィ; Map p736; www.facebook.com/barIWIofficial; 1-7 Motoshikkui-machi; 8pm-3am Mon-Sat; Shianbashi) Owned by Brynn, a friendly Kiwi, this cosy 'one-coin bar' has (mostly) ¥500 drinks and stays open to the wee hours, with an ever-changing mix of foreigners and primarily English-speaking locals. It's steps away from the Shianbashi tram stop.

DON'T MISS

NAGASAKI SPECIALITIES

Champon is a local take on ramen featuring squid, pork and vegetables in a milky, salt-based broth. *Sara-udon* nests the same toppings in a sauce over fried noodles. Chinese and Portuguese influences converge with Japanese in *shippoku-ryōri*, Nagasaki-style *kaiseki* (Japanese haute cuisine). *Kakuni-manju* is pork belly in a sweet sauce, a Chinese dish often found at street stalls. *Chirin-chirin* (flavoured shaved ice) is sold from tiny carts around town in warmer months.

And no visit to Nagasaki is complete without a taste of *castella*. This yellow brick-shaped sponge cake may have originated with the Portuguese, but has become a must-have Nagasaki treat and souvenir.

There seems to be a *castella* shop by every tourist attraction. Two of the finer shops are **Fukusaya** (福砂屋; Map p736; ☎095-821-2938; www.fukusaya.co.jp; 3-1 Funadaiku-machi; ⊙8.30am-8pm; Shianbashi), making the cakes since 1624, and **Shōkandō** (匠寛堂; Map p732; ☎095-826-1123; www.shokando.jp; 7-24 Uo-no-machi; ⊙9am-7pm; Megane-bashi), across from Megane-bashi, supplier to the Japanese imperial family.

Information

INTERNET ACCESS

Nagasaki offers free wi-fi in many public places including JR Nagasaki Station, Dejima Wharf and Shinchi Chinatown. Visit www.ninjin-area.net/sites/map to find locations, and look for ninjin.net in your browser to sign on (there's an option in English).

TOURIST INFORMATION

In addition to tourist brochures available at locations following, look for the free English-language magazine *Nagazasshi*, published by local expats, containing events, sightseeing tips and features. A new multilingual **call centre** (☎095-825-5175) caters to English-speaking visitors, and is being heavily pushed by the info desks – a shame, as speaking with a real person is often 10 times more effective than a phone call. This leads to a less-than-optimal tourist experience, but at the moment, if your questions run beyond which train to catch or whether there's a map available you'll likely be directed to call the number. It may be that your most frustrating moments will be there at the info desks – luckily, people are far friendlier and more eager to help once you're outside.

Nagasaki City Tourist Information Center (長崎市総合観光案内所; Map p732; ☎095-823-3631; www.at-nagasaki.jp/foreign/english; 1st fl, JR Nagasaki Station; ⊙8am-8pm) This often-busy office can assist with basic needs such as finding accommodation, and has brochures and maps in English. The English spoken is minimal, though.

Nagasaki Prefectural Tourism Association & Visitors Bureau (Map p732; ☎095-828-9407; www.visit-nagasaki.com; 8th fl, 14-10 Motofuna-machi; ⊙9am-5.30pm; Ōhato) Check the website for detailed info on tourism and activities.

Getting There & Away

AIR

Nagasaki's **airport** (☎0957-52-5555; www.nabic.co.jp; 593 Mishima-machi, Ōmura-shi) is located about 40km from the city. There are flights between Nagasaki and Tokyo (Haneda), Osaka (Itami), Okinawa and Nagoya, as well as Seoul and Shanghai. In addition, Skymark flies to Kobe, and Peach has a flight to Kansai International. Oriental Air Bridge (an ANA codeshare) flies to Nagasaki's island towns such as Iki, Tsushima and Goto-Fukue.

BUS

From the Kenei bus station opposite JR Nagasaki Station, buses depart for Unzen (¥1800, 1¾ hours), Sasebo (¥1500, 1½ hours), Fukuoka (¥2570, three hours), Kumamoto (¥3700, 3¼ hours) and Beppu (¥4630, 3½ hours). Night buses for Osaka (¥10,900, 10 hours) leave from both the **Kenei bus terminal** (県営バスターミナル; Map p732) and the **Shinchi bus terminal** (新地バスターミナル; Map p736).

TRAIN

JR lines from Nagasaki head for Sasebo (¥1650, 2¼ hours), Hirado (¥2990, four hours) and Fukuoka (Hakata Station; *tokkyū* ¥4500, two hours). Most other destinations require a change of train. Currently there's no *shinkansen* service to Nagasaki, but it's on the way, with completion expected in 2023.

Getting Around

The best way of getting around Nagasaki is by tram. There are four colour-coded routes numbered 1, 3, 4 and 5 (route 2 is for special events), and stops are signposted in English. It costs ¥120 to travel anywhere in town, but you can transfer for free at the Shinchi Chinatown (新地中華街) stop only: ask for a *noritsugi* (transfer pass). Alternatively, all day, unlimited tram passes are available for ¥500 from tourist information centres and many hotels. Most trams stop running around 11.30pm.

Buses cover a wider area than trams do, but they're less user-friendly for non-Japanese speakers.

Airport Bus Stop (Map p736) Services to the airport stop outside the Shinchi bus terminal.

Ropeway-mae Bus Stop (ロープウェイ前; Map p732) The bus stop closest to the ropeway.

Bicycles can be rented from JR Nagasaki Station at **Eki Rent-a-Car** (Map p732; 095-826-0480; 1-89 Onoemachi; per 2hr/day ¥500/1500; 8am-8pm). JR Pass holders receive a 20% discount. Bikes are electric; however, due to the hilly terrain, bikes are not the ideal way to get around.

Shimabara Peninsula

The hilly Shimabara Peninsula (島原半島), between the calm waters of Tachibana Bay and the Ariake Sea, can be visited en route from Nagasaki to Kumamoto. Highlights include hiking in the mountains and among the boiling hot springs of Unzen, and strolling the lovely town of Shimabara.

Getting There & Around

The peninsula is accessible by train and bus from Nagasaki. Rail service is a combination of JR Kyūshū and the Shimabara Railway. Ferry services connect Shimabara with Kumamoto.

While buses are available on the peninsula, times are infrequent. Your own rental car will save time and hassles.

Shimabara

0957 / POP 44,936

This relaxed castle town has a reconstructed castle, old samurai residence quarters and springs so clear that koi-filled waterways line the streets. The springs first appeared following the 1792 eruption of nearby Unzen-dake, and the town still vividly recalls the deadly 1991 eruption, commemorated with a harrowing museum.

Sights

★**Shimabara-jō** CASTLE

(島原城; 0957-62-4766; www.shimabarajou.com; 1-1183-1 Jonai; combined admission incl museums adult/child ¥540/270; 9am-5.30pm) This hilltop castle was ruled mostly by the Matsudaira clan from the 1660s and played a part in the Shimabara Rebellion. It was rebuilt in 1964. As well as lotus ponds, tangled gardens, almost 4km of massive stone walls overgrown with greenery, and staff dressed in period costume, the castle grounds house four museums. Most notable is the main castle, displaying arms, armour and items relating to local Christian history, with English explanations.

★**Samurai Houses** HISTORIC SITE

(武家屋敷) FREE In the Teppō-machi area, northwest of the castle, are *buke yashiki* (samurai residences) set along a pretty, 450m-long gravel road with a stream down the middle. Most of the houses are inhabited, but several are open to the public.

Teppō-machi is about a 10-minute walk from Shimabara Castle.

Koi no Uyogu Machi OLD TOWN

(鯉の泳ぐ街, City of Swimming Carp) FREE The spring water that flows into Shimabara from Mt Unzen is so pure that koi can swim in it, and in this district south of the castle you can see the fish in the drainage canals on the sides of the streets, and up close in teahouses like Shimeisō (p743).

Gamadas Dome Mt Unzen Disaster Memorial Hall MUSEUM

(がまだすドーム雲仙岳災害記念館; 0957-65-5555; www.udmh.or.jp; 1-1 Heisei-machi; adul ¥1000, student ¥500-700; 9am-6pm; P) About 4km south of the town centre, this excellent high-tech museum is larger than many a good-size city's town hall. It focuses on the 1991 eruption and vulcanology in general, and is plonked eerily at the base of the lava flow. Get the free English audio guide, and visit the disturbingly lifelike simulation theatre.

Sleeping & Eating

★**Hotel Nampūrō** HOTEL ¥¥

(ホテル南風楼; 0957-62-5111; www.nampuro.com; 2-7331-1 Bentenmachi; s from ¥10,000, d with/without 2 meals ¥17,600/11,600; P) This cheerful, busy resort is the place to stay, especially with kids in tow. English-speaking staff are welcoming, and there's a large family-friendly play area for young children, a pool (summer only), inflatable toys, and even a pen with goats and rabbits. For onsen bathers, multiple *rotemburo* (outdoor baths; day-use permitted) offer stunning sea views, especially at sunrise.

Shimabara

Top Sights

1 Samurai Houses A1
2 Shimabara-jō A1

Sights

3 Koi no Uyogu Machi B2

Eating

4 Himematsu-ya A1

Drinking & Nightlife

5 Shimabara Mizuyashiki B2
6 Shimeisō B2

Shopping

7 Inohara Kanamono-ten B1

Himematsu-ya JAPANESE ¥

(姫松屋; ☎0957-63-7272; 1-1208 Jōnai; dishes ¥500-1180, set meals ¥800-2100; ⏰11am-7pm, closed 2nd Tue of month) This venerable yet up-to-date restaurant across from the castle (p741) serves Shimabara's best-known dish, *guzōni*, a clear broth with *mochi* (pounded-rice dumplings), seafood and vegetables. There's more standard Japanese fare, too, and Unzen-raised *wagyū* beef goes for ¥1600.

Shopping

★ **Inohara Kanamono-ten** HOMEWARES

(猪原金物店; ☎0957-62-3117; www.inohara.jp; 912 Ueno-machi; ⏰11am-6pm Thu-Tue, closed 3rd Thu of month) Dating from the 1850s and a registered cultural property, this busy, rustic blade shop is filled with incredible knives, hatchets, swords and even ninja *shuriken* (throwing stars), plus just about anything you might need for a Japanese kitchen – *daikon* (radish) graters, bamboo strainers, *bentō* boxes and more. An enthusiastic owner helps you make sense of it all.

There's also a cafe, offering good Japanese curry (¥1000), *sōmen* (noodles; ¥680), *dango* (rice dumplings) and shaved ice (from ¥400), all made with fresh Shimabara water and using hand-sharpened blades.

Information

Tourist Information Office (島原温泉観光協会; ☎0957-62-3986; 7-5 Shimokawashirimachi; ⏰8.30am-5.30pm) Located inside the ferry-terminal bus station (note: not in the train station).

Getting There & Away

JR trains from Nagasaki to Isahaya (*futsū/tokkyū* ¥460/760, 34/17 minutes) connect with hourly private Shimabara-tetsudō line trains to Shimabara/Shimabara-gaikō Stations (¥1430/1510, 1/1¼ hours) by the castle/port respectively.

Ferries to Kumamoto Port depart frequently from Shimabara Port (7am to 7pm), including **Ocean Arrow Ferries** (オーシャンアロー; ☎0957-63-8008; www.kumamotoferry.co.jp; adult/child ¥1000/500, driver with economy-size car ¥3100; ⏰7.30am-5.30pm), which take 30 minutes, and slower (one hour) **Kyūshō Ferry Co** (九商フェリー; ☎Kumamoto 096-329-6111, Shimabara 0957-65-0456; www.kyusho-ferry.co.jp; 7-5 Shimokawashirimachi; adult/child ¥780/390, driver with economy-size car ¥2310; ⏰office 9am-7pm Mon-Fri, ticket office 6am-7.30pm daily) ferries. From Kumamoto Port, buses take you to the city (free to ¥480).

Getting Around

Local buses shuttle between Shimabara Station and the port (¥170) or train station (¥150). Bikes can also be rented at the castle or at Shimabara Gaikō Station (¥150 per hour).

Unzen

☎0957

In Unzen-Amakusa National Park, Japan's first national park, Unzen (雲仙) is off the beaten path but spectacularly worth a visit. It boasts dozens of onsen and woodsy trekking through volcanic landscapes. Unzen village is easily explored in an afternoon, and once the day trippers clear out you can enjoy a peaceful night's stay in some great hot-spring accommodation. The village also has the honour of being perhaps the last place in all of Japan without a convenience store.

Sights & Activities

A path just outside the village winds through the bubbling *jigoku* (literally 'hells'; boiling mineral hot springs). Unlike the touristy *jigoku* of Beppu, these natural wonders are broken up only by stands selling *onsen tamago* (onsen-steamed hard-cooked eggs). A few centuries ago these *jigoku* lived up to their infernal name when some 30 Christian martyrs were plunged alive into Oito Jigoku.

For a quick walk among the *jigoku* of Unzen village, start at **Gojū-shūnen Hiroba** (五十周年広場) near the tourist office.

From the town there are popular walks to Kinugasa, Takaiwa-san and Yadake, all situated within the national park. The Mt Unzen Visitors Centre (p744) has displays on volcanoes, flora and fauna, and information in English.

Nearby, via Nita-tōge (Nita Pass), is **Fugen-dake** (1359m), part of the Unzen-dake range. Its hiking trail has incredible views of the lava flow from the summit. A shared Heisei Taxi (p744) takes you to the Nita-tōge parking area (¥430), starting point for the Fugen-dake walk. A **cable car** (雲仙ロープウェイ; ☎0957-73-3572; 1 way ¥630; ⊙8.50am-5.20pm) gets you close to a shrine and the summit of **Myōken-dake** (1333m), from where the hike via **Kunimi-wakare** takes just under two hours return. Walk 3.5km back from the shrine to Nita via the village and valley of Azami-dani.

For a longer excursion (three hours), detour to **Kunimi-dake** (1347m) for a good glimpse of Japan's newest mountain, the smoking lava dome of **Heisei Shinzan** (1483m), created in November 1990 when Fugen-dake blew its stack.

Sleeping & Eating

Nearly all dining is done at hotels, so eating options are limited and close early. Along the hiking trail near the town centre you can snack on *onsen tamago*.

Tsudoi Guest House GUESTHOUSE ¥
(集; ☎0957-60-4225; 323-2-2 Unzen; dm ¥3300;) The name of this new guesthouse means 'to come together' in Japanese, and its relaxed, 20-bed facilities make that easy. The friendly owner leads activities like Nordic walking expeditions (¥1000 per person), and overnight stays include admission to local onsen. Prep your own simple meals in the guest-use kitchen.

★**Fukudaya** HOTEL ¥¥
(福田屋; ☎0957-73-2151; www.fukudaya.co.jp; 380-2 Unzen; r incl 2 meals from ¥12,800;) Fukudaya is a hip, stylish onsen hotel mixing Western and Japanese decor. The rooms with private *rotemburo* are gorgeous, with milky water and decks overlooking a small creek running below. The cafe-lounge in the lobby is a chill hang-out spot, and meals – in small, private rooms – vary between *kaiseki* and *teppan-yaki* of local *wagyū*.

★**Kyūshū Hotel** HOTEL ¥¥¥
(九州ホテル; ☎0957-73-3234; www.kyushuhtl.co.jp; 320 Unzen; r per person incl 2 meals from ¥30,240;) Unzen's *jigoku* make

DON'T MISS

SHIMABARA'S TEAHOUSES

With all the clear water flowing through town, Shimabara is known for its teahouses. For a quick break, stop for tea at **Shimeisō** (四明荘; ☎095-763-1121; 2-125 Shinmachi; ¥300; ⊙9am-6pm), a villa on stilts over a spring-fed pond. Off Shimabara's central arcade, the delightful Meiji-era **Shimabara Mizuyashiki** (しまばら水屋敷; ☎0957-62-8555; www.mizuyashiki.com; 513 Yorozumachi; tea & sweets ¥325-810; ⊙11am-5pm) features a lovely garden, a spring-fed pond and an obsessive collection of *maneki-neko* (lucky cat) figurines from all over Japan, some for sale. The enthusiastic owner has created a detailed walking map of sights and restaurants in town.

a dramatic backdrop for this eye-popping, ultra-luxe 'mountain resort', renovated in 2018 in the centre of the village. Behind the contemporary garden courtyard sit a stylish lobby and tempting, Japanese-Western-fusion rooms with walk-in closets and giant bathrooms with private onsen. There's beautiful wood and stone work throughout.

Information

Mt Unzen Visitors Centre (雲仙お山の情報館; 0957-73-3636; www.unzenvc.com; 320 Unzen; 9am-6pm Fri-Wed mid-Jul–Aug, to 5pm Sep–mid-Jul) Has information in English, and can store luggage for ¥300.

Unzen Tourist Association (雲仙観光協会; 0957-73-3434; 320 Unzen; 9am-5pm) Town maps and accommodation bookings.

Getting There & Around

Three buses run daily between Nagasaki and Unzen (¥1800, one hour and 40 minutes). Unzen is also a stop on the more frequent bus route from Shimabara (¥830, 54 minutes) to Isahaya (¥1350, one hour and 24 minutes), with train connections to Nagasaki (¥460, 34 minutes).

Unzen town is so small you can walk to most of the major hotels. If you want to get to the cable car or other hiking spots you'll need a **taxi** (0957-73-2010).

KUMAMOTO & AROUND

This beautiful region is firmly placed on the tourist map for its historic towns, towering mountains, active volcanoes, grassland plateaus, river-cut chasms and bubbling hot springs (including one of our favourite spots: Kurokawa Onsen).

The city of Kumamoto, known for its castle, is the main hub for central Kyūshū. In 2016 the Kumamoto region experienced several severe earthquakes that killed many people and destroyed thousands of homes. In October, Aso-san (Mt Aso) erupted, further damaging the area. At the time of writing, some sites and roads were still closed pending repair.

South of Aso-san, Takachiho is the mythical home of the sun goddess Amaterasu. (Note that it's not Takachiho-no-mine – Mt Takachiho – in nearby Kagoshima; the two are often confused.)

Kumamoto

096 / POP 737,812

Kumamoto (熊本) is deeply proud of its greatest landmark, Kumamoto-jō, the castle around which the city radiates. Even though the castle suffered significant damage in the April 2016 earthquake, it remains a focal point of the city. There's a lively and tempting collection of restaurants, bars and shops in the busy arcades east of the castle.

Kumamoto City is also the gateway to the popular Aso-san region, known for its cooler summer temperatures and impressive volcano.

The 2016 earthquakes resulted in several deaths, and severe damage to roads and buildings in addition to Kumamoto-jō; damage to the castle alone was estimated at ¥63.4 billion, and much of the castle and several nearby buildings remain closed for restoration. They are set to reopen as work is completed, but the dates are unclear; estimates are that some repairs will take 20 years. The city's tourism website (https://kumamoto-guide.jp) has the latest information about site closures, in English.

Sights

★Kumamoto-jō CASTLE

(熊本城; 096-322-5900; ¥500; 8.30am-6pm Mar-Nov, to 5pm Dec-Feb) Dominating the skyline, Kumamoto's robust castle is one of Japan's best, built in 1601–07 by *daimyō* Katō Kiyomasa, whose likeness is inescapable around the castle (look for the distinctive tall pointed hat). From 1632 it was the seat of the powerful Hosokawa clan. Unfortunately, the castle, many outbuildings and much of the grounds are closed indefinitely due to earthquake damage, but the site is still worth seeing from the street.

★Suizenji-jōjuen GARDENS

(水前寺成趣園, Suizenji Park; www.suizenji.or.jp; 8-1 Suizenji-kōen; ¥400; 7.30am-6pm Mar-Oct, 8.30am-5pm Nov-Feb; Suizenji Park) Southeast of the city centre, this photogenic lakeside garden was built between 1636 and 1716 for the ruling Hosokawa clan. The main path represents the 53 stations of the Tōkaidō (the feudal road that linked Tokyo and Kyoto). The miniature Mt Fuji is instantly recognisable, though much of the rest of the analogy is often lost in translation. Still, it's a lovely walk through groves of palms and hydrangeas and to a large Shintō shrine.

Central Kumamoto

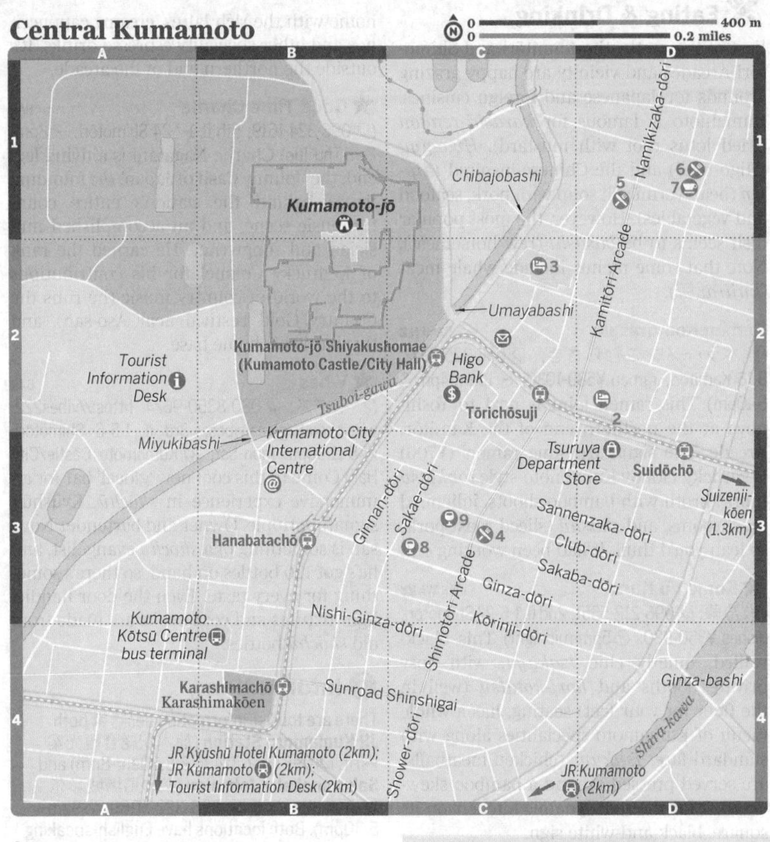

Central Kumamoto

Sleeping

★Kumamoto Hotel Castle HOTEL ¥¥¥
(熊本ホテルキャッスル; ☎096-326-3311; www.hotel-castle.co.jp; 4-2 Jōtō-machi; s/d/tw from ¥10,100/17,820/19,000, r Japanese style ¥35,640; P ⊖ ❄ ☎; ⓑ Kumamoto Castle/City Hall) Pride of place goes to this upmarket hotel overlooking the castle, with professional, friendly service, a beamed lobby ceiling inspired by its namesake, and rooms in muted browns and whites. It has received many VIPs, including imperial visitors, yet it's not above letting staff wear cheery Hawaiian shirts in Kumamoto's hot summers. Request a castle-view room.

Hotel Nikko Kumamoto HOTEL ¥¥¥
(ホテル日航熊本; ☎096-211-1111; www.nikko-kumamoto.co.jp; 2-1 Kamitōri-machi; s/d/tw from ¥17,820/47,520/32,080; P ⊖ ❄ @ ☎; ⓑ Torichōsuji) The classic Japanese-hotel experience, Kumamoto's premier place to stay has crisply uniformed staff, minimalist-cool design, soothing marble, fine-grained woods, and spacious rooms with big bathrooms and views to the castle or Aso-san. It's across from **Tsuruya Department Store** (鶴屋百貨店; www.tsuruya-dept.co.jp; 6-1 Tetori-honchō; ⌚ main building 10am-7pm Sun-Thu, to 7:30pm Fri & Sat) at the arcade entrance.

Eating & Drinking

East of the castle, the Kamitōri and Shimotōri Arcades and vicinity are happy grazing grounds for Japanese and foreign cuisines. Kumamoto is famous for *karashi-renkon* (fried lotus root with mustard), *Higo-gyū* (Higo beef) and the Chinese-inspired *taipien* (bean vermicelli soup with pork, seafood and vegetables). However, the most popular dish seems to be *basashi* (raw horsemeat). Note that some menus include whale meat (*kujira;* 鯨).

Ramen Komurasaki RAMEN ¥
(熊本ラーメンこむらさき; 096-325-8972; 8-16 Kamitōri; ramen ¥580-1030; 10am-4pm & 6-10pm) This ramen joint is next to Yoshinoya at the northern end of the Kamitōri Arcade. The signature 'king ramen' (¥700) is garlicky, cloudy Kumamoto-style *tonkotsu* (pork) broth with bamboo shoots, julienned mushrooms, and *chāshū* (sliced roast pork) so lean you'd think it had been working out.

★ Kome no Kura IZAKAYA ¥¥
(米乃蔵; 096-212-5551; 2nd fl, 1-6-27 Shimotōri; dishes ¥350-980; 5pm-midnight) This black-walled, quietly chic *izakaya*, with cosy private booths and *hori-kotatsu* (well in the floor for your feet) seating, has a whole menu of Kumamoto specialities along with standard fare. *Tsukune* (chicken meatballs) are served pressed around a bamboo skewer. Look for the red 'dynamic kitchen' on its square, black-and-white sign.

If you're having trouble finding it, look for Docomo: it's next door.

★ Yokobachi IZAKAYA ¥¥
(096-351-4581; 11-40 Kaminoura; small plates ¥480-1800; 5pm-midnight; Tōrichō-suji) Yokobachi's leafy courtyard and open kitchen are distinctive. Although some menu translations are head-scratchers, stand-out small plates include spicy *tebasaki* (chicken wings), Caesar salad with fried *gobo* (burdock root) chips, taro croquettes, delicately fried *mābō-doufu* ('bean curd Szechuan style'), beef skewers and, if you dare, *basashi* (¥880). There are 13 *shōchū* liquors to choose from. Reservations are recommended.

★ Andcoffeeroasters CAFE
(096-273-6178; www.andcoffeeroasters.com; 11-22 Kamitōri-machi; 8am-8pm) Delightful boutique coffee shop with freshly roasted beans and a 'tart of the day', such as persimmon or Earl Grey. Coffee nerds will feel right at home with the rich lattes, creamy cappuccinos and other speciality espresso drinks. It's outside the northern end of the arcade.

★ Good Time Charlie BAR
(096-324-1619; 5th fl, 1-7-24 Shimotōri; 8pm-2am Thu-Tue) Charlie Nagatani is a living legend, the 'Johnny Cash of Japan', *the* founding figure behind the nation's entire country-music scene, and an accomplished musician and songwriter. He earned the rank of Kentucky Colonel for his contributions to the world of country music (he runs the Country Gold Festival near Aso-san), and this bar is his home base.

★ Vibes BAR
(バイブス; 080-8350-9624; https://vibes222.wixsite.com/glocalvibes; 3rd fl, 1-5-6 Shimotōri; 8-11.30pm Mon-Sat; Kumamoto Castle/City Hall) Come to this cool new 'glocal' bar for an immersive experience in *shōchū,* Kyūshū's signature tipple. Owner and bartender Nori-san is something of a *shōchū* evangelist, and he's got 120 bottles on hand, so there's something for every taste. Even the door handle, light fixtures and coat hooks are made from old *shōchū* bottles.

Information

There are tourist-information desks at both **JR Kumamoto Station** (熊本駅総合観光案内所; 096-352-3743; 8.30am-8pm) and **Sakuranobaba Johsaien** (桜の馬場城彩苑総合観光案内所; 096-322-5060; 9am-5.30pm). Both locations have English-speaking assistants and accommodation listings.

Kumamoto City International Centre (熊本市国際交流会館; 096-359-2020; 4-18 Hanabata-chō; 9am-10pm, closed 2nd & 4th Mon of month; ; Hanabata-chō) has free wi-fi, plus BBC News and English-language magazines, international-themed classes and a cafe.

Visit www.kumamoto-icb.or.jp for city information.

Getting There & Away

AIR

Flights connect **Aso-Kumamoto Airport** (www.kmj-ab.co.jp) with Tokyo, Osaka, Nagoya and Seoul. Buses to and from the airport stop at JR Kumamoto Station (¥800, one hour), Kumamoto Kōtsū Centre bus terminal (¥730, 50 minutes) and Suizenji Park (¥600, 30 minutes).

BOAT

Kumamoto Port is about 25 minutes by road from Kumamoto Station. Kyūshō (p742) and Ocean Arrow (p742) ferries connect with Shimabara in Nagasaki Prefecture.

BUS

Highway buses depart from the **Kumamoto Kōtsū Centre bus terminal** (熊本交通センター; ☎096-325-0100; 7-20 Sakura-machi; ⏰7am-9.30pm). Routes include Fukuoka (¥2060, two hours), Kagoshima (¥3700, 3½ hours), Nagasaki (¥3700, 3¼ hours) and Miyazaki (¥4630, three hours).

CAR & MOTORCYCLE

Renting a car (from about ¥5250 per 12 hours) is recommended for trips to Aso and beyond. Rental services line the street across from JR Kumamoto Station.

TRAIN

JR Kumamoto Station is an inconvenient few kilometres southwest of the centre (though it's an easy tram ride away). It's a stop on the Kyūshū *shinkansen*, with destinations including Kagoshima-Chūō (¥6740, 45 minutes), Fukuoka (Hakata Station; ¥4930, 35 minutes), Hiroshima (¥13,340, 1¾ hours) and Shin-Osaka (¥18,340, 3¼ hours).

Getting Around

Kumamoto's tram service (Shiden) reaches the major sights for ¥170 per ride. One-day tram passes (¥500) can be bought on board and offer discounted admission to sights; use a coin to scratch off the day you're traveling. The tram's two lines mostly travel the same route, but they diverge south of the city centre, and only line A (red) goes to JR Kumamoto Station.

City buses are generally hard to manage without Japanese skills, with one exception: the Castle Loop Bus (Shiromegurin; ¥160/400 per ride/day pass), connecting the bus terminal with most sights in the castle area at least every half hour between 9am and 5pm daily.

Aso-san

☎0967 / POP 26,549

Halfway between Kumamoto and Beppu lies the volcanic caldera of Aso-san (阿蘇山). It's the world's third-largest (128km in circumference) and strikingly beautiful, yet its scale is so big that it's hard at first to comprehend. Formed through a series of eruptions over the past 300,000 years, the current outer crater is about 90,000 years old and now accommodates towns, villages and lush green farmland. Aso is the main town, and nearby Uchinomaki has inns, shops and dining. To the southeast, the town of Takamori is intimate and charming.

The Aso-san range is still active, and the summit is frequently off-limits due to toxic gas emissions or strong winds. In October 2016 the volcano had a major eruption, resulting in severe damage to surrounding areas. Be sure to check the latest access information with the tourist centre or at www.aso.ne.jp before planning a trip.

Sights

If you're driving, **Daikanbō Lookout** (大観峰; Ⓟ) is one of the best places to view the region from on high, although it's often crowded with tour buses. **Shiroyama Tembōjō** (城山展望所; Yamanami Hwy) is an appealing alternative.

★Naka-dake Crater VOLCANO

(中岳; www.aso.ne.jp) Naka-dake (1506m) is Aso's active volcano – very active in recent years, with fatal eruptions in 1958 and 1979, and other significant eruptions in 1989, 1990, 1993 and 2016. Access to the crater area may be closed when there's an increase in volcanic activity, such as dangerous sulphurous-gas emissions. Check the website for current conditions. People with asthma, bronchitis or head colds are advised to stay away.

If you make it to the top, you'll be rewarded by stark rock faces and a fluorescent-green lake inside the 100m-deep crater. With waters bubbling and steaming below, the crater varies in width from 400m to 1100m, and there's a walk around the southern edge of the rim. Arrive early in the morning to glimpse a sea of clouds hovering inside the crater, with Kujū-san (1791m) on the horizon.

A cable car served the crater until the most recent eruption, but operations have since been suspended. Nowadays, it's ¥800 for parking; alternatively, you can park at the former cable-car station (p751) and hike up in about 30 minutes, or take a shuttle bus (¥1200 return).

The most expensive, and perhaps most thrilling, way to see the crater is from way above, in a plane operated by Saga Aviation (p750).

Aso-gogaku MOUNTAIN

(阿蘇五岳) The Five Mountains of Aso are the smaller mountains within the Aso-san caldera's outer rim: Eboshi-dake (1337m); Kijima-dake (1321m); Naka-dake (1506m); Neko-dake (1408m), furthest east; and the highest, Taka-dake (1592m). Access roads were damaged in the 2016 earthquakes and at the time of writing were in the process of being repaired, although some areas may be closed due to toxic gas emissions.

Aso-San Area

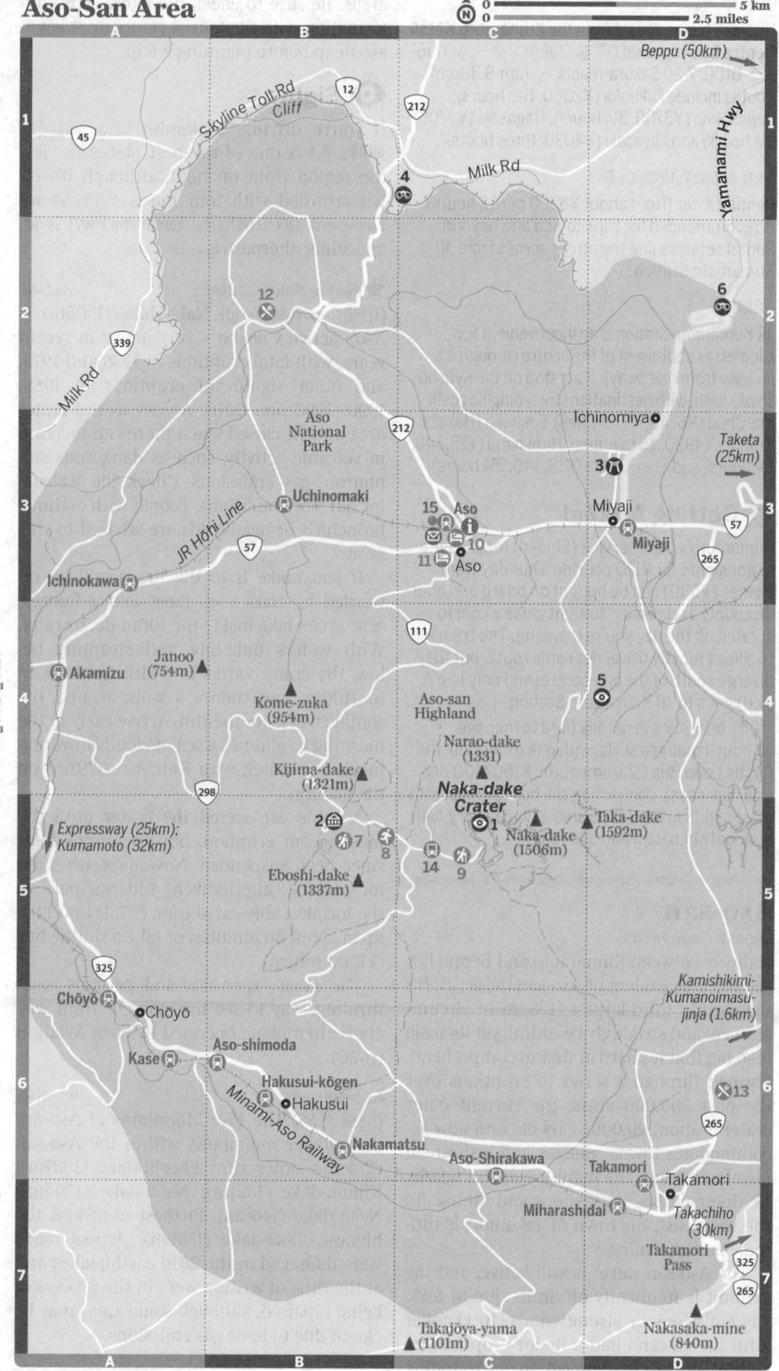

Beppu (50km)
Skyline Toll Rd
Cliff
Yamanami Hwy
Milk Rd
Aso National Park
Ichinomiya
Taketa (25km)
Uchinomaki
JR Hōhi Line
Aso
Miyaji
Ichinokawa
Akamizu
Janoo (754m)
Kome-zuka (954m)
Aso-san Highland
Narao-dake (1331)
Kijima-dake (1321m)
Naka-dake Crater
Naka-dake (1506m)
Taka-dake (1592m)
Expressway (25km); Kumamoto (32km)
Eboshi-dake (1337m)
Kamishikimi-Kumanoimasu-jinja (1.6km)
Chōyō
Kase
Aso-shimoda
Hakusui-kōgen
Hakusui
Minami-Aso Railway
Nakamatsu
Aso-Shirakawa
Takamori
Miharashidai
Takachiho (30km)
Takamori Pass
Takajōya-yama (1101m)
Nakasaka-mine (840m)
0 5 km
0 2.5 miles

Aso-San Area

Top Sights
1 Naka-dake Crater C5

Sights
2 Aso Volcano Museum B5
3 Aso-jinja D3
4 Daikanbō Lookout C1
5 Sensui Gorge D4
6 Shiroyama Tembōjō Lookout D2

Activities, Courses & Tours
7 Kusasenri B5
8 Saga Aviation B5
9 Sunasenri C5

Sleeping
10 Aso Base Backpackers C3
11 Shukubō Aso C3

Eating
Michi no Eki Aso .... (see 10)
12 Oshimaya Kagu Cafe B2
13 Takamori Dengaku-no-Sato D6
Yamaichi .... (see 12)

Transport
14 Mt Aso Ropeway Station C5
15 Toyota Rent-a-Car C3

Kamishikimi-Kumanoimasu-jinja SHINTŌ SHRINE
(上色見熊野座神社; 269 Kamishikimi; 24hr; P) FREE This gorgeous hilltop shrine and 'power spot' was pretty much left alone until it became the model for the set of the popular 2011 anime film *Hotarubi no Mori e*. It's easy to see why directors chose it. You ascend the approximately 230 (some uneven) steps along a lantern-lined path through an old-growth cedar forest to the main shrine. Continuing uphill (phew!), you eventually reach the ridge and a massive natural stone formation, with an opening (to heaven?) peeking through.

The shrine is about 6km from central Takamori, along Rte 265. Look for the post office across from the base of the stairs and a car park shortly thereafter.

Sensui Gorge GORGE
(仙酔峡, Sensui-kyō) In mid-May this gorge boasts a dramatic carpet of azalea blooms. Ask at tourist-information offices about trail conditions before setting out. Due to earthquake damage in 2016, this area had been inaccessible but it reopened in spring 2019.

Aso-jinja SHINTŌ SHRINE
(阿蘇神社; 3083-1 Miyaji, Ichinomiya) FREE Dedicated to the 12 gods of the mountain, this shrine, including its revered gate, suffered severe damage in the 2016 earthquakes; photos show the scale of the destruction. Some of the buildings are being gradually repaired and will reopen when rebuilt, but full completion isn't expected until 2030. People still come for the drinking water, which is so delicious that visitors fill canteens to take home.

The shrine is a 1.3km walk north of JR Miyaji Station.

Aso Volcano Museum MUSEUM
(阿蘇火山博物館; 0967-34-2111; www.asomuse.jp; 1930-1 Akamizu; ¥860, parking ¥410; 9am-5pm; P) This old-school museum has exhibits and dioramas about Aso, volcanos in general and the sometimes fraught relationship locals have with the volcano system. A free English-language audio guide describes the exhibits, video on a parabolic screen tells the story of the caldera's creation some 19,000 years ago, and you can see a real-time video feed from inside Naka-dake crater. Other exhibits cover the flora, fauna and customs of the region.

Activities

Saga Aviation SCENIC FLIGHTS
(0967-35-5030; www.sgc-air.co.jp/sightseeing/sightseeing_price; 3/7min flight ¥5000/10,000; 10am-5pm Fri-Mon) If you've got nerves of steel, this outfit will take you soaring over the Aso caldera and Naka-dake (p747) by helicopter. Cheap it isn't, but it's a good rush, the views are simply breathtaking, and it's often the only way to see Naka-dake when it's off-limits to earthbound travellers. Flights are first come, first served, so arrive early.

The heliport is on the side of the road between the Aso Volcano Museum and Naka-dake. Flights may be cancelled due to poor weather or volcanic activity.

Aso Kujyu Cycle Tour CYCLING
(阿蘇くじゅうサイクルツアー; 090-8666-1006; www.aso-cycletour.com; 2½/5hr tours per person ¥6000/10,000) This outfit offers a variety of cycling tours around the caldera, featuring friendly guides. There's no English on the website at the time of writing, but the welcoming owners make it work both for phone reservations and on the road.

Hiking

Although the Aso area has a wealth of walking and trekking routes, many were damaged by the 2016 earthquake and were in various stages of repair at research time. Others may become temporarily off-limits due to weather and volcanic conditions such as noxious gases. Be sure to check with tourism authorities before setting out.

If Naka-dake (p747) is accessible, you can walk around the crater rim and on to Taka-dake (a round trip of around 4½ to five hours). Or take the trail between Taka-dake and Neko-dake and on to Miyaji, the next train station east of Aso.

Shorter walks in the area include the easy ascent of Kijima-dake from the Aso Volcano Museum (p749), about 25 minutes to the top. You can then return to the museum or take the branch trail toward Naka-dake. The walk around the grassy plain of **Kusasenri** (草千里) takes about one hour, and can be combined with a climb to the top of Eboshi-dake (about 80 minutes). Kusasenri's sandier counterpart, **Sunasenri** (砂千里), is en route to Naka-dake.

If you're in the southeastern section of the caldera, the Shintō shrine Kamishikimi-Kumanoimasu-jinja (p749) is a profoundly spiritual place up the side of a mountain (some 200 steps get you there).

Sleeping

Aso Base Backpackers HOSTEL ¥
(阿蘇ベースバックパッカーズ; ☎0967-34-0408; www.aso-backpackers.com; 1498 Kurokawa; dm/s/tw/d without bathroom ¥2800/5500/6000/6600; ⊙closed early Jan-late Feb; P) A quick walk from JR Aso Station, this clean, modern, popular 30-bed hostel has English signage, a balcony with mountain views, a coin laundry, warm staff, and information about transport and sights. There are bicycles and motor-scooters for rent. Toilets, sinks and showers are down the hall; for baths, owners can direct you to nearby onsen.

Shukubō Aso RYOKAN ¥¥¥
(宿坊あそ; ☎0967-34-0194; 1076 Kurokawa; r per person incl 2 meals from ¥12,000; P) Less than 500m from Aso Station, this lovely, rustic ryokan in a 300-year-old samurai house has modern touches and a tree-lined setting. Its 12 rooms have private toilet and shared bathroom, and a dinner of local meats and fish is served around an *irori* (hearth). It's near pretty Saiganden-ji temple, which dates from 726. (Note: it's *not* nonsmoking.)

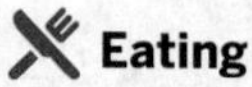

Eating

The area's specialities include *akaushi* (beef from local cows), *dangojiru* (dumpling soup), *takana gohan* (rice with mustard greens) and horse meat, most commonly served as *basashi* (raw). Eateries and food shops cluster around Hwy 57 near JR Aso Station; there are more in Uchinomaki and Takamori. Many restaurants open only for lunch, so unless you have dinner plans at your inn it's worth stocking up on snacks or *bentō* (boxed meals).

Yamaichi STEAK, JAPANESE ¥
(やまいち; ☎0967-32-2511; 235 Uchinomaki; mains ¥500-600, set meal ¥1700; ⊙11am-4pm) Aso *akaushi* is prized for its relatively low fat content. Get it here sliced over *donburi* (rice bowl). Set meals come with *dangojiru* and *takana gohan*. While other steak places have salad bars, Yamaichi stands out for its *tsukemono* (pickle) bar, with a dozen colourful house-made varieties.

Oshimaya Kagu Cafe CAFE ¥
(おしま屋家具カフェ; ☎0967-32-0041; 365 Uchinomaki; smoothies ¥450, dessert sets from ¥600; ⊙10am-5pm Wed-Sun, closed 3rd Thu of month) At this retro cafe you can sample coffees, cakes, smoothies and Aso-made ice creams while sitting on designy mid-century furniture (*kagu* in Japanese). Look for the giant metal chair on the corner just outside. Oshimaya also has an adorable gift shop.

★ **Takamori Dengaku-no-Sato** GRILL ¥¥
(高森田楽の里; ☎0967-62-1899; 2685-2 Ōaza-Takamori; set meals ¥1790-2850; ⊙10am-7.30pm late Mar-Nov, 10am-5pm Mon-Fri, to 6.30pm Sat & Sun Dec-late Mar; P) At this fantastic thatch-roofed ex-farmhouse the staff use oven mitts to grill *dengaku* (skewers of vegetables, meat including Aso beef, fish and tofu covered in the namesake *dengaku:* sweet miso paste) at your own *irori* embedded in the floor. It's a few minutes by car or taxi (about ¥600) from central Takamori. Cash only.

After lunch, stop by the restaurant's gift shop and cafe. Its atmospheric building was a Meiji period rice dealer's shop.

Information

Post office (⊙9am-5pm Mon-Fri, ATM 9am-6pm Mon-Fri, to 5pm Sat, to 12.30pm Sun) With ATM; lies 100m south of the tourist office, across Hwy 57.

DON'T MISS

TOP HIKING SPOTS

Hikers will discover that Kyūshū boasts some of Japan's most awe-inspiring treks – nearly every prefecture has great getaways. Below are some top spots, several of which follow still-active volcanoes, making for jaw-droppingly awesome vistas…and sometimes requiring special precautions. Look for the *Kyūshū Olle* brochure, available in many tourist booths, for trekking routes through towns and trails.

At research time, some Aso-san routes were closed due to volcanic damage, but these may reopen at any time.

- Kirishima-Kinkō-wan National Park (p777), Kagoshima
- Unzen (p743), Nagasaki
- Kaimon-dake (p775), Kagoshima
- Aso-san, Kumamoto
- Kujū-san (p759), Ōita

Tourist Information Center (道の駅阿蘇施設案内所, Michi no Eki Aso; ☎0967-35-5077; 1440-1 Kurokawa; 9am-6pm;) Inside **Michi no Eki Aso** (道の駅阿蘇; 1440-1 Kurokawa; 9am-6pm; P), next to JR Aso Station, this helpful centre offers free road and hiking maps, and local information in English, as well as coin lockers.

Getting There & Away

Aso lies on the JR Hōhi line between Kumamoto and Ōita, but at the time of writing trains from Kumamoto were not running all the way to Aso and were ending at Higo-Ōzu (¥2980, 3¼ hours) due to earthquake damage. Trains from Beppu *do* end in Aso (¥3050, 1¾ hours). Check the JR Kyushu website (www.jrkyushu.co.jp) for the latest conditions.

There is currently no Aso–Takamori train service. Buses from Takamori continue southeast to Takachiho (¥1320, 80 minutes, two daily).

Ōita-bound Yamabiko buses (¥1250, two hours, seven daily) run between Kumamoto Station and Aso Station (also stopping at Higo-Ōzu).

Buses usually operate every one to two hours from JR Aso Station via the volcano museum to Aso-nishi cable-car station (¥650, 40 minutes).

Getting Around

Best explored by car, the Aso-san region offers fabulous drives, diverse scenery and peaceful retreats. Routes 57, 265 and 325 encircle the outer caldera. The JR Hōhi line has historically run from Kumamoto across the northwestern section of the park, but it was closed due to earthquake damage and at research time a re-opening date had not been set. In the meantime, buses serve the Kumamoto–Aso route.

Conditions permitting, buses travel to the summit of Naka-dake. They stop at **Mt Aso Ropeway Station** (阿蘇山ロープウェー; 808-5 Kurokawa; 1 way/round trip ¥750/1200; 8.30am-6pm mid-Mar–Oct, 8.30am-5pm Nov, 9am-5pm Dec–mid-Mar); the ropeway was closed indefinitely at research time.

Rent electric bikes at JR Aso Station (¥400 for two hours), or cars at **Toyota Rent-a-Car** (☎096-735-5511; per day from ¥5600; 8am-6pm), adjacent to the train station (reserve in advance).

Kurokawa Onsen

☎0967 / POP 1700

Nestled on either side of a steep gorge about one hour northeast of Aso town, tranquil Kurokawa Onsen (黒川温泉) is one of Japan's prettiest hot-spring villages and has won top onsen honours year after year. Safely secluded from the rest of the world, it's the perfect spot to experience what an *onsen ryokan* getaway is all about.

It's well worth an overnight in Kurokawa Onsen for a relaxing stay, but for day trippers a *nyūtō tegata* (onsen passport; ¥1300) allows access to three baths among the town's 24 ryokan (open 8.30am to 9pm). Buy the pass at the tourist information desk (p752) and ask which locations are open during your visit.

Favourite baths include Yamamizuki, Kurokawa-sō and Shimmei-kan, with cave baths and riverside *rotemburo* (Kurokawa is especially famous for its *rotemburo*). Many places offer *konyoku* (mixed bathing) alongside women-only baths.

Sleeping & Eating

Kurokawa's *onsen ryokan* aren't cheap, but this isn't an experience you'll have every day. English is spoken to varying degrees. Many ryokan are a short walk across the gorge from Kurokawa Onsen's bus stop and tourist information centre, while some others can arrange pick-up from there.

If you're staying overnight, plan on eating ryokan meals. If you're a day visitor, note that there are few lunch places and they often close promptly.

★Sanga Ryokan RYOKAN ¥¥¥
(山河旅館; ☎0967-44-0906; www.sanga-ryokan.com; r per person incl 2 meals from ¥16,350; P ❄ 📶) Deep in the gorge, this romantic riverside ryokan is worth the 1.5km trip from the town centre for peace and pampering. Seven atmospheric common baths (in stone, cypress and more), 16 deluxe rooms (some with private onsen), exquisite *kaiseki* meals, attention to detail, heartfelt service and English-speaking staff make this a prime place to experience Japanese hospitality.

Okyakuya Ryokan RYOKAN ¥¥¥
(御客屋旅館; ☎0967-44-0454; www.okyakuya.jp; r per person incl 2 meals from ¥15,270; P ❄ 📶) At Kurokawa Onsen's oldest ryokan (in its seventh generation, run since 1722, though rebuilt in the mid-20th century) all 10 rooms have a rustic atmosphere and share onsen. The riverside *rotemburo* (enclosed for privacy) has a sound of rushing water that's enough to refresh you on its own. Some staff speak English.

Information

There's no ATM in Kurokawa Onsen, so prepare accordingly.

Tourist Information Desk (黒川温泉旅館組合, Ryokan Association; ☎0967-44-0076; www.kurokawaonsen.or.jp; Kurokawa-sakura-dōri; ⏲9am-6pm) Sells the *nyūtō tegata* (onsen passport; ¥1300) and dispenses friendly, helpful information. Signage around town points the way to inns and baths in Japanese and English.

DON'T MISS

BEST ONSEN

➜ Tamatebako Onsen (p774)
➜ Takegawara Onsen (p757)
➜ Musō-en (p762)
➜ Beppu Onsen Hoyōland (p757)
➜ Takeo Onsen (p727)

Getting There & Away

Experiencing this area is most enjoyable by car, but several daily buses connect Kurokawa Onsen with Aso (¥990, one hour) and Kumamoto (¥2060, 2½ hours). A couple also travel to Beppu (¥2980, 2½ hours) via Yufuin (¥2370). Check timetables if you intend to make this a day trip. These durations reflect route changes due to earthquake damage.

You can also take a three-hour express bus from Hakata Station (and the airport, too) for ¥3090; there are two departures in the morning and two from Kurokawa Onsen in the afternoon.

Takachiho

☎0982 / POP 12,300

In far northern Miyazaki Prefecture, the pretty mountain town of Takachiho (高千穂) is a remote but rewarding destination. There's a deep and dramatic gorge through the town centre, around which legend has it that Japan's sun goddess brought light back to the world, a story retold nightly through ancient performance art.

Sights

★Ama-no-Iwato-jinja SHINTŌ SHRINE
(天岩戸神社; 1073-1 Iwato; ⏲24hr, office 8.30am-5pm; P) FREE One of Shintō's loveliest shrines honours the cave where the goddess Amaterasu hid (p755). The cave itself is off-limits, but Nishi Hongū (the shrine's main building) sits right across the Iwato-gawa. Ask a staff member to show you the viewpoint behind the *honden* (main hall). Local 'Fureai' buses leave approximately hourly (¥300, 20 minutes) from Takachiho's Miyakō bus centre.

An approximately 10-minute walk beside a picturesque stream takes you to **Ama-no-Yasukawara**, a deep cave where tradition says that thousands of other deities discussed how to lure Amaterasu from the cave. Modern-day visitors have left innumerable *ishizumi* (stacks of stones) in tribute, imparting a sort of Indiana Jones feeling.

★Takachiho Gorge GORGE
(高千穂峡, Takachiho-kyō) Takachiho's magnificent gorge, with its waterfall, overhanging rocks and sheer walls, was formed over 120,000 years ago by a double volcanic eruption. There's a 1km-long nature trail above the gorge. Alternatively, view it up close from a **row boat** (貸しボート; ☎0982-73-1213; per 30min for up to 3 adults per boat ¥2000;

Takachiho

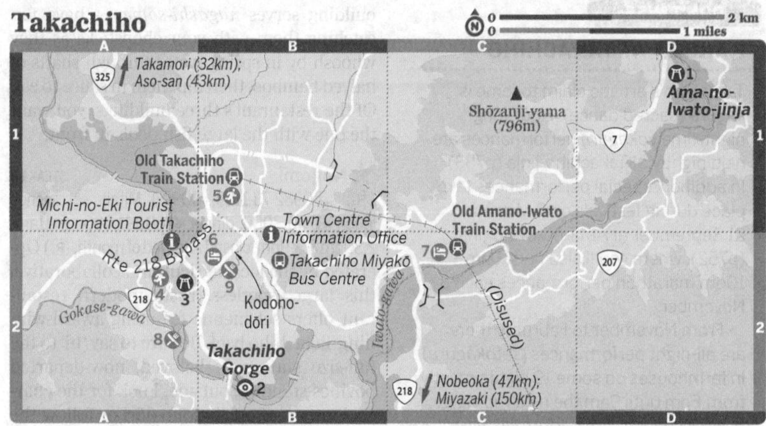

8am-5pm), though during high season it can be as busy as rush hour. For a different perspective, try the open-topped tourist train.

Takachiho-jinja SHINTŌ SHRINE

(高千穂神社) About 10 minutes' walk from the bus centre (p755), Takachiho-jinja is dramatically set in a grove of cryptomeria pines, including one that's over 800 years old. Some of the buildings here look as though they could almost be the same age. Yokagura (p754) performances are held nightly in the Kagura-den hall.

Activities

Takachiho Amaterasu Railway RAIL

(高千穂あまてらす鉄道; 0982-72-3216; www.amaterasu-railway.jp; Takachiho Station, 1425-1 Mitai; adult ¥1300, student ¥400-800; departures 9.40am-3.40pm, closed 3rd Thu of month;) After the local JR line was decommissioned and sat unused for years, some smart entrepreneurs converted it into a tourist railway. Nowadays, a pink-striped, open-topped (partly glass-bottomed), 30-passenger train leaves the former Takachiho Station on 5.1km, 30-minute rides. Passengers enjoy views across rice terraces to the distant mountains, and the train stops on Japan's tallest rail bridge, 105m above Takachiho Gorge.

There are 10 departures a day, with additional departures during peak seasons and on weekends and holidays March to November. Reservations not accepted. Operations may be suspended due to bad weather.

Takachiho

Top Sights

1 Ama-no-Iwato-jinja D1
2 Takachiho Gorge B2

Sights

3 Takachiho-jinja A2

Activities, Courses & Tours

4 Row Boats A2
5 Takachiho Amaterasu Railway B1

Sleeping

6 Solest Takachiho Hotel B2
7 Takachiho Youth Hostel C2

Eating

8 Chiho-no-ie A2
9 Nagomi B2

Festivals & Events

Yokagura DANCE

(夜神楽; Takachiho-jinja; tickets ¥700; 8pm) Designated an important intangible folk property of Japan, these night-time *kagura* (sacred dance) performances are held in the Kagura-den (Kagura Hall) at Takachiho-jinja. Reception opens at 7pm; it's cash only, and no reservations are accepted. Arrive early for your choice of seats.

Sleeping

Takachiho has about 30 hotels, ryokan, *minshuku* and pensions. Reserve early during festivals and the autumn foliage season.

Takachiho Youth Hostel HOSTEL ¥

(高千穂ユースホステル; 0982-72-3021; www.jyh.or.jp/e/i.php?jyhno=8602; 5899-2 Mitai;

DON'T MISS

KAGURA AT TAKACHIHO

Takachiho's artistic claim to fame is *kagura* (sacred dance). Hour-long night-time *yokagura* performances are held nightly at Takachiho-jinja (p753). In addition, special performances take place during festivals on 3 May and 21 September at Ama-no-Iwato-jinja (p752), where you'll also find 10am–10pm marathon performances each 3 November.

From November to February there are all-night performances *(satokagura)* in farmhouses on some 19 nights mostly from 6pm until 9am the next morning. In all, 33 dances are performed. If you brave the cold until morning, you'll be caught up in a wave of excitement. Contact the tourist information office for details.

dm HI member/nonmember ¥2800/3400; P ⊖ ❄ @) This large hostel is far from the sights, but it's clean, efficient and deep in the woods. Rooms are Japanese style, with breakfast on offer (¥500); laundry machines are available, as is pick-up from the bus centre if you call ahead.

★ **Solest Takachiho Hotel** HOTEL ¥¥
(ソレスト高千穂ホテル; ☎0982-83-0001; www.solest-takachiho.jp; 1261-1 Mitai; s/d/tw from ¥9000/14,980/16,500; P ❄ ☎) Crisp, comfy and contemporary, this stylish new hotel sits behind a black-box facade. Most of its 68 rooms are Western style (twin-bed rooms are significantly larger than doubles and have separate bathing and toilet areas), and all have rain showers and decent-size bathtubs.

Eating

Takachiho beef is much admired in Japan and available throughout town. Also popular is the Kyūshū speciality *nagashi-sōmen* (flowing noodles). Daytime restaurants and cafes dot the town centre, especially on Kodono-dōri, behind the tourist office. If you're not having dinner in your inn, there are several *izakaya* to choose from.

Chiho-no-ie NOODLES ¥
(千穂の家; ☎0982-72-2115; 62-1 Mukoyama; sōmen ¥500, set meals from ¥1500; ⏲9am-5pm; P) At the base of the gorge (p753) – though, sadly, with no water views – this simple building serves *nagashi-sōmen* – have fun catching them with your chopsticks as they whoosh by in spring water through shafts of halved bamboo, then dip them in sauce to eat. Of the restaurant's three buildings, you want the one with the large fish pools in front.

★ **Nagomi** STEAK ¥¥
(和; ☎0982-73-1109; 1099-1 Mitai; set menus lunch ¥1700-3000, dinner ¥2600-11,000; ⏲11am-2.30pm & 5-9pm, closed 2nd Wed of month; P) Operated by the local agricultural collaborative, this large, spotless, rustic-modern restaurant offers set menus featuring award-winning Takachiho beef. Be sure to say 'hi' to the full-size statues of beloved, now-departed bovines standing outside. Look for the charcoal-grey roof off Kodono-dōri or follow the signs to **Gamadase Ichiba** (がまだせ市場, Gamadase Market) next door, where local farm folk sell produce.

Information

Michi-no-Eki Tourist Information Booth (道の駅観光案内所; ☎098-272-4680; www.takachiho-kanko.jp; 1296-5 Mitai; ⏲8.30am-5.30pm) A well-stocked tourist info counter with friendly staff who can assist with making day plans or reservations.

Town Centre Information Office (町中案内所; ☎0982-72-3031; 802-3 Mitai; ⏲8.30am-5.30pm) Across from the bus station, this office has helpful staff and a variety of maps, brochures, info, postcards and souvenirs. You can also rent bicycles and cars here, and staff can assist with lodging reservations and restaurant advice.

Getting There & Away

Remote Takachiho is most easily reached by car from the Aso-san area in Kumamoto Prefecture. Two buses daily serve Takachiho's **Miyakō bus centre** (高千穂宮交バスセンター; ☎0982-72-4133; 804 Mitai) from Kumamoto (¥2370, 3½ hours), usually via Takamori (¥1320, 1¼ hours), plus there's one bus from Miyazaki (¥2500, three hours). There are no trains into Takachiho.

Getting Around

From the bus centre the gorge and Takachiho-jinja are within walking distance, but you'll need transport to reach other sights. Buses are infrequent, but the town-centre information office rents out electric bicycles (useful for the many hills; ¥300/1500 per hour/day) and can help with rental cars. If your time is limited, taxis can be chartered, starting at ¥6000 for 90 minutes.

ŌITA PREFECTURE

In northeast Kyūshū, Ōita Prefecture (大分県) is synonymous with onsen. It has two of the country's most famous hot spring resorts: Beppu and Yufuin. Less well known are the impressive Buddhist sites of the remote Kunisaki Peninsula and, south of Beppu, in Usuki.

Getting There & Around

Oita Airport, where you can pick up a rental car, is on the coast of the Kunisaki Peninsula. For public transport, Beppu is a regional hub, with rail access to other parts of Kyūshū. If you're coming here directly from Honshū, it's better to transfer at Kokura, in the city of Kitakyūshū, rather than going all the way to Hakata Station (in Fukuoka).

Beppu

0977 / POP 122,643

You don't have to look far in Beppu (別府) to see the reason for its popularity: steam rising from vents in the earth means there are onsen-bathing opportunities galore. Beppu is by turns quaint and touristy, modern and traditional, solid and rickety, but the charm of this hilly, hospitable city grows on visitors as sure as the waters are balmy. Winter visitors get the seasonal treat of seeing the entire town filled with warm escaping steam.

Beppu is also one of Kyūshū's more international cities, thanks to the large foreign-student population at Ritsumeikan Asia Pacific University, locally known as APU.

Sights

★Beppu Traditional Bamboo Crafts Centre MUSEUM

(別府市竹細工伝統産業会館; Map p756; 0977-23-1072; www.city.beppu.oita.jp; 8-3 Higashi-sōen; ¥300; 8.30am-5pm Tue-Sun) You may be blown away by the versatility of bamboo, which grows copiously in the Beppu region. In the ground-floor gallery, intricate, refined pieces span workers' baskets to museum-quality art, made by Edo-period artisans and modern masters. Upstairs, try crafting bamboo yourself (from ¥400, depending on the complexity of the item), with a reservation at least a week ahead. A new, modernist-minimalist shop and cafe sells bamboo toys, tableware, baskets and handbags, priced from inexpensive to head-spinning.

From Beppu Station, take bus 22 or 25 to Takezaiku-densankan-mae or bus 1 to Minami-baru (about 200m away).

Onsen Hells HOT SPRINGS

(温泉地獄, Onsen Jigoku; single/combination ticket ¥400/2000; 8am-5pm) Beppu's most-hyped attraction is the **jigoku meguri** ('hell circuit'; groups of boiling hot springs), where waters bubble forth from below the ground with unusual results. The circuit's eight stops have become mini amusement parks, each with a theme and some loaded with tourist kitsch; consider yourself warned. The hells are in two groups: six at Kannawa, over 4km northwest of Beppu Station, and two about 2.5km further north. Note: the combination ticket does not include Kannawa's **Yama Jigoku** (山地獄, Mountain Hell; Map p758; 0977-66-0647; http://yamajigoku.com; 6-kumi Miyuki Kannawa).

In the Kannawa group are steaming blue **Umi Jigoku** (海地獄, Sea Hell; Map p758; 0977-66-0121; 559-1 Kannawa); **Oniishibōzu Jigoku** (鬼石坊主地獄, Demon Monk Hell; Map p758; 0977-27-6655; 559-1 Kannawa), where the bubbling mud looks like a monk's shaved head; **Shira-ike Jigoku** (白池地獄, White Pond Hell; Map p758; 0977-66-0530; 278 Kannawa); and **Kamado Jigoku** (かまど地獄; Oven Hell; Map p758; 0977-66-0178; http://kamadojigoku.com; 621 Kannawa), so named because it was once used for cooking (*kamado* means stove in Japanese). At **Oni-yama Jigoku** (鬼山地獄, Devil's Mountain Hell; Map p758; 0977-67-1500; 625 Kannawa; ¥400; 8am-5pm) and Yama Jigoku, a variety of animals are kept in enclosures that look uncomfortably small. To get here, take a bus from Beppu Station to Umi-Jigoku-mae (¥330).

JAPAN'S SUN GODDESS

According to Shintō legend, the sun goddess Amaterasu, angered by the misbehaviour of her brother, exiled herself into a cave sealed by a boulder, plunging the world into darkness. Alarmed, other gods gathered at another nearby cave to discuss how to get her to re-emerge. Eventually the goddess Ame-no-Uzume performed a bawdy dance that aroused Amaterasu's curiosity; she emerged from the cave, and light was restored to the earth. *Iwato kagura* dances performed in Takachiho today re-enact this story.

Beppu

0 — 1 km
0 — 0.5 miles

A B C D

1 2 3 4 5 6 7

Kunisaki Peninsula (20km); Ōita (30km)

Kamegawa

2 3

Beppu-wan

See Kannawa Hells Area Map (p758)

KANNAWA HELLS AREA

11

Beppu Daigaku

500

Beppu Onsen Hoyōland (1km)

645

4

Yamanami Hwy

Matsuyama; Osaka

Haruki-gawa

Ferry Sunflower Kansai Kisen

Beppu Traditional Bamboo Crafts Centre

1

HORITA

Sakai-gawa

Yufuin (24km)

52

Fujimi-dori

Beppu-Koen

See Central Beppu Map (p760)

Beppu

5

10

Asami-gawa

Ōita (14km); Usuki (40km)

Ōita (12km)

Beppu

The smaller group of hells has **Chi-no-ike Jigoku** (血の池地獄; Blood Pool Hell; Map p756; 778 Noda; ¥400; 8am-5pm), named for the blood *(chi)* red of its photogenic water, and **Tatsumaki Jigoku** (龍巻地獄, Tornado Hell; Map p756; 0977-66-1854; 782 Noda; ¥400; 8am-5pm), where a geyser shoots off about every 35 minutes.

Activities

Beppu has eight onsen districts, **Beppu Hattō** (www.city.beppu.oita.jp/01onsen/english/index.html). Onsen aficionados spend their time in Beppu moving from one bath to another and consider at least three baths a day de rigueur; bathing costs from ¥100 to ¥1000. Bring your own soap, wash cloth and towel, as some places don't rent them.

★ Takegawara Onsen ONSEN
(竹瓦温泉; Map p761; 0977-23-1585; 16-23 Moto-machi; ¥100, sand bath ¥1030; 6.30am-10.30pm, sand bath 8am-9.30pm, sand bath closed 3rd Wed of month) On the south side of Beppu's downtown commercial district, this classic onsen dates from the Meiji era and is a local icon. Its bath is very simple and very hot; scoop out water with a bucket, pour it over yourself, and jump in! It also has a relaxing sand bath where a *yukata* (light cotton kimono) is provided.

The sand bath involves lying down in a shallow trench and being buried up to your neck in heated sand, followed by an onsen dip and a shower. The process takes about 40 minutes.

★ Beppu Onsen Hoyōland ONSEN
(別府温泉保養ランド; 0977-66-2221; 5-1 Myōban; ¥1100; 9am-8pm) These rustic 1960s-era shacks a few kilometres out of town lead to giant, open-air mud baths said to date from the 8th century. Although men's and women's changing facilities are separate and mud will generally cover your most intimate areas, it's wise to take a towel for certain locations if you value your privacy.

Myōban Yunosato ONSEN
(明礬湯の里; 0977-66-8166; www.yuno-hana.jp; 6-kumi Myōban Onsen; ¥600; 10am-9pm) On a hillside east of the city centre is this beautiful, rustic, gender-separate stone *rotemburo* (outdoor bath) with lovely views up and down. Nearby are thatched huts where onsen minerals are harvested using mid-18th-century methods into *yunohana* bath powder, which is available for purchase. The minerals accumulate inside the huts at a rate of 1mm per day.

Kannawa Mushi-yu ONSEN
(鉄輪蒸し湯; Map p758; 0977-67-3880; 1-kumi Kannawa-kami; ¥510; 6.30am-8pm) Downhill from Kannawa bus stop is Kannawa Mushi-yu, a super-heated room where wrapped in a *yukata* you'll steam at 65°C (ow!) on top of Japanese rush leaves. Eight to 10 minutes here is said to have the detoxifying power of up to 30 minutes in a sauna.

Kaihin Sand Bath ONSEN
(海浜砂湯; Map p756; 0977-66-5737; 9-kumi Shōnin-ga-hama; ¥1030; 8.30am-6pm Mar-Nov, 9am-5pm Dec-Feb) Between JR Beppu Station and the Kamegawa onsen area, this sand bath is at the very popular Shōnin-ga-hama beach; it has a great location, and some English is spoken. It closes early if the wait gets too long, so go sooner in the day to make sure you don't miss out.

Sleeping

Beppu is a dense town with a large variety of accommodation options. Be aware that rooms facing even the side streets can be noisy, as the city's nightlife is boisterous and doesn't end until the wee hours.

Guest House Rojiura GUESTHOUSE ¥
(ゲストハウス路地裏; Map p761; 0977-25-0100; www.gh-rojiura.com; 9-14 Ekimae-chō; dm/s/d/tr from ¥3000/4000/7000/9000; P @) This spanking-new guesthouse sits on a quiet side street near Beppu Station. Spotless, bunk-bedded dorms are mixed and female only, and there are some windowless private rooms. No meals are offered, but there is free coffee, tea and water, and an entire wall of manga. Showers are available, or staff will direct you to nearby onsen.

Kannawa Hells Area

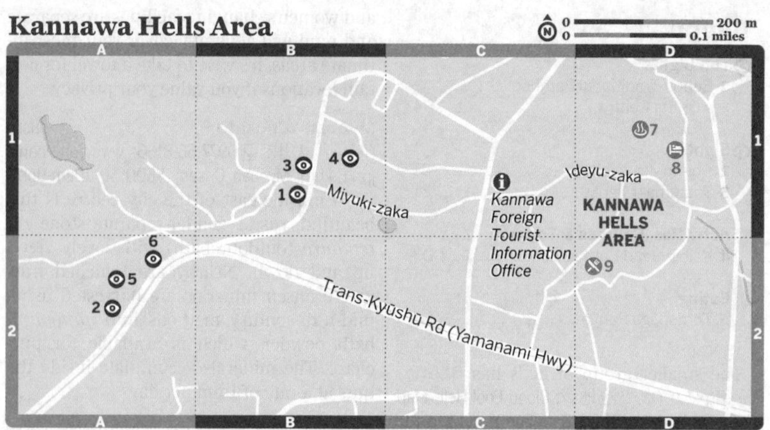

Kannawa Hells Area

Sights

1 Kamado Jigoku....B1
2 Oniishibōzu Jigoku....A2
3 Oni-yama Jigoku....B1
4 Shira-ike Jigoku....B1
5 Umi Jigoku....A2
6 Yama Jigoku....A2

Activities, Courses & Tours

7 Kannawa Mushi-yu....D1

Sleeping

8 Yanagi-ya....D1

Eating

9 Enma....D2

Cabosu House Beppu HOSTEL ¥
(かぼすハウス別府; Map p761; ☎0977-80-1315; www.facebook.com/cabosuhouse; 1-25 Minami-matogahama-chō; dm/s from ¥2000/3000; P ⊖ ❄ @ ᯤ) There's new-wave decor at this hostel, which is spread over two buildings about a two-minute walk from each other. There's an English-speaking staff, a well-stocked bar on the ground floor and some pleasant common areas for making friends. Doors are locked after 9pm, but you can enter with a code. The older building also has its own hot-spring bath.

In the newer building, all rooms have toilet and shower.

★**Yanagi-ya** RYOKAN ¥¥
(柳家; Map p758; ☎0977-66-4414; www.beppu-yanagiya.jp; 2-kumi Kannawa-ida; s/d from ¥7560/10,800; P ⊖ ❄ ᯤ) In a former Meiji-period curative spa, this intimate, dark-wood ryokan makes great use of Beppu's healing waters. Rooms (some with beds, others with futons; some with private facilities) are heated with onsen steam, and meals (Japanese or Italian) are cooked in onsen water (lunch ¥1400 to ¥2700, dinner from ¥5000); try cooking your own if you like.

★**Yamada Bessou** RYOKAN ¥¥
(山田別荘; Map p761; ☎0977-24-2121; www.yamadabessou.jp; 3-2-18 Kitahama; r per person with/without breakfast from ¥7500/6500; P ⊖ ❄ ᯤ) This sprawling, family-run 1930s inn has wonderfully preserved Japanese rooms and well-chosen art and furnishings evoking periods from art deco to today. The stone-and-tile onsen and private *rotemburo* are so lovely you'll hardly mind that only a couple of the eight rooms have full bath and toilet; two others have toilet only.

If you'd like to drop by just to use the baths, day use is ¥500 to ¥700; baths are open 11am to 3pm.

★**Beppu Hotel Umine** HOTEL ¥¥¥
(別府ホテルうみね; Map p761; ☎0977-26-0002; www.hotelumine.com; 3-8-3 Kitahama; r per person incl breakfast from ¥17,280; P ⊖ ❄ ᯤ) In-room onsen with water views, gorgeous common baths, savvy contemporary design, excellent restaurants and oodles of personal service make this Beppu's top stay. Rates are expensive but include snacks in the library lounge.

Eating

Beppu is renowned for *toriten* (chicken tempura), freshwater fish, *Bungō-gyū* (local beef), *fugu* (pufferfish), wild mountain vegetables and *dangojiru* (miso soup with thick-cut noodles). Your fish may be served with a wedge of *kabosu*, a tangy local citrus fruit that looks like a lime but is in the bitter-orange family. The arcades off Ekimae-dōri are great for restaurant browsing.

★Gyōza Kogetsu GYOZA ¥
(餃子湖月; Map p761; ☎0977-21-0226; 1-9-4 Kitahama; gyōza ¥600; ⊙2-8pm Wed-Mon) This seven-seat, 1940s time warp with a manic local following has only two things on the menu, both ¥600: generous plates of *gyōza* (dumplings) perfectly fried to a delicate crunch, and bottles of beer. It's in the tiny alley left of the Sol Paseo Ginza Arcade entrance; look for the display case filled with cat figurines. Unusually, it's nonsmoking.

Genova ICE CREAM ¥
(ジェノバ; Map p761; ☎0120-336-051; 1-10-5 Kitahama; cone/cup from ¥400/450; ⊙3pm-midnight Tue-Sat, to 10pm Sun) There always seems to be a queue at this ice-cream counter just inside Sol Paseo Ginza Arcade. Even if something seems to have been lost in the English translations of a few flavours ('Strawberry cubic'? 'Yogurt ice multiplied by the honey'?), they sure taste delish; try the Earl Grey and black-sesame varieties.

Tomonaga Panya BAKERY ¥
(友永パン屋; Map p756; ☎0977-23-0969; Chiyo-machi 2-29; pastries from ¥70; ⊙8.30am-5.30pm Mon-Sat) This charming, historic bakery has been in business since 1916, and people still happily queue for its ever-changing selection of oven-fresh breads and pastries. Take a number when you enter and peruse the English menu. The *wanchan* (doggie) bun (¥110) is filled with custard cream and uses raisins for the eyes and nose. The shop closes when sold out.

It's on the side street behind Ono Collection boutique.

Toyotsune Honten JAPANESE ¥¥
(とよ常本店; Map p761; ☎0977-22-3274; www.toyotsune.com; 2-12-24 Kitahama; mains ¥650-1650; ⊙11am-2pm & 5-10pm Thu-Tue; Ⓟ) Local favourite Toyotsune nails the Beppu specialities: *toriten, Bungō-gyū,* soy-marinated *Ryukyu* fish, plus tempura and lots of fresh fish. This recently renovated, brightly lit main branch is behind the Ōita Kōtsu bus stop; a **second branch** (とよ常別府駅前店; Map p761; ☎0977-23-74873-7 Ekimae-honmachi; mains ¥750-1650; ⊙11am-2pm & 5-10pm Fri-Wed) is across from Beppu Station.

Fugu Matsu SEAFOOD ¥¥¥
(ふぐ松; Map p761; ☎0977-21-1717; www.fugumatsu.jp; 3-6-14 Kitahama; fugu set meals from ¥8640; ⊙11am-9pm) This friendly shop has been serving simple *fugu* (pufferfish) since 1958. Sit on *hori-kotatsu* seating and sample sashimi, *karaage* (fried *fugu*) and *hirezake* (sake boiled with a grilled *fugu* fin). Reservations are required, at least a day ahead. It's behind the old-style grey-and-white lattice front.

Drinking & Nightlife

Beppu has a vibrant scene after dark and certainly knows how to party. While most of the clubs and bars cater to a Japanese clientele, there are a number of fun spots for tourists to meet fellow travellers or hang out with English-speaking locals, and there are plenty of *izakaya* in the arcades.

Creole Cafe BAR
(クレオールカフェ; Map p761; ☎0977-85-8322; www.creoledj.com; 1st fl, Beppu Tower, 3-10-2 Kitahama; ⊙noon-2pm & 6pm-1am Fri-Wed) On the ground floor of Beppu Tower (☎0977-21-3944; http://bepputower.co.jp) and with windows looking out onto the busy street, Creole Cafe brings together Beppu's Japanese and

WORTH A TRIP

KUJŪ-SAN

Tucked in Ōita Prefecture's southwestern corner lies its biggest mountain range, collectively known as Kujū-san, a favourite for hikers and mountaineering clubs. Accessed by car either from Ōita or from Kumamoto (via Aso National Park), it offers more than 20 peaks, including the island's highest, Naka-dake (1791m). Because of this, the range is known as the 'rooftop of Kyūshū'. One of the most popular climbs is from Makinotoi-tōge, which is an easy day hike thanks to access via a circuitous yet lovely road that goes most of the way. It's more peopled than other peak ascents. From there the avid can hike all the way to Naka-dake. The **Aso Kujū-Kōgen Youth Hostel** (阿蘇くじゅう高原ユースホステル; ☎0967-44-0157; www.asokujuuyh.sakura.ne.jp; 6332 Senomoto; dm/r per person from ¥3000/3800, HI discount ¥600; Ⓟ) near Kurokawa Onsen is a good base camp for excursions.

foreign communities over drinks, reasonably priced food (curry and pasta at lunch, European fusion at night) and special events like salsa dancing.

Basara House CAFE
(バサラハウス; Map p761; www.facebook.com/Basara-House-BEPPU-392113911278824; 3-2-2 Kitahama; ⏲11am-3pm Sun & Mon, 11am-6pm Thu-Sat) There's a handmade, arty feel to this renovated 1940s house, filled with exposed beams, period tile work and eclectic ephemera. All the better to sip coffee, chai or *ume* (Japanese plum) soda and appreciate occasional art exhibits or musical happenings. Round things out with curries or fried rice for lunch (¥800), including some veggie options.

Shopping

For over a century, the must-have souvenir for Japanese holidaymakers in Beppu was everyday-use products made from the region's plentiful bamboo. You can still find these around town, but nowadays the trend is towards art pieces such as baskets for flower arranging. **Chikugōgei Yamashō** (竹工芸山正; Map p761; ☎0977-22-6208; 4-9 Kusunoki-machi; ⏲10am-6pm), the Beppu Traditional Bamboo Crafts Centre (p755) and Oita-branded shops sell high-quality pieces by local artisans with prices to match. Elsewhere, you might want to ask *'Nihon-sei desu ka?'* (Is this made in Japan?).

DON'T MISS

ONSEN COOKING EXPERIENCE

Ingenious! Amid the hells of Kannawa a couple of restaurants offer the opportunity to cook your own meal in onsen steam. Purchase ingredients on the spot (or bring your own), and steam them in *kama* (vats) roiling from the onsen below. Kannawa Mushi-yu (p757) shares a building with the Foreign Tourist Information Office, so there's usually an English speaker on hand to help until 5pm. At **Enma** (縁間; Map p758; ☎0977-75-9592; 228-1 Furomoto Kannawa; dishes ¥300-950, plus steaming charge ¥500; ⏲10am-7pm) you have the bonus of a foot bath in which to soak your tootsies while you eat. Both places can be crowded at peak times, such as weekend lunch.

Information

Foreign Tourist Information Branches at **Beppu Station**(えきマチ一丁目別府インフォーメーション; Map p761; ☎0977-21-6220; 12-13 Ekimae-machi; ⏲8.30am-5pm; 📶) and **Kannawa** (Map p758; ☎0977-66-3855; 306-1 Kannawa; ⏲9am-5pm; 📶) are well equipped with helpful multilingual volunteers and an arsenal of local information and advice.

Be Beppu (www.bebeppu.com) is a local magazine covering mostly onsen. The print version (¥580) is filled with discount coupons.

Getting There & Away

AIR

Flights go to nearby **Ōita Airport** (☎0978-67-1174; www.oita-airport.jp) from Tokyo Haneda and Narita, Nagoya, and Osaka Itami Airports. Flights also operate to Seoul.

Beppu Airport buses (¥1500) from Ōita Airport stop **outside Tokiwa department store** (Map p761; 48 minutes) and Beppu Station (51 minutes).

BOAT

The **Ferry Sunflower Kansai Kisen** (Map p756; ☎0977-22-1311) makes an overnight run between Beppu and Osaka and Kōbe (one way/return ¥7900/15,500, 12 hours), stopping at Matsuyama (4½ hours). The evening boat departs between 6.45pm and 7.35pm to western Honshū and passes through the Inland Sea (Seto-nai-kai), arriving at 6.35am or 7.35am the next morning. For the port, take bus 20 or 26 from Beppu Station's **west exit** (Map p761).

BUS

There's a Kyūshū Odan (Trans-Kyūshū) bus to Aso Station (¥2980, 3¼ hours) and Kumamoto (¥3960, five hours). **Nishitetsu** buses from Fukuoka Airport run every hour to Kitahama Station (¥3190, two hours).

TRAIN

Beppu is not on any *shinkansen* lines, but from Hakata (Fukuoka), the fastest connection is by *shinkansen* to Kokura and connecting with the Sonic *tokkyū* on the JR Nippō line (*shinkansen* and *tokkyū* ¥5740, 100 minutes) to Beppu. Alternatively, Sonic trains go all the way to Hakata Station (¥5050, about two hours). The JR Nippō line continues to Miyazaki via Ōita (*tokkyū* ¥5480, 3¼ hours). To get to Kagoshima-Chūō, change to the Kyūshū *shinkansen* at Kokura (¥14,610, 3¼ hours).

Getting Around

Beppu centre is walkable and flat once you head downhill from the station area. Buses are a good way to reach the hells and outskirts. If you really

Central Beppu

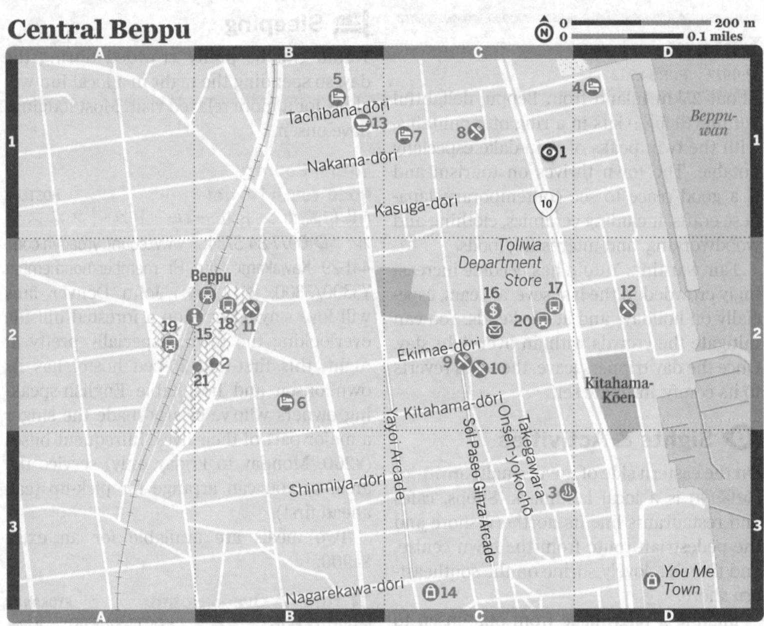

Central Beppu

Sights
1 Beppu Tower C1

Activities, Courses & Tours
2 Oita Kōtsū Bus B2
3 Takegawara Onsen C3

Sleeping
4 Beppu Hotel Umine D1
5 Cabosu House Beppu B1
6 Guest House Rojiura B2
7 Yamada Bessou C1

Eating
8 Fugu Matsu C1
9 Genova C2
10 Gyōza Kogetsu C2
11 Toyotsune Beppu Ekimae-ten B2
12 Toyotsune Honten D2

Drinking & Nightlife
13 Basara House B1
Creole Cafe .... (see 1)

Shopping
14 Chikugōgei Yamashō C3

Information
15 JR Beppu Station Information Office B2
16 Ōita Bank C2

Transport
17 Airport Bus Stop C2
18 Beppu Station Bus Stop (East Side) B2
19 Beppu Station Bus Stop (West Side) A2
20 Bus Stop for Kannawa Onsen C2
21 Eki Rent-a-Car B2

need to get away, **Eki Rent-a-Car** (Map p761; ☎0977-24-4428; www.ekiren.co.jp; 12-13 Ekimae-chō) is inside Beppu Station, with cars that start at about ¥5400 per day.

BUS

Kamenoi is the main bus company. An unlimited 'My Beppu Free' pass comes in two varieties: 'mini' (one day adult/student/child ¥900/700/450, two days adult/child ¥1500/750), which covers Beppu city (and offers discounts); and 'wide' (one/two days adult ¥1600/2400, child ¥800/1200), which extends to Yufuin. Passes are available from foreign tourist information offices, the train station and ferry terminal, and some lodgings. From JR Beppu Station, buses 2, 5, 7, 9, 20, 24, 25 and 41 go to Kannawa (15 to 25 minutes), and buses 26 and 26A serve Chi-no-ike and Tatsumaki *jigoku*. Kannawa-bound buses also leave from a **bus stop** (Map p761) near Rte 10.

Yufuin

☎0977 / POP 34,922

About 25km inland from Beppu, delightful Yufuin (由布院) sits in a ring of mountains, with the twin peaks of Yufu-dake especially notable. The town thrives on tourism and is a good place to see contemporary Japanese crafts, including ceramics, clothing and woodworking, and interesting foods.

Fair warning: Yufuin has become increasingly crowded in the last several years, especially on holidays and at weekends. You can mitigate the crowds with an overnight stay. Once the day trippers leave, the town reverts to its comfy, intimate self.

Sights & Activities

On the eastern side of town, small **Kinrin-ko** (金鱗湖) is a local landmark. Shops, cafes and restaurants line its northern shore and the pedestrian route from the town centre, and there's a lovely shrine on the southeastern shore.

Making a pilgrimage from one onsen to another is a popular activity. Alternatively, work up a sweat on double-peaked **Yufu-dake** (1584m) volcano, which overlooks Yufuin and takes about 90 minutes to climb. *Then* go and dip in the onsen.

★Musō-en ONSEN
(夢想園; ☎0977-84-2171; www.musouen.co.jp; 1243 Kawaminami; ¥700; ⊙10am-3pm) A little out of town (about 20 minutes on foot from the station or a moderate uphill bike ride), this *onsen ryokan* offers exceptionally clear waters for exceptionally clear reflections of Yufu-dake. Private 'family' baths are also available.

Nurukawa Onsen ONSEN
(ぬるかわ温泉; ☎0977-84-2869; 1490-1 Kawakami Takemoto; ¥430, private baths from ¥1650; ⊙7am-8pm) A short walk from Kinrin-ko and separated by gender, this cluster of small bathing rooms boasts lots of character and lovely mountain views.

Shitan-yu ONSEN
(下ん湯; ☎0977-84-3111; ¥200; ⊙10am-9pm) An atmospheric one-room thatched bathhouse with mixed bathing only, on the northern shore of Kinrin-ko. Deposit your payment in the slot outside.

Sleeping

Yufuin can be pretty crowded during the day, so spending the night in a local inn will allow for a more relaxed visit. Most lodgings have onsen.

Yufuin Country Road Youth Hostel HOSTEL ¥
(湯布院カントリーロードユースホステル; ☎0977-84-3734; www.countryroadyh.com; 441-29 Kawakami; dm HI member/nonmember ¥3300/3800; P⊖@🛜) John Denver fans will love staying here on a forested hillside overlooking the town. Especially pretty at night, this first-rate 25-bed hostel has its own onsen and hospitable English-speaking owners who've clearly made the singer a major part of their lives. Infrequent buses (¥200, Monday to Friday only) service the area, or you can arrange for pick-up (call ahead first).

Two meals are available for an extra ¥1900.

★Yufu-no-Oyado Hotaru RYOKAN ¥¥
(由布のお宿ほたる; ☎0977-84-5151; www.yufuin-hotaru.com; 1791-1 Kawakita; r per person incl 2 meals from ¥16,500; ⊙reception 7am-9pm; P❄🛜) This lovely, family-run traditional ryokan is nestled among cypress and bamboo. A variety of onsen make it a lovely spot for dippers, and one of the owners speaks excellent English. It's about ¥1200 by taxi from the Yufuin Station area.

★Makiba-no-ie RYOKAN ¥¥
(牧場の家; ☎0977-84-2138; 2870-1 Kawakami; r per person incl 2 meals from ¥16,350; P❄🛜) There's atmosphere aplenty in these dozen thatched-roof huts with Japanese rooms, sink and toilet surrounding a beautiful *rotemburo*. The antique-filled, garden-view restaurant offers *jidori* (local chicken) and *Bungō-gyū teishoku* (local-beef set meals) from ¥1600. Lunch, by reservation only, includes bath admission. Otherwise, visitors can use the *rotemburo* (¥600, until 5pm daily) and the eight family (private) baths (from ¥1800).

Eating

Most patrons have their meals while relaxing in their inn, but there's a concentration of eateries by the station and in the busy shopping streets around Kinrin-ko.

Kappō Satō JAPANESE ¥¥

(割烹サトウ; ☎0977-85-2550; 2955-18 Kawakami; lunch specials ¥950-1200, Bungō beef set ¥2300; ⊙11am-2pm & 4-8pm Wed-Mon) Get your fill of local specialities at this delightful old wooden house across from a river: *toriten* (chicken tempura), fried chicken with *yuzu* (citron) pepper, *Bungō-gyū* beef sets, sushi and sashimi. Lunch specials are a great deal.

Izumi Soba NOODLES ¥¥

(泉そば; ☎0977-85-2283; 1599-1 Kawakami; soba ¥1295-2160; ⊙11am-5pm) There are less expensive soba shops in town, but at this classy place with a view of Kinrin-ko you can often watch the noodles being made in the window before you sit down. The standard is *seirō-soba* (on a bamboo mat); *oroshi-soba* comes topped with grated *daikon* (radish).

Information

Yufuinfo (由布市ツーリストインフォメーションセンター; ☎0977-84-2446; ⊙9am-7pm; 📶) Next to the train station, this lovely new office has plenty of information in English, including detailed walking maps and brochures about natural sights, galleries, museums and onsen. Electric and ordinary bikes are available for rent.

Getting There & Away

Unless you're using a Japan Rail pass, bus is the cheaper way to travel from Beppu. It's also usually faster, and the route through the mountains is like a mini-sightseeing tour. Buses connect JR Beppu Station with Yufuin throughout the day (one way/return ¥900/1500, 65 minutes). One-way tickets are sold on board; buy return tickets at the Beppu Station tourist information office or Yufuin bus terminal.

Frequent express buses serve Fukuoka (¥2880, two hours), while a couple of departures a day go to Kurokawa Onsen (¥2000, 1½ hours), Aso (¥3000, 2½ hours) and Kumamoto (¥4200, 4½ hours).

Trains connect Beppu with Yufuin (*futsū* ¥1110, 90 minutes) via Ōita. A few daily Yufu or Yufuin-no-mori *tokkyū* trains cost ¥1930/2450 for non-reserved/reserved seats, and take about 65 minutes with no change of train; some trains have reserved seats only.

Getting Around

Some buses from Yufuin stop at the base of Yufu-dake at Yufu-tozanguchi (由布登山口; ¥360, 15 minutes, about hourly).

Electric bikes can be rented at the tourist office (two hours with/without JR pass ¥400/500); the assistance can be useful if you'll be heading uphill out of the town centre. Standard bikes are also available (¥250 per hour, up to ¥1250 per day) from 9am to 5pm.

Kunisaki Peninsula

It would be easy to overlook the Kunisaki Peninsula (国東半島), a remote corner of Kyūshū north of Beppu, under-served as it is by public transport, but you'd be missing some of the most undisturbed *pawā spotto* (power spots; Japanese slang for spiritual places) in the nation. The town of Bungo-Takada is nicknamed 'Buddha's Village' and the region is noted for its early Buddhist influence, including some rock-carved images linked to the more famous ones at Usuki. Your own car is useful for getting around the region efficiently.

The peninsula can be visited as a day trip from Beppu, where you'll find the best sleeping options.

Sights

★**Kumano Magaibutsu** BUDDHIST SITE

(熊野磨崖仏; ¥300; ⊙8am-5pm Apr-Oct, 8.30am-4.30pm Nov-Mar) Deep in a forest along a mossy riverbed are two Heian-period Buddha images carved into a cliff: a 6m figure of the Dainichi Buddha and an 8m figure of Fudō-Myō-o. Known as Kumano Magaibutsu, these are the largest Buddhist images of this type in Japan, reached via stone stairs said to have been built overnight by an ogre. If you thought the few hundred steps to the carvings were tough, wait until the next few hundred to the shrine at the top.

The entrance to the carvings is around 2km south of Maki Ōdō (p764) Hall.

Usa-jingū SHINTŌ SHRINE

(宇佐神宮; www.usajinguu.com; 2859 Minami, Usa) FREE The sprawling, wooded and water-crossed Usa-jingū, the original of which dates back some 1200 years, is the chief shrine among some 40,000 in Japan dedicated to the warrior-god Hachiman. An audio 'touch pen' guide (¥500), available at the tourist information office near the bus stop, offers detailed descriptions in English. Allow one to two hours to view the entire grounds, up to four hours if you listen to all the audio content.

It's a 4km bus (¥230, seven minutes, hourly) or taxi ride from Usa Station (get off at Usa-Hachiman-mae), on the JR Nippō line from Beppu. Parking costs ¥400. A monorail helps those with limited mobility.

Futago-ji BUDDHIST TEMPLE
(両子寺; www.futago.jp; 1548 Futago, Akimachi; ¥300; ⊙8am-5pm Apr-Nov, 8.30am-4.30pm Dec-Mar) In the centre of the Kunisaki Peninsula, near the summit of Futago-san (721m), this temple was founded in 718 and dedicated to Fudō-Myō-o, the fire-enshrouded, sword-wielding deity. It's a lovely climb up an uneven stone path, especially in spring or autumn, and there are plenty of subtemples to explore around the mountain's forested gorges. There's a lovely mossy stream and detours for hiking, especially when Japanese maples work their colourful magic.

Among the sub-buildings, Okun-no-in Hall has an unusual construction of a wooden front built around a cave. The temple offers unique *ema* (wooden votive plaques) with a cutout of a human body; use a marker to draw where healing is needed, detach, and leave the *ema* in a tray; it will be burnt as an offering inside the Goma-dō (fire hall).

Fuki-ji BUDDHIST TEMPLE
(富貴寺; ☎0978-26-3189; 2395 Tashibufuki, Bungo-takada; ¥300; ⊙8.30am-4.30pm) Located on the outskirts of Bungo-takada, this National Treasure, made of fragrant nutmeg wood, is the oldest wooden edifice in Kyūshū and one of the oldest wooden temples in Japan. Its overgrown grounds and moss-covered stupas complement the 11th-century structure beautifully. Use your smartphone to access information in English via wi-fi. Ōita Kōtsū buses from Usa Station go to Bungo-takada (¥810, 20 minutes); from there, it's a 10-minute taxi ride (around ¥1000).

Maki Ōdō BUDDHIST TEMPLE
(真木大堂; ☎0978-26-2075; 1796 Tashibumaki, Bungo-takada; ⊙8.30am-5pm) This temple's main hall dates from the Edo period, but the key reason to come here is to see the nine Heian-period sculptures designated important cultural properties, centred on the Amida Buddha and protector gods of the four directions, in a more recently built hall. A wi-fi system offers detailed descriptions in English. A stone-stepped path leads to an observation area to survey the plains below.

Taizō-ji BUDDHIST TEMPLE
(胎蔵寺; ☎0978-26-2901; 2579 Tashibuhirano, Bungo-takada; ⊙9am-5pm) FREE At this temple near the entrance to the Kumano Magaibutsu, monks will give you stickers to put on the statue of your Chinese birth year.

Eating

This area is quite spread out, and dining options are few and far between. There's a wonderfully casual seaside noodle shop and a few options in the former samurai district of Kitsuki. Otherwise, you may do well to pack a meal from Beppu or find a *conbini* (convenience store).

★ **Soba Cafe Yuuhi** CAFE ¥
(Soba Cafe ゆうひ; ☎0978-25-8533; www.facebook.com/sobacafeyuuhi; 5125 Usuno, Bungo-takada; soba dishes ¥750-1400; ⊙11am-sunset Wed-Mon; P) This beach-casual shop might offer the most spectacular sunset of your trip: the sun sinks into the ocean or behind mudflats that stretch to the horizon – on clear evenings you can even see the green flash. Yuuhi sells handmade soba, smoothies (¥700) and iced coffee (¥400), and rents such gear as stand-up paddleboards (¥2000 per hour) and clamming equipment (¥500).

Go for *kamo nanban* (duck soup) soba or the *koikana* (lover's wish) set meal (¥1200), with soba, fried side dishes and heart-shaped *onigiri* (rice balls).

It's on a roadside turnout by the little beach Matama-kaigan (真玉海岸).

ℹ Getting There & Around

Buses circle the peninsula, but getting to the temples using public transport is inconvenient and time-consuming. **Oita Kōtsū Bus** (大分交通バス; Map p761; ☎097-536-3655; www.oitakotsu.co.jp; Kunisaki Peninsula tour ¥5050; ⊙9am-5pm) runs daily bus tours from Beppu to view the main temples, but the best way to view this area is by car. Rentals are available in Beppu, or take transit to Ōita Airport and rent from there.

Usuki

☎0972 / POP 38,750

About 30km southeast of Beppu, Usuki (臼杵) is best known for the astounding thousand-year-old **Usuki Stone Buddhas** (臼杵石仏; ☎0972-65-3300; https://sekibutsu.com; 804-1 Oaza Fukata; ¥540; ⊙6am-6pm Oct-Mar, to 7pm Apr-Sep). Four clusters comprising 60-plus images (59 are designated National Treasures) lie in a series of niches in a ravine. They're largely made of lava rock from Aso-san (p747). Some are complete statues, whereas others have only the heads remaining. It's truly a spiritual place if it's uncrowded, although some of the magic can be lost in the touristy ambience just outside.

Information

Tourist Information Office (臼杵市観光情報協会; ☎0972-63-2366; JR Usuki Station; ⏱9am-3pm) Inside the JR Station.

Usuki City Tourism & Community Plaza (臼杵市観光交流プラザ; ☎097-263-1715; 100-2 Ōaza; ⏱9am-6pm; 📶) This sparkling-new tourist plaza is set inconveniently far from the station. It has maps, pamphlets and life-size figures of Usuki's mascot, 'Hotto-san', a cute stone Buddha cartoon character.

Getting There & Away

Usuki is 40km southeast of Beppu. Take the JR Nippō line to Usuki Station (*tokkyū/futsū* ¥2070/940, 45/60 minutes); you'll usually need to change in Ōita.

From the station, infrequent buses (¥310) take 20 minutes to reach the Buddha images (get off at Usuki Sekibutsu bus stop), or it's about ¥2020 in a taxi or 35 minutes by bike. You can rent standard bikes (free!) or electric bikes (¥300 per hour) at the station from 9am to 3pm, or from the Tourism & Community Plaza until 6pm.

SOUTHERN KYŪSHŪ

Including the prefectures of Kagoshima (鹿児島) to the west and Miyazaki (宮崎) to the east, with Kinkō-wan (Kinkō Bay) in the middle, balmy southern Kyūshū is the furthest south you can get in Japan without boarding a ferry.

Kagoshima features in the annals of history again and again: from ancient Jōmon-era dwellings to the feudal period, the beginnings of the Meiji Restoration, and the departure of thousands of WWII pilots. The prefecture also boasts the smouldering Kirishima mountain range – a draw for bird- and wildlife-watchers.

Miyazaki Prefecture is Kagoshima's 'hippie sibling': relaxed and quiet, with a renowned coastline that lures surfers from all over Japan. Coastal drives here may remind you of California or the Italian Riviera – until you detour inland and meet the resident bands of wild monkeys. Northern Miyazaki Prefecture is the land of legends, including the queen of them all, the sun goddess Amaterasu.

Getting There & Away

Southern Kyūshū is accessible by *shinkansen*, air and bus services from other parts of the island, or via international flights. Many travellers use Kagoshima International Airport as their entry/exit point.

Kagoshima

☎099 / POP 606,800

The southernmost big city on Japan's main islands, sunny Kagoshima (鹿児島) has a personality to match its climate and has been voted Japan's friendliest city nationwide. It's proud of its past as capital of the feudal Satsuma province, which holds an outsize place in Japanese history. Kagoshima's backdrop/deity is Sakurajima, a very active volcano *just* across the bay. Locals raise their umbrellas against the mountain's recurrent eruptions, when fine ash coats the landscape like snow and obscures the sun like fog – mystical and captivating.

History

Everywhere you go throughout central Kagoshima are reminders of the proud history of the city and prefecture. Capital of the feudal Satsuma domain, Kagoshima was ruled by the Shimazu clan for a remarkable 700 years. The province's location at the far southwest of the Japanese main islands helped it grow wealthy through trade, particularly with China. Contact was also made with Korea, whose pottery methods were influential in the creation of Satsuma-yaki.

When Japan opened to the world in the mid-19th century, Satsuma's government competed with the shogunate, engaging in war with Britain and hosting a Satsuma pavilion – independent from the Japanese pavilion – at the 1867 Paris Expo. In the late 19th century, 17 young men from

DON'T MISS

SOUTHERN KYŪSHŪ DISHES

Kagoshima's most famous food is *kurobuta*, pork from a species of 'black' pig prized for its flavourful meat. You may also find *inoshishi* (wild boar), which is a bit more gamey than regular pork and well worth a try. *Satsuma-age* is deep-fried fish cakes. The southern part of the prefecture is famous for *nagashi-sōmen*, noodles that diners fish out of spring water flowing through tabletop troughs. Miyazaki's speciality is *chikin nanban* (sweet fried chicken served with tartar sauce). *Sumiyaki jidori*, free-range chicken grilled over charcoal, is another popular dish.

Central Kagoshima

A
B
C
D
1
2
3
4
5
6
7
Shiroyama-kōen
Shinkan-bashi
Shinkanbashi
St Francis Xavier Church
St Xavier Park
Hirata-bashi
Ōgon-dōri
Sengokubaba-dōri
Nigiwai-dōri
9
5
Nishida-bashi
Takami-baba
Kajiya-chō
Miyako-dōri
Takami-bashi
Takamibashi
11
Kōtsuki-gawa
Museum of the Meiji Restoration
1
Kagoshima Chūō
21
22
Kagoshima Chūō Station
Amu Plaza
Napoli-dōri
20
Nanshū-bashi
Kōrai-bashi
Kōtsuki-bashi
Perth-dōri
Kyōken-kōen

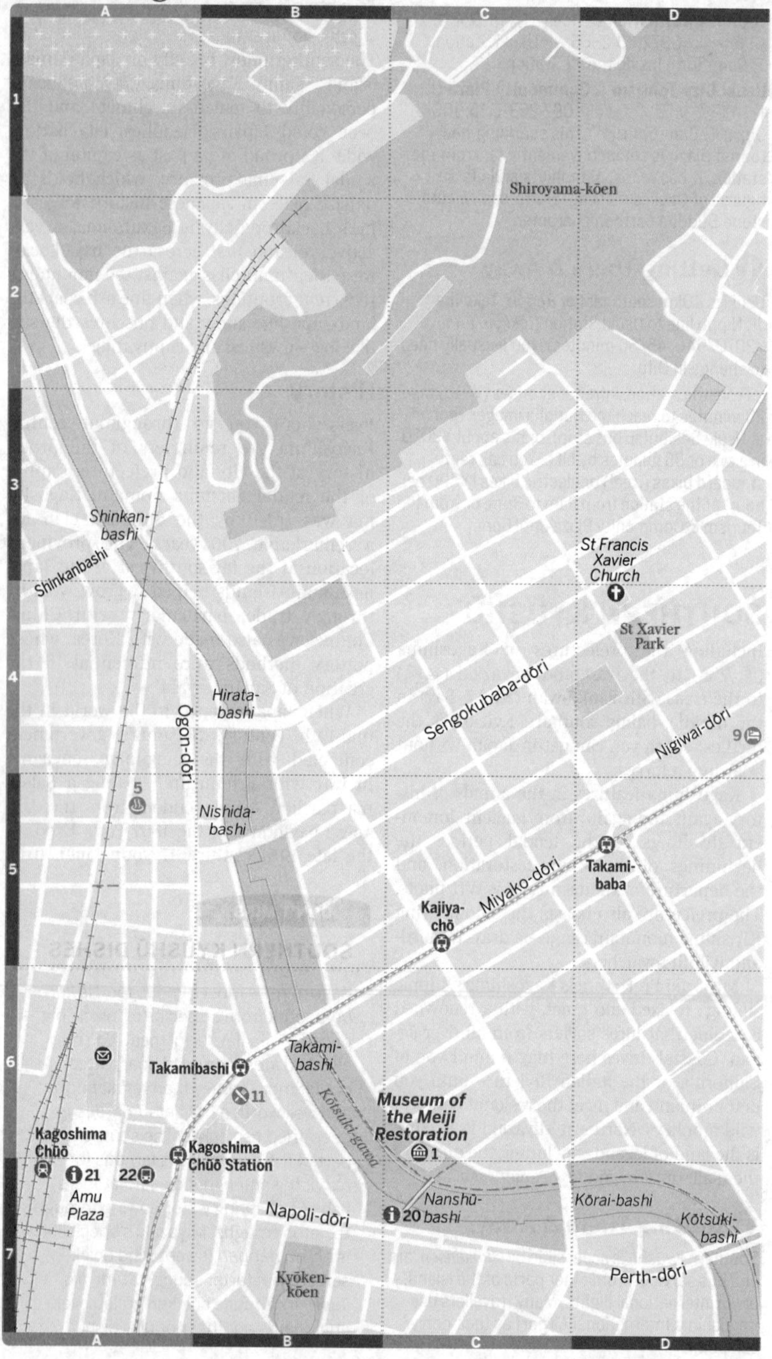

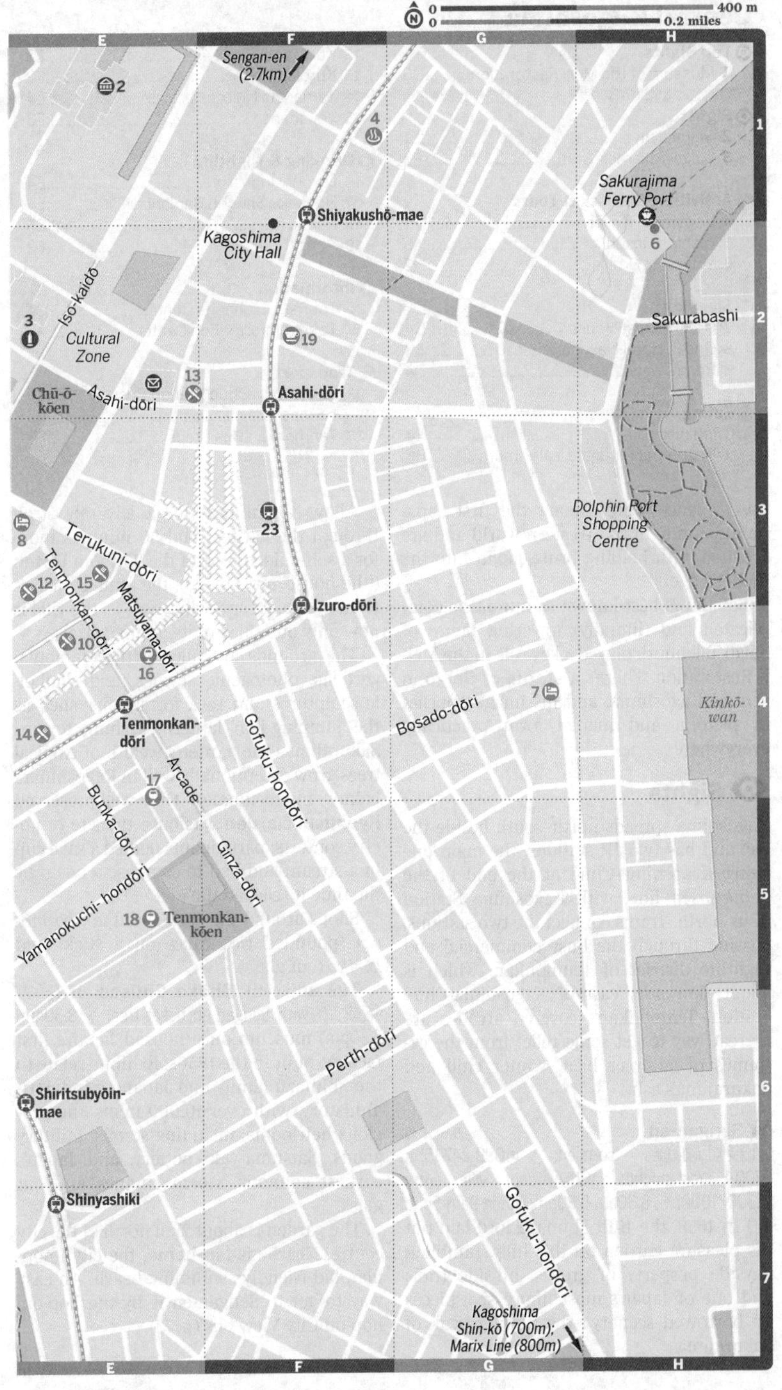

0 400 m
0 0.2 miles
E
F
G
H
Sengan-en (2.7km)
2
4
1
Sakurajima Ferry Port
Shiyakushō-mae
Kagoshima City Hall
6
Iso-kaidō
3
Cultural Zone
19
Sakurabashi
2
13
Chū-ō-kōen
Asahi-dōri
Asahi-dōri
3
23
8
Terukuni-dōri
Dolphin Port Shopping Centre
Tenmonkan-dōri
12
15
Matsuyama-dōri
Izuro-dōri
10
16
Kinkō-wan
4
7
Tenmonkan-dōri
Bosado-dōri
14
Gofuku-hondōri
Arcade
17
Bunka-dōri
Ginza-dōri
5
Yamanokuchi- hondōri
18
Tenmonkan-kōen
Perth-dōri
6
Shiritsubyōin-mae
Shinyashiki
Gofuku-hondōri
7
Kagoshima Shin-kō (700m); Marix Line (800m)

Central Kagoshima

Top Sights
1 Museum of the Meiji Restoration C6

Sights
2 Reimeikan E1
3 Saigō Takamori Statue E2

Activities, Courses & Tours
4 Kagomma Onsen F1
5 Nishida Onsen A5
6 Yorimichi Cruise H2

Sleeping
7 Green Guest House G4
8 Onsen Hotel Nakahara Bessō E3
9 Remm Kagoshima D4

Eating
10 Ichinisan E4
11 Kagomma Furusato Yatai-mura B6
12 Kumasotei E3
13 Kurokatsu-tei E2
14 Yamauchi Nōjō E4
15 Yokaban E3

Drinking & Nightlife
16 Dolphin Industry E4
17 Honkaku Shōchū Bar Ishizue E4
18 Karakara E5
19 Retroft F2

Information
20 Tourism Exchange Centre C7
21 Tourist Information Center A7

Transport
22 Kagoshima Chūō Station Bus Stops A7
23 Tenmonkan Bus Stops F3

the province were among the first Japanese to study in the Western world and are credited with helping bring Japan into the modern age.

Satsuma's best-known samurai, the complicated and (literally) towering figure of Saigō Takamori, played a key role in the Meiji Restoration. There's a **statue of Saigō** in central Kagoshima, and his image appears in pictoral and manga form practically everywhere.

Sights

Kagoshima spreads north–south beside the bay and has two JR stations, the main one being Kagoshima-Chūō at the end of the *shinkansen* line, with Kagoshima Station to its north. Trams connect the two stations, passing through the busy commercial and nightlife district of Tenmonkan, which is about 1km northeast of Kagoshima-Chūō Station. Tenmonkan's covered arcades are a great way to get some relief from the extremes of summer heat, winter chill and Sakurajima's ash.

★Sengan-en — GARDENS

(仙巌園·磯庭園, Iso-teien; ☎099-247-1551; 9700-1 Yoshinochō; with/without villa entry ¥1300/1000; ⌚8.30am-5.30pm, Goten 9am-5pm; P) In 1658, the 19th Shimazu lord laid out his pleasure garden on this hilly, rambling bayside property of groves, hillside trails and one of Japan's most impressive pieces of 'borrowed scenery': the fuming peak of Sakurajima.

Allow 45 minutes for a leisurely stroll through the garden, and 30 minutes more for a self-guided tour of the 25-room **Goten** ('the house' on signage), the Shimazu clan's former villa. As sprawling as it is, the villa is now only one-third of its original size!

The grounds are filled with ceremonial gardens, photogenic shrines, and symbolic sculptures and rock formations, such as the jumping-lion lantern, arching toward Sakurajima. The garden's wealth of tropical trees grow exceptionally well in Kagoshima's balmy microclimate. The well-preserved **Kyokusui Garden** was once the site of poetry contests; participants floated a sake cup in a stream and had to compose a poem by the time it reached the end.

Shops around the garden sell *jambo-mochi* (pounded rice cakes on a stick) and *kiriko* (cut glass).

The adjacent **Shōko Shūseikan** (尚古集成館; with Sengan-en ticket free; ⌚8.30am-5.30pm) museum once housed Japan's first factory, built in the 1850s. Exhibits relate to the Shimazu family and Japanese industrial history, with over 10,000 items and precious heirlooms, including scrolls, military goods, Satsuma-yaki pottery, and Japan's earliest cannons, steam engines and cut glass.

The garden is about 2km north of the city centre. Nearby is **Iso-hama**, the city's popular, kid-friendly swimming beach. An easy way to get to Sengan-en is by the hop-on, hop-off City View bus (p773).

★ Museum of the Meiji Restoration
MUSEUM

(維新ふるさと館; ☎099-239-7700; 23-1 Kaijiya-chō; ¥300; ⏰9am-5pm; 🚇JR Kagoshima-Chūō) This museum offers insights into the unique social system of education, samurai loyalty and sword techniques that made Satsuma one of Japan's leading provinces. There's a good smartphone app in English. Hourly audiovisual presentations – told by animatronic Meiji-era reformers, including Saigō Takamori and Sakamoto Ryōma – detail the Satsuma Rebellion and the ground-breaking visits of Satsuma students to the West.

Reimeikan
MUSEUM

(黎明館, Kagoshima Prefectural Museum of Culture; www.pref.kagoshima.jp/reimeikan; 7-2 Shiroyama-chō; ¥310; ⏰9am-6pm Tue-Sun, closed 25th of each month; 🚇Shiyakushō-mae) The Reimeikan has extensive displays on Satsuma history and ancient sword-making. It's inside the site of Kagoshima's castle, **Tsurumaru-jō** (1602); the walls and moat are all that remain, and bullet holes in the stones are still visible. It's behind Kagoshima's **City Hall** (鹿児島市役所) and government buildings.

Activities

Kagoshima boasts some 50 bathhouses, most meant for locals and recalling the humble, everyday *sentō* (public bath) of old. Examples include local favourite **Nishida Onsen** (西田温泉; 1-2-17 Takashi; ¥390; ⏰5.30am-10.30pm, closed 2nd Mon of month), just a few minutes' walk from JR Kagoshima-Chūō Station, and **Kagomma Onsen** (かごっま温泉; ☎099-226-2688; 3-28 Yasui-chō; ¥390; ⏰8am-midnight, closed 15th of month; 🚇Shiyakusho-mae), near City Hall. A great onsen brochure is available from most tourist info desks and in many hotel lobbies.

Tours

Yorimichi Cruise
CRUISE

(よりみちクルーズ船; ☎099-223-7271; adult/child ¥500/250; ⏰11.05am) The Yorimichi Cruise takes one of six circuitous sightseeing routes from Kagoshima Port to Sakurajima Port in about 50 minutes.

Sleeping

Kagoshima has plenty of good-value places to sleep. Kagoshima-Chūō Station is convenient for getting into and out of town, but if you're looking for nightlife, aim to stay nearer to Tenmonkan.

Green Guest House
HOSTEL ¥

(グリーンゲストハウス; ☎0998-02-4301; www.green-guesthouse.com; 5-7 Sumiyoshi-chō; dm/tw/private r ¥1900/2400/5600; 🚭❄@📶; 🚇Izuro-dōri) Clean and compact, this five-storey hostel is very convenient to the ferry docks, which is useful if you're planning a trip to Sakurajima. Separate-gender dorms and private rooms are available. Check out the views of Sakurajima from the roof deck. Some English is spoken at the front desk, and all important signage is in English and Japanese.

It's about a 10-minute walk to central Tenmonkan, on a main street lined with chain restaurants.

★ Onsen Hotel Nakahara Bessō
HOTEL ¥¥¥

(温泉ホテル中原別荘; ☎099-225-2800; www.nakahara-bessou.co.jp; 15-19 Terukuni-chō; r per person with/without 2 meals from ¥12,960/8640; P🚭❄@📶; 🚇Tenmonkan-dōri) Just outside Tenmonkan and across from a park, this family-owned inn traces its history to 1904, though the current building has a mid-20th-century feel, especially in its white-and-grey facade. Inside you'll find a modern *rotemburo*, 75 spacious Japanese-style rooms with traditional artwork and a good *Satsuma-ryōri* restaurant. Rooms and restaurants are strictly nonsmoking.

Remm Kagoshima
HOTEL ¥¥¥

(レム鹿児島; ☎099-224-0606; https://global.hankyu-hotel.com/remm-kagoshima; 1-32 Higashi-sengoku-chō; s/d/tw ¥10,800/15,120/19,980; P🚭❄@📶; 🚇Tenmonkan-dōri) At this

SAKURAJIMA'S ASH

The Sakurajima volcano erupts so frequently that weather reports in Kagoshima Prefecture have a special ash forecast. Once ash starts falling you'll understand why: it stings, coats your teeth with grit, dirties futons and laundry, and makes anyone who has just washed their car burst into tears.

In most of Japan, umbrellas are for rain, and many people carry parasols as shields from the summer heat. In Kagoshima there's a third use: protection from Sakurajima's ash. Don't have an umbrella? Pick up a loaner on a city tram and return it the next time you ride.

hotel in Tenmonkan, rooms are business-hotel-size but futuristic in style and amenities, with custom-designed beds, fluffy white duvets, massage chairs, rain showers, and glass windows in the bathrooms for natural light (and, thoughtfully, curtains). The ageless design in the public spaces incorporates ancient stones and hardwoods. It's worth springing for the extensive breakfast buffet (¥1000).

Eating

The JR Kagoshima-Chūō Station area, the backstreets of Tenmonkan and the Dolphin Port shopping centre near the ferry terminals all abound with restaurants.

Local friends will think you're really in the know if you venture into the narrow lanes of the Meizanbori neighbourhood southeast of City Hall (p769). These dilapidated-looking Shōwa-era blocks are crammed with tiny yet often chic purveyors of everything from *yakitori* and curry rice to French and Spanish cooking, plus cool bars. It's worth a wander, and you never know what you might find. Shop hours vary, but most are open nights only.

Kurokatsutei TONKATSU ¥

(黒かつ亭; ☎099-213-9600; www.kurokatutei.net; 2-2 Yamashita-chō; sets lunch ¥770-1080, dinner ¥960-1740, donburi ¥880-970; ⏰11am-3.30pm & 5-11.20pm; 🚋Asahi-dōri) If your favourite way to enjoy *kurobuta* (Kagoshima-style black pork) is deep-fried, this institution does it in prodigiously crunchy crust, as *tonkatsu* (cutlets) or *donburi* (rice bowls). Reasonably priced *teishoku* (set meals) come with generous sides of cabbage rice and delicate, pork-broth-based miso soup. The Kurokatsutei set lunch features two of the best-selling pork cuts: fillet and loin.

Look for the black storefront one block east of the Kagoshima East Post Office. Inside, the atmosphere is updated farm house.

Yamauchi Nōjō IZAKAYA ¥

(山内農場; ☎099-223-7488; 2nd fl, 1-26 Higashi-sengoku-chō; dishes ¥350-1180; ⏰5pm-2am Mon-Thu, to 3am Fri & Sat, to 1am Sun; 🚋Tenmonkan-dōri) *Kuro Satsuma-dori* (black Satsuma chicken) is the name of the bird served here, and also what it looks like after being grilled *sumibi-yaki*-style over open charcoal. Other local dishes: marinated *katsuo* (bonito) sashimi, *kurobuta* (black pork) salad, and *tsukune* (chicken meatballs) with cheese or raw egg. Decor is modern-meets-rustic. Enter around the corner from Lawson, by the Remm Kagoshima hotel.

Kagomma Furusato Yatai-mura JAPANESE ¥

(かごっまふるさと屋台村; ☎099-255-1588; 6-4 Chūō-chō; prices vary; ⏰lunch & dinner, stall hours vary; 🚋Takami-bashi, 🚉Kagoshima-Chūō) *Yatai-mura* means 'food-stall village', and some two dozen stalls near Kagoshima-Chūō Station offer a taste of Kagoshima of old. Follow your nose to your favourites, such as *sumibi-yaki* (coal-fired chicken), sashimi, *teppan-yaki* beef and fish dishes. Booth 16 serves delicious Kagoshima *kurobuta shabu-shabu* style (¥1280).

★Kumasotei JAPANESE ¥¥

(熊襲亭; ☎099-222-6356; 6-10 Higashi-Sengoku-chō; set meals lunch/dinner from ¥1500/3000; ⏰11am-2pm & 5-10pm; 🚋Tenmonkan-dōri) This atmospheric multistorey restaurant near central Tenmonkan covers all your *Satsuma-ryōri* needs: *Satsuma-age* (deep-fried fish cake), *tonkotsu* (pork ribs), *kurobuta shabu-shabu* (black-pork hotpot), and lots of fresh fish and seafood. Look for the vertical sign with red lettering and large wooden kanji above the entryway.

Yokaban IZAKAYA ¥¥

(よか晩; ☎099-227-1010; 17-17 Higashi Sengoku-chō; Yōgan-yaki ¥750, 'tulip' fried chicken per piece ¥200; ⏰6pm-midnight Tue-Sun; 🚋Tenmonkan-dōri) Owner Reina-san doesn't speak much English but is a bundle of energy, reflected in her cosy, spirited, home-style *izakaya* on a Tenmonkan side street. Start with self-serve drinks and continue with dishes like *yōgan-yaki* (chicken and vegetables grilled on Sakurajima-lava plates), house-made tofu (try the hot-sesame version) and 'tulip' *karaage* fried chicken, plus seasonal dishes. Cash only.

Look for the glass windows facing the narrow street, diagonally across from Blow antique shop.

Yokaban, by the way, is Kagoshima dialect for 'a fun evening'.

Ichinisan JAPANESE ¥¥

(いちにぃさん; ☎099-225-2123; 11-6 Higashi-Sengoku-chō; plates ¥300-850, black pork ¥800-1800; ⏰11am-10pm Mon-Sat, to 9.30pm Sun; 🚋Tenmonkan-dōri) Come here to try Kagoshima black pork at an affordable price. It's served several ways: *shabu-shabu* dipped in delectable broth with minced green onion; with black vinegar; *kakuni* (pork belly);

and (the best way) atop humble tofu. Try house-made soba, which comes with most *shabu-shabu* meals; fried, local *kibinago* (slender sprat); and the amazingly zingy condiment *yuzu-kosho* (citron-pepper paste).

Drinking & Nightlife

Tenmonkan is where most of the action happens – shot bars, clubs and karaoke boxes. Most dance clubs don't get going until around 11pm and many bars charge admission (¥500 to ¥1000 on average). Many also charge a 'table fee' or 'service' for the snacks or bar nuts they'll serve, whether you eat them or not.

★Honkaku Shōchū Bar Ishizue BAR
(本格焼酎Bar 礎; ☎099-227-0125; www.honkakushochu-bar-ishizue.com; 4th fl, Flower Bldg, 6-1 Sengoku-chō; ¥2000; ⏲8pm-3am; 🚊Tenmonkan-dōri) This chic, amber-and-wood *shōchū* bar has everything going for it, and it's one of the finest places to drink Kagoshima's prefectural liquor. There are more than 1500 choices from around the prefecture, each with its own story, and English-speaking staff to explain. Reserve ahead, especially Friday and Saturday nights.

It's across from Gacha Pon game parlour.

★Karakara BAR
(からから; ☎099-223-0214; 3rd fl, 7-27 Yamanokuchi; ⏲8pm-3am, irregular closures; 🚊Tenmonkan-dōri) On the 3rd floor of a generic bar building next to a 7-Eleven, a low door leads to another dimension. Enthusiastic owner Hiroshi-san has crammed every square millimetre with 30,000 (!) Shōwa-era toys, memorabilia and furniture, including some of questionable taste and refinement. Drinks are just as whimsical; the Garigari-kun highball plunks a popsicle into Japanese whisky.

Dolphin Industry CRAFT BEER
(☎099-295-4600; www.dolphintrip.net; 3rd fl, 4-15 Higashi-Sengoku-chō; ⏲5pm-midnight Sun-Thu, to 2am Fri & Sat; 📶; 🚊Tenmonkan-dōri) This new, surf-themed beer and burger bar brings the California wave across the Pacific. A friendly, just-off-Huntington-Beach vibe of surfboard art, reclaimed wood and corrugated metal accompanies the small but well-chosen rotating selection of Japanese craft brews on tap. Sample three in a 'triple pack' for ¥1200 while enjoying a burger (¥950 to ¥1200, Kagoshima *wagyū* ¥1800). Also Californian: it's nonsmoking.

SHŌCHŪ

Shōchū (焼酎) is a distilled spirit that can be made from a variety of raw materials, including potato, barley and sugarcane. It's quite potent, with an alcohol content of about 25% (but can be as much as 45%). The beverage is strongly associated with Kyūshū, and especially Kagoshima, where *imo-jōchū* (芋焼酎; *shōchū* made from sweet potatoes) predominates; in Ōita, it's *mugi-jōchū* (麦焼酎; *shōchū* made from barley).

Drink it straight (ストレート; *sutoraito*), with soda (ソーダ割り; *sōda-wari*) or on the rocks (ロックで; *rokku de*), but the most traditional way is *oyuwari* (お湯割り) – mixed with water heated in a stone pot over glowing coals. Drink until you yourself begin to glow. Honkaku Shōchū Bar Ishizue is a great place to start your *shōchū* education.

Retroft CAFE
(レトロフト; ☎099-223-5066; 2-1 Meizan-chō; ⏲11am-7pm Tue-Sat, to 4pm Sun, closed 1st & 4th Sun of month; 🚊Asahi-dōri) There's a lot going on in this retro-cool space c 1968: part cafe, part used bookshop, part artist gathering place. Coffee, hot dogs and local sweets are sold out of various nooks and crannies, each with different hours (lunch specials ¥700), while a gallery space upstairs holds occasional exhibitions. There's usually an English speaker on hand.

ℹ Information

Tourist information is available on the prefectural site, www.kagoshima-kankou.com. The city website (www.city.kagoshima.lg.jp) has detailed info on transport, sights and living in town. For sightseeing info, and arts and entertainment listings, see www.kic-update.com.

Tourist Information Center (鹿児島中央駅総合観光案内所; ☎099-253-2500; JR Kagoshima-Chūō Station; ⏲8am-8pm) Has plenty of information in English.

Tourism Exchange Centre (観光交流センター; ☎099-298-5111; 1-1 Uenosono-chō; ⏲9am-7pm; 🚊Takamibashi) Near the Museum of the Meiji Restoration (p769); has pamphlets and can make hotel reservations.

Getting There & Away

AIR

Kagoshima Airport (鹿児島空港; www.koj-ab.co.jp) has connections to Shanghai, Hong Kong, Taipei and Seoul, and convenient domestic flights, including to Tokyo, Osaka and Okinawa (Naha).

BOAT

Ferries depart from Minami-futō pier to Yakushima (jet foil/regular ferry ¥8300/4900, one hour and 40 minutes/four hours). From Kagoshima Shin-kō (Kagoshima New Port), **Marix Line** (☎099-225-1551) has ferries to Naha (Okinawa) via the Amami archipelago (¥14,610, 25 hours).

Frequent passenger and car ferries shuttle around the clock between Kagoshima and Sakurajima (¥160, 15 minutes). Reach the **ferry terminal**, near the aquarium, on the City View Bus or other buses headed for Suizokukan-mae, or by tram to Suizokukan-guchi.

The Yorimichi Cruise (p769) takes one of six circuitous sightseeing routes from Kagoshima Port to Sakurajima Port in about 50 minutes.

BUS

Long-distance buses depart from the express bus stops at **Kagoshima Chūō Station**, near the station's east exit, and from street-side stops at Takashima Plaza (aka 'Takapura') in **Tenmonkan**.

Routes include Miyazaki (¥2780, three hours), Fukuoka (¥5450, 4½ hours), Ōita (¥5660, 7½ hours) and Nagasaki (¥6690, 5½ hours).

CAR & MOTORCYCLE

Many outlets around JR Kagoshima-Chūō Station rent cars for trips around the region.

TRAIN

JR Kagoshima-Chūō Station is the terminus of the Kyūshū *shinkansen*, with stops including Kumamoto (¥6420, 52 minutes), Hakata (¥9930, 90 minutes), Hiroshima (¥17,150, 2½ hours) and Shin-Osaka (¥21,380, 3¾ hours). Also stopping at Kagoshima Station, the JR Nippō line goes to Miyazaki (*tokkyū* ¥3710, two hours) and Beppu (¥9090, five hours).

CUTE TRANSIT PASS

Visitors can take advantage of the Cute transit card (one/two days ¥1200/1800), covering city buses (including the City View and Sakurajima Island View buses), trams, Sakurajima ferries and the Yorimichi Cruise (p769). Cardholders also get discounted admission to many attractions. Pick the card up at tourist information offices.

Getting Around

BICYCLE

Bikes can be rented (¥500/1500 per two hours/day, with a 20% discount for JR users) at JR Kagoshima-Chūō Station.

BUS

Hop-on, hop-off City View Buses (¥190, every 30 minutes, 9am to 6.20pm) loop around the major sights in two routes. A one-day pass (¥600) is also valid on trams and city bus lines and offers discounted admission to many attractions. Otherwise, local buses tend to be inconvenient, particularly if you don't speak Japanese (you're better off with trams).

TRAM

If you're doing only a limited amount of sightseeing, trams are the easiest way around town. Rte 1 starts from Kagoshima Station and goes through the centre into the suburbs. Rte 2 diverges at Takami-baba (高見馬場) to JR Kagoshima-Chūō Station and terminates at Kōrimoto. Either pay the flat fare (¥170) or buy a one-day travel pass (¥600) from the tourist information centre or on board. A third line, Chokko-bin, runs from Kagoshima Station only at peak commuting times, bypassing Kōrimoto and ending in Taniyama.

Sakurajima

☎099

Kagoshima's iconic symbol, Sakurajima has been spewing an almost continuous stream of smoke and ash since 1955, and it's not uncommon for it to have more than 1000, mostly small, 'burps' per year. In 1914 more than 3 billion tonnes of lava swallowed numerous island villages – 1000-plus homes – and joined Sakurajima to the mainland to the southeast.

Despite its volatility, Sakurajima is currently friendly enough for visitors to get fairly close. Among the volcano's three peaks, only Minami-dake (South Peak; 1040m) is active. Climbing the mountain is prohibited, but there are several lookout points.

On the mainland, Kagoshima residents speak proudly of Sakurajima. As the light shifts on its surface throughout the day it's said to feature *nanairo* (seven colours), visible from across Kinkō-wan.

Sights

Arimura Lava Observatory VIEWPOINT
(有村溶岩展望所; ☎099-298-5111; 952 Arimura; ⏲24hr) FREE The name 'Observatory' is misleading, as there's no building here. The site is a shaded picnic area with some lava escape tunnels and walking trails that let you get up close to recent lava, much of it covered now with small pine trees. Smoky Minami-dake, the southernmost peak of Sakurajima, smoulders above you.

Buried Torii LANDMARK
(黒神埋没鳥居) Near Sakurajima's east coast, the top of a once-3m-high *torii* (shrine gate) emerges from the volcanic ash at Kurokami; the rest of it was buried in the 1914 eruption.

Yunohira Lookout VIEWPOINT
(湯之平展望所) A drive along the tranquil north coast and then inland will lead you to Yunohira Lookout, offering views of the mountain and back across the bay to central Kagoshima.

Karasujima Observation Point VIEWPOINT
(烏島展望台) South of the visitor centre is this observation point, where the 1914 lava flow engulfed a small island that had once been 500m offshore. There's now an *ashi-yu* (foot bath), Japan's second longest.

Sleeping & Eating

Options for staying here are limited, with just a couple of properties; otherwise, take the ferry to Kagoshima or circle north to Kirishima.

There are some convenience stores and food options near the ferry terminal.

Information

Sakurajima Visitors Centre (☎099-293-2443; www.sakurajima.gr.jp/svc; ⏲9am-5pm) Nearish the ferry terminal, with exhibits about the volcano, including a model showing its growth, and helpful English-speaking staff.

Getting There & Away

Frequent passenger and car ferries shuttle around the clock between Kagoshima and Sakurajima (¥160, 15 minutes).

The Yorimichi Cruise (p769) takes one of six circuitous sightseeing routes from Kagoshima Port to Sakurajima Port in about 50 minutes; you can then purchase a standard ferry ticket back from Sakurajima to Kagoshima.

Getting Around

Sakurajima Island View buses (1 way ¥120-440, day pass ¥500; ⏲8 per day 9am-4.30pm) loop around Sakurajima. Alternatively, try **Sakurajima Rentacar** (☎099-293-2162; 2hr/day from ¥4800/11,000), which also rents out bikes (¥300 per hour), though biking isn't recommended: if the volcano erupts during your ride, you may find yourself unprotected from breathing the ash.

Though there are buses, this volcanic island is best enjoyed by car; the drive around takes at least an hour, depending on stops. If travelling by bus, consider the Kagoshima Cute day pass, good on the Sakurajima Island View and Kagoshima City View buses, plus trams and the ferry to Sakurajima.

Satsuma Peninsula

The Satsuma Peninsula (薩摩半島) south of Kagoshima city has fine rural scenery, samurai houses, a haunting kamikaze museum, spectacular sand baths and a super-fun way to eat noodles. While the main towns of Ibusuki and Makurazaki are accessible by bus and train respectively, renting a car from Kagoshima will save time and hassles. Along Ibusuki Skyline Rd, you'll also find wonderful views of Kinkō Bay (錦江湾; Kinkō-wan) and the main islands' southernmost mountains. Time permitting, head all the way to the tip for great glimpses of Kaimon-dake (開聞岳), this area's Mt Fuji.

Ibusuki

☎0993 / POP 41,850

In southeastern Satsuma Peninsula, around 50km from Kagoshima, the palmy hot-spring resort of Ibusuki (指宿) is known for its 'sand baths', in which attendants bury guests up to their necks in beach sand heated by underground onsen.

Otherwise, Ibusuki is generally pretty quiet, particularly in the low season, and more especially after dark. A recent large influx of tourists from China may change that.

Ibusuki Station is located about 1km from the beachfront and most accommodation, but the few eateries are near the station.

Sights

Chiringashima ISLAND
(知林ヶ島) Lovely Chiringashima is connected to the mainland by a thin land bridge that appears only at low tide, when hikers, beachcombers and tide-pool explorers can

walk the coral and shell-strewn connector and visit a small shrine on the island itself. Hours vary with the tides, which you may have to race if you walk too slowly. A taxi from Ibusuki Station takes 10 minutes; the over-sand hike, one way, takes about half an hour, more if you stop along the way.

Satsuma Denshōkan MUSEUM
(薩摩伝承館; www.satsuma-denshokan.com; 12131-4 Higashikata, Hakusuikan; ¥1500; ⌚8.30am-7pm) This striking museum offers a history of Satsuma plus displays of Chinese ceramics and gleaming Satsuma-yaki in a temple-style building that seems to float on its own lake. There are English-language audio guides. It's about 3.5km from Ibusuki Station (taxi ¥1220, 10 minutes), at the Hakusuikan onsen hotel.

Activities

★Tamatebako Onsen ONSEN
(たまて箱温泉; ☎0993-35-3577; 3292 Fukumoto Yamakawa; bath/bath & sand bath ¥510/1130; ⌚9.30am-7.30pm Fri-Wed) Consistently topping lists of the world's best onsen, Tamatebako is in two parts: conventional, ocean-view baths on a cliffside and a *sunamushi* (sand bath). Gender-separated baths are Japanese (more popular) or Western style and switch daily; on odd-numbered days men get the Japanese bath, with a view of Kaimon-dake. Sand-bath admission includes *yukata*; towels can be rented.

Nearby is the site of an old salt works where geysers stream water from the earth. Stand in the spray and it will taste like salt.

Tamatebako Onsen is a 9.5km drive from Ibusuki Station; follow signs for 'Healthy Land'.

Ibusuki Sunamushi Kaikan Saraku ONSEN
(いぶすき砂むし会館 砂楽; ☎0993-23-3900; www.sa-raku.sakura.ne.jp; 5-25-18 Yunohama; bath/bath & sand bath ¥610/1080; ⌚8.30am-9pm, closed noon-1pm Mon-Fri) Pay at the entrance, change into a *yukata* and wander down to the beach where, under a canopy of bamboo-slat blinds, women with shovels bury you in hot volcanic sand. Reactions range from panic to euphoria. It's said that 10 minutes will get rid of impurities, but many people stay longer. Afterwards, soak in the onsen.

Private cabins also available.

Sleeping

Minshuku Takayoshi MINSHUKU ¥
(民宿たかよし; ☎0993-22-5982; 5-1-1 Yunohama; r with/without 2 meals ¥6630/3880; P ⊖ ❄ ⊜) This seven-room *minshuku* is no frills but spotless and has onsen baths and washlet toilets. Some rooms have balconies. It uses home-grown produce in its meals. Not much English is spoken, but the cheerful, animated owner is fun to be around. It's about 400m from the sand baths.

Tsukimi-sō RYOKAN ¥¥
(月見荘; ☎0993-22-4221; www.tsukimi.jp; 5-24-8 Yunohama; r per person incl 2 meals from ¥13,110; P ⊖ ❄ ⊜) Rooms at this spotless seven-room ryokan across from the sand baths have private facilities, in addition to pretty indoor and outdoor baths and meals featuring *Satsuma-ryōri* (Kagoshima's regional cuisine), such as *tonkotsu* and sashimi. Not much English is spoken, but the amenable staff makes it work. The whole place is nonsmoking.

★Hakusuikan HOTEL ¥¥¥
(白水館; ☎0993-22-3131; www.hakusuikan.co.jp; 12126-12 Higashi-kata; r per person incl 2 meals from ¥18,510; P ⊖ ❄ @ ⊜ ≋) Visiting dignitaries might stay in the sumptuous, 40-room Rikyū wing, but those of more modest means can splurge on the less expensive of Hakusuikan's 164 rooms. The opulent onsen/*rotemburo*/sand baths are worth the stay by themselves. There's a choice of Japanese or Italian meals; the Fenice Italian restaurant is as tasty as it is attractive.

Also on the property is the Satsuma Denshōkan, a striking museum of regional treasures.

Ryokan Ginshō RYOKAN ¥¥¥
(旅館吟松, Ginsyo; ☎0993-22-3231; www.ginsyou.co.jp; 5-26-27 Yunohama; r per person incl 2 meals from ¥15,120; P ⊖ ❄ ⊜) The exquisite 2nd- and 9th-floor *rotemburo* of this upmarket beachfront ryokan have expansive views and a lovely relaxation garden. There's a broad range of rates depending on room facilities and view (ocean-facing rooms are pricier). For meals, there's an onsen vent right in your dinner table, for genteel servers to cook *Satsuma-age* (deep-fried fish cake) before your eyes.

Nonguests can arrive between 6pm and 8pm to use the bath (¥1000).

WORTH A TRIP

IKEDA-KO & KAIMON-DAKE

Ikeda-ko is a volcanic caldera lake west of Ibusuki, inhabited by giant eels kept in tanks by the parking lot. South of the lake is **Cape Nagasaki-bana**, from where you can see offshore islands on a clear day.

The beautifully symmetrical 924m cone of Kaimon-dake, nicknamed 'Satsuma Fuji', dominates the southern skyline and can be climbed in two hours. An early start may reward you with views of Sakurajima (p773), the Sata Peninsula, and Yakushima (p789) and Tanegashima (p794) islands.

In a riverside gorge near Ikeda-ko, **Tōsenkyō Sōmen Nagashi** (唐船峡そうめん流し; 0993-32-2143; 5967 Jūchō; sōmen ¥570; 10am-8pm Aug, to 7.30pm Jul & Sep, to 5.30pm Mar-Jun & Oct, to 3.30pm Nov-Feb;) is the birthplace of *nagashi-sōmen* (flowing noodles). *Sōmen* (thin wheat-flour noodles) spin around tyre-shaped tabletop tanks of swiftly flowing 13°C water; catch the noodles with your chopsticks and dip them in sauce to eat. Lots of fun and ultra-refreshing on hot days. It gets an estimated 200,000 annual visitors (!), and is such a pilgrimage site that there's even a Shintō shrine here.

Eating

Although there's a smattering of restaurants around Ibusuki Station, dining choices are limited and your tastiest options may be the meals at your hotel.

Taketora RAMEN ¥

(たけとら; 0993-22-5338; 1-1-13 Omure; ramen ¥800-1200; 11.30am-2.30pm & 5.30-7pm Mon, Wed, Thu & Fri, 11.30am-4pm Sat & Sun; P) Even tiny Ibusuki has its own ramen style. This polished shop won a prefectural ramen competition for its Kaimon-dake ramen (¥950), filled with local ingredients like ground black pork and hot-spring-boiled egg. The standard soy-sauce ramen is made with broth from local bonito. Also try *tako yakimeshi* (fried rice with deep-fried octopus), topped with writhing fish flakes.

Aoba IZAKAYA ¥

(青葉; 0993-22-3356; 1-2-11 Minato; dishes from ¥480; 11am-3pm & 5.30-10pm Thu-Tue) A minute's walk left from the station, this cheery shop serves a satisfying and varied menu of local specialities like *katsuo-donburi* (bonito on a bowl of rice; ¥740), *kurobuta rōsukatsu* (black-pork cutlet) *teishoku* (set meal; ¥1420) or, if you dare, *kuro Satsuma dori sashimi* (raw sliced chicken; ¥850).

Information

Ibusuki Tourist Information (指宿駅総合観光案内所; 0993-22-4114; 9am-6pm;) The station's tourist info desk offers a variety of services beyond just maps, directions and brochures. It can help with hotel reservations and even deliver luggage to your lodging in town for ¥400 if you arrive by 3pm.

Getting There & Away

Ibusuki Station is about 1½ hours from Kagoshima by bus (¥950) or 51 minutes by train from Kagoshima-chūō (*tokkyū* ¥2130). Train geeks and sightseers will love the one-of-a-kind wood-panelled Ibutama *tokkyū* with specially angled seats for breathtaking bay views.

Getting Around

The Nottari-Oritari My Plan Bus (¥1100 per day) offers unlimited hop-on, hop-off service around Ibusuki highlights. Rent bikes (¥500 for two hours) from the station. Car-rental offices are steps away.

Chiran

0993

A river runs through Chiran (知覧), 34km south of Kagoshima, parallel to a collection of restored samurai houses, surrounded by placid green tea and sweet-potato fields. At the town's edge is a museum about WWII's kamikaze pilots.

Sights

★Chiran Peace Museum MUSEUM

(知覧特攻平和会館, Kamikaze Peace Museum; 0993-83-2525; www.chiran-tokkou.jp; 17881 Chiran-chō; ¥500; 9am-5pm) There is perhaps no more eloquent monument to the futility of war than this harrowing museum about WWII kamikaze pilots. Around 2km west of town, Chiran's air base was the point of departure for 1036 WWII *tokkō* ('special attack forces', as the pilots were formally known), the biggest percentage in the Japanese military. On the base's former site, this large, thought-provoking museum presents

WORTH A TRIP

ARCHAEOLOGICAL FINDS IN SOUTHERN KYŪSHŪ

Uenohara Jōmon no Mori

Archaeology enthusiasts will want to detour to this **museum** (上野原縄文の森; ☎0995-48-5701; 1-1 Uenohara Jōmon-no-mori, Kokubu; ¥310; ⏱9am-5pm Tue-Sun), on the site where the oldest authenticated Jōmon-era pottery shards were uncovered – during excavations for nearby office parks. Based on these findings, anthropologists began to conclude that the first humans may have come to Japan from the south, rather than the north as previously thought, via canoes or rafts along the Ryūkyū island chain. The futuristic main building offers lots of artefacts, with detailed English explanations via smartphone. Outside, about 1.5 km of trails through the park-like grounds connect recreated Jōmon-era dwellings. The museum can be reached by train from Kagoshima to Kokubu, from where it's about 8km (20 minutes) by taxi or private car.

Saitobaru Burial Mounds Park

North of Miyazaki, the Saitobaru Burial Mounds Park looks like a golf course at first glance, but the hillocks dotting the several square kilometres of fields and forests are actually more than 300 *kofun* (tumuli; burial mounds). These mostly keyhole-shaped mounds, dating from 300 to 600 CE, served much the same function as Egyptian pyramids for early Japanese nobility. Bike rental is free.

The large **Saitobaru Archaeological Museum** (西都原考古博物館; ☎0983-41-0041; 5670 Miyake; ⏱10am-6pm Tue-Sun) FREE displays excavated items such as Jōmon pottery, ancient swords, armour and *haniwa* (earthenware figures). Rent the English audio guide (¥400); signage is in Japanese. A hall nearby is built around an excavation site.

Buses run twice a day to Saitobaru from Miyakō bus terminal (¥1140, 70 minutes) in Miyazaki, but you'll need your own transport if you want to explore the tomb-strewn countryside. Saitobaru is not covered by the Visit Miyazaki Bus Pass (p781).

aircraft, mementos, photographs and footage of the fresh-faced young men selected for the ultimate sacrifice.

While much of the signage is in Japanese only, it's well worth investing in the English-language audio guide (rental ¥200), which offers details about many of the individual pilots. You'll need a heart of stone not to be moved by their stories.

Samurai Houses HISTORIC BUILDING
(武家屋敷; 6198 Chiran-chō; combined admission to all houses ¥500; ⏱9am-5pm) Seven of the mid-Edo-period residences along Chiran's 700m street of samurai houses have gardens open to the public. Water is usually symbolised in the gardens by sand, *shirasu* (volcanic ash) or gravel. Allow up to one leisurely hour to view them all.

Eating

Taki-An NOODLES ¥
(高城庵; ☎0993-83-3186; 6329 Chiran-chō; soba ¥660, set meals from ¥1080; ⏱10.30am-3pm) Just off the samurai street, Taki-An is a lovely restaurant in another traditional house where you can sit on tatami and admire the garden over hot or cold *ocha udon* (noodles made with green tea; ¥650) or Satsuma specialities such as *tonkotsu teishoku* (pork set meal; ¥1650) and Chiran's famous green tea. Picture menu available.

Information

Chiran Samurai Residence & Garden Preservation Association (知覧武家屋敷庭園事務所; ☎0993-58-7878; www.chiran-bukeyashiki.jp; 13731-1 Chiran-chō; ⏱9am-5pm) This tourist info office details everything you'll need to know about the samurai houses. There's even a helmet you can try on for size.

Getting There & Away

Kagoshima Kōtsū (鹿児島交通) buses to Chiran (samurai houses/Peace Museum ¥890/930, 80/85 minutes, hourly) stop in Tenmonkan and near JR Kagoshima-Chūō Station. From Chiran, buses run five times daily to Ibusuki (¥940, 69 minutes).

Kirishima-Kinkō-wan National Park

Pockmarked with volcanic craters, criss-crossed by hiking trails and boasting some lovely coastal scenery, Kirishima-Kinkō-wan National Park straddles northern Kagoshima and western Miyazaki Prefectures. There are excellent hikes of many lengths, although ash eruptions, toxic gases and other volcanic activity sometimes change accessibility. The area is known for its wild azaleas, hot springs and the 75m waterfall **Senriga-taki**. It's also famous in Japanese mythology as being the place where the gods first descended to earth and began the imperial dynasty, said to be unbroken to this day.

Hikers should monitor the weather closely before setting out. Apart from volcanic conditions, thunderstorms and fog are common during the rainy season (mid-May to June) and winters can be bitter; otherwise, the vistas are superb.

Daily weather updates are available at the visitor centres (p778).

Sights

Kirishima-jingū SHINTŌ SHRINE

(霧島神宮; 2608-5 Kirishima-Taguchi; 24hr) FREE Picturesque, tangerine Kirishima-jingū has a good vantage point. Though the original dates from the 6th century, the present shrine was built in 1715. It is dedicated to Ninigi-no-mikoto, who, according to *Kojiki* (a book compiled in 712), led the gods from the heavens to the Takachiho-no-mine summit. The shrine is accessible by bus (¥240, 15 minutes) from JR Kirishima-jingū Station.

There's a small village with inns and restaurants at the foot of the shrine.

Ebino-kōgen Eco Museum Centre NATURE CENTRE

(えびのエコミュージアムセンター; 0984-33-3002; 1-4 Suenaga, Ebino-shi; 9am-5pm) FREE This attractive, lodge-like tourist centre has information, maps, models of the area's wildlife, topography and nature (in easily understandable English) and helpful staff. There's a video of the 2011 eruption of the Shinmoe-dake volcano and important info about daily volcanic eruptions for hikers. If conditions don't permit you to get out into nature itself, this is a good stand-in.

Activities

This gorgeous area is blessed with great hiking and sublime onsen, both natural and artificial. Views from the peaks are particularly stunning – well worth taking time for.

Hiking

The **Ebino-kōgen circuit** is a relaxed 4km stroll around a series of volcanic lakes – **Rokkannon Mi-ike** is a stunning, intensely cyan lake. Across the road from the lake, **Fudō-ike**, at the base of Karakuni-dake, is a steaming *jigoku* (boiling hot spring). The stiffer climb to the 1700m summit of **Karakuni-dake** skirts the edge of the volcano's deep crater before arriving at the high point on the eastern side. The panoramic view south is outstanding, taking in the perfectly circular caldera lake of Ōnami-ike, **Shinmoe-dake** (the volcano that erupted in January 2011; parts remain inaccessible) and the perfect cone of **Takachiho-no-mine**. On a clear day, you can see Kagoshima and the smoking molar of Sakurajima. Friendly wild deer roam freely through the town of **Ebino-kōgen** and are happy to be photographed.

Onsen

This area has numerous onsen, both 'wild' ones (just hot spots in rivers!) to expansive onsen hotels. You will see steam rising from numerous places as you travel around. All of the hotels in this area have baths, and a number of hotels make their baths available to day visitors. Some onsen include mixed-gender bathing pools as well as segregated male and female baths.

Sleeping & Eating

Lodgings are clustered near Kirishima-jingū and in Ebino-kōgen village.

With towns so spread out, eating options are limited; most visitors eat at their hotels. Most village shops close by 5pm.

Kirishima Jingū-mae Youth Hostel HOSTEL ¥

(霧島神宮前ユースホステル; 0995-57-1188; 2459-83 Kirishima-Taguchi; dm HI member/nonmember ¥3390/3990, minshuku per person incl 2 meals ¥7710; P ❄ @ ⊜) A few minutes from Kirishima-jingū, this neat, comfy youth hostel has Japanese rooms, and mountain views from its onsen. Breakfast/dinner costs ¥540/1080. It also operates as a more expensive *minshuku*, with better meals and a *rotemburo*.

Minshuku Kirishima-ji MINSHUKU ¥¥
(民宿きりしま路; ☎0995-57-0272; 2459 Kirishima-Taguchi; r per person with/without 2 meals ¥7080/4500; P) This spartan but friendly six-room inn, just across the gorge from the shrine (p777), has forest views and shared onsen. Day visitors can stop here for a lunch of house-made soba dishes (¥480 to ¥880), including a house-special *champon* (Nagasaki-style ramen). Day use of the bath is possible for ¥300.

★ **Ebino-Kōgen Sō** HOTEL ¥¥¥
(えびの高原荘; ☎0984-33-0161; www.ebinokogenso.com; 1489 Ōaza Suenaga; r per person incl 2 meals & with/without bathroom from ¥10,500/9500; P) This friendly onsen hotel boasts some excellent facilities, including mountain-view rooms (mostly Japanese style), coin laundry, and English-speaking staff. The lovely *rotemburo* (¥520) is open to the public from 11.30am to 8pm, and there's a family-style bath deep in the forest (¥1030 per hour). The location, near Ebino-kōgen village, is superb and the restaurant makes tasty meals.

Rates may be lower depending on meals, which might include *kaiseki* dinners, so ask when you reserve. Also ask about shuttle-bus services serving trailheads and train stations.

Information

Nature centres at each end of the volcano walk have bilingual maps and hiking information, and exhibits on local wildlife.

Kirishima City Tourist Information (霧島市観光案内所; ☎0995-57-1588; 2459-6 Taguchi; 9am-6pm Apr-Sep, to 5pm Oct-Mar) Right near the giant *torii* at the entrance to Kirishima-jingū. There's a foot onsen steps from the entrance. Rental bikes are available but not cheap (¥1000 per two hours).

Takachiho-gawara Visitors Centre (高千穂河原ビジターセンター; ☎0995-57-2505; 9am-5pm) A small visitor centre at the base of Takachiho with hiking info, maps and safety suggestions.

Getting There & Around

The main train junctions are JR Kobayashi Station, northeast of Ebino Plateau, and Kirishima-jingū Station to the south.

Two buses per day connect the Kirishima-jingū area with Ebino-kōgen (¥990), but this region is vastly more accessible by car.

Miyazaki

☎0985 / POP 401,000

The prefectural capital of Miyazaki (宮崎) makes a convenient base for forays around the region, with a friendly, low-key vibe and fun, unique restaurants and night spots in the Nishitachi nightlife district, about 700m from the station.

Sights

Heiwadai-kōen PARK
(平和台公園, Peace Park; ☎098-535-3181; www.heiwadai-bunkakoen.info; 24hr) The park's centrepiece is the 37m-high **Peace Tower** monument constructed in 1940, a time when peace in Japan was about to disappear. Its timeless design may remind you of ancient Inca or Khmer monuments, and it's made of stones from all over the world. The **Haniwa Garden** is dotted with reproductions of clay *haniwa* (earthenware figures found in Kōfun-period tombs) excavated from the Saitobaru burial mounds, set among mossy hillocks.

Heiwadai-kōen is about 1km north of Miyazaki-jingū. Buses from Miyazaki Station stop along Tachibana-dōri (¥290, 20 minutes, at least two per hour).

Miyazaki-jingū SHINTŌ SHRINE
(宮崎神宮; 2-4-1 Jingū) FREE This shrine honours Emperor Jimmu, the semi-mythical first emperor of Japan and founder of the Yamato court. Spectacular centuries-old wisteria vines cover the thickly forested grounds and bloom in April. It's a 500m walk from Miyazaki-jingū Station, one stop (¥160, three minutes) north of Miyazaki Station.

Miyazaki Science Centre MUSEUM
(宮崎科学技術館; ☎0985-23-2700; 1-2-2 Miyazaki-eki Higashi; with/without sky show ¥750/540; 9am-4.30pm Tue-Sun) Steps away from Miyazaki Station, this family-friendly interactive science museum boasts one of the world's largest planetariums; some exhibits include English translations. Look for the life-size rocket replica outside the entrance. Inside, see robots and a spaceship lander.

Sleeping

Hotel Route Inn BUSINESS HOTEL ¥¥
(ホテルルートイン宮崎; ☎0985-61-1488; www.route-inn.co.jp; 4-1-27 Tachibana-dōri-nishi; s/d/tw incl breakfast ¥6800/12,800/13,550; P) Across from the Nishitachi

Miyazaki

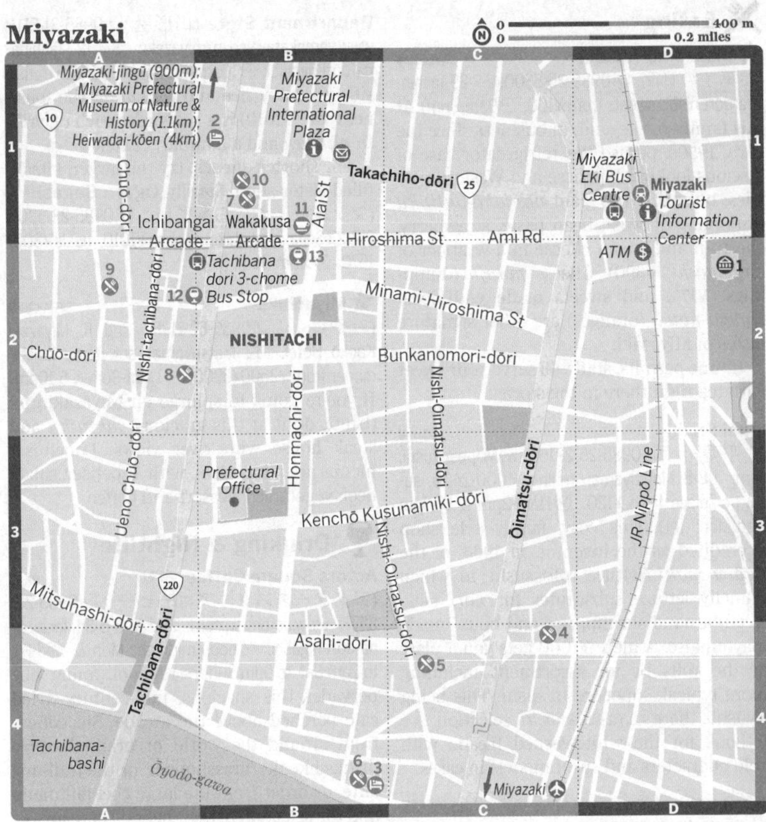

Miyazaki

Sights

1 Miyazaki Science Centre........D2

Sleeping

2 Hotel Route Inn........B1
3 Miyazaki Kankō Hotel........B4

Eating

4 Family Ogura Segashira-ten........C4
5 Ippei Sushi........C4
6 Miyachiku........B4
7 Ogura Honten........B1
8 Okashi no Hidaka........A2
9 Togakushi........A2
10 Yamakataya Department Store........B1

Drinking & Nightlife

11 Actors Square Coffee........B1
12 Igokochiya Anbai........A2
13 The Bar........B2

district, this 213-room hotel is excellent value, with a great breakfast buffet, spacious, decently appointed rooms, free coffee in the granite lobby and common baths (in addition to private bathrooms).

Miyazaki Kankō Hotel HOTEL ¥¥¥
(宮崎観光ホテル; ☎0985-27-1212; www.miyakan-h.com; 1-1-1 Matsuyama; s/tw from ¥9720/18,360; P ⊖ ❄ @ ☎) This towering hotel has two buildings: the west wing, and the more recently remodelled east wing (with room prices ¥2000 to ¥3000 more per person). Even if the decor in the public spaces is a little frilly and dated, rooms are relatively spacious, there are several fine restaurants, and there's an onsen with *rotemburo* (day use ¥1000).

The hotel is next to the river, which means some lovely views from rooms and nice strolls in the evening, but it's quite far to walk from the station and nightlife district.

Eating

★Okashi no Hidaka — SWEETS ¥

(お菓子の日高; ☎0985-25-5300; 2-7-25 Tachibana-dōri-nishi; sweets from ¥100; ⏱9am-9pm) At this family-run legend, in business since the early 1950s, peruse the refrigerator case of luscious-looking Japanese and Western pastries, but order the giant *nanjakō-daifuku* (dumpling of sweet bean paste, strawberry, chestnut and cream cheese in a wrapper of airy *mochi;* ¥390). Cheese *manju* (dumplings; ¥175) and sweets made with local *Hyūga-natsu* (oranges) are other signature tastes of Miyazaki.

If time permits, staff will serve your sweet with tea right there in the store.

Ippei Sushi — SUSHI ¥

(一平寿司; ☎0985-25-2215; www.ippei-sushi.com; 1-8-8 Matsuyama; mains ¥1000-2400, sushi per piece from ¥120; ⏱11am-3pm & 5-10pm Wed-Mon; P) This cosy, family-style shop is credited as the inventor, in 1966, of the *retasu maki* (lettuce roll) sushi, in which crunchy lettuce substitutes for *nori* (seaweed) around shrimp, rice and house-made mayonnaise. A mere ¥1000 gets you a plate of the rolls or an assortment including more typical, super-fresh, sushi. This being Kyūshū, there's a great *shōchū* selection.

Look for the whitewashed facade with gold characters and sushi models in cases.

Togakushi — NOODLES ¥

(戸隠; ☎0985-24-6864; www.miyazaki-togakushi.com; 7-10 Chūō-dōri; noodles ¥650-950; ⏱7pm-2am Mon-Sat) Togakushi has no English menu, but any difficulties this may present are worth it for the delicate, thin *kama-age udon* (barrel-boiled wheat noodles; ¥650), for dipping in a tangy *negi* (green onion) sauce, *tempura-ko* (tempura crispies) and refreshing *yuzu* (Japanese citron); pour the water from the noodles into the sauce to make soup. This is what locals crave after a bender.

Look for the giant red lantern in front of the traditional house.

★Ogura Honten — JAPANESE ¥¥

(おぐら本店; ☎0985-22-2296; 3-4-24 Tachibana-higashi; chikin nanban ¥1010, other mains ¥670-1300; ⏱11am-3pm & 5-8.30pm Wed-Mon) *Chikin nanban* (sweet fried chicken with tartar sauce; pictured on the menu) was invented here in 1961, and crowds still flock to this no-frills shop under a red-and-white awning, in the alley behind **Yamakataya Department Store** (山形屋; ☎0985-31-3111; www.yamakataya.co.jp/miyazaki; 3-4-12 Tachibana-dōri-higashi; ⏱10am-7.30pm). There are also riffs on curry rice and *tonkatsu*; the 'business set' (¥1010) is a half-order each of *chikin nanban* and a hamburger steak.

For shorter queues, try the larger, kitsch-filled sister shop, **Family Ogura Segashira** (ファミリーおぐら瀬頭店; ☎0985-23-5301; 2-2-23 Segashira; chikin nanban ¥1010, meals ¥800-1670; ⏱11am-9pm; 👪).

★Miyachiku — STEAK ¥¥¥

(みやちく; ☎0985-62-1129; 2nd fl, Miyazaki Kankō Hotel, 1-1-1 Matsuyama; set menu lunch/dinner from ¥2500/5900; ⏱11am-3pm & 5-10pm) If you're going to splurge on Miyazaki *gyū* (beef), do it at this gracious *yakiniku* and steak house with river views. Lunch set menus are a nice deal, with appetiser, salad, beef, vegetables, dessert and coffee.

Drinking & Nightlife

Actors Square Coffee — CAFE

(アクターズスクエアコーヒー; ☎0985-26-8577; www.actors-sq.com; 2nd fl, 3-6-34 Tachibana-dōri-higashi; ⏱noon-midnight Mon & Wed-Fri, to 2am Sat, to 9pm Sun; 📶) A cool, young vibe pervades this spacious, mid-century-styled cafe perched above the arcade. Sip coffees from around the world or original coffee drinks like the 'grasshopper' or the trail-mix latte, or order from the large cocktail menu and the selection of craft beers. There are occasional live music events, and food includes fried-chicken plates and curry rice.

Igokochiya Anbai — BAR

(いごこち屋 あんばい; ☎0985-27-4117; 3-3-33 Tachibanadōri-nishi; ⏱6pm-1am Mon-Sat) Anbai is a sophisticated *izakaya* with more than 350 varieties of *shōchū*, well-chosen local dishes and cool background music. Not much English is spoken, but the '*mama-san*' (hostess) is extremely kind, and if you order alcohol staff will bring the bottle so you can study the label as you sip.

Look for the giant ball of cedar fronds next door to Menya Katsumi.

The Bar — BAR

(ザ・バー; ☎0985-71-0423; www.thebarmiyazaki.info; 3rd fl, Paul Smith Bldg, 3-7-15 Tachibana-dōri-higashi; ⏱7pm-3am; 📶) This hub of the expat community and its local friends draws a cheery mixed crowd who are proud of the city and keen to welcome visitors over Miyazaki-brewed craft beers, mojitos made with mint from the owner's garden, giant Jenga and a well-used, full-size billiard table. Plus, it's nonsmoking, a rarity in Japan.

Note: there's another 'the Bar' across town, near the Tachibana arcade.

Information

Miyazaki Prefectural International Plaza (宮崎県国際交流協会; ☎0985-32-8457; 9th fl, Carino Bldg; ⏲10am-7pm Tue-Sat) Information good for longer-term visitors who need to make connections, find services or job hunt; walk to the back of the building to find this office on the 9th floor.

Tourist Information Center (宮崎市観光案内所; ☎0985-22-6469; ⏲9am-6pm) This helpful and ever-friendly centre inside JR Miyazaki Station has maps of the city and its surroundings.

Getting There & Away

AIR

Miyazaki is served by a variety of airlines that fly to Tokyo, Osaka, Nagoya, Fukuoka, Okinawa, Seoul, Taipei and Hong Kong. **Miyazaki Airport** (www.miyazaki-airport.co.jp) is connected to the city centre by bus (¥440, 26 minutes) or train (¥350, 10 minutes) from JR Miyazaki Station.

BOAT

Miyazaki Car Ferry (宮崎カーフェリー; ☎0985-29-5566; www.miyazakicarferry.com; 3-14 Minato; 2nd class from ¥9050) Links Miyazaki with Kōbe (12 hours).

BUS

Bus routes include Kagoshima (¥2780, three hours), Kumamoto (¥4630, 3½ hours), Nagasaki (¥6690, 5½ hours) and Fukuoka (¥4630, 4½ hours). Phone the **Miyazaki Eki Bus Centre** (宮崎駅バスセンター; ☎0985-23-0106) for more info.

CAR & MOTORCYCLE

Car rental (12 hours from about ¥5500) is the most convenient way to explore the coastal region outside the city. There are many agencies outside the station's west exit.

TRAIN

The JR Nippō line runs down to Kagoshima (*tokkyū* ¥4020, two hours) and up to Beppu (*tokkyū* ¥5790, 3¼ hours).

Getting Around

Most city bus services use the Miyazaki Eki Bus Centre diagonally opposite the train station.

For the Nishitachi nightlife district, the **Tachibana dori 3-chome bus stop** is the most convenient.

> **VISIT MIYAZAKI BUS PASS**
>
> For budget travellers not in a hurry, this bus pass (www.miyakoh.co.jp; ¥1500 per day) is a fabulous deal, covering *most* Miyazaki buses including those to Aoshima and Nichinan Coast; however, it does not include buses that go to Takachiho or Nobeoka. Buy the pass at tourist counters and some hotels.

Aoshima

☎0985

Aoshima (青島) is both a tiny palm-covered island (1.5km in circumference) and the name of the adjacent mainland town, one of Japan's more relaxed communities. Surfers and sunbathers come for its lovely beaches, strewn with sand dollars after rough storms, and it's also a training ground for Japanese sports teams. All in all, it's a laid-back alternative to staying in central Miyazaki.

The first thing you'll notice as you cross the Yayoibashi bridge (120m) to the island of Aoshima is the unique geological feature surrounding it. Called the 'devil's washboard' (*oni no sentaku-ita*; 鬼の洗濯板), the rows of rock formations look just like a washboard of centuries ago. They're best viewed at low tide. An estimated 200 plant and animal species (including some 5000 biro palm trees, up to 350 years old) can be found within the island's 1.6km circumference.

Besides its natural beauty, the island boasts the photogenic Shintō shrine **Aoshima-jinja** (青島神社; ☎0985-65-1262; https://aoshima-jinja.jp; 2-13-1 Aoshima; ⏲8am-5pm), reputedly good for matchmaking. To the right of the main shrine, a path lined with a few heart-shaped arches leads to a smaller shrine at the island's geographic centre. Next to it are twin palm trees called *meoto* (female and male) biro. Would-be lovers can purchase brightly coloured strings (¥100) to tie to ropes between the trees as an offering.

Visit the **Legend of Hyūga Hall** (日向神話館; ☎098-565-1262; ¥600; ⏲8am-6pm Jul & Aug, to 5pm Sep-Jun) here to learn about Japan's origin myths and stories.

Sleeping

★ Aoshima Fisherman's Beachside Hostel & Spa HOSTEL ¥
(青島フィッシャーマンズ・ビーチサイドホステル&スパ; ☎0985-77-5525; www.aoshima-hostel.com; 3-1-53 Aoshima; dm/s/tw/tr/q without bathroom ¥1980/5700/6200/9300/9960; P ❄ @ ☎; 🚉Aoshima) If this spanking-new, oceanfront hostel is the way things are going, that's an excellent sign. Built of Miyazaki cedar, its modern campus offers two dorms and 81 private rooms, all with access to shared kitchen spaces. There are three restaurants (Italian, seafood and Japanese), plus onsen with *rotemburo* and sauna (¥540 extra), though no ocean views. Day users of the spa pay once and can return all day.

★ Minshuku Misakisō MINSHUKU ¥¥
(民宿みさき荘; ☎0985-65-0038; www.misakisou.com; 1-5-4 Aoshima; s/d without bathroom ¥5000/8000; P ❄ ☎) Gracious and friendly, this modern *minshuku* is a one-stop shop: a place to stay, a (guests-only) bar, a lunchtime cafe and a surf-rental outlet (boards from ¥3000; cafe and rental closed Wednesday). Rooms are mainly Japanese style, with one Western option. All are clean and very convenient for surfers or sunbathers: just cross the street and you're at the beach. No English is spoken, but the owners are friendly and warm.

The cafe (mains ¥600 to ¥700, lunch set ¥850, open 11am to 3pm) does curry rice, *chikin nanban* (sweet fried chicken served with tartar sauce) and other simple dishes.

Eating

Aoshima Beach Park FOOD HALL ¥¥
(青島ビーチパーク; ☎0985-65-1055; www.aoshimabeachpark.com; 2-233 Aoshima; prices vary; ⏲11am-6pm Mon-Fri, to 7pm Sat & Sun late Apr-Jul & Sep-early Oct, 9am-9pm Aug; P 👪) In a nation with lots of sea coast but precious little recreational beachfront, this new spot along the promenade facing Aoshima Island is a breath of fresh air. There's a hipster-friendly outdoor food court of pop-up restaurants in renovated shipping containers (check website for current offerings) and picnic-table seating. In peak season, nighttime might bring DJ events and fireworks.

Minato Aoshima SEAFOOD ¥¥
(港あおしま; ☎0985-65-1044; 3-5-1 Aoshima; set menus ¥1100-1700; ⏲11am-2.30pm Tue-Sun) Overlooking the port, and owned and run by the local fishermen's collective, this take-your-shoes-off spot offers some of the finest and freshest seafood that Aoshima has to offer. Most meals are sets such as *kaisen-don* (raw seafood over rice) and *ise-ebi* (with several side dishes and miso soup).

Information

Aoshima Tourist Information (青島観光インフォメーション; ☎0985-65-1121; Aoshiymaya, 2-12-1 Aoshima; ⏲9.30am-3.30pm) Inside the new tourist complex Aoshimaya, which also offers restaurants and souvenir and snack shops.

Getting There & Away

Aoshima is on the JR Nichinan line from Miyazaki (¥370, 30 minutes). It's about 800m to the island from the station.

Buses from Miyazaki Station stop at Aoshima (¥720, 48 minutes, hourly) en route to Udo-jingū (¥1480); the Visit Miyazaki bus pass (p781) also covers Aoshima.

Nichinan Coast

The palm-lined stretch of coastal road from Aoshima to Toi-misaki (都井岬; Cape Toi) via the town of Nichinan (日南) is a rewarding drive, with seaside cliffs and views of the islands reminiscent of gumdrops and camels. On sunny days the light pierces the water and turns it an electric-blue colour, making for lovely photos at nearly every turn. Cape Toi and Kō-jima are popular destinations. En route is **Koigaura-hama** (Koigaura Beach), where the *surf-zoku* (surf tribe) hang out.

If you turn inland, drive slowly: several bands of wild monkeys inhabit the mountains, and it's often possible to see them. Earthworms the size of garter snakes are another curious denizen.

Udo-jingū SHINTŌ SHRINE
(鵜戸神宮; ☎0987-29-1001; 3232 Ōaza Miyaura) Reached via a coastal path, this brightly painted Shintō shrine occupies an open cavern overlooking unusual rock formations in the cove below. In 2017 the Japanese government designated it a site of special scenic beauty. It's protocol to buy five *undama* (luck stones; ¥100), make a wish, and try to hit the shallow depression on top of the turtle-shaped rock.

Men use their left hand, women their right, when making the throw. Wishes are usually related to marriage, childbirth and lactation, because the boulders in front of the cavern are said to represent Emperor Jimmu's grandmother's breasts (no, really!).

Hourly buses from Aoshima (¥1010, 36 minutes) and Miyazaki (¥1480, 1½ hours) stop on the highway. From the bus stop, it's about a 700m walk to the shrine past interesting rock formations and picturesque fishing boats.

Far and away the best transport option for this area is a rental car, as you'll want to stop at nearly every corner to take photographs. You can be dropped off by bus at Cape Toi, but the park is vast and driving is perhaps the best – or only realistic – way to get around.

Obi

☎0987

In the quaint town of Obi (飫肥), nicknamed 'Little Kyoto', the wealthy Ito clan ruled from Obi castle for 14 generations from 1587, somehow surviving the 'one kingdom, one castle' ruling in 1615. The castle-ruin area is now the main tourist attraction.

It's also worth exploring the *joka-machi* (area below the castle), which has photogenic streetscapes, streetside canals so clean that carp can swim in them, and a historic shopping thoroughfare.

Purchase the Eatabout/Walkabout Map (in Japanese: あゆみちゃんのマップ, Ayumi-chan no mappu; with/without museum combination ticket ¥1200/700), and at numbered buildings around town you can exchange tear-off tickets on the map for snacks or craft or gift items. The best part of it is getting to know the local people in the process.

Sleeping

Kiraku RENTAL HOUSE ¥¥¥

(季楽; ☎0987-25-1905; www.nazuna.co; 8-1-48 Obi; tw ¥29,000; P ❄ 📶) Cheap it isn't, but how often can you stay in a samurai house? This large (100 sq metre) former castle guard house has been renovated in Japanese minimalist-modernist style (dark wood, stone floors, kitchen, cypress bathtub) and sleeps up to six, with options for futons or beds. It's a real retreat, and the owner provides a list of local restaurants.

Arrangements are handled out of Komura Kinenkan Museum. Prices do not include tax.

Eating

Many of the historic buildings in the central area are now lovely restaurants and cafes, most with English menus. The region is Japan's largest source of line-caught *katsuo* (bonito), served in restaurants throughout town. Fried fish-paste 'tempura' is another local speciality, so tasty it's almost addictive. Most eating spots have English menus.

Obiten JAPANESE ¥

(おび天; ☎0987-25-5717; 9-1-8 Obi; mains ¥600-1050, set meals ¥1100-1360; ⏲9am-5pm) By **Obi-jō** (飫肥城; ☎0987-25-4533; single building/combined ticket/with eatabout-walkabout pass ¥200/610/1200; ⏲9am-4.30pm), this old-school shop makes and sells a local version of *Satsuma-age* (fried cakes of fish paste and vegetables, here called *tempura*). The signature Obiten with udon is ¥900.

Gallery Kodama JAPANESE ¥¥

(ギャラリーこだま; ☎0987-25-0602; 8-1-1 Obi; bonito set meal ¥1500; ⏲11am-3pm Wed-Mon) Try local bonito multiple ways in a set meal called *katsuoaburi-ju*. Bonito in two marinades can be eaten raw, grilled over your own tiny hibachi or nestled over broth with rice and condiments – or all three; instructions are provided in English. The antique-filled house has been in the same family for nine generations.

Look for the white-stucco-and-brown-lattice building on the main road, by the road sign for Nichinan Dam Park.

Information

Obi Castle Tourist Information (飫肥城観光案内; ☎0987-25-3308; ⏲9.30am-4.30pm)

Getting There & Away

The JR Nichinan line connects Obi with Miyazaki (*kaisoku* ¥940, 65 minutes) via Aoshima (¥560, 40 minutes). From Obi Station, it's a 10- to 15-minute walk to the castle. Buses from Miyazaki (¥2080, 2¼ hours, last return bus 4pm) stop below the castle entrance.

Rent bikes (¥500 per day) in the castle parking lot and at JR Obi Station.

AT A GLANCE

POPULATION
Naha: 319,000

SMALLEST INHABITED ISLAND
Tonaki-jima

BEST LOCAL MARKET
Daichi Makishi Kōsetsu Ichiba (p803)

BEST SURF LODGE
Pension Green Hill (p796)

BEST OKINAWAN FOOD
Yūnangi (p806)

WHEN TO GO

May–Jun Coincides with rainy season; while not too intense, sunshine may be scarce.

Jul–Sep Best time to enjoy the beaches, but expect big crowds and increasingly frequent typhoons.

Oct–Mar Water is cooler but swimmable, and you'll have entire beaches to yourself.

Kabira Bay (p822), Ishigaki-jima
LEUNGCHOPAN/SHUTTERSTOCK ©

Okinawa & the Southwest Islands

Collectively known as the Southwest Islands, the Nansei-shotō (南西諸島) comprises several chains of semitropical, coral-fringed isles far removed from the concerns of mainland life, where the slow pace and unique cultural heritage of the former Ryūkyū kingdom endures, offering a vibrant contrast to Japan's focus on modernity and technology.

Since WWII, Okinawa-hontō, the region's biggest island, has been appropriated by the US military for several key installations in the Pacific. Okinawa's bustling capital Naha and the sprawling resorts further north draw steady streams of shopping, sun-seeking and honeymooning tourists from neighbouring Asian nations.

INCLUDES

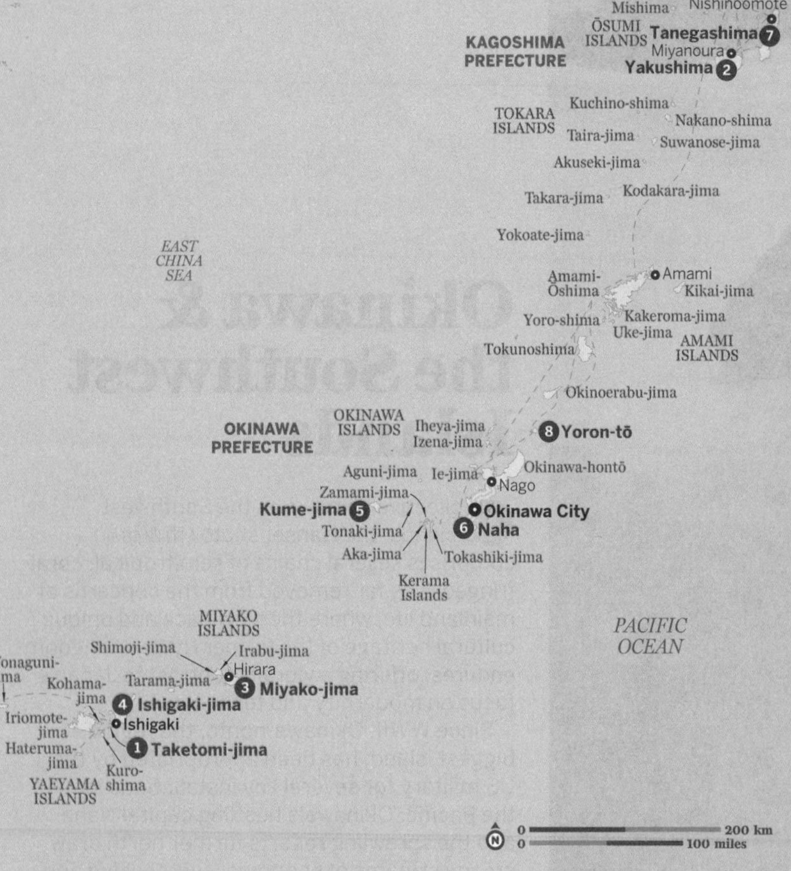

Okinawa & the Southwest Islands Highlights

1. **Kaiji-hama** (p828) Seeking star-sand on the time-warp island of Taketomi-jima.
2. **Jōmon-sugi** (p789) Hiking to this ancient cedar tree in Yakushima.
3. **Sunayama Beach** (p815) Snorkelling among corals on the most beautiful beach on Miyako-jima.
4. **Sunset Beach** (p822) Swimming in the azure waters of this Ishigaki-jima beach.
5. **Bade Haus Kumejima** (p813) Soaking in mineral-rich water in this oceanfront onsen (of sorts), on Kume-jima.
6. **Naha** (p800) Discovering Okinawa's wartime past, rich cultural heritage and significance in US-Japanese politics.
7. **Space Science & Technology Museum** (p794) Discovering the Japanese space programme on Tanegashima.
8. **Yoron Minzoku-mura** (p799) Learning the local lingo in this Ryūkyūan cultural centre on Yoron-tō.

History

After centuries ruled by *aji* (local chieftains), in 1429 Okinawa and the Southwest Islands were united by Sho Hashi of the Chūzan kingdom, which led to the establishment of the Ryūkyū dynasty. During this period, Sho Hashi increased contact with China, which contributed to the flourishing of Okinawan music, dance, literature and ceramics. In this 'Golden Era' weapons were prohibited, and the islands were rewarded with peace and tranquillity.

But the Ryūkyū kingdom was not prepared for war when the Shimazu clan of Satsuma (modern-day Kagoshima) invaded in 1609. The Shimazu conquered the kingdom easily and established severe controls over its trade. The islands were controlled with an iron fist, and taxed and exploited greedily for the next 250 years.

With the restoration of the Meiji emperor, the Ryūkyūs were annexed to Japan as Okinawa Prefecture in 1879. However, life hardly changed for the islanders as they were treated as foreign subjects by the Japanese government. Furthermore, the Meiji government stamped out local culture by outlawing the teaching of Ryūkyū history in schools, and establishing Japanese as the official language.

In the closing days of WWII, the Japanese military made a decision to use the islands of Okinawa as a shield against Allied forces. This cost the islanders dearly: more than 100,000 Okinawan civilians lost their lives in the Battle of Okinawa.

Following the war, the occupation of the Japanese mainland ended in 1952, but Okinawa remained under US control until 1972. Its return was contingent upon Japan agreeing to allow the Americans to maintain bases on the islands; and some 30,000 American military personnel remain today.

Climate

The Southwest Islands have a subtropical climate. With the exception of the peaks of Yakushima, which can be snow-capped between December and February, there's no real winter. You can comfortably travel the Southwest Islands any time of year, but swimming might be uncomfortable between late October and early May, unless you're the hardy sort.

In December the average daily temperature on Okinawa-hontō is 19°C, while it is 29.4°C in July. The islands of Kagoshima Prefecture average a few degrees cooler, while the Yaeyama and Miyako Islands are a few degrees warmer, although they often feel less hot and humid than Okinawa due to the prevailing sea breezes.

The islands are most crowded during June, July and August and during the Golden Week holiday in early May. Outside of these times, the islands are often blissfully quiet.

The main thing to keep in mind when planning a trip to the Southwest Islands is the possibility of typhoons, which have been increasing in frequency and intensity in recent years and can strike any time between June and October. If you go then, build flexibility into your schedule, as typhoons often cause transport delays.

Ideally purchase tickets that allow changes without incurring a fee. The website of the Japan Meteorological Agency (www.jma.go.jp/en/typh) has the latest details on typhoons approaching Japan.

Language

Although the Ryūkyū Islands used to have their own distinctive languages, by and large these have disappeared. Standard Japanese is spoken by most islanders, though perhaps with some strong regional dialects and intonations. You might also hear some Okinawan phrases, such as *mensōre* ('welcome') instead of the standard Japanese *yōkoso* – or *nifei dēbiru* instead of *arigatō*.

ℹ Information

SAFE TRAVEL

Every swimming beach you visit on any of the main islands will alert you to the potential dangers of marine stingers, the likes of box jellyfish (ハブくらげ; *habu kurage*) and venomous snakes – also called *habu* – the latter, being a kind of viper unique to the Ryūkyū islands whose bite can be deadly. But what are the risks? The answer to that question, of course, depends on who you talk to.

Between them the Southwest Islands have hundreds of kilometres of mostly spectacular coastline and visitors are told they should only swim in the netted areas of designated 'swimming' beaches, but that precludes many of the 'secret' beaches that you might come across on your own intrepid explorations. The venom of the box jellyfish is capable of causing paralysis and cardiac arrest in humans and, at least, an incredibly painful sting.

Deaths caused by both box jellyfish stings and *habu* snakebites are uncommon, but the threat is real and shouldn't be treated lightly. Wherever possible, do swim in netted areas, and if you just *must* swim in a non-patrolled zone, be sure to check with locals if jellyfish are about. Camp cautiously and wear covered shoes if you plan to be traipsing through long grass and if you find yourself feeling like you've been bitten or stung, seek help immediately.

Getting There & Away

AIR

There are flights on Japan's big two airlines, Japan Airlines (JAL) and All Nippon Airways (ANA) between major cities in mainland Japan and Amami-Ōshima, Okinawa-hontō, Miyako-jima and Ishigaki-jima. Kagoshima has flights to/from all these islands and many of the smaller islands as well. Other islands such as Yonaguni-jima and Kume-jima can be reached from Naha or Ishigaki. In recent years, a number of low-cost airlines have commenced services from a variety of cities into Naha and a handful of other island destinations. It pays to shop around and explore different route combinations before you travel.

BOAT

Ferries run from Osaka/Kōbe and Kagoshima to the Amami Islands and Okinawa-hontō, and are plentiful between Kagoshima and Yakushima and Tanegashima. Once you arrive in a port such as Naze on Amami-Ōshima or Naha on Okinawa-hontō, there are local ferry services to nearby islands. However, you cannot reach the Miyako Islands or Yaeyama Islands by ferry from mainland Japan or Okinawa-hontō; it's necessary to fly to these destinations.

OKINAWA AIR PASSES

If you are arriving in Japan by air, there are a number of flight passes available that offer excellent savings on flights to/from and around the Southwest Islands. As a general rule, tickets are non-changeable and non-refundable, though some exceptions apply. Some of the better passes and fares available at time of writing, include the below,

Japan Explorer Pass & ANA Experience Japan Fare

Carrier Japan Explorer Pass: Japan Airlines (JAL), Japan Transocean Air (JTA), Ryukyu Air Commuter (RAC); Experience Japan Fare: All Nippon Airways (ANA)

Restrictions Both JAL and ANA groups have a competitive pass with similar conditions. The passenger must provide evidence of an international ticket to & from Japan on any international carrier. Route restrictions apply, though many popular routes are available. Japan Explorer Pass tickets can be purchased online, even when you're in Japan, as they are issued by JAL's ticket office in the US. For ANA's offering, tickets must be issued at least 72hr prior to departure.

Popular routes Naha–Miyako-jima, Naha–Kumejima, Nagoya–Naha, Amami-Ōshima–Fukuoka (JAL); Takamatsu–Naha, Hiroshima–Naha (ANA)

Price Flight sectors ¥5400, ¥7560 and ¥10,800, route dependent.

Visit Japan Fare

Carrier All Nippon Airways (ANA)

Restrictions A minimum of 2 flights (sectors) and a maximum of 5 can be purchased at the discounted rate on any ANA route, by non-residents of Japan. Proof of inbound and outbound carriage on any airline is required. Ticket must be issued outside Japan. Routing restrictions do not apply.

Popular routes Sapporo–Naha, Osaka (Itami)–Naha, Nagoya–Ishigaki

Price ¥13,000 per sector (minimum 2 sectors = from ¥26,000).

ENJOY Japan Fare

Carrier Solaseed Air (SNJ)

Restrictions Passenger must not reside in Japan & must hold an outbound international ticket on any carrier.

Popular routes Kagoshima–Naha, Tokyo (Haneda)–Miyako-jima

Price Route specific and subject to availability; fares as low as ¥8900.

Getting Around

While regular ferry and hydrofoil services are the most common way to island-hop, air travel is becoming a more popular and affordable way to get between islands. Most inter-island services are operated by JTA/JAC – subsidiaries of Japan Airlines – and to a lesser extent, ANA.

JTA offers the Okinawa Island Pass, an inter-island air-pass that must be purchased outside Japan and with proof of onward travel – sorry, expats. It offers up to five inter-island flights (between Okinawa-hontō, Miyako-jima, Ishigaki-jima and Kume-jima only), representing substantial savings from standard domestic airfares purchased within Japan. Fares are route specific, have limited availability and must be issued by a travel agency or Japan Airlines branch office, outside Japan, at least 72 hours prior to departure.

While most islands have public bus systems, there are usually not more than a few buses per day on each route. We recommend bringing an International Driving Permit and renting a car or scooter, particularly on Ishigaki, Miyako, Kume and Yakushima.

On Okinawa-hontō, driving in Naha can be a real drag, with horrible traffic congestion and slow speed limits. If you're only planning on exploring the city itself, you'll find local public transport – although not as widespread and user-friendly as many other Japanese cities – is often the best option.

Renting a car is advised for exploration of the island beyond the city itself.

ŌSUMI ISLANDS

The Ōsumi Islands (大隈諸島) comprise the two main islands of Yakushima and Tanegashima and the seldom-visited triumvirate of islands known as Mishima-mura. The all-star attraction in the group is World Heritage–protected Yakushima, known in Japan as a 'power-spot' (パワースポット; *pawā supotto*) for its ancient cedar trees. The island, most easily accessed from Kagoshima city, is a paradise for hikers and nature lovers, enticing large numbers of domestic and international visitors every year.

Neighbouring Tanegashima's claim to fame is as the home of Japan's space program, but despite being a popular surfing destination for domestic surfers, the island sees relatively few foreign travellers.

Yakushima

0997 / POP 13,178

If you're a nature lover or an avid hiker, Yakushima (屋久島), designated a Unesco World Heritage Site in 1993, is one of the most rewarding islands in the Southwest Islands. The craggy mountain peaks of the island's interior are home to the world-famous *yakusugi* (屋久杉; *Cryptomeria japonica*), ancient cedar trees that are said to have been the inspiration for some of the scenes in Miyazaki Hayao's animation classic *Princess Mononoke*.

Keep in mind that Yakushima is a place of extremes: the mountains wring every last drop of moisture from the passing clouds and the interior of the island is one of the wettest places in Japan. In the winter the peaks may be covered in snow, while the coast is still relatively balmy. Whatever you do, come prepared and don't set off on a hike without a good map and the proper gear.

Sights

Yakushima's main port is **Miyanoura** (宮之浦), on the island's northeast coast. This is the most convenient place to be based, as most buses originate from here. From Miyanoura, a road runs around the perimeter of the island, passing through the secondary port of **Anbō** (安房), on the east coast, and then through the hot-springs town of **Onoaida** (尾之間) in the south. Heading north from Miyanoura, the road takes you to the town of **Nagata** (永田), which has a brilliant stretch of white-sand beach.

★ Jōmon-sugi LANDMARK

(縄文杉) FREE This enormous *yakusugi* tree is estimated to be between 3000 and 7000 years old, and though no longer living, it remains a majestic sight. Most hikers reach the tree via the 19.5km, eight to 10-hour round trip from **Arakawa-tozanguchi** (Arakawa trailhead; 荒川登山口).

Yakusugi Museum MUSEUM

(屋久杉自然館; 0997-46-3113; www.yakusugi-museum.com; 273 9343 Anbō; adult/child ¥600/400; 9am-5pm, closed 1st Tue of the month) In a forested spot with sea views, the Yakusugi Museum has informative, beautifully designed exhibits about *yakusugi* and the history of the islanders' relationship to these magnificent trees. The museum offers

Yakushima

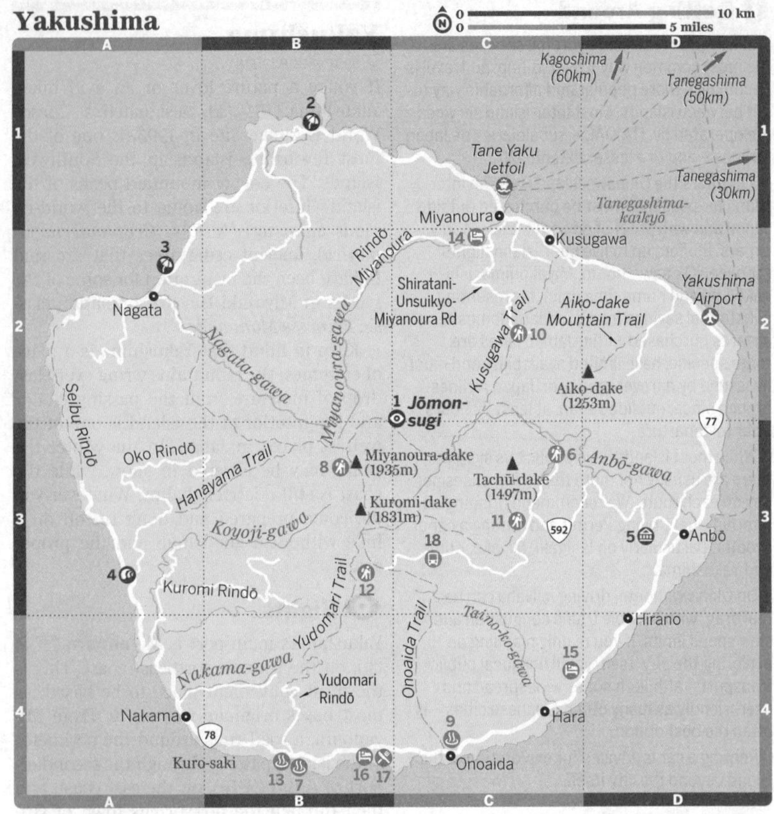

Yakushima

Top Sights
1 Jōmon-sugi C2

Sights
2 Issō-kaisuiyokujō B1
3 Nagata Inaka-hama A2
4 Ōko-no-taki A3
Umigame-kan .... (see 3)
5 Yakusugi Museum D3

Activities, Courses & Tours
6 Arakawa-tozanguchi Hike C3
7 Hirauchi Kaichū Onsen B4
8 Miyanoura-dake Hike B3
9 Onoaida Onsen C4
10 Shiratani-unsuikyō-tozanguchi Hike C2
11 Yakusugi Land C3
12 Yodogawa-tozanguchi Hike B3
13 Yudomari Onsen B4

Sleeping
14 Lodge Yaedake-sansō C2
15 Sankara Hotel & Spa C4
Sōyōtei .... (see 3)
16 Yakushima South Village B4

Eating
17 Naa Yuu Cafe B4

Transport
Arakawa Mountain Bus Stop .... (see 5)
18 Kigen-sugi Bus Stop C3

an excellent audio guide in English. It's conveniently located on the road leading up to Yakusugi Land. Two daily buses run to and from Miyanoura (¥960, 80 minutes, March to November).

Ōko-no-taki WATERFALL
(大川の滝) On the west coast is Yakushima's highest waterfall, at 88m. It's a five-minute walk from Ōko-no-taki bus stop, which is the last stop for some of the buses running south and west from Miyanoura and Anbō

(note that only two buses a day run all the way out here).

Nagata Inaka-hama BEACH

(永田いなか浜) On the island's northwest coast, Nagata Inaka-hama is a beautiful beach for sunsets, and it's where sea turtles lay their eggs from May to July. It's beside the Inaka-hama bus stop, served by Nagata-bound buses from Miyanoura.

Umigame-kan MUSEUM

(うみがめ館; ☎0997-49-6550; 489-8 Nagata; ¥300; ⏲9am-5pm Wed-Mon) This nonprofit organisation has displays and information about turtles, mostly in Japanese. During nesting (June and July) and hatching (August) seasons, it arranges night tours on the beach. In order to protect the nesting turtles, eggs and hatchlings, it is imperative that visitors go with a sanctioned tour.

Activities

Hiking

Hiking is the best way to experience Yakushima's beauty. The most popular hike is the long day trip up to Jōmon-sugi (p789) and back, but there are other attractive alternatives. Yakusugi Land is designed for casual hikers.

Even though trails can be very crowded during holidays, be sure to alert someone at your accommodation of your intended route and fill in a *tōzan todokede* (route plan) at the trailhead.

With Yakushima being one of the wettest places on Earth, it rains *a lot* in the island's interior. Be sure to prepare adequately for hiking rainforests in which you may find yourself slogging through torrential rain for a whole day. **Nakagawa Sports** (ナカガワスポーツ; ☎0997-42-0341; www.yakushima-sp.com; 421-6 Miyanoura; ⏲9am-7pm, closed every other Wed) in Miyanoura rents out everything from rainwear and waterproof hiking boots (also in large sizes) to tents and baby carriers.

★Shiratani-unsuikyō-tozanguchi Hike HIKING

(白谷雲水峡登山口; ¥300) Although the long day trek to Jōmon-sugi (p789) is the most famous in Yakushima, the shorter Shiratani-unsuikyō hike is arguably more beautiful, passing waterfalls, moss-lined rocks and towering *yakusugi* to the overlook at **Taiko-iwa**. The trailhead (622m) is served by up to 10 daily buses to and from Miyanoura (¥550, 40 minutes, March to November). Allow three or four hours for this hike.

The ¥300 entrance fee goes towards trail maintenance and gets you a walking map.

Yodogawa-tozanguchi Hike HIKING

(Yodogawa trailhead; 淀川登山口) Trailhead (1370m) for summiting Miyanoura-dake, the highest point in southern Japan. The trailhead is about 1.5km (about 30 minutes) beyond the Kigen-sugi bus stop, served by two buses a day to/from Anbō (¥940, one hour).

Miyanoura-dake Hike HIKING

The granddaddy of hikes here is the day-long outing to the 1935m summit of Miyanoura-dake, the highest point in southern Japan. Fit climbers should allow about seven hours return from Yodogawa-tozanguchi.

The Yodogawa trailhead is about 1.5km (about 30 minutes) beyond the **Kigen-sugi bus stop**, served by two buses a day to/from Anbō (¥940, one hour). The buses do not give you sufficient time to complete the round trip in a day – an early-morning taxi from Miyanoura (around ¥11,000) gives you time to make the second bus back to Anbō. Of course, renting a car gives you maximum flexibility on timing your hike.

Yakusugi Land HIKING

(ヤクスギランド; ☎0997-42-3508; www.y-rekumori.com; 1593 Miyanoura; ¥300; ⏲9am-5pm) A great way to see some *yakusugi* without a long trek into the forest, Yakusugi Land offers shorter hiking courses over wooden boardwalks, and longer hikes deep into the ancient cedar forest. There are four buses a day to and from Anbō (¥740, 40 minutes).

Onsen

Yakushima has several onsen, from beautifully desolate seaside pools to upmarket hotel facilities. Seaside onsen here are typically *konyoku* (mixed bathing) where swimsuits are not allowed; women traditionally wrap themselves in a thin towel for modesty.

★Yudomari Onsen ONSEN

(湯泊温泉; 1714-28 Yudomari; ¥100; ⏲24hr) This blissfully serene onsen at the ocean's edge can be entered at any tide. Get off at the Yudomari bus stop and take the road opposite the post office in the direction of the sea. Once you enter the village, the way is marked. It's a 300m walk and you pass a great banyan tree en route.

Hirauchi Kaichū Onsen ONSEN
(平内海中温泉; ☎0997-43-5900; Hirauchi, Kumage; ¥100; ⏲24hr) Onsen lovers will be in heaven here. The outdoor baths are in the rocks by the sea and can only be entered at or close to low tide. You can walk to the baths from the Kaichū Onsen bus stop, but the next stop, Nishikaikon, is actually closer. From Nishikaikon, walk downhill towards the sea for about 200m and take a right at the bottom of the hill.

Onoaida Onsen ONSEN
(尾之間温泉; ☎0997-47-2872; 1293 Onoaida; ¥200; ⏲7am-9.30pm May-Oct, to 9pm Nov-Apr, from noon Mon) In the village of Onoaida, about 350m uphill from the Onoaida Onsen bus stop, rub shoulders with the village elders at this rustic indoor bathhouse. BYO everything and ease slowly into the divine, naturally hot water.

Sleeping

The most convenient place to be based is Miyanoura. You'll also find lodgings in larger villages and several bare-bones *yama-goya* (mountain huts) in the mountains. In July, August and the spring Golden Week holiday, it's best to reserve ahead since places fill up early.

Yakushima South Village HOSTEL ¥
(屋久島サウスビレッジ; ☎0997-47-3751; www.yakushima-yh.net; 258-24 Hirauchi; dm/s/d from ¥3500/4500/6500; P❄@📶) This well-run youth hostel is about 3km west of Onoaida, nestled into the forest. Accommodation is in either Japanese- or Western-style dorms, and the shared kitchen and bathroom facilities are spotless. Get off any southbound buses from Miyanoura at the Hirauchi-iriguchi bus stop and take the road towards the sea for about 200m.

Yakushima Youth Hostel HOSTEL ¥
(屋久島ユースホステル; ☎0997-49-1316; www.yakushima-yh.net; 278-2 Miyanoura; dm/d from ¥3800/4400; P❄@📶) This simple and clean youth hostel doesn't offer meals, but there are several good restaurants close by. It's a 10-minute walk from Miyanoura port – turn left off the main port road and veer left after passing the portside park; it's about 100m further. Its sister property, Yakushima South Village is predictably on the south side.

★**Sōyōtei** RYOKAN ¥¥
(送陽邸; ☎0997-45-2819; www.soyotei.net; 521-4 Nagata; r per person incl meals from ¥13,650; P❄) On the northwest coast near Nagata Inaka-hama, this gorgeous, family-run guesthouse has a collection of semidetached units that boast private verandahs and ocean views. The traditional structures feature rooftops unique to Yakushima, with stones anchoring the roof tiles – you'll recognise the place immediately. There are several baths for private use, including an outdoor bath overlooking the crashing waves.

Lovely seafood-focused meals are served in a communal, open-air dining room that looks out over Inaka-hama and the sea.

Lodge Yaedake-sansō LODGE ¥¥
(ロッジ八重岳山荘; ☎0997-42-1551; www.yaedake.jp; Miyanoura; r per person incl meals from ¥8100; P⊖❄📶) This secluded accommodation features Japanese- and Western-style rooms in rustic riverside cabins connected by wooden walkways. Soak up the beauty of your surroundings in the communal baths; children will enjoy splashing in the river. Meals served in the tatami dining room are balanced and exquisite. The lodge is located inland on the Miyanoura-gawa; staff can pick you up in Miyanoura.

The lodge also runs the **Minshuku Yaedake Honkan** (民宿八重岳本館; ☎0997-42-2552; www.yaedake.jp/minshuku; 208 Miyanoura; r per person incl meals from ¥6800; P❄) in town.

Sankara Hotel & Spa HOTEL ¥¥¥
(☎0997-47-3488, toll-free 0800-800-6007; www.sankarahotel-spa.com; 553 Haginoue, Mugio; r per person incl breakfast from ¥39,000; P❄@📶≋) 🍃 Overlooking Yakushima's southeast coast, this stunning collection of luxury villas blends ocean views with Balinese design elements. Sustainable practices at Sankara include all water used on the property being sourced from mountain run-off, and the restaurant utilising as much local and organic produce as possible, much of which is grown expressly for the hotel. Guests 15 years and older only.

Eating

There are a few restaurants in each of the island's villages, with the best selection in Miyanoura. If you're staying anywhere but Miyanoura, request the set two-meal plan at your lodgings. If you're going hiking, you can ask your lodging to prepare a *bentō* (boxed meal) the night before you set out.

Naa Yuu Cafe CAFE ¥

(なーゆーカフェ; ☎0997-49-3195; http://charu.air-nifty.com/naayuu/naa-yuu-cafe.html; 349-109 Hirauchi; lunch sets ¥850-1280; ⊙11.30am-7pm Wed-Sun) Down a dirt road and facing a field of wild reeds, this cute cafe feels vaguely Hawaiian. The menu, however, leans more toward Thailand. Lunch sets range from red curry to Kagoshima black-pork-sausage pizza, and the fresh, homemade breads are dreamy. Look for a green sign in English, about 3km west of Onoaida.

Yakuden SUPERMARKET ¥

(ヤクデン; ☎997-42-1501; 1197-1 Miyanoura; ⊙9am-10pm) Stock up on provisions for camping or hiking at this supermarket on the main street in Miyanoura, just north of the entrance to the pier area.

Shiosai SEAFOOD ¥¥

(潮騒; ☎0997-42-2721; 305-3 Miyanoura; dishes ¥450-1100; ⊙11.30am-2pm & 5.30-9.30pm Fri-Wed) Find a full range of Japanese standards such as *sashimi teishoku* (sashimi set; ¥1700) or *ebi-furai teishoku* (fried shrimp set; ¥1400). Look for the blue and whitish building with automatic glass doors along the main road through Miyanoura.

Information

The best place to get money on Yakushima is at one of the island's post offices, the most convenient of which is **Kamiyaku Post Office** (上屋久郵便局; ☎0997-42-0042; 126 Miyanoura; ⊙9am-5pm Mon-Sat, to noon Sun) in Miyanoura.

Anbō Tourist Office (安房観光案内所; ☎0997-46-2333; www.yakukan.jp; 410-155 Anbō; ⊙9am-4pm) Just north of the river, this is full of helpful information.

Miyanoura Tourist Information Centre (宮之浦観光案内所; ☎0997-42-1019; www.yakukan.jp; 823-1 Miyanoura; ⊙9am-5pm) A helpful office on the road leading away from the port; you can't miss its dramatic architecture. Staff here can help you find lodgings and answer all questions about the island.

Getting There & Away

AIR

Flights to Yakushima are expensive and the island is often excluded as a potential routing on many low-cost air-passes.

Japan Air Commuter (JAC) has regular scheduled services between Yakushima and Osaka, Fukuoka and Kagoshima.

SEA TURTLES ON YAKUSHIMA

Loggerhead sea turtles and green sea turtles come ashore on the beaches of Yakushima to lay their eggs. Unfortunately, human activity can significantly interfere with the egg-laying process. Thus we recommend that you keep the following rules in mind when visiting the beaches of Yakushima (particularly those on the northwest coast):

- Never approach a sea turtle that has come ashore.
- Do not start fires on the beach as the light will confuse the hatchlings (who use moonlight to orient themselves). Likewise, do not shine torches (flashlights) or car headlights at or near the beach.
- Do not walk on the beach at night.
- Be extremely careful when you walk on the beach, as you might inadvertently step on a newly hatched turtle.
- If you want to observe the turtles, enquire at Umigame-kan (p791).

Yakushima Airport (屋久島空港; ☎0997-42-1200) is on the northeastern coast between Miyanoura and Anbō. Hourly buses stop at the airport, though you may be able to arrange pick-up in advance from your accommodation.

BOAT

Hydrofoil services operate between Kagoshima and Yakushima, some of which stop at Tanegashima en route. **Tane Yaku Jetfoil** (☎in Kagoshima 099-226-0128, in Miyanoura 0997-42-2003; www.tykousoku.jp; ⊙8.30am-5.30pm Mon-Fri, to 7pm Sat & Sun) runs six Toppy and Rocket hydrofoils per day between Kagoshima (leaving from the high-speed ferry terminal just to the south of Minamifutō pier) and Miyanoura (¥9000, one hour 50 minutes for direct sailings, two hours 40 minutes with a stop in Tanegashima). There are also two hydrofoils per day between Kagoshima and Anbō Port (2½ hours) on Yakushima. Booking ahead is wise.

The regular ferry **Yakushima 2** (屋久島２フェリー; ☎099-266-0731; www.ferryyakusima2.com/index.html) sails from Kagoshima's Minamifutō pier for Yakushima's Miyanoura port (one way/return ¥4900/8900). It leaves at 8.30am and takes four hours.

The **Hibiscus** (フェリーはいびすかす; ☎099-261-7000; www.yakushimaferry.com) also sails between Kagoshima and Yakushima, leaving at

6pm, stopping overnight in Tanegashima, and arriving at Miyanoura at 7am the following day. Fares vary by routing. Reservations aren't usually necessary for this ferry, which usually departs from Kagoshima's Taniyama pier.

Local buses travel the coastal road part way around Yakushima roughly every hour or two, though only a few head up into the interior. Your best bet is to rent a car from the port.

Getting Around

Local buses travel the coastal road part way around Yakushima roughly every hour or two, though only a few head up into the interior.

You'll save a lot of money by purchasing a Yakushima Kotsu Free Pass, which is good for unlimited travel on Yakushima Kotsu buses. One-/two-day passes cost ¥2000/3000 and are available at the airport, the Anbō port and the tourist information centre in Miyanoura.

Hikers should note that from March through November, in order to limit traffic congestion and environmental impact, all hikers must transfer to an **Arakawa Mountain Bus** (round trip ¥1740) from the Yakusugi Museum parking lot to get to the Arakawa-tozanguchi. You must buy a ticket at least a day in advance; also note that this fare is not covered by the one- or two-day bus passes.

Hitching is also possible, but an International Driving Permit will vastly increase your enjoyment here, as buses are few and far between. **Toyota Rent-a-Car** (トヨタレンタカー; 0997-42-2000; https://rent.toyota.co.jp; 8am-8pm) is north of the port in Miyanoura.

Tanegashima

0997 / POP 33,000

A long, narrow island about 20km northeast of Yakushima, Tanegashima (種子島) is a laid-back destination popular with Japanese surfers and beach lovers. Home to Japan's Space Centre, Tanegashima was where firearms were first introduced to Japan by shipwrecked Portuguese in 1543. Although good ferry connections make this island easy to pair with a trip to Yakushima, it's often overlooked by time-poor visitors making a beeline for the 'main event'.

The island's main port of **Nishi-no-Omote** (西之表) is on the northwest coast of the island, while the airport is about halfway down the island near the west coast. The best beaches and most of the surf breaks are on the east coast of the island, which is also home to an onsen.

Sights

★ Space Science & Technology Museum MUSEUM
(宇宙科学技術館; 0997-26-9244; http://fanfun.jaxa.jp/visit/tanegashima; Kukinaga, Minamitane-chō; 9.30am-5.30pm Tue-Sun, closed on launch days) FREE Reopened in 2017 after an extensive re-design, Tanegashima's Space Centre, on the spectacular southeastern coast of the island, is a large parklike complex with rocket-launch facilities. Its Space Science & Technology Museum details the history of Japan's space program, with models of Japan's rockets and some of the satellites it has launched (with some English interpretive signage).

Buses running from Nishi-no-Omote all the way to Tanegashima Space Centre take two hours.

Takezaki-kaigan BEACH
(竹崎海岸) Nearby to the Space Centre, this coastline is home to a beautiful stretch of white sand popular with surfers. The best spot to enjoy it is the beach in front of the Iwasaki Hotel (closest bus stop: Iwasaki Hotel), which has some impressive rock formations.

Nagahama-kaigan BEACH
(長浜海岸) The west coast of Tanegashima is home to a 12km stretch of beach known as the Nagahama-*kaigan* (coastline) that is equally popular with diehard surfers and egg-laying sea turtles.

Activities

Akaogi-no-Yu ONSEN
(赤尾木の湯; 0997-22-1555; www.araki-hotel.co.jp; 78 Nishimachi, Nishi-no-Omote; ¥1000; 6am-11pm) Just a five-minute walk from the Nishi-no-Omote port, this sparkling new onsen offers a soothing end to a day of surfing or sunning – BYO towel. Or simply soak your feet in the free foot bath before or after a ferry ride.

Nakatane-chō Onsen Center ONSEN
(中種子町温泉保養センター; 0997-27-9211; 5542 Sakai, Nakatane; ¥300; 11am-8pm Fri-Wed) Bring your own bathing supplies to this ocean-view hot spring at Kumano-kaigan. Floor-to-ceiling one-way glass allows you to soak while enjoying the views of rock formations offshore. The closest bus stop is Kumano-kaisuiyokujō; if driving, follow the signs to Kumano Onsen.

Sleeping & Eating

Most travellers base themselves in the port town of Nishi-no-Omote. If you're staying outside of the town, it's a good idea to book meals with your accommodation.

★ Miharu-sō RYOKAN ¥

(美春荘; ☎0997-22-1393; www.miharuso.jp; 7486-6 Nishi-no-Omote; r per person incl breakfast ¥5500; P ⊖ ❄ ☎) Tidy Japanese-style rooms in this family-run ryokan in Nishi-no-Omote are homely and full of natural light. If you speak Japanese, you can hit up the owner for local info on surf spots. If not, he's likely to point you in the right direction anyway.

Hotel Lexton HOTEL ¥¥

(ホテル・レクストン種子島; ☎0997-22-2000; www.nisikawa.net/lex-tane; 16069 Nishi-no-Omote; s/d from ¥6200/8200) Tanegashima's newest and smartest digs belong to this glorified business hotel, with dark-woody rooms, the latest tech and a convenient location not far from the port.

East Coast BUNGALOW ¥¥

(イーストコースト; ☎0997-25-0763; www.eastcoast.jp; 140-2 Anjō; s/d/tr from ¥2700/5400/8100, large cabin ¥12,960; P) With two homely, fully equipped bungalows near the local break, this place is (as you might guess) on the east coast of Tanegashima. Reservations are essential. The owner is an English-speaking Japanese surfer who also runs a great on-site cafe serving simple favourites like curry and fried shrimp with rice (open from 11am to 6pm, Thursday to Tuesday).

You'll need your own wheels to get to the coast as it's quite a way from town.

Koryōri Shirō IZAKAYA ¥¥

(小料理しろう; ☎0997-23-2117; 24-6 Higashi-chō; dishes ¥400-1100; ⊙5-11pm; ❄) Head to this friendly little *izakaya* (Japanese pub-eatery) in Nishi-no-Omote to sample tasty dishes such as the *sashimi teishoku* (sashimi set; ¥1200). There are plants out the front and blue-and-white *noren* (doorway curtains). It's along the main road east of the post office.

Information

The road from the Nishi-no-Omote pier dead-ends at the **post office** (種子島郵便局; 61-1 Nishimachi; ⊙9.30am-4pm Mon-Fri), which houses an international ATM.

Tanegashima Tourist Information Office (種子島観光案内所; ☎0997-23-0111; ⊙9am-5pm) This helpful office is located at the pier in Nishi-no-Omote, inside the ferry office/waiting room.

Getting There & Away

Six flights to and from Kagoshima (about 30 minutes) on Japan Air Commuter (JAC) land at the **airport** (種子島空港).

Depending on the season, Tane Yaku Jetfoil (p793) runs at least five daily high-speed ferries (¥7100, 1½ hours) between Kagoshima and Tanegashima. Yakushima Ferry operates the Ferry Hibiscus (p793) service each evening between Kagoshima and Tanegashima (¥3700, three hours and 40 minutes).

Getting Around

Unfortunately, the relative lack of buses makes it difficult to enjoy this island without a rental car or scooter, or, at least, a good touring bicycle.

There's a rental-car counter in the arrivals hall of the airport, and a couple of rental agencies outside Nishi-no-Omote port.

DON'T MISS

BEST BEACHES

- Sunset Beach, Ishigaki-jima (p822)
- Sunayama Beach, Miyako-jima (p815)
- Nishibama Beach, Aka-jima (p811)
- Furuzamami Beach, Zamami-jima (p812)

AMAMI ISLANDS

The Amami archipelago (奄美諸島) comprises Kagoshima Prefecture's southernmost islands and boasts excellent beaches and subtropical forests. The main gateway and transport hub, Amami-Ōshima, has seen a surge in popularity in recent years, due to new airline routes, improved ferry connections and tourism infrastructure. The latter includes a handful of fresh, appealing accommodation offerings for the discerning traveller.

Furthest south, tiny Yoron-tō – within sight of Okinawa-hontō – is an important hub for inter-island transport and for the preservation of local language and culture.

Amami-Ōshima

0997 / POP 73,000

Amami-Ōshima (奄美大島), Japan's third-largest offshore island after Okinawa-hontō and Sado-ga-shima, is enjoying a rise in visitor numbers due to improved access and tourism infrastructure. With a mild subtropical climate year-round, the island is home to some unusual flora and fauna, including the endemic Amami black rabbit, tree ferns and mangroves. The coastline of the island is incredibly convoluted – a succession of bays, points and inlets, punctuated by the occasional white-sand beach – and ascends into dense forest, making the island a more complex, interesting alternative to islands further south.

Sights

Amami-Ōshima's main city and port on the north coast is known by locals as both Amami-shi (奄美市) and Naze (名瀬), and it's from here that you'll set off to explore the island by touring bike or rental car. The coastal route to **Uken** (宇検) on the west coast has some lovely stretches. Another option is Rte 58 south to **Koniya** (古仁屋), from where you can continue southeast to the **Honohoshi-kaigan** (ホノホシ海岸), a rocky beach with incredible coastal formations, or catch a ferry to **Kakeroma-jima** (加計呂麻島), a small island with a few shallow beaches; the best beaches are at the northeast end.

Ōhama Seaside Park PARK

(大浜海浜公園, Ōhama-kaihin-kōen; www.michinoshima.jp; 701-1 Nagase Kojuku Ōhama) With forest rolling down to white sand and turquoise water, the Ōhama Seaside Park complex is best known for its lovely beach, which is popular for swimming, snorkelling, sea kayaking and fishing. As it's the closest beach to Naze, it can get crowded during the summer, but it's convenient and spacious. Take an Ōhama-bound bus from Naze and get off at the Ōhama stop (¥400).

Sakibaru Beach BEACH

(崎原ビーチ; 0997-63-0828; 3622 Ōaza Kise, Kasari-chō) This stunner of a beach lies about 4.5km up a point of land just north of Kise (about 20km northeast of Naze). Take a Sani-bound bus from Naze and get off at Kiseura (¥950), and then walk. If you're driving, it's marked in English off the main road (be prepared for *narrow* roads).

Tomori-kaigan BEACH

(土盛海岸; 0997-52-1111; Tomori, Kasari-chō) It's easy to get to this beach, which offers brilliant white sand and some great snorkelling with a channel leading outside the reef. It's about 3km north of the airport. Take a Sani-bound bus from Naze and get off at Tomori (¥1210).

Amami-no-Sato MUSEUM

(奄美の郷; 0997-55-2333; www.amamipark.com; 1834 Setta, Kasari-chō; ¥620; 9am-6pm, to 7pm Jul & Aug, closed 1st & 3rd Wed of the month) Though most displays are in Japanese, there's enough multimedia here to make this cultural and natural-history museum engaging, even for non-Japanese speakers. Musical exhibits, short films documenting island customs, colourful dioramas and an art museum showcasing the work of Tanaka Isson, famed for his paintings of local flora and bird life, bring Amami traditions to life.

Sleeping

Golden Mile Hostel HOSTEL ¥

(0997-58-8366; www.goldenmilehostel.com; 2-6 Naze Sawai-chō; dm/d from ¥2100/6000;) There's a great vibe surrounding this hostel near the ferry terminal, which has excellent dorm and private rooms and a funky bar attracting a friendly crowd. The hostel is located in an old building that has been given a new lease of life with some smart design choices made by young, forward-thinking minds.

Native Sea Amami HOTEL ¥¥

(ネイティブシー奄美; 0997-62-2385; www.native-sea.com; 835 Ashitoku, Tatusgō-chō; r per person incl 2 meals from ¥12,500; P@) This dive centre/resort has comfortable wood-floored Western-style accommodation perched on a promontory over a lovely bay. Guestrooms have gorgeous, sweeping views of the bay and access to a nice, shallow beach below. For a more romantic stay, opt for one of the spacious beachfront rooms at the annexe, the Petit Resort (プチリゾート), about 100m down the road.

Native Sea is about 28km east of Naze (or 3km from the Akaogi bus stop).

Pension Green Hill GUESTHOUSE ¥¥

(ペンショングリーンヒル; 0997-62-5180; www.greenhill-amami.com; 1728-2 Akaogi, Tatsugō-chō; s/d incl 2 meals ¥9720/17,280; P@) A favourite among Japanese surfers, convivial Green Hill has ocean views

Amami-Ōshima

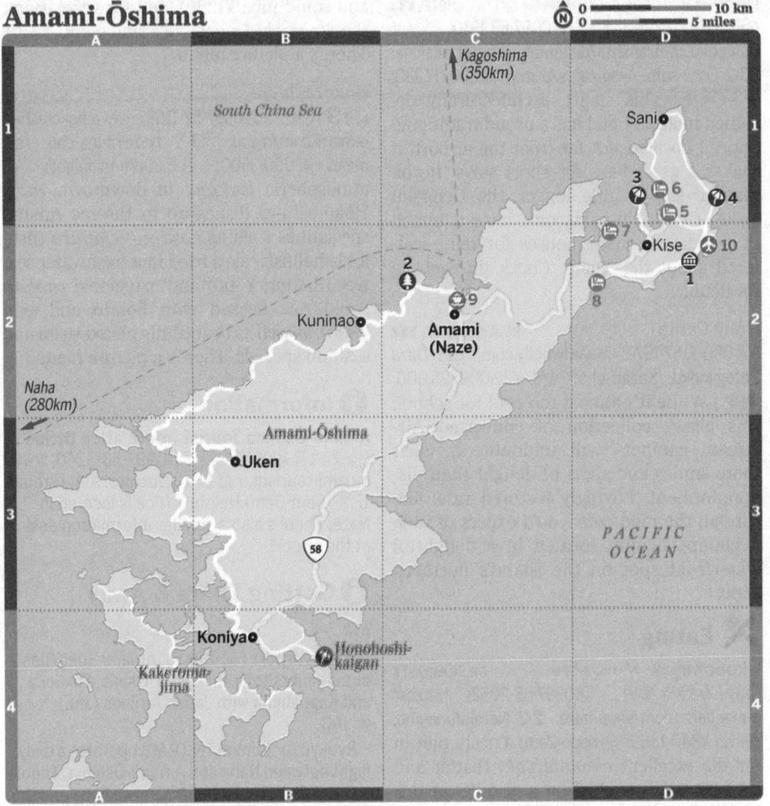

Amami-Ōshima

Sights

1 Amami-no-Sato D2
2 Ōhama Seaside Park C2
3 Sakibaru Beach D1
4 Tomori-kaigan D1

Sleeping

5 Denpaku Hotel Akagina D1
6 Holly Camp D1
7 Native Sea Amami D2
Nest at Amami .... (see 7)
8 Pension Green Hill D2

Transport

9 A Line Ferry C2
10 Amami Airport D2
Marix Line .... (see 9)
Nazeshinko Ferry Terminal .... (see 9)
Times Car Rental .... (see 10)

(including the local surf spot, Tebiro Point) and Japanese- and Western-style rooms, some with lofts. It's about 30 minutes from the airport and a few minutes' walk to the beach. If you ask nicely, you can arrange pick-up in advance.

★ **Nest at Amami** BOUTIQUE HOTEL ¥¥¥
(ネストアット奄美; ☎0997-55-4066; www.nestatamami.com; 800 Ashitoku; villas d per person from ¥19,000) While tightly knitted together, these stunning, architect-designed, fully self-contained waterfront villas retain a sense of privacy and rate among the most noteworthy accommodations in the Southwest Islands for the discerning romantic. They include three dreamy luxury pool villas. Tempted? Check the homepage for more details. A fancy on-site restaurant completes the picture. Priced accordingly.

Denpaku Hotel Akagina HOTEL ¥¥¥

(伝泊ホテル赤木名; ☎0997-63-1910; www.den-paku.com/amami/distinations/hotel_akakina; 50-2 Ōaza-sato, Akagina; s/d from ¥8100/17,280; P⊖❄☎) This smart, architecturally designed modern hotel has a proud traditional appeal. Located not far from the airport, it makes a great base for short stays. If you plan to stay a little longer, the Denpaku group (www.den-paku.com) have a bunch of wonderful, rustic houses for rent, scattered about the island. Check the website for details.

Holly Camp BOUTIQUE HOTEL ¥¥¥

(☎090-7167-1970; www.livholly.com; 815 Ōaza Sotoganeku, Kazari-chō; s/d ¥22,000/25,000; P☎) While it's almost too cool for school, this classy collection of converted Airstream campers will undoubtedly elicit more smiles and sighs of delight than disappointment. Lovingly restored vans feature all the mod-cons you'd expect of such a glampy facility, located in a delightful waterfront spot on the island's northern cape.

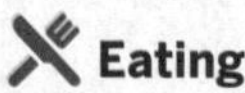

Eating

Okonomiyaki Mangetsu OKONOMIYAKI ¥

(お好み焼き満月; ☎0997-53-2052; https://o-mangetsu.com/shop-naze; 2-2 Nazeirifune-chō; dishes ¥840-1380; ⊙noon-2am) Locals pile in for the excellent *okonomiyaki* (batter and cabbage cakes cooked on a griddle) at this excellent Naze eatery. For carnivores, we recommend the *kurobuta* mix (pork, shrimp and squid mix; ¥1260), and for vegetarians, the *isobecchi* (*mochi* rice and *nori;* ¥750). There's a picture menu.

Hokorashi-ya IZAKAYA ¥¥

(誇羅司屋; ☎0997-52-1158; www.hokorashiya-amami.com/menu; 13-6 Nazeirifune-chō; set meals ¥2000-3500; ⊙5.30pm-midnight) An atmospheric *izakaya* in downtown Naze, Hokorashi-ya dishes up toothsome Amami specialities such as *aosa-no-tempura* (fish-and-shellfish cakes fried in a freshwater seaweed batter; ¥600) and a regional *chāhan* (fried rice flecked with bonito and egg; ¥800), as well as beautifully plated sushi and sashimi specials. There's a picture menu.

ℹ Information

Amami-Ōshima Tourist Information Office (奄美大島観光案内所; ☎0997-53-3240; www.amami-tourism.org; 14-10 Suehiro, AiAi Hiroba 1F; ⊙9am-6pm) Helpful office is located in Naze. There's also a smaller information desk at the airport.

ℹ Getting There & Away

AIR

Amami Airport (奄美空港; Amami Kūkō) has direct flights to/from Tokyo, Osaka, Fukuoka and Kagoshima with Japan Airlines (JAL) or JAC.

Ryukyu Air Commuter (RAC) operates a daily flight between Naha and Amami-Ōshima. There are also flights between Amami-Ōshima and the other islands in the Amami group.

THE SOUTHWEST ISLANDS IN...

Two Days

➡ Spend one day exploring Naha and the next beach-lounging and snorkelling on Aka-jima or Zamami-jima.

➡ Alternatively, fly directly to Miyako-jima and rent a car to explore the beaches of these bridge-linked islands.

Four Days

➡ Enjoy epic hikes and seaside onsen on Yakushima, then ferry over to Tanegashima for surfing and beach time.

➡ Bookend two days in the Yaeyama Islands with a day exploring Ishigaki-jima and a day cycling around Taketomi-jima.

One Week

➡ Spend a day or two on Okinawa-hontō then take your pick, splitting your time between the Amami Islands and the Yaeyama or Miyako Islands, spending two to three days on each.

BOAT

Travelling by sea, **Marix** (マリックスライン; ☎Amami office 0997-53-3112, Kagoshima office 099-225-1551; www.marix-line.co.jp; 2281 Naze Shiohama-chō) and **A Line** (☎Amami office 099-222-2338, Kagoshima office 099-226-4141; www.aline-ferry.com; 8-21 Naze Iroifune-chō, 1F Yūson Bldg) run their own ferries along the same routes for the same rates, but on alternating days, from the **Nazeshinko Ferry Terminal** (名瀬新港フェリーターミナル). If you find that one does not offer a route on the day you wish to travel, simply book with the other company.

Marix and A Line run four or five ferries a month from Osaka/Kōbe (¥15,120, 29 hours), as well as daily ferries to and from Kagoshima (¥9050, 11 hours) and Naha (¥9570, 13 hours).

Getting Around

Amami-Ōshima has a good bus system, but you will definitely appreciate a rental car if you have an International Driving Permit. **Times Car Rental** (タイムズレンタカー; ☎0997-63-0240; 467 Kasari-chō; 8am-7pm) has subcompacts from ¥5500, with a branch in Naze and another across from the airport.

The island's tiny airport is on the northeast end of the island; 55 minutes from Naze by bus (¥1100, almost hourly) with buses timed to meet flights.

Yoron-tō

☎0997 / POP 5263

Fringed with white, star-sand-speckled beaches and extensive coral reefs, Yoron-tō (与論島) is one of the most appealing islands in the Southwest Islands chain. A mere 5km across, it is the southernmost island in Kagoshima Prefecture. On a good day, Okinawa-hontō's northernmost point of Hedo-misaki is visible 23km to the southwest.

Lovely beaches border the island, with the best dive spots clustered off the northwest and southwest coasts.

The harbour is next to the airport on the western tip of the island, while the main town of Chabana (茶花) is 1km to the east.

Sights

★Yoron Minzoku-mura MUSEUM

(与論民族村; ☎0997-97-2934; www.minzokumura.jp; 693 Higashi-ku; adult/child ¥400/200; 9am-6pm) At the island's southeastern tip, the excellent Yoron Minzoku-mura is a collection of traditional thatch-roofed island dwellings and storehouses that contain exhibits on the island's culture and history. If at all possible, come with a Japanese speaker, as the owner is an incredible source of information on the island's heritage and dialect.

Oganeku-kaigan BEACH

(大金久海岸; Furusato) The popular Oganeku-kaigan is Yoron-tō's best beach, located on the eastern side of the island. About 500m offshore from here lies **Yurigahama** (百合ヶ浜), a stunning stretch of white sand that disappears completely at high tide and is rich with star sand, where each microscopic granule is in the form of star. Boats (¥2000 return) ferry visitors between the two beaches.

Terasaki-kaigan BEACH

(寺崎海岸; Nama) On the northeast coast, Terasaki-kaigan represents the archetypical Amami beach, with its white sand, rocky outcrops and aquamarine water.

Sleeping

Shiomi-sō MINSHUKU ¥

(汐見荘; ☎0997-97-2167; 2229-3 Chabana; r per person without bathroom incl 2 meals ¥6470; P❄@) This friendly and casual *minshuku* is popular with young people. Both Western- and Japanese-style rooms are available, and all share bathrooms. Starting from Chabana harbour, take the main road north (uphill) out of town and look for the cute little white house on the left after the turn. Staff will pick you up if you phone ahead.

★Pricia Resort HOTEL ¥¥¥

(プリシアリゾート; ☎0997-97-5060; www.pricia.co.jp; 358-1 Ricchō; r per person incl breakfast from ¥12,800; P❄@) These

> **DON'T MISS**
>
> **DIVING SPOTS**
>
> The Southwest Islands are stunning above the surface and just as appealing below, where whales sharks, turtles, corals and wrecks offer great opportunities for diving (p62).
>
> Our favourite places:
>
> ➡ Yonaguni-jima (p829)
>
> ➡ Kerama Islands (p810)
>
> ➡ Ishigaki-jima (p822)
>
> ➡ Iriomote-jima (p825)

relaxing whitewashed cottages by the airport evoke Yoron-tō's sister island, Mykonos, in Greece. The best cottages are the beachside 'B type' units. Breezy Western-style rooms and Jacuzzi baths are popular with Japanese divers and holidaying US service members from Okinawa. The hotel offers an entire menu of activities, including windsurfing, snorkelling and banana-boat rides. It also rents out bicycles and cars.

Eating & Drinking

Umi Café CAFE ¥

(海カフェ; ☎0997-97-4621; 2309 Chabana; light meals ¥650-900; ⏰11am-6pm Sun-Wed & Fri, 1-6pm Sat, closed Thu) This delightful terraced gallery-cafe with ocean views is something you'd expect to find perched on a Greek cliff; it's no surprise to find chicken gyros (¥700) on the menu. Go to the village office at the top of the main drag, turn left and then right at the end of the street. Look for small signs pointing uphill.

The owner also runs a small hostel (dorm beds ¥1500).

Bar Natural Reef BAR

(ナチュラルリーフ; ☎0997-97-3661; 16-1 Chabana; ⏰9pm-1am) This tiki bar on Chabana's main drag is the best watering hole on the island, with plenty of *yū sen*, a local *shōchū* (strong distilled alcohol) made from sugar cane, to keep everyone happy. Owner Kowaguchi-san has lots of tips about the best spots on Yoron-tō.

Information

At the **post office** (☎0997-97-2042; 68-6 Chabana; ⏰9am-5pm Mon-Fri, to 12.30pm Sat & Sun) in Chabana there is an international ATM.

Yoron-tō Tourism Association (ヨロン島観光協会; ☎0997-97-5151; www.yorontou.info; 32-1 Chabana; ⏰8.30am-5.30pm) This friendly place beside the city office in Chabana provides a basic English-language map of the island and can make accommodation bookings.

Getting There & Away

Yoron Airport (与論空港; Yoron-kūkō) has direct flights to/from Kagoshima, Amami-Ōshima (JAC) and Naha (RAC).

Yoron's **port** (与論港) is served by Marix (p799) and A Line Ferry (p799), which run between Kagoshima (some originating in Honshū) and Naha.

Getting Around

Yoron-tō has a bus system, but you'll definitely appreciate the convenience of a car, scooter or touring bicycle. **Yoron Rentacar** (ヨロンレンタカー; ☎0997-97-3633; 48-7 Chabana; ⏰8am-6pm), in Chabana, will meet car- or scooter-rental clients at the airport, and may even offer you an energy drink when sending you on your way. If you don't opt for a pick-up, find Yoron Rentacar on the road just east of the post office, off Chabana's main drag.

OKINAWA-HONTŌ

☎098

Depending on the suffix used, Okinawa (沖縄) can refer to the prefecture (-ken, 県), its enclosing archipelago (-rettō, 列島), the main island (-hontō, 本島) or the eponymous city on the main island (-shi, 市); but when most visitors say they're 'going to Okinawa', they mean they're visiting the Southwest Islands.

Formerly the seat of power of the Ryūkyū dynasty, Okinawa-hontō is the largest island in the Nansei-shotō (Southwest Islands) and its capital, Naha, the busiest city. If Tōkyō were a pie, and you cut a tiny slice, dropped it on an island in the Pacific, and served it with a dollop of Florida, Naha might be what you'd get. Most visible traces of Ryukyū culture were obliterated in WWII, and there remains a huge US military presence on the island.

In spite of this, the Ryūkyū lineage remains strong and is evident in Okinawa's unique culinary, artistic and musical traditions.

Getting There & Away

Naha is Okinawa's transport hub, with international flights to and from Hong Kong, Seoul, Shanghai, Singapore and Taipei, as well as domestic flights connecting to major cities in Japan, including Tokyo and Osaka.

Naha is also the maritime hub for jetfoils to the Kerama Islands, and long-distance ferries to Miyako-jima and the Yaeyama Islands.

Naha

☎098 / POP 319,000

Flattened during WWII, the prefectural capital of Naha (那覇) is now a thriving urban centre that looks like most other tidy, small-to-medium Japanese cities, except for the frequent splashes of leafy green, rows of palm trees, or glimpses of azure waters from

Okinawa-hontō

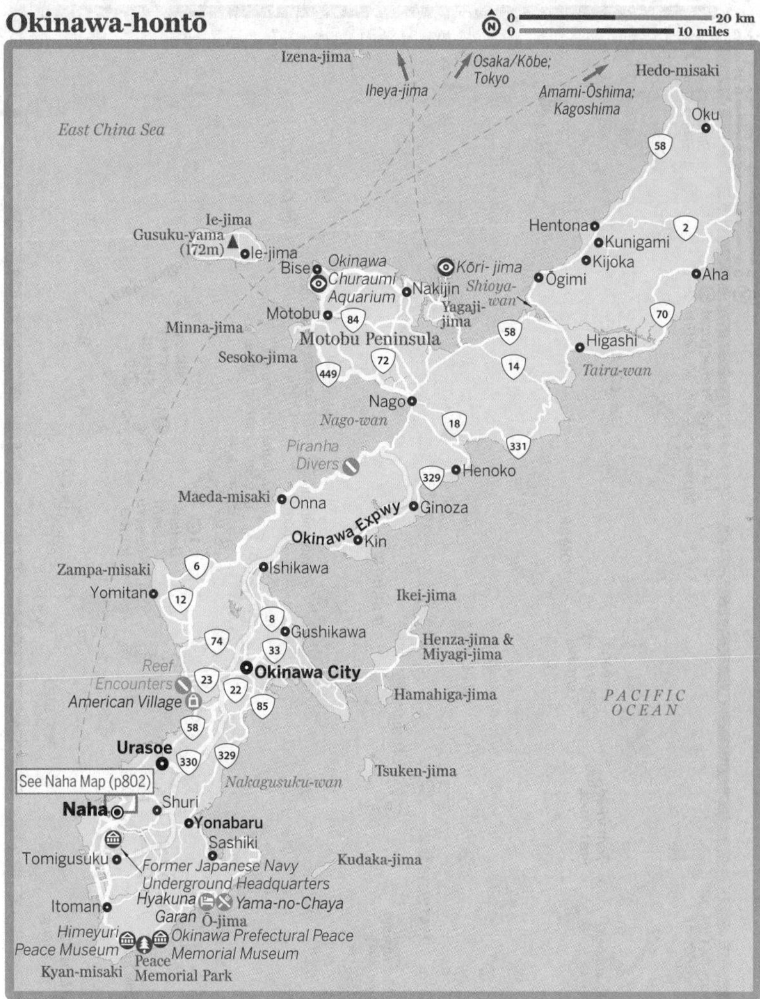

between the modern high-rises, which make up Naha's rapidly expanding skyline.

The city plays host to an interesting mix of young Japanese holidaymakers, American GIs looking for off-base fun and a growing number of foreign tourists. The action centres on Kokusai-dōri (International Blvd), and overlooking it all from a safe distance to the east is Shuri-jō, a wonderfully restored castle that was once the home of Ryūkyū royalty.

Thankfully, Naha's unique elevated monorail, the Yui Rail, makes getting around a breeze, because driving here can be quite the nightmare: despite its size, Naha's traffic jams make for slow going.

Sights

Naha is fairly easy to navigate, especially since the main sights and attractions are located in the city centre. The city's main artery is **Kokusai-dōri** (国際通り), a riot of neon, noise, souvenir shops, bustling restaurants and Japanese young things out strutting their stuff. It's a festival of tat and tackiness, but it's good fun if you're in the mood for it.

Many people prefer the atmosphere of the three covered shopping arcades that run south off Kokusai-dōri: **Ichibahon-dōri** (市場本道り), **Mutsumibashi-dōri** (むつみ橋通り) and **Heiwa-dōri** (平和通り).

Naha

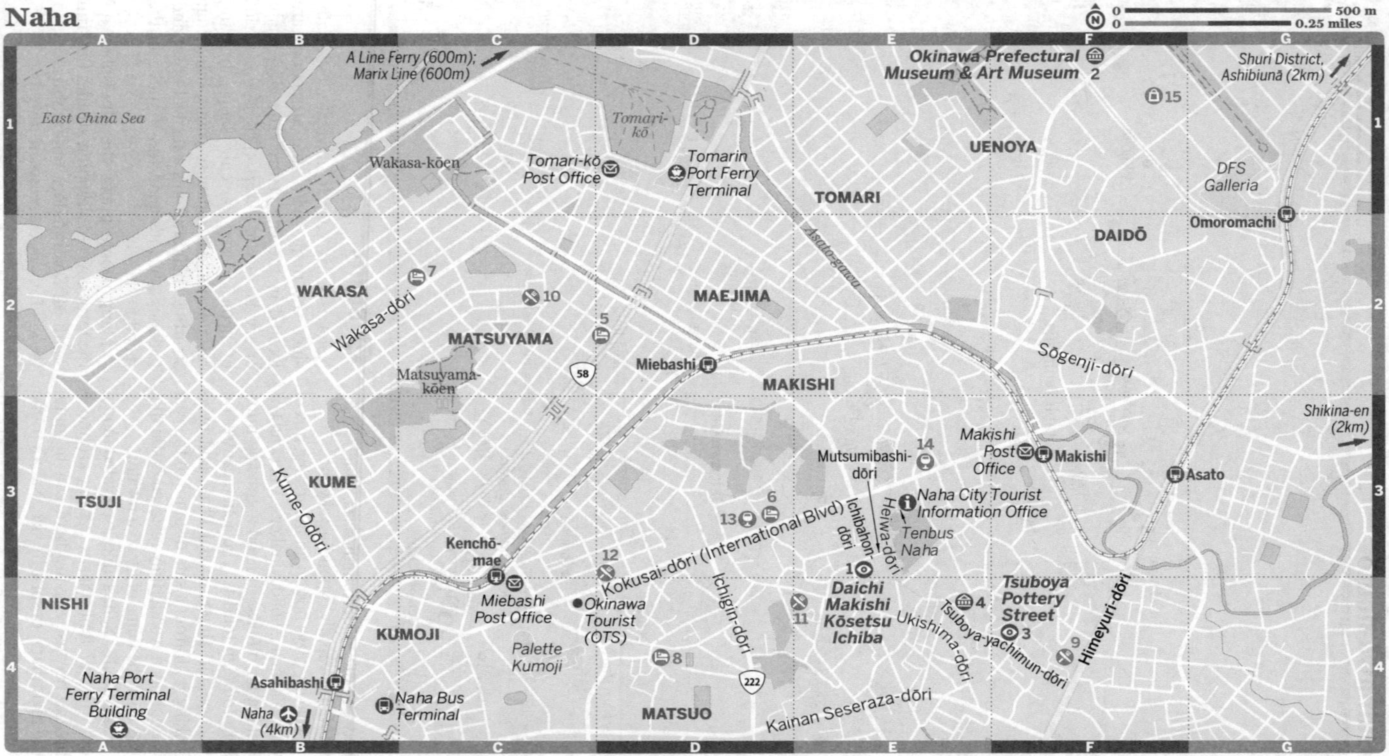

0 500 m
0 0.25 miles

A Line Ferry (600m); Marix Line (600m)
Okinawa Prefectural Museum & Art Museum 2
Shuri District, Ashibiunā (2km)
15
East China Sea
Tomari-kō
UENOYA
Wakasa-kōen
Tomari-kō Post Office
Tomarin Port Ferry Terminal
DFS Galleria
TOMARI
Omoromachi
DAIDŌ
Asato-gawa
7
WAKASA
10
MAEJIMA
Wakasa-dōri
5
MATSUYAMA
Sōgenji-dōri
58
Miebashi
Matsuyama-kōen
MAKISHI
Shikina-en (2km)
Makishi Post Office
Makishi
14
Mutsumibashi-dōri
Asato
KUME
6
Naha City Tourist Information Office
TSUJI
Kume-Ōdōri
13
Ichibahon-dōri
Heiwa-dōri
Tenbus Naha
Kokusai-dōri (International Blvd)
Kenchō-mae
12
1 Daichi Makishi Kōsetsu Ichiba
Tsuboya Pottery Street
4
Miebashi Post Office
Okinawa Tourist (OTS)
11
Ukishima-dōri
NISHI
Ichigin-dōri
Tsuboya-yachimun-dōri
3
KUMOJI
Palette Kumoji
9
Himeyuri-dōri
8
Naha Port Ferry Terminal Building
Asahibashi
222
Naha (4km)
Naha Bus Terminal
MATSUO
Kainan Seseraza-dōri

Naha

The Shuri district is about 3km to the east of the city centre.

★**Shuri-jō** CASTLE

(首里城; ☎098-886-2020; www.oki-park.jp; 1-2 Kinjō-chō, Shuri; ¥820, with 1- or 2-day monorail pass discounted to ¥660; ⏲8.30am-7pm Apr-Jun & Oct-Nov, to 8pm Jul-Sep, to 6pm Dec-Mar, closed 1st Wed & Thu Jul) This reconstructed castle was originally built in the 14th century and served as the administrative centre and royal residence of the Ryūkyū kingdom until the 19th century. Enter through the **Kankai-mon** (歓会門) and go up to the **Hōshin-mon** (奉神門), which forms the entryway to the inner sanctum of the castle. Visitors can enter the impressive **Seiden** (正殿), which has exhibits on the castle and the Okinawan royals.

About 200m west of the Seiden, the observation terrace **Iri-no-Azana** (西のアザナ) affords great views over Naha and the Kerama Islands. There is also a small collection of displays in the nearby **Hokuden** (北殿).

To reach the complex, which sits atop a hill overlooking Naha's urban sprawl, take the Yui Rail to Shuri Station. Exit to the west, go down the steps, walk straight ahead, cross one big street, then a smaller one and go right on the opposite side. From there, walk about 350m and look for the signs on the left.

★**Okinawa Prefectural Museum & Art Museum** MUSEUM

(沖縄県立博物館・美術館; Map p802; ☎098-941-8200; www.museums.pref.okinawa.jp; Omoromachi 3-1-1; prefectural/art museum ¥410/310; ⏲9am-6pm Tue-Thu & Sun, to 8pm Fri & Sat) Opened in 2007, this museum of Okinawa's history, culture and natural history is easily one of the best museums in Japan. Displays are well laid out, attractively presented and easy to understand, with excellent bilingual interpretive signage. The art-museum section holds interesting special exhibits (admission prices vary) with an emphasis on local artists. It's about 15 minutes' walk northwest of the Omoromachi monorail station.

★**Daichi Makishi Kōsetsu Ichiba** MARKET

(第一牧志公設市場; Map p802; 2-10-1 Matsuo; ⏲8am-8pm, restaurants 10am-7pm) In Naha, a great place to sample everyday Okinawan eats is at one of the 2nd-floor eateries in this covered food market just off Ichibahon-dōri, about 200m south of Kokusai-dōri. The colourful variety of fish and produce on offer here is amazing. Don't miss the wonderful local restaurants upstairs.

★**Tsuboya Pottery Street** AREA

(壷屋やちむん道り; Tsuboya Yachimun-dōri; Map p802) One of the best parts of Naha is this neighbourhood, a centre of ceramic production from 1682, when Ryūkyū kilns were consolidated here by royal decree. Most shops along this old-timey street sell all the popular Okinawan ceramics, including *shiisā* (lion-dog roof guardians) and containers for serving *awamori* (Okinawan liquor distilled from rice), the local firewater. The lanes off the main street here contain some classic crumbling old Okinawan houses. To get here from Kokusai-dōri, walk south through the entirety of Heiwa-dōri arcade (about 350m).

Tsuboya Pottery Museum MUSEUM

(壷屋焼物博物館; Map p802; ☎098-862-3761; www.edu.city.naha.okinawa.jp/tsuboya; 1-9-32 Tsuboya; adult/concession ¥350/280; ⏲10am-6pm Tue-Sun) The excellent Tsuboya Pottery Museum houses some fine examples of traditional Okinawan pottery. Here you can also inspect potters' wheels and *arayachi* (unglazed) and *jōyachi* (glazed) pieces. There's even a cross-section of a *noborigama* (kiln built on a slope) set in its original location, where crushed pieces of pottery that date back to the 17th century lie suspended in earth.

Shikina-en GARDENS
(識名園; ☎098-855-5936; 421-7 Aza Māji; ¥400; ⊙9am-6pm Thu-Tue Apr-Sep, to 5.30pm Oct-Mar) Around 4km east of the city centre is a Chinese-style garden containing stone bridges, a viewing pavilion and a villa that belonged to the Ryūkyū royal family. Despite its flawless appearance, everything here was painstakingly rebuilt after WWII. To reach the garden, take bus 2, 3 or 5 to the Shikinaen-mae stop (¥230, 20 minutes).

Activities

Ryūkyū Onsen Ryūjin-no-yu ONSEN
(琉球温泉龍神の湯[]; ☎098-851-7077; www.hotelwbf.com/senaga; 174-5 Senaga, Tomigusuku; ¥720) Near the airport, on tiny reclaimed, land-linked Senaga island, you'll find what could be one of Naha's most tempting attractions, with its selection of sea-view hot-spring pools and fabulous location with views out over the airstrip and the East China Sea. Words of warning: it's at times overwhelmingly popular, and its door policy refuses entry to persons with even the smallest tattoos. Entrance to the onsen is to the right of the hotel lobby.

Reef Encounters DIVING
(Map p801; ☎098-995-9414, 090-1940-3528; www.reefencounters.org; 1-493 Miyagi, Chatan-chō; 2-dive boat trips from ¥14,040, equipment rental ¥5000) The experienced, safety-oriented dive guides at this organised outfit – based in Chatan, 15km north of Naha – can, between the lot of them, speak fluent English, Spanish, Portuguese, Japanese, Mandarin and Cantonese.

Festivals & Events

Dragon-Boat Races CULTURAL
(⊙May) Held in early May, particularly in Itoman and Naha. These *hari* (races) are thought to bring luck and prosperity to fishers.

Naha Ōzunahiki SPORTS
(⊙Oct) Takes place in Naha on Sunday around the national Sports Day Holiday, and features large teams that compete in the world's biggest tug of war, using a gigantic 1m-thick rope weighing over 40 tonnes.

Sleeping

Minshuku Gettō MINSHUKU ¥
(民宿月桃; Map p802; ☎098-861-7555; 1-16-24 Matsuo; s with/without bathroom from ¥3500/3000; P ❄ @ ☎) Tucked into a small, quiet neighbourhood two minutes' walk from Kokusai-dōri, this spotless little *minshuku* offers secure, stand-alone apartments, some with private bathrooms and kitchenettes. Reserve well in advance for a coveted spot, as it's a steal.

★ **Hotel Pesquera** BOUTIQUE HOTEL ¥¥
(ホテルペスケーラ; Map p802; ☎098-894-8847; www.pesquera.okinawa.jp; 2-4-13 Wakasa; r from ¥6500; P ⊖ ❄ ☎) New in 2017, this lovable private hotel has simple polished concrete rooms with exceedingly comfortable full-sized beds, ample balconies, functional kitchenettes and full laundry facilities, including washer and dryer. Pesquera offers that contented feeling you get when, exhausted, you enter your room late, ready for bed, only to then wish you'd arrived earlier simply to enjoy the space.

★ **Hotel Estinate** BOUTIQUE HOTEL ¥¥
(エスティネートホテル; Map p802; ☎098-943-4900; www.estinate.com; 2-3-11 Matsuyama; s/d from ¥5500/9500; ⊖ ☎) There's a lot to love about this homely little design hotel, which could have been plucked from Tokyo's Omote-sandō and transplanted into Naha's up-and-coming entertainment district. Rooms are sparsely but freshly furnished with restrained bursts of colour that change the vibe from 'bed for a night' to 'home for a night'. Best of all: price.

The downstairs bar-restaurant and outdoor beer garden are lively smart-casual places to mingle with locals and fellow travellers.

Hotel JAL City Naha HOTEL ¥¥¥
(ホテルJALシティ那覇; Map p802; ☎098-866-2580; www.naha.jalcity.co.jp; 1-3-70 Makishi; s/d from ¥12,800/17,000; P ⊖ ❄ @ ☎) In the middle of the action on Kokusai-dōri, JAL City has 304 swish, modern rooms, in which even the single beds are wide enough to serve as snug doubles. Though staff here speak limited English, the service is excellent and the accommodation an elegant refuge from the noise of Kokusai-dōri.

Eating

★Shanghai Wantan Rō CHINESE ¥
(上海雲呑　樓; Map p802; ☎098-943-4865; 2-21-21 Matsuyama; small plates ¥450-1080; ⏲8pm-5am) If you can hold out for this little late-night eatery, you won't be disappointed. The standouts of the drool-worthy menu (which is, incidentally, perfectly paired with ice-cold beer) are the juicy, deep-fried wonton dumplings and, if you're going to do it right, Shanghai *yaki-soba* and a side of steamed Chinese greens.

Ashibiunā OKINAWAN ¥
(あしびうなぁ; ☎098-884-0035; www.ryoji-family.co.jp/ryukyusabo.html; 2-13 Shuri Tonokura-chō; lunch sets ¥800-1280; ⏲11.30am-3pm & 5.30pm-midnight) Perfect for lunch after touring Shuri-jō (p803), Ashibiunā has a traditional ambience and picturesque garden. Set meals feature local specialities such as *gōyā champurū*, *okinawa-soba* and *ikasumi yaki-soba*. On the road leading away from Shuri-jō, Ashibiunā is on the right, just before the intersection to the main road.

★Ryūkyū Ryōri Nuchigafū OKINAWAN ¥¥
(琉球料理ぬちがふう; Map p802; ☎098-861-2952; www.facebook.com/RyukyuCuisine.Nuchigafu; 1-28-3 Tsuboya; set dinner from ¥3000; ⏲11.30am-5pm & 5.30-10pm Wed-Mon) For a memorable, elegant meal in Naha, don't pass up dinner at the hilltop Nuchigafū, off the southern end of Tsuboya Pottery Street (p803). Formerly a lovely Okinawan teahouse, and before that a historic Ryūkyūan residence, Nuchigafū serves lunch and frothy *buku-buku* tea during the day and beautifully plated multi-course Okinawan dinners by night. Children aged 11 and older are welcome.

AMERICAN BASES IN OKINAWA

The US officially returned Okinawa to Japanese administration in 1972, but it negotiated a Status of Forces Agreement that guaranteed the Americans the right to use large tracts of Okinawan land for military bases, most of which are on Okinawa-hontō. These bases are home to some 30,000 American service members.

Although the bases have supported Okinawa's economic growth in the past, they now contribute only about 5% to the Okinawan GDP. The bases are a sore point for islanders due in part to occasional crimes committed by American servicemen. Antibase feelings peaked in 1995, after three American servicemen abducted and raped a 12-year-old Okinawan girl. Similar incidents in recent years have perpetuated animosity, including the death of a 20-year-old Okinawan woman in 2016 – a former Marine working at a US base has been charged with her rape and murder.

Plans to relocate the base from Futenma to the less densely populated Henoko district were officially approved by both the US and Japan in 1996, but have continually met with vocal opposition from Okinawan residents, the majority of whom would like to see the US military presence take leave of the island entirely.

In April 2010, 90,000 protesters gathered to call for an end to the bases, the biggest such demonstration in 15 years. That year, then prime minister Hatoyama Yukio fell on his sword after breaking a promise to move Futenma air base off the island; he finally admitted it would stay.

Though the USA formally agreed in early 2012 to move 9000 Marines (amounting to around half of the Marines on Okinawa) to bases on Guam, Hawaii and elsewhere in the Pacific, this plan will not begin manifesting until the mid-2020s.

As of December 2016 Okinawa's previous governor, Onaga Takeshi, was battling the Japanese government in court over his revocation of a landfill permit issued by his predecessor – this delay in construction represents Okinawan residents' wishes to see a significant reduction in the US military presence on the island.

During the same month, the US returned 4000 hectares of land to Okinawa – a move that, on the surface, appears to be a positive development. However, the return of land was made on the condition that helipad construction for controversial Osprey aircraft be completed. Many Okinawans oppose the presence of Osprey aircraft flying near residential areas, as the aircraft have had a string of accidents over the last several years, including a crash-landing in Nago as recently as mid-December 2016.

Following Governor Onaga's death in 2018, current governor Denny Tamaki was appointed, and is also an opponent of military presence in the islands.

A FOOD LOVER'S GUIDE TO OKINAWA

Reflecting the islands' geographic and historical isolation, Okinawa's food shares little in common with that of mainland Japan. The cuisine originated in the splendour of the Ryūkyū court and from the humble lives of the impoverished islanders. Healthy eating is considered to be extremely important; indeed, islanders have long held that medicine and food are essentially the same. And it must be noted that Okinawans are among the longest-lived people in the world.

Today one of the island's staple foods is pork, which is acidic and rich in protein. Every part of the pig is eaten. *Mimigā* (ミミガー) is thinly sliced pig's ears marinated in vinegar, perfect with a cold glass of local Orion beer (オリオンビール). *Rafutē* (ラフテー) is pork stewed with ginger, brown sugar, rice wine and soy sauce until it falls apart. If you need some stamina, try some *ikasumi-jiru* (イカスミ汁), which is stewed pork in black squid ink.

While stewing is common, Okinawans prefer stir-frying, and refer to the technique as *champurū* (チャンプルー). Perhaps the best-known stir-fry is *gōyā champurū* (ゴーヤーチャンプルー), a mix of pork, bitter melon and the island's uniquely sturdy tofu, *shima-dōfu* (島豆腐). Occasionally you'll come across an unusual tofu variant known as *tōfuyō* (豆腐痒), a type of *shima-dōfu* whose strong flavour is due to fermentation in *awamori* (Okinawan liquor distilled from rice).

The ubiquitous *okinawa-soba* (沖縄そば) is udon (thick white wheat noodles) served in a pork broth. The most common variants are *sōki-soba* (ソーキそば), topped with pork spare ribs, and *Yaeyama-soba* (八重山そば), which contains soba topped with tiny pieces of tender pork, bean sprouts and scallions.

Aside from *gōyā champurū,* bitter melon appears in all kinds of dishes, delivering a dose of antioxidants and holding promise for its potential to combat diabetes.

Finally, there's nothing quite like Blue Seal (ブルーシール) brand ice cream, an American favourite introduced here after WWII. It's best savoured at a shop rather than in prepacked containers.

★Yūnangi OKINAWAN ¥¥

(ゆうなんぎい; Map p802; ☎098-867-3765; 3-3-3 Kumoji; dishes ¥750-1400; ⏰noon-3pm & 5.30-10.30pm Mon-Sat) You'll be lucky to get a seat here, but if you do, you'll be treated to some of the best Okinawan food around, served in traditional but bustling surroundings. Try the *okinawa-soba* set (¥1400), or choose from the picture menu. It's on a side street off Kokusai-dōri – look for the wooden sign with white lettering above the doorway.

Ukishima Garden VEGETARIAN ¥¥

(浮島ガーデン; Map p802; ☎098-943-2100; www.ukishima-garden.com; 2-12-3 Matsuo; lunch/dinner set menus from ¥1300/4200; ⏰11.30am-3pm & 6-11pm; 🖉) With pork featuring prominently in traditional Okinawan cuisine, Ukishima Garden is a refreshing, cleansing change. Here vegetarian and vegan creations utilise as much organic and locally grown produce as possible, resulting in balanced and complex renditions of dishes from taco rice to spaghetti carbonara. Pair your meal with organic wine; end with an *amazake* (fermented rice milk) smoothie.

Drinking & Nightlife

Naha is the biggest and rowdiest city for hundreds of miles around, and most of its nightlife centres on Kokusai-dōri and the streets and lanes either side of Wakasa Ōdori.

Rehab BAR

(Map p802; ☎098-988-1198; www.facebook.com/RehabInternationalBar; 3rd fl, 2-4-14 Makishi; ⏰7pm-late) This 3rd-floor international bar on Kokusai-dōri attracts a friendly, mixed crowd and has cosy nook seating, imported beer and two-for-one drinks on Tuesdays. The cool bartenders here speak English.

Helios Pub PUB

(ヘリオスパブ; Map p802; ☎098-863-7227; www.helios-food-service.co.jp; 1-2-25 Makishi; ⏰11.30am-11pm Sun-Thu, to midnight Fri & Sat) Craft-beer lovers who tire of Orion can perk up bored palates with a sample flight of four house brews (¥900) and pints for ¥525. Edibles cover the pub-menu gamut, all very reasonably priced.

Shopping

★American Village CONCEPT STORE

(Map p801; ☎098-926-5678; www.okinawa-americanvillage.com; 15-69 Mihama, Chatan-cho) This amusement-park-esque, American-themed shopping mall is as kitsch as they come, but if you can resist your instinctive resistance, closer exploration will provide a fascinating glimpse into modern Okinawan life, where off-duty GIs shop for memories of home alongside Chinese tourists on the hunt for Americana. There are some excellent vintage-clothing stores, a bunch of fun dining options and a big-ass Ferris wheel to boot.

Take the 20, 28 or 29 bus from Naha to the Kuwae stop (40 minutes, ¥720).

★San-A Naha Main Place SHOPPING CENTRE

(サンエー那覇メインプレイス; Map p802; ☎098-951-3300; www.san-a.co.jp/nahamainplace; 4-4-9 Omoromachi; ⏲9am-11pm) Naha's busiest downtown mall is always a hive of activity for its many duty-free stores (including Tokyū Hands – great for, well, anything you can think of), cinema complex and array of enticing eateries where you should expect to queue, any time of day.

Information

Tourist Information Counter (☎098-857-6884; Naha International Airport, 1F Arrivals Terminal; ⏲9am-9pm) At Naha airport's helpful tourism branch pick up a copy of the *Naha Guide Map* or the *Okinawa Guide Map*.

Naha City Tourist Information Office (那覇市観光案内所; Map p802; ☎098-868-4887; www.visitokinawa.jp; 3-2-10 Makishi; ⏲9am-8pm) Located in the Tenbus Building, this gives out free maps and information.

Okinawa Tourist (沖縄ツーリストサービス; OTS; Map p802; ☎098-862-1111; www.otsinfo.co.jp; 1-2-3 Matsuo; ⏲9.30am-6pm Mon-Fri, to 3.30pm Sat) This competent travel agency, with English speakers, on Kokusai-dōri can help with all manner of ferry and flight bookings. With the wide variety of options on offer, Naha is one place where a travel agent can come in particularly handy.

Getting There & Away

AIR

Naha International Airport (那覇国際空港; Naha Kokusai-kūkō; OKA; ☎098-840-1151; www.naha-airport.co.jp/en) has direct international connections with Hong Kong, Seoul, Shanghai, Singapore and Taipei. Connections with mainland Japan include Fukuoka, Osaka, Nagoya and Tokyo; significant discounts (*tabiwari* on All Nippon Airways and *sakitoku* on JAL) can sometimes be had if you purchase tickets a month in advance. Note that this is only a partial list; services from most large Japanese cities fly into Naha.

Naha also has air connections with Ishigaki-jima, Kume-jima, Miyako-jima and Yoron-tō, among other Southwest Islands.

As well as JAL and ANA, try searching these low-cost carriers, which may well have discount flights between Naha and where you wish to fly:

Jetstar (www.jetstar.co.jp)

Peach Aviation (www.flypeach.com)

Solaseed Air (www.solaseedair.jp)

Skymark (www.skymark.co.jp)

BOAT

Naha has regular ferry connections with ports in Honshū (Tokyo and Osaka/Kōbe) and Kyūshū (Kagoshima).

Marix (☎in Kagoshima 099-225-1551, in Naha 098-868-9098; www.marix-line.co.jp; Tomarin Port) and **A Line** (☎in Naha 098-861-1886, in Tokyo 03-5643-6170; www.aline-ferry.com; Tomarin Port) operate four to six ferries a month to/from Tokyo (¥27,230, 47 hours) and Osaka/Kōbe (¥19,330, 42 hours), as well as daily ferries to/from Kagoshima (¥14,610, 25 hours).

There are three ports in Naha, and this can be confusing: Amami Islands ferries operate from **Naha Port** (那覇港ポートフェリーターミナルビル; Map p802); Tokyo/Osaka/Kōbe/Kagoshima ferries operate from **Naha Shin Port** (那覇新港フェリーターミナルビル); and Kume-jima and Kerama Islands ferries operate from **Tomarin Port** (とまりん港フェリーターミナル; Map p802).

Note that there is no ferry service to the Miyako or Yaeyama Islands from Naha.

Getting Around

The Yui Rail monorail conveniently runs from Naha International Airport in the south to Shuri in the north. Prices range from ¥200 to ¥290; one- and two-day passes cost ¥700 and ¥1200, respectively. Kenchō-mae Station sits at the western end of Kokusai-dōri, while Makishi Station is at its eastern end.

Naha Port is a 10-minute walk southwest from Asahibashi Station, while Tomarin Port is a similar distance north from Miebashi Station. Bus 101 from **Naha Bus Terminal** (那覇バスターミナル; Map p802; 1-20-1 Izumizaki) heads further north to Naha Shin Port, taking 20 minutes and leaving hourly.

When riding on local town buses, simply dump ¥200 into the slot next to the driver as you enter. For longer trips, take a ticket showing your starting point as you board and pay the appropriate fare as you disembark. Buses

OKINAWA'S SHIISĀ LION DOG

As you wander the streets of Naha, you'll notice these curious Chinese dragon-like stone statues, often painted red, ferociously guarding the entrances to homes and businesses. Known as *Shiisā* (guardian lion-dogs), the statues embody elements of both Chinese and Ryūkyūan cultures. Somewhat a symbol of Okinawan resilience, they're often seen in pairs, one with an open mouth swallowing good fortune for the house and the other, whose mouth is firmly shut, ensuring it won't escape. Together they symbolise strength and protection.

run from Naha to destinations all over the island. A handy English-language reference for deciphering the many local bus lines is www.kotsu-okinawa.org/en.

A rental car makes everything easier when exploring Okinawa-hontō, although traffic jams and low speed limits can be frustrating. The rental-car counter in the arrivals hall of Naha International Airport offers information on the dozen or so rental companies in Naha, allowing you to comparison shop.

Southern Okinawa-hontō

During the closing days of the Battle of Okinawa, the southern part of Okinawa-hontō served as one of the last holdouts of the Japanese military and an evacuation point for wounded Japanese soldiers.

Okinawa's most important war memorials are clustered in the Peace Memorial Park, located in the city of Itoman on the southern coast of the island.

A visit to the area as a day or half-day trip from Naha, is highly recommended for those with an interest in wartime history or seeking a deeper understanding of the modern Okinawan identity.

Sights

★Okinawa Prefectural Peace Memorial Museum MUSEUM

(沖縄県平和祈念資料館; Map p801; ☎098-997-3844; www.peace-museum.pref.okinawa.jp; 614-1 Aza Mabuni, Itoman; ¥300; ⊙9am-5pm) The centrepiece of the Peace Memorial Park focuses on the suffering of the Okinawan people during the island's invasion and under the subsequent American Occupation. While some material may stir debate, the museum's mission is to serve as a reminder of the horrors of war, so that such suffering is not repeated. There is a free English-language audio guide available, providing great detail on the 2nd-floor exhibit.

★Himeyuri Peace Museum MUSEUM

(ひめゆり平和祈念資料館; Map p801; ☎098-997-2100; www.himeyuri.or.jp; 671-1 Ihara, Itoman; ¥310; ⊙9am-5.30pm) Located above a cave that served as an emergency field hospital during the closing days of the Battle of Okinawa, the Himeyuri Peace Museum is a haunting monument whose mission is to promote peace, driven by survivors and alumnae of the school. Here 240 female high-school students were pressed into service as nurses for Japanese military wounded. As American forces closed in, the students were summarily dismissed and, thus abandoned, most perished. Excellent, comprehensive interpretive signage is provided in English.

Bus 82 stops outside.

Former Japanese Navy Underground Headquarters MUSEUM

(旧海軍司令部壕; Kyūkaigun Shireibu-gō; Map p801; ☎098-850-4055; http://kaigungou.ocvb.or.jp; 236 Tomishiro, Tomigusuku; ¥440; ⊙8.30am-5pm Oct-Jun, to 5.30pm Jul-Sep) Directly south of Naha in Kaigungo-kōen is the Former Japanese Navy Underground Headquarters, where 4000 men committed suicide or were killed as the Battle of Okinawa drew to its bloody conclusion. Only 250m of the tunnels are open, but you can wander through the maze of corridors, see the commander's final words on the wall of his room, and inspect the holes and scars in other walls from the grenade blasts that killed many of the men.

To reach the site, take bus 55 or 98 from Naha Bus Terminal to the Uebaru Danchimae stop (¥220, 10 minutes, several hourly). From there it's a five-minute walk – follow the English signs (the entrance is near the top of the hill).

Peace Memorial Park PARK

(平和祈念公園; Map p801; 550 Mabuni; ⊙dawn-dusk) Housing Okinawa's most important war memorials, including the Okinawa Prefectural Peace Memorial Museum, the Peace Memorial Park occupies an appropriately peaceful coastal location in the southern city of Itoman.

To reach the park, take bus 89 from Naha bus terminal to the Itoman bus terminal (¥580, one hour, every 20 minutes), then transfer to bus 82, and get off at Heiwa Kinendō Iriguchi (¥470, 30 minutes, hourly).

Cornerstone of Peace MONUMENT
(平和の礎; 614-1 Aza Mabuni, Itoman; dawn-dusk) FREE Outside the Okinawa Prefectural Peace Memorial Museum is the Cornerstone of Peace, inscribed with the names of everyone who died in the Battle of Okinawa.

Sleeping & Eating

Southern Beach Hotel and Resort RESORT ¥¥
(サザンビーチホテルアンドリゾート; 098-992-7500; www.southernbeachhotelresort.com; 1-6-1 Nishizaki, Itoman; d from ¥14,400; P) Located in Itoman city, south of Naha, this freshly updated resort offers an oasis from Naha's hustle and bustle while remaining within easy reach of the city. Its bright, light-filled rooms have a splash of colour and big, comfy beds, and guests enjoy the resort's pool, gym and dining facilities. Great value.

Hyakuna Garan RYOKAN ¥¥¥
(百名伽藍; Map p801; 098-949-1011; www.hyakunagaran.com; 1299-1 Hyakuna, Tamagusuku; d from ¥45,000; P) This exquisite ryokan is one for those whose wallets can stretch a little further than most, and who value the finer details of the culinary art of *kaiseki* course dining and the less-is-more concept of *wabi-sabi* in architecture and design. Supremely luxurious rooms are not to be forgotten.

Yama-no-Chaya OKINAWAN ¥¥
(山の茶屋; Map p801; 098-948-1227; http://yama.hamabenochaya.com; 19-1 Tamagusuku, Nanjō-shi; meals ¥800-1400; 11am-6pm Fri-Wed;) If you're exploring southern Okinawa-hontō, seek out this serene, ocean-view cafe nestled in the forest. This is a lovely place for refreshing vegetarian fare made with organic and local ingredients. It's a 10-minute walk from the Mibaru Beach stop on bus 39 from Naha.

Getting There & Away

Southern Okinawa-hontō is conveniently served by regular buses from Naha, but renting a car will give you more freedom to explore the area's diverse attractions.

Motobu Peninsula

It's about an hour's drive north of Naha to the city of Nago and the hilly Motobu Peninsula, which is home to some scenic vistas, islets and decent beaches, as well as an incredibly popular aquarium. Aside from that, there's not a lot to 'do' out here, other than to relax, read a good book and glimpse a more *authentic* Okinawan way of life than you might find among the colourful distractions of big-city Naha.

Sights

Okinawa Churaumi Aquarium AQUARIUM
(沖縄美ら海水族館; Map p801; 0980-48-3748, for GPS navigation systems 0980-48-2741; www.churaumi.okinawa; 424 Ishikawa, Motobu-chō; adult/child ¥1850/610; 8.30am-6.30pm Oct-Feb, to 8pm Mar-Sep) The centrepiece of Motobu's **Ocean Expo Park** (海洋博公園) is the Okinawa Churaumi Aquarium, which features the world's largest aquarium tank. The aquarium houses a wide variety of marine life, including whale sharks. Dolphins are also kept here, a practice widely acknowledged as harmful to the animals' health. The aquarium is on every visitor's checklist, so it's usually packed. From Nago, buses 65, 66 and 70 run directly to the park (¥860, 50 minutes).

Kōri-jima ISLAND
(古宇利島; Map p801; Kōri-jima, Motobu-chō) Aquariums and crowds not your cup of tea? If you've got your own wheels, drive out to Kōri-jima via **Yagaji-jima** (屋我地島). The bridge between the two islands is surrounded by picturesque turquoise water, and there's a decent beach on either side of the road as you reach Kōri-jima. The bridge to Yagaji-jima starts just north of the Motobu Peninsula off Rte 58.

Bise VILLAGE
(備瀬; Bise, Motobu-chō) At the northwestern tip of the peninsula is the quaintly preserved village of Bise, a leafy beachside community of traditional Okinawan houses. Stroll along **Fukugi-namiki-dōri** (フクギ並木通り), an atmospheric lane lined with old garcinia trees, taking a peek at the local beach on the northern end. Near the lane's southern end, find refreshment at beachside cafe Cahaya Bulan (p810).

Activities

Piranha Divers DIVING
(Map p801; ☎080-4277-1155, 098-967-8487; www.piranha-divers.jp; 2288-532 Aza-Nakama, Nago; 2-dive boat trips from ¥14,000, equipment rental ¥5000) In Onna Village in the Nago area, this excellent family-run operation caters to individuals and small groups. Dive guides speak fluent English, German and Japanese.

Sleeping

Nago city has plenty of decent dining options, including all the big Japanese chain-offerings you've grown to love. Beyond that, in the smaller hamlets of the Motobu Peninsula, you'll be limited to a sparse scattering of cafes and *izakaya* around the tourist sites.

Hotel Route-Inn Nago BUSINESS HOTEL ¥¥
(ホテルルートイン名護; ☎0980-54-8511; www.route-inn.co.jp; 5-11-3 Agarie; s/tw from ¥6600/11,700; P ❄ 📶) This stock-standard business hotel is a hop, skip and a jump from the waterfront. It benefits from its design palette – featuring natural, earthy tones that soften the fluorescent lighting and late-night vibe, which seem to be the decor downside to this otherwise great-value accommodation.

Class Inn Nago HOTEL ¥¥
(クラスイン名護; ☎0980-43-0020; www.class-inn.com; 875-25 Miyazato, Nago; s/d from ¥6700/9500; P ❄ 📶) The rooms of this smart condo tower, shiny new in December 2017, have a hybrid hotel-room/studio-apartment feel. Accommodations feature dark wood furnishings, comfortable bedding, and full kitchen and laundry facilities.

Cahaya Bulan OKINAWAN ¥
(チャハヤブラン; ☎098-051-7272; 429-1 Bise; ajian-soba ¥850; ⏰noon-sunset Thu-Tue, winter Fri-Tue; P 📶) Relax on the outdoor patio of this Bise cafe and slurp some noodles, such as *ajian-soba* (Asian-style soba), while enjoying views of Ie-jima.

Getting There & Away

By car, the drive from Naha to Nago takes about an hour; from there, it's about another hour to loop all the way around the peninsula.

The Motobu Peninsula is served by frequent loop lines from Nago – buses 66 and 65 respectively run anticlockwise and clockwise around the peninsula.

KERAMA ISLANDS

Depending on when you visit, the coral-fringed Kerama Islands (慶良間諸島) feel worlds apart from bustling Naha, a cheap and cheery boat ride away. Their azure waters provide sanctuary for sea turtles and breeding humpback whales, while safe white-sand beaches, ideal for swimming, snorkelling and lazy sun-bathing, are the main reasons to visit.

That said, since being declared a national park (Kerama Shotō Kokuritsu Kōen; 慶良間諸島国立公園) in 2014, their increased popularity with tour groups and day trippers from Naha means that during summer holidays, crowded ferries and beaches can make you feel like you've been transplanted into a pan-Asian spring break, instead of an idyllic island paradise.

Each of the three main islands – Zamami-jima, Aka-jima and Tokashiki-jima – can be visited as day trips from Naha, but to savour the slow-paced pleasures, visit in shoulder season and spend a night in a rustic island hostel or *minshuku*.

Sleeping & Eating

You won't find any fancy-pants luxury resorts in the Keramas, which is part of their charm. What you will find are diving-centric *minshuku* and sleepy island pensions – the bulk of which are concentrated on Zamami-jima.

On Aka-jima, you're best off reserving breakfast and dinner with your accommodation, as everything on this tiny island shuts down early, including the two basic shops selling food. Zamami-jima has some restaurants and cafes open for lunch and dinner, though it's a good idea to have breakfast at your accommodation.

Getting There & Around

Zamami Village Office (座間味村役場; ☎098-868-4567) operates two high-speed services per day on the *Queen Zamami 3* (¥3140, 70 minutes) and one daily service on the slower *Ferry Zamami* (¥2120, 1½ hours) between Zamami-jima and Naha's Tomari Port. The ferries usually stop at Aka-jima en route (same price). Advance reservations can be made online by following the link from www.zamamitouristinfo.wordpress.com/getting-here to the official ferry site.

The **Mitsu Shima** motorboat also makes four trips a day between Aka-jima and Zamami-jima (¥300, 15 minutes). For detailed information, refer to www.zamamienglishguide.com/ferries.

Aka-jima

098 / POP 300

A mere 2km in diameter, tiny Aka-jima (阿嘉島) makes up for in beauty what it lacks in size. Some of the best beaches in the Keramas and an extremely peaceful atmosphere mean it's easy to get stuck here for several days – and, of course, there's great snorkelling and diving offshore.

If you keep your eyes open around dusk you might spot a Kerama deer (慶良間シカ; *kerama shika*), descendants of deer that were brought by the Satsuma from Kagoshima when they conquered the Ryūkyūs in 1609. The deer are smaller and darker than their mainland cousins, and have been designated a National Treasure.

It's important to note that the main village on Aka-jima is Zamami-mura but Zamami-jima is the name of the slightly larger island just north of Aka-jima.

Sights & Activities

Both Marine House Seasir and Kawai Diving double as dive shops and *minshuku*. Both have English-speaking dive guides and friendly vibes.

★Nishibama Beach BEACH

(北浜ビーチ; Zamami-mura) Lovely beaches fringe every side of the island, but for sheer postcard-perfect beauty, it's hard to beat the 1km stretch of white sand on the northeast coast known as Nishibama Beach. It can be crowded in summer; if you want privacy, there are quieter beaches on the other sides of the island.

Sleeping

★Marine House Seasir MINSHUKU ¥¥

(マリンハウスシーサー; 090-8668-6544, in English 098-869-4022; www.seasir.com; 162 Aka; s/d incl 3 meals from ¥9800/17,600; P) At the west end of the main village, this diver-focused *minshuku* has good, clean Western- and Japanese-style rooms just a minute's amble from the beach. Credit cards are accepted, and a range of diving courses are available.

Hanamuro Inter-Islander's Hotel MINSHUKU ¥¥

(ハナムロインターアイランダーズホテル; 098-987-2301; http://hanamuroint.wixsite.com/keramablue; 179 Aka; r per person incl 2 meals from ¥9100;) Since the building that houses it is also a marine-biology research facility, this *minshuku* may look a little industrial from the outside. But the rooms are quiet, spacious and comfortable, with private terraces affording excellent sunrise views. Hire snorkelling equipment here (¥1000) and hop on the free shuttle to Nishibama Beach before returning for a creatively delicious dinner. Cash only.

Rates are reduced for stays longer than one night.

Hanamuro Inn GUESTHOUSE ¥¥

(ハナムロイン; 098-98-2301; www.geocities.jp/hanamuroint; 52 Aka; r per person incl 2 meals from ¥7500;) All six rooms at this cosy inn share bathrooms and a terrace with one-person soaker tubs. It's a one-minute walk to the beach if you dawdle. It closes completely after high season, but the innkeepers also run the Hanamuro Inter-Islander's Hotel at the back of the village, year-round.

Kawai Diving MINSHUKU ¥¥

(098-987-2219; www.oki-zamami.jp/~kawai; 153 Aka; s/d incl 2 meals from ¥7200/14,400; P@) Perched just above Maehama Beach on the south coast, this inn has simple rooms, a family atmosphere and a relaxed beachside location. English-speaking staff are happy to tell guests about the island and take them diving (one/two dives ¥7000/11,000, including equipment rental). Please note: cash payments only.

> **AWAMORI**
>
> While travelling through the Southwest Islands, be sure to sample the local firewater, *awamori* (泡盛), which is distilled from rice and has an alcohol content of 30% to 60%. Although it's usually served *mizu-wari* (水割; diluted with water), this is seriously lethal stuff, especially the *habushu* (ハブ酒), which comes with a small snake in the bottle. If you're hitting the *awamori* hard, take our advice and cancel your plans for the next day (or two).

Zamami-jima

098 / POP 924

Not to be confused with Zamami-mura, the village on Aka-jima, Zamami-jima (座間味島), just across the bay, is only *slightly* more developed. The island has its own share of lovely beaches, with great diving and snorkelling in the surrounding waters including a handful of delightful, even smaller offshore islands, which are accessible with the help of local guides. Plentiful tour options are available.

From January to March migrating humpback whales can be observed in these tropical waters, and Zamami is a popular spot for whale-watching expeditions.

Sights & Activities

Diving is one of the main draws of the gorgeous Keramas. It's always advisable to do your research online and book ahead, but if you've not been able to do that, drop into Joy Joy pension, which usually has helpful English-speaking guides on staff.

Whale-watching is possible between the months of December and April. For more information, either enquire at the tourist information office or call the **Zamami-mura Whale-Watching Association** (座間味村ホエールウォッチング協会; ☎098-896-4141; www.vill.zamami.okinawa.jp/whale; adult/child ¥5400/2700), which has one to two tours daily (two hours).

If you fancy a little solitude, you'll find picturesque empty beaches in the coves on the other sides of the island, away from the village. The best beaches, however, are on the islets of Gahi-jima (嘉比島) and Agenashiku-jima (安慶名敷島), which are located about a kilometre south of the port. Ringed by delightful white-sand beaches, they are perfect for a half-day Robinson Crusoe experience.

The tourist information office can help arrange boat tours (¥1500 per person round trip).

Rental cars, scooters and bicycles are available near the pier.

★Furuzamami Beach BEACH

(古座間味ビーチ; 1743 Zamami) Approximately 1km southeast from the port (over the hill) is this stunning 700m stretch of white sand, fronted by clear, shallow water and a bit of coral. The beach is well developed for day trippers, with toilets, showers and food stalls. You can also rent snorkelling gear here (¥1000).

Sleeping

Joy Joy PENSION ¥

(ジョイジョイ; ☎098-987-2445; www.keramajoyjoy.com; 434-2 Zamami; r per person without bathroom incl breakfast from ¥6000; ❄📶) This pension in the northwest corner of the village has Western- and Japanese-style rooms that surround a small garden area. It also runs a dive shop, with two-dive boat tours that include all equipment from ¥12,000.

Cha Villa GUESTHOUSE ¥¥

(チャーヴィラ; ☎098-987-3737; www.miniyon3737.sakura.ne.jp; 90 Zamami; s/d ¥8000/12,000; 🚭❄📶) *'Cha-bira'* means 'I'm home!' in the local dialect, and anchored by a shady tree in the garden out front, this friendly place feels just like home. Its attached cafe serves breakfast (should you crave toast and eggs rather than the usual Japanese spread) and light meals. Both Japanese- and Western-style rooms are available, all with private bathroom and kitchenette.

Marumiya OKINAWAN ¥¥

(まるみや; ☎098-987-3166; 432-2 Zamami; lunch special ¥700; ⏰11am-2.30pm & 6-10.30pm Thu-Tue; ❄) Cheap, delicious, friendly and therefore popular, the busy Marumiya offers a variety of Okinawan and Japanese dishes. Its inexpensive lunch specials are a great deal, but sell out fast.

Information

Maps and English-language information are dispensed at the port's **Zamami Village Tourist Information Center** (☎098-987-2277; www.zamamitouristinfo.wordpress.com; ⏰9am-5pm; 📶). An excellent online resource is www.zamamienglishguide.com.

KUME-JIMA

☎098 / POP 7647

Kume-jima (久米島), the furthest flung of the Okinawan islands – located about 90km west of Naha, from port to port, as the crow flies – is close enough for easy access and just far enough away to retain that real 'island' feel. Its location and transport connections, while convenient and affordable, mean that the island isn't really a day-trip destination, unlike the neighbouring Keramas. The plus side to this is that Kume-jima rarely feels crowded.

While there are some mountainous areas offering spectacular views, the island's 63.5 sq km of terrain is mostly flat and covered with sugar cane. Its shoreline boasts a few lovely beaches and the mother of all sandbars off its east coast. There's also a decent selection of interesting historic sites, vistas and activities beyond snorkelling and diving, making Kume-jima a worthy overnight or two-night stay.

For a moment at least, you might not want to leave.

Sights & Activities

★ Former

Uezu Residence HISTORIC BUILDING

(上江洲家; 816 Nishime; ¥300; ⏲10am-6pm) Built around 1750, this traditional Ryūkyūan dwelling was the former home of Kume-jima's dominant clan, the Uezu family. Lovingly maintained and set amid a beautiful subtropical garden, the grounds of this open house are a delight to stroll among – you can almost feel the ghosts of the past overseeing your visit, grateful for your interest in their lineage.

Uegusuku Castle Ruins RUINS

(宇江城城跡; Uegusukujo-ato; 2064-1 Uegusuku; P) FREE Perched atop the island's highest peak, at an elevation of around 310m, are the meticulously placed crumbling stone walls of what was once the stronghold of the ruling Kume lord, before the 16th century. Views from the tiered levels of the former castle, looking out over the East China Sea, and the whole of Kume-jima, are nothing short of spectacular.

Tatami-ishi BEACH

(畳石; Ōjima) On tiny **Ōjima** (奥武島), which is connected to Kume-jima's east coast by a causeway, you'll find the intriguing Tatami-ishi, a natural formation of flat pentagonal rocks that covers the seashore. When the water is calm, the beach around the rocks is a safe and pleasant place to frolic, swim and snorkel. Nearby you'll find Bade Haus Kumejima onsen and its delightful **Ōjima Campgrounds** (奥武島キャンプ場; ☎098-985-8600; www.bade-kumejima.co.jp/about/camp; 170-1 Ōjima; per night adult/child ¥540/270).

Eef Beach BEACH

(イーフビーチ) Kume-jima's most popular beach is also one of its nicest, though it sadly does receive its fair share of flotsam from the ocean. *Iifu (Eef)* means 'white' in the local Kume dialect, and not surprisingly, the beach is known for its powdery white sand. The mainstay of Kume-jima's accommodation, restaurants and facilities are found in the area alongside the beachfront.

Hate-no-hama BEACH

(はての浜) Kume-jima's most famous attraction is this 7km sandbar that extends from the eastern point of the island, pointing back towards Okinawa-hontō. If you arrive by air, you can't miss this coral-fringed strip of white framed by turquoise sea. Hatenohama Kankō Service runs three-hour tours out here.

Shinri-hama BEACH

(シンリ浜) As any local will tell you, this attractive beach is the best place on the island for watching the sunset over the East China Sea. Find it on the west coast near Cypress Resort (p814).

★ Bade Haus Kumejima ONSEN

(バーデハウス久米島; ☎098-985-8600; www.bade-kumejima.co.jp; 170-1 Ōjima; large pool only ¥2000, onsen bath & sauna only ¥1000; ⏲10am-9pm, last entry 8pm) On little Ōjima island, by the Tatami-ishi rock formations, you'll find this shiny seaside bathhouse, which has a slightly European vibe. A large indoor pool with jets is filled with mineral-rich sea water, pumped up from a depth of 612m. Swimwear is required in this section of the complex, but if you're looking for a more Japanese onsen-style experience, there's a quieter, clothing optional sauna and hot-tub area, which is refreshing after a skin-parching day in the sun.

Tours

Hatenohama Kankō Service BOATING

(はての浜観光サービス; ☎090-8292-8854; https://inhatenohama.wixsite.com/hatenohama; 172 Une; tours from adult/child ¥3500/2000) Hatenohama Kankō Service runs a range of tours to the sandbar, starting with the basic two-hour free-time plan, for ¥3500. Hotel pick-ups are available – enquire at your accommodation. Departure times, set by the captain in advance, are subject to tidal and weather conditions and may be cancelled at short notice due to unforgiving seas.

Sleeping & Eating

The majority of accommodation options are located along the 1.5km waterfront stretch of Eef Beach, but if you're looking for a more far-flung island feel, there are a number of decent options scattered about the island.

There are plenty of *izakaya* along Eef Beach as well as a supermarket and a 24-hour convenience store.

Minshuku Nankurunaisā MINSHUKU ¥
(民宿なんくるないさぁ; ☎098-985-7973; 160-68 Higa; r per person from ¥5500; P@) If you're looking for a clean, quiet, family-run *minshuku* in the Eef Beach area, this is a solid, no-frills option welcoming international guests.

★**Cypress Resort** RESORT ¥¥
(☎098-985-3700; www.cypresshotels.jp/kumejima; 803-1 Ōhara; s/d from ¥11,925/13,050; P) Kume-jima's nicest digs are found near the airport, fronting the lovely-at-sunset Shinri-hama (p813) beach. The resort boasts an attractive (though shallow and tepid) beachfront infinity pool; friendly, helpful staff; an excellent restaurant; and large, ocean-fronted rooms with deep balconies. Unless you have a car, you're limited to the resort's dining options as there are few facilities in the area, especially after dark.

Kumejima Eef Beach Hotel HOTEL ¥¥
(久米島イーフビーチホテル; ☎098-985-7111; www.courthotels.co.jp; 548 Janadō; s/d incl breakfast from ¥8800/14,600; P@) The somewhat dated though absolute waterfront Eef Beach Hotel is a good bet for budget-with-a-whiff-of-luxury stays on the island. It's *location, location, location* here, with beach and the island's mainstay of dining options and facilities mere steps away. An airport shuttle is available.

Yangwa Soba OKINAWAN ¥
(そば やん小~; ☎080-3226-3130; 509 Nakadomari; dishes ¥550-900; noon-2pm or until sold out Mon-Sat; P) Kume-jima's most famous soba shop is open for lunch only and is worth the trip. Serving handmade noodles out of his own home, the hospitable Nakasone-san cultivates a warm and nurturing island vibe. Enjoy your Kume-jima soba (with barbecued pork rib), or miso and bean-sprout soba, in the open-air tatami dining room or at the table in the front garden.

Information

Kumejima Tourism Association (久米島町観光協会; ☎098-851-7973; www.kanko-kumejima.com; 160-57 Higa, Eef Beach Information Plaza; 10am-4pm) Has offices are located near Eef Beach, and operates a helpful counter at the airport in summer (opens to meet incoming flights.)

Getting There & Away

The **airport** (久米島空港; Kumejima Kūkō; ☎098-985-4812; 566-2 Kitahara) is at the western extreme of the island, with the main port of Kanegusuku (兼城) just a few kilometres south. JTA and RAC operate five to six flights a day between Naha and Kume-jima.

Kume Shōsen (久米商船; ☎098-868-2686; www.kumeline.com) runs one or two daily ferries from Naha's Tomari Port to/from Kume-jima's Kanegusuku Port (¥3390, three hours).

Getting Around

The island has an efficient bus system, and there are several rental-car companies at the port and airport. Renting a car (from ¥5500 per day) is by far your best bet for uncovering the island's unsung charms.

MIYAKO ISLANDS

Just north of the Tropic of Cancer, the Miyako Islands (宮古諸島) have some of the most beautiful white-sand beaches in the Nansei-Shotō, with good diving, snorkelling and kiteboarding to boot. The island group consists of the main island of Miyako-jima, along with Ikema-jima, Irabu-jima, Shimoji-jima and Kurima-jima, plus a scattering of tiny islets.

In 2015, nine years of construction culminated in the opening of the 3540m **Irabu Bridge** (伊良部大橋), rendering the ferry obsolete and making Irabu-jima and Shimoji-jima much more accessible from Miyako-jima. Despite the increased ease of getting here, these islands retain a stuck-in-time feel and an unhurried pace, enhanced by abiding island congeniality.

One gets the feeling that the rush of tourism and development that was anticipated once the bridge was completed never really came, which makes the area, whose natural beauty sells itself, just that little bit more interesting.

Getting There & Away

Both JTA/RAC (Japan Airlines) and ANA fly into **Miyakojima Airport** (宮古島空港; Miyakojima-kūkō; MMY; Map p815; ☎0980-72-1212; 1657-128 Shimozato), which is centrally located, a short drive from most accommodation and the busy Hirara town centre.

Scheduled direct services connect the island with Tokyo's Haneda Airport (JTA/ANA), Osaka's Kansai Airport (ANA), Naha (JTA/RAC/ANA) and Ishigaki (RAC/ANA) airports.

Miyako Islands

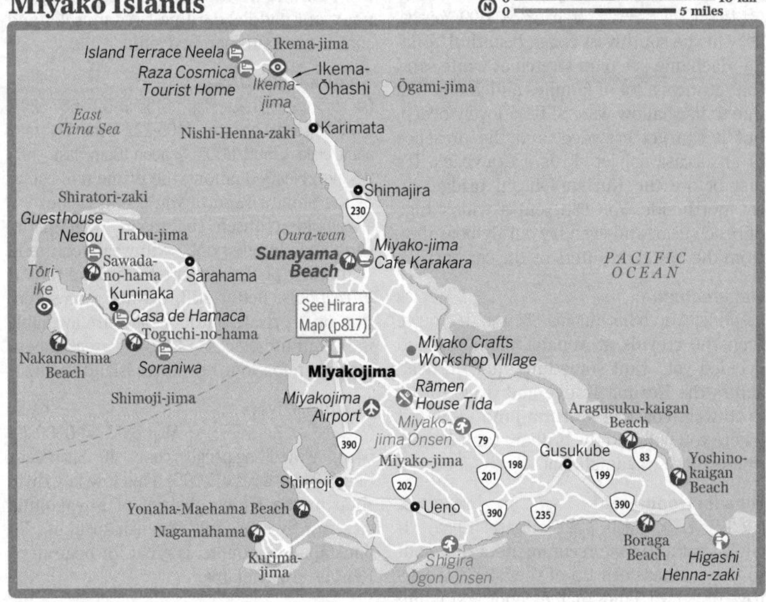

Getting Around

Miyako-jima has a limited bus network that operates from two bus stands in Miyakojima city's Hirara district. Buses run between the airport and Hirara (¥230, 10 minutes).

Buses also depart from Yachiyo bus terminal for Ikema-jima (¥510, 35 minutes), and from the Miyako Kyōei bus terminal, 700m east of town, to Yoshino-kaigan/Boraga Beach (¥510, 50 minutes). Yet another line runs between Hirara and Yoneha-Maehama/Kurima-jima (¥390, 30 minutes).

The island's flat terrain is perfectly suited to biking; hire bicycles from guesthouse Hiraraya (p816) or enquire at the Miyakojima Tourism Association (p818).

Most will find renting a car from the numerous car-rental outlets at the airport to be the most practical and efficient way to explore the islands.

Irabu-jima and Shimoji-jima are connected to Miyako-jima by a series of bridges.

Miyako-jima

0980 / POP 54,908

The main island in the Miyako group, Miyako-jima (宮古島) is a mostly flat expanse of sugar cane edged with excellent beaches and long fingers of land pointing out into the sea. Lying just offshore are four smaller islands, all of which are connected to the main island by bridges.

You can happily spend your days here hopping from one great beach to the next, with a spot of snorkelling, stand-up paddleboarding or even fly-boarding, if you fancy. If you tire of those, a seaside drive to the various capes and wetlands is a great way to spend a few hours.

If you're visiting another of the bigger islands beyond the pull of Okinawa-hontō, both Miyako-jima and Ishigaki-jima have their own merits. Miyako is a little rougher around the edges than its southern counterpart, but that adds to its charm. You'll feel a bit more like Robinson Crusoe here.

Sights

★Sunayama Beach BEACH

(砂山ビーチ; Map p815; 0980-73-2690; 7am-7pm; P) Just 4km north of the Hirara district of Miyakojima city, you'll find this little, archetypally tropical Japan beach, which lies at the bottom of a large sand dune (hence the name 'Sand Mountain Beach'). If you've only got one beach day to spend, or are getting around via bus, park yourself here. Find showers and toilets here, too.

Yonaha-Maehama Beach BEACH
(与那覇前浜ビーチ; Map p815; 1199 Yonaha; P) On the southwest coast, beautiful Yonaha-Maehama is a 6km stretch of white sand that attracts a lot of families and young folk due to its shallow waters. It's a lovely beach, but it can get crowded, and the presence of an occasional jet ski is a drawback. It's just before the Kurima-Ōhashi bridge, on the north side. You can rent a wide range of beach gear, and even try out fly-boarding, from the rental outfitters by the car park.

Nagamahama BEACH
(長間浜; Map p815; Kurima Shimoji) If you've seen the crowds at Yonaha-Maehama and decided you want something quieter, head across the Kurima Bridge and drive to the northwest coast of **Kurima-jima** (来間島), where you will find the brilliant (and usually uncrowded) Nagamahama.

Higashi Henna-zaki LIGHTHOUSE
(東平安名崎; Map p815; Higashi-henna) If you've got a car, we recommend a drive out to the southeastern tip of the island, a narrow finger of land that extends 2km into the Pacific Ocean. There are picnic tables, walking trails and a lighthouse at the point to explore.

Boraga Beach BEACH
(保良泉ビーチ; Map p815; Gusukube) On the southeast end of the island, this is a popular spot for snorkelling and kayaking (with a hair-raisingly steep access road).

Ikema-jima ISLAND
(池間島; Map p815) Head north to drive across **Ikema-Ōhashi** (池間大橋) to the little island of Ikema-jima. The shallow aquamarine water on either side of this 1.4km bridge is insanely beautiful on a sunny day (just try to keep your eyes on the road). You'll find several secluded pocket beaches around the coast of Ikema-jima.

Activities

Miyako-jima Onsen ONSEN
(宮古島温泉; Map p815; 0980-75-5151; https://miyakojima-onsen.co.jp; 1898-19 Higashi-nakasone; ¥900; 11am-10pm, last admission 9pm) More like a *sento* (public bath) than a typical mainland onsen, Miyako's original bathhouse, with attached hotel and treatment centre, has a chilled-out, communal vibe. Its earthy, mineral-rich waters are just the right temperature. Located in the middle of the island, about a 15-minute drive from Hirara, it's the perfect place to rejuvenate your paddleboarding-tired muscles and soothe your sun-parched skin.

Shigira Ōgon Onsen ONSEN
(シギラ黄金温泉; Map p815; 092-687-5294; www.nanseirakuen.com; 1405-223 Ueno Shinzato; adult/child ¥1500/800; noon-10pm, last entry 9.30pm) Nestled among the prime real estate of the Shigira Resorts you'll find this exclusive-looking onsen spa resort with its lagoon-style jungle pool (swimwear required), swimming pool and more traditional *rotemburo* pools. Better still, private rooms centred on a private outdoor bath are available in 90-minute blocks (¥4320). A great way to limber up for your next inter-island flight.

Penguin Divers DIVING
(ペンギンダイバーズ; Map p817; 0980-79-5433; www.diving-penguin.com; 40 Shimozato, Hirara; 2 boat dives ¥13,000) This low-key dive-shop in the Hirara district of Miyakojima city, run by a friendly, English-speaking Fijian-Japanese couple, is great for beginners. Rentals are available.

Courses

Miyako Crafts Workshop Village COURSE
(宮古島市体験工芸村; Map p815; 0980-73-4111; www.miyakotaiken.com; 1166-286 Higashi-nakasone, Hirara; workshops from ¥1500; 10am-6pm) At this crafts village adjoining the Miyako Botanical Garden, you can learn about Miyako-jima's traditional handicrafts with some hands-on creativity. Course offerings, most of which are suitable for kids, include making *shiisā* (lion-dog roof guardians) from clay, cooking Miyako specialities, and *Miyako-jōfu* (traditional weaving). Though some workshops accommodate walk-ins, it's best to make reservations beforehand.

Sleeping

Hiraraya GUESTHOUSE ¥
(ひららや; Map p817; 0980-75-3221; www.miyako-net.ne.jp/~hiraraya; 282-1 Higashi-nakasone, Hirara; dm per night/week ¥2500/15,000, s/d ¥3500/6000; P) The genial, English-speaking Hiro presides over this laid-back spot where young neighbours and friends cruise in to hang out. Accommodation is available in a dorm with huge curtained bunk beds, or a Japanese-style private room. All guests share the facilities, which include a big kitchen. Look for the doorway curtain that says 'Hiraraya' down the side of the quiet lane.

Hotel Peace Island Miyakojima HOTEL ¥¥
(ホテルピースアイランド宮古島; Map p817; ☎0980-74-1717; http://peace-k.jp/miyako; 310 Nishizato, Hirara; s/d incl breakfast from ¥7900/9500; P ❄ 📶) Peace Island has a bright, clean, welcoming vibe, even if the rooms are decidedly average – except for the luxury of washer-dryer units in every room. The hotel's brand-new annexe across the street (the 'Hotel Peacely In Miyakojima Nexus') has the best rooms, set up like mini-condos, with wood flooring, tiny kitchenettes and in-room laundry units.

Raza Cosmica Tourist Home HOTEL ¥¥
(ラザ・コスミカツーリストホーム; Map p815; ☎0980-75-2020; www.raza-cosmica.com; 309-1 Hirara-maezato; r per person without bathroom ¥7000; P ❄ 📶) This serene South Asian–themed inn sits above a lovely secluded beach on Ikema-jima. Wood-floored, Western-style rooms offer peace and quiet – especially as children under 12 are not permitted. Spotless bathroom facilities are shared. Because of its somewhat isolated location, it's best to rent a car. Reservations must be made in advance via email.

Island Terrace Neela BOUTIQUE HOTEL ¥¥¥
(アイランドテラス・ニーラ; Map p815; ☎0980-74-4678; www.neela.jp; 317-1 Hirara-maezato; s/d incl breakfast from ¥36,000/39,600; P ❄ 📶 🏊) Overlooking a serene white-sand beach on Ikema-jima, this intimate high-end resort looks like a whitewashed Mediterranean retreat airlifted to Japan. The private villas would make a decadent honeymoon destination. Rates are moderately less expensive during slower seasons.

Eating & Drinking

The downtown alleys of Miyakojima city's Hirara district come alive at night and offer the best dining variety, though there are numerous options further afield.

One of Miyako-jima's local specialities is the seaweed known as *umibudō* (literally 'sea grapes'), with a softly crunchy texture and sweet seawater flavour. Sea grapes don't travel so well, so it's a delicacy to enjoy almost exclusively here and in the Yaeyama Islands.

★ **Rāmen House Tida** NOODLES ¥
(ラーメンハウスてぃだ; Map p815; ☎0980-73-9113; 3107-325 Shimozato, Hirara; noodle bowls ¥550-850; ⏰11am-3pm & 5-9pm) This old-school family noodle joint exudes a Shōwa-era movie vibe if only for its fabulously faded original decor. Friendly hosts dish out hearty bowls of steaming broth, tasty fried rice and juicy *gyōza*. Many years of slow-paced island cooking, kids growing up at the counter, and locals visiting week after week have all helped to perfect the product.

It's on the way to Miyako-jima Onsen near the intersection of Rtes 78 and 194.

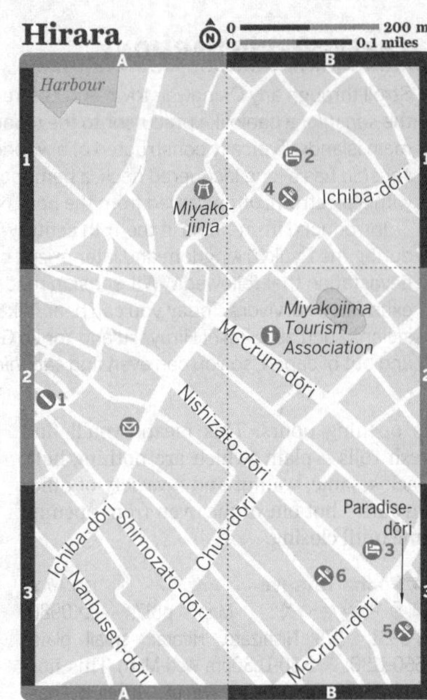

Hirara

Mojanopan BAKERY ¥
(モジャのパン; Map p817; ☎090-3977-6778; 20 Higashi-Nakasone, Hirara; bread ¥160-300, coffee ¥250-450; ⏰11am-3pm or until sold out Tue-Sat) If you couldn't see this hole-in-the-wall bakery, you'd smell it. It's unique for its owner's commitment to selling fresh bread throughout

THREE-STRING HARMONY

Stroll through any Okinawan town and before long you'll likely hear the tinkly sound of the *sanshin*, a banjolike precursor to the ubiquitous *shamisen* that is played on Japan's main islands. Typically constructed of a wooden frame covered with python skin, the *sanshin* has a long lacquered neck, a bamboo bridge and three strings that are struck with a plectrum, often carved from the horn of a water buffalo.

Introduced from China in the 16th century, the *sanshin* was used for court music during the Ryūkyū kingdom and later prized by commoners for its soothing sound; in the devastation that followed WWII, *sanshin* made of tin cans and nylon string cheered the exhausted survivors. Today you can hear folk songs featuring *sanshin* all over Japan. Musicians such as Takashi Hirayasu and Yoriko Ganeko have helped popularise the sound in and out of Japan, so you can even find *sanshin* groups overseas.

its opening hours. This means you'll find fresh rolls – plain (which are nothing but), black sesame, walnut and a variety of other flavours – hot out of the oven from opening time until closing.

★ Pōcha Tatsuya IZAKAYA ¥¥
(ぽうちゃたつや; Map p817; ☎0980-73-3931; 275 Nishizato, Hirara; small plates ¥560-1180; ⏲6.30-11.30pm Wed-Mon) This hospitable *izakaya* is a warm, efficient bastion of Miyako-jima quality, serving fresh, thoughtfully prepared local fare such as *kobushime-yawaraka-ni* (steamed cuttlefish; ¥730) and *sūchiki* (vinegared pork with bitter melon; ¥630). Its justified popularity necessitates reserving ahead. Some Japanese skills are helpful here, as the specials change often, but requesting *omakase* (chef's choice) will result in a succession of regional delights.

Nanraku IZAKAYA ¥¥
(南楽; Map p817; ☎0980-73-1855; Asahi Bldg 1F, 568 Nishizato, Hirara; small plates ¥650-1480; ⏲6pm-midnight, closed irregularly) Nanraku is Miyako-jima embodied in an *izakaya* – an earthy, convivial atmosphere, with ingredients sourced from local bounty. Chef Nanraku-san is a local boy, and his celebration of the island's cuisine and its provenance shines through in what he plates. He's famous for the *nekomanma* (*donburi* with bonito and *umibudō*). Splurge on Miyako beef sashimi (¥3500 for a small dish for two).

This is an excellent place for *osusume* (recommendation) – name your budget and food preferences.

★ Miyako-jima Cafe Karakara CAFE
(宮古島のカフェカラカラ; Map p815; ☎0980-73-8385; 130 Ōura, Hirara) Stop in to pay a visit to the inimitable and delightful Mr and Mrs Yamashita, who built this fabulously atmospheric sea-shanty cafe on the road to Ikema-jima, with their own love and gumption. Be sure to have a bowl of the special Miyako curry! The cafe is a few kilometres from gorgeous Sunayama Beach (p815).

ℹ Information

Miyakojima Tourism Association (宮古島観光協会; Map p817; ☎0980-73-1881; www.miyako-guide.net; 187-2 Nishizato; ⏲9am-6pm) Based opposite the Miyakojima City Hall, also operates an information desk in the arrivals hall of Miyakojima Airport (p814), where you can pick up one of several local sightseeing-related publications. Travellers who can read Japanese should also grab a copy of the Japanese-language versions of the tourist literature and maps, which have more detailed listings.

Irabu-jima & Shimoji-jima

Not much happens on Irabu-jima (伊良部島) and Shimoji-jima (下地島) aside from sugarcane cultivation and the 'touch-and-go' (landing and immediate take-off) exercises by ANA pilots. These islands are blessed with uncrowded beaches and a snail-paced vibe that make them worth a look-see: both now have easy road links from Miyakojima city.

Sights

Tōri-ike CAVE
(通り池; Map p815; Sawata, Irabu) An intriguing site for a stroll or dive is this pair of seawater pools on the west coast of Shimoji-jima, known by locals as 'dragon's eyes' – these are actually sinkholes in the coral that formed the island.

Toguchi-no-hama BEACH

(渡口の浜; Map p815; 1352-16 Irabu) On Irabu-jima's west coast, this is the island's best swimming beach, with showers, toilets and the delightful Blue Turtle bar-restaurant.

Nakanoshima Beach BEACH

(中の島ビーチ; Map p815; Shimoji-jima, Irabu) The best snorkelling beach on Shimoji and Irabu, Nakanoshima Beach is protected by a high-walled bay on the west coast of Shimoji-jima. You'll greatly enhance your experience by making your visit early in the morning, around lunchtime or in lower seasons, when buses and boats aren't descending on the beach all at once. Look for the sign reading 'Nakano Island The Beach'.

Sleeping & Eating

There's not much by way of dining options, save for a handful of daytime-only cafes on each of the islands, but you'll always find something open. It's a good idea to pack some snacks and sandwiches in Miyakojima city in preparation for a pop-up beach picnic should you find yourself peckish at a picturesque spot.

Guesthouse Nesou GUESTHOUSE ¥¥

(ゲストハウスねそう; Map p815; 0980-78-3380; 1436-1 Irabu; dm/s/d ¥2800/4000/6000, breakfast ¥300) A few blocks inland from the beach, this tiny guesthouse, formerly known as 'Birafuyaa', is run by a welcoming, clued-in couple who have created a kind of a social hub for local musicians and artists and visiting free spirits from around the globe. They offer inexpensive bike rental, snorkelling tours, sunset beers on the rooftop patio and an all-around serene vibe.

Casa de Hamaca GUESTHOUSE ¥¥

(カサ・デ・アマカ; Map p815; 080-3277-8941; www.casadehamaca.com; 621-3 Kuninaka; s/d without bathroom ¥3500/6300; closed Jan-Mar; P ❄ ᯤ) If you're seeking something out of the ordinary, opt to stay at the singular, utterly delightful Casa de Hamaca. Run by Japanese runner and world traveller Sekiyama Tadashi, this is probably the only accommodation in Japan outfitted solely with hammocks *and* with a Spanish-speaking proprietor. The inn is not suitable for families, which creates a more relaxed, kid-free vibe.

★ **Soraniwa** BOUTIQUE HOTEL ¥¥¥

(そらにわ; Map p815; 0980-74-5528; www.soraniwa.org; 721-1 Irabu-azairabu; s incl breakfast/2 meals from ¥15,000/19,500; P ❄ @) For a secluded and romantic experience, head to Soraniwa on the south coast. This small, stylish cafe-hotel is run by a young couple transplanted from the 'mainland'. The restaurant (open 11.30am to 6pm Friday to Tuesday; lunch ¥950 to ¥1400) uses local, organic ingredients, while the intimate, modern hotel features sumptuous beds, shelves made from repurposed wood and a rooftop Jacuzzi looking out to the sea.

The private 'side.B *sora*' condo offers 100 sq metres of refined luxury including an overflow pool off the balcony. *Shhh*... don't tell everyone, but it's quite reasonably priced. Check the website for details.

★ **Blue Turtle** BISTRO ¥¥

(0980-74-5333; www.blueturtle.jp; 1352-16 Irabu; mains ¥1200-2800) This blingy little bistro gets bonus points for its delightfully secluded location, resting atop a shaded grassy knoll on a white-sand beach, whose turquoise waters glimmer seductively while you sip your cocktail at the rooftop bar. Romantics might bypass the bar to dine on well-presented European and Japanese fare in the stylish air-conditioned bistro.

YAEYAMA ISLANDS

At the far southwestern end of the Southwest Islands are the gorgeous Yaeyama Islands (八重山諸島; Yaeyama-shotō), which include the main islands of Ishigaki-jima and Iriomote-jima as well as a spread of 17 isles. Located near the Tropic of Cancer, they are renowned for their lovely beaches, superb diving and lush landscapes.

The Yaeyama Islands are one of the most popular destinations in the Southwest Islands. They offer Japan's best snorkelling and diving, and some of the country's last intact subtropical jungles and mangrove swamps (both on Iriomote-jima). Perhaps the best feature of the Yaeyamas is their variety and the ease with which you can explore them: plentiful ferry services run between Ishigaki city and nearby islands such as Iriomote-jima and Taketomi-jima, and you can easily explore three or four islands in one trip.

Yaeyama Islands

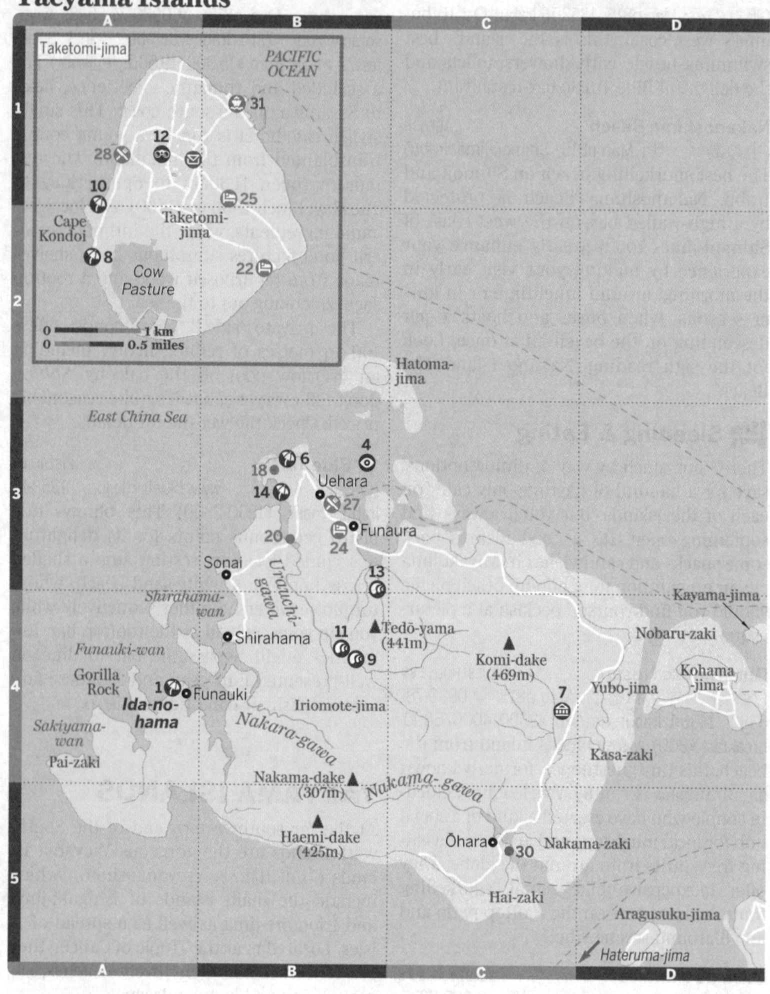

Yaeyama Islands

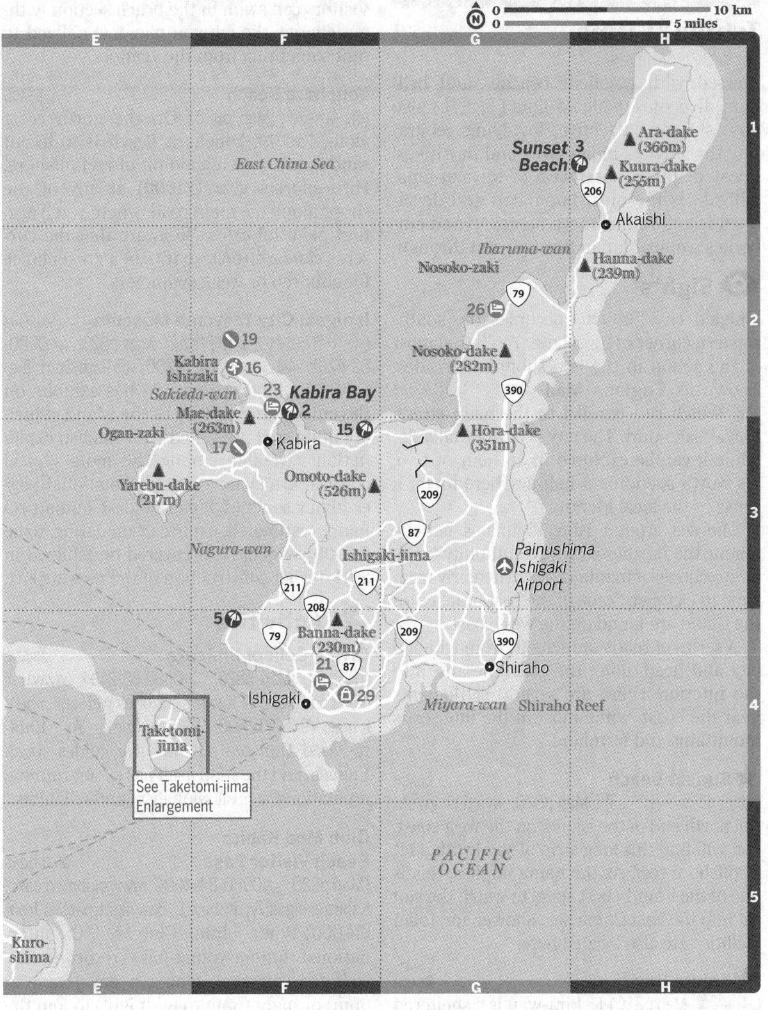

Sleeping

21 Art Hotel Isghigaki........................F4
Coral Garden..............................(see 6)
22 Hoshinoya Taketomi-jima.............B2
23 Iriwa..F2
24 Irumote-sō B3
25 Takana Ryokan..............................B1
26 Tsundara Beach Retreat.................G2

Eating

27 Densā Shokudō B3
Kitchen Inaba ....(see 14)
Oishiisā-gu................................(see 23)
28 Soba-dokoro Takenoko A1

Shopping

29 Minsā Kōgeikan...............................F4

Transport

30 Ōhara Port C5
31 Taketomi Higashi-ko B1
Uehara Port ....(see 27)
Yamaneko Rentacar..................(see 24)

Ishigaki-jima

0980 / POP 48,816

Blessed with excellent beaches and brilliant dive sites, Ishigaki-jima (石垣島) also possesses an attractive, low-lying geography that invites long drives and day hikes. Located 100km southwest of Miyako-jima, Ishigaki is the most populated and developed island in the Yaeyama group and embodies tropical Japan through and through.

Sights

Ishigaki city (石垣市) occupies the southwestern corner of the island. You'll find most of the action in the two shopping arcades, known as **Euglena Mall** (ユーグレナモール), which run parallel to the main street, Shiyakusho-dōri. The city is easily walkable; while it can be explored in an hour or two, it's worth spending a half-day here to get a sense of the local identity.

The sea around Ishigaki-jima is famous among the Japanese diving community for its large schools of manta rays, particularly from June to October. Some of the best beaches on the island are found on the west coast.

A series of roads branch out from Ishigaki city and head along the coastline and into the interior. There are several settlements near the coast, while most of the interior is mountains and farmland.

★Sunset Beach BEACH

(サンセットビーチ; Map p820; www.i-sb.jp) At the north end of the island, on the west coast, you will find this long strip of sand with a bit of offshore reef. As the name implies, this is one of the island's best spots to watch the sun set into the East China Sea. Shower and toilet facilities are also located here.

★Kabira Bay BEACH

(川平湾; Map p820) Kabira-wan is a sheltered bay with white-sand shores and a couple of interesting clumplike islets offshore. Swimming is not allowed in the bay, as pearls are cultivated here, but there's no shortage of glass-bottomed boats offering a look at the reef life below.

Fusaki Beach Aqua Garden BEACH

(フサキビーチアクアガーデン; Map p820; 0980-88-7000; www.fusaki.com/english; 1625 Arakawa; from ¥2000) Nonguests of the adjacent resort can pay to enter this massive 'aqua garden' complex with a beachfront pool, bar-restaurant, yoga lessons and a huge range of equipment rental options, from snorkels to stand-up paddleboards. Visitors can swim in the beach section without charge, though you may feel obliged to rent something from the vendors.

Yonehara Beach BEACH

(米原海岸; Map p820) On the north coast along Rte 79, Yonehara Beach is a decent sand beach with a good bit of reef offshore. Hire snorkel gear (¥1000) at any of the shops along the main road, where you'll also find plentiful cafes. Be aware that the currents can be strong, so it's not a great choice for children or weak swimmers.

Ishigaki City Yaeyama Museum MUSEUM

(石垣市立八重山博物館; Map p823; 0980-82-4712; 4-1 Tonoshiro; ¥200; 9am-5pm Tue-Sun) This modest museum has exhibits on the culture and history of the island, which are quite well presented with English explanations. Notable among the more typical cultural artefacts: a few informational pages about some of Japan's oldest human remains (estimated, using carbon dating, to be 24,000 years old), discovered on Ishigaki in 2011 during construction of the new airport.

Activities

Diving School Umicoza DIVING

(海講座; Map p820; 0980-88-2434; www.umicoza.com; 1287-97 Kabira; 1/2 dives with equipment rental ¥9450/12,600; 8am-6pm) At Kabira-based Umicoza, all the dive guides speak English, and the shop itself has a long-running reputation for professionalism and reliability.

Club Med Kabira Beach Visitor Pass OUTDOORS

(Map p820; 0980-84-4600; www.clubmed.ca/r/Kabira-Ishigaki/y; Kabira 1; day/night passes from ¥14,000) While joining Club Med, the international fun-for-young-folks resort group, isn't for everyone, taking a day (11am to 6pm) or night (6pm to midnight) to join the fun and enjoy this excellent resort's pool, private beach and extensive drinking and dining facilities might be music to the ears of many. The deal is kept fairly hush-hush... enquire at the front desk. Passes include facilities use, food and limited beverages.

Kabira Ishizaki Manta Scramble DIVING

(Map p820) The most popular dive spot on Ishigaki-jima is Manta Scramble, off the coast of Kabira Ishizaki. Although you'll probably be sharing it with a fair number of dive boats, you're almost guaranteed to see a manta (or four) in season. There are a number of dive shops on Ishigaki.

Ishigaki City

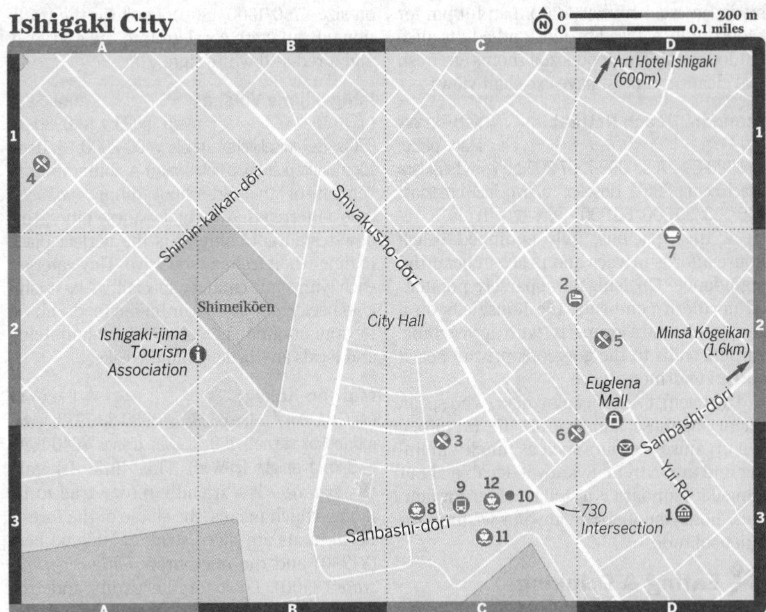

Sleeping

Rakutenya GUESTHOUSE ¥

(楽天屋; Map p823; ☎0980-83-8713; www3.big.or.jp/~erm8p3gi; 291 Ōkawa; r per person without bathroom ¥3600; P❄@☎) This quaint guesthouse is two blocks north of the shopping arcades in Ishigaki city, and has attractive Western- and Japanese-style rooms in a couple of rickety old wooden houses. The managers are a friendly Japanese couple who speak some English and are a fantastic source of local information.

Iriwa GUESTHOUSE ¥¥

(イリワ; Map p820; ☎0980-88-2563; http://iriwa.org; 599 Kabira; dm ¥2700, s/d from ¥7000/7600; P❄@☎) Just above Kabira-wan on the north coast, Iriwa is a comfortable guesthouse with dorm beds, two large private rooms, a small self-contained cottage and two converted trailers, all warmly decorated with a Hawaiian aesthetic. All but one trailer share bathroom facilities. It's run by a super-chilled, friendly young Korean-Japanese couple who like to share meals and snorkelling expeditions with guests.

The main house has a communal lounge room and spacious, sunny kitchen – the roof, the highest point in Kabira village, offers excellent views of the sea during the day and stars at night.

Ishigaki City

Sights

1 Ishigaki City Yaeyama Museum........D3

Sleeping

2 Rakutenya........C2

Eating

3 Ishigakijima Village........C3
4 Kamal Indian Nepal Food........A1
5 Mori-no-Kokage........D2
6 Shima-no-tabemonoya Paikaji........C3

Drinking & Nightlife

7 Cafe Taniwha........D2

Transport

8 Anei Kankō........C3
9 Ishigaki Bus Terminal........C3
10 Ishigaki Rentacar........C3
11 Ishigaki-jima Rittō Ferry Terminal........C3
12 Yaeyama Kankō Ferry........C3

★**Art Hotel Ishigaki** HOTEL ¥¥¥

(アートホテル石垣; Map p820; ☎0980-83-3311; www.art-ishigakijima.com; 559 Okawa; s/d from ¥14,800/18,900; P❄☎) Formerly the Hotel Nikkō Yaeyama, this thoroughly renovated and rebranded hilltop complex, though far from the shoreline, makes an excellent choice for its range of facilities, including a communal bathhouse (which can be visited by day guests between 4.30pm and 10pm for ¥1600) and a loved-by-kids-and-adults-alike outdoor pool. The good-sized rooms are fresh and clean, and most have excellent views.

Tsundara Beach Retreat APARTMENT ¥¥¥
(つんだらビーチ・リトリート; Map p820; ☎0980-89-2765, 090-7587-2029; www.tsundarabeach.com; 895-2 Nosoko; d/tr/q incl breakfast ¥40,000/50,000/60,000; P ❄ 📶) Truly a retreat, this spacious, fully equipped beach house affords privacy and peace in beautiful abundance. On Ishigaki's sparsely populated northern peninsula, the house sits on a grassy 1-hectare property with a vegetable garden, trails to the gorgeous private beach and an enormous tepee.

The pacifist American owners (who speak fluent Japanese and live on the premises) can organise ecotours such as jungle zip lining and are extremely knowledgeable about Ishigaki. Tsundara is a stellar refuge for families, honeymooners or anyone wishing for quiet solitude.

Eating & Drinking

Kamal Indian Nepal Food INDIAN ¥
(Map p823; ☎080-3753-1313; 2-6-31 Hamazaki-cho; dishes ¥600-1050, sets from ¥1200; ⏲11am-11pm; 🖉) There's lots to love about this spotless restaurant serving Indian and Nepali cuisine, from what appears to have been a former gas stand or car-rental office. Meals are authentic and full of flavour and a variety of set-menu options offer excellent value. Vegetarian friendly!

Oishiisā-gu NOODLES ¥
(おいシーサー遇; Map p820; ☎0980-88-2233; 906-1 Kabira; meals ¥600-1050; ⏲11am-5pm, summer to 7pm; P) This sunlit soba place in Kabira serves local dishes like chilled *yomogi-soba* (mugwort soba) served in a conch shell, or *tebichi soba* (Okinawan soba topped with stewed pork trotters). Even better, follow your lunch with homemade gelato in flavours like Ishigaki beer, *gōyā* or black sesame and soybean.

★ **Shima-no-tabemonoya Paikaji** IZAKAYA ¥¥
(島の食べものや 南風; Map p823; ☎0980-82-6027; 219 Ōkawa; small plates ¥580-1470; ⏲5pm-midnight Mon-Sat) This Ishigaki city favourite serves all the Okinawan and Yaeyama standards. The boisterous atmosphere and kitchen get top marks, although smokers detract from the experience. Try the *ikasumi chahan* (squid-ink fried rice; ¥700), *gōyā champurū* (¥750) or *sashimi moriawase* (sashimi assortment; depending on size ¥750/1300/1800). Look for the traditional front, with coral around the entryway and a red-and-white sign.

Ishigakijima Village JAPANESE ¥¥
(石垣島ヴィレッジ; Map p823; ☎0980-87-0708; 8-9 Misaki-chō; meals ¥400-2000; ⏲11am-10pm, individual shop hours vary) A contemporary version of the old-school dining *yokochō* (alleys) ferreted away in Japanese cities, this new restaurant complex is the perfect place to dine when feeling indecisive. Tiny eateries, each with some culinary speciality – be it Ishigaki beef, *izakaya* eats or Italian food – all vie for your attention here. Friendly restaurateurs and locals are the icing on the cake.

Mori-no-Kokage IZAKAYA ¥¥
(森のこかげ; Map p823; ☎0980-83-7933; www.morinokokage.net; 199 Ōkawa; dishes ¥640-1570; ⏲5pm-midnight Fri-Wed) This little Ishigaki city *izakaya* is a friendly refuge true to its name, which means 'the shade of the forest'. Local treats are sliced steak of Ishigaki beef (¥1280) and the microbrew *ishigaki-jima-zake* (¥500). Look for the plants and tree trunks outside, and meet some friendly locals under the canopy of an ersatz forest.

Cafe Taniwha CAFE
(カフェたにふぁ; Map p823; ☎0980-88-6352; http://youkoso.cafe-taniwha.com; 188 Ōkawa; ⏲11am-11pm Tue-Sat) You can't do better than Cafe Taniwha as a first stop in Ishigaki. Owners and citizens of the world, Kuri and Fusa have created a snug, welcoming space for local eccentrics and international travellers. They sometimes host live music, and it's a great place to start your evening or park yourself for the duration.

Shopping

Minsā Kōgeikan ART
(みんさー工芸館; Map p820; ☎0980-82-3473; www.minsah.co.jp; 909 Tonoshiro; ⏲9am-6pm) Minsā Kōgeikan is a weaving workshop and showroom with exhibits on Yaeyama Islands textiles. You can also try your hand at weaving a coaster (¥1500); you'll need to reserve ahead by phone. The building is located between the Ishigaki city centre and the airport, and can be reached via the airport bus (there's a Minsā Kōgeikan stop).

Information

Ishigaki-jima Tourism Association (石垣市観光協会; Map p823; ☎0980-82-2809; Ishigaki-shi Shōkō Kaikan 1F; ⏲8.30am-5.30pm Mon-Fri) Produces an English-language *Yaeyama*

Islands brochure and operates a small-but-helpful information counter in the airport arrivals hall. There is also the *Ishigaki Town Guide* and the *Yaeyama Navi* for Japanese readers

Ishigaki-jima Rittō Ferry Terminal Offers an array of publications and other material.

Getting There & Away

AIR

Painushima Ishigaki Airport (南ぬ島石垣空港; Map p820; ☎0980-87-0468; www.ishigaki-airport.co.jp; 7.30am-9pm) has direct flights to/from Tokyo's Narita Airport (Vanilla Air) and Haneda Airport (JTA/ANA), Osaka's Kansai International Airport (JTA/ANA/Peach Airlines), Naha (JTA/ANA), Miyako-jima (RAC/ANA) and Yonaguni-jima (RAC).

BOAT

Ishigaki-jima Rittō Ferry Terminal (石垣港離島ターミナル; Map p823; ☎0980-82-0043; 1 Misaki) serves islands including Iriomote-jima, Kohama-jima, Taketomi-jima and Hateruma-jima. Departures are frequent enough that you can usually just turn up in the morning and hop on the next ferry departing for your intended destination (except during the summer high season). To get to the ferry terminal, head southwest along the waterfront from the 730 Intersection.

Getting Around

The **bus terminal** (Map p823; Misaki-cho) is across the road from the ferry terminal in Ishigaki city. Several buses an hour go to the airport (¥540, 45 minutes). A few daily buses go to Kabira-wan (¥680, 50 minutes) and Yonehara Beach (¥820, one hour). One-/five-day (¥1000/2000) bus passes are available for purchase directly from the driver. Rental cars, scooters and bicycles are readily available at shops throughout the city centre. If you're comfortable on a scooter, it's a scenic four- to five-hour cruise around the island, though you should plan for longer if you want to spend some time relaxing on the island's beaches.

Gogoro Go Share (☎0980-87-5562; www.ridegoshare.jp/en; per hr from ¥1000) is a new and unique-to-Ishigaki ride-share system for eco-scooters that are 100% battery operated. There are stations at which to drop-off or recharge scooters dotted around the island. To see if it's right for you, stop into any Gogoro station that you pass for the explanatory tour: there's also a location at the ferry terminal. Look out for the cyan-blue bikes.

Ishigaki Rentacar (石垣島レンタカー; Map p823; ☎0980-82-8840; 25 Ōkawa; 8am-7pm) is located in the Ishigaki city centre and has reasonable rates.

Iriomote-jima

☎0980 / POP 2402

Although only 20km west of Ishigaki-jima, Iriomote-jima (西表島) could easily qualify as Japan's last frontier. Dense jungles and mangrove swamp blanket more than 90% of the island, and it's fringed by some of the most beautiful coral reefs in Japan. If you're super-lucky, you may spot one of the island's rare *yamaneko,* a nocturnal and rarely seen wildcat (they're most often seen crossing the road at night, so drive carefully).

Several rivers penetrate far into the lush interior of the island and these can be explored by riverboat or kayak. Add to the mix sun-drenched beaches and spectacular diving and snorkelling, and it's easy to see why Iriomote-jima is one of the best destinations in Japan for nature lovers. That said, if you're not an avid explorer of the great outdoors, you're likely to find the slow decline of Iriomote's tourist infrastructure (what little there is) somewhat disappointing.

Sights & Activities

Much of the brilliant coral fringing Iriomote's shores is accessible to proficient snorkellers. Most of the offshore dive sites around Iriomote are served by dive operators based on Ishigaki.

One spot worth noting is **Barasu-tō** (バラス島; Map p820) – an islet formed entirely of bits of broken coral – located between Iriomote-jima and Hatoma-jima; the reefs nearby are good for calm days.

★Ida-no-hama BEACH

(イダの浜; Map p820) From Shirahama, at the western end of the north coast road, there are four daily boats (¥500) to the isolated settlement of Funauki. Once there, it's a mere 10-minute walk on to the absolutely gorgeous Ida-no-hama.

Hoshisuna-no-hama BEACH

(星砂の浜, Star Sand Beach; Map p820) If you're looking to do a bit of snorkelling, head to this beach on the northwestern tip of the island. The beach is named after its star sand, which actually consists of the dried skeletons of marine protozoa.

Iriomote Wildlife Conservation Center MUSEUM

(西表野生生物保護センター; Map p820; ☎0980-85-5581; Komi Taketomi; 10am-4pm Tue-Sun, closed noon-1pm) FREE If you are at all intrigued by the *yamaneko* (Iriomote's

HIKING ON IRIOMOTE-JIMA

Iriomote has some great hikes, but do not head off into the jungle interior without registering with the police: the trails in the interior are hard to follow – many people have become lost and required rescue. We strongly suggest that you stick to well-marked tracks like the ones along the Urauchi-gawa, or arrange a guide through your accommodation (from ¥10,000).

endemic wildcat), whose critically endangered population hovers around 100, it's worth stopping by this small natural-history centre. Exhibits include English signage, and the museum also screens a short documentary in Japanese about the *yamaneko* and its population decline, due to hazards like human refuse and fast cars.

Pinaisāra-no-taki WATERFALL

(ピナイサーラの滝; Map p820) At the back of a mangrove-lined bay called **Funaura-wan**, a few kilometres east of Uehara, you can make out the lovely Pinaisāra-no-taki, Okinawa's highest waterfall at 55m. When the tide is right, you can paddle a kayak across the shallow lagoon and then follow the Hinai-gawa (on the left) to the base of the falls.

The short Māre-gawa (on the right) meets a trail where it narrows. This climbs to the top of the falls, from where there are superb views down to the coast. From the river, walk inland until you come to a pumping station, then turn around and take the right fork in the path. The walk takes less than two hours, and the river is great for a cooling dip.

Unfortunately, it is difficult to find a tour company that will rent you a kayak without requiring you to join a guided tour (half-/full days cost about ¥6000/10,000).

Tsuki-ga-hama BEACH

(月ヶ浜, Moon Beach; Map p820) The best swimming beach on the island is Tsuki-gahama, a crescent-shaped yellow-sand beach at the mouth of the Urauchi-gawa on the north coast.

Tours

Iriomote's number-one attraction is a boat trip up the **Urauchi-gawa** (浦内川), a winding brown river reminiscent of a tiny stretch of the Amazon. This is a great, accessible way to get a feel for Iriomote's inner-island wildness.

Iriomote Osanpo Kibun KAYAKING

(西表おさんぽ気分; Map p820; ☎0980-84-8178; www.iriomote-osanpo.com; half/full-day kayaking & trekking tours from ¥6000/10,000) Choose from trekking, kayaking and snorkelling tours with this reliable outfit, all with an English-speaking guide who will illuminate your experience with local knowledge. This is the easiest way to check out Pinaisāra-no-taki and Iriomote's other natural attractions on land and water. Tour prices normally include lunch and transfers.

Urauchi-gawa Kankō TOURS

(浦内川観光; Map p820; ☎0980-85-6154; www.urauchigawa.com; adult/child river tours ¥1800/900, full-day trekking & kayak tours ¥8400) From the river's mouth, Urauchi-gawa Kankō runs boat tours 8km up the river (round trip ¥1800, 30 minutes each way, multiple departures daily between 9.30am and 3.30pm). At the 8km point, the boat docks and you can walk a further 2km to the scenic waterfalls of **Mariyudō-no-taki** (マリユドゥの滝; Map p820), from where another 200m brings you to another waterfall, **Kanpire-no-taki** (カンピレーの滝; Map p820).

The walk from the dock to Kanpire-no-taki and back takes around two hours. You can also opt to just take the boat trip to the dock and back. The **pier** (浦内川遊覧船乗場) is about 6km west of Uehara; river trips don't require reservations, but the full-day kayaking trips do.

Sleeping

Iriomote-jima's accommodation is generally quite basic and spread out around the island. Most places will send a car to pick you up from the ferry terminal if you let them know what time you will be arriving.

Kanpira-sō MINSHUKU ¥

(カンピラ荘; ☎0980-85-6508; www.kanpira.com; 545 Uehara; r per person incl breakfast with/without bathroom from ¥4700/3700; P ❄ ☎) Two minutes' walk from the ferry landing in Uehara, this hospitable *minshuku* has basic Japanese-style rooms and an informative manager who produces extraordinarily good bilingual maps of the island (although little English is spoken here). From Uehara Port, turn right on the main road; you'll soon see it on the right.

Irumote-sō HOSTEL ¥

(いるもて荘; Map p820; ☎0980-85-6255; www.ishigaki.com/irumote; 870-95 Uehara; dm dinner from ¥5300/4000, r per person with/without dinner ¥7250/5900; P ❄ @ ☎) Between Uehara

Port (上原港) and Funaura Port (船浦港), this peaceful hillside hostel has comfortable dorms and simple Japanese-style private rooms. Meals are served in the large communal dining room. We recommend calling for a pick-up before you arrive as it's hard to find. Discounts available for Hostelling International members.

Coral Garden PENSION ¥¥
(コーラルガーデン; Map p820; ☎0980-85-6027; 289-17 Uehara; s/d incl breakfast from ¥8500/13,000; ⊙closed Dec-Feb; P ❄ @ ☜ ≋) A five-minute drive from Uehara, this beachside pension has simple Japanese- and Western-style rooms overlooking Hoshisuna-no-hama (p825). It has a small pool, and a path leading down to the beach, which is a great spot for snorkelling. Call ahead for pick-up from the port.

Eating

With few restaurants on the island, most travellers' only option is to take meals at their accommodation (or self-cater).

Densā Shokudō OKINAWAN ¥
(デンサー食堂; Map p820; ☎0980-85-6453; www.densa-syokudo.com; 558 Uehara; meals ¥650-950; ⊙11.30am-6pm Thu-Mon, to 4pm Tue) This comfy daytime eatery serves up Okinawan favourites, like *gōyā champurū teishoku* (¥850) and *Yaeyama soba* (¥500), in a homely dining room with an outdoor terrace. Browse a selection of manga while you wait. It's directly across the road once you head out of the Uehara Port.

Laugh La Garden OKINAWAN ¥
(ラフラガーデン; ☎0980-85-7088; 2nd fl, 550-1 Uehara; dishes ¥900; ⊙11.30am-2pm & 6-9pm Fri-Wed) Near the road from Uehara Port and beside the petrol station, this relaxed cafe-restaurant has sets such as *ishigakibuta-no-misokatsu teishoku* (miso-seasoned Ishigaki pork cutlets; ¥950) and Iriomote delicacies such as *inoshishi-sashimi* (wild boar sashimi; ¥600).

Kitchen Inaba OKINAWAN ¥¥
(キッチンイナバ; Map p820; ☎0980-84-8164; www.kitcheninaba.com; 742-6 Uehara; dishes ¥400-1800; ⊙11.30am-2.30pm & 6-8.30pm; P ❄) In the Tsuki-ga-hama area, the relatively upmarket Kitchen Inaba serves the usual local specialities in a spot where no other dining options exist. It's a lovely place for a meal if you're spending a day at the beach and are reliant on public transport; consider making reservations for the sometimes crowded dinner hours.

Getting There & Away

Yaeyama Kankō Ferry (八重山観光フェリー; Map p823; ☎0980-82-5010; www.yaeyama.co.jp), **Ishigaki Dream Kankō** (石垣島ドリーム観光; ☎0980-84-3178; www.ishigaki-dream.co.jp) and **Anei Kankō** (安栄観光; Map p823; ☎0980-83-0055; www.aneikankou.co.jp) operate ferries between Ishigaki city (on Ishigaki-jima) and Iriomote-jima. Ferries from Ishigaki sail to/from two main ports on Iriomote: **Uehara Port** (上原港; Map p820), one hour, up to 20 daily, convenient for most destinations; and **Ōhara Port** (大原港; Map p820), 40 minutes, up to 27 daily. Strong north winds will require Uehara-bound ferries to travel the safer route to Ōhara; in these cases, buses at the port will shuttle passengers to Uehara for free.

Getting Around

Iriomote-jima has a 58km-long perimeter road that runs about halfway around the coast. No roads run into the unspoiled interior.

Six to nine buses daily run between Ōhara Port and Shirahama (¥1240, 1½ hours); raise your hand to get on anywhere. There's a 'free pass' for buses (one-/three-day passes ¥1030/1540) that also gives you 10% off attractions such as the Urauchi-gawa cruise.

For self-driving, try **Yamaneko Rentacar** (やまねこレンタカー; Map p820; ☎0980-85-6111; 201-209 Haemi; ⊙8am-6pm), but don't forget your International Driving Permit. Otherwise, it's likely you'll be confronted by a trio of staff from rival car-rental companies brandishing placards as you arrive off the ferry.

Most of the island's accommodation also rents out bicycles to guests.

Taketomi-jima

☎0980 / POP 361

A mere 15-minute boat ride from Ishigaki-jima, the tiny island of Taketomi-jima (竹富島) is a living museum of Ryūkyū culture. Centred on a flower-decorated village of traditional houses complete with red *kawara* (tiled) roofs, coral walls and *shiisā* statues, Taketomi is a breath of fresh air if you're suffering from an overdose of modern Japan.

In order to preserve the island's historical ambience, residents have joined together to ban some signs of modernism. The island is criss-crossed by crushed-coral roads bedecked with bougainvillea and is free of chain convenience stores.

While Taketomi is besieged by Japanese day trippers in the busy summer months, the island remains blissfully quiet at night. This is true even in summer, as the island offers little in the way of after-dark entertainment. Taketomi truly weaves its spell after the sun dips below the horizon.

Sights

Ferries arrive at the small port on the northeast corner of the island, while Taketomi village is located in the centre of the island.

Kaiji-hama BEACH

(カイジ浜; 皆治浜; Map p820) This lovely stretch of beach is on the southwest coast, also happens to be the main *hoshi-suna* (star sand) hunting ground. If you don't arrive bearing some kind of container for the minuscule treasures, there's usually a stall here selling small vials of star sand.

Kondoi Beach BEACH

(コンドイビーチ; Map p820) Kondoi Beach, on the west coast, offers the best swimming on the island. At the entrance to the beach you'll find bike parking, picnic tables and toilets.

Nagomi-no-tō VIEWPOINT

(なごみの塔; Map p820; 24hr) FREE Roughly in the centre of the village, this modest lookout tower has good views over the red-tiled roofs of the pancake-flat island.

Sleeping & Eating

Many of the traditional houses around the island are Japanese-style ryokan. Note that Taketomi fills up quickly in the summer, so be sure to book ahead if you plan to stay overnight.

Takana Ryokan RYOKAN ¥¥

(高那旅館; Map p820; 0980-85-2151; www.kit.hi-ho.ne.jp/hayasaka-my; 499 Taketomi; dm with/without meals ¥5500/4000, r per person incl meals from ¥8800;) Opposite the tiny post office, Takana consists of a basic youth hostel and an attached upmarket ryokan. Simple Western-style dorms in the youth hostel are a great option if you're on a budget, though the Japanese-style tatami rooms in the ryokan are a bit more comfortable.

Hoshinoya Taketomi-jima LUXURY HOTEL ¥¥¥

(星のや竹富島; Map p820; 0980-84-5888; www.hoshinoya.com; Taketomi; d from ¥42,000;) This sumptuous offering from the renowned team at luxury brand Hoshinoya certainly delivers. The best part about these decadent digs is that after dark it's more blissfully quiet and peaceful than you probably ever thought possible in Japan.

Soba-dokoro Takenoko NOODLES ¥

(そば処竹の子; Map p820; 0980-85-2251; 101-1 Taketomi; dishes ¥600-900; 10.30am-4pm & 7-9pm) This tiny restaurant on the northwest side of the village (look for the blue banner and the umbrellas) serves up *sōki-soba* (¥800) and *Yaeyama soba* (¥600) in amazing broth.

Information

Tourist literature is available from stands in the **ferry terminal** (竹富東港; Map p820).

Getting There & Around

Yaeyama Kankō Ferry (p827) and Anei Kankō (p827) operate ferries between Ishigaki city (on Ishigaki-jima) and Taketomi-jima (¥600, 10 minutes, up to 45 daily).

Since the island is only 3km long and 2km wide, it is easily explored on foot or by bicycle. An assortment of bike-rental outfits meet arriving ferries at the port and run free shuttles between their shops and the port. The going rate for bike rentals is ¥300 per hour or ¥1500 for the day.

Hateruma-jima

0980 / POP 528

Forty-five kilometres south of Iriomote-jima is the tiny islet of Hateruma-jima (波照間島), Japan's southernmost inhabited island. Just 15km around, Hateruma-jima has a couple of beauteous beaches and a seriously laid-back vibe. If you come this far, plan to stay a night to get off the grid and get back to nature with the friendly locals; you'll be glad you did.

Ferries arrive at the small port on the northwest corner of the island, while Hateruma village is in the centre.

Sights

Japan's Southernmost Point LANDMARK

(日本最南端の碑) Cycling along roads criss-crossing fields of sugar cane and tracing kilometres of unspoiled coastline – the southernmost point of Japan's southernmost inhabited island, feels appropriately far-flung once you've arrived. There's also a monument marking the spot, a popular locale for photo ops.

Nishihama BEACH
(ニシ浜) Just to the west of the port is this perfect beach of snow-white sand with some good coral offshore. Here you will find free public showers, toilets and a camping ground.

Takanazaki NATURAL FEATURE
(高那崎) At the southeast corner of the island is this impressive 1km-long cliff of Ryūkyū limestone, pounded by the Pacific Ocean. There's a small observatory here, and at the western end of the cliffs is a small monument marking Japan's southernmost point, an extremely popular photo spot for Japanese visitors and a must-do if you've come all this way.

Sleeping & Eating

You can book meals at most *minshuku;* self-caterers will find a few small shops in town.

Pension Sainantan PENSION ¥¥
(ペンション最南端; ☎0980-85-8686; www.pensionsainantan.wixsite.com/hateruma; 886-1 Hateruma; r per person incl 2 meals from ¥8800; P ❄ @) This airy pension offers Japanese-style rooms with small terraces downstairs and Western-style rooms with balconies upstairs. There's also a rooftop terrace with spectacular views of the beach and sea, and a handy shared laundry. It's located three minutes' walk from Nishihama.

House Minami MINSHUKU ¥¥
(ハウス美波; ☎0980-85-8050; http://minami85.my.coocan.jp; 3138 Hateruma; r from ¥8000; P ❄ 📶) East of the town centre, these fully equipped, detached quarters are arranged around a cosy courtyard close to sugar-cane fields. Though the proprietors don't speak English, they are very foreigner-friendly.

Getting There & Around

Anei Kankō (p827) has three to four ferries a day from Ishigaki-jima to Hateruma-jima (¥3090, one hour).

There is no public transport on the island. Rental bicycles and scooters are readily available for hire near the port and from the local *minshuku*.

Yonaguni-jima

☎0980 / POP 1843

About 125km west of Ishigaki-jima and 110km east of Taiwan is the island of Yonaguni-jima (与那国島), Japan's westernmost inhabited island. Renowned for its strong sake, small horses and marlin fishing, the island is also home to the world's largest moth, the Yonaguni Atlas, but most come for the diving.

In 1985 a local diver discovered what appeared to be human-made 'ruins' off the south coast of the island, which came to be known as the Kaitei Iseki (海底遺跡), or Yonaguni Monument. Some claim the ruins, which look like the steps of a sunken pyramid, are the remains of a Pacific Atlantis, though science suggests they're the result of natural geological processes. Local dive-school operators can get you down there.

Adding to the underwater allure are the large schools of hammerhead sharks that frequent the waters off the west coast, making Yonaguni perhaps the most famous single diving destination in Japan.

Sights

Yonaguni has an extremely rugged, wind- and sea-battered landscape, and the coastline is marked with dramatic rock formations, much like those on the east coast of Taiwan. The island's most notable formations are off the southeast coast.

The ferry port of **Kubura** (久部良) is at the island's western extreme. The main settlement is around the secondary port of **Sonai** (祖納) on the north coast. In between, on the northwest coast, you'll find the airport.

Irizaki MONUMENT
(西崎) Just as Hateruma-jima has a monument to mark Japan's southernmost point, Yonaguni-jima has one to mark the country's **westernmost point** (日本最西端の碑), here at Irizaki. If the weather is perfect, the mountains of Taiwan are visible far over the sea (this happens only about twice a year – don't be disappointed if you can't see them).

Tachigami-iwa NATURAL FEATURE
(立神岩) Literally 'Standing-God Rock' (although another name might come to mind), this offshore obelisk can be viewed from several spots on the bluffs above.

Agarizaki VIEWPOINT
(東崎) At the eastern tip of the island, wild Yonaguni horses graze in the pastures leading out to the lighthouse at Agarizaki.

Activities

Yonaguni Diving Service DIVING
(与那国ダイビングサービス; ☎0980-87-2658; www.yonaguniyds.com; 3984-3 Yonaguni; 2-dive boat trips ¥12,500, equipment rental ¥4600) This dependable diving outfit on Yonaguni also runs the diver-friendly Minshuku Yoshimaru-sō in Kubura.

Diving Service MARLIN DIVING
(ダイビングサービスMARLIN; ☎0980-87-3365; www.yonagunidiving.com/iseki; 309 Yonaguni; 1/2 dives from ¥6500/11,000) This reputable diving service is well versed in the mysteries of, and science behind, the *Kaitei Iseki* rock formations discovered off Yonaguni in 1985 and can get you in the water to take a look for yourself. A variety of dive courses and programmes are available.

Yonaguni Fishing Co-operative FISHING
(与那国町漁協; ☎in Japanese 0980-87-2803) If you're interested in trolling, boats in Yonaguni's port town of Kubura can be chartered from ¥60,000 a day.

Sleeping & Eating

Your best bet is to book meals at your accommodation; self-caterers will find simple supermarkets in both Sonai and Kubura.

Minshuku Yoshimaru-sō MINSHUKU ¥
(民宿よしまる荘; ☎0980-87-2658; www.yonaguniyds.com/yoshimaru; 3984-3 Yonaguni; dm/r per person incl 2 meals ¥6000/7050; P ❄ ☎) Up the hill from the port in Kubura, Yoshimaru-sō is ideal for divers, as the friendly owners also operate the on-site and long-standing Yonaguni Diving Service. Simple Japanese- and Western-style rooms have nice views of the nearby port and spacious communal bathing facilities.

The real appeal of this *minshuku* is the owners' local diving expertise. Book ahead to get picked up at the airport or ferry terminal.

Villa Eden no Sachi RYOKAN ¥¥
(Villa エデンの幸旅館; ☎0980-87-2450; 4022-253 Yonaguni; r per person incl 2 meals ¥9000; P ❄ ☎) Uphill to the north of Kubura's port, this basic, no-frills ryokan offers a convenient and restful base for exploring Yonaguni.

Island Cuisine Isun IZAKAYA ¥¥
(島料理; ☎0980-87-2158; 4022 Yonaguni; dishes ¥500-1280; ⏰11.30am-2pm & 6-11pm Thu-Tue) In Kubura, this cosy *izakaya* is a local favourite. Though the menu is in Japanese only, we recommend the *kajiki* (locally caught swordfish) sashimi and the *sansai* (locally gathered wild mountain vegetables) salad. Ask a Japanese speaker to make reservations for you, as it's a small and popular spot that fills up quickly.

Dōurai IZAKAYA ¥¥
(どぅーらい; ☎0980-87-2909; 62 Yonaguni; dishes ¥450-1200; ⏰5pm-midnight Mon-Sat) In the centre of Sonai is this delightful little Okinawan *izakaya* that serves local specialities such as *Ishigakigyū-sutēki* (Ishigaki-style steak; ¥1300) and *rafutē* (gingered, stewed pork; ¥700). It's about 100m southeast of the post office in Sonai. Look for the small blue sign by the door.

Information

Each post office in Kubura and Sonai has an international ATM.

Yonaguni Tourism Association (与那国町観光協会; ☎0980-87-2402; http://yona-shoko.com/info/center; 437-17 Yonaguni; ⏰11am-6pm) Maintains a counter at the airport, which can help you find accommodation. You can also pick up the Japanese-language *Yonaguni-jima* map and an English-language version that includes set locations of the erstwhile TV drama *Dr Koto's Clinic,* which was set on Yonaguni.

For travel info online, be sure to check out www.welcome-yonaguni.jp.

Getting There & Away

RAC flies once daily between Yonaguni and Naha, and operates three flights a day between Yonaguni and Ishigaki-jima.

Fukuyama Kaiun (福山海運; ☎in Ishigaki 0980-82-4962, in Yonaguni 0980-87-2555) operates two ferries a week between Ishigaki-jima and Kubura Port on Yonaguni (¥3550, four hours). Be warned: these are not for the weak stomached.

Getting Around

There are public buses here, but they make only four trips around the island per day, so the best transport is rental car or scooter. **Yonehama Rentacar** (米浜レンタカー; ☎0980-87-2148; www.yonehama.com; ⏰open for flight arrivals) offers very reasonable rates and has a counter inside the airport terminal.

Understand Japan

History

Japan has been shaped by both its isolation as an island nation and its proximity to the massive Asian continent (particularly Korea and China). During times of openness, the country has absorbed ideas and cultures from abroad; in times of retreat, it has incubated its own way of doing things. Together, these trends created the fascinating Japan we know today – as has its times of power struggle, aggression, defeat and resurrection.

Ancient Japan

Early Settlers

The earliest traces of human life in Japan date to around 30,000 years ago, but it is possible that people were here much earlier. Until about 12,000 years ago, a number of land bridges linked Japan to the continent – Siberia to the north, Korea to the west and probably present-day Taiwan to the south.

The earliest identifiable culture was that of the neolithic Jōmon, who, from about 10,000 BCE, inhabited coastal areas, particularly in eastern Japan. Historians associate them with a distinct style of hand-formed pottery imprinted with twisted cords (Jōmon means 'cord markings'). They lived a quasi-nomadic life, gathering seaweed and wild mushrooms, hunting deer and bear, fishing and dry-farming crops like taro.

The museum at Aomori's Sannai Maruyama excavation site is the best place to learn more about Japan's early Jōmon culture; there are also artefacts on display at the Tokyo National Museum's Japanese Archaeological Gallery.

Sometime between 800 and 300 BCE a new culture began to take shape, that which is referred to as Yayoi (again after a distinctive form of pottery, this time created on a wheel). There remains much debate regarding the origin of this shift, whether it was brought about by settlers from China or Korea (or both); the earliest known Yayoi settlements were discovered in northern Kyūshū, which is close to the Korean Peninsula.

By the 1st century CE, the Yayoi had spread to the middle of Honshū, bringing with them a huge game-changer: wet-rice farming. Not only did this labour-intensive practice demand more stable settlement, it also encouraged population growth in fertile basins (and population growth in general). Agriculture-based settlement led to territories and boundaries being established. The Yayoi also introduced iron and bronze.

TIMELINE

c 13,000 BCE

First evidence of the hunter-gatherer Jōmon, neolithic peoples who migrated from mainland Asia.

c 400 BCE

Yayoi people appear in southwest Japan (probably via Korea), practising wet rice cultivation and using metal tools. They also promote a sense of territoriality.

3rd century CE

Queen Himiko reigns over a region called Yamatai and is recognised by Chinese visitors as 'over-queen' of Japan's more than 100 kingdoms.

The Rise of Yamato Culture

According to Chinese sources, by the end of the 3rd century CE there were more than a hundred kingdoms in Japan, organised into federations. The most powerful of these was ruled by a shamaness-queen named Himiko (in either present-day Nara prefecture or northwest Kyūshū; the location is unclear). Her land was called Yamatai. The Chinese called her state 'Wa'; through tributes, she acknowledged her allegiance to the Chinese emperor.

Over the next couple of centuries, administrative and military power began to coalesce around a polity called Yamato (which may or may not be related to Himiko's Yamatai), in Nara prefecture. Part of Yamato culture was the practice of burying leaders in mounded tombs (called *kofun*), whose shape and size corresponded to status – evidence of a burgeoning material culture and increasing societal stratification. By the end of the Kofun period (250–538 CE), tombs could be found as far north as Niigata and as far south as Tanegashima, an island off the coast of present-day Kagoshima (though the largest were around Nara), showing the extent of Yamato hegemony.

The Yamato did have their challengers: throughout these early centuries rival chiefdoms within the Yayoi cultural sphere made power plays of their own. There were also what historians call the Epi-Jōmon people, who had resisted Yayoi culture altogether. Likely descended from the earlier Jōmon people, the Epi-Jōmon lived in Tōhoku (northern Honshū) and traded with the Satsumon and Okhotsk people of Hokkaidō

Shintō is one of the few religions in the world with a female solar deity. Amaterasu (Light of Heaven), the Sun Goddess, is enshrined at Ise-jinja, the most important shrine in the country, where members of the imperial family serve as chief priest or priestess.

MYTHIC ORIGINS

Once upon a time, the male and female deities Izanagi and Izanami came down to a watery world from Takamagahara (the Plains of High Heaven), to create land. Droplets from Izanagi's 'spear' solidified into the land now known as Japan, and Izanami and Izanagi then populated it with gods. One of these was Japan's supreme deity, the Sun Goddess Amaterasu (Light of Heaven), whose great-great-grandson Jimmu became the first emperor of Japan, reputedly in 660 BCE. This is the story of Japan's creation, as told by the young empire's first written accounts, *Kojiki* (*Record of Old Things*; 712) and *Nihon Shoki* (*Record of Japan*; 720).

Scholars are sceptical of the existence of the earliest emperors. Some believe the 10th emperor, Sujin, was the first to really exist, and was perhaps the founder of the Yamato dynasty (some also think he led a clan of horsemen into Japan from the Korean Peninsula). Different accounts place his reign anywhere from the 1st century BCE to the 4th century CE. Emperor Kinmei (r 539–71 CE) is the first emperor of verifiable historical record. According to the lineage of legend, he would have been the 29th emperor. Either way, the Yamoto dynasty is the longest unbroken monarchy in the world.

mid-5th century

Writing – and thus record-keeping – is introduced into Japan by scholars from the Korean kingdom of Baekje (though based on the Chinese system of characters).

mid-6th century

Baekje scholars introduce Buddhism. Its texts can be read by a now-literate elite, who use it as a unifying tool.

710

Japan's first capital is established at Nara, based on Chinese models. By now, Japan, with its estimated five million people, has many characteristics of a nation-state.

740

Construction begins on the vast Tōdai-ji temple complex in Nara. It is thought the complex was built to provide a focus for the nation and to ward off smallpox.

and Sakhalin. The Yamato court called the Epi-Jōmon people Emishi and fought to subjugate them in wars that continued until the 8th century.

The Age of Courtiers

Buddhism Enters Japan

Buddhism entered Japan in the mid-6th century, introduced by the Korean kingdom of Baekji, considerably transforming Yamato culture. The religion itself was noteworthy for the cohesive world view it presented, but also powerful were the attendant technologies – used to create temples and statues that would confer on the court an undeniable gravitas. Buddhist rites were incorporated into the increasingly elaborate pageantry of courtly life. The era of *kofun* building was over.

Asuka, in southern Nara Prefecture, is the best place to learn about pre-Buddhist Japanese culture; there are several intact *kofun* (burial mounds) here, as well as The Museum, Archaeological Institute of Kashihara.

Imported concurrently with Buddhism, increasingly sophisticated techniques of statecraft would serve to bolster the Yamato state. Prince Shōtoku (573–620), the powerful regent to Empress Suiko (592–628), was an early champion of Buddhism and founded the temple Horyū-ji (607). He also enacted the first of a series of administrative reforms that regulated land distribution and official ranks, laying the groundwork for a bureaucratic society. From the 7th century onward, the court sent emissaries to Tang-dynasty China to further study Buddhism, government, medicine and art.

For centuries, Shintō tenets on purity had ordained that the court relocate following the death of an emperor or empress; however, in 710, a permanent capital was established at Nara, designed in the same grid pattern as the Tang dynasty capital, Chang'an (present-day Xi'an). The great temple Tōdai-ji (752) was symbolic of the Buddhist theocratic state that reached its peak during the Nara period (710–794). And yet, the court did not totally relinquish its older Shintō belief system; in fact, it doubled down on it, compiling record books that traced the lineage of Yamato's emperors to the realm of its native gods.

The Capital at Heian-kyō

By the end of the 8th century the Buddhist clergy at Nara had become so powerful that Emperor Kammu decided to move the capital to escape it. He first settled in Nagaoka (today a suburb of Kyoto), but following several inauspicious disasters, he relocated the capital to Heian-kyō, present-day Kyoto, where it would exist for the next 1000 years. The location was ideal: surrounded on three sides by gentle mountains, the site was both a natural fortress and a perfect embodiment of the principles of Chinese geomancy that were in vogue at the time. Like Nara, Heian-kyō was modelled after Chang'an.

Heian-kyō was an exclusive, insular world that revolved around the court. (Interestingly, the court had no practice of executions; to be transferred to the provinces was considered punishment enough.) It has been

794
The imperial capital moves to Heian-kyō, renamed Kyoto in the 11th century. It is laid out in a grid in accordance with Chinese geomancy principles.

804
After travelling to China to study Buddhism, Kūkai (also known as Kōbō Daishi) founds Shingon (Esoteric) Buddhism in Japan and establishes the famous Kōya-san religious centre.

early 1000s
Lady of the court, Murasaki Shikibu, writes *The Tale of Genji*, considered to be the world's first novel.

1100s
The Northern Fujiwara clan, largely independent of the court, wrests control of northeastern Honshū (present-day Tōhoku), pushing the native peoples (possible Jōmon descendants) north to Hokkaidō.

estimated that the number of courtiers and courtesans hovered around 5000 to 7000; including family members, servants, merchants and artisans, it is likely that the population of the capital was at least 10 times that. Rank, largely determined by bloodlines, was everything; it determined, for example, what clothes could be worn and what kind of house could be built. High-ranking clans were granted untaxed estates (called *shōen*) from which they derived their wealth (and which were worked by peasants). In Heian-era Japan, women could inherit land, which gave them a degree of independence.

In 894, as China's Tang dynasty was on the wane and political tensions in Heian-kyō were at a high, the imperial court ceased its practice of sending emissaries to China. For the next several centuries, Japan turned inward. On the one hand, from isolation was born a rich court culture – the first inklings of what we consider today to be Japanese culture – defined by refined aesthetic pursuits. Purely Japanese styles of Buddhism developed, in the Tendai and Shingon sects. On the other hand, the court grew increasingly stagnant and out of touch, removed from the realities of governing. By now much power was out of imperial hands, as court politics came to be largely manipulated by the powerful Fujiwara clan.

The Genpei War

Outside the capital, in the provinces, powerful military forces were developing. They were typically led by minor nobles, often sent on behalf of court-based major nobles to carry out tedious local administrative duties or to put out the flames of rebellions – particularly in northeast Japan, then the very edge of the court's sphere of influence. Some were distant imperial family members, barred from succession claims (they were given new names and farmed out to provincial clans) and hostile to the court. To build up their own power, they recruited local warriors, who would later become the samurai of the feudal period.

There were two prominent and increasingly influential clans of disenfranchised lesser nobles: the Minamoto (also known as Genji) and Taira (Heike) were hostile towards each other. In 1156 they were employed to help rival claimants to the Fujiwara family leadership, but these figures soon faded into the background when an all-out feud developed between the Minamoto and the Taira.

The Taira prevailed under their leader Kiyomori (1118–81), who based himself in the capital. Over the following 20 years he, too, became overly absorbed in courtly politics and society. In 1180 he enabled the enthroning of his two-year-old grandson, Antoku. When a rival claimant requested the help of the Minamoto family, who had spent those last two decades regrouping, their leader, Yoritomo (1147–99), was more than ready to agree.

The epic *Tale of the Heike* describes the battles of the Genpei War. It was recited by travelling monks to the accompaniment of the *biwa* (Japanese lute), spreading the Buddhist idea of impermanence (*mujō*) along with the story of the Heike's fall. It's available in translation by Royall Tyler (2014).

1156

The major provincial clans Taira and Minamoto are employed by rival court factions and engage in bitter warfare, with the Taira prevailing under its warrior-leader Kiyomori.

1185–92

Minamoto Yoritomo topples the Taira and fights to secure his authority by eliminating rivals (including his own half-brother). By defeating the Northern Fujiwara in 1189 he adds northeast Japan to his territory.

1192

Yoritomo takes the title shogun (generalissimo) from a largely powerless emperor and establishes the *bakufu* (shogunate) in his home territory at Kamakura, heralding the start of feudalism in Japan.

1200–50

Hōnen and Shinran promote the 'Pure Land' schools of Buddhism, which remain the country's most popular Buddhist sects.

HISTORICAL PERIODS

PERIOD	DATE	KEY EVENTS
Jōmon	c 10,000 BCE–c 400 BCE	Japan is populated by neolithic peoples, who migrated from mainland Asia.
Yayoi	c 400 BCE–c 250 CE	Technologically advanced immigrants – likely from the Korean Peninsula – arrive, introducing wet-rice farming and bronze tool-making.
Kofun	250–538	Burial mounds codified according to status indicate a society with increasing stratification.
Asuka	538–710	Buddhism takes hold; civil codes over a burgeoning empire are established by the ruling Yamato clan.
Nara	710–794	The first permanent capital of Japan is established in the city of Nara.
Heian	794–1185	A period of peace and cultural refinement thrives under the imperial court in its new capital, Kyoto.
Kamakura	1185–1333	Feudalism is imposed by a new military regime in Kamakura; it is led by a shogun, who is granted power from the (now largely powerless) emperor.
Muromachi	1333–1568	The shogunate, under new leadership, is removed to Kyoto; though a period of instability, culture influenced by Zen Buddhism flourishes.
Azuchi-Momoyama	1568–1603	Near-constant civil war rages until Tokugawa Ieyasu establishes a new shogunate in Edo (Tokyo).
Edo	1603–1868	The Tokugawa shogunate closes the country and ushers in a period of significant peace and prosperity.
Meiji	1868–1912	The shogunate is abolished and the emperor is reinstated as the supreme power; Japan, now open to the world, begins a wholesale importation of Western ideas.
Taishō	1912–26	Western-style democracy briefly takes hold, before giving way to militarisation.
Shōwa	1926–89	The first half of the era is marked by imperial aggression and war; the latter half sees remarkable postwar growth and the emergence of a substantial middle class.
Heisei	1989–2019	Growth screeches to a halt and inequality widens; the country reconsiders its role in the world and how to move forward.
Reiwa	2019–	The Covid-19 pandemic and the postponed 2020 Olympics dominate the early years of this era.

1223

The monk Dōgen studies Chang Buddhism in China and later returns to found the Sōtō school of Zen Buddhism. Zen proves popular with the warrior class and goes on to influence Japanese aesthetics.

1274 & 1281

Under Kublai Khan, the Mongols twice attempt to invade Japan, but fail due to poor planning, spirited Japanese resistance and, especially, the destruction of their fleets by typhoons.

1333

General Ashikaga Takauji, allied with Emperor Go-Daigo, topples the unpopular Hōjō shogunate. Takauji requests the title of shogun, but Go-Daigo declines and a rift develops.

1338–92

Takauji installs a new puppet emperor who names him shogun, establishing the Ashikaga shogunate in Kyoto's Muromachi district. Two rival emperors exist till Go-Daigo's line is betrayed by Takauji's grandson in 1392.

Both Kiyomori and the claimant died shortly afterwards, but Yoritomo and his younger half-brother Yoshitsune (1159–89) continued the campaign against the Taira. By 1185 Kyoto had fallen and the Taira had been pursued to the western tip of Honshū. A naval battle ensued – the famous Battle of Dan-no-ura, won by the Minamoto. In a well-known tragic tale, Kiyomori's widow leapt into the sea with her grandson Antoku (now aged seven), rather than have him surrender.

The Age of Warriors

The Kamakura Shoguns

Minamoto Yoritomo was now the most powerful figure in Japan, yet he did not seek to become emperor; instead, he asked the new emperor to legitimise his authority by conferring upon him the title *Sei-i Taishōgun* (Commander-in-Chief of Barbarian Subjugation) – or shogun, for short. This was granted in 1192.

Yoritomo left many existing offices and institutions in place in Kyoto and set up a base in his home territory of Kamakura (not far from present-day Tokyo). The shogun's government was called the *bakufu*, meaning the tent headquarters of a field general. In theory, the shogun represented the military arm of the emperor's government; in practice, the shogun held the real power. The feudal age had begun.

Yoritomo's government, and that of the Hōjō clan (his wife's family) who succeeded him, laid the groundwork for the loyalty-based lord-vassal system that would rule Japanese politics and society for the next seven centuries. With few exceptions, the emperor would now largely be a symbolic ruler.

Though influential, the Kamakura shogunate would be short-lived. The Mongols, under Kublai Khan and at the height of their power, reached Korea in 1259 and sent envoys to Japan seeking Japanese submission. When the envoys were expelled, the Mongols sent a fleet to invade the southern island of Kyūshū in 1274. This attack, and a more determined effort in 1281, were only barely repulsed after timely storms destroyed much of the Mongol fleet.

Despite having held off the Mongol invasion, the shogunate suffered. Its inability to make promised payments to the warriors involved in holding off the Mongols caused considerable discontent, while the payments it did make severely depleted its finances. Dissatisfaction towards the Kamakura regime came to a head under the unusually assertive emperor Go-Daigo (1288–1339). In 1333, following a failed coup that saw him exiled, Go-Daigo raised an army and toppled the government, ushering in a return of political authority to Kyoto.

People of the late Heian and early Kamakura periods were distressed by the idea of *mappō*, the 'age of the latter law', when civilisation would enter a 10,000-year period of degeneration. It was predicted to start 2000 years after the Buddha's death.

late 1300s

Kyoto's Kinkaku-ji (Golden Temple) is designed as a retreat for the shogun; in accordance with his will, it is transformed into a Zen temple on his death.

1400s

The Ōnin War (1467–77), ignited by succession claims, kicks off a near constant era of civil war, referred to as the Sengoku (Warring States) period, that lasts through the 16th century.

1543

Portuguese, the first Europeans, arrive by chance in Japan, bringing firearms and Christianity. Firearms prove popular among warlords; Christianity gets a mixed reception.

1568

The warlord Oda Nobunaga seizes Kyoto and becomes the supreme power, though he does not take the title of shogun. He is noted for his massive ego and brutality.

The Ashikaga Shoguns

Kamakura receded but feudalism did not. Go-Daigo, and the Kyoto nobility, sought a return to courtly rule, but the warriors who fought for him – notably his general, Ashikaga Takauji – had no intention of withdrawing quietly back to the provinces. When Go-Daigo refused to name Takauji shogun, the general revolted; Go-Daigo fled south to Yoshino (where he set up a court in exile that existed until 1392). Takauji installed a puppet emperor from a rival line, who returned the favour by declaring him shogun in 1338.

Takauji set up his base in Kyoto, at Muromachi. With few exceptions, the Ashikaga shoguns were relatively ineffective. They struggled to control the provincial warlords (called *daimyō*), who they relied on to maintain rule over the country. Buddhist populist revolts and vigilantism fed off and further exaggerated the lack of central authority.

By the 15th century, the warlords had succeeded in carving Japan into a patchwork of fiefdoms. Castles and fortresses were going up around the country. The Ōnin War (1467–77), between two rival clans who wielded much of the real power in the capital, all but destroyed Kyoto. For the next hundred years, the country was in a near-constant state of civil war – a time known as the Sengoku-jidai (Warring States period; 1467–1568).

The Bloody Road to Reunification

In the latter half of the 16th century, a series of powerful *daimyō* attempted to bring the country back under united rule: first Oda Nobunaga (1534–82), then Toyotomi Hideyoshi (1537–98) and finally Tokugawa Ieyasu (1543–1616). By now, Europeans had begun to arrive, bringing with them Christianity and firearms – another game changer.

One of the most successful of the warlords to take advantage of firearms was Oda Nobunaga. Starting from a relatively minor power base in what is now Aichi Prefecture, he managed to outmanoeuvre rivals (including several family members), seizing Kyoto in 1568. He installed a puppet shogun from the Ashikaga clan (Yoshiaki), only to drive him out in 1573. Although he did not take the title of shogun, Nobunaga held de-facto power. He was noted for his brutality and his disdain for Buddhist priests; he tolerated Christianity as a counterbalance to Buddhism's hegemony.

Following Nobunaga's assassination (by one of his generals), another of his generals, Toyotomi Hideyoshi – a foot soldier who had risen through the ranks to become Nobunaga's favourite – took up the torch of unification, succeeding over eight years in taking control of Japan.

Hideyoshi's power had been briefly contested by Tokugawa Ieyasu, son of a minor lord allied to Nobunaga. Ieyasu agreed to a truce with Hideyoshi; in return, Hideyoshi granted him eight provinces in eastern

The typhoon of 1281 that helped Japan repel Mongol invaders was thought of as a gift from the gods, a *kamikaze* (literally 'divine wind'). Later this term was used to describe Pacific War suicide pilots who, said to be infused with divine spirit, gave their lives to protect Japan from invasion.

1582

Nobunaga is betrayed and forced to commit suicide. Power transfers to one of his loyal generals, Toyotomi Hideyoshi, who takes the title of regent.

late 1500s

Sen-no-Rikyū lays down the form of the tea ceremony, the ritualised drinking of tea originally practised by nobility and later spreading to wealthy commoners.

1592 & 1597–98

Hideyoshi twice tries to conquer Korea as part of a plan to control Asia, the second attempt ending after his death in 1598. The invasions seriously damage relations between Japan and Korea.

1600

The warlord Tokugawa Ieyasu breaks an earlier promise to the dying Hideyoshi to protect his young son and heir Hideyori, and seizes power at the Battle of Sekigahara.

Japan (around present-day Tokyo). Hideyoshi intended this to weaken Ieyasu by separating him from his ancestral homeland Chūbu (now Aichi Prefecture); however Ieyasu looked upon the gift as an opportunity to strengthen his power.

Hideyoshi built his showy castle – which reputedly took some 100,000 workers three years to build – in Osaka. The emperor crowned him regent. In his later years, Hideyoshi became increasingly paranoid, cruel and megalomaniacal. He had grand plans for a pan-Asian conquest, and as a first step he attempted an invasion of Korea in 1592, which failed amid much bloodshed. He tried again in 1597, but the campaign was abandoned when Hideyoshi died of illness in 1598.

On his deathbed, Hideyoshi entrusted Ieyasu, who had proven to be one of his ablest generals, with safeguarding the country and the succession of his young son Hideyori (1593–1615). Ieyasu, however, soon went to war against those loyal to Hideyori, finally defeating them in the decisive Battle of Sekigahara in 1600. In 1603 the emperor named

In 1191 the Zen monk Eisai is said to have brought tea leaves from China, starting Japan's tradition of tea drinking.

SAMURAI: JAPAN'S FEUDAL-ERA WARRIORS

The prime duty of a samurai – a member of the warrior class from about the 12th century onward – was to give faithful service to his lord. In fact, the origin of the term 'samurai' is closely linked to a word meaning 'to serve'. Instantly recognisable with their plated armour knit with silken cords, terrifying face guards and helmets sprouting crests or horns, they are one of the most enduring images of Japan. The samurai's best-known weapon was the *katana* sword, which rendered them a formidable opponent in single combat.

Over the centuries samurai established a code of conduct that came to be known as *bushidō* (the way of the warrior). Above all, this meant loyal service to the lord. A samurai's honour was his life; disgrace and shame were to be avoided above all else, and all insults were to be avenged. *Seppuku*, also known as *hara-kiri*, was for the samurai an honourable death – far preferable to surrender. It required the samurai to ritually disembowel himself, watched by an aide, who then drew his own sword and lopped off the samurai's head. Subterfuge was to be despised, as were all commercial and financial transactions. Towards the oppressed, a samurai was expected to show benevolence and exercise justice.

Of course not all (and probably very few) samurai lived up to these strict standards. Some were professional mercenaries who were unreliable and often defected. Samurai indulging in double-crossing or subterfuge, or displaying outright cowardice, were popular themes in Japanese theatre. Those who became lordless were known as *rōnin* (wanderers or masterless samurai); they acted more like brigands and were a serious social problem.

Following the Meiji Restoration, the new government – itself comprising samurai – replaced the historic warriors with a conscript army.

1603

Ieyasu becomes shogun, establishing a new shogunate in the small castle town Edo (now Tokyo), beginning 250 years of relative peace under Tokugawa rule.

1606

Matsumae castle is erected in southern Hokkaidō giving Japan a toehold on the northern island, then called Ezo and populated by a people called Ainu.

1638

The *sakoku* policy of national isolation is enacted; shogunal forces massacre Japanese Christians in the Christian-led Shimabara Rebellion.

1689–91

Matsuo Bashō, the greatest name in haiku poetry, completes a journey around Japan that inspires his most famous collection of poems, *The Narrow Road to the Deep North*.

Ieyasu shogun. Breaking centuries of tradition, Tokugawa Ieyasu decided to locate his government not in Kyoto, but within his own stronghold in eastern Japan, choosing a small castle town called Edo (present day Tokyo) for his capital.

The Edo Period

Besides loyal samurai, Tokugawa Ieyasu stocked his capital with ninja. Their commander was Hattori Hanzō, renowned for his cunning, deadly tactics that helped Ieyasu at key moments in his career. The ninja master's legacy was enshrined in Hanzōmon, a gate that still exists today at the Imperial Palace.

Tokugawa Rule

The Tokugawa shoguns would rule for two and a half centuries – a period of relative peace known as the Edo period (1603–1868). Tokugawa Ieyasu was both an ambitious ruler and an ambitious city planner. He built the world's largest fortress, Edo-jō (Edo Castle); around the castle, a spiral of moats were dug (by samurai attached to the clans who had opposed Tokugawa), as well as a canal system to bring water to the population that had quickly swelled to 500,000 by 1650.

Much of Edo's stability and swift rise can be attributed to a canny move by the Tokugawa regime that ensured its hegemony: a system called *sankin kōtai* that demanded that all *daimyō* in Japan spend alternate years in Edo. Their wives and children remained in Edo (hostages, essentially) while the *daimyō* returned to administer their home provinces. This dislocating policy made it hard for ambitious *daimyō* to usurp the Tokugawas and the high costs of travelling back and forth (with sufficiently large retinues) eroded their finances.

Tokugawa-style micro-management extended to directly controlled ports, mines, major towns and other strategic areas. Movement was severely restricted by checkpoints; written authority was required for travel and wheel transport was outlawed.

The Tokugawa regime promoted a brand of neo-Confucianism that emphasised hierarchical order and had the effect of promoting literacy: by the end of the period of Tokugawa rule, up to a third of the 30 million Japanese were literate – far ahead of Western populations of the time.

Retreat from the World

Early on, the Tokugawa shogunate adopted a policy of *sakoku* (closure to the outside world). The regime was leery of Christianity's potential influence and expelled missionaries in 1614. All Westerners except the Protestant Dutch were expelled by 1638. The shogunate found Protestantism less threatening than Catholicism (knowing that the Vatican could muster one of the biggest military forces in the world) and would have let the British stay on if the Dutch had not convinced it that Britain was a Catholic country. Nevertheless, the Dutch were just a few dozen men confined to a tiny trading base on the artificial island of Dejima near Nagasaki.

Overseas travel for Japanese was banned (as well as the return of those already overseas). And yet, the country did not remain completely cut off: trade with Asia and the West continued through the Dutch and Ryūkyū empire (now Okinawa) – it was just tightly controlled and, along with the exchange of ideas, funnelled exclusively to the shogunate.

early to mid-19th century
The nation's isolation is threatened by increasing numbers of foreign whalers and other vessels entering Japanese waters. Treatment of those attempting to land is harsh.

1853–54
US commodore Matthew Perry's 'black ships' arrive off the coast of Shimoda, forcing Japan to open up for trade and reprovisioning.

1859
Five international ports are established in Yokohama, Hakodate, Kōbe, Niigata and Nagasaki, opening the way for foreign settlements.

1854–67
Opposition to the shogunate grows, led by samurai from the Satsuma and Chōshū domains, resulting in civil war; the last shogun retires in 1867.

Rise of the Merchant Class

Society under Tokugawa rule was made rigidly hierarchical, comprising (in descending order of importance): *shi* (samurai), *nō* (farmers), *kō* (artisans) and *shō* (merchants). Class dress, living quarters and even manner of speech were all strictly codified, and interclass movement was prohibited. Village and neighbourhood heads were enlisted to enforce rules at the local level, creating an atmosphere of surveillance. Punishments could be harsh, cruel and even deadly for minor offences.

Yet for all its constraints, the Tokugawa period had a considerable dynamism. Japan's cities grew enormously during this period: Edo's population topped one million in the early 1700s, dwarfing much older London and Paris. Kyoto, which evolved into a production centre for luxury goods, and Osaka, a centre for trade, each hovered around 400,000 for much of the period.

Though they sat at the bottom of the hierarchy, many merchants became fabulously wealthy, profiting from the great cost required of the *daimyō* for their processions and suitably grand lifestyles in Edo. Shut out from established status symbols by law – they were not allowed, for example, to wear embroidered silk – the *shōnin* (merchants) created their own culture, one that revolved around the Kabuki theatre, sumo tournaments and the pleasure quarters. The height of fashion was *iki*, a kind of rakish dandyism.

The feat of the 47 *rōnin* (masterless samurai), who plotted for over a year (1701–03) to avenge their master's death, is among Japan's most storied historical events. While sentenced to death, so great was the outpouring of respect, that the loyal samurai were allowed to keep their honour and commit *seppuku* (ritual suicide).

Modernisation

The Black Ships

By the mid-19th century, the Tokugawa shogunate was losing its grip. It is questionable how much longer it might have held on, but as it happened, external forces were to hasten its demise. A number of Western vessels – which the Japanese called *kurofune* (black ships), because they were cloaked in pitch – had begun appearing in Japanese waters since the start of the 19th century.

America in particular was keen to expand its interests across the Pacific. In 1853 and again the following year, US commodore Matthew Perry steamed into Edo-wan (now Tokyo Bay) with a show of gunships and demanded Japan open up to trade and provisioning. The shogunate was no match for Perry's firepower and had to agree to his demands. Soon an American consul arrived, and other Western powers followed suit. Japan was obliged to sign what came to be called the 'unequal treaties', opening ports and giving Western nations control over tariffs.

Despite last-ditch efforts by the Tokugawa regime to reassert their power, anti-shogun sentiment was high, particularly in the outer domains of Satsuma (southern Kyūshū) and Chōshū (western Honshū). A

1867–68

The Meiji Restoration reinstates imperial authority, installing 15-year-old emperor Mutsuhito as head of state (though real power is wielded by oligarchs). Japan's capital is moved to Edo, renamed Tokyo.

1869

Japan formally annexes Hokkaidō; in 1889 laws enforcing assimilation of the indigenous Ainu people are enacted.

1879

Japan annexes the Ryūkyū Kingdom (then a tributary of China) and renames it Okinawa; assimilation policies are also carried out against native Okinawans.

1895

Defeating China in the Sino-Japanese War, Japan, who initiated the conflict in 1894, gains Taiwan and its territorial expansion begins.

movement arose to 'revere the emperor and expel the barbarians' (*sonnō jōi*); in other words, to restore the emperor to a position of real power (rather than titular authority) and to kick the Westerners out.

After unsuccessfully skirmishing with the Western powers, however, the reformers realised that expelling the foreigners was not feasible. Restoring the emperor was, however, and following a series of military clashes between the shogun's armies and the rebels, the rebels proved victorious. The last shogun, Yoshinobu (1837–1913), agreed to retire in 1867. He lived out his remaining years peacefully in Shizuoka. Which is not to say Tokugawa loyalists went quietly into the night; fighting continued, especially in the northeast, through 1868–69, in what is known as the Boshin War.

CHRISTIANITY IN JAPAN

Japan's so-called 'Christian Century' began in 1549 with the arrival of Portuguese missionaries on the island of Kyūshū. Within decades, hundreds of thousands of Japanese, from peasants to *daimyō* (domain lords), were converted.

The rapid rise of Christian belief, as well as its association with trade, Western weaponry and possibly territory grabbing, came to be viewed as a threat by the *bakufu* (shogunate) under Toyotomi Hideyoshi. In 1597 Hideyoshi ordered the crucifixion of 26 Japanese and Spanish Franciscans in Nagasaki. Despite his death in 1598, an era of suppression of Christians had begun and, with the expulsion of missionaries ordered in 1614 by Tokugawa Hidetada (who succeeded his father, Tokugawa Ieyasu, in 1605), thousands of Christians were persecuted over the following six decades. One form of persecution was *fumi-e*, in which suspected Christians were forced to walk on images of Jesus. Many thousands of Christian peasants revolted in the 1637–38 Shimabara Rebellion, after which Christianity was outlawed completely.

Japanese Christians reacted by going undercover as *kakure Kirishitan* (hidden Christians). Without priests, they worshipped in services held in secret rooms inside private homes. On the surface, worship resembled other Japanese religions, including using *kamidana* (Shintō altars) and *butsudan* (Buddhist ancestor-worship chests) in homes, and ceremonial rice and sake. But *kakure Kirishitan* also kept hanging scrolls of Jesus, Mary and saints, as well as statues like the Maria-Kannon, depicting Mary in the form of the Buddhist deity of mercy holding an infant symbolising Jesus. The sounds of worship, too, mimicked Buddhist incantations. Scholars estimate there were about 150,000 hidden Christians.

It was not until 1865 – 12 years after the arrival of the American expedition led by Commodore Matthew Perry, who eventually forced Japan to reopen to the West – that Japan had its first large-scale church again: Ōura Cathedral in Nagasaki. The Meiji government officially declared freedom of religion in 1871. Today, there are estimated to be between one and two million Japanese Christians (about 1% of the population).

1902

Japan signs the Anglo-Japanese Alliance, the first-ever equal alliance between a Western and non-Western nation and an indicator of Japan's growing power.

1904–05

Japan wins the Russo-Japanese War. Antipathy towards Russia had developed after the Sino-Japanese War, when Russia pressured Japan to renounce Chinese territory that it then occupied.

1910

Free of any Russian threat, Japan formally annexes Korea, in which it had been increasingly interested since the 1870s. The international community makes no real protest.

1912

Emperor Meiji (Mutsuhito) dies, after seeing Japan rise from a remote pre-industrial nation to a world power in half a century. His mentally disabled son, Yoshihito, succeeds him.

Meiji Restoration

In 1868, the new teenage emperor Mutsuhito (1852–1912; later known as Meiji) was named the supreme leader of the land, commencing the Meiji period (1868–1912; Enlightened Rule). The institution of the shogun was abolished and the shogunal base at Edo was refashioned into the imperial capital and given the new name, Tokyo (Eastern Capital). In truth, the emperor still wielded little actual power: the new government was formed primarily of Satsuma or Chōshū samurai.

The Meiji Restoration heralded far-reaching social changes. The four-tier class system was scrapped; after centuries of having everything prescribed for them, citizens were now free to choose their occupation and place of residence. Many moved to the cities to join the growing workforce in the new manufacturing and white-collar sectors. In 1898, Tokyo's population was just shy of 1.5 million; by 1909 it had surpassed two million.

The new government sought to expand its rule: annexing Hokkaidō in 1869 and the Ryūkyū Kingdom (then a tributary of China; now present day Okinawa) in 1879, imposing strict assimilation policies.

The disorienting collapse of the regimented Tokugawa world produced a form of mass hysteria called *ee ja nai ka* (who cares?), that saw people dancing naked in the streets and giving away possessions.

Westernisation

Above all, the new leaders of Japan – keen observers of what was happening throughout Asia – feared colonisation by the West. They moved quickly to modernise, as defined by the Western powers, to prove they could stand on an equal footing with the colonisers. The government embarked on a grand project of industrialisation and militarisation. A great exchange began between Japan and the West: Japanese scholars were dispatched to Europe to study everything from literature and engineering to nation building and modern warfare. Western scholars were invited to teach in Japan's nascent universities.

The new Japanese establishment learned quickly: in 1872 the first railroad opened, connecting Tokyo with the new port of Yokohama, south along Tokyo Bay. By 1889 the country had a constitution, modelled after the government frameworks of England and Prussia. Banking systems, a new legal code and political parties were established. *Daimyō* were 'persuaded' to give their domain land to the government in return for governorships or other compensation, enabling a prefectural system to be set up.

Still, cronyism persisted: the government took responsibility for establishing major industries and then selling them off at bargain rates to chosen government-friendly industrial entrepreneurs – a factor in the formation of huge industrial conglomerates known as *zaibatsu*, many of which still exist today (such as Mitsubishi, Sumitomo and Mitsui).

1914–15

Japan sides with the Entente in WWI in 1914; in 1915 it presents China with 'Twenty-One Demands' for more control in China, earning rebuke from its new allies.

1923

The Great Kantō Earthquake strikes Japan near Tokyo, killing an estimated 100,000 to 140,000 people. Much of the destruction is caused by fires sweeping through Tokyo and Yokohama after the quake.

1931

Increasingly defiant of the West, Japan invades Manchuria and then dramatically withdraws from the League of Nations in response to criticism.

1937

During an attempted occupation of China, Japan commits grave atrocities in Nanjing, killing many thousands of people, mostly civilians.

By the 1920s, Western fashions and ideas, initially the domain of the elite, began to trickle down to the middle class. Women began to work outside the home, in offices, department stores and factories, enjoying a new freedom and disposable income. Like women around the world in the 1920s, they cut their hair short and wore pants – and became symbols for both the optimism and the dread that the new modern era inspired.

The World Stage

Imperialist Japan

A key element of Japan's aim to become a world power was military might. Following Prussian army and British navy models, Japan built up a formidable armed force. Using the same 'gunboat diplomacy' on Korea that Perry had used on the Japanese, in 1876 Japan was able to force on Korea an unequal treaty of its own, and increasingly meddled in Korean politics.

Using Chinese 'interference' in Korea as a justification, in 1894 Japan manufactured a war with China and emerged victorious. As a result, it gained Taiwan and the Liaotung Peninsula. Russia pressured Japan into renouncing the peninsula and then promptly occupied it, leading to the Russo-Japanese War of 1904–05, won by Japan. When Japan officially annexed Korea in 1910, there was little international protest.

By the time of Mutsuhito's death in 1912, Japan was recognised as a world power. Japan entered WWI on the side of the Allies, and was rewarded with a council seat in the newly formed League of Nations. It also acquired German possessions in East Asia and the Pacific. The war had been a boon for industry, creating a new stratum of wealth (though the vast majority of the population was left out).

David Mitchell's *Thousand Autumns of Jacob de Zoet: A Novel* (2010) tells about the Dutch living on the island of Dejima during the period of *sakoku*. Mitchell (who also wrote the award-winning novel *Cloud Atlas*) spent most of the 1990s teaching in Western Honshū, an early inspiration for the book.

Aggression in China

The early decades of the 20th century were a time of optimism, when democratic ideals seemed to be overtaking feudal-era loyalties. But there was a dark undercurrent of dissatisfaction, both among certain political and military factions (who felt they were still not held in equal esteem by Western powers) and by the poor (rural and urban alike, as the Great Depression hit Japan), appalled by what they saw as an elite under the sway of Western decadence.

The Washington Conference of 1921–22 set naval ratios of three capital ships for Japan to five American and five British, which upset the Japanese (despite being well ahead of France's 1.75). Around the same time, a racial-equality clause proposed by Japan to the League of Nations was rejected. And in 1924 America introduced race-based immigration policies that effectively targeted Japanese. The armed forces bristled at

1941

Japan enters WWII by striking Pearl Harbor without warning on 7 December, destroying much of the USA's Pacific fleet and drawing America into the war.

1942

After early military successes, Japan's expansion is thwarted at the Battle of Midway in June, with significant losses. From this time, Japan is largely in retreat.

1945

Following intensive firebombing of Tokyo in March, Hiroshima and Nagasaki become victims of an atomic bombing on 6 and 9 August, leading Japan's leader, Hirohito, to surrender on 15 August.

1945–52

Japan undergoes USA-led occupation and a rapid economic recovery follows. Hirohito is spared from prosecution as a war criminal, angering many American allies.

the humiliation of yet another round of capitulations. Prime Minister Hamaguchi Osachi, who favoured economic austerity over increased military spending, was shot in 1931 (dying some months later). By then, the military was acting of its own accord.

In the fall of 1931, members of the Japanese army stationed in Manchuria, who were there to guard rail lines leased by China to Japan, detonated explosives along the track and blamed the act on Chinese dissidents. This ruse, which gave the Japanese army an excuse for armed retaliation, became known as the Manchurian Incident. The Japanese easily overpowered Chinese forces and within months had taken control of Manchuria (present-day Heilongjiang, Jilin and Liaoning provinces) and installed a puppet government. The League of Nations refused to acknowledge the new Manchurian government; in 1933 Japan left the league.

When NHK, Japan's national broadcaster, played a message prerecorded by Emperor Hirohito declaring Japan's surrender to the Allies in WWII, it was the first time the people of Japan had heard their emperor speak.

Skirmishes continued between the Chinese and Japanese armies, leading to full-blown war in 1937. Following a hard-fought victory in Shanghai, Japanese troops advanced south to capture Nanjing. Over several months somewhere between 40,000 and 300,000 Chinese were killed in what has become known as the Nanjing Massacre or Rape of Nanjing. To this day, the number of deaths and the prevalence of rape, torture and looting by Japanese soldiers is hotly debated among historians (and government nationalists) on both sides. Japanese attempts to downplay this and other massacres in Asia remain to this day a stumbling block in Japan's relations with many Asian nations.

WWII

Encouraged by Germany's early WWII victories, Japan signed a pact with Germany and Italy in 1940 (though these European allies offered little actual cooperation). With France and the Netherlands distracted and weakened by the war in Europe, Japan quickly moved on their colonial territories – French Indo-China and the Dutch West Indies – in Southeast Asia. According to Japanese wartime rhetoric, the empire sought to create what it called a 'Greater East Asian Co-Prosperity Sphere' and to liberate other Asian peoples from European colonialism. While some locals may have been initially optimistic about the ousting of the European imperialists, their hopes quickly faded; millions, especially in Indonesia, were conscripted into harsh labour.

Meanwhile, tensions between Japan and the USA had been intensifying, as the Americans, alarmed by Japan's aggression, demanded Japan back down in China. When diplomacy failed, the USA (then still neutral) barred oil exports to Japan – a crucial blow. Japanese forces struck at Pearl Harbor on 7 December, 1941, damaging much of the USA's Pacific fleet and bringing the USA into the war.

1954

Godzilla makes his first appearance in an animated movie of the same name, directed by Honda Ishirō, with the premise that Godzilla was a monster created by the atomic bombings of WWII.

1955

The Liberal Democratic Party is formed; excepting the periods of 1993–94 and 2009–12, it will hold continuous power.

1960s

Protests against the signing of the 'Treaty of Mutual Cooperation and Security between the United States and Japan' (known as ANPO) erupt in 1960, ushering in a decade of social agitation.

1964

Tokyo hosts the Summer Olympics, an event that for many Japanese marked Japan's full re-entry into the international community and the completion of its recovery from WWII.

Despite initial successes, the tide started to turn against Japan at the Battle of Midway in June 1942, when much of its carrier fleet was destroyed. Japan had overextended itself, and over the next three years was subjected to an island-hopping counter-attack by the Allies. By mid-1945, Japan, ignoring the Potsdam Declaration calling for unconditional surrender, was preparing for a final Allied assault on its homeland. On 6 August the USA dropped the world's first atomic bomb on Hiroshima, killing 90,000 civilians. Russia, which Japan had hoped might mediate, declared war on 8 August. On 9 August another atomic bomb was dropped, this time on Nagasaki, causing another 50,000 deaths. The emperor formally surrendered on 15 August, 1945.

Post-War Japan

Occupation

The terms of Japan's surrender to the Allies allowed the country to hold on to the emperor as the ceremonial head of state, but he no longer had authority – nor could he be thought of as divine – and Japan was forced to give up its territorial claims in Korea and China. In addition, America occupied the country under General Douglas MacArthur, the Supreme Commander of Allied Powers (SCAP), a situation that would last until 1952 (and until 1972 in Okinawa).

Until Japan was occupied by the USA and other Allies following WWII, the nation had never been conquered or occupied by a foreign power.

MacArthur lead the drafting of a new constitution, one that laid out the emperor's new role as figurehead; dictated a separation of religion and state; and extended suffrage to women. Crucially, Article 9 of the constitution renounced war and the right to maintain a standing armed forces. In 1951, a security treaty was signed by the United States and Japan that stipulated Japan would fall under the umbrella of US military protection – a treaty (and source of contention) that remains to this day.

Following the end of occupation, Japan settled into a– if not happy, then stable – medium between the democratic ideals put forth in its new constitution and the top-down authority favoured by the government's reigning conservatives (who still bristled at Japan's defeat). In 1955, the Liberal Democratic Party (LDP) came to power; they would rule Japanese politics with few breaks until the present day, in cooperation with career bureaucrats and big business.

The Boom Years

In the 1950s Japan took off on a trajectory of phenomenal growth that is often described as miraculous (though it was jump-started by US procurement for the Korean War). Throughout the 1960s, Japan's GDP grew, on average, 10% a year. The new consumer class, inspired by the images of affluence introduced during the American occupation, yearned for the so-called 'three sacred treasures' of the modern era (a play on the three

1972
The USA returns administrative control of Okinawa to Japan, but keeps many bases in place, which is a continuing source of tension.

1990
The so-called 'Bubble Economy', based on overinflated land and stock prices, finally bursts in Japan. By the end of the year, the stock market has lost 48% of its value.

1995
The Great Hanshin Earthquake (magnitude 6.9) strikes Kōbe, killing over 6000; two months later a cult releases sarin gas on the Tokyo Metro, killing 12.

2005
Japan's population declines for the first year since WWII, a trend that will continue.

sacred treasures of the imperial family: the sword, the mirror and the jewel) – a refrigerator, a washing machine and a television. By 1964, 90% of the population had them.

The 1964 Tokyo Summer Olympics, were seen by many as a turning point in the nation's history, the moment when Japan finally recovered from the devastation of WWII to emerge as a fully fledged member of the modern world economy.

Growth continued through the '70s and reached a peak in the late '80s, when wildly inflated real-estate prices and stock speculation fuelled what is now known as the 'Bubble economy'. These were heady times, when it seemed like all the hard work of the postwar decades had paid off; many Japanese went overseas for the first time, famously snapping up Louis Vuitton handbags by the armful. It seemed like things could only go up – until they didn't.

Heisei & Reiwa

In 1991, just two years after the Heisei Emperor ascended the throne, the bubble burst and Japan's economy went into a tailspin. The 1990s were christened the 'Lost Decade', but that has since turned into two, and probably three, as the economy continues to slump along, despite government intervention. By now a whole generation has come of age in a Japan where lifelong employment – the backbone of the middle class – is no longer a guarantee. The Heisei era was also marked by a number of tragic events that signalled the end of Japan's feeling of omnipotence, born of the unlimited successes of the 1980s: the Great Hanshin Earthquake in Kōbe and the sarin gas attack on the Tokyo subway in 1995 and then the earthquake, tsunami and nuclear meltdown in northeastern Japan in 2011.

When Emperor Akihito abdicated and his son, Crown Prince Naruhito ascended the chrysanthemum throne in 2019, the Heisei era ended and a new one, the Reiwa era, began. Of course, the starts and ends of Japan's historic periods – in modern times determined by the passing of emperors – depend on nature, yet they really do seem to effectively bracket the culture's shifting moods. The Heisei era had become symbolic of economic stagnation and uncertainty; perhaps Reiwa would be better?

The country was looking with optimism to the 2020 Tokyo Summer Olympics, hoping that, like the 1964 games, it would reassert Japan's position on the global stage. Then the COVID-19 pandemic hit. Borders closed and the Olympics were postponed, eventually taking place in July and August 2021. Although the sporting events were a success, they were conducted without international spectators and against a backdrop of public unease, rising case numbers and a vaccination programme that lagged behind many other developed nations.

Based on the price paid for the most expensive real estate in the late 1980s, the land value of Tokyo exceeded that of the entire US.

2010
China surpasses Japan as the world's second-largest economy after the USA.

2011
On 11 March, the Great East Japan Earthquake strikes off the coast of northeast Japan (Tōhoku), generating a tsunami that kills many thousands and setting off a crisis at a nuclear power plant in Fukushima Prefecture.

2019
Emperor Akihito abdicates – the first emperor to do so since 1817 – ushering in a new era.

2021
Tokyo once again hosts the Summer Olympics; scheduled for 2020, the games were postponed due to the global COVID-19 pandemic.

The People of Japan

The people of Japan are depicted as inscrutable. Or reticent. Or shy. They often are these things, but often they are not. Japan is typically considered a homogeneous nation, and ethnically this is largely true (though there are minority cultures). But there are also deep divides between urban and rural, stubbornly persistent gendered spheres and growing social stratification. Increasingly, the Japanese are grappling with the problems faced by developed nations the world over.

Population

The population of Japan is approximately 126.5 million. That alone makes Japan a densely populated nation. But the population is unevenly distributed: about nine out of 10 people live in an area classified as urban. Roughly a quarter of the population (about 36 million) lives within the Greater Tokyo Metropolitan Area, which encompasses the cities of Tokyo, Kawasaki and Yokohama, plus the commuter towns stretching deep into the suburbs; it's the most heavily populated metropolitan area in the world. Another nearly 20 million live in the Kyoto–Osaka–Kōbe conurbation (often called Keihanshin). Japan has 13 cities in which the population exceeds one million.

But the population, in general, is shrinking and getting older: for the last two decades the country's birthrate has hovered consistently around 1.4 – among the lowest in the world. The population peaked at 128 million in 2007 and has been in decline since; the latest estimates see a decline of 20 million (roughly one sixth of the total population!) in the next 25 years. Currently over one in four Japanese is over the age of 65; in 25 years, if current trends hold, the number will be one in three and less than one in 10 will be a child under the age of 15.

Diversity

One notable feature of Japan's population is its relative ethnic and cultural homogeneity. This is particularly striking for visitors from the USA, Australia and other multicultural nations. The Japanese census does not ask questions pertaining to race, only nationality. As a result, discussions of diversity in Japan tend to fall on divisions of national identity – who is Japanese and who is not.

The 2015 census revealed 2.23 million foreigners living in Japan – an uptick of 5% from the year before; the count includes those holding permanent residence status as well as students and temporary workers. The largest non-Japanese group in the country is the Chinese, who number roughly 666,000, or almost 30% of Japan's foreign population; next are Koreans, who number 458,000 (20%) and Filipinos (229,600; 10%).

Zainichi Koreans

There are just under half a million Koreans living in Japan today, but that number masks layers of complexity. When Japan annexed Korea in 1910 many migrants came to Japan for work; during WWII hundreds of thousands were brought over by the Japanese government to work in

WE JAPANESE

It's common to hear Japanese begin explanations of their culture by saying, *ware ware nihonjin*, which means, 'we Japanese'. There's a strong sense of national cohesion, reinforced by the media which plays up images of Japan as a unique cultural Galapagos; TV programs featuring foreign visitors being awed and wowed by the curious Japanese way of doing things are popular with viewers. The Japanese, in turn, are often fascinated (and intimidated) by what they perceive as the otherness of outside cultures.

wartime factories or stand on the front lines. When the war ended and Korea regained its independence most Koreans returned home, but quite a few stayed. Some had established lives in Japan, others couldn't afford the trip home and still others were wary of instability on the peninsula.

Under the colonial empire Koreans were subjects of the Japanese emperor; however, after the war, the Japanese government did not automatically grant those Koreans who stayed citizenship. Instead they became Zainichi (temporary residents) and were effectively stateless. Up until the 1980s, Zainichi Koreans who wished to become naturalised citizens were required to adopt Japanese-sounding names. Zainichi Koreans who did not naturalise faced discrimination in the workplace and in marriage. Those who did were often accused of betrayal by those who hadn't; if outed, they would face discrimination anyway.

When Japan resumed diplomatic relations with South Korea in 1965, the latter allowed Zainichi Koreans to claim South Korean nationality, which would now be recognised in Japan. Those who chose not to (perhaps because their allegiance or family ties lay with North Korea) and had not become naturalised Japanese citizens, remained stateless. According to the 2015 census, there are still 34,000 of them. Japan does not grant citizenship automatically at birth unless one parent is already a Japanese citizen. There are now Zainichi Koreans who are fourth- or fifth-generation residents of Japan. Every year some choose to naturalise; if they don't, they remain shut out of certain social welfare benefits available only to citizens.

Minority Cultures

Hidden within the population stats are Japan's invisible minorities – those who are native-born Japanese, who appear no different from other native-born Japanese but who can trace their ancestry to historically disenfranchised peoples. Chief among these are the descendants of the Ainu, the native people of Hokkaidō, and Okinawans.

Prior to being annexed by Japan in the 19th century, Hokkaidō and Okinawa (formerly the Ryūkyū Empire) were independent territories. Following annexation, the Japanese government imposed assimilation policies that forbade many traditional customs and even the teaching of native languages.

The number of Japanese who identify as Ainu is estimated to be around 20,000, though it is likely that there are many more descendants of Hokkaido's indigenous people out there – some who may not know it, perhaps because their ancestors buried their identity so deep (for fear of discrimination) that it became hidden forever. There are maybe 10 native speakers of Ainu left; however, in recent decades movements have emerged among the younger generation to learn the language and other aspects of their culture.

Today's Okinawans have a strong regional identity, though it is less about their ties to the former Ryūkyū Empire and more about their shared recent history since WWII. The Okinawans shouldered an unequal burden, both of casualties and of occupation.

Japan has long prided itself on being a middle-class nation; however, income inequality has grown in recent years, especially affecting single-parent households. Today, one in six children is raised in relative poverty, in a household with an income of less than half the national average.

Shibuya Crossing (p109), Tokyo

Another group is the *burakumin*. Racially no different from other Japanese, they were the disenfranchised of the feudal-era social hierarchy, whose work included tanning, butchering, the handling of corpses, and other occupations that carried the taint of death. Shunned, they lived in isolated settlements (called *buraku*). When the old caste system was abolished and the country modernised, the stigma should have faded, but it didn't: official household registries (often required as proof of residence when applying for a job) tied the ancestors of the *burakumin* to towns known to be former *buraku*.

Discrimination in work and marriage was once common, though negative feelings towards *buraku* descendants appear to be diminishing with each generation.

Though English is slim, the Liberty Museum in Osaka has exhibits on Japan's minority cultures and their struggles for social justice.

Work Life

Over 70% of Japanese work in the service industry, a broad category that covers white-collar jobs, retail, care-giving and so on. A quarter of the population works in manufacturing, though these jobs are on the decline. Just 3.4% of Japanese today still work full-time in agriculture, forestry and fishing. It's a huge shift: until the beginning of last century, the majority of Japanese lived in close-knit rural farming communities.

For much of the 20th century, the backbone of the middle class was the Japanese corporation, which provided lifetime employment to the legions of blue-suited, white-collar workers, almost all of them men (and nicknamed 'salarymen'), who lived, worked, drank, ate and slept in the service of the companies for which they toiled. Families typically consisted of a salaryman father, a housewife mother, kids who studied dutifully in order to earn a place at one of Japan's elite universities and an elderly relative who had moved in.

Since the recession of the 1990s (which plagues the economy to this day), this system has faltered. Today, roughly 37% of employees are considered 'non-regular', meaning they are on temporary contracts, often through dispatch agencies. In many cases they are doing work that once would have been done by full-time, contracted staff – just now with less pay, less stability and fewer benefits. The percentage of non-regular workers is particularly high for young people, older people and women. For some, this is a conscientious rejection of their parents' lifestyles, but for most it is because they find themselves shut out of the full-time workforce. As in most developed countries, *tomobataraki* (both spouses working) is now increasingly common.

Religion

Shintō

Shintō, or 'the way of the gods', is the native religion of Japan. Its innumerable *kami* (gods) are located mostly in nature (in trees, rocks, waterfalls and mountains, for example), but also in the mundane objects of daily life, like hearths and wells. *Kami* can be summoned through rituals of dance and music in the shrines the Japanese have built for them, where they may be beseeched with prayers for a good harvest or a healthy pregnancy, for example; in modern times for success in business or school exams.

Shintō's origins are unclear. For ages it was a vague, amorphous set of practices and beliefs. It has no doctrine and no beginning or endgame; it simply is. One important concept is *musubi*, a kind of vital energy that animates everything (*kami* and mortals alike). Impurities (*tsumi*) interfere with *musubi* so purification rituals are part of all Shintō rites and practices. For this reason, visitors to shrines first wash their hands and mouth at the *temizu* (font). Some traditional rites include fire, which is also seen as a purifying force. In the late 19th and early 20th centuries, Shintō was reconfigured by the imperialist state into a national religion centred on emperor worship. This ended with Japan's defeat in WWII, when Emperor Hirohito himself publicly renounced his divinity. It's unclear what those who today identify as Shintō actually believe.

Regardless of belief, there are customs so ingrained in Japanese culture that many continue to perform them anyway, as a way of carrying on family and community traditions. Shrines are still the place to greet the New Year, a rite called Hatsu-mōde; to celebrate the milestones, such as Coming-of-Age Day (p30) and Shichi-go-san (p33); and where the lovelorn come to pray for a match. At the very least, many would say, doing such things can't hurt.

VISITING A SHINTŌ SHRINE

A visit to a shrine is a prescribed ritual. Upon entering a *torii* gate, it's the custom to bow, hands pressed together, and then proceed to the *temizuya* (font). Use the dipper to collect water from the spigot, pour it over your left hand and then your right (careful not to let the water drip back into the font). Fill your left hand with water and rinse out your mouth; then rinse your left hand a final time with the remaining water.

Next, head to the *haiden* (hall of worship), which sits in front of the *honden* (main hall) enshrining the *kami* (god of the shrine). Here you'll find a thick rope hanging from a gong, with an offerings box in front. Toss a coin – a ¥5 coin is considered lucky – into the box and ring the gong by pulling on the rope (to summon the deity). Then pray, clap your hands twice, bow and then back away from the shrine. Be sure to bow again at the gate on your way out.

Buddhism

A *butsudan* is a traditional Buddhist family altar, where candles or incense may be lit as an offering to one's ancestors. They're passed down through the male line, typically to the household of the oldest son. Many rural families still keep them up; increasingly city dwellers don't.

Buddhism in Japan is part of the Mahāyāna (Great Vehicle) tradition, which teaches that anyone (as opposed to just monks) can attain salvation in this lifetime. A key figure in Mahāyāna Buddhism is the bodhisattva, a compassionate being who, on the cusp of achieving Buddha-hood, delays transcendence in order to help others. By the time Buddhism arrived in Japan in the 6th century, having travelled from India via Tibet, China and Korea, it had acquired a whole pantheon of deities. More importantly, it didn't so much supplant Shintō as elaborate on it. Overtime, Shintō *kami* became integrated into the Buddhist cosmology while many new deities were adopted as *kami*; those with similar aspects were seen as two faces of the same being.

Over the centuries, several distinct sects developed in Japan. Zen is the most well-known internationally, for its meditative practice *zazen* (seated meditation), but there are others, too, like the older esoteric Shingon sect (which shares similarities with Tibetan Buddhism) and the populist Pure Land sect (which has the greatest number of adherents). Regardless of sect, the most popular deity in Japan is Kannon, a bodhisattva who embodies mercy and compassion and is believed to have the power to alleviate suffering in this world.

Given its association with the afterlife, many turn to Buddhism later in life. (And because of its role in funereal rites, many young Japanese have a dour view of the religion). But, like Shintō, there are certain practices carried out by believers and non-believers alike. The Buddhist festival of O-Bon (p32), in mid-summer, is when the souls of departed ancestors are believed to pay a short visit. Families return to their hometowns to sweep gravestones, an act called *ohaka-mairi*, and welcome them. Only the most staunch non-believer could avoid the creeping sense that skipping such rituals would be tempting fate.

Women in Japan

Women have historically been viewed as keepers of the home, responsible for overseeing the household budget, monitoring the children's education and taking care of the day-to-day tasks of cooking and cleaning. Of course this ideal was rarely matched by reality: labour shortfalls often resulted in women taking on factory work and, even before that, women often worked side by side with men in the fields.

Oya-koko is the Japanese expression for filial piety, though it more literally means something like 'making your parents happy'. This can mean taking care of them when they're older but also calling them up, taking them out to lunch or popping around to do some odd chores.

As might be expected, the contemporary situation is complex. There are women who prefer the traditionally neat division of labour. They tend to opt for shorter college courses, often at women's colleges. They may work for several years, enjoying a period of independence before settling down, leaving the role of breadwinner to the husband and becoming full-time mums.

While gender discrimination in the workforce is illegal, it remains pernicious. And while there is less societal resistance to women working, they still face enormous pressure to be doting mothers. Most women see the long hours that Japanese companies demand as incompatible with child-rearing, especially in the early years; few fathers are willing or, given their own work commitments, able to pick up the slack. Attempts at work-life balance, such as working from home, can result in guilt trips from colleagues or bosses. Working women have coined the phrase 'maternity harassment' to describe the remarks they hear in the office after announcing a pregnancy, the subtle suggestions that she quit so as not to cause trouble. Six out of 10 women quit work after having their first child.

And yet many return: women do in fact make up over 40% of the workforce – not far off the global average; however, over half of them

Women in kimono, Tokyo

are working part-time and often menial, low-paying jobs. They hold only 9.3% of managerial positions. Women in full-time positions make on average 73% of what their male counterparts make; up from 60% in the 1990s. Women also continue to spend far more time on unpaid labour (including childcare and housework duties): 3¾ hours per day, compared to men's 40 minutes. This is among the most dramatic imbalances in the developed world.

Taking all of this into account, the World Economic Forum in its Global Gender Gap Report for 2018 has given Japan the damning rating of 110 out of 144 countries – in between Mauritius at 109 and Belize at 111. Far and away the lowest of any G7 nation (the second-lowest, Italy, is ranked number 70), Japan scores particularly low in economic participation and opportunity, and political empowerment.

On the upside: Japanese women have an average life expectancy of 89 years, second only to Monaco.

BRIAN KENNEDY/GETTY IMAGES ©

Arts

Since the early days of the court and during periods of openness, Japan imported styles, techniques and themes from its nearest Asian neighbours, China and Korea. During times of retreat, Japan's artists refined these techniques, filtered styles through local sensibilities and tweaked themes to correspond with the times and materials at hand. The result is a sublime artistic tradition that goes beyond museums and monumental works, seeping into everyday life.

Classical Arts

Above Tea ceremony (p856)

Japan has a long artistic tradition of painting, calligraphy, lacquerware, ceramics, metalwork and textiles. Lacquerware, in particular, is very old: it's believed to go back 7000 years. These are all still very much living arts: you'll see historic works in museums, but also the works of contemporary artists in galleries and department stores, and in high-end restaurants and teahouses.

Temples are great repositories of Buddhist sculpture, which enjoyed a golden age during the Nara, Heian and Kamakura eras. Unlike paintings, which are fragile, sculptures are often on public display.

Shikki (Lacquerware)

Known in Japan as *shikki* or *nurimono,* lacquerware is made using the sap from the lacquer tree *(urushi),* a close relative of poison oak. Raw lacquer is actually toxic and causes severe skin irritation in those who have not developed immunity. Multiple layers of lacquer are painstakingly applied and left to dry, and finally polished to a luxurious shine; once hardened, it becomes extraordinarily durable.

Lacquer is naturally clear; pigments such as iron oxide (which produces vermilion) are added for colour. People in Japan have been using lacquer to protect and enhance the beauty of wood since at least 5000 BCE. During the Heian period, black lacquerware decorated with gold and silver powder (called *maki-e*) became popular with court nobles. More sophisticated techniques that developed include inlay (such as mother-of-pearl) and layering different colours then sanding away the top coat to create a worn appearance (*negoro* style).

Shodō (Calligraphy)

Shodō (the way of writing) is one of Japan's most valued arts, cultivated by nobles, priests and samurai alike, and is still studied by Japanese school children today as *shūji*. Like the characters of the Japanese kanji script, the art of *shodō* was imported from China. In the Heian period, a fluid, cursive, distinctly Japanese style of *shodō* called *wayō* evolved, though the Chinese style remained popular in Japan among Zen priests and the literati for some time.

In both Chinese and Japanese *shodō* there are three important types. Most common is *kaisho* (block-style script). Due to its clarity, this style is favoured when readability is key. *Gyōsho* (running hand) is semi-cursive and is often used in informal correspondence. *Sōsho* (grass hand) is a truly cursive style. *Sōsho* abbreviates and links the characters together to create a flowing, graceful effect.

Famous laquerware-producing areas include Wajima in Ishikawa Prefecture, where it takes over 100 steps to create pieces that are known for their sturdy elegance, and Okinawa, where the style known as Ryūkyū-shikki incorporates designs of flowers and dragons more common to Chinese art.

Painting

Traditionally, paintings were done in black ink or mineral pigments on *washi* (Japanese handmade paper; itself an art form), scrolls (that either unfurled horizontally or were designed to hang vertically), folding screens or sliding doors.

HAIKU: JAPAN'S SIGNATURE POETRY

Japan has a rich poetic tradition, and one that was historically social in nature. Poetry groups would come together to collaborate on long *renga* (linked verse), with each new verse playing off some word or association in the one that came before. *Renga* were composed in a game-like atmosphere and were more about witty repartee than about creating works to be preserved and read. Sometime in the 17th century, however, the opening stanza of a *renga* became accepted as a standalone poem – and the haiku was born. Today, the haiku is Japan's most widely known form of poetry; at just 17 sparse syllables, it is also the shortest.

Matsuo Bashō (1644–94) is considered the master of the form and is Japan's most famous poet. He's also the origin of the popular image of the haiku artist as a Zen-like ascetic figure. In 1689 Bashō left his home in Edo (Tokyo) to embark on a five-month, 2400km walk around northern Japan – then considered the ends of the earth. He returned to write his most famous work, *Oku no Hosomichi* (*The Narrow Road to the Deep North*; 1702), a poetic account of his journey.

Makura no Sōshi (*The Pillow Book*; 1002), written by Heian-era lady-in-waiting Sei Shōnagon feels oddly modern, like a blog, and is a fascinating peek into courtly life at the time.

Paintings of the Heian era (794–1185) depicted episodes of court life, like those narrated in the novel *Genji Monogatari (The Tale of Genji)*, or seasonal motifs, often on scrolls. Works such as these were later called *yamato-e* (Yamato referring to the imperial clan), as they distinguished themselves thematically from those that were mere copies of Chinese paintings. Gradually a series of style conventions evolved to further distinguish *yamato-e;* one of the most striking is the use of a not-quite-bird's-eye perspective peering into palace rooms without their roofs (the better to see the intrigue!).

With the rise of Zen Buddhism in the 14th century, minimalist monochrome ink paintings came into vogue; the painters themselves were priests and the quick, spontaneous brush strokes of this painting style were in harmony with their guiding philosophies.

It was during the Muromachi period (1333–1573) that the ruling class became great patrons of Japanese painters, giving them the space and the means to develop their own styles. Two styles emerged at this time; the Tosa school and the Kano school.

The Tosa clan of artists worked for the imperial house, and were torch-bearers for the now classic *yamato-e* style, using fine brushwork to create highly stylised figures and elegant scenes from history and of the four seasons; sometimes the scenes were half-cloaked in washes of wispy gold clouds.

The Kano painters were under the patronage of the Ashikaga shogunate and employed to decorate their castles and villas. It was they who created the kind of works most associated with Japanese painting: decorative polychromatic depictions of mythical Chinese creatures and scenes from nature, boldly outlined on large folding screens and sliding doors.

The Tea Ceremony

Chanoyu (literally 'water for tea') is usually translated as 'tea ceremony', but it's more like performance art, with each element – from the gestures of the host to the feel of the tea bowl in your hand – carefully designed to articulate an aesthetic experience. It's had a profound and lasting influence on the arts in Japan, one that has percolated through all the divergent arts wrapped up in it: architecture, landscape design, ikebana (flower arranging), ceramics and calligraphy.

The culture of drinking *matcha* (powdered green tea) entered Japan along with Zen Buddhism in the 12th century. Like everything else in monastic life – the sweeping of the temple grounds and the tending of the garden, for example – the preparation of tea was approached as a kind of working meditation. The practice was later taken up by the ruling class, and in the 16th century the famous tea master Sen no Rikkyū (1522–1591) is credited with laying down the foundations of *wabi-sabi* – and with raising tea to an art form.

Pottery Towns

Arita (p727)

Bizen (p477)

Hagi (p512)

Kanazawa (p258)

Wabi roughly means 'rustic' and connotes the loneliness of the wilderness, while *sabi* can be interpreted as 'weathered', 'waning' or 'altered with age'. Together the two words signify an object's natural imperfections, arising in its inception, and the acquired beauty that comes with the patina of time. Ceramics selected for tea ceremonies were often dented, misshapen or rough in texture, with drips of glaze running down the edges – and all the more prized for it. The most famous styles associated with the tea ceremony are *raku, shigaraki* and *bizen.*

The classic *chashitsu* (teahouse), as established by the old medieval masters, had an area of 4½ tatami mats, or nearly 7.5 sq metres (though they could be even smaller). Made of earth and wood, with a thatched roof, teahouses often look more like hastily thrown-together shelters

Shodō (calligraphy)

than intentional works of art – which was exactly the point. The most rustic extreme (and the truest embodiment of *wabi-sabi*) are called *sōan*, literally 'grass cottages'. More than just a place to drink tea, a Japanese teahouse is a distillation of an artistic vision; even today, no architect would turn down a commission to work on one.

Visitors to a teahouse approach via the *roji* ('dewy' path), formed by irregular stepping stones. The path represents a space of transition – a place to clear one's mind and calm one's spirit before entering the teahouse. The doorway is purposely low, causing those who enter to stoop, and thus humble themselves. All are considered equal inside the teahouse (swords were to remain outside). Inside, the sole decoration is a spray of seasonal flowers or leaves and a hanging scroll in the *tokanoma* (alcove).

Gardens all over Japan have *chashitsu* (tea houses); in Kyoto, sign up to experience a tea ceremony.

Ukiyo-e (Woodblock Prints)

Ukiyo was a play on words: spelt with one set of Chinese characters, it meant the 'fleeting world', our tenuous, temporary abode on earth and a pivotal concept in Japanese Buddhism for centuries. Change the first character, however, and you got the homophone, the 'floating world', which was used to describe the urban pleasure quarters of the Edo period. In this topsy-turvy world, the social hierarchies dictated by the Tokugawa shogunate were inverted: money meant more than rank, Kabuki actors were the arbitrators of style and courtesans were the most accomplished of artists.

Ukiyo-e were pictures of this floating world, capturing famed beauties, pleasure boats and outings under the cherry blossoms. They were also postcards from the world beyond; at a time when rigid laws prevented

One of the most famous *ukiyo-e* (woodblock prints) is *The Great Wave* by Hokusai (1760–1849), one of the great masters of the form. It's on permanent display at the Kyoto Ukiyo-e Museum.

Ikebana (literally 'living flowers') is the Japanese art of flower arranging; of key importance is the suggestion of space and the symbolism inherent in the choice and placement of the flowers and, in some cases, bare branches. There are classical schools of ikebana and also daring contemporary artists.

much of the populace from travelling, woodblock prints presented compelling scenes from around Japan. The famous *ukiyo-e* artists, Katsushika Hokusai (1760–1849) and Utagawa Hiroshige (1797–1858) are best known, respectively, for their series *Fifty Three Stations of the Tōkaidō* and *One Hundred Famous Views of Edo*.

The vivid colours, novel composition and flowing lines of *ukiyo-e* caused great excitement when they finally arrived in the West; the French came to dub it 'Japonisme'. *Ukiyo-e* was a key influence on Impressionists and post-Impressionists (including Toulouse-Lautrec, Manet and Degas). Yet among the Japanese, the prints were hardly given more than passing consideration – millions were produced annually in Edo, often thrown away or used as wrapping paper for pottery.

20th-Century Modernism

When Japan opened up to the world in the late 19th century, new forms and ideas came spilling in – oil painting, figurative sculpture, the novel – which was exciting, but also fraught. A painting tradition with a 1000-year history was flattened into the catchall term *nihonga* (Japanese-style painting) as a foil to the new *yōga* (Western-style painting). Making art now meant either a rejection or an embrace of Western influence, a choice that was hard to divorce from politics.

This shift raised a number of questions: should the old styles stay just that? And, if not, how could they possibly evolve organically without addressing the elephant (Western-influence) in the room? Could works in Western mediums ever transcend mere imitation? And who would be the new patrons of the arts, now that the old power structures had been dismantled? Some critics argue that these same questions haunt the arts to this day.

The plots of most modern Japanese horror films can be traced back to the popular *kaidan* (traditional horror or ghost stories) of the Edo and Meiji periods.

Literature and film, with their narrative qualities, were perhaps the best mediums in which to parse the profound disorientation that had settled upon Japan by the early 20th century. Novels such as Sōseki Natsume's *Kokoro* (1914) and Kawabata Yasunari's *Yukiguni* (*Snow Country*; 1935–37) address the conflict between Japan's nostalgia for the past and its rush towards the future, between its rural heartland and its burgeoning metropolises. These are themes still explored today: just watch recent anime hit *Your Name*.

Film, meanwhile, was as new to Japan as the rest of the world – which conferred upon the medium an enviable freedom. Ozu Yasujirō (1903–63), Japan's first great auteur, created family dramas of grace and depth, looking at the rapid change that left different generations all but isolated from each other. His *Tokyo Story* will break your heart. And it was with film that Japanese artists first achieved major international recognition in the 20th century, most notably Kurosawa Akira (1910–98), who won the Golden Lion at the Venice International Film Festival for the haunting *Rashōmon* (1950) and later an honorary Oscar. Kurosawa is an oft-cited influence for film-makers around the world.

Art Festivals

Echigo-Tsumari Art Triennale (www.echigo-tsumari.jp)

Sapporo International Arts Festival (http://siaf.jp)

Setouchi Triennale (www.setouchi-artfest.jp)

Yokohama Triennale (www.yokohamatriennale.jp)

Contemporary Art

The '90s was a big decade for Japanese contemporary art: love him or hate him, Murakami Takashi (b 1962) brought Japan back into an international spotlight it hadn't enjoyed since 19th-century collectors went wild for *ukiyo-e* (woodblock prints). His work makes fantastic use of the flat planes, clear lines and decorative techniques associated with *nihonga* (Japanese-style painting), while lifting motifs from the lowbrow subculture of manga (Japanese comics).

As much an artist as a clever theorist, Murakami proclaimed in his 'Superflat' manifesto that his work picked up where Japanese artists left off after the Meiji Restoration – and might just be the future of painting, given that most of us now view the world through the portals of two-dimensional screens. Murakami inspired a whole generation of artists who worked in his 'factory', Kaikai Kiki, and presented their works at his Geisai art fairs.

Murakami might have made the biggest splash, but he was just one of many artists from the '90s (and beyond) working to deconstruct Japanese art history and untangle it from the stubborn legacy of West-centric art criticism. For example, there's also Aida Makoto (b 1965), who revels in resurrecting the rather ribald tradition of *ukiyo-e* (many were rather racy or grotesque), creating sometimes shocking works; he also riffs on pop culture, including Japan's infatuation with cute mascots.

And there are also artists who have nothing to do with the old styles. The collective known as Chim-Pom (http://chimpom.jp), formed by a group of 20-somethings in the mid-aughts, is one of the more daring presences in Tokyo's art scene: their conceptual installations directly address (sometimes confrontationally, often cheekily) contemporary issues in Japanese, and global, society.

Tokyo is the centre of Japan's contemporary art world, though Kyoto has a thriving gallery scene as well. Travellers with a keen interest in contemporary art will also want to make a trip to Naoshima.

Manga & Anime

Whole generations have come of age reading classic manga, such as Tezuka Osamu's *Tetsuwan Atom* (*Astro Boy*; 1952–68) and *Black Jack* (1973–83); Toriyama Akira's *Dragon Ball* (1984–95); and Kishimoto Masashi's *Naruto* (1999–2014). Osamu (1928–89) is often known as *manga no kamisama* (the 'god of manga') for having brought a level of artistry and profundity to the form, raising it above mere pulp. ('Astro Boy' is a humanoid robot with empathetic powers and a champion of robots' rights.) He was also the first to draw characters with big eyes; though this look has come to define Japanese manga and anime, Osamu was in fact influenced by early Disney works (like *Bambi*) and the 1930s American cartoon character Betty Boop (animation's first pin-up).

An excellent introduction to the art of manga is the Kyoto International Manga Museum (p318).

Anime has a synergistic relationship with manga: many anime series are adapted from manga (*Full Metal Alchemist*, *Death Note* and *Jojo's Bizarre Adventure* are great examples; and of course there's the *One Piece* animated series). There are also hugely popular original anime series, like *Mobile Suit Gundam* (1979–1980) and *Neon Genesis Evangelion* (1995–1996), that have since spawned larger media franchises, including manga series feature-length movies. Both *Mobile Suit*

HIGHLIGHTS OF JAPANESE CINEMA

1950s

The golden age of Japanese film. **Watch** Kurosawa Akira's *Rashōmon* (1950); Mizoguchi's *Ugetsu Monogatari* (1953).

1960s

Colour and prosperity arrive. **Watch** Ozu's *Sanma no Aji* (*An Autumn Afternoon*; 1962).

1970s

Ōshima Nagisa brings new-wave visual techniques and raw sex. **Watch** *Ai no Korīda* (*In the Realm of the Senses*; 1976).

1980s

Imamura Shōhei and Itami Jūzō earn critical success for a new generation. **Watch** Imamura's *Narayama Bushiko* (*The Ballad of Narayama*; 1983); Itami's *Tampopo* (1986).

1990s

Actor and comedian Takeshi Kitano emerges as a director of merit and vision. **Watch** *Hana-bi* (*Fireworks*; 1997).

2000s

Anime and horror flicks are international hits. **Watch** Miyazaki Hayao's *Sen to Chihiro no Kamikakushi* (*Spirited Away*; 2001) and Fukasaku Kinji's *Battle Royale* (2000).

2010s

New voices and visions. **Watch** Shinkai Makoto's *Your Name* (2016); Hirokazu Kore-eda's *Shoplifters* (2018).

All Studio Ghibli fans will want to make a pilgrimage to the delightful Ghibli Museum in the Tokyo suburb of Mitaka. A Ghibli theme park is in the works in Nagoya, scheduled to open in 2022.

Gundam and *Neon Genesis Evangelion* belong to the genre of anime and manga called 'mecha', meaning they feature robots.

While anime, like film, can be about anything really, the form has proven to be particularly outstanding at world-building and imbuing post-humans and machines with a certain pathos. Classics include Ōtomo Katsuhiro's *Akira* (1988), a psychedelic fantasy set in a future Tokyo (actually 2019); Ōshii Mamoru's *Ghost in the Shell* (1995), with a sci-fi plot worthy of Philip K Dick involving cyborgs, hackers and the mother of all computer networks; and the works of Kon Satoshi (1963–2010), such as the Hitchcockian *Perfect Blue* (1997), the charming *Tokyo Godfathers* (2003) and the sci-fi thriller *Paprika* (2006).

Studio Ghibli (www.ghibli.jp) is Japan's most critically acclaimed and commercially successful producer of animated movies. Its films include *Nausicaä of the Valley of the Winds* (1984), *My Neighbor Totoro* (1988) and the Oscar-winning *Spirited Away* (2001), all directed by Miyazaki Hayao. In 2016 Miyazaki announced he was coming out of retirement to make one last film, to be called *How Do You Live?*. Based on a 1930s novel of the same name, it will likely be released in 2022 or 2023.

One new director to watch is Shinkai Makoto: his 2016 *Kimi no Na wa* (*Your Name*) was both a critical and box-office smash – the second-highest-grossing domestic film ever, after *Spirited Away*.

Performing Arts

Japan has a rich tradition of performing arts. Above all, there's kabuki – Japan's most famous form of performing arts, known for its exaggerated poses and fearsome expressions, dramatic stage makeup and boldly coloured costumes. It is this intensely visual nature and heightened sense of drama that makes kabuki so appealing to foreign audiences – you don't really have to know the story to enjoy the spectacle.

Other forms of traditional theatre that can be seen on Japan's stages include *nō* (an even older form of stylised dance-drama), *bunraku* (classic puppet theatre using huge puppets to portray dramas similar to kabuki) and *bugaku* (dance pieces played by court orchestras in ancient Japan).

Nō

Nō, which emerged in 14th-century Kyoto, is the oldest existent Japanese performing art. Its roots are likely older still: *nō* is believed to be a pastiche of earlier traditions, including Shintō rites, popular entertainments

BUTŌ: AVANT-GARDE DANCE

Butō is Japan's unique and fascinating contribution to contemporary dance. It was born out of a rejection of the excessive formalisation that characterises traditional forms of Japanese dance and of an intention to return to more ancient roots. Hijikata Tatsumi (1928–86), born in the remote northern province of Akita, is credited with giving the first *butō* performance in 1959; Ōno Kazuo (1906–2010) was also a key figure.

During a performance, dancers use their naked or seminaked bodies to express the most elemental and intense human emotions. Nothing is forbidden in *butō* and performances often deal with taboo topics such as sexuality and death. For this reason, critics often describe *butō* as scandalous, and *butō* dancers delight in pushing the boundaries of what can be considered beautiful in artistic performance. It's also entirely visual, meaning both Japanese and non-Japanese spectators are on level footing.

Though performers have toured internationally, in Japan *butō* has remained a largely underground scene. Check out Kyoto's Butoh-kan (www.butohkan.jp) for weekly performances; top Tokyo-based troupes include Sankai Juku (www.sankaijuku.com) and Dairakudakan Kochūten (www.dairakudakan.com).

Kabukiza (p150), Tokyo

like pantomime and acrobatics, and *gagaku* (the traditional music and dance of the imperial court).

Rather than a drama in the usual sense of a story in motion, *nō* seeks to express a poetic moment by symbolic and almost abstract means: glorious movements, sonorous chorus and music, and subtle expression. Its principal aesthetic, *yūgen* – a kind of gentle and mysterious, yet profound, grace – was laid down by the dramatist Zeami Motokiyo (1363–1443), who wrote many of the plays still performed today. Characters speak in the language of the medieval court.

The *nō* stage is furnished with only a single pine tree. There are two principal characters: the *shite*, who is sometimes a living person but more often a ghost whose soul cannot rest or a demon; and the *waki*, who leads the *shite* towards the play's climactic moment.

Haunting masks, carved from wood, are used to depict female and nonhuman characters. Often they are designed to appear differently when tilted at varying angles – an effect heightened by the lighting of the stage (traditionally torch-lit). Many still in use are hundreds of years old (the oil and sweat from the actors' faces keeps the wood supple). Adult male characters are played without masks.

Some viewers find this all captivating; others (including most Japanese today) find its subtlety all too subtle. As if anticipating this, comic vignettes known as *kyōgen* are part of the programs of *nō* plays, taking the spectator from the sublime realm to the ridiculous world of the everyday. Using the colloquial language of the time and a cast of stock characters, *kyōgen* poke fun at such subjects as cowardly samurai, depraved priests and faithless women.

The National Nō Theatre (p150) is located in Tokyo and there are several active schools that occasionally host performances. However, the

Contemporary theatre is at its most accessible during Tokyo's month-long theatre festival, Festival/Tokyo (http://festival-tokyo.jp/en; October to November), which features both domestic and international productions. Some of these have English subtitles or synopses, while others require no language ability to appreciate.

most evocative performances are those that are held outside at night, with only torches for lighting. This style is called *takagi-nō*; it is often performed at Shintō shrines. The island of Sado-ga-shima (p578) is especially famous for this.

Kabuki

Book tickets for kabuki in Tokyo and Kyoto at www.kabukiweb.net. For tickets to traditional performances (*nō*, *bunraku*) at Japan's national theatres, go through the Japan Arts Council (www.ntj.jac.go.jp/english.html).

Kabuki got its start in Kyoto: around the year 1600, a charismatic shrine priestess and her entourage began publicly performing a new (and a bit bawdy) style of dance. People dubbed it *kabuki*, a slang expression that meant 'cool' or 'in vogue' at the time. It was also a gateway to prostitution, which eventually led the shogunate to ban the female performers. Adolescent men took their place, though that didn't solve the problem. Finally, in 1653, the authorities mandated that only adult men with shorn forelocks could perform kabuki, which gave rise to one of kabuki's most fascinating elements, the *onnagata* (actors who specialise in portraying women).

But it was in the urbane circles of Edo that kabuki evolved into what we think of today. Those exaggerated moves? They're not-so-subtle references to the off-duty samurai or the dandyish merchant swaggering around the pleasure quarters – both characters lifted from everyday life. Kabuki deals in archetypes; the make-up signals whether a character is good or evil, noble or ruled by passion. But it is not simplistic: though much gets lost in translation (even for modern Japanese), many of the plays, and especially the confrontations, are meant to be funny.

More than by plot, however, kabuki is driven by its actors, who train for the profession from childhood. In its heyday, kabuki actors outshone even those swaggering samurai and merchants; they were the ultimate influencers. Sons (biological or adopted) follow their fathers into a *yago* (kabuki acting house); the leading families of modern kabuki (such as Bandō and Ichikawa) go back many generations. At pivotal moments in a performance, like when the actors pause in dramatic poses (called *mie*), enthusiastic fans shout out the actor's *yago* – an act called *kakegoe*.

See kabuki in Tokyo at Kabukiza (p150) or in Kyoto at Minamiza (p357).

Bunraku

Like kabuki, *bunraku*, Japan's classic puppet theatre, was an art form that developed during the Edo period. Many of the plays are similar, and in fact were first written for *bunraku* and then adopted by kabuki. The most famous playwright was Chikamatsu Monzaemon (1653–1724), who was largely responsible for popularising the form, especially in Osaka.

The puppets used in *bunraku* are sophisticated and large – nearly two-thirds life-sized. They're manipulated by up to three silent, black-robed puppeteers. The story is provided by a narrator performing *jōruri* (narrative chanting) to the accompaniment of a *shamisen* (a three-stringed instrument resembling a lute or banjo). The synchronisation required to pull this off is incredible.

See *bunraku* at Osaka's National Bunraku Theatre (p387).

Traditional Music

Japan's classical music is *gagaku*, the music played in the court from the 7th century onward, on the *koto* (zither) and *biwa* (short-neck lute), among other instruments brought over from China. Haunting and ancient-sounding, it is occasionally performed for the public in national theatres or at Shintō shrines.

More accessible (and admittedly way more fun), *min'yo* (folk music) is usually played on a *shamisen* (three-stringed instrument resembling a lute or banjo). Different regions have different styles, and even different structures; in some areas of Japan (particularly Aomori and Okinawa) you can find bars and restaurants with spirited live performances. The energetic performances of the Sado-ga-shima–based *taiko* (drum) troupe Kodo (www.kodo.or.jp) are also crowd-pleasers.

Music plays a big part in Japan's traditional performing arts: *nō* is punctuated by *taiko* and flute music; kabuki and *bunraku* are accompanied by *shamisen*.

Living Art of the Geisha

The word geisha literally means 'arts person'; in Kyoto the term used is *geiko* (child of the arts). Though dressed in the finest silks and often astonishingly beautiful, geisha are first and foremost accomplished musicians and dancers. On top of that, they are charming, skilled conversationalists. Kyoto is particularly known for its geisha districts and its culture of *maiko* (apprentice geisha), who wear showy kimono, dramatic makeup and elaborate hairstyles.

The novel *Geisha in Rivalry* (1918), by Nagai Kafu, chronicles the love lives of two Tokyo geisha with a penchant for drama. Kafu, a notorious dandy, did plenty of on-the-ground research for this one.

Geisha now live a dramatically different life to their predecessors. Prior to the mid-20th century, a girl might arrive at an *okiya* (geisha living quarters) still a young child, and indeed some were sold into service by desperate families, to work as a maid. Should she show promise, the owner of the *okiya* would send her to the *kaburenjō* (school for geisha arts). She would continue maid duty, waiting on the geisha of the house, while honing her skills and eventually specialising in one of the arts, such as playing the *shamisen* or dance. Training typically lasted about six years; those who passed exams would begin work as an apprentice under the wing of a senior geisha and eventually graduate to full-fledged geisha themselves.

Geisha were often indebted to the *okiya* who covered their board and training. Given the lack of bargaining chips that have historically been afforded women, there is no doubt that many geisha of the past, at some point in their careers, engaged in compensated relationships; this would be with a *danna* (a patron) with whom the geisha would enter a contractual relationship not unlike a marriage (one that could be terminated). A wealthy *danna* could help a woman pay off her debt to the *okiya* or help her start her own. Other geisha married, which required them to leave the profession; some were adopted by their *okiya* and inherited the role of house mother; still others worked until old age.

Mizoguchi Kenji's 1936 black-and-white film *Sisters of Gion* is a riveting portrayal of two very different sisters working in the famous Kyoto geisha district. The actress Yamada Isuzu, who plays one of the sisters, was herself the daughter of a geisha.

Today's geisha begin their training no earlier than in their teens – perhaps after being inspired by a school trip to Kyoto – while completing their compulsory education (in Japan, until age 15). Then they'll leave home for an *okiya* (they do still exist) and start work as an apprentice. While in the past, a *maiko* would never be seen out and about in anything but finery, today's apprentices act much like ordinary teens in their downtime. For some, the magic is in the *maiko* stage and they never proceed to become geisha; those who do are free to live where they choose, date as they like and change professions when they please.

Architecture & Gardens

Japan's traditional design aesthetic of clean lines, natural materials, heightened spatial awareness and subtle enhancement has long been an inspiration to creators around the world. The country's contemporary architects, riffing on old and contemplating the new, are among the most internationally acclaimed and influential. Since ancient times landscape design has been inseparable from architecture, and Japan has a wealth of gardens, both beautiful and meditative.

Traditional Architecture

Japan's abundant forests were an easy source of wood, which has historically been the building material of choice. Stone appears in foundations, bridges or castle ramparts; however, the frequency of earthquakes in Japan made it an unsuitable material for walls. Other natural materials also come into play: mulberry bark is fashioned into *washi* (Japanese traditional paper), which is employed in varying degrees of thickness on *shōji* (sliding wooden doors covered with translucent *washi*) and *fusama* (sliding screens covered with opaque *washi*, used to partition rooms and closets); dried reeds are woven into floor mats (tatami) and window shades.

Traditionally, Japanese constructions use a post-and-lintel system, which, when combined with the gridlike composition of latticed screens and tatami-mat floors, give buildings an overwhelmingly rectilinear appearance. Another hallmark of traditional architecture is a strong roof, with long overhanging eaves that shelter the verandahs from the elements.

Hōryū-ji (607) is commonly believed to have the two oldest wooden structures in the world, including a 32m-high pagoda. Tōdai-ji's main hall is among the world's biggest wooden buildings; the current structure (1709) is actually only two-thirds of its original 8th-century size.

Early architectural styles and techniques were greatly influenced by Korea and China, and well into the modern era (and possibly still today) building projects would begin by consulting a geomancer practised in the art of feng shui. Over the centuries the tastes of various ruling classes have left their mark, from the austere elegance favoured by the medieval warrior class to the more ostentatious styles that were in vogue during the Edo period. Even in the showiest buildings, however, the function of ornamentation was to draw out the beauty of the structure itself and that of the materials employed.

A prominent feature of any monumental structure is its *mon* (gate), which may be even more impressive than the structures behind it. Gates in Japan are rich in symbolism: their size and design elements correspond to strict regulations on rank and importance; in the case of temples or shrines, they represent the boundary between the sacred and the mundane. It is not uncommon for a structure to have more than one gate; perhaps counter-intuitively, the gates are usually freestanding, unconnected to border walls.

Traditional wooden structures were vulnerable to fire and few truly old, original structures remain – though many reconstructions follow the old patterns.

GLOSSARY OF TRADITIONAL JAPANESE ARCHITECTURE

fusama	papered sliding screens used to divide space into rooms
hinoki	Japanese cypress; the preferred material for monumental structures
kawara	slate roof tile
machiya	traditional Japanese townhouse, made of wood and usually of two storeys, with a shop on the ground floor and living quarters upstairs
mon	main entrance gate of a temple or castle constructed of several pillars or casements, joined at the top by a multitiered roof
shoin-zukuri	style of elegant and refined architecture for the ascendant warrior class, originating in the 14th century.
sukiya-zukuri	humbler than, though similar to, *shoin-zukuri*; shabby-chic style that developed in tandem with the tea ceremony in the 16th century
shōji	movable wooden screens, covered with mulberry paper, used as doors
tatami	mats of woven reeds that cover the floors in traditional Japanese buildings; the size is codified and area is often measured by the number of mats
torii	Shintō shrine gate composed of two upright pillars, joined at the top by two horizontal crossbars, the upper of which is normally slightly curved; often painted a bright vermilion

Foreign Influences

When Japan opened its doors to Western influence following the Meiji Restoration (1868), it ushered in new building materials, techniques and styles. The newly opened port cities, like Yokohama, Kōbe and Hakodate, with their foreign settlements and influence, acquired many Western-style buildings, often made of brick or stone. Foreign consulates, corporations and congregations built structures in the style of their native lands, meaning a Victorian-style manor might sit next to a Russian Orthodox church, around the corner from a neo-Baroque bank. Style conventions from any of the above could be sampled to make a building appear Western.

A century-long push and pull ensued, between enthusiasts and detractors: architects who embraced the new styles and materials and those who rejected them. In Tokyo for example – which the government wanted very much to be a modern showcase city – Tokyo Station (1914), with its brick facade and domes, looks very much like a European terminus. Meanwhile, the Tokyo National Museum (1938) was done in what was called the Imperial Style, a sturdy, modern rendering of traditional design. At the time, it was also the vogue for the wealthy elite to build hybrid homes, with Japanese- and European-style wings.

A pagoda (*to*) is a tower with stacked eaves, each one smaller than the one below. It is a style of Buddhist architecture that evolved in China from the Indian stupa, which originally functioned as a reliquary. Wooden pagodas may be anywhere from one to seven storeys tall.

As the mid-20th century approached, the International Style – characterised by sleek lines, cubic forms and materials such as glass, steel and brick – arrived in Japan, settling the debate and putting an end (mostly) to the idea that modern-style (ie Western) buildings needed to incorporate neo-classical flourishes. This particular style also squared more neatly with Japan's own architectural tradition.

Modern Icons

Modern Japanese architecture really came into its own in the 1960s. The best known of Japan's 20th-century builders was Tange Kenzō (1913–2005), who was influenced by traditional Japanese forms as well as the aggressively sculptural works of French architect Le Corbusier. One of his early commissions was the Hiroshima Peace Center and Memorial Park (1955). He also designed the National Gymnasium built for the 1964 Tokyo Olympics – a structure that looks vaguely like a samurai helmet

TEMPLE OR SHRINE?

Buddhist temples and Shintō shrines were historically intertwined, until they were forcibly separated by government decree in 1868. But centuries of coexistence means the two resemble each other architecturally; you'll also often find small temples within shrines and vice versa. The easiest way to tell the two apart is to check the gate: the main entrance of a shrine is a *torii* (gate) of two upright pillars, often painted red; a temple *mon* (main entrance gate) is often a much more substantial affair, with eaves, either natural wood or decoratively painted. Temple gates often contain guardian figures, usually Niō (*deva* kings).

and uses suspension-bridge technology – and later the Tokyo Metropolitan Government Offices (1991), a looming complex with the silhouette of a Gothic cathedral.

Concurrent with Tange were the 'metabolists', Shinohara Kazuo, Kurokawa Kishō, Maki Fumihiko and Kikutake Kiyonori. The Metabolism movement promoted flexible spaces and functions at the expense of fixed forms in building. Design-wise, they were a radical bunch who produced a number of fascinating sketches and plans, the majority of which went unbuilt. One that did go up is Kurokawa's Nakagin Capsule Tower (1972), an apartment complex in Tokyo, with apartments designed as pods that could be removed whole from a central core and replaced. Maki, the most realistic of the group, went on to have a celebrated career; his buildings, which make use of new and varied materials, have a geometric, uncentred composition. Tokyo's Spiral Building is a great example.

Contemporary Architecture

Since the 1980s a new generation of Japanese architects has emerged who continue to explore both modernism and postmodernism, while mining Japan's architectural heritage. Among the more influential ones are Tadao Ando (b 1941) and Itō Toyō (b 1941). Ando's works tend to be grounded and monumental, yet unobtrusive, with no unnecessary flourishes; he works in modern materials such as concrete and steel. He has many works in Tokyo and also on Naoshima.

In 1917 Frank Lloyd Wright, a noted Japanophile, visited Japan, bequeathing it six structures and a bevy of disciples schooled in the principles of modernism. Many Meiji-era structures, including part of Wright's original design for the Imperial Hotel (rebuilt in 1967), can be seen at Meiji-mura, outside Nagoya.

Itō's designs are lighter and more conceptual, meditating on the ideas of borders between inside and outside, public and private. Among his signature works is the Sendai Mediatheque. Two of his protégés, Sejima Kazuyo and Nishizawa Ryūe, went on to form the firm SANAA. Their own luminous form-follows-function creations have also been influential. See their work at the 21st Century Museum of Contemporary Art in Kanazawa and the other-worldly Teshima Art Museum.

Another name to know is Kengo Kuma, who has received many high-profile commissions over the last decade, including the new stadium for the Tokyo 2020 Olympics. Kengo is famous for his use of wood, employing cutting-edge computer drafting technology to mould that age-old staple of Japanese construction.

Landscape Design

Flowering plants are only one component of the Japanese garden, which may be composed of any combination of vegetation (including trees, shrubs and moss), stones of varying sizes, and water. Some gardens are not limited to that which falls within their walls, but take into account the scenery beyond (a technique called *shakkei* or 'borrowed scenery'). Often they are meant to evoke a landscape in miniature, with rocks standing in for famous mountains of myth or Chinese literature;

raked gravel may represent flowing water. Garden elements are arranged asymmetrically and shapes, such as the outline of a pond, are often irregular. The idea is that the garden should appear natural, or more like nature in its ideal state; in reality most gardens are meticulously maintained – and entirely by hand.

Gardens may be designed as spaces of beauty, for leisure and entertainment purposes, or they might be a designation of sacred space (most fall somewhere in between). The white gravel that appears in some temple gardens is rooted in Shintō tradition: there are gravel courtyards at Ise-jingū, which dates to the 3rd century and is considered Japan's most sacred spot.

Garden Books

Zen Gardens and Temples of Kyoto (John Dougill; 2017)

The Art of the Japanese Garden (David and Michiko Young; 2005)

Japanese Stone Gardens (Stephen Mansfield; 2009)

Kare-sansui: 'Dry' Landscape Gardens

Equally iconic and enigmatic, *kare-sansui* are gardens composed of rocks and raked gravel. They may also have moss or shrubbery, but there is no water element and none of the lushness that you might associate with gardens. They are designed to be viewed from a single vantage point – usually that of an adjacent hall; this style is known as *kanshō* (contemplation garden). *Kare-sansui* gardens are rooted in the culture of the Zen monastery. Monks would meditate on them and in them – as tending to the garden was also considered a form of meditation. Some bear a resemblance to nature scenes depicted in monochrome ink wash paintings; the garden of 15 stones at Kyoto's Ryōan-ji is famously abstract (and, like Zen, resists interpretation). Kyoto is the best place in Japan to see *kare-sansui*.

Strolling Gardens

Strolling gardens (*shūyū*) are meant to be entered and viewed from multiple vantage points along a meandering path. This style falls towards the leisure end of the spectrum and can often be found on imperial or feudal estates. In the Edo period, *kaiyū* (many pleasure) gardens came into fashion; these were like several gardens in one, set around a central pond. Such gardens have a number of interesting architectural elements, such as bridges, which may be a graceful sloping arch or a simple slab of stone, and pavilions, which were created as places for rest or for moon-viewing. Some may employ a technique called *shin-gyō-sō* (formal-semiformal-informal; the *sō* is the same as in *sōan*, the 'grass cottage' of the teahouse), meaning the garden takes on a more and more intimate feeling as the visitor heads deeper. The ideal garden is designed to be attractive in all seasons, though most are associated with a particular time of year (be it the blooming of the azaleas in April or the turning of the maples in November).

Environment

Stretching from the Sea of Okhotsk to the South China Sea, the Japanese archipelago is a fantastically diverse place. Few countries enjoy such a variety of climates and ecosystems, with everything from coral-reefed islands to snow-capped mountains. And few feel nature as acutely as Japan, which sits on the Pacific 'Ring of Fire', where earthquakes and volcanic eruptions are not uncommon. It's also a crowded country, where much of the land bears the imprint of human activity.

The Land

Japan has four main islands: Honshū (the largest, slightly smaller than Britain, and where the majority of the population lives), Hokkaidō (the second largest and northernmost), Kyūshū (the southernmost) and Shikoku (the smallest). These make up 95% of the country's landmass. In addition, there are some 6848 smaller islands. The archipelago stretches from northern Hokkaidō in the north at 45°N, (comparable to Montreal) to the southernmost of the Ryūkyū Islands, of which Okinawa is the largest, at around 25°N (comparable to Miami).

Japan identifies very strongly as a *shima-guni* (island nation), defined by its geographical independence and historical reliance on the ocean for both food and travel. Literally everywhere else in the world is referred to in Japan as *kaigai* (overseas). Within Japan, or rather specifically Honshū, the central spine of mountains is another sort of border. The large population centres are all located on the Pacific Coast. Until the last century regions on the other side of the mountains, the Sea of Japan side, were considered more remote and isolated, connected only by the Kitamae-bune, the trading ships that made a circuit of the coastal ports around the country. (Now tunnels make easy work of getting through the mountains).

It's estimated that 1500 or so earthquakes happen annually in Japan. Most go unfelt, though gentle rocks that can be felt are not uncommon. The last truly devastating earthquake to occur was the 9.0-magnitude Great East Japan Earthquake in 2011, the fourth-largest earthquake recorded in modern history.

Ring of Fire

Situated along the 'Ring of Fire', Japan occupies one of earth's most seismically active regions, which has deeply shaped both its geography and culture and continues to impact these today. Japan has 10% of the world's active volcanoes. Within Japan, Central Honshū is among the most active. Most of Japan's mountain ranges run parallel to the basic northeast to southwest direction of the island chain, but running through the middle of Central Honshū – almost at right-angles to the standard ranges – is the Fossa-Magna Tectonic Line (Fossa-Magna means great rift, and it's essentially a wide crack). This clash in the direction of the fault lines has produced the highest mountains in Japan, including the North, Central and South Alps. Central Honshū is home of all 21 of Japan's 3000m-plus peaks, including the volcanoes Fuji (which last erupted 300 years ago, but is now considered dormant), Ontake and Norikura. While the country's volcanoes are actively monitored and fatalities rare, an unexpected eruption of Ontake-san in Nagano killed 56 hikers in 2014.

Snow Country

In winter parts of Japan get extreme levels of snow. And yet, Sapporo, the country's northernmost city, sits at 43° North, the same latitude as Marseille in the south of France. So why all the snow? Winter weather and storms tend to come from the northwest, from frigid regions of Siberia and northern China. The cold air picks up moisture as it passes over the Sea of Japan, hits the land and the mountainous spine of Honshū, where the moisture-laden air is forced up to become even colder. This causes snow to fall heavily, particularly on the Japan Sea side of the mountains, in western Hokkaidō, the western side of Tōhoku, Nagano, the North Alps (the highest mountains) and along the Hokuriku coast – the areas where all the ski resorts are located. Japan calls the stretch on Honshū's Sea of Japan coast from Fukui to Aomori *yukiguni* (snow country). Here snow can get so deep that the ploughed roads feel like canyons, and buildings have a separate entrance on the second floor for use in winter. By contrast, Tokyo and other cities on the Pacific coast rarely have snow on the ground in winter.

Japan is home to the three snowiest major cities: Aomori is tops with an annual average of 790cm; Sapporo comes in second, with 485cm (a city of nearly two million, it has winter living down to a science); Toyama is third, with an average of 363cm of snow per year.

Wildlife

The latitudinal spread of Japan's islands makes for a wide diversity of flora and fauna. The Nansei and Ogasawara archipelagos in the far south are subtropical, and flora and fauna in this region are related to those found on the Malay peninsula. Mainland Japan (Honshū, Kyūshū and Shikoku) shows more similarities with Korea and China, while Hokkaidō shares many features with Russia's nearby Sakhalin Island. For more information on wildlife in Japan, visit the website of the Biodiversity Center of Japan at www.biodic.go.jp.

Animals

Land bridges to the Asian continent allowed the migration of animals from Korea and China (and in Hokkaidō from Sakhalin). There are also species that are unique to Japan, such as the Japanese serow (described as a goat-antelope, with short horns and bushy coats; rather cute) and the Japanese macaque (some of whom famously enjoy soaking in onsen). In addition, the Nansei archipelago, which has been separated from the mainland for longer than the rest of Japan, has a few examples of fauna that are classified by experts as 'living fossils', such as the Iriomote cat, found only on Iriomote-jima.

Japan's largest carnivorous mammals are its bears. Two species are found in Japan: the *higuma* (brown bear) of Hokkaidō, and the *tsukinowaguma* (Asiatic brown bear or 'moon bear' because of the white crescent on its chest) of Honshū, Shikoku and Kyūshū. Though not frequent, bear attacks do occur and hikers typically attach bells to their packs to ward them off.

The International Union for Conservation of Nature and Natural Resources (IUCN) 'Red List' currently tallies 36 critically endangered and 104 endangered fauna species in Japan, including Blakiston's fish eagle, the widely consumed Japanese eel, the red-crowned crane (an imperial emblem and symbol of longevity in Japan) and the Iriomote cat (critically endangered). The majority of the critically endangered species are located in the Ogasawara Islands, a remote island chain in the Pacific that's something like Japan's own Galapagos.

Plants

The flora of Japan today is, for the most part, not what the Japanese saw hundreds of years ago. The cool-to-temperate zones of central and northern Honshū and southern Hokkaidō were once home to broadleaf mixed deciduous forests. While roughly two-thirds of the country remains forested, natural forests make up only a fraction of that; the rest is planted forest, mainly of cedar and cypress, which have long been key materials in traditional architecture. It is also thought that 200 to 500 plant species have been introduced to Japan since the Meiji period, mainly from Europe, but also from North America.

The subtropical islands of Yakushima and Iriomote are part of the Nansei archipelago, which extends southwest from Kyūshū. The islands stand out for their largely untouched landscapes; Iriomote, in particular, is a mostly unexplored primordial jungle, home to numerous endemic plants. At the other end of the country, at the northeastern tip of Hokkaidō, Shiretoko National Park is home to old-growth temperate and sub-alpine forests of Erman's birch, Sakhalin fir and Mongolian oak.

National Parks

In 1931 Japan laid the groundwork for its national park system and today has 34 national parks, ranging from the far south (Iriomote National Park) to the northern tip of Hokkaidō (Rishiri-Rebun-Sarobetsu National Park), plus 57 awkwardly titled quasi-national parks. National parks cover 5.5% of Japan's landmass and are administered by the Ministry of the Environment. Including quasi-national parks and prefectural national parks, the total amount of protected land extends to 14.3%. The two most recently added parks are the Yambara National Park (2016), a sub-tropical forest on the northern end of Okinawa-hontō, and the Amami Guntō National Park (2017), comprising the Amami Islands chain, south of Kyūshū.

Unlike national parks in some other countries, the ones in Japan are not entirely government-owned land – the system was far too late for that. Shintō shrines, in particular, laid claim to many of Japan's mountains long ago. National parks also contain towns, farmland, onsen resorts, industry – anything really. Much of the land that is government-owned land is forested and instead overseen by the Forestry Agency (rather than the Ministry of the Environment). A convoluted multi-tier system is used to regulate development in such a way as to minimise environmental impact to varying degrees.

For descriptions of Japan's parks, see www.env.go.jp/en/np.

Environmental Issues

Energy & Emissions Post Fukushima

Japan is a high consumer of energy – ranked number five in the world; it is also the world's fifth biggest carbon-emitter. The country has historically invested heavily in nuclear power: it has 42 reactors and at its peak, nuclear was producing 30% of Japan's energy. Then the 2011 Great East Japan Earthquake hit, unleashing a tsunami that overwhelmed the seaside six-reactor Fukushima Dai-ichi nuclear power plant. The flooding knocked out backup generators which resulted in a catastrophic loss of essential cooling capacity, causing a core meltdown in three reactors. The incident was classified as a level seven 'major disaster' on the scale used by the International Atomic Energy Agency – the same level as Chernobyl.

Kamikatsu (pop 1580), a village on the island of Shikoku, has committed to becoming zero-waste. Food waste is already 100% composted and so far 80% of other waste is recycled, sorted into 45 different categories.

The real scope of the environmental and public health impact is largely still unknown. While it is thought that much of the toxic radioactive material remains contained on-site, a significant amount of radiation was initially dispersed in a plume to the northwest. As late as 2018, reports of leakages from the containment vessels were continuing to make headlines, suggesting the situation is far from stabilised. That same year, the government reported one death (the first of its kind) linked to the disaster: a plant worker who had been measuring radiation levels outside shortly after the incident and later died of lung cancer. Much of the initial 20km exclusion zone is still off-limits.

Though the central government promoted nuclear power as clean, sustainable and safe, following the meltdown in Fukushima there was significant push back from the public and local governments. In a country that tends to shy away from outright activism, this was a rare and forceful outcry. The reactors were taken offline and revamped safety measures were adopted. In the meantime, Japan resorted to burning more coal and by 2013 emissions were up by 14%, though they have since returned to pre-2011 levels. As of 2018, Japan had five reactors online and the ruling party had made clear its intention to bring the plants back; a 2016 public opinion poll showed a majority of Japanese oppose this decision.

Japan is only now seriously looking at making renewable energy happen. Though the country signed on to the 2016 Paris Agreement, pledging to cut emissions by 26% by 2030, it's largely the private sector that is leading the way.

Whaling

Commercial whaling was banned by the International Whaling Commission (IWC) in the 1980s, but exemptions exist for scientific research and subsistence hunting by indigenous communities. For decades, the Japanese government funded the Japan Institute of Cetacean Research (JICR), which conducted expeditions in the name of science in the Southern Ocean. Critics have long questioned the actual scientific aims of the program; in 30 years the research led to no notable discoveries and afterwards meat was sold on the commercial market. In 2014 the International Court of Justice ruled that Japan's whaling program was not scientific and ordered Japan to cease whaling; it did not. In 2018, Japan declared that it was leaving the IWC altogether and would resume commercial whaling in July 2019, a rare post-WWII example of the country exiting a major international organisation.

The government's stance is that whale populations have sufficiently recovered to the point where a controlled level of whaling should be permissible. Japan will cease its Antarctic missions and will instead hunt whales only in its own waters in select coastal areas, including: Abishiro and Hakodate (in Hokkaidō), Ayukawa (in Ishinomaki, Miyagi prefecture), Wadaura (in Chiba prefecture), Taiji (on the Kii Peninsula in Wakayama prefecture) and Shimonoseki (in Yamaguchi prefecture in western Honshū). Three species will be hunted in limited numbers: Bryde's, minke and sei. Sei whales are classified as endangered on the International Union for Conservation of Nature's Red List; the others are not.

Proponents of whaling in Japan claim that the country has a long history of whaling, and accuse opponents of cultural imperialism. Certain communities, like Taiji, have a documented history of hunting whales. Shimonoseki is the port from where the Antarctic missions departed and is the home district of prime minister Abe Shinzō.

Whale consumption in Japan peaked in the two decades following WWII, when it was a major source of protein for a nation starved by war. For this reason, some elderly Japanese feel fondly towards it. But consumption levels today are so low that much of the whale meat presented at auction goes unsold. Both whale and dolphin meat are known to have high levels of mercury.

Japan's local whaling traditions have come under fire since the release of the documentary *The Cove* (2009), by American producer Fisher Stevens. The film focuses on the annual dolphin hunt in Taiji, during which pods of dolphins are herded into a cove and either slaughtered for meat

SUSTAINABLE TRAVEL IN JAPAN

As a traveller, you can minimise your impact on the Japanese environment in several simple ways.

Refuse packaging At the cash register, you can say: *Fukuro wa irimasen* (I don't need a bag), or just hold up a reusable shopping bag to show you've already got one.

Carry your own chopsticks Buy a pair of *hashi* (chopsticks) with their own carrying case from a convenience store that you can wash in your accommodation to avoid relying on the disposable ones many restaurants use.

And your own water bottle Japanese tap water is potable so bring your own bottle to fill up. Kettles are standard in accommodations, so bring a thermos too and make tea or coffee to go.

Less tuna and eel, please Limit your consumption of seafood threatened by over-fishing, such as *unagi* (eel) and *maguro* (tuna) – including *toro* (fatty tuna belly).

Use public transport Japan's public transport system is among the best in the world; there's little reason not to use it. Many guesthouses and even some tourist information centres offer bike rentals (often for free).

Skip vending machines While ubiquitous vending machines are part of Japan's urban identity, they eat up a considerable amount of energy.

or sold to aquariums. It won the Academy Award for best documentary feature that year, drew attention to the region's whaling culture in general and brought a steady stream of activists to tiny Taiji (pop 3500). A more recent documentary, *A Whale of a Tale* (2018), by director Megumi Sasaki, who was born in Japan but lives in the US, looks at Taiji since *The Cove*, giving voice to both the local fishermen and the activists.

Japan's Construction Addiction

In the post-war period, Japan invested heavily in infrastructure; before then, many mountain villages didn't have paved roads, let alone tunnels and bridges that made easy work of connecting them to major hubs. Hillsides prone to landslides were shored up and riverbanks prone to flooding were encased in concrete. In a country long plagued by disasters, such measures made sense, and carried with them a sense of progress. They also provided comparatively lucrative new jobs for a rural population that had hitherto been eking out an existence in agriculture, fishing or forestry. But at some point, the projects became less about sensible infrastructure improvements and more about holding on to those jobs.

Rural areas yield enormous power in Japanese politics, as representation is determined more by area than by population. In order to ensure the support of their constituencies, rural politicians often take to lobbying for government spending on public-work projects – to keep jobs in their areas. And the government obliges: the rural vote has kept the ruling Liberal Democrat Party in power for most of the post-war period. As a result, Japan is number four in the world in dam construction and state-of-the-art bridges loom over depopulated villages. Alex Kerr writes extensively on this phenomenon in his 2001 book *Dogs and Demons*.

Many rural communities are now looking to tourism as a potential new source of jobs. It's a sad irony that the much heralded projects of the last century can now be seen as detractors, marring what might otherwise be more impressive natural scenery.

Sport

Sumo, steeped in ancient ritual, is Japan's national sport. While it has its devout followers, it's baseball that is the clear fan favourite; soccer is popular, too. Martial arts have a following among both spectators and participants, and get a boost every four years during the Olympics, as Japan excels at judo. Interest in sports in general is at a high, as Japan held the Rugby World Cup in 2019 and Tokyo hosted the Summer Olympics in 2021.

Sumo

Japan's national sport is a ritualistic form of wrestling that developed out of ancient Shintō rites for a good harvest. Two large and amply muscled men, clothed only in *mawashi* (loin cloths) with their hair slicked back into a topknot, battle it out in a packed earth *dōyo* (ring) over which hangs a roof that resembles that of a shrine. Before bouts, which typically last only seconds, the *rikishi* (wrestlers) rinse their mouths with water and toss salt into the ring – both purification rituals. They also perform the *shiko* movement, where they squat, clap their hands and alternately raise each leg as high as it can go before stamping it down – a show of strength and agility.

Tournaments *(bashō)* are held over a 15-day period, six times a year. These are all-day events, marked as much by pageantry as by sport. Doors open at 8am for the early matches that take place between junior wrestlers. The stakes (and pageantry) begin in earnest in the afternoon, when the *makuuchi* (top tier) wrestlers enter the ring wearing decorative *keshō-mawashi* aprons, followed by the *yokozuna* (the top of the top), complete with sword-bearing attendants. Many spectators skip the

Sumo Events

Tokyo: January, May and September

Osaka: March

Nagoya: July

Fukuoka: November

SUMO MOVES

Size is important in sumo, but woe betide any *rikishi* who relies solely on bulk as, more often than not, it's *kimari-te* (wrestling techniques) that win the day. There are 82 official *kimari-te* a *rikishi* may legitimately employ, including:

Abisetaoshi Using body weight to push an opponent backwards to the ground.

Oshidashi Pushing underneath an opponent's arms or in the chest to force them out of the ring.

Oshitaoshi Pushing an opponent to the ground either inside or outside the ring.

Shitatenage Tackling an opponent by grabbing inside their arms.

Tsukiotoshi Grabbing an opponent underneath the arm or on their side and forcing them down at an angle.

Uwatenage Grabbing an opponent's *mawashi* from outside the opponent's arms and throwing them to the ground.

Uwatedashinage As above but also dragging an opponent.

Yorikiri Lifting an opponent out of the ring by their *mawashi*.

Moves that will get a wrestler disqualified include punching with a closed fist, boxing ears, choking, grabbing an opponent in the crotch area and pulling hair.

Sumo contestant, Tokyo

morning, arriving around 2pm or 3pm. The final, most exciting, bouts of the day (featuring the *yokozuna*) finish around 6pm.

Baseball

The Japanese call it *yakyū;* it was introduced in 1873 by Horace Wilson, an American teacher in Tokyo. Games are played between April and October across the country in two pro leagues (Central and Pacific; www.npb.or.jp), each with six teams sponsored by big businesses. The victors in each league then duke it out in the end-of-season, seven-match Japan Series. The most successful team by a wide margin is Tokyo-based Yomiuri Giants, who have 35 Central League and 22 Japan Series titles to their name. In Kansai, the Hanshin Tigers are the hometown favourite. Other major cities with teams include Sapporo, Sendai, Nagoya, Hiroshima and Fukuoka. Regardless of your interest in baseball, it's worth catching a game just to watch the fans, who engage in elaborately choreographed cheering.

Martial Arts

Although they have their roots in the combat techniques honed over centuries by samurai and other warrior styles, the martial arts that are most closely associated with Japan today developed in the modern era. These *gendai budō* (modern martial arts) aim for self-improvement and self-protection rather than aggression. In Tokyo, tournaments are often held in the **Nippon Budōkan** (日本武道館; ☎03-3216-5100; www.nippon budokan.or.jp; 2-3 Kitanomaru-kōen, Chiyoda-ku; Ⓢ Hanzōmon line to Kudanshita, exit 2) – literally 'Martial Arts Hall' – the arena built to host the judo competitions in the 1964 Tokyo Summer Olympics.

Aikido

Developed in the early 20th century, this form of self-defence combines elements of judo, karate and kendō so that the practitioner uses, rather than opposes, an adversary's attack through techniques such as throws and controls. Tokyo's Hombu-dōjō is the headquarters of the International Aikido Federation (www.aikikai.or.jp); they offer beginner classes and longer training courses.

Five new sports were approved by the International Olympic Committee for inclusion in the 2020 Tokyo Summer Games: karate, skateboarding, surfing, climbing and – back for the first time since 2008 – baseball and softball. Two were added for the Paralympics: badminton and taekwondo.

Kendō

An evolution of *kenjutsu* (the art of sword fighting), kendō is a sport whose practitioners use *shinai* (blunt bamboo swords) and *bōgu* (light body armour). The sport is governed by the All-Japan Kendo Federation (www.kendo.or.jp).

Judo

An Olympic sport since 1964, judo (literally meaning 'the gentle way') is a wrestling style of martial art that developed at the end of the 19th century from the more harmful jujitsu fighting school. The controlling body is the Tokyo-based All-Japan Judo Federation (www.judo.or.jp); check their website for information on tournaments. The Kodokan Judo Institute (http://kodokanjudoinstitute.org/en) has training centres in Tokyo and Osaka; the former has a hostel at which recommended students can stay.

Karate

Meaning 'empty hand', karate came to mainland Japan from Okinawa and is a fusion of an Okinawan martial art known as *ke* and Chinese martial arts. Practitioners study *kata* (forms) and also engage in *kumite* (sparring). Today there are various styles of karate, with the Japan Karate Association (www.jka.or.jp) representing the most popular Shokotan tradition. The association's *dōjō* (practice hall) in Tokyo welcomes visitors who wish to join training sessions.

Soccer

Japan has had a professional soccer league (J-League; www.j-league.or.jp) since 1993. There are 18 clubs in the premier J1 division; the season runs March to October with top teams competing for the J-League Cup. On the national stage, the men's team made their World Cup debut in 1998 (losing all their games), but they've since made it to the quarter finals three times (most recently in 2018). More impressive is the women's team, nicknamed Nadeshiko Japan (*nadeshiko* meaning the feminine ideal). They won the 2011 Women's World Cup (defeating the US) and in 2015 came in second (losing to the the US).

Traditional Accommodation

A hotel is a hotel wherever you go. And while some of Japan's hotels are very nice indeed, staying in traditional-style accommodation offers an added cultural experience. Sleeping on futons (quilt-like mattresses), soaking in an *o-furo* (Japanese-style bath, often communal) or starting your day with grilled fish and rice are all opportunities to connect a little deeper with Japan. Options include ryokan (traditional inns), *minshuku* (traditional guesthouses) and *shukubō* (temple lodgings).

Ryokan

Ryokan (旅館) is the Japanese word for inn, but now refers specifically to a lodging where the majority of rooms are arranged in the traditional Japanese fashion, with tatami mats and futons (instead of beds). Beyond that simple definition, ryokan can vary widely. They can be rambling old wooden buildings that look straight out of a *ukiyo-e* (woodblock) print. Atmosphere-wise these are tops, though they do come with some drawbacks: facilities are often shared, luggage will have to be hauled upstairs, walls may be thin and the corridors drafty.

Others are modern concrete structures, which are more likely to have lifts, en suite bathrooms and a few rooms with beds (sometimes including a wheelchair-accessible room). While they may disappoint on first glance, contemporary ryokan can be beautifully designed inside. Or not: some really are just like ordinary, basic hotels where the rooms happen to be Japanese-style. Particularly luxurious ryokan (old and new) will have doting staff dressed in kimono. Some ryokan have onsen baths and beautiful gardens.

Another distinguishing feature of a ryokan is that they typically serve meals, both dinner and breakfast. In both cases the meal is a set course, using local ingredients, served in either a dining room or in your room. Meals can be quite lavish, similar to *kaiseki* (traditional haute cuisine) with numerous small dishes, and often outshine what is available in local restaurants. Though it is possible to book ryokan without meals, most guests do choose to eat in their lodgings, considering the meal part of the experience. (Ryokan are also often located in areas with few restaurants that are open outside of lunch hours).

The most basic ryokan can cost as little as ¥8000 per person (including meals) or ¥5000 without meals. For something with more amenities or charm, expect to pay between ¥12,000 and ¥20,000 per person – though truly luxurious ryokan can cost much, much more. Prices are based on double occupancy; ryokan sometimes charge a surcharge for single travellers, which varies greatly (from ¥1000 to near the cost of double occupancy). Per-person rates also go down slightly when rooms are used by three or four people.

Best Ryokan

- *Tawaraya (p342), Kyoto*
- *Nishimuraya Honkan (p450), Kinosaki Onsen*
- *Tsuru-no-yu Onsen (p566), Nyūtō Onsen*
- *Arai Ryokan (p204), Shuzen-ji Onsen*
- *Hōshi Onsen Chōjūkan (p307), Minakami*

Minshuku

Minshuku (民宿) are family-run private lodgings, rather like B&Bs in Europe or the USA. Rooms are typically smaller and simpler than those found in ryokan; en suite facilities are rare. Service is less formal, and much more a reflection of the inn owners' personality than Japan's exacting standards of hospitality. At some *minshuku* you may find yourself expected to lay out and put away your own bedding. Meals are simpler and more like home-cooking. Prices per night per person with two meals typically run from ¥5500 to ¥7500, or ¥3500 to ¥5000 without meals (again based on double occupancy; expect a small surcharge for single travellers).

Many *minshuku* are not on popular booking sites and require direct booking; in rural areas, local tourist information centres can often help, though note that it is often not possible to get dinner with same-day bookings.

According to government statistics there are roughly 40,000 ryokan in Japan; however the number decreases each year. Many young Japanese prefer the anonymous convenience of hotels; costly maintenance expenses for older buildings and inheritance taxes are also a factor.

Shukubō

Shukubō (宿坊) are lodgings offered at Buddhist temples. Historically they were created for pilgrims or official visitors to the temple, but these days many accept casual travellers. *Shukubō* vary tremendously in style and amenities: some are downright luxurious (rivalling high-end ryokan), while others offer bare tatami rooms (either communal or private) with shared facilities; most fall somewhere in between, or offer rooms of various grades. Many – though not all – *shukubō* allow visitors to observe the monks' morning prayer rituals.

Temples typically follow strict timelines and guests are expected to follow them: you may need to check in by a certain time, bathing times may be limited and there may be a curfew. The food served in *shukubō* is *shōjin-ryōri* (Buddhist vegetarian cuisine), which can be an excellent part of the experience (and a boon for vegetarians!). Breakfast is often served early, after morning prayers. There are *shukubō* all over Japan, though they can be difficult to find without some Japanese language ability.

The most popular destination for *shukubō* is the mountain monastery complex Kōya-san (p418), in Wakayama Prefecture (Kansai), about two hours by train south of Osaka. There are over 50 *shukubō* here and some are especially accommodating towards overseas guests, with English-speakers who can explain some of the monks' practices and beliefs. There are some quite beautiful temples here, too, with peaceful gardens. All rooms are private and prices are fixed: the minimum charge is ¥9720 per person including breakfast and dinner, and goes up from there (depending on the class of room and meals). Some places charge extra for solo travellers; others do not. For a list of temple accommodations in Kōya-san, visit Koyasan Shukubo Association (http://eng.shukubo.net).

At Kōya-san, temples offer guests few more experiences than attending morning prayer services (some also offer seated meditation sessions or sutra copying). For a more rigorous experience, look into the Sanzen Experience Program (p273), which includes four days (three nights) of 'proper' monk life at Daihonzan Eihei-ji (p272), a Zen Buddhism temple in Fukui. Note that here lodgings are communal and separated by gender.

Staying in Traditional Accommodation

Certain unspoken rules and rhythms apply to all traditional accommodations, be they simple *minshuku*, high-end ryokan or *shukubō*.

First things first: your shoes will come off at the entrance (called the *genkan*); the shoes-off zone is usually marked by a step. Most likely there will be slippers lined up for you to change into. At smaller, casual places, there will be a shelf or cupboard for you to stash your shoes (or, barring that, just leave them neatly to the side). At fancier places, you can just step out of your shoes and staff will whisk them away. The slippers are

NEED TO KNOW

Reservations A reservation is really a must, even if it's just a quick call a few hours before arriving. One easy way to do this is to have your present accommodation call ahead and reserve your next night's lodging.

Food If you have any dietary restrictions (or foods you wish to avoid) be upfront about this at the time of booking. Places that regularly welcome foreign guests may be able to accommodate certain requests, but others may not. If you'd prefer to forgo meals entirely, most inns offer *sudomari* (staying only) rates, but bear in mind that there may be no restaurants nearby. Traditional accommodations do not offer cooking facilities.

Luggage With the exception of higher-end ryokan, most traditional accommodations expect you to handle your own bags and, if you're staying in an older building, this will mean stairs. Ideally, your luggage should be carried (rather than rolled) to protect the floors, but if there is carpet laid down, roll away! Luggage should never be placed in the *tokonoma* (sacred alcove), usually decorated with a scroll. To avoid all this, consider packing a small overnight bag and sending your larger luggage on to your next destination, using Japan's new 'hands-free' travel service (www.jnto.go.jp/hands-free-travel). Alternatively, if you'll be backtracking, some accommodation will hold your bags for you overnight after check-out, allowing you to pick them up the next day.

for use in the corridors and are not to be worn on tatami (socks are OK). There will be separate slippers inside the toilet facilities; don't forget to slip back into your regular slippers on the way out! Given all this sharing of slippers, most guests prefer to wear socks.

For Japanese guests, a ryokan is a destination in and of itself, and as a result, most will check-in as early as possible (usually 3pm). Most places (ryokan, *minshuku* and *shukubō*) expect you to check-in by 6pm, unless you have arranged otherwise. Some request payment up front, others expect you to settle the bill at check-out (and many places will only take cash). After signing in (yes, by hand), you'll be escorted to your room and perhaps given a basic tour of the inn on the way, showing you where the baths and dining rooms are located. Staff will most likely enter the room with you, to show you where the robes and towels are stashed. If you've reserved meals, the staff may then ask what time you would like them. Dinner is typically early, at 6 or 7pm; breakfast is usually sometime between 7am and 8.30am.

The vast majority of traditional inns, regardless of whether they have en suite facilities, will have communal baths separated by gender. Inns that see a significant number of overseas guests may be an exception, having instead several small baths that can be used privately. The same etiquette rules apply as at public baths: wash yourself first in the shower area and then soak in the tub. Many Japanese guests will head right to the bath upon check-in. Soaking in the hot tubs can be uncomfortable after a big meal and especially after alcohol (be warned that this might have a dizzying effect).

All lodgings in Japan (save hostels) supply sleepwear and at ryokan and *minshuku* this will be a *yukata*, a light, cotton kimono-like robe (*shukubō* are more likely to supply some kind of pyjamas). Don't be insulted if you're given one marked extra large – they're sized by length, not by girth! Put it on over your underwear, left over right; women might want to wear a camisole, as the robes tend to creep open on top. Men typically tie the *obi* (sash) low on their hips while women tend to secure it snugly high at the waist. You can wear the *yukata* anywhere around the inn: to and from the baths and during meals (though of course this is optional). At some onsen resort towns, guests wear them around town as well, while going from bathhouse to bathhouse.

Survival Guide

Directory A–Z

Accessible Travel

Japan gets mixed marks in terms of accessibility, or what is called *bariafurī* (barrier free; バリアフリー) in Japanese. You'll find most service staff will go out of their way to be helpful, even if they don't speak much English. In cities, train stations usually have lifts and station staff will help you on and off the train with a temporary slope. Rural stations are harder to navigate.

Across the board, newer buildings are likely to have access ramps and wheelchair-accessible toilets. Major sights are often accessible, even if not obviously so: shrines and temples, for example, often have back entrances with ramps. That said, what is considered 'accessible' at many sights might still mean steep slopes or long gravel paths.

A fair number of hotels, from the higher end of midrange and above, offer a barrier-free room or two (book well in advance); note that what constitutes barrier free is not always consistent, so check the details carefully. Should you decide upon arrival that a wheelchair (車いす; *kuruma isu*) would be helpful, hotel staff can help you rent one.

Some downsides: many neighbourhoods in Japanese cities lack pavements, and restaurants are often too cramped to accommodate diners in wheelchairs. Look for *shōtengai* (商店街; market streets), which are often pedestrian-only, covered arcades; most cities have them.

Accessible Japan (www.accessible-japan.com) is the best resource; they also produce an ebook with lots of detail.

Download Lonely Planet's free Accessible Travel guide from http://lptravel.to/AccessibleTravel.

PRACTICALITIES

Smoking Many cities (including Tokyo, Osaka and Kyoto) prohibit smoking in public spaces except within designated smoking areas. From October 2019, smoking in Tokyo will be banned inside all bars and restaurants that employ staff (other than family), unless they can provide an air-tight smoking area – the strictest regulations in the country to date; elsewhere smoking is permissible inside bars and restaurants unless specifically prohibited by the establishment.

Weights and measures Japan uses the metric system.

Accommodation

Japan offers a wide range of accommodation, from cheap guesthouses to first-class hotels, and distinctive Japanese-style ryokan (traditional inns) and *minshuku* (guesthouses). Advance booking is highly recommended, especially in major tourist destinations.

Reservations

- Hotel and hostel bookings can be made online in English through booking sites and often directly from your lodging's homepage.
- Some traditional accommodation can also be easily booked online; others not so. Email is the next best bet, though you may have to call directly.
- Many smaller, independent inns and hostels offer slightly better rates if you book directly, rather than through a booking site.
- For hotels of all classes, rates can vary tremendously and discounts significantly below rack rates can be found online. Many hotels offer cheaper rates if you book two weeks or a month in advance.
- Not all tourist information centres can make bookings, but the ones in smaller towns and cities, where finding accommodation might be challenging, usually can.

Note that these can close as early as 5pm in rural areas.

Booking Services

Jalan (www.jalan.net) Popular Japanese discount accommodation site, searchable in English.

Japanese Inn Group (www.japaneseinngroup.com) Bookings for ryokan and other small, family-run inns.

Japanican (www.japanican.com) Booking site for foreign travellers run by JTB, Japan's largest travel agency; good for hotel and transport packages.

Lonely Planet (lonelyplanet.com/japan/hotels) Reviews, recommendations and bookings.

Accommodation Styles

APARTMENT RENTALS

Apartment rentals (*minpaku*) are strictly regulated in Japan. Very few places are currently able to meet the requirements to qualify. Those that appear on sites like AirBnB have completed the proper registration process. Options may increase in the near future, as more and more operators are able to get their paperwork through the approval process.

BUSINESS HOTELS

Functional and economical, business hotels have compact rooms, usually with semidouble beds (140cm across; roomy for one, a bit of a squeeze for two) and tiny en suite bathrooms. If cost performance is your chief deciding factor – and you don't plan to spend much time in your room – then a business hotel is your best bet.

They're famous for being deeply unfashionable, though many chains have updated their look in recent years. Expect to pay from ¥8000/12,000 for single/double occupancy (more in cities like Tokyo, Osaka and Kyoto).

Business hotels are usually clustered around train stations. Reliable chains include cheap and ubiquitous **Toyoko Inn** (www.toyoko-inn.com/eng) and **Dormy Inn** (www.hotespa.net/dormy-inn/english), which has some extra amenities like large communal baths, as well as in-room showers.

SLEEPING PRICE RANGES

The following price ranges refer to a double room for hotels, and per person without meals for ryokan. Unless otherwise stated, the national 8% consumption tax is included in the price, but note that some hotels quote exclusive of taxes.

¥ less than ¥6000 (less than ¥8000 in Tokyo and Kyoto)

¥¥ ¥6000 to ¥15,000 (¥8000 to ¥25,000 in Tokyo and Kyoto)

¥¥¥ more than ¥15,000 (more than ¥25,000 in Tokyo and Kyoto)

CAMPING

Japan has a huge number of campgrounds (キャンプ場; *kyampu-jō*), which are popular with students and families during the summer holidays; as such, many campgrounds are only open July through September. They're typically well maintained with showers and barbecue facilities. JNTO has a list of recommended campgrounds: www.jnto.go.jp/eng/location/rtg/pdf/pg-804.pdf.

Camping is also possible year-round (when conditions permit) at campgrounds – often more basic – in the mountains or around certain mountain huts. During summer holidays reservations are a good idea; otherwise you can usually just show up and register at the office. The fee is usually around ¥500 to ¥1000 per person or per tent.

'Guerrilla' or unofficial camping in rural Japan is not something we encourage unless you're able to work out where would be permissible by speaking with locals. Never set up camp on a river bed, as Japan is prone to flash floods.

CAPSULE & CABIN HOTELS

Capsule hotels offer a space the size of a single bed, with just enough headroom for you to sit up – like a bunk bed with more privacy: there's usually a curtain to seal off the entrance in addition to walls on three sides. Older capsule hotels have large communal baths (in which case visitors with visible tattoos are not allowed to stay); newer ones, geared more towards international travellers, often just have showers. Prices range from ¥3500 to ¥5000.

They're a neat experience as an alternative to a hostel, but bear in mind capsule hotels are not ideally set up for multiple-night stays. Most will allow you to stay consecutive days if you book and pay upfront, without having to check out and back in. They do, however, want you and your stuff to be out of the capsule for a few hours, usually around noon, when cleaning staff roll through. You can put your stuff in one of the lockers (typically big enough for a backpack); larger suitcases can usually be held at the front desk.

Some places will let you opt out of cleaning services, in which case you won't have to move out. Though, as capsules lack security, you might want to put your stuff in the locker anyway.

Cabin hotels are a new concept, falling somewhere in between capsule hotels and business hotels: they're not bunked so you have room to stand, but the 'door' is only a sliding curtain; facilities

PLAN YOUR STAY ONLINE

For more accommodation reviews by Lonely Planet authors, check out www.lonelyplanet.com. You'll find independent reviews, as well as recommendations on the best places to stay.

are shared. Price-wise, they also fall in between (¥5500 to ¥8000). The same caveats about cleaning time and security apply here.

In both capsule and cabin hotels, floors and facilities are sex-segregated and front-desk service is typically limited.

HOSTELS

Japan has an extensive network of hostels. These include official Japan Youth Hostel (JYH; www.jyh.or.jp/e/index.php) properties, as well as a growing number of independent, often quite stylish, hostels.

JYH lodgings are usually tightly run ships: guests are expected to check in between 3pm and 8pm or 9pm and there may be a curfew of 10pm or 11pm. Check-out is usually before 10am and dormitories may be closed between 10am and 3pm. Bath time is usually between 5pm and 9pm, dinner is between 6pm and 7.30pm, and breakfast is between 7am and 8am.

The price for members is usually around ¥3000 for a dorm room (around ¥3600 for nonmembers); a one-year membership costs ¥2500. Most of these hostels serve meals that are usually quite good and excellent value (about ¥1000 for dinner and ¥500 for breakfast); however, as meals are prepared in-house, kitchens are usually closed to guests. See the website for a list of properties and information on membership.

Independent hostels have a more laid-back atmosphere, with more flexible check-in times and no curfew (though less quality control). Staff, often travellers themselves, usually speak good English and are good sources of local information. These hostels usually don't provide meals so will have an open kitchen. Prices are similar to those charged by official hostels, sometimes even a bit cheaper. Among the more popular are the K's House (https://kshouse.jp/index_e.html) and J-Hoppers (http://j-hoppers.com) groups.

Hostels supply bedding, which you may need to make up yourself. Most are dorm-style but some have tatami rooms with futons. There will usually be some private and family rooms, too (costing about ¥1000 extra per person). Towels can be hired for about ¥100; basic toiletries (soap and shampoo) may or may not be supplied.

RIDER HOUSES

A rider house (ライダーハウス; *raidā hausu*) is bare-bones budget accommodation reserved for travellers on two wheels, usually on the outskirts of town. Nicer ones are similar to youth hostels; at the most basic, you might get a spare futon in a shed. Prices vary, but ¥1500 per person per night is about average. It's a good idea to have a sleeping bag, though you can ask to rent bedding from the owner. For bathing facilities, you will often be directed to the local *sentō* (public bath).

Many have been running for decades and have a devoted following. They can be a little tricky to find at first, as there's little information out there in English; but stay in one and you can tap into the local network of motorcyclists and cyclists, who can help you work out where to stay next.

Rider houses are most common in Hokkaidō, but there are some all over. Though it's in Japanese, the website Hatinosu (www.hatinosu.net/house) has info and a map of rider houses around Japan. As they're small they can fill up fast, so it's wise to call ahead during summer. Not all are open year-round, especially those in Hokkaidō.

TRADITIONAL ACCOMMODATION

A night (or several) in traditional accommodation (p876) is a highly recommended experience; in many rural areas, they might be the only lodgings in town. Types of accommodation include ryokan (traditional inns), *minshuku* (traditional guesthouses) and *shukubō* (temple lodgings). Sleeping is on futons and tatami mats; most provide two meals – breakfast and dinner – of local cuisine. Note that traditional accommodation tends to charge per person rather than per room; prices (including two meals) range from about ¥6000 for a simple *minshuku* to ¥12,000 or more (and possibly a lot more) for a night and two meals in a ryokan.

Climate

Japan is prone to disasters: earthquakes, tsunamis and volcanic eruptions. Sophisticated early-warning systems and strict building codes do much to mitigate impact, but are not foolproof.

Hot and humid summers present a real risk of heat stroke. Typhoon season runs from July to October (though may hit earlier or later). Severe typhoons can cause transportation delays or even shutdowns; at their worst, they can cause deadly flash floods and landslides.

Japan Meteorological Agency (www.jma.go.jp) Real-time weather and disaster warnings and up-to-date info concerning on-the-ground conditions in English.

JNTO Safety Tips (www.jnto.go.jp/safety-tips) Primer on what to do in the event of a disaster. Their app is clunky, but offers searchable and location-enabled weather and disaster alerts from the Japan Meteorological Agency, plus downloadable 'communication cards' with key phrases to help you get information in the event of an emergency.

Customs Regulations

- Japan has typical customs allowances for duty-free items; see Visit Japan Customs (www.customs.go.jp) for more information.
- Stimulant drugs, which include ADHD medication Adderall, are strictly prohibited in Japan. Narcotics (such as codeine) are controlled substances; in order to bring them for personal medical use you need to prepare a *yakkan shōmei* – an import certificate for pharmaceuticals. See the Ministry of Health, Labour & Welfare's website (www.mhlw.go.jp/english/policy/health-medical/pharmaceuticals/01.html) for more details.
- Pornography that clearly shows genitalia is illegal in Japan.
- To bring a sword out of the country, you will need to apply for a permit; reputable dealers will do this for you.

Electricity

The Japanese electricity supply is an unusual 100V AC. Appliances with a two-pin plug made for use in North America will work without an adaptor, but may be a bit sluggish. Tokyo and eastern Japan are on 50Hz, and western Japan, including Nagoya, Kyoto and Osaka, is on 60Hz.

DISCOUNT CARDS

Seniors Many sights in Japan offer discounted entry to seniors (usually over the age of 65). A passport is usually sufficient proof of age.

Students Discounts for students are common at sights though foreign cards – even the International Student Identity Card – are recognised inconsistently. A Japanese-university-issued student card will always work, and is the only one that qualifies for student fares on trains and ferries.

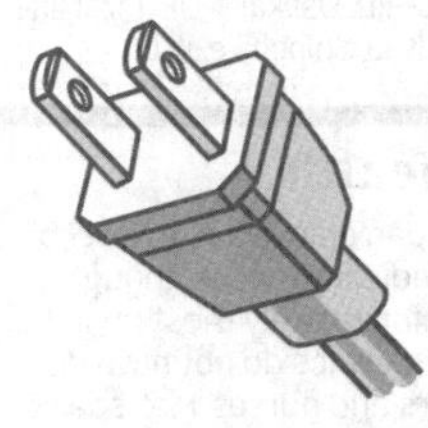

Type A
100V/50Hz

Embassies & Consulates

Australian Embassy (☎03-5232-4111; https://japan.embassy.gov.au; 2-1-14 Mita, Minato-ku; ⌚9am-12.30pm & 1.30-5pm Mon-Fri; Ⓢ Namboku line to Azabu-jūban, exit 2)

Australian Consulate (☎06-6941-9271; www.japan.embassy.gov.au; 16th fl, Twin 21 MID Tower, 2-1-61 Shiromi, Chūō-ku, Osaka; Ⓢ Nagahori Tsurumi-ryokuchi line to Osaka Business Park, exit 4)

Canadian Embassy (カナダ大使館; ☎03-5412-6200; www.canadainternational.gc.ca/japan-japon; 7-3-38 Akasaka, Minato-ku; ⌚9am-5.30pm Mon-Fri; Ⓢ Ginza line to Aoyama-itchōme, exit 4)

Chinese Embassy (☎03-3403-3388; www.china-embassy.or.jp; 3-4-33 Moto-Azabu, Minato-ku; ⌚9am-noon Mon-Fri; Ⓢ Hibya line to Hiro-o, exit 3)

Chinese Consulate (中華人民共和国駐大阪総領事館; ☎06-6445-9481; http://osaka.china-consulate.org/jpn; 3-9-2 Utsubo-Honmachi, Nishi-ku, Osaka; Ⓢ Chūō line to Awaza, exit 9)

French Embassy (☎03-5798-6000; www.ambafrance-jp.org; 4-11-44 Minami-Azabu, Minato-ku; ⌚9am-11.30am Mon-Fri; Ⓢ Hibiya line to Hiro-o, exit 1)

German Embassy (☎03-5791-7700; https://japan.diplo.de; 4-5-10 Minami-Azabu, Minato-ku; ⌚8am-11am Mon-Fri; Ⓢ Hibiya line to Hiro-o, exit 1)

German Consulate (☎06-6440-5070; www.japan.diplo.de; 35th fl, Umeda Sky Bldg Tower East, 1-1-88-3501 Ōyodo-naka, Kita-ku, Osaka; 🚇 JR Osaka, north central exit)

Irish Embassy (☎03-3263-0695; www.dfa.ie/irish-embassy/japan; Ireland House, 2-10-7 Kōji-machi, Chiyoda-ku; ⌚10am-12.30pm & 2-4pm Mon-Fri; Ⓢ Hanzōmon line to Hanzōmon, exit 4)

Netherlands Embassy (☎03-5776-5400; www.netherlandsandyou.nl; 3-6-3 Shiba-kōen, Minato-ku; ⌚9am-12.30pm Mon-Fri; Ⓢ Hibiya line to Kamiyachō, exit 1)

Netherlands Consulate (☎06-6484-6000; www.netherlandsandyou.nl; 8b, Kitahama

EATING PRICE RANGES

The following price ranges refer to a standard main meal.

¥ less than ¥1000 (less than ¥2000 in Tokyo and Kyoto)

¥¥ ¥1000 to ¥4000 (¥2000 to ¥5000 in Tokyo and Kyoto)

¥¥¥ more than ¥4000 (more than ¥5000 in Tokyo and Kyoto)

Itchōme Heiwa Bldg, 1-1-14 Kitahama, Chūō-ku, Osaka; S Sakai-suji line to Kitahama, exit 29)

New Zealand Embassy (03-3467-2271; www.nzembassy.com/japan; 20-40 Kamiyama-chō, Shibuya-ku, Tokyo; 9am-5.30pm Mon-Fri; JR Yamanote line to Shibuya, Hachikō exit)

New Zealand Consulate (06-6373-4583; www.mfat.govt.nz; Umeda Centre Bldg, 2-4-12 Nakazaki-nishi, Kita-ku, Osaka; S Tanimachi line to Nakazakichō, exit 4, Hankyū Umeda)

Russian Embassy (03-3583-4445; https://tokyo.mid.ru/web/tokyo-en; 2-1-1 Azabudai, Minato-ku; 9am-12.30pm & 2-5.30pm Mon-Fri; S Hibiya line to Roppongi, exit 3)

South Korean Embassy (03-3452-7611, emergency 090-1693-5773; http://overseas.mofa.go.kr/jp-ko/index.do; 1-2-5 Minami-Azabu, Minato-ku; 9am-noon & 1.30-6pm Mon-Fri; S Namboku line to Azabu-Jūban, exit 1)

South Korean Consulate (駐大阪大韓民国総領事館; 06-6213-1401; http://jpn-osaka.mofa.go.kr; 2-3-4 Shinsaibashi, Chūō-ku, Osaka; S Midō-suji line to Namba, exit 14)

UK Embassy (03-5211-1100; www.gov.uk/government/world/organisations/british-embassy-tokyo; 1 Ichibanchō, Chiyoda-ku; 9.30am-4.30pm Mon-Fri; S Hanzōmon line to Hanzōmon, exit 3A)

US Embassy (米国大使館; 03-3224-5000; http://japan.usembassy.gov; 1-10-5 Akasaka, Minato-ku; 8.30am-5.30pm Mon-Fri; S Ginza line to Tameike-sannō, exits 9, 12 & 13)

US Consulate (06-6315-5900; https://jp.usembassy.gov/embassy-consulates/osaka; 2-11-5 Nishi-Tenma, Kita-ku, Osaka; JR Tōzai line to Kita-Shinchi, exit 1)

Health

Japan enjoys a high level of medical services, though unfortunately most hospitals and clinics do not have doctors and nurses who speak English. Even for those that do, getting through reception can still be challenging. Enlist your accommodation's help to call ahead.

Even paid in full, the cost of medical care in Japan is low compared to countries like the US. Expect to pay about ¥3000 for a simple visit to an outpatient clinic and from around ¥20,000 and upwards for emergency care.

Insurance

The only insurance accepted at Japanese clinics and hospitals is Japan-issued health insurance; however, they cannot refuse treatment for lack of insurance. For any medical treatment you'll have to pay up front (credit cards are accepted at hospitals and may or may not be accepted at local clinics) and apply for reimbursement when you get home.

Medical Checklist

- Pharmacies in Japan carry very few recognisable foreign brands. Local substitutes of common medication such as ibuprofen and cough syrups are available, though the dosages may be less than what you're used to.
- Though no prescription is necessary, thrush pessaries are only stocked behind the counter (you'll have to ask) and many pharmacies don't carry them.
- Condoms and feminine hygiene products can be purchased at pharmacies.

Medical Services

Every city neighbourhood or town has at least one primary care clinic. Called *naika* (内科), these are often small – sometimes run by just one doctor – and are considered the first point of contact for common, non-urgent complaints, such as rashes, sinus infections, gastric upsets and the like. For additional care, the doctor can refer you to a specialist.

There is no requirement in the Japanese system to register with a particular primary care doctor or clinic. Most *naika* accept walk-ins; in fact, many do not take appointments. Be prepared to wait and note that most close for several hours during the early afternoon.

24-hour care is available at major hospitals.

Tap Water

Tap water is fine to drink in Japan; in some rural areas, locals swear by its health benefits.

Insurance

Basic emergency coverage is adequate.

Internet Access

Decent wi-fi is standard in accommodation in Japan (though exceptions exist). Many cities and even some prefectures and villages have free wi-fi networks; however, public signals are often weak and/or patchy. Some convenience stores, shopping centres and attractions also have wi-fi. To avoid having to sign up and log in to multiple networks, download the Japan Connected (www.ntt-bp.net/jcfw/en.html) app, which gives you access to all partner networks.

Some travellers do manage to get by solely on free wi-fi, but many find it too inconsistent. If staying connected is a priority (and it can be very useful to have online-access navigation apps), consider renting a pocket internet device, which can be shared among multiple devices.

Japan Wireless (www.japan-wireless.com) Pocket wi-fi rentals at reasonable prices and with reliable service; pre-order online.

Legal Matters

Japanese police have extraordinary powers compared with their Western counterparts: they have the right to detain a suspect without charging them for up to 48 hours. If the police can convince a judge of sufficient cause, they can detain you for a further 10 days (which can be extended for an additional 10 days). Bail is rarely granted.

You have the right to remain silent and the right to a lawyer. Note that police may begin questioning before a lawyer is present. If you do find yourself in police custody, you should first insist on speaking to your embassy and refuse to cooperate in any way until you are allowed to make such a call. Insist that a *tsuyakusha* (interpreter) be summoned (this is best, even if you can speak Japanese).

Japan takes a particularly hard-line approach to narcotics possession, with long sentences and fines even for first-time offenders. Japan has very strict drunk driving laws: the legal limit is 0.03% BAC.

Note that it is a legal requirement to have your passport (or, if you are staying longer than 90 days, your resident card) on you at all times. Though checks are not common, if you are stopped by police and caught without it, you could be hauled off to a police station to wait until someone fetches it for you.

JAPAN HELPLINE

Japan Helpline (☎0570-000-911; 24 hours) is an all-purpose, English-language information hotline for problems large and small; for data users, contact them via the web form online at jhelp.com.

LGBTIQ+ Travellers

LGBTIQ+ travellers are unlikely to encounter problems in Japan. There are no legal restraints on same-sex sexual activities here, apart from the usual age restrictions.

Outright discrimination is unusual; however, travellers have reported being turned away or grossly overcharged when checking into love hotels with a partner of the same sex. Such discrimination is illegal, but is rarely litigated.

One thing to keep in mind: Japanese people, regardless of their sexual orientation, do not typically engage in public displays of affection.

Tokyo has the largest gay and lesbian scene, centred around the neighbourhood Shinjuku-nichōme ('Nichōme' for short), followed by Osaka (centred in Dōyama-chō). Though there have been signs in recent years of growing acceptance, outside of these safe spaces many LGBT+ people in Japan remain fearful of the potential social and economic ramifications of living publicly out.

To keep up to date with issues concerning Japan's LGBT+ community, and to learn about events and meetups, follow Nijiro News (@nijinews) on twitter. Utopia Asia (www.utopia-asia.com) is also a great resource.

Akta Community Centre (☎03-3226-8998; http://akta.jp; 301 Nakae bldg No 2, 2-15-13 Shinjuku, Shinjuku-ku; ⊙6-10pm Thu-Mon; 🚇JR Yamanote line to Shinjuku, east exit) Free AIDS tests, counselling and any other information you might need, in Tokyo's Shinjuku-nichōme.

Media

Free Magazines English-language magazines made by and for the expat community, like *Tokyo Weekender* (www.tokyoweekender.com) and *Kansai Scene* (www.kansaiscene.com), can be good sources for events listings and dining and drinking recommendations; look for them at TICs and popular foreigner hangouts.

Newspapers The *Japan Times* (www.japantimes.co.jp), sold at convenience stores, train-station kiosks and select hotels, is Japan's long-running independent English-language daily. Also see Asia & Japan Watch (www.asahi.com/ajw), the online, English-language portal for Japan's just left-of-centre newspaper, the *Asahi Shimbun*, for news and commentary.

Radio Bilingual DJs on Tokyo's InterFM (76.1FM; www.interfm.co.jp) do news broadcasts and public service announcements in English; in Kansai, tune into multilingual FM Cocolo (76.5FM; www.cocolo.jp).

TV NHK World (www3.nhk.or.jp/nhkworld), the English-language version of Japan's national broadcaster NHK, has lots of shows on travel and food in addition to domestic and international news; watch it online or in select hotels.

Money

The currency in Japan is the yen (¥). The Japanese pronounce yen as 'en', with no 'y' sound. The kanji for yen is 円. With the exception of the ¥5 coin, all coins and banknote values are noted in Roman numerals.

Yen denominations:

¥1 coin; lightweight, silver colour

¥5 coin; bronze colour, hole in the middle

¥10 coin; copper colour

¥50 coin; silver colour, hole in the middle

¥100 coin; silver colour

¥500 coin; large, silver colour

¥1000 banknote

¥2000 banknote (rare)

¥5000 banknote

¥10,000 banknote

ATMs

Only a few branches of major Japanese banks – the big two are Sumitomo Mitsui (SMBC) and Tokyo-Mitsubishi UFJ (MUFG) – have ATMs that accept foreign-issued cards; there will be a sign in the window if the bank has an international ATM. Otherwise, even bank ATMs that display Visa and MasterCard logos only work with Japan-issued versions of these cards.

The easiest place to get cash in Japan is at one of the country's ubiquitous 7-Eleven convenience stores. Their **Seven Bank** (www.sevenbank.co.jp/english) ATMs consistently work with foreign-issued Visa, MasterCard, American Express, Plus, Cirrus, Maestro and Union Pay cards; have instructions in English; and are available 24 hours.

Other convenience-store chains have international ATMs, but Seven Bank is the most user-friendly.

Japan Post Bank (ゆうちょ銀行; www.jp-bank.japanpost.jp/en/ias/en_ias_index.html) ATMs, found inside post offices and sometimes at train stations, also accept most foreign-issued cards and have English instructions. The downside is that they have opening hours that are only slightly longer than regular post-office hours.

There is a withdrawal limit of ¥100,000 per transaction at Seven Bank ATMs (and ¥50,000 at Japan Post Bank ATMs). Bear in mind that your bank or card company may impose an even stricter limit; if your card is rejected, this might be the reason why.

Credit Cards

More places in Japan accept credit cards than they used to, and now many bookings can be paid for online. Businesses that do take credit cards will often display the logo for the cards they accept. Visa is the most widely accepted, followed by MasterCard, American Express and Diners Club. Foreign-issued cards should work fine.

Note that Japanese tend not to use credit cards for small or sundry purchases; some shops and restaurants have a minimum purchase requirement (of maybe ¥3000 or ¥5000 to use a card).

Exchanging Money

Major banks and post office main branches can usually exchange US, Canadian and Australian dollars, pounds sterling, euros, Swiss francs, Chinese yuan and Korean won.

MUFG operates **World Currency Shop** (www.tokyo-card.co.jp/wcs/wcs-shop-e.php) foreign-exchange counters in major cities that can handle a broader range of currencies, including Taiwan, Hong Kong, Singapore and New Zealand dollars. In all cases, you'll need to show your passport. Note that you receive a better exchange rate when withdrawing cash from ATMs than when exchanging cash or travellers cheques in Japan.

International Transfers

Western Union (www.wu-japan.com) has counters in most major cities.

Opening Hours

Note that some outdoor attractions (such as gardens) may close earlier in the winter. Standard opening hours:

Banks 9am to 3pm (some to 5pm) Monday to Friday

Bars 6pm to late, with no fixed closing hour

Boutiques noon to 8pm, irregularly closed

Cafes vary enormously; chains 7am to 10pm

Department stores 10am to 8pm

Museums 9am or 10am to 5pm; often closed Monday

Post offices 9am to 5pm Monday to Friday

Restaurants lunch 11.30am to 2pm; dinner 6pm to 10pm; last orders taken about half an hour before closing

Post

Japan Post (JP; www.post.japanpost.jp) is reliable, efficient and, for regular postcards and airmail letters, not markedly more expensive than in other developed countries. Even the smallest towns have post offices. Look for the symbol: a red T with a bar across the top on a white background (〒).

Mail can be sent to, from or within Japan when addressed in English (Roman script). If you want to ship purchases back, boxes are available for purchase at post offices. When presenting a package for shipping, staff will ask if there is a letter (*tegami*) inside, which will raise the shipping rate slightly.

Public Holidays

When a public holiday falls on a Sunday, the following Monday is taken as a holiday. If that Monday is already a holiday, the following day becomes a holiday as well. Note that while only 1 January is an official public holiday, most venues will remained closed (or with reduced hours) through 3 January.

Ganjitsu (New Year's Day) 1 January

Seijin-no-hi (Coming-of-Age Day) Second Monday in January

Kenkoku Kinem-bi (National Foundation Day) 11 February

Tennō Tanjōbi (Emperor's Birthday) 23 February

Shumbun-no-hi (spring equinox) 20 or 21 March

Shōwa-no-hi (Shōwa Emperor's Day) 29 April

Kempō Kinem-bi (Constitution Day) 3 May

Midori-no-hi (Green Day) 4 May

Kodomo-no-hi (Children's Day) 5 May

Umi-no-hi (Marine Day) Third Monday in July

Yama-no-hi (Mountain Day) 11 August

Keirō-no-hi (Respect-for-the-Aged Day) Third Monday in September

Shūbun-no-hi (autumn equinox) 22 or 23 September

Taiiku-no-hi (Health-Sports Day) Second Monday in October

Bunka-no-hi (Culture Day) 3 November

Kinrō Kansha-no-hi (Labour Thanksgiving Day) 23 November

Safe Travel

The biggest threat to travellers is Japan's general aura of safety. It's wise to keep up the same level of caution and common sense that you would back home.

➡ In certain nightlife districts with underground sex and/or drug industries, travellers may be harassed or solicited. These include Roppongi and Kabukichō (Tokyo), Susukino (Sapporo) and Nakasu (Fukuoka).

➡ Avoid touts or anyone who offers to 'help' you in such neighbourhoods, as the end result may be extortion.

➡ In the event of a non-emergency situation, in which you would like to consult with the police, call ☎9110.

GOVERNMENT TRAVEL ADVICE

The following government websites offer travel advisories and information on current hot spots.

Australian Department of Foreign Affairs (www.smartraveller.gov.au)

British Foreign Office (www.gov.uk/foreign-travel-advice)

US State Department (http://travel.state.gov/content/passports/english/country.html)

Taxes & Refunds

Japan's consumption tax is 8% (rising to 10% in October 2019). Many retailers (often noted by a sticker in English on the window) offer duty-free shopping for purchases totalling more than ¥5000. Only visitors on tourist visas are eligible; you'll need to show your passport.

Some shops will simply not charge you consumption tax at the point of sale. Others – particularly department stores – will charge you and then require you to go to the store's tax refund counter to get the money back; a small service fee may be deducted for this process.

Airports in Japan do not handle tax refunds so you do need to sort it out at the time of purchase. A form will be affixed to your passport then, which you'll simply hand over to customs officials at the airport when you depart.

For details, see https://tax-freeshop.jnto.go.jp.

Telephone

The country code for Japan is ☎81. Regional area codes vary from two to four digits (and always begin with a '0'); the total number of digits for landline numbers will always be 10, and 11 for mobile and IP phone numbers.

Mobile phone numbers start with ☎090, 080 or 070; IP phone numbers with ☎050; and toll-free numbers with ☎0120, 0070, 0077, 0088 and 0800.

When dialling Japan from abroad, dial the country code (☎81), drop the initial '0' and then dial the rest of the number.

Mobile Phones

Prepaid data-only SIM cards for unlocked smartphones are widely available and can be purchased at kiosks in the arrival halls at Narita, Haneda, Kansai and New Chitose airports, and also from dedicated desks at major electronics retailers like Bic Camera and Yodobashi Camera. You can reserve ahead online or purchase on arrival.

Two safe bets are the **Japan Travel SIM** (https://t.iijmio.jp/en) and **Japan Welcome SIM** (https://wow-j.com/en/sim_wifi). Getting the SIM to work may require some fiddling with settings, so make sure you've got a connection before you leave the counter. Staff usually speak some English.

Currently only Mobal (www.mobal.com) offers

SIMs that give you an actual phone number from which to make and receive calls; they offer English-language support and can ship to your accommodation. Otherwise, the variety is huge, and which provider to go with depends on the length of your stay and how much data you need.

Many mid- to high-end hotels in cities around Japan offer complementary Handy phones, which you can use free of charge for data and calls. For a list of properties that provide this service, see www.handy.travel.

Public Phones

Japan still has many public phones – a crucial lifeline when disasters wipe out the mobile network. Ordinary public phones are green; those that allow you to call abroad are grey and are usually marked 'International & Domestic Card/Coin Phone'. Public phones are most commonly located around train stations.

Local calls cost ¥10 per minute; note that you won't get change on a ¥100 coin. The minimum charge for international calls is ¥100, which buys you a fraction of a minute – good for a quick check-in but not economical for much more. Dial ☎001 010 (KDDI), ☎0061 010 (SoftBank Telecom) or ☎0033 010 (NTT), followed by the country code, area code and local number. There's very little difference in the rates from the different providers; all offer better rates at night. Reverse-charge (collect) international calls can be made by dialling ☎0051.

Time

All of Japan is in the same time zone: nine hours ahead of Greenwich Mean Time (GMT). Sydney and Wellington are ahead of Japan (by one and three hours, respectively), and most of the world's other big cities are behind: (London by nine, New York by 14 hours and Los Angeles by 17). Japan does not observe daylight saving time.

Toilets

- The word for toilet in Japanese is *toire* (トイレ, pronounced 'toy-rey') but many prefer to use the more politely evasive *o-te-arai* (お手洗い; wash room) or *keshōshitsu* (化粧室; powder room).
- Japan has few actual public toilets; most people prefer the privately maintained ones provided by train stations, tourist attractions, department stores, convenience stores and malls, which tend to be nicer.
- Toilets are typically marked with generic gendered pictograms; but just in case, note the characters for female (女) and male (男).
- Newer or recently redeveloped buildings may have 'multi-functional' (多機能; *takinō*) restrooms; these large, separate rooms are wheelchair accessible, may have nappy-changing or ostomate facilities, and are gender-neutral.
- Increasingly, Japan's toilets are western-style (*yōshiki*; 洋式), often with fancy bidet features (these are called 'washlets'); however, you may still encounter a traditional squat toilet (*washiki*; 和式), especially in rural areas. When using a squat toilet, the correct position is facing the hood.
- Toilet paper is usually present, but it's still a good idea to have a packet of tissues on hand.
- Paper towels and hand dryers may or may not be present; most Japanese carry a handkerchief for use after washing their hands.
- Separate toilet slippers will be provided in establishments where you take off your shoes at the entrance; they are typically just inside the toilet door. These are for use in the toilet area only, so remember to shuffle out of them when you leave.

Tourist Information

Even the smallest towns have tourist information counters (観光案内所; *kankō annai-sho*), located inside or in front of the main train station. In major cities, there should be at least one person on staff who can speak English. Outside of major cities, staff may or may not speak English (there is no consistency); however, there will usually be English-language materials, such as maps, and staff are accustomed to the usual concerns of travellers (food, lodging and transport schedules). Many tourist information centres have free wi-fi. While those in cities usually do not make bookings, rural ones can often call around for you.

Japan National Tourism Organization (JNTO; www.jnto.go.jp), Japan's government tourist bureau, produces lots of travel information; its website, with content available in many languages, is a useful planning tool.

Visas

Visitor Visas

Citizens of 68 countries/regions, including Australia, Canada, Hong Kong, Korea, New Zealand, Singapore, USA, UK and almost all European nations, will be automatically issued a temporary visitor visa on arrival. Typically this visa is good for 90 days. For a complete list of visa-exempt countries and visa durations, consult www.mofa.go.jp/j_info/visit/visa/short/novisa.html#list.

On entering Japan, all holders of foreign passports are photographed and fingerprinted. If asked, travellers arriving on a temporary visitor visa should be able to provide proof of onward travel or sufficient means to purchase an air or ferry ticket; in practice, this is rarely asked.

Visa Extensions

Citizens of Austria, Germany, Ireland, Lichtenstein, Mexico, Switzerland and the UK are able to extend their temporary visitor visa once, for another 90 days, but need to apply at a regional immigration bureau before the initial visa expires. For a list of immigration bureaus, see www.immi-moj.go.jp/english/soshiki/index.html.

For other nationalities, extending a temporary visa is difficult unless you have family or business contacts in Japan who can act as a guarantor on your behalf.

Resident Card

Anyone entering Japan on a visa for longer than the standard 90 days for tourists will be issued a resident card (在留カード; *zairyū kādo*). Those arriving at Narita, Haneda, Kansai or Chūbu airport will receive their cards at the airport (show your visa to airport staff to be directed to the correct counter); otherwise the card will be sent to a registered address.

Working-Holiday Visas

Citizens of 20 countries/regions are eligible for working-holiday visas: Argentina, Australia, Austria, Canada, Chile, Denmark, France, Germany, Ireland, Hong Kong, Hungary, Korea, New Zealand, Norway, Poland, Portugal, Slovakia, Spain, Taiwan and the UK.

To qualify you must be between the ages of 18 and 30 (or 18 and 25 for Australians, Canadians and Koreans) with no accompanying dependants. With few exceptions, the visa is valid for one year and you must apply from a Japanese embassy or consulate abroad.

The visa is designed to enable young people to travel during their stay, and there are legal restrictions about how long and where you can work; you may also be required to show proof of adequate funds.

For more details, see www.mofa.go.jp/j_info/visit/w_holiday.

Volunteering

Most meaningful volunteer work in Japan requires Japanese language ability or an ongoing commitment.

World Wide Opportunities on Organic Farms Japan (www.wwoofjapan.com) Popular with travellers, this organisation places volunteers on organic farms around the country, providing participants with a good look at Japanese rural life and the running of an organic farm.

Women Travellers

Japan is a relatively safe country for women travellers, though perhaps not quite as safe as some might think – crimes against women are believed to be widely under-reported. The best advice is to avoid being lulled into a false sense of security and to take the normal precautions you would in your home country.

Foreign women are occasionally subjected to some forms of verbal harassment or prying questions. The risk of harassment is highest in nightlife districts, especially for solo female travellers. Local women tend not to wear low-cut or form-fitting tops; wearing one may draw unsolicited attention. Physical attacks are very rare, but do occur.

Several train companies have women-only cars to protect female passengers from *chikan* (men who grope women and girls on packed trains). These cars are usually available during rush-hour periods on weekdays on busy urban lines. There are signs (usually in pink) on the platform indicating where you can board these cars; children of any gender may also ride these cars.

Work

It is illegal for non-Japanese to work in Japan without a proper visa. Holders of student or cultural visas who have filed for permission to work, or holders of working-holiday visas, can work legally in Japan under certain restrictions. A full-time job requires an employer-sponsored working visa. There are legal employment categories for foreigners that specify standards of experience and qualifications.

The most common job is English-teaching; however, it is increasingly difficult to find jobs while in Japan that offer visa sponsorship. If you do find one, know that the sponsorship process can be a lengthy one – typically taking at least three months.

The first step is to apply for a Certificate of Eligibility, which requires handing over any number of documents (depending on the desired visa status), at the nearest Japanese immigration office. Once this certificate has been issued, you can then apply for a visa. Some companies may handle some or all of this process for you.

Given the high cost of living in Japan, it makes sense to secure employment and a working visa while still in your home country or while in Japan on a visa that allows part-time work (such as a student or working-holiday visa). The Japan Exchange and Teaching (JET) Programme (jetprogramme.org), as well as some large English conversation school chains, sponsor qualified applicants.

Transport

GETTING THERE & AWAY

Flights, tours and rail tickets can be booked online at lonelyplanet.com/bookings.

Entering the Country

So long as you abide by the rules, entering and exiting Japan is usually hassle-free.

Visas (p888) are given on arrival for many nationalities. Foreigners are fingerprinted and photographed on arrival.

Air

Narita Airport, near Tokyo, is the main point of entry for international travellers; Tokyo has another smaller international airport, Haneda, which is closer to the city centre. If you plan to skip Tokyo or zero in on a specific region, international airports in Kansai (for Kyoto and Osaka), Hokkaidō, Kyūshū and Naha (for Okinawa) might be more time and cost effective. Unless you're flying from east or Southeast Asia, you'll most likely fly first to Tokyo and transfer from there.

Airports & Airlines

Japan's major international airports:

Fukuoka International Airport (www.fuk-ab.co.jp) At the northern end of Kyūshū, and the main arrival point for destinations in western Japan. The airport is conveniently located near the city and has direct flights to/from major cities in east and Southeast Asia.

Haneda Airport (www.tokyo-airport-bldg.co.jp) Tokyo's more convenient airport, about 30 minutes by train or monorail to the city centre. Haneda, also known as Tokyo International Airport, has direct flights to/from major cities in east and Southeast Asia, USA, Australia, Europe and the Middle East; domestic flights to/from Tokyo usually arrive/depart here.

Kansai International Airport (www.kansai-airport.or.jp) Serves the key Kansai cities of Kyoto, Osaka, Nara and Kōbe. Direct international flights to/from major cities in east and Southeast Asia, west coast USA and Australia.

Naha Airport (www.naha-airport.co.jp) On Okinawa-hontō (the main island of Okinawa), with direct flights to/from major cities in east Asia (including Beijing, Hong Kong, Busan, Seoul, Singapore, Shanghai and Taipei).

Narita International Airport (www.narita-airport.jp) About 75 minutes east of Tokyo by express train, Narita gets the bulk of

BAGGAGE FORWARDING

Baggage courier services (called *takkyūbin*) are popular in Japan and many domestic tourists use them to forward their bags, golf clubs, surfboards etc ahead to their destination, to avoid having to bring them on public transport. The tourism bureau has been working to open this service up to foreign travellers; see its guide, **Hands-Free Travel Japan** (www.jnto.go.jp/hands-free-travel), for a list of luggage forwarding counters, mostly at airports, train stations and shopping centres, set up for travellers.

This is a great service except for one caveat: in most cases, your bags won't get there until the following day. (So, for example, if you want to ship your luggage to or from the airport, you'll need a day pack with one night's worth of supplies.) On the other hand, this can free you from large luggage for a one-night detour to an onsen – just send your bags to the following night's destination.

Hotels can also often arrange this service for you (and the couriers will pick up the luggage from the lobby). Costs vary depending on the size and weight of the bag and where it's going, but it's typically around ¥2000.

international flights to Japan from around the world; most budget carriers flying to Tokyo arrive here.

New Chitose Airport (www.new-chitose-airport.jp) In central Hokkaidō, south of Sapporo, with direct flights to/from all major cities in east and Southeast Asia.

Japan's two main international carriers are **Japan Airlines** (JAL; ☎0570-025-121, 03-6733-3062; www.jal.co.jp/en) and **All Nippon Airways** (ANA; ☎0570-029-709, in Osaka 06-7637-6679, in Tokyo 03-6741-1120; www.ana.co.jp); both also operate extensive domestic networks.

GETTING AROUND

Air

Air services in Japan are extensive, reliable and safe. Flying is often faster and cheaper than *shinkansen* (bullet trains) and good for covering long distances or hopping islands.

All local carriers have websites in English on which you can check prices and book tickets.

Japan Airlines (JAL; ☎0570-025-121, 03-6733-3062; www.jal.co.jp/en), which includes **Hokkaidō Air System** (HAC) and Okinawa carrier **Japan Trans Ocean Air** (JTA), has the most extensive domestic network; **All Nippon Airways** (ANA; ☎0570-029-709, in Osaka 06-7637-6679, in Tokyo 03-6741-1120; www.ana.co.jp) is second.

Both All Nippon Airways (ANA) and Japan Airlines (JAL) offer discounts of up to 50% if you purchase your ticket a month or more in advance, with smaller discounts for purchases made one to three weeks in advance.

Budget airlines run between major regional airports, including Narita, Haneda, Kansai, Naha and New Chitose, and offer prices often lower than discounted fares on JAL and ANA for the same routes.

Air Do (www.airdo.jp) Flights from Hokkaidō's New Chitose Airport to Sendai, Haneda, Nagoya (Chubu), Kōbe and to Hokkaidō regional airports.

Jetstar (www.jetstar.com) Destinations from Tokyo's Narita Airport and Osaka's Kansai International Airport include Okinawa (Naha), Sapporo (New Chitose) and Fukuoka.

Peach (www.flypeach.com) Good for flights out of Kansai.

Skymark Airlines (www.skymark.co.jp) Connects many regional airports; Tokyo routes fly in/out of Haneda.

DEPARTURE TAX

Departure tax (¥1000) is included in the price of a ticket.

Vanilla Air (www.vanilla-air.com) Destinations from Tokyo (Narita) include Okinawa (Naha) and Sapporo (New Chitose).

Passes & Discounts

- Foreign travellers can purchase **ANA Experience Japan Fare** one-way domestic tickets for the flat rate of ¥10,800. For details, see www.ana.co.jp/wws/th/e/wws_common/promotions/share/experience_jp.
- JAL's **Visit Japan Fare** offers a similar ¥10,800 flat-rate ticket for domestic routes to foreign travellers flying inbound on any Oneworld carriers. For details, see www.jal.co.jp/yokosojapan.
- ANA Mileage Club members aged 12 to 25 years or over 65 can purchase discounted 'youth' and 'senior' same-day domestic tickets from ¥8000 (from ¥5200 for youth) to ¥22,000 per sector.
- JAL's **Okinawa Island Pass** (www.churashima.net/jta/company/island pass_en.html) makes

INTERNATIONAL FERRY FARES & DURATIONS

Ferries connect Japan to South Korea, China and Russia. Prices listed include fuel surcharges (which are subject to change).

ROUTE	2ND-CLASS FARE (¥)	DURATION (HR)	FREQUENCY
South Korea			
Fukuoka–Busan	10,310-14,000	3-6	3 daily
Osaka–Busan	15,120	19	3 weekly
Shimonoseki–Busan	10,310	12	1 daily
Sakai-Minato–Donghae	11,000	14	1 weekly
China			
Osaka–Shanghai	22,000	48	1-2 weekly
Russia			
Sakai Minato–Vladivostok	26,000	42	1 weekly

TRANSITING AT HANEDA AIRPORT

If you're flying international into Tokyo's Haneda Airport and then catching a domestic flight to elsewhere in Japan give yourself a good buffer (90 minutes as a minimum). Not only will you have to clear immigration (always a variable, even in efficient Japan), you'll have to take either the monorail or a shuttle bus between the international and domestic terminals – in totally different buildings.

island-hopping cheaper; it's only available for foreign visitors and must be purchased abroad.

➡ Early morning and late-night flights are usually the cheapest.

Bicycle

A few cities – including Tokyo, Osaka, Kōbe and Sapporo – have cycle-share schemes. They can be a little tricky to use, usually requiring advance registration online; follow the online directions. Many Japanese use bicycles to get around cities; by law bicycles should be ridden on the road but many people use the pavements. Cycle lanes are pretty much nonexistent. Drivers (and pedestrians) are generally courteous. In cities, bicycles should be parked at ports or designated bicycle parking areas.

Many tourist areas have bicycles for hire. These are almost always heavy-framed, single-speed shopping bikes, though some places have electric bicycles; child-sized bicycles are rarely available. They may be free as part of a local tourism initiative; otherwise private businesses, usually in the vicinity of train stations, rent them out for about ¥1000 per day. Ask at the local tourist information centre. Many youth hostels also have bicycles to rent or borrow.

Helmets are mandatory for children 12 years and under. Unless road touring, adults rarely wear them so rental shops don't provide them (unless they offer children's bicycles; then helmets for children will be included in the rental).

It is difficult to rent touring cycles in Japan; **Cycle Osaka** (☎080-5325-8975; www.cycleosaka.com; 2-12-1 Sagisu, Fukushima-ku; half-/full-day tour ¥5000/10,000; 🚊JR Loop line to Fukushima) is one operator that offers them. To take a bicycle on a train, it needs to be broken down and stored in a bike bag.

Boat

Ferries are pretty much never the cheapest way to get anywhere, and are always the least time-efficient, but the boat rides themselves can be fun: long-haul ferries in Japan have communal bathhouses, dining halls and even karaoke rooms.

DOMESTIC FERRY FARES & DURATIONS

Ferry fares fluctuate by season and by oil price; they change every three months.

ROUTE	2ND-CLASS FARE (¥)	DURATION (HR)
Honshū–Hokkaidō		
Hachinohe–Tomakomai	5000	7-9
Maizuru–Otaru	9570-16,350	20
Niigata–Otaru	6480-10,180	18
Ōarai–Tomakomai	8740-14,910	17
From Tokyo		
Shinmoji (Kitakyūshū)	16,110	35
Tokushima (Shikoku)	11,690	18-19½
From Osaka/Kōbe		
Beppu (Kyūshū)	11,200-12,000	12
Miyazaki (Kyūshū)	9460-10,700	12½
Naha (Okinawa)	19,330	40
Shibushi (Kyūshū)	12,880-13,400	15
Shinmoji (Kitakyūshū)	6170-6480	12½
Kyūshū–Okinawa		
Kagoshima–Naha	14,610	25

On overnight ferries, 2nd-class travel means sleeping in common rooms on plastic mats or the floor; however, you can pay a little extra to upgrade to a dorm room (or a lot extra for a suite).

Most major ferry companies have English websites for booking tickets; otherwise book through a travel agency like JTB (www.jtb.co.jp).

Bus

Japan has a comprehensive network of long-distance buses, connecting the islands of Honshū, Shikoku and Kyūshū. They're nowhere near as fast as the *shinkansen*, but they're significantly cheaper. Buses also travel routes that trains don't.

Japan Railways (JR) operates the largest network of highway buses in Japan; it tends to be a little pricier than other operators, but is reliable and buses tend to depart and arrive at train stations rather than bus stops elsewhere in the city.

Cheaper operators with large networks include **Willer Express** (☎050-5805-0383; http://willerexpress.com). You can book seats on Willer and other reputable operators through the company's Japan Bus Lines service (http://japanbuslines.com).

Most long-haul routes have a night bus option. Premium coaches have quite roomy seats that recline significantly; these can cost almost twice as much as ordinary coaches, but you're still saving on accommodation. They tend to arrive very early, around 6am or 7am. All buses have toilets on the bus.

Car & Motorcycle

For travel to rural areas a car is the best way to get around, especially for two or more people. Areas that are great for exploration by car include: Hokkaidō; Tōhoku; Hida, Shirakawa-gō, the Japan Alps and the Noto Peninsula (Central Honshū), the San-in Coast (Western Honshū); Shikoku; Kyūshū; and Okinawa.

Navigation systems have made driving in Japan much easier than it used to be. In remote mountain areas, however, these are not foolproof; be sure to give yourself plenty of time to find your destination.

For intercity travel, it's hard to compete with the trains – after taking into account expressway tolls, city traffic and parking.

Automobile Associations

If you're a member of an automobile association in your home country, you're eligible for reciprocal rights with the Japan Automobile Federation (JAF; www.jaf.or.jp)

Car & Motorcycle Hire

Prices are largely comparable among agencies: from around ¥7000 per day for a compact car, with reductions for rentals of more than one day.

The following rental agencies have large networks around Japan; vehicles with English-language navigation systems; and ETC cards for rent. Bookings can be completed online in English.

➡ Nippon (www.nrgroup-global.com)

➡ Toyota (https://rent.toyota.co.jp)

Agencies located at major international airports are most likely to have English-speaking staff. If you walk into a rental shop where the staff don't speak English, the best thing to do is first show them your international licence: whether or not you have a valid licence will be the primary concern.

Hiring a motorcycle for long-distance touring is not as easy as hiring a car. Rental 819 (www.rental819.com) is one of the few agencies that

SAMPLE BUS FARES

Typical long-distance one-way fares and travel times out of Tokyo include the following. Early booking often means discounts; prices usually rise on weekends.

DESTINATION	FARE (¥)	DURATION (HR)
Aomori	7000	11
Hiroshima	8600	12
Kanazawa	5500	8
Kōbe	5400	10
Kyoto	5400	8
Nagano	3200	4½
Nagoya	4100	5½
Nara	5980	8½
Osaka	5400	8½

DRIVING PHRASES

ENGLISH	PRONUNCIATION	SCRIPT
credit card	*kaado*	カード
cash	*genkin*	現金
expressway	*jidōshadō*	自動車道
full tank	*mantan*	満タン
high-octane gas	*hai-oku*	ハイオク
roadside station	*michi-no-eki*	道の駅
one-way street	*ippō tsūkō*	一方通行
petrol stand	*gasorin sutando*	ガソリンスタンド
regular gas	*regyuraa*	レギュラー
road closed	*tsūkō-dome*	通行止
self-service	*serufu*	セルフ

makes it possible to book in English. Crash helmets are compulsory for motorcyclists in Japan.

Scooter rentals are common on smaller islands; you'll still need an international licence (though not a motorcycle licence) to rent one of these.

Driving Licences

Travellers from most nations can drive (both cars and motorcycles) in Japan with an International Driving Permit backed up by their regular licence. The International Driving Permit is issued by your national automobile association. Make sure it is endorsed for cars and motorcycles if you're licensed for both.

Travellers from Switzerland, Germany, France, Belgium, Slovenia, Monaco, Estonia and Taiwan need to get an authorised translation of their licence (be sure to carry the original with you too). JAF branches do same-day translations for ¥3000.

Foreign licences and International Driving Permits are only valid in Japan for one year. If you are staying longer, you will have to get a Japanese licence from the local department of motor vehicles.

Expressways

Japan has an extensive, well-maintained expressway system. Expressways are numbered as well as named (the numbers are new and most locals know the roads only by name). Interchanges and exits are signposted in English, but make sure you know the name of your exit as it may not necessarily be the same as your destination.

Tolls are calculated at ¥24.60 per kilometre (plus a base fare and surcharges for some tunnels). Tokyo to Kyoto, for example, will cost about ¥10,500 in tolls. It adds up quickly: if you are going to be covering a lot of ground, it makes sense to get one of the expressway passes offered to foreign tourists.

Expressway toll booths accept credit cards; others will take only cash. Staffed toll booths will be marked in green with the characters 一般 *(ippan)* for drivers without ETC cards; automated ETC booths are marked ETC.

ETC CARDS

ETC cards (www.go-etc.jp), fitted into a reader inside the car, allow drivers to pass through the automated toll booths at 20km/h without stopping. The cards also save money: tolls for ETC users can be up to 30% less than standard tolls (depending on the time of day and distance travelled).

Rental cars have ETC card readers and major agencies will rent the cards for a small fee; you'll be presented with a bill for your tolls when you return the car.

EXPRESSWAY PASSES

These can save money if you plan to cover a lot of ground in a short time by relying on expressways to get around; they're less useful if you prefer to take more scenic roads.

Japan Expressway Pass (https://global.w-nexco.co.jp/en/jep) Seven-/14-day ¥20,000/34,000; covers the whole expressway system except for Hokkaidō, the Tokyo and Osaka metro areas and the bridges between Honshū and Shikoku.

Hokkaidō Expressway Pass (www.driveplaza.com/trip/drawari/hokkaido_expass/en.html) Available from two-day (¥3600) to 14-day (¥11,300); good for all Hokkaidō expressways.

JAPAN BUS PASS

Foreign travellers can purchase a **Japan Bus Pass** (http://willerexpress.com/st/3/en/pc/buspass), good for travel on non-consecutive days within two months. Only certain routes apply; make sure your itinerary doesn't involve having to double back to one of the hub cities.

DURATION (DAYS)	MON-THU (¥)	ALL DAYS (¥)
3	10,000	12,500
5	12,500	15,000
7	15,000	-

Kyūshū Expressway Pass (http://global.w-nexco.co.jp/en/kep) Available from two-day (¥3500) to 10-day (¥11,500); good for all Kyūshū expressways.

Fuel

Petrol stations can be found in almost every town and in service stations along the expressways. Petrol usually costs around ¥130 per litre for regular grade. Credit cards are accepted everywhere.

While self-serve petrol stations are increasing in number, full-service stations are still the most common.

To say 'fill 'er up' in Japanese, it's *mantan* (full tank). You will likely be asked how you intend to pay: *Oshiharai ha dono yō ni saremasu ka?* (How would you like to pay?) The two possible answers are *genkin* (cash) or *kaado* (credit card). Full service costs slightly more, but the service is excellent: staff will take any garbage you have, wipe your windshield inside and out and then wave you back into the traffic.

If you use a self service pump: the red pump is regular, the yellow is high-octane, and green is diesel.

Insurance

Mandatory coverage is included in the cost of the rental car and usually comes with a deductible fee of around ¥50,000. For an extra fee (about ¥1000 per day) you can add on extra coverage that includes the cost of the deductible as well.

Maps & Navigation

Kodansha's *Japan Atlas: A Bilingual Guide* has maps labelled in English and kanji.

Parking

In larger cities (like Tokyo, Osaka and Kyoto) parking is expensive and largely confined to car parks where you might pay anywhere from ¥300 to ¥600 per hour; metered street parking is rare in Japan. Car parks are easy to spot, as signs sport a big 'P' on them. Not all big city hotels have car parks; when they do, expect to pay from ¥500 to ¥1500 per night (the larger the city, the higher the cost).

In smaller cities and in the countryside, where locals rely on cars, parking is generally plentiful and free. Some sights will still charge for parking, often about ¥500 per day.

Rest Stops

There are regular service areas (SA) and parking areas (PA) along national expressways; the former usually have more amenities, including petrol, restaurants, cafes and souvenir shops. Only some are open 24 hours, but even those that aren't will always have a clean, well-lit restroom open for travellers.

Country roads have their own rest stops, called *michi-no-eki* (道の駅; road stations). In addition to toilets, these have restaurants or cafes run by community members and sometimes local produce and crafts for sale (but no petrol). For a list, see www.michi-no-eki.jp.

Road Conditions

Japanese roads are generally in excellent condition. You're far more likely to encounter roadworks in progress than a road in need of repair. Bear in mind that mountain roads tend to be narrow, as are many in the cities (where you'll also have to contend with one-way streets).

Winter driving in Japan can be treacherous if you don't have experience with snow and ice. Snow is possible in higher elevations as early as November (October in Hokkaidō) and may keep mountain passes closed as late as April, and while roads are signposted in English, weather warnings and road closures typically aren't. If you're driving through the mountains in winter, have someone (perhaps at your accommodation) check your route to make sure it's feasible under current conditions.

Car rental agencies rent vehicles with chains and snow tyres or four-wheel drive. Petrol stations in mountain areas will usually put the chains on for a charge (¥1000 to ¥2000). There may be police stops in these areas to make sure that cars have chains.

Road Rules

- Driving is on the left.
- There are no unusual rules, or interpretations of them, and most signposts follow international conventions.
- Stop signs are inverted red triangles.
- JAF publishes a *Rules of the Road* guide (digital/print ¥864/1404) in English, which is handy; it also has some useful information online.
- Speed limits tend to be low, though many local drivers ignore them (at their peril: patrol cars are often lurking).
- Japan takes a very hard line against drunk driving: a blood alcohol content of 0.03% can land you – and

> **USING CAR NAVIGATION SYSTEMS**
>
> Rental cars come equipped with satellite navigation systems that are generally very reliable; major agencies offer ones that have an English function. Japanese addresses can be confusing, so the best way to set your destination is to input the phone number. Many tourist organisations now also provide pamphlets with 'map codes' for major destinations, which you can use in car navigation systems.

ADDRESSES IN JAPAN

In Japan, finding a place from its address can be difficult, even for locals. Addresses are not designated by streets, but rather by concentric areas and blocks and then a building number, which may or may not be consecutive with the ones around it. Smartphones with navigation apps have been a real boon for travellers – probably the biggest reason to want a stable, consistent wi-fi connection at all times. In cities, ubiquitous *kōban* (police boxes) have maps, and officers are always happy to help with directions (though few speak English).

your passengers – a citation with a hefty fee.

➡ The law requires children under the age of six years to ride in a car seat; rental car agencies provide them for a small extra fee.

➡ Japanese drivers are generally safe and courteous. Be aware that they may use turn signals only after entering an intersection or initiating a lane change; they may also be slow to turn their lights on at dusk or in inclement weather (an issue mainly because the vast majority of cars in Japan are white, grey or black).

Hitching

Hitching is never entirely safe, and we don't recommend it. Travellers who decide to hitch should understand that they are taking a small but potentially serious risk.

Hitchhikers are a rare sight in Japan, but the practice is not illegal (so long as you don't stop traffic). Some hitchhikers have tales of extraordinary kindness from motorists who have picked them up.

The best places to look for rides are convenience stores and expressway service areas. At any service area look for a free map that shows all the interchanges (IC) and rest stops on the expressway network – important orientation points if you have a limited knowledge of Japanese.

Local Transport

Japan's larger cities are serviced by subways or trams, buses and taxis; indeed, many locals rely entirely on public transport.

Bus

All cities have public bus systems but it is unlikely that you will find yourself riding them often; Kyoto is the big exception. Smaller cities that don't have subway or tram services usually have a tourist bus that does a loop to the main sights starting and ending at the main train station. City buses typically have a flat fare; day passes are often the most economical way to get around.

Buses that head out of cities or traverse rural areas calculate fares based on distance. When you board (from the rear door most likely), pick up a paper ticket marked with a zone number from the dispenser; when you get off, match your zone number to the electric signboard in the front of the bus and put the posted fare and ticket into the fare box, or show the driver your ticket and a handful of coins and have him or her pick out the required fare; they're used to this.

All buses have change machines near the front door that can exchange ¥100 and ¥500 coins and ¥1000 notes.

Taxi

➡ Taxis are ubiquitous in big cities; they can be found in smaller cities and even on tiny islands, too, though usually just at transport hubs (train and bus stations and ferry ports) – otherwise you'll need to have one called.

➡ Transit stations and hotels have taxi stands where you are expected to queue. In the absence of a stand, you can hail a cab from the street, by standing on the curb and sticking your arm out.

➡ Use the JapanTaxi app to book taxis – including fixed fare ones to the airport. (In rural areas you're probably still better off having a local call a taxi for you.)

➡ Fares are fairly uniform throughout the country and all cabs run by the meter.

➡ Flagfall (posted on the taxi windows) is around ¥600 for the first 2km, after which it's around ¥100 for each 350m (approximately). Flagfall in Tokyo and Kyoto is ¥410 for the first 1km. There's also a time charge if the speed drops below 10km/h and a 20% surcharge between 10pm and 5am.

➡ Payment by credit card is usually accepted.

➡ A red light means the taxi is free and a green light means it's taken.

➡ The driver opens and closes the doors remotely – full service indeed!

➡ Drivers rarely speak English, though fortunately most taxis now have navigation systems. It's a good idea to have your destination written down in Japanese, or better yet, a business card with an address.

RIDE-SHARING APPS

Ride-sharing apps are regulated in Japan. A commercial licence is required to qualify as a driver, so an app like Uber will connect you with a private town car (and probably cost more than a taxi).

Train & Subway

Subway systems operate in Fukuoka, Kōbe, Kyoto, Nagoya, Osaka, Sapporo, Sendai, Tokyo and Yokohama. They are usually the fastest and most convenient way to get around the city. The Tokyo metro area and Kansai metro area are further linked by a network of JR and private rail lines. Stops and line names are posted in English. Rides cost from ¥160 to ¥200.

If you plan to zip around a city in a day, an unlimited-travel day ticket (called *ichi-nichi-jōsha-ken*) is a good deal; most cities offer them and they can be purchased at station windows. If you plan to spend more than a day or two, then getting a prepaid IC card is highly recommended.

Tram

Smaller cities have tram lines. These include Nagasaki, Kumamoto and Kagoshima on Kyūshū; Hiroshima on Honshū; Kōchi and Matsuyama on Shikoku; and Hakodate on Hokkaidō. These usually offer unlimited-travel day tickets.

Train

Japanese rail services are fast, frequent, clean and comfortable. Major stations are sign-posted in English and stops on long-haul trains are announced in English. The most challenging aspect of riding trains in Japan is navigating the sometimes enormous stations with their multiple routes. Give yourself plenty of time.

The predominant operator is Japan Railways, commonly known as 'JR', which is actually a number of distinct rail systems providing one linked service throughout the country. JR runs the *shinkansen* (bullet train) routes. A variety of rail pass schemes make the network very affordable.

IC CARDS

IC cards are prepaid travel cards with chips that work on subways, trams and buses in the Tokyo, Kansai, Sapporo, Niigata, Nagoya, Okayama, Hiroshima and Fukuoka metro areas. Each region has its own card, but they can be used interchangeably in any region where IC cards are used; however, they cannot be used for intercity travel.

The two most frequently used IC cards are **Suica** from JR East and **Icoca** from JR West; purchase them at JR travel counters at Narita and Haneda or Kansai airports, respectively. Cards can also be purchased and topped up from ticket vending machines in any of the cities that support them. A ¥500 deposit is required to purchase a card; you can get the deposit back by returning the card to a JR ticket window.

To use the card, simply swipe it over the reader at the ticket gates or near the doors on trams and buses. They can also be used to pay at some convenience stores and vending machines.

In addition to JR services, there is a huge network of private railways. Each large city usually has at least one private train line that services it and the surrounding area, or connects it to nearby cities. These are often a bit cheaper than equivalent JR services.

Intercity routes typically run local (called *futsū* or *kaku-eki-teisha*), express (called *kyūkō* or *kaisoku*) and limited express trains (called *tokkyū*). Most limited express trains, especially those travelling to resort areas, require seat reservations and a surcharge; in this case the trains will have comfortable reclining seats and toilets. All trains, save for a few *shinkansen* cars, are nonsmoking.

Intercity JR trains, including the *shinkansen*, have 'green car' carriages, which are akin to business class. Seats are a little more spacious and the carriages tend to be quieter and less crowded.

Shinkansen

Japan's *shinkansen* (bullet trains), which run at a maximum speed of 320km/h, connect almost every major city in the country. In some places, the *shinkansen* station is a fair distance from the main JR station (as is the case in Osaka and Hakodate), and a transfer is required to get into the city centre.

Some trains are faster than others, depending on how many stops they make en route. For example, the journey from Tokyo to Shin-Osaka on the Tōkaidō line takes 2½ hours on the Nozomi train, three hours on the Hikari train and nearly four hours on the Kodama train. There is no difference in fare.

Shinkansen passengers have the option of buying reserved seat or nonreserved seat tickets. Fares for reserved seats cost ¥320 to ¥720 more than nonreserved seats, depending on the time of year. If you purchase a non-reserved seat ticket and there are no seats in the allotted carriages, you will have to stand. JR Rail pass holders can reserve seats at no extra charge.

Travellers are allowed two pieces of luggage, but note that you'll have to put them up on the overhead racks.

TRAIN LINGO

ENGLISH	PRONUNCIATION	SCRIPT
local	*futsū*	普通
business-class car	*green-sha*	グリーン車
unreserved seat	*jiyū-seki*	自由席
JR rapid or express	*kaisoku*	快速
local	*kaku- eki-teisha*	各駅停車
one way	*katamichi*	片道
nonsmoking car	*kin'en-sha*	禁煙車
smoking car	*kitsuen-sha*	喫煙車
ordinary express	*kyūkō*	急行
round trip	*ōfuku*	往復
JR special rapid train	*shin-kaisoku*	新快速
bullet train	*shinkansen*	新幹線
reserved seat	*shitei-seki*	指定席
limited express	*tokkyū*	特急

Overnight Trains

The Sunrise Seto/Izumo runs between Tokyo and Okayama before splitting in two directions – one for Takamatsu on Shikoku (Sunrise Seto; from ¥15,750) and one for Izumo (Sunrise Izumo; from ¥15,070). Trains have private compartments and *nobi nobi* berths (partitioned person-sized patches of carpet); the latter are free of charge for Japan Rail Pass holders, while the former require a surcharge.

Tickets can be bought one month in advance at 10am from JR *midori-no-madoguchi* ticket counters; the *nobi nobi* berths, in particular, sell out fast.

Ticketing

Tickets can be purchased from touch-screen vending machines in major train stations; most have an English function and those for *shinkansen* journeys accept credit cards.

If you are booking a series of journeys, have questions or just want the reassurance of buying a ticket from a person, major JR stations have what are called *midori-no-madoguchi*, which function as JR's in-house travel agency; there are also locations at Narita and Kansai airports where staff speak good English. Private line trains will have their own ticket windows.

Tickets can also be purchased from travel agencies in Japan, which can also often be found within train stations. Japan Travel Bureau (JTB; www.jtb.co.jp) has branches everywhere.

Seat reservations can only be made for *shinkansen* services and certain limited express *(tokkyū)* lines (in which case they are required). Reserved-seat tickets can be bought any time from a month in advance to the day of departure.

MAKING RESERVATIONS

➡ Reservations are a good idea on weekends and all but necessary over long holiday weekends and during peak travel seasons – such as Golden Week (late April to early May), O-Bon (mid-August) and the New Year period.

➡ If you have a firm itinerary, you can reserve all your long-haul JR train tickets at once at a *midori-no-madoguchi*.

➡ JR East allows travellers (with or without rail passes) to make some reservations online via its website (www.jreast.co.jp/e/index.html), though only for lines within its network. Read the fine print and be sure to pick up your tickets the day before your planned journey begins.

➡ Tickets can be purchased for Tōkaidō and San'yō *shinkansen* journeys at a small discount through the app, Smart EX (https://smart-ex.jp/en); note that this service is not for rail pass holders.

➡ JR allows reservations to be changed once free of charge up to the time of departure; unused tickets can be refunded, minus a handling fee. Private lines have their own policies.

DISCOUNTED TICKETS

Platt Kodama (www.jrtours.co.jp/kodama) This is a discounted ticket (20% to 23% off) for the journey between Tokyo and Osaka (via Nagoya and Kyoto) on Kodama trains. These are the slowest trains on this *shinkansen* line, and make many stops. Tickets must be purchased at least one day before departure and are nonrefundable.

SEISHUN JŪHACHI KIPPU

With time, a sense of adventure and an affinity for slow travel, the **Seishun Jūhachi Kippu** (www.jreast.co.jp/e/pass/seishun18.html) is the best deal around and can be a really fun way to see the country. It literally means 'Youth 18 Ticket' and is designed for students to travel cheaply, but there are no actual age restrictions.

For ¥11,850 you get five one-day tickets valid for 24 hours each (starting at midnight) for travel anywhere in Japan on JR lines, which can also be shared. The only catch is that you can't travel on *tokkyū* (limited express) or *shinkansen* trains.

Purchase tickets at any JR ticket counter *(midori-no-madoguchi)*. As they're geared for students, travel time is limited to school holiday periods. Sale and validity periods are outlined in the following table:

SEASON	SALES PERIOD	VALIDITY PERIOD
Spring	20 Feb–31 Mar	1 Mar–10 Apr
Summer	1 Jul–31 Aug	20 Jul–10 Sep
Winter	1–31 Dec	10 Dec–10 Jan

Note that these periods are subject to change, so check online for the latest.

STUDENT DISCOUNTS

Students enrolled in Japanese universities (including foreign exchange students with a student ID issued by a Japanese university) can obtain 20% discount vouchers for *shinkansen*, JR limited express trains and some ferries from their university; unfortunately students enrolled in universities abroad are not able to obtain the vouchers.

Rail Passes

JAPAN RAIL PASS

The Japan Rail Pass (www.japanrailpass.net) is perfect for first-time visitors who want to zip around to see the highlights. It covers travel on all *shinkansen* trains except for the very fastest ones: the Nozomi and Mizuho trains on the Tōkaidō, San-yō and Kyūshū lines. A 'green' pass is good for rides in business-class 'green' train cars.

A one-way reserved-seat Tokyo–Kyoto *shinkansen* ticket costs ¥13,600, so you only need make one round trip between Tokyo and Kyoto on the *shinkansen* to make a seven-day pass come close to paying off (add a round trip between Narita Airport and Tokyo and you're already saving money).

DURATION	REGULAR (ADULT/CHILD)	GREEN (ADULT/CHILD)
7 days	¥29,110/14,550	¥38,880/19,440
14 days	¥46,390/23,190	¥62,950/31,470
21 days	¥59,350/29,670	¥81,870/40,930

Until recently, the countrywide Japan Rail Pass needed to be purchased outside of Japan prior to arrival through an authorised travel agency; it is currently available for purchase in country, but at a mark-up (a seven-day pass, for example, would cost ¥33,000). Note that the ability to purchase the pass within Japan is subject to change, so check online in advance.

If you purchase a pass outside of Japan, you will get an 'exchange order' that you should bring along with your passport to a JR Travel Service Centre (located at Narita, Haneda and Kansai international airports and at major train stations) to receive your pass.

When you validate the pass (at the same office), you select the date on which you want the pass to become valid. You can choose to make it valid immediately or on a later date. So, if you just plan to spend a few days in Kyoto or Tokyo before setting out to explore the country by rail, set the validity date to the day you start your journey outside the city.

Once you've validated your pass, you can make seat

SHINKANSEN ROUTES

SHINKANSEN	ROUTE	KEY STOPS	TRAIN NAMES
Tōkaidō	Tokyo–Shin-Osaka	Shinagawa, Shin-Yokohama, Odawara (Kodama only), Atami (Kodama only) Nagoya, Kyoto	Kodama, Hikari, Nozomi
San'yō	Shin-Osaka–Hakata	Shin-Kōbe, Himeji, Okayama, Hiroshima, Shin-Shimonoseki	Kodama, Hikari (to Okayama), Nozomi, Mizuho, Sakura
Kyūshū	Hakata–Kagoshima	Kumamoto	Mizuho, Sakura, Tsubame
Hokuriku	Tokyo–Kanazawa	Takasaki, Karuizawa, Nagano	Kagayaki, Asama (Tokyo–Nagano), Hakutaka (Nagano–Kanazawa)
Jōetsu	Tokyo–Niigata	Takasaki, Echigo-Yuzawa	Toki; Tanigawa (Tokyo–Echigo-Yuzawa)
Tōhoku	Tokyo–Shin-Aomori	Utsunomiya, Fukushima, Sendai, Morioka	Hayate, Yamabiko (Tokyo–Sendai)
Yamagata	Tokyo–Shinjō	Fukushima, Yamagata	Tsubasa
Akita	Tokyo–Akita	Utsunomiya, Fukushima, Morioka, Tazawa-ko, Kakunodate	Komachi
Hokkaidō	Tokyo–Shin-Hakodate-Hokuto	Utsunomiya, Fukushima, Sendai, Morioka, Shin-Aomori	Hayate, Hayabusa

reservations from any *midori-no-madoguchi* ('green window' ticket counters) at JR train stations. You can also just show your pass at the ticket gates and hop on any unreserved train car (though you'd be wise to book ahead during peak travel times).

For more information on the pass and overseas purchase locations, visit the Japan Rail Pass website.

HOKURIKU ARCH PASS

Slightly cheaper than the Japan Rail Pass (p899), the **Hokuriku Arch Pass** (adult/child ¥25,000/12,500; http://hokuriku-arch-pass.com/en) is valid for seven consecutive days and covers travel on the Hokuriku Shinkansen, which connects Tokyo to Kanazawa (via Nagano) and the Sea of Japan coast, and JR limited express trains that run from Kanazawa to and around the Kansai metro area (for Kyoto, Osaka, Nara and Kōbe).

Express train travel to and from Narita and Kansai airports is also included (but not direct *shinkansen* travel between Tokyo and Kansai), so this pass works well if you are flying into one airport and out the other and want to do a classic itinerary in a fixed amount of time. Purchased online for a ¥1000 discount.

JR EAST RAIL PASSES

JR East (www.jreast.co.jp) offers a few different rail passes that cover travel in different areas within eastern Honshū – a region that encompasses the Tokyo metro area, the Izu Peninsula, Nagano and the Japan Alps – Tōhoku (Northern Honshū) and southern Hokkaidō (up to Sapporo).

In addition to the routes outlined below, all of the following passes cover travel on JR limited express trains between Tokyo, Nikkō, Kofu (near Mt Fuji), Shimoda (at the tip of the Izu Peninsula) and Narita Airport.

The Tokyo Wide Pass is the only rail pass that can be used by foreign passport holders who are not on a tourist visa (foreign residents of Japan, for example). With the exception of the Tokyo Wide Pass, the following can be purchased online ahead of time for a ¥1000 discount.

Nagano & Niigata Area Pass (adult/child ¥18,000/9000) Flexible use for five days within 14 days; covers travel on the Jōetsu Shinkansen and the Hokuriku Shinkansen between Tokyo and Jōetsu-Myōkō (including Nagano). As these are mountain areas, this pass is good for skiers and hikers.

South Hokkaidō Rail Pass (adult/child ¥27,000/13,500) Flexible use for six days within 14 days; covers travel on the Tōhoku and Hokkaidō *shinkansen* lines. While only slightly cheaper than the country-wide JR pass, the flexibility here is a bonus.

Tōhoku Area Pass (adult/child ¥20,000/10,000) Flexible use for five days within 14 days; covers travel on the Tōhoku, Akita and Yamagata *shinkansen* lines and on the Jōetsu Shinkansen between Tokyo and ski resort Gala Yuzawa. Good for a tour of the rustic north (and some skiing).

Tokyo Wide Pass (adult/child ¥10,000/5000) Valid for three consecutive days for travel on the Jōetsu Shinkansen between Tokyo, Gala Yuzawa and Karuizawa. Good for sightseers with limited time.

JR CENTRAL RAIL PASSES

JR Central (http://english.jr-central.co.jp) has a few passes that are good for tackling mountain areas, including Takayama, Shirakawa-go, the Kiso Valley and the Kii Peninsula, without a

SAMPLE TRAIN FARES FROM TOKYO

JR fares are made up of the basic fare – what it would cost to take a local or express train on an ordinary trunk line – plus surcharges for limited express, *shinkansen* and sleeper trains.

The following are some typical fares from Tokyo (prices given for *shinkansen* are the total price of reserved seat ticket during mid-season, excluding Nozomi and Hayabusa trains).

DESTINATION	BASIC (¥)	SHINKANSEN (¥)
Hakata	13,820	22,330
Hiroshima	11,660	18,560
Kanazawa	7340	14,120
Kyoto	8210	13,600
Nagoya	6260	10,800
Niigata	5620	10,570
Okayama	10,480	16,820
Sendai	5940	10,890
Shin-Hakodate-Hokuto	11,560	22,180
Shin-Osaka	8750	14,140

CLIMATE CHANGE & TRAVEL

Every form of transport that relies on carbon-based fuel generates CO_2, the main cause of human-induced climate change. Modern travel is dependent on aeroplanes, which might use less fuel per kilometre per person than most cars but travel much greater distances. The altitude at which aircraft emit gases (including CO_2) and particles also contributes to their climate change impact. Many websites offer 'carbon calculators' that allow people to estimate the carbon emissions generated by their journey and, for those who wish to do so, to offset the impact of the greenhouse gases emitted with contributions to portfolios of climate-friendly initiatives throughout the world. Lonely Planet offsets the carbon footprint of all staff and author travel.

car. Purchase online ahead of time for a ¥1000 discount. For more pass details, see http://touristpass.jp/en.

Takayama-Hokuriku Pass (adult/child ¥15,000/7500) Valid for five consecutive days; covers travel on JR trains between Kansai International Airport, Osaka, Kyoto, Kanazawa, Takayama, Gero Onsen and Nagoya, plus buses around Shirakawa-go.

Alpine-Takayama-Matsumoto Pass (adult/child ¥18,500/9250) Valid for five consecutive days; covers travel on JR trains between Nagoya, the Kiso Valley, Matsumoto, Toyama and Takayama, including the Tateyama Kurobe Alpine Route.

Ise-Kumano-Wakayama Pass (adult/child ¥12,000/6000) Valid for five consecutive days; covers travel on JR trains between Kansai Airport, Osaka, Nara, Ise-Shima and around the Kii Peninsula, as well as local buses connecting towns along the Kumano Kodō.

JR WEST RAIL PASSES

JR West (www.westjr.co.jp) offers several different rail passes that cover travel in different areas within Western Honshū – a region that encompasses the Kansai metro area (Kyoto, Osaka, Kōbe and Nara), the Hokuriku area (Kanazawa and the Sea of Japan coast), the Okayama area (for Himeji and Kurashiki) and the Hiroshima area. Some also include Takamatsu (the northern gateway for Shikoku) and Hakata (the northern gateway for Kyūshū).

In addition to the routes outlined here, all Kansai area passes cover transport on JR lines to/from Kansai International Airport to Kyoto and Osaka. Pass holders can rent bicycles free of charge at Ekirin rental shops located at train stations covered within the scope of each pass.

Purchase online ahead of time for a ¥1000 discount. For a full list of currently available passes see: www.westjr.co.jp/global/en/ticket/pass

Kansai Wide Area Pass (adult/child ¥10,000/5000) Valid for five consecutive days; covers travel on JR intercity trains (excluding the *shinkansen*) between Osaka, Kyoto and Nara, plus travel on the San-yō Shinkansen between Osaka and Okayama (via Kōbe and Himeji) and limited express trains going north to the Sea of Japan coast (including Kinosaki Onsen) and south to the Kii Peninsula. Good for exploring the Kansai region in depth.

Kansai–Hiroshima Area Pass (adult/child ¥14,500/7250) Valid for five consecutive days; covers all JR limited express trains in Kansai, as well as the San-yō Shinkansen between Osaka and Hiroshima (via the castle town Himeji) and the ferry to Miyajima. Perfect for covering the highlights of Kansai and Western Honshū.

Kansai–Hokuriku Area Pass (adult/child ¥16,000/8000) Valid for seven consecutive days; covers all JR limited express trains in Kansai and Kanazawa (on the Sea of Japan coast), as well as the San-yō Shinkansen between Osaka and Okayama and the Hokuriku Shinkansen between Kanazawa and Jōetsu-Myōkō (in Niigata; good for skiing). The pass covers a good spread of well-travelled and less-travelled destinations.

San-yō-San'in Area Pass (adult/child ¥19,000/9500) Valid for seven consecutive days; covers all JR limited express trains in and around Kansai and to Takamatsu (Shikoku), as well as the San-yō Shinkansen between Osaka and Hakata in Kyūshū, via Okayama and Hiroshima. If you're skipping Tokyo and points east, this pass covers a good spread for significantly less than the classic JR Pass.

KANSAI THRU PASS

The **Kansai Thru Pass** (www.surutto.com/tickets/kansai_thru_english.html) is the best deal for hitting the highlights of the Kansai region. Good for two (adult/child ¥4000/2000) or three (adult/child ¥5200/2600) days, it covers city subways and buses and private railways (excluding JR lines) that connect Kyoto, Nara, Osaka, Kōbe, Himeji and the Kii Peninsula (including Kōya-san). It also entitles you to discounts at many attractions in the Kansai area.

Purchase it at Kansai International Airport or at any tourist information centre in the Kansai area.

JR KYŪSHŪ RAIL PASSES

JR Kyūshū's (www.jrkyushu.co.jp) **All Kyūshū Area Pass** (three-day adult/child ¥15,000/7500; five-day adult/child ¥18,000/9000) covers travel on the Kyūshū *shinkansen* between Hakata and Kagoshima (via Kumamoto) and limited express trains around the island, including routes to Nagasaki and the onsen towns of Beppu, Yufuin and Ibusuki. There are also cheaper passes covering just the northern or just the southern half of the island.

SHIKOKU RAIL PASS

The **All Shikoku Pass** (http://shikoku-railwaytrip.com/railpass.html) covers unlimited travel on the Shikoku intercity train network, including non-JR lines and scenic trains, and the ferry to Shodoshima.

DURATION	REGULAR (ADULT/CHILD)
3 days	¥9500/4750
4 days	¥10,500/5250
5 days	¥11,500/5750
7 days	¥12,500/6250

JR HOKKAIDŌ RAIL PASS

The **Hokkaidō Rail Pass** (www2.jrhokkaido.co.jp/global/english/ticket/railpass/index.html) covers all JR limited express trains on Hokkaidō (but not travel on the Hokkaidō *shinkansen*).

DURATION	REGULAR (ADULT/CHILD)
3 days	¥16,500/8250
4 days flexible	¥22,000/11,000
5 days	¥22,000/11,000
7 days	¥24,000/12,000

The four-day flexible pass is valid for 10 days.

Schedules & Information

Japan's extensive rail network is run by multiple operators (with their own websites), which makes searching timetables a chore. Train stations will have them posted for the lines running in and out of that particular station. You can also use the website HyperDia (www.hyperdia.com) to search routes and times in English.

For enquiries relating to JR, such as schedules, fares, fastest routes, lost baggage, discounts on rail travel, hotels and car hire, contact the **JR East Infoline** (☎from inside Japan 050-2016-1603, from overseas 81-50-2016-1603; www.jreast.co.jp/e/customer_support/infoline.html; ⏲10am-6pm). Information is available in English, Korean and Chinese.

Language

Japanese is spoken by more than 125 million people. While it bears some resemblance to Altaic languages such as Mongolian and Turkish and has grammatical similarities to Korean, its origins are unclear. Chinese is responsible for the existence of many Sino-Japanese words in Japanese, and for the originally Chinese kanji characters which the Japanese use in combination with the home-grown hiragana and katakana scripts.

Japanese pronunciation is easy to master for English speakers, as most of its sounds are also found in English – if you read our coloured pronunciation guides as if they were English, you'll be understood. Note though that in Japanese, it's important to make the distinction between short and long vowels, as vowel length can change the meaning of a word. The long vowels, shown in our pronunciation guides with a horizontal line on top of them (ā, ē, ī, ō, ū), should be held twice as long as the short ones. It's also important to make the distinction between single and double consonants, as this can produce a difference in meaning. Pronounce the double consonants with a slight pause between them, eg sak·ka (writer).

Note also that the vowel sound ai is pronounced as in 'aisle', air as in 'pair' and ow as in 'how'. As for the consonants, ts is pronounced as in 'hats', f sounds almost like 'fw' (with rounded lips), and r is halfway between 'r' and 'l'. All syllables in a word are pronounced fairly evenly in Japanese.

WANT MORE?

For in-depth language information and handy phrases, check out Lonely Planet's *Japanese Phrasebook*. You'll find it at **shop.lonelyplanet.com**, or you can buy Lonely Planet's iPhone phrasebooks at the Apple App Store.

BASICS

Japanese uses an array of registers of speech to reflect social and contextual hierarchy, but these can be simplified to the form most appropriate for the situation, which is what we've done in this language guide too.

Hello.	こんにちは。	kon·ni·chi·wa
Goodbye.	さようなら。	sa·yō·na·ra
Yes.	はい。	hai
No.	いいえ。	ī·e
Please. (when asking)	ください。	ku·da·sai
Please. (when offering)	どうぞ。	dō·zo
Thank you.	ありがとう。	a·ri·ga·tō
Excuse me. (to get attention)	すみません。	su·mi·ma·sen
Sorry.	ごめんなさい。	go·men·na·sai

You're welcome.
どういたしまして。 dō i·ta·shi·mash·te

How are you?
お元気ですか? o·gen·ki des ka

Fine. And you?
はい、元気です。 hai, gen·ki des
あなたは? a·na·ta wa

What's your name?
お名前は何ですか? o·na·ma·e wa nan des ka

My name is ...
私の名前は wa·ta·shi no na·ma·e wa
…です。 ... des

Do you speak English?
英語が話せますか? ē·go ga ha·na·se·mas ka

I don't understand.
わかりません。 wa·ka·ri·ma·sen

Does anyone speak English?
どなたか英語を do·na·ta ka ē·go o
話せますか? ha·na·se·mas ka

ACCOMMODATION

Where's a ...?	…がありますか?	... ga a·ri·mas ka
campsite	キャンプ場	kyam·pu·jō
guesthouse	民宿	min·shu·ku
hotel	ホテル	ho·te·ru
inn	旅館	ryo·kan
youth hostel	ユースホステル	yū·su·ho·su·te·ru

Do you have a ... room?	…ルームはありますか?	...rū·mu wa a·ri·mas ka
single	シングル	shin·gu·ru
double	ダブル	da·bu·ru

How much is it per ...?	…いくらですか?	... i·ku·ra des ka
night	1泊	ip·pa·ku
person	1人	hi·to·ri

air-con	エアコン	air·kon
bathroom	風呂場	fu·ro·ba
window	窓	ma·do

DIRECTIONS

Where's the ...?
…はどこですか? ... wa do·ko des ka

Can you show me (on the map)?
(地図で)教えてくれませんか? (chi·zu de) o·shi·e·te ku·re·ma·sen ka

What's the address?
住所は何ですか? jū·sho wa nan des ka

Could you please write it down?
書いてくれませんか? kai·te ku·re·ma·sen ka

behind ...	…の後ろ	... no u·shi·ro
in front of ...	…の前	... no ma·e
near ...	…の近く	... no chi·ka·ku
next to ...	…のとなり	... no to·na·ri
opposite ...	…の向かい側	... no mu·kai·ga·wa
straight ahead	この先	ko·no sa·ki

Turn ...	…まがってください。	... ma·gat·te ku·da·sai
at the corner	その角を	so·no ka·do o
at the traffic lights	その信号を	so·no shin·gō o
left	左へ	hi·da·ri e
right	右へ	mi·gi e

SIGNS

入口	**Entrance**
出口	**Exit**
営業中/開館	**Open**
閉店/閉館	**Closed**
インフォメーション	**Information**
危険	**Danger**
トイレ	**Toilets**
男	**Men**
女	**Women**

EATING & DRINKING

I'd like to reserve a table for (two people).
(2人)の予約をお願いします。 (fu·ta·ri) no yo·ya·ku o o·ne·gai shi·mas

What would you recommend?
なにがおすすめですか? na·ni ga o·su·su·me des ka

What's in that dish?
あの料理に何が入っていますか? a·no ryō·ri ni na·ni ga hait·te i·mas ka

Do you have any vegetarian dishes?
ベジタリアン料理がありますか? be·ji·ta·ri·an ryō·ri ga a·ri·mas ka

I'm a vegetarian.
私はベジタリアンです。 wa·ta·shi wa be·ji·ta·ri·an des

I'm a vegan.
私は厳格な菜食主義者です。 wa·ta·shi wa gen·ka·ku na sai·sho·ku·shu·gi·sha des

I don't eat ...	…は食べません。	... wa ta·be·ma·sen
dairy products	乳製品	nyū·sē·hin
(red) meat	(赤身の)肉	(a·ka·mi no) ni·ku
meat or dairy products	肉や乳製品は	ni·ku ya nyū·sē·hin
pork	豚肉	bu·ta·ni·ku
seafood	シーフード/海産物	shī·fū·do/kai·sam·bu·tsu

Is it cooked with pork lard or chicken stock?
これはラードか鶏のだしを使っていますか? ko·re wa rā·do ka to·ri no da·shi o tsu·kat·te i·mas ka

I'm allergic to (peanuts).
私は(ピーナッツ)にアレルギーがあります。 wa·ta·shi wa (pī·nat·tsu) ni a·re·ru·gī ga a·ri·mas

That was delicious!
おいしかった。 oy·shi·kat·ta

Cheers!
乾杯! kam·pai

Please bring the bill.
お勘定をください。 o·kan·jō o ku·da·sai

Key Words

appetisers	前菜	zen·sai
bottle	ビン	bin
bowl	ボール	bō·ru
breakfast	朝食	chō·sho·ku
cold	冷たい	tsu·me·ta·i
dinner	夕食	yū·sho·ku
fork	フォーク	fō·ku
glass	グラス	gu·ra·su
grocery	食料品	sho·ku·ryō·hin
hot (warm)	熱い	a·tsu·i
knife	ナイフ	nai·fu
lunch	昼食	chū·sho·ku
market	市場	i·chi·ba
menu	メニュー	me·nyū
plate	皿	sa·ra
spicy	スパイシー	spai·shī
spoon	スプーン	spūn
vegetarian	ベジタリアン	be·ji·ta·ri·an
with	いっしょに	is·sho ni
without	なしで	na·shi de

Meat & Fish

beef	牛肉	gyū·ni·ku
chicken	鶏肉	to·ri·ni·ku
duck	アヒル	a·hi·ru
eel	うなぎ	u·na·gi
fish	魚	sa·ka·na
lamb	子羊	ko·hi·tsu·ji
lobster	ロブスター	ro·bus·tā
meat	肉	ni·ku
pork	豚肉	bu·ta·ni·ku
prawn	エビ	e·bi
salmon	サケ	sa·ke
seafood	シーフード/海産物	shī·fū·do/kai·sam·bu·tsu
shrimp	小エビ	ko·e·bi
tuna	マグロ	ma·gu·ro
turkey	七面鳥	shi·chi·men·chō
veal	子牛	ko·u·shi

KEY PATTERNS

To get by in Japanese, mix and match these simple patterns with words of your choice:

When's (the next bus)?
(次のバスは)何時ですか? (tsu·gi no bas wa) nan·ji des ka

Where's (the station)?
(駅は)どこですか? (e·ki wa) do·ko des ka

Do you have (a map)?
(地図)がありますか? (chi·zu) ga a·ri·mas ka

Is there (a toilet)?
(トイレ)がありますか? (toy·re) ga a·ri·mas ka

I'd like (the menu).
(メニュー)をお願いします。 (me·nyū) o o·ne·gai shi·mas

Can I (sit here)?
(ここに座って)もいいですか? (ko·ko ni su·wat·te) mo ī des ka

I need (a can opener).
(缶切り)が必要です。 (kan·ki·ri) ga hi·tsu·yō des

Do I need (a visa)?
(ビザ)が必要ですか? (bi·za) ga hi·tsu·yō des ka

I have (a reservation).
(予約)があります。 (yo·ya·ku) ga a·ri·mas

I'm (a teacher).
私は(教師)です。 wa·ta·shi wa (kyō·shi) des

Fruit & Vegetables

apple	りんご	rin·go
banana	バナナ	ba·na·na
beans	豆	ma·me
capsicum	ピーマン	pī·man
carrot	ニンジン	nin·jin
cherry	さくらんぼ	sa·ku·ram·bo
cucumber	キュウリ	kyū·ri
fruit	果物	ku·da·mo·no
grapes	ブドウ	bu·dō
lettuce	レタス	re·tas
nut	ナッツ	nat·tsu
orange	オレンジ	o·ren·ji
peach	桃	mo·mo
peas	豆	ma·me
pineapple	パイナップル	pai·nap·pu·ru
potato	ジャガイモ	ja·ga·i·mo

QUESTION WORDS

How?	どのように?	do·no yō ni
What?	なに?	na·ni
When?	いつ?	i·tsu
Where?	どこ?	do·ko
Which?	どちら?	do·chi·ra
Who?	だれ?	da·re
Why?	なぜ?	na·ze

pumpkin	カボチャ	ka·bo·cha
spinach	ホウレンソウ	hō·ren·sō
strawberry	イチゴ	i·chi·go
tomato	トマト	to·ma·to
vegetables	野菜	ya·sai
watermelon	スイカ	su·i·ka

Other

bread	パン	pan
butter	バター	ba·tā
cheese	チーズ	chī·zu
chilli	唐辛子	tō·ga·ra·shi
egg	卵	ta·ma·go
honey	蜂蜜	ha·chi·mi·tsu
horseradish	わさび	wa·sa·bi
jam	ジャム	ja·mu
noodles	麺	men
pepper	コショウ	ko·shō
rice (cooked)	ごはん	go·han
salt	塩	shi·o
seaweed	のり	no·ri
soy sauce	しょう油	shō·yu
sugar	砂糖	sa·tō

Drinks

beer	ビール	bī·ru
coffee	コーヒー	kō·hī
(orange) juice	(オレンジ) ジュース	(o·ren·ji·) jū·su
lemonade	レモネード	re·mo·nē·do
milk	ミルク	mi·ru·ku
mineral water	ミネラル ウォーター	mi·ne·ra·ru· wō·tā
red wine	赤ワイン	a·ka wain
sake	酒	sa·ke
tea	紅茶	kō·cha
water	水	mi·zu
white wine	白ワイン	shi·ro wain
yogurt	ヨーグルト	yō·gu·ru·to

EMERGENCIES

Help!	
たすけて!	tas·ke·te
Go away!	
離れろ!	ha·na·re·ro
I'm lost.	
迷いました。	ma·yoy·mash·ta
Call the police.	
警察を呼んで。	kē·sa·tsu o yon·de
Call a doctor.	
医者を呼んで。	i·sha o yon·de
Where are the toilets?	
トイレはどこですか?	toy·re wa do·ko des ka
I'm ill.	
私は病気です。	wa·ta·shi wa byō·ki des
It hurts here.	
ここが痛いです。	ko·ko ga i·tai des
I'm allergic to ...	
私は… アレルギーです。	wa·ta·shi wa ... a·re·ru·gī des

SHOPPING & SERVICES

I'd like to buy ...	
…をください。	... o ku·da·sai
I'm just looking.	
見ているだけです。	mi·te i·ru da·ke des
Can I look at it?	
それを見ても いいですか?	so·re o mi·te mo ī des ka
How much is it?	
いくらですか?	i·ku·ra des ka
That's too expensive.	
高すぎます。	ta·ka·su·gi·mas
Can you give me a discount?	
ディスカウント できますか?	dis·kown·to de·ki·mas ka
There's a mistake in the bill.	
請求書に間違いが あります。	sē·kyū·sho ni ma·chi·gai ga a·ri·mas

ATM	ATM	ē·tī·e·mu
credit card	クレジット カード	ku·re·jit·to· kā·do
post office	郵便局	yū·bin·kyo·ku
public phone	公衆電話	kō·shū·den·wa
tourist office	観光案内所	kan·kō·an·nai·jo

TIME & DATES

What time is it?
何時ですか？ nan·ji des ka

It's (10) o'clock.
(10)時です。 (jū)·ji des

Half past (10).
(10)時半です。 (jū)·ji han des

am	午前	go·zen
pm	午後	go·go

Monday	月曜日	ge·tsu·yō·bi
Tuesday	火曜日	ka·yō·bi
Wednesday	水曜日	su·i·yō·bi
Thursday	木曜日	mo·ku·yō·bi
Friday	金曜日	kin·yō·bi
Saturday	土曜日	do·yō·bi
Sunday	日曜日	ni·chi·yō·bi

January	1月	i·chi·ga·tsu
February	2月	ni·ga·tsu
March	3月	san·ga·tsu
April	4月	shi·ga·tsu
May	5月	go·ga·tsu
June	6月	ro·ku·ga·tsu
July	7月	shi·chi·ga·tsu
August	8月	ha·chi·ga·tsu
September	9月	ku·ga·tsu
October	10月	jū·ga·tsu
November	11月	jū·i·chi·ga·tsu
December	12月	jū·ni·ga·tsu

TRANSPORT

boat	船	fu·ne
bus	バス	bas
metro	地下鉄	chi·ka·te·tsu
plane	飛行機	hi·kō·ki
train	電車	den·sha
tram	市電	shi·den

What time does it leave?
これは何時に 出ますか？ ko·re wa nan·ji ni de·mas ka

Does it stop at (...)?
(…)に 停まりますか？ (...) ni to·ma·ri·mas ka

Please tell me when we get to (...).
(…)に着いたら 教えてください。 (...) ni tsu·i·ta·ra o·shi·e·te ku·da·sai

A one-way/return ticket (to ...).
(. . . 行きの) 片道/往復 切符。 (...·yu·ki no) ka·ta·mi·chi/ō·fu·ku kip·pu

bus stop	バス停	bas·tē
first	始発の	shi·ha·tsu no
last	最終の	sai·shū no
ticket window	窓口	ma·do·gu·chi
timetable	時刻表	ji·ko·ku·hyō
train station	駅	e·ki

I'd like to hire a ... …を借りたいのですが。 ... o ka·ri·tai no des ga

4WD	四駆	yon·ku
bicycle	自転車	ji·ten·sha
car	自動車	ji·dō·sha
motorbike	オートバイ	ō·to·bai

Is this the road to ...?
この道は . . . まで行きますか？ ko·no mi·chi wa ... ma·de i·ki·mas ka

(How long) Can I park here?
(どのくらい)ここに 駐車できますか？ (do·no·ku·rai) ko·ko ni chū·sha de·ki·mas ka

NUMBERS

1	一	i·chi
2	二	ni
3	三	san
4	四	shi/yon
5	五	go
6	六	ro·ku
7	七	shi·chi/na·na
8	八	ha·chi
9	九	ku/kyū
10	十	jū
20	二十	ni·jū
30	三十	san·jū
40	四十	yon·jū
50	五十	go·jū
60	六十	ro·ku·jū
70	七十	na·na·jū
80	八十	ha·chi·jū
90	九十	kyū·jū
100	百	hya·ku
1000	千	sen

GLOSSARY

For lists of culinary terms, see p64-77; for useful words when visiting an onsen, see p60-62; and for train terminology, see p898.

Ainu – indigenous people of Hokkaidō and parts of Northern Honshū
Amaterasu – sun goddess and link to the imperial throne
ANA – All Nippon Airways
annai-sho – information office
asa-ichi – morning market

bama – beach; see also *hama*
bashō – *sumō* tournament
bonsai – the art of growing miniature trees by careful pruning of branches and roots
bugaku – dance piece played by court orchestra in ancient Japan
buke yashiki – *samurai* residence
bunraku – classical puppet theatre which uses huge puppets to portray dramas similar to *kabuki*
Burakumin – traditionally outcasts associated with lowly occupations such as leatherwork; literally 'village people'
bushidō – a set of values followed by the *samurai;* literally 'the way of the warrior'
butsudan – Buddhist altar in Japanese homes

chō – city area (in large cities) between a *ku* and a *chōme* in size; also a street
chōchin – paper lantern
chōme – city area of a few blocks

Daibutsu – Great Buddha
daimyō – regional lord under the *shōgun*
daira – plain; see also *taira*
dake – peak; see also *take*
dani – valley; see also *tani*
danjiri – festival float
dera – temple; see also *tera*
dō – temple or hall of a temple

eki – train station

fu – prefecture; see also *ken*
fusuma – sliding screen door
futsū – local train; literally 'ordinary'

gaijin – foreigner; literally 'outside people'
gasoreen sutando – petrol station
gasshō-zukuri – an architectural style (usually thatch-roofed); literally 'hands in prayer'
gawa – river; see also *kawa*
geiko – the Kyoto word for *geisha*
geisha – woman versed in arts and drama who entertains guests; *not* a prostitute
gekijō – theatre
genkan – foyer area where shoes are removed or replaced when entering or leaving a building
geta – traditional wooden sandals
gū – shrine
gun – county

habu – a venomous snake found in Okinawa
haiku – 17-syllable poem
hama – beach; see also *bama*
hanami – blossom viewing (usually cherry blossoms)
haniwa – earthenware figure found in tombs of the Kōfun period
hantō – peninsula
hara – uncultivated field or plain
hari – dragon-boat race
hatsu-mōde – first shrine visit of the new year
henro – pilgrim on the Shikoku 88 Temple Circuit
Hikari – the second-fastest type of *shinkansen*
hiragana – phonetic syllabary used to write Japanese words
hondō – main route or main hall
honsen – main rail line

ichi-nichi-jōsha-ken – day pass for unlimited travel on bus, tram or subway systems
ikebana – art of flower arrangement
irezumi – a tattoo or the art of tattooing
irori – hearth or fireplace
izakaya – pub-style eatery

JAF – Japan Automobile Federation
JAL – Japan Airlines
ji – temple
jigoku – boiling mineral hot spring, which is definitely not for bathing in; literally 'hells'
jikokuhyō – timetable or book of timetables
jima – island; see also *shima*
jingū – shrine
jinja – shrine
jizō – small stone statue of the Buddhist protector of travellers and children
JNTO – Japan National Tourism Organization
jō – castle
JR – Japan Railways
JTB – Japan Travel Bureau
juku – after-school 'cram' school
JYHA – Japan Youth Hostel Association

kabuki – a form of Japanese theatre based on popular legends, characterised by elaborate costumes, stylised acting and the use of male actors for all roles
kaikan – hall or building
kaikyō – channel/strait
kaisoku – rapid train
kaisū-ken – a book of transport tickets
kami – Shintō gods; spirits of natural phenomena
kamikaze – typhoon that sunk Kublai Khan's 13th-century invasion fleet and the name adopted by suicide pilots in the waning days of WWII; literally 'divine wind'
kana – the two phonetic syllabaries, *hiragana* and *katakana*
kanji – Chinese ideographic script used for writing Japanese; literally 'Chinese script'
Kannon – Bodhisattva of Compassion (commonly referred to as the Buddhist Goddess of Mercy)

karaoke – bar where you sing along with taped music; literally 'empty orchestra'
katakana – phonetic syllabary used to write foreign words
katamichi – one-way transport ticket
katana – Japanese sword
kawa – river; see also *gawa*
ken – prefecture; see also *fu*
kendo – oldest martial art; literally 'the way of the sword'
ki – life force, will
kimono – brightly coloured, robe-like traditional outer garment
kin'en-sha – nonsmoking train carriage
kippu – ticket
kissaten – coffee shop
ko – lake
kō – port
kōban – police box
kōen – park
kōgen – high plain (in the mountains); plateau
kokumin-shukusha – people's lodge; an inexpensive form of accommodation
kokuritsu kōen – national park
kotatsu – heated table with a quilt or cover over it to keep the legs and lower body warm
koto – 13-stringed instrument derived from a Chinese zither that is played flat on the floor
ku – ward
kūkō – airport
kura – earth-walled storehouse
kyō – gorge
kyūkō – ordinary express train (faster than a *futsū*, only stopping at certain stations)

machi – city area (in large cities) between a *ku* and *chōme* in size; also street
machiya – traditional Japanese townhouse or merchant house
maiko – apprentice *geisha*
mama-san – woman who manages a bar or club
maneki-neko – beckoning or welcoming cat figure frequently seen in restaurants and bars; it's supposed to attract customers and trade
manga – Japanese comics
matsuri – festival
meishi – business card
midori-no-madoguchi – ticket counter in large Japan Rail stations, where you can make more complicated bookings (look for the green band across the glass)
mikoshi – portable shrine carried during festivals
minato – harbour
minshuku – the Japanese equivalent of a B&B; family-run budget accommodation
misaki – cape; see also *saki*
mon – gate
mura – village

N'EX – Narita Express
NHK – Nihon Hōsō Kyōkai (Japan Broadcasting Corporation)
Nihon – Japanese word for 'Japan'; literally 'source of the sun'; also *Nippon*
ningyō – Japanese doll
Nippon – see *Nihon*
nō – classical Japanese drama performed on a bare stage
noren – cloth hung as a sunshade, typically carrying the name of the shop or premises; indicates that a restaurant is open for business
norikae-ken – transfer ticket (trams and buses)
NTT – Nippon Telegraph & Telephone Corporation

o- – prefix used to show respect to anything it is applied to
ōfuku – return ticket
o-furo – traditional Japanese bath
OL – 'office lady'; female clerical worker; pronounced 'ō-eru'
onnagata – male actor playing a woman's role (usually in *kabuki*)
onsen – hot spring; mineral-spa area, usually with accommodation
oshibori – hot towel provided in restaurants

pachinko – popular vertical pinball game, played in *pachinko* parlours

rakugo – Japanese raconteur, stand-up comic
rettō – island group; see also *shotō*
Rinzai – school of Zen Buddhism which places an emphasis on *kōan* (riddles)
romaji – Japanese roman script
rōnin – student who must resit university entrance exam; literally 'masterless *samurai*', sometimes referred to as 'wanderer'
ropeway – Japanese word for a cable car, tramway or funicular railway
rotemburo – open-air or outdoor bath
ryokan – traditional Japanese inn

saki – cape; see also *misaki*
sakoku – Japan's period of national seclusion prior to the Meiji Restoration
sakura – cherry blossom
salaryman – male white-collar worker, usually in a large firm
sama – even more respectful suffix than *san*; used in instances such as *o-kyaku-sama* – the 'honoured guest'
samurai – warrior class
san – mountain; also suffix which shows respect to the person it is applied to
san-sō – mountain hut or cottage
sentō – public bath
seppuku – ritual suicide by disembowelment
shamisen – a three-stringed traditional Japanese instrument that resembles a banjo or lute
shi – city (used to distinguish cities from prefectures of the same name, eg Kyoto-shi)
shikki – lacquerware
shima – island; see also *jima*
shinkaisoku – express train or special rapid train (usually on JR lines)
shinkansen – super-express train, known in the West as 'bullet train'
Shintō – the indigenous religion of Japan; literally 'the way of the gods'
shirabyōshi – traditional dancer
shitamachi – traditionally the low-lying, less affluent parts of Tokyo

shodō – Japanese calligraphy; literally the 'way of writing'
shōgekijō – small theatre
shōgi – a version of chess in which each player has 20 pieces and the object is to capture the opponent's king
shōgun – former military ruler of Japan
shōgunate – military government
shōji – sliding rice-paper screen
shōjin ryōri – Buddhist vegetarian meal (served at temple lodgings etc)
shokudō – all-round restaurant
shotō – archipelago or island group; see also *rettō*
Shugendō – offbeat Buddhist school, which incorporates ancient shamanistic rites, *Shintō* beliefs and ascetic Buddhist traditions
shūji – a lesser form of *shodō;* literally 'the practice of letters'
shukubō – temple lodging
soapland – Japanese euphemism for a bathhouse offering sexual services, eg massage parlour
Sōtō – a school of Zen Buddhism which places emphasis on *zazen*
sumi-e – black-ink brush painting
sumō – Japanese wrestling

tabi – split-toed Japanese socks used when wearing *geta*
taiko – drum
taira – plain; see also *daira*
taisha – great shrine
take – peak; see also *dake*
taki – waterfall
tani – valley; see also *dani*
tanuki – racoon or dog-like folklore character frequently represented in ceramic figures
tatami – tightly woven floor matting on which shoes are never worn; traditionally, room size is defined by the number of tatami mats
teien – garden
tera – temple; see also *dera*
to – metropolis, eg Tokyo-to
tō – island
tokkyū – limited express train; faster than a *kyūkō*
tokonoma – sacred alcove in a house in which flowers may be displayed or a scroll hung
torii – entrance gate to a Shintō shrine
tōsu – lavatory

uchiwa – paper fan
ukiyo-e – woodblock print; literally 'pictures of the floating world'

wa – harmony, team spirit; also the old *kanji* used to denote Japan, and still used in Chinese and Japanese as a prefix to indicate things of Japanese origin, eg *wafuku* (Japanese-style clothing)
wabi – enjoyment of peace and tranquillity
wan – bay
washi – Japanese handmade paper
yabusame – samurai-style horseback archery
yakimono – pottery or ceramic ware
yakuza – Japanese mafia
yama – mountain; see also *zan*
yamabushi – mountain priest (Shugendō Buddhism practitioner)
yama-goya – mountain hut
yamato – a term of much debated origins that refers to the Japanese world
yamato-e – traditional Japanese painting
yatai – festival float; hawker stall
yukata – light cotton summer *kimono,* worn for lounging or casual use; standard issue when staying at a *ryokan*

zaibatsu – industrial conglomerate; the term arose pre-WWII but the Japanese economy is still dominated by huge firms such as Mitsui, Marubeni and Mitsubishi, which are involved in many different industries
zaki – cape
zan – mountain; see also *yama*
zazen – seated meditation emphasised in the Sōtō school of Zen Buddhism
Zen – an offshoot of Buddhism, introduced to Japan in the 12th century from China, that emphasises a direct, intuitive approach to enlightenment rather than rational analysis

Behind the Scenes

SEND US YOUR FEEDBACK

We love to hear from travellers – your comments keep us on our toes and help make our books better. Our well-travelled team reads every word on what you loved or loathed about this book. Although we cannot reply individually to your submissions, we always guarantee that your feedback goes straight to the appropriate authors, in time for the next edition. Each person who sends us information is thanked in the next edition – the most useful submissions are rewarded with a selection of digital PDF chapters.

Visit **lonelyplanet.com/contact** to submit your updates and suggestions or to ask for help. Our award-winning website also features inspirational travel stories, news and discussions.

Note: We may edit, reproduce and incorporate your comments in Lonely Planet products such as guidebooks, websites and digital products, so let us know if you don't want your comments reproduced or your name acknowledged. For a copy of our privacy policy visit lonelyplanet.com/privacy.

OUR READERS

Many thanks to the travellers who used the last edition and wrote to us with helpful hints, useful advice and interesting anecdotes:

Daniel Ford, Danielle McLean, Jassie-Bree Salmond, Kate Davis, Kitty Rolfe, Noemi Passafiume, Peter Tannen, Rene Brouwer

WRITER THANKS

Rebecca Milner

Thank you to my family and friends, who are there for me through all the ups and downs and late nights; to my indefatigable co-author Simon, for his inspiration and guidance; to Lonely Planet for standing by me; and to all the chefs, curators, professors, baristas and total strangers who knowingly or unknowingly provided me with new insight into this city, which I must also thank, for always keeping me on my toes.

Ray Bartlett

Thanks first and always to my family and amazing friends, for letting me go on these adventures and still remembering me when I get back. To the great editorial staff at Lonely Planet for their wisdom and advice. To all people I met or who helped me along the way. Tamura-さん, Airi, Kurumi and Aya, Yamaguchi-さん, Ishikawa-さん, Saeki, Saika, Minori, Emi, Ōtani-さん, Sakiko-さん, the lovely Linh, Watanabe Ayaka-さん... and so many other great people I met along the way. Thanks so much. Can't wait to be back again soon.

Andrew Bender

Thanks to my excellent Kyushu spirit guides Yohko Scott, Sakaguchi Riho, Jeremy Chen, Fujiyoshi Jun, Horichi Shiori, Ide Masahiro, Kai Hiroshi, Kamimoto Eiko, Kono Shintaro, Kuroki Shinya, Matsukawa Akihiro, Sasaki Takeshi, Shibata Kayoko, Cameron Stadin, Takae Tomoko, Takatori Aki, Taniguchi Yukiko, Yamasaki Keiko and Yoshida Kenji, and former Lonely Planet staff members Laura Crawford, James Smart and Sarah Bailey, without whom none of this would have been possible.

Stephanie d'Arc Taylor

Thank you to the charming, clever and indefatigable Christine, who fed me soba as a child and gave me my first copy of the *Inland Sea*. Without your help I couldn't have done this, or anything. Thank you to Chieko, Hidemasa, and to Teruko for saying that I use chopsticks better than Christine. Thank you to my mentors Lauren Keith, Laura Crawford, Rebecca Milner, Craig McLachlan and James Smart. Thank you to Bethan, who helped me prematurely celebrate this assignment.

Samantha Forge

Thank you to the wonderful people I met throughout Tōhoku for your knowledge, patience and boundless kindness. I have never drunk so many cups of tea in my life. Huge thanks also to the other Team Japan authors for their generosity and friendship, and to everyone at Lonely Planet who has had a hand in this project, especially the lovely Laura Crawford.

Craig McLachlan

A hearty thanks to all those who helped out on the road, but most of all, to my living kanji dictionary and exceptionally beautiful wife, Yuriko.

Kate Morgan

Thank you again to Laura Crawford for the opportunity to work on Osaka and Kyoto, and to Jen Carey for your help throughout. Huge thanks to Kengo Nakao from the Kyoto Tourist Information office for your assistance. Thanks to my parents for joining me in Kyoto and keeping up the research pace in the extreme heat! And to my friend Yuki and my husband Trent for great nights out, loads of food and rock bar shenanigans. Thanks also to all the inhouse staff at Lonely Planet who make this book happen.

Thomas O'Malley

Thanks to my esteemed fellow authors Simon and Rebecca for assisting this Japan-guide noob in the ways of the road warrior. Thanks to Family Mart and its konbini cohorts for all those cut-price caffeine hits on the road. Thanks to Mt Fuji for finally showing your beautiful face after days cloaked in cloud (I almost wept). Thanks to the two Ō-shima Island Aussies, Chloe and Caitlin. And thanks, as ever, to Ophelia.

Simon Richmond

Many thanks to co-writer Rebecca and to the following: Will Andrews, Toshiko Ishii, Kenichi, Giles Murray, Chris Kirkland, Shoji Kobayashi, Jun Onuma, Sabrina Suljevic, Ken Gail Kato, Toyokuni Honda, Tim Hornyak and Tomoko Yoshizawa.

Phillip Tang

Warm thanks to patient tourism staffers and travellers who shared their experiences. Thanks Laura Crawford for having me again; Japan will miss you. Thanks to 'David' Tong Wai Chung for skewers and whiskey highballs in Okayama, and tips on Izumo. Huge thanks to Chizu Otsuka at Tomato in Hiroshima. In Tokyo, *arigato* Nic for craft beers and 'life' talks; and Ayako for incredible chicken, weird waiters and Korean 'husbands'. Thanks in spirit to Vek Lewis for running guidance.

Benedict Walker

Big thanks as always to my Japanese 'family' the Shimizus for their continued friendship and fun, to Laura Crawford for keeping me on the team, to James Smart for his patience at submission time, to Taku Yamada and Kei Nakamura for your guidance and advice; to Cheryl, Bruce, Jess and Casey for being very sticky soul-glue; to Mum and the Walkers for watching over me from afar, and to my brother Andy for coming through with the goods and shining like a beacon of inspiration when I least expected it. To the resilient people of these remote island communities, where mother nature rules: you've forever won a place in my heart: *ganbarō!*

ACKNOWLEDGEMENTS

Illustrations p100-1 and p402-3 by Michael Weldon.

Climate map data adapted from Peel MC, Finlayson BL & McMahon TA (2007) 'Updated World Map of the Köppen-Geiger Climate Classification', *Hydrology and Earth System Sciences*, 11, 1633–44.

Cover photograph: Woman in *yukata* (light cotton kimono), Kyoto, f11photo/Shutterstock ©.

THIS BOOK

This 17th edition of Lonely Planet's *Japan* guidebook was researched and written by Rebecca Milner, Ray Bartlett, Andrew Bender, Samantha Forge, Thomas O'Malley, Craig McLachlan, Kate Morgan, Simon Richmond, Phillip Tang, Stephanie d'Arc Taylor, Benedict Walker. The previous two editions were written by Rebecca, Ray, Andrew, Samantha, Thomas, Craig, Kate, Simon, Phillip, Stephanie, Benedict, Tom Spurling and Wendy Yanagihara. This guidebook was produced by the following:

Destination Editors Laura Crawford, James Smart

Senior Product Editors Kate Chapman, Sandie Kestell

Product Editors Shona Gray, James Appleton

Senior Cartographer Diana Von Holdt

Assisting Cartographers Michael Garrett, Alison Lyall, Julie Sheridan

Book Designers Mazzy Prinsep, Catalina Aragón

Assisting Editors Sarah Bailey, Andrew Bain, James Bainbridge, Judith Bamber, Heather Champion, Samantha Cook, Lucy Cowie, Emma Gibbs, Carly Hall, Victoria Harrison, Lauren O'Connell, Kristin Odijk, Gabrielle Stefanos, Ross Taylor, Simon Williamson

Cover Researcher Fergal Condon

Thanks to Naoko Akamatsu, William Allen, Jennifer Carey, Gwen Cotter, Karen Henderson, Liz Heynes, Kate James, Elizabeth Jones, Campbell McKenzie, Virginia Moreno, Wayne Murphy, Genna Patterson, Kirsten Rawlings, Brad Smith

Map Pages **000**
Photo Pages **000**

Index

Map Pages **000**
Photo Pages **000**

I

J

K

L

M

Map Pages **000**
Photo Pages **000**

P

R

S

Map Pages **000**
Photo Pages **000**

Y

Z

Map Legend

Sights
- Beach
- Bird Sanctuary
- Buddhist
- Castle/Palace
- Christian
- Confucian
- Hindu
- Islamic
- Jain
- Jewish
- Monument
- Museum/Gallery/Historic Building
- Ruin
- Shinto
- Sikh
- Taoist
- Winery/Vineyard
- Zoo/Wildlife Sanctuary
- Other Sight

Activities, Courses & Tours
- Bodysurfing
- Diving
- Canoeing/Kayaking
- Course/Tour
- Sento Hot Baths/Onsen
- Skiing
- Snorkelling
- Surfing
- Swimming/Pool
- Walking
- Windsurfing
- Other Activity

Sleeping
- Sleeping
- Camping
- Hut/Shelter

Eating
- Eating

Drinking & Nightlife
- Drinking & Nightlife
- Cafe

Entertainment
- Entertainment

Shopping
- Shopping

Information
- Bank
- Embassy/Consulate
- Hospital/Medical
- Internet
- Police
- Post Office
- Telephone
- Toilet
- Tourist Information
- Other Information

Geographic
- Beach
- Gate
- Hut/Shelter
- Lighthouse
- Lookout
- Mountain/Volcano
- Oasis
- Park
- Pass
- Picnic Area
- Waterfall

Population
- Capital (National)
- Capital (State/Province)
- City/Large Town
- Town/Village

Transport
- Airport
- Border crossing
- Bus
- Cable car/Funicular
- Cycling
- Ferry
- Metro/MTR/MRT station
- Monorail
- Parking
- Petrol station
- Skytrain/Subway station
- Taxi
- Train station/Railway
- Tram
- Underground station
- Other Transport

Routes
- Tollway
- Freeway
- Primary
- Secondary
- Tertiary
- Lane
- Unsealed road
- Road under construction
- Plaza/Mall
- Steps
- Tunnel
- Pedestrian overpass
- Walking Tour
- Walking Tour detour
- Path/Walking Trail

Boundaries
- International
- State/Province
- Disputed
- Regional/Suburb
- Marine Park
- Cliff
- Wall

Hydrography
- River, Creek
- Intermittent River
- Canal
- Water
- Dry/Salt/Intermittent Lake
- Reef

Areas
- Airport/Runway
- Beach/Desert
- Cemetery (Christian)
- Cemetery (Other)
- Glacier
- Mudflat
- Park/Forest
- Sight (Building)
- Sportsground
- Swamp/Mangrove

Note: Not all symbols displayed above appear on the maps in this book

Craig McLachlan

The Japan Alps & Central Honshū, Shikoku Craig has covered destinations all over the globe for Lonely Planet for two decades. Based in Queenstown, New Zealand for half the year, he runs an outdoor activities company and a sake brewery, then moonlights overseas for the other half, leading tours and writing for Lonely Planet. Craig has completed a number of adventures in Japan and his books are available on Amazon. Check out www.craigmclachlan.com.

Kate Morgan

Kansai, Kyoto Having worked for Lonely Planet for over a decade now, Kate has worked as a travel writer on destinations such as Shanghai, Japan, India, Russia, Zimbabwe, the Philippines and Phuket. She has done stints living in London, Paris and Osaka but these days is based in one of her favourite regions in the world – Victoria, Australia. In between travelling the world and writing about it, Kate enjoys spending time at home working as a freelance editor.

Thomas O'Malley

Mt Fuji & Around Tokyo A British writer based in Beijing, Tom is a world-leading connoisseur of cheap eats, dive bars, dark alleyways and hangovers. He has contributed travel stories to everyone from the BBC to *Playboy*, and reviews hotels for the *Telegraph*. Under another guise, he is a comedy scriptwriter. Follow him by walking behind at a distance.

Simon Richmond

Tokyo Journalist and photographer Simon Richmond has specialised as a travel writer since the early 1990s and first worked for Lonely Planet in 1999 on their Central Asia guide. He's long since stopped counting the number of guidebooks he's researched and written for the company, but countries covered include Australia, China, India, Iran, Korea, Malaysia, Mongolia, Myanmar (Burma), Russia, Singapore, South Africa and Turkey.

Phillip Tang

Hiroshima & Western Honshū Phillip Tang grew up on a typically Australian diet of pho and fish'n'chips before moving to Mexico City. A degree in Chinese and Latin-American cultures launched him into travel and then writing about it for Lonely Planet's *Canada*, *China*, *Korea*, *Mexico*, *Peru* and *Vietnam* guides. Writing at hellophillip.com, photos @mrtangtangtang, and tweets @philliptang.

Benedict Walker

Okinawa & the Southwest Islands A beach baby from Newcastle, Australia, Benedict turned 40 in 2017 and decided to start a new life in Leipzig, Germany. Writing for Lonely Planet was a childhood dream and he has covered big chunks of Australia, Canada, Germany, USA, Switzerland, Sweden and Japan. Follow him on Instagram @wordsandjourneys.

OUR STORY

A beat-up old car, a few dollars in the pocket and a sense of adventure. In 1972 that's all Tony and Maureen Wheeler needed for the trip of a lifetime – across Europe and Asia overland to Australia. It took several months, and at the end – broke but inspired – they sat at their kitchen table writing and stapling together their first travel guide, *Across Asia on the Cheap*. Within a week they'd sold 1500 copies. Lonely Planet was born.

Today, Lonely Planet has offices in the US, Ireland and China, with a network of over 2000 contributors in every corner of the globe. We share Tony's belief that 'a great guidebook should do three things: inform, educate and amuse'.

OUR WRITERS

Rebecca Milner

Tokyo, Kansai California-born, living in Tokyo since 2002. Freelance writer covering travel, food & culture. Published in the *Guardian*, the *Independent*, the *Sunday Times Travel Magazine*, the *Japan Times* and more.

Ray Bartlett

Hokkaidō Ray Bartlett has been travel writing for nearly two decades, bringing Japan, Korea, Mexico, Tanzania, Guatemala, Indonesia and many parts of the United States to life in rich detail for top-industry publishers, newspapers and magazines. Ray currently divides his time between homes in the USA, Japan and Mexico.

Andrew Bender

Kyūshū Award-winning travel and food writer Andrew Bender has written three dozen Lonely Planet guidebooks (from Amsterdam to Los Angeles, Germany to Taiwan and over a dozen titles about Japan), plus numerous articles for lonely planet.com. Speaking of Japan, Andy also is a tour leader and tour planner for visits to Japan. Follow him on Twitter @wheresandynow.

Stephanie d'Arc Taylor

The Japan Alps & Central Honshū, Sapporo & Hokkaidō A native Angeleno, Stephanie grew up with the west LA weekend ritual of going for Iranian sweets after *ten zaru soba* in Little Osaka. Later, she quit her PhD to move to Beirut and become a writer. She has published work with the *New York Times*, *Guardian*, *Roads & Kingdoms* and *Kinfolk Magazine*, and co-founded Jaleesa, a venture-capital funded social impact business in Beirut. Follow her on Instagram @zerodarctaylor.

Samantha Forge

Northern Honshū (Tōhoku) Samantha became hooked on travel at the age of 17, when she arrived in London with an overstuffed backpack and a copy of Lonely Planet's *Europe on a Shoestring*. After a stint in Paris, she moved back to Australia and began working as an editor for Lonely Planet. Eventually her wanderlust got the better of her, and she now works as a freelance writer and editor.

OVER PAGE MORE WRITERS

Published by Lonely Planet Global Limited
CRN 554153
17th edition – December 2021
ISBN 978 1 78868 381 4

10 9 8 7 6 5 4 3 2 1
Printed in Singapore